THE CARDINALS

THE CARDINALS

Introduction by Jack Buck
Cardinal Graphics by John Warner Davenport
Historical text by Jeffrey Neuman

COLLIER BOOKS
A Division of Macmillan Publishing Co., Inc.
NEW YORK

COLLIER MACMILLAN PUBLISHERS
LONDON

Macmillan Publishing Co., Inc.
866 Third Avenue, New York, N.Y. 10022
Collier Macmillan Canada, Inc.

Library of Congress Cataloging in Publication Data
Main entry under title:

The Cardinals.

1. St. Louis Cardinals (Baseball team) 2. Baseball
players—United States—Biography. I. Davenport, John
Warner, 1931-   . II. Neuman, Jeffrey.
GV875.S3C37   1983   796.357′64′0977866   83-1857
ISBN 0-02-029400-X

10 9 8 7 6 5 4 3 2 1

Printed in the United States of America

Contents

Contents

Introduction

From the time I first stepped into the St. Louis Cardinals' broadcasting booth some thirty years ago, I should have known that covering the colorful Cards was going to be a joy and a delight, full of more surprises than a box of ballpark Crackerjacks. My very first game showed me that, no matter what else you could say about the Cardinals, you could never call them boring!

It was back in 1953, and I was working in the Cardinals' old chain gang, as we used to call the legendary, notorious farm system that Branch Rickey developed to bring the club from rags to riches—both on and off the field. I was asked to join the big club in New York. They wanted to take a look-see to consider me for a job on the rather infrequent telecasts of Cardinal games.

That first game was one of the most remarkable I ever saw. Some say the Cards staged the greatest rally in the club's long history in that game. The Cardinals trailed the New York Giants 11–0, and they were facing Sal "The Barber" Maglie, then the National League's best righthander. What a horrible game to use to try to impress St. Louis management! What can you say after you say you're sorry? But the Cardinals began to peck away—a run here, another run there. . . .

By the time Solly Hemus came up in the top of the eighth inning, the score was tied, 11–11. Hemus, a pesky leadoff hitter who usually either slapped at the ball or tried to work a walk, called time and headed down toward third base, where manager Eddie Stanky coached. Should he try for a base on balls?

Stanky, aptly nicknamed "The Brat," snarled just one word at him. "Attack!"

Hemus attacked. He hit a home run that inning and another in the ninth, and the Cardinals won the game, 14–12. A year later, I won the job in St. Louis with the Redbirds, leading to a happy career in the community, working with KMOX and the Cardinals.

Hemus later became one of the nine managers with whom I've worked since Anheuser-Busch took over the Cards. Anheuser-Busch's sponsorship of the Cardinals' games has allowed me many a close moment with the beer baron-sportsman Gussie Busch, who learned to be as competitive in baseball as he was with his brewery, his show horses, and his gin rummy game. As shown in his many accomplishments, both civic and personal, Mr. Busch is as colorful as the ball club, and that is saying something. As Bob Broeg pointed out in a photographic history of the club, *Redbirds: A Century of Cardinals Baseball,* the Cardinals have had more than their share of characters and kooks, players as flamboyant and flashy as were Ozzie Smith's backflips before Game 7 of the 1982 World Series.

I didn't arrive in time to see Rogers Hornsby shake the fences with his line drives for the Cardinals' first World Championship team. I'd have loved to see old Pete Alexander amble in from the Yankee Stadium bullpen to save that 1926 Series. And Frankie Frisch, the Fordham Flash, would have to go some to outdo the diving stops of our Wizard of Oz, but many who saw him play say he could and did.

By the time I came along Pepper Martin's Mudcat Band was just a memory. Dizzy Dean was gone, too, but his rousing rendition of "The Wabash Cannonball" still echoed around the walls of Sportsman's Park. But Stan Musial showed he could play a harmonica almost as well as he could hit—*almost.* Orlando Cepeda had the clubhouse jumping to a Latin beat as "El Birdos" flew high in the mid-'60s. And even though Whitey Herzog is no musical maestro, the clubhouse hijinks starring young John Stuper on the post-game "John Cosell" show was a tribute to his wit and the high spirits of the club that rolled down the stretch to a World Series title.

Oh, it has been a joyride, all right. Early in my first full season, 1954, Stan Musial hit five home runs in a doubleheader, and I thought, does Stan do that *every* Sunday? Not quite, I learned, but damn near. . . . I watched a loose-limbed second baseman, Red Schoendienst, stand out there so relaxed, with his glove off between pitches, that I wondered if he'd forget to put it back on in time. . . . I saw a kid named Wally Moon come up from the minors and cope manfully with the task of filling the shoes of one of St. Louis's all-time favorites, Enos Slaughter.

I watched Eddie Stanky, a proponent of "Billy Ball" when Billy was just a Kid, teach the art of the delayed steal to slowpoke Ray Jablonski, who teamed with Steve Bilko and Rip Repulski as part of the "Polish Falcons" in a good-hit, no-pitch era for the Cardinals. . . . and I saw the McDaniel brothers, Lindy and Von, as they took the town by storm, almost helping the Cardinals to a surprise pennant in 1957. Just as fast as he came up, 18-year-old Von went back down, but Lindy lasted to become an early-day Al Hrabosky or Bruce Sutter in the bullpen.

And when I despaired almost as much as Mr. Busch himself over the long wait for a pennant, the Cardinals came up with an all-time great pitcher, and general manager Bing Devine pulled off one of the all-time great trades. Bob Gibson was already an established star when Devine pulled off the neatest heist this side of the Brinks' job, prying Lou Brock from the Cubs in '64.

If I sound prejudiced on Gibby's behalf, so be it. I've had my favorites, including, obviously, Musial and others too numerous to mention, but Gibson was the most competitive performer I ever saw. His 1.12 earned run average in 1968, incredible for a 300-inning pitcher, is a record that will live as long as Joe DiMaggio's 56-game hitting streak, which I saw end from my bleacher seat in Cleveland in August 1941.

When Gibson set a Series record by striking out 17 Detroit batters in the '68 Series opener, thoroughly outpitching the Tigers' 31-game winner, Denny McLain, I was as thrilled as if I'd done the pitching myself. And I got all choked up at the mike the night in August, 1971, when Gibby threw a no-hit game at Pittsburgh, mindful that this take-charge guy was sure he'd never get the chance to pitch a no-hitter. And I firmly believe that the Cardinals' maddening series of second-place finishes that made the wait for the '82 title seem so long would have been far shorter if Gibson hadn't been hurt in 1973 and 1974. Gibby missed nine or ten starts for us in '73, and we finished just a game and a half out. And if Gibby had been sound, I'm sure Mike Jorgensen wouldn't have homered off him for Montreal in the final game of the '74 season, leaving us just short again, a game and a half behind.

Although I make every effort to report objectively and fairly, I second-guessed a friend that night. Manager Red Schoendienst had the fierce Fu Manchued visage of southpaw Al Hrabosky loose in the pen and ready to face the lefthanded Jorgensen, and I thought Red should have brought him in. After all, a gimpy-kneed Gibson wasn't the Gibby of old. But Red led with his heart, which, as a sentimental Irishman, I find hard to dispute. To Schoendienst, as he was to Johnny Keane back in the '64 Series, Gibson was the meal ticket, the man you wanted with the ball in his hand and the season on the line.

I've let sentiment get in the way occasionally, too, like in 1978 when Vern Rapp told me he thought Ted Simmons was "a loser." Ordinarily, I hear many comments that are best kept to myself, but I couldn't accept that one. To me, Simmons was always one of the toughest players I'd known. He was a great hitter, a deep thinker, and, actually, a man who wanted to win too much. I felt I had to say what I'd heard.

One of the people who spoke to me about Rapp's comment was Mr. Busch. He didn't like it, either. He decided to make a managerial change. The boss doesn't ask my opinion often, fortunately for him, but he did this time, and I gave him an answer. "Hire Ken Boyer," I suggested. In light of Kenny's tragic death last September, I'm glad he got his chance. I only wish he could have lived to see his club win the championship. And if general manager John Claiborne had picked up Bruce Sutter a year earlier, who knows? It might have been Kenny rather than Whitey being doused with the victory champagne.

I've seen a lot of changes in my years of traveling the highways and byways doing baseball, football, and other sports on radio and TV. Not the least of the changes is in the setting of the games themselves. Fans no longer tramp into the battleship-gray parks where they have to crane their necks to see around pillars and posts. Instead they come to a clean, modern stadium like Busch Stadium, a picture-book ballpark built with an eye toward excellent sight-lines as well as physical beauty.

I've seen baseball go from a regional game to a national—make that international—one, from traveling on trains to planes, from grass and dirt to a variety of artificial turfs, from heavy flannel uniforms to form-fitting polyester, from hot-house clubhouses to air-conditioned comfort. And I've seen the players themselves go from unsophisticated country boys who were too often underpaid to better-educated, more independent men who are very often overpaid. Why, now they don't even always talk to the media, by George!

But despite all the changes, the Cardinals' character endures. Whether they're silent and smiling or talkative and angry, whether they're reading *The Sporting News* or *The Wall Street Journal*, they still wear that famous trademark of twin redbirds perched on a golden bat. And when they turn the corner in August, ears pinned back in a race to the wire, they sing a September song that is as enchanting and as exciting as the colorful history of the St. Louis Cardinals.

JACK BUCK
ST. LOUIS
DECEMBER, 1982

The All-Time
Cardinals Leaders

This section provides information on individual all-time single season and lifetime Cardinals leaders. Included for all the various categories are leaders in batting, base running, fielding, and pitching. All the information is self-explanatory with the possible exception of Home Run Percentage, which is the number of home runs per 100 times at bat.

LIFETIME LEADERS

Batting. The top ten men are shown in batting and base-running categories. For averages, a minimum of 1500 at bats is necessary to qualify, except for pinch-hit batting average where 45 pinch-hit at bats is the minimum necessary to qualify. If required by ties, 11 players are shown. If ties would require more than 11 men to be shown, none of the last tied group is included.

Pitching. The top ten pitchers are shown in various categories. For averages, a minimum of 750 innings pitched is necessary to qualify. If required by ties, 11 players are shown. If ties would require more than 11 men to be shown, none of the last tied group is included. For relief pitching categories, the top five are shown.

Fielding. The top five in each fielding category are shown for each position. For averages, the minimum for qualification at each position except pitcher is 350 games played. For pitchers, 750 innings pitched are necessary. If required by ties, six players are shown. If ties would require more than six men to be shown, none of the last tied group is shown.

ALL-TIME SINGLE SEASON LEADERS

Batting. The top ten men are shown in batting and base-running categories. For averages, a player must have a total of at least 3.1 plate appearances for every scheduled game to qualify, except for pinch-hit batting average where 30 pinch-hit at bats are the minimum necessary to qualify. If required by ties, 11 players are shown. If ties would require more than 11 men to be shown, none of the last tied group is included.

Pitching. The top ten pitchers are shown in various categories. For averages, innings pitched must equal or exceed the number of scheduled games in order for a pitcher to qualify. If required by ties, 11 players are shown. If ties would require more than 11 men to be shown, none of the last tied group is included.

Fielding. The top five in each fielding category are shown for each position. For averages, the minimum for qualification at first base, second base, shortstop, third base, and catcher is 100 games played. For outfield, games played must equal or exceed two-thirds of the number of scheduled games. For pitchers, innings pitched must equal or exceed the number of scheduled games. If required by ties, 6 players are shown. If ties would require more than 6 men to be shown, none of the last tied group is shown.

BATTING AVERAGE

1. Rogers Hornsby, 1924 424
2. Rogers Hornsby, 1925 403
3. Jesse Burkett, 1899 402
4. Rogers Hornsby, 1922 401
5. Rogers Hornsby, 1921 397
6. Rogers Hornsby, 1923 384
7. Jesse Burkett, 1901 382
8. Stan Musial, 1948 376
9. Joe Medwick, 1937 374
10. George Watkins, 1930 . . .373

SLUGGING AVERAGE

1. Rogers Hornsby, 1925 756
2. Rogers Hornsby, 1922 722
3. Stan Musial, 1948 702
4. Rogers Hornsby, 1924 696
5. Chick Hafey, 1930 652
6. Joe Medwick, 1937 641
7. Rogers Hornsby, 1921 639
8. Johnny Mize, 1940 636
9. Chick Hafey, 1929 632
10. Jim Bottomley, 1928 628

HITS

1. Rogers Hornsby, 1922 250
2. Joe Medwick, 1937 237
3. Rogers Hornsby, 1921 235
4. Stan Musial, 1948 230
4. Joe Torre, 1971 230
6. Jesse Burkett, 1899 228
6. Jesse Burkett, 1901 228
6. Stan Musial, 1946 228
9. Rogers Hornsby, 1924 227
9. Jim Bottomley, 1925 227

DOUBLES

1. Joe Medwick, 1936 64
2. Joe Medwick, 1937 56
3. Stan Musial, 1953 53
4. Enos Slaughter, 1939 52
5. Stan Musial, 1944 51
6. Stan Musial, 1946 50
7. Joe Medwick, 1939 48
7. Keith Hernandez, 1979 48
7. Stan Musial, 1943 48
10. Chick Hafey, 1929 47
10. Joe Medwick, 1938 47

TRIPLES

1. Perry Werden, 1893 33
2. Roger Connor, 1894 25
2. Tommy Long, 1915 25
4. Duff Cooley, 1895 21
5. Jim Bottomley, 1928 20
5. Rogers Hornsby, 1920 20
5. Stan Musial, 1943 20
5. Stan Musial, 1946 20
9. Garry Templeton, 1979 19

HOME RUNS

1. Johnny Mize, 1940 43
2. Rogers Hornsby, 1922 42
3. Rogers Hornsby, 1925 39
3. Stan Musial, 1948 39
5. Stan Musial, 1949 36
6. Stan Musial, 1954 35
6. Ripper Collins, 1934 35
8. Richie Allen, 1970 34
9. Stan Musial, 1955 33
10. Ken Boyer, 1960 32
10. Stan Musial, 1951 32

RUNS

1. Rogers Hornsby, 1922 . . . 141
2. Jesse Burkett, 1901 139
3. Stan Musial, 1948 135
4. Rogers Hornsby, 1925 . . . 133
5. Joe Medwick, 1935 132
6. Rogers Hornsby, 1921 . . . 131
7. Stan Musial, 1949 128
7. Taylor Douthit, 1929 128
9. Stan Musial, 1953 127
10. Lou Brock, 1971 126

RUNS BATTED IN

1. Joe Medwick, 1937 154
2. Rogers Hornsby, 1922 . . . 152
3. Rogers Hornsby, 1925 . . . 143
4. Joe Medwick, 1936 138
5. Jim Bottomley, 1929 137
5. Johnny Mize, 1940 137
5. Joe Torre, 1971 137
8. Jim Bottomley, 1928 136
9. Stan Musial, 1948 131
10. Enos Slaughter, 1946 130

STOLEN BASES

1. Lou Brock, 1974 118
2. Lou Brock, 1966 74
3. Lou Brock, 1973 70
4. Lonnie Smith, 1982 68
5. Lou Brock, 1971 64
6. Lou Brock, 1972 63
6. Lou Brock, 1965 63
8. Lou Brock, 1968 62
9. Lou Brock, 1976 56
9. Lou Brock, 1975 56

RUNS PER GAME

1. Jesse Burkett, 1901 98
2. Rogers Hornsby, 1925 96
3. Ray Blades, 1925 92
4. Rogers Hornsby, 1922 92
5. Frankie Frisch, 1930 91
6. Chick Hafey, 1930 90
7. Pepper Martin, 1935 90
8. Stan Musial, 1948 87
9. Tom Brown, 1895 87
10. Tommy Dowd, 1893 86

RUNS BATTED IN PER GAME

1. Rogers Hornsby, 1925 . . . 1.04
2. Joe Medwick, 1937 99
3. Rogers Hornsby, 1922 99
4. Jim Bottomley, 1929 94
5. Chick Hafey, 1929 93
6. Jim Bottomley, 1928 91
7. Chick Hafey, 1930 89
8. Joe Medwick, 1936 89
9. Johnny Mize, 1940 88
10. Frankie Frisch, 1930 86

HOME RUN PERCENTAGE

1. Rogers Hornsby, 1925 . . . 7.7
2. Johnny Mize, 1940 . . . . . . 7.4
3. Richie Allen, 1970 . . . . . . 7.4
4. Rogers Hornsby, 1922 . . . 6.7
5. Stan Musial, 1948 . . . . . . 6.4
6. Stan Musial, 1954 . . . . . . 5.9
7. Stan Musial, 1949 . . . . . . 5.9
8. Stan Musial, 1955 . . . . . . 5.9
9. Ripper Collins, 1934 . . . . . 5.8
10. Chick Hafey, 1930 . . . . . . 5.8

AT BATS

1. Lou Brock, 1967 689
2. Curt Flood, 1964 679
3. Garry Templeton, 1979 672
4. Taylor Douthit, 1930 664
5. Lou Brock, 1970 664
6. Curt Flood, 1963 662
7. Lou Brock, 1968 660
8. Red Schoendienst, 1947 .. 659
9. Bill White, 1963 658
10. Lou Brock, 1969 655

EXTRA BASE HITS

1. Stan Musial, 1948 103
2. Rogers Hornsby, 1922 102
3. Joe Medwick, 1937 97
4. Joe Medwick, 1936 95
5. Jim Bottomley, 1928 93
6. Stan Musial, 1953 92
7. Rogers Hornsby, 1925 90
8. Stan Musial, 1949 90
9. Johnny Mize, 1940 87
9. Ripper Collins, 1934 87

TOTAL BASES

1. Rogers Hornsby, 1922 450
2. Stan Musial, 1948 429
3. Joe Medwick, 1937 406
4. Stan Musial, 1949 382
5. Rogers Hornsby, 1925 .. 381
6. Rogers Hornsby, 1921 .. 378
7. Rogers Hornsby, 1924 373
8. Ripper Collins, 1934 369
9. Johnny Mize, 1940 368
10. Joe Medwick, 1936 367

BASES ON BALLS

1. John Crooks, 1892 136
2. John Crooks, 1893 121
3. Miller Huggins, 1910 116
4. Stan Musial, 1949 107
5. Miller Huggins, 1914 105
5. Stan Musial, 1953 105
7. Stan Musial, 1954 103
8. Keith Hernandez, 1982 100
9. Stan Musial, 1951 98

STRIKEOUTS

1. Lou Brock, 1966 134
2. Steve Bilko, 1953 125
3. Lou Brock, 1968 124
4. Hector Cruz, 1976 119
5. Richie Allen, 1970 118
6. Lou Brock, 1965 116
7. Lou Brock, 1969 115
8. Mike Shannon, 1968 114
9. Lou Brock, 1973 112
10. Lou Brock, 1967 109

HIGHEST STRIKEOUT AVERAGE

1. Richie Allen, 1970 .. ... .257
2. Hector Cruz, 1976 .... .226
3. Steve Bilko, 1953 ...... .219
4. Joe Orengo, 1940 ...... .217
5. Lou Brock, 1966 ...... .208
6. George Altman, 1963 ... ... .200
7. Mike Shannon, 1968 198
8. Joe Hague, 1970 ...... .193
9. Miller Huggins, 1915 .. .193
10. Lou Brock, 1968 .... .188

BB AVERAGE

1. John Crooks, 1892 .. .... .234
2. John Crooks, 1893 .... .213
3. John McGraw, 1900 .. .203
4. Miller Huggins, 1913 . .. .192
5. Tommy Glaviano, 1950 .. .180
6. Miller Huggins, 1910 ... .175
7. Miller Huggins, 1915 .. .173
8. Miller Huggins, 1914 ... .171
9. Miller Huggins, 1912 168
10. Joe Cunningham, 1959 .. .161

PINCH HITS

1. Vic Davalillo, 1970 24
2. Peanuts Lowrey, 1953 22
2. Red Schoendienst, 1962 .. 22
4. Frenchy Bordagaray, 1938 . 20
4. Joe Frazier, 1954 20
6. George Crowe, 1959 17
7. Red Schoendienst, 1961 .. 16
8. Bob Skinner, 1965 15
8. George Crowe, 1960 15
10. Bob Burda, 1971 14

PINCH HIT AT BATS

1. Vic Davalillo, 1970 73
2. Red Schoendienst, 1962 .. 72
3. George Crowe, 1959 63
4. Joe Frazier, 1954 62
5. George Crowe, 1960 61
6. Peanuts Lowrey, 1953 59
7. Art Butler, 1916 54
8. Peanuts Lowrey, 1954 53
9. Bob Burda, 1971 48
9. Red Schoendienst, 1961 .. . 48

PINCH HIT BATTING AVERAGE

1. Frenchy Bordagaray, 1938 .465
2. Peanuts Lowrey, 1953 . . .373
3. Ron Fairly, 1975 .... .343
4. Fred Whitfield, 1962 . . .333
4. Red Schoendienst, 1961 .333
6. Vic Davalillo, 1970 ..... .329
7. Joe Frazier, 1954 .... .323
8. Bob Skinner, 1965 .. .... .319
9. Red Schoendienst, 1962 .306
10. Bobby Tolan, 1967 .. ... .303

GAMES

1. Mark Littell, 1978   72
2. Bruce Sutter, 1982   70
3. Al Hrabosky, 1976   68
4. Don Hood, 1980   66
4. Mike Garman, 1975   66
6. Lindy McDaniel, 1960   65
6. Diego Segui, 1973   65
6. Al Hrabosky, 1975   65
6. Al Hrabosky, 1974   65
6. Al Hrabosky, 1977   65
6. Ron Willis, 1967   65

WINS

1. Dizzy Dean, 1934   30
2. Dizzy Dean, 1935   28
3. Ted Breitenstein, 1894   27
4. Cy Young, 1899   26
5. Jesse Haines, 1927   24
5. Dizzy Dean, 1936   24
7. Bob Gibson, 1970   23
7. Jack Harper, 1901   23
7. Bob Harmon, 1911   23
7. Jack Powell, 1899   23

LOSSES

1. Red Donahue, 1897   33
2. Ted Breitenstein, 1895   30
3. Bill Hart, 1896   29
3. Jack Taylor, 1898   29
5. Bill Hart, 1897   27
5. Willie Sudhoff, 1898   27
7. Ted Breitenstein, 1896   26
7. Pink Hawley, 1894   26

COMPLETE GAMES

1. Ted Breitenstein, 1895   46
1. Ted Breitenstein, 1894   46
3. Kid Gleason, 1892   43
4. Jack Taylor, 1898   42
5. Cy Young, 1899   40
5. Jack Powell, 1899   40
7. Jack Taylor, 1904   39
8. Ted Breitenstein, 1893   38
8. Red Donahue, 1897   38

WINNING PERCENTAGE

1. Dizzy Dean, 1934 811
2. Ted Wilks, 1944 810
3. Johnny Beazley, 1942 778
3. Harry Brecheen, 1945 778
5. Bill Doak, 1914 769
6. Bob Gibson, 1970 767
7. Jesse Haines, 1926 765
8. Harry Brecheen, 1944 762
8. George Munger, 1947 762
10. Mort Cooper, 1944 759
10. Mort Cooper, 1942 759

EARNED RUN AVERAGE

1. Bob Gibson, 1968 . . . .   1.12
2. Bill Doak, 1914 . . . .   1.72
3. Howie Pollet, 1943 . . . .   1.75
4. Mort Cooper, 1942 . . . .   1.78
5. Max Lanier, 1943 . . . .   1.90
6. Kid Nichols, 1904 . . . .   2.02
7. Bugs Raymond, 1908 . . . . . .   2.03
8. Ed Karger, 1907 . . . .   2.03
9. Mike O'Neill, 1904 . . . .   2.09
10. Howie Pollet, 1946 . . . .   2.10

INNINGS PITCHED

1. Ted Breitenstein, 1894   447
2. Ted Breitenstein, 1895   430
3. Kid Gleason, 1892   400
4. Jack Taylor, 1898   397
5. Pink Hawley, 1894   393
6. Ted Breitenstein, 1893   383
7. Kid Gleason, 1893   380
8. Jack Powell, 1899   373
9. Cy Young, 1899   369
10. Stoney McGlynn, 1907   352

STRIKEOUTS

1. Bob Gibson, 1970   274
2. Bob Gibson, 1965   270
3. Bob Gibson, 1969   269
4. Bob Gibson, 1968   268
5. Bob Gibson, 1964   245
6. Sam Jones, 1958   225
6. Bob Gibson, 1966   225
8. Steve Carlton, 1969   210
9. Bob Gibson, 1962   208
9. Bob Gibson, 1972   208

BASES ON BALLS

1. Ted Breitenstein, 1894   191
2. Kid Gleason, 1893   187
3. Bob Harmon, 1911   181
4. Ted Breitenstein, 1895   178
5. Ted Breitenstein, 1893   156
6. Kid Gleason, 1892   151
7. Pink Hawley, 1894   149
8. Ted Breitenstein, 1892   148
8. Bill Hart, 1897   148
10. Bill Hart, 1896 141

HITS PER 9 INNINGS

1. Bob Gibson, 1968 . . . .   5.85
2. Howie Pollet, 1943 . . . . . .   6.31
3. Fred Beebe, 1906 . . . .   6.44
4. Bugs Raymond, 1908 . .   6.55
5. Dick Hughes, 1967 . . . .   6.64
6. Mort Cooper, 1942 . . .   6.69
7. Bob Gibson, 1962 . . . .   6.70
8. Bob Gibson, 1966 . . . .   6.74
9. Bill Doak, 1914 . . . .   6.79
10. Ernie Broglio, 1960 . . . . . .   6.84

STRIKEOUTS PER 9 INNINGS

1. Bob Gibson, 1970 . . . .   8.39
2. Bob Gibson, 1965 . . . .   8.13
3. Sam Jones, 1958 . . . . . .   8.10
4. Bob Gibson, 1962 . . . .   8.01
5. Steve Carlton, 1969 . . . . . .   8.01
6. Bob Gibson, 1968 . . . .   7.92
7. Steve Carlton, 1967 . . . . . .   7.83
8. Bob Gibson, 1969 . . . .   7.71
9. Bob Gibson, 1964 . . . .   7.67
10. Sam Jones, 1957 . . . .   7.59

BASES ON BALLS PER 9 INNINGS

1. Cy Young, 1900 . . . .   1.01
2. Cy Young, 1899 . . . .   1.07
3. Grover Alexander, 1927 .   1.28
4. Jack Powell, 1901 . . . .   1.33
5. Nig Cuppy, 1899 . . . .   1.36
6. Grover Alexander, 1928 .   1.37
7. Bob Forsch, 1980 . . . .   1.38
8. Red Barrett, 1945 . . . .   1.39
9. Syl Johnson, 1931 . . . .   1.40
10. Kid Nichols, 1904 . . . .   1.42

SHUTOUTS

1. Bob Gibson, 1968   13
2. Mort Cooper, 1942   10
3. Harry Brecheen, 1948   7
3. Mort Cooper, 1944   7
3. Dizzy Dean, 1934   7
3. Bill Doak, 1914   7

RELIEF GAMES

1. Mark Littell, 1978   70
1. Bruce Sutter, 1982   70
3. Al Hrabosky, 1976   68
4. Mike Garman, 1975   66

RELIEF WINS

1. Al Hrabosky, 1975   13
1. Lindy McDaniel, 1959   13
3. Lindy McDaniel, 1960   12
4. Eddie Yuhas, 1952   11
5. Ted Wilks, 1949   10
5. Lindy McDaniel, 1961   10

SAVES

1. Bruce Sutter, 1982   36
2. Lindy McDaniel, 1960   26
3. Bruce Sutter, 1981   25
4. Al Hrabosky, 1975   22
5. Al Brazle, 1953   18

RELIEF WINS PLUS SAVES

1. Bruce Sutter, 1982   45
2. Lindy McDaniel, 1960   38
3. Al Hrabosky, 1975   35
4. Lindy McDaniel, 1959   28
4. Bruce Sutter, 1981   28

RELIEF WINNING PERCENTAGE

1. Eddie Yuhas, 1952 917
2. Al Hrabosky, 1974 889
3. Lindy McDaniel, 1960 857
4. Al Hrabosky, 1975 813

PUTOUTS	ASSISTS	FIELDING AVERAGE

1B

1. Jim Bottomley, 1927 1656	1. Keith Hernandez, 1979 146	1. Keith Hernandez, 1981 997
2. Ed Konetchy, 1911 1652	2. Keith Hernandez, 1982 135	2. Bill White, 1964 996
3. Ed Konetchy, 1908 1610	3. Steve Bilko, 1953 124	3. Joe Torre, 1969 996
4. Jim Bottomley, 1926 1607	4. Ed Konetchy, 1908 122	4. Ed Konetchy, 1913 995
5. Keith Hernandez, 1982 1586	5. Keith Hernandez, 1980 115	5. Keith Hernandez, 1979 . . .995

2B

1. Red Schoendienst, 1949 399	1. Frankie Frisch, 1927 641	1. Tommy Herr, 1981 992
1. Red Schoendienst, 1952 399	2. Rogers Hornsby, 1920 524	2. Red Schoendienst, 1951 . .990
3. Rogers Hornsby, 1922 398	3. Rogers Hornsby, 1924 517	3. Tommy Herr, 1982 987
3. Emil Verban, 1945 398	4. Don Blasingame, 1957 512	4. Red Schoendienst, 1949 . .987
5. Frankie Frisch, 1927 396	5. Rogers Hornsby, 1921 477	5. Red Schoendienst, 1955 . .985
	5. Red Schoendienst, 1954 . . 477	

3B

1. Lave Cross, 1898 215	1. Lave Cross, 1898 351	1. Ken Reitz, 1977 980
2. Bobby Byrne, 1907 211	2. Ken Boyer, 1958 350	2. Ken Reitz, 1980 979
3. John Crooks, 1893 210	3. Bobby Byrne, 1907 347	3. Don Gutteridge, 1937 978
4. Whitey Kurowski, 1944 188	4. Ken Boyer, 1961 346	4. Billy Johnson, 1951 976
5. Bobby Byrne, 1908 183	5. Ken Boyer, 1964 337	5. Ken Reitz, 1974 974

SS

1. Doc Lavan, 1921 382	1. Tommy Thevenow, 1926 597	1. Ozzie Smith, 1982 984
2. Tommy Thevenow, 1926 371	2. Bobby Wallace, 1901 542	2. Dal Maxvill, 1970 982
3. Charley Gelbert, 1929 338	3. Doc Lavan, 1921 540	3. Marty Marion, 1947 981
4. Marty Marion, 1947 329	4. Ozzie Smith, 1982 535	4. Dal Maxvill, 1971 979
	5. Rogers Hornsby, 1917 527	5. Marty Marion, 1950 978

OF

1. Taylor Douthit, 1928 547	1. John Heidrick, 1899 34	1. Curt Flood, 1966 . . . .1.000
2. Taylor Douthit, 1929 442	1. Owen Wilson, 1914 34	2. Tony Scott, 1980 997
3. Taylor Douthit, 1926 440	3. Patsy Donovan, 1902 30	3. Johnny Hopp, 1944 997
4. Tony Scott, 1979 427	4. Rube Ellis, 1909 28	4. Ken Boyer, 1957 996
5. Taylor Douthit, 1930 425	5. Tommy Dowd, 1893 27	5. Enos Slaughter, 1953 996

C

1. Tim McCarver, 1969 925	1. Frank Snyder, 1915 204	1. Tim McCarver, 1967 997
2. Ted Simmons, 1973 888	2. Ivy Wingo, 1912 148	2. Bill Sarni, 1954 996
3. Ted Simmons, 1972 842	3. Doc Marshall, 1907 142	3. Del Rice, 1948 996
4. Tim McCarver, 1966 841	4. Mike Gonzalez, 1916 136	4. Ken O'Dea, 1945 995
5. Tim McCarver, 1967 819	5. Jack O'Neill, 1903 135	5. Tim McCarver, 1965 995

P

1. Ted Breitenstein, 1895 45	1. Jack Taylor, 1898 144	
2. Ted Breitenstein, 1893 42	2. Cy Young, 1899 117	
2. Ted Breitenstein, 1894 42	3. Willie Sudhoff, 1898 114	
4. Ted Breitenstein, 1896 34	4. Jack Taylor, 1904 109	
5. Ernie Broglio, 1963 30	5. Bill Doak, 1915 108	
5. Kid Gleason, 1893 30	5. Bugs Raymond, 1908 108	

TOTAL CHANCES	TOTAL CHANCES PER GAME	DOUBLE PLAYS

1B

TOTAL CHANCES	TOTAL CHANCES PER GAME	DOUBLE PLAYS
1. Ed Konetchy, 1908 1756	1. Gene Paulette, 1917... ...12.7	1. Jim Bottomley, 1927.... ...149
2. Jim Bottomley, 1927... ... 1746	2. Gene Paulette, 1918... ...12.1	2. Keith Hernandez, 1980 146
3. Ed Konetchy, 1911 1739	3. Keith Hernandez, 1981... 11.7	2. Keith Hernandez, 1977 146
4. Keith Hernandez, 1982 1732	4. Jim Bottomley, 1927..... 11.5	4. Steve Bilko, 1953......... 145
5. Ed Konetchy, 1909 1707	5. Jake Beckley, 1905.... ... 11.5	4. Keith Hernandez, 1979 145

2B

TOTAL CHANCES	TOTAL CHANCES PER GAME	DOUBLE PLAYS
1. Frankie Frisch, 1927... ... 1059	1. Frankie Frisch, 1927... ... 6.9	1. Red Schoendienst, 1954... ...137
2. Rogers Hornsby, 1920... 901	2. Joe Quinn, 1894...... .... 6.7	2. Don Blasingame, 1957... ...128
3. Rogers Hornsby, 1922... 901	3. Frankie Frisch, 1930..... 6.5	3. Red Schoendienst, 1950... 124
4. Don Blasingame, 1957.. 898	4. John Farrell, 1902 .... 6.4	4. Red Schoendienst, 1951 113
5. Red Schoendienst, 1954.. ... 889	5. Frankie Frisch, 1928... ... 6.3	

3B

TOTAL CHANCES	TOTAL CHANCES PER GAME	DOUBLE PLAYS
1. Bobby Byrne, 1907 607	1. John Crooks, 1893 .... 4.4	1. Ken Boyer, 1958..... 41
2. Lave Cross, 1898 599	2. Lave Cross, 1899 .... 4.4	2. Les Bell, 1925 39
3. John Crooks, 1893 546	3. Bobby Byrne, 1909 .... 4.3	3. Ken Boyer, 1960.......... 37
4. Ken Boyer, 1958...... 526	4. Bobby Byrne, 1907 .... 4.1	3. Ken Boyer, 1956.......... 37
5. Mike Mowrey, 1910. 509	5. Lave Cross, 1898 .... 4.0	5. Ken Reitz, 1977......... .. 35

SS

TOTAL CHANCES	TOTAL CHANCES PER GAME	DOUBLE PLAYS
1. Tommy Thevenow, 1926.. ...1013	1. Bobby Wallace, 1901 .... 7.0	1. Mike Tyson, 1974......... ...108
2. Doc Lavan, 1921.......... 971	2. Monte Cross, 1897 ...... 7.0	1. Garry Templeton, 1978... .. 108
3. Bobby Wallace, 1901 934	3. Bobby Wallace, 1899 ...... 6.8	3. Alvin Dark, 1957......... 105
4. Monte Cross, 1897 913	4. Bobby Wallace, 1900 ...... 6.6	3. Marty Marion, 1946 105
5. Charley Gelbert, 1929... ... 883	5. Tommy Thevenow, 1926.. 6.5	

OF

TOTAL CHANCES	TOTAL CHANCES PER GAME	DOUBLE PLAYS
1. Taylor Douthit, 1928.... ... 566	1. Taylor Douthit, 1928... .. 3.7	1. Owen Wilson, 1914........ 11
2. Taylor Douthit, 1926.... ... 474	2. Taylor Douthit, 1926.... .. 3.4	2. Spike Shannon, 1904...... 10
3. Taylor Douthit, 1929.... ... 462	3. Taylor Douthit, 1927.... .. 3.4	2. Steve Evans, 1909......... 10
4. Taylor Douthit, 1930.... ... 449	4. Terry Moore, 1936......... 3.3	4. Tommy Dowd, 1893 9
5. Tony Scott, 1979 448	5. Terry Moore, 1935......... 3.2	4. Rube Ellis, 1909 9

C

TOTAL CHANCES	TOTAL CHANCES PER GAME	DOUBLE PLAYS
1. Tim McCarver, 1969.... ... 1005	1. Tim McCarver, 1969... .... 7.4	1. Mike Gonzalez, 1918....... 17
2. Ted Simmons, 1973 975	2. Tim McCarver, 1968... .. 7.1	2. Jimmie Wilson, 1929 16
3. Ted Simmons, 1972 928	3. Ted Simmons, 1972... ... 6.9	3. Jimmie Wilson, 1931 15
4. Tim McCarver, 1966...... 910	4. Tim McCarver, 1967... ... 6.8	3. Mike Gonzalez, 1924 15
5. Tim McCarver, 1967.... ... 889	5. Joe Torre, 1970.... .... 6.8	

P

TOTAL CHANCES	TOTAL CHANCES PER GAME	DOUBLE PLAYS
1. Jack Taylor, 1898...... 184	1. Wish Egan, 1905 .... 3.9	1. Bill Hallahan, 1932 10
2. Ted Breitenstein, 1895... .. 157	2. Chappie McFarland, 1904 3.9	2. Howie Pollet, 1946.... 9
3. Bill Hart, 1896........... 143	3. Jack Taylor, 1898...... .... 3.7	3. John Denny, 1978 8
4. Willie Sudhoff, 1898 141	4. Ed Karger, 1906.... .... 3.6	
5. Cy Young, 1899 139	5. Mike O'Neill, 1904.... ... 3.6	

PUTOUTS PER GAME		ASSISTS PER GAME	
1B			
1. Gene Paulette, 1917	12.2	1. Keith Hernandez, 1976	1.0
2. Gene Paulette, 1918	11.3	2. Keith Hernandez, 1979	.9
3. Jim Bottomley, 1927	10.9	3. Keith Hernandez, 1981	.9
4. Jake Beckley, 1905	10.8	4. Stan Musial, 1956	.9
5. Keith Hernandez, 1981	10.8	5. Keith Hernandez, 1982	.9
2B			
1. Joe Quinn, 1894	3.2	1. Frankie Frisch, 1927	4.2
2. Red Schoendienst, 1949	2.9	2. Frankie Frisch, 1930	3.8
3. Frankie Frisch, 1933	2.8	3. Tommy Herr, 1981	3.6
4. Red Schoendienst, 1952	2.8	4. Rogers Hornsby, 1924	3.6
5. John Crooks, 1892	2.8	5. John Farrell, 1902	3.6
3B			
1. John Crooks, 1893	1.7	1. Lave Cross, 1899	2.7
2. Bobby Byrne, 1909	1.6	2. Billy Johnson, 1951	2.5
3. Lave Cross, 1899	1.5	3. Doug Baird, 1917	2.5
4. Bobby Byrne, 1908	1.5	4. Ken Boyer, 1958	2.4
5. Jimmy Burke, 1903	1.5	5. Ken Oberkfell, 1981	2.4
SS			
1. Bobby Wallace, 1900	2.6	1. Bobby Wallace, 1901	4.0
2. Doc Lavan, 1921	2.5	2. Rogers Hornsby, 1918	4.0
3. Monte Cross, 1897	2.5	3. Garry Templeton, 1980	3.9
4. Bobby Wallace, 1901	2.4	4. Monte Cross, 1897	3.9
5. Monte Cross, 1896	2.4	5. Bobby Wallace, 1899	3.9
OF			
1. Taylor Douthit, 1928	3.6	1. Patsy Donovan, 1902	.2
2. Taylor Douthit, 1926	3.2	2. John Heidrick, 1899	.2
3. Taylor Douthit, 1927	3.2	3. Owen Wilson, 1914	.2
4. Terry Moore, 1936	3.1	4. Dick Harley, 1897	.2
5. Terry Moore, 1935	3.0	5. Frank Shugart, 1894	.2
C			
1. Tim McCarver, 1969	6.8	1. Jack O'Neill, 1903	1.8
2. Tim McCarver, 1968	6.5	2. Doc Marshall, 1907	1.7
3. Joe Torre, 1970	6.3	3. Ivy Wingo, 1912	1.6
4. Tim McCarver, 1967	6.3	4. Ed McFarland, 1896	1.5
5. Ted Simmons, 1972	6.2	5. Mike Gonzalez, 1916	1.5
P			
1. Ted Breitenstein, 1893	.9	1. Chappie McFarland, 1904	3.3
2. Murry Dickson, 1956	.9	2. Wish Egan, 1905	3.1
3. Ted Breitenstein, 1895	.8	3. Jack Taylor, 1906	3.0
4. John Denny, 1976	.8	4. Jack Taylor, 1898	2.9
5. Bob Gibson, 1967	.8	5. Bill Doak, 1915	2.8

GAMES

1. Stan Musial........ 3026
2. Lou Brock 2289
3. Enos Slaughter 1820
4. Red Schoendienst 1795
5. Curt Flood 1738
6. Ken Boyer 1667
7. Rogers Hornsby 1580
8. Julian Javier 1578
9. Ted Simmons........ 1564
10. Marty Marion........ 1502

AT BATS

1. Stan Musial........ 10972
2. Lou Brock 9125
3. Red Schoendienst 6841
4. Enos Slaughter 6775
5. Ken Boyer 6334
6. Curt Flood 6318
7. Rogers Hornsby 5881
8. Ted Simmons........ 5725
9. Julian Javier........ 5631
10. Jim Bottomley........ 5314

HITS

1. Stan Musial........ 3630
2. Lou Brock 2713
3. Rogers Hornsby 2110
4. Enos Slaughter 2064
5. Red Schoendienst 1980
6. Ken Boyer 1855
7. Curt Flood 1853
8. Jim Bottomley........ 1727
9. Ted Simmons........ 1704
10. Joe Medwick 1590

DOUBLES

1. Stan Musial........ 725
2. Lou Brock 434
3. Joe Medwick 377
4. Rogers Hornsby 367
5. Enos Slaughter 366
6. Red Schoendienst 352
7. Jim Bottomley........ 344
8. Ted Simmons........ 332
9. Frankie Frisch 286
10. Curt Flood 271

TRIPLES

1. Stan Musial........ 177
2. Rogers Hornsby 143
3. Enos Slaughter 135
4. Lou Brock 121
5. Jim Bottomley........ 119
6. Ed Konetchy........ 93
7. Joe Medwick 81
8. Pepper Martin 75
9. Garry Templeton 69
10. Johnny Mize........ 66

HOME RUNS

1. Stan Musial........ 475
2. Ken Boyer 255
3. Rogers Hornsby 193
4. Jim Bottomley........ 181
5. Ted Simmons........ 172
6. Johnny Mize........ 158
7. Joe Medwick 152
8. Enos Slaughter 146
9. Bill White 140
10. Lou Brock 129

BATTING AVERAGE

1. Jesse Burkett........ .382
2. Rogers Hornsby .... .359
3. Johnny Mize........ .336
4. Joe Medwick .... .335
5. Stan Musial........ .331
6. Chick Hafey .... .326
7. Jim Bottomley........ .325
8. Jack Fournier........ .317
9. Patsy Donovan .... .314
10. Frankie Frisch .... .312

SLUGGING AVERAGE

1. Johnny Mize........ .600
2. Rogers Hornsby ...... .568
3. Chick Hafey .... .568
4. Stan Musial........ .559
5. Joe Medwick .... .545
6. Jim Bottomley........ .537
7. Ripper Collins .... .517
8. Jesse Burkett........ .499
9. George Hendrick .... .477
10. Ken Boyer .... .475

HOME RUN PERCENTAGE

1. Johnny Mize........ 5.1
2. Stan Musial........ 4.3
3. Chick Hafey 4.3
4. George Hendrick 4.0
5. Ken Boyer 4.0
6. Ripper Collins 3.8
7. Orlando Cepeda 3.6
8. Jim Bottomley........ 3.4
9. Bill White 3.4
10. Whitey Kurowski........ 3.3

EXTRA BASE HITS

1. Stan Musial........ 1377
2. Rogers Hornsby 703
3. Lou Brock 684
4. Enos Slaughter 647
5. Jim Bottomley........ 644
6. Joe Medwick 610
7. Ken Boyer 585
8. Ted Simmons........ 541
9. Red Schoendienst 482
10. Johnny Mize........ 442

TOTAL BASES

1. Stan Musial........ 6134
2. Lou Brock 3776
3. Rogers Hornsby 3342
4. Enos Slaughter 3138
5. Ken Boyer 3011
6. Jim Bottomley........ 2852
7. Red Schoendienst 2657
8. Ted Simmons........ 2626
9. Joe Medwick 2585
10. Curt Flood 2464

STOLEN BASES

1. Lou Brock 888
2. Jack Smith 203
3. Frankie Frisch 195
4. Miller Huggins 174
5. Ed Konetchy........ 151
6. Pepper Martin 146
7. Garry Templeton 138
8. Julian Javier........ 134
9. Patsy Donovan 132
10. Rogers Hornsby 118

RUNS

1. Stan Musial..............1949
2. Lou Brock..............1427
3. Rogers Hornsby..........1089
4. Enos Slaughter..........1071
5. Red Schoendienst........1025
6. Ken Boyer...............988
7. Jim Bottomley...........921
8. Curt Flood.............845
9. Frankie Frisch.........831
10. Joe Medwick............811

RUNS BATTED IN

1. Stan Musial.............1951
2. Enos Slaughter..........1148
3. Jim Bottomley..........1105
4. Rogers Hornsby.........1072
5. Ken Boyer..............1001
6. Ted Simmons............929
7. Joe Medwick............923
8. Lou Brock..............814
9. Frankie Frisch.........720
10. Johnny Mize............653

RUNS PER GAME

1. Tommy Dowd.............71
2. Rogers Hornsby.........69
3. Taylor Douthit.........69
4. Chick Hafey...........67
5. Joe Medwick...........67
6. Jim Bottomley.........66
7. Stan Musial...........64
8. Johnny Mize...........64
9. Pepper Martin.........64
10. Frankie Frisch.......63

RUNS BATTED IN PER GAME

1. Jim Bottomley..........79
2. Johnny Mize...........76
3. Chick Hafey...........76
4. Joe Medwick...........76
5. Rogers Hornsby........68
6. Ripper Collins........66
7. George Hendrick.......66
8. Stan Musial...........64
9. Enos Slaughter........63
10. Joe Torre............61

BASES ON BALLS

1. Stan Musial.............1599
2. Enos Slaughter.........839
3. Lou Brock..............681
4. Rogers Hornsby.........660
5. Ken Boyer..............631
6. Ted Simmons...........624
7. Miller Huggins........571
8. Keith Hernandez.......561
9. Jim Bottomley.........509
10. Red Schoendienst......497

BB AVERAGE

1. Miller Huggins........172
2. Joe Cunningham........149
3. Solly Hemus...........147
4. Stan Musial...........127
5. Keith Hernandez.......127
6. Ray Sanders..........126
7. Ray Blades...........121
8. Johnny Mize..........120
9. Mike Mowrey..........110
10. Enos Slaughter.......110

STRIKEOUTS

1. Lou Brock..............1469
2. Ken Boyer..............859
3. Julian Javier.........801
4. Stan Musial...........696
5. Curt Flood............606
6. Bill White............601
7. Mike Shannon..........525
8. Marty Marion..........520
9. Keith Hernandez.......506
10. Rogers Hornsby.......480

HIGHEST STRIKEOUT AVERAGE

1. Mike Shannon...........189
2. Lou Brock.............161
3. Tony Scott............160
4. Dal Maxvill...........152
5. Orlando Cepeda........148
6. Bill White...........144
7. Julian Javier........142
8. Joe Torre............138
9. Ken Boyer............136
10. Mike Tyson...........133

LOWEST STRIKEOUT AVERAGE

1. Joe Quinn.............015
2. Frankie Frisch.......026
3. Jimmy Brown..........032
4. Red Schoendienst.....042
5. Milt Stock...........043
6. Tommy Dowd...........050
7. Lee Magee...........057
8. Jimmie Wilson........057
9. Specs Toporcer.......059
10. Walker Cooper.......061

PINCH HITS

1. Red Schoendienst.......53
2. Peanuts Lowrey........47
3. Dane Iorg.............40
4. Stan Musial...........35
5. Vic Davalillo.........33
6. George Crowe..........33
7. Tim McCarver..........31
8. Lou Brock............29
9. Bob Skinner..........28
10. Luis Melendez........27

PH BATTING AVERAGE

1. Roger Freed...........329
2. Red Schoendienst......312
3. Vic Davalillo.........308
4. Specs Toporcer........298
5. Peanuts Lowrey........296
6. Charlie James.........292
7. Lou Brock............290
8. Debs Garms...........289
9. Joe Cunningham.......287
10. Joe Schultz.........280

GAMES

1. Jesse Haines 554
2. Bob Gibson 528
3. Bill Sherdel 465
4. Al Brazle 441
5. Bill Doak 376
6. Lindy McDaniel 336
7. Larry Jackson 330
8. Al Hrabosky 329
9. Slim Sallee 316
10. Gerry Staley 301

WINS

1. Bob Gibson 251
2. Jesse Haines 210
3. Bill Sherdel 153
4. Bill Doak 145
5. Dizzy Dean 134
6. Harry Brecheen 127
7. Bob Forsch 108
8. Mort Cooper 105
8. Slim Sallee 105
10. Max Lanier 101
10. Larry Jackson 101

LOSSES

1. Bob Gibson 174
2. Jesse Haines 158
3. Bill Doak 136
4. Bill Sherdel 131
5. Ted Breitenstein 124
6. Slim Sallee 107
7. Larry Jackson 86
8. Bob Forsch 83
9. Bob Harmon 81
10. Harry Brecheen 79

COMPLETE GAMES

1. Bob Gibson 255
2. Jesse Haines 209
3. Ted Breitenstein 196
4. Bill Sherdel 144
4. Bill Doak 144
6. Dizzy Dean 141
7. Slim Sallee 122
7. Harry Brecheen 122
9. Mort Cooper 105
10. Jack Powell 101

WINNING PERCENTAGE

1. Mort Cooper .... .677
2. Dizzy Dean .... .641
3. Lon Warneke .... .629
4. Grover Alexander ... .618
5. Harry Brecheen ..... .617
6. Al Brazle .... .602
7. George Munger ...... .602
8. Howie Pollet ...... .599
9. Max Lanier .... .594
10. Bob Gibson .... .591

EARNED RUN AVERAGE

1. Slim Sallee 2.67
2. Jack Taylor 2.67
3. Johnny Lush 2.74
4. Red Ames 2.74
5. Mort Cooper 2.77
6. Fred Beebe 2.79
7. Max Lanier 2.84
8. Harry Brecheen 2.91
9. Bob Gibson 2.91
10. Bill Doak 2.93

INNINGS PITCHED

1. Bob Gibson 3885
2. Jesse Haines 3204
3. Bill Sherdel 2450
4. Bill Doak 2387
5. Slim Sallee 1902
6. Ted Breitenstein 1897
7. Harry Brecheen 1790
8. Bob Forsch 1766
9. Dizzy Dean 1736
10. Larry Jackson 1672

STRIKEOUTS

1. Bob Gibson 3117
2. Dizzy Dean 1087
3. Jesse Haines 979
4. Steve Carlton 951
5. Bill Doak 938
6. Larry Jackson 899
7. Harry Brecheen 857
8. Vinegar Bend Mizell . 789
9. Bill Hallahan 784
10. Bill Sherdel 779

BASES ON BALLS

1. Bob Gibson 1336
2. Jesse Haines 870
3. Ted Breitenstein 825
4. Bill Doak 740
5. Bill Hallahan 651
6. Bill Sherdel 595
7. Bob Harmon 594
8. Vinegar Bend Mizell . 568
9. Max Lanier 524
10. Bob Forsch 509

HITS PER 9 INNINGS

1.	Fred Beebe	7.29
2.	Bob Gibson	7.60
3.	Ernie Broglio	7.78
4.	Mort Cooper	7.95
5.	Jack Taylor	8.07
6.	Harry Brecheen	8.09
7.	Vinegar Bend Mizell	8.20
8.	Max Lanier	8.23
9.	Steve Carlton	8.32
10.	Murry Dickson	8.40

STRIKEOUTS PER 9 INNINGS

1.	Bob Gibson	7.22
2.	Steve Carlton	6.77
3.	Harvey Haddix	6.23
4.	Ernie Broglio	5.98
5.	Vinegar Bend Mizell	5.83
6.	Dizzy Dean	5.63
7.	Ray Sadecki	5.42
8.	Lindy McDaniel	5.32
9.	Nellie Briles	5.31
10.	Ray Washburn	5.22

BASES ON BALLS PER 9 INNINGS

1.	Grover Alexander	1.39
2.	Jack Powell	1.91
3.	Chappie McFarland	2.03
4.	Syl Johnson	2.05
5.	Dizzy Dean	2.14
6.	Curt Simmons	2.16
7.	Bill Sherdel	2.19
8.	Slim Sallee	2.20
9.	Jack Taylor	2.36
10.	Ray Washburn	2.41

SHUTOUTS

1.	Bob Gibson	56
2.	Bill Doak	32
3.	Mort Cooper	28
4.	Harry Brecheen	25
5.	Jesse Haines	24
6.	Dizzy Dean	23
7.	Max Lanier	20
7.	Howie Pollet	20
9.	Ernie Broglio	18
10.	Slim Sallee	17

RELIEF GAMES

1.	Al Hrabosky	328
2.	Al Brazle	324
3.	Lindy McDaniel	273
4.	Ted Wilks	239
5.	Bill Sherdel	222

RELIEF WINS

1.	Lindy McDaniel	45
2.	Al Brazle	41
3.	Al Hrabosky	40
4.	Bill Sherdel	38
5.	Ted Wilks	28

SAVES

1.	Lindy McDaniel	64
2.	Bruce Sutter	61
3.	Joe Hoerner	60
3.	Al Brazle	60
5.	Al Hrabosky	59

WINS PLUS SAVES

1.	Lindy McDaniel	109
2.	Al Brazle	101
3.	Al Hrabosky	99
4.	Joe Hoerner	79
5.	Bruce Sutter	73

RELIEF WINNING PERCENTAGE

1.	Ted Wilks	.778
2.	Howie Krist	.773
3.	Ron Taylor	.739
4.	Al Hrabosky	.667
4.	Max Lanier	.667

GAMES	CHANCES PER GAME	FIELDING AVERAGE

1B

GAMES	CHANCES PER GAME	FIELDING AVERAGE
1. Jim Bottomley ... 1340	1. Dots Miller ... 11.4	1. Keith Hernandez ... .994
2. Keith Hernandez ... 1064	2. Jake Beckley ... 11.3	2. Joe Torre ... .993
3. Stan Musial ... 1016	3. Ed Konetchy ... 11.1	3. Bill White ... .992
4. Ed Konetchy ... 979	4. Jim Bottomley ... 10.4	4. Ripper Collins ... .992
5. Bill White ... 972	5. Roger Connor ... 10.3	5. Stan Musial ... .992
		5. Ray Sanders ... .992

2B

GAMES	CHANCES PER GAME	FIELDING AVERAGE
1. Julian Javier ... 1547	1. John Farrell ... 6.2	1. Red Schoendienst ... .983
2. Red Schoendienst ... 1429	2. Frankie Frisch ... 5.9	2. Don Blasingame ... .978
3. Frankie Frisch ... 1153	3. Joe Quinn ... 5.9	3. Ted Sizemore ... .977
4. Rogers Hornsby ... 997	4. Rogers Hornsby ... 5.6	4. Mike Tyson ... .977
5. Miller Huggins ... 774	5. Don Blasingame ... 5.6	5. Frankie Frisch ... .975

3B

GAMES	CHANCES PER GAME	FIELDING AVERAGE
1. Ken Boyer ... 1539	1. Bobby Byrne ... 4.1	1. Ken Reitz ... .971
2. Ken Reitz ... 1081	2. Mike Mowrey ... 3.5	2. Whitey Kurowski ... .957
3. Whitey Kurowski ... 868	3. Whitey Kurowski ... 3.1	3. Ken Boyer ... .953
4. Milt Stock ... 661	4. Ken Boyer ... 3.1	4. Joe Torre ... .951
5. Mike Mowrey ... 515	5. Milt Stock ... 3.0	5. Don Gutteridge ... .948

SS

GAMES	CHANCES PER GAME	FIELDING AVERAGE
1. Marty Marion ... 1492	1. Bobby Wallace ... 6.7	1. Dal Maxvill ... .973
2. Dal Maxvill ... 1054	2. Doc Lavan ... 6.0	2. Marty Marion ... .968
3. Garry Templeton ... 700	3. Rogers Hornsby ... 5.9	3. Alex Grammas ... .966
4. Leo Durocher ... 681	4. Tommy Thevenow ... 5.9	4. Leo Durocher ... .962
5. Charley Gelbert ... 587	5. Charley Gelbert ... 5.6	5. Solly Hemus ... .962

OF

GAMES	CHANCES PER GAME	FIELDING AVERAGE
1. Lou Brock ... 2206	1. Taylor Douthit ... 3.2	1. George Hendrick ... .990
2. Stan Musial ... 1896	2. Terry Moore ... 2.7	2. Bake McBride ... .988
3. Enos Slaughter ... 1751	3. Bake McBride ... 2.7	3. Tony Scott ... .988
4. Curt Flood ... 1687	4. Cliff Heathcote ... 2.5	4. Curt Flood ... .987
5. Terry Moore ... 1189	5. Rebel Oakes ... 2.5	5. Mike Shannon ... .987

C

GAMES	CHANCES PER GAME	FIELDING AVERAGE
1. Ted Simmons ... 1440	1. Tim McCarver ... 6.5	1. Tim McCarver ... .990
2. Del Rice ... 1018	2. Ted Simmons ... 5.8	2. Hal Smith ... .989
3. Tim McCarver ... 960	3. Hal Smith ... 5.7	3. Del Rice ... .988
4. Jimmie Wilson ... 638	4. Frank Snyder ... 5.3	4. Ted Simmons ... .987
5. Frank Snyder ... 563	5. Walker Cooper ... 5.0	5. Verne Clemons ... .983

P

GAMES	CHANCES PER GAME
1. Jesse Haines ... 554	1. Jack Taylor ... 3.7
2. Bob Gibson ... 528	2. Clarence Currie ... 3.4
3. Bill Sherdel ... 465	3. Chappie McFarland ... 3.3
4. Al Brazle ... 441	4. Wish Egan ... 3.2
5. Bill Doak ... 376	5. Buster Brown ... 3.2

PUTOUTS	PUTOUTS PER GAME	ASSISTS

1B

PUTOUTS	PUTOUTS PER GAME	ASSISTS
1. Jim Bottomley 13160	1. Dots Miller........... 10.8	1. Keith Hernandez 828
2. Ed Konetchy......... 10086	2. Jake Beckley 10.7	2. Stan Musial........ 688
3. Keith Hernandez 9991	3. Ed Konetchy...... 10.3	3. Ed Konetchy........ 639
4. Stan Musial......... 8709	4. Jim Bottomley....... 9.8	4. Bill White 610
5. Bill White 8283	5. Roger Connor 9.4	5. Jim Bottomley........ 553

2B

PUTOUTS	PUTOUTS PER GAME	ASSISTS
1. Red Schoendienst ..... .3684	1. Joe Quinn 2.6	1. Red Schoendienst 4130
2. Julian Javier......... 3377	2. Red Schoendienst 2.6	2. Julian Javier......... 4107
3. Frankie Frisch 2879	3. Frankie Frisch 2.5	3. Frankie Frisch 3807
4. Rogers Hornsby .... .2144	4. Don Blasingame 2.5	4. Rogers Hornsby 3263
5. Miller Huggins....... 1675	5. John Farrell........ 2.4	5. Miller Huggins........ 2320

3B

PUTOUTS	PUTOUTS PER GAME	ASSISTS
1. Ken Boyer......... 1373	1. Bobby Byrne......... 1.5	1. Ken Boyer......... 3149
2. Whitey Kurowski....... 1025	2. Mike Mowrey........ 1.2	2. Ken Reitz......... 2011
3. Ken Reitz................ 799	3. Whitey Kurowski....... 1.2	3. Whitey Kurowski....... ...1569
4. Milt Stock 694	4. Don Gutteridge..... 1.1	4. Milt Stock 1188
5. Mike Mowrey........ 619	5. Milt Stock 1.0	5. Mike Mowrey......... 1071

SS

PUTOUTS	PUTOUTS PER GAME	ASSISTS
1. Marty Marion........... 2881	1. Bobby Wallace...... ......2.4	1. Marty Marion........... 4691
2. Dal Maxvill......... 1595	2. Doc Lavan 2.3	2. Dal Maxvill......... 3050
3. Leo Durocher......... 1450	3. Charley Gelbert...... 2.1	3. Garry Templeton 2396
4. Garry Templeton 1356	4. Leo Durocher........ 2.1	4. Leo Durocher........ 1958
5. Charley Gelbert....... 1256	5. Tommy Thevenow.... .... 2.1	5. Charley Gelbert....... ...1887

OF

PUTOUTS	PUTOUTS PER GAME	ASSISTS
1. Curt Flood........... .4005	1. Taylor Douthit....... 3.0	1. Enos Slaughter......... 142
2. Lou Brock........... .3790	2. Bake McBride....... 2.6	2. Stan Musial......... 130
3. Stan Musial......... 3730	3. Terry Moore....... 2.6	3. Jack Smith 122
4. Enos Slaughter........ .3457	4. Tony Scott........ 2.4	4. Curt Flood......... 114
5. Terry Moore......... ...3117	5. Curt Flood......... 2.4	5. Lou Brock 110

C

PUTOUTS	PUTOUTS PER GAME	ASSISTS
1. Ted Simmons......... 7460	1. Tim McCarver 6.0	1. Frank Snyder......... 758
2. Tim McCarver .... .5740	2. Ted Simmons....... 5.2	2. Ted Simmons........ 755
3. Del Rice............ .4311	3. Hal Smith 5.1	3. Mike Gonzalez........ 498
4. Hal Smith 2797	4. Walker Cooper 4.4	4. Del Rice 455
5. Jimmie Wilson........ 2582	5. Del Rice 4.2	5. Jimmie Wilson........ 417

P

PUTOUTS	PUTOUTS PER GAME	ASSISTS
1. Bob Gibson......... 291	1. Ted Breitenstein..... 8	1. Bill Doak.......... 808
2. Ted Breitenstein...... 187	2. Ed Karger 7	2. Jesse Haines 650
3. Bob Forsch 153	3. Lary Sorensen...... .7	3. Bill Sherdel 498
4. Larry Jackson 124	4. Joe Corbett........ .6	4. Bob Gibson........... 484
5. Jesse Haines 106	5. Bob Wicker 6	5. Slim Sallee......... 479

ASSISTS PER GAME	DOUBLE PLAYS	CHANCES

1B

1. Keith Hernandez .8	1. Jim Bottomley 1149	1. Jim Bottomley 13887
2. Stan Musial .7	2. Stan Musial 935	2. Keith Hernandez 10886
3. Roger Connor .7	3. Keith Hernandez 929	3. Ed Konetchy 10851
4. Ed Konetchy .7	4. Bill White 752	4. Stan Musial 9475
5. Ripper Collins .6	5. Johnny Mize 616	5. Bill White 8962

2B

1. John Farrell 3.4	1. Red Schoendienst 1087	1. Red Schoendienst 7951
2. Frankie Frisch 3.3	2. Julian Javier 907	2. Julian Javier 7703
3. Rogers Hornsby 3.3	3. Frankie Frisch 709	3. Frankie Frisch 6856
4. Don Blasingame 3.0	4. Rogers Hornsby 553	4. Rogers Hornsby 5614
5. Miller Huggins 3.0	5. Don Blasingame 419	5. Miller Huggins 4156

3B

1. Bobby Byrne 2.3	1. Ken Boyer 306	1. Ken Boyer 4747
2. Mike Mowrey 2.1	2. Ken Reitz 176	2. Ken Reitz 2895
3. Ken Boyer 2.0	3. Whitey Kurowski 137	3. Whitey Kurowski 2710
4. Ken Reitz 1.9	4. Milt Stock 105	4. Milt Stock 1993
5. Mike Shannon 1.8	5. Mike Mowrey 94	5. Mike Mowrey 1800

SS

1. Bobby Wallace 3.8	1. Marty Marion 937	1. Marty Marion 7819
2. Rogers Hornsby 3.5	2. Dal Maxvill 575	2. Dal Maxvill 4774
3. Tommy Thevenow 3.5	3. Garry Templeton 488	3. Garry Templeton 3929
4. Garry Templeton 3.4	4. Leo Durocher 383	4. Leo Durocher 3542
5. Doc Lavan 3.4	5. Charley Gelbert 377	5. Charley Gelbert 3308

OF

1. Owen Wilson .2	1. Jack Smith 42	1. Curt Flood 4172
2. Rube Ellis .2	2. Enos Slaughter 33	2. Lou Brock 4073
3. Patsy Donovan .2	3. Curt Flood 28	3. Stan Musial 3924
4. Austin McHenry .2	4. Stan Musial 27	4. Enos Slaughter 3673
5. Jesse Burkett .1	5. Homer Smoot 24	5. Terry Moore 3267

C

1. Frank Snyder 1.3	1. Ted Simmons 87	1. Ted Simmons 8319
2. Mike Gonzalez 1.1	2. Jimmie Wilson 77	2. Tim McCarver 6217
3. Verne Clemons 1.0	3. Del Rice 63	3. Del Rice 4825
4. Bob O'Farrell .7	4. Mike Gonzalez 54	4. Hal Smith 3077
5. Jimmie Wilson .7	4. Frank Snyder 54	5. Jimmie Wilson 3054
	4. Tim McCarver 54	

P

1. Jack Taylor 2.9	1. Bob Gibson 46	1. Bill Doak 935
2. Clarence Currie 2.8	2. Jesse Haines 32	2. Bob Gibson 817
3. Chappie McFarland 2.8	3. Bob Forsch 25	3. Jesse Haines 783
4. Wish Egan 2.6	4. Howie Pollet 24	4. Ted Breitenstein 658
5. Jake Thielman 2.6	4. Bill Hallahan 24	5. Bill Sherdel 593
	4. Bill Doak 24	

The Cardinals and Their Players
Year-by-Year

This section is a chronological listing of every Cardinals season through 1982. All format information and abbreviations are explained below.

ROSTER INFORMATION

POS	Fielding Position	R		Runs
B	Bats B(oth), L(eft), or	RBI		Runs Batted In
	R(ight)	BB		Bases on Balls
G	Games	SO		Strikeouts
AB	At Bats	SB		Stolen Bases
H	Hits			
2B	Doubles	*Pinch-Hit*		
3B	Triples		AB	Pinch-Hit At Bats
HR	Home Runs		H	Pinch Hits
HR%	Home Run Percentage			
	(the number of home	BA		Batting Average
	runs per 100 times at	SA		Slugging Average
	bat)			

Regulars. The men who appear first on the team roster are considered the regulars for that team at the positions indicated. There are several factors for determining regulars of which "most games played at a position" and "most fielding chances at a position," are the two prime considerations.

Substitutes. Appearing directly beneath the regulars are the substitutes for the team. Substitutes are listed by position: first infielders, then outfielders, then catchers. Within these areas, substitutes are listed in order of most at bats, and can be someone who played most of the team's games as a regular, but not at one position. The rules for determining the listed positions of substitutes are as follows:

21

One Position Substitutes. If a man played at least 70% of his games in the field at one position, then he is listed only at that position, except for outfielders, where all three outfield positions are included under one category.

Two Position Substitutes. If a man did not play at least 70% of his games in the field at one position, but did play more than 90% of his total games at two positions, then he is shown with a combination fielding position. For example, if a player has an "S2" shown in his position column, it would mean that he played at least 90% of his games at shortstop and second base. These combinations are always indicated by the first letter or number of the position. The position listed first is where the most games were played.

Utility Players. If a player has a "UT" shown in his position column, it means that he did not meet the above 70% or 90% requirement and is listed as a utility player.

Pinch Hitters. Men who played no games in the field are considered pinch hitters and are listed as "PH."

Individual League Leaders. (Applies to batting, fielding, and pitching.) Statistics that appear in bold-faced print indicate the player led or tied for the league lead in the particular statistical category.

Traded League Leaders. (Applies to batting, fielding, and pitching.) An asterisk (*) next to a particular figure indicates that the player led the league that year in the particular statistical category, but since he played for more than one team, the figure does not necessarily represent his league-leading total or average.

Meaningless Averages. Indicated by use of a dash (-). In batting, the dash may appear in averages. This means that the player had no official at bats even though he played in at least one game. A batting average of .000 would mean he had at least one at bat with no hits. In pitching, the dash may appear in winning percentage. This means that the pitcher never had a decision even though he pitched in at least one game. A percentage of .000 would mean that he had at least one loss.

Anytime the symbol "infinity" (∞) is shown for a pitching average, it means that the pitcher allowed at least one earned run, hit, or base on balls without retiring a batter.

INDIVIDUAL FIELDING INFORMATION

T	Throws L(eft) or R(ight)	E	Errors
	(blank if not available)	DP	Double Plays
G	Games	TC/G	Total Chances per
PO	Putouts		Game
A	Assists	FA	Fielding Average

Each man's fielding record is shown for each position he played during the year. Fielding information for pitchers is not included. .

TEAM AND LEAGUE INFORMATION

W	Wins	*Fielding*	
L	Losses	E	Errors
PCT	Winning Percentage	DP	Double Plays
GB	Games Behind the	FA	Fielding Average
	League Leader		
R	Runs Scored		
OR	Opponents' Runs	*Pitching*	
	(Runs Scored Against)	CG	Complete Games
		BB	Bases on Balls
Batting		SO	Strikeouts
2B	Doubles	ShO	Shutouts
3B	Triples	SV	Saves
HR	Home Runs	ERA	Earned Run Average
BA	Batting Average		
SA	Slugging Average		
SB	Stolen Bases		

Team League Leaders. Statistics that appear in bold-faced print indicate the team led or tied for the league lead in the particular statistical category. When teams are tied for league lead, the figures for all teams who tied are shown in boldface.

INDIVIDUAL PITCHING INFORMATION

T	Throws R(ight) or L(eft)	BB	Bases on Balls Allowed
W	Wins	SO	Strikeouts
L	Losses	R	Runs Allowed
PCT	Winning Percentage	ER	Earned Runs Allowed
ERA	Earned Run Average	ShO	Shutouts
SV	Saves	H/9	Hits Allowed Per 9
G	Games Pitched		Innings Pitched
GS	Games Started	BB/9	Bases on Balls Allowed
CG	Complete Games		Per 9 Innings Pitched
IP	Innings Pitched	SO/9	Strikeouts Per 9
H	Hits Allowed		Innings Pitched

The abbreviations for the teams appear as listed below.

ATL	Atlanta		MIL	Milwaukee
BAL	Baltimore		MON	Montreal
BOS	Boston		NY	New York
BKN	Brooklyn		PHI	Philadelphia
CHI	Chicago		PIT	Pittsburgh
CIN	Cincinnati		SD	San Diego
CLE	Cleveland		SF	San Francisco
HOU	Houston		STL	St. Louis
LA	Los Angeles		WAS	Washington
LOU	Louisville			

BEFORE THE BEGINNING

In 1876, when the National League was founded, St. Louis was one of eight charter members. The club forfeited its franchise the following year, however, and did not return to the league until 1885, only to disappear again two years later. It wasn't until 1892 that St. Louis joined the National League for good.

The game played in the early years of the league was different, but still recognizable. It was no longer legal to put a runner out by hitting him with the ball, but a foul ball caught on the first bounce was an out, and it took nine balls for a batter to draw a walk. The pitcher's box was 45 feet away, and all pitchers had to throw underhanded, while the batters could call for their pitches high or low, a practice that wasn't eliminated until 1887. Still, there were three outs to an inning, nine innings to a game, and nine players to a team, a level of standardization the two leagues seem incapable of today.

St. Louis finished that first season in second place, six games behind the Chicago White Stockings, who were led by two Hall of Famers: Cap Anson, the first man to amass 3,000 hits, and pitcher-manager Al Spalding, founder of the sporting goods company that bears his name. St. Louis's pitcher, George Washington Bradley, accounted for his team's entire 45-19 record, with a league-leading ERA of 1.23. Bradley pitched all but four innings of his team's 64-game schedule. Bradley also pitched the first National League no-hitter, a 2-0 victory against Hartford.

The St. Louis National League clubs of 1885 and 1886 finished eighth and sixth before folding. Their efforts were far overshadowed by the St. Louis entry in the rival American Association, which was just starting its run of four straight pennants. The Association used what we would today call aggressive marketing techniques in its fight with the National League, selling beer in all its ballparks, charging 25¢ for admission, half the National League price, and playing games on Sunday, an innovation which did not reach the National League until 1892.

The manager of the American Association's St. Louis Browns was first baseman Charles Comiskey, the same Comiskey for whom the White Sox park is named. St. Louis dominated the Association from 1885 to 1888, winning their pennants by an average margin of twelve games. The batting star was James Edward "Tip" O'Neill, who batted .347 in his six years with St. Louis. O'Neill had one of the greatest seasons in baseball history in 1887, as he batted .435 and became the only player ever to lead his league in doubles, triples, and home runs in the same year.

It was clear by 1891 that the club owners could profit substantially from a monopoly in the game, and so the National League and American Association merged into one twelve-team league, with Louisville, Washington, Baltimore, and St. Louis joining the National League. The treaty was largely the work of St. Louis owner and Association president Chris von der Ahe, who brought his club into the National League fold. Of the four, only St. Louis lasted in the league into the twentieth century.

MANAGER	W	L	PCT
Chris Von Der Ahe	56	94	.373

POS	Player	B	G	AB	H	2B	3B	HR	HR %	R	RBI	BB	SO	SB	Pinch Hit AB	Pinch Hit H	BA	SA
REGULARS																		
1B	Perry Werden	R	149	598	154	22	6	8	1.3	73	84	59	52	20	0	0	.258	.355
2B	John Crooks		128	445	95	7	4	7	1.6	82	38	136	52	23	0	0	.213	.294
SS	Jack Glasscock	R	139	566	151	27	5	3	0.5	83	72	44	19	26	0	0	.267	.348
3B	George Pinckney	R	78	290	50	3	2	0	0.0	31	25	36	26	4	0	0	.172	.197
RF	Bob Caruthers	L	143	513	142	16	8	3	0.6	76	69	86	29	24	0	0	.277	.357
CF	Steve Brodie	L	154	602	152	10	9	4	0.7	85	60	52	31	28	0	0	.252	.319
LF	Cliff Carroll	B	101	407	111	14	8	4	1.0	82	49	47	22	30	0	0	.273	.376
C	Dick Buckley		121	410	93	17	4	5	1.2	43	52	22	34	7	0	0	.227	.324
SUBSTITUTES																		
3B	Llewellyn Camp		42	145	30	3	1	2	1.4	19	13	17	27	12	0	0	.207	.283
SS	Frank Genins		15	51	10	1	0	0	0.0	5	4	1	11	3	0	0	.196	.216
3B	Willie Kuehne		7	28	4	1	0	0	0.0	1	0	0	4	1	0	0	.143	.179
23	Jim McCormick	R	3	11	0	0	0	0	0.0	0	0	1	5	0	0	0	.000	.000
3B	Harry DeMiller		1	4	0	0	0	0	0.0	0	0	0	0	0	0	0	.000	.000
3B	Hick Carpenter	R	1	3	1	0	0	0	0.0	0	0	1	1	0	0	0	.333	.333
3B	Mark McGrillis		1	3	0	0	0	0	0.0	0	0	0	1	0	0	0	.000	.000
UT	Kid Gleason	L	66	233	50	4	2	3	1.3	35	25	34	23	7	0	0	.215	.288
OF	Gene Moriarity		47	177	31	4	1	3	1.7	20	19	4	37	7	0	0	.175	.260
PO	Ted Breitenstein	L	47	131	16	1	1	0	0.0	16	6	16	20	4	0	0	.122	.145
OF	George Gore	L	20	73	15	0	1	0	0.0	9	4	18	6	2	0	0	.205	.233
OF	Bill Van Dyke	R	4	16	2	0	0	0	0.0	2	1	0	1	0	0	0	.125	.125
OF	Chicken Wolf	R	3	14	2	0	0	0	0.0	1	1	0	1	0	0	0	.143	.143
OF	Ed Haigh		1	4	1	0	0	0	0.0	0	0	0	2	0	0	0	.250	.250
OF	John Thornton		1	3	0	0	0	0	0.0	0	0	0	2	0	0	0	.000	.000
C	Bill Moran		24	81	11	1	0	0	0.0	2	5	2	12	0	0	0	.136	.148
CO	Grant Briggs		23	57	4	1	0	0	0.0	2	1	6	16	3	0	0	.070	.088
C	Frank Bird	R	17	50	10	3	1	1	2.0	9	1	6	11	2	0	0	.200	.360
C	Heinie Peitz	R	1	3	0	0	0	0	0.0	0	0	0	0	0	0	0	.000	.000
PITCHERS																		
P	Pink Hawley	L	20	71	12	0	0	1	1.4	3	5	1	8	0	0	0	.169	.225
P	Charlie Getzein	R	13	45	9	0	0	1	2.2	3	4	3	10	0	0	0	.200	.267
P	Bill Hawke		15	45	4	0	0	0	0.0	2	1	0	6	0	0	0	.089	.089
P	Pud Galvin	R	12	39	2	0	0	0	0.0	2	1	1	10	0	0	0	.051	.051
P	Frank Dwyer	R	10	25	2	0	0	0	0.0	4	0	4	2	0	0	0	.080	.080
P	Jack Easton		5	17	3	1	0	0	0.0	1	2	0	3	1	0	0	.176	.235
P	J. D. Young		1	1	0	0	0	0	0.0	0	0	0	0	0	0	0	.000	.000
	TEAM TOTAL			5161	1167	137	53	45	0.9	691	542	597	484	204	0	0	.226	.299

INDIVIDUAL FIELDING

POS	Player	T	G	PO	A	E	DP	TC/G	FA
1B	P. Werden	R	149	1467	102	28	81	10.7	.982
	K. Gleason	R	1	4	0	0	0	4.0	1.000
	B. Caruthers	R	4	35	1	3	4	9.8	.923
	D. Buckley	R	2	22	1	0	1	11.5	1.000
2B	J. Crooks		102	286	300	44	43	6.2	.930
	S. Brodie	R	16	29	36	7	8	4.5	.903
	K. Gleason	R	10	22	28	1	0	5.1	.980
	B. Caruthers	R	6	11	22	5	4	6.3	.868
	J. McCormick	R	2	3	5	0	0	4.0	1.000
SS	J. Glasscock	R	139	280	472	69	46	5.9	.916
	F. Genins	R	14	29	35	14	5	5.6	.821
	W. Kuehne	R	1	0	3	0	0	3.0	1.000
3B	G. Pinckney	R	78	84	161	31	12	3.5	.888
	L. Camp	R	39	37	62	28	4	3.3	.780
	J. Crooks		24	30	48	11	1	3.7	.876
	W. Kuehne	R	6	5	17	2	2	4.0	.917
	H. Carpenter	L	1	2	3	2	0	7.0	.714
	J. McCormick	R	1	1	3	0	0	4.0	1.000
	S. Brodie	R	2	1	2	0	0	1.5	1.000
	H. DeMiller		1	1	0	1	0	2.0	.500
	M. McGrillis		1	0	2	0	0	2.0	1.000

POS	Player	T	G	PO	A	E	DP	TC/G	FA
OF	S. Brodie	R	137	296	21	19	4	2.5	.943
	C. Carroll	R	101	181	19	22	1	2.2	.901
	B. Caruthers	R	122	159	14	21	2	1.6	.892
	G. Moriarity		47	96	9	23	0	2.7	.820
	G. Gore	R	20	35	3	7	0	2.3	.844
	E. Haigh		1	0	0	0	0	0.0	.000
	J. Thornton		1	0	0	0	0	0.0	.000
	J. Crooks		2	0	0	0	0	0.0	.000
	K. Gleason	R	11	14	2	3	0	1.7	.842
	Breitenstein	L	10	11	1	0	1	1.2	1.000
	B. Van Dyke	R	4	7	0	1	0	2.0	.875
	L. Camp	R	3	5	0	2	0	2.3	.714
	G. Briggs		9	4	0	3	0	0.8	.571
	B. Hawke		1	1	1	0	0	2.0	1.000
	J. Easton		1	1	0	0	0	1.0	1.000
	F. Genins	R	1	0	1	0	0	1.0	.000
	C. Wolf	R	3	1	0	0	0	0.3	1.000
C	D. Buckley	R	119	513	123	43	14	5.7	.937
	B. Moran		22	91	23	14	0	5.8	.891
	F. Bird	R	17	52	17	6	1	4.4	.920
	G. Briggs		15	42	13	6	0	4.1	.902
	K. Gleason	R	1	0	0	0	0	0.0	.000
	H. Peitz	R	1	3	0	0	0	3.0	1.000

With the merger of the National League and American Association, St. Louis joined the National League for the third time, this time for good. The two leagues had staged post-season series between their champions, but with just one league that was impossible. Their solution was a radical one: they elected to split the season and stage a playoff between the teams that won each half. Fortunately for the league, different teams won each half, with Boston taking the post-season series.

The format of the season made little difference to St. Louis; the Browns, as they were known, finished far back in both halves. They were weak offensively and defensively, finishing tenth in runs scored and eleventh in runs allowed. They batted .226, tied for last in the league, and no regular could crack the .280 mark.

THE SPLIT SEASON

FIRST HALF	W	L	PCT.	GB		SECOND HALF	W	L	PCT.	GB
BOS	52	22	.702			CLE	53	23	.697	
BKN	51	26	.662	2½		BOS	50	26	.658	3
PHI	46	30	.605	7		BKN	44	33	.571	9½
CIN	44	31	.587	8½		PIT	43	34	.558	10½
CLE	40	33	.548	11½		PHI	41	36	.532	12½
PIT	37	39	.487	16		NY	40	37	.519	13½
WAS	35	41	.461	18		CHI	39	37	.513	14
CHI	31	39	.443	21		CIN	38	37	.507	14½
STL	31	42	.425	22½		LOU	33	42	.440	19½
NY	31	43	.419	23		BAL	26	46	.361	25
LOU	30	47	.390	25½		STL	25	52	.325	28½
BAL	20	55	.267	34½		WAS	23	52	.307	29½

TEAM STATISTICS

	W	L	PCT	GB	R	OR	2B	3B	HR	BA	SA	SB	E	DP	FA	CG	BB	SO	ShO	SV	ERA
BOS	102	48	.680	–	862	649	203	51	34	.250	.327	338	454	128	.929	143	460	509	15	1	2.86
CLE	93	56	.624	8.5	855	613	196	96	26	.254	.340	225	407	95	.935	140	413	472	11	2	2.41
BKN	95	59	.617	9	935	733	183	105	30	.262	.350	409	398	98	.940	132	600	597	12	5	3.25
PHI	87	66	.569	16.5	860	690	225	95	50	.262	.367	216	393	128	.939	131	492	502	10	5	2.93
CIN	82	68	.547	20	766	731	155	75	44	.241	.322	270	402	140	.939	131	535	437	8	2	3.17
PIT	80	73	.523	23.5	802	796	143	108	38	.236	.322	222	483	113	.927	130	537	455	3	1	3.10
CHI	70	76	.479	30	635	735	149	92	26	.235	.316	233	424	85	.932	133	424	518	6	1	3.16
NY	71	80	.470	31.5	811	826	173	85	38	.251	.337	301	565	97	.912	139	635	641	5	1	3.29
LOU	63	89	.414	40	649	804	133	61	18	.226	.284	275	471	133	.928	147	447	430	9	0	3.34
WAS	58	93	.384	44.5	731	869	148	78	38	.239	.320	276	547	122	.916	129	556	479	5	3	3.46
STL	56	94	.373	46	703	922	138	53	45	.226	.298	209	452	100	.929	139	543	478	4	1	4.20
BAL	46	101	.313	54.5	779	1020	160	111	30	.254	.343	227	584	100	.910	131	536	437	2	1	4.28
LEAGUE TOTAL					9388	9388	2006	1010	417	.245	.327	3201	5580	1339	.928	1625	6178	5955	90	23	3.28

INDIVIDUAL PITCHING

PITCHER	T	W	L	PCT	ERA	SV	G	GS	CG	IP	H	BB	SO	R	ER	ShO	H/9	BB/9	SO/9
Kid Gleason	R	16	24	.400	3.33	0	47	45	43	400	389	151	133	244	148	2	8.75	3.40	2.99
Ted Breitenstein	L	14	20	.412	4.69	0	39	32	28	282.1	280	148	126	192	147	1	8.93	4.72	4.02
Pink Hawley	R	6	14	.300	3.19	0	20	20	18	166.1	160	63	63	116	59	0	8.66	3.41	3.41
Charlie Getzein	R	5	8	.385	5.67	0	13	13	12	108	159	31	32	87	68	0	13.25	2.58	2.67
Bob Caruthers	R	2	8	.200	5.84	1	16	10	10	101.2	131	27	21	75	66	0	11.60	2.39	1.86
Bill Hawke		4	5	.444	3.70	0	14	11	10	97.1	108	45	55	59	40	1	9.99	4.16	5.09
Pud Galvin	R	5	7	.417	3.23	0	12	12	10	92	102	26	27	47	33	0	9.98	2.54	2.64
Frank Dwyer	R	2	8	.200	5.63	0	10	10	6	64	90	24	16	58	40	0	12.66	3.38	2.25
Jack Easton		2	0	1.000	6.39	0	5	2	2	31	38	26	4	31	22	0	11.03	7.55	1.16
. D. Young		0	0	–	22.50	0	1	0	0	2	9	2	1	13	5	0	40.50	9.00	4.50
TEAM TOTAL		56	94	.373	4.20	1	177	155	139	1344.2	1466	543	478	922	628	4	9.81	3.63	3.20

MANAGER	W	L	PCT
Bill Watkins	57	75	.432

POS	Player	B	G	AB	H	2B	3B	HR	HR %	R	RBI	BB	SO	SB	Pinch Hit AB	Pinch Hit H	BA	SA
REGULARS																		
1B	Perry Werden	R	125	500	138	22	33	1	0.2	73	94	49	25	11	0	0	.276	.458
2B	Joe Quinn	R	135	547	126	18	6	0	0.0	68	71	33	7	24	0	0	.230	.285
SS	Jack Glasscock	R	48	195	56	8	1	1	0.5	32	26	25	3	20	0	0	.287	.354
3B	John Crooks		128	448	106	10	9	1	0.2	93	48	121	37	31	0	0	.237	.306
RF	Tommy Dowd	R	132	581	164	18	7	1	0.2	114	54	49	23	59	0	0	.282	.343
CF	Steve Brodie	L	107	469	149	16	8	2	0.4	71	79	33	16	41	0	0	.318	.399
LF	Charlie Frank		40	164	55	6	3	1	0.6	29	17	18	8	8	0	0	.335	.427
C	Heinie Peitz	R	96	362	92	12	9	1	0.3	53	45	54	20	12	0	0	.254	.345
SUBSTITUTES																		
SS	Bones Ely	R	44	178	45	1	6	0	0.0	25	16	17	13	2	0	0	.253	.326
1B	Dennie O'Neil		7	25	3	0	0	0	0.0	3	2	4	0	3	0	0	.120	.120
3B	Jud Smith	R	4	13	1	0	0	0	0.0	1	0	1	2	0	0	0	.077	.077
UT	Frank Shugart	L	59	246	69	10	4	0	0.0	41	28	22	10	13	0	0	.280	.354
OF	Jimmy Bannon	R	26	107	36	3	4	0	0.0	9	15	4	5	8	0	0	.336	.439
UT	Duff Cooley	L	29	107	37	2	3	0	0.0	20	21	8	9	8	1	0	.346	.421
OF	Sandy Griffin	R	23	92	18	1	1	0	0.0	9	9	16	2	2	0	0	.196	.228
OF	Lew Whistler		10	38	9	1	0	0	0.0	5	2	3	2	0	0	0	.237	.263
OF	Bill Goodenough		10	31	5	1	0	0	0.0	4	2	3	4	2	0	0	.161	.194
C	Joe Gunson		40	151	41	5	0	0	0.0	20	15	6	6	0	1	0	.272	.305
C	Old Hoss Twineham	L	14	48	15	2	0	0	0.0	8	11	1	2	0	0	0	.313	.354
C	Dick Buckley		9	23	4	1	0	0	0.0	2	1	0	0	0	0	0	.174	.217
C	Pat McCauley		5	16	1	0	0	0	0.0	0	0	0	1	0	0	0	.063	.063
CO	Kid Sommers		2	1	0	0	0	0	0.0	1	0	0	0	0	0	0	.000	.000
PITCHERS																		
P	Kid Gleason	L	59	199	51	6	4	0	0.0	25	20	19	8	2	2	1	.256	.327
P	Ted Breitenstein	L	49	160	29	1	1	1	0.6	20	14	18	15	3	0	0	.181	.219
P	Pink Hawley	L	31	91	26	7	3	0	0.0	10	17	11	16	1	0	0	.286	.429
P	Dad Clarkson	R	25	75	10	1	0	0	0.0	8	5	9	16	0	0	0	.133	.147
P	John Dolan		3	7	1	0	0	1	14.3	1	3	0	1	0	0	0	.143	.571
P	Bill Hawke		1	3	1	0	0	0	0.0	0	1	0	0	0	0	0	.333	.333
P	Frank Pears		1	2	0	0	0	0	0.0	0	0	0	0	0	0	0	.000	.000
	TEAM TOTAL			4879	1288	152	102	10	0.2	745	616	524	251	250	4	1	.264	.343

INDIVIDUAL FIELDING

POS	Player	T	G	PO	A	E	DP	TC/G	FA		POS	Player	T	G	PO	A	E	DP	TC/G	FA
1B	P. Werden	R	124	1194	81	42	75	10.6	.968		OF	S. Brodie	R	107	273	21	15	7	2.9	.951
	D. O'Neil		7	68	0	1	3	9.9	.986			T. Dowd	R	132	225	27	15	9	2.0	.944
	H. Peitz	R	5	50	1	1	4	10.4	.981			C. Frank		40	84	9	7	1	2.5	.930
	L. Whistler		1	10	0	0	1	10.0	1.000			F. Shugart	R	28	59	9	7	1	2.7	.907
												S. Griffin	R	23	46	2	5	0	2.3	.906
2B	J. Quinn	R	135	354	366	44	63	5.7	.942			J. Bannon	R	24	29	2	8	1	1.6	.795
	T. Dowd	R	1	0	0	1	0	1.0	.000			D. Cooley	R	15	17	1	1	0	1.3	.947
												D. Clarkson	R	1	0	0	0	0	0.0	.000
SS	J. Glasscock	R	48	85	159	25	19	5.6	.907			B. Goodenough		10	21	1	3	0	2.5	.880
	B. Ely	R	44	98	139	25	16	6.0	.905			K. Gleason	R	11	21	1	1	0	2.1	.957
	F. Shugart	R	23	35	76	22	8	5.8	.835			H. Peitz	R	10	17	1	2	0	2.0	.900
	H. Peitz	R	11	25	28	9	5	5.6	.855			L. Whistler		9	11	1	1	0	1.4	.923
	J. Crooks		4	9	12	3	2	6.0	.875			J. Gunson	R	5	8	1	0	1	1.8	1.000
	J. Bannon	R	2	2	8	7	2	8.5	.588			K. Sommers		1	1	0	1	0	2.0	.500
	D. Cooley	R	5	6	5	2	2	2.6	.846			P. Werden	R	1	0	1	1	0	2.0	.500
	K. Gleason	R	1	2	3	3	0	8.0	.625			Breitenstein	L	2	1	0	0	0	0.5	1.000
3B	J. Crooks		123	210	286	50	19	4.4	.908		C	H. Peitz	R	74	296	86	21	7	5.4	.948
	F. Shugart		9	13	16	5	2	3.8	.853			J. Gunson	R	35	130	36	13	4	5.1	.927
	J. Smith	R	4	7	9	2	2	4.5	.889			O. Twineham	R	14	48	16	5	1	4.9	.928
												D. Buckley	R	9	26	6	3	2	3.9	.914
												D. Cooley	R	10	23	6	1	0	3.0	.967
												P. McCauley	R	5	15	6	5	1	5.2	.808
												J. Crooks		1	4	2	0	0	6.0	1.000
												K. Sommers		1	0	1	1	0	2.0	.500

The club owners (or "magnates" as they preferred to be called) were concerned about low scoring. Before the '93 season, they made one of the first in a century-long series of moves to keep pitchers from dominating the game: they moved the mound back from 50 feet to 60 feet 6 inches. The move did indeed help the hitters, as the number of .300 hitters around the league (minimum 300 at bats) nearly tripled. Still, St. Louis had just one, centerfielder Steve Brodie, and they ranked eleventh in the league in team slugging, despite Perry Werden's all-time club record of 33 triples in a season.

St. Louis was the only team in the league whose ERA improved from 1892; the league ERA as a whole jumped from 3.28 to 4.66. Ted Breitenstein led the league in ERA, and was third in strikeouts. But while the team led the league in ERA as well, they trailed three clubs in runs allowed, thanks to a defense that had the fourth-highest number of errors, allowing a lot of unearned runs.

TEAM STATISTICS

	W	L	PCT	GB	R	OR	Batting 2B	3B	HR	BA	SA	SB	Fielding E	DP	FA	CG	BB	Pitching SO	ShO	SV	ERA
BOS	86	43	.667		1008	795	178	50	64	.290	.391	243	353	118	.936	115	402	253	2	2	4.43
PIT	81	48	.628	5	970	766	176	127	37	.299	.411	210	347	112	.938	104	504	280	8	1	4.08
CLE	73	55	.570	12.5	976	839	222	98	31	.300	.408	252	395	92	.929	110	356	242	2	2	4.20
PHI	72	57	.558	14	1011	841	246	90	79	.301	.430	202	318	121	.944	107	521	283	4	2	4.68
NY	68	64	.515	19.5	941	845	182	101	62	.293	.410	299	432	95	.927	111	581	395	6	4	4.29
BKN	65	63	.508	20.5	775	845	173	83	44	.266	.370	213	385	88	.930	109	547	297	3	3	4.55
CIN	65	63	.508	20.5	759	814	161	65	28	.259	.340	238	321	138	.943	97	549	258	4	5	4.59
BAL	60	70	.462	26.5	820	893	164	86	27	.275	.365	233	384	95	.929	104	534	275	1	2	4.97
CHI	56	71	.441	29	829	874	186	93	32	.279	.379	255	421	92	.922	101	553	273	4	5	4.81
STL	57	75	.432	30.5	745	829	152	98	10	.264	.341	250	398	110	.930	114	542	301	3	4	4.06
LOU	50	75	.400	34	759	942	178	73	18	.260	.342	203	330	111	.937	114	479	190	4	1	5.90
WAS	40	89	.310	46	722	1032	180	83	24	.266	.354	154	497	96	.912	110	574	292	2	0	5.56
LEAGUE TOTAL					10315	10315	2198	1047	456	.280	.379	2752	4581	1268	.931	1296	6142	3339	43	31	4.66

INDIVIDUAL PITCHING

PITCHER	T	W	L	PCT	ERA	SV	G	GS	CG	IP	H	BB	SO	R	ER	ShO	H/9	BB/9	SO/9
Ted Breitenstein	L	19	20	.487	3.18	1	48	42	38	382.2	359	156	102	197	135	1	8.44	3.67	2.40
Kid Gleason	R	21	25	.457	4.61	1	48	45	37	380.1	436	187	86	276	195	1	10.32	4.43	2.04
Pink Hawley	R	5	17	.227	4.60	1	31	24	21	227	249	103	73	184	116	0	9.87	4.08	2.89
Dad Clarkson	R	12	9	.571	3.48	0	24	21	17	186.1	194	79	37	116	72	1	9.37	3.82	1.79
John Dolan	R	0	2	.000	4.15	1	3	1	1	17.1	26	7	1	22	8	0	13.50	3.63	0.52
Bill Hawke		0	1	.000	5.06	0	1	1	0	5.1	9	3	1	9	3	0	15.19	5.06	1.69
Jimmy Bannon	R	0	1	.000	22.50	0	1	1	0	4	10	5	1	18	10	0	22.50	11.25	2.25
Frank Pears		0	0	-	13.50	0	1	0	0	4	9	2	0	7	6	0	20.25	4.50	0.00
TEAM TOTAL		57	75	.432	4.06	4	157	135	114	1207	1292	542	301	829	545	3	9.63	4.04	2.24

MANAGER	W	L	PCT
George Miller	56	76	.424

POS	Player	B	G	AB	H	2B	3B	HR	HR %	R	RBI	BB	SO	SB	Pinch Hit AB	Pinch Hit H	BA	SA
REGULARS																		
1B	Roger Connor	L	99	380	122	28	25	7	1.8	83	79	51	17	17	0	0	.321	.582
2B	Joe Quinn	R	106	405	116	18	1	4	1.0	59	61	24	8	25	0	0	.286	.365
SS	Bones Ely	R	127	510	156	20	12	12	2.4	85	89	30	34	23	0	0	.306	.463
3B	Doggie Miller	R	127	481	163	9	11	8	1.7	93	86	58	9	17	2	0	.339	.453
RF	Tommy Dowd	R	123	524	142	16	8	4	0.8	92	62	54	33	31	0	0	.271	.355
CF	Frank Shugart	L	133	527	154	19	18	7	1.3	103	72	38	37	21	0	0	.292	.436
LF	Charlie Frank		80	319	89	12	7	4	1.3	52	42	44	13	14	0	0	.279	.398
C	Heinie Peitz	R	99	338	89	19	9	3	0.9	52	49	43	21	14	0	0	.263	.399
SUBSTITUTES																		
3B	Tim O'Rourke		18	71	20	4	1	0	0.0	10	10	8	3	2	0	0	.282	.366
1B	Willard Brown	R	3	9	1	0	0	0	0.0	0	0	0	2	0	0	0	.111	.111
2B	Art Ball		1	3	1	0	0	0	0.0	0	0	0	1	0	0	0	.333	.333
3B	John Ricks		1	1	0	0	0	0	0.0	0	0	0	0	0	0	0	.000	.000
O3	Duff Cooley	L	54	206	61	3	1	1	0.5	35	21	12	16	7	0	0	.296	.335
OF	Marty Hogan		29	100	28	3	4	0	0.0	11	13	3	13	7	0	0	.280	.390
OF	Joe Peitz		7	26	11	2	3	0	0.0	10	3	6	1	2	0	0	.423	.731
UT	Paul Russell		3	10	1	0	0	0	0.0	1	0	0	2	0	0	0	.100	.100
OF	Pete Browning	R	2	7	1	0	0	0	0.0	1	0	0	0	0	0	0	.143	.143
OF	George Paynter	R	1	4	0	0	0	0	0.0	0	0	1	0	1	0	0	.000	.000
C	Old Hoss Twineham	L	38	127	40	4	1	1	0.8	22	16	9	11	2	0	0	.315	.386
C	Dick Buckley		29	89	16	1	2	1	1.1	5	3	6	3	1	1	0	.180	.270
PITCHERS																		
P	Ted Breitenstein	L	63	182	40	7	2	0	0.0	27	13	31	19	3	0	0	.220	.280
P	Pink Hawley	L	53	163	43	6	6	2	1.2	16	23	5	16	2	0	0	.264	.411
P	Dad Clarkson	R	33	88	16	0	1	0	0.0	11	7	16	28	1	1	0	.182	.205
P	Kid Gleason	L	9	28	7	0	1	0	0.0	3	1	2	1	0	0	0*	.250	.321
P	Ernie Mason		4	12	3	0	0	0	0.0	0	0	1	1	0	0	0	.250	.250
TEAM TOTAL				4610	1320	171	113	54	1.2	771	650	442	289	190	4	0	.286	.408

INDIVIDUAL FIELDING

POS	Player	T	G	PO	A	E	DP	TC/G	FA
1B	R. Connor	L	99	897	68	26	72*	10.0	.974
	D. Buckley	R	1	0	0	0	0	0.0	.000
	D. Miller	R	12	115	7	2	5	10.3	.984
	H. Peitz	R	14	107	12	4	11	8.8	.967
	C. Frank		3	30	1	0	0	10.3	1.000
	W. Brown	R	3	28	2	0	2	10.0	1.000
	K. Gleason	R	1	13	1	0	0	14.0	1.000
	D. Cooley	R	1	7	0	0	1	7.0	1.000
2B	J. Quinn	R	106	341	339	34	74	6.7	.952
	D. Miller	R	18	31	50	11	3	5.1	.880
	T. Dowd	R	7	20	19	4	2	6.1	.907
	B. Ely	R	1	3	4	2	0	9.0	.778
	P. Russell		1	3	3	1	0	7.0	.857
	A. Ball	R	1	2	0	1	0	3.0	.667
SS	B. Ely	R	126	273	442	79	51	6.3	.901
	D. Cooley	R	1	0	0	0	0	0.0	.000
	F. Shugart	R	7	25	16	5	2	6.6	.891
	D. Miller	R	1	2	1	2	0	5.0	.600
3B	D. Miller	R	52	68	96	33	6	3.8	.832
	H. Peitz	R	47	67	73	16	4	3.3	.897
	T. O'Rourke	R	18	29	33	10	3	4.0	.861
	T. Dowd	R	1	0	0	0	0	0.0	.000
	D. Cooley	R	13	10	21	12	1	3.3	.721
	F. Shugart	R	7	8	11	8	2	3.9	.704
	J. Ricks		1	1	0	3	0	4.0	.250
	P. Russell		1	1	2	1	0	4.0	.750
OF	F. Shugart	R	122	276	26	29	2	2.7	.912
	T. Dowd	R	117	199	14	16	4	2.0	.930
	C. Frank		77	161	11	26	4	2.6	.869
	D. Cooley	R	39	74	1	15	1	2.3	.833
	M. Hogan		29	42	5	6	5	1.8	.887
	P. Hawley	R	1	0	0	0	0	0.0	.000
	E. Mason		1	0	0	0	0	0.0	.000
	J. Peitz		7	17	1	4	1	3.1	.818
	D. Miller	R	4	5	1	1	0	1.8	.857
	Breitenstein	L	7	5	0	1	0	0.9	.833
	G. Paynter	R	1	1	2	0	0	3.0	1.000
	P. Russell		1	1	1	0	0	2.0	1.000
	P. Browning	R	2	2	0	0	0	1.0	1.000
C	H. Peitz	R	39	146	51	13	3	5.4	.938
	O. Twineham	R	38	147	38	12	1	5.2	.939
	D. Miller	R	41	140	36	11	3	4.6	.941
	D. Buckley	R	27	88	29	8	2	4.6	.936

Maybe it took the hitters a year to adjust to the new pitching distance. Whatever the reason, they put on an offensive show almost unparalleled in the history of the game. The league as a whole batted .309; Philadelphia's club batting average was .349, and they had three .400 hitters who finished 2-3-4 in batting, behind Boston's Hugh Duffy, who hit .438.

St. Louis broke well out of the gate, but quickly fell out of the pennant race, sitting comfortably in ninth place by the end of May. They lay tenth until the very last day of the season, when a doubleheader sweep against Cincinnati put them one percentage point ahead of the Red Stockings. Breitenstein set an all-time record by allowing 497 hits, but he still managed to stay over .500, and his 4.79 ERA is better than it looks; the league ERA for the year was 5.32.

TEAM STATISTICS

	W	L	PCT	GB	R	OR	2B	3B	HR	BA	SA	SB	E	DP	FA	CG	BB	SO	ShO	SV	ERA
								Batting						Fielding				Pitching			
BAL	89	39	.695		1171	820	271	150	33	.343	.483	324	293	105	.944	97	472	275	1	11	5.00
NY	88	44	.667	3	940	789	197	96	44	.301	.409	319	443	101	.924	111	539	395	5	5	3.83
BOS	83	49	.629	8	1222	1002	272	93	103	.331	.484	241	415	120	.925	108	262	262	3	1	5.41
PHI	71	57	.555	18	1143	966	252	131	40	.349	.476	273	338	111	.935	102	469	262	3	4	5.63
BKN	70	61	.534	20.5	1021	1007	228	130	42	.313	.440	282	390	85	.928	105	555	285	3	5	5.51
CLE	68	61	.527	21.5	932	896	241	90	37	.303	.414	220	344	107	.935	107	435	254	6	1	4.97
PIT	65	65	.500	25	955	972	222	123	49	.312	.443	220	354	106	.936	106	457	304	2	0	5.60
CHI	57	75	.432	34	1041	1066	265	86	65	.314	.441	327	452	113	.918	117	557	281	0	0	5.68
STL	56	76	.424	35	771	954	171	113	54	.286	.408	190	426	109	.923	114	500	319	2	0	5.29
CIN	55	75	.423	35	910	1085	224	68	60	.294	.410	215	423	119	.925	110	491	219	4	3	5.99
WAS	45	87	.341	46	882	1122	218	118	59	.287	.425	249	499	81	.908	102	446	190	1	4	5.51
LOU	36	94	.277	54	692	1001	173	88	42	.269	.375	217	428	130	.920	113	475	258	1	1	5.45
LEAGUE TOTAL					11680	11680	2734	1286	628	.309	.435	3113	4805	1287	.927	1292	5807	3304	32	35	5.32

INDIVIDUAL PITCHING

PITCHER	T	W	L	PCT	ERA	SV	G	GS	CG	IP	H	BB	SO	R	ER	ShO	H/9	BB/9	SO/9
Ted Breitenstein	L	27	25	.519	4.79	0	56	50	46	447.1	497	191	140	321	238	1	10.00	3.84	2.82
Pink Hawley	R	19	26	.422	4.90	0	53	41	36	392.2	481	149	120	306	214	0	11.02	3.42	2.75
Dad Clarkson	R	8	17	.320	6.36	0	32	32	24	233.1	318	117	46	236	165	1	12.27	4.51	1.77
Kid Gleason	R	2	6	.250	6.05	0	8	8	6	58	75	21	9	50	39	0	11.64	3.26	1.40
Ernie Mason		0	2	.000	7.15	0	4	2	2	22.2	34	10	3	29	18	0	13.50	3.97	1.19
Charlie Frank		0	0	–	15.00	0	2	0	0	3	6	7	1	5	5	0	18.00	21.00	3.00
Heinie Peitz	R	0	0	–	9.00	0	1	0	0	3	7	2	0	7	3	0	21.00	6.00	0.00
Bones Ely	R	0	0	–	0.00	0	1	0	0	1	0	3	0	0	0	0	0.00	27.00	0.00
TEAM TOTAL		56	76	.424	5.29	0	157	133	114	1161	1418	500	319	954	682	2	10.99	3.88	2.47

CARDINAL MVP WINNERS

1925	Rogers Hornsby	1944	Marty Marion
1926	Bob O'Farrell	1946	Stan Musial
1928	Jim Bottomley	1948	Stan Musial
1931	Frankie Frisch	1964	Ken Boyer
1934	Dizzy Dean	1967	Orlando Cepeda
1937	Joe Medwick	1968	Bob Gibson
1942	Mort Cooper	1971	Joe Torre
1943	Stan Musial	1979	Keith Hernandez (tied)

MANAGER	W	L	PCT
Al Buckenberger	16	32	.333
Joe Quinn	13	27	.325
Lew Phelan	8	21	.276
Chris Von Der Ahe	2	12	.143

POS	Player	B	G	AB	H	2B	3B	HR	HR %	R	RBI	BB	SO	SB	Pinch Hit AB	Pinch Hit H	BA	SA
REGULARS																		
1B	Roger Connor	L	104	402	131	29	9	8	2.0	78	77	63	10	9	0	0	.326	.502
2B	Joe Quinn	R	134	543	169	19	9	2	0.4	84	74	36	6	22	0	0	.311	.390
SS	Bones Ely	R	117	467	121	16	2	1	0.2	68	46	19	17	28	0	0	.259	.308
3B	Doggie Miller	R	121	490	143	15	4	5	1.0	81	74	25	12	18	0	0	.292	.369
RF	Tommy Dowd	R	129	505	163	19	17	6	1.2	95	74	30	31	30	2	0	.323	.463
CF	Tom Brown	L	83	350	76	11	4	1	0.3	72	31	48	44*	34	0	0	.217	.280
LF	Duff Cooley	L	132	563	191	9	21	6	1.1	106	75	36	29	27	1	0	.339	.462
C	Heinie Peitz	R	90	334	95	14	12	2	0.6	44	65	29	20	9	0	0	.284	.416
SUBSTITUTES																		
3B	Denny Lyons	R	33	129	38	6	0	2	1.6	24	25	14	5	3	0	0	.295	.388
3B	Ike Samuels	R	24	74	17	2	0	0	0.0	5	5	5	7	5	0	0	.230	.257
3O	Frank Bonner		15	59	8	0	1	1	1.7	3	8	1	8	2	0	0	.136	.220
1B	Guy McFadden		4	14	3	0	0	0	0.0	1	2	0	2	0	0	0	.214	.214
3B	Joe Connor		2	7	0	0	0	0	0.0	0	1	0	2	0	0	0	.000	.000
3B	Walt Kinlock		1	3	1	0	0	0	0.0	0	0	0	2	0	0	0	.333	.333
3B	J. Ryan		2	2	0	0	0	0	0.0	0	0	0	0	0	0	0	.000	.000
PO	Ted Breitenstein	L	72	218	42	2	0	0	0.0	25	18	29	22	5	1	1	.193	.202
O1	Biff Sheehan		52	180	57	3	6	1	0.6	24	18	20	6	7	0	0	.317	.417
UT	Bill Kissinger	R	33	97	24	6	1	0	0.0	8	8	0	11	1	0	0	.247	.330
OF	Marty Hogan		5	18	3	1	0	0	0.0	2	2	3	0	2	0	0	.167	.222
OF	Henry Adkinson		1	5	2	0	0	0	0.0	1	0	0	2	0	0	0	.400	.400
C	Joe Otten		26	87	21	0	0	0	0.0	8	8	5	8	2	0	0	.241	.241
C	Fred Fagin		1	3	1	0	0	0	0.0	0	2	0	0	0	0	0	.333	.333
PITCHERS																		
P	Red Ehret	R	37	96	21	2	1	1	1.0	13	9	6	12	0	0	0	.219	.292
P	Harry Staley	R	23	67	9	0	2	0	0.0	4	1	4	1	1	0	0	.134	.194
P	John McDougal		18	41	6	1	0	0	0.0	1	6	8	16	0	0	0	.146	.171
P	Dad Clarkson	R	7	23	1	0	0	0	0.0	0	0	3	4	0	0	0	.043	.043
P	John Coleman		1	5	1	0	0	0	0.0	0	0	0	1	0	0	0	.200	.200
P	Red Donahue	R	1	3	0	0	0	0	0.0	0	0	0	1	0	0	0	.000	.000
	TEAM TOTAL			4785	1344	155	89	36	0.8	747	629	384	279	205	4	1	.281	.373

INDIVIDUAL FIELDING

POS	Player	T	G	PO	A	E	DP	TC/G	FA	POS	Player	T	G	PO	A	E	DP	TC/G	FA
1B	R. Connor	L	103	953	62	14	60	10.0	.986	OF	D. Cooley	R	124	320	17	23	1	2.9	.936
	B. Sheehan	R	11	95	3	5	6	9.4	.951		T. Dowd	R	115	218	11	18	3	2.1	.927
	H. Peitz	R	11	76	7	4	6	7.9	.954		T. Brown	R	83	215	15	12	5	2.9	.950
	D. Miller	R	6	47	1	1	4	8.2	.980		B. Sheehan	R	41	56	7	4	1	1.6	.940
	G. McFadden		4	30	0	1	3	7.8	.968		D. Miller	R	21	28	4	10	1	2.0	.762
											Breitenstein	L	16	18	0	3	0	1.3	.857
2B	J. Quinn	R	134	359	390	43	63	5.9	.946		M. Hogan		5	13	2	3	0	3.6	.833
	T. Dowd	R	2	5	3	0	0	4.0	1.000		F. Bonner	R	5	10	0	0	0	2.0	1.000
											H. Adkinson		1	2	0	1	0	3.0	.667
SS	B. Ely	R	117	247	407	53	52	6.0	.925		J. Otten		2	1	0	1	0	1.0	.500
	D. Miller	R	9	10	27	5	1	4.7	.881		B. Kissinger	R	4	2	0	0	0	0.5	1.000
	B. Kissinger	R	4	3	14	5	0	5.5	.773										
	D. Cooley	R	3	5	10	4	0	6.3	.789	C	H. Peitz	R	71	260	80	23	10	5.1	.937
	I. Samuels	R	3	0	7	4	0	3.7	.636		D. Miller	R	46	137	41	13	5	4.2	.932
											J. Otten		24	74	15	5	3	3.9	.947
3B	D. Miller	R	46	54	72	26	5	3.3	.829		F. Fagin		1	4	3	4	0	11.0	.636
	D. Lyons	R	33	61	49	13	2	3.7	.894		D. Cooley	R	1	1	1	1	0	3.0	.667
	I. Samuels	R	21	22	38	20	1	3.8	.750		F. Bonner	R	1	1	0	0	0	1.0	1.000
	T. Dowd	R	17	15	26	9	0	2.9	.820										
	F. Bonner	R	10	8	13	11	0	3.2	.656										
	H. Peitz	R	10	12	6	5	1	2.3	.783										
	D. Cooley	R	5	10	10	1	2	4.2	.952										
	J. Connor		2	2	5	0	1	3.5	1.000										
	W. Kinlock		1	4	1	0	1	5.0	1.000										
	B. Kissinger	R	1	1	0	1	0	2.0	.500										
	J. Ryan		2	0	0	1	0	0.5	.000										

In an unusually exciting season, in which nine of the twelve teams finished above .500, it was inevitable that someone had to absorb a lot of losses. The Browns, along with Washington and Louisville, contributed mightily, dropping 92 of their 131 games. The Browns lost steadily and consistently, sitting in eleventh place almost from start to finish. They were eleventh in runs scored, tenth in runs allowed, and eleventh in ERA. Breitenstein led the league in complete games for the second straight year, and led the league in losses with 30. While they lost their season series with every other club, they somehow managed to split twelve games with the league champion Baltimore Orioles.

TEAM STATISTICS

	W	L	PCT	GB	R	OR	2B	3B	HR	BA	SA	SB	E	DP	FA	CG	BB	SO	ShO	SV	ERA
BAL	87	43	.669		1009	646	235	89	25	.324	.427	310	288	108	.946	104	430	244	10	4	3.80
CLE	84	46	.646	3	917	720	194	67	29	.305	.395	187	348	77	.936	108	346	326	6	3	3.90
PHI	78	53	.595	9.5	1068	957	272	73	61	.330	.450	276	369	93	.933	106	485	330	2	7	5.47
CHI	72	58	.554	15	866	854	171	85	55	.298	.405	260	401	113	.928	119	432	297	3	1	4.67
BKN	71	60	.542	16.5	867	834	189	77	39	.282	.379	183	325	96	.941	103	395	216	5	6	4.94
BOS	71	60	.542	16.5	907	826	197	57	54	.290	.391	199	364	104	.934	115	363	370	4	4	4.27
PIT	71	61	.538	17	811	787	190	89	26	.290	.386	257	392	95	.930	106	500	382	4	6	4.05
CIN	66	64	.508	21	903	854	235	107	33	.298	.415	326	377	112	.931	97	362	245	2	6	4.81
NY	66	65	.504	21.5	852	834	191	90	32	.288	.389	292	438	106	.922	115	415	409	6	1	4.51
WAS	43	85	.336	43	837	1048	207	101	55	.287	.412	237	447	96	.917	99	465	258	0	5	5.28
STL	39	92	.298	48.5	747	1032	155	89	36	.281	.373	205	380	94	.930	105	439	280	1	1	5.76
LOU	35	96	.267	52.5	698	1090	171	73	34	.279	.368	156	477	104	.913	104	469	245	3	1	5.90
LEAGUE TOTAL					10482	10482	2407	997	479	.296	.399	2888	4606	1198	.930	1281	5101	3602	46	45	4.78

INDIVIDUAL PITCHING

PITCHER	T	W	L	PCT	ERA	SV	G	GS	CG	IP	H	BB	SO	R	ER	ShO	H/9	BB/9	SO/9
Ted Breitenstein	L	18	30	.375	4.44	1	54	50	46	429.2	458	178	127	295	212	1	9.59	3.73	2.66
Ted Ehret	R	6	19	.240	6.02	0	37	32	18	231.2	360	88	55	223	155	0	13.99	3.42	2.14
Harry Staley	R	6	13	.316	5.22	0	23	16	13	158.2	223	39	28	136	92	0	12.65	2.21	1.59
Bill Kissinger	R	4	12	.250	6.72	0	24	14	9	140.2	222	51	31	145	105	0	14.20	3.26	1.98
John McDougal		4	10	.286	8.32	0	18	14	10	114.2	187	46	23	146	106	0	14.68	3.61	1.81
Dad Clarkson	R	1	6	.143	7.38	0	7	7	7	61	91	26	9	66	50	0	13.43	3.84	1.33
John Coleman		0	1	.000	13.50	0	1	1	1	8	12	8	5	15	12	0	13.50	9.00	5.63
Ted Donahue	R	0	1	.000	6.75	0	1	1	1	8	9	3	2	6	6	0	10.13	3.38	2.25
TEAM TOTAL		39	92	.298	5.76	1	165	135	105	1152.1	1562	439	280	1032	738	1	12.20	3.43	2.19

MANAGER	W	L	PCT
Harry Diddlebock	7	11	.389
Arlie Latham	0	2	.000
Chris Von Der Ahe	0	2	.000
Roger Connor	9	37	.196
Tommy Dowd	24	38	.387

POS	Player	B	G	AB	H	2B	3B	HR	HR %	R	RBI	BB	SO	SB	Pinch Hit AB	Pinch Hit H	BA	SA
REGULARS																		
1B	Roger Connor	L	126	483	137	21	9	11	2.3	71	72	52	14	10	0	0	.284	.433
2B	Tommy Dowd	R	126	521	138	17	11	5	1.0	93	46	42	19	40	0	0	.265	.369
SS	Monte Cross	R	125	427	104	10	6	6	1.4	66	52	58	48	40	0	0	.244	.337
3B	Bert Meyers		122	454	116	12	8	0	0.0	47	37	40	32	8	0	0	.256	.317
RF	Tuck Turner	L	51	203	50	7	8	1	0.5	30	27	14	21	6	0	0	.246	.374
CF	Tom Parrott	R	118	474	138	13	12	7	1.5	62	70	11	24	12	0	0	.291	.414
LF	Klondike Douglas	L	81	296	78	6	4	1	0.3	42	28	35	15	18	1	0	.264	.321
C	Ed McFarland	R	83	290	70	13	4	3	1.0	48	36	15	17	7	1	0	.241	.345
SUBSTITUTES																		
2B	Joe Quinn	R	48	191	40	6	1	1	0.5	19	17	9	5	8	0	0	.209	.267
3B	Arlie Latham	R	8	35	7	0	0	0	0.0	3	5	4	3	2	0	0	.200	.200
OF	Joe Sullivan		51	212	62	4	2	2	0.9	25	21	9	12	5	0	0	.292	.358
OF	Duff Cooley	L	40	166	51	5	3	0	0.0	29	13	7	3	12	0	0	.307	.373
OS	Tom Niland	R	18	68	12	0	1	0	0.0	3	3	5	4	0	0	0	.176	.206
OF	Biff Sheehan		6	19	3	0	0	0	0.0	0	1	4	0	0	0	0	.158	.158
C	Morgan Murphy	R	49	175	45	5	2	0	0.0	12	11	8	14	1	1	0	.257	.309
PITCHERS																		
P	Ted Breitenstein	L	51	162	42	5	2	0	0.0	21	12	13	26	8	1	1	.259	.315
P	Bill Hart		49	161	30	4	5	0	0.0	9	15	3	15	7	0	0	.186	.273
P	Red Donahue	R	33	107	17	2	0	0	0.0	5	9	3	23	1	0	0	.159	.178
P	Bill Kissinger	R	23	73	22	4	0	0	0.0	8	12	0	4	0	0	0	.301	.356
P	John McDougal		3	3	0	0	0	0	0.0	0	0	0	1	0	0	0	.000	.000
P	John Wood		1	0	0	0	0	0	–	0	0	0	0	0	0	0	–	–
	TEAM TOTAL			4520	1162	134	78	37	0.8	593	487	332	300	185	4	1	.257	.346

INDIVIDUAL FIELDING

POS	Player	T	G	PO	A	E	DP	TC/G	FA
1B	R. Connor	L	126	1217	94	16	48	10.5	.988
	T. Parrott	R	6	51	5	2	0	9.7	.966
2B	T. Dowd	R	78	182	220	35	22	5.6	.920
	J. Quinn	R	48	92	167	12	7	5.6	.956
	J. Sullivan		7	12	15	1	0	4.0	.964
SS	M. Cross	R	125	298	394	84	31	6.2	.892
	T. Niland	R	5	4	14	5	0	4.6	.783
	B. Meyers		1	3	1	0	0	4.0	1.000
	K. Douglas	R	2	0	4	0	0	2.0	1.000
3B	B. Meyers		121	162	242	62	16	3.9	.867
	A. Latham	R	8	14	15	10	2	4.9	.744
	B. Kissinger	R	1	0	2	3	0	5.0	.400
	J. Sullivan		1	2	2	0	0	4.0	1.000

POS	Player	T	G	PO	A	E	DP	TC/G	FA
OF	T. Parrott	R	108	276	16	15	7	2.8	.951
	K. Douglas	R	74	105	13	14	3	1.8	.894
	T. Dowd	R	48	111	4	8	2	2.6	.935
	D. Cooley	R	40	91	2	4	0	2.4	.959
	J. Sullivan		45	81	4	4	1	2.0	.955
	T. Turner		51	69	4	3	1	1.5	.961
	E. McFarland	R	2	0	0	0	0	0.0	.000
	T. Niland	R	13	19	2	2	1	1.8	.913
	Breitenstein	L	8	12	0	1	0	1.6	.923
	B. Sheehan	R	6	10	0	0	0	1.7	1.000
	B. Hart		8	9	0	0	0	1.1	1.000
	B. Kissinger	R	3	5	0	0	0	1.7	1.000
	R. Donahue	R	1	1	1	0	0	2.0	1.000
C	E. McFarland	R	80	276	117	16	6	5.1	.961
	M. Murphy	R	48	178	48	18	5	5.1	.926
	K. Douglas	R	6	18	5	1	2	4.0	.958

St. Louis started out strongly, but very quickly reclaimed their accustomed perch in eleventh place, suffering a 9–39 stretch that included a disastrous mark of 4–20 in the month of June. They won just 13 of 68 games on the road, and finished dead last in runs, batting average, slugging average, and ERA; they were also second to last in runs allowed. Their won-lost percentage against first division clubs was a woeful .211. Breitenstein improved his record all the way up to 18–26; Bill Hart picked up the slack with 29 losses. Their leading batter was centerfielder Tom Parrott, who ranked forty-eighth in the league among hitters who had played in a hundred or more games.

TEAM STATISTICS

	W	L	PCT	GB	R	OR	Batting 2B	3B	HR	BA	SA	SB	Fielding E	DP	FA	Pitching CG	BB	SO	ShO	SV	ERA
AL	90	39	.698		995	662	207	100	23	.328	.429	441	296	114	.945	115	339	302	9	1	3.67
LE	80	48	.625	9.5	840	650	207	72	28	.301	.391	175	288	117	.949	113	280	336	9	5	3.46
IN	77	50	.606	12	783	620	205	73	19	.294	.388	350	252	107	.951	105	310	219	12	4	3.67
OS	74	57	.565	17	860	761	175	74	36	.300	.392	241	368	94	.934	110	397	277	6	3	3.78
HI	71	57	.555	18.5	815	799	182	97	34	.286	.390	332	366	115	.934	118	467	353	2	1	4.41
IT	66	63	.512	24	787	741	169	94	27	.292	.385	217	317	103	.941	108	439	362	8	1	4.30
Y	64	67	.489	27	829	821	159	87	40	.297	.394	274	365	90	.933	104	403	312	1	2	4.54
HI	62	68	.477	28.5	890	891	234	84	49	.295	.413	191	313	112	.941	107	387	243	3	2	5.20
KN	58	73	.443	33	692	764	174	87	28	.284	.379	198	297	104	.945	97	400	259	3	1	4.25
AS	58	73	.443	33	818	920	179	79	45	.286	.388	258	398	99	.927	106	435	292	2	3	4.61
TL	40	90	.308	50.5	593	929	134	78	37	.257	.346	185	345	73	.936	115	456	279	1	1	5.33
OU	38	93	.290	53	653	997	142	80	37	.261	.351	195	475	110	.916	108	541	288	1	4	5.12
AGUE TOTAL					9555	9555	2167	1005	403	.290	.387	3057	4080	1238	.938	1306	4854	3522	57	28	4.36

INDIVIDUAL PITCHING

TCHER	T	W	L	PCT	ERA	SV	G	GS	CG	IP	H	BB	SO	R	ER	ShO	H/9	BB/9	SO/9
ed Breitenstein	L	18	26	.409	4.48	0	44	43	37	339.2	376	138	114	236	169	1	9.96	3.66	3.02
ll Hart		12	29	.293	5.12	0	42	41	37	336	411	141	65	271	191	0	11.01	3.78	1.74
ed Donahue	R	7	24	.226	5.80	0	32	32	28	267	376	98	70	235	172	0	12.67	3.30	2.36
ll Kissinger	R	2	9	.182	6.49	1	20	12	11	136	209	55	22	136	98	0	13.83	3.64	1.46
m Parrott	R	1	1	.500	6.21	0	7	2	2	42	62	18	8	39	29	0	13.29	3.86	1.71
hn McDougal		0	1	.000	8.10	0	3	1	0	10	13	4	0	11	9	0	11.70	3.60	0.00
AM TOTAL		40	90	.308	5.32	1	148	131	115	1130.2	1447	454	279	928	668	1	11.52	3.61	2.22

MANAGER	W	L	PCT
Tommy Dowd	6	25	.194
Hugh Nicol	9	29	.237
Bill Hallman	13	46	.220
Chris Von Der Ahe	1	2	.333

POS	Player	B	G	AB	H	2B	3B	HR	HR %	R	RBI	BB	SO	SB	Pinch Hit AB	Pinch Hit H	BA	SA
REGULARS																		
1B	Mike Grady	R	83	322	90	11	3	7	2.2*	48	55	26		7	0	0	.280	.398
2B	Bill Hallman	R	79	298	66	6	2	0	0.0	31	26	24		12	0	0	.221	.255
SS	Monte Cross	R	131	462	132	17	11	4	0.9	59	55	62		38	0	0	.286	.396
3B	Fred Hartman		124	516	158	21	8	2	0.4	67	67	26		18	0	0	.306	.390
RF	Tuck Turner	L	103	416	121	17	12	2	0.5	58	41	35		8	1	0	.291	.404
CF	Dick Harley	L	89	330	96	6	4	3	0.9	43	35	36		23	0	0	.291	.361
LF	Bud Lally	R	87	355	99	15	5	2	0.6	56	42	9		12	0	0	.279	.366
C	Klondike Douglas	L	125	516	170	15	3	6	1.2	77	50	52		12	1	1	.329	.405
SUBSTITUTES																		
2O	John Houseman		80	278	68	6	6	0	0.0	34	21	28		16	2	1	.245	.309
1B	Roger Connor	L	22	83	19	3	1	1	1.2	13	12	13		3	0	0	.229	.325
2B	Lou Bierbauer	R	12	46	10	0	0	0	0.0	1	1	0		2	0	0	.217	.217
OF	Tommy Dowd	R	35	145	38	9	1	0	0.0	25	9	6		11	0	0	.262	.338
PO	Bill Kissinger	R	14	39	13	3	2	0	0.0	7	6	3		0	0	0	.333	.513
OF	Ed Beecher		3	12	4	0	0	0	0.0	1	1	0		1	0	0	.333	.333
OF	Frank Huelsman	R	2	7	2	1	0	0	0.0	0	0	0		0	0	0	.286	.429
C	Morgan Murphy	R	62	207	35	2	0	0	0.0	13	12	6		1	0	0	.169	.179
UT	Ed McFarland	R	31	107	35	5	2	1	0.9	14	17	8		2	1	0	.327	.439
PITCHERS																		
P	Bill Hart		46	156	39	1	2	2	1.3	14	14	1		4	0	0	.250	.321
P	Red Donahue	R	49	155	33	7	2	1	0.6	11	14	4		1	0	0	.213	.303
P	Kid Carsey	R	13	43	13	2	2	0	0.0	2	5	1		1	1	1	.302	.442
P	Willie Sudhoff	R	11	42	10	1	0	0	0.0	7	3	1		0	0	0	.238	.262
P	Percy Coleman		12	28	6	0	0	0	0.0	2	3	1		0	0	0	.214	.214
P	Duke Esper		8	25	8	0	0	0	0.0	2	3	1		0	0	0	.320	.320
P	Bill Hutchison	R	6	18	5	0	1	0	0.0	1	0	1		0	0	0	.278	.389
P	Con Lucid		6	17	3	0	0	0	0.0	2	1	4		0	0	0	.176	.176
P	Mike McDermott		4	9	2	1	0	0	0.0	0	0	0		0	0	0	.222	.333
P	John Grimes	R	3	7	2	0	0	0	0.0	0	1	3		0	0	0	.286	.286
P	LeRoy Evans	R	3	3	0	0	0	0	0.0	0	0	3		0	0	0	.000	.000
	TEAM TOTAL			4642	1277	149	67	31	0.7	588	494	354		172	6	3	.275	.356

INDIVIDUAL FIELDING

POS	Player	T	G	PO	A	E	DP	TC/G	FA
1B	M. Grady	R	83	797	48	23	54	10.5	.974
	R. Connor	L	22	237	12	4	6	11.5	.984
	K. Douglas	R	17	140	6	2	5	8.7	.986
	M. Murphy	R	8	46	4	0	3	6.3	1.000
	B. Lally	R	3	31	3	2	1	12.0	.944
	E. McFarland	R	3	21	5	3	0	9.7	.897
	B. Hallman	R	3	21	3	1	0	8.3	.960
	R. Donahue	R	1	2	0	0	0	2.0	1.000
	B. Hart		1	1	0	0	0	1.0	1.000
2B	B. Hallman	R	77	189	244	28	35	6.0	.939
	J. Houseman		41	106	129	21	10	6.2	.918
	L. Bierbauer	R	12	25	33	5	4	5.3	.921
	T. Dowd	R	5	9	9	4	0	4.4	.818
	E. McFarland	R	1	4	3	2	0	9.0	.778
SS	M. Cross	R	131	327	513	73	47	7.0	.920
	K. Douglas	R	1	0	0	0	0	0.0	.000
	J. Houseman		5	5	8	1	0	2.8	.929
3B	F. Hartman	R	124	159	253	63	14	3.8	.867
	J. Houseman		3	1	10	2	0	4.3	.846
	K. Douglas	R	7	1	3	1	0	0.7	.800

POS	Player	T	G	PO	A	E	DP	TC/G	FA
OF	D. Harley	R	89	186	19	23	3	2.6	.899
	B. Lally	R	84	192	9	23	2	2.7	.897
	T. Turner		102	146	10	9	3	1.6	.945
	K. Douglas	R	43	81	7	5	1	2.2	.946
	T. Dowd	R	30	65	0	6	0	2.4	.915
	J. Houseman		33	62	2	3	0	2.0	.955
	B. Kissinger	R	7	11	0	3	0	2.0	.786
	B. Hart		6	9	0	2	0	1.8	.818
	R. Donahue	R	2	7	0	1	0	4.0	.875
	E. McFarland	R	3	6	0	1	0	2.3	.857
	E. Beecher		3	6	0	0	0	2.0	1.000
	M. Grady	R	1	1	0	0	0	1.0	1.000
	F. Huelsman	R	2	0	0	1	0	0.5	.000
C	K. Douglas	R	61	171	64	13	4	4.1	.948
	M. Murphy	R	53	145	62	11	3	4.1	.950
	E. McFarland	R	23	80	31	4	3	5.0	.965

The St. Louis club hit rock bottom in '97. They dropped 45 of their first 56, had their best month by far in July at 10–18, and then won just 8 of their final 50 to finish at 29–102, with the worst won-lost record recorded in the majors at that time. Their sole individual "highlight" was Red Donahue's tying for the league lead in complete games and starts—hardly helpful, since he allowed more than twelve and one-half hits per nine innings, had an ERA of 6.13, and set a modern record with 33 losses. Needless to say, he was gone before the following season, but that alone was not enough to solve their severe pitching problem. Their club ERA was 6.21; the combined ERA of the other eleven teams in the league was 4.14, over two runs a game better.

TEAM STATISTICS

	W	L	PCT	GB	R	OR	2B	3B	Batting HR	BA	SA	SB	E	Fielding DP	FA	CG	BB	Pitching SO	ShO	SV	ERA
OS	93	39	.705		1025	665	230	83	45	.319	.426	233	272	80	.951	115	393	329	8	7	3.65
AL	90	40	.692	2	964	674	243	66	20	.325	.414	401	277	110	.951	118	382	361	3	0	3.55
Y	83	48	.634	9.5	895	695	188	84	31	.299	.392	328	397	109	.930	118	486	456	8	3	3.47
IN	76	56	.576	17	763	705	219	69	22	.290	.383	194	273	100	.948	100	329	270	4	2	4.09
LE	69	62	.527	23.5	773	680	192	88	16	.298	.389	181	261	74	.950	111	277	277	6	0	3.95
KN	61	71	.462	32	802	845	202	72	22	.279	.365	187	364	99	.936	114	410	256	4	2	4.60
VAS	61	71	.462	32	781	793	194	77	36	.297	.395	208	369	103	.933	103	348	348	7	5	4.01
IT	60	71	.458	32.5	676	835	140	108	25	.276	.370	170	346	70	.936	112	318	342	2	2	4.67
HI	59	73	.447	34	832	894	189	97	38	.282	.386	264	393	112	.932	131	433	361	2	1	4.53
HI	55	77	.417	38	752	792	213	83	40	.293	.398	163	296	72	.944	115	364	253	4	2	4.60
OU	52	78	.400	40	669	859	160	70	40	.265	.358	195	395	85	.929	114	459	267	2	0	4.42
TL	29	102	.221	63.5	588	1083	149	67	31	.275	.356	172	375	84	.933	109	453	207	1	1	6.21
EAGUE TOTAL					9520	9520	2319	964	366	.292	.386	2696	4018	1098	.939	1360	4716	3727	51	25	4.31

INDIVIDUAL PITCHING

ITCHER	T	W	L	PCT	ERA	SV	G	GS	CG	IP	H	BB	SO	R	ER	ShO	H/9	BB/9	SO/9
ed Donahue	R	11	33	.250	6.13	1	46	42	38	348	484	106	64	306	237	1	12.52	2.74	1.66
ll Hart		9	27	.250	6.26	0	39	38	31	294.2	395	148	67	292	205	0	12.06	4.52	2.05
id Carsey	R	3	8	.273	6.00	0	12	11	11	99	133	31	14	81	66	0	12.09	2.82	1.27
illie Sudhoff	R	1	8	.111	4.47	0	11	9	9	92.2	126	21	19	72	46	0	12.24	2.04	1.85
uke Esper	L	1	6	.143	5.28	0	8	8	7	61.1	95	12	8	51	36	0	13.94	1.76	1.17
ercy Coleman		1	3	.250	8.16	0	12	4	2	57.1	99	32	10	71	52	0	15.54	5.02	1.57
on Lucid		1	5	.167	3.67	0	6	6	5	49	66	26	4	46	20	0	12.12	4.78	0.73
ll Hutchison	R	1	4	.200	6.08	0	6	5	2	40	55	22	5	41	27	0	12.38	4.95	1.13
ll Kissinger	R	0	4	.000	11.49	0	7	4	2	31.1	51	15	5	50	40	0	14.65	4.31	1.44
ike McDermott	R	1	2	.333	9.28	0	4	4	1	21.1	23	19	3	23	22	0	9.70	8.02	1.27
ohn Grimes	R	0	2	.000	5.95	0	3	1	1	19.2	24	8	4	23	13	0	10.98	3.66	1.83
eRoy Evans	R	0	0	–	9.69	0	3	0	0	13	33	13	4	27	14	0	22.85	9.00	2.77
EAM TOTAL		29	102	.221	6.21	1	157	132	109	1127.1	1584	453	207	1083	778	1	12.65	3.62	1.65

MANAGER	W	L	PCT
Tim Hurst	39	111	.260

POS	Player	B	G	AB	H	2B	3B	HR	HR %	R	RBI	BB	SO	SB	Pinch Hit AB	Pinch Hit H	BA	SA
REGULARS																		
1B	George Decker		76	286	74	10	0	1	0.3	26	45	20		4	1	0	.259	.304
2B	John Crooks		72	225	52	4	2	1	0.4	33	20	40		3	0	0	.231	.280
SS	Germany Smith	R	51	157	25	2	1	1	0.6	16	9	24		1	0	0	.159	.204
3B	Lave Cross	R	151	602	191	28	8	3	0.5	71	79	28		14	0	0	.317	.405
RF	Tommy Dowd	R	139	586	143	17	7	0	0.0	70	32	30		16	0	0	.244	.297
CF	Jake Stenzel	R	108	404	114	15	11	1	0.2	64	33	41		21	0	0	.282	.381
LF	Dick Harley	L	142	549	135	6	5	0	0.0	74	42	34		13	1	1	.246	.275
C	Jack Clements	L	99	335	86	19	5	3	0.9	39	41	21		1	12	1	.257	.370
SUBSTITUTES																		
2S	Joe Quinn	R	103	375	94	10	5	0	0.0	35	36	24		13	0	0	.251	.304
1B	Tommy Tucker	B	72	252	60	7	2	0	0.0	18	20	18		1	0	0	.238	.282
UT	Suter Sullivan		42	144	32	3	0	0	0.0	10	12	13		1	2	0	.222	.243
SS	Russ Hall		39	143	35	2	1	0	0.0	13	10	7		1	0	0	.245	.273
UT	Kid Carsey	R	38	105	21	0	1	1	1.0	8	10	10		3	0	0	.200	.248
UT	Lou Bierbauer	R	4	9	0	0	0	0	0.0	0	0	1		0	0	0	.000	.000
1B	Mike Mahoney		2	7	0	0	0	0	0.0	0	0	0		0	0	0	.000	.000
3B	Jim Donely	R	1	1	1	0	0	0	0.0	0	0	0		0	0	0	1.000	1.000
OF	Tuck Turner	L	35	141	28	8	0	0	0.0	20	7	14		1	1	0	.199	.255
OF	Ducky Holmes	L	23	101	24	1	1	0	0.0	9	0	2		4	1	1	.238	.267
CO	Joe Sugden	B	89	289	73	7	1	0	0.0	29	34	23		5	7	2	.253	.284
C	Tom Kinslow		14	53	15	2	1	0	0.0	5	4	1		0	0	0	.283	.358
PITCHERS																		
P	Jack Taylor	R	54	157	38	5	2	1	0.6	17	18	12		1	1	0	.242	.318
P	Willie Sudhoff	R	41	120	19	2	1	0	0.0	5	4	5		0	0	0	.158	.192
P	Jim Hughey		35	97	11	0	1	1	1.0	6	6	10		1	0	0	.113	.165
P	Duke Esper		11	27	10	0	0	0	0.0	1	5	1		0	1	0	.370	.370
P	Pete Daniels		10	17	3	1	0	0	0.0	1	1	3		0	0	0	.176	.235
P	George Gilpatrick		7	16	2	0	0	0	0.0	1	1	0		0	0	0	.125	.125
P	Harry Maupin		2	7	3	0	0	0	0.0	0	1	0		0	0	0	.429	.429
P	Jim Callahan		2	4	0	0	0	0	0.0	0	0	0		0	0	0	.000	.000
P	Bill Gannon		1	3	0	0	0	0	0.0	0	0	0		0	0	0	.000	.000
P	Tom Smith		1	2	1	0	0	0	0.0	0	0	1		0	0	0	.500	.500
TEAM TOTAL				5214	1290	149	55	13	0.2	571	470	383		104	27	5	.247	.305

INDIVIDUAL FIELDING

POS	Player	T	G	PO	A	E	DP	TC/G	FA
1B	T. Tucker	R	72	755*	36	22	40	11.3*	.973
	G. Decker		75	772	17	16	31	10.7	.980*
	S. Sullivan		1	0	0	0	0	0.0	.000
	J. Sugden	R	8	74	3	1	4	9.8	.987
	M. Mahoney		2	22	1	2	1	12.5	.920
2B	J. Crooks		66	192	209	17	23	6.3	.959
	J. Quinn	R	62	139	191	13	19	5.5	.962
	T. Dowd	R	11	23	28	6	3	5.2	.895
	K. Carsey	R	10	19	25	8	1	5.2	.846
	S. Sullivan		6	14	15	3	1	5.3	.906
	L. Bierbauer	R	2	0	3	4	0	3.5	.429
SS	G. Smith	R	51	79	167	26	14	5.3	.904
	J. Quinn	R	41	79	149	18	11	6.0	.927
	R. Hall	R	35	50	102	30	12	5.2	.835
	S. Sullivan		23	52	60	16	6	5.6	.875
	J. Crooks		2	5	8	2	1	7.5	.867
	L. Cross	R	2	3	7	2	2	6.0	.833
	L. Bierbauer	R	1	3	7	0	0	10.0	1.000
3B	L. Cross	R	149	215	351	33	20	4.0	.945
	L. Bierbauer	R	1	0	0	0	0	0.0	.000
	R. Hall	R	3	2	11	2	2	5.0	.867
	J. Crooks		3	1	7	0	0	2.7	1.000
	J. Donely	R	1	0	1	1	0	2.0	.500

POS	Player	T	G	PO	A	E	DP	TC/G	FA
OF	D. Harley	R	141	311	26	27	3	2.6	.926
	J. Stenzel	R	108	257	8	16	2	2.6	.943
	T. Dowd	R	129	208	11	19	3	1.8	.920
	T. Turner		34	50	2	4	1	1.6	.929
	D. Holmes	R	22	39	6	5	3	2.3	.900
	J. Sugden	R	15	17	0	2	1	1.3	.895
	S. Sullivan		10	9	3	0	0	1.2	1.000
	K. Carsey	R	8	6	1	2	0	1.1	.778
	J. Crooks		1	5	0	0	0	5.0	1.000
	R. Hall		1	1	1	0	0	2.0	1.000
	J. Quinn	R	1	2	0	0	0	2.0	1.000
	J. Taylor	R	2	1	0	0	0	0.5	1.000
C	J. Clements	L	86	287	81	11	8	4.4	.971
	J. Sugden	R	60	181	88	18	8	4.8	.937
	T. Kinslow	R	14	44	18	5	4	4.8	.925

The St. Louis club acquired a new sacrificial lamb in '98, as "Brewery Jack" Taylor led the league in games pitched, complete games, innings, and, naturally, losses for the club that finished in last place at 39–111. The pitching staff threw no shutouts, while the batters were shut out eleven times, and finished last in runs for the third straight year.

They also picked up a new owner. A fire gutted their ballpark in April, virtually breaking their owner, Chris von der Ahe. He was forced to sell the club to Frank and Stanley Robison, owners of the Cleveland club. When the Robisons ordered new uniforms for the team, they also earned a new nickname. According to legend, a female fan expressed her admiration for the new cardinal-colored trim on the uniforms within earshot of a sportswriter, who adopted the name "Cardinals" to replace the now obsolete "Browns." It was Branch Rickey who later developed the Redbird logo still used today.

TEAM STATISTICS

	W	L	PCT	GB	R	OR	Batting 2B	3B	HR	BA	SA	SB	Fielding E	DP	FA	CG	BB	Pitching SO	ShO	SV	ERA
OS	102	47	.685		872	614	190	55	53	.290	.377	172	310	102	.950	127	470	432	9	7	2.98
AL	96	53	.644	6	933	623	154	77	12	.302	.368	250	326	105	.947	138	400	422	12	0	2.90
IN	92	60	.605	11.5	831	740	207	101	19	.271	.359	165	325	128	.950	131	449	294	10	2	3.50
HI	85	65	.567	17.5	828	679	175	83	19	.274	.350	220	412	149	.936	137	364	323	13	0	2.83
LE	81	68	.544	21	730	683	162	56	18	.263	.325	93	301	95	.952	142	309	339	9	0	3.20
HI	78	71	.523	24	823	784	238	81	33	.280	.377	182	379	102	.937	129	399	325	10	0	3.72
Y	77	73	.513	25.5	837	800	190	86	33	.266	.352	214	447	113	.932	141	587	558	9	1	3.44
IT	72	76	.486	29.5	634	694	140	88	14	.258	.328	107	340	105	.946	131	346	330	10	3	3.41
OU	70	81	.464	33	728	833	150	71	32	.267	.342	235	382	114	.939	137	470	271	4	0	4.24
KN	54	91	.372	46	638	811	156	66	17	.256	.322	130	334	125	.947	134	476	294	1	0	4.01
VAS	51	101	.336	52.5	704	939	177	81	35	.271	.355	197	443	119	.929	129	450	371	0	1	4.52
TL	39	111	.260	63.5	571	929	149	55	13	.247	.305	104	388	97	.939	133	372	288	0	2	4.53
EAGUE TOTAL					9129	9129	2088	900	298	.271	.347	2069	4387	1354	.942	1609	5092	4247	87	16	3.60

INDIVIDUAL PITCHING

ITCHER	T	W	L	PCT	ERA	SV	G	GS	CG	IP	H	BB	SO	R	ER	ShO	H/9	BB/9	SO/9
ack Taylor	R	15	29	.341	3.90	1	50	47	42	397.1	465	83	89	259	172	0	10.53	1.88	2.02
illie Sudhoff	R	11	27	.289	4.34	1	41	38	35	315	355	102	65	205	152	0	10.14	2.91	1.86
m Hughey	R	7	24	.226	3.93	0	35	33	31	283.2	325	71	74	169	124	0	10.31	2.25	2.35
id Carsey	R	2	12	.143	6.33	0	20	13	10	123.2	177	37	10	112	87	0	12.88	2.69	0.73
uke Esper	L	3	5	.375	5.98	0	10	8	6	64.2	86	22	14	49	43	0	11.97	3.06	1.95
ete Daniels		1	6	.143	3.62	0	10	6	3	54.2	62	14	13	41	22	0	10.21	2.30	2.14
eorge Gilpatrick		0	2	.000	6.94	0	7	3	1	35	42	19	12	38	27	0	10.80	4.89	3.09
arry Maupin		0	2	.000	5.50	0	2	2	2	18	22	3	3	11	11	0	11.00	1.50	1.50
ll Gannon		0	1	.000	11.00	0	1	1	1	9	13	5	2	13	11	0	13.00	5.00	2.00
om Smith		0	1	.000	2.00	0	1	1	1	9	9	5	1	8	2	0	9.00	5.00	1.00
m Callahan		0	2	.000	16.20	0	2	2	1	8.1	18	7	2	20	15	0	19.44	7.56	2.16
ter Sullivan		0	0	—	1.50	0	1	0	0	6	10	4	3	4	1	0	15.00	6.00	4.50
EAM TOTAL		39	111	.260	4.53	2	180	154	133	1324.1	1584	372	288	929	667	0	10.76	2.53	1.96

MANAGER	W	L	PCT
Patsy Tebeau	84	67	.556

POS	Player	B	G	AB	H	2B	3B	HR	HR %	R	RBI	BB	SO	SB	Pinch Hit AB	Pinch Hit H	BA	SA
REGULARS																		
1B	Patsy Tebeau	R	77	281	69	10	3	1	0.4	27	26	18		5	0	0	.246	.313
2B	Cupid Childs	L	125	465	124	11	11	1	0.2	73	48	74		17	0	0	.267	.344
SS	Bobby Wallace	R	151	577	174	28	14	12	2.1	91	108	54		17	0	0	.302	.461
3B	Lave Cross	R	103	403	122	14	5	4	1.0	61	64	17		11	0	0	.303	.392
RF	John Heidrick		146	591	194	21	14	2	0.3	109	82	34		55	1	1	.328	.421
CF	Harry Blake	R	97	292	70	9	4	2	0.7	50	41	43		16	4	2	.240	.318
LF	Jesse Burkett	L	141	567	228	17	10	7	1.2	115	71	67		22	0	0	.402	.504
C	Lou Criger	R	77	258	66	4	5	2	0.8	39	44	28		14	2	1	.256	.333
SUBSTITUTES																		
UT	Ed McKean	R	67	277	72	7	3	3	1.1	40	40	20		4	0	0	.260	.339
1C	Ossee Schreckengost	R	72	277	77	12	2	2	0.7	42	37	15		14	4	0	.278	.357
2B	Tim Flood	R	10	31	9	0	0	0	0.0	0	3	4		1	0	0	.290	.290
2B	Freddy Parent	R	2	8	1	0	0	0	0.0	0	1	0		0	0	0	.125	.125
2B	John Burke		2	6	2	0	0	0	0.0	1	0	1		0	0	0	.333	.333
O1	Mike Donlin	L	66	267	88	9	6	6	2.2	49	27	17		20	0	0	.330	.476
OF	Jake Stenzel	R	35	128	35	9	0	1	0.8	21	19	16		8	1	0	.273	.367
OF	Dusty Miller	L	10	39	8	1	0	0	0.0	3	3	3		1	0	0	.205	.231
OF	Charlie Hemphill	L	11	37	9	0	0	1	2.7	4	3	6		0	1	1	.243	.324
C1	Jack O'Connor	R	84	289	73	5	6	0	0.0	33	43	15		7	2	0	.253	.311
CO	Fritz Buelow	R	7	15	7	0	2	0	0.0	4	2	2		0	1	0	.467	.733
PITCHERS																		
P	Cy Young	R	44	148	32	5	3	1	0.7	22	18	2		1	0	0	.216	.311
P	Jack Powell	R	49	134	27	0	2	0	0.0	13	6	12		0	0	0	.201	.231
P	Nig Cuppy	R	21	70	13	0	0	0	0.0	6	3	3		0	0	0	.186	.186
P	Willie Sudhoff	R	26	68	14	1	1	0	0.0	10	2	8		0	0	0	.206	.250
P	Cowboy Jones	L	12	29	5	3	0	0	0.0	1	0	4		0	0	0	.172	.276
P	Pete McBride	R	12	27	5	1	0	1	3.7	2	5	2		0	0	0	.185	.333
P	Tom Thomas	R	4	12	3	1	0	0	0.0	0	2	0		0	0	0	.250	.333
P	Zeke Wilson		5	10	0	0	0	0	0.0	0	0	1		0	0	0	.000	.000
P	Jack Sutthoff	R	2	6	0	0	0	0	0.0	0	0	0		0	0	0	.000	.000
P	Frank Bates		2	3	1	0	0	0	0.0	2	1	2		0	0	0	.333	.333
TEAM TOTAL				5315	1528	168	91	46	0.9	818	699	468		207	16	5	.287	.379

INDIVIDUAL FIELDING

POS	Player	T	G	PO	A	E	DP	TC/G	FA
1B	P. Tebeau	R	65	648	22	14	33	10.5	.980
	Schreckengost	R	42	441	9	17	30	11.1	.964
	J. O'Connor	R	26	242	13	3	17	9.9	.988
	E. McKean	R	15	162	10	5	8	11.8	.972
	M. Donlin	L	13	116	5	9	3	10.0	.931
	H. Blake	R	1	10	1	1	1	12.0	.917
2B	C. Childs	R	125	323	355	48	45	5.8	.934
	P. McBride	R	1	0	0	0	0	0.0	.000
	T. Flood	R	10	15	28	6	3	4.9	.878
	E. McKean	R	10	20	23	4	4	4.7	.915
	H. Blake	R	4	13	14	5	2	8.0	.844
	J. Burke		2	4	8	1	2	6.5	.923
	F. Parent	R	2	3	5	1	1	4.5	.889
	J. Burkett	L	1	2	3	2	0	7.0	.714
	P. Tebeau	R	1	5	2	0	0	7.0	1.000
	Schreckengost	R	1	2	1	1	0	4.0	.750
SS	B. Wallace	R	100	238	386	55	40	6.8	.919
	E. McKean	R	42	72	123	25	13	5.2	.886
	P. Tebeau	R	11	22	43	7	1	6.5	.903
	M. Donlin	L	3	2	4	5	1	3.7	.545
	H. Blake	R	1	0	0	0	0	1.0	1.000
3B	L. Cross	R	103	157	277	18	25*	4.4	.960*
	B. Wallace	R	52	84	150	18	13	4.8	.929
	P. Tebeau	R	1	1	1	1	0	3.0	.667

POS	Player	T	G	PO	A	E	DP	TC/G	FA
OF	J. Burkett	L	140	296	20	21	3	2.4	.938
	J. Heidrick		145	211	34	20	6	1.8	.925
	H. Blake	R	87	176	10	4	3	2.2	.979
	M. Donlin	L	51	96	7	15	2	2.3	.873
	J. Stenzel	R	33	71	3	4	1	2.4	.949
	J. Powell	R	1	0	0	0	0	0.0	.000
	Schreckengost	R	1	0	0	0	0	0.0	.000
	D. Miller	R	10	20	1	3	1	2.4	.875
	C. Hemphill	L	10	13	2	5	1	2.0	.750
	F. Buelow	R	2	1	0	1	0	1.0	.500
C	L. Criger	R	75	228	91	17	6	4.5	.949
	J. O'Connor	R	57	185	63	15	3	4.6	.943
	Schreckengost	R	25	75	40	6*	5	4.8	.950
	F. Buelow	R	4	11	1	0	0	3.0	1.000
	H. Blake	R	1	3	2	0	0	5.0	1.000

The Robison brothers took a long look at their two ball clubs before the '99 season and decided that a good team in St. Louis would draw far better than a good one in Cleveland. As a result, they simply shipped their fifth-place Cleveland club intact to St. Louis and sent most of the remaining St. Louis players to Cleveland. When Lave Cross and Willie Sudhoff proved effective performers for Cleveland, they were quickly returned to the Cardinals. Except for one player who was out of baseball, the entire Cleveland starting lineup from 1898 wore St. Louis uniforms in 1899. Among the gifts of the magnates were leftfielder Jesse Burkett, who batted .402 for the season, and pitcher Cy Young, who went 26–15 for the rejuvenated St. Louis nine. They finished in the first division for the first time, with their first record above .500. We can only pity the poor Cleveland fans ("cranks" in the words of the time), who saw a strong team taken away from them and replaced with a crew of lowlights who went 20–134, dropping 40 of their last 41 games before disappearing from the National League for good.

TEAM STATISTICS

	W	L	PCT	GB	R	OR	Batting 2B	3B	HR	BA	SA	SB	Fielding E	DP	FA	CG	BB	Pitching SO	ShO	SV	ERA
BKN	101	47	.682		892	658	178	97	26	.291	.382	271	314	125	.948	121	463	331	9	9	3.25
BOS	95	57	.625	8	858	645	178	89	40	.287	.377	185	303	124	.952	138	385		13	4	3.26
PHI	94	58	.618	9	916	743	241	84	30	.301	.395	212	379	110	.940	129	370	281	15	2	3.47
BAL	86	62	.581	15	827	691	204	71	17	.297	.376	364	308	96	.949	133	349	294	9	4	3.31
STL	84	67	.556	18.5	819	739	172	89	46	.285	.377	210	397	117	.939	134	321	331	7	1	3.36
CIN	83	67	.553	19	856	770	194	105	13	.275	.360	228	339	111	.947	130	370	360	8	5	3.70
PIT	76	73	.510	25.5	834	765	196	121	27	.289	.384	179	361	98	.945	117	437	334	9	4	3.60
CHI	75	73	.507	26	812	763	173	82	27	.277	.359	247	428	145	.935	147	330	313	8	1	3.37
LOU	75	77	.493	28	827	775	192	68	40	.280	.364	233	394	102	.939	134	323	287	5	2	3.45
NY	60	90	.400	42	734	863	161	65	23	.281	.352	234	433	140	.932	138	628	397	4	0	4.29
WAS	54	98	.355	49	743	983	162	87	17	.272	.363	176	403	99	.935	131	422	328	3	0	4.93
CLE	20	134	.130	84	529	1252	142	50	12	.253	.305	127	388	121	.937	138	527	215	0	0	6.37
LEAGUE TOTAL					9647	9647	2193	1008	348	.282	.366	2666	4447	1388	.942	1590	4972	3856	90	32	3.85

INDIVIDUAL PITCHING

PITCHER	T	W	L	PCT	ERA	SV	G	GS	CG	IP	H	BB	SO	R	ER	ShO	H/9	BB/9	SO/9
Jack Powell	R	23	21	.523	3.52	0	48	43	40	373	433	85	87	197	146	2	10.45	2.05	2.10
Cy Young	R	26	15	.634	2.58	1	44	42	40	369.1	368	44	111	173	106	4	8.97	1.07	2.70
Willie Sudhoff	R	13	10	.565	3.61	0	26	24	18	189.1	203	67	33	110	76	0	9.65	3.18	1.57
Nig Cuppy	R	11	8	.579	3.15	0	21	21	18	171.2	203	26	25	89	60	1	10.64	1.36	1.31
Cowboy Jones	L	6	5	.545	3.59	0	12	12	9	85.1	111	22	28	51	34	0	11.71	2.32	2.95
Pete McBride	R	2	4	.333	4.08	0	11	6	4	64	65	40	26	46	29	0	9.14	5.63	3.66
Zeke Wilson		1	1	.500	4.50	0	5	2	2	26	30	4	3	18	13	0	10.38	1.38	1.04
Tom Thomas	R	1	1	.500	2.52	0	4	2	2	25	22	4	8	14	7	0	7.92	1.44	2.88
Mike Donlin	L	0	1	.000	7.63	0	3	1	0	15.1	15	14	6	15	13	0	8.80	8.22	3.52
Jack Sutthoff	R	1	1	.500	10.38	0	2	2	1	13	19	10	4	24	15	0	13.15	6.92	2.77
Frank Bates		0	0	—	1.04	0	2	0	0	8.2	7	5	0	2	1	0	7.27	5.19	0.00
TEAM TOTAL		84	67	.556	3.36	1	178	155	134	1340.2	1476	321	331	739	500	7	9.91	2.15	2.22

MANAGER	W	L	PCT
Patsy Tebeau	48	55	.466
Louie Heilbroner	17	20	.459

POS	Player	B	G	AB	H	2B	3B	HR	HR %	R	RBI	BB	SO	SB	Pinch Hit AB	Pinch Hit H	BA	SA
REGULARS																		
1B	Dan McGann	B	124	450	136	14	9	4	0.9	79	58	32		26	0	0	.302	.400
2B	Bill Keister	R	126	497	149	26	10	1	0.2	78	72	25		32	1	1	.300	.398
SS	Bobby Wallace	R	129	489	133	25	9	4	0.8	70	70	40		7	0	0	.272	.384
3B	John McGraw	L	99	334	115	10	4	2	0.6	84	33	85		29	0	0	.344	.416
RF	Patsy Donovan	R	126	503	159	11	1	0	0.0	78	61	38		45	2	1	.316	.342
CF	John Heidrick		85	339	102	6	8	2	0.6	51	45	18		22	2	0	.301	.383
LF	Jesse Burkett	L	142	560	203	14	12	7	1.3	88	68	62		32	0	0	.363	.468
C	Lou Criger	R	80	288	78	8	6	2	0.7	31	38	4		5	4	1	.271	.361
SUBSTITUTES																		
2S	Joe Quinn	R	22	80	21	2	0	1	1.3	12	11	10		4	1	1	.263	.325
3B	Lave Cross	R	16	61	18	1	0	0	0.0	6	6	1		1	0	0	.295	.311
2B	Otto Krueger	R	12	35	14	3	2	1	2.9	8	3	10		0	0	0	.400	.686
SS	Patsy Tebeau	R	1	4	0	0	0	0	0.0	0	0	0		0	0	0	.000	.000
O1	Mike Donlin	L	78	276	90	8	6	10	3.6	40	48	14		14	10	4	.326	.507
O3	Pat Dillard		57	183	42	5	2	0	0.0	24	12	13		7	8	1	.230	.279
UT	Willie Sudhoff	R	35	106	20	1	1	0	0.0	15	6	11		8	1	0	.189	.217
C	Wilbert Robinson	R	60	210	52	5	1	0	0.0	26	28	11		7	5	1	.248	.281
C	Jack O'Connor	R	10	32	7	0	0	0	0.0	4	6	2		0	0	0	.219	.219
C	Fritz Buelow	R	6	17	4	0	0	0	0.0	2	3	0		0	1	1	.235	.235
C	Harry Stanton		1	0	0	0	0	0	—	0	0	0		0	0	0	—	—
PITCHERS																		
P	Cy Young	R	41	124	22	5	1	1	0.8	13	13	3		1	0	0	.177	.258
P	Cowboy Jones	L	39	117	21	0	2	0	0.0	12	7	7		0	0	0	.179	.214
P	Jack Powell	R	38	109	31	4	4	1	0.9	15	12	10		3	0	0	.284	.422
P	Jim Hughey		20	41	7	0	0	0	0.0	6	2	8		0	0	0	.171	.171
P	Gus Weyhing	R	7	21	2	0	0	0	0.0	1	0	0		0	0	0	.095	.095
P	Tom Thomas	R	5	11	1	0	0	0	0.0	1	0	2		0	0	0	.091	.091
P	Jack Harper	R	1	1	0	0	0	0	0.0	0	0	0		0	0	0	.000	.000
	TEAM TOTAL			4888	1427	148	78	36	0.7	744	602	406		243	35	11	.292	.376

INDIVIDUAL FIELDING

POS	Player	T	G	PO	A	E	DP	TC/G	FA
1B	D. McGann	R	121	1212	58	13	41	10.6	**.990**
	M. Donlin	L	21	209	4	12	9	10.7	.947
2B	B. Keister	R	116	206	315	41	26	4.8	.927
	J. Quinn	R	14	26	30	4	3	4.3	.933
	O. Krueger	R	12	20	26	8	2	4.5	.852
	D. McGann	R	1	3	1	0	0	4.0	1.000
SS	B. Wallace	R	126	327	447	55	31	6.6	.934
	B. Keister	R	7	14	21	8	1	6.1	.814
	J. Quinn	R	6	17	13	3	1	5.5	.909
	P. Tebeau	R	1	4	3	3	0	10.0	.700
	P. Dillard		3	2	4	2	0	2.7	.750
3B	J. McGraw	R	99	106	213	32	7	3.5	.909
	P. Dillard		21	29	43	11	2	4.0	.867
	L. Cross	R	16	11	39	2	1	3.3	.962*
	W. Sudhoff	R	7	6	21	6	0	4.7	.818
	B. Keister	R	3	4	9	1	0	4.7	.929
	L. Criger	R	1	1	3	1	0	5.0	.800
	J. Quinn	R	1	1	3	0	0	4.0	1.000
	B. Wallace	R	1	2	2	0	0	4.0	1.000

POS	Player	T	G	PO	A	E	DP	TC/G	FA
OF	J. Burkett	L	141	**337**	17	25	6	2.7	.934
	J. Heidrick		83	215	21	10	4	3.0	.959
	P. Donovan	L	124	180	13	10	4	1.6	.951
	M. Donlin	L	47	99	7	9	5	2.4	.922
	P. Dillard		26	45	4	3	0	2.0	.942
	F. Buelow	R	1	0	0	0	0	0.0	.000
	W. Sudhoff	R	12	15	1	2	1	1.5	.889
C	L. Criger	R	75	282	105	19	8	5.4	.953
	W. Robinson	R	54	189	72	7	3	5.0	.974
	H. Stanton	R	1	0	0	0	0	0.0	.000
	J. O'Connor	R	10	33	11	2	0	4.6	.957
	F. Buelow	R	4	13	6	3	0	5.5	.864

TEAM STATISTICS

	W	L	PCT	GB	R	OR	Batting 2B	Batting 3B	Batting HR	Batting BA	Batting SA	Batting SB	Fielding E	Fielding DP	Fielding FA	Pitching CG	Pitching BB	Pitching SO	Pitching ShO	Pitching SV	Pitching ERA
BKN	82	54	.603		816	722	199	81	26	**.293**	**.383**	**274**	303	102	.948	104	405	300	8	**4**	3.89
PIT	79	60	.568	4.5	733	612	185	**100**	25	.272	.368	174	322	106	.945	114	**295**	415	11	1	**3.06**
PHI	75	63	.543	8	810	792	187	82	29	.290	.378	205	330	**125**	.945	116	402	284	7	3	4.12
BOS	66	72	.478	17	778	739	163	68	**48**	.283	.373	182	**273**	86	**.953**	116	463	340	8	2	3.72
CHI	65	75	.464	19	635	751	**202**	51	33	.260	.342	189	418	98	.933	**137**	324	357	9	1	3.23
STL	65	75	.464	19	744	748	141	81	36	.291	.375	243	331	73	.943	117	299	325	**12**	0	3.75
CIN	62	77	.446	21.5	703	745	178	83	33	.266	.354	183	341	120	.945	118	404	399	9	1	3.83
NY	60	78	.435	23	713	823	177	61	23	.279	.357	236	439	124	.928	114	442	277	4	0	3.96
LEAGUE TOTAL					5932	5932	1432	607	253	.279	.366	1686	2757	834	.942	936	3034	2697	68	12	3.69

The National League owners reorganized the league before the 1900 season, dropping the four weakest franchises: Baltimore, Cleveland, Washington, and Louisville. They had hoped to improve their financial picture, but the decision backfired: they angered the fans in those cities and opened the door for a new major league, the American League, which quickly moved into three of the four abandoned cities for the 1901 season.

Expectations were high for the Cardinals following their strong showing in 1899, and with the addition of several players picked up from the Baltimore roster, including Bill Keister and John McGraw, they felt they were ready to fight for the pennant. Instead, they were never in the hunt at all, bouncing between sixth and seventh place for the last three months of the season, despite a beefed-up offense that included six .300 hitters in the starting lineup. Jesse Burkett again finished in the top five in batting; his .363 average was his lowest in three years with the Cardinals. Thirty-three-year-old Cy Young was 20–18 for the worst won-lost percentage of his career to that point. Far from being over the hill, he would average 30 wins a year for the next four; unfortunately for St. Louis, it would be with Boston in the American League.

INDIVIDUAL PITCHING

PITCHER	T	W	L	PCT	ERA	SV	G	GS	CG	IP	H	BB	SO	R	ER	ShO	H/9	BB/9	SO/9
Cy Young	R	20	18	.526	3.00	0	41	35	32	321.1	337	36	119	144	107	4	9.44	1.01	3.33
Cowboy Jones	L	13	19	.406	3.54	0	39	36	29	292.2	334	82	68	185	115	3	10.27	2.52	2.09
Jack Powell	R	17	17	.500	4.44	0	38	37	28	287.2	325	77	77	194	142	3	10.17	2.41	2.41
Willie Sudhoff	R	6	8	.429	2.76	0	16	14	13	127	128	37	29	62	39	2	9.07	2.62	2.06
Jim Hughey	R	5	7	.417	5.19	0	20	12	11	112.2	147	40	23	90	65	0	11.74	3.20	1.84
Gus Weyhing	R	3	4	.429	4.63	0	7	5	3	46.2	60	21	6	44	24	0	11.57	4.05	1.16
Tom Thomas	R	1	1	.500	3.76	0	5	1	1	26.1	38	4	7	22	11	0	12.99	1.37	2.39
Jack Harper	R	0	1	.000	12.00	0	1	1	0	3	4	2	0	7	4	0	12.00	6.00	0.00
TEAM TOTAL		65	75	.464	3.75	0	167	141	117	1217.1	1373	299	329	748	507	12	10.15	2.21	2.43

EAT YOUR HEART OUT, GEORGE STEINBRENNER

From *The Sporting News,* October 20, 1900:
"The St. Louis club withheld the last installment of salary due all of its players except McGraw, Robinson, Donovan, and Young, and notified them that their services in 1900 were unsatisfactory. . . . The letter of President Robison to the players reads as follows: '. . . . In your contract for the past playing season of nineteen hundred (1900) said contract called for —— per month for playing and producing first class base ball for the American Base Ball and Athletic Exhibition Company of St. Louis, Mo. This you have not done. . . .' "

MANAGER	W	L	PCT
Patsy Donovan	76	64	.543

POS	Player	B	G	AB	H	2B	3B	HR	HR %	R	RBI	BB	SO	SB	Pinch Hit AB	Pinch Hit H	BA	SA
REGULARS																		
1B	Dan McGann	B	103	426	123	14	10	6	1.4	73	56	16		17	0	0	.289	.411
2B	Dick Padden	R	123	489	125	17	7	2	0.4	71	62	31		26	0	0	.256	.331
SS	Bobby Wallace	R	135	556	179	34	15	2	0.4	69	91	20		15	0	0	.322	.448
3B	Otto Krueger	R	142	520	143	16	12	2	0.4	77	79	50		19	0	0	.275	.363
RF	Patsy Donovan	R	130	531	161	23	5	1	0.2	92	73	27		28	0	0	.303	.371
CF	John Heidrick		118	502	170	24	12	6	1.2	94	67	21		32	0	0	.339	.470
LF	Jesse Burkett	L	142	597	228	21	17	10	1.7	139	75	59		27	0	0	.382	.524
C	John Ryan	R	83	300	59	6	5	0	0.0	27	31	7		5	1	0	.197	.250
SUBSTITUTES																		
2B	Pete Childs		29	79	21	1	0	0	0.0	12	8	14		0	6	1	.266	.278
1B	Bill Richardson		15	52	11	2	0	2	3.8	7	7	6		1	0	0	.212	.365
CO	Art Nichols	R	93	308	75	11	3	1	0.3	50	33	10		14	6	1	.244	.308
C1	Pop Schriver	R	53	166	45	7	3	1	0.6	17	23	12		2	9	3	.271	.367
C	Mike Heydon		16	43	9	1	1	1	2.3	2	6	5		2	1	0	.209	.349
PITCHERS																		
P	Jack Powell	R	45	119	21	3	1	2	1.7	14	8	6		0	0	0	.176	.269
P	Jack Harper	R	39	116	20	1	1	1	0.9	13	10	10		1	0	0	.172	.224
P	Willie Sudhoff	R	38	108	19	2	3	1	0.9	11	17	10		0	0	0	.176	.278
P	Ed Murphy		23	64	16	3	0	1	1.6	11	9	3		0	0	0	.250	.344
P	Cowboy Jones	L	10	27	4	1	1	0	0.0	2	0	2		0	0	0	.148	.259
P	Mike O'Neill	L	6	15	6	0	0	0	0.0	3	2	3		0	1	1	.400	.400
P	Stan Yerkes		4	12	1	0	0	0	0.0	1	0	1		0	0	0	.083	.083
P	Ted Breitenstein	L	3	6	2	0	0	0	0.0	1	0	0		0	0	0	.333	.333
P	Bill Magee		1	4	2	0	1	0	0.0	1	0	0		0	0	0	.500	1.000
P	Bob Wicker	R	3	3	1	0	0	0	0.0	1	0	0		0	1	0	.333	.333
P	Chauncey Fisher	R	1	1	0	0	0	0	0.0	0	0	0		0	0	0	.000	.000
P	Farmer Burns		1	0	0	0	0	0	–	1	0			1	0	0	–	–
	TEAM TOTAL			5044	1441	187	97	39	0.8	789	657	314		190	25	6	.286	.384

INDIVIDUAL FIELDING

POS	Player	T	G	PO	A	E	DP	TC/G	FA
1B	D. McGann	R	103	1030	50	18	64	10.7	.984
	P. Schriver	R	19	182	18	6	11	10.8	.971
	B. Richardson		15	154	5	3	7	10.8	.981
	J. Ryan	R	5	50	5	0	7	11.0	1.000
2B	D. Padden	R	115	286	336	33	47	5.7	.950
	P. Childs	R	19	39	49	9	4	5.1	.907
	J. Ryan	R	9	17	28	6	3	5.7	.882
SS	B. Wallace	R	134	326	542	66	67	7.0	.929
	D. Padden	R	8	15	24	7	2	5.8	.848
	P. Childs	R	1	0	1	2	0	3.0	.333
3B	O. Krueger	R	142	171	275	60	11	3.6	.881

POS	Player	T	G	PO	A	E	DP	TC/G	FA
OF	J. Burkett	L	142	307	17	27	4	2.5	.923
	J. Heidrick		118	258	15	16	2	2.4	.945
	P. Donovan	L	129	215	19	5	8	1.9	.979
	A. Nichols	R	40	69	9	3	4	2.0	.963
	M. Heydon	R	1	0	0	0	0	0.0	.000
	J. Ryan	R	3	3	1	1	0	1.7	.800
	P. Childs	R	2	2	0	0	0	1.0	1.000
C	J. Ryan	R	65	292	84	7	7	5.9	.982
	A. Nichols	R	47	187	51	10	5	5.3	.960
	P. Schriver	R	24	91	43	4	2	5.8	.971
	M. Heydon	R	13	54	10	4	2	5.2	.941

Just ten years into its tenure in the National League, St. Louis was already starting to become the kind of team that would characterize the club throughout its history: strong on offense, loaded with batters for high average, but troubled by pitching worries. The biggest difference between the 1901 club and the historical profile is that this club led the league in home runs, a feat they've managed just five times in ninety-one years.

Jesse Burkett, in his last year before jumping to St. Louis's American League club, gave the Cardinals their first batting champion at .382; he also led the league in hits and runs scored. The team rose as high as second place in late August, but Pittsburgh pulled steadily out in front, and St. Louis fell back into fourth place, finishing 14½ games out of first.

TEAM STATISTICS

	W	L	PCT	GB	R	OR	2B	3B	HR	BA	SA	SB	E	DP	FA	CG	BB	SO	ShO	SV	ERA
PIT	90	49	.647		776	534	182	92	28	.286	.378	203	287	97	.950	119	244	505	15	4	2.58
PHI	83	57	.593	7.5	668	543	194	59	23	.266	.346	199	262	65	.954	125	259	480	15	0	2.87
BKN	79	57	.581	9.5	744	600	206	93	32	.287	.387	178	281	99	.950	111	435	583	7	3	3.14
STL	76	64	.543	14.5	792	689	187	94	39	.284	.381	190	305	108	.949	118	332	445	5	5	3.68
BOS	69	69	.500	20.5	530	556	135	36	28	.249	.310	158	282	89	.952	128	349	558	11	0	2.90
CHI	53	86	.381	37	578	698	153	61	17	.258	.325	204	336	87	.943	131	324	586	2	0	3.33
NY	52	85	.380	37	544	755	167	46	19	.253	.318	133	348	81	.941	118	377	542	11	1	3.87
CIN	52	87	.374	38	561	818	173	70	38	.251	.338	137	355	102	.940	126	365	542	4	0	4.17
LEAGUE TOTAL					5193	5193	1397	551	224	.267	.348	1402	2456	728	.947	976	2685	4241	70	13	3.32

INDIVIDUAL PITCHING

PITCHER	T	W	L	PCT	ERA	SV	G	GS	CG	IP	H	BB	SO	R	ER	ShO	H/9	BB/9	SO/9
Jack Powell	R	19	19	.500	3.54	3	45	37	33	338.1	351	50	133	168	133	2	9.34	1.33	3.54
Jack Harper	R	23	13	.639	3.62	0	39	37	28	308.2	294	99	128	135	124	1	8.57	2.89	3.73
Willie Sudhoff	R	17	11	.607	3.52	2	38	26	25	276.1	281	92	78	142	108	1	9.15	3.00	2.54
Ed Murphy	R	10	9	.526	4.20	0	23	21	16	165	201	32	42	105	77	0	10.96	1.75	2.29
Cowboy Jones	L	2	6	.250	4.48	0	10	9	7	76.1	97	22	25	51	38	0	11.44	2.59	2.95
Mike O'Neill	L	2	2	.500	1.32	0	5	4	4	41	29	10	16	12	6	1	6.37	2.20	3.51
Stan Yerkes		3	1	.750	3.18	0	4	4	4	34	35	6	15	14	12	0	9.26	1.59	3.97
Ted Breitenstein	L	0	3	.000	6.60	0	3	3	1	15	24	14	3	26	11	0	14.40	8.40	1.80
Bill Magee	R	0	0	–	4.50	0	1	1	0	8	8	4	3	4	4	0	9.00	4.50	3.38
Chauncey Fisher	R	0	0	–	15.00	0	1	0	0	3	7	1	0	5	5	0	21.00	3.00	0.00
Bob Wicker	R	0	0	–	0.00	0	1	0	0	3	4	1	2	3	0	0	12.00	3.00	6.00
Farmer Burns	R	0	0	–	9.00	0	1	0	0	1	2	1	0	1	1	0	18.00	9.00	0.00
TEAM TOTAL		76	64	.543	3.68	5	171	142	118	1269.2	1333	332	445	689	519	5	9.45	2.35	3.15

CARDINAL BATTING CHAMPIONS

1901	Jesse Burkett, .382	1943	Stan Musial, .357
1920	Rogers Hornsby, .370	1946	Stan Musial, .365
1921	Rogers Hornsby, .397	1948	Stan Musial, .376
1922	Rogers Hornsby, .401	1950	Stan Musial, .346
1923	Rogers Hornsby, .384	1951	Stan Musial, .355
1924	Rogers Hornsby, .424	1952	Stan Musial, .336
1925	Rogers Hornsby, .403	1957	Stan Musial, .351
1931	Chick Hafey, .349	1971	Joe Torre, .363
1937	Joe Medwick, .374	1979	Keith Hernandez, .344
1939	Johnny Mize, .349		

MANAGER	W	L	PCT
Patsy Donovan	56	78	.418

POS	Player	B	G	AB	H	2B	3B	HR	HR %	R	RBI	BB	SO	SB	Pinch Hit AB	H	BA	SA
REGULARS																		
1B	Kitty Brashear		110	388	107	8	2	1	0.3	36	40	32		9	3	1	.276	.314
2B	John Farrell		138	565	141	13	5	0	0.0	68	25	43		9	0	0	.250	.290
SS	Otto Krueger	R	128	467	124	7	8	0	0.0	55	46	29		14	3	0	.266	.315
3B	Fred Hartman		114	416	90	10	3	0	0.0	30	52	14		14	2	1	.216	.255
RF	Patsy Donovan	R	126	502	158	12	4	0	0.0	70	35	28		34	0	0	.315	.355
CF	Homer Smoot	L	129	518	161	19	4	3	0.6	58	48	23		20	0	0	.311	.380
LF	George Barclay		137	543	163	14	2	3	0.6	79	53	31		30	0	0	.300	.350
C	John Ryan	R	76	267	48	4	4	0	0.0	23	14	4		2	0	0	.180	.225
SUBSTITUTES																		
1C	Art Nichols	R	73	251	67	12	0	1	0.4	36	31	21		18	2	0	.267	.327
31	John Calhoun	R	20	64	10	2	1	0	0.0	3	8	8		1	2	0	.156	.219
1B	Doc Hazleton		7	23	3	0	0	0	0.0	0	0	2		0	0	0	.130	.130
SS	Rudy Kling	R	4	10	2	0	0	0	0.0	1	0	4		1	0	0	.200	.200
SS	Otto Williams	R	2	5	2	0	0	0	0.0	0	2	1		1	0	0	.400	.400
3B	Soldier Boy Murphy		1	3	2	1	0	0	0.0	1	1	1		0	0	0	.667	1.000
PO	Jim Hackett	R	6	21	6	1	0	0	0.0	2	4	2		1	0	0	.286	.333
C	Jack O'Neill	R	63	192	27	1	1	0	0.0	13	12	13		2	4	0	.141	.156
C	Art Weaver		11	33	6	2	0	0	0.0	2	3	1		0	0	0	.182	.242
PITCHERS																		
P	Mike O'Neill	L	51	135	43	5	3	2	1.5	21	15	2		0	12	1	.319	.444
P	Stan Yerkes		39	91	12	1	0	0	0.0	4	2	9		0	0	0	.132	.143
P	Bob Wicker	R	31	77	18	2	0	0	0.0	6	3	3		2	6	1	.234	.260
P	Ed Murphy		23	61	16	0	0	0	0.0	4	3	1		0	0	0	.262	.262
P	Clarence Currie	R	16	46	9	2	0	0	0.0	3	3	1		0	1	0	.196	.239
P	Alex Pearson	R	11	34	9	0	0	0	0.0	2	2	0		0	0	0	.265	.265
P	Bill Popp		9	21	1	0	0	0	0.0	0	0	0		0	0	0	.048	.048
P	Wiley Dunham		7	12	1	0	0	0	0.0	0	0	0		0	0	0	.083	.083
P	Chappie McFarland		2	4	0	0	0	0	0.0	0	0	0		0	0	0	.000	.000
P	Joe Adams	R	1	2	0	0	0	0	0.0	0	0	0		0	0	0	.000	.000
	TEAM TOTAL			4751	1226	116	37	10	0.2	517	402	273		158	35	4	.258	.304

INDIVIDUAL FIELDING

POS	Player	T	G	PO	A	E	DP	TC/G	FA
1B	K. Brashear		67	751	36	16	49	12.0	.980
	A. Nichols	R	56	577	24	10	26	10.9	.984
	D. Hazleton		7	67	4	2	8	10.4	.973
	J. Calhoun	R	5	42	2	3	3	9.4	.936
	J. Ryan	R	4	37	3	0	3	10.0	1.000
	F. Hartman	R	3	23	3	1	1	9.0	.963
2B	J. Farrell	R	118	297	422	40	72	6.4	.947
	K. Brashear		21	47	52	5	4	5.0	.952
	J. Ryan		2	5	6	0	0	5.5	1.000
SS	O. Krueger	R	107	184	390	66	47	6.0	.897
	J. Farrell	R	21	40	79	9	4	6.1	.930
	J. Ryan		1	0	0	0	0	0.0	.000
	F. Hartman	R	4	7	9	4	1	5.0	.800
	R. Kling	R	4	9	7	3	2	4.8	.842
	K. Brashear		3	8	8	2	1	6.0	.889
	O. Williams	R	2	5	8	3	0	8.0	.813
3B	F. Hartman	R	105	138	229	37	9	3.8	.908
	O. Krueger	R	18	22	36	9	1	3.7	.866
	J. Calhoun	R	12	15	20	1	1	3.0	.972
	J. Ryan	R	4	3	8	0	1	2.8	1.000
	S. Murphy		1	2	0	0	0	2.0	1.000

POS	Player	T	G	PO	A	E	DP	TC/G	FA
OF	H. Smoot	R	129	284	14	22	5	2.5	.931
	G. Barclay		137	247	16	28	3	2.1	.904
	P. Donovan	L	126	179	30	9	6	1.7	.959
	K. Brashear		16	22	1	1	0	1.5	.958
	B. Wicker	R	3	7	0	1	0	2.7	.875
	A. Nichols	R	4	7	0	0	0	1.8	1.000
	M. O'Neill	L	3	5	0	0	0	1.7	1.000
	J. Hackett	R	2	3	0	1	0	2.0	.750
	J. Calhoun	R	1	3	0	0	0	3.0	1.000
C	J. Ryan	R	66	258	86	12	8	5.4	.966
	J. O'Neill	R	59	246	79	9	5	5.7	.973
	A. Weaver	R	11	40	17	1	1	5.3	.983
	A. Nichols	R	11	31	9	3	2	3.9	.930

St. Louis was hit hard by raids from American League teams; of the eight starting players and three top pitchers from the 1900 club, only one, player-manager Patsy Donovan, was still with them in 1902.

With most of their offense scattered, St. Louis fell into the cellar in the early going, finally climbing out with a strong July showing, settling into sixth place. While they were never a factor in the pennant race, neither was anyone else but Pittsburgh, who opened a lead of eleven games by the end of June and rolled to the pennant by a 27½-game margin. Cardinal fans could console themselves with the showing by their outfield, which consisted of two rookies, George Barclay and Homer Smoot, and veteran Patsy Donovan. Each of the three finished over the .300 mark, a feat managed by just eleven other players in the league.

TEAM STATISTICS

	W	L	PCT	GB	R	OR	Batting 2B	3B	HR	BA	SA	SB	Fielding E	DP	FA	Pitching CG	BB	SO	ShO	SV	ERA
PIT	103	36	.741		775	440	189	94	19	.286	.374	222	247	87	.958	131	250	564	21	3	2.30
BKN	75	63	.543	27.5	564	519	147	50	18	.256	.318	145	275	79	.952	131	363	536	14	1	2.69
BOS	73	64	.533	29	571	515	142	39	14	.249	.305	189	240	90	.959	124	372	523	14	4	2.61
CIN	70	70	.500	33.5	632	566	188	77	18	.282	.362	131	322	118	.945	130	352	430	9	1	2.67
CHI	68	69	.496	34	530	501	131	40	6	.250	.298	222	327	111	.946	132	279	437	17	2	2.21
STL	56	78	.418	44.5	517	695	116	37	10	.258	.304	158	336	107	.944	112	338	400	7	2	3.47
PHI	56	81	.409	46	484	649	110	43	4	.247	.292	108	305	81	.946	118	334	504	8	2	3.50
NY	48	88	.353	53.5	401	589	147	34	8	.238	.290	187	330	104	.943	118	332	501	11	1	2.82
LEAGUE TOTAL					4474	4474	1170	414	97	.259	.319	1362	2382	777	.949	996	2620	3895	101	16	2.78

INDIVIDUAL PITCHING

PITCHER	T	W	L	PCT	ERA	SV	G	GS	CG	IP	H	BB	SO	R	ER	ShO	H/9	BB/9	SO/9
Stan Yerkes		11	20	.355	3.66	0	39	37	27	272.2	341	79	81	160	111	1	11.26	2.61	2.67
Mike O'Neill	L	17	13	.567	2.76	0	34	30	27	270.1	276	58	99	125	83	2	9.19	1.93	3.30
Ed Murphy	R	9	7	.563	3.02	1	23	17	12	164	187	31	37	86	55	1	10.26	1.70	2.03
Bob Wicker	R	5	13	.278	3.19	0	22	16	14	152.1	159	45	78	82	54	1	9.39	2.66	4.61
Clarence Currie	R	6	5	.545	2.75	0	14	11	9	117.2	122	31	29	54	36	1	9.33	2.37	2.22
Alex Pearson	R	2	6	.250	3.95	0	11	10	8	82	90	22	24	47	36	0	9.88	2.41	2.63
Bill Popp	R	2	6	.250	4.92	0	9	7	5	60.1	87	26	20	60	33	0	12.98	3.88	2.98
Wiley Dunham		2	3	.400	5.68	1	7	5	3	38	47	13	15	31	24	0	11.13	3.08	3.55
Jim Hackett	R	0	3	.000	6.23	0	4	3	3	30.1	46	16	7	26	21	0	13.65	4.75	2.08
Jack O'Neill	R	1	1	.500	5.00	0	2	2	2	18	21	8	6	11	10	0	10.50	4.00	3.00
Chappie McFarland	R	1	0	1.000	5.73	0	2	1	1	11	11	3	3	7	7	0	9.00	2.45	2.45
John Ryan	R	1	0	1.000	0.00	0	1	1	1	7	3	4	1	0	0	1	3.86	5.14	1.29
Joe Adams	L	0	0	–	9.00	0	1	0	0	4	9	2	0	6	4	0	20.25	4.50	0.00
TEAM TOTAL		56	78	.418	3.47	2	169	140	112	1227.2	1399	338	400	695	474	7	10.26	2.48	2.93

BUILDING A BALL CLUB, NEW YORK STYLE

In a remarkable turn of events that marked the peak of hostilities between the two leagues, a group of National League investors purchased the Baltimore club of the American League in midseason. They immediately shifted most of its assets, its best players, to the National League. The chief beneficiary was the New York Giants, who gained three future Hall of Famers: catcher Roger Bresnahan, pitcher Joe "Iron Man" McGinnity, and manager John McGraw. American League owners were forced to restock the Orioles to enable them to finish out the season. The war ended when a peace treaty was signed during the off-season. The Giants were rewarded for their enterprise with a new crosstown rival—the gutted Orioles were shifted to New York as the Highlanders (later the Yankees).

MANAGER	W	L	PCT
Patsy Donovan	43	94	.314

POS	Player	B	G	AB	H	2B	3B	HR	HR %	R	RBI	BB	SO	SB	Pinch Hit AB	Pinch Hit H	BA	SA
REGULARS																		
1B	Jim Hackett	R	99	351	80	13	8	0	0.0	24	36	19		2	3	0	.228	.311
2B	John Farrell		130	519	141	25	8	1	0.2	83	32	48		17	0	0	.272	.356
SS	Dave Brain	R	119	464	107	8	15	1	0.2	44	60	25		21	0	0	.231	.319
3B	Jimmy Burke	R	115	431	123	13	3	0	0.0	55	42	23		28	1	0	.285	.329
RF	Patsy Donovan	R	105	410	134	15	3	0	0.0	63	39	25		25	0	0	.327	.378
CF	Homer Smoot	L	129	500	148	22	8	4	0.8	67	49	32		17	0	0	.296	.396
LF	George Barclay		108	419	104	10	8	0	0.0	37	42	15		12	0	0	.248	.310
C	Jack O'Neill	R	75	246	58	9	1	0	0.0	23	27	13		11	1	0	.236	.280
SUBSTITUTES																		
SS	Otto Williams	R	53	187	38	4	2	0	0.0	10	9	9		6	0	0	.203	.246
1O	Art Nichols	R	36	120	23	2	0	0	0.0	13	9	12		9	1	0	.192	.208
S2	Lee DeMontreville	R	26	70	17	3	1	0	0.0	8	7	8		3	5	1	.243	.314
P1	Ed Murphy		24	64	13	1	0	0	0.0	4	6	1		0	0	0	.203	.219
2S	Harry Berte		4	15	5	0	0	0	0.0	1	1	1		0	0	0	.333	.333
PS	Charley Moran	R	4	14	6	0	0	0	0.0	2	1	0		1	0	0	.429	.429
1B	Lou Ury		2	7	1	0	0	0	0.0	0	0	0		0	0	0	.143	.143
OP	John Dunleavy		61	193	48	3	3	0	0.0	23	10	13		10	9	4	.249	.295
PO	Mike O'Neill	L	41	110	25	2	2	0	0.0	12	6	8		3	7	3	.227	.282
C1	John Ryan	R	67	227	54	5	1	1	0.4	18	10	10		2	0	0	.238	.282
C	Art Weaver		16	49	12	0	0	0	0.0	4	5	4		1	0	0	.245	.245
C	John Coveney		4	14	2	0	0	0	0.0	0	0	0		0	0	0	.143	.143
PITCHERS																		
P	Three Finger Brown	B	26	77	15	2	1	0	0.0	4	6	1		2	0	0	.195	.247
P	Chappie McFarland		28	74	8	1	0	0	0.0	3	2	7		1	0	0	.108	.122
P	Bob Rhoads	R	18	50	7	0	0	0	0.0	4	4	0		0	0	0	.140	.140
P	Clarence Currie	R	22	47	4	0	1	0	0.0	1	1	3		0	0	0	.085	.128
P	War Sanders	R	8	15	1	0	0	0	0.0	1	0	0		0	0	0	.067	.067
P	Hal Betts	R	1	3	0	0	0	0	0.0	0	0	0		0	0	0	.000	.000
P	Pat Hynes		1	3	0	0	0	0	0.0	0	0	0		0	0	0	.000	.000
P	John Lovett		3	3	1	0	0	0	0.0	0	0	0		0	0	0	.333	.333
P	Larry Milton		1	2	1	0	0	0	0.0	0	0	0		0	0	0	.500	.500
P	Bob Wicker	R	1	2	0	0	0	0	0.0	1	0	0		0	0	0	.000	.000
P	Stan Yerkes		1	2	0	0	0	0	0.0	0	0	0		0	0	0	.000	.000
P	Ed Taylor		1	1	0	0	0	0	0.0	0	0	0		0	0	0	.000	.000
TEAM TOTAL				4689	1176	138	65	7	0.1	505	404	277		171	27	8	.251	.312

INDIVIDUAL FIELDING

POS	Player	T	G	PO	A	E	DP	TC/G	FA
1B	J. Hackett	R	89	947	40	28	63	11.4	.972
	A. Nichols	R	25	276	3	8	11	11.5	.972
	J. Ryan	R	18	174	9	2	17	10.3	.989
	E. Murphy	R	8	68	3	4	3	9.4	.947
	L. Ury	R	2	23	1	0	1	12.0	1.000
2B	J. Farrell	R	118	281	394	53	52	6.2	.927
	J. Burke	R	15	25	58	6	0	5.9	.933
	DeMontreville	R	4	9	6	4	0	4.8	.789
	H. Berte	R	3	3	4	2	1	3.0	.778
	O. Williams	R	1	1	2	0	0	3.0	1.000
SS	D. Brain	R	72	163	244	41	34	6.2	.908
	O. Williams	R	52	94	161	33	16	5.5	.885
	DeMontreville	R	15	27	46	8	8	5.4	.901
	J. Ryan	R	2	1	7	1	0	4.5	.889
	H. Berte	R	1	0	2	2	0	4.0	.500
	C. Moran	R	1	1	1	0	0	2.0	1.000
3B	J. Burke	R	93	139	199	33	14	4.0	.911
	D. Brain	R	46	70	106	22	9	4.3	.889
OF	H. Smoot	R	129	231	14	15	3	2.0	.942
	G. Barclay		107	187	13	22	0	2.1	.901
	P. Donovan	L	105	142	16	8	5	1.6	.952
	J. Dunleavy		38	58	11	2	5	1.9	.972
	E. Murphy	R	1	0	0	0	0	0.0	.000
	J. Farrell	R	12	39	5	1	0	3.8	.978
	M. O'Neill	L	13	22	2	0	0	1.8	1.000
	A. Nichols	R	7	12	1	1	1	2.0	.929
	J. Burke	R	5	6	0	1	0	1.4	.857
	B. Rhoads	R	1	3	0	0	0	3.0	1.000
	DeMontreville		1	1	0	1	0	2.0	.500
C	J. O'Neill	R	74	348	135	14	8	6.7	.972
	J. Ryan	R	47	168	65	7	4	5.1	.971
	A. Weaver	R	16	63	31	3	0	6.1	.969
	J. Coveney	R	4	13	11	2	0	6.5	.923
	A. Nichols	R	2	6	5	1	0	6.0	.917

With the signing of the NL–AL peace treaty, the open market for ballplayers' services ended—at least until the 1970s. With the return to normal operations, St. Louis fell back into the cellar. The Cardinals fought the Phillies for seventh place until the last month of the season, but then fell securely back. They were last in both runs and runs allowed, and hit just seven home runs—two fewer than the league leader, Jimmy Sheckard of Brooklyn. No pitcher on the staff managed to win as many as ten games as an anemic offense combined with poor pitching for a dismal season. Only manager Patsy Donovan was able to crack the top twenty in batting.

TEAM STATISTICS

W	L	PCT	GB	R	OR	2B	3B	Batting HR	BA	SA	SB	E	Fielding DP	FA	CG	BB	Pitching SO	ShO	SV	ERA
91	49	.650		792	613	208	110	34	.287	.393	172	295	100	.951	117	384	454	15	5	2.91
84	55	.604	6.5	729	548	181	49	20	.272	.344	264	287	87	.951	115	371	628	8	8	2.95
82	56	.594	8	695	594	191	62	9	.275	.347	259	338	78	.942	117	354	451	6	6	2.77
74	65	.532	16.5	764	749	228	92	28	.288	.390	144	312	84	.946	126	378	480	11	1	3.07
70	66	.515	19	666	674	177	56	15	.265	.339	273	284	98	.951	118	377	438	11	4	3.44
58	80	.420	32	575	661	176	47	25	.245	.318	159	361	89	.937	125	460	516	5	0	3.34
49	86	.363	39.5	618	743	186	62	12	.268	.341	120	300	76	.947	126	425	381	5	2	3.97
43	94	.314	46.5	505	762	138	65	7	.251	.312	171	354	111	.940	111	430	419	4	2	3.76
AGUE TOTAL				5344	5344	1485	543	150	.269	.348	1562	2531	723	.946	955	3179	3767	65	28	3.27

INDIVIDUAL PITCHING

PITCHER	T	W	L	PCT	ERA	SV	G	GS	CG	IP	H	BB	SO	R	ER	ShO	H/9	BB/9	SO/9
appie McFarland	R	9	18	.333	3.07	0	28	26	25	229	253	48	76	133	78	1	9.94	1.89	2.99
ree Finger Brown	R	9	13	.409	2.60	0	26	24	19	201	201	59	83	105	58	1	10.34	2.64	3.72
arence Currie	R	4	12	.250	4.01	0	22	16	13	148	155	60	52	93	66	1	9.43	3.65	3.16
b Rhoads	R	5	8	.385	4.60	0	17	13	12	129	154	47	52	88	66	1	10.74	3.28	3.63
ke O'Neill	L	4	13	.235	4.77	0	19	17	12	115	184	43	39	124	61	0	14.40	3.37	3.05
Murphy	R	4	8	.333	3.31	0	15	12	9	106	108	38	16	62	39	0	9.17	3.23	1.36
hn Dunleavy		6	8	.429	4.06	0	14	13	9	102	101	57	51	59	46	0	8.91	5.03	4.50
n Hackett	R	1	4	.200	3.72	1	7	6	5	48.1	47	18	21	23	20	0	8.75	3.35	3.91
ar Sanders	L	1	5	.167	6.08	0	8	6	3	40	48	21	9	37	27	0	10.80	4.73	2.03
arley Moran	R	0	1	.000	5.25	0	3	2	2	24	30	19	7	29	14	0	11.25	7.13	2.63
l Betts	R	0	1	.000	10.00	0	1	1	1	9	11	5	2	10	10	0	11.00	5.00	2.00
t Hynes		0	1	.000	4.00	0	1	1	1	9	10	6	1	6	4	0	10.00	6.00	1.00
hn Lovett		0	1	.000	5.40	0	3	1	0	5	6	5	3	5	3	0	10.80	9.00	5.40
b Wicker	R	0	0	–	0.00	0	1	0	0	5	4	3	3	1	0	0	7.20	5.40	5.40
an Yerkes		0	1	.000	1.80	0	1	1	0	5	8	0	3	6	1	0	14.40	0.00	5.40
rry Milton		0	0	–	2.25	0	1	0	0	4	3	1	0	1	1	0	6.75	2.25	0.00
Taylor		0	0	–	0.00	0	1	0	0	3	0	0	1	0	0	0	0.00	0.00	3.00
AM TOTAL		43	94	.314	3.76	2	168	139	111	1182.1	1353	430	419	782	494	4	10.30	3.27	3.19

CARDINAL SLUGGING CHAMPIONS

1917 Rogers Hornsby, .484	1938 Johnny Mize, .614
1920 Rogers Hornsby, .559	1939 Johnny Mize, .626
1921 Rogers Hornsby, .639	1940 Johnny Mize, .636
1922 Rogers Hornsby, .722	1943 Stan Musial, .562
1923 Rogers Hornsby, .627	1944 Stan Musial, .549
1924 Rogers Hornsby, .696	1946 Stan Musial, .587
1925 Rogers Hornsby, .756	1948 Stan Musial, .702
1927 Chick Hafey, .590	1950 Stan Musial, .596
1934 Ripper Collins, .615	1952 Stan Musial, .538
1937 Joe Medwick, .641	

MANAGER	W	L	PCT
Kid Nichols	75	79	.487

POS	Player	B	G	AB	H	2B	3B	HR	HR %	R	RBI	BB	SO	SB	Pinch Hit AB	Pinch Hit H	BA	SA
REGULARS																		
1B	Jake Beckley	L	142	551	179	22	9	1	0.2	72	67	35		17	0	0	.325	.403
2B	John Farrell		131	509	130	23	3	0	0.0	72	20	46		16	1	0	.255	.312
SS	Danny Shay		99	340	87	11	1	1	0.3	45	18	39		36	1	0	.256	.303
3B	Jimmy Burke	R	118	406	92	10	3	0	0.0	37	37	15		17	0	0	.227	.266
RF	Spike Shannon		134	500	140	10	3	1	0.2	84	26	50		34	1	0	.280	.318
CF	Homer Smoot	L	137	520	146	23	6	3	0.6	58	66	37		23	0	0	.281	.365
LF	George Barclay		103	375	75	7	4	1	0.3	41	28	12		14	0	0	.200	.248
C	Mike Grady	R	101	323	101	15	11	5	1.5	44	43	31		6	7	1	.313	.474
SUBSTITUTES																		
UT	Dave Brain	R	127	488	130	24	12	7	1.4	57	72	17		18	2	0	.266	.408
23	Simmy Murch		13	51	7	1	0	0	0.0	3	1	1		0	0	0	.137	.157
2S	She Donahue	R	4	15	4	0	0	0	0.0	1	2	0		3	0	0	.267	.267
OF	John Dunleavy		51	172	40	7	3	1	0.6	23	14	16		8	0	0	.233	.326
OF	Hugh Hill		23	93	21	2	1	3	3.2	13	4	2		3	0	0	.226	.366
C	Larry McLean	R	27	84	14	2	1	0	0.0	5	4	4		1	2	0	.167	.214
C	Dave Zearfoss		27	80	17	2	0	0	0.0	7	9	10		0	1	0	.213	.238
C	Bill Byers		19	60	13	0	0	0	0.0	3	4	1		0	2	1	.217	.217
C	John Butler	R	12	37	6	1	0	0	0.0	0	1	4		0	0	0	.162	.189
C	Charlie Swindell		3	8	1	0	0	0	0.0	0	0	0		0	0	0	.125	.125
PITCHERS																		
P	Jack Taylor	R	42	133	28	3	3	1	0.8	9	8	4		3	0	0	.211	.301
P	Kid Nichols	R	36	109	17	1	2	0	0.0	7	5	7		0	0	0	.156	.202
P	Chappie McFarland		32	99	13	0	0	0	0.0	8	4	5		0	0	0	.131	.172
P	Mike O'Neill	L	30	91	21	7	2	0	0.0	9	16	5		0	2	1	.231	.352
P	Joe Corbett	R	14	43	9	4	0	0	0.0	4	6	2		0	0	0	.209	.302
P	Jim McGinley	R	3	11	1	0	0	0	0.0	0	1	0		0	0	0	.091	.091
P	War Sanders	R	4	6	0	0	0	0	0.0	0	0	0		0	0	0	.000	.000
	TEAM TOTAL			5104	1292	175	66	24	0.5	602	456	343		199	19	3	.253	.327

INDIVIDUAL FIELDING

POS	Player	T	G	PO	A	E	DP	TC/G	FA
1B	J. Beckley	L	142	**1526**	64	20	65	11.3	.988
	M. Grady	R	11	93	5	0	4	8.9	1.000
	D. Brain	R	4	40	3	2	1	11.3	.956
	B. Byers	R	1	6	0	1	0	7.0	.857
2B	J. Farrell	R	130	297	450	53	**55**	6.2	.934
	D. Brain	R	13	35	55	6	3	7.4	.938
	S. Murch	R	6	6	13	2	2	3.5	.905
	S. Donahue	R	3	5	6	2	1	4.3	.846
	M. Grady	R	3	5	7	0	0	4.0	1.000
	D. Shay	R	2	0	5	0	0	2.5	1.000
SS	D. Shay	R	97	153	319	46	30	5.3	.911
	D. Brain	R	59	109	182	23	21	5.3	.927
	S. Murch	R	1	2	2	0	0	4.0	1.000
	S. Donahue	R	1	0	0	1	0	1.0	.000
3B	J. Burke	R	118	148	217	42	10	3.4	.897
	D. Brain	R	30	40	68	14	1	4.1	.885
	S. Murch	R	6	5	12	0	0	2.8	1.000
	M. Grady	R	1	0	4	1	0	5.0	.800

POS	Player	T	G	PO	A	E	DP	TC/G	FA
OF	H. Smoot	R	137	270	17	10	6	2.2	.966
	S. Shannon	R	133	246	18	6	10	2.0	**.978**
	G. Barclay		103	170	7	10	2	1.8	.947
	J. Dunleavy		44	68	6	1	2	1.7	.987
	H. Hill		23	41	2	0	1	1.9	1.000
	D. Brain	R	19	35	0	0	0	1.8	1.000
	M. O'Neill	L	3	3	1	0	0	1.3	1.000
C	M. Grady	R	77	323	77	19	7	5.4	.955
	L. McLean	R	24	126	20	7	1	6.4	.954
	D. Zearfoss	R	25	107	33	5	1	5.8	.966
	B. Byers	R	16	84	15	3	1	6.4	.971
	J. Butler	R	12	49	11	2	2	5.2	.968
	C. Swindell	R	3	14	1	0	0	5.0	1.000

The Cardinals improved by 32 wins, aided somewhat by the extension of the season to a 154-game schedule. The improvement was welcome, but did not necessarily bode well for the future of the team. Even with their improvement, they were still 30½ games out of first place, and the main contributions came from two future Hall of Famers well past their primes: 36-year-old first baseman Jake Beckley, third in batting with a .325 average; and 34-year-old pitcher-manager Kid Nichols, who won 21 and had an ERA of 2.02. They were also helped by 34-year-old catcher Mike Grady, who ranked fourth in batting and second in slugging. The dead ball era was in full force; Dave Brain was second in the league with just seven homers, and Grady's five homers in 323 at bats was good enough for third place in the league in home-run percentage.

TEAM STATISTICS

	W	L	PCT	GB	R	OR	2B	3B	HR	BA	SA	SB	E	DP	FA	CG	BB	SO	ShO	SV	ERA
								Batting						Fielding				Pitching			
Y	106	47	.693		744	476	202	65	31	.262	.344	283	294	93	.956	127	349	707	12	14	2.17
HI	93	60	.608	13	597	517	157	62	22	.248	.315	227	298	89	.954	139	402	618	18	5	2.30
N	88	65	.575	18	692	547	189	92	21	.255	.338	179	301	81	.954	142	343	502	12	2	2.35
T	87	66	.569	19	675	586	164	102	15	.258	.338	178	291	93	.955	133	379	455	14	1	2.89
L	75	79	.487	31.5	602	595	175	66	24	.253	.327	199	307	83	.952	146	319	529	7	2	2.64
KN	56	97	.366	50	497	614	159	53	15	.232	.295	205	343	87	.945	135	414	453	12	2	2.70
OS	55	98	.359	51	491	752	153	50	24	.237	.300	143	348	91	.946	136	500	544	13	0	3.43
HI	52	100	.342	53.5	571	782	170	54	23	.248	.316	159	403	93	.937	131	425	469	9	2	3.39
AGUE TOTAL					4869	4869	1369	544	175	.249	.322	1573	2585	710	.950	1089	3131	4277	97	28	2.73

INDIVIDUAL PITCHING

CHER	T	W	L	PCT	ERA	SV	G	GS	CG	IP	H	BB	SO	R	ER	ShO	H/9	BB/9	SO/9
ck Taylor	R	21	19	.525	2.22	1	41	39	39	352	297	82	103	133	87	2	7.59	2.10	2.63
Nichols	R	21	13	.618	2.02	1	36	35	35	317	268	50	134	97	71	3	7.61	1.42	3.80
appie McFarland	R	14	17	.452	3.21	0	32	31	28	269.1	266	56	111	149	96	1	8.89	1.87	3.71
ke O'Neill	L	10	14	.417	2.09	0	25	24	23	220	229	50	68	86	51	1	9.37	2.05	2.78
e Corbett	R	5	9	.357	4.39	0	14	14	12	108.2	110	51	68	75	53	0	9.11	4.22	5.63
n Dunleavy		1	4	.200	4.42	0	7	5	5	55	63	23	28	32	27	0	10.31	3.76	4.58
McGinley	R	2	1	.667	2.00	0	3	3	3	27	28	6	6	8	6	0	9.33	2.00	2.00
r Sanders	L	1	2	.333	4.74	0	4	3	1	19	25	1	11	15	10	0	11.84	0.47	5.21
AM TOTAL		75	79	.487	2.64	2	162	154	146	1368	1286	319	529	595	401	7	8.46	2.10	3.48

MANAGER	W	L	PCT
Kid Nichols	19	29	.396
Jimmy Burke	17	32	.347
Stanley Robison	22	35	.386

POS	Player	B	G	AB	H	2B	3B	HR	HR %	R	RBI	BB	SO	SB	Pinch Hit AB	Pinch Hit H	BA	SA
REGULARS																		
1B	Jake Beckley	L	134	514	147	20	10	1	0.2	48	57	30		12	0	0	.286	.370
2B	Harry Arndt		113	415	101	11	6	2	0.5	40	36	24		13	2	1	.243	.313
SS	George McBride	R	81	281	61	1	2	2	0.7	22	34	14		10	0	0	.217	.256
3B	Jimmy Burke	R	122	431	97	9	5	1	0.2	34	30	21		15	0	0	.225	.276
RF	John Dunleavy		119	435	105	8	8	1	0.2	52	25	55		15	0	0	.241	.303
CF	Homer Smoot	L	139	534	166	21	16	4	0.7	73	58	33		21	1	0	.311	.433
LF	Spike Shannon		140	544	146	16	3	0	0.0	73	41	47		27	0	0	.268	.309
C	Mike Grady	R	100	311	89	20	7	4	1.3	41	41	33		15	9	2	.286	.434
SUBSTITUTES																		
S2	Danny Shay		78	281	67	12	1	0	0.0	30	28	35		11	0	0	.238	.288
UT	Dave Brain	R	44	158	36	4	5	1	0.6	11	17	8		4	3	1	.228	.335
3B	Art Hoelskoetter		24	83	20	2	1	0	0.0	7	5	3		1	0	0	.241	.289
2B	John Farrell		7	24	4	0	1	0	0.0	6	1	4		1	0	0	.167	.250
2S	Simmy Murch		3	9	1	0	0	0	0.0	0	0	0		0	1	0	.111	.111
O2	Josh Clarke	L	50	167	43	3	2	3	1.8	31	18	27		8	4	1	.257	.353
OF	Rube DeGroff		15	56	14	2	1	0	0.0	3	5	5		1	0	0	.250	.321
OF	John Himes		12	41	6	0	0	0	0.0	3	0	1		0	1	0	.146	.146
C	John Warner	L	41	137	35	2	2	1	0.7	9	12	6		2	0	0	.255	.321
C	Tom Leahy		35	97	22	1	3	0	0.0	3	7	8		0	6	1	.227	.299
C	Dave Zearfoss		20	51	8	0	1	0	0.0	2	2	4		0	1	0	.157	.196
C	Gerry Shea		2	6	2	0	0	0	0.0	0	0	0		0	0	0	.333	.333
PITCHERS																		
P	Jack Taylor	R	39	121	23	5	2	0	0.0	11	12	8		4	0	0	.190	.264
P	Jake Thielman		34	91	21	1	5	0	0.0	16	8	12		1	1	0	.231	.352
P	Chappie McFarland		31	85	14	2	1	0	0.0	8	4	6		0	0	0	.165	.212
P	Buster Brown	R	23	65	6	0	3	0	0.0	3	1	1		0	0	0	.092	.185
P	Wish Egan	R	23	59	6	0	0	0	0.0	5	0	3		1	0	0	.102	.102
P	Win Kellum	L	11	25	5	0	0	0	0.0	2	3	3		0	0	0	.200	.200
P	Kid Nichols	R	8	22	5	0	0	0	0.0	0	0	0		0	0	0	.227	.227
P	Sandy McDougal		5	15	2	0	0	0	0.0	0	1	0		0	0	0	.133	.133
P	Billy Campbell	L	2	7	1	0	0	0	0.0	1	0	0		0	0	0	.143	.143
P	Jim McGinley	R	1	1	1	0	0	0	0.0	0	0	0		0	0	0	1.000	1.000
	TEAM TOTAL			5066	1254	140	85	20	0.4	534	446	391		162	29	6	.248	.321

INDIVIDUAL FIELDING

POS	Player	T	G	PO	A	E	DP	TC/G	FA
1B	J. Beckley	L	134	1442	69	28	56	11.5	.982
	M. Grady	R	20	180	17	7	5	10.2	.966
	G. McBride	R	1	2	0	0	1	2.0	1.000
2B	H. Arndt		90	173	254	22	25	5.0	.951
	D. Shay	R	39	82	120	10	14	5.4	.953
	J. Clarke	R	16	26	48	9	3	5.2	.892
	J. Farrell	R	7	19	14	4	0	5.3	.892
	Hoelskoetter	R	3	10	3	2	1	5.0	.867
	S. Murch	R	2	3	0	1	0	2.0	.750
	J. Dunleavy		1	0	3	0	0	3.0	1.000
SS	G. McBride	R	80	147	273	28	29	5.6	.938
	D. Shay	R	39	90	110	25	8	5.8	.889
	D. Brain	R	29	58	74	13	4	5.0	.910
	H. Arndt		5	10	16	1	0	5.4	.963
	J. Clarke	R	4	7	7	1	0	3.8	.933
	S. Murch		1	3	1	1	0	5.0	.800
3B	J. Burke	R	122	174	238	34	13	3.7	.924
	Hoelskoetter	R	20	30	40	2	3	3.6	.972
	D. Brain	R	6	8	15	0	0	3.8	1.000
	H. Arndt		7	9	13	0	1	3.1	1.000
	J. Taylor	R	2	2	2	1	0	2.5	.800

POS	Player	T	G	PO	A	E	DP	TC/G	FA
OF	H. Smoot	R	138	295	18	8	6	2.3	.975
	S. Shannon	R	140	299	7	5	3	2.2	.984
	J. Dunleavy		118	177	25	8	7	1.8	.962
	J. Clarke	R	26	48	1	3	0	2.0	.942
	R. DeGroff		15	27	3	3	1	2.2	.909
	K. Nichols	R	1	0	0	0	0	0.0	.000
	J. Himes		11	17	1	0	0	1.6	1.000
	H. Arndt		9	14	2	0	0	1.8	1.000
	D. Brain	R	6	11	3	0	0	2.3	1.000
	J. Thielman		1	2	0	0	0	2.0	1.000
C	M. Grady	R	71	288	79	17	7	5.4	.956
	J. Warner	R	41	165	63	10	4	5.8	.958
	T. Leahy	R	29	91	31	7	1	4.4	.946
	D. Zearfoss	R	19	62	22	3	0	4.6	.966
	G. Shea		2	7	4	1	1	6.0	.917

The Cardinals sat in sixth place from mid-May to the end of the season. After pitcher-manager Kid Nichols was sent to Philadelphia, and third baseman Jimmy Burke failed to improve matters, co-owner Stanley Robison, following in the long-established path of Chris von der Ahe, took things into his own hands, managing the club himself for the remainder of the season. There were few real bright spots—Homer Smoot's .311 average placed him seventh in the league, but he managed just 58 RBIs, which nonetheless led the club. For the fourth consecutive season, Jack Taylor finished every game he started. When he was finally pulled for a reliever while pitching for the Cubs the next year, he ended an untouchable streak of 187 consecutive complete-game starts.

TEAM STATISTICS

W	L	PCT	GB	R	OR	2B	3B	Batting HR	BA	SA	SB	E	Fielding DP	FA	CG	BB	Pitching SO	ShO	SV	ERA
105	48	.686		780	504	191	88	39	.273	.368	291	258	93	.960	117	364	760	17	14	2.39
96	57	.627	9	692	569	190	91	22	.266	.350	202	255	112	.961	113	389	512	12	4	2.86
92	61	.601	13	667	442	157	82	12	.245	.314	267	248	99	.962	133	385	627	23	2	2.04
83	69	.546	21.5	708	603	187	82	16	.260	.336	180	275	99	.957	119	411	516	12	5	2.81
79	74	.516	26	736	691	160	101	27	.269	.354	181	310	122	.953	119	439	547	10	1	3.01
58	96	.377	47.5	534	741	140	85	20	.248	.321	162	274	83	.957	135	367	411	10	2	3.59
51	103	.331	54.5	467	733	148	52	17	.234	.293	132	325	89	.951	139	433	533	13	0	3.52
48	104	.316	56.5	506	807	154	60	29	.246	.317	186	411	101	.936	125	476	556	7	3	3.76
GUE TOTAL				5090	5090	1327	641	182	.255	.332	1601	2356	798	.954	1000	3264	4462	104	31	2.99

INDIVIDUAL PITCHING

CHER	T	W	L	PCT	ERA	SV	G	GS	CG	IP	H	BB	SO	R	ER	ShO	H/9	BB/9	SO/9
Taylor	R	15	21	.417	3.44	1	37	34	34	309	302	85	102	155	118	3	8.80	2.48	2.97
ppie McFarland	R	8	18	.308	3.82	1	31	28	22	250	281	65	85	145	106	3	10.12	2.34	3.06
e Thielman		15	16	.484	3.50	0	32	29	26	242	265	62	87	138	94	0	9.86	2.31	3.24
ter Brown	R	8	11	.421	2.97	0	23	21	17	179	172	62	57	80	59	3	8.65	3.12	2.87
h Egan	R	6	15	.286	3.58	0	23	19	18	171	189	39	29	93	68	0	9.95	2.05	1.53
Kellum	L	3	3	.500	2.92	0	11	7	5	74	70	10	19	30	24	1	8.51	1.22	2.31
Nichols	R	1	5	.167	5.37	0	7	7	5	52	64	18	16	47	31	0	11.08	3.12	2.77
dy McDougal		1	4	.200	3.43	0	5	5	5	44.2	50	12	10	24	17	0	10.07	2.42	2.01
Campbell	L	1	1	.500	7.41	0	2	2	2	17	27	7	2	17	14	0	14.29	3.71	1.06
Hoelskoetter	R	0	1	.000	1.50	0	1	1	1	6	6	5	4	6	1	0	9.00	7.50	6.00
McGinley	R	0	1	.000	15.00	0	1	1	0	3	5	2	0	6	5	0	15.00	6.00	0.00
M TOTAL		58	96	.377	3.59	2	173	154	135	1347.2	1431	367	411	741	537	10	9.56	2.45	2.74

CARDINAL HOME RUN CHAMPIONS

1921	Rogers Hornsby, 42	1939	Johnny Mize, 28
1925	Rogers Hornsby, 39	1940	Johnny Mize, 43
1937	Joe Medwick, 31		

MANAGER	W	L	PCT
John McCloskey	52	98	.347

POS	Player	B	G	AB	H	2B	3B	HR	HR %	R	RBI	BB	SO	SB	Pinch Hit AB	Pinch Hit H	BA	SA
REGULARS																		
1B	Jake Beckley	L	87	320	79	16	6	0	0.0	29	44	13		3	2	1	.247	.334
2B	Pug Bennett		153	595	156	16	7	1	0.2	66	34	56		20	0	0	.262	.318
SS	George McBride	R	90	313	53	8	2	0	0.0	24	13	17		5	0	0	.169	.208
3B	Harry Arndt		69	256	69	7	9	2	0.8	30	26	19		5	1	0	.270	.391
RF	Al Burch	L	91	335	89	5	1	0	0.0	40	11	37		15	0	0	.266	.287
CF	Homer Smoot	L	86	343	85	9	10	0	0.0	41	31	11		3	0	0	.248	.332
LF	Spike Shannon		80	302	78	4	0	0	0.0	36	25	36		15	0	0	.258	.272
C	Mike Grady	R	97	280	70	11	3	3	1.1	33	27	48		5	5	1	.250	.343
SUBSTITUTES																		
UT	Art Hoelskoetter		94	317	71	6	3	0	0.0	21	14	4		2	0	0	.224	.262
SS	Forrest Crawford		45	145	30	3	1	0	0.0	8	11	7		1	0	0	.207	.241
3B	Bill Phyle		22	73	13	3	1	0	0.0	6	4	5		2	0	0	.178	.247
SS	Ed Holly	R	10	34	2	0	0	0	0.0	1	7	5		0	0	0	.059	.059
3B	Eddie Zimmerman	R	5	14	3	0	0	0	0.0	0	1	0		0	0	0	.214	.214
O1	Shad Barry	R	62	237	59	9	1	0	0.0	26	12	15		6	0	0	.249	.295
OF	Sam Mertes	R	53	191	47	7	4	0	0.0	20	19	16		10	0	0	.246	.325
OF	John Himes		40	155	42	5	2	0	0.0	10	14	7		4	0	0	.271	.329
OF	Red Murray	R	46	144	37	9	7	1	0.7	18	16	9		5	5	0	.257	.438
OF	Joe Marshall		33	95	15	1	2	0	0.0	2	7	6		0	5	1	.158	.211
OF	Tom O'Hara		14	53	16	1	0	0	0.0	8	0	3		3	0	0	.302	.321
OF	Rube DeGroff		1	4	0	0	0	0	0.0	1	0	0		0	0	0	.000	.000
C1	Pete Noonan	R	44	125	21	1	3	1	0.8	8	9	11		1	5	1	.168	.248
C	Doc Marshall	R	39	123	34	4	1	0	0.0	6	10	6		1	1	0	.276	.325
C	Tommy Raub	R	24	78	22	2	4	0	0.0	9	2	4		2	0	0	.282	.410
C	Joe McCarthy	R	15	37	9	2	0	0	0.0	3	2	2		0	0	0	.243	.297
C	Ducky Holmes		9	27	5	0	0	0	0.0	2	2	2		0	0	0	.185	.185
C	Jack Slattery	R	3	7	2	0	0	0	0.0	0	0	1		0	1	0	.286	.286
PITCHERS																		
P	Buster Brown	R	32	85	14	3	0	1	1.2	4	4	4		0	0	0	.165	.235
P	Ed Karger	L	25	73	17	3	1	1	1.4	2	3	1		0	0	0	.233	.342
P	Fred Beebe	R	20	58	10	1	1	0	0.0	5	2	2		1	0	0	.172	.224
P	Carl Druhot	L	15	56	13	1	0	0	0.0	6	2	0		0	0	0	.232	.250
P	Jack Taylor	R	17	53	11	0	0	0	0.0	4	2	10		1	0	0	.208	.208
P	Gus Thompson	R	17	34	6	0	0	0	0.0	1	2	0		0	0	0	.176	.176
P	Wish Egan	R	16	29	2	0	0	0	0.0	0	1	2		0	0	0	.069	.069
P	Irv Higginbotham	R	7	18	4	0	0	0	0.0	2	0	1		0	0	0	.222	.222
P	Stoney McGlynn		6	17	1	0	0	0	0.0	0	0	1		0	0	0	.059	.059
P	Charlie Rhodes	R	9	16	3	0	0	0	0.0	0	1	0		0	0	0	.188	.188
P	Chappie McFarland		6	15	2	0	0	0	0.0	1	0	0		0	0	0	.133	.133
P	Art Fromme	R	3	9	2	0	0	0	0.0	1	1	0		0	0	0	.222	.222
P	Ambrose Puttman		4	6	2	0	0	0	0.0	1	0	0		0	0	0	.333	.333
P	Jake Thielman		1	2	1	0	0	0	0.0	0	2	0		0	0	0	.500	.500
P	Babe Adams	L	1	1	0	0	0	0	0.0	0	0	0		0	0	0	.000	.000
	TEAM TOTAL			5075	1195	137	69	10	0.2	475	362	361		110	25	4	.235	.296

INDIVIDUAL FIELDING

POS	Player	T	G	PO	A	E	DP	TC/G	FA	POS	Player	T	G	PO	A	E	DP	TC/G	FA
1B	J. Beckley	L	85	928	43	13	38	11.6	.987	OF	H. Smoot	R	86	174	8	9	4	2.2	.953
	M. Grady	R	38	299	18	6	7	8.5	.981		A. Burch	R	91	155	15	12	6	2.0	.934
	S. Barry	R	21	224	13	8	8	11.7	.967		S. Shannon	R	80	165	9	5	3	2.2	.972
	P. Noonan	R	16	152	11	7	5	10.6	.959		S. Mertes	R	53	77	4	10	0	1.7	.890
	J. Marshall		4	32	3	3	3	9.5	.921		J. Himes		40	76	10	2	2	2.2	.977
	H. Arndt		1	8	0	0	1	8.0	1.000		R. Murray	R	34	43	7	2	0	1.5	.962
											S. Barry	R	35	37	3	3	1	1.2	.930
2B	P. Bennett	R	153	295	447	41	43	5.1	.948		J. Marshall		23	22	6	3	0	1.3	.903
	Hoelskoetter		1	0	0	0	0	0.0	.000		H. Arndt		1	0	0	0	0	0.0	.000
											R. DeGroff		1	0	0	0	0	0.0	.000
SS	G. McBride	R	90	194	310	30	33	5.9	.944		T. O'Hara		14	24	0	3	0	1.9	.889
	F. Crawford	R	39	56	108	13	7	4.5	.927		Hoelskoetter	R	12	12	1	2	1	1.3	.867
	Hoelskoetter	R	16	24	45	5	2	4.6	.932										
	E. Holly	R	10	24	22	3	7	4.9	.939	C	D. Marshall	R	38	193	56	10	4	5.8	.961
											M. Grady	R	60	115	67	5	9	3.1	.973
3B	H. Arndt	R	65	108	139	9	15	3.9	.965		P. Noonan	R	23	118	37	7	0	7.0	.957
	Hoelskoetter	R	53	68	114	11	7	3.6	.943		T. Raub	R	22	81	30	5	1	5.3	.957
	B. Phyle	R	21	31	41	5	2	3.7	.935		J. McCarthy	R	15	47	14	1	2	4.1	.984
	F. Crawford	R	6	6	13	1	1	3.3	.950		D. Holmes	R	9	37	9	1	2	5.2	.979
	S. Barry	R	6	4	13	1	0	3.0	.944		R. Murray	R	7	30	10	3	2	6.1	.930
	E. Zimmerman	R	5	7	6	1	0	2.8	.929		J. Slattery	R	2	12	1	0	0	6.5	1.000

St. Louis stood near .500 at the end of May, the latest they had seen that level in several years, but a 3–19 June dropped them to seventh place. The dreadful offense, seventh in the league in runs and batting, ranked ahead of only the Boston Braves, who finished the season at 49–102. The highest average on the club among players with 300 at bats was .266 by leftfielder Al Burch. The pitching provided little comfort; they were never able to settle on a set rotation, as seven pitchers had at least ten starts, and no pitcher managed to win ten games. In their fifteen years in the league, St. Louis had never finished closer than 14½ games from first place. They had finished over .500 just twice, and it would be another five years before they topped that mark again.

TEAM STATISTICS

W	L	PCT	GB	R	OR	2B	3B	Batting HR	BA	SA	SB	E	Fielding DP	FA	CG	BB	Pitching SO	ShO	SV	ERA
116	36	.763		704	381	181	71	20	.262	.339	283	194	100	.969	125	446	702	28	9	1.76
96	56	.632	20	625	508	162	53	15	.255	.321	288	233	84	.963	105	394	639	16	16	2.49
93	60	.608	23.5	622	464	164	67	12	.261	.327	162	228	109	.964	116	309	532	26	2	2.21
71	82	.464	45.5	530	568	197	47	12	.241	.307	180	271	83	.956	108	436	500	20	5	2.58
66	86	.434	50	495	620	141	68	25	.236	.308	175	283	73	.955	119	453	476	22	9	3.13
64	87	.424	51.5	530	582	140	71	16	.238	.304	170	262	97	.959	126	470	567	11	5	2.69
52	98	.347	63	475	620	137	69	10	.235	.296	110	272	92	.957	118	479	559	4	2	3.04
49	102	.325	66.5	408	646	136	43	16	.226	.281	93	337	102	.947	137	436	562	10	0	3.17
AGUE TOTAL				4389	4389	1258	489	126	.244	.310	1461	2080	740	.959	954	3423	4537	137	48	2.63

INDIVIDUAL PITCHING

TCHER	T	W	L	PCT	ERA	SV	G	GS	CG	IP	H	BB	SO	R	ER	ShO	H/9	BB/9	SO/9
ster Brown	R	8	16	.333	2.64	0	32	27	21	238.1	208	112	109	98	70	0	7.85	4.23	4.12
Karger	L	5	16	.238	2.72	1	25	20	17	191.2	193	43	73	85	58	0	9.06	2.02	3.43
d Beebe	R	9	9	.500	3.02	0	20	19	16	160.2	115	68	109	65	54	1	6.44	3.81	6.50
k Taylor	R	8	9	.471	2.15	0	17	17	17	155	133	47	27	50	37	1	7.72	2.73	1.57
l Druhot	L	6	8	.429	2.62	0	15	13	12	130.1	117	46	45	55	38	1	8.08	3.18	3.11
s Thompson	R	2	10	.167	4.28	0	17	12	8	103	111	25	36	61	49	0	9.70	2.18	3.15
sh Egan	R	2	9	.182	4.59	0	16	12	7	86.1	97	27	23	45	44	0	10.11	2.81	2.40
Hoelskoetter	R	2	4	.333	4.63	0	12	3	2	58.1	53	34	20	37	30	0	8.18	5.25	3.09
ney McGlynn		2	2	.500	2.44	0	6	6	6	48	43	15	25	16	13	0	8.06	2.81	4.69
Higginbotham	R	1	4	.200	3.23	0	7	6	4	47.1	50	11	14	21	17	0	9.51	2.09	2.66
arlie Rhodes	R	3	4	.429	3.40	0	9	6	3	45	37	20	32	21	17	0	7.40	4.00	6.40
appie McFarland	R	2	1	.667	1.93	1	6	4	2	37.1	33	8	16	18	8	0	7.96	1.93	3.86
Fromme	R	1	2	.333	1.44	0	3	3	3	25	19	10	11	6	4	1	6.84	3.60	3.96
brose Puttman	L	1	2	.333	5.30	0	4	4	0	18.2	23	9	12	13	11	0	11.09	4.34	5.79
e Thielman		0	1	.000	3.60	0	1	1	0	5	5	2	0	6	2	0	9.00	3.60	0.00
e Adams	R	0	1	.000	13.50	0	1	1	0	4	9	2	0	8	6	0	20.25	4.50	0.00
AM TOTAL		52	98	.347	3.04	2	191	154	118	1354	1246	479	559	605	458	4	8.28	3.18	3.72

MANAGER	W	L	PCT
John McCloskey	52	101	.340

POS	Player	B	G	AB	H	2B	3B	HR	HR %	R	RBI	BB	SO	SB	Pinch Hit AB	Pinch Hit H	BA	SA
REGULARS																		
1B	Ed Konetchy	R	90	330	83	11	8	3	0.9	34	30	26		13	0	0	.252	.361
2B	Pug Bennett		87	324	72	8	2	0	0.0	20	21	21		7	1	0	.222	.259
SS	Ed Holly	R	149	544	125	18	3	1	0.2	55	40	36		16	0	0	.230	.279
3B	Bobby Byrne	R	148	558	143	11	5	0	0.0	55	29	35		21	0	0	.256	.294
RF	Shad Barry	R	80	292	72	5	2	0	0.0	30	19	28		4	0	0	.247	.277
CF	John Burnett		59	206	49	8	4	0	0.0	18	12	15		5	0	0	.238	.316
LF	Red Murray	R	132	485	127	10	10	7	1.4	46	46	24		23	1	1	.262	.367
C	Doc Marshall	R	84	268	54	8	2	2	0.7	19	18	12		2	1	0	.201	.269
SUBSTITUTES																		
UT	Art Hoelskoetter		119	396	98	6	3	2	0.5	21	28	27		5	2	0	.247	.293
1B	Jake Beckley	L	32	115	24	3	0	0	0.0	6	7	1		0	0	0	.209	.235
13	Harry Arndt		11	32	6	1	0	0	0.0	3	2	1		0	4	1	.188	.219
SS	Forrest Crawford		7	22	5	0	0	0	0.0	0	3	2		0	0	0	.227	.227
1B	John Baxter		6	21	4	0	0	0	0.0	1	0	0		0	0	0	.190	.190
OF	John Kelly		53	197	37	5	0	0	0.0	12	6	13		7	1	0	.188	.213
OF	Tom O'Hara		48	173	41	2	1	0	0.0	11	5	12		1	1	0	.237	.260
OF	Al Burch	L	48	154	35	3	1	0	0.0	18	5	17		7	0	0	.227	.260
PO	Johnny Lush	L	27	82	23	2	3	0	0.0	6	5	5		4	8	1	.280	.378
OP	Harry Wolter	L	16	47	16	0	0	0	0.0	4	6	3		1	4	0	.340	.340
OF	Sis Hopkins	R	15	44	6	3	0	0	0.0	7	3	10		2	0	0	.136	.205
OF	Al Shaw	L	8	23	7	0	0	0	0.0	2	1	3		1	0	0	.304	.304
OF	Joe Delahanty	R	6	21	7	0	0	1	4.8	3	2	0		3	0	0	.333	.476
C	Pete Noonan	R	74	236	53	7	3	1	0.4	19	16	9		3	5	1	.225	.292
PITCHERS																		
P	Stoney McGlynn		46	125	25	5	0	0	0.0	8	9	6		0	1	0	.200	.240
P	Ed Karger	L	38	111	19	2	0	2	1.8	9	9	2		0	0	0	.171	.243
P	Fred Beebe	R	31	86	11	1	1	0	0.0	4	6	1		0	0	0	.128	.163
P	Art Fromme	R	23	55	10	1	1	0	0.0	5	1	1		0	0	0	.182	.236
P	Buster Brown	R	9	26	7	1	1	0	0.0	1	1	0		0	0	0	.269	.385
P	Bugs Raymond	R	8	22	2	0	1	0	0.0	2	1	2		0	0	0	.091	.182
P	Charlie Shields	L	3	2	0	0	0	0	0.0	0	0	0		0	0	0	.000	.000
P	Carl Druhot	L	1	0	0	0	0	0	0.0	0	0	0		0	0	0	–	–
	TEAM TOTAL			4997	1161	121	51	19	0.4	419	331	312		125	29	4	.232	.288

INDIVIDUAL FIELDING

POS	Player	T	G	PO	A	E	DP	TC/G	FA	POS	Player	T	G	PO	A	E	DP	TC/G	FA
1B	E. Konetchy	R	90	920	71	25	46	11.3	.975	OF	R. Murray	R	131	232	25	18	4	2.1	.935
	J. Beckley	L	32	303	13	4	17	10.0	.988		J. Burnett		59	98	8	5	1	1.9	.955
	Hoelskoetter	R	27	263	18	6	13	10.6	.979		S. Barry	R	80	93	11	4	0	1.4	.963
	J. Baxter		6	54	4	5	1	10.5	.921		A. Burch	R	48	85	10	8	4	2.1	.922
	H. Arndt		4	33	3	0	2	9.0	1.000		J. Kelly		52	85	7	3	4	1.8	.968
2B	Hoelskoetter	R	72	149	233	30	26	5.7	.927		T. O'Hara		47	78	5	5	2	1.9	.943
	P. Bennett	R	83	175	208	25	26	4.9	.939		S. Hopkins	R	15	21	0	3	0	1.6	.875
	E. Holly	R	3	9	6	2	0	5.7	.882		A. Shaw	R	8	17	1	1	0	2.4	.947
SS	E. Holly	R	146	316	474	62	45	5.8	.927		J. Delahanty	R	6	14	0	1	0	2.5	.933
	F. Crawford	R	7	13	18	3	2	4.9	.912		H. Wolter	L	9	13	2	0	1	1.7	1.000
	B. Byrne	R	1	3	5	1	0	9.0	.889		Hoelskoetter		8	9	0	2	0	1.4	.818
3B	B. Byrne	R	147	211	347	49	24	4.1	.919		J. Lush	L	7	2	0	0	0	0.3	1.000
	H. Arndt		3	3	6	1	1	3.3	.900	C	D. Marshall	R	83	374	142	26	9	6.5	.952
	P. Bennett	R	3	3	6	0	1	3.0	1.000		P. Noonan	R	69	364	97	24	12	7.0	.951
	Hoelskoetter	R	2	1	5	1	1	3.5	.857		Hoelskoetter	R	8	27	11	3	0	5.1	.927

The fact that St. Louis managed to stay out of the cellar for the first few weeks of the season did not signal much improvement; they were kept in seventh place only by Brooklyn's horrendous 1–16 start. While the Dodgers steadied themselves, playing just under .500 for the rest of the season, the Cards continued to fall at an alarming rate. By the end of July they were 53 games under .500 with a record of 21–74, 48 games out of first. They ended up in eighth, last in the league in runs and fielding, seventh in runs allowed and ERA. Their staff led the league in complete games, but considering the quality of the staff, that was of very little benefit.

TEAM STATISTICS

W	L	PCT	GB	R	OR	2B	3B	Batting HR	BA	SA	SB	E	Fielding DP	FA	CG	BB	Pitching SO	ShO	SV	ERA
107	45	.704		570	390	160	48	13	.250	.310	235	211	110	.967	113	402	584	30	7	1.73
91	63	.591	17	634	507	133	78	19	.254	.324	264	256	75	.959	111	368	497	24	4	2.30
83	64	.565	21.5	514	481	162	65	12	.236	.305	154	256	104	.957	110	422	499	21	3	2.43
82	71	.536	25.5	573	511	160	48	23	.251	.317	205	232	75	.963	109	369	655	19	11	2.45
65	83	.439	40	446	522	142	63	18	.232	.298	121	262	94	.959	125	463	479	20	1	2.38
66	87	.431	41.5	524	514	126	90	15	.247	.318	158	227	118	.963	118	444	481	10	2	2.41
58	90	.392	47	503	651	142	61	22	.243	.309	120	249	128	.961	121	458	426	9	2	3.33
52	101	.340	55.5	419	607	121	51	19	.232	.288	125	339	105	.948	126	499	589	20	2	2.70
AGUE TOTAL				4183	4183	1146	504	141	.243	.309	1382	2032	809	.960	933	3425	4210	153	32	2.46

INDIVIDUAL PITCHING

TCHER	T	W	L	PCT	ERA	SV	G	GS	CG	IP	H	BB	SO	R	ER	ShO	H/9	BB/9	SO/9
ney McGlynn		14	25	.359	2.91	1	45	39	33	352.1	329	112	109	159	114	3	8.40	2.86	2.78
Karger	L	15	19	.441	2.03	1	38	31	28	310	251	64	132	100	70	6	7.29	1.86	3.83
d Beebe	R	7	19	.269	2.72	0	31	29	24	238.1	192	109	141	95	72	4	7.25	4.12	5.32
Fromme	R	5	13	.278	2.90	0	23	16	13	145.2	138	67	67	73	47	2	8.53	4.14	4.14
nny Lush	L	7	10	.412	2.50	0	20	19	15	144	132	42	71	63	40	4	8.25	2.63	4.44
gs Raymond	R	2	4	.333	1.67	0	8	6	6	64.2	56	21	34	34	12	1	7.79	2.92	4.73
ster Brown	R	1	6	.143	3.39	0	9	8	6	63.2	57	45	17	38	24	0	8.06	6.36	2.40
rry Wolter	L	1	2	.333	4.30	0	3	3	1	23	27	18	8	13	11	0	10.57	7.04	3.13
Hoelskoetter	R	0	0	–	5.73	0	2	0	0	11	9	10	8	16	7	0	7.36	8.18	6.55
arlie Shields	L	0	2	.000	9.45	0	3	2	0	6.2	12	7	1	11	7	0	16.20	9.45	1.35
l Druhot	L	0	1	.000	15.43	0	1	1	0	2.1	3	4	1	5	4	0	11.57	15.43	3.86
AM TOTAL		52	101	.340	2.70	2	183	154	126	1361.2	1206	499	589	607	408	20	7.97	3.30	3.89

CARDINAL STOLEN BASE CHAMPIONS

1900	Patsy Donovan, 45	1967	Lou Brock, 52
1927	Frankie Frisch, 48	1968	Lou Brock, 62
1931	Frankie Frisch, 28	1969	Lou Brock, 53
1933	Pepper Martin, 26	1971	Lou Brock, 64
1936	Pepper Martin, 23	1972	Lou Brock, 63
1945	Red Schoendienst, 26	1973	Lou Brock, 70
1966	Lou Brock, 74	1974	Lou Brock, 118

MANAGER	W	L	PCT
John McCloskey	49	105	.318

POS	Player	B	G	AB	H	2B	3B	HR	HR %	R	RBI	BB	SO	SB	Pinch Hit AB	Pinch Hit H	BA	SA
REGULARS																		
1B	Ed Konetchy	R	154	545	135	19	12	5	0.9	46	50	38		16	0	0	.248	.354
2B	Billy Gilbert	R	89	276	59	7	0	0	0.0	12	10	20		6	0	0	.214	.239
SS	Patsy O'Rourke	R	53	164	32	4	2	0	0.0	8	16	14		2	0	0	.195	.244
3B	Bobby Byrne	R	127	439	84	7	1	0	0.0	27	14	23		16	1	0	.191	.212
RF	Red Murray	R	154	593	167	19	15	7	1.2	64	62	37		48	0	0	.282	.400
CF	Al Shaw	L	107	367	97	13	4	1	0.3	40	19	25		9	10	5	.264	.330
LF	Joe Delahanty	R	140	499	127	14	11	1	0.2	37	44	32		11	1	0	.255	.333
C	Bill Ludwig	R	66	187	34	2	2	0	0.0	15	8	16		3	4	0	.182	.214
SUBSTITUTES																		
UT	Chappy Charles	R	121	454	93	14	3	1	0.2	39	17	19		15	2	0	.205	.256
S3	Champ Osteen	L	29	112	22	4	0	0	0.0	2	11	0		0	0	0	.196	.232
SS	Tom Reilly	R	29	81	14	1	0	1	1.2	5	3	2		4	0	0	.173	.222
SS	Walter Morris		23	73	13	1	1	0	0.0	1	2	0		1	1	0	.178	.219
OF	Shad Barry	R	74	268	61	8	1	0	0.0	24	11	19		9	3	0	.228	.265
OF	Wilbur Murdock		27	62	16	3	0	0	0.0	5	5	3		4	9	2	.258	.306
OF	Ralph McLaurin		8	22	5	0	0	0	0.0	2	0	0		0	2	0	.227	.227
C	Art Hoelskoetter		62	155	36	7	1	0	0.0	10	6	6		1	16	3	.232	.290
C	John Bliss	R	44	136	29	4	0	1	0.7	9	5	8		3	2	1	.213	.265
C	Charley Moran	R	21	63	11	1	2	0	0.0	2	2	0		0	5	2	.175	.254
C	Doc Marshall	R	6	14	1	0	0	0	0.0	0	1	0		0	0	0	.071	.071
PITCHERS																		
P	Bugs Raymond	R	48	90	17	2	0	0	0.0	3	6	5		0	0	0	.189	.211
P	Johnny Lush	L	45	89	15	2	0	0	0.0	7	2	7		1	6	1	.169	.191
P	Fred Beebe	R	29	56	7	0	1	0	0.0	1	1	0		0	0	0	.125	.161
P	Ed Karger	L	24	54	13	1	1	0	0.0	4	3	0		1	1	0	.241	.296
P	Slim Sallee	L	25	41	2	0	0	0	0.0	2	1	3		0	0	0	.049	.049
P	Irv Higginbotham	R	19	38	5	0	0	0	0.0	3	0	0		0	0	0	.132	.132
P	Art Fromme	R	20	36	5	0	0	0	0.0	2	2	1		0	0	0	.139	.139
P	Stoney McGlynn		16	26	2	0	0	0	0.0	0	0	4		0	0	0	.077	.077
P	Charlie Rhodes	R	4	12	3	1	0	0	0.0	2	0	0		0	0	0	.250	.333
P	O. F. Baldwin		4	6	0	0	0	0	0.0	0	0	0		0	0	0	.000	.000
P	Fred Gaiser		1	1	0	0	0	0	0.0	0	0	0		0	0	0	.000	.000
	TEAM TOTAL			4959	1105	134	57	17	0.3	372	301	282		150	63	14	.223	.283

INDIVIDUAL FIELDING

POS	Player	T	G	PO	A	E	DP	TC/G	FA		POS	Player	T	G	PO	A	E	DP	TC/G	FA
1B	E. Konetchy	R	154	1610	122	24	61	11.4	.986		OF	R. Murray	R	154	274	22	28	4	2.1	.914
	Hoelskoetter	R	1	1	1	0	1	2.0	1.000			J. Delahanty	R	138	243	11	6	1	1.9	.977
2B	B. Gilbert	R	89	222	254	24	23	5.6	.952			A. Shaw	R	91	179	23	15	7	2.4	.931
	C. Charles	R	65	123	182	26	5	5.1	.921			S. Barry	R	69	109	10	4	0	1.8	.967
	Hoelskoetter	R	1	1	5	1	0	7.0	.857			W. Murdock		16	21	0	2	0	1.4	.913
SS	P. O'Rourke	R	53	80	171	41	10	5.5	.860			R. McLaurin		6	14	0	2	0	2.7	.875
	C. Charles	R	31	57	95	15	20	5.4	.910		C	B. Ludwig	R	62	227	87	16	2	5.3	.952
	W. Morris	R	23	47	75	8	8	5.7	.938			J. Bliss	R	43	194	59	2	6	5.9	.992
	T. Reilly	R	29	34	69	16	10	4.1	.866			Hoelskoetter	R	41	182	56	13	6	6.1	.948
	C. Osteen	R	17	30	42	13	6	5.0	.847			C. Moran	R	16	58	26	9	1	5.8	.903
	B. Byrne	R	4	4	10	5	1	4.8	.737			D. Marshall	R	6	26	6	0	1	5.3	1.000
	A. Shaw	R	4	7	5	4	1	4.0	.750											
	S. Barry	R	2	3	2	3	1	4.0	.625											
3B	B. Byrne	R	122	183	248	35	14	3.8	.925											
	C. Charles	R	23	35	45	8	0	3.8	.909											
	A. Shaw	R	1	0	0	0	0	0.0	.000											
	C. Osteen	R	12	14	21	1	0	3.0	.972											
	Hoelskoetter	R	2	3	3	2	0	4.0	.750											

Unlike the 1907 campaign, the Dodgers stayed with the Cardinals through-out the year, and the two conducted a lively battle for last place, with St. Louis not clinching that spot until the final week of the season. They scored the fewest runs in the league and allowed the most, averaging fewer than two and one-half runs a game for and more than four against. They also committed the most errors in the league by far, leading the next-highest total by ninety-three. Only three Cardinals drove in as many as twenty runs. The beleaguered pitching staff was left in an impossible position. We can only imagine the frustration of Bugs Raymond, who pitched 324 innings with a 2.03 ERA, only to be rewarded with a 14–25 record as his club was shut out behind him eleven times.

TEAM STATISTICS

W	L	PCT	GB	R	OR	2B	3B	HR	BA	SA	SB	E	DP	FA	CG	BB	SO	ShO	SV	ERA
						Batting						**Fielding**					**Pitching**			
99	55	.643		625	457	197	56	19	.249	.321	212	205	76	.969	108	437	668	27	10	2.14
98	56	.636	1	652	458	182	43	20	.267	.333	181	250	79	.962	95	288	656	24	15	2.14
98	56	.636	1	585	474	162	98	25	.247	.332	186	226	74	.964	100	406	468	24	8	2.12
83	71	.539	16	503	446	194	68	11	.244	.316	200	238	75	.963	116	379	476	22	6	2.10
73	81	.474	26	488	542	129	77	14	.227	.294	196	255	72	.959	110	415	433	17	7	2.37
63	91	.409	36	537	621	137	43	17	.239	.293	134	253	90	.962	92	423	416	14	1	2.79
53	101	.344	46	375	515	110	60	28	.213	.277	113	247	66	.961	118	444	535	20	3	2.47
49	105	.318	50	372	624	134	57	17	.223	.283	150	348	68	.946	97	430	528	13	4	2.64
GUE TOTAL				4137	4137	1245	502	151	.239	.306	1372	2022	600	.961	836	3222	4180	161	54	2.35

INDIVIDUAL PITCHING

PITCHER	T	W	L	PCT	ERA	SV	G	GS	CG	IP	H	BB	SO	R	ER	ShO	H/9	BB/9	SO/9
gs Raymond	R	14	**25**	.359	2.03	2	48	37	23	324.1	236	95	145	116	73	5	6.55	2.64	4.02
nny Lush	L	11	19	.367	2.12	1	38	32	23	250.2	221	57	93	102	59	3	7.93	2.05	3.34
d Beebe	R	5	13	.278	2.63	0	29	19	12	174.1	134	66	72	88	51	0	6.92	3.41	3.72
Karger	L	4	8	.333	3.06	0	22	15	9	141.1	148	50	34	77	48	1	9.42	3.18	2.17
n Sallee	L	3	8	.273	3.15	0	25	12	7	128.2	144	36	39	65	45	1	10.07	2.52	2.73
Fromme	R	5	13	.278	2.72	0	20	14	9	116	102	50	62	59	35	2	7.91	3.88	4.81
Higginbotham	R	4	8	.333	3.20	0	19	11	7	107	113	33	38	51	38	1	9.50	2.78	3.20
ney McGlynn		1	6	.143	3.45	1	16	6	4	75.2	76	17	23	40	29	0	9.04	2.02	2.74
arlie Rhodes	R	1	2	.333	3.00	0	4	4	3	33	23	12	15	14	11	0	6.27	3.27	4.09
F. Baldwin		1	3	.250	6.14	0	4	4	0	14.2	16	11	5	10	10	0	9.82	6.75	3.07
d Gaiser		0	0	—	7.71	0	1	0	0	2.1	4	3	2	2	2	0	15.43	11.57	7.71
AM TOTAL		49	105	.318	2.64	4	226	154	97	1368	1217	430	528	624	401	13	8.01	2.83	3.47

MANAGER	W	L	PCT
Roger Bresnahan	54	98	.355

POS	Player	B	G	AB	H	2B	3B	HR	HR %	R	RBI	BB	SO	SB	Pinch Hit AB	Pinch Hit H	BA	SA
REGULARS																		
1B	Ed Konetchy	R	152	576	165	23	14	4	0.7	88	80	65		25	0	0	.286	.396
2B	Chappy Charles	R	99	339	80	7	3	0	0.0	33	29	31		7	0	0	.236	.274
SS	Rudy Hulswitt	R	82	289	81	8	3	0	0.0	21	29	19		7	4	1	.280	.329
3B	Bobby Byrne	R	105	421	90	13	6	1	0.2	61	33	46		21	0	0	.214	.280
RF	Steve Evans	L	143	498	129	17	6	2	0.4	67	56	66		14	0	0	.259	.329
CF	Al Shaw	L	114	331	82	12	7	2	0.6	45	34	55		15	15	3	.248	.344
LF	Rube Ellis	L	149	575	154	10	9	3	0.5	76	46	54		16	4	1	.268	.332
C	Ed Phelps	R	100	306	76	13	1	0	0.0	43	22	39		7	19	3	.248	.297
SUBSTITUTES																		
3B	Jap Barbeau	R	47	175	44	3	0	0	0.0	23	5	28		14	1	0	.251	.269
SS	Alan Storke		48	174	49	5	0	0	0.0	11	10	12		5	0	0	.282	.310
SS	Champ Osteen	L	16	45	9	1	0	0	0.0	6	7	7		1	0	0	.200	.222
2B	Billy Gilbert	R	12	29	5	0	0	0	0.0	4	1	4		1	0	0	.172	.172
23	Mike Mowrey	R	12	29	7	1	0	0	0.0	3	4	4		1	3	1	.241	.276
SS	Charlie Enwright	L	3	7	1	0	0	0	0.0	1	1	2		0	1	0	.143	.143
SS	Tom Reilly	R	5	7	2	0	1	0	0.0	0	2	0		0	0	0	.286	.571
O2	Joe Delahanty	R	123	411	88	16	4	2	0.5	28	54	42		10	10	3	.214	.287
OF	Howard Murphy	L	25	60	12	0	0	0	0.0	3	3	4		1	5	1	.200	.200
OF	Bob James	L	6	21	6	0	0	0	0.0	1	0	4		1	0	0	.286	.286
C	Roger Bresnahan	R	72	234	57	4	1	0	0.0	27	23	46		11	2	0	.244	.269
C	John Bliss	R	35	113	25	2	1	1	0.9	12	8	12		2	9	1	.221	.283
C	Coonie Blank		1	2	0	0	0	0	0.0	0	0	0		0	0	0	.000	.000
PITCHERS																		
P	Fred Beebe	R	44	108	18	2	0	0	0.0	4	10	1		0	0	0	.167	.185
P	Johnny Lush	L	45	92	22	5	0	0	0.0	11	14	6		2	7	0	.239	.293
P	Slim Sallee	L	32	71	8	2	0	0	0.0	5	3	5		0	0	0	.113	.141
P	Bob Harmon	B	21	51	13	1	0	0	0.0	3	1	6		0	0	0	.255	.275
P	Les Backman	R	21	39	4	0	0	0	0.0	1	2	4		0	0	0	.103	.103
P	John Raleigh	R	15	23	2	0	0	0	0.0	0	0	0		0	0	0	.087	.087
P	Festus Higgins	R	16	21	4	0	0	0	0.0	1	0	0		0	0	0	.190	.190
P	Charlie Rhodes	R	12	19	4	2	0	0	0.0	3	0	2		0	0	0	.211	.316
P	Steve Melter		23	15	2	1	0	0	0.0	1	1	1		0	0	0	.133	.200
P	Forrest More	R	15	13	2	0	0	0	0.0	1	1	3		0	0	0	.154	.154
P	Grover Lowdermilk	R	7	10	1	0	0	0	0.0	0	0	0		0	0	0	.100	.100
P	Irv Higginbotham	R	3	3	0	0	0	0	0.0	0	0	0		0	0	0	.000	.000
P	Harry Sullivan	L	2	1	0	0	0	0	0.0	0	0	0		0	0	0	.000	.000
P	Joe Bernard		1	0	0	0	0	0	0.0	0	0	0		0	0	0	—	—
TEAM TOTAL				5108	1242	148	56	15	0.3	583	479	568		161	80	14	.243	.303

INDIVIDUAL FIELDING

POS	Player	T	G	PO	A	E	DP	TC/G	FA
1B	E. Konetchy	R	152	**1584**	97	26	71	11.2	.985
	S. Evans	L	2	23	0	1	1	12.0	.958
	A. Storke	R	1	3	0	0	1	3.0	1.000
2B	C. Charles	R	71	162	186	31	28	5.3	.918
	J. Delahanty	R	48	77	113	20	9	4.4	.905
	B. Gilbert	R	12	19	28	4	1	4.3	.922
	R. Hulswitt	R	12	19	28	4	4	4.3	.922
	M. Mowrey	R	7	18	17	3	0	5.4	.921
	R. Bresnahan	R	9	11	25	2	6	4.2	.947
	A. Storke	R	4	7	17	1	1	6.3	.960
SS	R. Hulswitt	R	65	147	200	26	16	5.7	.930
	A. Storke	R	44	93	135	10	14	5.4	.958
	C. Charles	R	28	68	87	13	5	6.0	.923
	C. Osteen	R	16	17	41	8	1	4.1	.879
	C. Enwright	R	2	2	2	5	0	4.5	.444
	T. Reilly	R	5	2	7	0	0	1.8	1.000
3B	B. Byrne	R	105	164*	252*	35	11	4.3*	.922
	J. Barbeau	R	46	56	72	14*	7	3.1	.901
	C. Charles	R	2	6	6	1	0	6.5	.923
	R. Bresnahan	R	1	2	2	2	0	6.0	.667
	M. Mowrey	R	2	0	1	0	0	0.5	1.000

POS	Player	T	G	PO	A	E	DP	TC/G	FA
OF	R. Ellis	L	145	332	28	17	9	**2.6**	.955
	S. Evans	L	141	212	19	13	**10**	1.7	.947
	A. Shaw	R	92	189	14	13	1	2.3	.940
	J. Delahanty	R	63	126	8	2	2	2.2	.985
	H. Murphy	R	19	35	2	3	0	2.1	.925
	B. James	R	6	9	1	1	1	1.8	.909
	J. Lush	L	3	4	0	0	0	1.3	1.000
C	E. Phelps	R	82	330	87	20	11	5.3	.954
	R. Bresnahan	R	59	211	78	12	3	5.1	.960
	J. Bliss	R	32	138	37	9	10	5.8	.951
	C. Blank		1	2	0	0	0	2.0	1.000

Under new manager Roger Bresnahan, the Hall of Fame catcher who arrived from New York, St. Louis climbed out of the cellar for the first time in three years despite posting a 15-game losing streak, the longest in club history. Run production jumped by more than two hundred for the season. First baseman "Big Ed" Konetchy gave the Cardinals strong production from that position for the first time, hitting .288 and finishing third in the league in total bases, fifth in RBIs. Despite the improved offense, they were still giving up too many runs to begin to contend. They were last again in runs allowed; they had been last or next-to-last for the last five years, and would remain so for the next four. Their ERA of 3.41 would be a fine one today, but in 1909 it was nearly a run above the league average. Fred Beebe gave the Cards their fourth different 20-game loser in the last five years.

TEAM STATISTICS

W	L	PCT	GB	R	OR	Batting 2B	3B	HR	BA	SA	SB	Fielding E	DP	FA	CG	BB	Pitching SO	ShO	SV	ERA
110	42	.724		701	448	218	92	25	.260	.353	185	228	100	.964	93	320	490	20	9	2.07
104	49	.680	6.5	632	376	203	60	20	.245	.322	187	244	95	.961	111	364	680	31	9	1.75
92	61	.601	18.5	621	546	172	68	26	.254	.329	230	307	99	.954	104	396	735	16	12	2.27
77	76	.503	33.5	603	599	159	72	22	.250	.323	280	308	120	.952	91	510	477	10	9	2.52
74	79	.484	36.5	514	518	184	53	12	.244	.309	185	240	97	.961	88	470	610	17	6	2.44
55	98	.359	55.5	442	627	176	59	16	.229	.296	141	282	86	.954	126	528	594	17	2	3.10
54	98	.355	56	583	728	148	56	15	.243	.303	161	322	90	.950	84	483	435	4	2	3.41
45	108	.294	65.5	427	681	124	43	15	.223	.274	135	342	101	.947	98	543	414	12	6	3.20
LEAGUE TOTAL				4523	4523	1384	503	151	.244	.314	1504	2273	788	.955	795	3614	4435	127	55	2.59

INDIVIDUAL PITCHING

PITCHER	T	W	L	PCT	ERA	SV	G	GS	CG	IP	H	BB	SO	R	ER	ShO	H/9	BB/9	SO/9
d Beebe	R	15	21	.417	2.82	1	44	35	18	287.2	256	104	105	142	90	1	8.01	3.25	3.29
nny Lush	L	11	18	.379	3.13	0	34	28	21	221.1	215	69	66	96	77	2	8.74	2.81	2.68
n Sallee	L	10	10	.500	2.42	0	32	27	12	219	223	59	55	107	59	1	9.16	2.42	2.26
o Harmon	R	5	12	.294	3.68	0	21	17	10	159	155	65	48	85	65	0	8.77	3.68	2.72
s Backman	R	3	12	.200	4.14	0	21	15	8	128.1	146	39	35	69	59	0	10.24	2.74	2.45
n Raleigh	L	1	9	.100	3.79	0	15	10	3	80.2	85	21	26	42	34	0	9.48	2.34	2.90
tus Higgins	R	3	3	.500	4.50	0	16	5	5	66	68	17	15	36	33	0	9.27	2.32	2.05
ve Melter	R	2	1	.667	3.50	1	23	1	0	64.1	79	20	24	49	25	0	11.05	2.80	3.36
arlie Rhodes	R	2	5	.286	3.98	0	12	10	4	61	55	33	25	36	27	0	8.11	4.87	3.69
rest More	R	1	5	.167	5.04	0	15	3	1	50	48	20	17	33	28	0	8.64	3.60	3.06
ver Lowdermilk	R	0	2	.000	6.21	0	7	3	1	29	28	30	14	24	20	0	8.69	9.31	4.34
Higginbotham	R	1	0	1.000	1.59	0	3	1	1	11.1	5	2	2	3	2	0	3.97	1.59	1.59
Bernard		0	0	—	0.00	0	1	0	0	1	1	2	2	0	0	0	9.00	18.00	18.00
rry Sullivan	L	0	0	—	36.00	0	2	1	0	1	4	2	1	6	4	0	36.00	18.00	9.00
AM TOTAL		54	98	.355	3.41	2	246	156	84	1379.2	1368	483	435	728	523	4	8.92	3.15	2.84

MANAGER	W	L	PCT
Roger Bresnahan	63	90	.412

POS	Player	B	G	AB	H	2B	3B	HR	HR %	R	RBI	BB	SO	SB	Pinch Hit AB	Pinch Hit H	BA	SA
REGULARS																		
1B	Ed Konetchy	R	144	520	157	23	16	3	0.6	87	78	78	59	18	0	0	.302	.425
2B	Miller Huggins	B	151	547	145	15	6	1	0.2	101	36	116	46	34	0	0	.265	.320
SS	Arnold Hauser	R	119	375	77	7	2	2	0.5	37	36	49	39	15	1	0	.205	.251
3B	Mike Mowrey	R	143	489	138	24	6	2	0.4	69	70	67	38	21	0	0	.282	.368
RF	Steve Evans	L	151	506	122	21	8	2	0.4	73	73	78	63	10	0	0	.241	.326
CF	Rebel Oakes	L	131	468	118	14	6	0	0.0	50	43	38	38	18	3	1	.252	.308
LF	Rube Ellis	L	142	550	142	18	8	4	0.7	87	54	62	70	25	0	0	.258	.342
C	Ed Phelps	R	93	270	71	4	2	0	0.0	25	37	36	29	9	13	3	.263	.293
SUBSTITUTES																		
SS	Rudy Hulswitt	R	63	133	33	7	2	0	0.0	9	14	13	10	5	31	6	.248	.331
UT	Frank Betcher	B	35	89	18	2	0	0	0.0	7	6	7	14	1	8	2	.202	.225
3B	Jap Barbeau	R	7	21	4	0	1	0	0.0	4	2	3	3	0	0	0	.190	.286
OF	Elmer Zacher	R	47	132	28	5	1	0	0.0	7	10	10	19	3	9	2	.212	.265
OF	Ody Abbott	R	22	70	13	2	1	0	0.0	2	6	6	20	3	1	0	.186	.243
OF	Bill O'Hara	L	9	20	3	0	0	0	0.0	1	2	1	3	0	3	0	.150	.150
PO	Festus Higgins	R	3	5	2	0	1	0	0.0	1	1	0	2	0	0	0	.400	.800
OF	Ernie Lush		1	4	0	0	0	0	0.0	0	0	1	1	0	0	0	.000	.000
C	Roger Bresnahan	R	88	234	65	15	3	0	0.0	35	27	55	17	13	5	0	.278	.368
C	John Bliss	R	16	33	2	0	0	0	0.0	2	3	4	8	0	3	0	.061	.061
C	Bill Kelly	R	2	2	0	0	0	0	0.0	1	0	1	0	0	1	0	.000	.000
PITCHERS																		
P	Johnny Lush	L	47	93	21	1	3	0	0.0	8	10	8	11	2	10	4	.226	.301
P	Bob Harmon	B	43	76	14	4	1	0	0.0	11	6	8	23	2	0	0	.184	.263
P	Vic Willis	R	33	66	11	0	1	0	0.0	5	2	2	8	0	0	0	.167	.197
P	Frank Corridon	R	30	51	10	2	0	0	0.0	3	0	1	14	0	0	0	.196	.235
P	Slim Sallee	L	18	37	4	0	0	0	0.0	3	0	2	8	0	0	0	.108	.108
P	Les Backman	R	26	35	4	1	1	0	0.0	2	3	4	12	0	0	0	.114	.200
P	Bill Steele	R	9	31	8	1	1	0	0.0	3	3	0	4	0	0	0	.258	.355
P	Roy Golden		7	15	4	1	0	0	0.0	0	3	0	2	0	0	0	.267	.333
P	Bunny Hearn	L	5	15	2	0	0	1	6.7	2	1	0	6	0	0	0	.133	.333
P	Ed Zmich	L	9	13	1	0	0	0	0.0	0	1	0	7	0	0	0	.077	.077
P	Cy Alberts	R	4	7	0	0	0	0	0.0	0	0	2	3	0	0	0	.000	.000
P	Elmer Rieger	B	13	3	0	0	0	0	0.0	1	0	2	3	0	0	0	.000	.000
P	Rube Geyer		4	1	0	0	0	0	0.0	0	0	0	1	0	0	0	.000	.000
P	John Raleigh	R	3	1	0	0	0	0	0.0	0	0	0	0	0	0	0	.000	.000
P	Bill Chambers	R	1	0	0	0	0	0	−	0	0	0	0	0	0	0	−	−
P	Harry Patton		1	0	0	0	0	0	−	0	0	0	0	0	0	0	−	−
P	Charlie Pickett		2	0	0	0	0	0	−	1	0	1	0	0	0	0	−	−
TEAM TOTAL				4912	1217	167	70	15	0.3	637	527	655	581	179	88	18	.248	.319

INDIVIDUAL FIELDING

POS	Player	T	G	PO	A	E	DP	TC/G	FA	POS	Player	T	G	PO	A	E	DP	TC/G	FA
1B	E. Konetchy	R	144	**1499**	98	15	81	11.2	.991	OF	R. Ellis	L	141	268	25	18	4	2.2	.942
	E. Zacher	R	0	0	0	0	0	0.0	.000		R. Oakes	R	127	266	12	18	3	2.3	.939
	S. Evans	L	10	104	2	3	4	10.9	.972		S. Evans	L	141	226	16	8	3	1.8	.968
	B. O'Hara		1	7	0	0	0	7.0	1.000		E. Zacher	R	36	77	7	3	1	2.4	.966
											O. Abbott	R	21	52	2	1	2	2.6	.982
2B	M. Huggins	R	151	325	452	30	58	5.3	.963		F. Higgins	R	1	0	0	0	0	0.0	.000
	E. Zacher	R	1	0	0	0	0	0.0	.000		B. O'Hara		4	7	1	0	0	2.0	1.000
	F. Betcher	R	6	7	6	2	1	2.5	.867		E. Lush	L	1	1	0	0	0	1.0	1.000
	R. Hulswitt	R	2	1	2	1	0	2.0	.750		F. Betcher	R	2	1	0	0	0	0.5	1.000
	J. Barbeau	R	1	2	1	0	1	3.0	1.000		R. Bresnahan	R	2	1	0	0	0	0.5	1.000
SS	A. Hauser	R	117	212	345	41	31	5.1	.931	C	E. Phelps	R	80	320	84	10	10	5.2	.976
	R. Hulswitt	R	30	39	78	20	4	4.6	.854		R. Bresnahan	R	77	295	100	16	11	5.3	.961
	F. Betcher	R	12	24	40	5	4	5.8	.928		B. Kelly	R	1	0	0	0	0	0.0	.000
3B	M. Mowrey	R	141	171	**301**	37	30	3.6	.927		J. Bliss	R	13	39	10	1	0	3.8	.980
	J. Barbeau	R	6	4	18	2	0	4.0	.917										
	F. Betcher	R	7	5	15	1	0	3.0	.952										
	A. Hauser	R	1	0	1	0	0	1.0	1.000										

In 1910 Ed Konetchy gave the Cardinals something they hadn't had since 1905—a .300 hitter. The Cards were able to narrow the gap between their runs scored and allowed totals, but the club's improved offense could not compensate for their pitching weakness. They were last in ERA by more than a half a run per game, and were last again in runs allowed.

Miller Huggins, acquired in a pre-season trade with Cincinnati, played solid second base for the Cardinals, as he would for the next six years. His league-leading total of 119 walks gave him an on-base percentage (not including hit batsmen) of .394.

TEAM STATISTICS

	W	L	PCT	GB	R	OR	2B	3B	HR	BA	SA	SB	E	DP	FA	CG	BB	SO	ShO	SV	ERA
							Batting						Fielding			Pitching					
HI	104	50	.675		711	497	219	84	34	.268	.366	173	230	110	.963	99	474	609	25	11	2.51
Y	91	63	.591	13	715	545	204	83	31	.275	.366	282	291	117	.955	96	397	717	9	8	2.68
IT	86	67	.562	17.5	655	576	214	83	33	.266	.360	148	245	102	.961	73	392	479	13	11	2.83
HI	78	75	.510	25.5	674	682	223	71	22	.255	.338	199	258	132	.960	84	547	657	16	7	3.05
IN	75	79	.487	29	620	665	150	79	23	.259	.333	310	291	103	.955	86	528	497	15	9	3.08
KN	64	90	.416	40	497	622	166	73	25	.229	.305	151	235	125	.964	103	545	555	15	4	3.07
TL	63	90	.412	40.5	637	717	167	70	15	.248	.319	179	261	109	.959	83	541	466	3	12	3.78
OS	53	100	.346	50.5	495	700	173	49	31	.246	.317	152	305	137	.954	74	599	531	12	7	3.22
EAGUE TOTAL					5004	5004	1516	592	214	.256	.338	1594	2116	935	.959	698	4023	4511	108	69	3.02

INDIVIDUAL PITCHING

PITCHER	T	W	L	PCT	ERA	SV	G	GS	CG	IP	H	BB	SO	R	ER	ShO	H/9	BB/9	SO/9
ob Harmon	R	11	15	.423	4.46	2	43	33	15	236	227	133	87	128	117	0	8.66	5.07	3.32
ohnny Lush	L	14	13	.519	3.20	1	36	25	13	225.1	235	70	54	116	80	1	9.39	2.80	2.16
c Willis	R	9	12	.429	3.35	3	33	23	12	212	224	61	67	113	79	1	9.51	2.59	2.84
rank Corridon	R	7	15	.318	3.81	2	30	18	9	156	168	55	51	88	66	0	9.69	3.17	2.94
es Backman	R	7	6	.538	3.03	1	26	11	6	116	117	53	41	55	39	0	9.08	4.11	3.18
im Sallee	L	7	9	.438	2.97	2	18	13	9	115	112	24	46	44	38	1	8.77	1.88	3.60
ll Steele	R	4	4	.500	3.27	1	9	8	8	71.2	71	24	25	35	26	0	8.92	3.01	3.14
oy Golden	R	2	3	.400	4.43	0	7	6	3	42.2	44	33	31	28	21	0	11.31	3.69	3.23
nny Hearn	L	1	3	.250	5.08	0	5	5	4	39	49	16	14	27	22	0	9.50	7.25	4.75
d Zmich	L	0	5	.000	6.25	0	9	6	2	36	38	29	19	27	25	0	11.39	6.51	3.25
y Alberts	R	1	2	.333	6.18	0	4	3	2	27.2	35	20	10	21	19	0	11.39	2.95	3.80
mer Rieger	R	0	2	.000	5.48	0	13	2	0	21.1	26	7	9	16	13	0	10.97	2.95	3.80
estus Higgins	R	0	1	.000	4.35	0	2	0	0	10.1	15	7	1	8	5	0	13.06	6.10	0.87
harlie Pickett		0	0	–	1.50	0	2	0	0	6	7	2	2	2	1	0	10.50	3.00	3.00
ohn Raleigh	L	0	0	–	9.00	0	3	1	0	5	8	0	2	5	5	0	14.40	0.00	3.60
ube Geyer	R	0	0	–	4.50	0	4	0	0	4	5	3	5	3	2	0	11.25	6.75	11.25
d Konetchy	R	0	0	–	4.50	0	1	0	0	4	4	1	0	2	2	0	9.00	2.25	0.00
arry Patton		0	0	–	2.25	0	1	0	0	4	4	2	2	1	0	0	9.00	4.50	4.50
oger Bresnahan	R	0	0	–	0.00	0	1	0	0	3.1	6	1	0	1	0	0	16.20	2.70	0.00
ll Chambers	R	0	0	–	0.00	0	1	0	0	1	1	0	0	1	0	0	9.00	0.00	0.00
ll O'Hara		0	0	–	0.00	0	1	0	0	1	0	0	0	0	0	0	0.00	0.00	0.00
EAM TOTAL		63	90	.412	3.78	12	249	154	83	1337.1	1396	541	466	717	561	3	9.39	3.64	3.14

PRESENTED WITHOUT COMMENT

From the *Spalding Official Baseball Guide,* 1911: "December 14, 1910: The National League decided that it would be best to examine the eyes of umpires prior to the beginning of a season."

MANAGER	W	L	PCT
Roger Bresnahan	75	74	.503

POS	Player	B	G	AB	H	2B	3B	HR	HR %	R	RBI	BB	SO	SB	Pinch Hit AB	Pinch Hit H	BA	SA
REGULARS																		
1B	Ed Konetchy	R	158	571	165	38	13	6	1.1	90	88	81	63	27	0	0	.289	.433
2B	Miller Huggins	B	138	509	133	19	2	1	0.2	106	24	96	52	37	1	1	.261	.312
SS	Arnold Hauser	R	136	515	124	11	8	3	0.6	61	46	26	67	24	0	0	.241	.311
3B	Mike Mowrey	R	137	471	126	29	7	0	0.0	59	61	59	46	15	1	0	.268	.359
RF	Steve Evans	L	154	547	161	24	13	5	0.9	74	71	46	52	13	3	1	.294	.413
CF	Rebel Oakes	L	154	551	145	13	6	2	0.4	69	59	41	35	25	2	1	.263	.319
LF	Rube Ellis	L	155	555	139	20	10	3	0.5	69	66	66	64	9	6	1	.250	.339
C	John Bliss	R	97	258	59	6	4	1	0.4	36	27	42	25	5	8	1	.229	.295
SUBSTITUTES																		
UT	Wally Smith	R	81	194	42	6	5	2	1.0	23	19	21	33	5	16	2	.216	.330
2B	Lee Magee	B	26	69	18	1	1	0	0.0	9	8	8	8	4	2	0	.261	.304
2B	Dan McGeehan	R	3	9	2	0	0	0	0.0	0	1	0	1	0	0	0	.222	.222
SO	Hap Morse		4	8	0	0	0	0	0.0	0	0	1	2	0	1	0	.000	.000
3B	Ed Conwell	R	1	1	0	0	0	0	0.0	0	0	0	0	0	0	0	.000	.000
OF	Otto McIver	B	30	62	14	2	1	1	1.6	11	9	9	14	0	7	0	.226	.339
OF	Denney Wilie	L	28	51	12	3	1	0	0.0	10	3	8	11	3	10	1	.235	.333
OF	Jim Clark	R	14	18	3	0	1	0	0.0	2	3	3	4	2	6	1	.167	.278
OF	Frank Gilhooley	L	1	0	0	0	0	0	-	0	0	0	0	0	0	0	-	-
C	Roger Bresnahan	R	81	227	63	17	8	3	1.3	22	41	45	19	4	3	1	.278	.463
C	Ivy Wingo	L	25	57	12	2	0	0	0.0	4	3	3	7	0	6	0	.211	.246
PH	Milt Reed	L	1	1	0	0	0	0	0.0	0	0	0	0	0	1	0	.000	.000
PITCHERS																		
P	Bob Harmon	B	51	111	17	4	1	0	0.0	7	3	11	48	2	0	0	.153	.207
P	Bill Steele	R	43	101	21	2	2	0	0.0	8	15	11	21	0	0	0	.208	.267
P	Slim Sallee	L	36	89	15	0	1	0	0.0	5	9	3	28	0	0	0	.169	.191
P	Rube Geyer		29	57	13	2	1	0	0.0	3	2	0	7	0	0	0	.228	.298
P	Roy Golden		30	44	5	0	0	0	0.0	2	4	5	10	0	0	0	.114	.114
P	Lou Lowdermilk	R	16	18	2	0	0	0	0.0	0	2	2	14	0	0	0	.111	.111
P	Grover Lowdermilk	R	11	9	1	0	0	0	0.0	0	0	0	5	0	0	0	.111	.111
P	Gene Woodburn	R	11	6	1	0	0	0	0.0	1	3	5	3	0	0	0	.167	.167
P	Gene Dale	R	5	5	2	0	0	0	0.0	0	0	1	0	0	0	0	.400	.400
P	Joe Willis	R	2	5	0	0	0	0	0.0	0	0	0	0	0	0	0	.000	.000
P	Ed Zmich	L	4	4	0	0	0	0	0.0	0	0	3	0	0	0	0	.000	.000
P	Roy Radebaugh	R	2	3	0	0	0	0	0.0	0	0	2	0	0	0	0	.000	.000
P	Jack Reis	R	3	2	0	0	0	0	0.0	0	0	0	0	0	0	0	.000	.000
P	Bunny Hearn	L	2	1	0	0	0	0	0.0	0	0	0	1	0	0	0	.000	.000
P	Jack McAdams	R	6	1	0	0	0	0	0.0	0	0	0	1	0	0	0	.000	.000
P	Pete Standridge	R	2	1	0	0	0	0	0.0	0	0	0	0	0	0	0	.000	.000
P	George Zackert	L	4	1	0	0	0	0	0.0	0	0	0	1	0	0	0	.000	.000
P	Harry Camnitz	R	2	0	0	0	0	0	-	0	0	0	0	0	0	0	-	-
	TEAM TOTAL			5132	1295	199	85	27	0.5	671	567	592	650	175	73	10	.252	.340

INDIVIDUAL FIELDING

POS	Player	T	G	PO	A	E	DP	TC/G	FA
1B	E. Konetchy	R	158	1652	71	16	85	11.0	.991
2B	M. Huggins	R	136	281	439	29	62	5.5	.961
	L. Magee	R	18	42	35	2	6	4.4	.975
	W. Smith	R	8	9	14	1	0	3.0	.958
	D. McGeehan	R	3	4	5	2	0	3.7	.818
	R. Bresnahan	R	2	2	3	1	0	3.0	.833
SS	A. Hauser	R	134	223	400	56	51	5.1	.918
	W. Smith	R	25	26	80	8	6	4.6	.930
	L. Magee	R	3	3	9	3	0	5.0	.800
	H. Morse	R	2	4	5	3	0	6.0	.750
	J. Bliss	R	1	0	1	0	0	1.0	1.000
	M. Mowrey	R	1	1	0	0	0	1.0	1.000
3B	M. Mowrey	R	134	174	267	26	19	3.5	.944
	W. Smith	R	26	28	45	5	1	3.0	.936
	A. Hauser	R	2	2	2	0	1	2.0	1.000
	E. Conwell	R	1	0	0	1	0	1.0	.000

POS	Player	T	G	PO	A	E	DP	TC/G	FA
OF	R. Oakes	R	151	364	26	16	8	2.7	.961
	R. Ellis	L	148	297	21	21	3	2.3	.938
	S. Evans	L	150	258	17	8	5	1.9	.972
	O. McIver	L	17	24	1	2	0	1.6	.926
	D. Wilie	L	15	18	2	0	0	1.3	1.000
	F. Gilhooley	R	1	0	0	0	0	0.0	.000
	W. Smith	R	1	0	0	0	0	0.0	.000
	J. Clark	R	8	6	0	0	0	0.8	1.000
	H. Morse	R	1	2	0	0	0	2.0	1.000
C	J. Bliss	R	84	332	103	22	9	5.4	.952
	R. Bresnahan	R	77	323	100	13	9	5.7	.970
	I. Wingo	R	18	65	22	8	3	5.3	.916

St. Louis was the surprise team of the National League in 1911, staying in the pennant race until late in the running. They stood just six games out of first place at the beginning of August, but fell behind from there; nonetheless, they finished above the .500 mark for the first time since 1901. Manager Roger Bresnahan was given much of the credit for getting the club to play together as a team. Indeed, the team did far better than their records would lead us to expect, as they finished above .500 despite allowing seventy-four more runs than they scored. Bob Harmon gave the Cardinals their first 20-game winner in seven years with his 23–15 record, and Konetchy's 38 doubles made him the first St. Louis player to lead the league in any offensive category since Jesse Burkett in 1901.

TEAM STATISTICS

	W	L	PCT	GB	R	OR	2B	3B	HR	BA	SA	SB	E	DP	FA	CG	BB	SO	ShO	SV	ERA
							Batting						Fielding			Pitching					
Y	99	54	.647		756	542	225	105	39	.279	.390	347	256	86	.959	95	369	771	18	11	2.69
HI	92	62	.597	7.5	757	607	218	101	54	.260	.374	214	260	114	.960	85	525	582	11	16	2.90
IT	85	69	.552	14.5	744	560	206	106	48	.262	.371	160	232	131	.963	91	375	605	13	10	2.84
HI	79	73	.520	19.5	658	673	214	56	60	.259	.359	153	231	113	.963	90	598	697	20	9	3.30
TL	75	74	.503	22	671	745	199	85	27	.252	.340	175	261	106	.960	88	701	561	6	9	3.68
IN	70	83	.458	29	682	700	180	105	21	.261	.346	289	295	108	.955	77	476	557	4	10	3.26
KN	64	86	.427	33.5	539	659	151	71	28	.237	.311	184	241	112	.962	81	566	533	14	10	3.39
OS	44	107	.291	54	699	1020	249	54	37	.267	.355	169	347	110	.947	73	672	486	5	6	5.08
LEAGUE TOTAL					5506	5506	1642	683	314	.260	.356	1691	2123	880	.958	680	4282	4792	91	81	3.39

INDIVIDUAL PITCHING

PITCHER	T	W	L	PCT	ERA	SV	G	GS	CG	IP	H	BB	SO	R	ER	ShO	H/9	BB/9	SO/9
Bob Harmon	R	23	15	.605	3.13	4	51	41	28	348	290	181	144	155	121	2	7.50	4.68	3.72
Bill Steele	R	16	19	.457	3.73	3	43	34	23	287.1	287	113	115	153	119	1	8.99	3.54	3.60
Slim Sallee	L	16	9	.640	2.76	2	36	30	18	245	234	64	74	102	75	1	8.60	2.35	2.72
Rube Geyer	R	9	6	.600	3.27	0	29	11	7	148.2	141	56	46	80	54	1	8.54	3.39	2.78
Roy Golden	R	4	9	.308	5.02	0	30	25	6	148.2	127	129	81	90	83	0	7.69	7.81	4.90
Lou Lowdermilk	L	3	4	.429	3.46	0	16	3	3	65	72	29	20	39	25	0	9.97	4.02	2.77
Gene Woodburn	R	1	6	.143	5.40	0	11	6	1	38.1	22	40	23	32	23	0	5.17	9.39	5.40
Grover Lowdermilk	R	0	1	.000	7.29	0	11	2	1	33.1	37	33	15	30	27	0	9.99	8.91	4.05
Joe Willis	L	0	1	.000	4.20	0	2	1	0	15	13	4	5	9	7	0	7.80	2.40	3.00
Gene Dale	R	1	2	.333	6.75	0	5	2	0	14.2	13	16	13	12	11	0	7.98	9.82	7.98
Ed Zmich	L	1	0	1.000	2.13	0	4	0	0	12.2	8	8	4	5	3	0	5.68	5.68	2.84
Roy Radebaugh	R	0	0	–	2.70	0	2	1	0	10	6	4	1	3	3	0	5.40	3.60	0.90
Jack McAdams	R	0	0	–	3.72	0	6	0	0	9.2	7	5	4	5	4	0	6.52	4.66	3.72
Jack Reis	R	0	0	–	0.96	0	3	0	0	9.1	5	8	4	3	1	0	4.82	7.71	3.86
George Zackert	L	0	2	.000	11.05	0	4	1	0	7.1	17	6	6	13	9	0	20.86	7.36	7.36
Pete Standridge	R	0	0	–	9.64	0	2	0	0	4.2	10	4	3	10	5	0	19.29	7.71	5.79
Bunny Hearn	L	0	0	–	13.50	0	2	0	0	2.2	7	0	1	4	4	0	23.63	0.00	3.38
Harry Camnitz	R	1	0	1.000	0.00	0	2	0	0	2	0	1	2	0	0	0	0.00	4.50	9.00
TEAM TOTAL		75	74	.503	3.68	9	259	158	88	1402.1	1296	701	561	745	574	5	8.32	4.50	3.60

MANAGER	W	L	PCT
Roger Bresnahan	63	90	.412

POS	Player	B	G	AB	H	2B	3B	HR	HR %	R	RBI	BB	SO	SB	Pinch Hit AB	Pinch Hit H	BA	SA
REGULARS																		
1B	Ed Konetchy	R	143	538	169	26	13	8	1.5	81	82	62	66	25	0	0	.314	.455
2B	Miller Huggins	B	120	431	131	15	4	0	0.0	82	29	87	31	35	5	0	.304	.357
SS	Arnold Hauser	R	133	479	124	14	7	1	0.2	73	42	39	69	26	1	1	.259	.324
3B	Mike Mowrey	R	114	408	104	13	8	2	0.5	59	50	46	29	19	4	1	.255	.341
RF	Steve Evans	L	135	491	139	23	9	6	1.2	59	72	36	51	11	1	0	.283	.403
CF	Rebel Oakes	L	136	495	139	19	5	3	0.6	57	58	31	24	26	1	1	.281	.358
LF	Lee Magee	B	128	458	133	13	8	0	0.0	60	40	39	29	16	8	3	.290	.354
C	Ivy Wingo	L	100	310	82	18	8	2	0.6	38	44	23	45	8	9	1	.265	.394
SUBSTITUTES																		
3S	Wally Smith	R	75	219	56	5	5	0	0.0	22	26	29	27	4	12	0	.256	.324
2B	Bad News Galloway	B	21	54	10	2	0	0	0.0	4	4	5	8	2	3	0	.185	.222
3B	Possum Whitted	R	12	46	12	3	0	0	0.0	7	7	3	5	1	0	0	.261	.326
2B	Ray Rolling	R	5	15	3	0	0	0	0.0	0	0	0	5	0	0	0	.200	.200
3B	John Kelleher	R	8	12	4	1	0	0	0.0	0	1	0	2	0	4	1	.333	.417
1B	John Mercer	L	1	1	0	0	0	0	0.0	0	0	0	0	0	0	0	.000	.000
OF	Rube Ellis	L	109	305	82	18	2	4	1.3	47	33	34	36	6	27	8	.269	.380
OF	Frank Gilhooley	L	13	49	11	0	0	0	0.0	5	2	3	8	0	1	0	.224	.224
OF	Denney Wilie	L	30	48	11	0	1	0	0.0	2	6	7	9	0	8	2	.229	.271
OF	Elmer Miller	R	12	37	7	1	0	0	0.0	5	3	4	9	1	1	0	.189	.216
OF	Ted Cather	R	5	19	8	1	1	0	0.0	4	2	0	4	1	0	0	.421	.579
C	John Bliss	R	49	114	28	3	1	0	0.0	11	18	19	14	3	6	3	.246	.289
C	Roger Bresnahan	R	48	108	36	7	2	1	0.9	8	15	14	9	4	14	7	.333	.463
C	Frank Snyder	R	11	18	2	0	0	0	0.0	2	0	2	7	1	0	0	.111	.111
C	Ed Burns	R	1	1	0	0	0	0	0.0	0	1	0	0	0	0	0	.000	.000
C	Mike Murphy	R	1	1	0	0	0	0	0.0	0	1	0	0	0	0	0	.000	.000
PH	Jim Clark	R	2	1	0	0	0	0	0.0	0	0	0	1	0	1	0	.000	.000
PITCHERS																		
P	Slim Sallee	L	48	103	14	2	1	0	0.0	9	0	6	32	0	0	0	.136	.175
P	Bob Harmon	B	46	99	23	1	1	0	0.0	7	7	1	31	2	0	0	.232	.263
P	Bill Steele	R	41	61	11	2	1	0	0.0	5	8	9	15	0	1	0	.180	.246
P	Rube Geyer		41	53	11	1	0	0	0.0	5	3	3	10	1	0	0	.208	.226
P	Joe Willis	R	31	38	6	1	0	0	0.0	2	3	1	11	0	0	0	.158	.184
P	Gene Dale	R	20	22	6	1	0	0	0.0	0	0	0	7	0	1	0	.273	.318
P	Dan Griner	L	12	13	1	0	0	0	0.0	2	1	3	6	1	0	0	.077	.077
P	Gene Woodburn	R	20	13	0	0	0	0	0.0	1	1	1	9	0	0	0	.000	.000
P	Sandy Burk	R	12	11	0	0	0	0	0.0	0	0	0	3	0	0	0	.000	.000
P	Pol Perritt	R	6	9	2	0	0	0	0.0	1	1	0	6	0	0	0	.222	.222
P	Phil Redding	L	3	8	0	0	0	0	0.0	0	0	1	1	0	0	0	.000	.000
P	Lou Lowdermilk	R	4	4	1	0	0	0	0.0	1	1	0	1	0	0	0	.250	.250
P	George Zackert	L	2	1	0	0	0	0	0.0	0	0	0	0	0	0	0	.000	.000
P	Wheezer Dell	R	3	0	0	0	0	0	–	0	0	0	0	0	0	0	–	–
P	Bob Ewing	R	1	0	0	0	0	0	–	0	0	0	0	0	0	0	–	–
P	Roland Howell	R	3	0	0	0	0	0	–	0	0	0	0	0	0	0	–	–
	TEAM TOTAL			5093	1366	190	77	27	0.5	659	561	508	620	193	108	28	.268	.352

INDIVIDUAL FIELDING

POS	Player	T	G	PO	A	E	DP	TC/G	FA	POS	Player	T	G	PO	A	E	DP	TC/G	FA
1B	E. Konetchy	R	142	1392	90	13	77	10.5	.991	OF	R. Oakes	R	136	324	15	19	5	2.6	.947
	W. Smith	R	6	55	4	0	1	9.8	1.000		S. Evans	L	134	219	24	15	2	1.9	.942
	L. Magee	R	6	48	3	0	6	8.5	1.000		L. Magee	L	85	198	18	10	2	2.7	.956
	J. Mercer	L	1	1	0	1	0	2.0	.500		R. Ellis	L	76	173	10	14	5	2.6	.929
											D. Wilie	L	16	21	1	2	0	1.5	.917
2B	M. Huggins	R	114	272	337	37	50	5.7	.943		E. Miller	R	11	24	1	0	1	2.3	1.000
	L. Magee	R	23	52	79	8	9	6.0	.942		T. Cather	R	5	15	2	1	0	3.6	.944
	B. Galloway	R	16	26	42	2	5	4.4	.971		F. Gilhooley	R	11	16	1	0	0	1.5	1.000
	R. Rolling	R	4	9	9	1	0	4.8	.947		E. Konetchy	R	1	4	1	0	0	5.0	1.000
SS	A. Hauser	R	132	262	446	50	54	5.7	.934	C	I. Wingo	R	92	360	148	23	11	5.8	.957
	W. Smith	R	22	48	65	5	7	5.4	.958		R. Bresnahan	R	28	138	49	5	4	6.9	.974
	B. Galloway	R	1	1	4	0	0	5.0	1.000		J. Bliss	R	41	140	42	5	7	4.6	.973
	L. Magee	R	1	1	1	2	0	4.0	.500		E. Burns	R	1	0	0	0	0	0.0	.000
3B	M. Mowrey	R	108	131	220	26	22	3.5	.931		M. Murphy	R	1	0	0	0	0	0.0	.000
	W. Smith	R	32	33	61	5	3	3.1	.949		F. Snyder	R	11	25	9	3	0	3.4	.919
	P. Whitted	R	12	19	17	6	1	3.5	.857										
	J. Kelleher	R	3	3	4	0	1	2.3	1.000										

Poor pitching doomed the Cardinals yet again in the 1912 season. They gave up close to five and one-half runs per game as their pitchers posted the most walks and fewest strikeouts in the league. They were only two games under .500 through the end of May, but a 7–20 June knocked them deep into the second division, where they remained for the rest of the season. Konetchy and Huggins both topped .300, but only Cincinnati had fewer extra-base hits than the Cards, and they finished closer to the cellar than to the first division. The time had come for a managerial change; the new manager would be Miller Huggins, whose managerial skill in writing the names Ruth and Gehrig on his Yankee lineup card would one day land him in the Hall of Fame. Alas, he had no Ruths or Gehrigs in St. Louis, but the Cards still managed two first-division finishes in his five years at the helm.

TEAM STATISTICS

	W	L	PCT	GB	R	OR	2B	Batting 3B	HR	BA	SA	SB	E	Fielding DP	FA	CG	BB	Pitching SO	ShO	SV	ERA
NY	103	48	.682		823	571	231	88	48	.286	.395	319	280	123	.956	93	338	652	8	13	2.58
PIT	93	58	.616	10	751	565	222	129	39	.284	.398	177	169	125	.972	94	487	664	18	6	2.85
CHI	91	59	.607	11.5	756	666	245	91	42	.277	.386	164	249	125	.960	80	493	554	14	8	3.42
CIN	75	78	.490	29	656	722	183	91	19	.256	.339	248	249	102	.960	86	452	561	12	10	3.42
PHI	73	79	.480	30.5	670	689	245	68	42	.267	.367	159	231	98	.963	82	515	616	10	8	3.25
STL	63	90	.412	41	659	825	190	77	27	.268	.352	193	274	113	.957	62	560	487	6	11	3.85
BKN	58	95	.379	46	651	748	220	73	32	.268	.358	179	255	96	.959	71	510	553	10	7	3.64
BOS	52	101	.340	52	693	873	227	68	35	.273	.361	137	297	129	.954	92	521	542	4	3	4.17
LEAGUE TOTAL					5659	5659	1763	685	284	.272	.369	1576	2004	911	.960	660	3876	4629	82	66	3.40

INDIVIDUAL PITCHING

PITCHER	T	W	L	PCT	ERA	SV	G	GS	CG	IP	H	BB	SO	R	ER	ShO	H/9	BB/9	SO/9
Slim Sallee	L	15	17	.469	2.60	6	48	32	20	294	289	72	108	122	85	3	8.85	2.20	3.31
Bob Harmon	R	18	18	.500	3.93	0	43	34	15	268	284	116	73	156	117	3	9.54	3.90	2.45
Bill Steele	R	10	13	.435	4.69	1	40	25	7	194	245	66	67	143	101	0	11.37	3.06	3.11
Rube Geyer	R	7	14	.333	3.28	0	41	18	6	181	191	84	61	110	66	0	9.50	4.18	3.03
Joe Willis	L	4	9	.308	4.44	2	31	17	4	129.2	143	62	55	83	64	0	9.93	4.30	3.82
Gene Dale	R	0	5	.000	6.57	0	19	3	1	61.2	76	51	37	58	45	0	11.09	7.44	5.40
Dan Griner	R	3	4	.429	3.17	0	12	7	2	54	59	15	20	35	19	0	9.83	2.50	3.33
Gene Woodburn	R	1	4	.200	5.59	0	20	5	1	48.1	60	42	25	48	30	0	11.17	7.82	4.66
Sandy Burk	R	1	3	.250	2.42	1	12	4	2	44.2	37	12	17	19	12	0	7.46	2.42	3.43
Pol Perritt	R	1	1	.500	3.19	0	6	3	1	31	25	10	13	16	11	0	7.26	2.90	3.77
Phil Redding	R	2	1	.667	4.97	0	3	3	2	25.1	31	11	9	17	14	0	11.01	3.91	3.20
Lou Lowdermilk	L	1	1	.500	3.00	0	4	1	1	15	14	9	2	8	5	0	8.40	5.40	1.20
Wheezer Dell	R	0	0	–	11.57	0	3	0	0	2.1	3	3	0	3	3	0	11.57	11.57	0.00
Roland Howell	R	0	0	–	27.00	0	3	0	0	1.2	5	5	0	5	5	0	27.00	27.00	0.00
Bob Ewing	R	0	0	–	0.00	0	1	1	0	1.1	2	1	0	0	0	0	13.50	6.75	0.00
George Zackert	L	0	0	–	18.00	0	1	0	0	1	2	1	0	2	2	0	18.00	9.00	0.00
TEAM TOTAL		63	90	.412	3.85	11	287	153	62	1353	1466	560	487	825	579	6	9.75	3.73	3.24

MANAGER	W	L	PCT
Miller Huggins	51	99	.340

POS	Player	B	G	AB	H	2B	3B	HR	HR %	R	RBI	BB	SO	SB	Pinch Hit AB	Pinch Hit H	BA	SA
REGULARS																		
1B	Ed Konetchy	R	139	502	137	18	17	7	1.4	74	68	53	41	27	0	0	.273	.418
2B	Miller Huggins	B	120	382	109	12	0	0	0.0	74	27	91	49	23	5	1	.285	.317
SS	Charley O'Leary	R	120	404	88	15	5	0	0.0	32	31	20	34	3	1	0	.218	.280
3B	Mike Mowrey	R	131	449	116	18	4	0	0.0	61	33	53	40	21	0	0	.258	.316
RF	Steve Evans	L	97	245	61	15	6	1	0.4	18	31	20	28	5	20	4	.249	.371
CF	Rebel Oakes	L	146	537	156	14	5	0	0.0	59	49	43	32	22	2	1	.291	.335
LF	Lee Magee	B	136	529	140	13	7	2	0.4	53	31	34	30	23	0	0	.265	.327
C	Ivy Wingo	L	111	305	78	5	8	2	0.7	25	35	17	41	18	10	4	.256	.344
SUBSTITUTES																		
S2	Arnold Hauser	R	22	45	13	0	3	0	0.0	3	9	2	2	1	8	4	.289	.422
S3	Zinn Beck	R	10	30	5	1	0	0	0.0	4	2	4	10	1	0	0	.167	.200
SS	Wes Callahan	R	7	14	4	0	0	0	0.0	0	1	2	2	1	1	0	.286	.286
SS	Al Cabrera		1	2	0	0	0	0	0.0	0	0	0	0	0	0	0	.000	.000
2B	Doc Crandall	R	2	2	0	0	0	0	0.0	0	0	0	2	0	2	0	.000	.000
UT	Possum Whitted	R	122	402	89	10	5	0	0.0	44	38	31	44	9	15	3	.221	.271
OF	Ted Cather	R	67	183	39	8	4	0	0.0	16	12	9	24	7	7	3	.213	.301
OF	Jimmy Sheckard	L	52	136	27	2	1	0	0.0	18	17	41	25	5	4	2	.199	.228
OF	Finners Quinlan	L	13	50	8	0	0	0	0.0	1	1	1	9	0	1	0	.160	.160
OF	Charlie Miller	L	4	12	2	0	0	0	0.0	0	1	0	2	0	1	0	.167	.167
C	Larry McLean	R	48	152	41	9	0	0	0.0	7	12	6	9	0	6	1	.270	.329
C	Palmer Hildebrand	R	26	55	9	2	0	0	0.0	3	1	1	10	1	2	0	.164	.200
C	Skipper Roberts	L	26	41	6	2	0	0	0.0	4	3	3	13	1	7	0	.146	.195
C	Frank Snyder	R	7	21	4	0	1	0	0.0	1	2	0	4	0	0	0	.190	.286
CO	Heinie Peitz	R	3	4	1	0	1	0	0.0	1	0	0	0	0	0	0	.250	.750
PH	John Vann	R	1	1	0	0	0	0	0.0	0	0	0	1	0	1	0	.000	.000
PH	Jim Whelan	R	1	1	0	0	0	0	0.0	0	0	0	0	0	1	0	.000	.000
PITCHERS																		
P	Slim Sallee	L	49	94	19	3	0	2	2.1	6	5	1	15	1	0	0	.202	.298
P	Bob Harmon	B	46	92	24	1	2	0	0.0	7	3	6	22	2	1	0	.261	.315
P	Dan Griner	L	34	81	21	3	2	0	0.0	7	8	5	25	0	0	0	.259	.346
P	Pol Perritt	R	36	59	12	1	0	0	0.0	3	4	0	15	0	0	0	.203	.220
P	Bill Doak	R	15	31	1	0	0	0	0.0	0	0	1	18	0	0	0	.032	.032
P	Sandy Burk	R	19	22	2	0	0	0	0.0	1	0	1	9	0	0	0	.091	.091
P	Rube Geyer		30	22	2	0	0	0	0.0	1	1	3	3	0	0	0	.091	.091
P	Bill Steele	R	12	18	1	0	0	0	0.0	1	1	2	4	0	0	0	.056	.056
P	Harry Trekell	R	7	9	1	0	0	0	0.0	0	0	1	2	0	0	0	.111	.111
P	Bill Hopper	R	3	8	3	0	1	0	0.0	0	1	0	3	0	0	0	.375	.625
P	Dick Niehaus	L	3	7	2	0	0	0	0.0	0	0	2	3	0	0	0	.286	.286
P	Joe Willis	R	7	3	0	0	0	0	0.0	0	0	0	2	0	0	0	.000	.000
P	Ben Hunt	L	2	2	0	0	0	0	0.0	0	0	0	0	0	0	0	.000	.000
P	Phil Redding	L	1	1	0	0	0	0	0.0	0	0	0	0	0	0	0	.000	.000
P	Walt Marbet	R	3	0	0	0	0	0	–	0	0	0	0	0	0	0	–	–
	TEAM TOTAL			4953	1221	152	72	14	0.3	524	427	450	573	171	95	23	.247	.315

INDIVIDUAL FIELDING

POS	Player	T	G	PO	A	E	DP	TC/G	FA	POS	Player	T	G	PO	A	E	DP	TC/G	FA
1B	E. Konetchy	R	139	1429	90	7	71	11.0	.995	OF	R. Oakes	R	144	321	16	11	2	2.4	.968
	L. Magee	R	6	72	8	0	4	13.3	1.000		L. Magee	R	107	250	21	5	5	2.6	.982
	I. Wingo	R	5	47	7	3	2	11.4	.947		S. Evans	L	74	111	5	2	0	1.6	.983
	P. Whitted	R	2	26	1	0	2	13.5	1.000		P. Whitted	R	40	83	5	1	0	2.2	.989
	T. Cather	R	1	4	0	0	0	4.0	1.000		J. Sheckard	R	46	76	6	4	3	1.9	.953
	S. Evans	L	1	2	0	2	0	4.0	.500		T. Cather	R	57	67	8	7	0	1.4	.915
											P. Hildebrand	R	1	0	0	0	0	0.0	.000
2B	M. Huggins	R	112	265	339	14	44	5.5	.977		H. Peitz	R	1	0	0	0	0	0.0	.000
	L. Magee	R	21	48	56	4	8	5.1	.963		I. Wingo	R	1	0	0	0	0	0.0	.000
	C. O'Leary	R	15	25	41	3	11	4.6	.957		F. Quinlan	L	12	23	3	3	2	2.4	.897
	P. Whitted	R	7	9	24	4	0	5.3	.892		C. Miller	L	3	4	0	0	0	1.3	1.000
	A. Hauser	R	4	7	8	0	2	3.8	1.000										
	D. Crandall	R	1	2	3	0	1	5.0	1.000	C	I. Wingo	R	97	344	132	28	12	5.2	.944
											L. McLean	R	42	143	60	3	8	4.9	.985
SS	C. O'Leary	R	102	192	296	25	22	5.0	.951		P. Hildebrand	R	22	71	21	3	5	4.3	.968
	P. Whitted	R	37	77	122	16	16	5.8	.926		S. Roberts	R	16	44	11	9	2	4.0	.859
	A. Cabrera	R	1	0	0	0	0	0.0	.000		F. Snyder	R	7	31	12	2	0	6.4	.956
	A. Hauser	R	8	11	17	5	2	4.1	.848		H. Peitz	R	2	3	2	3	0	4.0	.625
	Z. Beck	R	5	7	18	5	2	6.0	.833										
	W. Callahan	R	6	8	15	2	2	4.2	.920										
	L. Magee	R	2	3	1	0	0	2.0	1.000										
3B	M. Mowrey	R	130	143	282	21	23	3.4	.953										
	P. Whitted	R	21	27	51	6	9	4.0	.929										
	Z. Beck	R	5	4	11	0	0	3.0	1.000										

Historians might call 1913 a rebuilding year in St. Louis. At the time, though, it simply looked dismal, as both its teams, the Cardinals and the Browns, finished in last place for the only time in St. Louis history. (This fate befell Boston three times, Chicago once, and Philadelphia a remarkable nine times, including three years in a row *twice*.) The Cards were once again last in both runs and runs allowed, with an ERA more than a run worse than the league average. There were rumors of dissension on the club, and in fact just three of the Cardinals from the 1913 starting lineup, including player-manager Huggins, would remain with the club for the 1914 season.

TEAM STATISTICS

	W	L	PCT	GB	R	OR	2B	Batting 3B	HR	BA	SA	SB	E	Fielding DP	FA	CG	BB	Pitching SO	ShO	SV	ERA
NY	101	51	.664		684	502	226	70	31	.273	.361	296	254	107	.961	82	315	651	11	16	2.43
PHI	88	63	.583	12.5	693	636	257	78	73	.265	.382	156	214	112	.968	77	512	667	18	11	3.15
CHI	88	65	.575	13.5	720	640	194	96	59	.257	.369	181	259	106	.959	89	478	556	12	14	3.13
PIT	78	71	.523	21.5	673	585	210	86	35	.263	.356	181	226	94	.964	74	434	590	9	7	2.90
BOS	69	82	.457	31.5	641	690	191	60	32	.256	.335	177	273	82	.957	105	419	597	12	3	2.09
BKN	65	84	.436	34.5	595	613	193	86	39	.270	.363	188	243	125	.961	70	439	548	9	6	3.13
CIN	64	89	.418	37.5	607	714	170	96	27	.261	.347	226	251	104	.961	71	456	522	10	10	3.46
STL	51	99	.340	49	523	756	152	72	14	.247	.315	171	219	113	.965	73	476	464	6	10	4.24
LEAGUE TOTAL					5136	5136	1593	644	310	.262	.354	1576	1939	843	.962	641	3529	4595	87	77	3.06

INDIVIDUAL PITCHING

PITCHER	T	W	L	PCT	ERA	SV	G	GS	CG	IP	H	BB	SO	R	ER	ShO	H/9	BB/9	SO/9
Bob Harmon	R	8	21	.276	3.92	1	42	27	16	273.1	291	99	66	135	119	1	9.58	3.26	2.17
Slim Sallee	L	18	15	.545	2.70	5	49	30	17	273	254	59	105	97	82	3	8.37	1.95	3.46
Dan Griner	R	10	22	.313	5.08	0	34	34	18	225	279	66	79	150	127	1	11.16	2.64	3.16
Pol Perritt	R	6	14	.300	5.25	0	36	21	8	175	205	64	64	123	102	0	10.54	3.29	3.29
Bill Doak	R	2	8	.200	3.10	1	15	12	5	93	79	39	51	42	32	1	7.65	3.77	4.94
Rube Geyer	R	1	5	.167	5.26	1	30	4	2	78.2	83	38	21	57	46	0	9.50	4.35	2.40
Sandy Burk	R	1	2	.333	5.14	1	19	4	0	70	81	33	29	45	40	0	10.41	4.24	3.73
Bill Steele	R	4	4	.500	5.00	0	12	9	2	54	58	18	10	31	30	0	9.67	3.00	1.67
Harry Trekell	R	0	1	.000	4.50	0	7	1	1	30	25	8	15	20	15	0	7.50	2.40	4.50
Bill Hopper	R	0	3	.000	3.75	0	3	3	2	24	20	8	3	14	10	0	7.50	3.00	1.13
Dick Niehaus	L	0	2	.000	4.13	0	3	3	2	24	20	13	4	17	11	0	7.50	4.88	1.50
Joe Willis	L	0	0	–	7.45	1	7	0	0	9.2	9	11	6	9	8	0	8.38	10.24	5.59
Ben Hunt	L	0	1	.000	3.38	0	2	1	0	8	6	9	6	5	3	0	6.75	10.13	6.75
Ed Konetchy	R	1	0	1.000	0.00	0	1	0	0	4.2	1	4	3	0	0	0	1.93	7.71	5.79
Walt Marbet	R	0	1	.000	16.20	0	3	1	0	3.1	9	4	1	7	6	0	24.30	10.80	2.70
Phil Redding	R	0	0	–	6.75	0	1	0	0	2.2	2	1	1	2	2	0	6.75	3.38	3.38
Ted Cather	R	0	0	–	54.00	0	1	0	0	.1	1	2	0	2	2	0	27.00	54.00	0.00
TEAM TOTAL		51	99	.340	4.24	10	265	150	73	1348.2	1423	476	464	756	635	6	9.50	3.18	3.10

MANAGER	W	L	PCT
Miller Huggins	81	72	.529

POS	Player	B	G	AB	H	2B	3B	HR	HR %	R	RBI	BB	SO	SB	Pinch Hit AB	Pinch Hit H	BA	SA
REGULARS																		
1B	Dots Miller	R	155	573	166	27	10	4	0.7	67	88	34	52	16	0	0	.290	.393
2B	Miller Huggins	B	148	509	134	17	4	1	0.2	85	24	105	63	32	1	0	.263	.318
SS	Art Butler	R	86	274	55	12	3	1	0.4	29	24	39	23	14	2	0	.201	.277
3B	Zinn Beck	R	137	457	106	15	11	3	0.7	42	45	28	32	14	0	0	.232	.333
RF	Owen Wilson	L	154	580	150	27	12	9	1.6	64	73	32	66	14	0	0	.259	.393
CF	Lee Magee	B	162	529	150	23	4	2	0.4	59	40	42	24	36	0	0	.284	.353
LF	Cozy Dolan	R	126	421	101	16	3	4	1.0	76	32	55	74	42	1	1	.240	.321
C	Frank Snyder	R	100	326	75	15	4	1	0.3	19	25	13	28	1	2	0	.230	.310
SUBSTITUTES																		
1B	Lee Dressen	L	46	103	24	2	1	0	0.0	16	7	11	20	2	7	1	.233	.272
UT	Ken Nash	B	24	51	14	3	1	0	0.0	4	6	6	10	0	5	1	.275	.373
3O	Possum Whitted	R	20	31	4	1	0	0	0.0	3	1	0	3	1	4	0	.129	.161
2B	Bruno Betzel	R	7	9	0	0	0	0	0.0	2	0	1	1	0	2	0	.000	.000
SS	Rolla Daringer	L	2	4	2	1	0	0	0.0	1	0	1	2	0	1	0	.500	.750
OF	Walt Cruise	L	95	256	58	9	3	4	1.6	20	28	25	42	3	11	3	.227	.332
OF	Ted Cather	R	39	99	27	7	0	0	0.0	11	13	3	15	4	10	1	.273	.343
OF	Joe Riggert	R	34	89	19	5	2	0	0.0	9	8	5	14	4	4	0	.213	.315
OF	Charlie Miller	L	36	36	7	1	0	0	0.0	4	2	3	9	2	11	2	.194	.222
C	Ivy Wingo	L	80	237	71	8	5	4	1.7	24	26	18	17	15	4	2	.300	.426
C	Paddy O'Connor	R	10	9	0	0	0	0	0.0	0	0	2	2	0	2	0	.000	.000
C	Jack Roche	R	12	9	6	2	1	0	0.0	1	3	0	1	1	6	5	.667	1.111
PITCHERS																		
P	Pol Perritt	R	41	92	13	1	1	0	0.0	4	3	3	30	2	0	0	.141	.174
P	Slim Sallee	L	46	91	21	1	0	0	0.0	6	3	3	17	0	0	0	.231	.242
P	Bill Doak	R	36	85	10	3	0	0	0.0	3	3	3	31	0	0	0	.118	.153
P	Dan Griner	L	37	55	14	4	0	0	0.0	4	2	6	18	1	0	0	.255	.327
P	Hub Perdue	R	22	48	8	0	0	0	0.0	0	2	2	11	0	0	0	.167	.167
P	Hank Robinson	R	26	35	6	0	0	0	0.0	3	1	2	4	0	0	0	.171	.171
P	Bill Steele	R	17	17	5	2	0	0	0.0	2	1	1	2	0	0	0	.294	.412
P	Casey Hageman	R	12	16	2	0	0	0	0.0	0	0	1	4	0	0	0	.125	.125
P	Dick Niehaus	L	8	4	1	1	0	0	0.0	0	0	0	2	0	0	0	.250	.500
P	Steamboat Williams	L	5	1	0	0	0	0	0.0	0	1	0	1	0	0	0	.000	.000
P	Bill Hopper	R	3	0	0	0	0	0	–	0	0	0	0	0	0	0	–	–
	TEAM TOTAL			5046	1249	203	65	33	0.7	558	461	445	618	204	73	16	.248	.333

INDIVIDUAL FIELDING

POS	Player	T	G	PO	A	E	DP	TC/G	FA		POS	Player	T	G	PO	A	E	DP	TC/G	FA
1B	D. Miller	R	98	1019	57	8	46	11.1	.993		OF	O. Wilson	R	154	312	34	6	11	2.3	**.983**
	L. Magee	R	40	412	28	1	20	11.0	.998			L. Magee	R	102	210	14	7	4	2.3	.970
	L. Dressen	L	38	258	13	5	15	7.3	.982			C. Dolan	R	97	182	10	9	2	2.1	.955
2B	M. Huggins	R	147	328	428	28	58	5.3	.964			W. Cruise	R	81	158	6	4	1	2.1	.976
	P. Whitted	R	1	0	0	0	0	0.0	.000			T. Cather	R	28	49	4	1	1	1.9	.981
	K. Nash	R	6	9	17	4	2	5.0	.867			J. Riggert	R	30	46	3	2	0	1.7	.961
	B. Betzel	R	5	4	22	0	0	5.2	1.000			C. Miller	L	19	11	1	0	0	0.6	1.000
	D. Miller	R	5	5	8	2	2	3.0	.867			A. Butler	R	1	0	0	0	0	0.0	.000
	L. Magee	R	6	4	9	0	1	2.2	1.000			P. Whitted	R	3	0	0	1	0	0.3	.000
SS	A. Butler	R	84	155	228	30	24	4.9	.927		C	F. Snyder	R	98	419	130	12	12	5.7	**.979**
	D. Miller	R	53	152	182	20	19	6.7	.944			I. Wingo	R	70	276	93	16	7	5.5	.958
	Z. Beck	R	16	41	54	7	6	6.4	.931			P. O'Connor	R	7	9	3	0	0	1.7	1.000
	R. Daringer	R	1	0	2	1	1	3.0	.667			J. Roche	R	9	2	0	1	1	0.3	.667
	K. Nash	R	3	0	0	2	0	0.7	.000											
3B	Z. Beck	R	122	141	264	28	24	3.5	.935											
	C. Dolan	R	29	23	49	14	1	3.0	.837											
	P. Whitted	R	11	6	10	2	1	1.6	.889											
	K. Nash	R	10	6	8	2	0	1.6	.875											

The last successful effort to form a third major league came in 1914 with the formation of the Federal League. While few major stars jumped to the Feds until the following year, the league may have had an effect on the National League standings, which saw many surprises. Most surprising of all was the Boston Braves' famous march from last place on the Fourth of July to the pennant. The Cardinals improved dramatically as well, shooting up to third place, with their best won-lost record since 1901. The pitching staff leaped from last in runs allowed to first, and the team ERA dropped from 4.24 to 2.38. The staff was led by a pair of youngsters: 21-year-old Pol Perritt, 16–13 with a 2.36 ERA, and 23-year-old righthander Bill Doak, who went 20–6 and led the league with his 1.72 ERA. In addition, southpaw Slim Sallee had his best ERA and led the league in saves for the second time.

TEAM STATISTICS

	W	L	PCT	GB	R	OR	2B	3B	HR	BA	SA	SB	E	DP	FA	CG	BB	SO	ShO	SV	ERA
							Batting						Fielding			Pitching					
OS	94	59	.614		657	548	213	60	35	.251	.335	139	246	143	.963	104	477	604	18	5	2.74
NY	84	70	.545	10.5	672	576	222	59	30	.265	.348	239	254	119	.961	88	367	563	20	9	2.94
TL	81	72	.529	13	558	540	203	65	33	.248	.333	204	239	109	.964	83	422	531	16	11	2.38
CHI	78	76	.506	16.5	605	638	199	74	41	.243	.336	164	310	87	.951	70	528	651	14	9	2.71
KN	75	79	.487	19.5	622	612	172	90	31	.269	.355	173	248	112	.961	80	466	605	11	10	2.82
HI	74	80	.481	20.5	651	673	211	52	62	.263	.361	145	324	81	.950	85	452	650	14	6	3.06
IT	69	85	.448	25.5	503	540	148	79	18	.233	.303	147	223	96	.966	86	392	488	10	9	2.70
IN	60	94	.390	34.5	530	671	142	64	16	.236	.300	224	314	113	.952	74	489	607	14	14	2.94
LEAGUE TOTAL					4798	4798	1510	543	266	.251	.334	1435	2158	860	.958	670	3593	4699	117	73	2.78

INDIVIDUAL PITCHING

PITCHER	T	W	L	PCT	ERA	SV	G	GS	CG	IP	H	BB	SO	R	ER	ShO	H/9	BB/9	SO/9
Pol Perritt	R	16	13	.552	2.36	2	41	32	18	286	248	93	115	106	75	3	7.80	2.93	3.62
Slim Sallee	L	18	17	.514	2.10	6	46	30	18	282.1	252	72	105	92	66	3	8.03	2.30	3.35
Bill Doak	R	20	6	.769	1.72	0	36	33	16	256	193	87	118	79	49	7	6.79	3.06	4.15
Dan Griner	R	9	13	.409	2.51	2	37	16	11	179	163	57	74	66	50	2	8.20	2.87	3.72
Hub Perdue	R	8	8	.500	2.82	1	22	19	12	153.1	160	35	43	60	48	0	9.39	2.05	2.52
Hank Robinson	L	6	8	.429	3.00	0	26	16	6	126	128	32	30	61	42	1	9.14	2.29	2.14
Casey Hageman	R	1	4	.200	2.44	0	12	7	1	55.1	43	20	21	24	15	0	6.99	3.25	3.42
Bill Steele	R	2	2	.500	2.70	0	17	2	0	53.1	55	7	16	30	16	0	9.28	1.18	2.70
Dick Niehaus	L	1	0	1.000	3.12	0	8	1	1	17.1	18	8	6	11	6	0	9.35	4.15	3.12
Steamboat Williams	R	0	1	.000	6.55	0	5	1	0	11	13	6	2	8	8	0	10.64	4.91	1.64
Bill Hopper	R	0	0	–	3.60	0	3	0	0	5	6	5	1	3	2	0	10.80	9.00	1.80
TEAM TOTAL		81	72	.529	2.38	11	253	157	83	1424.2	1279	422	531	540	377	16	8.08	2.67	3.35

CARDINAL ERA LEADERS

1893	Ted Breitenstein, 3.18	1946	Howie Pollett, 2.10
1914	Bill Doak, 1.72	1948	Harry Brecheen, 2.24
1921	Bill Doak, 2.59	1968	Bob Gibson, 1.12
1942	Mort Cooper, 1.78	1976	John Denny, 2.52
1943	Howie Pollett, 1.75		

MANAGER	W	L	PCT
Miller Huggins	72	81	.471

POS	Player	B	G	AB	H	2B	3B	HR	HR %	R	RBI	BB	SO	SB	Pinch Hit AB	Pinch Hit H	BA	SA
REGULARS																		
1B	Dots Miller	R	150	553	146	17	10	2	0.4	73	72	43	48	27	0	0	.264	.342
2B	Miller Huggins	B	107	353	85	5	2	2	0.6	57	24	74	68	13	0	0	.241	.283
SS	Art Butler	R	130	469	119	12	5	1	0.2	73	31	47	34	26	2	0	.254	.307
3B	Bruno Betzel	R	117	367	92	12	4	0	0.0	42	27	18	48	10	0	0	.251	.305
RF	Tommy Long	R	140	507	149	21	25	2	0.4	61	61	31	50	19	4	2	.294	.446
CF	Owen Wilson	L	107	348	96	13	6	3	0.9	33	39	19	43	8	2	0	.276	.374
LF	Bob Bescher	B	130	486	128	15	7	4	0.8	71	34	52	53	27	0	0	.263	.348
C	Frank Snyder	R	144	473	141	22	7	2	0.4	41	55	39	49	3	1	0	.298	.387
SUBSTITUTES																		
1O	Ham Hyatt	L	106	295	79	8	9	2	0.7	23	46	28	24	3	14	3	.268	.376
3B	Zinn Beck	R	70	223	52	9	4	0	0.0	21	15	12	31	3	2	0	.233	.309
SS	Rogers Hornsby	R	18	57	14	2	0	0	0.0	5	4	2	6	0	0	0	.246	.281
SS	Rolla Daringer	L	10	23	2	0	0	0	0.0	3	0	9	5	0	0	0	.087	.087
OF	Cozy Dolan	R	111	322	90	14	9	2	0.6	53	38	34	37	17	3	1	.280	.398
OF	Jack Smith	L	4	16	3	0	1	0	0.0	2	0	1	5	0	0	0	.188	.313
OF	Jim Brown	R	1	2	1	0	0	0	0.0	0	0	2	1	0	0	0	.500	.500
C1	Mike Gonzalez	R	51	97	22	2	2	0	0.0	12	10	8	9	4	6	1	.227	.289
C	Jack Roche	R	46	39	8	0	1	0	0.0	2	6	4	8	1	37	8	.205	.256
C	Harry Glenn	L	6	16	5	0	0	0	0.0	1	1	3	0	0	1	0	.313	.313
PITCHERS																		
P	Slim Sallee	L	46	92	11	0	0	0	0.0	0	5	6	27	0	0	0	.120	.120
P	Bill Doak	R	38	86	15	3	0	0	0.0	6	2	6	27	0	0	0	.174	.209
P	Lee Meadows	L	39	83	8	0	0	0	0.0	2	4	7	31	0	0	0	.096	.096
P	Dan Griner	L	39	52	14	4	0	0	0.0	4	5	4	17	0	2	0	.269	.346
P	Hank Robinson	R	32	47	5	0	0	0	0.0	1	0	2	4	0	0	0	.106	.106
P	Hub Perdue	R	31	36	4	0	0	0	0.0	2	0	3	8	0	0	0	.111	.111
P	Red Ames	B	15	35	4	0	0	0	0.0	0	2	2	17	0	0	0	.114	.114
P	Dick Niehaus	L	15	14	1	0	0	0	0.0	1	0	1	4	1	0	0	.071	.071
P	Fred Lamline	R	4	8	1	0	0	0	0.0	0	1	0	1	0	0	0	.125	.125
P	Charlie Boardman	L	3	7	2	0	0	0	0.0	1	1	0	3	0	0	0	.286	.286
TEAM TOTAL				5106	1297	159	92	20	0.4	590	483	457	658	162	77	16	.254	.333

INDIVIDUAL FIELDING

POS	Player	T	G	PO	A	E	DP	TC/G	FA	POS	Player	T	G	PO	A	E	DP	TC/G	FA
1B	D. Miller	R	83	1000	50	10	54	12.8	.991	OF	B. Bescher	L	130	257	12	8	1	2.1	.971
	H. Hyatt	R	81	616	21	6	31	7.9	.991		T. Long	R	140	236	18	20	1	2.0	.927
	M. Gonzalez	R	8	82	7	1	6	11.3	.989		O. Wilson	R	107	234	20	4	3	2.4	.984
2B	M. Huggins	R	107	194	315	23	44	5.0	.957		C. Dolan	R	98	179	14	14	0	2.0	.929
	D. Miller	R	55	136	156	9	28	5.5	.970		H. Hyatt	R	25	40	2	3	1	1.8	.933
	Z. Beck	R	2	1	2	1	0	2.0	.750		J. Smith	L	4	5	0	0	0	1.3	1.000
	B. Betzel	R	3	1	1	1	0	1.0	.667		J. Brown	R	1	1	0	0	0	1.0	1.000
SS	A. Butler	R	130	235	351	53	43	4.9	.917	C	F. Snyder	R	144	592	204	14	9	5.6	.983
	R. Hornsby	R	18	48	46	8	12	5.7	.922		M. Gonzalez	R	31	93	24	1	3	3.8	.992
	R. Daringer	R	10	13	23	2	5	3.8	.947		H. Glenn	R	5	22	4	2	0	5.6	.929
	D. Miller	R	3	6	8	1	1	5.0	.933		J. Roche	R	4	1	3	0	1	1.0	1.000
	Z. Beck	R	4	3	8	2	0	3.3	.846										
	B. Betzel	R	2	3	6	2	1	5.5	.818										
3B	B. Betzel	R	105	105	221	22	10	3.3	.937										
	Z. Beck	R	60	59	127	13	10	3.3	.935										
	D. Miller	R	9	0	1	0	0	0.1	1.000										

The Cardinals reversed their wins and losses from the previous year as they fell from third place to sixth, but just a game behind fourth-place Chicago. The Cards went from sixth in runs scored to first, but improved by just thirty-two runs. Club batting was up just six points, and the slugging average remained the same. The real action in St. Louis was in the Federal League, where its club was in a race with Chicago and Pittsburgh that ended up with the three clubs within a half-game in baseball's tightest three-team race ever. Chicago won it by one percentage point over St. Louis and a half-game over Pittsburgh. For the Cardinals, the '15 season included the first appearance in the majors for a 19-year-old shortstop who batted just .246 in an 18-game trial. By the time he ended his career twenty-two years later, though, Rogers Hornsby would be generally recognized as the greatest righthanded batter of all time.

TEAM STATISTICS

	W	L	PCT	GB	R	OR	2B	Batting 3B	HR	BA	SA	SB	Fielding E	DP	FA	CG	BB	Pitching SO	ShO	SV	ERA
HI	90	62	.592		589	463	202	39	58	.247	.340	121	216	99	.966	98	342	652	20	8	2.17
OS	83	69	.546	7	582	545	231	57	17	.240	.319	121	213	115	.966	95	366	630	15	9	2.57
KN	80	72	.526	10	536	560	165	75	14	.248	.317	131	238	96	.963	87	473	499	16	7	2.66
HI	73	80	.477	17.5	570	620	212	66	53	.244	.342	166	268	94	.958	71	480	657	18	6	3.11
T	73	81	.474	18	557	520	197	91	24	.246	.334	182	214	100	.966	91	384	544	18	10	2.60
TL	72	81	.471	18.5	590	601	159	92	20	.254	.333	162	235	109	.964	79	402	538	12	9	2.89
N	71	83	.461	20	516	585	194	84	15	.253	.331	156	222	148	.966	80	497	572	19	12	2.84
Y	69	83	.454	21	582	628	195	68	24	.251	.329	155	256	119	.960	78	325	637	15	8	3.11
EAGUE TOTAL					4522	4522	1555	572	225	.248	.331	1194	1862	880	.964	679	3269	4729	133	69	2.75

INDIVIDUAL PITCHING

ITCHER	T	W	L	PCT	ERA	SV	G	GS	CG	IP	H	BB	SO	R	ER	ShO	H/9	BB/9	SO/9
ll Doak	R	16	18	.471	2.64	1	38	36	19	276	263	85	124	103	81	3	8.58	2.77	4.04
im Sallee	L	13	17	.433	2.84	3	46	33	17	275.1	245	57	91	121	87	2	8.01	1.86	2.97
ee Meadows	R	13	11	.542	2.99	0	39	26	14	244	232	88	104	112	81	1	8.56	3.25	3.84
an Griner	R	5	11	.313	2.81	3	37	18	9	150.1	137	46	46	59	47	3	8.20	2.75	2.75
ank Robinson	L	7	8	.467	2.45	0	32	15	6	143	128	35	57	54	39	1	8.06	2.20	3.59
ub Perdue	R	6	12	.333	4.21	1	31	13	5	115.1	141	19	29	66	54	1	11.00	1.48	2.26
ed Ames	R	9	3	.750	2.46	1	15	14	8	113.1	93	32	48	35	31	2	7.39	2.54	3.81
ck Niehaus	L	2	1	.667	3.97	0	15	2	0	45.1	48	22	21	35	20	0	9.53	4.37	4.17
harlie Boardman	L	1	0	1.000	1.42	0	3	1	1	19	12	15	7	4	3	0	5.68	7.11	3.32
ed Lamline	R	0	0	–	2.84	0	4	0	0	19	21	3	11	12	6	0	9.95	1.42	5.21
EAM TOTAL		72	81	.471	2.89	9	260	158	79	1400.2	1320	402	538	601	449	13	8.48	2.58	3.46

MANAGER	W	L	PCT
Miller Huggins	60	93	.392

POS	Player	B	G	AB	H	2B	3B	HR	HR %	R	RBI	BB	SO	SB	Pinch Hit AB	Pinch Hit H	BA	SA
REGULARS																		
1B	Dots Miller	R	143	505	120	22	7	1	0.2	47	46	40	49	18	0	0	.238	.315
2B	Bruno Betzel	R	142	510	119	15	11	1	0.2	49	37	39	77	22	0	0	.233	.312
SS	Roy Corhan	R	92	295	62	6	3	0	0.0	30	18	20	31	15	7	3	.210	.251
3B	Rogers Hornsby	R	139	495	155	17	15	6	1.2	63	65	40	63	17	1	1	.313	.444
RF	Tommy Long	R	119	403	118	11	10	1	0.2	37	33	10	43	21	12	2	.293	.377
CF	Jack Smith	L	130	357	87	6	5	6	1.7	43	34	20	50	24	7	1	.244	.339
LF	Bob Bescher	B	151	561	132	24	8	6	1.1	78	43	60	50	39	0	0	.235	.339
C	Mike Gonzalez	R	118	331	79	15	4	0	0.0	33	29	28	18	5	10	0	.239	.308
SUBSTITUTES																		
3B	Zinn Beck	R	62	184	41	7	1	0	0.0	8	10	14	21	3	9	2	.223	.272
SS	Sammy Bohne	R	14	38	9	0	0	0	0.0	3	0	4	6	3	0	0	.237	.237
2B	Stuffy Stewart	R	9	17	3	0	0	0	0.0	0	1	0	3	0	0	0	.176	.176
2B	Miller Huggins	B	18	9	3	0	0	0	0.0	2	0	2	3	0	4	2	.333	.333
OF	Owen Wilson	L	120	355	85	8	2	3	0.8	30	32	20	46	4	6	0	.239	.299
O2	Art Butler	R	86	110	23	5	0	0	0.0	9	7	7	12	3	54	13	.209	.255
OF	Walt Cruise	L	3	3	2	0	0	0	0.0	0	0	1	0	0	1	1	.667	.667
C1	Frank Snyder	R	132	406	105	12	4	0	0.0	23	39	18	31	7	13	5	.259	.308
C	Tony Brottem	R	26	33	6	1	0	0	0.0	3	4	3	10	1	7	4	.182	.212
PITCHERS																		
P	Lee Meadows	L	51	95	15	3	2	0	0.0	3	4	0	32	0	0	0	.158	.232
P	Red Ames	B	45	68	12	0	1	0	0.0	3	1	3	19	0	0	0	.176	.206
P	Bill Doak	R	29	62	8	1	0	0	0.0	3	2	1	21	0	0	0	.129	.177
P	Bob Steele	R	24	51	10	0	0	0	0.0	0	0	0	11	0	0	0	.196	.196
P	Hi Jasper	R	21	33	7	0	0	1	3.0	2	3	0	16	0	0	0	.212	.303
P	Milt Watson	R	18	32	7	0	0	0	0.0	0	1	0	9	0	0	0	.219	.219
P	Steamboat Williams	L	36	24	5	1	0	0	0.0	3	1	3	6	0	0	0	.208	.250
P	Slim Sallee	L	16	18	3	0	0	0	0.0	2	0	1	9	0	0	0	.167	.167
P	Charley Hall	L	10	14	2	0	0	0	0.0	0	1	0	6	0	0	0	.143	.143
P	Joe Lotz	R	12	12	4	1	0	0	0.0	1	2	0	4	0	0	0	.333	.417
P	Dan Griner	L	4	4	1	0	0	0	0.0	1	0	0	2	0	0	0	.250	.250
P	Murphy Currie	R	6	3	0	0	0	0	0.0	0	0	1	1	0	0	0	.000	.000
P	Cy Warmoth	L	3	2	0	0	0	0	0.0	0	0	0	0	0	0	0	.000	.000
TEAM TOTAL				5030	1223	155	74	25	0.5	476	413	335	651	182	131	34	.243	.318

INDIVIDUAL FIELDING

POS	Player	T	G	PO	A	E	DP	TC/G	FA
1B	D. Miller	R	93	948	43	7	60	10.7	.993
	F. Snyder	R	46	421	23	7	24	9.8	.984
	R. Hornsby	R	15	150	5	2	6	10.5	.987
	M. Gonzalez	R	13	116	2	0	7	9.1	1.000
	Z. Beck	R	1	1	0	0	1	1.0	1.000
2B	B. Betzel	R	113	275	366	27	64	5.9	.960
	D. Miller	R	38	72	98	5	14	4.6	.971
	Z. Beck	R	1	0	0	0	0	0.0	.000
	S. Stewart	R	8	11	9	4	2	3.0	.833
	M. Huggins	R	7	10	10	0	0	2.9	1.000
	A. Butler	R	8	8	10	1	3	2.4	.947
	R. Hornsby	R	1	3	4	1	0	8.0	.875
SS	R. Corhan	R	84	153	278	39	35	5.6	.917
	R. Hornsby	R	45	90	132	22	22	5.4	.910
	D. Miller	R	21	36	58	7	10	4.8	.931
	A. Butler	R	1	0	0	0	0	0.0	.000
	F. Snyder	R	1	0	0	0	0	0.0	.000
	S. Bohne	R	14	15	32	7	3	3.9	.870
3B	R. Hornsby	R	83	82	174	20	7	3.3	.928
	Z. Beck	R	52	45	86	13	7	2.8	.910
	B. Betzel	R	33	34	69	13	3	3.5	.888
	A. Butler	R	1	0	0	0	0	0.0	.000
	D. Miller	R	1	0	1	0	0	1.0	1.000

POS	Player	T	G	PO	A	E	DP	TC/G	FA
OF	B. Bescher	L	151	284	18	15	2	2.1	.953
	J. Smith	L	120	212	12	12	4	2.0	.949
	O. Wilson	R	113	181	11	9	3	1.8	.955
	T. Long	R	106	143	13	9	2	1.6	.945
	A. Butler	R	15	15	0	2	0	1.1	.882
	T. Brottem	R	2	0	0	0	0	0.0	.000
	B. Betzel	R	7	10	0	0	0	1.4	1.000
	W. Cruise	R	2	2	0	0	0	1.0	1.000
C	M. Gonzalez	R	93	367	136	10	8	5.5	.981
	F. Snyder	R	72	310	115	12	11	6.1	.973
	T. Brottem	R	15	25	13	2	1	2.7	.950

The Federal League folded after the 1915 season, and its players returned to the National and American Leagues. Normalcy returned in St. Louis: the Cards were last again in the standings, tied with Cincinnati, and last in runs scored and allowed, ERA, and fielding percentage. Hornsby, shifted over to third for the season, showed promise, finishing fourth in the league in batting and slugging.

After the 1916 season, Helene Robison Briton, who inherited the club from her father, Frank Robison, decided to sell the club to a group of local investors. The group approached several sportswriters for recommendations on who should run the club's operations. The seven writers were unanimous: the only man for the job was the general manager of the Browns, Branch Rickey. Rickey came on as president of the club and began making the changes that would lead the Cardinals out of the basement—this time for good.

TEAM STATISTICS

	W	L	PCT	GB	R	OR	2B	3B	Batting HR	BA	SA	SB	E	Fielding DP	FA	CG	BB	Pitching SO	ShO	SV	ERA
BKN	94	60	.610		585	467	195	80	28	.261	.345	187	224	90	.965	96	372	634	22	7	2.12
PHI	91	62	.595	2.5	581	489	223	53	42	.250	.341	149	234	119	.963	97	295	601	24	9	2.36
BOS	89	63	.586	4	542	453	166	73	22	.233	.307	141	212	124	.967	97	325	644	21	11	2.19
NY	86	66	.566	7	597	503	188	74	42	.253	.343	206	217	108	.966	88	310	638	22	10	2.60
CHI	67	86	.438	26.5	520	541	194	56	46	.239	.325	133	286	104	.957	72	365	616	17	12	2.65
PIT	65	89	.422	29	484	586	147	91	20	.240	.316	173	260	97	.959	88	443	596	10	7	2.76
CIN	60	93	.392	33.5	505	622	187	88	14	.254	.331	157	228	126	.965	86	458	569	7	6	3.10
STL	60	93	.392	33.5	476	629	155	74	25	.243	.318	182	278	124	.957	58	445	529	11	14	3.14
LEAGUE TOTAL					4290	4290	1455	589	239	.247	.328	1328	1939	892	.963	682	3013	4827	134	76	2.61

INDIVIDUAL PITCHING

PITCHER	T	W	L	PCT	ERA	SV	G	GS	CG	IP	H	BB	SO	R	ER	ShO	H/9	BB/9	SO/9
Lee Meadows	R	12	23	.343	2.58	2	51	36	11	289	261	119	120	117	83	1	8.13	3.71	3.74
Red Ames	R	11	16	.407	2.64	7	45	22	10	228	225	57	98	100	67	2	8.88	2.25	3.87
Bill Doak	R	12	8	.600	2.63	0	29	26	11	192	177	55	82	76	56	3	8.30	2.58	3.84
Bob Steele	L	5	15	.250	3.41	0	29	22	7	148	156	42	67	74	56	1	9.49	2.55	4.07
Hi Jasper	R	5	6	.455	3.28	1	21	9	2	107	97	42	37	54	39	0	8.16	3.53	3.11
Steamboat Williams	R	6	7	.462	4.20	1	36	8	5	105	121	27	25	63	49	0	10.37	2.31	2.14
Milt Watson	R	4	6	.400	3.06	0	18	13	5	103	109	33	27	51	35	2	9.52	2.88	2.36
Slim Sallee	L	5	5	.500	3.47	1	16	7	4	70	75	23	28	28	27	2	9.64	2.96	3.60
Charley Hall	R	0	4	.000	5.48	1	10	5	2	42.2	45	14	15	27	26	0	9.49	2.95	3.16
Joe Lotz	R	0	3	.000	4.28	0	12	3	1	40	31	17	18	20	19	0	6.98	3.83	4.05
Murphy Currie	R	0	0	—	1.88	0	6	0	0	14.1	7	9	8	4	3	0	4.40	5.65	5.02
Dan Griner	R	0	0	—	4.09	1	4	0	0	11	15	3	3	5	5	0	12.27	2.45	2.45
Cy Warmoth	L	0	0	—	14.40	0	3	0	0	5	12	4	1	10	8	0	21.60	7.20	1.80
TEAM TOTAL		60	93	.392	3.14	14	280	151	58	1355	1331	445	529	629	473	11	8.84	2.96	3.51

MANAGER	W	L	PCT
Miller Huggins	82	70	.539

POS	Player	B	G	AB	H	2B	3B	HR	HR %	R	RBI	BB	SO	SB	Pinch Hit AB	Pinch Hit H	BA	SA
REGULARS																		
1B	Gene Paulette	R	95	332	88	21	7	0	0.0	32	34	16	16	9	2	0	.265	.370
2B	Dots Miller	R	148	544	135	15	9	2	0.4	61	45	33	52	14	0	0	.248	.320
SS	Rogers Hornsby	R	145	523	171	24	17	8	1.5	86	66	45	34	17	1	0	.327	**.484**
3B	Doug Baird	R	104	364	92	19	12	0	0.0	38	24	23	52	18	0	0	.253	.371
RF	Tommy Long	R	144	530	123	12	14	3	0.6	49	41	37	44	21	7	1	.232	.325
CF	Jack Smith	L	137	462	137	16	11	3	0.6	64	34	38	65	25	8	4	.297	.398
LF	Walt Cruise	L	153	529	156	20	10	5	0.9	70	59	38	73	16	1	1	.295	.399
C	Frank Snyder	R	115	313	74	9	2	1	0.3	18	33	27	43	4	18	6	.236	.288
SUBSTITUTES																		
2O	Bruno Betzel	R	106	328	71	4	3	1	0.3	24	17	20	47	9	3	2	.216	.256
3B	Fred Smith	R	56	165	30	0	2	1	0.6	11	17	17	22	4	1	0	.182	.224
3B	Tony DeFate	R	14	14	2	0	0	0	0.0	0	1	0	4	0	0	0	.143	.143
3S	Bobby Wallace	R	8	10	1	0	0	0	0.0	0	2	0	1	0	3	1	.100	.100
SS	Ike McAuley	R	3	7	2	0	0	0	0.0	0	1	0	1	0	0	0	.286	.286
OF	Bob Bescher	B	42	110	17	1	1	1	0.9	10	8	20	13	3	8	0	.155	.209
OF	Red Smyth	L	28	72	15	0	2	0	0.0	5	4	4	9	3	11	3	.208	.264
O2	Stuffy Stewart	R	13	9	0	0	0	0	0.0	4	0	0	4	0	1	0	.000	.000
C1	Mike Gonzalez	R	106	290	76	8	1	1	0.3	28	28	22	24	12	17	2	.262	.307
C	Paddy Livingston	R	7	20	4	0	0	0	0.0	0	2	0	1	2	1	0	.200	.200
C	John Brock	R	7	15	6	1	0	0	0.0	4	2	0	2	2	3	1	.400	.467
C	Jack Roche	R	1	1	0	0	0	0	0.0	0	0	0	0	0	0	0	.000	.000
PITCHERS																		
P	Bill Doak	R	44	95	12	1	0	0	0.0	5	3	3	34	0	0	0	.126	.137
P	Lee Meadows	L	43	89	9	1	0	0	0.0	5	4	1	32	0	0	0	.101	.112
P	Red Ames	B	43	64	12	1	2	0	0.0	3	7	6	23	0	0	0	.188	.266
P	Gene Packard	L	36	52	15	2	0	0	0.0	4	1	2	11	0	1	0	.288	.327
P	Milt Watson	R	41	51	5	1	0	0	0.0	5	1	0	15	0	0	0	.098	.118
P	Oscar Horstmann	R	35	46	9	2	0	0	0.0	1	2	2	13	0	0	0	.196	.239
P	Marv Goodwin	R	14	23	4	0	0	0	0.0	2	0	1	5	0	0	0	.174	.174
P	Bob Steele	R	12	13	5	1	0	0	0.0	2	0	0	0	0	0	0	.385	.462
P	Jakie May	R	15	4	0	0	0	0	0.0	0	0	0	3	0	0	0	.000	.000
P	George Pearce	L	5	4	0	0	0	0	0.0	0	0	0	4	0	0	0	.000	.000
P	Lou North	R	5	3	0	0	0	0	0.0	0	0	0	3	0	0	0	.000	.000
P	Bruce Hitt	R	2	1	0	0	0	0	0.0	0	0	0	1	0	0	0	.000	.000
P	Tim Murchison	R	1	0	0	0	0	0	0.0	0	0	0	0	0	0	0	—	—
TEAM TOTAL				5083	1271	159	93	26	0.5	531	436	359	652	159	92	22	.250	.333

INDIVIDUAL FIELDING

POS	Player	T	G	PO	A	E	DP	TC/G	FA		POS	Player	T	G	PO	A	E	DP	TC/G	FA
1B	G. Paulette	R	93	1130	45	8	82	12.7	.993		OF	W. Cruise	R	152	285	15	11	6	2.0	.965
	D. Miller	R	46	518	26	1	36	11.8	.998			J. Smith	L	128	233	12	10	6	2.0	.961
	M. Gonzalez	R	18	203	13	4	11	12.2	.982			T. Long	R	137	173	9	16	2	1.4	.919
2B	D. Miller	R	92	219	308	22	56	6.0	.960			B. Bescher	L	32	61	0	1	0	1.9	.984
	B. Betzel	R	75	159	217	15	40	5.2	.962			B. Betzel	R	23	32	3	1	1	1.6	.972
	F. Smith	R	2	0	2	0	0	1.0	1.000			R. Smyth	R	23	23	1	3	0	1.2	.889
	T. DeFate	R	1	0	1	0	1	1.0	1.000			M. Gonzalez	R	1	0	0	0	0	0.0	.000
	S. Stewart	R	2	1	0	0	0	0.5	1.000			D. Baird	R	2	0	0	0	0	0.0	.000
SS	R. Hornsby	R	144	268	527	52	82	5.9	.939			S. Stewart	R	7	2	1	0	0	0.4	1.000
	D. Miller	R	11	18	28	5	8	4.6	.902		C	F. Snyder	R	94	341	134	12	10	5.2	.975
	B. Wallace	R	2	4	6	1	0	5.5	.909			M. Gonzalez	R	68	241	97	8	8	5.1	.977
	I. McAuley	R	3	2	3	1	0	2.0	.833			P. Livingston	R	6	26	6	0	0	5.3	1.000
	F. Smith	R	1	1	1	0	1	2.0	1.000			J. Brock	R	4	13	4	1	0	4.5	.944
3B	D. Baird	R	103	110	259	23	24	3.8*	.941			J. Roche	R	1	0	0	1	0	1.0	.000
	F. Smith	R	51	62	110	9	5	3.5	.950											
	B. Betzel	R	4	2	5	1	1	2.0	.875											
	T. DeFate	R	5	1	4	0	0	1.0	1.000											
	B. Wallace	R	5	1	0	0	0	0.2	1.000											

The Cardinals' roller coaster swung up in 1917, as they improved by twenty-two wins and four places in the standings, reaching as high as second place for a brief time in mid-summer. Hornsby led the way, leading the league in slugging, triples, and total bases; he was also second in batting and third in home runs. The Cardinals' unusual feat of finishing 12 games over .500 while allowing 37 runs more than they scored convinced the New York Yankees that Miller Huggins was the manager they needed. Huggins joined the Yanks for the 1918 season, and posted a .597 won-lost record with six pennants in his twelve years at the helm.

TEAM STATISTICS

	W	L	PCT	GB	R	OR	Batting 2B	3B	HR	BA	SA	SB	Fielding E	DP	FA	CG	BB	Pitching SO	ShO	SV	ERA
NY	98	56	.636		635	457	170	71	39	.261	.343	162	208	122	.968	92	327	551	17	14	2.27
PHI	87	65	.572	10	578	501	225	60	38	.248	.339	109	212	112	.967	103	327	617	22	4	2.46
STL	82	70	.539	15	531	568	159	93	26	.250	.333	159	221	153	.967	66	421	502	16	10	3.03
CIN	78	76	.506	20	601	611	196	100	26	.264	.354	153	247	120	.962	94	404	492	11	6	2.66
CHI	74	80	.481	24	552	553	194	67	17	.239	.313	127	267	121	.959	79	374	654	14	8	2.62
BOS	72	81	.471	25.5	536	558	169	75	22	.246	.320	155	224	122	.966	105	371	593	19	2	2.77
BKN	70	81	.464	26.5	511	566	159	78	25	.247	.322	130	245	102	.962	99	405	582	7	9	2.78
PIT	51	103	.331	47	464	594	160	61	9	.238	.298	150	251	119	.961	84	432	509	17	6	3.01
LEAGUE TOTAL					4408	4408	1432	605	202	.249	.328	1145	1875	971	.964	722	3061	4500	123	59	2.70

INDIVIDUAL PITCHING

PITCHER	T	W	L	PCT	ERA	SV	G	GS	CG	IP	H	BB	SO	R	ER	ShO	H/9	BB/9	SO/9
Bill Doak	R	16	20	.444	3.10	2	44	37	16	281.1	257	85	111	123	97	3	8.22	2.72	3.55
Lee Meadows	R	15	9	.625	3.09	2	43	37	18	265.1	253	90	100	99	91	4	8.58	3.05	3.39
Red Ames	R	15	10	.600	2.71	3	43	19	10	209	189	57	62	75	63	2	8.14	2.45	2.67
Milt Watson	R	10	13	.435	3.51	0	41	20	5	161.1	149	51	45	74	63	3	8.31	2.85	2.51
Gene Packard	L	9	6	.600	2.47	2	34	11	6	153.1	138	25	44	48	42	0	8.10	1.47	2.58
Oscar Horstmann	R	9	4	.692	3.45	1	35	11	4	138.1	111	54	50	67	53	1	7.22	3.51	3.25
Marv Goodwin	R	6	4	.600	2.21	0	14	12	6	85.1	70	19	38	33	21	3	7.38	2.00	4.01
Bob Steele	L	1	3	.250	3.21	0	12	6	1	42	33	19	23	18	15	0	7.07	4.07	4.93
Jakie May	L	0	0	–	3.38	0	15	1	0	29.1	29	11	18	13	11	0	8.90	3.38	5.52
Lou North	R	0	0	–	3.97	0	5	0	0	11.1	14	4	4	5	5	0	11.12	3.18	3.18
George Pearce	L	1	1	.500	3.48	0	5	0	0	10.1	7	3	4	7	4	0	6.10	2.61	3.48
Bruce Hitt	R	0	0	–	9.00	0	2	0	0	4	7	1	1	6	4	0	15.75	2.25	2.25
Tim Murchison	L	0	0	–	0.00	0	1	0	0	1	0	2	2	0	0	0	0.00	18.00	18.00
TEAM TOTAL		82	70	.539	3.03	10	294	154	66	1392	1257	421	502	568	469	16	8.13	2.72	3.25

CARDINAL RBI CHAMPIONS

1920	Rogers Hornsby, 94	1938	Joe Medwick, 122
1921	Rogers Hornsby, 126	1940	Johnny Mize, 137
1922	Rogers Hornsby, 152	1946	Enos Slaughter, 130
1925	Rogers Hornsby, 143	1948	Stan Musial, 131
1926	Jim Bottomley, 120	1956	Stan Musial, 109
1927	Jim Bottomley, 136	1964	Ken Boyer, 119
1936	Joe Medwick, 138	1967	Orlando Cepeda, 111
1937	Joe Medwick, 154	1971	Joe Torre, 137

MANAGER	W	L	PCT
Jack Hendricks	51	78	.395

POS	Player	B	G	AB	H	2B	3B	HR	HR %	R	RBI	BB	SO	SB	Pinch Hit AB	Pinch Hit H	BA	SA
REGULARS																		
1B	Gene Paulette	R	125	461	126	15	3	0	0.0	33	52	27	16	11	3	0	.273	.319
2B	Bob Fisher	R	63	246	78	11	3	2	0.8	36	20	15	11	7	0	0	.317	.411
SS	Rogers Hornsby	R	115	416	117	19	11	5	1.2	51	60	40	43	8	4	2	.281	.416
3B	Doug Baird	R	82	316	78	12	8	2	0.6	41	25	42	25	0	0		.247	.354
RF	Walt Cruise	L	70	240	65	5	4	6	2.5	34	39	30	26	2	5	0	.271	.400
CF	Cliff Heathcote	L	88	348	90	12	3	4	1.1	37	32	20	40	12	0	0	.259	.345
LF	Austin McHenry	R	80	272	71	12	6	1	0.4	32	29	21	24	8	0	0	.261	.360
C	Mike Gonzalez	R	117	349	88	13	4	3	0.9	33	20	39	30	14	8	1	.252	.338
SUBSTITUTES																		
UT	Bruno Betzel	R	76	230	51	6	7	0	0.0	18	13	12	16	8	6	2	.222	.309
1B	Charlie Grimm	L	50	141	31	7	0	0	0.0	11	12	6	15	2	5	0	.220	.270
2S	Bobby Wallace	R	32	98	15	1	0	0	0.0	3	4	6	9	1	3	2	.153	.163
2B	Bert Niehoff	R	22	84	15	2	0	0	0.0	5	5	3	10	2	0	0	.179	.202
3B	Herman Bronkie	R	18	68	15	3	0	1	1.5	7	7	2	4	0	0	0	.221	.309
UT	Dutch Distel	R	8	17	3	1	1	0	0.0	3	1	2	3	0	1	0	.176	.353
SS	Bob Larmore	R	4	7	2	0	0	0	0.0	0	1	0	2	0	2	2	.286	.286
1B	Tony Brottem	R	2	4	0	0	0	0	0.0	0	0	1	0	0	1	0	.000	.000
OF	Jack Smith	L	42	166	35	2	1	0	0.0	24	4	7	21	5	0	0	.211	.235
OF	George Anderson	L	35	132	39	4	5	0	0.0	20	6	15	7	0	0	0	.295	.402
O2	Red Smyth	L	40	113	24	1	2	0	0.0	19	4	16	11	3	1	0	.212	.257
OF	Johnny Beall	L	19	49	11	1	0	0	0.0	2	6	3	6	0	5	2	.224	.245
O2	Marty Kavanagh	R	12	44	8	1	0	1	2.3	6	8	3	1	1	0	0	.182	.273
OF	Wally Mattick	R	8	14	2	0	0	0	0.0	0	1	2	3	0	5	1	.143	.143
OF	Dick Wheeler		3	6	0	0	0	0	0.0	0	0	0	3	0	1	0	.000	.000
OF	Ted Menze	R	1	3	0	0	0	0	0.0	0	0	0	2	0	0	0	.000	.000
C	Frank Snyder	R	39	112	28	7	1	0	0.0	5	10	6	13	4	9	2	.250	.330
C	John Brock	R	27	52	11	2	0	0	0.0	9	4	3	10	5	7	2	.212	.250
PITCHERS																		
P	Gene Packard	L	36	69	12	2	1	0	0.0	3	6	2	9	0	5	1	.174	.232
P	Bill Doak	R	31	66	12	3	2	0	0.0	5	1	3	21	0	0	0	.182	.288
P	Red Ames	B	27	64	10	1	0	0	0.0	1	4	7	14	1	0	0	.156	.172
P	Bill Sherdel	L	35	62	15	3	1	1	1.6	7	8	2	10	0	0	0	.242	.371
P	Lee Meadows	L	30	55	7	1	1	0	0.0	0	5	2	17	0	0	0	.127	.182
P	Jakie May	R	29	45	3	0	0	1	2.2	2	3	8	17	0	0	0	.067	.133
P	Oscar Tuero	R	12	12	3	0	0	0	0.0	2	0	1	0	0	0	0	.250	.250
P	Oscar Horstmann	R	9	4	0	0	0	0	0.0	0	0	1	2	0	0	0	.000	.000
P	Adam Johnson	R	6	4	1	0	0	0	0.0	0	0	0	2	0	0	0	.250	.250
P	Earl Howard	R	1	0	0	0	0	0	—	0	1	0	0	0	0	0	—	—
	TEAM TOTAL			4369	1066	147	64	27	0.6	454	388	329	461	119	71	17	.244	.325

INDIVIDUAL FIELDING

POS	Player	T	G	PO	A	E	DP	TC/G	FA
1B	G. Paulette	R	97	1093	59	20	64	12.1	.983
	C. Grimm	L	42	385	14	12	24	9.8	.971
	F. Snyder	R	3	23	3	0	1	8.7	1.000
	T. Brottem	R	2	11	3	0	0	7.0	1.000
	M. Gonzalez	R	2	4	0	0	1	2.0	1.000
	G. Packard	L	1	1	0	0	0	1.0	1.000
2B	B. Fisher	R	63	147	232	8	34	6.1	.979
	B. Niehoff	R	22	54	65	3	11	5.5	.975
	B. Wallace	R	17	40	54	4	8	5.8	.959
	B. Betzel	R	10	26	37	7	6	7.0	.900
	G. Paulette	R	7	24	23	1	1	6.9	.979
	R. Smyth	R	11	17	27	3	2	4.3	.936
	M. Kavanagh	R	4	11	12	2	0	6.3	.920
	D. Distel	R	5	5	13	2	1	4.0	.900
SS	R. Hornsby	R	109	208	434	46	55	6.3	.933
	D. Baird	R	1	0	0	0	0	0.0	.000
	G. Paulette	R	12	40	42	5	10	7.3	.943
	B. Wallace	R	12	20	27	5	5	4.3	.904
	B. Larmore	R	2	3	4	2	0	4.5	.778
	D. Distel	R	2	0	1	2	0	1.5	.333
3B	D. Baird	R	81	99	219	11	12	4.1	.967
	B. Betzel	R	34	32	64	9	3	3.1	.914
	H. Bronkie	R	18	18	43	1	2	3.4	.984
	B. Wallace	R	1	1	2	1	0	4.0	.750
	G. Paulette	R	2	0	2	0	0	1.0	1.000
	C. Grimm	L	1	0	1	0	0	1.0	1.000
OF	C. Heathcote	L	88	222	6	16	0	2.8	.934
	A. McHenry	R	80	145	14	8	3	2.1	.952
	W. Cruise	R	65	103	4	4	0	1.7	.964
	J. Smith	L	42	87	9	6	6	2.4	.941
	G. Anderson	R	35	62	3	3	1	1.9	.956
	B. Betzel	R	21	42	2	1	1	2.1	.978
	R. Smyth	R	25	39	4	2	0	1.8	.956
	J. Beall	R	18	26	2	0	1	1.6	1.000
	J. Brock	R	1	0	0	0	0	0.0	.000
	D. Wheeler	R	2	0	0	0	0	0.0	.000
	G. Paulette	R	6	14	2	0	2	2.7	1.000
	M. Kavanagh	R	8	14	0	0	0	1.8	1.000
	C. Grimm	L	2	4	2	0	0	3.0	1.000
	W. Mattick	R	3	5	1	0	0	2.0	1.000
	M. Gonzalez	R	5	4	0	0	0	0.8	1.000
	R. Hornsby	R	2	3	0	0	0	1.5	1.000
	D. Baird	R	1	2	0	0	0	2.0	1.000
	D. Distel	R	1	1	0	0	0	1.0	1.000
	T. Menze	R	1	1	0	0	0	1.0	1.000
C	M. Gonzalez	R	100	362	124	11	17	5.0	.978
	F. Snyder	R	27	104	37	6	3	5.4	.959
	J. Brock	R	18	38	20	3	1	3.4	.951

And the roller coaster swung back down. The war-shortened season ended on Labor Day with the Cards back in the cellar. They trailed from the start, not escaping last place from late June until the mercifully early end of the season. Only two Cardinal batters, Hornsby and Gene Paulette, were able to drive in as many as forty runs. The Cards were last again in runs, and as a result Red Ames and Bill Doak could only manage records of 9–14 and 9–15 despite ERAs of 2.31 and 2.43 respectively. It was the eighth time in their first twenty-seven years in the National League that St. Louis had finished in last place or tied for it. They have not done it since.

TEAM STATISTICS

	W	L	PCT	GB	R	OR	2B	3B	Batting HR	BA	SA	SB	E	Fielding DP	FA	CG	BB	Pitching SO	ShO	SV	ERA
CHI	84	45	.651		538	391	164	54	20	.265	.342	159	188	91	.966	92	296	472	23	6	2.18
NY	71	53	.573	10.5	480	423	150	53	13	.260	.330	130	152	78	.970	74	228	330	18	10	2.64
CIN	68	60	.531	15.5	538	496	165	84	15	.278	.366	128	192	127	.964	84	381	321	14	5	3.00
PIT	65	60	.520	17	466	411	107	72	15	.248	.321	108	179	108	.966	85	299	367	10	7	2.48
BKN	57	69	.452	25.5	360	459	121	62	10	.250	.315	113	193	74	.963	85	320	395	17	0	2.81
PHI	55	68	.447	26	430	507	158	28	25	.244	.313	97	211	91	.961	78	369	312	10	6	3.15
BOS	53	71	.427	28.5	424	469	107	59	13	.244	.307	83	184	89	.965	96	277	340	13	0	2.90
STL	51	78	.395	33	454	534	147	64	27	.244	.325	119	220	116	.962	72	352	361	3	5	2.96
LEAGUE TOTAL					3690	3690	1119	476	138	.254	.328	1029	1519	774	.965	666	2522	2898	108	39	2.76

INDIVIDUAL PITCHING

PITCHER	T	W	L	PCT	ERA	SV	G	GS	CG	IP	H	BB	SO	R	ER	ShO	H/9	BB/9	SO/9
Bill Doak	R	9	15	.375	2.43	1	31	23	16	211	191	60	74	76	57	1	8.15	2.56	3.16
Red Ames	R	9	14	.391	2.31	1	27	25	17	206.2	192	52	68	75	53	0	8.36	2.26	2.96
Gene Packard	L	12	12	.500	3.50	2	30	23	10	182.1	184	33	46	84	71	1	9.08	1.63	2.27
Bill Sherdel	L	6	12	.333	2.71	0	35	17	9	182.1	174	49	40	78	55	1	8.59	2.42	1.97
Lee Meadows	R	8	14	.364	3.59	1	30	22	12	165.1	176	56	49	91	66	0	9.58	3.05	2.67
Jakie May	L	5	6	.455	3.83	0	29	16	6	152.2	149	69	61	83	65	0	8.78	4.07	3.60
Oscar Tuero	R	1	2	.333	1.02	0	11	3	2	44.1	32	10	13	12	5	0	6.50	2.03	2.64
Oscar Horstmann	R	0	2	.000	5.48	0	9	2	0	23	29	14	6	18	14	0	11.35	5.48	2.35
Adam Johnson	R	1	1	.500	2.74	0	6	1	0	23	20	7	4	10	7	0	7.83	2.74	1.57
Earl Howard	R	0	0	–	0.00	0	1	0	0	2	0	2	0	0	0	0	0.00	9.00	0.00
Gene Paulette	R	0	0	–	0.00	0	1	0	0	.1	1	0	0	0	0	0	27.00	0.00	0.00
TEAM TOTAL		51	78	.395	2.96	5	210	132	72	1193	1148	352	361	527	393	3	8.66	2.66	2.72

MANAGER	W	L	PCT
Branch Rickey	54	83	.394

POS	Player	B	G	AB	H	2B	3B	HR	HR%	R	RBI	BB	SO	SB	Pinch Hit AB	Pinch Hit H	BA	SA
REGULARS																		
1B	Dots Miller	R	101	346	80	10	4	1	0.3	38	24	13	23	6	5	2	.231	.292
2B	Milt Stock	R	135	492	151	16	4	0	0.0	56	52	49	21	17	0	0	.307	.356
SS	Doc Lavan	R	100	356	86	12	2	1	0.3	25	25	11	30	4	1	0	.242	.295
3B	Rogers Hornsby	R	138	512	163	15	9	8	1.6	68	71	48	41	17	0	0	.318	.430
RF	Jack Smith	L	119	408	91	16	3	0	0.0	47	15	26	29	30	0	0	.223	.277
CF	Cliff Heathcote	L	114	401	112	13	4	1	0.2	53	29	20	41	26	9	3	.279	.339
LF	Austin McHenry	R	110	371	106	19	11	1	0.3	41	47	19	57	7	4	0	.286	.404
C	Verne Clemons	R	88	239	63	13	2	2	0.8	14	22	26	13	4	10	5	.264	.360
SUBSTITUTES																		
1B	Gene Paulette	R	43	144	31	6	0	0	0.0	11	11	9	6	4	3	0	.215	.257
1B	Fritz Mollwitz	R	25	83	19	3	0	0	0.0	7	5	7	3	2	0	0	.229	.265
3B	Doug Baird	R	16	33	7	0	1	0	0.0	4	4	2	3	2	4	1	.212	.273
1B	Roy Leslie	R	12	24	5	1	0	0	0.0	2	4	4	3	0	1	0	.208	.250
UT	Hal Janvrin	R	7	14	3	1	0	0	0.0	1	1	2	2	0	2	0	.214	.286
2B	Bob Fisher	R	3	11	3	1	0	0	0.0	0	1	0	2	0	0	0	.273	.364
12	Sam Fisburn	R	9	6	2	1	0	0	0.0	0	2	0	0	1	1	1	.333	.500
SS	Wally Kimmick	R	2	1	0	0	0	0	0.0	1	0	1	0	1	1	0	.000	.000
OF	Burt Shotton	L	85	270	77	13	5	1	0.4	35	20	22	25	17	14	1	.285	.381
OF	Joe Schultz	R	88	229	58	9	1	2	0.9	24	21	11	7	4	31	8	.253	.328
O1	Walt Cruise	L	9	21	2	1	0	0	0.0	0	0	1	6	0	3	1	.095	.143
C	Frank Snyder	R	50	154	28	4	2	0	0.0	7	14	5	13	2	1	0	.182	.234
C	Pickles Dillhoefer	R	45	108	23	3	2	0	0.0	11	12	8	6	5	1	1	.213	.278
PH	Mike Pasquriello	R	1	1	0	0	0	0	0.0	0	0	0	1	0	1	0	.000	.000
PITCHERS																		
P	Bill Doak	R	31	64	7	0	0	0	0.0	2	2	2	20	0	0	0	.109	.109
P	Marv Goodwin	R	34	60	12	0	1	0	0.0	7	2	6	6	0	0	0	.200	.233
P	Bill Sherdel	L	40	48	13	2	0	0	0.0	1	5	1	8	0	2	2	.271	.313
P	Oscar Tuero	R	45	39	8	1	0	0	0.0	4	6	4	9	0	0	0	.205	.231
P	Jakie May	R	28	37	6	0	0	0	0.0	0	0	1	11	0	0	0	.162	.162
P	Lee Meadows	L	22	29	3	1	0	0	0.0	2	0	1	8	0	0	0	.103	.138
P	Elmer Jacobs	R	17	23	8	2	1	0	0.0	0	0	1	4	0	0	0	.348	.522
P	Frank Woodward	R	17	21	1	0	0	0	0.0	0	0	1	5	0	0	0	.048	.048
P	Ferdie Schupp	R	10	20	1	0	0	1	5.0	2	2	3	7	0	0	0	.050	.200
P	Red Ames	B	23	18	4	0	0	0	0.0	0	1	0	7	0	0	0	.222	.222
P	Bill Bolden	R	3	3	1	0	0	0	0.0	0	0	0	0	0	0	0	.333	.333
P	Oscar Horstmann	R	6	2	1	0	0	0	0.0	0	0	0	1	0	0	0	.500	.500
P	Willis Koenigsmark	R	1	0	0	0	0	0	–	0	0	0	0	0	0	0	–	–
P	Roy Parker	R	2	0	0	0	0	0	–	0	0	0	0	0	0	0	–	–
P	Art Reinhart	L	1	0	0	0	0	0	–	0	0	0	0	0	0	0	–	–
	TEAM TOTAL			4588	1175	163	52	18	0.4	463	398	304	418	148	94	25	.256	.326

INDIVIDUAL FIELDING

POS	Player	T	G	PO	A	E	DP	TC/G	FA
1B	D. Miller	R	68	687	40	14	34	10.9	.981
	G. Paulette	R	35	392	24	4	23	12.0	.990
	F. Mollwitz	R	25	299	15	2	20	12.6	.994
	R. Leslie	R	9	62	4	3	5	7.7	.957
	R. Hornsby	R	5	48	0	0	3	9.6	1.000
	C. Heathcote	L	2	24	0	0	0	12.0	1.000
	F. Snyder	R	1	12	0	0	0	12.0	1.000
	S. Fisburn	R	1	8	0	0	0	8.0	1.000
	W. Cruise	R	2	6	1	0	0	3.5	1.000
2B	M. Stock	R	77	168	254	15	32	5.7	.966
	D. Miller	R	28	69	87	8	13	5.9	.951
	R. Hornsby	R	25	46	101	5	13	6.1	.967
	J. Schultz	R	5	12	9	4	1	5.0	.840
	B. Fisher	R	3	9	9	2	2	6.7	.900
	H. Janvrin	R	2	7	2	0	0	4.5	1.000
	S. Fisburn	R	1	3	0	0	1	3.0	1.000
	D. Baird	R	1	0	1	0	0	1.0	1.000
SS	D. Lavan	R	99	207	352	43	49	6.1	.929
	R. Hornsby	R	37	66	115	18	12	5.4	.910
	G. Paulette	R	3	6	11	2	3	6.3	.895
	H. Janvrin	R	1	1	2	1	0	4.0	.750
	W. Kimmick	R	1	0	1	0	0	1.0	1.000
3B	R. Hornsby	R	72	73	151	14	11	3.3	.941
	M. Stock	R	58	51	139	14	15	3.5	.931
	D. Baird	R	8	6	11	5	0	2.8	.773
	H. Janvrin	R	1	0	2	0	0	2.0	1.000

POS	Player	T	G	PO	A	E	DP	TC/G	FA
OF	C. Heathcote	L	101	225	10	8	3	2.4	.967
	J. Smith	L	111	197	19	9	6	2.0	.960
	A. McHenry	R	103	183	20	3	3	2.0	.985
	B. Shotton	R	67	104	10	9	2	1.8	.927
	J. Schultz	R	49	75	6	0	1	1.7	1.000
	D. Baird	R	1	0	0	0	0	0.0	.000
	W. Cruise	R	5	5	0	1	0	1.2	.833
C	V. Clemons	R	75	289	89	7	8	5.1	.982
	F. Snyder	R	48	149	80	4	4	4.9	.983
	P. Dillhoefer	R	39	122	35	5	6	4.2	.969

Branch Rickey took over as field manager of the club in '19, largely, he would later claim, in an effort to save the financially shaky club a manager's salary. He was not a notable success as a manager, infuriating his players by talking over their heads and boring them with lectures on strategy, often diagramming plays in football-style chalk talks. Fortunately for the Cardinals, Rickey was a better judge of talent than manager of it, and he had inherited a Hornsby to write on the lineup card every day. Hornsby played in every game, shifting among the four infield positions before being set for good as a second baseman in 1920. His .318 average was second in the league to Edd Roush's .321, and he was second in hits, third in RBIs, and fourth in slugging and home runs.

TEAM STATISTICS

	W	L	PCT	GB	R	OR	2B	3B	HR	BA	SA	SB	E	DP	FA	CG	BB	SO	ShO	SV	ERA
							Batting						Fielding					Pitching			
IN	96	44	.686		578	402	135	84	19	.263	.342	143	151	98	.974	89	298	407	23	9	2.23
NY	87	53	.621	9	605	470	204	64	40	.269	.366	157	216	96	.964	72	305	340	11	11	2.70
CHI	75	65	.536	21	454	407	166	58	21	.256	.332	150	186	87	.969	80	294	495	21	5	2.21
PIT	71	68	.511	24.5	472	466	130	82	17	.249	.325	196	166	89	.970	92	263	391	16	4	2.88
BKN	69	71	.493	27	525	513	167	66	25	.263	.340	112	218	84	.963	98	292	476	12	1	2.73
BOS	57	82	.410	38.5	465	563	142	62	24	.253	.324	145	204	111	.966	79	337	374	5	7	3.17
STL	54	83	.394	40.5	463	552	163	52	18	.256	.326	148	217	112	.963	55	415	414	6	7	3.23
PHI	47	90	.343	47.5	510	699	208	50	42	.251	.342	114	219	112	.963	93	408	397	6	2	4.17
LEAGUE TOTAL					4072	4072	1315	518	206	.258	.337	1165	1577	789	.966	658	2612	3294	100	46	2.91

INDIVIDUAL PITCHING

PITCHER	T	W	L	PCT	ERA	SV	G	GS	CG	IP	H	BB	SO	R	ER	ShO	H/9	BB/9	SO/9
ill Doak	R	13	14	.481	3.11	0	31	29	13	202.2	182	55	69	87	70	3	8.08	2.44	3.06
Marv Goodwin	R	11	9	.550	2.51	0	33	17	7	179	163	33	48	66	50	0	8.20	1.66	2.41
scar Tuero	R	5	7	.417	3.20	4	45	15	4	154.2	137	42	45	71	55	0	7.97	2.44	2.62
ill Sherdel	L	5	9	.357	3.47	1	36	10	7	137.1	137	42	52	66	53	0	8.98	2.75	3.41
akie May	L	3	12	.200	3.22	0	28	19	8	125.2	99	87	58	64	45	1	7.09	6.23	4.15
ee Meadows	R	4	10*	.286	3.03	0	22	12	3	92	100	30	28	44	31	1	9.78	2.93	2.74
lmer Jacobs	R	2	6	.250	2.53	1	17	8	4	85.1	81	25	31	30	24	1	8.54	2.64	3.27
rank Woodward	R	4	5	.444	2.63	0	17	7	2	72	65	28	18	27	21	0	8.13	3.50	2.25
ed Ames	R	3	5	.375	4.89	1	23	7	1	70	88	25	19	44	38	0	11.31	3.21	2.44
erdie Schupp	L	4	4	.500	3.75	0	10	9	6	69.2	55	30	37	31	29	0	7.11	3.88	4.78
scar Horstmann	R	0	1	.000	3.00	0	6	2	0	15	14	12	5	6	5	0	8.40	7.20	3.00
ill Bolden	R	0	1	.000	5.25	0	3	1	0	12	17	4	4	7	7	0	12.75	3.00	3.00
oy Parker	R	0	0	–	31.50	0	2	0	0	2	6	1	0	7	7	0	27.00	4.50	0.00
EAM TOTAL		54	83	.394	3.22	7	273	136	55	1217.1	1144	414	414	550	435	6	8.46	3.06	3.06

MANAGER	W	L	PCT
Branch Rickey	75	79	.487

POS	Player	B	G	AB	H	2B	3B	HR	HR %	R	RBI	BB	SO	SB	Pinch Hit AB	Pinch Hit H	BA	SA
REGULARS																		
1B	Jack Fournier	L	141	530	162	33	14	3	0.6	77	61	42	42	26	3	2	.306	.438
2B	Rogers Hornsby	R	149	589	218	44	20	9	1.5	96	94	60	50	12	0	0	.370	.559
SS	Doc Lavan	R	142	516	149	21	10	1	0.2	52	63	19	38	11	4	1	.289	.374
3B	Milt Stock	R	155	639	204	28	6	0	0.0	85	76	40	27	15	0	0	.319	.382
RF	Joe Schultz	R	99	320	84	5	5	0	0.0	38	32	21	11	5	14	2	.263	.309
CF	Cliff Heathcote	L	133	489	139	18	8	3	0.6	55	56	25	31	21	3	0	.284	.372
LF	Austin McHenry	R	137	504	142	19	11	10	2.0	66	65	25	73	8	3	1	.282	.423
C	Verne Clemons	R	112	338	95	10	6	1	0.3	17	36	30	12	1	7	1	.281	.355
SUBSTITUTES																		
UT	Hal Janvrin	R	87	270	74	8	4	1	0.4	33	28	17	19	5	4	1	.274	.344
OF	Jack Smith	L	91	313	104	22	5	1	0.3	53	28	25	23	14	4	1	.332	.444
OF	Burt Shotton	L	62	180	41	5	0	1	0.6	28	12	18	14	5	7	1	.228	.272
UT	Mike Knode	L	42	65	15	1	1	0	0.0	11	12	5	6	0	18	4	.231	.277
OF	Heinie Mueller	L	4	22	7	1	0	0	0.0	0	1	2	4	1	0	0	.318	.364
OF	Ed Hock	L	1	0	0	0	0	0	–	0	0	0	0	0	0	0	–	–
C	Pickles Dillhoefer	R	76	224	59	8	3	0	0.0	26	13	13	7	2	2	0	.263	.326
C	Lew McCarty	R	5	7	2	0	0	0	0.0	0	0	5	0	0	1	1	.286	.286
C	George Gilham	R	1	3	0	0	0	0	0.0	0	0	0	1	0	0	0	.000	.000
C	Tim Greisenbeck	R	5	3	1	0	0	0	0.0	1	0	0	0	0	1	0	.333	.333
C	Bill Schindler	R	1	2	0	0	0	0	0.0	0	0	0	1	0	0	0	.000	.000
PITCHERS																		
P	Jesse Haines	R	48	108	19	5	0	1	0.9	6	2	3	26	0	1	0	.176	.250
P	Bill Doak	R	39	88	10	0	0	0	0.0	4	5	5	37	0	0	0	.114	.114
P	Ferdie Schupp	R	39	86	22	7	1	0	0.0	11	6	6	18	0	0	0	.256	.360
P	Bill Sherdel	L	49	63	14	1	1	1	1.6	4	2	3	5	0	6	1	.222	.317
P	Marv Goodwin	R	32	35	7	0	0	0	0.0	4	1	3	8	0	0	0	.200	.200
P	Lou North	R	26	31	7	1	0	0	0.0	2	3	1	7	0	2	0	.226	.258
P	Elmer Jacobs	R	23	26	5	1	0	0	0.0	2	2	1	7	0	0	0	.192	.231
P	Jakie May	R	16	22	5	0	1	0	0.0	2	0	3	8	0	0	0	.227	.318
P	Mike Kircher	R	9	11	3	0	0	0	0.0	2	1	0	3	0	0	0	.273	.273
P	George Lyons	R	7	7	1	0	0	0	0.0	0	1	1	2	0	0	0	.143	.143
P	Walt Schulz	R	2	2	0	0	0	0	0.0	0	0	0	2	0	0	0	.000	.000
P	Hal Kime	L	4	1	0	0	0	0	0.0	0	0	0	1	0	0	0	.000	.000
P	George Scott	R	2	1	0	0	0	0	0.0	0	0	0	1	0	0	0	.000	.000
P	Bob Glenn		2	0	0	0	0	0	–	0	0	0	0	0	0	0	–	–
P	Oscar Tuero	R	2	0	0	0	0	0	–	0	0	0	0	0	0	0	–	–
	TEAM TOTAL			5495	1589	238	96	32	0.6	675	600	373	484	126	80	16	.289	.385

INDIVIDUAL FIELDING

POS	Player	T	G	PO	A	E	DP	TC/G	FA	POS	Player	T	G	PO	A	E	DP	TC/G	FA
1B	J. Fournier	R	138	1373	88	25	100	10.8	.983	OF	C. Heathcote	L	129	296	26	12	3	2.6	.964
	H. Janvrin	R	25	218	13	3	18	9.4	.987		A. McHenry	R	133	297	21	16	1	2.5	.952
2B	R. Hornsby	R	149	343	524	34	76	6.0	.962		J. Schultz	R	80	147	7	9	3	2.0	.945
	H. Janvrin	R	6	10	33	1	5	7.3	.977		J. Smith	L	83	144	12	6	1	2.0	.963
	M. Knode	R	4	4	6	0	0	2.5	1.000		B. Shotton	R	51	85	9	4	2	1.9	.959
SS	D. Lavan	R	138	327	489	50	77	6.3	.942		H. Janvrin	R	20	37	1	2	0	2.0	.950
	H. Janvrin	R	27	42	46	7	10	3.5	.926		E. Hock	R	1	0	0	0	0	0.0	.000
	M. Knode	R	2	4	10	2	0	8.0	.875		M. Knode	R	9	13	1	0	0	1.9	.824
3B	M. Stock	R	155	158	300	30	23	3.1	.939		H. Mueller	L	4	12	0	0	0	3.0	1.000
	M. Knode	R	2	1	0	0	0	0.5	1.000	C	V. Clemons	R	103	408	111	12	11	5.2	.977
											P. Dillhoefer	R	73	291	72	18	6	5.2	.953
											L. McCarty	R	3	5	4	0	1	3.0	1.000
											G. Gilham	R	1	2	1	1	0	4.0	.750
											B. Schindler	R	1	3	0	0	0	3.0	1.000
											Greisenbeck	R	3	2	0	0	0	0.7	1.000

During 1920, Sam Breadon purchased a majority interest in the Cardinals. He arrived at an opportune moment; Rickey was in the process of setting up his revolutionary system of farm teams, and the club needed a source of ready cash. On the field, they climbed to within a game of first at midseason, and ended up in a tie for fourth with the Cubs. Hornsby won the first of his six straight batting and slugging titles as the club led the league in batting and slugging averages. Hornsby was not a one-man team; third baseman Milt Stock tied for second in the league with 211 hits, and leftfielder Austin McHenry rapped ten homers, good for fifth in the league.

Rickey's faith in his judgment of talent led him to give a rotation spot to a 26-year-old pitcher with only one previous major league appearance. He lost 20 in '20, but Jesse "Pop" Haines became a mainstay of the Cardinal staff, winning over 200 games in a nineteen-year career that landed him in Cooperstown.

TEAM STATISTICS

W	L	PCT	GB	R	OR	Batting 2B	3B	HR	BA	SA	SB	Fielding E	DP	FA	CG	Pitching BB	SO	ShO	SV	ERA
N 93	61	.604		660	528	205	99	28	.277	.367	70	226	118	.966	89	327	553	17	10	2.62
86	68	.558	7	682	543	210	76	46	.269	.363	131	210	137	.969	86	297	380	18	9	2.80
N 82	71	.536	10.5	639	569	169	76	18	.277	.349	158	200	125	.968	90	393	435	12	9	2.84
79	75	.513	14	530	552	162	90	16	.257	.332	181	186	119	.971	92	280	444	17	10	2.89
75	79	.487	18	619	635	223	67	34	.264	.354	115	225	112	.965	95	382	508	13	9	3.27
75	79	.487	18	675	682	238	96	32	.289	.385	126	256	136	.961	72	479	529	9	12	3.43
S 62	90	.408	30	523	670	168	86	23	.260	.339	88	239	125	.964	93	415	368	13	6	3.54
62	91	.405	30.5	565	714	229	54	64	.263	.364	100	232	135	.964	77	444	419	8	11	3.63
AGUE TOTAL				4893	4893	1604	644	261	.270	.357	969	1774	1007	.966	694	3017	3636	107	76	3.13

INDIVIDUAL PITCHING

CHER	T	W	L	PCT	ERA	SV	G	GS	CG	IP	H	BB	SO	R	ER	ShO	H/9	BB/9	SO/9
se Haines	R	13	20	.394	2.98	2	47	37	19	301.2	303	80	120	136	100	4	9.04	2.39	3.58
Doak	R	20	12	.625	2.53	1	39	37	20	270	256	80	90	94	76	5	8.53	2.67	3.00
die Schupp	L	16	13	.552	3.52	0	38	37	17	250.2	246	127	119	118	98	0	8.83	4.56	4.27
Sherdel	L	11	10	.524	3.28	6	43	7	4	170	183	40	74	72	62	0	9.69	2.12	3.92
v Goodwin	R	3	8	.273	4.95	1	32	12	3	116.1	153	28	23	79	64	0	11.84	2.17	1.78
North	R	3	2	.600	3.27	1	24	6	3	88	90	32	37	42	32	0	9.20	3.27	3.78
er Jacobs	R	4	8	.333	5.21	1	23	9	1	77.2	91	33	21	56	45	0	10.55	3.82	2.43
e May	L	1	4	.200	3.06	0	16	5	3	70.2	65	37	33	38	24	0	8.28	4.71	4.20
e Kircher	L	2	1	.667	5.40	0	9	3	1	36.2	50	5	5	23	22	0	12.27	1.23	1.23
rge Lyons	R	2	1	.667	3.09	0	7	2	1	23.1	21	9	5	8	8	0	8.10	3.47	1.93
Kime	L	0	0	–	2.57	0	4	0	0	7	9	2	1	4	2	0	11.57	2.57	1.29
t Schulz	R	0	0	–	6.00	0	2	0	0	6	10	2	0	5	4	0	15.00	3.00	0.00
rge Scott	R	0	0	–	4.50	0	2	0	0	6	4	3	1	3	3	0	6.00	4.50	1.50
Glenn		0	0	–	0.00	0	2	0	0	2	2	0	0	0	0	0	9.00	0.00	0.00
ar Tuero	R	0	0	–	54.00	0	2	0	0	.2	5	1	0	4	4	0	67.50	13.50	0.00
M TOTAL		75	79	.487	3.43	12	290	155	72	1426.2	1488	479	529	682	544	9	9.39	3.02	3.34

MANAGER	W	L	PCT
Branch Rickey	87	66	.569

POS	Player	B	G	AB	H	2B	3B	HR	HR %	R	RBI	BB	SO	SB	Pinch Hit AB	Pinch Hit H	BA	SA
REGULARS																		
1B	Jack Fournier	L	149	574	197	27	9	16	2.8	103	86	56	48	20	0	0	.343	.505
2B	Rogers Hornsby	R	154	592	235	44	18	21	3.5	131	126	60	48	13	0	0	.397	.639
SS	Doc Lavan	R	150	560	145	23	11	2	0.4	58	82	23	30	7	0	0	.259	.350
3B	Milt Stock	R	149	587	180	27	6	3	0.5	96	84	48	26	11	0	0	.307	.388
RF	Jack Smith	L	116	411	135	22	9	7	1.7	86	33	21	24	11	4	0	.328	.477
CF	Les Mann	R	97	256	84	12	7	7	2.7	57	30	23	28	5	5	1	.328	.512
LF	Austin McHenry	R	152	574	201	37	8	17	3.0	92	102	38	48	10	0	0	.350	.531
C	Verne Clemons	R	117	341	109	16	2	2	0.6	29	48	33	17	0	8	2	.320	.396
SUBSTITUTES																		
2B	Specs Toporcer	L	22	53	14	1	0	0	0.0	4	2	3	4	1	6	1	.264	.283
2B	Hal Janvrin	R	18	32	9	1	0	0	0.0	5	5	1	0	1	7	1	.281	.313
1B	Herb Hunter	L	9	2	0	0	0	0	0.0	3	0	1	0	0	1	0	.000	.000
SS	Reuben Ewing	R	3	1	0	0	0	0	0.0	0	0	0	1	0	1	0	.000	.000
1P	Mike Kircher	R	3	0	0	0	0	0	–	0	0	0	0	0	0	0	–	–
OF	Joe Schultz	R	92	275	85	20	3	6	2.2	37	45	15	11	4	18	6	.309	.469
OF	Heinie Mueller	L	55	176	62	10	6	1	0.6	25	34	11	22	2	1	0	.352	.494
OF	Cliff Heathcote	L	62	156	38	6	2	0	0.0	18	9	10	9	7	7	1	.244	.308
OF	Burt Shotton	L	38	48	12	1	1	1	2.1	9	7	7	4	0	22	7	.250	.375
OF	Howie Jones	L	3	2	0	0	0	0	0.0	0	0	0	1	0	2	0	.000	.000
C	Pickles Dillhoefer	R	76	162	39	4	4	0	0.0	19	15	11	7	2	4	0	.241	.315
C	Eddie Ainsmith	R	27	62	18	0	1	0	0.0	5	5	3	4	0	3	0	.290	.323
C	Charlie Niebergall	R	5	6	1	0	0	0	0.0	1	0	0	0	0	2	1	.167	.167
PH	George Gilham	R	1	1	0	0	0	0	0.0	0	0	0	0	0	1	0	.000	.000
PH	Walt Irwin	R	4	1	0	0	0	0	0.0	0	0	0	1	0	1	0	.000	.000
PH	Lew McCarty	R	1	1	0	0	0	0	0.0	0	0	0	1	0	1	0	.000	.000
PITCHERS																		
P	Jesse Haines	R	39	94	17	1	0	0	0.0	9	6	1	23	0	2	0	.181	.191
P	Bill Doak	R	32	70	10	2	1	0	0.0	4	1	0	28	0	0	0	.143	.200
P	Bill Pertica	R	38	70	10	2	0	0	0.0	5	2	2	16	0	0	0	.143	.171
P	Roy Walker	R	38	54	11	2	0	0	0.0	2	2	2	20	0	0	0	.204	.241
P	Bill Sherdel	L	39	44	5	0	0	0	0.0	2	4	4	7	0	0	0	.114	.114
P	Jeff Pfeffer	R	18	29	4	1	0	0	0.0	2	1	2	7	0	0	0	.138	.172
P	Bill Bailey	L	19	22	2	0	0	0	0.0	0	0	1	5	0	0	0	.091	.091
P	Lou North	R	40	19	3	0	0	0	0.0	2	1	1	4	0	0	0	.158	.158
P	Ferdie Schupp	R	9	14	4	0	0	0	0.0	2	3	0	3	0	0	0	.286	.286
P	Tink Riviere	R	18	8	3	1	0	0	0.0	2	0	3	3	0	0	0	.375	.500
P	Marv Goodwin	R	14	6	0	0	0	0	0.0	0	0	1	2	0	0	0	.000	.000
P	Jakie May	R	5	6	2	0	0	0	0.0	0	0	1	0	0	0	0	.333	.333
TEAM TOTAL				5309	1635	260	88	83	1.6	809	733	382	452	94	96	20	.308	.437

INDIVIDUAL FIELDING

POS	Player	T	G	PO	A	E	DP	TC/G	FA	POS	Player	T	G	PO	A	E	DP	TC/G	FA
1B	J. Fournier	R	149	1416	73	19	91	10.1	.987	OF	A. McHenry	R	152	371	13	14	3	2.6	.965
	M. Kircher	L	9	58	3	2	5	7.0	.968		J. Smith	L	103	179	11	9	3	1.9	.955
	J. Schultz	R	2	14	0	0	0	7.0	1.000		L. Mann	R	79	174	11	6	2	2.4	.969
	E. Ainsmith	R	1	8	0	0	0	8.0	1.000		J. Schultz	R	67	120	7	3	4	1.9	.977
	R. Hornsby	R	1	8	0	0	0	8.0	1.000		H. Mueller	L	54	117	5	3	1	2.3	.976
	H. Hunter	R	1	3	0	0	1	3.0	1.000		C. Heathcote	L	51	83	5	7	0	1.9	.926
	B. Sherdel	L	1	2	0	0	0	2.0	1.000		H. Jones	L	1	0	0	0	0	0.0	.000
											B. Shotton	R	11	21	2	1	1	2.2	.958
2B	R. Hornsby	R	142	305	477	25	59	5.7	.969		R. Hornsby	R	6	14	0	0	0	2.3	1.000
	S. Toporcer	R	12	24	37	4	6	5.4	.938	C	V. Clemons	R	109	357	101	7	12	4.3	.985
	H. Janvrin	R	1	1	5	0	0	6.0	1.000		P. Dillhoefer	R	69	170	52	11	0	3.4	.953
SS	D. Lavan	R	150	382	540	49	88	6.5	.950		E. Ainsmith	R	23	70	17	4	2	4.0	.956
	R. Hornsby	R	3	11	8	1	3	6.7	.950		C. Niebergall	R	3	2	1	0	0	1.0	1.000
	S. Toporcer	R	2	1	5	0	0	3.0	1.000										
	R. Ewing	R	1	0	1	0	0	1.0	1.000										
3B	M. Stock	R	149	148	243	25	21	2.8	.940										
	J. Schultz	R	3	3	7	3	0	4.3	.769										
	R. Hornsby	R	3	2	2	1	1	1.7	.800										

The name on everyone's lips in the baseball world was Ruth. The Babe had hit 54 homers in 1920—35 more than his nearest competitor. Fans responded to the excitement of high scoring, and so the ball may have been "juiced up" a bit to enliven the game. Whatever the cause, the batting average for the National League was up from .270 to .289 in 1921, with the third-place Cardinals batting .308 as a team. They had eight .300 hitters with at least 250 at bats, and placed three men, Hornsby, McHenry, and Jack Fournier, in the top five in both batting and slugging. Hornsby just missed his first Triple Crown; he led in batting and RBIs, but finished second in homers with 21 behind New York's George Kelly, who hit 23. The Cardinals finished just seven games out of first, thanks to a late season charge that saw them go 28–6 from mid-August to mid-September. Their final record of 87–66 was their best yet.

TEAM STATISTICS

W	L	PCT	GB	R	OR	2B	3B	HR	BA	SA	SB	E	DP	FA	CG	BB	SO	ShO	SV	ERA
								Batting					Fielding				Pitching			
94	59	.614		840	637	237	93	75	.298	.421	137	187	155	.971	71	295	357	9	18	3.55
90	63	.588	4	692	595	231	104	37	.285	.387	134	172	129	.973	88	322	500	10	10	3.17
87	66	.569	7	809	681	260	88	83	.308	.437	94	219	130	.965	71	399	464	10	16	3.62
79	74	.516	15	721	697	209	100	61	.290	.400	94	199	122	.969	74	420	382	11	12	3.90
77	75	.507	16.5	667	681	209	85	59	.280	.386	91	232	142	.964	82	361	471	8	12	3.70
70	83	.458	24	618	649	221	94	20	.278	.370	117	193	139	.969	83	305	408	7	9	3.46
64	89	.418	30	668	773	234	56	37	.292	.378	70	166	129	.974	73	409	441	7	7	4.39
51	103	.331	43.5	617	919	238	50	88	.284	.397	66	295	127	.955	82	371	333	5	8	4.48
LEAGUE TOTAL				5632	5632	1839	670	460	.289	.397	803	1663	1073	.967	624	2882	3356	67	92	3.78

INDIVIDUAL PITCHING

PITCHER	T	W	L	PCT	ERA	SV	G	GS	CG	IP	H	BB	SO	R	ER	ShO	H/9	BB/9	SO/9
se Haines	R	18	12	.600	3.50	0	37	29	14	244.1	261	56	84	112	95	3	9.61	2.06	3.09
Doak	R	15	6	.714	2.59	1	32	28	13	208.2	224	37	83	85	60	1	9.66	1.60	3.58
Pertica	R	14	10	.583	3.37	2	38	31	15	208.1	212	70	67	104	78	2	9.16	3.02	2.89
Walker	R	11	12	.478	4.22	3	38	24	11	170.2	194	53	52	93	80	0	10.23	2.79	2.74
Sherdel	L	9	8	.529	3.18	1	38	8	5	144.1	137	38	57	62	51	1	8.54	2.37	3.55
Pfeffer	R	9	3	.750	4.29	0	18	13	7	98.2	115	28	22	51	47	1	10.49	2.55	2.01
North	R	4	4	.500	3.54	7	40	0	0	86.1	81	32	28	39	34	0	8.44	3.34	2.92
Bailey	L	2	5	.286	4.26	0	19	6	3	74	95	22	20	41	35	1	11.55	2.68	2.43
Riviere	R	1	0	1.000	6.10	0	18	2	0	38.1	45	20	15	30	26	0	10.57	4.70	3.52
die Schupp	L	2	0	1.000	4.10	1	9	4	1	37.1	42	21	22	26	17	0	10.13	5.06	5.30
v Goodwin	R	1	2	.333	3.72	1	14	4	1	36.1	47	9	7	21	15	0	11.64	2.23	1.73
e May	L	1	3	.250	4.71	0	5	5	1	21	29	12	5	14	11	0	12.43	5.14	2.14
e Kircher	L	0	1	.000	8.10	0	3	3	0	3.1	4	1	2	3	3	0	10.80	2.70	5.40
M TOTAL		87	66	.569	3.62	16	309	154	71	1371.2	1486	399	464	681	552	9	9.75	2.62	3.04

MANAGER	W	L	PCT
Branch Rickey	85	69	.552

POS	Player	B	G	AB	H	2B	3B	HR	HR %	R	RBI	BB	SO	SB	Pinch Hit AB	Pinch Hit H	BA	SA
REGULARS																		
1B	Jack Fournier	L	128	404	119	23	9	10	2.5	64	61	40	21	6	12	5	.295	.470
2B	Rogers Hornsby	R	154	623	**250**	46	14	42	6.7	141	152	65	50	17	0	0	**.401**	**.722**
SS	Specs Toporcer	L	116	352	114	25	6	3	0.9	56	36	24	18	2	15	6	.324	.455
3B	Milt Stock	R	151	581	177	33	9	5	0.9	85	79	42	29	7	1	0	.305	.418
RF	Max Flack	L	66	267	78	12	1	2	0.7	46	21	31	11	3	0	0	.292	.367
CF	Jack Smith	L	143	510	158	23	12	8	1.6	117	46	50	30	18	4	1	.310	.449
LF	Joe Schultz	R	112	344	108	13	4	2	0.6	50	64	19	10	3	22	8	.314	.392
C	Eddie Ainsmith	R	119	379	111	14	4	13	3.4	46	59	28	43	2	2	1	.293	.454
SUBSTITUTES																		
SS	Doc Lavan	R	89	264	60	8	1	0	0.0	24	27	13	10	3	1	0	.227	.265
1B	Jim Bottomley	L	37	151	49	8	5	5	3.3	29	35	6	13	3	3	1	.325	.543
1O	Del Gainor	R	43	97	26	7	4	2	2.1	19	23	14	6	0	9	1	.268	.485
S3	Howard Freigau	R	3	1	0	0	0	0	0.0	0	0	0	0	0	0	0	.000	.000
OF	Austin McHenry	R	64	238	72	18	3	5	2.1	31	43	14	27	2	2	1	.303	.466
OF	Heinie Mueller	L	61	159	43	7	2	3	1.9	20	26	14	18	2	17	5	.270	.396
OF	Les Mann	R	84	147	51	14	1	2	1.4	42	20	16	12	0	2	0	.347	.497
OF	Ray Blades	R	37	130	39	2	4	3	2.3	27	21	25	21	3	0	0	.300	.446
OF	Cliff Heathcote	L	34	98	24	5	2	0	0.0	11	14	9	4	0	0	0	.245	.337
OF	Burt Shotton	L	34	30	6	1	0	0	0.0	5	2	4	6	0	26	5	.200	.233
C	Verne Clemons	R	71	160	41	4	0	0	0.0	9	15	18	5	1	7	1	.256	.281
C	Harry McCurdy	L	13	27	8	2	2	0	0.0	3	5	1	1	0	3	0	.296	.519
C	Ernie Vick	R	3	6	2	2	0	0	0.0	1	0	0	0	0	0	0	.333	.667
PITCHERS																		
P	Jeff Pfeffer	R	45	98	24	6	0	0	0.0	3	12	4	17	0	1	0	.245	.306
P	Bill Sherdel	L	48	88	17	2	1	1	1.1	11	10	2	10	0	0	0	.193	.273
P	Jesse Haines	R	30	72	12	1	1	0	0.0	6	3	1	16	1	0	0	.167	.208
P	Bill Doak	R	37	54	7	0	0	0	0.0	2	2	1	20	0	0	0	.130	.130
P	Lou North	R	53	47	11	0	1	1	2.1	5	5	1	3	0	0	0	.234	.340
P	Clyde Barfoot	R	42	34	12	1	1	0	0.0	3	4	4	3	0	0	0	.353	.441
P	Bill Pertica	R	35	33	6	1	1	0	0.0	3	0	0	13	0	1	0	.182	.273
P	Epp Sell	R	7	12	4	1	0	0	0.0	3	1	1	4	0	0	0	.333	.417
P	Bill Bailey	L	12	7	2	0	0	0	0.0	0	0	0	1	0	0	0	.286	.286
P	Roy Walker	B	12	7	1	0	0	0	0.0	0	0	1	3	0	0	0	.143	.143
P	Eddie Dyer	L	6	3	1	1	0	0	0.0	1	0	0	0	0	1	1	.333	.667
P	Jack Knight	L	1	2	1	0	0	0	0.0	0	0	0	0	0	0	0	.500	.500
P	Sid Benton	R	0	0	0	0	0	0	–	0	0	0	0	0	0	0	–	–
P	Marv Goodwin	R	2	0	0	0	0	0	–	0	0	0	0	0	0	0	–	–
P	Johnny Stuart	R	2	0	0	0	0	0	0.0	0	0	0	0	0	0	0	–	–
TEAM TOTAL				5425	1634	280	88	107	2.0	863	787	447	425	73	129	36	.301	.444

INDIVIDUAL FIELDING

POS	Player	T	G	PO	A	E	DP	TC/G	FA
1B	J. Fournier	R	109	902	60	18	63	9.0	.982
	J. Bottomley	L	34	346	12	5	20	10.7	.986
	D. Gainor	R	26	175	9	4	6	7.2	.979
	H. McCurdy	R	2	0	0	0	0		.000
	J. Haines	R	1	1	0	0	0	1.0	1.000
2B	R. Hornsby	R	154	**398**	473	30	**81**	5.9	**.967**
	S. Toporcer	R	1	1	2	0	0	3.0	1.000
SS	D. Lavan	R	82	169	246	28	40	5.4	.937
	S. Toporcer	R	91	168	246	27	31	4.8	.939
	R. Blades	R	4	5	12	5	2	5.5	.773
	M. Stock	R	1	3	2	0	0	5.0	1.000
	H. Freigau	R	2	2	3	0	1	2.5	1.000
	B. Pertica	R	1	0	0	1	0	1.0	.000
3B	M. Stock	R	149	172	245	22	22	2.9	.950
	H. Freigau	R	1	0	0	0	0	0.0	.000
	D. Lavan	R	5	3	12	2	0	3.4	.882
	S. Toporcer	R	6	2	7	2	4	1.8	.818
	R. Blades	R	1	1	2	1	0	4.0	.750

POS	Player	T	G	PO	A	E	DP	TC/G	FA
OF	J. Smith	L	136	282	11	15	3	2.3	.951
	J. Schultz	R	89	195	7	5	1	2.3	.976
	A. McHenry	R	61	132	13	10	3	2.5	.935
	M. Flack	L	66	116	5	4	3	1.9	.968
	C. Heathcote	L	32	93	2	5	1	3.1	.950
	H. Mueller	L	44	83	6	5	2	2.1	.947
	L. Mann	R	57	87	3	2	1	1.6	.978
	R. Blades	R	29	61	6	5	0	2.5	.931
	D. Gainor	R	10	14	2	1	2	1.7	.941
	S. Toporcer	R	1	2	0	1	0	3.0	.667
	B. Shotton	R	3	1	0	0	0	0.3	1.000
C	E. Ainsmith	R	116	428	99	**20**	14	4.7	.963
	V. Clemons	R	63	172	50	1	2	3.5	.996
	H. McCurdy	R	9	24	5	1	2	3.3	.967
	E. Vick	R	3	7	0	1	1	2.7	.875

The Hornsby Era continued as the Rajah had what may have been his best season, winning the Triple Crown that eluded him the year before, and setting an NL record of 450 total bases that still stands. He was the first National Leaguer to top .400 since Burkett in 1899, and his 42 homers and 152 RBIs set National League records (though they would not last out the decade). He led the Cardinals into first place for a few dizzying days, but they then fell back into a three-team tangle behind the front-running Giants. The club batting average fell to .301, which was only good enough for third in the league.

In a Memorial Day oddity, Cliff Heathcote played for two teams in one day. Between games of a doubleheader, he was traded from St. Louis to Chicago, playing for the Cardinals in the opener and the Cubs in the nightcap.

TEAM STATISTICS

	W	L	PCT	GB	R	OR	Batting						Fielding			Pitching					
							2B	3B	HR	BA	SA	SB	E	DP	FA	CG	BB	SO	ShO	SV	ERA
Y	93	61	.604		852	658	253	90	80	.305	.428	116	194	145	.970	73	393	388	7	15	3.45
N	86	68	.558	7	766	677	226	99	45	.296	.401	130	205	147	.968	88	326	357	8	3	3.53
T	85	69	.552	8	865	736	239	110	52	.308	.419	145	187	126	.970	88	358	490	15	7	3.98
L	85	69	.552	8	863	819	280	88	107	.301	.444	73	239	122	.961	60	447	465	8	12	4.44
HI	80	74	.519	13	771	808	248	71	42	.293	.390	97	204	154	.968	74	475	402	8	12	4.34
KN	76	78	.494	17	743	754	235	76	56	.290	.392	79	208	139	.967	82	490	499	12	8	4.05
HI	57	96	.373	35.5	738	920	268	55	116	.282	.415	48	225	152	.965	73	460	394	6	5	4.64
OS	53	100	.346	39.5	596	822	162	73	32	.263	.341	67	215	121	.965	62	489	360	7	6	4.37
AGUE TOTAL					6194	6194	1911	662	530	.292	.404	755	1677	1106	.967	600	3438	3355	71	68	4.10

INDIVIDUAL PITCHING

TCHER	T	W	L	PCT	ERA	SV	G	GS	CG	IP	H	BB	SO	R	ER	ShO	H/9	BB/9	SO/9
ff Pfeffer	R	19	12	.613	3.58	2	44	32	19	261.1	286	58	83	126	104	1	9.85	2.00	2.86
l Sherdel	L	17	13	.567	3.88	2	47	31	15	241.1	298	62	79	132	104	3	11.11	2.31	2.95
sse Haines	R	11	9	.550	3.84	0	29	26	11	183	207	45	62	103	78	2	10.18	2.21	3.05
l Doak	R	11	13	.458	5.54	2	37	29	8	180.1	222	69	73	127	111	2	11.08	3.44	3.64
u North	R	10	-3	.769	4.45	4	53	11	4	149.2	164	64	84	90	74	0	9.86	3.85	5.05
yde Barfoot	R	4	5	.444	4.21	2	42	2	1	117.2	139	30	19	75	55	0	10.63	2.29	1.45
l Pertica	R	8	8	.500	5.91	0	34	14	2	117.1	153	65	30	94	77	0	11.74	4.99	2.30
p Sell	R	4	2	.667	6.82	0	7	5	0	33	47	6	5	26	25	0	12.82	1.64	1.36
y Walker	R	1	2	.333	4.78	0	12	2	0	32	34	15	14	20	17	0	9.56	4.22	3.94
l Bailey	L	0	2	.000	5.40	0	12	0	0	31.2	38	23	11	22	19	0	10.80	6.54	3.13
rv Goodwin	R	0	0	–	2.25	0	2	0	0	4	3	3	0	1	1	0	6.75	6.75	0.00
ck Knight	R	0	0	–	9.00	0	1	1	0	4	9	3	1	4	4	0	20.25	6.75	2.25
die Dyer	L	0	0	–	2.45	0	2	0	0	3.2	7	0	3	2	1	0	17.18	0.00	7.36
nny Stuart	R	0	0	–	9.00	0	2	1	0	2	2	2	1	4	2	0	9.00	9.00	4.50
ck Fournier	R	0	0	–	0.00	0	1	0	0	1	0	0	0	0	0	0	0.00	0.00	0.00
AM TOTAL		85	69	.552	4.44	12	325	154	60	1362	1609	445	465	826	672	8	10.63	2.94	3.07

MANAGER	W	L	PCT
Branch Rickey	79	74	.516

POS	Player	B	G	AB	H	2B	3B	HR	HR %	R	RBI	BB	SO	SB	Pinch Hit AB	Pinch Hit H	BA	SA
REGULARS																		
1B	Jim Bottomley	L	134	523	194	34	14	8	1.5	79	94	45	44	4	4	1	.371	.535
2B	Rogers Hornsby	R	107	424	163	32	10	17	4.0	89	83	55	29	3	1	0	**.384**	**.627**
SS	Howard Freigau	R	113	358	94	18	1	1	0.3	30	35	25	36	5	0	0	.263	.327
3B	Milt Stock	R	151	603	174	33	3	2	0.3	63	96	40	21	9	1	0	.289	.363
RF	Max Flack	L	128	505	147	16	9	3	0.6	82	28	41	16	7	6	3	.291	.376
CF	Hy Myers	R	96	330	99	18	2	2	0.6	29	48	12	19	5	6	1	.300	.385
LF	Jack Smith	L	124	407	126	16	6	5	1.2	98	41	27	20	32	3	0	.310	.415
C	Eddie Ainsmith	R	82	263	56	11	6	3	1.1	22	34	22	19	4	2	1	.213	.335
SUBSTITUTES																		
2S	Specs Toporcer	L	97	303	77	11	3	3	1.0	45	35	41	14	4	8	3	.254	.340
SS	Doc Lavan	R	50	111	22	6	0	1	0.9	10	12	9	7	0	2	1	.198	.279
SS	Les Bell	R	15	51	19	2	1	0	0.0	5	9	9	7	1	0	0	.373	.451
UT	Jake Flowers	R	13	32	3	1	0	0	0.0	0	2	2	7	1	1	0	.094	.125
12	Jimmy Hudgens	L	6	12	3	1	0	0	0.0	2	0	3	3	0	2	0	.250	.333
1B	Joe Walker	R	2	7	2	0	0	0	0.0	1	0	0	1	0	0	0	.286	.286
OF	Ray Blades	R	98	317	78	21	5	5	1.6	48	44	37	46	4	4	1	.246	.391
OF	Heinie Mueller	L	78	265	91	16	9	5	1.9	39	41	18	16	4	4	3	.343	.528
OF	Les Mann	R	38	89	33	5	2	5	5.6	20	11	9	5	0	0	0	.371	.640
OP	Eddie Dyer	L	35	45	12	3	0	2	4.4	17	5	3	5	1	14	3	.267	.467
OF	Taylor Douthit	R	9	27	5	0	2	0	0.0	3	0	0	4	1	2	0	.185	.333
OF	Joe Schultz	R	2	7	2	0	0	0	0.0	0	1	1	0	0	0	0	.286	.286
OF	Tige Stone	R	5	1	1	0	0	0	0.0	0	0	2	0	0	0	0	1.000	1.000
C	Harry McCurdy	L	67	185	49	11	2	0	0.0	17	15	11	11	3	9	0	.265	.346
C	Verne Clemons	R	57	130	37	9	1	0	0.0	6	13	10	11	0	13	4	.285	.369
C	Charlie Niebergall	R	9	28	3	1	0	0	0.0	2	1	2	2	0	1	0	.107	.143
C	George Kopshaw	R	2	5	1	1	0	0	0.0	1	0	0	1	0	0	0	.200	.400
PH	Burt Shotton	L	1	0	0	0	0	0	—	1	0	0	0	0	0	0	—	—
PITCHERS																		
P	Jesse Haines	R	37	99	20	1	0	0	0.0	8	8	1	20	0	0	0	.202	.212
P	Bill Sherdel	L	45	83	28	2	0	1	1.2	13	9	7	8	0	4	1	.337	.398
P	Fred Toney	R	29	69	8	0	0	0	0.0	2	2	2	11	1	0	0	.116	.116
P	Bill Doak	R	30	67	3	0	0	0	0.0	0	2	1	27	0	0	0	.045	.045
P	Johnny Stuart	R	37	57	14	2	0	0	0.0	7	3	1	7	0	0	0	.246	.281
P	Jeff Pfeffer	R	26	55	7	2	0	0	0.0	3	2	0	10	0	0	0	.127	.164
P	Clyde Barfoot	R	37	37	7	1	0	0	0.0	1	1	1	10	0	3	0	.189	.216
P	Lou North	R	34	22	4	0	0	0	0.0	3	3	1	5	0	0	0	.182	.182
P	Epp Sell	R	5	7	0	0	0	0	0.0	0	0	0	3	0	0	0	.000	.000
P	Bill Pertica	R	1	1	0	0	0	0	0.0	0	0	0	1	0	0	0	.000	.000
P	Fred Wigington	R	4	1	0	0	0	0	0.0	0	0	0	0	0	0	0	.000	.000
TEAM TOTAL				5526	1582	274	76	63	1.1	746	676	438	446	89	90	22	.286	.398

INDIVIDUAL FIELDING

POS	Player	T	G	PO	A	E	DP	TC/G	FA
1B	J. Bottomley	L	130	1264	43	18	95	10.2	.986
	S. Toporcer	R	1	0	0	0	0	0.0	.000
	R. Hornsby	R	10	131	16	2	14	14.9	.987
	H. Freigau	R	9	47	8	4	7	6.6	.932
	J. Hudgens	L	3	29	3	0	0	10.7	1.000
	J. Walker	R	2	19	0	0	1	9.5	1.000
	D. Lavan	R	3	14	1	1	0	5.3	.938
2B	R. Hornsby	R	96	192	283	19	47	5.1	.962
	S. Toporcer	R	52	130	162	17	41	5.9	.945
	H. Freigau	R	16	33	41	4	8	4.9	.949
	D. Lavan	R	1	0	0	0	0	0.0	.000
	J. Hudgens	L	1	8	0	1	1	9.0	.889
	J. Flowers	R	2	2	3	0	0	2.5	1.000
	M. Stock	R	1	1	0	0	0	1.0	1.000
SS	H. Freigau	R	87	193	290	37	42	6.0	.929
	D. Lavan	R	40	64	95	13	0	4.3	.924
	S. Toporcer	R	33	62	77	7	16	4.4	.952
	L. Bell	R	15	35	53	8	9	6.4	.917
	J. Flowers	R	7	10	24	1	1	5.0	.971
3B	M. Stock	R	150	165	261	20	24	3.0	.955
	D. Lavan	R	4	5	8	0	0	3.3	1.000
	J. Flowers	R	2	3	1	1	0	2.5	.800
	H. Freigau	R	1	0	1	1	0	2.0	.500
	S. Toporcer	R	1	1	1	0	0	2.0	1.000
	R. Blades	R	4	0	1	0	1	0.3	1.000
OF	J. Smith	L	107	247	11	7	3	2.5	.974
	M. Flack	L	121	242	8	13	4	2.2	.951
	H. Myers	R	87	239	15	6	0	3.0	.977
	H. Mueller	L	74	197	9	8	3	2.9	.963
	R. Blades	R	83	194	11	7	1	2.6	.967
	L. Mann	R	26	44	3	1	0	1.8	.979
	H. Freigau	R	1	0	0	0	0	0.0	.000
	T. Stone	R	4	0	0	0	0	0.0	.000
	E. Dyer	L	8	18	0	0	0	2.3	1.000
	T. Douthit	R	7	12	1	0	0	1.9	1.000
	J. Schultz	R	2	5	0	0	0	2.5	1.000
C	E. Ainsmith	R	80	235	57	6	3	3.7	.980
	H. McCurdy	R	58	157	30	6	4	3.3	.969
	V. Clemons	R	41	124	34	3	1	3.9	.981
	C. Niebergall	R	7	28	5	0	0	4.7	1.000
	G. Kopshaw	R	1	2	0	0	0	2.0	1.000

The cream of Branch Rickey's farm system was beginning to come up to the parent club. One of the first major stars to be produced was first baseman "Sunny Jim" Bottomley, who hit .371 in his first full season in the majors. Hornsby and Bottomley finished 1-2 in the league in batting, but Hornsby missed forty-seven games and the Cardinals were never really in the pennant hunt. They hovered within a few games of the .500 level all season, and ended up 16 games out of first. Their won-lost record was a bit inflated by the presence in the league of the Braves and the Phillies. It was one of just six times in National League history that two teams each dropped a hundred games.

TEAM STATISTICS

	W	L	PCT	GB	R	OR	Batting 2B	3B	HR	BA	SA	SB	Fielding E	DP	FA	CG	BB	Pitching SO	ShO	SV	ERA
Y	95	58	.621		854	679	248	76	85	.295	.415	106	176	141	.972	62	424	453	10	18	3.90
N	91	63	.591	4.5	708	629	237	95	45	.285	.392	96	202	144	.969	88	359	450	11	9	3.21
T	87	67	.565	8.5	786	696	224	111	49	.295	.404	154	179	157	.971	92	402	414	5	9	3.87
HI	83	71	.539	12.5	756	704	243	52	90	.288	.406	181	208	144	.967	80	435	408	8	11	3.82
L	79	74	.516	16	746	732	274	76	63	.286	.398	89	232	141	.963	77	456	398	9	7	3.87
KN	76	78	.494	19.5	753	741	214	81	62	.285	.387	71	293	137	.955	94	477	549	8	5	3.73
DS	54	100	.351	41.5	636	798	213	58	32	.273	.353	57	230	157	.964	55	394	351	13	7	4.22
HI	50	104	.325	45.5	748	1008	259	39	112	.278	.401	70	217	172	.966	68	549	385	3	8	5.30
AGUE TOTAL					5987	5987	1912	588	538	.286	.395	824	1737	1193	.966	616	3496	3408	67	74	3.99

INDIVIDUAL PITCHING

TCHER	T	W	L	PCT	ERA	SV	G	GS	CG	IP	H	BB	SO	R	ER	ShO	H/9	BB/9	SO/9
sse Haines	R	20	13	.606	3.11	0	37	36	23	266	283	75	73	125	92	1	9.58	2.54	2.47
Sherdel	L	15	13	.536	4.32	2	39	26	14	225	270	59	78	127	108	0	10.80	2.36	3.12
ed Toney	R	11	12	.478	3.84	0	29	28	16	196.2	211	61	48	104	84	1	9.66	2.79	2.20
Doak	R	8	13	.381	3.26	0	30	26	7	185	199	69	53	85	67	3	9.68	3.36	2.58
f Pfeffer	R	8	9	.471	4.02	0	26	18	7	152.1	171	40	32	80	68	1	10.10	2.36	1.89
nny Stuart	R	9	5	.643	4.27	3	37	10	7	149.2	139	70	55	82	71	1	8.36	4.21	3.31
de Barfoot	R	3	3	.500	3.73	1	33	2	1	101.1	112	27	23	49	42	1	9.95	2.40	2.04
North	R	3	4	.429	5.15	1	34	3	0	71.2	90	31	24	50	41	0	11.30	3.89	3.01
die Dyer	L	2	1	.667	4.09	0	4	3	2	22	30	5	7	10	10	1	12.27	2.05	2.86
Sell	R	0	1	.000	6.00	0	5	1	0	15	16	8	2	10	10	0	9.60	4.80	1.20
d Wigington	R	0	0	–	3.24	0	4	0	0	8.1	11	5	2	4	3	0	11.88	5.40	2.16
e Stone	R	0	0	–	12.00	0	1	0	0	3	5	3	1	4	4	0	15.00	9.00	3.00
Pertica	R	0	0	–	3.86	0	1	1	0	2.1	2	3	0	2	1	0	7.71	11.57	0.00
M TOTAL		79	74	.516	3.87	7	280	154	77	1398.1	1539	456	398	732	601	9	9.91	2.93	2.56

MANAGER	W	L	PCT
Branch Rickey	65	89	.422

POS	Player	B	G	AB	H	2B	3B	HR	HR %	R	RBI	BB	SO	SB	Pinch Hit AB	H	BA	SA
REGULARS																		
1B	Jim Bottomley	L	137	528	167	31	12	14	2.7	87	111	35	35	5	3	1	.316	.500
2B	Rogers Hornsby	R	143	536	227	43	14	25	4.7	121	94	89	32	5	0	0	.424	.696
SS	Jimmy Cooney	R	110	383	113	20	8	1	0.3	44	57	20	20	12	0	0	.295	.397
3B	Howard Freigau	R	98	376	101	17	6	2	0.5	35	39	19	24	10	0	0	.269	.362
RF	Jack Smith	L	124	459	130	18	6	2	0.4	91	33	33	27	24	6	1	.283	.362
CF	Wattie Holm	R	81	293	86	10	4	0	0.0	40	23	8	16	1	5	1	.294	.355
LF	Ray Blades	R	131	456	142	21	13	11	2.4	86	68	35	38	7	2	1	.311	.487
C	Mike Gonzalez	R	120	402	119	27	1	3	0.7	34	53	24	22	1	1	1	.296	.391
SUBSTITUTES																		
3S	Specs Toporcer	L	70	198	62	10	3	1	0.5	30	24	11	14	2	10	1	.313	.409
SS	Tommy Thevenow	R	23	89	18	4	1	0	0.0	4	7	1	6	1	0	0	.202	.270
SS	Les Bell	R	17	57	14	3	2	1	1.8	5	5	3	7	0	0	0	.246	.421
S2	Doc Lavan	R	4	6	0	0	0	0	0.0	0	0	0	0	0	0	0	.000	.000
O1	Heinie Mueller	L	92	296	78	12	6	2	0.7	39	37	19	16	8	10	1	.264	.365
OF	Max Flack	L	67	209	55	11	3	2	1.0	31	21	21	5	3	13	3	.263	.373
OF	Taylor Douthit	R	53	173	48	13	1	0	0.0	24	13	16	19	4	1	0	.277	.364
O3	Hy Myers	R	43	124	26	5	1	1	0.8	12	15	3	10	1	5	0	.210	.290
OF	Chick Hafey	R	24	91	23	5	2	2	2.2	10	22	4	8	1	0	0	.253	.418
OF	Ed Clough	L	7	14	1	0	0	0	0.0	0	1	0	3	0	1	0	.071	.071
OF	Joe Schultz	R	12	12	2	0	0	0	0.0	0	2	3	0	0	0	0	.167	.167
OF	Joe Bratcher	L	4	1	0	0	0	0	0.0	1	0	0	0	0	1	0	.000	.000
C	Charlie Niebergall	R	40	58	17	6	0	0	0.0	6	7	3	9	0	6	2	.293	.397
C	Verne Clemons	R	25	56	18	3	0	0	0.0	3	6	2	3	0	7	2	.321	.375
C	Ernie Vick	R	16	23	8	1	0	0	0.0	2	0	3	3	0	0	0	.348	.391
C	Ray Shepherdson	R	3	6	0	0	0	0	0.0	1	0	0	3	0	0	0	.000	.000
PITCHERS																		
P	Eddie Dyer	L	50	76	18	2	3	0	0.0	8	8	3	8	1	16	4	.237	.342
P	Bill Sherdel	L	49	75	15	4	0	0	0.0	4	8	13	9	0	6	1	.200	.253
P	Jesse Haines	R	35	74	14	1	0	0	0.0	3	7	2	20	0	0	0	.189	.203
P	Allen Sothoron	R	29	72	14	2	0	0	0.0	6	3	1	12	0	0	0	.194	.222
P	Johnny Stuart	R	30	54	11	1	0	0	0.0	5	3	2	6	0	0	0	.204	.222
P	Leo Dickerman	R	18	39	9	0	1	0	0.0	4	2	2	6	0	0	0	.231	.282
P	Hi Bell	R	28	31	2	0	0	0	0.0	1	0	5	14	0	0	0	.065	.065
P	Jeff Pfeffer	R	16	26	3	0	0	0	0.0	2	1	0	7	0	0	0	.115	.115
P	Flint Rhem	R	6	12	2	0	0	0	0.0	0	1	1	5	0	0	0	.167	.167
P	Jesse Fowler	R	13	9	2	0	0	0	0.0	1	0	1	2	0	0	0	.222	.222
P	Pea Ridge Day	R	3	8	1	0	0	0	0.0	0	0	0	2	0	0	0	.125	.125
P	Art Delaney	R	8	7	2	0	0	0	0.0	0	0	0	2	0	0	0	.286	.286
P	Bill Doak	R	11	5	1	0	0	0	0.0	0	0	0	1	0	0	0	.200	.200
P	Vince Shields	L	3	5	2	0	0	0	0.0	0	1	0	0	0	0	0	.400	.400
P	Lou North	R	6	4	1	0	0	0	0.0	0	0	0	1	0	0	0	.250	.250
P	Bob Vines	R	2	4	0	0	0	0	0.0	0	0	0	1	0	0	0	.000	.000
P	Jack Berly	R	4	2	0	0	0	0	0.0	0	0	0	2	0	0	0	.000	.000
TEAM TOTAL				5349	1552	270	87	67	1.3	740	672	382	418	86	101	21	.290	.411

INDIVIDUAL FIELDING

POS	Player	T	G	PO	A	E	DP	TC/G	FA		POS	Player	T	G	PO	A	E	DP	TC/G	FA
1B	J. Bottomley	L	133	1297	48	24	110	10.3	.982		OF	J. Smith	L	114	251	18	9	8	2.4	.968
	H. Mueller	L	27	213	11	4	16	8.4	.982			R. Blades	R	109	256	6	12	1	2.5	.956
2B	R. Hornsby	R	143	301	517	30	102	5.9	.965			W. Holm	R	64	162	9	2	1	2.7	.988
	R. Blades	R	7	12	16	0	2	4.0	1.000			H. Mueller	L	53	122	4	5	1	2.5	.962
	H. Myers	R	3	3	11	0	0	4.7	1.000			T. Douthit	R	50	118	5	3	2	2.5	.976
	S. Toporcer	R	3	2	2	1	0	1.7	.800			M. Flack	L	52	90	9	3	0	2.0	.971
	D. Lavan	R	2	1	3	0	0	2.0	1.000			H. Myers	R	22	50	2	3	1	2.5	.945
	J. Bottomley	L	1	0	1	0	0	1.0	1.000			C. Hafey	R	24	48	3	4	1	2.3	.927
	J. Cooney	R	1	1	0	0	0	1.0	1.000			J. Bratcher	R	1	0	0	0	0	0.0	.000
												E. Dyer	L	1	1	0	0	0	1.0	1.000
SS	J. Cooney	R	99	242	322	18	68	5.9	.969			E. Clough	L	6	12	1	0	0	2.2	1.000
	T. Thevenow	R	23	61	95	8	15	7.1	.951			B. Sherdel	L	2	3	0	0	0	1.5	1.000
	L. Bell	R	17	44	42	9	8	5.6	.905			J. Schultz	R	2	1	0	0	0	0.5	1.000
	S. Toporcer	R	25	32	49	5	5	3.4	.942		C	M. Gonzalez	R	119	413	96	7	15	4.3	.986
	D. Lavan	R	2	2	7	2	2	5.5	.818			C. Niebergall	R	34	57	20	4	1	2.4	.951
	H. Freigau	R	2	1	1	0	0	1.0	1.000			V. Clemons	R	17	46	11	1	0	3.4	.983
3B	H. Freigau	R	98	127	171	13	24	3.2	.958			E. Vick	R	16	26	11	1	4	2.4	.974
	S. Toporcer	R	33	22	54	2	3	2.4	.974			W. Holm	R	9	15	3	1	1	2.1	.947
	J. Stuart	R	1	0	0	0	0	0.0	.000			Shepherdson	R	3	5	2	0	0	2.3	1.000
	H. Myers	R	12	8	12	3	0	1.9	.870											
	R. Blades	R	7	7	8	1	0	2.3	.938											
	J. Cooney	R	7	3	9	0	0	1.7	1.000											
	W. Holm	R	4	1	0	1	0	0.5	.500											

Rogers Hornsby's astounding season at the plate was not enough to make a contender of the '24 Cardinals. Hornsby's .424 average is the highest in the majors since 1900, and he won his batting title by the widest margin in National League history: forty-nine points over Brooklyn's Zach Wheat. Other individual accomplishments that season included Bottomley's major league record 12 RBIs in one game, and Hi Bell's becoming the last National League pitcher to win two complete games in one day. These bright spots were few and far between, however, as the Cards slumped to sixth place, 28½ games out of first. Unlike previous seasons, the Cardinals were worse than their statistics would indicate, finishing 24 games below .500 while being outscored by just ten runs. A change was on the way.

TEAM STATISTICS

W	L	PCT	GB	R	OR	2B	3B	HR	BA	SA	SB	E	DP	FA	CG	BB	SO	ShO	SV	ERA
93	60	.608		857	641	269	81	95	.300	.432	82	186	160	.971	71	392	406	4	21	3.62
92	62	.597	1.5	717	675	227	54	72	.287	.391	34	196	121	.968	98	403	640	10	5	3.64
90	63	.588	3	724	588	222	122	43	.287	.399	181	183	161	.971	85	323	364	15	5	3.27
83	70	.542	10	649	579	236	111	36	.290	.397	103	217	142	.966	77	293	451	14	9	3.12
81	72	.529	12	698	699	207	59	66	.276	.378	137	218	153	.966	85	438	416	4	6	3.83
65	89	.422	28.5	740	750	270	87	67	.290	.411	86	191	162	.969	79	486	393	7	6	4.15
55	96	.364	37	676	849	256	56	94	.275	.397	57	175	168	.972	59	469	349	7	10	4.87
53	100	.346	40	520	800	194	52	25	.256	.327	74	168	154	.973	66	402	364	10	4	4.46
LEAGUE TOTAL				5581	5581	1881	622	498	.283	.392	754	1534	1221	.970	620	3206	3383	71	66	3.87

INDIVIDUAL PITCHING

PITCHER	T	W	L	PCT	ERA	SV	G	GS	CG	IP	H	BB	SO	R	ER	ShO	H/9	BB/9	SO/9
sse Haines	R	8	19	.296	4.41	0	35	31	16	222.2	275	66	69	129	109	1	11.12	2.67	2.79
en Sothoron	R	10	16	.385	3.57	0	29	28	16	196.2	209	84	62	102	78	4	9.56	3.84	2.84
Sherdel	L	8	9	.471	3.42	1	35	10	6	168.2	188	38	57	77	64	0	10.03	2.03	3.04
nny Stuart	R	9	11	.450	4.75	0	28	22	13	159	167	60	54	100	84	0	9.45	3.40	3.06
die Dyer	L	8	11	.421	4.61	0	29	15	7	136.2	174	51	28	82	70	1	11.46	3.36	1.51
Dickerman	R	7	4	.636	2.41	0	18	13	8	119.2	108	51	28	43	32	1	8.12	3.84	2.11
Bell	R	3	8	.273	4.92	1	28	11	5	113.1	124	29	29	68	62	0	9.85	2.30	2.30
Pfeffer	R	4	5	.444	5.31	0	16	12	3	78	102	30	20	52	46	0	11.77	3.46	2.31
se Fowler	L	1	1	.500	4.41	0	13	3	0	32.2	28	18	5	21	16	0	7.71	4.96	1.38
t Rhem	R	2	2	.500	4.45	0	6	3	3	32.1	31	17	20	18	16	0	8.63	4.73	5.57
Doak	R	2	1	.667	3.27	3	11	1	0	22	25	14	7	8	8	0	10.23	5.73	2.86
Delaney	R	1	0	1.000	1.80	0	8	1	1	20	19	6	2	4	4	0	8.55	2.70	0.90
a Ridge Day	R	1	1	.500	4.58	0	3	3	1	17.2	22	6	3	11	9	0	11.21	3.06	1.53
North	R	0	0	–	6.75	0	6	0	0	14.2	15	9	8	12	11	0	9.20	5.52	4.91
ce Shields	R	1	1	.500	3.00	0	2	1	0	12	10	3	4	5	4	0	7.50	2.25	3.00
Vines	R	0	0	–	9.28	0	2	0	0	10.2	23	0	0	13	11	0	19.41	0.00	0.00
k Berly	R	0	0	–	5.63	0	4	0	0	8	8	4	2	5	5	0	9.00	4.50	2.25
AM TOTAL		65	89	.422	4.15	6	273	154	79	1364.2	1528	486	393	750	629	7	10.08	3.21	2.59

NO-HITTERS BY CARDINAL PITCHERS

Jesse Haines	July 17, 1924 vs. Boston, 5-0 (3 walks, 2 errors)
Paul Dean	September 21, 1934 vs. Brooklyn, 3-0 (1 walk)
Lon Warneke	August 30, 1941 at Cincinnati, 2-0 (1 walk, 2 errors)
Ray Washburn	September 18, 1968 at San Francisco, 2-0 (5 walks)
Bob Gibson	August 14, 1971 at Pittsburgh, 11-0 (3 walks)
Bob Forsch	April 16, 1978 vs. Philadelphia, 5-0 (2 walks, 1 error)

MANAGER	W	L	PCT
Branch Rickey	13	25	.342
Rogers Hornsby	64	51	.557

POS	Player	B	G	AB	H	2B	3B	HR	HR %	R	RBI	BB	SO	SB	Pinch Hit AB	Pinch Hit H	BA	SA
REGULARS																		
1B	Jim Bottomley	L	153	619	227	44	12	21	3.4	92	128	47	36	3	0	0	.367	.578
2B	Rogers Hornsby	R	138	504	203	41	10	39	7.7	133	143	83	39	5	0	0	.403	.756
SS	Specs Toporcer	L	83	268	76	13	4	2	0.7	38	26	36	15	7	8	2	.284	.384
3B	Les Bell	R	153	586	167	29	9	11	1.9	80	88	43	47	4	0	0	.285	.422
RF	Chick Hafey	R	93	358	108	25	2	5	1.4	36	57	10	29	3	5	1	.302	.425
CF	Heinie Mueller	L	78	243	76	16	4	1	0.4	33	26	17	11	0	5	2	.313	.424
LF	Ray Blades	R	122	462	158	37	8	12	2.6	112	57	59	47	6	4	2	.342	.535
C	Bob O'Farrell	R	94	317	88	13	2	3	0.9	37	32	46	26	0	2	0	.278	.360
SUBSTITUTES																		
S2	Jimmy Cooney	R	54	187	51	11	2	0	0.0	27	18	4	5	1	1	0	.273	.353
SS	Tommy Thevenow	R	50	175	47	7	2	0	0.0	17	17	7	12	3	0	0	.269	.331
SS	Howard Freigau	R	9	26	4	0	0	0	0.0	2	0	2	1	0	0	0	.154	.154
OF	Ralph Shinners	R	74	251	74	9	2	7	2.8	39	36	12	19	8	7	3	.295	.430
OF	Jack Smith	L	80	243	61	11	4	4	1.6	53	31	19	13	20	10	4	.251	.379
OF	Max Flack	L	79	241	60	7	8	0	0.0	23	28	21	9	5	19	3	.249	.344
OF	Taylor Douthit	R	30	73	20	3	1	1	1.4	13	8	2	6	0	9	5	.274	.384
OF	Wattie Holm	R	13	58	12	1	1	0	0.0	10	2	3	1	1	0	0	.207	.259
C	Walter Schmidt	R	37	87	22	2	1	0	0.0	9	9	4	3	1	4	1	.253	.299
C	Mike Gonzalez	R	22	71	22	3	0	0	0.0	9	4	6	2	1	0	0	.310	.352
C	Bill Warwick	R	13	41	12	1	2	1	2.4	8	6	5	5	0	0	0	.293	.488
C	Ernie Vick	R	14	32	6	2	1	0	0.0	3	3	3	1	0	5	0	.188	.313
PH	Hy Myers	R	2	2	1	0	0	0	0.0	1	0	0	0	0	2	1	.500	.500
PITCHERS																		
P	Jesse Haines	R	29	74	13	1	1	0	0.0	8	5	3	15	0	0	0	.176	.216
P	Bill Sherdel	L	33	73	15	5	0	1	1.4	12	5	5	0	1	0	0	.205	.315
P	Art Reinhart	L	28	67	22	2	1	0	0.0	9	7	2	10	0	6	1	.328	.388
P	Flint Rhem	R	30	59	14	2	0	1	1.7	8	8	1	22	0	0	0	.237	.322
P	Allen Sothoron	R	28	56	11	2	1	0	0.0	5	3	0	7	0	0	0	.196	.268
P	Duster Mails	L	21	45	6	2	0	0	0.0	3	3	3	13	0	0	0	.133	.178
P	Leo Dickerman	R	29	44	5	1	1	0	0.0	1	2	0	12	0	0	0	.114	.182
P	Eddie Dyer	L	31	31	3	1	0	0	0.0	4	0	3	1	1	1	0	.097	.129
P	Johnny Stuart	R	15	16	4	1	1	0	0.0	2	0	0	1	0	0	0	.250	.438
P	Pea Ridge Day	R	17	13	2	0	0	0	0.0	1	0	0	5	0	0	0	.154	.154
P	Ed Clough	L	3	4	1	0	0	0	0.0	0	0	0	0	0	0	0	.250	.250
P	Bill Hallahan	R	6	3	1	0	0	0	0.0	0	0	0	1	0	0	0	.333	.333
P	Gil Paulsen	R	1	0	0	0	0	0	-	0	0	0	0	0	0	0	-	-
	TEAM TOTAL			5329	1592	292	80	109	2.0	828	752	446	414	70	88	25	.299	.445

INDIVIDUAL FIELDING

POS	Player	T	G	PO	A	E	DP	TC/G	FA
1B	J. Bottomley	L	153	1466	74	21	133	10.2	.987
2B	R. Hornsby	R	136	287	416	34	95	5.4	.954
	J. Cooney	R	15	27	43	2	9	4.8	.972
	S. Toporcer	R	7	8	16	1	1	3.6	.960
	H. Freigau	R	1	2	1	0	0	3.0	1.000
SS	S. Toporcer	R	66	141	215	15	40	5.6	.960
	T. Thevenow	R	50	98	169	14	18	5.6	.950
	J. Cooney	R	37	70	94	4	22	4.5	.976
	H. Freigau	R	7	17	27	3	5	6.7	.936
	L. Bell	R	1	0	1	0	0	1.0	1.000
3B	L. Bell	R	153	151	284	36	39	3.1	.924
	R. Blades	R	1	1	0	0	0	1.0	1.000

POS	Player	T	G	PO	A	E	DP	TC/G	FA
OF	R. Blades	R	114	266	13	6	4	2.5	.979
	C. Hafey	R	88	180	9	9	2	2.3	.955
	H. Mueller	L	72	165	6	8	3	2.5	.955
	J. Smith	L	64	152	7	7	2	2.6	.958
	R. Shinners	R	66	161	2	3	1	2.5	.982
	M. Flack	L	59	103	8	1	1	1.9	.991
	T. Douthit	R	21	50	1	1	0	2.5	.981
	J. Cooney	R	1	0	0	0	0	0.0	.000
	W. Holm	R	13	40	1	1	1	3.2	.976
C	B. O'Farrell	R	92	324	67	10	5	4.4	.975
	W. Schmidt	R	31	84	33	4	2	3.9	.967
	M. Gonzalez	R	22	92	16	2	3	5.0	.982
	E. Vick	R	9	34	5	3	0	4.7	.929
	B. Warwick	R	13	33	4	0	0	2.8	1.000

After the first thirty-eight games of the 1925 season, the Cardinals were stuck in eighth place and going nowhere. Sam Breadon responded as owners have since the beginning of baseball: he fired his manager, relieving Rickey of his on-field duties. Breadon gave the job to Hornsby, who rallied the club to a fourth place finish, nosing above the .500 mark on the last weekend of the season. Hornsby became the first Cardinal to be named the National League's Most Valuable Player as he won his second Triple Crown. He was also one of just five National Leaguers in history to have more RBIs than games played (with at least a hundred of each), and he and Bottomley were 1-2 in batting for the second time in three years.

TEAM STATISTICS

W	L	PCT	GB	R	OR	Batting 2B	3B	HR	BA	SA	SB	Fielding E	DP	FA	Pitching CG	BB	SO	ShO	SV	ERA
95	58	.621		912	715	316	105	77	.307	.448	159	224	171	.964	77	387	386	2	13	3.87
86	66	.566	8.5	736	702	239	61	114	.283	.415	79	199	129	.968	80	408	446	6	8	3.94
80	73	.523	15	690	643	221	90	44	.285	.387	108	203	161	.968	92	324	437	11	12	3.38
77	76	.503	18	828	764	292	80	109	.299	.445	70	204	156	.966	82	470	351	5	4	4.36
70	83	.458	25	708	802	260	70	41	.292	.390	77	221	145	.964	77	458	351	5	4	4.39
68	85	.444	27	786	866	250	80	64	.296	.406	37	210	130	.966	82	477	518	4	4	4.77
68	85	.444	27	812	930	288	58	100	.295	.425	48	211	147	.966	69	444	371	8	9	5.02
68	86	.442	27.5	723	773	254	70	85	.275	.396	94	198	161	.969	75	485	435	5	10	4.41
LEAGUE TOTAL				6195	6195	2120	614	634	.292	.414	672	1670	1200	.966	634	3453	3372	49	67	4.27

INDIVIDUAL PITCHING

PITCHER	T	W	L	PCT	ERA	SV	G	GS	CG	IP	H	BB	SO	R	ER	ShO	H/9	BB/9	SO/9
Jesse Haines	R	13	14	.481	4.57	0	29	25	15	207	234	52	63	116	105	0	10.17	2.26	2.74
Sherdel	L	15	6	.714	3.11	1	32	21	17	200	216	42	53	77	69	2	9.72	1.89	2.39
Flint Rhem	R	8	13	.381	4.92	1	30	23	8	170	204	58	66	114	93	1	10.80	3.07	3.49
Allen Sothoron	R	10	10	.500	4.05	0	28	23	8	155.2	173	63	67	86	70	2	10.00	3.64	3.87
Reinhart	L	11	5	.688	3.05	0	20	16	15	144.2	149	47	26	61	49	1	9.27	2.92	1.62
Chester Mails	L	7	7	.500	4.60	0	21	14	9	131	145	58	49	78	67	0	9.96	3.98	3.37
Leo Dickerman	R	4	11	.267	5.58	1	29	20	7	130.2	135	79	40	95	81	2	9.30	5.44	2.76
Eddie Dyer	L	4	3	.571	4.15	3	27	5	1	82.1	93	24	25	52	38	0	10.17	2.62	2.73
Johnny Stuart	R	2	2	.500	6.13	0	15	1	1	47	52	24	14	41	32	0	9.96	4.60	2.68
Ridge Day	R	2	4	.333	6.30	1	17	4	1	40	53	7	13	31	28	0	11.93	1.58	2.93
Hallahan	L	1	0	1.000	3.52	0	6	0	0	15.1	14	11	8	6	6	0	8.22	6.46	4.70
Clough	L	0	1	.000	8.10	0	3	1	0	10	11	5	3	9	9	0	9.90	4.50	2.70
Paulsen	R	0	0	—	0.00	0	1	0	0	2	1	0	1	0	0	0	4.50	0.00	4.50
TEAM TOTAL		77	76	.503	4.36	7	258	153	82	1335.2	1480	470	428	766	647	8	9.97	3.17	2.88

MANAGER	W	L	PCT
Rogers Hornsby	89	65	.578

POS	Player	B	G	AB	H	2B	3B	HR	HR %	R	RBI	BB	SO	SB	Pinch Hit AB	Pinch Hit H	BA	SA
REGULARS																		
1B	Jim Bottomley	L	154	603	180	40	14	19	3.2	98	120	58	52	4	0	0	.299	.506
2B	Rogers Hornsby	R	134	527	167	34	5	11	2.1	96	93	61	39	3	0	0	.317	.463
SS	Tommy Thevenow	R	156	563	144	15	5	2	0.4	64	63	27	26	8	0	0	.256	.311
3B	Les Bell	R	155	581	189	33	14	17	2.9	85	100	54	62	9	0	0	.325	.518
RF	Billy Southworth	L	99	391	124	22	6	11	2.8	76	69	26	9	13	0	0	.317	.488
CF	Taylor Douthit	R	139	530	163	20	4	3	0.6	96	52	55	46	23	1	0	.308	.377
LF	Ray Blades	R	107	416	127	17	12	8	1.9	81	43	62	57	6	1	0	.305	.462
C	Bob O'Farrell	R	147	492	144	30	9	7	1.4	63	68	61	44	1	1	1	.293	.433
SUBSTITUTES																		
2B	Specs Toporcer	L	64	88	22	3	2	0	0.0	13	9	8	9	1	23	9	.250	.330
21	Jake Flowers	R	40	74	20	1	0	3	4.1	13	9	5	9	1	23	6	.270	.405
OF	Chick Hafey	R	78	225	61	19	2	4	1.8	30	38	11	36	2	22	7	.271	.427
OF	Heinie Mueller	L	52	191	51	7	5	3	1.6	36	28	11	6	8	0	0	.267	.403
OF	Wattie Holm	R	55	144	41	5	1	0	0.0	18	21	18	14	3	15	5	.285	.333
C	Ernie Vick	R	24	51	10	2	0	0	0.0	6	4	3	4	0	1	0	.196	.235
C	Bill Warwick	R	9	14	5	0	0	0	0.0	0	2	0	2	0	0	0	.357	.357
PH	Jack Smith	L	1	1	0	0	0	0	0.0	0	0	0	1	0	1	0	.000	.000
PITCHERS																		
P	Flint Rhem	R	34	96	18	1	0	1	1.0	11	12	4	36	0	0	0	.188	.229
P	Bill Sherdel	L	36	90	22	5	1	1	1.1	9	8	1	9	0	0	0	.244	.356
P	Art Reinhart	L	40	63	20	2	2	0	0.0	7	11	1	3	1	4	2	.317	.413
P	Jesse Haines	R	33	61	13	1	0	0	0.0	4	1	3	5	0	0	0	.213	.230
P	Vic Keen	R	26	53	3	0	0	0	0.0	4	1	2	15	0	0	0	.057	.057
P	Grover Alexander	R	23	50	6	1	0	0	0.0	1	3	2	14	0	0	0	.120	.140
P	Hi Bell	R	27	25	3	0	0	0	0.0	3	1	3	5	0	0	0	.120	.120
P	Bill Hallahan	R	19	16	4	1	0	0	0.0	0	0	0	7	0	0	0	.250	.313
P	Allen Sothoron	R	15	13	3	0	0	0	0.0	2	0	1	1	0	0	0	.231	.231
P	Syl Johnson	R	19	12	0	0	0	0	0.0	0	0	0	5	0	0	0	.000	.000
P	Walter Huntzinger	R	9	8	0	0	0	0	0.0	0	0	1	2	0	0	0	.000	.000
P	Eddie Dyer	L	6	2	1	0	0	0	0.0	1	0	0	0	0	0	0	.500	.500
P	Ed Clough	L	1	1	0	0	0	0	0.0	0	0	0	0	0	0	0	.000	.000
P	Duster Mails	L	1	0	0	0	0	0	—	0	0	0	0	0	0	0	—	—
TEAM TOTAL				5381	1541	259	82	90	1.7	817	756	478	518	83	92	30	.286	.415

INDIVIDUAL FIELDING

POS	Player	T	G	PO	A	E	DP	TC/G	FA	POS	Player	T	G	PO	A	E	DP	TC/G	FA
1B	J. Bottomley	L	154	1607	54	19	118	10.9	.989	OF	T. Douthit	R	138	440	14	20	2	3.4	.958
	J. Flowers	R	3	20	2	1	1	7.7	.957		R. Blades	R	105	229	10	5	1	2.3	.980
2B	R. Hornsby	R	134	245	433	27	73	5.3	.962		B. Southworth	R	99	228	5	7	0	2.4	.971
	S. Toporcer	R	27	22	35	1	3	2.1	.983		H. Mueller	L	51	106	7	6	3	2.3	.950
	J. Flowers	R	11	17	43	1	4	5.5	.984		C. Hafey	R	54	106	6	3	1	2.1	.974
SS	T. Thevenow	R	156	371	597	45	98	6.5	.956		W. Holm	R	39	75	1	3	1	2.0	.962
	S. Toporcer	R	5	2	3	0	0	1.0	1.000	C	B. O'Farrell	R	146	466	117	10	12	4.1	.983
	J. Flowers	R	1	1	0	1	0	2.0	.500		E. Vick	R	23	40	11	3	1	2.3	.944
3B	L. Bell	R	155	165	254	22	25	2.8	.950		B. Warwick	R	9	19	5	2	0	2.9	.923
	S. Toporcer	R	1	0	2	0	0	2.0	1.000										

Mention the year 1926 within earshot of a Cardinal fan and you'll hear two names invoked: Alexander and Lazzeri. Grover Cleveland Alexander either was or was not still drunk from celebrating his victory the day before when called on to face Tony Lazzeri of the Yankees in Game 7 with the bases loaded and the World Series hanging in the balance. Everyone remembers that manager Hornsby scrutinized him carefully to see if he was up to pitching, and everyone remembers that Alexander threw strike three past Lazzeri to strand the three runners and protect the one run lead. Few remember, however, that it was just the seventh inning, and that "Old Pete" still had to get by some pretty fair hitters named Earle Combs and Babe Ruth before the victory was secure. Fewer still remember that Alexander was an early-season acquisition, picked up from the Cubs by Rickey for the waiver price. And not one fan in a thousand could correctly name the Cardinal who was named NL Most Valuable Player in 1926: it was catcher Bob O'Farrell, who was seventh among Redbird starters in batting and fifth in RBIs, but whose rifle arm threw out scores of would-be basestealers, including Babe Ruth for the final out of the Series.

TEAM STATISTICS

	W	L	PCT	GB	R	OR	Batting 2B	3B	HR	BA	SA	SB	Fielding E	DP	FA	CG	BB	Pitching SO	ShO	SV	ERA
'L	89	65	.578		817	678	259	82	90	.286	.415	83	198	141	.969	90	397	365	10	6	3.67
N	87	67	.565	2	747	651	242	120	35	.290	.400	51	183	160	.972	88	324	424	14	8	3.42
T	84	69	.549	4.5	769	689	243	106	44	.285	.396	91	220	161	.965	83	455	387	12	18	3.67
-I	82	72	.532	7	682	602	291	49	66	.278	.390	85	162	174	.974	77	486	508	13	14	3.26
/	74	77	.490	13.5	663	668	214	58	73	.278	.384	94	186	150	.970	61	427	419	4	15	3.77
N	71	82	.464	17.5	623	705	246	62	40	.263	.358	76	229	95	.963	83	472	517	5	9	3.82
S	66	86	.434	22	624	719	209	62	16	.277	.350	81	208	150	.967	60	455	408	9	9	4.03
-I	58	93	.384	29.5	687	900	244	50	75	.281	.390	47	224	153	.964	68	454	331	5	5	5.19
AGUE TOTAL					5612	5612	1948	589	439	.280	.386	608	1610	1184	.968	610	3470	3359	72	84	3.84

INDIVIDUAL PITCHING

PITCHER	T	W	L	PCT	ERA	SV	G	GS	CG	IP	H	BB	SO	R	ER	ShO	H/9	BB/9	SO/9
nt Rhem	R	20	7	.741	3.21	0	34	34	20	258	241	75	72	121	92	1	8.41	2.62	2.51
l Sherdel	L	16	12	.571	3.49	0	34	29	17	234.2	255	49	59	103	91	3	9.78	1.88	2.26
sse Haines	R	13	4	.765	3.25	1	33	21	14	183	186	48	46	76	66	3	9.15	2.36	2.26
: Keen	R	10	9	.526	4.56	0	26	21	12	152	179	42	29	89	77	1	10.60	2.49	1.72
over Alexander	R	9	7	.563	2.91	2	23	16	11	148.1	136	24	35	57	48	2	8.25	1.46	2.12
t Reinhart	L	10	5	.667	4.22	0	27	11	9	143	159	47	26	75	67	0	10.01	2.96	1.64
Bell	R	6	6	.500	3.18	2	27	8	3	85	82	17	27	41	30	0	8.68	1.80	2.86
Hallahan	L	1	4	.200	3.65	0	19	3	0	56.2	45	32	28	27	23	0	7.15	5.08	4.45
Johnson	R	0	3	.000	4.22	1	19	6	1	49	54	15	10	27	23	0	9.92	2.76	1.84
en Sothoron	R	3	3	.500	4.22	0	15	4	1	42.2	37	16	19	22	20	0	7.80	3.38	4.01
lter Huntzinger	R	0	4	.000	4.24	0	9	4	2	34	35	14	9	19	16	0	9.26	3.71	2.38
die Dyer	L	1	0	1.000	11.57	0	6	0	0	9.1	7	14	4	14	12	0	6.75	13.50	3.86
Clough	L	0	0	–	22.50	0	1	0	0	2	5	3	0	6	5	0	22.50	13.50	0.00
ster Mails	L	0	1	.000	0.00	0	1	0	0	1	2	1	1	1	0	0	18.00	9.00	9.00
AM TOTAL		89	65	.578	3.67	6	274	157	90	1398.2	1423	397	365	678	570	10	9.16	2.55	2.35

MANAGER	W	L	PCT
Bob O'Farrell	92	61	.601

POS	Player	B	G	AB	H	2B	3B	HR	HR %	R	RBI	BB	SO	SB	Pinch Hit AB	Pinch Hit H	BA	SA
REGULARS																		
1B	Jim Bottomley	L	152	574	174	31	15	19	3.3	95	124	74	49	8	0	0	.303	.509
2B	Frankie Frisch	B	153	617	208	31	11	10	1.6	112	78	43	10	48	0	0	.337	.472
SS	Heinie Schuble	R	65	218	56	6	2	4	1.8	29	28	7	27	0	0	0	.257	.358
3B	Les Bell	R	115	390	101	26	6	9	2.3	48	65	34	63	5	5	0	.259	.426
RF	Wattie Holm	R	110	419	120	27	8	3	0.7	55	66	24	29	4	4	2	.286	.411
CF	Taylor Douthit	R	130	488	128	29	6	5	1.0	81	50	52	45	6	4	2	.262	.377
LF	Chick Hafey	R	103	346	114	26	5	18	5.2	62	63	36	41	12	9	5	.329	.590
C	Frank Snyder	R	63	194	50	5	0	1	0.5	7	30	9	18	0	1	1	.258	.299
SUBSTITUTES																		
3S	Specs Toporcer	L	86	290	72	13	4	0	0.0	37	19	27	16	5	8	3	.248	.321
SS	Tommy Thevenow	R	59	191	37	6	1	0	0.0	23	4	14	8	2	0	0	.194	.236
SS	Rabbit Maranville	R	9	29	7	1	0	0	0.0	0	0	2	2	0	0	0	.241	.276
OF	Billy Southworth	L	92	306	92	15	5	2	0.7	52	39	23	7	10	9	2	.301	.402
OF	Ray Blades	R	61	180	57	8	5	2	1.1	33	29	28	22	3	9	4	.317	.450
OF	Ernie Orsatti	L	27	92	29	7	3	0	0.0	15	12	11	12	2	1	0	.315	.457
OF	Danny Clark	L	58	72	17	2	2	0	0.0	8	13	8	7	0	40	12	.236	.319
OF	Homer Peel	R	2	2	0	0	0	0	0.0	0	0	0	1	0	1	0	.000	.000
OF	Wally Roettger	R	5	1	0	0	0	0	0.0	0	0	1	0	0	0	0	.000	.000
C	Bob O'Farrell	R	61	178	47	10	1	0	0.0	19	18	23	22	3	6	2	.264	.331
C	Johnny Schulte	L	64	156	45	8	2	9	5.8	35	32	47	19	1	3	1	.288	.538
C	Bobby Schang	R	3	5	1	0	0	0	0.0	0	0	0	0	0	0	0	.200	.200
PITCHERS																		
P	Jesse Haines	R	38	114	23	3	0	0	0.0	6	8	3	30	0	0	0	.202	.228
P	Grover Alexander	R	37	94	23	3	1	0	0.0	7	6	5	14	0	0	0	.245	.298
P	Bill Sherdel	L	39	72	14	2	0	1	1.4	9	5	7	6	0	0	0	.194	.264
P	Flint Rhem	R	27	59	4	1	0	0	0.0	3	2	2	31	0	0	0	.068	.085
P	Bob McGraw	R	18	33	6	0	2	1	3.0	4	5	0	15	1	0	0	.182	.394
P	Art Reinhart	L	27	32	10	1	0	0	0.0	8	0	2	6	0	2	1	.313	.344
P	Fred Frankhouse	R	8	20	5	0	0	0	0.0	0	3	1	1	0	2	1	.250	.250
P	Carlisle Littlejohn	R	15	12	5	1	0	0	0.0	2	1	0	2	0	0	0	.417	.500
P	Hi Bell	R	25	11	1	0	0	0	0.0	1	0	0	4	0	0	0	.091	.091
P	Jimmy Ring	R	13	8	3	2	0	0	0.0	3	0	0	2	0	0	0	.375	.625
P	Vic Keen	R	21	4	1	0	0	0	0.0	0	0	0	2	0	0	0	.250	.250
P	Eddie Dyer	L	1	0	0	0	0	0	–	0	0	1	0	0	0	0	–	–
P	Syl Johnson	R	2	0	0	0	0	0	–	0	0	0	0	0	0	0	–	–
P	Tony Kaufmann	R	1	0	0	0	0	0	–	0	0	0	0	0	0	0	–	–
TEAM TOTAL				5207	1450	264	79	84	1.6	754	700	484	511	110	104	36	.278	.408

INDIVIDUAL FIELDING

POS	Player	T	G	PO	A	E	DP	TC/G	FA
1B	J. Bottomley	L	152	1656	70	20	149	11.5	.989
	S. Toporcer	R	1	9	1	1	1	11.0	.909
	A. Reinhart	L	1	1	0	0	0	1.0	1.000
2B	F. Frisch	R	153	396	641	22	104	6.9	.979
	S. Toporcer	R	2	3	2	0	1	2.5	1.000
SS	H. Schuble	R	65	120	192	29	36	5.2	.915
	T. Thevenow	R	59	111	199	18	38	5.6	.945
	S. Toporcer	R	27	37	62	9	13	4.0	.917
	L. Bell	R	10	16	41	6	8	6.3	.905
	R. Maranville	R	9	17	34	2	6	5.9	.962
	F. Frisch	R	1	0	2	0	0	2.0	1.000
3B	L. Bell	R	100	85	142	24	13	2.5	.904
	S. Toporcer	R	54	49	95	3	8	2.7	.980
	W. Holm	R	9	4	22	0	2	2.9	1.000
OF	T. Douthit	R	125	396	8	15	4	3.4	.964
	W. Holm	R	97	201	3	7	0	2.2	.967
	C. Hafey	R	94	179	19	4	7	2.1	.980
	B. Southworth	R	83	153	6	5	2	2.0	.970
	R. Blades	R	50	64	0	6	0	1.4	.914
	E. Orsatti	L	26	56	3	5	2	2.5	.922
	H. Peel	R	1	0	0	0	0	0.0	.000
	D. Clark	R	9	25	1	2	1	3.1	.929
	W. Roettger	R	3	2	0	2	0	1.3	.500
C	J. Schulte	R	59	172	45	10	6	3.8	.956
	F. Snyder	R	62	174	37	4	5	3.5	.981
	B. O'Farrell	R	53	141	45	4	5	3.6	.979
	B. Schang	R	3	3	1	0	0	1.3	1.000

The 1927 season got off to a shocking start when Breadon and Rickey, outraged by Hornsby's salary demands, traded the leader and manager of their pennant-winning club to the New York Giants. The Cardinals received second baseman Frankie Frisch and pitcher Jimmy Ring. Frisch batted .337 and covered far more ground at second than Hornsby had; Rickey had put in place the first piece of the club that would be known as the Gashouse Gang.

The Cardinals won three games more than they had in 1926, but 92 wins wasn't enough, as the Pirates edged the Cards and Giants in a tight three-team race. Forty-year-old Alexander won 21 with a 2.52 ERA, and Jesse Haines went 24–10 with the newly found knuckleball that revived his career.

TEAM STATISTICS

	W	L	PCT	GB	R	OR	2B	3B	Batting HR	BA	SA	SB	E	Fielding DP	FA	CG	BB	Pitching SO	ShO	SV	ERA
T	94	60	.610		817	659	258	78	54	.305	.412	65	187	130	.969	90	418	435	10	10	3.66
TL	92	61	.601	1.5	754	665	264	79	84	.278	.408	110	213	170	.966	89	363	394	14	11	3.57
Y	92	62	.597	2	817	720	251	62	109	.297	.427	73	195	160	.969	65	453	442	7	16	3.97
HI	85	68	.556	8.5	750	661	266	63	74	.284	.400	65	181	152	.971	75	514	465	11	5	3.65
N	75	78	.490	18.5	643	653	222	77	29	.278	.367	62	165	160	.973	87	316	407	12	12	3.54
KN	65	88	.425	28.5	541	619	195	74	39	.253	.342	106	229	117	.963	74	418	574	7	10	3.36
OS	60	94	.390	34	651	771	216	61	37	.279	.363	100	231	130	.963	52	468	402	3	11	4.22
HI	51	103	.331	43	678	903	216	46	57	.280	.370	68	169	152	.972	81	462	377	5	6	5.35
AGUE TOTAL					5651	5651	1888	540	483	.282	.386	649	1570	1171	.969	613	3412	3496	69	81	3.91

INDIVIDUAL PITCHING

TCHER	T	W	L	PCT	ERA	SV	G	GS	CG	IP	H	BB	SO	R	ER	ShO	H/9	BB/9	SO/9
sse Haines	R	24	10	.706	2.72	1	38	36	25	300.2	273	77	89	114	91	6	8.17	2.30	2.66
over Alexander	R	21	10	.677	2.52	3	37	30	22	268	261	38	48	94	75	2	8.76	1.28	1.61
l Sherdel	L	17	12	.586	3.53	6	39	28	18	232.1	241	48	59	109	91	0	9.34	1.86	2.29
nt Rhem	R	10	12	.455	4.41	0	27	26	9	169.1	189	54	51	102	83	2	10.05	2.87	2.71
b McGraw	R	4	5	.444	5.07	0	18	12	4	94	121	30	37	65	53	1	11.59	2.87	3.54
Reinhart	L	5	2	.714	4.19	1	21	9	4	81.2	82	36	15	47	38	2	9.04	3.97	1.65
Bell	R	1	3	.250	3.92	0	25	1	0	57.1	71	22	31	37	25	0	11.15	3.45	4.87
ed Frankhouse	R	5	1	.833	2.70	0	6	6	5	50	41	16	20	18	15	1	7.38	2.88	3.60
rlisle Littlejohn	R	3	1	.750	4.50	0	14	2	1	42	47	14	16	21	21	0	10.07	3.00	3.43
: Keen	R	2	1	.667	4.81	0	21	0	0	33.2	39	8	12	21	18	0	10.43	2.14	3.21
nmy Ring	R	0	4	.000	6.55	0	13	3	1	33	39	17	13	28	24	0	10.64	4.64	3.55
l Johnson	R	0	0	–	6.00	0	2	0	0	3	3	0	2	2	2	0	9.00	0.00	6.00
die Dyer	L	0	0	–	18.00	0	1	0	0	2	5	2	1	4	4	0	22.50	9.00	4.50
ny Kaufmann	R	0	0	–	81.00	0	1	0	0	.1	4	1	0	3	3	0	108.00	27.00	0.00
AM TOTAL		92	61	.601	3.57	11	263	153	89	1367.1	1416	363	394	665	543	14	9.32	2.39	2.59

MANAGER	W	L	PCT
Bill McKechnie	95	59	.617

POS	Player	B	G	AB	H	2B	3B	HR	HR %	R	RBI	BB	SO	SB	Pinch Hit AB	Pinch Hit H	BA	SA
REGULARS																		
1B	Jim Bottomley	L	149	576	187	42	20	31	5.4	123	136	71	54	10	0	0	.325	.628
2B	Frankie Frisch	B	141	547	164	29	9	10	1.8	107	86	64	17	29	2	1	.300	.441
SS	Rabbit Maranville	R	112	366	88	14	10	1	0.3	40	34	36	27	3	0	0	.240	.342
3B	Wattie Holm	R	102	386	107	24	6	3	0.8	61	47	32	17	1	9	4	.277	.394
RF	George Harper	L	99	272	83	8	2	17	6.3	41	58	51	15	2	13	4	.305	.537
CF	Taylor Douthit	R	154	648	191	35	3	3	0.5	111	43	84	36	11	0	0	.295	.372
LF	Chick Hafey	R	138	520	175	46	6	27	5.2	101	111	40	53	8	4	0	.337	.604
C	Jimmie Wilson	R	120	411	106	26	2	2	0.5	45	50	45	24	9	0	0	.258	.345
SUBSTITUTES																		
32	Andy High	L	111	368	105	14	3	6	1.6	58	37	37	10	2	17	4	.285	.389
SS	Tommy Thevenow	R	69	171	35	8	3	0	0.0	11	13	20	12	0	0	0	.205	.287
12	Specs Toporcer	L	8	14	0	0	0	0	0.0	0	0	0	3	0	6	0	.000	.000
OF	Wally Roettger	R	68	261	89	17	4	6	2.3	27	44	10	22	2	2	0	.341	.506
OF	Ray Blades	R	51	85	20	7	1	1	1.2	9	19	20	26	0	24	4	.235	.376
O1	Ernie Orsatti	L	27	69	21	6	0	3	4.3	10	15	10	11	0	3	0	.304	.522
OF	Pepper Martin	R	39	13	4	0	0	0	0.0	11	0	1	2	2	12	3	.308	.308
C	Earl Smith	L	24	58	13	2	0	0	0.0	3	7	5	4	0	5	0	.224	.259
C	Bob O'Farrell	R	16	52	11	1	0	0	0.0	6	4	13	9	2	0	0	.212	.231
C	Gus Mancuso	R	11	38	7	0	1	0	0.0	2	3	0	5	0	0	0	.184	.237
C	Spud Davis	R	2	5	1	0	0	0	0.0	1	1	1	0	0	0	0	.200	.200
PH	Howie Williamson	L	10	9	2	0	0	0	0.0	0	0	1	4	0	9	2	.222	.222
PITCHERS																		
P	Jesse Haines	R	33	87	16	2	0	0	0.0	4	10	4	13	0	0	0	.184	.207
P	Grover Alexander	R	34	86	25	2	0	1	1.2	13	11	4	8	0	0	0	.291	.349
P	Bill Sherdel	L	38	84	19	5	0	1	1.2	10	8	8	10	1	0	0	.226	.321
P	Flint Rhem	R	28	67	11	0	0	1	1.5	4	6	2	23	0	0	0	.164	.209
P	Clarence Mitchell	L	19	56	7	1	0	0	0.0	0	1	0	3	0	0	0	.125	.143
P	Syl Johnson	R	34	38	6	1	0	0	0.0	5	1	3	18	0	0	0	.158	.184
P	Fred Frankhouse	R	22	27	5	2	0	0	0.0	3	2	3	4	0	1	0	.185	.259
P	Art Reinhart	L	27	24	4	0	0	0	0.0	1	1	2	4	0	1	0	.167	.167
P	Carlisle Littlejohn	R	12	11	0	0	0	0	0.0	0	0	0	2	0	0	0	.000	.000
P	Hal Haid	R	27	8	3	0	0	0	0.0	0	1	1	2	0	0	0	.375	.375
P	Tony Kaufmann	R	5	0	0	0	0	0	–	0	0	0	0	0	0	0	–	–
TEAM TOTAL				5357	1505	292	70	113	2.1	807	749	568	438	82	108	22	.281	.425

INDIVIDUAL FIELDING

POS	Player	T	G	PO	A	E	DP	TC/G	FA
1B	J. Bottomley	L	148	1454	52	20	113	10.3	.987
	E. Orsatti	L	5	41	1	1	2	8.6	.977
	S. Toporcer	R	1	7	3	0	0	10.0	1.000
	T. Thevenow	R	1	0	1	0	0	1.0	1.000
2B	F. Frisch	R	139	383	474	21	80	6.3	.976
	A. High	R	19	35	47	2	10	4.4	.976
	S. Toporcer	R	1	5	0	0	1	5.0	1.000
	R. Maranville	R	2	1	2	0	1	1.5	1.000
SS	R. Maranville	R	112	236	362	19	57	5.5	.969
	T. Thevenow	R	64	100	158	19	29	4.3	.931
3B	W. Holm	R	83	100	145	22	9	3.2	.918
	A. High	R	73	56	117	12	10	2.5	.935
	T. Thevenow	R	3	4	7	0	0	3.7	1.000

POS	Player	T	G	PO	A	E	DP	TC/G	FA
OF	T. Douthit	R	154	547	10	9	4	3.7	.984
	C. Hafey	R	133	287	13	11	3	2.3	.965
	G. Harper	R	84	156	13	2	2	2.0	.988
	W. Roettger	R	66	152	2	3	1	2.4	.981
	R. Blades	R	19	34	1	1	1	1.9	.972
	E. Orsatti	L	17	29	2	0	0	1.8	1.000
	W. Holm	R	7	18	0	0	0	2.6	1.000
	P. Martin	R	4	2	0	0	0	0.5	1.000
C	J. Wilson	R	120	394*	82*	8	13*	4.0	.983
	E. Smith	R	18	52	6	0	2	3.2	1.000
	B. O'Farrell	R	14	61	4	1	1	4.7	.985
	G. Mancuso	R	11	54	7	1	0	5.6	.984
	S. Davis	R	2	6	0	2	0	4.0	.750

Another three-win improvement meant another pennant, this time by two games over the Giants. Jim Bottomley and Chick Hafey, another farm product converted from a pitcher to an outfielder by Rickey, were the offensive stars. Bottomley led the league in homers and RBIs, was second in slugging, and was named the league's MVP; Hafey finished fourth in RBIs and third in slugging.

This Cardinal club had an outstanding balance of hitting, pitching, and fielding; they were second in the league in runs scored, runs allowed, slugging average, fielding percentage, and ERA. It was the last year for their starting triumvirate of Jesse Haines, Bill Sherdel, and Flint Rhem. The three had averaged 48 wins a season in their four years in the rotation together. Rhem missed the 1929 season, and Sherdel was traded away in 1930.

The Cardinals found the Yankees waiting for them again in the World Series, and this time they were too much for the Redbirds, winning in four straight. Babe Ruth cracked three home runs in Game 4 for the Yanks, the second time he had hit three homers in a Series game. It was also the second time he had done it against the Cardinals; the first was in '26, also in Game 4.

TEAM STATISTICS

	W	L	PCT	GB	R	OR	Batting 2B	3B	HR	BA	SA	SB	Fielding E	DP	FA	CG	BB	Pitching SO	ShO	SV	ERA
TL	95	59	.617		807	636	292	70	113	.281	.425	82	160	134	.974	83	399	422	4	21	3.38
Y	93	61	.604	2	807	653	276	59	118	.293	.430	62	178	175	.972	79	405	399	7	16	3.67
HI	91	63	.591	4	714	615	251	64	92	.278	.402	83	156	176	.975	75	508	531	12	14	3.40
IT	85	67	.559	9	837	704	246	100	52	.309	.421	64	201	123	.967	82	446	385	8	11	3.95
IN	78	74	.513	16	648	686	229	67	32	.280	.368	83	162	194	.974	68	410	355	11	11	3.94
KN	77	76	.503	17.5	665	640	229	70	66	.266	.374	81	217	113	.965	75	468	551	16	15	3.25
OS	50	103	.327	44.5	631	878	241	41	52	.275	.367	60	193	141	.969	54	524	343	1	6	4.83
HI	43	109	.283	51	660	957	257	47	85	.267	.382	53	181	171	.971	42	671	403	4	11	5.52
EAGUE TOTAL					5769	5769	2021	518	610	.281	.397	568	1448	1227	.971	558	3831	3389	63	105	3.98

INDIVIDUAL PITCHING

PITCHER	T	W	L	PCT	ERA	SV	G	GS	CG	IP	H	BB	SO	R	ER	ShO	H/9	BB/9	SO/9
ll Sherdel	L	21	10	.677	2.86	5	38	27	20	248.2	251	56	72	96	79	0	9.08	2.03	2.61
rover Alexander	R	16	9	.640	3.36	2	34	31	18	243.2	262	37	91	107	91	1	9.68	1.37	2.18
sse Haines	R	20	8	.714	3.18	0	33	28	20	240.1	238	72	77	98	85	1	8.91	2.70	2.88
nt Rhem	R	11	8	.579	4.14	3	28	22	9	169.2	199	71	47	91	78	0	10.56	3.77	2.49
arence Mitchell	L	8	9	.471	3.30	0	19	18	9	150	149	38	31	59	55	1	8.94	2.28	1.86
l Johnson	R	8	4	.667	3.90	3	34	6	2	120	117	33	66	53	52	0	8.78	2.48	4.95
ed Frankhouse	R	3	2	.600	3.96	1	21	10	.1	84	91	36	29	47	37	0	9.75	3.86	3.11
t Reinhart	L	4	6	.400	2.87	2	23	9	3	75.1	80	27	12	39	24	1	9.56	3.23	1.43
al Haid	R	2	2	.500	2.30	5	27	0	0	47	39	11	21	24	12	0	7.47	2.11	4.02
arlisle Littlejohn	R	2	1	.667	3.66	0	12	2	1	32	36	14	6	16	13	0	10.13	3.94	1.69
ny Kaufmann	R	0	0	–	9.64	0	4	1	0	4.2	8	4	2	5	5	0	15.43	7.71	3.86
AM TOTAL		95	59	.617	3.38	21	273	154	83	1415.1	1470	399	422	635	531	4	9.35	2.54	2.68

MANAGER	W	L	PCT
Billy Southworth	43	45	.489
Gabby Street	2	0	1.000
Bill McKechnie	33	29	.532

POS	Player	B	G	AB	H	2B	3B	HR	HR %	R	RBI	BB	SO	SB	Pinch Hit AB	Pinch Hit H	BA	SA
REGULARS																		
1B	Jim Bottomley	L	146	560	176	31	12	29	5.2	108	137	70	54	3	1	0	.314	.568
2B	Frankie Frisch	B	138	527	176	40	12	5	0.9	93	74	53	12	24	3	2	.334	.484
SS	Charley Gelbert	R	146	512	134	29	8	3	0.6	60	65	51	46	8	0	0	.262	.367
3B	Andy High	L	146	603	178	32	4	10	1.7	95	63	38	18	7	1	1	.295	.411
RF	Ernie Orsatti	L	113	346	115	21	7	3	0.9	64	39	33	43	7	17	6	.332	.460
CF	Taylor Douthit	R	150	613	206	42	7	9	1.5	128	62	79	49	8	0	0	.336	.471
LF	Chick Hafey	R	134	517	175	47	9	29	5.6	101	125	45	42	7	3	0	.338	.632
C	Jimmie Wilson	R	120	394	128	27	8	4	1.0	59	71	43	19	4	1	1	.325	.464
SUBSTITUTES																		
3S	Johnny Butler	R	17	55	9	1	1	0	0.0	5	5	4	5	0	0	0	.164	.218
2B	Carey Selph	R	25	51	12	1	1	0	0.0	8	7	6	4	1	5	1	.235	.294
UT	Eddie Delker	R	22	40	6	0	1	0	0.0	5	3	2	12	0	2	0	.150	.200
3B	Fred Haney	R	10	26	3	1	1	0	0.0	4	2	1	2	0	2	1	.115	.231
OF	Wally Roettger	R	79	269	68	11	3	3	1.1	27	42	13	27	0	10	1	.253	.349
OF	Wattie Holm	R	64	176	41	5	6	0	0.0	21	14	12	8	1	17	3	.233	.330
OF	Billy Southworth	L	19	32	6	2	0	0	0.0	1	3	2	4	0	13	1	.188	.250
C	Earl Smith	L	57	145	50	8	0	1	0.7	9	22	18	6	0	7	2	.345	.421
C	Bubber Jonnard	R	18	31	3	0	0	0	0.0	0	2	0	6	0	0	0	.097	.097
PITCHERS																		
P	Bill Sherdel	L	33	70	16	1	1	1	1.4	5	8	2	4	0	0	0	.229	.314
P	Jesse Haines	R	28	69	11	0	0	1	1.4	5	3	1	22	1	0	0	.159	.203
P	Clarence Mitchell	L	26	66	18	3	1	0	0.0	9	9	4	6	1	0	0	.273	.348
P	Syl Johnson	R	42	60	7	2	1	1	1.7	4	5	1	23	0	0	0	.117	.233
P	Fred Frankhouse	R	34	52	15	3	0	1	1.9	7	8	1	6	0	2	0	.288	.404
P	Hal Haid	R	38	49	4	1	0	0	0.0	4	3	3	15	0	0	0	.082	.102
P	Grover Alexander	R	22	41	2	0	0	0	0.0	2	2	3	5	0	0	0	.049	.049
P	Bill Hallahan	R	20	26	4	0	0	0	0.0	2	3	2	13	0	0	0	.154	.154
P	Al Grabowski	L	6	16	4	2	1	0	0.0	3	1	1	0	0	0	0	.250	.500
P	Jim Lindsey	R	2	5	1	0	0	0	0.0	0	0	0	0	0	0	0	.200	.200
P	Mul Holland	R	8	4	1	0	0	0	0.0	0	1	1	0	0	0	0	.250	.250
P	Hi Bell	R	7	3	0	0	0	0	0.0	0	0	0	2	0	0	0	.000	.000
P	Carmen Hill	R	3	3	0	0	0	0	0.0	0	0	0	1	0	0	0	.000	.000
P	Bill Doak	R	3	2	0	0	0	0	0.0	0	0	1	0	0	0	0	.000	.000
P	Hal Goldsmith	R	2	1	0	0	0	0	0.0	0	0	0	1	0	0	0	.000	.000
TEAM TOTAL				5364	1569	310	84	100	1.9	831	779	490	455	72	84	19	.293	.438

INDIVIDUAL FIELDING

POS	Player	T	G	PO	A	E	DP	TC/G	FA
1B	J. Bottomley	L	145	1347	75	13	122	9.9	.991
	E. Orsatti	L	10	83	2	1	4	8.6	.988
2B	F. Frisch	R	121	295	374	21	66	5.7	.970
	A. High	R	22	59	61	3	16	5.6	.976
	C. Selph	R	16	23	29	1	3	3.3	.981
	E. Delker	R	7	8	9	1	1	2.6	.944
SS	C. Gelbert	R	146	338	499	46	95	6.0	.948
	J. Butler	R	8	17	19	1	2	4.6	.973
	E. Delker	R	9	4	5	3	0	1.3	.750
	F. Frisch	R	1	1	0	0	0	1.0	1.000
3B	A. High	R	123	91	204	10	17	2.5	.967
	F. Frisch	R	13	9	33	1	1	3.3	.977
	J. Butler	R	9	13	14	1	0	3.1	.964
	F. Haney	R	6	8	15	1	2	4.0	.958
	E. Delker	R	3	4	6	1	1	3.7	.909
	W. Holm	R	1	1	0	0	0	1.0	1.000

POS	Player	T	G	PO	A	E	DP	TC/G	FA
OF	T. Douthit	R	150	442	8	12	1	3.1	.974
	C. Hafey	R	130	278	8	10	1	2.3	.966
	E. Orsatti	L	77	176	12	5	5	2.5	.974
	W. Roettger	R	69	137	4	1	0	2.1	.993
	W. Holm	R	44	115	4	7	2	2.9	.944
	B. Southworth	R	5	12	0	0	0	2.4	1.000
C	J. Wilson	R	119	410	80	14	16	4.2	.972
	E. Smith	R	50	131	21	6	1	3.2	.962
	B. Jonnard	R	18	39	5	2	1	2.6	.957

Despite an offense that boasted six .300-hitting regulars, St. Louis slipped to fourth place. The Cardinals were capable of some violent explosions: they set a post-1900 National League record for scoring in a 28–6 pasting of the Phillies in July, and at one point Chick Hafey rapped out ten straight hits, tying the league record. But the team ERA jumped from 3.36 to 4.66—still below the league average, but half a run behind the pennant-winning Cubs. Sherdel and Haines had astronomical ERAs of 5.93 and 5.71 respectively, as St. Louis fell into the middle of the pack in virtually every statistical category. Was it time to make drastic changes? Were the Cards going downhill? Quite the opposite—their best years were just around the corner.

TEAM STATISTICS

	W	L	PCT	GB	R	OR	Batting 2B	3B	HR	BA	SA	SB	Fielding E	DP	FA	Pitching CG	BB	SO	ShO	SV	ERA
CHI	98	54	.645		982	758	310	45	140	.303	.452	103	154	169	.975	79	537	548	14	21	4.16
PIT	88	65	.575	10.5	904	780	285	116	60	.303	.430	94	181	136	.970	79	439	409	5	13	4.36
NY	84	67	.556	13.5	897	709	251	47	136	.296	.436	85	158	163	.975	68	387	431	9	13	3.97
STL	78	74	.513	20	831	806	310	84	100	.293	.438	72	174	149	.971	83	474	453	6	8	4.66
PHI	71	82	.464	27.5	897	1032	305	51	153	.309	.467	59	191	153	.969	45	616	369	5	24	6.13
BKN	70	83	.458	28.5	755	888	282	69	99	.291	.427	80	192	113	.968	59	549	549	7	16	4.92
CIN	66	88	.429	33	686	760	258	79	34	.281	.379	134	162	148	.974	75	413	347	5	8	4.41
BOS	56	98	.364	43	657	876	252	78	32	.280	.375	65	204	146	.967	78	530	366	4	12	5.12
LEAGUE TOTAL					6609	6609	2253	569	754	.294	.426	692	1416	1177	.971	566	3945	3472	55	115	4.71

INDIVIDUAL PITCHING

PITCHER	T	W	L	PCT	ERA	SV	G	GS	CG	IP	H	BB	SO	R	ER	ShO	H/9	BB/9	SO/9
Bill Sherdel	L	10	15	.400	5.93	0	33	22	11	195.2	278	58	69	144	129	1	12.79	2.67	3.17
Syl Johnson	R	13	7	.650	3.60	3	42	19	12	182.1	186	56	80	88	73	3	9.18	2.76	3.95
Jesse Haines	R	13	10	.565	5.71	0	28	25	12	179.2	230	73	59	123	114	0	11.52	3.66	2.96
Clarence Mitchell	L	8	11	.421	4.27	0	25	22	16	173	221	60	39	89	82	0	11.50	3.12	2.03
Hal Haid	R	9	9	.500	4.07	4	38	12	8	154.2	171	66	41	90	70	0	9.95	3.84	2.39
Fred Frankhouse	R	7	2	.778	4.12	1	30	12	6	133.1	149	43	37	70	61	0	10.06	2.90	2.50
Grover Alexander	R	9	8	.529	3.89	0	22	19	8	132	149	23	33	65	57	0	10.16	1.57	2.25
Bill Hallahan	L	4	4	.500	4.42	0	20	12	5	93.2	94	60	52	51	46	0	9.03	5.77	5.00
Al Grabowski	L	3	2	.600	2.52	0	6	6	4	50	44	8	22	18	14	2	7.92	1.44	3.96
Jim Lindsey	R	1	1	.500	5.51	0	2	2	1	16.1	20	2	8	11	10	0	11.02	1.10	4.41
Paul Holland	R	0	1	.000	9.42	0	8	0	0	14.1	13	7	5	15	15	0	8.16	4.40	3.14
Bell	R	0	2	.000	6.92	0	7	0	0	13	19	4	4	15	10	0	13.15	2.77	2.77
Bill Doak	R	1	2	.333	12.00	0	3	2	0	9	17	5	3	15	12	0	17.00	5.00	3.00
Carmen Hill	R	0	0	–	8.31	0	3	1	0	8.2	10	8	1	10	8	0	10.38	8.31	1.04
Hal Goldsmith	R	0	0	–	6.75	0	2	0	0	4	3	1	0	3	3	0	6.75	2.25	0.00
TEAM TOTAL		78	74	.513	4.66	8	269	154	83	1359.2	1604	474	453	807	704	6	10.62	3.14	3.00

MANAGER	W	L	PCT
Gabby Street	92	62	.597

POS	Player	B	G	AB	H	2B	3B	HR	HR %	R	RBI	BB	SO	SB	Pinch Hit AB	Pinch Hit H	BA	SA
REGULARS																		
1B	Jim Bottomley	L	131	487	148	33	7	15	3.1	92	97	44	36	5	7	2	.304	.493
2B	Frankie Frisch	B	133	540	187	46	9	10	1.9	121	114	55	16	15	0	0	.346	.520
SS	Charley Gelbert	R	139	513	156	39	11	3	0.6	92	72	43	41	6	0	0	.304	.441
3B	Sparky Adams	R	137	570	179	36	9	0	0.0	98	55	45	27	7	2	1	.314	.409
RF	George Watkins	L	119	391	146	32	7	17	4.3	85	87	24	49	5	15	5	.373	.621
CF	Taylor Douthit	R	154	664	201	41	10	7	1.1	109	93	60	38	4	0	0	.303	.426
LF	Chick Hafey	R	120	446	150	39	12	26	5.8	108	107	46	51	12	1	0	.336	.652
C	Jimmie Wilson	R	107	362	115	25	7	1	0.3	54	58	28	17	8	8	3	.318	.434
SUBSTITUTES																		
3B	Andy High	L	72	215	60	12	2	2	0.9	34	29	23	6	1	17	5	.279	.381
1O	Ernie Orsatti	L	48	131	42	8	4	1	0.8	24	15	12	18	1	12	3	.321	.466
S2	Doc Farrell	R	23	61	13	1	1	0	0.0	3	6	4	2	1	1	0	.213	.262
OF	Showboat Fisher	L	92	254	95	18	6	8	3.1	49	61	25	21	4	20	8	.374	.587
OF	Ray Blades	R	45	101	40	6	2	4	4.0	26	25	21	15	1	7	2	.396	.614
OF	Homer Peel	R	26	73	12	2	0	0	0.0	9	10	3	4	0	4	1	.164	.192
OF	George Puccinelli	R	11	16	9	1	0	3	18.8	5	8	0	1	0	8	4	.563	1.188
C	Gus Mancuso	R	76	227	83	17	2	7	3.1	39	59	18	16	1	12	3	.366	.551
C	Earl Smith	L	8	10	0	0	0	0	0.0	0	0	3	1	0	0	0	.000	.000
PH	Pepper Martin	R	6	1	0	0	0	0	0.0	5	0	0	0	0	1	0	.000	.000
PITCHERS																		
P	Bill Hallahan	R	35	81	10	1	0	0	0.0	8	4	5	41	0	0	0	.123	.136
P	Syl Johnson	R	32	70	15	4	0	0	0.0	9	5	4	28	1	0	0	.214	.271
P	Jesse Haines	R	29	65	16	3	0	0	0.0	3	12	4	15	0	0	0	.246	.292
P	Burleigh Grimes	R	23	57	15	4	0	0	0.0	9	10	5	12	0	0	0	.263	.333
P	Flint Rhem	R	26	52	12	2	0	0	0.0	7	6	0	7	0	0	0	.231	.269
P	Al Grabowski	L	35	33	12	2	0	0	0.0	7	5	0	11	0	0	0	.364	.424
P	Jim Lindsey	R	39	28	8	1	0	0	0.0	2	4	0	7	0	0	0	.286	.321
P	Hi Bell	R	39	26	2	0	0	0	0.0	1	0	2	11	0	0	0	.077	.077
P	Bill Sherdel	L	13	19	2	0	0	0	0.0	3	0	3	2	0	0	0	.105	.105
P	Fred Frankhouse	R	9	5	0	0	0	0	0.0	0	0	0	1	0	0	0	.000	.000
P	Dizzy Dean	R	1	3	1	0	0	0	0.0	1	0	0	0	0	0	0	.333	.333
P	Hal Haid	R	21	3	0	0	0	0	0.0	0	0	1	1	0	0	0	.000	.000
P	Carmen Hill	R	4	3	1	0	0	0	0.0	0	0	0	0	0	0	0	.333	.333
P	Tony Kaufmann	R	2	3	1	0	0	0	0.0	1	0	1	1	0	0	0	.333	.333
P	Clarence Mitchell	L	1	2	1	0	0	0	0.0	0	0	0	0	0	0	0	.500	.500
TEAM TOTAL				5512	1732	373	89	104	1.9	1004	942	479	496	72	115	37	.314	.471

INDIVIDUAL FIELDING

POS	Player	T	G	PO	A	E	DP	TC/G	FA	POS	Player	T	G	PO	A	E	DP	TC/G	FA
1B	J. Bottomley	L	124	1164	41	12	127	9.8	.990	OF	T. Douthit	R	154	425	8	16	3	2.9	.964
	E. Orsatti	L	22	188	15	3	17	9.4	.985		C. Hafey	R	116	189	11	5	0	1.8	.976
	G. Watkins	R	13	116	8	3	12	9.8	.976		G. Watkins	R	89	163	10	8	4	2.0	.956
	D. Farrell	R	1	3	0	0	0	3.0	1.000		S. Fisher	R	67	122	6	5	0	2.0	.962
2B	F. Frisch	R	123	307	473	25	93	6.5	.969		R. Blades	R	32	66	1	3	0	2.2	.957
	S. Adams	R	25	62	85	4	25	6.0	.974		H. Peel	R	21	30	0	1	0	1.5	.968
	G. Watkins	R	1	0	0	0	0	0.0	.000		E. Orsatti	L	11	22	4	0	2	2.4	1.000
	D. Farrell	R	6	11	14	0	2	4.2	1.000		G. Puccinelli	R	3	2	0	0	0	0.7	1.000
	A. High	R	3	3	3	0	0	2.0	1.000	C	J. Wilson	R	107	456	67	7	11	5.0	.987
SS	C. Gelbert	R	139	322	472	44	104	6.0	.947		G. Mancuso	R	61	277	33	10	2	5.2	.969
	D. Farrell	R	15	31	36	4	10	4.7	.944		E. Smith	R	6	18	3	2	0	3.8	.913
	S. Adams	R	7	12	20	4	3	5.1	.889										
3B	S. Adams	R	104	66	159	8	18	2.2	.966										
	A. High	R	48	34	68	1	5	2.1	.990										
	F. Frisch	R	10	8	20	2	3	3.0	.933										

This time the Cardinals swept to their pennant from far back; in early August they were in fourth place, more than ten games behind the Dodgers. From August 30 until their pennant-clinching victory on September 26, the Cardinals won 21 and lost just 3. Every regular hit over .300, including George Watkins, whose .373 is the highest average ever turned in by a rookie. The club hit .314 in one of the greatest years for hitters in baseball history, and was the first team since 1900 to score 1000 runs. Their rather high ERA of 4.40 was still half a run below the league average. The Philadelphia Athletics' pitching was able to stifle the Cardinal bats in the Series, however. Lefty Grove and George Earnshaw allowed just five earned runs in their 44 innings of work, and the Cards were held to a .200 batting average in Philadelphia's six-game victory. But St. Louis would not have to wait long for revenge.

TEAM STATISTICS

W	L	PCT	GB	R	OR	Batting 2B	3B	HR	BA	SA	SB	Fielding E	DP	FA	CG	BB	Pitching SO	ShO	SV	ERA
L	92	62	.597		1004	784	373	89	104	.314	.471	72	183	176	.970	63	477	641	5	21	4.40
ll	90	64	.584	2	998	870	305	72	171	.309	.481	70	170	167	.973	67	528	601	6	12	4.80
Y	87	67	.565	5	959	814	264	83	143	.319	.473	59	164	164	.974	64	439	522	6	19	4.59
KN	86	68	.558	6	871	738	303	73	122	.304	.454	53	174	167	.972	74	394	526	13	15	4.03
T	80	74	.519	12	891	928	285	119	86	.303	.449	76	216	164	.965	80	438	393	7	13	5.24
)S	70	84	.455	22	693	835	246	78	66	.281	.393	69	178	167	.971	71	475	424	6	11	4.91
N	59	95	.383	33	665	857	265	67	74	.281	.400	48	161	164	.973	61	394	361	6	11	5.08
Il	52	102	.338	40	944	1199	345	44	126	.315	.458	34	239	169	.962	54	543	384	3	7	6.71
AGUE TOTAL				7025	7025	2386	625	892	.303	.448	481	1485	1338	.970	534	3688	3852	52	109	4.97

INDIVIDUAL PITCHING

TCHER	T	W	L	PCT	ERA	SV	G	GS	CG	IP	H	BB	SO	R	ER	ShO	H/9	BB/9	SO/9
l Hallahan	L	15	9	.625	4.66	2	35	32	13	237.1	233	126	177	135	123	2	8.84	4.78	6.71
l Johnson	R	12	10	.545	4.65	2	32	24	9	187.2	215	38	92	105	97	2	10.31	1.82	4.41
sse Haines	R	13	8	.619	4.30	1	29	24	14	182	215	54	68	107	87	0	10.63	2.67	3.36
rleigh Grimes	R	13	6	.684	3.01	0	22	19	10	152.1	174	43	58	66	51	1	10.28	2.54	3.43
nt Rhem	R	12	8	.600	4.45	0	26	19	9	139.2	173	37	47	90	69	0	11.15	2.38	3.03
Bell	R	4	3	.571	3.90	8	39	9	2	115.1	143	23	42	65	50	0	11.16	1.79	3.28
Grabowski	L	6	4	.600	4.84	1	33	8	1	106	121	50	45	66	57	0	10.27	4.25	3.82
n Lindsey	R	7	5	.583	4.43	5	39	6	3	105.2	131	46	50	59	52	0	11.16	3.92	4.26
' Sherdel	L	3	2	.600	4.64	0	13	7	1	64	86	13	29	34	33	1	12.09	1.83	4.08
l Haid	R	3	2	.600	4.09	2	20	0	0	33	38	14	13	17	15	0	10.36	3.82	3.55
d Frankhouse	R	2	3	.400	7.32	0	8	1	0	19.2	31	11	4	16	16	0	14.19	5.03	1.83
rmen Hill	R	0	1	.000	7.36	0	4	2	0	14.2	12	13	8	12	12	0	7.36	7.98	4.91
ny Kaufmann	R	0	1	.000	7.84	0	2	1	0	10.1	15	4	2	9	9	0	13.06	3.48	1.74
zy Dean	R	1	0	1.000	1.00	0	1	1	1	9	3	3	5	1	1	0	3.00	3.00	5.00
rence Mitchell	L	1	0	1.000	6.00	0	1	1	0	3	5	2	1	2	2	0	15.00	6.00	3.00
AM TOTAL		92	62	.597	4.40	21	304	154	63	1379.2	1595	477	641	784	674	6	10.40	3.11	4.18

MANAGER	W	L	PCT
Gabby Street	101	53	.656

POS	Player	B	G	AB	H	2B	3B	HR	HR %	R	RBI	BB	SO	SB	Pinch Hit AB	Pinch Hit H	BA	SA
REGULARS																		
1B	Jim Bottomley	L	108	382	133	34	5	9	2.4	73	75	34	24	3	14	3	.348	.534
2B	Frankie Frisch	B	131	518	161	24	4	4	0.8	96	82	45	13	28	2	0	.311	.396
SS	Charley Gelbert	R	131	447	129	29	5	1	0.2	61	62	54	31	7	0	0	.289	.383
3B	Sparky Adams	R	143	608	178	46	5	1	0.2	97	40	42	24	16	1	0	.293	.390
RF	George Watkins	L	131	503	145	30	13	13	2.6	93	51	31	66	15	2	0	.288	.477
CF	Pepper Martin	R	123	413	124	32	8	7	1.7	68	75	30	40	16	7	4	.300	.467
LF	Chick Hafey	R	122	450	157	35	8	16	3.6	94	95	39	43	11	4	1	.349	.569
C	Jimmie Wilson	R	115	383	105	20	2	0	0.0	45	51	28	15	5	5	0	.274	.337
SUBSTITUTES																		
1B	Ripper Collins	B	89	279	84	20	10	4	1.4	34	59	18	24	1	16	2	.301	.487
S2	Jake Flowers	R	45	137	34	11	1	2	1.5	19	19	9	6	7	2	0	.248	.387
32	Andy High	L	63	131	35	6	1	0	0.0	20	19	24	4	0	19	5	.267	.328
UT	Joe Benes	R	10	12	2	0	0	0	0.0	1	0	2	1	0	0	0	.167	.167
3B	Ray Cunningham	R	3	4	0	0	0	0	0.0	0	1	0	0	0	0	0	.000	.000
3B	Eddie Delker	R	1	2	1	1	0	0	0.0	0	2	0	0	0	0	0	.500	1.000
OF	Ernie Orsatti	L	78	158	46	16	6	0	0.0	27	19	14	16	1	15	2	.291	.468
OF	Wally Roettger	R	45	151	43	12	2	0	0.0	16	17	9	14	0	3	1	.285	.391
OF	Taylor Douthit	R	36	133	44	11	2	1	0.8	21	21	11	9	1	0	0	.331	.466
OF	Ray Blades	R	35	67	19	4	0	1	1.5	10	5	10	7	1	14	4	.284	.388
OF	Joel Hunt	R	4	1	0	0	0	0	0.0	0	2	0	1	0	1	0	.000	.000
C	Gus Mancuso	R	67	187	49	16	1	1	0.5	13	23	18	13	2	10	1	.262	.374
C	Mike Gonzalez	R	15	19	2	0	0	0	0.0	1	3	0	3	0	3	0	.105	.105
C	Gabby Street	R	1	1	0	0	0	0	0.0	0	0	0	0	0	0	0	.000	.000
PITCHERS																		
P	Bill Hallahan	R	37	81	8	2	0	0	0.0	5	5	7	34	0	0	0	.099	.123
P	Burleigh Grimes	R	29	76	14	0	0	0	0.0	4	8	1	10	0	0	0	.184	.184
P	Paul Derringer	R	35	72	7	0	0	0	0.0	2	1	1	18	0	0	0	.097	.097
P	Flint Rhem	R	33	69	9	1	0	0	0.0	4	6	0	21	0	0	0	.130	.145
P	Syl Johnson	R	32	60	14	2	1	0	0.0	4	7	3	16	0	0	0	.233	.300
P	Jesse Haines	R	19	45	6	1	0	0	0.0	3	4	0	6	0	0	0	.133	.156
P	Allyn Stout	R	30	19	2	0	0	0	0.0	0	1	0	9	0	0	0	.105	.105
P	Tony Kaufmann	R	20	18	2	0	0	0	0.0	1	0	1	3	0	1	0	.111	.111
P	Jim Lindsey	R	35	9	1	0	0	0	0.0	1	0	1	4	0	0	0	.111	.111
	TEAM TOTAL			5435	1554	353	74	60	1.1	815	751	432	475	114	119	23	.286	.411

INDIVIDUAL FIELDING

POS	Player	T	G	PO	A	E	DP	TC/G	FA
1B	J. Bottomley	L	93	897	43	12	95	10.2	.987
	R. Collins	L	68	563	42	3	54	8.9	.995
	E. Orsatti	L	1	11	1	1	0	13.0	.923
2B	F. Frisch	R	129	290	424	19	93	5.7	.974
	J. Flowers	R	20	34	51	1	14	4.3	.988
	A. High	R	19	19	38	1	4	3.1	.983
	J. Benes	R	2	4	6	1	0	5.5	.909
SS	C. Gelbert	R	131	281	435	31	91	5.7	.959
	J. Flowers	R	22	35	66	3	13	4.7	.971
	S. Adams	R	6	9	16	5	1	5.0	.833
	J. Benes	R	6	4	7	0	1	1.8	1.000
3B	S. Adams	R	138	118	223	13	29	2.6	.963
	A. High	R	23	13	26	0	5	1.7	1.000
	J. Benes	R	1	0	0	0	0	0.000	.000
	R. Cunningham	R	3	0	5	0	0	1.7	1.000
	E. Delker	R	1	1	0	0	0	1.0	1.000
	J. Flowers	R	1	1	1	0	0	1.0	1.000
OF	P. Martin	R	110	282	10	10	2	2.7	.967
	G. Watkins	R	129	263	12	12	4	2.2	.958
	C. Hafey	R	118	226	4	4	1	2.0	.983
	T. Douthit	R	36	105	0	3	0	3.0	.972
	E. Orsatti	L	45	83	0	1	0	1.9	.988
	W. Roettger	R	42	73	1	2	0	1.8	.974
	R. Blades	R	20	26	1	4	0	1.6	.871
	J. Hunt	R	1	0	0	0	0	0.0	.000
	T. Kaufmann	R	1	0	0	0	0	0.0	.000
	R. Collins	L	3	9	0	1	0	3.3	.900
C	J. Wilson	R	110	498	75	9	15	5.3	.985
	G. Mancuso	R	56	239	40	8	6	5.1	.972
	M. Gonzalez	R	12	15	4	0	0	1.6	1.000
	G. Street	R	1	1	1	0	0	2.0	1.000

The Cardinals finally won an easy pennant, leading wire-to-wire, and winning a hundred games for the first time. Frankie Frisch was named the league MVP, and Chick Hafey led the league in batting in the tightest batting race ever. Seven-tenths of a point separated first from third, as Hafey's .3489 nosed out Bill Terry of the Giants, with .3486, and teammate Jim Bottomley's .3482. Rookie Paul Derringer led the league in won-lost percentage; Wild Bill Hallahan led in wins and strikeouts; and Burleigh Grimes, the last of the legal spitballers, won 17 and added two more in the World Series, including the Game 7 clincher. But the talk of baseball was rookie centerfielder Pepper Martin, who hit .300 for the year and ran the Athletics ragged in the Series. Martin stole five bases in six attempts against catcher Mickey Cochrane, batted .500 for the Series, and tied a Series record with twelve hits, including four doubles and a homer.

TEAM STATISTICS

	W	L	PCT	GB	R	OR	Batting 2B	3B	HR	BA	SA	SB	Fielding E	DP	FA	CG	BB	Pitching SO	ShO	SV	ERA
TL	101	53	.656		815	614	353	74	60	.286	.411	114	160	169	.974	80	449	626	17	20	3.45
Y	87	65	.572	13	768	599	251	64	101	.289	.416	83	159	126	.974	90	421	571	17	12	3.30
HI	84	70	.545	17	828	710	340	67	83	.289	.422	49	169	141	.973	80	524	541	8	8	3.97
KN	79	73	.520	21	681	673	240	77	71	.276	.390	45	187	154	.969	64	351	546	9	18	3.84
T	75	79	.487	26	636	691	243	70	41	.266	.360	59	194	167	.968	89	442	345	9	5	3.66
HI	66	88	.429	35	684	828	299	52	81	.279	.400	42	210	149	.966	60	499	499	4	16	4.58
OS	64	90	.416	37	533	680	221	59	34	.258	.341	46	170	141	.973	78	406	419	12	9	3.90
IN	58	96	.377	43	592	742	241	70	21	.269	.352	24	165	194	.973	70	399	317	4	6	4.22
AGUE TOTAL					5537	5537	2188	533	492	.277	.387	462	1414	1241	.971	611	3503	3864	80	94	3.86

INDIVIDUAL PITCHING

TCHER	T	W	L	PCT	ERA	SV	G	GS	CG	IP	H	BB	SO	R	ER	ShO	H/9	BB/9	SO/9
ll Hallahan	L	19	9	.679	3.29	4	37	30	16	248.2	242	112	159	102	91	3	8.76	4.05	5.75
urleigh Grimes	R	17	9	.654	3.65	0	35	28	17	212.1	240	59	67	97	86	3	10.17	2.50	2.84
aul Derringer	R	18	8	.692	3.36	2	35	23	15	211.2	225	65	134	88	79	4	9.57	2.76	5.70
nt Rhem	R	11	10	.524	3.56	1	33	26	10	207.1	214	60	72	100	82	2	9.29	2.60	3.13
yl Johnson	R	11	9	.550	3.00	2	32	24	12	186	186	29	82	73	62	2	9.00	1.40	3.97
sse Haines	R	12	3	.800	3.02	0	19	17	8	122.1	134	28	27	48	41	2	9.86	2.06	1.99
m Lindsey	R	6	4	.600	2.77	7	35	2	1	74.2	77	45	32	32	23	1	9.28	5.42	3.86
lyn Stout	R	6	0	1.000	4.21	3	30	3	1	72.2	87	34	40	40	34	0	10.78	4.21	4.95
ony Kaufmann	R	1	1	.500	6.06	1	15	1	0	49	65	17	13	34	33	0	11.94	3.12	2.39
AM TOTAL		101	53	.656	3.45	20	265	154	80	1384.2	1470	449	626	614	531	17	9.55	2.92	4.07

CARDINAL WIN LEADERS

1931 Bill Hallahan, 19	1945 Red Barrett (also with Boston), 23
1934 Dizzy Dean, 30	
1935 Dizzy Dean, 28	1946 Howie Pollett, 21
1942 Mort Cooper, 22	1960 Ernie Broglio, 21
1943 Mort Cooper, 21	1970 Bob Gibson, 23

MANAGER	W	L	PCT
Gabby Street	72	82	.468

POS	Player	B	G	AB	H	2B	3B	HR	HR %	R	RBI	BB	SO	SB	Pinch Hit AB	Pinch Hit H	BA	SA
REGULARS																		
1B	Ripper Collins	B	149	549	153	28	8	21	3.8	82	91	38	67	4	8	2	.279	.474
2B	Frankie Frisch	B	115	486	142	26	2	3	0.6	59	60	25	13	18	0	0	.292	.372
SS	Charley Gelbert	R	122	455	122	28	9	1	0.2	60	45	39	30	8	0	0	.268	.376
3B	Jake Flowers	R	67	247	63	11	1	2	0.8	35	18	31	18	7	4	2	.255	.332
RF	George Watkins	L	137	458	143	35	3	9	2.0	67	63	45	46	18	6	2	.312	.461
CF	Pepper Martin	R	85	323	77	19	6	4	1.2	47	34	30	31	9	0	0	.238	.372
LF	Ernie Orsatti	L	101	375	126	27	6	2	0.5	44	44	18	29	5	3	2	.336	.456
C	Gus Mancuso	R	103	310	88	23	1	5	1.6	25	43	30	15	0	19	6	.284	.413
SUBSTITUTES																		
2B	Jimmy Reese	L	90	309	82	15	0	2	0.6	38	26	20	19	4	10	4	.265	.333
1B	Jim Bottomley	L	91	311	92	16	3	11	3.5	45	48	25	32	2	16	7	.296	.473
3B	Sparky Adams	R	31	127	35	3	1	0	0.0	22	13	14	5	0	0	0	.276	.315
SS	Charlie Wilson	B	24	96	19	3	3	1	1.0	7	2	3	8	0	0	0	.198	.323
3O	Harvey Hendrick	L	28	72	18	2	0	1	1.4	8	5	5	9	0	9	3	.250	.319
UT	Eddie Delker	R	20	42	5	4	0	0	0.0	1	2	8	7	0	0	0	.119	.214
3B	Ray Cunningham	R	11	22	4	1	0	0	0.0	4	0	3	4	0	1	0	.182	.227
SS	Hod Ford	R	1	2	0	0	0	0	0.0	0	0	0	0	0	0	0	.000	.000
SS	Skeeter Webb	R	1	0	0	0	0	0	–	0	0	0	0	0	0	0	–	–
OF	Ray Blades	R	80	201	46	10	1	3	1.5	35	29	34	31	2	16	2	.229	.333
OF	George Puccinelli	R	31	108	30	8	0	3	2.8	17	11	12	13	1	1	0	.278	.435
OF	Joe Medwick	R	26	106	37	12	1	2	1.9	13	12	2	10	3	0	0	.349	.538
OF	Ray Pepper	R	21	57	14	2	1	0	0.0	3	7	5	13	1	4	0	.246	.316
OF	Joel Hunt	R	12	21	4	1	0	0	0.0	0	3	4	3	0	5	2	.190	.238
OF	Rube Bressler	R	10	19	3	0	0	0	0.0	0	2	0	1	0	6	1	.158	.158
OF	Wattie Holm	R	11	17	3	1	0	0	0.0	2	1	3	1	0	5	1	.176	.235
C	Jimmie Wilson	R	92	274	68	16	2	2	0.7	36	28	15	18	9	10	3	.248	.343
C	Bill DeLancey	L	8	26	5	0	2	0	0.0	1	2	2	1	0	0	0	.192	.346
C	Mike Gonzalez	R	17	14	2	0	0	0	0.0	0	3	0	2	0	10	2	.143	.143
PITCHERS																		
P	Dizzy Dean	R	47	97	25	5	0	2	2.1	10	12	0	10	0	0	0	.258	.371
P	Paul Derringer	R	39	73	13	4	0	0	0.0	8	4	2	11	0	0	0	.178	.233
P	Tex Carleton	B	44	60	9	0	0	1	1.7	5	6	1	18	0	0	0	.150	.200
P	Bill Hallahan	R	28	56	12	2	1	0	0.0	3	2	5	12	1	0	0	.214	.286
P	Syl Johnson	R	32	51	10	1	0	0	0.0	0	5	0	13	0	0	0	.196	.216
P	Jesse Haines	R	20	27	5	0	0	1	3.7	1	3	0	2	0	0	0	.185	.296
P	Jim Lindsey	R	33	21	3	0	0	0	0.0	1	1	0	4	0	0	0	.143	.143
P	Allyn Stout	R	36	20	2	0	0	0	0.0	0	1	1	11	0	0	0	.100	.100
P	Flint Rhem	R	6	16	3	2	0	0	0.0	2	0	0	3	0	0	0	.188	.313
P	Ray Starr	R	3	4	1	0	0	0	0.0	0	0	0	1	0	0	0	.250	.250
P	Jim Winford	R	4	3	2	1	0	0	0.0	2	0	0	1	0	0	0	.667	1.000
P	Benny Frey	R	2	1	0	0	0	0	0.0	0	0	0	1	0	0	0	.000	.000
P	Bill Sherdel	L	3	1	1	1	0	0	0.0	1	0	0	0	0	0	0	1.000	2.000
P	Dick Terwilliger	R	1	1	0	0	0	0	0.0	0	0	0	1	0	0	0	.000	.000
P	Bud Teachout	R	1	0	0	0	0	0	–	0	0	0	0	0	0	0	–	–
	TEAM TOTAL			5458	1467	307	51	76	1.4	684	626	420	514	92	133	39	.269	.385

INDIVIDUAL FIELDING

POS	Player	T	G	PO	A	E	DP	TC/G	FA
1B	R. Collins	L	81	701	46	1	72	9.2	.999
	J. Bottomley	L	74	662	41	10	67	9.6	.986
	J. Wilson	R	3	17	2	1	2	6.7	.950
	E. Orsatti	L	1	10	0	1	1	11.0	.909
2B	F. Frisch	R	75	214	250	14	53	6.4	.971
	J. Reese	R	77	209	220	9	48	5.7	.979
	E. Delker	R	10	20	22	0	5	4.2	1.000
	J. Flowers	R	2	6	7	0	2	6.5	1.000
	R. Cunningham	R	2	1	4	0	1	2.5	1.000
	J. Wilson	R	1	1	1	0	0	2.0	1.000
SS	C. Gelbert	R	122	246	389	37	69	5.5	.945
	C. Wilson	R	24	28	73	7	14	4.5	.935
	S. Webb	R	1	0	0	0	0	0.0	.000
	J. Flowers	R	7	10	8	1	2	2.7	.947
	F. Frisch	R	4	5	10	2	2	4.3	.882
	E. Delker	R	4	2	5	0	1	1.8	1.000
	H. Ford	R	1	2	1	1	2	4.0	.750
3B	J. Flowers	R	54	59	91	3	10	2.8	.980
	F. Frisch	R	37	38	59	0	5	2.6	1.000
	S. Adams	R	30	25	42	5	11	2.4	.931
	P. Martin	R	15	18	18	1	1	2.5	.973
	R. Blades	R	1	0	0	0	0	0.0	.000
	H. Hendrick	R	12	8	17	4	3	2.4	.862
	R. Cunningham	R	8	10	11	0	0	2.6	1.000
	E. Delker	R	5	6	7	2	0	3.0	.867

POS	Player	T	G	PO	A	E	DP	TC/G	FA
OF	G. Watkins	R	120	267	11	15	1	2.4	.949
	E. Orsatti	L	96	197	3	5	0	2.1	.976
	P. Martin	R	69	151	10	4	3	2.4	.976
	R. Blades	R	62	117	2	3	0	2.0	.975
	R. Collins	L	60	96	7	5	2	1.0	.954
	G. Puccinelli	R	30	59	6	4	1	2.3	.942
	J. Medwick	R	26	63	2	2	1	2.6	.970
	R. Pepper	R	17	33	1	1	0	2.1	.971
	J. Hunt	R	5	13	0	0	0	2.6	1.000
	W. Holm	R	4	9	0	0	0	2.3	1.000
	R. Bressler	L	4	8	0	0	0	2.0	1.000
	H. Hendrick	R	5	6	1	0	0	1.4	1.000
C	G. Mancuso	R	82	454	53	12	7	6.3	.977
	J. Wilson	R	75	326	55	7	9	5.2	.982
	B. DeLancey	R	8	32	8	3	3	5.4	.930
	M. Gonzalez	R	7	12	1	0	0	1.9	1.000

In a deep tumble from their World Championship heights, the Cardinals fell all the way from first to a tie for sixth place, fading by twenty-nine wins. Pepper Martin missed half the season with a broken finger as injuries and age caught up with them. The pennant-winning club of '31 had five players in the starting lineup over 30 years of age. They had reached that delicate stage when the stars of one great team must give way to the stars of the next. Fortunately, acting decisively was never a problem for Rickey, who strongly believed in trading players after good seasons when their market value was high, particularly if that player was over 30 and had an able replacement waiting on the farm. Chick Hafey was shipped off to Cincinnati, and Jim Bottomley was eased out of the lineup to make room for Ripper Collins, who led the club with 21 homers. The team leader in wins was a brash 21-year-old from Arkansas who also led the league in innings pitched and strikeouts—but more about Dizzy Dean later.

TEAM STATISTICS

	W	L	PCT	GB	R	OR	2B	3B	HR	BA	SA	SB	E	DP	FA	CG	BB	SO	ShO	SV	ERA
								Batting						**Fielding**				**Pitching**			
CHI	90	64	.584		720	633	296	60	69	.278	.392	48	173	146	.973	79	409	527	9	7	**3.44**
PIT	86	68	.558	4	701	711	274	**90**	47	.285	.394	71	185	124	.969	72	338	377	12	12	3.75
BKN	81	73	.526	9	752	747	296	59	109	.283	.419	61	183	**169**	.971	61	403	499	7	16	4.28
PHI	78	76	.506	12	**844**	796	**330**	67	**122**	**.292**	**.442**	71	194	133	.968	59	450	459	4	**17**	4.47
BOS	77	77	.500	13	649	655	262	53	63	.265	.366	36	**152**	145	**.976**	72	420	440	8	8	3.53
NY	72	82	.468	18	755	706	263	54	116	.276	.406	31	191	143	.969	57	387	**681**	**13**	9	3.83
STL	72	82	.468	18	684	717	307	51	76	.269	.385	**92**	175	155	.971	70	455	506	3	16	3.97
CIN	60	94	.390	30	575	715	265	68	47	.263	.362	35	178	129	.971	**83**	**276**	359	6	6	3.79
LEAGUE TOTAL					5680	5680	2293	502	649	.276	.396	445	1431	1144	.971	553	3138	3848	62	91	3.88

INDIVIDUAL PITCHING

PITCHER	T	W	L	PCT	ERA	SV	G	GS	CG	IP	H	BB	SO	R	ER	ShO	H/9	BB/9	SO/9
Dizzy Dean	R	18	15	.545	3.30	2	46	33	16	286	280	102	**191**	122	105	**4**	8.81	3.21	**6.01**
Paul Derringer	R	11	14	.440	4.05	0	39	30	14	233.1	296	67	78	133	105	1	11.42	2.58	3.01
Tex Carleton	R	10	13	.435	4.08	0	44	22	9	196.1	198	70	113	94	89	3	9.08	3.21	5.18
Bill Hallahan	L	12	7	.632	3.11	1	25	22	13	176.1	169	69	108	79	61	1	8.63	3.52	5.51
Syl Johnson	R	5	14	.263	4.92	2	32	22	7	164.2	199	35	70	103	90	1	10.88	1.91	3.83
Jim Lindsey	R	3	3	.500	4.94	3	33	5	0	89.1	96	38	31	53	49	0	9.67	3.83	3.12
Jesse Haines	R	3	5	.375	4.75	0	20	10	4	85.1	116	16	27	51	45	1	12.23	1.69	2.85
Allyn Stout	R	4	5	.444	4.40	1	36	3	1	73.2	87	28	32	40	36	0	10.63	3.42	3.91
Flint Rhem	R	4	2	.667	3.06	0	6	6	5	50	48	10	18	19	17	1	8.64	1.80	3.24
Ray Starr	R	1	1	.500	2.70	0	3	2	1	20	19	10	6	7	6	1	8.55	4.50	2.70
Jim Winford	R	1	1	.500	6.48	0	4	1	0	8.1	9	5	4	7	6	0	9.72	5.40	4.32
Bill Sherdel	L	0	0	—	4.76	0	3	0	0	5.2	7	1	1	3	3	0	11.12	1.59	1.59
Benny Frey	R	0	2	.000	12.00	0	2	0	0	3	6	2	0	5	4	0	18.00	6.00	0.00
Dick Terwilliger	R	0	0	—	0.00	0	1	0	0	3	1	2	2	0	0	0	3.00	6.00	6.00
Bud Teachout	L	0	0	—	0.00	0	1	0	0	1	2	0	0	1	0	0	18.00	0.00	0.00
TEAM TOTAL		72	82	.468	3.97	9	295	156	70	1396	1533	455	681	717	616	13	9.88	2.93	4.39

MANAGER	W	L	PCT
Gabby Street	46	45	.505
Frankie Frisch	36	26	.581

POS	Player	B	G	AB	H	2B	3B	HR	HR %	R	RBI	BB	SO	SB	Pinch Hit AB	Pinch Hit H	BA	SA
REGULARS
1B	Ripper Collins	B	132	493	153	26	7	10	2.0	66	68	38	49	7	8	3	.310	.452
2B	Frankie Frisch	B	147	585	177	32	6	4	0.7	74	66	48	16	18	4	2	.303	.398
SS	Leo Durocher	R	123	395	102	18	4	2	0.5	45	41	26	32	3	0	0	.258	.339
3B	Pepper Martin	R	145	599	189	36	12	8	1.3	122	57	67	46	26	0	0	.316	.456
RF	George Watkins	L	138	525	146	24	5	5	1.0	66	62	39	62	11	3	0	.278	.371
CF	Ernie Orsatti	L	120	436	130	21	6	0	0.0	55	38	33	33	14	9	3	.298	.374
LF	Joe Medwick	R	148	595	182	40	10	18	3.0	92	98	26	56	5	1	0	.306	.497
C	Jimmie Wilson	R	113	369	94	17	0	1	0.3	34	45	23	33	6	5	1	.255	.309
SUBSTITUTES
UT	Pat Crawford	L	91	224	60	8	2	0	0.0	24	21	14	9	1	38	9	.268	.321
2B	Rogers Hornsby	R	46	83	27	6	0	2	2.4	9	21	12	6	1	26	8	.325	.470
SS	Gordon Slade	R	39	62	7	1	0	0	0.0	6	3	6	7	1	3	0	.113	.129
S3	Sparky Adams	R	8	30	5	1	0	0	0.0	1	0	1	3	0	0	0	.167	.200
S2	Burgess Whitehead	R	12	7	2	0	0	0	0.0	2	1	0	1	0	0	0	.286	.286
SS	Charlie Wilson	B	1	1	0	0	0	0	0.0	0	0	0	1	0	0	0	.000	.000
OF	Ethan Allen	R	91	261	63	7	3	0	0.0	25	36	13	22	3	21	3	.241	.291
OF	Gene Moore	L	11	38	15	3	2	0	0.0	3	6	4	10	1	1	0	.395	.579
OF	Estel Crabtree	L	23	34	9	3	0	0	0.0	6	8	6	3	1	12	2	.265	.353
OF	Ray Pepper	R	3	9	2	0	0	1	11.1	2	2	0	1	0	1	0	.222	.556
C	Bob O'Farrell	R	55	163	39	4	2	2	1.2	16	20	15	25	0	4	1	.239	.325
C	Bill Lewis	R	15	35	14	1	0	1	2.9	8	8	2	3	0	6	2	.400	.514
C	Joe Sprinz	R	3	5	1	0	0	0	0.0	0	1	1	1	0	0	0	.200	.200
PITCHERS
P	Dizzy Dean	R	51	105	19	2	2	1	1.0	8	12	3	14	1	0	0	.181	.267
P	Tex Carleton	R	46	91	17	2	0	1	1.1	7	7	6	27	0	0	0	.187	.242
P	Bill Hallahan	R	37	80	12	1	0	0	0.0	6	4	9	28	0	0	0	.150	.163
P	Bill Walker	R	29	53	7	0	0	1	1.9	2	2	1	16	0	0	0	.132	.189
P	Jesse Haines	R	33	30	2	1	0	0	0.0	1	1	1	8	0	0	0	.067	.100
P	Dazzy Vance	R	28	28	5	1	0	0	0.0	1	3	0	8	0	0	0	.179	.214
P	Syl Johnson	R	35	21	5	0	0	0	0.0	0	1	0	4	0	0	0	.238	.238
P	Jim Mooney	R	21	20	1	0	0	0	0.0	1	0	1	2	0	0	0	.050	.050
P	Paul Derringer	R	3	5	0	0	0	0	0.0	0	0	0	1	0	0	0	.000	.000
P	Burleigh Grimes	R	4	5	1	1	0	0	0.0	1	1	0	1	0	0	0	.200	.400
P	Jim Lindsey	R	1	0	0	0	0	0	–	0	0	0	0	0	0	0	–	–
P	Allyn Stout	R	1	0	0	0	0	0	–	0	0	0	0	0	0	0	–	–
	TEAM TOTAL			5387	1486	256	61	57	1.1	687	629	391	528	99	142	34	.276	.378

INDIVIDUAL FIELDING

POS	Player	T	G	PO	A	E	DP	TC/G	FA
1B	R. Collins	L	123	1054	79	7	82	9.3	.994
	P. Crawford	L	29	256	22	4	21	9.7	.986
	E. Orsatti	L	3	25	0	1	2	8.7	.962
2B	F. Frisch	R	132	371	378	14	71	5.8	.982
	R. Hornsby	R	17	24	35	2	7	3.6	.967
	P. Crawford	R	15	21	28	0	4	3.3	1.000
	G. Slade	R	1	0	0	0	0	0.0	.000
	B. Whitehead	R	3	1	4	0	1	1.7	1.000
SS	L. Durocher	R	123	238	358	24	64	5.0	.961*
	G. Slade	R	31	34	61	6	11	3.3	.941
	F. Frisch	R	15	24	35	4	9	4.2	.937
	C. Wilson	R	1	0	0	0	0	0.0	.000
	S. Adams	R	5	5	16	1	2	4.4	.955
	B. Whitehead	R	9	3	3	0	1	0.7	1.000
3B	P. Martin	R	145	139	273	25	14	3.0	.943
	P. Crawford	R	7	10	12	2	0	3.4	.917
	S. Adams	R	3	0	6	2	1	2.7	.750

POS	Player	T	G	PO	A	E	DP	TC/G	FA
OF	J. Medwick	R	147	318	17	7	2	2.3	.980
	G. Watkins	R	135	295	9	15	3	2.4	.953
	E. Orsatti	L	101	274	5	4	1	2.8	.986
	E. Allen	R	67	179	8	3	1	2.8	.984
	G. Moore	L	10	29	0	1	0	3.0	.967
	E. Crabtree	R	7	18	0	1	0	2.7	.947
	R. Pepper	R	2	3	0	0	0	1.5	1.000
C	J. Wilson	R	107	498	58	10	13	5.3	.982
	B. O'Farrell	R	50	211	19	7	1	4.7	.970
	B. Lewis	R	8	44	4	0	0	6.0	1.000
	J. Sprinz	R	3	18	1	0	0	6.3	1.000

Two more important members of the Gashouse Gang joined the Cardinals in '33. An off-season hunting accident took shortstop Charlie Gelbert out of the lineup and out of the league for two years while he recuperated. This left a gaping hole in the infield, which was filled when Rickey pried Leo Durocher away from Cincinnati to steady the defense. Joe Medwick came up from the farm and hit .306 in his rookie year, with 18 homers and 98 RBIs; his .497 slugging average was fourth in the league. While the Redbirds finished in fifth, they were just nine games out of first.

The year 1933 saw the birth of baseball's Mid-Summer Classic, the All-Star Game. Four Cardinals made the National League squad, and all were in the starting lineup: Pepper Martin at third, Frankie Frisch at second, Jimmie Wilson catching, and Bill Hallahan on the mound. Frisch hit the first National League homer in All-Star play, a solo shot in the sixth, but Babe Ruth had already cracked the first All-Star homer, in the third off Hallahan. Ruth's homer led the American League to a 4–2 victory. Yes, the American League won an All-Star Game!

TEAM STATISTICS

	W	L	PCT	GB	R	OR	Batting 2B	3B	HR	BA	SA	SB	Fielding E	DP	FA	CG	BB	Pitching SO	ShO	SV	ERA
NY	91	61	.599		636	515	204	41	82	.263	.361	31	178	156	.973	75	400	555	22	15	2.71
PIT	87	67	.565	5	667	619	249	84	39	.285	.383	34	166	133	.972	70	313	401	16	12	3.27
CHI	86	68	.558	6	646	536	256	51	72	.271	.380	52	168	163	.973	95	413	488	16	9	2.93
BOS	83	71	.539	9	552	531	217	56	54	.252	.345	25	138	148	.978	85	355	383	14	16	2.96
STL	82	71	.536	9.5	687	609	256	61	57	.276	.378	99	162	119	.973	73	452	635	10	16	3.37
BKN	65	88	.425	26.5	617	695	224	51	62	.263	.359	82	177	120	.971	71	374	415	9	10	3.73
PHI	60	92	.395	31	607	760	240	41	60	.274	.369	55	183	156	.970	52	410	341	10	13	4.34
CIN	58	94	.382	33	496	643	208	37	34	.246	.320	30	177	139	.971	74	257	310	13	8	3.42
LEAGUE TOTAL					4908	4908	1854	422	460	.266	.362	408	1349	1134	.973	595	2974	3528	110	99	3.34

INDIVIDUAL PITCHING

PITCHER	T	W	L	PCT	ERA	SV	G	GS	CG	IP	H	BB	SO	R	ER	ShO	H/9	BB/9	SO/9
Dizzy Dean	R	20	18	.526	3.04	4	48	34	26	293	279	64	199	113	99	3	8.57	1.97	6.11
Tex Carleton	R	17	11	.607	3.38	3	44	33	15	277	263	97	147	117	104	4	8.55	3.15	4.78
Bill Hallahan	L	16	13	.552	3.50	0	36	32	16	244.1	245	98	93	114	95	2	9.02	3.61	3.43
Bill Walker	L	9	10	.474	3.42	0	29	20	6	158	168	67	41	71	60	2	9.57	3.82	2.34
Jesse Haines	R	9	6	.600	2.50	1	32	10	5	115.1	113	37	37	46	32	0	8.82	2.89	2.89
Dazzy Vance	R	6	2	.750	3.55	3	28	11	2	99	105	28	67	42	39	0	9.55	2.55	6.09
Syl Johnson	R	3	3	.500	4.29	3	35	1	0	84	89	16	28	45	40	0	9.54	1.71	3.00
Jim Mooney	L	2	5	.286	3.72	1	21	8	2	77:1	87	26	14	36	32	0	10.13	3.03	1.63
Paul Derringer	R	0	2*	.000	4.24	0	3	2	1	17	24	9	3	11	8	0	12.71	4.76	1.59
Burleigh Grimes	R	0	1	.000	5.27	1	4	3	0	13.2	15	8	4	13	8	0	9.88	5.27	2.63
Jim Lindsey	R	0	0	–	4.50	0	1	0	0	2	2	1	1	1	1	0	9.00	4.50	4.50
Allyn Stout	R	0	0	–	0.00	0	1	0	0	2	1	1	1	0	0	0	4.50	4.50	4.50
TEAM TOTAL		82	71	.536	3.37	16	282	154	73	1382.2	1391	452	635	609	518	11	9.05	2.94	4.13

MANAGER	W	L	PCT
Frankie Frisch	95	58	.621

POS	Player	B	G	AB	H	2B	3B	HR	HR %	R	RBI	BB	SO	SB	Pinch Hit AB	Pinch Hit H	BA	SA
REGULARS																		
1B	Ripper Collins	B	154	600	200	40	12	35	5.8	116	128	57	50	2	0	0	.333	**.615**
2B	Frankie Frisch	B	140	550	168	30	6	3	0.5	74	75	45	10	11	2	0	.305	.398
SS	Leo Durocher	R	146	500	130	26	5	3	0.6	62	70	33	40	2	0	0	.260	.350
3B	Pepper Martin	R	110	454	131	25	11	5	1.1	76	49	32	41	23	1	0	.289	.425
RF	Jack Rothrock	B	154	647	184	35	3	11	1.7	106	72	49	56	10	0	0	.284	.399
CF	Ernie Orsatti	L	105	337	101	14	4	0	0.0	39	31	27	31	6	10	2	.300	.365
LF	Joe Medwick	R	149	620	198	40	18	18	2.9	110	106	21	83	3	0	0	.319	.529
C	Spud Davis	R	107	347	104	22	4	9	2.6	45	65	34	27	0	11	3	.300	.464
SUBSTITUTES																		
UT	Burgess Whitehead	R	100	332	92	13	5	1	0.3	55	24	12	19	5	1	0	.277	.355
32	Pat Crawford	L	61	70	19	2	0	0	0.0	3	16	5	3	0	43	11	.271	.300
OF	Chick Fullis	R	69	199	52	9	1	0	0.0	21	26	14	11	4	14	5	.261	.317
OF	Buster Mills	R	29	72	17	4	1	1	1.4	7	8	4	11	0	9	3	.236	.361
OF	Kiddo Davis	R	16	33	10	3	0	1	3.0	6	4	3	1	1	5	2	.303	.485
OF	Gene Moore	L	9	18	5	1	0	0	0.0	2	1	2	2	0	6	2	.278	.333
C	Bill DeLancey	L	93	253	80	18	3	13	5.1	41	40	41	37	1	15	3	.316	.565
UT	Francis Healy	R	15	13	4	1	0	0	0.0	1	1	0	2	0	8	3	.308	.385
PH	Lew Riggs	L	2	1	0	0	0	0	0.0	0	0	0	1	0	1	0	.000	.000
PH	Red Worthington	R	1	1	0	0	0	0	0.0	0	0	0	1	0	1	0	.000	.000
PITCHERS																		
P	Dizzy Dean	R	51	118	29	3	1	2	1.7	15	9	1	15	1	0	0	.246	.339
P	Tex Carleton	R	41	88	17	2	1	1	1.1	7	10	5	27	0	0	0	.193	.273
P	Paul Dean	R	39	83	20	4	0	0	0.0	6	3	1	12	0	0	0	.241	.289
P	Bill Hallahan	R	32	55	10	1	0	0	0.0	3	6	2	16	0	0	0	.182	.200
P	Bill Walker	R	24	54	5	1	0	0	0.0	2	1	1	26	0	0	0	.093	.111
P	Jesse Haines	R	37	19	3	0	0	0	0.0	1	0	1	5	0	0	0	.158	.158
P	Jim Mooney	R	32	19	1	0	0	0	0.0	0	2	0	1	0	0	0	.053	.053
P	Dazzy Vance	R	19	15	2	0	0	1	6.7	1	1	0	6	0	0	0	.133	.333
P	Flint Rhem	R	5	2	0	0	0	0	0.0	0	0	0	0	0	0	0	.000	.000
P	Jim Lindsey	R	11	1	0	0	0	0	0.0	0	0	0	0	0	0	0	.000	.000
P	Jim Winford	R	5	1	0	0	0	0	0.0	0	0	2	1	0	0	0	.000	.000
P	Burleigh Grimes	R	4	0	0	0	0	0	–	0	0	0	0	0	0	0	–	–
P	Clarence Heise	L	0	0	0	0	0	0	–	0	0	0	0	0	0	0	–	–
TEAM TOTAL				5502	1582	294	75	104	1.9	799	748	392	535	69	127	34	.288	.425

INDIVIDUAL FIELDING

POS	Player	T	G	PO	A	E	DP	TC/G	FA
1B	R. Collins	L	154	1289	110	13	115	9.2	.991
2B	F. Frisch	R	115	294	351	15	74	5.7	.977
	B. Whitehead	R	48	88	140	9	27	4.9	.962
	P. Crawford	R	4	8	15	2	4	6.3	.920
	J. Rothrock	R	1	0	2	0	0	2.0	1.000
SS	L. Durocher	R	146	320	407	33	86	5.2	.957
	B. Whitehead	R	29	40	33	4	5	2.7	.948
3B	P. Martin	R	107	85	195	19	7	2.8	.936
	B. Whitehead	R	28	30	47	3	6	2.9	.963
	F. Frisch	R	25	31	37	5	6	2.9	.932
	F. Healy	R	1	0	0	0	0	0.0	.000
	P. Crawford	R	9	3	6	1	0	1.1	.900

POS	Player	T	G	PO	A	E	DP	TC/G	FA
OF	J. Rothrock	R	154	343	10	9	4	2.4	.975
	J. Medwick	R	149	322	10	14	1	2.3	.960
	E. Orsatti	L	90	207	5	3	0	2.4	.986
	C. Fullis	R	56	124	2	4	1	2.3	.969
	B. Mills	R	18	45	0	0	0	2.5	1.000
	K. Davis	R	9	23	1	1	0	2.8*	.960
	G. Moore	L	3	12	0	1	0	4.3	.923
	F. Healy	R	1	1	0	0	0	1.0	1.000
C	S. Davis	R	94	459	42	6	7	5.4	.988
	B. DeLancey	R	77	363	35	8	5	5.3	.980
	F. Healy	R	2	3	1	0	1	2.0	1.000

The legend of the Gashouse Gang, that hard-fightin', rip-snortin' assemblage of good old country ballplayers that made up the '34 Cardinals, has tended to obscure the drama of the season. The Cardinals won their pennant by just two games, and didn't move into first place until the hundred and fifty-first game of the season. Naturally enough, it was Dizzy Dean, the club's self-proclaimed king of the hill, who put them ahead on that final Friday of the season, and Diz again who clinched the pennant with another shutout on the last day for his thirtieth win. Dean turned in the spectacular season that landed him in the Hall of Fame: he led the league in wins, strikeouts, and shutouts, and finished second to New York's Carl Hubbell in ERA. No National League hurler has won 30 games in a season since Dean in '34. He was amply helped by his brother Paul, who won 19 games as a rookie and pitched a no-hitter against Brooklyn in the middle of the Cardinals' stretch drive. Their potent offense, league leader in batting, slugging, and scoring, was led by Collins at first, who tied Mel Ott for the league lead in homers, and ranked second in RBIs and fourth in batting. The Dean brothers also won all four games for the Cardinals in their seven-game Series victory over the Tigers, rallying from a 3–2 deficit to win the last two games in Detroit. Who won Game 7? Diz, of course, in an 11–0 laugher.

TEAM STATISTICS

	W	L	PCT	GB	R	OR	Batting 2B	3B	HR	BA	SA	SB	Fielding E	DP	FA	CG	BB	Pitching SO	ShO	SV	ERA
-	95	58	.621		799	656	294	75	104	.288	.425	69	166	141	.972	78	411	689	15	16	3.69
	93	60	.608	2	760	583	240	41	126	.275	.405	19	179	141	.972	66	351	499	12	30	3.19
I	86	65	.570	8	705	639	263	44	101	.279	.402	59	137	135	.977	73	417	633	11	9	3.76
S	78	73	.517	16	683	714	233	44	83	.272	.378	30	169	120	.972	62	405	462	11	20	4.11
	74	76	.493	19.5	735	713	281	77	52	.287	.398	44	145	118	.975	61	354	487	8	8	4.20
N	71	81	.467	23.5	748	795	284	52	79	.281	.396	55	180	141	.970	66	476	520	6	12	4.48
I	56	93	.376	37	675	794	286	35	56	.284	.384	52	197	140	.966	52	437	416	8	15	4.76
N	52	99	.344	42	590	801	227	65	55	.266	.364	34	181	136	.970	51	389	438	3	19	4.37
GUE TOTAL					5695	5695	2108	433	656	.279	.394	362	1354	1072	.972	509	3240	4144	74	129	4.06

INDIVIDUAL PITCHING

CHER	T	W	L	PCT	ERA	SV	G	GS	CG	IP	H	BB	SO	R	ER	ShO	H/9	BB/9	SO/9
zzy Dean	R	30	7	.811	2.66	7	50	33	24	311.2	288	75	195	110	92	7	8.32	2.17	5.63
x Carleton	R	16	11	.593	4.26	2	40	31	16	240.2	260	52	103	126	114	0	9.72	1.94	3.85
ul Dean	R	19	11	.633	3.43	2	39	26	16	233.1	225	52	150	93	89	5	8.68	2.01	5.79
Hallahan	L	8	12	.400	4.26	0	32	26	10	162.2	195	66	70	93	77	2	10.79	3.65	3.87
Walker	L	12	4	.750	3.12	0	24	19	10	153	160	66	76	59	53	1	9.41	3.88	4.47
sse Haines	R	4	4	.500	3.50	1	37	6	0	90	86	19	17	42	35	0	8.60	1.90	1.70
n Mooney	L	2	4	.333	5.47	1	32	7	1	82.1	114	49	27	59	50	0	12.46	5.36	2.95
zzy Vance	R	1	1	.500	3.66	1	19	4	1	59	62	14	33	31	24	0	9.46	2.14	5.03
nt Rhem	R	1	0	1.000	4.60	1	5	1	0	15.2	26	7	6	12	8	0	14.94	4.02	3.45
n Lindsey	R	0	1	.000	6.43	1	11	0	0	14	21	3	7	13	10	0	13.50	1.93	4.50
n Winford	R	0	2	.000	7.82	0	5	1	0	12.2	17	6	3	13	11	0	12.08	4.26	2.13
rleigh Grimes	R	2	1	.667	3.52	0	4	0	0	7.2	5	2	1	3	3	0	5.87	2.35	1.17
arence Heise	L	0	0	–	4.50	0	1	0	0	2	3	0	1	1	1	0	13.50	0.00	4.50
pper Martin	R	0	0	–	4.50	0	1	0	0	2	1	0	0	1	1	0	4.50	0.00	0.00
AM TOTAL		95	58	.621	3.69	16	300	154	78	1386.2	1463	411	689	656	568	15	9.50	2.67	4.47

MANAGER	W	L	PCT
Frankie Frisch	96	58	.623

POS	Player	B	G	AB	H	2B	3B	HR	HR %	R	RBI	BB	SO	SB	Pinch Hit AB	Pinch Hit H	BA	SA
REGULARS																		
1B	Ripper Collins	B	150	578	181	36	10	23	4.0	109	122	65	45	0	0	0	.313	.529
2B	Frankie Frisch	B	103	354	104	16	2	1	0.3	52	55	33	16	2	9	1	.294	.359
SS	Leo Durocher	R	143	513	136	23	5	8	1.6	62	78	29	46	4	0	0	.265	.376
3B	Pepper Martin	R	135	539	161	41	6	9	1.7	121	54	33	58	20	5	0	.299	.447
RF	Jack Rothrock	B	129	502	137	18	5	3	0.6	76	56	57	29	7	1	0	.273	.347
CF	Terry Moore	R	119	456	131	34	3	6	1.3	63	53	15	40	13	0	0	.287	.414
LF	Joe Medwick	R	154	634	224	46	13	23	3.6	132	126	30	59	4	0	0	.353	.576
C	Bill DeLancey	L	103	301	84	14	5	6	2.0	37	41	42	34	0	17	4	.279	.419
SUBSTITUTES																		
2B	Burgess Whitehead	R	107	338	89	10	2	0	0.0	45	33	11	14	5	12	2	.263	.305
3S	Charley Gelbert	R	62	168	49	7	2	2	1.2	24	21	17	18	0	5	1	.292	.393
3B	Charlie Wilson	B	16	31	10	0	0	0	0.0	1	1	2	2	0	7	4	.323	.323
2B	Lyle Judy	R	8	11	0	0	0	0	0.0	2	0	2	2	2	0	0	.000	.000
OF	Ernie Orsatti	L	90	221	53	9	3	1	0.5	28	24	18	25	10	23	5	.240	.321
OF	Lynn King	L	8	22	4	0	0	0	0.0	6	0	4	1	2	1	0	.182	.182
OF	Tom Winsett	L	7	12	6	1	0	0	0.0	2	2	2	3	0	5	2	.500	.583
C	Spud Davis	R	102	315	100	24	2	1	0.3	28	60	33	30	0	13	4	.317	.416
C	Bob O'Farrell	R	14	10	0	0	0	0	0.0	0	0	2	0	0	4	0	.000	.000
C	Sam Narron	R	4	7	3	0	0	0	0.0	0	0	0	0	0	3	2	.429	.429
PH	Gene Moore	L	3	3	0	0	0	0	0.0	0	0	0	1	0	3	0	.000	.000
PITCHERS																		
P	Dizzy Dean	R	53	128	30	4	0	2	1.6	18	21	1	16	2	2	0	.234	.313
P	Paul Dean	R	46	90	12	1	0	0	0.0	3	3	1	23	0	0	0	.133	.144
P	Bill Walker	R	38	59	6	1	0	0	0.0	4	3	2	21	0	0	0	.102	.119
P	Bill Hallahan	R	40	56	8	0	0	1	1.8	8	3	2	13	0	0	0	.143	.196
P	Ed Heusser	R	33	34	4	0	1	0	0.0	1	2	1	10	0	0	0	.118	.176
P	Jesse Haines	R	30	33	9	1	0	0	0.0	2	1	0	7	0	0	0	.273	.303
P	Phil Collins	R	26	25	4	0	0	0	0.0	3	0	1	2	0	0	0	.160	.160
P	Mike Ryba	R	2	5	2	0	0	0	0.0	0	3	1	0	0	0	0	.400	.400
P	Ray Harrell	R	11	4	0	0	0	0	0.0	0	0	0	3	0	0	0	.000	.000
P	Bill McGee	R	1	3	1	0	0	0	0.0	0	0	0	0	0	0	0	.333	.333
P	Nub Kleinke	R	6	2	0	0	0	0	0.0	0	0	0	2	0	0	0	.000	.000
P	Jim Winford	R	2	2	0	0	0	0	0.0	0	0	0	1	0	0	0	.000	.000
P	Bud Tinning	R	4	1	0	0	0	0	0.0	0	0	0	0	0	0	0	.000	.000
P	Mays Copeland	R	1	0	0	0	0	0	–	0	0	0	0	0	0	0	–	–
P	Al Eckert	L	2	0	0	0	0	0		0	0	0	0	0	0	0	–	–
P	Tony Kaufmann	R	7	0	0	0	0	0	–	0	0	0	0	0	0	0	–	–
P	Dick Ward	R	1	0	0	0	0	0	–	0	0	0	0	0	0	0	–	–
TEAM TOTAL				5457	1548	286	59	86	1.6	829	762	404	521	71	110	25	.284	.405

INDIVIDUAL FIELDING

POS	Player	T	G	PO	A	E	DP	TC/G	FA
1B	R. Collins	L	150	1269	95	18	107	9.2	.987
	S. Davis	R	5	48	0	0	4	9.6	1.000
2B	F. Frisch	R	88	193	252	8	48	5.1	.982
	B. Whitehead	R	80	172	218	8	43	5.0	.980
	L. Judy	R	5	9	7	0	2	3.2	1.000
	C. Gelbert	R	3	3	3	0	0	2.0	1.000
SS	L. Durocher	R	142	313	420	28	81	5.4	.963
	C. Gelbert	R	21	31	39	3	8	3.5	.959
	B. Whitehead	R	6	9	10	1	2	3.3	.950
3B	P. Martin	R	114	113	171	30	17	2.8	.904
	C. Gelbert	R	37	31	56	2	8	2.4	.978
	B. Whitehead	R	8	7	12	1	2	2.5	.950
	C. Wilson	R	8	6	8	1	1	1.9	.933
	F. Frisch	R	5	6	6	2	0	2.8	.857

POS	Player	T	G	PO	A	E	DP	TC/G	FA
OF	J. Medwick	R	154	352	8	13	0	2.4	.965
	T. Moore	R	117	354	11	6	3	3.2	.984
	J. Rothrock	R	127	283	5	6	1	2.3	.980
	E. Orsatti	L	60	115	3	3	2	2.0	.975
	P. Martin	R	16	32	0	2	0	2.1	.941
	T. Winsett	R	2	0	0	0	0	0.0	.000
	L. King	R	6	26	0	0	0	4.3	1.000
C	B. DeLancey	R	83	372	29	12	6	5.0	.971
	S. Davis	R	81	335	34	3	2	4.6	.992
	B. O'Farrell	R	8	12	0	0	0	1.5	1.000
	S. Narron	R	1	5	0	0	0	5.0	1.000

St. Louis improved by one game over '34 and set a club record with a 14-game winning streak, but it wasn't enough to catch the Cubs, who won one hundred games for the only time since 1910 (and it doesn't look like they'll be doing it again soon). The Cubs had a little winning streak of their own— 21 straight wins in September that carried them from two and a half games back of the Cards on Labor Day to their clinching victory more than three weeks later. The Redbirds actually improved on their totals of runs scored and allowed from '34, but the Cubs were not to be denied. Medwick and Collins were the big guns at the plate. Medwick ranked second in the league in batting, slugging, hits, doubles, runs, and RBIs; Collins was right behind him in RBIs and tied him for the club lead with 23 homers. The Dean brothers teamed up for 47 wins; their two-year total of 96 wins sets a rather esoteric record for wins by brothers in consecutive years.

TEAM STATISTICS

	W	L	PCT	GB	R	OR	Batting 2B	3B	HR	BA	SA	SB	Fielding E	DP	FA	Pitching CG	BB	SO	ShO	SV	ERA
HI	100	54	.649		847	597	303	62	88	.288	.414	66	186	163	.970	81	400	589	12	14	3.26
TL	96	58	.623	4	829	625	286	59	86	.284	.405	71	164	133	.972	73	382	594	9	18	3.54
Y	91	62	.595	8.5	770	675	248	56	123	.286	.416	32	174	129	.972	76	411	524	10	11	3.78
T	86	67	.562	13.5	743	647	255	90	66	.285	.402	30	190	94	.968	76	312	549	15	11	3.42
KN	70	83	.458	29.5	711	767	235	62	59	.277	.376	60	188	146	.969	62	436	480	11	20	4.22
N	68	85	.444	31.5	646	772	244	68	73	.265	.378	72	204	139	.966	59	438	500	9	12	4.30
HI	64	89	.418	35.5	685	871	249	32	92	.269	.378	52	228	145	.963	53	505	475	8	15	4.76
OS	38	115	.248	61.5	575	852	233	33	75	.263	.362	20	197	101	.967	54	404	355	6	5	4.93
AGUE TOTAL					5806	5806	2053	462	662	.277	.391	403	1531	1050	.968	534	3288	4066	80	106	4.02

INDIVIDUAL PITCHING

TCHER	T	W	L	PCT	ERA	SV	G	GS	CG	IP	H	BB	SO	R	ER	ShO	H/9	BB/9	SO/9
zzy Dean	R	28	12	.700	3.11	5	50	36	29	324.1	326	82	182	128	112	3	9.05	2.28	5.05
ul Dean	R	19	12	.613	3.37	5	46	33	19	269.2	261	55	143	109	101	2	8.71	1.84	4.77
l Walker	L	13	8	.619	3.82	1	37	25	8	193.1	222	78	79	93	82	2	10.33	3.63	3.68
l Hallahan	L	15	8	.652	3.42	1	40	23	8	181.1	196	57	73	91	69	2	9.73	2.83	3.62
Heusser	R	5	5	.500	2.92	2	33	11	2	123.1	125	27	39	50	40	0	9.12	1.97	2.85
sse Haines	R	6	5	.545	3.59	2	30	12	3	115.1	110	28	24	49	46	0	8.58	2.18	1.87
il Collins	R	7	6	.538	4.57	2	26	8	2	82.2	96	26	18	48	42	0	10.45	2.83	1.96
y Harrell	R	1	1	.500	6.67	0	11	1	0	29.2	39	11	13	26	22	0	11.83	3.34	3.94
ke Ryba	R	1	1	.500	3.38	0	2	1	1	16	15	1	6	6	6	0	8.44	0.56	3.38
b Kleinke	R	0	0	–	4.97	0	4	2	0	12.2	19	3	5	8	7	0	13.50	2.13	3.55
n Winford	R	0	0	–	3.97	0	2	1	0	11.1	13	5	7	5	5	0	10.32	3.97	5.56
McGee	R	1	0	1.000	1.00	0	1	1	1	9	3	1	2	1	1	0	3.00	1.00	2.00
d Tinning	R	0	0	–	5.87	0	4	0	0	7.2	9	5	2	6	5	0	10.57	5.87	2.35
ny Kaufmann	R	0	0	–	2.45	0	3	0	0	3.2	4	1	0	1	1	0	9.82	2.45	0.00
Eckert	L	0	0	–	12.00	0	2	0	0	3	7	1	1	4	4	0	21.00	3.00	3.00
ys Copeland	R	0	0	–	13.50	0	1	0	0	.2	2	0	0	1	1	0	27.00	0.00	0.00
AM TOTAL		96	58	.623	3.54	18	292	154	73	1383.2	1447	381	594	626	544	9	9.41	2.48	3.86

MANAGER	W	L	PCT
Frankie Frisch	87	67	.565

POS	Player	B	G	AB	H	2B	3B	HR	HR %	R	RBI	BB	SO	SB	Pinch Hit AB	Pinch Hit H	BA	SA
REGULARS																		
1B	Johnny Mize	L	126	414	136	30	8	19	4.6	76	93	50	32	1	15	7	.329	.577
2B	Stu Martin	L	92	332	99	21	4	6	1.8	63	41	29	27	17	4	0	.298	.440
SS	Leo Durocher	R	136	510	146	22	3	1	0.2	57	58	29	47	3	0	0	.286	.347
3B	Charley Gelbert	R	93	280	64	15	2	3	1.1	33	27	25	26	2	2	0	.229	.329
RF	Pepper Martin	R	143	572	177	36	11	11	1.9	121	76	58	66	23	1	0	.309	.469
CF	Terry Moore	R	143	590	156	39	4	5	0.8	85	47	37	52	9	7	2	.264	.369
LF	Joe Medwick	R	155	636	223	64	13	18	2.8	115	138	34	33	3	0	0	.351	.577
C	Spud Davis	R	112	363	99	26	2	4	1.1	24	59	35	34	0	7	2	.273	.388
SUBSTITUTES																		
23	Frankie Frisch	B	93	303	83	10	0	1	0.3	40	26	36	10	2	8	3	.274	.317
1B	Ripper Collins	B	103	277	81	15	3	13	4.7	48	48	48	30	1	26	8	.292	.509
32	Art Garibaldi	R	71	232	64	12	0	1	0.4	30	20	16	30	3	1	0	.276	.341
3B	Don Gutteridge	R	23	91	29	3	4	3	3.3	13	16	1	14	3	0	0	.319	.538
3B	Johnny Vergez	R	8	18	3	1	0	0	0.0	1	1	1	3	0	0	0	.167	.222
SS	Pat Ankenman	R	1	3	0	0	0	0	0.0	0	0	0	3	0	0	0	.000	.000
1B	Walter Alston	R	1	1	0	0	0	0	0.0	0	0	0	1	0	0	0	.000	.000
3B	Heinie Schuble	R	2	0	0	0	0	0	–	0	0	0	0	0	0	0	–	–
OF	Lynn King	L	78	100	19	2	1	0	0.0	12	10	9	14	2	25	5	.190	.230
OF	Chick Fullis	R	47	89	25	6	1	0	0.0	15	6	7	11	0	12	2	.281	.371
OF	Eddie Morgan	L	8	18	5	0	0	1	5.6	4	3	2	4	0	3	2	.278	.444
OF	Lou Scoffic	R	4	7	3	0	0	0	0.0	2	2	1	2	0	0	0	.429	.429
C	Brusie Ogrodowski	R	94	237	54	15	1	1	0.4	28	20	10	20	0	9	1	.228	.312
PC	Mike Ryba	R	18	18	3	0	0	0	0.0	2	3	1	7	0	0	0	.167	.167
PITCHERS																		
P	Dizzy Dean	R	51	121	27	6	1	0	0.0	7	15	0	27	0	0	0	.223	.289
P	Roy Parmelee	R	37	76	15	2	1	0	0.0	3	5	2	19	0	0	0	.197	.250
P	Jim Winford	R	39	59	5	0	0	0	0.0	1	1	5	20	0	0	0	.085	.085
P	Paul Dean	R	17	34	2	0	0	0	0.0	0	1	0	2	0	0	0	.059	.059
P	Jesse Haines	R	25	30	5	0	0	0	0.0	3	4	2	7	0	0	0	.167	.167
P	Ed Heusser	R	42	26	7	0	1	1	3.8	4	4	3	12	0	0	0	.269	.462
P	Bill Walker	R	22	25	7	1	0	0	0.0	2	0	1	7	0	0	0	.280	.320
P	Si Johnson	R	12	21	4	1	0	0	0.0	1	2	0	8	0	0	0	.190	.238
P	George Earnshaw	R	20	18	4	0	0	0	0.0	0	4	0	3	0	0	0	.222	.222
P	Bill Hallahan	R	9	9	5	3	0	0	0.0	2	1	0	2	0	0	0	.556	.889
P	Les Munns	R	8	9	1	0	0	0	0.0	1	0	0	2	0	0	0	.111	.111
P	Flint Rhem	R	10	8	1	1	0	0	0.0	1	2	0	2	0	0	0	.125	.250
P	Cotton Pippen	R	6	6	1	1	0	0	0.0	0	0	0	0	0	0	0	.167	.333
P	Bill McGee	R	7	4	1	0	0	0	0.0	1	0	0	0	0	0	0	.250	.250
P	Bill Cox	R	2	0	0	0	0	0	–	0	0	0	0	0	0	0	–	–
P	Nels Potter	L	1	0	0	0	0	0	–	0	0	0	0	0	0	0	–	–
TEAM TOTAL				5537	1554	332	60	88	1.6	795	733	442	577	69	120	32	.281	.410

INDIVIDUAL FIELDING

POS	Player	T	G	PO	A	E	DP	TC/G	FA	POS	Player	T	G	PO	A	E	DP	TC/G	FA
1B	J. Mize	R	97	897	66	6	63	10.0	.994	OF	T. Moore	R	133	**418**	14	10	7	**3.3**	.977
	R. Collins	L	61	475	37	5	48	8.5	.990		J. Medwick	R	155	367	16	6	4	2.5	.985
	W. Alston	R	1	1	0	1	0	2.0	.500		P. Martin	R	127	226	13	6	5	1.9	.976
2B	S. Martin	R	83	169	242	22	50	5.2	.949		L. King	R	34	59	1	1	1	1.8	.984
	F. Frisch	R	61	124	176	11	27	5.1	.965		C. Fullis	R	26	53	2	0	2	2.1	1.000
	A. Garibaldi	R	24	50	67	3	5	5.0	.975		R. Collins	L	9	13	1	1	0	1.7	.933
	C. Gelbert	R	8	9	5	0	10	1.8	1.000		J. Mize	R	8	12	1	0	0	1.6	1.000
SS	L. Durocher	R	136	300	392	21	80	5.2	**.971**		E. Morgan	L	4	8	0	1	0	2.3	.889
	C. Gelbert	R	28	38	53	4	10	3.4	.958		L. Scoffic	R	3	7	0	1	0	2.7	.875
	S. Martin	R	3	4	8	0	2	4.0	1.000	C	S. Davis	R	103	390	59	7	7	4.4	.985
	P. Ankenman	R	1	2	1	2	0	5.0	.600		B. Ogrodowski	R	85	314	32	4	6	4.1	.989
	F. Frisch	R	1	0	2	1	0	3.0	.667		M. Ryba	R	4	16	1	0	0	4.3	1.000
3B	C. Gelbert	R	60	60	104	6	11	2.8	.965										
	A. Garibaldi	R	46	47	52	8	2	2.3	.925										
	D. Gutteridge	R	23	25	34	2	3	2.7	.967										
	F. Frisch	R	22	35	16	3	5	2.5	.944										
	P. Martin	R	15	13	12	7	1	2.1	.781										
	H. Schuble	R	1	0	0	0	0	0.0	.000										
	J. Vergez	R	8	7	6	1	1	1.8	.929										
	S. Davis	R	2	1	4	0	0	2.5	1.000										

Though they ended the season in a tie for second place, the Cardinals of 1936 were a club on the start of a downswing. The key veterans of the Gashouse Gang were aging, and the stars of the next great era were still making their way through Rickey's farm system. Still, they were in first place as late as August before falling behind. Joe Medwick turned in the second of his three straight .350-plus seasons, including a club record 64 doubles, and was aided by the slugging of a 23-year-old rookie first baseman, Johnny Mize. Mize spent just six years with the Cards, but they were enough to land him in sixth place on their all-time home run list. Dizzy Dean turned in what would be, tragically, his last great season; he not only led the league in complete games, but made seventeen relief appearances and picked up a league-leading eleven saves.

One Cardinal farmhand who was not destined to play a big role in St. Louis history made his one appearance in a major league box score in '36. He struck out in his only at bat, and made an error in one of his two chances at first base. The next time he put on a big league uniform, it would be as manager of the Dodgers, a job Walt Alston would hold for twenty-three years.

TEAM STATISTICS

W	L	PCT	GB	R	OR	Batting						Fielding			Pitching					
						2B	3B	HR	BA	SA	SB	E	DP	FA	CG	BB	SO	ShO	SV	ERA
92	62	.597		742	621	237	48	97	.281	.395	31	168	164	.974	58	401	500	12	22	**3.46**
87	67	.565	5	755	**603**	275	36	76	.286	.392	68	**146**	156	**.976**	77	434	597	**18**	10	3.53
87	67	.565	5	795	794	**332**	60	88	.281	**.410**	**69**	156	134	.974	65	477	561	5	**24**	4.48
84	70	.545	8	**804**	718	283	**80**	60	**.286**	.397	37	199	113	.967	67	**379**	559	5	12	3.89
74	80	.481	18	722	760	224	73	82	.274	.388	68	191	150	.969	50	418	459	6	23	4.22
71	83	.461	21	631	715	207	44	68	.265	.356	23	189	**175**	.971	60	451	421	7	13	3.94
67	87	.435	25	662	752	263	43	33	.272	.353	55	208	107	.966	59	528	**654**	7	18	3.98
54	100	.351	38	726	874	250	46	**103**	.281	.401	50	252	144	.959	51	515	454	7	14	4.64
GUE TOTAL				5837	5837	2071	430	607	.278	.386	401	1509	1143	.969	487	3603	4205	67	136	4.02

INDIVIDUAL   PITCHING

CHER	T	W	L	PCT	ERA	SV	G	GS	CG	IP	H	BB	SO	R	ER	ShO	H/9	BB/9	SO/9
zy Dean	R	24	13	.649	3.17	11	51	34	28	315	310	53	195	128	111	2	8.86	1.51	5.57
y Parmelee	R	11	11	.500	4.56	2	37	28	9	221	226	107	112	125	112	0	9.20	4.36	3.22
Winford	R	11	10	.524	3.80	3	39	23	10	192	203	68	72	90	81	1	9.52	3.19	3.38
Heusser	R	7	3	.700	5.43	3	42	3	0	104.1	130	38	26	73	63	0	11.21	3.28	2.24
se Haines	R	7	5	.583	3.90	1	25	9	4	99.1	110	21	19	44	43	0	9.97	1.90	1.72
l Dean	R	5	5	.500	4.60	1	17	14	5	92	113	20	28	57	47	0	11.05	1.96	2.74
Walker	L	5	6	.455	5.87	1	21	13	4	79.2	106	27	22	62	52	1	11.97	3.05	2.49
ohnson	R	5	3	.625	4.38	0	12	9	3	61.2	82	11	21	30	30	1	11.97	1.61	3.06
rge Earnshaw	R	2	1	.667	6.40	1	20	6	1	57.2	80	20	28	43	41	0	12.49	3.12	4.37
e Ryba	R	5	1	.833	5.40	0	14	0	0	45	55	16	25	33	27	0	11.00	3.20	5.00
Hallahan	L	2	2	.500	6.32	0	9	6	1	37	28	20	16	28	26	0	6.81	4.86	3.89
t Rhem	R	2	1	.667	6.75	0	10	4	0	26.2	49	49	9	26	20	0	16.54	16.54	3.04
Munns	R	0	3	.000	3.00	1	7	1	0	24	23	12	4	18	8	0	8.63	4.50	1.50
ton Pippen	R	0	2	.000	7.71	0	6	3	0	21	37	8	8	18	18	0	15.86	3.43	3.43
McGee	R	1	1	.500	8.04	0	7	2	0	15.2	23	4	8	14	14	0	13.21	2.30	4.60
Cox	R	0	0	–	6.75	0	2	0	0	2.2	4	1	1	5	2	0	13.50	3.38	3.38
per Martin	R	0	0	–	0.00	0	1	0	0	2	1	2	0	0	0	0	4.50	9.00	0.00
s Potter	R	0	0	–	0.00	0	1	0	0	1	0	0	0	0	0	0	0.00	0.00	0.00
M TOTAL		87	67	.565	4.48	24	321	155	65	1397.2	1580	477	561	794	695	5	10.17	3.07	3.61

MANAGER	W	L	PCT
Frankie Frisch	81	73	.526

POS	Player	B	G	AB	H	2B	3B	HR	HR %	R	RBI	BB	SO	SB	Pinch Hit AB	Pinch Hit H	BA	SA
REGULARS																		
1B	Johnny Mize	L	145	560	204	40	7	25	4.5	103	113	56	57	2	1	0	.364	.595
2B	Jimmy Brown	B	138	525	145	20	9	2	0.4	86	53	27	29	10	6	1	.276	.360
SS	Leo Durocher	R	135	477	97	11	3	1	0.2	46	47	38	36	6	0	0	.203	.245
3B	Don Gutteridge	R	119	447	121	26	10	7	1.6	66	61	25	66	12	8	1	.271	.421
RF	Don Padgett	L	123	446	140	22	6	10	2.2	62	74	30	43	4	13	4	.314	.457
CF	Terry Moore	R	115	461	123	17	3	5	1.1	76	43	32	41	13	8	1	.267	.349
LF	Joe Medwick	R	156	**633**	**237**	56	10	31	4.9	111	**154**	41	50	4	0	0	**.374**	**.641**
C	Brusie Ogrodowski	R	90	279	65	10	3	3	1.1	37	31	11	17	2	3	2	.233	.323
SUBSTITUTES																		
3O	Frenchy Bordagaray	R	96	300	88	11	4	1	0.3	43	37	15	25	11	16	1	.293	.367
2B	Stu Martin	L	90	223	58	6	1	1	0.4	34	17	32	18	3	28	6	.260	.309
1B	Dick Siebert	L	22	38	7	2	0	0	0.0	3	2	4	8	1	13	3	.184	.237
2B	Frankie Frisch	B	17	32	7	2	0	0	0.0	3	4	1	0	0	12	2	.219	.281
OF	Pepper Martin	R	98	339	103	27	8	5	1.5	60	38	33	50	9	9	2	.304	.475
OF	Randy Moore	L	8	7	0	0	0	0	0.0	0	0	0	0	0	7	0	.000	.000
C	Mickey Owen	R	80	234	54	4	2	0	0.0	17	20	15	13	1	2	0	.231	.265
C	Herb Bremer	R	11	33	7	1	0	0	0.0	2	3	2	4	0	0	0	.212	.242
PITCHERS																		
P	Bob Weiland	L	41	89	15	1	1	2	2.2	5	10	3	35	0	0	0	.169	.270
P	Lon Warneke	R	36	80	21	3	0	0	0.0	10	10	7	12	0	0	0	.263	.300
P	Dizzy Dean	R	27	66	15	1	0	1	1.5	8	5	3	11	0	0	0	.227	.288
P	Si Johnson	R	38	65	9	1	0	0	0.0	5	1	2	20	0	0	0	.138	.154
P	Mike Ryba	R	41	48	15	2	0	0	0.0	6	7	5	5	0	0	0	.313	.354
P	Jesse Haines	R	16	22	4	1	0	0	0.0	3	1	0	6	0	0	0	.182	.227
P	Ray Harrell	R	35	22	1	0	0	0	0.0	1	0	2	8	0	0	0	.045	.045
P	Sheriff Blake	B	14	10	3	0	0	0	0.0	1	0	0	1	0	0	0	.300	.300
P	Howie Krist	L	6	9	0	0	0	0	0.0	0	0	0	5	0	0	0	.000	.000
P	Tom Sunkel	L	9	9	1	0	0	0	0.0	1	0	0	3	0	0	0	.111	.111
P	Nub Kleinke	R	5	8	0	0	0	0	0.0	0	0	0	3	0	0	0	.000	.000
P	Jim Winford	R	16	8	1	0	0	0	0.0	0	0	0	2	0	0	0	.125	.125
P	Bill McGee	R	4	5	1	0	0	0	0.0	0	0	0	1	0	0	0	.200	.200
P	Abe White	R	5	1	1	0	0	0	0.0	0	0	0	0	0	0	0	1.000	1.000
P	Nate Andrews	R	4	0	0	0	0	0	–	0	0	1	0	0	0	0	–	–
P	John Chambers	L	2	0	0	0	0	0	–	0	0	0	0	0	0	0	–	–
P	Paul Dean	R	1	0	0	0	0	0	–	0	0	0	0	0	0	0	–	–
TEAM TOTAL				5476	1543	264	67	94	1.7	789	731	385	569	78	126	23	.282	.406

INDIVIDUAL FIELDING

POS	Player	T	G	PO	A	E	DP	TC/G	FA
1B	J. Mize	R	144	1308	67	17	104	9.7	.988
	S. Martin	R	9	75	4	1	3	8.9	.988
	D. Siebert	L	7	44	3	1	2	6.9	.979
2B	J. Brown	R	112	235	360	22	57	5.5	.964
	S. Martin	R	48	93	134	13	27	5.0	.946
	F. Frisch	R	17	12	14	0	0	1.5	1.000
SS	L. Durocher	R	134	279	381	28	72	5.1	.959
	J. Brown	R	25	41	53	9	10	4.1	.913
	S. Martin	R	1	0	0	0	0	0.0	.000
	D. Gutteridge	R	8	12	16	2	2	3.8	.933
3B	D. Gutteridge	R	105	133	176	7	18	3.0	.978
	F. Bordagaray	R	50	59	71	8	2	2.8	.942
	P. Martin	R	5	6	8	1	2	3.0	.933
	J. Brown	R	1	1	2	0	0	3.0	1.000
OF	J. Medwick	R	156	329	9	4	1	2.2	**.988**
	T. Moore	R	106	307	9	4	2	3.0	.988
	D. Padgett	R	109	225	9	11	5	2.2	.955
	P. Martin	R	82	204	12	6	3	2.7	.973
	F. Bordagaray	R	28	46	1	1	0	1.7	.979
	R. Moore	R	1	0	0	0	0	0.0	.000
C	B. Ogrodowski	R	87	387	50	7	2	5.1	.984
	M. Owen	R	78	287	49	9	6	4.4	.974
	H. Bremer	R	10	40	6	1	2	4.7	.979
	M. Ryba	R	3	5	0	0	0	1.7	1.000

It was Joe Medwick's biggest season; he not only led the league in batting, homers (tied with Mel Ott), and RBIs for a Triple Crown, but added titles in hits, doubles, runs, and slugging as well. Mize had a pretty fair season too, finishing right behind Medwick, the league MVP, in batting, slugging, and total bases. Despite their efforts, the Cardinals were already fading from contention when Earl Averill of Cleveland blasted a line drive off Dizzy Dean's foot in the All-Star Game. The result was a broken toe and, when Dean rushed himself back into the rotation, an altered pitching motion which led to the sore arm which effectively ended Dean's career. Rickey warned Phil Wrigley that Dean was damaged goods, but the Cubs were still willing to meet Rickey's price of $185,000 and two pitchers for Diz. Dean was 7–1 with a 1.81 ERA in thirteen games for the pennant-winning Cubs in '38, but he won just nine more games in his too-short major league career.

TEAM STATISTICS

	W	L	PCT	GB	R	OR	2B	3B	Batting HR	BA	SA	SB	E	Fielding DP	FA	CG	BB	Pitching SO	ShO	SV	ERA
Y	95	57	.625		732	602	251	41	111	.278	.403	45	159	143	.974	67	404	653	11	17	3.43
HI	93	61	.604	3	811	682	253	74	96	.287	.416	71	151	141	.975	73	502	596	11	13	3.97
IT	86	68	.558	10	704	646	223	86	47	.285	.384	32	181	135	.970	67	428	643	12	17	3.56
TL	81	73	.526	15	789	733	264	67	94	.282	.406	78	164	127	.973	81	448	573	10	4	3.95
OS	79	73	.520	16	579	556	200	41	63	.247	.339	45	157	128	.975	85	372	387	16	10	3.22
KN	62	91	.405	33.5	616	772	258	53	37	.265	.354	69	217	127	.964	63	476	592	5	8	4.13
HI	61	92	.399	34.5	724	869	258	37	103	.273	.391	66	184	157	.970	59	501	529	6	15	5.06
N	56	98	.364	40	612	707	215	59	73	.254	.360	53	208	139	.966	64	533	581	10	18	3.94
AGUE TOTAL					5567	5567	1922	458	624	.272	.382	459	1421	1097	.971	559	3664	4554	81	102	3.91

INDIVIDUAL PITCHING

TCHER	T	W	L	PCT	ERA	SV	G	GS	CG	IP	H	BB	SO	R	ER	ShO	H/9	BB/9	SO/9
b Weiland	L	15	14	.517	3.54	0	41	34	21	264.1	283	94	105	127	104	2	9.64	3.20	3.58
n Warneke	R	18	11	.621	4.53	0	36	33	18	238.2	280	69	87	139	120	2	10.56	2.60	3.28
zzy Dean	R	13	10	.565	2.69	1	27	25	17	197.1	206	33	120	76	59	4	9.40	1.51	5.47
Johnson	R	12	12	.500	3.32	1	38	21	12	192.1	222	43	64	92	71	1	10.39	2.01	2.99
ke Ryba	R	9	6	.600	4.13	0	38	8	5	135	152	40	57	76	62	0	10.13	2.67	3.80
y Harrell	R	3	7	.300	5.87	1	35	15	1	96.2	99	59	41	73	63	1	9.22	5.49	3.82
sse Haines	R	3	3	.500	4.52	0	16	6	2	65.2	81	23	18	36	33	0	11.10	3.15	2.47
n Winford	R	2	4	.333	5.83	0	16	4	0	46.1	56	27	19	31	30	0	10.88	5.24	3.69
eriff Blake	R	0	3	.000	3.71	0	14	2	2	43.2	45	18	20	23	18	0	9.27	3.71	4.12
m Sunkel	L	0	0	–	2.06	1	9	1	0	39.1	24	11	9	11	9	0	5.49	2.52	2.06
wie Krist	R	3	1	.750	4.23	0	6	4	1	27.2	34	10	6	13	13	0	11.06	3.25	1.95
b Kleinke	R	1	1	.500	4.79	0	5	2	1	20.2	25	7	9	14	11	0	10.89	3.05	3.92
McGee	R	1	0	1.000	2.63	0	4	1	1	13.2	13	4	9	4	4	0	8.56	2.63	5.93
e White	L	0	1	.000	6.75	0	5	0	0	9.1	14	3	2	7	7	0	13.50	2.89	1.93
te Andrews	R	0	0	–	4.00	0	4	1	0	9	12	3	6	4	4	0	12.00	3.00	6.00
n Chambers	R	0	0	–	18.00	0	2	0	0	2	5	2	1	4	4	0	22.50	9.00	4.50
l Dean	R	0	0	–	∞	0	1	0	0	1	2	2	0	3	3	0	∞	∞	0.00
AM TOTAL		80	73	.523	3.95	4	297	157	81	1401.2	1552	448	573	733	615	10	9.97	2.88	3.68

CARDINAL STRIKEOUT LEADERS

1905 Fred Beebe (also with Chicago), 171	1934 Dizzy Dean, 195
1930 Bill Hallahan, 177	1935 Dizzy Dean, 182
1931 Bill Hallahan, 159	1948 Harry Brecheen, 149
1932 Dizzy Dean, 191	1958 Sam Jones, 225
1933 Dizzy Dean, 199	1968 Bob Gibson, 268

MANAGER	W	L	PCT
Frankie Frisch	62	72	.463
Mike Gonzalez	9	8	.529

POS	Player	B	G	AB	H	2B	3B	HR	HR %	R	RBI	BB	SO	SB	Pinch Hit AB	Pinch Hit H	BA	SA
REGULARS																		
1B	Johnny Mize	L	149	531	179	34	16	27	5.1	85	102	74	47	0	7	1	.337	**.614**
2B	Stu Martin	L	114	417	116	26	2	1	0.2	54	27	30	28	4	15	3	.278	.357
SS	Lynn Myers	R	70	227	55	10	2	1	0.4	18	19	9	25	9	0	0	.242	.317
3B	Don Gutteridge	R	142	552	141	21	15	9	1.6	61	64	29	49	14	2	0	.255	.397
RF	Enos Slaughter	L	112	395	109	20	10	8	2.0	59	58	32	38	1	20	2	.276	.438
CF	Terry Moore	R	94	312	85	21	3	4	1.3	49	21	46	19	9	9	1	.272	.397
LF	Joe Medwick	R	146	590	190	**47**	8	21	3.6	100	**122**	42	41	0	2	0	.322	.536
C	Mickey Owen	R	122	397	106	25	2	4	1.0	45	36	32	14	2	5	1	.267	.370
SUBSTITUTES																		
UT	Jimmy Brown	B	108	382	115	12	6	0	0.0	50	38	27	9	7	9	3	.301	.364
3B	Joe Stripp	R	54	199	57	7	0	0	0.0	24	18	18	10	0	3	1	.286	.322
2B	Jim Bucher	L	17	57	13	3	1	0	0.0	7	7	2	2	0	2	1	.228	.316
SS	Creepy Crespi	R	7	19	5	2	0	0	0.0	2	1	2	7	0	0	0	.263	.368
O1	Don Padgett	L	110	388	105	26	5	8	2.1	59	65	18	28	0	18	6	.271	.425
OF	Pepper Martin	R	91	269	79	18	2	2	0.7	34	38	18	34	4	23	5	.294	.398
OF	Frenchy Bordagaray	R	81	156	44	5	1	0	0.0	19	21	8	9	2	43	20	.282	.327
OF	Hal Epps	L	17	50	15	0	0	1	2.0	8	3	2	4	2	7	0	.300	.360
OF	Tuck Stainback	R	6	10	0	0	0	0	0.0	2	0	0	3	0	3	0	.000	.000
C	Herb Bremer	R	50	151	33	5	1	2	1.3	14	14	9	36	1	0	0	.219	.305
PH	Dick Siebert	L	1	1	1	0	0	0	0.0	0	0	0	0	0	1	1	1.000	1.000
PITCHERS																		
P	Bob Weiland	L	35	80	11	0	0	0	0.0	7	1	5	34	0	0	0	.138	.138
P	Lon Warneke	R	31	71	23	3	0	0	0.0	5	6	2	7	0	0	0	.324	.366
P	Bill McGee	R	47	67	14	2	0	0	0.0	4	2	3	7	0	0	0	.209	.239
P	Curt Davis	R	40	57	13	0	0	3	5.3	8	9	0	16	0	0	0	.228	.386
P	Roy Henshaw	R	27	41	9	0	0	0	0.0	1	2	1	6	0	0	0	.220	.220
P	Max Macon	L	46	36	11	0	0	0	0.0	5	3	2	4	0	2	0	.306	.306
P	Clyde Shoun	L	40	31	8	0	0	0	0.0	2	3	0	6	0	0	0	.258	.258
P	Paul Dean	R	5	11	2	0	0	0	0.0	1	0	0	1	0	0	0	.182	.182
P	Ray Harrell	R	32	10	0	0	0	0	0.0	1	0	0	4	0	0	0	.000	.000
P	Max Lanier	R	18	10	1	0	0	0	0.0	1	0	1	0	0	0	0	.100	.100
P	Mort Cooper	R	4	9	2	1	0	0	0.0	0	0	0	3	0	0	0	.222	.333
P	Si Johnson	R	6	1	0	0	0	0	0.0	0	0	0	1	0	0	0	.000	.000
P	Preacher Roe	R	1	1	0	0	0	0	0.0	0	0	0	0	0	0	0	.000	.000
P	Guy Bush	R	6	0	0	0	0	0	–	0	0	0	0	0	0	0	–	–
P	Howie Krist	L	2	0	0	0	0	0	–	0	0	0	0	0	0	0	–	–
P	Mike Ryba	R	3	0	0	0	0	0	–	0	0	0	0	0	0	0	–	–
	TEAM TOTAL			5528	1542	288	74	91	1.6	725	680	412	492	55	171	45	.279	.407

INDIVIDUAL FIELDING

POS	Player	T	G	PO	A	E	DP	TC/G	FA	POS	Player	T	G	PO	A	E	DP	TC/G	FA
1B	J. Mize	R	140	1297	93	15	117	10.0	.989	OF	J. Medwick	R	144	330	12	9	6	2.4	.974
	D. Padgett	R	16	138	11	0	12	9.3	1.000		T. Moore	R	75	219	5	3	1	3.0	.987
2B	S. Martin	R	99	225	301	18	59	5.5	.967		E. Slaughter	R	92	189	7	6	0	2.2	.970
	J. Brown	R	49	121	151	9	37	5.7	.968		D. Padgett	R	71	140	14	6	3	2.3	.963
	J. Bucher	R	14	32	31	3	9	4.7	.955		P. Martin	R	62	138	1	2	1	2.3	.986
SS	D. Gutteridge	R	68	150	196	31	39	5.5	.918		F. Bordagaray	R	29	67	3	3	0	2.5	.959
	L. Myers	R	69	110	195	18	36	4.7	.944		M. Macon	L	1	0	0	0	0	0.0	.000
	J. Brown	R	30	49	59	9	13	3.9	.923		H. Epps	L	10	26	0	1	0	2.7	.963
	C. Crespi	R	7	14	12	6	4	4.6	.813		T. Stainback	R	2	8	0	0	0	4.0	1.000
3B	D. Gutteridge	R	73	94	148	14	17	3.5	.945	C	M. Owen	R	116	463	67	11	8	4.7	.980
	J. Stripp	R	51	53	76	3	9	2.6	.977*		H. Bremer	R	50	186	30	5	2	4.4	.977
	J. Brown	R	24	25	54	3	5	3.4	.963		D. Padgett	R	6	17	2	3	0	3.7	.864
	T. Moore	R	6	9	16	3	1	4.7	.893										
	F. Bordagaray	R	4	5	6	3	0	3.5	.786										
	P. Martin	R	4	1	3	0	0	1.0	1.000										
	J. Bucher	R	1	1	0	0	0	1.0	1.000										

How important is pitching? Very. The Cardinals dropped to sixth place in 1938 despite leading the league in runs, batting, and slugging. Medwick topped the one hundred mark in runs and RBIs for the fifth straight season, and Mize belted 27 homers, including two three-homer games in one week. Nonetheless, the Cards finished nine games under .500. They had, however, fallen as far as they were going to. Help was on the way from below: Enos Slaughter broke into the starting lineup, and pitchers Max Lanier and Mort Cooper made their first appearances in Cardinal uniforms.

The Cardinals' farm system was even strong enough to survive a ruling by Commissioner Kenesaw Mountain Landis that made free agents of seventy-four players because the Cardinals had secret arrangements with their clubs in violation of baseball law. The big one that got away was hard-hitting outfielder Pete Reiser, National League batting champ for Brooklyn in 1941.

TEAM STATISTICS

	W	L	PCT	GB	R	OR	2B	3B	HR	BA	SA	SB	E	DP	FA	CG	BB	SO	ShO	SV	ERA
							Batting						Fielding					Pitching			
l	89	63	.586		713	598	242	70	65	.269	.377	49	135	151	.978	67	454	583	16	18	3.37
T	86	64	.573	2	707	630	265	66	65	.279	.388	47	163	168	.974	57	432	557	8	15	3.46
Y	83	67	.553	5	705	637	210	36	125	.271	.396	31	168	147	.973	59	389	497	8	18	3.62
N	82	68	.547	6	723	634	251	57	110	.277	.406	19	172	133	.971	72	463	542	11	16	3.62
)S	77	75	.507	12	561	618	199	39	54	.250	.333	49	173	136	.972	83	465	413	15	12	3.40
L	71	80	.470	17.5	725	721	288	74	91	.279	.407	55	199	145	.967	58	474	534	10	16	3.84
N	69	80	.463	18.5	704	710	225	79	61	.257	.367	66	157	148	.973	56	446	469	12	14	4.07
l	45	105	.300	43	550	840	233	29	40	.254	.333	38	201	135	.966	68	582	492	3	6	4.93
GUE TOTAL					5388	5388	1913	450	611	.267	.376	354	1368	1163	.972	520	3705	4087	83	115	3.78

INDIVIDUAL PITCHING

PITCHER	T	W	L	PCT	ERA	SV	G	GS	CG	IP	H	BB	SO	R	ER	ShO	H/9	BB/9	SO/9
o Weiland	L	16	11	.593	3.59	1	35	29	11	228.1	248	67	117	118	91	1	9.78	2.64	4.61
McGee	R	7	12	.368	3.21	5	47	25	10	216	216	78	104	100	77	1	9.00	3.25	4.33
Warneke	R	13	8	.619	3.97	0	31	26	12	197	199	64	89	102	87	4	9.09	2.92	4.07
t Davis	R	12	8	.600	3.63	3	40	21	8	173.1	187	27	36	80	70	2	9.71	1.40	1.87
Henshaw	L	5	11	.313	4.02	0	27	15	4	130	132	48	34	63	58	0	9.14	3.32	2.35
x Macon	L	4	11	.267	4.11	2	38	12	5	129.1	133	61	39	83	59	1	9.26	4.24	2.71
de Shoun	L	6	6	.500	4.14	1	40	12	3	117.1	130	43	37	58	54	0	9.97	3.30	2.84
Harrell	R	2	3	.400	4.86	2	32	3	1	63	78	29	32	37	34	0	11.14	4.14	4.57
x Lanier	L	0	3	.000	4.20	0	18	3	1	45	57	28	14	30	21	0	11.40	5.60	2.80
ul Dean	R	3	1	.750	2.61	0	5	4	2	31	37	5	14	12	9	1	10.74	1.45	4.06
t Cooper	R	2	1	.667	3.04	1	4	3	1	23.2	17	12	11	11	8	0	6.46	4.56	4.18
Johnson	R	0	3	.000	7.47	0	6	3	0	15.2	27	6	4	17	13	0	15.51	3.45	2.30
Bush	R	0	1	.000	5.06	1	6	0	0	5.1	6	3	1	3	3	0	10.13	5.06	1.69
e Ryba	R	1	1	.500	5.40	0	3	0	0	5	8	1	0	3	3	0	14.40	1.80	0.00
acher Roe	L	0	0	—	13.50	0	1	0	0	2.2	6	2	1	4	4	0	20.25	6.75	3.38
vie Krist	R	0	0	—	0.00	0	2	0	0	1.1	1	0	1	0	0	0	6.75	0.00	6.75
M TOTAL		71	80	.470	3.84	16	335	156	58	1384	1482	474	534	721	591	10	9.64	3.08	3.47

MANAGER	W	L	PCT
Ray Blades	92	61	.601

POS	Player	B	G	AB	H	2B	3B	HR	HR %	R	RBI	BB	SO	SB	Pinch Hit AB	Pinch Hit H	BA	SA
REGULARS																		
1B	Johnny Mize	L	153	564	197	44	14	28	5.0	104	108	92	49	0	1	0	.349	.626
2B	Stu Martin	L	120	425	114	26	7	3	0.7	60	30	33	40	4	11	0	.268	.384
SS	Jimmy Brown	B	147	645	192	31	8	3	0.5	88	51	32	18	4	1	0	.298	.384
3B	Don Gutteridge	R	148	524	141	27	4	7	1.3	71	54	27	70	5	2	0	.269	.376
RF	Enos Slaughter	L	149	604	193	52	5	12	2.0	95	86	44	53	2	0	0	.320	.482
CF	Terry Moore	R	130	417	123	25	2	17	4.1	65	77	43	38	6	7	2	.295	.487
LF	Joe Medwick	R	150	606	201	48	8	14	2.3	98	117	45	44	6	1	0	.332	.507
C	Mickey Owen	R	131	344	89	18	2	3	0.9	32	35	43	28	6	5	0	.259	.349
SUBSTITUTES																		
S2	Lynn Myers	R	74	117	28	6	1	0	0.0	24	10	12	23	1	5	3	.239	.308
SS	Lyn Lary	R	34	75	14	3	0	0	0.0	11	9	16	15	1	1	0	.187	.227
2S	Creepy Crespi	R	15	29	5	1	0	0	0.0	3	6	3	6	0	3	0	.172	.207
2B	Bob Repass	R	3	6	2	1	0	0	0.0	0	1	0	2	0	1	1	.333	.500
1B	Johnny Hopp	L	6	4	2	1	0	0	0.0	1	2	1	1	0	3	2	.500	.750
SS	Eddie Lake	R	2	4	1	0	0	0	0.0	0	0	1	0	0	0	0	.250	.250
SS	Joe Orengo	R	7	3	0	0	0	0	0.0	0	0	0	1	0	0	0	.000	.000
O3	Pepper Martin	R	88	281	86	17	7	3	1.1	48	37	30	35	6	10	0	.306	.448
OF	Lynn King	L	89	85	20	2	0	0	0.0	10	11	15	3	2	35	10	.235	.259
C	Don Padgett	L	92	233	93	15	3	5	2.1	38	53	18	11	1	21	4	.399	.554
C	Herman Franks	L	17	17	1	0	0	0	0.0	1	3	3	3	0	2	0	.059	.059
C	Herb Bremer	R	9	9	1	0	0	0	0.0	0	1	0	2	0	1	0	.111	.111
PH	Buster Adams	R	2	1	0	0	0	0	0.0	1	0	0	0	0	1	0	.000	.000
PH	Johnny Echols	R	2	0	0	0	0	0	-	0	0	0	0	0	0	0	-	-
PITCHERS																		
P	Curt Davis	R	63	105	40	5	0	1	1.0	10	17	3	22	0	14	5	.381	.457
P	Mort Cooper	R	47	69	16	3	0	2	2.9	4	11	1	13	0	0	0	.232	.362
P	Bill McGee	R	43	55	8	1	0	0	0.0	2	2	1	13	0	0	0	.145	.164
P	Lon Warneke	R	34	52	10	3	0	0	0.0	4	8	4	7	0	0	0	.192	.250
P	Bob Bowman	R	51	47	4	1	0	0	0.0	2	1	4	29	0	0	0	.085	.106
P	Bob Weiland	L	32	46	3	0	0	0	0.0	1	0	1	22	0	0	0	.065	.065
P	Tom Sunkel	L	20	28	9	2	0	0	0.0	5	1	1	7	0	0	0	.321	.393
P	Clyde Shoun	L	53	26	3	0	1	0	0.0	0	1	1	4	0	0	0	.115	.192
P	Max Lanier	R	7	14	4	0	0	0	0.0	1	0	1	1	0	0	0	.286	.286
P	Paul Dean	R	16	9	1	0	0	0	0.0	0	0	0	3	0	0	0	.111	.111
P	Nate Andrews	R	11	2	0	0	0	0	0.0	0	0	0	0	0	0	0	.000	.000
P	Murry Dickson	R	1	1	0	0	0	0	0.0	0	0	0	1	0	0	0	.000	.000
P	Frank Barrett	R	1	0	0	0	0	0	-	0	0	0	0	0	0	0	-	-
P	Ken Raffensberger	R	1	0	0	0	0	0	-	0	0	0	0	0	0	0	-	-
TEAM TOTAL				5447	1601	332	62	98	1.8	779	732	475	566	44	125	27	.294	.432

INDIVIDUAL FIELDING

POS	Player	T	G	PO	A	E	DP	TC/G	FA	POS	Player	T	G	PO	A	E	DP	TC/G	FA
1B	J. Mize	R	152	1348	90	19	123	9.6	.987	OF	E. Slaughter	R	149	348	18	12	5	2.5	.968
	D. Padgett	R	6	27	0	1	1	4.7	.964		J. Medwick	R	149	313	10	8	1	2.2	.976
	S. Martin	R	1	7	1	0	0	8.0	1.000		T. Moore	R	121	291	16	2	1	2.6	.994
	J. Hopp	L	1	6	1	0	1	7.0	1.000		P. Martin	R	51	113	4	3	0	2.4	.975
2B	S. Martin	R	107	242	304	13	62	5.2	.977		L. King	R	44	53	1	1	0	1.3	.982
	J. Brown	R	50	120	143	10	25	5.5	.963	C	M. Owen	R	126	452	52	9	7	4.1	.982
	C. Crespi	R	6	9	16	1	1	4.3	.962		D. Padgett	R	61	249	18	6	5	4.5	.978
	L. Myers	R	13	7	15	1	4	1.8	.957		H. Franks	R	13	34	2	1	0	2.8	.973
	B. Repass	R	2	1	5	0	1	3.0	1.000		H. Bremer	R	8	13	0	0	0	1.6	1.000
SS	J. Brown	R	104	208	349	25	67	5.6	.957										
	L. Myers	R	36	55	76	15	21	4.1	.897										
	L. Lary	R	30	51	71	5	9	4.2	.961										
	C. Crespi	R	4	0	9	1	0	2.5	.900										
	J. Orengo	R	7	3	3	3	0	1.3	.667										
	E. Lake	R	2	3	3	1	1	3.5	.857										
	D. Gutteridge	R	2	0	1	0	0	0.5	1.000										
3B	D. Gutteridge	R	143	136	203	24	24	2.5	.934										
	P. Martin	R	22	15	30	4	2	2.2	.918										
	L. Myers	R	5	3	3	1	0	1.4	.857										
	L. Lary	R	3	1	0	0	0	0.3	1.000										

Improved hitting and much improved pitching led to 92 wins in 1939 and a second-place finish. The Cardinals got added production from every position except second, led by Slaughter, Medwick, and Mize, who finished 1-2-3 in the league in two-base hits. Rickey was a firm believer in the value of speed; while his clubs did not necessarily steal many bases, their overall speed, particularly in the outfield, led to many extra-base hits and sound defense. His clubs would have fared quite well on artificial turf. The '39 Cardinals were first in the league in doubles and triples, and second in homers, leading the league in batting by sixteen points and slugging by twenty-seven. Even the pitchers got into the swing of things: Curt Davis, acquired in the Dizzy Dean trade, hit .381, the highest average for a 20-game winner in the National League since 1900.

TEAM STATISTICS

	W	L	PCT	GB	R	OR	Batting 2B	3B	HR	BA	SA	SB	Fielding E	DP	FA	CG	BB	Pitching SO	ShO	SV	ERA
N	97	57	.630		767	595	269	60	98	.278	.405	46	162	170	.974	86	499	637	13	9	3.27
TL	92	61	.601	4.5	779	633	332	62	98	.294	.432	44	177	140	.971	45	498	603	18	32	3.59
KN	84	69	.549	12.5	708	645	265	57	78	.265	.380	59	176	157	.972	69	399	528	9	13	3.64
HI	84	70	.545	13	724	678	263	62	91	.266	.391	61	186	126	.970	72	430	584	8	13	3.80
Y	77	74	.510	18.5	703	685	211	38	116	.272	.396	26	153	152	.975	55	478	505	6	20	4.07
T	68	85	.444	28.5	666	721	261	60	63	.276	.384	44	168	153	.972	53	423	524	10	15	4.15
DS	63	88	.417	32.5	572	659	199	39	56	.264	.348	41	181	178	.971	68	513	430	11	15	3.71
HI	45	106	.298	50.5	553	856	232	40	49	.261	.351	47	171	133	.970	67	579	447	3	12	5.17
AGUE TOTAL					5472	5472	2032	418	649	.272	.386	368	1374	1209	.972	515	3819	4258	78	129	3.92

INDIVIDUAL   PITCHING

TCHER	T	W	L	PCT	ERA	SV	G	GS	CG	IP	H	BB	SO	R	ER	ShO	H/9	BB/9	SO/9
urt Davis	R	22	16	.579	3.63	7	49	31	13	248	279	48	70	121	100	3	10.13	1.74	2.54
ort Cooper	R	12	6	.667	3.25	4	45	26	7	210.2	208	97	130	94	76	2	8.89	4.14	5.55
b Bowman	R	13	5	.722	2.60	9	51	15	4	169.1	141	60	78	54	49	2	7.49	3.19	4.15
n Warneke	R	13	7	.650	3.78	2	34	21	6	162	160	49	59	73	68	3	8.89	2.72	3.28
l McGee	R	12	5	.706	3.81	0	43	17	5	156	155	59	56	68	66	4	8.94	3.40	3.23
b Weiland	L	10	12	.455	3.57	1	32	23	6	146.1	146	50	63	69	58	3	8.98	3.08	3.87
yde Shoun	L	3	1	.750	3.76	9	53	2	0	103	98	42	50	51	43	0	8.56	3.67	4.37
m Sunkel	L	4	4	.500	4.22	0	20	11	2	85.1	79	56	54	47	40	1	8.33	5.91	5.70
ul Dean	R	0	1	.000	6.07	0	16	2	0	43	54	10	16	30	29	0	11.30	2.09	3.35
x Lanier	L	2	1	.667	2.39	0	7	6	2	37.2	29	13	14	11	10	0	6.93	3.11	3.35
te Andrews	R	1	2	.333	6.75	0	11	1	0	16	24	12	6	14	12	0	13.50	6.75	3.38
rry Dickson	R	0	0	—	0.00	0	1	0	0	3.2	1	1	2	0	0	0	2.45	2.45	4.91
nk Barrett	R	0	1	.000	5.40	0	1	0	0	1.2	1	1	3	1	1	0	5.40	5.40	16.20
ry Moore	R	0	0	—	0.00	0	1	0	0	1	0	0	1	0	0	0	0.00	0.00	9.00
n Raffensberger	L	0	0	—	0.00	0	1	0	0	1	2	0	1	0	0	0	18.00	0.00	9.00
AM TOTAL		92	61	.601	3.59	32	365	155	45	1384.2	1377	498	603	633	552	18	8.95	3.24	3.92

MANAGER	W	L	PCT
Ray Blades	15	24	.385
Mike Gonzalez	0	5	.000
Billy Southworth	69	40	.633

POS	Player	B	G	AB	H	2B	3B	HR	HR %	R	RBI	BB	SO	SB	Pinch Hit AB	H	BA	SA
REGULARS																		
1B	Johnny Mize	L	155	579	182	31	13	43	7.4	111	137	82	49	7	2	1	.314	.636
2B	Joe Orengo	R	129	415	119	23	4	7	1.7	58	56	65	90	9	0	0	.287	.412
SS	Marty Marion	R	125	435	121	18	1	3	0.7	44	46	21	34	9	0	0	.278	.345
3B	Stu Martin	L	112	369	88	12	6	4	1.1	45	32	33	35	4	9	1	.238	.336
RF	Enos Slaughter	L	140	516	158	25	13	17	3.3	96	73	50	35	8	7	2	.306	.504
CF	Terry Moore	R	136	537	163	33	4	17	3.2	92	64	42	44	18	3	0	.304	.475
LF	Ernie Koy	R	93	348	108	19	5	8	2.3	44	52	28	59	12	2	0	.310	.463
C	Mickey Owen	R	117	307	81	16	2	0	0.0	27	27	34	13	4	4	2	.264	.329
SUBSTITUTES																		
UT	Jimmy Brown	B	107	454	127	17	4	0	0.0	56	30	24	15	9	1	0	.280	.335
3B	Don Gutteridge	R	69	108	29	5	0	3	2.8	19	14	5	15	3	20	2	.269	.398
2S	Eddie Lake	R	32	66	14	3	0	2	3.0	12	7	12	17	1	5	0	.212	.348
3S	Creepy Crespi	R	3	11	3	1	0	0	0.0	2	0	1	2	1	0	0	.273	.364
OF	Pepper Martin	R	86	228	72	15	4	3	1.3	28	39	22	24	6	17	4	.316	.456
OF	Joe Medwick	R	37	158	48	12	0	3	1.9	21	20	6	8	0	0	0	.304	.437
O1	Johnny Hopp	L	80	152	41	7	4	1	0.7	24	14	9	21	3	23	4	.270	.388
OF	Harry Walker	L	7	27	5	2	0	0	0.0	2	6	0	2	0	0	0	.185	.259
OF	Carden Gillenwater	R	7	25	4	1	0	0	0.0	1	5	0	2	0	0	0	.160	.200
OF	Hal Epps	L	11	15	3	0	0	0	0.0	6	1	0	3	0	2	0	.200	.200
OF	Red Jones	L	12	11	1	0	0	0	0.0	0	1	1	2	0	10	1	.091	.091
C	Don Padgett	L	93	240	58	15	1	6	2.5	24	41	26	14	1	16	3	.242	.388
C	Walker Cooper	R	6	19	6	1	0	0	0.0	3	2	2	2	1	0	0	.316	.368
C	Bill DeLancey	L	15	18	4	0	0	0	0.0	0	2	0	2	0	1	0	.222	.222
PITCHERS																		
P	Lon Warneke	R	33	86	18	2	0	1	1.2	6	13	5	24	0	0	0	.209	.267
P	Mort Cooper	R	38	83	13	2	0	0	0.0	5	3	1	22	0	0	0	.157	.181
P	Bill McGee	R	38	73	13	3	0	0	0.0	5	11	1	17	0	0	0	.178	.219
P	Clyde Shoun	L	54	63	12	0	0	0	0.0	5	5	0	5	0	0	0	.190	.190
P	Bob Bowman	R	28	33	2	0	0	0	0.0	2	2	4	17	0	0	0	.061	.061
P	Carl Doyle	R	21	30	6	2	0	1	3.3	3	5	2	11	0	0	0	.200	.367
P	Max Lanier	R	35	30	6	0	0	0	0.0	3	0	1	5	0	0	0	.200	.200
P	Curt Davis	R	14	19	0	0	0	0	0.0	0	0	0	6	0	0	0	.000	.000
P	Ira Hutchinson	R	20	18	4	0	0	0	0.0	2	0	0	8	0	0	0	.222	.222
P	Jack Russell	R	26	13	0	0	0	0	0.0	0	0	0	6	0	0	0	.000	.000
P	Ernie White	R	9	7	3	0	0	0	0.0	1	0	1	0	1	0	0	.429	.429
P	Newt Kimball	R	2	6	2	1	0	0	0.0	0	1	0	1	0	0	0	.333	.500
P	Harry Brecheen	L	3	0	0	0	0	0	–	0	0	0	0	0	0	0	–	–
P	Murry Dickson	R	1	0	0	0	0	0	–	0	0	0	0	0	0	0	–	–
P	Gene Lillard	R	2	0	0	0	0	0	–	0	0	0	0	0	0	0	–	–
P	Bob Weiland	L	1	0	0	0	0	0	–	0	0	0	0	0	0	0	–	–
TEAM TOTAL				5499	1514	266	61	119	2.2	747	709	479	610	97	122	20	.275	.411

INDIVIDUAL FIELDING

POS	Player	T	G	PO	A	E	DP	TC/G	FA	POS	Player	T	G	PO	A	E	DP	TC/G	FA
1B	J. Mize	R	153	1376	80	14	105	9.6	.990	OF	T. Moore	R	133	**383**	11	5	4	**3.0**	.987
	J. Hopp	L	10	43	3	1	4	4.7	.979		E. Slaughter	R	132	267	8	3	**5**	2.1	.989
	D. Padgett	R	2	1	0	0	0	0.5	1.000		E. Koy	R	91	192	2	6	0	2.2	.970
2B	J. Orengo	R	77	204	216	21	45	5.7	.952		P. Martin	R	63	103	8	3	0	1.8	.974
	J. Brown	R	48	115	135	6	32	5.3	.977		J. Hopp	L	39	86	1	3	0	2.3	.967
	S. Martin	R	33	47	71	3	12	3.7	.975		J. Medwick	R	37	81	1	1	0	2.2	.988
	E. Lake	R	17	30	36	3	4	4.1	.957		H. Walker	R	7	21	2	0	0	3.3	1.000
SS	M. Marion	R	125	245	366	33	76	5.2	.949		Gillenwater	R	7	12	0	0	0	1.7	1.000
	J. Orengo	R	19	38	59	6	15	5.4	.942		H. Epps	L	3	4	0	1	0	1.7	.800
	J. Brown	R	28	36	50	7	5	3.3	.925		R. Jones	R	1	1	0	0	0	1.0	1.000
	E. Lake	R	6	5	3	0	0	1.3	1.000	C	M. Owen	R	113	378	56	9	8	3.9	.980
	C. Crespi	R	1	2	3	1	1	6.0	.833		D. Padgett	R	72	243	34	11	5	4.0	.962
3B	S. Martin	R	73	52	89	4	2	2.0	.972		B. DeLancey	R	12	24	2	2	0	2.3	.929
	J. Brown	R	41	47	58	9	5	2.8	.921		W. Cooper	R	6	19	4	0	0	3.8	1.000
	J. Orengo	R	34	39	43	2	5	2.5	.976										
	D. Gutteridge	R	39	24	33	8	3	1.7	.877										
	P. Martin	R	2	3	5	0	0	4.0	1.000										
	C. Crespi	R	2	4	1	0	0	2.5	1.000										

It was The Big Cat's biggest year to date—Johnny Mize slugged a Cardinal-record 43 homers, led the league in home-run percentage for the only time in his career, and capped a remarkably consistent three-year reign as slugging champ. His slugging averages for the three years were .614, .626, and .636. Thanks to Mize, the Cards led the league in homers for just the fourth time in their history. Even so, the Cardinals were in sixth place with a 15–29 record when Billy Southworth took over the reins of the club from interim manager Mike Gonzalez. They played .633 ball the rest of the way. Under Southworth's guidance, the club would average 102 victories a year for the next five years, with three pennants and two near misses.

TEAM STATISTICS

	W	L	PCT	GB	R	OR	Batting 2B	3B	HR	BA	SA	SB	Fielding E	DP	FA	CG	BB	Pitching SO	ShO	SV	ERA
IN	100	53	.654		707	528	264	38	89	.266	.379	72	117	158	.981	91	445	557	10	11	3.05
KN	88	65	.575	12	697	621	256	70	93	.260	.383	56	183	110	.970	65	393	634	17	14	3.50
TL	84	69	.549	16	747	699	266	61	119	.275	.411	97	174	134	.971	71	488	550	10	14	3.83
IT	78	76	.506	22.5	809	783	276	68	76	.276	.394	69	217	160	.966	49	492	491	8	24	4.36
HI	75	79	.487	25.5	681	636	272	48	86	.267	.384	63	199	143	.968	69	430	564	12	14	3.54
Y	72	80	.474	27.5	663	659	201	46	91	.267	.374	45	139	132	.977	57	473	606	11	18	3.79
OS	65	87	.428	34.5	623	745	219	50	59	.256	.349	48	184	169	.970	76	573	435	9	12	4.36
HI	50	103	.327	50	494	750	180	35	75	.238	.331	25	181	136	.970	66	475	485	5	8	4.40
EAGUE TOTAL					5421	5421	1934	416	688	.264	.376	475	1394	1142	.972	544	3769	4322	82	115	3.85

INDIVIDUAL PITCHING

TCHER	T	W	L	PCT	ERA	SV	G	GS	CG	IP	H	BB	SO	R	ER	ShO	H/9	BB/9	SO/9
on Warneke	R	16	10	.615	3.14	0	33	31	17	232	235	47	85	103	81	1	9.12	1.82	3.30
ort Cooper	R	11	12	.478	3.63	3	38	29	16	230.2	225	86	95	103	93	3	8.78	3.36	3.71
ll McGee	R	16	10	.615	3.80	0	38	31	11	217.2	222	96	78	108	92	3	9.18	3.97	3.23
lyde Shoun	L	13	11	.542	3.92	5	54	19	13	197.1	193	46	82	96	86	1	8.80	2.10	3.74
ob Bowman	R	7	5	.583	4.33	0	28	17	7	114.1	118	43	43	66	55	0	9.29	3.38	3.38
ax Lanier	L	9	6	.600	3.34	3	35	11	4	105	113	38	49	50	39	2	9.69	3.26	4.20
arl Doyle	R	3	3	.500	5.89	0	21	5	1	81	99	41	44	57	53	0	11.00	4.56	4.89
a Hutchinson	R	4	2	.667	3.13	1	20	2	1	63.1	68	19	19	27	22	0	9.66	2.70	2.70
rt Davis	R	0	4	.000	5.17	1	14	7	0	54	73	19	12	34	31	0	12.17	3.17	2.00
ck Russell	R	3	4	.429	2.50	1	26	0	0	54	53	26	16	22	15	0	8.83	4.33	2.67
nie White	L	1	1	.500	4.15	0	8	1	0	21.2	29	14	15	13	10	0	12.05	5.82	6.23
ewt Kimball	R	1	0	1.000	2.57	0	2	1	1	14	11	6	6	5	4	0	7.07	3.86	3.86
ene Lillard	R	0	1	.000	13.50	0	2	1	0	4.2	8	4	2	7	7	0	15.43	7.71	3.86
arry Brecheen	L	0	0	–	0.00	0	3	0	0	3.1	2	2	4	1	0	0	5.40	5.40	10.80
urry Dickson	R	0	0	–	16.20	0	1	1	0	1.2	5	1	0	4	3	0	27.00	5.40	0.00
ob Weiland	L	0	0	–	40.50	0	1	0	0	.2	3	0	0	3	3	0	40.50	0.00	0.00
AM TOTAL		84	69	.549	3.83	14	324	156	71	1395.1	1457	488	550	699	594	10	9.40	3.15	3.55

MANAGER	W	L	PCT
Billy Southworth	97	56	.634

POS	Player	B	G	AB	H	2B	3B	HR	HR %	R	RBI	BB	SO	SB	Pinch Hit AB	Pinch Hit H	BA	SA
REGULARS																		
1B	Johnny Mize	L	126	473	150	39	8	16	3.4	67	100	70	45	4	4	1	.317	.535
2B	Creepy Crespi	R	146	560	156	24	2	4	0.7	85	46	57	58	3	0	0	.279	.350
SS	Marty Marion	R	155	547	138	22	3	3	0.5	50	58	42	48	8	0	0	.252	.320
3B	Jimmy Brown	B	132	549	168	28	9	3	0.5	81	56	45	22	2	1	1	.306	.406
RF	Enos Slaughter	L	113	425	132	22	9	13	3.1	71	76	53	28	4	2	0	.311	.496
CF	Terry Moore	R	122	493	145	26	4	6	1.2	86	68	52	31	3	1	0	.294	.400
LF	Johnny Hopp	L	134	445	135	25	11	4	0.9	83	50	50	63	15	6	1	.303	.436
C	Gus Mancuso	R	106	328	75	13	1	2	0.6	25	37	37	19	0	1	0	.229	.293
SUBSTITUTES																		
UT	Eddie Lake	R	45	76	8	2	0	0	0.0	9	0	15	22	3	6	1	.105	.132
3B	Steve Mesner	R	24	69	10	1	0	0	0.0	8	10	5	6	0	1	0	.145	.159
3B	Whitey Kurowski	R	5	9	3	2	0	0	0.0	1	2	0	2	0	1	0	.333	.556
OC	Don Padgett	L	107	324	80	18	0	5	1.5	39	44	21	16	0	22	3	.247	.349
OF	Coaker Triplett	R	76	185	53	6	3	3	1.6	29	21	18	27	0	25	5	.286	.400
OF	Estel Crabtree	L	77	167	57	6	3	5	3.0	27	28	26	24	1	21	7	.341	.503
OF	Stan Musial	L	12	47	20	4	0	1	2.1	8	7	2	1	1	1	0	.426	.574
OF	Ernie Koy	R	13	40	8	1	0	2	5.0	5	4	1	8	0	0	0	.200	.375
OF	Harry Walker	L	7	15	4	1	0	0	0.0	3	1	2	1	0	0	0	.267	.333
OF	Erv Dusak	R	6	14	2	0	0	0	0.0	1	3	2	6	1	2	0	.143	.143
OF	Walter Sessi	L	5	13	0	0	0	0	0.0	2	0	1	2	0	2	0	.000	.000
C	Walker Cooper	R	68	200	49	9	1	1	0.5	19	20	13	14	1	5	2	.245	.315
C	Charlie Marshall	R	1	0	0	0	0	0	–	0	0	0	0	0	0	0	–	–
PH	Pep Young	R	2	2	0	0	0	0	0.0	0	0	0	2	0	2	0	.000	.000
PITCHERS																		
P	Ernie White	R	33	79	15	2	1	0	0.0	6	10	3	8	0	0	0	.190	.241
P	Lon Warneke	R	37	77	9	0	0	0	0.0	6	4	11	18	0	0	0	.117	.117
P	Mort Cooper	R	29	70	13	0	0	0	0.0	4	5	4	10	0	0	0	.186	.186
P	Harry Gumbert	R	34	53	17	1	0	2	3.8	7	6	2	11	0	1	1	.321	.453
P	Max Lanier	R	35	52	10	0	0	0	0.0	3	0	1	5	0	0	0	.192	.192
P	Howie Krist	L	37	38	9	1	0	0	0.0	5	4	2	11	0	0	0	.237	.263
P	Howie Pollet	L	9	28	5	1	0	0	0.0	0	3	1	12	0	0	0	.179	.214
P	Sam Nahem	R	26	23	4	0	0	0	0.0	1	0	0	5	0	0	0	.174	.174
P	Clyde Shoun	L	26	22	4	0	1	0	0.0	2	0	1	2	0	0	0	.182	.273
P	Bill Crouch	B	18	13	0	0	0	0	0.0	1	0	1	6	0	0	0	.000	.000
P	Ira Hutchinson	R	29	8	2	0	0	0	0.0	0	0	0	3	0	0	0	.250	.250
P	Hank Gornicki	R	4	4	1	0	0	0	0.0	0	1	0	1	0	0	0	.250	.250
P	Bill McGee	R	4	4	0	0	0	0	0.0	0	0	0	2	0	0	0	.000	.000
P	Johnny Beazley	R	1	3	0	0	0	0	0.0	0	0	0	3	0	0	0	.000	.000
P	Johnny Grodzicki	R	5	2	0	0	0	0	0.0	0	0	2	1	0	0	0	.000	.000
P	Hersh Lyons	R	1	0	0	0	0	0	–	0	0	1	0	0	1	0	–	–
	TEAM TOTAL			5457	1482	254	56	70	1.3	734	664	541	543	47	104	22	.272	.377

INDIVIDUAL FIELDING

POS	Player	T	G	PO	A	E	DP	TC/G	FA	POS	Player	T	G	PO	A	E	DP	TC/G	FA
1B	J. Mize	R	122	1157	82	8	104	10.2	.994	OF	T. Moore	R	121	293	14	5	3	2.6	.984
	J. Hopp	L	39	329	17	4	23	9.0	.989		J. Hopp	L	91	213	4	4	1	2.4	.982
	D. Padgett	R	2	12	1	0	1	6.5	1.000		E. Slaughter	R	108	173	5	10	1	1.7	.947
2B	C. Crespi	R	145	382	421	32	94	5.8	.962		D. Padgett	R	62	115	1	5	0	2.0	.959
	J. Brown	R	11	22	28	2	9	4.7	.962		C. Triplett	R	46	78	4	3	0	1.8	.965
	E. Lake	R	5	5	6	3	1	2.8	.786		E. Crabtree	R	50	71	2	0	0	1.5	1.000
											S. Musial	L	11	20	1	0	0	1.9	1.000
SS	M. Marion	R	155	299	489	38	85	5.3	.954		E. Koy	R	12	18	0	0	0	1.5	1.000
	E. Lake	R	15	15	13	3	4	2.1	.903		E. Dusak	R	4	10	0	0	0	2.5	1.000
											H. Walker	R	5	7	0	1	0	1.6	.875
3B	J. Brown	R	123	135	276	15	22	3.5	.965		W. Sessi	L	3	3	0	1	0	1.3	.750
	S. Mesner	R	22	23	45	3	8	3.2	.958										
	E. Lake	R	15	20	37	3	6	4.0	.950	C	G. Mancuso	R	105	482	58	6	6	5.2	.989
	W. Kurowski	R	4	2	3	0	1	1.3	1.000		W. Cooper	R	63	247	39	10	11	4.7	.966
	E. Crabtree	R	1	0	2	0	0	2.0	1.000		D. Padgett	R	18	62	5	4	0	3.9	.944
											C. Marshall	R	1	1	0	0	0	1.0	1.000

The Dodgers and Cardinals battled for first place from the opening bell, quickly opening a big margin on the rest of the league. They entered September tied for the lead, but the Dodgers edged ahead and clinched the pennant in their hundred and fifty-second game. The Cards had served notice to the league, however, by making the leap to 97 wins. What few holes that remained were about to be plugged by the cream of the farm crop. Shortstop Marty Marion was in his second year in the majors; the catching duties were entrusted to rookie Walker Cooper until he broke a bone in his shoulder; third base would be given over to 24-year-old Whitey Kurowski; and a 20-year-old converted pitcher named Stan Musial was about to make even the great Mize expendable.

TEAM STATISTICS

W	L	PCT	GB	R	OR	Batting						Fielding			Pitching					
						2B	3B	HR	BA	SA	SB	E	DP	FA	CG	BB	SO	ShO	SV	ERA
KN	100	54	.649		800	581	286	69	101	.272	.405	36	162	125	.974	66	495	603	17	22	3.14
L	97	56	.634	2.5	734	589	254	56	70	.272	.377	47	172	146	.973	64	502	659	15	20	3.19
N	88	66	.571	12	616	564	213	33	64	.247	.337	68	152	147	.975	89	510	627	19	10	3.17
T	81	73	.526	19	690	643	233	65	56	.268	.368	59	196	130	.968	71	492	410	8	12	3.48
Y	74	79	.484	25.5	667	706	248	35	95	.260	.371	36	160	144	.974	55	539	566	12	18	3.94
HI	70	84	.455	30	666	670	239	25	99	.253	.365	39	180	139	.970	74	449	548	8	9	3.72
)S	62	92	.403	38	592	720	231	38	48	.251	.334	61	191	174	.969	62	554	446	10	9	3.95
HI	43	111	.279	57	501	793	188	38	64	.244	.331	65	187	147	.969	35	606	552	4	9	4.50
AGUE TOTAL				5266	5266	1892	359	597	.258	.361	411	1400	1152	.972	516	4147	4411	93	109	3.63

INDIVIDUAL PITCHING

TCHER	T	W	L	PCT	ERA	SV	G	GS	CG	IP	H	BB	SO	R	ER	ShO	H/9	BB/9	SO/9
n Warneke	R	17	9	.654	3.15	0	37	30	12	246	227	82	83	100	86	4	8.30	3.00	3.04
ie White	L	17	7	.708	2.40	2	32	25	12	210	169	70	117	72	56	3	7.24	3.00	5.01
rt Cooper	R	13	9	.591	3.91	0	29	25	12	186.2	175	69	118	88	81	0	8.44	3.33	5.69
x Lanier	L	10	8	.556	2.82	3	35	18	8	153	126	59	93	59	48	2	7.41	3.47	5.47
rry Gumbert	R	11	5	.688	2.74	1	33	17	8	144.1	139	30	53	52	44	3	8.67	1.87	3.30
wie Krist	R	10	0	1.000	4.03	2	37	8	2	114	107	35	36	57	51	0	8.45	2.76	2.84
n Nahem	R	5	2	.714	2.98	1	26	8	2	81.2	76	38	31	35	27	0	8.38	4.19	3.42
wie Pollet	L	5	2	.714	1.93	0	9	8	6	70	55	27	37	18	15	2	7.07	3.47	4.76
de Shoun	L	3	5	.375	5.66	0	26	6	0	70	98	20	34	48	44	0	12.60	2.57	4.37
Hutchinson	R	1	5	.167	3.86	5	29	0	0	46.2	32	19	19	23	20	0	6.17	3.66	3.66
Crouch	R	1	2	.333	3.00	6	18	4	0	45	45	14	15	16	15	0	9.00	2.80	3.00
McGee	R	0	1	.000	5.02	0	4	3	0	14.1	17	13	2	9	8	0	10.67	8.16	1.26
nny Grodzicki	R	2	1	.667	1.35	0	5	1	0	13.1	6	11	10	7	2	0	4.05	7.43	6.75
nk Gornicki	R	1	0	1.000	3.18	0	4	1	1	11.1	6	9	6	4	4	1	4.76	7.15	4.76
nny Beazley	R	1	0	1.000	1.00	0	1	1	1	9	10	3	4	1	1	0	10.00	3.00	4.00
sh Lyons	R	0	0	—	0.00	0	1	0	0	1.1	1	3	1	0	0	0	6.75	20.25	6.75
AM TOTAL		97	56	.634	3.19	20	326	155	64	1416.2	1289	502	659	589	502	15	8.19	3.19	4.19

MANAGER	W	L	PCT
Billy Southworth	106	48	.688

POS	Player	B	G	AB	H	2B	3B	HR	HR %	R	RBI	BB	SO	SB	Pinch Hit AB	Pinch Hit H	BA	SA
REGULARS																		
1B	Johnny Hopp	L	95	314	81	16	7	3	1.0	41	37	36	40	14	3	1	.258	.382
2B	Jimmy Brown	B	145	606	155	28	4	1	0.2	75	71	52	11	.4	0	0	.256	.320
SS	Marty Marion	R	147	485	134	38	5	0	0.0	66	54	48	50	8	0	0	.276	.375
3B	Whitey Kurowski	R	115	366	93	17	3	9	2.5	51	42	33	60	7	9	0	.254	.391
RF	Enos Slaughter	L	152	591	188	31	17	13	2.2	100	98	88	30	9	1	0	.318	.494
CF	Terry Moore	R	130	489	141	26	3	6	1.2	80	49	56	26	10	4	2	.288	.391
LF	Stan Musial	L	140	467	147	32	10	10	2.1	87	72	62	25	6	2	0	.315	.490
C	Walker Cooper	R	125	438	123	32	7	7	1.6	58	65	29	29	4	10	5	.281	.434
SUBSTITUTES																		
2B	Creepy Crespi	R	93	292	71	4	2	0	0.0	33	35	27	29	4	4	1	.243	.271
1B	Ray Sanders	L	95	282	71	17	2	5	1.8	37	39	42	31	2	15	2	.252	.379
SS	Buddy Blattner	R	19	23	1	0	0	0	0.0	3	1	3	6	0	2	0	.043	.043
SS	Jeff Cross	R	1	4	1	0	0	0	0.0	0	1	0	0	0	0	0	.250	.250
OF	Harry Walker	L	74	191	60	12	2	0	0.0	38	16	11	14	2	16	0	.314	.398
OF	Coaker Triplett	R	64	154	42	7	4	1	0.6	18	23	17	15	1	16	2	.273	.390
OF	Erv Dusak	R	12	27	5	3	0	0	0.0	4	3	3	7	0	1	0	.185	.296
C	Ken O'Dea	L	58	192	45	7	1	5	2.6	22	32	17	23	0	9	1	.234	.359
C	Gus Mancuso	R	5	13	1	0	0	0	0.0	0	1	0	0	0	2	0	.077	.077
C	Sam Narron	R	10	10	4	0	0	0	0.0	0	1	0	2	0	8	3	.400	.400
PH	Estel Crabtree	L	10	9	3	2	0	0	0.0	1	2	1	3	0	9	3	.333	.556
PITCHERS																		
P	Mort Cooper	R	37	103	19	1	0	0	0.0	6	7	3	21	0	0	0	.184	.194
P	Johnny Beazley	R	43	73	10	2	2	0	0.0	6	9	3	37	0	0	0	.137	.219
P	Harry Gumbert	R	38	54	6	2	0	0	0.0	2	3	1	12	0	0	0	.111	.148
P	Max Lanier	R	34	47	12	0	0	0	0.0	6	4	5	5	0	0	0	.255	.255
P	Murry Dickson	R	37	42	8	2	0	0	0.0	6	1	0	3	0	0	0	.190	.238
P	Howie Krist	L	35	42	6	1	0	0	0.0	5	1	1	12	0	0	0	.143	.167
P	Ernie White	R	27	41	8	0	0	0	0.0	5	3	3	4	0	0	0	.195	.195
P	Howie Pollet	L	27	31	7	2	0	0	0.0	2	7	7	7	0	0	0	.226	.290
P	Lon Warneke	R	12	30	10	0	0	0	0.0	2	3	3	4	0	0	0	.333	.333
P	Bill Lohrman	R	5	3	2	0	0	0	0.0	1	0	0	0	0	0	0	.667	.667
P	Whitey Moore	R	9	2	0	0	0	0	0.0	0	0	0	1	0	0	0	.000	.000
P	Bill Beckmann	R	2	1	0	0	0	0	0.0	0	0	0	0	0	0	0	.000	.000
P	Clyde Shoun	L	2	0	0	0	0	0	–	0	0	0	0	0	0	0	–	–
TEAM TOTAL				5422	1454	282	69	60	1.1	755	680	551	507	71	111	20	.268	.379

INDIVIDUAL FIELDING

POS	Player	T	G	PO	A	E	DP	TC/G	FA	POS	Player	T	G	PO	A	E	DP	TC/G	FA
1B	J. Hopp	L	88	746	44	14	68	9.1	.983	OF	S. Musial	L	135	296	6	5	0	2.3	.984
	R. Sanders	R	77	626	35	6	54	8.7	.991		E. Slaughter	R	151	287	15	4	2	2.0	.987
2B	J. Brown	R	82	211	215	13	56	5.4	.970		T. Moore	R	126	271	9	4	0	2.3	.986
	C. Crespi	R	83	219	190	14	42	5.1	.967		H. Walker	R	56	115	6	4	0	2.2	.968
	B. Blattner	R	3	3	2	0	1	1.7	1.000		C. Triplett	R	46	82	2	3	0	1.9	.966
	H. Walker	R	2	1	0	0	0	0.5	1.000		W. Kurowski	R	1	0	0	0	0	0.0	.000
SS	M. Marion	R	147	296	448	31	87	5.3	.960		E. Dusak	R	8	14	0	0	0	1.8	1.000
	W. Kurowski	R	1	0	0	0	0	0.0	.000	C	W. Cooper	R	115	519	62	17	6	5.2	.972
	B. Blattner	R	13	11	16	3	2	2.3	.900		K. O'Dea	R	49	247	37	6	6	5.9	.979
	C. Crespi	R	5	8	11	2	1	4.2	.905		G. Mancuso	R	3	11	0	1	0	4.0	.917
	J. Brown	R	12	3	3	2	1	0.7	.750		S. Narron	R	2	2	0	0	0	1.0	1.000
	J. Cross	R	1	0	3	0	0	3.0	1.000										
3B	W. Kurowski	R	104	124	194	19	19	3.2	.944										
	J. Brown	R	66	85	111	11	9	3.1	.947										
	E. Dusak	R	1	0	5	0	1	5.0	1.000										
	T. Moore	R	1	0	0	1	0	1.0	.000										

It was Branch Rickey's final year in St. Louis, and it was the culmination of all of his efforts. The Cardinals won 106 games to beat out a Brooklyn club whose 104 wins tied a record for victories by a second-place team. The Redbirds stormed by the Dodgers with a sizzling 21–4 mark in September. It was a club without a weakness: strong hitting for average and power, air-tight defense, and pitching led by MVP Mort Cooper (with league-leading totals of 22 wins, a 1.77 ERA, and 10 shutouts) and Johnny Beazley (21–6, 2.13, 3 shutouts). They were best in the league in runs scored and allowed, and led in doubles, triples, batting, slugging, shutouts, and ERA. They kept up their remarkable late-season surge with a five-game victory over the Yankees in the World Series, capped by Whitey Kurowski's ninth-inning game-winning homer in the fifth and final game.

TEAM STATISTICS

	W	L	PCT	GB	R	OR	Batting 2B	3B	HR	BA	SA	SB	Fielding E	DP	FA	CG	BB	Pitching SO	ShO	SV	ERA
STL	106	48	.688		755	482	282	69	60	.268	.379	71	169	137	.972	70	473	651	18	15	2.55
BKN	104	50	.675	2	742	510	263	34	62	.265	.362	79	138	150	.977	67	493	612	16	24	2.84
NY	85	67	.559	20	675	600	162	35	109	.254	.361	39	138	128	.977	70	493	497	12	13	3.31
CIN	76	76	.500	29	527	545	198	39	66	.231	.321	42	177	158	.971	80	526	616	12	8	2.82
PIT	66	81	.449	36.5	585	631	173	49	54	.245	.330	41	184	129	.969	64	435	426	13	11	3.58
CHI	68	86	.442	38	591	665	224	41	75	.254	.353	61	170	169	.973	71	525	507	10	14	3.60
BOS	59	89	.399	44	515	645	210	19	68	.240	.329	49	142	138	.976	68	518	414	9	8	3.76
PHI	42	109	.278	62.5	394	706	168	37	44	.232	.306	37	194	147	.968	51	605	472	2	6	4.12
LEAGUE TOTAL					4784	4784	1680	323	538	.249	.343	419	1312	1156	.973	541	4068	4195	92	99	3.31

INDIVIDUAL PITCHING

PITCHER	T	W	L	PCT	ERA	SV	G	GS	CG	IP	H	BB	SO	R	ER	ShO	H/9	BB/9	SO/9
Mort Cooper	R	22	7	.759	1.78	0	37	35	22	278.2	207	68	152	73	55	10	6.69	2.20	4.91
Johnny Beazley	R	21	6	.778	2.13	3	43	23	13	215.1	181	73	91	67	51	3	7.57	3.05	3.80
Harry Gumbert	R	9	5	.643	3.26	5	38	19	5	163	156	59	52	67	59	0	8.61	3.26	2.87
Max Lanier	L	13	8	.619	2.98	2	34	20	8	160	137	60	93	55	53	2	7.71	3.38	5.23
Ernie White	L	7	5	.583	2.52	2	26	19	7	128.1	113	41	67	57	36	1	7.92	2.88	4.70
Murry Dickson	R	6	3	.667	2.91	2	36	7	2	120.2	91	61	66	41	39	0	6.79	4.55	4.92
Howie Krist	R	13	3	.813	2.51	1	34	8	3	118.1	103	43	47	34	33	0	7.83	3.27	3.57
Howie Pollet	L	7	5	.583	2.88	0	27	13	5	109.1	102	39	42	43	35	2	8.40	3.21	3.46
Lon Warneke	R	6	4	.600	3.29	0	12	12	5	82	76	15	31	34	30	0	8.34	1.65*	3.40
Bill Lohrman	R	1	1	.500	1.42	0	5	0	0	12.2	11	2	6	3	2	0	7.82	1.42	4.26
Whitey Moore	R	0	1	.000	4.38	0	9	0	0	12.1	10	11	1	6	6	0	7.30	8.03	0.73
Bill Beckmann	R	1	0	1.000	0.00	0	2	0	0	7	4	1	3	0	0	0	5.14	1.29	3.86
Clyde Shoun	L	0	0	–	0.00	0	2	0	0	1.2	1	0	0	0	0	0	5.40	0.00	0.00
TEAM TOTAL		106	48	.688	2.55	15	305	156	70	1409.1	1192	473	651	480	399	18	7.61	3.02	4.16

MANAGER	W	L	PCT
Billy Southworth	105	49	.682

POS	Player	B	G	AB	H	2B	3B	HR	HR %	R	RBI	BB	SO	SB	Pinch Hit AB	Pinch Hit H	BA	SA
REGULARS																		
1B	Ray Sanders	L	144	478	134	21	5	11	2.3	69	73	77	33	1	3	0	.280	.414
2B	Lou Klein	R	154	627	180	28	14	7	1.1	91	62	50	70	9	0	0	.287	.410
SS	Marty Marion	R	129	418	117	15	3	1	0.2	38	52	32	37	1	1	0	.280	.337
3B	Whitey Kurowski	R	139	522	150	24	8	13	2.5	69	70	31	54	3	1	0	.287	.439
RF	Stan Musial	L	157	617	**220**	48	20	13	2.1	108	81	72	18	9	2	1	**.357**	**.562**
CF	Harry Walker	L	148	564	166	28	6	2	0.4	76	53	40	24	5	4	1	.294	.376
LF	Danny Litwhiler	R	80	258	72	14	3	7	2.7	40	31	19	31	1	8	0	.279	.438
C	Walker Cooper	R	122	449	143	30	4	9	2.0	52	81	19	19	1	10	1	.318	.463
SUBSTITUTES																		
UT	Jimmy Brown	B	34	110	20	4	2	0	0.0	6	8	6	1	0	1	0	.182	.255
2B	George Fallon	R	36	78	18	1	0	0	0.0	6	5	2	9	0	0	0	.231	.244
O3	Debs Garms	L	90	249	64	10	2	0	0.0	26	22	13	8	1	20	6	.257	.313
O1	Johnny Hopp	L	91	241	54	10	2	2	0.8	33	25	24	22	8	4	0	.224	.307
OF	Frank Demaree	R	39	86	25	2	0	0	0.0	5	9	8	4	1	13	1	.291	.314
OF	Coaker Triplett	R	9	25	2	0	0	1	4.0	1	4	1	6	0	3	1	.080	.200
OF	Buster Adams	R	8	11	1	1	0	0	0.0	1	1	4	4	0	0	0	.091	.182
C	Ken O'Dea	L	71	203	57	11	2	3	1.5	15	25	19	25	0	14	4	.281	.399
C	Sam Narron	R	10	11	1	0	0	0	0.0	0	0	1	2	0	7	1	.091	.091
PITCHERS																		
P	Mort Cooper	R	37	100	17	3	0	1	1.0	7	11	2	14	0	0	0	.170	.230
P	Max Lanier	R	32	73	12	0	0	0	0.0	8	5	1	5	0	0	0	.164	.164
P	Howie Krist	L	34	60	10	1	0	0	0.0	7	2	1	13	0	0	0	.167	.183
P	Harry Gumbert	R	21	45	7	0	0	0	0.0	1	1	1	11	0	0	0	.156	.156
P	Howie Pollet	L	16	43	7	1	0	0	0.0	3	1	1	9	0	0	0	.163	.186
P	Harry Brecheen	L	29	42	8	2	0	0	0.0	4	3	2	8	0	0	0	.190	.238
P	Murry Dickson	R	31	34	9	2	0	0	0.0	1	6	0	1	0	0	0	.265	.324
P	Al Brazle	L	13	32	9	1	1	0	0.0	4	4	0	2	0	0	0	.281	.375
P	George Munger	R	32	28	6	2	0	0	0.0	3	3	1	5	0	0	0	.214	.286
P	Ernie White	R	21	28	6	0	0	0	0.0	5	0	1	2	0	0	0	.214	.214
P	Bud Byerly	R	2	3	0	0	0	0	0.0	0	0	0	0	0	0	0	.000	.000
TEAM TOTAL				5435	1515	259	72	70	1.3	679	638	428	437	40	91	16	.279	.392

INDIVIDUAL FIELDING

POS	Player	T	G	PO	A	E	DP	TC/G	FA
1B	R. Sanders	R	141	1302	71	7	142	9.8	.995
	J. Hopp	L	27	173	16	6	23	7.2	.969
2B	L. Klein	R	126	301	356	18	99	5.4	.973
	G. Fallon	R	36	65	86	5	18	4.3	.968
	J. Brown	R	19	44	45	2	9	4.8	.978
	H. Walker	R	1	1	0	1	0	2.0	.500
SS	M. Marion	R	128	232	424	20	93	5.3	.970
	L. Klein	R	51	55	88	9	19	3.0	.941
	J. Brown	R	6	9	16	0	1	4.2	1.000
	W. Kurowski	R	2	1	2	0	0	1.5	1.000
	D. Garms	R	1	1	0	0	0	1.0	1.000
3B	W. Kurowski	R	137	**166**	255	21	29	3.2	.952
	D. Garms	R	23	18	22	7	5	2.0	.851
	J. Brown	R	9	12	15	0	4	3.0	1.000

POS	Player	T	G	PO	A	E	DP	TC/G	FA
OF	S. Musial	L	155	376	15	7	4	2.6	.982
	H. Walker	R	144	321	14	**12**	4	2.4	.965
	D. Litwhiler	R	70	139	7	0	1	2.1	1.000*
	J. Hopp	L	52	113	1	6	0	2.3	.950
	D. Garms	R	47	93	3	2	0	2.1	.980
	F. Demaree	R	23	35	1	0	0	1.6	1.000
	C. Triplett	R	6	13	0	0	0	2.2	1.000
	B. Adams	R	6	11	0	0	0*	1.8	1.000
C	W. Cooper	R	112	504	49	**14**	5	5.1	.975
	K. O'Dea	R	56	237	32	3	6	4.9	.989
	S. Narron	R	3	8	1	0	0	3.0	1.000

"The War Years" is a phrase baseball fans associate with substandard play, faceless players, and the spectacle of spring training in the frozen north. The Cardinals also lost players to the military, but the depth of their farm system allowed them to keep on winning. They lost the services of Terry Moore, Enos Slaughter, and Johnny Beazley for the '43 season, but kept on rolling, racking up 105 wins in winning the pennant by an 18-game margin. Stan Musial won the first of his seven batting titles, and Howie Pollett, Max Lanier, and Mort Cooper finished 1-2-3 in ERA. The season ended on a down note, though, as the Yankees got revenge for the '42 Series with a five-game victory of their own. Yankee pitchers allowed just nine runs in the five games, and held the potent Cardinal order to a .224 average.

TEAM STATISTICS

W	L	PCT	GB	R	OR	2B	3B	Batting HR	BA	SA	SB	E	Fielding DP	FA	CG	BB	Pitching SO	ShO	SV	ERA
105	49	.682		679	475	259	72	70	.279	.391	40	151	183	.976	94	477	639	21	15	2.57
87	67	.565	18	608	543	229	47	43	.256	.340	49	125	193	.980	78	581	498	18	17	3.13
81	72	.529	23.5	716	674	263	35	39	.272	.357	58	168	137	.972	50	585	588	12	22	3.88
80	74	.519	25	669	605	240	73	42	.262	.357	64	170	159	.973	74	421	396	11	12	3.06
74	79	.484	30.5	632	600	207	56	52	.261	.351	53	168	138	.973	67	394	513	12	14	3.24
68	85	.444	36.5	465	612	202	36	39	.233	.309	56	176	139	.972	87	440	409	13	4	3.25
64	90	.416	41	571	676	186	36	66	.249	.335	29	189	143	.969	66	456	431	11	14	3.79
55	98	.359	49.5	558	713	153	33	81	.247	.335	35	166	140	.973	35	626	588	6	19	4.08
GUE TOTAL				4898	4898	1739	388	432	.258	.347	384	1313	1232	.974	551	3980	4062	104	117	3.37

INDIVIDUAL PITCHING

CHER	T	W	L	PCT	ERA	SV	G	GS	CG	IP	H	BB	SO	R	ER	ShO	H/9	BB/9	SO/9
t Cooper	R	21	8	.724	2.30	3	37	32	24	274	228	79	141	81	70	6	7.49	2.59	4.63
Lanier	L	15	7	.682	1.90	3	32	25	14	213.1	195	75	123	62	45	2	8.23	3.16	5.19
ie Krist	R	11	5	.688	2.90	3	34	17	9	164.1	141	62	57	57	53	3	7.72	3.40	3.12
y Brecheen	L	9	6	.600	2.26	4	29	13	8	135.1	98	39	68	41	34	1	6.52	2.59	4.52
y Gumbert	R	10	5	.667	2.84	0	21	19	7	133	115	32	40	46	42	2	7.78	2.17	2.71
ie Pollet	L	8	4	.667	1.75	0	16	14	12	118.1	83	32	61	26	23	5	6.31	2.43	4.64
ry Dickson	R	8	2	.800	3.58	0	31	7	2	115.2	114	49	44	51	46	0	8.87	3.81	3.42
rge Munger	R	9	5	.643	3.95	2	32	9	5	93.1	101	42	45	47	41	0	9.74	4.05	4.34
razle	L	8	2	.800	1.53	0	13	9	8	88	74	29	26	18	15	1	7.57	2.97	2.66
e White	L	5	5	.500	3.78	0	14	10	5	78.2	78	33	28	38	33	1	8.92	3.78	3.20
Byerly	R	1	0	1.000	3.46	0	2	2	0	13	14	5	6	6	5	0	9.69	3.46	4.15
M TOTAL		105	49	.682	2.57	15	261	157	94	1427	1241	477	639	473	407	21	7.83	3.01	4.03

MANAGER	W	L	PCT
Billy Southworth	105	49	.682

POS	Player	B	G	AB	H	2B	3B	HR	HR %	R	RBI	BB	SO	SB	Pinch Hit AB	Pinch Hit H	BA	SA
REGULARS																		
1B	Ray Sanders	L	154	601	177	34	9	12	2.0	87	102	71	50	2	3	1	.295	.441
2B	Emil Verban	R	146	498	128	14	2	0	0.0	51	43	19	14	0	0	0	.257	.293
SS	Marty Marion	R	144	506	135	26	2	6	1.2	50	63	43	50	1	0	0	.267	.362
3B	Whitey Kurowski	R	149	555	150	25	7	20	3.6	95	87	58	40	2	2	0	.270	.449
RF	Stan Musial	L	146	568	**197**	51	14	12	2.1	112	94	90	28	7	0	0	.347	**.549**
CF	Johnny Hopp	L	139	527	177	35	9	11	2.1	106	72	58	47	15	2	0	.336	.499
LF	Danny Litwhiler	R	140	492	130	25	5	15	3.0	53	82	37	56	2	3	1	.264	.427
C	Walker Cooper	R	112	397	126	25	5	13	3.3	56	72	20	19	4	15	5	.317	.504
SUBSTITUTES																		
2S	George Fallon	R	69	141	28	6	0	1	0.7	16	9	16	11	1	0	0	.199	.262
UT	John Antonelli	R	8	21	4	1	0	0	0.0	0	1	0	4	0	0	0	.190	.238
OF	Augie Bergamo	L	80	192	55	6	3	2	1.0	35	19	35	23	0	26	4	.286	.380
O3	Debs Garms	L	73	149	30	3	0	0	0.0	17	5	13	8	0	30	6	.201	.221
OF	Pepper Martin	R	40	86	24	4	0	2	2.3	15	4	15	11	2	5	1	.279	.395
C	Ken O'Dea	L	85	265	66	11	2	6	2.3	35	37	37	29	1	14	4	.249	.374
C	Bob Keely	R	1	0	0	0	0	0	0.0	0	0	0	0	0	0	0	–	–
PITCHERS																		
P	Mort Cooper	R	34	94	19	3	0	0	0.0	9	13	7	12	0	0	0	.202	.234
P	Max Lanier	R	33	77	14	1	0	0	0.0	11	2	4	2	0	0	0	.182	.195
P	Harry Brecheen	L	31	68	11	0	1	0	0.0	8	4	9	12	0	0	0	.162	.191
P	Ted Wilks	R	36	64	9	2	0	0	0.0	6	6	5	15	0	0	0	.141	.172
P	Al Jurisich	R	30	45	8	1	0	0	0.0	2	1	1	13	0	0	0	.178	.200
P	George Munger	R	21	44	5	1	0	0	0.0	2	0	0	4	0	0	0	.114	.136
P	Freddy Schmidt	R	37	34	7	0	0	0	0.0	3	3	1	16	0	0	0	.206	.206
P	Harry Gumbert	R	10	21	4	0	0	0	0.0	2	2	1	1	0	0	0	.190	.190
P	Blix Donnelly	R	27	16	1	0	0	0	0.0	0	0	3	2	0	0	0	.063	.063
P	Bud Byerly	R	9	12	2	0	0	0	0.0	1	1	0	3	0	0	0	.167	.167
P	Bill Trotter	R	1	1	0	0	0	0	0.0	0	0	0	1	0	0	0	.000	.000
P	Mike Naymick	R	1	0	0	0	0	0	–	0	0	0	0	0	0	0	–	–
TEAM TOTAL				5474	1507	274	59	100	1.8	772	722	543	471	37	100	22	.275	.402

INDIVIDUAL FIELDING

POS	Player	T	G	PO	A	E	DP	TC/G	FA
1B	R. Sanders	R	152	1370	64	8	**142**	9.5	**.994**
	J. Hopp	L	6	36	2	0	0	6.3	1.000
	J. Antonelli	R	3	23	3	0	2	8.7	1.000
	A. Bergamo	L	2	4	0	0	0	2.0	1.000
2B	E. Verban	R	146	319	380	23	**105**	4.9	.968
	G. Fallon	R	38	57	53	3	11	3.0	.973
	W. Kurowski	R	9	4	7	0	1	1.2	1.000
	J. Antonelli	R	2	2	2	0	0	2.0	1.000
SS	M. Marion	R	144	268	461	21	90	5.2	**.972**
	G. Fallon	R	24	38	57	3	14	4.1	.969
	W. Kurowski	R	1	0	2	0	0	2.0	1.000
3B	W. Kurowski	R	146	**188**	281	17	20	3.3	.965
	D. Garms	R	21	14	16	1	1	1.5	.968
	G. Fallon	R	6	5	10	0	3	2.5	1.000
	J. Antonelli	R	3	3	5	0	0	2.7	1.000
OF	S. Musial	L	146	353	16	5	2	2.6	.987
	J. Hopp	L	131	316	2	1	1	2.4	**.997**
	D. Litwhiler	R	136	294	6	8	1	2.3	.974
	A. Bergamo	L	50	83	0	1	0	1.7	.988
	P. Martin	R	29	48	1	1	0	1.7	.980
	D. Garms	R	23	34	0	0	0	1.5	1.000
C	W. Cooper	R	97	442	40	10	7	**5.1**	.980
	K. O'Dea	R	69	326	34	2	4	5.2	.994
	B. Keely	R	1	1	0	0	0	1.0	1.000

It's a shame the quality of play had deteriorated so far by the 1944 season. The Cardinals fielded an outstanding club that could have won in any season; the lack of competition made it a runaway. They were one of just six clubs in baseball history to lead their league in runs, batting, fielding, and ERA—and one of the other five is the Cardinals of '46, substantially the same club playing in a tougher league. To make the year even more memorable, their hometown rivals, the Browns, won their only pennant on the season's final day, setting up the only all-St. Louis World Series, captured by the Cardinals in six games. All six were played at Sportsman's Park, only the third time that all the World Series games were played at the same site. (The first two were in 1921 and 1922, when the New York Giants opposed the Yankees in the Polo Grounds, where the Yankees played while awaiting construction of Yankee Stadium.)

TEAM STATISTICS

	W	L	PCT	GB	R	OR	2B	3B	HR	BA	SA	SB	E	DP	FA	CG	BB	SO	ShO	SV	ERA
TL	105	49	.682		772	490	274	59	100	.275	.402	37	112	162	.982	89	468	637	26	12	2.67
IT	90	63	.588	14.5	744	662	248	80	70	.265	.379	87	191	122	.970	77	435	452	10	19	3.44
IN	89	65	.578	16	573	537	229	31	51	.254	.338	51	137	153	.978	93	384	359	17	12	2.97
HI	75	79	.487	30	702	669	236	46	71	.261	.360	53	186	151	.970	70	452	535	11	13	3.59
Y	67	87	.435	38	682	773	191	47	93	.263	.370	38	179	128	.971	47	587	499	4	21	4.29
OS	65	89	.422	40	593	674	250	39	79	.246	.353	37	182	160	.971	70	527	454	13	12	3.67
KN	63	91	.409	42	690	832	255	51	56	.269	.366	43	197	112	.966	50	660	487	4	13	4.68
HI	61	92	.399	43.5	539	658	199	42	55	.251	.336	32	177	138	.972	66	459	496	11	6	3.64
EAGUE TOTAL					5295	5295	1882	395	575	.261	.363	378	1361	1126	.972	562	3972	3919	96	108	3.61

INDIVIDUAL PITCHING

ITCHER	T	W	L	PCT	ERA	SV	G	GS	CG	IP	H	BB	SO	R	ER	ShO	H/9	BB/9	SO/9
lort Cooper	R	22	7	.759	2.46	1	34	33	22	252.1	227	60	97	74	69	7	8.10	2.14	3.46
lax Lanier	L	17	12	.586	2.65	0	33	30	16	224.1	192	71	141	82	66	5	7.70	2.85	5.66
ed Wilks	R	17	4	.810	2.65	0	36	21	16	207.1	173	49	70	61	61	4	7.51	2.13	3.04
arry Brecheen	L	16	5	.762	2.85	0	30	22	13	189.1	174	46	88	67	60	3	8.27	2.19	4.18
I Jurisich	R	7	9	.438	3.39	1	30	14	5	130	102	65	53	53	49	2	7.06	4.50	3.67
eorge Munger	R	11	3	.786	1.34	2	21	12	7	121	92	41	55	23	18	2	6.84	3.05	4.09
reddy Schmidt	R	7	3	.700	3.15	5	37	9	3	114.1	94	58	58	48	40	2	7.40	4.57	4.57
lix Donnelly	R	2	1	.667	2.12	2	27	4	2	76.1	61	34	45	26	18	1	7.19	4.01	5.31
arry Gumbert	R	4	2	.667	2.49	1	10	7	3	61.1	60	19	16	23	17	0	8.80	2.79	2.35
ud Byerly	R	2	2	.500	3.40	0	9	4	2	42.1	37	20	13	18	16	0	7.87	4.25	2.76
Il Trotter	R	0	1	.000	13.50	0	2	1	0	6	14	4	0	14	9	0	21.00	6.00	0.00
ike Naymick	R	0	0	—	4.50	0	1	0	0	2	2	1	1	1	1	0	9.00	4.50	4.50
EAM TOTAL		105	49	.682	2.67	12	270	157	89	1426.2	1228	468	637	490	424	26	7.75	2.95	4.02

MANAGER	W	L	PCT
Billy Southworth	95	59	.617

POS	Player	B	G	AB	H	2B	3B	HR	HR%	R	RBI	BB	SO	SB	Pinch Hit AB	Pinch Hit H	BA	SA
REGULARS																		
1B	Ray Sanders	L	143	537	148	29	3	8	1.5	85	78	83	55	3	1	0	.276	.385
2B	Emil Verban	R	155	597	166	22	8	0	0.0	59	72	19	15	4	0	0	.278	.342
SS	Marty Marion	R	123	430	119	27	5	1	0.2	63	59	39	39	2	0	0	.277	.370
3B	Whitey Kurowski	R	133	511	165	27	3	21	4.1	84	102	45	45	1	1	0	.323	.511
RF	Johnny Hopp	L	124	446	129	22	8	3	0.7	67	44	49	24	14	6	1	.289	.395
CF	Buster Adams	R	140	578	169	26	0	20	3.5	98	101	57	75	3	0	0	.292	.441
LF	Red Schoendienst	B	137	565	157	22	6	1	0.2	89	47	21	17	26	7	2	.278	.343
C	Ken O'Dea	L	100	307	78	18	2	4	1.3	36	43	50	31	0	8	0	.254	.365
SUBSTITUTES																		
3O	Debs Garms	L	74	146	49	7	2	0	0.0	23	18	31	3	0	26	10	.336	.411
SS	George Fallon	R	24	55	13	2	1	0	0.0	4	7	6	6	1	0	0	.236	.309
UT	Pep Young	R	27	47	7	1	0	1	2.1	5	4	1	8	0	5	0	.149	.234
3B	John Antonelli	R	2	3	0	0	0	0	0.0	0	0	0	1	0	2	0	.000	.000
OF	Augie Bergamo	L	94	304	96	17	2	3	1.0	51	44	43	21	0	15	4	.316	.414
OF	Art Rebel	R	26	72	25	4	0	0	0.0	12	5	6	4	1	8	1	.347	.403
UT	Lou Klein	R	19	57	13	4	1	1	1.8	12	6	14	9	0	0	0	.228	.386
OF	Dave Bartosch	R	24	47	12	1	0	0	0.0	9	1	6	3	0	13	5	.255	.277
OF	Jim Mallory	R	13	43	10	2	0	0	0.0	3	5	0	2	0	2	1	.233	.279
OF	Glenn Crawford	L	4	3	0	0	0	0	0.0	0	0	0	1	0	2	0	.000	.000
C	Del Rice	R	83	253	66	17	3	1	0.4	27	28	16	33	0	6	1	.261	.364
C	Walker Cooper	R	4	18	7	0	0	0	0.0	3	1	0	0	0	0	0	.389	.389
C	Gene Crumling	R	6	12	1	0	0	0	0.0	0	1	0	1	0	0	0	.083	.083
C	Bob Keely	R	1	1	0	0	0	0	0.0	0	0	0	0	0	0	0	.000	.000
PITCHERS																		
P	Red Barrett	R	36	89	10	2	0	0	0.0	1	5	1	22	0	0	0	.112	.135
P	Ken Burkhart	R	42	72	13	2	0	0	0.0	5	5	4	14	0	0	0	.181	.208
P	Harry Brecheen	L	24	57	7	2	0	0	0.0	1	7	4	11	0	0	0	.123	.158
P	Blix Donnelly	R	31	54	7	1	0	0	0.0	3	4	2	5	0	0	0	.130	.148
P	George Dockins	L	31	34	6	0	0	0	0.0	4	1	6	11	0	0	0	.176	.176
P	Ted Wilks	R	18	30	4	0	0	0	0.0	2	1	4	7	0	0	0	.133	.133
P	Jack Creel	R	35	26	2	1	0	0	0.0	2	1	1	7	0	0	0	.077	.115
P	Bud Byerly	R	33	23	5	0	0	0	0.0	4	4	3	5	0	0	0	.217	.217
P	Al Jurisich	R	27	23	2	0	0	0	0.0	1	1	0	7	0	0	0	.087	.087
P	Glenn Gardner	R	17	21	7	0	0	0	0.0	1	2	1	2	0	0	0	.333	.333
P	Max Lanier	R	4	11	2	0	0	0	0.0	0	0	0	1	0	0	0	.182	.182
P	Mort Cooper	R	4	6	2	0	0	0	0.0	2	1	2	1	0	0	0	.333	.333
P	Art Lopatka	L	4	4	1	0	0	0	0.0	0	0	0	1	0	0	0	.250	.250
P	Stan Partenheimer	B	8	3	0	0	0	0	0.0	0	0	0	1	0	0	0	.000	.000
P	Bill Crouch	B	6	2	0	0	0	0	0.0	0	0	0	0	0	0	0	.000	.000
TEAM TOTAL				5487	1498	256	44	64	1.2	756	698	515	488	55	102	25	.273	.371

INDIVIDUAL FIELDING

POS	Player	T	G	PO	A	E	DP	TC/G	FA
1B	R. Sanders	R	142	1259	90	19	113	9.6	.986
	J. Hopp	L	15	131	11	2	11	9.6	.986
	A. Bergamo	L	2	14	0	0	1	7.0	1.000
2B	E. Verban	R	155	398	406	18	95	5.3	.978
	P. Young	R	3	5	4	0	1	3.0	1.000
	G. Fallon	R	4	5	2	0	1	1.8	1.000
	L. Klein	R	2	2	0	0	0	1.0	1.000
	Schoendienst	R	1	0	1	0	0	1.0	1.000
SS	M. Marion	R	122	237	372	21	70	5.2	.967
	G. Fallon	R	20	34	39	4	8	3.9	.948
	P. Young	R	11	23	21	1	3	4.1	.978
	Schoendienst	R	10	16	19	5	10	4.0	.875
	L. Klein	R	7	12	14	2	3	4.0	.929
	W. Kurowski	R	6	2	3	1	0	1.0	.833
3B	W. Kurowski	R	131	172	235	15	28	3.2	.964
	D. Garms	R	32	23	42	3	4	2.1	.956
	L. Klein	R	4	5	8	1	0	3.5	.929
	P. Young	R	9	3	5	1	0	1.0	.889
	J. Antonelli	R	1	2	0	1	0	3.0	.667
OF	B. Adams	R	140	382	9	9	3	2.9	.978
	Schoendienst	R	118	286	10	5	1	2.6	.983
	J. Hopp	L	104	244	5	5	2	2.4	.980
	A. Bergamo	R	77	146	9	5	3	2.1	.969
	A. Rebel	L	18	37	4	1	0	2.3	.976
	G. Crawford	R	1	0	0	0	0	0.0	.000
	D. Bartosch	R	11	26	1	1	0	2.5	.964
	J. Mallory	R	11	23	1	2	0	2.4	.923
	L. Klein	R	7	19	1	0	1	2.9	1.000
	D. Garms	R	10	7	1	0	0	0.8	1.000
C	K. O'Dea	R	91	321	50	2	14	4.1	.995
	D. Rice	R	77	284	39	2	6	4.2	.994
	W. Cooper	R	4	27	1	1	0	7.3	.966
	G. Crumling	R	6	16	4	0	0	3.3	1.000
	B. Keely	R	1	1	0	0	0	1.0	1.000

The siren call of military induction finally proved too much for the Redbirds in 1945 as they lost Musial, Walker Cooper, and Danny Litwhiler to the service. They also lost Mort Cooper to an elbow injury. They still managed 95 wins, but it wasn't enough to catch the Cubs, who were in the process of winning their last pennant. The Cards kept the race close, trailing by just a game and a half before splitting a crucial two-game set with the Cubs that was their last real chance to make up ground. Harry Brecheen had a 14–4 record for the season, raising his lifetime mark to 39–15, a .722 won-lost percentage. The latest farmhand to crack the lineup was a 22-year-old redhead who led the league in stolen bases as a regular in right field, but would soon become a fixture at second base: Albert "Red" Schoendienst.

TEAM STATISTICS

	W	L	PCT	GB	R	OR	2B	3B	HR	BA	SA	SB	E	DP	FA	CG	BB	SO	ShO	SV	ERA
CHI	98	56	.636		735	532	229	52	57	.277	.372	69	121	124	.980	86	385	541	15	14	2.98
STL	95	59	.617	3	756	583	256	44	64	.273	.371	55	137	150	.977	77	497	510	18	9	3.24
BKN	87	67	.565	11	795	724	257	71	57	.271	.376	75	230	144	.962	61	586	557	7	18	3.70
PIT	82	72	.532	16	753	686	259	56	72	.267	.377	81	178	141	.971	73	455	518	8	16	3.76
NY	78	74	.513	19	668	700	175	35	114	.269	.379	38	166	112	.973	53	529	530	13	21	4.06
BOS	67	85	.441	30	721	728	229	25	101	.267	.374	82	193	160	.969	57	557	404	7	13	4.04
CIN	61	93	.396	37	536	694	221	26	56	.249	.333	71	146	138	.976	77	534	372	11	6	4.00
PHI	46	108	.299	52	548	865	197	27	56	.246	.326	54	234	150	.962	31	608	433	4	26	4.64
LEAGUE TOTAL					5512	5512	1823	336	577	.265	.364	525	1405	1119	.971	515	4151	3865	83	123	3.80

INDIVIDUAL PITCHING

PITCHER	T	W	L	PCT	ERA	SV	G	GS	CG	IP	H	BB	SO	R	ER	ShO	H/9	BB/9	SO/9
Red Barrett	R	21*	9	.700	2.74	0	36	29	22*	246.2*	244*	38	63	84	75	3	8.90	1.39	2.30
Ken Burkhart	R	19	8	.704	2.90	2	42	22	12	217.1	206	66	67	76	70	4	8.53	2.73	2.77
Blix Donnelly	R	8	10	.444	3.52	2	31	23	9	166.1	157	87	76	79	65	4	8.49	4.71	4.11
Harry Brecheen	L	14	4	.778	2.52	2	24	18	13	157.1	136	44	63	48	44	3	7.78	2.52	3.60
George Dockins	L	8	6	.571	3.21	0	31	12	5	126.1	132	38	33	53	45	2	9.40	2.71	2.35
Ted Wilks	R	4	7	.364	2.93	0	18	16	4	98.1	103	29	28	39	32	1	9.43	2.65	2.56
Bud Byerly	R	4	5	.444	4.74	0	33	8	2	95	111	41	39	61	50	0	10.52	3.88	3.69
Jack Creel	R	5	4	.556	4.14	2	26	8	2	87	78	45	34	41	40	0	8.07	4.66	3.52
Al Jurisich	R	3	3	.500	5.15	0	27	6	1	71.2	61	45	41	45	41	0	7.66	5.15	5.27
Glenn Gardner	R	3	1	.750	3.29	1	17	4	2	54.2	50	27	20	21	20	1	8.23	4.45	3.29
Max Lanier	L	2	2	.500	1.73	0	4	3	3	26	22	8	16	10	5	0	7.62	2.77	5.54
Mort Cooper	R	2	0	1.000	1.52	0	4	3	1	23.2	20	7	14	7	4	0	7.61	2.66	5.32
Bill Crouch	R	1	0	1.000	3.38	0	6	0	0	13.1	12	7	4	5	5	0	8.10	4.73	2.70
Stan Partenheimer	L	0	0	—	6.08	0	8	2	0	13.1	12	16	6	9	9	0	8.10	10.80	4.05
Art Lopatka	L	1	0	1.000	1.54	0	4	1	1	11.2	7	3	5	4	2	0	5.40	2.31	3.86
TEAM TOTAL		95	59	.617	3.24	9	311	155	77	1408.2	1351	497	510	582	507	18	8.63	3.18	3.26

MANAGER	W	L	PCT
Eddie Dyer	98	58	.628

POS	Player	B	G	AB	H	2B	3B	HR	HR %	R	RBI	BB	SO	SB	Pinch Hit AB	Pinch Hit H	BA	SA
REGULARS																		
1B	Stan Musial	L	156	624	228	50	20	16	2.6	124	103	73	31	7	0	0	.365	.587
2B	Red Schoendienst	B	142	606	170	28	5	0	0.0	94	34	37	27	12	1	0	.281	.343
SS	Marty Marion	R	146	498	116	29	4	3	0.6	51	46	59	53	1	1	0	.233	.325
3B	Whitey Kurowski	R	142	519	156	32	5	14	2.7	76	89	72	47	2	3	1	.301	.462
RF	Enos Slaughter	L	156	609	183	30	8	18	3.0	100	130	69	41	9	0	0	.300	.465
CF	Harry Walker	L	112	346	82	14	6	3	0.9	53	27	30	29	12	11	3	.237	.338
LF	Erv Dusak	R	100	275	66	9	1	9	3.3	38	42	33	63	7	7	2	.240	.378
C	Joe Garagiola	L	74	211	50	4	1	3	1.4	21	22	23	25	0	4	2	.237	.308
SUBSTITUTES																		
1O	Dick Sisler	L	83	235	61	11	2	3	1.3	17	42	14	28	0	13	4	.260	.362
2B	Lou Klein	R	23	93	18	3	0	1	1.1	12	4	9	7	1	0	0	.194	.258
S2	Jeff Cross	R	49	69	15	3	0	0	0.0	17	6	10	8	4	3	0	.217	.261
2B	Nippy Jones	R	16	12	4	0	0	0	0.0	3	1	2	2	0	9	4	.333	.333
OF	Terry Moore	R	91	278	73	14	1	3	1.1	32	28	18	26	0	25	6	.263	.353
OF	Buster Adams	R	81	173	32	6	0	5	2.9	21	22	29	27	3	21	6	.185	.306
OF	Bill Endicott	L	20	20	4	3	0	0	0.0	2	3	4	4	0	14	3	.200	.350
C	Del Rice	R	55	139	38	8	1	1	0.7	10	12	8	16	0	2	0	.273	.367
C	Clyde Kluttz	R	52	136	36	7	0	0	0.0	8	14	10	10	0	2	2	.265	.316
C	Ken O'Dea	L	22	57	7	2	0	1	1.8	2	3	8	8	0	0	0	.123	.211
C	Del Wilber	R	4	4	0	0	0	0	0.0	0	0	1	0	0	0	0	.000	.000
PH	Walter Sessi	L	15	14	2	0	0	1	7.1	2	2	1	4	0	14	2	.143	.357
PH	Danny Litwhiler	R	6	5	0	0	0	0	0.0	0	0	1	1	0	5	0	.000	.000
PH	Emil Verban	R	1	1	0	0	0	0	0.0	0	0	0	0	0	1	0	.000	.000
PITCHERS																		
P	Howie Pollet	L	40	87	14	4	0	0	0.0	2	7	6	23	0	0	0	.161	.207
P	Harry Brecheen	L	37	83	11	1	0	0	0.0	2	6	3	17	0	0	0	.133	.145
P	Murry Dickson	R	47	65	18	5	1	0	0.0	8	6	1	6	0	0	0	.277	.385
P	Al Brazle	L	37	52	11	0	0	0	0.0	5	2	0	2	0	0	0	.212	.212
P	Ken Burkhart	R	25	34	5	1	1	0	0.0	2	3	1	8	0	0	0	.147	.235
P	Johnny Beazley	R	19	33	8	1	0	0	0.0	2	4	2	9	0	0	0	.242	.273
P	Max Lanier	R	6	25	5	0	0	0	0.0	1	2	1	1	0	0	0	.200	.200
P	Ted Wilks	R	40	24	5	0	0	0	0.0	5	1	1	5	0	0	0	.208	.208
P	Red Barrett	R	23	17	1	0	0	0	0.0	1	1	1	4	0	0	0	.059	.059
P	George Munger	R	10	16	4	0	0	0	0.0	1	3	2	3	0	0	0	.250	.250
P	Freddie Martin	R	6	11	3	0	0	0	0.0	0	0	0	1	0	0	0	.273	.273
P	Freddy Schmidt	R	16	1	0	0	0	0	0.0	0	0	0	1	0	0	0	.000	.000
P	Blix Donnelly	R	13	0	0	0	0	0	–	0	0	1	0	0	0	0	–	–
P	Johnny Grodzicki	R	3	0	0	0	0	0	–	0	0	0	0	0	0	0	–	–
P	Howie Krist	L	15	0	0	0	0	0	–	0	0	0	0	0	0	0	–	–
TEAM TOTAL				5372	1426	265	56	81	1.5	712	665	530	537	58	136	35	.265	.381

INDIVIDUAL FIELDING

POS	Player	T	G	PO	A	E	DP	TC/G	FA
1B	S. Musial	L	114	1056	65	13	119	9.9	.989
	D. Sisler	R	37	292	28	4	31	8.8	.988
	H. Walker	R	8	58	4	1	3	7.9	.984
2B	Schoendienst	R	128	340	354	11	87	5.5	.984
	L. Klein	R	23	58	60	3	18	5.3	.975
	J. Cross	R	8	16	9	2	0	3.4	.926
	N. Jones	R	3	2	2	1	1	1.7	.800
	E. Dusak	R	2	1	1	0	1	1.0	1.000
SS	M. Marion	R	145	290	480	21	105	5.5	.973
	J. Cross	R	17	25	40	2	10	3.9	.970
	Schoendienst	R	4	5	6	0	3	2.8	1.000
3B	W. Kurowski	R	138	175	249	15	17	3.2	.966
	Schoendienst	R	12	18	19	2	6	3.3	.949
	E. Dusak	R	11	6	19	1	3	2.4	.962
	J. Cross	R	1	0	1	0	0	1.0	1.000
OF	E. Slaughter	R	156	284	23	6	6	2.0	.981
	H. Walker	R	92	215	11	6	2	2.5	.974
	T. Moore	R	66	158	5	3	0	2.5	.982
	E. Dusak	R	77	139	12	1	1	2.0	.993
	S. Musial	L	42	110	4	2	0	2.8	.983
	B. Adams	R	58	95	1	1	1	1.7	.990
	D. Sisler	R	29	42	3	2	0	1.6	.957
	B. Endicott	L	2	4	0	0	0	2.0	1.000
C	J. Garagiola	R	70	260	25	3	6	4.1	.990
	D. Rice	R	53	196	12	5	0	4.0	.977
	C. Kluttz	R	49	177	24	4	4	4.2	.980
	K. O'Dea	R	22	99	14	1	0	5.2	.991
	D. Wilber	R	4	0	0	0	0	0.0	.000

With the major leagues back at full strength after the end of the war, the Cardinals showed their ability in a great pennant race. For the first time, 154 games were not enough to determine a champion; the Cardinals and Dodgers tied with identical 96–58 records. St. Louis swept the two-game playoff to win the pennant. They then topped this remarkable season with a memorable seven-game World Series triumph over the Boston Red Sox. Harry "The Cat" Brecheen won three games in the Series and posted a 0.45 ERA, including two innings of relief in Game 7 on one day's rest. But the unforgettable image of the Series is Enos Slaughter scoring the winning run from first on Harry Walker's eighth-inning, seventh-game double, as Boston shortstop Johnny Pesky held the ball—for a fraction of a second—before firing his too-late relay to the plate.

TEAM STATISTICS

	W	L	PCT	GB	R	OR	2B	3B	HR	BA	SA	SB	E	DP	FA	CG	BB	SO	ShO	SV	ERA
TL	98	58	.628		712	545	265	56	81	.265	.381	58	124	167	.980	75	493	607	18	15	3.01
KN	96	60	.615	2	701	570	233	66	55	.260	.361	100	174	154	.972	52	671	647	14	28	3.05
HI	82	71	.536	14.5	626	581	223	50	56	.254	.346	43	146	119	.976	59	527	609	14	11	3.24
OS	81	72	.529	15.5	630	592	238	48	44	.264	.353	60	169	129	.972	74	478	531	10	12	3.37
HI	69	85	.448	28	560	705	209	40	80	.258	.359	41	148	144	.975	55	542	490	11	23	3.99
IN	67	87	.435	30	523	570	206	33	65	.239	.327	82	155	192	.975	69	467	506	16	11	3.07
IT	63	91	.409	34	552	668	202	52	60	.250	.344	48	184	127	.970	61	541	458	10	6	3.72
Y	61	93	.396	36	612	685	176	37	121	.255	.374	46	159	121	.973	48	660	581	8	13	3.92
EAGUE TOTAL					4916	4916	1752	382		562	.256	.355	478	1259	1153	.974	493	4379	4429	101	119	3.42

INDIVIDUAL PITCHING

PITCHER	T	W	L	PCT	ERA	SV	G	GS	CG	IP	H	BB	SO	R	ER	ShO	H/9	BB/9	SO/9
owie Pollet	L	21	10	.677	2.10	5	40	32	22	266	228	86	107	84	62	4	7.71	2.91	3.62
arry Brecheen	L	15	15	.500	2.49	3	36	30	14	231.1	212	67	117	73	64	5	8.25	2.61	4.55
urry Dickson	R	15	6	.714	2.88	1	47	19	12	184.1	160	56	82	71	59	2	7.81	2.73	4.00
Brazle	L	11	10	.524	3.29	0	37	15	6	153.1	152	55	58	69	56	2	8.92	3.23	3.40
hnny Beazley	R	7	5	.583	4.46	0	19	18	5	103	109	55	36	55	51	0	9.52	4.81	3.15
en Burkhart	R	6	3	.667	2.88	2	25	13	5	100	111	36	32	34	32	2	9.99	3.24	2.88
ed Wilks	R	8	0	1.000	3.41	1	40	4	0	95	88	38	40	41	36	0	8.34	3.60	3.79
ed Barrett	R	3	2	.600	4.03	2	23	9	1	67	75	24	22	35	30	0	10.07	3.22	2.96
ax Lanier	L	6	0	1.000	1.93	0	6	6	6	56	45	19	36	13	12	2	7.23	3.05	5.79
eorge Munger	R	2	2	.500	3.33	1	10	7	2	48.2	47	12	28	19	18	0	8.69	2.22	5.18
eddie Martin	R	2	1	.667	4.08	0	6	3	2	28.2	29	8	19	13	13	0	9.10	2.51	5.97
eddie Schmidt	R	1	0	1.000	3.29	0	16	0	0	27.1	27	15	14	11	10	0	8.89	4.94	4.61
owie Krist	R	0	2	.000	6.75	0	15	0	0	18.2	22	8	3	14	14	0	10.61	3.86	1.45
ix Donnelly	R	1	2	.333	3.95	0	13	0	0	13.2	17	10	11	7	6	0	11.20	6.59	7.24
hnny Grodzicki	R	0	0	–	9.00	0	3	0	0	4	4	4	2	5	4	0	9.00	9.00	4.50
AM TOTAL		98	58	.628	3.01	15	336	156	75	1397	1326	493	607	545	467	18	8.54	3.18	3.91

MANAGER	W	L	PCT
Eddie Dyer	89	65	.578

POS	Player	B	G	AB	H	2B	3B	HR	HR %	R	RBI	BB	SO	SB	Pinch Hit AB	Pinch Hit H	BA	SA
REGULARS																		
1B	Stan Musial	L	149	587	183	30	13	19	3.2	113	95	80	24	4	0	0	.312	.504
2B	Red Schoendienst	B	151	659	167	25	9	3	0.5	91	48	48	27	6	3	1	.253	.332
SS	Marty Marion	R	149	540	147	19	6	4	0.7	57	74	49	58	3	0	0	.272	.352
3B	Whitey Kurowski	R	146	513	159	27	6	27	5.3	108	104	87	56	4	4	1	.310	.544
RF	Erv Dusak	R	111	328	93	7	3	6	1.8	56	28	50	34	1	13	1	.284	.378
CF	Terry Moore	R	127	460	130	17	1	7	1.5	61	45	38	39	1	6	1	.283	.370
LF	Enos Slaughter	L	147	551	162	31	13	10	1.8	100	86	59	27	4	4	0	.294	.452
C	Del Rice	R	97	261	57	7	3	12	4.6	28	44	36	40	1	3	0	.218	.406
SUBSTITUTES																		
1O	Dick Sisler	L	46	74	15	2	1	0	0.0	4	9	3	8	0	30	4	.203	.257
2B	Nippy Jones	R	23	73	18	4	0	1	1.4	6	5	2	10	0	7	1	.247	.342
3S	Jeff Cross	R	51	49	5	1	0	0	0.0	4	3	10	6	0	1	0	.102	.122
SS	Bernie Creger	R	15	16	3	1	0	0	0.0	3	0	1	3	1	0	0	.188	.250
OF	Ron Northey	L	110	311	91	19	3	15	4.8	52	63	48	29	0	13	3	.293	.518
OF	Joe Medwick	R	75	150	46	12	0	4	2.7	19	28	16	12	0	31	7	.307	.467
OF	Chuck Diering	R	105	74	16	3	1	2	2.7	22	11	19	22	3	8	1	.216	.365
OF	Harry Walker	L	10	25	5	1	0*	0	0.0	0	0	4	2	0	0	0	.200*	.240
C	Joe Garagiola	L	77	183	47	10	2	5	2.7	20	25	40	14	0	4	1	.257	.415
C	Del Wilber	R	51	99	23	8	1	0	0.0	7	12	5	13	0	15	5	.232	.333
PITCHERS																		
P	Harry Brecheen	L	29	83	20	2	1	0	0.0	5	8	7	7	0	0	0	.241	.289
P	George Munger	R	40	81	15	3	0	0	0.0	3	7	4	28	0	0	0	.185	.222
P	Murry Dickson	R	47	80	17	2	0	0	0.0	4	9	1	5	0	0	0	.213	.238
P	Howie Pollet	L	37	65	15	1	2	0	0.0	5	5	1	13	0	0	0	.231	.308
P	Al Brazle	L	44	64	14	1	0	0	0.0	6	5	1	5	0	0	0	.219	.234
P	Jim Hearn	R	37	55	8	2	0	0	0.0	1	3	2	19	0	0	0	.145	.182
P	Ken Burkhart	R	34	24	3	0	0	0	0.0	1	1	1	6	0	0	0	.125	.125
P	Gerry Staley	R	18	6	0	0	0	0	0.0	1	0	1	0	0	0	0	.000	.000
P	Ted Wilks	R	37	6	1	0	0	0	0.0	1	0	1	2	0	0	0	.167	.167
P	Ken Johnson	L	2	4	2	0	0	0	0.0	1	0	0	1	0	0	0	.500	.500
P	Johnny Grodzicki	R	16	1	0	0	0	0	0.0	0	0	0	0	0	0	0	.000	.000
P	Freddy Schmidt	R	2	0	0	0	0	0	0.0	0	0	0	0	0	0	0	–	–
TEAM TOTAL				5422	1462	235	65	115	2.1	780	718	612	511	28	142	26	.270	.401

INDIVIDUAL FIELDING

POS	Player	T	G	PO	A	E	DP	TC/G	FA
1B	S. Musial	L	149	1360	77	8	138	9.7	.994
	D. Sisler	R	10	76	6	2	3	8.4	.976
2B	Schoendienst	R	142	357	404	19	109	5.5	.976
	N. Jones	R	13	32	40	5	5	5.9	.935
	J. Cross	R	2	4	4	0	0	4.0	1.000
SS	M. Marion	R	149	329	452	15	104	5.3	.981
	J. Cross	R	14	15	30	4	9	3.5	.918
	B. Creger	R	13	6	18	5	2	2.2	.828
3B	W. Kurowski	R	141	140	250	19	17	2.9	.954
	J. Cross	R	15	5	13	1	1	1.3	.947
	Schoendienst	R	5	6	13	0	2	3.8	1.000
	E. Dusak	R	7	3	11	0	1	2.0	1.000
	R. Northey	R	2	2	7	1	0	5.0	.900

POS	Player	T	G	PO	A	E	DP	TC/G	FA
OF	E. Slaughter	R	142	306	15	6	5	2.3	.982
	T. Moore	R	120	292	6	5	2	2.5	.983
	E. Dusak	R	89	178	13	6	2	2.2	.970
	R. Northey	R	94	122	8	7	1	1.5	.949
	J. Medwick	R	43	56	3	0	2	1.4	1.000
	C. Diering	R	75	55	3	0	1	0.8	1.000
	H. Walker	R	9	15	0	1*	0	1.8	.938
	D. Sisler	R	5	8	0	0	0	1.6	1.000
	N. Jones	R	2	2	0	0	0	1.0	1.000
	Schoendienst	R	1	1	0	0	0	1.0	1.000
C	D. Rice	R	94	380	33	8	7	4.5	.981
	J. Garagiola	R	74	281	23	4	2	4.2	.987
	D. Wilber	R	34	108	10	2	2	3.5	.983

The Brooklyn challenge in '46 was a bad omen for St. Louis fans. The top products of Rickey's Cardinal farm system were already in the majors, and he was now working his magic for the Dodgers. Rickey's greatest accomplishment, the signing of Jackie Robinson and subsequent breaking of baseball's color barrier, would take the Cardinals by surprise. They were slow to react to Rickey's revolution; their first black player, Tom Alston, would not appear until 1954, long after the cream of the black talent was in the majors on other teams. The talent on hand was considerable, and good enough to average 90 wins while finishing second in '47, '48, and '49, but the team Rickey was building would dominate the team he had built, and it would be seventeen long years before St. Louis won another pennant. Significantly, that pennant would be won with help from three black players acquired in trades (Bill White, Curt Flood, and Lou Brock), and one great black pitcher from the farm system (Bob Gibson).

TEAM STATISTICS

	W	L	PCT	GB	R	OR	2B	3B	Batting HR	BA	SA	SB	E	Fielding DP	FA	CG	BB	Pitching SO	ShO	SV	ERA
BKN	94	60	.610		774	668	241	50	83	.272	.384	88	129	164	.978	47	626	592	14	34	3.82
STL	89	65	.578	5	780	634	235	65	115	.270	.401	28	128	169	.979	65	495	642	13	20	3.53
BOS	86	68	.558	8	701	622	265	42	85	.275	.390	58	153	124	.974	74	453	486	14	13	3.62
NY	81	73	.526	13	830	761	220	48	221	.271	.454	29	155	136	.974	58	590	553	6	14	4.44
CIN	73	81	.474	21	681	755	242	43	95	.259	.375	46	138	134	.977	54	589	633	13	13	4.41
CHI	69	85	.448	25	567	722	231	48	71	.259	.361	22	150	159	.975	46	618	571	8	15	4.10
PHI	62	92	.403	32	589	687	210	52	60	.258	.352	60	152	140	.974	70	501	514	8	14	3.96
PIT	62	92	.403	32	744	817	216	44	156	.261	.406	30	149	131	.975	44	592	501	9	13	4.68
LEAGUE TOTAL					5666	5666	1860	392	886	.265	.390	361	1154	1157	.976	458	4464	4492	85	136	4.07

INDIVIDUAL PITCHING

PITCHER	T	W	L	PCT	ERA	SV	G	GS	CG	IP	H	BB	SO	R	ER	ShO	H/9	BB/9	SO/9
Murry Dickson	R	13	16	.448	3.07	3	47	25	11	231.2	211	88	111	101	79	4	8.20	3.42	4.31
George Munger	R	16	5	.762	3.37	3	40	31	13	224.1	218	76	123	94	84	6	8.75	3.05	4.93
Harry Brecheen	L	16	11	.593	3.30	1	29	28	18	223.1	220	66	89	92	82	1	8.87	2.66	3.59
Howie Pollet	L	9	11	.450	4.34	2	37	24	9	176.1	195	87	73	96	85	0	9.95	4.44	3.73
Al Brazle	L	14	8	.636	2.84	4	44	19	7	168	186	48	85	65	53	0	9.96	2.57	4.55
Jim Hearn	R	12	7	.632	3.22	1	37	21	4	162	151	63	57	67	58	1	8.39	3.50	3.17
Ken Burkhart	R	3	6	.333	5.21	1	34	6	1	95	108	23	44	55	55	0	10.23	2.18	4.17
Ted Wilks	R	4	0	1.000	5.01	5	37	0	0	50.1	57	11	28	33	28	0	10.19	1.97	5.01
Gerry Staley	R	1	0	1.000	2.76	0	18	1	1	29.1	33	8	14	11	9	0	10.13	2.45	4.30
Johnny Grodzicki	R	0	1	.000	5.40	0	16	0	0	23.1	21	19	8	17	14	0	8.10	7.33	3.09
Ken Johnson	L	1	0	1.000	0.00	0	2	1	1	10	2	5	8	1	0	0	1.80	4.50	7.20
Freddy Schmidt	R	0	0	–	2.25	0	2	0	0	4	5	1	2	2	1	0	11.25	2.25	4.50
TEAM TOTAL		89	65	.578	3.53	20	343	156	65	1397.2	1407	495	642	634	548	12	9.06	3.19	4.13

MANAGER	W	L	PCT
Eddie Dyer	85	69	.552

POS	Player	B	G	AB	H	2B	3B	HR	HR %	R	RBI	BB	SO	SB	Pinch Hit AB	Pinch Hit H	BA	SA
REGULARS																		
1B	Nippy Jones	R	132	481	122	21	9	10	2.1	58	81	36	45	2	2	0	.254	.397
2B	Red Schoendienst	B	119	408	111	21	4	4	1.0	64	36	28	16	1	17	4	.272	.373
SS	Marty Marion	R	144	567	143	26	4	4	0.7	70	43	37	54	1	2	0	.252	.333
3B	Don Lang	R	117	323	87	14	1	4	1.2	30	31	47	38	2	16	1	.269	.356
RF	Enos Slaughter	L	146	549	176	27	11	11	2.0	91	90	81	29	4	0	0	.321	.470
CF	Terry Moore	R	91	207	48	11	0	4	1.9	30	18	27	12	0	17	4	.232	.343
LF	Stan Musial	L	155	611	**230**	46	18	39	6.4	**135**	131	79	34	7	0	0	.**376**	**.702**
C	Del Rice	R	100	290	57	10	1	4	1.4	24	34	37	46	1	0	0	.197	.279
SUBSTITUTES																		
2S	Ralph LaPointe	R	87	222	50	3	0	0	0.0	27	15	18	19	1	2	0	.225	.239
3B	Whitey Kurowski	R	77	220	47	8	0	2	0.9	34	33	42	28	0	9	1	.214	.277
1B	Babe Young	L	41	111	27	5	2	1	0.9	14	13	16	6	0	4	0	.243	.351
3B	Eddie Kazak	R	6	22	6	3	0	0	0.0	1	2	0	2	0	0	0	.273	.409
3B	Bobby Young	L	3	1	0	0	0	0	0.0	0	0	0	1	0	1	0	.000	.000
UT	Erv Dusak	R	114	311	65	9	2	6	1.9	60	19	49	55	3	9	3	.209	.309
OF	Ron Northey	L	96	246	79	10	1	13	5.3	40	64	38	25	0	25	11	.321	.528
OF	Hal Rice	L	8	31	10	1	2	0	0.0	3	3	2	4	0	0	0	.323	.484
OF	Joe Medwick	R	20	19	4	0	0	0	0.0	0	2	1	2	0	18	4	.211	.211
OF	Chuck Diering	R	7	7	0	0	0	0	0.0	2	0	2	2	1	0	0	.000	.000
C	Bill Baker	R	45	119	35	10	1	0	0.0	13	15	15	7	1	7	2	.294	.395
C	Del Wilber	R	27	58	11	2	0	0	0.0	5	10	4	9	0	1	0	.190	.224
C	Joe Garagiola	L	24	56	6	1	0	2	3.6	9	7	12	9	0	1	0	.107	.232
C	Johnny Bucha	R	2	1	0	0	0	0	0.0	0	0	1	0	0	0	0	.000	.000
PH	Larry Miggins	R	1	1	0	0	0	0	0.0	1	0	0	0	0	1	0	.000	.000
PH	Jeff Cross	R	2	0	0	0	0	0	–	0	0	0	0	0	0	0	–	–
PITCHERS																		
P	Murry Dickson	R	43	96	27	2	0	0	0.0	7	11	1	1	0	1	0	.281	.302
P	Harry Brecheen	L	33	82	12	1	1	0	0.0	4	2	5	20	0	0	0	.146	.183
P	Howie Pollet	L	38	68	8	1	0	0	0.0	6	4	3	9	0	0	0	.118	.132
P	Al Brazle	L	45	55	8	1	0	0	0.0	5	7	1	9	0	1	0	.145	.164
P	George Munger	R	39	50	8	1	1	0	0.0	2	2	4	15	0	0	0	.160	.220
P	Ted Wilks	R	57	30	5	1	0	0	0.0	2	4	3	7	0	0	0	.167	.200
P	Jim Hearn	R	36	25	5	0	0	0	0.0	1	1	0	7	0	0	0	.200	.200
P	Ken Johnson	L	20	20	6	2	0	0	0.0	2	1	0	7	0	5	2	.300	.400
P	Gerry Staley	R	31	9	2	0	0	1	11.1	1	1	1	2	0	0	0	.222	.556
P	Ken Burkhart	R	21	4	1	1	0	0	0.0	0	2	0	2	0	0	0	.250	.500
P	Al Papai	R	11	2	0	0	0	0	0.0	0	0	0	1	0	0	0	.000	.000
P	Clarence Beers	R	1	0	0	0	0	0	–	0	0	0	0	0	0	0	–	–
P	Ray Yochim	R	1	0	0	0	0	0	–	0	0	0	0	0	0	0	–	–
	TEAM TOTAL			5302	1396	238	58	105	2.0	742	680	590	523	24	140	32	.263	.389

INDIVIDUAL FIELDING

POS	Player	T	G	PO	A	E	DP	TC/G	FA
1B	N. Jones	R	128	1148	63	17	98	9.6	.986
	B. Young	L	35	266	8	1	23	7.9	.996
	S. Musial	L	2	7	1	0	0	4.0	1.000
2B	Schoendienst	R	96	230	269	10	57	5.3	.980
	R. LaPointe	R	44	114	108	8	24	5.2	.965
	E. Dusak	R	29	56	63	3	11	4.2	.975
	D. Lang	R	2	5	3	1	2	4.5	.889
SS	M. Marion	R	142	263	445	19	80	5.1	**.974**
	R. LaPointe	R	25	28	50	4	12	3.3	.951
	E. Dusak	R	1	1	2	0	1	3.0	1.000
3B	D. Lang	R	95	81	188	10	13	2.9	.964
	W. Kurowski	R	65	55	100	10	10	2.5	.939
	E. Kazak	R	6	7	11	2	2	3.3	.900
	E. Dusak	R	9	6	12	1	0	2.1	.947
	B. Young	R	1	2	0	0	0	2.0	1.000
	R. LaPointe	R	1	1	0	0	0	1.0	1.000

POS	Player	T	G	PO	A	E	DP	TC/G	FA
OF	S. Musial	L	155	347	10	7	3	2.3	.981
	E. Slaughter	R	146	330	9	10	1	2.4	.971
	T. Moore	R	71	131	2	1	0	1.9	.993
	E. Dusak	R	68	128	3	1	2	1.9	.992
	R. Northey	R	67	85	2	1	0	1.3	.989
	J. Medwick	R	1	0	0	0	0	0.0	.000
	H. Rice	R	8	16	0	0	0	2.0	1.000
	C. Diering	R	5	4	1	0	0	1.0	1.000
C	D. Rice	R	99	447	46	2	5	5.0	**.996**
	B. Baker	R	36	152	15	1	2	4.7	.994
	J. Garagiola	R	23	83	14	1	1	4.3	.990
	D. Wilber	R	26	67	7	4	1	3.0	.949
	J. Bucha	R	1	1	0	0	0	1.0	1.000

In Boston was heard the melodic refrain, "Spahn, Sain, and pray for rain," and the rains came often enough to keep St. Louis six and a half games behind the pennant-winning Braves. Stan the Man gave the Cards another MVP season, probably the finest of his career. He missed a Triple Crown by just one home run, leading the league in batting and RBIs, but trailing in homers with 39 to Johnny Mize's and Ralph Kiner's 40. He set career highs in hits, homers, runs, RBIs, batting, and slugging; his .702 slugging average and 429 total bases are tops in the National League since World War II. He also achieved the rare feat of having more home runs than strikeouts for the season. Pitching kept the Cardinals down, though. Despite Brecheen's league-leading 2.24 ERA, the team ERA was up sharply from '47, while the league ERA was coming down.

TEAM STATISTICS

	W	L	PCT	GB	R	OR	Batting 2B	3B	HR	BA	SA	SB	Fielding E	DP	FA	CG	BB	Pitching SO	ShO	SV	ERA
BOS	91	62	.595		739	584	272	49	95	.275	.399	43	143	132	.976	70	430	579	10	17	3.38
STL	85	69	.552	6.5	742	646	238	58	105	.263	.389	24	119	138	.980	60	476	635	13	18	3.91
BKN	84	70	.545	7.5	744	667	256	54	91	.261	.381	114	161	151	.973	52	633	670	9	22	3.75
PIT	83	71	.539	8.5	706	699	191	54	108	.263	.380	68	137	150	.977	65	564	519	5	19	4.15
NY	78	76	.506	13.5	780	704	210	49	164	.256	.408	51	156	134	.974	54	551	552	6	15	3.93
PHI	66	88	.429	25.5	591	729	227	39	91	.259	.368	68	210	126	.964	61	561	552	6	15	4.08
CIN	64	89	.418	27	588	752	221	37	104	.247	.365	42	158	135	.973	40	572	599	9	20	4.47
CHI	64	90	.416	27.5	597	706	225	44	87	.262	.369	39	172	152	.972	51	609	636	7	10	4.00
LEAGUE TOTAL					5487	5487	1840	384	845	.261	.383	449	1256	1118	.974	453	4396	4717	74	142	3.95

INDIVIDUAL PITCHING

PITCHER	T	W	L	PCT	ERA	SV	G	GS	CG	IP	H	BB	SO	R	ER	ShO	H/9	BB/9	SO/9
Murry Dickson	R	12	16	.429	4.14	1	42	29	11	252.1	257	85	113	121	116	1	9.17	3.03	4.03
Harry Brecheen	L	20	7	.741	2.24	1	33	30	21	233.1	193	49	149	62	58	7	7.44	1.89	5.75
Howie Pollet	L	13	8	.619	4.54	0	36	26	11	186.1	216	67	80	102	94	0	10.43	3.24	3.86
George Munger	R	10	11	.476	4.50	0	39	25	7	166	179	74	72	91	83	2	9.70	4.01	3.90
Al Brazle	L	10	6	.625	3.80	1	42	23	6	156.1	171	50	55	77	66	3	9.84	2.88	3.17
Ted Wilks	R	6	6	.500	2.62	13	57	2	1	130.2	113	39	71	40	38	0	7.78	2.69	4.89
Jim Hearn	R	8	6	.571	4.22	1	34	13	3	89.2	92	35	27	44	42	0	9.23	3.51	2.71
Gerry Staley	R	4	4	.500	6.92	0	31	3	0	52	61	21	23	44	40	0	10.56	3.63	3.98
Ken Johnson	L	2	4	.333	4.76	0	13	4	0	45.1	43	30	20	27	24	0	8.54	5.96	3.97
Ken Burkhart	R	0	0	–	5.54	1	20	0	0	37.1	50	14	16	24	23	0	12.05	3.38	3.86
Al Papai	R	0	1	.000	5.06	0	10	0	0	16	14	7	8	10	9	0	7.88	3.94	4.50
Erv Dusak	R	0	0	–	0.00	0	1	0	0	1	0	1	0	0	0	0	0.00	9.00	0.00
Ray Yochim	R	0	0	–	0.00	0	1	0	0	1	0	3	1	0	0	0	0.00	27.00	0.00
Clarence Beers	R	0	0	–	13.50	0	1	0	0	.2	3	1	0	4	1	0	40.50	13.50	0.00
TEAM TOTAL		85	69	.552	3.91	18	360	155	60	1368	1392	476	635	646	594	13	9.16	3.13	4.18

MANAGER	W	L	PCT
Eddie Dyer	96	58	.623

POS	Player	B	G	AB	H	2B	3B	HR	HR %	R	RBI	BB	SO	SB	Pinch Hit AB	Pinch Hit H	BA	SA
REGULARS																		
1B	Nippy Jones	R	110	380	114	20	2	8	2.1	51	62	16	20	1	11	2	.300	.426
2B	Red Schoendienst	B	151	640	190	25	2	3	0.5	102	54	51	18	8	1	1	.297	.356
SS	Marty Marion	R	134	515	140	31	2	5	1.0	61	70	37	42	0	0	0	.272	.369
3B	Eddie Kazak	R	92	326	99	15	3	6	1.8	43	42	29	17	0	7	2	.304	.423
RF	Stan Musial	L	157	612	207	41	13	36	5.9	128	123	107	38	3	0	0	.338	.624
CF	Chuck Diering	R	131	369	97	21	8	3	0.8	60	38	35	49	1	1	0	.263	.388
LF	Enos Slaughter	L	151	568	191	34	13	13	2.3	92	96	79	37	3	1	0	.336	.511
C	Del Rice	R	92	284	67	16	1	4	1.4	25	29	30	40	0	0	0	.236	.342
SUBSTITUTES																		
3B	Tommy Glaviano	R	87	258	69	16	1	6	2.3	32	36	41	35	0	7	3	.267	.407
1B	Rocky Nelson	L	82	244	54	8	4	4	1.6	28	32	11	12	1	8	2	.221	.336
UT	Lou Klein	R	58	114	25	6	0	2	1.8	25	12	22	20	0	18	3	.219	.325
2B	Solly Hemus	L	20	33	11	1	0	0	0.0	8	2	7	3	0	2	0	.333	.364
1B	Steve Bilko	R	6	17	5	2	0	0	0.0	3	2	5	6	0	1	0	.294	.412
3B	Whitey Kurowski	R	10	14	2	0	0	0	0.0	0	0	1	0	0	8	2	.143	.143
OF	Ron Northey	L	90	265	69	18	2	7	2.6	28	50	31	15	0	12	0	.260	.423
OF	Hal Rice	R	40	46	9	2	1	1	2.2	3	9	3	7	0	27	6	.196	.348
OF	Ed Sauer	R	24	45	10	2	1	0	0.0	5	1	3	8	0	11	1	.222	.311
OF	Bill Howerton	L	9	13	4	1	0	0	0.0	1	1	0	2	0	3	1	.308	.385
C	Joe Garagiola	L	81	241	63	14	0	3	1.2	25	26	31	19	0	2	1	.261	.357
C	Bill Baker	R	20	30	4	1	0	0	0.0	2	4	2	2	0	10	0	.133	.167
C	Del Wilber	R	2	4	1	0	0	0	0.0	0	0	0	0	0	0	0	.250	.250
PH	Russ Derry	L	2	2	0	0	0	0	0.0	0	0	0	2	0	2	0	.000	.000
PH	Erv Dusak	R	1	0	0	0	0	0	–	1	0	0	0	0	0	0	–	–
PITCHERS																		
P	Al Brazle	L	39	82	11	0	0	0	0.0	7	2	0	6	0	0	0	.134	.134
P	Howie Pollet	L	39	82	16	1	0	0	0.0	10	6	8	18	0	0	0	.195	.207
P	Harry Brecheen	L	32	77	21	3	1	0	0.0	8	6	4	14	0	0	0	.273	.338
P	George Munger	R	35	66	17	2	0	1	1.5	6	10	4	16	0	0	0	.258	.333
P	Gerry Staley	R	45	41	5	0	0	0	0.0	5	0	7	12	0	0	0	.122	.122
P	Max Lanier	R	15	27	2	0	0	0	0.0	1	1	3	1	0	0	0	.074	.074
P	Ted Wilks	R	59	27	1	0	0	0	0.0	0	1	1	15	0	0	0	.037	.037
P	Freddie Martin	R	21	20	6	0	0	0	0.0	2	2	0	3	0	0	0	.300	.300
P	Jim Hearn	R	17	10	1	0	0	0	0.0	1	1	1	3	0	0	0	.100	.100
P	Ken Johnson	L	21	8	2	1	0	0	0.0	3	2	0	1	0	0	0	.250	.375
P	Bill Reeder	R	21	3	0	0	0	0	0.0	0	0	0	1	0	0	0	.000	.000
P	Cloyd Boyer	R	4	0	0	0	0	0	–	0	0	0	0	0	0	0	–	–
P	Kurt Krieger	R	1	0	0	0	0	0	–	0	0	0	0	0	0	0	–	–
P	Ray Yochim	R	3	0	0	0	0	0	–	0	0	0	0	0	0	0	–	–
TEAM TOTAL				5463	1513	281	54	102	1.9	766	720	569	482	17	132	24	.277	.404

INDIVIDUAL FIELDING

POS	Player	T	G	PO	A	E	DP	TC/G	FA	POS	Player	T	G	PO	A	E	DP	TC/G	FA
1B	N. Jones	R	98	876	40	15	85	9.5	.984	OF	E. Slaughter	R	150	330	10	6	1	2.3	.983
	R. Nelson	L	70	564	24	0	48	8.4	1.000		S. Musial	L	156	326	10	3	5	2.2	.991
	S. Bilko	R	5	42	3	0	1	9.0	1.000		C. Diering	R	124	300	7	4	1	2.5	.987
	S. Musial	L	1	11	1	0	0	12.0	1.000		R. Northey	R	73	93	4	2	2	1.4	.980
2B	Schoendienst	R	138	399	424	11	105	6.0	.987		E. Sauer	R	10	12	1	0	0	1.3	1.000
	S. Hemus	R	16	29	24	1	4	3.4	.981		B. Howerton	R	6	9	0	1	0	1.7	.900
	L. Klein	R	9	14	13	0	3	3.0	1.000		H. Rice	R	10	8	1	0	0	0.9	1.000
	E. Kazak	R	5	10	12	4	2	5.2	.846		Schoendienst	R	2	4	0	1	0	2.5	.800
	T. Glaviano	R	7	14	9	1	3	3.4	.958	C	D. Rice	R	92	355	29	3	4	4.2	.992
SS	M. Marion	R	134	242	441	17	74	5.2	.976		J. Garagiola	R	80	332	35	6	1	4.7	.984
	L. Klein	R	21	17	64	10	7	4.3	.890		B. Baker	R	10	16	1	0	1	1.7	1.000
	Schoendienst	R	14	21	33	2	5	4.0	.964		D. Wilber	R	2	5	1	0	0	3.0	1.000
3B	T. Glaviano	R	73	67	181	19	15	3.7	.929										
	E. Kazak	R	80	64	175	19	20	3.2	.926										
	Schoendienst	R	6	4	14	2	0	3.3	.900										
	L. Klein	R	7	2	8	1	0	1.6	.909										
	W. Kurowski	R	2	3	2	0	0	2.5	1.000										

Both leagues produced dazzling pennant races in 1949, each one decided by a one-game margin. On September 21, the Cards led the Dodgers by one and a half games as the two clubs began a three-game set. The Cardinals won the first game 1–0, but the Dodgers returned the favor with a 5–0 win, and blasted the Redbirds in the rubber game by 19–6 to pull within a half-game. St. Louis then took two from Chicago, but lost four straight on the road to the Pirates and Cubs to give the Dodgers the lead. It all came down to the last day. The Cards won their game in Chicago, but the Dodgers eked out a 10-inning win over the Phils for the title. The Cardinal pitching staff gave up the fewest runs in the league, rebounding from its disappointing '48 season with very little change in personnel. The most dramatic change was in Howie Pollett's record, as he went from 13–8 with a 4.54 ERA to 20–9 and 2.77.

TEAM STATISTICS

	W	L	PCT	GB	R	OR	2B	3B	HR	BA	SA	SB	E	DP	FA	CG	BB	SO	ShO	SV	ERA
BKN	97	57	.630		879	651	236	47	152	.274	.419	117	122	162	.980	62	582	743	15	17	3.80
STL	96	58	.623	1	766	616	281	54	102	.277	.404	17	146	149	.976	64	506	606	13	19	3.45
PHI	81	73	.526	16	662	668	232	55	122	.254	.388	27	156	141	.974	58	502	495	12	15	3.89
BOS	75	79	.487	22	706	719	246	33	103	.258	.374	28	148	144	.976	68	520	591	12	11	3.99
NY	73	81	.474	24	736	693	203	52	147	.261	.401	43	161	134	.973	68	544	516	10	9	3.82
PIT	71	83	.461	26	681	760	191	41	126	.259	.384	48	132	173	.978	53	535	556	9	15	4.57
CIN	62	92	.403	35	627	770	264	35	86	.260	.368	31	138	150	.977	55	640	538	10	6	4.33
CHI	61	93	.396	36	593	773	212	53	97	.256	.373	53	186	160	.970	44	564	532	8	17	4.50
LEAGUE TOTAL					5650	5650	1865	370	935	.262	.389	364	1189	1213	.975	472	4393	4577	89	109	4.04

INDIVIDUAL PITCHING

PITCHER	T	W	L	PCT	ERA	SV	G	GS	CG	IP	H	BB	SO	R	ER	ShO	H/9	BB/9	SO/9
Howie Pollet	L	20	9	.690	2.77	1	39	28	17	230.2	228	59	108	80	71	5	8.90	2.30	4.21
Harry Brecheen	L	14	11	.560	3.35	1	32	31	14	214.2	207	65	88	96	80	2	8.68	2.73	3.69
Al Brazle	L	14	8	.636	3.18	0	39	25	9	206.1	208	61	75	85	73	1	9.07	2.66	3.27
George Munger	R	15	8	.652	3.87	2	35	28	12	188.1	179	87	82	86	81	2	8.55	4.16	3.92
Gerry Staley	R	10	10	.500	2.73	6	45	17	5	171.1	154	41	55	65	52	2	8.09	2.15	2.89
Ted Wilks	R	10	3	.769	3.73	9	59	0	0	118.1	105	38	71	52	49	0	7.99	2.89	5.40
Max Lanier	L	5	4	.556	3.82	0	15	15	4	92	92	35	37	42	39	1	9.00	3.42	3.62
Freddie Martin	R	6	0	1.000	2.44	0	21	5	3	70	65	20	30	24	19	0	8.36	2.57	3.86
Jim Hearn	R	1	3	.250	5.14	0	17	4	0	42	48	23	18	27	24	0	10.29	4.93	3.86
Ken Johnson	L	0	1	.000	6.42	0	14	2	0	33.2	29	35	18	28	24	0	7.75	9.36	4.81
Bill Reeder	R	1	1	.500	5.08	0	21	1	0	33.2	33	30	21	22	19	0	8.82	8.02	5.61
Cloyd Boyer	R	0	0	–	10.80	0	3	1	0	3.1	5	7	0	4	4	0	13.50	18.90	0.00
Ray Yochim	R	0	0	–	15.43	0	3	0	0	2.1	3	4	3	4	4	0	11.57	15.43	11.57
Kurt Krieger	R	0	0	–	0.00	0	1	0	0	1	0	1	0	0	0	0	0.00	9.00	0.00
TEAM TOTAL		96	58	.623	3.45	19	344	157	64	1407.2	1356	506	606	615	539	13	8.67	3.24	3.87

MANAGER	W	L	PCT
Eddie Dyer	78	75	.510

POS	Player	B	G	AB	H	2B	3B	HR	HR %	R	RBI	BB	SO	SB	Pinch Hit AB	Pinch Hit H	BA	SA
REGULARS																		
1B	Stan Musial	L	146	555	192	41	7	28	5.0	105	109	87	36	5	1	0	.346	.596
2B	Red Schoendienst	B	153	642	177	43	9	7	1.1	81	63	33	32	3	0	0	.276	.403
SS	Marty Marion	R	106	372	92	10	2	4	1.1	36	40	44	55	1	5	1	.247	.317
3B	Tommy Glaviano	R	115	410	117	29	2	11	2.7	92	44	90	74	6	4	0	.285	.446
RF	Enos Slaughter	L	148	556	161	26	7	10	1.8	82	101	66	33	3	3	2	.290	.415
CF	Chuck Diering	R	89	204	51	12	0	3	1.5	34	18	35	38	1	0	0	.250	.353
LF	Bill Howerton	L	110	313	88	20	8	10	3.2	50	59	47	60	0	17	5	.281	.492
C	Del Rice	R	130	414	101	20	3	9	2.2	39	54	43	65	0	0	0	.244	.372
SUBSTITUTES																		
1B	Rocky Nelson	L	76	235	58	10	4	1	0.4	27	20	26	9	4	4	1	.247	.336
3B	Eddie Kazak	R	93	207	53	2	2	5	2.4	21	23	18	19	0	42	10	.256	.357
SS	Eddie Miller	R	64	172	39	8	0	3	1.7	17	22	19	21	0	11	1	.227	.326
UT	Peanuts Lowrey	R	17	56	15	0	0	1	1.8	10	4	6	1	0	1	0	.268	.321
1B	Steve Bilko	R	10	33	6	1	0	0	0.0	1	2	4	10	0	1	1	.182	.212
1B	Nippy Jones	R	13	26	6	1	0	0	0.0	0	6	3	1	0	4	2	.231	.269
3B	Solly Hemus	L	11	15	2	1	0	0	0.0	1	0	2	4	0	5	0	.133	.200
1B	Don Bollweg	L	4	11	2	0	0	0	0.0	1	1	1	1	0	0	0	.182	.182
1B	Ed Mickelson	R	5	10	1	0	0	0	0.0	1	0	2	3	0	1	0	.100	.100
OF	Harry Walker	L	60	150	31	5	0	0	0.0	17	7	18	12	0	6	0	.207	.240
OF	Hal Rice	L	44	128	27	3	1	2	1.6	12	11	10	10	0	6	1	.211	.297
OF	Johnny Lindell	R	36	113	21	5	2	5	4.4	16	16	15	24	0	3	0	.186	.398
OF	Johnny Blatnik	R	7	20	3	0	0	0	0.0	0	1	3	2	0	1	0	.150	.150
C	Joe Garagiola	L	34	88	28	6	1	2	2.3	8	20	10	7	0	4	0	.318	.477
C	Johnny Bucha	R	22	36	5	1	0	0	0.0	1	1	4	7	0	5	2	.139	.167
PH	Danny Gardella	L	1	1	0	0	0	0	0.0	0	0	0	0	0	1	0	.000	.000
PH	Ed Mierkowicz	R	1	1	0	0	0	0	0.0	0	0	0	1	0	1	0	.000	.000
PITCHERS																		
P	Howie Pollet	L	38	84	12	2	0	0	0.0	7	3	5	18	0	0	0	.143	.167
P	Max Lanier	R	27	68	11	1	1	0	0.0	5	10	3	10	0	0	0	.162	.206
P	Al Brazle	L	47	61	13	0	0	0	0.0	6	5	0	8	0	0	0	.213	.213
P	Harry Brecheen	L	27	58	14	0	1	1	1.7	8	2	5	6	0	0	0	.241	.328
P	Gerry Staley	R	42	55	8	2	0	0	0.0	5	0	3	9	0	0	0	.145	.182
P	George Munger	R	32	51	7	1	0	0	0.0	4	1	2	10	0	0	0	.137	.157
P	Cloyd Boyer	R	36	33	6	2	0	0	0.0	3	1	2	8	0	0	0	.182	.242
P	Freddie Martin	R	31	15	4	2	0	0	0.0	2	2	0	5	0	0	0	.267	.400
P	Erv Dusak	R	23	12	1	1	0	0	0.0	0	0	0	3	0	0	0	.083	.167
P	Ted Wilks	R	18	4	0	0	0	0	0.0	0	0	0	1	0	0	0	.000	.000
P	Al Papai	R	13	3	0	0	0	0	0.0	0	0	0	1	0	0	0	.000	.000
P	Tom Poholsky	R	5	2	0	0	0	0	0.0	0	0	0	0	0	0	0	.000	.000
P	Jim Hearn	R	6	1	1	0	0	0	0.0	1	0	0	0	0	0	0	1.000	1.000
P	Cot Deal	B	3	0	0	0	0	0	–	0	0	0	0	0	0	0	–	–
P	Ken Johnson	L	2	0	0	0	0	0	–	0	0	0	0	0	0	0	–	–
	TEAM TOTAL			5215	1353	255	50	102	2.0	693	646	606	604	23	126	26	.259	.386

INDIVIDUAL FIELDING

POS	Player	T	G	PO	A	E	DP	TC/G	FA
1B	S. Musial	L	69	628	37	3	66	9.7	.996
	R. Nelson	L	70	596	51	5	66	9.3	.992
	S. Bilko	R	9	81	7	1	8	9.9	.989
	N. Jones	R	8	54	3	1	8	7.3	.983
	E. Mickelson	R	4	36	4	0	1	10.0	1.000
	D. Bollweg	L	4	26	0	0	3	6.5	1.000
	H. Walker	R	2	10	0	0	1	5.0	1.000
2B	Schoendienst	R	143	393	403	12	124	5.7	.985
	P. Lowrey	R	6	21	16	0	4	6.2	1.000
	T. Glaviano	R	5	15	13	0	4	5.6	1.000
	E. Miller	R	1	3	3	0	2	6.0	1.000
SS	M. Marion	R	101	180	313	11	73	5.0	.978
	E. Miller	R	51	72	173	5	29	4.9	.980
	Schoendienst	R	10	30	33	2	10	6.5	.969
	T. Glaviano	R	1	1	1	0	1	2.0	1.000
3B	T. Glaviano	R	106	103	255	25	16	3.6	.935
	E. Kazak	R	48	36	95	9	7	2.9	.936
	P. Lowrey	R	5	5	15	1	2	4.2	.952
	S. Hemus	R	5	2	8	0	1	2.0	1.000
	Schoendienst	R	1	2	1	0	0	3.0	1.000

POS	Player	T	G	PO	A	E	DP	TC/G	FA
OF	E. Slaughter	R	145	260	9	6	1	1.9	.978
	B. Howerton	R	94	183	2	6	0	2.0	.969
	C. Diering	R	81	178	8	2	2	2.3	.989
	S. Musial	L	77	132	2	5	1	1.8	.964
	H. Walker	R	46	92	3	3	0	2.1	.969
	H. Rice	R	37	67	3	2	0	1.9	.972
	J. Lindell	R	33	61	1	1	1	1.9	.984
	J. Blatnik	R	7	6	1	1	0	1.1	.875
	P. Lowrey	R	4	5	0	1	1	1.5	.833
	E. Dusak	R	2	5	0	0	0	2.5	1.000
C	D. Rice	R	130	572	63	10	12	5.0	.984
	J. Garagiola	R	30	99	8	0	2	3.6	1.000
	J. Bucha	R	17	42	5	2	0	2.9	.959

The decade of the 1950s did not start well for the Cardinals. While they were just a half-game behind the front-running Phillies in July, they faded badly and wound up in fifth place, just three games over .500. They had not finished in the second division since 1938, and there were more bad times to come. Musial continued his habit of leading the league in batting and slugging in even-numbered years; he would accomplish this in '46, '48, '50, and '52, with '43 thrown in for good measure. (His career record shows all five as alternate seasons, since he missed the 1945 season when he was in the service.) Another St. Louis institution played his last game for the Cardinals in 1950: it was announced that Marty Marion, five-time All-Star shortstop and the league MVP in 1944, would succeed Eddie Dyer as nonplaying manager for the '51 season.

TEAM STATISTICS

	W	L	PCT	GB	R	OR	2B	3B	Batting HR	BA	SA	SB	E	Fielding DP	FA	CG	BB	Pitching SO	ShO	SV	ERA
HI	91	63	.591		722	624	225	55	125	.265	.396	33	151	155	.975	57	530	620	13	27	3.50
KN	89	65	.578	2	847	724	247	46	194	.272	.444	77	127	183	.979	62	591	772	10	21	4.28
NY	86	68	.558	5	735	643	204	50	133	.258	.392	42	137	181	.977	70	536	596	19	15	3.71
OS	83	71	.539	8	785	736	246	36	148	.263	.405	71	182	146	.970	88	554	615	7	10	4.14
TL	78	75	.510	12.5	693	670	255	50	102	.259	.386	23	130	172	.978	57	535	603	10	14	3.97
IN	66	87	.431	24.5	654	734	257	27	99	.260	.376	37	140	132	.976	67	582	686	7	13	4.32
HI	64	89	.418	26.5	643	772	224	47	161	.248	.401	46	201	169	.968	55	593	559	9	19	4.28
IT	57	96	.373	33.5	681	857	227	59	138	.264	.406	43	136	165	.977	42	616	556	6	16	4.96
LEAGUE TOTAL					5760	5760	1885	370	1100	.261	.401	372	1204	1303	.975	498	4537	5007	81	135	4.14

INDIVIDUAL PITCHING

PITCHER	T	W	L	PCT	ERA	SV	G	GS	CG	IP	H	BB	SO	R	ER	ShO	H/9	BB/9	SO/9
owie Pollet	L	14	13	.519	3.29	2	37	30	14	232.1	228	68	117	103	85	2	8.83	2.63	4.53
ax Lanier	L	11	9	.550	3.13	0	27	27	10	181.1	173	68	89	70	63	2	8.59	3.38	4.42
erry Staley	R	13	13	.500	4.99	3	42	22	7	169.2	201	61	62	101	94	1	10.66	3.24	3.29
Brazle	L	11	9	.550	4.10	6	46	12	3	164.2	188	80	47	81	75	0	10.28	4.37	2.57
arry Brecheen	L	8	11	.421	3.80	1	27	23	12	163.1	151	45	80	77	69	2	8.32	2.48	4.41
eorge Munger	R	7	8	.467	3.90	0	32	20	5	154.2	158	70	61	73	67	1	9.19	4.07	3.55
loyd Boyer	R	7	7	.500	3.52	1	36	14	6	120.1	105	49	82	52	47	2	7.85	3.66	6.13
eddie Martin	R	4	2	.667	5.12	0	30	2	0	63.1	87	30	19	43	36	0	12.36	4.26	2.70
v Dusak	R	0	2	.000	3.72	1	14	2	0	36.1	27	27	16	17	15	0	6.69	6.69	3.96
d Wilks	R	2	0	1.000	6.66	0	18	0	0	24.1	27	9	15	18	18	0	9.99	3.33	5.55
Papai	R	1	0	1.000	5.21	0	13	0	0	19	21	14	7	12	11	0	9.95	6.63	3.32
m Poholsky	R	0	0	–	3.68	0	5	1	0	14.2	16	3	2	6	6	0	9.82	1.84	1.23
n Hearn	R	0	1	.000	10.00*	0	6	0	0	9	12	6	4	11	10	0*	12.00*	6.00	4.00
en Johnson	L	0	0	–	0.00	0	2	0	0	2	1	3	1	1	0	0	4.50	13.50	4.50
ot Deal	R	0	0	–	18.00	0	3	0	0	1	3	2	1	5	2	0	27.00	18.00	9.00
EAM TOTAL		78	75	.510	3.97	14	338	153	57	1356	1398	535	603	670	598	10	9.28	3.55	4.00

MANAGER	W	L	PCT
Marty Marion	81	73	.526

POS	Player	B	G	AB	H	2B	3B	HR	HR %	R	RBI	BB	SO	SB	Pinch Hit AB	Pinch Hit H	BA	SA
REGULARS																		
1B	Nippy Jones	R	80	300	79	12	0	3	1.0	20	41	9	13	1	9	1	.263	.333
2B	Red Schoendienst	B	135	553	160	32	7	6	1.1	88	54	35	23	0	1	1	.289	.405
SS	Solly Hemus	L	128	420	118	18	9	2	0.5	68	32	75	31	7	4	0	.281	.381
3B	Billy Johnson	R	124	442	116	23	1	14	3.2	52	64	46	49	5	0	0	.262	.414
RF	Enos Slaughter	L	123	409	115	17	8	4	1.0	48	64	68	25	7	11	2	.281	.391
CF	Peanuts Lowrey	R	114	370	112	19	5	5	1.4	52	40	35	12	0	19	5	.303	.422
LF	Stan Musial	L	152	578	205	30	12	32	5.5	124	108	98	40	4	1	1	.355	.614
C	Del Rice	R	122	374	94	13	1	9	2.4	34	47	34	26	0	3	0	.251	.364
SUBSTITUTES																		
SS	Stan Rojek	R	51	186	51	7	3	0	0.0	21	14	10	10	0	0	0	.274	.344
1B	Steve Bilko	R	21	72	16	4	0	2	2.8	5	12	9	10	0	2	1	.222	.361
3O	Vern Benson	L	13	46	12	3	1	1	2.2	8	7	6	8	0	0	0	.261	.435
2B	Dick Cole	R	15	36	7	1	0	0	0.0	4	3	6	5	0	0	0	.194	.222
3B	Don Richmond	L	12	34	3	1	0	1	2.9	3	4	3	3	0	0	0	.088	.206
3B	Eddie Kazak	R	11	33	6	2	0	0	0.0	2	4	5	5	0	1	0	.182	.242
1B	Rocky Nelson	L	9	18	4	1	0	0	0.0	3	1	1	0	0	5	1	.222	.278
1B	Don Bollweg	L	6	9	1	1	0	0	0.0	1	2	0	1	0	4	1	.111	.222
OF	Wally Westlake	R	73	267	68	8	5	6	2.2	36	39	24	42	1	4	0	.255	.390
OF	Hal Rice	L	69	236	60	12	1	4	1.7	20	38	24	22	0	5	1	.254	.364
O2	Tommy Glaviano	R	54	104	19	4	0	1	1.0	20	4	26	18	3	23	4	.183	.250
OF	Chuck Diering	R	64	85	22	5	1	0	0.0	9	8	6	15	0	8	3	.259	.341
OF	Bill Howerton	R	24	65	17	4	1	1	1.5	10	4	10	12	0	7	1	.262	.400
OF	Harry Walker	L	8	26	8	1	0	0	0.0	6	2	2	1	0	0	0	.308	.346
OF	Jay Van Noy	L	6	7	0	0	0	0	0.0	1	0	1	6	0	4	0	.000	.000
OF	Larry Ciaffone	R	5	5	0	0	0	0	0.0	0	0	1	2	0	3	0	.000	.000
C	Bill Sarni	R	36	86	15	1	0	0	0.0	7	2	9	13	1	1	0	.174	.186
C	Joe Garagiola	L	27	72	14	3	2	2	2.8	9	9	9	7	0	3	0	.194	.375
C	Bob Scheffing	R	12	18	2	0	0	0	0.0	0	2	3	5	0	2	0	.111	.111
PITCHERS																		
P	Gerry Staley	R	42	81	13	1	0	0	0.0	3	5	3	14	0	0	0	.160	.173
P	Tom Poholsky	R	38	67	14	1	0	0	0.0	5	3	1	14	1	0	0	.209	.224
P	Harry Brecheen	L	24	55	12	2	0	1	1.8	4	3	0	11	0	0	0	.218	.309
P	Max Lanier	R	31	53	8	0	0	0	0.0	2	1	1	5	0	0	0	.151	.151
P	Cliff Chambers	L	21	49	8	1	0	0	0.0	3	4	2	13	0	0	0	.163	.184
P	Al Brazle	L	56	46	5	0	0	0	0.0	1	2	0	2	0	0	0	.109	.109
P	Joe Presko	R	15	37	6	1	0	0	0.0	2	1	0	5	0	0	0	.162	.189
P	George Munger	R	23	29	5	1	0	0	0.0	2	2	1	4	0	0	0	.172	.207
P	Cloyd Boyer	R	19	20	4	1	0	0	0.0	5	2	0	9	0	0	0	.200	.250
P	Dick Bokelmann	R	20	14	0	0	0	0	0.0	0	2	0	6	0	0	0	.000	.000
P	Jackie Collum	L	3	7	3	0	0	0	0.0	0	0	0	1	0	0	0	.429	.429
P	Jack Crimian	R	11	3	1	0	0	0	0.0	0	0	0	0	0	0	0	.333	.333
P	Erv Dusak	R	5	2	1	0	0	1	50.0	1	1	0	1	0	0	0	.500	2.000
P	Bob Habenicht	R	3	1	0	0	0	0	0.0	1	0	0	1	0	0	0	.000	.000
P	Howie Pollet	L	6	1	0	0	0	0	0.0	0	0	3	1	0	0	0	.000	.000
P	Ted Wilks	R	17	1	0	0	0	0	0.0	0	0	0	1	0	0	0	.000	.000
P	Kurt Krieger	R	2	0	0	0	0	0	–	0	0	0	0	0	0	0	–	–
P	Dan Lewandowski	R	2	0	0	0	0	0	–	0	0	0	0	0	0	0	–	–
TEAM TOTAL			.	5317	1404	230	57	95	1.8	683	629	569	492	30	120	22	.264	.382

INDIVIDUAL FIELDING

POS	Player	T	G	PO	A	E	DP	TC/G	FA	POS	Player	T	G	PO	A	E	DP	TC/G	FA
1B	N. Jones	R	71	698	48	7	7	10.6	.991	OF	S. Musial	L	91	216	13	6	4	2.6	.974
	S. Musial	L	60	600	32	4	60	10.6	.994		P. Lowrey	R	85	220	6	4	3	2.7	.983
	S. Bilko	R	19	170	13	3	18	9.8	.984		E. Slaughter	R	106	198	10	1	3	2.0	.995
	R. Nelson	R	4	29	1	0	5	7.5	1.000		W. Westlake	R	68	154	7	3	1	2.4	.982
	D. Bollweg	L	2	16	0	1	2	8.5	.941		H. Rice	R	63	116	6	6	0	2.0	.953
	H. Walker	R	1	10	1	0	2	11.0	1.000		C. Diering	R	44	67	3	0	0	1.6	1.000
											B. Howerton	R	17	35	2	2	1	2.3	.949
2B	Schoendienst	R	124	339	386	7	113	5.9	.990		T. Glaviano	R	35	35	0	1	0	1.0	.972
	S. Hemus	R	12	40	32	2	14	6.2	.973		R. Nelson	L	1	0	0	0	0	0.0	.000
	D. Cole	R	14	21	41	2	10	4.6	.969		V. Benson	R	4	9	1	1	0	2.8	.909
	T. Glaviano	R	9	18	25	1	6	4.9	.977		H. Walker	R	6	10	0	0	0	1.7	1.000
	P. Lowrey	R	3	5	1	0	0	2.0	1.000		J. Van Noy	R	1	2	0	0	0	2.0	1.000
											L. Ciaffone	R	1	1	0	0	0	1.0	1.000
SS	S. Hemus	R	105	181	344	19	72	5.2	.965										
	S. Rojek	R	51	95	131	6	36	4.5	.974	C	D. Rice	R	120	447	66	8	12	4.3	.985
	Schoendienst	R	8	15	33	3	7	6.4	.941		B. Sarni	R	35	107	13	2	3	3.5	.984
3B	B. Johnson	R	124	99	316	10	32	3.4	.976		J. Garagiola	R	23	81	6	0	2	3.8	1.000
	D. Richmond	R	11	14	28	0	3	3.8	1.000		B. Scheffing	R	11	32	2	0	0	3.1	1.000
	E. Kazak	R	10	11	17	2	1	3.0	.933										
	P. Lowrey	R	11	5	18	5	2	2.5	.821										
	V. Benson	R	9	1	18	1	3	2.2	.950										

While the Giants and Dodgers fought out their epic pennant duel, capped by Bobby Thomson's homer, Marty Marion quietly brought the Cardinals into third place with a club that ranked fifth in runs and runs allowed, fifth in slugging, sixth in ERA, and seventh in home runs. As would be true so often through the '50s, their one main asset was Musial, who won his fifth batting title and led the league in triples for the fifth time. Owner Fred Saigh wasn't satisfied with the club's performance, however. Baseball tradition calls for firing the manager in such cases, and Saigh acted, trading Max Lanier and Chuck Diering to the Giants for Eddie Stanky, who became manager for the '52 season. Marion joined a parade of Cardinal greats that included such stars as Brecheen, Lanier, and Hornsby who went to work in the carnival atmosphere of Bill Veeck's Browns. It was a world of fireworks, giveaways, and a midget pinch-hitter named Eddie Gaedel.

TEAM STATISTICS

	W	L	PCT	GB	R	OR	2B	3B	HR	BA	SA	SB	E	DP	FA	CG	BB	SO	ShO	SV	ERA
								Batting						Fielding				Pitching			
'Y	98	59	.624		781	641	201	53	179	.260	.418	55	171	175	.972	64	482	625	9	18	3.48
KN	97	60	.618	1	855	672	249	37	184	.275	.434	89	129	192	.979	64	549	693	10	13	3.88
TL	81	73	.526	15.5	683	671	230	37	95	.264	.382	30	125	187	.980	58	568	546	9	23	3.95
OS	76	78	.494	20.5	723	662	234	37	130	.262	.394	78	145	157	.976	73	595	604	10	12	3.75
HI	73	81	.474	23.5	648	644	199	47	108	.260	.375	64	138	146	.977	57	496	570	19	15	3.81
IN	68	86	.442	28.5	559	667	215	33	88	.248	.351	44	140	141	.977	55	490	584	14	23	3.70
T	64	90	.416	32.5	689	845	218	56	137	.258	.397	26	170	178	.972	40	627	582	9	22	4.78
HI	62	92	.403	34.5	614	750	200	47	103	.250	.364	63	181	161	.971	48	572	544	10	10	4.34
AGUE TOTAL					5552	5552	1746	367	1024	.260	.390	449	1199	1337	.975	459	4379	4748	90	136	3.96

INDIVIDUAL PITCHING

TCHER	T	W	L	PCT	ERA	SV	G	GS	CG	IP	H	BB	SO	R	ER	ShO	H/9	BB/9	SO/9
erry Staley	R	19	13	.594	3.81	3	42	30	10	227	244	74	67	108	96	4	9.67	2.93	2.66
m Poholsky	R	7	13	.350	4.43	1	38	26	10	195	204	68	70	106	96	1	9.42	3.14	3.23
ax Lanier	L	11	9	.550	3.26	1	31	23	9	160	149	50	59	60	58	2	8.38	2.81	3.32
Brazle	L	6	5	.545	3.09	7	56	8	5	154.1	139	61	66	61	53	0	8.11	3.56	3.85
arry Brecheen	L	8	4	.667	3.25	2	24	16	5	138.2	134	54	57	54	50	0	8.70	3.50	3.70
iff Chambers	L	11	6	.647	3.83	0	21	16	9	129.1	120	56	45	59	55	1	8.35	3.90	3.13
eorge Munger	R	4	6	.400	5.32	0	23	11	3	94.2	106	46	44	58	56	0	10.08	4.37	4.18
e Presko	R	7	4	.636	3.45	2	15	12	5	88.2	86	20	38	36	34	0	8.73	2.03	3.86
oyd Boyer	R	2	5	.286	5.26	1	19	8	1	63.1	68	46	40	42	37	0	9.66	6.54	5.68
ck Bokelmann	R	3	3	.500	3.78	3	20	1	0	52.1	49	31	22	30	22	0	8.43	5.33	3.78
d Wilks	R	0	0	–	3.00	1*	17*	0	0	18	19	5	5	7	6	0	9.50	2.50	2.50
ckie Collum	L	2	1	.667	1.59	0	3	2	1	17	11	10	5	3	3	1	5.82	5.29	2.65
ck Crimian	R	1	0	1.000	9.00	0	11	0	0	17	24	8	5	17	17	0	12.71	4.24	2.65
wie Pollet	L	0	3	.000	4.38	1	6	2	0	12.1	10	8	10	10	6	0	7.30	5.84	7.30
y Dusak	R	0	0	–	7.20	0	5	0	0	10	14	7	8	8	8	0	12.60	6.30	7.20
b Habenicht	R	0	0	–	7.20	0	3	0	0	5	5	9	1	4	4	0	9.00	16.20	1.80
rt Krieger	R	0	0	–	15.75	0	2	0	0	4	6	5	3	7	7	0	13.50	11.25	6.75
n Lewandowski	R	0	1	.000	9.00	0	2	0	0	2	1	1	1	1	0	0	9.00	9.00	9.00
AM TOTAL		81	73	.526	3.95	23	338	155	58	1387.2	1389	559	546	671	609	9	9.01	3.63	3.54

MANAGER	W	L	PCT
Eddie Stanky	88	66	.571

POS	Player	B	G	AB	H	2B	3B	HR	HR %	R	RBI	BB	SO	SB	Pinch Hit AB	Pinch Hit H	BA	SA
REGULARS																		
1B	Dick Sisler	L	119	418	109	14	5	13	3.1	48	60	29	35	3	4	1	.261	.411
2B	Red Schoendienst	B	152	620	188	40	7	7	1.1	91	67	42	30	9	0	0	.303	.424
SS	Solly Hemus	L	151	570	153	28	8	15	2.6	105	52	96	55	1	1	0	.268	.425
3B	Billy Johnson	R	94	282	71	10	2	2	0.7	23	34	34	21	1	5	0	.252	.323
RF	Enos Slaughter	L	140	510	153	17	12	11	2.2	73	101	70	25	6	3	1	.300	.445
CF	Stan Musial	L	154	578	194	42	6	21	3.6	105	91	96	29	7	0	0	.336	.538
LF	Peanuts Lowrey	R	132	374	107	18	2	1	0.3	48	48	34	13	3	27	13	.286	.353
C	Del Rice	R	147	495	128	27	2	11	2.2	43	65	33	38	0	1	0	.259	.388
SUBSTITUTES																		
3B	Tommy Glaviano	R	80	162	39	5	1	3	1.9	30	19	27	26	0	10	2	.241	.340
2B	Eddie Stanky	R	53	83	19	4	0	0	0.0	13	7	19	9	0	26	9	.229	.277
1B	Steve Bilko	R	20	72	19	6	1	1	1.4	7	6	4	15	0	0	0	.264	.417
3B	Vern Benson	L	20	47	9	2	0	2	4.3	6	5	5	9	0	5	2	.191	.362
SS	Virgil Stallcup	R	29	31	4	1	0	0	0.0	4	1	1	5	0	13	3	.129	.161
1B	Neal Hertweck	L	2	6	0	0	0	0	0.0	0	0	1	1	0	0	0	.000	.000
SS	Gene Mauch	R	7	3	0	0	0	0	0.0	0	0	1	2	0	1	0	.000	.000
3B	Eddie Kazak	R	3	2	0	0	0	0	0.0	1	0	0	0	0	1	0	.000	.000
OF	Hal Rice	L	98	295	85	14	5	7	2.4	37	45	16	26	1	19	3	.288	.441
OF	Larry Miggins	R	42	96	22	5	1	2	2.1	7	10	3	19	0	16	4	.229	.365
OF	Wally Westlake	R	21	74	16	3	0	0	0.0	7	10	8	11	1	1	0	.216	.257
C	Les Fusselman	R	32	63	10	3	0	1	1.6	5	3	0	9	0	1	0	.159	.254
C	Bill Sarni	R	3	5	1	0	0	0	0.0	0	0	0	1	0	0	0	.200	.200
PH	Herb Gorman	L	1	1	0	0	0	0	0.0	0	0	0	0	0	1	0	.000	.000
PITCHERS																		
P	Gerry Staley	R	35	85	13	0	0	0	0.0	6	1	2	10	0	0	0	.153	.153
P	Vinegar Bend Mizell	R	30	68	3	1	1	0	0.0	2	1	0	31	0	0	0	.044	.088
P	Joe Presko	R	28	43	4	0	0	0	0.0	1	1	2	14	0	0	0	.093	.093
P	Cloyd Boyer	R	24	38	8	2	1	0	0.0	2	5	2	8	0	0	0	.211	.316
P	Al Brazle	L	46	32	4	1	0	0	0.0	1	3	0	2	0	0	0	.125	.156
P	Cliff Chambers	L	26	32	9	3	0	0	0.0	4	1	3	8	0	0	0	.281	.375
P	Harry Brecheen	L	25	29	6	0	0	0	0.0	3	1	4	5	0	0	0	.207	.207
P	Stu Miller	R	12	25	3	0	0	0	0.0	0	3	1	3	0	0	0	.120	.120
P	Eddie Yuhas	R	54	21	4	1	0	0	0.0	0	1	2	6	0	0	0	.190	.238
P	Harvey Haddix	L	9	14	3	0	0	0	0.0	3	2	1	5	1	0	0	.214	.214
P	Bill Werle	L	19	9	1	0	0	0	0.0	1	0	0	3	0	0	0	.111	.111
P	Willard Schmidt	R	18	8	1	0	0	0	0.0	0	0	0	1	0	0	0	.125	.125
P	Mike Clark	R	12	5	0	0	0	0	0.0	0	0	0	3	0	0	0	.000	.000
P	George Munger	R	1	2	0	0	0	0	0.0	0	0	0	0	0	0	0	.000	.000
P	Jack Crimian	R	5	1	0	0	0	0	0.0	0	0	1	1	0	0	0	.000	.000
P	Bobby Tiefenauer	R	6	1	0	0	0	0	0.0	1	0	0	0	0	0	0	.000	.000
P	Dick Bokelmann	R	11	0	0	0	0	0	–	0	0	0	0	0	0	0	–	–
P	Jackie Collum	L	2	0	0	0	0	0	–	0	0	0	0	0	0	0	–	–
P	Fred Hahn	R	1	0	0	0	0	0	–	0	0	0	0	0	0	0	–	–
	TEAM TOTAL			5200	1386	247	54	97	1.9	677	643	537	479	33	135	38	.267	.391

INDIVIDUAL FIELDING

POS	Player	T	G	PO	A	E	DP	TC/G	FA	POS	Player	T	G	PO	A	E	DP	TC/G	FA
1B	D. Sisler	R	114	1022	84	17*	116	9.9	.985	OF	S. Musial	L	135	298	6	4	2	2.3	.987
	S. Musial	L	25	204	12	1	13	8.7	.995		E. Slaughter	R	137	250	11	3	3	1.9	.989
	S. Bilko	R	20	177	24	1	14	10.1	.995		P. Lowrey	R	106	174	3	4	1	1.7	.978
	N. Hertweck	R	2	20	1	0	4	10.5	1.000		H. Rice	R	81	132	5	4	0	1.7	.972
	L. Miggins	R	1	1	0	0	0	1.0	1.000		W. Westlake	R	20	60	3	0	0	3.2	1.000
											L. Miggins	R	25	29	0	1	0	1.2	.967
2B	Schoendienst	R	142	399	424	19	108	5.9	.977		H. Haddix	L	1	0	0	0	0	0.0	.000
	E. Stanky	R	20	41	44	0	9	4.3	1.000										
	T. Glaviano	R	1	1	0	0	0	1.0	1.000	C	D. Rice	R	147	677	81	6	8	5.2	.992
											L. Fusselman	R	32	97	11	1	1	3.4	.991
SS	S. Hemus	R	148	253	452	29	104	5.0	.960		B. Sarni	R	3	19	0	0	0	6.3	1.000
	V. Stallcup	R	12	5	16	0	4	1.8	1.000										
	Schoendienst	R	3	3	7	1	1	3.7	.909										
	G. Mauch	R	2	1	0	1	0	1.0	.500										
3B	B. Johnson	R	89	56	177	12	10	2.8	.951										
	T. Glaviano	R	52	46	95	10	5	2.9	.934										
	V. Benson	R	15	5	27	4	3	2.4	.889										
	Schoendienst	R	11	15	29	0	2	4.0	1.000										
	P. Lowrey	R	6	2	17	3	1	3.7	.864										
	S. Hemus	R	3	3	7	1	0	5.5	.909										
	E. Kazak	R	1	0	1	0	0	1.0	1.000										

Under new manager Eddie Stanky the Cards won 88 games in '52, their highest win total of the '50s. They led the league in batting average, but scored almost a hundred runs fewer than the pennant-winning Dodgers. Despite their won-lost record, they were never in the pennant race, not pulling within five games of first from May on. Like everyone else in the league, their won-lost record was padded by the efforts of the Pirates, whose 112 losses was the second-highest total in the National League since 1900, B.T.M. (before the Mets).

During the 1952 season Fred Saigh was indicted for income tax evasion and was forced to sell the club. According to later reports, he met with a group of investors from Houston who may have wanted to move the club, but it was eventually bought by Anheuser-Busch, and August A. Busch, Jr., took over as club president in February 1953.

TEAM STATISTICS

	W	L	PCT	GB	R	OR	Batting						Fielding			CG	BB	Pitching			
							2B	3B	HR	BA	SA	SB	E	DP	FA			SO	ShO	SV	ERA
KN	96	57	.627		775	603	199	32	153	.262	.399	90	106	169	.982	45	544	773	11	24	3.53
Y	92	62	.597	4.5	722	639	186	56	151	.256	.399	30	158	175	.974	49	538	655	11	31	3.59
TL	88	66	.571	8.5	677	630	247	54	97	.267	.391	33	141	159	.977	49	501	712	11	27	3.66
HI	87	67	.565	9.5	657	552	237	45	93	.260	.376	60	150	145	.975	80	373	609	16	16	3.07
HI	77	77	.500	19.5	628	631	223	45	107	.264	.383	50	146	123	.976	59	534	661	15	15	3.58
N	69	85	.448	27.5	615	659	212	45	104	.249	.366	32	107	145	.982	56	517	579	11	12	4.01
DS	64	89	.418	32	569	651	187	31	110	.233	.343	58	154	143	.975	63	525	687	11	13	3.78
T	42	112	.273	54.5	515	793	181	30	92	.231	.331	43	182	167	.970	43	615	564	4	8	4.65
AGUE TOTAL					5158	5158	1672	338	907	.253	.374	396	1144	1226	.976	444	4147	5240	90	146	3.73

INDIVIDUAL PITCHING

TCHER	T	W	L	PCT	ERA	SV	G	GS	CG	IP	H	BB	SO	R	ER	ShO	H/9	BB/9	SO/9
rry Staley	R	17	14	.548	3.27	0	35	33	15	239.2	238	52	93	101	87	0	8.94	1.95	3.49
negar Bend Mizell	L	10	8	.556	3.65	0	30	30	7	190	171	103	146	89	77	2	8.10	4.88	6.92
e Presko	R	7	10	.412	4.05	0	28	18	5	146.2	140	57	63	74	66	1	8.59	3.50	3.87
oyd Boyer	R	6	6	.500	4.24	0	23	14	4	110.1	108	47	44	56	52	2	8.81	3.83	3.59
Brazle	L	12	5	.706	2.72	16	46	6	3	109.1	75	42	55	38	33	2	6.17	3.46	4.53
rry Brecheen	L	7	5	.583	3.32	2	25	13	4	100.1	82	28	54	39	37	1	7.36	2.51	4.84
die Yuhas	R	12	2	.857	2.72	6	54	2	0	99.1	90	35	39	35	30	0	8.15	3.17	3.53
ff Chambers	L	4	4	.500	4.12	1	26	13	2	98.1	110	33	47	51	45	1	10.07	3.02	4.30
J Miller	R	6	3	.667	2.05	0	12	11	6	88	63	26	64	25	20	2	6.44	2.66	6.55
rvey Haddix	L	2	2	.500	2.79	0	7	6	3	42	31	10	31	18	13	0	6.64	2.14	6.64
Werle	L	1	2	.333	4.85	1	19	0	0	39	40	15	23	23	21	0	9.23	3.46	5.31
lard Schmidt	R	2	3	.400	5.19	1	18	3	0	34.2	36	18	30	20	20	0	9.35	4.67	7.79
ke Clark	R	2	0	1.000	6.04	0	12	4	0	25.1	32	14	10	18	17	0	11.37	4.97	3.55
k Bokelmann	R	0	1	.000	9.24	0	11	0	0	12.2	20	7	5	17	13	0	14.21	4.97	3.55
ck Crimian	R	0	0	—	9.72	0	5	0	0	8.1	15	4	4	9	9	0	16.20	4.32	4.32
oby Tiefenauer	R	0	0	—	7.88	0	6	0	0	8	12	7	3	8	7	0	13.50	7.88	3.38
orge Munger	R	0	1	.000	12.46	0	1	1	0	4.1	7	1	1	6	6	0	14.54	2.08	2.08
kie Collum	L	0	0	—	0.00	0	2	0	0	3	2	1	0	1	0	0	6.00	3.00	0.00
d Hahn	L	0	0	—	0.00	0	1	0	0	2	2	1	0	2	0	0	9.00	4.50	0.00
AM TOTAL		88	66	.571	3.66	27	361	154	49	1361.1	1274	501	712	630	553	11	8.42	3.31	4.71

MANAGER	W	L	PCT
Eddie Stanky	83	71	.539

POS	Player	B	G	AB	H	2B	3B	HR	HR %	R	RBI	BB	SO	SB	Pinch Hit AB	Pinch Hit H	BA	SA
REGULARS																		
1B	Steve Bilko	R	154	570	143	23	3	21	3.7	72	84	70	125	0	0	0	.251	.412
2B	Red Schoendienst	B	146	564	193	35	5	15	2.7	107	79	60	23	3	6	4	.342	.502
SS	Solly Hemus	L	154	585	163	32	11	14	2.4	110	61	86	40	2	2	1	.279	.443
3B	Ray Jablonski	R	157	604	162	23	5	21	3.5	64	112	34	61	2	0	0	.268	.427
RF	Enos Slaughter	L	143	492	143	34	9	6	1.2	64	89	80	28	4	7	2	.291	.433
CF	Rip Repulski	R	153	567	156	25	4	15	2.6	75	66	33	71	3	0	0	.275	.413
LF	Stan Musial	L	157	593	200	53	9	30	5.1	127	113	105	32	3	0	0	.337	.609
C	Del Rice	R	135	419	99	22	1	6	1.4	32	37	48	49	0	0	0	.236	.337
SUBSTITUTES																		
3B	Pete Castiglione	R	67	52	9	2	0	0	0.0	9	3	2	5	0	7	3	.173	.212
1B	Dick Sisler	L	32	43	11	1	1	0	0.0	3	4	1	4	0	22	5	.256	.326
SS	Dick Schofield	B	33	39	7	0	0	2	5.1	9	4	2	11	0	1	0	.179	.333
2B	Eddie Stanky	R	17	30	8	0	0	0	0.0	5	1	6	4	0	5	0	.267	.267
3B	Billy Johnson	R	11	5	1	1	0	0	0.0	0	1	1	1	0	0	0	.200	.400
1B	Fred Marolewski	R	1	0	0	0	0	0	–	0	0	0	0	0	0	0	–	–
O2	Peanuts Lowrey	R	104	182	49	9	2	5	2.7	26	27	15	21	1	59	22	.269	.423
OF	Harry Elliott	R	24	59	15	6	1	1	1.7	6	6	3	8	0	6	0	.254	.441
OF	Grant Dunlap	R	16	17	6	0	1	1	5.9	2	3	0	2	0	15	5	.353	.647
C	Sal Yvars	R	30	57	14	2	0	1	1.8	4	6	4	6	0	6	1	.246	.333
C	Ferrell Anderson	R	18	35	10	2	0	0	0.0	1	1	0	4	0	7	0	.286	.343
C	Dick Rand	R	9	31	9	1	0	0	0.0	3	1	2	6	0	0	0	.290	.323
C	Les Fusselman	R	11	8	2	1	0	0	0.0	1	0	0	0	0	0	0	.250	.375
PH	Hal Rice	L	8	8	2	0	0	0	0.0	0	0	0	3	0	8	2	.250	.250
PH	Vern Benson	L	13	4	0	0	0	0	0.0	2	0	1	2	0	4	0	.000	.000
PH	Virgil Stallcup	R	1	1	0	0	0	0	0.0	0	0	0	0	0	1	0	.000	.000
PH	Ed Phillips	B	9	0	0	0	0	0	–	4	0	0	0	0	0	0	–	–
PITCHERS																		
P	Harvey Haddix	L	48	97	28	3	3	1	1.0	21	11	5	19	0	2	1	.289	.412
P	Vinegar Bend Mizell	R	33	83	7	1	1	1	1.2	4	8	3	42	0	0	0	.084	.157
P	Gerry Staley	R	40	78	8	0	0	0	0.0	4	2	4	21	0	0	0	.103	.103
P	Joe Presko	R	35	59	13	1	0	0	0.0	6	2	4	5	0	0	0	.220	.237
P	Stu Miller	R	42	43	8	2	0	0	0.0	4	1	3	2	0	0	0	.186	.233
P	Cliff Chambers	L	32	17	2	1	0	0	0.0	1	0	0	4	0	0	0	.118	.176
P	Hal White	L	49	16	0	0	0	0	0.0	0	0	1	8	0	0	0	.000	.000
P	Al Brazle	L	60	15	5	1	0	0	0.0	2	0	0	1	0	0	0	.333	.400
P	Mike Clark	R	23	6	0	0	0	0	0.0	0	0	0	1	0	0	0	.000	.000
P	Eddie Erautt	R	20	6	1	0	0	0	0.0	0	0	0	3	0	0	0	.167	.167
P	Willard Schmidt	R	6	4	0	0	0	0	0.0	0	0	0	2	0	0	0	.000	.000
P	Jackie Collum	L	7	3	0	0	0	0	0.0	0	0	1	0	0	0	0	.000	.000
P	Jack Faszholz	R	4	3	0	0	0	0	0.0	0	0	0	2	0	0	0	.000	.000
P	John Romonosky	R	2	2	0	0	0	0	0.0	0	0	0	1	0	0	0	.000	.000
P	Dick Bokelmann	R	3	0	0	0	0	0	–	0	0	0	0	0	0	0	–	–
P	Eddie Yuhas	R	2	0	0	0	0	0	–	0	0	0	0	0	0	0	–	–
	TEAM TOTAL			5397	1474	281	56	140	2.6	768	722	574	617	18	158	46	.273	.424

INDIVIDUAL FIELDING

POS	Player	T	G	PO	A	E	DP	TC/G	FA	POS	Player	T	G	PO	A	E	DP	TC/G	FA
1B	S. Bilko	R	154	**1446**	124	15	145	**10.3**	.991	OF	R. Repulski	R	153	361	7	5	1	2.4	.987
	F. Marolewski	R	1	0	0	0	0	0.0	.000		S. Musial	L	157	294	9	5	1	2.0	.984
	D. Sisler	R	10	42	6	0	5	4.8	1.000		E. Slaughter	R	137	235	2	1	0	1.7	**.996**
2B	Schoendienst	R	140	**365**	430	14	**109**	5.8	**.983**		P. Lowrey	R	38	42	1	0	0	1.1	1.000
	P. Lowrey	R	10	22	19	3	6	4.4	.932		H. Elliott	R	17	34	1	0	0	2.1	1.000
	E. Stanky	R	8	16	22	0	4	4.8	1.000		G. Dunlap	R	1	0	0	0	0	0.0	.000
	Castiglione	R	9	14	15	2	3	3.4	.935	C	D. Rice	R	135	627	60	8	6	5.1	.988
	S. Hemus	R	3	0	1	0	0	0.3	1.000		S. Yvars	R	26	76	12	1	3	3.4	.989
SS	S. Hemus	R	150	257	476	**27**	90	5.1	.964		D. Rand	R	9	56	7	1	0	7.1	.984
	D. Schofield	R	15	19	36	5	8	4.0	.917		F. Anderson	R	12	32	4	0	0	3.0	1.000
	Castiglione	R	3	3	7	1	1	3.7	.909		L. Fusselman	R	11	20	2	0	0	2.0	1.000
3B	R. Jablonski	R	157	94	278	27	27	2.5	.932										
	Castiglione	R	51	7	22	1	4	0.6	.967										
	P. Lowrey	R	1	0	0	0	0	0.0	.000										
	B. Johnson	R	11	1	8	0	1	0.8	1.000										

Cardinal fans in 1953 said farewell to the Cat and hello to the Kitten, as Harry Brecheen moved over to the Browns as player-coach, and Harvey Haddix joined the pitching rotation. Haddix won 20 for the third-place Redbirds, and led the league in shutouts with six. For the first time since his rookie year, Stan Musial did not lead the team in batting; that honor went to Red Schoendienst, whose .342 average was second in the league behind Carl Furillo of the Dodgers. Thirty-nine-year-old relief specialist Al Brazle led the National League in saves despite posting a 4.21 ERA and allowing more than a hit per inning. It was the second straight year he had led the league in saves; the only other Cardinal pitchers to accomplish this are Bill Sherdel, Lindy McDaniel, and Bruce Sutter.

TEAM STATISTICS

W	L	PCT	GB	R	OR	Batting						Fielding			CG	BB	Pitching			
						2B	3B	HR	BA	SA	SB	E	DP	FA			SO	ShO	SV	ERA
KN	105	49	.682		955	689	274	59	208	.285	.474	90	118	161	.980	51	509	819	11	29	4.10
IL	92	62	.597	13	738	589	227	52	156	.266	.415	46	143	169	.976	72	539	738	14	15	**3.30**
HI	83	71	.539	22	716	666	228	62	115	.265	.396	42	147	161	.975	76	410	637	13	15	3.80
TL	83	71	.539	22	768	713	281	56	140	.273	.424	18	138	161	.977	51	533	732	11	**36**	4.23
Y	70	84	.455	35	768	747	195	45	176	.271	.424	31	151	151	.975	46	610	647	10	20	4.25
IN	68	86	.442	37	714	788	190	34	166	.261	.403	25	129	176	.978	47	488	506	7	15	4.64
HI	65	89	.422	40	633	835	204	57	137	.260	.399	49	193	141	.967	38	554	623	3	22	4.79
T	50	104	.325	55	622	887	178	49	99	.247	.356	41	163	139	.973	49	577	607	4	10	5.22
AGUE TOTAL				5914	5914	1777	414	1197	.266	.411	342	1182	1259	.975	430	4220	5309	73	162	4.29

INDIVIDUAL PITCHING

TCHER	T	W	L	PCT	ERA	SV	G	GS	CG	IP	H	BB	SO	R	ER	ShO	H/9	BB/9	SO/9
arvey Haddix	L	20	9	.690	3.06	1	36	33	19	253	220	69	163	97	86	6	7.83	2.45	5.80
erry Staley	R	18	9	.667	3.99	4	40	32	10	230	243	54	88	118	102	1	9.51	2.11	3.44
negar Bend Mizell	L	13	11	.542	3.49	0	33	33	10	224.1	193	114	173	93	87	1	7.74	4.57	**6.94**
e Presko	R	6	13	.316	5.01	1	34	25	4	161.2	165	65	56	95	90	0	9.19	3.62	3.12
u Miller	R	7	8	.467	5.56	4	40	18	8	137.2	161	47	79	86	85	2	10.53	3.07	5.16
Brazle	L	6	7	.462	4.21	18	60	0	0	92	101	43	57	47	43	0	9.88	4.21	5.58
l White	R	6	5	.545	2.98	7	49	0	0	84.2	84	39	32	32	28	0	8.93	4.15	3.40
ff Chambers	L	3	6	.333	4.86	0	32	8	0	79.2	82	43	26	50	43	0	9.26	4.86	2.94
ke Clark	R	1	0	1.000	4.79	1	23	2	0	35.2	46	21	17	21	19	0	11.61	5.30	4.29
die Erautt	R	3	1	.750	6.31	0	20	1	0	35.2	43	16	15	25	25	0	10.85	4.04	3.79
lard Schmidt	R	0	2	.000	9.17	0	6	2	0	17.2	21	13	11	20	18	0	10.70	6.62	5.60
ck Faszholz	R	0	0	–	6.94	0	4	1	0	11.2	16	1	7	9	9	0	12.34	0.77	5.40
ckie Collum	L	0	0	–	6.35	0	7	0	0	11.1	15	4	5	10	8	0	11.91	3.18	3.97
n Romonosky	R	0	0	–	4.70	0	2	2	0	7.2	9	4	3	6	4	0	10.57	4.70	3.52
k Bokelmann	R	0	0	–	6.00	0	3	0	0	3	4	0	0	2	2	0	12.00	0.00	0.00
die Yuhas	R	0	0	–	18.00	0	2	0	0	1	3	0	0	2	2	0	27.00	0.00	0.00
AM TOTAL		83	71	.539	4.23	36	391	157	51	1386.2	1406	533	732	713	651	10	9.13	3.46	4.75

MANAGER	W	L	PCT
Eddie Stanky	72	82	.468

POS	Player	B	G	AB	H	2B	3B	HR	HR %	R	RBI	BB	SO	SB	Pinch Hit AB	Pinch Hit H	BA	SA
REGULARS																		
1B	Joe Cunningham	L	85	310	88	11	3	11	3.5	40	50	43	40	1	0	0	.284	.445
2B	Red Schoendienst	B	148	610	192	38	8	5	0.8	98	79	54	22	4	4	1	.315	.428
SS	Alex Grammas	R	142	401	106	17	4	2	0.5	57	29	40	29	6	0	0	.264	.342
3B	Ray Jablonski	R	152	611	181	33	3	12	2.0	80	104	49	42	9	2	2	.296	.419
RF	Stan Musial	L	153	591	195	41	9	35	5.9	120	126	103	39	1	0	0	.330	.607
CF	Wally Moon	L	151	635	193	29	9	12	1.9	106	76	71	73	18	2	0	.304	.435
LF	Rip Repulski	R	152	619	175	39	5	19	3.1	99	79	43	75	8	0	0	.283	.454
C	Bill Sarni	R	123	380	114	18	4	9	2.4	40	70	25	42	3	6	3	.300	.439
SUBSTITUTES																		
1B	Tom Alston	L	66	244	60	14	2	4	1.6	28	34	24	41	3	2	1	.246	.369
UT	Solly Hemus	L	124	214	65	15	3	2	0.9	43	27	55	27	5	38	10	.304	.430
1B	Steve Bilko	R	8	14	2	0	0	0	0.0	1	1	3	1	0	1	0	.143	.143
SS	Dick Schofield	B	43	7	1	0	1	0	0.0	17	1	0	3	1	3	1	.143	.429
3B	Pete Castiglione	R	5	0	0	0	0	0	–	1	0	0	0	0	0	0	–	–
OF	Joe Frazier	L	81	88	26	5	2	3	3.4	8	18	13	17	0	62	20	.295	.500
OF	Peanuts Lowrey	R	74	61	7	1	2	0	0.0	6	5	9	9	0	53	7	.115	.197
OF	Tom Burgess	L	17	21	1	1	0	0	0.0	2	1	3	9	0	11	0	.048	.095
C	Del Rice	R	56	147	37	10	1	2	1.4	13	16	16	21	0	4	2	.252	.374
C	Sal Yvars	R	38	57	14	4	0	2	3.5	8	8	6	5	1	18	4	.246	.421
PITCHERS																		
P	Harvey Haddix	L	61	93	18	4	2	0	0.0	16	4	5	11	2	0	0	.194	.280
P	Vic Raschi	R	30	64	9	0	0	0	0.0	3	3	3	18	0	0	0	.141	.141
P	Brooks Lawrence	R	35	53	10	0	0	0	0.0	2	4	3	15	0	0	0	.189	.189
P	Gerry Staley	R	48	36	5	1	0	0	0.0	3	1	4	8	0	0	0	.139	.167
P	Tom Poholsky	R	25	27	4	1	0	0	0.0	1	4	0	4	0	0	0	.148	.185
P	Gordon Jones	R	11	24	3	1	0	0	0.0	0	1	1	4	0	0	0	.125	.167
P	Cot Deal	B	33	20	2	1	0	1	5.0	4	3	1	7	0	0	0	.100	.300
P	Ralph Beard	R	13	17	1	0	0	0	0.0	1	0	1	8	0	0	0	.059	.059
P	Joe Presko	R	38	16	4	0	0	0	0.0	0	1	0	2	0	0	0	.250	.250
P	Al Brazle	L	58	14	0	0	0	0	0.0	0	1	0	3	0	0	0	.000	.000
P	Stu Miller	R	20	13	4	0	0	0	0.0	1	0	1	5	0	0	0	.308	.308
P	Royce Lint	L	31	10	1	1	0	0	0.0	1	2	6	3	1	0	0	.100	.200
P	Ben Wade	R	13	3	0	0	0	0	0.0	0	0	0	2	0	0	0	.000	.000
P	Carl Scheib	R	3	2	0	0	0	0	0.0	0	0	0	0	0	0	0	.000	.000
P	Bill Greason	R	3	1	0	0	0	0	0.0	0	0	0	0	0	0	0	.000	.000
P	Hal White	L	4	1	0	0	0	0	0.0	0	0	0	1	0	0	0	.000	.000
P	Mel Wright	R	9	1	0	0	0	0	0.0	0	0	0	0	0	0	0	.000	.000
P	Memo Luna	L	1	0	0	0	0	0	–	0	0	0	0	0	0	0	–	–
	TEAM TOTAL			5405	1518	285	58	119	2.2	799	748	582	586	63	206	51	.281	.421

INDIVIDUAL FIELDING

POS	Player	T	G	PO	A	E	DP	TC/G	FA		POS	Player	T	G	PO	A	E	DP	TC/G	FA
1B	J. Cunningham	L	85	814	68	10	96	10.5	.989		OF	W. Moon	R	148	387	11	9	2	2.8	.978
	T. Alston	R	65	552	72	7	57	9.7	.989			R. Repulski	R	152	302	4	8	0	2.1	.975
	S. Musial	L	10	36	2	2	4	4.0	.950			S. Musial	L	152	271	13	3	4	1.9	.990
	S. Bilko	R	6	21	7	0	3	4.7	1.000			J. Frazier	R	11	15	0	1	0	1.5	.938
	R. Jablonski	R	1	5	1	0	0	6.0	1.000			P. Lowrey	R	12	5	0	0	0	0.4	1.000
	J. Frazier	R	1	1	1	0	0	2.0	1.000			T. Burgess	L	4	3	0	1	0	1.0	.750
2B	Schoendienst	R	144	394	477	18	137	6.2	.980		C	B. Sarni	R	118	486	41	2	12	4.5	.996
	S. Hemus	R	12	27	25	0	8	4.3	1.000			D. Rice	R	52	248	20	4	2	5.2	.985
SS	A. Grammas	R	142	252	432	24	100	5.0	.966			S. Yvars	R	21	46	9	0	1	2.6	1.000
	S. Hemus	R	66	49	102	9	18	2.4	.944											
	D. Schofield	R	11	4	3	0	1	0.6	1.000											
3B	R. Jablonski	R	149	122	298	34	25	3.0	.925											
	S. Hemus	R	27	9	24	1	3	1.3	.971											
	A. Grammas	R	1	1	0	0	0	1.0	1.000											
	Castiglione	R	5	0	1	0	0	0.2	1.000											

The back-to-back third-place finishes in 1952 and 1953 had masked the fact that the Cardinals were becoming an old ball club. The '53 starting lineup included five players over 30 years of age; in 1954 there were just two: Schoendienst and Musial. Just before the start of the season, the Cards sent 38-year-old Enos Slaughter to the Yankees for a four-player package including catcher Hal Smith and outfielder Bill Virdon. Among the new young starters, National League Rookie of the Year Wally Moon came through with a .304 average, and catcher Bill Sarni had 70 RBIs in fewer than 400 at bats. The Cards led the league in runs, as Musial scored over 100 runs for the eleventh straight season, but they finished in sixth place, 25 games out, thanks largely to a pitching staff that was next-to-last in runs allowed.

TEAM STATISTICS

	W	L	PCT	GB	R	OR	Batting 2B	3B	HR	BA	SA	SB	Fielding E	DP	FA	CG	BB	Pitching SO	ShO	SV	ERA
NY	97	57	.630		732	550	194	42	186	.264	.424	30	154	172	.975	45	613	692	19	33	3.09
BKN	92	62	.597	5	778	740	246	56	186	.270	.444	46	129	138	.978	39	533	762	8	36	4.31
MIL	89	65	.578	8	670	556	217	41	139	.265	.401	54	116	171	.981	63	553	698	13	21	3.19
PHI	75	79	.487	22	659	614	243	58	102	.267	.395	30	145	133	.975	78	450	570	14	12	3.59
CIN	74	80	.481	23	729	763	221	46	147	.262	.406	47	137	194	.977	34	547	537	8	27	4.50
STL	72	82	.468	25	799	790	285	58	119	.281	.421	63	146	178	.976	40	535	680	11	18	4.50
CHI	64	90	.416	33	700	766	229	45	159	.263	.412	46	154	164	.974	41	619	622	6	19	4.51
PIT	53	101	.344	44	557	845	181	57	76	.248	.350	21	173	136	.971	37	564	525	4	15	4.92
LEAGUE TOTAL					5624	5624	1816	403	1114	.265	.407	337	1154	1286	.976	377	4414	5086	83	181	4.07

INDIVIDUAL PITCHING

PITCHER	T	W	L	PCT	ERA	SV	G	GS	CG	IP	H	BB	SO	R	ER	ShO	H/9	BB/9	SO/9
Harvey Haddix	L	18	13	.581	3.57	4	43	35	13	259.2	247	77	184	114	103	3	8.56	2.67	6.38
Vic Raschi	R	8	9	.471	4.73	0	30	29	6	179	182	71	73	99	94	2	9.15	3.57	3.67
Brooks Lawrence	R	15	6	.714	3.74	1	35	18	8	158.2	141	72	72	71	66	0	8.00	4.08	4.08
Gerry Staley	R	7	13	.350	5.26	2	48	20	3	155.2	198	47	50	107	91	1	11.45	2.72	2.89
Tom Poholsky	R	5	7	.417	3.06	0	25	13	4	106	101	20	55	43	36	0	8.58	1.70	4.67
Al Brazle	L	5	4	.556	4.16	8	58	0	0	84.1	93	24	30	48	39	0	9.92	2.56	3.20
Gordon Jones	R	4	4	.500	2.00	0	11	10	4	81	78	19	48	25	18	2	8.67	2.11	5.33
Cot Deal	R	2	3	.400	6.28	1	33	0	0	71.2	85	36	25	56	50	0	10.67	4.52	3.14
Joe Presko	R	4	9	.308	6.91	0	37	6	1	71.2	97	41	36	56	55	1	12.18	5.15	4.52
Royce Lint	L	2	3	.400	4.86	0	30	4	1	70.1	75	30	36	46	38	1	9.60	3.84	4.61
Ralph Beard	R	0	4	.000	3.72	0	13	10	0	58	62	28	17	32	24	0	9.62	4.34	2.64
Stu Miller	R	2	3	.400	5.79	2	19	4	0	46.2	55	29	22	36	30	0	10.61	5.59	4.24
Ken Wade	R	0	0	–	5.48	0	13	0	0	23	27	15	19	15	14	0	10.57	5.87	7.43
Mel Wright	R	0	0	–	10.45	0	9	0	0	10.1	16	11	4	15	12	0	13.94	9.58	3.48
Hal White	R	0	0	–	19.80	0	4	0	0	5	11	4	2	11	11	0	19.80	7.20	3.60
Carl Scheib	R	0	1	.000	11.57	0	3	1	0	4.2	6	5	5	6	6	0	11.57	9.64	9.64
Bill Greason	R	0	1	.000	13.50	0	3	2	0	4	8	4	2	8	6	0	18.00	9.00	4.50
Memo Luna	L	0	1	.000	27.00	0	1	1	0	.2	2	2	0	2	2	0	27.00	27.00	0.00
TEAM TOTAL		72	81	.471	4.50	18	415	153	40	1390.1	1484	535	680	790	695	10	9.61	3.46	4.40

MANAGER	W	L	PCT
Eddie Stanky	17	19	.472
Harry Walker	51	67	.432

POS	Player	B	G	AB	H	2B	3B	HR	HR %	R	RBI	BB	SO	SB	Pinch Hit AB	Pinch Hit H	BA	SA
REGULARS																		
1B	Stan Musial	L	154	562	179	30	5	33	5.9	97	108	80	39	5	0	0	.319	.566
2B	Red Schoendienst	B	145	553	148	21	3	11	2.0	68	51	54	28	7	2	0	.268	.376
SS	Alex Grammas	R	128	366	88	19	2	3	0.8	32	25	33	36	4	1	0	.240	.328
3B	Ken Boyer	R	147	530	140	27	2	18	3.4	78	62	37	67	22	1	0	.264	.425
RF	Wally Moon	L	152	593	175	24	8	19	3.2	86	76	47	65	11	8	2	.295	.459
CF	Bill Virdon	L	144	534	150	18	6	17	3.2	58	68	36	64	2	9	1	.281	.433
LF	Rip Repulski	R	147	512	138	28	2	23	4.5	64	73	49	66	5	10	3	.270	.467
C	Bill Sarni	R	107	325	83	15	2	3	0.9	32	34	27	33	1	11	3	.255	.342
SUBSTITUTES																		
32	Solly Hemus	L	96	206	50	10	2	5	2.4	36	21	27	22	1	37	4	.243	.383
SS	Bobby Stephenson	R	67	111	27	3	0	0	0.0	19	6	5	18	2	6	0	.243	.270
2S	Don Blasingame	L	5	16	6	1	0	0	0.0	4	0	6	0	1	0	0	.375	.438
1B	Tom Alston	L	13	8	1	0	0	0	0.0	0	0	0	0	0	6	1	.125	.125
SS	Dick Schofield	B	12	4	0	0	0	0	0.0	3	0	0	1	0	2	0	.000	.000
OF	Harry Elliott	R	68	117	30	4	0	1	0.9	9	12	11	9	0	38	7	.256	.316
OF	Pete Whisenant	R	58	115	22	5	1	2	1.7	10	9	5	29	2	20	5	.191	.304
OF	Joe Frazier	L	58	70	14	1	0	4	5.7	12	9	6	12	0	45	4	.200	.386
OF	Harry Walker	L	11	14	5	2	0	0	0.0	2	1	1	0	0	9	4	.357	.500
C	Nels Burbrink	R	58	170	47	8	1	0	0.0	11	15	14	13	1	3	2	.276	.335
C	Del Rice	R	20	59	12	3	0	1	1.7	6	7	7	6	0	2	0	.203	.305
C	Dick Rand	R	3	10	3	0	0	1	10.0	1	3	1	1	0	0	0	.300	.600
PITCHERS																		
P	Harvey Haddix	L	37	73	12	2	2	1	1.4	10	7	4	15	0	0	0	.164	.288
P	Larry Jackson	R	37	57	3	0	0	0	0.0	1	0	2	17	0	0	0	.053	.053
P	Luis Arroyo	L	35	56	13	0	0	1	1.8	2	6	0	13	0	0	0	.232	.286
P	Tom Poholsky	R	30	44	8	3	0	0	0.0	6	3	1	6	0	0	0	.182	.250
P	Willard Schmidt	R	20	42	5	1	0	0	0.0	1	4	0	15	0	0	0	.119	.143
P	Brooks Lawrence	R	46	21	2	0	0	0	0.0	1	2	1	0	0	0	0	.095	.095
P	Paul LaPalme	L	56	19	4	1	0	0	0.0	1	2	1	1	0	0	0	.211	.263
P	Floyd Wooldridge	R	18	18	4	1	0	0	0.0	1	1	0	4	0	0	0	.222	.278
P	Gordon Jones	R	15	14	1	0	0	0	0.0	2	1	1	3	0	0	0	.071	.071
P	Ben Flowers	R	4	10	1	0	0	0	0.0	0	0	0	4	0	0	0	.100	.100
P	Al Gettel	R	8	6	3	1	0	0	0.0	1	2	0	1	0	0	0	.500	.667
P	Mel Wright	R	29	6	0	0	0	0	0.0	0	0	0	2	0	0	0	.000	.000
P	Lindy McDaniel	R	4	5	1	0	0	0	0.0	0	0	0	3	0	0	0	.200	.200
P	Bobby Tiefenauer	R	18	5	0	0	0	0	0.0	0	0	1	1	0	0	0	.000	.000
P	Johnny Mackinson	R	9	4	0	0	0	0	0.0	0	0	1	0	0	0	0	.000	.000
P	Barney Schultz	R	19	4	0	0	0	0	0.0	0	0	0	1	0	0	0	.000	.000
P	Frank Smith	R	28	4	0	0	0	0	0.0	0	0	0	2	0	0	0	.000	.000
P	Herb Moford	R	14	2	0	0	0	0	0.0	0	0	0	0	0	0	0	.000	.000
P	Tony Jacobs	B	1	1	0	0	0	0	0.0	0	0	0	0	0	0	0	.000	.000
P	Vic Raschi	R	1	0	0	0	0	0	–	0	0	0	0	0	0	0	–	–
	TEAM TOTAL			5266	1375	228	36	143	2.7	654	608	458	597	64	210	36	.261	.400

INDIVIDUAL FIELDING

POS	Player	T	G	PO	A	E	DP	TC/G	FA
1B	S. Musial	L	110	925	92	8	93	9.3	.992
	W. Moon	R	51	445	34	7	40	9.5	.986
	T. Alston	R	7	14	1	0	1	2.1	1.000
2B	Schoendienst	R	142	296	381	10	96	4.8	.985
	S. Hemus	R	40	18	20	0	3	1.0	1.000
	B. Stephenson	R	7	11	12	0	1	3.3	1.000
	D. Blasingame	R	3	8	13	1	1	7.3	.955
SS	A. Grammas	R	126	235	340	19	76	4.7	.968
	B. Stephenson	R	48	54	68	8	20	2.7	.938
	K. Boyer	R	18	31	42	2	10	4.2	.973
	D. Blasingame	R	2	2	6	1	1	4.5	.889
	D. Schofield	R	3	1	1	0	0	0.7	1.000
	S. Hemus	R	2	0	1	0	0	0.5	1.000
3B	K. Boyer	R	139	124	253	19	24	2.8	.952
	S. Hemus	R	43	38	70	5	7	2.6	.956
	B. Stephenson	R	1	0	0	0	0	0.0	.000

POS	Player	T	G	PO	A	E	DP	TC/G	FA
OF	B. Virdon	R	142	339	7	12	1	2.5	.966
	R. Repulski	R	141	260	5	7	1	1.9	.974
	W. Moon	R	100	188	5	5	1	2.0	.975
	P. Whisenant	R	40	76	4	3	1	2.1	.964
	S. Musial	L	51	75	2	1	0	1.5	.987
	H. Elliott	R	28	44	1	1	0	1.6	.978
	T. Poholsky	R	1	0	0	0	0	0.0	.000
	J. Frazier	R	14	16	0	0	0	1.1	1.000
	H. Walker	R	1	2	1	0	1	3.0	1.000
C	B. Sarni	R	99	482	39	7	8	5.3	.987
	N. Burbrink	R	55	261	24	6	4	5.3	.979
	D. Rice	R	18	74	6	3	1	4.6	.964
	D. Rand	R	3	9	1	0	0	3.3	1.000

For the second year in a row, the National League Rookie of the Year played centerfield for the Cardinals. This year it was Bill Virdon, who spent just the one season with St. Louis before being shipped to Pittsburgh in yet another Cardinal trade that did not pan out. A more significant rookie regular for the Cards' future was third baseman Ken Boyer, but his best years were still far ahead of him. Offensive production was down at every position, as their scoring total fell by almost a run a game. Harvey Haddix led the pitching staff with just 12 wins. Of the four starters used most often, only Tom Poholsky had an ERA below 4.00. Sixty-eight wins was their lowest total since 1924, and the last time they had fallen as low as seventh place was 1919, before the years of glory began.

TEAM STATISTICS

	W	L	PCT	GB	R	OR	Batting 2B	3B	HR	BA	SA	SB	Fielding E	DP	FA	CG	BB	Pitching SO	ShO	SV	ERA
N	98	55	.641		857	650	230	44	201	.271	.448	79	133	156	.978	46	483	773	11	37	3.68
-	85	69	.552	13.5	743	668	219	55	182	.261	.427	42	152	155	.975	61	591	654	5	12	3.85
	80	74	.519	18.5	702	673	173	34	169	.260	.402	38	142	165	.976	52	560	721	6	14	3.77
	77	77	.500	21.5	675	666	214	50	132	.255	.395	44	110	117	.981	58	477	657	11	21	3.93
	75	79	.487	23.5	761	684	216	28	181	.270	.425	51	139	169	.977	38	443	576	12	22	3.95
	72	81	.471	26	626	713	187	55	164	.247	.398	37	147	147	.975	47	601	686	10	23	4.17
-	68	86	.442	30.5	654	757	228	36	143	.261	.400	64	146	152	.975	42	549	730	10	15	4.56
	60	94	.390	38.5	560	767	210	60	91	.244	.361	22	166	175	.972	41	536	622	5	16	4.39
GUE TOTAL					5578	5578	1677	362	1263	.259	.407	377	1135	1236	.976	385	4240	5419	70	160	4.04

INDIVIDUAL PITCHING

CHER	T	W	L	PCT	ERA	SV	G	GS	CG	IP	H	BB	SO	R	ER	ShO	H/9	BB/9	SO/9
vey Haddix	L	12	16	.429	4.46	1	37	30	9	208	216	62	150	111	103	2	9.35	2.68	6.49
ry Jackson	R	9	14	.391	4.31	2	37	25	4	177.1	189	72	88	93	85	1	9.59	3.65	4.47
Arroyo	L	11	8	.579	4.19	0	35	24	9	159	162	63	68	80	74	1	9.17	3.57	3.85
Poholsky	R	9	11	.450	3.81	0	30	24	8	151	143	35	66	71	64	2	8.52	2.09	3.93
ard Schmidt	R	7	6	.538	2.78	0	20	15	8	129.2	89	57	86	40	40	1	6.18	3.96	5.97
ks Lawrence	R	3	8	.273	6.56	1	46	10	2	96	102	58	52	73	70	1	9.56	5.44	4.88
LaPalme	L	4	3	.571	2.75	3	56	0	0	91.2	76	34	39	36	28	0	7.46	3.34	3.83
d Wooldridge	R	2	4	.333	4.84	0	18	8	2	57.2	64	27	14	36	31	0	9.99	4.21	2.18
don Jones	R	1	4	.200	5.84	0	15	9	0	57	66	28	46	38	37	0	10.42	4.42	7.26
k Smith	R	3	1	.750	3.23	1	28	0	0	39	27	23	17	18	14	0	6.23	5.31	3.92
Wright	R	2	2	.500	6.19	1	29	0	0	36.1	44	9	18	26	25	0	10.90	2.23	4.46
y Tiefenauer	R	1	4	.200	4.41	0	18	0	0	32.2	31	10	16	19	16	0	8.54	2.76	4.41
ey Schultz	R	1	2	.333	7.89	4	19	0	0	29.2	28	15	19	27	26	0	8.49	4.55	5.76
Flowers	R	1	0	1.000	3.62	0	4	4	0	27.1	27	12	19	12	11	0	8.89	3.95	6.26
Moford	R	1	1	.500	7.88	2	14	1	0	24	29	15	8	23	21	0	10.88	5.63	3.00
ny Mackinson	R	0	1	.000	7.84	0	8	1	0	20.2	24	10	8	18	18	0	10.45	4.35	3.48
McDaniel	R	0	0	–	4.74	0	4	2	0	19	22	7	7	10	10	0	10.42	3.32	3.32
ettel	R	1	0	1.000	9.00	0	8	0	0	17	26	10	7	18	17	0	13.76	5.29	3.71
Jacobs	R	0	0	–	18.00	0	1	0	0	2	6	1	1	4	4	0	27.00	4.50	4.50
aschi	R	0	1	.000	21.60	0	1	1	0	1.2	5	1	1	4	4	0	27.00	5.40	5.40
M TOTAL		68	86	.442	4.56	15	428	154	42	1376.2	1376	549	730	757	698	8	9.00	3.59	4.77

MANAGER	W	L	PCT
Fred Hutchinson	76	78	.494

POS	Player	B	G	AB	H	2B	3B	HR	HR %	R	RBI	BB	SO	SB	Pinch Hit AB	Pinch Hit H	BA	SA
REGULARS																		
1B	Stan Musial	L	156	594	184	33	6	27	4.5	87	109	75	39	2	0	0	.310	.522
2B	Don Blasingame	L	150	587	153	22	7	0	0.0	94	27	72	52	8	2	0	.261	.322
SS	Alvin Dark	R	100	413	118	14	7	4	1.0	54	37	21	33	3	1	0	.286	.383
3B	Ken Boyer	R	150	595	182	30	2	26	4.4	91	98	38	65	8	1	0	.306	.494
RF	Wally Moon	L	149	540	161	22	11	16	3.0	86	68	80	50	12	0	0	.298	.469
CF	Bobby Del Greco	R	102	270	58	16	2	5	1.9	29	18	32	50	1	4	0	.215	.344
LF	Rip Repulski	R	112	376	104	18	3	11	2.9	44	55	24	46	2	17	7	.277	.428
C	Hal Smith	R	75	227	64	12	0	5	2.2	27	23	15	22	1	9	3	.282	.401
SUBSTITUTES																		
2B	Red Schoendienst	B	40	153	48	9	0	0	0.0	22	15	13	5	0	3	1	.314	.373
UT	Bobby Morgan	R	61	113	22	7	0	3	2.7	14	20	15	24	0	29	5	.195	.336
2B	Grady Hatton	L	44	73	18	1	2	0	0.0	10	7	13	7	1	28	6	.247	.315
1O	Rocky Nelson	L	38	56	13	5	0	3	5.4	6	8	6	6	0	19	3	.232	.482
SS	Dick Schofield	B	16	30	3	2	0	0	0.0	3	1	0	6	0	4	0	.100	.167
SS	Alex Grammas	R	6	12	3	0	0	0	0.0	1	1	1	2	0	1	1	.250	.250
1B	Joe Cunningham	L	4	3	0	0	0	0	0.0	1	0	1	1	0	2	0	.000	.000
1B	Tom Alston	L	3	2	0	0	0	0	0.0	0	0	0	0	0	0	0	.000	.000
OF	Whitey Lockman	L	70	193	48	0	2	0	0.0	14	10	18	8	2	13	4	.249	.269
OF	Hank Sauer	R	75	151	45	4	0	5	3.3	11	24	25	31	0	31	6	.298	.424
OF	Bill Virdon	L	24	71	15	2	0	2	2.8	10	9	5	8	0	1	0	.211	.324
OF	Charlie Peete	L	23	52	10	2	2	0	0.0	3	6	6	10	0	4	1	.192	.308
OF	Jackie Brandt	R	27	42	12	3	0	1	2.4	9	3	4	5	0	2	1	.286	.452
OF	Joe Frazier	L	14	19	4	2	0	1	5.3	1	4	3	3	0	7	1	.211	.474
O1	Chuck Harmon	R	20	15	0	0	0	0	0.0	2	0	2	2	0	3	0	.000	.000
C	Ray Katt	R	47	158	41	4	0	6	3.8	11	20	6	24	0	0	0	.259	.399
C	Bill Sarni	R	43	148	43	7	2	5	3.4	12	22	8	15	1	2	0	.291	.466
C	Walker Cooper	R	40	68	18	5	1	2	2.9	5	14	3	8	0	22	3	.265	.456
PH	Solly Hemus	L	8	5	1	0	0	0	0.0	1	2	1	0	0	5	1	.200	.200
PITCHERS																		
P	Murry Dickson	R	32	77	19	2	2	0	0.0	6	6	1	9	0	0	0	.247	.325
P	Vinegar Bend Mizell	R	33	75	8	1	0	0	0.0	5	4	4	16	0	0	0	.107	.120
P	Tom Poholsky	R	33	69	11	2	0	0	0.0	7	3	1	14	0	0	0	.159	.188
P	Herm Wehmeier	R	42	58	13	3	0	2	3.4	6	8	2	17	0	0	0	.224	.379
P	Willard Schmidt	R	33	43	10	1	0	0	0.0	3	0	2	16	0	0	0	.233	.256
P	Lindy McDaniel	R	39	32	7	4	0	0	0.0	1	2	1	10	0	0	0	.219	.344
P	Jackie Collum	L	38	14	3	0	0	0	0.0	1	1	2	1	0	0	0	.214	.214
P	Bob Blaylock	R	14	11	1	0	0	0	0.0	0	0	0	4	0	0	0	.091	.091
P	Larry Jackson	R	51	11	1	0	0	0	0.0	0	1	1	5	0	0	0	.091	.091
P	Harvey Haddix	L	5	9	2	1	0	0	0.0	1	1	2	3	0	0	0	.222	.333
P	Ben Flowers	R	3	3	0	0	0	0	0.0	0	0	0	0	0	0	0	.000	.000
P	Gordon Jones	R	5	2	0	0	0	0	0.0	0	0	0	1	0	0	0	.000	.000
P	Ellis Kinder	R	22	2	0	0	0	0	0.0	0	0	0	2	0	0	0	.000	.000
P	Don Liddle	L	15	2	0	0	0	0	0.0	0	0	0	1	0	0	0	.000	.000
P	Dick Littlefield	L	3	2	0	0	0	0	0.0	0	0	0	0	0	0	0	.000	.000
P	Stu Miller	R	4	1	0	0	0	0	0.0	0	0	0	1	0	0	0	.000	.000
P	Max Surkont	R	5	1	0	0	0	0	0.0	0	0	0	0	0	0	0	–	–
P	Jim Konstanty	R	27	0	0	0	0	0	–	0	1	0	0	0	0	0	–	–
P	Paul LaPalme	L	1	0	0	0	0	0	–	0	0	0	0	0	0	0	–	–
TEAM TOTAL				5378	1443	234	49	124	2.3	678	628	503	622	41	210	43	.268	.399

INDIVIDUAL FIELDING

POS	Player	T	G	PO	A	E	DP	TC/G	FA
1B	S. Musial	L	103	870	90	7	96	9.4	.993
	W. Moon	R	52	498	47	9	52	10.7	.984
	R. Nelson	L	14	54	7	0	6	4.4	1.000
	W. Lockman	R	2	14	0	2	1	8.0	.875
	T. Alston	R	3	4	1	0	1	1.7	1.000
	C. Harmon	R	2	4	0	0	1	2.0	1.000
	J. Cunningham	L	1	2	0	0	0	2.0	1.000
2B	D. Blasingame	R	98	280	303	8	89	6.0	.986
	Schoendienst	R	36	99	93	1	22	5.4	.995*
	G. Hatton	R	13	24	34	3	8	4.7	.951
	B. Morgan	R	13	25	25	1	3	3.9	.980
SS	A. Dark	R	99	178	292	20	66	4.9	.959
	D. Blasingame	R	49	93	135	13	31	4.9	.946
	D. Schofield	R	9	11	13	2	4	2.9	.923
	B. Morgan	R	6	8	8	1	2	2.8	.941
	A. Grammas	R	5	3	9	0	1	2.4	1.000
3B	K. Boyer	R	149	130	309	18	37	3.1	.961
	C. Harmon	R	1	0	0	0	0	0.0	.000
	G. Hatton	R	1	0	0	0	0	0.0	.000
	B. Morgan	R	11	9	23	4	1	3.3	.889
	D. Blasingame	R	2	0	4	0	0	2.0	1.000

POS	Player	T	G	PO	A	E	DP	TC/G	FA
OF	B. Del Greco	R	99	217	3	3	0	2.3	.987
	R. Repulski	R	100	187	3	5	0	2.0	.974
	W. Moon	R	97	159	8	2	2	1.7	.988
	W. Lockman	R	57	103	2	5	0	1.9	.955
	S. Musial	L	53	84	5	1	0	1.7	.989
	H. Sauer	R	37	55	2	0	1	1.5	1.000
	B. Virdon	R	24	53	2	1	0	2.3	.982
	C. Peete	R	21	37	3	0	1	1.9	1.000
	J. Brandt	R	26	33	1	0	1	1.3	1.000
	R. Nelson	L	8	11	0	0	0	1.4	1.000
	C. Harmon	R	11	7	0	0	0	0.6	1.000
	J. Frazier	R	3	4	0	1	0	1.7	.800
C	H. Smith	R	66	300	34	6	3	5.2	.982
	R. Katt	R	47	231	16	4	0	5.3	.984
	B. Sarni	R	41	219	25*	2	1*	6.0	.992
	W. Cooper	R	16	56	4	1	0	3.8	.984

The extent of the Cardinals' improvement in 1956 is better indicated by stating that they won eight games more than in '55 than by saying they jumped from seventh place to fourth. Fourth place in 1956 was nothing more than "the best of the rest," as the three top teams far outdistanced the lower five. Under new manager Fred Hutchinson, the Cards turned over much of their pitching staff; of their five most frequent starters of 1955, Haddix and Luis Arroyo were traded away, and Larry Jackson was moved to the bullpen. They were replaced by Herm Wehmeier, Murry Dickson (acquired from the Phillies in the Haddix deal), and Wilmer "Vinegar Bend" Mizell, who rejoined the club after two years of military service. The shake-up continued as they sent Red Schoendienst to the Giants in a deal in which they received shortstop Alvin Dark. It was a trade they would soon regret.

TEAM STATISTICS

W	L	PCT	GB	R	OR	2B	3B	HR	BA	SA	SB	E	DP	FA	CG	BB	SO	ShO	SV	ERA
						Batting						Fielding			Pitching					
93	61	.604		720	601	212	36	179	.258	.419	65	111	149	.981	46	441	772	12	30	3.57
92	62	.597	1	709	569	212	54	177	.259	.423	29	130	159	.979	64	467	639	12	27	3.11
91	63	.591	2	775	658	201	32	221	.266	.441	45	113	147	.981	47	458	653	4	29	3.85
76	78	.494	17	678	698	234	49	124	.268	.399	41	134	172	.978	41	546	709	12	30	3.97
71	83	.461	22	668	738	207	49	121	.252	.381	45	144	140	.975	57	437	750	4	15	4.20
67	87	.435	26	540	650	192	45	145	.244	.382	67	144	143	.976	31	551	765	9	28	3.78
66	88	.429	27	588	653	199	57	110	.257	.380	24	162	140	.973	37	469	662	8	24	3.74
60	94	.390	33	597	708	202	50	142	.244	.382	55	144	141	.976	37	613	744	6	17	3.96
AGUE TOTAL				5275	5275	1659	372	1219	.256	.401	371	1082	1191	.977	360	3982	5694	67	200	3.77

INDIVIDUAL PITCHING

TCHER	T	W	L	PCT	ERA	SV	G	GS	CG	IP	H	BB	SO	R	ER	ShO	H/9	BB/9	SO/9
negar Bend Mizell	L	14	14	.500	3.62	0	33	33	11	208.2	172	92	153	93	84	3	7.42	3.97	6.60
m Poholsky	R	9	14	.391	3.59	0	33	29	7	203	210	44	95	100	81	2	9.31	1.95	4.21
rry Dickson	R	13	8	.619	3.07	0	28	27	12	196.1	175	57	109	75	67	3	8.02	2.61	5.00
rm Wehmeier	R	12	9	.571	3.69	1	34	19	7	170.2	150	71	68	80	70	2	7.91	3.74	3.59
llard Schmidt	R	6	8	.429	3.84	0	33	21	2	147.2	131	78	52	69	63	0	7.98	4.75	3.17
dy McDaniel	R	7	6	.538	3.40	0	39	7	1	116.1	121	42	59	60	44	0	9.36	3.25	4.56
rry Jackson	R	2	2	.500	4.11	9	51	1	0	85.1	75	45	50	44	39	0	7.91	4.05	2.55
ckie Collum	L	6	2	.750	4.20	7	38	1	0	60	63	27	17	29	28	0	9.45	4.05	2.55
b Blaylock	R	1	6	.143	6.37	0	14	6	0	41	45	24	39	32	29	0	9.88	5.27	8.56
n Konstanty	R	1	1	.500	4.58	5	27	0	0	39.1	46	6	7	20	20	0	10.53	1.37	1.60
s Kinder	R	2	0	1.000	3.51	6	22	0	0	25.2	23	9	4	11	10	0	8.06	3.16	1.40
n Liddle	L	1	2	.333	8.39	0	14	2	0	24.2	36	18	14	25	23	0	13.14	6.57	5.11
rvey Haddix	L	1	0	1.000	5.32	0	4	4	1	23.2	28	10	16	15	14	1	10.65	3.80	6.08
n Flowers	R	1	1	.500	6.94	0	3	3	0	11.2	15	5	5	9	9	0	11.57	3.86	3.86
rdon Jones	R	0	2	.000	5.56	0	5	1	0	11.1	14	5	6	9	7	0	11.12	3.97	4.76
k Littlefield	L	0	2	.000	7.45	0	3	2	0	9.2	9	4	5	9	8	0	8.38	3.72	4.66
Miller	R	0	1	.000	4.91	1	3	0	0	7.1	12	5	5	6	4	0	14.73	6.14	6.14
x Surkont	R	0	0	–	9.53	0	5	0	0	5.2	10	2	5	6	6	0	15.88	3.18	7.94
l LaPalme	L	0	0	–	81.00	0	1	0	0	.2	4	2	0	6	6	0	54.00	27.00	0.00
AM TOTAL		76	78	.494	3.97	30	390	156	41	1388.2	1339	546	709	698	612	11	8.68	3.54	4.60

MANAGER	W	L	PCT
Fred Hutchinson	87	67	.565

POS	Player	B	G	AB	H	2B	3B	HR	HR %	R	RBI	BB	SO	SB	Pinch Hit AB	Pinch Hit H	BA	SA
REGULARS																		
1B	Stan Musial	L	134	502	176	38	3	29	5.8	82	102	66	34	1	4	2	.351	.612
2B	Don Blasingame	L	154	650	176	25	7	8	1.2	108	58	71	49	21	0	0	.271	.368
SS	Alvin Dark	R	140	583	169	25	8	4	0.7	80	64	29	56	3	1	0	.290	.381
3B	Eddie Kasko	R	134	479	131	16	5	1	0.2	59	35	33	53	6	5	1	.273	.334
RF	Del Ennis	R	136	490	140	24	3	24	4.9	61	105	37	50	1	8	3	.286	.494
CF	Ken Boyer	R	142	544	144	18	3	19	3.5	79	62	44	77	12	1	0	.265	.414
LF	Wally Moon	L	142	516	152	28	5	24	4.7	86	73	62	57	5	9	1	.295	.508
C	Hal Smith	R	100	333	93	12	3	2	0.6	25	37	18	18	2	4	2	.279	.351
SUBSTITUTES																		
1O	Joe Cunningham	L	122	261	83	15	0	9	3.4	50	52	56	29	3	29	11	.318	.479
SS	Dick Schofield	B	65	56	9	0	0	0	0.0	10	1	7	13	1	11	1	.161	.161
1B	Tom Alston	L	9	17	5	1	0	0	0.0	2	2	1	5	0	3	2	.294	.353
OF	Bobby Gene Smith	R	93	185	39	7	1	3	1.6	24	18	13	35	1	11	1	.211	.308
OF	Eddie Miksis	R	49	38	8	0	0	1	2.6	3	2	7	7	0	14	3	.211	.289
OF	Jim King	L	22	35	11	0	0	0	0.0	1	2	4	2	0	16	4	.314	.314
OF	Irv Noren	L	17	30	11	4	1	1	3.3	3	10	4	6	0	9	3	.367	.667
OF	Gene Green	R	6	15	3	1	0	0	0.0	0	2	0	3	0	3	0	.200	.267
OF	Don Lassetter	R	4	13	2	0	1	0	0.0	2	0	1	3	0	1	0	.154	.308
OF	Chuck Harmon	R	9	3	1	0	1	0	0.0	2	1	0	0	1	1	0	.333	1.000
C	Hobie Landrith	L	75	214	52	6	0	3	1.4	18	26	25	27	1	10	1	.243	.313
C	Walker Cooper	R	48	78	21	5	1	3	3.8	7	10	5	10	0	30	7	.269	.474
PITCHERS																		
P	Lindy McDaniel	R	31	74	19	5	0	1	1.4	7	5	0	24	0	0	0	.257	.365
P	Larry Jackson	R	41	72	13	1	0	0	0.0	5	2	4	20	0	0	0	.181	.194
P	Sam Jones	R	28	63	10	1	0	0	0.0	2	3	1	25	0	0	0	.159	.175
P	Herm Wehmeier	R	40	59	12	0	1	0	0.0	9	3	0	14	0	1	0	.203	.237
P	Vinegar Bend Mizell	R	33	45	4	2	0	0	0.0	1	3	3	17	0	0	0	.089	.133
P	Willard Schmidt	R	40	33	7	0	0	0	0.0	3	3	0	8	0	0	0	.212	.212
P	Murry Dickson	R	14	27	6	1	0	0	0.0	4	4	0	6	0	0	0	.222	.259
P	Von McDaniel	R	17	26	0	0	0	0	0.0	0	0	0	10	0	0	0	.000	.000
P	Lloyd Merritt	R	44	7	0	0	0	0	0.0	2	0	2	3	0	0	0	.000	.000
P	Billy Muffett	R	23	7	0	0	0	0	0.0	0	0	0	4	0	0	0	.000	.000
P	Hoyt Wilhelm	R	40	6	0	0	0	0	0.0	0	0	0	4	0	0	0	.000	.000
P	Frank Barnes	R	4	2	0	0	0	0	0.0	1	0	0	1	0	0	0	.000	.000
P	Tom Cheney	R	4	2	0	0	0	0	0.0	0	0	0	0	0	0	0	.000	.000
P	Lynn Lovenguth	L	3	2	0	0	0	0	0.0	1	0	0	0	0	0	0	.000	.000
P	Morrie Martin	L	4	2	0	0	0	0	0.0	0	0	0	1	0	0	0	.000	.000
P	Bob Smith	R	6	2	0	0	0	0	0.0	0	0	0	0	0	0	0	.000	.000
P	Jim Davis	B	10	1	0	0	0	0	0.0	0	0	0	1	0	0	0	.000	.000
P	Bob Kuzava	B	3	0	0	0	0	0	–	0	0	0	0	0	0	0	–	–
P	Bob Miller	R	7	0	0	0	0	0	–	0	0	0	0	0	0	0	–	–
	TEAM TOTAL			5472	1497	235	43	132	2.4	737	685	493	672	58	171	42	.274	.405

INDIVIDUAL FIELDING

POS	Player	T	G	PO	A	E	DP	TC/G	FA	POS	Player	T	G	PO	A	E	DP	TC/G	FA
1B	S. Musial	L	130	1167	99	10	131	9.8	.992	OF	K. Boyer	R	105	275	2	1	1	2.6	.996
	J. Cunningham	L	57	279	17	0	17	5.2	1.000		W. Moon	R	133	245	8	9	1	2.0	.966
	T. Alston	R	6	35	1	2	4	6.3	.947		D. Ennis	R	127	180	3	11	0	1.5	.943
2B	D. Blasingame	R	154	372	512	14	128	5.8	.984		B. Smith	R	79	138	6	4	4	1.9	.973
	E. Kasko	R	1	0	0	0	0	0.0	.000		J. Cunningham	L	46	81	1	3	0	1.8	.965
SS	A. Dark	R	139	276	419	25	105	5.2	.965		E. Miksis	R	31	13	0	0	0	0.4	1.000
	D. Schofield	R	23	21	34	3	8	2.5	.948		D. Lassetter	R	3	9	0	0	0	3.0	1.000
	E. Kasko	R	13	18	24	2	5	3.4	.955		J. King	R	8	7	0	0	0	0.9	1.000
3B	E. Kasko	R	120	100	224	13	21	2.8	.961		I. Noren	L	8	6	0	0	0	0.8	1.000
	K. Boyer	R	41	41	93	13	7	3.6	.912		C. Harmon	R	8	4	0	0	0	0.5	1.000
	A. Dark	R	1	0	2	0	0	2.0	1.000		G. Green	R	3	2	0	0	0	0.7	1.000
										C	H. Smith	R	97	468	42	5	8	5.3	.990
											H. Landrith	R	67	339	29	5	3	5.6	.987
											W. Cooper	R	13	62	5	3	0	5.4	.957

From also-rans in 1956 to surprising contenders in 1957, the Cardinals even edged into first place in July and stayed close to the Braves until a late September skid dropped them eight games back. Del Ennis, picked up from the Phillies, added some needed punch to the lineup. The shift of Ken Boyer from third base to center field may have affected his hitting, as he dropped from .306 with 26 homers to .265 and 19 (only to jump back to .307 and 23 in 1958, back at third). Nonetheless, the outfield trio of Ennis, Boyer, and Moon combined for more homers than any previous Cardinal outfield. Musial's .351 average gave him his seventh and last batting title, but St. Louis could not overcome Milwaukee's advantage in both hitting and pitching. Sadly for Cardinal fans, the man who solidified the Braves' infield while leading the league in base hits was old friend Red Schoendienst, acquired from the Giants in mid-June.

TEAM STATISTICS

W	L	PCT	GB	R	OR	2B	3B	HR	BA	SA	SB	E	DP	FA	CG	BB	SO	ShO	SV	ERA
95	59	.617		772	613	221	62	199	.269	.442	35	120	173	.981	60	570	693	9	24	3.47
87	67	.565	8	737	666	235	43	132	.274	.405	58	131	168	.979	46	506	778	11	29	3.78
84	70	.545	11	690	591	188	38	147	.253	.387	60	127	136	.979	44	456	891	18	29	3.35
80	74	.519	15	747	781	251	33	187	.269	.432	51	107	139	.982	40	429	707	5	29	4.62
77	77	.500	18	623	656	213	44	117	.250	.375	57	136	117	.976	54	412	858	9	23	3.80
69	85	.448	26	643	701	171	54	157	.252	.393	64	161	180	.974	35	471	701	9	20	4.01
62	92	.403	33	628	722	223	31	147	.244	.380	28	149	140	.975	30	601	859	5	26	4.13
62	92	.403	33	586	696	231	60	92	.268	.384	46	170	143	.972	47	421	663	9	15	3.88
LEAGUE TOTAL				5426	5426	1733	365	1178	.260	.400	399	1101	1196	.977	356	3866	6150	75	195	3.88

INDIVIDUAL PITCHING

PITCHER	T	W	L	PCT	ERA	SV	G	GS	CG	IP	H	BB	SO	R	ER	ShO	H/9	BB/9	SO/9
arry Jackson	R	15	9	.625	3.47	1	41	22	6	210.1	196	57	96	84	81	2	8.39	2.44	4.11
ndy McDaniel	R	15	9	.625	3.49	0	30	26	10	191	196	53	75	87	74	1	9.24	2.50	3.53
am Jones	R	12	9	.571	3.60	0	28	27	10	182.2	164	71	154	77	73	2	8.08	3.50	7.59
erm Wehmeier	R	10	7	.588	4.31	0	36	18	5	165	165	54	91	91	79	0	9.00	2.95	4.96
negar Bend Mizell	L	8	10	.444	3.74	0	33	21	7	149.1	136	51	87	69	62	2	8.20	3.07	5.24
llard Schmidt	R	10	3	.769	4.78	0	40	8	1	116.2	146	49	63	67	62	0	11.26	3.78	4.86
on McDaniel	R	7	5	.583	3.22	0	17	13	4	86.2	71	31	45	37	31	2	7.37	3.22	4.67
urry Dickson	R	5	3	.625	4.14	0	14	13	3	74	87	25	29	41	34	1	10.58	3.04	3.53
oyd Merritt	R	1	2	.333	3.31	7	44	0	0	65.1	60	28	35	29	24	0	8.27	3.86	4.82
oyt Wilhelm	R	1	4	.200	4.25	11	40	0	0	55	52	21	29	28	26	0	8.51	3.44	4.75
ly Muffett	R	3	2	.600	2.25	8	23	0	0	44	35	13	21	11	11	0	7.16	2.66	4.30
m Davis	L	0	1	.000	5.27	0	10	0	0	13.2	18	6	5	8	8	0	11.85	3.95	3.29
orrie Martin	L	0	0	—	2.53	0	4	1	0	10.2	5	4	7	3	3	0	4.22	3.38	5.91
ank Barnes	R	0	1	.000	4.50	0	3	1	0	10	13	9	5	5	5	0	11.70	8.10	4.50
ob Smith	L	0	0	—	4.66	1	6	0	0	9.2	12	6	11	10	5	0	11.17	5.59	10.24
m Cheney	R	0	1	.000	5.00	0	4	3	0	9	6	15	10	6	5	0	6.00	15.00	10.00
nn Lovenguth	R	0	1	.000	2.00	0	2	1	0	9	6	6	6	3	2	0	6.00	6.00	6.00
b Miller	R	0	0	—	7.00	0	5	0	0	9	13	5	7	9	7	0	13.00	5.00	7.00
b Kuzava	L	0	0	—	3.86	0	3	0	0	2.1	4	2	2	1	1	0	15.43	7.71	7.71
EAM TOTAL		87	67	.565	3.78	29	383	154	46	1413.1	1385	506	778	666	593	10	8.82	3.22	4.95

MANAGER	W	L	PCT
Fred Hutchinson	69	75	.479
Stan Hack	3	7	.300

POS	Player	B	G	AB	H	2B	3B	HR	HR %	R	RBI	BB	SO	SB	Pinch Hit AB	Pinch Hit H	BA	SA
REGULARS																		
1B	Stan Musial	L	135	472	159	35	2	17	3.6	64	62	72	26	0	12	5	.337	.528
2B	Don Blasingame	L	143	547	150	19	10	2	0.4	71	36	57	47	20	4	0	.274	.356
SS	Eddie Kasko	R	104	259	57	8	1	2	0.8	20	22	21	25	1	10	3	.220	.282
3B	Ken Boyer	R	150	570	175	21	9	23	4.0	101	90	49	53	11	1	0	.307	.496
RF	Wally Moon	L	108	290	69	10	3	7	2.4	36	38	47	30	2	23	2	.238	.366
CF	Curt Flood	R	121	422	110	17	2	10	2.4	50	41	31	56	2	0	0	.261	.382
LF	Del Ennis	R	106	329	86	18	1	3	0.9	22	47	15	35	0	22	2	.261	.350
C	Hal Smith	R	77	220	50	4	1	1	0.5	13	24	14	14	0	5	0	.227	.268
SUBSTITUTES																		
1O	Joe Cunningham	L	131	337	105	20	3	12	3.6	61	57	82	23	4	19	5	.312	.496
S2	Gene Freese	R	62	191	49	11	1	6	3.1	28	16	10	32	1	14	3	.257	.419
SS	Dick Schofield	B	39	108	23	4	0	1	0.9	16	8	23	15	0	7	3	.213	.278
SS	Ruben Amaro	R	40	76	17	2	1	0	0.0	8	0	5	8	0	1	0	.224	.276
S3	Alvin Dark	R	18	64	19	0	0	1	1.6	7	5	2	6	0	5	4	.297	.344
SS	Lee Tate	R	10	35	7	2	0	0	0.0	4	1	4	3	0	1	0	.200	.257
3B	Benny Valenzuela	R	10	14	3	1	0	0	0.0	0	0	1	0	0	5	2	.214	.286
UT	Johnny O'Brien	R	12	2	0	0	0	0	0.0	3	0	1	0	0	1	0	.000	.000
OC	Gene Green	R	137	442	124	18	3	13	2.9	47	55	37	48	2	13	1	.281	.423
OF	Irv Noren	L	117	178	47	9	1	4	2.2	24	22	13	21	0	43	8	.264	.393
OF	Bobby Gene Smith	R	28	88	25	3	0	2	2.3	8	5	2	18	1	1	0	.284	.386
OF	Ellis Burton	B	8	30	7	0	1	2	6.7	5	4	3	8	0	1	0	.233	.500
OF	Joe Taylor	L	18	23	7	3	0	1	4.3	2	2	2	4	0	12	4	.304	.565
C	Hobie Landrith	L	70	144	31	4	0	3	2.1	9	13	26	21	0	24	5	.215	.306
C	Ray Katt	R	19	41	7	1	0	1	2.4	1	4	4	6	0	5	0	.171	.268
PITCHERS																		
P	Sam Jones	R	35	90	9	0	0	0	0.0	2	4	2	26	0	0	0	.100	.100
P	Vinegar Bend Mizell	R	30	61	7	1	0	0	0.0	3	1	1	25	0	0	0	.115	.131
P	Larry Jackson	R	50	60	9	1	0	0	0.0	4	2	1	20	0	0	0	.150	.167
P	Jim Brosnan	R	33	31	3	2	0	0	0.0	2	1	3	11	0	0	0	.097	.161
P	Lindy McDaniel	R	26	30	2	0	0	0	0.0	0	3	0	14	0	0	0	.067	.067
P	Bob Mabe	R	32	24	1	0	0	0	0.0	2	1	1	15	0	0	0	.042	.042
P	Billy Muffett	R	35	20	4	1	0	0	0.0	2	2	1	4	0	0	0	.200	.250
P	Sal Maglie	R	10	16	2	0	0	0	0.0	1	0	1	6	0	0	0	.125	.125
P	Bill Wight	L	28	10	1	0	0	0	0.0	0	0	1	6	0	0	0	.100	.100
P	Phil Paine	R	46	7	2	0	0	0	0.0	1	1	0	1	0	0	0	.286	.286
P	Frank Barnes	R	13	6	1	0	0	0	0.0	2	0	0	2	0	0	0	.167	.167
P	Morrie Martin	L	17	5	0	0	0	0	0.0	0	0	0	3	0	0	0	.000	.000
P	Nels Chittum	R	13	4	1	0	0	0	0.0	0	1	0	2	0	0	0	.250	.250
P	Chuck Stobbs	L	17	4	1	0	0	0	0.0	1	0	1	1	0	0	0	.250	.250
P	Bill Smith	L	2	2	0	0	0	0	0.0	0	0	0	1	0	0	0	.000	.000
P	Herm Wehmeier	R	3	2	1	1	0	0	0.0	0	0	0	0	0	0	0	.500	1.000
P	Phil Clark	R	8	1	0	0	0	0	0.0	0	0	0	1	0	0	0	.000	.000
P	Tom Flanigan	R	2	0	0	0	0	0	–	0	0	0	0	0	0	0	–	–
P	Von McDaniel	R	2	0	0	0	0	0	–	0	0	0	0	0	0	0	–	–
TEAM TOTAL				5255	1371	216	39	111	2.1	619	567	533	637	44	229	47	.261	.380

INDIVIDUAL FIELDING

POS	Player	T	G	PO	A	E	DP	TC/G	FA	POS	Player	T	G	PO	A	E	DP	TC/G	FA
1B	S. Musial	L	124	1019	100	13	127	9.1	.989	OF	C. Flood	R	120	346	18	8	3	3.1	.978
	J. Cunningham	L	67	328	23	1	19	5.3	.997		G. Green	R	75	141	12	7	3	2.1	.956
2B	D. Blasingame	R	137	312	380	26	97	5.2	.964		D. Ennis	R	84	122	11	1	2	1.6	.993
	G. Freese	R	14	32	25	4	4	4.4	.934		W. Moon	R	82	122	5	2	0	1.6	.984
	E. Kasko	R	12	25	31	1	7	4.8	.982		J. Cunningham	L	66	90	3	2	2	1.4	.979
	R. Amaro	R	1	1	1	0	0	2.0	1.000		I. Noren	L	77	75	1	2	0	1.0	.974
	J. O'Brien	R	1	2	0	0	0	2.0	1.000		B. Smith	R	27	57	2	0	0	2.2	1.000
SS	E. Kasko	R	77	111	186	12	47	4.0	.961		E. Burton	R	7	12	0	0	0	1.7	1.000
	D. Schofield	R	27	43	81	9	13	4.9	.932		K. Boyer	R	6	11	0	0	0	1.8	1.000
	R. Amaro	R	36	44	65	6	18	3.2	.948		J. Taylor	L	5	10	0	0	0	2.0	1.000
	G. Freese	R	28	45	52	8	10	3.8	.924										
	L. Tate	R	9	16	22	2	5	4.4	.950	C	H. Smith	R	71	346	22	4	4	5.2	.989
	A. Dark	R	8	10	23	2	6	4.4	.943		G. Green	R	48	287	23	2	2	6.5	.994
	J. O'Brien	R	5	1	1	0	0	0.4	1.000		H. Landrith	R	45	227	16	2	3	5.4	.992
	K. Boyer	R	1	1	0	0	0	1.000			R. Katt	R	14	63	4	2	2	4.9	.971
3B	K. Boyer	R	144	156	350	20	41	3.7	.962										
	C. Flood	R	1	0	0	0	0	0.0	.000										
	A. Dark	R	8	4	12	1	0	2.1	.941										
	G. Freese	R	3	5	6	0	0	3.7	1.000										
	B. Valenzuela	R	3	3	4	1	0	2.7	.875										
	E. Kasko	R	1	0	1	0	0	1.0	1.000										

Was the second-place finish in 1957 an illusion? St. Louis fans had to be asking themselves that as the Cards limped out of the gate, falling quickly into the cellar in '58. They rallied to third place by the end of June, but fell off again, finishing in a dense four-team cluster, with just three games separating the top of the second division from the bottom. The plunge resulted from an uncharacteristic offensive failure; they were dead last in runs for the first time in over forty years. One of the few highlights came on May 13, when Musial cracked a double into the left field corner off Moe Drabowsky of the Cubs to become the eighth player to reach the 3,000-hit plateau. The Cardinals unveiled their third rookie centerfielder in four years, a 20-year-old acquired (stolen might be a better word) from Cincinnati: Curt Flood, picked up for three pitchers, only one of whom appeared in even one game for the Reds.

TEAM STATISTICS

	W	L	PCT	GB	R	OR	2B	3B	HR	BA	SA	SB	E	DP	FA	CG	BB	SO	ShO	SV	ERA
IL	92	62	.597		675	541	221	21	167	**.266**	.412	26	120	152	.980	**72**	426	773	**16**	17	3.21
T	84	70	.545	8	662	607	229	**68**	134	.264	.410	30	133	173	.978	43	470	679	10	**41**	3.56
	80	74	.519	12	**727**	698	250	42	170	.263	.422	64	152	156	.975	38	512	775	7	25	3.98
IN	76	78	.494	16	695	621	242	40	123	.258	.389	61	100	148	**.983**	50	419	705	7	20	3.73
HI	72	82	.468	20	709	725	207	49	**182**	.265	**.426**	39	150	161	.975	27	619	805	5	24	4.22
L	72	82	.468	20	619	704	216	39	111	.261	.380	44	153	163	.974	45	567	822	6	25	4.12
A	71	83	.461	21	668	761	166	50	172	.251	.402	**73**	146	**198**	.975	30	606	**855**	7	31	4.47
HI	69	85	.448	23	664	762	238	56	124	.266	.400	51	129	136	.978	51	446	778	6	15	4.32
AGUE TOTAL					5419	5419	1769	365	1183	.262	.405	388	1083	1287	.977	356	4065	6192	64	198	3.95

INDIVIDUAL PITCHING

TCHER	T	W	L	PCT	ERA	SV	G	GS	CG	IP	H	BB	SO	R	ER	ShO	H/9	BB/9	SO/9
m Jones	R	14	13	.519	2.88	0	35	35	14	250	204	107	225	95	80	2	7.34	3.85	8.10
rry Jackson	R	13	13	.500	3.68	8	49	23	11	198	211	51	124	93	81	1	9.59	2.32	5.64
negar Bend Mizell	L	10	14	.417	3.42	0	30	29	8	189.2	178	91	80	81	72	2	8.45	4.32	3.80
n Brosnan	R	8	4	.667	3.44	7	33	12	2	115	107	50	65	46	44	0	8.37	3.91	5.09
b Mabe	R	3	9	.250	4.51	0	31	13	4	111.2	113	41	74	66	56	0	9.11	3.30	5.96
ndy McDaniel	R	5	7	.417	5.80	0	26	17	2	108.2	139	31	47	76	70	1	11.51	2.57	3.89
ly Muffett	R	4	6	.400	4.93	5	35	6	1	84	107	42	41	52	46	0	11.46	4.50	4.39
il Paine	R	5	1	.833	3.56	1	46	0	0	73.1	70	31	45	33	29	0	8.59	3.80	5.52
l Wight	L	3	0	1.000	5.02	2	28	1	1	57.1	64	32	18	35	32	0	10.05	5.02	2.83
l Maglie	R	2	6	.250	4.75	0	10	10	2	53	46	25	21	31	28	0	7.81	4.25	3.57
uck Stobbs	L	1	3	.250	3.63	0	17	0	0	39.2	40	14	25	16	16	0	9.08	3.18	5.67
ls Chittum	R	0	1	.000	6.44	0	13	2	0	29.1	31	7	13	21	21	0	9.51	2.15	3.99
rrie Martin	L	3	1	.750	4.74	0	17	0	0	24.2	19	12	16	13	13	0	6.93	4.38	5.84
ank Barnes	R	1	1	.500	7.58	0	8	1	0	19	19	16	17	16	16	0	9.00	7.58	8.05
l Smith	L	0	1	.000	6.52	0	2	1	0	9.2	12	4	4	7	7	0	11.17	3.72	3.72
il Clark	R	0	1	.000	3.52	1	7	0	0	7.2	11	3	1	5	3	0	12.91	3.52	1.17
rm Wehmeier	R	0	1	.000	13.50	0	3	3	0	6	13	2	4	9	9	0	19.50	3.00	6.00
n McDaniel	R	0	0	–	13.50	0	2	1	0	2	5	5	0	3	3	0	22.50	22.50	0.00
hnny O'Brien	R	0	0	–	22.50	0	1	0	0	2	7	2	2	5	5	0	31.50	9.00	9.00
m Flanigan	L	0	0	–	9.00	0	1	0	0	1	2	1	1	1	1	0	18.00	9.00	0.00
AM TOTAL		72	82	.468	4.12	25	394	154	45	1381.2	1398	567	822	704	632	6	9.11	3.69	5.35

MANAGER	W	L	PCT
Solly Hemus	71	83	.461

POS	Player	B	G	AB	H	2B	3B	HR	HR %	R	RBI	BB	SO	SB	Pinch Hit AB	Pinch Hit H	BA	SA
REGULARS																		
1B	Stan Musial	L	115	341	87	13	2	14	4.1	37	44	60	25	0	22	5	.255	.428
2B	Don Blasingame	L	150	615	178	26	7	1	0.2	90	24	67	42	15	1	0	.289	.359
SS	Alex Grammas	R	131	368	99	14	2	3	0.8	43	30	38	26	3	1	1	.269	.342
3B	Ken Boyer	R	149	563	174	18	5	28	5.0	86	94	67	77	12	1	0	.309	.508
RF	Joe Cunningham	L	144	458	158	28	6	7	1.5	65	60	88	47	2	8	2	.345	.478
CF	Gino Cimoli	R	143	519	145	40	7	8	1.5	61	72	37	83	7	3	1	.279	.430
LF	Bill White	L	138	517	156	33	9	12	2.3	77	72	34	61	15	5	1	.302	.470
C	Hal Smith	R	142	452	122	15	3	13	2.9	35	50	15	28	2	1	0	.270	.403
SUBSTITUTES																		
1B	George Crowe	L	77	103	31	6	0	8	7.8	14	29	5	12	0	63	17	.301	.592
S2	Wally Shannon	L	47	95	27	5	0	0	0.0	5	5	0	12	0	28	9	.284	.337
3B	Ray Jablonski	R	60	87	22	4	0	3	3.4	11	14	8	19	1	44	7	.253	.402
UT	Dick Gray	R	36	51	16	1	0	1	2.0	9	6	6	8	3	17	4	.314	.392
SS	Lee Tate	R	41	50	7	1	1	1	2.0	5	4	5	7	0	0	0	.140	.260
23	Solly Hemus	L	24	17	4	2	0	0	0.0	2	1	7	2	0	14	2	.235	.353
OF	Curt Flood	R	121	208	53	7	3	7	3.4	24	26	16	35	2	10	5	.255	.418
OC	Gene Oliver	R	68	172	42	9	0	6	3.5	14	28	7	41	3	18	4	.244	.401
OC	Gene Green	R	30	74	14	6	0	1	1.4	8	3	5	18	0	2	0	.189	.311
OF	Bobby Gene Smith	R	43	60	13	1	1	1	1.7	11	7	1	9	0	7	2	.217	.317
OF	Chuck Essegian	R	17	39	7	2	1	0	0.0	2	5	1	13	0	9	1	.179	.282
OF	Duke Carmel	L	10	23	3	1	0	0	0.0	2	3	1	6	0	0	0	.130	.174
O1	Irv Noren	L	8	8	1	1	0	0	0.0	0	0	0	0	0	5	0	.125	.250
OF	Charlie King	R	5	7	3	0	0	0	0.0	0	1	0	2	0	0	0	.429	.429
OF	Joe Durham	R	6	5	0	0	0	0	0.0	0	0	0	1	0	2	0	.000	.000
C	J W Porter	R	23	33	7	3	0	1	3.0	5	2	1	4	0	3	1	.212	.394
C	Ray Katt	R	15	24	7	2	0	0	0.0	0	2	0	8	0	1	0	.292	.375
C	Tim McCarver	L	8	24	4	1	0	0	0.0	3	0	2	1	0	1	0	.167	.208
PH	Charlie O'Rourke	R	2	2	0	0	0	0	0.0	0	0	0	0	0	2	0	.000	.000
PITCHERS																		
P	Larry Jackson	R	54	80	9	1	0	0	0.0	9	2	2	25	0	0	0	.113	.125
P	Vinegar Bend Mizell	R	31	75	14	1	1	0	0.0	7	7	3	29	0	0	0	.187	.227
P	Ernie Broglio	R	35	61	6	0	0	0	0.0	3	4	3	18	0	0	0	.098	.098
P	Gary Blaylock	R	31	34	4	0	0	2	5.9	4	4	0	17	0	0	0	.118	.294
P	Lindy McDaniel	R	62	29	1	0	0	0	0.0	2	0	3	16	0	0	0	.034	.034
P	Bob Gibson	R	21	26	3	2	0	0	0.0	1	1	0	10	0	0	0	.115	.192
P	Bob Miller	R	11	24	5	0	0	0	0.0	1	1	1	13	0	0	0	.208	.208
P	Marshall Bridges	B	27	23	5	1	0	1	4.3	3	4	1	6	0	0	0	.217	.391
P	Dick Ricketts	L	12	18	1	0	0	0	0.0	0	0	0	6	0	0	0	.056	.056
P	Alex Kellner	R	12	9	2	0	0	0	0.0	0	0	0	7	0	0	0	.222	.222
P	Jim Brosnan	R	20	7	2	0	1	0	0.0	0	0	0	2	0	0	0	.286	.571
P	Bob Duliba	R	11	4	0	0	0	0	0.0	0	0	0	3	0	0	0	.000	.000
P	Dean Stone	L	18	4	0	0	0	0	0.0	0	0	0	0	0	0	0	.000	.000
P	Hal Jeffcoat	R	12	3	0	0	0	0	0.0	0	0	0	3	0	0	0	.000	.000
P	Bob Blaylock	R	3	1	0	0	0	0	0.0	0	0	0	0	0	0	0	.000	.000
P	Tom Hughes	L	2	1	0	0	0	0	0.0	0	0	0	1	0	0	0	.000	.000
P	Howie Nunn	R	16	1	0	0	0	0	0.0	0	0	0	0	0	0	0	.000	.000
P	Bill Smith	L	6	1	0	0	0	0	0.0	0	0	0	0	0	0	0	.000	.000
P	Jack Urban	R	8	1	0	0	0	0	0.0	0	0	0	0	0	0	0	.000	.000
P	Tom Cheney	R	11	0	0	0	0	0	—	0	0	0	0	0	0	0	—	—
P	Phil Clark	R	7	0	0	0	0	0	—	0	0	0	0	0	0	0	—	—
P	Marv Grissom	R	3	0	0	0	0	0	—	0	0	0	0	0	0	0	—	—
TEAM TOTAL				5317	1432	244	49	118	2.2	641	605	485	747	65	268	62	.269	.400

INDIVIDUAL FIELDING

POS	Player	T	G	PO	A	E	DP	TC/G	FA	POS	Player	T	G	PO	A	E	DP	TC/G	FA
1B	S. Musial	L	90	623	63	7	72	7.7	.990	OF	G. Cimoli	R	141	267	12	6	2	2.0	.979
	B. White	L	71	404	25	2	32	6.1	.995		J. Cunningham	L	121	201	5	6	1	1.8	.972
	J. Cunningham	L	35	158	9	1	22	4.8	.994		B. White	L	92	175	2	7	1	2.0	.962
	J. Porter	R	1	0	0	0	0	0.0	.000		C. Flood	R	106	147	1	5	1	1.4	.967
	G. Crowe	L	14	82	12	0	9	6.7	1.000		G. Oliver	R	42	62	1	3	0	1.6	.955
	G. Oliver	R	5	39	2	0	1	8.2	1.000		G. Green	R	19	28	6	2	2	1.9	.944
	I. Noren	L	1	1	0	0	1	1.0	1.000		B. Smith	R	32	31	3	1	1	1.1	.971
											D. Gray	R	1	0	0	0	0	0.0	.000
2B	D. Blasingame	R	150	362	439	17	104	5.5	.979		I. Noren	L	2	0	0	0	0	0.0	.000
	C. Flood	R	1	0	0	0	0	0.0	.000		D. Carmel	L	10	15	0	0	0	1.5	1.000
	W. Shannon	R	10	13	18	3	2	3.4	.912		C. Essegian	R	9	8	1	0	0	1.0	1.000
	L. Tate	R	2	2	3	0	1	2.5	1.000		C. King	R	4	7	0	0	0	1.8	1.000
	S. Hemus	R	1	0	3	0	0	3.0	1.000		J. Durham	R	1	2	0	0	0	2.0	1.000
	D. Gray	R	2	1	0	0	0	0.5	1.000		S. Musial	L	3	1	0	0	0	0.3	1.000
SS	A. Grammas	R	130	216	373	22	80	4.7	.964	C	H. Smith	R	141	758	60	9	13	5.9	.989
	L. Tate	R	39	31	45	6	9	2.1	.927		J. Porter	R	19	53	4	0	1	3.0	1.000
	W. Shannon	R	21	27	17	0	7	2.1	1.000		R. Katt	R	14	38	2	1	0	2.9	.976
	R. Jablonski	R	1	0	0	0	0	0.0	.000		G. Green	R	11	34	3	0	0	3.4	1.000
	D. Gray	R	13	10	13	1	3	1.8	.958		T. McCarver	R	6	32	2	1	0	5.8	.971
	K. Boyer	R	12	9	10	2	1	1.8	.905		G. Oliver	R	9	24	2	1	0	3.0	.963
3B	K. Boyer	R	143	134	300	20	32	3.2	.956										
	R. Jablonski	R	19	7	20	3	2	1.6	.900										
	D. Gray	R	6	1	4	2	0	1.2	.714										
	S. Hemus	R	1	0	2	0	0	2.0	1.000										
	L. Tate	R	2	0	1	0	0	0.5	1.000										

Slowly, very slowly, a team was starting to come together. Their next pennant was still a few years away, though, and there were more tough years ahead. The Cardinals concluded the '59 season 15 games out of first (before the Dodgers-Braves playoff); nothing to be proud of, but better than a seventh-place finish would indicate. The Cards picked up Bill White from the Giants, and brought a young fireballer named Bob Gibson up from the minors. They also acquired Ernie Broglio, whose role in Cardinal history will be forever secure. Joe Cunningham's .345 average placed him second in the league behind Hank Aaron, and White and Boyer gave them three .300 hitters for the first time since '54. Stan Musial, now 38, slipped to .255, and began to hear whispers that the time had come for him to retire.

TEAM STATISTICS

	W	L	PCT	GB	R	OR	2B	3B	Batting HR	BA	SA	SB	E	Fielding DP	FA	CG	BB	Pitching SO	ShO	SV	ERA
A	88	68	.564		705	670	196	46	148	.257	.396	84	114	154	.981	43	614	1077	14	26	3.79
IL	86	70	.551	2	724	623	216	36	177	.265	.417	41	127	138	.979	69	429	775	18	18	3.51
	83	71	.539	4	705	613	239	35	167	.261	.414	81	152	118	.974	52	500	873	12	23	3.47
T	78	76	.506	9	651	680	230	42	112	.263	.384	32	154	165	.975	48	418	730	7	17	3.90
HI	74	80	.481	13	673	688	209	44	163	.249	.398	32	140	142	.977	30	519	765	11	25	4.01
N	74	80	.481	13	764	738	258	34	161	.274	.427	65	126	157	.978	44	456	690	7	26	4.31
L	71	83	.461	16	641	725	244	49	118	.269	.400	65	146	158	.975	36	564	846	8	21	4.34
HI	64	90	.416	23	599	725	196	38	113	.242	.362	39	154	132	.973	54	474	769	8	15	4.27
AGUE TOTAL					5462	5462	1788	324	1159	.260	.400	439	1113	1164	.977	376	3974	6525	85	171	3.95

INDIVIDUAL PITCHING

TCHER	T	W	L	PCT	ERA	SV	G	GS	CG	IP	H	BB	SO	R	ER	ShO	H/9	BB/9	SO/9
rry Jackson	R	14	13	.519	3.30	0	40	37	12	256	271	64	145	103	94	3	9.53	2.25	5.10
negar Bend Mizell	L	13	10	.565	4.20	0	31	30	8	201.1	196	89	108	104	94	1	8.76	3.98	4.83
nie Broglio	R	7	12	.368	4.72	0	35	25	6	181.1	174	89	118	104	95	0	8.64	4.42	6.60
ndy McDaniel	R	14	12	.538	3.82	15	62	7	1	132	144	41	86	61	56	0	9.82	2.80	5.86
ary Blaylock	R	4	5	.444	5.13	0	26	12	3	100	117	43	61	61	57	0	10.53	3.87	5.49
arshall Bridges	L	6	3	.667	4.26	1	27	4	1	76	67	37	76	38	36	0	7.93	4.38	9.00
b Gibson	R	3	5	.375	3.33	0	13	9	2	75.2	77	39	48	35	28	1	9.16	4.64	5.71
b Miller	R	4	3	.571	3.31	0	11	10	3	70.2	66	21	43	31	26	0	8.41	2.67	5.48
ck Ricketts	R	1	6	.143	5.82	0	12	9	0	55.2	68	30	25	42	36	0	10.99	4.85	4.04
ex Kellner	L	2	1	.667	3.16	0	12	4	0	37	31	10	19	17	13	0	7.54	2.43	4.62
n Brosnan	R	1	3	.250	4.91	2	20	1	0	33	34	15	18	18	18	0	9.27	4.09	4.91
an Stone	L	0	1	.000	4.20	1	18	1	0	30	30	16	17	15	14	0	9.00	4.80	5.10
b Duliba	R	0	1	.000	2.78	1	11	0	0	22.2	19	12	14	7	7	0	7.54	4.76	5.56
wie Nunn	R	2	2	.500	7.59	0	16	0	0	21.1	23	15	20	18	18	0	9.70	6.33	8.44
l Jeffcoat	R	0	1	.000	9.17	0	11	0	0	17.2	33	9	7	18	18	0	16.81	4.58	3.57
m Cheney	R	0	1	.000	6.94	0	11	2	0	11.2	17	11	8	9	9	0	13.11	8.49	6.17
ck Urban	R	0	0	–	9.28	0	8	0	0	10.2	18	7	4	11	11	0	15.19	5.91	3.38
b Blaylock	R	0	1	.000	4.00	0	3	1	0	9	8	3	3	5	4	0	8.00	3.00	3.00
l Smith	L	0	0	–	1.08	1	6	0	0	8.1	11	3	4	3	1	0	11.88	3.24	4.32
l Clark	R	0	1	.000	12.86	0	7	0	0	7	8	8	5	11	10	0	10.29	10.29	6.43
n Hughes	R	0	2	.000	15.75	0	2	2	0	4	9	2	2	9	7	0	20.25	4.50	4.50
rv Grissom	R	0	0	–	22.50	0	3	0	0	2	6	0	0	5	5	0	27.00	0.00	0.00
AM TOTAL		71	83	.461	4.34	21	385	154	36	1363	1427	564	846	725	657	8	9.42	3.72	5.59

MANAGER	W	L	PCT
Solly Hemus	86	68	.558

POS	Player	B	G	AB	H	2B	3B	HR	HR %	R	RBI	BB	SO	SB	Pinch Hit AB	Pinch Hit H	BA	SA
REGULARS																		
1B	Bill White	L	144	554	157	27	10	16	2.9	81	79	42	83	12	3	0	.283	.455
2B	Julian Javier	R	119	451	107	19	8	4	0.9	55	21	21	72	19	0	0	.237	.341
SS	Daryl Spencer	R	148	507	131	20	3	16	3.2	70	58	81	74	1	2	1	.258	.404
3B	Ken Boyer	R	151	552	168	26	10	32	5.8	95	97	56	77	8	5	1	.304	.562
RF	Joe Cunningham	L	139	492	138	28	3	6	1.2	68	39	59	59	1	9	2	.280	.386
CF	Curt Flood	R	140	396	94	20	1	8	2.0	37	38	35	54	0	2	0	.237	.354
LF	Stan Musial	L	116	331	91	17	1	17	5.1	49	63	41	34	1	28	4	.275	.486
C	Hal Smith	R	127	337	77	16	0	2	0.6	20	28	29	33	1	5	1	.228	.294
SUBSTITUTES																		
UT	Alex Grammas	R	102	196	48	4	1	4	2.0	20	17	12	15	0	7	2	.245	.337
1B	George Crowe	L	73	72	17	3	0	4	5.6	5	13	5	16	0	61	15	.236	.444
2B	Wally Shannon	L	18	23	4	0	0	0	0.0	2	1	3	6	0	9	1	.174	.174
S3	Julio Gotay	R	3	8	3	0	0	0	0.0	1	0	0	2	1	1	1	.375	.375
2B	Dick Gray	R	9	5	0	0	0	0	0.0	1	1	2	2	0	3	0	.000	.000
2B	Ed Olivares	R	3	5	0	0	0	0	0.0	0	0	0	3	0	2	0	.000	.000
1O	Duke Carmel	L	4	3	0	0	0	0	0.0	0	0	1	1	1	0	0	.000	.000
2B	Bob Sadowski	L	1	1	0	0	0	0	0.0	0	0	1	0	0	0	0	.000	.000
2B	Rocky Bridges	R	3	0	0	0	0	0	–	0	0	0	0	0	0	0	–	–
OF	Walt Moryn	L	75	200	49	4	3	11	5.5	24	35	17	38	0	14	1	.245	.460
OF	Bob Nieman	R	81	188	54	13	5	4	2.1	19	31	24	31	0	26	4	.287	.473
OF	Leon Wagner	L	39	98	21	2	0	4	4.1	12	11	17	17	0	7	1	.214	.357
OF	Charlie James	R	43	50	9	1	0	2	4.0	5	5	1	12	0	9	1	.180	.320
OF	Don Landrum	L	13	49	12	0	1	2	4.1	7	3	4	6	3	0	0	.245	.408
OF	John Glenn	R	32	31	8	0	1	0	0.0	4	5	0	9	0	3	0	.258	.323
OF	Ellis Burton	B	29	28	6	1	0	0	0.0	5	2	4	14	0	5	2	.214	.250
OF	Gary Kolb	L	9	3	0	0	0	0	0.0	1	0	0	0	0	0	0	.000	.000
OF	Doug Clemens	L	1	0	0	0	0	0	–	0	0	0	0	0	0	0	–	–
C	Carl Sawatski	L	78	179	41	4	0	6	3.4	16	27	22	24	0	27	7	.229	.352
C	Tim McCarver	L	10	10	2	0	0	0	0.0	3	0	0	2	0	4	1	.200	.200
C	Chris Cannizzaro	R	7	9	2	0	0	0	0.0	0	1	1	3	0	0	0	.222	.222
C	Darrell Johnson	R	8	3	0	0	0	0	0.0	0	0	1	0	0	0	0	.000	.000
C	Del Rice	R	1	2	0	0	0	0	0.0	0	0	1	0	0	0	0	.000	.000
PITCHERS																		
P	Larry Jackson	R	52	95	20	1	0	0	0.0	10	3	6	21	0	0	0	.211	.232
P	Ernie Broglio	R	52	68	14	4	0	0	0.0	7	5	7	22	0	0	0	.206	.265
P	Ray Sadecki	L	29	57	12	0	0	0	0.0	5	2	1	6	0	0	0	.211	.211
P	Curt Simmons	L	29	47	10	1	0	0	0.0	8	1	4	9	0	0	0	.213	.234
P	Ron Kline	R	34	35	5	0	0	0	0.0	1	1	0	13	0	0	0	.143	.143
P	Bob Gibson	R	40	28	5	1	0	0	0.0	4	1	0	7	0	0	0	.179	.214
P	Lindy McDaniel	R	65	26	6	0	0	0	0.0	0	0	1	7	0	0	0	.231	.269
P	Vinegar Bend Mizell	R	9	18	2	1	0	0	0.0	1	2	1	10	0	0	0	.111	.167
P	Bob Miller	R	17	14	2	0	0	0	0.0	1	1	1	6	0	0	0	.143	.143
P	Marshall Bridges	B	20	6	0	0	0	0	0.0	1	0	1	1	0	0	0	.000	.000
P	Bob Duliba	R	27	5	1	0	0	0	0.0	1	0	0	2	0	0	0	.200	.200
P	Frank Barnes	R	4	2	0	0	0	0	0.0	0	0	0	0	0	0	0	.000	.000
P	Mel Nelson	R	2	2	1	0	0	0	0.0	0	1	0	1	0	0	0	.500	.500
P	Ed Bauta	R	9	1	0	0	0	0	0.0	0	0	0	0	0	0	0	.000	.000
P	Bob Grim	R	15	0	0	0	0	0	0.0	0	0	0	0	0	0	0	.000	.000
P	Cal Browning	L	1	0	0	0	0	0	–	0	0	0	0	0	0	0	–	–
TEAM TOTAL				5187	1317	213	48	138	2.7	639	592	501	792	48	232	45	.254	.393

INDIVIDUAL FIELDING

POS	Player	T	G	PO	A	E	DP	TC/G	FA
1B	B. White	L	123	994	65	11	109	8.7	.990
	S. Musial	L	29	203	17	2	16	7.7	.991
	J. Cunningham	L	15	114	10	0	7	8.3	1.000
	G. Crowe	L	5	21	2	0	1	4.6	1.000
	D. Carmel	L	2	10	2	0	1	6.0	1.000
2B	J. Javier	R	119	272	338	24	71	5.3	.962
	A. Grammas	R	38	38	63	4	16	2.8	.962
	D. Spencer	R	16	27	36	1	8	4.0	.984
	W. Shannon	R	15	9	23	0	4	2.1	1.000
	D. Gray	R	4	2	4	0	2	1.5	1.000
	R. Bridges	R	3	4	1	0	1	1.7	1.000
	E. Olivares	R	1	0	1	1	0	2.0	.500
	B. Sadowski	R	1	0	0	1	0	1.0	.000
SS	D. Spencer	R	138	215	323	31	66	4.1	.946
	A. Grammas	R	40	56	81	4	12	3.5	.972
	J. Gotay	R	2	1	2	1	0	2.0	.750
	W. Shannon	R	1	1	0	0	0	1.0	1.000
3B	K. Boyer	R	146	140	300	19	37	3.1	.959
	A. Grammas	R	13	8	27	1	5	2.8	.972
	C. Flood	R	1	1	0	0	0	1.0	1.000
	J. Gotay	R	1	0	1	0	0	1.0	1.000
	D. Gray	R	1	0	1	0	0	1.0	1.000
OF	C. Flood	R	134	290	7	2	0	2.2	.993
	J. Cunningham	L	116	184	6	10	1	1.7	.950
	W. Moryn	R	62	100	4	1	0	1.7	.990
	S. Musial	L	59	97	2	1	0	1.7	.990
	B. White	L	29	64	1	2	0	2.3	.970
	B. Nieman	R	55	63	0	4	0	1.2	.940
	L. Wagner	R	32	48	4	2	0	1.7	.963
	C. James	R	37	21	1	2	1	0.6	.917
	J. Glenn	R	28	19	0	0	0	0.7	1.000
	E. Burton	R	23	8	0	0	0	0.3	1.000
	D. Carmel	L	1	0	0	0	0	0.0	1.000
	D. Landrum	R	13	34	1	0	0	2.7	1.000
	G. Kolb	R	2	4	0	0	0	2.0	1.000
	D. Clemens	R	1	2	0	0	0	2.0	1.000
C	H. Smith	R	124	664	61	7	9	5.9	.990
	C. Sawatski	R	67	279	25	2	5	4.6	.993
	C. Cannizzaro	R	6	19	3	0	1	3.7	1.000
	D. Johnson	R	8	10	1	0	0	1.4	1.000
	T. McCarver	R	5	9	0	0	0	1.8	1.000
	D. Rice	R	1	4	0	0	0	4.0	1.000

Even considering the fact that 1960 was a pitcher's year, the improvement in the Redbird staff was dramatic. They went from a tie for sixth in runs allowed to third, and cut seven-tenths of a run from their ERA. Ernie Broglio tied Warren Spahn for the league lead in wins, gave up the fewest hits per nine innings, and ranked second in ERA behind Mike McCormick's 2.70. Lindy McDaniel, at age 24, had his second straight outstanding season in relief, leading the league with 26 saves, and posting a 12–4 record and 2.09 ERA. Offense was still a problem, though, as they ranked sixth in runs despite Ken Boyer's fine season. Boyer had a career-high 32 homers, and ranked third in slugging, fourth in homers, and fifth in RBIs. Three more players who would play important roles in the '64 championship club joined the Cardinals: Curt Simmons came over from the Phillies, and Ray Sadecki and Julian Javier came up from the minor leagues.

TEAM STATISTICS

W	L	PCT	GB	R	OR	2B	3B	HR	BA	SA	SB	E	DP	FA	CG	BB	SO	ShO	SV	ERA
95	59	.617		734	593	236	56	120	.276	.407	34	128	163	.979	47	386	811	11	33	3.49
88	66	.571	7	724	658	198	48	170	.265	.417	69	141	137	.976	55	518	807	13	28	3.76
86	68	.558	9	639	616	213	48	138	.254	.393	48	141	152	.976	37	511	906	11	30	3.64
82	72	.532	13	662	593	216	38	126	.255	.383	95	125	142	.979	46	564	1122	13	20	3.40
79	75	.513	16	671	631	220	62	130	.255	.393	86	166	117	.972	55	512	897	16	26	3.44
67	87	.435	28	640	692	230	40	140	.250	.388	73	125	155	.979	33	442	740	8	35	4.00
60	94	.390	35	634	776	213	48	119	.243	.369	51	143	133	.977	36	565	805	6	25	4.35
59	95	.383	36	546	691	196	44	99	.239	.351	45	155	129	.974	45	439	736	6	16	4.01
AGUE TOTAL				5250	5250	1722	384	1042	.255	.388	501	1124	1128	.977	354	3937	6824	84	213	3.76

INDIVIDUAL PITCHING

TCHER	T	W	L	PCT	ERA	SV	G	GS	CG	IP	H	BB	SO	R	ER	ShO	H/9	BB/9	SO/9
rry Jackson	R	18	13	.581	3.48	0	43	38	14	282	277	70	171	123	109	3	8.84	2.23	5.46
nie Broglio	R	21	9	.700	2.74	0	52	24	9	226.1	172	100	188	76	69	3	6.84	3.98	7.48
y Sadecki	L	9	9	.500	3.78	0	26	26	7	157.1	148	86	95	76	66	1	8.47	4.92	5.43
rt Simmons	L	7	4	.636	2.66	0	23	17	3	152	149	31	63	50	45	1	8.82	1.84	3.73
n Kline	R	4	9	.308	6.04	1	34	17	1	117.2	133	43	54	86	79	0	10.17	3.29	4.13
dy McDaniel	R	12	4	.750	2.09	26	65	2	1	116.1	85	24	105	28	27	0	6.58	1.86	8.12
b Gibson	R	3	6	.333	5.61	0	27	12	2	86.2	97	48	69	61	54	0	10.07	4.98	7.17
negar Bend Mizell	L	1	3	.250	4.55	0	9	9	0	55.1	64	28	42	31	28	0	10.41	4.55	6.83
b Miller	R	4	3	.571	3.42	0	15	7	0	52.2	53	17	33	21	20	0	9.06	2.91	5.64
b Duliba	R	4	4	.500	4.20	0	27	0	0	40.2	49	16	23	20	19	0	10.84	3.54	5.09
arshall Bridges	L	2	2	.500	3.45	1	20	1	0	31.1	33	16	27	15	12	0	9.48	4.60	7.76
b Grim	R	1	0	1.000	3.05	0	15	0	0	20.2	22	9	15	7	7	0	9.58	3.92	6.53
Bauta	R	0	0	—	6.32	1	9	0	0	15.2	14	11	6	11	11	0	8.04	6.32	3.45
el Nelson	L	0	1	.000	3.38	0	2	1	0	8	7	2	7	3	3	0	7.88	2.25	7.88
ank Barnes	R	0	1	.000	3.52	1	4	1	0	7.2	8	9	8	5	3	0	9.39	10.57	9.39
al Browning	L	0	0	—	40.50	0	1	0	0	.2	5	1	0	3	3	0	67.50	13.50	0.00
AM TOTAL		86	68	.558	3.64	30	372	155	37	1371	1316	511	906	616	555	8	8.64	3.35	5.95

MANAGER	W	L	PCT
Solly Hemus	33	41	.446
Johnny Keane	47	33	.588

POS	Player	B	G	AB	H	2B	3B	HR	HR %	R	RBI	BB	SO	SB	Pinch Hit AB	Pinch Hit H	BA	SA
REGULARS																		
1B	Bill White	L	153	591	169	28	11	20	3.4	89	90	64	84	8	3	0	.286	.472
2B	Julian Javier	R	113	445	124	14	3	2	0.4	58	41	30	51	11	0	0	.279	.337
SS	Alex Grammas	R	89	170	36	10	1	0	0.0	23	21	19	21	0	5	1	.212	.282
3B	Ken Boyer	R	153	589	194	26	11	24	4.1	109	95	68	91	6	0	0	.329	.533
RF	Charlie James	R	108	349	89	19	2	4	1.1	43	44	15	59	2	19	3	.255	.355
CF	Curt Flood	R	132	335	108	15	5	2	0.6	53	21	35	33	6	12	4	.322	.415
LF	Stan Musial	L	123	372	107	22	4	15	4.0	46	70	52	35	0	19	5	.288	.489
C	Jimmie Schaffer	R	68	153	39	7	0	1	0.7	15	16	9	29	0	1	1	.255	.320
SUBSTITUTES																		
S2	Bob Lillis	R	86	230	50	4	0	0	0.0	24	21	7	13	3	0	0	.217	.235
SS	Daryl Spencer	R	37	130	33	4	0	4	3.1	19	21	23	17	1	0	0	.254	.377
2B	Red Schoendienst	B	72	120	36	9	0	1	0.8	9	12	12	6	1	48	16	.300	.400
SS	Jerry Buchek	R	31	90	12	2	0	0	0.0	6	9	0	28	0	0	0	.133	.156
SS	Julio Gotay	R	10	45	11	4	0	0	0.0	5	5	3	5	0	0	0	.244	.333
OF	Joe Cunningham	L	113	322	92	11	2	7	2.2	60	40	53	32	1	20	5	.286	.398
OF	Don Taussig	R	98	188	54	14	5	2	1.1	27	25	16	34	2	8	2	.287	.447
OF	Carl Warwick	R	55	152	38	6	2	4	2.6	27	16	18	33	3	7	3	.250	.395
OF	Don Landrum	L	28	66	11	2	0	1	1.5	5	3	5	14	1	1	0	.167	.242
OF	Walt Moryn	L	17	32	4	2	0	0	0.0	0	2	1	5	0	10	1	.125	.188
OF	Ed Olivares	R	21	30	5	0	0	0	0.0	2	1	0	4	1	11	1	.167	.167
OF	Bob Nieman	R	6	17	8	1	0	0	0.0	0	2	0	2	0	2	1	.471	.529
OF	Doug Clemens	L	6	12	2	1	0	0	0.0	1	0	3	1	0	3	1	.167	.250
C	Carl Sawatski	L	86	174	52	8	0	10	5.7	23	33	25	17	0	39	10	.299	.517
C	Hal Smith	R	45	125	31	4	1	0	0.0	6	10	11	12	0	1	0	.248	.296
C	Tim McCarver	L	22	67	16	2	1	1	1.5	5	6	0	5	0	2	2	.239	.343
C	Gene Oliver	R	22	52	14	2	0	4	7.7	8	9	6	10	0	5	1	.269	.538
C	Chris Cannizzaro	R	6	2	1	0	0	0	0.0	0	0	0	0	0	1	1	.500	.500
PH	George Crowe	L	7	7	1	0	0	0	0.0	0	0	0	1	0	7	1	.143	.143
PITCHERS																		
P	Ray Sadecki	L	36	87	22	4	0	0	0.0	6	12	1	7	0	1	0	.253	.299
P	Larry Jackson	R	34	74	13	3	2	0	0.0	9	6	2	14	0	0	0	.176	.270
P	Bob Gibson	R	40	66	13	5	0	1	1.5	4	10	3	23	0	0	0	.197	.318
P	Curt Simmons	L	32	66	20	3	0	0	0.0	9	6	8	22	0	0	0	.303	.348
P	Ernie Broglio	R	29	62	9	1	0	0	0.0	3	5	3	11	0	0	0	.145	.161
P	Al Cicotte	R	29	21	6	1	0	0	0.0	2	2	0	6	0	0	0	.286	.333
P	Lindy McDaniel	R	55	17	4	0	0	0	0.0	1	0	0	5	0	0	0	.235	.235
P	Mickey McDermott	L	22	14	1	1	0	0	0.0	1	3	0	4	0	6	1	.071	.143
P	Bob Miller	R	35	14	5	0	1	0	0.0	2	0	2	5	0	0	0	.357	.500
P	Craig Anderson	R	25	9	3	1	0	0	0.0	2	0	1	0	0	0	0	.333	.444
P	Ray Washburn	R	3	8	1	0	0	0	0.0	1	0	0	4	0	0	0	.125	.125
P	Ed Bauta	R	13	4	2	0	0	0	0.0	0	0	0	1	0	0	0	.500	.500
P	Bobby Tiefenauer	R	3	0	0	0	0	0	0.0	0	0	0	0	0	0	0	–	–
TEAM TOTAL				5307	1436	236	51	103	1.9	703	657	494	745	46	231	60	.271	.393

INDIVIDUAL FIELDING

POS	Player	T	G	PO	A	E	DP	TC/G	FA
1B	B. White	L	151	1373	104	17	125	9.9	.989
	J. Cunningham	L	10	69	1	0	8	7.0	1.000
2B	J. Javier	R	113	239	332	20	82	5.2	.966
	B. Lillis	R	24	43	62	2	13	4.5	.981
	Schoendienst	R	32	43	42	4	10	2.8	.955
	A. Grammas	R	18	31	43	1	11	4.2	.987
	D. Landrum	R	1	0	0	0	0	0.0	.000
SS	A. Grammas	R	65	81	136	9	29	3.5	.960
	B. Lillis	R	56	73	134	16	19	4.0	.928
	D. Spencer	R	37	66	109	8	26	4.9	.956
	J. Buchek	R	31	42	62	10	20	3.7	.912
	J. Gotay	R	10	16	25	10	6	5.1	.804
3B	K. Boyer	R	153	117	346	24	23	3.2	.951
	A. Grammas	R	3	0	3	0	0	1.0	1.000

POS	Player	T	G	PO	A	E	DP	TC/G	FA
OF	C. Flood	R	119	241	13	4	4	2.2	.984
	C. James	R	90	151	3	6	1	1.8	.963
	S. Musial	L	103	149	9	1	0	1.5	.994
	J. Cunningham	L	86	131	2	5	1	1.6	.964
	D. Taussig	R	87	123	6	1	2	1.5	.992
	C. Warwick	L	48	94	2	3	1	2.1	.970
	D. Landrum	R	25	42	3	0	1	1.8	1.000
	C. Sawatski	R	1	0	0	0	0	0.0	.000
	W. Moryn	R	7	8	0	1	0	1.3	.889
	E. Olivares	R	10	8	0	0	0	0.8	1.000
	G. Oliver	R	1	2	0	1	0	3.0	.667
	D. Clemens	R	3	2	0	1	0	1.0	.667
	B. Nieman	R	4	2	0	0	0	0.5	1.000
C	H. Smith	R	45	261	28	2	6	6.5	.993
	J. Schaffer	R	68	244	23	1	6	3.9	.996
	C. Sawatski	R	60	218	19	1	3	4.0	.996
	T. McCarver	R	20	86	9	3	0	4.9	.969
	G. Oliver	R	15	75	6	0	4	5.4	1.000
	C. Cannizzaro	R	5	5	0	0	0	1.0	1.000

While all the attention in baseball was on the Yankees and Roger Maris's assault on Babe Ruth's home run record, the Cardinals were quietly rebuilding their pitching staff. The ERAs for their pitchers may look unremarkable, but the league leader in ERA was Warren Spahn at 3.02, and the Cardinals' team ERA of 3.74 was the lowest in the league. A midseason managerial change turned the club around, and they played .588 ball under Johnny Keane after their 33–41 start. Ken Boyer had another outstanding season at third, winding up third in the league in batting behind Roberto Clemente and Vada Pinson. Curt Flood showed that he could hit in the majors, with a .322 average following three disappointing seasons. From 1961 on, Flood batted .301 over nine full seasons.

TEAM STATISTICS

W	L	PCT	GB	R	OR	2B	Batting 3B	HR	BA	SA	SB	Fielding E	DP	FA	CG	BB	Pitching SO	ShO	SV	ERA
93	61	.604		710	653	247	35	158	.270	.421	70	134	124	.977	46	500	829	12	40	3.78
89	65	.578	4	735	697	193	40	157	.262	.405	86	144	162	.975	40	544	1105	10	35	4.04
85	69	.552	8	773	655	219	32	183	.258	.417	79	102	102	.977	39	502	924	9	30	3.77
83	71	.539	10	712	656	199	34	188	.258	.415	70	111	152	.982	57	493	652	8	16	3.89
80	74	.519	13	703	668	236	51	103	.271	.393	46	166	165	.972	49	570	823	10	24	3.74
75	79	.487	18	694	675	232	57	128	.273	.410	26	150	187	.975	34	400	759	9	29	3.92
64	90	.416	29	689	800	238	51	176	.255	.418	35	183	175	.970	34	465	755	6	25	4.48
47	107	.305	46	584	796	185	50	103	.243	.357	56	146	179	.976	29	521	775	9	13	4.61
GUE TOTAL				5600	5600	1749	350	1196	.261	.404	468	1136	1246	.976	328	3995	6622	73	212	4.03

INDIVIDUAL PITCHING

CHER	T	W	L	PCT	ERA	SV	G	GS	CG	IP	H	BB	SO	R	ER	ShO	H/9	BB/9	SO/9
Sadecki	L	14	10	.583	3.72	0	31	31	13	222.2	196	102	114	100	92	0	7.92	4.12	4.61
Gibson	R	13	12	.520	3.24	1	35	27	10	211.1	186	119	166	91	76	2	7.92	5.07	7.07
ry Jackson	R	14	11	.560	3.75	0	33	28	12	211	203	56	113	99	88	3	8.66	2.39	4.82
t Simmons	L	9	10	.474	3.13	0	30	29	6	195.2	203	64	99	91	68	2	9.34	2.94	4.55
ie Broglio	R	9	12	.429	4.12	0	29	26	7	174.2	166	75	113	97	80	2	8.55	3.86	5.82
dy McDaniel	R	10	6	.625	4.87	9	55	0	0	94.1	117	31	65	57	51	0	11.16	2.96	6.20
Cicotte	R	2	6	.250	5.28	1	29	7	0	75	83	34	51	47	44	0	9.96	4.08	6.12
Miller	R	1	3	.250	4.24	3	34	5	0	74.1	82	46	39	41	35	0	9.93	5.57	4.72
ig Anderson	R	4	3	.571	3.26	1	25	0	0	38.2	38	12	21	15	14	0	8.84	2.79	4.89
key McDermott	L	1	0	1.000	3.67	4	19	0	0	27	29	15	15	17	11	0	9.67	5.00	5.00
Washburn	R	1	1	.500	1.77	0	3	2	1	20.1	10	7	12	4	4	0	4.43	3.10	5.31
Bauta	R	2	0	1.000	1.40	5	13	0	0	19.1	12	5	12	5	3	0	5.59	2.33	5.59
bby Tiefenauer	R	0	0	–	6.23	0	3	0	0	4.1	9	4	3	4	3	0	18.69	8.31	6.23
AM TOTAL		80	74	.519	3.74	24	339	155	49	1368.2	1334	570	823	668	569	9	8.77	3.75	5.41

MANAGER	W	L	PCT
Johnny Keane	84	78	.519

POS	Player	B	G	AB	H	2B	3B	HR	HR %	R	RBI	BB	SO	SB	Pinch Hit AB	Pinch Hit H	BA	SA
REGULARS																		
1B	Bill White	L	159	614	199	31	3	20	3.3	93	102	58	69	9	1	0	.324	.482
2B	Julian Javier	R	155	598	157	25	5	7	1.2	97	39	47	73	26	0	0	.263	.356
SS	Julio Gotay	R	127	369	94	12	1	2	0.5	47	27	27	47	7	1	0	.255	.309
3B	Ken Boyer	R	160	611	178	27	5	24	3.9	92	98	75	104	12	0	0	.291	.470
RF	Charlie James	R	129	388	107	13	4	8	2.1	50	59	10	58	3	12	4	.276	.392
CF	Curt Flood	R	151	635	188	30	5	12	1.9	99	70	42	57	8	0	0	.296	.416
LF	Stan Musial	L	135	433	143	18	1	19	4.4	57	82	64	46	3	13	8	.330	.508
C	Gene Oliver	R	122	345	89	19	1	14	4.1	42	45	50	59	5	19	6	.258	.441
SUBSTITUTES																		
SS	Dal Maxvill	R	79	189	42	3	1	1	0.5	20	18	17	39	1	3	0	.222	.265
1B	Fred Whitfield	L	73	158	42	7	1	8	5.1	20	34	7	30	1	33	11	.266	.475
2B	Red Schoendienst	B	98	143	43	4	0	2	1.4	21	12	9	12	0	72	22	.301	.371
SS	Alex Grammas	R	21	18	2	0	0	0	0.0	0	1	1	6	0	1	0	.111	.111
OF	Bobby Gene Smith	R	91	130	30	9	0	0	0.0	13	12	7	14	1	10	1	.231	.300
OF	Minnie Minoso	R	39	97	19	5	0	1	1.0	14	10	7	11	4	6	0	.196	.278
OF	Doug Clemens	L	48	93	22	1	1	1	1.1	12	12	17	19	0	15	5	.237	.301
OF	Don Landrum	L	32	35	11	0	0	0	0.0	11	3	4	2	2	3	0	.314	.314
OF	Carl Warwick	R	13	23	8	0	0	1	4.3	4	4	2	2	2	5	2	.348	.478
OF	Mike Shannon	R	10	15	2	0	0	0	0.0	3	0	1	3	0	0	0	.133	.133
OF	Bob Burda	L	7	14	1	0	0	0	0.0	0	0	3	1	1	0	0	.071	.071
OF	Gary Kolb	L	6	14	5	0	0	0	0.0	1	0	1	3	0	0	0	.357	.357
C	Carl Sawatski	L	85	222	56	9	1	13	5.9	26	42	36	38	0	15	2	.252	.477
C	Jimmie Schaffer	R	70	66	16	2	1	0	0.0	7	6	6	16	1	1	0	.242	.303
PITCHERS																		
P	Larry Jackson	R	36	89	15	3	1	0	0.0	10	4	7	20	0	0	0	.169	.225
P	Bob Gibson	R	42	76	20	0	0	2	2.6	11	5	4	28	0	0	0	.263	.342
P	Ernie Broglio	R	34	72	10	0	0	0	0.0	5	5	3	18	0	0	0	.139	.139
P	Ray Washburn	R	34	56	10	2	0	0	0.0	8	7	4	21	0	0	0	.179	.214
P	Curt Simmons	L	31	50	8	1	0	0	0.0	4	4	5	11	0	0	0	.160	.180
P	Ray Sadecki	L	24	37	3	0	0	1	2.7	4	1	0	6	0	1	0	.081	.162
P	Lindy McDaniel	R	55	21	2	0	0	0	0.0	1	1	1	11	0	0	0	.095	.095
P	Bobby Shantz	R	28	13	2	0	0	0	0.0	0	0	0	7	0	0	0	.154	.154
P	Don Ferrarese	R	38	5	1	0	0	1	20.0	1	2	0	3	0	0	0	.200	.800
P	Paul Toth	R	6	5	2	0	0	0	0.0	1	0	0	1	0	0	0	.400	.400
P	Ed Bauta	R	20	4	1	0	0	0	0.0	0	0	0	0	0	0	0	.250	.250
P	Bob Duliba	R	28	4	0	0	0	0	0.0	0	0	0	4	0	0	0	.000	.000
P	Harvey Branch	R	1	1	0	0	0	0	0.0	0	0	0	1	0	0	0	.000	.000
P	John Anderson	R	5	0	0	0	0	0	–	0	0	0	0	0	0	0	–	–
P	Larry Locke	R	1	0	0	0	0	0	–	0	0	0	0	0	0	0	–	–
TEAM TOTAL				5643	1528	221	31	137	2.4	774	707	515	846	86	212	61	.271	.394

INDIVIDUAL FIELDING

POS	Player	T	G	PO	A	E	DP	TC/G	FA	POS	Player	T	G	PO	A	E	DP	TC/G	FA
1B	B. White	L	146	1221	94	9	114	9.1	.993	OF	C. Flood	R	151	387	12	4	5	2.7	.990
	F. Whitfield	L	38	282	25	4	32	8.2	.987		S. Musial	L	119	164	6	4	1	1.5	.977
	G. Oliver	R	3	14	1	0	2	5.0	1.000		C. James	R	116	156	7	2	1	1.4	.988
2B	J. Javier	R	151	344	414	18	96	5.1	.977		B. Smith	R	80	65	4	0	1	0.9	1.000
	Schoendienst	R	21	30	42	1	10	3.5	.986		B. White	L	27	39	3	1	2	1.6	.977
	A. Grammas	R	2	0	0	0	0	0.0	.000		D. Clemens	R	34	38	0	1	0	1.1	.974
	J. Gotay	R	8	11	21	1	5	4.1	.970		M. Minoso	R	27	33	2	1	0	1.3	.972
SS	J. Gotay	R	120	179	339	24	65	4.5	.956		D. Landrum	R	26	19	0	0	0	0.7	1.000
	D. Maxvill	R	76	111	169	11	41	3.8	.962		J. Gotay	R	2	0	0	0	0	0.0	.000
	A. Grammas	R	16	11	17	2	2	1.9	.933		B. Burda	L	6	11	0	1	0	2.0	.917
	J. Javier	R	4	0	2	1	0	0.8	.667		C. Warwick	R	10	9	1	0	0	1.0	1.000
3B	K. Boyer	R	160	158	318	22	34	3.1	.956		G. Kolb	R	6	9	0	0	0	1.5	1.000
	J. Gotay	R	1	0	0	0	0	0.0	.000		M. Shannon	R	7	7	1	0	0	1.1	1.000
	D. Maxvill	R	1	0	0	0	0	0.0	.000		G. Oliver	R	8	6	0	0	0	0.8	1.000
	Schoendienst	R	4	3	6	0	0	2.3	1.000	C	G. Oliver	R	98	494	46	5	7	5.6	.991
											C. Sawatski	R	70	354	24	1	4	5.4	.997
											J. Schaffer	R	69	134	10	1	1	2.1	.993

Stan Musial had his third straight sub-.300 average in 1961, and he turned 41 during the off-season. The time had come for him to seriously consider retirement. But the time had also come for the National League to expand to ten teams. The thought of thirty-six games against the two expansion clubs must have made him feel ten years younger, because Musial, in his forty-second year, batted .330 and ranked third in the league. He also hit 19 homers, including four in a row (three in one game) against the Mets at the Polo Grounds. Gibson showed the first signs that he would become a dominating pitcher as he led the league in shutouts with five, and recorded 200 strikeouts for the first of nine times. In an important off-season trade, the Cardinals added shortstop Dick Groat in exchange for Don Cardwell and Julio Gotay. Groat was just two years removed from his MVP season in Pittsburgh, and would play an important role in the next two seasons.

TEAM STATISTICS

	W	L	PCT	GB	R	OR	2B	3B	HR	BA	SA	SB	E	DP	FA	CG	BB	SO	ShO	SV	ERA
SF	103	62	.624		878	690	235	32	204	.278	.441	73	142	153	.977	62	503	886	10	39	3.79
LA	102	63	.618	1	842	697	192	65	140	.268	.400	198	193	144	.970	44	588	1104	8	46	3.62
CIN	98	64	.605	3.5	802	685	252	40	167	.270	.417	66	145	144	.977	51	567	964	13	35	3.75
PIT	93	68	.578	8	706	626	240	65	108	.268	.394	50	152	177	.976	40	466	897	13	41	3.37
MIL	86	76	.531	15.5	730	665	204	38	181	.252	.403	57	124	154	.980	59	407	802	10	24	3.68
STL	84	78	.519	17.5	774	664	221	31	137	.271	.394	86	132	170	.979	53	517	914	17	25	3.55
PHI	81	80	.503	20	705	759	199	39	142	.260	.390	79	138	167	.977	43	574	863	7	24	4.28
HOU	64	96	.400	36.5	592	717	170	47	105	.246	.351	42	173	149	.973	34	471	1047	4	26	3.83
CHI	59	103	.364	42.5	632	827	196	56	126	.253	.377	78	146	171	.977	29	601	783	4	26	4.54
NY	40	120	.250	60.5	617	948	166	40	139	.240	.361	59	210	167	.967	43	571	772	4	10	5.04
LEAGUE TOTAL					7278	7278	2075	453	1449	.261	.393	788	1555	1596	.975	458	5265	9032	95	289	3.94

INDIVIDUAL PITCHING

PITCHER	T	W	L	PCT	ERA	SV	G	GS	CG	IP	H	BB	SO	R	ER	ShO	H/9	BB/9	SO/9
Larry Jackson	R	16	11	.593	3.75	0	36	35	11	252.1	267	64	112	121	105	2	9.52	2.28	3.99
Bob Gibson	R	15	13	.536	2.85	1	32	30	15	233.2	174	95	208	84	74	5	6.70	3.66	8.01
Ernie Broglio	R	12	9	.571	3.00	0	34	30	11	222.1	193	93	132	80	74	4	7.81	3.76	5.34
Ray Washburn	R	12	9	.571	4.10	0	34	25	2	175.2	187	58	109	90	80	1	9.58	2.97	5.58
Curt Simmons	L	10	10	.500	3.51	0	31	22	9	154	167	32	74	78	60	4	9.76	1.87	4.32
Lindy McDaniel	R	3	10	.231	4.12	14	55	2	0	107	96	29	79	53	49	0	8.07	2.44	6.64
Ray Sadecki	L	6	8	.429	5.54	1	22	17	4	102.1	121	43	50	74	63	1	10.64	3.78	4.40
Bobby Shantz	L	5	3	.625	2.18	4	28	0	0	57.2	45	20	47	22	14	0	7.02	3.12	7.34
Don Ferrarese	L	1	4	.200	2.70	1	38	0	0	56.2	55	31	45	19	17	0	8.74	4.92	7.15
Bob Duliba	R	2	0	1.000	2.06	2	28	0	0	39.1	33	17	22	11	9	0	7.55	3.89	5.03
Ed Bauta	R	1	0	1.000	5.01	1	20	0	0	32.1	28	21	25	18	18	0	7.79	5.85	6.96
Paul Toth	R	1	0	1.000	5.40	0	6	1	1	16.2	18	4	5	10	10	0	9.72	2.16	2.70
John Anderson	R	0	0	—	1.42	1	5	0	0	6.1	4	3	3	1	1	0	5.68	4.26	4.26
Harvey Branch	L	0	1	.000	5.40	0	1	1	0	5	5	5	2	3	3	0	9.00	9.00	3.60
Larry Locke	R	0	0	—	0.00	0	1	0	0	2	1	2	1	0	0	0	4.50	9.00	4.50
TEAM TOTAL		84	78	.519	3.55	25	371	163	53	1463.1	1394	517	914	664	577	17	8.57	3.18	5.62

MANAGER	W	L	PCT
Johnny Keane	93	69	.574

POS	Player	B	G	AB	H	2B	3B	HR	HR %	R	RBI	BB	SO	SB	Pinch Hit AB	Pinch Hit H	BA	SA
REGULARS																		
1B	Bill White	L	162	658	200	26	8	27	4.1	106	109	59	100	10	0	0	.304	.491
2B	Julian Javier	R	161	609	160	27	9	9	1.5	82	46	24	86	18	0	0	.263	.381
SS	Dick Groat	R	158	631	201	43	11	6	1.0	85	73	56	58	3	1	0	.319	.450
3B	Ken Boyer	R	159	617	176	28	2	24	3.9	86	111	70	90	1	0	0	.285	.454
RF	George Altman	L	135	464	127	18	7	9	1.9	62	47	47	93	13	12	3	.274	.401
CF	Curt Flood	R	158	662	200	34	9	5	0.8	112	63	42	57	17	1	0	.302	.403
LF	Charlie James	R	116	347	93	14	2	10	2.9	34	45	10	64	2	18	10	.268	.406
C	Tim McCarver	L	127	405	117	12	7	4	1.0	39	51	27	43	5	5	1	.289	.383
SUBSTITUTES																		
S2	Dal Maxvill	R	53	51	12	2	0	0	0.0	12	3	6	11	0	3	0	.235	.275
23	Phil Gagliano	R	10	5	2	0	0	0	0.0	1	1	1	1	0	2	0	.400	.400
SS	Jerry Buchek	R	3	4	1	0	0	0	0.0	0	0	0	2	0	2	0	.250	.250
3B	Clyde Bloomfield	R	1	0	0	0	0	0	–	0	0	0	0	0	0	0	–	–
OF	Stan Musial	L	124	337	86	10	2	12	3.6	34	58	35	43	2	21	4	.255	.404
OF	Gary Kolb	L	75	96	26	1	5	3	3.1	23	10	22	26	2	6	0	.271	.479
O3	Leo Burke	R	30	49	10	2	1	1	2.0	6	5	4	12	0	16	4	.204	.347
OF	Duke Carmel	L	57	44	10	1	0	1	2.3	9	2	9	11	0	12	3	.227	.318
OF	Mike Shannon	R	32	26	8	0	0	1	3.8	3	2	0	6	0	4	1	.308	.423
OF	Corky Withrow	R	6	9	0	0	0	0	0.0	0	1	0	2	0	4	0	.000	.000
OF	Doug Clemens	L	5	6	1	0	0	1	16.7	1	2	1	2	0	1	0	.167	.667
O2	Jack Damaska	R	5	5	1	0	0	0	0.0	1	1	0	4	0	4	1	.200	.200
C	Carl Sawatski	L	56	105	25	0	0	6	5.7	12	14	15	28	2	31	4	.238	.410
C	Gene Oliver	R	39	102	23	4	0	6	5.9	10	18	13	19	0	9	1	.225	.441
C	Dave Ricketts	B	3	8	2	0	0	0	0.0	0	0	0	2	0	0	0	.250	.250
C	Moe Thacker	R	3	4	0	0	0	0	0.0	0	0	0	3	0	0	0	.000	.000
PH	Jeoff Long	R	5	5	1	0	0	0	0.0	0	0	0	1	0	5	1	.200	.200
PH	Red Schoendienst	B	6	5	0	0	0	0	0.0	0	0	0	1	0	5	0	.000	.000
PH	Jim Beauchamp	R	4	3	0	0	0	0	0.0	0	0	0	2	0	3	0	.000	.000
PITCHERS																		
P	Ernie Broglio	R	39	89	10	2	0	0	0.0	6	2	2	28	0	0	0	.112	.135
P	Bob Gibson	R	41	87	18	3	1	3	3.4	12	20	8	35	0	1	0	.207	.368
P	Curt Simmons	L	32	81	13	2	1	0	0.0	4	5	2	32	1	0	0	.160	.210
P	Ray Sadecki	L	39	64	9	0	1	0	0.0	6	3	1	11	0	0	0	.141	.172
P	Ron Taylor	R	54	32	1	0	0	0	0.0	0	1	0	22	0	0	0	.031	.031
P	Lew Burdette	R	21	31	3	1	0	0	0.0	0	1	0	6	1	0	0	.097	.129
P	Ray Washburn	R	11	19	1	0	0	0	0.0	1	0	1	11	0	0	0	.053	.053
P	Bobby Shantz	R	55	7	1	0	0	0	0.0	0	1	2	1	0	0	0	.143	.143
P	Ed Bauta	R	38	5	0	0	0	0	0.0	0	0	0	1	0	0	0	.000	.000
P	Harry Fanok	B	12	5	2	1	0	0	0.0	0	2	0	1	0	0	0	.400	.600
P	Sam Jones	R	11	1	0	0	0	0	0.0	0	0	1	0	0	0	0	.000	.000
P	Bob Humphreys	R	9	0	0	0	0	0	–	0	0	0	0	0	0	0	–	–
P	Ken MacKenzie	R	8	0	0	0	0	0	–	0	0	0	0	0	0	0	–	–
P	Diomedes Olivo	L	19	0	0	0	0	0	–	0	0	0	0	0	0	0	–	–
P	Barney Schultz	R	24	0	0	0	0	0	–	0	0	0	0	0	0	0	–	–
	TEAM TOTAL			5678	1540	231	66	128	2.3	747	697	458	915	77	166	33	.271	.403

INDIVIDUAL FIELDING

POS	Player	T	G	PO	A	E	DP	TC/G	FA
1B	B. White	L	162	1389	105	13	126	9.3	.991
	D. Carmel	L	1	0	0	0	0	0.0	.000
2B	J. Javier	R	161	377	415	25	93	5.1	.969
	J. Damaska	R	1	0	0	0	0	0.0	.000
	D. Maxvill	R	9	8	19	1	5	3.1	.964
	P. Gagliano	R	3	5	2	0	0	2.3	1.000
SS	D. Groat	R	158	257	448	26	91	4.6	.964
	D. Maxvill	R	24	17	21	1	5	1.6	.974
	J. Buchek	R	1	1	1	0	1	2.0	1.000
3B	K. Boyer	R	159	129	293	34	23	2.9	.925
	C. Bloomfield	R	1	0	0	0	0	0.0	.000
	G. Kolb	R	1	0	0	0	0	0.0	.000
	D. Maxvill	R	3	0	0	0	0	0.0	.000
	L. Burke	R	5	6	6	2	0	2.8	.857
	P. Gagliano	R	1	0	1	0	0	1.0	1.000

POS	Player	T	G	PO	A	E	DP	TC/G	FA
OF	C. Flood	R	158	401	12	5	2	2.6	.988
	G. Altman	R	124	220	8	5	1	1.9	.979
	C. James	R	101	169	4	1	1	1.7	.994
	S. Musial	L	96	121	1	4	0	1.3	.968
	G. Kolb	R	58	50	1	1	1	0.9	.981
	D. Carmel	L	38	38	0	1	0	1.0	.974
	M. Shannon	R	26	15	2	1	0	0.7	.944
	J. Damaska	R	1	0	0	0	0	0.0	.000
	L. Burke	R	11	13	0	0	0	1.2	1.000
	D. Clemens	R	3	3	1	0	0	1.3	1.000
	C. Withrow	R	2	3	0	0	0	1.5	1.000
C	T. McCarver	R	126	722	55	5	7	6.2	.994
	G. Oliver	R	35	197	14	4	1	6.1	.981
	C. Sawatski	R	27	125	11	2	0	5.1	.986
	D. Ricketts	R	3	14	0	0	0	4.7	1.000
	M. Thacker	R	3	9	1	0	0	3.3	1.000
	G. Kolb	R	1	2	0	0	0	2.0	1.000

With the addition of Groat at short, the Cardinals made a great leap forward to 93 wins. They led the league in runs scored, but, in sharp contrast to 1961, their 3.35 ERA was *higher* than the league average. The offense was led by three .300 hitters, Flood, Groat, and White, all of whom hit the 200-hit mark. A 19–1 stretch brought them within one game of Los Angeles in September, but they fell back and wound up six games behind the Dodgers. In addition to Groat, the Cardinals added knuckleballer Barney Schultz to the relief staff, and in a post-season trade picked up a fourth starter, Roger Craig, from the Mets. Craig was fresh off a 5–22 season which included 18 straight losses, but gave the Cardinals the pitching depth that would allow them to trade away Broglio. Tim McCarver broke into the starting lineup behind the plate, and Mike Shannon saw brief action in the outfield. But the most important player change was the retirement of Stan Musial after a glorious 22-year career. Only two men, Brooks Robinson and Carl Yastrzemski, have spent longer careers with just one club.

TEAM STATISTICS

	W	L	PCT	GB	R	OR	2B	3B	Batting HR	BA	SA	SB	E	Fielding DP	FA	CG	BB	Pitching SO	ShO	SV	ERA
LA	99	63	.611		640	550	178	34	110	.251	.357	124	159	129	.975	51	402	1095	24	29	2.85
STL	93	69	.574	6	747	628	231	66	128	.271	.403	77	147	136	.976	49	463	978	17	32	3.32
SF	88	74	.543	11	725	641	206	35	197	.258	.414	55	156	113	.975	46	464	954	9	30	3.35
PHI	87	75	.537	12	642	578	228	54	126	.252	.381	56	142	147	.978	45	553	1052	12	31	3.09
CIN	86	76	.531	13	648	594	225	44	122	.246	.371	92	135	127	.978	55	425	1048	22	36	3.29
MIL	84	78	.519	15	677	603	204	39	139	.244	.370	75	129	161	.980	56	489	924	18	25	3.26
CHI	82	80	.506	17	570	578	205	44	127	.238	.363	68	155	172	.976	45	400	851	15	28	3.08
PIT	74	88	.457	25	567	595	181	49	108	.250	.359	57	182	195	.972	34	457	900	16	33	3.10
HOU	66	96	.407	33	464	640	170	39	62	.220	.301	39	162	100	.974	36	378	937	16	20	3.44
NY	51	111	.315	48	501	774	156	35	96	.219	.315	41	210	151	.967	42	529	806	5	12	4.12
LEAGUE TOTAL					6181	6181	1984	439	1215	.245	.364	684	1577	1431	.975	459	4560	9545	154	276	3.29

INDIVIDUAL PITCHING

PITCHER	T	W	L	PCT	ERA	SV	G	GS	CG	IP	H	BB	SO	R	ER	ShO	H/9	BB/9	SO/9
Bob Gibson	R	18	9	.667	3.39	0	36	33	14	254.2	224	96	204	110	96	2	7.92	3.39	7.21
Ernie Broglio	R	18	8	.692	2.99	0	39	35	11	250	202	90	145	97	83	5	7.27	3.24	5.22
Curt Simmons	L	15	9	.625	2.48	0	32	32	11	232.2	209	48	127	82	64	6	8.08	1.86	4.91
Ray Sadecki	L	10	10	.500	4.10	1	36	28	4	193.1	198	78	136	100	88	0	9.22	3.63	6.33
Ron Taylor	R	9	7	.563	2.84	11	54	9	2	133.1	119	30	91	44	42	0	8.03	2.03	6.14
Lew Burdette	R	3	8	.273	3.75	2	21	14	3	98.1	106	16	45	50	41	0	9.70	1.46	4.12
Bobby Shantz	L	6	4	.600	2.61	11	55	0	0	79.1	55	17	70	28	23	0	6.24	1.93	7.94
Ray Washburn	R	5	3	.625	3.08	0	11	11	4	64.1	50	14	47	25	22	2	6.99	1.96	6.58
Ed Bauta	R	3	4	.429	3.93	3	38	0	0	52.2	55	21	30	26	23	0	9.40	3.59	5.13
Barney Schultz	R	2	0	1.000	3.57	1	24	0	0	35.1	36	8	26	15	14	0	9.17	2.04	6.62
Harry Fanok	R	2	1	.667	5.26	1	12	0	0	25.2	24	21	25	16	15	0	8.42	7.36	8.77
Diomedes Olivo	L	0	5	.000	5.40	0	19	0	0	13.1	16	9	9	9	8	0	10.80	6.08	6.08
Sam Jones	R	2	0	1.000	9.00	2	11	0	0	11	15	5	8	12	11	0	12.27	4.09	6.55
Bob Humphreys	R	0	1	.000	5.06	0	9	0	0	10.2	11	7	8	8	6	0	9.28	5.91	6.75
Ken MacKenzie	L	0	0	–	4.15	0	8	0	0	8.2	9	3	7	6	4	0	9.35	3.12	7.27
TEAM TOTAL		93	69	.574	3.32	32	405	162	49	1463.1	1329	463	978	628	540	16	8.17	2.85	6.02

MANAGER	W	L	PCT
Johnny Keane	93	69	.574

POS	Player	B	G	AB	H	2B	3B	HR	HR %	R	RBI	BB	SO	SB	Pinch Hit AB	Pinch Hit H	BA	SA
REGULARS																		
1B	Bill White	L	160	631	191	37	4	21	3.3	92	102	52	103	7	0	0	.303	.474
2B	Julian Javier	R	155	535	129	19	5	12	2.2	66	65	30	82	9	0	0	.241	.363
SS	Dick Groat	R	161	636	186	35	6	1	0.2	70	70	44	42	2	1	0	.292	.371
3B	Ken Boyer	R	162	628	185	30	10	24	3.8	100	119	70	85	3	0	0	.295	.489
RF	Mike Shannon	R	88	253	66	8	2	9	3.6	30	43	19	54	4	2	0	.261	.415
CF	Curt Flood	R	162	679	211	25	3	5	0.7	97	46	43	53	8	1	0	.311	.378
LF	Lou Brock	L	103	419	146	21	9	12	2.9	81	44	27	87	33	1	0	.348	.527
C	Tim McCarver	L	143	465	134	19	3	9	1.9	53	52	40	44	2	7	1	.288	.400
SUBSTITUTES																		
UT	Phil Gagliano	R	40	58	15	4	0	1	1.7	5	9	3	10	0	19	3	.259	.379
S2	Jerry Buchek	R	35	30	6	0	2	0	0.0	7	1	3	11	0	2	0	.200	.333
2S	Dal Maxvill	R	37	26	6	0	0	0	0.0	4	4	0	7	1	1	0	.231	.231
OF	Charlie James	R	88	233	52	9	1	5	2.1	24	17	11	58	0	31	8	.223	.335
OF	Carl Warwick	R	88	158	41	7	1	3	1.9	14	15	11	30	2	43	11	.259	.373
OF	Bob Skinner	L	55	118	32	5	0	1	0.8	10	16	11	20	0	24	6	.271	.339
OF	Johnny Lewis	L	40	94	22	2	2	2	2.1	10	7	13	23	2	3	0	.234	.362
OF	Doug Clemens	L	33	78	16	4	3	1	1.3	8	9	6	16	0	8	2	.205	.372
O1	Jeoff Long	R	28	43	10	1	0	1	2.3	5	4	6	18	0	16	3	.233	.326
C	Bob Uecker	R	40	106	21	1	0	1	0.9	8	6	17	24	0	0	0	.198	.236
PH	Ed Spiezio	R	12	12	4	0	0	0	0.0	0	0	0	1	0	12	4	.333	.333
PH	Joe Morgan	L	3	3	0	0	0	0	0.0	0	0	0	2	0	3	0	.000	.000
PITCHERS																		
P	Bob Gibson	R	40	96	15	3	1	0	0.0	8	4	3	38	0	0	0	.156	.208
P	Curt Simmons	L	34	94	10	0	0	0	0.0	6	6	4	32	0	0	0	.106	.106
P	Ray Sadecki	L	39	75	12	6	1	0	0.0	7	6	2	14	0	0	0	.160	.267
P	Roger Craig	R	39	48	10	1	0	0	0.0	4	3	5	24	0	0	0	.208	.229
P	Ernie Broglio	R	11	21	2	1	0	0	0.0	1	3	2	8	0	0	0	.095	.143
P	Mike Cuellar	L	32	18	0	0	0	0	0.0	0	0	0	8	0	0	0	.000	.000
P	Ron Taylor	R	63	15	2	0	0	0	0.0	0	0	0	9	0	0	0	.133	.133
P	Ray Washburn	R	15	15	2	1	0	0	0.0	2	1	0	7	0	0	0	.133	.200
P	Glen Hobbie	R	13	13	2	1	0	1	7.7	1	1	0	2	0	0	0	.154	.462
P	Gordie Richardson	R	19	13	1	0	0	0	0.0	0	0	2	9	0	0	0	.077	.077
P	Barney Schultz	R	30	6	1	0	0	0	0.0	0	0	0	2	0	0	0	.167	.167
P	Bob Humphreys	R	28	4	1	0	0	0	0.0	2	1	2	1	0	0	0	.250	.250
P	Lew Burdette	R	8	1	0	0	0	0	0.0	0	0	0	0	0	0	0	.000	.000
P	Harry Fanok	B	4	1	0	0	0	0	0.0	0	0	0	1	0	0	0	.000	.000
P	Dave Bakenhaster	R	2	0	0	0	0	0	–	0	0	0	0	0	0	0	–	–
P	Dave Dowling	R	1	0	0	0	0	0	–	0	0	0	0	0	0	0	–	–
P	Bobby Shantz	R	16	0	0	0	0	0	–	0	0	1	0	0	0	0	–	–
P	Jack Spring	R	2	0	0	0	0	0	–	0	0	0	0	0	0	0	–	–
TEAM TOTAL				5625	1531	240	53	109	1.9	715	654	427	925	73	174	38	.272	.392

INDIVIDUAL FIELDING

POS	Player	T	G	PO	A	E	DP	TC/G	FA
1B	B. White	L	160	1513	101	6	125	10.1	.996
	J. Long	R	3	30	0	0	4	10.0	1.000
	P. Gagliano	R	1	5	0	0	1	5.0	1.000
2B	J. Javier	R	154	360	401	27	97	5.1	.966
	D. Maxvill	R	15	21	14	1	5	2.4	.972
	P. Gagliano	R	12	17	28	4	5	4.1	.918
	J. Buchek	R	9	16	17	3	3	4.0	.917
SS	D. Groat	R	160	249	499	40	91	4.9	.949
	J. Buchek	R	20	8	18	2	2	1.4	.929
	D. Maxvill	R	13	5	4	0	0	0.7	1.000
3B	K. Boyer	R	162	131	337	24	30	3.0	.951
	J. Buchek	R	1	0	0	0	0	0.0	.000
	P. Gagliano	R	1	0	0	0	0	0.0	.000
	D. Maxvill	R	1	0	1	0	0	1.0	1.000

POS	Player	T	G	PO	A	E	DP	TC/G	FA
OF	C. Flood	R	162	391	10	5	2	2.5	.988
	L. Brock	L	102	180	7	10*	0	1.9	.949
	M. Shannon	R	88	110	7	2	1	1.4	.983
	C. James	R	60	76	3	3	0	1.4	.963
	C. Warwick	L	49	53	3	4	2	1.2	.933
	J. Lewis	R	36	53	3	2	1	1.6	.966
	B. Skinner	R	31	42	3	3	0	1.5	.938
	D. Clemens	R	22	30	2	1	0	1.5	.970
	J. Long	R	4	5	0	1	0	1.5	.833
	P. Gagliano	R	2	4	0	0	0	2.0	1.000
	D. Maxvill	R	1	1	0	0	0	1.0	1.000
C	T. McCarver	R	137	762	43	11	9	6.0	.987
	B. Uecker	R	40	201	20	3	2	5.6	.987

Ninety-three wins again, but this time it was enough in a year that saw the best trade in Cardinals history win them a pennant after the total collapse of the front-running Phillies. The Cardinals were sitting in seventh place when they pulled off The Trade: Ernie Broglio, Bobby Shantz and outfielder Doug Clemens to the Cubs for Lou Brock and two journeymen pitchers, Paul Toth and Jack Spring. Brock hit .348 and stole 33 bases in his 103 games with St. Louis, providing the offensive catalyst at the top of the order they had lacked. Still, the Cards and Reds stood tied for second, six and a half games behind the Phillies with two weeks to go. The Phillies then dropped ten straight games while the Cards won nine of ten. It wasn't until the last day of the season, though, when the Cards beat the Mets and Philadelphia rallied to knock off the Reds that the title was clinched. The Cardinals then raised their post-season record againt the Yankees to 3–2 with an exciting seven-game World Series victory, sparked by Bob Gibson's two wins and National League MVP Ken Boyer's Game 4 grand-slam homer. The Cardinals are the only team in baseball history with a winning record in World Series play against the Yanks.

TEAM STATISTICS

	W	L	PCT	GB	R	OR	Batting 2B	3B	HR	BA	SA	SB	Fielding E	DP	FA	Pitching CG	BB	SO	ShO	SV	ERA
STL	93	69	.574		715	652	240	53	109	.272	.392	73	172	147	.973	47	410	877	10	38	3.43
CIN	92	70	.568	1	660	566	220	38	130	.249	.372	90	130	137	.979	54	436	1122	14	35	3.07
PHI	92	70	.568	1	693	632	241	51	130	.258	.391	30	157	150	.975	37	440	1009	17	41	3.36
SF	90	72	.556	3	656	587	185	38	165	.246	.382	64	159	136	.975	48	480	1023	17	30	3.19
MIL	88	74	.543	5	803	744	274	32	159	.272	.418	53	143	139	.977	45	452	906	14	39	4.12
LA	80	82	.494	13	614	572	180	39	79	.250	.340	141	170	126	.973	47	458	1062	19	27	2.95
PIT	80	82	.494	13	663	636	225	54	121	.264	.389	39	177	179	.972	42	476	951	14	29	3.52
CHI	76	86	.469	17	649	724	239	50	145	.251	.390	70	162	147	.975	58	423	737	11	19	4.08
HOU	66	96	.407	27	495	628	162	41	70	.229	.315	40	149	124	.976	30	353	852	9	31	3.41
NY	53	109	.327	40	569	776	195	31	103	.246	.348	36	167	154	.974	40	466	717	10	15	4.25
LEAGUE TOTAL					6517	6517	2161	427	1211	.254	.374	636	1586	1439	.975	448	4394	9256	135	304	3.54

INDIVIDUAL PITCHING

PITCHER	T	W	L	PCT	ERA	SV	G	GS	CG	IP	H	BB	SO	R	ER	ShO	H/9	BB/9	SO/9
Bob Gibson	R	19	12	.613	3.01	1	40	36	17	287.1	250	86	245	106	96	2	7.83	2.69	7.67
Curt Simmons	L	18	9	.667	3.43	0	34	34	12	244	233	49	104	104	93	3	8.59	1.81	3.84
Ray Sadecki	L	20	11	.645	3.68	1	37	32	9	220	232	60	119	104	90	2	9.49	2.45	4.87
Roger Craig	R	7	9	.438	3.25	5	39	19	3	166	180	35	84	76	60	0	9.76	1.90	4.55
Ron Taylor	R	8	4	.667	4.62	7	63	2	0	101.1	109	33	69	56	52	0	9.68	2.93	6.13
Mike Cuellar	L	5	5	.500	4.50	4	32	7	1	72	80	33	56	43	36	0	10.00	4.13	7.00
Ernie Broglio	R	3	5	.375	3.50	0	11	11	3	69.1	65	26	36	33	27	1	8.44	3.38	4.67
Ray Washburn	R	3	4	.429	4.05	2	15	10	0	60	60	17	28	29	27	0	9.00	2.55	4.20
Barney Schultz	R	1	3	.250	1.64	14	30	0	0	49.1	35	11	29	14	9	0	6.39	2.01	5.29
Gordie Richardson	L	4	2	.667	2.30	1	37	0	0	47	40	15	28	18	12	0	7.66	2.87	5.36
Glen Hobbie	R	1	2	.333	4.26	1	13	5	1	44.1	41	15	18	23	21	0	8.32	3.05	3.65
Bob Humphreys	R	2	0	1.000	2.53	2	28	0	0	42.2	32	15	36	14	12	0	6.75	3.16	7.59
Bobby Shantz	L	1	3	.250	3.12	0	16	0	0	17.1	14	7	12	6	6	0	7.27	3.63	6.23
Lew Burdette	R	1	0	1.000	1.80	0	8	0	0	10	10	3	3	3	2	0	9.00	2.70	2.70
Harry Fanok	R	0	0	–	5.87	0	4	0	0	7.2	5	3	10	6	5	0	5.87	3.52	11.74
Dave Bakenhaster	R	0	0	–	6.00	0	2	0	0	3	9	1	0	6	2	0	27.00	3.00	0.00
Jack Spring	L	0	0	–	3.00	0	2	0	0	3	8	1	0	9	1	0	24.00	3.00	0.00
Dave Dowling	L	0	0	–	0.00	0	1	0	0	1	2	0	0	0	0	0	18.00	0.00	0.00
TEAM TOTAL		93	69	.574	3.43	38	394	162	47	1445.1	1405	410	877	652	551	8	8.75	2.55	5.46

MANAGER	W	L	PCT
Red Schoendienst	80	81	.497

POS	Player	B	G	AB	H	2B	3B	HR	HR %	R	RBI	BB	SO	SB	Pinch Hit AB	H	BA	SA
REGULARS																		
1B	Bill White	L	148	543	157	26	3	24	4.4	82	73	63	86	3	4	1	.289	.481
2B	Julian Javier	R	77	229	52	6	4	2	0.9	34	23	8	44	5	0	0	.227	.314
SS	Dick Groat	R	153	587	149	26	5	0	0.0	55	52	56	50	1	6	3	.254	.315
3B	Ken Boyer	R	144	535	139	18	2	13	2.4	71	75	57	73	2	3	0	.260	.374
RF	Mike Shannon	R	124	244	54	17	3	3	1.2	32	25	28	46	2	19	2	.221	.352
CF	Curt Flood	R	156	617	191	30	3	11	1.8	90	83	51	50	9	5	0	.310	.421
LF	Lou Brock	L	155	631	182	35	8	16	2.5	107	69	45	116	63	1	0	.288	.445
C	Tim McCarver	L	113	409	113	17	2	11	2.7	48	48	31	26	5	5	2	.276	.408
SUBSTITUTES																		
UT	Phil Gagliano	R	122	363	87	14	2	8	2.2	46	53	40	45	2	26	5	.240	.355
2S	Jerry Buchek	R	55	166	41	8	3	3	1.8	17	21	13	46	1	5	0	.247	.386
2B	Dal Maxvill	R	68	89	12	2	2	0	0.0	10	10	7	15	0	2	0	.135	.202
1B	George Kernek	L	10	31	9	3	1	0	0.0	6	3	2	4	0	3	0	.290	.452
3B	Ed Spiezio	R	10	18	3	0	0	0	0.0	0	5	1	4	0	7	2	.167	.167
O1	Tito Francona	L	81	174	45	6	2	5	2.9	15	19	17	30	0	35	9	.259	.402
OF	Bob Skinner	L	80	152	47	5	4	5	3.3	25	26	12	30	1	47	15	.309	.493
OF	Carl Warwick	R	50	77	12	2	1	0	0.0	3	6	4	18	1	30	4	.156	.208
OF	Bobby Tolan	L	17	69	13	2	0	0	0.0	8	6	0	4	2	0	0	.188	.217
OF	Ted Savage	R	30	63	10	3	0	1	1.6	7	4	6	9	1	7	2	.159	.254
C	Bob Uecker	R	53	145	33	7	0	2	1.4	17	10	24	27	0	5	0	.228	.317
C	Dave Ricketts	B	11	29	7	0	0	0	0.0	1	0	1	3	0	1	0	.241	.241
PITCHERS																		
P	Bob Gibson	R	42	104	25	2	0	5	4.8	14	19	3	26	2	1	1	.240	.404
P	Tracy Stallard	R	40	68	6	0	0	0	0.0	2	1	0	26	0	0	0	.088	.088
P	Curt Simmons	L	34	64	3	1	0	0	0.0	2	1	0	30	0	0	0	.047	.063
P	Ray Sadecki	L	36	55	11	2	1	0	0.0	6	4	2	11	0	0	0	.200	.273
P	Bob Purkey	R	32	35	1	0	0	0	0.0	3	3	1	21	0	0	0	.029	.029
P	Ray Washburn	R	28	33	5	1	0	0	0.0	3	1	2	19	0	0	0	.152	.182
P	Nellie Briles	R	37	15	2	0	0	0	0.0	0	2	1	8	0	0	0	.133	.133
P	Larry Jaster	L	4	10	2	0	0	0	0.0	1	2	1	5	0	0	0	.200	.200
P	Hal Woodeshick	R	51	8	0	0	0	0	0.0	0	1	1	4	0	0	0	.000	.000
P	Don Dennis	R	41	5	2	0	0	0	0.0	0	0	0	1	0	0	0	.400	.400
P	Ron Taylor	R	25	5	2	1	0	0	0.0	0	0	0	2	0	0	0	.400	.600
P	Steve Carlton	L	15	2	0	0	0	0	0.0	0	0	0	1	0	0	0	.000	.000
P	Barney Schultz	R	34	2	0	0	0	0	0.0	1	0	0	0	0	0	0	.000	.000
P	Dennis Aust	R	6	1	0	0	0	0	0.0	0	0	0	1	0	0	0	.000	.000
P	Earl Francis	R	2	1	0	0	0	0	0.0	0	0	0	1	0	0	0	.000	.000
	TEAM TOTAL			5579	1415	234	46	109	2.0	707	645	477	882	100	212	46	.254	.371

INDIVIDUAL FIELDING

POS	Player	T	G	PO	A	E	DP	TC/G	FA
1B	B. White	L	144	1308	109	11	114	9.9	.992
	T. Francona	L	13	102	3	1	8	8.2	.991
	G. Kernek	L	7	65	5	2	9	10.3	.972
	C. Warwick	L	4	23	0	0	4	5.8	1.000
2B	J. Javier	R	69	128	179	8	40	4.6	.975
	P. Gagliano	R	57	130	134	11	31	4.8	.960
	J. Buchek	R	33	65	91	1	22	4.8	.994
	D. Maxvill	R	49	64	76	1	22	2.9	.993
SS	D. Groat	R	148	242	450	27	86	4.9	.962
	J. Buchek	R	18	27	63	4	16	5.2	.957
	D. Maxvill	R	12	10	10	1	1	1.8	.952
3B	K. Boyer	R	143	113	250	12	18	2.6	**.968**
	P. Gagliano	R	19	20	35	3	3	3.1	.948
	E. Spiezio	R	3	1	7	0	0	2.7	1.000
	D. Groat	R	2	0	5	0	1	2.5	1.000
	J. Buchek	R	1	1	0	0	0	1.0	1.000

POS	Player	T	G	PO	A	E	DP	TC/G	FA
OF	C. Flood	R	151	349	7	5	3	2.4	.986
	L. Brock	L	153	272	11	12	1	1.9	.959
	M. Shannon	R	101	170	5	1	1	1.7	.994
	P. Gagliano	R	25	51	0	2	0	2.1	.962
	B. Skinner	R	33	43	0	3	0	1.4	.935
	T. Francona	L	34	35	0	1	0	1.1	.972
	B. Tolan	L	17	32	0	1	0	1.9	.970
	T. Savage	R	20	29	1	2	0	1.6	.938
	C. Warwick	L	21	23	1	1	0	1.2	.960
C	T. McCarver	R	111	687	43	4	4	6.6	**.995**
	B. Uecker	R	49	240	29	4	1	5.6	.985
	D. Ricketts	R	11	41	2	1	0	4.0	.977
	M. Shannon	R	4	23	1	0	1	6.0	1.000

In a startling change of command, the Yankees fired their manager, Yogi Berra, during the off-season and replaced him with the Cardinals' manager, Johnny Keane. Keane was replaced by Red Schoendienst, but the Cards fell to seventh place at 80–81. They were never able to get untracked, and were hurt by the abrupt turnaround by starters Ray Sadecki and Curt Simmons. Simmons went from 18–9 with a 3.43 ERA to 9–15 and 4.08. Sadecki, the Cards' only 20-game winner in '64, fell to 6–15, and his ERA ballooned to 5.21. Team batting declined by eighteen points as everyone but Flood fell off: Brock fell by sixty points compared to his St. Louis average, Boyer by thirty-five (and forty-six RBIs), and Groat by thirty-eight. The front office responded in a very traditional Cardinal manner: they cashed in their aging veterans, sending 34-year-old Ken Boyer to the Mets, and 31-year-old Bill White to Philadelphia.

TEAM STATISTICS

	W	L	PCT	GB	R	OR	2B	3B	Batting HR	BA	SA	SB	E	Fielding DP	FA	CG	BB	Pitching SO	ShO	SV	ERA
A	97	65	.599		608	521	193	32	78	.245	.335	172	134	135	.979	58	425	1079	23	34	2.81
F	95	67	.586	2	682	593	169	43	159	.252	.385	47	148	124	.976	42	408	1060	17	42	3.20
PIT	90	72	.556	7	675	580	217	57	111	.265	.382	51	152	189	.977	49	469	882	17	27	3.01
CIN	89	73	.549	8	825	704	268	61	183	.273	.439	82	117	142	.981	43	587	1113	9	34	3.88
MIL	86	76	.531	11	708	633	243	28	196	.256	.416	64	140	145	.978	43	541	966	4	38	3.52
TL	80	81	.497	16.5	707	674	205	53	144	.250	.384	46	157	153	.975	50	466	1071	18	21	3.53
PHI	85	76	.528	11.5	654	667	234	46	109	.254	.371	100	130	152	.979	40	467	916	11	35	3.77
CHI	72	90	.444	25	635	723	202	33	134	.238	.358	65	171	166	.974	33	481	855	9	35	3.78
HOU	65	97	.401	32	569	711	188	42	97	.237	.340	90	166	130	.974	29	388	931	7	26	3.84
NY	50	112	.309	47	495	752	203	27	107	.221	.327	28	171	153	.974	29	498	776	11	14	4.06
LEAGUE TOTAL					6558	6558	2122	422	1318	.249	.374	745	1486	1489	.977	416	4730	9649	126	306	3.54

INDIVIDUAL PITCHING

PITCHER	T	W	L	PCT	ERA	SV	G	GS	CG	IP	H	BB	SO	R	ER	ShO	H/9	BB/9	SO/9
Bob Gibson	R	20	12	.625	3.07	1	38	36	20	299	243	103	270	110	102	6	7.31	3.10	8.13
Curt Simmons	L	9	15	.375	4.08	0	34	32	5	203	229	54	96	104	92	0	10.15	2.39	4.26
Tracy Stallard	R	11	8	.579	3.38	0	40	26	4	194.1	172	70	99	83	73	1	7.97	3.24	4.58
Ray Sadecki	L	6	15	.286	5.21	1	36	28	4	172.2	192	64	122	107	100	0	10.01	3.34	6.36
Bob Purkey	R	10	9	.526	5.79	2	32	17	3	124.1	148	33	39	83	80	1	10.71	2.39	2.82
Ray Washburn	R	9	11	.450	3.62	2	28	16	1	119.1	114	28	67	57	48	1	8.60	2.11	5.05
Nellie Briles	R	3	3	.500	3.50	4	37	2	0	82.1	79	26	52	33	32	0	8.64	2.84	5.68
Hal Woodeshick	L	3	2	.600	1.81	15	51	0	0	59.2	47	27	37	14	12	0	7.09	4.07	5.58
Don Dennis	R	2	3	.400	2.29	6	41	0	0	55	47	16	29	17	14	0	7.69	2.62	4.75
Don Taylor	R	2	1	.667	4.53	1	25	0	0	43.2	43	15	26	24	22	0	8.86	3.09	5.36
Barney Schultz	R	2	2	.500	3.83	2	34	0	0	42.1	39	11	38	22	18	0	8.29	2.34	8.08
Larry Jaster	L	3	0	1.000	1.61	0	4	3	0	28	21	7	10	5	5	0	6.75	2.25	3.21
Steve Carlton	L	0	0	—	2.52	0	15	2	0	25	27	8	21	7	7	0	9.72	2.88	7.56
Dennis Aust	R	0	0	—	4.91	0	6	0	0	7.1	6	2	7	4	4	0	7.36	2.45	8.59
Carl Francis	R	0	0	—	5.06	0	2	0	0	5.1	7	3	3	4	3	0	11.81	5.06	5.06
TEAM TOTAL		80	81	.497	3.77	35	423	162	40	1461.1	1414	467	916	674	612	9	8.71	2.88	5.64

MANAGER	W	L	PCT
Red Schoendienst	83	79	.512

POS	Player	B	G	AB	H	2B	3B	HR	HR %	R	RBI	BB	SO	SB	Pinch Hit AB	Pinch Hit H	BA	SA
REGULARS																		
1B	Orlando Cepeda	R	123	452	137	24	0	17	3.8	65	58	34	68	9	3	2	.303	.469
2B	Julian Javier	R	147	460	105	13	5	7	1.5	52	31	26	63	11	0	0	.228	.324
SS	Dal Maxvill	R	134	394	96	14	3	0	0.0	25	24	37	61	3	2	0	.244	.294
3B	Charley Smith	R	116	391	104	13	4	10	2.6	34	43	22	81	0	8	3	.266	.396
RF	Mike Shannon	R	137	459	132	20	6	16	3.5	61	64	37	106	8	9	2	.288	.462
CF	Curt Flood	R	160	626	167	21	5	10	1.6	64	78	26	50	14	0	0	.267	.364
LF	Lou Brock	L	156	643	183	24	12	15	2.3	94	46	31	134	74	1	0	.285	.429
C	Tim McCarver	L	150	543	149	19	13	12	2.2	50	68	36	38	9	5	1	.274	.424
SUBSTITUTES																		
2S	Jerry Buchek	R	100	284	67	10	4	4	1.4	23	25	23	71	0	9	1	.236	.342
UT	Phil Gagliano	R	90	213	54	8	2	2	0.9	23	15	24	29	2	36	4	.254	.338
1O	Tito Francona	L	83	156	33	4	1	4	2.6	14	17	7	27	0	41	7	.212	.327
3B	Ed Spiezio	R	26	73	16	5	1	2	2.7	4	10	5	11	1	6	0	.219	.397
1B	George Kernek	L	20	50	12	0	1	0	0.0	5	3	4	9	1	4	1	.240	.280
S2	Jim Williams	R	13	11	3	0	0	0	0.0	1	1	1	5	0	1	0	.273	.273
OF	Bobby Tolan	L	43	93	16	5	1	1	1.1	10	6	6	15	1	12	3	.172	.280
OF	Alex Johnson	R	25	86	16	0	1	2	2.3	7	6	5	18	1	2	0	.186	.279
OF	Ted Savage	R	16	29	5	2	1	0	0.0	4	3	4	7	4	9	2	.172	.310
C	Pat Corrales	R	28	72	13	2	0	0	0.0	5	3	2	17	1	1	0	.181	.208
PH	Bob Skinner	L	49	45	7	1	0	1	2.2	2	5	2	17	0	45	7	.156	.244
PITCHERS																		
P	Bob Gibson	R	46	100	20	4	0	1	1.0	11	8	3	35	3	6	2	.200	.270
P	Al Jackson	L	51	74	13	4	1	0	0.0	6	5	3	30	2	0	0	.176	.257
P	Ray Washburn	R	27	54	5	1	0	1	1.9	2	6	2	25	0	0	0	.093	.167
P	Larry Jaster	L	26	45	8	0	0	1	2.2	4	3	2	8	0	0	0	.178	.244
P	Nellie Briles	R	49	38	3	0	0	0	0.0	2	0	2	16	0	0	0	.079	.079
P	Steve Carlton	L	9	15	4	0	0	0	0.0	0	0	0	3	0	0	0	.267	.267
P	Tracy Stallard	R	20	14	0	0	0	0	0.0	0	0	0	7	0	0	0	.000	.000
P	Don Dennis	R	38	12	1	0	0	0	0.0	0	0	0	3	0	0	0	.083	.083
P	Joe Hoerner	R	57	8	1	0	0	1	12.5	1	3	0	5	0	0	0	.125	.500
P	Curt Simmons	L	10	8	1	1	0	0	0.0	0	0	1	3	0	0	0	.125	.250
P	Art Mahaffey	R	12	7	0	0	0	0	0.0	0	0	0	3	0	0	0	.000	.000
P	Ray Sadecki	L	6	7	3	0	0	1	14.3	2	2	0	2	0	0	0	.429	.857
P	Dick Hughes	R	6	5	2	0	0	0	0.0	0	0	0	0	0	0	0	.400	.400
P	Hal Woodeshick	R	59	5	1	1	0	0	0.0	0	0	0	4	0	0	0	.200	.400
P	Ron Piche	R	20	4	0	0	0	0	0.0	0	0	0	2	0	0	0	.000	.000
P	Jim Cosman	R	1	3	0	0	0	0	0.0	0	0	0	3	0	0	0	.000	.000
P	Dennis Aust	R	9	1	0	0	0	0	0.0	0	0	0	1	0	0	0	.000	.000
P	Ron Willis	R	4	0	0	0	0	0	—	0	0	0	0	0	0	0	—	—
TEAM TOTAL				5480	1377	196	61	108	2.0	571	533	345	977	144	200	35	.251	.368

INDIVIDUAL FIELDING

POS	Player	T	G	PO	A	E	DP	TC/G	FA
1B	O. Cepeda	R	120	1109	62	13	111	9.9	.989
	T. Francona	L	30	210	18	3	20	7.7	.987
	G. Kernek	L	16	114	8	2	14	7.8	.984
	P. Gagliano	R	8	59	9	0	9	8.5	1.000
	B. Tolan	L	1	2	0	0	0	2.0	1.000
2B	J. Javier	R	145	306	364	13	89	4.7	.981
	J. Buchek	R	49	79	107	5	30	3.9	.974
	P. Gagliano	R	1	0	0	0	0	0.0	.000
	J. Williams	R	3	0	0	0	0	0.0	.000
	D. Maxvill	R	5	4	6	0	3	2.0	1.000
SS	D. Maxvill	R	128	219	428	22	88	5.2	.967
	J. Buchek	R	48	69	113	13	22	4.1	.933
	C. Smith	R	1	5	3	0	1	8.0	1.000
	J. Williams	R	7	2	5	0	1	1.0	1.000
3B	C. Smith	R	107	84	213	11	26	2.9	.964
	P. Gagliano	R	41	30	77	2	7	2.7	.982
	E. Spiezio	R	19	14	32	6	3	2.7	.885
	J. Buchek	R	4	3	8	1	0	3.0	.917

POS	Player	T	G	PO	A	E	DP	TC/G	FA
OF	C. Flood	R	159	391	5	0	1	2.5	1.000
	L. Brock	L	154	269	9	19	1	1.9	.936
	M. Shannon	R	129	247	10	4	4	2.0	.985
	B. Tolan	L	26	39	1	2	0	1.6	.952
	A. Johnson	R	22	23	2	1	0	1.2	.962
	D. Maxvill	R	1	0	0	0	0	0.0	.000
	T. Francona	L	9	14	0	0	0	1.6	1.000
	T. Savage	R	7	9	0	0	0	1.3	1.000
	P. Gagliano	R	5	6	0	0	0	1.2	1.000
C	T. McCarver	R	148	841	62	7	7	6.1	.992
	P. Corrales	R	27	133	23	4	2	5.9	.975
	M. Shannon	R	1	1	0	0	0	1.0	1.000

TEAM STATISTICS

	W	L	PCT	GB	R	OR	Batting 2B	Batting 3B	Batting HR	Batting BA	Batting SA	SB	Fielding E	Fielding DP	FA	Pitching CG	Pitching BB	Pitching SO	ShO	SV	ERA
LA	95	67	.586		606	490	201	27	108	.256	.362	94	133	128	.979	52	356	1084	20	35	2.62
SF	93	68	.578	1.5	675	626	195	31	181	.248	.392	29	168	131	.974	52	359	973	14	27	3.24
PIT	92	70	.568	3	759	641	238	66	158	.279	.428	64	141	215	.978	35	463	898	12	43	3.52
PHI	87	75	.537	8	696	640	224	49	117	.258	.378	56	113	147	.982	52	412	928	15	23	3.57
ATL	85	77	.525	10	782	683	220	32	207	.263	.424	64	154	139	.976	37	485	884	10	36	3.68
STL	83	79	.512	12	571	577	196	61	108	.251	.368	144	145	166	.977	47	448	892	19	32	3.11
CIN	76	84	.475	18	692	702	232	33	149	.260	.395	70	122	133	.980	28	490	1043	10	35	4.08
HOU	72	90	.444	23	612	695	203	35	112	.255	.365	90	174	126	.972	34	391	929	13	26	3.76
NY	66	95	.410	28.5	587	761	187	35	98	.239	.342	55	159	171	.975	37	521	773	9	22	4.17
CHI	59	103	.364	36	644	809	203	43	140	.254	.380	76	166	132	.974	28	479	908	6	24	4.33
LEAGUE TOTAL					6624	6624	2099	412	1378	.256	.384	737	1475	1488	.977	402	4404	9312	128	303	3.61

The traditional form of the Cardinal ball clubs has been adequate pitching, strong hitting for average, and excellent speed for extra-base hits and defense. In 1966, the speed was still there: the Cards led the league in stolen bases, paced by Brock's league-leading 74. The defense was still effective, led by Curt Flood, who played 159 games in center field without making an error. But the offense slumped badly as the club finished last in runs with their lowest total since 1919. It was the pitching that brought them 83 wins; the club ERA was an excellent 3.11. The ace of the staff was Bob Gibson, who ranked third in the league in wins, complete games, and hits per nine innings; fourth in strikeouts; and fifth in ERA. Even Nellie Briles, with a 4–15 record, had a fine 3.21 ERA. In an effort to shore up the offense, the Cardinals acquired Orlando Cepeda from the Giants for Ray Sadecki, and sent Charlie Smith to the Yankees for Roger Maris.

INDIVIDUAL PITCHING

PITCHER	T	W	L	PCT	ERA	SV	G	GS	CG	IP	H	BB	SO	R	ER	ShO	H/9	BB/9	SO/9
Bob Gibson	R	21	12	.636	2.44	0	35	35	20	280.1	210	78	225	90	76	5	6.74	2.50	7.22
Al Jackson	L	13	15	.464	2.51	0	36	30	11	232.2	222	45	90	82	65	3	8.59	1.74	3.48
Ray Washburn	R	11	9	.550	3.76	0	27	26	4	170	183	44	98	75	71	1	9.69	2.33	5.19
Nellie Briles	R	4	15	.211	3.21	6	49	17	0	154	162	54	100	65	55	0	9.47	3.16	5.84
Larry Jaster	L	11	5	.688	3.26	0	26	21	6	151.2	124	45	92	57	55	5	7.36	2.67	5.46
Joe Hoerner	L	5	1	.833	1.54	13	57	0	0	76	57	21	63	16	13	0	6.75	2.49	7.46
Hal Woodeshick	L	2	1	.667	1.92	4	59	0	0	70.1	57	23	30	17	15	0	7.29	2.94	3.84
Don Dennis	R	4	2	.667	4.98	2	38	1	0	59.2	73	17	25	36	33	0	11.01	2.56	3.77
Tracy Stallard	R	1	5	.167	5.68	1	20	7	0	52.1	65	25	35	40	33	0	11.18	4.30	6.02
Steve Carlton	L	3	3	.500	3.12	0	9	9	2	52	56	18	25	22	18	1	9.69	3.12	4.33
Art Mahaffey	R	1	4	.200	6.43	1	12	5	0	35	37	21	19	27	25	0	9.51	5.40	4.89
Curt Simmons	L	1	1	.500	4.59	0	10	5	1	33.1	35	14	14	17	17	0	9.45	3.78	3.78
Ron Piche	R	1	3	.250	4.26	2	20	0	0	25.1	21	18	21	13	12	0	7.46	6.39	7.46
Ray Sadecki	L	2	1	.667	2.22	0	5	3	1	24.1	16	9	21	9	6	0	5.92	3.33	7.77
Dick Hughes	R	2	1	.667	1.71	1	6	2	1	21	12	7	20	4	4	1	5.14	3.00	8.57
Dennis Aust	R	0	1	.000	6.52	1	9	0	0	9.2	12	6	7	7	7	0	11.17	5.59	6.52
Jim Cosman	R	1	0	1.000	0.00	0	1	1	1	9	2	2	5	0	0	1	2.00	2.00	5.00
Ron Willis	R	0	0	–	0.00	1	4	0	0	3	1	1	2	0	0	0	3.00	3.00	6.00
TEAM TOTAL		83	79	.512	3.11	32	423	162	47	1459.2	1345	448	892	577	505	17	8.29	2.76	5.50

THE TRIANGULAR TRADE

What three players had exactly equal trade value? The answer is Orlando Cepeda, Joe Torre, and Ray Sadecki. Watch:

May 8, 1966: The Cardinals trade Ray Sadecki to San Francisco for Orlando Cepeda.

March 17, 1969: The Cardinals trade Orlando Cepeda to Atlanta for Joe Torre.

October 13, 1974: The Cardinals trade Joe Torre to the Mets for Ray Sadecki (and Tommy Moore, who did little other than break up the perfect symmetry).

MANAGER	W	L	PCT
Red Schoendienst	101	60	.627

POS	Player	B	G	AB	H	2B	3B	HR	HR %	R	RBI	BB	SO	SB	Pinch Hit AB	Pinch Hit H	BA	SA
REGULARS																		
1B	Orlando Cepeda	R	151	563	183	37	0	25	4.4	91	111	62	75	11	1	1	.325	.524
2B	Julian Javier	R	140	520	146	16	3	14	2.7	68	64	25	92	6	2	0	.281	.404
SS	Dal Maxvill	R	152	476	108	14	4	1	0.2	37	41	48	66	0	0	0	.227	.279
3B	Mike Shannon	R	130	482	118	18	3	12	2.5	53	77	37	89	2	2	1	.245	.369
RF	Roger Maris	L	125	410	107	18	7	9	2.2	64	55	52	61	0	19	2	.261	.405
CF	Curt Flood	R	134	514	172	24	1	5	1.0	68	50	37	46	2	8	4	.335	.414
LF	Lou Brock	L	159	689	206	32	12	21	3.0	113	76	24	109	52	4	0	.299	.472
C	Tim McCarver	L	138	471	139	26	3	14	3.0	68	69	54	32	8	11	4	.295	.452
SUBSTITUTES																		
UT	Phil Gagliano	R	73	217	48	7	0	2	0.9	20	21	19	26	0	17	0	.221	.281
3O	Ed Spiezio	R	55	105	22	2	0	3	2.9	9	10	7	18	2	27	8	.210	.314
SS	Ed Bressoud	R	52	67	9	1	1	1	1.5	8	1	9	18	0	3	1	.134	.224
2B	Steve Huntz	B	3	6	1	0	0	0	0.0	1	0	1	2	0	1	1	.167	.167
SS	Jim Williams	R	1	2	0	0	0	0	0.0	0	0	0	1	0	0	0	.000	.000
OF	Bobby Tolan	L	110	265	67	7	3	6	2.3	35	32	19	43	12	33	10	.253	.370
OF	Alex Johnson	R	81	175	39	9	2	1	0.6	20	12	9	26	6	20	5	.223	.314
C	Dave Ricketts	B	52	99	27	8	0	1	1.0	11	14	4	7	0	32	7	.273	.384
C	Johnny Romano	R	24	58	7	1	0	0	0.0	1	2	13	15	1	4	0	.121	.138
PH	Ted Savage	R	9	8	1	0	0	0	0.0	1	0	.1			8	1	.125	.125
PITCHERS																		
P	Dick Hughes	R	40	78	10	0	0	0	0.0	3	4	2	36	0	0	0	.128	.128
P	Steve Carlton	L	30	72	11	2	0	0	0.0	5	3	3	28	0	0	0	.153	.181
P	Ray Washburn	R	27	66	6	1	1	0	0.0	0	3	1	41	0	0	0	.091	.136
P	Bob Gibson	R	27	60	8	0	0	0	0.0	7	3	8	26	0	0	0	.133	.133
P	Larry Jaster	L	35	50	5	0	0	0	0.0	3	2	3	11	0	1	0	.100	.100
P	Nellie Briles	R	49	40	6	0	0	0	0.0	5	0	3	20	0	0	0	.150	.150
P	Al Jackson	L	41	31	8	1	0	0	0.0	4	2	2	9	0	0	0	.258	.290
P	Joe Hoerner	R	57	11	2	0	0	0	0.0	0	0	0	5	0	0	0	.182	.182
P	Jack Lamabe	R	23	10	2	0	0	0	0.0	0	1	0	6	0	0	0	.200	.200
P	Jim Cosman	R	10	8	1	0	0	0	0.0	0	1	0	3	0	0	0	.125	.125
P	Ron Willis	R	65	8	3	1	0	0	0.0	0	2	0	2	0	0	0	.375	.500
P	Hal Woodeshick	R	36	4	0	0	0	0	0.0	0	0	0	3	0	0	0	.000	.000
P	Mike Torrez	R	3	1	0	0	0	0	0.0	0	0	0	0	0	0	0	.000	.000
TEAM TOTAL				5566	1462	225	40	115	2.1	695	656	443	919	102	193	45	.263	.379

INDIVIDUAL FIELDING

POS	Player	T	G	PO	A	E	DP	TC/G	FA
1B	O. Cepeda	R	151	1304	90	10	103	9.3	.993
	B. Tolan	.L	13	107	5	0	7	8.6	1.000
	P. Gagliano	R	4	39	1	0	3	10.0	1.000
2B	J. Javier	R	138	311	352	24	72	5.0	.965
	P. Gagliano	R	27	55	51	3	9	4.0	.972
	D. Maxvill	R	7	5	16	0	4	3.0	1.000
	S. Huntz	R	2	3	2	0	0	2.5	1.000
SS	D. Maxvill	R	148	236	470	19	74	4.9	.974
	E. Bressoud	R	48	34	58	7	12	2.1	.929
	J. Williams	R	1	6	1	0	0	7.0	1.000
	P. Gagliano	R	2	1	1	0	0	1.0	1.000
3B	M. Shannon	R	122	88	239	29	18	2.9	.919
	P. Gagliano	R	25	20	46	5	4	2.8	.930
	E. Spiezio	R	19	15	35	2	4	2.7	.962
	E. Bressoud	R	1	0	0	0	0	0.0	.000

POS	Player	T	G	PO	A	E	DP	TC/G	FA
OF	C. Flood	R	126	314	4	4	1	2.6	.988
	L. Brock	L	157	272	12	13	2	1.9	.956
	R. Maris	R	118	224	5	2	1	2.0	.991
	B. Tolan	L	80	118	4	1	1	1.5	.992
	A. Johnson	R	57	91	7	3	2	1.8	.970
	M. Shannon	R	6	10	2	0	0	2.0	1.000
	E. Spiezio	R	7	9	0	0	0	1.3	1.000
C	T. McCarver	R	130	819	67	3	10	6.8	.997
	D. Ricketts	R	21	111	10	0	0	5.8	1.000
	J. Romano	R	20	111	3	2	1	5.8	.983

The 1967 season saw an astounding four-team pennant race in the American League, with three teams still in contention on the final Sunday. The Redbirds had a much easier time of it, opening up a margin of ten games by early August. "El Birdos," as they were called, were led by Orlando Cepeda's MVP season, as he led the league in RBIs, ranked second in doubles, and was fifth in slugging. The offense vaulted from last in the league in runs scored to second, behind the surprising Cubs. Lou Brock became the first player to hit 20 home runs and steal 50 bases in a season, and Curt Flood's .335 average was a career high. The pitching picked up where it left off the year before, despite losing Gibson for the second half of the season to a broken leg. The young mound crew had seven pitchers who won nine or more games, three of whom—Larry Jaster, Nellie Briles, and Steve Carlton—were under 24 years of age. The Cards then won, yes, another exciting seven-game World Series against Boston. (Of St. Louis's thirteen Series appearances, seven went the full seven games.) Gibson's leg healed in time for him to rudely awaken the Red Sox from their "Impossible Dream," as he pitched and won three complete games, striking out 26 in 27 innings.

TEAM STATISTICS

	W	L	PCT	GB	R	OR	2B	3B	HR	BA	SA	SB	E	DP	FA	CG	BB	SO	ShO	SV	ERA
STL	101	60	.627		695	557	225	40	115	.263	.379	102	140	127	.978	44	431	956	17	45	3.05
SF	91	71	.562	10.5	652	551	201	39	140	.245	.372	22	134	149	.979	64	453	990	17	25	**2.92**
CHI	87	74	.540	14	**702**	624	211	49	128	.251	.378	63	121	143	**.981**	47	463	888	7	28	3.48
CIN	87	75	.537	14.5	604	563	251	54	109	.248	.372	92	121	124	.980	34	498	888	17	23	3.05
PHI	82	80	.506	19.5	612	581	221	47	103	.242	.357	79	137	174	.978	46	403	967	17	23	3.10
PIT	81	81	.500	20.5	679	693	193	**62**	91	**.277**	**.380**	79	141	**186**	.978	35	561	820	5	35	3.74
ATL	77	85	.475	24.5	631	640	191	29	**158**	.240	.372	55	138	148	.978	35	449	862	5	32	3.47
LA	73	89	.451	28.5	519	595	203	38	82	.236	.332	56	160	144	.975	41	**393**	967	17	24	3.21
HOU	69	93	.426	32.5	626	742	**259**	46	93	.249	.364	88	159	120	.974	35	485	1060	8	21	4.03
NY	61	101	.377	40.5	498	672	178	23	83	.238	.325	58	157	147	.975	36	536	893	10	19	3.73
LEAGUE TOTAL					6218	6218	2133	427	1102	.249	.363	694	1408	1462	.978	417	4672	9468	121	291	3.38

INDIVIDUAL PITCHING

PITCHER	T	W	L	PCT	ERA	SV	G	GS	CG	IP	H	BB	SO	R	ER	ShO	H/9	BB/9	SO/9
Dick Hughes	R	16	6	**.727**	2.67	3	37	27	12	222.1	164	48	161	72	66	3	**6.64**	1.94	6.52
Steve Carlton	L	14	9	.609	2.98	1	30	28	11	193	173	62	168	71	64	2	8.07	2.89	7.83
Ray Washburn	R	10	7	.588	3.53	0	27	27	3	186.1	190	42	98	78	73	1	9.18	2.03	4.73
Bob Gibson	R	13	7	.650	2.98	0	24	24	10	175.1	151	40	147	62	58	2	7.75	2.05	7.55
Nellie Briles	R	14	5	.737	2.43	6	49	14	4	155.1	139	40	94	45	42	2	8.05	2.32	5.45
Larry Jaster	L	9	7	.563	3.01	3	34	23	2	152.1	141	44	87	57	51	1	8.33	2.60	5.14
Al Jackson	L	9	4	.692	3.95	1	38	11	1	107	117	29	43	61	47	1	9.84	2.44	3.62
Ron Willis	R	6	5	.545	2.67	10	65	0	0	81	76	43	42	27	24	0	8.44	4.78	4.67
Joe Hoerner	L	4	4	.500	2.59	15	57	0	0	66	52	20	50	25	19	0	7.09	2.73	6.82
Jack Lamabe	R	3	4	.429	2.83	4	23	1	1	47.2	43	10	30	16	15	1	8.12	1.89	5.66
Hal Woodeshick	L	2	1	.667	5.18	2	36	0	0	41.2	41	28	20	29	24	0	8.86	6.05	4.32
Jim Cosman	R	1	0	1.000	3.16	0	10	5	0	31.1	21	24	11	12	11	0	6.03	6.89	3.16
Mike Torrez	R	0	1	.000	3.18	0	3	1	0	5.2	5	1	5	2	2	0	7.94	1.59	7.94
TEAM TOTAL		101	60	.627	3.05	45	433	161	44	1465	1313	431	956	557	496	13	8.07	2.65	5.87

MANAGER	W	L	PCT
Red Schoendienst	97	65	.599

POS	Player	B	G	AB	H	2B	3B	HR	HR %	R	RBI	BB	SO	SB	Pinch Hit AB	Pinch Hit H	BA	SA
REGULARS																		
1B	Orlando Cepeda	R	157	600	149	26	2	16	2.7	71	73	43	96	8	3	1	.248	.378
2B	Julian Javier	R	139	519	135	25	4	4	0.8	54	52	24	61	10	0	0	.260	.347
SS	Dal Maxvill	R	151	459	116	8	5	1	0.2	51	24	52	71	0	0	0	.253	.298
3B	Mike Shannon	R	156	576	153	29	2	15	2.6	62	79	37	114	1	0	0	.266	.401
RF	Roger Maris	L	100	310	79	18	2	5	1.6	25	45	24	38	0	21	6	.255	.374
CF	Curt Flood	R	150	618	186	17	4	5	0.8	71	60	33	58	11	2	0	.301	.366
LF	Lou Brock	L	159	660	184	46	14	6	0.9	92	51	46	124	62	3	1	.279	.418
C	Tim McCarver	L	128	434	110	15	6	5	1.2	35	48	26	31	4	19	4	.253	.350
SUBSTITUTES																		
S2	Dick Schofield	B	69	127	28	7	1	1	0.8	14	8	13	31	1	11	0	.220	.315
UT	Phil Gagliano	R	53	105	24	4	2	0	0.0	13	13	7	12	0	17	4	.229	.305
OF	Bobby Tolan	L	92	278	64	12	1	5	1.8	28	17	13	42	9	23	2	.230	.335
OF	Ron Davis	R	33	79	14	4	2	0	0.0	11	5	5	17	1	0	0	.177	.278
OF	Dick Simpson	R	26	56	13	0	0	3	5.4	11	8	8	21	0	2	0	.232	.393
OF	Ed Spiezio	R	29	51	8	0	0	0	0.0	1	2	5	6	1	14	4	.157	.157
O1	Joe Hague	L	7	17	4	0	0	1	5.9	2	1	2	2	0	1	0	.235	.412
C	Johnny Edwards	L	85	230	55	9	1	3	1.3	14	29	16	20	1	26	7	.239	.326
C	Dave Ricketts	B	20	22	3	0	0	0	0.0	1	1	0	3	0	19	2	.136	.136
C	Ted Simmons	B	2	3	1	0	0	0	0.0	0	0	1	1	0	0	0	.333	.333
PH	Floyd Wicker	L	5	4	2	0	0	0	0.0	2	0	0	0	0	4	2	.500	.500
PITCHERS																		
P	Bob Gibson	R	35	94	16	5	0	0	0.0	3	6	7	32	1	0	0	.170	.223
P	Nellie Briles	R	33	80	11	2	0	0	0.0	5	5	4	21	0	0	0	.138	.163
P	Steve Carlton	L	35	73	12	0	1	2	2.7	6	3	0	25	0	0	0	.164	.274
P	Ray Washburn	R	31	60	5	0	1	0	0.0	5	5	8	38	0	0	0	.083	.117
P	Larry Jaster	L	31	43	6	0	0	1	2.3	2	1	1	9	0	0	0	.140	.209
P	Dick Hughes	R	25	15	0	0	0	0	0.0	0	0	1	7	0	0	0	.000	.000
P	Mel Nelson	R	18	12	2	0	0	0	0.0	2	2	1	4	0	0	0	.167	.167
P	Ron Willis	R	48	11	0	0	0	0	0.0	1	0	1	4	0	0	0	.000	.000
P	Mike Torrez	R	5	7	2	0	0	0	0.0	1	1	0	2	0	0	0	.286	.286
P	Joe Hoerner	R	47	6	0	0	0	0	0.0	0	0	0	3	0	0	0	.000	.000
P	Wayne Granger	R	34	5	1	0	0	0	0.0	0	0	0	2	0	0	0	.200	.200
P	Hal Gilson	R	13	4	0	0	0	0	0.0	0	0	0	2	0	0	0	.000	.000
P	Pete Mikkelsen	R	5	3	0	0	0	0	0.0	0	0	0	0	0	0	0	.000	.000
TEAM TOTAL				5561	1383	227	48	73	1.3	583	539	378	897	110	165	33	.249	.346

INDIVIDUAL FIELDING

POS	Player	T	G	PO	A	E	DP	TC/G	FA		POS	Player	T	G	PO	A	E	DP	TC/G	FA
1B	O. Cepeda	R	154	1362	90	17	109	9.5	.988		OF	C. Flood	R	149	386	11	7	4	2.7	.983
	B. Tolan	L	9	83	9	0	7	10.2	1.000			L. Brock	L	156	269	9	14	1	1.9	.952
	J. Hague	L	2	15	1	0	1	8.0	1.000			R. Maris	R	84	169	4	3	1	2.1	.983
2B	J. Javier	R	139	304	339	16	68	4.7	.976			B. Tolan	L	67	116	3	4	1	1.8	.967
	D. Schofield	R	23	65	50	3	15	5.1	.975			R. Davis	R	25	44	3	1	1	1.9	.979
	P. Gagliano	R	17	24	32	1	6	3.4	.982			D. Simpson	R	22	26	1	0	0	1.2	1.000
SS	D. Maxvill	R	151	232	458	22	81	4.7	.969			E. Spiezio	R	11	19	1	0	1	1.8	1.000
	D. Schofield	R	43	44	66	3	7	2.6	.973			J. Hague	L	3	4	0	1	0	1.7	.800
3B	M. Shannon	R	156	110	310	21	25	2.8	.952			P. Gagliano	R	5	2	1	0	0	0.6	1.000
	P. Gagliano	R	10	5	19	0	2	2.4	1.000		C	T. McCarver	R	109	708	54	11	6	7.1	.986
	E. Spiezio	R	2	1	4	0	0	2.5	1.000			J. Edwards	R	54	350	25	3	2	7.0	.992
												D. Ricketts	R	1	5	0	0	0	5.0	1.000
												T. Simmons	R	2	3	1	0	0	2.0	1.000

Nineteen sixty-eight was The Year of the Pitcher. Batting averages tumbled, and the league ERA fell below 3.00. Just six batters topped .300, only one of them in the American League (Carl Yastrzemski at .301). The plight of the hitter was brought home in September as Gaylord Perry pitched a no-hitter against St. Louis, only to watch Ray Washburn pitch one against the Giants the very next day. Of all the gaudy stats turned in by pitchers, the gaudiest belonged to Bob Gibson: an astounding 1.12 ERA with 13 shutouts. Between May 28 and August 24, Gibson won fifteen straight, ten of them shutouts. His overpowering season won him the Cy Young and MVP awards, as the Cardinals won the pennant going away. They lost the Series, however, when the Tigers beat Gibson 4–1 in Game 7, breaking his World Series streak of seven consecutive complete-game wins going back to 1964.

TEAM STATISTICS

	W	L	PCT	GB	R	OR	Batting						Fielding			Pitching					
							2B	3B	HR	BA	SA	SB	E	DP	FA	CG	BB	SO	ShO	SV	ERA
L	97	65	.599		583	472	227	48	73	.249	.346	110	140	135	.978	63	375	971	30	32	2.49
	88	74	.543	9	599	529	162	33	108	.239	.341	50	162	125	.975	77	344	942	20	16	2.71
Hl	84	78	.519	13	612	611	203	43	130	.242	.366	41	119	149	.981	46	392	894	12	32	3.41
N	83	79	.512	14	690	673	281	36	106	.273	.389	59	144	144	.978	24	573	963	16	38	3.56
L	81	81	.500	16	514	549	179	31	80	.252	.339	83	125	139	.980	44	362	871	16	29	2.92
r	80	82	.494	17	583	532	180	44	80	.252	.343	130	139	162	.979	42	485	897	19	30	2.74
	76	86	.469	21	470	509	202	36	67	.230	.319	57	144	144	.977	38	414	994	23	31	2.69
Hl	76	86	.469	21	543	615	178	30	100	.233	.333	58	127	163	.980	42	421	935	12	27	3.36
'	73	89	.451	24	473	499	178	30	81	.228	.315	72	133	142	.979	45	430	1014	25	32	2.72
)U	72	90	.444	25	510	588	205	28	66	.231	.317	44	156	129	.975	50	479	1021	12	23	3.26
AGUE TOTAL					5577	5577	1995	359	891	.243	.341	704	1389	1432	.978	471	4275	9502	185	290	2.99

INDIVIDUAL PITCHING

CHER	T	W	L	PCT	ERA	SV	G	GS	CG	IP	H	BB	SO	R	ER	ShO	H/9	BB/9	SO/9
) Gibson	R	22	9	.710	1.12	0	34	34	28	304.2	198	62	268	49	38	13	5.85	1.83	7.92
llie Briles	R	19	11	.633	2.81	0	33	33	13	243.2	251	55	141	90	76	4	9.27	2.03	5.21
ve Carlton	L	13	11	.542	2.99	0	34	33	10	232	214	61	162	87	77	5	8.30	2.37	6.28
y Washburn	R	14	8	.636	2.26	0	31	30	8	215.1	191	47	124	67	54	4	7.98	1.96	5.18
ry Jaster	L	9	13	.409	3.51	0	31	21	3	153.2	153	38	70	63	60	1	8.96	2.23	4.10
k Hughes	R	2	2	.500	3.53	4	25	5	0	63.2	45	21	49	25	25	0	6.36	2.97	6.93
n Willis	R	2	3	.400	3.39	4	48	0	0	63.2	50	28	39	25	24	0	7.07	3.96	5.51
Nelson	L	2	1	.667	2.91	1	18	4	1	52.2	49	9	16	20	17	0	8.37	1.54	2.73
Hoerner	L	8	2	.800	1.47	17	47	0	0	49	34	12	42	9	8	0	6.24	2.20	7.71
yne Granger	R	4	2	.667	2.25	4	34	0	0	44	40	12	27	14	11	0	8.18	2.45	5.52
Gilson	L	0	2	.000	4.57	2	13	0	0	21.2	27	11	19	11	11	0	11.22	4.57	7.89
e Torrez	R	2	1	.667	2.84	0	5	2	0	19	20	12	6	7	6	0	9.47	5.68	2.84
e Mikkelsen	R	0	0	—	1.13	0	5	0	0	16	10	7	8	5	2	0	5.63	3.94	4.50
AM TOTAL		97	65	.599	2.49	32	358	162	63	1479	1282	375	971	472	409	27	7.80	2.28	5.91

MANAGER	W	L	PCT
Red Schoendienst	87	75	.537

POS	Player	B	G	AB	H	2B	3B	HR	HR %	R	RBI	BB	SO	SB	Pinch Hit AB	Pinch Hit H	BA	SA
REGULARS																		
1B	Joe Torre	R	159	602	174	29	6	18	3.0	72	101	66	85	0	1	0	.289	.447
2B	Julian Javier	R	143	493	139	28	2	10	2.0	59	42	40	74	8	4	1	.282	.408
SS	Dal Maxvill	R	132	372	65	10	2	2	0.5	27	32	44	52	1	0	0	.175	.228
3B	Mike Shannon	R	150	551	140	15	5	12	2.2	51	55	49	87	1	2	1	.254	.365
RF	Vada Pinson	L	132	495	126	22	6	10	2.0	58	70	35	63	4	8	1	.255	.384
CF	Curt Flood	R	153	606	173	31	3	4	0.7	80	57	48	57	9	2	1	.285	.366
LF	Lou Brock	L	157	655	195	33	10	12	1.8	97	47	50	115	53	2	1	.298	.434
C	Tim McCarver	L	138	515	134	27	3	7	1.4	46	51	49	26	4	1	0	.260	.365
SUBSTITUTES																		
S2	Steve Huntz	B	71	139	27	4	0	3	2.2	13	13	27	34	0	3	0	.194	.288
UT	Phil Gagliano	R	62	128	29	2	0	1	0.8	7	10	14	12	0	21	2	.227	.266
1B	Bill White	L	49	57	12	1	0	0	0.0	7	4	11	15	1	31	5	.211	.228
SS	Jerry Davanon	R	16	40	12	3	0	1	2.5	7	7	6	8	0	0	0	.300	.450
3B	Bob Johnson	R	19	29	6	0	0	1	3.4	1	2	2	4	0	12	1	.207	.310
2B	Tom Coulter	L	6	19	6	1	1	0	0.0	3	4	2	6	0	0	0	.316	.474
O1	Joe Hague	L	40	100	17	2	1	2	2.0	8	8	12	23	0	14	1	.170	.270
OF	Vic Davalillo	L	63	98	26	3	0	2	2.0	15	10	7	8	1	34	9	.265	.357
OF	Byron Browne	R	22	53	12	0	1	1	1.9	9	7	11	14	0	7	0	.226	.321
OF	Jim Hicks	R	19	44	8	0	2	1	2.3	5	3	4	14	0	1	0	.182	.341
OF	Leron Lee	L	7	23	5	1	0	0	0.0	3	0	3	8	0	0	0	.217	.261
OF	Boots Day	L	11	6	0	0	0	0	0.0	1	0	1	1	0	5	0	.000	.000
OF	Joe Nossek	R	9	5	1	0	0	0	0.0	2	0	0	3	0	4	1	.200	.200
C	Dave Ricketts	B	30	44	12	1	0	0	0.0	2	5	4	5	0	18	5	.273	.295
C	Ted Simmons	B	5	14	3	0	1	0	0.0	0	3	1	1	0	1	0	.214	.357
PITCHERS																		
P	Bob Gibson	R	37	118	29	6	0	1	0.8	11	8	3	36	5	1	0	.246	.322
P	Steve Carlton	L	32	80	17	4	1	1	1.3	5	7	3	27	0	0	0	.213	.325
P	Nellie Briles	R	36	76	8	0	0	1	1.3	1	5	4	26	0	0	0	.105	.145
P	Mike Torrez	R	24	41	3	1	0	0	0.0	3	0	1	13	0	0	0	.073	.098
P	Chuck Taylor	R	27	39	7	2	0	0	0.0	0	2	1	14	0	0	0	.179	.231
P	Ray Washburn	R	28	37	3	0	0	0	0.0	0	0	1	25	0	0	0	.081	.081
P	Dave Giusti	R	22	25	5	1	0	0	0.0	1	1	3	6	0	0	0	.200	.240
P	Mudcat Grant	R	31	17	5	0	0	0	0.0	1	3	1	7	0	0	0	.294	.294
P	Joe Hoerner	R	45	5	0	0	0	0	0.0	0	0	0	4	0	0	0	.000	.000
P	Jerry Reuss	L	1	3	1	0	0	0	0.0	0	1	0	2	0	0	0	.333	.333
P	Santiago Guzman	R	1	3	1	0	0	0	0.0	0	0	0	1	0	0	0	.333	.333
P	Ron Willis	R	26	1	0	0	0	0	0.0	0	1	0	0	0	1	0	1.000	1.000
P	Gary Waslewski	R	12	1	0	0	0	0	0.0	0	0	0	0	0	0	0	.000	.000
P	Tom Hilgendorf	B	6	1	1	1	0	0	0.0	0	1	0	0	0	1	0	1.000	2.000
P	Reggie Cleveland	R	1	1	0	0	0	0	0.0	0	0	0	0	0	0	0	.000	.000
P	Mel Nelson	R	8	0	0	0	0	0	–	0	0	0	0	0	0	0	–	–
P	Dennis Ribant	R	2	0	0	0	0	0	–	0	0	0	0	0	0	0	–	–
P	Jim Ellis	R	2	0	0	0	0	0	–	0	1	0	0	0	0	0	–	–
P	Sal Campisi	R	7	0	0	0	0	0	0.0	0	0	0	0	0	0	0	–	–
	TEAM TOTAL			5536	1403	228	44	90	1.6	595	561	503	876	87	172	29	.253	.359

INDIVIDUAL FIELDING

POS	Player	T	G	PO	A	E	DP	TC/G	FA	POS	Player	T	G	PO	A	E	DP	TC/G	FA
1B	J. Torre	R	144	1270	83	6	117	9.4	.996	OF	C. Flood	R	152	362	14	4	2	2.5	.989
	B. White	L	15	81	7	0	7	5.9	1.000		L. Brock	L	157	255	7	14	2	1.8	.949
	J. Hague	L	9	73	5	0	3	8.7	1.000		V. Pinson	L	124	218	6	1	2	1.8	.996
	P. Gagliano	R	9	47	5	1	5	5.9	.981		B. Browne	R	16	35	3	0	1	2.4	1.000
	B. Johnson	R	1	1	0	0	0	1.0	1.000		V. Davalillo	L	23	37	0	0	0	1.6	1.000
2B	J. Javier	R	141	244	374	21	70	4.5	.967		J. Hague	L	17	31	0	2	0	1.9	.939
	P. Gagliano	R	20	50	41	0	11	4.6	.989		J. Hicks	R	15	24	2	0	0	1.7	1.000
	S. Huntz	R	12	10	21	0	2	2.6	1.000		B. Day	L	1	0	0	0	0	0.0	.000
	T. Coulter	R	6	8	16	1	5	4.2	.960		L. Lee	R	7	7	1	0	0	1.1	1.000
SS	D. Maxvill	R	131	216	408	20	78	4.9	.969		J. Nossek	R	1	2	0	0	0	2.0	1.000
	S. Huntz	R	52	65	91	9	20	3.2	.945		P. Gagliano	R	2	1	1	0	0	1.0	1.000
	J. Davanon	R	16	29	39	3	6	4.4	.958	C	T. McCarver	R	136	925	66	14	10	7.4	.986
3B	M. Shannon	R	149	123	258	22	22	2.7	.945		J. Torre	R	17	90	8	1	0	5.8	.990
	P. Gagliano	R	9	10	8	0	0	2.0	1.000		D. Ricketts	R	8	57	1	1	0	7.4	.983
	B. Johnson	R	4	3	7	2	1	3.0	.833		T. Simmons	R	4	22	0	1	0	5.8	.957
	S. Huntz	R	6	2	9	0	0	1.8	1.000										

When the National League expanded to twelve teams in 1969, it gave a great deal of thought to the proper alignment. It settled on the geographically incorrect one that placed St. Louis and Chicago in the East, and Cincinnati and Atlanta in the West, using the Cardinals to strengthen the relatively weak East. Naturally, the Cardinals ended up as spectators as the Miracle Mets blew by the Cubs for the title. The problem was their offense: while their scoring rose by 12 runs from '68, the other nine clubs improved by an average of 139. The pitching was still strong, leading in runs allowed and ERA, as Steve Carlton proved an excellent southpaw complement to Gibson. But the pre-season trade of Cepeda for Joe Torre may have hurt; while Cepeda fell off in 1968, so did everyone, and it is always dangerous to trade away one of a club's acknowledged leaders.

TEAM STATISTICS

	W	L	PCT	GB	R	OR	2B	3B	HR	BA	SA	SB	E	DP	FA	CG	BB	SO	ShO	SV	ERA
EAST																					
NY	100	62	.617		632	541	184	41	109	.242	.351	66	122	146	.980	51	517	1012	**28**	35	2.99
CHI	92	70	.568	8	720	611	215	40	142	.253	.384	30	136	149	.979	58	475	1017	22	27	3.34
PIT	88	74	.543	12	725	652	220	52	119	**.277**	.398	74	155	169	.975	39	553	1124	9	33	3.61
STL	87	75	.537	13	595	**540**	**228**	44	90	.253	.359	87	138	144	.978	63	511	1004	12	26	**2.94**
PHI	63	99	.389	37	645	745	227	35	137	.241	.372	73	136	157	.978	47	570	921	14	21	4.17
MON	52	110	.321	48	582	791	202	33	125	.240	.359	52	184	**179**	.971	26	702	973	8	21	4.33
WEST																					
ATL	93	69	.574		691	631	195	22	141	.258	.380	59	**115**	114	**.981**	38	438	893	7	42	3.53
SF	90	72	.556	3	713	636	187	28	136	.242	.361	71	169	155	.974	**71**	461	906	15	17	3.25
CIN	89	73	.549	4	**798**	768	224	42	**171**	.277	**.422**	79	168	158	.973	23	611	818	11	**44**	4.13
LA	85	77	.525	8	645	561	185	**52**	97	.254	.359	80	126	130	.980	47	**420**	975	20	31	3.09
HOU	81	81	.500	12	676	668	208	40	104	.240	.352	**101**	153	136	.975	52	547	**1221**	11	34	3.60
SD	52	110	.321	41	468	746	180	42	99	.225	.329	45	156	140	.975	16	592	764	9	25	4.24
LEAGUE TOTAL					7890	7890	2455	471	1470	.250	.369	817	1758	1777	.977	531	6397	11628	166	356	3.60

INDIVIDUAL PITCHING

PITCHER	T	W	L	PCT	ERA	SV	G	GS	CG	IP	H	BB	SO	R	ER	ShO	H/9	BB/9	SO/9
Bob Gibson	R	20	13	.606	2.18	0	35	35	**28**	314	251	95	269	84	76	4	7.19	2.72	7.71
Steve Carlton	L	17	11	.607	2.17	0	31	31	12	236	185	93	210	66	57	2	7.06	3.55	8.01
Nellie Briles	R	15	13	.536	3.51	0	36	33	10	228	218	63	126	104	89	3	8.61	2.49	4.97
Ray Washburn	R	3	8	.273	3.07	1	28	16	2	132	133	49	80	59	45	0	9.07	3.34	5.45
Chuck Taylor	R	7	5	.583	2.55	0	27	13	5	127	108	30	62	39	36	1	7.65	2.13	4.39
Mike Torrez	R	10	4	.714	3.58	0	24	15	3	108	96	62	61	47	43	0	8.00	5.17	5.08
Dave Giusti	R	3	7	.300	3.60	0	22	12	2	100	96	37	62	46	40	1	8.64	3.33	5.58
Mudcat Grant	R	7	5	.583	4.12	7	30	3	1	63.1	62	22	35	31	29	0	8.81	3.13	4.97
Joe Hoerner	L	2	3	.400	2.89	15	45	0	0	53	44	9	35	18	17	0	7.47	1.53	5.94
Ron Willis	R	1	2	.333	4.18	0	26	0	0	32.1	26	19	23	16	15	0	7.24	5.29	6.40
Gary Waslewski	R	0	2	.000	3.92	1	12	0	0	20.2	19	8	16	9	9	0	8.27	3.48	6.97
Sal Campisi	R	1	0	1.000	0.90	0	7	0	0	10	4	6	7	1	1	0	3.60	5.40	6.30
Jerry Reuss	L	1	0	1.000	0.00	0	1	1	0	7	2	3	3	0	0	0	2.57	3.86	3.86
Santiago Guzman	R	0	1	.000	5.14	0	1	1	0	7	9	3	7	4	4	0	11.57	3.86	9.00
Tom Hilgendorf	L	0	0	—	1.50	2	6	0	0	6	3	2	2	1	1	0	4.50	3.00	3.00
Mel Nelson	L	0	1	.000	12.60	0	8	0	0	5	13	3	3	7	7	0	23.40	5.40	5.40
Jim Ellis	L	0	0	—	1.80	0	2	1	0	5	7	3	0	1	1	0	12.60	5.40	0.00
Reggie Cleveland	R	0	0	—	9.00	0	1	1	0	4	7	1	3	4	4	0	15.75	2.25	6.75
Dennis Ribant	R	0	0	—	13.50	0	1	0	0	1.1	4	1	0	2	2	0	27.00	6.75	0.00
Vic Davalillo	L	0	0	—	∞	0	2	0	0		2	2	0	1	1	0	∞	∞	0.00
TEAM TOTAL		87	75	.537	2.94	26	345	162	63	1459.2	1289	511	1004	540	477	11	7.95	3.15	6.19

ONE FOR THE HISTORY BOOKS

In a post-season trade that shook the baseball world, the Cardinals sent Tim McCarver, Curt Flood, Byron Browne, and Joe Horner to the Phillies for Dick Allen, Cookie Rojas, and Jerry Johnson. Flood refused to report to Philadelphia, choosing to challenge baseball's reserve clause in court. One year later, in *Kuhn v. Flood,* the U. S. Supreme Court ruled against Flood, upholding baseball's antitrust exemption as an anomaly, but one that could only be eliminated by Congress. (In the meantime, the Cardinals sent Willie Montanez to Philadelphia to take Flood's place.)

MANAGER	W	L	PCT
Red Schoendienst	76	86	.469

POS	Player	B	G	AB	H	2B	3B	HR	HR %	R	RBI	BB	SO	SB	Pinch Hit AB	Pinch Hit H	BA	SA
REGULARS																		
1B	Joe Hague	L	139	451	122	16	4	14	3.1	58	68	63	87	2	17	7	.271	.417
2B	Julian Javier	R	139	513	129	16	3	2	0.4	62	42	24	70	6	3	2	.251	.306
SS	Dal Maxvill	R	152	399	80	5	2	0	0.0	35	28	51	56	0	0	0	.201	.223
3B	Joe Torre	R	161	624	203	27	9	21	3.4	89	100	70	91	2	0	0	.325	.498
RF	Leron Lee	L	121	264	60	13	1	6	2.3	28	23	24	66	5	38	9	.227	.352
CF	Jose Cardenal	R	148	552	162	32	6	10	1.8	73	74	45	70	26	16	8	.293	.428
LF	Lou Brock	L	155	664	202	29	5	13	2.0	114	57	60	99	51	3	2	.304	.422
C	Ted Simmons	B	82	284	69	8	2	3	1.1	29	24	37	37	2	4	1	.243	.317
SUBSTITUTES																		
13	Richie Allen	R	122	459	128	17	5	34	7.4	88	101	71	118	5	3	1	.279	.560
3B	Mike Shannon	R	52	174	37	9	2	0	0.0	18	22	16	20	1	5	1	.213	.287
SS	Ed Crosby	L	38	95	24	4	1	0	0.0	9	6	7	5	0	2	1	.253	.316
SS	Milt Ramirez	R	62	79	15	2	1	0	0.0	8	3	8	9	0	1	0	.190	.241
UT	Cookie Rojas	R	23	47	5	0	0	0	0.0	2	2	3	4	0	10	2	.106	.106
UT	Phil Gagliano	R	18	32	6	0	0	0	0.0	0	2	1	3	0	8	2	.188	.188
S2	Jim Kennedy	L	12	24	3	0	0	0	0.0	1	0	0	0	0	1	0	.125	.125
32	Jerry Davanon	R	11	18	2	1	0	0	0.0	2	0	2	5	0	3	0	.111	.167
O1	Carl Taylor	R	104	245	61	12	2	6	2.4	39	45	41	30	5	42	11	.249	.388
OF	Vic Davalillo	L	111	183	57	14	3	1	0.5	29	33	13	19	4	73	24	.311	.437
OF	Luis Melendez	R	21	70	21	1	0	0	0.0	11	8	2	12	3	3	0	.300	.314
O1	Jim Beauchamp	R	44	58	15	2	0	1	1.7	8	6	8	11	2	23	7	.259	.345
OF	Jose Cruz	L	6	17	6	1	0	0	0.0	2	1	4	0	0	1	1	.353	.412
OF	Jorge Roque	R	5	1	0	0	0	0	0.0	2	0	0	1	0	1	0	.000	.000
C	Bart Zeller	R	1	0	0	0	0	0	—	0	0	0	0	0	0	0	—	—
PH	Jim Campbell	L	13	13	3	0	0	0	0.0	0	1	0	3	0	13	3	.231	.231
PH	Joe Nossek	R	1	1	0	0	0	0	0.0	0	0	0	0	0	1	0	.000	.000
PITCHERS																		
P	Bob Gibson	R	40	109	33	3	1	2	1.8	14	19	8	25	0	2	0	.303	.404
P	Steve Carlton	L	34	80	16	2	0	0	0.0	4	4	1	28	1	0	0	.200	.225
P	Mike Torrez	R	30	63	17	2	1	0	0.0	4	5	0	18	0	0	0	.270	.333
P	Jerry Reuss	L	20	40	2	0	0	0	0.0	3	1	3	32	1	0	0	.050	.050
P	Nellie Briles	R	30	39	7	1	2	0	0.0	4	3	1	14	0	0	0	.179	.308
P	Chuck Taylor	R	56	26	3	1	0	0	0.0	3	3	1	7	0	0	0	.115	.154
P	George Culver	R	11	17	3	0	1	0	0.0	2	6	0	5	1	0	0	.176	.294
P	Harry Parker	R	7	8	2	0	0	0	0.0	1	0	0	2	0	0	0	.250	.250
P	Frank Bertaina	L	8	7	1	0	0	0	0.0	0	0	0	0	0	0	0	.143	.143
P	Frank Linzy	R	47	7	0	0	0	0	0.0	0	0	0	5	0	0	0	.000	.000
P	Santiago Guzman	R	8	5	1	0	0	0	0.0	1	1	0	1	0	0	0	.200	.200
P	Billy McCool	R	18	4	0	0	0	0	0.0	0	0	0	1	0	0	0	.000	.000
P	Reggie Cleveland	R	16	4	1	0	0	0	0.0	0	0	0	2	0	0	0	.250	.250
P	Ted Abernathy	R	11	3	0	0	0	0	0.0	0	0	0	0	0	0	0	.000	.000
P	Al Hrabosky	R	16	3	0	0	0	0	0.0	0	0	0	2	0	0	0	.000	.000
P	Chuck Hartenstein	R	6	2	0	0	0	0	0.0	0	0	1	2	0	0	0	.000	.000
P	Rich Nye	L	6	2	1	0	0	0	0.0	0	0	1	0	0	0	0	.500	.500
P	Jerry Johnson	R	7	1	0	0	0	0	0.0	1	0	1	0	0	0	0	.000	.000
P	Sal Campisi	R	37	1	0	0	0	0	0.0	0	0	0	1	0	0	0	.000	.000
P	Tom Hilgendorf	B	23	1	0	0	0	0	0.0	0	0	0	0	0	0	0	.000	.000
P	Fred Norman	L	1	0	0	0	0	0	—	0	0	0	0	0	0	0	—	—
P	Bob Chlupsa	R	14	0	0	0	0	0	—	0	0	0	0	0	0	0	—	—
TEAM TOTAL				5689	1497	218	51	113	2.0	744	688	569	961	117	273	82	.263	.379

INDIVIDUAL FIELDING

POS	Player	T	G	PO	A	E	DP	TC/G	FA
1B	J. Hague	L	82	672	48	4	65	8.8	.994
	R. Allen	R	79	676	41	5	67	9.1	.993
	C. Taylor	R	15	109	6	2	10	7.8	.983
	J. Beauchamp	R	5	26	3	0	1	5.8	1.000
	P. Gagliano	R	3	16	0	0	2	5.3	1.000
	J. Torre	R	1	12	0	0	0	12.0	1.000
2B	J. Javier	R	137	329	413	15	84	5.5	.980
	D. Maxvill	R	22	44	59	1	11	4.7	.990
	C. Rojas	R	10	22	30	0	9	5.2	1.000
	J. Kennedy	R	5	10	9	2	3	4.2	.905
	P. Gagliano	R	2	5	4	1	1	5.0	.900
	J. Davanon	R	3	2	8	0	0	3.3	1.000
	E. Crosby	R	2	4	1	1	1	3.0	.833
SS	D. Maxvill	R	136	216	426	12	80	4.8	**.982**
	M. Ramirez	R	59	63	92	13	25	2.8	.923
	E. Crosby	R	35	37	87	6	15	3.7	.954
	J. Kennedy	R	7	9	11	2	2	3.1	.909
	C. Rojas	R	2	1	0	0	0	0.5	1.000
3B	J. Torre	R	73	68	133	11	12	2.9	.948
	R. Allen	R	38	27	67	11	3	2.8	.895
	M. Shannon	R	51	32	59	8	4	1.9	.919
	J. Davanon	R	5	6	6	0	3	2.4	1.000
	P. Gagliano	R	6	3	4	0	1	1.2	1.000
	E. Crosby	R	3	3	3	0	1	2.0	1.000
	C. Taylor	R	1	1	2	0	0	3.0	1.000
	M. Ramirez	R	1	0	0	1	0	1.0	.000

POS	Player	T	G	PO	A	E	DP	TC/G	FA
OF	J. Cardenal	R	134	276	6	9	0	2.2	.969
	L. Brock	L	152	247	9	10	2	1.8	.962
	L. Lee	R	77	120	3	4	0	1.6	.969
	J. Hague	L	52	77	3	1	1	1.6	.988
	V. Davalillo	L	54	67	3	2	1	1.3	.972
	C. Taylor	R	46	66	3	1	1	1.5	.986
	L. Melendez	R	18	31	2	0	0	1.8	1.000
	J. Roque	R	1	0	0	0	0	0.0	.000
	J. Beauchamp	R	10	16	1	0	1	1.7	1.000
	J. Cruz	L	4	16	0	0	0	4.0	1.000
	R. Allen	R	3	5	1	2	0	2.7	.750
	C. Rojas	R	3	1	0	0	0	0.3	1.000
C	J. Torre	R	90	571	29	8	4	6.8	.987
	T. Simmons	R	79	466	37	5	2	6.4	.990
	B. Zeller	R	1	1	0	0	0	1.0	1.000

The Cardinals' moves to repair their offense, including the acquisition of Dick Allen in the Flood trade, worked as run production jumped by nearly a run a game. Unfortunately, so did runs allowed, and the club slumped to ten games below .500. They lost 16 of 18 at one stretch, and fell to last place before climbing out, just three games ahead of Montreal. The leaders of the offense were Joe Torre, second in the league in batting with his .325 average, and Allen, with 34 homers and 101 RBIs. Allen's power, though, could not outweigh his idiosyncratic personality, and he was unloaded in the off-season for Ted Sizemore and Bob Stinson. Gibson had a typical Gibson season: sixteen games over .500 for a team that finished ten under, fourth in the league in ERA, second with 274 strikeouts and 23 complete games, and another Cy Young Award. He was also the last National League pitcher to win 20 and hit .300 in the same year. Behind Gibson, though, was trouble—Carlton's 19 losses led the league, Mike Torrez and Jerry Reuss had ERAs over 4.00 (though not much over the league average), and Briles shot up to 6.22.

TEAM STATISTICS

W	L	PCT	GB	R	OR	2B	3B	HR	BA	SA	SB	E	DP	FA	CG	BB	SO	ShO	SV	ERA
									Batting				Fielding				Pitching			
T	89	73	.549		729	664	235	70	130	.270	.406	66	137	195	.979	36	625	990	13	43	3.70
HI	84	78	.519	5	806	679	228	44	179	.259	.415	39	137	146	.978	59	475	1000	9	25	3.76
Y	83	79	.512	6	695	630	211	42	120	.249	.370	118	124	136	.979	47	575	1064	10	32	3.46
L	76	86	.469	13	744	747	218	51	113	.263	.379	117	150	159	.977	51	632	960	11	20	4.05
HI	73	88	.453	15.5	594	730	224	58	101	.238	.356	72	114	134	.981	24	538	1047	8	36	4.17
ON	73	89	.451	16	687	807	211	35	136	.237	.365	65	141	193	.977	29	716	914	10	32	4.50
EST																					
N	102	60	.630		775	681	253	45	191	.270	.436	115	151	173	.976	32	592	843	15	60	3.71
A	87	74	.540	14.5	749	684	233	42	170	.270	.382	138	135	135	.978	37	496	880	17	42	3.82
	86	76	.531	16	831	826	257	35	165	.262	.409	83	170	153	.973	50	604	931	7	30	4.50
OU	79	83	.488	23	744	763	250	47	160	.259	.391	114	140	144	.978	36	577	942	6	35	4.23
L	76	86	.469	26	736	772	215	24	160	.270	.404	58	141	118	.977	45	478	960	9	24	4.35
	63	99	.389	39	681	788	208	36	172	.246	.391	60	158	159	.975	24	611	886	9	32	4.38
AGUE TOTAL					8771	8771	2743	554	1683	.258	.392	1045	1698	1845	.977	470	6919	11417	124	411	4.05

INDIVIDUAL PITCHING

TCHER	T	W	L	PCT	ERA	SV	G	GS	CG	IP	H	BB	SO	R	ER	ShO	H/9	BB/9	SO/9
b Gibson	R	23	7	.767	3.12	0	34	34	23	294	262	88	274	111	102	3	8.02	2.69	8.39
eve Carlton	L	10	19	.345	3.72	0	34	33	13	254	239	109	193	123	105	2	8.47	3.86	6.84
ke Torrez	R	8	10	.444	4.22	0	30	28	5	179	168	103	100	96	84	1	8.45	5.18	5.03
rry Reuss	L	7	8	.467	4.11	0	20	20	5	124	132	49	74	62	58	2	9.35	3.47	5.24
uck Taylor	R	6	7	.462	3.12	8	56	7	1	124	116	31	64	47	43	1	8.42	2.25	4.65
lie Briles	R	6	7	.462	6.22	0	30	19	1	107	129	36	59	84	74	1	10.85	3.03	4.96
ank Linzy	R	3	5	.375	3.67	2	47	0	0	61.1	66	23	19	26	25	0	9.68	3.38	2.79
orge Culver	R	3	3	.500	4.61	0	11	7	2	56.2	64	24	23	31	29	0	10.16	3.81	3.65
l Campisi	R	2	2	.500	2.94	4	37	0	0	49	53	37	26	19	16	0	9.73	6.80	4.78
ank Bertaina	L	1	2	.333	3.19	0	8	5	0	31	36	15	14	16	11	0	10.45	4.35	4.06
ggie Cleveland	R	0	4	.000	7.62	0	16	1	0	26	31	18	22	27	22	0	10.73	6.23	7.62
y McCool	L	0	3	.000	6.14	1	18	0	0	22	20	16	12	15	15	0	8.18	6.55	4.91
rry Parker	R	1	1	.500	3.27	0	7	4	0	22	24	15	9	13	8	0	9.82	6.14	3.68
m Hilgendorf	L	0	4	.000	3.86	0	16	0	0	21	22	13	13	11	9	0	9.43	5.57	5.57
Hrabosky	L	2	1	.667	4.74	0	16	1	0	19	22	7	12	10	10	0	10.42	3.32	5.68
d Abernathy	R	1	0	1.000	2.95	1	11	0	0	18.1	15	12	8	6	6	0	7.36	5.89	3.93
o Chlupsa	R	0	2	.000	9.00	0	14	0	0	16	26	9	10	16	16	0	14.63	5.06	5.63
ntiago Guzman	R	1	1	.500	7.07	0	8	3	1	14	14	13	9	12	11	0	9.00	8.36	5.79
uck Hartenstein	R	0	0	—	8.78	0	6	0	0	13.1	24	5	9	13	13	0	16.20	3.38	6.08
ry Johnson	R	2	0	1.000	3.18	1	7	0	0	11.1	6	3	5	4	4	0	4.76	2.38	3.97
n Nye	L	0	0	—	4.50	0	6	0	0	8	13	6	5	5	4	0	14.63	6.75	5.63
d Norman	L	0	0	—	0.00	0	1	0	0	1	1	0	0	0	0	0	9.00	0.00	0.00
AM TOTAL		76	86	.469	4.06	20	440	162	51	1475	1483	632	960	747	665	10	9.05	3.86	5.86

MANAGER		W	L	PCT
Red Schoendienst		90	72	.556

POS	Player	B	G	AB	H	2B	3B	HR	HR %	R	RBI	BB	SO	SB	Pinch Hit AB	Pinch Hit H	BA	SA
REGULARS																		
1B	Joe Hague	L	129	380	86	9	3	16	4.2	46	54	58	69	0	17	2	.226	.392
2B	Ted Sizemore	R	135	478	126	14	5	3	0.6	53	42	42	26	4	6	3	.264	.333
SS	Dal Maxvill	R	142	356	80	10	1	0	0.0	31	24	43	45	1	1	0	.225	.258
3B	Joe Torre	R	161	634	230	34	8	24	3.8	97	137	63	70	4	0	0	.363	.555
RF	Matty Alou	L	149	609	192	28	6	7	1.1	85	74	34	27	19	6	2	.315	.415
CF	Jose Cruz	L	83	292	80	13	2	9	3.1	46	27	49	35	6	2	1	.274	.425
LF	Lou Brock	L	157	640	200	37	7	7	1.1	126	61	76	107	64	2	1	.313	.425
C	Ted Simmons	B	133	510	155	32	4	7	1.4	64	77	36	50	1	6	1	.304	.424
SUBSTITUTES																		
2B	Julian Javier	R	90	259	67	6	4	3	1.2	32	28	9	33	5	9	2	.259	.347
1B	Jim Beauchamp	R	77	162	38	8	3	2	1.2	24	16	9	26	3	32	8	.235	.358
S2	Ted Kubiak	L	32	72	18	3	2	1	1.4	8	10	11	12	1	6	1	.250	.389
1B	Bob Burda	L	65	71	21	0	0	1	1.4	6	12	10	11	0	48	14	.296	.338
S2	Dick Schofield	B	34	60	13	2	0	1	1.7	7	6	10	9	0	7	2	.217	.300
SS	Milt Ramirez	R	4	11	3	0	0	0	0.0	2	0	2	1	0	0	0	.273	.273
OF	Jose Cardenal	R	89	301	73	12	4	7	2.3	37	48	29	35	12	7	4	.243	.379
OF	Luis Melendez	R	88	173	39	3	1	0	0.0	25	11	24	29	2	22	4	.225	.254
OF	Leron Lee	L	25	28	5	1	0	1	3.6	3	2	4	12	0	17	3	.179	.321
OF	Jorge Roque	R	3	10	3	0	0	0	0.0	2	1	0	3	1	0	0	.300	.300
C	Jerry McNertney	R	56	128	37	4	2	4	3.1	15	22	12	14	0	16	5	.289	.445
CO	Bob Stinson	B	17	19	4	1	0	0	0.0	3	1	1	7	0	2	1	.211	.263
PITCHERS																		
P	Steve Carlton	L	37	96	17	4	0	0	0.0	5	8	4	31	0	0	0	.177	.219
P	Bob Gibson	R	31	87	15	0	1	2	2.3	5	10	3	24	1	0	0	.172	.264
P	Reggie Cleveland	R	34	82	14	2	0	0	0.0	5	7	1	16	0	0	0	.171	.195
P	Jerry Reuss	L	36	65	8	1	0	0	0.0	6	4	10	36	0	0	0	.123	.138
P	Chris Zachary	L	24	33	8	0	0	0	0.0	3	0	0	5	0	0	0	.242	.242
P	Chuck Taylor	R	43	12	2	0	1	0	0.0	1	2	0	5	0	0	0	.167	.333
P	Al Santorini	R	19	10	3	0	0	0	0.0	0	1	0	4	0	0	0	.300	.300
P	Mike Torrez	R	9	7	1	1	0	0	0.0	0	1	2	2	0	0	0	.143	.286
P	Moe Drabowsky	R	51	6	1	0	0	0	0.0	0	0	0	3	0	0	0	.167	.167
P	Daryl Patterson	L	13	5	0	0	0	0	0.0	0	0	0	3	0	0	0	.000	.000
P	Frank Linzy	R	50	4	2	0	0	0	0.0	0	1	0	2	0	0	0	.500	.500
P	George Brunet	R	7	3	1	0	0	0	0.0	0	0	0	1	0	0	0	.333	.333
P	Dennis Higgins	R	3	1	0	0	0	0	0.0	0	0	0	0	0	0	0	.000	.000
P	Stan Williams	R	10	1	0	0	0	0	0.0	0	0	0	1	0	0	0	.000	.000
P	Don Shaw	L	45	1	0	0	0	0	0.0	0	0	0	0	0	0	0	.000	.000
P	Bob Reynolds	R	4	1	0	0	0	0	0.0	0	0	0	1	0	0	0	.000	.000
P	Santiago Guzman	R	2	1	0	0	0	0	0.0	0	0	0	0	0	0	0	.000	.000
P	Rudy Arroyo	R	9	1	0	0	0	0	0.0	0	0	0	1	0	0	0	.000	.000
P	Mike Jackson	R	1	1	0	0	0	0	0.0	0	0	0	1	0	0	0	.000	.000
P	Fred Norman	L	4	0	0	0	0	0	–	0	0	0	0	0	0	0	–	–
P	Bob Chlupsa	R	1	0	0	0	0	0	–	0	0	0	0	0	0	0	–	–
P	Al Hrabosky	R	1	0	0	0	0	0	–	0	0	0	0	0	0	0	–	–
P	Harry Parker	R	4	0	0	0	0	0	–	0	0	0	0	0	0	0	–	–
TEAM TOTAL				5610	1542	225	54	95	1.7	739	686	543	757	124	206	54	.275	.385

INDIVIDUAL FIELDING

POS	Player	T	G	PO	A	E	DP	TC/G	FA	POS	Player	T	G	PO	A	E	DP	TC/G	FA
1B	J. Hague	L	91	618	50	3	63	7.4	.996	OF	L. Brock	L	157	262	7	14	3	1.8	.951
	M. Alou	L	57	507	27	5	42	9.5	.991		M. Alou	L	94	203	8	4	0	2.3	.981
	J. Beauchamp	R	44	311	19	6	27	7.6	.982		J. Cruz	L	83	197	2	5	1	2.5	.975
	B. Burda	L	13	62	6	0	4	5.2	1.000		J. Cardenal	R	83	181	9	6	1	2.4	.969
2B	T. Sizemore	R	93	206	237	11	55	4.9	.976		L. Melendez	R	66	90	4	0	1	1.5	.959
	J. Javier	R	80	163	186	8	45	4.5	.978		J. Hague	L	36	58	0	2	0	1.7	.967
	T. Kubiak	R	14	25	33	2	4	4.3	.967		T. Sizemore	R	15	19	1	0	0	1.3	1.000
	D. Schofield	R	13	17	26	0	6	3.3	1.000		J. Beauchamp	R	1	0	0	0	0	0.0	.000
SS	D. Maxvill	R	140	188	413	13	71	4.4	.979		B. Burda	L	1	0	0	0	0	0.0	.000
	T. Sizemore	R	39	52	140	7	24	5.1	.965		J. Roque	R	3	6	0	0	0	2.0	1.000
	T. Kubiak	R	17	24	23	2	4	2.9	.959		L. Lee	R	8	4	0	1	0	0.6	.800
	D. Schofield	R	17	12	31	3	6	2.7	.935		B. Stinson	R	3	2	0	0	0	0.7	1.000
	M. Ramirez	R	4	11	7	1	1	4.8	.947	C	T. Simmons	R	130	747	52	9	11	6.2	.989
3B	J. Torre	R	161	136	271	21	22	2.7	.951		J. McNertney	R	36	192	7	3	1	5.6	.985
	D. Schofield	R	3	0	4	0	0	1.3	1.000		B. Stinson	R	6	34	0	1	0	5.8	.971
	J. Javier	R	1	1	2	0	0	3.0	1.000										
	T. Sizemore	R	1	0	1	0	0	1.0	1.000										

TEAM STATISTICS

	W	L	PCT	GB	R	OR	Batting 2B	Batting 3B	Batting HR	Batting BA	Batting SA	Batting SB	Fielding E	Fielding DP	Fielding FA	Pitching CG	Pitching BB	Pitching SO	Pitching ShO	Pitching SV	Pitching ERA
EAST																					
PIT	97	65	.599		788	599	223	61	154	.274	.416	65	133	164	.979	43	470	813	15	48	3.3
STL	90	72	.556	7	739	699	225	54	95	.275	.385	124	142	155	.978	56	576	911	14	22	3.8
CHI	83	79	.512	14	637	648	202	34	128	.258	.378	44	126	150	.980	75	411	900	17	13	3.6
NY	83	79	.512	14	588	550	203	29	98	.249	.351	89	114	135	.981	42	529	1157	13	22	3.0
MON	71	90	.441	25.5	622	729	197	29	88	.246	.343	51	150	164	.976	49	658	829	8	25	4.1
PHI	67	95	.414	30	558	688	209	35	123	.233	.350	63	122	158	.981	31	525	838	10	25	3.7
WEST																					
SF	90	72	.556		706	644	224	36	140	.247	.378	101	179	153	.972	45	471	831	14	30	3.3
LA	89	73	.549	1	663	587	213	38	95	.266	.370	76	131	159	.979	48	399	853	18	33	3.2
ATL	82	80	.506	8	643	699	192	30	153	.257	.385	57	146	180	.977	40	485	823	11	31	3.7
CIN	79	83	.488	11	586	581	203	28	138	.241	.366	59	103	174	.984	27	501	750	11	38	3.3
HOU	79	83	.488	11	585	567	230	52	71	.240	.340	101	106	152	.983	43	475	914	10	25	3.1
SD	61	100	.379	28.5	486	610	184	31	96	.233	.332	70	161	144	.974	47	559	923	10	17	3.2
LEAGUE TOTAL					7601	7601	2505	457	1379	.252	.366	900	1613	1888	.979	546	6059	10542	151	329	3.4

The Cardinals rode a roller coaster through the 1970s: up one year, down the next. The year 1971 was an up year, though their pennant hopes vanished in a 9–22 June that dropped them from first to fourth. The club was led by National League MVP Joe Torre, who had the season of his life with a .363 average, 24 homers, and 137 RBIs. His RBI total was the most on the club by sixty. Lou Brock took back the stolen base lead he had relinquished to Bobby Tolan the year before. The inconsistency of the offense, though, can be read in the records of Gibson and Carlton. Carlton was 20–9 with an ERA above the league average; Gibson was 16–13 with an ERA more than half a run lower than Carlton's. Something in this inspired the Cardinals to trade away their ace lefthander, one of a series of unprofitable trades involving pitchers.

THE STAFF THAT MIGHT HAVE BEEN

Over a fifteen-month period, the Cardinals made the following trades (the won-lost records in parentheses indicate the pitchers' records since the trade was made):

DATE	TRADE WITH	ACQUIRED	GAVE UP
January 29, 1971	Pittsburgh	Matty Alou and George Brunet (0–1)	Nellie Briles (68–58) and Vic Davalillo
June 14, 1971	San Diego	Al Santorini (8–13)	Fred Norman (102–98) and Leron Lee
June 15, 1971	Montreal	Bob Reynolds (12–15)	Mike Torrez (154–120)
February 25, 1972	Philadelphia	Rick Wise (113–105)	Steve Carlton (208–122)
April 15, 1972	Houston	Scipio Spinks (6–10) and Lance Clemons (1–1)	Jerry Reuss (139–107)

This method distorts the picture a little, and the Cards did get Reggie Smith in partial return for Wise, but the pitchers they traded away went 671–505, while the ones they got in return went 140–145.

INDIVIDUAL PITCHING

:HER	T	W	L	PCT	ERA	SV	G	GS	CG	IP	H	BB	SO	R	ER	ShO	H/9	BB/9	SO/9
e Carlton	L	20	9	.690	3.56	0	37	36	18	273	275	98	172	120	108	4	9.07	3.23	5.67
Gibson	R	16	13	.552	3.04	0	31	31	20	246	215	76	185	96	83	5	7.87	2.78	6.77
ie Cleveland	R	12	12	.500	4.01	0	34	34	10	222	238	53	148	107	99	2	9.65	2.15	6.00
Reuss	L	14	14	.500	4.78	0	36	35	7	211	228	109	131	125	112	2	9.73	4.65	5.59
Zachary	R	3	10	.231	5.30	0	23	12	1	90	114	26	48	58	53	1	11.40	2.60	4.80
k Taylor	R	3	1	.750	3.55	3	43	1	0	71	72	25	46	32	28	0	9.13	3.17	5.83
Drabowsky	R	6	1	.857	3.45	8	51	0	0	60	45	33	49	23	23	0	6.75	4.95	7.35
k Linzy	R	4	3	.571	2.14	6	50	0	0	59	49	27	24	18	14	0	7.47	4.12	3.66
Shaw	L	7	2	.778	2.65	2	45	0	0	51	45	31	19	19	15	0	7.94	5.47	3.35
ntorini	R	0	2	.000	3.81	2	19	5	0	49.2	51	19	21	21	21	0	9.24	3.44	3.81
Torrez	R	1	2	.333	6.00	0	9	6	0	36	41	30	8	27	24	0	10.25	7.50	2.00
Patterson	R	0	1	.000	4.33	1	13	2	0	27	20	15	11	14	13	0	6.67	5.00	3.67
Williams	R	3	0	1.000	1.38	0	10	0	0	13	13	2	8	2	2	0	9.00	1.38	5.54
Arroyo	L	0	1	.000	5.25	0	9	0	0	12	18	5	5	8	7	0	13.50	3.75	3.75
ago Guzman	R	0	0	—	4.50	0	2	1	0	10	6	2	13	1	0	0	5.40	1.80	11.70
ie Brunet	L	0	1	.000	6.00	0	7	0	0	9	12	7	4	6	6	0	12.00	7.00	4.00
s Higgins	R	1	0	1.000	3.86	0	3	0	0	7	6	2	6	3	3	0	7.71	2.57	7.71
Reynolds	R	0	0	—	10.29	0	4	0	0	7	15	6	4	8	8	0	19.29	7.71	5.14
Parker	R	0	0	—	7.20	0	4	0	0	5	6	2	2	4	4	0	10.80	3.60	3.60
Norman	L	0	0	—	12.27	0	4	0	0	3.2	7	7	4	5	5	0	17.18	17.18	9.82
Chlupsa	R	0	0	—	9.00	0	1	0	0	2	3	0	1	2	2	0	13.50	0.00	4.50
abosky	L	0	0	—	9.00	0	1	0	0	2	2	0	2	0	0	0	9.00	0.00	9.00
Jackson	L	0	0	—	0.00	0	1	0	0	1	1	1	0	0	0	0	9.00	9.00	0.00
TOTAL		90	72	.556	3.86	22	437	163	56	1467.1	1482	576	911	699	630	14	9.09	3.53	5.59

MANAGER	W	L	PCT
Red Schoendienst	75	81	.481

POS	Player	B	G	AB	H	2B	3B	HR	HR %	R	RBI	BB	SO	SB	Pinch Hit AB	Pinch Hit H	BA	SA
REGULARS																		
1B	Matty Alou	L	108	404	127	17	2	3	0.7	46	31	24	23	11	9	1	.314	.389
2B	Ted Sizemore	R	120	439	116	17	4	2	0.5	53	38	37	36	8	13	1	.264	.335
SS	Dal Maxvill	R	105	276	61	6	1	1	0.4	22	23	31	47	0	1	0	.221	.261
3B	Joe Torre	R	149	544	157	26	6	11	2.0	71	81	54	64	3	6	4	.289	.419
RF	Luis Melendez	R	118	332	79	11	3	5	1.5	32	28	25	34	5	21	2	.238	.334
CF	Jose Cruz	L	117	332	78	14	4	2	0.6	33	23	36	54	9	13	5	.235	.319
LF	Lou Brock	L	153	621	193	26	8	3	0.5	81	42	47	93	63	4	1	.311	.393
C	Ted Simmons	B	152	594	180	36	6	16	2.7	70	96	29	57	1	2	0	.303	.465
SUBSTITUTES																		
UT	Ed Crosby	L	101	276	60	9	1	0	0.0	27	19	18	27	1	15	0	.217	.257
1B	Donn Clendenon	R	61	136	26	4	0	4	2.9	13	9	17	37	1	20	4	.191	.309
S3	Dwain Anderson	R	57	135	36	4	1	1	0.7	12	8	8	23	0	0	0	.267	.333
3B	Ken Reitz	R	21	78	28	4	0	0	0.0	5	10	2	4	0	1	0	.359	.410
1B	Joe Hague	L	27	76	18	5	1	3	3.9	8	11	17	18	0	3	1	.237	.447
SS	Mick Kelleher	R	23	63	10	2	1	0	0.0	5	1	6	15	0	0	0	.159	.222
2B	Mike Tyson	R	13	37	7	1	0	0	0.0	1	0	1	9	0	0	0	.189	.216
1B	Ron Allen	B	7	11	1	0	0	1	9.1	2	1	3	5	0	0	0	.091	.364
1B	Mike Fiore	L	17	10	1	0	0	0	0.0	0	1	2	3	0	10	1	.100	.100
UT	Marty Martinez	B	9	7	3	0	0	0	0.0	0	2	0	1	0	3	1	.429	.429
OF	Bernie Carbo	L	99	302	78	13	1	7	2.3	42	34	57	56	0	6	1	.258	.377
OF	Jorge Roque	R	32	67	7	2	1	1	1.5	3	5	6	19	1	6	1	.104	.209
O3	Bill Stein	R	14	35	11	0	1	2	5.7	2	3	0	7	1	6	3	.314	.543
OF	Brant Alyea	R	13	19	3	1	0	0	0.0	0	1	0	6	0	11	2	.158	.211
OF	Bill Voss	L	11	15	4	2	0	0	0.0	1	3	2	2	0	7	1	.267	.400
C	Skip Jutze	R	21	71	17	2	0	0	0.0	1	5	1	16	0	4	0	.239	.268
C	Jerry McNertney	R	39	48	10	3	1	0	0.0	3	9	6	16	0	28	4	.208	.313
PITCHERS																		
P	Bob Gibson	R	34	103	20	6	0	5	4.9	12	12	1	25	0	0	0	.194	.398
P	Rick Wise	R	35	93	16	2	0	1	1.1	8	9	1	30	0	0	0	.172	.226
P	Reggie Cleveland	R	33	71	17	0	0	0	0.0	0	3	7	13	0	0	0	.239	.239
P	Scipio Spinks	R	21	42	7	0	0	0	0.0	4	1	0	21	0	0	0	.167	.167
P	Al Santorini	R	30	40	3	0	0	0	0.0	2	1	3	13	0	0	0	.075	.075
P	Don Durham	R	14	14	7	0	0	2	14.3	3	4	0	4	0	0	0	.500	.929
P	Jim Bibby	R	6	8	1	0	0	0	0.0	0	0	2	3	0	0	0	.125	.125
P	Diego Segui	R	33	7	1	1	0	0	0.0	0	0	0	3	0	0	0	.143	.286
P	John Cumberland	R	14	5	0	0	0	0	0.0	0	0	0	2	0	0	0	.000	.000
P	Lowell Palmer	R	17	5	0	0	0	0	0.0	0	1	0	0	0	0	0	.000	.000
P	Tony Cloninger	R	17	3	0	0	0	0	0.0	0	0	0	2	0	0	0	.000	.000
P	Moe Drabowsky	R	30	1	0	0	0	0	0.0	0	0	0	0	0	0	0	.000	.000
P	Joe Grzenda	R	30	1	0	0	0	0	0.0	0	0	0	0	0	0	0	.000	.000
P	Dennis Higgins	R	15	1	0	0	0	0	0.0	0	0	0	0	0	0	0	.000	.000
P	Don Shaw	L	8	1	0	0	0	0	0.0	0	0	0	1	0	0	0	.000	.000
P	Lance Clemons	L	3	1	0	0	0	0	0.0	0	1	0	0	0	0	0	.000	.000
P	Rich Folkers	L	9	1	0	0	0	0	0.0	0	0	0	0	0	0	0	.000	.000
P	Al Hrabosky	R	9	1	0	0	0	0	0.0	0	0	0	1	0	0	0	.000	.000
P	Santiago Guzman	R	1	0	0	0	0	0	–	0	0	0	0	0	0	0	–	–
P	Ray Bare	R	14	0	0	0	0	0		0	0	0	0	0	9	0	–	–
P	Charles Hudson	L	12	0	0	0	0	0	–	0	0	0	0	0	0	0	–	–
P	Tim Plodinec	R	1	0	0	0	0	0	–	0	0	0	0	0	0	0	–	–
TEAM TOTAL				5326	1383	214	42	70	1.3	568	518	437	793	104	198	33	.260	.355

INDIVIDUAL FIELDING

POS	Player	T	G	PO	A	E	DP	TC/G	FA
1B	M. Alou	L	66	535	40	7	53	8.8	.988
	D. Clendenon	R	36	259	26	4	34	8.0	.986
	J. Torre	R	27	234	16	4	17	9.4	.984
	J. Hague	L	22	188	10	0	16	9.0	1.000
	T. Simmons	R	15	125	15	5	9	9.7	.966
	R. Allen	R	5	29	1	1	1	6.2	.968
	M. Fiore	L	6	7	0	0	2	1.2	1.000
2B	T. Sizemore	R	111	222	342	14	68	5.2	.976
	E. Crosby	R	38	68	92	6	21	4.4	.964
	D. Maxvill	R	11	28	30	2	4	5.5	.967
	M. Tyson	R	11	20	31	1	3	4.7	.981
	D. Anderson	R	1	2	1	0	1	3.0	1.000
	M. Martinez	R	2	2	1	0	1	1.5	1.000
SS	D. Maxvill	R	95	145	243	8	56	4.2	.980
	D. Anderson	R	43	59	80	7	14	3.4	.952
	E. Crosby	R	43	51	86	3	20	3.3	.979
	M. Kelleher	R	23	60	61	2	14	5.3	.984
	M. Tyson	R	2	6	5	2	1	6.5	.846
	M. Martinez	R	3	0	1	0	0	0.3	1.000
3B	J. Torre	R	117	102	182	11	17	2.5	.963
	K. Reitz	R	20	17	26	2	3	2.3	.956
	E. Crosby	R	14	11	19	1	1	2.2	.968
	D. Anderson	R	13	9	16	1	3	2.0	.962
	B. Stein	R	4	1	4	0	0	1.3	1.000
	M. Martinez	R	1	1	0	0	0	1.0	1.000
	B. Carbo	R	1	0	1	0	0	1.0	1.000

POS	Player	T	G	PO	A	E	DP	TC/G	FA
OF	L. Brock	L	149	253	6	13	1	1.8	.952
	J. Cruz	L	102	220	9	5	5	2.3	.979
	L. Melendez	R	105	206	5	9	0	2.1	.959
	B. Carbo	R	92	162	15*	6	3	2.0	.967
	M. Alou	L	39	52	4	0	0	1.4	1.000
	J. Roque	R	24	50	0	1	0	2.1	.980
	M. Fiore	L	1	0	0	0	0	0.0	.000
	B. Alyea	R	3	5	1	0	1	2.0	1.000
	B. Voss	L	2	4	0	0	0	2.0	1.000
	B. Stein	R	4	4	0	0	0	1.0	1.000
	J. Hague	L	3	2	1	0	0	1.0	1.000
C	T. Simmons	R	135	842	78	8	6	6.9	.991
	S. Jutze	R	17	93	15	4	1	6.6	.964
	J. McNertney	R	10	50	4	1	0	5.5	.982

For the first time in baseball history, a player strike forced cancellation of the first thirteen days of the season. St. Louis lost six games to the strike, but it made little difference in their season as they finished in fourth place, 21½ games out. (The Red Sox were not so lucky; they lost seven games to the strike, one more than Detroit, and ended up a half-game behind the Tigers.) The Redbirds gave up a half a run per game fewer than in '71, but scored nearly a run less. On the plus side, 22-year-old catcher Ted Simmons had his second straight .300 season as the full-time catcher. Minuses included the bullpen, where Diego Segui was the team leader with just nine saves. In addition, Cardinal fans had to watch as Steve Carlton turned in an astounding performance, going 27–10 for Philadelphia, a club that finished in last place, 38 games under .500.

TEAM STATISTICS

	W	L	PCT	GB	R	OR	2B	3B	HR	BA	SA	SB	E	DP	FA	CG	BB	SO	ShO	SV	ERA
AST																					
T	96	59	.619		691	512	251	47	110	.274	.397	49	136	171	.978	39	433	838	15	48	2.81
HI	85	70	.548	11	685	567	206	40	133	.257	.387	69	132	148	.979	54	421	824	19	32	3.22
Y	83	73	.532	13.5	528	578	175	31	105	.225	.332	41	116	122	.980	32	486	1059	12	41	3.27
L	75	81	.481	21.5	568	600	214	42	70	.260	.355	104	141	146	.977	64	531	912	13	13	3.42
ON	70	86	.449	26.5	513	609	156	22	91	.234	.325	68	134	141	.978	39	579	888	11	23	3.60
HI	59	97	.378	37.5	503	635	200	36	98	.236	.344	42	116	142	.981	43	536	927	13	15	3.67
EST																					
N	95	59	.617		707	557	214	44	124	.251	.380	140	110	143	.982	25	435	806	15	60	3.21
OU	84	69	.549	10.5	708	636	233	38	134	.258	.393	111	116	151	.980	38	498	971	14	31	3.77
	85	70	.548	10.5	584	527	178	39	98	.256	.360	82	162	145	.974	50	429	856	23	29	2.78
L	70	84	.455	25	628	730	186	17	144	.258	.382	47	156	130	.974	40	512	732	4	27	4.27
	69	86	.445	26.5	662	649	211	36	150	.244	.384	123	156	121	.974	44	507	771	8	23	3.70
	58	95	.379	36.5	488	665	168	38	102	.227	.332	78	144	146	.976	39	618	960	17	19	3.78
AGUE TOTAL					7265	7265	2392	430	1359	.248	.365	954	1619	1706	.978	507	5985	10544	164	361	3.46

INDIVIDUAL PITCHING

TCHER	T	W	L	PCT	ERA	SV	G	GS	CG	IP	H	BB	SO	R	ER	ShO	H/9	BB/9	SO/9
o Gibson	R	19	11	.633	2.46	0	34	34	23	278	226	88	208	83	76	4	7.32	2.85	6.73
k Wise	R	16	16	.500	3.11	0	35	35	20	269	250	71	142	98	93	2	8.36	2.38	4.75
ggie Cleveland	R	14	15	.483	3.94	0	33	33	11	230.2	229	60	153	120	101	3	8.93	2.34	5.97
Santorini	R	8	11	.421	4.11	0	30	19	3	133.2	136	46	72	63	61	3	9.16	3.10	4.85
pio Spinks	R	5	5	.500	2.67	0	16	16	6	118	96	59	93	39	35	0	7.32	4.50	7.09
go Segui	R	3	1	.750	3.07	9	33	0	0	55.2	47	32	54	23	19	0	7.60	5.17	8.73
n Durham	R	2	7	.222	4.34	0	10	8	1	47.2	42	22	35	28	23	0	7.93	4.15	6.61
Bibby	R	1	3	.250	3.35	0	6	6	0	40.1	29	19	28	18	15	0	6.47	4.24	6.25
vell Palmer	R	0	3	.000	3.86	0	16	2	0	35	30	26	25	16	15	0	7.71	6.69	6.43
Grzenda	L	1	0	1.000	5.71	0	30	0	0	34.2	46	17	15	24	22	0	11.94	4.41	3.89
e Drabowsky	R	1	1	.500	2.60	2	30	0	0	27.2	29	14	22	13	8	0	9.43	4.55	7.16
y Cloninger	R	0	2	.000	5.19	0	17	0	0	26	29	19	11	17	15	0	10.04	6.58	3.81
nnis Higgins	R	1	2	.333	3.97	1	15	1	0	22.2	19	22	20	14	10	0	7.54	8.74	7.94
n Cumberland	L	1	1	.500	6.65	0	14	1	0	21.2	23	7	7	17	16	0	9.55	2.91	2.91
Bare	R	0	1	.000	0.54	1	14	0	0	16.2	12	6	5	2	1	0	9.72	3.24	2.70
n Folkers	L	1	0	1.000	3.38	0	9	0	0	13.1	12	5	7	5	5	0	8.10	3.38	4.73
arles Hudson	L	1	0	1.000	5.11	0	12	0	0	12.1	10	7	4	8	7	0	7.30	5.11	2.92
rabosky	L	1	0	1.000	0.00	0	5	0	0	7	4	3	9	0	0	0	2.57	3.86	11.57
ce Clemons	L	0	1	.000	10.13	0	3	1	0	5.1	8	5	2	7	6	0	13.50	8.44	3.38
Shaw	L	0	1	.000	9.00	0	8	0	0	3	5	3	0	3	3	0	15.00	9.00	0.00
tiago Guzman	R	0	0	—	9.00	0	1	0	0	1	1	0	0	1	1	0	9.00	0.00	0.00
Plodinec	R	0	0	—	27.00	0	1	0	0	.1	3	0	0	1	1	0	81.00	0.00	0.00
M TOTAL		75	81	.481	3.43	13	372	156	64	1399.2	1290	531	912	600	533	12	8.29	3.41	5.86

MANAGER	W	L	PCT
Red Schoendienst	81	81	.500

POS	Player	B	G	AB	H	2B	3B	HR	HR %	R	RBI	BB	SO	SB	Pinch Hit AB	Pinch Hit H	BA	SA
REGULARS																		
1B	Joe Torre	R	141	519	149	17	2	13	2.5	67	69	65	78	2	0	0	.287	.403
2B	Ted Sizemore	R	142	521	147	22	1	1	0.2	69	54	68	34	6	1	0	.282	.334
SS	Mike Tyson	R	144	469	114	15	4	1	0.2	48	33	23	66	2	0	0	.243	.299
3B	Ken Reitz	R	147	426	100	20	2	6	1.4	40	42	9	25	0	12	2	.235	.333
RF	Luis Melendez	R	121	341	91	18	1	2	0.6	35	35	27	50	2	21	8	.267	.343
CF	Jose Cruz	L	132	406	92	22	5	10	2.5	51	57	51	66	10	14	3	.227	.379
LF	Lou Brock	L	160	650	193	29	8	7	1.1	110	63	71	112	70	1	0	.297	.398
C	Ted Simmons	B	161	619	192	36	2	13	2.1	62	91	61	47	0	2	1	.310	.438
SUBSTITUTES																		
1B	Tim McCarver	L	130	331	88	16	4	3	0.9	30	49	38	31	2	39	8	.266	.366
SS	Ray Busse	R	24	70	10	4	2	2	2.9	6	5	5	21	0	0	0	.143	.343
UT	Ed Crosby	L	22	39	5	2	1	0	0.0	4	1	4	4	0	10	3	.128	.231
SS	Mick Kelleher	R	43	38	7	2	0	0	0.0	4	2	4	11	0	0	0	.184	.237
2B	Tom Heintzelman	R	23	29	9	0	0	0	0.0	5	0	3	3	0	15	4	.310	.310
2B	Dave Campbell	R	13	21	0	0	0	0	0.0	1	1	1	6	0	7	0	.000	.000
SO	Dwain Anderson	R	18	17	2	0	0	0	0.0	5	0	4	4	0	10	1	.118	.118
3B	Terry Hughes	R	11	14	3	1	0	0	0.0	1	1	1	4	0	4	1	.214	.286
UT	Matty Alou	L	11	11	3	0	0	0	0.0	1	1	1	0	0	10	3	.273	.273
2B	Bobby Fenwick	R	5	6	1	0	0	0	0.0	0	0	0	2	0	2	0	.167	.167
OF	Bernie Carbo	L	111	308	88	18	0	8	2.6	42	40	58	52	2	17	5	.286	.422
OF	Bake McBride	L	40	63	19	3	0	0	0.0	8	5	4	10	0	17	6	.302	.349
OF	Tommie Agee	R	26	62	11	3	1	3	4.8	8	7	5	13	1	8	1	.177	.403
OF	Jim Dwyer	L	28	57	11	1	1	0	0.0	7	0	1	5	0	8	1	.193	.246
O1	Bill Stein	R	32	55	12	2	0	0	0.0	4	2	7	18	0	18	3	.218	.255
OF	Hector Cruz	R	11	11	0	0	0	0	0.0	1	0	1	3	0	4	0	.000	.000
OF	Cirilio Cruz	L	3	0	0	0	0	0	–	1	0	0	0	0	0	0	–	–
C	Marc Hill	R	1	3	0	0	0	0	0.0	0	0	0	1	0	0	0	.000	.000
C	Larry Haney	R	2	1	0	0	0	0	0.0	0	0	0	1	0	0	0	.000	.000
PITCHERS																		
P	Rick Wise	R	35	88	17	3	1	3	3.4	12	14	5	36	0	0	0	.193	.352
P	Reggie Cleveland	R	32	74	17	4	0	0	0.0	5	3	4	19	0	0	0	.230	.284
P	Alan Foster	R	35	68	13	1	0	0	0.0	4	2	2	17	0	0	0	.191	.206
P	Bob Gibson	R	25	65	12	0	0	2	3.1	8	8	3	17	1	0	0	.185	.277
P	Tom Murphy	R	19	23	4	1	0	0	0.0	1	1	1	5	0	0	0	.174	.217
P	Rich Folkers	L	34	20	2	0	0	0	0.0	0	1	0	6	0	0	0	.100	.100
P	Mike Nagy	R	9	11	1	0	0	0	0.0	0	1	0	7	0	0	0	.091	.091
P	Scipio Spinks	R	8	11	2	0	0	1	9.1	2	1	1	7	0	0	0	.182	.455
P	Diego Segui	R	65	10	0	0	0	0	0.0	0	0	1	6	0	0	0	.000	.000
P	Orlando Pena	R	42	7	1	0	0	0	0.0	0	1	0	4	0	0	0	.143	.143
P	Al Hrabosky	R	44	4	0	0	0	0	0.0	0	0	0	2	0	0	0	.000	.000
P	Wayne Granger	R	33	3	0	0	0	0	0.0	0	0	1	0	0	0	0	.000	.000
P	Jim Bibby	R	6	2	0	0	0	0	0.0	1	0	1	1	0	0	0	.000	.000
P	John Andrews	L	16	2	1	0	0	0	0.0	0	0	0	0	0	0	0	.500	.500
P	Eddie Fisher	R	6	1	1	0	0	0	0.0	0	1	0	0	0	0	0	1.000	1.000
P	Al Santorini	R	6	1	0	0	0	0	0.0	0	0	0	0	0	0	0	.000	.000
P	Mike Thompson	R	2	1	0	0	0	0	0.0	0	0	0	1	0	0	0	.000	.000
P	Lew Krausse	R	1	0	0	0	0	0	–	0	0	0	0	0	0	0	–	–
P	Ed Sprague	R	8	0	0	0	0	0	–	0	0	0	0	0	0	0	–	–
TEAM TOTAL				5478	1418	240	35	75	1.4	643	592	531	796	100	219	49	.259	.357

INDIVIDUAL FIELDING

POS	Player	T	G	PO	A	E	DP	TC/G	FA
1B	J. Torre	R	114	833	60	6	80	7.9	.993
	T. McCarver	R	77	545	30	8	47	7.6	.986
	T. Simmons	R	6	38	4	1	1	7.2	.977
	B. Stein	R	2	21	0	0	1	10.5	1.000
	T. Hughes	R	1	8	0	0	0	8.0	1.000
	M. Alou	L	1	3	0	0	0	3.0	1.000
2B	T. Sizemore	R	139	312	463	15	83	5.7	.981
	M. Tyson	R	16	37	49	0	12	5.4	1.000
	D. Campbell	R	6	6	18	1	1	4.2	.960
	E. Crosby	R	5	5	16	2	2	4.6	.913
	Heintzelman	R	6	8	13	0	3	3.5	1.000
	B. Fenwick	R	3	2	1	1	2	1.3	.750
SS	M. Tyson	R	128	202	352	33	68	4.6	.944
	R. Busse	R	23	32	65	11	16	4.7	.898
	M. Kelleher	R	42	30	55	4	10	2.1	.955
	E. Crosby	R	7	6	9	1	2	2.3	.938
	K. Reitz	R	1	3	2	0	1	5.0	1.000
	D. Anderson	R	3	2	0	2	0	1.3	.500
3B	K. Reitz	R	135	85	211	8	19	2.3	.974
	J. Torre	R	58	48	68	6	3	2.1	.951
	T. Hughes	R	5	1	4	0	1	1.0	1.000
	E. Crosby	R	4	0	1	1	0	0.5	.500
	B. Stein	R	1	0	1	0	0	1.0	1.000
	T. Sizemore	R	3	1	0	0	1	0.3	1.000

POS	Player	T	G	PO	A	E	DP	TC/G	FA
OF	L. Brock	L	159	310	3	12	1	2.0	.963
	J. Cruz	L	118	276	2	6	1	2.4	.979
	L. Melendez	R	95	196	8	2	4	2.2	.990
	B. Carbo	R	94	171	11	4	3	2.0	.978
	T. Agee	R	19	50	1	1	0	2.7	.981
	B. McBride	R	17	39	1	1	0	2.4	.976
	J. Dwyer	L	20	32	0	0	0	1.6	1.000
	C. Cruz	L	1	0	0	0	0	0.0	.000
	B. Stein	R	10	16	0	0	0	1.6	1.000
	H. Cruz	R	5	7	0	0	0	1.4	1.000
	T. Simmons	R	2	6	0	0	0	3.0	1.000
	D. Anderson	R	2	2	0	0	0	1.0	1.000
	M. Alou	L	1	0	1	0	0	1.0	1.000
C	T. Simmons	R	153	888	74	13	13	6.4	.987
	T. McCarver	R	11	63	4	1	1	6.2	.985
	M. Hill	R	1	5	0	0	0	5.0	1.000
	L. Haney	R	2	2	0	0	0	1.0	1.000

A .500 record is nothing to brag about, but in the wild National League East of 1973, 81–81 was good enough for second place, just a game and a half behind the pennant-winning Mets. Even after their season ended at .500, the Cards still had a chance to tie if the Cubs could sweep a doubleheader from the Mets, but the Mets won the first game to clinch the cheapest title in baseball history. It was a year of unimpressive statistics all around; St. Louis had just one .300 hitter, Ted Simmons, who also led the club with just 13 homers. The whole team hit 75 homers which, coupled with the previous year's 70, was their lowest two-year total since the 1940s. Rick Wise was the only Cardinal pitcher to win fifteen games. A blow was struck for managerial stability, though, as Red Schoendienst made it through his eighth straight year, passing Branch Rickey to become the longest-tenured manager in club history.

TEAM STATISTICS

W	L	PCT	GB	R	OR	2B	3B	HR	BA	SA	SB	E	DP	FA	CG	BB	SO	ShO	SV	ERA
								Batting					Fielding				Pitching			
ST																				
82	79	.509		608	588	198	24	85	.246	.338	27	126	140	.980	47	490	1027	15	40	3.27
81	81	.500	1.5	643	603	240	35	75	.259	.357	100	159	149	.975	42	486	867	14	36	3.25
80	82	.494	2.5	704	693	257	44	154	.261	.405	23	151	156	.976	26	564	839	11	44	3.74
N 79	83	.488	3.5	668	702	190	23	125	.251	.364	77	163	156	.974	26	681	866	6	38	3.73
77	84	.478	5	614	655	201	21	117	.247	.357	65	157	155	.975	27	438	885	13	40	3.66
71	91	.438	11.5	642	717	218	29	134	.249	.371	51	134	179	.979	49	632	919	11	22	4.00
ST																				
99	63	.611		741	621	232	34	137	.254	.383	148	115	162	.982	39	518	801	17	43	3.43
95	66	.590	3.5	675	565	219	29	110	.263	.371	109	125	166	.981	45	461	961	15	38	3.00
88	74	.543	11	739	702	212	52	161	.262	.407	112	163	138	.974	33	485	787	8	44	3.78
J 82	80	.506	17	681	672	216	35	134	.251	.376	92	116	140	.981	45	575	907	14	26	3.79
76	85	.472	22.5	799	774	219	34	206	.266	.427	84	166	142	.974	34	548	845	10	35	4.25
60	102	.370	39	548	770	198	26	112	.244	.351	88	170	152	.973	34	548	845	10	23	4.16
GUE TOTAL				8062	8062	2600	386	1550	.254	.376	976	1745	1835	.977	447	6453	10507	143	429	3.67

INDIVIDUAL PITCHING

CHER	T	W	L	PCT	ERA	SV	G	GS	CG	IP	H	BB	SO	R	ER	ShO	H/9	BB/9	SO/9
Wise	R	16	12	.571	3.37	0	35	34	14	259	259	59	144	113	97	5	9.00	2.05	5.00
gie Cleveland	R	14	10	.583	3.01	0	32	32	6	224	211	61	122	88	75	3	8.48	2.45	4.90
Foster	R	13	9	.591	3.14	0	35	29	6	203.2	195	63	106	82	71	2	8.62	2.78	4.68
Gibson	R	12	10	.545	2.77	0	25	25	13	195	159	57	142	71	60	1	7.34	2.63	6.55
go Segui	R	7	6	.538	2.78	17	65	0	0	100.1	78	53	93	35	31	0	7.00	4.75	8.34
Murphy	R	3	7	.300	3.76	0	19	13	2	88.2	89	22	42	38	37	0	9.03	2.23	4.26
Folkers	L	4	4	.500	3.61	3	34	9	1	82.1	74	34	44	34	33	0	8.09	3.72	4.81
ndo Pena	R	4	4	.500	2.18	6	42	0	0	62	60	14	38	17	15	0	8.71	2.03	5.52
rabosky	L	2	4	.333	2.09	5	44	0	0	56	45	21	57	15	13	0	7.23	3.38	9.16
ne Granger	R	2	4	.333	4.24	5	33	0	0	46.2	50	21	14	29	22	0	9.64	4.05	2.70
e Nagy	R	0	2	.000	4.20	0	9	7	0	40.2	44	15	14	21	19	0	9.74	3.32	3.10
io Spinks	R	1	5	.167	4.89	0	8	8	0	38.2	39	25	25	25	21	0	9.08	5.82	5.82
Andrews	L	1	1	.500	4.42	0	16	0	0	18.1	16	11	5	10	9	0	7.85	5.40	2.45
Bibby	R	0	2	.000	9.56	0	6	3	0	16	19	17	12	17	17	0	10.69	9.56	6.75
antorini	R	0	0	–	5.40	0	6	0	0	8.1	14	2	2	5	5	0	15.12	2.16	2.16
prague	R	0	0	–	2.25	0	8	0	0	8	8	4	2	2	2	0	9.00	4.50	2.25
e Fisher	R	2	1	.667	1.29	0	6	0	0	7	3	1	1	1	1	0	3.86	1.29	1.29
e Thompson	R	0	0	–	0.00	0	2	0	0	4	1	5	3	0	0	0	2.25	11.25	6.75
Krausse	R	0	0	–	0.00	0	1	0	0	2	2	1	1	0	0	0	9.00	4.50	4.50
M TOTAL		81	81	.500	3.25	36	426	162	42	1460.2	1366	486	867	603	528	11	8.42	2.99	5.34

MANAGER	W	L	PCT
Red Schoendienst	86	75	.534

POS	Player	B	G	AB	H	2B	3B	HR	HR %	R	RBI	BB	SO	SB	Pinch Hit AB	Pinch Hit H	BA	SA
REGULARS																		
1B	Joe Torre	R	147	529	149	28	1	11	2.1	59	70	69	88	1	4	2	.282	.401
2B	Ted Sizemore	R	129	504	126	17	0	2	0.4	68	47	70	37	8	2	0	.250	.296
SS	Mike Tyson	R	151	422	94	14	5	1	0.2	35	37	22	70	4	0	0	.223	.287
3B	Ken Reitz	R	154	579	157	28	2	7	1.2	48	54	23	63	0	3	1	.271	.363
RF	Reggie Smith	B	143	517	160	26	9	23	4.4	79	100	71	70	4	10	4	.309	.528
CF	Bake McBride	L	150	559	173	19	5	6	1.1	81	56	43	57	30	7	3	.309	.394
LF	Lou Brock	L	153	635	194	25	7	3	0.5	105	48	61	88	118	3	1	.306	.381
C	Ted Simmons	B	152	599	163	33	6	20	3.3	66	103	47	35	0	2	1	.272	.447
SUBSTITUTES																		
2B	Tom Heintzelman	R	38	74	17	4	0	1	1.4	10	6	9	14	0	7	1	.230	.324
SS	Jack Heidemann	R	47	70	19	1	0	0	0.0	8	3	5	10	0	4	0	.271	.286
1B	Jim Hickman	R	50	60	16	0	0	2	3.3	5	4	8	10	0	30	6	.267	.367
UT	Jerry Davanon	R	30	40	6	1	0	0	0.0	4	4	4	5	0	1	0	.150	.175
SS	Luis Alvarado	R	17	36	5	2	0	0	0.0	3	1	2	6	0	0	0	.139	.194
1B	Keith Hernandez	L	14	34	10	1	2	0	0.0	3	2	7	8	0	3	1	.294	.441
2B	Ron Hunt	R	12	23	4	0	0	0	0.0	1	0	3	2	0	4	2	.174	.174
2B	Bob Heise	R	3	7	1	0	0	0	0.0	0	0	0	0	0	0	0	.143	.143
SS	Stan Papi	R	8	4	1	0	0	0	0.0	0	1	0	0	0	1	0	.250	.250
OF	Jose Cruz	L	107	161	42	4	3	5	3.1	24	20	20	27	4	47	11	.261	.416
OF	Luis Melendez	R	83	124	27	4	3	0	0.0	15	8	11	9	2	31	4	.218	.298
OF	Jim Dwyer	L	74	86	24	1	0	2	2.3	13	11	11	16	0	41	10	.279	.360
OF	Danny Godby	R	13	13	2	0	0	0	0.0	2	1	3	4	0	6	1	.154	.154
OF	Jerry Mumphrey	B	5	2	0	0	0	0	0.0	2	0	0	0	0	0	0	.000	.000
OF	Larry Herndon	R	12	1	1	0	0	0	0.0	3	0	0	0	0	1	0	1.000	1.000
C1	Tim McCarver	L	74	106	23	0	1	0	0.0	13	11	22	6	0	40	7	.217	.236
C	Marc Hill	R	10	21	5	1	0	0	0.0	2	2	4	5	0	1	0	.238	.286
C	Dick Billings	R	1	5	1	0	0	0	0.0	0	0	0	1	0	0	0	.200	.200
PITCHERS																		
P	Lynn McGlothen	L	31	83	15	1	0	0	0.0	3	4	2	19	0	0	0	.181	.193
P	Bob Gibson	R	33	81	17	4	1	0	0.0	6	6	3	19	0	0	0	.210	.284
P	John Curtis	L	34	63	10	1	0	0	0.0	7	2	4	30	0	0	0	.159	.175
P	Alan Foster	R	33	48	8	0	0	0	0.0	4	2	2	7	0	0	0	.167	.167
P	Sonny Siebert	R	28	44	5	0	0	0	0.0	3	3	3	17	0	0	0	.114	.114
P	Bob Forsch	R	20	29	7	1	0	0	0.0	1	1	2	11	1	0	0	.241	.276
P	Al Hrabosky	R	66	13	4	0	1	0	0.0	2	2	0	2	0	0	0	.308	.462
P	Mike Garman	R	64	10	1	0	0	0	0.0	1	0	0	2	0	0	0	.100	.100
P	Rich Folkers	L	55	10	1	0	0	0	0.0	0	0	0	3	0	0	0	.100	.100
P	Mike Thompson	R	19	8	0	0	0	0	0.0	0	0	0	4	0	0	0	.000	.000
P	Claude Osteen	L	8	7	0	0	0	0	0.0	0	0	0	1	0	0	0	.000	.000
P	Ray Bare	R	10	5	1	0	0	0	0.0	1	1	0	0	0	0	0	.200	.200
P	Orlando Pena	R	42	2	1	0	0	0	0.0	0	0	0	1	0	0	0	.500	.500
P	Pete Richert	L	13	0	0	0	0	0	–	0	0	0	0	0	0	0	–	–
P	Barry Lersch	R	1	0	0	0	0	0	–	0	0	0	0	0	0	0	–	–
P	John Denny	R	2	0	0	0	0	0	–	0	0	0	0	0	0	0	–	–
TEAM TOTAL				5614	1490	216	46	83	1.5	677	610	531	751	172	247	55	.265	.365

INDIVIDUAL FIELDING

POS	Player	T	G	PO	A	E	DP	TC/G	FA
1B	J. Torre	R	139	1165	102	10	144	9.2	.992
	T. Simmons	R	12	96	5	4	5	8.8	.962
	K. Hernandez	L	9	70	1	2	8	8.1	.973
	J. Hickman	R	14	64	7	1	13	5.1	.986
	T. McCarver	R	6	40	2	1	1	7.2	.977
	R. Smith	R	1	11	0	0	0	11.0	1.000
	J. Dwyer	L	3	4	2	0	2	2.0	1.000
	J. Cruz	L	1	5	0	0	2	5.0	1.000
2B	T. Sizemore	R	128	335	412	15	109	6.0	.980
	Heintzelman	R	28	39	51	2	12	3.3	.978
	S. Papi	R	1	0	0	0	0	0.0	.000
	M. Tyson	R	12	16	24	1	7	3.4	.976
	J. Davanon	R	7	9	19	0	5	4.0	1.000
	R. Hunt	R	5	10	13	0	3	4.6	1.000
	B. Heise	R	3	7	8	0	2	5.0	1.000
SS	M. Tyson	R	143	231	410	30	108	4.7	.955
	J. Heidemann	R	45	42	46	3	9	2.0	.967
	L. Alvarado	R	17	16	33	1	8	2.9	.980
	Heintzelman	R	1	0	0	0	0	0.0	.000
	J. Davanon	R	14	8	13	4	3	1.8	.840
	S. Papi	R	7	6	3	0	3	1.3	1.000
	K. Reitz	R	2	0	3	1	0	2.0	.750
	T. Sizemore	R	1	0	0	1	0	1.0	.000
	L. Melendez	R	1	0	1	0	0	1.0	1.000
3B	K. Reitz	R	151	131	278	11	29	2.8	.974
	J. Torre	R	18	8	19	4	1	1.7	.871
	J. Heidemann	R	1	0	0	0	0	0.0	.000
	Heintzelman	R	2	2	5	0	0	3.5	1.000
	J. Davanon	R	8	2	3	1	0	0.8	.833
	J. Hickman	R	1	1	0	0	1	1.0	1.000

POS	Player	T	G	PO	A	E	DP	TC/G	FA
OF	B. McBride	R	144	395	9	4	1	2.8	.990
	L. Brock	L	152	283	8	10	2	2.0	.967
	R. Smith	R	132	275	9	7	3	2.2	.976
	L. Melendez	R	46	84	0	2	0	1.9	.977
	J. Cruz	L	53	76	2	2	1	1.5	.975
	J. Dwyer	L	25	27	1	0	0	1.1	1.000
	J. Davanon	R	1	0	0	0	0	0.0	.000
	J. Mumphrey	R	1	0	0	0	0	0.0	.000
	D. Godby	R	4	8	1	0	0	2.3	1.000
	T. Sizemore	R	1	1	0	0	0	1.0	1.000
	L. Herndon	R	1	1	0	0	0	1.0	1.000
C	T. Simmons	R	141	717	82	11	13	5.7	.986
	T. McCarver	R	21	86	9	3	0	4.7	.969
	M. Hill	R	9	41	5	0	0	5.1	1.000
	D. Billings	R	1	8	0	0	0	8.0	1.000

The decline in stolen bases in the 1940s and 1950s led many sportswriters to describe Ty Cobb's record of 96 steals in a season as unbreakable; in a class with Joe DiMaggio's 56-game hitting streak, or Hornsby's .424 average. Maury Wills broke the unbreakable record with his 104 steals in 1962, and then Lou Brock shattered Wills's mark with his astounding 118 in 1974, a remarkable performance for a 35-year-old ballplayer. Relying on his guile more than raw speed, Brock used his knowledge of pitchers' moves to pioneer his rolling start off first. Brock was part of the most recent .300-hitting outfield along with Reggie Smith, acquired over the winter from Boston, and Bake McBride, the National League Rookie of the Year. The Cards and Pirates battled through September, with St. Louis taking over first place on the strength of a six-game winning streak that began with a 25-inning 4–3 victory over the Mets, but for the second straight year they were eliminated on the season's final day.

TEAM STATISTICS

	W	L	PCT	GB	R	OR	2B	3B	HR	BA	SA	SB	E	DP	FA	CG	BB	SO	ShO	SV	ERA
EAST																					
PIT	88	74	.543		751	657	238	46	114	.274	.391	55	162	154	.975	51	543	721	9	17	3.49
STL	86	75	.534	1.5	677	643	216	46	83	.265	.365	172	147	192	.977	37	616	794	13	20	3.48
PHI	80	82	.494	8	676	701	233	50	95	.261	.373	115	148	168	.976	46	682	892	4	19	3.92
MON	79	82	.491	8.5	662	657	201	29	86	.254	.350	124	153	157	.976	35	544	822	8	27	3.60
NY	71	91	.438	17	572	646	183	22	96	.235	.329	43	158	150	.975	46	504	908	15	14	3.42
CHI	66	96	.407	22	669	826	221	42	110	.251	.365	78	199	141	.969	23	576	895	6	26	4.28
WEST																					
LA	102	60	.630		798	561	231	34	139	.272	.401	149	157	122	.975	33	464	943	19	23	2.97
CIN	98	64	.605	4	776	631	271	35	135	.260	.394	146	134	151	.979	34	536	875	11	27	3.42
ATL	88	74	.543	14	661	563	202	37	120	.249	.363	72	132	161	.979	46	488	772	21	22	3.05
HOU	81	81	.500	21	653	632	222	41	110	.263	.378	108	113	161	.982	36	601	738	18	18	3.48
SF	72	90	.444	30	634	723	228	38	93	.252	.358	107	175	153	.972	27	559	756	11	25	3.80
SD	60	102	.370	42	541	830	196	27	99	.229	.330	85	170	126	.973	25	715	855	7	19	4.61
LEAGUE TOTAL					8070	8070	2642	447	1280	.255	.367	1254	1848	1836	.976	439	6828	9971	142	257	3.62

INDIVIDUAL PITCHING

PITCHER	T	W	L	PCT	ERA	SV	G	GS	CG	IP	H	BB	SO	R	ER	ShO	H/9	BB/9	SO/9
Bob Gibson	R	11	13	.458	3.83	0	33	33	9	240	236	104	129	111	102	1	8.85	3.90	4.84
Lynn McGlothen	R	16	12	.571	2.70	0	31	31	8	237	212	89	142	80	71	3	8.05	3.38	5.39
John Curtis	L	10	14	.417	3.78	1	33	29	5	195	199	83	89	91	82	2	9.18	3.83	4.11
Alan Foster	R	7	10	.412	3.89	0	31	25	5	162	167	61	78	81	70	1	9.28	3.39	4.33
Sonny Siebert	R	8	8	.500	3.83	0	28	20	5	134	150	51	68	66	57	3	10.07	3.43	4.57
Bob Forsch	R	7	4	.636	2.97	0	19	14	5	100	84	34	39	38	33	2	7.56	3.06	3.51
Rich Folkers	L	6	2	.750	3.00	2	55	0	0	90	65	38	57	31	30	0	6.50	3.80	5.70
Al Hrabosky	L	8	1	.889	2.97	9	65	0	0	88	71	38	82	34	29	0	7.26	3.89	8.39
Mike Garman	R	7	2	.778	2.63	6	64	0	0	82	66	27	45	26	24	0	7.24	2.96	4.94
Orlando Pena	R	5	2	.714	2.60	1	42	0	0	45	45	20	23	15	13	0	9.00	4.00	4.60
Mike Thompson	R	0	3	.000	5.63	0	19	4	0	38.1	37	35	25	24	24	0	8.69	8.22	5.87
Ray Bare	R	1	2	.333	6.00	0	10	3	0	24	25	9	6	17	16	0	9.38	3.38	2.25
Claude Osteen	L	0	2	.000	4.37	0	8	2	0	22.2	26	11	6	14	11	0	10.32	4.37	2.38
Pete Richert	L	0	0	–	2.38	1	13	0	0	11.1	10	11	4	7	3	0	7.94	8.74	3.18
John Denny	R	0	0	–	0.00	0	2	0	0	2	3	0	1	2	0	0	13.50	0.00	4.50
Barry Lersch	R	0	0	–	54.00	0	1	0	0	1	3	5	0	6	6	0	27.00	45.00	0.00
TEAM TOTAL		86	75	.534	3.49	20	454	161	37	1472.1	1399	616	794	643	571	12	8.55	3.77	4.85

MANAGER	W	L	PCT
Red Schoendienst	82	80	.506

POS	Player	B	G	AB	H	2B	3B	HR	HR %	R	RBI	BB	SO	SB	Pinch Hit AB	Pinch Hit H	BA	SA
REGULARS																		
1B	Reggie Smith	B	135	477	144	26	3	19	4.0	67	76	63	59	9	7	3	.302	.488
2B	Ted Sizemore	R	153	562	135	23	1	3	0.5	56	49	45	37	1	1	1	.240	.301
SS	Mike Tyson	R	122	368	98	16	3	2	0.5	45	37	24	39	5	2	0	.266	.342
3B	Ken Reitz	R	161	592	159	25	1	5	0.8	43	63	22	54	1	1	0	.269	.340
RF	Bake McBride	L	116	413	124	10	9	5	1.2	70	36	34	52	26	11	3	.300	.404
CF	Willie Davis	L	98	350	102	19	6	6	1.7	41	50	14	27	10	12	3	.291	.431
LF	Lou Brock	L	136	528	163	27	6	3	0.6	78	47	38	64	56	8	3	.309	.400
C	Ted Simmons	B	157	581	193	32	3	18	3.1	80	100	63	35	1	5	1	.332	.491
SUBSTITUTES																		
1O	Ron Fairly	L	107	229	69	13	2	7	3.1	32	37	45	22	0	35	12	.301	.467
1B	Keith Hernandez	L	64	188	47	8	2	3	1.6	20	20	17	26	0	9	3	.250	.362
SS	Mario Guerrero	R	64	184	44	9	0	0	0.0	17	11	10	7	0	0	0	.239	.288
SS	Ed Brinkman	R	28	75	18	4	0	1	1.3	6	6	7	10	0	4	1	.240	.333
3O	Hector Cruz	R	23	48	7	2	2	0	0.0	7	6	2	4	0	6	1	.146	.271
1B	Danny Cater	R	22	35	8	2	0	0	0.0	3	2	1	3	0	13	2	.229	.286
1B	Doug Howard	R	17	29	6	0	0	1	3.4	1	1	0	7	0	10	3	.207	.310
S2	Larry Lintz	R	27	18	5	1	0	0	0.0	6	1	3	2	4	0	0	.278	.333
SS	Mick Kelleher	R	7	4	0	0	0	0	0.0	0	0	0	1	0	0	0	.000	.000
OF	Luis Melendez	R	110	291	77	8	5	2	0.7	33	27	16	25	3	35	8	.265	.347
OF	Buddy Bradford	R	50	81	22	1	0	4	4.9	12	15	12	24	0	23	6	.272	.432
OF	Jim Dwyer	L	21	31	6	1	0	0	0.0	4	1	4	6	0	11	2	.194	.226
UT	Teddy Martinez	R	16	21	4	2	0	0	0.0	1	2	0	2	0	6	1	.190	.286
OF	Jerry Mumphrey	B	11	16	6	2	0	0	0.0	2	1	4	3	0	4	2	.375	.500
OF	Don Hahn	R	7	8	1	0	0	0	0.0	3	0	1	1	0	0	0	.125	.125
C	Ken Rudolph	R	44	80	16	2	0	1	1.3	5	6	3	10	0	14	1	.200	.263
PH	Dick Billings	R	3	3	0	0	0	0	0.0	0	0	0	2	0	3	0	.000	.000
PITCHERS																		
P	Lynn McGlothen	L	35	80	7	0	0	0	0.0	3	0	0	25	0	0	0	.088	.088
P	Bob Forsch	R	35	78	24	3	3	1	1.3	9	5	3	20	0	0	0	.308	.462
P	Ron Reed	R	24	56	9	3	0	0	0.0	4	3	1	19	0	0	0	.161	.214
P	John Denny	R	26	44	10	0	0	0	0.0	4	3	0	17	0	0	0	.227	.227
P	John Curtis	L	39	38	8	0	0	0	0.0	6	1	5	16	0	0	0	.211	.211
P	Bob Gibson	R	22	28	5	0	0	0	0.0	1	4	3	9	0	0	0	.179	.179
P	Eric Rasmussen	R	14	26	4	0	0	0	0.0	1	3	1	8	0	0	0	.154	.154
P	Al Hrabosky	R	65	15	3	0	0	0	0.0	2	4	2	5	0	0	0	.200	.200
P	Elias Sosa	R	14	8	1	0	0	0	0.0	0	1	0	4	0	0	0	.125	.125
P	Greg Terlecky	R	20	3	1	0	0	0	0.0	0	0	0	2	0	0	0	.333	.333
P	Mike Garman	R	66	2	0	0	0	0	0.0	0	0	0	1	0	0	0	.000	.000
P	Ken Reynolds	L	10	2	0	0	0	0	0.0	0	0	0	0	0	0	0	.000	.000
P	Tommy Moore	R	10	2	1	0	0	0	0.0	0	0	0	1	0	0	0	.500	.500
P	Ron Bryant	B	10	1	0	0	0	0	0.0	0	1	0	0	0	0	0	.000	.000
P	Ryan Kurosaki	R	7	1	0	0	0	0	0.0	0	0	0	0	0	0	0	.000	.000
P	Harry Parker	R	14	1	0	0	0	0	0.0	0	0	1	0	0	0	0	.000	.000
P	Ray Sadecki	L	8	0	0	0	0	0	–	0	0	0	0	0	0	0	–	–
P	Mike Barlow	L	9	0	0	0	0	0	–	0	0	0	0	0	0	0	–	–
P	Mike Wallace	L	9	0	0	0	0	0	–	0	0	0	0	0	0	0	–	–
TEAM TOTAL				5597	1527	239	46	81	1.4	662	619	444	649	116	220	56	.273	.375

INDIVIDUAL FIELDING

POS	Player	T	G	PO	A	E	DP	TC/G	FA	POS	Player	T	G	PO	A	E	DP	TC/G	FA
1B	R. Smith	R	66	524	33	10	51	8.6	.982	OF	B. McBride	R	107	289	4	3	1	2.8	.990
	K. Hernandez	L	56	469	36	2	34	9.1	.996		L. Brock	L	128	247	5	9	0	2.0	.966
	R. Fairly	L	56	351	33	8	33	7.0	.980		W. Davis	L	89	187	5	6	2	2.2	.970
	D. Howard	R	7	60	6	0	5	9.4	1.000		L. Melendez	R	89	169	3	3	1	2.0	.983
	D. Cater	R	12	49	4	1	4	4.5	.981		R. Smith	R	69	126	3	5	0	1.9	.963
	T. Simmons	R	2	10	2	0	0	6.0	1.000		B. Bradford	R	25	42	1	3	0	1.8	.935
2B	T. Sizemore	R	153	329	405	21	82	4.9	.972		R. Fairly	L	20	32	0	0	0	1.6	1.000
	M. Tyson	R	24	29	57	3	8	3.7	.966		J. Dwyer	L	9	18	0	0	0	2.0	1.000
	L. Lintz	R	6	5	11	2	0	3.0	.889		H. Cruz	R	6	16	0	1	0	2.8	.941
	T. Martinez	R	2	1	0	0	0	0.5	1.000		J. Mumphrey	R	3	9	0	0	0	3.0	1.000
SS	M. Tyson	R	95	154	246	12	44	4.3	.971		T. Martinez	R	7	9	0	0	0	1.3	1.000
	M. Guerrero	R	64	76	198	13	29	4.5	.955		T. Simmons	R	2	5	0	0	0	2.5	1.000
	E. Brinkman	R	24	40	69	6	15	4.8	.948		D. Hahn	R	4	4	0	0	0	1.0	1.000
	L. Lintz	R	6	5	12	1	3	3.0	.944										
	M. Kelleher	R	7	3	7	1	1	1.6	.909	C	T. Simmons	R	154	803	62	15	5	5.7	.983
	T. Martinez	R	1	0	1	1	0	2.0	.500		K. Rudolph	R	31	93	11	3	1	3.5	.972
3B	K. Reitz	R	160	124	279	23	21	2.7	.946										
	H. Cruz	R	12	4	4	2	0	0.8	.800										
	M. Tyson	R	5	1	5	0	0	1.2	1.000										
	R. Smith	R	1	0	3	0	0	3.0	1.000										
	T. Martinez	R	1	1	2	0	0	3.0	1.000										

Nineteen seventy-five produced very little in the way of pennant races in any of the four divisions. The Cardinals lagged far back early, then charged to within three games of first in August, only to fall back into a tie for third, 10½ games behind the Pirates. The Cards led the league in batting, but their lack of power left them sixth in runs scored. Ted Simmons hit a career-high .332, and topped 100 RBIs for the second straight season, showing few ill effects from a summer spent catching 154 games. The Cards had a new star in the bullpen, Al Hrabosky, "The Mad Hungarian," who went 13–3 in relief with a league-leading 22 saves. Bob Forsch spent his first full season in the majors, compiling a 15–10 record, and Keith Hernandez played 56 games at first after being called up from Tulsa, where he was hitting .330. But it was a disappointing final season for 39-year-old Bob Gibson, who struggled to a 3–10 record with a 5.04 ERA and just one complete game in fourteen starts. Gibson ended his career as the Cardinals' all-time leader in wins, strikeouts, complete games, and shutouts. After the minimum five-year wait, Gibson was elected to the Hall of Fame.

TEAM STATISTICS

W	L	PCT	GB	R	OR	2B	3B	HR	BA	SA	SB	E	DP	FA	CG	BB	SO	ShO	SV	ERA
AST																				
T	92	69	.571		712	565	255	47	**138**	.263	.402	49	151	147	.976	43	551	768	14	31	3.02
HI	86	76	.531	6.5	735	694	**283**	42	125	.269	.402	126	152	156	.976	33	546	897	11	30	3.82
Y	82	80	.506	10.5	646	625	217	34	101	.256	.361	32	151	144	.976	40	580	**989**	14	31	3.39
L	82	80	.506	10.5	662	689	239	46	81	**.273**	.375	116	171	140	.973	33	551	824	13	36	3.58
HI	75	87	.463	17.5	712	827	229	41	95	.259	.368	67	179	152	.972	27	551	850	8	33	4.57
ON	75	87	.463	17.5	601	690	216	31	98	.244	.348	108	180	**179**	.973	30	665	831	12	25	3.73
EST																				
N	108	54	.667		**840**	586	278	37	124	.271	.401	**168**	**102**	173	**.984**	22	487	663	8	**50**	3.37
A	88	74	.543	20	648	**534**	217	31	118	.248	.365	138	127	106	.979	**51**	**448**	894	**18**	21	**2.92**
	80	81	.497	27.5	659	671	235	45	84	.259	.365	99	146	164	.976	37	612	856	9	24	3.74
O	71	91	.438	37	552	683	215	22	78	.244	.335	85	188	163	.971	40	521	713	12	20	3.51
L	67	94	.416	40.5	583	739	179	28	107	.244	.346	55	175	147	.972	32	519	669	4	25	3.93
OU	64	97	.398	43.5	664	711	218	**54**	84	.254	.359	133	137	166	.979	39	679	839	6	25	4.05
AGUE TOTAL					8014	8014	2781	458	1233	.257	.369	1176	1859	1837	.976	427	6730	9793	129	351	3.63

INDIVIDUAL PITCHING

TCHER	T	W	L	PCT	ERA	SV	G	GS	CG	IP	H	BB	SO	R	ER	ShO	H/9	BB/9	SO/9
nn McGlothen	R	15	13	.536	3.92	0	35	34	9	239	231	97	146	110	104	2	8.70	3.65	5.50
b Forsch	R	15	10	.600	2.86	0	34	34	7	230	213	70	108	89	73	4	8.33	2.74	4.23
n Reed	R	9	8	.529	3.23	0	24	24	7	175.2	181	37	99	79	63	2	9.27	1.90	5.07
nn Curtis	L	8	9	.471	3.43	1	39	18	4	147	151	65	67	73	56	0	9.24	3.98	4.10
nn Denny	R	10	7	.588	3.97	0	25	24	3	136	149	51	72	73	60	2	9.86	3.38	4.76
b Gibson	R	3	10	.231	5.04	2	22	14	0	109	120	62	60	66	61	0	9.91	5.12	4.95
Hrabosky	L	13	3	.813	1.67	**22**	65	0	0	97	72	33	82	27	18	0	6.68	3.06	7.61
c Rasmussen	R	5	5	.500	3.78	0	14	13	2	81	86	20	59	44	34	1	9.56	2.22	6.56
ke Garman	R	3	8	.273	2.39	10	66	0	0	79	73	48	48	31	21	0	8.32	5.47	5.47
eg Terlecky	R	0	1	.000	4.50	0	20	0	0	30	38	12	13	16	15	0	11.40	3.60	3.90
as Sosa	R	0	3	.000	3.95	0	14	1	0	27.1	22	14	15	14	12	0	7.24	4.61	4.94
mmy Moore	R	0	0	–	3.79	0	10	0	0	19	15	12	6	10	8	0	7.11	5.68	2.84
rry Parker	R	0	1	.000	6.27	1	14	0	0	18.2	21	10	13	13	13	0	10.13	4.82	6.27
n Reynolds	L	0	1	.000	1.59	0	10	0	0	17	12	11	7	4	3	0	6.35	5.82	3.71
an Kurosaki	R	0	0	–	7.62	0	7	0	0	13	15	7	6	11	11	0	10.38	4.85	4.15
y Sadecki	L	1	0	1.000	3.27	0	8	0	0	11	13	7	8	7	4	0	10.64	5.73	6.55
n Bryant	L	0	1	.000	16.00	0	10	1	0	9	20	7	7	17	16	0	20.00	7.00	7.00
ke Wallace	L	0	0	–	2.00	0	9	0	0	9	9	5	6	2	2	0	9.00	5.00	6.00
ke Barlow	L	0	0	–	4.50	0	9	0	0	8	11	3	2	6	4	0	12.38	3.38	2.25
AM TOTAL		82	80	.506	3.57	36	435	163	33	1455.2	1452	571	824	689	578	11	8.98	3.53	5.09

MANAGER	W	L	PCT
Red Schoendienst	72	90	.444

POS	Player	B	G	AB	H	2B	3B	HR	HR %	R	RBI	BB	SO	SB	Pinch Hit AB	Pinch Hit H	BA	SA
REGULARS																		
1B	Keith Hernandez	L	129	374	108	21	5	7	1.9	54	46	49	53	4	17	4	.289	.428
2B	Mike Tyson	R	76	245	70	12	9	3	1.2	26	28	16	34	3	1	0	.286	.445
SS	Don Kessinger	B	145	502	120	22	6	1	0.2	55	40	61	51	3	1	0	.239	.313
3B	Hector Cruz	R	151	526	120	17	1	13	2.5	54	71	42	119	1	3	0	.228	.338
RF	Willie Crawford	L	120	392	119	17	5	9	2.3	49	50	37	53	2	16	5	.304	.441
CF	Jerry Mumphrey	B	112	384	99	15	5	1	0.3	51	26	37	53	22	10	5	.258	.331
LF	Lou Brock	L	133	498	150	24	5	4	0.8	73	67	35	75	56	12	3	.301	.394
C	Ted Simmons	B	150	546	159	35	3	5	0.9	60	75	73	35	0	7	4	.291	.394
SUBSTITUTES																		
UT	Vic Harris	B	97	259	59	12	3	1	0.4	21	19	16	55	1	23	4	.228	.309
SS	Garry Templeton	B	53	213	62	8	2	1	0.5	32	17	7	33	11	1	0	.291	.362
UT	Reggie Smith	B	47	170	37	7	1	8	4.7	20	23	14	28	1	3	1	.218	.412
1B	Ron Fairly	L	73	110	29	4	0	0	0.0	13	21	23	12	0	46	10	.264	.300
2S	Lee Richard	R	66	91	16	4	2	0	0.0	12	5	4	9	1	3	0	.176	.264
2B	Luis Alvarado	R	16	42	12	1	0	0	0.0	5	3	3	6	0	0	0	.286	.310
2B	Doug Clarey	R	9	4	1	0	0	1	25.0	2	2	0	1	0	2	1	.250	1.000
OF	Bake McBride	L	72	272	91	13	4	3	1.1	40	24	18	28	10	7	2	.335	.445
OF	Mike Anderson	R	86	199	58	8	1	1	0.5	17	12	26	30	1	21	7	.291	.357
OF	Luis Melendez	R	20	24	3	0	0	0	0.0	0	0	0	3	0	11	1	.125	.125
OF	Sam Mejias	R	18	21	3	1	0	0	0.0	1	0	2	2	1	1	0	.143	.190
OF	Mike Potter	R	9	16	0	0	0	0	0.0	0	0	1	6	0	5	0	.000	.000
OF	Charlie Chant	R	15	14	2	0	0	0	0.0	0	0	0	4	0	1	0	.143	.143
CO	Joe Ferguson	R	71	189	38	8	4	4	2.1	22	21	32	40	4	12	2	.201	.349
C	Ken Rudolph	R	27	50	8	3	0	0	0.0	1	5	1	7	0	13	4	.160	.220
C	John Tamargo	B	10	10	3	0	0	0	0.0	2	1	3	0	0	7	2	.300	.300
PITCHERS																		
P	Lynn McGlothen	L	33	71	15	3	0	0	0.0	3	11	1	15	0	0	0	.211	.254
P	John Denny	R	30	67	15	2	0	0	0.0	3	4	1	27	1	0	0	.224	.254
P	Bob Forsch	R	35	62	11	2	0	1	1.6	6	5	1	17	0	0	0	.177	.258
P	Pete Falcone	L	32	62	8	1	0	0	0.0	3	2	1	23	0	0	0	.129	.145
P	Eric Rasmussen	R	43	38	4	1	0	0	0.0	0	0	2	15	0	0	0	.105	.132
P	John Curtis	L	38	35	7	1	1	0	0.0	3	0	2	13	0	0	0	.200	.286
P	Al Hrabosky	R	68	7	0	0	0	0	0.0	0	0	2	4	0	0	0	.000	.000
P	Lerrin LaGrow	R	8	5	0	0	0	0	0.0	0	0	0	3	0	0	0	.000	.000
P	Tom Walker	R	10	5	2	0	0	0	0.0	0	0	0	0	0	0	0	.400	.400
P	Eddie Solomon	R	26	5	2	1	0	0	0.0	0	4	0	3	0	0	0	.400	.600
P	Bill Greif	B	47	4	0	0	0	0	0.0	0	0	2	2	0	0	0	.000	.000
P	Mike Wallace	L	49	3	1	0	0	0	0.0	1	0	0	1	0	0	0	.333	.333
P	Danny Frisella	L	18	1	0	0	0	0	0.0	0	0	0	0	0	0	0	.000	.000
P	Doug Capilla	L	7	0	0	0	0	0	–	0	0	0	0	0	0	0	–	–
P	Mike Proly	R	14	0	0	0	0	0	–	0	0	0	0	0	0	0	–	–
P	Steve Waterbury	R	5	0	0	0	0	0	–	0	0	0	0	0	0	0	–	–
TEAM TOTAL				5516	1432	243	57	63	1.1	629	584	512	860	123	223	53	.260	.359

INDIVIDUAL FIELDING

POS	Player	T	G	PO	A	E	DP	TC/G	FA
1B	K. Hernandez	L	110	862	107	10	87	8.9	.990
	T. Simmons	R	30	219	21	3	21	8.1	.988
	R. Fairly	L	27	174	21	1	19	7.3	.995
	R. Smith	R	17	128	10	2	16	8.2	.986
	M. Anderson	R	5	30	2	1	3	6.6	.970
2B	M. Tyson	R	74	158	237	12	54	5.5	.971
	V. Harris	R	37	91	97	11	21	5.4	.945
	D. Kessinger	R	31	53	85	6	21	4.6	.958
	L. Richard	R	26	59	59	3	14	4.7	.975
	L. Alvarado	R	16	22	22	3	3	2.9	.936
	D. Clarey	R	7	3	1	0	0	0.6	1.000
SS	D. Kessinger	R	113	212	350	18	84	5.1	.969
	G. Templeton	R	53	111	172	24	41	5.8	.922
	V. Harris	R	1	0	0	0	0	0.0	.000
	L. Richard	R	12	12	12	4	4	2.3	.857
3B	H. Cruz	R	148	100	270	26	19	2.7	.934
	L. Richard	R	1	0	0	0	0	0.0	.000
	R. Smith	R	13	14	30	0	2	3.4	1.000
	T. Simmons	R	2	3	1	3	0	3.5	.571
	V. Harris	R	12	1	5	1	0	0.6	.857
	D. Kessinger	R	2	1	0	0	0	0.5	1.000

POS	Player	T	G	PO	A	E	DP	TC/G	FA
OF	J. Mumphrey	R	94	261	6	2	1	2.9	.993
	L. Brock	L	123	221	6	4	0	1.9	.983
	W. Crawford	L	107	209	6	4	1	2.0	.982
	B. McBride	R	66	201	5	4	0	3.2	.981
	M. Anderson	R	58	106	5	2	1	1.9	.982
	V. Harris	R	35	81	1	2	0	2.4	.976
	R. Smith	R	16	42	4	0	0	2.9	1.000
	S. Mejias	R	17	19	1	0	0	1.2	1.000
	J. Ferguson	R	14	15	0	2	0	1.2	.882
	C. Chant	R	14	15	1	0	0	1.1	1.000
	L. Melendez	R	8	14	0	0	0	1.8	1.000
	T. Simmons	R	7	11	0	0	0	1.6	1.000
	M. Potter	R	4	9	0	0	0	2.3	1.000
C	T. Simmons	R	113	493	66	4	4	5.0	.993
	J. Ferguson	R	48	238	32	6	6	5.8	.978
	K. Rudolph	R	14	61	2	4	1	4.8	.940
	J. Tamargo	R	1	4	0	0	0	4.0	1.000

Red Schoendienst's last full season as Cardinals' manager was a distinct downer, as the Cardinals lost 90 games, the most since 1916. Their only battle was with the Cubs for fourth place, which they ended up losing by three games. Third baseman Hector Cruz was the only Cardinal in double figures in homers, and just three players drove in more than fifty runs. Reggie Smith was clearly out of his element with this club; he hit three home runs in one game in May (almost 5 percent of the club's season total!), and was traded to the Dodgers three weeks later. Just three Cardinal pitchers won ten or more games, but one of them, John Denny, led the league in ERA, despite a won-lost record of just 11–9. There were a few bright spots: Hernandez took hold of the first base job, batting .289, and a 20-year-old shortstop, Garry Templeton, hit .291 in a 53-game trial. And Lou Brock kept rolling along, swiping 56 bases for this twelfth straight season of 50 or more steals.

TEAM STATISTICS

	W	L	PCT	GB	R	OR	2B	3B	HR	BA	SA	SB	E	DP	FA	CG	BB	SO	ShO	SV	ERA
EAST																					
PHI	101	61	.623		770	557	259	45	110	.272	.395	127	115	148	.981	34	397	918	9	44	3.10
PIT	92	70	.568	9	708	630	249	56	110	.267	.391	130	163	142	.975	45	460	762	12	35	3.37
NY	86	76	.531	15	615	538	198	34	102	.246	.352	66	131	116	.979	53	419	1025	18	25	2.94
CHI	75	87	.463	26	611	728	216	24	105	.251	.356	74	140	145	.978	27	490	850	12	33	3.93
STL	72	90	.444	29	629	671	243	57	63	.260	.359	123	174	163	.973	35	581	731	15	26	3.61
MON	55	107	.340	46	531	734	224	32	94	.235	.340	86	155	179	.976	26	659	783	10	21	3.99
WEST																					
CIN	102	60	.630		857	633	271	63	141	.280	.424	210	102	157	.984	33	491	790	12	45	3.51
LA	92	70	.568	10	608	543	200	34	91	.251	.349	144	128	154	.980	47	479	747	17	28	3.02
HOU	80	82	.494	22	625	657	195	50	66	.256	.347	150	140	155	.978	42	662	780	17	29	3.55
SF	74	88	.457	28	595	686	211	37	85	.246	.345	88	186	153	.971	27	518	746	18	31	3.53
SD	73	89	.451	29	570	662	216	37	64	.247	.337	92	141	148	.978	47	543	652	11	18	3.65
ATL	70	92	.432	32	620	700	170	30	82	.245	.334	74	167	151	.973	33	564	818	13	27	3.87
LEAGUE TOTAL					7739	7739	2652	499	1113	.255	.361	1364	1742	1811	.977	449	6263	9602	164	362	3.50

INDIVIDUAL PITCHING

PITCHER	T	W	L	PCT	ERA	SV	G	GS	CG	IP	H	BB	SO	R	ER	ShO	H/9	BB/9	SO/9
Pete Falcone	L	12	16	.429	3.23	0	32	32	9	212	173	93	138	87	76	2	7.34	3.95	5.86
John Denny	R	11	9	.550	2.52	0	30	30	8	207	189	74	74	71	58	3	8.22	3.22	3.22
Lynn McGlothen	R	13	15	.464	3.91	0	33	32	10	205	209	68	106	96	89	4	9.18	2.99	4.65
Bob Forsch	R	8	10	.444	3.94	0	33	32	2	194	209	71	76	112	85	0	9.70	3.29	3.53
Eric Rasmussen	R	6	12	.333	3.53	0	43	17	2	150.1	139	54	76	67	59	1	8.32	3.23	4.55
John Curtis	L	6	11	.353	4.50	1	37	15	3	134	139	65	52	68	67	1	9.34	4.37	3.49
Al Hrabosky	L	8	6	.571	3.30	13	68	0	0	95.1	89	39	73	42	35	0	8.40	3.68	6.89
Mike Wallace	L	3	2	.600	4.07	2	49	0	0	66.1	66	39	40	34	30	0	8.95	5.29	5.43
Bill Greif	R	1	5	.167	4.12	6	47	0	0	54.2	60	26	32	28	25	0	9.88	4.28	5.27
Eddie Solomon	R	1	1	.500	4.86	0	26	2	0	37	45	16	19	24	20	0	10.95	3.89	4.62
Terrin LaGrow	R	0	1	.000	1.48	0	8	2	1	24.1	21	7	10	4	4	0	7.77	2.59	3.70
Danny Frisella	R	0	0	–	3.97	1	18	0	0	22.2	19	13	11	10	10	0	7.54	5.16	4.37
Tom Walker	R	1	2	.333	4.12	3	10	0	0	19.2	22	3	11	10	9	0	10.07	1.37	5.03
Mike Proly	R	1	0	1.000	3.71	0	14	0	0	17	21	6	4	9	7	0	11.12	3.18	2.12
Doug Capilla	L	1	0	1.000	5.40	0	7	0	0	8.1	8	4	5	5	5	0	8.64	4.32	5.40
Steve Waterbury	R	0	0	–	6.00	0	5	0	0	6	7	3	4	4	4	0	10.50	4.50	6.00
TEAM TOTAL		72	90	.444	3.61	26	460	162	35	1453.2	1416	581	731	671	583	11	8.77	3.60	4.53

MANAGER	W	L	PCT
Vern Rapp	83	79	.512

POS	Player	B	G	AB	H	2B	3B	HR	HR %	R	RBI	BB	SO	SB	Pinch Hit AB	Pinch Hit H	BA	SA
REGULARS																		
1B	Keith Hernandez	L	161	560	163	41	4	15	2.7	90	91	79	88	7	6	1	.291	.459
2B	Mike Tyson	R	138	418	103	15	2	7	1.7	42	57	30	48	3	2	0	.246	.342
SS	Garry Templeton	B	153	621	200	19	18	8	1.3	94	79	15	70	28	2	0	.322	.449
3B	Ken Reitz	R	157	587	153	36	1	17	2.9	58	79	19	74	2	0	0	.261	.412
RF	Hector Cruz	R	118	339	80	19	2	6	1.8	50	42	46	56	2	15	2	.236	.357
CF	Jerry Mumphrey	B	145	463	133	20	10	2	0.4	73	38	47	70	22	16	3	.287	.387
LF	Lou Brock	L	141	489	133	22	6	2	0.4	69	46	30	74	35	18	7	.272	.354
C	Ted Simmons	B	150	516	164	25	3	21	4.1	82	95	79	37	2	17	2	.318	.500
SUBSTITUTES																		
S2	Don Kessinger	B	59	134	32	4	0	0	0.0	14	7	14	26	0	15	0	.239	.269
UT	Mike Phillips	L	48	87	21	3	2	0	0.0	17	9	9	13	1	9	0	.241	.322
1O	Roger Freed	R	49	83	33	2	1	5	6.0	10	21	11	9	0	23	9	.398	.627
3B	Taylor Duncan	R	8	12	4	0	0	1	8.3	2	2	2	1	0	2	0	.333	.583
2B	Ken Oberkfell	L	9	9	1	0	0	0	0.0	0	1	0	3	0	3	0	.111	.111
2B	Jerry Davanon	R	9	8	0	0	0	0	0.0	2	0	1	2	0	1	0	.000	.000
OF	Tony Scott	B	95	292	85	16	3	3	1.0	38	41	33	48	13	10	1	.291	.397
OF	Mike Anderson	R	94	154	34	4	1	4	2.6	18	17	14	31	2	20	5	.221	.338
OF	Bake McBride	L	43	122	32	5	1	4	3.3	21	20	7	19	9	8	3	.262	.418
OF	Rick Bosetti	R	41	69	16	0	0	0	0.0	12	3	6	11	4	2	0	.232	.232
OF	Dane Iorg	L	30	32	10	1	0	0	0.0	2	4	5	4	0	18	6	.313	.344
OF	Jim Dwyer	L	13	31	7	1	0	0	0.0	3	2	4	5	0	2	1	.226	.258
O3	Joel Youngblood	R	25	27	5	2	0	0	0.0	1	1	3	5	0	7	2	.185	.259
OF	Mike Potter	R	5	7	0	0	0	0	0.0	0	0	0	2	0	5	0	.000	.000
OF	Benny Ayala	R	1	3	1	0	0	0	0.0	0	0	0	1	0	0	0	.333	.333
C	Dave Rader	L	66	114	30	7	1	1	0.9	15	16	9	10	3	28	9	.263	.368
C	John Tamargo	B	4	4	0	0	0	0	0.0	0	0	0	2	0	3	0	.000	.000
PITCHERS																		
P	Bob Forsch	R	35	72	12	4	0	0	0.0	6	4	2	29	0	0	0	.167	.222
P	Eric Rasmussen	R	34	72	10	5	0	0	0.0	4	3	5	27	0	0	0	.139	.208
P	John Denny	R	26	51	5	0	0	0	0.0	4	2	1	15	1	0	0	.098	.098
P	Pete Falcone	L	27	41	10	0	1	0	0.0	3	2	2	12	0	0	0	.244	.293
P	Tom Underwood	R	19	30	4	1	0	0	0.0	4	2	3	7	0	0	0	.133	.167
P	John Urrea	R	41	29	4	0	0	0	0.0	2	1	9	6	0	0	0	.138	.138
P	Buddy Schultz	R	41	12	2	0	0	0	0.0	1	0	2	5	0	0	0	.167	.167
P	Clay Carroll	R	51	11	1	0	0	0	0.0	0	0	0	2	0	0	0	.091	.091
P	Larry Dierker	R	11	8	0	0	0	0	0.0	0	0	0	4	0	0	0	.000	.000
P	Al Hrabosky	R	65	8	0	0	0	0	0.0	0	0	0	1	0	1	0	.000	.000
P	Rawley Eastwick	R	41	5	2	0	0	0	0.0	0	0	0	0	0	0	0	.400	.400
P	Clarence Metzger	R	58	4	0	0	0	0	0.0	0	1	2	3	0	0	0	.000	.000
P	John D'Acquisto	R	3	2	0	0	0	0	0.0	0	0	0	1	0	0	0	.000	.000
P	Johnny Sutton	R	14	1	0	0	0	0	0.0	0	0	0	0	0	0	0	.000	.000
P	Doug Capilla	L	2	0	0	0	0	0	–	0	0	0	0	0	0	0	–	–
TEAM TOTAL				5527	1490	252	56	96	1.7	737	686	489	823	134	233	51	.270	.388

INDIVIDUAL FIELDING

POS	Player	T	G	PO	A	E	DP	TC/G	FA	POS	Player	T	G	PO	A	E	DP	TC/G	FA
1B	K. Hernandez	L	158	1453	106	12	146	9.9	.992	OF	J. Mumphrey	R	133	291	8	9	1	2.7	.971
	R. Freed	R	18	102	7	0	13	6.1	1.000		T. Scott	R	89	223	5	1	0	2.6	.996
2B	M. Tyson	R	135	267	423	15	99	5.2	.979		L. Brock	L	130	184	2	9	1	2.0	.954
	M. Phillips	R	31	42	57	3	15	3.3	.971		H. Cruz	R	106	154	9	6	1	1.6	.964
	D. Kessinger	R	24	32	63	5	9	4.2	.950		M. Anderson	R	77	96	4	2	0	1.3	.980
	J. Davanon	R	5	4	8	1	0	2.6	.923		B. McBride	R	33	48	2	0	0	1.5	1.000
	K. Oberkfell	R	6	3	4	0	1	1.2	1.000		R. Bosetti	R	35	42	5	0	0	1.3	1.000
SS	G. Templeton	R	151	285	453	32	98	5.1	.958		T. Simmons	R	1	0	0	0	0	0.0	.000
	D. Kessinger	R	26	37	54	2	15	3.6	.978		M. Potter	R	1	0	0	0	0	0.0	.000
	M. Phillips	R	5	11	11	1	6	4.6	.957		J. Dwyer	L	12	16	0	0	0	1.3	1.000
3B	K. Reitz	R	157	121	320	9	35	2.9	.980		D. Iorg	R	7	7	0	1	0	1.1	.875
	M. Phillips	R	5	4	6	1	0	2.2	.909		B. Ayala	R	1	6	1	0	1	7.0	1.000
	J. Youngblood	R	6	1	6	1	0	1.3	.875		J. Youngblood	R	11	7	0	0	0	0.6	1.000
	D. Kessinger	R	4	0	2	1	0	0.8	.667		R. Freed	R	6	5	0	1	0	1.0	.833
	H. Cruz	R	2	0	1	1	1	1.0	.500	C	T. Simmons	R	144	683	75	10	5	5.3	.987
	T. Duncan	R	5	0	2	0	0	0.4	1.000		D. Rader	R	38	147	13	4	2	4.3	.976
											J. Tamargo	R	1	1	0	0	0	1.0	1.000

St. Louis pulled back up over the .500 mark under a new manager, disciplinarian Vern Rapp. The Cardinals fought the Cubs again in '77, this time for third place, and this time they were victorious by a two-game margin. The new star was shortstop Garry Templeton, who hit .322 to rank second in the league behind Dave Parker, had 200 hits, and led the league with 18 triples. Simmons had another excellent year behind the plate, leading the club with 21 homers and 95 RBIs, and Hernandez knocked in 91 runs while scoring 90. Bob Forsch won 20 games, but the pitching staff was hurt by Al Hrabosky's woes, as he saved just ten games and had an ERA of 4.40. Hrabosky was then shipped off to Kansas City for Mark Littell and George Frazier. Pitching help for '78 came in two good trades by which the Cardinals added Silvio Martinez and Pete Vuckovich.

TEAM STATISTICS

	W	L	PCT	GB	R	OR	2B	3B	HR	BA	SA	SB	E	DP	FA	CG	BB	SO	ShO	SV	ERA
EAST																					
PHI	101	61	.623		847	668	266	56	186	.279	.448	135	120	168	.981	31	482	856	4	47	3.71
PIT	96	66	.593	5	734	665	278	57	133	.274	.413	260	145	137	.977	25	485	890	15	39	3.61
STL	83	79	.512	18	737	688	252	56	96	.270	.388	134	139	147	.978	16	532	768	10	31	3.81
CHI	81	81	.500	20	692	739	271	37	111	.266	.387	64	153	147	.977	16	489	942	10	44	4.01
MON	75	87	.463	26	665	736	294	50	138	.260	.402	88	129	128	.980	31	579	856	11	33	4.01
NY	64	98	.395	37	587	663	227	30	88	.244	.346	98	134	132	.978	27	490	911	12	28	3.77
WEST																					
LA	98	64	.605		769	582	223	28	191	.266	.418	114	124	160	.981	34	438	930	13	39	3.22
CIN	88	74	.543	10	802	725	269	42	181	.274	.436	170	95	154	.984	33	544	868	12	32	4.22
HOU	81	81	.500	17	680	650	263	60	114	.254	.385	187	142	136	.978	37	545	871	11	28	3.54
SF	75	87	.463	23	673	711	227	41	134	.253	.383	90	179	136	.972	27	529	854	10	33	3.75
SD	69	93	.426	29	692	834	245	49	120	.249	.375	133	189	142	.971	6	673	827	5	44	4.43
ATL	61	101	.377	37	678	895	218	20	139	.254	.376	82	175	127	.972	28	701	915	5	31	4.85
LEAGUE TOTAL					8556	8556	3033	526	1631	.262	.396	1555	1724	1741	.977	321	6487	10488	118	429	3.91

INDIVIDUAL PITCHING

PITCHER	T	W	L	PCT	ERA	SV	G	GS	CG	IP	H	BB	SO	R	ER	ShO	H/9	BB/9	SO/9
Eric Rasmussen	R	11	17	.393	3.48	0	34	34	11	233	223	63	120	103	90	3	8.61	2.43	4.64
Bob Forsch	R	20	7	.741	3.48	0	35	35	8	217	210	69	95	97	84	2	8.71	2.86	3.94
John Denny	R	8	8	.500	4.50	0	26	26	3	150	165	62	60	85	75	1	9.90	3.72	3.60
John Urrea	R	7	6	.538	3.15	4	41	12	2	140	126	35	81	56	49	1	8.10	2.25	5.21
Pete Falcone	L	4	8	.333	5.44	1	27	22	1	124	130	61	75	79	75	1	9.44	4.43	5.44
Tom Underwood	L	6	9	.400	4.95	0	19	17	1	100	104	57	66	61	55	0	9.36	5.13	5.94
Clarence Metzger	R	4	2	.667	3.11	7	58	0	0	92.2	78	38	48	36	32	0	7.58	3.69	4.66
Clay Carroll	R	4	2	.667	2.50	4	51	1	0	90	77	24	34	28	25	0	7.70	2.40	3.40
Al Hrabosky	L	6	5	.545	4.40	10	65	0	0	86	82	41	68	44	42	0	8.58	4.29	7.12
Buddy Schultz	L	6	1	.857	2.33	1	40	3	0	85	76	24	66	26	22	0	8.05	2.54	6.99
Rawley Eastwick	R	3	7	.300	4.70	4	41	1	0	53.2	74	21	30	34	28	0	12.41	3.52	5.03
Larry Dierker	R	2	6	.250	4.62	0	11	9	0	39	40	16	6	21	20	0	9.23	3.69	1.38
Johnny Sutton	R	2	1	.667	2.63	0	14	0	0	24	28	9	9	10	7	0	10.50	3.38	3.38
John D'Acquisto	R	0	0	–	4.32	0	3	2	0	8.1	5	10	9	4	4	0	5.40	10.80	9.72
Doug Capilla	L	0	0	–	15.43	0	2	0	0	2.1	2	2	1	4	4	0	7.71	7.71	3.86
TEAM TOTAL		83	79	.512	3.81	31	467	162	26	1445	1420	532	768	688	612	8	8.84	3.31	4.78

MANAGER	W	L	PCT
Vern Rapp	5	10	.333
Jack Krol	2	1	.667
Ken Boyer	62	82	.431

POS	Player	B	G	AB	H	2B	3B	HR	HR %	R	RBI	BB	SO	SB	Pinch Hit AB	Pinch Hit H	BA	SA
REGULARS																		
1B	Keith Hernandez	L	159	542	138	32	4	11	2.0	90	64	82	68	13	5	1	.255	.389
2B	Mike Tyson	R	125	377	88	16	0	3	0.8	26	26	24	41	2	4	1	.233	.300
SS	Garry Templeton	B	155	647	181	31	13	2	0.3	82	47	22	87	34	2	0	.280	.377
3B	Ken Reitz	R	150	540	133	26	2	10	1.9	41	75	23	61	1	4	4	.246	.357
RF	Jerry Morales	R	130	457	109	19	8	4	0.9	44	46	33	44	4	8	1	.239	.341
CF	George Hendrick	R	102	382	110	27	1	17	4.5	55	67	28	44	1	1	1	.288	.497
LF	Jerry Mumphrey	B	125	367	96	13	4	2	0.5	41	37	30	40	14	16	5	.262	.335
C	Ted Simmons	B	152	516	148	40	5	22	4.3	71	80	77	39	1	10	3	.287	.512
SUBSTITUTES																		
2B	Mike Phillips	L	76	164	44	8	1	1	0.6	14	28	13	25	0	19	1	.268	.348
1O	Roger Freed	R	52	92	22	6	0	2	2.2	3	20	8	17	1	29	11	.239	.370
3B	Wayne Garrett	L	33	63	21	4	0	1	1.6	11	10	11	16	1	12	4	.333	.444
2B	Ken Oberkfell	L	24	50	6	1	0	0	0.0	7	0	3	1	0	3	0	.120	.140
2B	Gary Sutherland	R	10	6	1	0	0	0	0.0	1	0	0	0	0	6	1	.167	.167
SS	Mike Ramsey	B	12	5	1	0	0	0	0.0	4	0	1	1	0	1	0	.200	.200
OF	Lou Brock	L	92	298	66	9	0	0	0.0	31	12	17	29	17	15	4	.221	.252
OF	Tony Scott	B	96	219	50	5	2	1	0.5	28	14	14	41	5	30	6	.228	.283
OF	Dane Iorg	L	35	85	23	4	1	0	0.0	6	4	4	10	0	11	2	.271	.341
OF	Jim Dwyer	L	34	65	14	3	0	1	1.5	8	4	9	3	1	12	2	.215	.308
OF	Jim Lentine	R	8	11	2	0	0	0	0.0	1	1	0	1	1	1	0	.182	.182
OF	Bob Coluccio	R	5	3	0	0	0	0	0.0	0	0	1	2	0	3	0	.000	.000
C	Steve Swisher	R	45	115	32	5	1	1	0.9	11	10	8	14	1	3	1	.278	.365
C	Terry Kennedy	L	10	29	5	0	0	0	0.0	0	2	4	3	0	1	0	.172	.172
C	John Tamargo	B	6	6	0	0	0	0	0.0	0	0	0	2	0	6	0	.000	.000
PITCHERS																		
P	Bob Forsch	R	34	83	15	7	0	1	1.2	2	8	1	26	0	0	0	.181	.301
P	John Denny	R	33	73	13	3	1	0	0.0	10	3	4	21	0	0	0	.178	.247
P	Pete Vuckovich	R	45	58	8	1	0	0	0.0	4	3	1	22	0	0	0	.138	.155
P	Silvio Martinez	R	22	47	8	2	0	0	0.0	4	3	0	21	0	0	0	.170	.213
P	John Urrea	R	27	24	3	0	0	0	0.0	0	2	1	8	0	0	0	.125	.125
P	Pete Falcone	L	19	21	5	1	0	0	0.0	0	0	0	2	0	0	0	.238	.286
P	Eric Rasmussen	R	10	18	2	0	0	0	0.0	1	1	0	8	0	0	0	.111	.111
P	Aurelio Lopez	R	25	14	3	0	0	0	0.0	0	0	0	0	0	0	0	.214	.214
P	Tom Bruno	R	18	12	1	0	0	0	0.0	0	0	0	3	0	0	0	.083	.083
P	Mark Littell	L	72	7	0	0	0	0	0.0	0	0	1	1	0	0	0	.000	.000
P	Buddy Schultz	R	62	5	1	0	1	0	0.0	1	0	1	2	0	0	0	.200	.600
P	Roy Thomas	R	16	4	1	0	0	0	0.0	0	1	0	1	0	0	0	.250	.250
P	Rob Dressler	R	3	3	0	0	0	0	0.0	0	0	0	2	0	0	0	.000	.000
P	George Frazier	R	14	3	1	0	0	0	0.0	0	0	0	1	0	0	0	.333	.333
P	Dan O'Brien	R	7	3	0	0	0	0	0.0	0	0	0	0	0	0	0	.000	.000
P	Dave Hamilton	L	13	1	0	0	0	0	0.0	0	0	0	1	0	0	0	.000	.000
TEAM TOTAL				5415	1351	263	44	79	1.5	600	568	420	713	97	202	48	.249	.358

INDIVIDUAL FIELDING

POS	Player	T	G	PO	A	E	DP	TC/G	FA
1B	K. Hernandez	L	158	1436	96	10	124	9.8	.994
	R. Freed	R	15	110	10	1	13	8.1	.992
2B	M. Tyson	R	124	246	306	13	78	4.6	.977
	M. Phillips	R	55	93	110	6	24	3.8	.971
	K. Oberkfell	R	17	30	48	1	8	4.6	.987
	G. Sutherland	R	1	0	3	0	0	3.0	1.000
SS	G. Templeton	R	155	285	523	40	108	5.5	.953
	M. Phillips	R	10	14	25	1	7	4.0	.975
	M. Ramsey	R	4	4	6	1	3	2.8	.909
3B	K. Reitz	R	150	111	314	12	18	2.9	.973
	W. Garrett	R	19	12	26	3	5	2.2	.927
	M. Phillips	R	1	0	0	0	0	0.0	.000
	K. Oberkfell	R	4	0	0	0	0	0.0	.000

POS	Player	T	G	PO	A	E	DP	TC/G	FA
OF	J. Morales	R	126	254	5	6	0	2.1	.977
	G. Hendrick	R	101	241	5	1	0	2.4	.996
	J. Mumphrey	R	116	178	10	1	1	1.6	.995
	L. Brock	L	79	114	2	3	0	1.5	.975
	T. Scott	R	77	100	6	6	0	1.5	.975
	D. Iorg	R	25	33	5	0	0	1.5	1.000
	T. Simmons	R	23	33	0	1	0	1.5	.971
	J. Dwyer	L	22	19	1	1	0	1.0	.952
	J. Lentine	R	3	4	0	0	0	1.3	1.000
	R. Freed	R	6	3	0	0	0	0.5	1.000
	B. Coluccio	R	2	1	0	0	0	0.5	1.000
C	T. Simmons	R	134	670	88	9	6	5.7	.988
	S. Swisher	R	42	202	13	2	0	5.2	.991
	J. Tamargo	R	9	0	0	0	0	0.0	.000
	T. Kennedy	R	10	46	4	1	1	5.1	.980

Bob Forsch's no-hitter against Philadelphia in April was one of the few bright spots for the Cardinals in 1978. They fell quickly into the cellar, and did not climb out until August, long after Ken Boyer, the Cardinals' 1964 MVP and Series hero, had taken over the club from the much-disliked Rapp. The club batting average of .249 was their lowest since 1968, "The Year of the Pitcher"; before that, it had not been so low since World War I. Everyone in the lineup suffered, as the club was unable to settle on any starting outfield, shuffling Morales, Hendrick, Mumphrey, Brock, and Scott in and out of the lineup. Brock raised some eyebrows with his determination to play one more season; most fans looked at his .221 average and felt that the time had come for him to retire.

TEAM STATISTICS

	W	L	PCT	GB	R	OR	Batting 2B	3B	HR	BA	SA	SB	Fielding E	DP	FA	CG	BB	Pitching SO	ShO	SV	ERA
AST																					
HI	90	72	.556		708	586	248	32	133	.258	.388	152	104	155	.983	38	393	813	9	29	3.33
IT	88	73	.547	1.5	684	637	239	54	115	.257	.385	213	167	133	.973	30	499	880	13	44	3.41
HI	79	83	.488	11	664	724	224	48	72	.264	.361	110	144	154	.978	24	539	768	7	38	4.05
ON	76	86	.469	14	633	611	269	31	121	.254	.379	80	134	150	.979	42	572	740	13	32	3.42
TL	69	93	.426	21	600	657	263	44	79	.249	.358	97	136	155	.978	32	600	859	13	22	3.58
Y	66	96	.407	24	607	690	227	47	86	.245	.352	100	132	159	.979	21	531	775	7	26	3.87
EST																					
A	95	67	.586		727	573	251	27	149	.264	.402	137	140	138	.978	46	440	800	16	38	3.12
N	92	69	.571	2.5	710	688	270	32	136	.256	.393	137	134	120	.978	16	567	908	10	46	3.81
	89	73	.549	6	613	594	240	41	117	.248	.374	87	146	118	.977	42	453	840	17	29	3.30
	84	78	.519	11	591	598	208	42	75	.252	.348	152	160	171	.975	21	483	744	10	55	3.28
OU	74	88	.457	21	605	634	231	45	70	.258	.355	178	133	109	.978	48	578	930	17	23	3.63
TL	69	93	.426	26	600	750	191	39	123	.244	.363	90	153	126	.975	29	624	848	12	32	4.08
AGUE TOTAL					7742	7742	2861	482	1276	.254	.372	1533	1683	1688	.978	389	6279	9905	144	414	3.58

INDIVIDUAL PITCHING

TCHER	T	W	L	PCT	ERA	SV	G	GS	CG	IP	H	BB	SO	R	ER	ShO	H/9	BB/9	SO/9
hn Denny	R	14	11	.560	2.96	0	33	33	11	234	200	74	103	81	77	2	7.69	2.85	3.96
b Forsch	R	11	17	.393	3.69	0	34	34	7	234	205	97	114	110	96	3	7.88	3.73	4.38
te Vuckovich	R	12	12	.500	2.55	1	45	23	6	198	187	59	149	65	56	2	8.50	2.68	6.77
vio Martinez	R	9	8	.529	3.65	0	22	22	5	138	114	71	45	65	56	2	7.43	4.63	2.93
ark Littell	R	4	8	.333	2.80	11	72	2	0	106	80	59	130	38	33	0	6.79	5.01	11.04
hn Urrea	R	4	9	.308	5.36	0	27	12	1	99	108	47	61	75	59	0	9.82	4.27	5.55
ddy Schultz	L	2	4	.333	3.80	6	62	0	0	83	68	36	70	36	35	0	7.37	3.90	7.59
te Falcone	L	2	7	.222	5.76	0	19	14	0	75	94	48	28	52	48	0	11.28	5.76	3.36
relio Lopez	R	4	2	.667	4.29	0	25	4	0	65	52	32	46	35	31	0	7.20	4.43	6.37
c Rasmussen	R	2	5	.286	4.18	0	10	10	2	60.1	61	20	32	32	28	1	9.10	2.98	4.77
m Bruno	R	4	3	.571	1.98	0	18	3	0	50	38	17	33	12	11	0	6.84	3.06	5.94
y Thomas	R	1	1	.500	3.86	3	16	1	0	28	21	16	16	14	12	0	6.75	5.14	5.14
orge Frazier	R	0	3	.000	4.09	0	14	0	0	22	22	6	8	14	10	0	9.00	2.45	3.27
n O'Brien	R	0	2	.000	4.50	0	7	2	0	18	22	8	12	12	9	0	11.00	4.00	6.00
ve Hamilton	L	0	0	—	6.43	0	13	0	0	14	16	6	8	13	10	0	10.29	3.86	5.14
b Dressler	R	0	1	.000	2.08	0	3	2	0	13	12	4	4	3	3	0	8.31	2.77	2.77
AM TOTAL		69	93	.426	3.59	22	420	162	32	1437.1	1300	600	859	657	574	10	8.14	3.76	5.38

MANAGER	W	L	PCT
Ken Boyer	86	76	.531

POS	Player	B	G	AB	H	2B	3B	HR	HR %	R	RBI	BB	SO	SB	Pinch Hit AB	Pinch Hit H	BA	SA
REGULARS																		
1B	Keith Hernandez	L	161	610	210	48	11	11	1.8	116	105	80	78	11	2	2	.344	.513
2B	Ken Oberkfell	L	135	369	111	19	5	1	0.3	53	35	57	35	4	13	3	.301	.388
SS	Garry Templeton	B	154	672	211	32	19	9	1.3	105	62	18	91	26	1	0	.301	.388
3B	Ken Reitz	R	159	605	162	41	2	8	1.3	42	73	25	85	1	2	0	.268	.382
RF	George Hendrick	R	140	493	148	27	1	16	3.2	67	75	49	62	2	7	2	.300	.456
CF	Tony Scott	B	153	587	152	22	10	6	1.0	69	68	34	92	37	3	1	.259	.361
LF	Lou Brock	L	120	405	123	15	4	5	1.2	56	38	23	43	21	22	5	.304	.398
C	Ted Simmons	B	123	448	127	22	0	26	5.8	68	87	61	34	0	4	0	.283	.507
SUBSTITUTES																		
2B	Mike Tyson	R	75	190	42	8	2	5	2.6	18	20	13	28	2	9	2	.221	.363
S2	Mike Phillips	L	44	97	22	3	1	1	1.0	10	6	10	9	0	1	0	.227	.309
1B	Roger Freed	R	34	31	8	2	0	2	6.5	2	8	5	7	0	27	6	.258	.516
2B	Tommy Herr	B	14	10	2	0	0	0	0.0	4	1	2	2	1	1	0	.200	.200
OF	Jerry Mumphrey	B	124	339	100	10	3	3	0.9	53	32	26	39	8	16	5	.295	.369
O1	Dane Iorg	L	79	179	52	11	1	1	0.6	12	21	12	28	1	39	11	.291	.380
OF	Bernie Carbo	L	52	64	18	1	0	3	4.7	6	12	10	22	1	32	6	.281	.438
OF	Jim Lentine	R	11	23	9	1	0	0	0.0	2	1	3	6	0	3	2	.391	.435
OF	Tom Grieve	R	9	15	3	1	0	0	0.0	1	0	4	1	0	1	0	.200	.267
OF	Keith Smith	R	6	13	3	0	0	0	0.0	1	0	0	1	0	0	0	.231	.231
OF	Mike Dimmel	R	6	3	1	0	0	0	0.0	1	0	0	0	0	0	0	.333	.333
C	Terry Kennedy	L	33	109	31	7	0	2	1.8	11	17	6	20	0	5	1	.284	.404
C	Steve Swisher	R	38	73	11	1	1	1	1.4	4	3	6	17	0	5	0	.151	.233
PITCHERS																		
P	Pete Vuckovich	R	34	79	12	0	0	0	0.0	7	3	1	14	0	0	0	.152	.152
P	Bob Forsch	R	33	73	8	2	2	0	0.0	7	5	5	17	0	0	0	.110	.192
P	John Denny	R	31	70	9	2	1	0	0.0	5	3	1	21	1	0	0	.129	.186
P	Silvio Martinez	R	33	62	8	1	0	0	0.0	5	4	1	26	0	0	0	.129	.145
P	John Fulgham	R	22	42	6	2	0	0	0.0	3	4	6	21	0	0	0	.143	.190
P	Bob Sykes	L	13	21	2	0	0	0	0.0	2	0	1	11	0	0	0	.095	.095
P	Roy Thomas	R	26	17	1	1	0	0	0.0	0	0	0	11	0	0	0	.059	.118
P	Mark Littell	L	63	14	0	0	0	0	0.0	1	1	1	11	0	0	0	.000	.000
P	Tom Bruno	R	27	5	1	0	0	0	0.0	0	0	0	2	0	0	0	.200	.200
P	Buddy Schultz	R	31	4	0	0	0	0	0.0	0	1	0	1	0	0	0	.000	.000
P	John Urrea	R	3	4	1	0	0	0	0.0	0	0	0	1	0	0	0	.250	.250
P	Will McEnaney	L	45	3	0	0	0	0	0.0	0	0	0	2	0	0	0	.000	.000
P	Darold Knowles	L	48	2	0	0	0	0	0.0	0	0	0	0	0	0	0	.000	.000
P	Dan O'Brien	R	6	2	0	0	0	0	0.0	0	0	0	0	0	0	0	.000	.000
P	George Frazier	R	25	1	0	0	0	0	0.0	0	0	0	0	0	0	0	.000	.000
P	Kim Seaman	L	1	0	0	0	0	0	–	0	0	0	0	0	0	0	–	–
TEAM TOTAL				5734	1594	279	63	100	1.7	731	685	460	838	116	193	46	.278	.401

INDIVIDUAL FIELDING

POS	Player	T	G	PO	A	E	DP	TC/G	FA	POS	Player	T	G	PO	A	E	DP	TC/G	FA
1B	K. Hernandez	L	160	1489	146	8	145	10.3	.995	OF	T. Scott	R	151	427	14	7	5	3.0	.984
	D. Iorg	R	10	70	5	0	2	7.5	1.000		G. Hendrick	R	138	254	20	2	7	2.0	.993
	R. Freed	R	1	7	1	1	0	9.0	.889		J. Mumphrey	R	114	180	3	3	0	1.6	.984
2B	K. Oberkfell	R	117	213	323	8	65	4.6	.985		L. Brock	L	98	152	7	7	2	1.7	.958
	M. Tyson	R	71	125	184	8	42	4.5	.975		D. Iorg	R	39	51	2	2	0	1.4	.964
	M. Phillips	R	16	21	30	1	5	3.3	.981		B. Carbo	R	17	10	0	0	0	0.6	1.000
	T. Herr	R	6	12	11	0	3	3.8	1.000		K. Smith	R	5	14	1	0	0	3.0	1.000
SS	G. Templeton	R	150	292	525	34	102	5.7	.960		J. Lentine	R	8	12	1	0	1	1.6	1.000
	M. Phillips	R	25	33	76	3	11	4.5	.973		T. Grieve	R	5	7	0	1	0	1.6	.875
	K. Oberkfell	R	2	0	1	0	0	0.5	1.000		M. Dimmel	R	5	3	0	0	0	0.6	1.000
3B	K. Reitz	R	158	124	290	12	26	2.7	.972	C	T. Simmons	R	122	606	69	10	10	5.6	.985
	K. Oberkfell	R	17	10	19	1	2	1.8	.967		T. Kennedy	R	32	135	7	1	1	4.5	.993
	M. Phillips	R	1	0	1	0	0	1.0	1.000		S. Swisher	R	33	105	6	3	2	3.5	.974

It was Lou Brock's final season, and he went out in style: a .304 average for the season, the last of his record 938 stolen bases, and his 3,000th hit off Dennis Lamp of Chicago—literally "off Lamp," as the ball rebounded off his leg. Brock's fine season could not completely overshadow the efforts of Keith Hernandez, who hit .344, drove in 105 runs while scoring 116, and was named co-MVP with Willie Stargell of the Pirates. Besides Brock and Hernandez, the Cards had three other .300 hitters in the lineup, and regained the league lead in team batting with just two lineup changes from 1978, Tony Scott replacing Morales, and Ken Oberkfell replacing Mike Tyson. The pitching staff, though, was just average—their ERA matched the league average for the second straight season.

TEAM STATISTICS

	W	L	PCT	GB	R	OR	Batting 2B	3B	HR	BA	SA	SB	Fielding E	DP	FA	CG	BB	Pitching SO	ShO	SV	ERA
EAST																					
PIT	98	64	.605		775	643	264	52	148	.272	.416	180	134	163	.979	24	504	904	7	52	3.41
MON	95	65	.594	2	701	581	273	42	143	.264	.408	121	131	123	.979	33	450	813	18	39	3.14
STL	86	76	.531	12	731	693	279	63	100	.278	.401	116	132	166	.980	38	501	788	10	25	3.72
PHI	84	78	.519	14	683	718	250	53	119	.266	.396	128	106	148	.983	33	477	787	14	29	4.16
CHI	80	82	.494	18	706	707	250	43	135	.269	.403	73	159	163	.980	20	521	933	11	44	3.88
NY	63	99	.389	35	593	706	255	41	74	.250	.350	135	140	168	.978	16	607	819	10	36	3.84
WEST																					
CIN	90	71	.559		731	644	266	31	132	.264	.396	99	124	152	.980	27	485	773	10	40	3.58
HOU	89	73	.549	1.5	583	582	224	52	49	.256	.344	190	138	146	.978	55	504	854	19	31	3.19
LA	79	83	.488	11.5	739	717	220	24	183	.263	.412	106	118	123	.981	30	555	811	6	34	3.83
SF	71	91	.438	19.5	672	751	192	36	125	.246	.365	140	163	138	.974	25	577	880	6	34	4.16
SD	68	93	.422	22	603	681	193	53	93	.242	.348	100	141	154	.978	29	513	779	7	25	3.69
ATL	66	94	.413	23.5	669	763	220	28	126	.256	.377	98	183	139	.970	32	494	779	3	34	4.18
LEAGUE TOTAL					8186	8186	2886	518	1427	.261	.385	1486	1669	1783	.978	362	6188	9920	121	423	3.73

INDIVIDUAL PITCHING

PITCHER	T	W	L	PCT	ERA	SV	G	GS	CG	IP	H	BB	SO	R	ER	ShO	H/9	BB/9	SO/9
Pete Vuckovich	R	15	10	.600	3.59	0	34	32	9	233	229	64	145	108	93	0	8.85	2.47	5.60
Bob Forsch	R	11	11	.500	3.82	0	33	32	7	219	215	52	92	102	93	1	8.84	2.14	3.78
Silvio Martinez	R	15	8	.652	3.26	0	32	29	7	207	204	67	102	92	75	2	8.87	2.91	4.43
John Denny	R	8	11	.421	4.85	0	31	31	5	206	206	100	99	116	111	2	9.00	4.37	4.33
John Fulgham	R	10	6	.625	2.53	0	20	19	10	146	123	26	75	47	41	2	7.58	1.60	4.62
Mark Littell	R	9	4	.692	2.20	13	63	0	0	82	60	39	67	22	20	0	6.59	4.28	7.35
Roy Thomas	R	3	4	.429	2.92	1	26	6	0	77	66	24	44	29	25	0	7.71	2.81	5.14
Bob Sykes	L	4	3	.571	6.18	0	13	11	0	67	86	34	35	49	46	0	11.55	4.57	4.70
Will McEnaney	L	0	3	.000	2.95	2	45	0	0	64	60	16	15	26	21	0	8.44	2.25	2.11
Darold Knowles	L	2	5	.286	4.04	6	48	0	0	49	54	17	22	27	22	4	9.92	3.12	4.04
Buddy Schultz	L	4	3	.571	4.50	3	31	0	0	40	44	14	38	21	21	0	8.57	3.00	8.14
Tom Bruno	R	2	3	.400	4.26	0	27	1	0	38	37	22	27	18	18	0	8.76	5.21	6.39
George Frazier	R	2	4	.333	4.50	0	25	0	0	32	35	12	14	19	16	0	9.84	3.38	3.94
John Urrea	R	0	0	—	4.09	0	3	2	0	11	13	9	5	7	5	0	10.64	7.36	4.09
Dan O'Brien	R	1	1	.500	8.18	0	6	0	0	11	21	3	5	10	10	0	17.18	2.45	4.09
Kim Seaman	L	0	0	—	0.00	0	1	0	0	2	0	2	3	0	0	0	0.00	9.00	13.50
TEAM TOTAL		86	76	.531	3.74	25	438	163	38	1486	1449	501	788	693	617	7	8.78	3.03	4.77

MANAGER	W	L	PCT	MANAGER	W	L	PCT
Ken Boyer	18	33	.353	Whitey Herzog	38	35	.521
Jack Krol	0	1	.000	Red Schoendienst	18	19	.486

POS	Player	B	G	AB	H	2B	3B	HR	HR%	R	RBI	BB	SO	SB	Pinch Hit AB	Pinch Hit H	BA	SA
REGULARS																		
1B	Keith Hernandez	L	159	595	191	39	8	16	2.7	111	99	86	73	14	2	0	.321	.494
2B	Ken Oberkfell	L	116	422	128	27	6	3	0.7	58	46	51	23	4	1	0	.303	.417
SS	Garry Templeton	B	118	504	161	19	9	4	0.8	83	43	18	43	31	2	0	.319	.417
3B	Ken Reitz	R	151	523	141	33	0	8	1.5	39	58	22	44	0	1	0	.270	.379
RF	George Hendrick	R	150	572	173	33	2	25	4.4	73	109	32	67	6	3	0	.302	.498
CF	Tony Scott	B	143	415	104	19	3	0	0.0	51	28	35	68	22	8	2	.251	.311
LF	Leon Durham	L	96	303	82	15	4	8	2.6	42	42	18	55	8	16	5	.271	.426
C	Ted Simmons	B	145	495	150	33	2	21	4.2	84	98	59	45	1	15	3	.303	.505
SUBSTITUTES																		
2B	Tommy Herr	B	76	222	55	12	6	0	0.0	29	15	16	21	9	9	2	.248	.347
UT	Mike Phillips	L	63	128	30	5	0	0	0.0	13	7	9	17	0	9	2	.234	.273
UT	Mike Ramsey	B	59	126	33	8	1	0	0.0	11	8	3	17	0	18	6	.262	.341
3B	Ty Waller	R	5	12	1	0	0	0	0.0	3	0	1	5	0	0	0	.083	.083
OF	Dane Iorg	L	105	251	76	23	1	3	1.2	33	36	20	34	1	38	10	.303	.438
OF	Bobby Bonds	R	86	231	47	5	3	5	2.2	37	24	33	74	15	15	2	.203	.316
OF	Tito Landrum	R	35	77	19	2	2	0	0.0	6	7	6	17	3	5	1	.247	.325
OF	Keith Smith	R	24	31	4	1	0	0	0.0	3	2	2	2	0	17	3	.129	.161
O1	Joe DeSa	L	7	11	3	0	0	0	0.0	0	0	0	2	0	5	2	.273	.273
OF	Jim Lentine	R	9	10	1	0	0	0	0.0	1	1	0	2	0	3	0	.100	.100
CO	Terry Kennedy	L	84	248	63	12	3	4	1.6	28	34	28	34	0	12	2	.254	.375
C	Steve Swisher	R	18	24	6	1	0	0	0.0	2	2	1	7	0	9	2	.250	.292
PITCHERS																		
P	Bob Forsch	R	32	78	23	5	0	3	3.8	11	10	2	18	1	0	0	.295	.474
P	Pete Vuckovich	R	32	71	13	6	0	0	0.0	4	7	1	13	1	0	0	.183	.268
P	Bob Sykes	L	27	39	4	0	0	0	0.0	2	2	1	14	0	0	0	.103	.103
P	Jim Kaat	L	49	35	5	1	0	1	2.9	4	2	2	13	1	0	0	.143	.257
P	Silvio Martinez	R	25	35	3	0	0	0	0.0	3	1	2	19	0	0	0	.086	.086
P	John Fulgham	R	16	27	0	0	0	0	0.0	1	0	0	17	0	0	0	.000	.000
P	Don Hood	L	35	20	4	0	0	0	0.0	3	1	0	9	0	0	0	.200	.200
P	Roy Thomas	R	24	13	2	0	0	0	0.0	0	0	1	4	0	0	0	.154	.154
P	John Urrea	R	30	13	3	0	0	0	0.0	0	0	0	4	0	0	0	.231	.231
P	Andy Rincon	R	4	12	3	0	0	0	0.0	0	0	0	5	0	0	0	.250	.250
P	John Littlefield	R	52	11	0	0	0	0	0.0	0	0	0	3	0	0	0	.000	.000
P	John Martin	B	9	11	3	0	0	0	0.0	0	1	1	3	0	0	0	.273	.273
P	Alan Olmsted	R	5	11	2	0	0	0	0.0	0	1	0	3	0	0	0	.182	.182
P	Jeff Little	R	7	6	1	0	0	0	0.0	1	0	0	2	0	0	0	.167	.167
P	Jim Otten	R	31	5	1	0	0	0	0.0	0	0	0	1	0	0	0	.200	.200
P	Pedro Borbon	R	10	4	1	0	0	0	0.0	0	0	0	0	0	0	0	.250	.250
P	Donnie Moore	L	11	4	3	1	0	0	0.0	0	2	0	0	0	0	0	.750	1.000
P	Mark Littell	L	14	1	0	0	0	0	0.0	0	0	0	0	0	0	0	.000	.000
P	Kim Seaman	L	26	1	0	0	0	0	0.0	0	0	0	1	0	0	0	.000	.000
P	Darold Knowles	L	2	0	0	0	0	0	—	0	0	0	0	0	0	0	—	—
P	George Frazier	R	22	0	0	0	0	0	—	0	0	0	0	0	0	0	—	—
	TEAM TOTAL			5597	1539	300	49	101	1.8	738	688	450	781	117	188	42	.275	.400

INDIVIDUAL FIELDING

POS	Player	T	G	PO	A	E	DP	TC/G	FA	POS	Player	T	G	PO	A	E	DP	TC/G	FA
1B	K. Hernandez	L	157	1572	115	9	146	10.8	.995	OF	G. Hendrick	R	149	322	10	2	2	2.2	.994
	L. Durham	L	8	44	8	1	6	6.6	.981		T. Scott	R	134	324	5	1	2	2.5	.997
	D. Iorg	R	5	25	0	0	2	5.0	1.000		L. Durham	L	78	136	14	2	2	1.9	.987
	J. DeSa	L	1	2	0	0	0	2.0	1.000		B. Bonds	R	70	114	5	4	2	1.8	.967
2B	K. Oberkfell	R	101	223	310	6	62	5.3	.989		D. Iorg	R	63	108	2	1	0	1.8	.991
	T. Herr	R	58	107	136	4	37	4.3	.984		T. Kennedy	R	28	49	1	0	0	1.8	1.000
	M. Ramsey	R	24	36	59	4	13	4.1	.960		T. Landrum	R	29	40	1	1	0	1.4	.976
	M. Phillips	R	9	13	6	1	0	2.2	.950		K. Smith	R	7	10	0	0	0	1.4	1.000
SS	G. Templeton	R	115	223	451	29	85	6.1	.959		T. Simmons	R	5	8	0	1	0	1.8	.889
	M. Phillips	R	37	49	117	5	26	4.6	.971		J. Lentine	R	6	4	0	0	0	0.7	1.000
	M. Ramsey	R	20	25	29	5	6	3.0	.915		J. DeSa	L	1	1	0	0	0	1.0	1.000
	T. Herr	R	14	17	48	3	10	4.9	.956	C	T. Simmons	R	129	520	71	9	12	4.7	.985
3B	K. Reitz	R	150	86	293	8	25	2.6	.979		T. Kennedy	R	41	182	21	7	3	5.1	.967
	K. Oberkfell	R	16	4	30	1	2	2.2	.971		S. Swisher	R	8	21	1	1	0	2.9	.957
	M. Phillips	R	8	1	7	3	1	1.4	.727										
	M. Ramsey	R	8	1	6	0	0	0.9	1.000										
	T. Waller	R	5	1	2	0	0	0.6	1.000										
	D. Iorg	R	1	1	0	0	0	1.0	1.000										

TEAM STATISTICS

	W	L	PCT	GB	R	OR	Batting 2B	Batting 3B	Batting HR	BA	SA	SB	Fielding E	Fielding DP	FA	Pitching CG	Pitching BB	Pitching SO	ShO	SV	ERA
EAST																					
PHI	91	71	.562		728	639	272	54	117	.270	.400	140	136	136	.979	25	530	889	8	40	3.43
MON	90	72	.556	1	694	629	250	61	114	.257	.388	237	144	126	.977	33	460	823	15	36	3.48
PIT	83	79	.512	8	666	646	249	38	116	.266	.388	209	137	154	.978	25	451	832	8	43	3.58
STL	74	88	.457	17	738	710	300	49	101	.275	.400	117	122	174	.981	34	495	664	9	27	3.93
NY	67	95	.414	24	611	702	218	41	61	.257	.345	158	154	132	.975	17	510	886	9	33	3.85
CHI	64	98	.395	27	614	728	251	35	107	.251	.365	93	174	149	.974	13	589	923	6	35	3.89
WEST																					
HOU	93	70	.571		637	589	231	67	75	.261	.367	194	140	145	.978	31	466	929	18	41	3.10
LA	92	71	.564	1	663	591	209	24	148	.263	.388	123	123	149	.981	24	480	835	19	42	3.24
CIN	89	73	.549	3.5	707	670	256	45	113	.262	.386	156	106	144	.983	30	506	833	12	37	3.85
ATL	81	80	.503	11	630	660	226	22	144	.250	.380	73	162	156	.975	29	454	696	9	37	3.77
SF	75	86	.466	17	573	634	199	44	80	.244	.342	100	159	124	.975	27	492	811	10	35	3.46
SD	73	89	.451	19.5	591	654	195	43	67	.255	.342	239	132	157	.980	19	536	728	9	39	3.65
LEAGUE TOTAL					7852	7852	2856	523	1243	.259	.374	1839	1689	1746	.978	307	5969	9849	132	445	3.60

"Whitey Shuffles the Cards" runs the inevitable headline after the post-season baseball meetings in 1980. New general manager Whitey Herzog saw a club in need of a shake-up, and he made wholesale changes in an unstable club that had gone 74–88.

The 1980 Cardinal club was not nearly as good as its statistics. They finished 14 games below .500 despite outscoring their opponents by 28 runs. They led the league in scoring, batting, and slugging, but had just two pitchers in double figures in wins. While they had five .300 hitters (six including part-timer Dane Iorg), they suffered through intermittent batting slumps and lacked the pitching, especially relief pitching, to win when they weren't hitting.

In a span of six days, Herzog added nine players and unloaded thirteen, rebuilding the club to emphasize speed, defense, and pitching. Herzog paid particular attention to the bullpen, at one point holding the two best relievers in baseball, Rollie Fingers and Bruce Sutter, before trading Fingers away in the big deal with Milwaukee.

INDIVIDUAL PITCHING

PITCHER	T	W	L	PCT	ERA	SV	G	GS	CG	IP	H	BB	SO	R	ER	ShO	H/9	BB/9	SO/9
Pete Vuckovich	R	12	9	.571	3.41	1	32	30	7	222	203	68	132	96	84	3	8.23	2.76	5.35
Bob Forsch	R	11	10	.524	3.77	0	31	31	8	215	225	33	87	102	90	0	9.42	1.38	3.64
Jim Kaat	L	8	7	.533	3.81	4	49	14	6	130	140	33	36	61	55	1	9.69	2.28	2.49
Bob Sykes	L	6	10	.375	4.64	0	27	19	4	126	134	54	50	67	65	3	9.57	3.86	3.57
Silvio Martinez	R	5	10	.333	4.80	0	25	20	2	120	127	48	39	75	64	0	9.53	3.60	2.93
John Fulgham	R	4	6	.400	3.39	0	15	14	4	85	66	32	48	33	32	1	6.99	3.39	5.08
Don Hood	L	4	6	.400	3.40	0	33	8	1	82	90	34	35	39	31	0	9.88	3.73	3.84
John Littlefield	R	5	5	.500	3.14	9	52	0	0	66	71	20	22	31	23	0	9.68	2.73	3.00
John Urrea	R	4	1	.800	3.46	3	30	1	0	65	57	41	36	28	25	0	7.89	5.68	4.98
Jim Otten	R	0	5	.000	5.56	0	31	4	0	55	71	26	38	38	34	0	11.62	4.25	6.22
Roy Thomas	R	2	3	.400	4.75	0	24	5	0	55	59	25	22	32	29	0	9.65	4.09	3.60
John Martin	L	2	3	.400	4.29	0	9	5	1	42	39	9	23	20	20	0	8.36	1.93	4.93
Alan Olmsted	L	1	1	.500	2.83	0	5	5	0	35	32	14	14	13	11	0	8.23	3.60	3.60
Andy Rincon	R	3	1	.750	2.61	0	4	4	1	31	23	7	22	9	9	0	6.68	2.03	6.39
Kim Seaman	L	3	2	.600	3.38	4	26	0	0	24	16	13	10	10	9	0	6.00	4.88	3.75
George Frazier	R	1	4	.200	2.74	3	22	0	0	23	24	7	11	10	7	0	9.39	2.74	4.30
Donnie Moore	R	1	1	.500	6.14	0	11	0	0	22	25	5	10	15	15	0	10.23	2.05	4.09
Pedro Borbon	R	1	0	1.000	3.79	1	10	0	0	19	17	10	4	10	8	0	8.05	4.74	1.89
Jeff Little	L	1	1	.500	3.79	0	7	2	0	19	18	9	17	9	8	0	8.53	4.26	8.05
Mark Littell	R	0	2	.000	9.00	2	14	0	0	11	14	7	7	11	11	0	11.45	5.73	5.73
Darold Knowles	L	0	1	.000	9.00	0	2	0	0	2	3	0	1	2	2	0	13.50	0.00	4.50
TEAM TOTAL		74	88	.457	3.93	27	459	162	34	1449	1454	495	664	710	632	8	9.03	3.07	4.12

WHITEY'S BIG WEEK

DATE	TRADE WITH	ACQUIRED	GAVE UP
December 7	—	Darrell Porter (free agent signing)	—
December 8	San Diego	Rollie Fingers, Bob Shirley, Gene Tenace	Terry Kennedy, Steve Swisher, Mike Phillips, John Littlefield, John Urrea, Kim Seaman, Al Olmstead
December 9	Chicago	Bruce Sutter	Leon Durham, Ken Reitz, Ty Waller
December 12	Milwaukee	Sixto Lezcano, David Green, Lary Sorensen, Dave LaPoint	Rollie Fingers, Pete Vuckovich, Ted Simmons

MANAGER

	W	L	PCT	
Whitey Herzog	30	20	.600	(1st)
Whitey Herzog	29	23	.558	(2nd)

POS	Player	B	G	AB	H	2B	3B	HR	HR %	R	RBI	BB	SO	SB	Pinch Hit AB	Pinch Hit H	BA	SA
REGULARS																		
1B	Keith Hernandez	L	103	376	115	27	4	8	2.1	65	48	61	45	12	2	0	.306	.463
2B	Tommy Herr	B	103	411	110	14	9	0	0.0	50	46	39	30	23	0	0	.268	.345
SS	Garry Templeton	B	80	333	96	16	8	1	0.3	47	33	14	55	8	4	0	.288	.393
3B	Ken Oberkfell	L	102	376	110	12	6	2	0.5	43	45	37	28	13	1	0	.293	.372
RF	Sixto Lezcano	R	72	214	57	8	2	5	2.3	26	28	40	40	0	4	1	.266	.393
CF	George Hendrick	R	101	394	112	19	3	18	4.6	67	61	41	44	4	0	0	.284	.485
LF	Dane Iorg	L	75	217	71	11	2	2	0.9	23	39	7	9	2	14	4	.327	.424
C	Darrell Porter	L	61	174	39	10	2	6	3.4	22	31	39	32	1	6	0	.224	.408
SUBSTITUTES																		
SS	Mike Ramsey	B	47	124	32	3	0	0	0.0	19	9	8	16	4	7	1	.258	.282
UT	Julio Gonzalez	R	20	22	7	1	0	1	4.5	2	3	1	3	0	10	2	.318	.500
OF	Tony Scott	B	45	176	40	5	2	2	1.1	21	17	5	22	10	0	0	.227	.313
OF	Tito Landrum	R	81	119	31	5	4	0	0.0	13	10	6	14	4	11	3	.261	.370
OF	Gene Roof	B	23	60	18	6	0	0	0.0	11	3	12	16	5	2	0	.300	.400
OF	Steve Braun	L	44	46	9	2	1	0	0.0	9	2	15	7	1	25	5	.196	.283
OF	David Green	R	21	34	5	1	0	0	0.0	6	2	6	5	0	2	0	.147	.176
C	Gene Tenace	R	58	129	30	7	0	5	3.9	26	22	38	26	0	12	3	.233	.403
C	Orlando Sanchez	L	27	49	14	2	1	0	0.0	5	6	2	6	1	11	3	.286	.367
C	Glenn Brummer	R	21	30	6	1	0	0	0.0	2	2	1	2	0	2	0	.200	.233
PITCHERS																		
P	Lary Sorensen	R	23	46	3	1	0	0	0.0	0	0	0	21	0	0	0	.065	.087
P	Bob Forsch	R	20	41	5	1	0	0	0.0	0	3	1	10	0	0	0	.122	.146
P	Silvio Martinez	R	18	35	7	2	0	0	0.0	1	2	1	12	0	0	0	.200	.257
P	John Martin	B	18	33	7	2	1	0	0.0	2	8	2	14	0	0	0	.212	.333
P	Bob Shirley	L	28	22	3	0	0	0	0.0	0	1	0	7	0	0	0	.136	.136
P	Joaquin Andujar	R	12	19	0	0	0	0	0.0	0	0	0	9	0	0	0	.000	.000
P	Andy Rincon	R	5	13	3	1	0	0	0.0	1	5	1	6	0	0	0	.231	.308
P	Bruce Sutter	R	48	9	0	0	0	0	0.0	0	1	0	4	0	0	0	.000	.000
P	Jim Kaat	L	41	8	3	1	0	0	0.0	0	2	1	0	0	0	0	.375	.500
P	Mark Littell	L	28	8	2	0	0	0	0.0	0	2	0	2	0	0	0	.250	.250
P	Dave LaPoint	L	3	5	0	0	0	0	0.0	0	0	0	3	0	0	0	.000	.000
P	Doug Bair	R	11	3	0	0	0	0	0.0	0	0	0	3	0	0	0	.000	.000
P	Joe Edelen	R	13	3	1	0	0	0	0.0	0	0	0	1	0	0	0	.333	.333
P	Jim Otten	R	24	2	0	0	0	0	0.0	0	0	0	0	0	0	0	.000	.000
P	Bob Sykes	L	22	2	0	0	0	0	0.0	0	0	1	2	0	0	0	.000	.000
P	Luis DeLeon	R	10	1	0	0	0	0	0.0	0	0	0	0	0	0	0	.000	.000
TEAM TOTAL				3534	936	158	45	50	1.4	464	431	379	494	88	113	22	.265	.377

INDIVIDUAL FIELDING

POS	Player	T	G	PO	A	E	DP	TC/G	FA
1B	K. Hernandez	L	98	1054	86	3	99	11.7	.997
	D. Iorg	R	8	47	5	0	1	6.5	1.000
	G. Tenace	R	7	39	4	0	3	6.1	1.000
2B	T. Herr	R	103	211	374	5	74	5.7	.992
	J. Gonzalez	R	4	3	5	1	0	2.3	.889
	M. Ramsey	R	1	2	2	0	0	4.0	1.000
SS	G. Templeton	R	76	160	272	18	54	5.9	.960
	M. Ramsey	R	35	52	118	6	20	5.0	.966
	J. Gonzalez	R	5	3	7	0	1	2.0	1.000
	K. Oberkfell	R	1	0	1	0	0	1.0	1.000
3B	K. Oberkfell	R	102	77	246	15	23	3.3	.956
	S. Braun	R	1	0	0	0	0	0.0	.000
	M. Ramsey	R	5	2	6	0	1	1.6	1.000
	J. Gonzalez	R	2	1	1	0	0	1.0	1.000
	D. Iorg	R	2	0	2	0	0	1.0	1.000
OF	G. Hendrick	R	101	227	6	4	0	2.3	.983
	T. Scott	R	44	120	2	0	0	2.8	1.000
	S. Lezcano	R	65	103	5	3	1	1.7	.973
	D. Iorg	R	57	78	0	3	0	1.4	.963
	T. Landrum	R	67	72	6	0	1	1.2	1.000
	G. Roof	R	20	38	0	2	0	2.0	.950
	D. Green	R	18	31	1	1	0	1.8	.970
	M. Ramsey	R	1	0	0	0	0	0.0	.000
	S. Braun	R	12	15	2	0	1	1.4	1.000
	K. Hernandez	L	3	2	0	0	0	0.7	1.000
C	D. Porter	R	52	206	31	5	2	4.7	.979
	G. Tenace	R	38	126	18	3	1	3.9	.980
	O. Sanchez	R	18	50	0	4	1	3.0	.926
	G. Brummer	R	19	43	3	0	1	2.4	1.000

TEAM STATISTICS

	W	L	PCT	GB	R	OR	Batting 2B	3B	HR	BA	SA	SB	Fielding E	DP	FA	CG	BB	Pitching SO	ShO	SV	ERA
EAST																					
STL	59	43	.578		464	417	158	45	50	.265	.377	88	82	108	.981	11	290	388	5	33	3.63
MON	60	48	.556	2	443	394	146	28	81	.246	.370	138	81	88	.980	20	268	520	12	23	3.30
PHI	59	48	.551	2.5	491	472	165	25	69	.273	.389	103	86	90	.980	19	347	580	5	23	4.05
PIT	46	56	.451	13	407	425	176	30	55	.257	.369	122	86	106	.979	11	346	492	5	29	3.55
NY	41	62	.398	18.5	348	432	136	35	57	.248	.356	103	130	89	.968	7	336	490	3	24	3.55
CHI	38	65	.369	21.5	370	483	138	29	57	.236	.340	72	113	103	.974	6	388	532	2	20	4.01
WEST																					
CIN	66	42	.611		464	440	190	24	64	.267	.385	58	80	99	.981	25	393	593	14	20	3.73
LA	63	47	.573	4	450	356	133	20	82	.262	.374	73	87	101	.980	26	302	603	19	24	3.01
HOU	61	49	.555	6	394	331	160	35	45	.257	.356	81	87	81	.980	23	300	610	19	25	2.66
SF	56	55	.505	11.5	427	414	161	26	63	.250	.357	81	102	102	.977	8	393	561	9	33	3.42
ATL	50	56	.472	15	395	416	148	22	64	.243	.349	98	102	93	.976	11	330	471	4	24	3.45
SD	41	69	.373	26	382	455	170	35	32	.256	.346	83	102	117	.977	9	414	492	6	23	3.72
LEAGUE TOTAL					5035	5035	1881	354	719	.255	.364	1108	1138	1177	.978	176	4107	6332	103	301	3.49

The lengthy player strike of 1981 caused the first split season in eighty-nine years. In any such season, there are winners and losers. The biggest losers were the Reds and Cardinals, who had the best overall records in their divisions, but did not qualify for the playoffs.

Herzog's moves paid immediate dividends. The club rose to second in the division in runs, and Sutter contributed 25 saves. Herzog did not rest, though. In June, he traded Tony Scott to Houston for Joaquin Andujar. Over the winter, he dealt away Sorensen and Martinez, picking up Lonnie Smith from Philadelphia in a three-way deal. In a quiet minor-league trade, he sent Bob Sykes to the Yankees for Willie McGee. And in an extremely protracted deal, Sixto Lezcano and a player to be named went to San Diego for Steve Mura and a player to be named. The unnamed players, pending the players' approval, were shortstops Ozzie Smith and Garry Templeton. Templeton had sealed his fate with an obscene outburst in September, and Herzog believed Smith's defense would make up for the 74-point difference in their lifetime batting averages. The 1982 season would show how right he was.

INDIVIDUAL PITCHING

PITCHER	T	W	L	PCT	ERA	SV	G	GS	CG	IP	H	BB	SO	R	ER	ShO	H/9	BB/9	SO/9
Lary Sorensen	R	7	7	.500	3.28	0	23	23	3	140	149	26	52	59	51	1	9.58	1.67	3.34
Bob Forsch	R	10	5	.667	3.19	0	20	20	1	124	106	29	41	47	44	0	7.69	2.10	2.98
John Martin	L	8	5	.615	3.41	0	17	15	4	103	85	26	36	43	39	0	7.43	2.27	3.15
Silvio Martinez	R	2	5	.286	3.99	0	18	16	0	97	95	39	34	48	43	0	8.81	3.62	3.15
Bruce Sutter	R	3	5	.375	2.63	25	48	0	0	82	64	24	57	24	24	0	7.02	2.63	6.26
Bob Shirley	L	6	4	.600	4.10	1	28	11	1	79	78	34	36	42	36	0	8.89	3.87	4.10
Joaquin Andujar	R	6	1	.857	3.74	0	11	8	1	55.1	56	11	19	24	23	0	9.11	1.79	3.09
Jim Kaat	L	6	6	.500	3.40	4	41	1	0	53	60	17	8	25	20	0	10.19	2.89	1.36
Mark Littell	R	1	3	.250	4.39	2	28	1	0	41	36	31	22	21	20	0	7.90	6.80	4.83
Bob Sykes	L	2	0	1.000	4.62	0	22	1	0	37	37	18	14	20	19	0	9.00	4.38	3.41
Jim Otten	R	1	0	1.000	5.25	0	24	0	0	36	44	20	20	23	21	0	11.00	5.00	5.00
Andy Rincon	R	3	1	.750	1.75	0	5	5	1	36	27	5	13	8	7	1	6.75	1.25	3.25
Joe Edelen	R	1	0	1.000	9.35	0	13	0	0	17.1	29	3	10	18	18	0	15.06	1.56	5.19
Doug Bair	R	2	0	1.000	3.45	1	11	0	0	15.2	13	2	14	6	6	0	7.47	1.15	8.04
Luis DeLeon	R	0	1	.000	2.40	0	11	0	0	15	11	3	8	4	4	0	6.60	1.80	4.80
Dave LaPoint	L	1	0	1.000	4.09	0	3	2	0	11	12	2	4	5	5	0	9.82	1.64	3.27
TEAM TOTAL		59	43	.578	3.63	33	322	103	11	942.1	902	290	388	417	380	2	8.61	2.77	3.71

THE SPLIT SEASON

EAST					WEST				
First Half									
PHI	34	21	.618		LA	36	21	.632	
STL	30	20	.600	1½	CIN	35	21	.625	½
MON	30	25	.545	4	HOU	28	29	.491	8
PIT	25	23	.521	5½	ATL	25	29	.463	9½
NY	17	34	.333	15	SF	27	32	.458	10
CHI	15	37	.288	17½	SD	23	33	.411	12½
Second Half									
MON	30	23	.566		HOU	33	20	.633	
STL	29	23	.558	½	CIN	31	21	.596	1½
PHI	25	27	.481	4½	SF	29	23	.558	3½
NY	24	28	.462	5½	LA	27	26	.509	6
CHI	23	28	.451	6	ATL	25	27	.481	7½
PIT	21	33	.389	9½	SD	18	36	.333	15½

MANAGER	W	L	PCT
Whitey Herzog	92	70	.568

POS	Player	B	G	AB	H	2B	3B	HR	HR %	R	RBI	BB	SO	SB	Pinch Hit AB	Pinch Hit H	BA	SA
REGULARS																		
1B	Keith Hernandez	L	160	579	173	33	6	7	1.2	79	94	100	67	19	1	1	.299	.413
2B	Tommy Herr	B	135	493	131	19	4	0	0.0	83	36	57	56	25	5	2	.266	.320
SS	Ozzie Smith	B	140	488	121	24	1	2	0.4	58	43	68	32	25	1	0	.248	.314
3B	Ken Oberkfell	L	137	470	136	22	5	2	0.4	55	34	40	31	11	3	1	.289	.370
RF	George Hendrick	R	136	515	145	20	5	19	3.7	65	104	37	80	3	2	1	.282	.450
CF	Willie McGee	B	123	422	125	12	8	4	0.9	43	56	12	58	24	15	6	.296	.391
LF	Lonnie Smith	R	156	592	182	35	8	8	1.4	120	69	64	74	68	9	1	.307	.434
C	Darrell Porter	L	120	373	86	18	5	12	3.2	46	48	66	66	1	8	1	.231	.402
SUBSTITUTES																		
UT	Mike Ramsey	B	112	256	59	8	2	1	0.4	18	21	22	34	6	16	4	.230	.289
32	Julio Gonzalez	R	42	87	21	3	2	1	1.1	9	7	1	24	1	12	1	.241	.356
3S	Kelly Paris	B	12	29	3	0	0	0	0.0	1	1	0	7	0	3	1	.103	.103
OF	Dane Iorg	L	102	238	70	14	1	0	0.0	17	34	23	23	0	27	7	.294	.361
OF	David Green	R	76	166	47	7	1	2	1.2	21	23	8	29	11	12	4	.283	.373
OF	Tito Landrum	R	79	72	20	3	0	2	2.8	12	14	8	18	0	18	4	.278	.403
O3	Steve Braun	L	58	62	17	4	0	0	0.0	6	4	11	10	0	41	12	.274	.339
OF	Gene Roof	B	11	15	4	0	0	0	0.0	3	2	1	4	2	7	2	.267	.267
C	Gene Tenace	R	66	124	32	9	0	7	5.6	18	18	36	31	1	12	3	.258	.500
C	Glenn Brummer	R	35	64	15	4	0	0	0.0	4	8	0	12	2	1	1	.234	.297
C	Orlando Sanchez	L	26	37	7	0	1	0	0.0	6	3	5	5	0	9	2	.189	.243
PITCHERS																		
P	Joaquin Andujar	R	38	95	15	1	1	0	0.0	3	4	0	44	1	0	0	.158	.189
P	Bob Forsch	R	36	73	15	3	1	0	0.0	7	3	3	20	0	0	0	.205	.274
P	Steve Mura	R	35	53	3	0	0	0	0.0	3	3	1	10	0	0	0	.057	.057
P	John Stuper	R	23	42	5	0	1	0	0.0	1	0	1	24	0	0	0	.119	.167
P	Dave LaPoint	L	42	38	2	0	0	0	0.0	1	1	1	18	0	0	0	.053	.053
P	Doug Bair	R	63	13	1	0	0	0	0.0	0	0	0	3	0	0	0	.077	.077
P	Jeff Lahti	R	33	13	1	0	0	0	0.0	0	0	0	8	0	0	0	.077	.077
P	Jim Kaat	L	62	12	0	0	0	0	0.0	0	0	1	4	0	0	0	.000	.000
P	John Martin	B	24	11	1	0	0	0	0.0	1	0	1	3	0	0	0	.091	.091
P	Andy Rincon	R	11	10	1	0	0	0	0.0	3	1	1	6	0	0	0	.100	.100
P	Bruce Sutter	R	70	8	1	0	0	0	0.0	1	1	0	1	0	0	0	.125	.125
P	Eric Rasmussen	R	8	3	0	0	0	0	0.0	0	0	1	1	0	0	0	.000	.000
P	Mark Littell	L	16	2	0	0	0	0	0.0	0	0	0	2	0	0	0	.000	.000
P	Jeff Keener	L	19	0	0	0	0	0	0.0	0	0	0	0	0	0	0	–	–
	TEAM TOTAL			5455	1439	239	52	67	1.2	685	632	569	805	200	202	54	.264	.364

INDIVIDUAL FIELDING

POS	Player	T	G	PO	A	E	DP	TC/G	FA
1B	K. Hernandez	L	158	1586	135	11	140	11.0	.994
	D. Iorg	R	10	77	5	0	6	8.2	1.000
	G. Tenace	R	7	39	3	0	4	6.0	1.000
2B	T. Herr	R	128	263	427	9	97	5.5	.987
	M. Ramsey	R	43	93	115	8	25	5.0	.963
	J. Gonzalez	R	9	10	13	0	4	2.6	1.000
	K. Oberkfell	R	1	2	1	0	0	3.0	1.000
SS	O. Smith	R	139	279	535	13	101	5.9	.984
	M. Ramsey	R	22	37	73	1	15	5.0	.991
	K. Paris	R	4	4	17	2	2	5.8	.913
	J. Gonzalez	R	1	1	2	0	0	3.0	1.000
3B	K. Oberkfell	R	135	78	304	11	23	2.9	.972
	J. Gonzalez	R	21	10	29	4	1	2.0	.907
	M. Ramsey	R	28	5	31	1	2	1.3	.973
	K. Paris	R	5	5	8	2	2	3.0	.867
	S. Braun	R	5	2	5	1	0	1.6	.875
	D. Iorg	R	2	1	3	0	0	2.0	1.000

POS	Player	T	G	PO	A	E	DP	TC/G	FA
OF	L. Smith	R	149	303	16	10	3	2.2	.970
	W. McGee	R	117	245	3	11	0	2.2	.958
	G. Hendrick	R	134	238	6	5	1	1.9	.980
	D. Green	R	68	111	4	1	1	1.7	.991
	D. Iorg	R	63	99	2	3	0	1.7	.971
	T. Landrum	R	56	50	2	0	1	0.9	1.000
	M. Ramsey	R	2	0	0	0	0	0.0	.000
	K. Hernandez	L	4	5	0	0	0	1.3	1.000
	G. Roof	R	5	5	0	0	0	1.0	1.000
	S. Braun	R	8	4	0	0	0	0.5	1.000
C	D. Porter	R	111	469	64	9	8	4.9	.983
	G. Tenace	R	37	149	21	1	0	4.6	.994
	G. Brummer	R	32	88	8	3	1	3.1	.970
	O. Sanchez	R	15	34	4	0	1	2.5	1.000

They called it "Whitey Ball" in honor of their manager, but it was really the traditional Cardinal formula: speed in the field, speed on the basepaths, and solid if unspectacular pitching. The Cardinals were second in the league in batting, but a distant last in home runs; they hit just 67, with only two players, George Hendrick and Darrell Porter, in double figures. But how they could fly! They led the league in triples and stolen bases, paced by Lonnie Smith, who was second in steals with 68, tied for fifth in triples, ranked fourth in batting at .307, and led the league with 120 runs scored. But it was the surprising pitching that led them to the pennant. The pitchers did not amass impressive statistics, as only two of them managed fifteen wins, but they allowed the fewest runs in the league by keeping the ball in the park and letting their swift fielders track it down. In one mid-September week, the Cards went from half a game behind Philadelphia to four and one-half games up with an eight-game winning streak in which they allowed just seven runs. Andujar became a top-flight stopper, and Bruce Sutter did everything asked of him, leading the league with 36 saves. The Cards swept Atlanta in the Championship Series, and rallied after trailing three games to two to win an exciting seven-game World Series against the Milwaukee Brewers. And most exciting of all, this was a young ball club whose lineup averaged just 27 years old—and was very likely to get even better.

TEAM STATISTICS

	W	L	PCT	GB	R	OR	Batting 2B	3B	HR	BA	SA	SB	Fielding E	DP	FA	CG	BB	Pitching SO	ShO	SV	ERA
AST																					
TL	92	70	.568		685	609	239	52	67	.264	.364	200	124	169	.981	25	502	689	10	47	3.37
HI	89	73	.549	3	664	654	245	25	112	.260	.376	128	121	138	.981	38	472	1002	13	33	3.61
ION	86	76	.531	6	697	616	270	38	133	.262	.396	156	122	117	.980	34	448	936	10	43	3.31
IT	84	78	.519	8	724	696	272	40	134	.273	.408	161	145	133	.977	19	521	933	7	39	3.81
HI	73	89	.451	19	676	709	239	46	102	.260	.375	132	132	110	.979	9	452	764	7	43	3.92
IY	65	97	.401	27	609	723	227	26	97	.247	.350	137	175	134	.972	15	582	759	5	37	3.88
EST																					
TL	89	73	.549		739	702	215	22	146	.256	.383	151	137	186	.979	15	502	813	11	51	3.82
A	88	74	.543	1	691	612	222	32	138	.264	.388	151	139	131	.979	37	468	932	16	28	3.26
F	87	75	.537	2	673	687	213	30	133	.253	.376	130	173	125	.973	18	466	810	4	45	3.64
D	81	81	.500	8	675	658	217	52	81	.257	.359	165	152	142	.976	20	502	765	11	41	3.52
OU	77	85	.475	12	569	620	236	48	74	.247	.349	140	136	154	.978	37	479	899	16	31	3.41
IN	61	101	.377	28	545	661	228	34	82	.251	.350	131	128	158	.980	22	570	998	7	31	3.66
EAGUE TOTAL					7947	7947	2823	445	1299	.258	.373	1782	1684	1697	.978	289	5964	10300	117	469	3.60

INDIVIDUAL PITCHING

ITCHER	T	W	L	PCT	ERA	SV	G	GS	CG	IP	H	BB	SO	R	ER	ShO	H/9	BB/9	SO/9
)aquin Andujar	R	15	10	.600	2.47	0	38	37	9	265.2	237	50	137	85	73	5	8.03	1.69	4.64
ob Forsch	R	15	9	.625	3.48	0	36	34	6	233	238	54	69	95	90	2	9.19	2.09	2.67
teve Mura	R	12	11	.522	4.05	0	35	30	7	184.1	196	80	84	89	83	1	9.57	3.91	4.10
ave LaPoint	L	9	3	.750	3.42	0	42	21	0	152.2	170	52	81	63	58	0	10.02	3.07	4.78
)hn Stuper	R	9	7	.563	3.36	0	23	21	2	136.2	137	55	53	55	51	0	9.02	3.62	3.49
ruce Sutter	R	9	8	.529	2.90	36	70	0	0	102.1	88	34	61	38	33	0	7.74	2.99	5.36
oug Bair	R	5	3	.625	2.55	8	63	0	0	91.2	69	36	68	27	26	0	6.77	3.53	6.68
n Kaat	L	5	3	.625	4.08	2	62	2	0	75	79	23	35	40	34	0	9.48	2.76	4.20
)hn Martin	L	4	5	.444	4.23	0	24	7	0	66	56	30	21	33	31	0	7.64	4.09	2.86
ff Lahti	R	5	4	.556	3.81	0	33	1	0	56.2	53	21	22	27	24	0	8.42	3.34	3.49
ndy Rincon	R	2	3	.400	4.73	0	11	6	1	40	35	25	11	22	21	0	7.88	5.63	2.48
ff Keener	R	1	1	.500	1.61	0	11	0	0	22.1	19	19	25	8	4	0	7.66	7.66	10.07
ark Littell	R	0	1	.000	5.23	0	16	0	0	20.2	22	15	7	14	12	0	9.58	6.53	3.05
ic Rasmussen	R	1	2	.333	4.42	0	8	3	0	18.1	21	8	15	13	9	0	10.31	3.93	7.36
EAM TOTAL		92	70	.568	3.37	47	480	162	25	1465.1	1420	502	689	609	549	8	8.72	3.08	4.23

Cardinal Graphics

Graphs are not everyone's cup of tea. That's a shame because a clear, well-drawn graph can present an enormous amount of information faster than any other method. And baseball is the perfect subject for a graphic treatment that can make quick sense of the wealth of statistics and measures generated by that most measured of all sports.

The beauty of John Warner Davenport's work is that it paints a clear, visual picture of more than eighty years of accumulated results and communicates it in a glance. A very clear pattern emerges from a look at Davenport's graphic history of the St. Louis Cardinals: a bad period in the first two decades of the century, followed by a sharp rise capped by three straight pennants in the early 1940s, with a falling off thereafter into the late 1970s, interrupted by the three pennants in the 1960s. It's also clear that the 1981 and 1982 seasons mark a sharp upturn, and may well lead to a new glory period, comparable to that of the '40s.

If the graphic treatment of baseball history in this section strikes your fancy, you will definitely be interested in Davenport's two books, *Baseball Graphics* and *Baseball's Pennant Races: A Graphic Look,* published by First Impressions of Madison, Wisconsin.

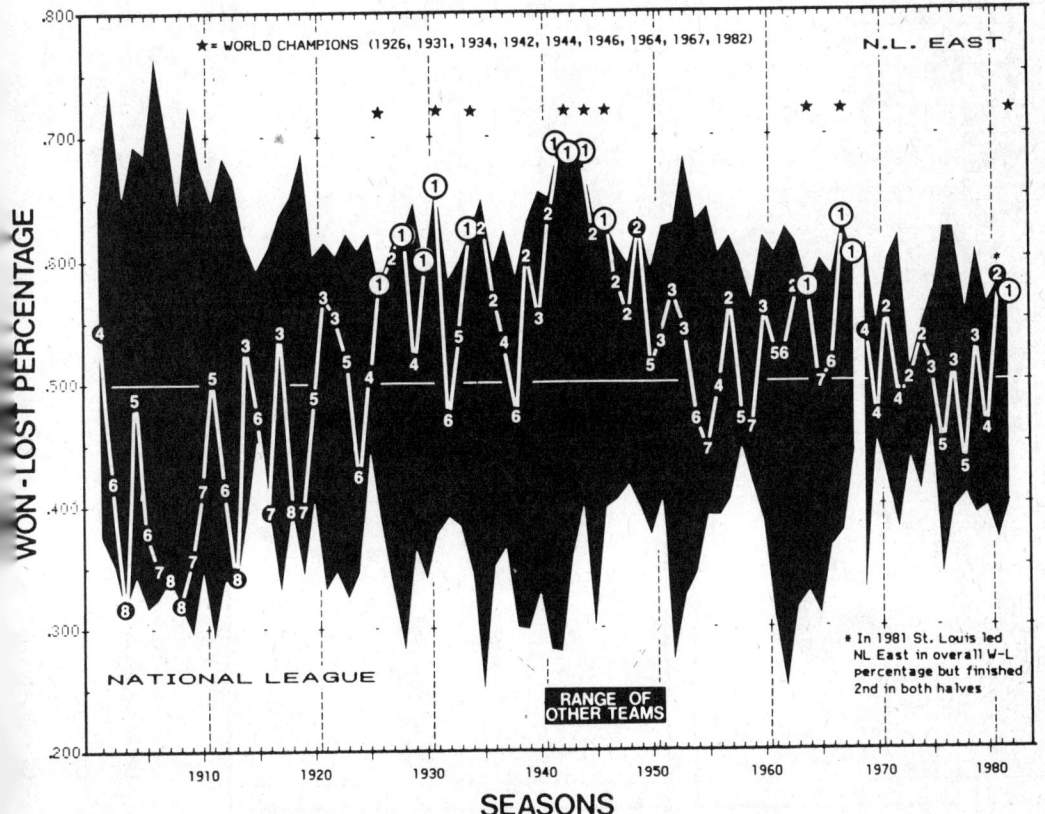

The black space indicates the range of won-lost percentages for all the teams in the league in each season; the white numbers represent the Cardinals' finish in each season. Notice, from 1939 to 1953, their period of fifteen straight years above .500.

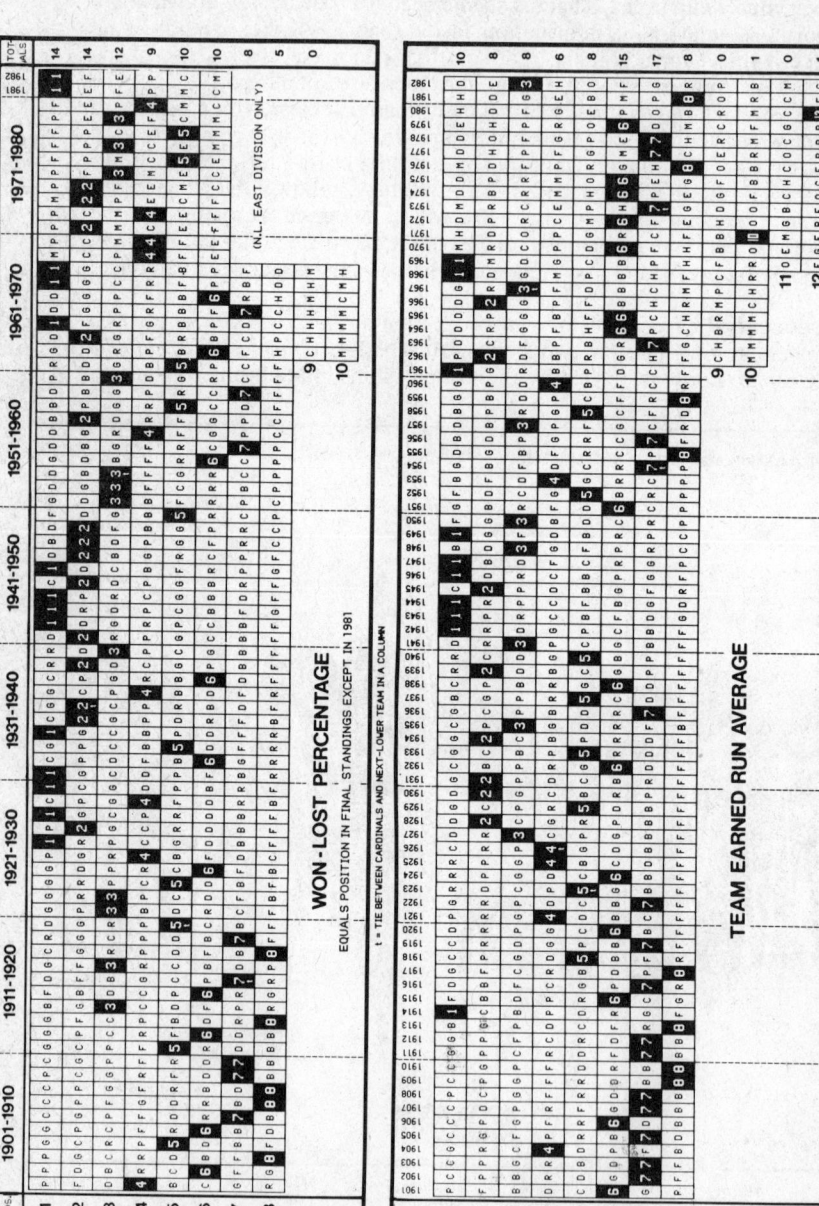

WON-LOST PERCENTAGE

EQUALS POSITION IN FINAL STANDINGS EXCEPT IN 1981

t = TIE BETWEEN CARDINALS AND NEXT-LOWER TEAM IN A COLUMN

(N.L. EAST DIVISION ONLY)

TEAM EARNED RUN AVERAGE

ABBREVIATIONS: B = BRAVES C = CUBS D = DODGERS E = EXPOS F = PHILLIES G = GIANTS H = ASTROS M = METS O = PADRES P = PIRATES R = REDS

Is it a graph or a table? It's really a little of both—these "grables" give all the detailed information of a table with the visual impact of a graph. The black numbered boxes show where the Cardinals finished in these categories in each season. The white lettered boxes show the finish of every other team in the league. Following the black boxes through their pattern in the white field gives a graph-like look at how the Cardinals have fared.

These two grables help demonstrate the old adage that pitching wins pennants. The won-lost percentage pattern closely mirrors that of the earned run average. Also notice that in the last three years, Herzog has

TEAM BATTING AVERAGE

t = TIE BETWEEN CARDINALS AND NEXT-LOWER TEAM IN A COLUMN

TEAM HOME RUNS TOTAL

These two graphs demonstrate forcefully that the Cardinals have *always* been a club of high-average, low-home-run hitters. In the last sixty-two years, the Cards have been in the bottom half of the league in batting average just eleven times. The period in which the Cardinals were in the top half in home runs coincides almost exactly with Branch Rickey's tenure with the club (1917-1942). The drop-off in Cardinal home runs since 1950 is truly startling. It's hardly surprising that no Cardinal has won a league home run title since Johnny Mize in 1940.

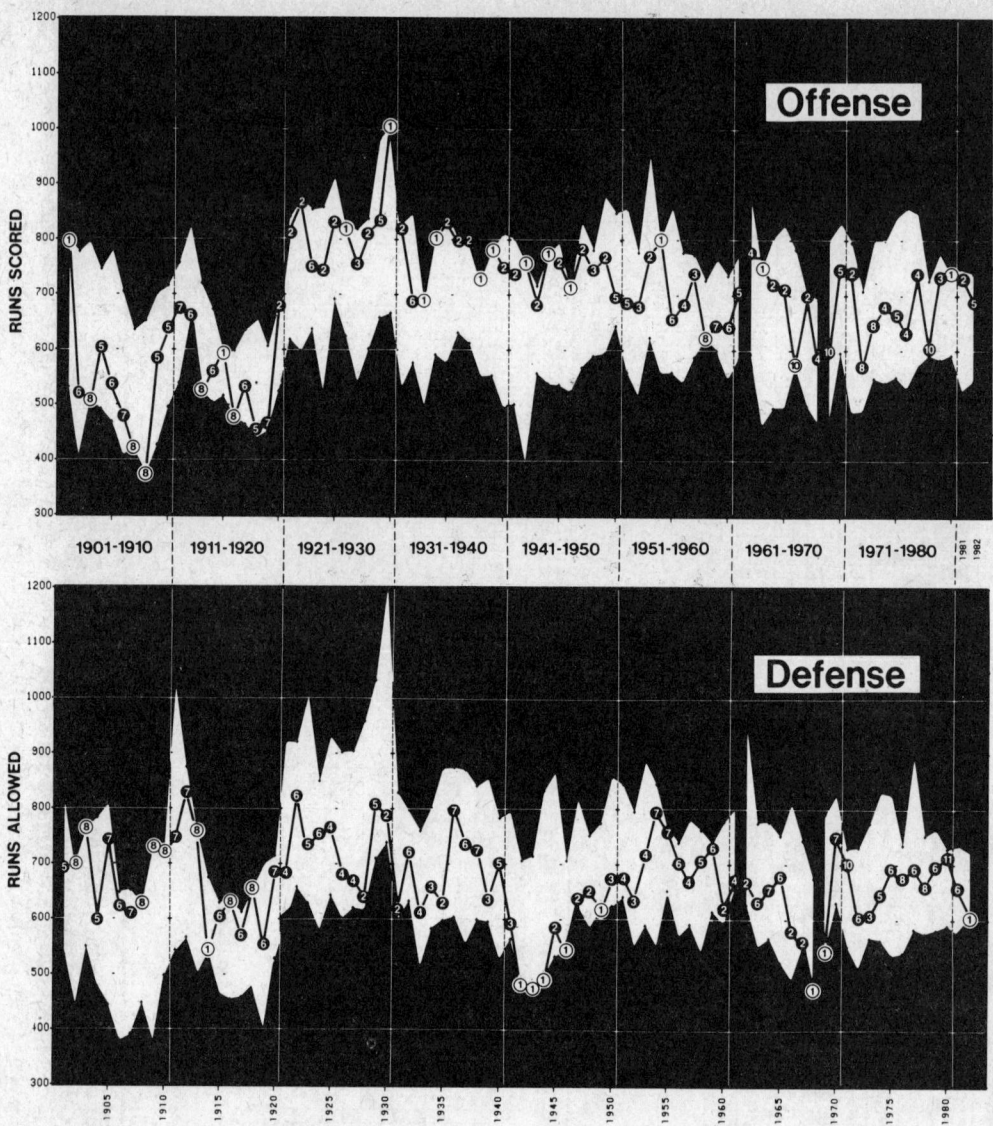

As Bill James has amply argued in his *Baseball Abstracts,* baseball games are measured in
runs. The mark of an offense is the number of runs it scores; the mark of the defense is the
number of runs it allows. (On the Defense graph above, first place in runs allowed is at the
bottom of the range for all teams, represented by the white area on the graph.)
Has any one team ever dominated a league in a category as the Cardinals did in runs from
1933 to 1949? In that period, the Cardinals put together a seventeen-year run of finishing
first, second, or third (just once!) in the league in runs scored.

THE PENNANT RACES

Graphs provide an excellent way of showing the patterns and results of a pennant race. Davenport's method is to chart each team's progress above or below the .500 mark. That way each win is a movement up, each loss a step down. It takes a two-game difference in record over or under .500 to make a one-game difference in the standings: A team with a 10–1 mark, nine games over .500, is one game ahead of one with a 9–2 mark, seven over .500.

The two "close-up" graphs below show two Cardinal pennant victories down the stretch. In 1934 the Gashouse Gang stood six and a half games behind the Giants on September 3. The Giants went 11–13 the rest of the way, while the Cardinals came charging with a 20–5 finish. The steep rise of the Cardinals' line reflects the way the Cardinals rose to battle the Giants, whose five-game losing streak came at the worst possible time.

In 1964, there was a very different kind of race. The Phillies had it all locked up with a six-and-a-half-game lead on September 20, before it all fell apart. They lost ten straight while the Reds were going 7–2 and the Cardinals 9–1 to knock the Phils into third place.

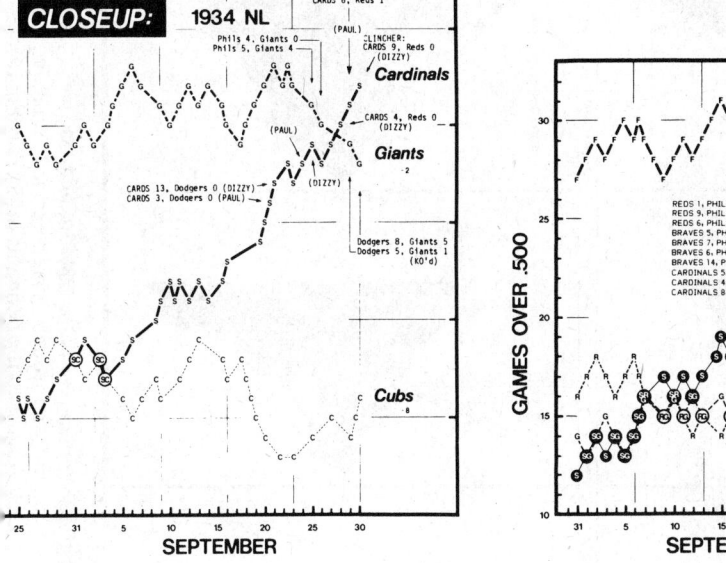

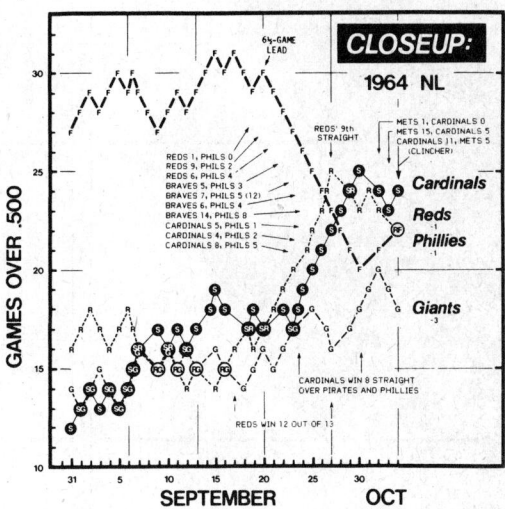

The graphs on the following pages track the Cardinals' standing from start to finish for every season since 1925. The black space shows the range of all the clubs in the league (or division, since 1969).

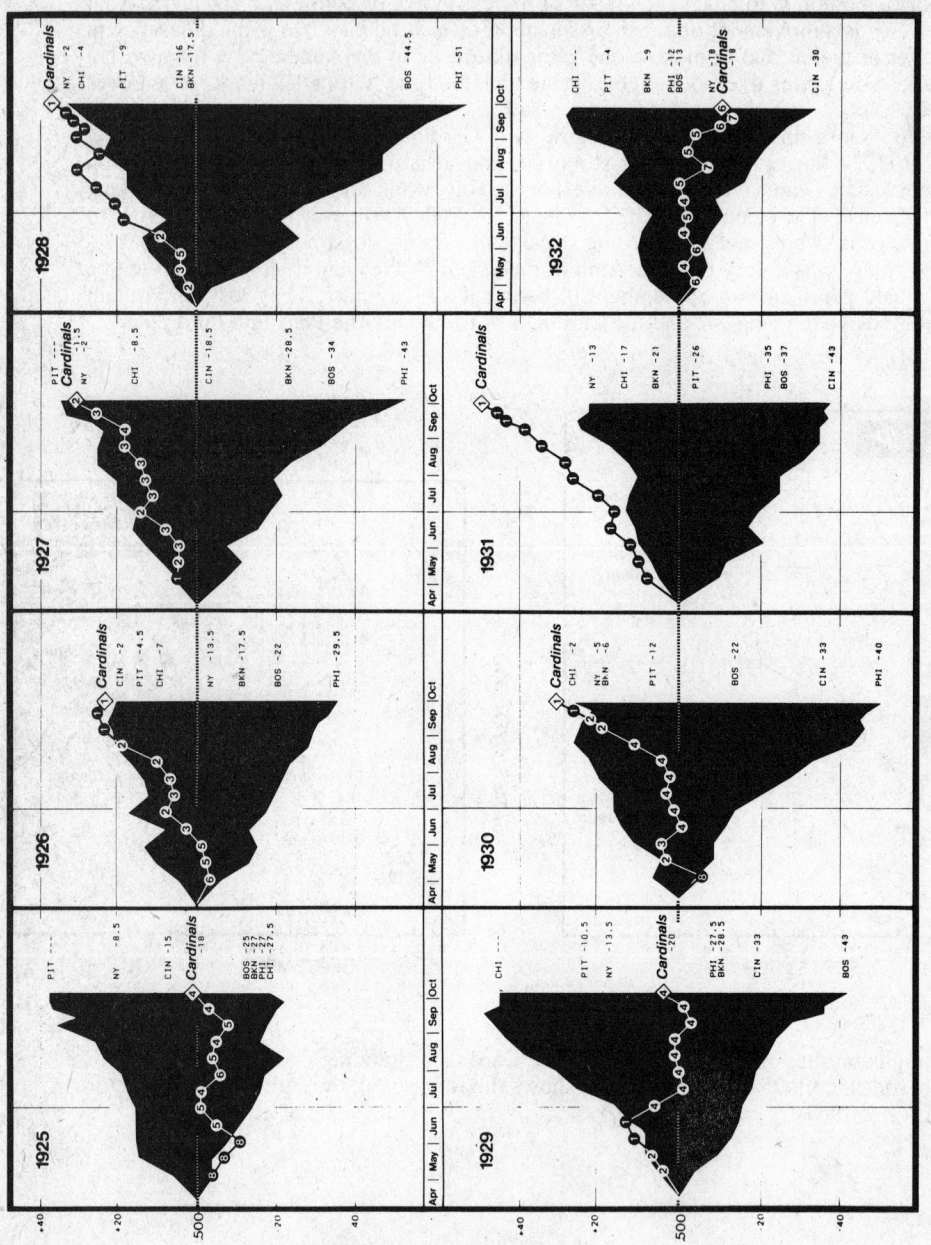

The Cardinals' first four pennants, in '26, '28, '30, and '31, were won in very different ways: in '26, a steady rise to the lead, hanging on through September; in '28, an early lead clung to through the finish; in '30, a sharp rise from early August to the pennant; in '31, a romp from the first week of the season.

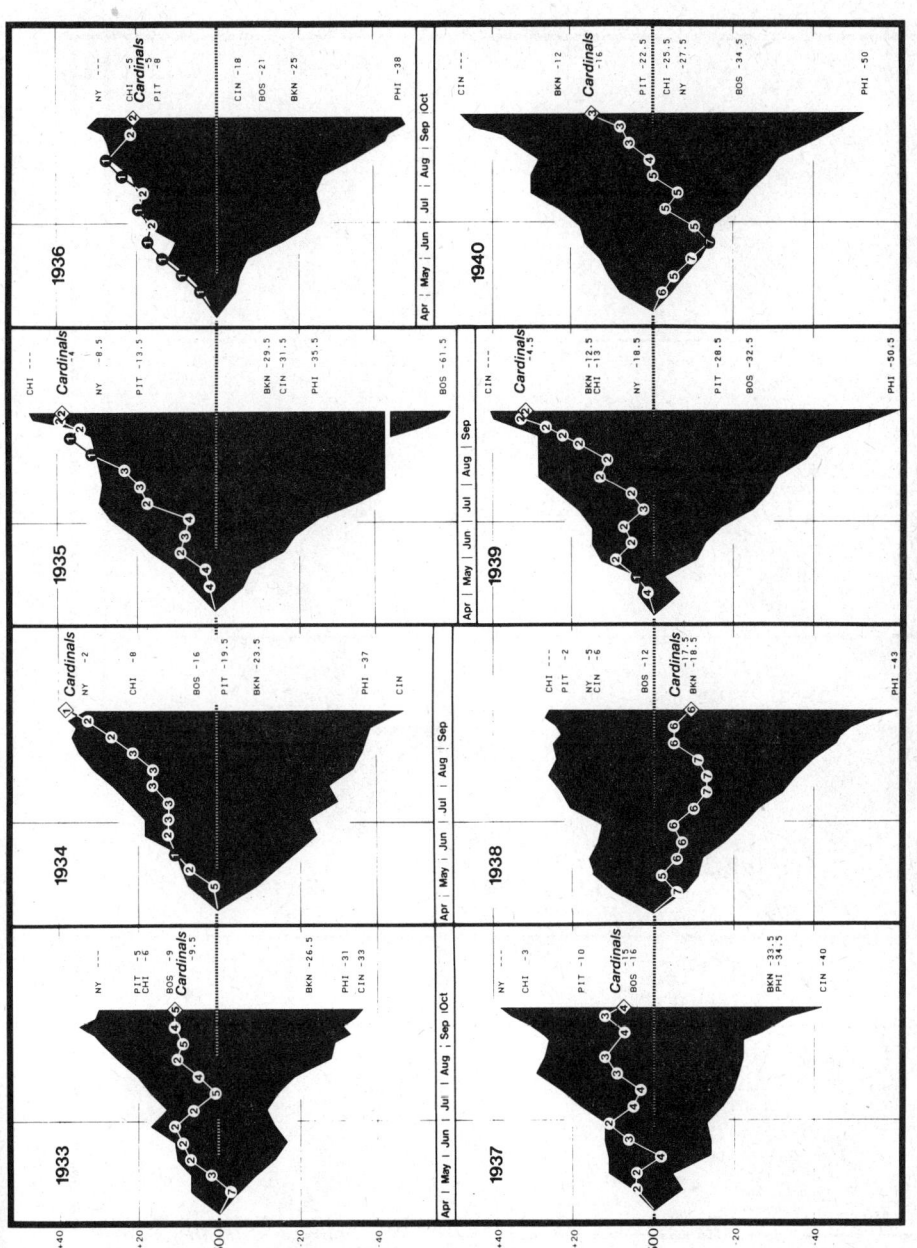

Games over or under .500

Just one pennant, but two near-misses the next two years, and another strong showing in 1939. The break at the bottom of the 1935 graph, condensed for space, indicates how far the Braves fell behind the rest of the league; their actual finish was 77 games below .500.

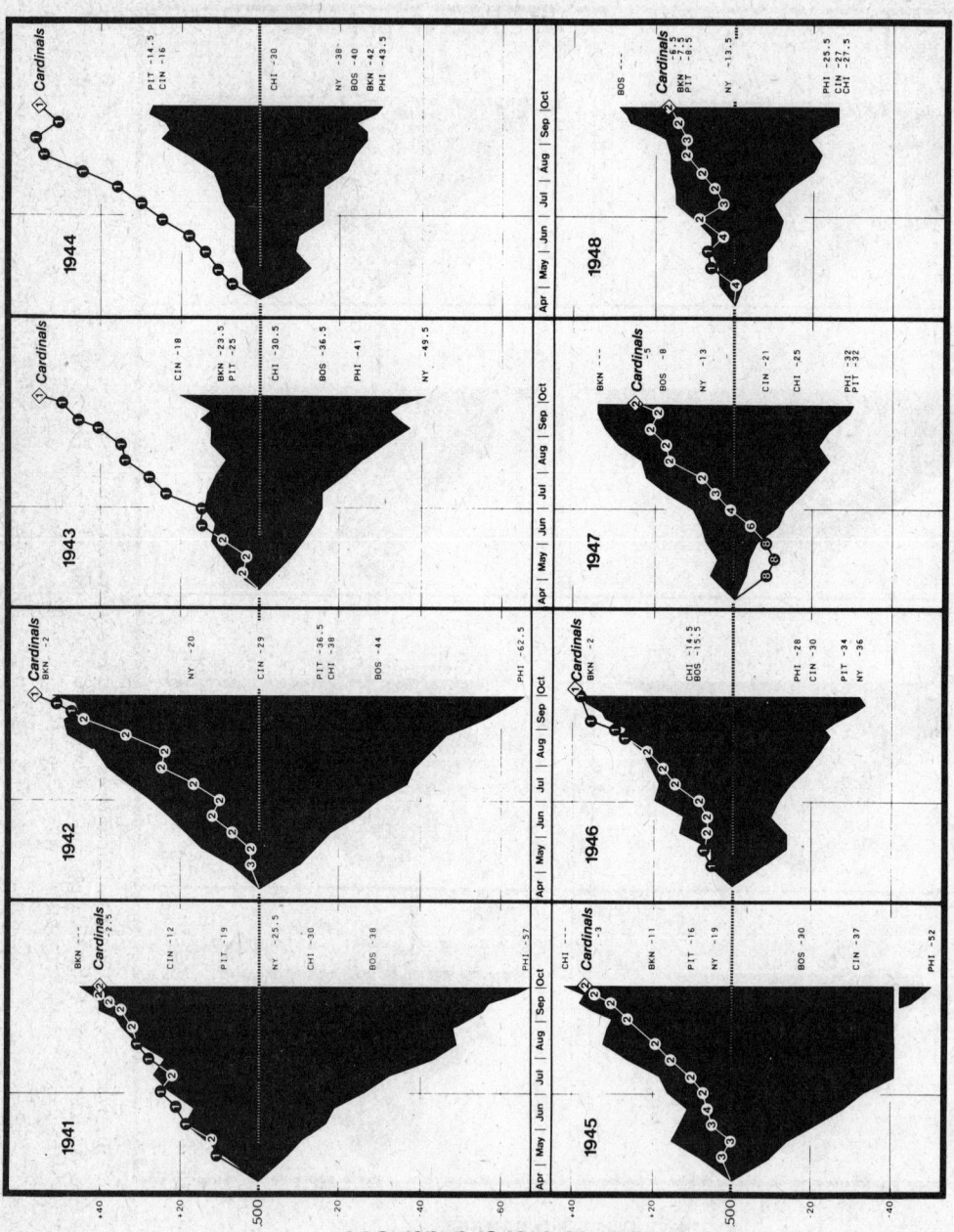

Games over or under .500

The glory years of the Cardinals: four pennants and four seconds in eight years. The 1941 graph shows just what a tight, season-long pennant race there was between the Cardinals and Dodgers, seesawing back and

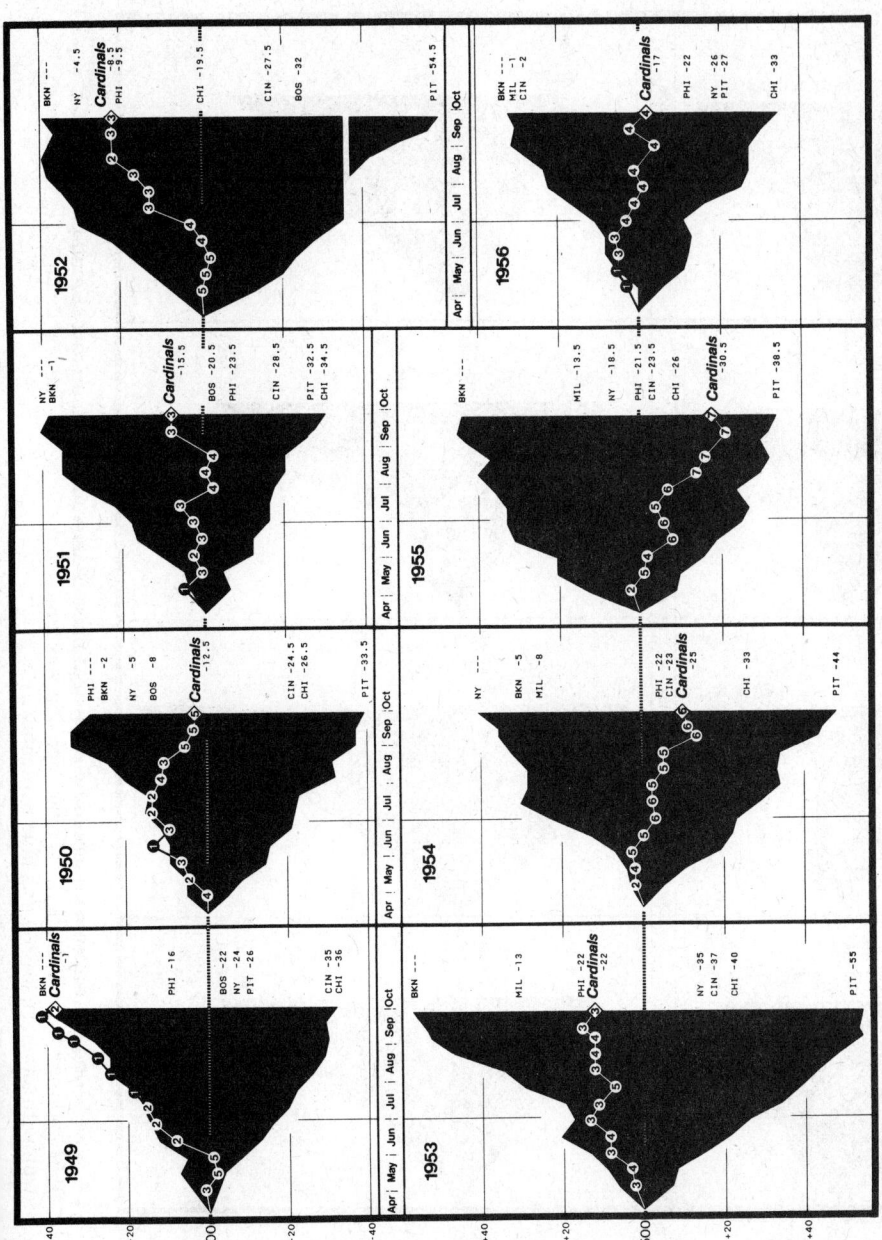

After a loss in 1949, a lean period for St. Louis fans, as the Cardinals were usually out of the pennant race from the start, mired in the middle of the pack.

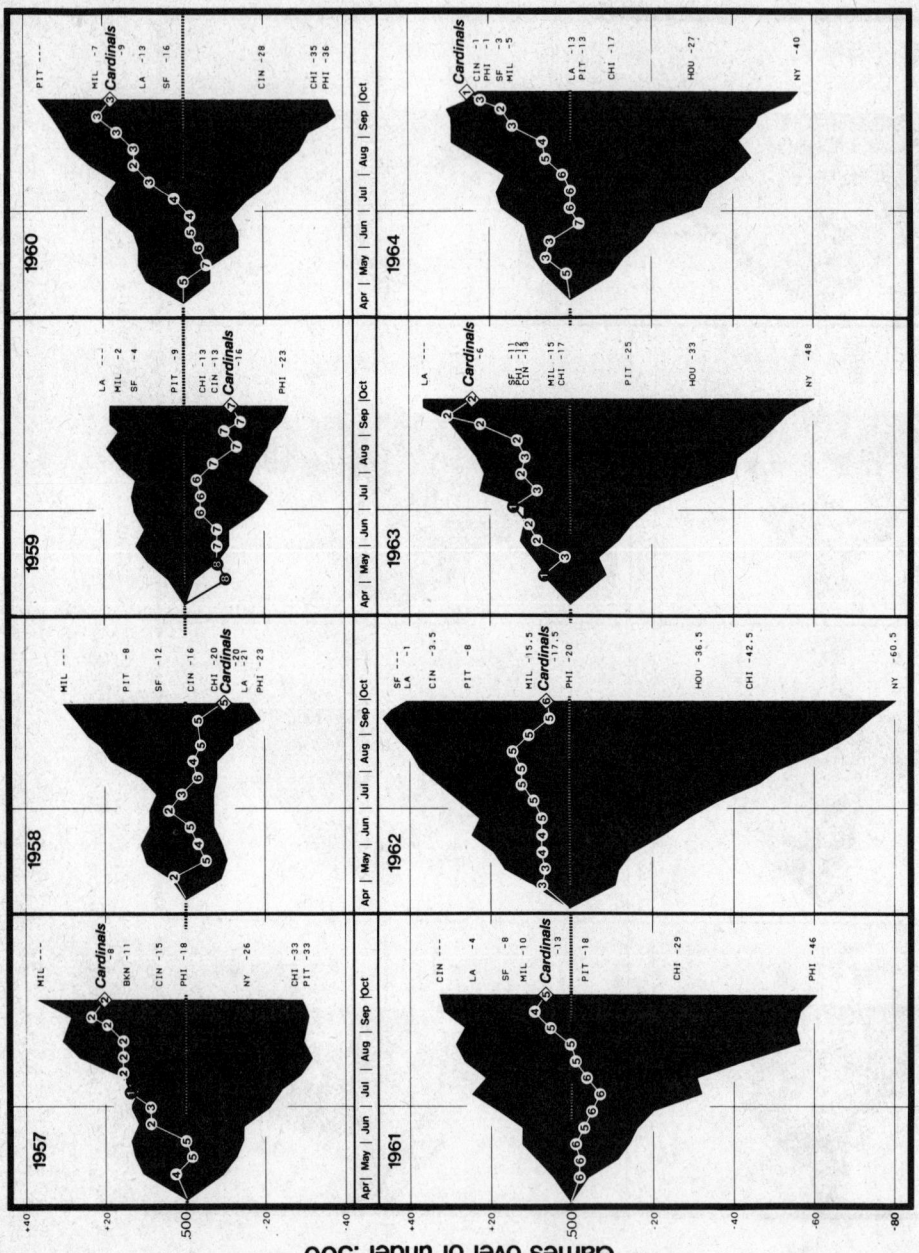

A slow period of awakening, marked by consistent finishes above .500, led up to a second-place finish in 1963 and the title in 1964. The '64 championship was largely a result of the Phillies' collapse, as the Cards won with an unusually low winning percentage.

219

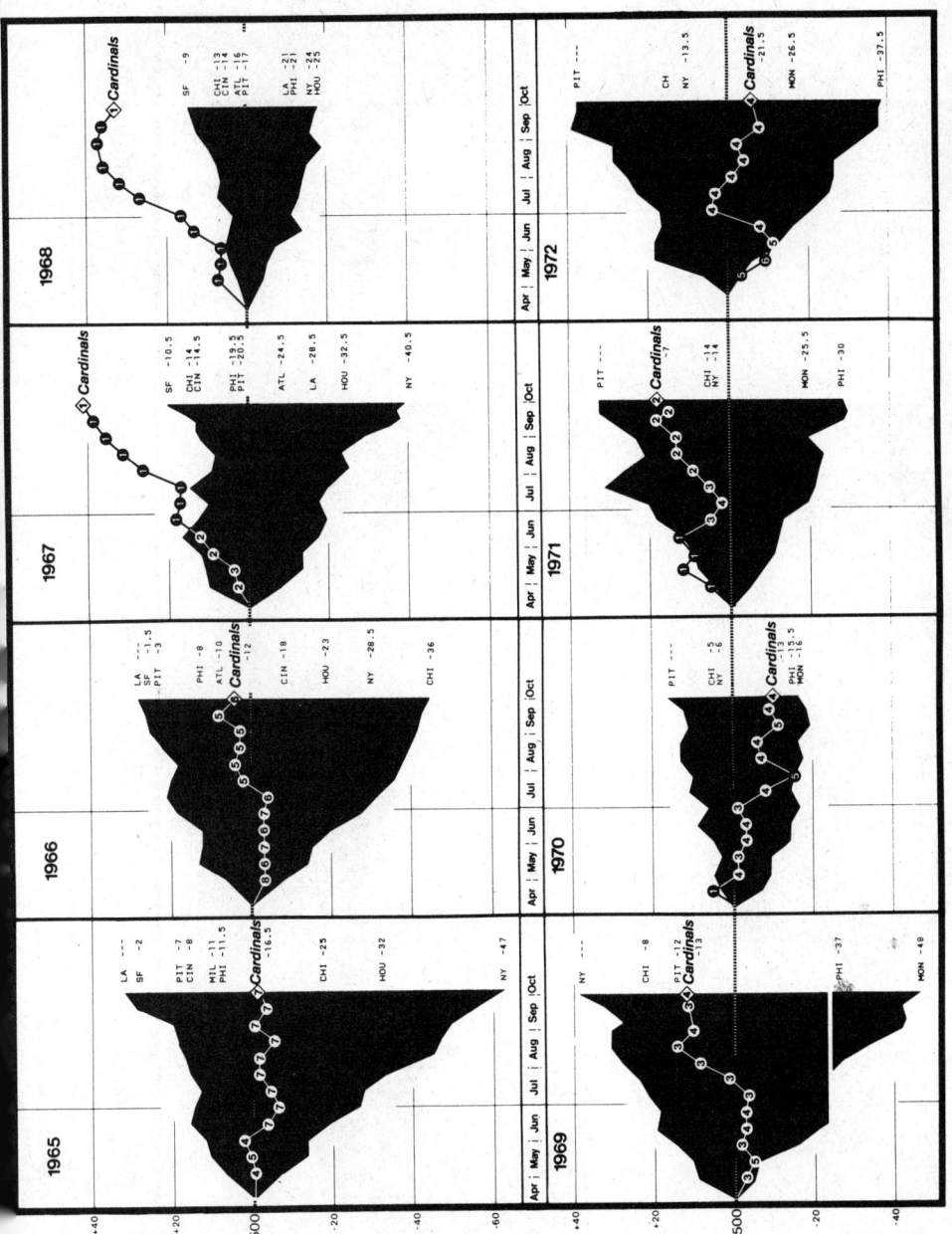

The Cardinals hugged the .500 mark through 1965 and 1966, before exploding to their two big victories in '67 and '68. Besides those two, however, there was little to cheer about, even with the reduced competition of the six-team Eastern Division from 1969 on.

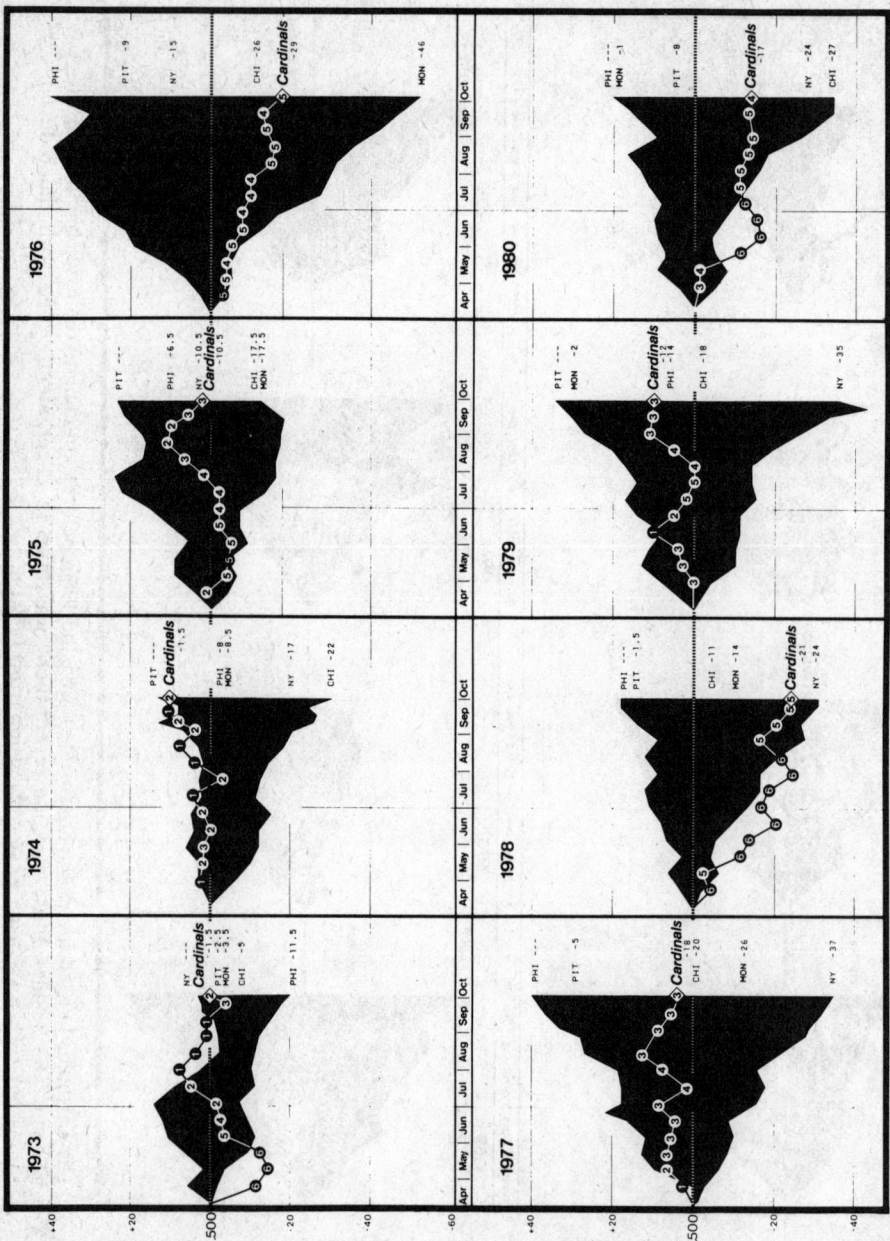

Two pennants were lost by a total of three games in '73 and '74, and the division showed an unusually tight spread from top to bottom. After that, the Cards bounced above and below the .500 mark in alternate seasons through 1980. It was this talented but woefully inconsistent club that Whitey Herzog took over and remade in his image.

1981 TITLE RACES

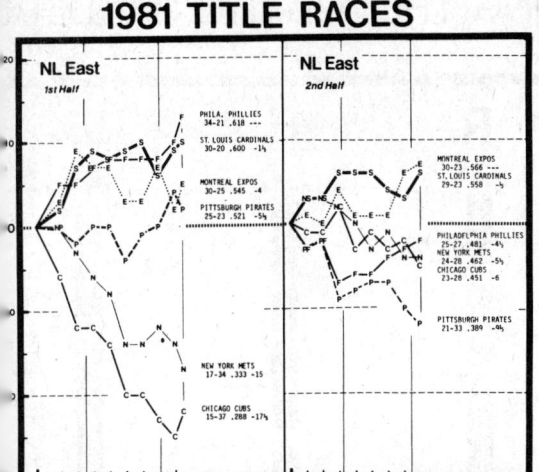

Two views of the 1981 season—the split and the combined. The Cardinals won the unified season, but could not catch either the Phils in the first half or the Expos in the second.

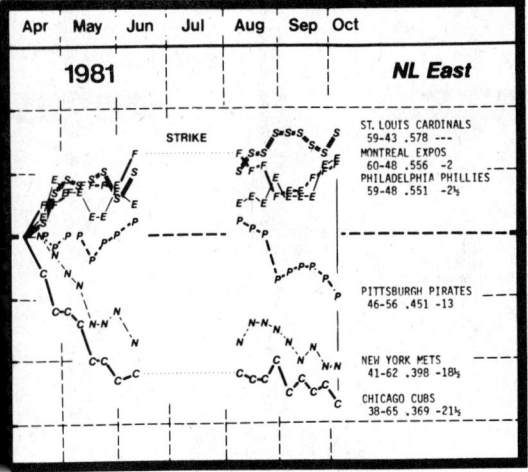

he race for the pennant in 1982. The bi-weekly plotting conceals the fact that the Cardinals actually trailed Philadelphia in arly September before breaking away.

CLIMBING THE ALL-TIME LADDERS

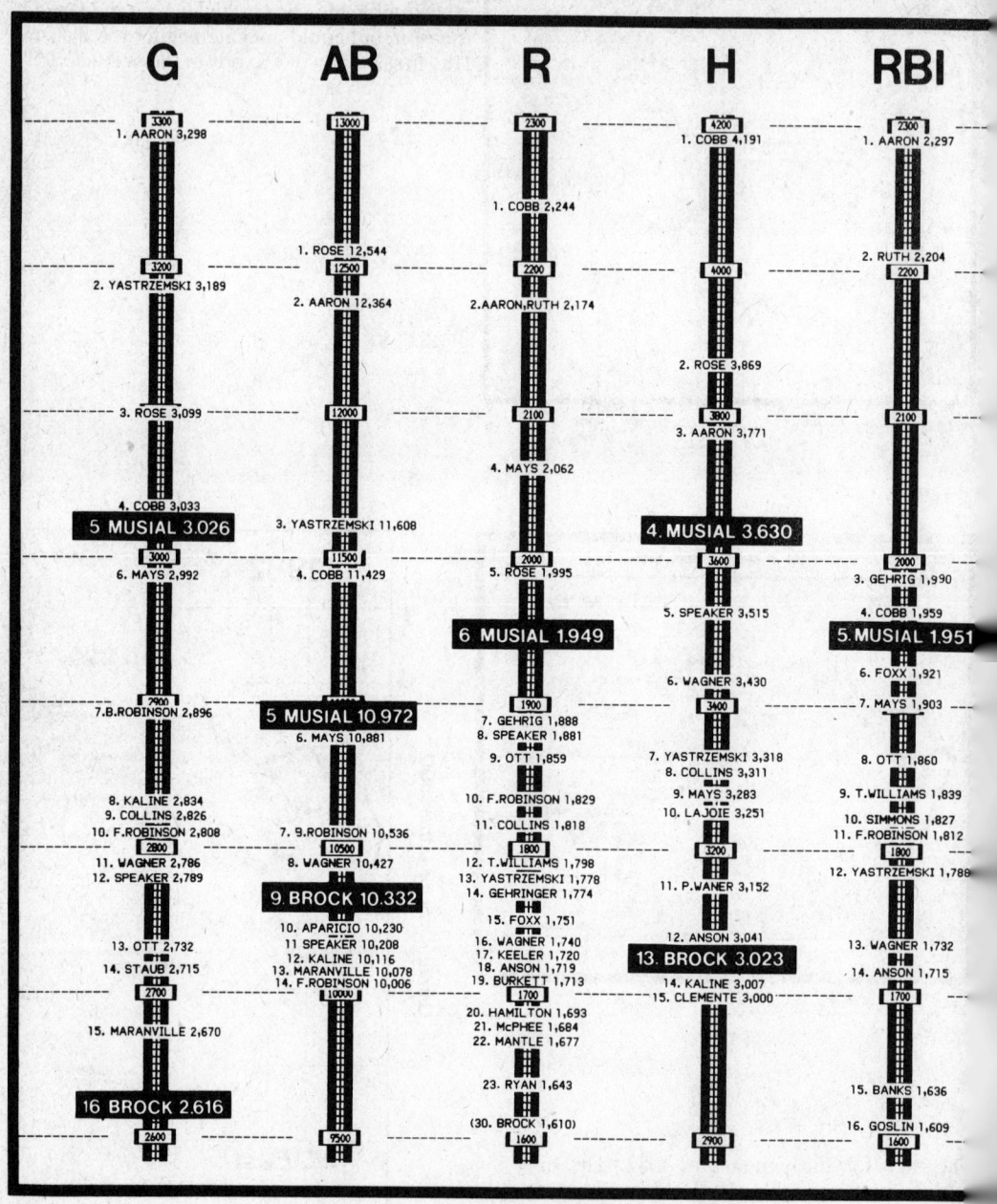

G

3300	
1. AARON 3,298	
1200	
2. YASTRZEMSKI 3,189	
3. ROSE 3,099	
4. COBB 3,033	
5 MUSIAL 3,026	
3000	
6. MAYS 2,992	
2900	
7. B.ROBINSON 2,896	
8. KALINE 2,834	
9. COLLINS 2,826	
10. F.ROBINSON 2,808	
2800	
11. WAGNER 2,786	
12. SPEAKER 2,789	
13. OTT 2,732	
14. STAUB 2,715	
2700	
15. MARANVILLE 2,670	
16 BROCK 2,616	
2600	

AB

13000	
1. ROSE 12,544	
12500	
2. AARON 12,364	
12000	
3. YASTRZEMSKI 11,608	
11500	
4. COBB 11,429	
5 MUSIAL 10,972	
6. MAYS 10,881	
7. 9.ROBINSON 10,536	
10500	
8. WAGNER 10,427	
9. BROCK 10,332	
10. APARICIO 10,230	
11 SPEAKER 10,208	
12. KALINE 10,116	
13. MARANVILLE 10,078	
14. F.ROBINSON 10,006	
10000	
9500	

R

2300	
1. COBB 2,244	
2200	
2.AARON,RUTH 2,174	
2100	
4. MAYS 2,062	
2000	
5. ROSE 1,995	
6 MUSIAL 1,949	
1900	
7. GEHRIG 1,888	
8. SPEAKER 1,881	
9. OTT 1,859	
10. F.ROBINSON 1,829	
11. COLLINS 1,818	
1800	
12. T.WILLIAMS 1,798	
13. YASTRZEMSKI 1,778	
14. GEHRINGER 1,774	
15. FOXX 1,751	
16. WAGNER 1,740	
17. KEELER 1,720	
18. ANSON 1,719	
19. BURKETT 1,713	
1700	
20. HAMILTON 1,693	
21. McPHEE 1,684	
22. MANTLE 1,677	
23. RYAN 1,643	
(30. BROCK 1,610)	
1600	

H

4200	
1. COBB 4,191	
4000	
2. ROSE 3,869	
3800	
3. AARON 3,771	
4. MUSIAL 3,630	
3600	
5. SPEAKER 3,515	
6. WAGNER 3,430	
3400	
7. YASTRZEMSKI 3,318	
8. COLLINS 3,311	
9. MAYS 3,283	
10. LAJOIE 3,251	
3200	
11. P.WANER 3,152	
12. ANSON 3,041	
13. BROCK 3,023	
14. KALINE 3,007	
15. CLEMENTE 3,000	
2900	

RBI

2300	
1. AARON 2,297	
2. RUTH 2,204	
2200	
3. GEHRIG 1,990	
2100	
4. COBB 1,959	
5. MUSIAL 1,951	
6. FOXX 1,921	
7. MAYS 1,903	
8. OTT 1,860	
9. T.WILLIAMS 1,839	
10. SIMMONS 1,827	
11. F.ROBINSON 1,812	
1800	
12. YASTRZEMSKI 1,788	
13. WAGNER 1,732	
14. ANSON 1,715	
1700	
15. BANKS 1,636	
16. GOSLIN 1,609	
1600	

HERE THE CARDINALS' ALL-STARS STAND

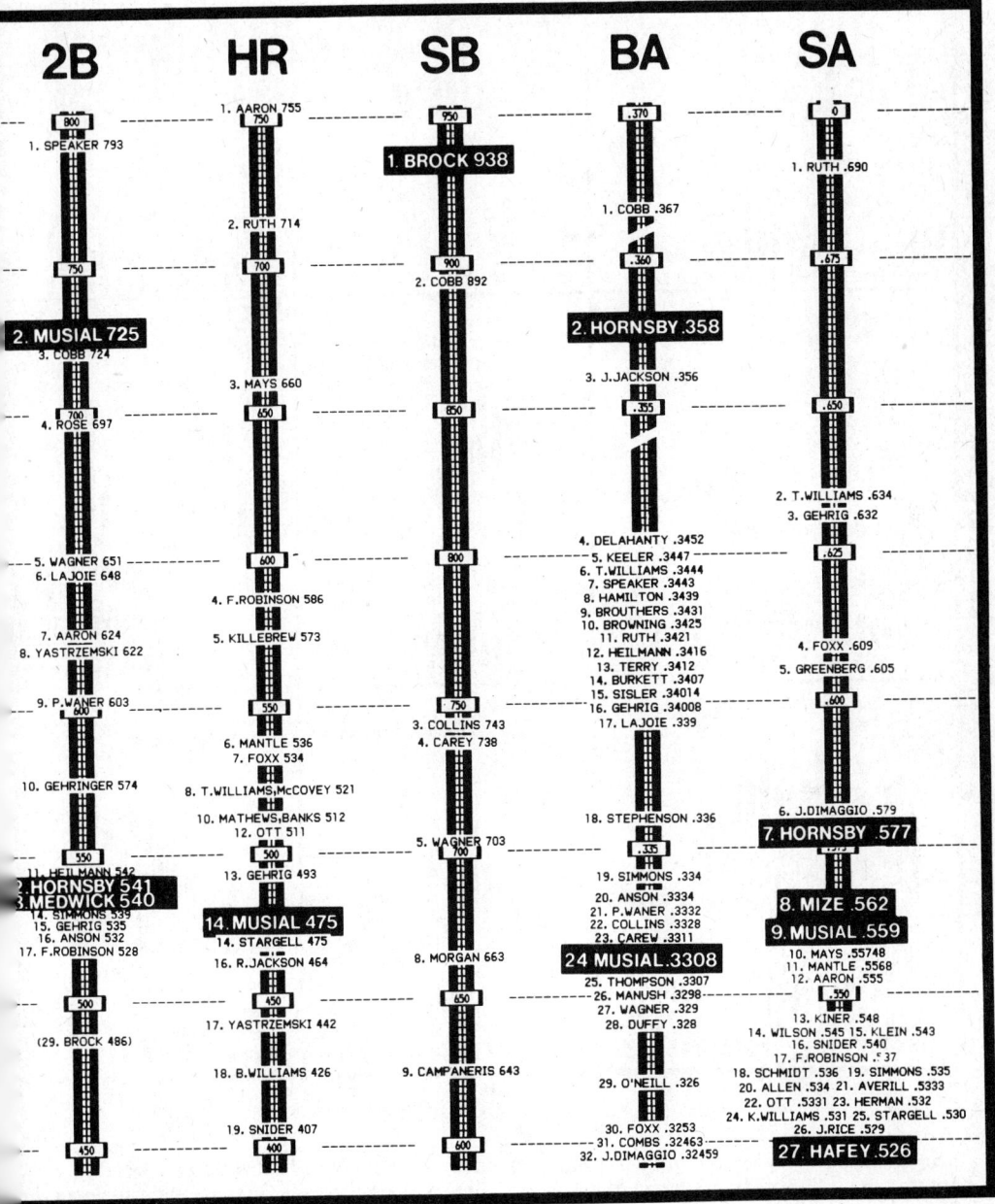

2B

- 800
- 1. SPEAKER 793
- 750
- 2. MUSIAL 725
- 3. COBB 724
- 700
- 4. ROSE 697
- 5. WAGNER 651
- 6. LAJOIE 648
- 7. AARON 624
- 8. YASTRZEMSKI 622
- 9. P.WANER 603
- 600
- 10. GEHRINGER 574
- 550
- 11. HEILMANN 542
- 12. HORNSBY 541
- 13. MEDWICK 540
- 14. SIMMONS 539
- 15. GEHRIG 535
- 16. ANSON 532
- 17. F.ROBINSON 528
- 500
- (29. BROCK 486)
- 450

HR

- 1. AARON 755
- 750
- 2. RUTH 714
- 700
- 3. MAYS 660
- 650
- 4. F.ROBINSON 586
- 5. KILLEBREW 573
- 600
- 550
- 6. MANTLE 536
- 7. FOXX 534
- 8. T.WILLIAMS,McCOVEY 521
- 10. MATHEWS,BANKS 512
- 12. OTT 511
- 500
- 13. GEHRIG 493
- 14. MUSIAL 475
- 14. STARGELL 475
- 16. R.JACKSON 464
- 450
- 17. YASTRZEMSKI 442
- 18. B.WILLIAMS 426
- 19. SNIDER 407
- 400

SB

- 950
- 1. BROCK 938
- 900
- 2. COBB 892
- 850
- 800
- 750
- 3. COLLINS 743
- 4. CAREY 738
- 5. WAGNER 703
- 700
- 8. MORGAN 663
- 650
- 9. CAMPANERIS 643
- 600

BA

- .370
- 1. COBB .367
- .360
- 2. HORNSBY .358
- 3. J.JACKSON .356
- .355
- 4. DELAHANTY .3452
- 5. KEELER .3447
- 6. T.WILLIAMS .3443
- 7. SPEAKER .3439
- 8. HAMILTON .3439
- 9. BROUTHERS .3431
- 10. BROWNING .3425
- 11. RUTH .3421
- 12. HEILMANN .3416
- 13. TERRY .3412
- 14. BURKETT .3407
- 15. SISLER .34014
- 16. GEHRIG .34008
- 17. LAJOIE .339
- 18. STEPHENSON .336
- .335
- 19. SIMMONS .334
- 20. ANSON .3334
- 21. P.WANER .3332
- 22. COLLINS .3328
- 23. CAREW .3311
- 24. MUSIAL .3308
- 25. THOMPSON .3307
- 26. MANUSH .3298
- 27. WAGNER .329
- 28. DUFFY .328
- 29. O'NEILL .326
- 30. FOXX .3253
- 31. COMBS .32463
- 32. J.DIMAGGIO .32459

SA

- 0
- 1. RUTH .690
- .675
- .650
- 2. T.WILLIAMS .634
- 3. GEHRIG .632
- .625
- 4. FOXX .609
- 5. GREENBERG .605
- .600
- 6. J.DIMAGGIO .579
- 7. HORNSBY .577
- 8. MIZE .562
- 9. MUSIAL .559
- 10. MAYS .55748
- 11. MANTLE .5568
- 12. AARON .555
- .550
- 13. KINER .548
- 14. WILSON .545 15. KLEIN .543
- 16. SNIDER .540
- 17. F.ROBINSON .537
- 18. SCHMIDT .536 19. SIMMONS .535
- 20. ALLEN .534 21. AVERILL .5333
- 22. OTT .5331 23. HERMAN .532
- 24. K.WILLIAMS .531 25. STARGELL .530
- 26. J.RICE .529
- 27. HAFEY .526

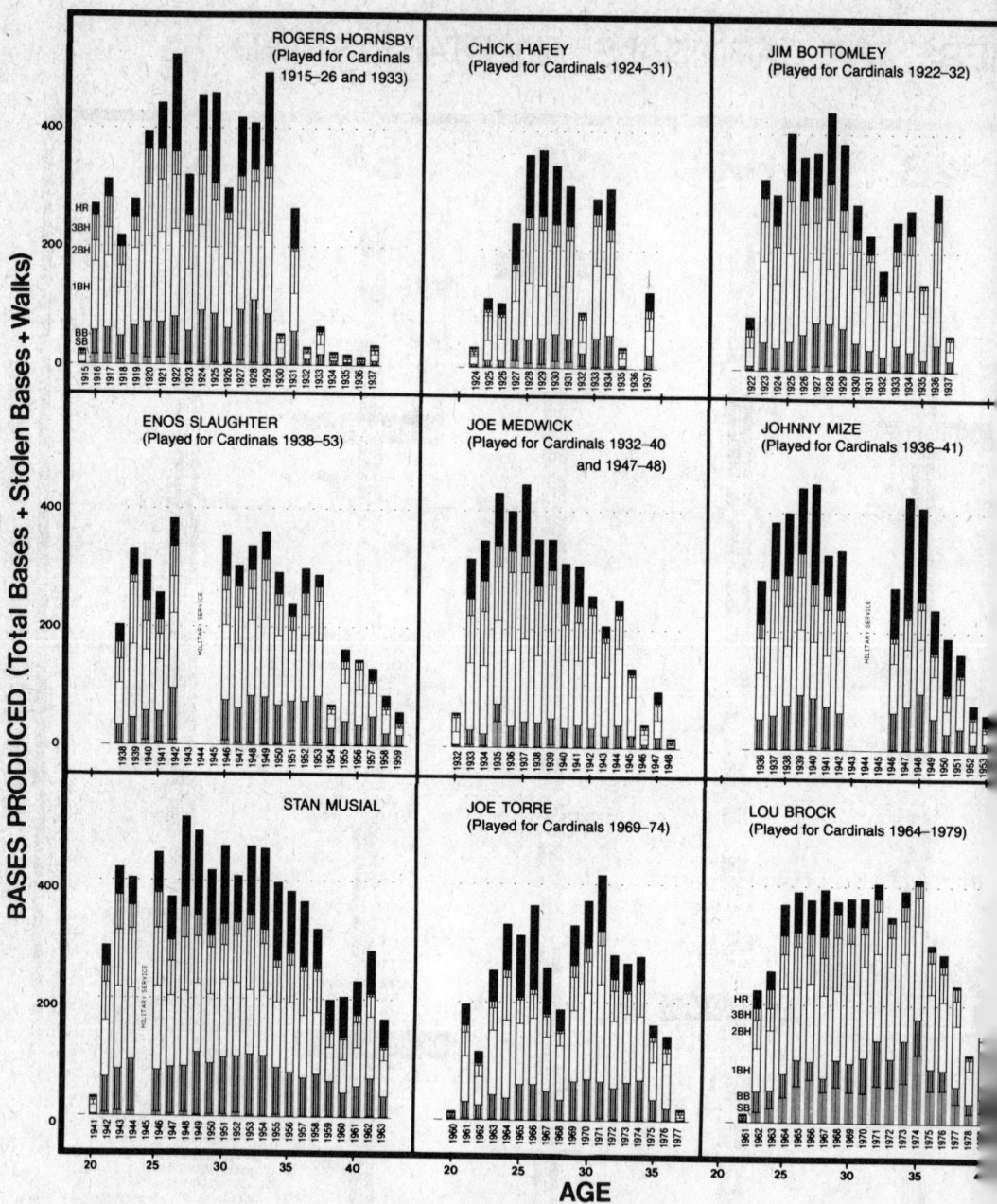

How do you compare the offensive statistics of great ballplayers? How do you weigh the power of Johnny Mize against the base-stealing of Lou Brock? One useful way is to examine Bases Produced: Total Bases, Stolen Bases, and Walks all treated equally. These offensive graphs show how the Bases Produced totals for each player, year-by-year, stack up. Some valuable patterns emerge: while Brock never reached the heights scaled by Hornsby or Mize, his ability to do so many things offensively gave him a remarkably consistent pattern throughout his career. And the graphs of Bottomley, Hornsby, Hafey, and Medwick are a testament to Branch Rickey's ability to get the best years out of a ballplayer's career, and then trade him away while his market value was still high.

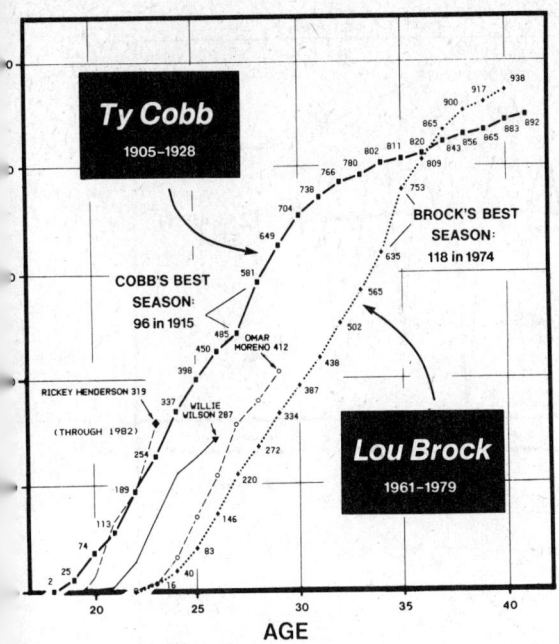

The pursuit of a legend: Lou Brock's chase of Ty Cobb's career stolen base record. Brock's pattern is unusual in that he picked up his pace as he got older; Cobb's line shows a more normal tailing off. And the career lines of Willie Wilson and Omar Moreno are beginning to look like that of Cobb, but Rickey Henderson is building up such a big lead over Brock at comparable ages that he can probably fall off quite a bit and still break Brock's career record.

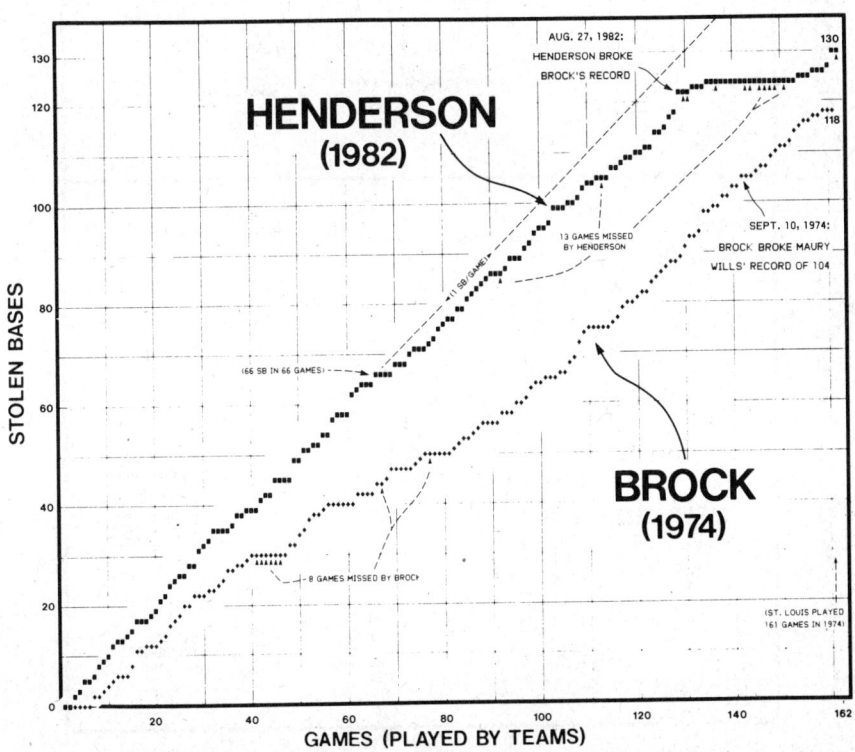

Lou Brock's other record, his 118 stolen bases, wasn't unbreakable for long. Rickey Henderson was ahead of his pace from the first game of the season, and established a serious shot at an unbelievable 162 steals in a season before falling off, as the toll of a season's pounding began to show on his legs. After breaking Brock's record, Henderson stole just two bases in Oakland's next twenty-four games, ten of which he sat out. A steal-a-game pace is the next goal.

GIBSON IN 1968

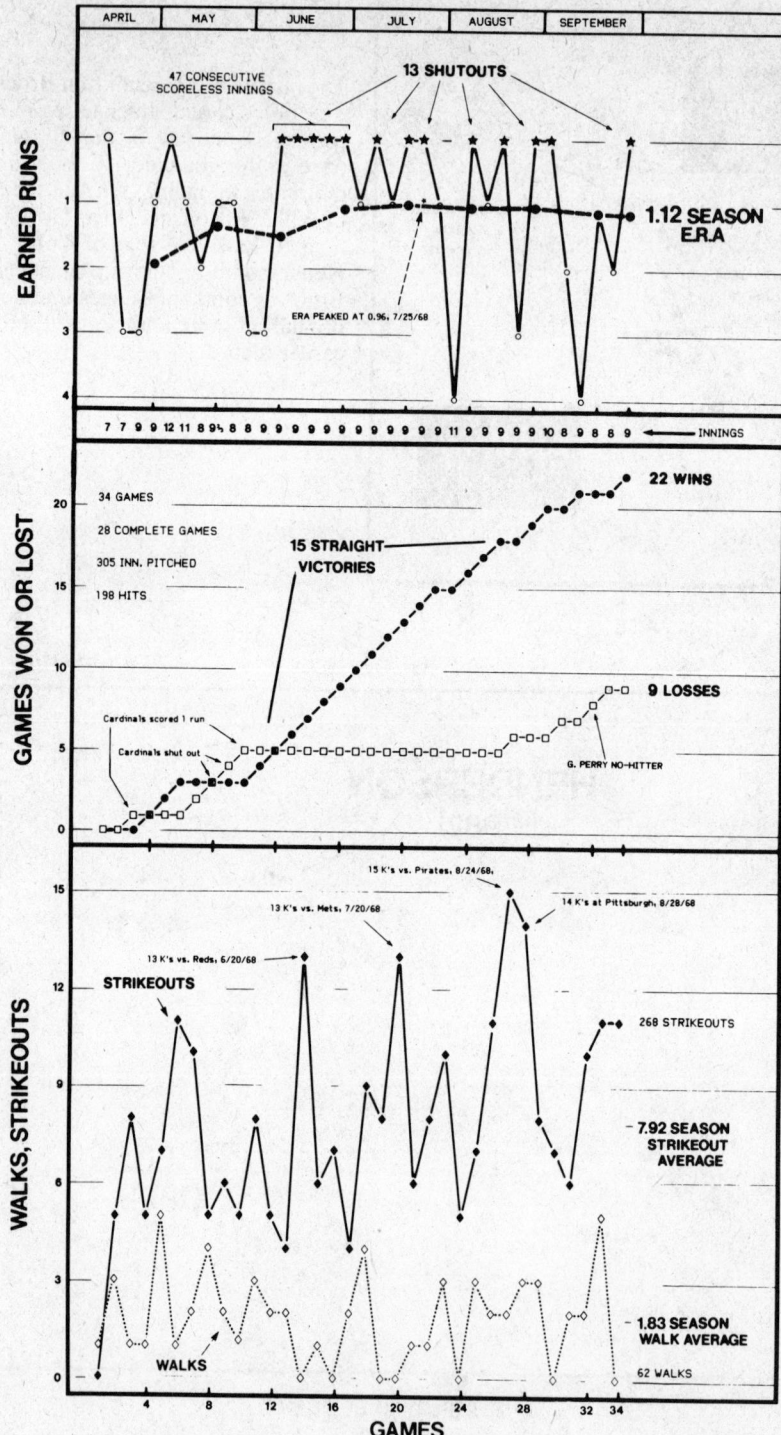

Gibson's 1968 season deserves game-by-game treatment. He never allowed more than four earned runs in a game, holding opponents to none or one in 21 of 34 starts. Of his nine losses, five were by one run, including Gaylord Perry's 1–0 no-hitter in September. From June 2 to July 30, Gibson pitched twelve consecutive complete game victories, allowing a total of six runs in 108 innings, lowering his season's ERA to a hallucinatory 0.96.

Player Register

The Player Register is an alphabetical listing of every man who has played in the major leagues and played or managed for the St. Louis Cardinals from 1892 through today, except those players who were primarily pitchers. However, pitchers who pinch-hit and played in other positions for a total of 25 games or more are listed in this Player Register. Included are facts about the players and their year-by-year batting records and their lifetime totals of League Championship Series and World Series.

Much of this information has never been compiled, especially for the period 1876 through 1919. For certain other years some statistics are still missing or incomplete. Research in this area is still in progress, and the years that lack complete information are indicated. In fact, all information and abbreviations that may appear unfamiliar are explained in the sample format presented below. John Doe, the player used in the sample, is fictitious and serves only to illustrate the information.

	G	AB	H	2B	3B	HR	HR %	R	RBI	BB	SO	SB	BA	SA	Pinch Hit AB	Pinch Hit H	G by POS

John Doe

DOE, JOHN LEE (Slim)
Played as John Cherry part of 1900.
Born John Lee Doughnut.   Brother of Bill Doe.
B. Jan. 1,1850, New York, N. Y.   D. July 1, 1855, New York, N. Y.
Manager.1908-15.
Hall of Fame 1946.

BR TR 6'2"   165 lbs.
BB 1884 BL 1906

	G	AB	H	2B	3B	HR	HR %	R	RBI	BB	SO	SB	BA	SA	PH AB	PH H	G by POS
1884 STL U	125	435	121	18	1	3	0.7	44		37	42	7	.278	.345	9	2	SS-99, P-26
1885 LOU AA	155	547	138	22	3	3	0.6	50	58	42	48	8	.252	.320	8	4	SS-115, P-40
1886 CLE N	147	485	134	38	5	0	0.0	66	54	48	50	8	.276	.375	7	1	SS-107, P-40
1887 BOS N	129	418	117	15	3	1	0.2	38	52	32	37	1	.280	.337	1	0	SS-102, P-27
1888 NY N	144	506	135	26	2	6	1.2	50	63	43	50	1	.267	.362	10	8	SS-105, P-39
1889 3 teams	DET N (10G – .300)				PIT N (32G – .241)				PHI N (41G – .364)								
" total	83	237	75	31	16	7	3.0	90	42	25	35	3	.316	.671	6	3	SS-61, P-22
1890 NY P	123	430	119	27	5	1	0.2	63	59	39	39	2	.277	.370	12	10	SS-85, P-38
1900 CHI N	146	498	116	29	4	3	0.6	51	46	59	53	1	.233	.325	13	8	SS-111, P-35
1901 NY N	149	540	147	19	6	4	0.7	57	74	49	58	3	.272	.352	23	15	SS-114, P-35
1906 STL N	144	567	143	26	4	4	0.7	70	43	37	54	1	.252	.333	7	1	SS-113, P-31
1907	134	515	140	31	2	5	1.0	61	70	37	42	0	.272	.369	13	8	SS-97, P-37
1908	106	372	92	10	2	4	1.1	36	40	4	55	1	.247	.317	1	0	SS-105, P-1
1914 CHI F	6	6	0	0	0	0	0.0	0	0	0	0	0	.000	.000	0	0	P-6
1915 NY A	1	0	0	0	0	0	–	0	0	0	0	0	–	–	0	0	SS-1
14 yrs.	1592	5556	1927	292 (4th)	53	41	0.7	676	601	452	564	36	.266	.360	110	60	SS-1215, P-377
3 yrs.	384	1454	375	67	8	13	0.9	167	153	78	151	2	.258	.342	21 (6th)	9	SS-315, P-96

LEAGUE CHAMPIONSHIP SERIES

	G	AB	H	2B	3B	HR	HR %	R	RBI	BB	SO	SB	BA	SA	PH AB	PH H	G by POS
1901 NY N	3	14	5	2	0	3	21.4	3	7	0	1	0	.357	1.143	0	0	OF-3

WORLD SERIES

	G	AB	H	2B	3B	HR	HR %	R	RBI	BB	SO	SB	BA	SA	PH AB	PH H	G by POS
1901 NY N	7	28	9	1	0	6	21.4	12	14	3	4	0	.321	1.000	0	0	SS-5, P-2
1906 STL N	5	10	5	1	0	1	10.0	3	2	0	2	0	.500	.900	2	0	P-4, SS-1
2 yrs.	12	38	14	2	0 (5th)	7	18.4	15	16 (9th)	3	6	0	.368	.974	2	0	SS-6, P-6

PLAYER INFORMATION

John Doe	This shortened version of the player's full name is the name most familiar to the fans. All players in this section are alphabetically arranged by the last name part of this name.
DOE, JOHN LEE	Player's full name. The arrangement is last name first, then first and middle name(s).
(Slim)	Player's nickname. Any name or names appearing in parentheses indicates a nickname.

The player's main batting and throwing style. Doe, for instance, batted and threw righthanded. The information listed directly below the main batting information indicates that at various times in a player's career he changed his batting style. The "BB" for Doe in 1884 means he was a switch hitter that year, and the "BL" means he batted lefthanded in 1906. For the years that are not shown it can be assumed that Doe batted right, as his main batting information indicates.

BR TR
BB 1884
BL 1906

Player's height.

6'2"

Player's average playing weight.

165 lbs

The player at one time in his major league career played under another name and can be found only in box scores or newspaper stories under that name.

Played as John Cherry part of 1900

The name the player was given at birth. (For the most part, the player never used this name while playing in the major leagues, but, if he did, it would be listed as "played as," which is explained above under the heading "Played as John Cherry part of 1900.")

Born John Lee Doughnut

The player's brother. (Relatives indicated here are fathers, sons, brothers, grandfathers, and grandsons who played or managed in the major leagues and the National Association.)

Brother of Bill Doe

Date and place of birth.   B. Jan. 1, 1850,

Date and place of death. (For those players who are   New York, N.Y.
listed simply as "deceased," it means that, although no   D. July 1, 1955,
certification of death or other information is presently   New York, N.Y.
available, it is reasonably certain they are dead.)

Doe also served as a major league manager. All men who   Manager
were managers for the Cardinals can be found in the   1908–5
Manager Register, where their complete managerial record is shown.

Doe was elected to the Baseball Hall of Fame in 1946.   Hall of Fame
                                                          1946

COLUMN HEADINGS INFORMATION

G	AB	H	2B	3B	HR	HR %	R	RBI	BB	SO	SB	BA	SA	Pinch Hit AB H	G by POS

G — Games
AB — At Bats
H — Hits
2B — Doubles
3B — Triples
HR — Home Runs
HR % — Home Run Percentage (the number of home runs per 100 times at bat)
R — Runs Scored
RBI — Runs Batted In
BB — Bases on Balls
SO — Strikeouts
SB — Stolen Bases
BA — Batting Average
SA — Slugging Average

Pinch Hit
AB — Pinch Hit At Bats
H — Pinch Hits

G by POS — Games by Position. (All fielding positions a man played within the given year are shown. The position where the most games were played is listed first. Any man who pitched, as Doe did, is listed also in the alphabetically arranged Pitcher Register, where his complete pitching record can be found.) If no fielding positions are shown in a particular year, it means the player only pinch-hit, pinch-ran, or was a "designated hitter."

TEAM AND LEAGUE INFORMATION

Doe's record has been exaggerated so that his playing career spans all the years of the six different major leagues. Directly alongside the year and team information is the symbol for the league:

N National League (1876 to date)
A American League (1901 to date)
F Federal League (1914–15)
AA American Association (1882–91)
P Players' League (1890)
U Union Association (1884)

STL—The abbreviation of the city in which the team played. Doe, for example, played for St. Louis in 1884. All teams in this section are listed by an abbreviation of the city in which the team played. The abbreviations follow:

ALT	Altoona		NWK	Newark
ATL	Atlanta		NY	New York
BAL	Baltimore		OAK	Oakland
BOS	Boston		PHI	Philadelphia
BKN	Brooklyn		PIT	Pittsburgh
BUF	Buffalo		PRO	Providence
CAL	California		RIC	Richmond
CHI	Chicago		ROC	Rochester
CIN	Cincinnati		SD	San Diego
CLE	Cleveland		SEA	Seattle
COL	Columbus		SF	San Francisco
DET	Detroit		STL	St. Louis
HAR	Hartford		STP	St. Paul
HOU	Houston		SYR	Syracuse
IND	Indianapolis		TEX	Texas
KC	Kansas City		TOL	Toledo
LA	Los Angeles		TOR	Toronto
LOU	Louisville		TRO	Troy
MIL	Milwaukee		WAS	Washington
MIN	Minnesota		WIL	Wilmington
MON	Montreal		WOR	Worcester

Three franchises in the history of major league baseball changed their location during the season. These teams are designated by the first letter of the two cities they represented. They are:

B-B   Brooklyn-Baltimore (American Association, 1890)
C-M   Cincinnati-Milwaukee (American Association, 1891)
C-P   Chicago-Pittsburgh (Union Association, 1884)

Blank space appearing beneath a team and league indicates that the team and league are the same. Doe, for example, played for St. Louis in the National League from 1906 through 1908.

3 Teams Total. Indicates a player played for more than one team in the same year. Doe played for three teams in 1889. The number of games he played and his batting average for each team are also shown. Directly beneath this line, following the word "total," is Doe's combined record for all three teams for 1889.

Total Playing Years. This information, which appears as the first item on the player's lifetime total line, indicates the total number of years in which he played at least one game. Doe, for example, played in at least one game for fourteen years.

Cardinals Playing Years. This information, which appears as the first item on the player's Cardinals career total line, indicates the total number of years in which he played at least one game for the Cardinals.

STATISTICAL INFORMATION

League Leaders. Statistics that appear in bold-faced print indicate the player led his league that year in a particular statistical category. Doe, for example, led the National League in doubles in 1889. When there is a tie for league lead, the figures for all the men who tied are shown in boldface.

All-Time Single Season Leaders. Indicated by the small number that appears next to the statistic. Doe, for example, is shown with a small number "1" next to his doubles total in 1889. This means he is first on the all-time major league list for hitting the most doubles in a single season. All players who tied for first are also shown by the same number.

Lifetime Leaders. Indicated by the figure that appears beneath the line showing the player's lifetime totals. Doe has a "4th" shown below his lifetime triples total. This means that, lifetime, Doe ranks fourth among major league players for hitting the most triples. Once again, only the top ten are indicated, and players who are tied receive the same number.

Unavailable Information. Any time a blank space is shown in a particular statistical column, such as in Doe's 1884 RBI total, it indicates the information was unavailable or incomplete.

Meaningless Averages. Indicated by use of a dash (—). In the case of Doe, a dash is shown for his 1915 batting average. This means that, although he played one game, he had no official at bats. A batting average of .000 would mean he had at least one at bat with no hits.

Cardinals Career Totals. The statistical line appearing below Doe's major league career totals indicates his totals for his career with the St. Louis Cardinals. In Doe's case, the totals are for the years 1906—1908.

Cardinals Lifetime Leaders. Indicated by the figure that appears beneath his Cardinals career total. Doe has a "6th" shown below his Cardinal career pinch hit at bats total. This means that he ranks sixth among Cardinals in that category, counting only his years with the club.

World Series Lifetime Leaders. Indicated by the figure that appears beneath the player's lifetime World Series totals. Doe has a "5th" shown below his lifetime home run total. This means that, lifetime, Doe ranks fifth among major league players for hitting the most home runs in total World Series play. Players who tied for a position in the top ten are shown by the same number, so that, if two men tied for fourth and fifth place, the appropriate information for both men would be followed by the small number "4," and the next man would be considered sixth in the ranking. Cardinals career totals are not provided for post-season play; the indicated totals are for Doe's entire career.

	G	AB	H	2B	3B	HR	HR %	R	RBI	BB	SO	SB	BA	SA	Pinch Hit AB	Pinch Hit H	G by POS

Ody Abbott

ABBOTT, ODY CLEON (Toby)
B. Sept. 5, 1886, New Eagle, Pa.   D. Apr. 13, 1933, Washington, D. C.
BR TR 6'2"   180 lbs.

	G	AB	H	2B	3B	HR	HR %	R	RBI	BB	SO	SB	BA	SA	PH AB	PH H	G by POS
1910 STL N	22	70	13	2	1	0	0.0	2	6	6	20	3	.186	.243	1	0	OF-21

Buster Adams

ADAMS, ELVIN CLARK
B. June 24, 1915, Trinidad, Colo.
BR TR 6'   180 lbs.

	G	AB	H	2B	3B	HR	HR %	R	RBI	BB	SO	SB	BA	SA	PH AB	PH H	G by POS
1939 STL N	2	1	0	0	0	0	0.0	1	0	0	0	0	.000	.000	1	0	
1943 2 teams	STL N (8G – .091)			PHI N (111G – .256)													
" Total	119	429	108	15	7	4	0.9	49	39	43	71	2	.252	.347	2	1	OF-113
1944 PHI N	151	584	165	35	3	17	2.9	86	64	74	74	2	.283	.440	0	0	OF-151
1945 2 teams	PHI N (14G – .232)			STL N (140G – .292)													
" Total	154	634	182	29	1	22	3.5	104	109	62	80	3	.287	.440	0	0	OF-153
1946 STL N	81	173	32	6	0	5	2.9	21	22	29	27	3	.185	.306	21	6	OF-58
1947 PHI N	69	182	45	11	1	2	1.1	21	15	26	29	2	.247	.352	15	6	OF-51
6 yrs.	576	2003	532	96	12	50	2.5	282	249	234	281	12	.266	.400	39	13	OF-526
4 yrs.	231	763	202	33	0	25	3.3	121	124	90	106	6	.265	.406	22	6	OF-204

Sparky Adams

ADAMS, EARL JOHN
B. Aug. 26, 1894, Newtown, Pa.
BR TR 5'5½"   151 lbs.

	G	AB	H	2B	3B	HR	HR %	R	RBI	BB	SO	SB	BA	SA	PH AB	PH H	G by POS
1922 CHI N	11	44	11	0	0	0	0.0	5	3	4	3	1	.250	.295	0	0	2B-11
1923	95	311	90	12	0	4	1.3	40	35	26	10	20	.289	.367	10	4	SS-79, OF-1
1924	117	418	117	11	5	1	0.2	66	27	40	20	15	.280	.337	7	2	SS-88, 2B-19
1925	149	627	180	29	8	2	0.3	95	48	44	15	26	.287	.368	0	0	2B-144, SS-5
1926	154	624	193	35	3	0	0.0	95	39	52	27	27	.309	.375	2	0	2B-136, 3B-19, SS-2
1927	146	647	189	17	7	0	0.0	100	49	42	26	26	.292	.340	0	0	2B-60, 3B-53, SS-40
1928 PIT N	135	539	149	14	6	0	0.0	91	38	64	18	8	.276	.325	1	0	2B-107, SS-27, OF-1
1929	74	196	51	8	1	0	0.0	37	11	15	5	3	.260	.311	4	2	SS-30, 2B-20, 3B-15, OF-2
1930 STL N	137	570	179	36	9	0	0.0	98	55	45	27	7	.314	.409	2	1	3B-104, 2B-25, SS-7
1931	143	608	178	46	5	1	0.2	97	40	42	24	16	.293	.390	1	0	3B-138, SS-6
1932	31	127	35	3	1	0	0.0	22	13	14	5	0	.276	.315	0	0	3B-30
1933 2 teams	STL N (8G – .167)			CIN N (137G – .262)													
" Total	145	568	146	22	1	1	0.2	60	22	45	33	3	.257	.305	0	0	3B-135, SS-13
1934 CIN N	87	278	70	16	1	0	0.0	38	14	20	10	2	.252	.317	12	4	3B-38, 2B-29
13 yrs.	1424	5557	1588	249	48	9	0.2	844	394	453	223	154	.286	.353	39	13	2B-551, 3B-532, SS-297, OF-4
4 yrs.	319	1335	397	86	15	1	0.1	218	108	102	59	23	.297	.387	3	1	3B-275, 2B-25, SS-18
WORLD SERIES																	
1930 STL N	6	21	3	0	0	0	0.0	0	1	0	4	0	.143	.143	0	0	3B-6
1931	2	4	1	0	0	0	0.0	0	0	0	1	0	.250	.250	0	0	3B-2
2 yrs.	8	25	4	0	0	0	0.0	0	1	0	5	0	.160	.160	0	0	3B-8

Henry Adkinson

ADKINSON, HENRY MAGEE
B. Sept. 1, 1874, Chicago, Ill.   D. May 1, 1923, Salt Lake City, Utah

	G	AB	H	2B	3B	HR	HR %	R	RBI	BB	SO	SB	BA	SA	PH AB	PH H	G by POS
1895 STL N	1	5	2	0	0	0	0.0	1	0	0	2	0	.400	.400	0	0	OF-1

Tommie Agee

AGEE, TOMMIE LEE
B. Aug. 9, 1942, Magnolia, Ala.
BR TR 5'11"   195 lbs.

	G	AB	H	2B	3B	HR	HR %	R	RBI	BB	SO	SB	BA	SA	PH AB	PH H	G by POS
1962 CLE A	5	14	3	0	0	0	0.0	2	2	0	4	0	.214	.214	2	0	OF-3
1963	13	27	4	1	0	1	3.7	3	3	2	9	0	.148	.296	0	0	OF-13
1964	13	12	2	0	0	0	0.0	0	0	0	3	0	.167	.167	0	0	OF-12
1965 CHI A	10	19	3	1	0	0	0.0	2	3	2	6	0	.158	.211	1	0	OF-9
1966	160	629	172	27	8	22	3.5	98	86	41	127	44	.273	.447	0	0	OF-159
1967	158	529	124	26	2	14	2.6	73	52	44	129	28	.234	.371	2	1	OF-152
1968 NY N	132	368	80	12	3	5	1.4	30	17	15	103	13	.217	.307	3	1	OF-127
1969	149	565	153	23	4	26	4.6	97	76	59	137	12	.271	.464	3	1	OF-146
1970	153	636	182	30	7	24	3.8	107	75	55	156	31	.286	.469	3	1	OF-150
1971	113	425	121	19	0	14	3.3	58	50	50	84	28	.285	.428	6	3	OF-107
1972	114	422	96	23	0	13	3.1	52	47	53	92	8	.227	.374	4	0	OF-109
1973 2 teams	HOU N (83G – .235)			STL N (26G – .177)													
" Total	109	266	59	8	3	11	4.1	38	22	21	68	3	.222	.398	19	4	OF-86
12 yrs.	1129	3912	999	170	27	130	3.3	558	433	342	918	167	.255	.412	43	11	OF-1073
1 yr.	26	62	11	3	1	3	4.8	8	7	5	13	1	.177	.403	8	1	OF-19
LEAGUE CHAMPIONSHIP SERIES																	
1969 NY N	3	14	5	1	0	2	14.3	4	4	2	5	2	.357	.857	0	0	OF-3
WORLD SERIES																	
1969 NY N	5	18	3	0	0	1	5.6	1	1	2	5	1	.167	.333	0	0	OF-5

Eddie Ainsmith

AINSMITH, EDWARD WILBUR
B. Feb. 4, 1890, Cambridge, Mass.   D. Sept. 6, 1981, Ft. Lauderdale, Fla.
BR TR 5'11"   180 lbs.

	G	AB	H	2B	3B	HR	HR %	R	RBI	BB	SO	SB	BA	SA	PH AB	PH H	G by POS
1910 WAS A	33	104	20	1	2	0	0.0	4	9	6		0	.192	.240	0	0	C-30
1911	61	149	33	2	3	0	0.0	12	14	10		5	.221	.275	7	1	C-49
1912	60	186	42	7	2	0	0.0	22	22	14		4	.226	.285	2	0	C-58
1913	79	229	49	4	4	2	0.9	26	20	12	41	17	.214	.293	0	0	C-79, P-1
1914	58	151	34	7	0	0	0.0	11	13	9	28	8	.225	.272	3	2	C-51
1915	47	120	24	4	2	0	0.0	13	6	10	18	7	.200	.267	3	0	C-42
1916	51	100	17	4	0	0	0.0	11	8	8	14	3	.170	.210	4	0	C-46
1917	125	350	67	17	4	0	0.0	38	42	40	48	16	.191	.263	5	0	C-119
1918	96	292	62	10	9	0	0.0	22	20	29	44	6	.212	.308	4	1	C-89
1919 DET A	114	364	99	17	12	3	0.8	45	32	45	30	9	.272	.409	8	1	C-106
1920	69	186	43	5	3	1	0.5	19	19	14	19	4	.231	.306	7	2	C-61
1921 2 teams	DET A (35G – .276)			STL N (27G – .290)													
" Total	62	160	45	5	3	0	0.0	11	17	16	11	1	.281	.350	4	0	C-57, 1B-1

	G	AB	H	2B	3B	HR	HR %	R	RBI	BB	SO	SB	BA	SA	Pinch Hit AB	Pinch Hit H	G by POS

Eddie Ainsmith continued

	G	AB	H	2B	3B	HR	HR %	R	RBI	BB	SO	SB	BA	SA	AB	H	G by POS
1922 STL N	119	379	111	14	4	13	3.4	46	59	28	43	2	.293	.454	2	1	C-116
1923 2 teams		STL N	(82G –	.213)		BKN N	(2G –	.200)									
" Total	84	273	58	11	6	3	1.1	22	36	22	19	4	.212	.330	2	1	C-82
1924 NY N	10	5	3	0	0	0	0.0	0	0	0	0	0	.600	.600	1	1	C-9
15 yrs.	1068	3048	707	108	54	22	0.7	299	317	263	315	86	.232	.324	49	10	C-994, 1B-1, P-1
3 yrs.	228	704	185	25	11	16	2.3	73	98	53	66	6	.263	.398	7	2	C-219, 1B-1

Ethan Allen

ALLEN, ETHAN NATHAN
B. Jan. 1, 1904, Cincinnati, Ohio   BR TR 6'1"   180 lbs.

	G	AB	H	2B	3B	HR	HR %	R	RBI	BB	SO	SB	BA	SA	AB	H	G by POS
1926 CIN N	18	13	4	1	0	0	0.0	3	0	0	3	0	.308	.385	2	0	OF-9
1927	111	359	106	26	4	2	0.6	54	20	14	23	12	.295	.407	2	1	OF-98
1928	129	485	148	30	7	1	0.2	55	62	27	29	6	.305	.402	0	0	OF-129
1929	143	538	157	27	11	6	1.1	69	64	20	21	21	.292	.416	2	0	OF-137
1930 2 teams		CIN N	(21G –	.217)		NY N	(76G –	.307)									
" Total	97	284	83	10	2	10	3.5	58	38	17	25	6	.292	.447	18	5	OF-77
1931 NY N	94	298	98	18	2	5	1.7	58	43	15	15	6	.329	.453	14	8	OF-77
1932	54	103	18	6	2	1	1.0	13	7	1	12	0	.175	.301	22	1	OF-24
1933 STL N	91	261	63	7	3	0	0.0	25	36	13	22	3	.241	.291	21	3	OF-67
1934 PHI N	145	581	192	42	4	10	1.7	87	85	33	47	6	.330	.468	0	0	OF-145
1935	156	645	198	46	1	8	1.2	90	63	43	54	5	.307	.419	0	0	OF-156
1936 2 teams		PHI N	(30G –	.296)		CHI N	(91G –	.295)									
" Total	121	498	147	21	7	4	0.8	68	48	17	38	16	.295	.390	0	0	OF-119
1937 STL A	103	320	101	18	1	0	0.0	39	31	21	17	3	.316	.378	23	8	OF-78
1938	19	33	10	3	1	0	0.0	4	4	2	4	0	.303	.455	12	3	OF-7
13 yrs.	1281	4418	1325	255	45	47	1.1	623	501	223	310	84	.300	.410	116	29	OF-1123
1 yr.	91	261	63	7	3	0	0.0	25	36	13	22	3	.241	.291	21	3	OF-67

Richie Allen

ALLEN, RICHARD ANTHONY
Brother of Hank Allen.   Brother of Ron Allen.
B. Mar. 8, 1942, Wampum, Pa.   BR TR 5'11"   187 lbs.

	G	AB	H	2B	3B	HR	HR %	R	RBI	BB	SO	SB	BA	SA	AB	H	G by POS
1963 PHI N	10	24	7	2	1	0	0.0	6	2	0	5	0	.292	.458	2	0	OF-7, 3B-1
1964	162	632	201	38	13	29	4.6	125	91	67	138	3	.318	.557	0	0	3B-162
1965	161	619	187	31	14	20	3.2	93	85	74	150	15	.302	.494	1	0	3B-160, SS-5
1966	141	524	166	25	10	40	7.6	112	110	68	136	10	.317	.632	4	1	3B-91, OF-47
1967	122	463	142	31	10	23	5.0	89	77	75	117	20	.307	.566	1	0	3B-121, SS-1, 2B-1
1968	152	521	137	17	9	33	6.3	87	90	74	161	7	.263	.520	8	0	OF-139, 3B-10
1969	118	438	126	23	3	32	7.3	79	89	64	144	9	.288	.573	1	1	1B-117
1970 STL N	122	459	128	17	5	34	7.4	88	101	71	118	5	.279	.560	3	1	1B-79, 3B-38, OF-3
1971 LA N	155	549	162	24	1	23	4.2	82	90	93	113	8	.295	.468	3	0	3B-67, OF-60, 1B-28
1972 CHI A	148	506	156	28	5	37	7.3	90	113	99	126	19	.308	.603	7	1	1B-143, 3B-2
1973	72	250	79	20	3	16	6.4	39	41	33	51	7	.316	.612	3	0	1B-67, 2B-2
1974	128	462	139	23	1	32	6.9	84	88	57	89	7	.301	.563	4	0	1B-125, 2B-1
1975 PHI N	119	416	97	21	3	12	2.9	54	62	58	109	11	.233	.385	5	0	1B-113
1976	85	298	80	16	1	15	5.0	52	49	37	63	11	.268	.480	2	1	1B-85
1977 OAK A	54	171	41	4	0	5	2.9	19	31	24	36	1	.240	.351	2	0	1B-50
15 yrs.	1749	6332	1848	320	79	351	5.5	1099	1119	894	1556	133	.292	.534	46	5	1B-807, 3B-652, OF-256, 2B-4, SS-3
											9th						
1 yr.	122	459	128	17	5	34	7.4	88	101	71	118	5	.279	.560	3	1	1B-79, 3B-38, OF-3

LEAGUE CHAMPIONSHIP SERIES

	G	AB	H	2B	3B	HR	HR %	R	RBI	BB	SO	SB	BA	SA	AB	H	G by POS
1976 PHI N	3	9	2	0	0	0	0.0	1	0	3	2	0	.222	.222	0	0	1B-3

Ron Allen

ALLEN, RONALD FREDERICK
Brother of Hank Allen.   Brother of Richie Allen.
B. Dec. 23, 1943, Ellwood City, Pa.   BB TR 6'3"   205 lbs.

	G	AB	H	2B	3B	HR	HR %	R	RBI	BB	SO	SB	BA	SA	AB	H	G by POS
1972 STL N	7	11	1	0	0	1	9.1	2	1	3	5	0	.091	.364	0	0	1B-5

Matty Alou

ALOU, MATEO ROJAS
Brother of Jesus Alou.   Brother of Felipe Alou.
B. Dec. 22, 1938, Haina, Dominican Republic   BL TL 5'9"   160 lbs.

	G	AB	H	2B	3B	HR	HR %	R	RBI	BB	SO	SB	BA	SA	AB	H	G by POS
1960 SF N	4	3	1	0	0	0	0.0	1	0	0	0	0	.333	.333	3	1	OF-1
1961	81	200	62	7	2	6	3.0	38	24	15	18	3	.310	.455	22	5	OF-58
1962	78	195	57	8	1	3	1.5	28	14	14	17	3	.292	.390	24	9	OF-57
1963	63	76	11	1	0	0	0.0	4	2	2	13	0	.145	.158	45	4	OF-20
1964	110	250	66	4	2	1	0.4	28	14	11	25	5	.264	.308	30	4	OF-80
1965	117	324	75	12	2	2	0.6	37	18	17	28	10	.231	.299	19	1	OF-103, P-1
1966 PIT N	141	535	183	18	9	2	0.4	86	27	24	44	23	.342	.421	7	4	OF-136
1967	139	550	186	21	7	2	0.4	87	28	24	42	16	.338	.413	10	2	OF-134, 1B-1
1968	146	558	185	28	4	0	0.0	59	52	27	26	18	.332	.396	2	1	OF-144
1969	162	698	231	41	6	1	0.1	105	48	42	35	22	.331	.411	0	0	OF-162
1970	155	677	201	21	8	1	0.1	97	47	30	18	19	.297	.356	2	0	OF-153
1971 STL N	149	609	192	28	6	7	1.1	85	74	34	27	19	.315	.415	6	2	OF-94, 1B-57
1972 2 teams		STL N	(108G –	.314)		OAK A	(32G –	.281)									
" Total	140	525	161	22	2	4	0.8	57	47	35	35	13	.307	.379	9	1	OF-71, 1B-67
1973 2 teams		NY A	(123G –	.296)		STL N	(11G –	.273)									
" Total	134	508	150	22	1	2	0.4	60	29	31	43	4	.295	.354	10	2	OF-86, 1B-41
1974 SD N	48	81	16	3	0	0	0.0	8	3	5	6	0	.198	.235	30	5	OF-13, 1B-2
15 yrs.	1667	5789	1777	236	50	31	0.5	780	427	311	377	155	.307	.381	219	46	OF-1312, 1B-168, P-1
3 yrs.	268	1024	322	45	8	10	0.4	132	106	59	50	30	.314	.403	25	6	OF-134, 1B-124

LEAGUE CHAMPIONSHIP SERIES

	G	AB	H	2B	3B	HR	HR %	R	RBI	BB	SO	SB	BA	SA	AB	H	G by POS
1970 PIT N	3	12	3	1	0	0	0.0	1	0	2	1	0	.250	.333	0	0	OF-3
1972 OAK A	5	21	8	4	0	0	0.0	2	2	0	2	1	.381	.571	0	0	OF-5
2 yrs.	8	33	11	5	0	0	0.0	3	2	2	3	1	.333	.485	0	0	OF-8

	G	AB	H	2B	3B	HR	HR %	R	RBI	BB	SO	SB	BA	SA	Pinch Hit AB	Pinch Hit H	G by POS

Matty Alou continued

WORLD SERIES

	G	AB	H	2B	3B	HR	HR %	R	RBI	BB	SO	SB	BA	SA	AB	H	G by POS
1962 SF N	6	12	4	1	0	0	0.0	2	1	0	1	0	.333	.417	3	2	OF-4
1972 OAK A	7	24	1	0	0	0	0.0	0	0	3	0	1	.042	.042	0	0	OF-7
2 yrs.	13	36	5	1	0	0	0.0	2	1	3	1	1	.139	.167	3	2	OF-11

Tom Alston

ALSTON, THOMAS EDISON
B. Jan. 31, 1931, Greensboro, N. C.

BL TR 6'5" 210 lbs.

	G	AB	H	2B	3B	HR	HR %	R	RBI	BB	SO	SB	BA	SA	AB	H	G by POS
1954 STL N	66	244	60	14	2	4	1.6	28	34	24	41	3	.246	.369	2	1	1B-65
1955	13	8	1	0	0	0	0.0	0	0	0	0	0	.125	.125	6	1	1B-7
1956	3	2	0	0	0	0	0.0	0	0	0	0	0	.000	.000	0	0	1B-3
1957	9	17	5	1	0	0	0.0	2	2	1	5	0	.294	.353	3	2	1B-6
4 yrs.	91	271	66	15	2	4	1.5	30	36	25	46	3	.244	.358	11	4	1B-81
4 yrs.	91	271	66	15	2	4	1.5	30	36	25	46	3	.244	.358	11	4	1B-81

Walter Alston

ALSTON, WALTER EMMONS (Smokey)
B. Dec. 1, 1911, Venice, Ohio
Manager 1954-76.

BR TR 6'2" 195 lbs.

	G	AB	H	2B	3B	HR	HR %	R	RBI	BB	SO	SB	BA	SA	AB	H	G by POS
1936 STL N	1	1	0	0	0	0	0.0	0	0	0	1	0	.000	.000	0	0	1B-1

George Altman

ALTMAN, GEORGE LEE
B. Mar. 20, 1933, Goldsboro, N. C.

BL TR 6'4" 200 lbs.

	G	AB	H	2B	3B	HR	HR %	R	RBI	BB	SO	SB	BA	SA	AB	H	G by POS
1959 CHI N	135	420	103	14	4	12	2.9	54	47	34	80	1	.245	.383	15	4	OF-121
1960	119	334	89	16	4	13	3.9	50	51	32	67	4	.266	.455	20	8	OF-79, 1B-21
1961	138	518	157	28	12	27	5.2	77	96	40	92	6	.303	.560	6	0	OF-130, 1B-3
1962	147	534	170	27	5	22	4.1	74	74	62	89	19	.318	.511	6	1	OF-129, 1B-16
1963 STL N	135	464	127	18	7	9	1.9	62	47	47	93	13	.274	.401	12	3	OF-124
1964 NY N	124	422	97	14	1	9	2.1	48	47	18	70	4	.230	.332	18	6	OF-109
1965 CHI N	90	196	46	7	1	4	2.0	24	23	19	36	3	.235	.342	43	6	OF-45, 1B-2
1966	88	185	41	6	0	5	2.7	19	17	14	37	2	.222	.335	44	9	OF-42, 1B-4
1967	15	18	2	2	0	0	0.0	1	1	2	8	0	.111	.222	9	2	OF-4, 1B-1
9 yrs.	991	3091	832	132	34	101	3.3	409	403	268	572	52	.269	.432	173	39	OF-783, 1B-47
1 yr.	135	464	127	18	7	9	1.9	62	47	47	93	13	.274	.401	12	3	OF-124

Luis Alvarado

ALVARADO, LUIS CESAR (Pimba)
B. Jan. 15, 1949, La Jas, Puerto Rico

BR TR 5'9" 162 lbs.

	G	AB	H	2B	3B	HR	HR %	R	RBI	BB	SO	SB	BA	SA	AB	H	G by POS
1968 BOS A	11	46	6	2	0	0	0.0	3	1	1	11	0	.130	.174	0	0	SS-11
1969	6	5	0	0	0	0	0.0	0	0	0	2	0	.000	.000	1	0	SS-5
1970	59	183	41	11	0	1	0.5	19	10	9	30	1	.224	.301	1	0	3B-29, SS-27
1971 CHI A	99	264	57	14	1	0	0.0	22	8	11	34	1	.216	.277	9	0	SS-71, 2B-16
1972	103	254	54	4	1	4	1.6	30	29	13	36	2	.213	.283	7	2	SS-81, 2B-16, 3B-2
1973	79	203	47	7	2	0	0.0	21	20	4	20	6	.232	.286	7	4	2B-45, SS-18, 3B-10
1974 3 teams		CHI A (8G – .100)				CLE A (61G – .219)				STL N (17G – .139)							
" Total	86	160	31	4	0	0	0.0	16	13	8	21	1	.194	.219	5	1	2B-47, SS-28, 3B-1
1976 STL N	16	42	12	1	0	0	0.0	5	3	3	6	0	.286	.310	0	0	2B-16
1977 2 teams		DET A (2G – .000)				NY N (1G – .000)											
" Total	3	3	0	0	0	0	0.0	0	0	0	0	0	.000	.000	0	0	3B-2, 2B-1
9 yrs.	462	1160	248	43	4	5	0.4	116	84	49	160	11	.214	.271	30	7	SS-241, 2B-141, 3B-44
2 yrs.	33	78	17	3	0	0	0.0	8	4	5	12	0	.218	.256	0	0	SS-17, 2B-16

Brant Alyea

ALYEA, GARRABRANT RYERSON
B. Dec. 8, 1940, Passaic, N. J.

BR TR 6'3" 215 lbs.

	G	AB	H	2B	3B	HR	HR %	R	RBI	BB	SO	SB	BA	SA	AB	H	G by POS
1965 WAS A	8	13	3	0	0	2	15.4	3	6	1	4	0	.231	.692	5	1	1B-3, OF-1
1968	53	150	40	11	1	6	4.0	18	23	10	39	0	.267	.473	18	3	OF-39
1969	104	237	59	4	0	11	4.6	29	40	34	67	1	.249	.405	41	8	OF-69, 1B-3
1970 MIN A	94	258	75	12	1	16	6.2	34	61	28	51	3	.291	.531	18	7	OF-75
1971	79	158	28	4	0	2	1.3	13	15	24	38	1	.177	.241	25	4	OF-48
1972 2 teams		OAK A (20G – .194)				STL N (13G – .158)											
" Total	33	50	9	2	0	1	2.0	3	3	3	11	0	.180	.280	20	3	OF-11
6 yrs.	371	866	214	33	2	38	4.4	100	148	100	210	5	.247	.421	127	26	OF-243, 1B-6
1 yr.	13	19	3	1	0	0	0.0	0	1	0	6	0	.158	.211	11	2	OF-3

LEAGUE CHAMPIONSHIP SERIES

	G	AB	H	2B	3B	HR	HR %	R	RBI	BB	SO	SB	BA	SA	AB	H	G by POS
1970 MIN A	3	7	0	0	0	0	0.0	1	0	2	3	0	.000	.000	1	0	OF-2

Ruben Amaro

AMARO, RUBEN MORA
B. Jan. 6, 1936, Vera Cruz, Mexico

BR TR 5'11" 170 lbs.

	G	AB	H	2B	3B	HR	HR %	R	RBI	BB	SO	SB	BA	SA	AB	H	G by POS
1958 STL N	40	76	17	2	1	0	0.0	8	0	5	8	0	.224	.276	1	0	SS-36, 2B-1
1960 PHI N	92	264	61	9	1	0	0.0	25	16	21	32	0	.231	.273	0	0	SS-92
1961	135	381	98	14	9	1	0.3	34	32	53	59	1	.257	.349	0	0	SS-132, 1B-3, 2B-1
1962	79	226	55	10	0	0	0.0	24	19	30	28	5	.243	.288	0	0	SS-78, 1B-1
1963	115	217	47	9	2	2	0.9	25	19	19	31	0	.217	.304	7	0	SS-63, 3B-45, 1B-5
1964	129	299	79	11	0	4	1.3	31	34	16	37	1	.264	.341	9	1	SS-79, 1B-58, 3B-3, 2B-3, OF-1
1965	118	184	39	7	0	0	0.0	26	15	27	22	1	.212	.250	7	0	SS-60, 1B-60, 2B-6
1966 NY A	14	23	5	0	0	0	0.0	0	3	0	2	0	.217	.217	0	0	SS-14
1967	130	417	93	12	0	1	0.2	31	17	43	49	3	.223	.259	2	0	SS-123, 3B-3, 1B-2
1968	47	41	5	1	0	0	0.0	3	0	9	6	0	.122	.146	1	0	SS-23, 1B-22
1969 CAL A	41	27	6	0	0	0	0.0	4	1	4	6	0	.222	.222	5	1	1B-18, 2B-9, SS-5, 3B-2
11 yrs.	940	2155	505	75	13	8	0.4	211	156	227	280	11	.234	.292	32	2	SS-705, 1B-169, 3B-53, 2B-20, OF-1
1 yr.	40	76	17	2	1	0	0.0	8	0	5	8	0	.224	.276	1	0	SS-36, 2B-1

	G	AB	H	2B	3B	HR	HR %	R	RBI	BB	SO	SB	BA	SA	Pinch Hit AB	Pinch Hit H	G by POS

Dwain Anderson
ANDERSON, DWAIN CLEAVEN
B. Nov. 23, 1947, Berkeley, Calif. BR TR 5'11" 165 lbs.

	G	AB	H	2B	3B	HR	HR%	R	RBI	BB	SO	SB	BA	SA	AB	H	G by POS
1971 OAK A	16	37	10	2	1	0	0.0	3	3	5	9	0	.270	.378	0	0	SS-10, 2B-5, 3B-1
1972 2 teams	OAK A	(3G – .000)				STL N	(57G – .267)										
" Total	60	142	36	4	1	1	0.7	14	8	9	27	0	.254	.317	1	0	SS-44, 3B-14, 2B-1
1973 2 teams	STL N	(18G – .118)				SD N	(53G – .121)										
" Total	71	124	15	0	0	0	0.0	16	3	18	33	2	.121	.121	15	1	SS-42, 3B-6, OF-2
1974 CLE A	2	3	1	0	0	0	0.0	0	0	0	1	0	.333	.333	0	0	2B-1
4 yrs.	149	306	62	6	2	1	0.3	33	14	32	70	2	.203	.245	16	1	SS-96, 3B-21, 2B-7, OF-2
2 yrs.	75	152	38	4	1	1	0.7	17	8	12	27	0	.250	.309	10	1	SS-46, 3B-13, OF-2, 2B-1

Ferrell Anderson
ANDERSON, FERRELL JACK
B. Jan. 9, 1918, Maple City, Kans.   D. Mar. 12, 1978, Joplin, Mo.   BR TR 6'1" 200 lbs.

	G	AB	H	2B	3B	HR	HR%	R	RBI	BB	SO	SB	BA	SA	AB	H	G by POS
1946 BKN N	70	199	51	10	0	2	1.0	19	14	18	21	1	.256	.337	8	2	C-70
1953 STL N	18	35	10	2	0	0	0.0	1	1	0	4	0	.286	.343	7	0	C-12
2 yrs.	88	234	61	12	0	2	0.9	20	15	18	25	1	.261	.338	15	2	C-82
1 yr.	18	35	10	2	0	0	0.0	1	1	0	4	0	.286	.343	7	0	C-12

George Anderson
ANDERSON, GEORGE ANDREW JENDRUS
B. Sept. 26, 1889, Cleveland, Ohio   D. May 28, 1962, Warrensville Hts., Ohio   BL TR 5'8½" 160 lbs.

	G	AB	H	2B	3B	HR	HR%	R	RBI	BB	SO	SB	BA	SA	AB	H	G by POS
1914 BKN F	98	364	115	13	3	3	0.8	58	24	31		16	.316	.393	5	0	OF-92
1915	136	511	135	23	9	2	0.4	70	39	52		20	.264	.356	1	0	OF-134
1918 STL N	35	132	39	4	5	0	0.0	20	6	15	7	0	.295	.402	0	0	OF-35
3 yrs.	269	1007	289	40	17	5	0.5	148	69	98	7	36	.287	.375	6	0	OF-261
1 yr.	35	132	39	4	5	0	0.0	20	6	15	7	0	.295	.402	0	0	OF-35

Mike Anderson
ANDERSON, MICHAEL ALLEN
B. June 22, 1951, Florence, S. C.   BR TR 6'2" 200 lbs.

	G	AB	H	2B	3B	HR	HR%	R	RBI	BB	SO	SB	BA	SA	AB	H	G by POS
1971 PHI N	26	89	22	5	1	2	2.2	11	5	13	28	0	.247	.393	0	0	OF-26
1972	36	103	20	5	1	2	1.9	8	5	19	36	1	.194	.320	0	0	OF-35
1973	87	193	49	9	1	9	4.7	32	28	19	53	0	.254	.451	26	4	OF-67
1974	145	395	99	22	2	5	1.3	35	34	37	75	2	.251	.354	19	5	OF-133, 1B-1
1975	115	247	64	10	3	4	1.6	24	28	17	66	1	.259	.372	16	5	OF-105, 1B-3
1976 STL N	86	199	58	8	1	1	0.5	17	12	26	30	1	.291	.357	21	7	OF-58, 1B-5
1977	94	154	34	4	1	4	2.6	18	17	14	31	2	.221	.338	20	5	OF-77
1978 BAL A	53	32	3	0	1	0	0.0	2	3	3	10	0	.094	.156	6	0	OF-47
1979 PHI N	79	78	18	4	0	1	1.3	12	2	13	14	1	.231	.321	11	0	OF-70, P-1
9 yrs.	721	1490	367	67	11	28	1.9	159	134	161	343	8	.246	.362	119	26	OF-618, 1B-9, P-1
2 yrs.	180	353	92	12	2	5	1.4	35	29	40	61	3	.261	.348	41	12	OF-135, 1B-5

Pat Ankenman
ANKENMAN, FRED NORMAN
B. Dec. 23, 1912, Houston, Tex.   BR TR 5'4" 125 lbs.

	G	AB	H	2B	3B	HR	HR%	R	RBI	BB	SO	SB	BA	SA	AB	H	G by POS
1936 STL N	1	3	0	0	0	0	0.0	0	0	0	3	0	.000	.000	0	0	SS-1
1943 BKN N	1	2	1	0	0	0	0.0	1	0	0	0	0	.500	.500	0	0	SS-1
1944	13	24	6	1	0	0	0.0	1	3	0	2	0	.250	.292	1	0	2B-11, SS-2
3 yrs.	15	29	7	1	0	0	0.0	2	3	0	5	0	.241	.276	1	0	2B-11, SS-4
1 yr.	1	3	0	0	0	0	0.0	0	0	0	3	0	.000	.000	0	0	SS-1

John Antonelli
ANTONELLI, JOHN LAWRENCE
B. July 15, 1915, Memphis, Tenn.   BR TR 5'10½" 165 lbs.

	G	AB	H	2B	3B	HR	HR%	R	RBI	BB	SO	SB	BA	SA	AB	H	G by POS
1944 STL N	8	21	4	1	0	0	0.0		1	0	4	0	.190	.238	0	0	3B-3, 1B-3, 2B-2
1945 2 teams	STL N	(2G – .000)				PHI N	(125G – .256)										
" Total	127	507	129	27	2	1	0.2	50	28	24	25	1	.254	.321	2	0	3B-109, 2B-23, SS-1, 1B-1
2 yrs.	135	528	133	28	2	1	0.2	50	29	24	29	1	.252	.318	2	0	3B-112, 2B-25, 1B-4, SS-1
2 yrs.	10	24	4	1	0	0	0.0			0	5	0	.167	.208	2	0	3B-4, 1B-3, 2B-2

Harry Arndt
ARNDT, HARRY A.
B. Feb. 12, 1879, South Bend, Ind.   D. Mar. 25, 1921, South Bend, Ind.

	G	AB	H	2B	3B	HR	HR%	R	RBI	BB	SO	SB	BA	SA	AB	H	G by POS
1902 2 teams	DET A	(10G – .147)				BAL A	(68G – .254)										
" Total	78	282	68	7	5	2	0.7	45	35	41		9	.241	.323	0	0	OF-72, 2B-4, 3B-2, SS-1, 1B-1
1905 STL N	113	415	101	11	6	2	0.5	40	36	24		13	.243	.313	2	1	2B-90, OF-9, 3B-7, SS-5
1906	69	256	69	7	9	2	0.8	30	26	19		5	.270	.391	4	1	3B-65, OF-1, 1B-1
1907	11	32	6	1	0	0	0.0	3	2	1		0	.188	.219	4	1	1B-4, 3B-3
4 yrs.	271	985	244	26	20	6	0.6	118	99	85		27	.248	.333	7	2	2B-94, OF-82, 3B-77, SS-6, 1B-6
3 yrs.	193	703	176	19	15	4	0.6	73	64	44		18	.250	.337	7	2	2B-90, 3B-75, OF-10, SS-5, 1B-5

Benny Ayala
AYALA, BENIGO FELIX
B. Feb. 7, 1951, Yavco, Puerto Rico   BR TR 6'1" 185 lbs.

	G	AB	H	2B	3B	HR	HR%	R	RBI	BB	SO	SB	BA	SA	AB	H	G by POS
1974 NY N	23	68	16	1	0	2	2.9	9	8	7	17	0	.235	.338	4	0	OF-20
1976	22	26	3	0	0	1	3.8	2	2	2	6	0	.115	.231	15	2	OF-7
1977 STL N	1	3	1	0	0	0	0.0	0	0	0	1	0	.333	.333	0	0	OF-1
1979 BAL A	42	86	22	5	0	6	7.0	15	13	6	9	0	.256	.523	13	3	OF-24
1980	76	170	45	8	1	10	5.9	28	33	19	21	0	.265	.500	28	5	OF-19
1981	44	86	24	2	0	3	3.5	12	13	11	9	0	.279	.407	16	5	OF-4
1982	64	128	39	6	0	6	4.7	17	24	5	14	1	.305	.492	24	9	OF-25, 1B-3
7 yrs.	272	567	150	22	1	28	4.9	83	93	50	77	1	.265	.455	100	24	OF-100, 1B-3
1 yr.	1	3	1	0	0	0	0.0	0	0	0	1	0	.333	.333	0	0	OF-1

WORLD SERIES

	G	AB	H	2B	3B	HR	HR%	R	RBI	BB	SO	SB	BA	SA	AB	H	G by POS
1979 BAL A	4	6	2	0	0	1	16.7	1	2	1	0	0	.333	.833	0	0	OF-3

	G	AB	H	2B	3B	HR	HR%	R	RBI	BB	SO	SB	BA	SA	Pinch Hit AB	H	G by POS

Doug Baird

BAIRD, HOWARD DOUGLASS
B. Sept. 27, 1891, St. Charles, Mo.   D. June 13, 1967, Thomasville, Ga.
BR TR 5'9½" 148 lbs.

	G	AB	H	2B	3B	HR	HR%	R	RBI	BB	SO	SB	BA	SA	AB	H	G by POS
1915 PIT N	145	512	112	26	12	1	0.2	49	53	37	88	29	.219	.322	2	0	3B-131, OF-20, 2B-3
1916	128	430	93	10	7	1	0.2	41	28	24	49	20	.216	.279	3	0	3B-80, 2B-29, OF-16
1917 2 teams		PIT	N	(43G –	.259)			STL	N	(104G –	.253)						
" Total	147	499	127	25	13	0	0.0	55	42	43	71	26	.255	.357	0	0	3B-144, OF-2, 2B-2
1918 STL N	82	316	78	12	8	2	0.6	41	25	25	42	25	.247	.354	0	0	3B-81, OF-1, SS-1
1919 3 teams		PHI	N	(66G –	.252)			STL	N	(16G –	.212)		BKN	N	(20G –	.183)
" Total	102	335	79	13	5	2	0.6	43	42	25	41	18	.236	.322	5	1	3B-91, OF-1, 2B-1
1920 2 teams		BKN	N	(6G –	.333)			NY	N	(7G –	.125)						
" Total	13	14	3	0	0	0	0.0	1	1	3	4	0	.214	.214	3	1	3B-6
6 yrs.	617	2106	492	86	45	6	0.3	230	191	157	295	118	.234	.326	13	2	3B-533, OF-40, 2B-35, SS-1
3 yrs.	202	713	177	31	21	2	0.3	83	53	50	97	45	.248	.359	4	1	3B-192, OF-4, SS-1, 2B-1

Bill Baker

BAKER, WILLIAM PRESLEY
B. Feb. 22, 1911, Paw Creek, N. C.
BR TR 6' 200 lbs.

	G	AB	H	2B	3B	HR	HR%	R	RBI	BB	SO	SB	BA	SA	AB	H	G by POS
1940 CIN N	27	69	15	1	1	0	0.0	5	7	4	8	2	.217	.261	3	0	C-24
1941 2 teams		CIN	N	(2G –	.000)			PIT	N	(35G –	.224)						
" Total	37	68	15	3	0	0	0.0	5	6	12	1	0	.221	.265	3	0	C-34
1942 PIT N	18	17	2	0	0	0	0.0	1	2	1	0	0	.118	.118	7	2	C-11
1943	63	172	47	6	3	1	0.6	12	26	22	6	3	.273	.360	7	1	C-56
1946	53	113	27	4	0	1	0.9	7	8	12	6	0	.239	.301	9	2	C-41, 1B-1
1948 STL N	45	119	35	10	1	0	0.0	13	15	15	7	1	.294	.395	7	2	C-36
1949	20	30	4	1	0	0	0.0	2	4	2	2	0	.133	.167	10	0	C-10
7 yrs.	263	588	145	25	5	2	0.3	45	68	68	30	6	.247	.316	46	7	C-212, 1B-1
2 yrs.	65	149	39	11	1	0	0.0	15	19	17	9	1	.262	.349	17	2	C-46

WORLD SERIES

	G	AB	H	2B	3B	HR	HR%	R	RBI	BB	SO	SB	BA	SA	AB	H	G by POS
1940 CIN N	3	4	1	0	0	0	0.0	1	0	0	1	0	.250	.250	1	0	C-3

Art Ball

BALL, ARTHUR
B. Chicago, Ill.   D. Dec. 26, 1915, Chicago, Ill.
TR

	G	AB	H	2B	3B	HR	HR%	R	RBI	BB	SO	SB	BA	SA	AB	H	G by POS
1894 STL N	1	3	1	0	0	0	0.0	0	0	0		1	.333	.333	0	0	2B-1
1898 BAL N	32	81	15	2	0	0	0.0	7	8	7		2	.185	.210	0	0	3B-15, SS-14, 2B-2, OF-1
2 yrs.	33	84	16	2	0	0	0.0	7	8	7	1	2	.190	.214	0	0	3B-15, SS-14, 2B-3, OF-1
1 yr.	1	3	1	0	0	0	0.0	0	0	0		1	.333	.333	0	0	2B-1

Jimmy Bannon

BANNON, JAMES HENRY (Foxy Grandpa)
Brother of Tom Bannon.
B. May 5, 1871, Amesbury, Mass.   D. Mar. 24, 1948, Glenrock, N. J.
BR TR 5'5" 160 lbs.

	G	AB	H	2B	3B	HR	HR%	R	RBI	BB	SO	SB	BA	SA	AB	H	G by POS
'1893 STL N	26	107	36	3	4	0	0.0	9	15	4	5	8	.336	.439	0	0	OF-24, SS-2, P-1
1894 BOS N	128	494	166	29	10	13	2.6	130	114	62	42	47	.336	.514	0	0	OF-128, P-1
1895	123	489	171	35	5	6	1.2	101	74	54	31	28	.350	.479	1	0	OF-122, P-1
1896	89	343	86	9	5	0	0.0	52	50	32	23	16	.251	.306	1	0	OF-76, 2B-6, SS-5, 3B-3
4 yrs.	366	1433	459	76	24	19	1.3	292	253	152	101	99	.320	.447	2	0	OF-350, SS-7, 2B-6, 3B-3, P-3
1 yr.	26	107	36	3	4	0	0.0	9	15	4	5	8	.336	.439	0	0	OF-24, SS-2, P-1

Jap Barbeau

BARBEAU, WILLIAM JOSEPH
B. June 10, 1882, New York, N. Y.   D. Sept. 10, 1969, Milwaukee, Wis.
BR TR 5'5" 140 lbs.

	G	AB	H	2B	3B	HR	HR%	R	RBI	BB	SO	SB	BA	SA	AB	H	G by POS
1905 CLE A	11	37	10	1	1	0	0.0	1	2	1		1	.270	.351	0	0	2B-11
1906	42	129	25	5	3	0	0.0	8	12	9		5	.194	.279	3	0	3B-32, SS-6
1909 2 teams		PIT	N	(91G –	.220)			STL	N	(47G –	.251)						
" Total	138	525	121	19	3	0	0.0	83	30	65		33	.230	.278	7	0	3B-131
1910 STL N	7	21	4	0	1	0	0.0	4	2	3	3	0	.190	.286	0	0	3B-6, 2B-1
4 yrs.	198	712	160	25	8	0	0.0	96	46	78	3	39	.225	.282	10	0	3B-169, 2B-12, SS-6
2 yrs.	54	196	48	3	1	0	0.0	27	7	31	3	4	.245	.270	1	0	3B-52, 2B-1

George Barclay

BARCLAY, GEORGE OLIVER (Deerfoot)
B. May 16, 1875, Millville, Pa.   D. Apr. 2, 1909, Philadelphia, Pa.
5'10" 162 lbs.

	G	AB	H	2B	3B	HR	HR%	R	RBI	BB	SO	SB	BA	SA	AB	H	G by POS
1902 STL N	137	543	163	14	2	3	0.6	79	53	31		30	.300	.350	0	0	OF-137
1903	108	419	104	10	8	0	0.0	37	42	15		12	.248	.310	0	0	OF-107
1904 2 teams		STL	N	(103G –	.200)			BOS	N	(24G –	.226)						
" Total	127	468	96	10	5	1	0.2	46	38	14		17	.205	.254	0	0	OF-127
1905 BOS N	29	108	19	1	0	0	0.0	5	7	2		2	.176	.185	1	0	OF-28
4 yrs.	401	1538	382	35	15	4	0.3	167	140	62		61	.248	.298	1	0	OF-399
3 yrs.	348	1337	342	31	14	4	0.3	157	123	58		56	.256	.309	0	0	OF-347

Shad Barry

BARRY, JOHN C.
B. Sept. 28, 1876, Newburgh, N. Y.   D. Nov. 27, 1936, Los Angeles, Calif.
BR TR

	G	AB	H	2B	3B	HR	HR%	R	RBI	BB	SO	SB	BA	SA	AB	H	G by POS
1899 WAS N	78	247	71	7	5	1	0.4	31	33	12		11	.287	.368	3	0	OF-23, 1B-22, SS-13, 3B-13, 2B-7
1900 BOS N	81	254	66	10	7	1	0.4	40	37	13		9	.260	.366	14	3	OF-24, SS-18, 2B-16, 1B-10, 3B-1
1901 2 teams		BOS	N	(11G –	.175)			PHI	N	(67G –	.246)						
" Total	78	292	69	12	0	1	0.3	38	28	17		14	.236	.288	4	0	2B-35, OF-24, 3B-16, SS-1
1902 PHI N	138	543	156	20	6	2	0.4	65	57	44		14	.287	.357	0	0	OF-137, 1B-1
1903	138	550	152	24	5	1	0.2	75	60	30		26	.276	.344	0	0	OF-107, 1B-30, 3B-1
1904 2 teams		PHI	N	(35G –	.205)			CHI	N	(73G –	.262)						
" Total	108	385	94	9	2	1	0.3	44	29	28		14	.244	.286	3	0	OF-62, 1B-18, 3B-17, SS-8, 2B-2
1905 2 teams		CHI	N	(27G –	.212)			CIN	N	(125G –	.324)						
" Total	152	598	182	13	12	1	0.2	100	66	38		21	.304	.371	1	0	1B-149, OF-2
1906 2 teams		CIN	N	(73G –	.287)			STL	N	(62G –	.249)						
" Total	135	516	139	19	6	1	0.2	64	45	41		17	.269	.335	0	0	OF-65, 1B-64, 3B-6

	G	AB	H	2B	3B	HR	HR %	R	RBI	BB	SO	SB	BA	SA	Pinch Hit AB	Pinch Hit H	G by POS

Shad Barry *continued*

	G	AB	H	2B	3B	HR	HR%	R	RBI	BB	SO	SB	BA	SA	PH AB	PH H	G by POS
1907 STL N	80	292	72	5	2	0	0.0	30	19	28		4	.247	.277	0	0	OF-80
1908 2 teams	STL N (74G – .228)				NY N (37G – .149)												
" Total	111	335	71	9	2	0	0.0	29	16	28		10	.212	.251	7	1	OF-100, SS-2
10 yrs.	1099	4012	1072	128	47	9	0.2	516	390	279		140	.267	.329	32	4	OF-624, 1B-294, 2B-60, 3B-54, SS-42
3 yrs.	216	797	192	22	4	0	0.0	80	42	62		19	.241	.279	3	0	OF-184, 1B-21, 3B-6, SS-2

Dave Bartosch

BARTOSCH, DAVID ROBERT
B. Mar. 24, 1917, St. Louis, Mo. BR TR 6'1" 190 lbs.

	G	AB	H	2B	3B	HR	HR%	R	RBI	BB	SO	SB	BA	SA	PH AB	PH H	G by POS
1945 STL N	24	47	12	1	0	0	0.0	9	1	6	3	0	.255	.277	13	5	OF-11

John Baxter

BAXTER, JOHN
B. Spokane, Wash.

	G	AB	H	2B	3B	HR	HR%	R	RBI	BB	SO	SB	BA	SA	PH AB	PH H	G by POS
1907 STL N	6	21	4	0	0	0	0.0	1	0	0		0	.190	.190	0	0	1B-6

Johnny Beall

BEALL, JOHN WOOLF
B. Mar. 12, 1882, Beltsville, Md. D. June 13, 1926, Beltsville, Md. BL TR 6' 180 lbs.

	G	AB	H	2B	3B	HR	HR%	R	RBI	BB	SO	SB	BA	SA	PH AB	PH H	G by POS
1913 2 teams	CLE A (6G – .167)				CHI A (17G – .267)												
" Total	23	66	17	0	1	2	3.0	10	4	0	2	1	.258	.379	6	1	OF-17
1915 CIN N	10	34	8	1	0	0	0.0	3	3	5	10	0	.235	.265	0	0	OF-10
1916	6	21	7	2	0	1	4.8	3	4	3	7	1	.333	.571	1	0	OF-6
1918 STL N	19	49	11	1	0	0	0.0	2	6	3	6	0	.224	.245	5	2	OF-18
4 yrs.	58	170	43	4	1	3	1.8	18	17	11	25	2	.253	.341	12	3	OF-51
1 yr.	19	49	11	1	0	0	0.0	2	6	3	6	0	.224	.245	5	2	OF-18

Jim Beauchamp

BEAUCHAMP, JAMES EDWARD
B. Aug. 21, 1939, Vinita, Okla. BR TR 6'2" 190 lbs.

	G	AB	H	2B	3B	HR	HR%	R	RBI	BB	SO	SB	BA	SA	PH AB	PH H	G by POS
1963 STL N	4	3	0	0	0	0	0.0	0	0	0	2	0	.000	.000	3	0	
1964 HOU N	23	55	9	2	0	2	3.6	6	4	5	16	0	.164	.309	6	1	OF-15, 1B-2
1965 2 teams	HOU N (24G – .189)				MIL N (4G – .000)												
" Total	28	56	10	1	0	0	0.0	5	4	6	12	0	.179	.196	13	2	OF-9, 1B-5
1967 ATL N	4	3	0	0	0	0	0.0	0	1	0	0	0	.000	.000	3	0	
1968 CIN N	31	57	15	2	0	2	3.5	10	14	4	19	0	.263	.404	17	4	OF-13, 1B-1
1969	43	60	15	1	0	1	1.7	8	8	5	13	0	.250	.317	32	7	OF-9, 1B-3
1970 2 teams	HOU N (31G – .192)				STL N (44G – .259)												
" Total	75	84	20	2	0	2	2.4	11	10	11	18	2	.238	.333	37	9	OF-26, 1B-5
1971 STL N	77	162	38	8	3	2	1.2	24	16	9	26	3	.235	.358	32	8	1B-44, OF-1
1972 NY N	58	120	29	1	0	5	4.2	10	19	7	33	0	.242	.375	21	6	1B-35, OF-3
1973	50	61	17	1	1	0	0.0	5	14	7	11	1	.279	.328	34	9	1B-11
10 yrs.	393	661	153	18	4	14	2.1	79	90	54	150	6	.231	.334	198	46	1B-106, OF-76
3 yrs.	125	223	53	10	3	3	1.3	32	22	17	39	5	.238	.350	58	15	1B-49, OF-11

WORLD SERIES

	G	AB	H	2B	3B	HR	HR%	R	RBI	BB	SO	SB	BA	SA	PH AB	PH H	G by POS
1973 NY N	4	4	0	0	0	0	0.0	0	0		1	0	.000	.000	4	0	

Zinn Beck

BECK, ZINN BERTRAM
B. Sept. 30, 1885, Steubenville, Ohio BR TR 5'10½" 160 lbs.

	G	AB	H	2B	3B	HR	HR%	R	RBI	BB	SO	SB	BA	SA	PH AB	PH H	G by POS
1913 STL N	10	30	5	1	0	0	0.0	4	2	4	10	1	.167	.200	0	0	SS-5, 3B-5
1914	137	457	106	15	11	3	0.7	42	45	28	32	14	.232	.333	0	0	3B-122, SS-16
1915	70	223	52	9	4	0	0.0	21	15	12	31	3	.233	.309	2	0	3B-60, SS-4, 2B-2
1916	62	184	41	7	1	0	0.0	8	10	14	21	3	.223	.272	9	2	3B-52, 2B-1, 1B-1
1918 NY A	11	8	0	0	0	0	0.0	0	1	0	1	0	.000	.000	4	0	1B-5
5 yrs.	290	902	204	32	16	3	0.3	75	73	58	95	21	.226	.307	15	2	3B-239, SS-25, 1B-6, 2B-3
4 yrs.	279	894	204	32	16	3	0.3	75	72	58	94	21	.228	.310	11	2	3B-239, SS-25, 2B-3, 1B-1

Jake Beckley

BECKLEY, JACOB PETER (Eagle Eye)
B. Aug. 4, 1867, Hannibal, Mo. D. June 25, 1918, Kansas City, Mo.
Hall of Fame 1971. BL TL 5'10" 200 lbs.

	G	AB	H	2B	3B	HR	HR%	R	RBI	BB	SO	SB	BA	SA	PH AB	PH H	G by POS
1888 PIT N	71	283	97	15	3	0	0.0	35	27	7	22	20	.343	.417	0	0	1B-71
1889	123	522	157	24	10	9	1.7	91	97	29	29	11	.301	.437	0	0	1B-122, OF-1
1890 PIT P	121	516	167	38	22	10	1.9	109	120	42	32	18	.324	.541	0	0	1B-121
1891 PIT N	133	554	162	20	20	4	0.7	94	73	44	46	13	.292	.422	0	0	1B-133
1892	151	614	145	21	19	10	1.6	102	96	31	44	30	.236	.381	0	0	1B-151
1893	131	542	164	32	19	5	0.9	108	106	54	26	15	.303	.459	0	0	1B-131
1894	131	533	183	36	17	8	1.5	121	120	43	16	21	.343	.520	0	0	1B-131
1895	129	530	174	30	20	5	0.9	104	110	24	20	20	.328	.489	0	0	1B-129
1896 2 teams	PIT N (59G – .253)				NY N (46G – .302)												
" Total	105	399	110	15	9	8	2.0	81	70	31	35	19	.276	.419	0	0	1B-101, OF-5, 2B-1
1897 2 teams	NY N (17G – .250)				CIN N (97G – .345)												
" Total	114	433	143	19	12	8	1.8	84	87	20		25	.330	.485	0	0	1B-114
1898 CIN N	118	459	135	20	12	4	0.9	86	72	28		6	.294	.416	0	0	1B-118
1899	134	513	171	27	16	3	0.6	87	99	40		20	.333	.466	0	0	1B-134
1900	141	558	190	26	10	2	0.4	98	94	40		23	.341	.434	1	0	1B-140
1901	140	580	178	39	13	3	0.5	78	79	28		4	.307	.434	0	0	1B-140
1902	129	531	175	23	7	5	0.9	82	69	34		15	.330	.427	0	0	1B-129, P-1
1903	120	459	150	29	10	2	0.4	85	81	42		23	.327	.447	1	1	1B-119
1904 STL N	142	551	179	22	9	1	0.2	72	67	35		17	.325	.403	0	0	1B-142
1905	134	514	147	20	10	1	0.2	48	57	30		12	.286	.370	0	0	1B-134
1906	87	320	79	16	6	0	0.0	29	44	13		3	.247	.334	2	1	1B-85
1907	32	115	24	3	0	0	0.0	6	7	1		0	.209	.235	0	0	1B-32
20 yrs.	2386	9526	2930	475	244 4th	88	0.9	1600	1575	616	270	315	.308	.436	4	2	1B-2377, OF-6, 2B-1, P-1
4 yrs.	395	1500	429	61	25	2	0.1	155	175	79		32	.286	.364	2	1	1B-393

	G	AB	H	2B	3B	HR	HR %	R	RBI	BB	SO	SB	BA	SA	Pinch Hit AB	Pinch Hit H	G by POS

Ed Beecher

BEECHER, EDWARD (Scrap Iron)
B. Aug. 27, 1873   Deceased.

	G	AB	H	2B	3B	HR	HR %	R	RBI	BB	SO	SB	BA	SA	AB	H	G by POS
1897 STL N	3	12	4	0	0	0	0.0	1	1	0		1	.333	.333	0	0	OF-3
1898 CLE N	8	25	5	2	0	0	0.0	1	0	0		0	.200	.280	0	0	OF-8
2 yrs.	11	37	9	2	0	0	0.0	2	1	0		1	.243	.297	0	0	OF-11
1 yr.	3	12	4	0	0	0	0.0	1	1	0		1	.333	.333	0	0	OF-3

Les Bell

BELL, LESTER ROWLAND   BR TR 5'11" 165 lbs.
B. Dec. 14, 1901, Harrisburg, Pa.

	G	AB	H	2B	3B	HR	HR %	R	RBI	BB	SO	SB	BA	SA	AB	H	G by POS
1923 STL N	15	51	19	2	1	0	0.0	5	9	9	7	1	.373	.451	0	0	SS-15
1924	17	57	14	3	2	1	1.8	5	5	3	7	0	.246	.421	0	0	SS-17
1925	153	586	167	29	9	11	1.9	80	88	43	47	4	.285	.422	0	0	3B-153, SS-1
1926	155	581	189	33	14	17	2.9	85	100	54	62	9	.325	.518	0	0	3B-155
1927	115	390	101	26	6	9	2.3	48	65	34	63	5	.259	.426	5	0	3B-100, SS-10
1928 BOS N	153	591	164	36	7	10	1.7	58	91	40	45	1	.277	.413	0	0	3B-153
1929	139	483	144	23	5	9	1.9	58	72	50	42	4	.298	.422	9	2	3B-127, SS-1, 2B-1
1930 CHI N	74	248	69	15	4	5	2.0	35	47	24	27	1	.278	.431	2	0	3B-70, 1B-2
1931	75	252	71	17	1	4	1.6	30	32	19	22	0	.282	.405	5	1	3B-70
9 yrs.	896	3239	938	184	49	66	2.0	404	509	276	322	25	.290	.438	21	3	3B-828, SS-44, 1B-2, 2B-1
5 yrs.	455	1665	490	93	32	38	2.3	223	267	143	186	19	.294	.457	5	0	3B-408, SS-43

WORLD SERIES
	G	AB	H	2B	3B	HR	HR %	R	RBI	BB	SO	SB	BA	SA	AB	H	G by POS
1926 STL N	7	27	7	1	0	1	3.7	4	6	2	5	0	.259	.407	0	0	3B-7

Joe Benes

BENES, JOSEPH ANTHONY (Bananas)   BR TR 5'8½" 158 lbs.
B. Jan. 1, 1901, Long Island City, N. Y.

	G	AB	H	2B	3B	HR	HR %	R	RBI	BB	SO	SB	BA	SA	AB	H	G by POS
1931 STL N	10	12	2	0	0	0	0.0	1	0	2	1	0	.167	.167	0	0	SS-6, 2B-2, 3B-1

Pug Bennett

BENNETT, JUSTIN TITUS   TR
B. Feb. 20, 1874, Ponca, Neb.   D. Sept. 12, 1935, Kirkland, Wash.

	G	AB	H	2B	3B	HR	HR %	R	RBI	BB	SO	SB	BA	SA	AB	H	G by POS
1906 STL N	153	595	156	16	7	1	0.2	66	34	56		20	.262	.318	0	0	2B-153
1907	87	324	72	8	2	0	0.0	20	21	21		7	.222	.259	1	0	2B-83, 3B-3
2 yrs.	240	919	228	24	9	1	0.1	86	55	77		27	.248	.297	1	0	2B-236, 3B-3
2 yrs.	240	919	228	24	9	1	0.1	86	55	77		27	.248	.297	1	0	2B-236, 3B-3

Vern Benson

BENSON, VERNON ADAIR   BL TR 5'10" 160 lbs.
B. Sept. 19, 1924, Granite Quarry, N. C.

	G	AB	H	2B	3B	HR	HR %	R	RBI	BB	SO	SB	BA	SA	AB	H	G by POS
1943 PHI A	2	2	0	0	0	0	0.0	0	0	0	0	0	.000	.000	2	0	
1946	7	5	0	0	0	0	0.0	1	0	1	3	0	.000	.000	0	0	OF-2
1951 STL N	13	46	12	3	1	1	2.2	8	7	6	8	0	.261	.435	0	0	3B-9, OF-4
1952	20	47	9	2	0	2	4.3	6	5	5	9	0	.191	.362	5	2	3B-15
1953	13	4	0	0	0	0	0.0	2	0	1	2	0	.000	.000	4	0	
5 yrs.	55	104	21	5	1	3	2.9	17	12	13	22	0	.202	.356	11	2	3B-24, OF-6
3 yrs.	46	97	21	5	1	3	3.1	16	12	12	19	0	.216	.381	9	2	3B-24, OF-4

Augie Bergamo

BERGAMO, AUGUST SAMUEL   BL TL 5'9" 165 lbs.
B. Feb. 14, 1918, Detroit, Mich.

	G	AB	H	2B	3B	HR	HR %	R	RBI	BB	SO	SB	BA	SA	AB	H	G by POS
1944 STL N	80	192	55	6	3	2	1.0	35	19	35	23	0	.286	.380	26	4	OF-50, 1B-2
1945	94	304	96	17	2	3	1.0	51	44	43	21	0	.316	.414	15	4	OF-77, 1B-2
2 yrs.	174	496	151	23	5	5	1.0	86	63	78	44	0	.304	.401	41	8	OF-127, 1B-4
2 yrs.	174	496	151	23	5	5	1.0	86	63	78	44	0	.304	.401	41	8	OF-127, 1B-4

WORLD SERIES
	G	AB	H	2B	3B	HR	HR %	R	RBI	BB	SO	SB	BA	SA	AB	H	G by POS
1944 STL N	3	6	0	0	0	0	0.0	0	1	2	3	0	.000	.000	0	0	OF-2

Harry Berte

BERTE, HARRY   TR
B. May 10, 1872, Covington, Ky.

	G	AB	H	2B	3B	HR	HR %	R	RBI	BB	SO	SB	BA	SA	AB	H	G by POS
1903 STL N	4	15	5	0	0	0	0.0	1	1	1		0	.333	.333	0	0	2B-3, SS-1

Bob Bescher

BESCHER, ROBERT HENRY   BB TL 6'1" 200 lbs.
B. Feb. 25, 1884, London, Ohio   D. Nov. 29, 1942, London, Ohio

	G	AB	H	2B	3B	HR	HR %	R	RBI	BB	SO	SB	BA	SA	AB	H	G by POS
1908 CIN N	32	114	31	5	5	0	0.0	16	17	9		10	.272	.404	0	0	OF-32
1909	124	446	107	17	6	1	0.2	73	34	56		54	.240	.312	6	1	OF-117
1910	150	589	147	20	10	4	0.7	95	48	81	75	70	.250	.338	0	0	OF-150
1911	153	599	165	32	10	1	0.2	106	45	102	78	81	.275	.367	0	0	OF-153
1912	145	548	154	29	12	3	0.5	120	38	83	61	67	.281	.394	2	1	OF-143
1913	141	511	132	22	11	1	0.2	86	37	94	68	38	.258	.350	2	0	OF-138
1914 NY N	135	512	138	23	4	6	1.2	82	35	45	48	36	.270	.365	8	3	OF-126
1915 STL N	130	486	128	15	7	4	0.8	71	34	52	53	27	.263	.370	0	0	OF-130
1916	151	561	132	24	8	6	1.1	78	43	60	50	39	.235	.339	0	0	OF-151
1917	42	110	17	1	1	1	0.9	10	8	20	13	3	.155	.209	8	0	OF-32
1918 CLE A	25	60	20	2	1	0	0.0	12	6	17	5	3	.333	.400	4	3	OF-17
11 yrs.	1228	4536	1171	190	75	27	0.6	749	345	619	451	428	.258	.351	30	8	OF-1189
3 yrs.	323	1157	277	40	16	11	1.0	159	85	132	116	69	.239	.330	8	0	OF-313

Frank Betcher

BETCHER, FRANKLIN LYLE   BB TR 5'11" 173 lbs.
Born Franklin Lyle Bettger.
B. Feb. 15, 1888, Philadelphia, Pa.

	G	AB	H	2B	3B	HR	HR %	R	RBI	BB	SO	SB	BA	SA	AB	H	G by POS
1910 STL N	35	89	18	2	0	0	0.0	7	6	7	14	1	.202	.225	8	2	SS-12, 3B-7, 2B-6, OF-2

	G	AB	H	2B	3B	HR	HR%	R	RBI	BB	SO	SB	BA	SA	Pinch Hit AB	Pinch Hit H	G by POS

Bruno Betzel

BETZEL, CHRISTIAN FREDERICK ALBERT JOHN HENRY DAVID
BR TR 5'9" 158 lbs.
B. Dec. 6, 1894, Chattanooga, Ohio   D. Feb. 7, 1965, West Hollywood, Fla.

	G	AB	H	2B	3B	HR	HR%	R	RBI	BB	SO	SB	BA	SA	PH AB	PH H	G by POS
1914 STL N	7	9	0	0	0	0	0.0	2	0	1	1	0	.000	.000	2	0	2B-5
1915	117	367	92	12	4	0	0.0	42	27	18	48	10	.251	.305	3	1	3B-105, 2B-3, SS-2
1916	142	510	119	15	11	1	0.2	49	37	39	77	22	.233	.312	0	0	2B-113, 3B-33, OF-7
1917	106	328	71	4	3	1	0.3	24	17	20	47	9	.216	.256	3	2	2B-75, OF-23, 3B-4
1918	76	230	51	6	7	0	0.0	18	13	12	16	8	.222	.309	6	2	3B-34, OF-21, 2B-10
5 yrs.	448	1444	333	37	25	2	0.1	135	94	90	189	49	.231	.295	14	5	2B-206, 3B-176, OF-51, SS-2
5 yrs.	448	1444	333	37	25	2	0.1	135	94	90	189	49	.231	.295	14	5	2B-206, 3B-176, OF-51, SS-2

Lou Bierbauer

BIERBAUER, LOUIS W.
Also appeared in box score as Bauer
B. Sept. 28, 1865, Erie, Pa.   D. Jan. 31, 1926, Erie, Pa.
BR TR

	G	AB	H	2B	3B	HR	HR%	R	RBI	BB	SO	SB	BA	SA	PH AB	PH H	G by POS
1886 PHI AA	137	522	118	17	5	2	0.4	56		21			.226	.289	0	0	2B-133, C-4, SS-2, P-2
1887	126	530	144	19	7	1	0.2	74		13		40	.272	.340	0	0	2B-126, P-1
1888	134	535	143	20	9	0	0.0	83	80	25		34	.267	.338	0	0	2B-121, 3B-13, P-1
1889	130	549	167	27	7	7	1.3	80	105	29	30	17	.304	.417	0	0	2B-130, C-1
1890 BKN P	133	589	180	31	11	7	1.2	128	99	40	15	16	.306	.431	0	0	2B-133
1891 PIT N	121	500	103	13	6	1	0.2	60	47	28	19	12	.206	.262	0	0	2B-121
1892	152	649	153	20	9	8	1.2	81	65	25	29	11	.236	.331	0	0	2B-152
1893	128	528	150	19	11	4	0.8	84	94	36	12	11	.284	.384	0	0	2B-128
1894	130	525	159	14	13	3	0.6	86	107	26	9	19	.303	.406	0	0	2B-130
1895	117	466	120	13	11	0	0.0	53	69	19	8	18	.258	.333	0	0	2B-117
1896	59	258	74	10	6	0	0.0	33	39	5	7	1	.287	.372	0	0	2B-59
1897 STL N	12	46	10	0	0	0	0.0	1	1	0		2	.217	.217	0	0	2B-12
1898	4	9	0	0	0	0	0.0	0	0	1		0	.000	.000	0	0	2B-2, SS-1, 3B-1
13 yrs.	1383	5706	1521	208	95	33	0.6	819	705	268	129	187	.267	.354	0	0	2B-1364, 3B-14, C-5, P-4, SS-3
2 yrs.	16	55	10	0	0	0	0.0	1	1		2	.182	.182	0	0	2B-14, SS-1, 3B-1

Steve Bilko

BILKO, STEPHEN
BR TR 6'1" 230 lbs.
B. Nov. 13, 1928, Nanticoke, Pa.   D. Mar. 7, 1978, Wilkes Barre, Pa.

	G	AB	H	2B	3B	HR	HR%	R	RBI	BB	SO	SB	BA	SA	PH AB	PH H	G by POS
1949 STL N	6	17	5	2	0	0	0.0	3	2	5	6	0	.294	.412	1	0	1B-5
1950	10	33	6	1	0	0	0.0	1	2	4	10	0	.182	.212	1	1	1B-9
1951	21	72	16	4	0	2	2.8	5	12	9	10	0	.222	.361	2	1	1B-19
1952	20	72	19	6	1	1	1.4	7	6	4	15	0	.264	.417	0	0	1B-20
1953	154	570	143	23	3	21	3.7	72	84	70	125	0	.251	.412	0	0	1B-154
1954 2 teams	STL N (8G – .143)						CHI N (47G – .239)										
" Total	55	106	24	8	1	4	3.8	12	13	14	25	0	.226	.434	24	6	1B-28
1958 2 teams	CIN N (31G – .264)						LA N (47G – .208)										
" Total	78	188	44	5	4	11	5.9	25	35	18	57	0	.234	.479	27	5	1B-46
1960 DET A	78	222	46	11	2	9	4.1	20	25	27	31	0	.207	.396	17	1	1B-62
1961 LA A	114	294	82	16	1	20	6.8	49	59	58	81	1	.279	.544	24	8	1B-86, OF-3
1962	64	164	47	9	1	8	4.9	26	38	25	35	1	.287	.500	14	3	1B-50
10 yrs.	600	1738	432	85	13	76	4.4	220	276	234	395	2	.249	.444	110	25	1B-479, OF-3
6 yrs.	219	778	191	36	4	24	3.1	89	107	95	167	0	.246	.395	5	2	1B-213

Dick Billings

BILLINGS, RICHARD ARLIN
BR TR 6'1" 195 lbs.
B. Dec. 4, 1942, Detroit, Mich.

	G	AB	H	2B	3B	HR	HR%	R	RBI	BB	SO	SB	BA	SA	PH AB	PH H	G by POS
1968 WAS A	12	33	6	1	0	1	3.0	3	3	5	13	0	.182	.303	3	1	OF-8, 3B-4
1969	27	37	5	0	0	0	0.0	3	0	6	8	0	.135	.135	15	1	OF-6, 3B-1
1970	11	24	6	2	0	1	4.2	3	1	2	3	0	.250	.458	3	0	C-8
1971	116	349	86	14	0	6	1.7	32	48	21	54	2	.246	.338	24	8	C-62, OF-32, 3B-2
1972 TEX A	133	469	119	15	1	5	1.1	41	58	29	77	1	.254	.322	10	1	C-92, OF-41, 3B-5, 1B-1
1973	81	280	50	11	0	3	1.1	17	32	20	43	1	.179	.250	5	1	C-72, OF-4, 1B-3
1974 2 teams	TEX A (16G – .226)						STL N (1G – .200)										
" Total	17	36	8	1	0	0	0.0	0	0	4	7	2	.222	.250	1	0	C-14, OF-1
1975 STL N	3	3	0	0	0	0	0.0	0	0	0	2	0	.000	.000	3	0	C-1
8 yrs.	400	1231	280	44	1	16	1.3	101	142	87	207	6	.227	.304	64	12	C-248, OF-92, 3B-12, 1B-4
2 yrs.	4	8	1	0	0	0	0.0	0	0	0	3	0	.125	.125	3	0	C-1

Frank Bird

BIRD, FRANK ZEPHERIN (Dodo)
BR TR 5'10" 195 lbs.
B. Mar. 10, 1869, Spencer, Mass.   D. May 20, 1958, Worcester, Mass.

	G	AB	H	2B	3B	HR	HR%	R	RBI	BB	SO	SB	BA	SA	PH AB	PH H	G by POS
1892 STL N	17	50	10	3	1	1	2.0	9	1	6	11	2	.200	.360	0	0	C-17

Ray Blades

BLADES, FRANCIS RAYMOND
BR TR 5'7½" 163 lbs.
B. Aug. 6, 1896, Mt. Vernon, Ill.   D. May 18, 1979, Lincoln, Ill.
Manager 1939-40.

	G	AB	H	2B	3B	HR	HR%	R	RBI	BB	SO	SB	BA	SA	PH AB	PH H	G by POS
1922 STL N	37	130	39	2	4	3	2.3	27	21	25	21	3	.300	.446	0	0	OF-29, SS-4, 3B-1
1923	98	317	78	21	5	5	1.6	48	44	37	46	4	.246	.391	4	1	OF-83, 3B-4
1924	131	456	142	21	13	11	2.4	86	68	35	38	7	.311	.487	2	1	OF-109, 3B-7, 2B-7
1925	122	462	158	37	8	12	2.6	112	57	59	47	6	.342	.535	4	2	OF-114, 3B-1
1926	107	416	127	17	12	8	1.9	81	43	62	57	6	.305	.462	1	0	OF-105
1927	61	180	57	8	5	2	1.1	33	29	28	22	3	.317	.450	9	4	OF-50
1928	51	85	20	7	1	1	1.2	9	19	20	26	0	.235	.376	24	4	OF-19
1930	45	101	40	6	2	4	4.0	26	25	21	15	1	.396	.614	7	2	OF-32
1931	35	67	19	4	0	1	1.5	10	5	10	7	1	.284	.388	14	4	OF-20
1932	80	201	46	10	1	3	1.5	35	29	34	31	2	.229	.333	16	2	OF-62, 3B-1
10 yrs.	767	2415	726	133	51	50	2.1	467	340	331	310	33	.301	.460	81	20	OF-623, 3B-14, 2B-7, SS-4
10 yrs.	767	2415	726	133	51	50	2.1	467	340	331	310	33	.301	.460	81	20	OF-623, 3B-14, 2B-7, SS-4

	G	AB	H	2B	3B	HR	HR %	R	RBI	BB	SO	SB	BA	SA	Pinch Hit AB	Pinch Hit H	G by POS

Ray Blades continued

WORLD SERIES

	G	AB	H	2B	3B	HR	HR %	R	RBI	BB	SO	SB	BA	SA	AB	H	G by POS
1928 STL N	1	1	0	0	0	0	0.0	0	0	0	1	0	.000	.000	1	0	
1930	5	9	1	0	0	0	0.0	2	0	2	2	0	.111	.111	1	0	OF-3
1931	2	2	0	0	0	0	0.0	0	0	0	2	0	.000	.000	2	0	
3 yrs.	8	12	1	0	0	0	0.0	2	0	2	5	0	.083	.083	4	0	OF-3

Harry Blake

BLAKE, HARRY COOPER (Dude) BR TR 5'7" 165 lbs.
B. June 16, 1874, Portsmouth, Ohio   D. Oct. 14, 1919, Chicago, Ill.

	G	AB	H	2B	3B	HR	HR %	R	RBI	BB	SO	SB	BA	SA	AB	H	G by POS
1894 CLE N	73	296	78	15	4	1	0.3	51	51	30	22	1	.264	.351	0	0	OF-73
1895	84	315	87	10	1	3	1.0	50	45	30	33	11	.276	.343	1	0	OF-83
1896	104	383	92	12	5	1	0.3	66	43	46	30	10	.240	.305	0	0	OF-103, SS-1
1897	32	117	30	3	1	1	0.9	17	15	12		5	.256	.325	0	0	OF-32
1898	136	474	116	18	7	0	0.0	65	58	69		12	.245	.312	0	0	OF-136, 1B-2
1899 STL N	97	292	70	9	4	2	0.7	50	41	43		16	.240	.318	4	2	OF-87, 2B-4, SS-1, 1B-1, C-1
6 yrs.	526	1877	473	67	22	8	0.4	299	253	230	85	55	.252	.324	5	2	OF-514, 2B-4, 1B-3, SS-2, C-1
1 yr.	97	292	70	9	4	2	0.7	50	41	43		16	.240	.318	4	2	OF-87, 2B-4, SS-1, 1B-1, C-1

Coonie Blank

BLANK, FRANK IGNATZ
D. Dec. 8, 1961

	G	AB	H	2B	3B	HR	HR %	R	RBI	BB	SO	SB	BA	SA	AB	H	G by POS
1909 STL N	1	2	0	0	0	0	0.0	0	0	0		0	.000	.000	0	0	C-1

Don Blasingame

BLASINGAME, DON LEE (The Blazer) BL TR 5'10" 160 lbs.
B. Mar. 16, 1932, Corinth, Miss.

	G	AB	H	2B	3B	HR	HR %	R	RBI	BB	SO	SB	BA	SA	AB	H	G by POS
1955 STL N	5	16	6	1	0	0	0.0	4	0	6	0	1	.375	.438	0	0	2B-3, SS-2
1956	150	587	153	22	7	0	0.0	94	27	72	52	8	.261	.322	2	0	2B-98, SS-49, 3B-2
1957	154	650	176	25	7	8	1.2	108	58	71	49	21	.271	.368	0	0	2B-154
1958	143	547	150	19	10	2	0.4	71	36	57	47	20	.274	.356	4	0	2B-137
1959	150	615	178	26	7	1	0.2	90	24	67	42	15	.289	.359	1	0	2B-150
1960 SF N	136	523	123	12	8	2	0.4	72	31	49	53	14	.235	.300	3	0	2B-133
1961 2 teams		SF	N	(3G – .000)		CIN	N	(123G – .222)									
" Total	126	451	100	18	4	1	0.2	60	21	41	39	4	.222	.286	8	2	2B-116
1962 CIN N	141	494	139	9	7	2	0.4	77	35	63	44	4	.281	.340	6	2	2B-137
1963 2 teams		CIN	N	(18G – .161)		WAS	A	(69G – .256)									
" Total	87	285	70	12	2	2	0.7	33	12	31	23	3	.246	.323	9	2	2B-75, 3B-2
1964 WAS A	143	506	135	17	2	1	0.2	56	34	40	44	8	.267	.314	17	0	2B-135
1965	129	403	90	8	8	1	0.2	47	18	35	45	5	.223	.290	13	2	2B-110
1966 2 teams		WAS	A	(68G – .215)		KC	A	(12G – .158)									
" Total	80	219	46	9	0	1	0.5	19	12	20	24	2	.210	.265	10	1	2B-62, SS-1
12 yrs.	1444	5296	1366	178	62	21	0.4	731	308	552	462	105	.258	.327	73	9	2B-1310, SS-52, 3B-4
5 yrs.	602	2415	663	93	31	11	0.5	367	145	273	190	65	.275	.352	7	0	2B-542, SS-51, 3B-2

WORLD SERIES

	G	AB	H	2B	3B	HR	HR %	R	RBI	BB	SO	SB	BA	SA	AB	H	G by POS
1961 CIN N	3	7	1	0	0	0	0.0	1	0	3		0	.143	.143	0	0	2B-3

Johnny Blatnik

BLATNIK, JOHN LOUIS (Chief) BR TR 6' 195 lbs.
B. Mar. 10, 1921, Bridgeport, Ohio

	G	AB	H	2B	3B	HR	HR %	R	RBI	BB	SO	SB	BA	SA	AB	H	G by POS
1948 PHI N	121	415	108	27	8	6	1.4	56	45	31	77	3	.260	.407	15	4	OF-105
1949	6	8	1	0	0	0	0.0	3	0	4	1	0	.125	.125	3	1	OF-2
1950 2 teams		PHI	N	(4G – .250)		STL	N	(7G – .150)									
" Total	11	24	4	0	0	0	0.0	0	1	5	5	0	.167	.167	4	1	OF-8
3 yrs.	138	447	113	27	8	6	1.3	59	46	40	83	3	.253	.389	22	6	OF-115
1 yr.	7	20	3	0	0	0	0.0	0	1	3	2	0	.150	.150	1	0	OF-7

Buddy Blattner

BLATTNER, ROBERT GARNETT BR TR 6'½" 180 lbs.
B. Feb. 8, 1920, St. Louis, Mo.

	G	AB	H	2B	3B	HR	HR %	R	RBI	BB	SO	SB	BA	SA	AB	H	G by POS
1942 STL N	19	23	1	0	0	0	0.0	3	1	3	6	0	.043	.043	2	0	SS-13, 2B-3
1946 NY N	126	420	107	18	6	11	2.6	63	49	56	52	12	.255	.405	2	0	2B-114, 1B-1
1947	55	153	40	9	2	0	0.0	28	13	21	19	4	.261	.346	2	0	2B-34, 3B-4
1948	8	20	4	1	0	0	0.0	3	0	3	2	2	.200	.250	0	0	2B-7
1949 PHI N	64	97	24	6	0	5	5.2	15	21	19	17	0	.247	.464	29	7	3B-62, 2B-15, SS-7
5 yrs.	272	713	176	34	8	16	2.2	112	84	102	96	18	.247	.384	35	7	2B-173, 3B-66, SS-20, 1B-1
1 yr.	19	23	1	0	0	0	0.0	3	1	3	6	0	.043	.043	2	0	SS-13, 2B-3

John Bliss

BLISS, JOHN JOSEPH ALFRED BR TR 5'9" 185 lbs.
B. Jan. 9, 1882, Vancouver, Wash.   D. Oct. 23, 1968, Temple City, Calif.

	G	AB	H	2B	3B	HR	HR %	R	RBI	BB	SO	SB	BA	SA	AB	H	G by POS
1908 STL N	44	136	29	4	0	1	0.7	9	5	8		3	.213	.265	2	1	C-43
1909	35	113	25	2	1	1	0.9	12	8	12		2	.221	.283	9	1	C-32
1910	16	33	2	0	0	0	0.0	2	3	4	8	0	.061	.061	3	0	C-13
1911	97	258	59	6	4	1	0.4	36	27	42	25	5	.229	.295	8	1	C-84, SS-1
1912	49	114	28	3	1	0	0.0	11	18	19	14	3	.246	.289	6	3	C-41
5 yrs.	241	654	143	15	6	3	0.5	70	61	85	47	13	.219	.274	28	6	C-213, SS-1
5 yrs.	241	654	143	15	6	3	0.5	70	61	85	47	13	.219	.274	28	6	C-213, SS-1

Clyde Bloomfield

BLOOMFIELD, CLYDE STALCUP (Bud) BR TR 5'11½" 175 lbs.
B. Jan. 5, 1937, Oklahoma City, Okla.

	G	AB	H	2B	3B	HR	HR %	R	RBI	BB	SO	SB	BA	SA	AB	H	G by POS
1963 STL N	1	0	0	0	0	0	–	0	0	0	0	0	–	–	0	0	3B-1
1964 MIN A	7	7	1	0	0	0	0.0	1	0	0	0	0	.143	.143	0	0	2B-3, SS-2
2 yrs.	8	7	1	0	0	0	0.0	1	0	0	0	0	.143	.143	0	0	2B-3, SS-2, 3B-1
1 yr.	1	0	0	0	0	0	–	0	0	0	0	0	–	–	0	0	3B-1

	G	AB	H	2B	3B	HR	HR %	R	RBI	BB	SO	SB	BA	SA	Pinch Hit AB	Pinch Hit H	G by POS

Sammy Bohne

BOHNE, SAMMY ARTHUR
Born Sammy Arthur Cohen.
B. Oct. 22, 1896, San Francisco, Calif.   D. May 23, 1977, Palo Alto, Calif.
BR TR 5'8½" 175 lbs.

	G	AB	H	2B	3B	HR	HR %	R	RBI	BB	SO	SB	BA	SA	AB	H	G by POS
1916 STL N	14	38	9	0	0	0	0.0	3	0	4	6	3	.237	.237	0	0	SS-14
1921 CIN N	153	613	175	28	16	3	0.5	98	44	54	38	26	.285	.398	0	0	2B-102, 3B-53
1922	112	383	105	14	5	3	0.8	53	51	39	18	13	.274	.360	2	0	2B-85, SS-22
1923	139	539	136	18	10	3	0.6	77	47	48	37	16	.252	.340	0	0	2B-96, 3B-35, SS-9, 1B-1
1924	100	349	89	15	9	4	1.1	42	46	18	24	9	.255	.384	0	0	2B-48, SS-40, 3B-12
1925	73	214	55	9	1	2	0.9	24	24	14	14	6	.257	.336	3	1	SS-49, 2B-10, OF-4, 3B-2, 1B-2
1926 2 teams	CIN N (25G – .204)					BKN N (47G – .200)											
" Total	72	179	36	3	4	1	0.6	12	16	16	17	2	.201	.279	0	0	2B-31, SS-20, 3B-15
7 yrs.	663	2315	605	87	45	16	0.7	309	228	193	154	75	.261	.359	5	1	2B-372, SS-154, 3B-117, OF-4, 1B-3
1 yr.	14	38	9	0	0	0	0.0	3	0	4	6	3	.237	.237	0	0	SS-14

Don Bollweg

BOLLWEG, DONALD RAYMOND
B. Feb. 12, 1921, Wheaton, Ill.
BL TL 6'1" 190 lbs.

	G	AB	H	2B	3B	HR	HR %	R	RBI	BB	SO	SB	BA	SA	AB	H	G by POS
1950 STL N	4	11	2	0	0	0	0.0	1	1	1	1	0	.182	.182	0	0	1B-4
1951	6	9	1	1	0	0	0.0	1	2	0	1	0	.111	.222	4	1	1B-2
1953 NY A	70	155	46	6	4	6	3.9	24	24	21	31	1	.297	.503	21	5	1B-43
1954 PHI A	103	268	60	15	3	5	1.9	35	24	35	33	1	.224	.358	29	6	1B-71
1955 KC A	12	9	1	0	0	0	0.0	1	2	3	2	0	.111	.111	9	1	1B-3
5 yrs.	195	452	110	22	7	11	2.4	62	53	60	68	2	.243	.396	63	13	1B-123
2 yrs.	10	20	3	1	0	0	0.0	2	3	1	2	0	.150	.200	4	1	1B-6

WORLD SERIES

	G	AB	H	2B	3B	HR	HR %	R	RBI	BB	SO	SB	BA	SA	AB	H	G by POS
1953 NY A	3	2	0	0	0	0	0.0	0	0	0	2	0	.000	.000	2	0	1B-1

Bobby Bonds

BONDS, BOBBY LEE
B. Mar. 15, 1946, Riverside, Calif.
BR TR 6'1" 190 lbs.

	G	AB	H	2B	3B	HR	HR %	R	RBI	BB	SO	SB	BA	SA	AB	H	G by POS
1968 SF N	81	307	78	10	5	9	2.9	55	35	38	84	16	.254	.407	0	0	OF-80
1969	158	622	161	25	6	32	5.1	120	90	81	187	45	.259	.473	1	0	OF-155
1970	157	663	200	36	10	26	3.9	134	78	77	189	48	.302	.504	2	0	OF-157
1971	155	619	178	32	4	33	5.3	110	102	62	137	26	.288	.512	3	1	OF-154
1972	153	626	162	29	5	26	4.2	118	80	60	137	44	.259	.446	0	0	OF-153
1973	160	643	182	34	4	39	6.1	131	96	87	148	43	.283	.530	2	1	OF-158
1974	150	567	145	22	8	21	3.7	97	71	95	134	41	.256	.434	3	1	OF-148
1975 NY A	145	529	143	26	3	32	6.0	93	85	89	137	30	.270	.512	4	1	OF-129
1976 CAL A	99	378	100	10	3	10	2.6	48	54	41	90	30	.265	.386	1	0	OF-98
1977	158	592	156	23	9	37	6.3	103	115	74	141	41	.264	.520	1	0	OF-140
1978 2 teams	CHI A (26G – .278)					TEX A (130G – .265)											
" Total	156	565	151	19	4	31	5.5	93	90	79	120	43	.267	.480	2	1	OF-133
1979 CLE A	146	538	148	24	1	25	4.6	93	85	74	135	34	.275	.463	1	0	OF-116
1980 STL N	86	231	47	5	3	5	2.2	37	24	33	74	15	.203	.316	15	2	OF-70
1981 CHI N	45	163	35	7	1	6	3.7	26	19	24	44	5	.215	.380	0	0	OF-45
14 yrs.	1849	7043	1886	302	66	332	4.7	1258	1024	914	1757 3rd	461	.268	.471	35	7	OF-1736
1 yr.	86	231	47	5	3	5	2.2	37	24	33	74	15	.203	.316	15	2	OF-70

LEAGUE CHAMPIONSHIP SERIES

	G	AB	H	2B	3B	HR	HR %	R	RBI	BB	SO	SB	BA	SA	AB	H	G by POS
1971 SF N	3	8	2	0	0	0	0.0	0	2	4	0	0	.250	.250	0	0	OF-3

Frank Bonner

BONNER, FRANK J. (The Human Flea)
B. Aug. 20, 1869, Lowell, Mass.   D. Dec. 31, 1905, Kansas City, Mo.
TR

	G	AB	H	2B	3B	HR	HR %	R	RBI	BB	SO	SB	BA	SA	AB	H	G by POS
1894 BAL N	33	118	38	10	2	0	0.0	27	24	17	5	12	.322	.441	1	0	2B-27, OF-4, 3B-2, SS-1
1895 2 teams	BAL N (11G – .333)					STL N (15G – .136)											
" Total	26	101	22	1	2	1	1.0	12	15	6	9	6	.218	.297	0	0	3B-21, OF-5, C-1
1896 BKN N	9	34	6	2	0	0	0.0	8	5	2	8	1	.176	.235	0	0	2B-9
1899 WAS N	85	347	95	20	4	2	0.6	41	44	18		6	.274	.372	0	0	2B-85
1902 2 teams	CLE A (34G – .280)					PHI A (11G – .182)											
" Total	45	176	45	6	0	0	0.0	16	17	5		1	.256	.290	0	0	2B-45
1903 BOS N	48	173	38	5	0	1	0.6	11	10	7		2	.220	.266	2	1	2B-24, SS-22
6 yrs.	246	949	244	44	8	4	0.4	115	115	55	22	28	.257	.333	3	1	2B-190, SS-23, 3B-23, OF-9, C-1
1 yr.	15	59	8	0	1	1	1.7	3	8	1	8	2	.136	.220	0	0	3B-10, OF-5, C-1

Frenchy Bordagaray

BORDAGARAY, STANLEY GEORGE
B. Jan. 3, 1912, Coalinga, Calif.
BR TR 5'7½" 175 lbs.

	G	AB	H	2B	3B	HR	HR %	R	RBI	BB	SO	SB	BA	SA	AB	H	G by POS
1934 CHI A	29	87	28	3	1	0	0.0	12	2	3	8	1	.322	.379	12	8	OF-17
1935 BKN N	120	422	119	19	6	1	0.2	69	39	17	29	18	.282	.363	9	2	OF-105
1936	125	372	117	21	3	4	1.1	63	31	17	42	12	.315	.419	6	2	OF-92, 2B-11
1937 STL N	96	300	88	11	4	1	0.3	43	37	15	25	11	.293	.367	16	1	3B-50, OF-28
1938	81	156	44	5	1	0	0.0	19	21	8	9	2	.282	.327	43	20	OF-29, 3B-4
1939 CIN N	63	122	24	5	1	0	0.0	19	12	9	10	3	.197	.254	11	0	OF-43, 2B-2
1941 NY N	36	73	19	1	0	0	0.0	10	4	6	8	1	.260	.274	13	4	OF-19
1942 BKN N	48	58	14	2	0	0	0.0	11	5	3	3	2	.241	.276	15	4	OF-17
1943	89	268	81	18	2	0	0.0	47	19	30	15	6	.302	.384	6	2	OF-53, 3B-25
1944	130	501	141	26	4	6	1.2	85	51	36	22	2	.281	.385	10	3	3B-98, OF-25
1945	113	273	70	9	6	2	0.7	32	49	29	15	7	.256	.355	32	8	3B-57, OF-22
11 yrs.	930	2632	745	120	28	14	0.5	410	270	173	186	65	.283	.366	173	54	OF-450, 3B-234, 2B-13
2 yrs.	177	456	132	16	5	1	0.2	62	58	23	34	13	.289	.353	59	21	OF-57, 3B-54

WORLD SERIES

	G	AB	H	2B	3B	HR	HR %	R	RBI	BB	SO	SB	BA	SA	AB	H	G by POS
1939 CIN N	2	0	0	0	0	0	–	0	0	0	0	0	–	–	0	0	
1941 NY A	1	0	0	0	0	0	–	0	0	0	0	0	–	–	0	0	
2 yrs.	3	0	0	0	0	0	–	0	0	0	0	0	–	–	0	0	

	G	AB	H	2B	3B	HR	HR %	R	RBI	BB	SO	SB	BA	SA	Pinch Hit AB	Pinch Hit H	G by POS

Rick Bosetti

BOSETTI, RICHARD ALAN
B. Aug. 5, 1953, Redding, Calif.   BR TR 5'11" 185 lbs.

	G	AB	H	2B	3B	HR	HR %	R	RBI	BB	SO	SB	BA	SA	PH AB	PH H	G by POS
1976 PHI N	13	18	5	1	0	0	0.0	6	0	1	3	3	.278	.333	1	0	OF-6
1977 STL N	41	69	16	0	0	0	0.0	12	3	6	11	4	.232	.232	2	0	OF-35
1978 TOR A	136	568	147	25	5	5	0.9	61	42	30	65	6	.259	.347	0	0	OF-135
1979	162	619	161	35	2	8	1.3	59	65	22	70	13	.260	.362	0	0	OF-162
1980	53	188	40	7	1	4	2.1	24	18	15	29	4	.213	.324	1	0	OF-51
1981 2 teams	TOR A (25G – .234)			OAK A (9G – .105)													
" Total	34	66	13	2	0	0	0.0	9	5	5	9	0	.197	.227	3	1	OF-24
1982 OAK A	6	15	3	0	0	0	0.0	1	0	0	1	0	.200	.200	0	0	OF-6
7 yrs.	445	1543	385	70	8	17	1.1	172	133	79	188	30	.250	.338	7	1	OF-419
1 yr.	41	69	16	0	0	0	0.0	12	3	6	11	4	.232	.232	2	0	OF-35

DIVISIONAL PLAYOFF SERIES

	G	AB	H	2B	3B	HR	HR %	R	RBI	BB	SO	SB	BA	SA	PH AB	PH H	G by POS
1981 OAK A	1	0	0	0	0	0	–	0	0	0	0	0	–	–	0	0	OF-1

LEAGUE CHAMPIONSHIP SERIES

	G	AB	H	2B	3B	HR	HR %	R	RBI	BB	SO	SB	BA	SA	PH AB	PH H	G by POS
1981 OAK A	2	4	1	1	0	0	0.0	1	0	0	1	0	.250	.500	1	0	OF-1

Jim Bottomley

BOTTOMLEY, JAMES LeROY (Sunny Jim)
B. Apr. 23, 1900, Oglesby, Ill.   D. Dec. 11, 1959, St. Louis, Mo.
Manager 1937.
Hall of Fame 1974.   BL TL 6' 180 lbs.

	G	AB	H	2B	3B	HR	HR %	R	RBI	BB	SO	SB	BA	SA	PH AB	PH H	G by POS
1922 STL N	37	151	49	8	5	5	3.3	29	35	6	13	3	.325	.543	3	1	1B-34
1923	134	523	194	34	14	8	1.5	79	94	45	44	4	.371	.535	4	1	1B-130
1924	137	528	167	31	12	14	2.7	87	111	35	35	5	.316	.500	3	1	1B-133, 2B-1
1925	153	619	227	44	12	21	3.4	92	128	47	36	3	.367	.578	0	0	1B-153
1926	154	603	180	40	14	19	3.2	98	120	58	52	4	.299	.506	0	0	1B-154
1927	152	574	174	31	15	19	3.3	95	124	74	49	8	.303	.509	0	0	1B-152
1928	149	576	187	42	20	31	5.4	123	136	71	54	10	.325	.628	0	0	1B-148
1929	146	560	176	31	12	29	5.2	108	137	70	54	3	.314	.568	1	0	1B-145
1930	131	487	148	33	7	15	3.1	92	97	44	36	5	.304	.493	7	2	1B-124
1931	108	382	133	34	5	9	2.4	73	75	34	24	3	.348	.534	14	3	1B-93
1932	91	311	92	16	3	11	3.5	45	48	25	32	2	.296	.473	16	7	1B-74
1933 CIN N	145	549	137	23	9	13	2.4	57	83	42	28	3	.250	.395	0	0	1B-145
1934	142	556	158	31	11	11	2.0	72	78	33	40	1	.284	.439	3	0	1B-139
1935	107	399	103	21	1	1	0.3	44	49	18	24	3	.258	.323	10	5	1B-97
1936 STL A	140	544	162	39	11	12	2.2	72	95	44	55	0	.298	.476	0	0	1B-140
1937	65	109	26	7	0	1	0.9	11	12	18	15	1	.239	.330	38	7	1B-24
16 yrs.	1991	7471	2313	465	151	219	2.9	1177	1422	664	591	58	.310	.500	99	27	1B-1885, 2B-1
11 yrs.	1392	5314	1727	344	119	181	3.4	921	1105	509	429	50	.325	.537	48	15	1B-1340, 2B-1
		10th	8th	7th	5th	4th	8th		7th	3rd	9th			7th	6th		

WORLD SERIES

	G	AB	H	2B	3B	HR	HR %	R	RBI	BB	SO	SB	BA	SA	PH AB	PH H	G by POS
1926 STL N	7	29	10	3	0	0	0.0	4	5	1	2	0	.345	.448	0	0	1B-7
1928	4	14	3	0	1	1	7.1	1	3	2	6	0	.214	.571	0	0	1B-4
1930	6	22	1	1	0	0	0.0	1	0	2	9	0	.045	.091	0	0	1B-6
1931	7	25	4	1	0	0	0.0	2	2	2	5	0	.160	.200	0	0	1B-7
4 yrs.	24	90	18	5	1	1	1.1	8	10	7	22	0	.200	.311	0	0	1B-24

Ken Boyer

BOYER, KENTON LLOYD
Brother of Cloyd Boyer. Brother of Clete Boyer.
B. May 20, 1931, Liberty, Mo.   D. Sept. 7, 1982, St. Louis, Mo.
Manager 1978-80.   BR TR 6'1½" 190 lbs.

	G	AB	H	2B	3B	HR	HR %	R	RBI	BB	SO	SB	BA	SA	PH AB	PH H	G by POS
1955 STL N	147	530	140	27	2	18	3.4	78	62	37	67	22	.264	.425	1	0	3B-139, SS-18
1956	150	595	182	30	2	26	4.4	91	98	38	65	8	.306	.494	1	0	3B-149
1957	142	544	144	18	3	19	3.5	79	62	44	77	12	.265	.414	1	0	OF-105, 3B-41
1958	150	570	175	21	9	23	4.0	101	90	49	53	11	.307	.496	1	0	3B-144, OF-6, SS-1
1959	149	563	174	18	5	28	5.0	86	94	67	77	12	.309	.508	1	0	3B-143, SS-12
1960	151	552	168	26	10	32	5.8	95	97	56	77	8	.304	.562	5	1	3B-146
1961	153	589	194	26	11	24	4.1	109	95	68	91	6	.329	.533	0	0	3B-153
1962	160	611	178	27	5	24	3.9	92	98	75	104	12	.291	.470	0	0	3B-160
1963	159	617	176	28	2	24	3.9	86	111	70	90	1	.285	.454	0	0	3B-159
1964	162	628	185	30	10	24	3.8	100	119	70	85	3	.295	.489	0	0	3B-162
1965	144	535	139	18	2	13	2.4	71	75	57	73	2	.260	.374	3	0	3B-143
1966 NY N	136	496	132	28	2	14	2.8	62	61	30	64	4	.266	.415	7	3	3B-130, 1B-2
1967 2 teams	NY N (56G – .235)			CHI A (57G – .261)													
" Total	113	346	86	12	3	7	2.0	34	34	33	47	2	.249	.361	15	4	3B-77, 1B-26
1968 2 teams	CHI A (10G – .125)			LA N (83G – .271)													
" Total	93	245	63	7	2	6	2.4	20	41	17	40	2	.257	.376	29	6	3B-39, 1B-33
1969 LA N	25	34	7	2	0	0	0.0	4		2	7	0	.206	.265	19	4	1B-14
15 yrs.	2034	7455	2143	318	68	282	3.8	1104	1141	713	1017	105	.287	.462	83	18	3B-1785, OF-111, 1B-65, SS-31
11 yrs.	1667	6334	1855	269	61	255	4.0	988	1001	631	859	97	.293	.475	13	1	3B-1539, OF-111, SS-31
		6th	5th	6th		2nd	5th		6th	5th	5th	5th	2nd		10th		

WORLD SERIES

	G	AB	H	2B	3B	HR	HR %	R	RBI	BB	SO	SB	BA	SA	PH AB	PH H	G by POS
1964 STL N	7	27	6	1	0	2	7.4	5	6	1	5	0	.222	.481	0	0	3B-7

Buddy Bradford

BRADFORD, CHARLES WILLIAM
B. July 25, 1944, Mobile, Ala.   BR TR 5'11" 170 lbs.

	G	AB	H	2B	3B	HR	HR %	R	RBI	BB	SO	SB	BA	SA	PH AB	PH H	G by POS
1966 CHI A	14	28	4	0	0	0	0.0	3	0	2	6	0	.143	.143	0	0	OF-9
1967	24	20	2	1	0	0	0.0	6	1	1	7	1	.100	.150	3	1	OF-10
1968	103	281	61	11	0	5	1.8	32	24	23	67	8	.217	.310	6	1	OF-99
1969	93	273	70	8	2	11	4.0	36	27	34	75	5	.256	.421	5	0	OF-88
1970 2 teams	CHI A (32G – .187)			CLE A (75G – .196)													
" Total	107	254	49	9	1	9	3.5	33	31	31	73	1	.193	.343	18	3	OF-91, 3B-1
1971 2 teams	CLE A (20G – .158)			CIN N (79G – .200)													
" Total	99	138	26	5	1	2	1.4	21	15	20	33	4	.188	.283	14	2	OF-84

	G	AB	H	2B	3B	HR	HR %	R	RBI	BB	SO	SB	BA	SA	Pinch Hit AB	Pinch Hit H	G by POS

Buddy Bradford   continued

	G	AB	H	2B	3B	HR	HR %	R	RBI	BB	SO	SB	BA	SA	AB	H	G by POS
1972 CHI A	35	48	13	2	0	2	4.2	13	8	4	13	3	.271	.438	10	4	OF-28
1973	53	168	40	3	1	8	4.8	24	15	17	43	4	.238	.411	5	0	OF-51
1974	39	96	32	2	0	5	5.2	16	10	13	11	1	.333	.510	7	2	OF-32
1975 2 teams		CHI	A	(25G –	.155)		STL	N	(50G –	.272)							
" Total	75	139	31	4	1	6	4.3	20	30	20	46	3	.223	.396	27	6	OF-43
1976 CHI A	55	160	35	5	2	4	2.5	20	14	19	37	6	.219	.350	9	0	OF-48
11 yrs.	697	1605	363	50	8	52	3.2	224	175	184	411	36	.226	.364	104	19	OF-587, 3B-1
1 yr.	50	81	22	1	0	4	4.9	12	15	12	24	0	.272	.432	23	6	OF-25

Dave Brain

BRAIN, DAVID LEONARD   BR TR 5'10"   170 lbs.
B. Jan. 24, 1879, Hereford, England   D. May 25, 1959, Los Angeles, Calif.

	G	AB	H	2B	3B	HR	HR %	R	RBI	BB	SO	SB	BA	SA	AB	H	G by POS
1901 CHI A	5	20	7	1	0	0	0.0	2	5	1		0	.350	.400	0	0	2B-5
1903 STL N	119	464	107	8	15	1	0.2	44	60	25		21	.231	.319	0	0	SS-72, 3B-46
1904	127	488	130	24	12	7	1.4	57	72	17		18	.266	.408	2	0	SS-59, 3B-30, OF-19, 2B-13, 1B-4
1905 2 teams		STL	N	(44G –	.228)		PIT	N	(85G –	.257)							
" Total	129	465	115	21	11	4	0.9	42	63	23		12	.247	.366	3	1	3B-84, SS-33, OF-6
1906 BOS N	139	525	131	19	5	5	1.0	43	45	29		11	.250	.333	0	0	3B-139
1907	133	509	142	24	9	10	2.0	60	56	29		10	.279	.420	0	0	3B-130, OF-3
1908 2 teams		CIN	N	(16G –	.109)		NY	N	(11G –	.176)							
" Total	27	72	9	0	0	0	0.0	6	2	10		1	.125	.125	2	0	OF-19, 2B-3, 3B-2, SS-1
7 yrs.	679	2543	641	97	52	27	1.1	254	303	134		73	.252	.363	7	1	3B-431, SS-165, OF-47, 2B-21, 1B-4
3 yrs.	290	1110	273	36	32	9	0.8	112	149	50		43	.246	.360	5	1	SS-160, 3B-82, OF-25, 2B-13, 1B-4

Jackie Brandt

BRANDT, JOHN GEORGE   BR TR 5'11"   165 lbs.
B. Apr. 28, 1934, Omaha, Neb.

	G	AB	H	2B	3B	HR	HR %	R	RBI	BB	SO	SB	BA	SA	AB	H	G by POS
1956 2 teams		STL	N	(27G –	.286)		NY	N	(98G –	.299)							
" Total	125	393	117	19	8	12	3.1	54	50	21	36	3	.298	.478	4	2	OF-122
1958 SF N	18	52	13	1	0	0	0.0	7	3	6	5	1	.250	.269	5	1	OF-14
1959	137	429	116	16	5	12	2.8	63	57	35	69	11	.270	.415	16	4	OF-116, 3B-18, 1B-3, 2B-1
1960 BAL A	145	511	130	24	6	15	2.9	73	65	47	69	5	.254	.413	4	0	OF-142, 3B-2, 1B-1
1961	139	516	153	18	5	16	3.1	93	72	62	51	10	.297	.444	0	0	OF-136, 3B-1
1962	143	505	129	29	5	19	3.8	76	75	55	64	9	.255	.446	6	1	OF-138, 3B-2
1963	142	451	112	15	5	15	3.3	49	61	34	85	4	.248	.404	8	1	OF-134, 3B-1
1964	137	523	127	25	1	13	2.5	66	47	45	104	1	.243	.369	4	0	OF-134
1965	96	243	59	17	0	8	3.3	35	24	21	40	1	.243	.412	14	2	OF-84
1966 PHI N	82	164	41	6	1	1	0.6	16	15	17	36	0	.250	.317	15	4	OF-71
1967 2 teams		PHI	N	(16G –	.105)		HOU	N	(41G –	.236)							
" Total	57	108	23	5	1	1	0.9	8	16	8	15	0	.213	.306	33	9	1B-14, OF-9, 3B-1
11 yrs.	1221	3895	1020	175	37	112	2.9	540	485	351	574	45	.262	.412	109	24	OF-1100, 3B-25, 1B-18, 2B-1
1 yr.	27	42	12	3	0	1	2.4	9	3	4	5	0	.286	.429	2	1	OF-26

Kitty Brashear

BRASHEAR, ROBERT NORMAN
Brother of Roy Brashear.
B. Aug. 12, 1878, Mansfield, Ohio   D. Dec. 23, 1934, Los Angeles, Calif.

	G	AB	H	2B	3B	HR	HR %	R	RBI	BB	SO	SB	BA	SA	AB	H	G by POS
1902 STL N	110	388	107	8	2	1	0.3	36	40	32		9	.276	.314	3	1	1B-67, 2B-21, OF-16, SS-3

Joe Bratcher

BRATCHER, JOSEPH WARLICK (Goobers)   BL TR 5'8½"   140 lbs.
B. July 22, 1898, Grand Saline, Tex.

	G	AB	H	2B	3B	HR	HR %	R	RBI	BB	SO	SB	BA	SA	AB	H	G by POS
1924 STL N	4	1	0	0	0	0	0.0	1	0	0	0	0	.000	.000	1	0	OF-1

Steve Braun

BRAUN, STEPHEN RUSSELL   BL TR 5'10"   180 lbs.
B. May 8, 1948, Trenton, N. J.

	G	AB	H	2B	3B	HR	HR %	R	RBI	BB	SO	SB	BA	SA	AB	H	G by POS
1971 MIN A	128	343	87	12	2	5	1.5	51	35	48	50	8	.254	.344	26	7	3B-73, 2B-28, SS-10, OF-2
1972	121	402	116	21	0	2	0.5	40	50	45	38	4	.289	.356	14	4	3B-74, 2B-20, SS-11, OF-9
1973	115	361	102	28	5	6	1.7	46	42	74	48	4	.283	.438	5	1	3B-102, OF-6
1974	129	453	127	12	1	8	1.8	53	40	56	51	4	.280	.364	6	1	OF-108, 3B-17
1975	136	453	137	18	3	11	2.4	70	45	66	55	0	.302	.428	11	6	OF-106, 1B-9, 3B-2, 2B-1
1976	122	417	120	12	3	3	0.7	73	61	67	43	12	.288	.353	9	5	OF-32, 3B-16
1977 SEA A	139	451	106	19	1	5	1.1	51	31	80	59	8	.235	.315	11	0	OF-100, 3B-1
1978 2 teams		SEA	A	(32G –	.230)		KC	A	(64G –	.263)							
" Total	96	211	53	14	1	3	1.4	27	29	37	21	4	.251	.370	38	11	OF-37, 3B-11
1979 KC A	58	116	31	2	0	4	3.4	15	10	22	11	0	.267	.388	28	8	OF-18, 3B-2
1980 2 teams		KC	A	(14G –	.043)		TOR	A	(37G –	.273)							
" Total	51	78	16	2	1	1	1.3	4	10	10	7	0	.205	.269	35	10	OF-5, 3B-1
1981 STL N	44	46	9	2	1	0	0.0	9	2	15	7	1	.196	.283	25	5	OF-12, 3B-1
1982	58	62	17	4	0	0	0.0	6	4	11	10	0	.274	.339	41	12	OF-8, 3B-5
12 yrs.	1197	3393	921	146	17	48	1.4	445	359	531	400	45	.271	.367	249	70	OF-443, 3B-305, 2B-49, SS-21, 1B-9
2 yrs.	102	108	26	6	1	0	0.0	15	6	26	17	1	.241	.315	66	17	OF-20, 3B-6

LEAGUE CHAMPIONSHIP SERIES

	G	AB	H	2B	3B	HR	HR %	R	RBI	BB	SO	SB	BA	SA	AB	H	G by POS
1978 KC A	2	5	0	0	0	0	0.0	0	1	0	0	0	.000	.000	1	0	OF-1
1982 STL N	1	1	0	0	0	0		0	0	0	0	0	.000	.000	1	0	
2 yrs.	3	6	0	0	0	0	0.0	0	1	0	0	0	.000	.000	2	0	OF-1

WORLD SERIES

	G	AB	H	2B	3B	HR	HR %	R	RBI	BB	SO	SB	BA	SA	AB	H	G by POS
1982 STL N	2	2	1	0	0	0	0.0	0	1	0	0	0	.500	.500	1	0	

	G	AB	H	2B	3B	HR	HR%	R	RBI	BB	SO	SB	BA	SA	Pinch Hit AB	Pinch Hit H	G by POS

ed Breitenstein

BREITENSTEIN, THEODORE P.   BL TL 5'9" 167 lbs.
B. June 1, 1869, St. Louis, Mo.   D. May 3, 1935, St. Louis, Mo.

	G	AB	H	2B	3B	HR	HR%	R	RBI	BB	SO	SB	BA	SA	AB	H	G by POS
91 STL AA	6	12	0	0	0	0	0.0	2	0	2	0	1	.000	.000	0	0	P-6, OF-1
92 STL N	47	131	16	1	1	0	0.0	16	6	16	20	4	.122	.145	0	0	P-39, OF-10
93	49	160	29	1	1	1	0.6	20	14	18	15	3	.181	.219	0	0	P-48, OF-2
94	63	182	40	7	2	0	0.0	27	13	31	19	3	.220	.280	0	0	P-56, OF-7
95	72	218	42	2	0	0	0.0	25	18	29	22	5	.193	.202	1	1	P-54, OF-16
96	51	162	42	5	2	0	0.0	21	12	13	26	8	.259	.315	1	1	P-44, OF-8
97 CIN N	41	124	33	4	0	0	0.0	16	23	6		5	.266	.395	1	0	P-40
98	41	121	26	2	1	0	0.0	16	17	16		0	.215	.248	0	0	P-39, OF-2
99	33	105	37	4	1	1	1.0	18	11	10		1	.352	.438	0	0	P-26, OF-7
00	41	126	24	1	1	2	1.6	12	12	9		0	.190	.262	5	1	P-24, OF-12
01 STL N	3	6	2	0	0	0	0.0	1	0	0		0	.333	.333	0	0	P-3
11 yrs.	447	1347	291	27	15	4	0.3	174	126	150	102	30	.216	.267	8	3	P-379, OF-65
6 yrs.	285	859	171	16	6	1	0.1	110	63	107	102	23	.199	.235	2	2	P-244, OF-43

erb Bremer

BREMER, HERBERT FREDERICK   BR TR 6' 195 lbs.
B. Oct. 25, 1913, Chicago, Ill.   D. Nov. 28, 1979, Chicago, Ill.

	G	AB	H	2B	3B	HR	HR%	R	RBI	BB	SO	SB	BA	SA	AB	H	G by POS
37 STL N	11	33	7	1	0	0	0.0	2	3	2	4	0	.212	.242	0	0	C-10
38	50	151	33	5	1	2	1.3	14	14	9	36	1	.219	.305	0	0	C-50
39	9	9	1	0	0	0	0.0	0	1	0	2	0	.111	.111	1	0	C-8
3 yrs.	70	193	41	6	1	2	1.0	16	18	11	42	1	.212	.285	1	0	C-68
3 yrs.	70	193	41	6	1	2	1.0	16	18	11	42	1	.212	.285	1	0	C-68

oger Bresnahan

BRESNAHAN, ROGER PHILIP (The Duke of Tralee)   BR TR 5'9" 200 lbs.
B. June 11, 1879, Toledo, Ohio   D. Dec. 4, 1944, Toledo, Ohio
Manager 1909-12, 1915.
Hall of Fame 1945.

	G	AB	H	2B	3B	HR	HR%	R	RBI	BB	SO	SB	BA	SA	AB	H	G by POS
97 WAS N	6	16	6	0	0	0	0.0	1	3	1		0	.375	.375	0	0	P-6, OF-1
00 CHI N	2	2	0	0	0	0	0.0	0	0	0		0	.000	.000	0	0	C-1
01 BAL A	86	295	79	9	9	1	0.3	40	32	23		10	.268	.369	1	0	C-69, OF-8, 3B-4, 2B-2, P-2
02 2 teams		BAL A	(65G – .272)		NY N	(51G – .292)											
Total	116	413	116	22	9	5	1.2	47	56	37		18	.281	.414	2	2	OF-42, C-38, 3B-31, SS-4, 1B-4
03 NY N	113	406	142	30	8	4	1.0	87	55	61		34	.350	.493	1	1	OF-84, 1B-13, C-11, 3B-4
04	109	402	114	21	8	5	1.2	81	33	58		13	.284	.413	3	1	OF-93, 1B-10, SS-4, 3B-1, 2B-1
05	104	331	100	18	3	0	0.0	58	46	50		11	.302	.375	6	0	C-87, OF-8
06	124	405	114	22	4	0	0.0	69	43	81		25	.281	.356	0	0	C-82, OF-40
07	110	328	83	9	7	4	1.2	57	38	61		15	.253	.360	6	2	C-95, 1B-6, OF-2, 3B-1
08	140	449	127	25	3	1	0.2	70	54	83		14	.283	.359	1	1	C-139
09 STL N	72	234	57	4	1	0	0.0	27	23	46		11	.244	.269	2	0	C-59, 2B-9, 3B-1
0	88	234	65	15	3	0	0.0	35	27	55	17	13	.278	.368	5	0	C-77, OF-2, P-1
1	81	227	63	17	8	3	1.3	22	41	45	19	4	.278	.463	3	1	C-77, 2B-2
2	48	108	36	7	2	1	0.9	8	15	14	9	4	.333	.463	14	7	C-28
3 CHI N	68	161	37	5	2	1	0.6	20	21	21	11	7	.230	.304	9	4	C-58
4	86	248	69	10	4	0	0.0	42	24	49	20	14	.278	.351	4	1	C-85, 2B-14, OF-1
5	77	221	45	8	1	1	0.5	19	19	29	23	19	.204	.262	6	0	C-68
7 yrs.	1430	4480	1253	222	72	26	0.6	683	530	714	99	212	.280	.379	63	20	C-974, OF-281, 3B-42, 1B-33, 2B-28, P-9, SS-8
4 yrs.	289	803	221	43	14	4	0.5	92	106	160	45	32	.275	.379	24	8	C-241, 2B-11, OF-2, 3B-1, P-1

WORLD SERIES

	G	AB	H	2B	3B	HR	HR%	R	RBI	BB	SO	SB	BA	SA	AB	H	G by POS
05 NY N	5	16	5	2	0	0	0.0	3	1	4	0	1	.313	.438	0	0	C-5

ube Bressler

BRESSLER, RAYMOND BLOOM   BR TL 6' 187 lbs.
B. Oct. 23, 1894, Coder, Pa.   D. Nov. 7, 1966, Cincinnati, Ohio

	G	AB	H	2B	3B	HR	HR%	R	RBI	BB	SO	SB	BA	SA	AB	H	G by POS
14 PHI A	29	51	11	1	1	0	0.0	6	4	6	7	0	.216	.275	0	0	P-29
5	33	55	8	0	1	1	1.8	9	4	9	13	0	.145	.236	1	0	P-32
6	4	5	1	0	1	0	0.0	1	1	0	0	0	.200	.600	0	0	P-4
7 CIN N	3	5	1	0	0	0	0.0	0	0	0	2	0	.200	.200	1	0	P-2
8	23	62	17	5	0	0	0.0	10	6	5	4	0	.274	.355	1	0	P-17, OF-3
9	61	165	34	3	4	2	1.2	22	17	23	15	2	.206	.309	1	0	OF-48, P-13
0	21	30	8	1	0	0	0.0	4	3	1	4	1	.267	.300	6	0	P-10, OF-3, 1B-2
1	109	323	99	18	6	1	0.3	41	54	39	20	5	.307	.409	12	4	OF-85, 1B-6
2	52	53	14	0	2	0	0.0	7	8	4	4	1	.264	.340	43	13	1B-3, OF-2
3	54	119	33	3	1	0	0.0	25	18	20	4	3	.277	.319	24	9	1B-22, OF-6
4	115	383	133	14	13	4	1.0	41	49	22	20	9	.347	.483	16	3	1B-50, OF-49
5	97	319	111	17	6	4	1.3	43	61	40	16	9	.348	.476	6	3	1B-52, OF-38
6	86	297	106	15	9	1	0.3	58	51	37	20	3	.357	.478	4	0	OF-80, 1B-4
7	124	467	136	14	8	3	0.6	43	77	32	22	4	.291	.375	3	0	OF-120
8 BKN N	145	501	148	29	13	4	0.8	78	70	80	33	2	.295	.429	7	3	OF-137
9	136	456	145	22	8	9	2.0	72	77	67	27	4	.318	.461	12	3	OF-122
0	109	335	100	12	8	3	0.9	53	52	51	19	4	.299	.409	8	0	OF-90, 1B-7
1	67	153	43	4	5	0	0.0	22	26	11	10	0	.281	.373	29	2	OF-35, 1B-1
2 2 teams		PHI N	(27G – .229)		STL N	(10G – .158)											
Total	37	102	22	6	1	0	0.0	9	8	2	6	0	.216	.294	14	5	OF-22
19 yrs.	1305	3881	1170	164	87	32	0.8	544	586	449	246	47	.301	.413	188	45	OF-840, 1B-147, P-107
1 yr.	10	19	3	0	0	0	0.0	0	2	0	1	0	.158	.158	6	1	OF-4

d Bressoud

BRESSOUD, EDWARD FRANCIS   BR TR 6'1" 175 lbs.
B. May 2, 1932, Los Angeles, Calif.

	G	AB	H	2B	3B	HR	HR%	R	RBI	BB	SO	SB	BA	SA	AB	H	G by POS
56 NY N	49	163	37	4	2	0	0.0	15	9	12	20	1	.227	.276	1	0	SS-48
7	49	127	34	2	2	5	3.9	11	10	4	19	0	.268	.433	2	0	SS-33, 3B-12

	G	AB	H	2B	3B	HR	HR %	R	RBI	BB	SO	SB	BA	SA	Pinch Hit AB	Pinch Hit H	G by POS

Ed Bressoud continued

	G	AB	H	2B	3B	HR	HR %	R	RBI	BB	SO	SB	BA	SA	AB	H	G by POS
1958 SF N	66	137	36	5	3	0	0.0	19	8	14	22	0	.263	.343	0	0	2B-57, 3B-6, SS-4
1959	104	315	79	17	2	9	2.9	36	26	28	55	0	.251	.403	5	0	SS-92, 3B-1, 2B-1, 1B-1
1960	116	386	87	19	6	9	2.3	37	43	35	72	1	.225	.376	1	0	SS-115
1961	59	114	24	6	0	3	2.6	14	11	11	23	1	.211	.342	20	4	SS-34, 3B-3, 2B-1
1962 BOS A	153	599	166	40	9	14	2.3	79	68	46	118	2	.277	.444	0	0	SS-153
1963	140	497	129	23	6	20	4.0	61	60	52	93	1	.260	.451	2	0	SS-137
1964	158	566	166	41	3	15	2.7	86	55	72	99	1	.293	.456	0	0	SS-158
1965	107	296	67	11	1	8	2.7	29	25	29	77	0	.226	.351	21	7	SS-86, 3B-2, OF-1
1966 NY N	133	405	91	15	5	10	2.5	48	49	47	107	2	.225	.360	12	2	SS-94, 3B-32, 1B-9, 2B-7
1967 STL N	52	67	9	1	1	1	1.5	8	1	9	18	0	.134	.224	3	1	SS-48, 3B-1
12 yrs.	1186	3672	925	184	40	94	2.6	443	365	359	723	9	.252	.401	67	14	SS-1002, 2B-66, 3B-57, 1B-10, OF-1
1 yr.	52	67	9	1	1	1	1.5	8	1	9	18	0	.134	.224	3	1	SS-48, 3B-1

WORLD SERIES

	G	AB	H	2B	3B	HR	HR %	R	RBI	BB	SO	SB	BA	SA	AB	H	G by POS
1967 STL N	2	0	0	0	0	0	–	0	0	0	0	0	–	–	0	0	SS-2

Rocky Bridges

BRIDGES, EVERETT LAMAR
B. Aug. 7, 1927, Refugio, Tex.
BR TR 5'8" 170 lbs.

	G	AB	H	2B	3B	HR	HR %	R	RBI	BB	SO	SB	BA	SA	AB	H	G by POS
1951 BKN N	63	134	34	7	0	1	0.7	13	15	10	10	0	.254	.328	2	0	3B-40, 2B-10, SS-9
1952	51	56	11	3	0	0	0.0	9	2	7	9	0	.196	.250	3	1	2B-24, SS-13, 3B-6
1953 CIN N	122	432	98	13	2	1	0.2	52	21	37	42	6	.227	.273	4	0	2B-115, SS-6, 3B-3
1954	53	52	12	1	0	0	0.0	4	2	7	7	0	.231	.250	1	0	SS-20, 2B-19, 3B-13
1955	95	168	48	4	0	1	0.6	20	18	15	19	1	.286	.327	0	0	3B-59, SS-26, 2B-9
1956	71	19	4	0	0	0	0.0	9	1	4	3	1	.211	.211	2	0	3B-51, 2B-8, SS-7, OF-1
1957 2 teams	CIN N	(5G –	.000)		WAS A	(120G –	.228)										
" Total	125	392	89	17	2	3	0.8	41	47	41	33	0	.227	.304	0	0	SS-109, 2B-16, 3B-2
1958 WAS A	116	377	99	14	3	5	1.3	38	28	27	32	0	.263	.355	4	0	SS-112, 3B-3, 2B-3
1959 DET A	116	381	102	16	3	3	0.8	38	35	30	35	1	.268	.349	2	0	SS-110, 2B-5
1960 3 teams	DET A	(10G –	.200)		CLE A	(10G –	.333)		STL N	(3G –	.000)						
" Total	23	32	10	0	0	0	0.0	1	3	1	2	0	.313	.313	0	0	SS-10, 3B-10, 2B-3
1961 LA A	84	229	55	5	1	2	0.9	20	15	26	37	1	.240	.297	1	0	2B-58, SS-25, 3B-4
11 yrs.	919	2272	562	80	11	16	0.7	245	187	205	229	10	.247	.313	19	1	SS-447, 2B-270, 3B-191, OF-1
1 yr.	3	0	0	0	0	0	–	0	0	0	0	0	–	–	0	0	2B-3

Grant Briggs

BRIGGS, GRANT
B. Philadelphia, Pa. Deceased.

	G	AB	H	2B	3B	HR	HR %	R	RBI	BB	SO	SB	BA	SA	AB	H	G by POS
1890 SYR AA	86	316	57	6	5	0	0.0	44		16		7	.180	.231	0	0	C-46, OF-33, 3B-5, SS-4
1891 LOU AA	1	4	1	0	0	0	0.0	0	0	0	0	0	.250	.250	0	0	C-1
1892 STL N	23	57	4	1	0	0	0.0	2	1	6	16	3	.070	.088	0	0	C-15, OF-9
1895 LOU N	1	3	0	0	0	0	0.0	0		0	1		.000	.000	0	0	C-1
4 yrs.	111	380	62	7	5	0	0.0	46	2	22	17	10	.163	.208	0	0	C-63, OF-42, 3B-5, SS-4
1 yr.	23	57	4	1	0	0	0.0	2	1	6	16	3	.070	.088	0	0	C-15, OF-9

Ed Brinkman

BRINKMAN, EDWIN ALBERT
Brother of Chuck Brinkman.
B. Dec. 8, 1941, Cincinnati, Ohio
BR TR 6' 170 lbs.

	G	AB	H	2B	3B	HR	HR %	R	RBI	BB	SO	SB	BA	SA	AB	H	G by POS
1961 WAS A	4	11	1	0	0	0	0.0	0	0	1	1	0	.091	.091	1	0	3B-3
1962	54	133	22	7	1	0	0.0	8	4	11	28	1	.165	.233	0	0	SS-38, 3B-10
1963	145	514	117	20	3	7	1.4	44	45	31	86	5	.228	.319	2	1	SS-143
1964	132	447	100	20	3	8	1.8	54	34	26	99	2	.224	.336	7	1	SS-125
1965	154	444	82	13	2	5	1.1	35	35	38	82	1	.185	.257	3	0	SS-150
1966	158	582	133	18	9	7	1.2	42	48	29	105	7	.229	.326	0	0	SS-158
1967	109	320	60	9	2	1	0.3	21	18	24	58	1	.188	.238	0	0	SS-109
1968	77	193	36	3	0	0	0.0	12	6	19	31	0	.187	.202	2	0	SS-74, 2B-2, OF-1
1969	151	576	153	18	5	2	0.3	71	43	50	42	2	.266	.325	1	1	SS-150
1970	158	625	164	17	2	1	0.2	63	40	60	41	8	.262	.301	0	0	SS-157
1971 DET A	159	527	120	18	2	1	0.2	40	37	44	54	1	.228	.275	0	0	SS-159
1972	156	516	105	19	1	6	1.2	42	49	38	51	0	.203	.279	0	0	SS-156
1973	162	515	122	16	4	7	1.4	55	40	34	79	0	.237	.324	0	0	SS-162
1974	153	502	111	15	3	14	2.8	55	54	29	71	2	.221	.347	0	0	SS-151, 3B-2
1975 3 teams	STL N	(28G –	.240)		TEX A	(1G –	.000)		NY A	(44G –	.175)						
" Total	73	140	29	8	1	0	0.7	8	8	10	17	0	.207	.300	4	1	SS-63, 3B-4, 2B-3
15 yrs.	1845	6045	1355	201	38	60	1.0	550	461	444	845	30	.224	.300	22	5	SS-1795, 3B-19, 2B-5, OF-1
1 yr.	28	75	18	4	0	1	1.3	6	6	7	10	0	.240	.333	4	1	SS-24

LEAGUE CHAMPIONSHIP SERIES

	G	AB	H	2B	3B	HR	HR %	R	RBI	BB	SO	SB	BA	SA	AB	H	G by POS
1972 DET A	1	4	1	1	0	0	0.0	0	0	0	0	0	.250	.500	0	0	SS-1

John Brock

BROCK, JOHN ROY
B. Oct. 19, 1896, Hamilton, Ill. D. Oct. 27, 1951, St. Louis, Mo.
BR TR 5'6½" 165 lbs.

	G	AB	H	2B	3B	HR	HR %	R	RBI	BB	SO	SB	BA	SA	AB	H	G by POS
1917 STL N	7	15	6	1	0	0	0.0	4	2	0	2	2	.400	.467	3	1	C-4
1918	27	52	11	2	0	0	0.0	9	4	3	10	5	.212	.250	7	2	C-18, OF-1
2 yrs.	34	67	17	3	0	0	0.0	13	6	3	12	7	.254	.299	10	3	C-22, OF-1
2 yrs.	34	67	17	3	0	0	0.0	13	6	3	12	7	.254	.299	10	3	C-22, OF-1

Lou Brock

BROCK, LOUIS CLARK
B. June 18, 1939, El Dorado, Ark.
BL TL 5'11½" 170 lbs.

	G	AB	H	2B	3B	HR	HR %	R	RBI	BB	SO	SB	BA	SA	AB	H	G by POS
1961 CHI N	4	11	1	0	0	0	0.0	1	0	1	3	0	.091	.091	0	0	OF-3
1962	123	434	114	24	7	9	2.1	73	35	35	96	16	.263	.412	15	2	OF-106
1963	148	547	141	19	11	9	1.6	79	37	31	122	24	.258	.382	10	2	OF-140
1964 2 teams	CHI N	(52G –	.251)		STL N	(103G –	.348)										
" Total	155	634	200	30	11	14	2.2	111	58	40	127	43	.315	.464	1	0	OF-154

	G	AB	H	2B	3B	HR	HR %	R	RBI	BB	SO	SB	BA	SA	Pinch Hit AB	Pinch Hit H	G by POS

Lou Brock continued

	G	AB	H	2B	3B	HR	HR%	R	RBI	BB	SO	SB	BA	SA	PH AB	PH H	G by POS
1965 STL N	155	631	182	35	8	16	2.5	107	69	45	116	63	.288	.445	1	0	OF-153
1966	156	643	183	24	12	15	2.3	94	46	31	134	74	.285	.429	1	0	OF-154
1967	159	**689**	206	32	12	21	3.0	**113**	76	24	109	52	.299	.472	4	0	OF-157
1968	159	660	184	**46**	**14**	6	0.9	92	51	46	124	62	.279	.418	3	1	OF-156
1969	157	655	195	33	10	12	1.8	97	47	50	115	53	.298	.434	2	1	OF-157
1970	155	664	202	29	5	13	2.0	114	57	60	99	51	.304	.422	3	2	OF-152
1971	157	640	200	37	7	7	1.1	**126**	42	76	107	64	.313	.425	2	1	OF-157
1972	153	621	193	26	8	3	0.5	81	42	47	93	63	.311	.393	4	1	OF-149
1973	160	650	193	29	8	7	1.1	110	63	71	112	70	.297	.398	1	0	OF-159
1974	153	635	194	25	7	3	0.5	105	48	61	88	**118**	.306	.381	3	1	OF-152
1975	136	528	163	27	6	3	0.6	78	47	38	64	56	.309	.400	8	3	OF-128
1976	133	498	150	24	5	4	0.8	73	67	35	75	56	.301	.394	12	3	OF-123
1977	141	489	133	22	6	2	0.4	69	46	30	74	35	.272	.354	18	7	OF-130
1978	92	298	66	9	0	0	0.0	31	12	17	29	17	.221	.252	15	4	OF-79
1979	120	405	123	15	4	5	1.2	56	38	23	43	21	.304	.398	22	5	OF-98
19 yrs.	2616	10332	3023	486	141	149	1.4	1610	900	761	1730	938	.293	.410	125	33	OF-2507
		9th									5th	1st					
16 yrs.	2289	9125	2713	434	121	129	1.4	1427	814	681	1469	888	.297	.414	100	29	OF-2206
	2nd	2nd	2nd	2nd	4th	10th		2nd		8th	3rd	1st	1st			8th	

WORLD SERIES

	G	AB	H	2B	3B	HR	HR%	R	RBI	BB	SO	SB	BA	SA	PH AB	PH H	G by POS
1964 STL N	7	30	9	2	0	1	3.3	2	5	0	3	0	.300	.467	0	0	OF-7
1967	7	29	12	2	1	1	3.4	8	3	2	3	7	.414	.655	0	0	OF-7
1968	7	28	13	3	1	2	7.1	6	5	3	4	7	.464	.857	0	0	OF-7
3 yrs.	21	87	34	7	2	4	4.6	16	13	5	10	14	.391	.655	0	0	OF-21
			8th								1st	2nd	5th				

Steve Brodie

BRODIE, WALTER SCOTT   BL TR 5'9½" 176 lbs.
B. Sept. 11, 1868, Warrenton, Va.   D. Oct. 30, 1935, Baltimore, Md.

	G	AB	H	2B	3B	HR	HR%	R	RBI	BB	SO	SB	BA	SA	PH AB	PH H	G by POS
1890 BOS N	132	514	152	19	9	0	0.0	77	67	66	20	29	.296	.368	0	0	OF-132
1891	133	523	136	13	6	2	0.4	84	78	63	39	25	.260	.319	0	0	OF-133
1892 STL N	154	602	152	10	9	4	0.7	85	60	52	31	28	.252	.319	0	0	OF-137, 2B-16, 3B-2
1893 2 teams	STL	N	(107G –	.318)	BAL	N	(25G –	.361)									
" Total	132	566	184	23	10	2	0.4	89	98	45	18	49	.325	.412	0	0	OF-132
1894 BAL N	129	573	210	25	11	3	0.5	134	113	18	8	42	.366	.464	0	0	OF-129
1895	131	528	184	27	10	2	0.4	85	134	26	15	35	.348	.449	0	0	OF-131
1896	132	516	153	19	11	2	0.4	98	87	36	17	25	.297	.388	0	0	OF-132
1897 PIT N	100	370	108	7	12	2	0.5	47	53	25		11	.292	.392	0	0	OF-100
1898 2 teams	PIT	N	(42G –	.263)	BAL	N	(23G –	.306)									
" Total	65	254	71	8	2	0	0.0	27	40	11		6	.280	.327	0	0	OF-65
1899 BAL N	137	531	164	26	1	3	0.6	82	87	31		19	.309	.379	0	0	OF-137
1901 BAL A	84	306	95	6	6	2	0.7	41	41	25		9	.310	.389	0	0	OF-83
1902 NY N	109	416	117	8	2	3	0.7	37	42	22		11	.281	.332	0	0	OF-109
12 yrs.	1438	5699	1726	191	89	25	0.4	886	900	420	148	289	.303	.381	0	0	OF-1420, 2B-16, 3B-2
2 yrs.	261	1071	301	26	17	6	0.6	156	139	85	47	69	.281	.354	0	0	OF-244, 2B-16, 3B-2

Herman Bronkie

BRONKIE, HERMAN CHARLES (Dutch)   BR TR 5'9" 165 lbs.
B. Mar. 30, 1885, S. Manchester, Conn.   D. May 27, 1968, Somers, Conn.

	G	AB	H	2B	3B	HR	HR%	R	RBI	BB	SO	SB	BA	SA	PH AB	PH H	G by POS
1910 CLE A	4	9	2	0	0	0	0.0	1	0	1		1	.222	.222	0	0	3B-3, SS-1
1911	2	6	1	0	0	0	0.0	0	0	0		0	.167	.167	0	0	3B-2
1912	6	16	0	0	0	0	0.0	1	0	1		0	.000	.000	0	0	3B-6
1914 CHI N	1	1	1	1	0	0	0.0	1	1	0	0	0	1.000	2.000	0	0	3B-1
1918 STL N	18	68	15	3	0	1	1.5	7	7	2	4	0	.221	.309	0	0	3B-18
1919 STL A	67	196	50	6	4	0	0.0	23	14	23	23	2	.255	.327	12	3	3B-34, 2B-16, 1B-2
1922	23	64	18	4	1	0	0.0	7	2	6	7	0	.281	.375	4	1	3B-18
7 yrs.	121	360	87	14	5	1	0.3	40	24	33	34	3	.242	.317	16	4	3B-82, 2B-16, 1B-2, SS-1
1 yr.	18	68	15	3	0	1	1.5	7	7	2	4	0	.221	.309	0	0	3B-18

Tony Brottem

BROTTEM, ANTON CHRISTIAN   BR TR 6'½" 176 lbs.
B. Apr. 30, 1892, Halstead, Minn.   D. Aug. 5, 1929, Chicago, Ill.

	G	AB	H	2B	3B	HR	HR%	R	RBI	BB	SO	SB	BA	SA	PH AB	PH H	G by POS
1916 STL N	26	33	6	1	0	0	0.0	3	4	3	10	1	.182	.212	7	4	C-15, OF-2
1918	2	4	0	0	0	0	0.0	0	1	0		0	.000	.000	1	0	1B-2
1921 2 teams	WAS	A	(4G –	.143)	PIT	N	(30G –	.242)									
" Total	34	98	23	2	0	0	0.0	7	9	5	12	0	.235	.255	1	0	C-33
3 yrs.	62	135	29	3	0	0	0.0	10	13	9	22	1	.215	.237	9	4	C-48, OF-2, 1B-2
2 yrs.	28	37	6	1	0	0	0.0	3	4	4	10	1	.162	.189	8	4	C-15, OF-2, 1B-2

Jim Brown

BROWN, JAMES DONALDSON (Moose)   BR TR
B. Mar. 31, 1897, Laurel, Ind.

	G	AB	H	2B	3B	HR	HR%	R	RBI	BB	SO	SB	BA	SA	PH AB	PH H	G by POS
1915 STL N	1	2	1	0	0	0	0.0	0	0	2	1	0	.500	.500	0	0	OF-1
1916 PHI A	14	42	10	2	1	1	2.4	6	5	4	9	0	.238	.405	2	0	OF-12
2 yrs.	15	44	11	2	1	1	2.3	6	5	6	10	0	.250	.409	2	0	OF-13
1 yr.	1	2	1	0	0	0	0.0	0	0	2	1	0	.500	.500	0	0	OF-1

Jimmy Brown

BROWN, JAMES ROBERSON   BB TR 5'8½" 165 lbs.
B. Apr. 25, 1910, Jamesville, N.C.   D. Dec. 29, 1977, Bath, N.C.

	G	AB	H	2B	3B	HR	HR%	R	RBI	BB	SO	SB	BA	SA	PH AB	PH H	G by POS
1937 STL N	138	525	145	20	9	2	0.4	86	53	27	29	10	.276	.360	6	1	2B-112, SS-25, 3B-1
1938	108	382	115	12	6	0	0.0	50	38	27	9	7	.301	.364	9	3	2B-49, SS-30, 3B-24
1939	147	**645**	192	31	8	3	0.5	88	51	32	18	4	.298	.384	1	0	SS-104, 2B-50
1940	107	454	127	17	4	0	0.0	56	30	24	15	9	.280	.335	1	0	2B-48, 3B-41, SS-28
1941	132	549	168	28	9	3	0.5	81	56	45	22	2	.306	.406	1	1	3B-123, 2B-11
1942	145	**606**	155	28	4	1	0.2	75	71	52	11	4	.256	.320	0	0	2B-82, 3B-66, SS-12
1943	34	110	20	4	2	0	0.0	6	8	6	1	0	.182	.255	1	0	2B-19, 3B-9, SS-6
1946 PIT N	79	241	58	6	0	0	0.0	23	12	18	5	3	.241	.266	20	7	SS-30, 2B-21, 3B-9

	G	AB	H	2B	3B	HR	HR %	R	RBI	BB	SO	SB	BA	SA	Pinch Hit AB	Pinch Hit H	G by POS

Jimmy Brown continued

	G	AB	H	2B	3B	HR	HR%	R	RBI	BB	SO	SB	BA	SA	AB	H	G by POS
8 yrs.	890	3512	980	146	42	9	0.3	465	319	231	110	39	.279	.352	39	12	2B-392, 3B-273, SS-235
7 yrs.	811	3271	922	140	42	9	0.3	442	307	213	105	36	.282	.359	19	5	2B-371, 3B-264, SS-205

WORLD SERIES

	G	AB	H	2B	3B	HR	HR%	R	RBI	BB	SO	SB	BA	SA	AB	H	G by POS
1942 STL N	5	20	6	0	0	0	0.0	2	1	3	0	0	.300	.300	0	0	2B-5

Tom Brown

BROWN, THOMAS T.   BL TR 5'10"   168 lbs.
B. Sept. 21, 1860, Liverpool, England   D. Oct. 27, 1927, Washington, D. C.
Manager 1897-98.

	G	AB	H	2B	3B	HR	HR%	R	RBI	BB	SO	SB	BA	SA	AB	H	G by POS
1883 COL AA	97	420	115	12	7	5	1.2	69		20			.274	.371	0	0	OF-96, P-3
1884	107	451	123	9	11	5	1.1	93		24			.273	.375	0	0	OF-107, P-4
1885 PIT AA	108	437	134	16	12	4	0.9	81		34			.307	.426	0	0	OF-108, P-2
1886	115	460	131	11	11	1	0.2	106		56			.285	.363	0	0	OF-115, P-1
1887 2 teams		PIT	N	(47G –	.245)		IND	N	(36G –	.179)							
" Total	83	332	72	6	4	2	0.6	50	15	19	65	25	.217	.277	0	0	OF-83
1888 BOS N	107	420	104	10	7	9	2.1	62	49	30	68	46	.248	.369	0	0	OF-107
1889	90	362	84	10	5	2	0.6	93	24	59	56	63	.232	.304	0	0	OF-90
1890 BOS P	128	543	150	23	14	4	0.7	146	61	86	84	79	.276	.392	0	0	OF-128
1891 BOS AA	137	589	189	30	21	5	0.8	177	71	70	96	106	.321	.469	0	0	OF-137
1892 LOU N	153	660	150	16	8	2	0.3	105	45	47	94	78	.227	.285	0	0	OF-153
1893	122	529	127	15	7	5	0.9	104	54	56	63	66	.240	.323	0	0	OF-122
1894	129	536	136	22	14	9	1.7	122	57	60	73	66	.254	.397	0	0	OF-129
1895 2 teams		STL	N	(83G –	.217)		WAS	N	(34G –	.239)							
" Total	117	484	108	19	7	3	0.6	97	47	66	60	42	.223	.310	0	0	OF-117
1896 WAS N	116	435	128	17	6	2	0.5	87	59	58	49	28	.294	.375	0	0	OF-116
1897	116	469	137	17	2	5	1.1	91	45	52		25	.292	.369	0	0	OF-115
1898	16	55	9	1	0	0	0.0	8	2	5		3	.164	.182	0	0	OF-15
16 yrs.	1741	7182	1897	234	136	63	0.9	1491	528	742	708	627	.264	.361	0	0	OF-1738, P-10
1 yr.	83	350	76	11	4	1	0.3	50	72	31	48	44	.217	.280	0	0	OF-83

Willard Brown

BROWN, WILLARD (Big Bill, California Brown)   BR TR 6'2"
B. 1866, San Francisco, Calif.   D. Dec. 20, 1897, San Francisco, Calif.

	G	AB	H	2B	3B	HR	HR%	R	RBI	BB	SO	SB	BA	SA	AB	H	G by POS
1887 NY N	49	170	37	3	2	0	0.0	17	25	10	15	10	.218	.259	0	0	C-46, 3B-3, OF-2
1888	20	59	16	1	0	0	0.0	4	6	1	8	1	.271	.288	0	0	C-20
1889	40	139	36	10	0	1	0.7	16	29	9	9	6	.259	.353	0	0	C-37, OF-3
1890 NY P	60	230	64	8	4	4	1.7	47	43	13	13	5	.278	.400	0	0	C-34, OF-13, 1B-9, 3B-3, 2B-2
1891 PHI N	115	441	107	20	4	0	0.0	62	50	34	35	7	.243	.306	0	0	1B-97, C-19, OF-2
1893 2 teams		BAL	N	(7G –	.125)		LOU	N	(111G –	.304)							
" Total	118	493	144	26	1	1	0.2	85	90	51	35	9	.292	.379	0	0	1B-118, C-1
1894 2 teams		LOU	N	(13G –	.208)		STL	N	(3G –	.111)							
" Total	16	57	11	2	0	0	0.0	5	9	5	9	1	.193	.228	0	0	1B-16
7 yrs.	418	1589	415	70	17	6	0.4	236	252	123	124	39	.261	.338	0	0	1B-240, C-157, OF-20, 3B-6, 2B-2
1 yr.	3	9	1	0	0	0	0.0	0	0	0	2	0	.111	.111	0	0	1B-3

Byron Browne

BROWNE, BYRON ELLIS   BR TR 6'2"   190 lbs.
B. Dec. 27, 1942, St. Joseph, Mo.

	G	AB	H	2B	3B	HR	HR%	R	RBI	BB	SO	SB	BA	SA	AB	H	G by POS
1965 CHI N	4	6	0	0	0	0	0.0	0	0	0	2	0	.000	.000	1	0	OF-4
1966	120	419	102	15	7	16	3.8	46	51	40	143	3	.243	.427	5	0	OF-114
1967	10	19	3	2	0	0	0.0	3	2	4	5	1	.158	.263	2	0	OF-8
1968 HOU N	10	13	3	0	0	0	0.0	0	1	4	6	0	.231	.231	6	1	OF-2
1969 STL N	22	53	12	0	1	1	1.9	9	7	11	14	0	.226	.321	7	0	OF-16
1970 PHI N	104	270	67	17	2	10	3.7	29	36	33	72	1	.248	.437	18	4	OF-88
1971	58	68	14	3	0	3	4.4	5	5	8	23	0	.206	.382	27	7	OF-30
1972	21	21	4	0	0	0	0.0	2	0	1	8	0	.190	.190	14	3	OF-9
8 yrs.	349	869	205	37	10	30	3.5	94	102	101	273	5	.236	.405	80	15	OF-271
1 yr.	22	53	12	0	1	1	1.9	9	7	11	14	0	.226	.321	7	0	OF-16

Pete Browning

BROWNING, LOUIS ROGERS (The Gladiator)   BR TR 6'   180 lbs.
B. July 17, 1858, Louisville, Ky.   D. Sept. 10, 1905, Louisville, Ky.

	G	AB	H	2B	3B	HR	HR%	R	RBI	BB	SO	SB	BA	SA	AB	H	G by POS
1882 LOU AA	69	288	110	19	3	5	1.7	67		26			.382	.521	0	0	2B-42, SS-18, 3B-13
1883	84	360	121	14	11	4	1.1	95		23			.336	.469	0	0	OF-48, SS-26, 3B-10, 2B-3, 1B-1
1884	105	454	150	34	8	4	0.9	101		13			.330	.467	0	0	3B-52, OF-24, 1B-23, 2B-4, P-1
1885	112	481	174	34	10	9	1.9	98		25			.362	.530	0	0	OF-112
1886	112	467	159	29	6	3	0.6	86		30			.340	.448	0	0	OF-112
1887	134	547	220	36	18	4	0.7	137		55		103	.402	.556	0	0	OF-134
1888	99	383	120	23	8	3	0.8	58	72	37		36	.313	.439	0	0	OF-99
1889	83	324	83	19	5	2	0.6	39	32	34	30	21	.256	.364	0	0	OF-83
1890 CLE P	118	493	191	40	8	5	1.0	114	93	75	36	35	.387	.531	0	0	OF-118
1891 2 teams		PIT	N	(50G –	.291)		CIN	N	(55G –	.343)							
" Total	105	419	133	24	4	4	1.0	64	61	51	54	16	.317	.422	0	0	OF-105
1892 2 teams		LOU	N	(21G –	.247)		CIN	N	(83G –	.303)							
" Total	104	384	112	16	5	3	0.8	57	56	52	32	13	.292	.383	0	0	OF-103, 1B-2
1893 LOU N	57	220	78	11	3	1	0.5	38	37	44	15	8	.355	.445	0	0	OF-57
1894 2 teams		STL	N	(2G –	.143)		BKN	N	(1G –	1.000)							
" Total	3	9	3	0	0	0	0.0	2	1	1	0	0	.333	.333	0	0	OF-3
13 yrs.	1185	4829	1654	299	89	47	1.0	956	352	466	167	232	.343 10th	.470	0	0	OF-998, 3B-75, 2B-49, SS-44, 1B-26, P-1
1 yr.	2	7	1	0	0	0	0.0	1	0	0	0	0	.143	.143	0	0	OF-2

	G	AB	H	2B	3B	HR	HR %	R	RBI	BB	SO	SB	BA	SA	Pinch Hit AB	Pinch Hit H	G by POS

Glenn Brummer

BRUMMER, GLENN EDWARD   B. Nov. 23, 1954, Olney, Ill.   BR TR 6' 185 lbs.

	G	AB	H	2B	3B	HR	HR %	R	RBI	BB	SO	SB	BA	SA	PH AB	PH H	G by POS
1981 STL N	21	30	6	1	0	0	0.0	2	2	1	2	0	.200	.233	2	0	C-19
1982	35	64	15	4	0	0	0.0	4	8	0	12	2	.234	.297	1	1	C-32
2 yrs.	56	94	21	5	0	0	0.0	6	10	1	14	2	.223	.277	3	1	C-51
2 yrs.	56	94	21	5	0	0	0.0	6	10	1	14	2	.223	.277	3	1	C-51

WORLD SERIES

	G	AB	H	2B	3B	HR	HR %	R	RBI	BB	SO	SB	BA	SA	PH AB	PH H	G by POS
1982 STL N	1	0	0	0	0	0	–	0	0	0	0	0	–	–	0	0	C-1

Johnny Bucha

BUCHA, JOHN GEORGE   B. Jan. 22, 1925, Allentown, Pa.   BR TR 5'11" 190 lbs.

	G	AB	H	2B	3B	HR	HR %	R	RBI	BB	SO	SB	BA	SA	PH AB	PH H	G by POS
1948 STL N	2	1	0	0	0	0	0.0	0	0	1	0	0	.000	.000	1	0	C-1
1950	22	36	5	1	0	0	0.0	1	1	4	7	0	.139	.167	5	2	C-17
1953 DET A	60	158	35	9	0	1	0.6	17	14	20	14	1	.222	.297	2	0	C-56
3 yrs.	84	195	40	10	0	1	0.5	18	15	25	21	1	.205	.272	8	2	C-74
2 yrs.	24	37	5	1	0	0	0.0	1	1	5	7	0	.135	.162	6	2	C-18

Jerry Buchek

BUCHEK, GERALD PETER   B. May 9, 1942, St. Louis, Mo.   BR TR 5'11" 185 lbs.

	G	AB	H	2B	3B	HR	HR %	R	RBI	BB	SO	SB	BA	SA	PH AB	PH H	G by POS
1961 STL N	31	90	12	2	0	0	0.0	6	9	0	28	0	.133	.156	0	0	SS-31
1963	3	4	1	0	0	0	0.0	0	0	0	2	0	.250	.250	2	0	SS-1
1964	35	30	6	0	2	0	0.0	7	1	3	11	0	.200	.333	2	0	SS-20, 2B-9, 3B-1
1965	55	166	41	8	3	3	1.8	17	21	13	46	1	.247	.386	5	0	2B-33, SS-18, 3B-1
1966	100	284	67	10	4	4	1.4	23	25	23	71	0	.236	.342	9	1	2B-49, SS-48, 3B-4
1967 NY N	124	411	97	11	2	14	3.4	35	41	26	101	3	.236	.375	9	2	2B-95, 3B-17, SS-9
1968	73	192	35	4	0	1	0.5	8	11	10	53	1	.182	.219	18	3	3B-37, 2B-12, OF-9
7 yrs.	421	1177	259	35	11	22	1.9	96	108	75	312	5	.220	.325	45	6	2B-198, SS-127, 3B-60, OF-9
5 yrs.	224	574	127	20	9	7	1.2	53	56	39	158	1	.221	.324	18	1	SS-118, 2B-91, 3B-6

WORLD SERIES

	G	AB	H	2B	3B	HR	HR %	R	RBI	BB	SO	SB	BA	SA	PH AB	PH H	G by POS
1964 STL N	4	1	1	0	0	0	0.0	1	0	0	0	0	1.000	1.000	0	0	2B-4

Jim Bucher

BUCHER, JAMES QUINTER   B. Mar. 11, 1911, Manassas, Va.   BL TR 5'11" 170 lbs.

	G	AB	H	2B	3B	HR	HR %	R	RBI	BB	SO	SB	BA	SA	PH AB	PH H	G by POS
1934 BKN N	47	84	19	5	2	0	0.0	12	8	4	7	1	.226	.333	18	8	2B-20, 3B-6
1935	123	473	143	22	1	7	1.5	72	58	10	33	4	.302	.397	12	0	2B-41, 3B-39, OF-37
1936	110	370	93	12	8	2	0.5	49	41	29	27	5	.251	.343	10	3	3B-39, 2B-32, OF-30
1937	125	380	96	11	2	4	1.1	44	37	20	18	5	.253	.324	23	3	2B-49, 3B-43, OF-6
1938 STL N	17	57	13	3	1	0	0.0	7	7	2	2	0	.228	.316	2	1	2B-14, 3B-1
1944 BOS A	80	277	76	9	2	4	1.4	39	31	19	13	3	.274	.365	15	5	3B-44, 2B-21
1945	52	151	34	4	3	0	0.0	19	11	7	13	1	.225	.291	17	2	3B-32, 2B-21
7 yrs.	554	1792	474	66	19	17	0.9	242	193	91	113	19	.265	.351	97	22	3B-204, 2B-179, OF-73
1 yr.	17	57	13	3	1	0	0.0	7	7	2	2	0	.228	.316	2	1	2B-14, 3B-1

Dick Buckley

BUCKLEY, RICHARD D.   B. Sept. 21, 1858, Troy, N.Y.   D. Dec. 12, 1929, Pittsburgh, Pa.   TR

	G	AB	H	2B	3B	HR	HR %	R	RBI	BB	SO	SB	BA	SA	PH AB	PH H	G by POS
1888 IND N	71	260	71	9	3	5	1.9	28	22	6	24	4	.273	.388	0	0	C-51, 3B-22, OF-1, 1B-1
1889	68	260	67	11	0	8	3.1	35	41	15	32	5	.258	.392	0	0	C-55, 3B-12, OF-1, 1B-1
1890 NY N	70	266	68	11	0	2	0.8	39	26	23	35	3	.256	.320	0	0	C-62, 3B-8
1891	75	253	55	9	1	4	1.6	23	31	11	30	1	.217	.308	0	0	C-74, 3B-1
1892 STL N	121	410	93	17	4	5	1.2	43	52	22	34	7	.227	.324	0	0	C-119, 1B-2
1893	9	23	4	1	0	0	0.0	2	1	0		0	0	.174	.217	0	0	C-9
1894 2 teams			STL N (29G – .180)		PHI N (43G – .294)												
Total	72	249	63	8	5	2	0.8	23	29	12	16	1	.253	.349	1	0	C-69, 1B-2
1895 PHI N	38	112	28	6	1	0	0.0	20	14	9	17	2	.250	.321	0	0	C-38
8 yrs.	524	1833	449	72	14	26	1.4	213	216	98	188	25	.245	.342	1	0	C-477, 3B-43, 1B-6, OF-2
3 yrs.	159	522	113	19	6	6	1.1	50	56	28	37	8	.216	.310	1	0	C-155, 1B-3

Fritz Buelow

BUELOW, FREDERICK WILLIAM   B. Feb. 13, 1876, Berlin, Germany   D. Dec. 27, 1933, Detroit, Mich.   BR TR

	G	AB	H	2B	3B	HR	HR %	R	RBI	BB	SO	SB	BA	SA	PH AB	PH H	G by POS
1899 STL N	7	15	7	0	2	0	0.0	4	2	2		0	.467	.733	1	0	C-4, OF-2
1900	6	17	4	0	0	0	0.0	2	3	0		0	.235	.235	1	0	C-4, OF-1
1901 DET A	70	231	52	5	5	2	0.9	28	29	11		2	.225	.316	1	0	C-69
1902	66	224	50	5	2	2	0.9	23	29	9		3	.223	.290	0	0	C-63, 1B-2
1903	63	192	41	3	6	1	0.5	24	13	6		4	.214	.307	0	0	C-60, 1B-2
1904 2 teams			DET A (42G – .110)		CLE A (42G – .176)												
Total	84	255	36	5	2	0	0.0	17	10	19		4	.141	.176	0	0	C-84
1905 CLE A	74	236	41	4	1	1	0.4	11	18	6		7	.174	.212	2	1	C-59, OF-8, 1B-3, 3B-2
1906	34	86	14	2	0	0	0.0	7	7	9		0	.163	.186	0	0	C-33, 1B-1
1907 STL A	26	75	11	1	0	0	0.0	9	1	7		0	.147	.160	1	0	C-25
9 yrs.	430	1331	256	25	18	6	0.5	125	112	69		20	.192	.252	6	1	C-401, OF-11, 1B-8, 3B-2
2 yrs.	13	32	11	0	2	0	0.0	6	5	2		0	.344	.469	2	1	C-8, OF-3

Nels Burbrink

BURBRINK, NELSON EDWARD   B. Dec. 28, 1921, Cincinnati, Ohio   BR TR 5'10" 195 lbs.

	G	AB	H	2B	3B	HR	HR %	R	RBI	BB	SO	SB	BA	SA	PH AB	PH H	G by POS
1955 STL N	58	170	47	8	1	0	0.0	11	15	14	13	1	.276	.335	3	2	C-55

Al Burch

BURCH, ALBERT WILLIAM   B. Oct. 7, 1883, Albany, N.Y.   D. Oct. 5, 1926, Brooklyn, N.Y.   BL TR 5'8½" 160 lbs.

	G	AB	H	2B	3B	HR	HR %	R	RBI	BB	SO	SB	BA	SA	PH AB	PH H	G by POS
1906 STL N	91	335	89	5	5	0	0.0	40	11	37		15	.266	.287	0	0	OF-91
1907 2 teams			STL N (48G – .227)		BKN N (40G – .292)												
Total	88	274	70	5	3	0	0.0	30	17	28		12	.255	.296	3	0	OF-84, 2B-1
1908 BKN N	123	456	111	8	4	2	0.4	45	18	33		15	.243	.292	6	1	OF-116

	G	AB	H	2B	3B	HR	HR %	R	RBI	BB	SO	SB	BA	SA	Pinch Hit AB	Pinch Hit H	G by POS

Al Burch continued

	G	AB	H	2B	3B	HR	HR %	R	RBI	BB	SO	SB	BA	SA	PH AB	PH H	G by POS
1909	152	601	163	20	6	1	0.2	80	30	51		38	.271	.329	0	0	OF-151, 1B-1
1910	103	352	83	8	3	1	0.3	41	20	22	30	13	.236	.284	18	7	OF-70, 1B-13
1911	54	167	38	2	3	0	0.0	18	7	15	22	3	.228	.275	6	0	OF-43, 2B-3
6 yrs.	611	2185	554	48	20	4	0.2	254	103	186	52	96	.254	.299	33	8	OF-555, 1B-14, 2B-4
2 yrs.	139	489	124	8	2	0	0.0	58	16	54		22	.254	.278	0	0	OF-139

Bob Burda

BURDA, EDWARD ROBERT BL TL 5'11" 174 lbs.
B. July 16, 1938, St. Louis, Mo.

	G	AB	H	2B	3B	HR	HR %	R	RBI	BB	SO	SB	BA	SA	PH AB	PH H	G by POS
1962 STL N	7	14	1	0	0	0	0.0	0	0	3	1	1	.071	.071	1	0	OF-6
1965 SF N	31	27	3	0	0	0	0.0	0	5	5	6	0	.111	.111	12	1	1B-11, OF-1
1966	37	43	7	3	0	0	0.0	3	2	2	5	0	.163	.233	25	4	1B-7, OF-4
1969	97	161	37	8	0	6	3.7	20	27	21	12	0	.230	.391	35	8	1B-45, OF-19
1970 2 teams	SF	N	(28G – .261)		MIL	A	(78G – .248)										
" Total	106	245	61	9	0	4	1.6	20	23	21	19	1	.249	.335	27	8	OF-65, 1B-15
1971 STL N	65	71	21	0	0	1	1.4	6	12	10	11	0	.296	.338	48	14	1B-13, OF-1
1972 BOS A	45	73	12	1	0	2	2.7	4	9	8	11	0	.164	.260	27	2	1B-15, OF-1
7 yrs.	388	634	142	21	0	13	2.1	53	78	70	65	2	.224	.319	175	37	1B-106, OF-97
2 yrs.	72	85	22	0	0	1	1.2	6	12	12	13	1	.259	.294	49	14	1B-13, OF-7

Tom Burgess

BURGESS, THOMAS ROLAND (Tim) BL TL 6' 180 lbs.
B. Sept. 1, 1927, London Ont., Canada

	G	AB	H	2B	3B	HR	HR %	R	RBI	BB	SO	SB	BA	SA	PH AB	PH H	G by POS
1954 STL N	17	21	1	1	0	0	0.0	2	1	3	9	0	.048	.095	11	0	OF-4
1962 LA A	87	143	28	7	1	2	1.4	17	13	36	20	2	.196	.301	43	7	1B-35, OF-2
2 yrs.	104	164	29	8	1	2	1.2	19	14	39	29	2	.177	.274	54	7	1B-35, OF-6
1 yr.	17	21	1	1	0	0	0.0	2	1	3	9	0	.048	.095	11	0	OF-4

Jimmy Burke

BURKE, JAMES TIMOTHY (Sunset Jimmy) BR TR
B. Oct. 12, 1874, St. Louis, Mo. D. Mar. 26, 1942, St. Louis, Mo.
Manager 1905, 1918-20.

	G	AB	H	2B	3B	HR	HR %	R	RBI	BB	SO	SB	BA	SA	PH AB	PH H	G by POS
1898 CLE N	13	38	4	1	0	0	0.0	1	1	2		1	.105	.132	0	0	3B-13
1901 MIL A	(64G – .206)		CHI	A	(42G – .264)		PIT	N	(14G – .196)								
" Total	120	432	97	13	0	0	0.0	48	51	33		17	.225	.255	0	0	3B-89, SS-31
1902 PIT N	60	203	60	12	2	0	0.0	24	26	17		9	.296	.374	2	0	2B-27, OF-18, 3B-9, SS-4
1903 STL N	115	431	123	13	3	0	0.0	55	42	23		28	.285	.329	1	0	3B-93, 2B-15, OF-5
1904	118	406	92	10	3	0	0.0	37	37	15		17	.227	.266	0	0	3B-118
1905	122	431	97	9	5	1	0.2	34	30	21		15	.225	.276	0	0	3B-122
6 yrs.	548	1941	473	58	13	1	0.1	199	187	111		87	.244	.289	3	0	3B-444, 2B-42, SS-35, OF-23
3 yrs.	355	1268	312	32	11	1	0.1	126	109	59		60	.246	.291	1	0	3B-333, 2B-15, OF-5

John Burke

BURKE, JOHN PATRICK
B. Jan. 27, 1877, Hazleton, Pa. D. Aug. 4, 1950, Jersey City, N. J.

	G	AB	H	2B	3B	HR	HR %	R	RBI	BB	SO	SB	BA	SA	PH AB	PH H	G by POS
1899 STL N	2	6	2	0	0	0	0.0	1	0	1		0	.333	.333	0	0	2B-2
1902 NY N	4	13	2	0	0	0	0.0	0	0	0		0	.154	.154	0	0	OF-2, P-2
2 yrs.	6	19	4	0	0	0	0.0	1	0	1		0	.211	.211	0	0	OF-2, 2B-2, P-2
1 yr.	2	6	2	0	0	0	0.0	1	0	1		0	.333	.333	0	0	2B-2

Leo Burke

BURKE, LEO PATRICK BR TR 5'11" 185 lbs.
B. May 6, 1934, Hagerstown, Md.

	G	AB	H	2B	3B	HR	HR %	R	RBI	BB	SO	SB	BA	SA	PH AB	PH H	G by POS
1958 BAL A	7	11	5	1	0	1	9.1	4	4	1	2	0	.455	.818	3	1	OF-3, 3B-1
1959	5	10	2	0	0	0	0.0	0	1	0	5	0	.200	.200	2	0	3B-2, 2B-2
1961 LA A	6	5	0	0	0	0	0.0	0	0	0	1	0	.000	.000	5	0	
1962	19	64	17	1	0	4	6.3	8	14	5	11	0	.266	.469	2	0	OF-12, 3B-4, SS-1
1963 2 teams	STL	N	(30G – .204)		CHI	N	(27G – .184)										
" Total	57	98	19	2	1	3	3.1	10	12	8	25	0	.194	.327	28	8	OF-11, 2B-10, 3B-5, 1B-4
1964 CHI N	59	103	27	3	1	1	1.0	11	14	7	31	0	.262	.340	34	10	OF-18, 2B-5, 3B-4, 1B-2, C-1
1965	12	10	2	0	0	0	0.0	0	0	0	4	0	.200	.200	9	1	C-2, OF-1
7 yrs.	165	301	72	7	2	9	3.0	33	45	21	79	0	.239	.365	83	20	OF-45, 2B-17, 3B-16, 1B-6, C-3, SS-1
1 yr.	30	49	10	2	1	1	2.0	6	5	4	12	0	.204	.347	16	4	OF-11, 3B-5

Jesse Burkett

BURKETT, JESSE CAIL (The Crab) BL TL 5'8" 155 lbs.
B. Dec. 4, 1868, Wheeling, W. Va. D. May 27, 1953, Worcester, Mass.
Hall of Fame 1946.

	G	AB	H	2B	3B	HR	HR %	R	RBI	BB	SO	SB	BA	SA	PH AB	PH H	G by POS
1890 NY N	101	401	124	23	13	4	1.0	67	60	33	52	14	.309	.461	0	0	OF-90, P-21
1891 CLE N	42	167	45	7	4	0	0.0	29	13	23	19	1	.269	.359	0	0	OF-42
1892	145	608	167	15	14	6	1.0	119	66	67	59	36	.275	.375	0	0	OF-145
1893	125	511	178	25	15	6	1.2	145	82	98	23	39	.348	.491	0	0	OF-125
1894	125	523	187	27	14	8	1.5	138	94	84	27	28	.358	.509	0	0	OF-125, P-1
1895	132	555	235	21	15	5	0.9	149	83	74	31	47	.423	.542	0	0	OF-132
1896	133	586	240	27	16	6	1.0	160	72	49	19	34	.410	.541	0	0	OF-133
1897	128	519	199	28	8	2	0.4	128	60	76		28	.383	.480	0	0	OF-127
1898	150	624	215	18	9	0	0.0	115	42	69		19	.345	.402	0	0	OF-150
1899 STL N	141	567	228	17	10	7	1.2	115	71	67		22	.402	.504	0	0	OF-140, 2B-1
1900	142	560	203	14	12	7	1.3	88	68	62		32	.363	.468	0	0	OF-141
1901	142	597	228	21	17	10	1.7	139	75	59		27	.382	.524	0	0	OF-142
1902 STL A	138	553	169	29	9	5	0.9	97	52	71		23	.306	.418	0	0	OF-137, SS-1, 3B-1, P-1
1903	132	515	152	20	7	3	0.6	74	40	52		25	.295	.379	0	0	OF-132
1904	147	576	157	15	9	2	0.3	72	27	78		12	.273	.340	0	0	OF-147
1905 BOS A	149	573	147	13	13	4	0.7	78	47	67		13	.257	.346	0	0	OF-149
16 yrs.	2072	8435	2874	320	185	75	0.9	1713	952	1029	230	392	.341	.449	0	0	OF-2057, P-23, SS-1, 3B-1, 2B-1
3 yrs.	425	1724	659	52	39	24	1.4	342	214	188		81	.382 1st	.499 8th	0	0	OF-423, 2B-1

THE ALL-TIME ALL-STARS

Jesse Burkett (*left*) was one of the outstanding hitters of the 1890s, topping the .400 mark three times, once as a Cardinal. *Right:* Miller Huggins's sharp eye and small strike zone helped him lead the National League in walks four times, but it was his managerial skill that landed him in the Hall of Fame.

They were called "The Gashouse Gang"—the hard-drinking, hard-fighting St. Louis
Cardinal crew of 1934. Among these stalwarts were (*above left, left to right*):
rightfielder Jack Rothrock, second baseman/manager Frankie Frisch, third baseman
Pepper Martin, first baseman Ripper Collins, leftfielder Joe Medwick, and pitcher
Dizzy Dean. *Above right:* Frisch and Detroit's Mickey Cochrane led their respective
clubs into the Series, where St. Louis emerged with a seven-game victory.

Left: Paul Dean and his brother Jerome. Paul was as quiet as Dizzy was boisterous,
but both were nearly unbeatable down the stretch in '34. In one doubleheader in late
September, Dizzy shut out Brooklyn in the first game, and Paul beat them with a no-
hitter in the nightcap. "If I'd a knowed Paul was gonna pitch a no-hitter," Diz told
reporters, "I'd a pitched one, too."

Branch Rickey pulled all the strings and built an unprecedented baseball empire in St. Louis, then moved on to Brooklyn and built another one. He was known for his keen eye for talent and his tight grip on a dollar. Addressing a reunion of the Gashouse Gang, Rickey recalled, "They loved the game so much, I believe those boys would have played for nothing." "Thanks to you, Mr. Rickey," Pepper Martin added, "we almost did!"

Joe Medwick and Johnny Mize provided the power for the Cardinals in the late 1930s. Medwick (*left*) averaged 215 hits, 52 doubles, and 131 RBIs in one five-year stretch. Mize (*below*) may be the one player Rickey traded away too soon; he hit 91 home runs for the Giants in '47-'48, and became a great pinch hitter on the Yankee teams of the early 1950s.

Three key pitchers from the Cardinals of the '40s—(*clockwise from top left*) Mort Cooper, National League MVP in '42; Murry Dickson, 15-6 for the '46 pennant winner; and Harry Brecheen, second in career World Series ERA at 0.83.

Shortstop Marty Marion (*left*) anchored the Cardinal infield from 1940 to 1950, when he took over the reins of the club from Eddie Dyer. *Below:* Enos Slaughter's full-speed, all-out approach to the game was epitomized by his dash around the bases with the Series-winning run on Harry Walker's bloop double in 1946.

Left: He started out as a sore-armed southpaw pitcher, and ended up, twenty-two years later, as St. Louis's best-loved ballplayer. In between, he hit .300 seventeen times, topped 40 doubles nine times, drove in 100 runs nine times, and scored 100 eleven times. His name is Stanley Frank Musial, and for those twenty-two years, he *was* the Cardinals.

Albert "Red" Schoendienst played outstanding second base for the Cards for ten years, always swung the bat well from both sides of the plate, and returned to manage the Cardinals longer than anyone else in their history.

Ken Boyer (*left*) provided power and consistency in the heart of the order for the Cards through the late '50s and early '60s, and was a part of the Cardinals family until his untimely death in 1982 at age fifty-one.

Orlando Cepeda (*right*) starred for the Cards in their pennant-winning years of 1967 and 1968. (*Photo courtesy of St. Louis Cardinals*)

The Cardinals all but stole him from the Cubs in 1964, and then he stole everything in sight, controlling a game from the basepaths as few players since Jackie Robinson could. Lou Brock retired with baseball's all-time stolen base record, and topped the 3,000-hit mark thanks to a gallant final season in which he hit .304 in 405 at bats at age forty.

Bob Gibson was a consummate power pitcher, and probably the most competitive athlete in sports. In nine World Series starts, he struck out 10.2 batters per nine innings, including a record seventeen in one game. Asked by reporters if he was surprised by that performance, he replied, "I'm never surprised at anything I do."

	G	AB	H	2B	3B	HR	HR %	R	RBI	BB	SO	SB	BA	SA	Pinch Hit AB	Pinch Hit H	G by POS

John Burnett

BURNETT, JOHN P.
B. Unknown.

	G	AB	H	2B	3B	HR	HR %	R	RBI	BB	SO	SB	BA	SA	PH AB	PH H	G by POS
1907 STL N	59	206	49	8	4	0	0.0	18	12	15		5	.238	.316	0	0	OF-59

Ed Burns

BURNS, EDWARD JAMES   BR TR 5'6"   165 lbs.
B. Oct. 31, 1887, San Francisco, Calif.   D. June 1, 1942, Monterey, Calif.

	G	AB	H	2B	3B	HR	HR %	R	RBI	BB	SO	SB	BA	SA	PH AB	PH H	G by POS
1912 STL N	1	1	0	0	0	0	0.0	0	1	0	0	0	.000	.000	0	0	C-1
1913 PHI N	17	30	6	3	0	0	0.0	3	3	6	3	2	.200	.300	1	0	C-15
1914	70	139	36	3	4	0	0.0	8	16	20	12	5	.259	.338	14	3	C-55
1915	67	174	42	5	0	0	0.0	11	16	20	12	1	.241	.270	5	2	C-67
1916	78	219	51	8	1	0	0.0	14	14	16	18	3	.233	.279	2	0	C-75, OF-1, SS-1
1917	20	49	10	1	0	0	0.0	2	6	1	5	2	.204	.224	5	0	C-15
1918	68	184	38	1	1	0	0.0	10	9	20	9	1	.207	.223	0	0	C-68
7 yrs.	321	796	183	21	6	0	0.0	48	65	83	59	14	.230	.271	27	5	C-296, OF-1, SS-1
1 yr.	1	1	0	0	0	0	0.0	0	1	0	0	0	.000	.000	0	0	C-1

WORLD SERIES
| 1915 PHI N | 5 | 16 | 3 | 0 | 0 | 0 | 0.0 | 1 | 0 | 1 | 2 | 0 | .188 | .188 | 0 | 0 | C-5 |

Ellis Burton

BURTON, ELLIS NARRINGTON   BB TR 5'11" 160 lbs.
B. Aug. 12, 1936, Los Angeles, Calif.

	G	AB	H	2B	3B	HR	HR %	R	RBI	BB	SO	SB	BA	SA	PH AB	PH H	G by POS
1958 STL N	8	30	7	0	1	2	6.7	5	4	3	8	0	.233	.500	1	0	OF-7
1960	29	28	6	1	0	0	0.0	5	2	4	14	0	.214	.250	5	2	OF-23
1963 2 teams	STL A	(26G – .194)				CHI N	(93G – .230)										
" Total	119	353	80	19	1	13	3.7	51	42	40	63	6	.227	.397	9	2	OF-106
1964 CHI N	42	105	20	3	2	2	1.9	12	7	17	22	4	.190	.314	12	2	OF-29
1965	17	40	7	1	0	0	0.0	6	4	1	10	1	.175	.200	8	2	OF-12
5 yrs.	215	556	120	24	4	17	3.1	79	59	65	117	11	.216	.365	35	8	OF-177
2 yrs.	37	58	13	1	1	2	3.4	10	6	7	22	0	.224	.379	6	2	OF-30

Ray Busse

BUSSE, RAYMOND EDWARD   BR TR 6'4"   175 lbs.
B. Sept. 25, 1948, Daytona Beach, Fla.

	G	AB	H	2B	3B	HR	HR %	R	RBI	BB	SO	SB	BA	SA	PH AB	PH H	G by POS
1971 HOU N	10	34	5	3	0	0	0.0	2	4	2	9	0	.147	.235	2	0	SS-5, 3B-3
1973 2 teams	STL N	(24G – .143)				HOU N	(15G – .059)										
" Total	39	87	11	4	2	2	2.3	7	5	6	33	0	.126	.287	6	0	SS-28, 3B-3
1974 HOU N	19	34	7	1	0	0	0.0	3	0	3	12	0	.206	.235	11	1	3B-8
3 yrs.	68	155	23	8	2	2	1.3	12	9	11	54	0	.148	.265	19	1	SS-33, 3B-14
1 yr.	24	70	10	4	2	2	2.9	6	5	5	21	0	.143	.343	0	0	SS-23

Art Butler

BUTLER, ARTHUR EDWARD   BR TR 5'9"   160 lbs.
Born Arthur Edward Bouthillier.
B. Dec. 19, 1887, Fall River, Mass.

	G	AB	H	2B	3B	HR	HR %	R	RBI	BB	SO	SB	BA	SA	PH AB	PH H	G by POS
1911 BOS N	27	68	12	2	0	0	0.0	11	2	6	6	0	.176	.206	7	1	3B-14, 2B-4, SS-1
1912 PIT N	43	154	42	4	2	1	0.6	19	17	15	11	2	.273	.344	0	0	2B-43
1913	82	214	60	9	3	0	0.0	40	20	32	14	9	.280	.350	18	6	2B-27, SS-24, OF-2, 3B-2
1914 STL N	86	274	55	12	3	1	0.4	29	24	39	23	14	.201	.277	2	0	SS-84, OF-1
1915	130	469	119	12	5	1	0.2	73	31	47	34	26	.254	.307	2	0	SS-130
1916	86	110	23	5	0	0	0.0	9	7	7	12	3	.209	.255	54	13	OF-15, 2B-8, SS-1, 3B-1
6 yrs.	454	1289	311	44	13	3	0.2	181	101	146	100	54	.241	.303	83	20	SS-240, 2B-82, OF-18, 3B-17
3 yrs.	302	853	197	29	8	2	0.2	111	62	93	69	43	.231	.291	58	13	SS-215, OF-16, 2B-8, 3B-1

John Butler

BUTLER, JOHN ALBERT   BR TR 5'7"   170 lbs.
B. July 26, 1879, Boston, Mass.   D. Feb. 2, 1950, Boston, Mass.

	G	AB	H	2B	3B	HR	HR %	R	RBI	BB	SO	SB	BA	SA	PH AB	PH H	G by POS
1904 STL N	12	37	6	1	0	0	0.0	0	1	4		0	.162	.189	0	0	C-12
1906 BKN N	1	0	0	0	0	0	–	0	0	0		0	–	–	0	0	C-1
1907	30	79	10	1	0	0	0.0	6	2	9		0	.127	.139	1	0	C-28, OF-1
3 yrs.	43	116	16	2	0	0	0.0	6	3	13		0	.138	.155	1	0	C-41, OF-1
1 yr.	12	37	6	1	0	0	0.0	0	1	4		0	.162	.189	0	0	C-12

Johnny Butler

BUTLER, JOHN STEPHEN (Trolley Line)   BR TR 6'   175 lbs.
B. Mar. 20, 1894, Eureka, Kans.   D. Apr. 29, 1967, Long Beach, Calif.

	G	AB	H	2B	3B	HR	HR %	R	RBI	BB	SO	SB	BA	SA	PH AB	PH H	G by POS
1926 BKN N	147	501	135	27	5	1	0.2	54	68	54	44	6	.269	.349	0	0	SS-102, 3B-42, 2B-8
1927	149	521	124	13	6	2	0.4	39	57	34	33	9	.238	.298	1	0	SS-90, 3B-60
1928 CHI N	62	174	47	7	0	0	0.0	17	16	19	7	2	.270	.310	1	0	3B-59, SS-2
1929 STL N	17	55	9	1	1	0	0.0	5	5	4	5	0	.164	.218	0	0	3B-9, SS-8
4 yrs.	375	1251	315	48	12	3	0.2	115	146	111	89	17	.252	.317	2	0	SS-202, 3B-170, 2B-8
1 yr.	17	55	9	1	1	0	0.0	5	5	4	5	0	.164	.218	0	0	3B-9, SS-8

Bill Byers

BYERS, JOHN WILLIAM (Big Bill)   TR
B. Baltimore, Md.

	G	AB	H	2B	3B	HR	HR %	R	RBI	BB	SO	SB	BA	SA	PH AB	PH H	G by POS
1904 STL N	19	60	13	0	0	0	0.0	3	4	1		0	.217	.217	2	1	C-16, 1B-1

Bobby Byrne

BYRNE, ROBERT MATTHEW   BR TR 5'7½" 145 lbs.
B. Dec. 31, 1884, St. Louis, Mo.   D. Dec. 31, 1964, Wayne, Pa.

	G	AB	H	2B	3B	HR	HR %	R	RBI	BB	SO	SB	BA	SA	PH AB	PH H	G by POS
1907 STL N	148	558	143	11	5	0	0.0	55	29	35		21	.256	.294	0	0	3B-147, SS-1
1908	127	439	84	7	1	0	0.0	27	14	23		16	.191	.212	1	0	3B-122, SS-4
1909 2 teams	STL N	(105G – .214)				PIT N	(46G – .256)										
" Total	151	589	133	19	8	1	0.2	92	40	78		29	.226	.290	0	0	3B-151

	G	AB	H	2B	3B	HR	HR %	R	RBI	BB	SO	SB	BA	SA	Pinch Hit AB	Pinch Hit H	G by POS

Bobby Byrne continued

	G	AB	H	2B	3B	HR	HR %	R	RBI	BB	SO	SB	BA	SA	AB	H	G by POS
1910 PIT N	148	602	178	43	12	2	0.3	101	52	66	27	36	.296	.417	0	0	3B-148
1911	153	598	155	24	17	2	0.3	96	52	67	41	23	.259	.366	1	0	3B-152
1912	130	528	152	31	11	3	0.6	99	35	54	40	20	.288	.405	0	0	3B-130
1913 2 teams	PIT	N	(113G –	.270)		PHI	N	(19G –	.224)								
" Total	132	506	134	23	0	2	0.4	63	51	34	31	12	.265	.322	5	1	3B-125
1914 PHI N	126	467	127	12	1	0	0.0	61	26	45	44	9	.272	.302	4	2	2B-101, 3B-22
1915	105	387	81	6	4	0	0.0	50	21	39	28	4	.209	.245	0	0	3B-105
1916	48	141	33	10	1	0	0.0	22	9	14	7	6	.234	.319	6	1	3B-40
1917 2 teams	PHI	N	(13G –	.357)		CHI	A	(1G –	.000)								
" Total	14	15	5	0	0	0	0.0	1	0	1	2	0	.333	.333	9	2	3B-4, 2B-1
11 yrs.	1282	4830	1225	186	60	10	0.2	667	329	456	220	176	.254	.323	26	6	3B-1146, 2B-102, SS-5
3 yrs.	380	1418	317	31	12	1	0.1	143	76	104		58	.224	.264	1	0	3B-374, SS-5

WORLD SERIES

	G	AB	H	2B	3B	HR	HR %	R	RBI	BB	SO	SB	BA	SA	AB	H	G by POS
1909 PIT N	7	24	6	1	0	0	0.0	5	0	1	4	1	.250	.292	0	0	3B-7
1915 PHI N	1	1	0	0	0	0	0.0	0	0	0	0	0	.000	.000	1	0	
2 yrs.	8	25	6	1	0	0	0.0	5	0	1	4	1	.240	.280	1	0	3B-7

Al Cabrera

CABRERA, ALFREDO A. TR
B. 1883, Canary Islands   D. Havana, Cuba

	G	AB	H	2B	3B	HR	HR %	R	RBI	BB	SO	SB	BA	SA	AB	H	G by POS
1913 STL N	1	2	0	0	0	0	0.0	0	0	0	0	0	.000	.000	0	0	SS-1

John Calhoun

CALHOUN, JOHN CHARLES (Red) BR TR 6'   185 lbs.
B. Dec. 14, 1879, Pittsburgh, Pa.   D. Feb. 27, 1947, Cincinnati, Ohio

	G	AB	H	2B	3B	HR	HR %	R	RBI	BB	SO	SB	BA	SA	AB	H	G by POS
1902 STL N	20	64	10	2	1	0	0.0	3	8	8		1	.156	.219	2	0	3B-12, 1B-5, OF-1

Wes Callahan

CALLAHAN, WESLEY LeROY BR TR 5'7½" 155 lbs.
B. July 3, 1888, Lyons, Ind.   D. Sept. 13, 1953, Dayton, Ohio

	G	AB	H	2B	3B	HR	HR %	R	RBI	BB	SO	SB	BA	SA	AB	H	G by POS
1913 STL N	7	14	4	0	0	0	0.0	2	2	2	1	1	.286	.286	1	0	SS-6

Llewellyn Camp

CAMP, LLEWELLYN ROBERT TR
Brother of Kid Camp.
B. Feb. 22, 1868, Columbus, Ohio   D. Oct. 1, 1948, Omaha, Neb.

	G	AB	H	2B	3B	HR	HR %	R	RBI	BB	SO	SB	BA	SA	AB	H	G by POS
1892 STL N	42	145	30	3	1	2	1.4	19	13	17	27	12	.207	.283	0	0	3B-39, OF-3
1893 CHI N	38	156	41	7	7	2	1.3	37	17	19	19	30	.263	.436	0	0	3B-16, OF-11, 2B-9, SS-3
1894	8	33	6	2	0	0	0.0	1	1	1	6	0	.182	.242	0	0	2B-8
3 yrs.	88	334	77	12	8	4	1.2	57	31	37	52	42	.231	.350	0	0	3B-55, 2B-17, OF-14, SS-3
1 yr.	42	145	30	3	1	2	1.4	19	13	17	27	12	.207	.283	0	0	3B-39, OF-3

Dave Campbell

CAMPBELL, DAVID WILSON BR TR 6'1" 180 lbs.
B. Jan. 14, 1942, Manistee, Mich.

	G	AB	H	2B	3B	HR	HR %	R	RBI	BB	SO	SB	BA	SA	AB	H	G by POS
1967 DET A	2	2	0	0	0	0	0.0	0	0	0	1	0	.000	.000	1	0	1B-1
1968	9	8	1	0	0	1	12.5	1	2	1	3	0	.125	.500	3	0	2B-5
1969	32	39	4	1	0	0	0.0	4	2	4	15	0	.103	.128	14	2	1B-13, 2B-5, 3B-1
1970 SD N	154	581	127	28	2	12	2.1	71	40	40	115	18	.219	.336	1	0	2B-153
1971	108	365	83	14	2	7	1.9	38	29	37	75	9	.227	.334	1	0	2B-69, 3B-40, SS-4, OF-2, 1B-2
1972	33	100	24	5	0	0	0.0	6	3	11	12	0	.240	.290	0	0	3B-31, 2B-1
1973 3 teams	SD	N	(33G –	.224)		STL	N	(13G –	.000)		HOU	N	(9G –	.267)			
" Total	55	134	26	5	0	0	0.0	4	11	9	25	1	.194	.231	10	0	2B-33, 3B-7, 1B-5, OF-1
1974 HOU N	35	23	2	1	0	0	0.0	4	2	1	8	1	.087	.130	13	0	2B-9, 1B-6, 3B-2, OF-1
8 yrs.	428	1252	267	54	4	20	1.6	128	89	102	254	29	.213	.311	43	2	2B-275, 3B-81, 1B-27, OF-4, SS-4
1 yr.	13	21	0	0	0	0	0.0	1	1	1	6	0	.000	.000	7	0	2B-6

Jim Campbell

CAMPBELL, JAMES ROBERT JR BL TR 6'   205 lbs.
B. Jan. 10, 1943, Hartsville, S. C.

	G	AB	H	2B	3B	HR	HR %	R	RBI	BB	SO	SB	BA	SA	AB	H	G by POS
1970 STL N	13	13	3	0	0	0	0.0	0	1	0	3	0	.231	.231	13	3	

Chris Cannizzaro

CANNIZZARO, CHRISTOPHER JOHN BR TR 6'   190 lbs.
B. May 3, 1938, Oakland, Calif.

	G	AB	H	2B	3B	HR	HR %	R	RBI	BB	SO	SB	BA	SA	AB	H	G by POS
1960 STL N	7	9	2	0	0	0	0.0	0	1	1	3	0	.222	.222	0	0	C-6
1961	6	2	1	0	0	0	0.0	0	0	0	0	0	.500	.500	1	1	C-5
1962 NY N	59	133	32	2	1	0	0.0	9	9	19	26	1	.241	.271	3	1	C-56, OF-1
1963	16	33	8	1	0	0	0.0	4	4	1	8	0	.242	.273	1	1	C-15
1964	60	164	51	10	0	0	0.0	11	10	14	28	0	.311	.372	5	1	C-53
1965	114	251	46	8	2	0	0.0	17	7	28	60	0	.183	.231	2	0	C-112
1968 PIT N	25	58	14	2	1	1	1.7	5	7	9	13	0	.241	.397	0	0	C-25
1969 SD N	134	418	92	14	3	4	1.0	23	33	42	81	0	.220	.297	2	0	C-132
1970	111	341	95	13	3	5	1.5	27	42	48	49	2	.279	.378	2	0	C-110
1971 2 teams	SD	N	(21G –	.190)		CHI	N	(71G –	.213)								
" Total	92	260	54	6	1	6	2.3	20	31	39	34	0	.208	.319	2	0	C-89
1972 LA N	73	200	48	6	0	2	1.0	14	18	31	38	0	.240	.300	5	2	C-72
1973	17	21	4	0	0	0	0.0	0	3	3	3	0	.190	.190	3	0	C-13
1974 SD N	26	60	11	0	0	0	0.0	2	4	6	11	0	.183	.200	0	0	C-26
13 yrs.	740	1950	458	66	12	18	0.9	132	169	241	354	3	.235	.309	26	6	C-714, OF-1
2 yrs.	13	11	3	0	0	0	0.0	0	1	1	3	0	.273	.273	1	1	C-11

Bernie Carbo

CARBO, BERNARDO BL TR 5'11" 173 lbs.
B. Aug. 5, 1947, Detroit, Mich.

	G	AB	H	2B	3B	HR	HR %	R	RBI	BB	SO	SB	BA	SA	AB	H	G by POS
1969 CIN N	4	3	0	0	0	0	0.0	0	0	0	2	0	.000	.000	3	0	

	G	AB	H	2B	3B	HR	HR %	R	RBI	BB	SO	SB	BA	SA	Pinch Hit AB	Pinch Hit H	G by POS

Bernie Carbo continued

	G	AB	H	2B	3B	HR	HR %	R	RBI	BB	SO	SB	BA	SA	PH AB	PH H	G by POS
1970	125	365	113	19	3	21	5.8	54	63	94	77	10	.310	.551	7	3	OF-119
1971	106	310	68	20	1	5	1.6	33	20	54	56	2	.219	.339	12	3	OF-90
1972 2 teams	CIN N (19G – .143)							STL N (99G – .258)									
" Total	118	323	81	13	1	7	2.2	44	34	63	59	0	.251	.362	17	1	OF-96, 3B-1
1973 STL N	111	308	88	18	0	8	2.6	42	40	58	52	2	.286	.422	17	5	OF-94
1974 BOS A	117	338	84	20	0	12	3.6	40	61	58	90	4	.249	.414	12	6	OF-87
1975	107	319	82	21	3	15	4.7	64	50	83	69	2	.257	.483	8	2	OF-85
1976 2 teams	BOS A (17G – .236)							MIL A (69G – .235)									
" Total	86	238	56	11	0	5	2.1	25	21	41	72	2	.235	.345	12	2	OF-34
1977 BOS A	86	228	66	6	1	15	6.6	36	34	47	72	1	.289	.522	14	4	OF-67
1978 2 teams	BOS A (17G – .261)							CLE A (60G – .287)									
" Total	77	220	62	11	0	5	2.3	28	22	28	39	2	.282	.400	8	0	OF-13
1979 STL N	52	64	18	1	0	3	4.7	6	12	10	22	1	.281	.438	32	6	OF-17
1980 2 teams	STL N (14G – .182)							PIT N (7G – .333)									
" Total	21	17	4	0	0	0	0.0	0	1	2	1	0	.235	.235	17	4	
12 yrs.	1010	2733	722	140	9	96	3.5	372	358	538	611	26	.264	.427	159	36	OF-702, 3B-1
4 yrs.	276	685	186	32	1	18	2.6	90	86	126	130	3	.272	.400	66	14	OF-203, 3B-1
LEAGUE CHAMPIONSHIP SERIES																	
1970 CIN N	2	6	0	0	0	0	0.0	0	0	0	3	0	.000	.000	1	0	OF-2
WORLD SERIES																	
1970 CIN N	4	8	0	0	0	0	0.0	0	0	2	3	0	.000	.000	2	0	OF-2
1975 BOS A	4	7	3	1	0	2	28.6	3	4	1	1	0	.429	1.429	3	2	OF-2
2 yrs.	8	15	3	1	0	2	13.3	3	4	3	4	0	.200	.667	5	2	OF-4

Jose Cardenal

CARDENAL, JOSE DOMEC   BR TR 5'10" 150 lbs.
B. Oct. 7, 1943, Matanzas, Cuba

	G	AB	H	2B	3B	HR	HR %	R	RBI	BB	SO	SB	BA	SA	PH AB	PH H	G by POS
1963 SF N	9	5	1	0	0	0	0.0	1	2	1	1	0	.200	.200	4	1	OF-2
1964	20	15	0	0	0	0	0.0	3	0	2	3	2	.000	.000	2	0	OF-16
1965 CAL A	134	512	128	23	2	11	2.1	58	57	27	72	37	.250	.367	1	1	OF-129, 3B-2, 2B-1
1966	154	561	155	15	3	16	2.9	67	48	34	69	24	.276	.399	10	2	OF-146
1967	108	381	90	13	5	6	1.6	40	27	15	63	10	.236	.344	8	0	OF-101
1968 CLE A	157	583	150	21	7	7	1.2	78	44	39	74	40	.257	.353	7	1	OF-153
1969	146	557	143	26	3	11	2.0	75	45	49	58	36	.257	.373	4	1	OF-142, 3B-5
1970 STL N	148	552	162	32	6	10	1.8	73	74	45	70	26	.293	.428	16	8	OF-134
1971 2 teams	STL N (89G – .243)							MIL A (53G – .258)									
" Total	142	499	124	22	4	10	2.0	57	80	42	55	21	.248	.369	9	5	OF-135
1972 CHI N	143	533	155	24	6	17	3.2	96	70	55	58	25	.291	.454	5	2	OF-137
1973	145	522	158	33	2	11	2.1	80	68	58	62	19	.303	.437	2	1	OF-142
1974	143	542	159	35	3	13	2.4	75	72	56	67	23	.293	.441	8	2	OF-136
1975	154	574	182	30	2	9	1.6	85	68	77	50	34	.317	.423	5	1	OF-151
1976	136	521	156	25	2	8	1.5	64	47	32	39	23	.299	.401	8	1	OF-128
1977	100	226	54	12	1	3	1.3	33	18	28	30	5	.239	.341	31	10	OF-62, 3B-1, 2B-1
1978 PHI N	87	201	50	12	0	4	2.0	27	33	23	16	2	.249	.368	33	9	1B-50, OF-13
1979 2 teams	PHI N (29G – .208)							NY N (11G – .297)									
" Total	40	85	21	7	0	2	2.4	12	13	14	11	2	.247	.400	17	4	OF-21, 1B-3
1980 2 teams	NY N (26G – .167)							KC A (25G – .340)									
" Total	51	95	25	3	0	0	0.0	12	9	11	9	0	.263	.295	17	1	OF-29, 1B-5
18 yrs.	2017	6964	1913	333	46	138	2.0	936	775	608	807	329	.275	.395	187	50	OF-1777, 1B-58, 3B-8, 2B-2
2 yrs.	237	853	235	44	10	17	2.0	110	122	74	105	38	.275	.410	23	12	OF-217
LEAGUE CHAMPIONSHIP SERIES																	
1978 PHI N	2	6	1	0	0	0	0.0	0	0	1	1	0	.167	.167	1	0	1B-2
WORLD SERIES																	
1980 KC A	4	10	2	0	0	0	0.0	0	0	0	3	0	.200	.200	1	0	OF-4

Duke Carmel

CARMEL, LEON JAMES   BL TL 6'3" 202 lbs.
B. Apr. 23, 1937, New York, N. Y.

	G	AB	H	2B	3B	HR	HR %	R	RBI	BB	SO	SB	BA	SA	PH AB	PH H	G by POS
1959 STL N	10	23	3	1	0	0	0.0	2	3	1	6	0	.130	.174	0	0	OF-10
1960	4	3	0	0	0	0	0.0	0	0	1	1	1	.000	.000	0	0	1B-2, OF-1
1963 2 teams	STL N (57G – .227)							NY N (47G – .235)									
" Total	104	193	45	6	3	4	2.1	20	20	25	48	2	.233	.358	19	4	OF-59, 1B-19
1965 NY A	6	8	0	0	0	0	0.0	0	0	0	5	0	.000	.000	4	0	1B-2
4 yrs.	124	227	48	7	3	4	1.8	22	23	27	60	3	.211	.322	23	4	OF-70, 1B-23
3 yrs.	71	70	13	2	0	1	1.4	11	5	11	18	1	.186	.257	12	3	OF-49, 1B-3

Hick Carpenter

CARPENTER, WARREN WILLIAM   BR TL 5'11" 186 lbs.
B. Aug. 16, 1855, Grafton, Mass.   D. Apr. 18, 1937, San Diego, Calif.

	G	AB	H	2B	3B	HR	HR %	R	RBI	BB	SO	SB	BA	SA	PH AB	PH H	G by POS
1879 SYR N	65	261	53	6	0	0	0.0	30	20	2	15		.203	.226	0	0	1B-34, 3B-18, OF-11, 2B-3
1880 CIN N	77	300	72	6	4	0	0.0	32	23	2	15		.240	.287	0	0	3B-67, 1B-9, SS-1
1881 WOR N	83	347	75	12	2	2	0.6	40	31	3	19		.216	.280	0	0	3B-83
1882 CIN AA	80	351	120	15	5	1	0.3	78		10			.342	.422	0	0	3B-80
1883	95	436	129	18	4	3	0.7	99		18			.296	.376	0	0	3B-95
1884	108	474	121	16	2	4	0.8	80		6			.255	.323	0	0	3B-108, OF-1
1885	112	473	131	12	8	2	0.4	89		9			.277	.349	0	0	3B-112
1886	111	458	101	8	5	2	0.4	67		18			.221	.273	0	0	3B-111
1887	127	498	124	12	6	1	0.2	70		19		44	.249	.303	0	0	3B-127
1888	136	551	147	14	5	3	0.5	68	67	5		59	.267	.327	0	0	3B-136
1889	123	486	127	23	6	0	0.0	67	63	18		47	.261	.333	0	0	3B-121, 1B-2
1892 STL N	1	3	1	0	0	0	0.0	0	0	0	1	0	.333	.333	0	0	3B-1
12 yrs.	1118	4638	1201	142	47	18	0.4	720	204	111	91	150	.259	.321	0	0	3B-1059, 1B-45, OF-12, 2B-3, SS-1
1 yr.	1	3	1	0	0	0	0.0	0	0	0	1	0	.333	.333	0	0	3B-1

	G	AB	H	2B	3B	HR	HR %	R	RBI	BB	SO	SB	BA	SA	Pinch Hit AB	H	G by POS

Cliff Carroll

CARROLL, SAMUEL CLIFFORD
B. Oct. 18, 1859, Clay Grove, Iowa   D. June 12, 1923, Portland, Ore.
BB TR 5'8"   163 lbs.

	G	AB	H	2B	3B	HR	HR %	R	RBI	BB	SO	SB	BA	SA	AB	H	G by POS
1882 PRO N	10	41	5	0	0	0	0.0	4		0	4		.122	.122	0	0	OF-10
1883	58	238	63	12	3	1	0.4	37		4	28		.265	.353	0	0	OF-58
1884	113	452	118	16	4	3	0.7	90		29	39		.261	.334	0	0	OF-113
1885	104	426	99	12	3	1	0.2	62	40	29	29		.232	.282	0	0	OF-104
1886 WAS N	111	433	99	11	6	2	0.5	73	22	44	26		.229	.296	0	0	OF-111
1887	103	420	104	17	4	4	1.0	79	37	17	30	40	.248	.336	0	0	OF-103
1888 PIT N	5	20	0	0	0	0	0.0	1	0	0	8	2	.000	.000	0	0	OF-5
1890 CHI N	136	582	166	16	6	7	1.2	134	65	53	34	34	.285	.369	0	0	OF-136
1891	130	515	132	20	8	7	1.4	87	80	50	42	31	.256	.367	0	0	OF-130
1892 STL N	101	407	111	14	8	4	1.0	82	49	47	22	30	.273	.376	0	0	OF-101
1893 BOS N	120	438	98	7	5	2	0.5	80	54	88	28	29	.224	.276	0	0	OF-120
11 yrs.	991	3972	995	125	47	31	0.8	729	346	361	290	166	.251	.329	0	0	OF-991
1 yr.	101	407	111	14	8	4	1.0	82	49	47	22	30	.273	.376	0	0	OF-101

Kid Carsey

CARSEY, WILFRED
B. Oct. 22, 1870, New York, N.Y.   Deceased.
BR TR 5'7"   168 lbs.

	G	AB	H	2B	3B	HR	HR %	R	RBI	BB	SO	SB	BA	SA	AB	H	G by POS
1891 WAS AA	61	187	28	5	2	0	0.0	25	15	19	38	2	.150	.198	0	0	P-54, OF-7, SS-2
1892 PHI N	44	131	20	2	1	1	0.8	8	10	9	24	1	.153	.206	0	0	P-43, OF-2
1893	39	145	27	1	1	0	0.0	12	10	5	14	2	.186	.207	0	0	P-39
1894	35	125	34	2	2	0	0.0	30	18	16	11	3	.272	.320	0	0	P-35
1895	44	141	41	2	0	0	0.0	24	20	15	12	2	.291	.305	0	0	P-44
1896	27	81	18	2	2	0	0.0	13	7	11	12	1	.222	.296	0	0	P-27
1897 2 teams			PHI	N	(4G –	.231)		STL	N	(13G –	.302)						
" Total	17	56	16	2	2	0	0.0	3	6	1		1	.286	.393	1	1	P-16
1898 STL N	38	105	21	0	1	1	1.0	8	10	10		3	.200	.248	0	0	P-20, 2B-10, OF-8
1899 3 teams			CLE	N	(11G –	.278)		WAS	N	(4G –	.000)		NY	N	(5G –	.333)	
" Total	20	65	16	1	0	0	0.0	8	5	5		2	.246	.262	0	0	P-14, SS-3, 3B-3
1901 BKN N	2	0	0	0	0	0	0.0	0	0	0		0	.000	.000	0	0	P-2
10 yrs.	327	1038	221	17	11	2	0.2	131	101	91	111	17	.213	.256	1	1	P-294, OF-17, 2B-10, SS-5, 3B-3
2 yrs.	51	148	34	2	3	1	0.7	10	15	11		4	.230	.304	1	1	P-32, 2B-10, OF-8

Bob Caruthers

CARUTHERS, ROBERT LEE (Parisian Bob)
B. Jan. 5, 1864, Memphis, Tenn.   D. Aug. 5, 1911, Peoria, Ill.
BL TR 5'7"   138 lbs.

	G	AB	H	2B	3B	HR	HR %	R	RBI	BB	SO	SB	BA	SA	AB	H	G by POS
1884 STL AA	23	82	21	2	0	2	2.4	15		4			.256	.354	0	0	OF-16, P-13
1885	60	222	50	10	2	1	0.5	37		20			.225	.302	0	0	P-53, OF-7
1886	87	317	106	21	14	4	1.3	91		64			.334	.527	0	0	P-44, OF-43, 2B-2
1887	98	364	130	23	11	8	2.2	102		66		49	.357	.547	0	0	OF-54, P-39, 1B-7
1888 BKN AA	94	335	77	10	5	5	1.5	58	53	45		23	.230	.334	0	0	OF-51, P-44
1889	59	172	43	8	3	2	1.2	45	31	44	17	9	.250	.366	0	0	P-56, OF-3, 1B-2
1890 BKN N	71	238	63	7	4	1	0.4	46	29	47	18	13	.265	.340	0	0	OF-39, P-37
1891	56	171	48	5	3	2	1.2	24	23	25	13	4	.281	.380	1	1	P-38, OF-17, 2B-1
1892 STL N	143	513	142	16	8	3	0.6	76	69	86	29	24	.277	.357	0	0	OF-122, P-16, 2B-6, 1B-4
1893 2 teams			CHI	N	(1G –	.000)		CIN	N	(13G –	.292)						
" Total	14	51	14	2	0	1	2.0	14	8	16	2	4	.275	.373	0	0	OF-14
10 yrs.	705	2465	694	104	50	29	1.2	508	212	417	79	126	.282	.400	1	0	OF-366, P-340, 1B-13, 2B-9
1 yr.	143	513	142	16	8	3	0.6	76	69	86	29	24	.277	.357	0	0	OF-122, P-16, 2B-6, 1B-4

Pete Castiglione

CASTIGLIONE, PETER PAUL
B. Feb. 13, 1921, Greenwich, Conn.
BR TR 5'11"   175 lbs.

	G	AB	H	2B	3B	HR	HR %	R	RBI	BB	SO	SB	BA	SA	AB	H	G by POS
1947 PIT N	13	50	14	0	0	0	0.0	6	1	2	5	0	.280	.280	0	0	SS-13
1948	4	2	0	0	0	0	0.0	0	0	0	0	1	.000	.000	1	0	SS-1
1949	118	448	120	20	2	6	1.3	57	43	20	43	2	.268	.362	5	1	3B-98, SS-17, OF-2
1950	94	263	67	10	3	3	1.1	29	22	23	23	1	.255	.350	22	7	3B-35, SS-29, 2B-9, 1B-3
1951	132	482	126	19	4	7	1.5	62	42	34	28	2	.261	.361	9	2	3B-99, SS-28
1952	67	214	57	9	1	4	1.9	27	18	17	8	3	.266	.374	9	2	3B-57, OF-1, 1B-1
1953 2 teams			PIT	N	(45G –	.208)		STL	N	(67G –	.173)						
" Total	112	211	42	4	1	4	1.9	23	24	7	19	1	.199	.284	8	4	3B-94, 2B-9, SS-3
1954 STL N	5	0	0	0	0	0	–	1	0	0	0	0	–	–	0	0	3B-5
8 yrs.	545	1670	426	62	11	24	1.4	205	150	103	126	10	.255	.349	54	16	3B-388, SS-91, 2B-18, 1B-4, OF-3
2 yrs.	72	52	9	2	0	0	0.0	10	3	2	5	0	.173	.212	7	3	3B-56, 2B-9, SS-3

Danny Cater

CATER, DANNY ANDERSON
B. Feb. 25, 1940, Austin, Tex.
BR TR 6'   170 lbs.

	G	AB	H	2B	3B	HR	HR %	R	RBI	BB	SO	SB	BA	SA	AB	H	G by POS
1964 PHI N	60	152	45	9	1	1	0.7	13	13	7	15	1	.296	.388	18	6	OF-39, 1B-7, 3B-1
1965 CHI A	142	514	139	18	4	14	2.7	74	55	33	65	3	.270	.403	7	2	OF-127, 3B-11, 1B-3
1966 2 teams			CHI	A	(21G –	.183)		KC	A	(116G –	.292)						
" Total	137	485	135	17	4	7	1.4	50	56	28	47	4	.278	.373	5	1	1B-53, 3B-42, OF-40
1967 KC A	142	529	143	17	4	0	0.8	55	46	34	56	4	.270	.340	2	1	3B-56, OF-55, 1B-44
1968 OAK A	147	504	146	28	3	6	1.2	53	62	35	43	8	.290	.393	11	4	1B-121, OF-20, 2B-1
1969	152	584	153	24	2	10	1.7	64	76	28	40	1	.262	.361	8	1	1B-132, OF-20, 2B-4
1970 NY A	155	582	175	26	5	6	1.0	64	76	34	44	4	.301	.393	3	0	1B-131, 3B-42, OF-7
1971	121	428	118	16	5	4	0.9	39	50	19	25	0	.276	.364	10	3	1B-78, 3B-52
1972 BOS A	92	317	75	17	1	8	2.5	32	39	15	33	0	.237	.372	6	1	1B-90
1973	63	195	61	12	0	1	0.5	30	24	10	22	0	.313	.390	7	2	1B-37, 3B-21
1974	56	126	31	5	0	5	4.0	14	20	10	13	1	.246	.405	18	5	1B-23
1975 STL N	22	35	8	2	0	0	0.0	3	2	1	3	0	.229	.286	13	2	1B-12
12 yrs.	1289	4451	1229	191	29	66	1.5	491	519	254	406	26	.276	.377	108	28	1B-731, OF-308, 3B-225, 2B-5
1 yr.	22	35	8	2	0	0	0.0	3	2	1	3	0	.229	.286	13	2	1B-12

	G	AB	H	2B	3B	HR	HR %	R	RBI	BB	SO	SB	BA	SA	Pinch Hit AB	Pinch Hit H	G by POS

Ted Cather

CATHER, THEODORE P   BR TR 5'10½" 178 lbs.
B. May 20, 1889, Chester, Pa.   D. Apr. 9, 1945, Charlestown, Md.

	G	AB	H	2B	3B	HR	HR %	R	RBI	BB	SO	SB	BA	SA	AB	H	G by POS
1912 STL N	5	19	8	1	1	0	0.0	4	2	0	4	1	.421	.579	0	0	OF-5
1913	67	183	39	8	4	0	0.0	16	12	9	24	7	.213	.301	7	3	OF-57, 1B-1, P-1
1914 2 teams		STL N (39G – .273)				BOS N (50G – .297)											
" Total	89	244	70	18	2	0	0.0	30	40	10	43	11	.287	.377	12	1	OF-76
1915 BOS N	40	102	21	3	1	2	2.0	10	18	15	19	2	.206	.314	7	1	OF-40
4 yrs.	201	548	138	30	8	2	0.4	60	72	34	90	21	.252	.347	26	5	OF-178, 1B-1, P-1
3 yrs.	111	301	74	16	5	0	0.0	31	27	12	43	12	.246	.332	17	4	OF-90, 1B-1, P-1

WORLD SERIES

	G	AB	H	2B	3B	HR	HR %	R	RBI	BB	SO	SB	BA	SA	AB	H	G by POS
1914 BOS N	1	5	0	0	0	0	0.0	0	0	0	1	0	.000	.000	0	0	OF-1

Orlando Cepeda

CEPEDA, ORLANDO MANUEL (The Baby Bull, Cha-Cha)   BR TR 6'2" 210 lbs.
B. Sept. 17, 1937, Ponce, Puerto Rico

	G	AB	H	2B	3B	HR	HR %	R	RBI	BB	SO	SB	BA	SA	AB	H	G by POS
1958 SF N	148	603	188	**38**	4	25	4.1	88	96	29	84	15	.312	.512	1	0	1B-147
1959	151	605	192	35	4	27	4.5	92	105	33	100	23	.317	.522	0	0	1B-122, OF-44, 3B-4
1960	151	569	169	36	3	24	4.2	81	96	34	91	15	.297	.497	4	0	OF-91, 1B-63
1961	152	585	182	28	4	**46**	7.9	105	**142**	39	91	12	.311	.609	1	0	1B-81, OF-80
1962	162	625	191	26	1	35	5.6	105	114	37	97	10	.306	.518	4	1	1B-160, OF-2
1963	156	579	183	33	4	34	5.9	100	97	37	70	8	.316	.563	8	2	1B-150, OF-3
1964	142	529	161	27	2	31	5.9	75	97	43	83	9	.304	.539	2	0	1B-139, OF-1
1965	33	34	6	1	0	1	2.9	1	5	3	9	0	.176	.294	21	4	1B-4, OF-2
1966 2 teams		SF N (19G – .286)				STL N (123G – .303)											
" Total	142	501	151	26	0	20	4.0	70	73	38	79	9	.301	.473	7	4	1B-126, OF-8
1967 STL N	151	563	183	37	0	25	4.4	91	**111**	62	75	11	.325	.524	1	1	1B-151
1968	157	600	149	26	2	16	2.7	71	73	43	96	8	.248	.378	3	1	1B-154
1969 ATL N	154	573	147	28	2	22	3.8	74	88	55	76	12	.257	.428	1	0	1B-153
1970	148	567	173	33	0	34	6.0	87	111	47	75	6	.305	.543	1	1	1B-148
1971	71	250	69	10	1	14	5.6	31	44	22	29	3	.276	.492	8	1	1B-63
1972 2 teams		ATL N (28G – .298)				OAK A (3G – .000)											
" Total	31	87	25	3	0	4	4.6	6	9	7	17	0	.287	.460	8	0	1B-22
1973 BOS A	142	550	159	25	0	20	3.6	51	86	50	81	0	.289	.444	0	0	
1974 KC A	33	107	23	5	0	1	0.9	3	18	9	16	1	.215	.290	7	2	
17 yrs.	2124	7927	2351	417	27	379	4.8	1131	1365	588	1169	142	.297	.499	77	17	1B-1683, OF-231, 3B-4
3 yrs.	431	1615	469	87	2	58	3.6	227	242	139	239	28	.290	.454	7	4	1B-425
						7th											

LEAGUE CHAMPIONSHIP SERIES

	G	AB	H	2B	3B	HR	HR %	R	RBI	BB	SO	SB	BA	SA	AB	H	G by POS
1969 ATL N	3	11	5	2	0	1	9.1	2	3	1	2	1	.455	.909	0	0	1B-3

WORLD SERIES

	G	AB	H	2B	3B	HR	HR %	R	RBI	BB	SO	SB	BA	SA	AB	H	G by POS
1962 SF N	5	19	3	1	0	0	0.0	1	2	0	4	0	.158	.211	0	0	1B-5
1967 STL N	7	29	3	2	0	0	0.0	1	1	0	4	0	.103	.172	0	0	1B-7
1968	7	28	7	0	0	2	7.1	2	6	2	3	0	.250	.464	0	0	1B-7
3 yrs.	19	76	13	3	0	2	2.6	4	9	2	11	0	.171	.289	0	0	1B-19

Charlie Chant

CHANT, CHARLES JOSEPH   BR TR 6' 190 lbs.
B. Aug. 7, 1951, Bell Gardens, Calif.

	G	AB	H	2B	3B	HR	HR %	R	RBI	BB	SO	SB	BA	SA	AB	H	G by POS
1975 OAK A	5	5	0	0	0	0	0.0	0	0	0	0	0	.000	.000	0	0	OF-5
1976 STL N	15	14	2	0	0	0	0.0	0	0	0	4	0	.143	.143	1	0	OF-14
2 yrs.	20	19	2	0	0	0	0.0	1	0	0	4	0	.105	.105	1	0	OF-19
1 yr.	15	14	2	0	0	0	0.0	0	0	0	4	0	.143	.143	1	0	OF-14

Chappy Charles

CHARLES, RAYMOND   BR TR
Born Charles S. Aschenbach.
B. 1883, Phillipsburg, N. J.   D. Aug. 4, 1959, Bethlehem, Pa.

	G	AB	H	2B	3B	HR	HR %	R	RBI	BB	SO	SB	BA	SA	AB	H	G by POS
1908 STL N	121	454	93	14	3	1	0.2	39	17	19		15	.205	.256	2	0	2B-65, SS-31, 3B-23
1909 2 teams		STL N (99G – .236)				CIN N (13G – .256)											
" Total	112	382	91	9	3	0	0.0	36	34	35		9	.238	.277	0	0	2B-81, SS-31, 3B-2
1910 CIN N	4	15	2	0	1	0	0.0	1	0	0		0	.133	.267	0	0	SS-4
3 yrs.	237	851	186	23	7	1	0.1	76	51	54		24	.219	.266	2	0	2B-146, SS-66, 3B-25
2 yrs.	220	793	173	21	6	1	0.1	72	46	50		22	.218	.264	2	0	2B-136, SS-59, 3B-25

Cupid Childs

CHILDS, CLARENCE ALGERNON   BL TR 5'8" 185 lbs.
B. Aug. 14, 1868, Calvert County, Md.   D. Nov. 8, 1912, Baltimore, Md.

	G	AB	H	2B	3B	HR	HR %	R	RBI	BB	SO	SB	BA	SA	AB	H	G by POS
1888 PHI N	2	4	0	0	0	0	0.0	0	0	0	0	0	.000	.000	0	0	2B-2
1890 SYR AA	136	493	170	**33**	14	2	0.4	109		72		56	.345	.481	0	0	2B-125, SS-1
1891 CLE N	141	551	155	21	12	2	0.4	120	83	97	32	39	.281	.374	0	0	2B-141
1892	145	558	177	14	11	3	0.5	**136**	53	117	20	26	.317	.398	0	0	2B-145
1893	124	485	158	19	10	3	0.6	145	65	120	12	23	.326	.425	0	0	2B-123
1894	118	479	169	21	12	2	0.4	143	52	107	11	17	.353	.459	0	0	2B-118
1895	119	462	133	15	3	4	0.9	96	90	74	24	20	.288	.359	0	0	2B-119
1896	132	498	177	24	9	1	0.2	106	106	100	18	25	.355	.446	0	0	2B-132
1897	114	444	150	15	9	1	0.2	105	61	74		25	.338	.419	0	0	2B-114
1898	110	422	122	9	4	1	0.2	91	31	69		9	.289	.336	0	0	2B-110
1899 STL N	125	465	124	11	11	1	0.2	73	48	74		11	.267	.344	0	0	2B-125
1900 CHI N	138	538	131	14	5	0	0.0	70	44	57		15	.243	.288	0	0	2B-137
1901	63	237	61	9	0	0	0.0	24	21	29		3	.257	.295	0	0	2B-62
13 yrs.	1467	5636	1727	205	100	20	0.4	1218	653	990	117	269	.306	.389	0	0	2B-1453, SS-1
1 yr.	125	465	124	11	11	1	0.2	73	48	74		11	.267	.344	0	0	2B-125

Pete Childs

CHILDS, GEORGE PETER   TR
B. Nov. 15, 1871, Philadelphia, Pa.   D. Feb. 15, 1922, Philadelphia, Pa.

	G	AB	H	2B	3B	HR	HR %	R	RBI	BB	SO	SB	BA	SA	AB	H	G by POS
1901 2 teams		STL N (29G – .266)				CHI N (61G – .225)											
" Total	90	292	69	6	1	0	0.0	35	22	41		4	.236	.264	6	1	2B-80, OF-2, SS-1
1902 PHI N	123	403	78	5	0	0	0.0	25	25	34		6	.194	.206	0	0	2B-123

	G	AB	H	2B	3B	HR	HR %	R	RBI	BB	SO	SB	BA	SA	Pinch Hit AB	Pinch Hit H	G by POS

Pete Childs continued

	G	AB	H	2B	3B	HR	HR%	R	RBI	BB	SO	SB	BA	SA	AB	H	G by POS
2 yrs.	213	695	147	11	1	0	0.0	60	47	75		10	.212	.230	6	1	2B-203, OF-2, SS-1
1 yr.	29	79	21	1	0	0	0.0	12	8	14		0	.266	.278	6	1	2B-19, OF-2, SS-1

Larry Ciaffone

CIAFFONE, LAWRENCE THOMAS (Symphony)   BR TR 5'9½" 185 lbs.
B. Aug. 17, 1924, Brooklyn, N. Y.

	G	AB	H	2B	3B	HR	HR%	R	RBI	BB	SO	SB	BA	SA	AB	H	G by POS
1951 STL N	5	5	0	0	0	0	0.0	0	0	1	2	0	.000	.000	3	0	OF-1

Gino Cimoli

CIMOLI, GINO NICHOLAS   BR TR 6'1" 180 lbs.
B. Dec. 18, 1929, San Francisco, Calif.

	G	AB	H	2B	3B	HR	HR%	R	RBI	BB	SO	SB	BA	SA	AB	H	G by POS
1956 BKN N	73	36	4	1	0	0	0.0	3	4	1	8	1	.111	.139	4	1	OF-62
1957	142	532	156	22	5	10	1.9	88	57	39	86	3	.293	.410	3	2	OF-138
1958 LA N	109	325	80	6	3	9	2.8	35	27	18	49	3	.246	.366	8	0	OF-104
1959 STL N	143	519	145	40	7	8	1.5	61	72	37	83	7	.279	.430	3	1	OF-141
1960 PIT N	101	307	82	14	4	0	0.0	36	28	32	43	1	.267	.339	10	2	OF-91
1961 2 teams	PIT N	(21G –	.299)		MIL N	(37G –	.197)										
" Total	58	184	43	8	1	3	1.6	16	10	13	28	1	.234	.337	7	1	OF-50
1962 KC A	152	550	151	20	15	10	1.8	67	71	40	89	2	.275	.420	7	2	OF-147
1963	145	529	139	19	11	4	0.8	56	48	39	72	3	.263	.363	9	4	OF-136
1964 2 teams	KC A	(4G –	.000)		BAL A	(38G –	.138)										
" Total	42	67	8	3	2	0	0.0	7	3	2	14	0	.119	.224	6	1	OF-39
1965 CAL A	4	5	0	0	0	0	0.0	1	1	0	2	0	.000	.000	3	0	OF-1
10 yrs.	969	3054	808	133	48	44	1.4	370	321	221	474	21	.265	.383	60	14	OF-909
1 yr.	143	519	145	40	7	8	1.5	61	72	37	83	7	.279	.430	3	1	OF-141

WORLD SERIES

	G	AB	H	2B	3B	HR	HR%	R	RBI	BB	SO	SB	BA	SA	AB	H	G by POS
1956 BKN N	1	0	0	0	0	0	–	0	0	0	0	0	–	–	0	0	OF-1
1960 PIT N	7	20	5	0	0	0	0.0	4	1	2	4	0	.250	.250	1	1	OF-6
2 yrs.	8	20	5	0	0	0	0.0	4	1	2	4	0	.250	.250	1	1	OF-7

Doug Clarey

CLAREY, DOUGLAS WILLIAM   BR TR 6' 180 lbs.
B. Apr. 20, 1954, Los Angeles, Calif.

	G	AB	H	2B	3B	HR	HR%	R	RBI	BB	SO	SB	BA	SA	AB	H	G by POS
1976 STL N	9	4	1	0	0	1	25.0	2	2	0	1	0	.250	1.000	2	1	2B-7

Danny Clark

CLARK, DANIEL CURRAN   BL TR 5'9" 167 lbs.
B. Jan. 18, 1895, Meridian, Miss.   D. May 23, 1937, Meridian, Miss.

	G	AB	H	2B	3B	HR	HR%	R	RBI	BB	SO	SB	BA	SA	AB	H	G by POS
1922 DET A	83	185	54	11	3	3	1.6	31	26	15	11	1	.292	.432	36	8	2B-38, OF-5, 3B-1
1924 BOS A	104	325	90	23	3	2	0.6	36	54	50	18	4	.277	.385	10	1	3B-93
1927 STL N	58	72	17	2	2	0	0.0	8	13	8	7	0	.236	.319	40	12	OF-9
3 yrs.	245	582	161	36	8	5	0.9	75	93	73	36	5	.277	.392	86	21	3B-94, 2B-38, OF-14
1 yr.	58	72	17	2	2	0	0.0	8	13	8	7	0	.236	.319	40	12	OF-9

Jim Clark

CLARK, JAMES F.   BR TR 5'11" 175 lbs.
B. Dec. 26, 1887, Brooklyn, N. Y.

	G	AB	H	2B	3B	HR	HR%	R	RBI	BB	SO	SB	BA	SA	AB	H	G by POS
1911 STL N	14	18	3	0	1	0	0.0	2	3	3	4	2	.167	.278	6	1	OF-8
1912	2	1	0	0	0	0	0.0	0	0	0	1	0	.000	.000	1	0	
2 yrs.	16	19	3	0	1	0	0.0	2	3	3	5	2	.158	.263	7	1	OF-8
2 yrs.	16	19	3	0	1	0	0.0	2	3	3	5	2	.158	.263	7	1	OF-8

Josh Clarke

CLARKE, JOSHUA BALDWIN (Pepper)   BL TR 5'10" 180 lbs.
Brother of Fred Clarke.
B. Mar. 8, 1879, Winfield, Kans.   D. July 2, 1962, Ventura, Calif.

	G	AB	H	2B	3B	HR	HR%	R	RBI	BB	SO	SB	BA	SA	AB	H	G by POS
1898 LOU N	6	18	3	0	0	0	0.0	0	0	1		0	.167	.167	1	0	OF-5
1905 STL N	50	167	43	3	2	3	1.8	31	18	27		8	.257	.353	4	1	OF-26, 2B-16, SS-4
1908 CLE A	131	492	119	8	4	1	0.2	70	21	76		37	.242	.280	0	0	OF-131
1909	4	12	0	0	0	0	0.0	1	0	2		0	.000	.000	0	0	OF-4
1911 BOS N	32	120	28	7	3	1	0.8	16	4	29	22	6	.233	.367	2	0	OF-30
5 yrs.	223	809	193	18	9	5	0.6	118	43	135	22	51	.239	.302	7	1	OF-196, 2B-16, SS-4
1 yr.	50	167	43	3	2	3	1.8	31	18	27		8	.257	.353	4	1	OF-26, 2B-16, SS-4

Doug Clemens

CLEMENS, DOUGLAS HORACE   BL TR 6' 180 lbs.
B. June 9, 1939, Leesport, Pa.

	G	AB	H	2B	3B	HR	HR%	R	RBI	BB	SO	SB	BA	SA	AB	H	G by POS
1960 STL N	1	0	0	0	0	0	–	0	0	0	0	0	–	–	0	0	OF-1
1961	6	12	2	1	0	0	0.0	1	0	3	1	0	.167	.250	3	1	OF-3
1962	48	93	22	1	1	1	1.1	12	12	17	19	0	.237	.301	15	5	OF-34
1963	5	6	1	0	0	1	16.7	1	2	1	2	0	.167	.667	1	0	OF-3
1964 2 teams	STL N	(33G –	.205)		CHI N	(54G –	.279)										
" Total	87	218	55	14	5	3	1.4	31	21	24	38	0	.252	.404	19	3	OF-62
1965 CHI N	128	340	75	11	0	4	1.2	36	26	38	53	5	.221	.288	25	6	OF-105
1966 PHI N	79	121	31	1	0	1	0.8	10	15	16	25	1	.256	.289	49	12	OF-28, 1B-1
1967	69	73	13	5	0	0	0.0	2	4	8	15	0	.178	.247	54	11	OF-10
1968	29	57	12	1	1	2	3.5	6	8	7	13	0	.211	.368	13	3	OF-17
9 yrs.	452	920	211	34	7	12	1.3	99	88	114	166	6	.229	.321	179	41	OF-263, 1B-1
5 yrs.	93	189	41	6	4	3	1.6	22	23	27	38	0	.217	.339	27	8	OF-63

Jack Clements

CLEMENTS, JOHN T.   BL TL 5'8½" 204 lbs.
B. June 24, 1864, Philadelphia, Pa.   D. May 23, 1941, Philadelphia, Pa.

	G	AB	H	2B	3B	HR	HR%	R	RBI	BB	SO	SB	BA	SA	AB	H	G by POS
1884 2 teams	PHI U	(41G –	.282)		PHI N	(9G –	.233)										
" Total	50	207	57	13	2	3	1.4	40		13	8		.275	.401	0	0	C-29, OF-22, SS-1
1885 PHI N	52	188	36	11	3	1	0.5	14		2	30		.191	.298	0	0	C-41, OF-11
1886	54	185	38	5	1	0	0.0	15	11	7	34		.205	.243	0	0	C-47, OF-7
1887	66	246	69	13	7	1	0.4	48	47	9	24	7	.280	.402	0	0	C-59, 3B-4, SS-3
1888	86	326	80	8	4	1	0.3	26	32	10	36	3	.245	.304	0	0	C-85, OF-1
1889	78	310	88	17	1	4	1.3	51	35	29	21	3	.284	.384	0	0	C-78

	G	AB	H	2B	3B	HR	HR %	R	RBI	BB	SO	SB	BA	SA	Pinch Hit AB	Pinch Hit H	G by POS

Jack Clements continued

	G	AB	H	2B	3B	HR	HR %	R	RBI	BB	SO	SB	BA	SA	PH AB	PH H	G by POS
1890	97	381	120	23	8	7	1.8	64	74	45	30	10	.315	.472	0	0	C-91, 1B-5
1891	107	423	131	29	4	4	0.9	58	75	43	19	3	.310	.426	0	0	C-107, 1B-2
1892	109	402	106	25	6	8	2.0	50	76	43	40	7	.264	.415	0	0	C-109
1893	94	376	107	20	3	17	4.5	64	80	39	29	3	.285	.489	2	0	C-92, 1B-1
1894	45	159	55	6	5	3	1.9	26	36	24	7	6	.346	.503	0	0	C-45
1895	88	322	127	27	2	13	4.0	64	75	22	7	3	.394	.612	0	0	C-88
1896	57	184	66	5	7	5	2.7	35	45	17	14	2	.359	.543	3	0	C-53
1897	55	185	44	4	2	6	3.2	18	36	12		3	.238	.378	5	1	C-49
1898 STL N	99	335	86	19	5	3	0.9	39	41	21		1	.257	.370	12	1	C-86
1899 CLE N	4	12	3	0	0	0	0.0	1	0	0		0	.250	.250	0	0	C-4
1900 BOS N	16	42	13	1	0	1	2.4	6	10	3		0	.310	.405	6	0	C-12
17 yrs.	1157	4283	1226	226	60	77	1.8	619	672	339	299	51	.286	.421	28	2	C-1073, OF-41, 1B-8, SS-4, 3B-4
1 yr.	99	335	86	19	5	3	0.9	39	41	21		1	.257	.370	12	1	C-86

Verne Clemons

CLEMONS, VERNE JAMES (Fats)
Brother of Bob Clemons.
B. Sept. 8, 1891   D. May 5, 1959, St. Petersburg, Fla.
BR TR 5'9½" 190 lbs.

	G	AB	H	2B	3B	HR	HR %	R	RBI	BB	SO	SB	BA	SA	PH AB	PH H	G by POS
1916 STL A	4	7	1	1	0	0	0.0	0	0	0	1	0	.143	.286	2	0	C-2
1919 STL N	88	239	63	13	2	2	0.8	14	22	26	13	4	.264	.360	10	5	C-75
1920	112	338	95	10	6	1	0.3	17	36	30	12	1	.281	.355	7	1	C-103
1921	117	341	109	16	2	2	0.6	29	48	33	17	0	.320	.396	8	2	C-109
1922	71	160	41	4	0	0	0.0	9	15	18	5	1	.256	.281	7	1	C-63
1923	57	130	37	9	1	0	0.0	6	13	10	11	0	.285	.369	13	4	C-41
1924	25	56	18	3	0	0	0.0	3	6	2	3	0	.321	.375	7	2	C-17
7 yrs.	474	1271	364	56	11	5	0.4	78	140	119	62	6	.286	.360	54	15	C-410
6 yrs.	470	1264	363	55	11	5	0.4	78	140	119	61	6	.287	.360	52	15	C-408

Donn Clendenon

CLENDENON, DONN ALVIN
B. July 15, 1935, Neosho, Mo.
BR TR 6'4" 209 lbs.

	G	AB	H	2B	3B	HR	HR %	R	RBI	BB	SO	SB	BA	SA	PH AB	PH H	G by POS
1961 PIT N	9	35	11	1	0	0	0.0	7	2	5	10	0	.314	.400	1	0	OF-8
1962	80	222	67	8	5	7	3.2	39	28	26	58	16	.302	.477	6	1	1B-52, OF-19
1963	154	563	155	28	7	15	2.7	65	57	39	136	22	.275	.430	5	0	1B-151
1964	133	457	129	23	8	12	2.6	53	64	26	96	12	.282	.446	15	7	1B-119
1965	162	612	184	32	14	14	2.3	89	96	48	128	9	.301	.467	3	1	1B-158, 3B-1
1966	155	571	171	22	10	28	4.9	80	98	52	142	8	.299	.520	4	1	1B-152
1967	131	478	119	15	2	13	2.7	46	56	34	107	4	.249	.370	8	1	1B-123
1968	158	584	150	20	6	17	2.9	63	87	47	163	10	.257	.399	2	1	1B-155
1969 2 teams	MON N	(38G – .240)		NY N	(72G – .252)												
" Total	110	331	82	11	1	16	4.8	45	51	25	94	3	.248	.432	24	2	1B-82, OF-12
1970 NY N	121	396	114	18	3	22	5.6	65	97	39	91	4	.288	.515	22	5	1B-100
1971	88	263	65	10	0	11	4.2	29	37	21	78	1	.247	.411	27	2	1B-72
1972 STL N	61	136	26	4	0	4	2.9	13	9	17	37	1	.191	.309	20	4	1B-36
12 yrs.	1362	4648	1273	192	57	159	3.4	594	682	379	1140	90	.274	.442	137	25	1B-1200, OF-39, 3B-1
1 yr.	61	136	26	4	0	4	2.9	13	9	17	37	1	.191	.309	20	4	1B-36

WORLD SERIES																	
1969 NY N	4	14	5	1	0	3	21.4	4	4	2	6	0	.357	1.071	0	0	1B-4

Ed Clough

CLOUGH, EDGAR GEORGE (Spec)
B. Oct. 11, 1905, Wiconisco, Pa.   D. Jan. 30, 1944, Harrisburg, Pa.
BL TL 6' 188 lbs.

	G	AB	H	2B	3B	HR	HR %	R	RBI	BB	SO	SB	BA	SA	PH AB	PH H	G by POS
1924 STL N	7	14	1	0	0	0	0.0	0	1	0	3	0	.071	.071	1	0	OF-6
1925	3	4	1	0	0	0	0.0	0	0	0	0	0	.250	.250	0	0	P-3
1926	1	1	0	0	0	0	0.0	0	0	0	0	0	.000	.000	0	0	P-1
3 yrs.	11	19	2	0	0	0	0.0	0	1	0	3	0	.105	.105	1	0	OF-6, P-4
3 yrs.	11	19	2	0	0	0	0.0	0	1	0	3	0	.105	.105	1	0	OF-6, P-4

Dick Cole

COLE, RICHARD ROY
B. May 6, 1926, Long Beach, Calif.
BR TR 6'2" 175 lbs.

	G	AB	H	2B	3B	HR	HR %	R	RBI	BB	SO	SB	BA	SA	PH AB	PH H	G by POS
1951 2 teams	STL N	(15G – .194)		PIT N	(42G – .236)												
" Total	57	142	32	5	0	1	0.7	13	14	21	14	0	.225	.282	0	0	2B-48, SS-8
1953 PIT N	97	235	64	13	1	0	0.0	29	23	38	26	2	.272	.336	9	6	SS-77, 2B-7, 1B-1
1954	138	486	131	22	5	1	0.0	42	40	41	48	0	.270	.342	7	1	SS-66, 3B-55, 2B-17
1955	77	239	54	8	3	0	0.0	16	21	18	22	0	.226	.285	11	2	3B-33, 2B-24, SS-12
1956	72	99	21	2	1	0	0.0	7	9	11	9	0	.212	.253	40	7	3B-18, 2B-12, SS-6
1957 MIL N	15	14	1	0	0	0	0.0	1	0	3	5	0	.071	.071	2	0	2B-10, 3B-1, 1B-1
6 yrs.	456	1215	303	50	10	2	0.2	106	107	132	124	2	.249	.312	69	16	SS-169, 2B-118, 3B-107, 1B-2
1 yr.	15	36	7	1	0	0	0.0	4	3	6	5	0	.194	.222	0	0	2B-14

Ripper Collins

COLLINS, JAMES ANTHONY
B. Mar. 30, 1904, Altoona, Pa.   D. Apr. 16, 1970, New Haven, N. Y.
BB TL 5'9" 165 lbs.

	G	AB	H	2B	3B	HR	HR %	R	RBI	BB	SO	SB	BA	SA	PH AB	PH H	G by POS
1931 STL N	89	279	84	20	10	4	1.4	34	59	18	24	1	.301	.487	16	2	1B-68, OF-3
1932	149	549	153	28	8	21	3.8	82	91	38	67	4	.279	.474	8	2	1B-81, OF-60
1933	132	493	153	26	7	10	2.0	66	68	38	49	7	.310	.452	8	3	1B-123
1934	154	600	200	40	12	35	5.8	116	128	57	50	2	.333	.615	0	0	1B-154
1935	150	578	181	36	10	23	4.0	109	122	65	45	0	.313	.529	0	0	1B-150
1936	103	277	81	15	3	13	4.7	48	48	48	30	1	.292	.509	26	8	1B-61, OF-9
1937 CHI N	115	456	125	16	5	16	3.5	77	71	32	46	2	.274	.436	4	0	1B-111
1938	143	490	131	22	8	13	2.7	78	61	54	48	1	.267	.424	7	0	1B-135
1941 PIT N	49	62	13	2	2	0	0.0	5	11	6	14	0	.210	.306	32	4	1B-11, OF-3
9 yrs.	1084	3784	1121	205	65	135	3.6	615	659	356	373	18	.296	.492	101	19	1B-894, OF-75
6 yrs.	777	2776	852	165	50	106	3.8	455	516	264	265	15	.307	.517	58	15	1B-637, OF-72
						6th								7th			

	G	AB	H	2B	3B	HR	HR %	R	RBI	BB	SO	SB	BA	SA	Pinch Hit AB	Pinch Hit H	G by POS

Ripper Collins continued

WORLD SERIES

	G	AB	H	2B	3B	HR	HR %	R	RBI	BB	SO	SB	BA	SA	AB	H	G by POS
1931 STL N	2	2	0	0	0	0	0.0	0	0	0	1	0	.000	.000	2	0	
1934	7	30	11	1	0	0	0.0	4	4	1	2	0	.367	.400	0	0	1B-7
1938 CHI N	4	15	2	0	0	0	0.0	1	0	0	3	0	.133	.133	0	0	1B-4
3 yrs.	13	47	13	1	0	0	0.0	5	4	1	6	0	.277	.298	2	0	1B-11

Bob Coluccio

COLUCCIO, ROBERT PASQUALI
B. Oct. 2, 1951, Centralia, Wash.

BR TR 5'11" 183 lbs.

	G	AB	H	2B	3B	HR	HR %	R	RBI	BB	SO	SB	BA	SA	AB	H	G by POS
1973 MIL A	124	438	98	21	8	15	3.4	64	58	54	92	13	.224	.411	5	0	OF-108
1974	138	394	88	13	4	6	1.5	42	31	43	61	15	.223	.322	2	0	OF-131
1975 2 teams			MIL	A	(22G –	.194)		CHI	A	(61G –	.205)						
" Total	83	223	45	4	3	5	2.2	30	18	24	45	5	.202	.314	4	0	OF-81
1977 CHI A	20	37	10	0	0	0	0.0	4	7	6	2	0	.270	.270	0	0	OF-19
1978 STL N	5	3	0	0	0	0	0.0	0	0	1	2	0	.000	.000	3	0	OF-2
5 yrs.	370	1095	241	38	15	26	2.4	140	114	128	202	33	.220	.353	14	0	OF-341
1 yr.	5	3	0	0	0	0	0.0	0	0	1	2	0	.000	.000	3	0	OF-2

Joe Connor

CONNOR, JOSEPH
Deceased.

	G	AB	H	2B	3B	HR	HR %	R	RBI	BB	SO	SB	BA	SA	AB	H	G by POS
1895 STL N	2	7	0	0	0	0	0.0	0	1	0	2	0	.000	.000	0	0	3B-2

Roger Connor

CONNOR, ROGER
Brother of Joe Connor.
B. July 1, 1857, Waterbury, Conn.   D. Jan. 4, 1931, Waterbury, Conn.
Manager 1896.
Hall of Fame 1976.

BL TL 6'3" 220 lbs.

	G	AB	H	2B	3B	HR	HR %	R	RBI	BB	SO	SB	BA	SA	AB	H	G by POS
1880 TRO N	83	340	113	18	8	3	0.9	53		13	21		.332	.459	0	0	3B-83
1881	85	367	107	17	6	2	0.5	55	31	15	20		.292	.387	0	0	1B-85
1882	81	349	115	22	18	4	1.1	65	42	13	20		.330	.530	0	0	1B-43, OF-24, 3B-14
1883 NY N	98	409	146	28	15	1	0.2	80		25	16		.357	.506	0	0	1B-98
1884	116	477	151	28	4	4	0.8	98		38	32		.317	.417	0	0	2B-67, OF-37, 3B-12
1885	110	455	169	23	15	1	0.2	102		51	8		.371	.495	0	0	1B-110
1886	118	485	172	29	20	7	1.4	105	71	41	15		.355	.540	0	0	1B-118
1887	127	471	134	26	22	17	3.6	113	104	75	50	43	.285	.541	0	0	1B-127
1888	134	481	140	15	17	14	2.9	98	71	73	44	27	.291	.480	0	0	1B-133, 2B-1
1889	131	496	157	32	17	13	2.6	117	130	93	46	21	.317	.528	0	0	1B-131, 3B-1
1890 NY P	123	484	180	25	15	13	2.7	134	103	88	32	22	.372	.566	0	0	1B-123
1891 NY N	129	479	139	29	13	6	1.3	112	94	83	39	27	.290	.443	0	0	1B-129
1892 PHI N	155	564	166	37	11	12	2.1	123	73	116	39	22	.294	.463	0	0	1B-155
1893 NY N	135	511	158	25	8	11	2.2	111	105	91	26	24	.309	.454	0	0	1B-135, 3B-1
1894 2 teams			NY	N	(22G –	.293)		STL	N	(99G –	.321)						
" Total	121	462	146	35	25	8	1.7	93	93	59	17	19	.316	.552	0	0	1B-120, OF-1
1895 STL N	104	402	131	29	9	8	2.0	78	77	63	10	9	.326	.502	0	0	1B-103
1896	126	483	137	21	9	11	2.3	71	72	52	14	10	.284	.433	0	0	1B-126
1897	22	83	19	3	1	1	1.2	13	12	13		3	.229	.325	0	0	1B-22
18 yrs.	1998	7798	2480	442	233	136	1.7	1621	1077	1002	449	227	.318	.487	0	0	1B-1758, 3B-111, 2B-68, OF-62
					5th												
4 yrs.	351	1348	409	81	44	27	2.0	245	240	179	41	39	.303	.489	0	0	1B-350

Ed Conwell

CONWELL, EDWARD JAMES (Irish)
B. Jan. 29, 1890, Chicago, Ill.

BR TR 5'11" 155 lbs.

	G	AB	H	2B	3B	HR	HR %	R	RBI	BB	SO	SB	BA	SA	AB	H	G by POS
1911 STL N	1	1	0	0	0	0	0.0	0	0	0	1	0	.000	.000	0	0	3B-1

Duff Cooley

COOLEY, DUFF C. (Sir Richard)
B. Mar. 29, 1873, Leavenworth, Kans.   D. Aug. 9, 1937, Dallas, Tex.

BL TR

	G	AB	H	2B	3B	HR	HR %	R	RBI	BB	SO	SB	BA	SA	AB	H	G by POS
1893 STL N	29	107	37	2	3	0	0.0	20	21	8	9	8	.346	.421	1	0	OF-15, C-10, SS-5
1894	54	206	61	3	1	1	0.5	35	21	12	16	7	.296	.335	0	0	OF-39, 3B-13, SS-1, 1B-1
1895	132	563	191	9	21	6	1.1	106	75	36	29	27	.339	.462	1	0	OF-124, 3B-5, SS-3, C-1
1896 2 teams			STL	N	(40G –	.307)		PHI	N	(64G –	.307)						
" Total	104	453	139	11	7	2	0.4	92	35	25	19	30	.307	.375	0	0	OF-104
1897 PHI N	133	566	186	14	13	4	0.7	124	40	51		31	.329	.420	0	0	OF-131, 1B-2
1898	149	629	196	24	12	4	0.6	123	55	48		17	.312	.407	0	0	OF-149
1899	94	406	112	15	8	0	0.0	75	31	29		15	.276	.360	1	0	1B-79, OF-14, 2B-1
1900 PIT N	66	249	50	8	1	0	0.0	30	22	14		9	.201	.257	0	0	1B-66
1901 BOS N	63	240	62	13	3	0	0.0	27	27	14		5	.258	.338	0	0	OF-53, 1B-10
1902	135	548	162	26	8	0	0.0	73	58	34		27	.296	.372	1	0	OF-127, 1B-7
1903	138	553	160	26	10	1	0.2	76	70	44		27	.289	.378	0	0	OF-126, 1B-13
1904	122	467	127	18	7	5	1.1	41	70	24		14	.272	.373	0	0	OF-116, 1B-6
1905 DET A	99	377	93	11	9	1	0.3	25	32	26		7	.247	.332	1	1	OF-97
13 yrs.	1318	5364	1576	180	103	25	0.5	847	557	365	73	224	.294	.380	5	1	OF-1095, 1B-184, 3B-18, C-11, SS-9, 2B-1
4 yrs.	255	1042	340	19	28	7	0.7	190	130	63	57	54	.326	.418	2	0	OF-218, 3B-18, C-11, SS-9, 1B-1

Jimmy Cooney

COONEY, JAMES EDWARD (Scoops)
Son of Jimmy Cooney.   Brother of Johnny Cooney.
B. Aug. 24, 1894, Cranston, R. I.

BR TR 5'11" 160 lbs.

	G	AB	H	2B	3B	HR	HR %	R	RBI	BB	SO	SB	BA	SA	AB	H	G by POS
1917 BOS A	11	36	8	1	0	0	0.0	4	3	6	2	0	.222	.250	0	0	2B-10, SS-1
1919 NY N	5	14	3	0	0	0	0.0	3	1	0	0	0	.214	.214	0	0	SS-4, 2B-1
1924 STL N	110	383	113	20	8	1	0.3	44	57	20	20	12	.295	.397	0	0	SS-99, 3B-7, 2B-1
1925	54	187	51	11	2	0	0.0	27	18	4	5	1	.273	.353	1	0	SS-37, 2B-15, OF-1
1926 CHI N	141	513	129	18	5	1	0.2	52	47	23	10	11	.251	.312	0	0	SS-141

	G	AB	H	2B	3B	HR	HR %	R	RBI	BB	SO	SB	BA	SA	Pinch Hit AB	Pinch Hit H	G by POS

Jimmy Cooney continued

	G	AB	H	2B	3B	HR	HR %	R	RBI	BB	SO	SB	BA	SA	PH AB	PH H	G by POS
1927 2 teams	CHI N (33G – .242)							PHI N (76G – .270)									
" Total	109	391	102	14	1	0	0.0	49	21	21	16	5	.261	.302	1	0	SS-107
1928 BOS N	18	51	7	0	0	0	0.0	2	3	2	5	1	.137	.137	4	0	SS-11, 2B-4
7 yrs.	448	1575	413	64	16	2	0.1	181	150	76	58	30	.262	.327	6	0	SS-400, 2B-31, 3B-7, OF-1
2 yrs.	164	570	164	31	10	1	0.2	71	75	24	25	13	.288	.382	1	0	SS-136, 2B-16, 3B-7, OF-1

Walker Cooper

COOPER, WILLIAM WALKER
Brother of Mort Cooper.
B. Jan. 8, 1915, Atherton, Mo.

BR TR 6'3" 210 lbs.

	G	AB	H	2B	3B	HR	HR %	R	RBI	BB	SO	SB	BA	SA	PH AB	PH H	G by POS
1940 STL N	6	19	6	1	0	0	0.0	3	2	2	2	1	.316	.368	0	0	C-6
1941	68	200	49	9	1	1	0.5	19	20	13	14	1	.245	.315	5	2	C-63
1942	125	438	123	32	7	7	1.6	58	65	29	29	4	.281	.434	10	5	C-115
1943	122	449	143	30	4	9	2.0	52	81	19	19	1	.318	.463	10	1	C-112
1944	112	397	126	25	5	13	3.3	56	72	20	19	4	.317	.504	15	5	C-97
1945	4	18	7	0	0	0	0.0	3	1	0	1	0	.389	.389	0	0	C-4
1946 NY N	87	280	75	10	1	8	2.9	29	46	17	12	0	.268	.396	13	3	C-73
1947	140	515	157	24	8	35	6.8	79	122	24	43	2	.305	.586	6	1	C-132
1948	91	290	77	12	0	16	5.5	40	54	28	29	1	.266	.472	12	2	C-79
1949 2 teams	NY N (42G – .211)							CIN N (82G – .280)									
" Total	124	454	117	13	4	20	4.4	48	83	28	32	0	.258	.436	5	1	C-117
1950 2 teams	CIN N (15G – .191)							BOS N (102G – .329)									
" Total	117	384	120	22	3	14	3.6	55	64	30	31	1	.313	.495	12	6	C-101
1951 BOS N	109	342	107	14	1	18	5.3	42	59	28	18	1	.313	.518	18	2	C-90
1952	102	349	82	12	1	10	2.9	33	55	22	32	1	.235	.361	13	4	C-89
1953 MIL N	53	137	30	6	0	3	2.2	12	16	12	15	1	.219	.328	17	3	C-35
1954 2 teams	PIT N (14G – .200)							CHI N (57G – .310)									
" Total	71	173	52	12	2	7	4.0	21	33	23	24	0	.301	.514	23	5	C-50
1955 CHI N	54	111	31	8	1	7	6.3	11	15	6	19	0	.279	.559	28	6	C-31
1956 STL N	40	68	18	5	1	2	2.9	5	14	3	8	0	.265	.456	22	3	C-16
1957	48	78	21	5	1	3	3.8	7	10	5	10	0	.269	.474	30	7	C-13
18 yrs.	1473	4702	1341	240	40	173	3.7	573	812	309	357	18	.285	.464	239	56	C-1223
8 yrs.	525	1667	493	107	19	35	2.1	203	265	91	102	11	.296	.446	92	23	C-426

WORLD SERIES																	
1942 STL N	5	21	6	1	0	0	0.0	3	4	0	1	0	.286	.333	0	0	C-5
1943	5	17	5	0	0	0	0.0	1	0	0	1	0	.294	.294	0	0	C-5
1944	6	22	7	2	1	0	0.0	1	2	3	2	0	.318	.500	0	0	C-6
3 yrs.	16	60	18	3	1	0	0.0	5	6	3	4	0	.300	.383	0	0	C-16

Roy Corhan

CORHAN, ROY GEORGE (Irish)
B. Oct. 21, 1887, Indianapolis, Ind. D. Nov. 24, 1958, San Francisco, Calif.

BR TR 5'9½" 165 lbs.

	G	AB	H	2B	3B	HR	HR %	R	RBI	BB	SO	SB	BA	SA	PH AB	PH H	G by POS
1911 CHI A	43	131	28	6	2	0	0.0	14	8	15		2	.214	.290	0	0	SS-43
1916 STL N	92	295	62	6	3	0	0.0	30	18	20	31	15	.210	.251	7	3	SS-84
2 yrs.	135	426	90	12	5	0	0.0	44	26	35	31	17	.211	.263	7	3	SS-127
1 yr.	92	295	62	6	3	0	0.0	30	18	20	31	15	.210	.251	7	3	SS-84

Pat Corrales

CORRALES, PATRICK
B. Mar. 20, 1941, Los Angeles, Calif.
Manager 1978-80, 1982

BR TR 6' 180 lbs.

	G	AB	H	2B	3B	HR	HR %	R	RBI	BB	SO	SB	BA	SA	PH AB	PH H	G by POS
1964 PHI N	2	1	0	0	0	0	0.0	0	1	0	0	0	.000	.000	1	0	
1965	63	174	39	8	1	2	1.1	16	15	25	42	0	.224	.316	2	0	C-62
1966 STL N	28	72	13	2	0	0	0.0	5	3	2	17	1	.181	.208	1	0	C-27
1968 CIN N	20	56	15	4	0	0	0.0	3	6	6	16	0	.268	.339	0	0	C-20
1969	29	72	19	5	0	1	1.4	10	5	8	17	0	.264	.375	0	0	C-29
1970	43	106	25	5	1	1	0.9	9	10	8	22	0	.236	.330	3	0	C-42
1971	40	94	17	2	0	0	0.0	6	6	6	17	0	.181	.202	1	0	C-39
1972 2 teams	CIN N (2G – .000)							SD N (44G – .193)									
" Total	46	120	23	0	0	0	0.0	6	6	13	26	0	.192	.192	1	0	C-45
1973 SD N	29	72	15	2	1	0	0.0	7	3	6	10	0	.208	.264	1	0	C-28
9 yrs.	300	767	166	28	3	4	0.5	63	54	75	167	1	.216	.276	10	0	C-292
1 yr.	28	72	13	2	0	0	0.0	5	3	2	17	1	.181	.208	1	0	C-27

WORLD SERIES																	
1970 CIN N	1	1	0	0	0	0	0.0	0	0	0	0	0	.000	.000	1	0	

Tom Coulter

COULTER, THOMAS LEE
B. June 5, 1945, Steubenville, Ohio

BL TR 5'10" 172 lbs.

	G	AB	H	2B	3B	HR	HR %	R	RBI	BB	SO	SB	BA	SA	PH AB	PH H	G by POS
1969 STL N	6	19	6	1	1	0	0.0	3	4	2	6	0	.316	.474	0	0	2B-6

John Coveney

COVENEY, JOHN PATRICK
B. 1880, S. Natick, Mass.

TR

	G	AB	H	2B	3B	HR	HR %	R	RBI	BB	SO	SB	BA	SA	PH AB	PH H	G by POS
1903 STL N	4	14	2	0	0	0	0.0	0	0	0		0	.143	.143	0	0	C-4

Estel Crabtree

CRABTREE, ESTEL CRAYTON (Crabby)
B. Aug. 19, 1903, Crabtree, Ohio D. Jan. 4, 1967, Logan, Ohio

BL TR 6' 168 lbs.

	G	AB	H	2B	3B	HR	HR %	R	RBI	BB	SO	SB	BA	SA	PH AB	PH H	G by POS
1929 CIN N	1	1	0	0	0	0	0.0	0	0	0	0	0	.000	.000	1	0	
1931	117	443	119	12	12	4	0.9	70	37	23	33	3	.269	.377	10	3	OF-101, 3B-4, 1B-2
1932	108	402	110	14	9	2	0.5	38	35	23	26	2	.274	.368	7	3	OF-95
1933 STL N	23	34	9	3	0	0	0.0	6	3	2	3	1	.265	.353	12	2	OF-7
1941	77	167	57	6	3	5	3.0	27	28	26	24	1	.341	.503	21	7	OF-50, 3B-1
1942	10	9	3	2	0	0	0.0	1	2	1	3	0	.333	.556	9	3	

	G	AB	H	2B	3B	HR	HR %	R	RBI	BB	SO	SB	BA	SA	Pinch Hit AB	H	G by POS

Estel Crabtree continued

	G	AB	H	2B	3B	HR	HR%	R	RBI	BB	SO	SB	BA	SA	PH AB	PH H	G by POS
1943 CIN N	95	254	70	12	0	2	0.8	25	26	25	17	1	.276	.346	24	10	OF-64
1944	58	98	28	4	1	0	0.0	7	11	13	3	0	.286	.347	32	9	OF-19, 1B-2
8 yrs.	489	1408	396	53	25	13	0.9	174	142	113	109	8	.281	.382	116	37	OF-336, 3B-5, 1B-4
3 yrs.	110	210	69	11	3	5	2.4	34	33	29	30	2	.329	.481	42	12	OF-57, 3B-1

Doc Crandall

CRANDALL, JAMES OTIS B. Oct. 8, 1887, Wadena, Ind. D. Aug. 17, 1951, Bell, Calif. BR TR 5'10½" 180 lbs.

	G	AB	H	2B	3B	HR	HR%	R	RBI	BB	SO	SB	BA	SA	PH AB	PH H	G by POS
1908 NY N	34	72	16	4	0	2	2.8	8	6	4		0	.222	.361	2	0	P-32, 2B-1
1909	30	41	10	0	1	1	2.4	4	1	1		0	.244	.366	0	0	P-30
1910	45	73	25	2	4	1	1.4	10	13	5	7	0	.342	.521	1	0	P-42, SS-1
1911	61	113	27	1	4	2	1.8	12	21	8	16	2	.239	.372	11	2	P-41, SS-4, 2B-3
1912	50	80	25	6	2	0	0.0	9	19	6	7	0	.313	.438	10	4	P-37, 2B-2, 1B-1
1913 2 teams	NY	N	(46G – .319)		STL	N	(2G – .000)										
" Total	48	49	15	4	1	0	0.0	7	4	3	10	0	.306	.429	10	2	P-35, 2B-1
1914 STL F	118	278	86	16	5	2	0.7	40	41	58		3	.309	.424	17	6	2B-63, P-27, OF-1, SS-1
1915	84	141	40	2	2	1	0.7	18	19	27		4	.284	.348	28	5	P-51
1916 STL A	16	12	1	0	0	0	0.0	0	0	2	4	0	.083	.083	12	1	P-2
1918 BOS N	14	28	8	0	0	0	0.0	1	2	4	3	0	.286	.286	5	2	P-5, OF-3
10 yrs.	500	887	253	35	19	9	1.0	109	126	118	47	9	.285	.398	96	22	P-302, 2B-70, SS-8, OF-4, 1B-1
1 yr.	2	2	0	0	0	0	0.0	0	0	0	2	0	.000	.000	2	0	2B-1

WORLD SERIES

	G	AB	H	2B	3B	HR	HR%	R	RBI	BB	SO	SB	BA	SA	PH AB	PH H	G by POS
1911 NY N	3	2	1	1	0	0	0.0	1	1	2	0	0	.500	1.000	0	0	P-2
1912	1	1	0	0	0	0	0.0	0	0	0	1	0	.000	.000	0	0	P-1
1913	4	4	0	0	0	0	0.0	0	0	0	0	0	.000	.000	2	0	P-2
3 yrs.	8	7	1	1	0	0	0.0	1	1	2	1	0	.143	.286	2	0	P-5

Forrest Crawford

CRAWFORD, FORREST B. May 10, 1881, Rockdale, Tex. D. Mar. 27, 1908, Austin, Tex. TR

	G	AB	H	2B	3B	HR	HR%	R	RBI	BB	SO	SB	BA	SA	PH AB	PH H	G by POS
1906 STL N	45	145	30	3	1	0	0.0	8	11	7		1	.207	.241	0	0	SS-39, 3B-6
1907	7	22	5	0	0	0	0.0	0	3	2		0	.227	.227	0	0	SS-7
2 yrs.	52	167	35	3	1	0	0.0	8	14	9		1	.210	.240	0	0	SS-46, 3B-6
2 yrs.	52	167	35	3	1	0	0.0	8	14	9		1	.210	.240	0	0	SS-46, 3B-6

Glenn Crawford

CRAWFORD, GLENN MARTIN (Shorty) B. Dec. 2, 1913, North Branch, Mich. D. Jan. 2, 1972, Saginaw, Mich. BL TR 5'9" 165 lbs.

	G	AB	H	2B	3B	HR	HR%	R	RBI	BB	SO	SB	BA	SA	PH AB	PH H	G by POS
1945 2 teams	STL	N	(4G – .000)		PHI	N	(82G – .295)										
" Total	86	305	89	13	2	2	0.7	41	24	37	15	5	.292	.367	4	0	OF-39, SS-34, 2B-14
1946 PHI N	1	1	0	0	0	0	0.0	0	0	0	0	0	.000	.000	1	0	
2 yrs.	87	306	89	13	2	2	0.7	41	24	37	15	5	.291	.366	5	0	OF-39, SS-34, 2B-14
1 yr.	4	3	0	0	0	0	0.0	0	0	1	0	0	.000	.000	2	0	OF-1

Pat Crawford

CRAWFORD, CLIFFORD RANKIN B. Jan. 28, 1902, Society Hill, S. C. BL TR 5'11" 170 lbs.

	G	AB	H	2B	3B	HR	HR%	R	RBI	BB	SO	SB	BA	SA	PH AB	PH H	G by POS
1929 NY N	65	57	17	3	0	5	5.3	13	24	11	5	1	.298	.509	44	10	1B-7, 3B-1
1930 2 teams	NY	N	(25G – .276)		CIN	N	(76G – .290)										
" Total	101	300	86	10	3	6	2.0	35	43	30	12	2	.287	.400	14	3	2B-72, 1B-14
1933 STL N	91	224	60	8	2	0	0.0	24	21	14	9	1	.268	.321	38	9	1B-29, 2B-15, 3B-7
1934	61	70	19	2	0	0	0.0	3	16	5	3	0	.271	.300	43	11	3B-9, 2B-4
4 yrs.	318	651	182	23	5	9	1.4	75	104	60	29	4	.280	.372	139	33	2B-91, 1B-50, 3B-17
2 yrs.	152	294	79	10	2	0	0.0	27	37	19	12	1	.269	.316	81	20	1B-29, 2B-19, 3B-16

WORLD SERIES

	G	AB	H	2B	3B	HR	HR%	R	RBI	BB	SO	SB	BA	SA	PH AB	PH H	G by POS
1934 STL N	2	2	0	0	0	0	0.0	0	0	0	0	0	.000	.000	2	0	

Willie Crawford

CRAWFORD, WILLIE MURPHY B. Sept. 7, 1946, Los Angeles, Calif. BL TL 6'1" 197 lbs.

	G	AB	H	2B	3B	HR	HR%	R	RBI	BB	SO	SB	BA	SA	PH AB	PH H	G by POS
1964 LA N	10	16	5	1	0	0	0.0	3	0	1	7	1	.313	.375	3	1	OF-4
1965	52	27	4	0	0	0	0.0	10	0	2	8	2	.148	.148	13	0	OF-8
1966	6	0	0	0	0	0	–	1	0	0	0	0	–	–	0	0	
1967	4	4	1	0	0	0	0.0	0	0	1	3	0	.250	.250	3	1	OF-1
1968	61	175	44	12	1	4	2.3	25	14	20	64	1	.251	.400	12	2	OF-48
1969	129	389	96	17	5	11	2.8	64	41	49	85	4	.247	.401	21	6	OF-113
1970	109	299	70	8	6	8	2.7	48	40	33	88	4	.234	.381	15	3	OF-94
1971	114	342	96	16	6	9	2.6	64	40	28	49	5	.281	.442	19	8	OF-97
1972	96	243	61	7	3	8	3.3	28	27	35	55	4	.251	.403	18	4	OF-74
1973	145	457	135	26	2	14	3.1	75	66	78	91	12	.295	.453	7	2	OF-138
1974	139	468	138	23	4	11	2.4	73	61	64	88	7	.295	.432	8	1	OF-133
1975	124	373	98	15	2	9	2.4	46	46	49	43	5	.263	.386	16	3	OF-113
1976 STL N	120	392	119	17	5	9	2.3	49	50	37	53	2	.304	.441	16	5	OF-107
1977 2 teams	HOU	N	(42G – .254)		OAK	A	(59G – .184)										
" Total	101	250	54	10	1	3	1.2	21	34	34	30	0	.216	.300	22	3	OF-52
14 yrs.	1210	3435	921	152	35	86	2.5	507	419	431	664	47	.268	.408	173	39	OF-982
1 yr.	120	392	119	17	5	9	2.3	49	50	37	53	2	.304	.441	16	5	OF-107

LEAGUE CHAMPIONSHIP SERIES

	G	AB	H	2B	3B	HR	HR%	R	RBI	BB	SO	SB	BA	SA	PH AB	PH H	G by POS
1974 LA N	2	4	1	0	0	0	0.0	1	1	1	1	0	.250	.250	1	1	OF-2

WORLD SERIES

	G	AB	H	2B	3B	HR	HR%	R	RBI	BB	SO	SB	BA	SA	PH AB	PH H	G by POS
1965 LA N	2	2	1	0	0	0	0.0	0	0	0	1	0	.500	.500	2	1	
1974	3	6	2	0	0	1	16.7	1	0	1	0	0	.333	.833	2	1	OF-2
2 yrs.	5	8	3	0	0	1	12.5	1	0	1	1	0	.375	.750	4	2	OF-2

	G	AB	H	2B	3B	HR	HR %	R	RBI	BB	SO	SB	BA	SA	Pinch Hit AB	Pinch Hit H	G by POS

Bernie Creger

CREGER, BERNARD ODELL   BR TR 6'   175 lbs.
B. Mar. 21, 1927, Wytheville, Va.

	G	AB	H	2B	3B	HR	HR %	R	RBI	BB	SO	SB	BA	SA	PH AB	PH H	G by POS
1947 STL N	15	16	3	1	0	0	0.0	3	0	1	3	1	.188	.250	0	0	SS-13

Creepy Crespi

CRESPI, FRANK ANGELO JOSEPH   BR TR 5'8½"   175 lbs.
B. Feb. 16, 1918, St. Louis, Mo.

	G	AB	H	2B	3B	HR	HR %	R	RBI	BB	SO	SB	BA	SA	PH AB	PH H	G by POS
1938 STL N	7	19	5	2	0	0	0.0	2	1	2	7	0	.263	.368	0	0	SS-7
1939	15	29	5	1	0	0	0.0	3	6	3	6	0	.172	.207	3	0	2B-6, SS-4
1940	3	11	3	1	0	0	0.0	2	0	1	2	1	.273	.364	0	0	3B-2, SS-1
1941	146	560	156	24	2	4	0.7	85	46	57	58	3	.279	.350	0	0	2B-145
1942	93	292	71	4	2	0	0.0	33	35	27	29	4	.243	.271	4	1	2B-83, SS-5
5 yrs.	264	911	240	32	4	4	0.4	125	88	90	102	8	.263	.321	7	1	2B-234, SS-17, 3B-2
5 yrs.	264	911	240	32	4	4	0.4	125	88	90	102	8	.263	.321	7	1	2B-234, SS-17, 3B-2
WORLD SERIES																	
1942 STL N	1	0	0	0	0	0	–	1	0	0	0	0	–	–	0	0	

Lou Criger

CRIGER, LOUIS   BR TR
B. Feb. 6, 1872, Elkhart, Ind.   D. May 14, 1934, Tucson, Ariz.

	G	AB	H	2B	3B	HR	HR %	R	RBI	BB	SO	SB	BA	SA	PH AB	PH H	G by POS
1896 CLE N	2	5	0	0	0	0	0.0	0	0		1	0	1	.000	.000	1	0	C-1
1897	39	138	31	4	1	0	0.0	15	22	23		5	.225	.268	0	0	C-37, 1B-2
1898	84	287	80	13	4	1	0.3	43	32	40		2	.279	.362	1	0	C-82
1899 STL N	77	258	66	4	5	2	0.8	39	44	28		14	.256	.333	2	1	C-75
1900	80	288	78	8	6	2	0.7	31	38	4		5	.271	.361	4	1	C-75, 3B-1
1901 BOS A	76	268	62	6	3	0	0.0	26	24	11		7	.231	.276	0	0	C-68, 1B-8
1902	83	266	68	16	6	0	0.0	32	28	27		7	.256	.361	1	0	C-80, OF-1
1903	96	317	61	7	10	3	0.9	41	31	26		5	.192	.306	0	0	C-96
1904	98	299	63	10	5	2	0.7	34	34	27		1	.211	.298	3	1	C-95
1905	109	313	62	6	7	1	0.3	33	36	54		5	.198	.272	0	0	C-109
1906	7	17	3	1	0	0	0.0	0	1	1		1	.176	.235	1	0	C-6
1907	75	226	41	4	0	0	0.0	12	14	19		2	.181	.199	1	0	C-75
1908	84	237	45	4	2	0	0.0	12	25	13		1	.190	.224	0	0	C-84
1909 STL A	74	212	36	1	1	0	0.0	15	9	25		2	.170	.184	1	0	C-73
1910 NY A	27	69	13	2	0	0	0.0	3	4	10		0	.188	.217	1	0	C-27
1912 STL A	1	0	0	0	0	0	0.0	1	0	0		0	.000	.000	0	0	C-1
16 yrs.	1012	3202	709	86	50	11	0.3	337	342	309		58	.221	.290	15	3	C-984, 1B-10, OF-1, 3B-1
2 yrs.	157	546	144	12	11	4	0.7	70	82	32		19	.264	.348	6	2	C-150, 3B-1
WORLD SERIES																	
1903 BOS A	8	26	6	0	0	0	0.0	1	4	2	3	0	.231	.231	0	0	C-8

John Crooks

CROOKS, JOHN CHARLES
B. Nov. 9, 1866, St. Paul, Minn.   D. Jan. 29, 1918, St. Louis, Mo.

	G	AB	H	2B	3B	HR	HR %	R	RBI	BB	SO	SB	BA	SA	PH AB	PH H	G by POS
1889 COL AA	12	43	14	2	3	0	0.0	13	7	10	4	10	.326	.512	0	0	2B-12
1890	135	485	107	5	4	1	0.2	86		96		57	.221	.254	0	0	2B-133, 3B-2, OF-1
1891	138	519	127	19	13	0	0.0	110	46	103	47	50	.245	.331	0	0	2B-138
1892 STL N	128	445	95	7	4	7	1.6	82	38	136	52	23	.213	.294	0	0	2B-102, 3B-24, OF-2
1893	128	448	106	10	9	1	0.2	93	48	121	37	31	.237	.306	0	0	3B-123, SS-4, C-1
1895 WAS N	117	409	114	19	8	6	1.5	80	57	68	39	36	.279	.408	0	0	2B-117
1896 2 teams			WAS N (25G – .286)			LOU N (39G – .238)											
" Total	64	206	53	8	1	5	2.4	39	35	36	16	10	.257	.379	1	0	2B-59, 3B-4
1898 STL N	72	225	52	4	2	1	0.4	33	20	40		3	.231	.280	1	0	2B-66, 3B-3, SS-2, OF-1
8 yrs.	794	2780	668	74	44	21	0.8	536	251	610	195	220	.240	.321	1	0	2B-627, 3B-156, SS-6, OF-4, C-1
3 yrs.	328	1118	253	21	15	9	0.8	208	106	297	89	57	.226	.296	0	0	2B-168, 3B-150, SS-6, OF-3, C-1

Ed Crosby

CROSBY, EDWARD CARLTON   BL TR 6'2"   175 lbs.
B. May 26, 1949, Long Beach, Calif.

	G	AB	H	2B	3B	HR	HR %	R	RBI	BB	SO	SB	BA	SA	PH AB	PH H	G by POS
1970 STL N	38	95	24	4	1	0	0.0	9	6	7	5	0	.253	.316	2	1	SS-35, 3B-3, 2B-2
1972	101	276	60	9	1	0	0.0	27	19	18	27	1	.217	.257	15	0	SS-43, 2B-38, 3B-14
1973 2 teams			STL N (22G – .128)			CIN N (36G – .216)											
" Total	58	90	16	3	2	0	0.0	8	6	11	16	0	.178	.256	13	4	SS-36, 2B-10, 3B-4
1974 CLE A	37	86	18	3	0	0	0.0	11	6	6	12	0	.209	.244	9	3	3B-18, SS-13, 2B-3
1975	61	128	30	3	0	0	0.0	12	7	13	14	0	.234	.258	0	0	SS-30, 2B-19, 3B-13
1976	2	2	1	0	0	0	0.0	0	0	0	0	0	.500	.500	0	0	3B-1
6 yrs.	297	677	149	22	4	0	0.0	67	44	55	74	1	.220	.264	39	8	SS-157, 2B-72, 3B-53
3 yrs.	161	340	89	15	3	0	0.0	40	26	29	36	1	.217	.268	27	4	SS-85, 2B-45, 3B-21
LEAGUE CHAMPIONSHIP SERIES																	
1973 CIN N	3	2	1	0	0	0	0.0	0	0	0	1	0	.500	.500	1	0	SS-2

Jeff Cross

CROSS, JOFFRE JAMES   BR TR 5'11"   160 lbs.
B. Aug. 28, 1918, Tulsa, Okla.

	G	AB	H	2B	3B	HR	HR %	R	RBI	BB	SO	SB	BA	SA	PH AB	PH H	G by POS
1942 STL N	1	4	1	0	0	0	0.0	0	0	0	0	0	.250	.250	0	0	SS-1
1946	49	69	15	3	0	0	0.0	17	6	10	8	4	.217	.261	3	0	SS-17, 2B-8, 3B-1
1947	51	49	5	1	0	0	0.0	4	3	10	6	0	.102	.122	1	0	3B-15, SS-14, 2B-2
1948 2 teams			STL N (2G – .000)			CHI N (16G – .100)											
" Total	18	20	2	0	0	0	0.0	1	0	4	4	0	.100	.100	4	0	SS-9, 2B-1
4 yrs.	119	142	23	4	0	0	0.0	22	10	20	18	4	.162	.190	8	0	SS-41, 3B-16, 2B-11
4 yrs.	103	122	21	4	0	0	0.0	21	10	20	14	4	.172	.205	4	0	SS-32, 3B-16, 2B-10

Lave Cross

CROSS, LAFAYETTE NAPOLEON   BR TR 5'8½"   155 lbs.
Brother of Frank Cross.   Brother of Amos Cross.
B. May 11, 1867, Milwaukee, Wis.   D. Sept. 4, 1927, Toledo, Ohio
Manager 1899.

	G	AB	H	2B	3B	HR	HR %	R	RBI	BB	SO	SB	BA	SA	PH AB	PH H	G by POS
1887 LOU AA	54	203	54	8	3	0	0.0	32		15		15	.266	.335	0	0	C-44, OF-10
1888	47	181	41	3	0	0	0.0	20	15	2		10	.227	.243	0	0	C-37, OF-12, SS-2

	G	AB	H	2B	3B	HR	HR %	R	RBI	BB	SO	SB	BA	SA	Pinch Hit AB	Pinch Hit H	G by POS

Lave Cross continued

	G	AB	H	2B	3B	HR	HR%	R	RBI	BB	SO	SB	BA	SA	PH AB	PH H	G by POS
1889 PHI AA	55	199	44	8	2	0	0.0	22	23	14	9	11	.221	.281	0	0	C-55
1890 PHI P	63	245	73	7	8	3	1.2	42	47	12	6	5	.298	.429	0	0	C-49, OF-15
1891 PHI AA	110	402	121	20	14	5	1.2	66	52	38	23	14	.301	.458	0	0	OF-43, C-43, 3B-24, SS-1, 2B-1
1892 PHI N	140	541	149	15	10	4	0.7	84	69	39	16	18	.275	.362	0	0	3B-65, C-39, OF-25, 2B-14, SS-5
1893	96	415	124	17	6	4	1.0	81	78	26	7	18	.299	.398	1	1	C-40, 3B-30, OF-10, SS-10, 1B-6
1894	119	529	204	34	9	7	1.3	123	125	29	7	21	.386	.524	0	0	3B-100, C-16, SS-7, 2B-1
1895	125	535	145	26	9	2	0.4	95	101	35	8	21	.271	.364	0	0	3B-125
1896	106	406	104	23	5	1	0.2	63	73	32	14	8	.256	.345	0	0	3B-61, SS-37, 2B-6, OF-2, C-1
1897	88	344	89	17	5	3	0.9	37	51	10		10	.259	.363	0	0	3B-47, 2B-38, OF-2, SS-1
1898 STL N	151	602	191	28	8	3	0.5	71	79	28		14	.317	.405	0	0	3B-149, SS-2
1899 2 teams		CLE	N	(38G –	.286)		STL	N	(103G –	.303)							
" Total	141	557	166	19	5	5	0.9	76	84	25		13	.298	.377	0	0	3B-141
1900 2 teams		STL	N	(16G –	.295)		BKN	N	(117G –	.293)							
" Total	133	522	153	15	6	4	0.8	79	73	26		21	.293	.368	0	0	3B-133
1901 PHI A	100	424	139	28	12	2	0.5	82	73	19		23	.328	.465	0	0	3B-100
1902	137	559	191	39	8	0	0.0	90	108	27		25	.342	.440	0	0	3B-137
1903	137	559	163	22	4	2	0.4	60	90	10		14	.292	.356	0	0	3B-136, 1B-1
1904	155	607	176	31	10	1	0.2	73	71	13		10	.290	.379	0	0	3B-155
1905	147	583	155	29	5	0	0.0	68	77	26		8	.266	.333	0	0	3B-147
1906 WAS A	130	494	130	14	6	1	0.2	55	46	28		19	.263	.322	0	0	3B-130
1907	41	161	32	8	0	0	0.0	13	10	10		3	.199	.248	0	0	3B-41
21 yrs.	2275	9068	2644	411	135	47	0.5	1332	1344	464	90	301	.292	.382	1	1	3B-1721, C-324, OF-119, SS-65, 2B-60, 1B-7
3 yrs.	270	1066	331	43	13	7	0.7	138	149	46		26	.311	.395	0	0	3B-268, SS-2

WORLD SERIES

	G	AB	H	2B	3B	HR	HR%	R	RBI	BB	SO	SB	BA	SA	PH AB	PH H	G by POS
1905 PHI A	5	19	2	0	0	0	0.0	0	0	1	1	0	.105	.105	0	0	3B-5

Monte Cross

CROSS, MONTFORD MONTGOMERY
B. Aug. 31, 1869, Philadelphia, Pa.   D. June 21, 1934, Philadelphia, Pa.   BR TR

	G	AB	H	2B	3B	HR	HR%	R	RBI	BB	SO	SB	BA	SA	PH AB	PH H	G by POS
1892 BAL N	15	50	8	0	0	0	0.0	5	2	4	10	2	.160	.160	0	0	SS-15
1894 PIT N	13	43	19	1	5	2	4.7	14	13	5	4	6	.442	.837	0	0	SS-13
1895	108	393	101	14	13	3	0.8	67	54	38	38	39	.257	.382	0	0	SS-107, 2B-1
1896 STL N	125	427	104	10	6	6	1.4	66	52	58	48	40	.244	.337	0	0	SS-125
1897	131	462	132	17	11	4	0.9	59	55	62		38	.286	.396	0	0	SS-131
1898 PHI N	149	525	135	25	5	1	0.2	68	50	55		20	.257	.330	0	0	SS-149
1899	154	557	143	25	6	3	0.5	85	65	56		26	.257	.339	0	0	SS-154
1900	131	466	94	11	3	3	0.6	59	62	51		19	.202	.258	0	0	SS-131
1901	139	483	95	14	1	1	0.2	49	44	52		24	.197	.236	0	0	SS-139
1902 PHI A	137	497	115	22	2	3	0.6	72	59	32		17	.231	.302	0	0	SS-137
1903	137	470	116	21	2	3	0.6	44	45	49		31	.247	.319	0	0	SS-137, 2B-1
1904	153	503	95	23	4	1	0.2	33	38	46		19	.189	.256	0	0	SS-153
1905	78	248	67	17	2	0	0.0	28	24	19		8	.270	.355	0	0	SS-76, 2B-2
1906	134	445	89	23	3	0	0.0	32	40	50		22	.200	.265	0	0	SS-134
1907	77	248	51	9	5	0	0.0	37	18	39		17	.206	.282	1	0	SS-74
15 yrs.	1681	5817	1364	232	68	30	0.5	718	621	616	100	328	.234	.313	1	0	SS-1675, 2B-4
2 yrs.	256	889	236	27	17	10	1.1	125	107	120	48	78	.265	.368	0	0	SS-256

WORLD SERIES

	G	AB	H	2B	3B	HR	HR%	R	RBI	BB	SO	SB	BA	SA	PH AB	PH H	G by POS
1905 PHI A	5	17	3	0	0	0	0.0	0	0	0	7	0	.176	.176	0	0	SS-5

George Crowe

CROWE, GEORGE DANIEL
B. Mar. 22, 1923, Whiteland, Ind.   BL TL 6'2"   210 lbs.

	G	AB	H	2B	3B	HR	HR%	R	RBI	BB	SO	SB	BA	SA	PH AB	PH H	G by POS
1952 BOS N	73	217	56	13	1	4	1.8	25	20	18	25	0	.258	.382	17	5	1B-55
1953 MIL N	47	42	12	2	0	2	4.8	6	6	2	7	0	.286	.476	37	9	1B-9
1955	104	303	85	12	4	15	5.0	41	55	44	1	.281	.495	21	5	1B-79
1956 CIN N	77	144	36	2	1	10	6.9	22	23	11	28	0	.250	.486	43	11	1B-32
1957	133	494	134	20	1	31	6.3	71	92	32	62	1	.271	.504	13	5	1B-120
1958	111	345	95	12	5	7	2.0	31	61	41	51	1	.275	.400	20	8	1B-93, 2B-1
1959 STL N	77	103	31	6	0	8	7.8	14	29	5	12	0	.301	.592	63	17	1B-14
1960	73	72	17	3	0	4	5.6	5	13	5	16	0	.236	.444	61	15	1B-5
1961	7	7	1	0	0	0	0.0	0	0	0	1	0	.143	.143	7	1	
9 yrs.	702	1727	467	70	12	81	4.7	215	299	159	246	3	.270	.466	282	76	1B-407, 2B-1
3 yrs.	157	182	49	9	0	12	6.6	19	42	10	29	0	.269	.516	131	33	1B-19
															7th	5th	

Walt Cruise

CRUISE, WALTON EDWIN
B. May 6, 1890, Childersburg, Ala.   D. Jan. 9, 1975, Sylacauga, Ala.   BL TR 6'   175 lbs.

	G	AB	H	2B	3B	HR	HR%	R	RBI	BB	SO	SB	BA	SA	PH AB	PH H	G by POS
1914 STL N	95	256	58	9	3	4	1.6	20	28	25	42	3	.227	.332	11	3	OF-81
1916	3	3	2	0	0	0	0.0	0	0	1	0	0	.667	.667	1	1	OF-2
1917	153	529	156	20	10	5	0.9	70	59	38	73	16	.295	.399	1	1	OF-152
1918	70	240	65	5	4	6	2.5	34	39	30	26	2	.271	.400	5	0	OF-65
1919 2 teams		STL	N	(9G –	.095)		BOS	N	(73G –	.216)							
" Total	82	262	54	8	0	1	0.4	23	21	18	35	8	.206	.248	9	2	OF-71, 1B-3
1920 BOS N	91	288	80	7	5	1	0.3	40	21	31	26	5	.278	.347	6	1	OF-82
1921	108	344	119	16	7	8	2.3	47	55	48	24	10	.346	.503	2	0	OF-102, 1B-2
1922	104	352	98	15	10	4	1.1	51	46	44	20	4	.278	.412	2	0	OF-100, 1B-2
1923	21	38	8	2	0	0	0.0	4	0	3	2	1	.211	.263	9	2	OF-9
1924	9	9	4	1	0	1	11.1	4	3	0	2	0	.444	.889	9	4	

	G	AB	H	2B	3B	HR	HR %	R	RBI	BB	SO	SB	BA	SA	Pinch Hit AB	H	G by POS

Walt Cruise continued

	G	AB	H	2B	3B	HR	HR%	R	RBI	BB	SO	SB	BA	SA	PH AB	H	G by POS
10 yrs.	736	2321	644	83	39	30	1.3	293	272	238	250	49	.277	.386	56	16	OF-664, 1B-6
5 yrs.	330	1049	283	35	17	15	1.4	124	126	95	147	21	.270	.378	21	6	OF-305, 1B-2

Gene Crumling

CRUMLING, EUGENE LEON   BR TR 6'   180 lbs.
B. Apr. 5, 1922, Wrightsville, Pa.

	G	AB	H	2B	3B	HR	HR%	R	RBI	BB	SO	SB	BA	SA	PH AB	H	G by POS
1945 STL N	6	12	1	0	0	0	0.0	0	0	1	0	0	.083	.083	0	0	C-6

Cirilio Cruz

CRUZ, CIRILIO DILAN (Tommy)   BL TL 5'9"   165 lbs.
Brother of Jose Cruz.   Brother of Hector Cruz.
B. Feb. 15, 1951, Arroyo, Puerto Rico

	G	AB	H	2B	3B	HR	HR%	R	RBI	BB	SO	SB	BA	SA	PH AB	H	G by POS
1973 STL N	3	0	0	0	0	0	—	1	0	0	0	0	—	—	0	0	OF-1
1977 CHI A	4	2	0	0	0	0	0.0	1	0	0	0	0	.000	.000	1	0	OF-2
2 yrs.	7	2	0	0	0	0	0.0	2	0	0	0	0	.000	.000	1	0	OF-3
1 yr.	3	0	0	0	0	0	—	1	0	0	0	0	—	—	0	0	OF-1

Hector Cruz

CRUZ, HECTOR DILAN   BR TR 5'11"   170 lbs.
Brother of Jose Cruz.   Brother of Cirilio Cruz.
B. Apr. 2, 1953, Arroyo, Puerto Rico

	G	AB	H	2B	3B	HR	HR%	R	RBI	BB	SO	SB	BA	SA	PH AB	H	G by POS
1973 STL N	11	11	0	0	0	0	0.0	1	0	1	3	0	.000	.000	4	0	OF-5
1975	23	48	7	2	0	0	0.0	7	6	2	4	0	.146	.271	6	1	3B-12, OF-6
1976	151	526	120	17	1	13	2.5	54	71	42	119	1	.228	.338	3	0	3B-148
1977	118	339	80	19	2	6	1.8	50	42	46	56	2	.236	.357	15	2	OF-106, 3B-2
1978 2 teams			CHI	N	(30G –	.237)		SF	N	(79G –	.223)						
" Total	109	273	62	13	1	8	2.9	27	33	24	45	0	.227	.370	30	7	OF-67, 3B-21
1979 2 teams			SF	N	(16G –	.120)		CIN	N	(74G –	.242)						
" Total	90	207	47	10	2	4	1.9	26	28	34	46	0	.227	.353	16	2	OF-75, 3B-2
1980 CIN N	52	75	16	4	1	1	1.3	5	5	8	16	0	.213	.333	22	1	OF-29
1981 CHI N	53	109	25	5	0	7	6.4	15	15	17	24	2	.229	.468	17	3	3B-18, OF-16
1982	17	19	4	1	0	0	0.0	1	0	2	4	0	.211	.263	15	3	OF-4
9 yrs.	624	1607	361	71	9	39	2.4	186	200	176	317	5	.225	.353	128	19	OF-308, 3B-203
4 yrs.	303	924	207	38	5	19	2.1	112	119	91	182	3	.224	.338	28	3	3B-162, OF-117

LEAGUE CHAMPIONSHIP SERIES

	G	AB	H	2B	3B	HR	HR%	R	RBI	BB	SO	SB	BA	SA	PH AB	H	G by POS
1979 CIN N	2	5	1	1	0	0	0.0	1	0	0	1	0	.200	.400	1	1	OF-1

Jose Cruz

CRUZ, JOSE DILAN   BL TL 6'   170 lbs.
Brother of Cirilio Cruz.   Brother of Hector Cruz.
B. Aug. 8, 1947, Arroyo, Puerto Rico

	G	AB	H	2B	3B	HR	HR%	R	RBI	BB	SO	SB	BA	SA	PH AB	H	G by POS
1970 STL N	6	17	6	1	0	0	0.0	2	1	4	0	0	.353	.412	1	1	OF-4
1971	83	292	80	13	2	9	3.1	46	27	49	35	6	.274	.425	2	1	OF-83
1972	117	332	78	14	4	2	0.6	33	23	36	54	9	.235	.319	13	5	OF-102
1973	132	406	92	22	5	10	2.5	51	57	51	66	10	.227	.379	14	3	OF-118
1974	107	161	42	4	3	5	3.1	24	20	20	27	4	.261	.416	47	11	OF-53, 1B-1
1975 HOU N	120	315	81	15	2	9	2.9	44	49	52	44	6	.257	.403	28	6	OF-94
1976	133	439	133	21	5	4	0.9	49	61	53	46	28	.303	.401	10	3	OF-125
1977	157	579	173	31	10	17	2.9	87	87	69	67	44	.299	.475	4	1	OF-155
1978	153	565	178	34	9	10	1.8	79	83	57	57	37	.315	.460	1	0	OF-152, 1B-2
1979	157	558	161	33	7	9	1.6	73	72	72	66	36	.289	.421	1	0	OF-156
1980	160	612	185	29	7	11	1.8	79	91	60	66	36	.302	.426	2	0	OF-158
1981	107	409	109	16	5	13	3.2	53	55	35	49	5	.267	.425	2	1	OF-105
1982	155	570	157	27	2	9	1.6	62	68	60	67	21	.275	.377	2	1	OF-155
13 yrs.	1587	5255	1475	260	61	108	2.1	682	694	618	644	242	.281	.415	127	33	OF-1460, 1B-3
5 yrs.	445	1208	298	54	14	26	2.2	156	128	160	182	29	.247	.379	77	21	OF-360, 1B-1

DIVISIONAL PLAYOFF SERIES

	G	AB	H	2B	3B	HR	HR%	R	RBI	BB	SO	SB	BA	SA	PH AB	H	G by POS
1981 HOU N	5	20	6	1	0	0	0.0	0	0	1	3	1	.300	.350	0	0	OF-5

LEAGUE CHAMPIONSHIP SERIES

	G	AB	H	2B	3B	HR	HR%	R	RBI	BB	SO	SB	BA	SA	PH AB	H	G by POS
1980 HOU N	5	15	6	1	1	0	0.0	3	4	8	1	0	.400	.600	0	0	OF-5

Joe Cunningham

CUNNINGHAM, JOSEPH ROBERT   BL TL 6'   180 lbs.
B. Aug. 27, 1931, Paterson, N. J.

	G	AB	H	2B	3B	HR	HR%	R	RBI	BB	SO	SB	BA	SA	PH AB	H	G by POS
1954 STL N	85	310	88	11	3	11	3.5	40	50	43	40	1	.284	.445	0	0	1B-85
1956	4	3	0	0	0	0	0.0	1	0	1	1	0	.000	.000	2	0	1B-1
1957	122	261	83	15	0	9	3.4	50	52	56	29	3	.318	.479	29	11	1B-57, OF-46
1958	131	337	105	20	3	12	3.6	61	57	82	23	4	.312	.496	19	5	1B-67, OF-66
1959	144	458	158	28	6	7	1.5	65	60	88	47	2	.345	.478	8	2	OF-121, 1B-35
1960	139	492	138	28	3	6	1.2	68	39	59	59	1	.280	.386	9	2	OF-116, 1B-15
1961	113	322	92	11	2	7	2.2	60	40	53	32	1	.286	.398	20	5	OF-86, 1B-10
1962 CHI A	149	526	155	32	7	8	1.5	91	70	101	59	3	.295	.428	1	1	1B-143, OF-5
1963	67	210	60	12	1	1	0.5	32	31	33	23	1	.286	.367	6	4	1B-58
1964 2 teams			CHI	A	(40G –	.250)		WAS	A	(49G –	.214)						
" Total	89	234	54	11	0	0	0.0	28	17	37	27	0	.231	.278	14	1	1B-74
1965 WAS A	95	201	46	9	1	3	1.5	29	20	46	27	0	.229	.328	27	5	1B-59
1966	3	8	1	0	0	0	0.0	0	0	0	1	0	.125	.125	0	0	1B-3
12 yrs.	1141	3362	980	177	26	64	1.9	525	436	599	368	16	.291	.417	137	36	1B-607, OF-440
7 yrs.	738	2183	664	113	17	52	2.4	345	298	382	231	12	.304	.443	87	25	OF-435, 1B-270

Ray Cunningham

CUNNINGHAM, RAYMOND LEE   BR TR 5'7½"   150 lbs.
B. Jan. 17, 1908, Mesquite, Tex.

	G	AB	H	2B	3B	HR	HR%	R	RBI	BB	SO	SB	BA	SA	PH AB	H	G by POS
1931 STL N	3	4	0	0	0	0	0.0	1	0	0	0	0	.000	.000	0	0	3B-3
1932	11	22	4	1	0	0	0.0	4	0	3	4	0	.182	.227	1	0	3B-8, 2B-2
2 yrs.	14	26	4	1	0	0	0.0	4	1	3	4	0	.154	.192	1	0	3B-11, 2B-2
2 yrs.	14	26	4	1	0	0	0.0	4	1	3	4	0	.154	.192	1	0	3B-11, 2B-2

	G	AB	H	2B	3B	HR	HR %	R	RBI	BB	SO	SB	BA	SA	Pinch Hit AB	Pinch Hit H	G by POS

Jack Damaska

DAMASKA, JACK LLOYD
B. Aug. 21, 1937, Beaver Falls, Pa.
BR TR 5'11" 168 lbs.

	G	AB	H	2B	3B	HR	HR %	R	RBI	BB	SO	SB	BA	SA	AB	H	G by POS
1963 STL N	5	5	1	0	0	0	0.0	1	1	0	4	0	.200	.200	4	1	OF-1, 2B-1

Rolla Daringer

DARINGER, ROLLA HARRISON
Brother of Cliff Daringer.
B. Nov. 15, 1889, North Vernon, Ind.   D. May 23, 1974, Seymour, Ind.
BL TR 5'10" 155 lbs.

	G	AB	H	2B	3B	HR	HR %	R	RBI	BB	SO	SB	BA	SA	AB	H	G by POS
1914 STL N	2	4	2	1	0	0	0.0	1	0	1	2	0	.500	.750	1	0	SS-1
1915	10	23	2	0	0	0	0.0	3	0	9	5	0	.087	.087	0	0	SS-10
2 yrs.	12	27	4	1	0	0	0.0	4	0	10	7	0	.148	.185	1	0	SS-11
2 yrs.	12	27	4	1	0	0	0.0	4	0	10	7	0	.148	.185	1	0	SS-11

Alvin Dark

DARK, ALVIN RALPH (Blackie)
B. Jan. 7, 1922, Comanche, Okla.
Manager 1961-64, 1966-71, 1974-75, 1977
BR TR 5'11" 185 lbs.

	G	AB	H	2B	3B	HR	HR %	R	RBI	BB	SO	SB	BA	SA	AB	H	G by POS
1946 BOS N	15	13	3	3	0	0	0.0	0	1	0	3	0	.231	.462	0	0	SS-12, OF-1
1948	137	543	175	39	6	3	0.6	85	48	24	36	4	.322	.433	4	3	SS-133
1949	130	529	146	23	5	3	0.6	74	53	31	43	5	.276	.355	0	0	SS-125, 3B-4
1950 NY N	154	587	164	36	5	16	2.7	79	67	39	60	9	.279	.440	0	0	SS-154
1951	156	646	196	41	7	14	2.2	114	69	42	39	12	.303	.454	0	0	SS-156
1952	151	589	177	29	3	14	2.4	92	73	47	39	6	.301	.431	1	0	SS-150
1953	155	647	194	41	6	23	3.6	126	88	28	34	7	.300	.488	1	0	SS-110, 2B-26, OF-17, 3B-8, P-1
1954	154	644	189	26	6	20	3.1	98	70	27	40	1	.293	.446	0	0	SS-154
1955	115	475	134	20	3	9	1.9	77	45	22	32	2	.282	.394	1	0	SS-115
1956 2 teams	NY	N	(48G –	.252)		STL	N	(100G –	.286)								
" Total	148	619	170	26	7	6	1.0	73	54	29	46	3	.275	.368	1	0	SS-147
1957 STL N	140	583	169	25	8	4	0.7	80	64	29	56	3	.290	.381	1	0	SS-139, 3B-3
1958 2 teams	STL	N	(18G –	.297)		CHI	N	(114G –	.295)								
" Total	132	528	156	16	4	4	0.8	61	48	31	29	1	.295	.364	8	5	3B-119, SS-8
1959 CHI N	136	477	126	22	9	6	1.3	60	45	55	50	1	.264	.386	1	0	3B-131, 1B-4, SS-1
1960 2 teams	PHI	N	(55G –	.242)		MIL	N	(50G –	.298)								
" Total	105	339	90	11	3	4	1.2	45	32	26	27	1	.265	.351	17	3	3B-57, OF-25, 1B-11, 2B-3
14 yrs.	1828	7219	2089	358	72	126	1.7	1064	757	430	534	59	.289	.411	35	11	SS-1404, 3B-320, OF-43, 2B-29, 1B-15, P-1
3 yrs.	258	1060	306	39	15	9	0.8	141	106	52	95	6	.289	.379	7	4	SS-246, 3B-9

WORLD SERIES

	G	AB	H	2B	3B	HR	HR %	R	RBI	BB	SO	SB	BA	SA	AB	H	G by POS
1948 BOS N	6	24	4	1	0	0	0.0	0	0	0	2	0	.167	.208	0	0	SS-6
1951 NY N	6	24	10	3	0	1	4.2	5	4	2	3	0	.417	.667	0	0	SS-6
1954	4	17	7	0	0	0	0.0	2	0	1	1	0	.412	.412	0	0	SS-4
3 yrs.	16	65	21	4	0	1	1.5	9	4	3	6	0	.323	.431	0	0	SS-16

Vic Davalillo

DAVALILLO, VICTOR JOSE
Brother of Yo-Yo Davalillo.
B. July 31, 1939, Cabimas, Venezuela
BL TL 5'7" 150 lbs.

	G	AB	H	2B	3B	HR	HR %	R	RBI	BB	SO	SB	BA	SA	AB	H	G by POS
1963 CLE A	90	370	108	18	5	7	1.9	44	36	16	41	3	.292	.424	2	2	OF-89
1964	150	577	156	26	2	6	1.0	64	51	34	77	21	.270	.354	5	0	OF-143
1965	142	505	152	19	1	5	1.0	67	40	35	50	26	.301	.372	8	1	OF-134
1966	121	344	86	6	4	3	0.9	42	19	24	37	8	.250	.317	18	3	OF-108
1967	139	359	103	17	5	2	0.6	47	22	10	30	6	.287	.379	20	4	OF-125
1968 2 teams	CLE	A	(51G –	.239)		CAL	A	(93G –	.298)								
" Total	144	519	144	17	7	3	0.6	49	31	18	53	25	.277	.355	7	3	OF-135
1969 2 teams	CAL	A	(33G –	.155)		STL	N	(63G –	.265)								
" Total	96	169	37	4	2	1	1.2	25	11	13	13	4	.219	.290	43	10	OF-45, 1B-3, P-2
1970 STL N	111	183	57	14	3	1	0.5	29	33	13	19	4	.311	.437	73	24	OF-54
1971 PIT N	99	295	84	14	6	1	0.3	48	33	11	31	10	.285	.383	27	9	OF-61, 1B-16
1972	117	368	117	19	2	4	1.1	59	28	26	44	14	.318	.413	12	5	OF-97, 1B-8
1973 2 teams	PIT	N	(59G –	.181)		OAK	A	(38G –	.188)								
" Total	97	147	27	2	0	1	0.7	14	7	5	11	0	.184	.218	49	10	OF-29, 1B-18
1974 OAK A	17	23	4	0	0	0	0.0	0	1	2	2	0	.174	.174	6	1	OF-6
1977 LA N	24	48	15	2	0	0	0.0	3	4	0	6	0	.313	.354	14	4	OF-12
1978	75	77	24	1	1	1	1.3	15	11	3	7	2	.312	.390	47	12	OF-25, 1B-2
1979	29	27	7	1	0	0	0.0	2	2	2	0	2	.259	.296	24	6	OF-3
1980	7	6	1	0	0	0	0.0	1	0	1	0	0	.167	.167	5	1	1B-1
16 yrs.	1458	4017	1122	160	37	36	0.9	509	329	212	422	125	.279	.364	360	95 9th	OF-1066, 1B-48, P-2
2 yrs.	174	281	83	17	3	3	1.1	44	43	20	27	5	.295	.409	107	33 5th	OF-77, P-2

LEAGUE CHAMPIONSHIP SERIES

	G	AB	H	2B	3B	HR	HR %	R	RBI	BB	SO	SB	BA	SA	AB	H	G by POS
1971 PIT N	2	2	0	0	0	0	0.0	0	0	0	1	0	.000	.000	2	0	
1972	1	0	0	0	0	0	–	0	0	1	0	0	–	–	0	0	
1973 OAK A	4	8	5	1	1	0	0.0	2	0	1	0	0	.625	1.000	1	1	OF-2
1977 LA N	1	1	1	0	0	0	0.0	0	1	0	0	0	1.000	1.000	1	1	
4 yrs.	8	11	6	1	1	0	0.0	3	1	2	1	0	.545	.818	4	2	OF-2

WORLD SERIES

	G	AB	H	2B	3B	HR	HR %	R	RBI	BB	SO	SB	BA	SA	AB	H	G by POS
1971 PIT N	3	3	1	0	0	0	0.0	1	0	0	0	0	.333	.333	3	1	OF-2
1973 OAK A	6	11	1	0	0	0	0.0	0	0	2	1	0	.091	.091	2	0	1B-1
1977 LA N	3	3	1	0	0	0	0.0	0	0	0	1	0	.333	.333	3	1	
1978	2	3	1	0	0	0	0.0	0	0	0	0	0	.333	.333	1	0	
4 yrs.	14	20	4	0	0	0	0.0	1	0	2	2	0	.200	.200	9 1st	2	OF-2, 1B-1

Jerry Davanon

DAVANON, FRANK GERALD
B. Aug. 21, 1945, Oceanside, Calif.
BR TR 5'11" 175 lbs.

	G	AB	H	2B	3B	HR	HR %	R	RBI	BB	SO	SB	BA	SA	AB	H	G by POS
1969 2 teams	SD	N	(24G –	.136)		STL	N	(16G –	.300)								
" Total	40	99	20	4	0	1	1.0	11	10	9	20	0	.202	.273	2	0	SS-23, 2B-15

	G	AB	H	2B	3B	HR	HR %	R	RBI	BB	SO	SB	BA	SA	Pinch Hit AB	Pinch Hit H	G by POS

Jerry Davanon continued

	G	AB	H	2B	3B	HR	HR %	R	RBI	BB	SO	SB	BA	SA	PH AB	PH H	G by POS
1970 STL N	11	18	2	1	0	0	0.0	2	0	2	5	0	.111	.167	3	0	3B-5, 2B-3
1971 BAL A	38	81	19	5	0	0	0.0	14	4	12	20	0	.235	.296	0	0	2B-20, SS-11, 3B-3, 1B-1
1973 CAL A	41	49	12	3	0	0	0.0	6	2	3	9	1	.245	.306	0	0	SS-14, 2B-12, 3B-7
1974 STL N	30	40	6	1	0	0	0.0	4	4	4	5	0	.150	.175	1	0	SS-14, 3B-8, 2B-7, OF-1
1975 HOU N	32	97	27	4	2	1	1.0	15	10	16	7	2	.278	.392	3	0	SS-21, 2B-9, 3B-3
1976	61	107	31	3	3	1	0.9	19	20	21	12	0	.290	.402	15	2	SS-17, 2B-17, 3B-9
1977 STL N	9	8	0	0	0	0	0.0	2	0	1	2	0	.000	.000	1	0	2B-5
8 yrs.	262	499	117	21	5	3	0.6	73	50	68	80	3	.234	.315	25	2	SS-100, 2B-88, 3B-35, OF-1, 1B-1
4 yrs.	66	106	20	5	0	1	0.9	15	11	13	20	0	.189	.264	5	0	SS-30, 2B-15, 3B-13, OF-1

Kiddo Davis

DAVIS, GEORGE WILLIS   BR TR 5'11"   178 lbs.
B. Feb. 12, 1902, Bridgeport, Conn.

	G	AB	H	2B	3B	HR	HR %	R	RBI	BB	SO	SB	BA	SA	PH AB	PH H	G by POS
1926 NY A	1	0	0	0	0	0	–	0	0	0	0	0	–	–	0	0	OF-1
1932 PHI N	137	576	178	39	6	5	0.9	100	57	44	56	16	.309	.424	0	0	OF-133
1933 NY N	126	434	112	20	4	7	1.6	61	37	25	30	10	.258	.371	5	1	OF-120
1934 2 teams	STL	N	(16G –	.303)		PHI N	(100G –	.293)									
" Total	116	426	125	28	5	4	0.9	56	52	30	29	2	.293	.411	5	2	OF-109
1935 NY N	47	91	24	7	1	2	2.2	16	6	10	4	2	.264	.429	21	5	OF-21
1936	47	67	16	1	0	0	0.0	6	5	6	5	0	.239	.254	9	1	OF-22
1937 2 teams	NY	N	(56G –	.263)		CIN N	(40G –	.257)									
" Total	96	212	55	16	0	1	0.5	39	14	26	13	2	.259	.349	13	4	OF-72
1938 CIN N	5	18	5	1	0	0	0.0	3	0	1	4	0	.278	.333	0	0	OF-5
8 yrs.	575	1824	515	112	16	19	1.0	281	171	142	141	32	.282	.393	53	13	OF-483
1 yr.	16	33	10	3	0	1	3.0	6	4	3	1	1	.303	.485	5	2	OF-9

WORLD SERIES

	G	AB	H	2B	3B	HR	HR %	R	RBI	BB	SO	SB	BA	SA	PH AB	PH H	G by POS
1933 NY N	5	19	7	1	0	0	0.0	1	0	0	3	0	.368	.421	0	0	OF-5
1936	4	2	1	0	0	0	0.0	2	0	0	0	0	.500	.500	2	1	
2 yrs.	9	21	8	1	0	0	0.0	3	0	0	3	0	.381	.429	2	1	OF-5

Ron Davis

DAVIS, RONALD EVERETTE   BR TR 6'   175 lbs.
B. Oct. 21, 1941, Roanoke Rapids, N. C.

	G	AB	H	2B	3B	HR	HR %	R	RBI	BB	SO	SB	BA	SA	PH AB	PH H	G by POS
1962 HOU N	6	14	3	0	0	0	0.0	1	1	1	7	1	.214	.214	0	0	OF-5
1966	48	194	48	10	1	2	1.0	21	19	13	26	2	.247	.340	0	0	OF-48
1967	94	285	73	19	1	7	2.5	31	38	17	48	5	.256	.404	15	3	OF-80
1968 2 teams	HOU	N	(52G –	.212)		STL N	(33G –	.177)									
" Total	85	296	60	14	3	1	0.3	33	17	18	65	1	.203	.280	0	0	OF-77
1969 PIT N	62	64	15	1	0	0	0.0	10	4	7	14	0	.234	.281	8	3	OF-51
5 yrs.	295	853	199	44	6	10	1.2	96	79	56	160	9	.233	.334	23	6	OF-261
1 yr.	33	79	14	4	2	0	0.0	11	5	5	17	1	.177	.278	0	0	OF-25

WORLD SERIES

	G	AB	H	2B	3B	HR	HR %	R	RBI	BB	SO	SB	BA	SA	PH AB	PH H	G by POS
1968 STL N	2	7	0	0	0	0	0.0	0	0	0	2	0	.000	.000	0	0	OF-2

Spud Davis

DAVIS, VIRGIL LAWRENCE   BR TR 6'1"   197 lbs.
B. Dec. 20, 1904, Birmingham, Ala.
Manager 1946.

	G	AB	H	2B	3B	HR	HR %	R	RBI	BB	SO	SB	BA	SA	PH AB	PH H	G by POS
1928 2 teams	STL	N	(2G –	.200)		PHI N	(67G –	.282)									
" Total	69	168	47	2	0	3	1.8	17	19	16	11	0	.280	.345	17	4	C-51
1929 PHI N	98	263	90	18	0	7	2.7	31	48	19	17	1	.342	.490	7	3	C-98
1930	106	329	103	16	1	14	4.3	41	65	17	20	1	.313	.495	9	2	C-96
1931	120	393	128	32	1	4	1.0	30	51	36	28	0	.326	.443	5	0	C-114
1932	125	402	135	23	5	14	3.5	44	70	40	39	1	.336	.522	5	3	C-120
1933	141	495	173	28	3	9	1.8	51	65	32	24	2	.349	.473	6	2	C-132
1934 STL N	107	347	104	22	4	9	2.6	45	65	34	27	0	.300	.464	11	3	C-94
1935	102	315	100	24	2	1	0.3	28	60	33	30	0	.317	.416	13	4	C-81, 1B-5
1936	112	363	99	26	2	4	1.1	24	59	35	34	0	.273	.388	7	2	C-103, 3B-2
193? CIN N	76	209	56	10	1	3	1.4	19	33	23	15	0	.268	.368	13	5	C-59
1938 2 teams	CIN	N	(12G –	.167)		PHI N	(70G –	.247)									
" Total	82	251	59	8	0	2	0.8	14	24	19	20	1	.235	.291	4	1	C-74
1939 PHI N	87	202	62	8	1	0	0.0	10	23	24	20	0	.307	.356	2	1	C-85
1940 PIT N	99	285	93	14	1	5	1.8	23	39	35	20	0	.326	.435	10	3	C-87
1941	57	107	27	4	1	0	0.0	3	6	11	11	0	.252	.308	7	2	C-49
1944	54	93	28	7	0	2	2.2	6	14	10	8	0	.301	.441	17	8	C-35
1945	23	33	8	2	0	0	0.0	2	6	2	2	0	.242	.303	9	2	C-13
16 yrs.	1458	4255	1312	244	22	77	1.8	388	647	386	326	6	.308	.430	146	45	C-1291, 1B-5, 3B-2
4 yrs.	323	1030	304	72	8	14	1.4	98	185	103	91	0	.295	.421	31	9	C-280, 1B-5, 3B-2

WORLD SERIES

	G	AB	H	2B	3B	HR	HR %	R	RBI	BB	SO	SB	BA	SA	PH AB	PH H	G by POS
1934 STL N	2	2	2	0	0	0	0.0	0	1	0	0	0	1.000	1.000	2	2	

Willie Davis

DAVIS, WILLIE HENRY   BL TL 5'11"   180 lbs.
B. Apr. 15, 1940, Mineral Springs, Ark.

	G	AB	H	2B	3B	HR	HR %	R	RBI	BB	SO	SB	BA	SA	PH AB	PH H	G by POS
1960 LA N	22	88	28	6	1	2	2.3	12	10	4	12	3	.318	.477	0	0	OF-22
1961	128	339	86	19	6	12	3.5	56	45	27	46	12	.254	.451	9	1	OF-114
1962	157	600	171	18	10	21	3.5	103	85	42	72	32	.285	.453	0	0	OF-156
1963	156	515	126	19	8	9	1.7	60	60	25	61	25	.245	.365	4	2	OF-153
1964	157	613	180	23	7	12	2.0	91	77	22	59	42	.294	.413	1	0	OF-155
1965	142	558	133	24	3	10	1.8	52	57	14	81	25	.238	.346	2	1	OF-141
1966	153	624	177	31	6	11	1.8	74	61	15	68	21	.284	.405	0	0	OF-152
1967	143	569	146	27	9	6	1.1	65	41	29	65	20	.257	.367	6	1	OF-138
1968	160	643	161	24	10	7	1.1	86	31	31	88	36	.250	.351	2	1	OF-158
1969	129	498	155	23	8	11	2.2	66	59	33	39	24	.311	.456	4	0	OF-125
1970	146	593	181	23	16	8	1.3	92	93	29	54	38	.305	.438	4	0	OF-143

	G	AB	H	2B	3B	HR	HR %	R	RBI	BB	SO	SB	BA	SA	Pinch Hit AB	Pinch Hit H	G by POS

Willie Davis continued

	G	AB	H	2B	3B	HR	HR%	R	RBI	BB	SO	SB	BA	SA	PH AB	PH H	G by POS
1971	158	641	198	33	10	10	1.6	84	74	23	47	20	.309	.438	3	1	OF-157
1972	149	615	178	22	7	19	3.1	81	79	27	61	20	.289	.441	2	1	OF-146
1973	152	599	171	29	9	16	2.7	82	77	29	62	17	.285	.444	7	3	OF-146
1974 MON N	153	611	180	27	9	12	2.0	86	89	27	69	25	.295	.427	5	2	OF-151
1975 2 teams	TEX A	(42G –	.249)		STL N	(98G –	.291)										
" Total	140	519	144	27	8	11	2.1	57	67	18	52	23	.277	.424	12	3	OF-131
1976 SD N	141	493	132	18	10	5	1.0	61	46	19	34	14	.268	.375	12	2	OF-128
1979 CAL A	43	56	14	2	1	0	0.0	9	2	4	7	1	.250	.321	24	5	OF-7
18 yrs.	2429	9174	2561	395	138	182	2.0	1217	1053	418	977	398	.279	.412	97	23	OF-2323
1 yr.	98	350	102	19	6	6	1.7	41	50	14	27	10	.291	.431	12	3	OF-89
LEAGUE CHAMPIONSHIP SERIES																	
1979 CAL A	2	2	1	1	0	0	0.0	1	0	0	0	0	.500	1.000	2	1	
WORLD SERIES																	
1963 LA N	4	12	2	2	0	0	0.0	2	3	0	6	0	.167	.333	0	0	OF-4
1965	7	26	6	0	0	0	0.0	3	0	0	2	3	.231	.231	0	0	OF-7
1966	4	16	1	0	0	0	0.0	0	0	0	4	0	.063	.063	0	0	OF-4
3 yrs.	15	54	9	2	0	0	0.0	5	3	0	12	3	.167	.204	0	0	OF-15

Boots Day

DAY, CHARLES FREDERICK
B. Aug. 31, 1947, Ilion, N. Y.
BL TL 5'9" 160 lbs.

	G	AB	H	2B	3B	HR	HR%	R	RBI	BB	SO	SB	BA	SA	PH AB	PH H	G by POS
1969 STL N	11	6	0	0	0	0	0.0	1	0	1	1	0	.000	.000	5	0	OF-1
1970 2 teams	CHI N	(11G –	.250)		MON N	(41G –	.269)										
" Total	52	116	31	4	0	0	0.0	16	5	6	21	3	.267	.302	13	4	OF-42
1971 MON N	127	371	105	10	2	4	1.1	53	33	33	39	9	.283	.353	15	5	OF-120
1972	128	386	90	7	4	0	0.0	32	30	29	44	3	.233	.272	17	5	OF-117
1973	101	207	57	7	0	4	1.9	36	28	21	28	0	.275	.367	48	13	OF-51
1974	52	65	12	0	0	0	0.0	8	2	5	8	0	.185	.185	31	3	OF-16
6 yrs.	471	1151	295	28	6	8	0.7	146	98	95	141	15	.256	.312	129	30	OF-347
1 yr.	11	6	0	0	0	0	0.0	1	0	1	1	0	.000	.000	5	0	OF-1

George Decker

DECKER, GEORGE A.
B. June 1, 1869, York, Pa.   D. June 9, 1909, Compton, Calif.

	G	AB	H	2B	3B	HR	HR%	R	RBI	BB	SO	SB	BA	SA	PH AB	PH H	G by POS
1892 CHI N	78	291	66	6	7	1	0.3	32	28	20	49	9	.227	.306	0	0	OF-62, 2B-16
1893	81	328	89	9	8	2	0.6	57	48	24	22	22	.271	.366	0	0	OF-33, 1B-27, 2B-20, SS-2
1894	91	384	120	17	6	8	2.1	74	92	24	17	23	.313	.451	4	1	1B-48, OF-29, 3B-7, 2B-2, SS-1
1895	73	297	82	9	7	2	0.7	51	41	17	22	11	.276	.374	0	0	OF-57, 1B-11, 3B-3, SS-1, 2B-1
1896	107	421	118	23	11	5	1.2	68	61	23	14	20	.280	.423	0	0	OF-71, 1B-36
1897	111	428	124	12	7	5	1.2	72	63	24		11	.290	.386	1	0	OF-75, 1B-38, 2B-1
1898 2 teams	STL N	(76G –	.259)		LOU N	(42G –	.297)										
" Total	118	434	118	14	3	1	0.2	53	64	29		13	.272	.325	5	2	1B-107, OF-6
1899 2 teams	LOU N	(38G –	.267)		WAS N	(4G –	.000)										
" Total	42	144	36	8	0	1	0.7	13	18	12		3	.250	.326	1	0	1B-40, OF-1
8 yrs.	701	2727	753	98	49	25	0.9	420	415	173	124	112	.276	.376	11	3	OF-334, 1B-307, 2B-40, 3B-10, SS-4
1 yr.	76	286	74	10	0	1	0.3	26	45	20		4	.259	.304	1	0	1B-75

Tony DeFate

DeFATE, CLYDE HERMAN
B. Feb. 22, 1898, Kansas City, Mo.   D. Sept. 3, 1963, New Orleans, La.
BR TR 5'8½" 158 lbs.

	G	AB	H	2B	3B	HR	HR%	R	RBI	BB	SO	SB	BA	SA	PH AB	PH H	G by POS
1917 2 teams	STL N	(14G –	.143)		DET A	(3G –	.000)										
" Total	17	16	2	0	0	0	0.0	1	1	4	6	0	.125	.125	6	1	3B-5, 2B-2

Rube DeGroff

DeGROFF, EDWARD ARTHUR
B. Sept. 2, 1879, Hyde Park, N. Y.   D. Dec. 17, 1955, Poughkeepsie, N. Y.

	G	AB	H	2B	3B	HR	HR%	R	RBI	BB	SO	SB	BA	SA	PH AB	PH H	G by POS
1905 STL N	15	56	14	2	1	0	0.0	3	5	5		1	.250	.321	0	0	OF-15
1906	1	4	0	0	0	0	0.0	1	0	0		0	.000	.000	0	0	OF-1
2 yrs.	16	60	14	2	1	0	0.0	4	5	5		1	.233	.300	0	0	OF-16
2 yrs.	16	60	14	2	1	0	0.0	4	5	5		1	.233	.300	0	0	OF-16

Joe Delahanty

DELAHANTY, JOSEPH NICHOLAS
Brother of Tom Delahanty.   Brother of Jim Delahanty.
Brother of Frank Delahanty.   Brother of Ed Delahanty.
B. Oct. 18, 1875, Cleveland, Ohio   D. Jan. 9, 1936, Cleveland, Ohio
BR TR 5'9" 168 lbs.

	G	AB	H	2B	3B	HR	HR%	R	RBI	BB	SO	SB	BA	SA	PH AB	PH H	G by POS
1907 STL N	6	21	7	0	0	1	4.8	3	2	0		3	.333	.476	0	0	OF-6
1908	140	499	127	14	11	1	0.2	37	44	32		11	.255	.333	1	0	OF-138
1909	123	411	88	16	4	2	0.5	28	54	42		10	.214	.287	10	3	OF-63, 2B-48
3 yrs.	269	931	222	30	15	4	0.4	68	100	74		24	.238	.316	11	3	OF-207, 2B-48
3 yrs.	269	931	222	30	15	4	0.4	68	100	74		24	.238	.316	11	3	OF-207, 2B-48

Bill DeLancey

DeLANCEY, WILLIAM PINKNEY
B. Nov. 28, 1901, Greensboro, N. C.   D. Nov. 28, 1946, Phoenix, Ariz.
BL TR 5'11½" 185 lbs.

	G	AB	H	2B	3B	HR	HR%	R	RBI	BB	SO	SB	BA	SA	PH AB	PH H	G by POS
1932 STL N	8	26	5	0	2	0	0.0	1	2	2	1	0	.192	.346	0	0	C-8
1934	93	253	80	18	3	13	5.1	41	40	41	37	1	.316	.565	15	3	C-77
1935	103	301	84	14	5	6	2.0	37	41	42	34	0	.279	.419	17	4	C-83
1940	15	18	4	0	0	0	0.0	0	2	0	2	0	.222	.222	1	0	C-12
4 yrs.	219	598	173	32	10	19	3.2	79	85	85	74	1	.289	.472	33	7	C-180
4 yrs.	219	598	173	32	10	19	3.2	79	85	85	74	1	.289	.472	33	7	C-180
WORLD SERIES																	
1934 STL N	7	29	5	3	0	1	3.4	3	4	2	8	0	.172	.379	0	0	C-7

	G	AB	H	2B	3B	HR	HR %	R	RBI	BB	SO	SB	BA	SA	Pinch Hit AB	Pinch Hit H	G by POS

Bobby Del Greco

DEL GRECO, ROBERT GEORGE
B. Apr. 7, 1933, Pittsburgh, Pa.
BR TR 5'10½" 185 lbs.

	G	AB	H	2B	3B	HR	HR %	R	RBI	BB	SO	SB	BA	SA	PH AB	PH H	G by POS
1952 PIT N	99	341	74	14	2	1	0.3	34	20	38	70	6	.217	.279	4	1	OF-93
1956 2 teams		PIT N (14G – .200)				STL N (102G – .215)											
" Total	116	290	62	16	2	7	2.4	33	21	35	53	1	.214	.355	7	0	OF-107, 3B-3
1957 2 teams		CHI N (20G – .200)				NY A (8G – .429)											
" Total	28	47	11	2	0	0	0.0	5	3	12	19	2	.234	.277	6	1	OF-22
1958 NY A	12	5	1	0	0	0	0.0	1	0	1	1	0	.200	.200	0	0	OF-12
1960 PHI N	100	300	71	16	4	10	3.3	48	26	54	64	1	.237	.417	11	3	OF-89
1961 2 teams		PHI N (41G – .259)				KC A (74G – .230)											
" Total	115	351	84	19	1	7	2.0	48	32	42	48	1	.239	.359	9	1	OF-105, 3B-1, 2B-1
1962 KC A	132	338	86	21	1	9	2.7	61	38	49	62	4	.254	.402	6	1	OF-124
1963	121	306	65	7	1	8	2.6	40	29	40	52	1	.212	.320	8	2	OF-110, 3B-2
1965 PHI N	8	4	0	0	0	0	0.0	1	0	0	3	0	.000	.000	2	0	OF-4
9 yrs.	731	1982	454	95	11	42	2.1	271	169	271	372	16	.229	.352	53	9	OF-666, 3B-6, 2B-1
1 yr.	102	270	58	16	2	5	1.9	29	18	32	50	1	.215	.344	4	0	OF-99

Eddie Delker

DELKER, EDWARD ALBERTS
B. Apr. 17, 1907, Palo Alto, Pa.
BR TR 5'10½" 170 lbs.

	G	AB	H	2B	3B	HR	HR %	R	RBI	BB	SO	SB	BA	SA	PH AB	PH H	G by POS
1929 STL N	22	40	6	0	1	0	0.0	5	3	2	12	0	.150	.200	2	0	SS-9, 2B-7, 3B-3
1931	1	2	1	1	0	0	0.0	0	2	0	0	0	.500	1.000	0	0	3B-1
1932 2 teams		STL N (20G – .119)				PHI N (30G – .161)											
" Total	50	104	15	5	1	1	1.0	8	9	14	21	0	.144	.240	1	0	2B-37, 3B-5, SS-4
1933 PHI N	25	41	7	3	1	0	0.0	6	1	0	12	0	.171	.293	3	0	2B-17, 3B-4
4 yrs.	98	187	29	9	3	1	0.5	19	15	16	45	0	.155	.251	6	0	2B-61, SS-13, 3B-13
3 yrs.	43	84	12	5	1	0	0.0	6	7	10	19	0	.143	.226	2	0	2B-17, SS-13, 3B-9

Frank Demaree

DEMAREE, JOSEPH FRANKLIN
Born Joseph Franklin Dimaria.
B. June 10, 1910, Winters, Calif.   D. Aug. 30, 1958, Los Angeles, Calif.
BR TR 5'11½" 185 lbs.

	G	AB	H	2B	3B	HR	HR %	R	RBI	BB	SO	SB	BA	SA	PH AB	PH H	G by POS
1932 CHI N	23	56	14	3	0	0	0.0	4	6	2	7	0	.250	.304	5	1	OF-17
1933	134	515	140	24	6	6	1.2	68	51	22	42	4	.272	.377	0	0	OF-133
1935	107	385	125	19	4	2	0.5	60	66	26	23	6	.325	.410	8	2	OF-98
1936	154	605	212	34	3	16	2.6	93	96	49	30	4	.350	.496	0	0	OF-154
1937	154	615	199	36	6	17	2.8	104	115	57	31	6	.324	.485	0	0	OF-154
1938	129	476	130	15	7	8	1.7	63	62	45	34	1	.273	.384	4	1	OF-125
1939 NY N	150	560	170	27	2	11	2.0	68	79	66	40	2	.304	.418	0	0	OF-150
1940	121	460	139	18	6	7	1.5	68	61	45	39	5	.302	.413	2	1	OF-119
1941 2 teams		NY N (16G – .171)				BOS N (48G – .230)											
" Total	64	148	32	5	2	1	1.4	23	16	16	6	2	.216	.318	22	3	OF-38
1942 BOS N	64	187	42	5	0	3	1.6	18	24	17	10	2	.225	.299	13	1	OF-49
1943 STL N	39	86	25	2	0	0	0.0	5	9	8	4	1	.291	.314	13	1	OF-23
1944 STL A	16	51	13	2	0	0	0.0	4	6	6	3	0	.255	.294	0	0	OF-16
12 yrs.	1155	4144	1241	190	36	72	1.7	578	591	359	269	33	.299	.415	67	10	OF-1076
1 yr.	39	86	25	2	0	0	0.0	5	9	8	4	1	.291	.314	13	1	OF-23
WORLD SERIES																	
1932 CHI N	2	7	2	0	0	1	14.3	1	4	1	0	0	.286	.714	0	0	OF-2
1935	6	24	6	1	0	2	8.3	2	2	1	4	0	.250	.542	0	0	OF-6
1938	3	10	1	0	0	0	0.0	1	0	1	2	0	.100	.100	0	0	OF-3
1943 STL N	1	1	0	0	0	0	0.0	0	0	0	0	0	.000	.000	1	0	
4 yrs.	12	42	9	1	0	3	7.1	4	6	3	6	0	.214	.452	1	0	OF-11

Harry DeMiller

DeMILLER, HARRY
B. Nov. 12, 1867, Wooster, Ohio   D. Oct. 19, 1928, Santa Ana, Calif.

	G	AB	H	2B	3B	HR	HR %	R	RBI	BB	SO	SB	BA	SA	PH AB	PH H	G by POS
1892 STL N	1	4	0	0	0	0	0.0	0	0	0	0	0	.000	.000	0	0	3B-1

Lee DeMontreville

DeMONTREVILLE, LEON
Brother of Gene DeMontreville.
B. Sept. 23, 1879, St. Paul, Minn.   D. Mar. 22, 1962, Pelham Manor, N. Y.
BR TR 5'7" 140 lbs.

	G	AB	H	2B	3B	HR	HR %	R	RBI	BB	SO	SB	BA	SA	PH AB	PH H	G by POS
1903 STL N	26	70	17	3	1	0	0.0	8	7	8		3	.243	.314	5	1	SS-15, 2B-4, OF-1

Russ Derry

DERRY, ALVA RUSSELL
B. Oct. 7, 1916, Princeton, Mo.
BL TR 6'1" 180 lbs.

	G	AB	H	2B	3B	HR	HR %	R	RBI	BB	SO	SB	BA	SA	PH AB	PH H	G by POS
1944 NY A	38	114	29	3	0	4	3.5	14	14	20	19	1	.254	.386	7	5	OF-28
1945	78	253	57	6	2	13	5.1	37	45	31	49	1	.225	.419	9	3	OF-68
1946 PHI N	69	184	38	8	5	0	0.0	17	14	27	54	0	.207	.304	16	3	OF-50
1949 STL N	2	2	0	0	0	0	0.0	0	0	0	2	0	.000	.000	2	0	
4 yrs.	187	553	124	17	7	17	3.1	68	73	78	124	2	.224	.373	34	11	OF-146
1 yr.	2	2	0	0	0	0	0.0	0	0	0	2	0	.000	.000	2	0	

Joe DeSa

DeSA, JOSEPH
B. July 7, 1959, Honolulu, Hawaii
BL TL 5'11" 170 lbs.

	G	AB	H	2B	3B	HR	HR %	R	RBI	BB	SO	SB	BA	SA	PH AB	PH H	G by POS
1980 STL N	7	11	3	0	0	0	0.0	0	0	0	2	0	.273	.273	5	2	OF-1, 1B-1

Chuck Diering

DIERING, CHARLES EDWARD ALLEN
B. Feb. 5, 1923, St. Louis, Mo.
BR TR 5'10" 165 lbs.

	G	AB	H	2B	3B	HR	HR %	R	RBI	BB	SO	SB	BA	SA	PH AB	PH H	G by POS
1947 STL N	105	74	16	3	1	2	2.7	22	11	19	22	3	.216	.365	8	1	OF-75
1948	7	7	0	0	0	0	0.0	2	0	2	2	1	.000	.000	0	0	OF-5
1949	131	369	97	21	8	3	0.8	60	38	35	49	1	.263	.388	1	0	OF-124
1950	89	204	51	12	0	3	1.5	34	18	35	38	1	.250	.353	0	0	OF-81
1951	64	85	22	5	1	0	0.0	9	8	16	15	0	.259	.341	8	3	OF-44
1952 NY N	41	23	4	1	1	0	0.0	2	2	4	3	0	.174	.304	0	0	OF-36
1954 BAL A	128	418	108	14	1	2	0.5	35	29	56	57	3	.258	.311	6	2	OF-119
1955	137	371	95	16	2	3	0.8	38	31	57	45	5	.256	.334	4	1	OF-107, 3B-34, SS-12
1956	50	97	18	4	0	1	1.0	15	4	23	19	2	.186	.258	4	0	OF-40, 3B-2

	G	AB	H	2B	3B	HR	HR %	R	RBI	BB	SO	SB	BA	SA	Pinch Hit AB	Pinch Hit H	G by POS

Chuck Diering continued

	G	AB	H	2B	3B	HR	HR%	R	RBI	BB	SO	SB	BA	SA	AB	H	G by POS
9 yrs.	752	1648	411	76	14	14	0.8	217	141	237	250	16	.249	.338	31	7	OF-631, 3B-36, SS-12
5 yrs.	396	739	186	41	10	8	1.1	127	75	97	126	6	.252	.367	17	4	OF-329

Pat Dillard

DILLARD, ROBERT LEE
B. June 12, 1874, Chattanooga, Tenn.   D. July 22, 1907, Denver, Colo.

	G	AB	H	2B	3B	HR	HR%	R	RBI	BB	SO	SB	BA	SA	AB	H	G by POS
1900 STL N	57	183	42	5	2	0	0.0	24	12	13		7	.230	.279	8	1	OF-26, 3B-21, SS-3

Pickles Dillhoefer

DILLHOEFER, WILLIAM MARTIN   BR TR 5'7"   154 lbs.
B. Oct. 13, 1894, Cleveland, Ohio   D. Feb. 22, 1922, St. Louis, Mo.

	G	AB	H	2B	3B	HR	HR%	R	RBI	BB	SO	SB	BA	SA	AB	H	G by POS
1917 CHI N	42	95	12	1	1	0	0.0	3	8	2	9	1	.126	.158	4	0	C-37
1918 PHI N	8	11	1	0	0	0	0.0	0	0	1	1	2	.091	.091	2	0	C-6
1919 STL N	45	108	23	3	2	0	0.0	11	12	8	6	5	.213	.278	1	1	C-39
1920	76	224	59	8	3	0	0.0	26	13	13	7	2	.263	.326	2	0	C-73
1921	76	162	39	4	4	0	0.0	19	15	11	7	2	.241	.315	4	0	C-69
5 yrs.	247	600	134	16	10	0	0.0	59	48	35	30	12	.223	.283	13	1	C-224
3 yrs.	197	494	121	15	9	0	0.0	56	40	32	20	9	.245	.312	7	1	C-181

Mike Dimmel

DIMMEL, MICHAEL WAYNE   BR TR 6'   180 lbs.
B. Oct. 18, 1954, Albert Lea, Minn.

	G	AB	H	2B	3B	HR	HR%	R	RBI	BB	SO	SB	BA	SA	AB	H	G by POS
1977 BAL A	25	5	0	0	0	0	0.0	8	0	0	1	1	.000	.000	0	0	OF-23
1978	8	0	0	0	0	0	–	2	0	0	0	0	–	–	0	0	OF-7
1979 STL N	6	3	1	0	0	0	0.0	1	0	0	0	0	.333	.333	0	0	OF-5
3 yrs.	39	8	1	0	0	0	0.0	11	0	0	1	1	.125	.125	0	0	OF-35
1 yr.	6	3	1	0	0	0	0.0	1	0	0	0	0	.333	.333	0	0	OF-5

Dutch Distel

DISTEL, GEORGE ADAM   BR TR 5'9"   165 lbs.
B. Apr. 15, 1896, Madison, Ind.   D. Feb. 12, 1967, Madison, Ind.

	G	AB	H	2B	3B	HR	HR%	R	RBI	BB	SO	SB	BA	SA	AB	H	G by POS
1918 STL N	8	17	3	1	1	0	0.0	1	2	3	0	1	.176	.353	1	0	2B-5, SS-2, OF-1

Cozy Dolan

DOLAN, ALVIN JAMES   BR TR 5'10"   160 lbs.
Born James Alberts.
B. Dec. 6, 1882, Oshkosh, Wis.   D. Dec. 10, 1958, Chicago, Ill.

	G	AB	H	2B	3B	HR	HR%	R	RBI	BB	SO	SB	BA	SA	AB	H	G by POS
1909 CIN N	3	6	1	0	0	0	0.0	0		2		0	.167	.167	0	0	3B-3
1911 NY A	19	69	21	1	2	1	1.4	19	6	8		12	.304	.420	0	0	3B-19
1912 2 teams	NY A (17G – .200)					PHI N	(11G – .280)										
" Total	28	110	26	3	5	0	0.0	23	18	6	10	8	.236	.355	0	0	3B-28
1913 2 teams	PHI N (55G – .262)					PIT N	(35G – .203)										
" Total	90	259	60	9	4	0	0.0	37	17	16	35	23	.232	.282	13	3	3B-39, OF-12, SS-10, 2B-9, 1B-1
1914 STL N	126	421	101	16	3	4	1.0	76	32	55	74	42	.240	.321	1	1	OF-97, 3B-29
1915	111	322	90	14	9	2	0.6	53	38	34	37	17	.280	.398	3	1	OF-98
1922 NY N	1	0	0	0	0	0	–	0	0	0	0	0	–	–	0	0	
7 yrs.	378	1187	299	43	21	7	0.6	210	111	121	156	102	.252	.341	17	5	OF-207, 3B-118, SS-10, 2B-9, 1B-1
2 yrs.	237	743	191	30	12	6	0.8	129	70	89	111	59	.257	.354	4	2	OF-195, 3B-29

She Donahue

DONAHUE, CHARLES MICHAEL   BR TR
B. June 29, 1877, Oswego, N.Y.   D. Aug. 28, 1947, New York, N.Y.

	G	AB	H	2B	3B	HR	HR%	R	RBI	BB	SO	SB	BA	SA	AB	H	G by POS
1904 2 teams	STL N (4G – .267)					PHI N	(58G – .215)										
" Total	62	215	47	4	0	0	0.0	22	16	3		10	.219	.237	0	0	SS-30, 3B-24, 2B-5, 1B-3

Jim Donely

DONELY, JAMES B.   BR TR
B. July 19, 1865, New Haven, Conn.   D. Mar. 5, 1915, New Haven, Conn.

	G	AB	H	2B	3B	HR	HR%	R	RBI	BB	SO	SB	BA	SA	AB	H	G by POS
1884 2 teams	KC U (6G – .130)					IND AA	(40G – .254)										
" Total	46	157	37	3	2	0	0.0	24		6			.236	.280	0	0	3B-29, SS-8, OF-6, 2B-2, C-1
1885 DET N	56	211	49	4	3	1	0.5	24	22	10	29		.232	.294	0	0	3B-55, 1B-1
1886 KC N	113	438	88	11	3	0	0.0	51	38	36	57		.201	.240	0	0	3B-113
1887 WAS N	117	425	85	9	6	1	0.2	51	46	16	26	42	.200	.256	0	0	3B-115, SS-2
1888	122	428	86	9	4	0	0.0	43	23	20	16	44	.201	.241	0	0	3B-117, SS-5
1889	4	13	2	0	0	0	0.0	3	0	2	0	1	.154	.154	0	0	3B-4
1890 STL AA	11	42	14	0	0	0	0.0	11		8		5	.333	.333	0	0	3B-11
1891 COL AA	17	54	13	0	0	0	0.0	6	9	13	5	7	.241	.241	0	0	3B-17
1896 BAL N	106	396	130	14	10	0	0.0	70	71	34	11	38	.328	.414	0	0	3B-106
1897 2 teams	PIT N (44G – .193)					NY N	(23G – .188)										
" Total	67	246	47	7	0	0	0.0	41	25	25		20	.191	.220	0	0	3B-67
1898 STL N	1	1	1	0	0	0	0.0	0	0	0		0	1.000	1.000	0	0	3B-1
11 yrs.	660	2411	552	57	28	2	0.1	324	233	170	144	157	.229	.278	0	0	3B-635, SS-15, OF-6, 2B-2, 1B-1, C-1
1 yr.	1	1	1	0	0	0	0.0	0	0	0		0	1.000	1.000	0	0	3B-1

Mike Donlin

DONLIN, MICHAEL JOSEPH (Turkey Mike)   BL TL 5'9"   170 lbs.
B. May 30, 1878, Erie, Pa.   D. Sept. 24, 1933, Hollywood, Calif.

	G	AB	H	2B	3B	HR	HR%	R	RBI	BB	SO	SB	BA	SA	AB	H	G by POS
1899 STL N	66	267	88	9	6	6	2.2	49	27	17		20	.330	.476	0	0	OF-51, 1B-13, SS-3, P-3
1900	78	276	90	8	6	10	3.6	40	48	14		14	.326	.507	10	4	OF-47, 1B-21
1901 BAL A	122	481	164	23	13	5	1.0	108	67	53		33	.341	.474	1	1	OF-74, 1B-47
1902 CIN N	34	143	42	5	4	0	0.0	30	9	9		9	.294	.385	1	0	OF-32, SS-1, P-1
1903	126	496	174	25	18	7	1.4	110	67	56		26	.351	.516	2	1	OF-118, 1B-7
1904 2 teams	CIN N (60G – .356)					NY N	(42G – .280)										
" Total	102	368	121	18	10	3	0.8	59	52	28		22	.329	.457	6	0	OF-90, 1B-6
1905 NY N	150	606	216	31	16	7	1.2	124	80	56		33	.356	.495	0	0	OF-150
1906	37	121	38	5	1	1	0.8	18	15	14		9	.314	.397	6	0	OF-29, 1B-1

	G	AB	H	2B	3B	HR	HR %	R	RBI	BB	SO	SB	BA	SA	Pinch Hit AB	Pinch Hit H	G by POS

Mike Donlin continued

	G	AB	H	2B	3B	HR	HR%	R	RBI	BB	SO	SB	BA	SA	PH AB	PH H	G by POS
1908	155	593	198	26	13	6	1.0	71	106	23		30	.334	.452	0	0	OF-155
1911 2 teams	NY N (12G – .333)					BOS N (56G – .315)											
" Total	68	234	74	16	1	3	1.3	36	35	22	18	9	.316	.432	9	2	OF-59
1912 PIT N	77	244	77	9	8	2	0.8	27	35	20	16	8	.316	.443	13	2	OF-62
1914 NY N	35	31	5	1	1	1	3.2	1	3	3	5	0	.161	.355	31	5	
12 yrs.	1050	3860	1287	176	97	51	1.3	670	543	312	39	213	.333	.469	79	15	OF-867, 1B-95, SS-4, P-4
2 yrs.	144	543	178	17	12	16	2.9	89	75	31		34	.328	.492	10	4	OF-98, 1B-34, SS-3, P-3

WORLD SERIES

	G	AB	H	2B	3B	HR	HR%	R	RBI	BB	SO	SB	BA	SA	PH AB	PH H	G by POS
1905 NY N	5	19	6	1	0	0	0.0	4	1	2	1	2	.316	.368	0	0	OF-5

Patsy Donovan

DONOVAN, PATRICK JOSEPH   BR TL 5'11½" 175 lbs.
Brother of Wild Bill Donovan.
B. Mar. 16, 1865, County Cork, Ireland   D. Dec. 25, 1953, Lawrence, Mass.
Manager 1897, 1899, 1901-04, 1906-08, 1910-11.

	G	AB	H	2B	3B	HR	HR%	R	RBI	BB	SO	SB	BA	SA	PH AB	PH H	G by POS
1890 2 teams	BOS N (32G – .179)					BKN N (28G – .352)											
" Total	60	245	62	6	1	0	0.0	34	17	13	22	13	.253	.286	0	0	OF-60
1891 2 teams	LOU AA (105G – .321)					WAS AA (17G – .200)											
" Total	122	509	155	11	3	2	0.4	82	56	34	23	28	.305	.350	0	0	OF-122
1892 2 teams	WAS N (40G – .239)					PIT N (90G – .294)											
" Total	130	551	153	18	6	2	0.4	106	38	31	29	56	.278	.343	0	0	OF-130
1893 PIT N	113	499	158	5	8	2	0.4	114	56	42	8	46	.317	.371	1	0	OF-112
1894	132	576	174	21	10	4	0.7	145	76	33	12	41	.302	.394	0	0	OF-132
1895	125	519	160	17	6	1	0.2	114	58	47	19	36	.308	.370	0	0	OF-125
1896	131	573	183	20	5	3	0.5	113	59	35	18	48	.319	.387	0	0	OF-131
1897	120	479	154	16	7	0	0.0	82	57	25		34	.322	.384	0	0	OF-120
1898	147	610	184	16	9	0	0.0	112	37	34		41	.302	.357	0	0	OF-147
1899	121	531	156	11	7	1	0.2	82	55	17		26	.294	.347	0	0	OF-121
1900 STL N	126	503	159	11	1	0	0.0	78	61	38		45	.316	.342	2	1	OF-124
1901	130	531	161	23	5	1	0.2	92	73	27		28	.303	.371	0	0	OF-129
1902	126	502	158	12	4	0	0.0	70	35	28		34	.315	.355	0	0	OF-126
1903	105	410	134	15	3	0	0.0	63	39	25		25	.327	.378	0	0	OF-105
1904 WAS A	125	436	100	6	0	0	0.0	30	19	24		17	.229	.243	3	0	OF-6
1906 BKN N	7	21	5	0	0	0	0.0	1	0	0		0	.238	.238	1	0	OF-1
1907	1	1	0	0	0	0	0.0	0	0	0		0	.000	.000	0	0	
17 yrs.	1821	7496	2256	208	75	16	0.2	1318	736	453	131	518	.301	.355	7	1	OF-1813
4 yrs.	487	1946	612	61	13	1	0.1	303	208	118		132	.314	.361	2	1	OF-484
											9th	9th					

Klondike Douglas

DOUGLAS, WILLIAM B.   BL TR
B. May 10, 1872, Boston, Pa.   D. Dec. 13, 1953, Bend, Ore.

	G	AB	H	2B	3B	HR	HR%	R	RBI	BB	SO	SB	BA	SA	PH AB	PH H	G by POS
1896 STL N	81	296	78	6	4	1	0.3	42	28	35	15	18	.264	.321	1	0	OF-74, C-6, SS-2
1897	125	516	170	15	3	6	1.2	77	50	52		12	.329	.405	1	1	C-61, OF-43, 1B-17, 3B-7, SS-1
1898 PHI N	146	582	150	26	4	2	0.3	105	48	55		18	.258	.326	0	0	1B-146
1899	77	275	70	6	6	0	0.0	26	27	10		7	.255	.320	1	0	C-66, 3B-4, 1B-4, OF-1
1900	50	160	48	9	4	0	0.0	23	25	13		7	.300	.406	2	1	C-47, 3B-2
1901	51	173	56	6	1	0	0.0	14	23	11		10	.324	.370	3	1	C-41, 1B-6, OF-2
1902	109	408	95	12	3	0	0.0	37	37	23		6	.233	.277	1	0	1B-69, C-29, OF-10
1903	105	377	96	5	4	1	0.3	43	36	28		6	.255	.297	5	1	1B-97
1904	3	3	0	0	0	0	0.0	1	1	0		0	.300	.300	0	0	1B-3
9 yrs.	747	2797	766	85	29	10	0.4	368	275	227	15	84	.274	.336	14	3	1B-342, C-250, OF-130, 3B-13, SS-3
2 yrs.	206	812	248	21	7	7	0.9	119	78	87	15	30	.305	.374	2	1	OF-117, C-67, 1B-17, 3B-7, SS-3

Taylor Douthit

DOUTHIT, TAYLOR LEE   BR TR 5'11½" 175 lbs.
B. Apr. 22, 1901, Little Rock, Ark.

	G	AB	H	2B	3B	HR	HR%	R	RBI	BB	SO	SB	BA	SA	PH AB	PH H	G by POS
1923 STL N	9	27	5	0	2	0	0.0	3	0	0	4	1	.185	.333	2	0	OF-7
1924	53	173	48	13	1	0	0.0	24	13	16	19	4	.277	.364	1	0	OF-50
1925	30	73	20	3	1	1	1.4	13	8	2	6	0	.274	.384	9	5	OF-21
1926	139	530	163	20	4	3	0.6	96	52	55	46	23	.308	.377	1	0	OF-138
1927	130	488	128	29	6	5	1.0	81	50	52	45	6	.262	.377	4	2	OF-125
1928	154	648	191	35	3	3	0.5	111	43	84	36	11	.295	.372	0	0	OF-154
1929	150	613	206	42	7	9	1.5	128	62	79	49	8	.336	.471	0	0	OF-150
1930	154	664	201	41	10	7	1.1	109	93	60	38	4	.303	.426	0	0	OF-154
1931 2 teams	STL N (36G – .331)					CIN N (95G – .262)											
" Total	131	507	142	20	3	1	0.2	63	45	53	33	5	.280	.337	0	0	OF-131
1932 CIN N	96	333	81	12	1	0	0.0	28	25	31	29	3	.243	.285	2	0	OF-88
1933 2 teams	CIN N (1G – .000)					CHI N (27G – .225)											
" Total	28	71	16	5	0	0	0.0	9	5	11	7	2	.225	.296	1	0	OF-18
11 yrs.	1074	4127	1201	220	38	29	0.7	665	396	443	312	67	.291	.384	20	7	OF-1036
9 yrs.	855	3349	1006	194	36	29	0.9	586	342	359	252	58	.300	.406	17	7	OF-835

WORLD SERIES

	G	AB	H	2B	3B	HR	HR%	R	RBI	BB	SO	SB	BA	SA	PH AB	PH H	G by POS
1926 STL N	4	15	4	2	0	0	0.0	3	1	3	2	0	.267	.400	0	0	OF-4
1928	3	11	1	0	0	0	0.0	1	0	1	1	0	.091	.091	0	0	OF-3
1930	6	24	2	0	0	1	4.2	1	2	0	2	0	.083	.208	0	0	OF-6
3 yrs.	13	50	7	2	0	1	2.0	5	3	4	5	0	.140	.240	0	0	OF-13

Tommy Dowd

DOWD, THOMAS JEFFERSON (Buttermilk Tommy)   BR TR
B. Apr. 20, 1869, Holyoke, Mass.   D. July 2, 1933, Holyoke, Mass.
Manager 1896-97.

	G	AB	H	2B	3B	HR	HR%	R	RBI	BB	SO	SB	BA	SA	PH AB	PH H	G by POS
1891 2 teams	BOS AA (4G – .091)					WAS AA (112G – .259)											
" Total	116	475	121	9	10	1	0.2	67	44	19	45	39	.255	.322	0	0	2B-107, OF-9

	G	AB	H	2B	3B	HR	HR %	R	RBI	BB	SO	SB	BA	SA	Pinch Hit AB	Pinch Hit H	G by POS

Tommy Dowd continued

	G	AB	H	2B	3B	HR	HR %	R	RBI	BB	SO	SB	BA	SA	PH AB	PH H	G by POS
1892 WAS N	144	584	142	9	10	1	0.2	94	50	34	49	49	.243	.298	0	0	2B-98, OF-23, 3B-18, SS-6
1893 STL N	132	581	164	18	7	1	0.2	114	54	49	23	59	.282	.343	0	0	OF-132, 2B-1
1894	123	524	142	16	8	4	0.8	92	62	54	33	31	.271	.355	0	0	OF-117, 2B-7, 3B-1
1895	129	505	163	19	17	6	1.2	95	74	30	31	30	.323	.463	2	0	OF-115, 3B-17, 2B-2
1896	126	521	138	17	11	5	1.0	93	46	42	19	40	.265	.369	0	0	2B-78, OF-48
1897 2 teams	STL	N	(35G –	.262)		PHI	N	(91G –	.292)								
" Total	126	536	152	23	5	0	0.0	93	52	25		41	.284	.345	0	0	OF-103, 2B-24
1898 STL N	139	586	143	17	7	0	0.0	70	32	30		16	.244	.297	0	0	OF-129, 2B-11
1899 CLE N	147	605	168	17	6	2	0.3	81	35	48		28	.278	.336	0	0	OF-147
1901 BOS A	138	594	159	18	7	3	0.5	104	52	38		33	.268	.337	0	0	OF-137, 1B-2, 3B-1
10 yrs.	1320	5511	1492	163	88	23	0.4	903	501	369	200	366	.271	.345	2	0	OF-960, 2B-328, 3B-37, SS-6, 1B-2
6 yrs.	684	2862	788	96	51	16	0.6	489	277	211	106	187	.275	.361	2	0	OF-571, 2B-104, 3B-18

Lee Dressen

DRESSEN, LEE AUGUST
B. July 23, 1889, Ellinwood, Kans.   D. June 30, 1931, Diller, Neb.
BL TL 6'   165 lbs.

	G	AB	H	2B	3B	HR	HR %	R	RBI	BB	SO	SB	BA	SA	PH AB	PH H	G by POS
1914 STL N	46	103	24	2	1	0	0.0	16	7	11	20	2	.233	.272	7	1	1B-38
1918 DET A	31	107	19	1	2	0	0.0	10	3	21	10	2	.178	.224	1	0	1B-30
2 yrs.	77	210	43	3	3	0	0.0	26	10	32	30	4	.205	.248	8	1	1B-68
1 yr.	46	103	24	2	1	0	0.0	16	7	11	20	2	.233	.272	7	1	1B-38

Taylor Duncan

DUNCAN, TAYLOR McDOWELL
B. May 12, 1953, Memphis, Tenn.
BR TR 6'   170 lbs.

	G	AB	H	2B	3B	HR	HR %	R	RBI	BB	SO	SB	BA	SA	PH AB	PH H	G by POS
1977 STL N	8	12	4	0	0	1	8.3	2	2	2	1	0	.333	.583	2	0	3B-5
1978 OAK A	104	319	82	15	2	2	0.6	25	37	19	38	1	.257	.335	13	1	3B-84, 2B-11, SS-1
2 yrs.	112	331	86	15	2	3	0.9	27	39	21	39	1	.260	.344	15	1	3B-89, 2B-11, SS-1
1 yr.	8	12	4	0	0	1	8.3	2	2	2	1	0	.333	.583	2	0	3B-5

Grant Dunlap

DUNLAP, GRANT LESTER (Snap)
B. Dec. 20, 1923, Stockton, Calif.
BR TR 6'2"   180 lbs.

	G	AB	H	2B	3B	HR	HR %	R	RBI	BB	SO	SB	BA	SA	PH AB	PH H	G by POS
1953 STL N	16	17	6	0	1	1	5.9	2	3	0	2	0	.353	.647	15	5	OF-1

John Dunleavy

DUNLEAVY, JOHN FRANCIS
B. Sept. 14, 1879, Harrison, N. J.   D. Apr. 12, 1944, South Norwalk, Conn.

	G	AB	H	2B	3B	HR	HR %	R	RBI	BB	SO	SB	BA	SA	PH AB	PH H	G by POS
1903 STL N	61	193	48	3	3	0	0.0	23	10	13		10	.249	.295	9	4	OF-38, P-14
1904	51	172	40	7	3	1	0.6	23	14	16		8	.233	.326	0	0	OF-44, P-7
1905	119	435	105	8	8	1	0.2	52	25	55		15	.241	.303	0	0	OF-118, 2B-1
3 yrs.	231	800	193	18	14	2	0.3	98	49	84		33	.241	.306	9	4	OF-200, P-21, 2B-1
3 yrs.	231	800	193	18	14	2	0.3	98	49	84		33	.241	.306	9	4	OF-200, P-21, 2B-1

Joe Durham

DURHAM, JOSEPH VANN (Pop)
B. July 31, 1931, Newport News, Va.
BR TR 6'1"   186 lbs.

	G	AB	H	2B	3B	HR	HR %	R	RBI	BB	SO	SB	BA	SA	PH AB	PH H	G by POS
1954 BAL A	10	40	9	0	0	1	2.5	4	3	4	7	0	.225	.300	0	0	OF-10
1957	77	157	29	2	0	4	2.5	19	17	16	42	1	.185	.274	15	1	OF-59
1959 STL N	6	5	0	0	0	0	0.0	2	0	0	1	0	.000	.000	2	0	OF-1
3 yrs.	93	202	38	2	0	5	2.5	25	20	20	50	1	.188	.272	17	1	OF-70
1 yr.	6	5	0	0	0	0	0.0	2	0	0	1	0	.000	.000	2	0	OF-1

Leon Durham

DURHAM, LEON (Bull)
B. July 31, 1957, Cincinnati, Ohio
BL TL 6'1"   185 lbs.

	G	AB	H	2B	3B	HR	HR %	R	RBI	BB	SO	SB	BA	SA	PH AB	PH H	G by POS
1980 STL N	96	303	82	15	4	8	2.6	42	42	18	55	8	.271	.426	16	5	OF-78, 1B-8
1981 CHI N	87	328	95	14	6	10	3.0	42	35	27	53	25	.290	.460	3	1	OF-83, 1B-3
1982	148	539	168	33	7	22	4.1	84	90	66	77	28	.312	.521	5	2	OF-143, 1B-1
3 yrs.	331	1170	345	62	17	40	3.4	168	167	111	185	61	.295	.479	24	8	OF-304, 1B-12
1 yr.	96	303	82	15	4	8	2.6	42	42	18	55	8	.271	.426	16	5	OF-78, 1B-8

Leo Durocher

DUROCHER, LEO ERNEST (The Lip)
B. July 27, 1905, W. Springfield, Mass.
Manager 1939-46, 1948-55, 1966-73.
BR TR 5'10"   160 lbs.
BB 1929

	G	AB	H	2B	3B	HR	HR %	R	RBI	BB	SO	SB	BA	SA	PH AB	PH H	G by POS
1925 NY A	2	1	0	0	0	0	0.0	1	0	0	0	0	.000	.000	1	0	
1928	102	296	80	8	6	0	0.0	46	31	22	52	1	.270	.338	3	1	2B-66, SS-29
1929	106	341	84	4	5	0	0.0	53	32	34	33	3	.246	.287	1	0	SS-93, 2B-12
1930 CIN N	119	354	86	15	3	3	0.8	31	32	20	45	0	.243	.328	0	0	SS-103, 2B-13
1931	121	361	82	11	5	1	0.3	26	29	18	32	0	.227	.294	0	0	SS-120
1932	143	457	99	22	5	1	0.2	43	33	36	40	3	.217	.293	0	0	SS-142
1933 2 teams	CIN	N	(16G –	.216)		STL	N	(123G –	.258)								
" Total	139	446	113	19	4	3	0.7	51	44	30	37	3	.253	.334	0	0	SS-139
1934 STL N	146	500	130	26	5	3	0.6	62	70	33	40	2	.260	.350	0	0	SS-146
1935	143	513	136	23	5	8	1.6	62	78	29	46	4	.265	.376	0	0	SS-142
1936	136	510	146	22	3	1	0.2	57	58	29	47	3	.286	.347	0	0	SS-136
1937	135	477	97	11	3	1	0.2	46	47	38	36	6	.203	.245	0	0	SS-134
1938 BKN N	141	479	105	18	5	1	0.2	41	56	47	30	3	.219	.284	0	0	SS-141
1939	116	390	108	21	6	1	0.3	42	34	27	24	2	.277	.369	2	0	SS-113, 3B-1
1940	62	160	37	9	1	1	0.6	10	14	12	13	1	.231	.319	1	0	SS-53, 2B-4
1941	18	42	12	1	0	0	0.0	2	6	1	3	0	.286	.310	5	1	SS-12, 2B-1
1943	6	18	4	0	0	0	0.0	1	1	1	2	0	.222	.222	0	0	SS-6
1945	2	5	1	0	0	0	0.0	0	0	1	0	0	.200	.200	0	0	2B-2
17 yrs.	1637	5350	1320	210	56	24	0.4	575	567	377	480	31	.247	.320	13	2	SS-1509, 2B-98, 3B-1
5 yrs.	683	2395	611	100	20	15	0.6	272	294	155	201	18	.255	.332	0	0	SS-681

WORLD SERIES

	G	AB	H	2B	3B	HR	HR %	R	RBI	BB	SO	SB	BA	SA	PH AB	PH H	G by POS
1928 NY A	4	2	0	0	0	0	0.0	0	0	1	0	0	.000	.000	0	0	2B-4

	G	AB	H	2B	3B	HR	HR %	R	RBI	BB	SO	SB	BA	SA	Pinch Hit AB	Pinch Hit H	G by POS

Leo Durocher continued

1934 STL N	7	27	7	1	1	0	0.0	4	0	0	0	0	.259	.370	0	0	SS-7
2 yrs.	11	29	7	1	1	0	0.0	4	0	0	1	0	.241	.345	0	0	SS-7, 2B-4

Erv Dusak

DUSAK, ERVIN FRANK (Four Sack)
B. July 29, 1920, Chicago, Ill.
BR TR 6'2" 185 lbs.

1941 STL N	6	14	2	0	0	0	0.0	1	3	2	6	1	.143	.143	2	0	OF-4
1942	12	27	5	3	0	0	0.0	4	3	3	7	0	.185	.296	1	0	OF-8, 3B-1
1946	100	275	66	9	1	9	3.3	38	42	33	63	7	.240	.378	7	2	OF-77, 3B-11, 2B-2
1947	111	328	93	7	3	6	1.8	56	28	50	34	1	.284	.378	13	1	OF-89, 3B-7
1948	114	311	65	9	2	6	1.9	60	19	49	55	3	.209	.309	9	3	OF-68, 2B-29, 3B-9, SS-1, P-1
1949	1	0	0	0	0	0	–	1	0	0	0	0	–	–	0	0	
1950	23	12	1	1	0	0	0.0	0	0	0	3	0	.083	.167	0	0	P-14, OF-2
1951 2 teams	STL N	(5G – .500)		PIT N	(21G – .308)												
" Total	26	41	13	3	0	2	4.9	7	8	3	12	0	.317	.537	1	0	OF-12, P-8, 3B-2, 2B-2
1952 PIT N	20	27	6	0	0	1	3.7	1	3	2	8	0	.222	.333	11	2	OF-11
9 yrs.	413	1035	251	32	6	24	2.3	168	106	142	188	12	.243	.355	44	8	OF-271, 2B-33, 3B-30, P-23, SS-1
8 yrs.	372	969	233	29	6	22	2.3	161	96	137	169	12	.240	.351	32	6	OF-248, 2B-31, 3B-28, P-20, SS-1

WORLD SERIES
1946 STL N	4	4	1	1	0	0	0.0	0	0	2	2	0	.250	.500	1	0	OF-4

Frank Dwyer

DWYER, JOHN FRANCIS
B. Mar. 25, 1868, Lee, Mass.   D. Feb. 4, 1943, Pittsfield, Mass.
Manager 1902.
BR TR 5'8" 145 lbs.

1888 CHI N	5	21	4	1	0	0	0.0	2	2	0	5	0	.190	.238	0	0	P-5
1889	36	135	27	1	1	1	0.7	14	6	4	8	0	.200	.244	0	0	P-32, OF-3, SS-2
1890 CHI P	16	53	14	2	0	0	0.0	10	11	0	2	1	.264	.302	0	0	P-12, OF-4
1891 C-M AA	48	181	49	5	3	0	0.0	25	20	6	16	5	.271	.331	0	0	P-45, OF-4, 2B-2
1892 2 teams	STL N	(10G – .080)		CIN N	(40G – .163)												
" Total	50	154	23	0	2	0	0.0	19	6	8	11	2	.149	.175	1	0	P-43, OF-6
1893 CIN N	38	120	24	1	2	1	0.8	22	17	9	5	2	.200	.267	0	0	P-37, OF-1, 1B-1
1894	54	172	46	9	2	2	1.2	31	28	15	13	0	.267	.378	1	0	P-45, OF-10, SS-2
1895	37	113	30	3	5	1	0.9	14	16	5	5	2	.265	.407	0	0	P-37
1896	36	110	29	4	4	0	0.0	17	15	11	15	3	.264	.373	0	0	P-36
1897	37	94	25	1	1	0	0.0	13	10	5		0	.266	.298	0	0	P-37
1898	31	85	12	1	1	0	0.0	11	5	7		1	.141	.176	0	0	P-31
1899	5	11	4	0	0	0	0.0	0	0	0		0	.364	.364	0	0	P-5
12 yrs.	393	1249	287	28	21	5	0.4	178	136	70	80	16	.230	.298	2	0	P-365, OF-28, SS-4, 2B-2, 1B-1
1 yr.	10	25	2	0	0	0	0.0	4	0	4	2	0	.080	.080	0	0	P-10

Jim Dwyer

DWYER, JAMES EDWARD
B. Jan. 3, 1950, Evergreen Park, Ill.
BL TL 5'10" 165 lbs.

1973 STL N	28	57	11	1	1	0	0.0	7	0	1	5	0	.193	.246	8	1	OF-20
1974	74	86	24	1	0	2	2.3	13	11	11	16	0	.279	.360	41	10	OF-25, 1B-3
1975 2 teams	STL N	(21G – .194)		MON N	(60G – .286)												
" Total	81	206	56	8	1	3	1.5	26	21	27	36	4	.272	.364	21	6	OF-61
1976 2 teams	MON N	(50G – .185)		NY N	(11G – .154)												
" Total	61	105	19	3	1	0	0.0	9	5	13	11	0	.181	.229	38	6	OF-21
1977 STL N	13	31	7	1	0	0	0.0	3	2	4	5	0	.226	.258	2	1	OF-12
1978 2 teams	STL N	(34G – .215)		SF N	(73G – .225)												
" Total	107	238	53	12	2	6	2.5	30	26	37	32	7	.223	.366	24	5	OF-58, 1B-29
1979 BOS A	76	113	30	7	0	2	1.8	19	14	17	9	3	.265	.381	22	7	1B-25, OF-19
1980	93	260	74	11	1	9	3.5	41	38	28	23	3	.285	.438	11	2	OF-65, 1B-9
1981 BAL A	68	134	30	0	1	3	2.2	16	10	20	19	0	.224	.306	6	0	OF-59, 1B-3
1982	71	148	45	4	3	6	4.1	28	15	27	24	2	.304	.493	23	6	OF-49, 1B-1
10 yrs.	672	1378	349	48	10	31	2.2	192	142	185	180	19	.253	.370	196	44	OF-389, 1B-70
5 yrs.	170	270	62	7	1	3	1.1	36	18	29	35	1	.230	.296	74	16	OF-88, 1B-3

Eddie Dyer

DYER, EDWIN HAWLEY
B. Oct. 11, 1900, Morgan City, La.   D. Apr. 20, 1964, Houston, Tex.
Manager 1946-50.
BL TL 5'11½" 168 lbs.

1922 STL N	6	3	1	1	0	0	0.0	1	0	0	0	0	.333	.667	1	1	P-2
1923	35	45	12	3	0	2	4.4	17	5	3	5	1	.267	.467	14	3	OF-8, P-4
1924	50	76	18	2	3	0	0.0	8	8	3	8	1	.237	.342	16	4	P-29, OF-1
1925	31	31	3	1	0	0	0.0	4	0	3	1	1	.097	.129	1	0	P-31
1926	6	2	1	0	0	0	0.0	1	0	0	0	0	.500	.500	0	0	P-6
1927	1	0	0	0	0	0	–	0	0	1	0	0	–	–	0	0	P-1
6 yrs.	129	157	35	7	3	2	1.3	31	13	10	14	3	.223	.344	32	8	P-73, OF-9
6 yrs.	129	157	35	7	3	2	1.3	31	13	10	14	3	.223	.344	32	8	P-73, OF-9

Johnny Echols

ECHOLS, JOHN GRESHAM
B. Jan. 9, 1917, Atlanta, Ga.   D. Nov. 13, 1972, Atlanta, Ga.
BR TR 5'10½" 175 lbs.

1939 STL N	2	0	0	0	0	0	–	0	0	0	0	0	–	–	0	0	

Johnny Edwards

EDWARDS, JOHN ALBAN
B. June 10, 1938, Columbus, Ohio
BL TR 6'4" 220 lbs.

1961 CIN N	52	145	27	5	0	2	1.4	14	14	18	28	1	.186	.262	2	0	C-52
1962	133	452	115	28	5	8	1.8	47	50	45	70	1	.254	.392	7	4	C-130
1963	148	495	128	19	4	11	2.2	46	67	45	93	1	.259	.380	2	2	C-148
1964	126	423	119	23	1	7	1.7	47	55	34	65	1	.281	.390	8	0	C-120

Johnny Edwards continued

	G	AB	H	2B	3B	HR	HR %	R	RBI	BB	SO	SB	BA	SA	Pinch Hit AB	Pinch Hit H	G by POS
1965	114	371	99	22	2	17	4.6	47	51	50	45	0	.267	.474	11	5	C-110
1966	98	282	54	8	0	6	2.1	24	39	31	42	1	.191	.284	1	0	C-98
1967	80	209	43	6	0	2	1.0	10	20	16	28	1	.206	.263	7	1	C-73
1968 STL N	85	230	55	9	1	3	1.3	14	29	16	20	1	.239	.326	26	7	C-54
1969 HOU N	151	496	115	20	6	6	1.2	52	50	53	69	2	.232	.333	1	0	C-151
1970	140	458	101	16	4	7	1.5	46	49	51	63	1	.221	.319	2	2	C-139
1971	106	317	74	13	4	1	0.3	18	23	26	38	1	.233	.309	7	2	C-104
1972	108	332	89	16	2	5	1.5	33	40	50	39	2	.268	.373	6	0	C-105
1973	79	250	61	10	2	5	2.0	24	27	19	23	1	.244	.360	7	1	C-76
1974	50	117	26	7	1	1	0.9	8	10	11	12	1	.222	.325	17	5	C-32
14 yrs.	1470	4577	1106	202	32	81	1.8	430	524	465	635	15	.242	.353	104	29	C-1392
1 yr.	85	230	55	9	1	3	1.3	14	29	16	20	1	.239	.326	26	7	C-54

WORLD SERIES

	G	AB	H	2B	3B	HR	HR %	R	RBI	BB	SO	SB	BA	SA	Pinch Hit AB	Pinch Hit H	G by POS
1961 CIN N	3	11	4	2	0	0	0.0	1	2	0	0	0	.364	.545	0	0	C-3
1968 STL N	1	1	0	0	0	0	0.0	0	0	0	1	0	.000	.000	1	0	
2 yrs.	4	12	4	2	0	0	0.0	1	2	0	1	0	.333	.500	1	0	C-3

Red Ehret

EHRET, PHILIP SYDNEY BR TR 6' 175 lbs.
B. Aug. 31, 1868, Louisville, Ky. D. July 28, 1940, Cincinnati, Ohio

	G	AB	H	2B	3B	HR	HR %	R	RBI	BB	SO	SB	BA	SA	Pinch Hit AB	Pinch Hit H	G by POS
1888 KC AA	17	63	12	4	0	0	0.0	4	4	1		1	.190	.254	0	0	OF-10, P-7, 2B-1, 1B-1
1889 LOU AA	67	258	65	6	6	1	0.4	27	31	4	23	4	.252	.333	0	0	P-45, OF-22, SS-1, 3B-1, 2B-1
1890	43	146	31	2	1	0	0.0	11		1		1	.212	.240	0	0	P-43
1891	26	91	22	2	1	0	0.0	9	9	5	15	3	.242	.286	0	0	P-26
1892 PIT N	40	132	34	2	0	0	0.0	12	19	7	22	1	.258	.273	1	0	P-39
1893	40	136	24	3	0	1	0.7	16	17	10	18	1	.176	.221	0	0	P-39
1894	46	135	23	4	1	0	0.0	6	11	8	22	0	.170	.215	0	0	P-46
1895 STL N	37	96	21	2	1	1	1.0	13	9	6	12	0	.219	.292	0	0	P-37
1896 CIN N	34	102	20	2	0	1	1.0	10	20	10		2	.196	.245	0	0	P-34, 1B-1
1897	34	66	13	2	0	0	0.0	6	6	4		2	.197	.227	0	0	P-34
1898 LOU N	13	40	9	3	1	0	0.0	3	4	1		0	.225	.350	1	0	P-12
11 yrs.	397	1265	274	32	11	4	0.3	117	130	57	124	15	.217	.269	2	0	P-362, OF-32, 2B-2, 1B-2, SS-1, 3B-1
1 yr.	37	96	21	2	1	1	1.0	13	9	6	12	0	.219	.292	0	0	P-37

Harry Elliott

ELLIOTT, HARRY LEWIS BR TR 5'10" 175 lbs.
B. Dec. 30, 1925, San Francisco, Calif.

	G	AB	H	2B	3B	HR	HR %	R	RBI	BB	SO	SB	BA	SA	Pinch Hit AB	Pinch Hit H	G by POS
1953 STL N	24	59	15	6	1	1	1.7	6	6	3	8	0	.254	.441	6	0	OF-17
1955	68	117	30	4	0	1	0.9	9	12	11	9	0	.256	.316	38	7	OF-28
2 yrs.	92	176	45	10	1	2	1.1	15	18	14	17	0	.256	.358	44	7	OF-45
2 yrs.	92	176	45	10	1	2	1.1	15	18	14	17	0	.256	.358	44	7	OF-45

Rube Ellis

ELLIS, GEORGE WILLIAM BL TL
B. Nov. 17, 1885, Los Angeles, Calif. D. Mar. 13, 1938, Rivera, Calif.

	G	AB	H	2B	3B	HR	HR %	R	RBI	BB	SO	SB	BA	SA	Pinch Hit AB	Pinch Hit H	G by POS
1909 STL N	149	575	154	10	9	3	0.5	76	46	54		16	.268	.332	4	1	OF-145
1910	142	550	142	18	8	4	0.7	87	54	62	70	25	.258	.342	0	0	OF-141
1911	155	555	139	20	10	3	0.5	69	66	66	64	9	.250	.339	6	1	OF-148
1912	109	305	82	18	2	4	1.3	47	33	34	36	6	.269	.380	27	8	OF-76
4 yrs.	555	1985	517	66	29	14	0.7	279	199	216	170	56	.260	.344	37	10	OF-510
4 yrs.	555	1985	517	66	29	14	0.7	279	199	216	170	56	.260	.344	37	10	OF-510

Bones Ely

ELY, FREDERICK WILLIAM BR TR 6'1" 155 lbs.
B. June 7, 1863, Girard, Pa. D. Jan. 10, 1952, Imola, Calif.

	G	AB	H	2B	3B	HR	HR %	R	RBI	BB	SO	SB	BA	SA	Pinch Hit AB	Pinch Hit H	G by POS
1884 BUF N	1	4	0	0	0	0	0.0			0	2		.000	.000	0	0	OF-1, P-1
1886 LOU AA	10	32	5	0	0	0	0.0	5		2			.156	.156	0	0	P-6, OF-5
1890 SYR AA	119	496	130	16	6	0	0.0	72		31		44	.262	.319	0	0	OF-78, SS-36, 1B-4, 2B-2, 3B-1, P-1
1891 BKN N	31	111	17	0	1	0	0.0	9	11	7	9	4	.153	.171	0	0	SS-28, 3B-2, 2B-1
1892 BAL N	1	3	0	0	0	0	0.0	0	0	0	1	0	.000	.000	0	0	P-1
1893 STL N	44	178	45	1	6	0	0.0	25	16	17	13	2	.253	.326	0	0	SS-44
1894	127	510	156	20	12	12	2.4	85	89	30	34	23	.306	.463	0	0	SS-126, 2B-1, P-1
1895	117	467	121	16	2	1	0.2	68	46	19	17	28	.259	.308	0	0	SS-117
1896 PIT N	128	537	153	15	9	3	0.6	85	77	33	33	18	.285	.363	0	0	SS-128
1897	133	516	146	20	8	2	0.4	63	74	25		10	.283	.364	0	0	SS-133
1898	148	519	110	14	5	2	0.4	49	44	24		6	.212	.270	0	0	SS-148
1899	138	522	145	18	6	3	0.6	66	72	22		8	.278	.352	0	0	SS-132, 2B-6
1900	130	475	116	6	6	0	0.0	60	51	17		6	.244	.282	0	0	SS-130
1901 2 teams	PIT	N	(65G – .208)		PHI	A	(45G – .216)										
" Total	110	411	87	12	5	0	0.0	29	44	9		11	.212	.265	1	0	SS-109, 3B-1
1902 WAS A	105	381	100	11	2	1	0.3	40	62	21		3	.262	.310	0	0	SS-105
15 yrs.	1342	5162	1331	149	68	24	0.5	656	585	257	109	163	.258	.327	1	0	SS-1236, OF-84, 2B-10, P-10, 3B-4, 1B-4
3 yrs.	288	1155	322	37	20	13	1.1	178	151	66	64	53	.279	.379	1	0	SS-287, 2B-1, P-1

Bill Endicott

ENDICOTT, WILLIAM FRANKLIN BL TL 5'11½" 175 lbs.
B. Sept. 4, 1918, Acorn, Mo.

	G	AB	H	2B	3B	HR	HR %	R	RBI	BB	SO	SB	BA	SA	Pinch Hit AB	Pinch Hit H	G by POS
1946 STL N	20	20	4	3	0	0	0.0	2	3	4	4	0	.200	.350	14	3	OF-2

Del Ennis

ENNIS, DELMER BR TR 6' 195 lbs.
B. June 8, 1925, Philadelphia, Pa.

	G	AB	H	2B	3B	HR	HR %	R	RBI	BB	SO	SB	BA	SA	Pinch Hit AB	Pinch Hit H	G by POS
1946 PHI N	141	540	169	30	6	17	3.1	70	73	39	65	5	.313	.485	3	0	OF-138
1947	139	541	149	25	6	12	2.2	71	81	37	51	9	.275	.410	4	1	OF-135

	G	AB	H	2B	3B	HR	HR %	R	RBI	BB	SO	SB	BA	SA	Pinch Hit AB	Pinch Hit H	G by POS

Del Ennis continued

1948	152	589	171	40	4	30	5.1	86	95	47	58	2	.290	.525	2	1	OF-151
1949	154	610	184	39	11	25	4.1	92	110	59	61	2	.302	.525	0	0	OF-154
1950	153	595	185	34	8	31	5.2	92	126	56	59	2	.311	.551	4	0	OF-149
1951	144	532	142	20	5	15	2.8	76	73	68	42	4	.267	.408	8	2	OF-144
1952	151	592	171	30	10	20	3.4	90	107	47	65	6	.289	.475	2	0	OF-149
1953	152	578	165	22	3	29	5.0	79	125	57	53	1	.285	.484	2	0	OF-150
1954	145	556	145	23	2	25	4.5	73	119	50	60	2	.261	.444	1	0	OF-142, 1B-1
1955	146	564	167	24	7	29	5.1	82	120	46	46	4	.296	.518	1	0	OF-145
1956	153	630	164	23	3	26	4.1	80	95	33	62	7	.260	.430	0	0	OF-153
1957 STL N	136	490	140	24	3	24	4.9	61	105	37	50	1	.286	.494	8	3	OF-127
1958	106	329	86	18	1	3	0.9	22	47	15	35	0	.261	.350	22	2	OF-84
1959 2 teams	CIN	N	(5G –	.333)		CHI	A	(26G –	.219)								
" Total	31	108	25	6	0	2	1.9	11	8	6	12	0	.231	.343	3	1	OF-28
14 yrs.	1903	7254	2063	358	69	288	4.0	985	1284	597	719	45	.284	.472	60	10	OF-1849, 1B-1
2 yrs.	242	819	226	42	4	27	3.3	83	152	52	85	1	.276	.436	30	5	OF-211

WORLD SERIES

1950 PHI N	4	14	2	1	0	0	0.0	1	0	0	1	0	.143	.214	0	0	OF-4

Charlie Enwright
ENWRIGHT, CHARLES MICHAEL BL TR
B. Oct. 6, 1887, Sacramento, Calif. D. Jan. 19, 1917, Sacramento, Calif.

1909 STL N	3	7	1	0	0	0	0.0	1	1	2		0	.143	.143	1	0	SS-2

Hal Epps
EPPS, HAROLD FRANKLIN BL TL 6' 175 lbs.
B. Mar. 26, 1914, Athens, Ga.

1938 STL N	17	50	15	0	0	1	2.0	8	3	2	4	2	.300	.360	7	0	OF-10
1940	11	15	3	0	0	0	0.0	6	1	0	3	0	.200	.200	2	0	OF-3
1943 STL A	8	35	10	4	0	0	0.0	2	1	3	4	1	.286	.400	0	0	OF-8
1944 2 teams	STL	A	(22G –	.177)		PHI	A	(67G –	.262)								
" Total	89	291	71	9	9	0	0.0	42	16	32	32	2	.244	.337	10	3	OF-78
4 yrs.	125	391	99	13	9	1	0.3	58	21	37	43	5	.253	.340	19	3	OF-99
2 yrs.	28	65	18	0	0	1	1.5	14	4	2	7	2	.277	.323	9	0	OF-13

Chuck Essegian
ESSEGIAN, CHARLES ABRAHAM BR TR 5'11" 200 lbs.
B. Aug. 9, 1931, Boston, Mass.

1958 PHI N	39	114	28	5	2	5	4.4	15	16	12	34	0	.246	.456	9	2	OF-30
1959 2 teams	STL	N	(17G –	.179)		LA	N	(24G –	.304)								
" Total	41	85	21	8	1	1	1.2	8	10	5	24	0	.247	.400	22	5	OF-19
1960 LA N	52	79	17	3	0	3	3.8	8	11	8	24	0	.215	.367	37	8	OF-18
1961 3 teams	BAL	A	(1G –	.000)	KC	A	(4G –	.333)	CLE	A	(60G –	.289)					
" Total	65	173	50	8	1	12	6.9	26	36	11	35	0	.289	.555	20	7	OF-50
1962 CLE A	106	336	92	12	0	21	6.3	59	50	42	68	0	.274	.497	14	2	OF-90
1963 KC A	101	231	52	9	0	5	2.2	23	27	19	48	0	.225	.329	40	9	OF-53
6 yrs.	404	1018	260	45	4	47	4.6	139	150	97	233	0	.255	.446	142	33	OF-260
1 yr.	17	39	7	2	1	0	0.0	2	5	1	13	0	.179	.282	9	1	OF-9

WORLD SERIES

1959 LA N	4	3	2	0	0	2	66.7	2	2	1	1	0	.667	2.667	4	2	

Steve Evans
EVANS, LOUIS RICHARD BL TL
B. Feb. 17, 1885, Cleveland, Ohio D. Dec. 28, 1943, Cleveland, Ohio

1908 NY N	2	2	1	0	0	0	0.0	0	0	0		0	.500	.500	1	0	OF-1
1909 STL N	143	498	129	17	6	2	0.4	67	56	66		14	.259	.329	0	0	OF-141, 1B-2
1910	151	506	122	21	8	2	0.4	73	73	78	63	10	.241	.326	0	0	OF-141, 1B-10
1911	154	547	161	24	13	5	0.9	74	71	46	52	13	.294	.413	3	1	OF-150
1912	135	491	139	23	9	6	1.2	59	72	36	51	11	.283	.403	1	0	OF-134
1913	97	245	61	15	6	1	0.4	18	31	20	28	5	.249	.371	20	4	OF-74, 1B-1
1914 BKN F	145	514	179	41	15	12	2.3	93	96	50		18	.348	.556	7	1	OF-112, 1B-27
1915 2 teams	BKN	F	(63G –	.296)	BAL	F	(88G –	.315)									
" Total	151	556	171	34	10	4	0.7	94	67	63		15	.308	.426	1	0	OF-149, 1B-5
8 yrs.	978	3359	963	175	67	32	1.0	478	466	359	194	86	.287	.407	33	6	OF-902, 1B-45
5 yrs.	680	2287	612	100	42	16	0.7	291	303	246	194	53	.268	.369	24	5	OF-640, 1B-13

Reuben Ewing
EWING, REUBEN BR TR 5'4½" 150 lbs.
Born Reuben Cohen.
B. Nov. 30, 1899, Odessa, Russia D. Oct. 5, 1970, W. Hartford, Conn.

1921 STL N	3	1	0	0	0	0	0.0	0		0	1	0	.000	.000	1	0	SS-1

Fred Fagin
FAGIN, FREDERICK H.
B. Cincinnati, Ohio Deceased.

1895 STL N	1	3	1	0	0	0	0.0	0		2	0	0	.333	.333	0	0	C-1

Ron Fairly
FAIRLY, RONALD RAY BL TL 5'10" 175 lbs.
B. July 12, 1938, Macon, Ga.

1958 LA N	15	53	15	1	0	2	3.8	6	8	6	7	0	.283	.415	0	0	OF-15
1959	118	244	58	12	1	4	1.6	27	23	31	29	0	.238	.344	31	7	OF-88
1960	14	37	4	0	3	1	2.7	6	3	7	12	0	.108	.351	1	0	OF-13
1961	111	245	79	15	2	10	4.1	42	48	48	22	0	.322	.522	20	6	OF-71, 1B-23
1962	147	460	128	15	7	14	3.0	80	71	75	59	1	.278	.433	7	0	1B-120, OF-48
1963	152	490	133	21	0	12	2.4	62	77	58	69	5	.271	.388	5	2	1B-119, OF-45
1964	150	454	116	19	5	10	2.2	62	74	65	59	4	.256	.385	9	2	1B-141
1965	158	555	152	28	1	9	1.6	73	70	76	72	2	.274	.377	3	0	OF-148, 1B-13

	G	AB	H	2B	3B	HR	HR %	R	RBI	BB	SO	SB	BA	SA	Pinch Hit AB	Pinch Hit H	G by POS

Ron Fairly *continued*

	G	AB	H	2B	3B	HR	HR%	R	RBI	BB	SO	SB	BA	SA	AB	H	G by POS
1966	117	351	101	20	0	14	4.0	53	61	52	38	3	.288	.464	6	2	OF-98, 1B-25
1967	153	486	107	19	0	10	2.1	45	55	54	51	1	.220	.321	9	1	OF-97, 1B-68
1968	141	441	103	15	1	4	0.9	32	43	41	61	0	.234	.299	12	4	OF-105, 1B-36
1969 2 teams	LA	N	(30G –	.219)		MON	N	(70G –	.289)								
" Total	100	317	87	16	6	12	3.8	38	47	37	28	1	.274	.476	10	3	1B-64, OF-31
1970 MON N	119	385	111	19	0	15	3.9	54	61	72	64	10	.288	.455	7	2	1B-118, OF-4
1971	146	447	115	23	0	13	2.9	58	71	81	65	1	.257	.396	17	5	1B-135, OF-10
1972	140	446	124	15	1	17	3.8	51	68	46	45	3	.278	.430	13	4	OF-70, 1B-68
1973	142	413	123	13	1	17	4.1	70	49	86	33	2	.298	.458	25	5	OF-121, 1B-5
1974	101	282	69	9	1	12	4.3	35	43	57	28	2	.245	.411	15	1	1B-67, OF-20
1975 STL N	107	229	69	13	2	7	3.1	32	37	45	22	0	.301	.467	35	12	1B-56, OF-20
1976 2 teams	STL	N	(73G –	.264)		OAK	A	(15G –	.239)								
" Total	88	156	40	5	0	3	1.9	22	31	32	24	0	.256	.346	47	11	1B-42
1977 TOR A	132	458	128	24	2	19	4.1	60	64	58	58	0	.279	.465	4	2	1B-40, OF-33
1978 CAL A	91	235	51	5	0	10	4.3	23	40	25	31	0	.217	.366	13	1	1B-78
21 yrs.	2442	7184	1913	307	33	215	3.0	931	1044	1052	877	35	.266	.408	289	68	1B-1218, OF-1037
2 yrs.	180	339	98	17	2	7	2.1	45	58	68	34	0	.289	.413	81	22	1B-83, OF-20

WORLD SERIES

	G	AB	H	2B	3B	HR	HR%	R	RBI	BB	SO	SB	BA	SA	AB	H	G by POS
1959 LA N	6	3	0	0	0	0	0.0	0	0	0	1	0	.000	.000	2	0	OF-4
1963	4	1	0	0	0	0	0.0	0	0	3	0	0	.000	.000	0	0	OF-4
1965	7	29	11	3	0	2	6.9	7	6	0	1	0	.379	.690	0	0	OF-7
1966	3	7	1	0	0	0	0.0	0	0	2	4	0	.143	.143	1	0	OF-2
4 yrs.	20	40	12	3	0	2	5.0	7	6	5	6	0	.300	.525	3	0	OF-17

George Fallon

FALLON, GEORGE DECATUR (Flash)
B. July 8, 1916, Jersey City, N. J.   BR TR 5'9"   155 lbs.

	G	AB	H	2B	3B	HR	HR%	R	RBI	BB	SO	SB	BA	SA	AB	H	G by POS
1937 BKN N	4	8	2	1	0	0	0.0	0	0	1	0	0	.250	.375	0	0	2B-4
1943 STL N	36	78	18	1	0	0	0.0	6	5	2	9	0	.231	.244	0	0	2B-36
1944	69	141	28	6	0	1	0.7	16	9	16	11	1	.199	.262	0	0	2B-38, SS-24, 3B-6
1945	24	55	13	2	1	0	0.0	4	7	6	6	1	.236	.309	0	0	SS-20, 2B-4
4 yrs.	133	282	61	10	1	1	0.4	26	21	25	26	2	.216	.270	0	0	2B-82, SS-44, 3B-6
3 yrs.	129	274	59	9	1	1	0.4	26	21	24	26	2	.215	.266	0	0	2B-78, SS-44, 3B-6

WORLD SERIES

	G	AB	H	2B	3B	HR	HR%	R	RBI	BB	SO	SB	BA	SA	AB	H	G by POS
1944 STL N	2	2	0	0	0	0	0.0	0	0	0	1	0	.000	.000	0	0	2B-2

Doc Farrell

FARRELL, EDWARD STEPHEN   BR TR 5'8"   160 lbs.
B. Dec. 26, 1901, Johnson City, N. Y.   D. Dec. 20, 1966, Livingston, N. J.

	G	AB	H	2B	3B	HR	HR%	R	RBI	BB	SO	SB	BA	SA	AB	H	G by POS
1925 NY N	27	56	12	1	0	0	0.0	6	4	4	6	0	.214	.232	3	0	SS-13, 3B-7, 2B-1
1926	67	171	49	10	1	2	1.2	19	23	12	17	4	.287	.392	8	2	SS-53, 2B-3
1927 2 teams	NY	N	(42G –	.387)		BOS	N	(110G –	.292)								
" Total	152	566	179	23	3	4	0.7	57	92	26	32	4	.316	.389	4	2	SS-93, 2B-40, 3B-20
1928 BOS N	134	483	104	14	2	3	0.6	36	43	26	26	3	.215	.271	1	0	SS-132, 2B-1
1929 2 teams	BOS	N	(5G –	.125)		NY	N	(63G –	.213)								
" Total	68	186	39	6	0	0	0.0	18	18	9	18	2	.210	.242	8	1	3B-28, 2B-26, SS-5
1930 2 teams	STL	N	(23G –	.213)		CHI	N	(46G –	.292)								
" Total	69	174	46	7	1	1	0.6	24	22	13	7	1	.264	.333	2	0	SS-53, 2B-7, 1B-1
1932 NY A	26	63	11	1	1	0	0.0	4	4	2	8	0	.175	.222	0	0	2B-16, SS-5, 1B-2, 3B-1
1933	44	93	25	0	0	0	0.0	16	6	16	6	0	.269	.269	0	0	SS-22, 2B-20
1935 BOS A	4	7	2	1	0	0	0.0	1	1	1	0	0	.286	.429	0	0	2B-4
9 yrs.	591	1799	467	63	8	10	0.6	181	213	109	120	14	.260	.320	26	5	SS-376, 2B-118, 3B-56, 1B-3
1 yr.	23	61	13	1	1	0	0.0	3	6	4	2	1	.213	.262	1	0	SS-15, 2B-6, 1B-1

John Farrell

FARRELL, JOHN STEPHEN   TR
B. Dec. 4, 1876, Covington, Ky.   D. May 14, 1921, Kansas City, Mo.

	G	AB	H	2B	3B	HR	HR%	R	RBI	BB	SO	SB	BA	SA	AB	H	G by POS
1901 WAS A	135	555	151	32	11	3	0.5	100	63	52		25	.272	.386	0	0	2B-72, OF-62, 3B-1
1902 STL N	138	565	141	13	5	0	0.0	68	25	43		9	.250	.290	0	0	2B-118, SS-21
1903	130	519	141	25	8	1	0.2	83	32	48		17	.272	.356	0	0	2B-118, OF-12
1904	131	509	130	23	3	0	0.0	72	20	46		16	.255	.312	1	0	2B-130
1905	7	24	4	0	1	0	0.0	6	1	4		1	.167	.250	0	0	2B-7
5 yrs.	541	2172	567	93	28	4	0.2	329	141	193		68	.261	.335	1	0	2B-445, OF-74, SS-21, 3B-1
4 yrs.	406	1617	416	61	17	1	0.1	229	78	141		43	.257	.318	1	0	2B-373, SS-21, OF-12

Bobby Fenwick

FENWICK, ROBERT RICHARD (Bloop)   BR TR 5'9"   165 lbs.
B. Dec. 10, 1946, Okinawa

	G	AB	H	2B	3B	HR	HR%	R	RBI	BB	SO	SB	BA	SA	AB	H	G by POS
1972 HOU N	36	50	9	3	0	0	0.0	7	4	3	13	0	.180	.240	5	0	2B-17, SS-4, 3B-2
1973 STL N	5	6	1	0	0	0	0.0	0	1	0	2	0	.167	.167	2	0	2B-3
2 yrs.	41	56	10	3	0	0	0.0	7	5	3	15	0	.179	.232	7	0	2B-20, SS-4, 3B-2
1 yr.	5	6	1	0	0	0	0.0	0	1	0	2	0	.167	.167	2	0	2B-3

Joe Ferguson

FERGUSON, JOE VANCE   BR TR 6'2"   200 lbs.
B. Sept. 19, 1946, San Francisco, Calif.

	G	AB	H	2B	3B	HR	HR%	R	RBI	BB	SO	SB	BA	SA	AB	H	G by POS
1970 LA N	5	4	1	0	0	0	0.0	1	2	0	2	0	.250	.250	0	0	C-3
1971	36	102	22	3	0	2	2.0	13	7	12	15	1	.216	.304	2	1	C-35
1972	8	24	7	3	0	1	4.2	2	5	2	4	0	.292	.542	0	0	C-7, OF-2
1973	136	487	128	26	0	25	5.1	84	88	87	81	1	.263	.470	1	1	C-122, OF-20
1974	111	349	88	14	1	16	4.6	54	57	75	73	2	.252	.436	6	0	C-82, OF-32
1975	66	202	42	1	1	5	2.5	15	15	35	47	2	.208	.302	8	4	C-35, OF-34
1976 2 teams	LA	N	(54G –	.222)		STL	N	(71G –	.201)								
" Total	125	374	79	15	4	10	2.7	46	39	57	81	6	.211	.353	14	2	C-65, OF-53
1977 HOU N	132	421	108	21	3	16	3.8	59	61	85	79	6	.257	.435	12	2	C-122, 1B-1
1978 2 teams	HOU	N	(51G –	.207)		LA	N	(67G –	.237)								
" Total	118	348	78	16	0	14	4.0	40	50	71	71	6	.224	.391	5	1	C-113, OF-3

	G	AB	H	2B	3B	HR	HR %	R	RBI	BB	SO	SB	BA	SA	Pinch Hit AB	Pinch Hit H	G by POS

Joe Ferguson continued

	G	AB	H	2B	3B	HR	HR%	R	RBI	BB	SO	SB	BA	SA	AB	H	G by POS
1979 LA N	122	363	95	14	0	20	5.5	54	69	70	68	1	.262	.466	9	1	C-67, OF-52
1980	77	172	41	3	2	9	5.2	20	29	38	46	2	.238	.436	14	2	C-66, OF-1
1981 2 teams		LA	N	(17G –	.143)		CAL	A	(12G –	.233)							
" Total	29	44	9	2	0	1	2.3	7	6	11	13	0	.205	.318	13	0	C-8, OF-5
1982 CAL A	36	84	19	2	0	3	3.6	10	8	12	19	0	.226	.357	0	0	C-32, OF-2
13 yrs.	1001	2974	717	121	11	122	4.1	404	443	557	599	22	.241	.412	84	14	C-757, OF-204, 1B-1
1 yr.	71	189	38	8	4	4	2.1	22	21	32	40	4	.201	.349	12	2	C-48, OF-14

LEAGUE CHAMPIONSHIP SERIES

	G	AB	H	2B	3B	HR	HR%	R	RBI	BB	SO	SB	BA	SA	AB	H	G by POS
1974 LA N	4	13	3	0	0	0	0.0	3	2	5	1	0	.231	.231	0	0	OF-3
1978	2	2	0	0	0	0	0.0	0	0	0	1	0	.000	.000	2	0	
2 yrs.	6	15	3	0	0	0	0.0	3	2	5	2	0	.200	.200	2	0	OF-3

WORLD SERIES

	G	AB	H	2B	3B	HR	HR%	R	RBI	BB	SO	SB	BA	SA	AB	H	G by POS
1974 LA N	5	16	2	0	0	1	6.3	2	2	4	6	1	.125	.313	0	0	C-2
1978	2	4	2	2	0	0	0.0	1	0	0	1	0	.500	1.000	0	0	C-2
2 yrs.	7	20	4	2	0	1	5.0	3	2	4	7	1	.200	.450	0	0	C-4

Neil Fiala

FIALA, NEIL STEPHEN
B. Aug. 24, 1956, St. Louis, Mo.   BL TR 6'1" 185 lbs.

	G	AB	H	2B	3B	HR	HR%	R	RBI	BB	SO	SB	BA	SA	AB	H	G by POS
1981 2 teams		STL	N	(3G –	.000)		CIN	N	(2G –	.500)							
" Total	5	5	1	0	0	0	0.0	1	1	0	2	0	.200	.200	5	1	

Mike Fiore

FIORE, MICHAEL GARRY JOSEPH (Lefty)
B. Oct. 11, 1944, Brooklyn, N.Y.   BL TL 6' 175 lbs.

	G	AB	H	2B	3B	HR	HR%	R	RBI	BB	SO	SB	BA	SA	AB	H	G by POS
1968 BAL A	6	17	1	0	0	0	0.0	2	0	4	4	0	.059	.059	0	0	1B-5, OF-1
1969 KC A	107	339	93	14	1	12	3.5	53	35	84	63	4	.274	.428	5	4	1B-91, OF-13
1970 2 teams		KC	A	(25G –	.181)		BOS	A	(41G –	.140)							
" Total	66	122	20	2	0	0	0.0	11	8	21	28	1	.164	.180	26	5	1B-37, OF-2
1971 BOS A	51	62	11	2	0	1	1.6	9	6	12	14	0	.177	.258	33	8	1B-12
1972 2 teams		STL	N	(17G –	.100)		SD	N	(7G –	.000)							
" Total	24	16	1	0	0	0	0.0	0	1	3	6	0	.063	.063	16	1	1B-6, OF-1
5 yrs.	254	556	126	18	1	13	2.3	75	50	124	115	5	.227	.333	80	18	1B-151, OF-17
1 yr.	17	10	1	0	0	0	0.0	0	1	2	3	0	.100	.100	10	1	1B-6, OF-1

Sam Fisburn

FISBURN, SAMUEL
B. May 18, 1893, Haverhill, Mass.   D. Apr. 11, 1965, Bethlehem, Pa.   BR TR 5'9" 157 lbs.

	G	AB	H	2B	3B	HR	HR%	R	RBI	BB	SO	SB	BA	SA	AB	H	G by POS
1919 STL N	9	6	2	1	0	0	0.0	0	0	2	0	0	.333	.500	1	1	2B-1, 1B-1

Bob Fisher

FISHER, ROBERT TECUMSEH
Brother of Newt Fisher.
B. Nov. 3, 1887, Nashville, Tenn.   D. Aug. 4, 1963, Jacksonville, Fla.   BR TR 5'9½" 170 lbs.

	G	AB	H	2B	3B	HR	HR%	R	RBI	BB	SO	SB	BA	SA	AB	H	G by POS
1912 BKN N	82	257	60	10	3	0	0.0	27	26	14	32	7	.233	.296	4	0	SS-74, 3B-1, 2B-1
1913	132	474	124	11	10	4	0.8	42	54	10	43	16	.262	.352	11	2	SS-131
1914 CHI N	15	50	15	2	2	0	0.0	5	5	3	4	2	.300	.420	0	0	SS-15
1915	147	568	163	22	5	5	0.9	70	53	30	51	9	.287	.370	2	0	SS-147
1916 CIN N	61	136	37	4	3	0	0.0	9	11	8	14	7	.272	.346	25	6	SS-29, 2B-6, OF-1
1918 STL N	63	246	78	11	3	2	0.8	36	20	15	11	7	.317	.411	0	0	2B-63
1919	3	11	3	1	0	0	0.0	0	1	0	2	0	.273	.364	0	0	2B-3
7 yrs.	503	1742	480	61	26	11	0.6	189	170	80	157	48	.276	.359	42	8	SS-396, 2B-73, OF-1, 3B-1
2 yrs.	66	257	81	12	3	2	0.8	36	21	15	13	7	.315	.409	0	0	2B-66

Showboat Fisher

FISHER, GEORGE ALOYS
B. Jan. 16, 1899, Jennings, Iowa   BL TR 5'10" 170 lbs.

	G	AB	H	2B	3B	HR	HR%	R	RBI	BB	SO	SB	BA	SA	AB	H	G by POS
1923 WAS A	13	23	6	2	0	0	0.0	4	2	4	3	0	.261	.348	4	1	OF-5
1924	15	41	9	1	0	0	0.0	7	6	6	6	2	.220	.244	4	2	OF-11
1930 STL N	92	254	95	18	6	8	3.1	49	61	25	21	4	.374	.587	20	8	OF-67
1932 STL A	18	22	4	0	0	0	0.0	2	2	2	5	0	.182	.182	11	2	OF-5
4 yrs.	138	340	114	21	6	8	2.4	62	71	37	35	6	.335	.503	39	13	OF-88
1 yr.	92	254	95	18	6	8	3.1	49	61	25	21	4	.374	.587	20	8	OF-67

WORLD SERIES

	G	AB	H	2B	3B	HR	HR%	R	RBI	BB	SO	SB	BA	SA	AB	H	G by POS
1930 STL N	2	2	1	1	0	0	0.0	0	0	0	1	0	.500	1.000	2	1	

Max Flack

FLACK, MAX JOHN
B. Feb. 5, 1890, Belleville, Ill.   D. July 31, 1975, Belleville, Ill.   BL TL 5'7" 148 lbs.

	G	AB	H	2B	3B	HR	HR%	R	RBI	BB	SO	SB	BA	SA	AB	H	G by POS
1914 CHI F	134	502	124	15	3	2	0.4	66	39	51		37		.247	.301	1	0	OF-133
1915	141	523	164	20	14	3	0.6	88	45	40		37		.314	.423	3	2	OF-138
1916 CHI N	141	465	120	14	3	3	0.6	65	20	42	43	24	.258	.320	3	0	OF-136
1917	131	447	111	18	7	0	0.0	65	21	51	34	17	.248	.320	10	3	OF-117
1918	123	478	123	17	10	4	0.8	74	41	56	19	17	.257	.360	0	0	OF-121
1919	116	469	138	20	4	6	1.3	71	35	34	13	18	.294	.392	0	0	OF-116
1920	135	520	157	30	6	4	0.8	85	49	52	15	13	.302	.406	2	0	OF-132
1921	133	572	172	31	6	1	0.2	80	37	32	15	17	.301	.400	3	1	OF-130
1922 2 teams		CHI	N	(17G –	.222)		STL	N	(66G –	.292)							
" Total	83	321	90	13	1	2	0.6	55	27	33	15	5	.280	.346	1	0	OF-83
1923 STL N	128	505	147	16	9	3	0.6	82	28	41	16	7	.291	.376	6	3	OF-121
1924	67	209	55	11	3	2	1.0	31	21	21	5	3	.263	.373	13	3	OF-52
1925	79	241	60	7	8	0	0.0	23	28	21	9	5	.249	.344	19	3	OF-59
12 yrs.	1411	5252	1461	212	72	35	0.7	783	391	474	184	200	.278	.366	61	15	OF-1338
4 yrs.	340	1222	340	46	21	7	0.6	182	98	114	41	18	.278	.367	38	9	OF-298

WORLD SERIES

	G	AB	H	2B	3B	HR	HR%	R	RBI	BB	SO	SB	BA	SA	AB	H	G by POS
1918 CHI N	6	19	5	0	0	0	0.0	2	1	4	1	1	.263	.263	0	0	OF-6

	G	AB	H	2B	3B	HR	HR %	R	RBI	BB	SO	SB	BA	SA	Pinch Hit AB	Pinch Hit H	G by POS

Curt Flood

FLOOD, CURTIS CHARLES
B. Jan. 18, 1938, Houston, Tex. BR TR 5'9" 165 lbs.

	G	AB	H	2B	3B	HR	HR %	R	RBI	BB	SO	SB	BA	SA	PH AB	PH H	G by POS
1956 CIN N	5	1	0	0	0	0	0.0	0	0	0	1	0	.000	.000	1	0	
1957	3	3	1	0	0	1	33.3	2	1	0	0	0	.333	1.333	1	0	3B-2, 2B-1
1958 STL N	121	422	110	17	2	10	2.4	50	41	31	56	2	.261	.382	0	0	OF-120, 3B-1
1959	121	208	53	7	3	7	3.4	24	26	16	35	2	.255	.418	10	5	OF-106, 2B-1
1960	140	396	94	20	1	8	2.0	37	38	35	54	0	.237	.354	2	0	OF-134, 3B-1
1961	132	335	108	15	5	2	0.6	53	21	35	33	6	.322	.415	12	4	OF-119
1962	151	635	188	30	5	12	1.9	99	70	42	57	8	.296	.416	0	0	OF-151
1963	158	662	200	34	9	5	0.8	112	63	42	57	17	.302	.403	1	0	OF-158
1964	162	679	211	25	3	5	0.7	97	46	43	53	8	.311	.378	1	0	OF-162
1965	156	617	191	30	3	11	1.8	90	83	51	50	9	.310	.421	5	0	OF-151
1966	160	626	167	21	5	10	1.6	64	78	26	50	14	.267	.364	2	0	OF-159
1967	134	514	172	24	1	5	1.0	68	50	37	46	2	.335	.414	8	4	OF-126
1968	150	618	186	17	4	5	0.8	71	60	33	58	11	.301	.366	2	0	OF-149
1969	153	606	173	31	3	4	0.7	80	57	48	57	9	.285	.366	2	1	OF-152
1971 WAS A	13	35	7	0	0	0	0.0	4	2	5	2	0	.200	.200	1	0	OF-10
15 yrs.	1759	6357	1861	271	44	85	1.3	851	636	444	609	88	.293	.389	46	14	OF-1697, 3B-4, 2B-2
12 yrs.	1738	6318	1853	271	44	84	1.3	845	633	439	606	88	.293	.390	43	14	OF-1687, 3B-2, 2B-1
	5th	6th	7th	10th					8th						5th		

WORLD SERIES

	G	AB	H	2B	3B	HR	HR %	R	RBI	BB	SO	SB	BA	SA	PH AB	PH H	G by POS
1964 STL N	7	30	6	0	1	0	0.0	5	3	3	1	0	.200	.267	0	0	OF-7
1967	7	28	5	1	0	0	0.0	2	3	3	3	0	.179	.214	0	0	OF-7
1968	7	28	8	1	0	0	0.0	4	2	2	2	3	.286	.321	0	0	OF-7
3 yrs.	21	86	19	2	1	0	0.0	11	8	8	6	3	.221	.267	0	0	OF-21

Tim Flood

FLOOD, TIMOTHY A.
B. Mar. 13, 1877, Montgomery City, Mo. D. June 15, 1929, St. Louis, Mo. BR TR

	G	AB	H	2B	3B	HR	HR %	R	RBI	BB	SO	SB	BA	SA	PH AB	PH H	G by POS
1899 STL N	10	31	9	0	0	0	0.0	0	3	4		1	.290	.290	0	0	2B-10
1902 BKN N	132	476	104	11	5	2	0.4	43	50	23		8	.218	.275	0	0	2B-132, OF-1
1903	89	309	77	15	2	0	0.0	27	32	15		14	.249	.311	2	0	2B-84, SS-2, OF-1
3 yrs.	231	816	190	26	7	2	0.2	70	85	42		23	.233	.289	2	0	2B-226, OF-2, SS-2
1 yr.	10	31	9	0	0	0	0.0	0	3	4		1	.290	.290	0	0	2B-10

Jake Flowers

FLOWERS, D'ARCY RAYMOND
B. Mar. 16, 1902, Cambridge, Md. D. Dec. 27, 1962, Clearwater, Fla. BR TR 5'11½" 170 lbs.

	G	AB	H	2B	3B	HR	HR %	R	RBI	BB	SO	SB	BA	SA	PH AB	PH H	G by POS
1923 STL N	13	32	3	1	0	0	0.0	0	2	2	7	1	.094	.125	1	0	SS-7, 3B-2, 2B-2
1926	40	74	20	1	0	3	4.1	13	9	5	9	1	.270	.405	23	6	2B-11, 1B-3, SS-1
1927 BKN N	67	231	54	5	5	2	0.9	26	20	21	25	3	.234	.325	1	0	SS-65, 2B-1
1928	103	339	93	11	6	2	0.6	51	44	47	30	10	.274	.360	3	1	2B-94, SS-6
1929	46	130	26	6	0	1	0.8	16	16	22	6	9	.200	.269	5	2	2B-39
1930	89	253	81	18	3	2	0.8	37	50	21	18	5	.320	.439	16	6	2B-65, OF-1
1931 2 teams		BKN N	(22G – .226)			STL N	(45G – .248)										
" Total	67	168	41	11	1	2	1.2	22	20	16	10	8	.244	.357	12	3	2B-26, SS-23, 3B-1
1932 STL N	67	247	63	11	1	2	0.8	35	18	31	18	7	.255	.332	4	2	SS-54, SS-7, 2B-2
1933 BKN N	78	210	49	11	2	2	1.0	28	22	24	15	13	.233	.333	7	2	SS-36, 2B-19, 3B-8, OF-1
1934 CIN N	13	9	3	0	0	0	0.0	1	0	1	1	1	.333	.333	9	3	
10 yrs.	583	1693	433	75	18	16	0.9	229	201	190	139	58	.256	.350	81	25	2B-259, SS-145, 3B-65, 1B-3, OF-2
4 yrs.	165	490	120	24	2	7	1.4	67	48	47	40	16	.245	.345	30	8	3B-57, SS-37, 2B-35, 1B-3

WORLD SERIES

	G	AB	H	2B	3B	HR	HR %	R	RBI	BB	SO	SB	BA	SA	PH AB	PH H	G by POS
1926 STL N	3	3	0	0	0	0	0.0	0	0	0	1	0	.000	.000	3	0	
1931	5	11	1	1	0	0	0.0	1	0	1	0	0	.091	.182	1	0	3B-4
2 yrs.	8	14	1	1	0	0	0.0	1	0	1	1	0	.071	.143	4	0	3B-4

Hod Ford

FORD, HORACE HILLS
B. July 23, 1897, New Haven, Conn. D. Jan. 29, 1977, Winchester, Mass. BR TR 5'10" 165 lbs.

	G	AB	H	2B	3B	HR	HR %	R	RBI	BB	SO	SB	BA	SA	PH AB	PH H	G by POS
1919 BOS N	10	28	6	0	1	0	0.0	4	3	2	6	0	.214	.286	0	0	SS-8, 3B-2
1920	88	257	62	12	5	1	0.4	16	30	18	25	3	.241	.339	6	0	2B-59, SS-18, 1B-4
1921	152	555	155	29	5	2	0.4	50	61	36	49	2	.279	.360	0	0	2B-119, SS-33
1922	143	515	140	23	9	2	0.4	58	60	30	36	2	.272	.363	0	0	SS-115, 2B-28
1923	111	380	103	16	7	2	0.5	27	50	31	30	1	.271	.366	0	0	2B-95, SS-19
1924 PHI N	145	530	144	27	5	3	0.6	58	53	27	40	1	.272	.358	0	0	2B-145
1925 BKN N	66	216	59	11	0	1	0.5	32	15	26	15	0	.273	.338	0	0	SS-66
1926 CIN N	57	197	55	6	1	0	0.0	14	18	14	12	1	.279	.320	0	0	SS-57
1927	115	409	112	16	2	1	0.2	45	46	33	34	0	.274	.330	0	0	SS-104, 2B-12
1928	149	506	122	17	4	0	0.0	49	54	47	31	1	.241	.291	0	0	SS-149
1929	148	529	146	14	6	3	0.6	68	50	41	25	8	.276	.342	0	0	SS-108, 2B-42
1930	132	424	98	16	7	1	0.2	36	34	24	28	2	.231	.309	1	0	SS-74, 2B-66
1931	84	175	40	8	1	0	0.0	18	13	13	13	0	.229	.286	7	1	SS-73, 2B-3, 3B-1
1932 2 teams		STL N	(1G – .000)			BOS N	(40G – .274)										
" Total	41	97	26	5	2	0	0.0	9	6	9	0	0	.268	.361	2	0	2B-20, SS-17, 3B-2
1933 BOS N	5	15	1	0	0	0	0.0	0	1	3	1	0	.067	.067	0	0	SS-5
15 yrs.	1446	4833	1269	200	55	16	0.3	484	494	351	354	21	.263	.337	16	1	SS-846, 2B-589, 3B-5, 1B-4
1 yr.	1	2	0	0	0	0	0.0	0	0	0	0	0	.000	.000	0	0	SS-1

Jack Fournier

FOURNIER, JOHN FRANK (Jacques)
B. Sept. 28, 1892, Au Sable, Mich. D. Sept. 5, 1973, Tacoma, Wash. BL TR 6' 195 lbs.

	G	AB	H	2B	3B	HR	HR %	R	RBI	BB	SO	SB	BA	SA	PH AB	PH H	G by POS
1912 CHI A	35	73	14	5	2	0	0.0	5	2	4		1	.192	.315	18	5	1B-17
1913	68	172	40	8	5	1	0.6	20	23	21	23	9	.233	.355	13	1	1B-29, OF-23
1914	109	379	118	14	9	6	1.6	44	44	31	44	10	.311	.443	6	0	1B-97, OF-6
1915	126	422	136	20	18	5	1.2	86	77	64	37	21	.322	.491	4	2	1B-65, OF-57
1916	105	313	75	13	9	3	1.0	36	44	36	40	19	.240	.367	14	2	1B-85, OF-1

	G	AB	H	2B	3B	HR	HR %	R	RBI	BB	SO	SB	BA	SA	Pinch Hit AB	Pinch Hit H	G by POS

Jack Fournier continued

	G	AB	H	2B	3B	HR	HR %	R	RBI	BB	SO	SB	BA	SA	AB	H	G by POS
1917	1	1	0	0	0	0	0.0	0	0	0	1	0	.000	.000	1	0	
1918 NY A	27	100	35	6	1	0	0.0	9	12	7	7	7	.350	.430	0	0	1B-27
1920 STL N	141	530	162	33	14	3	0.6	77	61	42	42	26	.306	.438	3	2	1B-138
1921	149	574	197	27	9	16	2.8	103	86	56	48	20	.343	.505	0	0	1B-149
1922	128	404	119	23	9	10	2.5	64	61	40	21	6	.295	.470	12	5	1B-109, P-1
1923 BKN N	133	515	181	30	13	22	4.3	91	102	43	28	11	.351	.588	0	0	1B-133
1924	154	563	188	25	4	27	4.8	93	116	83	46	7	.334	.536	1	0	1B-153
1925	145	545	191	21	16	22	4.0	99	130	86	39	4	.350	.569	0	0	1B-145
1926	87	243	69	9	2	11	4.5	39	48	30	16	0	.284	.473	18	4	1B-64
1927 BOS N	122	374	106	18	2	10	2.7	55	53	44	16	4	.283	.422	19	8	1B-102
15 yrs.	1530	5208	1631	252	113	136	2.6	821	859	587	408	145	.313	.483	109	29	1B-1313, OF-87, P-1
3 yrs.	418	1508	478	83	32	29	1.9	244	208	138	111	52	.317	.472	15	7	1B-396, P-1
												8th					

Tito Francona

FRANCONA, JOHN PATSY
Father of Terry Francona.
B. Nov. 4, 1933, Aliquippa, Pa.   BL TL 5'11" 190 lbs.

	G	AB	H	2B	3B	HR	HR %	R	RBI	BB	SO	SB	BA	SA	AB	H	G by POS
1956 BAL A	139	445	115	16	4	9	2.0	62	57	51	60	11	.258	.373	18	4	OF-122, 1B-21
1957	97	279	65	8	3	7	2.5	35	38	29	48	7	.233	.358	23	3	OF-73, 1B-4
1958 2 teams		CHI	A	(41G –	.258)		DET	A	(45G –	.246)							
" Total	86	197	50	8	2	1	0.5	21	20	29	40	2	.254	.330	29	11	OF-72
1959 CLE A	122	399	145	17	2	20	5.0	68	79	35	42	2	.363	.566	20	5	OF-64, 1B-35
1960	147	544	159	36	2	17	3.1	84	79	67	67	4	.292	.460	3	0	OF-138, 1B-13
1961	155	592	178	30	8	16	2.7	87	85	56	52	2	.301	.459	7	1	OF-138, 1B-14
1962	158	621	169	28	5	14	2.3	82	70	47	74	3	.272	.401	0	0	1B-158
1963	142	500	114	29	0	10	2.0	57	41	47	77	9	.228	.346	13	4	OF-122, 1B-11
1964	111	270	67	13	2	8	3.0	35	24	44	46	1	.248	.400	29	6	OF-69, 1B-17
1965 STL N	81	174	45	6	2	5	2.9	15	19	17	30	0	.259	.402	35	9	OF-34, 1B-13
1966	83	156	33	4	1	4	2.6	14	17	7	27	0	.212	.327	41	7	1B-30, OF-9
1967 2 teams		PHI	N	(27G –	.205)		ATL	N	(82G –	.248)							
" Total	109	327	78	6	1	6	1.8	35	28	27	44	1	.239	.318	27	3	1B-80, OF-7
1968 ATL N	122	346	99	13	1	2	0.6	32	47	51	45	3	.286	.347	24	5	OF-65, 1B-33
1969 2 teams		ATL	N	(51G –	.295)		OAK	A	(32G –	.341)							
" Total	83	173	55	7	1	5	2.9	17	42	25	21	0	.318	.457	32	8	1B-26, OF-16
1970 2 teams		OAK	A	(32G –	.242)		MIL	A	(52G –	.231)							
" Total	84	98	23	3	0	1	1.0	6	10	12	21	1	.235	.296	64	15	1B-19, OF-1
15 yrs.	1719	5121	1395	224	34	125	2.4	650	656	544	694	46	.272	.403	365	81	OF-930, 1B-474
2 yrs.	164	330	78	10	3	9	2.7	29	36	24	57	0	.236	.367	76	16	OF-43, 1B-43

Charlie Frank

FRANK, CHARLES
B. May 30, 1870, Mobile, Ala.   D. May 24, 1922, Memphis, Tenn.

	G	AB	H	2B	3B	HR	HR %	R	RBI	BB	SO	SB	BA	SA	AB	H	G by POS
1893 STL N	40	164	55	6	3	1	0.6	29	17	18	8	8	.335	.427	0	0	OF-40
1894	80	319	89	12	7	4	1.3	52	42	44	13	14	.279	.398	0	0	OF-77, 1B-3, P-2
2 yrs.	120	483	144	18	10	5	1.0	81	59	62	21	22	.298	.408	0	0	OF-117, 1B-3, P-2
2 yrs.	120	483	144	18	10	5	1.0	81	59	62	21	22	.298	.408	0	0	OF-117, 1B-3, P-2

Herman Franks

FRANKS, HERMAN LOUIS
B. Jan. 4, 1914, Price, Utah
Manager 1965-68, 1977-79.   BL TR 5'10½" 187 lbs.

	G	AB	H	2B	3B	HR	HR %	R	RBI	BB	SO	SB	BA	SA	AB	H	G by POS
1939 STL N	17	17	1	0	0	0	0.0	1	3	3	3	0	.059	.059	2	0	C-13
1940 BKN N	65	131	24	4	0	1	0.8	11	14	20	6	2	.183	.237	19	3	C-43
1941	59	139	28	7	0	1	0.7	10	11	14	13	0	.201	.273	2	1	C-54, OF-1
1947 PHI A	8	15	3	0	1	0	0.0	2	1	4	4	0	.200	.333	2	0	C-4
1948	40	98	22	7	1	1	1.0	10	14	16	11	0	.224	.347	9	1	C-27
1949 NY N	1	3	2	0	0	0	0.0	1	0	0	0	0	.667	.667	0	0	C-1
6 yrs.	190	403	80	18	2	3	0.7	35	43	57	37	2	.199	.275	34	5	C-142, OF-1
1 yr.	17	17	1	0	0	0	0.0	1	3	3	3	0	.059	.059	2	0	C-13
WORLD SERIES																	
1941 BKN N	1	1	0	0	0	0	0.0	0	0	0	0	0	.000	.000	0	0	C-1

Joe Frazier

FRAZIER, JOSEPH FILMORE (Cobra Joe)
B. Oct. 6, 1922, Liberty, N. C.
Manager 1976-77.   BL TR 6' 180 lbs.

	G	AB	H	2B	3B	HR	HR %	R	RBI	BB	SO	SB	BA	SA	AB	H	G by POS
1947 CLE A	9	14	1	1	0	0	0.0	1	0	1	1	0	.071	.143	2	0	OF-5
1954 STL N	81	88	26	5	2	3	3.4	8	18	13	17	0	.295	.500	62	20	OF-11, 1B-1
1955	58	70	14	1	0	4	5.7	12	9	6	12	0	.200	.386	45	4	OF-14
1956 3 teams		STL	N	(14G –	.211)		CIN	N	(10G –	.235)		BAL	A	(45G –	.257)		
" Total	69	110	27	8	0	3	2.7	10	18	15	16	0	.245	.400	40	9	OF-26
4 yrs.	217	282	68	15	2	10	3.5	31	45	35	46	0	.241	.415	149	33	OF-56, 1B-1
3 yrs.	153	177	44	8	2	8	4.5	21	31	22	32	0	.249	.452	114	24	OF-28, 1B-1
												10th					

Roger Freed

FREED, ROGER VERNON
B. June 2, 1946, Los Angeles, Calif.   BR TR 6' 190 lbs.

	G	AB	H	2B	3B	HR	HR %	R	RBI	BB	SO	SB	BA	SA	AB	H	G by POS
1970 BAL A	4	13	2	0	0	0	0.0	1	3	4	0	.154	.154	0	0	1B-3, OF-1
1971 PHI N	118	348	77	12	1	6	1.7	23	37	44	86	0	.221	.313	14	2	OF-106, C-1
1972	73	129	29	4	0	6	4.7	10	18	23	39	0	.225	.395	27	4	OF-46
1974 CIN N	6	6	2	0	0	1	16.7	1	3	1	1	0	.333	.833	6	2	1B-1
1976 MON N	8	15	3	1	0	0	0.0	0	1	0	3	0	.200	.267	5	1	1B-3, OF-1
1977 STL N	49	83	33	2	1	5	6.0	10	21	11	9	0	.398	.627	23	9	1B-18, OF-6
1978	52	92	22	6	0	2	2.2	3	20	8	17	1	.239	.370	29	11	1B-15, OF-6
1979	34	31	8	2	0	2	6.5	2	8	5	7	0	.258	.516	27	6	1B-1
8 yrs.	344	717	176	27	2	22	3.1	49	109	95	166	1	.245	.381	131	35	OF-166, 1B-41, C-1
3 yrs.	135	206	63	10	1	9	4.4	15	49	24	33	1	.306	.495	79	26	1B-34, OF-12

	G	AB	H	2B	3B	HR	HR %	R	RBI	BB	SO	SB	BA	SA	Pinch Hit AB	Pinch Hit H	G by POS

Gene Freese

FREESE, EUGENE LEWIS (Augie)   BR TR 5'11" 175 lbs.
Brother of George Freese.
B. Jan. 8, 1934, Wheeling, W. Va.

	G	AB	H	2B	3B	HR	HR %	R	RBI	BB	SO	SB	BA	SA	PH AB	PH H	G by POS
1955 PIT N	134	455	115	21	8	14	3.1	69	44	34	57	5	.253	.426	12	3	3B-65, 2B-57
1956	65	207	43	9	0	3	1.4	17	14	16	45	2	.208	.295	10	0	3B-47, 2B-26
1957	114	346	98	18	2	6	1.7	44	31	17	42	9	.283	.399	30	9	3B-74, OF-10, 2B-10
1958 2 teams	PIT N (17G – .167)				STL N (62G – .257)												
" Total	79	209	52	11	1	7	3.3	29	18	11	34	1	.249	.411	29	6	SS-28, 2B-14, 3B-4
1959 PHI N	132	400	107	14	5	23	5.8	60	70	43	61	8	.268	.500	20	7	3B-109, 2B-6
1960 CHI A	127	455	124	32	6	17	3.7	60	79	29	65	10	.273	.481	6	1	3B-122
1961 CIN N	152	575	159	27	2	26	4.5	78	87	27	78	8	.277	.466	1	0	3B-151, 2B-1
1962	18	42	6	1	0	0	0.0	2	1	6	8	0	.143	.167	5	0	3B-10
1963	66	217	53	9	1	6	2.8	20	26	17	42	4	.244	.378	3	0	3B-62, OF-1
1964 PIT N	99	289	65	13	2	9	3.1	33	40	19	45	1	.225	.377	30	5	3B-72
1965 2 teams	PIT N (43G – .263)				CHI A (17G – .281)												
" Total	60	112	30	4	1	1	0.9	8	12	11	27	0	.268	.348	31	12	3B-27
1966 2 teams	CHI A (48G – .208)				HOU N (21G – .091)												
" Total	69	139	25	2	0	3	2.2	9	10	13	31	3	.180	.259	29	2	3B-38, 2B-3, OF-1
12 yrs.	1115	3446	877	161	28	115	3.3	429	432	243	535	51	.254	.418	206	45	3B-781, 2B-117, SS-28, OF-12
1 yr.	62	191	49	11	1	6	3.1	28	16	10	32	1	.257	.419	14	3	SS-28, 2B-14, 3B-3

WORLD SERIES

	G	AB	H	2B	3B	HR	HR %	R	RBI	BB	SO	SB	BA	SA	PH AB	PH H	G by POS
1961 CIN N	5	16	1	1	0	0	0.0	0	0	3	4	0	.063	.125	0	0	3B-5

Howard Freigau

FREIGAU, HOWARD EARL (Ty)   BR TR 5'10½" 160 lbs.
B. Aug. 1, 1902, Dayton, Ohio.   D. July 18, 1932, Chattanooga, Tenn.

	G	AB	H	2B	3B	HR	HR %	R	RBI	BB	SO	SB	BA	SA	PH AB	PH H	G by POS
1922 STL N	3	1	0	0	0	0	0.0	0	0	0	0	0	.000	.000	0	0	SS-2, 3B-1
1923	113	358	94	18	1	1	0.3	30	35	25	36	5	.263	.327	0	0	SS-87, 2B-16, 1B-9, OF-1, 3B-1
1924	98	376	101	17	6	2	0.5	35	39	19	24	10	.269	.362	0	0	3B-98, SS-2
1925 2 teams	STL N (9G – .154)				CHI N (117G – .307)												
" Total	126	502	150	22	10	8	1.6	79	71	32	32	10	.299	.430	0	0	3B-96, SS-24, 1B-7, 2B-1
1926 CHI N	140	508	137	27	7	3	0.6	51	51	43	42	6	.270	.368	4	2	3B-135, SS-2, OF-1
1927	30	86	20	5	0	0	0.0	12	10	9	10	0	.233	.291	0	0	3B-30
1928 2 teams	BKN N (17G – .206)				BOS N (52G – .257)												
" Total	69	143	35	10	1	1	0.7	17	20	10	17	1	.245	.350	26	8	SS-15, 2B-11, 3B-10
7 yrs.	579	1974	537	99	25	15	0.8	224	226	138	161	32	.272	.370	30	10	3B-371, SS-132, 2B-28, 1B-16, OF-2
4 yrs.	223	761	199	35	7	3	0.4	67	74	46	61	15	.261	.338	0	0	3B-100, SS-98, 2B-17, 1B-9, OF-1

Frankie Frisch

FRISCH, FRANK FRANCIS (The Fordham Flash)   BB TR 5'11" 165 lbs.
B. Sept. 9, 1898, Queens, N. Y.   D. Mar. 12, 1973, Wilmington, Del.
Manager 1933-38, 1940-46, 1949-51.
Hall of Fame 1947.

	G	AB	H	2B	3B	HR	HR %	R	RBI	BB	SO	SB	BA	SA	PH AB	PH H	G by POS
1919 NY N	54	190	43	3	2	2	1.1	21	24	4	14	15	.226	.295	3	0	2B-29, 3B-28, SS-1
1920	110	440	123	10	10	4	0.9	57	77	20	18	34	.280	.375	1	0	3B-110, SS-2
1921	153	618	211	31	17	8	1.3	121	100	42	28	49	.341	.485	0	0	3B-93, 2B-61
1922	132	514	168	16	13	5	1.0	101	51	47	13	31	.327	.438	0	0	2B-85, 3B-53, SS-1
1923	151	641	**223**	32	10	12	1.9	116	111	46	12	29	.348	.485	0	0	2B-135, 3B-17
1924	145	603	198	33	15	7	1.2	**121**	69	56	24	22	.328	.468	0	0	2B-143, SS-10, 3B-2
1925	120	502	166	26	6	11	2.2	89	48	32	14	21	.331	.472	0	0	3B-46, 2B-42, SS-39
1926	135	545	171	29	4	5	0.9	75	44	33	16	23	.314	.409	1	1	2B-127, 3B-7
1927 STL N	153	617	208	31	11	10	1.6	112	78	43	10	**48**	.337	.472	0	0	2B-153, SS-1
1928	141	547	164	29	9	10	1.8	107	86	64	17	29	.300	.441	2	1	2B-139
1929	138	527	176	40	12	5	0.9	93	74	53	12	24	.334	.484	3	2	2B-121, 3B-13, SS-1
1930	133	540	187	46	9	10	1.9	121	114	55	16	15	.346	.520	0	0	2B-123, 3B-10
1931	131	518	161	24	4	4	0.8	96	82	45	13	**28**	.311	.396	2	0	2B-129
1932	115	486	142	26	2	3	0.6	59	60	25	13	18	.292	.372	0	0	2B-75, 3B-37, SS-4
1933	147	585	177	32	6	4	0.7	74	66	48	16	18	.303	.398	4	3	2B-132, SS-15
1934	140	550	168	30	6	3	0.5	74	75	45	10	11	.305	.398	2	0	2B-115, 3B-25
1935	103	354	104	16	2	1	0.3	52	55	33	14	2	.294	.359	9	1	2B-88, 3B-5
1936	93	303	83	10	0	1	0.3	40	26	36	10	2	.274	.317	8	3	2B-61, 3B-22, SS-1
1937	17	32	7	2	0	0	0.0	3	4	1	0	0	.219	.281	12	2	2B-17
19 yrs.	2311	9112	2880	466	138	105	1.2	1532	1244	728	272	419	.316	.432	47	12	2B-1775, 3B-468, SS-75
			9th														
11 yrs.	1311	5059	1577	286	61	51	1.0	831	720	448	133	195	.312	.423	42	11	2B-1153, 3B-112, SS-22
								9th	9th			3rd	10th				

WORLD SERIES

	G	AB	H	2B	3B	HR	HR %	R	RBI	BB	SO	SB	BA	SA	PH AB	PH H	G by POS
1921 NY N	8	30	9	0	1	0	0.0	5	1	4	3	3	.300	.367	0	0	3B-8
1922	5	17	8	1	0	0	0.0	3	2	1	0	1	.471	.529	0	0	2B-5
1923	6	25	10	0	1	0	0.0	2	1	0	0	0	.400	.480	0	0	2B-6
1924	7	30	10	4	1	0	0.0	1	0	4	1	1	.333	.533	0	0	2B-7
1928 STL N	4	13	3	0	0	0	0.0	1	1	2	2	2	.231	.231	0	0	2B-4
1930	6	24	5	2	0	0	0.0	0	0	0	0	1	.208	.292	0	0	2B-6
1931	7	27	7	2	0	0	0.0	2	1	2	1	2	.259	.333	0	0	2B-7
1934	7	31	6	1	0	0	0.0	2	4	1	0	1	.194	.226	0	0	2B-7
8 yrs.	50	197	58	10	3	0	0.0	16	10	12	9	9	.294	.376	0	0	2B-42, 3B-8
		8th	4th	3rd	1st	4th						6th					

	G	AB	H	2B	3B	HR	HR %	R	RBI	BB	SO	SB	BA	SA	Pinch Hit AB	Pinch Hit H	G by POS

Chick Fullis

FULLIS, CHARLES PHILIP   BR TR 5'9"   170 lbs.
B. Feb. 27, 1904, Girardville, Pa.   D. Mar. 28, 1946, Ashland, Pa.

	G	AB	H	2B	3B	HR	HR %	R	RBI	BB	SO	SB	BA	SA	AB	H	G by POS
1928 NY N	11	1	0	0	0	0	0.0	5	0	1	1	0	.000	.000	1	0	
1929	86	274	79	11	1	7	2.6	67	29	30	26	7	.288	.412	2	0	OF-78
1930	13	6	0	0	0	0	0.0	2	0	0	1	1	.000	.000	5	0	OF-2
1931	89	302	99	15	2	3	1.0	61	28	23	13	13	.328	.421	6	3	OF-68, 2B-9
1932	96	235	70	14	3	1	0.4	35	21	11	12	1	.298	.396	32	7	OF-55, 2B-1
1933 PHI N	151	647	200	31	6	1	0.2	91	45	36	34	18	.309	.380	0	0	OF-151, 3B-1
1934 2 teams		PHI N	(28G – .225)			STL N	(69G – .261)										
" Total	97	301	75	15	1	0	0.0	29	38	24	15	6	.249	.306	15	6	OF-83
1936 STL N	47	89	25	6	1	0	0.0	15	6	7	11	0	.281	.371	12	2	OF-26
8 yrs.	590	1855	548	92	14	12	0.6	305	167	132	113	46	.295	.380	73	18	OF-463, 2B-10, 3B-1
2 yrs.	116	288	77	15	2	0	0.0	36	32	21	22	4	.267	.333	26	7	OF-82

WORLD SERIES

	G	AB	H	2B	3B	HR	HR %	R	RBI	BB	SO	SB	BA	SA	AB	H	G by POS
1934 STL N	3	5	2	0	0	0	0.0	0	0	0	0	0	.400	.400	0	0	OF-3

Les Fusselman

FUSSELMAN, LESTER LeROY   BR TR 6'1"   195 lbs.
B. Mar. 7, 1921, Pryor, Okla.   D. May 21, 1970, Cleveland, Ohio

	G	AB	H	2B	3B	HR	HR %	R	RBI	BB	SO	SB	BA	SA	AB	H	G by POS
1952 STL N	32	63	10	3	0	1	1.6	5	3	0	9	0	.159	.254	1	0	C-32
1953	11	8	2	1	0	0	0.0	1	0	0	0	0	.250	.375	0	0	C-11
2 yrs.	43	71	12	4	0	1	1.4	6	3	0	9	0	.169	.268	1	0	C-43
2 yrs.	43	71	12	4	0	1	1.4	6	3	0	9	0	.169	.268	1	0	C-43

Phil Gagliano

GAGLIANO, PHILIP JOSEPH   BR TR 6'1"   180 lbs.
Brother of Ralph Gagliano.
B. Dec. 27, 1941, Memphis, Tenn.

	G	AB	H	2B	3B	HR	HR %	R	RBI	BB	SO	SB	BA	SA	AB	H	G by POS
1963 STL N	10	5	2	0	0	0	0.0	1	1	1	1	0	.400	.400	2	0	2B-3, 3B-1
1964	40	58	15	4	0	1	1.7	5	9	3	10	0	.259	.379	19	3	2B-12, OF-2, 3B-1, 1B-1
1965	122	363	87	14	2	8	2.2	46	53	40	45	2	.240	.355	26	5	2B-57, OF-25, 3B-19
1966	90	213	54	8	2	2	0.9	23	15	24	29	2	.254	.338	36	4	3B-41, 1B-8, OF-5, 2B-1
1967	73	217	48	7	0	2	0.9	20	21	19	26	0	.221	.281	17	0	2B-27, 3B-25, 1B-4, SS-2
1968	53	105	24	4	2	0	0.0	13	13	7	12	0	.229	.305	17	4	2B-17, 3B-10, OF-5
1969	62	128	29	2	0	1	0.8	7	10	14	12	0	.227	.266	21	2	2B-20, 3B-9, 1B-9, OF-2
1970 2 teams		STL N	(18G – .188)			CHI N	(26G – .150)										
" Total	44	72	12	0	0	0	0.0	5	7	6	8	0	.167	.167	16	3	2B-18, 3B-7, 1B-4
1971 BOS A	47	68	22	5	0	0	0.0	11	13	11	5	0	.324	.397	22	8	OF-11, 2B-7, 3B-4
1972	52	82	21	4	1	0	0.0	9	10	10	13	1	.256	.329	26	9	OF-12, 3B-5, 2B-4, 1B-2
1973 CIN N	63	69	20	2	0	0	0.0	8	7	13	16	0	.290	.319	41	15	2B-4, 3B-2, OF-1, 1B-1
1974	46	31	2	0	0	0	0.0	2	0	15	7	0	.065	.065	29	2	2B-2, 3B-1, 1B-1
12 yrs.	702	1411	336	50	7	14	1.0	150	159	163	184	5	.238	.313	272	55	2B-172, 3B-125, OF-63, 1B-30, SS-2
8 yrs.	468	1121	265	39	6	14	1.2	115	124	109	138	4	.236	.319	146 4th	20	2B-139, 3B-112, OF-39, 1B-25, SS-2

LEAGUE CHAMPIONSHIP SERIES

	G	AB	H	2B	3B	HR	HR %	R	RBI	BB	SO	SB	BA	SA	AB	H	G by POS
1973 CIN N	3	3	0	0	0	0	0.0	0	0	0	2	0	.000	.000	3	0	

WORLD SERIES

	G	AB	H	2B	3B	HR	HR %	R	RBI	BB	SO	SB	BA	SA	AB	H	G by POS
1967 STL N	1	1	0	0	0	0	0.0	0	0	0	0	0	.000	.000	1	0	
1968	3	3	0	0	0	0	0.0	0	0	0	0	0	.000	.000	3	0	
2 yrs.	4	4	0	0	0	0	0.0	0	0	0	0	0	.000	.000	4	0	

Del Gainor

GAINOR, DELOS CHARLES (Sheriff)   BR TR 6'   180 lbs.
B. Nov. 10, 1886, Elkins, W. Va.   D. Jan. 29, 1947, Elkins, W. Va.

	G	AB	H	2B	3B	HR	HR %	R	RBI	BB	SO	SB	BA	SA	AB	H	G by POS
1909 DET A	2	5	1	0	0	0	0.0	0	0	0		0	.200	.200	0	0	1B-2
1911	70	248	75	11	4	2	0.8	32	25	20		10	.302	.403	0	0	1B-69
1912	51	179	43	5	6	0	0.0	28	20	18		14	.240	.335	0	0	1B-50
1913	104	363	97	16	8	2	0.6	47	25	30	45	10	.267	.372	2	1	1B-102
1914 2 teams		DET A	(1G – .000)			BOS A	(38G – .238)										
" Total	39	84	20	9	2	2	2.4	11	13	8	14	2	.238	.464	8	1	1B-19, 2B-11
1915 BOS A	82	200	59	5	8	1	0.5	30	29	21	31	7	.295	.415	14	4	1B-56, OF-6
1916	56	142	36	6	0	3	2.1	14	18	10	24	5	.254	.359	4	0	1B-48, 2B-2
1917	52	172	53	10	2	2	1.2	28	19	15	21	1	.308	.424	1	0	1B-50
1919	47	118	28	6	2	0	0.0	9	13	13	15	5	.237	.322	6	1	1B-21, OF-18
1922 STL N	43	97	26	7	4	2	2.1	19	23	14	6	0	.268	.485	9	1	1B-26, OF-10
10 yrs.	546	1608	438	75	36	14	0.9	218	185	149	156	54	.272	.390	44	8	1B-443, OF-34, 2B-13
1 yr.	43	97	26	7	4	2	2.1	19	23	14	6	0	.268	.485	9	1	1B-26, OF-10

WORLD SERIES

	G	AB	H	2B	3B	HR	HR %	R	RBI	BB	SO	SB	BA	SA	AB	H	G by POS
1915 BOS A	1	3	1	0	0	0	0.0	1	0	0	0	0	.333	.333	1	0	1B-1
1916	1	1	1	0	0	0	0.0	0	1	0	0	0	1.000	1.000	1	1	
2 yrs.	2	4	2	0	0	0	0.0	1	1	0	0	0	.500	.500	2	1	1B-1

Bad News Galloway

GALLOWAY, JAMES CATO   BB TR 6'3"   187 lbs.
B. Sept. 16, 1887, Iredell, Tex.   D. May 3, 1950, Fort Worth, Tex.

	G	AB	H	2B	3B	HR	HR %	R	RBI	BB	SO	SB	BA	SA	AB	H	G by POS
1912 STL N	21	54	10	2	0	0	0.0	4	4	5	8	2	.185	.222	3	0	2B-16, SS-1

Pud Galvin

GALVIN, JAMES FRANCIS (Gentle Jeems, The Little Steam Engine)
                                                                        BR TR 5'8"   190 lbs.
Brother of Lou Galvin.
B. Dec. 25, 1855, St. Louis, Mo.   D. Mar. 7, 1902, Pittsburgh, Pa.
Manager 1885.
Hall of Fame 1965.

	G	AB	H	2B	3B	HR	HR %	R	RBI	BB	SO	SB	BA	SA	AB	H	G by POS
1879 BUF N	67	265	66	11	6	0	0.0	34	27	1	56		.249	.336	0	0	P-66, SS-1
1880	66	241	51	9	2	0	0.0	25	12	5	57		.212	.266	0	0	P-58, OF-19
1881	62	236	50	12	4	0	0.0	19	21	3	70		.212	.297	0	0	P-56, OF-14, SS-1
1882	54	206	44	7	4	0	0.0	21		2	49		.214	.286	0	0	P-52, OF-6

	G	AB	H	2B	3B	HR	HR %	R	RBI	BB	SO	SB	BA	SA	Pinch Hit AB	Pinch Hit H	G by POS

Pud Galvin continued

	G	AB	H	2B	3B	HR	HR %	R	RBI	BB	SO	SB	BA	SA	AB	H	G by POS
1883	80	322	71	11	2	1	0.3	41		3	79		.220	.276	0	0	P-76, OF-8
1884	72	274	49	6	1	0	0.0	34		2	80		.179	.208	0	0	P-72, OF-1
1885 2 teams	BUF	N	(33G –	.189)		PIT	AA	(11G –	.105)								
" Total	44	160	27	4	2	1	0.6	16	10	1	27		.169	.238	0	0	P-44, OF-1
1886 PIT AA	50	194	49	7	2	0	0.0	24		3			.253	.309	0	0	P-50
1887 PIT N	49	193	41	7	3	2	1.0	10	22	2	47	5	.212	.311	0	0	P-49, OF-1
1888	50	175	25	1	1	1	0.6	6	3	1	51	4	.143	.177	0	0	P-50, OF-1
1889	41	150	28	7	2	0	0.0	15	16	3	46	2	.187	.260	0	0	P-41
1890 PIT P	26	97	20	2	1	0	0.0	8	12	6	20	1	.206	.247	0	0	P-26
1891 PIT N	33	109	18	0	0	0	0.0	11	7	3	29	0	.165	.165	0	0	P-33
1892 2 teams	PIT	N	(12G –	.122)		STL	N	(12G –	.051)								
" Total	24	80	7	1	0	0	0.0	6	5	3	19	0	.088	.100	0	0	P-24
14 yrs.	718	2702	546	85	30	5	0.2	270	135	38	630	12	.202	.261	0	0	P-697, OF-51, SS-2
1 yr.	12	39	2	0	0	0	0.0	2	1	1	10	0	.051	.051	0	0	P-12

Bill Gannon

GANNON, WILLIAM G.
B. New Haven, Conn.   D. Apr. 26, 1927, Ft. Worth, Tex.

	G	AB	H	2B	3B	HR	HR %	R	RBI	BB	SO	SB	BA	SA	AB	H	G by POS
1898 STL N	1	3	0	0	0	0	0.0	0	0	0		0	.000	.000	0	0	P-1
1901 CHI N	15	61	9	0	0	0	0.0	2	0	1		5	.148	.148	0	0	OF-15
2 yrs.	16	64	9	0	0	0	0.0	2	0	1		5	.141	.141	0	0	OF-15, P-1
1 yr.	1	3	0	0	0	0	0.0	0	0	0		0	.000	.000	0	0	P-1

Joe Garagiola

GARAGIOLA, JOSEPH HENRY
B. Feb. 12, 1926, St. Louis, Mo.   BL TR 6'   190 lbs.

	G	AB	H	2B	3B	HR	HR %	R	RBI	BB	SO	SB	BA	SA	AB	H	G by POS
1946 STL N	74	211	50	4	1	3	1.4	21	22	23	25	0	.237	.308	4	2	C-70
1947	77	183	47	10	2	5	2.7	20	25	40	14	0	.257	.415	4	1	C-74
1948	24	56	6	1	0	2	3.6	9	7	12	9	0	.107	.232	1	0	C-23
1949	81	241	63	14	0	3	1.2	25	26	31	19	0	.261	.357	2	1	C-80
1950	34	88	28	6	1	2	2.3	8	20	10	7	0	.318	.477	4	0	C-30
1951 2 teams	STL	N	(27G –	.194)		PIT	N	(72G –	.255)								
" Total	99	284	68	11	4	11	3.9	33	44	41	27	4	.239	.423	12	0	C-84
1952 PIT N	118	344	94	15	4	8	2.3	35	54	50	24	0	.273	.410	12	4	C-105
1953 2 teams	PIT	N	(27G –	.233)		CHI	N	(74G –	.272)								
" Total	101	301	79	14	4	3	1.0	30	35	31	34	1	.262	.365	13	3	C-90
1954 2 teams	CHI	N	(63G –	.281)		NY	N	(5G –	.273)								
" Total	68	164	46	7	0	5	3.0	17	22	29	14	0	.280	.415	11	2	C-58
9 yrs.	676	1872	481	82	16	42	2.2	198	255	267	173	5	.257	.385	63	13	C-614
6 yrs.	317	851	208	38	6	17	2.0	92	109	125	81	0	.244	.363	18	4	C-300

WORLD SERIES

	G	AB	H	2B	3B	HR	HR %	R	RBI	BB	SO	SB	BA	SA	AB	H	G by POS
1946 STL N	5	19	6	2	0	0	0.0	2	4	0	3	0	.316	.421	0	0	C-5

Danny Gardella

GARDELLA, DANIEL LEWIS
Brother of Al Gardella.
B. Feb. 26, 1920, New York, N. Y.   BL TL 5'7½"   160 lbs.

	G	AB	H	2B	3B	HR	HR %	R	RBI	BB	SO	SB	BA	SA	AB	H	G by POS
1944 NY N	47	112	28	2	2	6	5.4	20	14	11	13	0	.250	.464	16	4	OF-25
1945	121	430	117	10	1	18	4.2	54	71	46	55	2	.272	.426	11	4	OF-94, 1B-15
1950 STL N	1	1	0	0	0	0	0.0	0	0	0	0	0	.000	.000	1	0	
3 yrs.	169	543	145	12	3	24	4.4	74	85	57	68	2	.267	.433	28	8	OF-119, 1B-15
1 yr.	1	1	0	0	0	0	0.0	0	0	0	0	0	.000	.000	1	0	

Art Garibaldi

GARIBALDI, ARTHUR E.
B. Aug. 21, 1907, San Francisco, Calif.   D. Oct. 20, 1967, Sacramento, Calif.   BR TR 5'8"   165 lbs.

	G	AB	H	2B	3B	HR	HR %	R	RBI	BB	SO	SB	BA	SA	AB	H	G by POS
1936 STL N	71	232	64	12	0	1	0.4	30	20	16	30	3	.276	.341	1	0	3B-46, 2B-24

Debs Garms

GARMS, DEBS
B. June 26, 1908, Bangs, Tex.   BL TR 5'8½"   165 lbs.

	G	AB	H	2B	3B	HR	HR %	R	RBI	BB	SO	SB	BA	SA	AB	H	G by POS
1932 STL A	34	134	38	7	1	1	0.7	20	8	17	7	4	.284	.373	1	0	OF-33
1933	78	189	60	10	2	4	2.1	35	24	30	21	2	.317	.455	23	5	OF-47
1934	91	232	68	14	4	0	0.0	25	31	27	19	0	.293	.388	27	7	OF-56
1935	10	15	4	0	0	0	0.0	1	0	2	2	0	.267	.267	6	1	OF-2
1937 BOS N	125	478	124	15	8	2	0.4	60	37	37	33	2	.259	.337	10	3	OF-81, 3B-36
1938	117	428	135	19	1	0	0.0	62	47	34	22	4	.315	.364	4	1	OF-63, 3B-54, 2B-1
1939	132	513	153	24	9	2	0.4	68	37	39	20	2	.298	.392	2	0	OF-96, 3B-37
1940 PIT N	103	358	127	23	7	5	1.4	76	57	23	6	3	.355	.500	18	5	3B-64, OF-19
1941	83	220	58	9	3	3	1.4	25	42	22	12	0	.264	.373	31	10	3B-29, OF-24
1943 STL N	90	249	64	10	2	0	0.0	26	22	13	8	1	.257	.313	20	6	OF-47, 3B-23, SS-1
1944	73	149	30	3	0	0	0.0	17	5	13	8	0	.201	.221	30	6	OF-23, 3B-21
1945	74	146	49	7	2	0	0.0	23	18	31	3	0	.336	.411	26	10	3B-32, OF-10
12 yrs.	1010	3111	910	141	39	17	0.5	438	328	288	161	18	.293	.379	198	54	OF-501, 3B-296, SS-1, 2B-1
3 yrs.	237	544	143	20	4	0	0.0	66	45	57	19	1	.263	.314	76	22	OF-80, 3B-76, SS-1

WORLD SERIES

	G	AB	H	2B	3B	HR	HR %	R	RBI	BB	SO	SB	BA	SA	AB	H	G by POS
1943 STL N	2	5	0	0	0	0	0.0	0	0	0	0	0	.000	.000	1	0	OF-1
1944	2	2	0	0	0	0	0.0	0	0	0	2	0	.000	.000	2	0	
2 yrs.	4	7	0	0	0	0	0.0	0	0	0	2	0	.000	.000	3	0	OF-1

Wayne Garrett

GARRETT, RONALD WAYNE
Brother of Adrian Garrett.
B. Dec. 3, 1947, Sarasota, Fla.   BL TR 5'11"   175 lbs.

	G	AB	H	2B	3B	HR	HR %	R	RBI	BB	SO	SB	BA	SA	AB	H	G by POS
1969 NY N	124	400	87	11	3	1	0.3	38	39	40	75	4	.218	.268	14	1	3B-72, 2B-47, SS-9
1970	114	366	93	17	4	12	3.3	74	45	81	60	5	.254	.421	5	0	3B-70, 2B-45, SS-1

Wayne Garrett continued

	G	AB	H	2B	3B	HR	HR%	R	RBI	BB	SO	SB	BA	SA	Pinch Hit AB	Pinch Hit H	G by POS
1971	56	202	43	2	0	1	0.5	20	11	28	31	1	.213	.238	2	0	3B-53, 2B-9
1972	111	298	69	13	3	2	0.7	41	29	70	58	3	.232	.315	8	0	3B-82, 2B-22
1973	140	504	129	20	3	16	3.2	76	58	72	74	6	.256	.403	4	4	3B-130, SS-9, 2B-6
1974	151	522	117	14	3	13	2.5	55	53	89	96	4	.224	.337	3	2	3B-144, SS-9
1975	107	274	73	8	3	6	2.2	49	34	50	45	3	.266	.383	12	6	3B-94, SS-3
1976 2 teams NY N (80G – .223) MON N (59G – .243)																	
" Total	139	428	99	12	2	6	1.4	51	37	82	46	9	.231	.311	17	3	3B-66, 2B-64, SS-1
1977 MON N	68	159	43	6	1	2	1.3	17	22	30	18	2	.270	.358	18	1	3B-49, 2B-1
1978 2 teams MON N (49G – .174) STL N (33G – .333)																	
" Total	82	132	33	4	0	2	1.5	17	12	19	26	1	.250	.326	43	9	3B-32
10 yrs.	1092	3285	786	107	22	61	1.9	438	340	561	529	38	.239	.341	126	26	3B-792, 2B-194, SS-32
1 yr.	33	63	21	4	0	1	1.6	11	10	11	16	1	.333	.444	12	4	3B-19
LEAGUE CHAMPIONSHIP SERIES																	
1969 NY N	3	13	5	2	0	1	7.7	3	3	2	2	1	.385	.769	0	0	3B-3
1973	5	23	2	1	0	0	0.0	1	1	0	5	0	.087	.130	0	0	3B-5
2 yrs.	8	36	7	3	0	1	2.8	4	4	2	7	1	.194	.361	0	0	3B-8
WORLD SERIES																	
1969 NY N	2	1	0	0	0	0	0.0	0	0	2	1	0	.000	.000	0	0	3B-2
1973	7	30	5	0	0	2	6.7	4	2	5	11	0	.167	.367	0	0	3B-7
2 yrs.	9	31	5	0	0	2	6.5	4	2	7	12	0	.161	.355	0	0	3B-9

Charley Gelbert

GELBERT, CHARLES MAGNUS   BR TR 5'11" 170 lbs.
B. Jan. 26, 1906, Scranton, Pa.   D. Jan. 13, 1967, Easton, Pa.

	G	AB	H	2B	3B	HR	HR%	R	RBI	BB	SO	SB	BA	SA	Pinch Hit AB	Pinch Hit H	G by POS
1929 STL N	146	512	134	29	8	3	0.6	60	65	51	46	8	.262	.367	0	0	SS-146
1930	139	513	156	39	11	3	0.6	92	72	43	41	6	.304	.441	0	0	SS-139
1931	131	447	129	29	5	1	0.2	61	62	54	31	7	.289	.383	0	0	SS-131
1932	122	455	122	28	9	1	0.2	60	45	39	30	8	.268	.376	0	0	SS-122
1935	62	168	49	7	2	2	1.2	24	21	17	18	0	.292	.393	5	1	3B-37, SS-21, 2B-3
1936	93	280	64	15	2	3	1.1	33	27	25	26	2	.229	.329	2	0	3B-60, SS-28, 2B-8
1937 2 teams CIN N (43G – .193) DET A (20G – .085)																	
" Total	63	161	26	6	0	1	0.6	16	14	19	23	1	.161	.217	6	0	SS-53, 2B-9, 3B-1
1939 WAS A	68	188	48	7	5	3	1.6	36	29	30	11	2	.255	.394	16	2	SS-28, 3B-20, 2B-1
1940 2 teams WAS A (22G – .370) BOS A (30G – .198)																	
" Total	52	145	38	9	1	0	0.0	16	15	12	19	0	.262	.338	4	0	3B-29, SS-13, P-2, 2B-1
9 yrs.	876	2869	766	169	43	17	0.6	398	350	290	245	34	.267	.374	33	3	SS-681, 3B-147, 2B-22, P-2
6 yrs.	693	2375	654	147	37	13	0.5	330	292	229	192	31	.275	.385	7	1	SS-587, 3B-97, 2B-11
WORLD SERIES																	
1930 STL N	6	17	6	0	1	0	0.0	2	2	3	3	0	.353	.471	0	0	SS-6
1931	7	23	6	1	0	0	0.0	0	0	3	4	0	.261	.304	0	0	SS-7
2 yrs.	13	40	12	1	1	0	0.0	5	3		7	0	.300	.375	0	0	SS-13

Frank Genins

GENINS, C. FRANK (Frenchy)   TR
B. Nov. 2, 1866, St. Louis, Mo.   D. Sept. 30, 1922, St. Louis, Mo.

	G	AB	H	2B	3B	HR	HR%	R	RBI	BB	SO	SB	BA	SA	Pinch Hit AB	Pinch Hit H	G by POS
1892 2 teams CIN N (35G – .182) STL N (15G – .196)																	
" Total	50	161	30	5	0	0	0.0	17	11	13	23	10	.186	.217	0	0	SS-31, OF-15, 3B-4
1895 PIT N	73	252	63	8	0	2	0.8	43	24	22	14	19	.250	.306	3	0	OF-29, 3B-16, 2B-16, SS-8, 1B-2
1901 CLE A	26	101	23	5	0	0	0.0	15	9	8		3	.228	.277	0	0	OF-26
3 yrs.	149	514	116	18	0	2	0.4	75	44	43	37	32	.226	.272	3	0	OF-70, SS-39, 3B-20, 2B-16, 1B-2
1 yr.	15	51	10	0	0	0	0.0	5	4	1	11	3	.196	.216	0	0	SS-14, OF-1

Billy Gilbert

GILBERT, WILLIAM OLIVER   BR TR
B. June 21, 1876, Trenton, N. J.   D. Aug. 8, 1927, New York, N. Y.

	G	AB	H	2B	3B	HR	HR%	R	RBI	BB	SO	SB	BA	SA	Pinch Hit AB	Pinch Hit H	G by POS
1901 MIL A	127	492	133	14	7	0	0.0	77	43	31		19	.270	.327	0	0	2B-127
1902 BAL A	129	445	109	12	3	2	0.4	74	38	45		38	.245	.299	0	0	SS-129
1903 NY N	128	413	104	9	0	1	0.2	62	40	41		37	.252	.281	0	0	2B-128
1904	146	478	121	13	3	1	0.2	57	54	46		33	.253	.299	0	0	2B-146
1905	115	376	93	11	3	0	0.0	45	24	41		11	.247	.293	0	0	2B-115
1906	104	307	71	6	1	1	0.3	44	27	42		22	.231	.267	4	1	2B-98
1908 STL N	89	276	59	7	0	0	0.0	12	10	20		6	.214	.239	0	0	2B-89
1909	12	29	5	0	0	0	0.0	1	4	1			.172	.172	0	0	2B-12
8 yrs.	850	2816	695	72	17	5	0.2	375	237	270		167	.247	.290	4	1	2B-715, SS-129
2 yrs.	101	305	64	7	0	0	0.0	16	11	24		7	.210	.233	0	0	2B-101
WORLD SERIES																	
1905 NY N	5	17	4	0	0	0	0.0	1	1	0		2	1	.235	.235	0	0	2B-5

George Gilham

GILHAM, GEORGE LEWIS   BR TR 5'11" 164 lbs.
B. Sept. 8, 1899, Shamokin, Pa.   D. Apr. 25, 1937, Lansdowne, Pa.

	G	AB	H	2B	3B	HR	HR%	R	RBI	BB	SO	SB	BA	SA	Pinch Hit AB	Pinch Hit H	G by POS
1920 STL N	1	3	0	0	0	0	0.0	0	0	0	1	0	.000	.000	0	0	C-1
1921	1	1	0	0	0	0	0.0	0	0	0	0	0	.000	.000	1	0	
2 yrs.	2	4	0	0	0	0	0.0	0	0	0	1	0	.000	.000	1	0	C-1
2 yrs.	2	4	0	0	0	0	0.0	0	0	0	1	0	.000	.000	1	0	C-1

Frank Gilhooley

GILHOOLEY, FRANK PATRICK (Flash)   BL TR 5'8" 155 lbs.
B. June 10, 1892, Toledo, Ohio   D. July 11, 1959, Toledo, Ohio

	G	AB	H	2B	3B	HR	HR%	R	RBI	BB	SO	SB	BA	SA	Pinch Hit AB	Pinch Hit H	G by POS
1911 STL N	1	0	0	0	0	0	–	0	0	0	0	0	—	—	0	0	OF-1
1912	13	49	11	0	0	0	0.0	5	2	3	8	0	.224	.224	1	0	OF-11
1913 NY A	24	85	29	2	1	0	0.0	10	14	4	9	6	.341	.388	0	0	OF-24
1914	1	3	2	0	0	0	0.0	1	0	1	0	0	.667	.667	0	0	OF-1
1915	1	4	0	0	0	0	0.0	0	0	1	0	0	.000	.000	0	0	OF-1

	G	AB	H	2B	3B	HR	HR%	R	RBI	BB	SO	SB	BA	SA	Pinch Hit AB	H	G by POS

Frank Gilhooley continued

	G	AB	H	2B	3B	HR	HR%	R	RBI	BB	SO	SB	BA	SA	PH AB	PH H	G by POS
1916	58	223	62	5	4	0	0.0	40	10	37	17	16	.278	.336	1	1	OF-57
1917	54	165	40	6	1	0	0.0	14	8	30	13	6	.242	.291	2	1	OF-46
1918	112	427	118	13	5	1	0.2	58	23	53	24	7	.276	.337	1	0	OF-111
1919 BOS A	48	112	27	4	0	0	0.0	14	1	12	8	2	.241	.277	10	2	OF-33
9 yrs.	312	1068	289	30	11	1	0.1	141	58	140	80	37	.271	.322	15	4	OF-285
2 yrs.	14	49	11	0	0	0	0.0	5	2	3	8	0	.224	.224	1	0	OF-12

Carden Gillenwater

GILLENWATER, CARDEN EDISON BR TR 6'1" 175 lbs.
B. May 13, 1918, Riceville, Tenn.

	G	AB	H	2B	3B	HR	HR%	R	RBI	BB	SO	SB	BA	SA	PH AB	PH H	G by POS
1940 STL N	7	25	4	1	0	0	0.0	1	5	0	2	0	.160	.200	0	0	OF-7
1943 BKN N	8	17	3	0	0	0	0.0	1	2	2	3	0	.176	.176	3	0	OF-5
1945 BOS N	144	517	149	20	2	7	1.4	74	72	73	70	13	.288	.375	3	1	OF-140
1946	99	224	51	10	1	1	0.4	30	14	39	27	3	.228	.295	14	2	OF-78
1948 WAS A	77	221	54	10	4	3	1.4	23	21	39	36	4	.244	.367	11	0	OF-67
5 yrs.	335	1004	261	41	7	11	1.1	129	114	153	138	20	.260	.348	31	3	OF-297
1 yr.	7	25	4	1	0	0	0.0	1	5	0	2	0	.160	.200	0	0	OF-7

Jack Glasscock

GLASSCOCK, JOHN WESLEY (Pebbly Jack) BR TR 5'8" 160 lbs.
B. July 22, 1859, Wheeling, W. Va. D. Feb. 24, 1947, Wheeling, W. Va.
Manager 1889.

	G	AB	H	2B	3B	HR	HR%	R	RBI	BB	SO	SB	BA	SA	PH AB	PH H	G by POS
1879 CLE N	80	325	68	9	3	0	0.0	31	29	6	24		.209	.255	0	0	2B-66, 3B-14
1880	77	296	72	13	3	0	0.0	37		2	21		.243	.307	0	0	SS-77
1881	85	335	86	9	5	0	0.0	49	33	15	8		.257	.313	0	0	SS-79, 2B-6
1882	84	358	104	27	9	4	1.1	66	46	13	9		.291	.450	0	0	SS-83, 3B-1
1883	96	383	110	19	6	0	0.0	67		13	23		.287	.368	0	0	SS-93, 2B-3
1884 2 teams			CLE N (72G – .249)				CIN U (38G – .419)										
" Total	110	453	142	13	9	3	0.7	93	22	33	16		.313	.402	0	0	SS-105, 2B-5, P-2
1885 STL N	111	446	125	18	3	1	0.2	66	40	29	10		.280	.341	0	0	SS-110, 2B-1
1886	121	486	158	29	7	3	0.6	96	40	38	13		.325	.432	0	0	SS-120, OF-1
1887 IND N	122	483	142	18	7	0	0.0	91	40	41	8	62	.294	.360	0	0	SS-122, P-1
1888	113	442	119	17	3	1	0.2	63	45	14	17	48	.269	.328	0	0	SS-110, 2B-3, P-1
1889	134	582	205	40	3	7	1.2	128	85	31	10	57	.352	.467	0	0	SS-132, 2B-2, P-1
1890 NY N	124	512	172	32	9	1	0.2	91	66	41	8	54	.336	.439	0	0	SS-124
1891	97	369	89	12	6	0	0.0	46	55	36	11	29	.241	.306	0	0	SS-97
1892 STL N	139	566	151	27	5	3	0.5	83	72	44	19	26	.267	.348	0	0	SS-139
1893 2 teams			STL N (48G – .287)				PIT N (66G – .341)										
" Total	114	488	156	15	12	2	0.4	81	100	42	7	36	.320	.412	0	0	SS-114
1894 PIT N	86	332	93	10	7	1	0.3	46	63	31	4	18	.280	.361	1	0	SS-85
1895 2 teams			LOU N (18G – .338)				WAS N (25G – .230)										
" Total	43	174	48	5	1	1	0.6	29	16	10	4	4	.276	.333	0	0	SS-38, 1B-5
17 yrs.	1736	7030	2040	313	98	27	0.4	1163	752	439	212	334	.290	.374	1	0	SS-1628, 2B-86, 3B-15, 1B-5, P-5, OF-1
4 yrs.	419	1693	490	82	16	8	0.5	277	178	136	45	46	.289	.371	0	0	SS-417, OF-1, 2B-1

Tommy Glaviano

GLAVIANO, THOMAS GIATANO (Rabbit) BR TR 5'9" 175 lbs.
B. Oct. 26, 1923, Sacramento, Calif.

	G	AB	H	2B	3B	HR	HR%	R	RBI	BB	SO	SB	BA	SA	PH AB	PH H	G by POS
1949 STL N	87	258	69	16	1	6	2.3	32	36	41	35	0	.267	.407	7	3	3B-73, 2B-7
1950	115	410	117	29	2	11	2.7	92	44	90	74	6	.285	.446	4	0	3B-106, 2B-5, SS-1
1951	54	104	19	4	0	1	1.0	20	4	26	18	3	.183	.250	23	4	OF-35, 2B-9
1952	80	162	39	5	1	3	1.9	30	19	27	26	0	.241	.340	10	2	3B-52, 2B-1
1953 PHI N	53	74	15	1	2	3	4.1	17	5	24	20	2	.203	.392	20	2	3B-14, 2B-12, SS-1
5 yrs.	389	1008	259	55	6	24	2.4	191	108	208	173	11	.257	.395	64	11	3B-245, OF-35, 2B-34, SS-2
4 yrs.	336	934	244	54	4	21	2.2	174	103	184	153	9	.261	.395	44	9	3B-231, OF-35, 2B-22, SS-1

Kid Gleason

GLEASON, WILLIAM J. BL TR 5'7" 158 lbs.
Brother of Harry Gleason.
B. Oct. 26, 1866, Camden, N. J. D. Jan. 2, 1933, Philadelphia, Pa.
Manager 1919-23.

	G	AB	H	2B	3B	HR	HR%	R	RBI	BB	SO	SB	BA	SA	PH AB	PH H	G by POS
1888 PHI N	24	83	17	2	0	0	0.0	4	5	3	16	3	.205	.229	0	0	P-24, OF-1
1889	30	99	25	5	0	0	0.0	11	8	8	12	4	.253	.303	0	0	P-28, OF-3, 2B-2
1890	63	224	47	3	0	0	0.0	22	17	12	21	10	.210	.223	0	0	P-60, 2B-2
1891	65	214	53	5	2	0	0.0	31	17	20	17	6	.248	.290	0	0	P-53, OF-9, SS-4
1892 STL N	66	233	50	4	2	3	1.3	35	25	34	23	7	.215	.288	0	0	P-47, OF-11, 2B-10, 1B-1, C-1
1893	59	199	51	6	4	0	0.0	25	20	19	8	2	.256	.327	2	1	P-48, OF-11, SS-1
1894 2 teams			STL N (9G – .250)				BAL N (26G – .349)										
" Total	35	114	37	5	2	0	0.0	25	18	9	3	1	.325	.404	4	2	P-29, 1B-2
1895 BAL N	112	421	130	14	12	0	0.0	90	74	33	18	19	.309	.399	3	0	2B-85, 3B-12, P-9, OF-4
1896 NY N	133	541	162	17	5	4	0.7	79	89	42	13	46	.299	.372	0	0	2B-130, 3B-3, P-1
1897	131	540	172	16	4	1	0.2	85	106	26		43	.319	.369	0	0	2B-129, SS-3
1898	150	570	126	8	5	0	0.0	78	62	39		21	.221	.253	0	0	2B-144, SS-6
1899	146	576	152	14	4	0	0.0	72	59	24		29	.264	.302	0	0	2B-146
1900	111	420	104	11	3	1	0.2	60	29	17		23	.248	.295	0	0	2B-111, SS-1
1901 DET A	135	547	150	16	12	3	0.5	82	75	41		32	.274	.364	0	0	2B-135
1902	118	441	109	11	4	1	0.2	42	38	25		17	.247	.297	0	0	2B-118
1903 PHI N	106	412	117	19	6	1	0.2	65	49	23		12	.284	.367	0	0	2B-102, OF-4
1904	153	587	161	23	6	0	0.0	61	42	37		17	.274	.334	0	0	2B-152, 3B-1
1905	155	608	150	17	7	1	0.2	95	50	45		16	.247	.303	0	0	2B-155
1906	135	494	112	17	2	0	0.0	47	34	36		17	.227	.269	0	0	2B-135
1907	36	126	18	3	0	0	0.0	11	6	7		3	.143	.167	1	0	2B-26, SS-4, 1B-4, OF-1
1908	2	1	0	0	0	0	0.0	0	0	0		0	.000	.000	0	0	OF-1, 2B-1
1912 CHI A	1	2	1	0	0	0	0.0	0	0	0		0	.500	.500	0	0	2B-1

	G	AB	H	2B	3B	HR	HR %	R	RBI	BB	SO	SB	BA	SA	Pinch Hit AB	Pinch Hit H	G by POS

...id Gleason continued

	G	AB	H	2B	3B	HR	HR %	R	RBI	BB	SO	SB	BA	SA	Pinch Hit AB	Pinch Hit H	G by POS
2 yrs.	1966	7452	1944	216	80	15	0.2	1020	823	500	131	328	.261	.317	10	3	2B-1584, P-298, OF-46, SS-19, 3B-16, 1B-7, C-1
3 yrs.	134	460	108	10	7	3	0.7	63	46	55	32	9	.235	.307	2	1	P-103, OF-22, 2B-10, 1B-2, SS-1, C-1

...arry Glenn   GLENN, HARRY MELVILLE   BL TR 6'1"   200 lbs.
B. June 9, 1890, Shelburn, Ind.   D. Oct. 12, 1918, St. Paul, Minn.

	G	AB	H	2B	3B	HR	HR %	R	RBI	BB	SO	SB	BA	SA	Pinch Hit AB	Pinch Hit H	G by POS
5 STL N	6	16	5	0	0	0	0.0	1	1	3	0	0	.313	.313	1	0	C-5

...ohn Glenn   GLENN, JOHN   BR TR 6'3"   180 lbs.
B. July 10, 1928, Moultrie, Ga.

	G	AB	H	2B	3B	HR	HR %	R	RBI	BB	SO	SB	BA	SA	Pinch Hit AB	Pinch Hit H	G by POS
0 STL N	32	31	8	0	1	0	0.0	4	5	0	9	0	.258	.323	3	0	OF-28

...anny Godby   GODBY, DANNY RAY   BR TR 6'   185 lbs.
B. Nov. 4, 1946, Logan, W. Va.

	G	AB	H	2B	3B	HR	HR %	R	RBI	BB	SO	SB	BA	SA	Pinch Hit AB	Pinch Hit H	G by POS
4 STL N	13	13	2	0	0	0	0.0	2	1	3	4	0	.154	.154	6	1	OF-4

...lio Gonzalez   GONZALEZ, JULIO CESAR   BR TR 5'11"   162 lbs.
Also known as Julio Cesar Hernandez.
B. Dec. 25, 1953, Caguas, Puerto Rico

	G	AB	H	2B	3B	HR	HR %	R	RBI	BB	SO	SB	BA	SA	Pinch Hit AB	Pinch Hit H	G by POS
7 HOU N	110	383	94	18	3	1	0.3	34	27	19	45	3	.245	.316	7	1	SS-63, 2B-45
8	78	223	52	3	1	1	0.4	24	16	8	31	6	.233	.269	12	1	2B-54, SS-17, 3B-4
9	68	181	45	5	2	0	0.0	16	10	5	14	2	.249	.298	7	3	2B-32, SS-21, 3B-9
0	40	52	6	1	0	0	0.0	5	1	1	8	1	.115	.135	10	0	SS-16, 3B-11, 2B-2
1 STL N	20	22	7	1	0	1	4.5	2	3	1	3	0	.318	.500	2	2	SS-5, 2B-4, 3B-2
2	42	87	21	3	2	1	1.1	9	7	1	24	1	.241	.356	12	1	3B-21, 2B-9, SS-1
6 yrs.	358	948	225	31	8	4	0.4	90	64	35	125	13	.237	.300	58	8	2B-146, SS-123, 3B-47
2 yrs.	62	109	28	4	2	2	1.8	11	10	2	27	1	.257	.385	22	3	3B-23, 2B-13, SS-6

...like Gonzalez   GONZALEZ, MIGUEL ANGEL   BR TR 6'1"   200 lbs.
B. Sept. 24, 1890, Havana, Cuba   D. Havana, Cuba
Manager 1938, 1940.

	G	AB	H	2B	3B	HR	HR %	R	RBI	BB	SO	SB	BA	SA	Pinch Hit AB	Pinch Hit H	G by POS
2 BOS N	1	2	0	0	0	0	0.0	0	0	1	1	0	.000	.000	0	0	C-1
4 CIN N	95	176	41	6	0	0	0.0	19	10	13	16	2	.233	.267	9	2	C-83
5 STL N	51	97	22	2	2	0	0.0	12	10	8	9	4	.227	.289	6	1	C-31, 1B-8
6	118	331	79	15	4	0	0.0	33	29	28	18	5	.239	.308	10	0	C-93, 1B-13
7	106	290	76	8	1	1	0.3	28	28	22	24	12	.262	.307	17	2	C-68, 1B-18, OF-1
8	117	349	88	13	4	3	0.9	33	20	39	30	14	.252	.338	8	1	C-100, OF-5, 1B-2
9 NY N	58	158	30	6	0	0	0.0	18	8	20	9	3	.190	.228	3	0	C-52, 1B-4
0	11	13	3	0	0	0	0.0	1	0	3	1	1	.231	.231	2	0	C-8
1	13	24	9	1	0	0	0.0	3	0	1	0	0	.375	.417	4	1	1B-6, C-2
4 STL N	120	402	119	27	1	3	0.7	34	53	24	22	1	.296	.391	1	1	C-119
5 2 teams	STL	N	(22G –	.310)		CHI	N	(70G –	.264)								
Total	92	268	74	16	1	3	1.1	35	22	19	17	3	.276	.377	9	2	C-72, 1B-9
6 CHI N	80	253	63	13	3	1	0.4	24	23	13	17	3	.249	.336	2	0	C-78
7	39	108	26	4	1	1	0.9	15	15	10	8	1	.241	.324	3	1	C-36
8	49	158	43	9	2	1	0.6	12	21	12	7	2	.272	.373	4	0	C-45
9	60	167	40	3	0	0	0.0	15	18	18	14	1	.240	.257	0	0	C-60
1 STL N	15	19	2	0	0	0	0.0	1	3	0	3	0	.105	.105	3	0	C-12
2	17	14	2	0	0	0	0.0	0	3	0	2	0	.143	.143	10	2	C-7
7 yrs.	1042	2829	717	123	19	13	0.5	283	263	231	198	52	.253	.324	91	13	C-867, 1B-60, OF-6
8 yrs.	566	1573	410	68	12	7	0.4	150	150	127	110	37	.261	.332	55	7	C-452, 1B-41, OF-6
WORLD SERIES																	
9 CHI N	2	1	0	0	0	0	0.0	0	0	0	1	0	.000	.000	1	0	C-1

...ill Goodenough   GOODENOUGH, WILLIAM B.
B. St. Louis, Mo.   D. May 24, 1905, St. Louis, Mo.

	G	AB	H	2B	3B	HR	HR %	R	RBI	BB	SO	SB	BA	SA	Pinch Hit AB	Pinch Hit H	G by POS
3 STL N	10	31	5	1	0	0	0.0	4	2	3	4	2	.161	.194	0	0	OF-10

...eorge Gore   GORE, GEORGE F.   BL TR 5'11"   195 lbs.
B. May 3, 1852, Saccarappa, Me.   D. Sept. 16, 1933, Utica, N. Y.

	G	AB	H	2B	3B	HR	HR %	R	RBI	BB	SO	SB	BA	SA	Pinch Hit AB	Pinch Hit H	G by POS
9 CHI N	63	266	70	17	4	0	0.0	43	32	8	30		.263	.357	0	0	OF-54, 1B-9
0	77	322	116	23	2	2	0.6	70	47	21	10		.360	.463	0	0	OF-74, 1B-7
1	73	309	92	18	9	1	0.3	86	44	27	23		.298	.424	0	0	OF-72, 3B-1, 1B-1
2	84	367	117	15	7	3	0.8	99	51	29	19		.319	.422	0	0	OF-84
3	92	392	131	30	9	2	0.5	105		27	13		.334	.472	0	0	OF-92
4	103	422	134	18	4	5	1.2	104		61	26		.318	.415	0	0	OF-103
5	109	441	138	21	13	5	1.1	115	51	68	25		.313	.454	0	0	OF-109
6	118	444	135	20	12	6	1.4	150	63	102	30		.304	.444	0	0	OF-118
7 NY N	111	459	133	16	5	1	0.2	95	49	42	18	39	.290	.353	0	0	OF-111
8	64	254	56	4	4	2	0.8	37	17	30	31	11	.220	.291	0	0	OF-64
9	120	488	149	21	7	7	1.4	132	54	84	28	28	.305	.420	0	0	OF-120
0 NY P	93	399	127	26	8	10	2.5	132	55	77	23	28	.318	.499	0	0	OF-93
1 NY N	130	528	150	22	7	2	0.4	103	48	74	34	19	.284	.364	0	0	OF-130
2 2 teams	NY	N	(53G –	.254)		STL	N	(20G –	.205)								
Total	73	266	64	11	3	0	0.0	56	15	67	22	22	.241	.305	0	0	OF-73
4 yrs.	1310	5357	1612	262	94	46	0.9	1327	526	717	332	147	.301	.411	0	0	OF-1297, 1B-17, 3B-1
1 yr.	20	73	15	0	1	0	0.0	9	4	18	6	2	.205	.233	0	0	OF-20

	G	AB	H	2B	3B	HR	HR %	R	RBI	BB	SO	SB	BA	SA	Pinch Hit AB	Pinch Hit H	G by POS

Herb Gorman

GORMAN, HERBERT ALLEN
B. Dec. 18, 1924, San Francisco, Calif.   D. Apr. 5, 1953, San Diego, Calif.
BL TL 5'11"   180 lbs.

	G	AB	H	2B	3B	HR	HR %	R	RBI	BB	SO	SB	BA	SA	AB	H	G by POS
1952 STL N	1	1	0	0	0	0	0.0	0	0	0	0	0	.000	.000	1	0	

Julio Gotay

GOTAY, JULIO SANCHEZ
B. June 9, 1939, Fajardo, Puerto Rico
BR TR 6'   180 lbs.

	G	AB	H	2B	3B	HR	HR %	R	RBI	BB	SO	SB	BA	SA	AB	H	G by POS
1960 STL N	3	8	3	0	0	0	0.0	1	0	0	2	1	.375	.375	1	1	SS-2, 3B-1
1961	10	45	11	4	0	0	0.0	5	5	3	5	0	.244	.333	0	0	SS-10
1962	127	369	94	12	1	2	0.5	47	27	27	47	7	.255	.309	1	0	SS-120, 2B-8, OF-2, 3B-1
1963 PIT N	4	2	1	0	0	0	0.0	0	0	0	0	0	.500	.500	1	1	2B-1
1964	3	2	1	0	0	0	0.0	1	0	1	0	0	.500	.500	2	1	
1965 CAL A	40	77	19	4	0	1	1.3	6	3	4	9	0	.247	.338	8	2	2B-23, 3B-9, SS-1
1966 HOU N	4	5	0	0	0	0	0.0	0	0	0	0	0	.000	.000	3	0	3B-1
1967	77	234	66	10	2	2	0.9	30	15	15	30	1	.282	.368	19	6	2B-30, SS-20, 3B-3
1968	75	165	41	3	0	1	0.6	9	11	4	21	1	.248	.285	25	8	2B-48, 3B-1
1969	46	81	21	5	0	0	0.0	7	9	7	13	2	.259	.321	30	6	2B-16, 3B-1
10 yrs.	389	988	257	38	3	6	0.6	106	70	61	127	12	.260	.323	90	25	SS-153, 2B-126, 3B-17, OF-2
3 yrs.	140	422	108	16	1	2	0.5	53	32	30	54	8	.256	.313	2	1	SS-132, 2B-8, OF-2, 3B-2

Mike Grady

GRADY, MICHAEL WILLIAM
B. Dec. 23, 1869, Kennett Square, Pa.   D. Dec. 3, 1943, Kennett Square, Pa.
BR TR 5'11"   190 lbs.

	G	AB	H	2B	3B	HR	HR %	R	RBI	BB	SO	SB	BA	SA	AB	H	G by POS
1894 PHI N	60	190	69	13	8	0	0.0	45	40	14	13	3	.363	.516	3	2	C-44, 1B-11, OF-2
1895	46	123	40	3	1	1	0.8	21	23	14	8	5	.325	.390	2	1	C-38, OF-5, 3B-1, 1B-1
1896	72	242	77	20	7	1	0.4	49	44	16	19	10	.318	.471	4	0	C-61, 3B-7
1897 2 teams	PHI	N	(4G – .154)		STL	N	(83G – .280)										
" Total	87	335	92	11	3	7	2.1	49	55	27			7	.275	.388	1	0	1B-83, C-3, OF-1
1898 NY N	93	287	85	19	5	3	1.0	64	49	38			20	.296	.429	2	0	C-57, OF-30, 1B-11, SS-3
1899	86	311	104	18	8	2	0.6	47	54	29			20	.334	.463	1	1	C-43, 3B-35, OF-4, 1B-4
1900	83	251	55	8	4	0	0.0	36	27	34			9	.219	.283	6	2	C-41, 1B-12, SS-11, 3B-7, OF-5, 2B-2
1901 WAS A	94	347	99	17	10	9	2.6	57	56	27			14	.285	.470	2	0	1B-59, C-30, OF-3
1904 STL N	101	323	101	15	11	5	1.5	44	43	31			6	.313	.474	7	1	C-77, 1B-11, 2B-3, 3B-1
1905	100	311	89	20	7	4	1.3	41	41	33			15	.286	.434	9	2	C-71, 1B-20
1906	97	280	70	11	3	3	1.1	33	27	48			5	.250	.343	5	1	C-60, 1B-38
11 yrs.	919	3000	881	155	67	35	1.2	486	459	311	40	114	.294	.425	42	10	C-525, 1B-246, 3B-51, OF-50, SS-14, 2B-5
4 yrs.	381	1236	350	57	24	19	1.5	166	166	138		33	.283	.414	21	4	C-208, 1B-152, 2B-3, OF-1, 3B-1

Alex Grammas

GRAMMAS, ALEXANDER PETER
B. Apr. 3, 1927, Birmingham, Ala.
Manager 1969, 1976-77.
BR TR 6'   175 lbs.

	G	AB	H	2B	3B	HR	HR %	R	RBI	BB	SO	SB	BA	SA	AB	H	G by POS
1954 STL N	142	401	106	17	4	2	0.5	57	29	40	29	6	.264	.342	0	0	SS-142, 3B-1
1955	128	366	88	19	2	3	0.8	32	25	33	36	4	.240	.328	1	0	SS-126
1956 2 teams	STL	N	(6G – .250)		CIN	N	(77G – .243)										
" Total	83	152	37	11	0	0	0.0	18	17	17	20	0	.243	.316	2	1	3B-58, SS-17, 2B-5
1957 CIN N	73	99	30	4	0	0	0.0	14	8	10	6	1	.303	.343	2	0	SS-42, 2B-20, 3B-9
1958	105	216	47	8	0	0	0.0	25	12	34	24	2	.218	.255	1	0	SS-61, 3B-38, 2B-14
1959 STL N	131	368	99	14	2	3	0.8	43	30	38	26	3	.269	.342	1	1	SS-130
1960	102	196	48	4	1	4	2.0	20	17	12	15	0	.245	.337	7	2	SS-40, 2B-38, 3B-13
1961	89	170	36	10	1	0	0.0	23	21	19	21	0	.212	.282	5	1	SS-65, 2B-18, 3B-3
1962 2 teams	STL	N	(21G – .111)		CHI	N	(23G – .233)										
" Total	44	78	16	3	0	0	0.0	3	4	13	13	1	.205	.244	4	0	SS-29, 2B-5, 3B-1
1963 CHI N	16	27	5	0	0	0	0.0	1	0	0	3	0	.185	.185	3	0	SS-13
10 yrs.	913	2073	512	90	10	12	0.6	236	163	206	193	17	.247	.317	26	5	SS-665, 2B-123, 3B-100
7 yrs.	619	1531	382	64	10	12	0.8	176	124	144	135	13	.250	.328	16	5	SS-524, 2B-58, 3B-17

Dick Gray

GRAY, RICHARD BENJAMIN
B. July 11, 1931, Jefferson, Pa.
BR TR 5'11"   165 lbs.

	G	AB	H	2B	3B	HR	HR %	R	RBI	BB	SO	SB	BA	SA	AB	H	G by POS
1958 LA N	58	197	49	5	6	9	4.6	25	30	19	30	1	.249	.472	4	2	3B-55
1959 2 teams	LA	N	(21G – .154)		STL	N	(36G – .314)										
" Total	57	103	24	2	0	3	2.9	17	10	12	20	3	.233	.340	25	5	3B-17, SS-13, 2B-2, OF-1
1960 STL N	9	5	0	0	0	0	0.0	1	1	2	2	0	.000	.000	3	0	2B-4, 3B-1
3 yrs.	124	305	73	7	6	12	3.9	43	41	33	52	4	.239	.420	32	7	3B-73, SS-13, 2B-6, OF-1
2 yrs.	45	56	16	1	0	1	1.8	10	7	8	10	3	.286	.357	20	4	SS-13, 3B-7, 2B-6, OF-1

David Green

GREEN, DAVID ALEJANDRO
B. Dec. 4, 1960, Managua, Venezuela
BR TR 6'3"   170 lbs.

	G	AB	H	2B	3B	HR	HR %	R	RBI	BB	SO	SB	BA	SA	AB	H	G by POS
1981 STL N	21	34	5	1	0	0	0.0	6	2	6	5	0	.147	.176	2	0	OF-18
1982	76	166	47	7	1	2	1.2	21	23	8	29	11	.283	.373	12	4	OF-68
2 yrs.	97	200	52	8	1	2	1.0	27	25	14	34	11	.260	.340	14	4	OF-86
2 yrs.	97	200	52	8	1	2	1.0	27	25	14	34	11	.260	.340	14	4	OF-86

LEAGUE CHAMPIONSHIP SERIES

	G	AB	H	2B	3B	HR	HR %	R	RBI	BB	SO	SB	BA	SA	AB	H	G by POS
1982 STL N	2	1	1	0	0	0	0.0	1	0	0	0	0	1.000	1.000	0	0	OF-2

WORLD SERIES

	G	AB	H	2B	3B	HR	HR %	R	RBI	BB	SO	SB	BA	SA	AB	H	G by POS
1982 STL N	7	10	2	1	0	0	0.0	3	0	1	3	0	.200	.500	1	0	OF-5

Gene Green

GREEN, GENE LEROY
B. June 26, 1933, Los Angeles, Calif.   D. May 23, 1981, St. Louis, Mo.
BR TR 6'2½"   200 lbs.

	G	AB	H	2B	3B	HR	HR %	R	RBI	BB	SO	SB	BA	SA	AB	H	G by POS
1957 STL N	6	15	3	1	0	0	0.0	2	0	0	3	0	.200	.267	0	0	OF-3
1958	137	442	124	18	3	13	2.9	47	55	37	48	2	.281	.423	13	1	OF-75, C-48
1959	30	74	14	6	0	1	1.4	8	3	5	18	0	.189	.311	2	0	OF-19, C-11
1960 BAL A	1	4	1	0	0	0	0.0	0	0	0	0	0	.250	.250	0	0	OF-1

	G	AB	H	2B	3B	HR	HR %	R	RBI	BB	SO	SB	BA	SA	Pinch Hit AB	Pinch Hit H	G by POS

Gene Green continued

	G	AB	H	2B	3B	HR	HR %	R	RBI	BB	SO	SB	BA	SA	AB	H	G by POS
1961 WAS A	110	364	102	16	3	18	4.9	52	62	35	65	0	.280	.489	11	2	C-79, OF-21
1962 CLE A	66	143	40	4	1	11	7.7	16	28	8	21	0	.280	.552	30	10	OF-33, 1B-2
1963 2 teams		CLE	A	(43G –	.205)		CIN	N	(15G –	.226)							
" Total	58	109	23	4	0	3	2.8	7	10	4	30	0	.211	.330	31	5	OF-18, C-8
7 yrs.	408	1151	307	49	7	46	4.0	130	160	89	185	2	.267	.441	90	18	OF-170, C-146, 1B-2
3 yrs.	173	531	141	25	3	14	2.6	55	60	42	69	2	.266	.403	18	1	OF-97, C-59

Tim Greisenbeck

GREISENBECK, CARLOS TIMOTHY   BR TR 5'10½" 190 lbs.
B. Dec. 10, 1898, San Antonio, Tex.   D. Mar. 25, 1953, San Antonio, Tex.

	G	AB	H	2B	3B	HR	HR %	R	RBI	BB	SO	SB	BA	SA	AB	H	G by POS
1920 STL N	5	3	1	0	0	0	0.0	1	0	0	0	0	.333	.333	1	0	C-3

Tom Grieve

GRIEVE, THOMAS ALAN   BR TR 6'2" 190 lbs.
B. Mar. 4, 1948, Pittsfield, Mass.

	G	AB	H	2B	3B	HR	HR %	R	RBI	BB	SO	SB	BA	SA	AB	H	G by POS
1970 WAS A	47	116	23	5	1	3	2.6	12	10	14	38	0	.198	.336	12	2	OF-39
1972 TEX A	64	142	29	2	1	3	2.1	12	11	11	39	1	.204	.296	17	4	OF-49
1973	66	123	38	6	0	7	5.7	22	21	7	25	1	.309	.528	5	2	OF-59
1974	84	259	66	10	4	9	3.5	30	32	20	48	0	.255	.429	7	2	OF-38, 1B-1
1975	118	369	102	17	1	14	3.8	46	61	22	74	0	.276	.442	14	1	OF-63
1976	149	546	139	23	3	20	3.7	57	81	35	119	4	.255	.418	3	1	OF-52
1977	79	236	53	9	0	7	3.0	24	30	13	57	1	.225	.352	12	4	OF-60
1978 NY N	54	101	21	3	0	2	2.0	5	8	9	23	0	.208	.297	25	2	OF-26
1979 STL N	9	15	3	1	0	0	0.0	1	0	4	1	0	.200	.267	1	0	OF-5
9 yrs.	670	1907	474	76	10	65	3.4	209	254	135	424	7	.249	.401	96	18	OF-391, 1B-1
1 yr.	9	15	3	1	0	0	0.0	1	0	4	1	0	.200	.267	1	0	OF-5

Sandy Griffin

GRIFFIN, TOBIAS CHARLES   BR TR 5'10" 160 lbs.
B. July 19, 1858, Fayetteville, N. Y.   D. June 5, 1926, Fayetteville, N. Y.
Manager 1891.

	G	AB	H	2B	3B	HR	HR %	R	RBI	BB	SO	SB	BA	SA	AB	H	G by POS
1884 NY N	16	62	11	2	0	0	0.0	7		1	19		.177	.210	0	0	OF-16
1890 ROC AA	107	407	125	28	4	5	1.2	85		50		21	.307	.432	0	0	OF-107, 2B-1
1891 WAS AA	20	69	19	4	2	0	0.0	15	10	10	3	2	.275	.391	0	0	OF-20
1893 STL N	23	92	18	1	1	0	0.0	9	9	16	2	2	.196	.228	0	0	OF-23
4 yrs.	166	630	173	35	7	5	0.8	116	18	77	24	25	.275	.376	0	0	OF-166, 2B-1
1 yr.	23	92	18	1	1	0	0.0	9	9	16	2	2	.196	.228	0	0	OF-23

Charlie Grimm

GRIMM, CHARLES JOHN (Jolly Cholly)   BL TL 5'11½" 173 lbs.
B. Aug. 28, 1898, St. Louis, Mo.
Manager 1932-38, 1944-49, 1952-56, 1960.

	G	AB	H	2B	3B	HR	HR %	R	RBI	BB	SO	SB	BA	SA	AB	H	G by POS
1916 PHI A	12	22	2	0	0	0	0.0	0	0	2	4	0	.091	.091	4	0	OF-7
1918 STL N	50	141	31	7	0	0	0.0	11	12	6	15	2	.220	.270	5	0	1B-42, OF-2, 3B-1
1919 PIT N	12	44	14	1	3	0	0.0	6	6	2	4	1	.318	.477	0	0	1B-11
1920	148	533	121	13	7	2	0.4	38	54	30	40	7	.227	.289	0	0	1B-148
1921	151	562	154	21	17	7	1.2	62	71	31	38	6	.274	.409	1	0	1B-150
1922	154	593	173	28	13	0	0.0	64	76	43	15	6	.292	.383	0	0	1B-154
1923	152	563	194	29	13	7	1.2	78	99	41	43	6	.345	.480	0	0	1B-152
1924	151	542	156	25	12	2	0.4	53	63	37	22	3	.288	.389	0	0	1B-151
1925 CHI N	141	519	159	29	5	10	1.9	73	76	38	25	4	.306	.439	2	0	1B-139
1926	147	524	145	30	6	8	1.5	58	82	49	25	3	.277	.403	0	0	1B-147
1927	147	543	169	29	6	2	0.4	68	74	45	21	3	.311	.398	0	0	1B-147
1928	147	547	161	25	5	5	0.9	67	62	39	20	7	.294	.386	0	0	1B-147
1929	120	463	138	28	3	10	2.2	66	91	42	25	3	.298	.436	0	0	1B-120
1930	114	429	124	27	2	6	1.4	58	66	41	26	1	.289	.403	1	0	1B-113
1931	146	531	176	33	11	4	0.8	65	66	53	29	1	.331	.458	1	0	1B-144
1932	149	570	175	42	2	7	1.2	66	80	35	22	2	.307	.425	0	0	1B-149
1933	107	384	95	15	2	3	0.8	38	37	23	15	1	.247	.320	2	0	1B-104
1934	75	267	79	8	1	5	1.9	24	47	16	12	1	.296	.390	1	0	1B-74
1935	2	8	0	0	0	0	0.0	0	0	0	1	0	.000	.000	0	0	1B-2
1936	39	132	33	4	0	1	0.8	13	16	5	8	0	.250	.303	4	1	1B-35
20 yrs.	2164	7917	2299	394	108	79	1.0	908	1078	578	410	57	.290	.397	21	1	1B-2129, OF-9, 3B-1
1 yr.	50	141	31	7	0	0	0.0	11	12	6	15	2	.220	.270	5	0	1B-42, OF-2, 3B-1

WORLD SERIES

	G	AB	H	2B	3B	HR	HR %	R	RBI	BB	SO	SB	BA	SA	AB	H	G by POS
1929 CHI N	5	18	7	0	0	1	5.6	2	4	1	2	0	.389	.556	0	0	1B-5
1932	4	15	5	2	0	0	0.0	2	1	2	2	0	.333	.467	0	0	1B-4
2 yrs.	9	33	12	2	0	1	3.0	4	5	3	4	0	.364	.515	0	0	1B-9

Dick Groat

GROAT, RICHARD MORROW   BR TR 5'11½" 180 lbs.
B. Nov. 4, 1930, Wilkinsburg, Pa.

	G	AB	H	2B	3B	HR	HR %	R	RBI	BB	SO	SB	BA	SA	AB	H	G by POS
1952 PIT N	95	384	109	6	1	1	0.3	38	29	19	27	2	.284	.313	1	0	SS-94
1955	151	521	139	28	2	4	0.8	45	51	38	26	0	.267	.351	1	0	SS-149
1956	142	520	142	19	3	0	0.0	40	37	35	25	0	.273	.321	0	0	SS-141, 3B-2
1957	125	501	158	30	5	7	1.4	58	54	27	28	0	.315	.437	0	0	SS-123, 3B-2
1958	151	584	175	36	9	3	0.5	67	66	23	32	2	.300	.408	1	0	SS-149
1959	147	593	163	22	7	5	0.8	74	51	32	35	0	.275	.361	2	0	SS-145
1960	138	573	186	26	4	2	0.3	85	50	39	35	0	.325	.394	1	0	SS-136
1961	148	596	164	25	6	6	1.0	71	55	40	44	0	.275	.367	2	0	SS-146, 3B-1
1962	161	678	199	34	2	2	0.3	76	61	31	61	2	.294	.361	0	0	SS-161
1963 STL N	158	631	201	43	11	6	1.0	85	73	56	58	3	.319	.450	1	0	SS-158
1964	161	636	186	35	6	1	0.2	70	70	44	42	2	.292	.371	1	0	SS-160
1965	153	587	149	26	5	0	0.0	55	52	56	50	1	.254	.315	6	3	SS-148, 3B-2
1966 PHI N	155	584	152	21	4	2	0.3	58	53	40	38	2	.260	.320	2	1	SS-139, 3B-20, 1B-1
1967 2 teams		PHI	N	(10G –	.115)		SF	N	(34G –	.171)							
" Total	44	96	15	1	1	0	0.0	7	5	10	11	0	.156	.188	14	1	SS-30, 2B-1

	G	AB	H	2B	3B	HR	HR %	R	RBI	BB	SO	SB	BA	SA	Pinch Hit AB	H	G by POS

Dick Groat continued

	G	AB	H	2B	3B	HR	HR%	R	RBI	BB	SO	SB	BA	SA	PH AB	PH H	G by POS
14 yrs.	1929	7484	2138	352	67	39	0.5	829	707	490	512	14	.286	.366	32	5	SS-1877, 3B-27, 2B-1, 1B-1
3 yrs.	472	1854	536	104	22	7	0.4	210	195	156	150	6	.289	.380	8	3	SS-466, 3B-2

WORLD SERIES

	G	AB	H	2B	3B	HR	HR%	R	RBI	BB	SO	SB	BA	SA	PH AB	PH H	G by POS
1960 PIT N	7	28	6	2	0	0	0.0	3	2	0	1	0	.214	.286	0	0	SS-7
1964 STL N	7	26	5	1	1	0	0.0	3	1	4	3	0	.192	.308	0	0	SS-7
2 yrs.	14	54	11	3	1	0	0.0	6	3	4	4	0	.204	.296	0	0	SS-14

Mario Guerrero

GUERRERO, MARIO MIGUEL
B. Sept. 28, 1949, Santo Domingo, Dominican Republic
BR TR 5'10" 155 lbs.

	G	AB	H	2B	3B	HR	HR%	R	RBI	BB	SO	SB	BA	SA	PH AB	PH H	G by POS
1973 BOS A	66	219	51	5	2	0	0.0	19	11	10	21	2	.233	.274	0	0	SS-46, 2B-24
1974	93	284	70	6	2	0	0.0	18	23	13	22	3	.246	.282	0	0	SS-93
1975 STL N	64	184	44	9	0	0	0.0	17	11	10	7	0	.239	.288	0	0	SS-64
1976 CAL A	83	268	76	12	0	1	0.4	24	18	7	12	0	.284	.340	1	0	SS-41, 2B-41
1977	86	244	69	8	2	1	0.4	17	28	4	16	0	.283	.344	27	4	SS-31, 2B-12
1978 OAK A	143	505	139	18	4	3	0.6	27	38	15	35	0	.275	.345	2	0	SS-142
1979	46	166	38	5	0	0	0.0	12	18	6	7	0	.229	.259	3	0	SS-43
1980	116	381	91	16	2	2	0.5	32	23	19	32	3	.239	.307	0	0	SS-116
8 yrs.	697	2251	578	79	12	7	0.3	166	170	84	152	8	.257	.312	33	4	SS-576, 2B-77
1 yr.	64	184	44	9	0	0	0.0	17	11	10	7	0	.239	.288	0	0	SS-64

Joe Gunson

GUNSON, JOSEPH BROOK
B. Mar. 23, 1863, Philadelphia, Pa.   D. Nov. 15, 1942, Philadelphia, Pa.
TR

	G	AB	H	2B	3B	HR	HR%	R	RBI	BB	SO	SB	BA	SA	PH AB	PH H	G by POS
1884 WAS U	45	166	23	2	0	0	0.0	15		3			.139	.151	0	0	C-33, OF-18
1889 KC AA	34	122	24	3	1	0	0.0	15	12	3	17	2	.197	.238	0	0	C-32, OF-1, 3B-1
1892 BAL N	89	314	67	10	5	0	0.0	35	32	16	17	2	.213	.277	0	0	C-67, OF-20, 1B-2, 2B-1
1893 2 teams		STL	N	(40G –	.272)		CLE	N	(21G –	.260)							
" Total	61	224	60	6	0	0	0.0	31	24	12	6	0	.268	.295	2	1	C-55, OF-5
4 yrs.	229	826	174	21	6	0	0.0	96	67	34	40	4	.211	.251	2	1	C-187, OF-44, 1B-2, 3B-1, 2B-1
1 yr.	40	151	41	5	0	0	0.0	20	15	6	6	0	.272	.305	1	0	C-35, OF-5

Don Gutteridge

GUTTERIDGE, DONALD JOSEPH
B. June 19, 1912, Pittsburg, Kans.
Manager 1969-70.
BR TR 5'10½" 165 lbs.

	G	AB	H	2B	3B	HR	HR%	R	RBI	BB	SO	SB	BA	SA	PH AB	PH H	G by POS
1936 STL N	23	91	29	3	4	3	3.3	13	16	1	14	3	.319	.538	0	0	3B-23
1937	119	447	121	26	10	7	1.6	66	61	25	66	12	.271	.421	8	1	3B-105, SS-8
1938	142	552	141	21	15	9	1.6	61	64	29	49	14	.255	.397	2	0	3B-73, SS-68
1939	148	524	141	27	4	7	1.3	71	54	27	70	5	.269	.376	2	0	3B-143, SS-2
1940	69	108	29	5	0	3	2.8	19	14	5	15	3	.269	.398	20	2	3B-39
1942 STL A	147	616	157	27	11	1	0.2	90	50	59	54	16	.255	.339	1	1	2B-145, 3B-2
1943	132	538	147	35	6	1	0.2	77	36	50	46	10	.273	.366	1	0	2B-132
1944	148	603	148	27	11	3	0.5	89	36	51	63	20	.245	.342	1	0	2B-146
1945	143	543	129	24	3	2	0.4	72	49	43	46	9	.238	.304	1	0	2B-128, OF-14
1946 BOS A	22	47	11	3	0	1	2.1	8	6	2	7	0	.234	.362	1	0	2B-9, 3B-8
1947	54	131	22	2	0	2	1.5	20	5	17	13	3	.168	.229	5	1	2B-20, 3B-19
1948 PIT N	4	2	0	0	0	0	0.0	0	0	0	1	0	.000	.000	2	0	
12 yrs.	1151	4202	1075	200	64	39	0.9	586	391	309	444	95	.256	.362	44	5	2B-580, 3B-412, SS-78, OF-14
5 yrs.	501	1722	461	82	33	29	1.7	230	209	87	214	37	.268	.404	32	3	3B-383, SS-78

WORLD SERIES

	G	AB	H	2B	3B	HR	HR%	R	RBI	BB	SO	SB	BA	SA	PH AB	PH H	G by POS
1944 STL A	6	21	3	1	0	0	0.0	1	0	3	5	0	.143	.190	0	0	2B-6
1946 BOS A	3	5	2	0	0	0	0.0	1	1	0	0	0	.400	.400	0	0	2B-2
2 yrs.	9	26	5	1	0	0	0.0	2	1	3	5	0	.192	.231	0	0	2B-8

Stan Hack

HACK, STANLEY CAMFIELD (Smiling Stan)
B. Dec. 6, 1909, Sacramento, Calif.   D. Dec. 15, 1979, Dickson, Ill.
Manager 1954-56, 1958.
BL TR 6' 170 lbs.

	G	AB	H	2B	3B	HR	HR%	R	RBI	BB	SO	SB	BA	SA	PH AB	PH H	G by POS
1932 CHI N	72	178	42	5	6	2	1.1	32	19	17	16	5	.236	.365	14	2	3B-51
1933	20	60	21	3	1	1	1.7	10	2	8	3	4	.350	.483	0	0	3B-17
1934	111	402	116	16	6	1	0.2	54	21	45	42	11	.289	.366	2	0	3B-109
1935	124	427	133	23	9	4	0.9	75	64	65	17	14	.311	.436	5	2	3B-111, 1B-7
1936	149	561	167	27	4	6	1.1	102	78	89	39	17	.298	.392	0	0	3B-140, 1B-11
1937	154	582	173	27	6	2	0.3	106	63	83	42	16	.297	.375	1	0	3B-150, 1B-4
1938	152	609	195	34	11	4	0.7	109	67	94	39	16	.320	.432	0	0	3B-152
1939	156	641	191	28	6	8	1.2	112	56	65	35	17	.298	.398	0	0	3B-156
1940	149	603	191	38	6	8	1.3	101	40	75	24	21	.317	.439	0	0	3B-148, 1B-1
1941	151	586	186	33	5	7	1.2	111	45	99	40	10	.317	.427	0	0	3B-150, 1B-1
1942	140	553	166	36	3	6	1.1	91	39	94	40	9	.300	.409	0	0	3B-139
1943	144	533	154	24	4	3	0.6	78	35	82	27	5	.289	.366	7	0	3B-136
1944	98	383	108	16	1	3	0.8	65	32	53	21	5	.282	.352	4	1	3B-75, 1B-18
1945	150	597	193	29	7	2	0.3	110	43	99	30	12	.323	.405	0	0	3B-146, 1B-5
1946	92	323	92	13	4	0	0.0	55	26	83	32	3	.285	.350	2	0	3B-90
1947	76	240	65	11	2	0	0.0	28	12	41	19	0	.271	.333	10	2	3B-66
16 yrs.	1938	7278	2193	363	81	57	0.8	1239	642	1092	466	165	.301	.397	45	7	3B-1836, 1B-47

WORLD SERIES

	G	AB	H	2B	3B	HR	HR%	R	RBI	BB	SO	SB	BA	SA	PH AB	PH H	G by POS
1932 CHI N	1	0	0	0	0	0	–	0	0	0	0	0	–	–	0	0	
1935	6	22	5	1	1	0	0.0	2	0	2	2	1	.227	.364	0	0	SS-1
1938	4	17	8	1	0	0	0.0	3	1	1	2	0	.471	.529	0	0	3B-4
1945	7	30	11	3	0	0	0.0	1	4	4	2	0	.367	.467	0	0	3B-7
4 yrs.	18	69	24	5	1	0	0.0	6	5	7	6	1	.348	.449	0	0	3B-11, SS-1

	G	AB	H	2B	3B	HR	HR %	R	RBI	BB	SO	SB	BA	SA	Pinch Hit AB	Pinch Hit H	G by POS

Jim Hackett

HACKETT, JAMES JOSEPH (Sunny Jim)   BR TR 6'2"   185 lbs.
B. Oct. 1, 1877, Jacksonville, Ill.   D. Mar. 28, 1961, Douglas, Mich.

	G	AB	H	2B	3B	HR	HR %	R	RBI	BB	SO	SB	BA	SA	PH AB	PH H	G by POS
1902 STL N	6	21	6	1	0	0	0.0	2	4	2		1	.286	.333	0	0	P-4, OF-2
1903	99	351	80	13	8	0	0.0	24	36	19		2	.228	.311	3	0	1B-89, P-7
2 yrs.	105	372	86	14	8	0	0.0	26	40	21		3	.231	.312	3	0	1B-89, P-11, OF-2
2 yrs.	105	372	86	14	8	0	0.0	26	40	21		3	.231	.312	3	0	1B-89, P-11, OF-2

Harvey Haddix

HADDIX, HARVEY (The Kitten)   BL TL 5'9½"   170 lbs.
B. Sept. 18, 1925, Medway, Ohio

	G	AB	H	2B	3B	HR	HR %	R	RBI	BB	SO	SB	BA	SA	PH AB	PH H	G by POS
1952 STL N	9	14	3	0	0	0	0.0	3	2	1	5	1	.214	.214	0	0	P-7, OF-1
1953	48	97	28	3	3	1	1.0	21	11	5	19	0	.289	.412	2	1	P-36
1954	61	93	18	4	2	0	0.0	16	4	5	11	2	.194	.280	0	0	P-43
1955	37	73	12	2	2	1	1.4	10	7	4	15	0	.164	.288	0	0	P-37
1956 2 teams		STL	N	(5G –	.222)		PHI	N	(46G –	.237)							
" Total	51	102	24	5	0	0	0.0	7	11	7	13	0	.235	.284	15	4	P-35
1957 PHI N	41	68	21	3	1	0	0.0	6	6	3	12	1	.309	.382	7	1	P-27
1958 CIN N	42	61	11	4	0	1	1.6	11	1	8	18	0	.180	.295	2	0	P-29
1959 PIT N	31	83	12	4	0	0	0.0	3	5	3	17	0	.145	.193	0	0	P-31
1960	29	67	17	4	0	0	0.0	7	7	3	15	0	.254	.313	0	0	P-29
1961	31	56	8	3	0	0	0.0	2	3	6	14	0	.143	.196	0	0	P-29
1962	28	52	13	3	1	1	1.9	9	5	1	11	0	.250	.404	0	0	P-28
1963	50	11	2	2	0	0	0.0	0	2	0	1	0	.182	.364	1	1	P-49
1964 BAL A	49	19	0	0	0	0	0.0	0	0	0	10	0	.000	.000	1	0	P-49
1965	24	2	0	0	0	0	0.0	0	0	0	1	0	.000	.000	0	0	P-24
14 yrs.	531	798	169	37	9	4	0.5	95	64	46	162	4	.212	.296	28	7	P-453, OF-1
5 yrs.	160	286	63	10	7	2	0.7	51	25	17	53	3	.220	.325	2	1	P-127, OF-1
WORLD SERIES																	
1960 PIT N	2	3	1	0	0	0	0.0	0	0	0	1	0	.333	.333	0	0	P-2

Chick Hafey

HAFEY, CHARLES JAMES   BR TR 6'   185 lbs.
B. Feb. 12, 1903, Berkeley, Calif.   D. July 2, 1973, Calistoga, Calif.
Hall of Fame 1971.

	G	AB	H	2B	3B	HR	HR %	R	RBI	BB	SO	SB	BA	SA	PH AB	PH H	G by POS
1924 STL N	24	91	23	5	2	2	2.2	10	22	4	8	1	.253	.418	0	0	OF-24
1925	93	358	108	25	2	5	1.4	36	57	10	29	3	.302	.425	5	1	OF-88
1926	78	225	61	19	2	4	1.8	30	38	11	36	2	.271	.427	22	7	OF-54
1927	103	346	114	26	5	18	5.2	62	63	36	41	12	.329	**.590**	9	5	OF-94
1928	138	520	175	46	6	27	5.2	101	111	40	53	8	.337	.604	4	0	OF-133
1929	134	517	175	47	9	29	5.6	101	125	45	42	7	.338	.632	3	0	OF-130
1930	120	446	150	39	12	26	5.8	108	107	46	51	12	.336	.652	1	0	OF-116
1931	122	450	157	35	8	16	3.6	94	95	39	43	11	**.349**	.569	4	1	OF-118
1932 CIN N	83	253	87	19	3	2	0.8	34	36	22	20	4	.344	.466	18	5	OF-83
1933	144	568	172	34	6	7	1.2	77	62	40	44	3	.303	.421	0	0	OF-144
1934	140	535	157	29	6	18	3.4	75	67	52	63	4	.293	.471	0	0	OF-140
1935	15	59	20	6	1	1	1.7	10	9	4	5	1	.339	.525	0	0	OF-15
1937	89	257	67	11	5	9	3.5	39	41	23	42	2	.261	.447	22	3	OF-64
13 yrs.	1283	4625	1466	341	67	164	3.5	777	833	372	477	70	.317	.526	88	22	OF-1203
8 yrs.	812	2953	963	242	46	127	4.3	542	618	231	303	56	.326	.568	48	14	OF-757
										3rd				**6th**	**3rd**		
WORLD SERIES																	
1926 STL N	7	27	5	2	0	0	0.0	2	0	0	7	0	.185	.259	0	0	OF-7
1928	4	15	3	0	0	0	0.0	0	0	1	4	0	.200	.200	0	0	OF-4
1930	6	22	6	5	0	0	0.0	2	2	1	3	0	.273	.500	0	0	OF-6
1931	6	24	4	0	0	0	0.0	1	0	0	5	1	.167	.167	0	0	OF-6
4 yrs.	23	88	18	7	0	0	0.0	5	2	2	19	1	.205	.284	0	0	OF-23
				8th													

Joe Hague

HAGUE, JOE CLARENCE   BL TL 6'   195 lbs.
B. Apr. 25, 1944, Huntington, W. Va.

	G	AB	H	2B	3B	HR	HR %	R	RBI	BB	SO	SB	BA	SA	PH AB	PH H	G by POS
1968 STL N	7	17	4	0	0	1	5.9	2	1	2	2	0	.235	.412	1	0	OF-3, 1B-2
1969	40	100	17	2	1	2	2.0	8	8	12	23	0	.170	.270	14	1	OF-17, 1B-9
1970	139	451	122	16	4	14	3.1	58	68	63	87	2	.271	.417	17	7	1B-82, OF-52
1971	129	380	86	9	3	16	4.2	46	54	58	69	0	.226	.392	17	2	1B-91, OF-36
1972 2 teams		STL	N	(27G –	.237)		CIN	N	(69G –	.246)							
" Total	96	214	52	12	2	7	3.3	25	31	37	36	1	.243	.416	32	11	1B-44, OF-22
1973 CIN N	19	33	5	2	0	0	0.0	2	1	5	5	1	.152	.212	8	3	OF-5, 1B-4
6 yrs.	430	1195	286	41	10	40	3.3	141	163	177	222	4	.239	.391	89	24	1B-232, OF-135
5 yrs.	342	1024	247	32	9	36	3.5	122	142	152	199	2	.241	.396	52	11	1B-206, OF-111
LEAGUE CHAMPIONSHIP SERIES																	
1972 CIN N	3	1	0	0	0	0	0.0	0	0	0	1	0	.000	.000	1	0	
WORLD SERIES																	
1972 CIN N	3	3	0	0	0	0	0.0	0	0	0	0	0	.000	.000	3	0	OF-1

Don Hahn

HAHN, DONALD ANTONE   BR TR 6'1"   180 lbs.
B. Nov. 16, 1948, San Francisco, Calif.

	G	AB	H	2B	3B	HR	HR %	R	RBI	BB	SO	SB	BA	SA	PH AB	PH H	G by POS
1969 MON N	4	9	1	0	0	0	0.0	0	2	0	5	0	.111	.111	0	0	OF-3
1970	82	149	38	8	0	0	0.0	22	8	27	27	4	.255	.309	18	5	OF-61
1971 NY N	98	178	42	5	1	1	0.6	16	11	21	32	2	.236	.292	8	2	OF-80
1972	17	37	6	0	0	0	0.0	0	1	4	12	0	.162	.162	6	0	OF-10
1973	93	262	60	10	0	2	0.8	22	21	22	43	1	.229	.290	9	2	OF-87
1974	110	323	81	14	1	4	1.2	34	28	37	34	2	.251	.337	8	3	OF-106
1975 3 teams		PHI	N	(9G –	.000)		STL	N	(7G –	.125)		SD	N	(34G –	.231)		
" Total	50	39	7	1	2	0	0.0	10	3	11	5	1	.179	.308	5	0	OF-37
7 yrs.	454	997	235	38	4	7	0.7	104	74	122	158	11	.236	.303	54	12	OF-384
1 yr.	7	8	1	0	0	0	0.0	3	0	1	1	0	.125	.125	0	0	OF-4

	G	AB	H	2B	3B	HR	HR %	R	RBI	BB	SO	SB	BA	SA	Pinch Hit AB	Pinch Hit H	G by POS

Don Hahn continued

LEAGUE CHAMPIONSHIP SERIES
| 1973 NY N | 5 | 17 | 4 | 0 | 0 | 0 | 0.0 | 2 | 1 | 2 | 4 | 0 | .235 | .235 | 0 | 0 | OF-5 |

WORLD SERIES
| 1973 NY N | 7 | 29 | 7 | 1 | 1 | 0 | 0.0 | 2 | 2 | 1 | 6 | 0 | .241 | .345 | 0 | 0 | OF-7 |

Ed Haigh

HAIGH, EDWARD E.
B. Feb. 5, 1867, Philadelphia, Pa.   D. Feb. 14, 1953, Atlantic City, N. J.

| 1892 STL N | 1 | 4 | 1 | 0 | 0 | 0 | 0.0 | 0 | 0 | 0 | 2 | 0 | .250 | .250 | 0 | 0 | OF-1 |

Charley Hall

HALL, CHARLES LOUIS (Sea Lion)   BL TR 6'1" 187 lbs.
Born Carlos Clolo.
B. July 27, 1885, Ventura, Calif.   D. Dec. 6, 1943, Ventura, Calif.

1906 CIN N	17	47	6	2	0	0	0.0	7	2	2		0	.128	.170	1	0	P-14, 1B-2
1907	12	26	7	0	1	0	0.0	1	1	0		0	.269	.346	1	0	P-11
1909 BOS A	11	19	3	0	0	0	0.0	0	4	0		0	.158	.158	0	0	P-11
1910	47	82	17	2	4	0	0.0	6	8	6		1	.207	.329	8	1	P-35, OF-3
1911	39	64	9	1	1	1	1.6	6	8	4		0	.141	.234	7	1	P-32
1912	34	75	20	4	2	1	1.3	10	14	4		0	.267	.413	0	0	P-34
1913	43	42	9	1	1	0	0.0	2	2	1	10	0	.214	.286	7	0	P-35, 3B-1
1916 STL N	10	14	2	0	0	0	0.0	0	1	0	6	0	.143	.143	0	0	P-10
1918 DET A	6	2	0	0	0	0	0.0	0	0	0	0	0	.000	.000	0	0	P-6
9 yrs.	219	371	73	10	9	2	0.5	32	40	17	16	1	.197	.288	24	2	P-188, OF-3, 1B-2, 3B-1
1 yr.	10	14	2	0	0	0	0.0	0	1	0	6	0	.143	.143	0	0	P-10

WORLD SERIES
| 1912 BOS A | 2 | 4 | 3 | 1 | 0 | 0 | 0.0 | 1 | 0 | 1 | 0 | 0 | .750 | 1.000 | 0 | 0 | P-2 |

Russ Hall

HALL, RUSSELL P.   TR
B. Sept. 29, 1871, Shelbyville, Ky.   D. July 1, 1937, Los Angeles, Calif.

1898 STL N	39	143	35	2	1	0	0.0	13	10	7		1	.245	.273	0	0	SS-35, 3B-3, OF-1
1901 CLE A	1	4	2	0	0	0	0.0	2	0	0		0	.500	.500	0	0	SS-1
2 yrs.	40	147	37	2	1	0	0.0	15	10	7		1	.252	.279	0	0	SS-36, 3B-3, OF-1
1 yr.	39	143	35	2	1	0	0.0	13	10	7		1	.245	.273	0	0	SS-35, 3B-3, OF-1

Bill Hallman

HALLMAN, WILLIAM WHITE   BR TR
B. Mar. 30, 1867, Pittsburgh, Pa.   D. Sept. 11, 1920, Philadelphia, Pa.
Manager 1897.

1888 PHI N	18	63	13	4	1	0	0.0	5	6	1	12	1	.206	.302	0	0	C-10, 2B-4, OF-3, SS-1, 3B-1
1889	119	462	117	21	8	2	0.4	67	60	36	54	20	.253	.346	0	0	SS-106, 2B-13, C-1
1890 PHI P	84	356	95	16	7	1	0.3	59	37	33	24	6	.267	.360	0	0	OF-34, C-26, 2B-14, 3B-10, SS-2
1891 PHI AA	141	587	166	21	13	6	1.0	112	69	38	56	18	.283	.394	0	0	2B-141
1892 PHI N	138	586	171	27	10	2	0.3	106	84	32	52	19	.292	.382	0	0	2B-138
1893	132	596	183	28	7	4	0.7	119	76	51	27	22	.307	.398	0	0	2B-120, 1B-12
1894	119	505	156	19	7	0	0.0	107	66	36	15	36	.309	.374	0	0	2B-119
1895	124	539	169	26	5	1	0.2	94	91	34	20	16	.314	.386	0	0	2B-122, SS-3
1896	120	469	150	21	3	0	0.0	82	83	45	23	16	.320	.390	0	0	2B-120, P-1
1897 2 teams			PHI	N	(31G –	.262)		STL	N	(79G –	.221)						
" Total	110	424	99	9	2	0	0.0	47	41	32		13	.233	.264	0	0	2B-108, 1B-3
1898 BKN N	134	509	124	10	7	2	0.4	57	63	29		9	.244	.303	0	0	2B-124, 3B-10
1901 2 teams			CLE	A	(5G –	.211)		PHI	N	(123G –	.184)						
" Total	128	464	86	13	5	0	0.0	48	41	28		13	.185	.235	0	0	2B-90, 3B-33, SS-5
1902 PHI N	73	254	63	8	4	0	0.0	14	35	14		9	.248	.311	1	1	3B-72
1903	63	198	42	11	2	0	0.0	20	17	16		2	.212	.288	6	0	2B-22, 3B-19, 1B-9, OF-4, SS-3
14 yrs.	1503	6012	1634	234	81	20	0.3	937	769	425	283	200	.272	.348	7	1	2B-1135, 3B-145, SS-120, OF-41, C-37, 1B-24, P-1
1 yr.	79	298	66	6	2	0	0.0	31	26	24		12	.221	.255	0	0	2B-77, 1B-3

Fred Haney

HANEY, FRED GIRARD (Pudge)   BR TR 5'6" 170 lbs.
B. Apr. 25, 1898, Albuquerque, N. M.   D. Nov. 9, 1977, Beverly Hills, Calif.
Manager 1939-41, 1953-59.

1922 DET A	81	213	75	7	4	0	0.0	41	25	32	14	3	.352	.423	9	3	3B-42, 1B-11, SS-2
1923	142	503	142	13	4	4	0.8	85	67	45	23	12	.282	.348	0	0	2B-69, 3B-55, SS-16
1924	86	256	79	11	1	1	0.4	54	30	39	13	7	.309	.371	13	4	3B-59, SS-4, 2B-3
1925	114	398	111	15	3	0	0.0	84	40	66	29	11	.279	.332	5	1	3B-107
1926 BOS A	138	462	102	15	7	0	0.0	47	52	74	28	13	.221	.284	1	0	3B-137
1927 2 teams			BOS	A	(47G –	.276)		CHI	N	(4G –	.000)						
" Total	51	119	32	4	1	3	2.5	23	12	25	14	4	.269	.395	14	4	3B-34, OF-1
1929 STL N	10	26	3	1	1	0	0.0	4	2	1	2	0	.115	.231	2	1	3B-6
7 yrs.	622	1977	544	66	21	8	0.4	338	228	282	123	50	.275	.342	44	13	3B-440, 2B-72, SS-22, 1B-11, OF-1
1 yr.	10	26	3	1	1	0	0.0	4	2	1	2	0	.115	.231	2	1	3B-6

Larry Haney

HANEY, WALLACE LARRY   BR TR 6'2" 195 lbs.
B. Nov. 19, 1942, Charlottesville, Va.

1966 BAL A	20	56	9	1	0	1	1.8	3	3	1	15	0	.161	.232	1	0	C-20
1967	58	164	44	11	0	3	1.8	13	20	6	28	1	.268	.390	1	0	C-57
1968	38	89	21	3	1	1	1.1	5	5	0	19	0	.236	.326	6	2	C-32
1969 2 teams			SEA	A	(22G –	.254)		OAK	A	(53G –	.151)						
" Total	75	145	28	7	0	4	2.8	11	19	13	31	1	.193	.324	1	0	C-73
1970 OAK A	2	2	0	0	0	0	0.0	0	0	0	2	1	.000	.000	1	0	C-1

	G	AB	H	2B	3B	HR	HR %	R	RBI	BB	SO	SB	BA	SA	Pinch Hit AB	Pinch Hit H	G by POS

Larry Haney continued

	G	AB	H	2B	3B	HR	HR %	R	RBI	BB	SO	SB	BA	SA	PH AB	PH H	G by POS
1972	5	4	0	0	0	0	0.0	0	0	0	1	0	.000	.000	1	0	C-4, 2B-1
1973 2 teams	OAK A (2G – .500)				STL N (2G – .000)												
" Total	4	3	1	0	0	0	0.0	0	0	0	1	0	.333	.333	0	0	C-4
1974 OAK A	76	121	20	4	0	2	1.7	12	3	3	18	1	.165	.248	1	0	C-73, 3B-3, 1B-2
1975	47	26	5	0	0	1	3.8	3	2	1	4	0	.192	.308	0	0	C-43, 3B-4
1976	88	177	40	2	0	0	0.0	12	10	13	26	0	.226	.237	1	0	C-87
1977 MIL A	63	127	29	2	0	0	0.0	7	10	5	30	0	.228	.244	0	0	C-63
1978	4	5	1	0	0	0	0.0	0	1	0	1	0	.200	.200	0	0	C-4
12 yrs.	480	919	198	30	1	12	1.3	68	73	44	175	3	.215	.289	14	3	C-461, 3B-7, 1B-2, 2B-1
1 yr.	2	1	0	0	0	0	0.0	0	0	0	1	0	.000	.000	0	0	C-2

WORLD SERIES

	G	AB	H	2B	3B	HR	HR %	R	RBI	BB	SO	SB	BA	SA	PH AB	PH H	G by POS
1974 OAK A	2	0	0	0	0	0	–	0	0	0	0	0	–	–	0	0	C-2

Dick Harley

HARLEY, RICHARD JOSEPH
B. Sept. 25, 1872, Philadelphia, Pa. D. Apr. 3, 1952, Philadelphia, Pa. BL TR 5'10½" 165 lbs.

	G	AB	H	2B	3B	HR	HR %	R	RBI	BB	SO	SB	BA	SA	PH AB	PH H	G by POS
1897 STL N	89	330	96	6	4	3	0.9	43	35	36		23	.291	.361	0	0	OF-89
1898	142	549	135	6	5	0	0.0	74	42	34		13	.246	.275	1	1	OF-141
1899 CLE N	142	567	142	15	7	1	0.2	70	50	40		15	.250	.307	0	0	OF-143
1900 CIN N	5	21	9	1	0	0	0.0	2	5	1		4	.429	.476	0	0	OF-5
1901	133	535	146	13	2	4	0.7	69	27	31		37	.273	.327	0	0	OF-133
1902 DET A	125	491	138	9	8	2	0.4	59	44	36		20	.281	.344	0	0	OF-125
1903 CHI N	104	386	89	9	1	0	0.0	72	33	45		27	.231	.259	2	2	OF-103
7 yrs.	740	2879	755	59	27	10	0.3	389	236	223		139	.262	.312	3	3	OF-739
2 yrs.	231	879	231	12	9	3	0.3	117	77	70		36	.263	.307	1	1	OF-230

Chuck Harmon

HARMON, CHARLES BYRON
B. Apr. 23, 1926, Washington, Ind. BR TR 6'2" 175 lbs.

	G	AB	H	2B	3B	HR	HR %	R	RBI	BB	SO	SB	BA	SA	PH AB	PH H	G by POS
1954 CIN N	94	286	68	7	3	2	0.7	39	25	17	27	7	.238	.304	23	3	3B-67, 1B-3
1955	96	198	50	6	3	5	2.5	31	28	26	24	9	.253	.389	15	4	3B-39, OF-32, 1B-4
1956 2 teams	CIN N (13G – .000)				STL N (20G – .000)												
" Total	33	19	0	0	0	0	0.0	4	0	2	2	1	.000	.000	3	0	OF-17, 1B-4, 3B-1
1957 2 teams	STL N (9G – .333)				PHI N (57G – .256)												
" Total	66	89	23	2	0	0	0.0	16	6	1	4	8	.258	.326	10	3	OF-33, 3B-5, 1B-2
4 yrs.	289	592	141	15	8	7	1.2	90	59	46	57	25	.238	.326	51	10	3B-112, OF-82, 1B-13
2 yrs.	29	18	1	0	1	0	0.0	4	1	2	2	1	.056	.167	4	0	OF-19, 1B-2, 3B-1

George Harper

HARPER, GEORGE WASHINGTON
B. June 24, 1892, Arlington, Ky. D. Aug. 18, 1978, Magnolia, Ark. BL TR 5'8" 167 lbs.

	G	AB	H	2B	3B	HR	HR %	R	RBI	BB	SO	SB	BA	SA	PH AB	PH H	G by POS
1916 DET A	44	56	9	1	0	0	0.0	4	3	5	8	0	.161	.179	24	4	OF-14
1917	47	117	24	3	0	0	0.0	6	12	11	15	2	.205	.231	16	4	OF-31
1918	69	227	55	5	2	0	0.0	19	16	18	14	3	.242	.282	3	0	OF-64
1922 CIN N	128	430	146	22	8	2	0.5	67	68	35	22	11	.340	.442	14	3	OF-109
1923	61	125	32	4	2	3	2.4	14	16	11	9	0	.256	.392	28	7	OF-29
1924 2 teams	CIN N (28G – .270)				PHI N (109G – .294)												
" Total	137	485	141	29	6	16	3.3	75	58	51	28	11	.291	.474	2	0	OF-131
1925 PHI N	132	495	173	35	7	18	3.6	86	97	28	32	10	.349	.558	6	3	OF-126
1926	56	194	61	6	5	7	3.6	32	38	16	7	6	.314	.505	1	1	OF-55
1927 NY N	145	483	160	19	6	16	3.3	85	87	84	27	7	.331	.505	3	1	OF-142
1928 2 teams	NY N (19G – .228)				STL N (99G – .305)												
" Total	118	329	96	9	2	19	5.8	52	65	61	19	3	.292	.505	13	4	OF-103
1929 BOS N	136	457	133	25	5	10	2.2	65	68	69	27	5	.291	.433	5	0	OF-130
11 yrs.	1073	3398	1030	158	43	91	2.7	505	528	389	208	58	.303	.455	115	27	OF-934
1 yr.	99	272	83	8	2	17	6.3	41	58	51	15	2	.305	.537	13	4	OF-84

WORLD SERIES

	G	AB	H	2B	3B	HR	HR %	R	RBI	BB	SO	SB	BA	SA	PH AB	PH H	G by POS
1928 STL N	3	9	1	0	0	0	0.0	1	0	2	2	0	.111	.111	0	0	OF-3

Vic Harris

HARRIS, VICTOR LANIER
B. Mar. 27, 1950, Los Angeles, Calif. BB TR 5'11" 165 lbs.

	G	AB	H	2B	3B	HR	HR %	R	RBI	BB	SO	SB	BA	SA	PH AB	PH H	G by POS
1972 TEX A	61	186	26	5	1	0	0.0	8	10	12	39	7	.140	.177	4	0	2B-58, SS-1
1973	152	555	138	14	7	8	1.4	71	44	55	81	13	.249	.342	1	0	OF-113, 3B-25, 2B-18
1974 CHI N	62	200	39	6	3	0	0.0	18	11	29	26	9	.195	.255	4	0	2B-56
1975	51	56	10	0	0	0	0.0	6	5	6	7	0	.179	.179	24	4	OF-11, 3B-7, 2B-5
1976 STL N	97	259	59	12	3	1	0.4	21	19	16	55	1	.228	.309	23	4	2B-37, OF-35, 3B-12, SS-1
1977 SF N	69	165	43	12	0	2	1.2	28	14	19	36	2	.261	.370	25	3	2B-27, SS-11, 3B-9, OF-3
1978	53	100	15	4	0	1	1.0	8	11	11	24	0	.150	.220	16	1	SS-22, 2B-10, OF-6
1980 MIL A	34	89	19	4	1	1	1.1	8	7	12	13	4	.213	.315	1	0	OF-31, 3B-2, 2B-1
8 yrs.	579	1610	349	57	15	13	0.8	168	121	160	281	36	.217	.295	98	12	2B-212, OF-199, 3B-55, SS-35
1 yr.	97	259	59	12	3	1	0.4	21	19	16	55	1	.228	.309	23	4	2B-37, OF-35, 3B-12, SS-1

Bill Hart

HART, WILLIAM FRANKLIN
B. July 19, 1865, Louisville, Ky. D. Sept. 19, 1936, Cincinnati, Ohio

	G	AB	H	2B	3B	HR	HR %	R	RBI	BB	SO	SB	BA	SA	PH AB	PH H	G by POS
1886 PHI AA	22	73	10	1	1	0	0.0	3		3			.137	.178	0	0	P-22
1887	3	13	1	0	0	0	0.0	0		0		0	.077	.077	0	0	P-3
1892 BKN N	37	125	24	3	4	2	1.6	14	17	7	22	4	.192	.328	0	0	P-28, OF-12
1895 PIT N	36	106	25	5	2	0	0.0	8	11	1	12	1	.236	.321	0	0	P-36
1896 STL N	49	161	30	4	5	0	0.0	9	15	3	15	7	.186	.273	0	0	P-42, OF-8
1897	46	156	39	1	2	2	1.3	14	14	1		4	.250	.321	0	0	P-39, OF-6, 1B-1
1898 PIT N	16	50	12	0	1	0	0.0	4	3	1		0	.240	.280	0	0	P-16
1901 CLE A	20	64	14	0	1	0	0.0	7	6	1		0	.219	.219	0	0	P-20
8 yrs.	229	748	155	14	15	4	0.5	59	65	17	49	17	.207	.282	0	0	P-206, OF-26, 1B-1
2 yrs.	95	317	69	5	7	2	0.6	23	29	4	15	11	.218	.297	0	0	P-81, OF-14, 1B-1

	G	AB	H	2B	3B	HR	HR%	R	RBI	BB	SO	SB	BA	SA	Pinch Hit AB	Pinch Hit H	G by POS

Fred Hartman

HARTMAN, FREDERICK ORRIN (Dutch)   TR
B. Apr. 25, 1868, Pittsburgh, Pa.   D. Nov. 11, 1938, McKeesport, Pa.

	G	AB	H	2B	3B	HR	HR%	R	RBI	BB	SO	SB	BA	SA	PH AB	PH H	G by POS
1894 PIT N	49	182	58	4	7	2	1.1	41	20	16	11	12	.319	.451	0	0	3B-49
1897 STL N	124	516	158	21	8	2	0.4	67	67	26		18	.306	.390	0	0	3B-124
1898 NY N	123	475	129	16	11	2	0.4	57	88	25		11	.272	.364	0	0	3B-123
1899	50	174	41	3	5	1	0.6	25	16	12		2	.236	.328	0	0	3B-50
1901 CHI N	120	473	146	23	13	3	0.6	77	89	25		31	.309	.431	1	1	3B-119
1902 STL N	114	416	90	10	3	0	0.0	30	52	14		14	.216	.255	2	1	3B-105, SS-4, 1B-3
6 yrs.	580	2236	622	77	47	10	0.4	297	332	118	11	88	.278	.368	3	2	3B-570, SS-4, 1B-3
2 yrs.	238	932	248	31	11	2	0.2	97	119	40		32	.266	.329	2	1	3B-229, SS-4, 1B-3

Grady Hatton

HATTON, GRADY EDGEBERT   BL TR 5'8½" 170 lbs.
B. Oct. 7, 1922, Beaumont, Tex.
Manager 1966-68.

	G	AB	H	2B	3B	HR	HR%	R	RBI	BB	SO	SB	BA	SA	PH AB	PH H	G by POS
1946 CIN N	116	436	118	18	3	14	3.2	56	69	66	53	6	.271	.422	0	0	3B-116, OF-2
1947	146	524	147	24	8	16	3.1	91	77	81	50	7	.281	.448	7	2	3B-136
1948	133	458	110	17	2	9	2.0	58	44	72	50	7	.240	.345	3	1	3B-123, 2B-3, SS-2, OF-1
1949	137	537	141	38	5	11	2.0	71	69	62	48	4	.263	.413	1	0	3B-136
1950	130	438	114	17	1	11	2.5	67	54	70	39	6	.260	.379	4	1	3B-126, SS-1, 2B-1
1951	96	331	84	9	3	4	1.2	41	37	33	32	4	.254	.335	7	2	3B-87, OF-2
1952	128	433	92	14	1	9	2.1	48	57	66	60	5	.212	.312	7	1	2B-120
1953	83	159	37	3	1	7	4.4	22	22	29	24	0	.233	.396	38	7	2B-35, 1B-10, 3B-5
1954 3 teams	CIN N (1G – .000)			CHI A (13G – .167)				BOS A (99G – .281)									
" Total	113	333	90	13	3	5	1.5	43	36	63	28	2	.270	.372	8	0	3B-103, 1B-4, SS-1
1955 BOS A	126	380	93	11	4	4	1.1	48	49	76	28	0	.245	.326	12	1	3B-111, 2B-1
1956 3 teams	BOS A (5G – .400)			STL N (44G – .247)				BAL A (27G – .148)									
" Total	76	139	29	2	2	1	0.7	14	12	26	13	1	.209	.273	35	9	2B-28, 3B-13
1960 CHI N	28	38	13	0	0	0	0.0	3	7	2	5	0	.342	.342	16	3	2B-8
12 yrs.	1312	4206	1068	166	33	91	2.2	562	533	646	430	42	.254	.374	138	27	3B-956, 2B-196, 1B-14, OF-5, SS-4
1 yr.	44	73	18	1	2	0	0.0	10	7	13	7	1	.247	.315	28	6	2B-13, 3B-1

Arnold Hauser

HAUSER, ARNOLD GEORGE (Pee Wee)   BR TR
B. Sept. 25, 1888, Chicago, Ill.   D. May 22, 1956, Aurora, Ill.

	G	AB	H	2B	3B	HR	HR%	R	RBI	BB	SO	SB	BA	SA	PH AB	PH H	G by POS
1910 STL N	119	375	77	7	2	2	0.5	37	36	49	39	15	.205	.251	1	0	SS-117, 3B-1
1911	136	515	124	11	8	3	0.6	61	46	26	67	24	.241	.311	0	0	SS-134, 3B-2
1912	133	479	124	14	7	1	0.2	73	42	39	69	26	.259	.324	1	1	SS-132
1913	22	45	13	0	3	0	0.0	3	9	2	2	1	.289	.422	8	4	SS-8, 2B-4
1915 CHI F	23	54	11	1	0	0	0.0	6	4	5		2	.204	.222	0	0	SS-16, 3B-6
5 yrs.	433	1468	349	33	20	6	0.4	180	137	121	177	68	.238	.300	10	5	SS-407, 3B-9, 2B-4
4 yrs.	410	1414	338	32	20	6	0.4	174	133	116	177	66	.239	.303	10	5	SS-391, 2B-4, 3B-3

Doc Hazleton

HAZLETON, WILLARD CARPENTER
B. Aug. 28, 1876, Strafford, Vt.   D. Mar. 17, 1941, Burlington, Vt.

	G	AB	H	2B	3B	HR	HR%	R	RBI	BB	SO	SB	BA	SA	PH AB	PH H	G by POS
1902 STL N	7	23	3	0	0	0	0.0	0	0	2		0	.130	.130	0	0	1B-7

Francis Healy

HEALY, FRANCIS PAUL   BR TR 5'9½" 175 lbs.
B. June 29, 1910, Holyoke, Mass.

	G	AB	H	2B	3B	HR	HR%	R	RBI	BB	SO	SB	BA	SA	PH AB	PH H	G by POS
1930 NY N	7	2	0	0	0	0	0.0	2	0	0	0	0	.000	.000	2	0	C-1
1931	6	7	1	0	0	0	0.0	1	0	0	0	0	.143	.143	0	0	C-6
1932	14	32	8	2	0	0	0.0	5	4	2	8	0	.250	.313	2	0	C-11
1934 STL N	15	13	4	1	0	0	0.0	1	1	0	2	0	.308	.385	8	3	C-2, OF-1, 3B-1
4 yrs.	42	54	13	3	0	0	0.0	9	5	2	10	0	.241	.296	12	3	C-20, OF-1, 3B-1
1 yr.	15	13	4	1	0	0	0.0	1	1	0	2	0	.308	.385	8	3	C-2, OF-1, 3B-1

Cliff Heathcote

HEATHCOTE, CLIFTON EARL   BL TL 5'10½" 160 lbs.
B. Jan. 24, 1898, Glen Rock, Pa.   D. Jan. 19, 1939, York, Pa.

	G	AB	H	2B	3B	HR	HR%	R	RBI	BB	SO	SB	BA	SA	PH AB	PH H	G by POS
1918 STL N	88	348	90	12	3	4	1.1	37	32	20	40	12	.259	.345	0	0	OF-88
1919	114	401	112	13	4	1	0.2	53	29	20	41	26	.279	.339	9	3	OF-101, 1B-2
1920	133	489	139	18	8	3	0.6	55	56	25	31	21	.284	.372	3	0	OF-129
1921	62	156	38	6	2	0	0.0	18	9	10	9	7	.244	.308	7	1	OF-51
1922 2 teams	STL N (34G – .245)			CHI N (76G – .280)													
" Total	110	341	92	13	9	1	0.3	48	48	27	19	5	.270	.370	12	3	OF-92
1923 CHI N	117	393	98	14	3	1	0.3	48	27	25	22	32	.249	.308	2	0	OF-112
1924	113	392	121	19	7	0	0.0	66	30	28	28	26	.309	.393	1	0	OF-111
1925	109	380	100	14	5	5	1.3	57	39	39	26	15	.263	.366	10	1	OF-99
1926	139	510	141	33	3	10	2.0	98	53	58	30	18	.276	.412	3	1	OF-133
1927	83	228	67	12	4	2	0.9	28	25	20	16	6	.294	.408	17	4	OF-57
1928	67	137	39	8	0	3	2.2	26	18	17	12	6	.285	.409	21	5	OF-39
1929	82	224	70	17	0	2	0.9	45	31	25	17	9	.313	.415	22	7	OF-52
1930	70	150	39	10	1	9	6.0	30	18	18	15	4	.260	.520	31	5	OF-35
1931 CIN N	90	252	65	15	6	0	0.0	24	28	32	16	3	.258	.365	25	6	OF-59
1932 2 teams	CIN N (8G – .000)			PHI N (30G – .282)													
" Total	38	42	11	2	0	1	2.4	10	5	3	3	0	.262	.381	20	4	1B-7
15 yrs.	1415	4443	1222	206	55	42	0.9	643	448	367	325	190	.275	.375	183	36	OF-1158, 1B-9
5 yrs.	431	1492	403	54	19	8	0.5	174	140	84	125	66	.270	.348	19	4	OF-401, 1B-2

WORLD SERIES

	G	AB	H	2B	3B	HR	HR%	R	RBI	BB	SO	SB	BA	SA	PH AB	PH H	G by POS
1929 CHI N	2	1	0	0	0	0	0.0	0	0	0	0	0	.000	.000	1	0	

	G	AB	H	2B	3B	HR	HR %	R	RBI	BB	SO	SB	BA	SA	Pinch Hit AB	Pinch Hit H	G by POS

Jack Heidemann

HEIDEMANN, JACK SEALE
B. July 11, 1949, Brenham, Tex.   BR TR 6'   175 lbs.

	G	AB	H	2B	3B	HR	HR%	R	RBI	BB	SO	SB	BA	SA	PH AB	PH H	G by POS
1969 CLE A	3	3	0	0	0	0	0.0	0	0	0	2	0	.000	.000	0	0	SS-3
1970	133	445	94	14	2	6	1.3	44	37	34	88	2	.211	.292	1	0	SS-132
1971	81	240	50	7	0	0	0.0	16	9	12	46	1	.208	.238	0	0	SS-81
1972	10	20	3	0	0	0	0.0	0	0	2	3	0	.150	.150	0	0	SS-10
1974 2 teams	CLE	A	(12G –	.091)		STL	N	(47G –	.271)								
" Total	59	81	20	1	0	0	0.0	10	3	5	12	0	.247	.259	5	0	SS-49, 3B-7, 2B-1, 1B-1
1975 NY N	61	145	31	4	2	1	0.7	12	16	17	28	1	.214	.290	18	1	SS-44, 3B-4, 2B-1
1976 2 teams	NY	N	(5G –	.083)		MIL	A	(69G –	.219)								
" Total	74	158	33	1	0	2	1.3	11	10	7	24	1	.209	.253	6	0	3B-40, 2B-25, SS-3
1977 MIL A	5	1	0	0	0	0	0.0	1	0	1	0	0	.000	.000	1	0	2B-1
8 yrs.	426	1093	231	27	4	9	0.8	94	75	78	203	5	.211	.268	31	1	SS-322, 3B-51, 2B-28, 1B-1
1 yr.	47	70	19	1	0	0	0.0	8	3	5	10	0	.271	.286	4	0	SS-45, 3B-1

John Heidrick

HEIDRICK, JOHN EMMETT (Snags)
B. July 6, 1876, Queenstown, Pa.   D. Jan. 20, 1916, Clarion, Pa.

	G	AB	H	2B	3B	HR	HR%	R	RBI	BB	SO	SB	BA	SA	PH AB	PH H	G by POS
1898 CLE N	19	76	23	2	2	0	0.0	10	8	3		3	.303	.382	0	0	OF-19
1899 STL N	146	591	194	21	14	2	0.3	109	82	34		55	.328	.421	1	1	OF-145
1900	85	339	102	6	8	2	0.6	51	45	18		22	.301	.383	2	0	OF-83
1901	118	502	170	24	12	6	1.2	94	67	21		32	.339	.470	0	0	OF-118
1902 STL A	110	447	129	19	10	3	0.7	75	56	34		17	.289	.396	0	0	OF-109, SS-1, 3B-1, P-1
1903	120	461	129	20	15	1	0.2	55	42	19		19	.280	.395	1	0	OF-119, C-1
1904	133	538	147	14	10	1	0.2	66	36	16		35	.273	.342	3	0	OF-130
1908	26	93	20	2	2	1	1.1	8	6	1		3	.215	.312	1	0	OF-25
8 yrs.	757	3047	914	108	73	16	0.5	468	342	146		186	.300	.399	8	1	OF-748, SS-1, 3B-1, C-1, P-1
3 yrs.	349	1432	466	51	34	10	0.7	254	194	73		109	.325	.429	3	1	OF-346

Tom Heintzelman

HEINTZELMAN, THOMAS KENNETH
Son of Ken Heintzelman.
B. Nov. 3, 1946, St. Charles, Mo.   BR TR 6'1"   180 lbs.

	G	AB	H	2B	3B	HR	HR%	R	RBI	BB	SO	SB	BA	SA	PH AB	PH H	G by POS
1973 STL N	23	29	9	0	0	0	0.0	5	5	3	3	0	.310	.310	15	4	2B-6
1974	38	74	17	4	0	1	1.4	10	6	9	14	0	.230	.324	7	1	2B-28, 3B-2, SS-1
1977 SF N	2	2	0	0	0	0	0.0	0	0	0	0	0	.000	.000	2	0	
1978	27	35	8	1	0	2	5.7	2	6	2	5	0	.229	.429	19	4	2B-5, 3B-3, 1B-2
4 yrs.	90	140	34	5	0	3	2.1	17	12	14	22	0	.243	.343	43	9	2B-39, 3B-5, 1B-2, SS-1
2 yrs.	61	103	26	4	0	1	1.0	15	6	12	17	0	.252	.320	22	5	2B-34, 3B-2, SS-1

Bob Heise

HEISE, ROBERT LOWELL
B. May 12, 1947, San Antonio, Tex.   BR TR 6'   175 lbs.

	G	AB	H	2B	3B	HR	HR%	R	RBI	BB	SO	SB	BA	SA	PH AB	PH H	G by POS
1967 NY N	16	62	20	4	0	0	0.0	7	3	3	1	0	.323	.387	0	0	2B-12, SS-3, 3B-2
1968	6	23	5	0	0	0	0.0	3	1	1	1	0	.217	.217	0	0	SS-6, 2B-1
1969	4	10	3	1	0	0	0.0	1	0	3	2	0	.300	.400	1	1	SS-3
1970 SF N	67	154	36	5	1	1	0.6	15	22	5	13	0	.234	.299	7	2	SS-33, 2B-28, 3B-2
1971 2 teams	SF	N	(13G –	.000)		MIL	A	(68G –	.254)								
" Total	81	200	48	7	0	0	0.0	12	7	7	16	1	.240	.275	10	1	SS-54, 3B-13, 2B-4, OF-1
1972 MIL A	95	271	72	10	1	0	0.0	23	12	12	14	1	.266	.310	18	5	2B-49, 3B-24, SS-9
1973	49	98	20	2	0	0	0.0	8	4	4	4	1	.204	.224	0	0	SS-29, 3B-9, 2B-4, 1B-4
1974 2 teams	STL	N	(3G –	.143)		CAL	A	(29G –	.267)								
" Total	32	82	21	7	0	0	0.0	7	6	5	10	0	.256	.341	2	0	2B-20, 3B-6, SS-3
1975 BOS A	63	126	27	3	0	0	0.0	12	21	4	6	0	.214	.238	2	0	3B-45, 2B-14, SS-4, 1B-1
1976	32	56	15	2	0	0	0.0	5	5	1	2	0	.268	.304	0	0	3B-22, SS-9, 2B-1
1977 KC A	54	62	16	2	1	0	0.0	11	5	2	8	0	.258	.323	1	0	SS-21, 2B-21, 3B-12, 1B-1
11 yrs.	499	1144	283	43	3	1	0.1	104	86	47	77	3	.247	.293	41	9	SS-174, 2B-154, 3B-135, 1B-6, OF-1
1 yr.	3	7	1	0	0	0	0.0	0	0	0	0	0	.143	.143	0	0	2B-3

Charlie Hemphill

HEMPHILL, CHARLES JUDSON (Eagle Eye)
Brother of Frank Hemphill.
B. Apr. 20, 1876, Greenville, Mich.   D. June 22, 1953, Detroit, Mich.   BL TL 5'9"   160 lbs.

	G	AB	H	2B	3B	HR	HR%	R	RBI	BB	SO	SB	BA	SA	PH AB	PH H	G by POS
1899 2 teams	STL	N	(11G –	.243)		CLE	N	(55G –	.277)								
" Total	66	239	65	3	5	3	1.3	27	26	12		3	.272	.364	1	1	OF-64
1901 BOS A	136	545	142	10	10	3	0.6	71	62	39		11	.261	.332	0	0	OF-136
1902 2 teams	CLE	A	(25G –	.266)		STL	A	(103G –	.317)								
" Total	128	510	157	16	11	6	1.2	81	69	49		27	.308	.418	6	2	OF-120, 2B-2
1903 STL A	105	383	94	6	3	3	0.8	36	29	23		16	.245	.300	1	0	OF-104
1904	114	438	112	13	2	2	0.5	47	45	35		23	.256	.308	4	1	OF-108, 2B-1
1906	154	585	169	19	12	4	0.7	90	62	43		33	.289	.383	0	0	OF-154
1907	153	603	156	20	9	0	0.0	66	38	51		14	.259	.322	0	0	OF-153
1908 NY A	142	505	150	12	9	0	0.0	62	44	59		42	.297	.356	0	0	OF-142
1909	73	181	44	5	1	0	0.0	23	10	32		10	.243	.282	24	6	OF-45
1910	102	351	84	9	4	0	0.0	45	20	55		19	.239	.288	4	1	OF-94
1911	69	201	57	4	2	1	0.5	32	15	37		9	.284	.338	9	0	OF-56
11 yrs.	1242	4541	1230	117	68	22	0.5	580	421	435		207	.271	.341	49	11	OF-1176, 2B-3
1 yr.	11	37	9	0	0	1	2.7	4	3	6		0	.243	.324	1	1	OF-10

Solly Hemus

HEMUS, SOLOMON JOSEPH
B. Apr. 17, 1923, Phoenix, Ariz.
Manager 1959-61.   BL TR 5'9"   165 lbs.

	G	AB	H	2B	3B	HR	HR%	R	RBI	BB	SO	SB	BA	SA	PH AB	PH H	G by POS
1949 STL N	20	33	11	1	0	0	0.0	8	2	7	3	0	.333	.364	2	0	2B-16
1950	11	15	2	1	0	0	0.0	1	0	2	4	0	.133	.200	5	0	3B-5
1951	128	420	118	18	9	2	0.5	68	32	75	31	7	.281	.381	4	0	SS-105, 2B-12
1952	151	570	153	28	8	15	2.6	105	52	96	55	1	.268	.425	1	0	SS-148, 3B-2
1953	154	585	163	32	11	14	2.4	110	61	86	40	2	.279	.443	2	1	SS-150, 2B-3

	G	AB	H	2B	3B	HR	HR %	R	RBI	BB	SO	SB	BA	SA	Pinch Hit AB	Pinch Hit H	G by POS

Solly Hemus *continued*

		G	AB	H	2B	3B	HR	HR%	R	RBI	BB	SO	SB	BA	SA	AB	H	G by POS
1954		124	214	65	15	3	2	0.9	43	27	55	27	5	.304	.430	38	10	SS-66, 3B-27, 2B-12
1955		96	206	50	10	2	5	2.4	36	21	27	22	1	.243	.383	37	4	3B-43, 2B-40, SS-2
1956 2 teams	STL N (8G – .200)					PHI N	(78G – .289)											
" Total		86	192	55	10	4	5	2.6	25	26	29	21	1	.286	.458	33	9	2B-49, 3B-1
1957 PHI N		70	108	20	6	1	0	0.0	8	5	20	8	1	.185	.259	33	2	2B-24
1958		105	334	95	14	3	8	2.4	53	36	51	34	3	.284	.416	20	3	2B-84, 3B-1
1959 STL N		24	17	4	2	0	0	0.0	2	1	8	2	0	.235	.353	14	2	3B-1, 2B-1
11 yrs.		969	2694	736	137	41	51	1.9	459	263	456	247	21	.273	.411	189	31	SS-471, 2B-241, 3B-80
9 yrs.		716	2065	567	107	33	38	1.8	374	198	357	184	16	.275	.414	108	18	SS-471, 2B-84, 3B-78

George Hendrick

HENDRICK, GEORGE ANDREW
B. Oct. 18, 1949, Los Angeles, Calif.

BR TR 6'3" 195 lbs.

		G	AB	H	2B	3B	HR	HR%	R	RBI	BB	SO	SB	BA	SA	AB	H	G by POS
1971 OAK A		42	114	27	4	1	0	0.0	8	8	3	20	0	.237	.289	5	2	OF-36
1972		58	121	22	1	1	4	3.3	10	15	3	22	3	.182	.306	19	5	OF-41
1973 CLE A		113	440	118	18	0	21	4.8	64	61	25	71	7	.268	.452	3	1	OF-110
1974		139	495	138	23	1	19	3.8	65	67	33	73	6	.279	.444	5	0	OF-133
1975		145	561	145	21	2	24	4.3	82	86	40	78	6	.258	.431	2	1	OF-143
1976		149	551	146	20	3	25	4.5	72	81	51	82	4	.265	.448	1	1	OF-146
1977 SD N		152	541	168	25	2	23	4.3	75	81	61	74	11	.311	.492	9	2	OF-142
1978 2 teams	SD N (36G – .243)					STL N	(102G – .288)											
" Total		138	493	137	31	2	20	4.1	64	75	40	60	2	.278	.467	5	3	OF-134
1979 STL N		140	493	148	27	1	16	3.2	67	75	49	62	2	.300	.456	7	2	OF-138
1980		150	572	173	33	2	25	4.4	73	109	32	67	6	.302	.498	3	0	OF-149
1981		101	394	112	19	3	18	4.6	67	61	41	44	4	.284	.485	0	0	OF-101
1982		136	515	145	20	5	19	3.7	65	104	37	80	3	.282	.450	2	1	OF-134
12 yrs.		1463	5290	1479	242	22	214	4.0	712	823	415	733	54	.280	.455	61	18	OF-1407
5 yrs.		629	2356	688	126	12	95	4.0	327	416	187	297	16	.292	.477	13	4	OF-623
								4th							**9th**			

LEAGUE CHAMPIONSHIP SERIES

		G	AB	H	2B	3B	HR	HR%	R	RBI	BB	SO	SB	BA	SA	AB	H	G by POS
1972 OAK A		5	7	1	0	0	0	0.0	2	0	0	1	0	.143	.143	4	1	OF-1
1982 STL N		3	13	4	0	0	0	0.0	2	2	1	2	0	.308	.308	0	0	OF-3
2 yrs.		8	20	5	0	0	0	0.0	4	2	1	3	0	.250	.250	4	1	OF-4

WORLD SERIES

		G	AB	H	2B	3B	HR	HR%	R	RBI	BB	SO	SB	BA	SA	AB	H	G by POS
1972 OAK A		5	15	2	0	0	0	0.0	3	0	1	0	0	.133	.133	0	0	OF-5
1982 STL N		7	28	9	0	0	0	0.0	1	5	2	1	0	.321	.321	0	0	OF-7
2 yrs.		12	43	11	0	0	0	0.0	4	5	3	1	0	.256	.256	0	0	OF-12

Harvey Hendrick

HENDRICK, HARVEY LEE (Gink)
B. Nov. 9, 1897, Mason, Tenn.   D. Oct. 29, 1941, Covington, Tenn.

BL TR 6'2" 190 lbs.

		G	AB	H	2B	3B	HR	HR%	R	RBI	BB	SO	SB	BA	SA	AB	H	G by POS
1923 NY A		37	66	18	3	1	3	4.5	9	12	2	8	3	.273	.485	24	6	OF-12
1924		40	76	20	0	0	1	1.3	7	11	2	7	1	.263	.303	21	4	OF-17
1925 CLE A		25	28	8	1	2	0	0.0	2	9	3	5	0	.286	.464	16	6	1B-3
1927 BKN N		128	458	142	18	11	4	0.9	55	50	24	40	29	.310	.424	10	3	OF-64, 1B-53, 2B-1
1928		126	425	135	15	10	11	2.6	83	59	54	34	16	.318	.478	13	5	3B-91, OF-17
1929		110	384	136	25	6	14	3.6	69	82	31	20	14	.354	.560	13	7	OF-42, 1B-39, 3B-7, SS-4
1930		68	167	43	10	1	5	3.0	29	28	20	19	2	.257	.419	16	4	OF-42, 1B-7
1931 2 teams	BKN N (1G – .000)					CIN N	(137G – .315)											
" Total		138	531	167	32	9	1	0.2	74	75	53	40	3	.315	.414	1	0	1B-137
1932 2 teams	STL N (28G – .250)					CIN N	(94G – .302)											
" Total		122	470	138	32	3	5	1.1	64	45	28	38	3	.294	.406	9	3	1B-94, 3B-12, OF-5
1933 CHI N		69	189	55	13	3	4	2.1	30	23	13	17	4	.291	.455	19	6	1B-38, OF-8, 3B-1
1934 PHI N		59	116	34	8	0	0	0.0	12	19	9	15	0	.293	.362	31	7	OF-12, 3B-7, 1B-7
11 yrs.		922	2910	896	157	46	48	1.6	434	413	239	243	75	.308	.443	173	51	1B-378, OF-219, 3B-118, SS-4, 2B-1
1 yr.		28	72	18	2	0	1	1.4	8	5	5	9	0	.250	.319	9	3	3B-12, OF-5

WORLD SERIES

		G	AB	H	2B	3B	HR	HR%	R	RBI	BB	SO	SB	BA	SA	AB	H	G by POS
1923 NY A		1	1	0	0	0	0	0.0	0	0	0	0	0	.000	.000	1	0	

Jack Hendricks

HENDRICKS, JOHN CHARLES
B. Apr. 9, 1875, Joliet, Ill.   D. May 13, 1943, Chicago, Ill.
Manager 1918, 1924-29.

BL TL 5'11½" 160 lbs.

		G	AB	H	2B	3B	HR	HR%	R	RBI	BB	SO	SB	BA	SA	AB	H	G by POS
1902 2 teams	NY N (8G – .231)					CHI N	(2G – .571)											
" Total		10	33	10	2	1	0	0.0	1	0	2		2	.303	.424	1	0	OF-9
1903 WAS A		32	112	20	1	3	0	0.0	10	4	13		3	.179	.241	0	0	OF-32
2 yrs.		42	145	30	3	4	0	0.0	11	4	15		5	.207	.283	1	0	OF-41
yrs.		0	0	0	0	0	0	–	0	0	0	0	0	–	–	0	0	

Keith Hernandez

HERNANDEZ, KEITH
B. Oct. 20, 1953, San Francisco, Calif.

BL TL 6' 180 lbs.

		G	AB	H	2B	3B	HR	HR%	R	RBI	BB	SO	SB	BA	SA	AB	H	G by POS
1974 STL N		14	34	10	1	2	0	0.0	3	2	7	8	0	.294	.441	3	1	1B-9
1975		64	188	47	8	2	3	1.6	20	20	17	26	0	.250	.362	9	3	1B-56
1976		129	374	108	21	5	7	1.9	54	46	49	53	4	.289	.428	17	4	1B-110
1977		161	560	163	41	4	15	2.7	90	91	79	88	7	.291	.459	6	1	1B-158
1978		159	542	138	32	4	11	2.0	90	64	82	68	13	.255	.389	5	1	1B-158
1979		161	610	210	**48**	11	11	1.8	116	105	80	78	11	**.344**	.513	2	2	1B-160
1980		159	595	191	39	8	16	2.7	111	99	86	73	14	.321	.494	2	0	1B-157
1981		103	376	115	27	4	8	2.1	65	48	61	45	12	.306	.463	2	0	1B-98, OF-3
1982		160	579	173	33	6	7	1.2	79	94	100	67	19	.299	.413	1	1	1B-158, OF-4
9 yrs.		1110	3858	1155	250	46	78	2.0	628	569	561	506	80	.299	.449	47	13	1B-1064, OF-7
9 yrs.		1110	3858	1155	250	46	78	2.0	628	569	561	506	80	.299	.449	47	13	1B-1064, OF-7
											8th	**9th**						

LEAGUE CHAMPIONSHIP SERIES

		G	AB	H	2B	3B	HR	HR%	R	RBI	BB	SO	SB	BA	SA	AB	H	G by POS
1982 STL N		3	12	4	0	0	0	0.0	3	1	2	3	0	.333	.333	0	0	1B-3

	G	AB	H	2B	3B	HR	HR %	R	RBI	BB	SO	SB	BA	SA	Pinch Hit AB	Pinch Hit H	G by POS

Keith Hernandez continued

WORLD SERIES

	G	AB	H	2B	3B	HR	HR%	R	RBI	BB	SO	SB	BA	SA	AB	H	G by POS
1982 STL N	7	27	7	2	0	1	3.7	4	8	4	2	0	.259	.444	0	0	1B-7

Larry Herndon

HERNDON, LARRY DARNELL
B. Nov. 3, 1953, Sunflower, Miss.   BR TR 6'3"   190 lbs.

	G	AB	H	2B	3B	HR	HR%	R	RBI	BB	SO	SB	BA	SA	AB	H	G by POS
1974 STL N	12	1	1	0	0	0	0.0	3	0	0	0		1.000	1.000	0	0	OF-1
1976 SF N	115	337	97	11	3	2	0.6	42	23	23	45	12	.288	.356	6	2	OF-110
1977	49	109	26	4	3	1	0.9	13	5	5	20	4	.239	.358	5	1	OF-44
1978	151	471	122	15	9	1	0.2	52	32	35	71	13	.259	.335	4	2	OF-149
1979	132	354	91	14	5	7	2.0	35	36	29	70	8	.257	.384	19	7	OF-122
1980	139	493	127	17	11	8	1.6	54	49	19	91	8	.258	.385	21	6	OF-122
1981	96	364	105	15	8	5	1.4	48	41	20	55	15	.288	.415	4	0	OF-93
1982 DET A	157	614	179	21	13	23	3.7	92	88	38	92	12	.292	.480	3	0	OF-155
8 yrs.	851	2743	748	97	52	47	1.7	339	274	169	444	72	.273	.397	62	18	OF-796
1 yr.	12	1	1	0	0	0	0.0	3	0	0	0		1.000	1.000	0	0	OF-1

Tommy Herr

HERR, THOMAS MITCHELL
B. Apr. 4, 1956, Lancaster, Pa.   BB TR 6'   175 lbs.

	G	AB	H	2B	3B	HR	HR%	R	RBI	BB	SO	SB	BA	SA	AB	H	G by POS
1979 STL N	14	10	2	0	0	0	0.0	4	1	2	2	1	.200	.200	1	0	2B-6
1980	76	222	55	12	5	0	0.0	29	15	16	21	9	.248	.347	9	2	2B-58, SS-14
1981	103	411	110	14	9	0	0.0	50	46	39	30	23	.268	.345	0	0	2B-103
1982	135	493	131	19	4	0	0.0	83	36	57	56	25	.266	.320	5	2	2B-128
4 yrs.	328	1136	298	45	18	0	0.0	166	98	114	109	58	.262	.334	15	4	2B-295, SS-14
4 yrs.	328	1136	298	45	18	0	0.0	166	98	114	109	58	.262	.334	15	4	2B-295, SS-14

LEAGUE CHAMPIONSHIP SERIES

	G	AB	H	2B	3B	HR	HR%	R	RBI	BB	SO	SB	BA	SA	AB	H	G by POS
1982 STL N	3	13	3	1	0	0	0.0	1	0	1	2	0	.231	.308	0	0	2B-3

WORLD SERIES

	G	AB	H	2B	3B	HR	HR%	R	RBI	BB	SO	SB	BA	SA	AB	H	G by POS
1982 STL N	7	25	4	2	0	0	0.0	2	5	3	3	0	.160	.240	0	0	2B-7

Neal Hertweck

HERTWECK, NEAL CHARLES
B. Nov. 22, 1931, St. Louis, Mo.   BL TL 6'1½"   175 lbs.

	G	AB	H	2B	3B	HR	HR%	R	RBI	BB	SO	SB	BA	SA	AB	H	G by POS
1952 STL N	2	6	0	0	0	0	0.0	0	1	1	0	.000	.000	0	0	1B-2

Whitey Herzog

HERZOG, DORREL NORMAN ELVERT
B. Nov. 9, 1931, New Athens, Ill.
Manager 1973, 1975-82.   BL TL 5'11"   182 lbs.

	G	AB	H	2B	3B	HR	HR%	R	RBI	BB	SO	SB	BA	SA	AB	H	G by POS
1956 WAS A	117	421	103	13	7	4	1.0	49	35	35	74	8	.245	.337	11	5	OF-103, 1B-5
1957	36	78	13	3	0	0	0.0	7	4	13	12	1	.167	.205	10	0	OF-28
1958 2 teams	WAS A (8G – .000)					KC A	(88G – .240)										
" Total	96	101	23	1	2	0	0.0	11	9	17	26	0	.228	.277	32	7	OF-44, 1B-22
1959 KC A	38	123	36	7	1	1	0.8	25	9	34	23	1	.293	.390	2	1	OF-34, 1B-1
1960	83	252	67	10	2	8	3.2	43	38	40	32	0	.266	.417	12	5	OF-69, 1B-2
1961 BAL A	113	323	94	11	6	5	1.5	39	35	50	41	1	.291	.409	18	6	OF-98
1962	99	263	70	13	1	7	2.7	34	35	41	36	2	.266	.403	26	5	OF-70
1963 DET A	52	53	8	2	1	0	0.0	5	7	11	17	0	.151	.226	35	4	1B-7, OF-4
8 yrs.	634	1614	414	60	20	25	1.5	213	172	241	261	13	.257	.365	146	33	OF-450, 1B-37

Mike Heydon

HEYDON, MICHAEL EDWARD
B. July 15, 1874, Indianapolis, Ind.   D. Oct. 13, 1913, Indianapolis, Ind.   TR

	G	AB	H	2B	3B	HR	HR%	R	RBI	BB	SO	SB	BA	SA	AB	H	G by POS
1898 BAL N	3	9	1	0	0	0	0.0	2	1	2		0	.111	.111	0	0	C-3
1899 WAS N	3	3	0	0	0	0	0.0	0	0	2		0	.000	.000	0	0	C-2
1901 STL N	16	43	9	1	1	1	2.3	2	6	5		2	.209	.349	1	0	C-13, OF-1
1904 CHI A	4	10	1	1	0	0	0.0	0	1	1		0	.100	.200	0	0	C-4
1905 WAS A	77	245	47	7	4	1	0.4	20	26	21		5	.192	.265	0	0	C-77
1906	49	145	23	7	1	0	0.0	14	10	14		2	.159	.221	0	0	C-49
1907	62	164	30	3	0	0	0.0	14	9	25		3	.183	.201	4	0	C-57
7 yrs.	214	619	111	19	6	2	0.3	52	53	70		12	.179	.239	6	0	C-205, OF-1
1 yr.	16	43	9	1	1	1	2.3	2	6	5		2	.209	.349	1	0	C-13, OF-1

Jim Hickman

HICKMAN, JAMES LUCIUS
B. May 10, 1937, Henning, Tenn.   BR TR 6'3"   192 lbs.

	G	AB	H	2B	3B	HR	HR%	R	RBI	BB	SO	SB	BA	SA	AB	H	G by POS
1962 NY N	140	392	96	18	2	13	3.3	54	46	47	96	4	.245	.401	13	3	OF-124
1963	146	494	113	21	6	17	3.4	53	51	44	120	0	.229	.399	11	1	OF-82, 3B-59
1964	139	409	105	14	1	11	2.7	48	57	36	90	0	.257	.377	31	8	OF-113, 3B-1
1965	141	369	87	18	0	15	4.1	32	40	27	76	3	.236	.407	29	5	OF-91, 1B-30, 3B-14
1966	58	160	38	7	0	4	2.5	15	16	13	34	2	.238	.356	11	1	OF-45, 1B-17
1967 LA N	65	98	16	6	1	0	0.0	7	10	14	28	1	.163	.245	25	3	OF-37, 3B-2, 1B-2, P-1
1968 CHI N	75	188	42	6	3	5	2.7	22	23	18	38	1	.223	.367	12	2	OF-66
1969	134	338	80	11	2	21	6.2	38	54	47	74	2	.237	.467	18	5	OF-125
1970	149	514	162	33	4	32	6.2	102	115	93	99	0	.315	.582	2	0	OF-79, 1B-74
1971	117	383	98	13	2	19	5.0	50	60	50	61	0	.256	.449	12	2	OF-69, 1B-44
1972	115	368	100	15	2	17	4.6	65	64	52	64	3	.272	.462	13	3	1B-77, OF-27
1973	92	201	49	1	2	3	1.5	27	20	42	42	1	.244	.313	34	6	1B-51, OF-13
1974 STL N	50	60	16	0	0	2	3.3	5	4	8	10	0	.267	.367	30	6	1B-14, 3B-1
13 yrs.	1421	3974	1002	163	25	159	4.0	518	560	491	832	17	.252	.426	241	45	OF-871, 1B-309, 3B-77, P-1
1 yr.	50	60	16	0	0	2	3.3	5	4	8	10	0	.267	.367	30	6	1B-14, 3B-1

	G	AB	H	2B	3B	HR	HR %	R	RBI	BB	SO	SB	BA	SA	Pinch Hit AB	Pinch Hit H	G by POS

Jim Hicks

HICKS, JAMES EDWARD
B. May 18, 1940, East Chicago, Ind.   BR TR 6'3" 205 lbs.

	G	AB	H	2B	3B	HR	HR %	R	RBI	BB	SO	SB	BA	SA	PH AB	PH H	G by POS
1964 CHI A	2	0	0	0	0	0	–	0	0	0	0	0	–	–	0	0	
1965	13	19	5	1	0	1	5.3	2	2	0	9	0	.263	.474	8	2	OF-5
1966	18	26	5	0	1	0	0.0	3	1	1	5	0	.192	.269	2	0	OF-10, 1B-2
1969 2 teams	STL	N	(19G –	.182)		CAL	A	(37G –	.083)								
" Total	56	92	12	0	2	4	4.3	11	11	17	32	0	.130	.304	17	0	OF-25, 1B-8
1970 CAL A	4	4	1	0	0	0	0.0	0	0	0	2	0	.250	.250	4	1	
5 yrs.	93	141	23	1	3	5	3.5	16	14	18	48	0	.163	.319	31	3	OF-40, 1B-10
1 yr.	19	44	8	0	2	1	2.3	5	3	4	14	0	.182	.341	1	0	OF-15

Andy High

HIGH, ANDREW AIRD (Handy Andy)
Brother of Charlie High. Brother of Hugh High.   BL TR 5'6" 155 lbs.
B. Nov. 21, 1897, Ava, Ill.   D. Feb. 22, 1981, Toledo, Ohio

	G	AB	H	2B	3B	HR	HR %	R	RBI	BB	SO	SB	BA	SA	PH AB	PH H	G by POS
1922 BKN N	153	579	164	27	10	6	1.0	82	65	59	26	3	.283	.396	0	0	3B-130, SS-22, 2B-1
1923	123	426	115	23	9	3	0.7	51	37	47	13	4	.270	.387	0	0	3B-80, SS-45, 2B-5
1924	144	582	191	26	13	6	1.0	98	61	57	16	3	.328	.448	0	0	2B-133, SS-17, 3B-1
1925 2 teams	BKN	N	(44G –	.200)		BOS	N	(60G –	.288)								
" Total	104	334	86	15	2	4	1.2	42	34	38	7	3	.257	.350	17	5	3B-71, 2B-12, SS-3
1926 BOS N	130	476	141	17	10	2	0.4	55	66	39	9	4	.296	.387	4	2	3B-81, 2B-49
1927	113	384	116	15	9	4	1.0	59	46	26	11	4	.302	.419	13	6	3B-89, 2B-8, SS-2
1928 STL N	111	368	105	14	3	6	1.6	58	37	37	10	2	.285	.389	17	4	3B-73, 2B-19
1929	146	603	178	32	4	10	1.7	95	63	38	18	7	.295	.411	1	1	3B-123, 2B-22
1930	72	215	60	12	2	2	0.9	34	29	23	6	1	.279	.381	17	5	3B-48, 2B-3
1931	63	131	35	6	1	0	0.0	20	19	24	4	0	.267	.328	19	5	3B-23, 2B-19
1932 CIN N	84	191	36	4	2	0	0.0	16	12	23	6	1	.188	.230	23	7	3B-46, 2B-12
1933	24	43	9	2	0	1	2.3	4	6	5	1	0	.209	.326	10	2	3B-11, 2B-2
1934 PHI N	47	68	14	2	0	0	0.0	4	7	9	3	1	.206	.235	23	5	3B-14, 2B-2
13 yrs.	1314	4400	1250	195	65	44	1.0	618	482	425	130	33	.284	.388	144	42	3B-790, 2B-287, SS-89
4 yrs.	392	1317	378	64	10	18	1.4	207	148	122	38	10	.287	.392	54	15	3B-267, 2B-63
WORLD SERIES																	
1928 STL N	4	17	5	2	0	0	0.0	1	1	1	3	0	.294	.412	0	0	3B-4
1930	1	2	1	0	0	0	0.0	1	0	0	0	0	.500	.500	0	0	3B-1
1931	4	15	4	0	0	0	0.0	3	0	0	2	0	.267	.267	0	0	3B-4
3 yrs.	9	34	10	2	0	0	0.0	5	1	1	5	0	.294	.353	0	0	3B-9

Palmer Hildebrand

HILDEBRAND, PALMER MARION (Pete)
B. Dec. 23, 1884, Schauck, Ohio   D. Jan. 25, 1960, Canton, Ohio   BR TR 5'10" 170 lbs.

	G	AB	H	2B	3B	HR	HR %	R	RBI	BB	SO	SB	BA	SA	PH AB	PH H	G by POS
1913 STL N	26	55	9	2	0	0	0.0	3	1	1	10	1	.164	.200	2	0	C-22, OF-1

Hugh Hill

HILL, HUGH ELLIS
Brother of Still Bill Hill.
B. July 21, 1879, Ringgold, Ga.   D. Sept. 6, 1958, Cincinnati, Ohio

	G	AB	H	2B	3B	HR	HR %	R	RBI	BB	SO	SB	BA	SA	PH AB	PH H	G by POS
1903 CLE A	1	1	0	0	0	0	0.0	0		0		0	.000	.000	1	0	
1904 STL N	23	93	21	2	1	3	3.2	13	4	2		3	.226	.366	0	0	OF-23
2 yrs.	24	94	21	2	1	3	3.2	13	4	2		3	.223	.362	1	0	OF-23
1 yr.	23	93	21	2	1	3	3.2	13	4	2		3	.226	.366	0	0	OF-23

Marc Hill

HILL, MARC KEVIN
B. Feb. 18, 1952, Louisiana, Mo.   BR TR 6'3" 205 lbs.

	G	AB	H	2B	3B	HR	HR %	R	RBI	BB	SO	SB	BA	SA	PH AB	PH H	G by POS
1973 STL N	1	3	0	0	0	0	0.0	0	0	0	1	0	.000	.000	0	0	C-1
1974	10	21	5	1	0	0	0.0	2	2	4	5	0	.238	.286	1	0	C-9
1975 SF N	72	182	39	4	0	5	2.7	14	23	25	27	0	.214	.319	16	3	C-60, 3B-1
1976	54	131	24	5	0	3	2.3	11	15	10	19	0	.183	.290	4	1	C-49, 1B-1
1977	108	320	80	10	0	9	2.8	28	50	34	34	0	.250	.366	7	2	C-102
1978	117	358	87	15	1	3	0.8	20	36	45	39	1	.243	.316	5	3	C-116, 1B-2
1979	63	169	35	3	0	3	1.8	20	15	26	25	0	.207	.278	6	1	C-58, 1B-1
1980 2 teams	SF	N	(17G –	.171)		SEA	A	(29G –	.229)								
" Total	46	111	23	4	1	2	1.8	9	9	4	17	0	.207	.315	3	0	C-43
1981 CHI A	16	6	0	0	0	0	0.0	0	0	0	1	0	.000	.000	3	0	C-14, 3B-1, 1B-1
1982	53	88	23	2	0	3	3.4	9	13	6	13	0	.261	.386	2	1	C-49, 3B-1, 1B-1
10 yrs.	540	1389	316	44	2	28	2.0	113	163	154	181	1	.228	.323	47	11	C-501, 1B-6, 3B-3
2 yrs.	11	24	5	1	0	0	0.0	2	2	4	6	0	.208	.250	1	0	C-10

John Himes

HIMES, JOHN HERB
D. Dec. 16, 1949, Joliet, Ill.

	G	AB	H	2B	3B	HR	HR %	R	RBI	BB	SO	SB	BA	SA	PH AB	PH H	G by POS
1905 STL N	12	41	6	0	0	0	0.0	3	1	1		0	.146	.146	1	0	OF-11
1906	40	155	42	5	2	0	0.0	10	14	7		4	.271	.329	0	0	OF-40
2 yrs.	52	196	48	5	2	0	0.0	13	14	8		4	.245	.291	1	0	OF-51
2 yrs.	52	196	48	5	2	0	0.0	13	14	8		4	.245	.291	1	0	OF-51

Ed Hock

HOCK, EDWARD FRANCIS
B. Mar. 27, 1899, Franklin Furnace, Ohio   D. Nov. 21, 1963, Portsmouth, Ohio   BL TR 5'10½" 165 lbs.

	G	AB	H	2B	3B	HR	HR %	R	RBI	BB	SO	SB	BA	SA	PH AB	PH H	G by POS
1920 STL N	1	0	0	0	0	0	–	0	0	0	0	0	–	–	0	0	OF-1
1923 CIN N	2	0	0	0	0	0	–	0	0	0	0	0	–	–	0	0	OF-1
1924	16	10	1	0	0	0	0.0	7	0	0	2	0	.100	.100	4	1	OF-2
3 yrs.	19	10	1	0	0	0	0.0	7	0	0	2	0	.100	.100	4	1	OF-3
1 yr.	1	0	0	0	0	0	–	0	0	0	0	0	–	–	0	0	OF-1

Art Hoelskoetter

HOELSKOETTER, ARTHUR H.
Played as Art Hostetter 1907-08.   TR
B. Sept. 30, 1882, St. Louis, Mo.   D. Aug. 3, 1954, St. Louis, Mo.

	G	AB	H	2B	3B	HR	HR %	R	RBI	BB	SO	SB	BA	SA	PH AB	PH H	G by POS
1905 STL N	24	83	20	2	1	0	0.0	7	5	3		1	.241	.289	0	0	3B-20, 2B-3, P-1
1906	94	317	71	6	3	0	0.0	21	14	4		2	.224	.262	0	0	3B-53, SS-16, OF-12, P-12, 2B-1

	G	AB	H	2B	3B	HR	HR %	R	RBI	BB	SO	SB	BA	SA	Pinch Hit AB	H	G by POS

Art Hoelskoetter continued

	G	AB	H	2B	3B	HR	HR%	R	RBI	BB	SO	SB	BA	SA	PH AB	H	G by POS
1907	119	396	98	6	3	2	0.5	21	28	27		5	.247	.293	2	0	2B-72, 1B-27, OF-8, C-8, 3B-2, P-2
1908	62	155	36	7	1	0	0.0	10	6	6		1	.232	.290	16	3	C-41, 3B-2, 2B-1, 1B-1
4 yrs.	299	951	225	21	8	2	0.2	59	53	40		9	.237	.282	18	3	3B-77, 2B-77, C-49, 1B-28, OF-20, SS-16, P-15
4 yrs.	299	951	225	21	8	2	0.2	59	53	40		9	.237	.282	18	3	3B-77, 2B-77, C-49, 1B-28, OF-20, SS-16, P-15

Marty Hogan

HOGAN, MARTIN T.
B. Oct. 25, 1871, Wensbury, England   D. Aug. 16, 1923, Youngstown, Ohio

	G	AB	H	2B	3B	HR	HR%	R	RBI	BB	SO	SB	BA	SA	PH AB	H	G by POS
1894 2 teams	CIN N	(6G – .130)			STL N	(29G – .280)											
" Total	35	123	31	3	4	0	0.0	15	16	4	17	9	.252	.341	0	0	OF-35
1895 STL N	5	18	3	1	0	0	0.0	2	2	3	0	2	.167	.222	0	0	OF-5
2 yrs.	40	141	34	4	4	0	0.0	17	18	7	17	11	.241	.326	0	0	OF-40
2 yrs.	34	118	31	4	4	0	0.0	13	15	6	13	9	.263	.364	0	0	OF-34

Ed Holly

HOLLY, EDWARD WILLIAM   BR TR 5'10" 165 lbs.
B. July 6, 1879, Chicago, Ill.   D. Nov. 27, 1973, Williamsport, Pa.

	G	AB	H	2B	3B	HR	HR%	R	RBI	BB	SO	SB	BA	SA	PH AB	H	G by POS
1906 STL N	10	34	2	0	0	0	0.0	1	7	5		0	.059	.059	0	0	SS-10
1907	149	544	125	18	3	1	0.2	55	40	36		16	.230	.279	0	0	SS-146, 2B-3
1914 PIT F	100	350	86	9	4	0	0.0	28	26	17		14	.246	.294	3	2	SS-94, OF-2, 2B-1
1915	16	42	11	2	0	0	0.0	8	5	5		3	.262	.310	1	1	SS-11, 3B-3
4 yrs.	275	970	224	29	7	1	0.1	92	78	63		33	.231	.278	4	3	SS-261, 2B-4, 3B-3, OF-2
2 yrs.	159	578	127	18	3	1	0.2	56	47	41		16	.220	.266	0	0	SS-156, 2B-3

Wattie Holm

HOLM, ROSCOE ALBERT   BR TR 5'9½" 160 lbs.
B. Dec. 28, 1901, Peterson, Iowa   D. May 19, 1950, Everly, Iowa

	G	AB	H	2B	3B	HR	HR%	R	RBI	BB	SO	SB	BA	SA	PH AB	H	G by POS
1924 STL N	81	293	86	10	4	0	0.0	40	23	8	16	1	.294	.355	5	1	OF-64, C-9, 3B-4
1925	13	58	12	1	1	0	0.0	10	2	3	1	1	.207	.259	0	0	OF-13
1926	55	144	41	5	1	0	0.0	18	21	18	14	3	.285	.333	15	5	OF-39
1927	110	419	120	27	8	3	0.7	55	66	24	29	4	.286	.411	4	2	OF-97, 3B-9
1928	102	386	107	24	6	3	0.8	61	47	32	17	1	.277	.394	9	4	3B-83, OF-7
1929	64	176	41	5	6	0	0.0	21	14	12	8	1	.233	.330	17	3	OF-44, 3B-1
1932	11	17	3	1	0	0	0.0	2	1	3	1	0	.176	.235	5	1	OF-4
7 yrs.	436	1493	410	73	26	6	0.4	207	174	100	86	11	.275	.370	55	16	OF-268, 3B-97, C-9
7 yrs.	436	1493	410	73	26	6	0.4	207	174	100	86	11	.275	.370	55	16	OF-268, 3B-97, C-9

WORLD SERIES

	G	AB	H	2B	3B	HR	HR%	R	RBI	BB	SO	SB	BA	SA	PH AB	H	G by POS
1926 STL N	5	16	2	0	0	0	0.0	1	1	1	2	0	.125	.125	1	0	OF-4
1928	3	6	1	0	0	0	0.0	0	1	0	1	0	.167	.167	2	0	OF-1
2 yrs.	8	22	3	0	0	0	0.0	1	2	1	3	0	.136	.136	3	0	OF-5

Ducky Holmes

HOLMES, HOWARD ELBERT   TR
B. July 8, 1883, Dayton, Ohio   D. Sept. 18, 1945, Dayton, Ohio

	G	AB	H	2B	3B	HR	HR%	R	RBI	BB	SO	SB	BA	SA	PH AB	H	G by POS
1906 STL N	9	27	5	0	0	0	0.0	2	2	2		0	.185	.185	0	0	C-9

Ducky Holmes

HOLMES, JAMES WILLIAM   BL TR 5'6" 170 lbs.
B. Jan. 28, 1869, Des Moines, Iowa   D. Aug. 6, 1932, Truro, Iowa

	G	AB	H	2B	3B	HR	HR%	R	RBI	BB	SO	SB	BA	SA	PH AB	H	G by POS
1895 LOU N	40	161	60	10	2	3	1.9	33	20	12	9	9	.373	.516	0	0	OF-29, SS-8, 3B-4, P-2
1896	47	141	38	3	2	0	0.0	22	18	13	5	8	.270	.319	10	3	OF-33, P-2, SS-1, 2B-1
1897 2 teams	LOU N	(2G – .000)			NY N	(79G – .268)											
" Total	81	310	82	8	6	1	0.3	51	44	19		30	.265	.339	2	0	OF-77, SS-2
1898 2 teams	STL N	(23G – .238)			BAL N	(113G – .285)											
" Total	136	543	150	11	10	1	0.2	63	64	25		29	.276	.339	1	1	OF-135
1899 BAL N	138	553	177	31	7	4	0.7	80	66	39		50	.320	.423	0	0	OF-138
1901 DET A	131	537	158	28	10	4	0.7	90	62	37		35	.294	.406	0	0	OF-131
1902	92	362	93	15	4	2	0.6	50	33	28		16	.257	.337	0	0	OF-92
1903 2 teams	WAS A	(21G – .225)			CHI A	(86G – .279)											
" Total	107	415	112	10	6	1	0.2	66	26	30		35	.270	.330	3	0	OF-96, 3B-7, 2B-2
1904 CHI A	68	251	78	11	9	1	0.4	42	19	14		13	.311	.438	5	2	OF-63
1905	92	328	66	15	2	0	0.0	42	22	19		11	.201	.259	3	2	OF-89
10 yrs.	932	3601	1014	142	58	17	0.5	539	374	236	14	236	.282	.367	24	8	OF-883, SS-11, 3B-11, P-4, 2B-3
1 yr.	23	101	24	1	1	0	0.0	9	0	2		4	.238	.267	1	1	OF-22

Sis Hopkins

HOPKINS, JOHN HINTON   BR TR
B. Jan. 3, 1883, Phoebus, Va.   D. Oct. 2, 1929, Phoebus, Va.

	G	AB	H	2B	3B	HR	HR%	R	RBI	BB	SO	SB	BA	SA	PH AB	H	G by POS
1907 STL N	15	44	6	3	0	0	0.0	7	3	10		2	.136	.205	0	0	OF-15

Johnny Hopp

HOPP, JOHN LEONARD (Hippity)   BL TL 5'10" 170 lbs.
B. July 18, 1916, Hastings, Neb.

	G	AB	H	2B	3B	HR	HR%	R	RBI	BB	SO	SB	BA	SA	PH AB	H	G by POS
1939 STL N	6	4	2	1	0	0	0.0	1	2	1	1	0	.500	.750	3	2	1B-1
1940	80	152	41	7	4	1	0.7	24	14	9	21	3	.270	.388	23	4	OF-39, 1B-10
1941	134	445	135	25	11	4	0.9	83	50	50	63	15	.303	.436	6	1	OF-91, 1B-39
1942	95	314	81	16	7	3	1.0	41	37	36	40	14	.258	.382	3	1	1B-88
1943	91	241	54	10	2	2	0.8	33	25	24	22	8	.224	.307	4	0	OF-52, 1B-27
1944	139	527	177	35	9	11	2.1	106	72	58	47	15	.336	.499	2	0	OF-131, 1B-6
1945	124	446	129	22	8	3	0.7	67	44	49	24	14	.289	.395	6	1	OF-104, 1B-15
1946 BOS N	129	445	148	23	8	3	0.7	71	48	34	34	21	.333	.440	8	3	1B-68, OF-58
1947	134	430	124	20	2	2	0.5	74	32	58	30	13	.288	.358	7	0	OF-125
1948 PIT N	120	392	109	15	12	1	0.3	64	31	40	25	5	.278	.385	14	7	OF-80, 1B-25

	G	AB	H	2B	3B	HR	HR %	R	RBI	BB	SO	SB	BA	SA	Pinch Hit AB	Pinch Hit H	G by POS

Johnny Hopp continued

		G	AB	H	2B	3B	HR	HR %	R	RBI	BB	SO	SB	BA	SA	PH AB	PH H	G by POS
1949	2 teams	PIT N (105G – .318)					BKN N (8G – .000)											
"	Total	113	385	118	14	5	5	1.3	55	39	37	32	9	.306	.408	13	5	1B-79, OF-20
1950	2 teams	PIT N (106G – .340)					NY A (19G – .333)											
"	Total	125	345	117	26	6	9	2.6	60	55	52	18	7	.339	.528	28	8	1B-82, OF-13
1951	NY A	46	63	13	1	0	2	3.2	10	4	9	11	2	.206	.317	19	4	1B-25
1952	2 teams	NY A (15G – .160)					DET A (42G – .217)											
"	Total	57	71	14	1	0	0	0.0	9	5	8	10	2	.197	.211	33	8	1B-13, OF-4
14 yrs.		1393	4260	1262	216	74	46	1.1	698	458	465	378	128	.296	.414	169	44	OF-717, 1B-478
7 yrs.		669	2129	619	116	41	24	1.1	355	244	227	218	69	.291	.418	47	9	OF-417, 1B-186
WORLD SERIES																		
1942	STL N	5	17	3	0	0	0	0.0	3	0	1	1	0	.176	.176	0	0	1B-5
1943		1	4	0	0	0	0	0.0	0	0	0	1	0	.000	.000	0	0	OF-1
1944		6	27	5	0	0	0	0.0	2	0	0	8	0	.185	.185	0	0	OF-6
1950	NY A	3	2	0	0	0	0	0.0	0	0	0	0	0	.000	.000	0	0	1B-3
1951		1	0	0	0	0	0	–	0	0	1	0	0	–	–	0	0	
5 yrs.		16	50	8	0	0	0	0.0	5	0	2	10	0	.160	.160	0	0	1B-8, OF-7

Rogers Hornsby

HORNSBY, ROGERS (Rajah)
B. Apr. 27, 1896, Winters, Tex.   D. Jan. 5, 1963, Chicago, Ill.
Manager 1925-26, 1928, 1930-37, 1952-53.
Hall of Fame 1942.

BR TR 5'11"   175 lbs.

		G	AB	H	2B	3B	HR	HR %	R	RBI	BB	SO	SB	BA	SA	PH AB	PH H	G by POS
1915	STL N	18	57	14	2	0	0	0.0	5	4	2	6	0	.246	.281	0	0	SS-18
1916		139	495	.155	17	15	6	1.2	63	65	40	63	17	.313	.444	1	1	3B-83, SS-45, 1B-15, 2B-1
1917		145	523	171	24	17	8	1.5	86	66	45	34	17	.327	.484	1	0	SS-144
1918		115	416	117	19	11	5	1.2	51	60	40	43	8	.281	.416	4	2	SS-109, OF-2
1919		138	512	163	15	9	8	1.6	68	71	48	41	17	.318	.430	0	0	3B-72, SS-37, 2B-25, 1B-5
1920		149	589	218	44	20	9	1.5	96	94	60	50	12	.370	.559	0	0	2B-149
1921		154	592	235	44	18	21	3.5	131	126	60	48	13	.397	.639	0	0	2B-142, OF-6, SS-3, 3B-3, 1B-1
1922		154	623	250	46	14	42	6.7	141	152	65	50	17	.401	.722	0	0	2B-154
1923		107	424	163	32	10	17	4.0	89	83	55	29	3	.384	.627	1	0	2B-96, 1B-10
1924		143	536	227	43	14	25	4.7	121	94	89	32	5	.424	.696	0	0	2B-143
1925		138	504	203	41	10	39	7.7	133	143	83	39	5	.403	.756	0	0	2B-136
1926		134	527	167	34	5	11	2.1	96	93	61	39	3	.317	.463	0	0	2B-134
1927	NY N	155	568	205	32	9	26	4.6	133	125	86	38	9	.361	.586	0	0	2B-155
1928	BOS N	140	486	188	42	7	21	4.3	99	94	107	41	5	.387	.632	0	0	2B-140
1929	CHI N	156	602	229	47	8	39	6.5	156	149	87	65	2	.380	.679	0	0	2B-156
1930		42	104	32	5	1	2	1.9	15	18	12	12	0	.308	.433	15	2	2B-25
1931		100	357	118	37	1	16	4.5	64	90	56	23	1	.331	.574	4	2	2B-69, 3B-26
1932		19	58	13	2	0	1	1.7	10	7	10	4	0	.224	.310	3	1	OF-10, 3B-6
1933	2 teams	STL N (46G – .325)					STL A (11G – .333)											
"	Total	57	92	30	7	0	3	3.3	11	23	14	7	1	.326	.500	35	11	2B-17
1934	STL A	24	23	7	2	0	1	4.3	2	11	7	4	0	.304	.522	15	5	OF-1, 3B-1
1935		10	24	5	3	0	0	0.0	1	3	3	6	0	.208	.333	3	1	1B-3, 2B-2, 3B-1
1936		2	5	2	0	0	0	0.0	1	2	1	0	0	.400	.400	1	1	1B-1
1937		20	56	18	3	0	1	1.8	7	11	7	5	0	.321	.429	3	0	2B-17
23 yrs.		2259	8173	2930	541	169	301	3.7	1579	1584	1038	679	135	.358 2nd	.577 7th	86	26	2B-1561, SS-356, 3B-192, 1B-35, OF-19
13 yrs.		1580 7th	5881 7th	2110 3rd	367 4th	143 2nd	193 3rd	3.3	1089 3rd	1072 4th	660 4th	480 10th	118 10th	.359 2nd	.568 2nd	33	11	2B-997, SS-356, 3B-158, 1B-31, OF-8
WORLD SERIES																		
1926	STL N	7	28	7	1	0	0	0.0	2	4	2	2	1	.250	.286	0	0	2B-7
1929	CHI N	5	21	5	1	1	0	0.0	4	1	1	8	0	.238	.381	0	0	2B-5
2 yrs.		12	49	12	2	1	0	0.0	6	5	3	10	1	.245	.327	0	0	2B-12

Art Hostetter

Playing record listed under Art Hoelskoetter

John Houseman

HOUSEMAN, JOHN FRANKLIN
B. Jan. 10, 1870, Holland, Mich.   D. Nov. 4, 1922, Chicago, Ill.

		G	AB	H	2B	3B	HR	HR %	R	RBI	BB	SO	SB	BA	SA	PH AB	PH H	G by POS
1894	CHI N	4	15	6	3	1	0	0.0	5	4	5	3	2	.400	.733	0	0	SS-3, 2B-1
1897	STL N	80	278	68	6	6	0	0.0	34	21	28		16	.245	.309	2	1	2B-41, OF-33, SS-5, 3B-3
2 yrs.		84	293	74	9	7	0	0.0	39	25	33	3	18	.253	.331	2	1	2B-42, OF-33, SS-5, 3B-3
1 yr.		80	278	68	6	6	0	0.0	34	21	28		16	.245	.309	2	1	2B-41, OF-33, SS-5, 3B-3

Doug Howard

HOWARD, DOUGLAS LYN
B. Feb. 6, 1948, Salt Lake City, Utah

BR TR 6'3"   185 lbs.

		G	AB	H	2B	3B	HR	HR %	R	RBI	BB	SO	SB	BA	SA	PH AB	PH H	G by POS
1972	CAL A	11	38	10	1	0	0	0.0	4	2	1	3	0	.263	.289	1	0	OF-8, 3B-1, 1B-1
1973		8	21	2	0	0	0	0.0	2	1	1	6	0	.095	.095	2	0	OF-6, 3B-1, 1B-1
1974		22	39	9	0	1	0	0.0	5	5	2	1	1	.231	.282	9	3	OF-8, 1B-5
1975	STL N	17	29	6	0	0	1	3.4	1	1	0	7	0	.207	.310	10	3	1B-7
1976	CLE A	39	90	19	4	0	0	0.0	7	13	3	13	1	.211	.256	4	1	1B-32, OF-2
5 yrs.		97	217	46	5	1	1	0.5	19	22	7	30	2	.212	.258	26	7	1B-46, OF-24, 3B-2
1 yr.		17	29	6	0	0	1	3.4	1	1	0	7	0	.207	.310	10	3	1B-7

Bill Howerton

HOWERTON, WILLIAM RAY (Hopalong)
B. Dec. 12, 1921, Lompoc, Calif.

BL TR 5'11"   185 lbs.

		G	AB	H	2B	3B	HR	HR %	R	RBI	BB	SO	SB	BA	SA	PH AB	PH H	G by POS
1949	STL N	9	13	4	0	0	0	0.0	1	1	0	2	0	.308	.385	3	1	OF-6
1950		110	313	88	20	8	10	3.2	50	59	47	60	0	.281	.492	17	5	OF-94
1951	2 teams	STL N (24G – .262)					PIT N (80G – .274)											
"	Total	104	284	77	16	3	12	4.2	39	41	36	56	1	.271	.475	29	4	OF-70, 3B-4
1952	2 teams	PIT N (13G – .320)					NY N (11G – .067)											
"	Total	24	40	9	2	0	0	0.0	5	5	9	7	0	.225	.325	13	2	OF-8, 3B-1

	G	AB	H	2B	3B	HR	HR %	R	RBI	BB	SO	SB	BA	SA	Pinch Hit AB	H	G by POS

Bill Howerton continued

	G	AB	H	2B	3B	HR	HR %	R	RBI	BB	SO	SB	BA	SA	Pinch Hit AB	H	G by POS
4 yrs.	247	650	178	39	12	22	3.4	95	106	92	125	1	.274	.472	62	12	OF-178, 3B-5
3 yrs.	143	391	109	25	9	11	2.8	61	64	57	74	0	.279	.473	27	7	OF-117

Jimmy Hudgens

HUDGENS, JAMES PRICE   BL TL 6'   180 lbs.
B. Aug. 24, 1902, Newburg, Mo.   D. Aug. 26, 1955, St. Louis, Mo.

	G	AB	H	2B	3B	HR	HR %	R	RBI	BB	SO	SB	BA	SA	Pinch Hit AB	H	G by POS
1923 STL N	6	12	3	1	0	0	0.0	2	0	3	3	0	.250	.333	2	0	1B-3, 2B-1
1925 CIN N	3	7	3	1	1	0	0.0	0	0	1	1	0	.429	.857	0	0	1B-3
1926	17	20	5	1	0	0	0.0	2	1	1	0	0	.250	.300	10	3	1B-6
3 yrs.	26	39	11	3	1	0	0.0	4	1	5	4	0	.282	.410	12	3	1B-12, 2B-1
1 yr.	6	12	3	1	0	0	0.0	2	0	3	3	0	.250	.333	2	0	1B-3, 2B-1

Frank Huelsman

HUELSMAN, FRANK ELMER   BR TR 6'2"   210 lbs.
B. June 5, 1874, St. Louis, Mo.   D. June 9, 1959, Affton, Mo.

	G	AB	H	2B	3B	HR	HR %	R	RBI	BB	SO	SB	BA	SA	Pinch Hit AB	H	G by POS
1897 STL N	2	7	2	1	0	0	0.0	0	0	0		0	.286	.429	0	0	OF-2
1904 4 teams	CHI A (4G – .143)				DET A (4G – .333)				STL A (20G – .221)				WAS A (84G – .248)				
" Total	112	396	97	23	5	2	0.5	28	35	31		7	.245	.343	4	0	OF-107
1905 WAS A	126	421	114	28	8	3	0.7	48	62	31		11	.271	.397	4	1	OF-123
3 yrs.	240	824	213	52	13	5	0.6	76	97	62		18	.258	.371	8	1	OF-232
1 yr.	2	7	2	1	0	0	0.0	0	0	0		0	.286	.429	0	0	OF-2

Miller Huggins

HUGGINS, MILLER JAMES (Hug, The Mighty Mite)   BB TR 5'6½"   140 lbs.
B. Mar. 27, 1879, Cincinnati, Ohio   D. Sept. 25, 1929, New York, N. Y.
Manager 1913-29.
Hall of Fame 1964.

	G	AB	H	2B	3B	HR	HR %	R	RBI	BB	SO	SB	BA	SA	Pinch Hit AB	H	G by POS
1904 CIN N	140	491	129	12	7	2	0.4	96	30	88		13	.263	.328	0	0	2B-140
1905	149	564	154	11	8	1	0.2	117	38	103		27	.273	.326	0	0	2B-149
1906	146	545	159	11	7	0	0.0	81	26	71		41	.292	.338	0	0	2B-146
1907	156	561	139	12	4	1	0.2	64	41	83		28	.248	.289	0	0	2B-156
1908	135	498	119	14	5	0	0.0	65	23	58		30	.239	.287	4	1	2B-135
1909	57	159	34	3	1	0	0.0	18	6	28		11	.214	.245	10	1	2B-31, 3B-15
1910 STL N	151	547	145	15	6	1	0.2	101	36	116	46	34	.265	.320	0	0	2B-151
1911	138	509	133	19	2	1	0.2	106	24	96	52	37	.261	.312	1	1	2B-136
1912	120	431	131	15	4	0	0.0	82	29	87	31	35	.304	.357	5	0	2B-114
1913	120	382	109	12	0	0	0.0	74	27	91	49	23	.285	.317	5	1	2B-112
1914	148	509	134	17	4	1	0.2	85	24	105	63	32	.263	.318	1	0	2B-147
1915	107	353	85	5	2	2	0.6	57	24	74	68	13	.241	.283	0	0	2B-107
1916	18	9	3	0	0	0	0.0	2	2	3	0	2	.333	.333	4	2	2B-7
13 yrs.	1585	5558	1474	146	50	9	0.2	948	328	1002	312	324	.265	.314	30	6	2B-1531, 3B-15
7 yrs.	802	2740	740	83	18	5	0.2	507	164	571	312	174	.270	.319	16	4	2B-774
										7th		4th					

Terry Hughes

HUGHES, TERRY WAYNE   BR TR 6'1"   185 lbs.
B. May 13, 1949, Spartanburg, S. C.

	G	AB	H	2B	3B	HR	HR %	R	RBI	BB	SO	SB	BA	SA	Pinch Hit AB	H	G by POS
1970 CHI N	2	3	1	0	0	0	0.0	0	0	0	0	0	.333	.333	1	1	OF-1, 3B-1
1973 STL N	11	14	3	1	0	0	0.0	1	1	1	4	0	.214	.286	4	1	3B-5, 1B-1
1974 BOS A	41	69	14	2	0	1	1.4	5	6	6	18	0	.203	.275	1	0	3B-36
3 yrs.	54	86	18	3	0	1	1.2	6	7	7	22	0	.209	.279	6	2	3B-42, OF-1, 1B-1
1 yr.	11	14	3	1	0	0	0.0	1	1	1	4	0	.214	.286	4	1	3B-5, 1B-1

Rudy Hulswitt

HULSWITT, RUDOLPH EDWARD   BR TR 5'8½"   165 lbs.
B. Feb. 23, 1877, Newport, Ky.   D. Jan. 16, 1950, Louisville, Ky.

	G	AB	H	2B	3B	HR	HR %	R	RBI	BB	SO	SB	BA	SA	Pinch Hit AB	H	G by POS
1899 LOU N	1	0	0	0	0	0	–	0	0	0		0	–	–	0	0	SS-1
1902 PHI N	128	497	135	11	7	0	0.0	59	38	30		12	.272	.322	0	0	SS-125, 3B-3
1903	138	519	128	22	9	1	0.2	56	58	28		10	.247	.329	0	0	SS-138
1904	113	406	99	11	4	1	0.2	36	36	16		8	.244	.298	0	0	SS-113
1908 CIN N	119	386	88	5	7	1	0.3	27	28	30		7	.228	.285	0	0	SS-118, 2B-1
1909 STL N	82	289	81	8	3	0	0.0	21	29	19		7	.280	.329	4	1	SS-65, 2B-12
1910	63	133	33	7	2	0	0.0	9	14	13	10	5	.248	.331	31	6	SS-30, 2B-2
7 yrs.	644	2230	564	64	32	3	0.1	208	203	136	10	49	.253	.314	35	7	SS-590, 2B-15, 3B-3
2 yrs.	145	422	114	15	5	0	0.0	30	43	32	10	12	.270	.329	35	7	SS-95, 2B-14

Joel Hunt

HUNT, OLIVER JOEL (Jodie)   BR TR 5'10"   165 lbs.
B. Oct. 11, 1905, Texico, N. M.   D. July 24, 1978, Teague, Tex.

	G	AB	H	2B	3B	HR	HR %	R	RBI	BB	SO	SB	BA	SA	Pinch Hit AB	H	G by POS
1931 STL N	4	1	0	0	0	0	0.0	2	0	0	1	0	.000	.000	1	0	OF-1
1932	12	21	4	1	0	0	0.0	0	3	4	3	0	.190	.238	5	2	OF-5
2 yrs.	16	22	4	1	0	0	0.0	2	3	4	4	0	.182	.227	6	2	OF-6
2 yrs.	16	22	4	1	0	0	0.0	2	3	4	4	0	.182	.227	6	2	OF-6

Ron Hunt

HUNT, RONALD KENNETH   BR TR 6'   186 lbs.
B. Feb. 23, 1941, St. Louis, Mo.

	G	AB	H	2B	3B	HR	HR %	R	RBI	BB	SO	SB	BA	SA	Pinch Hit AB	H	G by POS
1963 NY N	143	533	145	28	4	10	1.9	64	42	40	50	5	.272	.396	1	1	2B-142, 3B-1
1964	127	475	144	19	6	6	1.3	59	42	29	30	6	.303	.406	6	2	2B-109, 3B-12
1965	57	196	47	12	1	1	0.5	21	10	14	19	2	.240	.327	4	0	2B-46, 3B-6
1966	132	479	138	19	2	3	0.6	63	33	41	34	8	.288	.355	2	2	2B-123, SS-1, 3B-1
1967 LA N	110	388	102	17	3	3	0.8	44	33	39	24	2	.263	.345	10	1	2B-90, 3B-8
1968 SF N	148	529	132	19	0	2	0.4	79	28	78	41	6	.250	.297	2	1	2B-147
1969	128	478	125	23	3	3	0.6	72	41	51	47	9	.262	.341	3	0	2B-125, 3B-1
1970	117	367	103	17	1	6	1.6	70	41	44	29	1	.281	.381	23	7	2B-85, 3B-16
1971 MON N	152	520	145	20	3	5	1.0	89	38	58	41	5	.279	.358	5	0	2B-133, 3B-19
1972	129	443	112	20	0	0	0.0	56	18	51	29	9	.253	.298	5	0	2B-122, 3B-5
1973	113	401	124	14	0	0	0.0	61	18	52	19	10	.309	.344	6	2	2B-102, 3B-14

	G	AB	H	2B	3B	HR	HR %	R	RBI	BB	SO	SB	BA	SA	Pinch Hit AB	H	G by POS

Ron Hunt continued

1974 **2 teams**		**MON N** (115G – .268)				**STL N** (12G – .174)											
" Total	127	426	112	15	0	0	0.0	67	26	58	19	2	.263	.298	10	3	3B-75, 2B-36, SS-1
12 yrs.	1483	5235	1429	223	23	39	0.7	745	370	555	382	65	.273	.347	83	20	2B-1260, 3B-158, SS-2
1 yr.	12	23	4	0	0	0	0.0	1	0	3	2	0	.174	.174	4	2	2B-5

Herb Hunter

HUNTER, HERBERT HARRISON
B. Dec. 25, 1895, Boston, Mass. D. July 25, 1970, Orlando, Fla. BL TR 6'½" 165 lbs.

1916 **2 teams**		**NY N** (21G – .250)				**CHI N** (2G – .000)											
" Total	23	32	7	0	0	1	3.1	3	4	0	5	0	.219	.313	11	2	3B-7, 1B-2
1917 CHI N	3	3	0	0	0	0	0.0	0	0	0	0	0	.000	.000	1	0	3B-1, 2B-1
1920 BOS A	4	12	1	0	0	0	0.0	2	0	1	1	0	.083	.083	1	0	OF-4
1921 STL N	9	2	0	0	0	0	0.0	3	0	1	0	0	.000	.000	1	0	1B-1
4 yrs.	39	49	8	0	0	1	2.0	8	4	2	6	0	.163	.224	13	2	3B-8, OF-4, 1B-3, 2B-1
1 yr.	9	2	0	0	0	0	0.0	3	0	1	0	0	.000	.000	1	0	1B-1

Steve Huntz

HUNTZ, STEPHEN MICHAEL
B. Dec. 3, 1945, Cleveland, Ohio BB TR 6'1" 204 lbs.

1967 STL N	3	6	1	0	0	0	0.0	1	0	1	2	0	.167	.167	1	1	2B-2
1969	71	139	27	4	0	3	2.2	13	13	27	34	0	.194	.288	3	0	SS-52, 2B-12, 3B-6
1970 SD N	106	352	77	8	0	11	3.1	54	37	66	69	0	.219	.335	9	1	SS-57, 3B-51
1971 CHI A	35	86	18	3	1	2	2.3	10	6	7	9	1	.209	.337	12	0	2B-14, SS-7, 3B-6
1975 SD N	22	53	8	4	0	0	0.0	3	4	7	8	0	.151	.226	6	0	3B-16, 2B-2
5 yrs.	237	636	131	19	1	16	2.5	81	60	108	122	1	.206	.314	31	2	SS-116, 3B-79, 2B-30
2 yrs.	74	145	28	4	0	3	2.1	14	13	28	36	0	.193	.283	4	1	SS-52, 2B-14, 3B-6

Fred Hutchinson

HUTCHINSON, FREDERICK CHARLES
B. Aug. 12, 1919, Seattle, Wash. D. Nov. 12, 1964, Bradenton, Fla. BL TR 6'2" 190 lbs.
Manager 1952-54, 1956-64.

1939 DET A	13	34	13	1	0	0	0.0	5	6	2	0	0	.382	.412	0	0	P-13
1940	17	30	8	1	0	0	0.0	1	2	0	0	0	.267	.300	0	0	P-17
1941	2	2	0	0	0	0	0.0	0	0	0	2	0	.000	.000	2	0	
1946	40	89	28	4	0	0	0.0	11	13	6	1	0	.315	.360	9	2	P-28
1947	56	106	32	5	2	2	1.9	8	15	6	6	2	.302	.443	22	6	P-33
1948	76	112	23	1	0	1	0.9	11	12	23	9	3	.205	.241	32	7	P-33
1949	38	73	18	2	1	0	0.0	12	7	8	5	1	.247	.301	4	1	P-33
1950	44	95	31	7	0	0	0.0	15	20	12	3	0	.326	.400	4	1	P-39
1951	47	85	16	2	0	0	0.0	7	7	7	4	0	.188	.212	13	2	P-31
1952	17	18	1	0	0	0	0.0	0	0	3	0	0	.056	.056	5	1	P-12
1953	4	6	1	0	0	1	16.7	1	1	0	0	0	.167	.667	4	1	P-3, 1B-1
11 yrs.	354	650	171	23	3	4	0.6	71	83	67	30	6	.263	.326	91	20	P-242, 1B-1

WORLD SERIES

1940 DET A	1	0	0	0	0	0	–	0	0	0	0	0	–	–	0	0	P-1

Ham Hyatt

HYATT, ROBERT HAMILTON
B. Nov. 1, 1884, Buncombe County, N. C. D. Sept. 11, 1963, Liberty Lake, Wash. BL TR 6'1" 185 lbs.

1909 PIT N	48	67	20	3	4	0	0.0	9	7	3		1	.299	.463	37	9	OF-6, 1B-2
1910	74	175	46	5	6	1	0.6	19	30	8	14	3	.263	.377	31	6	1B-38, OF-4
1912	46	97	28	3	1	0	0.0	13	22	6	8	2	.289	.340	27	6	OF-15, 1B-3
1913	63	81	27	6	2	4	4.9	8	16	3	8	0	.333	.605	52	15	OF-5, 1B-5
1914	74	79	17	3	1	1	1.3	2	15	7	14	1	.215	.316	58	14	1B-7, C-1
1915 STL N	106	295	79	8	9	2	0.7	23	46	28	24	3	.268	.376	14	3	1B-81, OF-25
1918 NY A	53	131	30	8	0	2	1.5	11	10	8	8	1	.229	.336	21	4	OF-25, 1B-5
7 yrs.	464	925	247	36	23	10	1.1	85	146	63	76	11	.267	.388	240	57	1B-141, OF-80, C-1
1 yr.	106	295	79	8	9	2	0.7	23	46	28	24	3	.268	.376	14	3	1B-81, OF-25

WORLD SERIES

1909 PIT N	2	4	0	0	0	0	0.0	1	1	1	0	0	.000	.000	1	0	OF-1

Pat Hynes

HYNES, PATRICK J.
B. Mar. 12, 1884, St. Louis, Mo. D. Mar. 12, 1907, St. Louis, Mo.

1903 STL N	1	3	0	0	0	0	0.0	0	0	0		0	.000	.000	0	0	P-1
1904 STL A	66	254	60	7	3	0	0.0	23	15	3		3	.236	.287	0	0	OF-63, P-5
2 yrs.	67	257	60	7	3	0	0.0	23	15	3		3	.233	.284	0	0	OF-63, P-6
1 yr.	1	3	0	0	0	0	0.0	0	0	0		0	.000	.000	0	0	P-1

Dane Iorg

IORG, DANE CHARLES
Brother of Garth Iorg.
B. May 11, 1950, Calif. BL TR 6' 180 lbs.

1977 **2 teams**		**PHI N** (12G – .167)				**STL N** (30G – .313)											
" Total	42	62	15	2	0	0	0.0	5	6	6	7	0	.242	.274	21	6	1B-9, OF-7
1978 STL N	35	85	23	4	1	0	0.0	6	4	4	10	0	.271	.341	11	2	OF-25
1979	79	179	52	11	1	1	0.6	12	21	12	28	1	.291	.380	39	11	OF-39, 1B-10
1980	105	251	76	23	1	3	1.2	33	36	20	34	1	.303	.438	38	10	OF-57, 1B-5, 3B-1
1981	75	217	71	11	2	2	0.9	23	39	7	9	2	.327	.424	14	4	OF-57, 1B-8, 3B-2
1982	102	238	70	14	1	0	0.0	17	34	23	23	0	.294	.361	27	7	OF-63, 1B-10, 3B-2
6 yrs.	438	1032	307	65	6	6	0.6	96	140	72	111	4	.297	.390	150	40	OF-254, 1B-42, 3B-5
6 yrs.	426	1002	302	64	6	6	0.6	93	138	71	108	4	.301	.395	147	40	OF-254, 1B-33, 3B-5
															3rd	3rd	

WORLD SERIES

1982 STL N	5	17	9	4	1	0	0.0	4	1	0	0	0	.529	.882	0	0	

	G	AB	H	2B	3B	HR	HR %	R	RBI	BB	SO	SB	BA	SA	Pinch Hit AB	Pinch Hit H	G by POS

Walt Irwin

IRWIN, WALTER KINGSLEY (Lightning)   BR TR 5'10½" 170 lbs.
B. Sept. 23, 1897, Henrietta, Pa.   D. Aug. 18, 1976, Spring Lake, Mich.

	G	AB	H	2B	3B	HR	HR %	R	RBI	BB	SO	SB	BA	SA	PH AB	PH H	G by POS
1921 STL N	4	1	0	0	0	0	0.0	1	0	0	1	0	.000	.000	1	0	

Ray Jablonski

JABLONSKI, RAYMOND LEO (Jabbo)   BR TR 5'10" 175 lbs.
B. Dec. 17, 1926, Chicago, Ill.

	G	AB	H	2B	3B	HR	HR %	R	RBI	BB	SO	SB	BA	SA	PH AB	PH H	G by POS
1953 STL N	157	604	162	23	5	21	3.5	64	112	34	61	2	.268	.427	0	0	3B-157
1954	152	611	181	33	3	12	2.0	80	104	49	42	9	.296	.419	2	2	3B-149, 1B-1
1955 CIN N	74	221	53	9	0	9	4.1	28	28	13	35	0	.240	.403	17	4	OF-28, 3B-28
1956	130	407	104	25	1	15	3.7	42	66	37	57	2	.256	.432	14	5	3B-127, 2B-1
1957 NY N	107	305	88	15	1	9	3.0	37	57	31	47	0	.289	.433	28	6	3B-70, 1B-6, OF-1
1958 SF N	82	230	53	15	1	12	5.2	28	46	17	50	2	.230	.461	31	9	3B-57
1959 2 teams		STL N	(60G –	.253)		KC	A	(25G –	.262)								
" Total	85	152	39	5	0	5	3.3	15	22	11	30	1	.257	.388	53	8	3B-36, SS-1
1960 KC A	21	32	7	1	0	0	0.0	3	4	8	0	0	.219	.250	13	3	3B-6
8 yrs.	808	2562	687	126	11	83	3.2	297	438	196	330	16	.268	.423	158	37	3B-630, OF-29, 1B-7, SS-1, 2B-1
3 yrs.	369	1302	365	60	8	36	2.8	155	230	91	122	12	.280	.422	46	9	3B-325, SS-1, 1B-1

Bob James

JAMES, BERTON HULON   BL TR 5'11" 175 lbs.
B. July 7, 1886, Adamsville, Ky.   D. Jan. 2, 1959, Adairville, Ky.

	G	AB	H	2B	3B	HR	HR %	R	RBI	BB	SO	SB	BA	SA	PH AB	PH H	G by POS
1909 STL N	6	21	6	0	0	0	0.0	1	0	4		1	.286	.286	0	0	OF-6

Charlie James

JAMES, CHARLES WESLEY   BR TR 6'1" 195 lbs.
B. Dec. 22, 1937, St. Louis, Mo.

	G	AB	H	2B	3B	HR	HR %	R	RBI	BB	SO	SB	BA	SA	PH AB	PH H	G by POS
1960 STL N	43	50	9	1	0	2	4.0	5	5	1	12	0	.180	.320	9	1	OF-37
1961	108	349	89	19	2	4	1.1	43	44	15	59	2	.255	.355	19	3	OF-90
1962	129	388	107	13	4	8	2.1	50	59	10	58	3	.276	.392	12	4	OF-116
1963	116	347	93	14	2	10	2.9	34	45	10	64	2	.268	.406	18	10	OF-101
1964	88	233	52	9	1	5	2.1	24	17	11	58	0	.223	.335	31	8	OF-60
1965 CIN N	26	39	8	0	0	0	0.0	2	2	1	9	0	.205	.205	19	4	OF-7
6 yrs.	510	1406	358	56	9	29	2.1	158	172	48	260	7	.255	.369	108	30	OF-411
5 yrs.	484	1367	350	56	9	29	2.1	156	170	47	251	7	.256	.374	89	26	OF-404

WORLD SERIES

	G	AB	H	2B	3B	HR	HR %	R	RBI	BB	SO	SB	BA	SA	PH AB	PH H	G by POS
1964 STL N	3	3	0	0	0	0	0.0	0	0	0	1	0	.000	.000	3	0	

Hal Janvrin

JANVRIN, HAROLD CHANDLER (Childe Harold)   BR TR 5'11½" 168 lbs.
B. Aug. 27, 1892, Haverhill, Mass.   D. Mar. 2, 1962, Boston, Mass.

	G	AB	H	2B	3B	HR	HR %	R	RBI	BB	SO	SB	BA	SA	PH AB	PH H	G by POS
1911 BOS A	9	27	4	1	0	0	0.0	2	1	3		0	.148	.185	0	0	3B-5, 1B-4
1913	86	276	57	5	1	3	1.1	18	25	23	27	17	.207	.264	5	0	SS-48, 3B-19, 2B-8, 1B-6
1914	143	492	117	18	6	1	0.2	65	51	38	50	29	.238	.305	0	0	2B-57, 1B-56, SS-20, 3B-6
1915	99	316	85	9	1	0	0.0	41	37	14	27	8	.269	.304	3	1	SS-64, 3B-20, 2B-8
1916	117	310	69	11	4	0	0.0	32	26	32	32	6	.223	.284	7	1	SS-59, 2B-39, 1B-4, 3B-3
1917	55	127	25	3	0	0	0.0	21	8	11	13	2	.197	.220	4	1	2B-38, SS-10, 1B-1
1919 2 teams		WAS A	(61G –	.178)		STL N	(7G –	.214)									
" Total	68	222	40	5	1	1	0.5	18	14	21	19	8	.180	.225	3	1	2B-58, SS-3, 3B-1
1920 STL N	87	270	74	8	4	1	0.4	33	28	17	19	5	.274	.344	4	1	SS-27, 1B-25, OF-20, 2B-6
1921 2 teams		STL N	(18G –	.281)		BKN N	(44G –	.196)									
" Total	62	124	27	5	0	0	0.0	13	19	8	6	4	.218	.258	8	1	SS-17, 2B-11, 1B-8, 3B-5, OF-1
1922 BKN N	30	57	17	3	1	0	0.0	7	1	4	4	0	.298	.386	5	2	2B-15, SS-4, 3B-2, OF-1, 1B-1
10 yrs.	756	2221	515	68	18	6	0.3	250	210	171	197	79	.232	.287	39	8	SS-252, 2B-240, 1B-105, 3B-61, OF-22
3 yrs.	112	316	86	10	4	1	0.3	39	34	20	21	6	.272	.339	13	2	SS-28, 1B-25, OF-20, 2B-9, 3B-1

WORLD SERIES

	G	AB	H	2B	3B	HR	HR %	R	RBI	BB	SO	SB	BA	SA	PH AB	PH H	G by POS
1915 BOS A	1	1	0	0	0	0	0.0	0	0	0	0	0	.000	.000	0	0	SS-1
1916	5	23	5	3	0	0	0.0	2	1	0	6	0	.217	.348	0	0	2B-5
2 yrs.	6	24	5	3	0	0	0.0	2	1	0	6	0	.208	.333	0	0	2B-5, SS-1

Julian Javier

JAVIER, MANUEL JULIAN LIRANZO (Hoolie, The Phantom)   BR TR 6'1" 175 lbs.
B. Aug. 9, 1936, San Francisco De Macoris, Dominican Republic

	G	AB	H	2B	3B	HR	HR %	R	RBI	BB	SO	SB	BA	SA	PH AB	PH H	G by POS
1960 STL N	119	451	107	19	8	4	0.9	55	21	21	72	19	.237	.341	0	0	2B-119
1961	113	445	124	14	3	2	0.4	58	41	30	51	11	.279	.337	0	0	2B-113
1962	155	598	157	25	5	7	1.2	97	39	47	73	26	.263	.356	0	0	2B-151, SS-4
1963	161	609	160	27	9	9	1.5	82	46	24	86	18	.263	.381	0	0	2B-161
1964	155	535	129	19	5	12	2.2	66	65	30	84	9	.241	.363	0	0	2B-154
1965	77	229	52	6	4	2	0.9	34	23	8	44	5	.227	.314	0	0	2B-69
1966	147	460	105	13	5	7	1.5	52	31	26	63	11	.228	.324	0	0	2B-145
1967	140	520	146	16	3	14	2.7	68	64	25	92	6	.281	.404	2	0	2B-138
1968	139	519	135	25	4	8	1.5	54	52	24	61	10	.260	.347	0	0	2B-139
1969	143	493	139	28	2	10	2.0	59	42	40	74	8	.282	.408	4	1	2B-141
1970	139	513	129	16	3	2	0.4	62	42	24	70	6	.251	.306	3	2	2B-137
1971	90	259	67	6	4	3	1.2	32	28	9	33	5	.259	.347	9	2	2B-80, 3B-1
1972 CIN N	44	91	19	2	0	2	2.2	3	12	6	11	1	.209	.297	20	4	3B-19, 2B-5, 1B-1
13 yrs.	1622	5722	1469	216	55	78	1.4	722	506	314	812	135	.257	.355	38	9	2B-1552, 3B-20, SS-4, 1B-1
12 yrs.	1578	5631	1450	214	55	76	1.3	719	494	308	801	134	.258	.356	18	5	2B-1547, SS-4, 3B-1
	8th	9th								3rd	8th						

WORLD SERIES

	G	AB	H	2B	3B	HR	HR %	R	RBI	BB	SO	SB	BA	SA	PH AB	PH H	G by POS
1964 STL N	1	0	0	0	0	0	–	1	0	0	0	0	–	–	0	0	2B-1

	G	AB	H	2B	3B	HR	HR %	R	RBI	BB	SO	SB	BA	SA	Pinch Hit AB	Pinch Hit H	G by POS

Julian Javier continued

	G	AB	H	2B	3B	HR	HR %	R	RBI	BB	SO	SB	BA	SA	PH AB	PH H	G by POS
1967	7	25	9	3	0	1	4.0	2	4	0	6	0	.360	.600	0	0	2B-7
1968	7	27	9	1	0	0	0.0	1	3	3	4	1	.333	.370	0	0	2B-7
1972 CIN N	4	2	0	0	0	0	0.0	0	0	0	0	0	.000	.000	2	0	
4 yrs.	19	54	18	4	0	1	1.9	4	7	3	10	1	.333	.463	2	0	2B-15

Hal Jeffcoat

JEFFCOAT, HAROLD BENTLEY
Brother of George Jeffcoat.
B. Sept. 6, 1924, West Columbia, S. C.
BR TR 5'10½" 185 lbs.

	G	AB	H	2B	3B	HR	HR %	R	RBI	BB	SO	SB	BA	SA	PH AB	PH H	G by POS
1948 CHI N	134	473	132	16	4	4	0.8	53	42	24	68	8	.279	.355	14	6	OF-119
1949	108	363	89	18	6	2	0.6	43	26	20	48	12	.245	.344	5	2	OF-101
1950	66	179	42	13	1	2	1.1	21	18	6	23	7	.235	.352	8	1	OF-53
1951	113	278	76	20	2	4	1.4	44	27	16	23	8	.273	.403	9	3	OF-87
1952	102	297	65	17	2	4	1.3	29	30	15	40	7	.219	.330	1	0	OF-95
1953	106	183	43	3	1	4	2.2	22	22	21	26	5	.235	.328	2	0	OF-100
1954	56	31	8	2	1	1	3.2	13	6	1	7	2	.258	.484	0	0	P-43, OF-3
1955	52	23	4	0	0	1	4.3	3	1	2	9	0	.174	.304	0	0	P-50
1956 CIN N	49	54	8	2	0	0	0.0	5	5	3	20	0	.148	.185	0	0	P-38
1957	53	69	14	3	1	4	5.8	13	11	5	20	0	.203	.449	0	0	P-37
1958	50	9	5	0	0	0	0.0	2	0	1	2	0	.556	.556	0	0	P-49, OF-1
1959 2 teams				CIN N (17G – 1.000)				STL N (12G – .000)									
" Total	29	4	1	1	0	0	0.0	0	0	0	3	0	.250	.500	0	0	P-28
12 yrs.	918	1963	487	95	18	26	1.3	249	188	114	289	49	.248	.355	39	12	OF-559, P-245
1 yr.	12	3	0	0	0	0	0.0	0	0	0	3	0	.000	.000	0	0	P-11

Alex Johnson

JOHNSON, ALEXANDER
B. Dec. 7, 1942, Helena, Ark.
BR TR 6' 205 lbs.

	G	AB	H	2B	3B	HR	HR %	R	RBI	BB	SO	SB	BA	SA	PH AB	PH H	G by POS
1964 PHI N	43	109	33	7	1	4	3.7	18	18	6	26	1	.303	.495	7	2	OF-35
1965	97	262	77	9	3	8	3.1	27	28	15	60	4	.294	.443	27	8	OF-82
1966 STL N	25	86	16	0	1	2	2.3	7	6	5	18	1	.186	.279	2	0	OF-22
1967	81	175	39	9	2	1	0.6	20	12	9	26	6	.223	.314	20	5	OF-57
1968 CIN N	149	603	188	32	6	2	0.3	79	58	26	71	16	.312	.395	9	1	OF-140
1969	139	523	165	18	4	17	3.3	86	88	25	69	11	.315	.463	9	2	OF-132
1970 CAL A	156	614	202	26	6	14	2.3	85	86	35	68	17	.329	.459	0	0	OF-156
1971	65	242	63	8	0	2	0.8	19	21	15	34	5	.260	.318	5	0	OF-61
1972 CLE A	108	356	85	10	1	8	2.2	31	37	22	40	6	.239	.340	0	0	OF-95
1973 TEX A	158	624	179	26	3	8	1.3	62	68	32	82	10	.287	.377	1	1	OF-47
1974 2 teams				TEX A (114G – .291)				NY A (10G – .214)									
" Total	124	481	138	15	3	5	1.0	60	43	28	62	20	.287	.362	6	0	OF-82
1975 NY A	52	119	31	5	1	1	0.8	15	15	7	21	2	.261	.345	14	5	OF-7
1976 DET A	125	429	115	15	2	6	1.4	41	45	19	49	14	.268	.354	16	5	OF-90
13 yrs.	1322	4623	1331	180	33	78	1.7	550	525	244	626	113	.288	.392	126	30	OF-1006
2 yrs.	106	261	55	9	3	3	1.1	27	18	14	44	7	.211	.303	22	5	OF-79

Billy Johnson

JOHNSON, WILLIAM RUSSELL (Bull)
B. Aug. 30, 1918, Montclair, N. J.
BR TR 5'10" 180 lbs.

	G	AB	H	2B	3B	HR	HR %	R	RBI	BB	SO	SB	BA	SA	PH AB	PH H	G by POS
1943 NY A	155	592	166	24	6	5	0.8	70	94	53	30	3	.280	.367	0	0	3B-155
1946	85	296	77	14	5	4	1.4	51	35	31	42	1	.260	.382	10	1	3B-74
1947	132	494	141	19	8	10	2.0	67	95	44	43	1	.285	.417	0	0	3B-132
1948	127	446	131	20	6	12	2.7	59	64	41	30	0	.294	.446	8	2	3B-118
1949	113	329	82	11	3	8	2.4	48	56	48	44	1	.249	.374	13	6	3B-81, 1B-21, 2B-1
1950	108	327	85	16	2	6	1.8	44	40	42	30	1	.260	.376	4	1	3B-100, 1B-5
1951 2 teams				NY A (15G – .300)				STL N (124G – .262)									
" Total	139	482	128	26	1	14	2.9	57	68	53	49	5	.266	.411	1	0	3B-137
1952 STL N	94	282	71	10	2	2	0.7	23	34	34	21	1	.252	.323	5	0	3B-89
1953	11	5	1	1	0	0	0.0	0	1	1	1	0	.200	.400	0	0	3B-11
9 yrs.	964	3253	882	141	33	61	1.9	419	487	347	290	13	.271	.391	41	10	3B-897, 1B-26, 2B-1
3 yrs.	229	729	188	34	3	16	2.2	75	99	81	71	6	.258	.379	5	0	3B-224

WORLD SERIES

	G	AB	H	2B	3B	HR	HR %	R	RBI	BB	SO	SB	BA	SA	PH AB	PH H	G by POS
1943 NY A	5	20	6	1	1	0	0.0	3	3	0	3	0	.300	.450	0	0	3B-5
1947	7	26	7	0	3	0	0.0	8	2	3	4	0	.269	.500	0	0	3B-7
1949	2	7	1	0	0	0	0.0	0	0	0	2	1	.143	.143	0	0	3B-2
1950	4	6	0	0	0	0	0.0	0	0	0	3	0	.000	.000	0	0	3B-4
4 yrs.	18	59	14	1	4	0	0.0	11	5	3	12	1	.237	.390	0	0	3B-18

1st

Bob Johnson

JOHNSON, ROBERT WALLACE
B. Mar. 4, 1936, Omaha, Neb.
BR TR 5'10" 175 lbs.

	G	AB	H	2B	3B	HR	HR %	R	RBI	BB	SO	SB	BA	SA	PH AB	PH H	G by POS
1960 KC A	76	146	30	4	0	1	0.7	12	9	19	23	2	.205	.253	5	0	SS-30, 2B-27, 3B-11
1961 WAS A	61	224	66	13	1	6	2.7	27	28	19	26	4	.295	.442	1	0	SS-57, 3B-2, 2B-2
1962	135	466	134	20	2	12	2.6	58	43	32	50	9	.288	.416	12	0	3B-72, SS-50, 2B-3, OF-1
1963 BAL A	82	254	75	10	0	8	3.1	34	32	18	35	5	.295	.429	14	6	2B-50, 1B-8, SS-7, 3B-5
1964	93	210	52	8	2	3	1.4	18	29	9	37	0	.248	.348	45	15	SS-18, 2B-15, 1B-15, OF-1, 3B-1
1965	87	273	66	13	2	5	1.8	36	27	15	34	1	.242	.359	15	1	1B-34, SS-23, 3B-13, 2B-5
1966	71	157	34	5	0	1	0.6	13	10	12	24	0	.217	.268	30	7	2B-20, 1B-17, 3B-3
1967 2 teams				BAL A (4G – .333)				NY N (90G – .348)									
" Total	94	233	81	8	3	5	2.1	27	27	13	30	1	.348	.472	34	13	2B-39, 1B-23, SS-14, 3B-1
1968 2 teams				CIN N (16G – .267)				ATL N (59G – .262)									
" Total	75	202	53	5	1	0	0.0	17	12	11	22	0	.262	.297	18	3	3B-48, 2B-4, SS-2, 1B-1
1969 2 teams				STL N (19G – .207)				OAK A (51G – .343)									
	70	96	29	1	0	2	2.1	6	11	5	8	0	.302	.375	50	14	1B-8, 3B-4, 2B-2
1970 OAK A	30	46	8	1	0	2	2.2	6	6	3	2	2	.174	.261	19	3	3B-6, SS-2, 1B-1
11 yrs.	874	2307	628	88	11	44	1.9	254	230	156	291	24	.272	.377	243	66	SS-203, 2B-167, 3B-166, 1B-107, OF-2
1 yr.	19	29	6	0	0	1	3.4	1	2	2	4	0	.207	.310	12	1	3B-4, 1B-1

	G	AB	H	2B	3B	HR	HR %	R	RBI	BB	SO	SB	BA	SA	Pinch Hit AB	H	G by POS

Darrell Johnson

JOHNSON, DARRELL DEAN
B. Aug. 25, 1928, Horace, Neb.
Manager 1974-80, 1982.

BR TR 6'1" 180 lbs.

	G	AB	H	2B	3B	HR	HR %	R	RBI	BB	SO	SB	BA	SA	AB	H	G by POS
1952 2 teams	STL A (29G – .282)					CHI A (22G – .108)											
" Total	51	115	26	2	1	0	0.0	12	10	16	13	1	.226	.261	10	4	C-43
1957 NY A	21	46	10	1	0	1	2.2	4	8	3	10	0	.217	.304	1	0	C-20
1958	5	16	4	0	0	0	0.0	1	0	0	2	0	.250	.250	1	0	C-4
1960 STL N	8	2	0	0	0	0	0.0	0	0	1	0	0	.000	.000	0	0	C-8
1961 2 teams	PHI N (21G – .230)					CIN N (20G – .315)											
" Total	41	115	31	3	0	1	0.9	7	9	4	10	0	.270	.322	0	0	C-41
1962 2 teams	CIN N (2G – .000)					BAL A (6G – .182)											
" Total	8	26	4	0	0	0	0.0	0	1	2	4	0	.154	.154	0	0	C-8
6 yrs.	134	320	75	6	1	2	0.6	24	28	26	39	1	.234	.278	12	4	C-124
1 yr.	8	2	0	0	0	0	0.0	0	0	1	0	0	.000	.000	0	0	C-8
WORLD SERIES																	
1961 CIN N	2	4	2	0	0	0	0.0	0	0	0	0	0	.500	.500	0	0	C-2

Howie Jones

JONES, HOWARD
B. Jan. 1, 1889, Irwin, Pa.   D. July 15, 1972, Jeanette, Pa.

BL TL 5'11" 165 lbs.

	G	AB	H	2B	3B	HR	HR %	R	RBI	BB	SO	SB	BA	SA	AB	H	G by POS
1921 STL N	3	2	0	0	0	0	0.0	0	0	0	1	0	.000	.000	2	0	OF-1

Nippy Jones

JONES, VERNAL LEROY
B. June 29, 1925, Los Angeles, Calif.

BR TR 6'1" 185 lbs.

	G	AB	H	2B	3B	HR	HR %	R	RBI	BB	SO	SB	BA	SA	AB	H	G by POS
1946 STL N	16	12	4	0	0	0	0.0	3	1	2	2	0	.333	.333	9	4	2B-3
1947	23	73	18	4	0	1	1.4	6	5	2	10	0	.247	.342	7	1	2B-13, OF-2
1948	132	481	122	21	9	10	2.1	58	81	36	45	2	.254	.397	2	0	1B-128
1949	110	380	114	20	2	8	2.1	51	62	16	20	1	.300	.426	11	2	1B-98
1950	13	26	6	1	0	0	0.0	0	6	3	1	0	.231	.269	4	2	1B-8
1951	80	300	79	12	0	3	1.0	20	41	9	13	1	.263	.333	9	1	1B-71
1952 PHI N	8	30	5	0	0	1	3.3	3	5	0	4	0	.167	.267	0	0	1B-8
1957 MIL N	30	79	21	2	1	2	2.5	5	8	3	7	0	.266	.392	10	2	1B-20, OF-1
8 yrs.	412	1381	369	60	12	25	1.8	146	209	71	102	4	.267	.382	52	12	1B-333, 2B-16, OF-3
6 yrs.	374	1272	343	58	11	22	1.7	138	196	68	91	4	.270	.384	42	10	1B-305, 2B-16, OF-2
WORLD SERIES																	
1946 STL N	1	1	0	0	0	0	0.0	0	0	0	1	0	.000	.000	1	0	
1957 MIL N	3	2	0	0	0	0	0.0	0	0	0	0	0	.000	.000	2	0	
2 yrs.	4	3	0	0	0	0	0.0	0	0	0	1	0	.000	.000	3	0	

Red Jones

JONES, MAURICE MORRIS
B. Nov. 2, 1914, Timpson, Tex.

BL TR 6'3" 190 lbs.

	G	AB	H	2B	3B	HR	HR %	R	RBI	BB	SO	SB	BA	SA	AB	H	G by POS
1940 STL N	12	11	1	0	0	0	0.0	0	1	1	2	0	.091	.091	10	1	OF-1

Bubber Jonnard

JONNARD, CLARENCE JAMES
Brother of Claude Jonnard.
B. Nov. 23, 1897, Nashville, Tenn.   D. Aug. 23, 1977, New York, N. Y.

BR TR 6'1" 185 lbs.

	G	AB	H	2B	3B	HR	HR %	R	RBI	BB	SO	SB	BA	SA	AB	H	G by POS
1920 CHI A	2	5	0	0	0	0	0.0	0	0	0	1	0	.000	.000	1	0	C-1
1922 PIT N	10	21	5	0	1	0	0.0	4	2	2	4	0	.238	.333	0	0	C-10
1926 PHI N	19	34	4	1	0	0	0.0	3	2	3	4	0	.118	.147	4	0	C-15
1927	53	143	42	6	0	0	0.0	18	14	7	7	0	.294	.336	7	5	C-41
1929 STL N	18	31	3	0	0	0	0.0	1	2	0	6	0	.097	.097	0	0	C-18
1935 PHI N	1	1	0	0	0	0	0.0	0	0	0	1	0	.000	.000	0	0	C-1
6 yrs.	103	235	54	7	1	0	0.0	26	20	12	23	0	.230	.268	12	5	C-86
1 yr.	18	31	3	0	0	0	0.0	1	2	0	6	0	.097	.097	0	0	C-18

Mike Joyce

Playing record listed under Mike O'Neill

Lyle Judy

JUDY, LYLE LeROY (Punch)
B. Nov. 15, 1913, Lawrenceville, Ill.

BR TR 5'10" 150 lbs.

	G	AB	H	2B	3B	HR	HR %	R	RBI	BB	SO	SB	BA	SA	AB	H	G by POS
1935 STL N	8	11	0	0	0	0	0.0	2	0	2	2	2	.000	.000	0	0	2B-5

Skip Jutze

JUTZE, ALFRED HENRY
B. May 28, 1946, Bayside, N. Y.

BR TR 5'11" 190 lbs.

	G	AB	H	2B	3B	HR	HR %	R	RBI	BB	SO	SB	BA	SA	AB	H	G by POS
1972 STL N	21	71	17	2	0	0	0.0	1	5	1	16	0	.239	.268	4	0	C-17
1973 HOU N	90	278	62	6	0	0	0.0	18	18	19	37	0	.223	.245	3	0	C-86
1974	8	13	3	0	0	0	0.0	0	1	1	1	0	.231	.231	0	0	C-7
1975	51	93	21	2	0	0	0.0	9	6	2	4	1	.226	.247	2	0	C-47
1976	42	92	14	2	3	0	0.0	7	6	4	16	0	.152	.239	2	1	C-40
1977 SEA A	42	109	24	2	0	3	2.8	10	15	7	12	0	.220	.321	3	0	C-42
6 yrs.	254	656	141	14	3	3	0.5	45	51	34	86	1	.215	.259	14	1	C-239
1 yr.	21	71	17	2	0	0	0.0	1	5	1	16	0	.239	.268	4	0	C-17

Eddie Kasko

KASKO, EDWARD MICHAEL
B. June 27, 1932, Linden, N. J.
Manager 1970-73.

BR TR 6' 180 lbs.

	G	AB	H	2B	3B	HR	HR %	R	RBI	BB	SO	SB	BA	SA	AB	H	G by POS
1957 STL N	134	479	131	16	5	1	0.2	59	35	33	53	6	.273	.334	5	1	3B-120, SS-13, 2B-1
1958	104	259	57	8	1	2	0.8	20	22	21	25	1	.220	.282	10	3	SS-77, 2B-12, 3B-1
1959 CIN N	118	329	93	14	1	2	0.6	39	31	14	38	2	.283	.350	2	0	SS-84, 3B-31, 2B-2

	G	AB	H	2B	3B	HR	HR %	R	RBI	BB	SO	SB	BA	SA	Pinch Hit AB	H	G by POS

Eddie Kasko continued

	G	AB	H	2B	3B	HR	HR%	R	RBI	BB	SO	SB	BA	SA	Pinch Hit AB	H	G by POS
1960	126	479	140	21	1	6	1.3	56	51	46	37	9	.292	.378	7	2	3B-86, 2B-33, SS-15
1961	126	469	127	22	1	2	0.4	64	27	32	36	4	.271	.335	7	2	SS-112, 3B-12, 2B-6
1962	134	533	148	26	2	4	0.8	74	41	35	44	3	.278	.356	4	1	3B-114, SS-21
1963	76	199	48	9	0	3	1.5	25	10	21	29	0	.241	.332	14	3	3B-48, SS-15, 2B-1
1964 HOU N	133	448	109	16	1	0	0.0	45	22	37	52	4	.243	.283	4	2	SS-128, 3B-2
1965	68	215	53	7	1	1	0.5	18	10	11	20	1	.247	.302	8	2	SS-59, 3B-2
1966 BOS A	58	136	29	7	0	1	0.7	11	12	15	19	1	.213	.287	20	3	SS-20, 3B-10, 2B-8
10 yrs.	1077	3546	935	146	13	22	0.6	411	261	265	353	31	.264	.331	81	19	SS-544, 3B-426, 2B-63
2 yrs.	238	738	188	24	6	3	0.4	79	57	54	78	7	.255	.316	15	4	3B-121, SS-90, 2B-13
WORLD SERIES																	
1961 CIN N	5	22	7	0	0	0	0.0	1	1	0	2	0	.318	.318	0	0	SS-5

Ray Katt

KATT, RAYMOND FREDERICK BR TR 6'2" 190 lbs.
B. May 9, 1927, New Braunfels, Tex.

	G	AB	H	2B	3B	HR	HR%	R	RBI	BB	SO	SB	BA	SA	Pinch Hit AB	H	G by POS
1952 NY N	9	27	6	0	0	0	0.0	4	1	1	5	0	.222	.222	0	0	C-8
1953	8	29	5	1	0	0	0.0	2	1	3	3	0	.172	.207	0	0	C-8
1954	86	200	51	7	1	9	4.5	26	33	19	29	1	.255	.435	5	0	C-82
1955	124	326	70	7	2	7	2.1	27	28	22	38	0	.215	.313	3	2	C-122
1956 2 teams	NY	N	(37G –	.228)		STL	N	(47G –	.259)								
" Total	84	259	64	8	0	13	5.0	21	34	12	40	0	.247	.429	0	0	C-84
1957 NY N	72	165	38	3	1	2	1.2	11	17	15	35	1	.230	.297	7	2	C-68
1958 STL N	19	41	7	1	0	1	2.4	1	4	4	6	0	.171	.268	5	0	C-14
1959	15	24	7	2	0	0	0.0	0	2	0	8	0	.292	.375	1	0	C-14
8 yrs.	417	1071	248	29	4	32	3.0	92	120	74	164	2	.232	.356	21	4	C-400
3 yrs.	81	223	55	7	0	7	3.1	12	26	10	38	0	.247	.372	6	0	C-75

Marty Kavanagh

KAVANAGH, MARTIN JOSEPH BR TR 6' 187 lbs.
B. June 13, 1891, Harrison, N. J.   D. July 28, 1960, Taylor, Mich.

	G	AB	H	2B	3B	HR	HR%	R	RBI	BB	SO	SB	BA	SA	Pinch Hit AB	H	G by POS
1914 DET A	127	439	109	21	6	4	0.9	60	35	41	42	16	.248	.351	8	1	2B-115, 1B-4
1915	113	332	98	14	13	4	1.2	55	49	42	44	8	.295	.452	20	10	1B-44, 2B-42, OF-2, SS-2
1916 2 teams	DET	A	(58G –	.141)		CLE	A	(19G –	.250)								
" Total	77	122	22	6	1	1	0.8	10	15	11	20	0	.180	.270	46	7	OF-11, 2B-11, 3B-3, 1B-1
1917 CLE A	14	14	0	0	0	0	0.0	1	0	0	3	0	.000	.000	9	0	OF-2
1918 3 teams	CLE	A	(13G –	.211)		STL	N	(12G –	.182)		DET	A	(13G –	.273)			
" Total	38	126	28	6	0	1	0.8	12	23	21	14	2	.222	.294	2	0	1B-24, OF-8, 2B-4
5 yrs.	369	1033	257	47	20	10	1.0	138	122	118	122	26	.249	.362	85	18	2B-172, 1B-73, OF-23, 3B-3, SS-2
1 yr.	12	44	8	1	0	1	2.3	6	8	3	1	1	.182	.273	0	0	OF-8, 2B-4

Eddie Kazak

KAZAK, EDWARD TERRANCE BR TR 6' 175 lbs.
Born Edward Terrance Tkaczuk.
B. July 18, 1920, Steubenville, Ohio

	G	AB	H	2B	3B	HR	HR%	R	RBI	BB	SO	SB	BA	SA	Pinch Hit AB	H	G by POS
1948 STL N	6	22	6	3	0	0	0.0	1	2	0	2	0	.273	.409	0	0	3B-6
1949	92	326	99	15	3	6	1.8	43	42	29	17	0	.304	.423	7	2	3B-80, 2B-5
1950	93	207	53	2	2	5	2.4	21	23	18	19	0	.256	.357	42	10	3B-48
1951	11	33	6	2	0	0	0.0	2	4	5	5	0	.182	.242	1	0	3B-10
1952 2 teams	STL	N	(3G –	.000)		CIN	N	(13G –	.067)								
" Total	16	17	1	0	0	0	0.0	0	0	2	2	0	.059	.176	9	1	3B-4, 1B-1
5 yrs.	218	605	165	22	6	11	1.8	69	71	52	45	0	.273	.383	59	13	3B-148, 2B-5, 1B-1
5 yrs.	205	590	164	22	5	11	1.9	68	71	52	43	0	.278	.388	51	12	3B-145, 2B-5

Bob Keely

KEELY, ROBERT WILLIAM BR TR 6' 175 lbs.
B. Aug. 22, 1909, St. Louis, Mo.

	G	AB	H	2B	3B	HR	HR%	R	RBI	BB	SO	SB	BA	SA	Pinch Hit AB	H	G by POS
1944 STL N	1	0	0	0	0	0	–	0	0	0	0	0	–	–	0	0	C-1
1945	1	1	0	0	0	0	0.0	0	0	0	0	0	.000	.000	0	0	C-1
2 yrs.	2	1	0	0	0	0	0.0	0	0	0	0	0	.000	.000	0	0	C-2
2 yrs.	2	1	0	0	0	0	0.0	0	0	0	0	0	.000	.000	0	0	C-2

Bill Keister

KEISTER, WILLIAM HOFFMAN (Wagon Tongue) BR TR
B. Aug. 17, 1874, Baltimore, Md.   D. Aug. 19, 1924, Baltimore, Md.

	G	AB	H	2B	3B	HR	HR%	R	RBI	BB	SO	SB	BA	SA	Pinch Hit AB	H	G by POS
1896 BAL N	15	58	14	3	0	0	0.0	8	5	3		5	.241	.293	1	0	2B-8, 3B-6
1898 BOS N	10	30	5	2	0	0	0.0	5	4	0		0	.167	.233	1	0	SS-4, 2B-4, OF-1
1899 BAL N	136	523	172	22	16	3	0.6	96	73	16		33	.329	.449	0	0	SS-90, 2B-46, OF-1
1900 STL N	126	497	149	26	10	1	0.2	78	72	25		32	.300	.398	1	1	2B-116, SS-7, 3B-3
1901 BAL A	115	442	145	20	21	2	0.5	78	93	18		24	.328	.482	2	0	SS-112
1902 WAS A	119	483	145	33	9	9	1.9	82	90	14		27	.300	.462	1	0	OF-65, 2B-40, 3B-14, SS-2
1903 PHI N	100	400	128	27	7	3	0.8	53	63	14		11	.320	.445	0	0	OF-100
7 yrs.	621	2433	758	133	63	18	0.7	400	400	90	5	131	.312	.440	6	1	SS-215, 2B-214, OF-167, 3B-23
1 yr.	126	497	149	26	10	1	0.2	78	72	25		32	.300	.398	1	1	2B-116, SS-7, 3B-3

John Kelleher

KELLEHER, JOHN PATRICK BR TR 5'11" 150 lbs.
B. Sept. 13, 1893, Brookline, Mass.   D. Aug. 21, 1960, Boston, Mass.

	G	AB	H	2B	3B	HR	HR%	R	RBI	BB	SO	SB	BA	SA	Pinch Hit AB	H	G by POS
1912 STL N	8	12	4	1	0	0	0.0	0	1	0	2	0	.333	.417	4	1	3B-3
1916 BKN N	2	3	0	0	0	0	0.0	0	0	0	0	0	.000	.000	0	0	SS-1, 3B-1
1921 CHI N	95	301	93	11	7	4	1.3	31	47	16	16	2	.309	.432	9	5	3B-37, 2B-27, SS-11, 1B-11, OF-1
1922	63	193	50	7	1	0	0.0	23	20	15	14	5	.259	.306	6	0	3B-46, SS-7, 1B-4
1923	66	193	59	10	0	6	3.1	27	21	14	9	2	.306	.451	15	6	1B-22, SS-14, 3B-11, 2B-6
1924 BOS N	1	1	0	0	0	0	0.0	0	0	0	1	0	.000	.000	1	0	
6 yrs.	235	703	206	29	8	10	1.4	81	89	45	42	9	.293	.400	35	12	3B-98, 1B-37, SS-33, 2B-33, OF-1
1 yr.	8	12	4	1	0	0	0.0	0	1	0	2	0	.333	.417	4	1	3B-3

	G	AB	H	2B	3B	HR	HR %	R	RBI	BB	SO	SB	BA	SA	Pinch Hit AB	Pinch Hit H	G by POS

Mick Kelleher

KELLEHER, MICHAEL DENNIS
B. July 25, 1947, Seattle, Wash.
BR TR 5'9" 176 lbs.

	G	AB	H	2B	3B	HR	HR %	R	RBI	BB	SO	SB	BA	SA	PH AB	PH H	G by POS
1972 STL N	23	63	10	2	1	0	0.0	5	1	6	15	0	.159	.222	0	0	SS-23
1973	43	38	7	2	0	0	0.0	4	2	4	11	0	.184	.237	0	0	SS-42
1974 HOU N	19	57	9	0	0	0	0.0	4	2	5	10	1	.158	.158	0	0	SS-18
1975 STL N	7	4	0	0	0	0	0.0	0	0	0	1	0	.000	.000	0	0	SS-7
1976 CHI N	124	337	77	12	1	0	0.0	28	22	15	32	0	.228	.270	3	1	SS-101, 3B-22, 2B-5
1977	63	122	28	5	2	0	0.0	14	11	9	12	0	.230	.303	0	0	2B-40, SS-14, 3B-1
1978	68	95	24	1	0	0	0.0	8	6	7	11	4	.253	.263	3	1	3B-37, 2B-17, SS-10
1979	73	142	36	4	1	0	0.0	14	10	7	9	2	.254	.296	0	1	3B-32, 2B-29, SS-14
1980	105	96	14	1	1	0	0.0	12	4	9	17	1	.146	.177	3	1	2B-57, 3B-31, SS-17
1981 DET A	61	77	17	4	0	0	0.0	10	6	7	10	0	.221	.273	3	1	3B-39, 2B-11, SS-9
1982 2 teams			DET A (2G – .000)			CAL A (34G – .163)											
" Total	36	50	8	1	0	0	0.0	9	1	5	5	1	.160	.180	1	0	SS-28, 3B-7, 2B-1
11 yrs.	622	1081	230	32	6	0	0.0	108	65	74	133	9	.213	.253	13	4	SS-283, 3B-169, 2B-160
3 yrs.	73	105	17	4	1	0	0.0	9	3	10	27	0	.162	.219	0	0	SS-72

Bill Kelly

KELLY, WILLIAM JOSEPH
B. May 18, 1886, Baltimore, Md.   D. June 3, 1940, Detroit, Mich.
BR TR 6'½" 183 lbs.

	G	AB	H	2B	3B	HR	HR %	R	RBI	BB	SO	SB	BA	SA	PH AB	PH H	G by POS
1910 STL N	2	2	0	0	0	0	0.0	1	0	1	0	0	.000	.000	1	0	C-1
1911 PIT N	6	8	1	0	0	0	0.0	0	0	0	2	0	.125	.125	5	1	C-1
1912	48	132	42	3	2	1	0.8	20	11	2	16	8	.318	.394	3	0	C-39
1913	48	82	22	2	2	0	0.0	11	9	2	12	1	.268	.341	5	2	C-40
4 yrs.	104	224	65	5	4	1	0.4	32	20	5	30	9	.290	.362	14	3	C-81
1 yr.	2	2	0	0	0	0	0.0	1	0	1	0	0	.000	.000	1	0	C-1

John Kelly

KELLY, JOHN B.
B. Mar. 13, 1879, Clifton Heights, Pa.   D. Mar. 19, 1944, Baltimore, Md.
5'9" 165 lbs.

	G	AB	H	2B	3B	HR	HR %	R	RBI	BB	SO	SB	BA	SA	PH AB	PH H	G by POS
1907 STL N	53	197	37	5	0	0	0.0	12	6	13		7	.188	.213	1	0	OF-52

Jim Kennedy

KENNEDY, JAMES EARL
Brother of Junior Kennedy.
B. Nov. 1, 1946, Tulsa, Okla.
BL TR 5'9" 160 lbs.

	G	AB	H	2B	3B	HR	HR %	R	RBI	BB	SO	SB	BA	SA	PH AB	PH H	G by POS
1970 STL N	12	24	3	0	0	0	0.0	1	0	0	0	0	.125	.125	1	0	SS-7, 2B-5

Terry Kennedy

KENNEDY, TERRENCE EDWARD
B. June 4, 1956, Euclid, Ohio
BL TR 6'3" 220 lbs.

	G	AB	H	2B	3B	HR	HR %	R	RBI	BB	SO	SB	BA	SA	PH AB	PH H	G by POS
1978 STL N	10	29	5	0	0	0	0.0	0	2	4	3	0	.172	.172	1	0	C-10
1979	33	109	31	7	0	2	1.8	11	17	6	20	0	.284	.404	5	1	C-32
1980	84	248	63	12	3	4	1.6	28	34	28	34	0	.254	.375	12	2	C-41, OF-28
1981 SD N	101	382	115	24	1	2	0.5	32	41	22	53	0	.301	.385	3	0	C-100
1982	153	562	166	42	1	21	3.7	75	97	26	91	1	.295	.486	5	2	C-139, 1B-12
5 yrs.	381	1330	380	85	5	29	2.2	146	191	86	201	1	.286	.423	26	5	C-322, OF-28, 1B-12
3 yrs.	127	386	99	19	3	6	1.6	39	53	38	57	0	.256	.368	18	3	C-83, OF-28

George Kernek

KERNEK, GEORGE BOYD
B. Jan. 12, 1940, Holdenville, Okla.
BL TL 6'3" 170 lbs.

	G	AB	H	2B	3B	HR	HR %	R	RBI	BB	SO	SB	BA	SA	PH AB	PH H	G by POS
1965 STL N	10	31	9	3	1	0	0.0	6	3	2	4	0	.290	.452	3	0	1B-7
1966	20	50	12	0	1	0	0.0	5	3	4	9	1	.240	.280	4	1	1B-16
2 yrs.	30	81	21	3	2	0	0.0	11	6	6	13	1	.259	.346	7	1	1B-23
2 yrs.	30	81	21	3	2	0	0.0	11	6	6	13	1	.259	.346	7	1	1B-23

Don Kessinger

KESSINGER, DONALD EULON
B. July 17, 1942, Forrest City, Ark.
Manager 1979.
BB TR 6'1" 170 lbs.
BR 1964-65

	G	AB	H	2B	3B	HR	HR %	R	RBI	BB	SO	SB	BA	SA	PH AB	PH H	G by POS
1964 CHI N	4	12	2	0	0	0	0.0	1	0	0	1	0	.167	.167	2	0	SS-4
1965	106	309	62	4	3	0	0.0	19	14	20	44	1	.201	.233	0	0	SS-105
1966	150	533	146	8	2	1	0.2	50	43	26	46	13	.274	.302	0	0	SS-148
1967	145	580	134	10	7	0	0.0	61	42	33	80	6	.231	.272	0	0	SS-143
1968	160	655	157	14	7	1	0.2	63	32	38	86	9	.240	.287	1	0	SS-159
1969	158	664	181	38	6	4	0.6	109	53	61	70	11	.273	.366	1	0	SS-157
1970	154	631	168	21	14	1	0.2	100	39	66	59	12	.266	.349	0	0	SS-154
1971	155	617	159	18	6	2	0.3	77	38	52	54	15	.258	.316	2	0	SS-154
1972	149	577	158	20	6	1	0.2	77	39	67	44	8	.274	.334	3	0	SS-146
1973	160	577	151	22	3	0	0.0	52	43	57	44	6	.262	.310	2	0	SS-158
1974	153	599	155	20	7	1	0.2	83	42	62	54	7	.259	.321	3	0	SS-150
1975	154	601	146	26	10	0	0.0	77	46	68	47	4	.243	.319	2	0	SS-140, 3B-13
1976 STL N	145	502	120	22	6	1	0.2	55	40	61	51	3	.239	.313	1	0	SS-113, 2B-31, 3B-2
1977 2 teams			STL N (59G – .239)			CHI A (39G – .235)											
" Total	98	253	60	7	2	0	0.0	26	18	27	33	2	.237	.281	15	0	SS-47, 2B-37, 3B-13
1978 CHI A	131	431	110	18	1	1	0.2	35	31	36	34	2	.255	.309	1	0	SS-123, 2B-9
1979	56	110	22	6	0	1	0.9	14	7	10	12	1	.200	.282	0	0	SS-54, 2B-1, 1B-1
16 yrs.	2078	7651	1931	254	80	14	0.2	899	527	684	759	100	.252	.312	33	0	SS-1955, 2B-78, 3B-28, 1B-1
2 yrs.	204	636	152	26	6	1	0.2	69	47	75	77	3	.239	.303	16	0	SS-139, 2B-55, 3B-6

Wally Kimmick

KIMMICK, WALTER LYONS
B. May 30, 1897, Turtle Creek, Pa.
BR TR 5'11" 174 lbs.

	G	AB	H	2B	3B	HR	HR %	R	RBI	BB	SO	SB	BA	SA	PH AB	PH H	G by POS
1919 STL N	2	1	0	0	0	0	0.0	1	0	1	0	1	.000	.000	1	0	SS-1

	G	AB	H	2B	3B	HR	HR %	R	RBI	BB	SO	SB	BA	SA	Pinch Hit AB	Pinch Hit H	G by POS

Wally Kimmick continued

	G	AB	H	2B	3B	HR	HR %	R	RBI	BB	SO	SB	BA	SA	AB	H	G by POS
1921 CIN N	3	6	1	0	0	0	0.0	0	1	0	1	0	.167	.167	1	0	3B-2
1922	39	89	22	2	1	0	0.0	11	12	3	12	0	.247	.292	3	0	SS-30, 2B-3, 3B-1
1923	29	80	18	2	1	0	0.0	11	6	5	15	3	.225	.275	2	0	2B-17, 3B-4, SS-1
1925 PHI N	70	141	43	3	2	1	0.7	16	10	22	26	0	.305	.376	11	4	SS-28, 3B-21, 2B-13
1926	20	28	6	2	1	0	0.0	0	2	3	7	0	.214	.357	6	1	1B-5, SS-4, 3B-4, 2B-1
6 yrs.	163	345	90	9	5	1	0.3	39	31	34	61	4	.261	.325	24	5	SS-64, 2B-34, 3B-32, 1B-5
1 yr.	2	1	0	0	0	0	0.0	0	0	1	0	1	.000	.000	1	0	SS-1

Charlie King

KING, CHARLES GILBERT (Chick)
B. Nov. 10, 1930, Paris, Tenn.   BR TR 6'2"   190 lbs.

	G	AB	H	2B	3B	HR	HR %	R	RBI	BB	SO	SB	BA	SA	AB	H	G by POS
1954 DET A	11	28	6	0	1	0	0.0	4	3	3	8	0	.214	.286	4	0	OF-7
1955	7	21	5	0	0	0	0.0	3	0	1	2	0	.238	.238	0	0	OF-6
1956	7	9	2	0	0	0	0.0	0	0	1	4	0	.222	.222	2	0	OF-4
1958 CHI N	8	8	2	0	0	0	0.0	1	1	3	1	0	.250	.250	1	0	OF-7
1959 2 teams			CHI N	(7G –	.000)		STL N	(5G –	.429)								
" Total	12	10	3	0	0	0	0.0	3	1	0	3	0	.300	.300	0	0	OF-5
5 yrs.	45	76	18	0	1	0	0.0	11	5	8	18	0	.237	.263	7	0	OF-29
1 yr.	5	7	3	0	0	0	0.0	1	0	2	0	0	.429	.429	0	0	OF-4

Jim King

KING, JAMES HUBERT
B. Aug. 27, 1932, Elkins, Ark.   BL TR 6'   185 lbs.

	G	AB	H	2B	3B	HR	HR %	R	RBI	BB	SO	SB	BA	SA	AB	H	G by POS
1955 CHI N	113	301	77	12	3	11	3.7	43	45	24	39	2	.256	.425	18	4	OF-93
1956	118	317	79	13	2	15	4.7	32	54	30	40	1	.249	.445	34	6	OF-82
1957 STL N	22	35	11	0	0	0	0.0	1	2	4	2	0	.314	.314	16	4	OF-8
1958 SF N	34	56	12	2	1	2	3.6	8	8	10	8	0	.214	.393	14	3	OF-15
1961 WAS A	110	263	71	12	1	11	4.2	43	46	38	45	4	.270	.449	17	1	OF-91, C-1
1962	132	333	81	15	0	11	3.3	39	35	55	37	4	.243	.387	31	8	OF-101
1963	136	459	106	16	5	24	5.2	61	62	45	43	3	.231	.444	22	4	OF-123
1964	134	415	100	15	1	18	4.3	46	56	55	65	3	.241	.412	22	7	OF-121
1965	120	258	55	10	2	14	5.4	46	49	44	50	1	.213	.430	37	8	OF-88
1966	117	310	77	14	2	10	3.2	41	30	38	41	4	.248	.403	34	7	OF-85
1967 3 teams			WAS A	(47G –	.210)		CHI A	(23G –	.120)		CLE A	(19G –	.143)				
" Total	89	171	30	3	2	1	0.6	14	14	20	31	1	.175	.234	42	11	OF-44, C-1
11 yrs.	1125	2918	699	112	19	117	4.0	374	401	363	401	23	.240	.411	287	63	OF-851, C-2
1 yr.	22	35	11	0	0	0	0.0	1	2	4	2	0	.314	.314	16	4	OF-8

Lynn King

KING, LYNN PAUL (Dig)
B. Nov. 28, 1907, Villisca, Iowa   D. May 11, 1972, Iowa   BL TR 5'9"   165 lbs.

	G	AB	H	2B	3B	HR	HR %	R	RBI	BB	SO	SB	BA	SA	AB	H	G by POS
1935 STL N	8	22	4	0	0	0	0.0	6	0	4	1	2	.182	.182	1	0	OF-6
1936	78	100	19	2	1	0	0.0	12	10	9	14	2	.190	.230	25	5	OF-34
1939	89	85	20	2	0	0	0.0	10	11	15	3	2	.235	.259	35	10	OF-44
3 yrs.	175	207	43	4	1	0	0.0	28	21	28	18	6	.208	.237	61	15	OF-84
3 yrs.	175	207	43	4	1	0	0.0	28	21	28	18	6	.208	.237	61	15	OF-84

Walt Kinlock

KINLOCK, WALTER
B. 1878, St. Joseph, Mo.   Deceased.

	G	AB	H	2B	3B	HR	HR %	R	RBI	BB	SO	SB	BA	SA	AB	H	G by POS
1895 STL N	1	3	1	0	0	0	0.0	0	0	0	2	0	.333	.333	0	0	3B-1

Tom Kinslow

KINSLOW, THOMAS F.
B. Jan. 12, 1866, Washington, D. C.   D. Feb. 22, 1901, Washington, D. C.   TR

	G	AB	H	2B	3B	HR	HR %	R	RBI	BB	SO	SB	BA	SA	AB	H	G by POS
1886 WAS N	3	8	2	0	0	0	0.0	1	1	0	1		.250	.250	0	0	C-3
1887 NY AA	2	6	0	0	0	0	0.0	0		0		0	.000	.000	0	0	C-2
1890 BKN P	64	242	64	11	6	4	1.7	30	46	10	22	2	.264	.409	0	0	C-64
1891 BKN N	61	228	54	6	0	0	0.0	22	33	9	22	3	.237	.263	0	0	C-61
1892	66	246	75	6	11	2	0.8	37	40	13	16	4	.305	.443	0	0	C-66
1893	78	312	76	8	4	4	1.3	38	45	11	13	4	.244	.333	0	0	C-76, OF-2
1894	62	223	68	5	6	2	0.9	39	41	20	11	4	.305	.408	0	0	C-61, 1B-1
1895 PIT N	19	62	14	2	0	0	0.0	10	5	2	2	1	.226	.258	1	0	C-18
1896 LOU N	8	25	7	0	1	0	0.0	4	7	1		5	0	.280	.360	2	0	C-5, 1B-1
1898 2 teams			WAS N	(3G –	.111)		STL N	(14G –	.283)								
" Total	17	62	16	2	1	0	0.0	5	4	1			0	.258	.323	0	0	C-17, 1B-1
10 yrs.	380	1414	376	40	29	12	0.8	186	222	67	92	18	.266	.361	3	0	C-373, 1B-2, OF-2
1 yr.	14	53	15	2	1	0	0.0	5	4	1		0	.283	.358	0	0	C-14

Bill Kissinger

KISSINGER, WILLIAM FRANCIS (Shang)
B. Aug. 15, 1871, Dayton, Ky.   D. Apr. 20, 1929, Cincinnati, Ohio   BR TR

	G	AB	H	2B	3B	HR	HR %	R	RBI	BB	SO	SB	BA	SA	AB	H	G by POS
1895 2 teams			BAL N	(2G –	.200)		STL N	(33G –	.247)								
" Total	35	102	25	6	1	0	0.0	9	8	0	12	1	.245	.324	0	0	P-26, OF-4, SS-4, 3B-1
1896 STL N	23	73	22	4	0	0	0.0	8	12	0	4	0	.301	.356	0	0	P-20, OF-3, 3B-1
1897	14	39	13	3	2	0	0.0	7	6	3		0	.333	.513	0	0	OF-7, P-7
3 yrs.	72	214	60	13	3	0	0.0	24	26	3	16	1	.280	.369	0	0	P-53, OF-14, SS-4, 3B-2
3 yrs.	70	209	59	13	3	0	0.0	23	26	3	15	1	.282	.373	0	0	P-51, OF-14, SS-4, 3B-2

Lou Klein

KLEIN, LOUIS FRANK
B. Oct. 22, 1918, New Orleans, La.   D. June 20, 1976, Metairie, La.   BR TR 5'11"   167 lbs.
Manager 1961-62, 1965.

	G	AB	H	2B	3B	HR	HR %	R	RBI	BB	SO	SB	BA	SA	AB	H	G by POS
1943 STL N	154	627	180	28	14	7	1.1	91	62	50	70	9	.287	.410	0	0	2B-126, SS-51
1945	19	57	13	4	1	1	1.8	12	6	14	9	0	.228	.386	0	0	OF-7, SS-7, 3B-4, 2B-2
1946	23	93	18	3	0	1	1.1	12	4	9	7	1	.194	.258	0	0	2B-23
1949	58	114	25	6	0	2	1.8	25	12	22	20	0	.219	.325	18	3	SS-21, 2B-9, 3B-7
1951 2 teams			CLE A	(2G –	.000)		PHI A	(49G –	.229)								
" Total	51	146	33	7	0	5	3.4	22	17	10	13	0	.226	.377	9	0	2B-42

	G	AB	H	2B	3B	HR	HR %	R	RBI	BB	SO	SB	BA	SA	Pinch Hit AB	Pinch Hit H	G by POS

Lou Klein continued

	G	AB	H	2B	3B	HR	HR %	R	RBI	BB	SO	SB	BA	SA	PH AB	PH H	G by POS
5 yrs.	305	1037	269	48	15	16	1.5	162	101	105	119	10	.259	.381	27	3	2B-202, SS-79, 3B-11, OF-7
4 yrs.	254	891	236	41	15	11	1.2	140	84	95	106	10	.265	.382	18	3	2B-160, SS-79, 3B-11, OF-7

WORLD SERIES

	G	AB	H	2B	3B	HR	HR %	R	RBI	BB	SO	SB	BA	SA	PH AB	PH H	G by POS
1943 STL N	5	22	3	0	0	0	0.0	0	0	1	2	0	.136	.136	0	0	2B-5

Rudy Kling

KLING, RUDOLPH A.   B. Mar. 23, 1875, St. Louis, Mo.   D. Mar. 14, 1937, St. Louis, Mo.   BR TR

	G	AB	H	2B	3B	HR	HR %	R	RBI	BB	SO	SB	BA	SA	PH AB	PH H	G by POS
1902 STL N	4	10	2	0	0	0	0.0	1	0	4		1	.200	.200	0	0	SS-4

Clyde Kluttz

KLUTTZ, CLYDE FRANKLIN   B. Dec. 12, 1917, Rockwell, N.C.   D. May 12, 1979, Salisbury, N.C.   BR TR 6' 193 lbs.

	G	AB	H	2B	3B	HR	HR %	R	RBI	BB	SO	SB	BA	SA	PH AB	PH H	G by POS
1942 BOS N	72	210	56	10	1	1	0.5	21	31	7	13	0	.267	.338	15	6	C-57
1943	66	207	51	7	0	0	0.0	13	20	15	9	0	.246	.280	9	1	C-55
1944	81	229	64	12	2	2	0.9	20	19	13	14	0	.279	.376	23	4	C-58
1945 2 teams	BOS N (25G – .296)				NY N (73G – .279)												
" Total	98	303	86	18	1	4	1.3	34	31	17	16	1	.284	.389	20	3	C-76
1946 2 teams	NY N (5G – .375)				STL N (52G – .265)												
" Total	57	144	39	7	0	0	0.0	8	15	10	11	0	.271	.319	5	3	C-51
1947 PIT N	73	232	70	9	2	6	2.6	26	42	17	18	1	.302	.435	4	1	C-69
1948	94	271	60	12	2	4	1.5	26	20	20	19	3	.221	.325	3	1	C-91
1951 2 teams	STL A (4G – .500)				WAS A (53G – .308)												
" Total	57	163	51	10	0	1	0.6	17	23	21	8	0	.313	.393	9	2	C-47
1952 WAS A	58	144	33	5	0	1	0.7	7	11	12	11	0	.229	.285	6	1	C-52
9 yrs.	656	1903	510	90	8	19	1.0	172	212	132	119	5	.268	.354	94	22	C-556
1 yr.	52	136	36	7	0	0	0.0	8	14	10	10	0	.265	.316	2	2	C-49

Mike Knode

KNODE, KENNETH THOMSON   Brother of Ray Knode.   B. Nov. 8, 1895, Westminister, Md.   BL TR 5'10" 160 lbs.

	G	AB	H	2B	3B	HR	HR %	R	RBI	BB	SO	SB	BA	SA	PH AB	PH H	G by POS
1920 STL N	42	65	15	1	1	0	0.0	11	12	5	6	0	.231	.277	18	4	OF-9, 2B-4, SS-2, 3B-2

Gary Kolb

KOLB, GARY ALAN   B. Mar. 13, 1940, Rock Falls, Ill.   BL TR 6' 194 lbs.

	G	AB	H	2B	3B	HR	HR %	R	RBI	BB	SO	SB	BA	SA	PH AB	PH H	G by POS
1960 STL N	9	3	0	0	0	0	0.0	1	0	0	0	0	.000	.000	0	0	OF-2
1962	6	14	5	0	0	0	0.0	1	0	1	3	0	.357	.357	0	0	OF-6
1963	75	96	26	1	5	3	3.1	23	10	22	26	2	.271	.479	6	0	OF-58, 3B-1, C-1
1964 MIL N	36	64	12	1	0	0	0.0	7	2	6	10	3	.188	.203	5	0	OF-14, 3B-7, 2B-6, C-2
1965 2 teams	MIL N (24G – .259)				NY N (40G – .167)												
" Total	64	117	22	2	0	1	0.9	11	8	4	34	3	.188	.231	20	5	OF-42, 3B-1, 1B-1
1968 PIT N	74	119	26	4	1	2	1.7	16	6	11	17	2	.218	.319	31	6	OF-25, C-10, 3B-4, 2B-1
1969	29	37	3	1	0	0	0.0	4	3	2	14	0	.081	.108	20	1	C-7
7 yrs.	293	450	94	9	6	6	1.3	63	29	46	104	10	.209	.296	82	12	OF-147, C-20, 3B-13, 2B-7, 1B-1
3 yrs.	90	113	31	1	5	3	2.7	25	10	23	29	2	.274	.451	6	0	OF-66, 3B-1, C-1

Ed Konetchy

KONETCHY, EDWARD JOSEPH (Big Ed)   Also appeared in box score as Koney.   B. Sept. 3, 1885, LaCrosse, Wis.   D. May 27, 1947, Fort Worth, Tex.   BR TR 6'2½" 195 lbs.

	G	AB	H	2B	3B	HR	HR %	R	RBI	BB	SO	SB	BA	SA	PH AB	PH H	G by POS
1907 STL N	90	330	83	11	8	3	0.9	34	30	26		13	.252	.361	0	0	1B-90
1908	154	545	135	19	12	5	0.9	46	50	38		16	.248	.354	0	0	1B-154
1909	152	576	165	23	14	4	0.7	88	80	65		25	.286	.396	0	0	1B-152
1910	144	520	157	23	16	3	0.6	87	78	78	59	18	.302	.425	0	0	1B-144, P-1
1911	158	571	165	38	13	6	1.1	90	88	81	63	27	.289	.433	0	0	1B-158
1912	143	538	169	26	13	8	1.5	81	82	62	66	25	.314	.455	0	0	1B-142, OF-1
1913	139	502	137	18	17	7	1.4	74	68	53	41	27	.273	.418	0	0	1B-139, P-1
1914 PIT N	154	563	140	23	9	4	0.7	56	51	32	48	20	.249	.343	0	0	1B-154
1915 PIT F	152	576	181	31	18	10	1.7	79	93	41		27	.314	.483	0	0	1B-152
1916 BOS N	158	566	147	29	13	3	0.5	76	70	43	46	13	.260	.373	0	0	1B-158
1917	130	474	129	19	13	2	0.4	56	54	36	40	16	.272	.380	1	0	1B-129
1918	119	437	103	15	5	2	0.5	33	56	32	35	5	.236	.307	0	0	1B-112, OF-6, P-1
1919 BKN N	132	486	145	24	9	1	0.2	46	47	29	39	14	.298	.391	0	0	1B-132
1920	131	497	153	22	12	5	1.0	62	63	33	18	3	.308	.431	1	0	1B-130
1921 2 teams	BKN N (55G – .269)				PHI N (72G – .321)												
" Total	127	465	139	23	9	11	2.4	63	82	40	35	4	.299	.458	2	0	1B-125
15 yrs.	2083	7646	2148 (6th)	344	181	74	1.0	971	992	689 (5th)	493	255	.281	.402	4	0	1B-2071, OF-7, P-3
7 yrs.	980	3582	1011	158	93	36	1.0	500	476	403	229	151	.282	.408	0	0	1B-979, P-2, OF-1

WORLD SERIES

	G	AB	H	2B	3B	HR	HR %	R	RBI	BB	SO	SB	BA	SA	PH AB	PH H	G by POS
1920 BKN N	7	23	4	0	1	0	0.0	0	2	3	2	0	.174	.261	0	0	1B-7

George Kopshaw

KOPSHAW, GEORGE KARL   B. July 5, 1895, Passaic, N.J.   D. Dec. 26, 1934, Lynchburg, Va.   BR TR 5'11½" 176 lbs.

	G	AB	H	2B	3B	HR	HR %	R	RBI	BB	SO	SB	BA	SA	PH AB	PH H	G by POS
1923 STL N	2	5	1	1	0	0	0.0	1	0	0	1	0	.200	.400	0	0	C-1

Ernie Koy

KOY, ERNEST ANYZ (Chief)   B. Sept. 17, 1909, Sealy, Tex.   BR TR 6' 200 lbs.

	G	AB	H	2B	3B	HR	HR %	R	RBI	BB	SO	SB	BA	SA	PH AB	PH H	G by POS
1938 BKN N	142	521	156	29	13	11	2.1	78	76	38	76	15	.299	.468	3	1	OF-135, 3B-1
1939	123	425	118	37	5	8	1.9	57	67	39	64	11	.278	.445	9	1	OF-114
1940 2 teams	BKN N (24G – .229)				STL N (93G – .310)												
" Total	117	396	119	21	6	9	2.3	53	60	31	62	13	.301	.452	7	0	OF-110

	G	AB	H	2B	3B	HR	HR %	R	RBI	BB	SO	SB	BA	SA	Pinch Hit AB	Pinch Hit H	G by POS

Ernie Koy continued

		G	AB	H	2B	3B	HR	HR%	R	RBI	BB	SO	SB	BA	SA	AB	H	G by POS
1941	2 teams	STL N (13G – .200)							CIN N	(67G – .250)								
"	Total	80	244	59	12	2	4	1.6	29	31	15	30	1	.242	.357	13	3	OF-61
1942	2 teams	CIN N (3G – .000)							PHI N	(91G – .244)								
"	Total	94	260	63	9	3	4	1.5	21	26	14	52	0	.242	.346	9	2	OF-78
5 yrs.		556	1846	515	108	29	36	2.0	238	260	137	284	40	.279	.427	41	7	OF-498, 3B-1
2 yrs.		106	388	116	20	5	10	2.6	49	56	29	67	12	.299	.454	2	0	OF-103

Otto Krueger

KRUEGER, ARTHUR WILLIAM (Oom Paul)   BR TR 5'7" 165 lbs.
B. Sept. 17, 1876, Chicago, Ill.   D. Feb. 20, 1961, St. Louis, Mo.

		G	AB	H	2B	3B	HR	HR%	R	RBI	BB	SO	SB	BA	SA	AB	H	G by POS
1899	CLE N	13	44	10	1	0	0	0.0	4	2	8		1	.227	.250	0	0	3B-9, SS-2, 2B-2
1900	STL N	12	35	14	3	2	1	2.9	8	3	10		0	.400	.686	0	0	2B-12
1901		142	520	143	16	12	2	0.4	77	79	50		19	.275	.363	0	0	3B-142
1902		128	467	124	7	8	0	0.0	55	46	29		14	.266	.315	3	0	SS-107, 3B-18
1903	PIT N	80	256	63	6	8	1	0.4	42	28	21		5	.246	.344	4	1	SS-29, OF-28, 3B-13, 2B-3
1904		86	268	52	6	2	1	0.4	34	26	29		8	.194	.243	8	1	OF-33, SS-32, 3B-10
1905	PHI N	46	114	21	1	0	0	0.0	10	12	13		1	.184	.211	16	3	SS-23, OF-6, 3B-1
7 yrs.		507	1704	427	40	33	5	0.3	230	196	160		48	.251	.322	31	5	SS-193, 3B-193, OF-67, 2B-17
3 yrs.		282	1022	281	26	22	3	0.3	140	128	89		33	.275	.352	3	0	3B-160, SS-107, 2B-12

Ted Kubiak

KUBIAK, THEODORE RODGER   BL TR 6' 175 lbs.
B. May 12, 1942, New Brunswick, N. J.   BB 1968

		G	AB	H	2B	3B	HR	HR%	R	RBI	BB	SO	SB	BA	SA	AB	H	G by POS
1967	KC A	53	102	16	2	1	0	0.0	6	5	12	20	0	.157	.196	15	2	SS-20, 2B-10, 3B-5
1968	OAK A	48	120	30	5	2	0	0.0	10	8	8	18	1	.250	.325	13	2	2B-24, SS-12
1969		92	305	76	9	1	2	0.7	38	27	25	35	2	.249	.305	14	3	SS-42, 2B-33
1970	MIL A	158	540	136	9	6	4	0.7	63	41	72	51	4	.252	.313	0	0	2B-91, SS-73
1971	2 teams	MIL A (89G – .227)							STL N	(32G – .250)								
"	Total	121	332	77	9	7	4	1.2	34	27	52	43	1	.232	.337	12	2	2B-62, SS-56
1972	2 teams	TEX A (46G – .224)							OAK A	(51G – .181)								
"	Total	97	210	43	7	1	0	0.0	19	15	21	23	0	.205	.248	9	1	2B-74, SS-15, 3B-2
1973	OAK A	106	182	40	6	1	3	1.6	15	17	12	19	1	.220	.313	4	1	2B-83, SS-26, 3B-2
1974		99	220	46	3	0	0	0.0	22	18	18	15	1	.209	.223	4	0	2B-71, SS-19, 3B-14
1975	2 teams	OAK A (20G – .250)							SD N	(87G – .224)								
"	Total	107	224	51	6	0	0	0.0	15	18	26	20	3	.228	.254	13	2	3B-71, 2B-17, SS-7, 1B-1
1976	SD N	96	212	50	5	2	0	0.0	16	26	25	28	0	.236	.278	39	6	3B-27, 2B-25, SS-6, 1B-1
10 yrs.		977	2447	565	61	21	13	0.5	238	202	271	272	13	.231	.289	123	15	2B-490, SS-276, 3B-121, 1B-2
1 yr.		32	72	18	3	2	1	1.4	8	10	11	12	1	.250	.389	6	1	SS-17, 2B-14

LEAGUE CHAMPIONSHIP SERIES

		G	AB	H	2B	3B	HR	HR%	R	RBI	BB	SO	SB	BA	SA	AB	H	G by POS
1972	OAK A	4	4	2	0	0	0	0.0	0	1	0	0	0	.500	.500	0	0	2B-3
1973		3	2	0	0	0	0	0.0	0	0	0	1	0	.000	.000	0	0	2B-3
2 yrs.		7	6	2	0	0	0	0.0	0	1	0	1	0	.333	.333	0	0	2B-6

WORLD SERIES

		G	AB	H	2B	3B	HR	HR%	R	RBI	BB	SO	SB	BA	SA	AB	H	G by POS
1972	OAK A	4	3	1	0	0	0	0.0	0	0	0	0	0	.333	.333	0	0	2B-4
1973		4	3	0	0	0	0	0.0	1	0	1	1	0	.000	.000	0	0	2B-4
2 yrs.		8	6	1	0	0	0	0.0	1	0	1	1	0	.167	.167	0	0	2B-8

Willie Kuehne

KUEHNE, WILLIAM J.   TR 185 lbs.
Born William J. Knelme.
B. Oct. 24, 1858, Liepzig, Germany   D. Oct. 27, 1921, Sulphur Springs, Ohio

		G	AB	H	2B	3B	HR	HR%	R	RBI	BB	SO	SB	BA	SA	AB	H	G by POS
1883	COL AA	95	374	85	8	14	1	0.3	38		2			.227	.332	0	0	3B-69, 2B-18, SS-7, OF-3
1884		110	415	98	13	16	5	1.2	48		9			.236	.381	0	0	3B-109, OF-1
1885	PIT AA	104	411	93	9	19	0	0.0	54		15			.226	.341	0	0	3B-97, SS-7
1886		117	481	98	16	17	1	0.2	73		19			.204	.314	0	0	OF-54, 3B-47, 1B-18
1887	PIT N	102	402	120	18	15	1	0.2	68	41	14	39	17	.299	.425	0	0	SS-91, 3B-4, 1B-4, OF-3
1888		138	524	123	22	11	3	0.6	60	62	9	68	34	.235	.336	0	0	3B-75, SS-63
1889		97	390	96	20	5	5	1.3	43	57	9	36	15	.246	.362	0	0	3B-75, OF-13, 2B-5, SS-2, 1B-2
1890	PIT P	126	528	126	21	12	5	0.9	66	73	28	37	21	.239	.352	0	0	3B-126
1891	2 teams	COL AA (68G – .215)							LOU AA	(41G – .277)								
"	Total	109	420	100	12	1	3	0.7	60	40	18	35	31	.238	.293	0	0	3B-109
1892	3 teams	LOU N (76G – .167)							STL N (7G – .143)		CIN N	(6G – .208)						
"	Total	89	339	57	6	5	1	0.3	26	40	14	45	7	.168	.224	0	0	3B-86, 2B-2, SS-1
10 yrs.		1087	4284	996	145	115	25	0.6	536	312	137	260	125	.232	.338	0	0	3B-797, SS-171, OF-74, 2B-25, 1B-24
1 yr.		7	28	4	1	0	0	0.0	1	0	0	4	1	.143	.179	0	0	3B-6, SS-1

Whitey Kurowski

KUROWSKI, GEORGE JOHN   BR TR 5'11" 193 lbs.
B. Apr. 19, 1918, Reading, Pa.

		G	AB	H	2B	3B	HR	HR%	R	RBI	BB	SO	SB	BA	SA	AB	H	G by POS
1941	STL N	5	9	3	2	0	0	0.0	1	2	0	2	0	.333	.556	1	0	3B-4
1942		115	366	93	17	3	9	2.5	51	42	33	60	7	.254	.391	9	0	3B-104, OF-1, SS-1
1943		139	522	150	24	8	13	2.5	69	70	31	54	3	.287	.439	1	0	3B-137, SS-2
1944		149	555	150	25	7	20	3.6	95	87	58	40	2	.270	.449	2	0	3B-146, 2B-9, SS-1
1945		133	511	165	27	3	21	4.1	84	102	45	45	1	.323	.511	0	0	3B-131, SS-6
1946		142	519	156	32	5	14	2.7	76	89	72	47	2	.301	.462	3	1	3B-138
1947		146	513	159	27	6	27	5.3	108	104	87	56	4	.310	.544	4	1	3B-141
1948		77	220	47	8	0	2	0.9	34	33	42	28	0	.214	.277	9	1	3B-65
1949		10	14	2	0	0	0	0.0	0	0	1	0	0	.143	.143	8	2	3B-2
9 yrs.		916	3229	925	162	32	106	3.3	518	529	369	332	19	.286	.455	38	5	3B-868, SS-10, 2B-9, OF-1
9 yrs.		916	3229	925	162	32	106	3.3 10th	518	529	369	332	19	.286	.455	38	5	3B-868, SS-10, 2B-9, OF-1

WORLD SERIES

		G	AB	H	2B	3B	HR	HR%	R	RBI	BB	SO	SB	BA	SA	AB	H	G by POS
1942	STL N	5	15	4	0	1	1	6.7	3	5	2	3	0	.267	.600	0	0	3B-5

	G	AB	H	2B	3B	HR	HR %	R	RBI	BB	SO	SB	BA	SA	Pinch Hit AB	Pinch Hit H	G by POS

Whitey Kurowski continued

	G	AB	H	2B	3B	HR	HR %	R	RBI	BB	SO	SB	BA	SA	AB	H	G by POS
1943	5	18	4	1	0	0	0.0	2	1	0	3	0	.222	.278	0	0	3B-5
1944	6	23	5	1	0	0	0.0	2	1	1	4	0	.217	.261	0	0	3B-6
1946	7	27	8	3	0	0	0.0	5	2	0	3	0	.296	.407	0	0	3B-7
4 yrs.	23	83	21	5	1	1	1.2	12	9	3	13	0	.253	.373	0	0	3B-23

Eddie Lake

LAKE, EDWARD ERVING
B. Mar. 18, 1916, Antioch, Calif.
BR TR 5'7" 159 lbs.

	G	AB	H	2B	3B	HR	HR %	R	RBI	BB	SO	SB	BA	SA	AB	H	G by POS
1939 STL N	2	4	1	0	0	0	0.0	0	0	1	0	0	.250	.250	0	0	SS-2
1940	32	66	14	3	0	2	3.0	12	7	12	17	1	.212	.348	5	0	2B-17, SS-6
1941	45	76	8	2	0	0	0.0	9	0	15	22	3	.105	.132	6	1	SS-15, 3B-15, 2B-5
1943 BOS A	75	216	43	10	0	3	1.4	26	16	47	35	3	.199	.287	2	0	SS-63
1944	57	126	26	5	0	0	0.0	21	8	23	22	5	.206	.246	1	0	SS-41, P-6, 2B-3, 3B-1
1945	133	473	132	27	1	11	2.3	81	51	106	37	9	.279	.410	1	0	SS-130, 2B-1
1946 DET A	155	587	149	24	1	8	1.4	105	31	103	69	15	.254	.339	0	0	SS-155
1947	158	602	127	19	6	12	2.0	96	46	120	54	11	.211	.322	0	0	SS-158
1948	64	198	52	6	0	2	1.0	51	18	57	20	3	.263	.323	0	0	2B-45, 3B-17
1949	94	240	47	9	1	1	0.4	38	15	61	33	2	.196	.254	12	3	SS-38, 2B-19, 3B-18
1950	20	7	0	0	0	0	0.0	3	1	1	3	0	.000	.000	7	0	SS-1, 3B-1
11 yrs.	835	2595	599	105	9	39	1.5	442	193	546	312	52	.231	.323	34	3	SS-609, 2B-90, 3B-52, P-6
3 yrs.	79	146	23	5	0	2	1.4	21	7	28	39	4	.158	.233	11	1	SS-23, 2B-22, 3B-15

Bud Lally

LALLY, DANIEL J.
B. Aug. 12, 1867, Jersey City, N. J.   D. Apr. 14, 1936, Milwaukee, Wis.
BR TR 5'11½" 210 lbs.

	G	AB	H	2B	3B	HR	HR %	R	RBI	BB	SO	SB	BA	SA	AB	H	G by POS
1891 PIT N	41	143	32	6	2	1	0.7	24	17	16	20		.224	.315	0	0	OF-41
1897 STL N	87	355	99	15	5	2	0.6	56	42	9		12	.279	.366	0	0	OF-84, 1B-3
2 yrs.	128	498	131	21	7	3	0.6	80	59	25	20	12	.263	.351	0	0	OF-125, 1B-3
1 yr.	87	355	99	15	5	2	0.6	56	42	9		12	.279	.366	0	0	OF-84, 1B-3

Hobie Landrith

LANDRITH, HOBERT NEAL
B. Mar. 16, 1930, Decatur, Ill.
BL TR 5'10" 170 lbs.

	G	AB	H	2B	3B	HR	HR %	R	RBI	BB	SO	SB	BA	SA	AB	H	G by POS
1950 CIN N	4	14	3	0	0	0	0.0	1	2	1	1	0	.214	.214	0	0	C-4
1951	4	13	5	1	0	0	0.0	3	0	1	1	0	.385	.462	0	0	C-4
1952	15	50	13	4	0	0	0.0	1	4	0	4	0	.260	.340	1	1	C-14
1953	52	154	37	3	1	3	1.9	15	16	12	8	2	.240	.331	4	2	C-47
1954	48	81	16	0	0	5	6.2	12	14	18	9	1	.198	.383	5	2	C-42
1955	43	87	22	3	0	4	4.6	9	7	10	14	0	.253	.425	16	3	C-27
1956 CHI N	111	312	69	10	3	4	1.3	22	32	39	38	0	.221	.311	15	4	C-99
1957 STL N	75	214	52	6	0	3	1.4	18	26	25	27	1	.243	.313	10	1	C-67
1958	70	144	31	4	0	3	2.1	9	13	26	21	0	.215	.306	24	5	C-45
1959 SF N	109	283	71	14	0	3	1.1	30	29	43	23	0	.251	.332	2	1	C-109
1960	71	190	46	10	0	1	0.5	18	20	23	11	1	.242	.311	2	0	C-70
1961	43	71	17	4	0	2	2.8	11	10	12	7	0	.239	.380	13	2	C-30
1962 2 teams	NY N	(23G – .289)			BAL A	(60G – .222)											
" Total	83	212	50	7	1	5	2.4	24	24	27	12	0	.236	.349	2	0	C-81
1963 2 teams	BAL	A	(2G – .000)		WAS	A	(42G – .175)										
" Total	44	104	18	3	0	1	1.0	6	7	15	12	0	.173	.231	7	0	C-38
14 yrs.	772	1929	450	69	5	34	1.8	179	203	253	188	5	.233	.327	101	21	C-677
2 yrs.	145	358	83	10	0	6	1.7	27	39	51	48	1	.232	.310	34	6	C-112

Don Landrum

LANDRUM, DONALD LeROY
B. Feb. 16, 1936, Santa Rosa, Calif.
BL TR 6' 180 lbs.

	G	AB	H	2B	3B	HR	HR %	R	RBI	BB	SO	SB	BA	SA	AB	H	G by POS
1957 PHI N	2	7	1	1	0	0	0.0	1	0	2	1	0	.143	.286	0	0	OF-2
1960 STL N	13	49	12	0	1	2	4.1	7	3	4	6	3	.245	.408	0	0	OF-13
1961	28	66	11	2	0	1	1.5	5	3	5	14	1	.167	.242	1	0	OF-25, 2B-1
1962 2 teams	STL N	(32G – .314)		CHI N	(83G – .282)												
" Total	115	273	78	5	2	1	0.4	40	18	34	33	11	.286	.330	20	2	OF-85
1963 CHI N	84	227	55	4	1	1	0.4	27	10	13	42	6	.242	.282	24	3	OF-57
1964	11	11	0	0	0	0	0.0	2	0	1	2	0	.000	.000	8	0	OF-1
1965	131	425	96	20	4	6	1.4	60	34	36	84	14	.226	.334	15	2	OF-115
1966 SF N	72	102	19	4	0	1	1.0	9	7	9	18	1	.186	.255	18	2	OF-54
8 yrs.	456	1160	272	36	8	12	1.0	151	75	104	200	36	.234	.310	86	9	OF-352, 2B-1
3 yrs.	73	150	34	2	1	3	2.0	23	9	13	22	6	.227	.313	4	0	OF-64, 2B-1

Tito Landrum

LANDRUM, TERRY LEE
B. Oct. 25, 1954, Joplin, Mo.
BR TR 5'11" 175 lbs.

	G	AB	H	2B	3B	HR	HR %	R	RBI	BB	SO	SB	BA	SA	AB	H	G by POS
1980 STL N	35	77	19	2	2	0	0.0	6	7	6	17	3	.247	.325	5	1	OF-29
1981	81	119	31	5	4	0	0.0	13	10	6	14	4	.261	.370	11	3	OF-67
1982	79	72	20	3	0	2	2.8	12	14	8	18	0	.278	.403	18	4	OF-56
3 yrs.	195	268	70	10	6	2	0.7	31	31	20	49	7	.261	.366	34	8	OF-152
3 yrs.	195	268	70	10	6	2	0.7	31	31	20	49	7	.261	.366	34	8	OF-152

Don Lang

LANG, DONALD CHARLES
B. Mar. 15, 1915, Selma, Calif.
BR TR 6' 175 lbs.

	G	AB	H	2B	3B	HR	HR %	R	RBI	BB	SO	SB	BA	SA	AB	H	G by POS
1938 CIN N	21	50	13	3	1	1	2.0	5	11	2	7	0	.260	.420	2	2	3B-15, SS-1, 2B-1
1948 STL N	117	323	87	14	1	4	1.2	30	31	47	38	2	.269	.356	16	1	3B-95, 2B-2
2 yrs.	138	373	100	17	2	5	1.3	35	42	49	45	2	.268	.365	18	3	3B-110, 2B-3, SS-1
1 yr.	117	323	87	14	1	4	1.2	30	31	47	38	2	.269	.356	16	1	3B-95, 2B-2

Ralph LaPointe

LaPOINTE, RALPH ROBERT
B. Jan. 8, 1922, Winooski, Vt.   D. Sept. 13, 1967, Burlington, Vt.
BR TR 5'11" 185 lbs.

	G	AB	H	2B	3B	HR	HR %	R	RBI	BB	SO	SB	BA	SA	AB	H	G by POS
1947 PHI N	56	211	65	7	0	1	0.5	33	15	17	15	8	.308	.355	2	1	SS-54
1948 STL N	87	222	50	3	0	0	0.0	27	15	18	19	1	.225	.239	2	0	2B-44, SS-25, 3B-1

	G	AB	H	2B	3B	HR	HR %	R	RBI	BB	SO	SB	BA	SA	Pinch Hit AB	Pinch Hit H	G by POS

Ralph LaPointe continued

	G	AB	H	2B	3B	HR	HR%	R	RBI	BB	SO	SB	BA	SA	AB	H	G by POS
2 yrs.	143	433	115	10	0	1	0.2	60	30	35	34	9	.266	.296	4	1	SS-79, 2B-44, 3B-1
1 yr.	87	222	50	3	0	0	0.0	27	15	18	19	1	.225	.239	2	0	2B-44, SS-25, 3B-1

Bob Larmore

LARMORE, ROBERT McCAHAN (Red) BR TR 5'10½" 185 lbs.
B. Dec. 6, 1896, Anderson, Ind. D. Jan. 15, 1964, St. Louis, Mo.

	G	AB	H	2B	3B	HR	HR%	R	RBI	BB	SO	SB	BA	SA	AB	H	G by POS
1918 STL N	4	7	2	0	0	0	0.0	1	0	2	0	.286	.286	2	2	SS-2

Lyn Lary

LARY, LYNFORD HOBART BR TR 6' 165 lbs.
B. Jan. 28, 1906, Armona, Calif. D. Jan. 9, 1973, Downey, Calif.

	G	AB	H	2B	3B	HR	HR%	R	RBI	BB	SO	SB	BA	SA	AB	H	G by POS
1929 NY A	80	236	73	9	2	5	2.1	48	26	24	15	4	.309	.428	7	0	3B-55, SS-14, 2B-2
1930	117	464	134	20	8	3	0.6	93	52	45	40	14	.289	.386	3	0	SS-113
1931	155	610	171	35	9	10	1.6	100	107	88	54	13	.280	.416	0	0	SS-155
1932	91	280	65	14	4	3	1.1	56	39	52	28	9	.232	.343	1	0	SS-80, 1B-5, 3B-2, 2B-2, OF-1
1933	52	127	28	3	3	0	0.0	25	13	28	17	2	.220	.291	4	0	3B-28, SS-16, 1B-3, OF-1
1934 2 teams		NY	A	(1G – .000)				BOS	A	(129G – .241)							
" Total	130	419	101	20	4	2	0.5	58	54	67	51	12	.241	.322	0	0	SS-129, 1B-1
1935 2 teams		WAS	A	(39G – .194)				STL	A	(93G – .288)							
" Total	132	474	127	29	7	2	0.4	86	42	76	53	28	.268	.371	3	1	SS-123
1936 STL A	155	620	179	30	6	2	0.3	112	52	117	54	37	.289	.366	0	0	SS-155
1937 CLE A	156	644	187	46	7	8	1.2	110	77	88	64	18	.290	.421	0	0	SS-156
1938	141	568	152	36	4	3	0.5	94	51	88	65	23	.268	.361	0	0	SS-141
1939 3 teams		CLE	A	(3G – .000)				BKN	N	(29G – .161)			STL	N	(34G – .187)	
" Total	66	108	19	4	1	0	0.0	18	10	28	22	2	.176	.231	3	0	SS-44, 3B-10
1940 STL A	27	54	3	1	1	0	0.0	5	3	4	7	0	.056	.111	6	0	SS-12, 2B-1
12 yrs.	1302	4604	1239	247	56	38	0.8	805	526	705	470	162	.269	.372	27	1	SS-1138, 3B-95, 1B-9, 2B-5, OF-2
1 yr.	34	75	14	3	0	0	0.0	11	9	16	15	1	.187	.227	1	0	SS-30, 3B-3

Don Lassetter

LASSETTER, DONALD O'NEAL BR TR 6'3" 200 lbs.
B. Mar. 27, 1933, Newnan, Ga.

	G	AB	H	2B	3B	HR	HR%	R	RBI	BB	SO	SB	BA	SA	AB	H	G by POS
1957 STL N	4	13	2	0	1	0	0.0	2	0	1	3	0	.154	.308	1	0	OF-3

Arlie Latham

LATHAM, WALTER ARLINGTON (The Freshest Man on Earth) BR TR 5'8" 150 lbs.
B. Mar. 15, 1859, W. Lebanon, N. H. D. Nov. 29, 1952, Garden City, N. Y.
Manager 1896.

	G	AB	H	2B	3B	HR	HR%	R	RBI	BB	SO	SB	BA	SA	AB	H	G by POS
1880 BUF N	22	79	10	3	1	0	0.0	9	3	1	8		.127	.190	0	0	SS-12, OF-10, C-1
1883 STL AA	98	406	96	12	7	0	0.0	86		18			.236	.300	0	0	3B-98, C 1
1884	110	474	130	17	12	1	0.2	115		19			.274	.367	0	0	3B-110, C-1
1885	110	485	100	15	3	1	0.2	84		18			.206	.256	0	0	3B-109, C-2
1886	134	578	174	23	8	1	0.2	152		55			.301	.374	0	0	3B-133, 2B-1
1887	136	627	198	35	10	2	0.3	163		45		129	.316	.413	0	0	3B-132, 2B-5, C-2
1888	133	570	151	19	5	2	0.4	119	31	43		109	.265	.326	0	0	3B-133, SS-1
1889	118	512	126	13	3	4	0.8	110	49	42	30	69	.246	.307	0	0	3B-116, 2B-3
1890 2 teams		CHI	P	(52G – .229)				CIN	N	(41G – .250)							
" Total	93	378	90	13	4	1	0.3	82	35	45	40	52	.238	.302	0	0	3B-93, OF-1
1891 CIN N	135	533	145	20	10	7	1.3	119	53	74	35	87	.272	.386	0	0	3B-135, C-1
1892	152	622	148	20	4	0	0.0	111	44	60	54	66	.238	.283	0	0	3B-142, 2B-9, OF-1
1893	127	531	150	18	6	2	0.4	101	49	62	20	57	.282	.350	0	0	3B-127
1894	129	524	164	23	6	4	0.8	129	60	60	24	59	.313	.403	0	0	3B-127, 2B-2
1895	112	460	143	14	6	2	0.4	93	69	42	25	48	.311	.380	0	0	3B-108, 1B-3, 2B-1
1896 STL N	8	35	7	0	0	0	0.0	3	5	4	3	2	.200	.200	0	0	3B-8
1899 WAS N	6	6	1	0	0	0	0.0	1	0	1		0	.167	.167	2	1	OF-1, 2B-1
1909 NY N	4	2	0	0	0	0	0.0	1				0	.000	.000	1	0	2B-2
17 yrs.	1627	6822	1833	245	85	27	0.4	1478	398	589	239	679	.269	.341	3	1	3B-1571, 2B-24, OF-13, SS-13, C-8, 1B-3
1 yr.	8	35	7	0	0	0	0.0	3	5	4	3	2	.200	.200	0	0	3B-8

Doc Lavan

LAVAN, JOHN LEONARD BR TR 5'8½" 151 lbs.
B. Oct. 28, 1890, Grand Rapids, Mich. D. May 30, 1952, Detroit, Mich.

	G	AB	H	2B	3B	HR	HR%	R	RBI	BB	SO	SB	BA	SA	AB	H	G by POS
1913 2 teams		STL	A	(46G – .141)				PHI	A	(5G – .071)							
" Total	51	163	22	2	2	0	0.0	9	5	10	46	3	.135	.172	0	0	SS-51
1914 STL A	74	239	63	7	4	1	0.4	21	21	17	39	6	.264	.339	0	0	SS-73
1915	157	514	112	17	7	1	0.2	44	48	42	83	13	.218	.284	0	0	SS-157
1916	110	343	81	13	1	0	0.0	32	19	32	38	7	.236	.280	3	1	SS-106
1917	118	355	85	8	5	0	0.0	19	30	19	34	5	.239	.290	1	0	SS-110, 2B-7
1918 WAS A	117	464	129	17	2	0	0.0	44	45	14	21	12	.278	.323	0	0	SS-117, OF-1
1919 STL N	100	356	86	12	2	1	0.3	25	25	11	30	4	.242	.295	1	0	SS-99
1920	142	516	149	21	10	1	0.2	52	63	19	38	11	.289	.374	4	0	SS-138
1921	150	560	145	23	11	2	0.4	58	82	23	30	7	.259	.350	0	0	SS-150
1922	89	264	60	8	1	0	0.0	24	27	13	10	3	.227	.265	1	0	SS-82, 3B-5
1923	50	111	22	6	0	1	0.9	10	12	9	7	0	.198	.279	2	1	SS-40, 3B-4, 1B-3, 2B-1
1924	4	6	0	0	0	0	0.0	0	0	0	0	0	.000	.000	0	0	SS-2, 3B-2
12 yrs.	1162	3891	954	134	45	7	0.2	338	377	209	376	71	.245	.308	12	3	SS-1125, 2B-10, 3B-9, 1B-3, OF-1
6 yrs.	535	1813	462	70	24	5	0.3	169	209	75	115	25	.255	.328	8	2	SS-555, 3B-9, 2B-3, 1B-3

Tom Leahy

LEAHY, THOMAS JOSEPH TR
B. June 2, 1869, New Haven, Conn. D. June 12, 1951, New Haven, Conn.

	G	AB	H	2B	3B	HR	HR%	R	RBI	BB	SO	SB	BA	SA	AB	H	G by POS
1897 2 teams		PIT	N	(24G – .261)				WAS	N	(19G – .385)							
" Total	43	144	44	5	4	0	0.0	22	19	16		9	.306	.396	0	0	OF-23, 3B-11, C-7, 2B-3
1898 WAS N	15	55	10	2	0	0	0.0	10	5	8			.182	.218	0	0	3B-12, 2B-3

	G	AB	H	2B	3B	HR	HR %	R	RBI	BB	SO	SB	BA	SA	Pinch Hit AB	Pinch Hit H	G by POS

Tom Leahy continued

	G	AB	H	2B	3B	HR	HR%	R	RBI	BB	SO	SB	BA	SA	PH AB	PH H	G by POS
1901 2 teams	MIL A (33G – .242)					PHI A (5G – .333)											
" Total	38	114	29	7	2	0	0.0	19	11	12		3	.254	.351	3	2	C-29, OF-4, SS-1, 2B-1
1905 STL N	35	97	22	1	3	0	0.0	3	7	8		0	.227	.299	6	1	C-29
4 yrs.	131	410	105	15	9	0	0.0	54	42	44		18	.256	.337	9	3	C-65, OF-27, 3B-23, 2B-7, SS-1
1 yr.	35	97	22	1	3	0	0.0	3	7	8		0	.227	.299	6	1	C-29

Leron Lee
LEE, LERON
B. Mar. 4, 1948, Bakersfield, Calif.   BL TR 6' 196 lbs.

	G	AB	H	2B	3B	HR	HR%	R	RBI	BB	SO	SB	BA	SA	PH AB	PH H	G by POS
1969 STL N	7	23	5	1	0	0	0.0	3	0	3	8	0	.217	.261	0	0	OF-7
1970	121	264	60	13	1	6	2.3	28	23	24	66	5	.227	.352	38	9	OF-77
1971 2 teams	STL N (25G – .179)					SD N (79G – .273)											
" Total	104	284	75	21	2	5	1.8	32	23	22	57	4	.264	.405	26	3	OF-76
1972 SD N	101	370	111	23	7	12	3.2	50	47	29	58	2	.300	.497	4	2	OF-96
1973	118	333	79	7	2	3	0.9	36	30	33	61	4	.237	.297	30	7	OF-84
1974 CLE A	79	232	54	13	0	5	2.2	18	25	15	42	3	.233	.353	17	2	OF-62
1975 2 teams	CLE A (13G – .130)					LA N (48G – .256)											
" Total	61	66	14	5	0	0	0.0	5	2	5	14	1	.212	.288	46	10	OF-9
1976 LA N	23	45	6	0	1	0	0.0	1	2	2	9	0	.133	.178	14	3	OF-10
8 yrs.	614	1617	404	83	13	31	1.9	173	152	133	315	19	.250	.375	175	36	OF-421
3 yrs.	153	315	70	15	1	7	2.2	34	25	31	86	5	.222	.343	55	12	OF-92

Jim Lentine
LENTINE, JAMES MATTHEW
B. July 16, 1954, Los Angeles, Calif.   BR TR 6' 175 lbs.

	G	AB	H	2B	3B	HR	HR%	R	RBI	BB	SO	SB	BA	SA	PH AB	PH H	G by POS
1978 STL N	8	11	2	0	0	0	0.0	1	1	0	0	1	.182	.182	1	0	OF-3
1979	11	23	9	1	0	0	0.0	2	1	3	6	0	.391	.435	3	2	OF-8
1980 2 teams	STL N (9G – .100)					DET A (67G – .261)											
" Total	76	171	43	8	1	1	0.6	20	18	28	32	2	.251	.327	10	2	OF-61
3 yrs.	95	205	54	9	1	1	0.5	23	20	31	38	3	.263	.332	14	4	OF-72
3 yrs.	28	44	12	1	0	0	0.0	4	3	3	8	1	.273	.295	7	2	OF-17

Roy Leslie
LESLIE, ROY REID
B. Aug. 23, 1894, Bailey, Tex.   D. Apr. 10, 1972, Sherman, Tex.   BR TR 6'1" 175 lbs.

	G	AB	H	2B	3B	HR	HR%	R	RBI	BB	SO	SB	BA	SA	PH AB	PH H	G by POS
1917 CHI N	7	19	4	0	0	0	0.0	1	1	1	5	1	.211	.211	1	0	1B-6
1919 STL N	12	24	5	1	0	0	0.0	2	4	4	3	0	.208	.250	1	0	1B-9
1922 PHI N	141	513	139	23	2	6	1.2	44	50	37	49	3	.271	.359	2	2	1B-139
3 yrs.	160	556	148	24	2	6	1.1	47	55	42	57	4	.266	.349	4	2	1B-154
1 yr.	12	24	5	1	0	0	0.0	2	4	4	3	0	.208	.250	1	0	1B-9

Bill Lewis
LEWIS, WILLIAM HENRY (Buddy)
B. Oct. 15, 1904, Ripley, Tenn.   D. Oct. 24, 1977, Memphis, Tenn.   BR TR 5'9" 165 lbs.

	G	AB	H	2B	3B	HR	HR%	R	RBI	BB	SO	SB	BA	SA	PH AB	PH H	G by POS
1933 STL N	15	35	14	1	0	1	2.9	8	8	2	3	0	.400	.514	6	2	C-8
1935 BOS N	6	4	0	0	0	0	0.0	1	0	1	1	0	.000	.000	4	0	C-1
1936	29	62	19	2	0	0	0.0	11	3	12	7	0	.306	.339	8	2	C-21
3 yrs.	50	101	33	3	0	1	1.0	20	11	15	11	0	.327	.386	18	4	C-30
1 yr.	15	35	14	1	0	1	2.9	8	8	2	3	0	.400	.514	6	2	C-8

Johnny Lewis
LEWIS, JOHNNY JOE
B. Aug. 10, 1939, Greenville, Ala.   BL TR 6'1" 189 lbs.

	G	AB	H	2B	3B	HR	HR%	R	RBI	BB	SO	SB	BA	SA	PH AB	PH H	G by POS
1964 STL N	40	94	22	2	2	2	2.1	10	7	13	23	2	.234	.362	3	0	OF-36
1965 NY N	148	477	117	15	3	15	3.1	64	45	59	117	4	.245	.384	14	4	OF-142
1966	65	166	32	6	1	5	3.0	21	20	21	43	2	.193	.331	16	2	OF-49
1967	13	34	4	1	0	0	0.0	2	2	2	11	0	.118	.147	4	0	OF-10
4 yrs.	266	771	175	24	6	22	2.9	97	74	95	194	8	.227	.359	37	6	OF-237
1 yr.	40	94	22	2	2	2	2.1	10	7	13	23	2	.234	.362	3	0	OF-36

Sixto Lezcano
LEZCANO, SIXTO
B. Nov. 28, 1953, Manati, Puerto Rico   BR TR 5'10" 165 lbs.

	G	AB	H	2B	3B	HR	HR%	R	RBI	BB	SO	SB	BA	SA	PH AB	PH H	G by POS
1974 MIL A	15	54	13	2	0	2	3.7	5	9	4	9	1	.241	.389	0	0	OF-15
1975	134	429	106	19	3	11	2.6	55	43	46	93	5	.247	.382	4	0	OF-129
1976	145	513	146	19	5	7	1.4	53	56	51	112	14	.285	.382	0	0	OF-142
1977	109	400	109	21	4	21	5.3	50	49	52	78	6	.273	.503	0	0	OF-108
1978	132	442	129	21	4	15	3.4	62	61	64	83	3	.292	.459	2	1	OF-127
1979	138	473	152	29	3	28	5.9	84	101	77	74	4	.321	.573	1	0	OF-135
1980	112	411	94	19	3	18	4.4	51	55	39	76	1	.229	.421	0	0	OF-108
1981 STL N	72	214	57	8	2	5	2.3	26	28	40	40	4	.266	.393	4	1	OF-65
1982 SD N	138	470	136	26	6	16	3.4	73	84	78	69	2	.289	.472	2	0	OF-134
9 yrs.	995	3406	942	164	30	123	3.6	459	486	451	634	36	.277	.451	13	2	OF-963
1 yr.	72	214	57	8	2	5	2.3	26	28	40	40	4	.266	.393	4	1	OF-65

Gene Lillard
LILLARD, ROBERT EUGENE
Brother of Bill Lillard.
B. Nov. 12, 1913, Santa Barbara, Calif.   BR TR 5'10½" 178 lbs.

	G	AB	H	2B	3B	HR	HR%	R	RBI	BB	SO	SB	BA	SA	PH AB	PH H	G by POS
1936 CHI N	19	34	7	1	0	0	0.0	6	2	3	8	0	.206	.235	10	3	SS-4, 3B-3
1939	23	10	1	0	0	0	0.0	3	0	6	3	0	.100	.100	0	0	P-20
1940 STL N	2	0	0	0	0	0	–	0	0	0	0	0	–	–	0	0	P-2
3 yrs.	44	44	8	1	0	0	0.0	9	2	9	11	0	.182	.205	10	3	P-22, SS-4, 3B-3
1 yr.	2	0	0	0	0	0	–	0	0	0	0	0	–	–	0	0	P-2

	G	AB	H	2B	3B	HR	HR %	R	RBI	BB	SO	SB	BA	SA	Pinch Hit AB	Pinch Hit H	G by POS

Bob Lillis

LILLIS, ROBERT PERRY
B. June 2, 1930, Altadena, Calif.
Manager 1982

BR TR 5'11"   160 lbs.

	G	AB	H	2B	3B	HR	HR %	R	RBI	BB	SO	SB	BA	SA	PH AB	PH H	G by POS
1958 LA N	20	69	27	3	1	1	1.4	10	5	4	2	1	.391	.507	1	1	SS-19
1959	30	48	11	2	0	0	0.0	7	2	3	4	0	.229	.271	1	1	SS-20
1960	48	60	16	4	0	0	0.0	6	6	2	6	2	.267	.333	3	0	SS-23, 3B-14, 2B-1
1961 2 teams	LA	N	(19G –	.111)		STL	N	(86G –	.217)								
" Total	105	239	51	4	0	0	0.0	24	22	8	14	3	.213	.230	3	0	SS-57, 2B-25, 3B-12
1962 HOU N	129	457	114	12	4	1	0.2	38	30	28	23	7	.249	.300	1	1	SS-99, 2B-33, 3B-9
1963	147	469	93	13	1	1	0.2	31	19	15	35	3	.198	.237	3	0	SS-124, 2B-19, 3B-6
1964	109	332	89	11	2	0	0.0	31	17	11	10	4	.268	.313	13	3	2B-52, SS-43, 3B-12
1965	124	408	90	12	1	0	0.0	34	20	20	10	2	.221	.255	5	3	SS-104, 3B-9, 2B-6
1966	68	164	38	6	0	0	0.0	14	11	7	4	1	.232	.268	8	1	2B-35, SS-18, 3B-6
1967	37	82	20	1	0	0	0.0	3	5	1	8	0	.244	.256	9	1	SS-23, 2B-3, 3B-2
10 yrs.	817	2328	549	68	9	3	0.1	198	137	99	116	23	.236	.277	47	11	SS-530, 2B-174, 3B-70
1 yr.	86	230	50	4	0	0	0.0	24	21	7	13	3	.217	.235	0	0	SS-56, 2B-24

Johnny Lindell

LINDELL, JOHN HARLAN
B. Aug. 30, 1916, Greeley, Colo.

BR TR 6'4½"   217 lbs.

	G	AB	H	2B	3B	HR	HR %	R	RBI	BB	SO	SB	BA	SA	PH AB	PH H	G by POS
1941 NY A	1	1	0	0	0	0	0.0	0	0	0	0	0	.000	.000	1	0	
1942	27	24	6	1	0	0	0.0	1	4	0	5	0	.250	.292	5	2	P-23
1943	122	441	108	17	12	4	0.9	53	51	51	55	2	.245	.365	1	0	OF-122
1944	149	594	178	33	16	18	3.0	91	103	44	56	5	.300	.500	0	0	OF-149
1945	41	159	45	6	3	1	0.6	26	20	17	10	2	.283	.377	0	0	OF-41
1946	102	332	86	10	5	10	3.0	41	40	32	47	4	.259	.410	14	3	OF-74, 1B-14
1947	127	476	131	18	7	11	2.3	66	67	32	70	1	.275	.412	7	3	OF-118
1948	88	309	98	17	2	13	4.2	58	55	35	50	0	.317	.511	7	0	OF-79
1949	78	211	51	10	0	6	2.8	33	27	35	27	3	.242	.374	13	2	OF-65
1950 2 teams	NY	A	(7G –	.190)		STL	N	(36G –	.186)								
" Total	43	134	25	5	2	5	3.7	18	18	19	26	0	.187	.366	4	0	OF-39
1953 2 teams	PIT	N	(58G –	.286)		PHI	N	(11G –	.389)								
" Total	69	109	33	7	1	4	3.7	14	17	22	17	0	.303	.495	26	8	P-32, OF-2, 1B-2
1954 PHI N	7	5	1	0	0	0	0.0	2	2	3	3	0	.200	.200	5	1	
12 yrs.	854	2795	762	124	48	72	2.6	401	404	289	366	17	.273	.429	83	19	OF-689, P-55, 1B-16
1 yr.	36	113	21	5	2	5	4.4	16	16	15	24	0	.186	.398	3	0	OF-33

WORLD SERIES

	G	AB	H	2B	3B	HR	HR %	R	RBI	BB	SO	SB	BA	SA	PH AB	PH H	G by POS
1943 NY A	4	9	1	0	0	0	0.0	1	0	1	4	0	.111	.111	0	0	OF-4
1947	6	18	9	3	1	0	0.0	3	7	5	2	0	.500	.778	0	0	OF-6
1949	2	7	1	0	0	0	0.0	0	0	0	2	0	.143	.143	0	0	OF-2
3 yrs.	12	34	11	3	1	0	0.0	4	7	6	8	0	.324	.471	0	0	OF-12

Larry Lintz

LINTZ, LARRY
B. Oct. 10, 1949, Martinez, Calif.

BR TR 5'9"   150 lbs.

	G	AB	H	2B	3B	HR	HR %	R	RBI	BB	SO	SB	BA	SA	PH AB	PH H	G by POS
1973 MON N	52	116	29	1	0	0	0.0	20	3	17	18	12	.250	.259	2	1	2B-34, SS-15
1974	113	319	76	10	1	0	0.0	60	20	44	50	50	.238	.276	0	0	2B-67, SS-31, 3B-1
1975 2 teams	MON	N	(46G –	.197)		STL	N	(27G –	.278)								
" Total	73	150	31	1	0	0	0.0	24	4	26	20	21	.207	.213	0	0	2B-45, SS-8
1976 OAK A	68	1	0	0	0	0	0.0	21	0	2	0	31	.000	.000	0	0	2B-5, OF-3
1977	41	30	4	1	0	0	0.0	11	0	8	13	13	.133	.167	0	0	2B-28, SS-2, 3B-1
1978 CLE A	3	0	0	0	0	0	–	1	0	0	0	1	–	–	0	0	
6 yrs.	350	616	140	13	1	0	0.0	137	27	97	101	128	.227	.252	2	1	2B-179, SS-56, OF-3, 3B-2
1 yr.	27	18	5	1	0	0	0.0	6	1	3	2	4	.278	.333	0	0	SS-6, 2B-6

Danny Litwhiler

LITWHILER, DANIEL WEBSTER
B. Aug. 31, 1916, Ringtown, Pa.

BR TR 5'10½"   198 lbs.

	G	AB	H	2B	3B	HR	HR %	R	RBI	BB	SO	SB	BA	SA	PH AB	PH H	G by POS
1940 PHI N	36	142	49	2	2	5	3.5	10	17	3	13	1	.345	.493	2	0	OF-36
1941	151	590	180	29	6	18	3.1	72	66	39	43	1	.305	.466	1	0	OF-150
1942	151	591	160	25	9	9	1.5	59	56	27	42	2	.271	.389	0	0	OF-151
1943 2 teams	PHI	N	(36G –	.259)		STL	N	(80G –	.279)								
" Total	116	397	108	20	3	12	3.0	63	48	30	45	2	.272	.428	8	0	OF-104
1944 STL N	140	492	130	25	5	15	3.0	53	82	37	56	2	.264	.427	3	1	OF-136
1946 2 teams	STL	N	(6G –	.000)		BOS	N	(79G –	.291)								
" Total	85	252	72	12	2	8	3.2	29	38	20	24	1	.286	.444	17	5	OF-65, 3B-2
1947 BOS N	91	226	59	5	2	7	3.1	38	31	25	43	1	.261	.394	23	4	OF-66
1948 2 teams	BOS	N	(13G –	.273)		CIN	N	(106G –	.275)								
" Total	119	371	102	21	2	14	3.8	51	50	52	43	1	.275	.456	15	5	OF-91, 3B-15
1949 CIN N	102	292	85	18	1	11	3.8	35	48	44	42	0	.291	.473	14	3	OF-82, 3B-3
1950	54	112	29	4	0	6	5.4	15	12	20	21	0	.259	.455	19	4	OF-29
1951	12	29	8	1	0	2	6.9	3	3	2	5	0	.276	.517	4	2	OF-7
11 yrs.	1057	3494	982	162	32	107	3.1	428	451	299	377	11	.281	.438	106	24	OF-917, 3B-20
3 yrs.	226	755	202	39	8	22	2.9	93	113	57	88	3	.268	.428	16	1	OF-206

WORLD SERIES

	G	AB	H	2B	3B	HR	HR %	R	RBI	BB	SO	SB	BA	SA	PH AB	PH H	G by POS
1943 STL N	5	15	4	1	0	1	6.7	2	2	2	4	0	.267	.333	1	1	OF-4
1944	5	20	4	1	0	1	5.0	2	1	2	7	0	.200	.400	0	0	OF-5
2 yrs.	10	35	8	2	0	2	2.9	2	3	4	11	0	.229	.371	1	1	OF-9

Paddy Livingston

LIVINGSTON, PATRICK JOSEPH
B. Jan. 14, 1880, Cleveland, Ohio   D. Sept. 19, 1977, Cleveland, Ohio

BR TR 5'8"   197 lbs.

	G	AB	H	2B	3B	HR	HR %	R	RBI	BB	SO	SB	BA	SA	PH AB	PH H	G by POS
1901 CLE A	1	2	0	0	0	0	0.0	0		0		0	.000	.000	0	0	C-1
1906 CIN N	50	139	22	1	4	0	0.0	8	8	12		0	.158	.223	3	0	C-47
1909 PHI A	64	175	41	6	4	0	0.0	15	15	15		4	.234	.314	0	0	C-64
1910	37	120	25	4	3	0	0.0	11	9	6		0	.208	.292	0	0	C-37
1911	27	71	17	4	0	0	0.0	9	8	7		1	.239	.296	1	0	C-26
1912 CLE A	19	47	11	2	1	0	0.0	5	3	1		0	.234	.319	6	0	C-13
1917 STL N	7	20	4	0	0	0	0.0	1	2	0	1	0	.200	.200	1	0	C-6

	G	AB	H	2B	3B	HR	HR %	R	RBI	BB	SO	SB	BA	SA	Pinch Hit AB	Pinch Hit H	G by POS

Paddy Livingston continued

	G	AB	H	2B	3B	HR	HR %	R	RBI	BB	SO	SB	BA	SA	AB	H	G by POS
7 yrs.	205	574	120	17	12	0	0.0	48	45	41	1	9	.209	.280	11	0	C-194
1 yr.	7	20	4	0	0	0	0.0	0	2	0	1	2	.200	.200	1	0	C-6

Whitey Lockman

LOCKMAN, CARROLL WALTER   BL TR 6'1"   175 lbs.
B. July 25, 1926, Lowell, N. C.
Manager 1972-74.

		G	AB	H	2B	3B	HR	HR %	R	RBI	BB	SO	SB	BA	SA	AB	H	G by POS
1945	NY N	32	129	44	9	0	3	2.3	16	18	13	10	1	.341	.481	0	0	OF-32
1947		2	2	1	0	0	0	0.0	0	1	0	0	0	.500	.500	2	1	
1948		146	584	167	24	10	18	3.1	117	59	68	63	8	.286	.454	1	0	OF-144
1949		151	617	186	32	7	11	1.8	97	65	62	31	12	.301	.429	0	0	OF-151
1950		129	532	157	28	5	6	1.1	72	52	42	29	1	.295	.400	1	0	OF-128
1951		153	614	173	27	7	12	2.0	85	73	50	32	4	.282	.407	0	0	1B-119, OF-34
1952		154	606	176	17	4	13	2.1	99	58	67	52	2	.290	.396	0	0	1B-154
1953		150	607	179	22	4	9	1.5	85	61	52	36	3	.295	.389	3	1	1B-120, OF-30
1954		148	570	143	17	3	16	2.8	73	60	59	31	2	.251	.375	1	0	1B-145, OF-2
1955		147	576	157	19	0	15	2.6	76	49	39	34	3	.273	.384	2	0	OF-81, 1B-68
1956 2 teams	NY N (48G – .272)					STL N	(70G – .249)											
" Total		118	362	94	7	3	1	0.3	27	20	34	25	2	.260	.304	17	4	OF-96, 1B-9
1957 NY N		133	456	113	9	4	7	1.5	51	30	39	19	5	.248	.331	8	0	1B-102, OF-27
1958 SF N		92	122	29	5	0	2	1.6	15	7	13	8	0	.238	.328	45	11	OF-25, 2B-15, 1B-7
1959 2 teams	BAL A (38G – .217)					CIN N	(52G – .262)											
" Total		90	153	37	6	2	0	0.0	17	9	12	10	0	.242	.307	33	4	1B-42, 2B-11, OF-2, 3B-1
1960 CIN N		21	10	2	0	0	1	10.0	6	1	2	3	0	.200	.500	8	1	1B-5
15 yrs.		1666	5940	1658	222	49	114	1.9	836	563	552	383	43	.279	.391	121	22	1B-771, OF-752, 2B-26, 3B-1
1 yr.		70	193	48	0	2	0	0.0	14	10	18	8	2	.249	.269	13	4	OF-57, 1B-2
WORLD SERIES																		
1951 NY N		6	25	6	2	0	1	4.0	1	4	1	2	0	.240	.440	0	0	1B-6
1954		4	18	2	0	0	0	0.0	2	0	1	2	0	.111	.111	0	0	1B-4
2 yrs.		10	43	8	2	0	1	2.3	3	4	2	4	0	.186	.302	0	0	1B-10

Jeoff Long

LONG, JEOFFREY KEITH   BR TR 6'1"   200 lbs.
B. Oct. 9, 1941, Covington, Ky.

		G	AB	H	2B	3B	HR	HR %	R	RBI	BB	SO	SB	BA	SA	AB	H	G by POS
1963 STL N		5	5	1	0	0	0	0.0	0	0	0	1	0	.200	.200	5	1	
1964 2 teams	STL N (28G – .233)					CHI A	(23G – .143)											
" Total		51	78	15	1	0	1	1.3	5	9	10	33	0	.192	.244	28	4	OF-9, 1B-8
2 yrs.		56	83	16	1	0	1	1.2	5	9	10	34	0	.193	.241	33	5	OF-9, 1B-8
2 yrs.		33	48	11	1	0	1	2.1	5	4	6	19	0	.229	.313	21	4	OF-4, 1B-3

Tommy Long

LONG, THOMAS AUGUSTUS   BR TR 5'10½" 165 lbs.
B. June 1, 1890, Mitchum, Ala.   D. June 15, 1972, Jackson, Ala.

		G	AB	H	2B	3B	HR	HR %	R	RBI	BB	SO	SB	BA	SA	AB	H	G by POS
1911 WAS A		14	48	11	3	0	0	0.0	1	5	1		4	.229	.292	1	0	OF-13
1912		1	1	0	0	0	0	0.0	0	0	0		0	.000	.000	1	0	
1915 STL N		140	507	149	21	25	2	0.4	61	61	31	50	19	.294	.446	4	2	OF-140
1916		119	403	118	11	10	1	0.2	37	33	10	43	21	.293	.377	12	2	OF-106
1917		144	530	123	12	14	3	0.6	49	41	37	44	21	.232	.325	7	1	OF-137
5 yrs.		418	1489	401	47	49	6	0.4	148	140	79	137	65	.269	.379	25	5	OF-396
3 yrs.		403	1440	390	44	49	6	0.4	147	135	78	137	61	.271	.382	23	5	OF-383

Peanuts Lowrey

LOWREY, HARRY LEE   BR TR 5'8½" 170 lbs.
B. Aug. 27, 1918, Culver City, Calif.

		G	AB	H	2B	3B	HR	HR %	R	RBI	BB	SO	SB	BA	SA	AB	H	G by POS
1942 CHI N		27	58	11	0	0	1	1.7	4	4	4	4	0	.190	.241	3	0	OF-19
1943		130	480	140	25	12	1	0.2	59	63	35	24	13	.292	.400	4	1	OF-113, SS-16, 2B-3
1945		143	523	148	22	7	7	1.3	72	89	48	27	11	.283	.392	5	1	OF-138, SS-2
1946		144	540	139	24	5	4	0.7	75	54	56	22	10	.257	.343	0	0	OF-126, 3B-20
1947		115	448	126	17	5	5	1.1	56	37	38	26	2	.281	.375	1	0	3B-91, OF-25, 2B-6
1948		129	435	128	21	2	0.5	47	54	34	31	2	.294	.349	13	3	OF-103, 3B-9, 2B-2, SS-1
1949 2 teams	CHI N (38G – .270)					CIN N	(89G – .275)											
" Total		127	420	115	21	2	4	1.0	66	35	46	19	4	.274	.362	16	6	OF-109, 3B-1
1950 2 teams	CIN N (91G – .227)					STL N	(17G – .268)											
" Total		108	320	75	14	0	2	0.6	44	15	42	8	0	.234	.297	14	2	OF-76, 2B-7, 3B-5
1951 STL N		114	370	112	19	5	5	1.4	52	40	35	12	0	.303	.422	19	5	OF-85, 3B-11, 2B-3
1952		132	374	107	18	2	1	0.3	48	48	34	13	3	.286	.353	27	13	OF-106, 3B-6
1953		104	182	49	9	2	5	2.7	26	27	15	21	1	.269	.423	59	22	OF-38, 2B-10, 3B-1
1954		74	61	7	1	2	0	0.0	6	5	9	9	0	.115	.197	53	7	OF-12
1955 PHI N		54	106	20	4	0	0	0.0	9	8	7	10	2	.189	.226	16	2	OF-28, 2B-2, 1B-1
13 yrs.		1401	4317	1177	186	45	37	0.9	564	479	403	226	48	.273	.362	230	62	OF-978, 3B-144, 2B-33, SS-19, 1B-1
5 yrs.		441	1043	290	47	11	12	1.2	142	124	99	56	4	.278	.379	159 2nd	47 2nd	OF-245, 3B-23, 2B-19
WORLD SERIES																		
1945 CHI N		7	29	9	1	0	0	0.0	4	0	1	2	1	.310	.345	0	0	OF-7

Bill Ludwig

LUDWIG, WILLIAM LAWRENCE   BR TR
B. May 27, 1882, Louisville, Ky.   D. Sept. 5, 1947, Louisville, Ky.

		G	AB	H	2B	3B	HR	HR %	R	RBI	BB	SO	SB	BA	SA	AB	H	G by POS
1908 STL N		66	187	34	2	2	0	0.0	15	8	16		3	.182	.214	4	0	C-62

Ernie Lush

LUSH, ERNEST BENJAMIN   TL
Brother of Billy Lush.
B. Oct. 31, 1884, Bridgeport, Conn.   D. Feb. 26, 1937, Detroit, Mich.

		G	AB	H	2B	3B	HR	HR %	R	RBI	BB	SO	SB	BA	SA	AB	H	G by POS
1910 STL N		1	4	0	0	0	0	0.0	0	0	1		0	.000	.000	0	0	OF-1

	G	AB	H	2B	3B	HR	HR%	R	RBI	BB	SO	SB	BA	SA	Pinch Hit AB	Pinch Hit H	G by POS

Johnny Lush

LUSH, JOHN CHARLES
B. Oct. 8, 1885, Williamsport, Pa.   D. Nov. 18, 1946, Beverly Hills, Calif.   BL TL 5'9½" 165 lbs.

	G	AB	H	2B	3B	HR	HR%	R	RBI	BB	SO	SB	BA	SA	PH AB	PH H	G by POS
1904 PHI N	106	369	102	22	3	2	0.5	39	42	27		12	.276	.369	4	1	1B-62, OF-33, P-7
1905	6	16	5	0	0	0	0.0	3	1	1		0	.313	.313	1	1	OF-3, P-2
1906	76	212	56	7	1	0	0.0	28	15	14		6	.264	.307	14	1	P-37, OF-22, 1B-2
1907 2 teams	PHI	N	(17G –	.200)		STL	N	(27G –	.280)								
" Total	44	122	31	3	4	0	0.0	11	10	6		5	.254	.344	13	2	P-28, OF-11
1908 STL N	45	89	15	2	0	0	0.0	7	2	7		1	.169	.191	6	1	P-38
1909	45	92	22	5	0	0	0.0	11	14	6		2	.239	.293	7	0	P-34, OF-3
1910	47	93	21	1	3	0	0.0	8	10	8	11	2	.226	.301	10	4	P-36
7 yrs.	369	993	252	40	11	2	0.2	107	94	69	11	28	.254	.322	55	10	P-182, OF-72, 1B-64
4 yrs.	164	356	81	10	6	0	0.0	32	31	26	11	9	.228	.289	31	6	P-128, OF-10

Denny Lyons

LYONS, DENNIS PATRICK ALOYSIUS
B. Mar. 12, 1866, Cincinnati, Ohio   D. Jan. 2, 1929, West Covington, Ky.   BR TR 5'10" 185 lbs.

	G	AB	H	2B	3B	HR	HR%	R	RBI	BB	SO	SB	BA	SA	PH AB	PH H	G by POS
1885 PRO N	4	16	2	1	0	0	0.0	3	1	0		3	.125	.188	0	0	3B-4
1886 PHI AA	32	123	26	3	1	0	0.0	22		8			.211	.252	0	0	3B-32
1887	137	570	209	43	14	6	1.1	128		47		73	.367	.523	0	0	3B-137
1888	111	456	135	22	5	6	1.3	93	83	41		39	.296	.406	0	0	3B-111
1889	131	510	168	36	4	9	1.8	135	82	79	44	10	.329	.469	0	0	3B-130, 1B-1
1890	88	339	120	29	5	7	**2.1**	79		57		21	.354	**.531**	0	0	3B-88
1891 STL AA	120	451	142	24	3	11	2.4	124	84	88	58	9	.315	.455	0	0	3B-120
1892 NY N	108	389	100	16	7	8	2.1	71	51	59	36	11	.257	.396	0	0	3B-108
1893 PIT N	131	490	150	19	16	3	0.6	103	105	97	29	19	.306	.429	0	0	3B-131
1894	71	254	82	14	4	4	1.6	51	50	42	12	14	.323	.457	0	0	3B-71
1895 STL N	33	129	38	6	0	2	1.6	24	25	14	5	3	.295	.388	0	0	3B-33
1896 PIT N	118	436	134	25	6	4	0.9	77	71	67	25	13	.307	.420	2	0	3B-116
1897	37	131	27	6	4	2	1.5	22	17	22			.206	.359	0	0	1B-35, 3B-2
13 yrs.	1121	4294	1333	244	69	62	1.4	932	569	621	212	217	.310	.443	2	0	3B-1083, 1B-36
1 yr.	33	129	38	6	0	2	1.6	24	25	14	5	3	.295	.388	0	0	3B-33

Max Macon

MACON, MAX CULLEN
B. Oct. 14, 1915, Pensacola, Fla.   BL TL 6'3" 175 lbs.

	G	AB	H	2B	3B	HR	HR%	R	RBI	BB	SO	SB	BA	SA	PH AB	PH H	G by POS
1938 STL N	46	36	11	0	0	0	0.0	5	3	2	4	0	.306	.306	2	0	P-38, OF-1
1940 BKN N	2	1	1	0	0	0	0.0	0	0	0	0	0	1.000	1.000	0	0	P-2
1942	26	43	12	2	1	0	0.0	4	1	2	4	1	.279	.372	11	5	P-14
1943	45	55	9	0	0	0	0.0	7	6	0	1	1	.164	.164	13	1	P-25, 1B-3
1944 BOS N	106	366	100	15	3	3	0.8	38	36	12	23	7	.273	.355	10	2	1B-72, OF-22, P-1
1947	1	1	0	0	0	0	0.0	0	0	0	0	0	.000	.000	0	0	P-1
6 yrs.	226	502	133	17	4	3	0.6	54	46	16	32	9	.265	.333	36	8	P-81, 1B-75, OF-23
1 yr.	46	36	11	0	0	0	0.0	5	3	2	4	0	.306	.306	2	0	P-38, OF-1

Lee Magee

MAGEE, LEO CHRISTOPHER
Born Leopold Christopher Hoernschemeyer.
B. June 4, 1889, Cincinnati, Ohio   D. Mar. 14, 1966, Columbus, Ohio
Manager 1915.   BB TR 5'11" 165 lbs.

	G	AB	H	2B	3B	HR	HR%	R	RBI	BB	SO	SB	BA	SA	PH AB	PH H	G by POS
1911 STL N	26	69	18	1	1	0	0.0	9	8	8	4	2	.261	.304	2	0	2B-18, SS-3
1912	128	458	133	13	8	0	0.0	60	40	39	29	16	.290	.354	8	3	OF-85, 2B-23, 1B-6, SS-1
1913	136	529	140	13	7	2	0.4	53	31	34	30	23	.265	.327	0	0	OF-107, 2B-21, 1B-6, SS-2
1914	162	529	150	23	4	2	0.4	59	40	42	24	36	.284	.353	0	0	OF-102, 1B-40, 2B-6
1915 BKN F	121	452	146	19	10	4	0.9	87	49	22		34	.323	.436	4	0	2B-115, 1B-2
1916 NY A	131	510	131	18	4	3	0.6	57	45	50	31	29	.257	.325	1	0	OF-128, 2B-2
1917 2 teams	NY	A	(51G –	.220)		STL	A	(36G –	.170)								
" Total	87	285	57	5	1	0	0.0	28	12	19	24	6	.200	.225	3	1	OF-51, 3B-20, 2B-6, 1B-5
1918 CIN N	119	459	133	22	13	0	0.0	62	28	28	19	19	.290	.394	1	0	2B-114, 3B-3
1919 2 teams	BKN	N	(45G –	.238)		CHI	N	(79G –	.292)								
" Total	124	448	121	19	6	1	0.2	52	24	23	24	19	.270	.346	7	2	OF-44, 2B-43, 3B-19, SS-13
9 yrs.	1034	3739	1029	133	54	12	0.3	467	277	265	189	186	.275	.349	26	6	OF-517, 2B-348, 1B-59, 3B-42, SS-19
4 yrs.	452	1585	441	50	20	4	0.3	181	119	123	91	79	.278	.343	10	3	OF-294, 2B-68, 1B-52, SS-6

Mike Mahoney

MAHONEY, GEORGE W.
B. Dec. 5, 1873, Boston, Mass.   D. Jan. 3, 1940, Boston, Mass.

	G	AB	H	2B	3B	HR	HR%	R	RBI	BB	SO	SB	BA	SA	PH AB	PH H	G by POS
1897 BOS N	2	2	1	0	0	0	0.0	1	1	0		0	.500	.500	0	0	C-1, P-1
1898 STL N	2	7	0	0	0	0	0.0	0	0	0		0	.000	.000	0	0	1B-2
2 yrs.	4	9	1	0	0	0	0.0	1	1	0		0	.111	.111	0	0	1B-2, C-1, P-1
1 yr.	2	7	0	0	0	0	0.0	0	0	0		0	.000	.000	0	0	1B-2

Jim Mallory

MALLORY, JAMES BAUGH (Sunny Jim)
B. Sept. 1, 1918, Lawrenceville, Va.   BR TR 6'1" 170 lbs.

	G	AB	H	2B	3B	HR	HR%	R	RBI	BB	SO	SB	BA	SA	PH AB	PH H	G by POS
1940 WAS A	4	12	2	0	0	0	0.0	2	0	1	1	0	.167	.167	0	0	OF-3
1945 2 teams	STL	N	(13G –	.233)		NY	N	(37G –	.298)								
" Total	50	137	38	3	0	0	0.0	13	14	6	9	1	.277	.299	11	3	OF-32
2 yrs.	54	149	40	3	0	0	0.0	15	14	7	10	1	.268	.289	11	3	OF-35
1 yr.	13	43	10	2	0	0	0.0	3	5	2	2	1	.233	.279	2		OF-11

Gus Mancuso

MANCUSO, AUGUST RODNEY (Blackie)
Brother of Frank Mancuso.
B. Dec. 5, 1905, Galveston, Tex.   BR TR 5'10" 185 lbs.

	G	AB	H	2B	3B	HR	HR%	R	RBI	BB	SO	SB	BA	SA	PH AB	PH H	G by POS
1928 STL N	11	38	7	0	1	0	0.0	3	5	0	5	0	.184	.237	0	0	C-11
1930	76	227	83	17	2	7	3.1	39	59	18	16	1	.366	.551	12	3	C-61
1931	67	187	49	16	1	1	0.5	13	23	18	13	2	.262	.374	10	1	C-56

	G	AB	H	2B	3B	HR	HR %	R	RBI	BB	SO	SB	BA	SA	Pinch Hit AB	Pinch Hit H	G by POS

Gus Mancuso continued

	G	AB	H	2B	3B	HR	HR %	R	RBI	BB	SO	SB	BA	SA	PH AB	PH H	G by POS
1932	103	310	88	23	1	5	1.6	25	43	30	15	0	.284	.413	19	6	C-82
1933 NY N	144	481	127	17	2	6	1.2	39	56	48	21	0	.264	.345	2	1	C-142
1934	122	383	94	14	0	7	1.8	32	46	27	19	0	.245	.337	0	0	C-122
1935	128	447	133	18	2	5	1.1	33	56	30	16	1	.298	.380	2	0	C-126
1936	139	519	156	21	3	9	1.7	55	63	39	28	0	.301	.405	1	0	C-138
1937	86	287	80	17	1	4	1.4	30	39	17	20	1	.279	.387	5	0	C-81
1938	52	158	55	8	0	2	1.3	19	15	17	13	0	.348	.437	8	2	C-44
1939 CHI N	80	251	58	10	0	2	0.8	17	17	24	19	0	.231	.295	3	0	C-76
1940 BKN N	60	144	33	8	0	0	0.0	16	16	13	7	0	.229	.285	4	1	C-56
1941 STL N	106	328	75	13	1	2	0.6	25	37	37	19	0	.229	.293	1	0	C-105
1942 2 teams	STL	N	(5G –	.077)		NY	N	(39G –	.193)								
" Total	44	122	22	1	1	0	0.0	4	9	14	7	1	.180	.205	3	0	C-41
1943 NY N	94	252	50	5	0	2	0.8	11	20	28	16	0	.198	.242	15	3	C-77
1944	78	195	49	4	1	1	0.5	15	25	30	20	0	.251	.297	4	2	C-72
1945 PHI N	70	176	35	5	0	0	0.0	11	16	28	10	2	.199	.227	0	0	C-70
17 yrs.	1460	4505	1194	197	16	53	1.2	386	543	418	264	8	.265	.351	89	19	C-1360
6 yrs.	368	1103	303	69	6	15	1.4	104	166	103	68	3	.275	.389	44	10	C-318

WORLD SERIES

	G	AB	H	2B	3B	HR	HR %	R	RBI	BB	SO	SB	BA	SA	PH AB	PH H	G by POS
1930 STL N	2	7	2	0	0	0	0.0	1	0	1	2	0	.286	.286	0	0	C-2
1931	2	1	0	0	0	0	0.0	0	0	0	0	0	.000	.000	1	0	C-1
1933 NY N	5	17	2	1	0	0	0.0	2	2	3	0	0	.118	.176	0	0	C-5
1936	6	19	5	2	0	0	0.0	3	1	3	3	0	.263	.368	0	0	C-6
1937	3	8	0	0	0	0	0.0	0	1	0	1	0	.000	.000	1	0	C-2
5 yrs.	18	52	9	3	0	0	0.0	6	4	7	6	0	.173	.231	2	0	C-16

Les Mann

MANN, LESLIE
B. Nov. 18, 1893, Lincoln, Neb.   D. Jan. 14, 1962, Pasadena, Calif.   BR TR 5'9" 172 lbs.

	G	AB	H	2B	3B	HR	HR %	R	RBI	BB	SO	SB	BA	SA	PH AB	PH H	G by POS
1913 BOS N	120	407	103	24	7	3	0.7	54	51	18	73	7	.253	.369	0	0	OF-120
1914	126	389	96	16	11	4	1.0	44	40	24	50	9	.247	.375	3	0	OF-123
1915 CHI N	135	470	144	12	19	4	0.9	74	58	36		18	.306	.438	4	2	OF-130, SS-1
1916 CHI N	127	415	113	13	9	2	0.5	46	29	19	31	11	.272	.361	9	1	OF-115
1917	117	444	121	19	10	1	0.2	63	44	27	46	14	.273	.367	1	0	OF-116
1918	129	489	141	27	7	2	0.4	69	55	38	45	21	.288	.384	0	0	OF-129
1919 2 teams	CHI	N	(80G –	.227)		BOS	N	(40G –	.283)								
" Total	120	444	109	14	12	4	0.9	46	42	20	43	19	.245	.358	1	0	OF-118
1920 BOS N	110	424	117	7	8	3	0.7	48	32	38	42	7	.276	.351	3	0	OF-110
1921 STL N	97	256	84	12	7	7	2.7	57	30	23	28	5	.328	.512	5	1	OF-79
1922	84	147	51	14	1	2	1.4	42	20	16	12	0	.347	.497	2	0	OF-57
1923 2 teams	STL	N	(38G –	.371)		CIN	N	(8G –	.000)								
" Total	46	90	33	5	2	5	5.6	21	11	9	5	0	.367	.633	1	0	OF-26
1924 BOS N	32	102	28	7	4	0	0.0	13	10	8	10	1	.275	.422	3	1	OF-28
1925	60	184	63	11	4	2	1.1	27	20	5	11	6	.342	.478	2	1	OF-57
1926	50	129	39	8	2	1	0.8	23	20	9	9	5	.302	.419	3	0	OF-46
1927 2 teams	BOS	N	(29G –	.258)		NY	N	(29G –	.328)								
" Total	58	133	39	7	2	2	1.5	21	16	16	10	4	.293	.421	5	1	OF-46
1928 NY N	82	193	51	7	1	2	1.0	29	25	18	9	2	.264	.342	1	0	OF-68
16 yrs.	1493	4716	1332	203	106	44	0.9	677	503	324	424	129	.282	.398	43	7	OF-1368, SS-1
3 yrs.	219	492	168	31	10	14	2.8	119	61	48	45	5	.341	.530	7	1	OF-162

WORLD SERIES

	G	AB	H	2B	3B	HR	HR %	R	RBI	BB	SO	SB	BA	SA	PH AB	PH H	G by POS
1914 BOS N	3	7	2	0	0	0	0.0	1	1	0	1	0	.286	.286	1	0	OF-2
1918 CHI N	6	22	5	2	0	0	0.0	0	2	0	0	0	.227	.318	0	0	OF-6
2 yrs.	9	29	7	2	0	0	0.0	1	3	0	1	0	.241	.310	1	0	OF-8

Rabbit Maranville

MARANVILLE, WALTER JAMES VINCENT
B. Nov. 11, 1891, Springfield, Mass.   D. Jan. 5, 1954, New York, N. Y.   BR TR 5'5" 155 lbs.
Manager 1925.
Hall of Fame 1954.

	G	AB	H	2B	3B	HR	HR %	R	RBI	BB	SO	SB	BA	SA	PH AB	PH H	G by POS
1912 BOS N	26	86	18	2	0	0	0.0	8	8	9	14	1	.209	.233	0	0	SS-26
1913	143	571	141	13	8	2	0.4	68	48	68	62	25	.247	.308	0	0	SS-143
1914	156	586	144	23	6	4	0.7	74	78	45	56	28	.246	.326	0	0	SS-156
1915	149	509	124	23	6	2	0.4	51	43	45	65	18	.244	.324	0	0	SS-149
1916	155	604	142	16	13	4	0.7	79	38	50	69	32	.235	.325	0	0	SS-155
1917	142	561	146	19	13	3	0.5	69	43	40	47	27	.260	.357	0	0	SS-142
1918	11	38	12	0	1	0	0.0	3	3	4	0	0	.316	.368	0	0	SS-11
1919	131	480	128	18	10	5	1.0	44	43	36	23	12	.267	.377	0	0	SS-131
1920	134	493	131	19	15	1	0.2	48	43	28	24	14	.266	.371	1	0	SS-133
1921 PIT N	153	612	180	25	12	1	0.2	90	70	47	38	25	.294	.379	0	0	SS-153
1922	155	672	198	26	15	0	0.0	115	63	61	43	24	.295	.378	0	0	SS-138, 2B-18
1923	141	581	161	19	9	1	0.2	78	41	42	34	14	.277	.346	0	0	SS-141
1924	152	594	158	33	20	2	0.3	62	71	35	53	18	.266	.399	0	0	2B-152
1925 CHI N	75	266	62	10	3	0	0.0	37	23	29	20	6	.233	.293	1	0	SS-74
1926 BKN N	78	234	55	8	5	0	0.0	32	24	26	24	7	.235	.312	0	0	SS-60, 2B-18
1927 STL N	9	29	7	1	0	0	0.0	0	0	2	2	0	.241	.276	0	0	SS-9
1928	112	366	88	14	10	1	0.3	40	34	36	27	3	.240	.342	0	0	SS-112, 2B-2
1929 BOS N	146	560	159	26	10	0	0.0	87	55	47	33	13	.284	.366	0	0	SS-146, 2B-1
1930	142	558	157	26	8	2	0.4	85	43	48	23	9	.281	.367	0	0	SS-138, 3B-4
1931	145	562	146	22	5	0	0.0	69	33	56	34	9	.260	.317	1	0	SS-137, 2B-11
1932	149	571	134	20	4	0	0.0	67	37	46	28	4	.235	.284	0	0	2B-149
1933	143	478	104	15	4	0	0.0	46	38	36	34	2	.218	.266	1	1	2B-142
1935	23	67	10	2	0	0	0.0	3	5	3	3	0	.149	.179	3	0	2B-20
23 yrs.	2670	10078	2605	380	177	28	0.3	1255	884	839	756	291	.258	.340	7	1	SS-2154, 2B-513, 3B-4
2 yrs.	121	395	95	15	10	1	0.3	40	34	38	29	3	.241	.337	0	0	SS-121, 2B-2

WORLD SERIES

	G	AB	H	2B	3B	HR	HR %	R	RBI	BB	SO	SB	BA	SA	PH AB	PH H	G by POS
1914 BOS N	4	13	4	0	0	0	0.0	1	3	1	1	2	.308	.308	0	0	SS-4

	G	AB	H	2B	3B	HR	HR %	R	RBI	BB	SO	SB	BA	SA	Pinch Hit AB	Pinch Hit H	G by POS

Rabbit Maranville continued

	G	AB	H	2B	3B	HR	HR %	R	RBI	BB	SO	SB	BA	SA	AB	H	G by POS
1928 STL N	4	13	4	1	0	0	0.0	2	0	1	1	1	.308	.385	0	0	SS-4
2 yrs.	8	26	8	1	0	0	0.0	3	3	2	2	3	.308	.346	0	0	SS-8

Marty Marion

MARION, MARTIN WHITFORD (Slats, The Octopus)   BR TR 6'2"   170 lbs.
Brother of Red Marion.
B. Dec. 1, 1917, Richburg, S. C.
Manager 1951-56.

	G	AB	H	2B	3B	HR	HR %	R	RBI	BB	SO	SB	BA	SA	AB	H	G by POS
1940 STL N	125	435	121	18	1	3	0.7	44	46	21	34	9	.278	.345	0	0	SS-125
1941	155	547	138	22	3	3	0.5	50	58	42	48	8	.252	.320	0	0	SS-155
1942	147	485	134	38	5	0	0.0	66	54	48	50	8	.276	.375	0	0	SS-147
1943	129	418	117	15	3	1	0.2	38	52	32	37	1	.280	.337	1	0	SS-128
1944	144	506	135	26	2	6	1.2	50	63	43	50	1	.267	.362	0	0	SS-144
1945	123	430	119	27	5	1	0.2	63	59	39	39	2	.277	.370	0	0	SS-122
1946	146	498	116	29	4	3	0.6	51	46	59	53	1	.233	.325	1	0	SS-145
1947	149	540	147	19	6	4	0.7	57	74	49	58	3	.272	.352	0	0	SS-149
1948	144	567	143	26	4	4	0.7	70	43	37	54	1	.252	.333	2	0	SS-142
1949	134	515	140	31	2	5	1.0	61	70	37	42	0	.272	.369	0	0	SS-134
1950	106	372	92	10	2	4	1.1	36	40	44	55	1	.247	.317	5	1	SS-101
1952 STL A	67	186	46	11	0	2	1.1	16	19	19	17	0	.247	.339	4	2	SS-63
1953	3	7	0	0	0	0	0.0	0	0	0	0	0	.000	.000	1	0	3B-2
13 yrs.	1572	5506	1448	272	37	36	0.7	602	624	470	537	35	.263	.345	14	3	SS-1555, 3B-2
11 yrs.	1502	5313	1402	261	37	34	0.6	586	605	451	520	35	.264	.346	9	1	SS-1492
	10th										**8th**						

WORLD SERIES

	G	AB	H	2B	3B	HR	HR %	R	RBI	BB	SO	SB	BA	SA	AB	H	G by POS
1942 STL N	5	18	2	0	1	0	0.0	2	3	1	2	0	.111	.222	0	0	SS-5
1943	5	14	5	2	0	1	7.1	1	2	3	1	1	.357	.714	0	0	SS-5
1944	6	22	5	3	0	0	0.0	1	2	2	3	0	.227	.364	0	0	SS-6
1946	7	24	6	2	0	0	0.0	1	4	1	1	0	.250	.333	0	0	SS-7
4 yrs.	23	78	18	7	1	1	1.3	5	11	7	7	1	.231	.385	0	0	SS-23
				8th													

Roger Maris

MARIS, ROGER EUGENE   BL TR 6'   197 lbs.
B. Sept. 10, 1934, Fargo, N. D.

	G	AB	H	2B	3B	HR	HR %	R	RBI	BB	SO	SB	BA	SA	AB	H	G by POS
1957 CLE A	116	358	84	9	5	14	3.9	61	51	60	79	8	.235	.405	5	2	OF-112
1958 2 teams		CLE A	(51G – .225)			KC A	(99G – .247)										
" Total	150	583	140	19	4	28	4.8	87	80	45	85	4	.240	.431	6	0	OF-146
1959 KC A	122	433	118	21	7	16	3.7	69	72	58	53	2	.273	.464	5	2	OF-117
1960 NY A	136	499	141	18	7	39	7.8	98	112	70	65	2	.283	.581	4	1	OF-131
1961	161	590	159	16	4	61	10.3	132	142	94	67	0	.269	.620	1	0	OF-160
1962	157	590	151	34	1	33	5.6	92	100	87	78	1	.256	.485	5	2	OF-154
1963	90	312	84	14	1	23	7.4	53	53	35	40	1	.269	.542	5	2	OF-86
1964	141	513	144	12	2	26	5.1	86	71	62	78	3	.281	.464	6	1	OF-137
1965	46	155	37	7	0	8	5.2	22	27	29	29	0	.239	.439	4	1	OF-43
1966	119	348	81	9	2	13	3.7	37	43	36	60	0	.233	.382	20	6	OF-95
1967 STL N	125	410	107	18	7	9	2.2	64	55	52	61	0	.261	.405	19	2	OF-118
1968	100	310	79	18	2	5	1.6	25	45	24	38	0	.255	.374	21	6	OF-84
12 yrs.	1463	5101	1325	195	42	275	5.4	826	851	652	733	21	.260	.476	99	23	OF-1383
2 yrs.	225	720	186	36	9	14	1.9	89	100	76	99	0	.258	.392	40	8	OF-202

WORLD SERIES

	G	AB	H	2B	3B	HR	HR %	R	RBI	BB	SO	SB	BA	SA	AB	H	G by POS
1960 NY A	7	30	8	1	0	2	6.7	6	2	2	4	0	.267	.500	0	0	OF-7
1961	5	19	2	1	0	1	5.3	4	2	4	6	0	.105	.316	0	0	OF-5
1962	7	23	4	1	0	1	4.3	4	5	5	2	0	.174	.348	0	0	OF-7
1963	2	5	0	0	0	0	0.0	0	0	0	1	0	.000	.000	0	0	OF-2
1964	7	30	6	0	0	1	3.3	4	1	1	4	0	.200	.300	0	0	OF-7
1967 STL N	7	26	10	1	0	1	3.8	3	7	3	1	0	.385	.538	0	0	OF-7
1968	6	19	3	1	0	0	0.0	5	1	3	3	0	.158	.211	1	0	OF-5
7 yrs.	41	152	33	5	0	6	3.9	26	18	18	21	0	.217	.368	1	0	OF-40
	10th	**10th**						**6th**									

Fred Marolewski

MAROLEWSKI, FRED DANIEL (Fritz)   BR TR 6'2½" 205 lbs.
B. Oct. 6, 1928, Chicago, Ill.

	G	AB	H	2B	3B	HR	HR %	R	RBI	BB	SO	SB	BA	SA	AB	H	G by POS
1953 STL N	1	0	0	0	0	0	–	0	0	0	0	0	–	–	0	0	1B-1

Charlie Marshall

MARSHALL, CHARLES ANTHONY   BR TR 5'10½" 178 lbs.
Born Charles Anthony Marczlewicz.
B. Aug. 28, 1919, Wilmington, Del.

	G	AB	H	2B	3B	HR	HR %	R	RBI	BB	SO	SB	BA	SA	AB	H	G by POS
1941 STL N	1	0	0	0	0	0	–	0	0	0	0	0	–	–	0	0	C-1

Doc Marshall

MARSHALL, WILLIAM RIDDLE   BR TR 6'1"   185 lbs.
B. Sept. 22, 1875, Butler, Pa.   D. Dec. 11, 1959, Clinton, Ill.

	G	AB	H	2B	3B	HR	HR %	R	RBI	BB	SO	SB	BA	SA	AB	H	G by POS
1904 3 teams		PHI N	(8G – .100)			NY N	(11G – .353)			BOS N	(13G – .209)						
" Total	32	80	17	1	1	0	0.0	7	5	3		2	.213	.250	7	0	C-20, OF-3, 2B-1
1906 2 teams		NY N	(38G – .167)			STL N	(39G – .276)										
" Total	77	225	51	7	3	0	0.0	14	17	13		8	.227	.284	9	1	C-51, OF-16, 1B-1
1907 STL N	84	268	54	8	2	2	0.7	19	18	12		7	.201	.269	1	0	C-83
1908 2 teams		STL N	(6G – .071)			CHI N	(12G – .300)										
" Total	18	34	7	0	1	0	0.0	4	4	0		0	.206	.265	2	1	C-10, OF-3
1909 BKN N	50	149	30	7	1	0	0.0	7	10	6		3	.201	.262	1	0	C-49, OF-1
5 yrs.	261	756	159	23	8	2	0.3	51	54	34		15	.210	.270	20	2	C-213, OF-23, 1B-2, 2B-1
3 yrs.	129	405	89	15	3	2	0.5	25	29	18		2	.220	.279	2	0	C-127

	G	AB	H	2B	3B	HR	HR %	R	RBI	BB	SO	SB	BA	SA	Pinch Hit AB	Pinch Hit H	G by POS

Joe Marshall

MARSHALL, JOSEPH HELMER
B. Troy, N. Y.   D. May 4, 1934, Walla Walla, Wash.

	G	AB	H	2B	3B	HR	HR %	R	RBI	BB	SO	SB	BA	SA	PH AB	PH H	G by POS
1903 PIT N	10	23	6	1	2	0	0.0	2	2	0		0	.261	.478	3	0	OF-3, SS-3, 2B-1
1906 STL N	33	95	15	1	2	0	0.0	2	7	6		0	.158	.211	5	1	OF-23, 1B-4
2 yrs.	43	118	21	2	4	0	0.0	4	9	6		0	.178	.263	8	1	OF-26, 1B-4, SS-3, 2B-1
1 yr.	33	95	15	1	2	0	0.0	2	7	6		0	.158	.211	5	1	OF-23, 1B-4

Pepper Martin

MARTIN, JOHNNY LEONARD ROOSEVELT (The Wild Hoss Of The Osage)
BR TR 5'8"   170 lbs.
B. Feb. 29, 1904, Temple, Okla.   D. Mar. 5, 1965, McAlester, Okla.

	G	AB	H	2B	3B	HR	HR %	R	RBI	BB	SO	SB	BA	SA	PH AB	PH H	G by POS
1928 STL N	39	13	4	0	0	0	0.0	11	0	1	2	2	.308	.308	12	3	OF-4
1930	1	1	0	0	0	0	0.0	5	0	0	0	0	.000	.000	1	0	
1931	123	413	124	32	8	7	1.7	68	75	30	40	16	.300	.467	7	4	OF-110
1932	85	323	77	19	6	4	1.2	47	34	30	31	9	.238	.372	0	0	OF-69, 3B-15
1933	145	599	189	36	12	8	1.3	122	57	67	46	26	.316	.456	0	0	3B-145
1934	110	454	131	25	11	5	1.1	76	49	32	41	23	.289	.425	1	0	3B-107, P-1
1935	135	539	161	41	6	9	1.7	121	54	33	58	20	.299	.447	5	0	3B-114, OF-16
1936	143	572	177	36	11	11	1.9	121	76	58	66	23	.309	.469	1	0	OF-127, 3B-15, P-1
1937	98	339	103	27	8	5	1.5	60	38	33	50	9	.304	.475	9	2	OF-82, 3B-5
1938	91	269	79	18	2	2	0.7	34	38	18	34	4	.294	.398	23	5	OF-62, 3B-4
1939	88	281	86	17	7	3	1.1	48	37	30	35	6	.306	.448	10	0	OF-51, 3B-22
1940	86	228	72	15	4	3	1.3	28	39	22	24	6	.316	.456	17	4	OF-63, 3B-2
1944	40	86	24	4	0	2	2.3	15	4	15	11	2	.279	.395	5	1	OF-29
13 yrs.	1189	4117	1227	270	75	59	1.4	756	501	369	438	146	.298	.443	91	19	OF-613, 3B-429, P-2
13 yrs.	1189	4117	1227	270	75	59	1.4	756	501	369	438	146	.298	.443	91	19	OF-613, 3B-429, P-2
				8th							6th						

WORLD SERIES

	G	AB	H	2B	3B	HR	HR %	R	RBI	BB	SO	SB	BA	SA	PH AB	PH H	G by POS
1928 STL N	1	0	0	0	0	0	–	1	0	0	0	0	–	–	0	0	
1931	7	24	12	4	0	1	4.2	5	5	2	3	5	.500	.792	0	0	OF-7
1934	7	31	11	3	1	0	0.0	8	3	3	3	2	.355	.516	0	0	3B-7
3 yrs.	15	55	23	7	1	1	1.8	14	8	5	6	7	.418	.636	0	0	OF-7, 3B-7
				8th							9th	1st	6th				

Stu Martin

MARTIN, STUART McGUIRE
BL TR 6'   155 lbs.
B. Nov. 17, 1913, Rich Square, N. C.

	G	AB	H	2B	3B	HR	HR %	R	RBI	BB	SO	SB	BA	SA	PH AB	PH H	G by POS
1936 STL N	92	332	99	21	4	6	1.8	63	41	29	27	17	.298	.440	4	0	2B-83, SS-3
1937	90	223	58	6	1	1	0.4	34	17	32	18	3	.260	.309	28	6	2B-48, 1B-9, SS-1
1938	114	417	116	26	2	1	0.2	54	27	30	28	4	.278	.357	15	3	2B-99
1939	120	425	114	26	7	3	0.7	60	30	33	40	4	.268	.384	11	0	2B-107, 1B-1
1940	112	369	88	12	6	4	1.1	45	32	33	35	4	.238	.336	9	1	3B-73, 2B-33
1941 PIT N	88	233	71	13	2	0	0.0	37	19	10	17	2	.305	.378	28	6	2B-53, 3B-2, 1B-1
1942	42	120	27	4	2	1	0.8	16	12	8	10	1	.225	.317	10	0	2B-30, SS-1, 1B-1
1943 CHI N	64	118	26	4	0	0	0.0	13	5	15	10	1	.220	.254	25	5	2B-22, 3B-8, 1B-2
8 yrs.	722	2237	599	112	24	16	0.7	322	183	190	185	36	.268	.361	130	21	2B-475, 3B-83, 1B-14, SS-5
5 yrs.	528	1766	475	91	20	15	0.8	256	147	157	148	32	.269	.369	67	10	2B-370, 3B-73, 1B-10, SS-4

Marty Martinez

MARTINEZ, ORLANDO OLIVO
BB TR 6'   170 lbs.
B. Aug. 23, 1941, Havana, Cuba
BR 1962

	G	AB	H	2B	3B	HR	HR %	R	RBI	BB	SO	SB	BA	SA	PH AB	PH H	G by POS
1962 MIN A	37	18	3	0	1	0	0.0	13	3	3	4	0	.167	.278	0	0	SS-11, 3B-1
1967 ATL N	44	73	21	2	1	0	0.0	14	5	11	11	0	.288	.342	0	0	SS-25, 2B-9, C-3, 3B-2, 1B-1
1968	113	356	82	5	3	0	0.0	34	12	29	28	6	.230	.261	1	0	SS-54, 3B-37, 2B-16, C-14
1969 HOU N	78	198	61	5	4	0	0.0	14	15	10	21	0	.308	.374	18	4	OF-21, SS-17, 3B-15, C-7, 2B-1, P-1
1970	75	150	33	3	0	0	0.0	12	12	9	22	0	.220	.240	38	9	SS-29, 3B-10, C-6, 2B-4
1971	32	62	16	3	1	0	0.0	4	4	3	6	1	.258	.339	13	4	2B-9, SS-7, 1B-4, 3B-3
1972 3 teams	STL N (9G – .429)			TEX A (26G – .146)				OAK A (22G – .125)									
" Total	57	88	14	1	1	0	0.0	6	6	5	15	0	.159	.193	19	4	2B-20, SS-14, 3B-6
7 yrs.	436	945	230	19	11	0	0.0	97	57	70	107	7	.243	.287	89	21	SS-157, 3B-74, 2B-59, C-30, OF-21, 1B-5, P-1
1 yr.	9	7	3	0	0	0	0.0	0		2	0	1	0	.429	.429	3	1	SS-3, 2B-2, 3B-1

Teddy Martinez

MARTINEZ, TEODORO NOEL
BR TR 6'   165 lbs.
B. Dec. 10, 1947, Central Barahona, Dominican Republic

	G	AB	H	2B	3B	HR	HR %	R	RBI	BB	SO	SB	BA	SA	PH AB	PH H	G by POS
1970 NY N	4	16	1	0	0	0	0.0			0	3	0	.063	.063	0	0	2B-4, SS-1
1971	38	125	36	5	2	1	0.8	16	10	4	22	6	.288	.384	1	0	2B-13, 3B-3, OF-1
1972	103	330	74	5	5	1	0.3	22	19	12	49	7	.224	.279	4	0	2B-47, SS-42, OF-15, 3B-2
1973	92	263	67	11	0	1	0.4	34	14	13	38	3	.255	.308	1	0	SS-44, OF-21, 3B-14, 2B-5
1974	116	334	73	15	7	2	0.6	32	43	14	40	1	.219	.323	8	1	SS-75, 3B-12, 2B-11, OF-10
1975 2 teams	STL N (16G – .190)			OAK A (86G – .172)													
" Total	102	108	19	2	0	0	0.0	8	5	2	11	1	.176	.194	11	1	SS-46, 2B-33, 3B-15, OF-7
1977 LA N	67	137	41	6	1	1	0.7	21	10	2	20	3	.299	.380	4	0	SS-27, SS-13, 3B-12
1978	54	55	14	1	0	1	1.8	13	5	4	14	3	.255	.327	4	0	SS-17, 3B-16, 2B-10
1979	81	112	30	5	1	0	0.0	19	2	4	16	3	.268	.330	4	0	3B-23, SS-14, 2B-18
9 yrs.	657	1480	355	50	16	7	0.5	165	108	55	213	29	.240	.309	37	2	SS-282, 2B-168, 3B-97, OF-54
1 yr.	16	21	4	0	0	0	0.0	1		2		0	.190	.286	6	1	OF-7, 2B-2, SS-1, 3B-1

LEAGUE CHAMPIONSHIP SERIES

	G	AB	H	2B	3B	HR	HR %	R	RBI	BB	SO	SB	BA	SA	PH AB	PH H	G by POS
1975 OAK A	3	0	0	0	0	0	–	0	0	0	0	0	–	–	0	0	2B-3

	G	AB	H	2B	3B	HR	HR %	R	RBI	BB	SO	SB	BA	SA	Pinch Hit AB	Pinch Hit H	G by POS

Teddy Martinez continued

WORLD SERIES

	G	AB	H	2B	3B	HR	HR %	R	RBI	BB	SO	SB	BA	SA	AB	H	G by POS
1973 NY N	2	0	0	0	0	0	–	0	0	0	0	0	–	–	0	0	

Wally Mattick

MATTICK, WALTER JOSEPH (Chick)
Father of Bobby Mattick.
B. Mar. 12, 1887, St. Louis, Mo.   D. Nov. 5, 1968, Los Altos, Calif.   BR TR 5'10'' 180 lbs.

	G	AB	H	2B	3B	HR	HR %	R	RBI	BB	SO	SB	BA	SA	AB	H	G by POS
1912 CHI A	88	285	74	7	9	1	0.4	45	35	27		15	.260	.358	8	3	OF-78
1913	68	207	39	8	1	0	0.0	15	11	18	16	3	.188	.237	3	1	OF-63
1918 STL N	8	14	2	0	0	0	0.0	0	1	2	3	0	.143	.143	5	1	OF-3
3 yrs.	164	506	115	15	10	1	0.2	60	47	47	19	18	.227	.302	16	5	OF-144
1 yr.	8	14	2	0	0	0	0.0	0	1	2	3	0	.143	.143	5	1	OF-3

Gene Mauch

MAUCH, GENE WILLIAM (Skip)
B. Nov. 18, 1925, Salina, Kans.
Manager 1960-82.   BR TR 5'10'' 165 lbs.

	G	AB	H	2B	3B	HR	HR %	R	RBI	BB	SO	SB	BA	SA	AB	H	G by POS
1944 BKN N	5	15	2	1	0	0	0.0	2	2	2	3	0	.133	.200	0	0	SS-5
1947 PIT N	16	30	9	0	0	0	0.0	8	1	7	6	0	.300	.300	0	0	2B-6, SS-4
1948 2 teams	BKN N (12G – .154)						CHI N (53G – .203)										
" Total	65	151	30	3	2	1	0.7	19	7	27	14	1	.199	.265	11	0	2B-33, SS-20
1949 CHI N	72	150	37	6	2	1	0.7	15	7	21	15	3	.247	.333	13	4	2B-25, SS-19, 3B-7
1950 BOS N	48	121	28	5	0	1	0.8	17	15	14	9	1	.231	.298	3	2	2B-28, 3B-7, SS-5
1951	19	20	2	0	0	0	0.0	5	1	7	4	0	.100	.100	2	0	SS-10, 3B-3, 2B-2
1952 STL N	7	3	0	0	0	0	0.0	0	0	1	2	0	.000	.000	1	0	SS-2
1956 BOS A	7	25	8	0	0	0	0.0	4	1	3	3	0	.320	.320	1	0	2B-6
1957	65	222	60	10	3	2	0.9	23	28	22	26	1	.270	.369	7	3	2B-58
9 yrs.	304	737	176	25	7	5	0.7	93	62	104	82	6	.239	.312	38	9	2B-158, SS-65, 3B-17
1 yr.	7	3	0	0	0	0	0.0	0	0	1	2	0	.000	.000	1	0	SS-2

Dal Maxvill

MAXVILL, CHARLES DALLAN
B. Feb. 18, 1939, Granite City, Ill.   BR TR 5'11'' 157 lbs.

	G	AB	H	2B	3B	HR	HR %	R	RBI	BB	SO	SB	BA	SA	AB	H	G by POS
1962 STL N	79	189	42	3	1	1	0.5	20	18	17	39	1	.222	.265	3	0	SS-76, 3B-1
1963	53	51	12	2	0	0	0.0	12	3	6	11	0	.235	.275	3	0	SS-24, 2B-9, 3B-3
1964	37	26	6	0	0	0	0.0	4	4	0	7	1	.231	.231	1	0	2B-15, SS-13, OF-1, 3B-1
1965	68	89	12	2	2	0	0.0	10	10	7	15	0	.135	.202	2	0	2B-49, SS-12
1966	134	394	96	14	3	0	0.0	25	24	37	61	3	.244	.294	2	0	SS-128, 2B-5, OF-1
1967	152	476	108	14	4	1	0.2	37	41	48	66	0	.227	.279	0	0	SS-148, 2B-7
1968	151	459	116	8	5	1	0.2	51	24	52	71	0	.253	.298	0	0	SS-151
1969	132	372	65	10	2	2	0.5	27	32	44	52	1	.175	.228	0	0	SS-131
1970	152	399	80	5	2	0	0.0	35	28	51	56	0	.201	.223	0	0	SS-136, 2B-22
1971	142	356	80	10	1	0	0.0	31	24	43	45	1	.225	.258	1	0	SS-140
1972 2 teams	STL N (105G – .221)						OAK A (27G – .250)										
" Total	132	312	70	7	1	1	0.3	24	24	32	58	0	.224	.263	1	0	SS-99, 2B-35
1973 2 teams	OAK A (29G – .211)						PIT N (74G – .189)										
" Total	103	236	45	4	3	0	0.0	19	18	23	43	0	.191	.233	2	0	SS-92, 2B-11, 3B-1
1974 2 teams	PIT N (8G – .182)						OAK A (60G – .192)										
" Total	68	74	14	0	0	0	0.0	6	2	10	14	0	.189	.189	0	0	SS-37, 2B-30, 3B-1
1975 OAK A	20	10	2	0	0	0	0.0	0	0	2	4	0	.200	.200	0	0	SS-20, 2B-2
14 yrs.	1423	3443	748	79	24	6	0.2	302	252	370	538	7	.217	.259	15	0	SS-1207, 2B-185, 3B-7, OF-2
11 yrs.	1205	3087	678	74	21	6	0.2	274	231	336	470	7	.220	.263	13	0	SS-1054, 2B-118, 3B-5, OF-2

LEAGUE CHAMPIONSHIP SERIES

	G	AB	H	2B	3B	HR	HR %	R	RBI	BB	SO	SB	BA	SA	AB	H	G by POS
1972 OAK A	5	8	1	0	0	0	0.0	0	0	1	2	1	.125	.125	0	0	SS-4
1974	1	1	0	0	0	0	0.0	0	0	0	1	0	.000	.000	0	0	2B-1
2 yrs.	6	9	1	0	0	0	0.0	0	0	1	3	1	.111	.111	0	0	SS-4, 2B-1

WORLD SERIES

	G	AB	H	2B	3B	HR	HR %	R	RBI	BB	SO	SB	BA	SA	AB	H	G by POS
1964 STL N	7	20	4	1	0	0	0.0	0	1	1	4	0	.200	.250	0	0	2B-7
1967	7	19	3	0	1	0	0.0	1	1	4	1	0	.158	.263	0	0	SS-7
1968	7	22	0	0	0	0	0.0	1	0	3	5	0	.000	.000	0	0	SS-7
1974 OAK A	2	0	0	0	0	0	–	0	0	0	0	0	–	–	0	0	2B-2
4 yrs.	23	61	7	1	1	0	0.0	2	2	8	10	0	.115	.164	0	0	SS-14, 2B-9

Ike McAuley

McAULEY, JAMES EARL
B. Aug. 19, 1893, Wichita, Kans.   D. Apr. 6, 1928, Des Moines, Iowa   BR TR 5'9½'' 150 lbs.

	G	AB	H	2B	3B	HR	HR %	R	RBI	BB	SO	SB	BA	SA	AB	H	G by POS
1914 PIT N	15	24	3	0	0	0	0.0	3	0	0	8	0	.125	.125	1	0	SS-5, 3B-3, 2B-2
1915	5	15	2	1	0	0	0.0	0	0	0	6	0	.133	.200	2	0	SS-5
1916	4	8	2	0	0	0	0.0	1	1	0	1	0	.250	.250	0	0	SS-4
1917 STL N	3	7	2	0	0	0	0.0	0	1	0	1	0	.286	.286	0	0	SS-3
1925 CHI N	37	125	35	7	2	0	0.0	10	11	11	12	1	.280	.368	0	0	SS-37
5 yrs.	64	179	44	8	2	0	0.0	14	13	11	28	1	.246	.313	3	0	SS-54, 3B-3, 2B-2
1 yr.	3	7	2	0	0	0	0.0	0	1	0	1	0	.286	.286	0	0	SS-3

Bake McBride

McBRIDE, ARNOLD RAY
B. Feb. 3, 1949, Fulton, Mo.   BL TR 6'2'' 190 lbs.

	G	AB	H	2B	3B	HR	HR %	R	RBI	BB	SO	SB	BA	SA	AB	H	G by POS
1973 STL N	40	63	19	3	0	0	0.0	8	5	4	10	0	.302	.349	17	6	OF-17
1974	150	559	173	19	5	6	1.1	81	56	43	57	30	.309	.394	7	3	OF-144
1975	116	413	124	10	9	5	1.2	70	36	34	52	26	.300	.404	11	3	OF-107
1976	72	272	91	13	4	3	1.1	40	24	18	28	10	.335	.445	7	2	OF-66
1977 2 teams	STL N (43G – .262)						PHI N (85G – .339)										
" Total	128	402	127	25	6	15	3.7	76	61	32	44	36	.316	.520	21	5	OF-106
1978 PHI N	122	472	127	20	4	10	2.1	68	49	28	68	28	.269	.392	6	1	OF-119
1979	151	582	163	16	12	12	2.1	82	60	41	77	25	.280	.411	9	3	OF-147
1980	137	554	171	33	10	9	1.6	68	87	26	58	13	.309	.453	3	2	OF-133

	G	AB	H	2B	3B	HR	HR %	R	RBI	BB	SO	SB	BA	SA	Pinch Hit AB	Pinch Hit H	G by POS

Bake McBride continued

	G	AB	H	2B	3B	HR	HR%	R	RBI	BB	SO	SB	BA	SA	PH AB	PH H	G by POS
1981	58	221	60	17	1	2	0.9	26	21	11	25	5	.271	.385	9	3	OF-56
1982 CLE A	27	85	31	3	3	0	0.0	8	13	2	12	2	.365	.471	5	2	OF-22
10 yrs.	1001	3623	1086	159	54	62	1.7	527	412	239	431	175	.300	.425	95	30	OF-917
5 yrs.	421	1429	439	50	19	18	1.3	220	141	106	166	75	.307	.407	50	17	OF-367

DIVISIONAL PLAYOFF SERIES

	G	AB	H	2B	3B	HR	HR%	R	RBI	BB	SO	SB	BA	SA	PH AB	PH H	G by POS
1981 PHI N	4	15	3	1	0	0	0.0	1	0	0	5	0	.200	.267	0	0	OF-4

LEAGUE CHAMPIONSHIP SERIES

	G	AB	H	2B	3B	HR	HR%	R	RBI	BB	SO	SB	BA	SA	PH AB	PH H	G by POS
1977 PHI N	4	18	4	0	0	1	5.6	2	2	0	2	0	.222	.389	0	0	OF-4
1978	3	9	2	0	0	1	11.1	2	1	0	2	0	.222	.556	1	1	OF-2
1980	5	21	5	0	0	0	0.0	0	0	1	5	2	.238	.238	0	0	OF-5
3 yrs.	12	48	11	0	0	2	4.2	4	3	1	9	2	.229	.354	1	1	OF-11

WORLD SERIES

	G	AB	H	2B	3B	HR	HR%	R	RBI	BB	SO	SB	BA	SA	PH AB	PH H	G by POS
1980 PHI N	6	23	7	1	0	1	4.3	3	5	2	1	0	.304	.478	0	0	OF-6

George McBride

McBRIDE, GEORGE FLORIAN
B. Nov. 20, 1880, Milwaukee, Wis.   D. July 2, 1973, Milwaukee, Wis.
Manager 1921.
BR TR 5'11" 170 lbs.

	G	AB	H	2B	3B	HR	HR%	R	RBI	BB	SO	SB	BA	SA	PH AB	PH H	G by POS
1901 MIL A	3	12	2	0	0	0	0.0	0	0	1		0	.167	.167	0	0	SS-3
1905 2 teams					PIT N (27G – .218)					STL N (81G – .217)							
" Total	108	368	80	5	2	2	0.5	31	41	20		12	.217	.258	2	0	SS-88, 3B-17, 1B-1
1906 STL N	90	313	53	8	2	0	0.0	24	13	17		5	.169	.208	0	0	SS-90
1908 WAS A	155	518	120	10	6	0	0.0	47	34	41		12	.232	.274	0	0	SS-155
1909	155	504	118	16	0	0	0.0	38	34	36		17	.234	.266	0	0	SS-155
1910	154	514	118	19	4	1	0.2	54	55	61		11	.230	.288	0	0	SS-154
1911	154	557	131	11	4	0	0.0	58	59	52		15	.235	.269	0	0	SS-154
1912	152	521	118	13	7	1	0.0	56	52	38		17	.226	.284	0	0	SS-152
1913	150	499	107	18	7	1	0.2	52	52	43	46	12	.214	.285	0	0	SS-150
1914	156	503	102	12	4	0	0.0	49	24	43	70	12	.203	.243	0	0	SS-156
1915	146	476	97	8	6	1	0.2	54	30	29	60	10	.204	.252	0	0	SS-146
1916	139	466	106	15	4	1	0.2	36	36	23	58	8	.227	.283	0	0	SS-139
1917	50	141	27	3	0	0	0.0	6	9	10	17	1	.191	.213	1	0	SS-41, 3B-6, 2B-2
1918	18	53	7	0	0	0	0.0	2	1	0	11	1	.132	.132	1	0	SS-14, 2B-2
1919	15	40	8	1	1	0	0.0	3	4	3	6	0	.200	.275	0	0	SS-15
1920	13	41	9	1	0	0	0.0	6	3	2	3	0	.220	.244	0	0	SS-13
16 yrs.	1658	5526	1203	140	47	7	0.1	516	447	419	271	133	.218	.264	4	0	SS-1625, 3B-23, 2B-4, 1B-1
2 yrs.	171	594	114	9	4	2	0.3	46	47	31		15	.192	.231	0	0	SS-170, 1B-1

Joe McCarthy

McCARTHY, JOSEPH N.
B. Dec. 25, 1881, Syracuse, N. Y.   D. Jan. 12, 1937, Syracuse, N. Y.
BR TR

	G	AB	H	2B	3B	HR	HR%	R	RBI	BB	SO	SB	BA	SA	PH AB	PH H	G by POS
1905 NY A	1	2	0	0	0	0	0.0	0	0	0		0	.000	.000	0	0	C-1
1906 STL N	15	37	9	2	0	0	0.0	3	2	2		0	.243	.297	0	0	C-15
2 yrs.	16	39	9	2	0	0	0.0	3	2	2		0	.231	.282	0	0	C-16
1 yr.	15	37	9	2	0	0	0.0	3	2	2		0	.243	.297	0	0	C-15

Lew McCarty

McCARTY, GEORGE LEWIS
B. Nov. 17, 1888, Milton, Pa.   D. June 9, 1930, Reading, Pa.
BR TR 5'11½" 192 lbs.

	G	AB	H	2B	3B	HR	HR%	R	RBI	BB	SO	SB	BA	SA	PH AB	PH H	G by POS
1913 BKN N	9	26	6	0	0	0	0.0	1	2	2	0	0	.231	.231	0	0	C-9
1914	90	284	72	14	2	0	0.4	20	30	14	22	1	.254	.327	6	2	C-84
1915	84	276	66	9	4	0	0.0	19	19	7	23	7	.239	.301	3	1	C-84
1916 2 teams					BKN N (55G – .313)					NY N (25G – .397)							
" Total	80	218	74	9	5	0	0.0	23	22	21	25	4	.339	.427	10	4	C-51, 1B-17
1917 NY N	56	162	40	3	2	2	1.2	15	19	14	6	1	.247	.327	2	1	C-54
1918	86	257	69	7	3	0	0.0	16	24	17	13	3	.268	.319	7	2	C-75
1919	85	210	59	5	4	2	1.0	17	21	18	15	2	.281	.371	24	7	C-59
1920 2 teams					NY N (36G – .132)					STL N (5G – .286)							
" Total	41	45	7	0	0	0	0.0	9	2	2		2	.156	.156	29	5	C-8
1921 STL N	1	1	0	0	0	0	0.0	0	0	0		0	.000	.000	1	0	
9 yrs.	532	1479	393	47	20	5	0.3	113	137	102	107	20	.266	.335	82	22	C-424, 1B-17
2 yrs.	6	8	2	0	0	0	0.0	0	0	5		1	.250	.250	2	1	C-3

WORLD SERIES

	G	AB	H	2B	3B	HR	HR%	R	RBI	BB	SO	SB	BA	SA	PH AB	PH H	G by POS
1917 NY N	3	5	2	0	1	0	0.0	1	1	0	0	0	.400	.800	1	0	C-2

Tim McCarver

McCARVER, JAMES TIMOTHY
B. Oct. 16, 1941, Memphis, Tenn.
BL TR 6' 183 lbs.

	G	AB	H	2B	3B	HR	HR%	R	RBI	BB	SO	SB	BA	SA	PH AB	PH H	G by POS
1959 STL N	8	24	4	1	0	0	0.0	3	0	2	1	0	.167	.208	1	0	C-6
1960	10	10	2	0	0	0	0.0	3	0	0	2	0	.200	.200	4	1	C-5
1961	22	67	16	2	1	1	1.5	5	6	0	5	0	.239	.343	2	2	C-20
1963	127	405	117	12	7	4	1.0	39	51	27	43	5	.289	.383	5	1	C-126
1964	143	465	134	19	3	9	1.9	53	52	40	44	2	.288	.400	7	1	C-137
1965	113	409	113	17	2	11	2.7	48	48	31	26	5	.276	.408	5	2	C-111
1966	150	543	149	19	13	12	2.2	50	68	36	38	9	.274	.424	5	1	C-148
1967	138	471	139	26	3	14	3.0	68	69	54	32	8	.295	.452	11	4	C-130
1968	128	434	110	15	6	5	1.2	35	48	26	31	4	.253	.350	19	4	C-109
1969	138	515	134	27	3	7	1.4	46	51	49	26	4	.260	.365	1	0	C-136
1970 PHI N	44	164	47	11	4	2	1.2	16	14	14	10	2	.287	.439	0	0	C-44
1971	134	474	132	20	5	8	1.7	51	46	43	26	5	.278	.392	14	3	C-125
1972 2 teams					PHI N (45G – .237)					MON N (77G – .251)							
" Total	122	391	96	11	7	1	0.3	33	34	36	29	5	.246	.338	18	2	C-85, OF-14, 3B-6
1973 STL N	130	331	88	16	4	3	0.9	30	49	38	31	2	.266	.366	39	8	1B-77, C-11
1974 2 teams					STL N (74G – .217)					BOS A (11G – .250)							
" Total	85	134	30	1	1	0	0.0	16	12	26	7	1	.224	.246	43	7	C-29, 1B-6

	G	AB	H	2B	3B	HR	HR %	R	RBI	BB	SO	SB	BA	SA	Pinch Hit AB	H	G by POS

Tim McCarver continued

1975 2 teams	**BOS** A	(12G –	.381)		**PHI** N	(47G –	.254)										
" Total	59	80	23	4	1	1	1.3	7	10	15	10	0	.288	.400	39	10	C-17, 1B-2
1976 PHI N	90	155	43	11	2	3	1.9	26	29	35	14	2	.277	.432	42	9	C-41, 1B-2
1977	93	169	54	13	2	6	3.6	28	30	28	11	3	.320	.527	36	9	C-42, 1B-3
1978	90	146	36	9	1	1	0.7	18	14	28	24	2	.247	.342	41	8	C-34, 1B-11
1979	79	137	33	5	1	1	0.7	13	12	19	12	2	.241	.314	39	10	C-31, OF-1
1980	6	5	1	1	0	0	0.0	2	2	1	0	0	.200	.400	2	0	1B-2
21 yrs.	1909	5529	1501	242	57	97	1.8	590	645	548	422	61	.271	.388	373 **10th**	82	C-1387, 1B-103, OF-15, 3B-6
12 yrs.	1181	3780	1029	154	43	66	1.7	393	453	325	285	39	.272	.388	139 **6th**	31 **7th**	C-960, 1B-83

LEAGUE CHAMPIONSHIP SERIES

1976 PHI N	2	4	0	0	0	0	0.0	0	0	0	1	0	.000	.000	1	0	C-1
1977	3	6	1	0	0	0	0.0	1	0	1	3	0	.167	.167	1	0	C-2
1978	2	4	0	0	0	0	0.0	2	1	2	0	0	.000	.000	1	0	C-1
3 yrs.	7	14	1	0	0	0	0.0	3	1	3	4	0	.071	.071	3	0	C-4

WORLD SERIES

1964 STL N	7	23	11	1	1	1	4.3	4	5	5	1	1	.478	.739	0	0	C-7
1967	7	24	3	1	0	0	0.0	3	2	2	2	0	.125	.167	0	0	C-7
1968	7	27	9	0	2	1	3.7	3	4	3	2	0	.333	.593	0	0	C-7
3 yrs.	21	74	23	2	3 **4th**	2	2.7	10	11	10	5	1	.311	.500	0	0	C-21

Pat McCauley

McCAULEY, PATRICK M.
B. June 10, 1870, Ware, Mass.   D. Jan. 23, 1917, Newark, N. J.   TR

1893 STL N	5	16	1	0	0	0	0.0	0	0	0	1	0	.063	.063	0	0	C-5
1896 WAS N	26	84	21	3	0	2	2.4	14	11	7	8	3	.250	.357	1	0	C-24, OF-1
1903 NY A	6	19	1	0	0	0	0.0	0	1	0		0	.053	.053	0	0	C-6
3 yrs.	37	119	23	3	0	2	1.7	14	12	7	9	3	.193	.269	1	0	C-35, OF-1
1 yr.	5	16	1	0	0	0	0.0	0	0	0	1	0	.063	.063	0	0	C-5

Jim McCormick

McCORMICK, JAMES AMBROSE
B. Nov. 2, 1868, Spencer, Mass.   D. Feb. 1, 1948, Saco, Me.   BR TR 6'1" 160 lbs.

1892 STL N	3	11	0	0	0	0	0.0	1	5	0	.000	.000	0	0	2B-2, 3B-1

Harry McCurdy

McCURDY, HARRY HENRY
B. Sept. 15, 1900, Stevens Point, Wis.   D. July 21, 1972, Houston, Tex.   BL TR 5'11" 187 lbs.

1922 STL N	13	27	8	2	2	0	0.0	3	5	1	1	0	.296	.519	3	0	C-9, 1B-2
1923	67	185	49	11	2	0	0.0	17	15	11	11	3	.265	.346	9	0	C-58
1926 CHI A	44	86	28	7	2	1	1.2	16	11	6	10	0	.326	.488	11	2	C 25, 1B 8
1927	86	262	75	19	3	1	0.4	34	27	32	24	6	.286	.393	3	0	C-82
1928	49	103	27	10	0	2	1.9	12	13	8	15	1	.262	.417	14	3	C-34
1930 PHI N	80	148	49	6	2	1	0.7	23	25	15	12	0	.331	.419	32	8	C-41
1931	66	150	43	9	0	1	0.7	21	25	23	16	2	.287	.367	17	7	C-45
1932	62	136	32	6	1	1	0.7	13	14	17	13	0	.235	.316	15	2	C-42
1933	73	54	15	1	0	2	3.7	9	12	16	6	0	.278	.407	52	15	C-2
1934 CIN N	3	6	0	0	0	0	0.0	0	1	0	0	0	.000	.000	2	0	1B-3
10 yrs.	543	1157	326	71	12	9	0.8	148	148	129	108	12	.282	.387	158	37	C-338, 1B-13
2 yrs.	80	212	57	13	4	0	0.0	20	20	12	12	3	.269	.368	12	0	C-67, 1B-2

Mickey McDermott

McDERMOTT, MAURICE JOSEPH
B. Aug. 29, 1928, Poughkeepsie, N. Y.   BL TL 6'2" 170 lbs.

1948 BOS A	7	8	3	1	0	0	0.0	2	0	0	0	0	.375	.500	0	0	P-7
1949	13	33	7	3	0	0	0.0	3	6	3	6	0	.212	.303	0	0	P-12
1950	39	44	16	5	0	0	0.0	11	12	9	3	0	.364	.477	0	0	P-38
1951	43	66	18	1	1	1	1.5	8	6	3	14	0	.273	.364	3	0	P-34
1952	36	62	14	1	1	1	1.6	10	7	4	11	0	.226	.323	1	0	P-30
1953	45	93	28	8	0	1	1.1	9	13	2	13	0	.301	.419	12	1	P-32
1954 WAS A	54	95	19	3	0	0	0.0	7	4	7	12	0	.200	.232	19	3	P-31
1955	70	95	25	4	0	1	1.1	10	10	6	16	1	.263	.337	38	9	P-31
1956 NY A	46	52	11	0	0	1	1.9	4	4	8	13	0	.212	.269	19	4	P-23
1957 KC A	58	49	12	1	0	4	8.2	6	7	9	16	0	.245	.510	24	5	P-29, 1B-2
1958 DET A	4	3	1	0	0	0	0.0	0	1	0	2	0	.333	.333	2	1	P-2
1961 2 teams	**STL** N	(22G –	.071)		**KC** A	(7G –	.200)										
" Total	29	19	2	2	0	0	0.0	1	4	1	6	0	.105	.211	9	2	P-23
12 yrs.	444	619	156	29	2	9	1.5	71	74	52	112	1	.252	.349	127	25	P-291, 1B-2
1 yr.	22	14	1	1	0	0	0.0	1	3	0	4	0	.071	.143	6	1	P-19

WORLD SERIES

1956 NY A	1	1	1	0	0	0	0.0	0	0	0	0	0	1.000	1.000	0	0	P-1

Guy McFadden

McFADDEN, GUY
Deceased.

1895 STL N	4	14	3	0	0	0	0.0	1	2	0	2	0	.214	.214	0	0	1B-4

Ed McFarland

McFARLAND, EDWARD WILLIAM
B. Aug. 3, 1874, Cleveland, Ohio   D. Nov. 28, 1959, Cleveland, Ohio   BR TR 5'10" 180 lbs.

1893 CLE N	8	22	9	2	1	0	0.0	5	6	1	2	0	.409	.591	0	0	OF-5, 3B-2, C-1
1896 STL N	83	290	70	13	4	3	1.0	48	36	15	17	7	.241	.345	1	0	C-80, OF-2
1897 2 teams	**STL** N	(31G –	.327)		**PHI** N	(38G –	.223)										
" Total	69	237	64	8	7	2	0.8	32	33	22			4	.270	.388	2	0	C-60, OF-3, 1B-3, 2B-1
1898 PHI N	121	429	121	21	5	3	0.7	65	71	44			4	.282	.375	0	0	C-121

	G	AB	H	2B	3B	HR	HR %	R	RBI	BB	SO	SB	BA	SA	Pinch Hit AB	Pinch Hit H	G by POS

Ed McFarland continued

	G	AB	H	2B	3B	HR	HR%	R	RBI	BB	SO	SB	BA	SA	PH AB	PH H	G by POS
1899	96	324	108	22	10	1	0.3	59	57	36		9	.333	.472	2	0	C-94
1900	94	344	105	14	8	0	0.0	50	38	29		9	.305	.392	1	0	C-93, 3B-1
1901	74	295	84	14	2	1	0.3	33	32	18		11	.285	.356	0	0	C-74
1902 CHI A	73	244	56	9	2	1	0.4	29	25	19		8	.230	.295	2	0	C-69, 1B-1
1903	61	201	42	7	2	1	0.5	15	19	14		3	.209	.279	4	1	C-56, 1B-1
1904	50	160	44	11	3	0	0.0	22	20	17		2	.275	.381	1	1	C-49
1905	80	250	70	13	4	0	0.0	24	31	23		5	.280	.364	9	4	C-70
1906	7	22	3	1	0	0	0.0	0	3	3		0	.136	.182	3	1	C-3
1907	52	138	39	9	1	0	0.0	11	8	12		3	.283	.362	7	2	C-43
1908 BOS A	19	48	10	2	1	0	0.0	5	4	1		0	.208	.292	6	2	C-13
14 yrs.	887	3004	825	146	50	12	0.4	398	383	254	19	65	.275	.369	38	11	C-826, OF-10, 1B-5, 3B-3, 2B-1
2 yrs.	114	397	105	18	6	4	1.0	62	53	23	17	9	.264	.370	2	0	C-103, OF-5, 1B-3, 2B-1

WORLD SERIES

	G	AB	H	2B	3B	HR	HR%	R	RBI	BB	SO	SB	BA	SA	PH AB	PH H	G by POS
1906 CHI A	1	1	0	0	0	0	0.0	0	0	0		0	.000	.000	1	0	

Dan McGann

McGANN, DENNIS L.
B. July 15, 1872, Shelbyville, Ky.   D. Dec. 13, 1910, Louisville, Ky.

BB TR 6'   190 lbs.

	G	AB	H	2B	3B	HR	HR%	R	RBI	BB	SO	SB	BA	SA	PH AB	PH H	G by POS
1895 LOU N	20	73	21	5	2	0	0.0	9	9	8		6	.288	.411	1	0	SS-8, 3B-6, OF-5
1896 BOS N	43	171	55	6	7	2	1.2	25	30	12	10	2	.322	.474	0	0	2B-43
1898 BAL N	145	535	161	18	8	5	0.9	99	106	53		33	.301	.393	0	0	1B-145
1899 2 teams		BKN	N	(63G –	.243)		WAS	N	(76G –	.343)							
" Total	139	494	148	20	12	7	1.4	114	90	35		27	.300	.431	2	0	1B-137
1900 STL N	124	450	136	14	9	4	0.9	79	58	32		26	.302	.400	0	0	1B-121, 2B-1
1901	103	426	123	14	10	6	1.4	73	56	16		17	.289	.411	0	0	1B-103
1902 2 teams		BAL	A	(68G –	.316)		NY	N	(61G –	.300)							
" Total	129	477	147	15	15	0	0.0	65	63	31		29	.308	.403	0	0	1B-129
1903 NY N	129	482	130	21	6	3	0.6	75	50	32		36	.270	.357	0	0	1B-129
1904	141	517	148	22	6	6	1.2	81	71	36		42	.286	.387	0	0	1B-141
1905	136	491	147	23	14	5	1.0	88	75	55		22	.299	.434	0	0	1B-136
1906	134	451	107	14	8	0	0.0	62	37	60		30	.237	.304	1	0	1B-133
1907	81	262	78	9	1	2	0.8	29	36	29		9	.298	.363	0	0	1B-81
1908 BOS N	135	475	114	8	5	2	0.4	52	55	38		9	.240	.291	5	1	1B-121, 2B-9
13 yrs.	1459	5304	1515	189	103	42	0.8	851	736	437	16	288	.286	.384	9	1	1B-1376, 2B-53, SS-8, 3B-6, OF-5
2 yrs.	227	876	259	28	19	10	1.1	152	114	48		43	.296	.405	0	0	1B-224, 2B-1

WORLD SERIES

	G	AB	H	2B	3B	HR	HR%	R	RBI	BB	SO	SB	BA	SA	PH AB	PH H	G by POS
1905 NY N	5	17	4	2	0	0	0.0	1	4	2	7	0	.235	.353	0	0	1B-5

Willie McGee

McGEE, WILLIE DEAN
B. Nov. 2, 1958, San Francisco, Calif.

BB TR 6'1"   176 lbs.

	G	AB	H	2B	3B	HR	HR%	R	RBI	BB	SO	SB	BA	SA	PH AB	PH H	G by POS
1982 STL N	123	422	125	12	8	4	0.9	43	56	12	58	24	.296	.391	15	6	OF-117

LEAGUE CHAMPIONSHIP SERIES

	G	AB	H	2B	3B	HR	HR%	R	RBI	BB	SO	SB	BA	SA	PH AB	PH H	G by POS
1982 STL N	3	13	4	0	2	1	7.7	4	5	0	5	0	.308	.846	0	0	OF-3

WORLD SERIES

	G	AB	H	2B	3B	HR	HR%	R	RBI	BB	SO	SB	BA	SA	PH AB	PH H	G by POS
1982 STL N	6	25	6	0	0	2	8.0	6	5	1	3	2	.240	.480	0	0	OF-6

Dan McGeehan

McGEEHAN, DANIEL DeSALES
Brother of Conny McGeehan.
B. June 7, 1885, Jeddo, Pa.   D. July 12, 1955, Hazleton, Pa.

BR TR 5'6"   135 lbs.

	G	AB	H	2B	3B	HR	HR%	R	RBI	BB	SO	SB	BA	SA	PH AB	PH H	G by POS
1911 STL N	3	9	2	0	0	0	0.0	0	1	0	1	0	.222	.222	0	0	2B-3

John McGraw

McGRAW, JOHN JOSEPH (Little Napoleon)
B. Apr. 7, 1873, Truxton, N. Y.   D. Feb. 25, 1934, New Rochelle, N. Y.
Manager 1899, 1901-32.
Hall of Fame 1937.

BL TR 5'7"   155 lbs.

	G	AB	H	2B	3B	HR	HR%	R	RBI	BB	SO	SB	BA	SA	PH AB	PH H	G by POS
1891 BAL AA	33	115	31	3	5	0	0.0	17	14	12	17	4	.270	.383	0	0	SS-21, OF-9, 2B-3
1892 BAL N	79	286	77	14	2	1	0.3	41	26	32	21	15	.269	.343	0	0	OF-34, 2B-34, SS-8, 3B-3
1893	127	480	154	10	8	5	1.0	123	64	101	11	38	.321	.406	0	0	SS-117, OF-11
1894	124	512	174	20	14	1	0.2	156	92	91	12	78	.340	.439	0	0	3B-118, 2B-6
1895	96	388	143	15	6	2	0.5	110	48	60	9	61	.369	.454	0	0	3B-95, 2B-1
1896	23	77	25	2	2	0	0.0	20	14	11	4	13	.325	.403	3	0	3B-18, 1B-1
1897	106	391	127	15	3	0	0.0	90	48	99		44	.325	.379	1	0	3B-105
1898	143	515	176	8	10	0	0.0	143	53	112		43	.342	.396	1	0	3B-137, OF-3
1899	117	399	156	13	3	1	0.3	140	33	124		73	.391	.446	0	0	3B-117
1900 STL N	99	334	115	10	4	2	0.6	84	33	85		29	.344	.416	0	0	3B-99
1901 BAL A	73	232	81	14	9	0	0.0	71	28	61		24	.349	.487	3	0	3B-69
1902 2 teams		BAL	A	(20G –	.286)		NY	N	(35G –	.234)							
" Total	55	170	43	3	2	1	0.6	27	8	43		12	.253	.312	2	0	SS-34, 3B-19
1903 NY N	12	11	3	0	0	0	0.0	2	1	1		1	.273	.273	6	2	OF-2, 2B-2, SS-1, 3B-1
1904	5	12	4	0	0	0	0.0	1	0	3		0	.333	.333	1	0	SS-2, 2B-2
1905	3	0	0	0	0	0	–	0	0	1		1	–	–	0	0	OF-1
1906	4	2	0	0	0	0	0.0	0	0	0		0	.000	.000	2	0	3B-1
16 yrs.	1099	3924	1309	127	68	13	0.3	1024	462	836	74	436	.334	.411	19	2	3B-782, SS-183, OF-60, 2B-48, 1B-1
1 yr.	99	334	115	10	4	2	0.6	84	33	85		29	.344	.416	0	0	3B-99

Mark McGrillis

McGRILLIS, MARK
Deceased.

	G	AB	H	2B	3B	HR	HR%	R	RBI	BB	SO	SB	BA	SA	PH AB	PH H	G by POS
1892 STL N	1	3	0	0	0	0	0.0	0	0	0	1	0	.000	.000	0	0	3B-1

	G	AB	H	2B	3B	HR	HR %	R	RBI	BB	SO	SB	BA	SA	Pinch Hit AB	Pinch Hit H	G by POS

Austin McHenry

McHENRY, AUSTIN BUSH
B. Sept. 22, 1895, Stout, Ohio   D. Nov. 27, 1922, Mt. Orab, Ohio   BR TR 5'11" 152 lbs.

	G	AB	H	2B	3B	HR	HR %	R	RBI	BB	SO	SB	BA	SA	AB	H	G by POS
1918 STL N	80	272	71	12	6	1	0.4	32	29	21	24	8	.261	.360	0	0	OF-80
1919	110	371	106	19	11	1	0.3	41	47	19	57	7	.286	.404	4	0	OF-103
1920	137	504	142	19	11	10	2.0	66	65	25	73	8	.282	.423	3	1	OF-133
1921	152	574	201	37	8	17	3.0	92	102	38	48	10	.350	.531	0	0	OF-152
1922	64	238	72	18	3	5	2.1	31	43	14	27	2	.303	.466	2	1	OF-61
5 yrs.	543	1959	592	105	39	34	1.7	262	286	117	229	35	.302	.448	9	2	OF-529
5 yrs.	543	1959	592	105	39	34	1.7	262	286	117	229	35	.302	.448	9	2	OF-529

Otto McIver

McIVER, EDWARD OTTO
B. July 26, 1884, Greenville, Tex.   D. May 4, 1954, Dallas, Tex.   BB TL 5'11½" 175 lbs.

	G	AB	H	2B	3B	HR	HR %	R	RBI	BB	SO	SB	BA	SA	AB	H	G by POS
1911 STL N	30	62	14	2	1	1	1.6	11	9	9	14	0	.226	.339	7	0	OF-17

Ed McKean

McKEAN, EDWARD JOHN
B. June 6, 1864, Grafton, Ohio   D. Aug. 16, 1919, Cleveland, Ohio   BR TR 5'9" 160 lbs.

	G	AB	H	2B	3B	HR	HR %	R	RBI	BB	SO	SB	BA	SA	AB	H	G by POS
1887 CLE AA	132	539	154	16	13	2	0.4	97		60		76	.286	.375	0	0	SS-123, 2B-8, OF-4
1888	131	548	164	21	15	6	1.1	94	68	28		52	.299	.425	0	0	SS-78, OF-48, 2B-9, 3B-1
1889 CLE N	123	500	159	22	8	4	0.8	88	75	42	25	35	.318	.418	0	0	SS-122, 2B-1
1890	136	530	157	15	14	7	1.3	95	61	87	25	23	.296	.417	0	0	SS-134, 2B-3
1891	141	603	170	13	12	6	1.0	115	69	64	19	14	.282	.373	0	0	SS-141
1892	129	531	139	14	10	0	0.0	76	93	49	28	19	.262	.326	0	0	SS-129
1893	125	545	169	29	24	4	0.7	103	133	50	14	16	.310	.473	0	0	SS-125
1894	130	554	198	30	15	8	1.4	116	128	49	12	33	.357	.509	0	0	SS-130
1895	131	565	193	32	17	8	1.4	131	119	45	25	12	.342	.501	0	0	SS-131
1896	133	571	193	29	12	7	1.2	100	112	45	9	13	.338	.468	0	0	SS-133
1897	125	523	143	21	14	2	0.4	83	78	40		15	.273	.379	0	0	SS-125
1898	151	604	172	23	1	9	1.5	89	94	56		11	.285	.371	0	0	SS-151
1899 STL N	67	277	72	7	3	3	1.1	40	40	20		4	.260	.339	0	0	SS-42, 1B-15, 2B-10
13 yrs.	1654	6890	2083	272	158	66	1.0	1227	1069	635	157	323	.302	.416	0	0	SS-1564, OF-52, 2B-31, 1B-15, 3B-1
1 yr.	67	277	72	7	3	3	1.1	40	40	20		4	.260	.339	0	0	SS-42, 1B-15, 2B-10

Bill McKechnie

McKECHNIE, WILLIAM BOYD (Deacon)
B. Aug. 7, 1886, Wilkinsburg, Pa.   D. Oct. 29, 1965, Bradenton, Fla.   BB TR 5'10" 160 lbs.
Manager 1915, 1922-26, 1928-46.
Hall of Fame 1962.

	G	AB	H	2B	3B	HR	HR %	R	RBI	BB	SO	SB	BA	SA	AB	H	G by POS
1907 PIT N	3	8	1	0	0	0	0.0	0	0	0		0	.125	.125	0	0	3B-2, 2B-1
1910	71	212	46	1	2	0	0.0	23	12	11	23	4	.217	.241	8	2	2B-36, SS-14, 3B-8, 1B-4
1911	104	321	73	8	7	2	0.6	40	37	28	18	9	.227	.315	5	2	1B-57, 2B-17, SS-12, 3B-8
1912	24	73	18	0	1	0	0.0	8	4	2	1	2	.247	.274	1	0	3B-15, SS-4, 2B-3, 1B-2
1913 2 teams	BOS N (1G – .000)					NY A (44G – .134)											
" Total	45	116	15	0	0	0	0.0	8	8	8	18	2	.129	.129	4	0	2B-27, SS-7, 3B-2, OF-1
1914 IND F	149	570	173	24	6	2	0.4	107	38	53		47	.304	.377	0	0	3B-149
1915 NWK F	127	451	113	22	5	1	0.2	49	43	41		28	.251	.328	8	3	3B-117, OF-1
1916 2 teams	NY N (71G – .246)					CIN N (37G – .277)											
" Total	108	390	100	12	1	0	0.0	26	27	10	32	11	.256	.292	2	0	3B-106
1917 CIN N	48	134	34	3	1	0	0.0	11	15	7	7	5	.254	.291	4	1	2B-26, SS-13, 3B-4
1918 PIT N	126	435	111	13	9	2	0.5	34	43	24	22	12	.255	.340	0	0	3B-126
1920	40	133	29	3	1	0	0.8	13	13	4	7	7	.218	.278	3	0	3B-20, SS-10, 2B-6, 1B-1
11 yrs.	845	2843	713	86	33	8	0.3	319	240	188	128	127	.251	.313	35	8	3B-555, 2B-116, 1B-64, SS-60, OF-2

Ralph McLaurin

McLAURIN, RALPH EDGAR
B. May 23, 1885, Kissimmee, Fla.   D. Feb. 11, 1943, McColl, S. C.

	G	AB	H	2B	3B	HR	HR %	R	RBI	BB	SO	SB	BA	SA	AB	H	G by POS
1908 STL N	8	22	5	0	0	0	0.0	2	0	0		0	.227	.227	2	0	OF-6

Larry McLean

McLEAN, JOHN BANNERMAN
B. July 18, 1881, Cambridge, Mass.   D. Mar. 14, 1921, Boston, Mass.   BR TR 6'5" 228 lbs.

	G	AB	H	2B	3B	HR	HR %	R	RBI	BB	SO	SB	BA	SA	AB	H	G by POS
1901 BOS A	9	19	4	1	0	0	0.0	4	2	0		1	.211	.263	4	2	1B-5
1903 CHI N	1	4	0	0	0	0	0.0	0	1	1		0	.000	.000	0	0	C-1
1904 STL N	27	84	14	2	1	0	0.0	5	4	4		1	.167	.214	2	0	C-24
1906 CIN N	12	35	7	2	0	0	0.0	3	2	4		0	.200	.257	0	0	C-12
1907	113	374	108	9	9	0	0.0	35	54	13		4	.289	.361	11	2	C-89, 1B-13
1908	99	309	67	9	4	1	0.3	24	28	15		2	.217	.282	10	2	C-69, 1B-19
1909	95	324	83	12	2	2	0.6	26	36	21		1	.256	.324	0	0	C-95
1910	127	423	126	14	7	2	0.5	27	71	26	23	4	.298	.378	9	2	C-119
1911	107	328	94	7	2	0	0.0	24	34	20	18	1	.287	.320	8	0	C-98
1912	102	333	81	15	1	1	0.3	17	27	18	15	1	.243	.303	4	2	C-98
1913 2 teams	STL N (48G – .270)					NY N (30G – .320)											
" Total	78	227	65	13	0	0	0.0	10	21	10	13	1	.286	.344	8	2	C-70
1914 NY N	79	154	40	6	0	0	0.0	8	14	4	9	4	.260	.299	4	0	C-74
1915	13	33	5	0	0	0	0.0	0	1	0	1	0	.152	.152	1	0	C-12
13 yrs.	862	2647	694	90	26	6	0.2	183	298	136	79	20	.262	.323	61	12	C-761, 1B-37
2 yrs.	75	236	55	11	1	0	0.0	12	16	10	9	1	.233	.288	8	1	C-66
WORLD SERIES																	
1913 NY N	5	12	6	0	0	0	0.0	0	2	0	0	0	.500	.500	1	0	C-4

Jerry McNertney

McNERTNEY, GERALD EDWARD
B. Aug. 7, 1936, Boone, Iowa   BR TR 6' 180 lbs.

	G	AB	H	2B	3B	HR	HR %	R	RBI	BB	SO	SB	BA	SA	AB	H	G by POS
1964 CHI A	73	186	40	5	0	3	1.6	16	23	19	24	0	.215	.290	6	0	C-69
1966	44	59	13	0	0	0	0.0	3	1	7	6	1	.220	.220	5	0	C-37
1967	56	123	28	6	0	3	2.4	8	13	6	14	0	.228	.350	1	1	C-52

	G	AB	H	2B	3B	HR	HR %	R	RBI	BB	SO	SB	BA	SA	Pinch Hit AB	Pinch Hit H	G by POS

Jerry McNertney continued

	G	AB	H	2B	3B	HR	HR %	R	RBI	BB	SO	SB	BA	SA	AB	H	G by POS
1968	74	169	37	4	1	3	1.8	18	18	18	29	0	.219	.308	11	3	C-64, 1B-1
1969 SEA A	128	410	99	18	1	8	2.0	39	55	29	63	1	.241	.349	7	3	C-122
1970 MIL A	111	296	72	11	1	6	2.0	27	22	22	33	1	.243	.348	18	4	C-94, 1B-13
1971 STL N	56	128	37	4	2	4	3.1	15	22	12	14	0	.289	.445	16	5	C-36
1972	39	48	10	3	1	0	0.0	3	9	6	16	0	.208	.313	28	4	C-10
1973 PIT N	9	4	1	0	0	0	0.0	0	0	0	0	0	.250	.250	6	0	C-9
9 yrs.	590	1423	337	51	6	27	1.9	129	163	119	199	3	.237	.338	92	20	C-493, 1B-14
2 yrs.	95	176	47	7	3	4	2.3	18	31	18	30	0	.267	.409	44	9	C-46

Joe Medwick

MEDWICK, JOSEPH MICHAEL (Ducky, Muscles)   BR TR 5'10" 187 lbs.
B. Nov. 24, 1911, Carteret, N. J.   D. Mar. 21, 1975, Petersburg, Fla.
Hall of Fame 1968.

	G	AB	H	2B	3B	HR	HR %	R	RBI	BB	SO	SB	BA	SA	AB	H	G by POS
1932 STL N	26	106	37	12	1	2	1.9	13	12	2	10	3	.349	.538	0	0	OF-26
1933	148	595	182	40	10	18	3.0	92	98	26	56	5	.306	.497	1	0	OF-147
1934	149	620	198	40	18	18	2.9	110	106	21	83	3	.319	.529	0	0	OF-149
1935	154	634	224	46	13	23	3.6	132	126	30	59	4	.353	.576	0	0	OF-154
1936	155	636	223	64	13	18	2.8	115	138	34	33	3	.351	.577	0	0	OF-155
1937	156	633	237	56	10	31	4.9	111	154	41	50	4	.374	.641	0	0	OF-156
1938	146	590	190	47	8	21	3.6	100	122	42	41	0	.322	.536	2	0	OF-144
1939	150	606	201	48	8	14	2.3	98	117	45	44	6	.332	.507	1	0	OF-149
1940 2 teams			STL	N	(37G –	.304)		BKN	N	(106G –	.300)						
" Total	143	581	175	30	12	17	2.9	83	86	32	36	2	.301	.482	3	0	OF-140
1941 BKN N	133	538	171	33	10	18	3.3	100	88	38	35	2	.318	.517	2	1	OF-131
1942	142	553	166	37	4	4	0.7	69	96	32	25	2	.300	.403	2	0	OF-140
1943 2 teams			BKN	N	(48G –	.272)		NY	N	(78G –	.281)						
" Total	126	497	138	30	3	5	1.0	54	70	19	22	1	.278	.380	6	2	OF-117, 1B-3
1944 NY N	128	490	165	24	7	7	1.4	64	85	38	24	2	.337	.441	6	1	OF-122
1945 2 teams			NY	N	(26G –	.304)		BOS	N	(66G –	.284)						
" Total	92	310	90	17	0	3	1.0	31	37	14	14	5	.290	.374	17	3	OF-61, 1B-15
1946 BKN N	41	77	24	4	0	2	2.6	7	18	6	5	0	.312	.442	18	4	OF-18, 1B-1
1947 STL N	75	150	46	12	0	4	2.7	19	28	16	12	0	.307	.467	31	7	OF-43
1948	20	19	4	0	0	0	0.0	0	2	1	2	0	.211	.211	18	4	OF-1
17 yrs.	1984	7635	2471	540	113	205	2.7	1198	1383	437	551	42	.324	.505	107	22	OF-1853, 1B-19
11 yrs.	1216	4747	1590	377	81	152	3.2	811	923	264	398	28	.335	.545	53	11	OF-1161
				10th	3rd	7th	7th		10th	7th				4th	5th			

WORLD SERIES

	G	AB	H	2B	3B	HR	HR %	R	RBI	BB	SO	SB	BA	SA	AB	H	G by POS
1934 STL N	7	29	11	0	1	1	3.4	4	5	1	7	0	.379	.552	0	0	OF-7
1941 BKN N	5	17	4	1	0	0	0.0	1	0	1	2	0	.235	.294	0	0	OF-5
2 yrs.	12	46	15	1	1	1	2.2	5	5	2	9	0	.326	.457	0	0	OF-12

Sam Mejias

MEJIAS, SAMUEL ELIAS   BR TR 6' 170 lbs.
B. May 9, 1953, Santiago, Dominican Republic

	G	AB	H	2B	3B	HR	HR %	R	RBI	BB	SO	SB	BA	SA	AB	H	G by POS
1976 STL N	18	21	3	1	0	0	0.0	1	0	2	2	2	.143	.190	1	0	OF-17
1977 MON N	74	101	23	4	1	3	3.0	14	8	2	17	1	.228	.376	20	4	OF-56
1978	67	56	13	1	0	0	0.0	9	6	2	5	0	.232	.250	10	3	OF-52, P-1
1979 2 teams			CHI	N	(31G –	.182)		CIN	N	(7G –	.500)						
" Total	38	13	3	0	0	0	0.0	5	0	2	5	0	.231	.231	7	1	OF-28
1980 CIN N	71	108	30	5	.1	1	0.9	16	10	6	13	4	.278	.370	7	2	OF-67
1981	66	49	14	2	0	0	0.0	6	7	2	9	1	.286	.327	8	2	OF-58
6 yrs.	334	348	86	13	2	4	1.1	51	31	16	51	8	.247	.330	53	12	OF-278, P-1
1 yr.	18	21	3	1	0	0	0.0	1	0	2	2	2	.143	.190	1	0	OF-17

Luis Melendez

MELENDEZ, LUIS ANTONIO   BR TR 6' 165 lbs.
B. Aug. 11, 1949, Aibonito, Puerto Rico

	G	AB	H	2B	3B	HR	HR %	R	RBI	BB	SO	SB	BA	SA	AB	H	G by POS
1970 STL N	21	70	21	1	0	0	0.0	11	8	2	12	3	.300	.314	3	0	OF-18
1971	88	173	39	3	1	0	0.0	25	11	24	29	2	.225	.254	22	4	OF-66
1972	118	332	79	11	3	5	1.5	32	28	25	34	5	.238	.334	21	2	OF-105
1973	121	341	91	18	1	2	0.6	35	35	27	50	2	.267	.343	21	8	OF-95
1974	83	124	27	4	3	0	0.0	15	8	11	9	2	.218	.298	31	4	OF-46, SS-1
1975	110	291	77	8	5	2	0.7	33	27	16	25	3	.265	.347	35	8	OF-89
1976 2 teams			STL	N	(20G –	.125)		SD	N	(72G –	.244)						
" Total	92	143	32	5	0	0	0.0	15	5	3	15	1	.224	.259	25	4	OF-68
1977 SD N	8	3	0	0	0	0	0.0	1	0	1	1	0	.000	.000	3	0	OF-2
8 yrs.	641	1477	366	50	13	9	0.6	167	122	109	175	18	.248	.318	161	30	OF-489, SS-1
7 yrs.	561	1355	337	45	13	9	0.7	151	.117	105	162	17	.249	.321	144	27	OF-427, SS-1
															5th	10th	

Ted Menze

MENZE, THEODORE CHARLES   BR TR 5'9" 172 lbs.
B. Nov. 4, 1897, St. Louis, Mo.   D. Dec. 23, 1969, St. Louis, Mo.

	G	AB	H	2B	3B	HR	HR %	R	RBI	BB	SO	SB	BA	SA	AB	H	G by POS
1918 STL N	1	3	0	0	0	0	0.0	0	0	0	2	0	.000	.000	0	0	OF-1

John Mercer

MERCER, JOHN LOCKE   BL TL 5'10½" 155 lbs.
B. June 22, 1890, Taylortown, La.

	G	AB	H	2B	3B	HR	HR %	R	RBI	BB	SO	SB	BA	SA	AB	H	G by POS
1910 PIT N	1	0	0	0	0	0	–	0	0	0	0	0	–	–	0	0	P-1
1912 STL N	1	1	0	0	0	0	0.0	0	0	0	0	0	.000	.000	0	0	1B-1
2 yrs.	2	1	0	0	0	0	0.0	0	0	0	0	0	.000	.000	0	0	1B-1, P-1
1 yr.	1	1	0	0	0	0	0.0	0	0	0	0	0	.000	.000	0	0	1B-1

Sam Mertes

MERTES, SAMUEL BLAIR (Sandow)   BR TR 5'10" 185 lbs.
B. Aug. 6, 1872, San Francisco, Calif.   D. Mar. 11, 1945, San Francisco, Calif.

	G	AB	H	2B	3B	HR	HR %	R	RBI	BB	SO	SB	BA	SA	AB	H	G by POS
1896 PHI N	37	143	34	4	4	0	0.0	20	14	8	10	19	.238	.322	1	0	OF-35, SS-1, 2B-1
1898 CHI N	83	269	80	4	8	1	0.4	45	47	34		27	.297	.383	5	0	OF-60, SS-14, 2B-4, 1B-2

	G	AB	H	2B	3B	HR	HR %	R	RBI	BB	SO	SB	BA	SA	Pinch Hit AB	Pinch Hit H	G by POS

Sam Mertes continued

	G	AB	H	2B	3B	HR	HR%	R	RBI	BB	SO	SB	BA	SA	AB	H	G by POS
1899	117	426	127	13	16	9	2.1	83	81	33		45	.298	.467	5	1	OF-108, 1B-3, SS-1
1900	127	481	142	25	4	7	1.5	72	60	42		38	.295	.407	0	0	OF-88, 1B-33, SS-7
1901 CHI A	137	545	151	16	17	5	0.9	94	98	52		46	.277	.396	0	0	2B-132, OF-5
1902	129	497	140	23	7	1	0.2	60	79	37		46	.282	.362	0	0	OF-120, SS-5, C-2, 3B-1, 2B-1, 1B-1, P-1
1903 NY N	138	517	145	32	14	7	1.4	100	104	61		45	.280	.437	0	0	OF-137, 1B-1, C-1
1904	148	532	147	28	11	4	0.8	83	78	54		47	.276	.393	0	0	OF-147, SS-1
1905	150	551	154	27	17	5	0.9	81	108	56		52	.279	.417	0	0	OF-150
1906 2 teams	NY N (71G – .237)					STL N	(53G – .246)										
" Total	124	444	107	16	10	1	0.2	57	52	45		31	.241	.329	0	0	OF-124
10 yrs.	1190	4405	1227	188	108	40	0.9	695	721	422	10	396	.279	.398	11	1	OF-974, 2B-138, 1B-40, SS-29, C-3, 3B-1, P-1
1 yr.	53	191	47	7	4	0	0.0	20	19	16		10	.246	.325	0	0	OF-53

WORLD SERIES

	G	AB	H	2B	3B	HR	HR%	R	RBI	BB	SO	SB	BA	SA	AB	H	G by POS
1905 NY N	5	17	3	1	0	0	0.0	2	3	2	5	0	.176	.235	0	0	OF-5

Steve Mesner

MESNER, STEPHAN MATHIAS
B. Jan. 13, 1918, Los Angeles, Calif.   D. Apr. 6, 1981, San Diego, Calif.
BR TR 5'9"   178 lbs.

	G	AB	H	2B	3B	HR	HR%	R	RBI	BB	SO	SB	BA	SA	AB	H	G by POS
1938 CHI N	2	4	1	0	0	0	0.0	2	0	1	1	0	.250	.250	1	0	SS-1
1939	17	43	12	4	0	0	0.0	7	6	3	4	0	.279	.372	3	0	SS-12, 3B-1, 2B-1
1941 STL N	24	69	10	1	0	0	0.0	8	10	5	6	0	.145	.159	1	0	3B-22
1943 CIN N	137	504	137	26	1	0	0.0	53	52	26	20	6	.272	.327	7	4	3B-130
1944	121	414	100	17	4	1	0.2	31	47	34	20	1	.242	.309	1	0	3B-120
1945	150	540	137	19	1	1	0.2	52	52	52	18	4	.254	.298	0	0	3B-148, 2B-3
6 yrs.	451	1574	397	67	6	2	0.1	153	167	121	69	11	.252	.306	13	4	3B-421, SS-13, 2B-4
1 yr.	24	69	10	1	0	0	0.0	8	10	5	6	0	.145	.159	1	0	3B-22

Bert Meyers

MEYERS, JAMES ALBERT
B. Washington, D. C.   D. Dec. 12, 1915, Washington, D. C.

	G	AB	H	2B	3B	HR	HR%	R	RBI	BB	SO	SB	BA	SA	AB	H	G by POS
1896 STL N	122	454	116	12	8	0	0.0	47	37	40	32	8	.256	.317	0	0	3B-121, SS-1
1898 WAS N	31	110	29	1	4	0	0.0	14	13	13		2	.264	.345	0	0	3B-31
1900 PHI N	7	28	5	1	0	0	0.0	5	2	3		1	.179	.214	0	0	3B-7
3 yrs.	160	592	150	14	12	0	0.0	66	52	56	32	11	.253	.318	0	0	3B-159, SS-1
1 yr.	122	454	116	12	8	0	0.0	47	37	40	32	8	.256	.317	0	0	3B-121, SS-1

Ed Mickelson

MICKELSON, EDWARD ALLEN
B. Sept. 9, 1926, Ottawa, Ill.
BR TR 6'3"   205 lbs.

	G	AB	H	2B	3B	HR	HR%	R	RBI	BB	SO	SB	BA	SA	AB	H	G by POS
1950 STL N	5	10	1	0	0	0	0.0	0	2	3	0		.100	.100	1	0	1B-4
1953 STL A	7	15	2	1	0	0	0.0	1	2	2	6	0	.133	.200	3	0	1B-3
1957 CHI N	6	12	0	0	0	0	0.0	1		0	4	0	.000	.000	4	0	1B-2
3 yrs.	18	37	3	1	0	0	0.0	2	3	4	13	0	.081	.108	8	0	1B-9
1 yr.	5	10	1	0	0	0	0.0	0	2	3	0		.100	.100	1	0	1B-4

Ed Mierkowicz

MIERKOWICZ, EDWARD FRANK (Butch)
B. Mar. 6, 1924, Wyandotte, Mich.
BR TR 6'4"   205 lbs.

	G	AB	H	2B	3B	HR	HR%	R	RBI	BB	SO	SB	BA	SA	AB	H	G by POS
1945 DET A	10	15	2	2	0	0	0.0	2		1	3	0	.133	.267	3	1	OF-6
1947	21	42	8	1	0	1	2.4	6	1	1	12	1	.190	.286	9	1	OF-10
1948	3	5	1	0	0	0	0.0	0	1	2	2	0	.200	.200	2	0	OF-1
1950 STL N	1	1	0	0	0	0	0.0	0		0	1	0	.000	.000	1	0	
4 yrs.	35	63	11	3	0	1	1.6	6	4	4	18	1	.175	.270	15	2	OF-17
1 yr.	1	1	0	0	0	0	0.0	0		0	1	0	.000	.000	1	0	

WORLD SERIES

	G	AB	H	2B	3B	HR	HR%	R	RBI	BB	SO	SB	BA	SA	AB	H	G by POS
1945 DET A	1	0	0	0	0	0	–	0	0	0	0	0	–	–	0	0	OF-1

Larry Miggins

MIGGINS, LAWRENCE EDWARD (Irish)
B. Aug. 20, 1925, Bronx, N. Y.
BR TR 6'4"   198 lbs.

	G	AB	H	2B	3B	HR	HR%	R	RBI	BB	SO	SB	BA	SA	AB	H	G by POS
1948 STL N	1	1	0	0	0	0	0.0	1	0	0	0	0	.000	.000	1	0	
1952	42	96	22	5	1	2	2.1	7	10	3	19	0	.229	.365	16	4	OF-25, 1B-1
2 yrs.	43	97	22	5	1	2	2.1	8	10	3	19	0	.227	.361	17	4	OF-25, 1B-1
2 yrs.	43	97	22	5	1	2	2.1	8	10	3	19	0	.227	.361	17	4	OF-25, 1B-1

Eddie Miksis

MIKSIS, EDWARD THOMAS
B. Sept. 11, 1926, Burlington, N. J.
BR TR 6'½"   185 lbs.

	G	AB	H	2B	3B	HR	HR%	R	RBI	BB	SO	SB	BA	SA	AB	H	G by POS
1944 BKN N	26	91	20	2	0	0	0.0	12	11	6	11	4	.220	.242	1	0	3B-15, SS-10
1946	23	48	7	0	0	0	0.0	3	5	3	3	0	.146	.146	3	0	3B-13, 2B-1
1947	45	86	23	1	0	4	4.7	18	10	9	8	0	.267	.419	12	1	2B-13, OF-11, 3B-5, SS-2
1948	86	221	47	7	1	2	0.9	28	16	19	27	5	.213	.281	3	1	2B-54, 3B-22, SS-5
1949	50	113	25	5	0	1	0.9	17	6	7	8	3	.221	.292	8	0	3B-29, SS-4, 2B-3, 1B-1
1950	51	76	19	2	1	2	2.6	13	10	5	10	3	.250	.382	4	1	SS-15, 2B-15, 3B-7
1951 2 teams	BKN N (19G – .200)					CHI N	(102G – .266)										
" Total	121	431	114	14	3	4	0.9	54	35	34	38	11	.265	.339	5	1	2B-103, 3B-6
1952 CHI N	93	383	89	20	1	2	0.5	44	19	20	32	4	.232	.305	1	0	2B-54, SS-40
1953	142	577	145	17	6	8	1.4	61	39	33	59	13	.251	.343	0	0	2B-92, SS-53
1954	38	99	20	3	0	2	2.0	9	3	3	9	1	.202	.293	10	0	2B-21, 3B-2, OF-1
1955	131	481	113	14	2	9	1.9	52	41	32	55	3	.235	.328	2	0	OF-111, 3B-18
1956	114	356	85	10	3	9	2.5	54	27	32	40	4	.239	.360	6	3	3B-48, OF-33, 2B-19, SS-2
1957 2 teams	STL N (49G – .211)					BAL A	(1G – .000)										
" Total	50	39	8	0	0	1	2.6	3	2	7	7	0	.205	.282	15	3	OF-31
1958 2 teams	BAL A (3G – .000)					CIN N	(69G – .140)										
" Total	72	52	7	0	0	0	0.0	15	4	6	1		.135	.135	5	0	OF-32, 3B-14, 2B-7, SS-6, 1B-1

	G	AB	H	2B	3B	HR	HR %	R	RBI	BB	SO	SB	BA	SA	Pinch Hit AB	Pinch Hit H	G by POS

Eddie Miksis continued

	G	AB	H	2B	3B	HR	HR%	R	RBI	BB	SO	SB	BA	SA	AB	H	G by POS
14 yrs.	1042	3053	722	95	17	44	1.4	383	228	215	313	52	.236	.322	82	13	2B-382, OF-219, 3B-179, SS-137, 1B-2
1 yr.	49	38	8	0	0	1	2.6	3	2	7	7	0	.211	.289	14	3	OF-31
WORLD SERIES																	
1947 BKN N	5	4	1	0	0	0	0.0	1	0	0	1	0	.250	.250	3	0	OF-2
1949	3	7	2	1	0	0	0.0	0	0	0	1	0	.286	.429	1	1	3B-2
2 yrs.	8	11	3	1	0	0	0.0	1	0	0	2	0	.273	.364	4	1	OF-2, 3B-2

Charlie Miller

MILLER, CHARLES MARION   BL TL 5'8½" 155 lbs.
B. 1892   D. June 16, 1961, Houston, Tex.

	G	AB	H	2B	3B	HR	HR%	R	RBI	BB	SO	SB	BA	SA	AB	H	G by POS
1913 STL N	4	12	2	0	0	0	0.0	0	1	0	2	0	.167	.167	1	0	OF-3
1914	36	36	7	1	0	0	0.0	4	2	3	9	2	.194	.222	11	2	OF-19
2 yrs.	40	48	9	1	0	0	0.0	4	3	3	11	2	.188	.208	12	2	OF-22
2 yrs.	40	48	9	1	0	0	0.0	4	3	3	11	2	.188	.208	12	2	OF-22

Doggie Miller

MILLER, GEORGE FREDERICK (Foghorn, Calliope)   BR TR 5'6"
B. Aug. 15, 1864, Brooklyn, N. Y.   D. Apr. 6, 1909, Brooklyn, N. Y.

	G	AB	H	2B	3B	HR	HR%	R	RBI	BB	SO	SB	BA	SA	AB	H	G by POS
1884 PIT AA	89	347	78	10	2	0	0.0	46		13			.225	.265	0	0	OF-49, C-36, 3B-3, 2B-1
1885	42	166	27	3	1	0	0.0	19		4			.163	.193	0	0	C-33, OF-6, SS-2, 3B-2
1886	83	317	80	15	1	2	0.6	70		43			.252	.325	0	0	C-61, OF-23, 2B-1
1887 PIT N	87	342	83	17	4	1	0.3	58	34	35	13	33	.243	.325	0	0	C-73, OF-14, 3B-1
1888	103	404	112	17	5	0	0.0	50	36	18	16	27	.277	.344	0	0	C-68, OF-32, 3B-4
1889	104	422	113	25	3	6	1.4	77	56	31	11	16	.268	.384	0	0	C-76, OF-27, 3B-3
1890	138	549	150	24	3	4	0.7	85	66	68	11	32	.273	.350	0	0	3B-88, OF-25, SS-13, C-10, 2B-6
1891	135	548	156	19	6	4	0.7	80	57	59	26	35	.285	.363	0	0	C-41, SS-37, 3B-34, OF-24, 1B-1
1892	149	623	158	15	12	2	0.3	103	59	69	14	28	.254	.326	0	0	OF-76, C-63, SS-19, 3B-2
1893	41	154	28	6	1	0	0.0	23	17	17	8	3	.182	.234	1	0	C-40
1894 STL N	127	481	163	9	11	8	1.7	93	86	58	9	17	.339	.453	2	0	3B-52, C-41, 2B-18, 1B-12, OF-4, SS-1
1895	121	490	143	15	4	5	1.0	81	74	25	12	18	.292	.369	0	0	3B-46, C-46, OF-21, SS-9, 1B-6
1896 LOU N	98	324	89	17	4	1	0.3	54	33	27	9	16	.275	.361	9	6	C-48, 2B-25, OF-8, 3B-8, 1B-3, SS-2
13 yrs.	1317	5167	1380	192	57	33	0.6	839	517	467	129	225	.267	.345	12	6	C-636, OF-309, 3B-243, SS-83, 2B-51, 1B-22
2 yrs.	248	971	306	24	15	13	1.3	174	160	83	21	35	.315	.411	2	0	3B-98, C-87, OF-25, 2B-18, 1B-18, SS-10

Dots Miller

MILLER, JOHN BARNEY   BR TR 5'11½" 170 lbs.
B. Sept. 9, 1886, Kearny, N. J.   D. Sept. 5, 1923, Saranac Lake, N. Y.

	G	AB	H	2B	3B	HR	HR%	R	RBI	BB	SO	SB	BA	SA	AB	H	G by POS
1909 PIT N	151	560	156	31	13	3	0.5	71	87	39		14	.279	.396	1	0	2B-150
1910	120	444	101	13	10	1	0.2	45	48	33	41	11	.227	.309	1	0	2B-117, SS-2
1911	137	470	126	17	8	6	1.3	82	78	51	48	17	.268	.377	5	1	2B-129
1912	148	567	156	33	12	4	0.7	74	87	37	45	18	.275	.397	1	0	1B-147
1913	154	580	158	24	20	7	1.2	75	90	37	52	20	.272	.419	0	0	1B-150, SS-3
1914 STL N	155	573	166	27	10	4	0.7	67	88	34	52	16	.290	.393	0	0	1B-98, SS-53, 2B-5
1915	150	553	146	17	10	2	0.4	73	72	43	48	27	.264	.342	0	0	1B-83, 2B-55, 3B-9, SS-3
1916	143	505	120	22	7	1	0.2	47	46	40	49	18	.238	.315	0	0	1B-93, 2B-38, SS-21, 3B-1
1917	148	544	135	15	9	2	0.4	61	45	33	52	14	.248	.320	0	0	2B-92, 1B-46, SS-11
1918	101	346	80	10	4	1	0.3	38	24	13	23	6	.231	.292	5	2	1B-68, 2B-28
1920 PHI N	98	343	87	12	2	1	0.3	41	27	16	17	13	.254	.309	2	0	2B-59, 3B-17, SS-12, 1B-9, OF-1
1921	84	320	95	11	3	0	0.0	37	23	15	27	3	.297	.350	1	0	3B-41, 1B-38, 2B-8
12 yrs.	1589	5805	1526	232	108	32	0.6	711	715	391	454	177	.263	.357	16	3	1B-732, 2B-679, SS-105, 3B-68, OF-1
5 yrs.	697	2521	647	91	40	10	0.4	286	275	163	224	81	.257	.336	5	2	1B-388, 2B-218, SS-88, 3B-10
WORLD SERIES																	
1909 PIT N	7	28	7	1	0	0	0.0	2	4	2	4	3	.250	.286	0	0	2B-7

Dusty Miller

MILLER, CHARLES BRADLEY   BL TR 5'11½" 170 lbs.
B. Sept. 10, 1868, Oil City, Pa.   D. Sept. 3, 1945, Memphis, Tenn.

	G	AB	H	2B	3B	HR	HR%	R	RBI	BB	SO	SB	BA	SA	AB	H	G by POS
1889 BAL AA	11	40	6	1	1	0	0.0	4	6	2	11	3	.150	.225	0	0	SS-8, OF-3
1890 STL AA	26	96	21	5	3	1	1.0	17		8		4	.219	.365	0	0	OF-24, SS-3
1895 CIN N	132	529	177	31	18	8	1.5	103	112	33	34	43	.335	.507	0	0	OF-132
1896	125	504	162	38	12	4	0.8	91	93	33	30	76	.321	.468	0	0	OF-125
1897	119	440	139	27	1	4	0.9	83	70	48		29	.316	.409	0	0	OF-119
1898	152	586	175	24	12	3	0.5	99	90	38		32	.299	.396	0	0	OF-152
1899 2 teams			CIN N	(80G –	.251)		STL N	(10G –	.205)								
" Total	90	362	89	13	5	0	0.0	47	40	12		19	.246	.309	0	0	OF-90
7 yrs.	655	2557	769	139	52	20	0.8	444	411	174	75	206	.301	.419	0	0	OF-645, SS-11
1 yr.	10	39	8	1	0	0	0.0	3	3	3		1	.205	.231	0	0	OF-10

Eddie Miller

MILLER, EDWARD ROBERT (Eppie)   BR TR 5'9"   180 lbs.
B. Nov. 26, 1916, Pittsburgh, Pa.

	G	AB	H	2B	3B	HR	HR%	R	RBI	BB	SO	SB	BA	SA	AB	H	G by POS
1936 CIN N	5	10	1	0	0	0	0.0	0	0	1	1	0	.100	.100	0	0	SS-4, 2B-1
1937	36	60	9	3	1	0	0.0	3	5	3	8	0	.150	.233	2	0	SS-30, 3B-4
1939 BOS N	77	296	79	12	2	4	1.4	32	31	16	21	0	.267	.361	0	0	SS-77
1940	151	569	157	33	3	14	2.5	78	79	41	43	8	.276	.418	0	0	SS-151
1941	154	585	140	27	3	6	1.0	54	68	35	72	8	.239	.326	0	0	SS-154

Eddie Miller continued

	G	AB	H	2B	3B	HR	HR%	R	RBI	BB	SO	SB	BA	SA	PH AB	PH H	G by POS
1942	144	534	130	28	2	6	1.1	47	47	22	42	11	.243	.337	0	0	SS-144
1943 CIN N	154	576	129	26	4	2	0.3	49	71	33	43	8	.224	.293	0	0	SS-154
1944	155	536	112	21	5	4	0.7	48	55	41	41	9	.209	.289	0	0	SS-155
1945	115	421	100	27	2	13	3.1	46	49	18	38	4	.238	.404	0	0	SS-115
1946	91	299	58	10	0	6	2.0	30	36	25	34	5	.194	.288	3	1	SS-88
1947	151	545	146	38	4	19	3.5	69	87	49	40	5	.268	.457	0	0	SS-151
1948 PHI N	130	468	115	20	1	14	3.0	45	61	19	40	1	.246	.382	7	0	SS-122
1949	85	266	55	10	1	6	2.3	21	29	29	21	1	.207	.320	3	1	2B-82, SS-1
1950 STL N	64	172	39	8	0	3	1.7	17	22	19	21	0	.227	.326	11	1	SS-51, 2B-1
14 yrs.	1512	5337	1270	263	28	97	1.8	539	640	351	465	64	.238	.352	26	3	SS-1397, 2B-84, 3B-4
1 yr.	64	172	39	8	0	3	1.7	17	22	19	21	0	.227	.326	11	1	SS-51, 2B-1

Elmer Miller

MILLER, ELMER BR TR 6' 175 lbs.
B. July 28, 1890, Sandusky, Ohio D. Nov. 28, 1944, Beloit, Wis.

	G	AB	H	2B	3B	HR	HR%	R	RBI	BB	SO	SB	BA	SA	PH AB	PH H	G by POS
1912 STL N	12	37	7	1	0	0	0.0	5	3	4	9	1	.189	.216	1	0	OF-11
1915 NY A	26	83	12	1	0	0	0.0	4	3	4	14	0	.145	.157	0	0	OF-26
1916	43	152	34	3	2	1	0.7	12	18	11	18	8	.224	.289	0	0	OF-42
1917	114	379	95	11	3	3	0.8	43	35	40	44	11	.251	.319	1	0	OF-112
1918	67	202	49	9	2	1	0.5	18	22	19	17	2	.243	.322	4	0	OF-62
1921	56	242	72	9	8	4	1.7	41	36	19	16	2	.298	.450	0	0	OF-56
1922 2 teams	NY A (51G – .267)						BOS A (44G – .190)										
" Total	95	319	74	9	5	2	2.2	47	34	16	22	5	.232	.357	9	1	OF-83
7 yrs.	413	1414	343	43	20	16	1.1	170	151	113	140	29	.243	.335	15	1	OF-392
1 yr.	12	37	7	1	0	0	0.0	5	3	4	9	1	.189	.216	1	0	OF-11

WORLD SERIES

	G	AB	H	2B	3B	HR	HR%	R	RBI	BB	SO	SB	BA	SA	PH AB	PH H	G by POS
1921 NY A	8	31	5	1	0	0	0.0	3	2	2	5	0	.161	.194	0	0	OF-8

George Miller

MILLER, GEORGE BR TR 5'5" 160 lbs.
B. Feb. 19, 1853, Newport, Ky. D. July 25, 1929, Cincinnati, Ohio

	G	AB	H	2B	3B	HR	HR%	R	RBI	BB	SO	SB	BA	SA	PH AB	PH H	G by POS
1877 CIN N	11	37	6	1	0	0	0.0	4	3	5	2		.162	.189	0	0	C-11
1884 CIN AA	6	20	5	1	1	0	0.0	6		1			.250	.400	0	0	C-6
2 yrs.	17	57	11	2	1	0	0.0	10	3	6	2		.193	.263	0	0	C-17

Buster Mills

MILLS, COLONEL BUSTER BR TR 5'11½" 195 lbs.
B. Sept. 16, 1908, Ranger, Tex.
Manager 1953.

	G	AB	H	2B	3B	HR	HR%	R	RBI	BB	SO	SB	BA	SA	PH AB	PH H	G by POS
1934 STL N	29	72	17	4	1	1	1.4	7	8	4	11	0	.236	.361	9	3	OF-18
1935 BKN N	17	56	12	2	1	1	1.8	12	7	5	11	1	.214	.339	0	0	OF-17
1937 BOS A	123	505	149	25	8	7	1.4	85	58	46	41	11	.295	.418	3	1	OF-120
1938 STL A	123	466	133	24	4	3	0.6	66	46	43	46	7	.285	.373	10	1	OF-113
1940 NY A	34	63	25	3	3	1	1.6	10	15	7	5	0	.397	.587	18	6	OF-14
1942 CLE A	80	195	54	4	2	1	0.5	19	26	23	18	5	.277	.333	24	4	OF-53
1946	9	22	6	0	0	0	0.0	1	3	3	5	0	.273	.273	3	0	OF-6
7 yrs.	415	1379	396	62	19	14	1.0	200	163	131	137	24	.287	.390	67	15	OF-341
1 yr.	29	72	17	4	1	1	1.4	7	8	4	11	0	.236	.361	9	3	OF-18

Minnie Minoso

MINOSO, SATURNINO ORESTES ARRIETA ARMAS BR TR 5'10" 175 lbs.
B. Nov. 29, 1922, Havana, Cuba

	G	AB	H	2B	3B	HR	HR%	R	RBI	BB	SO	SB	BA	SA	PH AB	PH H	G by POS
1949 CLE A	9	16	3	0	0	1	6.3	2	1	2	2	0	.188	.375	1	0	OF-7
1951 2 teams	CLE A (8G – .429)						CHI A (138G – .324)										
" Total	146	530	173	34	14	10	1.9	112	76	72	42	31	.326	.500	2	0	OF-82, 3B-68, 1B-7, SS-1
1952 CHI A	147	569	160	24	9	13	2.3	96	61	71	46	22	.281	.424	0	0	OF-143, 3B-9, SS-1
1953	157	556	174	24	8	15	2.7	104	104	74	43	25	.313	.466	0	0	OF-147, 3B-10
1954	153	568	182	29	18	19	3.3	119	116	77	46	18	.320	.535	0	0	OF-146, 3B-9
1955	139	517	149	26	7	10	1.9	79	70	76	43	19	.288	.424	1	0	OF-138, 3B-2
1956	151	545	172	29	11	21	3.9	106	88	86	40	12	.316	.525	3	1	OF-148, 3B-8, 1B-1
1957	153	568	176	36	5	12	2.1	96	103	79	54	18	.310	.454	0	0	OF-152, 3B-1
1958 CLE A	149	556	168	25	2	24	4.3	94	80	59	53	14	.302	.484	3	1	OF-147, 3B-1
1959	148	570	172	32	0	21	3.7	92	92	54	46	8	.302	.468	0	0	OF-148
1960 CHI A	154	591	184	32	4	20	3.4	89	105	52	63	17	.311	.481	0	0	OF-154
1961	152	540	151	28	3	14	2.6	91	82	67	46	9	.280	.420	1	0	OF-147
1962 STL N	39	97	19	5	0	1	1.0	14	10	7	17	4	.196	.278	6	0	OF-27
1963 WAS A	109	315	72	12	2	4	1.3	38	30	33	38	8	.229	.317	26	4	OF-74, 3B-8
1964 CHI A	30	31	7	0	0	1	3.2	4	5	5	3	0	.226	.323	22	4	OF-5
1976	3	8	1	0	0	0	0.0	0	0	0	2	0	.125	.125	0	0	
1980	2	2	0	0	0	0	0.0	0	0	0	0	0	.000	.000	2	0	
17 yrs.	1841	6579	1963	336	83	186	2.8	1136	1023	814	584	205	.298	.459	67	11	OF-1665, 3B-116, 1B-8, SS-2
1 yr.	39	97	19	5	0	1	1.0	14	10	7	17	4	.196	.278	6	0	OF-27

Clarence Mitchell

MITCHELL, CLARENCE ELMER BL TL 5'11½" 190 lbs.
B. Feb. 22, 1891, Franklin, Neb. D. Nov. 6, 1963, Grand Island, Neb.

	G	AB	H	2B	3B	HR	HR%	R	RBI	BB	SO	SB	BA	SA	PH AB	PH H	G by POS
1911 DET A	5	4	2	0	0	0	0.0	2	0	1		0	.500	.500	0	0	P-5
1916 CIN N	56	117	28	2	1	0	0.0	11	11	4	6	1	.239	.274	14	4	P-29, 1B-9, OF-3
1917	47	90	25	3	0	0	0.0	13	5	5	5	0	.278	.311	1	0	P-32, 1B-6, OF-5
1918 BKN N	10	24	6	1	1	0	0.0	2	2	0	3	0	.250	.375	2	0	OF-6, 1B-2, P-1
1919	34	49	18	1	0	1	2.0	7	2	4	4	0	.367	.449	9	3	P-23
1920	55	107	25	2	0	0	0.0	9	11	8	9	1	.234	.290	18	6	P-19, 1B-11, OF-4
1921	46	91	24	5	0	0	0.0	11	12	5	7	3	.264	.319	3	0	P-37, 1B-4
1922	55	155	45	6	3	3	1.9	21	28	19	6	0	.290	.426	9	4	1B-42, P-5

	G	AB	H	2B	3B	HR	HR %	R	RBI	BB	SO	SB	BA	SA	Pinch Hit AB	Pinch Hit H	G by POS

Clarence Mitchell continued

	G	AB	H	2B	3B	HR	HR %	R	RBI	BB	SO	SB	BA	SA	PH AB	PH H	G by POS
1923 PHI N	53	78	21	3	2	1	1.3	10	9	4	11	0	.269	.397	24	6	P-29
1924	69	102	26	3	0	0	0.0	7	13	2	7	1	.255	.284	37	6	P-30
1925	52	92	18	2	0	0	0.0	7	13	5	9	2	.196	.217	17	1	P-32, 1B-2
1926	39	78	19	4	0	0	0.0	8	6	5	5	0	.244	.295	7	1	P-28, 1B-4
1927	18	42	10	2	0	1	2.4	5	6	2	1	0	.238	.357	3	0	P-13
1928 2 teams	PHI	N (5G – .250)			STL	N	(19G – .125)										
" Total	24	60	8	1	0	0	0.0			0	3	0	.133	.150	1	0	P-22
1929 STL N	26	66	18	3	1	0	0.0	9	9	4	6	1	.273	.348	0	0	P-25
1930 2 teams	STL	N (1G – .500)			NY	N	(24G – .255)										
" Total	25	49	13	1	0	0	0.0	9	1	1	5	0	.265	.286	0	0	P-25
1931 NY N	27	73	16	2	0	1	1.4	5	4	2	4	0	.219	.288	0	0	P-27
1932	8	10	2	0	0	0	0.0	2	0	1	1	0	.200	.200	0	0	P-8
18 yrs.	649	1287	324	41	10	7	0.5	138	133	72	92	9	.252	.315	145	31	P-390, 1B-80, OF-18
3 yrs.	46	124	26	4	1	0	0.0	9	10	4	9	1	.210	.258	0	0	P-45

WORLD SERIES

	G	AB	H	2B	3B	HR	HR %	R	RBI	BB	SO	SB	BA	SA	PH AB	PH H	G by POS
1920 BKN N	2	3	1	0	0	0	0.0	0	0	0	0	0	.333	.333	1	1	P-1
1928 STL N	1	2	0	0	0	0	0.0	0	0	0	0	0	.000	.000	0	0	P-1
2 yrs.	3	5	1	0	0	0	0.0	0	0	0	0	0	.200	.200	1	1	P-2

Johnny Mize

MIZE, JOHN ROBERT (The Big Cat)   BL TR 6'2"   215 lbs.
B. Jan. 7, 1913, Demorest, Ga.
Hall of Fame 1981.

	G	AB	H	2B	3B	HR	HR %	R	RBI	BB	SO	SB	BA	SA	PH AB	PH H	G by POS
1936 STL N	126	414	136	30	8	19	4.6	76	93	50	32	1	.329	.577	15	7	1B-97, OF-8
1937	145	560	204	40	7	25	4.5	103	113	56	57	2	.364	.595	1	0	1B-144
1938	149	531	179	34	16	27	5.1	85	102	74	47	0	.337	.614	7	1	1B-140
1939	153	564	197	44	14	28	5.0	104	108	92	49	0	.349	.626	1	0	1B-152
1940	155	579	182	31	13	43	7.4	111	137	82	49	7	.314	.636	2	1	1B-153
1941	126	473	150	39	8	16	3.4	67	100	70	45	4	.317	.535	4	1	1B-122
1942 NY N	142	541	165	25	7	26	4.8	97	110	60	39	3	.305	.521	3	0	1B-138
1946	101	377	127	18	3	22	5.8	70	70	62	26	3	.337	.576	0	0	1B-101
1947	154	586	177	26	2	51	8.7	137	138	74	42	2	.302	.614	0	0	1B-154
1948	152	560	162	26	4	40	7.1	110	125	94	37	4	.289	.564	0	0	1B-152
1949 2 teams	NY	N (106G – .263)			NY	A	(13G – .261)										
" Total	119	411	108	16	0	19	4.6	63	64	54	21	1	.263	.440	8	2	1B-107
1950 NY A	90	274	76	12	0	25	9.1	43	72	29	24	0	.277	.595	16	3	1B-72
1951	113	332	86	14	1	10	3.0	37	49	36	24	1	.259	.398	21	9	1B-93
1952	78	137	36	9	0	4	2.9	9	29	11	15	0	.263	.416	48	10	1B-27
1953	81	104	26	3	0	4	3.8	6	27	12	17	0	.250	.394	61	19	1B-15
15 yrs.	1884	6443	2011	367	83	359	5.6	1118	1337	856	524	28	.312	.562 8th		187	53	1B-1667, OF-8
6 yrs.	854	3121	1048	218 10th	66 6th	158 1st	5.1	546	653 10th	424	279	14	.336 3rd	.600 1st	30	10	1B-808, OF-8

WORLD SERIES

	G	AB	H	2B	3B	HR	HR %	R	RBI	BB	SO	SB	BA	SA	PH AB	PH H	G by POS
1949 NY A	2	2	2	0	0	0	0.0	0	2	0	0	0	1.000	1.000	2	2	
1950	4	15	2	0	0	0	0.0	0	0	0	1	0	.133	.133	0	0	1B-2
1951	4	7	2	1	0	0	0.0	2	1	2	0	0	.286	.429	2	0	1B-2
1952	5	15	6	1	0	3	20.0	3	6	3	1	0	.400	1.067	1	1	1B-4
1953	3	3	0	0	0	0	0.0	0	0	0	1	0	.000	.000	3	0	
5 yrs.	18	42	12	2	0	3	7.1	5	9	5	3	0	.286 3rd	.548 1st	8	3	1B-10

Fritz Mollwitz

MOLLWITZ, FREDERICK AUGUST (Zip)   BR TR 6'2"   170 lbs.
B. June 16, 1890, Kolberg, Germany   D. Oct. 3, 1967, Bradenton, Fla.

	G	AB	H	2B	3B	HR	HR %	R	RBI	BB	SO	SB	BA	SA	PH AB	PH H	G by POS
1913 CHI N	2	7	3	0	0	0	0.0	1	0	0	0	0	.429	.429	0	0	1B-2
1914 2 teams	CHI	N (13G – .150)			CIN	N	(32G – .162)										
" Total	45	131	21	2	0	0	0.0	12	6	3	12	3	.160	.176	6	0	1B-36, OF-1
1915 CIN N	153	525	136	21	3	1	0.2	36	51	15	49	19	.259	.316	0	0	1B-155
1916 2 teams	CIN	N (65G – .224)			CHI	N	(33G – .268)										
" Total	98	254	60	6	4	0	0.0	13	27	12	18	10	.236	.291	20	5	1B-73, OF-6
1917 PIT N	36	140	36	4	1	0	0.0	15	12	8	8	4	.257	.300	0	0	1B-36, 2B-1
1918	119	432	116	12	7	0	0.0	43	45	23	24	23	.269	.329	0	0	1B-119
1919 2 teams	PIT	N (56G – .173)			STL	N	(25G – .229)										
" Total	81	251	48	5	4	0	0.0	18	17	22	21	11	.191	.243	2	1	1B-77, OF-2
7 yrs.	534	1740	420	50	19	1	0.1	138	158	83	132	70	.241	.294	28	6	1B-498, OF-9, 2B-1
1 yr.	25	83	19	3	0	0	0.0	7	5	7	3	2	.229	.265	0	0	1B-25

Wally Moon

MOON, WALLACE WADE   BL TR 6'   169 lbs.
B. Apr. 3, 1930, Bay, Ark.

	G	AB	H	2B	3B	HR	HR %	R	RBI	BB	SO	SB	BA	SA	PH AB	PH H	G by POS
1954 STL N	151	635	193	29	9	12	1.9	106	76	71	73	18	.304	.435	2	0	OF-148
1955	152	593	175	24	8	19	3.2	86	76	47	65	11	.295	.459	8	2	OF-100, 1B-51
1956	149	540	161	22	11	16	3.0	86	68	80	50	12	.298	.469	0	0	OF-97, 1B-52
1957	142	516	152	28	5	24	4.7	86	73	62	57	5	.295	.508	9	5	OF-133
1958	108	290	69	10	3	7	2.4	36	38	47	30	2	.238	.366	23	2	OF-82
1959 LA N	145	543	164	26	11	19	3.5	93	74	81	64	15	.302	.495	3	2	OF-143, 1B-1
1960	138	469	140	21	6	13	2.8	74	69	67	53	6	.299	.452	12	3	OF-127
1961	134	463	152	25	3	17	3.7	79	88	89	79	7	.328	.505	3	0	OF-133
1962	95	244	59	9	1	4	1.6	36	31	30	33	5	.242	.336	32	6	OF-36, 1B-32
1963	122	343	90	13	2	8	2.3	41	48	45	43	5	.262	.382	25	6	OF-96
1964	68	118	26	2	1	2	1.7	8	9	12	22	1	.220	.305	43	8	OF-23
1965	53	89	18	3	0	1	1.1	6	11	13	22	2	.202	.270	25	5	OF-23
12 yrs.	1457	4843	1399	212	60	142	2.9	737	661	644	591	89	.289	.445	185	35	OF-1141, 1B-136
5 yrs.	702	2574	750	113	36	78	3.0	400	331	307	275	48	.291	.454	42	5	OF-560, 1B-103

WORLD SERIES

	G	AB	H	2B	3B	HR	HR %	R	RBI	BB	SO	SB	BA	SA	PH AB	PH H	G by POS
1959 LA N	6	23	6	0	0	1	4.3	3	2	2	2	1	.261	.391	0	0	OF-6

	G	AB	H	2B	3B	HR	HR%	R	RBI	BB	SO	SB	BA	SA	Pinch Hit AB	Pinch Hit H	G by POS

Wally Moon continued

	G	AB	H	2B	3B	HR	HR%	R	RBI	BB	SO	SB	BA	SA	PH AB	PH H	G by POS
1965	2	2	0	0	0	0	0.0	0	0	0	0	0	.000	.000	2	0	
2 yrs.	8	25	6	0	0	1	4.0	3	2	2	2	1	.240	.360	2	0	OF-6

Gene Moore

MOORE, EUGENE, JR. (Rowdy)
Son of Gene Moore.
B. Aug. 26, 1909, Lancaster, Tex.

BL TL 5'11" 175 lbs.

	G	AB	H	2B	3B	HR	HR%	R	RBI	BB	SO	SB	BA	SA	PH AB	PH H	G by POS
1931 CIN N	4	14	2	1	0	0	0.0	2	1	0	0	0	.143	.214	1	0	OF-3
1933 STL N	11	38	15	3	2	0	0.0	6	8	4	10	1	.395	.579	1	0	OF-10
1934	9	18	5	1	0	0	0.0	2	1	2	2	0	.278	.333	6	2	OF-3
1935	3	3	0	0	0	0	0.0	0	0	0	1	0	.000	.000	3	0	
1936 BOS N	151	637	185	38	12	13	2.0	91	67	40	80	6	.290	.449	0	0	OF-151
1937	148	561	159	29	10	16	2.9	88	70	61	73	11	.283	.456	0	0	OF-148
1938	54	180	49	8	3	3	1.7	27	19	16	20	1	.272	.400	5	1	OF-47
1939 BKN N	107	306	69	13	6	3	1.0	45	39	40	50	4	.225	.337	18	3	OF-86, 1B-1
1940 2 teams		BKN N	(10G –	.269)			BOS N	(103G –	.292)								
" Total	113	389	113	26	1	5	1.3	49	41	26	35	2	.290	.401	11	4	OF-100
1941 BOS N	129	397	108	17	8	5	1.3	42	43	45	37	5	.272	.393	16	3	OF-110
1942 WAS A	1	2	0	0	0	0	0.0	0	0	0	1	0	.000	.000	0	0	OF-1
1943	92	254	68	14	3	2	0.8	41	39	19	29	0	.268	.370	30	12	OF-57, 1B-1
1944 STL A	110	390	93	13	6	6	1.5	56	58	24	37	0	.238	.349	11	5	OF-98, 1B-1
1945	110	354	92	16	2	5	1.4	48	50	40	26	1	.260	.359	10	0	OF-100
14 yrs.	1042	3543	958	179	53	58	1.6	497	436	317	401	31	.270	.400	112	27	OF-914, 1B-3
3 yrs.	23	59	20	4	2	0	0.0	8	9	6	13	1	.339	.475	10	2	OF-13
WORLD SERIES																	
1944 STL A	6	22	4	0	0	0	0.0	4	0	3	6	0	.182	.182	0	0	OF-6

Randy Moore

MOORE, RANDOLPH EDWARD
B. June 21, 1905, Naples, Tex.

BL TR 6' 185 lbs.

	G	AB	H	2B	3B	HR	HR%	R	RBI	BB	SO	SB	BA	SA	PH AB	PH H	G by POS
1927 CHI A	6	15	0	0	0	0	0.0	0	0	0	2	0	.000	.000	2	0	OF-4
1928	24	61	13	4	1	0	0.0	6	5	3	5	0	.213	.311	6	2	OF-16
1930 BOS N	83	191	55	9	0	2	1.0	24	34	10	13	3	.288	.366	30	6	OF-34, 3B-13
1931	83	192	50	8	1	3	1.6	19	34	13	3	1	.260	.359	32	6	OF-29, 3B-22, 2B-1
1932	107	351	103	21	2	3	0.9	41	43	15	11	1	.293	.390	14	4	OF-41, 3B-31, 1B-22, C-1
1933	135	497	150	23	7	8	1.6	64	70	40	16	3	.302	.425	6	1	OF-122, 1B-10
1934	123	422	120	21	2	7	1.7	55	64	40	16	2	.284	.393	13	5	OF-72, 1B-37
1935	125	407	112	20	4	4	1.0	42	42	26	16	1	.275	.373	23	5	OF-78, 1B-21
1936 BKN N	42	88	21	3	0	0	0.0	4	14	8	1	0	.239	.273	18	7	OF-21
1937 2 teams		BKN N	(13G –	.136)			STL N	(8G –	.000)								
" Total	21	29	3	1	0	0	0.0	3	2	3	2	0	.103	.138	9	0	C-10, OF-1
10 yrs.	749	2253	627	110	17	27	1.2	258	308	158	85	11	.278	.378	153	36	OF-418, 1B-90, 3B-66, C-11, 2B-1
1 yr.	8	7	0	0	0	0	0.0	0	0	0	0	0	.000	.000	7	0	OF-1

Terry Moore

MOORE, TERRY BLUFORD
B. May 27, 1912, Vernon, Ala.
Manager 1954.

BR TR 5'11" 195 lbs.

	G	AB	H	2B	3B	HR	HR%	R	RBI	BB	SO	SB	BA	SA	PH AB	PH H	G by POS
1935 STL N	119	456	131	34	3	6	1.3	63	53	15	40	13	.287	.414	0	0	OF-117
1936	143	590	156	39	4	5	0.8	85	47	37	52	9	.264	.369	7	2	OF-133
1937	115	461	123	17	3	5	1.1	76	43	32	41	13	.267	.349	8	1	OF-106
1938	94	312	85	21	3	4	1.3	49	21	46	19	9	.272	.397	9	1	OF-75, 3B-6
1939	130	417	123	25	2	17	4.1	65	77	43	38	6	.295	.487	7	2	OF-121, P-1
1940	136	537	163	33	4	17	3.2	92	64	42	44	18	.304	.475	3	0	OF-133
1941	122	493	145	26	4	6	1.2	86	68	52	31	3	.294	.400	1	0	OF-121
1942	130	489	141	26	3	6	1.2	80	49	56	26	10	.288	.391	4	2	OF-126, 3B-1
1946	91	278	73	14	1	3	1.1	32	28	18	26	0	.263	.353	25	6	OF-66
1947	127	460	130	17	1	7	1.5	61	45	38	39	1	.283	.370	6	1	OF-120
1948	91	207	48	11	0	4	1.9	30	18	27	12	0	.232	.343	17	4	OF-71
11 yrs.	1298	4700	1318	263	28	80	1.7	719	513	406	368	82	.280	.399	87	19	OF-1189, 3B-7, P-1
11 yrs.	1298	4700	1318	263	28	80	1.7	719	513	406	368	82	.280	.399	87	19	OF-1189, 3B-7, P-1
WORLD SERIES																	
1942 STL N	5	17	5	1	0	0	0.0	2	2	2	3	0	.294	.353	0	0	OF-5
1946	7	27	4	0	0	0	0.0	1	2	2	6	0	.148	.148	0	0	OF-7
2 yrs.	12	44	9	1	0	0	0.0	3	4	4	9	0	.205	.227	0	0	OF-12

Jerry Morales

MORALES, JULIO RUBEN
B. Feb. 18, 1949, Yabucoa, Puerto Rico

BR TR 5'10" 155 lbs.

	G	AB	H	2B	3B	HR	HR%	R	RBI	BB	SO	SB	BA	SA	PH AB	PH H	G by POS
1969 SD N	19	41	8	2	0	1	2.4	5	6	5	7	0	.195	.317	0	0	OF-19
1970	28	58	9	0	1	1	1.7	6	4	3	11	0	.155	.241	2	0	OF-26
1971	12	17	2	0	0	0	0.0	1	1	2	2	1	.118	.118	2	0	OF-7
1972	115	347	83	15	7	4	1.2	38	18	35	54	4	.239	.357	19	3	OF-96, 3B-4
1973	122	388	109	23	2	9	2.3	47	34	27	55	6	.281	.420	22	9	OF-100
1974 CHI N	151	534	146	21	7	15	2.8	70	82	46	63	2	.273	.423	8	2	OF-143
1975	153	578	156	21	0	12	2.1	62	91	50	65	3	.270	.369	2	2	OF-151
1976	140	537	147	17	0	16	3.0	66	67	41	49	3	.274	.395	5	1	OF-136
1977	136	490	142	34	5	11	2.2	56	69	43	75	0	.290	.447	11	3	OF-128
1978 STL N	130	457	109	19	8	4	0.9	44	46	33	44	4	.239	.341	8	1	OF-126
1979 DET A	129	440	93	23	1	14	3.2	50	56	30	56	10	.211	.364	7	0	OF-119
1980 NY N	94	193	49	7	1	3	1.6	19	30	13	31	2	.254	.347	30	7	OF-63
1981 CHI N	84	245	70	6	2	1	0.4	27	25	22	29	1	.286	.339	12	3	OF-72
1982	65	116	33	2	2	4	3.4	14	30	9	7	1	.284	.440	30	10	OF-41
14 yrs.	1378	4441	1156	190	36	95	2.1	505	559	359	548	37	.260	.383	158	41	OF-1227, 3B-4
1 yr.	130	457	109	19	8	4	0.9	44	46	33	44	4	.239	.341	8	1	OF-126

	G	AB	H	2B	3B	HR	HR %	R	RBI	BB	SO	SB	BA	SA	Pinch Hit AB	Pinch Hit H	G by POS

Bill Moran

MORAN, WILLIAM L.
B. Oct. 10, 1869, Joliet, Ill.   D. Apr. 8, 1916, Joliet, Ill.

	G	AB	H	2B	3B	HR	HR %	R	RBI	BB	SO	SB	BA	SA	AB	H	G by POS
1892 STL N	24	81	11	1	0	0	0.0	2	5	2	12	0	.136	.148	0	0	C-22
1895 CHI N	15	55	9	2	1	1	1.8	8	9	3	2	2	.164	.291	0	0	C-15
2 yrs.	39	136	20	3	1	1	0.7	10	14	5	14	2	.147	.206	0	0	C-37
1 yr.	24	81	11	1	0	0	0.0	2	5	2	12	0	.136	.148	0	0	C-22

Charley Moran

MORAN, CHARLES BARTHELL (Uncle Charlie)   BR TR 5'8" 180 lbs.
B. Feb. 22, 1878, Nashville, Tenn.   D. June 13, 1949, Horse Cave, Ky.

	G	AB	H	2B	3B	HR	HR %	R	RBI	BB	SO	SB	BA	SA	AB	H	G by POS
1903 STL N	4	14	6	0	0	0	0.0	2	1	0		1	.429	.429	0	0	P-3, SS-1
1908	21	63	11	1	2	0	0.0	2	2	0		0	.175	.254	5	2	C-16
2 yrs.	25	77	17	1	2	0	0.0	4	3	0		1	.221	.286	5	2	C-16, P-3, SS-1
2 yrs.	25	77	17	1	2	0	0.0	4	3	0		1	.221	.286	5	2	C-16, P-3, SS-1

Bobby Morgan

MORGAN, ROBERT MORRIS   BR TR 5'9" 175 lbs.
B. June 29, 1926, Oklahoma City, Okla.

	G	AB	H	2B	3B	HR	HR %	R	RBI	BB	SO	SB	BA	SA	AB	H	G by POS
1950 BKN N	67	199	45	10	3	7	3.5	38	21	32	43	0	.226	.412	5	1	3B-52, SS-10
1952	67	191	45	8	0	7	3.7	36	16	46	35	2	.236	.387	2	0	3B-60, 2B-5, SS-4
1953	69	196	51	6	2	7	3.6	35	33	33	47	2	.260	.418	9	0	3B-36, SS-21
1954 PHI N	135	455	119	25	2	14	3.1	58	50	70	68	3	.262	.418	0	0	SS-129, 3B-8, 2B-5
1955	136	483	112	20	2	10	2.1	61	49	73	72	6	.232	.344	6	2	2B-88, SS-41, 3B-6, 1B-1
1956 2 teams	PHI	N	(8G –	.200)		STL	N	(61G –	.195)								
" Total	69	138	27	7	0	3	2.2	15	21	21	28	0	.196	.312	29	5	3B-16, 2B-16, SS-6
1957 2 teams	PHI	N	(2G –	.000)		CHI	N	(125G –	.207)								
" Total	127	425	88	20	2	5	1.2	43	27	52	87	5	.207	.299	0	0	2B-118, 3B-12
1958 CHI N	1	1	0	0	0	0	0.0	0	0	0	1	0	.000	.000	1	0	
8 yrs.	671	2088	487	96	11	53	2.5	286	217	327	381	18	.233	.366	52	8	2B-232, SS-211, 3B-190, 1B-1
1 yr.	61	113	22	7	0	3	2.7	14	20	15	24	0	.195	.336	29	5	2B-13, 3B-11, SS-6

WORLD SERIES

	G	AB	H	2B	3B	HR	HR %	R	RBI	BB	SO	SB	BA	SA	AB	H	G by POS
1952 BKN N	2	1	0	0	0	0	0.0	0	0	0	0	0	.000	.000	1	0	3B-2
1953	1	1	0	0	0	0	0.0	0	0	0	0	0	.000	.000	1	0	
2 yrs.	3	2	0	0	0	0	0.0	0	0	0	0	0	.000	.000	2	0	3B-2

Eddie Morgan

MORGAN, EDWIN WILLIS (Pepper)   BL TL 5'10" 160 lbs.
B. Nov. 19, 1914, Brady Lake, Ohio

	G	AB	H	2B	3B	HR	HR %	R	RBI	BB	SO	SB	BA	SA	AB	H	G by POS
1936 STL N	8	18	5	0	0	1	5.6	4	3	2	4	0	.278	.444	3	2	OF-4
1937 BKN N	31	48	9	3	0	0	0.0	4	5	9	7	0	.188	.250	8	1	OF-7, 1B-7
2 yrs.	39	66	14	3	0	1	1.5	8	8	11	11	0	.212	.303	11	3	OF-11, 1B-7
1 yr.	8	18	5	0	0	1	5.6	4	3	2	4	0	.278	.444	3	2	OF-4

Joe Morgan

MORGAN, JOSEPH MICHAEL   BL TR 5'10" 170 lbs.
B. Nov. 19, 1930, Walpole, Mass.

	G	AB	H	2B	3B	HR	HR %	R	RBI	BB	SO	SB	BA	SA	AB	H	G by POS
1959 2 teams	MIL	N	(13G –	.217)		KC	A	(20G –	.190)								
" Total	33	44	9	1	1	0	0.0	4	4	5	11	0	.205	.273	22	5	2B-7, 3B-2
1960 2 teams	PHI	N	(26G –	.133)		CLE	A	(22G –	.298)								
" Total	48	130	25	4	2	2	1.5	11	6	12	15	0	.192	.300	10	1	3B-36, OF-2
1961 CLE A	4	10	2	0	0	0	0.0	0	0	1	3	0	.200	.200	2	0	OF-2
1964 STL N	3	3	0	0	0	0	0.0	0	0	0	2	0	.000	.000	3	0	
4 yrs.	88	187	36	5	3	2	1.1	15	10	18	31	0	.193	.283	37	6	3B-38, 2B-7, OF-4
1 yr.	3	3	0	0	0	0	0.0	0	0	0	2	0	.000	.000	3	0	

Gene Moriarity

MORIARITY, EUGENE JOHN   5'8" 190 lbs.
B. Holyoke, Mass.   Deceased.

	G	AB	H	2B	3B	HR	HR %	R	RBI	BB	SO	SB	BA	SA	AB	H	G by POS
1884 2 teams	BOS	N	(4G –	.063)		IND	AA	(10G –	.216)								
" Total	14	53	9	0	2	0	0.0	5		0	8		.170	.245	0	0	OF-11, P-2, 3B-1
1885 DET N	11	39	1	1	0	0	0.0	1	0	0	10		.026	.051	0	0	OF-6, 3B-4, SS-1, P-1
1892 STL N	47	177	31	4	1	3	1.7	20	19	4	37	7	.175	.260	0	0	OF-47
3 yrs.	72	269	41	5	3	3	1.1	26	18	4	55	7	.152	.227	0	0	OF-64, 3B-5, P-3, SS-1
1 yr.	47	177	31	4	1	3	1.7	20	19	4	37	7	.175	.260	0	0	OF-47

Walter Morris

MORRIS, JOHN WALTER   TR
B. Jan. 31, 1881, Rockwall, Tex.   D. Aug. 2, 1961, Dallas, Tex.

	G	AB	H	2B	3B	HR	HR %	R	RBI	BB	SO	SB	BA	SA	AB	H	G by POS
1908 STL N	23	73	13	1	1	0	0.0	1	2	0		1	.178	.219	1	0	SS-23

Hap Morse

MORSE, PETER RAYMOND   TR
B. St. Paul, Minn.   D. June 19, 1974, St. Paul, Minn.

	G	AB	H	2B	3B	HR	HR %	R	RBI	BB	SO	SB	BA	SA	AB	H	G by POS
1911 STL N	4	8	0	0	0	0	0.0	0		1	2	0	.000	.000	1	0	SS-2, OF-1

Walt Moryn

MORYN, WALTER JOSEPH (Moose)   BL TR 6'2" 205 lbs.
B. Apr. 12, 1926, St. Paul, Minn.

	G	AB	H	2B	3B	HR	HR %	R	RBI	BB	SO	SB	BA	SA	AB	H	G by POS
1954 BKN N	48	91	25	4	2	2	2.2	16	14	7	11	0	.275	.429	23	5	OF-21
1955	11	19	5	1	0	1	5.3	3	3	5	4	0	.263	.474	4	0	OF-7
1956 CHI N	147	529	151	27	3	23	4.3	69	67	50	67	4	.285	.478	4	0	OF-141
1957	149	568	164	33	0	19	3.3	76	88	50	90	0	.289	.447	4	1	OF-147
1958	143	512	135	26	7	26	5.1	77	77	62	83	1	.264	.494	6	4	OF-141
1959	117	381	89	14	1	14	3.7	41	48	44	66	0	.234	.386	13	5	OF-104
1960 2 teams	CHI	N	(38G –	.294)		STL	N	(75G –	.245)								
" Total	113	309	81	8	3	13	4.2	36	46	30	57	2	.262	.434	22	3	OF-92
1961 2 teams	STL	N	(17G –	.125)		PIT	N	(40G –	.200)								
" Total	57	97	17	3	0	3	3.1	6	11	3	15	0	.175	.299	36	6	OF-18
8 yrs.	785	2506	667	116	16	101	4.0	324	354	251	393	7	.266	.446	114	24	OF-671
2 yrs.	92	232	53	6	3	11	4.7	24	37	18	43	0	.228	.422	24	2	OF-69

	G	AB	H	2B	3B	HR	HR %	R	RBI	BB	SO	SB	BA	SA	Pinch Hit AB	Pinch Hit H	G by POS

Mike Mowrey

MOWREY, HARRY HARLAN
B. Mar. 24, 1884, Brown's Mill, Pa.   D. Mar. 20, 1947, Chambersburg, Pa.
BR TR 5'10" 180 lbs.

	G	AB	H	2B	3B	HR	HR %	R	RBI	BB	SO	SB	BA	SA	AB	H	G by POS
1905 CIN N	7	30	8	1	0	0	0.0	4	6	1		0	.267	.300	0	0	3B-7
1906	21	53	17	3	0	0	0.0	3	6	5		2	.321	.377	4	1	3B-15, SS-1, 2B-1
1907	138	448	113	16	6	1	0.2	43	44	35		10	.252	.321	0	0	3B-127, SS-11
1908	77	227	50	9	1	0	0.0	17	23	12		5	.220	.269	12	2	3B-56, OF-3, SS-3
1909 2 teams	CIN	N	(38G –	.191)		STL	N	(12G –	.241)								
" Total	50	144	29	6	0	0	0.0	13	9	24		3	.201	.243	6	1	3B-24, SS-13, 2B-7
1910 STL N	143	489	138	24	6	2	0.4	69	70	67	38	21	.282	.368	0	0	3B-141
1911	137	471	126	29	7	0	0.0	59	61	59	46	15	.268	.359	1	0	3B-134, SS-1
1912	114	408	104	13	8	2	0.5	59	50	46	29	19	.255	.341	4	1	3B-108
1913	131	449	116	18	4	0	0.0	61	33	53	40	21	.258	.316	0	0	3B-130
1914 PIT N	79	284	72	7	5	1	0.4	24	25	22	20	8	.254	.324	0	0	3B-78
1915 PIT F	151	521	146	26	6	1	0.2	56	49	66		40	.280	.359	0	0	3B-151
1916 BKN N	144	495	121	22	6	0	0.0	57	60	50	60	16	.244	.313	0	0	3B-144
1917	83	271	58	9	5	0	0.0	20	25	29	25	7	.214	.284	1	0	3B-80, 2B-2
13 yrs.	1275	4290	1098	183	54	7	0.2	485	461	469	258	167	.256	.329	28	5	3B-1195, SS-29, 2B-10, OF-3
5 yrs.	537	1846	491	85	25	4	0.2	251	218	229	153	77	.266	.346	8	2	3B-515, 2B-7, SS-1
WORLD SERIES																	
1916 BKN N	5	17	3	0	0	0	0.0	2	1	3	2	0	.176	.176	0	0	3B-5

Heinie Mueller

MUELLER, CLARENCE FRANCIS
Brother of Walter Mueller.
B. Sept. 16, 1899, Creve Coeur, Mo.   D. Jan. 23, 1974, Desoto, Mo.
BL TL 5'8" 158 lbs.

	G	AB	H	2B	3B	HR	HR %	R	RBI	BB	SO	SB	BA	SA	AB	H	G by POS
1920 STL N	4	22	7	1	0	0	0.0	0	2	4	1	.318	.364	0	0	OF-4
1921	55	176	62	10	6	1	0.6	25	34	11	22	2	.352	.494	1	0	OF-54
1922	61	159	43	7	2	3	1.9	20	26	14	18	2	.270	.396	17	5	OF-44
1923	78	265	91	16	9	5	1.9	39	41	18	16	4	.343	.528	4	3	OF-74
1924	92	296	78	12	6	2	0.7	39	37	19	16	8	.264	.365	10	1	OF-53, 1B-27
1925	78	243	76	16	4	1	0.4	33	26	17	11	0	.313	.424	5	2	OF-72
1926 2 teams	STL	N	(52G –	.267)		NY	N	(85G –	.249)								
" Total	137	496	127	13	7	7	1.4	72	57	32	23	15	.256	.353	3	2	OF-133
1927 NY N	84	190	55	6	1	3	1.6	33	19	25	12	2	.289	.379	18	3	OF-56, 1B-1
1928 BOS N	42	151	34	3	1	0	0.0	25	19	17	9	1	.225	.258	1	1	OF-41
1929	46	93	19	2	1	0	0.0	10	11	12	12	2	.204	.247	16	4	OF-24
1935 STL A	16	27	5	1	0	0	0.0	0	1	1	4	0	.185	.222	11	3	1B-3, OF-2
11 yrs.	693	2118	597	87	37	22	1.0	296	272	168	147	37	.282	.389	86	24	OF-557, 1B-31
7 yrs.	420	1352	408	69	32	15	1.1	192	193	92	93	25	.302	.433	37	11	OF-352, 1B-27

Jerry Mumphrey

MUMPHREY, JERRY WAYNE
B. Sept. 9, 1952, Tyler, Tex.
BB TR 6'2" 185 lbs.

	G	AB	H	2B	3B	HR	HR %	R	RBI	BB	SO	SB	BA	SA	AB	H	G by POS
1974 STL N	5	2	0	0	0	0	0.0	0	0	0	0	0	.000	.000	0	0	OF-1
1975	11	16	6	2	0	0	0.0	2	1	4	3	0	.375	.500	4	2	OF-3
1976	112	384	99	15	5	1	0.3	51	26	37	53	22	.258	.331	10	3	OF-94
1977	145	463	133	20	10	2	0.4	73	38	47	70	22	.287	.387	16	3	OF-133
1978	125	367	96	13	4	2	0.5	41	37	30	40	14	.262	.335	16	5	OF-116
1979	124	339	100	10	3	3	0.9	53	32	26	39	8	.295	.369	16	5	OF-114
1980 SD N	160	564	168	24	3	4	0.7	61	59	49	90	52	.298	.372	6	1	OF-153
1981 NY A	80	319	98	11	5	6	1.9	44	32	24	27	13	.307	.429	0	0	OF-79
1982	123	477	143	24	10	9	1.9	76	68	50	66	11	.300	.449	0	0	OF-123
9 yrs.	885	2931	843	119	40	27	0.9	403	293	267	388	142	.288	.383	68	19	OF-816
6 yrs.	522	1571	434	60	22	8	0.5	222	134	144	205	66	.276	.358	62	18	OF-461
DIVISIONAL PLAYOFF SERIES																	
1981 NY A	5	21	2	0	0	0	0.0	2	0	0	1	1	.095	.095	0	0	OF-5
LEAGUE CHAMPIONSHIP SERIES																	
1981 NY A	3	12	6	1	0	0	0.0	2	0	3	2	0	.500	.583	0	0	OF-3
WORLD SERIES																	
1981 NY A	5	15	3	0	0	0	0.0	2	0	3	2	1	.200	.200	0	0	OF-5

Simmy Murch

MURCH, SIMEON T.
B. Nov. 21, 1880, Castine, Me.   D. June 6, 1939, Exeter, N. H.
TR 6'4" 220 lbs.

	G	AB	H	2B	3B	HR	HR %	R	RBI	BB	SO	SB	BA	SA	AB	H	G by POS
1904 STL N	13	51	7	1	0	0	0.0	3	1	1		0	.137	.157	0	0	3B-6, 2B-6, SS-1
1905	3	9	1	0	0	0	0.0	0	0	0		0	.111	.111	1	0	2B-2, SS-1
1908 BKN N	6	11	2	1	0	0	0.0	1	0	1		0	.182	.273	4	0	1B-2
3 yrs.	22	71	10	2	0	0	0.0	4	1	2		0	.141	.169	5	0	2B-8, 3B-6, SS-2, 1B-2
2 yrs.	16	60	8	1	0	0	0.0	3	1	1		0	.133	.150	1	0	2B-8, 3B-6, SS-2

Wilbur Murdock

MURDOCK, WILBUR E.
B. Unknown.

	G	AB	H	2B	3B	HR	HR %	R	RBI	BB	SO	SB	BA	SA	AB	H	G by POS
1908 STL N	27	62	16	3	0	0	0.0	5	5	3		4	.258	.306	9	2	OF-16

Howard Murphy

MURPHY, HOWARD
B. 1882, Milton, Okla.   D. Sept. 5, 1926, Riverside, Tex.
BL TR 5'8½" 150 lbs.

	G	AB	H	2B	3B	HR	HR %	R	RBI	BB	SO	SB	BA	SA	AB	H	G by POS
1909 STL N	25	60	12	0	0	0	0.0	3	3	4		1	.200	.200	5	1	OF-19

Mike Murphy

MURPHY, MICHAEL JEROME
B. Aug. 19, 1888, Forestville, Pa.   D. Oct. 27, 1952, Johnson City, N. Y.
BR TR

	G	AB	H	2B	3B	HR	HR %	R	RBI	BB	SO	SB	BA	SA	AB	H	G by POS
1912 STL N	1	1	0	0	0	0	0.0	0	0	0	0	0	.000	.000	0	0	C-1
1916 PHI A	14	27	3	0	0	0	0.0	0	1	1	3	0	.111	.111	2	0	C-12
2 yrs.	15	28	3	0	0	0	0.0	0	1	1	3	0	.107	.107	2	0	C-13
1 yr.	1	1	0	0	0	0	0.0	0	0	0	0	0	.000	.000	0	0	C-1

	G	AB	H	2B	3B	HR	HR %	R	RBI	BB	SO	SB	BA	SA	Pinch Hit AB	H	G by POS

Kid Nichols

NICHOLS, CHARLES AUGUSTUS
B. Sept. 14, 1869, Madison, Wis.   D. Apr. 11, 1953, Kansas City, Mo.
Manager 1904-05.
Hall of Fame 1949.   BR TR 5'10½" 175 lbs.

	G	AB	H	2B	3B	HR	HR %	R	RBI	BB	SO	SB	BA	SA	Pinch Hit AB	H	G by POS
1890 BOS N	49	174	43	5	1	0	0.0	18	23	11	36	2	.247	.287	0	0	P-48, OF-2
1891	52	183	36	6	0	0	0.0	21	27	12	31	1	.197	.230	0	0	P-52
1892	57	197	39	6	2	2	1.0	21	21	16	51	3	.198	.279	0	0	P-53, OF-5
1893	53	177	39	3	2	2	1.1	25	26	15	22	4	.220	.294	0	0	P-52, OF-1
1894	51	170	50	11	2	0	0.0	39	34	16	24	1	.294	.382	0	0	P-50, OF-1
1895	49	157	37	3	2	0	0.0	23	18	14	28	0	.236	.280	0	0	P-48, OF-1
1896	51	147	28	3	3	1	0.7	27	24	12	18	2	.190	.272	0	0	P-49, OF-2
1897	46	147	39	5	0	3	2.0	20	28	7		4	.265	.361	0	0	P-46
1898	51	158	38	3	3	2	1.3	26	23	4		0	.241	.335	0	0	P-50, 1B-1
1899	42	136	26	3	0	1	0.7	13	12	6		1	.191	.235	0	0	P-42
1900	29	90	18	0	0	1	1.1	14	7	7		1	.200	.233	0	0	P-29
1901	55	163	46	8	7	4	2.5	16	28	8		0	.282	.491	4	2	P-38, OF-7, 1B-5
1904 STL N	36	109	17	1	2	0	0.0	7	5	7		0	.156	.202	0	0	P-36
1905 2 teams		STL	N	(8G –	.227)		PHI	N	(17G –	.189)							
" Total	25	75	15	1	0	0	0.0	3	2	2		0	.200	.213	0	0	P-24, OF-1
1906 PHI N	4	3	0	0	0	0	0.0	0	0	0		0	.000	.000	0	0	P-4
15 yrs.	650	2086	471	58	24	16	0.8	273	278	137	210	19	.226	.300	4	2	P-621, OF-20, 1B-6
2 yrs.	44	131	22	1	2	0	0.0	7	5	7		0	.168	.206	0	0	P-43, OF-1

Hugh Nicol

NICOL, HUGH N.
B. Jan. 1, 1858, Campsie, Scotland   D. June 27, 1921, Lafayette, Ind.
Manager 1897.   BR TR 5'4" 145 lbs.

	G	AB	H	2B	3B	HR	HR %	R	RBI	BB	SO	SB	BA	SA	Pinch Hit AB	H	G by POS
1881 CHI N	26	108	22	2	0	0	0.0	13	7	4	12		.204	.222	0	0	OF-26, SS-1
1882	47	186	37	9	1	1	0.5	19	16	7	29		.199	.274	0	0	OF-47, SS-8
1883 STL AA	94	368	106	13	3	0	0.0	73		18			.288	.340	0	0	OF-84, 2B-11
1884	110	442	115	14	5	0	0.0	79		22			.260	.314	0	0	OF-87, 2B-23, SS-1, 3B-1
1885	112	425	88	11	1	0	0.0	59		34			.207	.238	0	0	OF-111, 3B-1
1886	67	253	52	6	3	0	0.0	44		26			.206	.253	0	0	OF-57, SS-8, 2B-4
1887 CIN AA	125	475	102	18	2	1	0.2	122		86		138	.215	.267	0	0	OF-125
1888	135	548	131	10	2	1	0.2	112	35	67		103	.239	.270	0	0	OF-125, 2B-12, SS-1
1889	122	474	121	7	8	2	0.4	82	58	54	35	80	.255	.316	0	0	OF-115, 2B-7, 3B-3
1890 CIN N	50	186	39	1	4	0	0.0	28	19	19	12	24	.210	.258	0	0	OF-46, SS-3, 2B-1
10 yrs.	888	3465	813	91	29	5	0.1	631	135	337	88	345	.235	.282	0	0	OF-823, 2B-58, SS-22, 3B-5

Charlie Niebergall

NIEBERGALL, CHARLES ARTHUR (Nig)
B. May 23, 1899, New York, N. Y.   BR TR 5'10" 160 lbs.

	G	AB	H	2B	3B	HR	HR %	R	RBI	BB	SO	SB	BA	SA	Pinch Hit AB	H	G by POS
1921 STL N	5	6	1	0	0	0	0.0	1	0	0	0	0	.167	.167	2	1	C-3
1923	9	28	3	1	0	0	0.0	2	1	2	2	0	.107	.143	1	0	C-7
1924	40	58	17	6	0	0	0.0	6	7	3	9	0	.293	.397	6	2	C-34
3 yrs.	54	92	21	7	0	0	0.0	9	8	5	11	0	.228	.304	9	3	C-44
3 yrs.	54	92	21	7	0	0	0.0	9	8	5	11	0	.228	.304	9	3	C-44

Bert Niehoff

NIEHOFF, JOHN ALBERT
B. May 13, 1884, Louisville, Colo.   D. Dec. 8, 1974, Inglewood, Calif.   BR TR 5'10½" 170 lbs.

	G	AB	H	2B	3B	HR	HR %	R	RBI	BB	SO	SB	BA	SA	Pinch Hit AB	H	G by POS
1913 CIN N	2	8	0	0	0	0	0.0	0	0	0	2	0	.000	.000	0	0	3B-2
1914	142	484	117	16	9	4	0.8	46	49	38	77	20	.242	.337	5	2	3B-134, 2B-3
1915 PHI N	148	529	126	27	2	2	0.4	61	49	30	63	21	.238	.308	0	0	2B-148
1916	146	548	133	42	4	4	0.7	65	61	37	57	20	.243	.356	0	0	2B-146, 3B-1
1917	114	361	92	17	4	2	0.6	30	42	23	29	8	.255	.341	7	0	2B-96, 1B-7, 3B-6
1918 2 teams		STL	N	(22G –	.179)		NY	N	(7G –	.261)							
" Total	29	107	21	2	0	0	0.0	8	6	3	14	2	.196	.215	0	0	2B-29
6 yrs.	581	2037	489	104	19	12	0.6	210	207	131	242	71	.240	.327	12	2	2B-422, 3B-143, 1B-7
1 yr.	22	84	15	2	0	0	0.0	5	5	3	10	2	.179	.202	0	0	2B-22

WORLD SERIES

	G	AB	H	2B	3B	HR	HR %	R	RBI	BB	SO	SB	BA	SA	Pinch Hit AB	H	G by POS
1915 PHI N	5	16	1	0	0	0	0.0	1	0	1	5	0	.063	.063	0	0	2B-5

Bob Nieman

NIEMAN, ROBERT CHARLES
B. Jan. 26, 1927, Cincinnati, Ohio   BR TR 5'11" 195 lbs.

	G	AB	H	2B	3B	HR	HR %	R	RBI	BB	SO	SB	BA	SA	Pinch Hit AB	H	G by POS
1951 STL A	12	43	16	3	1	2	4.7	6	8	3	5	0	.372	.628	1	1	OF-11
1952	131	478	138	22	2	18	3.8	66	74	46	73	0	.289	.456	9	1	OF-125
1953 DET A	142	508	143	32	5	15	3.0	72	69	57	57	0	.281	.453	7	1	OF-135
1954	91	251	66	14	1	8	3.2	24	35	22	32	0	.263	.422	26	8	OF-62
1955 CHI A	99	272	77	11	2	11	4.0	36	53	36	37	1	.283	.460	24	7	OF-78
1956 2 teams		CHI	A	(14G –	.300)		BAL	A	(114G –	.322)							
" Total	128	428	137	21	6	14	3.3	63	68	90	63	1	.320	.495	1	1	OF-124
1957 BAL A	129	445	123	17	6	13	2.9	61	70	63	86	4	.276	.429	9	0	OF-120
1958	105	366	119	20	2	16	4.4	56	60	44	57	2	.325	.522	6	1	OF-100
1959	118	360	105	18	2	21	5.8	49	60	42	55	1	.292	.528	17	4	OF-97
1960 STL N	81	188	54	13	5	4	2.1	19	31	24	31	0	.287	.473	26	4	OF-55
1961 2 teams		STL	N	(6G –	.471)		CLE	A	(39G –	.354)							
" Total	45	82	31	7	0	2	2.4	2	12	7	6	1	.378	.537	27	9	OF-16
1962 2 teams		CLE	A	(2G –	.000)		SF	N	(30G –	.300)							
" Total	32	31	9	2	0	1	3.2	1	4	1	10	0	.290	.452	30	8	OF-3
12 yrs.	1113	3452	1018	180	32	125	3.6	455	544	435	512	10	.295	.474	183	45	OF-926
2 yrs.	87	205	62	14	5	4	2.0	19	33	24	33	0	.302	.478	28	5	OF-59

WORLD SERIES

	G	AB	H	2B	3B	HR	HR %	R	RBI	BB	SO	SB	BA	SA	Pinch Hit AB	H	G by POS
1962 SF N	1	0	0	0	0	0	–	0	0	1	0	0	–	–	0	0	

	G	AB	H	2B	3B	HR	HR %	R	RBI	BB	SO	SB	BA	SA	Pinch Hit AB	Pinch Hit H	G by POS

Tom Niland

NILAND, THOMAS JAMES (Honest Tom)   BR TR 5'11"   160 lbs.
B. Apr. 14, 1870, Brookfield, Mass.   D. Apr. 30, 1950, Lynn, Mass.

	G	AB	H	2B	3B	HR	HR%	R	RBI	BB	SO	SB	BA	SA	PH AB	PH H	G by POS
1896 STL N	18	68	12	0	1	0	0.0	3	3	5	4	0	.176	.206	0	0	OF-13, SS-5

Pete Noonan

NOONAN, PETER JOHN   BR TR 6'   180 lbs.
B. Nov. 24, 1881, W. Stockbridge, Mass.   D. Jan. 11, 1965, Pittsfield, Mass.

	G	AB	H	2B	3B	HR	HR%	R	RBI	BB	SO	SB	BA	SA	PH AB	PH H	G by POS
1904 PHI A	39	114	23	3	1	2	1.8	13	13	1		1	.202	.298	6	1	C-22, 1B-10
1906 2 teams	CHI N	(5G – .333)		STL	N	(44G – .168)											
" Total	49	128	22	1	3	1	0.8	8	9	11		1	.172	.250	8	2	C-23, 1B-17
1907 STL N	74	236	53	7	3	1	0.4	19	16	9		3	.225	.292	5	1	C-69
3 yrs.	162	478	98	11	7	4	0.8	40	38	21		5	.205	.282	19	4	C-114, 1B-27
2 yrs.	118	361	74	8	6	2	0.6	27	25	20		4	.205	.277	10	2	C-92, 1B-16

Irv Noren

NOREN, IRVING ARNOLD   BL TL 6'   190 lbs.
B. Nov. 29, 1924, Jamestown, N. Y.

	G	AB	H	2B	3B	HR	HR%	R	RBI	BB	SO	SB	BA	SA	PH AB	PH H	G by POS
1950 WAS A	138	542	160	27	10	14	2.6	80	98	67	77	5	.295	.459	0	0	OF-121, 1B-17
1951	129	509	142	33	5	8	1.6	82	86	51	35	10	.279	.411	3	0	OF-126
1952 2 teams	WAS	A	(12G – .245)		NY	A	(93G – .235)										
" Total	105	321	76	16	3	5	1.6	40	23	32	37	5	.237	.352	18	3	OF-72, 1B-19
1953 NY A	109	345	92	12	6	6	1.7	55	46	42	39	3	.267	.388	15	3	OF-96
1954	125	426	136	21	6	12	2.8	70	66	43	38	4	.319	.481	12	5	OF-116, 1B-1
1955	132	371	94	19	1	8	2.2	49	59	43	33	5	.253	.375	11	1	OF-126
1956	29	37	8	1	0	0	0.0	4	6	12	7	0	.216	.243	13	4	OF-10, 1B-1
1957 2 teams	KC	A	(81G – .213)		STL	N	(17G – .367)										
" Total	98	190	45	12	1	3	1.6	11	26	15	25	0	.237	.358	54	13	1B-25, OF-14
1958 STL N	117	178	47	9	1	4	2.2	24	22	13	21	0	.264	.393	43	8	OF-77
1959 2 teams	STL	N	(8G – .125)		CHI	N	(65G – .321)										
" Total	73	164	51	7	2	4	2.4	27	19	13	26	2	.311	.451	29	12	OF-42, 1B-2
1960 2 teams	CHI	N	(12G – .091)		LA	N	(26G – .200)										
" Total	38	36	6	0	0	1	2.8	2	7	4	12	0	.167	.250	32	5	OF-1, 1B-1
11 yrs.	1093	3119	857	157	35	65	2.1	443	453	335	350	34	.275	.410	230	52	OF-801, 1B-66
3 yrs.	142	216	59	14	2	5	2.3	27	32	17	29	0	.273	.426	57	11	OF-87, 1B-1

WORLD SERIES

	G	AB	H	2B	3B	HR	HR%	R	RBI	BB	SO	SB	BA	SA	PH AB	PH H	G by POS
1952 NY A	4	10	3	0	0	0	0.0	0	1	1	3	0	.300	.300	1	1	OF-3
1953	2	1	0	0	0	0	0.0	0	0	1	0	0	.000	.000	1	0	
1955	5	16	1	0	0	0	0.0	0	1	1	1	0	.063	.063	0	0	OF-5
3 yrs.	11	27	4	0	0	0	0.0	0	2	3	4	0	.148	.148	2	1	OF-8

Ron Northey

NORTHEY, RONALD JAMES (The Round Man)   BL TR 5'10"   195 lbs.
Father of Scott Northey.
B. Apr. 26, 1920, Mahanoy City, Pa.   D. Apr. 16, 1971, Pittsburgh, Pa.

	G	AB	H	2B	3B	HR	HR%	R	RBI	BB	SO	SB	BA	SA	PH AB	PH H	G by POS
1942 PHI N	127	402	101	13	2	5	1.2	31	31	28	33	2	.251	.331	17	4	OF-109
1943	147	586	163	31	5	16	2.7	72	68	51	52	2	.278	.430	2	0	OF-145
1944	152	570	164	35	9	22	3.9	72	104	67	51	1	.288	.496	1	0	OF-151
1946	128	438	109	24	6	16	3.7	55	62	39	59	1	.249	.441	14	5	OF-111
1947 2 teams	PHI	N	(13G – .255)		STL	N	(110G – .293)										
" Total	123	358	103	22	3	15	4.2	59	66	54	32	1	.288	.492	13	3	OF-107, 3B-2
1948 STL N	96	246	79	10	1	13	5.3	40	64	38	25	0	.321	.528	25	11	OF-67
1949	90	265	69	18	2	7	2.6	28	50	31	15	0	.260	.423	12	0	OF-73
1950 2 teams	CIN	N	(27G – .260)		CHI	N	(53G – .281)										
" Total	80	191	52	14	0	9	4.7	22	29	25	15	0	.272	.487	27	5	OF-51
1952 CHI N	1	1	0	0	0	0	0.0	0	0	0	0	0	.000	.000	1	0	
1955 CHI A	14	14	5	2	0	1	7.1	1	4	3	3	0	.357	.714	10	4	OF-2
1956	53	48	17	2	0	3	6.3	4	23	8	1	0	.354	.583	39	15	OF-4
1957 2 teams	CHI	A	(40G – .185)		PHI	N	(33G – .269)										
" Total	73	53	12	1	0	1	1.9	1	12	17	11	0	.226	.302	53	12	
12 yrs.	1084	3172	874	172	28	108	3.4	385	513	361	297	7	.276	.450	214	59	OF-820, 3B-2
3 yrs.	296	822	239	47	6	35	4.3	120	177	117	69	0	.291	.490	50	14	OF-234, 3B-2

Joe Nossek

NOSSEK, JOSEPH RUDOLPH   BR TR 6'   178 lbs.
B. Nov. 8, 1940, Cleveland, Ohio

	G	AB	H	2B	3B	HR	HR%	R	RBI	BB	SO	SB	BA	SA	PH AB	PH H	G by POS
1964 MIN A	7	1	0	0	0	0	0.0	0	0	0	0	0	.000	.000	1	0	OF-2
1965	87	170	37	9	0	2	1.2	19	16	7	22	2	.218	.306	28	7	OF-48, 3B-9
1966 2 teams	MIN	A	(4G – .000)		KC	A	(87G – .261)										
" Total	91	230	60	10	3	1	0.4	13	27	8	21	4	.261	.343	17	8	OF-80, 3B-1
1967 KC A	87	166	34	6	1	0	0.0	12	10	4	26	2	.205	.253	28	1	OF-63
1969 2 teams	OAK	A	(13G – .000)		STL	N	(9G – .200)										
" Total	22	11	1	0	0	0	0.0	2	0	0	3	0	.091	.091	4	1	OF-13
1970 STL N	1	1	0	0	0	0	0.0	0	0	0	0	0	.000	.000	1	0	
6 yrs.	295	579	132	25	4	3	0.5	47	53	19	72	8	.228	.301	79	17	OF-206, 3B-10
2 yrs.	10	6	1	0	0	0	0.0	2	0	0	3	0	.167	.167	5	1	OF-1

WORLD SERIES

	G	AB	H	2B	3B	HR	HR%	R	RBI	BB	SO	SB	BA	SA	PH AB	PH H	G by POS
1965 MIN A	6	20	4	0	0	0	0.0	0	0	0	1	0	.200	.200	1	1	OF-5

Rebel Oakes

OAKES, ENNIS TALMADGE   BL TR 5'8"   170 lbs.
B. Dec. 17, 1886, Homer, La.   D. Feb. 8, 1948, Shreveport, La.
Manager 1914-15.

	G	AB	H	2B	3B	HR	HR%	R	RBI	BB	SO	SB	BA	SA	PH AB	PH H	G by POS
1909 CIN N	120	415	112	10	5	3	0.7	55	31	40		23	.270	.340	7	2	OF-113
1910 STL N	131	468	118	14	6	0	0.0	50	43	38	38	18	.252	.308	3	1	OF-127
1911	154	551	145	13	6	2	0.4	69	59	41	35	25	.263	.319	2	1	OF-151
1912	136	495	139	19	5	3	0.6	57	58	31	24	26	.281	.358	1	1	OF-136
1913	146	537	156	14	5	0	0.0	59	49	43	32	22	.291	.335	2	1	OF-144
1914 PIT F	145	571	178	18	10	7	1.2	82	75	35		28	.312	.415	0	0	OF-145
1915	153	580	161	24	5	0	0.0	55	82	37		21	.278	.336	0	0	OF-153
7 yrs.	985	3617	1009	112	42	15	0.4	427	397	265	129	163	.279	.346	15	6	OF-969
4 yrs.	567	2051	558	60	22	5	0.2	235	209	153	129	91	.272	.330	8	4	OF-558

	G	AB	H	2B	3B	HR	HR %	R	RBI	BB	SO	SB	BA	SA	Pinch Hit AB	Pinch Hit H	G by POS

Ken Oberkfell

OBERKFELL, KENNETH RAY
B. May 4, 1956, Maryville, Ill.
BL TR 6'   175 lbs.

	G	AB	H	2B	3B	HR	HR%	R	RBI	BB	SO	SB	BA	SA	AB	H	G by POS
1977 STL N	9	9	1	0	0	0	0.0	0	1	0	3	0	.111	.111	3	0	2B-6
1978	24	50	6	1	0	0	0.0	7	0	3	1	0	.120	.140	3	0	2B-17, 3B-4
1979	135	369	111	19	5	1	0.3	53	35	57	35	4	.301	.388	13	3	2B-117, 3B-17, SS-2
1980	116	422	128	27	6	3	0.7	58	46	51	23	4	.303	.417	1	0	2B-101, 3B-16
1981	102	376	110	12	6	2	0.5	43	45	37	28	13	.293	.372	1	0	3B-102, SS-1
1982	137	470	136	22	5	2	0.4	55	34	40	31	11	.289	.370	3	1	3B-135, 2B-1
6 yrs.	523	1696	492	81	22	8	0.5	216	161	188	121	32	.290	.378	24	4	3B-274, 2B-242, SS-3
6 yrs.	523	1696	492	81	22	8	0.5	216	161	188	121	32	.290	.378	24	4	3B-274, 2B-242, SS-3
LEAGUE CHAMPIONSHIP SERIES																	
1982 STL N	3	15	3	0	0	0	0.0	1	2	0	0	0	.200	.200	0	0	3B-3
WORLD SERIES																	
1982 STL N	7	24	7	1	0	0	0.0	4	1	2	1	2	.292	.333	0	0	3B-7

Johnny O'Brien

O'BRIEN, JOHN THOMAS
Brother of Eddie O'Brien.
B. Dec. 11, 1930, South Amboy, N. J.
BR TR 5'9"   170 lbs.

	G	AB	H	2B	3B	HR	HR%	R	RBI	BB	SO	SB	BA	SA	AB	H	G by POS
1953 PIT N	89	279	69	13	2	2	0.7	28	22	21	36	1	.247	.330	5	0	2B-77, SS-1
1955	84	278	83	15	2	1	0.4	22	25	20	19	1	.299	.378	5	0	2B-78
1956	73	104	18	1	0	0	0.0	13	3	5	7	0	.173	.183	8	1	2B-53, P-8, SS-1
1957	34	35	11	2	1	0	0.0	7	1	1	4	0	.314	.429	3	1	P-16, SS-8, 2B-2
1958 2 teams	PIT N (3G – .000)			STL N (12G – .000)													
" Total	15	3	0	0	0	0	0.0	4	0	1	1	0	.000	.000	2	0	SS-5, 2B-1, P-1
1959 MIL N	44	116	23	4	0	1	0.9	16	8	11	15	0	.198	.259	0	0	2B-37
6 yrs.	339	815	204	35	5	4	0.5	90	59	59	82	2	.250	.320	23	2	2B-248, P-25, SS-15
1 yr.	12	2	0	0	0	0	0.0	3	0	1	0	0	.000	.000	1	0	SS-5, 2B-1, P-1

Jack O'Connor

O'CONNOR, JOHN JOSEPH (Peach Pie)
B. Mar. 3, 1867, St. Louis, Mo.   D. Nov. 14, 1937, St. Louis, Mo.
Manager 1910.
BR TR 5'10"   170 lbs.

	G	AB	H	2B	3B	HR	HR%	R	RBI	BB	SO	SB	BA	SA	AB	H	G by POS
1887 CIN AA	12	40	4	0	0	0	0.0	4		2		3	.100	.100	0	0	OF-7, C-5
1888	36	137	28	3	1	1	0.7	14	17	6		12	.204	.263	0	0	OF-34, C-2
1889 COL AA	107	398	107	17	7	4	1.0	69	60	33	37	26	.269	.377	0	0	C-84, OF-19, 2B-4, 1B-3
1890	121	457	148	14	10	2	0.4	89		38		29	.324	.411	0	0	C-106, OF-9, SS-8, 2B-2, 3B-1
1891	56	229	61	12	3	0	0.0	28	37	11	14	10	.266	.345	0	0	OF-40, C-21
1892 CLE N	140	572	142	22	5	1	0.2	71	58	25	48	17	.248	.309	1	0	OF-106, C-34
1893	96	384	110	23	1	3	0.8	72	75	29	12	29	.286	.375	0	0	C-56, OF-44
1894	86	330	104	23	7	2	0.6	67	51	15	7	15	.315	.445	1	0	C-45, OF-33, 1B-7
1895	89	340	99	14	10	0	0.0	51	58	30	22	11	.291	.391	0	0	C-47, 1B-41, 3B-1
1896	68	256	76	11	1	1	0.4	41	43	15	12	15	.297	.359	3	2	C-37, 1B-17, OF-12
1897	103	397	115	21	4	2	0.5	49	69	26		20	.290	.378	4	3	OF-52, 1B-36, C-13
1898	131	478	119	17	4	1	0.2	50	56	26		8	.249	.308	1	0	1B-69, C-48, OF-15
1899 STL N	84	289	73	5	6	0	0.0	33	43	15		7	.253	.311	2	0	C-57, 1B-26
1900 2 teams	STL N (10G – .219)			PIT N (43G – .238)													
" Total	53	179	42	4	1	0	0.0	19	25	5		5	.235	.268	1	0	C-50, 1B-2
1901 PIT N	61	202	39	7	3	0	0.0	16	22	10		2	.193	.257	2	0	C-59
1902	49	170	50	1	2	1	0.6	13	28	3		2	.294	.341	0	0	C-42, 1B-6, OF-1
1903 NY A	64	212	43	4	1	0	0.0	13	12	8		4	.203	.231	0	0	C-63, 1B-1
1904 STL A	14	47	10	1	0	0	0.0	4	2	2		0	.213	.234	0	0	C-14
1906	58	174	33	0	0	0	0.0	8	11	2		4	.190	.190	4	0	C-54
1907	25	89	14	2	0	0	0.0	2	4	0		0	.157	.180	0	0	C-25
1910	1	0	0	0	0	0	–	0	0	0		0	–	–	0	0	C-1
21 yrs.	1454	5380	1417	201	66	18	0.3	713	670	301	152	219	.263	.335	19	5	C-863, OF-372, 1B-208, SS-8, 2B-6, 3B-2
2 yrs.	94	321	80	5	6	0	0.0	37	49	17		7	.249	.302	2	0	C-67, 1B-26

Paddy O'Connor

O'CONNOR, PATRICK FRANCIS
B. Aug. 4, 1879, Windsor Locks, Conn.   D. Aug. 17, 1950, Springfield, Mass.
BR TR 5'8"   168 lbs.

	G	AB	H	2B	3B	HR	HR%	R	RBI	BB	SO	SB	BA	SA	AB	H	G by POS
1908 PIT N	12	16	3	0	0	0	0.0	1	2	0		0	.188	.188	7	2	C-4
1909	9	16	5	1	0	0	0.0	1	3	0		0	.313	.375	5	0	C-3, 3B-1
1910	6	4	1	0	0	0	0.0	0	0	1	1	0	.250	.250	4	1	C-1
1914 STL N	10	9	0	0	0	0	0.0	0	0	2	2	0	.000	.000	2	0	C-7
1915 PIT F	70	219	50	10	1	0	0.0	15	16	14		4	.228	.283	4	1	C-66
1918 NY A	1	3	1	0	0	0	0.0	0	0	0		0	.333	.333	0	0	C-1
6 yrs.	108	267	60	11	1	0	0.0	17	21	17	4	4	.225	.273	22	4	C-82, 3B-1
1 yr.	10	9	0	0	0	0	0.0	0	0	2	2	0	.000	.000	2	0	C-7
WORLD SERIES																	
1909 PIT N	1	1	0	0	0	0	0.0	0	0	0	1	0	.000	.000	1	0	

Ken O'Dea

O'DEA, JAMES KENNETH
B. Mar. 16, 1913, Lima, N. Y.
BL TR 6'   180 lbs.

	G	AB	H	2B	3B	HR	HR%	R	RBI	BB	SO	SB	BA	SA	AB	H	G by POS
1935 CHI N	76	202	52	13	2	6	3.0	30	38	26	18	0	.257	.431	9	1	C-63
1936	80	189	58	10	3	2	1.1	36	38	38	18	0	.307	.423	22	7	C-55
1937	83	219	66	7	5	4	1.8	31	32	24	26	1	.301	.434	13	3	C-64
1938	86	247	65	12	1	3	1.2	22	33	12	18	1	.263	.356	13	2	C-71
1939 NY N	52	97	17	1	0	3	3.1	7	11	10	16	0	.175	.278	26	3	C-30
1940	48	96	23	4	1	0	0.0	9	12	16	15	0	.240	.302	14	2	C-31
1941	59	89	19	5	1	3	3.4	13	17	8	20	0	.213	.393	42	9	C-14

	G	AB	H	2B	3B	HR	HR %	R	RBI	BB	SO	SB	BA	SA	Pinch Hit AB	H	G by POS

Ken O'Dea continued

	G	AB	H	2B	3B	HR	HR %	R	RBI	BB	SO	SB	BA	SA	PH AB	PH H	G by POS
1942 STL N	58	192	45	7	1	5	2.6	22	32	17	23	0	.234	.359	9	1	C-49
1943	71	203	57	11	2	3	1.5	15	25	19	25	0	.281	.399	14	4	C-56
1944	85	265	66	11	2	6	2.3	35	37	37	29	1	.249	.374	14	4	C-69
1945	100	307	78	18	2	4	1.3	36	43	50	31	0	.254	.365	8	0	C-91
1946 2 teams	STL	N	(22G –	.123)		BOS	N	(12G –	.219)								
" Total	34	89	14	2	0	1	1.1	6	5	16	12	0	.157	.213	0	0	C-34
12 yrs.	832	2195	560	101	20	40	1.8	262	323	273	251	3	.255	.374	184	36	C-627
5 yrs.	336	1024	253	49	7	19	1.9	110	140	131	116	1	.247	.364	45	9	C-287
WORLD SERIES																	
1935 CHI N	1	1	1	0	0	0	0.0	0	1	0	0	0	1.000	1.000	1	1	
1938	3	5	1	0	0	1	20.0	1	2	1	0	0	.200	.800	2	0	C-1
1942 STL N	1	1	1	0	0	0	0.0	0	1	0	0	0	1.000	1.000	1	1	
1943	2	3	2	0	0	0	0.0	0	0	0	0	0	.667	.667	1	0	C-1
1944	3	3	1	0	0	0	0.0	0	2	0	0	0	.333	.333	3	1	
5 yrs.	10	13	6	0	0	1	7.7	1	6	1	0	0	.462	.692	8	3	C-2

3rd 1st

Bob O'Farrell

O'FARRELL, ROBERT ARTHUR
B. Oct. 19, 1896, Waukegan, Ill.
Manager 1927, 1934.

BR TR 5'9½" 180 lbs.

	G	AB	H	2B	3B	HR	HR %	R	RBI	BB	SO	SB	BA	SA	PH AB	PH H	G by POS
1915 CHI N	2	3	1	0	0	0	0.0	0	0	0	0	0	.333	.333	0	0	C-2
1916	1	0	0	0	0	0	–	0	0	0	0	0	–	–	0	0	C-1
1917	3	8	3	2	0	0	0.0	1	1	1	0	1	.375	.625	0	0	C-3
1918	52	113	32	7	3	1	0.9	9	14	10	15	0	.283	.425	7	2	C-45
1919	49	125	27	4	2	0	0.0	11	9	7	10	2	.216	.280	9	1	C-38
1920	94	270	67	11	4	3	1.1	29	19	34	23	1	.248	.352	8	0	C-86
1921	96	260	65	12	7	4	1.5	32	32	18	14	2	.250	.396	6	1	C-90
1922	128	392	127	18	8	4	1.0	68	60	79	34	5	.324	.441	2	1	C-125
1923	131	452	144	25	4	12	2.7	73	84	67	38	10	.319	.471	6	3	C-124
1924	71	183	44	6	2	3	1.6	25	28	30	13	2	.240	.344	10	3	C-57
1925 2 teams	CHI	N	(17G –	.182)		STL	N	(94G –	.278)								
" Total	111	339	92	13	3	3	0.9	39	35	48	31	0	.271	.354	14	4	C-95
1926 STL N	147	492	144	30	9	7	1.4	63	68	61	44	1	.293	.433	1	1	C-146
1927	61	178	47	10	1	0	0.0	19	18	23	22	3	.264	.331	6	2	C-53
1928 2 teams	STL	N	(16G –	.212)		NY	N	(75G –	.195)								
" Total	91	185	37	7	0	2	1.1	29	24	47	25	4	.200	.270	1	1	C-77
1929 NY N	91	248	76	14	3	4	1.6	35	42	28	30	3	.306	.435	4	2	C-84
1930	94	249	75	16	4	4	1.6	37	54	31	21	1	.301	.446	23	6	C-69
1931	85	174	39	8	3	1	0.6	11	19	21	23	0	.224	.322	5	0	C-80
1932	50	67	16	3	0	0	0.0	7	8	11	10	0	.239	.284	5	1	C-41
1933 STL N	55	163	39	4	2	2	1.2	16	20	15	25	0	.239	.325	4	1	C-50
1934 2 teams	CIN	N	(44G –	.244)		CHI	N	(22G –	.224)								
" Total	66	190	45	11	3	1	0.5	13	14	14	30	0	.237	.342	2	0	C-64
1935 STL N	14	10	0	0	0	0	0.0	0	0	2	0	0	.000	.000	4	0	C-8
21 yrs.	1492	4101	1120	201	58	51	1.2	517	549	547	408	35	.273	.388	125	29	C-1338
6 yrs.	387	1212	329	58	14	12	1.0	141	142	160	126	6	.271	.372	17	4	C-363
WORLD SERIES																	
1918 CHI N	3	3	0	0	0	0	0.0	0	0	0	0	0	.000	.000	3	0	C-1
1926 STL N	7	23	7	1	0	0	0.0	2	2	2	2	0	.304	.348	0	0	C-7
2 yrs.	10	26	7	1	0	0	0.0	2	2	2	2	0	.269	.308	3	0	C-8

Brusie Ogrodowski

OGRODOWSKI, AMBROSE FRANCIS
B. Feb. 17, 1912, Hoytville, Pa.   D. Mar. 5, 1956, San Francisco, Calif.

BR TR 5'11" 175 lbs.

	G	AB	H	2B	3B	HR	HR %	R	RBI	BB	SO	SB	BA	SA	PH AB	PH H	G by POS
1936 STL N	94	237	54	15	1	1	0.4	28	20	10	20	0	.228	.312	9	1	C-85
1937	90	279	65	10	3	3	1.1	37	31	11	17	2	.233	.323	3	2	C-87
2 yrs.	184	516	119	25	4	4	0.8	65	51	21	37	2	.231	.318	12	3	C-172
2 yrs.	184	516	119	25	4	4	0.8	65	51	21	37	2	.231	.318	12	3	C-172

Bill O'Hara

O'HARA, WILLIAM ALEXANDER
B. Aug. 14, 1883, Toronto, Ont., Canada   D. June 15, 1931, Jersey City, N. J.

BL

	G	AB	H	2B	3B	HR	HR %	R	RBI	BB	SO	SB	BA	SA	PH AB	PH H	G by POS
1909 NY N	115	360	85	9	3	1	0.3	48	30	41		31	.236	.286	0	0	OF-115
1910 STL N	9	20	3	0	0	0	0.0	1	2	1		0	.150	.150	3	0	OF-4, 1B-1
2 yrs.	124	380	88	9	3	1	0.3	49	32	42		31	.232	.279	3	0	OF-119, 1B-1
1 yr.	9	20	3	0	0	0	0.0	1	2	1		0	.150	.150	3	0	OF-4, 1B-1

Tom O'Hara

O'HARA, THOMAS F.
B. July 13, 1885, Waverly, N. Y.   D. June 8, 1954, Denver, Colo.

	G	AB	H	2B	3B	HR	HR %	R	RBI	BB	SO	SB	BA	SA	PH AB	PH H	G by POS
1906 STL N	14	53	16	1	0	0	0.0	8	0	3		3	.302	.321	0	0	OF-14
1907	48	173	41	2	1	0	0.0	11	5	12		1	.237	.260	1	0	OF-47
2 yrs.	62	226	57	3	1	0	0.0	19	5	15		4	.252	.274	1	0	OF-61
2 yrs.	62	226	57	3	1	0	0.0	19	5	15		4	.252	.274	1	0	OF-61

Charley O'Leary

O'LEARY, CHARLES TIMOTHY
B. Oct. 15, 1881, Chicago, Ill.   D. Jan. 6, 1941, Chicago, Ill.

BR TR 5'7" 165 lbs.

	G	AB	H	2B	3B	HR	HR %	R	RBI	BB	SO	SB	BA	SA	PH AB	PH H	G by POS
1904 DET A	135	456	97	10	3	1	0.2	39	16	21		9	.213	.254	0	0	SS-135
1905	148	512	109	13	1	1	0.2	47	33	29		13	.213	.248	0	0	SS-148
1906	128	443	97	13	2	2	0.5	34	34	17		8	.219	.271	1	1	SS-127
1907	139	465	112	19	1	0	0.0	61	34	32		11	.241	.286	1	0	SS-138
1908	65	211	53	9	3	0	0.0	21	17	9		4	.251	.322	0	0	SS-64, 2B-1
1909	76	261	53	10	0	0	0.0	29	13	6		9	.203	.241	0	0	3B-54, 2B-15, SS-4, OF-2
1910	65	211	51	7	1	0	0.0	23	9	9		7	.242	.284	2	0	2B-38, SS-16, 3B-6
1911	74	256	68	8	2	0	0.0	29	25	11		10	.266	.313	0	0	2B-67, 3B-6

	G	AB	H	2B	3B	HR	HR %	R	RBI	BB	SO	SB	BA	SA	Pinch Hit AB	Pinch Hit H	G by POS

Charley O'Leary continued

	G	AB	H	2B	3B	HR	HR %	R	RBI	BB	SO	SB	BA	SA	PH AB	PH H	G by POS
1912	3	10	2	0	0	0	0.0	1	1	0		0	.200	.200	0	0	2B-3
1913 STL N	120	404	88	15	5	0	0.0	32	31	20	34	3	.218	.280	1	0	SS-102, 2B-15
1934 STL A	1	1	1	0	0	0	0.0	1	0	0	0	0	1.000	1.000	1	1	
11 yrs.	954	3230	731	104	18	4	0.1	317	213	164	34	74	.226	.273	6	2	SS-734, 2B-139, 3B-66, OF-2
1 yr.	120	404	88	15	5	0	0.0	32	31	20	34	3	.218	.280	1	0	SS-102, 2B-15
WORLD SERIES																	
1907 DET A	5	17	1	0	0	0	0.0	0	0	1	3	0	.059	.059	0	0	SS-5
1908	5	19	3	0	0	0	0.0	2	0	0	3	0	.158	.158	0	0	SS-5
1909	1	3	0	0	0	0	0.0	0	0	0	0	0	.000	.000	0	0	3B-1
3 yrs.	11	39	4	0	0	0	0.0	2	0	1	6	0	.103	.103	0	0	SS-10, 3B-1

Ed Olivares

OLIVARES, EDWARD BALZAC
B. Nov. 5, 1938, Mayaguez, Puerto Rico   BR TR 5'11"   180 lbs.

	G	AB	H	2B	3B	HR	HR %	R	RBI	BB	SO	SB	BA	SA	PH AB	PH H	G by POS
1960 STL N	3	5	0	0	0	0	0.0	0	0	0	3	0	.000	.000	2	0	2B-1
1961	21	30	5	0	0	0	0.0	2	1	0	4	1	.167	.167	11	1	OF-10
2 yrs.	24	35	5	0	0	0	0.0	2	1	0	7	1	.143	.143	13	1	OF-10, 2B-1
2 yrs.	24	35	5	0	0	0	0.0	2	1	0	7	1	.143	.143	13	1	OF-10, 2B-1

Gene Oliver

OLIVER, EUGENE GEORGE
B. Mar. 22, 1936, Moline, Ill.   BR TR 6'2"   225 lbs.

	G	AB	H	2B	3B	HR	HR %	R	RBI	BB	SO	SB	BA	SA	PH AB	PH H	G by POS
1959 STL N	68	172	42	9	0	6	3.5	14	28	7	41	3	.244	.401	18	4	OF-42, C-9, 1B-5
1961	22	52	14	2	0	4	7.7	8	9	6	10	0	.269	.538	5	1	C-15, OF-1
1962	122	345	89	19	1	14	4.1	42	45	50	59	5	.258	.441	19	6	C-98, OF-8, 1B-3
1963 2 teams	STL N (39G – .225) MIL N (95G – .250)																
" Total	134	398	97	16	2	17	4.3	44	65	40	78	4	.244	.422	16	2	1B-55, C-37, OF-35
1964 MIL N	93	279	77	15	1	13	4.7	45	49	17	41	3	.276	.477	23	3	1B-76, C-1
1965	122	392	106	20	0	21	5.4	56	58	36	61	5	.270	.482	12	3	C-64, 1B-52, OF-1
1966 ATL N	76	191	37	9	1	8	4.2	19	24	16	43	2	.194	.377	24	5	C-48, 1B-5, OF-2
1967 2 teams	ATL N (17G – .196) PHI N (85G – .224)																
" Total	102	314	69	18	0	10	3.2	37	40	35	64	2	.220	.373	11	0	C-93, 1B-2
1968 2 teams	BOS A (16G – .143) CHI N (8G – .364)																
" Total	24	46	9	0	0	0	0.0	3	2	7	14	0	.196	.196	10	3	C-11, OF-2, 1B-2
1969 CHI N	23	27	6	3	0	0	0.0	0	0	1	9	0	.222	.333	14	4	C-6
10 yrs.	786	2216	546	111	5	93	4.2	268	320	215	420	24	.246	.427	152	31	C-382, 1B-200, OF-91
4 yrs.	251	671	168	34	1	30	4.5	74	100	76	129	8	.250	.438	51	12	C-157, OF-51, 1B-8

Dennie O'Neil

O'NEIL, DENNIS
B. 1861, Ireland   Deceased.

	G	AB	H	2B	3B	HR	HR %	R	RBI	BB	SO	SB	BA	SA	PH AB	PH H	G by POS
1893 STL N	7	25	3	0	0	0	0.0	3	2	4		3	.120	.120	0	0	1B-7

Jack O'Neill

O'NEILL, JOHN JOSEPH
Brother of Jim O'Neill.   Brother of Steve O'Neill.
Brother of Mike O'Neill.
B. Jan. 10, 1873, Maam, Ireland   D. June 29, 1935, Scranton, Pa.   BR TR 5'10"   165 lbs.

	G	AB	H	2B	3B	HR	HR %	R	RBI	BB	SO	SB	BA	SA	PH AB	PH H	G by POS
1902 STL N	63	192	27	1	1	0	0.0	13	12	13		2	.141	.156	4	0	C-59
1903	75	246	58	9	1	0	0.0	23	27	13		11	.236	.280	1	0	C-74
1904 CHI N	51	168	36	5	0	1	0.6	8	19	6		1	.214	.262	2	0	C-49
1905	53	172	34	4	2	0	0.0	16	12	8		6	.198	.244	3	0	C-50
1906 BOS N	61	167	30	5	1	0	0.0	14	4	12		0	.180	.222	7	2	C-48, 1B-2, OF-1
5 yrs.	303	945	185	24	5	1	0.1	74	74	52		20	.196	.235	17	2	C-280, 1B-2, OF-1
2 yrs.	138	438	85	10	2	0	0.0	36	39	26		13	.194	.226	5	0	C-133

Mike O'Neill

O'NEILL, MICHAEL JOYCE
Played as Mike Joyce 1901.   Brother of Jim O'Neill.
Brother of Jack O'Neill.   Brother of Steve O'Neill.
B. Sept. 7, 1877, Galway, Ireland   D. Aug. 12, 1959, Scranton, Pa.   BL TL 5'11"   185 lbs.

	G	AB	H	2B	3B	HR	HR %	R	RBI	BB	SO	SB	BA	SA	PH AB	PH H	G by POS
1901 STL N	6	15	6	0	0	0	0.0	3	2	3		0	.400	.400	1	1	P-5
1902	51	135	43	5	3	2	1.5	21	15	2		0	.319	.444	12	1	P-36, OF-3
1903	41	110	25	2	2	0	0.0	12	6	8		3	.227	.282	7	3	P-19, OF-13
1904	30	91	21	7	2	0	0.0	9	16	5		0	.231	.352	2	1	P-25, OF-3
1907 CIN N	9	29	2	0	2	0	0.0	5	2	2		1	.069	.207	0	0	OF-9
5 yrs.	137	380	97	14	9	2	0.5	50	41	20		4	.255	.355	22	6	P-85, OF-28
4 yrs.	128	351	95	14	7	2	0.6	45	39	18		3	.271	.368	22	6	P-85, OF-19

Joe Orengo

ORENGO, JOSEPH CHARLES
B. Nov. 29, 1914, San Francisco, Calif.   BR TR 6'   185 lbs.

	G	AB	H	2B	3B	HR	HR %	R	RBI	BB	SO	SB	BA	SA	PH AB	PH H	G by POS
1939 STL N	7	3	0	0	0	0	0.0	0	0	0	1	0	.000	.000	0	0	SS-7
1940	129	415	119	23	4	7	1.7	58	56	65	90	9	.287	.412	0	0	2B-77, 3B-34, SS-19
1941 NY N	77	252	54	11	2	4	1.6	23	25	28	49	1	.214	.321	3	1	3B-59, SS-9, 2B-6
1943 2 teams	NY N (83G – .218) BKN N (7G – .200)																
" Total	90	281	61	10	2	6	2.1	29	30	40	48	1	.217	.331	2	2	1B-82, 3B-6
1944 DET A	46	154	31	10	0	0	0.0	14	10	20	29	1	.201	.266	1	0	SS-29, 3B-11, 1B-5, 2B-2
1945 CHI A	17	15	1	0	0	0	0.0	5	1	3	2	0	.067	.067	5	0	3B-7, 2B-1
6 yrs.	366	1120	266	54	8	17	1.5	129	122	156	219	12	.238	.346	11	3	3B-117, 1B-87, 2B-86, SS-64
2 yrs.	136	418	119	23	4	7	1.7	58	56	65	91	9	.285	.409	0	0	2B-77, 3B-34, SS-26

Charlie O'Rourke

O'ROURKE, JAMES PATRICK
B. June 22, 1937, Walla Walla, Wash.   BR TR 6'2"   195 lbs.

	G	AB	H	2B	3B	HR	HR %	R	RBI	BB	SO	SB	BA	SA	PH AB	PH H	G by POS
1959 STL N	2	2	0	0	0	0	0.0	0	0	0	0	0	.000	.000	2	0	

	G	AB	H	2B	3B	HR	HR %	R	RBI	BB	SO	SB	BA	SA	Pinch Hit AB	Pinch Hit H	G by POS

Patsy O'Rourke

O'ROURKE, JOSEPH LEO, SR.
Father of Joe O'Rourke.
B. Apr. 13, 1881, Philadelphia, Pa.   D. Apr. 18, 1956, Philadelphia, Pa.
BR TR 5'7" 160 lbs.

	G	AB	H	2B	3B	HR	HR %	R	RBI	BB	SO	SB	BA	SA	PH AB	PH H	G by POS
1908 STL N	53	164	32	4	2	0	0.0	8	16	14		2	.195	.244	0	0	SS-53

Tim O'Rourke

O'ROURKE, TIMOTHY PATRICK (Voiceless Tim)
B. May 18, 1864, Chicago, Ill.   D. Apr. 20, 1938, Seattle, Wash.
TR

	G	AB	H	2B	3B	HR	HR %	R	RBI	BB	SO	SB	BA	SA	PH AB	PH H	G by POS
1890 SYR AA	87	332	94	13	6	1	0.3	48		36		22	.283	.367	0	0	3B-87
1891 COL AA	34	136	38	1	3	0	0.0	22	12	15	7	9	.279	.331	0	0	3B-34
1892 BAL N	63	239	74	8	4	0	0.0	40	35	24	19	12	.310	.377	0	0	SS-58, OF-4, 3B-1
1893 2 teams			BAL N	(31G –	.363)			LOU N	(92G –	.281)							
" Total	123	487	148	12	5	0	0.0	102	72	89	19	27	.304	.349	0	0	SS-61, OF-51, 3B-11
1894 3 teams			LOU N	(55G –	.277)			STL N	(18G –	.282)		WAS N	(7G –	.200)			
" Total	80	316	86	9	5	0	0.0	60	39	33	13	11	.272	.332	0	0	1B-30, 3B-21, OF-18, SS-6, 2B-5
5 yrs.	387	1510	440	43	23	1	0.1	272	157	197	58	81	.291	.352	0	0	3B-154, SS-125, OF-73, 1B-30, 2B-5
1 yr.	18	71	20	4	1	0	0.0	10	10	8	3	2	.282	.366	0	0	3B-18

Ernie Orsatti

ORSATTI, ERNESTO RALPH
B. Sept. 8, 1903, Los Angeles, Calif.   D. Sept. 4, 1968, Canoga Park, Calif.
BL TL 5'7½" 154 lbs.

	G	AB	H	2B	3B	HR	HR %	R	RBI	BB	SO	SB	BA	SA	PH AB	PH H	G by POS
1927 STL N	27	92	29	7	3	0	0.0	15	12	11	12	2	.315	.457	1	0	OF-26
1928	27	69	21	6	0	3	4.3	10	15	10	11	0	.304	.522	3	0	OF-17, 1B-5
1929	113	346	115	21	7	3	0.9	64	39	33	43	7	.332	.460	17	6	OF-77, 1B-10
1930	48	131	42	8	4	1	0.8	24	15	12	18	1	.321	.466	12	3	1B-22, OF-11
1931	78	158	46	16	6	0	0.0	27	19	14	16	1	.291	.468	15	2	OF-45, 1B-1
1932	101	375	126	27	6	2	0.5	44	44	18	29	5	.336	.456	2	0	OF-96, 1B-1
1933	120	436	130	21	6	0	0.0	55	38	33	33	14	.298	.374	9	3	OF-101, 1B-3
1934	105	337	101	14	4	0	0.0	39	31	27	31	6	.300	.365	10	2	OF-90
1935	90	221	53	9	3	1	0.5	28	24	18	25	10	.240	.321	23	5	OF-60
9 yrs.	709	2165	663	129	39	10	0.5	306	237	176	218	46	.306	.416	93	23	OF-523, 1B-42
9 yrs.	709	2165	663	129	39	10	0.5	306	237	176	218	46	.306	.416	93	23	OF-523, 1B-42

WORLD SERIES

	G	AB	H	2B	3B	HR	HR %	R	RBI	BB	SO	SB	BA	SA	PH AB	PH H	G by POS
1928 STL N	4	7	2	1	0	0	0.0	1		1	3	0	.286	.429	2	0	OF-1
1930	1	1	0	0	0	0	0.0	0		0	0	0	.000	.000	1	0	
1931	1	3	0	0	0	0	0.0	0	0	0	3	0	.000	.000	0	0	OF-1
1934	7	22	7	0	1	0	0.0	3	2	3	1	0	.318	.409	1	0	OF-6
4 yrs.	13	33	9	1	1	0	0.0	4	2	4	7	0	.273	.364	4	0	OF-8

Champ Osteen

OSTEEN, JAMES CHAMPLIN
B. Feb. 24, 1877, Hendersonville, N.C.   D. Dec. 14, 1962, Greenville, S.C.
BL TR 5'8" 150 lbs.

	G	AB	H	2B	3B	HR	HR %	R	RBI	BB	SO	SB	BA	SA	PH AB	PH H	G by POS
1903 WAS A	10	40	8	0	2	0	0.0	4	4	2		0	.200	.300	0	0	SS-10
1904 NY A	28	107	21	1	4	2	1.9	15	9	1		0	.196	.336	0	0	3B-17, SS-8, 1B-4
1908 STL N	29	112	22	4	0	0	0.0	2	11	0		0	.196	.232	0	0	SS-17, 3B-12
1909	16	45	9	1	0	0	0.0	6	7	7		1	.200	.222	0	0	SS-16
4 yrs.	83	304	60	6	6	2	0.7	27	31	10		1	.197	.276	0	0	SS-51, 3B-29, 1B-4
2 yrs.	45	157	31	5	0	0	0.0	8	18	7		1	.197	.229	0	0	SS-33, 3B-12

Joe Otten

OTTEN, JOSEPH G.
B. Murphysboro, Ill.   Deceased.

	G	AB	H	2B	3B	HR	HR %	R	RBI	BB	SO	SB	BA	SA	PH AB	PH H	G by POS
1895 STL N	26	87	21	0	0	0	0.0	8	8	5	8	2	.241	.241	0	0	C-24, OF-2

Mickey Owen

OWEN, ARNOLD MALCOLM
B. Apr. 4, 1916, Nixa, Mo.
BR TR 5'10" 190 lbs.

	G	AB	H	2B	3B	HR	HR %	R	RBI	BB	SO	SB	BA	SA	PH AB	PH H	G by POS
1937 STL N	80	234	54	4	2	0	0.0	17	20	15	13	1	.231	.265	2	0	C-78
1938	122	397	106	25	2	4	1.0	45	36	32	14	2	.267	.370	5	1	C-116
1939	131	344	89	18	2	3	0.9	32	35	43	28	6	.259	.349	5	0	C-126
1940	117	307	81	16	2	0	0.0	27	27	34	13	4	.264	.329	4	2	C-113
1941 BKN N	128	386	89	15	2	1	0.3	32	44	34	14	1	.231	.288	0	0	C-128
1942	133	421	109	16	3	0	0.0	53	44	44	17	10	.259	.311	0	0	C-133
1943	106	365	95	11	2	0	0.0	31	54	25	15	4	.260	.301	5	1	C-100, 3B-3, SS-1
1944	130	461	126	20	3	1	0.2	43	42	36	17	4	.273	.336	4	1	C-125, 2B-1
1945	24	84	24	9	0	0	0.0	5	11	10	2	0	.286	.393	0	0	C-24
1949 CHI N	62	198	54	9	3	2	1.0	15	18	12	13	1	.273	.379	3	0	C-59
1950	86	259	63	11	0	2	0.8	22	21	13	16	2	.243	.309	1	0	C-86
1951	58	125	23	6	0	0	0.0	10	15	19	13	1	.184	.232	1	0	C-57
1954 BOS A	32	68	16	3	0	1	1.5	6	11	9	6	0	.235	.324	1	1	C-30
13 yrs.	1209	3649	929	163	21	14	0.4	338	378	326	181	36	.255	.322	31	7	C-1175, 3B-3, SS-1, 2B-1
4 yrs.	450	1282	330	63	8	7	0.5	121	118	124	68	13	.257	.335	16	3	C-433

WORLD SERIES

	G	AB	H	2B	3B	HR	HR %	R	RBI	BB	SO	SB	BA	SA	PH AB	PH H	G by POS
1941 BKN N	5	12	2	0	1	0	0.0	1	2	3	0	0	.167	.333	0	0	C-5

Dick Padden

PADDEN, RICHARD J.
B. Sept. 17, 1870, Martins Ferry, Ohio   D. Oct. 31, 1922, Martins Ferry, Ohio
BR TR

	G	AB	H	2B	3B	HR	HR %	R	RBI	BB	SO	SB	BA	SA	PH AB	PH H	G by POS
1896 PIT N	61	219	53	4	8	2	0.9	33	24	14	9	8	.242	.361	0	0	2B-61
1897	134	517	146	16	10	2	0.4	84	58	38		18	.282	.364	0	0	2B-134
1898	128	463	119	7	6	2	0.4	61	43	35		11	.257	.311	0	0	2B-128
1899 WAS N	134	451	125	20	7	2	0.4	66	61	24		27	.277	.366	1	1	SS-85, 2B-48
1901 STL N	123	489	125	17	7	2	0.4	71	62	31		26	.256	.331	0	0	2B-115, SS-8
1902 STL A	117	413	109	26	3	1	0.2	54	40	30		11	.264	.349	0	0	2B-117
1903	29	94	19	3	0	0	0.0	7	6	9		5	.202	.234	0	0	2B-29
1904	132	453	108	19	4	0	0.0	42	36	40		23	.238	.298	0	0	2B-132
1905	16	58	10	1	1	0	0.0	5	4	3		1	.172	.224	0	0	2B-16

	G	AB	H	2B	3B	HR	HR %	R	RBI	BB	SO	SB	BA	SA	Pinch Hit AB	Pinch Hit H	G by POS

Dick Padden continued

	G	AB	H	2B	3B	HR	HR %	R	RBI	BB	SO	SB	BA	SA	PH AB	PH H	G by POS
9 yrs.	874	3157	814	113	46	11	0.3	423	334	224		9	132	.258	.333	1	1	2B-780, SS-93
1 yr.	123	489	125	17	7	2	0.4	71	62	31			26	.256	.331	0	0	2B-115, SS-8

Don Padgett

PADGETT, DON WILSON (Red)
B. Dec. 5, 1911, Caroleen, N. C.　　D. Dec. 9, 1980, High Point, N. C.　　BL TR 6'　190 lbs.

	G	AB	H	2B	3B	HR	HR %	R	RBI	BB	SO	SB	BA	SA	PH AB	PH H	G by POS
1937 STL N	123	446	140	22	6	10	2.2	62	74	30	43	4	.314	.457	13	4	OF-109
1938	110	388	105	26	5	8	2.1	59	65	18	28	0	.271	.425	18	6	OF-71, 1B-16, C-6
1939	92	233	93	15	3	5	2.1	38	53	18	11	1	.399	.554	21	4	C-61, 1B-6
1940	93	240	58	15	1	6	2.5	24	41	26	14	1	.242	.388	16	3	C-72, 1B-2
1941	107	324	80	18	0	5	1.5	39	44	21	16	0	.247	.349	22	3	OF-62, C-18, 1B-2
1946 2 teams		BKN	N	(19G – .167)		BOS	N	(44G – .255)									
" Total	63	128	30	4	0	3	2.3	8	30	9	11	0	.234	.336	27	4	C-36
1947 PHI N	75	158	50	8	1	0	0.0	14	24	16	5	0	.316	.380	31	8	C-39
1948	36	74	17	3	0	0	0.0	3	7	3	2	0	.230	.270	13	2	C-19
8 yrs.	699	1991	573	111	16	37	1.9	247	338	141	130	6	.288	.415	161	34	C-251, OF-242, 1B-26
5 yrs.	525	1631	476	96	15	34	2.1	222	277	113	112	6	.292	.432	90	20	OF-242, C-157, 1B-26

Stan Papi

PAPI, STANLEY GERARD
B. Feb. 4, 1951, Fresno, Calif.　　BR TR 6'　170 lbs.

	G	AB	H	2B	3B	HR	HR %	R	RBI	BB	SO	SB	BA	SA	PH AB	PH H	G by POS
1974 STL N	8	4	1	0	0	0	0.0	0	1	0	0	0	.250	.250	1	0	SS-7, 2B-1
1977 MON N	13	43	10	2	1	0	0.0	5	4	1	9	.1	.233	.326	0	0	3B-10, SS-2, 2B-1
1978	67	152	35	11	0	0	0.0	15	11	10	28	0	.230	.303	24	3	SS-22, 3B-15, 2B-5
1979 BOS A	50	117	22	8	0	1	0.9	9	6	5	20	0	.188	.282	3	0	2B-26, SS-21
1980 2 teams		BOS	A	(1G – .000)		DET	A	(46G – .237)									
" Total	47	114	27	3	4	3	2.6	12	17	5	24	0	.237	.412	4	1	2B-31, 3B-12, SS-5, 1B-1
1981 DET A	40	93	19	2	1	3	3.2	8	12	3	18	1	.204	.344	4	1	3B-32, OF-1, 2B-1, 1B-1
6 yrs.	225	523	114	26	6	7	1.3	49	51	24	99	2	.218	.331	36	5	3B-69, 2B-65, SS-57, 1B-2, OF-1
1 yr.	8	4	1	0	0	0	0.0	0	1	0	0	0	.250	.250	1	0	SS-7, 2B-1

Freddy Parent

PARENT, FREDERICK ALFRED
B. Nov. 25, 1875, Biddeford, Me.　　D. Nov. 2, 1972, Sanford, Me.　　BR TR 5'5½"　148 lbs.

	G	AB	H	2B	3B	HR	HR %	R	RBI	BB	SO	SB	BA	SA	PH AB	PH H	G by POS
1899 STL N	2	8	1	0	0	0	0.0	0	1	0		0	.125	.125	0	0	2B-2
1901 BOS A	138	517	158	23	9	4	0.8	87	59	41		16	.306	.408	0	0	SS-138
1902	138	567	156	31	8	3	0.5	91	62	24		16	.275	.374	0	0	SS-138
1903	139	560	170	31	17	4	0.7	83	80	13		24	.304	.441	0	0	SS-139
1904	155	591	172	22	9	6	1.0	85	77	28		20	.291	.389	0	0	SS-155
1905	153	602	141	16	5	0	0.0	55	33	47		25	.234	.277	0	0	SS-153
1906	149	600	141	14	10	1	0.2	67	49	31		16	.235	.297	0	0	SS-143, 2B-6
1907	114	409	113	19	5	1	0.2	51	26	22		12	.276	.355	12	2	OF-47, SS-43, 3B-7, 2B-5
1908 CHI A	119	391	81	7	5	0	0.0	28	35	50		9	.207	.251	0	0	SS-118
1909	136	472	123	10	5	0	0.0	61	30	46		32	.261	.303	0	0	SS-98, OF-37, 2B-1
1910	81	258	46	6	1	1	0.4	23	16	29		14	.178	.221	0	0	OF-62, 2B-11, SS-4, 3B-1
1911	3	9	4	1	0	0	0.0	2	3	2		0	.444	.556	0	0	2B-3
12 yrs.	1327	4984	1306	180	74	20	0.4	633	471	333		184	.262	.340	12	2	SS-1129, OF-146, 2B-28, 3B-8
1 yr.	2	8	1	0	0	0	0.0	0	1	0		0	.125	.125	0	0	2B-2

WORLD SERIES

	G	AB	H	2B	3B	HR	HR %	R	RBI	BB	SO	SB	BA	SA	PH AB	PH H	G by POS
1903 BOS A	8	32	9	0	3	0	0.0	8	3	1	1	0	.281	.469	0	0	SS-8
					4th												

Kelly Paris

PARIS, KELLY JAY
B. Oct. 17, 1957, Encino, Calif.　　BB TR 6'　175 lbs.

	G	AB	H	2B	3B	HR	HR %	R	RBI	BB	SO	SB	BA	SA	PH AB	PH H	G by POS
1982 STL N	12	29	3	0	0	0	0.0	1	1	0	7	0	.103	.103	3	1	3B-5, SS-4

Tom Parrott

PARROTT, THOMAS WILLIAM (Tacky Tom)
Brother of Jiggs Parrott.
B. Apr. 10, 1868, Portland, Ore.　　D. Jan. 1, 1932, Newberg, Ore.　　BR TR 5'10½"　170 lbs.

	G	AB	H	2B	3B	HR	HR %	R	RBI	BB	SO	SB	BA	SA	PH AB	PH H	G by POS
1893 2 teams		CHI	N	(7G – .259)		CIN	N	(24G – .191)									
" Total	31	95	20	2	1	1	1.1	9	12	2	11	0	.211	.284	1	0	P-26, 3B-2, OF-1, 2B-1
1894 CIN N	68	229	74	12	6	4	1.7	51	40	17	10	4	.323	.480	3	2	P-41, OF-13, 1B-12, SS-1, 3B-1, 2B-1
1895	64	201	69	13	7	3	1.5	35	41	11	8	10	.343	.522	0	0	P-41, 1B-14, OF-9
1896 STL N	118	474	138	13	12	7	1.5	62	70	11	24	12	.291	.414	0	0	OF-108, P-7, 1B-6
4 yrs.	281	999	301	40	26	15	1.5	157	163	41	53	26	.301	.438	4	2	OF-131, P-115, 1B-32, 3B-3, 2B-2, SS-1
1 yr.	118	474	138	13	12	7	1.5	62	70	11	24	12	.291	.414	0	0	OF-108, P-7, 1B-6

Mike Pasquriello

PASQURIELLO, MICHAEL JOHN
B. Nov. 7, 1898, Philadelphia, Pa.　　D. Apr. 5, 1965, Bridgeport, Conn.　　BR TR 5'11"　167 lbs.

	G	AB	H	2B	3B	HR	HR %	R	RBI	BB	SO	SB	BA	SA	PH AB	PH H	G by POS
1919 2 teams		PHI	N	(1G – 1.000)		STL	N	(1G – .000)									
" Total	2	2	1	0	0	0	0.0	1	0	0	1	0	.500	.500	1	0	1B-1

Gene Paulette

PAULETTE, EUGENE EDWARD
B. May 26, 1891, Centralia, Ill.　　D. Feb. 8, 1966, Little Rock, Ark.　　BR TR 6'　150 lbs.

	G	AB	H	2B	3B	HR	HR %	R	RBI	BB	SO	SB	BA	SA	PH AB	PH H	G by POS
1911 NY N	10	12	2	0	0	0	0.0	1	1	0	1	0	.167	.167	0	0	1B-7, SS-1, 3B-1
1916 STL A	5	4	2	0	0	0	0.0	1	0	1	1	0	.500	.500	4	2	
1917 2 teams		STL	A	(12G – .182)		STL	N	(95G – .265)									
" Total	107	354	92	21	7	0	0.0	35	34	19	19	9	.260	.359	6	1	1B-98, 2B-3, 3B-1
1918 STL N	125	461	126	15	3	0	0.0	33	52	27	16	11	.273	.319	3	0	1B-97, SS-12, 2B-7, OF-6, 3B-2, P-1
1919 2 teams		STL	N	(43G – .215)		PHI	N	(67G – .259)									
" Total	110	387	94	14	3	1	0.3	31	42	28	16	14	.243	.302	3	0	2B-53, 1B-36, OF-10, SS-3

	G	AB	H	2B	3B	HR	HR %	R	RBI	BB	SO	SB	BA	SA	Pinch Hit AB	Pinch Hit H	G by POS

Gene Paulette continued

	G	AB	H	2B	3B	HR	HR%	R	RBI	BB	SO	SB	BA	SA	AB	H	G by POS
1920 PHI N	143	562	162	16	6	1	0.2	59	36	33	16	9	.288	.343	2	1	1B-139, SS-2
6 yrs.	500	1780	478	66	19	2	0.1	160	165	108	69	43	.269	.330	18	4	1B-377, 2B-63, SS-18, OF-16, 3B-4, P-1
3 yrs.	263	937	245	42	10	0	0.0	76	97	52	38	24	.261	.328	8	0	1B-225, SS-15, 2B-7, OF-6, 3B-2, P-1

George Paynter

PAYNTER, GEORGE WASHINGTON BR TR 5'9" 125 lbs.
Born George Washington Paner.
B. July 6, 1871, Cincinnati, Ohio   D. Oct. 1, 1950, Cincinnati, Ohio

	G	AB	H	2B	3B	HR	HR%	R	RBI	BB	SO	SB	BA	SA	AB	H	G by POS
1894 STL N	1	4	0	0	0	0	0.0	0		0		1	.000	.000	0	0	OF-1

Homer Peel

PEEL, HOMER HEFNER BR TR 5'9½" 170 lbs.
B. Oct. 10, 1902, Port Sullivan, Tex.

	G	AB	H	2B	3B	HR	HR%	R	RBI	BB	SO	SB	BA	SA	AB	H	G by POS
1927 STL N	2	2	0	0	0	0	0.0	0	0	0	1	0	.000	.000	1	0	OF-1
1929 PHI N	53	156	42	12	1	0	0.0	16	19	12	7	1	.269	.359	13	1	OF-39, 1B-1
1930 STL N	26	73	12	2	0	0	0.0	9	10	3	4	0	.164	.192	4	1	OF-21
1933 NY N	84	148	38	1	1	1	0.7	16	12	14	10	0	.257	.297	35	9	OF-45
1934	21	41	8	0	0	1	2.4	7	3	1	2	0	.195	.268	10	2	OF-10
5 yrs.	186	420	100	15	2	2	0.5	48	44	30	24	1	.238	.298	63	13	OF-116, 1B-1
2 yrs.	28	75	12	2	0	0	0.0	9	10	3	5	0	.160	.187	5	1	OF-22

WORLD SERIES
| 1933 NY N | 2 | 2 | 1 | 0 | 0 | 0 | 0.0 | 0 | 0 | 0 | 0 | 0 | .500 | .500 | 1 | 1 | OF-1 |

Charlie Peete

PEETE, CHARLES (Mule) BL TR 5'9½" 190 lbs.
B. Feb. 22, 1931, Franklin, Va.   D. Nov. 27, 1956, Caracas, Venezuela

	G	AB	H	2B	3B	HR	HR%	R	RBI	BB	SO	SB	BA	SA	AB	H	G by POS
1956 STL N	23	52	10	2	2	0	0.0	3	6	6	10	0	.192	.308	4	1	OF-21

Heinie Peitz

PEITZ, HENRY CLEMENT BR TR 5'11" 165 lbs.
Brother of Joe Peitz.
B. Nov. 28, 1870, St. Louis, Mo.   D. Oct. 23, 1943, Cincinnati, Ohio

	G	AB	H	2B	3B	HR	HR%	R	RBI	BB	SO	SB	BA	SA	AB	H	G by POS
1892 STL N	1	3	0	0	0	0	0.0	0	0	0	0	0	.000	.000	0	0	C-1
1893	96	362	92	12	9	1	0.3	53	45	54	20	12	.254	.345	0	0	C-74, SS-11, OF-10, 1B-5
1894	99	338	89	19	9	3	0.9	52	49	43	21	14	.263	.399	0	0	3B-47, C-39, 1B-14, P-1
1895	90	334	95	14	12	2	0.6	44	65	29	20	9	.284	.416	0	0	C-71, 1B-11, 3B-10
1896 CIN N	68	211	63	12	5	2	0.9	33	34	30	15	7	.299	.431	1	0	C-67
1897	77	266	78	11	7	1	0.4	35	44	18		3	.293	.398	4	0	C-71, P-2
1898	105	330	90	15	5	1	0.3	49	43	35		9	.273	.358	3	1	C-101
1899	93	290	79	13	2	1	0.3	45	43	45		11	.272	.341	2	0	C-91, P-1
1900	91	294	75	14	1	2	0.7	34	34	20		5	.255	.330	4	0	C-80, 1B-8
1901	82	269	82	13	5	1	0.4	24	24	23		3	.305	.401	6	4	C-49, 2B-21, 3B-6, 1B-2
1902	112	387	122	22	5	1	0.3	54	60	24		7	.315	.406	5	1	2B-48, C-47, 3B-6, 1B-6
1903	105	358	93	15	3	0	0.0	45	42	37		7	.260	.318	2	1	C-78, 1B-11, 3B-9, 2B-4
1904	84	272	66	13	2	1	0.4	32	30	14		1	.243	.316	2	1	C-64, 1B-18, 3B-1
1905 PIT N	88	278	62	10	0	0	0.0	18	27	24		2	.223	.259	2	0	C-87, 2B-1
1906	40	125	30	8	0	0	0.0	13	20	13		1	.240	.304	2	0	C-38
1913 STL N	3	4	1	0	1	0	0.0	1	0	0	0	0	.250	.750	0	0	C-2, OF-1
16 yrs.	1234	4121	1117	191	66	16	0.4	532	560	409	76	91	.271	.361	33	6	C-960, 3B-79, 1B-75, 2B-74, OF-11, SS-11, P-4
5 yrs.	289	1041	277	45	31	6	0.6	150	159	126	61	35	.266	.386	0	0	C-187, 3B-57, 1B-30, OF-11, SS-11, P-1

Joe Peitz

PEITZ, JOSEPH
Brother of Heinie Peitz.
Deceased.

	G	AB	H	2B	3B	HR	HR%	R	RBI	BB	SO	SB	BA	SA	AB	H	G by POS
1894 STL N	7	26	11	2	3	0	0.0	10	3	6		2	.423	.731	0	0	OF-7

Ray Pepper

PEPPER, RAYMOND WATSON BR TR 6'2" 195 lbs.
B. Aug. 5, 1905, Decatur, Ala.

	G	AB	H	2B	3B	HR	HR%	R	RBI	BB	SO	SB	BA	SA	AB	H	G by POS
1932 STL N	21	57	14	2	1	0	0.0	3	7	5	13	1	.246	.316	4	0	OF-17
1933	3	9	2	0	0	1	11.1	2	2	0	1	0	.222	.556	1	0	OF-2
1934 STL A	148	564	168	24	6	7	1.2	71	101	29	67	1	.298	.399	12	2	OF-136
1935	92	261	66	15	3	4	1.5	20	37	20	32	0	.253	.379	34	7	OF-57
1936	75	124	35	5	0	2	1.6	13	23	5	23	0	.282	.371	54	18	OF-18
5 yrs.	339	1015	285	46	10	14	1.4	109	170	59	136	2	.281	.387	105	27	OF-230
2 yrs.	24	66	16	2	1	1	1.5	5	9	5	14	1	.242	.348	5	0	OF-19

Ed Phelps

PHELPS, EDWARD JOSEPH BR TR 5'11" 185 lbs.
B. Mar. 3, 1879, Albany, N. Y.   D. Jan. 31, 1942, Albany, N. Y.

	G	AB	H	2B	3B	HR	HR%	R	RBI	BB	SO	SB	BA	SA	AB	H	G by POS
1902 PIT N	18	61	13	1	0	0	0.0	5	6	4		2	.213	.230	0	0	C-13, 1B-5
1903	81	273	77	7	3	2	0.7	32	31	17		2	.282	.352	1	0	C-76, 1B-3
1904	94	302	73	5	3	0	0.0	29	28	15		2	.242	.278	1	0	C-91, 1B-1
1905 CIN N	44	156	36	5	3	0	0.0	18	18	12		4	.231	.301	0	0	C-44
1906 2 teams	55		CIN N (12G – .275)			PIT N (43G – .237)											
" Total	55	158	39	3	3	1	0.6	12	17	12		3	.247	.323	2	0	C-52
1907 PIT N	43	113	24	0	0	0	0.0	11	12	9		1	.212	.221	6	0	C-35, 1B-1
1908	34	64	15	2	0	0	0.0	3	11	2		1	.234	.328	12	7	C-20
1909 STL N	100	306	76	13	1	0	0.0	43	22	39		7	.248	.297	19	3	C-82
1910	93	270	71	4	2	0	0.0	25	37	36	29	9	.263	.293	13	3	C-80
1912 BKN N	52	111	32	4	3	0	0.0	8	23	16	15	1	.288	.378	20	4	C-32
1913	15	18	4	0	0	0	0.0	0	1	2	0	1	.222	.222	10	2	C-4

	G	AB	H	2B	3B	HR	HR %	R	RBI	BB	SO	SB	BA	SA	Pinch Hit AB	H	G by POS

Ed Phelps continued

	G	AB	H	2B	3B	HR	HR %	R	RBI	BB	SO	SB	BA	SA	Pinch Hit AB	H	G by POS
11 yrs.	629	1832	460	45	20	3	0.2	186	205	163	46	31	.251	.302	84	19	C-529, 1B-10
2 yrs.	193	576	147	17	3	0	0.0	68	59	75	29	16	.255	.295	32	6	C-162

WORLD SERIES

| 1903 PIT N | 8 | 26 | 6 | 2 | 0 | 0 | 0.0 | 1 | 2 | 1 | 6 | 0 | .231 | .308 | 1 | 0 | C-7 |

Ed Phillips

PHILLIPS, HOWARD EDWARD
B. July 8, 1931, St. Louis, Mo.   BB TR 6'1"   180 lbs.

| 1953 STL N | 9 | 0 | 0 | 0 | 0 | 0 | – | 4 | 0 | 0 | 0 | 0 | – | – | 0 | 0 | |

Mike Phillips

PHILLIPS, MICHAEL DWAINE
B. Aug. 19, 1950, Beaumont, Tex.   BL TR 6'   170 lbs.

1973 SF N	63	104	25	3	4	1	1.0	18	9	6	17	0	.240	.375	5	1	3B-28, SS-20, 2B-7
1974	100	283	62	6	1	2	0.7	19	20	14	37	4	.219	.269	13	2	3B-34, 2B-30, SS-23
1975 2 teams		SF	N	(10G – .194)		NY	N	(116G – .256)									
" Total	126	414	104	10	7	1	0.2	34	29	31	51	4	.251	.316	3	0	SS-115, 2B-7, 3B-6
1976 NY N	87	262	67	4	6	4	1.5	30	29	25	29	2	.256	.363	13	3	SS-53, 2B-19, 3B-10
1977 2 teams		NY	N	(38G – .209)		STL	N	(48G – .241)									
" Total	86	173	39	5	3	1	0.6	22	12	20	36	1	.225	.306	24	0	2B-35, SS-29, 3B-14
1978 STL N	76	164	44	8	1	1	0.6	14	28	13	25	0	.268	.348	19	1	2B-55, SS-10, 3B-1
1979	44	97	22	3	1	1	1.0	10	6	10	9	0	.227	.309	1	0	SS-25, 2B-16, 3B-1
1980	63	128	30	5	0	0	0.0	13	7	9	17	0	.234	.273	9	2	SS-37, 2B-9, 3B-8
1981 2 teams		SD	N	(14G – .207)		MON	N	(34G – .218)									
" Total	48	84	18	2	1	0	0.0	6	4	5	18	1	.214	.262	5	1	SS-27, 2B-15
1982 MON N	14	8	1	0	0	0	0.0	0	1	0	3	0	.125	.125	1	0	2B-10, SS-2
10 yrs.	707	1717	412	46	24	11	0.6	166	145	133	242	12	.240	.314	93	10	SS-341, 2B-203, 3B-102
4 yrs.	231	476	117	19	4	2	0.4	54	50	41	64	1	.246	.315	38	3	2B-111, SS-77, 3B-15

DIVISIONAL PLAYOFF SERIES

| 1981 MON N | 1 | 1 | 0 | 0 | 0 | 0 | 0.0 | 0 | 0 | 0 | 0 | 0 | .000 | .000 | 0 | 0 | 2B-1 |

Bill Phyle

PHYLE, WILLIAM JOSEPH
B. June 25, 1875, Duluth, Minn.   D. Aug. 7, 1953, Los Angeles, Calif.   TR

1898 CHI N	4	9	1	0	0	0	0.0	1	0	2		0	.111	.111	0	0	P-3
1899	10	34	6	0	0	0	0.0	2	1	0		0	.176	.176	0	0	P-10
1901 NY N	25	66	12	2	0	0	0.0	8	3	2		0	.182	.212	0	0	P-24, SS-1
1906 STL N	22	73	13	3	1	0	0.0	6	4	5		2	.178	.247	0	0	3B-21
4 yrs.	61	182	32	5	1	0	0.0	17	8	9		2	.176	.214	0	0	P-37, 3B-21, SS-1
1 yr.	22	73	13	3	1	0	0.0	6	4	5		2	.178	.247	0	0	3B-21

George Pinckney

PINCKNEY, GEORGE BURTON
B. Jan. 11, 1862, Peoria, Ill.   D. Nov. 9, 1926, Peoria, Ill.   BR TR

1884 CLE N	36	144	45	9	0	0	0.0	18	16	10	7		.313	.375	0	0	2B-25, SS-11
1885 BKN AA	110	447	124	16	5	0	0.0	77		27			.277	.336	0	0	2B-57, 3B-51, SS-3
1886	141	597	156	22	7	0	0.0	119		70			.261	.322	0	0	3B-141, P-1
1887	138	580	155	26	6	3	0.5	133		61		59	.267	.348	0	0	3B-136, SS-2
1888	143	575	156	18	8	4	0.7	134	52	66		51	.271	.351	0	0	3B-143
1889	138	545	134	25	7	4	0.7	103	82	59	43	47	.246	.339	0	0	3B-138
1890 BKN N	126	485	150	20	9	7	1.4	115	83	80	19	47	.309	.431	0	0	3B-126
1891	135	501	137	19	6	2	0.4	80	71	66	32	44	.273	.347	0	0	3B-130, SS-5
1892 STL N	78	290	50	3	2	0	0.0	31	25	36	26	4	.172	.197	0	0	3B-78
1893 LOU N	118	446	105	12	6	1	0.2	64	62	50	8	12	.235	.296	0	0	3B-118
10 yrs.	1163	4610	1212	170	56	21	0.5	874	391	525	135	264	.263	.338	0	0	3B-1061, 2B-82, SS-21, P-1
1 yr.	78	290	50	3	2	0	0.0	31	25	36	26	4	.172	.197	0	0	3B-78

Vada Pinson

PINSON, VADA EDWARD
B. Aug. 8, 1938, Memphis, Tenn.   BL TL 5'11"   170 lbs.

1958 CIN N	27	96	26	7	0	1	1.0	20	8	11	18	2	.271	.375	0	0	OF-27
1959	154	648	205	47	9	20	3.1	131	84	55	98	21	.316	.509	0	0	OF-154
1960	154	652	187	37	12	20	3.1	107	61	47	96	32	.287	.472	0	0	OF-154
1961	154	607	208	34	8	16	2.6	101	87	39	63	23	.343	.504	1	1	OF-153
1962	155	619	181	31	7	23	3.7	107	100	45	68	26	.292	.477	3	1	OF-152
1963	162	652	204	37	14	22	3.4	96	106	36	80	27	.313	.514	0	0	OF-162
1964	156	625	166	23	11	23	3.7	99	84	42	99	8	.266	.448	1	0	OF-156
1965	159	669	204	34	10	22	3.3	97	94	43	81	21	.305	.484	0	0	OF-159
1966	156	618	178	35	6	16	2.6	70	76	33	83	18	.288	.442	3	2	OF-154
1967	158	650	187	28	13	18	2.8	90	66	26	86	26	.288	.454	1	0	OF-157
1968	130	499	135	29	6	5	1.0	60	48	32	59	17	.271	.383	10	2	OF-123
1969 STL N	132	495	126	22	6	10	2.0	58	70	35	63	4	.255	.384	8	1	OF-124
1970 CLE A	148	574	164	28	6	24	4.2	74	82	28	69	7	.286	.481	8	1	OF-141, 1B-7
1971	146	566	149	23	4	11	1.9	60	35	21	58	25	.263	.376	7	2	OF-141, 1B-3
1972 CAL A	136	484	133	24	2	7	1.4	56	49	30	54	17	.275	.376	7	1	OF-134, 1B-1
1973	124	466	121	14	6	8	1.7	56	57	20	55	5	.260	.367	4	1	OF-120
1974 KC A	115	406	112	18	6	6	1.5	46	41	21	45	21	.276	.374	9	3	OF-110, 1B-1
1975	103	319	71	14	5	4	1.3	38	22	10	21	5	.223	.335	17	2	OF-82, 1B-4
18 yrs.	2469	9645	2757	485	127	256	2.7	1366	1170	574	1196	305	.286	.442	80	17	OF-2403, 1B-16
1 yr.	132	495	126	22	6	10	2.0	58	70	35	63	4	.255	.384	8	1	OF-124

WORLD SERIES

| 1961 CIN N | 5 | 22 | 2 | 1 | 0 | 0 | 0.0 | 0 | 0 | 0 | 1 | 0 | .091 | .136 | 0 | 0 | OF-5 |

	G	AB	H	2B	3B	HR	HR %	R	RBI	BB	SO	SB	BA	SA	Pinch Hit AB	Pinch Hit H	G by POS

Darrell Porter

PORTER, DARRELL RAY
B. Jan. 17, 1952, Joplin, Mo.   BL TR 6'   193 lbs.

	G	AB	H	2B	3B	HR	HR %	R	RBI	BB	SO	SB	BA	SA	PH AB	PH H	G by POS
1971 MIL A	22	70	15	2	0	2	2.9	4	9	9	20	2	.214	.329	1	0	C-22
1972	18	56	7	1	0	1	1.8	2	2	5	21	0	.125	.196	0	0	C-18
1973	117	350	89	19	2	16	4.6	50	67	57	85	5	.254	.457	9	4	C-90
1974	131	432	104	15	4	12	2.8	59	56	50	88	8	.241	.377	5	1	C-117
1975	130	409	95	12	5	18	4.4	66	60	89	77	2	.232	.418	2	0	C-124
1976	119	389	81	14	1	5	1.3	43	32	51	61	2	.208	.288	7	1	C-111
1977 KC A	130	425	117	21	3	16	3.8	61	60	53	70	1	.275	.452	5	2	C-125
1978	150	520	138	27	6	18	3.5	77	78	75	75	0	.265	.444	5	2	C-145
1979	157	533	155	23	10	20	3.8	101	112	121	65	3	.291	.484	0	0	C-141
1980	118	418	104	14	2	7	1.7	51	51	69	50	1	.249	.342	4	0	C-81
1981 STL N	61	174	39	10	2	6	3.4	22	31	39	32	1	.224	.408	6	0	C-52
1982	120	373	86	18	5	12	3.2	46	48	66	66	1	.231	.402	8	1	C-111
12 yrs.	1273	4149	1030	176	40	133	3.2	582	606	684	710	26	.248	.406	52	11	C-1137
2 yrs.	181	547	125	28	7	18	3.3	68	79	105	98	2	.229	.404	14	1	C-163

LEAGUE CHAMPIONSHIP SERIES

	G	AB	H	2B	3B	HR	HR %	R	RBI	BB	SO	SB	BA	SA	PH AB	PH H	G by POS
1977 KC A	5	15	5	0	0	0	0.0	3	0	3	0	0	.333	.333	0	0	C-5
1978	4	14	5	1	0	0	0.0	1	3	2	0	0	.357	.429	0	0	C-4
1980	3	10	1	0	0	0	0.0	2	0	1	0	0	.100	.100	0	0	C-3
1982 STL N	3	9	5	3	0	0	0.0	3	1	5	2	0	.556	.889	0	0	C-3
4 yrs.	15	48	16	4	0	0	0.0	9	4	11	2	0	.333	.417	0	0	C-15

WORLD SERIES

	G	AB	H	2B	3B	HR	HR %	R	RBI	BB	SO	SB	BA	SA	PH AB	PH H	G by POS
1980 KC A	5	14	2	0	0	0	0.0	1	0	3	4	0	.143	.143	1	0	C-4
1982 STL N	7	28	8	2	0	1	3.6	1	5	1	4	0	.286	.464	0	0	C-7
2 yrs.	12	42	10	2	0	1	2.4	2	5	4	8	0	.238	.357	1	0	C-11

J W Porter

PORTER, J W (Jay)
B. Jan. 17, 1933, Shawnee, Okla.   BR TR 6'2"   180 lbs.

	G	AB	H	2B	3B	HR	HR %	R	RBI	BB	SO	SB	BA	SA	PH AB	PH H	G by POS
1952 STL A	33	104	26	4	1	0	0.0	12	7	10	10	4	.250	.308	1	0	OF-29, 3B-2
1955 DET A	24	55	13	2	0	0	0.0	6	3	8	15	0	.236	.273	8	2	1B-6, OF-4, C-4
1956	14	21	2	0	0	0	0.0	0	3	0	8	0	.095	.095	10	0	OF-2, C-2
1957	58	140	35	8	0	2	1.4	14	18	14	20	0	.250	.350	17	4	OF-27, C-12, 1B-3
1958 CLE A	40	85	17	1	0	4	4.7	13	19	9	23	0	.200	.353	17	3	C-20, 1B-4, 3B-1
1959 2 teams		WAS A	(37G –	.226)		STL N	(23G –	.212)									
" Total	60	139	31	7	0	2	1.4	13	12	12	20	0	.223	.317	6	2	C-53, 1B-3
6 yrs.	229	544	124	22	1	8	1.5	58	62	53	96	4	.228	.316	59	11	C-91, OF-62, 1B-16, 3B-3
1 yr.	23	33	7	3	0	1	3.0	5	2	1	4	0	.212	.394	3	1	C-19, 1B-1

Mike Potter

POTTER, MICHAEL GARY
B. May 16, 1951, Montebello, Calif.   BR TR 6'1"   195 lbs.

	G	AB	H	2B	3B	HR	HR %	R	RBI	BB	SO	SB	BA	SA	PH AB	PH H	G by POS
1976 STL N	9	16	0	0	0	0	0.0	0	0	1	6	0	.000	.000	5	0	OF-4
1977	5	7	0	0	0	0	0.0	0	0	0	2	0	.000	.000	5	0	OF-1
2 yrs.	14	23	0	0	0	0	0.0	0	0	1	8	0	.000	.000	10	0	OF-5
2 yrs.	14	23	0	0	0	0	0.0	0	0	1	8	0	.000	.000	10	0	OF-5

George Puccinelli

PUCCINELLI, GEORGE LAWRENCE (Count)
B. June 22, 1906, San Francisco, Calif.   D. Apr. 16, 1956, San Francisco, Calif.   BR TR 6'½"   190 lbs.

	G	AB	H	2B	3B	HR	HR %	R	RBI	BB	SO	SB	BA	SA	PH AB	PH H	G by POS
1930 STL N	11	16	9	1	0	3	18.8	5	8	0	1	0	.563	1.188	8	4	OF-3
1932	31	108	30	8	0	3	2.8	17	11	12	13	1	.278	.435	1	0	OF-30
1934 STL A	10	26	6	1	0	2	7.7	4	5	1	8	0	.231	.500	4	0	OF-6
1936 PHI A	135	457	127	30	3	11	2.4	83	78	65	70	2	.278	.429	17	3	OF-117
4 yrs.	187	607	172	40	3	19	3.1	109	102	78	92	3	.283	.453	30	7	OF-156
2 yrs.	42	124	39	9	0	6	4.8	22	19	12	14	1	.315	.532	9	4	OF-33

WORLD SERIES

	G	AB	H	2B	3B	HR	HR %	R	RBI	BB	SO	SB	BA	SA	PH AB	PH H	G by POS
1930 STL N	1	1	0	0	0	0	0.0	0	0	0	0	0	.000	.000	1	0	

Finners Quinlan

QUINLAN, THOMAS ALOYSIUS
B. Oct. 21, 1887, Scranton, Pa.   D. Feb. 17, 1966, Scranton, Pa.   BL TL 5'8"   154 lbs.

	G	AB	H	2B	3B	HR	HR %	R	RBI	BB	SO	SB	BA	SA	PH AB	PH H	G by POS
1913 STL N	13	50	8	0	0	0	0.0	1	1	1	9	0	.160	.160	1	0	OF-12
1915 CHI A	42	114	22	3	0	0	0.0	11	7	4	11	3	.193	.219	4	0	OF-32
2 yrs.	55	164	30	3	0	0	0.0	12	8	5	20	3	.183	.201	5	0	OF-44
1 yr.	13	50	8	0	0	0	0.0	1	1	1	9	0	.160	.160	1	0	OF-12

Joe Quinn

QUINN, JOSEPH J.
B. Dec. 25, 1864, Sydney, Australia   D. Nov. 12, 1940, St. Louis, Mo.   BR TR 5'7"   158 lbs.
Manager 1895, 1899.

	G	AB	H	2B	3B	HR	HR %	R	RBI	BB	SO	SB	BA	SA	PH AB	PH H	G by POS
1884 STL U	103	429	116	21	1	0	0.0	74		9				.270	.324	0	0	1B-100, OF-3, SS-1
1885 STL N	97	343	73	8	2	0	0.0	27	15	9	38		.213	.248	0	0	OF-57, 3B-31, 1B-11
1886	75	271	63	11	3	1	0.4	33	21	8	31		.232	.306	0	0	OF-48, 2B-15, 1B-7, 3B-4, SS-2
1888 BOS N	38	156	47	8	3	4	2.6	19	29	2	5	12	.301	.468	0	0	2B-38
1889	112	444	116	13	5	2	0.5	57	69	25	21	24	.261	.327	0	0	SS-63, 2B-47, 3B-2
1890 BOS P	130	509	153	19	8	7	1.4	87	82	44	24	29	.301	.411	0	0	2B-130
1891 BOS N	124	508	122	8	10	3	0.6	70	63	28	28	24	.240	.313	0	0	2B-124
1892	143	532	116	14	1	1	0.2	63	59	35	40	17	.218	.254	0	0	2B-143
1893 STL N	135	547	126	18	6	0	0.0	68	71	33	7	21	.230	.285	0	0	2B-135
1894	106	405	116	18	1	4	1.0	59	61	24	8	25	.286	.365	0	0	2B-106
1895	134	543	169	18	8	2	0.4	84	74	36	6	22	.311	.390	0	0	2B-134
1896 2 teams		STL	N	(48G –	.209)		BAL	N	(24G –	.329)							
" Total	72	281	67	7	2	1	0.4	41	22	5	14	14	.245	.297	2	0	2B-56, OF-8, 3B-5, SS-1
1897 BAL N	75	285	74	11	4	1	0.4	33	45	13		12	.260	.337	2	0	3B-37, SS-21, 2B-11, OF-6, 1B-2
1898 2 teams		BAL	N	(12G –	.250)		STL	N	(103G –	.251)							
" Total	115	407	102	11	5	0	0.0	40	41	25		13	.251	.302	1	0	2B-63, SS-41, 3B-8, OF-2

	G	AB	H	2B	3B	HR	HR %	R	RBI	BB	SO	SB	BA	SA	Pinch Hit AB	Pinch Hit H	G by POS

Joe Quinn continued

		G	AB	H	2B	3B	HR	HR %	R	RBI	BB	SO	SB	BA	SA	PH AB	PH H	G by POS
1899	CLE N	147	615	176	24	6	0	0.0	73	72	21		22	.286	.345	0	0	2B-147
1900	2 teams	STL N (22G – .263)					CIN N	(74G – .274)										
"	Total	96	346	94	7	2	1	0.3	30	36	26		11	.272	.312	1	1	2B-88, SS-6, 3B-1
1901	WAS A	66	266	67	11	2	3	1.1	33	36	11		7	.252	.342	0	0	2B-66
17 yrs.		1768	6879	1797	228	70	30	0.4	891	795	364	214	256	.261	.328	6	1	2B-1303, SS-135, OF-124, 1B-120, 3B-88
8 yrs.		720	2755	702	92	27	9	0.3	337	306	153	95	96	.255	.318	1		2B-514, OF-106, SS-49, 3B-36, 1B-18

Dave Rader

RADER, DAVID MARTIN   BL TR 5'11"   165 lbs.
B. Dec. 26, 1948, Claremore, Okla.

		G	AB	H	2B	3B	HR	HR %	R	RBI	BB	SO	SB	BA	SA	PH AB	PH H	G by POS
1971	SF N	3	4	0	0	0	0	0.0	0	0	0	0	0	.000	.000	3	0	C-1
1972		133	459	119	14	1	6	1.3	44	41	29	31	1	.259	.333	9	2	C-127
1973		148	462	106	15	4	9	1.9	59	41	63	22	0	.229	.338	4	3	C-148
1974		113	323	94	16	2	1	0.3	26	26	31	21	1	.291	.362	13	4	C-109
1975		98	292	85	15	0	5	1.7	39	31	32	30	1	.291	.394	7	1	C-94
1976		88	255	67	15	0	1	0.4	25	22	27	21	2	.263	.333	12	2	C-81
1977	STL N	66	114	30	7	1	1	0.9	15	16	9	10	3	.263	.368	28	9	C-38
1978	CHI N	116	305	62	13	3	3	1.0	29	36	34	26	1	.203	.295	13	4	C-114
1979	PHI N	31	54	11	1	1	1	1.9	3	5	6	7	0	.204	.315	7	1	C-25
1980	BOS A	50	137	45	11	0	3	2.2	14	17	14	12	1	.328	.474	9	2	C-34
10 yrs.		846	2405	619	107	12	30	1.2	254	235	245	180	10	.257	.349	105	28	C-771
1 yr.		66	114	30	7	1	1	0.9	15	16	9	10	3	.263	.368	28	9	C-38

Milt Ramirez

RAMIREZ, MILTON   BR TR 5'9"   150 lbs.
B. Apr. 2, 1950, Mayaguez, Puerto Rico

		G	AB	H	2B	3B	HR	HR %	R	RBI	BB	SO	SB	BA	SA	PH AB	PH H	G by POS
1970	STL N	62	79	15	2	1	0	0.0	8	3	8	9	0	.190	.241	1	0	SS-59, 3B-1
1971		4	11	3	0	0	0	0.0	2	0	2	1	0	.273	.273	0	0	SS-4
1979	OAK A	28	62	10	1	1	0	0.0	4	3	3	8	0	.161	.210	0	0	3B-12, 2B-11, SS-8
3 yrs.		94	152	28	3	2	0	0.0	14	6	13	18	0	.184	.230	1	0	SS-71, 3B-13, 2B-11
2 yrs.		66	90	18	2	1	0	0.0	10	3	10	10	0	.200	.244	1	0	SS-63, 3B-1

Mike Ramsey

RAMSEY, MICHAEL JEFFREY   BB TR 6'1"   170 lbs.
B. May 29, 1954, Roanoke, Va.

		G	AB	H	2B	3B	HR	HR %	R	RBI	BB	SO	SB	BA	SA	PH AB	PH H	G by POS
1978	STL N	12	5	1	0	0	0	0.0	4	0	0	1	0	.200	.200	1	0	SS-4
1980		59	126	33	8	1	0	0.0	11	8	3	17	0	.262	.341	18	6	2B-24, SS-20, 3B-8
1981		47	124	32	3	0	0	0.0	19	9	8	16	4	.258	.282	7	1	SS-35, 3B-5, OF-1, 2B-1
1982		112	256	59	8	2	1	0.4	18	21	22	34	6	.230	.289	16	4	2B-43, 3B-28, SS-22, OF-2
4 yrs.		230	511	125	19	3	1	0.2	52	38	33	68	10	.245	.299	42	11	SS-81, 2B-68, 3B-41, OF-3
4 yrs.		230	511	125	19	3	1	0.2	52	38	33	68	10	.245	.299	42	11	SS-81, 2B-68, 3B-41, OF-3

WORLD SERIES

		G	AB	H	2B	3B	HR	HR %	R	RBI	BB	SO	SB	BA	SA	PH AB	PH H	G by POS
1982	STL N	3	1	0	0	0	0	0.0	1	0	0	1	0	.000	.000	0	0	3B-2

Dick Rand

RAND, RICHARD HILTON   BR TR 6'2"   185 lbs.
B. Mar. 7, 1931, South Gate, Calif.

		G	AB	H	2B	3B	HR	HR %	R	RBI	BB	SO	SB	BA	SA	PH AB	PH H	G by POS
1953	STL N	9	31	9	1	0	0	0.0	3	1	2	6	0	.290	.323	0	0	C-9
1955		3	10	3	0	0	1	10.0	1	3	1	1	0	.300	.600	0	0	C-3
1957	PIT N	60	105	23	2	1	1	1.0	7	9	11	24	0	.219	.286	3	1	C-57
3 yrs.		72	146	35	3	1	2	1.4	11	13	14	31	0	.240	.315	3	1	C-69
2 yrs.		12	41	12	1	0	1	2.4	4	4	3	7	0	.293	.390	0	0	C-12

Tommy Raub

RAUB, THOMAS JEFFERSON   BR TR 5'10"   155 lbs.
B. Dec. 1, 1870, Raubsville, Pa.   D. Feb. 16, 1949, Phillipsburg, N. J.

		G	AB	H	2B	3B	HR	HR %	R	RBI	BB	SO	SB	BA	SA	PH AB	PH H	G by POS
1903	CHI N	36	84	19	3	2	0	0.0	6	7	5		3	.226	.310	8	3	C-12, 1B-6, OF-5, 3B-4
1906	STL N	24	78	22	2	4	0	0.0	9	2	4		2	.282	.410	0	0	C-22
2 yrs.		60	162	41	5	6	0	0.0	15	9	9		5	.253	.358	8	3	C-34, 1B-6, OF-5, 3B-4
1 yr.		24	78	22	2	4	0	0.0	9	2	4		2	.282	.410	0	0	C-22

Art Rebel

REBEL, ARTHUR ANTHONY   BL TL 5'8"   180 lbs.
B. Mar. 4, 1915, Cincinnati, Ohio

		G	AB	H	2B	3B	HR	HR %	R	RBI	BB	SO	SB	BA	SA	PH AB	PH H	G by POS
1938	PHI N	7	9	2	0	0	0	0.0	2	1	1	1	0	.222	.222	4	0	OF-3
1945	STL N	26	72	25	4	0	0	0.0	12	5	6	4	1	.347	.403	8	1	OF-18
2 yrs.		33	81	27	4	0	0	0.0	14	6	7	5	1	.333	.383	12	1	OF-21
1 yr.		26	72	25	4	0	0	0.0	12	5	6	4	1	.347	.403	8	1	OF-18

Milt Reed

REED, MILTON D.   BL TR 5'9½"   150 lbs.
B. July 4, 1890, Atlanta, Ga.   D. July 27, 1938, Atlanta, Ga.

		G	AB	H	2B	3B	HR	HR %	R	RBI	BB	SO	SB	BA	SA	PH AB	PH H	G by POS
1911	STL N	1	1	0	0	0	0	0.0	0	0	0	0	0	.000	.000	1	0	
1913	PHI N	13	24	6	1	0	0	0.0	4	0	1	5	1	.250	.292	1	1	SS-9, 2B-3
1914		44	107	22	2	1	0	0.0	10	2	10	13	4	.206	.243	6	2	SS-22, 2B-11, 3B-1
1915	BKN F	10	31	9	1	1	0	0.0	2	8	2		2	.290	.387	0	0	SS-10
4 yrs.		68	163	37	4	2	0	0.0	16	10	13	18	7	.227	.276	8	3	SS-41, 2B-14, 3B-1
1 yr.		1	1	0	0	0	0	0.0	0	0	0	0	0	.000	.000	1	0	

Jimmy Reese

REESE, JAMES HYMIE   BL TR 5'11½"   165 lbs.
Born James Hymie Soloman.
B. Oct. 1, 1904, Los Angeles, Calif.

		G	AB	H	2B	3B	HR	HR %	R	RBI	BB	SO	SB	BA	SA	PH AB	PH H	G by POS
1930	NY A	77	188	65	14	2	3	1.6	44	18	11	8	1	.346	.489	20	10	2B-48, 3B-5

	G	AB	H	2B	3B	HR	HR %	R	RBI	BB	SO	SB	BA	SA	Pinch Hit AB	Pinch Hit H	G by POS

Jimmy Reese continued

	G	AB	H	2B	3B	HR	HR%	R	RBI	BB	SO	SB	BA	SA	AB	H	G by POS
1931	65	245	59	10	2	3	1.2	41	26	17	10	2	.241	.335	3	1	2B-61
1932 STL N	90	309	82	15	0	2	0.6	38	26	20	19	4	.265	.333	10	4	2B-77
3 yrs.	232	742	206	39	4	8	1.1	123	70	48	37	7	.278	.373	33	15	2B-186, 3B-5
1 yr.	90	309	82	15	0	2	0.6	38	26	20	19	4	.265	.333	10	4	2B-77

Tom Reilly

REILLY, THOMAS H. BR TR
B. Aug. 3, 1884, St. Louis, Mo.   D. Oct., 1918, New Orleans, La.

	G	AB	H	2B	3B	HR	HR%	R	RBI	BB	SO	SB	BA	SA	AB	H	G by POS
1908 STL N	29	81	14	1	0	1	1.2	5	3	2		4	.173	.222	0	0	SS-29
1909	5	7	2	0	1	0	0.0	0	2	0	0	0	.286	.571	0	0	SS-5
1914 CLE A	1	1	0	0	0	0	0.0	0	0	0	0	0	.000	.000	1	0	
3 yrs.	35	89	16	1	1	1	1.1	5	5	2	0	4	.180	.247	1	0	SS-34
2 yrs.	34	88	16	1	1	1	1.1	5	5	2	0	4	.182	.250	0	0	SS-34

Ken Reitz

REITZ, KENNETH JOHN BR TR 6'   180 lbs.
B. June 24, 1951, San Francisco, Calif.

	G	AB	H	2B	3B	HR	HR%	R	RBI	BB	SO	SB	BA	SA	AB	H	G by POS
1972 STL N	21	78	28	4	0	0	0.0	5	10	2	4	0	.359	.410	1	0	3B-20
1973	147	426	100	20	2	6	1.4	40	42	9	25	0	.235	.333	12	2	3B-135, SS-1
1974	154	579	157	28	2	7	1.2	48	54	23	63	0	.271	.363	3	1	3B-151, SS-2
1975	161	592	159	25	1	5	0.8	43	63	22	54	1	.269	.340	1	0	3B-160
1976 SF N	155	577	154	21	1	5	0.9	40	66	24	48	5	.267	.333	0	0	3B-155, SS-1
1977 STL N	157	587	153	36	1	17	2.9	58	79	19	74	2	.261	.412	0	0	3B-157
1978	150	540	133	26	2	10	1.9	41	75	23	61	1	.246	.357	4	4	3B-150
1979	159	605	162	41	2	8	1.3	42	73	25	85	1	.268	.382	2	0	3B-158
1980	151	523	141	33	0	8	1.5	39	58	22	44	0	.270	.379	1	0	3B-150
1981 CHI N	82	260	56	9	1	2	0.8	10	28	15	56	0	.215	.281	1	0	3B-81
1982 PIT N	7	10	0	0	0	0	0.0	0	0	0	4	0	.000	.000	1	0	3B-4
11 yrs.	1344	4777	1243	243	12	68	1.4	366	548	184	518	10	.260	.359	28	7	3B-1321, SS-4
8 yrs.	1100	3930	1033	213	10	61	1.6	316	454	145	410	5	.263	.369	24	7	3B-1081, SS-3

Bob Repass

REPASS, ROBERT WILLIS BR TR 6'1"   185 lbs.
B. Nov. 6, 1917, West Pittston, Pa.

	G	AB	H	2B	3B	HR	HR%	R	RBI	BB	SO	SB	BA	SA	AB	H	G by POS
1939 STL N	3	6	2	1	0	0	0.0	0	1	0	2	0	.333	.500	1	1	2B-2
1942 WAS A	81	259	62	11	1	2	0.8	30	23	33	30	6	.239	.313	6	1	2B-33, 3B-29, SS-11
2 yrs.	84	265	64	12	1	2	0.8	30	24	33	32	6	.242	.317	7	2	2B-35, 3B-29, SS-11
1 yr.	3	6	2	1	0	0	0.0	0	1	0	2	0	.333	.500	1	1	2B-2

Rip Repulski

REPULSKI, ELDON JOHN BR TR 6'   195 lbs.
B. Oct. 4, 1927, Sauk Rapids, Minn.

	G	AB	H	2B	3B	HR	HR%	R	RBI	BB	SO	SB	BA	SA	AB	H	G by POS
1953 STL N	153	567	156	25	4	15	2.6	75	66	33	71	3	.275	.413	0	0	OF-153
1954	152	619	175	39	5	19	3.1	99	79	43	75	8	.283	.454	0	0	OF-152
1955	147	512	138	28	2	23	4.5	64	73	49	66	5	.270	.467	10	3	OF-141
1956	112	376	104	18	3	11	2.9	44	55	24	46	2	.277	.428	17	7	OF-100
1957 PHI N	134	516	134	23	4	20	3.9	65	68	19	74	7	.260	.436	3	0	OF-130
1958	85	238	58	9	4	13	5.5	33	40	15	47	0	.244	.479	30	8	OF-56
1959 LA N	53	94	24	4	0	2	2.1	11	14	13	23	0	.255	.362	25	8	OF-31
1960 2 teams		LA	N	(4G –	.200)			BOS	A	(73G –	.243)						
" Total	77	141	34	6	1	3	2.1	14	20	10	26	0	.241	.362	39	9	OF-35
1961 BOS A	15	25	7	1	0	0	0.0	2	1	1	5	0	.280	.320	10	3	OF-4
9 yrs.	928	3088	830	153	23	106	3.4	407	416	207	433	25	.269	.436	134	38	OF-802
4 yrs.	564	2074	573	110	14	68	3.3	282	273	149	258	18	.276	.441	27	10	OF-546

WORLD SERIES

	G	AB	H	2B	3B	HR	HR%	R	RBI	BB	SO	SB	BA	SA	AB	H	G by POS
1959 LA N	1	0	0	0	0	0	–	0	0	1	0	0	–	–	0	0	OF-1

Del Rice

RICE, DELBERT W. BR TR 6'2"   190 lbs.
B. Oct. 27, 1922, Portsmouth, Ohio
Manager 1972

	G	AB	H	2B	3B	HR	HR%	R	RBI	BB	SO	SB	BA	SA	AB	H	G by POS
1945 STL N	83	253	66	17	3	1	0.4	27	28	16	33	0	.261	.364	6	1	C-77
1946	55	139	38	8	1	1	0.7	10	12	8	16	0	.273	.367	2	0	C-53
1947	97	261	57	7	3	12	4.6	28	44	36	40	1	.218	.406	3	0	C-94
1948	100	290	57	10	1	4	1.4	24	34	37	46	1	.197	.279	0	0	C-99
1949	92	284	67	16	1	4	1.4	25	29	30	40	0	.236	.342	0	0	C-92
1950	130	414	101	20	3	9	2.2	39	54	43	65	0	.244	.372	0	0	C-130
1951	122	374	94	13	1	9	2.4	34	47	34	26	0	.251	.364	3	0	C-120
1952	147	495	128	27	2	11	2.2	43	65	33	38	0	.259	.388	1	0	C-147
1953	135	419	99	22	1	6	1.4	32	37	48	49	0	.236	.337	0	0	C-135
1954	56	147	37	10	1	2	1.4	13	16	16	21	0	.252	.374	4	2	C-52
1955 2 teams		STL	N	(20G –	.203)			MIL	N	(27G –	.197)						
" Total	47	130	26	3	1	3	2.3	11	14	13	18	0	.200	.308	7	0	C-40
1956 MIL N	71	188	40	9	1	3	1.6	15	17	18	34	0	.213	.319	5	1	C-65
1957	54	144	33	1	1	9	6.3	15	20	17	37	0	.229	.438	6	1	C-48
1958	43	121	27	7	0	1	0.8	10	8	8	30	0	.223	.306	6	2	C-38
1959	13	29	6	0	0	0	0.0	3	1	2	3	0	.207	.207	4	1	C-9
1960 3 teams		CHI	N	(18G –	.231)			STL	N	(1G –	.000)		BAL	A	(1G –	.000)	
" Total	20	55	12	3	0	0	0.0	2	4	3	7	0	.218	.273	0	0	C-20
1961 LA A	44	83	20	4	0	4	4.8	11	11	20	19	0	.241	.434	15	4	C-30
17 yrs.	1309	3826	908	177	20	79	2.1	342	441	382	522	2	.237	.356	62	12	C-1249
12 yrs.	1038	3137	756	153	17	60	1.9	281	373	309	380	2	.241	.358	21	3	C-1018

WORLD SERIES

	G	AB	H	2B	3B	HR	HR%	R	RBI	BB	SO	SB	BA	SA	AB	H	G by POS
1946 STL N	3	6	3	1	0	0	0.0	2	0	1	0	0	.500	.667	0	0	C-3
1957 MIL N	2	6	1	0	0	0	0.0	0	0	1	2	0	.167	.167	0	0	C-2
2 yrs.	5	12	4	1	0	0	0.0	2	0	2	2	0	.333	.417	0	0	C-5

	G	AB	H	2B	3B	HR	HR %	R	RBI	BB	SO	SB	BA	SA	Pinch Hit AB	Pinch Hit H	G by POS

Hal Rice

RICE, HAROLD HOUSTEN (Hoot)
B. Feb. 11, 1924, Morganette, W. Va.   BL TR 6'1"   195 lbs.

	G	AB	H	2B	3B	HR	HR%	R	RBI	BB	SO	SB	BA	SA	PH AB	PH H	G by POS
1948 STL N	8	31	10	1	2	0	0.0	3	3	2	4	0	.323	.484	0	0	OF-8
1949	40	46	9	2	1	1	2.2	3	9	3	7	0	.196	.348	27	6	OF-10
1950	44	128	27	3	1	2	1.6	12	11	10	10	0	.211	.297	6	1	OF-37
1951	69	236	60	12	1	4	1.7	20	38	24	22	0	.254	.364	5	1	OF-63
1952	98	295	85	14	5	7	2.4	37	45	16	26	1	.288	.441	19	3	OF-81
1953 2 teams	STL	N	(8G –	.250)		PIT	N	(78G –	.311)								
" Total	86	294	91	16	1	4	1.4	39	42	17	25	0	.310	.412	17	3	OF-70
1954 2 teams	PIT	N	(28G –	.173)		CHI	N	(51G –	.153)								
" Total	79	153	25	4	1	1	0.7	15	14	22	39	0	.163	.222	29	2	OF-48
7 yrs.	424	1183	307	52	12	19	1.6	129	162	94	133	1	.260	.372	103	16	OF-317
6 yrs.	267	744	193	32	10	14	1.9	75	106	55	72	1	.259	.386	65	13	OF-199

Lee Richard

RICHARD, LEE EDWARD (Bee Bee)
B. Sept. 18, 1948, Lafayette, La.   BR TR 5'11"   165 lbs.

	G	AB	H	2B	3B	HR	HR%	R	RBI	BB	SO	SB	BA	SA	PH AB	PH H	G by POS
1971 CHI A	87	260	60	7	3	2	0.8	38	17	20	46	8	.231	.304	6	0	SS-68, OF-16
1972	11	29	7	0	0	0	0.0	5	1	0	7	1	.241	.241	1	1	OF-6, SS-1
1974	32	67	11	1	0	0	0.0	5	1	5	8	0	.164	.179	0	0	3B-12, SS-6, 2B-3, OF-1
1975	43	45	9	0	1	0	0.0	11	5	4	7	2	.200	.244	0	0	3B-12, SS-9, 2B-5
1976 STL N	66	91	16	4	2	0	0.0	12	5	4	9	1	.176	.264	3	0	2B-26, SS-12, 3B-1
5 yrs.	239	492	103	12	6	2	0.4	71	29	33	77	12	.209	.270	10	1	SS-96, 2B-34, 3B-25, OF-23
1 yr.	66	91	16	4	2	0	0.0	12	5	4	9	1	.176	.264	3	0	2B-26, SS-12, 3B-1

Bill Richardson

RICHARDSON, WILLIAM HEZEKIAH
B. Oct. 8, 1877, Decatur County, Ind.   D. Apr. 11, 1954, Batesville, Ind.

	G	AB	H	2B	3B	HR	HR%	R	RBI	BB	SO	SB	BA	SA	PH AB	PH H	G by POS
1901 STL N	15	52	11	2	0	2	3.8	7	7	6		1	.212	.365	0	0	1B-15

Don Richmond

RICHMOND, DONALD LESTER
B. Oct. 27, 1919, Gillett, Pa.   D. May 24, 1981, Elmira, N. Y.   BL TR 6'1"   175 lbs.

	G	AB	H	2B	3B	HR	HR%	R	RBI	BB	SO	SB	BA	SA	PH AB	PH H	G by POS
1941 PHI A	9	35	7	1	1	0	0.0	3	5	0	1	0	.200	.286	0	0	3B-9
1946	16	62	18	3	0	1	1.6	3	9	0	10	1	.290	.387	0	0	3B-16
1947	19	21	4	1	1	0	0.0	2	4	3	3	0	.190	.333	11	2	3B-4, 2B-1
1951 STL N	12	34	3	1	0	1	2.9	3	4	3	3	0	.088	.206	0	0	3B-11
4 yrs.	56	152	32	6	2	2	1.3	11	22	6	17	1	.211	.316	11	2	3B-40, 2B-1
1 yr.	12	34	3	1	0	1	2.9	3	4	3	3	0	.088	.206	0	0	3B-11

Dave Ricketts

RICKETTS, DAVID WILLIAM
Brother of Dick Ricketts.
B. July 12, 1935, Pottstown, Pa.   BB TR 6'   190 lbs.

	G	AB	H	2B	3B	HR	HR%	R	RBI	BB	SO	SB	BA	SA	PH AB	PH H	G by POS
1963 STL N	3	8	2	0	0	0	0.0	0	0	0	2	0	.250	.250	0	0	C-3
1965	11	29	7	0	0	0	0.0	1	0	1	3	0	.241	.241	1	0	C-11
1967	52	99	27	8	0	1	1.0	11	14	4	7	0	.273	.384	32	7	C-21
1968	20	22	3	0	0	0	0.0	1	1	0	3	0	.136	.136	19	2	C-1
1969	30	44	12	1	0	0	0.0	2	5	4	5	0	.273	.295	18	5	C-8
1970 PIT N	14	11	2	0	0	0	0.0	0	0	1	3	0	.182	.182	7	1	C-7
6 yrs.	130	213	53	9	0	1	0.5	15	20	10	23	0	.249	.305	77	15	C-51
5 yrs.	116	202	51	9	0	1	0.5	15	20	9	20	0	.252	.312	70	14	C-44
WORLD SERIES																	
1967 STL N	3	3	0	0	0	0	0.0	0	0	0	0	0	.000	.000	3	0	
1968	1	1	1	0	0	0	0.0	0	0	0	0	0	1.000	1.000	1	1	
2 yrs.	4	4	1	0	0	0	0.0	0	0	0	0	0	.250	.250	4	1	

Branch Rickey

RICKEY, WESLEY BRANCH (The Mahatma)
B. Dec. 20, 1881, Stockdale, Ohio   D. Dec. 9, 1965, Columbia, Mo.   BL TR 5'9"   175 lbs.
Manager 1913-15, 1919-25.
Hall of Fame 1967.

	G	AB	H	2B	3B	HR	HR%	R	RBI	BB	SO	SB	BA	SA	PH AB	PH H	G by POS
1905 STL A	1	3	0	0	0	0	0.0	0	0	0		0	.000	.000	0	0	C-1
1906	64	201	57	7	3	3	1.5	22	24	16		4	.284	.393	7	2	C-54, OF-1
1907 NY A	52	137	25	2	3	0	0.0	16	15	11		4	.182	.241	12	1	OF-22, C-11, 1B-9
1914 STL A	2	2	0	0	0	0	0.0	0	0	0		0	.000	.000	2	0	
4 yrs.	119	343	82	9	6	3	0.9	38	39	27		8	.239	.327	21	3	C-66, OF-23, 1B-9

John Ricks

RICKS, JOHN
Deceased.

	G	AB	H	2B	3B	HR	HR%	R	RBI	BB	SO	SB	BA	SA	PH AB	PH H	G by POS
1891 STL AA	5	18	3	0	0	0	0.0	3	0	0	2	0	.167	.167	0	0	3B-5
1894 STL N	1	1	0	0	0	0	0.0	0	0	0	0	0	.000	.000	0	0	3B-1
2 yrs.	6	19	3	0	0	0	0.0	3	0	0	2	0	.158	.158	0	0	3B-6
1 yr.	1	1	0	0	0	0	0.0	0	0	0	0	0	.000	.000	0	0	3B-1

Joe Riggert

RIGGERT, JOSEPH ALOYSIUS
B. Dec. 11, 1886, Janesville, Wis.   D. Dec. 10, 1973, Kansas City, Mo.   BR TR 5'9½"   170 lbs.

	G	AB	H	2B	3B	HR	HR%	R	RBI	BB	SO	SB	BA	SA	PH AB	PH H	G by POS
1911 BOS A	50	146	31	4	2	1.4	19	13	12		5	.212	.336	8	3	OF-38
1914 2 teams	BKN	N	(27G –	.193)		STL	N	(34G –	.213)								
" Total	61	172	35	6	5	2	1.2	15	14	9	34	6	.203	.331	8	0	OF-50
1919 BOS N	63	240	68	8	7	6	2.5	34	17	25	30	9	.283	.408	0	0	OF-61
3 yrs.	174	558	134	18	14	8	1.4	68	44	46	64	20	.240	.366	16	3	OF-149
1 yr.	34	89	19	5	2	0	0.0	9	8	5	14	4	.213	.315	4	0	OF-30

	G	AB	H	2B	3B	HR	HR %	R	RBI	BB	SO	SB	BA	SA	Pinch Hit AB	Pinch Hit H	G by POS
Lew Riggs														**RIGGS, LEWIS SIDNEY** B. Apr. 22, 1910, Mebane, N. C.			BL TR 6' 175 lbs.
1934 STL N	2	1	0	0	0	0	0.0	0	0	0	1	0	.000	.000	1	0	
1935 CIN N	142	532	148	26	8	5	0.9	73	46	43	32	8	.278	.385	2	0	3B-135
1936	141	538	138	20	12	6	1.1	69	57	38	33	5	.257	.372	1	1	3B-140
1937	122	384	93	17	5	6	1.6	43	45	24	17	4	.242	.359	17	4	3B-100, 2B-4, SS-1
1938	142	531	134	21	13	2	0.4	53	55	40	28	3	.252	.352	2	0	3B-142
1939	22	38	6	1	0	0	0.0	5	1	5	4	1	.158	.184	6	1	3B-11
1940	41	72	21	7	1	1	1.4	8	9	2	4	0	.292	.458	27	8	3B-11
1941 BKN N	77	197	60	13	4	5	2.5	27	36	16	12	1	.305	.487	29	10	3B-43, 2B-1, 1B-1
1942	70	180	50	5	0	3	1.7	20	22	13	9	0	.278	.356	21	8	3B-46, 1B-1
1946	1	4	0	0	0	0	0.0	0	0	0	0	0	.000	.000	0	0	3B-1
10 yrs.	760	2477	650	110	43	28	1.1	298	271	181	140	22	.262	.375	106	32	3B-629, 2B-5, 1B-2, SS-1
1 yr.	2	1	0	0	0	0	0.0	0	0	0	1	0	.000	.000	1	0	
WORLD SERIES																	
1940 CIN N	3	3	0	0	0	0	0.0	1	0	0	2	0	.000	.000	3	0	
1941 BKN N	3	8	2	0	0	0	0.0	0	1	1	1	0	.250	.250	1	1	3B-2
2 yrs.	6	11	2	0	0	0	0.0	1	1	1	3	0	.182	.182	4	1	3B-2
Skipper Roberts														**ROBERTS, CLARENCE ASHLEY** B. Jan. 11, 1888, Wardner, Ida. D. Dec. 24, 1963, Long Beach, Calif.			BL TR 5'10½" 175 lbs.
1913 STL N	26	41	6	2	0	0	0.0	4	3	3	13	1	.146	.195	7	0	C-16
1914 2 teams	PIT F (52G – .234)				CHI F (4G – .333)												
" Total	56	97	23	4	2	1	1.0	12	9	3			3	.237	.351	29	8	C-23, OF-1
2 yrs.	82	138	29	6	2	1	0.7	16	12	6	13	4	.210	.304	36	8	C-39, OF-1
1 yr.	26	41	6	2	0	0	0.0	4	3	3	13	1	.146	.195	7	0	C-16
Wilbert Robinson														**ROBINSON, WILBERT (Uncle Robbie)** Brother of Fred Robinson. B. June 2, 1863, Bolton, Mass. D. Aug. 8, 1934, Atlanta, Ga. Manager 1902, 1914-31. Hall of Fame 1945.			BR TR 5'8½" 215 lbs.
1886 PHI AA	87	342	69	11	3	1	0.3	57		21				.202	.260	0	0	C-61, 1B-22, OF-5
1887	68	264	60	6	2	1	0.4	28		14		15		.227	.277	0	0	C-67, 1B-3, OF-1
1888	66	254	62	7	2	1	0.4	32	31	9		11		.244	.299	0	0	C-65, 1B-1
1889	69	264	61	13	2	0	0.0	31	28	6	34	9		.231	.295	0	0	C-69
1890 2 teams	PHI AA (82G – .237)				B-B AA (14G – .271)												
" Total	96	377	91	14	4	4	1.1	39		19		21		.241	.332	0	0	C-93, 1B-3
1891 BAL AA	93	334	72	8	5	2	0.6	25	46	16	37	18	.216	.287	0	0	C-92, OF-1
1892 BAL N	90	330	88	14	4	2	0.6	36	57	15	35	5	.267	.352	0	0	C-87, 1B-2, OF-1
1893	95	359	120	21	3	3	0.8	49	57	26	22	17	.334	.435	1	0	C-93, 1B-1
1894	109	414	146	21	4	1	0.2	69	98	46	18	12	.353	.430	0	0	C-109
1895	77	282	74	19	1	0	0.0	38	48	12	19	11	.262	.337	2	1	C-75
1896	67	245	85	9	6	2	0.8	43	38	14	13	9	.347	.457	0	0	C-67
1897	48	181	57	9	0	0	0.0	25	23	8		0	.315	.365	0	0	C-48
1898	79	289	80	12	2	0	0.0	29	38	16		3	.277	.332	1	1	C-77
1899	108	356	101	15	2	0	0.0	40	47	31		5	.284	.337	3	2	C-105
1900 STL N	60	210	52	5	1	0	0.0	26	28	11		7	.248	.281	5	1	C-54
1901 BAL A	68	239	72	12	3	0	0.0	32	26	10		9	.301	.377	1	0	C-67
1902	91	335	98	16	7	1	0.3	38	57	12		11	.293	.391	4	2	C-87
17 yrs.	1371	5075	1388	212	51	18	0.4	637	621	286	178	163	.273	.346	17	7	C-1316, 1B-32, OF-8
1 yr.	60	210	52	5	1	0	0.0	26	28	11		7	.248	.281	5	1	C-54
Jack Roche														**ROCHE, JOHN JOSEPH (Red)** B. Nov. 22, 1890, Los Angeles, Calif.			BR TR 6'1" 178 lbs.
1914 STL N	12	9	6	2	1	0	0.0	1	3	0	1	1	.667	1.111	6	5	C-9
1915	46	39	8	0	1	0	0.0	2	6	4	8	1	.205	.256	37	8	C-4
1917	1	1	0	0	0	0	0.0	0	0	0	0	0	.000	.000	0	0	C-1
3 yrs.	59	49	14	2	2	0	0.0	3	9	4	9	2	.286	.408	43	13	C-14
3 yrs.	59	49	14	2	2	0	0.0	3	9	4	9	2	.286	.408	43	13	C-14
Wally Roettger														**ROETTGER, WALTER HENRY** Brother of Oscar Roettger. B. Aug. 28, 1902, St. Louis, Mo. D. Sept. 14, 1951, Champaign, Ill.			BR TR 6'1½" 190 lbs.
1927 STL N	5	1	0	0	0	0	0.0	0		1	0	0	.000	.000	0	0	OF-3
1928	68	261	89	17	4	6	2.3	27	44	10	22	2	.341	.506	2	0	OF-66
1929	79	269	68	11	3	3	1.1	27	42	13	27	0	.253	.349	10	1	OF-69
1930 NY N	121	420	119	15	5	5	1.2	51	51	25	29	1	.283	.379	7	3	OF-114
1931 2 teams	CIN N (44G – .351)				STL N (45G – .285)												
" Total	89	336	108	23	6	1	0.3	41	37	16	23	1	.321	.435	3	1	OF-86
1932 CIN N	106	347	96	18	3	3	0.9	26	43	23	24	0	.277	.372	10	3	OF-94
1933	84	209	50	7	1	0	0.0	13	17	8	10	0	.239	.297	28	8	OF-55
1934 PIT N	47	106	26	5	1	0	0.0	7	11	3	8	0	.245	.311	23	7	OF-23
8 yrs.	599	1949	556	96	23	19	1.0	192	245	99	143	4	.285	.387	83	23	OF-510
4 yrs.	197	682	200	40	9	9	1.3	70	103	33	63	2	.293	.418	15	2	OF-180
WORLD SERIES																	
1931 STL N	3	14	4	1	0	0	0.0	1	0	0	3	0	.286	.357	0	0	OF-3
Cookie Rojas														**ROJAS, OCTAVIO RIVAS** B. Mar. 6, 1939, Havana, Cuba			BR TR 5'10" 160 lbs.
1962 CIN N	39	86	19	2	0	0	0.0	9	6	9	4	1	.221	.244	2	0	2B-30, 3B-1
1963 PHI N	64	77	17	0	1	1	1.3	18	2	3	8	4	.221	.286	8	3	2B-25, OF-1
1964	109	340	99	19	5	2	0.6	58	31	22	17	1	.291	.394	16	1	OF-70, 2B-20, SS-18, 3B-1, C-1

	G	AB	H	2B	3B	HR	HR %	R	RBI	BB	SO	SB	BA	SA	Pinch Hit AB	Pinch Hit H	G by POS

Cookie Rojas continued

	G	AB	H	2B	3B	HR	HR %	R	RBI	BB	SO	SB	BA	SA	AB	H	G by POS
1965	142	521	158	25	3	3	0.6	78	42	42	33	5	.303	.380	11	2	2B-84, OF-55, SS-11, C-2, 1B-1
1966	156	626	168	18	1	6	1.0	77	55	35	46	4	.268	.329	1	0	2B-106, OF-56, SS-2
1967	147	528	137	21	2	4	0.8	60	45	30	58	8	.259	.330	5	2	2B-137, OF-9, C-3, SS-2, 3B-1, P-1
1968	152	621	144	19	0	9	1.4	53	48	16	55	4	.232	.306	2	0	2B-150, C-1
1969	110	391	89	11	1	4	1.0	35	30	23	28	1	.228	.292	11	1	2B-95, OF-2
1970 2 teams	STL	N	(23G –	.106)		KC	A	(98G –	.260)								
" Total	121	431	105	13	3	2	0.5	38	30	23	33	3	.244	.302	12	2	2B-107, OF-6, SS-2
1971 KC A	115	414	124	22	2	6	1.4	56	59	39	35	8	.300	.406	2	0	2B-111, SS-2, OF-1
1972	137	487	127	25	0	3	0.6	49	53	41	35	2	.261	.331	2	0	2B-133, 3B-6, SS-2
1973	139	551	152	29	3	6	1.1	78	69	37	38	18	.276	.372	3	2	2B-137
1974	144	542	147	17	1	6	1.1	52	60	30	43	8	.271	.339	8	1	2B-141
1975	120	406	103	18	2	2	0.5	34	37	30	24	4	.254	.323	8	3	2B-117
1976	63	132	32	6	0	0	0.0	11	16	8	15	2	.242	.288	28	7	2B-40, 3B-6, 1B-1
1977	64	156	39	9	1	0	0.0	8	10	8	17	1	.250	.321	17	3	3B-31, 2B-16
16 yrs.	1822	6309	1660	254	25	54	0.9	714	593	396	489	74	.263	.337	136	27	2B-1449, OF-200, 3B-46, SS-39, C-7, 1B-2, P-1
1 yr.	23	47	5	0	0	0	0.0	2	2	3	4	0	.106	.106	10	2	2B-10, OF-3, SS-2
LEAGUE CHAMPIONSHIP SERIES																	
1976 KC A	4	9	3	0	0	0	0.0	2	1	0	0	1	.333	.333	2	0	2B-4
1977	1	4	1	0	0	0	0.0	0	0	0	1	1	.250	.250	0	0	
2 yrs.	5	13	4	0	0	0	0.0	2	1	0	1	2	.308	.308	2	0	2B-4

Stan Rojek

ROJEK, STANLEY ANDREW
B. Apr. 21, 1919, North Tonawanda, N. Y.   BR TR 5'10" 170 lbs.

	G	AB	H	2B	3B	HR	HR %	R	RBI	BB	SO	SB	BA	SA	AB	H	G by POS
1942 BKN N	1	0	0	0	0	0	–	1	0	0	0	0	–	–	0	0	
1946	45	47	13	2	1	0	0.0	11	2	4	1	1	.277	.362	10	3	SS-15, 2B-6, 3B-4
1947	32	80	21	0	1	0	0.0	7	7	7	3	1	.263	.288	1	0	SS-17, 3B-9, 2B-7
1948 PIT N	156	641	186	27	5	4	0.6	85	51	61	41	24	.290	.367	0	0	SS-156
1949	144	557	136	19	2	0	0.0	72	31	50	31	4	.244	.285	0	0	SS-144
1950	76	230	59	12	1	0	0.0	28	17	18	13	2	.257	.317	4	0	SS-68, 2B-3
1951 2 teams	PIT	N	(8G –	.188)		STL	N	(51G –	.274)								
" Total	59	202	54	7	3	0	0.0	21	14	10	11	0	.267	.332	0	0	SS-59
1952 STL A	9	7	1	0	0	0	0.0	2	0	2	0	0	.143	.143	2	0	SS-4, 2B-1
8 yrs.	522	1764	470	67	13	4	0.2	225	122	152	100	32	.266	.326	17	3	SS-463, 2B-17, 3B-13
1 yr.	51	186	51	7	3	0	0.0	21	14	10	10	0	.274	.344	0	0	SS-51

Ray Rolling

ROLLING, RAYMOND COPELAND
B. Sept. 8, 1886, Martinsburg, Mo.   D. Aug. 25, 1966, St. Paul, Minn.   BR TR 5'10½" 160 lbs.

	G	AB	H	2B	3B	HR	HR %	R	RBI	BB	SO	SB	BA	SA	AB	H	G by POS
1912 STL N	5	15	3	0	0	0	0.0	0	0	0		5	.200	.200	0	0	2B-4

Johnny Romano

ROMANO, JOHN ANTHONY (Honey)
B. Aug. 23, 1934, Hoboken, N. J.   BR TR 5'11" 205 lbs.

	G	AB	H	2B	3B	HR	HR %	R	RBI	BB	SO	SB	BA	SA	AB	H	G by POS
1958 CHI A	4	7	2	0	0	0	0.0	1	1	1	0	0	.286	.286	2	0	C-2
1959	53	126	37	5	1	5	4.0	20	25	23	18	0	.294	.468	13	8	C-38
1960 CLE A	108	316	86	12	2	16	5.1	40	52	37	50	0	.272	.475	11	0	C-99
1961	142	509	152	29	1	21	4.1	76	80	61	60	0	.299	.483	2	0	C-141
1962	135	459	120	19	3	25	5.4	71	81	73	64	0	.261	.479	4	3	C-130
1963	89	255	55	5	2	10	3.9	28	34	38	49	4	.216	.369	16	4	C-71, OF-4
1964	106	352	85	18	1	19	5.4	46	47	51	83	2	.241	.460	10	2	C-96, 1B-1
1965 CHI A	122	356	86	11	0	18	5.1	39	48	59	74	0	.242	.424	8	1	C-111, OF-4, 1B-2
1966	122	329	76	12	0	15	4.6	33	47	58	72	0	.231	.404	16	4	C-102
1967 STL N	24	58	7	1	0	0	0.0	1	2	13	15	1	.121	.138	4	0	C-20
10 yrs.	905	2767	706	112	10	129	4.7	355	417	414	485	7	.255	.443	86	22	C-810, OF-8, 1B-3
1 yr.	24	58	7	1	0	0	0.0	1	2	13	15	1	.121	.138	4	0	C-20
WORLD SERIES																	
1959 CHI A	2	1	0	0	0	0	0.0	0	0	0	0	0	.000	.000	1	0	

Gene Roof

ROOF, EUGENE LAWRENCE
Brother of Phil Roof.
B. Jan. 13, 1958, Mayfield, Ky.   BB TR 6'2" 180 lbs.

	G	AB	H	2B	3B	HR	HR %	R	RBI	BB	SO	SB	BA	SA	AB	H	G by POS
1981 STL N	23	60	18	6	0	0	0.0	11	3	12	16	5	.300	.400	2	0	OF-20
1982	11	15	4	0	0	0	0.0	3	2	1	4	2	.267	.267	7	2	OF-5
2 yrs.	34	75	22	6	0	0	0.0	14	5	13	20	7	.293	.373	9	2	OF-25
2 yrs.	34	75	22	6	0	0	0.0	14	5	13	20	7	.293	.373	9	2	OF-25

Jorge Roque

ROQUE, JORGE
B. Apr. 28, 1950, Ponce, Puerto Rico   BR TR 5'10" 158 lbs.

	G	AB	H	2B	3B	HR	HR %	R	RBI	BB	SO	SB	BA	SA	AB	H	G by POS
1970 STL N	5	1	0	0	0	0	0.0	2	0	0	1	0	.000	.000	1	0	OF-1
1971	3	10	3	0	0	0	0.0	2	1	0	3	1	.300	.300	0	0	OF-3
1972	32	67	7	2	1	1	1.5	3	5	6	19	1	.104	.209	6	1	OF-24
1973 MON N	25	61	9	2	0	1	1.6	7	6	4	17	2	.148	.230	0	0	OF-24
4 yrs.	65	139	19	4	1	2	1.4	14	12	10	40	4	.137	.223	7	1	OF-52
3 yrs.	40	78	10	2	1	1	1.3	7	6	6	23	2	.128	.218	7	1	OF-28

Jack Rothrock

ROTHROCK, JOHN HOUSTON
B. Mar. 14, 1905, Long Beach, Calif.   BB TR 5'11½" 165 lbs.
D. Feb. 2, 1980, San Bernardino, Calif.   BR 1925-27

	G	AB	H	2B	3B	HR	HR %	R	RBI	BB	SO	SB	BA	SA	AB	H	G by POS
1925 BOS A	22	55	19	3	3	0	0.0	6	7	3	7	0	.345	.509	0	0	SS-22
1926	15	17	5	1	0	0	0.0	3	2	3	1	0	.294	.353	10	4	SS-2

	G	AB	H	2B	3B	HR	HR %	R	RBI	BB	SO	SB	BA	SA	Pinch Hit AB	H	G by POS

Jack Rothrock continued

	G	AB	H	2B	3B	HR	HR %	R	RBI	BB	SO	SB	BA	SA	PH AB	PH H	G by POS
1927	117	428	111	24	8	1	0.2	61	36	24	46	5	.259	.360	6	1	SS-40, 2B-36, 3B-20, 1B-13
1928	117	344	92	9	4	3	0.9	52	22	33	40	12	.267	.343	9	2	OF-53, 3B-17, 1B-16, SS-13, 2B-2, C-1, P-1
1929	143	473	142	19	7	6	1.3	70	59	43	47	23	.300	.408	10	2	OF-128
1930	45	65	18	3	1	0	0.0	4	4	2	9	0	.277	.354	32	9	OF-9, 3B-1
1931	133	475	132	32	3	4	0.8	81	42	47	48	13	.278	.383	20	9	OF-79, 2B-23, 1B-8, 3B-2, SS-1
1932 2 teams		BOS	A	(12G –	.208)		CHI	A	(39G –	.188)							
" Total	51	112	22	3	1	0	0.0	11	6	10	14	4	.196	.241	7	1	OF-31, 3B-8, 1B-1
1934 STL N	154	647	184	35	3	11	1.7	106	72	49	56	10	.284	.399	0	0	OF-154, 2B-1
1935	129	502	137	18	5	3	0.6	76	56	57	29	7	.273	.347	1	0	OF-127
1937 PHI A	88	232	62	15	0	0	0.0	28	21	28	15	1	.267	.332	29	8	OF-58, 2B-1
11 yrs.	1014	3350	924	162	35	28	0.8	498	327	299	312	75	.276	.370	124	36	OF-639, SS-78, 2B-63, 3B-48, 1B-38, C-1, P-1
2 yrs.	283	1149	321	53	8	14	1.2	182	128	106	85	17	.279	.376	1	0	OF-281, 2B-1
WORLD SERIES																	
1934 STL N	7	30	7	3	1	0	0.0	3	6	1	2	0	.233	.400	0	0	OF-7

Ken Rudolph

RUDOLPH, KENNETH VICTOR
B. Dec. 29, 1946, Rockford, Ill.   BR TR 6'1"   180 lbs.

	G	AB	H	2B	3B	HR	HR %	R	RBI	BB	SO	SB	BA	SA	PH AB	PH H	G by POS
1969 CHI N	27	34	7	1	0	1	2.9	7	6	6	11	0	.206	.324	10	3	C-11, OF-3
1970	20	40	4	1	0	0	0.0	1	2	1	12	0	.100	.125	3	0	C-16
1971	25	76	15	3	0	0	0.0	5	7	6	20	0	.197	.237	0	0	C-25
1972	42	106	25	1	1	2	1.9	10	9	6	14	1	.236	.321	1	0	C-41
1973	64	170	35	8	1	2	1.2	12	17	7	25	1	.206	.300	0	0	C-64
1974 SF N	57	158	41	3	0	0	0.0	11	10	21	15	0	.259	.278	0	0	C-56
1975 STL N	44	80	16	2	0	1	1.3	5	6	3	10	0	.200	.263	14	1	C-31
1976	27	50	8	3	0	0	0.0	1	5	1	7	0	.160	.220	13	4	C-14
1977 2 teams		SF	N	(11G –	.200)		BAL	A	(11G –	.286)							
" Total	22	29	7	1	0	0	0.0	3	2	1	7	0	.241	.276	5	0	C-22
9 yrs.	328	743	158	23	2	6	0.8	55	64	52	121	2	.213	.273	46	8	C-280, OF-3
2 yrs.	71	130	24	5	0	1	0.8	6	11	4	17	0	.185	.246	27	5	C-45

Paul Russell

RUSSELL, BENJAMIN PAUL
B. 1870, Reading, Pa.   D. Pottstown, Pa.

	G	AB	H	2B	3B	HR	HR %	R	RBI	BB	SO	SB	BA	SA	PH AB	PH H	G by POS
1894 STL N	3	10	1	0	0	0	0.0	1	0	1	0	2	0	.100	.100	0	0	OF-1, 3B-1, 2B-1

J. Ryan

RYAN, J.
Deceased.

	G	AB	H	2B	3B	HR	HR %	R	RBI	BB	SO	SB	BA	SA	PH AB	PH H	G by POS
1895 STL N	2	2	0	0	0	0	0.0	0	0	0	0	0	.000	.000	0	0	3B-2

John Ryan

RYAN, JOHN BENNETT
B. Nov. 12, 1868, Haverhill, Mass.   Deceased.   BR TR 5'10½" 165 lbs.

	G	AB	H	2B	3B	HR	HR %	R	RBI	BB	SO	SB	BA	SA	PH AB	PH H	G by POS
1889 LOU AA	21	79	14	1	0	0	0.0	8	2	3	17	2	.177	.190	0	0	C-15, OF-4, 3B-2
1890	93	337	73	16	4	0	0.0	43		12		6	.217	.288	0	0	C-89, OF-3, SS-1, 1B-1
1891	75	253	57	5	4	2	0.8	24	25	15	40	3	.225	.300	0	0	C-56, 1B-11, 3B-6, OF-4, 2B-3
1894 BOS N	53	201	54	12	7	1	0.5	39	29	13	16	3	.269	.413	0	0	C-51, 1B-2
1895	49	189	55	7	0	0	0.0	22	18	6	6	3	.291	.328	0	0	C-43, 2B-5, OF-1
1896	8	32	3	1	0	0	0.0	2	0	0	1	0	.094	.125	0	0	C-8
1898 BKN N	87	301	57	11	4	0	0.0	39	24	15		5	.189	.252	0	0	C-84, 3B-4, 1B-1
1899 BAL N	2	4	2	1	0	0	0.0	0	1	0		1	.500	.750	0	0	C-2
1901 STL N	83	300	59	6	5	0	0.0	27	31	7		5	.197	.250	1	0	C-65, 2B-9, 1B-5, OF-3
1902	76	267	48	4	4	0	0.0	23	14	4		2	.180	.225	0	0	C-66, 3B-4, 1B-4, 2B-2, SS-1, P-1
1903	67	227	54	5	1	0	0.4	18	10	10		2	.238	.282	0	0	C-47, 1B-18, SS-2
1912 WAS A	1	1	0	0	0	0	0.0	0	0	0		0	.000	.000	0	0	3B-1
1913	1	1	0	0	0	0	0.0	0	0	0	0	0	.000	.000	0	0	C-1
13 yrs.	616	2192	476	69	29	4	0.2	245	154	85	80	32	.217	.281	1	0	C-527, 1B-42, 2B-19, 3B-17, OF-15, SS-4, P-1
3 yrs.	226	794	161	15	10	1	0.1	68	55	21		9	.203	.251	1	0	C-178, 1B-27, 2B-11, 3B-4, OF-3, SS-3, P-1

Bob Sadowski

SADOWSKI, ROBERT FRANK (Sid)
B. Jan. 15, 1937, St. Louis, Mo.   BL TR 6'   175 lbs.

	G	AB	H	2B	3B	HR	HR %	R	RBI	BB	SO	SB	BA	SA	PH AB	PH H	G by POS
1960 STL N	1	1	0	0	0	0	0.0	0	0	1	0	0	.000	.000	0	0	2B-1
1961 PHI N	16	54	7	0	0	0	0.0	4	0	4	7	1	.130	.130	3	0	3B-14
1962 CHI A	79	130	30	3	3	6	4.6	22	24	13	22	0	.231	.438	44	10	3B-16, 2B-12
1963 LA A	88	144	36	6	0	1	0.7	12	22	15	34	2	.250	.313	50	12	OF-25, 3B-6, 2B-4
4 yrs.	184	329	73	9	3	7	2.1	38	46	33	63	3	.222	.331	97	22	3B-36, OF-25, 2B-17
1 yr.	1	1	0	0	0	0	0.0	0	0	1	0	0	.000	.000	0	0	2B-1

Ike Samuels

SAMUELS, SAMUEL EARL
B. Feb. 20, 1876, Chicago, Ill.   Deceased.   BR TR

	G	AB	H	2B	3B	HR	HR %	R	RBI	BB	SO	SB	BA	SA	PH AB	PH H	G by POS
1895 STL N	24	74	17	2	0	0	0.0	5	5	5	7	5	.230	.257	0	0	3B-21, SS-3

Orlando Sanchez

SANCHEZ, ORLANDO
B. Sept. 7, 1956, Canovanas, Puerto Rico   BL TR 6'   185 lbs.

	G	AB	H	2B	3B	HR	HR %	R	RBI	BB	SO	SB	BA	SA	PH AB	PH H	G by POS
1981 STL N	27	49	14	2	1	0	0.0	5	6	2	6	1	.286	.367	11	3	C-18
1982	26	37	7	0	1	0	0.0	6	3	5	5	0	.189	.243	9	2	C-15
2 yrs.	53	86	21	2	2	0	0.0	11	9	7	11	1	.244	.314	20	5	C-33
2 yrs.	53	86	21	2	2	0	0.0	11	9	7	11	1	.244	.314	20	5	C-33

	G	AB	H	2B	3B	HR	HR %	R	RBI	BB	SO	SB	BA	SA	Pinch Hit AB	Pinch Hit H	G by POS

Ray Sanders

SANDERS, RAYMOND FLOYD
B. Dec. 4, 1916, Bonne Terre, Mo. BL TR 6'2" 185 lbs.

Year/Team	G	AB	H	2B	3B	HR	HR%	R	RBI	BB	SO	SB	BA	SA	PH AB	PH H	G by POS
1942 STL N	95	282	71	17	2	5	1.8	37	39	42	31	2	.252	.379	15	2	1B-77
1943	144	478	134	21	5	11	2.3	69	73	77	33	1	.280	.414	3	0	1B-141
1944	154	601	177	34	9	12	2.0	87	102	71	50	2	.295	.441	3	1	1B-152
1945	143	537	148	29	3	8	1.5	85	78	83	55	3	.276	.385	1	0	1B-142
1946 BOS N	80	259	63	12	0	6	2.3	43	35	50	38	0	.243	.359	2	1	1B-77
1948	5	4	1	0	0	0	0.0	0	2	1	0	0	.250	.250	4	1	
1949	9	21	3	1	0	0	0.0	0	0	4	9	0	.143	.190	1	0	1B-7
7 yrs.	630	2182	597	114	19	42	1.9	321	329	328	216	8	.274	.401	29	5	1B-596
4 yrs.	536	1898	530	101	19	36	1.9	278	292	273	169	8	.279	.409	22	3	1B-512

WORLD SERIES

Year/Team	G	AB	H	2B	3B	HR	HR%	R	RBI	BB	SO	SB	BA	SA	PH AB	PH H	G by POS
1942 STL N	2	1	0	0	0	0	0.0	0	1	0	1	0	.000	.000	1	0	
1943	5	17	5	0	0	1	5.9	3	2	3	4	0	.294	.471	0	0	1B-5
1944	6	21	6	0	0	1	4.8	5	1	5	8	0	.286	.429	0	0	1B-6
1948 BOS N	1	1	0	0	0	0	0.0	0	0	0	0	0	.000	.000	1	0	
4 yrs.	14	40	11	0	0	2	5.0	9	3	9	12	0	.275	.425	2	0	1B-11

Bill Sarni

SARNI, WILLIAM F.
B. Sept. 19, 1927, Los Angeles, Calif. BR TR 5'11" 180 lbs.

Year/Team	G	AB	H	2B	3B	HR	HR%	R	RBI	BB	SO	SB	BA	SA	PH AB	PH H	G by POS
1951 STL N	36	86	15	1	0	0	0.0	7	2	9	13	1	.174	.186	1	0	C-35
1952	3	5	1	0	0	0	0.0	0	0	0	1	0	.200	.200	0	0	C-3
1954	123	380	114	18	4	9	2.4	40	70	25	42	3	.300	.439	6	3	C-118
1955	107	325	83	15	2	3	0.9	32	34	27	33	1	.255	.342	11	3	C-99
1956 2 teams		STL N (43G – .291)				NY N (78G – .231)											
" Total	121	386	98	16	5	10	2.6	28	45	28	46	1	.254	.399	6	1	C-116
5 yrs.	390	1182	311	50	11	22	1.9	107	151	89	135	6	.263	.380	24	7	C-371
5 yrs.	312	944	256	41	8	17	1.8	91	128	69	104	6	.271	.386	20	6	C-296

Ed Sauer

SAUER, EDWARD (Horn)
Brother of Hank Sauer.
B. Jan. 3, 1920, Pittsburgh, Pa. BR TR 6'1" 188 lbs.

Year/Team	G	AB	H	2B	3B	HR	HR%	R	RBI	BB	SO	SB	BA	SA	PH AB	PH H	G by POS
1943 CHI N	14	55	15	3	0	0	0.0	3	9	3	6	1	.273	.327	0	0	OF-13, 3B-1
1944	23	50	11	4	0	0	0.0	3	5	2	6	0	.220	.300	9	2	OF-12
1945	49	93	24	4	1	2	2.2	8	11	8	23	2	.258	.387	15	3	OF-26
1949 2 teams		STL N (24G – .222)				BOS N (79G – .266)											
" Total	103	259	67	14	1	3	1.2	31	32	20	42	0	.259	.355	19	4	OF-81, 3B-2
4 yrs.	189	457	117	25	2	5	1.1	45	57	33	77	3	.256	.352	43	9	OF-132, 3B-3
1 yr.	24	45	10	2	1	0	0.0	5	1	3	8	0	.222	.311	11	1	OF-10

WORLD SERIES

Year/Team	G	AB	H	2B	3B	HR	HR%	R	RBI	BB	SO	SB	BA	SA	PH AB	PH H	G by POS
1945 CHI N	2	2	0	0	0	0	0.0	0	0	0	2	0	.000	.000	2	0	

Hank Sauer

SAUER, HENRY JOHN
Brother of Ed Sauer.
B. Mar. 17, 1919, Pittsburgh, Pa. BR TR 6'2" 198 lbs.

Year/Team	G	AB	H	2B	3B	HR	HR%	R	RBI	BB	SO	SB	BA	SA	PH AB	PH H	G by POS
1941 CIN N	9	33	10	4	0	0	0.0	4	5	1	4	0	.303	.424	1	1	OF-8
1942	7	20	5	0	0	2	10.0	4	4	2	2	0	.250	.550	3	1	1B-4
1945	31	116	34	1	0	5	4.3	18	20	6	16	2	.293	.431	1	0	OF-28, 1B-3
1948	145	530	138	22	1	35	6.6	78	97	60	85	2	.260	.504	2	0	OF-132, 1B-12
1949 2 teams		CIN N (42G – .237)				CHI N (96G – .291)											
" Total	138	509	140	23	1	31	6.1	81	99	55	66	0	.275	.507	3	0	OF-135, 1B-1
1950 CHI N	145	540	148	32	2	32	5.9	85	103	60	67	1	.274	.519	3	2	OF-125, 1B-18
1951	141	525	138	19	4	30	5.7	77	89	45	77	2	.263	.486	8	1	OF-132
1952	151	567	153	31	3	37	6.5	89	121	77	92	1	.270	.531	0	0	OF-151
1953	108	395	104	16	5	19	4.8	61	60	50	56	0	.263	.473	5	0	OF-105
1954	142	520	150	18	1	41	7.9	98	103	70	68	2	.288	.563	1	0	OF-141
1955	79	261	55	8	1	12	4.6	29	28	26	47	0	.211	.387	10	0	OF-68
1956 STL N	75	151	45	4	0	5	3.3	11	24	25	31	0	.298	.424	31	6	OF-37
1957 NY N	127	378	98	14	1	26	6.9	46	76	49	59	1	.259	.508	24	7	OF-98
1958 SF N	88	236	59	8	0	12	5.1	27	46	35	37	0	.250	.436	19	2	OF-67
1959	13	15	1	0	0	1	6.7	1	7	1	7	0	.067	.267	12	1	OF-1
15 yrs.	1399	4796	1278	200	19	288	6.0	709	876	561	714	11	.266	.496	123	22	OF-1228, 1B-38
1 yr.	75	151	45	4	0	5	3.3	11	24	25	31	0	.298	.424	31	6	OF-37

Ted Savage

SAVAGE, THEODORE EPHESIAN
B. Feb. 21, 1937, Venice, Ill. BR TR 6'1" 185 lbs.

Year/Team	G	AB	H	2B	3B	HR	HR%	R	RBI	BB	SO	SB	BA	SA	PH AB	PH H	G by POS
1962 PHI N	127	335	89	11	2	7	2.1	54	39	40	66	16	.266	.373	21	3	OF-109
1963 PIT N	85	149	29	2	1	5	3.4	22	14	14	31	4	.195	.322	33	5	OF-47
1965 STL N	30	63	10	3	0	1	1.6	7	4	6	9	1	.159	.254	7	2	OF-20
1966	16	29	5	2	1	0	0.0	4	3	4	7	4	.172	.310	9	2	OF-7
1967 2 teams		STL N (9G – .125)				CHI N (96G – .218)											
" Total	105	233	50	10	1	5	2.1	41	33	41	57	7	.215	.330	17	4	OF-86, 3B-1
1968 2 teams		CHI N (3G – .250)				LA N (61G – .206)											
" Total	64	134	28	6	1	2	1.5	7	7	10	21	1	.209	.313	22	4	OF-41
1969 CIN N	68	110	25	7	0	2	1.8	20	11	20	27	3	.227	.345	27	5	OF-17, 2B-1
1970 MIL A	114	276	77	10	5	12	4.3	43	50	57	44	10	.279	.482	31	6	OF-82, 1B-1
1971 2 teams		MIL A (14G – .176)				KC A (19G – .172)											
" Total	33	46	8	0	0	0	0.0	4	2	8	10	3	.174	.174	18	2	OF-15
9 yrs.	642	1375	321	51	11	34	2.5	202	163	200	272	49	.233	.361	185	33	OF-424, 3B-1, 2B-1, 1B-1
3 yrs.	55	100	16	5	1	1	1.0	12	7	11	19	5	.160	.260	24	5	OF-27

	G	AB	H	2B	3B	HR	HR%	R	RBI	BB	SO	SB	BA	SA	Pinch Hit AB	Pinch Hit H	G by POS

Carl Sawatski
SAWATSKI, CARL ERNEST (Swats)
B. Nov. 4, 1927, Shickshinny, Pa.   BL TR 5'10" 210 lbs.

	G	AB	H	2B	3B	HR	HR%	R	RBI	BB	SO	SB	BA	SA	PH AB	PH H	G by POS
1948 CHI N	2	2	0	0	0	0	0.0	0	0	0	0	0	.000	.000	2	0	
1950	38	103	18	1	0	1	1.0	4	7	11	19	0	.175	.214	7	0	C-32
1953	43	59	13	3	0	1	1.7	5	5	7	7	0	.220	.322	29	6	C-15
1954 CHI A	43	109	20	3	1	0	0.9	6	12	15	20	0	.183	.294	8	1	C-33
1957 MIL N	58	105	25	4	0	6	5.7	13	17	10	15	0	.238	.448	31	6	C-28
1958 2 teams MIL N (10G - .100) PHI N (60G - .230)																	
" Total	70	193	43	4	1	5	2.6	13	13	18	47	0	.223	.332	13	4	C-56
1959 PHI N	74	198	58	10	0	9	4.5	15	43	32	36	0	.293	.480	7	1	C-69
1960 STL N	78	179	41	4	0	6	3.4	16	27	22	24	0	.229	.352	27	7	C-67
1961	86	174	52	8	0	10	5.7	23	33	25	17	0	.299	.517	39	10	C-60, OF-1
1962	85	222	56	9	1	13	5.9	26	42	36	38	0	.252	.477	15	2	C-70
1963	56	105	25	0	0	6	5.7	12	14	15	28	2	.238	.410	31	4	C-27
11 yrs.	633	1449	351	46	5	58	4.0	133	213	191	251	2	.242	.401	209	41	C-457, OF-1
4 yrs.	305	680	174	21	1	35	5.1	77	116	98	107	2	.256	.444	112	23	C-224, OF-1
WORLD SERIES																	
1957 MIL N	2	2	0	0	0	0	0.0	0	0	0	2	0	.000	.000	2	0	

Jimmie Schaffer
SCHAFFER, JIMMIE RONALD
B. Apr. 5, 1936, Limeport, Pa.   BR TR 5'9" 170 lbs.

	G	AB	H	2B	3B	HR	HR%	R	RBI	BB	SO	SB	BA	SA	PH AB	PH H	G by POS
1961 STL N	68	153	39	7	1	1	0.7	15	16	9	29	0	.255	.320	1	1	C-68
1962	70	66	16	2	1	0	0.0	7	6	6	16	1	.242	.303	1	0	C-69
1963 CHI N	57	142	34	7	0	7	4.9	17	19	11	35	0	.239	.437	1	0	C-54
1964	54	122	25	6	1	2	1.6	9	9	17	17	2	.205	.320	9	3	C-43
1965 2 teams CHI A (17G - .194) NY N (24G - .135)																	
" Total	41	68	11	5	1	0	0.0	2	1	4	19	0	.162	.265	7	0	C-35
1966 PHI N	18	15	2	1	0	1	6.7	2	4	1	7	0	.133	.400	2	0	C-6
1967	2	2	0	0	0	0	0.0	1	0	1	1	0	.000	.000	0	0	C-1
1968 CIN N	4	6	1	0	0	0	0.0	0	1	0	3	0	.167	.167	2	0	C-2
8 yrs.	314	574	128	28	3	11	1.9	53	56	49	127	3	.223	.340	23	4	C-278
2 yrs.	138	219	55	9	1	1	0.5	22	22	15	45	1	.251	.315	2	1	C-137

Bobby Schang
SCHANG, ROBERT MARTIN
Brother of Wally Schang.
B. Dec. 7, 1886, Wales Center, N. Y.   D. Aug. 29, 1966, Sacramento, Calif.   BR TR 5'7" 165 lbs.

	G	AB	H	2B	3B	HR	HR%	R	RBI	BB	SO	SB	BA	SA	PH AB	PH H	G by POS
1914 PIT N	11	35	8	1	1	0	0.0	0	0	0	10	0	.229	.314	1	0	C-10
1915 2 teams PIT N (56G - .184) NY N (12G - .143)																	
" Total	68	146	26	6	3	0	0.0	14	5	18	37	3	.178	.260	9	0	C-50
1927 STL N	3	5	1	0	0	0	0.0	0	1	0	0	0	.200	.200	0	0	C-3
3 yrs.	82	186	35	7	4	0	0.0	14	6	18	47	3	.188	.269	10	0	C-63
1 yr.	3	5	1	0	0	0	0.0	0	1	0	0	0	.200	.200	0	0	C-3

Bob Scheffing
SCHEFFING, ROBERT BODEN
B. Aug. 11, 1915, Overland, Mo.
Manager 1957-59, 1961-63.   BR TR 6'2" 180 lbs.

	G	AB	H	2B	3B	HR	HR%	R	RBI	BB	SO	SB	BA	SA	PH AB	PH H	G by POS
1941 CHI N	51	132	32	8	0	1	0.8	9	20	5	19	2	.242	.326	17	3	C-34
1942	44	102	20	3	0	2	2.0	7	12	7	11	2	.196	.284	12	1	C-32
1946	63	115	32	4	1	0	0.0	8	18	12	18	0	.278	.330	19	7	C-43
1947	110	363	96	11	5	5	1.4	33	50	25	25	2	.264	.364	13	5	C-97
1948	102	293	88	18	2	5	1.7	23	45	22	27	0	.300	.427	23	6	C-78
1949	55	149	40	6	1	3	2.0	12	19	9	9	0	.268	.383	14	3	C-40
1950 2 teams CHI N (12G - .188) CIN N (21G - .277)																	
" Total	33	63	16	1	0	2	3.2	4	7	4	4	0	.254	.365	19	5	C-14
1951 2 teams CIN N (47G - .254) STL N (12G - .111)																	
" Total	59	140	33	2	0	2	1.4	9	16	19	14	0	.236	.293	7	3	C-52
8 yrs.	517	1357	357	53	9	20	1.5	105	187	103	127	6	.263	.360	124	33	C-390
1 yr.	12	18	2	0	0	0	0.0	2	3	3	5	0	.111	.111	2	0	C-11

Carl Scheib
SCHEIB, CARL ALVIN
B. Jan. 1, 1927, Gratz, Pa.   BR TR 6'1" 192 lbs.

	G	AB	H	2B	3B	HR	HR%	R	RBI	BB	SO	SB	BA	SA	PH AB	PH H	G by POS
1943 PHI A	6	5	0	0	0	0	0.0	0	0	0	3	0	.000	.000	0	0	P-6
1944	15	10	3	2	0	0	0.0	1	0	0	2	0	.300	.500	0	0	P-15
1945	4	2	0	0	0	0	0.0	0	0	0	0	0	.000	.000	0	0	P-4
1947	22	45	6	0	0	0	0.0	4	3	1	3	0	.133	.133	1	0	P-21
1948	52	104	31	8	3	2	1.9	14	21	8	17	0	.298	.490	16	7	P-32, OF-2
1949	47	72	17	2	0	0	0.0	9	10	8	10	0	.236	.264	9	2	P-38
1950	50	52	13	0	1	1	1.9	6	6	1	9	0	.250	.346	7	1	P-43
1951	48	53	21	2	2	2	3.8	9	8	1	5	0	.396	.623	2	1	P-46
1952	44	82	18	0	0	0	0.0	4	7	0	9	1	.220	.220	14	2	P-30
1953	35	41	8	0	0	0	0.0	4	2		1	0	.195	.195	8	2	P-28
1954 2 teams PHI A (1G - .000) STL N (3G - .000)																	
" Total	4	2	0	0	0	0	0.0	0	0	0	0	0	.000	.000	0	0	P-4
11 yrs.	327	468	117	14	6	5	1.1	51	59	21	59	1	.250	.338	57	15	P-267, OF-2
1 yr.	3	2	0	0	0	0	0.0	0	0	0	0	0	.000	.000	0	0	P-3

Richie Scheinblum
SCHEINBLUM, RICHARD ALAN
B. Nov. 5, 1942, New York, N. Y.   BB TR 6'1" 180 lbs.

	G	AB	H	2B	3B	HR	HR%	R	RBI	BB	SO	SB	BA	SA	PH AB	PH H	G by POS
1965 CLE A	4	1	0	0	0	0	0.0	1	0	0	0	0	.000	.000	1	0	
1967	18	66	21	4	2	0	0.0	8	6	5	10	0	.318	.439	0	0	OF-18
1968	19	55	12	5	0	0	0.0	3	5	5	8	0	.218	.309	2	0	OF-16
1969	102	199	37	5	1	1	0.5	13	13	19	30	0	.186	.236	54	14	OF-50
1971 WAS A	27	49	7	3	0	0	0.0	5	4	8	5	0	.143	.204	13	3	OF-13
1972 KC A	134	450	135	21	4	8	1.8	60	66	58	40	0	.300	.418	16	7	OF-119
1973 2 teams CIN N (29G - .222) CAL A (77G - .328)																	
" Total	106	283	87	12	4	4	1.4	33	29	45	31	0	.307	.406	21	6	OF-73

	G	AB	H	2B	3B	HR	HR %	R	RBI	BB	SO	SB	BA	SA	Pinch Hit AB	Pinch Hit H	G by POS

Richie Scheinblum continued

1974 3 teams	CAL A (10G – .154)					KC A (36G – .181)			STL N (6G – .333)								
" Total	52	115	21	2	0	0	0.0	8	4	9	11	0	.183	.200	27	5	OF-10
8 yrs.	462	1218	320	52	9	13	1.1	131	127	149	135	0	.263	.352	134	35	OF-299
1 yr.	6	6	2	0	0	0	0.0	0	0	0	1	0	.333	.333	6	2	

Bill Schindler

SCHINDLER, WILLIAM GIBBONS
B. July 10, 1896, Perryville, Mo.

BR TR 5'11" 160 lbs.

	G	AB	H	2B	3B	HR	HR %	R	RBI	BB	SO	SB	BA	SA	AB	H	G by POS
1920 STL N	1	2	0	0	0	0	0.0	0	0	0	1	0	.000	.000	0	0	C-1

Walter Schmidt

SCHMIDT, WALTER JOSEPH
Brother of Boss Schmidt.
B. Mar. 20, 1887, Coal Hill, Ark.   D. July 4, 1973, Modesto, Calif.

BR TR 5'9" 159 lbs.

	G	AB	H	2B	3B	HR	HR %	R	RBI	BB	SO	SB	BA	SA	AB	H	G by POS
1916 PIT N	64	184	35	1	2	2	1.1	16	15	10	13	3	.190	.250	3	1	C-57
1917	75	183	45	7	0	0	0.0	9	17	11	11	4	.246	.284	7	1	C-61
1918	105	323	77	6	3	0	0.0	31	27	17	19	7	.238	.276	1	1	C-104
1919	85	267	67	9	2	0	0.0	23	29	23	9	5	.251	.300	0	0	C-85
1920	94	310	86	8	4	0	0.0	22	20	24	15	9	.277	.329	1	0	C-92
1921	114	393	111	9	3	0	0.0	30	38	12	13	10	.282	.321	3	0	C-111
1922	40	152	50	11	1	0	0.0	21	22	1	5	2	.329	.414	0	0	C-40
1923	97	335	83	7	2	0	0.0	39	37	22	12	10	.248	.281	1	1	C-96
1924	58	177	43	3	2	1	0.6	16	20	13	5	6	.243	.299	0	0	C-57
1925 STL N	37	87	22	2	1	0	0.0	9	9	4	3	1	.253	.299	4	1	C-31
10 yrs.	769	2411	619	63	20	3	0.1	216	234	137	105	57	.257	.303	20	5	C-734
1 yr.	37	87	22	2	1	0	0.0	9	9	4	3	1	.253	.299	4	1	C-31

Red Schoendienst

SCHOENDIENST, ALBERT FRED
B. Feb. 2, 1923, Germantown, Ill.
Manager 1965-76, 1980

BB TR 6' 170 lbs.

	G	AB	H	2B	3B	HR	HR %	R	RBI	BB	SO	SB	BA	SA	AB	H	G by POS
1945 STL N	137	565	157	22	6	1	0.2	89	47	21	17	26	.278	.343	7	2	OF-118, SS-10, 2B-1
1946	142	606	170	28	5	0	0.0	94	34	37	27	12	.281	.343	1	0	2B-128, 3B-12, SS-4
1947	151	659	167	25	9	3	0.5	91	48	48	27	6	.253	.332	3	1	2B-142, 3B-5, OF-1
1948	119	408	111	21	4	4	1.0	64	36	28	16	1	.272	.373	17	4	2B-96
1949	151	640	190	25	2	3	0.5	102	54	51	18	8	.297	.356	1	1	2B-138, SS-14, 3B-6, OF-2
1950	153	642	177	43	9	7	1.1	81	63	33	32	3	.276	.403	0	0	2B-143, SS-10, 3B-1
1951	135	553	160	32	7	6	1.1	88	54	35	23	0	.289	.405	1	1	2B-124, SS-8
1952	152	620	188	40	7	7	1.1	91	67	42	30	9	.303	.424	0	0	2B-142, 3B-11, SS-3
1953	146	564	193	35	5	15	2.7	107	79	60	23	3	.342	.502	6	4	2B-140
1954	148	610	192	38	8	5	0.8	98	79	54	22	4	.315	.428	4	1	2B-144
1955	145	553	148	21	3	11	2.0	68	51	54	28	7	.268	.376	2	0	2B-142
1956 2 teams	STL N (40G – .314)					NY N (92G – .296)											
" Total	132	487	147	21	3	2	0.4	61	29	41	15	1	.302	.370	10	4	2B-121
1957 2 teams	NY N (57G – .307)					MIL N (93G – .310)											
" Total	150	648	200	31	8	15	2.3	91	65	33	15	4	.309	.451	1	0	2B-149, OF-2
1958 MIL N	106	427	112	23	1	1	0.2	47	24	31	21	3	.262	.328	2	0	2B-105
1959	5	3	0	0	0	0	0.0	0	0	0	0	0	.000	.000	1	0	2B-4
1960	68	226	58	9	1	1	0.4	21	19	17	13	1	.257	.319	4	0	2B-62
1961 STL N	72	120	36	9	0	1	0.8	9	12	12	6	1	.300	.400	48	16	2B-32
1962	98	143	43	4	0	2	1.4	21	12	9	12	0	.301	.371	72	22	2B-21, 3B-4
1963	6	5	0	0	0	0	0.0	0	0	0	1	0	.000	.000	5	0	
19 yrs.	2216	8479	2449	427	78	84	1.0	1223	773	606	346	89	.289	.387	185	56	2B-1834, OF-123, SS-49, 3B-39
15 yrs.	1795	6841	1980	352	65	65	1.0	1025	651	497	287	80	.289	.388	170	53	2B-1429, OF-121, SS-49, 3B-39
		4th	3rd	5th	6th					5th		10th			1st	1st	
WORLD SERIES																	
1946 STL N	7	30	7	1	0	0	0.0	3	1	0	2	1	.233	.267	0	0	2B-7
1957 MIL N	5	18	5	1	0	0	0.0	0	2	0	1	0	.278	.333	0	0	2B-5
1958	7	30	9	3	1	0	0.0	5	0	2	1	0	.300	.467	0	0	2B-7
3 yrs.	19	78	21	5	1	0	0.0	8	3	2	4	1	.269	.359	0	0	2B-19

Dick Schofield

SCHOFIELD, JOHN RICHARD (Ducky)
B. Jan. 7, 1935, Springfield, Ill.

BB TR 5'9" 163 lbs.

	G	AB	H	2B	3B	HR	HR %	R	RBI	BB	SO	SB	BA	SA	AB	H	G by POS
1953 STL N	33	39	7	0	0	2	5.1	9	4	2	11	0	.179	.333	1	0	SS-15
1954	43	7	1	0	0	0	0.0	17	1	0	3	1	.143	.429	3	1	SS-11
1955	12	4	0	0	0	0	0.0	3	0	0	1	0	.000	.000	2	0	SS-3
1956	16	30	3	2	0	0	0.0	3	1	0	6	0	.100	.167	4	0	SS-9
1957	65	56	9	0	0	0	0.0	10	1	7	13	1	.161	.161	11	1	SS-23
1958 2 teams	STL N (39G – .213)					PIT N (26G – .148)											
" Total	65	135	27	4	1	1	0.7	20	10	26	21	0	.200	.267	14	3	SS-32, 3B-2
1959 PIT N	81	145	34	10	1	1	0.7	21	9	16	22	1	.234	.338	14	3	2B-28, SS-8, OF-3
1960	65	102	34	4	1	0	0.0	9	10	16	20	0	.333	.392	19	5	SS-23, 2B-10, 3B-1
1961	60	78	15	2	1	0	0.0	16	2	10	19	0	.192	.244	18	3	3B-11, SS-9, 2B-5, OF-3
1962	54	104	30	3	0	2	1.9	19	10	17	22	0	.288	.375	26	8	3B-20, 2B-2, SS-1
1963	138	541	133	18	2	3	0.6	54	32	69	83	2	.246	.303	0	0	SS-117, 2B-20, 3B-1
1964	121	398	98	22	5	3	0.8	50	36	54	60	1	.246	.349	10	0	SS-111
1965 2 teams	PIT N (31G – .229)					SF N (101G – .203)											
" Total	132	488	102	15	1	2	0.4	52	25	48	69	3	.209	.256	11	1	SS-121
1966 3 teams	SF N (11G – .063)					NY A (25G – .155)			LA N (20G – .257)								
" Total	56	144	28	2	0	0	0.0	19	6	19	18	1	.194	.208	4	1	SS-30, 3B-19
1967 LA N	84	232	50	10	1	2	0.9	23	15	31	40	1	.216	.293	6	0	SS-69, 2B-4, 3B-2
1968 STL N	69	127	28	7	1	1	0.8	14	8	13	31	1	.220	.315	11	0	SS-43, 2B-23
1969 BOS A	94	226	58	9	3	2	0.9	30	20	29	44	0	.257	.350	33	11	2B-37, SS-11, 3B-9, OF-5
1970	76	139	26	1	2	1	0.7	16	14	21	26	0	.187	.245	43	7	3B-15, 2B-15, SS-3

	G	AB	H	2B	3B	HR	HR%	R	RBI	BB	SO	SB	BA	SA	Pinch Hit AB	H	G by POS

Dick Schofield continued

		G	AB	H	2B	3B	HR	HR%	R	RBI	BB	SO	SB	BA	SA	PH AB	PH H	G by POS
1971 2 teams	STL N (34G – .217)	MIL A (23G – .107)																
" Total	57	88	16	4	0	1	1.1	9	7	12	17	0	.182	.261	17	5	SS-21, 3B-15, 2B-15
19 yrs.	1321	3083	699	113	20	21	0.7	394	211	390	526	12	.227	.297	247	49	SS-660, 2B-159, 3B-95, OF-11
8 yrs.	311	431	84	15	2	5	1.2	79	29	55	89	3	.195	.274	46	7	SS-148, 2B-36, 3B-3

WORLD SERIES

	G	AB	H	2B	3B	HR	HR%	R	RBI	BB	SO	SB	BA	SA	PH AB	PH H	G by POS
1960 PIT N	3	3	1	0	0	0	0.0	0	0	1	0	0	.333	.333	3	1	SS-2
1968 STL N	2	0	0	0	0	0	–	0	0	0	0	0	–	–	0	0	
2 yrs.	5	3	1	0	0	0	0.0	0	0	1	0	0	.333	.333	3	1	SS-2

Ossee Schreckengost

SCHRECKENGOST, OSSEE FREEMAN BR TR
Also appeared in box score as Schreck
B. Apr. 11, 1875, New Bethlehem, Pa. D. July 9, 1914, Philadelphia, Pa.

		G	AB	H	2B	3B	HR	HR%	R	RBI	BB	SO	SB	BA	SA	PH AB	PH H	G by POS
1897 LOU N		1	3	0	0	0	0	0.0	0	0	0		0	.000	.000	0	0	C-1
1898 CLE N		10	35	11	2	3	0	0.0	5	10	0		1	.314	.543	1	0	C-9
1899 2 teams	STL N (72G – .278)							CLE N (43G – .313)										
" Total		115	427	124	20	5	2	0.5	57	47	21		18	.290	.375	6	0	C-64, 1B-43, OF-2, SS-1, 2B-1
1901 BOS A		86	280	85	13	5	0	0.0	37	38	19		6	.304	.386	9	3	C-72, 1B-4
1902 2 teams	CLE A (18G – .338)							PHI A (79G – .324)										
" Total		97	358	117	17	2	2	0.6	50	52	9		5	.327	.402	2	0	C-71, 1B-24, OF-1
1903 PHI A		92	306	78	13	4	3	1.0	26	30	11		0	.255	.353	5	1	C-77, 1B-10
1904		95	311	58	9	1	1	0.3	23	21	5		3	.186	.232	3	1	C-84, 1B-9
1905		121	416	113	19	6	0	0.0	30	45	3		9	.272	.346	7	1	C-112, 1B-2
1906		98	338	96	20	1	1	0.3	29	41	10		5	.284	.358	5	0	C-89, 1B-4
1907		101	356	97	16	3	0	0.0	30	38	17		4	.272	.334	2	0	C-99, 1B-2
1908 2 teams	PHI A (71G – .222)							CHI A (6G – .188)										
" Total		77	223	49	7	1	0	0.0	17	16	7		1	.220	.260	5	3	C-72, 1B-1
11 yrs.		893	3053	828	136	31	9	0.3	304	338	102		52	.271	.345	45	9	C-750, 1B-99, OF-3, SS-1, 2B-1
1 yr.		72	277	77	12	2	2	0.7	42	37	15		14	.278	.357	4	0	1B-42, C-25, OF-1, 2B-1

WORLD SERIES

	G	AB	H	2B	3B	HR	HR%	R	RBI	BB	SO	SB	BA	SA	PH AB	PH H	G by POS
1905 PHI A	3	9	2	1	0	0	0.0	2	0	0		0	.222	.333	0	0	C-3

Pop Schriver

SCHRIVER, WILLIAM F. BR TR 5'9½" 172 lbs.
B. June 11, 1866, Brooklyn, N. Y. D. Dec. 27, 1932, Brooklyn, N. Y.

	G	AB	H	2B	3B	HR	HR%	R	RBI	BB	SO	SB	BA	SA	PH AB	PH H	G by POS
1886 BKN AA	8	21	1	0	0	0	0.0	2		2			.048	.048	0	0	OF-5, C-3
1888 PHI N	40	134	26	5	2	1	0.7	15	23	7	21	2	.194	.284	0	0	C-27, SS-6, 3B-6, OF-1
1889	55	211	56	10	0	1	0.5	24	19	16	8	5	.265	.327	0	0	C-48, 2B-6, 3B-1
1890	57	223	61	9	6	0	0.0	37	35	22	15	9	.274	.368	0	0	C-34, 1B-10, 3B-8, 2B-3, OF-2
1891 CHI N	27	90	30	1	4	1	1.1	15	21	10	9	1	.333	.467	0	0	C-27, 1B-2
1892	92	326	73	10	6	1	0.3	40	34	27	25	4	.224	.301	0	0	C-82, OF-10
1893	64	229	65	8	3	4	1.7	49	34	14	9	4	.284	.397	3	0	C-56, OF-5
1894	96	349	96	12	3	3	0.9	55	47	29	21	9	.275	.352	1	0	C-88, SS-3, 3B-3, 1B-2
1895 NY N	24	92	29	2	1	1	1.1	16	16	9	10	3	.315	.391	0	0	C-18, 1B-6
1897 CIN N	61	178	54	12	4	1	0.6	29	30	19		3	.303	.433	5	1	C-53
1898 PIT N	95	315	72	15	3	0	0.0	25	32	23		0	.229	.295	2	0	C-92, 1B-1
1899	91	301	85	19	5	1	0.3	31	49	23		4	.282	.389	5	1	C-78, 1B-8
1900	37	92	27	7	0	1	1.1	12	12	10		0	.293	.402	9	3	C-24, 1B-1
1901 STL N	53	166	45	7	3	1	0.6	17	23	12		2	.271	.367	9	3	C-24, 1B-19
14 yrs.	800	2727	720	117	40	16	0.6	367	374	223	118	46	.264	.354	34	8	C-654, 1B-49, OF-23, 3B-18, SS-9, 2B-9
1 yr.	53	166	45	7	3	1	0.6	17	23	12		2	.271	.367	9	3	C-24, 1B-19

Heinie Schuble

SCHUBLE, HENRY GEORGE BR TR 5'9" 152 lbs.
B. Nov. 1, 1906, Houston, Tex.

	G	AB	H	2B	3B	HR	HR%	R	RBI	BB	SO	SB	BA	SA	PH AB	PH H	G by POS
1927 STL N	65	218	56	6	2	4	1.8	29	28	7	27	0	.257	.358	0	0	SS-65
1929 DET A	92	258	60	11	7	2	0.8	35	28	19	23	3	.233	.353	1	0	SS-86, 3B-2
1932	101	340	92	20	6	5	1.5	57	52	24	37	14	.271	.409	2	0	3B-76, SS-15
1933	49	96	21	4	1	0	0.0	12	6	5	17	2	.219	.281	9	4	3B-23, SS-2, 2B-1
1934	11	15	4	2	0	0	0.0	2	2	1	4	0	.267	.400	4	0	SS-3, 3B-2, 2B-1
1935	11	8	2	0	0	0	0.0	3	0	1	0	0	.250	.250	2	1	3B-2, 2B-1
1936 STL N	2	0	0	0	0	0	–	0	0	0	0	0	–	–	0	0	3B-1
7 yrs.	331	935	235	43	16	11	1.2	138	116	57	108	19	.251	.367	18	5	SS-171, 3B-106, 2B-3
2 yrs.	67	218	56	6	2	4	1.8	29	28	7	27	0	.257	.358	0	0	SS-65, 3B-1

Johnny Schulte

SCHULTE, JOHN CLEMENT BL TR 5'11" 190 lbs.
B. Sept. 8, 1896, Fredericktown, Mo. D. June 28, 1978, St. Louis, Mo.

		G	AB	H	2B	3B	HR	HR%	R	RBI	BB	SO	SB	BA	SA	PH AB	PH H	G by POS
1923 STL A		7	3	0	0	0	0	0.0	1	1	4	0	0	.000	.000	2	0	1B-1, C-1
1927 STL N		64	156	45	8	2	9	5.8	35	32	47	19	1	.288	.538	3	1	C-59
1928 PHI N		65	113	28	2	2	4	3.5	14	17	15	12	0	.248	.407	26	6	C-34
1929 CHI N		31	69	18	3	0	0	0.0	6	9	7	11	0	.261	.304	1	1	C-30
1932 2 teams	STL A (15G – .208)							BOS N (10G – .222)										
" Total		25	33	7	2	0	1	3.0	3	5	3	7	0	.212	.364	8	1	C-16
5 yrs.		192	374	98	15	4	14	3.7	59	64	76	49	1	.262	.436	40	9	C-140, 1B-1
1 yr.		64	156	45	8	2	9	5.8	35	32	47	19	1	.288	.538	3	1	C-59

Joe Schultz

SCHULTZ, JOSEPH CHARLES (Germany) BR TR 5'11½" 172 lbs.
Father of Joe Schultz.
B. July 24, 1893, Pittsburgh, Pa. D. Apr. 13, 1941, Columbia, S. C.

	G	AB	H	2B	3B	HR	HR%	R	RBI	BB	SO	SB	BA	SA	PH AB	PH H	G by POS
1912 BOS N	4	12	3	1	0	0	0.0	1	4	0	2	0	.250	.333	0	0	2B-4

	G	AB	H	2B	3B	HR	HR %	R	RBI	BB	SO	SB	BA	SA	Pinch Hit AB	Pinch Hit H	G by POS

Joe Schultz continued

	G	AB	H	2B	3B	HR	HR %	R	RBI	BB	SO	SB	BA	SA	PH AB	PH H	G by POS
1913	9	18	4	0	0	0	0.0	2	1	2	7	0	.222	.222	1	0	OF-5, 2B-1
1915 2 teams	BKN N (56G – .292)				CHI N (7G – .250)												
" Total	63	128	37	3	2	0	0.0	14	7	10	20	3	.289	.344	29	8	3B-55, 2B-2, SS-1
1916 PIT N	77	204	53	8	2	0	0.0	18	22	7	14	6	.260	.319	20	5	3B-24, 2B-24, OF-6, SS-1
1919 STL N	88	229	58	9	1	2	0.9	24	21	11	7	4	.253	.328	31	8	OF-49, 2B-5
1920	99	320	84	5	5	0	0.0	38	32	21	11	5	.263	.309	14	2	OF-80
1921	92	275	85	20	3	6	2.2	37	45	15	11	4	.309	.469	18	6	OF-67, 3B-3, 2B-2
1922	112	344	108	13	4	2	0.6	50	64	19	10	3	.314	.392	22	8	OF-89
1923	2	7	2	0	0	0	0.0	0	1	1	0	0	.286	.286	0	0	OF-2
1924 2 teams	STL N (12G – .167)				PHI N (88G – .282)												
" Total	100	296	82	15	1	5	1.7	35	31	23	18	6	.277	.385	17	6	OF-78
1925 2 teams	PHI N (24G – .344)				CIN N (33G – .323)												
" Total	57	126	42	9	1	0	0.0	16	21	7	2	4	.333	.421	18	3	OF-35, 2B-1
11 yrs.	703	1959	558	83	19	15	0.8	235	249	116	102	35	.285	.370	170	46	OF-411, 3B-82, 2B-37, SS-2, 1B-2
6 yrs.	405	1187	339	47	13	10	0.8	149	165	70	39	16	.286	.372	93	26	OF-289, 2B-5, 3B-3, 1B-2

Lou Scoffic

SCOFFIC, LOUIS (Weaser)
B. May 20, 1913, Herrin, Ill.　　　　　　　BR TR 5'10" 182 lbs.

	G	AB	H	2B	3B	HR	HR %	R	RBI	BB	SO	SB	BA	SA	PH AB	PH H	G by POS
1936 STL N	4	7	3	0	0	0	0.0	2	2	1	2	0	.429	.429	0	0	OF-3

Tony Scott

SCOTT, ANTHONY
B. Sept. 18, 1951, Cincinnati, Ohio　　　　BB TR 6' 164 lbs.

	G	AB	H	2B	3B	HR	HR %	R	RBI	BB	SO	SB	BA	SA	PH AB	PH H	G by POS
1973 MON N	11	1	0	0	0	0	0.0	2	0	0	1	0	.000	.000	1	0	OF-3
1974	19	7	2	0	0	0	0.0	2	1	1	3	1	.286	.286	1	1	OF-16
1975	92	143	26	4	2	0	0.0	19	11	12	38	5	.182	.238	8	1	OF-71
1977 STL N	95	292	85	16	3	3	1.0	38	41	33	48	13	.291	.397	10	1	OF-89
1978	96	219	50	5	2	1	0.5	28	14	14	41	5	.228	.283	30	6	OF-77
1979	153	587	152	22	10	6	1.0	69	68	34	92	37	.259	.361	3	1	OF-151
1980	143	415	104	19	3	0	0.0	51	28	35	68	22	.251	.311	8	2	OF-134
1981 2 teams	STL N (45G – .227)				HOU N (55G – .293)												
" Total	100	401	106	18	4	4	1.0	49	39	20	54	18	.264	.359	0	0	OF-99
1982 HOU N	132	460	110	16	3	1	0.2	43	29	15	56	18	.239	.293	10	2	OF-129
9 yrs.	841	2525	635	100	27	15	0.6	301	231	164	401	119	.251	.330	71	14	OF-769
5 yrs.	532	1689	431	67	20	12	0.7	207	168	121	271	87	.255	.340	51	10	OF-495

DIVISIONAL PLAYOFF SERIES

	G	AB	H	2B	3B	HR	HR %	R	RBI	BB	SO	SB	BA	SA	PH AB	PH H	G by POS
1981 HOU N	5	20	3	0	0	0	0.0	0	2	1	6	0	.150	.150	0	0	OF-5

Carey Selph

SELPH, CAREY ISUM
B. Dec. 5, 1901, Donaldson, Ark.　　D. Feb. 24, 1976, Houston, Tex.　　BR TR 5'9½" 175 lbs.

	G	AB	H	2B	3B	HR	HR %	R	RBI	BB	SO	SB	BA	SA	PH AB	PH H	G by POS
1929 STL N	25	51	12	1	1	0	0.0	8	7	6	4	1	.235	.294	5	1	2B-16
1932 CHI A	116	396	112	19	8	0	0.0	50	51	31	9	7	.283	.371	18	2	3B-71, 2B-26
2 yrs.	141	447	124	20	9	0	0.0	58	58	37	13	8	.277	.362	23	3	3B-71, 2B-42
1 yr.	25	51	12	1	1	0	0.0	8	7	6	4	1	.235	.294	5	1	2B-16

Walter Sessi

SESSI, WALTER ANTHONY (Watsie)
B. July 23, 1918, Finleyville, Pa.　　　　BL TL 6'3" 225 lbs.

	G	AB	H	2B	3B	HR	HR %	R	RBI	BB	SO	SB	BA	SA	PH AB	PH H	G by POS
1941 STL N	5	13	0	0	0	0	0.0	2	0	1	2	0	.000	.000	2	0	OF-3
1946	15	14	2	0	0	1	7.1	2	2	1	4	0	.143	.357	14	2	
2 yrs.	20	27	2	0	0	1	3.7	4	2	2	6	0	.074	.185	16	2	OF-3
2 yrs.	20	27	2	0	0	1	3.7	4	2	2	6	0	.074	.185	16	2	OF-3

Mike Shannon

SHANNON, THOMAS MICHAEL (Moonman)
B. July 15, 1939, St. Louis, Mo.　　　　BR TR 6'3" 195 lbs.

	G	AB	H	2B	3B	HR	HR %	R	RBI	BB	SO	SB	BA	SA	PH AB	PH H	G by POS
1962 STL N	10	15	2	0	0	0	0.0	3	0	1	3	0	.133	.133	0	0	OF-7
1963	32	26	8	0	0	1	3.8	3	2	0	6	0	.308	.423	4	1	OF-26
1964	88	253	66	8	2	9	3.6	30	43	19	54	4	.261	.415	2	0	OF-88
1965	124	244	54	17	3	3	1.2	32	25	28	46	2	.221	.352	19	2	OF-101, C-4
1966	137	459	132	20	6	16	3.5	61	64	37	106	8	.288	.462	9	2	OF-129, C-1
1967	130	482	118	18	3	12	2.5	53	77	37	89	2	.245	.369	2	1	3B-122, OF-6
1968	156	576	153	29	2	15	2.6	62	79	37	114	1	.266	.401	0	0	3B-156
1969	150	551	140	15	5	12	2.2	51	55	49	87	1	.254	.365	2	1	3B-149
1970	52	174	37	9	2	0	0.0	18	22	16	20	1	.213	.287	5	1	3B-51
9 yrs.	879	2780	710	116	23	68	2.4	313	367	224	525	19	.255	.387	43	8	3B-478, OF-357, C-5
9 yrs.	879	2780	710	116	23	68	2.4	313	367	224	525	19	.255	.387	43	8	3B-478, OF-357, C-5
											7th						

WORLD SERIES

	G	AB	H	2B	3B	HR	HR %	R	RBI	BB	SO	SB	BA	SA	PH AB	PH H	G by POS
1964 STL N	7	28	6	0	0	1	3.6	6	2	0	9	1	.214	.321	0	0	OF-7
1967	7	24	5	1	0	1	4.2	3	2	1	4	0	.208	.375	0	0	3B-7
1968	7	29	8	1	0	1	3.4	3	4	1	5	0	.276	.414	0	0	3B-7
3 yrs.	21	81	19	2	0	3	3.7	12	8	2	18	1	.235	.370	0	0	3B-14, OF-7

Spike Shannon

SHANNON, WILLIAM PORTER
B. Feb. 7, 1878, Pittsburgh, Pa.　　D. May 16, 1940, Minneapolis, Minn.　　TR

	G	AB	H	2B	3B	HR	HR %	R	RBI	BB	SO	SB	BA	SA	PH AB	PH H	G by POS
1904 STL N	134	500	140	10	3	1	0.2	84	26	50		34	.280	.318	1	0	OF-133
1905	140	544	146	16	3	0	0.0	73	41	47		27	.268	.309	0	0	OF-140
1906 2 teams	STL N (80G – .258)				NY N (76G – .254)												
" Total	156	589	151	9	1	0	0.0	78	50	70		33	.256	.275	0	0	OF-156
1907 NY N	155	585	155	12	5	1	0.2	104	33	82		33	.265	.308	0	0	OF-155
1908 2 teams	NY N (77G – .224)				PIT N (32G – .197)												
" Total	109	395	85	2	3	1	0.3	44	33	37		18	.215	.243	2	0	OF-106

	G	AB	H	2B	3B	HR	HR %	R	RBI	BB	SO	SB	BA	SA	Pinch Hit AB	Pinch Hit H	G by POS

Spike Shannon continued

	G	AB	H	2B	3B	HR	HR %	R	RBI	BB	SO	SB	BA	SA	AB	H	G by POS
5 yrs.	694	2613	677	49	15	3	0.1	383	183	286		145	.259	.293	3	0	OF-690
3 yrs.	354	1346	364	30	6	1	0.1	193	92	133		76	.270	.304	1	0	OF-353

Wally Shannon

SHANNON, WALTER CHARLES   BL TR 6'   178 lbs.
B. Jan. 23, 1934, Cleveland, Ohio

	G	AB	H	2B	3B	HR	HR %	R	RBI	BB	SO	SB	BA	SA	AB	H	G by POS
1959 STL N	47	95	27	5	0	0	0.0	5	5	0	12	0	.284	.337	28	9	SS-21, 2B-10
1960	18	23	4	0	0	0	0.0	2	1	3	6	0	.174	.174	9	1	2B-15, SS-1
2 yrs.	65	118	31	5	0	0	0.0	7	6	3	18	0	.263	.305	37	10	2B-25, SS-22
2 yrs.	65	118	31	5	0	0	0.0	7	6	3	18	0	.263	.305	37	10	2B-25, SS-22

Al Shaw

SHAW, ALBERT SIMPSON   BL TR 5'8½"   165 lbs.
B. Mar. 1, 1881, Toledo, Ill.   D. Dec. 30, 1974, Danville, Ill.

	G	AB	H	2B	3B	HR	HR %	R	RBI	BB	SO	SB	BA	SA	AB	H	G by POS
1907 STL N	8	23	7	0	0	0	0.0	2	1	3		1	.304	.304	0	0	OF-8
1908	107	367	97	13	4	1	0.3	40	19	25		9	.264	.330	10	5	OF-91, SS-4, 3B-1
1909	114	331	82	12	7	2	0.6	45	34	55		15	.248	.344	15	3	OF-92
1914 BKN F	112	376	122	27	7	5	1.3	81	49	44		24	.324	.473	7	5	OF-102
1915 KC F	132	448	126	22	10	6	1.3	67	67	46		15	.281	.415	6	1	OF-124
5 yrs.	473	1545	434	74	28	14	0.9	235	170	173		64	.281	.392	38	14	OF-417, SS-4, 3B-1
3 yrs.	229	721	186	25	11	3	0.4	87	54	83		25	.258	.336	25	8	OF-191, SS-4, 3B-1

Danny Shay

SHAY, DANIEL C.   TR
B. Nov. 8, 1876, Kansas City, Mo.   D. Dec. 1, 1927, Kansas City, Mo.

	G	AB	H	2B	3B	HR	HR %	R	RBI	BB	SO	SB	BA	SA	AB	H	G by POS
1901 CLE A	19	75	17	2	2	0	0.0	4	10	2		0	.227	.307	0	0	SS-19
1904 STL N	99	340	87	11	1	1	0.3	45	18	39		36	.256	.303	1	0	SS-97, 2B-2
1905	78	281	67	12	1	0	0.0	30	28	35		11	.238	.288	0	0	SS-39, 2B-39
1907 NY N	35	79	15	1	1	1	1.3	10	6	12		5	.190	.266	11	2	2B-13, SS-9, OF-2
4 yrs.	231	775	186	26	5	2	0.3	89	62	88		52	.240	.294	12	2	SS-164, 2B-54, OF-2
2 yrs.	177	621	154	23	2	1	0.2	75	46	74		47	.248	.296	1	0	SS-136, 2B-41

Gerry Shea

SHEA, GERALD J.
B. 1881, St. Louis, Mo.   D. May 4, 1964, St. Louis, Mo.

	G	AB	H	2B	3B	HR	HR %	R	RBI	BB	SO	SB	BA	SA	AB	H	G by POS
1905 STL N	2	6	2	0	0	0	0.0	0	0	0		0	.333	.333	0	0	C-2

Jimmy Sheckard

SHECKARD, SAMUEL JAMES TILDEN   BL TR 5'9"   175 lbs.
B. Nov. 23, 1878, Upper Chanceford, Pa.   D. Jan. 15, 1947, Lancaster, Pa.

	G	AB	H	2B	3B	HR	HR %	R	RBI	BB	SO	SB	BA	SA	AB	H	G by POS
1897 BKN N	13	49	16	3	2	3	6.1	12	14	6		5	.327	.653	0	0	SS-11, OF-2
1898	105	409	119	17	9	4	1.0	51	64	37		8	.291	.406	0	0	OF-105, 3B-1
1899 BAL N	147	536	158	18	10	3	0.6	104	75	56		77	.295	.382	0	0	OF-146, 1B-1
1900 BKN N	85	273	82	19	10	1	0.4	74	39	42		30	.300	.454	6	1	OF-78
1901	133	558	197	30	21	11	2.0	116	104	47		35	.353	.541	0	0	OF-121, 3B-12
1902 2 teams	BAL A	(4G – .267)		BKN N	(123G – .265)												
" Total	127	501	133	21	10	4	0.8	89	37	58		25	.265	.371	0	0	OF-127
1903 BKN N	139	515	171	29	9	9	1.7	99	75	75		67	.332	.476	0	0	OF-139
1904	143	507	121	23	6	1	0.2	70	46	56		21	.239	.314	0	0	OF-141, 2B-2
1905	130	480	140	20	11	3	0.6	58	41	61		23	.292	.398	0	0	OF-129
1906 CHI N	149	549	144	27	10	1	0.2	90	45	67		30	.262	.353	0	0	OF-149
1907	142	482	127	22	1	1	0.2	75	36	76		31	.263	.320	1	0	OF-141
1908	115	403	93	18	3	2	0.5	54	22	62		18	.231	.305	0	0	OF-115
1909	148	525	134	29	5	1	0.2	81	43	72		15	.255	.335	0	0	OF-148
1910	144	507	130	27	6	5	1.0	82	51	83	53	22	.256	.363	1	1	OF-143
1911	156	539	149	26	11	4	0.7	121	50	147	58	32	.276	.388	0	0	OF-156
1912	146	523	128	22	10	3	0.6	85	47	122	81	16	.245	.342	0	0	OF-146
1913 2 teams	STL N	(52G – .199)		CIN N	(47G – .190)												
" Total	99	252	49	3	4	0	0.0	34	24	68	41	11	.194	.238	12	2	OF-84
17 yrs.	2121	7608	2091	354	138	56	0.7	1295	813	1135	233	465	.275	.380	20	4	OF-2070, 3B-13, SS-11, 2B-2, 1B-1
1 yr.	52	136	27	2	1	0	0.0	18	17	41	25	5	.199	.228	4	2	OF-46
WORLD SERIES																	
1906 CHI N	6	21	0	0	0	0	0.0	0	1	2	4	1	.000	.000	0	0	OF-6
1907	5	21	5	2	0	0	0.0	0	2	0	1	1	.238	.333	0	0	OF-5
1908	5	21	5	2	0	0	0.0	2	1	2	3	1	.238	.333	0	0	OF-5
1910	5	14	4	2	0	0	0.0	5	1	7	2	1	.286	.429	0	0	OF-5
4 yrs.	21	77	14	6	0	0	0.0	7	5	11	10	4	.182	.260	0	0	OF-21

Biff Sheehan

SHEEHAN, TIMOTHY JAMES   TR
B. Feb. 13, 1868, Hartford, Conn.   D. Oct. 21, 1923, Hartford, Conn.

	G	AB	H	2B	3B	HR	HR %	R	RBI	BB	SO	SB	BA	SA	AB	H	G by POS
1895 STL N	52	180	57	3	6	1	0.6	24	18	20	6	7	.317	.417	0	0	OF-41, 1B-11
1896	6	19	3	0	0	0	0.0	0	1	4		0	.158	.158	0	0	OF-6
2 yrs.	58	199	60	3	6	1	0.5	24	19	24	6	7	.302	.392	0	0	OF-47, 1B-11
2 yrs.	58	199	60	3	6	1	0.5	24	19	24	6	7	.302	.392	0	0	OF-47, 1B-11

Ray Shepherdson

SHEPHERDSON, RAYMOND FRANCIS   BR TR 5'11½" 170 lbs.
B. May 3, 1897, Little Falls, N. Y.

	G	AB	H	2B	3B	HR	HR %	R	RBI	BB	SO	SB	BA	SA	AB	H	G by POS
1924 STL N	3	6	0	0	0	0	0.0	1	0	0	3	0	.000	.000	0	0	C-3

Ralph Shinners

SHINNERS, RALPH PETER   BR TR 6'   180 lbs.
B. Oct. 4, 1895, Monches, Wis.   D. July 23, 1962, Milwaukee, Wis.

	G	AB	H	2B	3B	HR	HR %	R	RBI	BB	SO	SB	BA	SA	AB	H	G by POS
1922 NY N	56	135	34	4	2	0	0.0	16	15	5	22	3	.252	.311	12	2	OF-37
1923	33	13	2	1	0	0	0.0	5	0	2	1	0	.154	.231	9	1	OF-6
1925 STL N	74	251	74	9	2	7	2.8	39	36	12	19	8	.295	.430	7	3	OF-66
3 yrs.	163	399	110	14	4	7	1.8	60	51	19	42	11	.276	.383	28	6	OF-109
1 yr.	74	251	74	9	2	7	2.8	39	36	12	19	8	.295	.430	7	3	OF-66

	G	AB	H	2B	3B	HR	HR %	R	RBI	BB	SO	SB	BA	SA	Pinch Hit AB	Pinch Hit H	G by POS

Burt Shotton

SHOTTON, BURTON EDWIN (Barney)   BL TR 5'11" 175 lbs.
B. Oct. 18, 1884, Brownhelm, Ohio   D. July 29, 1962, Lake Wales, Fla.
Manager 1928-34, 1947-50.

	G	AB	H	2B	3B	HR	HR %	R	RBI	BB	SO	SB	BA	SA	PH AB	PH H	G by POS
1909 STL A	17	61	16	0	1	0	0.0	5	0	5		3	.262	.295	0	0	OF-17
1911	139	572	146	11	8	0	0.0	85	36	51		26	.255	.302	0	0	OF-139
1912	154	580	168	15	8	2	0.3	87	40	86		35	.290	.353	0	0	OF-154
1913	147	549	163	23	8	1	0.2	105	28	99	63	43	.297	.373	1	0	OF-146
1914	154	579	156	19	9	0	0.0	82	38	64	66	40	.269	.333	2	0	OF-152
1915	156	559	158	18	11	1	0.2	93	30	118	62	43	.283	.360	2	0	OF-154
1916	157	618	174	23	6	1	0.2	97	36	111	67	41	.282	.343	0	0	OF-157
1917	118	398	89	9	1	1	0.3	47	20	62	47	16	.224	.259	5	0	OF-107
1918 WAS A	126	505	132	16	7	0	0.0	68	21	67	28	25	.261	.321	3	1	OF-122
1919 STL N	85	270	77	13	5	1	0.4	35	20	22	25	17	.285	.381	14	1	OF-67
1920	62	180	41	5	0	1	0.6	28	12	18	14	5	.228	.272	7	1	OF-51
1921	38	48	12	1	1	1	2.1	9	7	7	4	0	.250	.375	22	7	OF-11
1922	34	30	6	1	0	0	0.0	5	2	4	6	0	.200	.233	26	5	OF-3
1923	1	0	0	0	0	0	–	1	0	0	0	0	–	–	0	0	
14 yrs.	1388	4949	1338	154	65	9	0.2	747	290	714	382	294	.270	.333	82	15	OF-1280
5 yrs.	220	528	136	20	6	3	0.6	78	41	51	49	22	.258	.335	69	14	OF-132

Frank Shugart

SHUGART, WILLIAM FRANK   BL TR
B. 1867, Chicago, Ill.   Deceased.

	G	AB	H	2B	3B	HR	HR %	R	RBI	BB	SO	SB	BA	SA	PH AB	PH H	G by POS
1890 CHI P	29	106	20	5	5	0	0.0	8	15	5	13	5	.189	.330	0	0	SS-25, OF-5
1891 PIT N	75	320	88	19	8	2	0.6	57	33	20	26	21	.275	.403	0	0	SS-75
1892	137	554	148	19	14	0	0.0	94	62	47	48	28	.267	.352	0	0	SS-134, C-2, OF-1
1893 2 teams		PIT	N (52G – .262)				STL	N	(59G – .280)								
" Total	111	456	124	17	7	1	0.2	78	60	41	25	25	.272	.346	0	0	SS-74, OF-29, 3B-9
1894 STL N	133	527	154	19	18	7	1.3	103	72	38	37	21	.292	.436	0	0	OF-122, SS-7, 3B-7
1895 LOU N	113	473	125	14	13	4	0.8	61	70	31	25	14	.264	.374	0	0	SS-88, OF-27
1897 PHI N	40	163	41	8	2	5	3.1	20	25	8		5	.252	.417	0	0	SS-40
1901 CHI A	107	415	104	9	12	2	0.5	62	47	28		12	.251	.345	0	0	SS-107
8 yrs.	745	3014	804	110	79	21	0.7	483	384	218	174	131	.267	.377	0	0	SS-550, OF-184, 3B-16, C-2
2 yrs.	192	773	223	29	22	7	0.9	144	100	60	47	34	.288	.410	0	0	OF-150, SS-30, 3B-16

Dick Siebert

SIEBERT, RICHARD WALTER   BL TL 6' 170 lbs.
Father of Paul Siebert.
B. Feb. 19, 1912, Fall River, Mass.   D. Nov. 9, 1978, Minneapolis, Minn.

	G	AB	H	2B	3B	HR	HR %	R	RBI	BB	SO	SB	BA	SA	PH AB	PH H	G by POS
1932 BKN N	6	7	2	0	0	0	0.0	1	0	2	2	0	.286	.286	3	1	1B-6
1936	2	2	0	0	0	0	0.0	0	0	0	0	0	.000	.000	1	0	OF-1
1937 STL N	22	38	7	2	0	0	0.0	3	2	4	8	1	.184	.237	13	3	1B-7
1938 2 teams		STL	N (1G – 1.000)				PHI	A	(48G – .284)								
" Total	49	195	56	8	3	0	0.0	24	28	10	9	2	.287	.359	3	2	1B-46
1939 PHI A	101	402	118	28	3	6	1.5	58	47	21	22	4	.294	.423	2	0	1B-99
1940	154	595	170	31	6	5	0.8	69	77	33	34	8	.286	.383	0	0	1B-154
1941	123	467	156	28	8	5	1.1	63	79	37	22	1	.334	.460	0	0	1B-123
1942	153	612	159	25	7	2	0.3	57	74	24	17	4	.260	.333	0	0	1B-152
1943	146	558	140	26	7	1	0.2	50	72	33	21	6	.251	.328	1	0	1B-145
1944	132	468	143	27	5	6	1.3	52	52	62	17	2	.306	.423	0	0	1B-74, OF-58
1945	147	573	153	29	1	7	1.2	62	51	50	33	2	.267	.358	0	0	1B-147
11 yrs.	1035	3917	1104	204	40	32	0.8	439	482	276	185	30	.282	.379	23	6	1B-953, OF-59
2 yrs.	23	39	8	2	0	0	0.0	3	2	4	8	1	.205	.256	14	4	1B-7

Ted Simmons

SIMMONS, TED LYLE   BB TR 5'11" 193 lbs.
B. Aug. 9, 1949, Highland Park, Mich.

	G	AB	H	2B	3B	HR	HR %	R	RBI	BB	SO	SB	BA	SA	PH AB	PH H	G by POS
1968 STL N	2	3	1	0	0	0	0.0	0	0	1	1	0	.333	.333	0	0	C-2
1969	5	14	3	0	1	0	0.0	0	3	1	1	0	.214	.357	1	0	C-4
1970	82	284	69	8	2	3	1.1	29	24	37	37	2	.243	.317	4	1	C-79
1971	133	510	155	32	4	7	1.4	64	77	36	50	1	.304	.424	6	1	C-130
1972	152	594	180	36	6	16	2.7	70	96	29	57	1	.303	.465	2	0	C-135, 1B-15
1973	161	619	192	36	2	13	2.1	62	91	61	47	2	.310	.438	1	0	C-153, 1B-6, OF-2
1974	152	599	163	33	6	20	3.3	66	103	47	35	0	.272	.447	2	1	C-141, 1B-12
1975	157	581	193	32	3	18	3.1	80	100	63	35	1	.332	.491	5	1	C-154, OF-2, 1B-2
1976	150	546	159	35	3	5	0.9	60	75	73	35	0	.291	.394	7	4	C-113, 1B-30, OF-7, 3B-2
1977	150	516	164	25	3	21	4.1	82	95	79	37	2	.318	.500	17	2	C-144, OF-1
1978	152	516	148	40	5	22	4.3	71	80	77	39	1	.287	.512	10	3	C-134, OF-23
1979	123	448	127	22	0	26	5.8	68	87	61	34	0	.283	.507	4	0	C-122
1980	145	495	150	33	2	21	4.2	84	98	59	45	1	.303	.505	15	3	C-129, OF-5
1981 MIL A	100	380	82	13	3	14	3.7	45	61	23	32	0	.216	.376	3	1	C-75, 1B-4
1982	137	539	145	29	0	23	4.3	73	97	32	40	0	.269	.451	2	1	C-121
15 yrs.	1801	6644	1931	374	40	209	3.1	854	1087	679	525	11	.291	.453	79	18	C-1636, 1B-69, OF-40, 3B-2
13 yrs.	1564	5725	1704	332	37	172	3.0	736	929	624	453	11	.298	.459	74	16	C-1440, 1B-65, OF-40, 3B-2
	9th	8th	9th	8th		5th			6th	6th							

DIVISIONAL PLAYOFF SERIES

	G	AB	H	2B	3B	HR	HR %	R	RBI	BB	SO	SB	BA	SA	PH AB	PH H	G by POS
1981 MIL A	5	19	4	1	0	1	5.3	1	4	2	1	0	.211	.421	0	0	C-5

LEAGUE CHAMPIONSHIP SERIES

	G	AB	H	2B	3B	HR	HR %	R	RBI	BB	SO	SB	BA	SA	PH AB	PH H	G by POS
1982 MIL A	5	18	3	0	0	0	0.0	3	1	1	4	0	.167	.167	0	0	C-5

WORLD SERIES

	G	AB	H	2B	3B	HR	HR %	R	RBI	BB	SO	SB	BA	SA	PH AB	PH H	G by POS
1982 MIL A	7	23	4	0	0	2	8.7	2	3	5	3	0	.174	.435	0	0	C-7

	G	AB	H	2B	3B	HR	HR %	R	RBI	BB	SO	SB	BA	SA	Pinch Hit AB	Pinch Hit H	G by POS

Dick Simpson

SIMPSON, RICHARD CHARLES
B. July 28, 1943, Washington, D. C.

BR TR 6'4" 176 lbs.

	G	AB	H	2B	3B	HR	HR %	R	RBI	BB	SO	SB	BA	SA	PH AB	PH H	G by POS
1962 LA A	6	8	2	1	0	0	0.0	1	1	2	3	0	.250	.375	2	0	OF-4
1964	21	50	7	1	0	2	4.0	11	4	8	15	2	.140	.280	0	0	OF-16
1965 CAL A	8	27	6	1	0	0	0.0	2	3	2	8	1	.222	.259	0	0	OF-8
1966 CIN N	92	84	20	2	0	4	4.8	26	14	10	32	0	.238	.405	18	2	OF-64
1967	44	54	14	3	0	1	1.9	8	6	7	11	0	.259	.370	9	4	OF-26
1968 2 teams		STL N	(26G –	.232)				HOU N	(59G –	.186)							
" Total	85	233	46	7	2	6	2.6	36	19	28	82	4	.197	.322	3	0	OF-71
1969 2 teams		NY A	(6G –	.273)				SEA A	(26G –	.176)							
" Total	32	62	12	4	0	2	3.2	10	9	7	23	3	.194	.355	8	0	OF-22
7 yrs.	288	518	107	19	2	15	2.9	94	56	64	174	10	.207	.338	40	6	OF-211
1 yr.	26	56	13	0	0	3	5.4	11	8	8	21	0	.232	.393	2	0	OF-22

Dick Sisler

SISLER, RICHARD ALLAN
Son of George Sisler.   Brother of Dave Sisler.
B. Nov. 2, 1920, St. Louis, Mo.
Manager 1964-65.

BL TR 6'2" 205 lbs.

	G	AB	H	2B	3B	HR	HR %	R	RBI	BB	SO	SB	BA	SA	PH AB	PH H	G by POS
1946 STL N	83	235	61	11	2	3	1.3	17	42	14	28	0	.260	.362	13	4	1B-37, OF-29
1947	46	74	15	2	1	0	0.0	4	9	3	8	0	.203	.257	30	4	1B-10, OF-5
1948 PHI N	121	446	122	21	3	11	2.5	60	56	47	46	1	.274	.408	2	0	1B-120
1949	121	412	119	19	6	7	1.7	42	50	25	38	0	.289	.415	23	6	1B-96
1950	141	523	155	29	4	13	2.5	79	83	64	50	1	.296	.442	2	1	OF-137
1951	125	428	123	20	5	8	1.9	46	52	40	39	1	.287	.414	11	4	OF-111
1952 2 teams		CIN N	(11G –	.185)				STL N	(119G –	.261)							
" Total	130	445	114	15	6	13	2.9	51	64	32	40	3	.256	.404	6	1	1B-114, OF-7
1953 STL N	32	43	11	1	1	0	0.0	3	4	1	4	0	.256	.326	22	5	1B-10
8 yrs.	799	2606	720	118	28	55	2.1	302	360	226	253	6	.276	.406	109	25	1B-387, OF-289
4 yrs.	280	770	196	28	9	16	2.1	72	115	47	75	3	.255	.377	69	14	1B-171, OF-34

WORLD SERIES

	G	AB	H	2B	3B	HR	HR %	R	RBI	BB	SO	SB	BA	SA	PH AB	PH H	G by POS
1946 STL N	2	2	0	0	0	0	0.0	0	0	0	0	0	.000	.000	2	0	
1950 PHI N	4	17	1	0	0	0	0.0	0	1	0	5	0	.059	.059	0	0	OF-4
2 yrs.	6	19	1	0	0	0	0.0	0	1	0	5	0	.053	.053	2	0	OF-4

Ted Sizemore

SIZEMORE, TED CRAWFORD
B. Apr. 15, 1946, Gadsden, Ala.

BR TR 5'10" 165 lbs.

	G	AB	H	2B	3B	HR	HR %	R	RBI	BB	SO	SB	BA	SA	PH AB	PH H	G by POS
1969 LA N	159	590	160	20	5	4	0.7	69	46	45	40	5	.271	.342	0	0	2B-118, SS-46, OF-1
1970	96	340	104	10	1	3	0.3	40	34	34	19	5	.306	.350	3	2	2B-86, OF-9, SS-2
1971 STL N	135	478	126	14	5	3	0.6	53	42	42	26	4	.264	.333	6	3	2B-93, SS-39, OF-15, 3B-1
1972	120	439	116	17	4	2	0.5	53	38	37	36	8	.264	.335	13	1	2B-111
1973	142	521	147	22	1	1	0.2	69	54	68	34	6	.282	.334	1	0	2B-139, 3B-3
1974	129	504	126	17	0	2	0.4	68	47	70	37	8	.250	.296	2	0	2B-128, OF-1, SS-1
1975	153	562	135	23	1	3	0.5	56	49	45	37	1	.240	.301	1	1	2B-153
1976 LA N	84	266	64	8	1	0	0.0	18	18	15	22	2	.241	.278	13	5	2B-71, 3B-3, C-2
1977 PHI N	152	519	146	20	3	4	0.8	64	47	52	40	8	.281	.355	1	0	2B-152
1978	108	351	77	12	0	0	0.0	38	25	25	29	8	.219	.254	1	0	2B-107
1979 2 teams		CHI N	(98G –	.248)				BOS A	(26G –	.261)							
" Total	124	418	105	24	0	3	0.7	48	30	36	30	4	.251	.330	3	0	2B-122, C-2
1980 BOS A	9	23	5	1	0	0	0.0	0	1	0	0	0	.217	.261	1	0	2B-8
12 yrs.	1411	5011	1311	188	21	23	0.5	577	430	469	350	59	.262	.321	45	12	2B-1288, SS-88, OF-26, 3B-7, C-4
5 yrs.	679	2504	650	93	11	11	0.4	299	230	262	170	27	.260	.319	23	5	2B-624, SS-40, OF-16, 3B-4

LEAGUE CHAMPIONSHIP SERIES

	G	AB	H	2B	3B	HR	HR %	R	RBI	BB	SO	SB	BA	SA	PH AB	PH H	G by POS
1977 PHI N	4	13	3	0	0	0	0.0	1	0	2	0	0	.231	.231	0	0	2B-4
1978	4	13	5	0	1	0	0.0	3	1	1	0	0	.385	.538	0	0	2B-4
2 yrs.	8	26	8	0	1	0	0.0	4	1	3	0	0	.308	.385	0	0	2B-8

Bob Skinner

SKINNER, ROBERT RALPH
B. Oct. 3, 1931, La Jolla, Calif.
Manager 1968-69, 1977

BL TR 6'4" 190 lbs.

	G	AB	H	2B	3B	HR	HR %	R	RBI	BB	SO	SB	BA	SA	PH AB	PH H	G by POS
1954 PIT N	132	470	117	15	9	8	1.7	67	46	47	59	4	.249	.370	11	6	1B-118, OF-2
1956	113	233	47	8	3	5	2.1	29	29	26	50	1	.202	.326	54	9	OF-36, 1B-24, 3B-1
1957	126	387	118	12	6	13	3.4	58	45	38	50	10	.305	.468	27	8	OF-93, 1B-9, 3B-1
1958	144	529	170	33	9	13	2.5	93	70	58	55	12	.321	.491	3	1	OF-141
1959	143	547	153	18	4	13	2.4	78	61	67	65	10	.280	.399	1	0	OF-142, 1B-1
1960	145	571	156	33	6	15	2.6	83	86	59	86	11	.273	.431	5	2	OF-141
1961	119	381	102	20	3	3	0.8	61	42	51	49	3	.268	.360	18	4	OF-97
1962	144	510	154	29	7	20	3.9	87	75	76	89	10	.302	.504	4	3	OF-139
1963 2 teams		PIT N	(34G –	.270)				CIN N	(72G –	.253)							
" Total	106	316	82	15	7	3	0.9	43	25	34	64	5	.259	.380	22	6	OF-83
1964 2 teams		CIN N	(25G –	.220)				STL N	(55G –	.271)							
" Total	80	177	45	8	0	4	2.3	16	21	15	32	0	.254	.367	37	8	OF-43
1965 STL N	80	152	47	5	4	5	3.3	25	26	12	30	1	.309	.493	47	15	OF-33
1966	49	45	7	1	0	1	2.2	2	5	2	17	0	.156	.244	45	7	
12 yrs.	1381	4318	1198	197	58	103	2.4	642	531	485	646	67	.277	.421	274	69	OF-950, 1B-152, 3B-2
3 yrs.	184	315	86	11	4	7	2.2	37	47	25	67	1	.273	.400	116	28	OF-64
															9th	9th	

WORLD SERIES

	G	AB	H	2B	3B	HR	HR %	R	RBI	BB	SO	SB	BA	SA	PH AB	PH H	G by POS
1960 PIT N	2	5	1	0	0	0	0.0	2	1	1	0	1	.200	.200	0	0	OF-2
1964 STL N	4	3	2	1	0	0	0.0	0	1	1	0	0	.667	1.000	3	2	
2 yrs.	6	8	3	1	0	0	0.0	2	2	2	0	1	.375	.500	3	2	OF-2

	G	AB	H	2B	3B	HR	HR %	R	RBI	BB	SO	SB	BA	SA	Pinch Hit AB	H	G by POS

Gordon Slade

SLADE, GORDON (Oskie)
B. Oct. 9, 1904, Salt Lake City, Utah   D. Jan. 2, 1974, Long Beach, Calif.   BR TR 5'10½" 160 lbs.

	G	AB	H	2B	3B	HR	HR %	R	RBI	BB	SO	SB	BA	SA	AB	H	G by POS
1930 BKN N	25	37	8	2	0	1	2.7	8	2	3	5	0	.216	.351	0	0	SS-21
1931	85	272	65	13	2	1	0.4	27	29	23	28	2	.239	.313	0	0	SS-82, 3B-2
1932	79	250	60	15	1	1	0.4	23	23	11	26	3	.240	.320	1	1	SS-55, 3B-23
1933 STL N	39	62	7	1	0	0	0.0	6	3	6	7	1	.113	.129	3	0	SS-31, 2B-1
1934 CIN N	138	555	158	19	8	4	0.7	61	52	25	34	6	.285	.369	1	0	SS-97, 2B-39
1935	71	196	55	10	0	1	0.5	22	14	16	16	0	.281	.347	7	2	SS-30, 2B-19, OF-8, 3B-7
6 yrs.	437	1372	353	60	11	8	0.6	147	123	84	116	12	.257	.335	12	3	SS-316, 2B-59, 3B-32, OF-8
1 yr.	39	62	7	1	0	0	0.0	6	3	6	7	1	.113	.129	3	0	SS-31, 2B-1

Jack Slattery

SLATTERY, JOHN TERRENCE
B. Jan. 6, 1877, Boston, Mass.   D. July 17, 1949, Boston, Mass.   BR TR 6'2" 191 lbs.
Manager 1928.

	G	AB	H	2B	3B	HR	HR %	R	RBI	BB	SO	SB	BA	SA	AB	H	G by POS
1901 BOS A	1	3	1	0	0	0	0.0	1	1	1		0	.333	.333	0	0	C-1
1903 2 teams		CLE A	(4G –	.000)		CHI A	(63G –	.218)									
" Total	67	222	46	3	2	0	0.0	9	20	2		2	.207	.239	4	0	C-56, 1B-7
1906 STL N	3	7	2	0	0	0	0.0	0	0	1		0	.286	.286	1	0	C-2
1909 WAS A	32	56	12	2	0	0	0.0	4	6	2		1	.214	.250	15	4	1B-11, C-5
4 yrs.	103	288	61	5	2	0	0.0	14	27	6		3	.212	.243	20	4	C-64, 1B-18
1 yr.	3	7	2	0	0	0	0.0	0	0	1		0	.286	.286	1	0	C-2

Enos Slaughter

SLAUGHTER, ENOS BRADSHER (Country)
B. Apr. 27, 1916, Roxboro, N. C.   BL TR 5'9½" 180 lbs.

	G	AB	H	2B	3B	HR	HR %	R	RBI	BB	SO	SB	BA	SA	AB	H	G by POS
1938 STL N	112	395	109	20	10	8	2.0	59	58	32	38	1	.276	.438	20	2	OF-92
1939	149	604	193	**52**	5	12	2.0	95	86	44	53	2	.320	.482	0	0	OF-149
1940	140	516	158	25	13	17	3.3	96	73	50	35	8	.306	.504	7	2	OF-132
1941	113	425	132	22	9	13	3.1	71	76	53	28	4	.311	.496	2	0	OF-108
1942	152	591	**188**	31	**17**	13	2.2	100	98	88	30	9	.318	.494	1	0	OF-151
1946	156	609	183	30	8	18	3.0	100	**130**	69	41	9	.300	.465	0	0	OF-156
1947	147	551	162	31	13	10	1.8	100	86	59	27	4	.294	.452	4	0	OF-142
1948	146	549	176	27	11	11	2.0	91	90	81	29	4	.321	.470	0	0	OF-146
1949	151	568	191	34	**13**	13	2.3	92	96	79	37	3	.336	.511	1	0	OF-150
1950	148	556	161	26	7	10	1.8	82	101	66	33	3	.290	.415	3	2	OF-145
1951	123	409	115	17	8	4	1.0	48	64	68	25	7	.281	.391	11	2	OF-106
1952	140	510	153	17	12	11	2.2	73	101	70	25	6	.300	.445	3	1	OF-137
1953	143	492	143	34	9	6	1.2	64	89	80	28	4	.291	.433	7	2	OF-137
1954 NY A	69	125	31	4	2	1	0.8	19	19	28	8	0	.248	.336	31	11	OF-30
1955 2 teams		NY	A	(10G –	.111)		KC	A	(108G –	.322)							
" Total	118	276	87	12	4	5	1.8	50	35	41	18	2	.315	.442	42	**16**	OF-77
1956 2 teams		KC	A	(91G –	.278)		NY	A	(24G –	.289)							
" Total	115	306	86	18	5	2	0.7	52	27	34	26	2	.281	.392	45	11	OF-76
1957 NY A	96	209	53	7	1	5	2.4	24	34	40	19	0	.254	.368	33	8	OF-64
1958	77	138	42	4	1	4	2.9	21	19	21	16	2	.304	.435	**48**	13	OF-35
1959 2 teams		NY	A	(74G –	.172)		MIL	N	(11G –	.167)							
" Total	85	117	20	2	0	6	5.1	10	22	16	22	1	.171	.342	48	7	OF-32
19 yrs.	2380	7946	2383	413	148	169	2.1	1247	1304	1019	538	71	.300	.453	306	77	OF-2065
13 yrs.	1820	6775	2064	366	135	146	2.2	1071	1148	839	429	64	.305	.463	59	11	OF-1751
	3rd	**4th**	**4th**	**5th**	**3rd**	**8th**		**4th**	**2nd**	**2nd**							

WORLD SERIES

	G	AB	H	2B	3B	HR	HR %	R	RBI	BB	SO	SB	BA	SA	AB	H	G by POS
1942 STL N	5	19	5	1	0	1	5.3	3	2	3	2	0	.263	.474	0	0	OF-5
1946	7	25	8	1	1	1	4.0	5	2	4	3	1	.320	.560	0	0	OF-7
1956 NY A	6	20	7	0	0	1	5.0	6	4	4	0	0	.350	.500	0	0	OF-6
1957	5	12	3	1	0	0	0.0	2	0	3	2	0	.250	.333	1	0	OF-5
1958	4	3	0	0	0	0	0.0	1	0	1	1	0	.000	.000	3	0	
5 yrs.	27	79	23	3	1	3	3.8	17	8	15	8	1	.291	.468	3	0	OF-23

Bobby Gene Smith

SMITH, BOBBY GENE
B. May 28, 1934, Hood River, Ore.   BR TR 5'11" 180 lbs.

	G	AB	H	2B	3B	HR	HR %	R	RBI	BB	SO	SB	BA	SA	AB	H	G by POS
1957 STL N	93	185	39	7	1	3	1.6	24	18	13	35	1	.211	.308	11	1	OF-79
1958	28	88	25	3	0	2	2.3	8	5	2	18	1	.284	.386	1	0	OF-27
1959	43	60	13	1	1	1	1.7	11	7	1	9	0	.217	.317	7	2	OF-32
1960 PHI N	98	217	62	5	2	4	1.8	24	27	10	28	2	.286	.382	35	11	OF-70, 3B-1
1961	79	174	44	7	0	2	1.1	16	18	15	32	0	.253	.328	31	6	OF-47
1962 3 teams		NY	(8G –	.136)		CHI	N	(13G –	.172)		STL	N	(91G –	.231)			
" Total	112	181	38	9	1	1	0.6	17	16	12	22	1	.210	.287	18	2	OF-93
1965 CAL A	23	57	13	3	0	0	0.0	1	5	2	10	0	.228	.281	7	2	OF-15
7 yrs.	476	962	234	35	5	13	1.4	101	96	55	154	5	.243	.331	110	24	OF-363, 3B-1
4 yrs.	255	463	107	20	2	6	1.3	56	42	23	76	3	.231	.322	29	4	OF-218

Charley Smith

SMITH, CHARLES WILLIAM
B. Sept. 15, 1937, Charleston, S. C.   BR TR 6'1" 170 lbs.

	G	AB	H	2B	3B	HR	HR %	R	RBI	BB	SO	SB	BA	SA	AB	H	G by POS
1960 LA N	18	60	10	1	1	0	0.0	2	5	1	15	0	.167	.217	0	0	3B-18
1961 2 teams		LA	N	(9G –	.250)		PHI	N	(112G –	.248)							
" Total	121	435	108	14	4	11	2.5	47	50	24	82	3	.248	.375	5	1	3B-98, SS-17
1962 CHI A	65	145	30	4	0	2	1.4	11	17	9	32	0	.207	.276	13	2	3B-54
1963	4	7	2	0	0	0	0.0	0	1	0	2	0	.286	.571	3	1	SS-1
1964 2 teams		CHI	A	(2G –	.143)		NY	N	(127G –	.239)							
" Total	129	450	107	12	1	20	4.4	45	58	20	102	2	.238	.402	7	2	3B-87, SS-36, OF-13
1965 NY N	135	499	122	20	3	16	3.2	49	62	17	123	2	.244	.393	3	0	3B-131, SS-6, 2B-1
1966 STL N	116	391	104	13	4	10	2.6	34	43	22	81	0	.266	.396	8	3	3B-107, SS-1
1967 NY A	135	425	95	15	3	9	2.1	38	38	32	110	0	.224	.336	20	6	3B-115
1968	46	70	16	4	1	1	1.4	2	7	5	18	0	.229	.357	31	10	3B-13
1969 CHI N	2	2	0	0	0	0	0.0	0	0	0	0	0	.000	.000	2	0	
10 yrs.	771	2484	594	83	18	69	2.8	228	281	130	565	7	.239	.370	92	25	3B-623, SS-61, OF-13, 2B-1
1 yr.	116	391	104	13	4	10	2.6	34	43	22	81	0	.266	.396	8	3	3B-107, SS-1

	G	AB	H	2B	3B	HR	HR %	R	RBI	BB	SO	SB	BA	SA	Pinch Hit AB	Pinch Hit H	G by POS

Earl Smith

SMITH, EARL SUTTON (Oil)
B. Feb. 14, 1897, Sheridan, Ark.   D. June 9, 1963, Little Rock, Ark.
BL TR 5'10½" 180 lbs.

Year/Team	G	AB	H	2B	3B	HR	HR%	R	RBI	BB	SO	SB	BA	SA	PH AB	PH H	G by POS
1919 NY N	21	36	9	2	1	0	0.0	5	8	3	3	1	.250	.361	6	0	C-14, 2B-1
1920	91	262	77	7	1	1	0.4	20	30	18	16	5	.294	.340	8	4	C-82
1921	89	229	77	8	4	10	4.4	35	51	27	8	4	.336	.537	8	3	C-78
1922	90	234	65	11	4	9	3.8	29	39	37	12	1	.278	.474	12	3	C-75
1923 2 teams	NY	N	(24G –	.206)		BOS	N	(72G –	.288)								
" Total	96	225	62	16	2	4	1.8	24	23	26	11	0	.276	.418	35	6	C-46
1924 2 teams	BOS	N	(33G –	.271)		PIT	N	(39G –	.369)								
" Total	72	170	57	13	1	4	2.4	13	29	19	7	2	.335	.494	21	10	C-48
1925 PIT N	109	329	103	22	3	8	2.4	34	64	31	13	4	.313	.471	12	5	C-96
1926	105	292	101	17	2	2	0.7	29	46	28	7	1	.346	.438	7	5	C-98
1927	66	189	51	3	1	5	2.6	16	25	21	11	0	.270	.376	5	3	C-61
1928 2 teams	PIT	N	(32G –	.247)		STL	N	(24G –	.224)								
" Total	56	143	34	8	0	2	1.4	11	18	16	11	0	.238	.336	8	0	C-46
1929 STL N	57	145	50	8	0	1	0.7	9	22	18	6	0	.345	.421	7	2	C-50
1930	8	10	0	0	0	0	0.0	0	0	3	1	0	.000	.000	0	0	C-6
12 yrs.	860	2264	686	115	19	46	2.0	225	355	247	106	18	.303	.432	129	41	C-700, 2B-1
3 yrs.	89	213	63	10	0	1	0.5	12	29	26	11	0	.296	.357	12	2	C-74
WORLD SERIES																	
1921 NY N	3	7	0	0	0	0	0.0	0	0	1	0	0	.000	.000	1	0	C-2
1922	4	7	1	0	0	0	0.0	0	0	0	2	0	.143	.143	3	0	C-1
1925 PIT N	6	20	7	1	0	0	0.0	0	0	1	2	0	.350	.400	0	0	C-6
1927	3	8	0	0	0	0	0.0	0	0	0	0	0	.000	.000	1	0	C-2
1928 STL N	1	4	3	0	0	0	0.0	0	0	0	0	0	.750	.750	0	0	C-1
5 yrs.	17	46	11	1	0	0	0.0	0	0	2	4	0	.239	.261	5	0	C-12

Fred Smith

SMITH, FREDERICK VINCENT
Brother of Charlie Smith.
B. July 29, 1891, Cleveland, Ohio   D. May 28, 1961, Cleveland, Ohio
BR TR 5'11½" 185 lbs.

Year/Team	G	AB	H	2B	3B	HR	HR%	R	RBI	BB	SO	SB	BA	SA	PH AB	PH H	G by POS
1913 BOS N	92	285	65	9	3	0	0.0	35	27	29	55	7	.228	.281	2	1	3B-59, 2B-14, SS-11, OF-4
1914 BUF F	145	473	104	12	10	2	0.4	48	45	49		24	.220	.300	0	0	3B-127, SS-19, 1B-1
1915 2 teams	BUF	F	(35G –	.237)		BKN	F	(110G –	.247)								
" Total	145	499	122	18	10	5	1.0	49	69	38		23	.244	.351	2	0	SS-126, 3B-16
1917 STL N	56	165	30	0	2	1	0.6	11	17	17	22	4	.182	.224	1	0	3B-51, 2B-2, SS-1
4 yrs.	438	1422	321	39	25	8	0.6	143	158	133	77	58	.226	.305	5	1	3B-253, SS-157, 2B-16, OF-4, 1B-1
1 yr.	56	165	30	0	2	1	0.6	11	17	17	22	4	.182	.224	1	0	3B-51, 2B-2, SS-1

Germany Smith

SMITH, GEORGE J.
B. Apr. 21, 1863, Pittsburgh, Pa.   D. Dec. 1, 1927, Altoona, Pa.
BR TR 6' 175 lbs.

Year/Team	G	AB	H	2B	3B	HR	HR%	R	RBI	BB	SO	SB	BA	SA	PH AB	PH H	G by POS
1884 2 teams	ALT	U	(25G –	.315)		CLE	N	(72G –	.254)								
" Total	97	399	108	22	5	4	1.0	40	26	3	45		.271	.381	0	0	SS-55, 2B-42, P-1
1885 BKN AA	108	419	108	17	11	4	1.0	63		10			.258	.379	0	0	SS-108
1886	105	426	105	17	6	2	0.5	66		19			.246	.329	0	0	SS-105, OF-1, C-1
1887	103	435	128	19	16	4	0.9	79		13		26	.294	.439	0	0	SS-101, 3B-2
1888	103	402	86	10	7	3	0.7	47	61	22		27	.214	.296	0	0	SS-103, 2B-1
1889	121	446	103	22	3	3	0.7	89	53	40	42	15	.231	.314	0	0	SS-120, OF-1
1890 BKN N	129	481	92	6	5	1	0.2	76	47	42	23	24	.191	.231	0	0	SS-129
1891 CIN N	138	512	103	11	5	3	0.6	50	53	38	32	16	.201	.260	0	0	SS-138
1892	139	506	121	13	6	8	1.6	58	63	42	52	19	.239	.336	0	0	SS-139
1893	130	500	118	18	6	3	0.6	63	56	38	20	14	.236	.314	0	0	SS-130
1894	127	482	127	33	5	3	0.7	73	76	41	28	15	.263	.371	0	0	SS-127
1895	127	503	151	23	6	4	0.8	75	74	34	24	13	.300	.394	0	0	SS-127
1896	120	456	131	22	9	2	0.4	65	71	28	22	22	.287	.388	0	0	SS-120
1897 BKN N	112	428	86	17	3	0	0.0	47	29	14		1	.201	.255	0	0	SS-112
1898 STL N	51	157	25	2	1	1	0.6	16	9	24			.159	.204	0	0	SS-51
15 yrs.	1710	6552	1592	252	94	45	0.7	907	618	408	288	213	.243	.331	0	0	SS-1665, 2B-43, OF-2, 3B-2, C-1, P-1
1 yr.	51	157	25	2	1	1	0.6	16	9	24		1	.159	.204	0	0	SS-51

Hal Smith

SMITH, HAROLD RAYMOND (Cura)
B. June 1, 1931, Barling, Ark.
BR TR 5'10½" 186 lbs.

Year/Team	G	AB	H	2B	3B	HR	HR%	R	RBI	BB	SO	SB	BA	SA	PH AB	PH H	G by POS
1956 STL N	75	227	64	12	0	5	2.2	27	23	15	22	1	.282	.401	9	3	C-66
1957	100	333	93	12	3	2	0.6	25	37	18	18	2	.279	.351	4	2	C-97
1958	77	220	50	4	1	1	0.5	13	24	14	14	0	.227	.268	5	0	C-71
1959	142	452	122	15	3	13	2.9	35	50	15	28	2	.270	.403	1	0	C-141
1960	127	337	77	16	0	2	0.6	20	28	29	33	1	.228	.294	5	1	C-124
1961	45	125	31	4	1	0	0.0	6	10	11	12	0	.248	.296	1	0	C-45
1965 PIT N	4	3	0	0	0	0	0.0	0	0	0	1	0	.000	.000	0	0	C-4
7 yrs.	570	1697	437	63	8	23	1.4	126	172	102	128	6	.258	.345	25	6	C-548
6 yrs.	566	1694	437	63	8	23	1.4	126	172	102	127	6	.258	.345	25	6	C-544

Jack Smith

SMITH, JOHN W.
Born Jan Smadt.
B. June 23, 1895, Chicago, Ill.   D. May 2, 1972, Westchester, Ill.
BL TL 5'8" 165 lbs.

Year/Team	G	AB	H	2B	3B	HR	HR%	R	RBI	BB	SO	SB	BA	SA	PH AB	PH H	G by POS
1915 STL N	4	16	3	0	1	0	0.0	2	0	1	5	0	.188	.313	0	0	OF-4
1916	130	357	87	6	5	6	1.7	43	34	20	50	24	.244	.339	7	1	OF-120
1917	137	462	137	16	11	3	0.6	64	34	38	65	25	.297	.398	8	4	OF-128
1918	42	166	35	2	1	0	0.0	24	4	7	21	5	.211	.235	0	0	OF-42

	G	AB	H	2B	3B	HR	HR %	R	RBI	BB	SO	SB	BA	SA	Pinch Hit AB	Pinch Hit H	G by POS

Jack Smith continued

	G	AB	H	2B	3B	HR	HR%	R	RBI	BB	SO	SB	BA	SA	AB	H	G by POS
1919	119	408	91	16	3	0	0.0	47	15	26	29	30	.223	.277	0	0	OF-111
1920	91	313	104	22	5	1	0.3	53	28	25	23	14	.332	.444	4	1	OF-83
1921	116	411	135	22	9	7	1.7	86	33	21	24	11	.328	.477	4	0	OF-103
1922	143	510	158	23	12	8	1.6	117	46	50	30	18	.310	.449	4	1	OF-136
1923	124	407	126	16	6	5	1.2	98	41	27	20	32	.310	.415	3	0	OF-107
1924	124	459	130	18	6	2	0.4	91	33	33	27	24	.283	.362	6	1	OF-114
1925	80	243	61	11	4	4	1.6	53	31	19	13	20	.251	.379	10	4	OF-64
1926 2 teams	STL	N	(1G –	.000)		BOS	N	(96G –	.311)								
" Total	97	323	100	15	2	2	0.6	46	25	28	13	11	.310	.387	9	0	OF-83
1927 BOS N	84	183	58	6	4	1	0.5	27	24	16	12	8	.317	.410	30	8	OF-48
1928	96	254	71	9	2	1	0.4	30	32	21	14	6	.280	.343	25	9	OF-65
1929	19	20	5	0	0	0	0.0	2	2	2	2	0	.250	.250	3	0	OF-9
15 yrs.	1406	4532	1301	182	71	40	0.9	783	382	334	348	228	.287	.385	113	29	OF-1217
12 yrs.	1111	3753	1067	152	63	36	1.0	678	299	267	308	203	.284	.387	47	12	OF-1012
											2nd						

Jud Smith

SMITH, JUDSON GRANT
B. Jan. 13, 1869, Green Oak, Mich.   D. Dec. 7, 1947, Los Angeles, Calif.   BR TR

	G	AB	H	2B	3B	HR	HR%	R	RBI	BB	SO	SB	BA	SA	AB	H	G by POS
1893 2 teams	CIN	N	(17G –	.233)		STL	N	(4G –	.077)								
" Total	21	56	11	1	0	1	1.8	8	5	10	7	1	.196	.268	0	0	3B-10, OF-9, SS-1
1896 PIT N	10	35	12	2	1	0	0.0	6	4	2	2	3	.343	.457	0	0	3B-10
1898 WAS N	66	234	71	7	5	3	1.3	33	28	22		11	.303	.415	0	0	3B-47, SS-10, 1B-7, 2B-1
1901 PIT N	6	21	3	1	0	0	0.0	1	0	3		0	.143	.190	0	0	3B-6
4 yrs.	103	346	97	11	6	4	1.2	48	37	37	9	15	.280	.382	0	0	3B-73, SS-11, OF-9, 1B-7, 2B-1
1 yr.	4	13	1	1	0	0	0.0	1	0	1	2	0	.077	.077	0	0	3B-4

Keith Smith

SMITH, KEITH LAVARNE
B. May 3, 1953, Palmetto, Fla.   BR TR 5'9" 178 lbs.

	G	AB	H	2B	3B	HR	HR%	R	RBI	BB	SO	SB	BA	SA	AB	H	G by POS
1977 TEX A	23	67	16	4	0	2	3.0	13	6	4	7	2	.239	.388	3	1	OF-22
1979 STL N	6	13	3	0	0	0	0.0	1	0	0	1	0	.231	.231	0	0	OF-5
1980	24	31	4	1	0	0	0.0	3	2	2	2	0	.129	.161	17	3	OF-7
3 yrs.	53	111	23	5	0	2	1.8	17	8	6	10	2	.207	.306	20	4	OF-34
2 yrs.	30	44	7	1	0	0	0.0	4	2	2	3	0	.159	.182	17	3	OF-12

Lonnie Smith

SMITH, LONNIE
B. Dec. 22, 1955, Chicago, Ill.   BR TR 5'9" 170 lbs.

	G	AB	H	2B	3B	HR	HR%	R	RBI	BB	SO	SB	BA	SA	AB	H	G by POS
1978 PHI N	17	4	0	0	0	0	0.0	6	0	4	3	4	.000	.000	1	0	OF-11
1979	17	30	5	2	0	0	0.0	4	3	1	7	2	.167	.233	4	0	OF-11
1980	100	298	101	14	4	3	1.0	69	20	26	48	33	.339	.443	8	2	OF-82
1981	62	176	57	14	3	2	1.1	40	11	18	14	21	.324	.472	5	3	OF-51
1982 STL N	156	592	182	35	8	8	1.4	120	69	64	74	68	.307	.434	9	1	OF-149
5 yrs.	352	1100	345	65	15	13	1.2	239	103	113	146	128	.314	.435	27	6	OF-304
1 yr.	156	592	182	35	8	8	1.4	120	69	64	74	68	.307	.434	9	1	OF-149

DIVISIONAL PLAYOFF SERIES

	G	AB	H	2B	3B	HR	HR%	R	RBI	BB	SO	SB	BA	SA	AB	H	G by POS
1981 PHI N	5	19	5	1	0	0	0.0	1	0	0	4	0	.263	.316	0	0	OF-5

LEAGUE CHAMPIONSHIP SERIES

	G	AB	H	2B	3B	HR	HR%	R	RBI	BB	SO	SB	BA	SA	AB	H	G by POS
1980 PHI N	3	5	3	0	0	0	0.0	2	0	0	0	1	.600	.600	0	0	OF-2
1982 STL N	3	11	3	0	0	0	0.0	1	1	0	1	0	.273	.273	0	0	OF-3
2 yrs.	6	16	6	0	0	0	0.0	3	1	0	1	1	.375	.375	0	0	OF-5

WORLD SERIES

	G	AB	H	2B	3B	HR	HR%	R	RBI	BB	SO	SB	BA	SA	AB	H	G by POS
1980 PHI N	6	19	5	1	0	0	0.0	2	1	1	1	0	.263	.316	0	0	OF-4
1982 STL N	7	28	9	4	1	0	0.0	6	1	1	5	2	.321	.536	0	0	OF-10
2 yrs.	13	47	14	5	1	0	0.0	8	2	2	6	2	.298	.447	0	0	

Ozzie Smith

SMITH, OSBORNE EARL
B. Dec. 26, 1954, Mobile, Ala.   BB TR 5'11" 150 lbs.

	G	AB	H	2B	3B	HR	HR%	R	RBI	BB	SO	SB	BA	SA	AB	H	G by POS
1978 SD N	159	590	152	17	6	1	0.2	69	46	47	43	40	.258	.312	1	0	SS-159
1979	156	587	124	18	6	0	0.0	77	27	37	37	28	.211	.262	0	0	SS-155
1980	158	609	140	18	5	0	0.0	67	35	71	49	57	.230	.276	0	0	SS-158
1981	110	450	100	11	2	0	0.0	53	21	41	37	22	.222	.256	0	0	SS-110
1982 STL N	140	488	121	24	1	2	0.4	58	43	68	32	25	.248	.314	1	0	SS-139
5 yrs.	723	2724	637	88	20	3	0.1	324	172	264	198	172	.234	.284	2	0	SS-721
1 yr.	140	488	121	24	1	2	0.4	58	43	68	32	25	.248	.314	1	0	SS-139

LEAGUE CHAMPIONSHIP SERIES

	G	AB	H	2B	3B	HR	HR%	R	RBI	BB	SO	SB	BA	SA	AB	H	G by POS
1982 STL N	3	9	5	0	0	0	0.0	0	3	3	0	1	.556	.556	0	0	SS-3

WORLD SERIES

	G	AB	H	2B	3B	HR	HR%	R	RBI	BB	SO	SB	BA	SA	AB	H	G by POS
1982 STL N	7	24	5	0	0	0	0.0	3	1	3	0	1	.208	.208	0	0	SS-7

Reggie Smith

SMITH, CARL REGINALD
B. Apr. 2, 1945, Shreveport, La.   BB TR 6' 180 lbs.

	G	AB	H	2B	3B	HR	HR%	R	RBI	BB	SO	SB	BA	SA	AB	H	G by POS
1966 BOS A	6	26	4	1	0	0	0.0	1	0	0	5	0	.154	.192	0	0	OF-6
1967	158	565	139	24	6	15	2.7	78	61	57	95	16	.246	.389	10	1	OF-144, 2B-6
1968	155	558	148	37	5	15	2.7	78	69	64	77	22	.265	.430	0	0	OF-155
1969	143	543	168	29	7	25	4.6	87	93	54	67	7	.309	.527	4	1	OF-139
1970	147	580	176	32	7	22	3.8	109	74	51	60	10	.303	.497	2	0	OF-145
1971	159	618	175	33	2	30	4.9	85	96	83	82	11	.283	.489	0	0	OF-159
1972	131	467	126	25	4	21	4.5	75	74	68	63	15	.270	.475	2	0	OF-129
1973	115	423	128	23	2	21	5.0	79	69	68	49	3	.303	.515	1	0	OF-104, 1B-8
1974 STL N	143	517	160	26	9	23	4.4	79	100	63	70	4	.309	.528	10	4	OF-132, 1B-8
1975	135	477	144	26	3	19	4.0	67	76	63	59	9	.302	.488	7	3	OF-69, 1B-66, 3B-1

	G	AB	H	2B	3B	HR	HR %	R	RBI	BB	SO	SB	BA	SA	Pinch Hit AB	Pinch Hit H	G by POS

Reggie Smith continued

1976 **2 teams**				STL **N**	(47G –	.218)		LA **N**	(65G –	.280)							
" **Total**	112	395	100	15	5	18	4.6	55	49	32	70	3	.253	.453	8	4	OF-74, 1B-17, 3B-14
1977 LA **N**	148	488	150	27	4	32	6.6	104	87	104	76	7	.307	.576	6	1	OF-140
1978	128	447	132	27	2	29	6.5	82	93	70	90	12	.295	.559	2	0	OF-126
1979	68	234	64	13	1	10	4.3	41	32	31	50	6	.274	.466	5	2	OF-62
1980	92	311	100	13	0	15	4.8	47	55	41	63	5	.322	.508	6	3	OF-84
1981	41	35	7	1	0	1	2.9	5	8	7	8	0	.200	.314	31	6	1B-2
1982 SF **N**	106	349	99	11	0	18	5.2	51	56	46	46	7	.284	.470	6	1	1B-99
17 yrs.	1987	7033	2020	363	57	314	4.5	1123	1092	890	1030	137	.287	.489	100	26	OF-1668, 1B-186, 3B-15, 2B-6
3 yrs.	325	1164	341	59	13	50	4.3	166	199	148	157	14	.293	.495	20	8	OF-217, 1B-84, 3B-14

DIVISIONAL PLAYOFF SERIES

1981 LA **N**	2	1	0	0	0	0	0.0	0	1	0	1	0	.000	.000	1	0	

LEAGUE CHAMPIONSHIP SERIES

1977 LA **N**	4	16	3	0	1	0	0.0	2	1	2	5	1	.188	.313	0	0	OF-4
1978	4	16	3	1	0	0	0.0	2	1	0	2	0	.188	.250	0	0	OF-4
1981	1	1	1	0	0	0	0.0	0	1	0	0	0	1.000	1.000	1	1	
3 yrs.	9	33	7	1	1	0	0.0	4	3	2	7	1	.212	.303	1	1	OF-8

WORLD SERIES

1967 BOS **A**	7	24	6	1	0	2	8.3	3	3	2	2	0	.250	.542	0	0	OF-7
1977 LA **N**	6	22	6	1	0	3	13.6	7	5	4	3	0	.273	.727	0	0	OF-6
1978	6	25	5	0	0	1	4.0	3	5	2	6	0	.200	.320	0	0	OF-6
1981	2	2	1	0	0	0	0.0	0	0	0	1	0	.500	.500	2	1	
4 yrs.	21	73	18	2	0	6	8.2	13	13	8	12	0	.247	.521	2	1	OF-19
							6th										

Wally Smith

SMITH, WALLACE H.
B. Mar. 13, 1889, Philadelphia, Pa.   D. June 10, 1930, Florence, Ariz.   BR TR 5'11½" 180 lbs.

1911 STL **N**	81	194	42	6	5	2	1.0	23	19	21	33	5	.216	.330	16	2	3B-26, SS-25, 2B-8, OF-1
1912	75	219	56	5	5	0	0.0	22	26	29	27	4	.256	.324	12	0	3B-32, SS-22, 1B-6
1914 WAS **A**	45	97	19	4	1	0	0.0	11	8	3	12	3	.196	.258	11	1	2B-12, SS-7, 1B-7, 3B-5, OF-1
3 yrs.	201	510	117	15	11	2	0.4	56	53	53	72	12	.229	.314	39	3	3B-63, SS-54, 2B-20, 1B-13, OF-2
2 yrs.	156	413	98	11	10	2	0.5	45	45	50	60	9	.237	.327	28	2	3B-58, SS-47, 2B-8, 1B-6, OF-1

Homer Smoot

SMOOT, HOMER
B. Mar. 23, 1878, Galestown, Md.   D. Mar. 25, 1928, Salisbury, Md.   BL TR 5'10" 180 lbs.

1902 STL **N**	129	518	161	19	4	3	0.6	58	48	23		20	.311	.380	0	0	OF-129
1903	129	500	148	22	8	4	0.8	67	49	32		17	.296	.396	0	0	OF-129
1904	137	520	146	23	6	3	0.6	58	66	37		23	.281	.365	0	0	OF-137
1905	139	534	166	21	16	4	0.7	73	58	33		21	.311	.433	1	0	OF-138
1906 **2 teams**	146					STL **N**	(86G –	.248)		CIN **N**	(60G –	.259)					
" **Total**	146	563	142	17	11	1	0.2	52	48	24		3	.252	.327	1	0	OF-145
5 yrs.	680	2635	763	102	45	15	0.6	308	269	149		84	.290	.380	2	0	OF-678
5 yrs.	620	2415	706	94	44	14	0.6	297	252	136		84	.292	.385	1	0	OF-619

Red Smyth

SMYTH, JAMES DANIEL
B. Jan. 30, 1893, Holly Springs, Miss.   D. Apr. 14, 1958, Inglewood, Calif.   BL TR 5'9" 152 lbs.

1915 BKN **N**	19	22	3	1	0	0	0.0	3	3	4	2	1	.136	.182	4	0	OF-9
1916	2	5	0	0	0	0	0.0	0	0	0	3	0	.000	.000	1	0	2B-2
1917 **2 teams**				BKN **N**	(29G –	.125)		STL **N**	(28G –	.208)							
" **Total**	57	96	18	0	2	0	0.0	10	5	8	15	3	.188	.229	24	5	OF-25, 3B-4
1918 STL **N**	40	113	24	1	2	0	0.0	19	4	16	11	3	.212	.257	1	0	OF-25, 2B-11
4 yrs.	118	236	45	2	4	0	0.0	32	12	28	31	7	.191	.233	30	5	OF-59, 2B-13, 3B-4
2 yrs.	68	185	39	1	4	0	0.0	24	8	20	20	6	.211	.259	12	3	OF-48, 2B-11

Frank Snyder

SNYDER, FRANK ELTON (Pancho)
B. May 27, 1893, San Antonio, Tex.   D. Jan. 5, 1962, San Antonio, Tex.   BR TR 6'2" 185 lbs.

1912 STL **N**	11	18	2	0	0	0	0.0	2	0	2	7	1	.111	.111	0	0	C-11
1913	7	21	4	0	1	0	0.0	1	2	0	4	0	.190	.286	0	0	C-7
1914	100	326	75	15	4	1	0.3	19	25	13	28	1	.230	.310	2	0	C-98
1915	144	473	141	22	7	2	0.4	41	55	39	49	3	.298	.387	1	0	C-144
1916	132	406	105	12	4	0	0.0	23	39	18	31	7	.259	.308	13	5	C-72, 1B-46, SS-1
1917	115	313	74	9	2	1	0.3	18	33	27	43	4	.236	.288	18	6	C-94
1918	39	112	28	7	1	0	0.0	5	10	6	13	4	.250	.330	9	2	C-27, 1B-3
1919 **2 teams**				STL **N**	(50G –	.182)		NY **N**	(32G –	.228)							
" **Total**	82	246	49	10	2	0	0.0	14	25	13	22	3	.199	.256	2	1	C-79, 1B-1
1920 NY **N**	87	264	66	13	4	3	1.1	26	27	17	18	2	.250	.364	3	0	C-84
1921	108	309	99	13	2	8	2.6	36	45	27	24	3	.320	.453	5	2	C-101
1922	104	318	109	21	5	5	1.6	34	51	23	25	1	.343	.487	5	2	C-97
1923	120	402	103	13	6	5	1.2	37	63	24	29	5	.256	.356	8	5	C-112
1924	118	354	107	18	3	5	1.4	37	53	30	43	3	.302	.412	3	0	C-110
1925	107	325	78	9	1	11	3.4	21	51	20	49	0	.240	.375	11	5	C-96
1926	55	148	32	3	2	5	3.4	10	16	13	13	0	.216	.365	0	0	C-55
1927 STL **N**	63	194	50	5	0	1	0.5	7	30	9	18	0	.258	.299	1	1	C-62
16 yrs.	1392	4229	1122	170	44	47	1.1	331	525	281	416	37	.265	.360	86	32	C-1249, 1B-50, SS-1
9 yrs.	661	2017	507	74	21	5	0.2	123	208	119	206	22	.251	.316	45	14	C-563, 1B-50, SS-1

WORLD SERIES

1921 NY **N**	7	22	8	1	0	1	4.5	4	3	0	2	0	.364	.545	1	0	C-6
1922	4	15	5	0	0	0	0.0	1	0	1	0	0	.333	.333	0	0	C-4

	G	AB	H	2B	3B	HR	HR %	R	RBI	BB	SO	SB	BA	SA	Pinch Hit AB	Pinch Hit H	G by POS

Frank Snyder continued

	G	AB	H	2B	3B	HR	HR %	R	RBI	BB	SO	SB	BA	SA	PH AB	PH H	G by POS
1923	5	17	2	0	0	1	5.9	1	2	0	2	0	.118	.294	0	0	C-5
1924	1	1	0	0	0	0	0.0	0	0	0	0	0	.000	.000	1	0	
4 yrs.	17	55	15	1	0	2	3.6	6	5	0	5	0	.273	.400	2	0	C-15

Kid Sommers

SOMMERS, WILLIAM
B. Toronto, Ont., Canada   D. Oct. 16, 1895, Toronto, Ont., Canada

	G	AB	H	2B	3B	HR	HR %	R	RBI	BB	SO	SB	BA	SA	PH AB	PH H	G by POS
1893 STL N	2	1	0	0	0	0	0.0	1	0	0	0	0	.000	.000	0	0	OF-1, C-1

Billy Southworth

SOUTHWORTH, WILLIAM HARRISON   BL TR 5'9"   170 lbs.
B. Mar. 9, 1893, Harvard, Neb.   D. Nov. 15, 1969, Columbus, Ohio
Manager 1929, 1940-51.

	G	AB	H	2B	3B	HR	HR %	R	RBI	BB	SO	SB	BA	SA	PH AB	PH H	G by POS
1913 CLE A	1	0	0	0	0	0	—	0	0	0	0	0	—	—	0	0	OF-1
1915	60	177	39	2	5	0	0.0	25	8	36	12	2	.220	.288	8	0	OF-44
1918 PIT N	64	246	84	5	7	2	0.8	37	43	26	9	19	.341	.443	0	0	OF-64
1919	121	453	127	14	14	4	0.9	56	61	32	22	23	.280	.400	0	0	OF-121
1920	146	546	155	17	13	2	0.4	64	53	52	20	23	.284	.374	2	0	OF-142
1921 BOS N	141	569	175	25	15	7	1.2	86	79	36	13	22	.308	.441	0	0	OF-141
1922	43	158	51	4	4	4	2.5	27	18	18	1	4	.323	.475	2	0	OF-41
1923	153	611	195	29	16	6	1.0	95	78	61	23	14	.319	.448	0	0	OF-151, 2B-2
1924 NY N	94	281	72	13	0	3	1.1	40	36	32	16	1	.256	.335	16	2	OF-75
1925	123	473	138	19	5	6	1.3	79	44	51	11	6	.292	.391	1	0	OF-120
1926 2 teams		NY	N	(36G –	.328)		STL	N	(99G –	.317)							
" Total	135	507	162	28	7	16	3.2	99	99	33	10	14	.320	.497	5	4	OF-127
1927 STL N	92	306	92	15	5	2	0.7	52	39	23	7	10	.301	.402	9	2	OF-83
1929	19	32	6	2	0	0	0.0	1	3	2	4	0	.188	.250	13	1	OF-5
13 yrs.	1192	4359	1296	173	91	52	1.2	661	561	402	148	138	.297	.415	56	9	OF-1115, 2B-2
3 yrs.	210	729	222	39	11	13	1.8	129	111	51	20	23	.305	.442	22	3	OF-187

WORLD SERIES

	G	AB	H	2B	3B	HR	HR %	R	RBI	BB	SO	SB	BA	SA	PH AB	PH H	G by POS
1924 NY N	5	1	0	0	0	0	0.0	1	0	0	0	1	.000	.000	1	0	OF-2
1926 STL N	7	29	10	1	1	1	3.4	6	4	0	0	1	.345	.552	0	0	OF-7
2 yrs.	12	30	10	1	1	1	3.3	7	4	0	0	1	.333	.533	1	0	OF-9

Daryl Spencer

SPENCER, DARYL DEAN (Big Dee)   BR TR 6'2½"   185 lbs.
B. July 13, 1929, Wichita, Kans.

	G	AB	H	2B	3B	HR	HR %	R	RBI	BB	SO	SB	BA	SA	PH AB	PH H	G by POS
1952 NY N	7	17	5	1	0	0	0.0	0	3	1	4	0	.294	.412	1	0	SS-3, 3B-3
1953	118	408	85	18	5	20	4.9	55	56	42	74	0	.208	.424	3	0	SS-53, 3B-36, 2B-32
1956	146	489	108	13	2	14	2.9	46	42	35	65	1	.221	.342	2	0	2B-70, SS-66, 3B-12
1957	148	534	133	31	2	11	2.1	65	50	50	50	3	.249	.376	2	0	SS-110, 2B-36, 3B-6
1958 SF N	148	539	138	20	5	17	3.2	71	74	73	60	1	.256	.406	0	0	SS-134, 2B-17
1959	152	555	147	20	1	12	2.2	59	62	58	67	5	.265	.369	1	0	2B-151, SS-4
1960 STL N	148	507	131	20	3	16	3.2	70	58	81	74	1	.258	.404	2	1	SS-138, 2B-16
1961 2 teams		STL	N	(37G –	.254)		LA	N	(60G –	.243)							
" Total	97	319	79	11	0	12	3.8	46	48	43	52	1	.248	.395	4	0	3B-57, SS-40
1962 LA N	77	157	37	5	1	2	1.3	24	12	32	31	0	.236	.318	13	1	3B-57, SS-10
1963 2 teams		LA	N	(7G –	.111)		CIN	N	(50G –	.239)							
" Total	57	164	38	7	0	1	0.6	21	23	34	39	1	.232	.293	7	0	3B-51
10 yrs.	1098	3689	901	145	20	105	2.8	457	428	449	516	13	.244	.380	32	2	SS-558, 2B-322, 3B-222
2 yrs.	185	637	164	24	3	20	3.1	89	79	104	91	2	.257	.399	2	1	SS-175, 2B-16

Ed Spiezio

SPIEZIO, EDWARD WAYNE   BR TR 5'11"   180 lbs.
B. Oct. 31, 1941, Joliet, Ill.

	G	AB	H	2B	3B	HR	HR %	R	RBI	BB	SO	SB	BA	SA	PH AB	PH H	G by POS
1964 STL N	12	12	4	0	0	0	0.0	0	0	0	1	0	.333	.333	12	4	3B-3
1965	10	18	3	0	0	0	0.0	0	5	1	4	0	.167	.167	7	2	3B-19
1966	26	73	16	5	1	2	2.7	4	10	5	11	1	.219	.397	6	0	3B-19
1967	55	105	22	2	0	3	2.9	9	10	7	18	2	.210	.314	27	8	3B-19, OF-7
1968	29	51	8	0	0	0	0.0	1	2	5	6	1	.157	.157	14	4	OF-11, 3B-2
1969 SD N	121	355	83	9	0	13	3.8	29	43	38	64	1	.234	.369	23	5	3B-98, OF-1
1970	111	315	90	18	1	12	3.8	45	42	43	42	4	.285	.462	21	7	3B-93
1971	97	308	71	10	1	7	2.3	16	36	22	50	6	.231	.338	7	2	3B-91, OF-1
1972 2 teams		SD	N	(20G –	.138)		CHI	A	(74G –	.238)							
" Total	94	306	70	12	1	2	0.7	22	26	14	49	1	.229	.294	17	1	3B-79
9 yrs.	554	1544	367	56	4	39	2.5	126	174	135	245	16	.238	.355	134	33	3B-404, OF-20
5 yrs.	132	259	53	7	1	5	1.9	14	27	18	40	4	.205	.297	66	18	3B-43, OF-18

WORLD SERIES

	G	AB	H	2B	3B	HR	HR %	R	RBI	BB	SO	SB	BA	SA	PH AB	PH H	G by POS
1967 STL N	1	1	0	0	0	0	0.0	0	0	0	0	0	.000	.000	1	0	
1968	1	1	1	0	0	0	0.0	0	0	0	0	0	1.000	1.000	1	1	
2 yrs.	2	2	1	0	0	0	0.0	0	0	0	0	0	.500	.500	2	1	

Joe Sprinz

SPRINZ, JOSEPH CONRAD (Mule)   BR TR 5'11"   185 lbs.
B. Aug. 3, 1902, St. Louis, Mo.

	G	AB	H	2B	3B	HR	HR %	R	RBI	BB	SO	SB	BA	SA	PH AB	PH H	G by POS
1930 CLE A	17	45	8	1	0	0	0.0	5	2	4	4	0	.178	.200	0	0	C-17
1931	1	3	0	0	0	0	0.0	0	0	0	0	0	.000	.000	0	0	C-1
1933 STL N	3	5	1	0	0	0	0.0	1	0	1	1	0	.200	.200	0	0	C-3
3 yrs.	21	53	9	1	0	0	0.0	6	2	5	5	0	.170	.189	0	0	C-21
1 yr.	3	5	1	0	0	0	0.0	1	0	1	1	0	.200	.200	0	0	C-3

Tuck Stainback

STAINBACK, GEORGE TUCKER   BR TR 5'11½"   175 lbs.
B. Aug. 4, 1910, Los Angeles, Calif.

	G	AB	H	2B	3B	HR	HR %	R	RBI	BB	SO	SB	BA	SA	PH AB	PH H	G by POS
1934 CHI N	104	359	110	14	3	2	0.6	47	46	8	42	7	.306	.379	8	3	OF-96, 3B-1
1935	47	94	24	4	0	3	3.2	16	11	0	13	1	.255	.394	10	3	OF-28
1936	44	75	13	3	0	1	1.3	13	5	6	14	1	.173	.253	9	1	OF-26

Tuck Stainback continued

	G	AB	H	2B	3B	HR	HR%	R	RBI	BB	SO	SB	BA	SA	Pinch Hit AB	H	G by POS
1937	72	160	37	7	1	0	0.0	18	14	7	16	3	.231	.288	10	2	OF-49
1938 3 teams	STL N (6G – .000)			PHI N (30G – .259)				BKN N (35G – .327)									
" Total	71	195	55	9	3	1	0.5	26	31	5	10	2	.282	.374	17	4	OF-50
1939 BKN N	168	201	54	7	0	3	1.5	22	19	4	23	0	.269	.348	10	2	OF-55
1940 DET A	15	40	9	2	0	0	0.0	4	1	1	9	0	.225	.275	5	1	OF-9
1941	94	200	49	8	1	2	1.0	19	10	3	21	6	.245	.325	8	1	OF-80
1942 NY A	15	10	2	0	0	0	0.0	0	2	0			.200	.200	1	0	OF-3
1943	71	231	60	11	2	0	0.0	31	10	7	16	3	.260	.325	5	3	OF-61
1944	30	78	17	3	0	0	0.0	13	5	3	7	1	.218	.256	5	1	OF-24
1945	95	327	84	12	2	5	1.5	40	32	13	20	0	.257	.352	9	2	OF-83
1946 PHI A	91	291	71	10	2	0	0.0	35	20	7	20	3	.244	.292	23	5	OF-66
13 yrs.	917	2261	585	90	14	17	0.8	284	204	64	213	27	.259	.333	120	28	OF-630, 3B-1
1 yr.	6	10	0	0	0	0	0.0	2	0	0	3	0	.000	.000	3	0	OF-2

WORLD SERIES

	G	AB	H	2B	3B	HR	HR%	R	RBI	BB	SO	SB	BA	SA	Pinch Hit AB	H	G by POS
1942 NY A	2	0	0	0	0	0	–	0	0	0	0	0	–	–	0	0	
1943	5	17	3	0	0	0	0.0	0	0	0	2	0	.176	.176	0	0	OF-5
2 yrs.	7	17	3	0	0	0	0.0	0	0	0	2	0	.176	.176	0	0	OF-5

Virgil Stallcup

STALLCUP, THOMAS VIRGIL (Red)
B. Jan. 3, 1922, Ravensford, N. C.   BR TR 6'3" 185 lbs.

	G	AB	H	2B	3B	HR	HR%	R	RBI	BB	SO	SB	BA	SA	Pinch Hit AB	H	G by POS
1947 CIN N	8	1	0	0	0	0	0.0	1	0		1	0	.000	.000	0	0	SS-1
1948	149	539	123	30	4	3	0.6	40	65	18	52	2	.228	.315	1	1	SS-148
1949	141	575	146	28	5	3	0.5	49	45	9	44	1	.254	.336	0	0	SS-141
1950	136	483	121	23	2	8	1.7	44	54	17	39	4	.251	.356	0	0	SS-136
1951	121	428	103	17	2	8	1.9	33	49	6	40	2	.241	.346	4	0	SS-117
1952 2 teams	CIN N (2G – .000)			STL N (29G – .129)													
" Total	31	32	4	1	0	0	0.0	4	1	1	5	0	.125	.156	14	3	SS-13
1953 STL N	1	0	0	0	0	0	0.0	0	0	0	0	0	.000	.000	1	0	
7 yrs.	587	2059	497	99	13	22	1.1	171	214	51	181	9	.241	.334	20	4	SS-556
2 yrs.	30	32	4	1	0	0	0.0	4	1	1	5	0	.125	.156	14	3	SS-12

Eddie Stanky

STANKY, EDWARD RAYMOND (The Brat, Muggsy)
B. Sept. 3, 1916, Philadelphia, Pa.
Manager 1952-55, 1966-68, 1977   BR TR 5'8" 170 lbs.

	G	AB	H	2B	3B	HR	HR%	R	RBI	BB	SO	SB	BA	SA	Pinch Hit AB	H	G by POS
1943 CHI N	142	510	125	15	1	0	0.0	92	47	92	42	4	.245	.278	0	0	2B-131, SS-12, 3B-2
1944 2 teams	CHI N (13G – .240)			BKN N (89G – .276)													
" Total	102	286	78	9	3	0	0.0	36	16	46	15	4	.273	.325	5	0	2B-61, SS-38, 3B-4
1945 BKN N	153	555	143	29	5	1	0.2	128	39	148	42	6	.258	.333	0	0	2B-153, SS-1
1946	144	483	132	24	7	0	0.0	98	36	137	56	8	.273	.352	2	0	2B-141
1947	146	559	141	24	5	3	0.5	97	53	103	39	3	.252	.329	0	0	2B-146
1948 BOS N	67	247	79	14	2	2	0.8	49	29	61	13	1	.320	.417	1	1	2B-66
1949	138	506	144	24	5	1	0.2	90	42	113	41	3	.285	.358	3	0	2B-135
1950 NY N	152	527	158	25	5	8	1.5	115	51	144	50	9	.300	.412	0	0	2B-151
1951	145	515	127	17	2	14	2.7	88	43	127	63	8	.247	.369	4	0	2B-140
1952 STL N	53	83	19	4	0	0	0.0	13	7	19	9	0	.229	.277	26	9	2B-20
1953	17	30	8	0	0	0	0.0	5	1	6	4	0	.267	.267	5	0	2B-8
11 yrs.	1259	4301	1154	185	35	29	0.7	811	364	996	374	48	.268	.348	46	10	2B-1152, SS-51, 3B-6
2 yrs.	70	113	27	4	0	0	0.0	18	8	25	13	0	.239	.274	31	9	2B-28

WORLD SERIES

	G	AB	H	2B	3B	HR	HR%	R	RBI	BB	SO	SB	BA	SA	Pinch Hit AB	H	G by POS
1947 BKN N	7	25	6	1	0	0	0.0	4	2	3	2	0	.240	.280	0	0	2B-7
1948 BOS N	6	14	4	1	0	0	0.0	0	1	7	1	0	.286	.357	0	0	2B-6
1951 NY N	6	22	3	0	0	0	0.0	3	1	3	2	0	.136	.136	0	0	2B-6
3 yrs.	19	61	13	2	0	0	0.0	7	4	13	5	0	.213	.246	0	0	2B-19

Harry Stanton

STANTON, HARRY ANDREW
B. St. Louis, Mo.   TR

	G	AB	H	2B	3B	HR	HR%	R	RBI	BB	SO	SB	BA	SA	Pinch Hit AB	H	G by POS
1900 STL N	1	0	0	0	0	0	–	0	0	0	0	0	–	–	0	0	C-1
1904 CHI N	1	3	0	0	0	0	0.0	0	0	0	0	0	.000	.000	0	0	C-1
2 yrs.	2	3	0	0	0	0	0.0	0	0	0	0	0	.000	.000	0	0	C-2
1 yr.	1	0	0	0	0	0	–	0	0	0	0	0	–	–	0	0	C-1

Bill Stein

STEIN, WILLIAM ALLEN
B. Jan. 21, 1947, Battle Creek, Mich.   BR TR 5'10" 170 lbs.

	G	AB	H	2B	3B	HR	HR%	R	RBI	BB	SO	SB	BA	SA	Pinch Hit AB	H	G by POS
1972 STL N	14	35	11	0	1	2	5.7	2	3	0	7	1	.314	.543	6	3	OF-4, 3B-4
1973	32	55	12	2	0	0	0.0	4	2	7	18	0	.218	.255	18	3	OF-10, 1B-2, 3B-1
1974 CHI A	13	43	12	1	0	0	0.0	5	5	7	8	0	.279	.302	6	0	3B-11
1975	76	226	61	7	1	3	1.3	23	21	18	32	2	.270	.350	6	0	2B-28, 3B-24, OF-1
1976	117	392	105	15	2	4	1.0	32	36	22	67	4	.268	.347	8	2	3B-58, 2B-58, OF-1, SS-1, 1B-1
1977 SEA A	151	556	144	26	5	13	2.3	53	67	29	79	3	.259	.394	1	0	3B-147, SS-2
1978	114	403	105	24	4	4	1.0	41	37	37	56	1	.261	.370	2	0	3B-111
1979	88	250	62	9	2	7	2.8	28	27	17	28	1	.248	.384	8	0	3B-67, 2B-17, SS-3
1980	67	198	53	5	1	5	2.5	16	27	16	25	1	.268	.379	11	1	3B-34, 2B-14, 1B-8
1981 TEX A	53	115	38	6	0	2	1.7	21	22	7	15	1	.330	.435	20	9	1B-20, OF-8, 3B-7, 2B-3, SS-1
1982	85	184	44	8	0	1	0.5	14	16	12	23	0	.239	.299	34	10	3B-28, 2B-28, SS-6, 1B-2, OF-1
11 yrs.	810	2457	647	103	16	41	1.7	239	263	172	358	14	.263	.368	120	28	3B-492, 2B-154, 1B-33, OF-25, SS-13
2 yrs.	46	90	23	2	1	2	2.2	6	5	7	25	1	.256	.367	24	6	OF-14, 3B-5, 1B-2

	G	AB	H	2B	3B	HR	HR %	R	RBI	BB	SO	SB	BA	SA	Pinch Hit AB	Pinch Hit H	G by POS

Jake Stenzel

STENZEL, JACOB CHARLES
Born Jacob Charles Stelzle.
B. June 24, 1867, Cincinnati, Ohio   D. Jan. 6, 1919, Cincinnati, Ohio
     BR TR 5'10" 168 lbs.

	G	AB	H	2B	3B	HR	HR %	R	RBI	BB	SO	SB	BA	SA	PH AB	PH H	G by POS
1890 CHI N	11	41	11	1	0	0	0.0	3	3	1		0	.268	.293	0	0	OF-6, C-6
1892 PIT N	3	9	0	0	0	0	0.0	0	0	1	3	1	.000	.000	0	0	OF-2, C-1
1893	60	224	81	13	4	4	1.8	57	37	24	17	16	.362	.509	6	1	OF-45, C-12, SS-1, 2B-1
1894	131	522	185	39	20	13	2.5	148	121	75	13	61	.354	.580	0	0	OF-131
1895	129	514	192	38	13	7	1.4	114	97	57		25	.374	.539	0	0	OF-129
1896	114	479	173	26	14	2	0.4	104	82	32	13	57	.361	.486	0	0	OF-114, 1B-1
1897 BAL N	131	536	189	**43**	7	5	0.9	113	116	36		69	.353	.487	0	0	OF-131
1898 2 teams	BAL N (35G – .254)				STL N (108G – .282)												
" Total	143	542	149	20	13	1	0.2	97	55	53		25	.275	.365	0	0	OF-143
1899 2 teams	STL N (35G – .273)				CIN N (9G – .310)												
" Total	44	157	44	10	0	1	0.6	26	22	20		10	.280	.363	3	0	OF-40
9 yrs.	766	3024	1024	190	71	33	1.1	662	533	299	71	292	.339	.481	9	1	OF-741, C-19, SS-1, 2B-1, 1B-1
2 yrs.	143	532	149	24	11	2	0.4	85	52	57		29	.280	.378	0	0	OF-141

Bobby Stephenson

STEPHENSON, ROBERT LLOYD
B. Aug. 11, 1928, Blair, Okla.
     BR TR 6' 165 lbs.

	G	AB	H	2B	3B	HR	HR %	R	RBI	BB	SO	SB	BA	SA	PH AB	PH H	G by POS
1955 STL N	67	111	27	3	0	0	0.0	19	6	5	18	2	.243	.270	6	0	SS-48, 2B-7, 3B-1

Stuffy Stewart

STEWART, JOHN FRANKLIN
B. Jan. 31, 1894, Jasper, Fla.   D. Sept. 30, 1930, Lake City, Fla.
     BR TR 5'9½" 160 lbs.

	G	AB	H	2B	3B	HR	HR %	R	RBI	BB	SO	SB	BA	SA	PH AB	PH H	G by POS
1916 STL N	9	17	3	0	0	0	0.0	0	1	0	3	0	.176	.176	0	0	2B-8
1917	13	9	0	0	0	0	0.0	4	0	0	4	0	.000	.000	1	0	OF-7, 2B-2
1922 PIT N	3	13	2	0	0	0	0.0	3	0	0	1	0	.154	.154	0	0	2B-3
1923 BKN N	4	11	4	1	0	1	9.1	3	1	1	1	0	.364	.727	0	0	2B-3
1925 WAS A	7	17	6	1	0	0	0.0	3	3	1	2	1	.353	.412	0	0	3B-5, 2B-1
1926	62	63	17	6	1	0	0.0	27	9	6	6	8	.270	.397	3	1	2B-25, 3B-1
1927	56	129	31	6	2	0	0.0	24	4	8	15	12	.240	.318	3	0	2B-37, 3B-2
1929	22	6	0	0	0	0	0.0	10	0	1	0	0	.000	.000	0	0	2B-3
8 yrs.	176	265	63	14	3	1	0.4	74	18	17	32	21	.238	.325	9	1	2B-82, 3B-8, OF-7
2 yrs.	22	26	3	0	0	0	0.0	4	1	0	7	0	.115	.115	1	0	2B-10, OF-7

Bob Stinson

STINSON, GORRELL ROBERT
B. Oct. 11, 1945, Elkin, N. C.
     BB TR 5'11" 180 lbs.

	G	AB	H	2B	3B	HR	HR %	R	RBI	BB	SO	SB	BA	SA	PH AB	PH H	G by POS
1969 LA N	4	8	3	0	0	0	0.0	1	2	0	2	0	.375	.375	0	0	C-4
1970	4	3	0	0	0	0	0.0	1	0	0	1	0	.000	.000	0	0	C-3
1971 STL N	17	19	4	1	0	0	0.0	3	1	1	7	0	.211	.263	2	1	C-6, OF-3
1972 HOU N	27	35	6	1	0	0	0.0	3	2	1	6	0	.171	.200	15	1	C-12, OF-3
1973 MON N	48	111	29	6	1	3	2.7	12	12	17	15	0	.261	.414	10	3	C-35, 3B-1
1974	38	87	15	2	0	1	1.1	4	6	15	16	1	.172	.230	12	3	C-29
1975 KC A	63	147	39	9	1	1	0.7	18	9	18	29	1	.265	.361	4	0	C-59, OF-1, 2B-1, 1B-1
1976	79	209	55	7	1	2	1.0	26	25	25	29	3	.263	.335	2	0	C-79
1977 SEA A	105	297	80	11	1	8	2.7	27	32	37	50	0	.269	.394	11	2	C-99
1978	124	364	94	14	3	11	3.0	46	55	45	42	2	.258	.404	7	1	C-123
1979	95	247	60	8	0	6	2.4	19	28	33	38	1	.243	.348	7	1	C-91
1980	48	107	23	2	0	1	0.9	6	8	9	19	0	.215	.262	12	1	C-45
12 yrs.	652	1634	408	61	7	33	2.0	166	180	201	254	8	.250	.356	82	13	C-585, OF-7, 3B-1, 2B-1, 1B-1
1 yr.	17	19	4	1	0	0	0.0	3	1	1	7	0	.211	.263	2	1	C-6, OF-3

LEAGUE CHAMPIONSHIP SERIES

	G	AB	H	2B	3B	HR	HR %	R	RBI	BB	SO	SB	BA	SA	PH AB	PH H	G by POS
1976 KC A	2	1	0	0	0	0	0.0	0	0	0	0	0	.000	.000	1	0	C-1

Milt Stock

STOCK, MILTON JOSEPH
B. July 11, 1893, Chicago, Ill.   D. July 16, 1977, Montrose, Ala.
     BR TR 5'8" 154 lbs.

	G	AB	H	2B	3B	HR	HR %	R	RBI	BB	SO	SB	BA	SA	PH AB	PH H	G by POS
1913 NY N	7	17	3	1	0	0	0.0	2	1	2	1	2	.176	.235	0	0	SS-1
1914	115	365	96	17	1	3	0.8	52	41	34	21	11	.263	.340	0	0	3B-113, SS-1
1915 PHI N	69	227	59	7	3	1	0.4	37	15	22	26	6	.260	.330	10	1	3B-55, SS-4
1916	132	509	143	25	6	1	0.2	61	43	27	33	21	.281	.360	3	1	3B-117, SS-15
1917	150	564	149	27	6	3	0.5	76	53	51	34	25	.264	.349	0	0	3B-133, SS-19
1918	123	481	132	14	1	1	0.2	62	42	35	22	20	.274	.314	1	0	3B-123
1919 STL N	135	492	151	16	4	0	0.0	56	52	49	21	17	.307	.356	0	0	2B-77, 3B-58
1920	155	**639**	204	28	6	0	0.0	85	76	40	27	15	.319	.382	0	0	3B-155
1921	149	587	180	27	6	3	0.5	96	84	48	26	11	.307	.388	0	0	3B-149
1922	151	581	177	33	9	5	0.9	85	79	42	29	7	.305	.418	1	0	3B-149, SS-1
1923	151	603	174	33	3	2	0.3	63	96	40	21	9	.289	.363	1	0	3B-150, 2B-1
1924 BKN N	142	561	136	14	2	2	0.4	66	52	26	32	3	.242	.292	0	0	3B-142
1925	146	615	202	28	9	1	0.2	98	62	38	28	8	.328	.408	0	0	2B-141, 3B-5
1926	3	8	0	0	0	0	0.0	0	0	0	0	0	.000	.000	0	0	2B-3
14 yrs.	1628	6249	1806	270	58	22	0.4	839	696	455	321	155	.289	.361	16	2	3B-1349, 2B-222, SS-41
5 yrs.	741	2902	886	137	28	10	0.3	385	387	219	124	59	.305	.382	2	0	3B-661, 2B-78, SS-1

WORLD SERIES

	G	AB	H	2B	3B	HR	HR %	R	RBI	BB	SO	SB	BA	SA	PH AB	PH H	G by POS
1915 PHI N	5	17	2	1	0	0	0.0	1	0	1	0	0	.118	.176	0	0	3B-5

Tige Stone

STONE, WILLIAM ARTHUR
B. Sept. 18, 1901, Macon, Ga.   D. Jan. 1, 1960, Jacksonville, Fla.
     BR TR 5'8" 145 lbs.

	G	AB	H	2B	3B	HR	HR %	R	RBI	BB	SO	SB	BA	SA	PH AB	PH H	G by POS
1923 STL N	5	1	1	0	0	0	0.0	0	0	2	0	0	1.000	1.000	0	0	OF-4, P-1

	G	AB	H	2B	3B	HR	HR %	R	RBI	BB	SO	SB	BA	SA	Pinch Hit AB	H	G by POS

Alan Storke

STORKE, ALAN MARSHALL   TR
B. Sept. 27, 1884, Auburn, N.Y.   D. Mar. 18, 1910, Newton, Mass.

	G	AB	H	2B	3B	HR	HR %	R	RBI	BB	SO	SB	BA	SA	PH AB	PH H	G by POS
1906 PIT N	5	12	3	1	0	0	0.0		1	1		1	.250	.333	2	1	3B-2, SS-1
1907	112	357	92	6	6	1	0.3	24	39	16		6	.258	.317	10	3	3B-67, 1B-23, 2B-7, SS-5
1908	64	202	51	5	3	1	0.5	20	12	9		4	.252	.322	8	0	1B-49, 3B-6, 2B-1
1909 2 teams				PIT	N	(37G –	.254)		STL	N	(48G –	.282)					
" Total	85	292	79	10	2	0		23	22	19		6	.271	.318	4	1	SS-44, 1B-19, 3B-14, 2B-4
4 yrs.	266	863	225	22	11	2	0.2	68	74	45		17	.261	.319	24	5	1B-91, 3B-89, SS-50, 2B-12
1 yr.	48	174	49	5	0	0	0.0	11	10	12		5	.282	.310	0	0	SS-44, 2B-4, 1B-1

Gabby Street

STREET, CHARLES EVARD (Old Sarge)   BR TR 5'11" 180 lbs.
B. Sept. 30, 1882, Huntsville, Ala.   D. Feb. 6, 1951, Joplin, Mo.
Manager 1929-33, 1938.

	G	AB	H	2B	3B	HR	HR %	R	RBI	BB	SO	SB	BA	SA	PH AB	PH H	G by POS
1904 CIN N	11	33	4	1	0	0	0.0	1	0	1		2	.121	.152	0	0	C-11
1905 3 teams			CIN	N	(2G –	.000)		BOS	N	(3G –	.167)		CIN	N	(29G –	.253)	
" Total	34	105	25	5	1	0	0.0	8	8	8		2	.238	.305	3	0	C-30
1908 WAS A	131	394	81	12	7	1	0.3	31	32	40		5	.206	.279	3	2	C-128
1909	137	407	86	12	1	0	0.0	25	29	26		2	.211	.246	0	0	C-137
1910	89	257	52	6	0	1	0.4	13	16	23		1	.202	.237	3	1	C-86
1911	72	216	48	7	1	0	0.0	16	14	14		4	.222	.264	1	0	C-71
1912 NY A	28	88	16	1	1	0	0.0	4	6	7		1	.182	.216	0	0	C-28
1931 STL N	1	1	0	0	0	0	0.0	0	0	0	0	0	.000	.000	0	0	C-1
8 yrs.	503	1501	312	44	11	2	0.1	98	105	119	0	17	.208	.256	10	3	C-492
1 yr.	1	1	0	0	0	0	0.0	0	0	0	0	0	.000	.000	0	0	C-1

Cub Stricker

STRICKER, JOHN A.   BR TR
Born John A. Streaker.
B. June 8, 1859, Philadelphia, Pa.   Deceased.

	G	AB	H	2B	3B	HR	HR %	R	RBI	BB	SO	SB	BA	SA	PH AB	PH H	G by POS
1882 PHI AA	72	272	59	6	1	0	0.0	34		15			.217	.246	0	0	2B-72, P-2, OF-1
1883	89	330	90	8	0	1	0.3	67		19			.273	.306	0	0	2B-88, C-2
1884	107	399	92	16	11	1	0.3	59		19			.231	.333	0	0	2B-107, OF-1, C-1, P-1
1885	106	398	93	9	3	1	0.3	71		21			.234	.279	0	0	2B-106
1887 CLE AA	131	534	141	19	4	2	0.4	122		53		86	.264	.326	0	0	2B-126, SS-6, P-3
1888	127	493	115	13	1	0	0.2	80	33	50		60	.233	.290	0	0	2B-122, OF-6, P-2
1889 CLE N	136	566	142	10	4	1	0.2	83	47	58	18	32	.251	.288	0	0	2B-135, SS-1
1890 CLE P	127	544	133	19	8	2	0.4	93	65	54	16	24	.244	.320	0	0	2B-109, SS-20
1891 BOS AA	139	514	111	15	4	0	0.0	96	46	63	34	54	.216	.261	0	0	2B 139
1892 2 teams			STL	N	(28G –	.204)		BAL	N	(75G –	.264)						
" Total	103	367	91	6	5	3	0.0	57	48	42	25	18	.248	.316	0	0	2B-75
1893 WAS N	59	218	40	7	1	0	0.0	28	20	20	12	4	.183	.225	0	0	2B-39, OF-12, SS-4, 3B-4
11 yrs.	1196	4635	1107	128	47	12	0.3	790	258	414	105	278	.239	.294	0	0	2B-1118, SS-31, OF-20, P-8, 3B-4, C-3
1 yr.	28	98	20	1	0	0	0.0	12	11	10	7	5	.204	.214	0	0	

Joe Stripp

STRIPP, JOSEPH VALENTINE (Jersey Joe)   BR TR 5'11½" 175 lbs.
B. Feb. 3, 1903, Harrison, N. J.

	G	AB	H	2B	3B	HR	HR %	R	RBI	BB	SO	SB	BA	SA	PH AB	PH H	G by POS
1928 CIN N	42	139	40	7	3	1	0.7	18	17	8	8	0	.288	.403	2	1	OF-21, 3B-17, SS-1
1929	64	187	40	3	2	3	1.6	24	20	24	15	2	.214	.299	7	2	3B-55, 2B-3
1930	130	464	142	37	6	3	0.6	74	64	51	37	15	.306	.431	6	0	1B-75, 3B-48
1931	105	426	138	26	2	3	0.7	71	42	21	31	5	.324	.415	1	1	3B-96, 1B-9
1932 BKN N	138	534	162	36	9	6	1.1	94	64	36	30	14	.303	.438	0	0	3B-93, 1B-43
1933	141	537	149	20	7	1	0.2	69	51	26	23	5	.277	.346	1	1	3B-140
1934	104	384	121	19	6	1	0.3	50	40	22	20	2	.315	.404	1	0	3B-96, 1B-7, SS-1
1935	109	373	114	13	5	3	0.8	44	43	22	15	2	.306	.391	4	2	3B-88, 1B-15, OF-1
1936	110	439	139	31	1	1	0.2	51	60	22	12	2	.317	.399	3	1	3B-106
1937	90	300	73	10	2	1	0.3	37	26	20	18	1	.243	.300	9	3	3B-66, 1B-14, SS-3
1938 2 teams			STL	N	(54G –	.286)		BOS	N	(59G –	.275)						
" Total	113	428	120	17	0	1	0.2	43	37	28	17	2	.280	.327	4	2	3B-109
11 yrs.	1146	4211	1238	219	43	24	0.6	575	464	280	226	50	.294	.384	38	13	3B-914, 1B-163, OF-22, SS-5, 2B-2
1 yr.	54	199	57	7	0	0	0.0	24	18	18	10	1	.286	.322	3	1	3B-51

Willie Sudhoff

SUDHOFF, JOHN WILLIAM (Wee Willie)   BR TR 5'7" 165 lbs.
B. Sept. 17, 1874, St. Louis, Mo.   D. May 25, 1917, St. Louis, Mo.

	G	AB	H	2B	3B	HR	HR %	R	RBI	BB	SO	SB	BA	SA	PH AB	PH H	G by POS
1897 STL N	11	42	10	1	0	0	0.0	7	3	1		0	.238	.262	0	0	P-11
1898	41	120	19	2	1	0	0.0	5	4	5		0	.158	.192	0	0	P-41
1899 2 teams			CLE	N	(11G –	.065)		STL	N	(26G –	.206)						
" Total	37	99	16	1	2	0	0.0	11	8	12		0	.162	.212	0	0	P-37
1900 STL N	35	106	20	1	1	0	0.0	15	6	11		8	.189	.217	1	0	P-16, OF-12, 3B-7
1901	38	108	19	2	3	1	0.9	11	17	10		0	.176	.278	0	0	P-38
1902 STL A	31	77	13	2	0	0	0.0	6	5	4		3	.169	.195	0	0	P-30, OF-1
1903	41	110	20	1	2	0	0.0	12	6	3		1	.182	.227	2	0	P-41
1904	30	85	14	3	0	0	0.0	5	7	6		0	.165	.200	0	0	P-27, OF-3
1905	32	86	16	3	1	0	0.0	6	3	7		0	.186	.244	0	0	P-32
1906 WAS A	9	7	3	0	0	0	0.0	0	0	0		0	.429	.429	0	0	P-9
10 yrs.	305	840	150	16	10	1	0.1	78	59	59		13	.179	.225	3	0	P-241, OF-16, 3B-7
5 yrs.	151	444	82	7	6	1	0.2	48	32	35		8	.185	.234	1	0	P-132, OF-12, 3B-7

Joe Sugden

SUGDEN, JOSEPH   BB TR 5'10" 180 lbs.
B. July 31, 1870, Philadelphia, Pa.   D. June 28, 1959, Philadelphia, Pa.

	G	AB	H	2B	3B	HR	HR %	R	RBI	BB	SO	SB	BA	SA	PH AB	PH H	G by POS
1893 PIT N	27	92	24	4	3	0	0.0	20	12	10	11	1	.261	.370	0	0	C-27
1894	39	139	46	13	2	2	1.4	23	23	14	2	3	.331	.496	0	0	C-31, 3B-4, SS-3, OF-1
1895	49	155	48	4	1	0	0.6	28	17	16	12	4	.310	.368	0	0	C-49
1896	80	301	89	5	7	0	0.0	42	36	19	9	5	.296	.359	0	0	C-70, 1B-7, OF-4

	G	AB	H	2B	3B	HR	HR %	R	RBI	BB	SO	SB	BA	SA	Pinch Hit AB	Pinch Hit H	G by POS

Joe Sugden continued

	G	AB	H	2B	3B	HR	HR %	R	RBI	BB	SO	SB	BA	SA	AB	H	G by POS
1897	84	288	64	6	4	0	0.0	31	38	18		9	.222	.271	0	0	C-81, 1B-3
1898 STL N	89	289	73	7	1	0	0.0	29	34	23		5	.253	.284	7	2	C-60, OF-15, 1B-8
1899 CLE N	76	250	69	5	1	0	0.0	19	14	11		2	.276	.304	2	1	C-66, OF-4, 1B-3, 3B-1
1901 CHI A	48	153	42	7	1	0	0.0	21	19	13		4	.275	.333	2	0	C-42, 1B-5
1902 STL A	68	200	50	7	2	0	0.0	25	15	20		2	.250	.305	3	1	C-61, 1B-4, P-1
1903	79	241	51	4	0	0	0.0	18	22	25		4	.212	.228	5	0	C-66, 1B-8
1904	105	348	93	6	3	0	0.0	25	30	28		6	.267	.302	1	0	C-79, 1B-28
1905	85	266	46	4	0	0	0.0	21	23	23		3	.173	.188	4	0	C-71, 1B-9
1912 DET A	1	4	1	0	0	0	0.0	1	0	0		0	.250	.250	0	0	1B-1
13 yrs.	830	2726	696	72	25	3	0.1	303	283	220	34	48	.255	.303	24	4	C-703, 1B-76, OF-24, 3B-5, SS-3, P-1
1 yr.	89	289	73	7	1	0	0.0	29	34	23		5	.253	.284	7	2	C-60, OF-15, 1B-8

Joe Sullivan

SULLIVAN, JOSEPH DANIEL
B. Jan. 6, 1870, Charlestown, Mass.   D. Nov. 2, 1897, Charlestown, Mass.

	G	AB	H	2B	3B	HR	HR %	R	RBI	BB	SO	SB	BA	SA	AB	H	G by POS
1893 WAS N	128	508	135	16	13	2	0.4	72	64	36	24	7	.266	.360	0	0	SS-128
1894 2 teams		WAS N	(17G –	.250)		PHI N	(75G –	.352)									
" Total	92	364	122	13	8	3	0.8	70	68	29	12	13	.335	.440	1	0	SS-81, 2B-8, OF-1, 3B-1
1895 PHI N	94	373	126	7	3	2	0.5	75	50	24	20	15	.338	.389	0	0	SS-89, OF-6
1896 2 teams		PHI N	(48G –	.251)		STL N	(51G –	.292)									
" Total	99	403	110	9	5	4	1.0	70	45	27	24	14	.273	.350	0	0	OF-90, 2B-7, SS-2, 3B-2
4 yrs.	413	1648	493	45	29	11	0.7	287	227	116	80	49	.299	.382	1	0	SS-300, OF-97, 2B-15, 3B-3
1 yr.	51	212	62	4	2	2	0.9	25	21	9	12	5	.292	.358	0	0	OF-45, 2B-7, 3B-1

Suter Sullivan

SULLIVAN, SUTER G.
B. 1872, Baltimore, Md.   Deceased.

	G	AB	H	2B	3B	HR	HR %	R	RBI	BB	SO	SB	BA	SA	AB	H	G by POS
1898 STL N	42	144	32	3	0	0	0.0	10	12	13		1	.222	.243	2	0	SS-23, OF-10, 2B-6, 1B-1, P-1
1899 CLE N	127	473	116	16	3	0	0.0	37	55	25		16	.245	.292	0	0	3B-101, OF-20, SS-3, 1B-3, 2B-2
2 yrs.	169	617	148	19	3	0	0.0	47	67	38		17	.240	.280	2	0	3B-101, OF-30, SS-26, 2B-8, 1B-4, P-1
1 yr.	42	144	32	3	0	0	0.0	10	12	13		1	.222	.243	2	0	SS-23, OF-10, 2B-6, 1B-1, P-1

Gary Sutherland

SUTHERLAND, GARY LYNN   BR TR 6'   185 lbs.
Brother of Darrell Sutherland.
B. Sept. 27, 1944, Glendale, Calif.

	G	AB	H	2B	3B	HR	HR %	R	RBI	BB	SO	SB	BA	SA	AB	H	G by POS
1966 PHI N	3	3	0	0	0	0	0.0	0	0	0	0	0	.000	.000	2	0	SS-1
1967	103	231	57	12	1	1	0.4	23	19	17	22	0	.247	.320	22	4	SS-66, OF-25
1968	67	138	38	7	0	0	0.0	16	15	8	15	0	.275	.326	31	9	2B-17, SS-10, 3B-10, OF-7
1969 MON N	141	544	130	26	1	3	0.6	63	35	37	31	5	.239	.307	1	0	2B-139, SS-15, OF-1
1970	116	359	74	10	0	3	0.8	37	26	31	22	2	.206	.259	23	4	2B-97, SS-15, 3B-1
1971	111	304	78	7	2	4	1.3	25	26	18	12	3	.257	.332	19	3	2B-56, SS-46, OF-4, 3B-2
1972 HOU N	5	8	1	0	0	0	0.0	0	1	0	0	0	.125	.125	4	0	3B-1, 2B-1
1973	16	54	14	5	0	0	0.0	8	3	3	5	0	.259	.352	2	1	2B-14, SS-1
1974 DET A	149	619	157	20	1	5	0.8	60	49	26	37	1	.254	.313	2	1	2B-147, SS-10, 3B-4
1975	129	503	130	12	3	6	1.2	51	39	45	41	0	.258	.330	1	0	2B-128
1976 2 teams		DET A	(42G –	.205)		MIL A	(59G –	.217)									
" Total	101	232	49	7	2	1	0.4	19	15	15	19	0	.211	.272	12	2	2B-87, 1B-2
1977 SD N	80	103	25	3	0	1	1.0	5	11	7	15	0	.243	.301	38	12	2B-30, 3B-21, 1B-4
1978 STL N	10	6	1	0	0	0	0.0	1	0	0	0	0	.167	.167	6	1	2B-1
13 yrs.	1031	3104	754	109	10	24	0.8	308	239	207	219	11	.243	.308	163	37	2B-717, SS-164, 3B-39, OF-37, 1B-6
1 yr.	10	6	1	0	0	0	0.0	1	0	0	0	0	.167	.167	6	1	2B-1

Charlie Swindell

SWINDELL, CHARLES J.   TR
B. Oct. 26, 1877, Rockford, Ill.   D. July 22, 1940, Portland, Ore.

	G	AB	H	2B	3B	HR	HR %	R	RBI	BB	SO	SB	BA	SA	AB	H	G by POS
1904 STL N	3	8	1	0	0	0	0.0	0	0			0	.125	.125	0	0	C-3

Steve Swisher

SWISHER, STEVEN EUGENE   BR TR 6'2"   205 lbs.
B. Aug. 9, 1951, Parkersburg, W. Va.

	G	AB	H	2B	3B	HR	HR %	R	RBI	BB	SO	SB	BA	SA	AB	H	G by POS
1974 CHI N	90	280	60	5	0	5	1.8	21	27	37	63	0	.214	.286	0	0	C-90
1975	93	254	54	16	2	1	0.4	20	22	30	57	1	.213	.303	0	0	C-93
1976	109	377	89	13	3	5	1.3	25	42	20	82	2	.236	.326	4	1	C-107
1977	74	205	39	7	0	5	2.4	21	15	9	47	0	.190	.298	4	1	C-72
1978 STL N	45	115	32	5	1	1	0.9	11	10	8	14	1	.278	.365	3	1	C-42
1979	38	73	11	1	1	1	1.4	4	3	6	17	0	.151	.233	5	0	C-33
1980	18	24	6	1	0	0	0.0	2	2	1	7	0	.250	.292	9	2	C-8
1981 SD N	16	28	4	0	0	0	0.0	2	0	2	11	0	.143	.143	7	1	C-10
1982	26	58	10	1	0	2	3.4	2	3	5	24	0	.172	.293	0	0	C-26
9 yrs.	509	1414	305	49	7	20	1.4	108	124	118	322	4	.216	.303	32	6	C-481
3 yrs.	101	212	49	7	2	2	0.9	17	15	15	38	1	.231	.311	17	3	C-83

John Tamargo

TAMARGO, JOHN FELIX   BB TR 5'10"   170 lbs.
B. Nov. 7, 1951, Tampa, Fla.

	G	AB	H	2B	3B	HR	HR %	R	RBI	BB	SO	SB	BA	SA	AB	H	G by POS
1976 STL N	10	10	3	0	0	0	0.0	1	3	0	0	0	.300	.300	7	2	C-1
1977	4	4	0	0	0	0	0.0	0	0	0	2	0	.000	.000	3	0	C-1
1978 2 teams		STL N	(6G –	.000)		SF N	(36G –	.239)									
" Total	42	98	22	4	1	1	1.0	6	8	18	9	1	.224	.316	11	1	C-32

	G	AB	H	2B	3B	HR	HR %	R	RBI	BB	SO	SB	BA	SA	Pinch Hit AB	Pinch Hit H	G by POS

John Tamargo continued

	G	AB	H	2B	3B	HR	HR %	R	RBI	BB	SO	SB	BA	SA	PH AB	PH H	G by POS
1979 2 teams		SF N (30G – .200)			MON N (12G – .381)												
" Total	42	81	20	5	0	2	2.5	7	11	7	11	0	.247	.383	21	6	C-21
1980 MON N	37	51	14	3	0	1	2.0	4	13	6	5	0	.275	.392	23	7	C-12
5 yrs.	135	244	59	12	1	4	1.6	19	33	34	27	1	.242	.348	65	16	C-67
3 yrs.	20	20	3	0	0	0	0.0	2	1	3	4	0	.150	.150	16	2	C-3

Lee Tate

TATE, LEE WILLIE (Skeeter)
B. Mar. 18, 1932, Black Rock, Ark.   BR TR 5'10" 165 lbs.

	G	AB	H	2B	3B	HR	HR %	R	RBI	BB	SO	SB	BA	SA	PH AB	PH H	G by POS
1958 STL N	10	35	7	2	0	0	0.0	4	1	4	3	0	.200	.257	1	0	SS-9
1959	41	50	7	1	1	1	2.0	5	4	5	7	0	.140	.260	0	0	SS-39, 3B-2, 2B-2
2 yrs.	51	85	14	3	1	1	1.2	9	5	9	10	0	.165	.259	1	0	SS-48, 3B-2, 2B-2
2 yrs.	51	85	14	3	1	1	1.2	9	5	9	10	0	.165	.259	1	0	SS-48, 3B-2, 2B-2

Don Taussig

TAUSSIG, DONALD FRANKLIN
B. Feb. 19, 1932, New York, N. Y.   BR TR 6' 190 lbs.

	G	AB	H	2B	3B	HR	HR %	R	RBI	BB	SO	SB	BA	SA	PH AB	PH H	G by POS
1958 SF N	39	50	10	0	0	1	2.0	10	4	3	8	0	.200	.260	3	1	OF-36
1961 STL N	98	188	54	14	5	2	1.1	27	25	16	34	2	.287	.447	8	2	OF-87
1962 HOU N	16	25	5	0	0	1	4.0	1	1	2	11	0	.200	.320	11	3	OF-4
3 yrs.	153	263	69	14	5	4	1.5	38	30	21	53	2	.262	.399	22	6	OF-127
1 yr.	98	188	54	14	5	2	1.1	27	25	16	34	2	.287	.447	8	2	OF-87

Carl Taylor

TAYLOR, CARL MEANS
B. Jan. 20, 1944, Sarasota, Fla.   BR TR 6'2" 200 lbs.

	G	AB	H	2B	3B	HR	HR %	R	RBI	BB	SO	SB	BA	SA	PH AB	PH H	G by POS
1968 PIT N	44	71	15	1	0	0	0.0	5	7	10	10	1	.211	.225	10	1	C-29, OF-2
1969	104	221	77	10	1	4	1.8	30	33	31	36	0	.348	.457	41	17	OF-36, 1B-24
1970 STL N	104	245	61	12	2	6	2.4	39	45	41	30	5	.249	.388	42	11	OF-46, 1B-15, 3B-1
1971 2 teams		KC A (20G – .179)			PIT N (7G – .167)												
" Total	27	51	9	0	1	0	0.0	4	3	5	18	0	.176	.216	13	2	OF-18
1972 KC A	63	113	30	2	1	0	0.0	17	11	17	16	4	.265	.301	26	8	C-21, OF-7, 1B-6, 3B-5
1973	69	145	33	6	1	0	0.0	18	16	32	20	2	.228	.283	1	0	C-63, 1B-2
6 yrs.	411	846	225	31	6	10	1.2	113	115	136	130	12	.266	.352	133	39	C-113, OF-109, 1B-47, 3B-6
1 yr.	104	245	61	12	2	6	2.4	39	45	41	30	5	.249	.388	42	11	OF-46, 1B-15, 3B-1

Jack Taylor

TAYLOR, JOHN W.
B. Sept. 13, 1873, Straightville, Ohio   D. Mar. 4, 1938, Columbus, Ohio   BR TR 5'10" 170 lbs.

	G	AB	H	2B	3B	HR	HR %	R	RBI	BB	SO	SB	BA	SA	PH AB	PH H	G by POS
1898 CHI N	5	15	3	2	0	0	0.0	4	2	3		0	.200	.333	0	0	P-5
1899	42	139	37	9	2	0	0.0	25	17	16		0	.266	.360	1	1	P-41
1900	28	81	19	3	1	1	1.2	7	6	3		1	.235	.333	0	0	P-28
1901	35	106	23	6	0	0	0.0	12	2	4		0	.217	.274	2	0	P-33
1902	55	186	44	6	1	0	0.0	18	17	8		6	.237	.280	1	0	P-36, 3B-12, OF-3, 1B-2, 2B-1
1903	40	126	28	3	4	0	0.0	13	17	6		3	.222	.310	0	0	P-37, 3B-1, 2B-1
1904 STL N	42	133	28	3	3	1	0.8	9	8	4		3	.211	.301	0	0	P-41
1905	39	121	23	3	1	0	0.0	11	12	8		4	.190	.264	0	0	P-37, 3B-2
1906 2 teams		STL N (17G – .208)			CHI N (17G – .208)												
" Total	34	106	22	3	0	0	0.0	9	5	14		1	.208	.236	0	0	P-34
1907 CHI N	18	47	9	2	0	0	0.0	2	1	0		0	.191	.234	0	0	P-18
10 yrs.	338	1060	236	42	13	2	0.2	110	87	66		18	.223	.292	4	1	P-310, 3B-15, OF-3, 2B-2, 1B-2
3 yrs.	98	307	62	8	5	1	0.3	24	22	22		8	.202	.270	0	0	P-95, 3B-2

Joe Taylor

TAYLOR, WILLIAM MICHAEL (Moose)
B. Dec. 30, 1929, Alhambra, Calif.   BL TL 6'3" 212 lbs.

	G	AB	H	2B	3B	HR	HR %	R	RBI	BB	SO	SB	BA	SA	PH AB	PH H	G by POS
1954 PHI A	18	58	13	1	1	1	1.7	5	8	2	9	0	.224	.328	3	2	OF-16
1957 CIN N	33	107	28	7	0	4	3.7	14	9	6	24	0	.262	.439	6	2	OF-27
1958 2 teams		STL N (18G – .304)			BAL A (36G – .273)												
" Total	54	100	28	7	0	3	3.0	13	9	9	23	0	.280	.440	25	7	OF-26
1959 BAL A	14	32	5	1	0	1	3.1	2	2	11	15	0	.156	.281	1	0	OF-12
4 yrs.	119	297	74	16	1	9	3.0	34	28	28	71	0	.249	.401	35	11	OF-81
1 yr.	18	23	7	1	0	1	4.3	2	0	2	4	0	.304	.565	12	4	OF-5

Patsy Tebeau

TEBEAU, OLIVER WENDELL
Brother of White Wings Tebeau.
B. Dec. 5, 1864, St. Louis, Mo.   D. May 15, 1918, St. Louis, Mo.   BR TR
Manager 1890-1900.

	G	AB	H	2B	3B	HR	HR %	R	RBI	BB	SO	SB	BA	SA	PH AB	PH H	G by POS
1887 CHI N	20	68	11	3	0	0	0.0	8	10	4	4	8	.162	.206	0	0	3B-20
1889 CLE N	136	521	147	20	6	8	1.5	72	76	37	41	26	.282	.390	0	0	3B-136
1890 CLE P	110	450	135	26	6	5	1.1	86	74	34	20	14	.300	.418	0	0	3B-110
1891 CLE N	61	249	65	8	3	1	0.4	38	41	16	13	12	.261	.329	0	1	3B-61, OF-1
1892	86	340	83	13	3	2	0.6	47	49	23	34	6	.244	.318	0	0	3B-74, 2B-5, 1B-4, SS-3
1893	116	486	160	32	8	2	0.4	90	102	32	11	19	.329	.440	0	0	1B-57, 3B-56, 2B-3
1894	125	523	158	23	7	3	0.6	82	89	35	35	30	.302	.390	0	0	1B-115, 2B-10, 3B-2, SS-1
1895	63	264	84	13	2	2	0.8	50	52	16	18	8	.318	.405	0	0	1B-49, 2B-9, 3B-6
1896	132	543	146	22	6	2	0.4	56	94	21	22	20	.269	.343	0	0	1B-122, 3B-7, 2B-5, SS-1, P-1
1897	109	412	110	15	9	0	0.0	62	59	30		11	.267	.347	0	0	1B-92, 2B-18, 3B-2, SS-1
1898	131	477	123	11	4	1	0.2	53	63	53		5	.258	.304	0	0	1B-91, 2B-34, SS-7, 3B-3
1899 STL N	77	281	69	10	3	1	0.4	27	26	18		5	.246	.313	0	0	1B-65, SS-11, 3B-1, 2B-1
1900	1	4	0	0	0	0	0.0	0	0	0			.000	.000	0	0	SS-1
13 yrs.	1167	4618	1291	196	57	27	0.6	671	735	319	198	164	.280	.364	0	0	1B-595, 3B-478, 2B-85, SS-25, OF-1, P-1
2 yrs.	78	285	69	10	3	1	0.4	27	26	18		5	.242	.309	0	0	1B-65, SS-12, 3B-1, 2B-1

	G	AB	H	2B	3B	HR	HR %	R	RBI	BB	SO	SB	BA	SA	Pinch Hit AB	Pinch Hit H	G by POS

Garry Templeton

TEMPLETON, GARRY LEWIS BB TR 5'11" 175 lbs.
B. Mar. 24, 1956, Lockey, Tex.

	G	AB	H	2B	3B	HR	HR %	R	RBI	BB	SO	SB	BA	SA	PH AB	PH H	G by POS
1976 STL N	53	213	62	8	2	1	0.5	32	17	7	33	11	.291	.362	1	0	SS-53
1977	153	621	200	19	18	8	1.3	94	79	15	70	28	.322	.449	2	0	SS-151
1978	155	647	181	31	13	2	0.3	82	47	22	87	34	.280	.377	2	0	SS-155
1979	154	672	211	32	19	9	1.3	105	62	18	91	26	.314	.458	1	0	SS-150
1980	118	504	161	19	9	4	0.8	83	43	18	43	31	.319	.417	2	0	SS-115
1981	80	333	96	16	8	1	0.3	47	33	14	55	8	.288	.393	4	0	SS-76
1982 SD N	141	563	139	25	8	6	1.1	76	64	26	82	27	.247	.352	6	1	SS-136
7 yrs.	854	3553	1050	150	77	31	0.9	519	345	120	461	165	.296	.407	18	1	SS-836
6 yrs.	713	2990	911	125	69	25	0.8	443	281	94	379	138	.305	.418	12	0	SS-700
				9th													

Gene Tenace

TENACE, FURY GENE BR TR 6' 190 lbs.
B. Oct. 10, 1946, Russellton, Pa.

	G	AB	H	2B	3B	HR	HR %	R	RBI	BB	SO	SB	BA	SA	PH AB	PH H	G by POS
1969 OAK A	16	38	6	0	0	1	2.6	1	2	1	15	0	.158	.237	5	0	C-13
1970	38	105	32	6	0	7	6.7	19	20	23	30	0	.305	.562	7	2	C-30
1971	65	179	49	7	0	7	3.9	26	25	29	34	2	.274	.430	13	4	C-52, OF-1
1972	82	227	51	5	3	5	2.2	22	32	24	42	0	.225	.339	17	7	C-49, OF-9, 1B-7, 3B-2, 2B-2
1973	160	510	132	18	2	24	4.7	83	84	101	94	2	.259	.443	2	0	1B-134, C-33, 2B-1
1974	158	484	102	17	1	26	5.4	71	73	110	105	2	.211	.411	0	0	1B-106, C-79, 2B-3
1975	158	498	127	17	0	29	5.8	83	87	106	127	7	.255	.464	0	0	C-125, 1B-68
1976	128	417	104	19	1	22	5.3	64	66	81	91	5	.249	.458	3	0	1B-70, C-65
1977 SD N	147	437	102	24	4	15	3.4	66	61	125	119	5	.233	.410	5	0	C-99, 1B-36, 3B-14
1978	142	401	90	18	4	16	4.0	60	61	101	98	6	.224	.409	7	1	1B-80, C-71, 3B-1
1979	151	463	122	16	4	20	4.3	61	67	105	106	2	.263	.445	7	2	C-94, 1B-72
1980	133	316	70	11	1	17	5.4	46	50	92	63	4	.222	.424	16	2	C-104, 1B-19
1981 STL N	58	129	30	7	0	5	3.9	26	22	38	26	0	.233	.403	12	3	C-38, 1B-7
1982	66	124	32	9	0	7	5.6	18	18	36	31	1	.258	.500	12	3	C-37, 1B-7
14 yrs.	1502	4328	1049	174	20	201	4.6	646	668	972	981	36	.242	.431	106	24	C-889, 1B-606, 3B-17, OF-10, 2B-6
2 yrs.	124	253	62	16	0	12	4.7	44	40	74	57	1	.245	.451	24	6	C-75, 1B-14

LEAGUE CHAMPIONSHIP SERIES

	G	AB	H	2B	3B	HR	HR %	R	RBI	BB	SO	SB	BA	SA	PH AB	PH H	G by POS
1971 OAK A	1	3	0	0	0	0	0.0	0	0	1	1	0	.000	.000	0	0	C-1
1972	5	17	1	0	0	0	0.0	1	1	3	5	0	.059	.059	0	0	C-5
1973	5	17	4	1	0	0	0.0	3	0	2	4	1	.235	.294	0	0	1B-5
1974	4	11	0	0	0	0	0.0	0	1	4	4	1	.000	.000	0	0	1B-4
1975	3	9	0	0	0	0	0.0	0	0	3	2	0	.000	.000	0	0	C-3
5 yrs.	18	57	5	1	0	0	0.0	5	2	13	16	2	.088	.105	0	0	1B-9, C-9

WORLD SERIES

	G	AB	H	2B	3B	HR	HR %	R	RBI	BB	SO	SB	BA	SA	PH AB	PH H	G by POS
1972 OAK A	7	23	8	1	0	4	17.4	5	9	2	4	0	.348	.913	0	0	C-6
1973	7	19	3	1	0	0	0.0	0	3	11	7	0	.158	.211	0	0	C-3
1974	5	9	2	0	0	0	0.0	0	0	3	4	0	.222	.222	0	0	1B-5
1982 STL N	5	6	0	0	0	0	0.0	0	0	1	2	0	.000	.000	4	0	
4 yrs.	24	57	13	2	0	4	7.0	5	12	17	17	0	.228	.474	4	0	C-9, 1B-5
							9th										

Moe Thacker

THACKER, MORRIS BENTON BR TR 6'3" 205 lbs.
B. May 21, 1934, Louisville, Ky.

	G	AB	H	2B	3B	HR	HR %	R	RBI	BB	SO	SB	BA	SA	PH AB	PH H	G by POS
1958 CHI N	11	24	6	1	0	2	8.3	4	3	1	7	0	.250	.542	2	1	C-9
1960	54	90	14	1	0	0	0.0	5	6	14	20	1	.156	.167	4	1	C-50
1961	25	35	6	0	0	0	0.0	3	2	11	11	0	.171	.171	0	0	C-25
1962	65	107	20	5	0	0	0.0	8	9	14	40	0	.187	.234	1	0	C-65
1963 STL N	3	4	0	0	0	0	0.0	0	0	0	3	0	.000	.000	0	0	C-3
5 yrs.	158	260	46	7	0	2	0.8	20	20	40	81	1	.177	.227	7	2	C-152
1 yr.	3	4	0	0	0	0	0.0	0	0	0	3	0	.000	.000	0	0	C-3

Tommy Thevenow

THEVENOW, THOMAS JOSEPH BR TR 5'10" 155 lbs.
B. Sept. 6, 1903, Madison, Ind. D. July 29, 1957, Madison, Ind.

	G	AB	H	2B	3B	HR	HR %	R	RBI	BB	SO	SB	BA	SA	PH AB	PH H	G by POS
1924 STL N	23	89	18	4	1	0	0.0	4	7	1	6	1	.202	.270	0	0	SS-23
1925	50	175	47	7	2	0	0.0	17	17	7	12	3	.269	.331	0	0	SS-50
1926	156	563	144	15	5	2	0.4	64	63	27	26	8	.256	.311	0	0	SS-156
1927	59	191	37	6	1	0	0.0	23	4	14	8	2	.194	.236	0	0	SS-59
1928	69	171	35	8	3	0	0.0	11	13	20	12	0	.205	.287	0	0	SS-64, 3B-3, 1B-1
1929 PHI N	90	317	72	11	0	0	0.0	30	35	25	25	3	.227	.262	0	0	SS-90
1930	156	573	164	21	1	0	0.0	57	78	23	26	1	.286	.326	0	0	SS-156
1931 PIT N	120	404	86	12	1	0	0.0	35	38	28	22	0	.213	.248	6	0	SS-120
1932	59	194	46	3	3	0	0.0	12	26	7	12	0	.237	.284	6	1	2B-61, SS-3, 3B-1
1933	73	253	79	5	1	0	0.0	20	34	3	5	2	.312	.340	9	1	2B-64, 3B-1
1934	122	446	121	16	2	0	0.0	37	54	20	20	0	.271	.316	6	2	2B-75, 3B-44, SS-1
1935	110	408	97	9	9	0	0.0	38	47	12	23	1	.238	.304	7	1	3B-82, SS-13, 2B-8
1936 CIN N	106	321	75	7	2	0	0.0	25	36	15	23	2	.234	.268	1	0	SS-68, 2B-33, 3B-12
1937 BOS N	21	34	4	0	1	0	0.0	5	2	4	2	0	.118	.176	1	0	SS-12, 3B-6, 2B-2
1938 PIT N	15	25	5	0	0	0	0.0	2	2	4	0	0	.200	.200	1	0	2B-9, SS-4, 3B-1
15 yrs.	1229	4164	1030	124	32	2	0.0	380	456	210	222	23	.247	.294	31	4	SS-848, 2B-188, 3B-171, 1B-1
5 yrs.	357	1189	281	40	12	2	0.2	119	104	69	64	14	.236	.295	0	0	SS-352, 3B-3, 2B-1

WORLD SERIES

	G	AB	H	2B	3B	HR	HR %	R	RBI	BB	SO	SB	BA	SA	PH AB	PH H	G by POS
1926 STL N	7	24	10	1	0	1	4.2	5	4	0	1	0	.417	.583	0	0	SS-7
1928	1	0	0	0	0	0	—	0	0	0	0	0	—	—	0	0	SS-1
2 yrs.	8	24	10	1	0	1	4.2	5	4	0	1	0	.417	.583	0	0	SS-8

	G	AB	H	2B	3B	HR	HR %	R	RBI	BB	SO	SB	BA	SA	Pinch Hit AB	Pinch Hit H	G by POS

Bobby Tolan

TOLAN, ROBERT
B. Nov. 19, 1945, Los Angeles, Calif.   BL TL 5'11"   170 lbs.

	G	AB	H	2B	3B	HR	HR %	R	RBI	BB	SO	SB	BA	SA	PH AB	PH H	G by POS
1965 STL N	17	69	13	2	0	0	0.0	8	6	0	4	2	.188	.217	0	0	OF-17
1966	43	93	16	5	1	1	1.1	10	6	6	15	1	.172	.280	12	3	OF-26, 1B-1
1967	110	265	67	7	3	6	2.3	35	32	19	43	12	.253	.370	33	10	OF-80, 1B-13
1968	92	278	64	12	1	5	1.8	28	17	13	42	9	.230	.335	23	2	OF-67, 1B-9
1969 CIN N	152	637	194	25	10	21	3.3	104	93	27	92	26	.305	.474	2	0	OF-150
1970	152	589	186	34	6	16	2.7	112	80	62	94	57	.316	.475	5	1	OF-150
1972	149	604	171	28	5	8	1.3	88	82	44	88	42	.283	.386	1	0	OF-149
1973	129	457	94	14	2	9	2.0	42	51	27	68	15	.206	.304	12	3	OF-120
1974 SD N	95	357	95	16	1	8	2.2	45	40	20	41	7	.266	.384	4	0	OF-88
1975	147	506	129	19	4	5	1.0	58	43	28	45	11	.255	.338	14	2	OF-120, 1B-27
1976 PHI N	110	272	71	7	0	5	1.8	32	35	7	39	10	.261	.342	33	4	1B-50, OF-35
1977 2 teams	PHI	N	(15G –	.125)	PIT	N	(49G –	.203)									
" Total	64	90	17	4	0	2	2.2	8	10	5	14	1	.189	.300	40	8	1B-25, OF-2
1979 SD N	22	21	4	0	1	0	0.0	2	2	0	2	0	.190	.286	13	5	1B-5, OF-1
13 yrs.	1282	4238	1121	173	34	86	2.0	572	497	258	587	193	.265	.382	192	36	OF-1005, 1B-130
4 yrs.	262	705	160	26	5	12	1.7	81	61	38	104	24	.227	.329	68	15	OF-190, 1B-23

LEAGUE CHAMPIONSHIP SERIES

	G	AB	H	2B	3B	HR	HR %	R	RBI	BB	SO	SB	BA	SA	PH AB	PH H	G by POS
1970 CIN N	3	12	5	0	0	1	8.3	3	2	1	1	1	.417	.667	0	0	OF-3
1972	5	21	5	1	1	0	0.0	3	4	0	4	0	.238	.381	0	0	OF-5
1976 PHI N	3	2	0	0	0	0	0.0	0	0	1	0	0	.000	.000	2	0	OF-1
3 yrs.	11	35	10	1	1	1	2.9	6	6	2	5	1	.286	.457	2	0	OF-9

WORLD SERIES

	G	AB	H	2B	3B	HR	HR %	R	RBI	BB	SO	SB	BA	SA	PH AB	PH H	G by POS
1967 STL N	3	2	0	0	0	0	0.0	1	0	0	1	0	.000	.000	2	0	
1968	1	1	0	0	0	0	0.0	0	0	0	1	0	.000	.000	1	0	
1970 CIN N	5	19	4	1	0	1	5.3	5	1	3	2	1	.211	.421	0	0	OF-5
1972	7	26	7	1	0	0	0.0	2	6	1	4	5	.269	.308	0	0	OF-7
4 yrs.	16	48	11	2	0	1	2.1	8	7	5	8	6	.229	.333	3	0	OF-12

10th

Specs Toporcer

TOPORCER, GEORGE
B. Feb. 9, 1899, New York, N. Y.   BL TR 5'10½"   165 lbs.

	G	AB	H	2B	3B	HR	HR %	R	RBI	BB	SO	SB	BA	SA	PH AB	PH H	G by POS
1921 STL N	22	53	14	1	0	0	0.0	4	2	3	4	1	.264	.283	6	1	2B-12, SS-2
1922	116	352	114	25	6	3	0.9	56	36	24	18	2	.324	.455	15	6	SS-91, 3B-6, OF-1, 2B-1
1923	97	303	77	11	3	3	1.0	45	35	41	14	4	.254	.340	8	3	2B-52, SS-33, 3B-1, 1B-1
1924	70	198	62	10	3	1	0.5	30	24	11	14	2	.313	.409	10	1	3B-33, SS-25, 2B-3
1925	83	268	76	13	4	2	0.7	38	26	36	15	7	.284	.384	8	2	SS-66, 2B-7
1926	64	88	22	3	2	0	0.0	13	9	8	9	1	.250	.330	23	9	2B-27, SS-5, 3B-1
1927	86	290	72	13	4	0	0.0	37	19	27	16	5	.248	.321	8	3	3B-54, SS-27, 2B-2, 1B-1
1928	8	14	0	0	0	0	0.0	0	0	0	3	0	.000	.000	6	0	2B-1, 1B-1
8 yrs.	546	1566	437	76	22	9	0.6	223	151	150	93	22	.279	.373	84	25	SS-249, 2B-105, 3B-95, 1B-3, OF-1
8 yrs.	546	1566	437	76	22	9	0.6	223	151	150	93	22	.279	.373	84	25	SS-249, 2B-105, 3B-95, 1B-3, OF-1

WORLD SERIES

	G	AB	H	2B	3B	HR	HR %	R	RBI	BB	SO	SB	BA	SA	PH AB	PH H	G by POS
1926 STL N	1	0	0	0	0	0	–	0	1	0	0	0	–	–	0	0	

Joe Torre

TORRE, JOSEPH PAUL
Brother of Frank Torre.
B. July 18, 1940, Brooklyn, N. Y.   BR TR 6'2"   212 lbs.
Manager 1977-82.

	G	AB	H	2B	3B	HR	HR %	R	RBI	BB	SO	SB	BA	SA	PH AB	PH H	G by POS
1960 MIL N	2	2	1	0	0	0	0.0	0	0	0	1	0	.500	.500	2	1	
1961	113	406	113	21	4	10	2.5	40	42	28	60	3	.278	.424	3	2	C-112
1962	80	220	62	8	1	5	2.3	23	26	24	24	1	.282	.395	16	6	C-63
1963	142	501	147	19	4	14	2.8	57	71	42	79	1	.293	.431	7	1	C-105, 1B-37, OF-2
1964	154	601	193	36	5	20	3.3	87	109	36	67	2	.321	.498	2	1	C-96, 1B-70
1965	148	523	152	21	1	27	5.2	68	80	61	79	0	.291	.489	5	2	C-100, 1B-49
1966 ATL N	148	546	172	20	3	36	6.6	83	101	60	61	0	.315	.560	3	1	C-114, 1B-36
1967	135	477	132	18	1	20	4.2	67	68	49	75	2	.277	.444	6	1	C-114, 1B-23
1968	115	424	115	11	2	10	2.4	45	55	34	72	1	.271	.377	1	0	C-92, 1B-29
1969 STL N	159	602	174	29	6	18	3.0	72	101	66	85	0	.289	.447	1	0	1B-144, C-17
1970	161	624	203	27	9	21	3.4	89	100	70	91	2	.325	.498	0	0	C-90, 3B-73, 1B-1
1971	161	634	230	34	8	24	3.8	97	137	63	70	4	.363	.555	0	0	3B-161
1972	149	544	157	26	6	11	2.0	71	81	54	64	3	.289	.419	6	4	3B-117, 1B-27
1973	141	519	149	17	2	13	2.5	67	69	65	78	2	.287	.403	0	0	1B-114, 3B-58
1974	147	529	149	28	1	11	2.1	59	70	69	88	1	.282	.401	4	2	1B-139, 3B-18
1975 NY N	114	361	89	16	3	6	1.7	33	35	35	55	0	.247	.357	22	5	3B-83, 1B-24
1976	114	310	95	10	3	5	1.6	36	31	21	35	1	.306	.406	35	8	1B-78, 3B-4
1977	26	51	9	3	0	1	2.0	2	9	2	10	0	.176	.294	11	2	1B-16, 3B-1
18 yrs.	2209	7874	2342	344	59	252	3.2	996	1185	779	1094	23	.297	.452	124	36	C-903, 1B-787, 3B-515, OF-2
6 yrs.	918	3452	1062	161	32	98	2.8	455	558	387	476	12	.308	.458	11	6	3B-427, 1B-425, C-107

Coaker Triplett

TRIPLETT, HERMAN COAKER
B. Dec. 18, 1911, Boone, N. C.   BR TR 5'11"   185 lbs.

	G	AB	H	2B	3B	HR	HR %	R	RBI	BB	SO	SB	BA	SA	PH AB	PH H	G by POS
1938 CHI N	12	36	9	2	1	0	0.0	4	2	0	9	0	.250	.361	3	0	OF-9
1941 STL N	76	185	53	6	3	3	1.6	29	21	18	27	0	.286	.400	25	5	OF-46
1942	64	154	42	9	1	1	0.6	18	23	17	15	1	.273	.390	16	2	OF-46
1943 2 teams	STL	N	(9G –	.080)	PHI	N	(105G –	.272)									
" Total	114	385	100	16	4	15	3.9	46	56	29	34	2	.260	.439	16	4	OF-96
1944 PHI N	84	184	43	5	1	1	0.5	15	25	19	10	1	.234	.288	36	8	OF-44
1945	120	363	87	11	1	7	1.9	36	46	40	27	6	.240	.333	28	5	OF-92
6 yrs.	470	1307	334	47	14	27	2.1	148	173	123	114	10	.256	.375	124	24	OF-333
3 yrs.	149	364	97	13	7	5	1.4	48	48	36	48	1	.266	.382	44	8	OF-98

	G	AB	H	2B	3B	HR	HR %	R	RBI	BB	SO	SB	BA	SA	Pinch Hit AB	H	G by POS

Tommy Tucker

TUCKER, THOMAS JOSEPH
B. Oct. 28, 1863, Holyoke, Mass.   D. Oct. 22, 1935, Montague, Mass.

BB TR 5'11"   165 lbs.

	G	AB	H	2B	3B	HR	HR %	R	RBI	BB	SO	SB	BA	SA	PH AB	H	G by POS
1887 BAL AA	136	524	144	15	9	6	1.1	114		29		85	.275	.372	0	0	1B-136
1888	136	520	149	17	12	6	1.2	74	61	16		43	.287	.400	0	0	1B-129, OF-7, P-1
1889	134	527	196	22	11	5	0.9	103	99	42	26	63	.372	.484	0	0	1B-123, OF-12
1890 BOS N	132	539	159	17	8	1	0.2	104	62	56	22	43	.295	.362	0	0	1B-132
1891	140	548	148	16	5	2	0.4	103	69	37	30	26	.270	.328	0	0	1B-140, P-1
1892	149	542	153	15	7	1	0.2	85	62	45	35	22	.282	.341	0	0	1B-149
1893	121	486	138	13	2	7	1.4	83	91	27	31	8	.284	.362	0	0	1B-121
1894	123	500	165	16	24	6	0.6	112	100	53	21	18	.330	.420	0	0	1B-123, OF-1
1895	125	462	115	19	6	3	0.6	87	73	61	29	15	.249	.335	0	0	1B-125
1896	122	474	144	27	5	2	0.4	74	72	30	29	6	.304	.395	0	0	1B-122
1897 2 teams		BOS	N	(4G –	.214)			WAS	N	(93G –	.338)						
" Total	97	366	122	20	5	5	1.4	52	65	29		18	.333	.456	0	0	1B-97
1898 2 teams		BKN	N	(73G –	.279)			STL	N	(72G –	.238)						
" Total	145	535	139	16	6	1	0.2	53	54	30		2	.260	.318	0	0	1B-145
1899 CLE N	127	456	110	19	3	0	0.0	40	40	24		3	.241	.296	0	0	1B-127
13 yrs.	1687	6479	1882	240	85	42	0.6	1084	847	479	223	352	.290	.373	0	0	1B-1669, OF-20, P-2
1 yr.	72	252	60	7	2	0	0.0	18	20	18		1	.238	.282	0	0	1B-72

Tuck Turner

TURNER, GEORGE A.
B. 1870, Staten Island, N. Y.   D. July 16, 1945, Staten Island, N. Y.

BL

	G	AB	H	2B	3B	HR	HR %	R	RBI	BB	SO	SB	BA	SA	PH AB	H	G by POS
1893 PHI N	36	155	50	4	3	1	0.6	32	13	9	19	7	.323	.406	0	0	OF-36
1894	80	339	141	21	9	1	0.3	91	82	23	13	11	.416	.540	1	0	OF-78, P-1
1895	59	210	81	8	6	2	1.0	51	43	25	11	14	.386	.510	4	2	OF-55
1896 2 teams		PHI	N	(13G –	.219)			STL	N	(51G –	.246)						
" Total	64	235	57	9	8	1	0.4	42	27	22	26	12	.243	.362	4	0	OF-59
1897 STL N	103	416	121	17	12	2	0.5	58	41	35		8	.291	.404	1	0	OF-102
1898	35	141	28	8	0	0	0.0	20	7	14		1	.199	.255	1	0	OF-34
6 yrs.	377	1496	478	67	38	7	0.5	294	213	128	69	53	.320	.429	11	2	OF-364, P-1
3 yrs.	189	760	199	32	20	3	0.4	108	75	63	21	15	.262	.368	2	0	OF-187

Old Hoss Twineham

TWINEHAM, ARTHUR W.
B. Nov. 26, 1866, Galesburg, Ill.   Deceased.

BL TR 6'1½"   190 lbs.

	G	AB	H	2B	3B	HR	HR %	R	RBI	BB	SO	SB	BA	SA	PH AB	H	G by POS
1893 STL N	14	48	15	2	0	0	0.0	8	11	1	2	0	.313	.354	0	0	C-14
1894	38	127	40	4	1	1	0.8	22	16	9	11	2	.315	.386	0	0	C-38
2 yrs.	52	175	55	6	1	1	0.6	30	27	10	13	2	.314	.377	0	0	C-52
2 yrs.	52	175	55	6	1	1	0.6	30	27	10	13	2	.314	.377	0	0	C-52

Mike Tyson

TYSON, MICHAEL RAY
B. Jan. 13, 1950, Rocky Mount, N. C.

BR TR 5'9"   170 lbs.

	G	AB	H	2B	3B	HR	HR %	R	RBI	BB	SO	SB	BA	SA	PH AB	H	G by POS
1972 STL N	13	37	7	1	0	0	0.0	1	0	1	9	0	.189	.216	0	0	2B-11, SS-2
1973	144	469	114	15	4	1	0.2	48	33	23	66	2	.243	.299	0	0	SS-128, 2B-16
1974	151	422	94	14	5	1	0.2	35	37	22	70	4	.223	.287	0	0	SS-143, 2B-12
1975	122	368	98	16	3	2	0.5	45	37	24	39	5	.266	.342	2	0	SS-95, 2B-24, 3B-5
1976	76	245	70	12	9	3	1.2	26	28	16	34	3	.286	.445	1	0	2B-74
1977	138	418	103	15	2	7	1.7	42	57	30	48	3	.246	.342	2	0	2B-135
1978	125	377	88	16	0	3	0.8	26	26	24	41	4	.233	.300	4	1	2B-124
1979	75	190	42	8	2	5	2.6	18	20	13	28	2	.221	.363	9	2	2B-71
1980 CHI N	123	341	81	19	3	3	0.9	34	23	15	61	1	.238	.337	6	2	2B-117
1981	50	92	17	2	0	2	2.2	6	8	7	15	1	.185	.272	13	4	2B-36, SS-1
10 yrs.	1017	2959	714	118	28	27	0.9	281	269	175	411	23	.241	.327	37	9	2B-620, SS-369, 3B-5
8 yrs.	844	2526	616	97	25	22	0.9	241	238	153	335	21	.244	.328	18	3	2B-467, SS-368, 3B-5

Bob Uecker

UECKER, ROBERT GEORGE
B. Jan. 26, 1935, Milwaukee, Wis.

BR TR 6'1"   190 lbs.

	G	AB	H	2B	3B	HR	HR %	R	RBI	BB	SO	SB	BA	SA	PH AB	H	G by POS
1962 MIL N	33	64	16	2	0	1	1.6	5	8	7	15	0	.250	.328	7	2	C-24
1963	13	16	4	2	0	0	0.0	3	0	2	5	0	.250	.375	7	2	C-6
1964 STL N	40	106	21	1	0	1	0.9	8	6	17	24	0	.198	.236	4	0	C-40
1965	53	145	33	7	0	2	1.4	17	10	24	27	0	.228	.317	5	0	C-49
1966 PHI N	78	207	43	6	0	7	3.4	15	30	22	36	0	.208	.338	4	0	C-76
1967 2 teams		PHI	N	(18G –	.171)			ATL	N	(62G –	.146)						
" Total	80	193	29	4	0	3	1.6	17	20	24	60	0	.150	.218	6	1	C-76
6 yrs.	297	731	146	22	0	14	1.9	65	74	96	167	0	.200	.287	29	5	C-271
2 yrs.	93	251	54	8	0	3	1.2	25	16	41	51	0	.215	.283	5	0	C-89

Lou Ury

URY, LOUIS NEWTON
B. Fort Smith, Ark.   D. Mar. 4, 1918, Kansas City, Mo.

TR

	G	AB	H	2B	3B	HR	HR %	R	RBI	BB	SO	SB	BA	SA	PH AB	H	G by POS
1903 STL N	2	7	1	0	0	0	0.0	0	0	0		0	.143	.143	0	0	1B-2

Benny Valenzuela

VALENZUELA, BENJAMIN BELTRAN (Papelero)
B. June 2, 1933, Los Mochis, Mexico

BR TR 5'10"   175 lbs.

	G	AB	H	2B	3B	HR	HR %	R	RBI	BB	SO	SB	BA	SA	PH AB	H	G by POS
1958 STL N	10	14	3	1	0	0	0.0	0	0	1	0	0	.214	.286	5	2	3B-3

Bill Van Dyke

VAN DYKE, WILLIAM JENNINGS
B. Dec. 15, 1863, Paris, Ill.   D. May 5, 1933, El Paso, Tex.

BR TR 5'8"   170 lbs.

	G	AB	H	2B	3B	HR	HR %	R	RBI	BB	SO	SB	BA	SA	PH AB	H	G by POS
1890 TOL AA	129	502	129	14	11	2	0.4	74		25		73	.257	.341	0	0	OF-110, 3B-18, 2B-2, C-1
1892 STL N	4	16	2	0	0	0	0.0	2	1	0	1	0	.125	.125	0	0	OF-4
1893 BOS N	3	12	3	1	0	0	0.0	2	1	0	1	1	.250	.333	0	0	OF-3
3 yrs.	136	530	134	15	11	2	0.4	78	1	25	2	74	.253	.334	0	0	OF-117, 3B-18, 2B-2, C-1
1 yr.	4	16	2	0	0	0	0.0	2	1	0	1	0	.125	.125	0	0	OF-4

	G	AB	H	2B	3B	HR	HR %	R	RBI	BB	SO	SB	BA	SA	Pinch Hit AB	Pinch Hit H	G by POS

John Vann

VANN, JOHN SILAS
B. June 7, 1893, Fairland, Okla.   D. June 10, 1958, Shreveport, La.   BR TR

	G	AB	H	2B	3B	HR	HR %	R	RBI	BB	SO	SB	BA	SA	PH AB	PH H	G by POS
1913 STL N	1	1	0	0	0	0	0.0	0	0	0	1	0	.000	.000	1	0	

Jay Van Noy

VAN NOY, JAY LOWELL
B. Nov. 4, 1928, Garland, Utah   BL TR 6'1"   200 lbs.

	G	AB	H	2B	3B	HR	HR %	R	RBI	BB	SO	SB	BA	SA	PH AB	PH H	G by POS
1951 STL N	6	7	0	0	0	0	0.0	1	0	1	6	0	.000	.000	4	0	OF-1

Emil Verban

VERBAN, EMIL MATTHEW (Dutch, The Antelope)
B. Aug. 27, 1915, Lincoln, Ill.   BR TR 5'11"   165 lbs.

	G	AB	H	2B	3B	HR	HR %	R	RBI	BB	SO	SB	BA	SA	PH AB	PH H	G by POS
1944 STL N	146	498	128	14	2	0	0.0	51	43	19	14	0	.257	.293	0	0	2B-146
1945	155	597	166	22	8	0	0.0	59	72	19	15	4	.278	.342	0	0	2B-155
1946 2 teams		STL	N	(1G –	.000)		PHI	N	(138G –	.275)							
" Total	139	474	130	17	5	0	0.0	44	34	21	18	5	.274	.331	1	0	2B-138
1947 PHI N	155	540	154	14	8	0	0.0	50	42	23	8	5	.285	.341	0	0	2B-155
1948 2 teams		PHI	N	(55G –	.231)		CHI	N	(56G –	.294)							
" Total	111	417	112	20	2	1	0.2	51	27	15	12	4	.269	.333	1	0	2B-110
1949 CHI N	98	343	99	11	1	0	0.0	38	22	8	2	3	.289	.327	7	1	2B-88
1950 2 teams		CHI	N	(45G –	.108)		BOS	N	(4G –	.000)							
" Total	49	42	4	1	0	0	0.0	8	3	5	0	0	.095	.119	13	1	2B-10, SS-3, OF-1, 3B-1
7 yrs.	853	2911	793	99	26	1	0.0	301	241	108	74	21	.272	.325	22	2	2B-802, SS-3, OF-1, 3B-1
3 yrs.	302	1096	294	36	10	0	0.0	110	115	38	29	4	.268	.319	1	0	2B-301

WORLD SERIES

	G	AB	H	2B	3B	HR	HR %	R	RBI	BB	SO	SB	BA	SA	PH AB	PH H	G by POS
1944 STL N	6	17	7	0	0	0	0.0	1	2	2	0	0	.412	.412	0	0	2B-6

Johnny Vergez

VERGEZ, JOHN LEWIS
B. July 9, 1906, Oakland, Calif.   BR TR 5'8"   165 lbs.

	G	AB	H	2B	3B	HR	HR %	R	RBI	BB	SO	SB	BA	SA	PH AB	PH H	G by POS
1931 NY N	152	565	157	24	2	13	2.3	67	81	29	65	11	.278	.396	0	0	3B-152
1932	118	376	98	21	3	6	1.6	42	43	25	36	1	.261	.380	3	1	3B-111, SS-1
1933	123	458	124	21	6	16	3.5	57	72	39	66	1	.271	.448	0	0	3B-123
1934	108	320	64	18	1	7	2.2	31	27	28	55	1	.200	.328	3	0	3B-104
1935 PHI N	148	546	136	27	4	9	1.6	56	63	46	67	8	.249	.363	0	0	3B-148, SS-2
1936 2 teams		PHI	N	(15G –	.275)		STL	N	(8G –	.167)							
" Total	23	58	14	3	0	1	1.7	5	6	4	14	0	.241	.345	2	0	3B-20
6 yrs.	672	2323	593	114	16	52	2.2	258	292	171	303	22	.255	.385	8	1	3B-658, SS-3
1 yr.	8	18	3	1	0	0	0.0	1	1	1	3	0	.167	.222	0	0	3B-8

Ernie Vick

VICK, HENRY ARTHUR
B. July 2, 1900, Toledo, Ohio   D. July 18, 1980, Ann Arbor, Mich.   BR TR 5'9½"   185 lbs.

	G	AB	H	2B	3B	HR	HR %	R	RBI	BB	SO	SB	BA	SA	PH AB	PH H	G by POS
1922 STL N	3	6	2	2	0	0	0.0	1	0	0	0	0	.333	.667	0	0	C-3
1924	16	23	8	1	0	0	0.0	2	0	3	3	0	.348	.391	0	0	C-16
1925	14	32	6	2	1	0	0.0	3	3	3	1	0	.188	.313	5	0	C-9
1926	24	51	10	2	0	0	0.0	6	4	3	4	0	.196	.235	1	0	C-23
4 yrs.	57	112	26	7	1	0	0.0	12	7	9	8	0	.232	.313	6	0	C-51
4 yrs.	57	112	26	7	1	0	0.0	12	7	9	8	0	.232	.313	6	0	C-51

Bill Virdon

VIRDON, WILLIAM CHARLES
B. June 9, 1931, Hazel Park, Mich.
Manager 1972-82.   BL TR 6'   175 lbs.

	G	AB	H	2B	3B	HR	HR %	R	RBI	BB	SO	SB	BA	SA	PH AB	PH H	G by POS
1955 STL N	144	534	150	18	6	17	3.2	58	68	36	64	2	.281	.433	9	1	OF-142
1956 2 teams		STL	N	(24G –	.211)		PIT	N	(133G –	.334)							
" Total	157	580	185	23	10	10	1.7	77	46	38	71	6	.319	.445	6	0	OF-154
1957 PIT N	144	561	141	28	11	8	1.4	59	50	33	69	3	.251	.383	5	1	OF-141
1958	144	604	161	24	11	9	1.5	75	46	52	70	5	.267	.387	1	0	OF-143
1959	144	519	132	24	2	8	1.5	67	41	55	65	7	.254	.355	0	0	OF-144
1960	120	409	108	16	9	8	2.0	60	40	40	44	8	.264	.406	9	3	OF-109
1961	146	599	156	22	8	9	1.5	81	58	49	45	5	.260	.369	1	0	OF-145
1962	156	663	164	27	10	6	0.9	82	47	36	65	5	.247	.345	0	0	OF-156
1963	142	554	149	22	6	8	1.4	58	53	43	55	1	.269	.374	0	0	OF-142
1964	145	473	115	11	3	3	0.6	59	27	30	48	1	.243	.298	10	2	OF-134
1965	135	481	134	22	5	4	0.8	58	24	30	49	4	.279	.370	11	1	OF-128
1968	6	3	1	0	0	1	33.3	1	2	0	2	0	.333	1.333	2	1	OF-4
12 yrs.	1583	5980	1596	237	81	91	1.5	735	502	442	647	47	.267	.379	54	9	OF-1542
2 yrs.	168	605	165	20	6	19	3.1	68	77	41	72	2	.273	.420	10	1	OF-166

WORLD SERIES

	G	AB	H	2B	3B	HR	HR %	R	RBI	BB	SO	SB	BA	SA	PH AB	PH H	G by POS
1960 PIT N	7	29	7	3	0	0	0.0	2	5	1	3	1	.241	.345	0	0	OF-7

Bill Voss

VOSS, WILLIAM EDWARD
B. Oct. 31, 1945, Glendale, Calif.   BL TL 6'2"   160 lbs.

	G	AB	H	2B	3B	HR	HR %	R	RBI	BB	SO	SB	BA	SA	PH AB	PH H	G by POS
1965 CHI A	11	33	6	0	1	1	3.0	4	3	3	5	0	.182	.333	0	0	OF-10
1966	2	2	0	0	0	0	0.0	0	0	0	2	0	.000	.000	1	0	OF-1
1967	13	22	2	0	0	0	0.0	4	0	0	1	1	.091	.091	0	0	OF-11
1968	61	167	26	2	1	2	1.2	14	15	16	34	5	.156	.216	7	2	OF-55
1969 CAL A	133	349	91	11	4	2	0.6	33	40	35	40	5	.261	.332	16	6	OF-111, 1B-2
1970	80	181	44	4	3	3	1.7	21	30	23	18	2	.243	.348	26	6	OF-55
1971 MIL A	97	275	69	4	0	10	3.6	31	30	34	45	2	.251	.375	20	5	OF-79
1972 3 teams		MIL	A	(27G –	.083)		OAK	A	(40G –	.227)		STL	N	(11G –	.267)		
" Total	78	148	29	8	1	1	0.7	12	9	16	22	0	.196	.284	30	5	OF-47
8 yrs.	475	1177	267	29	10	19	1.6	119	127	117	167	15	.227	.317	100	24	OF-369, 1B-2
1 yr.	11	15	4	2	0	0	0.0	3	2	2	0	0	.267	.400	7	1	OF-2

	G	AB	H	2B	3B	HR	HR %	R	RBI	BB	SO	SB	BA	SA	Pinch Hit AB	Pinch Hit H	G by POS

Leon Wagner

WAGNER, LEON LAMAR (Daddy Wags)
B. May 13, 1934, Chattanooga, Tenn.   BL TR 6'1"   195 lbs.

	G	AB	H	2B	3B	HR	HR %	R	RBI	BB	SO	SB	BA	SA	PH AB	PH H	G by POS
1958 SF N	74	221	70	9	0	13	5.9	31	35	18	34	1	.317	.534	18	4	OF-57
1959	87	129	29	4	3	5	3.9	20	22	25	24	0	.225	.419	52	10	OF-28
1960 STL N	39	98	21	2	0	4	4.1	12	11	17	17	0	.214	.357	7	1	OF-32
1961 LA A	133	453	127	19	2	28	6.2	74	79	48	65	5	.280	.517	16	3	OF-116
1962	160	612	164	21	5	37	6.0	96	107	50	87	7	.268	.500	3	1	OF-156
1963	149	550	160	11	1	26	4.7	73	90	49	73	5	.291	.456	9	2	OF-141
1964 CLE A	163	641	162	19	2	31	4.8	94	100	56	121	14	.253	.434	2	1	OF-163
1965	144	517	152	18	1	28	5.4	91	79	60	52	12	.294	.495	11	3	OF-134
1966	150	549	153	20	0	23	4.2	70	66	46	69	5	.279	.441	10	3	OF-139
1967	135	433	105	15	1	15	3.5	56	54	37	76	3	.242	.386	15	4	OF-117
1968 2 teams	CLE A	(38G –	.184)		CHI A	(69G –	.284)										
" Total	107	211	55	12	0	1	0.5	19	24	27	37	2	.261	.332	46	11	OF-56
1969 SF N	11	12	4	0	0	0	0.0	0	2	2	1	0	.333	.333	7	3	OF-1
12 yrs.	1352	4426	1202	150	15	211	4.8	636	669	435	656	54	.272	.455	196	46	OF-1140
1 yr.	39	98	21	2	0	4	4.1	12	11	17	17	0	.214	.357	7	1	OF-32

Harry Walker

WALKER, HARRY WILLIAM (The Hat)
Son of Dixie Walker.   Brother of Dixie Walker.   BL TR 6'2"   175 lbs.
B. Oct. 22, 1918, Pascagoula, Miss.
Manager 1955, 1965-72.

	G	AB	H	2B	3B	HR	HR %	R	RBI	BB	SO	SB	BA	SA	PH AB	PH H	G by POS
1940 STL N	7	27	5	2	0	0	0.0	2	6	0	2	0	.185	.259	0	0	OF-7
1941	7	15	4	1	0	0	0.0	3	1	2	1	0	.267	.333	0	0	OF-5
1942	74	191	60	12	2	0	0.0	38	16	11	14	2	.314	.398	16	6	OF-56, 2B-2
1943	148	564	166	28	6	2	0.4	76	53	40	24	5	.294	.376	4	1	OF-144, 2B-1
1946	112	346	82	14	6	3	0.9	53	27	30	29	12	.237	.338	11	3	OF-92, 1B-8
1947 2 teams	STL N	(10G –	.200)		PHI N	(130G –	.371)										
" Total	140	513	186	29	16	1	0.2	81	41	63	39	13	.363	.487	2	0	OF-136, 1B-1
1948 PHI N	112	332	97	11	2	2	0.6	34	23	33	30	4	.292	.355	26	6	OF-81, 1B-4, 3B-1
1949 2 teams	CHI N	(42G –	.264)		CIN N	(86G –	.318)										
" Total	128	473	142	21	5	2	0.4	73	37	45	23	6	.300	.378	11	2	OF-116, 1B-2
1950 STL N	60	150	31	5	0	0	0.0	17	7	18	12	0	.207	.240	6	0	OF-46, 1B-1
1951	8	26	8	1	0	0	0.0	6	2	2	1	0	.308	.346	0	0	OF-6, 1B-1
1955	11	14	5	2	0	0	0.0	2	1	1	0	0	.357	.500	9	4	OF-1
11 yrs.	807	2651	786	126	37	10	0.4	385	214	245	175	42	.296	.383	85	17	OF-690, 1B-20, 2B-3, 3B-1
9 yrs.	437	1358	366	66	14	5	0.4	199	113	108	85	19	.270	.350	46	8	OF-366, 1B-11, 2B-3

WORLD SERIES

	G	AB	H	2B	3B	HR	HR %	R	RBI	BB	SO	SB	BA	SA	PH AB	PH H	G by POS
1942 STL N	1	1	0	0	0	0	0.0	0	0	0	1	0	.000	.000	1	0	
1943	5	18	3	1	0	0	0.0	0	2	0	2	0	.167	.222	1	0	OF-5
1946	7	17	7	2	0	0	0.0	3	6	4	2	0	.412	.529	1	0	OF-7
3 yrs.	13	36	10	3	0	0	0.0	3	6	4	5	0	.278	.361	3	0	OF-12

Joe Walker

WALKER, JOSEPH RICHARD
B. Jan. 23, 1901, Munhall, Pa.   D. June 20, 1959, West Mifflin, Pa.   BR TR 6'   170 lbs.

	G	AB	H	2B	3B	HR	HR %	R	RBI	BB	SO	SB	BA	SA	PH AB	PH H	G by POS
1923 STL N	2	7	2	0	0	0	0.0	1	0	1	1	0	.286	.286	0	0	1B-2

Bobby Wallace

WALLACE, RODERICK JOHN (Rhody)
B. Nov. 4, 1873, Pittsburgh, Pa.   D. Nov. 3, 1960, Torrance, Calif.   BR TR 5'8"   170 lbs.
Manager 1911-12, 1937.
Hall of Fame 1953.

	G	AB	H	2B	3B	HR	HR %	R	RBI	BB	SO	SB	BA	SA	PH AB	PH H	G by POS
1894 CLE N	4	13	2	1	0	0	0.0	0	1	0	1	0	.154	.231	0	0	P-4
1895	30	98	21	2	3	0	0.0	16	10	6	17	0	.214	.296	0	0	P-30
1896	45	149	35	6	3	1	0.7	19	17	11	21	2	.235	.336	0	0	OF-23, P-22, 1B-1
1897	131	522	177	35	21	4	0.8	99	112	48		14	.339	.510	0	0	3B-130, OF-1
1898	154	593	160	25	13	3	0.5	81	99	63		7	.270	.371	0	0	3B-141, 2B-13
1899 STL N	151	577	174	28	14	12	2.1	91	108	54		17	.302	.461	0	0	SS-100, 3B-52
1900	129	489	133	25	9	4	0.8	70	70	40		15	.272	.384	0	0	SS-126, 3B-1
1901	135	556	179	34	15	2	0.4	69	91	20		15	.322	.448	0	0	SS-134
1902 STL A	133	495	142	32	9	1	0.2	71	63	45		18	.287	.394	1	0	SS-131, OF-1, P-1
1903	136	519	127	21	17	1	0.2	63	54	28		10	.245	.356	0	0	SS-135
1904	139	550	150	29	4	2	0.4	57	69	42		20	.273	.351	0	0	SS-139
1905	156	587	159	25	9	1	0.2	67	59	45		13	.271	.349	0	0	SS-156
1906	139	476	123	21	7	2	0.4	64	67	58		24	.258	.345	1	1	SS-147
1907	147	538	138	20	7	0	0.0	56	70	54		16	.257	.320	0	0	SS-137
1908	137	487	123	24	4	1	0.2	59	60	52		5	.253	.324	0	0	SS-137
1909	116	403	96	12	2	1	0.2	36	35	38		7	.238	.285	0	0	SS-87, 3B-29
1910	138	508	131	19	7	0	0.0	47	37	49		12	.258	.323	0	0	SS-98, 3B-40
1911	125	410	95	12	2	0	0.0	35	31	46		8	.232	.271	0	0	SS-124, 2B-1
1912	99	323	78	14	5	0	0.0	39	31	43		3	.241	.316	1	0	SS-86, 3B-10, 2B-2
1913	53	147	31	5	0	0	0.0	11	21	14	16	1	.211	.245	7	0	SS-38, 3B-7
1914	26	73	16	2	1	0	0.0	3	5	5	13	1	.219	.274	5	1	SS-19, 3B-2
1915	9	13	3	0	1	0	0.0	1	4	5	0	0	.231	.385	0	0	SS-9
1916	14	18	5	0	0	0	0.0	0	1	2	1	0	.278	.278	0	0	3B-9, SS-5
1917 STL N	8	10	1	0	0	0	0.0	0	2	0	1	0	.100	.100	1	0	3B-5, SS-2
1918	32	98	15	1	0	0	0.0	3	4	6	9	1	.153	.163	3	2	2B-17, SS-12, 3B-1
25 yrs.	2386	8652	2314	393	153	35	0.4	1057	1121	774	79	201	.267	.360	21	5	SS-1823, 3B-427, P-57, 2B-33, OF-25, 1B-1
5 yrs.	455	1730	502	88	38	18	1.0	233	275	120	10	40	.290	.416	6	3	SS-374, 3B-59, 2B-17

Ty Waller

WALLER, ELLIOTT TYRONE
B. Mar. 14, 1957, Fresno, Calif.   BR TR 6'   180 lbs.

	G	AB	H	2B	3B	HR	HR %	R	RBI	BB	SO	SB	BA	SA	PH AB	PH H	G by POS
1980 STL N	5	12	1	0	0	0	0.0	3	0	1	5	0	.083	.083	0	0	3B-5
1981 CHI N	30	71	19	2	1	3	4.2	10	13	4	18	2	.268	.451	1	1	3B-22, OF-3, 2B-3
1982	17	21	5	0	0	0	0.0	4	1	2	5	0	.238	.238	6	2	OF-7, 3B-1

	G	AB	H	2B	3B	HR	HR %	R	RBI	BB	SO	SB	BA	SA	Pinch Hit AB	Pinch Hit H	G by POS

Ty Waller continued

	G	AB	H	2B	3B	HR	HR %	R	RBI	BB	SO	SB	BA	SA	AB	H	G by POS
3 yrs.	52	104	25	2	1	3	2.9	17	14	7	28	2	.240	.365	7	3	3B-28, OF-10, 2B-3
1 yr.	5	12	1	0	0	0	0.0	3	0	1	5	0	.083	.083	0	0	3B-5

John Warner

WARNER, JOHN JOSEPH
B. Aug. 15, 1872, New York, N. Y. D. Dec. 21, 1943, New York, N. Y. BL TR

	G	AB	H	2B	3B	HR	HR %	R	RBI	BB	SO	SB	BA	SA	AB	H	G by POS
1895 2 teams		BOS	N	(3G –	.143)	LOU	N	(67G –	.267)								
" Total	70	239	63	4	2	1	0.4	22	21	12	16	10	.264	.310	0	0	C-67, 1B-3, 2B-1
1896 2 teams		LOU	N	(33G –	.227)	NY	N	(19G –	.259)								
" Total	52	164	39	2	1	0	0.0	18	13	13	17	4	.238	.262	0	0	C-51, 1B-1
1897 NY N	110	397	109	6	3	2	0.5	50	51	26		8	.275	.320	0	0	C-110
1898	110	373	96	14	5	0	0.0	40	42	22		9	.257	.322	0	0	C-109, OF-1
1899	88	293	78	8	1	0	0.0	38	19	15		15	.266	.300	3	0	C-82, 1B-3
1900	34	108	27	4	0	0	0.0	15	13	8		1	.250	.287	3	1	C-31
1901	87	291	70	6	1	0	0.0	19	20	3		3	.241	.268	3	0	C-84
1902 BOS A	65	222	52	5	7	0	0.0	19	12	13		0	.234	.320	0	0	C-64
1903 NY N	89	285	81	8	5	0	0.0	38	34	7		5	.284	.347	3	1	C-85
1904	86	287	57	5	1	0	0.3	29	15	14		7	.199	.233	0	0	C-86
1905 2 teams		STL	N	(41G –	.255)	DET	A	(36G –	.202)								
" Total	77	256	59	4	5	1	0.4	21	19	14		4	.230	.297	0	0	C-77
1906 2 teams		DET	A	(50G –	.242)	WAS	A	(32G –	.204)								
" Total	82	256	58	8	3	1	0.4	20	19	14		7	.227	.293	1	0	C-81
1907 WAS A	72	207	53	5	0	0	0.0	11	17	12		3	.256	.280	8	1	C-64
1908	51	116	28	2	1	0	0.0	8	8	8		1	.241	.276	8	1	C-41, 1B-1
14 yrs.	1073	3494	870	81	35	6	0.2	348	303	181	33	83	.249	.297	29	4	C-1032, 1B-8, OF-1, 2B-1
1 yr.	41	137	35	2	2	1	0.7	9	12	6		2	.255	.321	0	0	C-41

Bill Warwick

WARWICK, FIRMAN NEWTON
B. Nov. 26, 1897, Philadelphia, Pa. BR TR 6'½" 180 lbs.

	G	AB	H	2B	3B	HR	HR %	R	RBI	BB	SO	SB	BA	SA	AB	H	G by POS
1921 PIT N	1	1	0	0	0	0	0.0	0	0	0	0	0	.000	.000	0	0	C-1
1925 STL N	13	41	12	1	2	1	2.4	8	6	5	5	0	.293	.488	0	0	C-13
1926	9	14	5	0	0	0	0.0	0	2	0	2	0	.357	.357	0	0	C-9
3 yrs.	23	56	17	1	2	1	1.8	8	8	5	7	0	.304	.446	0	0	C-23
2 yrs.	22	55	17	1	2	1	1.8	8	8	5	7	0	.309	.455	0	0	C-22

Carl Warwick

WARWICK, CARL WAYNE
B. Feb. 27, 1937, Dallas, Tex. BR TL 5'10" 170 lbs.

	G	AB	H	2B	3B	HR	HR %	R	RBI	BB	SO	SB	BA	SA	AB	H	G by POS
1961 2 teams		LA	N	(19G –	.091)	STL	N	(55G –	.250)								
" Total	74	163	39	6	2	4	2.5	29	17	20	36	3	.239	.374	13	4	OF-60
1962 2 teams		STL	N	(13G –	.348)	HOU	N	(130G –	.260)								
" Total	143	500	132	17	1	17	3.4	67	64	40	79	4	.264	.404	13	4	OF-138
1963 HOU N	150	528	134	19	5	7	1.3	49	47	49	70	3	.254	.348	10	2	OF-141, 1B-2
1964 STL N	88	158	41	7	1	3	1.9	14	15	11	30	2	.259	.373	43	11	OF-49
1965 2 teams		STL	N	(50G –	.156)	BAL	A	(9G –	.000)								
" Total	59	91	12	2	1	0	0.0	6	6	7	20	1	.132	.176	36	4	OF-24, 1B-4
1966 CHI N	16	22	5	0	0	0	0.0	3	0	0	6	0	.227	.227	7	2	OF-10
6 yrs.	530	1462	363	51	10	31	2.1	168	149	127	241	13	.248	.360	122	27	OF-422, 1B-6
4 yrs.	206	410	99	15	4	8	2.0	48	41	35	83	8	.241	.356	85	20	OF-128, 1B-4
WORLD SERIES																	
1964 STL N	5	4	3	0	0	0	0.0	2	1	1	0	0	.750	.750	4	3 (1st)	

Bill Watkins

WATKINS, WILLIAM HENRY
B. May 5, 1859, Brantford, Ont., Canada D. June 9, 1937, Port Huron, Mich. 5'10" 156 lbs.
Manager 1884-89, 1893, 1898-99.

	G	AB	H	2B	3B	HR	HR %	R	RBI	BB	SO	SB	BA	SA	AB	H	G by POS
1884 IND AA	34	127	26	4	0	0	0.0	16		5			.205	.236	0	0	3B-23, 2B-9, SS-2

George Watkins

WATKINS, GEORGE ARCHIBALD
B. June 4, 1902, Palestine, Tex. D. June 1, 1970, Houston, Tex. BL TR 6' 175 lbs.

	G	AB	H	2B	3B	HR	HR %	R	RBI	BB	SO	SB	BA	SA	AB	H	G by POS
1930 STL N	119	391	146	32	7	17	4.3	85	87	24	49	5	.373	.621	15	5	OF-89, 1B-13, 2B-1
1931	131	503	145	30	13	13	2.6	93	51	31	66	15	.288	.477	2	0	OF-129
1932	137	458	143	35	4	9	2.0	67	63	45	46	18	.312	.461	6	2	OF-120
1933	138	525	146	24	5	5	1.0	66	62	39	62	11	.278	.371	3	0	OF-135
1934 NY N	105	296	73	18	3	6	2.0	38	33	24	34	2	.247	.389	16	3	OF-81
1935 PHI N	150	600	162	25	5	17	2.8	80	76	40	78	3	.270	.413	2	1	OF-148
1936 2 teams		PHI	N	(19G –	.243)	BKN	N	(105G –	.255)								
" Total	124	434	110	28	4	6	1.4	61	48	43	47	7	.253	.387	8	2	OF-115
7 yrs.	904	3207	925	192	42	73	2.3	490	420	246	382	61	.288	.443	52	13	OF-817, 1B-13, 2B-1
4 yrs.	525	1877	580	121	28	44	2.3	311	263	139	223	49	.309	.474	26	7	OF-473, 1B-13, 2B-1
WORLD SERIES																	
1930 STL N	4	12	2	0	0	1	8.3	2	1	1	3	0	.167	.417	0	0	OF-4
1931	5	14	4	1	0	1	7.1	4	2	2	1	1	.286	.571	0	0	OF-5
2 yrs.	9	26	6	1	0	2	7.7	6	3	3	4	1	.231	.500	0	0	OF-9

Art Weaver

WEAVER, ARTHUR COGGSHALL
B. Apr. 7, 1879, Wichita, Kans. D. Mar. 23, 1917, Denver, Colo. TR

	G	AB	H	2B	3B	HR	HR %	R	RBI	BB	SO	SB	BA	SA	AB	H	G by POS
1902 STL N	11	33	6	2	0	0	0.0	2		3	1		0	.182	.242	0	0	C-11
1903 2 teams		STL	N	(16G –	.245)	PIT	N	(16G –	.229)								
" Total	32	97	23	0	1	0	0.0	12	8	6		1	.237	.258	0	0	C-27, 1B-5
1905 STL A	28	92	11	2	1	0	0.0	5	3	1		0	.120	.163	0	0	C-28
1908 CHI A	15	35	7	1	0	0	0.0	1	1	1		0	.200	.229	0	0	C-15
4 yrs.	86	257	47	5	2	0	0.0	20	15	9		1	.183	.218	0	0	C-81, 1B-5
2 yrs.	27	82	18	2	0	0	0.0	8		5		1	.220	.244	0	0	C-27

	G	AB	H	2B	3B	HR	HR %	R	RBI	BB	SO	SB	BA	SA	Pinch Hit AB	Pinch Hit H	G by POS

Skeeter Webb

WEBB, JAMES LAVERNE
B. Nov. 4, 1909, Meridian, Miss.
BR TR 5'9½" 150 lbs.

	G	AB	H	2B	3B	HR	HR %	R	RBI	BB	SO	SB	BA	SA	AB	H	G by POS
1932 STL N	1	0	0	0	0	0	–	0	0	0	0	0	–	–	0	0	SS-1
1938 CLE A	20	58	16	2	0	0	0.0	11	2	8	7	1	.276	.310	0	0	SS-13, 3B-3, 2B-2
1939	81	269	71	14	1	2	0.7	28	26	15	24	1	.264	.346	0	0	SS-81
1940 CHI A	84	334	79	11	2	1	0.3	33	29	30	33	3	.237	.290	2	0	2B-74, SS-7, 3B-1
1941	29	84	16	2	0	0	0.0	7	6	3	9	1	.190	.214	3	1	2B-18, SS-5, 3B-3
1942	32	94	16	2	1	0	0.0	5	4	4	13	1	.170	.213	0	0	2B-29
1943	58	213	50	5	2	0	0.0	15	22	6	19	5	.235	.277	3	0	2B-54
1944	139	513	108	19	6	0	0.0	44	30	20	39	7	.211	.271	0	0	SS-135, 2B-5
1945 DET A	118	407	81	12	2	0	0.0	43	21	30	35	8	.199	.238	0	0	SS-104, 2B-11
1946	64	169	37	1	1	0	0.0	12	17	9	18	3	.219	.237	1	0	2B-50, SS-8
1947	50	79	16	3	0	0	0.0	13	6	7	9	3	.203	.241	2	0	2B-30, SS-6
1948 PHI A	23	54	8	2	0	0	0.0	5	3	0	9	0	.148	.185	0	0	2B-9, SS-8
12 yrs.	699	2274	498	73	15	3	0.1	216	166	132	215	33	.219	.268	11	1	SS-368, 2B-282, 3B-7
1 yr.	1	0	0	0	0	0	–	0	0	0	0	0	–	–	0	0	SS-1

WORLD SERIES

	G	AB	H	2B	3B	HR	HR %	R	RBI	BB	SO	SB	BA	SA	AB	H	G by POS
1945 DET A	7	27	5	0	0	0	0.0	4	1	3	1	0	.185	.185	0	0	SS-7

Perry Werden

WERDEN, PERCIVAL WHERITT
B. July 21, 1865, St. Louis, Mo.   D. Jan. 9, 1934, Minneapolis, Minn.
BR TR

	G	AB	H	2B	3B	HR	HR %	R	RBI	BB	SO	SB	BA	SA	AB	H	G by POS
1884 STL U	18	76	18	2	0	0	0.0	7		2			.237	.263	0	0	P-16, OF-6
1888 WAS N	3	10	3	0	0	0	0.0	0	2	1	4	0	.300	.300	0	0	OF-3
1890 TOL AA	128	498	147	22	20	6	1.2	113		78		59	.295	.456	0	0	1B-124, OF-5
1891 BAL AA	139	552	160	20	18	6	1.1	102	104	52	59	46	.290	.424	0	0	1B-139
1892 STL N	149	598	154	22	6	8	1.3	73	84	59	52	20	.258	.355	0	0	1B-149
1893	125	500	138	22	33	1	0.2	73	94	49	25	11	.276	.458	0	0	1B-124, OF-1
1897 LOU N	131	506	153	21	14	5	1.0	76	83	40		14	.302	.429	0	0	1B-131
7 yrs.	693	2740	773	109	91	26	0.9	444	366	281	140	150	.282	.417	0	0	1B-667, P-16, OF-15
2 yrs.	274	1098	292	44	39	9	0.8	146	178	108	77	31	.266	.402	0	0	1B-273, OF-1

Wally Westlake

WESTLAKE, WALDON THOMAS
Brother of Jim Westlake.
B. Nov. 8, 1920, Gridley, Calif.
BR TR 6' 186 lbs.

	G	AB	H	2B	3B	HR	HR %	R	RBI	BB	SO	SB	BA	SA	AB	H	G by POS
1947 PIT N	112	407	111	17	4	17	4.2	59	69	27	63	5	.273	.459	2	0	OF-109
1948	132	428	122	10	6	17	4.0	78	65	46	40	2	.285	.456	8	2	OF-125
1949	147	525	148	24	8	23	4.4	77	104	45	69	6	.282	.490	4	0	OF-143
1950	139	477	136	15	6	24	5.0	69	95	48	78	1	.285	.493	15	3	OF-123
1951 2 teams			PIT	N	(50G –	.282)		STL	N	(73G –	.255)						
" Total	123	448	119	12	5	22	4.9	64	84	33	68	1	.266	.462	9	1	OF-79, 3B-34
1952 3 teams			STL	N	(21G –	.216)		CIN	N	(59G –	.202)		CLE	A	(29G –	.232)	
" Total	109	326	69	11	4	4	1.2	47	33	47	56	2	.212	.288	6	0	OF-104
1953 CLE A	82	218	72	7	1	9	4.1	42	46	35	29	2	.330	.495	7	0	OF-72
1954	85	240	63	9	2	11	4.6	36	42	26	37	0	.263	.454	11	2	OF-70
1955 2 teams			CLE	A	(16G –	.250)		BAL	A	(8G –	.125)						
" Total	24	44	8	2	0	0	0.0	2	1	9	10	0	.182	.227	5	1	OF-14
1956 PHI N	5	4	0	0	0	0	0.0	0	0	1	3	0	.000	.000	4	0	
10 yrs.	958	3117	848	107	33	127	4.1	474	539	317	453	19	.272	.450	71	9	OF-839, 3B-34
2 yrs.	94	341	84	11	5	6	1.8	43	49	32	53	2	.246	.361	5	0	OF-88

WORLD SERIES

	G	AB	H	2B	3B	HR	HR %	R	RBI	BB	SO	SB	BA	SA	AB	H	G by POS
1954 CLE A	2	7	1	0	0	0	0.0	0	0	1	3	0	.143	.143	0	0	OF-2

Dick Wheeler

WHEELER, RICHARD
Also known as Richard Wheeler Maynard.
D. Feb. 12, 1962, Lexington, Mass.
TR

	G	AB	H	2B	3B	HR	HR %	R	RBI	BB	SO	SB	BA	SA	AB	H	G by POS
1918 STL N	3	6	0	0	0	0	0.0	0	0	0	3	0	.000	.000	1	0	OF-2

Jim Whelan

WHELAN, JAMES FRANK
B. 1890
BR TR 5'8½" 165 lbs.

	G	AB	H	2B	3B	HR	HR %	R	RBI	BB	SO	SB	BA	SA	AB	H	G by POS
1913 STL N	1	1	0	0	0	0	0.0	0	0	0	0	0	.000	.000	1	0	

Pete Whisenant

WHISENANT, THOMAS PETER
B. Dec. 14, 1929, Asheville, N. C.
BR TR 6'2" 190 lbs.

	G	AB	H	2B	3B	HR	HR %	R	RBI	BB	SO	SB	BA	SA	AB	H	G by POS
1952 BOS N	24	52	10	2	0	0	0.0	3	7	4	13	1	.192	.231	9	1	OF-14
1955 STL N	58	115	22	5	1	2	1.7	10	9	5	29	2	.191	.304	20	5	OF-40
1956 CHI N	103	314	75	16	3	11	3.5	37	46	24	53	8	.239	.414	8	2	OF-93
1957 CIN N	67	90	19	3	2	5	5.6	18	11	5	24	0	.211	.456	20	8	OF-43
1958	85	203	48	9	2	11	5.4	33	40	18	37	3	.236	.463	25	6	OF-66, 2B-1
1959	36	71	17	2	0	5	7.0	13	11	8	18	0	.239	.479	14	1	OF-21
1960 3 teams			CIN	N	(1G –	.000)		CLE	A	(7G –	.167)		WAS	A	(58G –	.226)	
" Total	66	122	27	9	0	3	2.5	19	9	19	16	2	.221	.369	15	2	OF-49
1961 2 teams			MIN	A	(10G –	.000)		CIN	N	(26G –	.200)						
" Total	36	21	3	0	0	0	0.0	7	1	3	6	1	.143	.143	13	1	OF-17, 3B-1, C-1
8 yrs.	475	988	221	46	8	37	3.7	140	134	86	196	17	.224	.399	124	26	OF-343, 3B-1, 2B-1, C-1
1 yr.	58	115	22	5	1	2	1.7	10	9	5	29	2	.191	.304	20	5	OF-40

Lew Whistler

WHISTLER, LEWIS
Born Lewis Wissler.
B. Mar. 10, 1868, St. Louis, Mo.   D. Dec. 30, 1959, St. Louis, Mo.

	G	AB	H	2B	3B	HR	HR %	R	RBI	BB	SO	SB	BA	SA	AB	H	G by POS
1890 NY N	45	170	49	9	7	2	1.2	27	29	20	37	8	.288	.459	0	0	1B-45
1891	72	265	65	8	7	4	1.5	39	38	24	45	4	.245	.374	0	0	SS-33, OF-22, 1B-7, 2B-6, 3B-5
1892 2 teams			BAL	N	(52G –	.225)		LOU	N	(80G –	.235)						
" Total	132	494	114	10	13	7	1.4	74	55	48	67	26	.231	.346	0	0	1B-123, 2B-10, OF-1

	G	AB	H	2B	3B	HR	HR %	R	RBI	BB	SO	SB	BA	SA	Pinch Hit AB	Pinch Hit H	G by POS

Lew Whistler continued

	G	AB	H	2B	3B	HR	HR %	R	RBI	BB	SO	SB	BA	SA	AB	H	G by POS
1893 2 teams	LOU	N	(13G – .213)		STL	N	(10G – .237)										
" Total	23	85	19	2	1	0	0.0	10	11	8	7	1	.224	.271	0	0	1B-14, OF-9
4 yrs.	272	1014	247	29	28	13	1.3	150	133	100	156	39	.244	.366	0	0	1B-189, SS-33, OF-32, 2B-16, 3B-5
1 yr.	10	38	9	1	0	0	0.0	5	2	3	2	0	.237	.263	0	0	OF-9, 1B-1

Bill White

WHITE, WILLIAM DeKOVA
B. Jan. 28, 1934, Lakewood, Fla.

BL TL 6' 185 lbs.

	G	AB	H	2B	3B	HR	HR %	R	RBI	BB	SO	SB	BA	SA	AB	H	G by POS
1956 NY N	138	508	130	23	7	22	4.3	63	59	47	72	15	.256	.459	0	0	1B-138, OF-2
1958 SF N	26	29	7	1	0	1	3.4	5	4	7	5	1	.241	.379	16	4	1B-3, OF-2
1959 STL N	138	517	156	33	9	12	2.3	77	72	34	61	15	.302	.470	5	1	OF-92, 1B-71
1960	144	554	157	27	10	16	2.9	81	79	42	83	12	.283	.455	3	0	1B-123, OF-29
1961	153	591	169	28	11	20	3.4	89	90	64	84	8	.286	.472	3	0	1B-151
1962	159	614	199	31	3	20	3.3	93	102	58	69	9	.324	.482	1	0	1B-146, OF-27
1963	162	658	200	26	8	27	4.1	106	109	59	100	10	.304	.491	0	0	1B-162
1964	160	631	191	37	4	21	3.3	92	102	52	103	7	.303	.474	0	0	1B-160
1965	148	543	157	26	3	24	4.4	82	73	63	86	3	.289	.481	4	1	1B-144
1966 PHI N	159	577	159	23	6	22	3.8	85	103	68	109	16	.276	.451	0	0	1B-158
1967	110	308	77	6	2	8	2.6	29	33	52	61	6	.250	.360	14	0	1B-95
1968	127	385	92	16	2	9	2.3	34	40	39	79	0	.239	.361	20	5	1B-111
1969 STL N	49	57	12	1	0	0	0.0	7	4	11	15	1	.211	.228	31	5	1B-15
13 yrs.	1673	5972	1706	278	65	202	3.4	843	870	596	927	103	.286	.455	101	16	1B-1477, OF-152
8 yrs.	1113	4165	1241	209	48	140	3.4	627	631	383	601	65	.298	.472	47	7	1B-972, OF-148
				9th	9th						6th						

WORLD SERIES

	G	AB	H	2B	3B	HR	HR %	R	RBI	BB	SO	SB	BA	SA	AB	H	G by POS
1964 STL N	7	27	3	1	0	0	0.0	2	2	2	6	1	.111	.148	0	0	1B-7

Burgess Whitehead

WHITEHEAD, BURGESS URQUHART (Whitey)
B. June 29, 1910, Tarboro, N. C.

BR TR 5'10½" 160 lbs.

	G	AB	H	2B	3B	HR	HR %	R	RBI	BB	SO	SB	BA	SA	AB	H	G by POS
1933 STL N	12	7	2	0	0	0	0.0	2	1	0	1	0	.286	.286	0	0	SS-9, 2B-3
1934	100	332	92	13	5	1	0.3	55	24	12	19	5	.277	.355	1	0	2B-48, SS-29, 3B-28
1935	107	338	89	10	2	0	0.0	45	33	11	14	5	.263	.305	12	2	2B-80, 3B-8, SS-6
1936 NY N	154	632	176	31	3	4	0.6	99	47	29	32	14	.278	.356	0	0	2B-153
1937	152	574	164	15	6	5	0.9	64	52	28	20	7	.286	.359	0	0	2B-152
1939	95	335	80	6	3	2	0.6	31	24	24	19	1	.239	.293	0	0	2B-91, SS-4, 3B-1
1940	133	568	160	9	6	4	0.7	68	36	26	17	9	.282	.340	0	0	3B-74, 2B-57, SS-4
1941	116	403	92	15	4	1	0.2	41	23	14	10	7	.228	.293	0	0	2B-104, 3B-1
1946 PIT N	55	127	28	1	2	0	0.0	10	5	6	6	3	.220	.260	12	2	2B-30, 3B-4, SS-1
9 yrs.	924	3316	883	100	31	17	0.5	415	245	150	138	51	.266	.331	25	4	2B-718, 3B-116, SS-53
3 yrs.	219	677	183	23	7	1	0.1	102	58	23	34	10	.270	.329	13	2	2B-131, SS-44, 3B-36

WORLD SERIES

	G	AB	H	2B	3B	HR	HR %	R	RBI	BB	SO	SB	BA	SA	AB	H	G by POS
1934 STL N	1	0	0	0	0	0	–	0	0	0	0	0	–	–	0	0	SS-1
1936 NY N	6	21	1	0	0	0	0.0	1	2	1	3	0	.048	.048	0	0	2B-6
1937	5	16	4	2	0	0	0.0	1	0	2	0	1	.250	.375	0	0	2B-5
3 yrs.	12	37	5	2	0	0	0.0	2	2	3	3	1	.135	.189	0	0	2B-11, SS-1

Fred Whitfield

WHITFIELD, FRED DWIGHT
B. Jan. 7, 1938, Vandiver, Ala.

BL TL 6'1" 190 lbs.

	G	AB	H	2B	3B	HR	HR %	R	RBI	BB	SO	SB	BA	SA	AB	H	G by POS
1962 STL N	73	158	42	7	1	8	5.1	20	34	7	30	1	.266	.475	33	11	1B-38
1963 CLE A	109	346	87	17	3	21	6.1	44	54	24	61	0	.251	.500	17	4	1B-92
1964	101	293	79	13	1	10	3.4	29	29	12	58	0	.270	.423	24	4	1B-79
1965	132	468	137	23	1	26	5.6	49	90	16	42	2	.293	.513	18	9	1B-122
1966	137	502	121	15	2	27	5.4	59	78	27	76	1	.241	.440	4	0	1B-132
1967	100	257	56	10	0	9	3.5	24	31	25	45	3	.218	.362	32	9	1B-66
1968 CIN N	87	171	44	8	0	6	3.5	15	32	9	29	0	.257	.409	46	11	1B-41
1969	74	74	11	0	0	1	1.4	2	8	18	27	0	.149	.189	51	8	1B-14
1970 MON N	4	15	1	0	0	0	0.0	0	0	1	3	0	.067	.067	0	0	1B-4
9 yrs.	817	2284	578	93	8	108	4.7	242	356	139	371	7	.253	.443	225	56	1B-588
1 yr.	73	158	42	7	1	8	5.1	20	34	7	30	1	.266	.475	33	11	1B-38

Possum Whitted

WHITTED, GEORGE BOSTIC
B. Feb. 4, 1890, Durham, N. C.   D. Oct. 16, 1962, Wilmington, N. C.

BR TR 5'8½" 168 lbs.

	G	AB	H	2B	3B	HR	HR %	R	RBI	BB	SO	SB	BA	SA	AB	H	G by POS
1912 STL N	12	46	12	3	0	0	0.0	7	3	3	5	1	.261	.326	0	0	3B-12
1913	122	402	89	10	5	0	0.0	44	38	31	44	9	.221	.271	15	3	OF-40, SS-37, 3B-21, 2B-7, 1B-2
1914 2 teams	STL	N	(20G – .129)		BOS	N	(66G – .261)										
" Total	86	249	61	12	4	2	0.8	39	32	18	21	11	.245	.349	6	1	OF-41, 3B-16, 2B-16, 1B-4, SS-3
1915 PHI N	125	448	126	17	3	1	0.2	46	43	29	47	24	.281	.339	1	0	OF-109, 1B-7
1916	147	526	148	20	12	6	1.1	68	68	19	46	29	.281	.399	1	0	OF-136, 1B-16
1917	149	553	155	24	9	3	0.5	69	70	30	56	10	.280	.373	1	0	OF-141, 1B-10, 3B-6, 2B-1
1918	24	86	21	4	0	0	0.0	7	7	4	10	4	.244	.291	2	1	OF-22, 1B-1
1919 2 teams	PHI	N	(78G – .249)		PIT	N	(35G – .389)										
" Total	113	420	123	21	8	3	0.7	47	53	20	24	12	.293	.402	2	1	OF-48, 3B-35, 2B-20, 3B-3
1920 PIT N	134	494	129	11	12	1	0.2	53	74	35	36	11	.261	.338	0	0	3B-125, 1B-10, OF-1
1921	108	403	114	23	7	7	1.7	60	63	26	21	5	.283	.427	1	0	OF-102, 1B-7
1922 BKN N	1	1	0	0	0	0	0.0	0	0	0	0	0	.000	.000	1	0	
11 yrs.	1021	3628	978	145	60	23	0.6	440	451	215	310	116	.270	.362	29	6	OF-640, 3B-182, 1B-92, 2B-44, SS-40
3 yrs.	154	479	105	14	5	0	0.0	54	46	34	52	11	.219	.269	19	3	3B-44, OF-43, SS-37, 2B-8, 1B-2

WORLD SERIES

	G	AB	H	2B	3B	HR	HR %	R	RBI	BB	SO	SB	BA	SA	AB	H	G by POS
1914 BOS N	4	14	3	0	1	0	0.0	2	2	3	1	1	.214	.357	0	0	OF-4

	G	AB	H	2B	3B	HR	HR%	R	RBI	BB	SO	SB	BA	SA	PH AB	PH H	G by POS

Possum Whitted continued

	G	AB	H	2B	3B	HR	HR%	R	RBI	BB	SO	SB	BA	SA	PH AB	PH H	G by POS
1915 PHI N	5	15	1	0	0	0	0.0	0	1	1	0	1	.067	.067	0	0	OF-5
2 yrs.	9	29	4	0	1	0	0.0	2	3	4	1	2	.138	.207	0	0	OF-9

Bob Wicker

WICKER, ROBERT KITRIDGE
B. May 25, 1878, Lawrence County, Ind.   D. Jan. 22, 1955, Evanston, Ill.   BR TR 5'11½" 180 lbs.

	G	AB	H	2B	3B	HR	HR%	R	RBI	BB	SO	SB	BA	SA	PH AB	PH H	G by POS
1901 STL N	3	3	1	0	0	0	0.0	0		0		0	.333	.333	1	0	P-1
1902	31	77	18	2	0	0	0.0	6	3	3		2	.234	.260	6	1	P-22, OF-3
1903 2 teams	STL	N	(1G –	.000)	CHI	N	(32G –	.245)									
" Total	33	100	24	5	0	0	0.0	19	8	4		1	.240	.330	0	0	P-33
1904 CHI N	50	155	34	1	0	0	0.0	17	9	4		4	.219	.226	0	0	P-30, OF-20
1905	25	72	10	0	0	0	0.0	5	3	4		1	.139	.139	0	0	P-22, OF-3
1906 2 teams	CHI	N	(10G –	.100)	CIN	N	(20G –	.180)									
" Total	30	70	11	1	2	0	0.0	6	4	7		2	.157	.229	0	0	P-30
6 yrs.	172	477	98	9	4	0	0.0	54	27	22		10	.205	.241	7	1	P-138, OF-26
3 yrs.	35	82	19	2	0	0	0.0	8	3	3		2	.232	.256	7	1	P-24, OF-3

Floyd Wicker

WICKER, FLOYD EULISS
B. Sept. 12, 1943, Burlington, N. C.   BL TR 6'2" 175 lbs.

	G	AB	H	2B	3B	HR	HR%	R	RBI	BB	SO	SB	BA	SA	PH AB	PH H	G by POS
1968 STL N	5	4	2	0	0	0	0.0	2	0	0	0	0	.500	.500	4	2	
1969 MON N	41	39	4	0	0	0	0.0	2	2	2	20	0	.103	.103	29	3	OF-11
1970 MIL A	15	41	8	1	0	1	2.4	3	3	1	8	0	.195	.293	6	1	OF-12
1971 2 teams	MIL	A	(11G –	.125)	SF	N	(9G –	.143)									
" Total	20	29	4	0	0	0	0.0	3	1	4	5	0	.138	.138	10	1	OF-7
4 yrs.	81	113	18	1	0	1	0.9	10	6	7	33	0	.159	.195	49	7	OF-30
1 yr.	5	4	2	0	0	0	0.0	2	0	0	0	0	.500	.500	4	2	

Del Wilber

WILBER, DELBERT QUENTIN (Babe)
B. Feb. 24, 1919, Lincoln Park, Mich.
Manager 1973   BR TR 6'3" 200 lbs.

	G	AB	H	2B	3B	HR	HR%	R	RBI	BB	SO	SB	BA	SA	PH AB	PH H	G by POS
1946 STL N	4	4	0	0	0	0	0.0	0	0	1	0	0	.000	.000	0	0	C-4
1947	51	99	23	8	1	0	0.0	7	12	5	13	0	.232	.333	15	5	C-34
1948	27	58	11	2	0	0	0.0	5	10	4	9	0	.190	.224	1	0	C-26
1949	2	4	1	0	0	0	0.0	0	0	0	0	0	.250	.250	0	0	C-2
1951 PHI N	84	245	68	7	3	8	3.3	30	34	17	26	0	.278	.429	10	1	C-73
1952 2 teams	PHI	N	(2G –	.000)	BOS	A	(47G –	.267)									
" Total	49	137	36	10	1	3	2.2	7	23	7	21	1	.263	.416	10	4	C-39
1953 BOS A	58	112	27	6	1	7	6.3	16	29	6	21	0	.241	.500	28	4	C-28, 1B-2
1954	24	61	8	2	1	1	1.6	2	7	4	6	0	.131	.246	6	1	C-18
8 yrs.	299	720	174	35	7	19	2.6	67	115	44	96	1	.242	.389	70	15	C-224, 1B-2
4 yrs.	84	165	35	10	1	0	0.0	12	22	10	22	0	.212	.285	16	5	C-66

Denney Wilie

WILIE, DENNEY EARNEST
B. Sept. 22, 1890, Mt. Calm, Tex.   D. June 20, 1966, Hayward, Calif.   BL TL 5'8" 155 lbs.

	G	AB	H	2B	3B	HR	HR%	R	RBI	BB	SO	SB	BA	SA	PH AB	PH H	G by POS
1911 STL N	28	51	12	3	1	0	0.0	10	3	8	11	3	.235	.333	10	1	OF-15
1912	30	48	11	0	1	0	0.0	2	6	7	9	0	.229	.271	8	2	OF-16
1915 CLE A	45	131	33	4	1	2	1.5	14	10	26	18	2	.252	.344	8	0	OF-35
3 yrs.	103	230	56	7	3	2	0.9	26	19	41	38	5	.243	.326	26	3	OF-66
2 yrs.	58	99	23	3	2	0	0.0	12	9	15	20	3	.232	.303	18	3	OF-31

Jim Williams

WILLIAMS, JAMES FRANCIS
B. Oct. 4, 1943, Santa Maria, Calif.   BR TR 5'10" 170 lbs.

	G	AB	H	2B	3B	HR	HR%	R	RBI	BB	SO	SB	BA	SA	PH AB	PH H	G by POS
1966 STL N	13	11	3	0	0	0	0.0	1	1	1	5	0	.273	.273	1	0	SS-7, 2B-3
1967	1	2	0	0	0	0	0.0	0	0	0	1	0	.000	.000	0	0	SS-1
2 yrs.	14	13	3	0	0	0	0.0	1	1	1	6	0	.231	.231	1	0	SS-8, 2B-3
2 yrs.	14	13	3	0	0	0	0.0	1	1	1	6	0	.231	.231	1	0	SS-8, 2B-3

Otto Williams

WILLIAMS, OTTO GEORGE
B. Nov. 2, 1877, Newark, N. J.   D. Mar. 19, 1937, Omaha, Neb.   BR TR

	G	AB	H	2B	3B	HR	HR%	R	RBI	BB	SO	SB	BA	SA	PH AB	PH H	G by POS
1902 STL N	2	5	2	0	0	0	0.0	0	2	1		1	.400	.400	0	0	SS-2
1903 2 teams	STL	N	(53G –	.203)	CHI	N	(38G –	.223)									
" Total	91	317	67	9	2	0	0.0	24	22	13		14	.211	.252	0	0	SS-78, 2B-8, 1B-3, 3B-1
1904 CHI N	57	185	37	4	1	0	0.0	21	8	13		9	.200	.232	2	1	OF-21, 1B-11, SS-10, 3B-6, 2B-6
1906 WAS A	20	51	7	0	0	0	0.0	3	2	2		0	.137	.137	3	0	SS-8, 2B-6, 1B-2, 3B-1
4 yrs.	170	558	113	13	3	0	0.0	48	34	29		24	.203	.237	5	1	SS-98, OF-21, 2B-20, 1B-16, 3B-8
2 yrs.	55	192	40	4	2	0	0.0	10	11	10		7	.208	.250	0	0	SS-54, 2B-1

Howie Williamson

WILLIAMSON, NATHANIEL HOWARD
B. Dec. 23, 1904, Little Rock, Ark.   BL TL 6' 170 lbs.

	G	AB	H	2B	3B	HR	HR%	R	RBI	BB	SO	SB	BA	SA	PH AB	PH H	G by POS
1928 STL N	10	9	2	0	0	0	0.0	0	0		4	0	.222	.222	9	2	

Charlie Wilson

WILSON, CHARLES WOODROW (Swamp Baby)
B. Jan. 13, 1905, Clinton, S. C.   BB TR 5'10½" 178 lbs.

	G	AB	H	2B	3B	HR	HR%	R	RBI	BB	SO	SB	BA	SA	PH AB	PH H	G by POS
1931 BOS N	16	58	11	4	0	1	1.7	7	11	3	5	0	.190	.310	0	0	3B-14
1932 STL N	24	96	19	3	3	1	1.0	7	2	3	8	0	.198	.323	0	0	SS-24
1933	1	1	0	0	0	0	0.0	0	0	0	1	0	.000	.000	0	0	SS-1
1935	16	31	10	0	0	0	0.0	1	1	2	2	0	.323	.323	7	4	3B-8
4 yrs.	57	186	40	7	3	2	1.1	15	14	8	16	0	.215	.317	7	4	SS-25, 3B-22
3 yrs.	41	128	29	3	3	1	0.8	8	3	5	11	0	.227	.320	7	4	SS-25, 3B-8

	G	AB	H	2B	3B	HR	HR %	R	RBI	BB	SO	SB	BA	SA	Pinch Hit AB	Pinch Hit H	G by POS

Jimmie Wilson

WILSON, JAMES (Ace)   BR TR 6'1½" 200 lbs.
B. July 23, 1900, Philadelphia, Pa.   D. May 31, 1947, Bradenton, Fla.
Manager 1934-38, 1941-44.

	G	AB	H	2B	3B	HR	HR %	R	RBI	BB	SO	SB	BA	SA	PH AB	PH H	G by POS
1923 PHI N	85	252	66	9	0	1	0.4	27	25	4	17	4	.262	.310	10	3	C-69, OF-2
1924	95	280	78	16	3	6	2.1	32	39	17	12	5	.279	.421	11	2	C-82, 1B-2, OF-1
1925	108	335	110	19	3	3	0.9	42	54	32	25	5	.328	.430	16	4	C-89, OF-1
1926	90	279	85	10	2	4	1.4	40	32	25	20	3	.305	.398	11	3	C-79
1927	128	443	122	15	2	2	0.5	50	45	34	15	13	.275	.332	4	1	C-124
1928 2 teams		PHI N (21G – .300)			STL N (120G – .258)												
" Total	141	481	127	30	3	2	0.4	56	63	54	32	12	.264	.351	0	0	C-140
1929 STL N	120	394	128	27	8	4	1.0	59	71	43	19	4	.325	.464	1	1	C-119
1930	107	362	115	25	7	1	0.3	54	58	28	17	8	.318	.434	8	3	C-107
1931	115	383	105	20	2	0	0.0	45	51	28	15	5	.274	.337	5	0	C-110
1932	92	274	68	16	2	2	0.7	36	28	15	18	9	.248	.343	10	3	C-75, 1B-3, 2B-1
1933	113	369	94	17	0	1	0.3	34	45	23	33	6	.255	.309	5	1	C-107
1934 PHI N	91	277	81	11	0	3	1.1	25	35	14	10	1	.292	.365	13	4	C-77, 2B-1, 1B-1
1935	93	290	81	20	0	1	0.3	38	37	19	19	4	.279	.359	14	4	C-78, 2B-1
1936	85	230	64	12	0	1	0.4	25	27	12	21	5	.278	.343	20	8	C-63, 1B-1
1937	39	87	24	3	0	1	1.1	15	8	6	4	1	.276	.345	16	0	C-22, 1B-2
1938	3	2	0	0	0	0	0.0	0	0	0	1	0	.000	.000	2	0	C-1
1939 CIN N	4	3	1	0	0	0	0.0	0	0	0	1	0	.333	.333	2	1	C-1
1940	16	37	9	2	0	0	0.0	2	3	2	1	1	.243	.297	0	0	C-16
18 yrs.	1525	4778	1358	252	32	32	0.7	580	621	356	280	86	.284	.370	148	38	C-1359, 1B-9, OF-4, 2B-3
6 yrs.	667	2193	616	131	21	10	0.5	273	303	182	126	41	.281	.373	29	8	C-638, 1B-3, 2B-1

WORLD SERIES

	G	AB	H	2B	3B	HR	HR %	R	RBI	BB	SO	SB	BA	SA	PH AB	PH H	G by POS
1928 STL N	3	11	1	1	0	0	0.0	1	1	0	3	0	.091	.182	0	0	C-3
1930	4	15	4	1	0	0	0.0	0	2	0	1	0	.267	.333	0	0	C-4
1931	7	23	5	0	0	0	0.0	2	2	1	1	0	.217	.217	0	0	C-7
1940 CIN N	6	17	6	0	0	0	0.0	0	0	1	2	1	.353	.353	0	0	C-6
4 yrs.	20	66	16	2	0	0	0.0	3	5	2	7	1	.242	.273	0	0	C-20

Owen Wilson

WILSON, JOHN OWEN (Chief)   BL TR 6'2" 185 lbs.
B. Aug. 21, 1883, Austin, Tex.   D. Feb. 22, 1954, Bertram, Tex.

	G	AB	H	2B	3B	HR	HR %	R	RBI	BB	SO	SB	BA	SA	PH AB	PH H	G by POS
1908 PIT N	144	529	120	8	7	3	0.6	47	43	22		12	.227	.285	0	0	OF-144
1909	154	569	155	22	12	4	0.7	64	59	19		17	.272	.374	0	0	OF-154
1910	146	536	148	14	13	4	0.7	59	50	21	68	8	.276	.373	0	0	OF-146
1911	148	544	163	34	12	12	2.2	72	107	41	55	10	.300	.472	1	1	OF-146
1912	152	583	175	19	36¹	11	1.9	80	95	35	67	16	.300	.513	0	0	OF-152
1913	155	580	154	12	14	10	1.7	71	73	32	62	9	.266	.386	0	0	OF-155
1914 STL N	154	580	150	27	12	9	1.6	64	73	32	66	14	.259	.393	0	0	OF-154
1915	107	348	96	13	6	3	0.9	33	39	19	43	8	.276	.374	2	0	OF-107
1916	120	355	85	8	2	3	0.8	30	32	20	46	4	.239	.299	6	0	OF-113
9 yrs.	1280	4624	1246	157	114	59	1.3	520	571	241	407	98	.269	.391	9	1	OF-1271
3 yrs.	381	1283	331	48	20	15	1.2	127	144	71	155	26	.258	.362	8	0	OF-374

WORLD SERIES

	G	AB	H	2B	3B	HR	HR %	R	RBI	BB	SO	SB	BA	SA	PH AB	PH H	G by POS
1909 PIT N	7	26	4	1	0	0	0.0	2	1	0	2	1	.154	.192	0	0	OF-7

Ivy Wingo

WINGO, IVEY BROWN   BL TR 5'10" 160 lbs.
Brother of Al Wingo.
B. July 8, 1890, Gainesville, Ga.   D. Mar. 1, 1941, Norcross, Ga.
Manager 1916.

	G	AB	H	2B	3B	HR	HR %	R	RBI	BB	SO	SB	BA	SA	PH AB	PH H	G by POS
1911 STL N	25	57	12	2	0	0	0.0	4	3	3	7	0	.211	.246	6	0	C-18
1912	100	310	82	18	8	2	0.6	38	44	23	45	8	.265	.394	9	1	C-92
1913	111	305	78	5	8	2	0.7	25	35	17	41	18	.256	.344	10	4	C-97, 1B-5, OF-1
1914	80	237	71	8	5	4	1.7	24	26	18	17	15	.300	.426	4	2	C-70
1915 CIN N	119	339	75	11	6	3	0.9	26	29	13	33	10	.221	.316	17	2	C-97, OF-1
1916	119	347	85	8	11	2	0.6	30	40	25	27	4	.245	.349	10	5	C-107
1917	121	399	106	16	11	2	0.5	37	39	25	13	9	.266	.376	1	0	C-120
1918	100	323	82	15	6	0	0.0	36	31	19	18	6	.254	.337	2	1	C-93, OF-5
1919	76	245	67	12	6	0	0.0	30	27	23	19	4	.273	.371	1	0	C-75
1920	108	364	96	11	5	2	0.5	32	38	19	13	6	.264	.338	0	0	C-107, 2B-2
1921	97	295	79	7	6	3	1.0	20	38	21	14	3	.268	.363	4	1	C-92, OF-1
1922	80	260	74	13	3	3	1.2	24	45	23	11	1	.285	.392	2	0	C-78
1923	61	171	45	9	2	1	0.6	10	24	9	11	1	.263	.357	4	1	C-57
1924	66	192	55	5	4	1	0.5	21	23	14	8	1	.286	.370	1	0	C-65, 1B-1
1925	55	146	30	7	0	0	0.0	6	12	11	8	1	.205	.253	0	0	C-55
1926	7	10	2	0	0	0	0.0	1	1	0	1	0	.200	.200	0	0	C-7
1929	1	1	0	0	0	0	0.0	0	0	0	0	0	.000	.000	0	0	C-1
17 yrs.	1326	4001	1039	147	81	25	0.6	363	455	264	285	87	.260	.356	71	17	C-1231, OF-8, 1B-6, 2B-2
4 yrs.	316	909	243	33	21	8	0.9	91	108	61	110	41	.267	.376	29	7	C-277, 1B-5, OF-1

WORLD SERIES

	G	AB	H	2B	3B	HR	HR %	R	RBI	BB	SO	SB	BA	SA	PH AB	PH H	G by POS
1919 CIN N	3	7	4	0	0	0	0.0	1	1	3	1	0	.571	.571	0	0	C-3

Tom Winsett

WINSETT, JOHN THOMAS (Long Tom)   BL TR 6'2" 190 lbs.
B. Nov. 24, 1909, McKenzie, Tenn.

	G	AB	H	2B	3B	HR	HR %	R	RBI	BB	SO	SB	BA	SA	PH AB	PH H	G by POS
1930 BOS A	1	1	0	0	0	0	0.0	0	0	0	1	0	.000	.000	0	0	
1931	64	76	15	1	0	1	1.3	6	7	4	21	0	.197	.250	52	11	OF-8
1933	6	12	1	0	0	0	0.0	1	0	1	6	0	.083	.083	2	0	OF-4
1935 STL N	7	12	6	1	0	0	0.0	2	2	2	3	0	.500	.583	5	2	OF-2
1936 BKN N	22	85	20	7	0	1	1.2	13	18	11	14	0	.235	.353	1	1	OF-21
1937	118	350	83	15	5	5	1.4	32	42	45	64	3	.237	.351	15	5	OF-101, P-1
1938	12	30	9	1	0	1	3.3	4	6	6	4	0	.300	.433	2	0	OF-9
7 yrs.	230	566	134	25	5	8	1.4	60	76	69	113	3	.237	.341	77	19	OF-145, P-1
1 yr.	7	12	6	1	0	0	0.0	2	2	2	3	0	.500	.583	5	2	OF-2

	G	AB	H	2B	3B	HR	HR %	R	RBI	BB	SO	SB	BA	SA	Pinch Hit AB	Pinch Hit H	G by POS

Corky Withrow

WITHROW, RAYMOND WALLACE
B. Nov. 28, 1937, High Coal, W. Va.

BR TR 6'3½" 197 lbs.

	G	AB	H	2B	3B	HR	HR %	R	RBI	BB	SO	SB	BA	SA	AB	H	G by POS
1963 STL N	6	9	0	0	0	0	0.0	0	1	0	2	0	.000	.000	4	0	OF-2

Chicken Wolf

WOLF, WILLIAM VAN WINKLE
B. May 12, 1862, Louisville, Ky.   D. May 16, 1903, Louisville, Ky.
Manager 1889.

BR TR

	G	AB	H	2B	3B	HR	HR %	R	RBI	BB	SO	SB	BA	SA	AB	H	G by POS
1882 LOU AA	78	318	95	11	8	0	0.0	46		9			.299	.384	0	0	OF-70, SS-9, 1B-1, P-1
1883	98	389	102	17	9	1	0.3	59		5			.262	.360	0	0	OF-78, C-20, SS-5, 2B-1
1884	110	486	146	24	11	3	0.6	79		4			.300	.414	0	0	OF-101, C-11, SS-1, 3B-1, 1B-1
1885	112	483	141	23	17	1	0.2	79		11			.292	.416	0	0	OF-111, C-2, 3B-1, P-1
1886	130	545	148	17	12	3	0.6	93		27			.272	.363	0	0	OF-122, 1B-8, C-3, 2B-1, P-1
1887	137	569	160	28	13	1	0.2	103		34		45	.281	.381	0	0	OF-128, 1B-11
1888	128	538	154	28	11	0	0.0	80	67	25		41	.286	.379	0	0	OF-85, SS-39, 3B-4, C-3, 1B-1
1889	130	546	159	20	9	3	0.5	72	57	29	34	18	.291	.377	0	0	OF-88, 1B-16, 2B-13, SS-10, 3B-7
1890	134	543	197	29	11	4	0.7	100		43		46	.363	.479	0	0	OF-123, 3B-12
1891	138	537	136	17	8	1	0.2	67	82	42	36	13	.253	.320	0	0	OF-133, 1B-5, 3B-1
1892 STL N	3	14	2	0	0	0	0.0	1	1	0	1	0	.143	.143	0	0	OF-3
11 yrs.	1198	4968	1440	214	109	17	0.3	779	206	229	71	163	.290	.387	0	0	OF-1042, SS-64, 1B-43, C-39, 3B-26, 2B-15, P-3
1 yr.	3	14	2	0	0	0	0.0	1	1	0	1	0	.143	.143	0	0	OF-3

Harry Wolter

WOLTER, HARRY MEIGS
B. July 11, 1884, Monterey, Calif.   D. July 7, 1970, Palo Alto, Calif.

BL TL 5'10"   175 lbs.

	G	AB	H	2B	3B	HR	HR %	R	RBI	BB	SO	SB	BA	SA	AB	H	G by POS
1907 3 teams	CIN N	(4G – .133)		PIT N	(1G – .000)		STL N	(16G – .340)									
" Total	21	63	18	0	0	0	0.0	5	7	3		1	.286	.286	4	0	OF-13, P-4
1909 BOS A	54	119	29	2	4	2	1.7	14	10	9		2	.244	.378	13	1	1B-17, P-10, OF-9
1910 NY A	135	479	128	15	9	4	0.8	84	42	66		39	.267	.361	2	0	OF-130
1911	122	434	132	17	15	4	0.9	78	36	62		28	.304	.440	3	2	OF-113, 1B-2
1912	12	32	11	2	1	0	0.0	8	1	10		5	.344	.469	3	0	OF-9
1913	126	425	108	18	6	2	0.5	53	43	80	50	13	.254	.339	3	1	OF-121
1917 CHI N	117	353	88	15	7	0	0.0	44	28	38	40	7	.249	.331	16	7	OF-97, 1B-1
7 yrs.	587	1905	514	69	42	12	0.6	286	167	268	90	95	.270	.369	44	11	OF-492, 1B-20, P-14
1 yr.	16	47	16	0	0	0	0.0	4	6	3		1	.340	.340	4	0	OF-9, P-3

Red Worthington

WORTHINGTON, ROBERT LEE (Bob)
B. Apr. 24, 1906, Alhambra, Calif.   D. Dec. 8, 1963, Sawtelle, Calif.

BR TR 5'11"   170 lbs.

	G	AB	H	2B	3B	HR	HR %	R	RBI	BB	SO	SB	BA	SA	AB	H	G by POS
1931 BOS N	128	491	143	25	10	4	0.8	47	44	26	38	1	.291	.407	4	0	OF-124
1932	105	435	132	35	8	8	1.8	62	61	15	24	1	.303	.476	1	0	OF-104
1933	17	45	7	4	0	0	0.0	3	0	1	3	0	.156	.244	7	0	OF-10
1934 2 teams	BOS N	(41G – .246)		STL N	(1G – .000)												
" Total	42	66	16	5	0	0	0.0	6	6	6	6	0	.242	.318	27	8	OF-11
4 yrs.	292	1037	298	69	18	12	1.2	118	111	48	71	2	.287	.423	39	8	OF-249
1 yr.	1	1	0	0	0	0	0.0	0	0	0	1	0	.000	.000	1	0	

Babe Young

YOUNG, NORMAN ROBERT
B. July 1, 1915, Astoria, N. Y.

BL TL 6'2½"   185 lbs.

	G	AB	H	2B	3B	HR	HR %	R	RBI	BB	SO	SB	BA	SA	AB	H	G by POS
1936 NY N	1	1	0	0	0	0	0.0	0	0	0	0	0	.000	.000	1	0	
1939	22	75	23	4	0	3	4.0	8	14	5	6	0	.307	.480	0	0	1B-22
1940	149	556	159	27	4	17	3.1	75	101	69	28	4	.286	.441	2	0	1B-147
1941	152	574	152	28	5	25	4.4	90	104	66	39	1	.265	.462	1	1	1B-150
1942	101	287	80	17	1	11	3.8	37	59	34	22	1	.279	.460	27	6	OF-54, 1B-18
1946	104	291	81	11	0	7	2.4	30	33	30	21	3	.278	.388	32	5	1B-49, OF-24
1947 2 teams	NY N	(14G – .071)		CIN N	(95G – .283)												
" Total	109	378	104	22	3	14	3.7	55	79	35	27	0	.275	.460	16	2	1B-93
1948 2 teams	CIN N	(49G – .231)		STL N	(41G – .243)												
" Total	90	241	57	12	4	2	0.8	25	25	35	18	0	.237	.344	18	3	1B-66, OF-1
8 yrs.	728	2403	656	121	17	79	3.3	320	415	274	161	9	.273	.436	97	17	1B-545, OF-79
1 yr.	41	111	27	5	2	1	0.9	14	13	16	6	0	.243	.351	4	0	1B-35

Bobby Young

YOUNG, ROBERT GEORGE
B. Jan. 22, 1925, Granite, Md.

BL TR 6'1"   175 lbs.

	G	AB	H	2B	3B	HR	HR %	R	RBI	BB	SO	SB	BA	SA	AB	H	G by POS
1948 STL N	3	1	0	0	0	0	0.0	0	0	0	1	0	.000	.000	1	0	3B-1
1951 STL A	147	611	159	13	9	1	0.2	75	31	44	51	8	.260	.316	0	0	2B-147
1952	149	575	142	15	9	4	0.7	59	39	56	48	3	.247	.325	1	1	2B-149
1953	148	537	137	22	2	4	0.7	48	25	41	40	2	.255	.326	0	0	2B-148
1954 BAL A	130	432	106	13	6	4	0.9	44	24	54	42	4	.245	.331	8	1	2B-127
1955 2 teams	BAL A	(59G – .199)		CLE A	(18G – .311)												
" Total	77	231	51	4	1	1	0.4	12	14	12	25	1	.221	.260	7	2	2B-69, 3B-1
1956 CLE A	1	0	0	0	0	0	–	0	0	0	0	0	–	–	0	0	
1958 PHI N	32	60	14	1	0	1	1.7	7	4	1	5	0	.233	.333	9	2	2B-21
8 yrs.	687	2447	609	68	28	15	0.6	244	137	208	212	18	.249	.318	26	6	2B-661, 3B-2
1 yr.	3	1	0	0	0	0	0.0	0	0	0	1	0	.000	.000	1	0	3B-1

	G	AB	H	2B	3B	HR	HR %	R	RBI	BB	SO	SB	BA	SA	Pinch Hit AB	Pinch Hit H	G by POS

Pep Young

YOUNG, LEMUEL FLOYD
B. Aug. 29, 1907, Jamestown, N. C.   D. Jan. 14, 1962, Jamestown, N. C.
BR TR 5'9"   162 lbs.

	G	AB	H	2B	3B	HR	HR %	R	RBI	BB	SO	SB	BA	SA	PH AB	PH H	G by POS
1933 PIT N	25	20	6	1	1	0	0.0	3	0	0	5	0	.300	.450	20	5	SS-1, 2B-1
1934	19	17	4	0	0	0	0.0	3	2	0	6	0	.235	.235	4	0	SS-2, 2B-2
1935	128	494	131	25	10	7	1.4	60	82	21	59	2	.265	.399	0	0	2B-107, OF-6, 3B-6, SS-4
1936	125	475	118	23	10	6	1.3	47	77	29	52	3	.248	.377	1	0	2B-123
1937	113	408	106	20	3	9	2.2	43	54	26	63	4	.260	.390	2	1	SS-45, 3B-39, 2B-30
1938	149	562	156	36	5	4	0.7	58	79	40	64	7	.278	.381	0	0	2B-149
1939	84	293	81	14	3	3	1.0	34	29	23	29	1	.276	.375	0	0	2B-84
1940	54	136	34	8	2	2	1.5	19	20	12	23	1	.250	.382	7	1	2B-33, SS-7, 3B-5
1941 2 teams	CIN N	(4G – .167)		STL N	(2G – .000)												
" Total	6	14	2	0	0	0	0.0	2	0	0	3	0	.143	.143	3	0	3B-3
1945 STL N	27	47	7	1	0	1	2.1	5	4	1	8	0	.149	.234	5	0	SS-11, 3B-9, 2B-3
10 yrs.	730	2466	645	128	34	32	1.3	274	347	152	312	18	.262	.380	42	7	2B-532, SS-70, 3B-62, OF-6
2 yrs.	29	49	7	1	0	1	2.0	5	4	1	10	0	.143	.224	7	0	SS-11, 3B-9, 2B-3

Joel Youngblood

YOUNGBLOOD, JOEL RANDOLPH
B. Aug. 28, 1951, Houston, Tex.
BR TR 6'

	G	AB	H	2B	3B	HR	HR %	R	RBI	BB	SO	SB	BA	SA	PH AB	PH H	G by POS
1976 CIN N	55	57	11	1	1	0	0.0	8	1	2	8	1	.193	.246	33	5	OF-9, 3B-6, 2B-1, C-1
1977 2 teams	STL N	(25G – .185)		NY N	(70G – .253)												
" Total	95	209	51	13	1	0	0.0	17	12	16	45	1	.244	.316	22	5	OF-33, 2B-33, 3B-16
1978 NY N	113	266	67	12	8	7	2.6	40	30	16	39	4	.252	.436	23	7	OF-50, 2B-39, 3B-9, SS-1
1979	158	590	162	37	5	16	2.7	90	60	60	84	18	.275	.436	4	1	OF-147, 2B-13, 3B-12
1980	146	514	142	26	2	8	1.6	58	69	52	69	14	.276	.381	13	7	OF-121, 3B-21, 2B-6
1981	43	143	50	10	2	4	2.8	16	25	12	19	2	.350	.531	3	0	OF-41
1982 2 teams	NY N	(80G – .257)		MON N	(40G – .200)												
" Total	120	292	70	14	0	3	1.0	37	29	17	58	2	.240	.318	15	2	OF-98, 2B-8, SS-1, 3B-1
7 yrs.	730	2071	553	113	19	38	1.8	266	226	175	322	42	.267	.395	113	27	OF-499, 2B-100, 3B-65, SS-2, C-1
1 yr.	25	27	5	2	0	0	0.0	1	1	3	5	0	.185	.259	7	2	OF-11, 3B-6

Sal Yvars

YVARS, SALVADOR ANTHONY
B. Feb. 20, 1924, New York, N. Y.
BR TR 5'10"   187 lbs.

	G	AB	H	2B	3B	HR	HR %	R	RBI	BB	SO	SB	BA	SA	PH AB	PH H	G by POS
1947 NY N	1	5	1	0	0	0	0.0	0	0	0	2	0	.200	.200	0	0	C-1
1948	15	38	8	1	0	1	2.6	4	6	3	1	0	.211	.316	0	0	C-15
1949	3	8	0	0	0	0	0.0	0	1	1	0	0	.000	.000	1	0	C-2
1950	9	14	2	0	0	0	0.0	0	1	1	2	0	.143	.143	0	0	C-9
1951	25	41	13	2	0	2	4.9	9	3	5	7	0	.317	.512	2	0	C-23
1952	66	151	37	3	0	4	2.6	15	18	10	16	0	.245	.344	7	1	C-59
1953 2 teams	NY N	(23G – .277)		STL N	(30G – .246)												
" Total	53	104	27	2	0	1	1.0	5	7	11	7	0	.260	.308	9	1	C-46
1954 STL N	38	57	14	4	0	2	3.5	8	8	6	5	1	.246	.421	18	4	C-21
8 yrs.	210	418	102	12	0	10	2.4	41	42	37	41	1	.244	.344	37	6	C-176
2 yrs.	68	114	28	6	0	3	2.6	12	14	10	11	1	.246	.377	24	5	C-47

WORLD SERIES

	G	AB	H	2B	3B	HR	HR %	R	RBI	BB	SO	SB	BA	SA	PH AB	PH H	G by POS
1951 NY N	1	1	0	0	0	0	0.0	0	0	0	0	0	.000	.000	1	0	

Elmer Zacher

ZACHER, ELMER HENRY (Silver)
B. Sept. 17, 1883, Buffalo, N. Y.   D. Dec. 20, 1944, Buffalo, N. Y.
BR TR

	G	AB	H	2B	3B	HR	HR %	R	RBI	BB	SO	SB	BA	SA	PH AB	PH H	G by POS
1910 2 teams	NY N	(1G – .000)		STL N	(47G – .212)												
" Total	48	132	28	5	1	0	0.0	10	10	19		3	.212	.265	9	2	OF-37, 2B-1

Dave Zearfoss

ZEARFOSS, DAVID WILLIAM TILDEN
B. Jan. 1, 1868, Schenectady, N. Y.   D. Sept. 12, 1945, Wilmington, Del.
TR

	G	AB	H	2B	3B	HR	HR %	R	RBI	BB	SO	SB	BA	SA	PH AB	PH H	G by POS
1896 NY N	19	60	13	1	1	0	0.0	5	6	5	5	2	.217	.267	0	0	C-19
1897	5	10	3	0	1	0	0.0	1	0	0		0	.300	.500	0	0	C-5
1898	1	1	1	0	0	0	0.0	0	0	0		0	1.000	1.000	0	0	C-1
1904 STL N	27	80	17	2	0	0	0.0	7	9	10		0	.213	.238	1	0	C-25
1905	20	51	8	0	1	0	0.0	2	2	4		0	.157	.196	1	0	C-19
5 yrs.	72	202	42	3	3	0	0.0	15	17	19	5	2	.208	.252	2	0	C-69
2 yrs.	47	131	25	2	1	0	0.0	9	11	14		0	.191	.221	2	0	C-44

Bart Zeller

ZELLER, BARTON WALLACE
B. July 22, 1941, Chicago Heights, Ill.
BR TR 6'1"   185 lbs.

	G	AB	H	2B	3B	HR	HR %	R	RBI	BB	SO	SB	BA	SA	PH AB	PH H	G by POS
1970 STL N	1	0	0	0	0	0	–	0	0	0	0	0	–	–	0	0	C-1

Eddie Zimmerman

ZIMMERMAN, EDWARD DESMOND
B. Jan. 4, 1883, Oceanic, N. J.   D. May 6, 1945, Emmaus, Pa.
BR TR

	G	AB	H	2B	3B	HR	HR %	R	RBI	BB	SO	SB	BA	SA	PH AB	PH H	G by POS
1906 STL N	5	14	3	0	0	0	0.0	0	1	0		0	.214	.214	0	0	3B-5
1911 BKN N	122	417	77	10	7	3	0.7	31	36	34	37	9	.185	.264	0	0	3B-122
2 yrs.	127	431	80	10	7	3	0.7	31	37	34	37	9	.186	.262	0	0	3B-127
1 yr.	5	14	3	0	0	0	0.0	0	1	0		0	.214	.214	0	0	3B-5

Pitcher Register

The Pitcher Register is an alphabetical list of every man who pitched in the major leagues and played or managed for the St. Louis Cardinals from 1892 through today. Included are lifetime totals of League Championship Series and World Series.

The player and team information for the Pitcher Register is the same as that for the Player Register explained on page 228.

	W	L	PCT	ERA	G	GS	CG	IP	H	BB	SO	ShO	Relief Pitching W	L	SV	BATTING AB	H	HR	BA

John Doe

DOE, JOHN LEE (Slim)
Played as John Cherry part of 1900.
Born John Lee Doughnut.   Brother of Bill Doe.
B. Jan. 1,1850, New York, N. Y.   D. July 1, 1955, New York, N. Y.
Hall of Fame 1946.

TR   6'2"   165 lbs.

	W	L	PCT	ERA	G	GS	CG	IP	H	BB	SO	ShO	Relief W	Relief L	Relief SV	AB	H	HR	BA
1884 STL U	4	2	.667	3.40	26	0	0	54.2	41	38	40	0	1	0	0	4	0	0	.000
1885 LOU AA	14	10	.583	4.12	40	19	10	207.2	193	76	70	0	1	0	1	16	2	0	.111
1886 CLE N	10	5	.667	4.08	40	8	4	117	110	55	77	0	0	1	0	10	0	0	.000
1887 BOS N	9	3	.750	3.38	27	5	2	88	90	36	34	0	2	2	5	44	3	0	.214
1888 NY N	13	4	.765	4.17	39	4	0	110	121	50	236	0	0	0	0	3	0	0	—
1889 3 teams DET N (10G 4-2) PIT N (2G 0-0) PHI N (10G 4-0)																			
" total	8	2	.800	4.25	22	2	2	91.1	90	41	43	0	2	1	10	37	1	0	.036
1890 NY P	13	6	.684	4.43	38	0	0	61.1	57	28	30	0	4	4	8	45	0	0	.000
1900 CHI N	18	4	.818	3.71	35	1	0	63.1	58	15	23	0	4	2	3	42	2	0	.027
1901 BAL A	18	4	.818	1.98¹	35	0	0	77.1	68	40	29	0	0	2	0	38	10	0	.132
1906 STL N	14	10	.583	3.41	31	0	0	58	66	23	24	0	0	0	1	32	3	0	.057
1907	13	4	.765	2.51	37	0	0	68	44	30	31	0	0	1	0	31	1	0	.500
1908	0	0	–	3.38	1	1	0	8	8	1	1	0	1	2	3	25	0	0	.000
1914 CHI F	3	1	.750	2.78	6	0	0	54.2	41	28	9	0	1	0	1	41	2	0	.400
13 yrs.	137	55	.714	3.50	377	40	18	1059.1	987	461	647 8th	0	16	18	32	*			
3 yrs.	27	14	.659	2.96	69	1	0	134	118	54	56	0	5	5	3	79	25	1	.316
LEAGUE CHAMPIONSHIP SERIES																			
1901 BAL A	1	1	.500	4.76	4	0	0	22.2	26	8	16	8	0	0	0	0	0	0	—
WORLD SERIES																			
1901 BAL A	2	0	1.000	1.00	2	2	2	18	14	7	31	0	0	0	1	7	1	0	.143
1908 STL N	2	0	.500	2.30	4	4	3	30	20	3	24	0	0	0	0	4	1	0	.250
2 yrs.	4	0	1.000	1.15	6	6	5	48	34	10	55 9th	0	0	0	1	11	2	0	.182

COLUMN HEADINGS INFORMATION

	W	L	PCT	ERA	G	GS	CG	IP	H	BB	SO	ShO	Relief Pitching W	L	SV	BATTING AB	H	HR	BA

Total Pitching (including all starting and relief appearances)

W	Wins
L	Losses
PCT	Winning Percentage
ERA	Earned Run Average
G	Games Pitched
GS	Games Started
CG	Complete Games
IP	Innings Pitched
H	Hits Allowed
BB	Bases on Balls Allowed
SO	Strikeouts
ShO	Shutouts

Relief Pitching

W	Wins
L	Losses
SV	Saves

Batting

AB	At Bats
H	Hits
HR	Home Runs
BA	Batting Average

Partial Innings Pitched. These are shown in the Innings Pitched column, and are indicated by a ".1" or ".2" after the total. Doe, for example, pitched 54⅔ innings in 1884.

All-Time Single Season Leaders. (Starts with 1893, the first year that the pitcher's box was moved to its present distance of 60 feet 6 inches.) Indicated by the small number that appears next to the statistic. Doe, for example, is shown by a small number "1" next to his earned run average in 1901. This means he is first on the all-time major league list for having the lowest earned run average in a single season. All pitchers who tied for first are also shown by the same number.

Meaningless Averages. Indicated by the use of a dash (—). In the case of Doe, a dash is shown for his 1908 winning percentage. This means that although he pitched in one game he never had a decision. A percentage of .000 would mean that he had at least one loss.

Estimated Earned Run Averages. Any time an earned run average appears in italics, it indicates that not all the earned runs allowed by the pitcher are known, and the information had to be estimated. Doe's 1885 earned run average, for example, appears in italics. It is known that Doe's team, Louisville, allowed 560 runs in 112 games. Of these games, it is known that in 90 of them Louisville allowed 420 runs of which 315 or 75% were earned. Doe pitched 207⅔ innings in 40 games and allowed 134 runs. In 35 of these games, it is known that he allowed 118 runs of which 83 were earned. By multiplying the team's known ratio of earned runs to total runs (75%), by Doe's 16 (134 minus 118) remaining runs allowed, a figure of 12 additional estimated earned runs is calculated. This means that Doe allowed an estimated total of 95 earned runs in 207⅔ innings, for an estimated earned run average of 4.12. In all cases at least 50% of the runs allowed by the team were "known" as a basis for estimating earned run averages. (Any time the symbol "infinity" (∞) is shown for a pitcher's earned run average, it means that the pitcher allowed one or more earned runs during a season without retiring a batter.)

Batting Statistics. Because a pitcher's batting statistics are of relatively minor importance—and the Designated Hitter rule may eliminate pitchers' batting entirely—only the most significant statistics are given; number of hits, home runs, and batting average.

An asterisk (*) shown in the lifetime batting totals means that the pitcher's complete year-by-year and lifetime batting record is listed in the Player Register.

	W	L	PCT	ERA	G	GS	CG	IP	H	BB	SO	ShO	Relief Pitching W	L	SV	BATTING AB	H	HR	BA

Ted Abernathy

ABERNATHY, THEODORE WADE
B. Mar. 6, 1933, Stanley, N. C.   BR TR 6'4"   215 lbs.

	W	L	PCT	ERA	G	GS	CG	IP	H	BB	SO	ShO	W	L	SV	AB	H	HR	BA
1955 WAS A	5	9	.357	5.96	40	14	3	119.1	136	67	79	2	1	1	0	26	4	0	.154
1956	1	3	.250	4.15	5	4	2	30.1	35	10	18	0	0	0	0	11	2	0	.182
1957	2	10	.167	6.78	26	16	2	85	100	65	50	0	1	0	0	24	4	0	.167
1960	0	0	—	12.00	2	0	0	3	4	4	1	0	0	0	0	1	1	0	1.000
1963 CLE A	7	2	.778	2.88	43	0	0	59.1	54	29	47	0	7	2	12	5	2	0	.400
1964	2	6	.250	4.33	53	0	0	72.2	66	46	57	0	2	6	11	6	0	0	.000
1965 CHI N	4	6	.400	2.57	84	0	0	136.1	113	56	104	0	4	6	31	18	3	0	.167
1966 2 teams			CHI	N	(20G 1–3)		ATL	N	(38G 4–4)										
" total	5	7	.417	4.55	58	0	0	93	84	53	60	0	5	7	8	12	2	0	.167
1967 CIN N	6	3	.667	1.27	70	0	0	106.1	63	41	88	0	6	3	28	17	1	0	.059
1968	10	7	.588	2.46	78	0	0	135.1	111	55	64	0	10	7	13	17	0	0	.000
1969 CHI N	4	3	.571	3.18	56	0	0	85	75	42	55	0	4	3	3	8	2	0	.250
1970 3 teams			CHI	N	(11G 0–0)		STL	N	(11G 1–0)		KC	A	(36G 9–3)						
" total	10	3	.769	2.59	58	0	0	83.1	65	55	59	0	10	3	14	17	3	0	.176
1971 KC A	4	6	.400	2.56	63	0	0	81	60	50	55	0	4	6	23	13	1	0	.077
1972	3	4	.429	1.71	45	0	0	58	44	19	28	0	3	4	5	6	0	0	.000
14 yrs.	63	69	.477	3.46	681	34	7	1148	1010	592	765	2	57	48	148	181	25	0	.138
1 yr.	1	0	1.000	2.95	11	0	0	18.1	15	12	8	0	1	0	1	3	0	0	.000

Babe Adams

ADAMS, CHARLES BENJAMIN
B. May 18, 1882, Tipton, Ind.   D. July 27, 1968, Silver Spring, Md.   BL TR 5'11½" 185 lbs.

	W	L	PCT	ERA	G	GS	CG	IP	H	BB	SO	ShO	W	L	SV	AB	H	HR	BA
1906 STL N	0	1	.000	13.50	1	1	0	4	9	2	0	0	0	0	0	1	0	0	.000
1907 PIT N	0	2	.000	6.95	4	3	1	22	40	3	11	0	0	0	0	7	2	0	.286
1909	12	3	.800	1.11	25	12	7	130	88	23	65	3	6	0	2	39	2	0	.051
1910	18	9	.667	2.24	34	30	16	245	217	60	101	3	0	1	0	83	16	0	.193
1911	22	12	.647	2.33	40	37	24	293.1	253	42	133	7	0	0	0	103	26	0	.252
1912	11	8	.579	2.91	28	21	11	170.1	169	35	63	2	1	1	0	53	12	0	.226
1913	21	10	.677	2.15	43	37	24	313.2	271	49	144	4	0	1	0	114	33	0	.289
1914	13	16	.448	2.51	40	35	19	283	253	39	91	3	0	1	1	97	16	1	.165
1915	14	14	.500	2.87	40	30	17	245	229	34	62	2	2	3	2	85	12	0	.141
1916	2	9	.182	5.72	16	10	4	72.1	91	12	22	1	0	1	0	22	6	0	.273
1918	1	1	.500	1.19	3	3	2	22.2	15	4	6	1	0	0	0	9	3	0	.333
1919	17	10	.630	1.98	34	29	23	263.1	213	23	92	7	1	0	1	92	17	0	.185
1920	17	13	.567	2.16	35	33	19	263	240	18	84	8	0	0	2	89	13	1	.146
1921	14	5	.737	2.64	25	20	11	160	155	18	55	2	3	0	0	63	16	0	.254
1922	8	11	.421	3.57	27	19	12	171.1	191	15	39	4	1	3	0	56	16	1	.286
1923	13	7	.650	4.42	26	22	11	158.2	196	25	38	0	1	1	1	55	15	0	.273
1924	3	1	.750	1.13	9	3	2	39.2	31	3	5	0	1	1	0	11	2	0	.182
1925	6	5	.545	5.42	33	10	3	101.1	129	17	18	0	3	1	3	31	7	0	.226
1926	2	3	.400	6.14	19	0	0	36.2	51	8	7	0	2	3	3	9	2	0	.222
19 yrs.	194	140	.581	2.76	482	355	206	2995.1	2841	430	1036	47	21	17	15	1019	216	3	.212
1 yr.	0	1	.000	13.50	1	1	0	4	9	2	0	0	0	0	0	1	0	0	.000

WORLD SERIES

	W	L	PCT	ERA	G	GS	CG	IP	H	BB	SO	ShO	W	L	SV	AB	H	HR	BA
1909 PIT N	3	0	1.000	1.33	3	3	3	27	18	6	11	1	0	0	0	9	0	0	.000
1925	0	0	—	0.00	1	0	0	1	2	0	0	0	0	0	0	0	0	0	—
2 yrs.	3	0	1.000	1.29	4	3	3	28	20	6	11	1	0	0	0	9	0	0	.000
				1st			9th												

Joe Adams

ADAMS, JOSEPH EDWARD (Wagon Tongue)
B. Oct. 28, 1877, Cowden, Ill.   D. Oct. 8, 1952, Montgomery City, Mo.   BR TL 6'   190 lbs.

	W	L	PCT	ERA	G	GS	CG	IP	H	BB	SO	ShO	W	L	SV	AB	H	HR	BA
1902 STL N	0	0	—	9.00	1	0	0	4	9	2	0	0	0	0	0	2	0	0	.000

Eddie Ainsmith

AINSMITH, EDWARD WILBUR
B. Feb. 4, 1890, Cambridge, Mass.   D. Sept. 6, 1981, Ft. Lauderdale, Fla.   BR TR 5'11"   180 lbs.

	W	L	PCT	ERA	G	GS	CG	IP	H	BB	SO	ShO	W	L	SV	AB	H	HR	BA
1913 WAS A	0	0	—	54.00	1	0	0	.1	2	0	0	0	0	0	0		*		

Cy Alberts

ALBERTS, FREDERICK JOSEPH
B. Jan. 14, 1882, Grand Rapids, Mich.   D. Aug. 27, 1917, Fort Wayne, Ind.   BR TR 6'   230 lbs.

	W	L	PCT	ERA	G	GS	CG	IP	H	BB	SO	ShO	W	L	SV	AB	H	HR	BA
1910 STL N	1	2	.333	6.18	4	3	2	27.2	35	20	10	0	0	0	0	7	0	0	.000

Grover Alexander

ALEXANDER, GROVER CLEVELAND (Pete)
B. Feb. 26, 1887, Elba, Neb.   D. Nov. 4, 1950, St. Paul, Neb.   BR TR 6'1"   185 lbs.
Hall of Fame 1938.

	W	L	PCT	ERA	G	GS	CG	IP	H	BB	SO	ShO	W	L	SV	AB	H	HR	BA
1911 PHI N	28	13	.683	2.57	48	37	31	367	285	129	227	7	4	2	3	138	24	0	.174
1912	19	17	.528	2.81	46	34	26	310.1	289	105	195	3	3	2	2	102	19	2	.186
1913	22	8	.733	2.79	47	35	23	306.1	288	75	159	9	4	2	2	103	13	0	.126
1914	27	15	.643	2.38	46	39	32	355	327	76	214	6	4	1	1	137	32	0	.234
1915	31	10	.756	1.22	49	42	36	376.1	253	64	241	12	1	1	3	130	22	1	.169
1916	33	12	.733	1.55	48	45	38	388.2	323	50	167	16¹	0	0	3	138	33	0	.239
1917	30	13	.698	1.86	45	44	35	387.2	336	58	201	8	0	0	0	139	30	1	.216
1918 CHI N	2	1	.667	1.73	3	3	3	26	19	3	15	0	0	0	0	10	1	0	.100
1919	16	11	.593	1.72	30	27	20	235	180	38	121	9	1	0	1	70	12	0	.171
1920	27	14	.659	1.91	46	40	33	363.1	335	69	173	7	1	0	5	118	27	1	.229
1921	15	13	.536	3.39	31	29	21	252	286	33	77	3	0	0	1	95	29	1	.305
1922	16	13	.552	3.63	33	31	20	245.2	283	34	48	1	1	0	1	85	15	0	.176
1923	22	12	.647	3.19	39	36	26	305	308	30	72	3	0	1	2	111	24	0	.216
1924	12	5	.706	3.03	21	20	12	169.1	183	25	33	0	0	1	0	65	15	1	.231
1925	15	11	.577	3.39	32	30	20	236	270	29	63	1	0	1	0	79	19	2	.241
1926 2 teams			CHI	N	(7G 3–3)		STL	N	(23G 9–7)										
" total	12	10	.545	3.05	30	23	15	200.1	191	31	47	2	2	1	3	65	13	0	.200
1927 STL N	21	10	.677	2.52	37	30	22	268	261	38	48	2	2	1	3	94	23	0	.245

	W	L	PCT	ERA	G	GS	CG	IP	H	BB	SO	ShO	Relief Pitching W	L	SV	BATTING AB	H	HR	BA

Grover Alexander continued

	W	L	PCT	ERA	G	GS	CG	IP	H	BB	SO	ShO	W	L	SV	AB	H	HR	BA
1928	16	9	.640	3.36	34	31	18	243.2	262	37	59	1	0	0	2	86	25	1	.291
1929	9	8	.529	3.89	22	19	8	132	149	23	33	0	1	1	0	41	2	0	.049
1930 PHI N	0	3	.000	9.14	9	3	0	21.2	40	6	6	0	0	2	0	4	0	0	.000
20 yrs.	373 3rd	208	.642	2.56	696	598	439	5189.1 .5th	4868	953	2199	90 2nd	23	17	31	1810	378	11	.209
4 yrs.	55	34	.618 4th	3.08	116	96	59	792	808	122	175	5	5	3	7	271	56	1	.207

WORLD SERIES

	W	L	PCT	ERA	G	GS	CG	IP	H	BB	SO	ShO	W	L	SV	AB	H	HR	BA
1915 PHI N	1	1	.500	1.53	2	2	2	17.2	14	4	10	1	0	0	0	5	1	0	.200
1926 STL N	2	0	1.000	0.89	3	2	2	20.1	12	4	17	0	0	0	1	7	0	0	.000
1928	0	1	.000	19.80	2	1	0	5	10	4	2	0	0	0	0	1	0	0	.000
3 yrs.	3	2	.600	3.35	7	5	4	43	36	12	29	0	0	0	1	13	1	0	.077

Matty Alou

ALOU, MATEO ROJAS
Brother of Jesus Alou.   Brother of Felipe Alou.
B. Dec. 22, 1938, Haina, Dominican Republic   BL TL 5'9" 160 lbs.

	W	L	PCT	ERA	G	GS	CG	IP	H	BB	SO	ShO	W	L	SV	AB	H	HR	BA
1965 SF N	0	0	–	0.00	1	0	0	2	3	1	3	0	0	0	0	*			

Red Ames

AMES, LEON KESSLING
B. Aug. 2, 1882, Warren, Ohio   D. Oct. 8, 1936, Warren, Ohio   BB TR 5'10½" 185 lbs.

	W	L	PCT	ERA	G	GS	CG	IP	H	BB	SO	ShO	W	L	SV	AB	H	HR	BA
1903 NY N	2	0	1.000	1.29	2	2	2	14	5	8	14	1	0	0	0	6	0	0	.000
1904	4	6	.400	2.27	16	13	11	115	94	38	93	1	0	0	3	40	5	0	.125
1905	22	8	.733	2.74	34	31	21	263	220	105	198	2	1	0	0	97	14	0	.144
1906	12	10	.545	2.66	31	25	15	203.1	166	93	156	1	1	0	1	61	4	0	.066
1907	10	12	.455	2.16	39	26	17	233.1	184	108	146	2	0	3	1	69	12	1	.174
1908	7	4	.636	1.81	18	15	5	114.1	96	27	81	0	1	0	0	36	7	0	.194
1909	15	10	.600	2.70	34	25	20	240	214	81	156	2	1	0	1	80	6	0	.075
1910	12	11	.522	2.22	33	23	13	190.1	161	63	94	3	0	3	0	62	11	1	.177
1911	11	10	.524	2.68	34	23	13	205	170	54	118	1	2	1	1	64	6	0	.094
1912	11	5	.688	2.46	33	22	9	179	194	35	83	2	1	0	2	58	13	0	.224
1913 2 teams	13	14	.481	2.78	NY N (8G 2–1)			CIN N (31G 11–13)											
" total	13	14	.481	2.78	39	29	14	227	220	78	110	1	2	1	3	72	8	0	.111
1914 CIN N	15	23	.395	2.64	47	36	18	297	274	94	128	4	1	4	6	94	12	1	.128
1915 2 teams					CIN N (17G 2–4)			STL N (15G 9–3)											
" total	11	7	.611	3.23	32	21	12	181.1	175	56	74	3	0	0	2	55	5	0	.091
1916 STL N	11	16	.407	2.64	45	22	10	228	225	57	98	2	4	5	7	68	12	0	.176
1917	15	10	.600	2.71	43	19	10	209	189	57	62	2	8	2	3	64	12	0	.188
1918	9	14	.391	2.31	27	25	17	206.2	192	52	68	0	0	0	0	64	10	0	.156
1919 2 teams					STL N (23G 3–5)			PHI N (3G 0–2)											
" total	3	7	.300	5.13	26	9	2	86	114	28	23	0	2	0	2	23	6	0	.261
17 yrs.	183	167	.523	2.63	533	366	209	3192.1	2893	1034	1702	27	24	19	33	1013	143	3	.141
5 yrs.	47	48	.495	2.74 4th	153	87	46	827	787	223	295	6	14	7	13	249	42	0	.169

WORLD SERIES

	W	L	PCT	ERA	G	GS	CG	IP	H	BB	SO	ShO	W	L	SV	AB	H	HR	BA
1905 NY N	0	0	–	0.00	1	0	0	1	1	1	1	0	0	0	0	0	0	0	–
1911	0	1	.000	2.25	2	1	0	8	6	1	6	0	0	0	0	2	1	0	.500
1912	0	0	–	4.50	1	0	0	2	3	1	0	0	0	0	0	0	0	0	–
3 yrs.	0	1	.000	2.45	4	1	0	11	10	3	7	0	0	0	0	2	1	0	.500

Craig Anderson

ANDERSON, NORMAN CRAIG
B. July 1, 1938, Washington, D. C.   BR TR 6'2" 205 lbs.

	W	L	PCT	ERA	G	GS	CG	IP	H	BB	SO	ShO	W	L	SV	AB	H	HR	BA
1961 STL N	4	3	.571	3.26	25	0	0	38.2	38	12	21	0	4	3	1	9	3	0	.333
1962 NY N	3	17	.150	5.35	50	14	2	131.1	150	63	62	0	3	6	4	32	3	0	.094
1963	0	2	.000	8.68	3	2	0	9.1	17	3	6	0	0	0	0	3	1	0	.333
1964	0	1	.000	5.54	4	1	0	13	21	3	5	0	0	0	0	3	0	0	.000
4 yrs.	7	23	.233	5.10	82	17	2	192.1	226	81	94	0	7	9	5	47	7	0	.149
1 yr.	4	3	.571	3.26	25	0	0	38.2	38	12	21	0	4	3	1	9	3	0	.333

John Anderson

ANDERSON, JOHN CHARLES
B. Nov. 23, 1932, St. Paul, Minn.   BR TR 6'1" 190 lbs.

	W	L	PCT	ERA	G	GS	CG	IP	H	BB	SO	ShO	W	L	SV	AB	H	HR	BA
1958 PHI N	0	0	–	7.88	5	1	0	16	26	4	9	0	0	0	0	3	0	0	.000
1960 BAL A	0	0	–	13.50	4	0	0	4.2	8	4	1	0	0	0	0	0	0	0	–
1962 2 teams					STL N (5G 0–0)			HOU N (10G 0–0)											
" total	0	0	–	4.13	15	0	0	24	30	6	9	0	0	0	1	2	0	0	.000
3 yrs.	0	0	–	6.45	24	1	0	44.2	64	14	19	0	0	0	1	5	0	0	.000
1 yr.	0	0	–	1.42	5	0	0	6.1	4	3	3	0	0	0	1	0	0	0	–

Mike Anderson

ANDERSON, MICHAEL ALLEN
B. June 22, 1951, Florence, S. C.   BR TR 6'2" 200 lbs.

	W	L	PCT	ERA	G	GS	CG	IP	H	BB	SO	ShO	W	L	SV	AB	H	HR	BA
1979 PHI N	0	0	–	0.00	1	0	0	1	2	0	2	0	0	0	0	*			

John Andrews

ANDREWS, JOHN RICHARD
B. Feb. 9, 1949, Monterey Park, Calif.   BL TL 5'10" 175 lbs.

	W	L	PCT	ERA	G	GS	CG	IP	H	BB	SO	ShO	W	L	SV	AB	H	HR	BA
1973 STL N	1	1	.500	4.42	16	1	0	18.1	16	11	5	0	1	1	0	2	1	0	.500

Nate Andrews

ANDREWS, NATHAN HARDY
B. Sept. 30, 1913, Pembroke, N. C.   BR TR 6' 195 lbs.

	W	L	PCT	ERA	G	GS	CG	IP	H	BB	SO	ShO	W	L	SV	AB	H	HR	BA
1937 STL N	0	0	–	4.00	4	1	0	9	12	3	6	0	0	0	0	2	0	0	–
1939	1	2	.333	6.75	11	1	0	16	24	12	6	0	1	1	0	2	0	0	.000
1940 CLE A	0	1	.000	6.00	6	0	0	12	16	6	3	0	0	1	0	0	0	0	–
1941	0	0	–	11.57	2	0	0	2.1	3	2	1	0	0	0	0	0	0	0	.000

	W	L	PCT	ERA	G	GS	CG	IP	H	BB	SO	ShO	W	L	SV	AB	H	HR	BA
													Relief Pitching			BATTING			

Nate Andrews continued

	W	L	PCT	ERA	G	GS	CG	IP	H	BB	SO	ShO	W	L	SV	AB	H	HR	BA
1943 BOS N	14	20	.412	2.57	36	34	23	283.2	253	75	80	3	0	2	0	90	14	0	.156
1944	16	15	.516	3.22	37	34	16	257.1	263	74	76	3	1	0	2	88	10	0	.114
1945	7	12	.368	4.58	21	19	8	137.2	160	52	26	0	0	1	0	43	9	0	.209
1946 2 teams			CIN N	(7G 2–4)			NY	N	(3G 1–0)										
" total	3	4	.429	4.39	10	9	4	55.1	67	12	18	0	0	0	0	16	2	0	.125
8 yrs.	41	54	.432	3.46	127	98	51	773.1	798	236	216	6	2	5	2	240	35	0	.146
2 yrs.	1	2	.333	5.76	15	2	0	25	36	15	12	0	1	1	0	2	0	0	.000

Joaquin Andujar

ANDUJAR, JOACHIN
B. Dec. 21, 1952, San Pedro, Dominican Republic   BR TR 6'   170 lbs.

	W	L	PCT	ERA	G	GS	CG	IP	H	BB	SO	ShO	W	L	SV	AB	H	HR	BA
1976 HOU N	9	10	.474	3.61	28	25	9	172	163	75	59	4	0	0	0	57	8	0	.140
1977	11	8	.579	3.68	26	25	4	159	149	64	69	1	0	0	0	53	10	0	.189
1978	5	7	.417	3.41	35	13	2	111	88	58	55	0	2	3	1	23	3	0	.130
1979	12	12	.500	3.43	46	23	8	194	168	88	77	0	3	2	4	57	5	2	.088
1980	3	8	.273	3.91	35	14	0	122	132	43	75	0	0	2	2	29	5	1	.172
1981 2 teams			HOU	N	(9G 2–3)			STL	N	(11G 6–1)									
" total	8	4	.667	4.10	20	11	1	79	85	23	37	0	1	1	0	23	0	0	.000
1982 STL N	15	10	.600	2.47	38	37	9	265.2	237	50	137	5	0	0	0	95	15	0	.158
7 yrs.	63	59	.516	3.36	228	148	33	1102.2	1022	401	509	10	6	8	7	337	46	3	.136
2 yrs.	21	11	.656	2.69	49	45	10	321	293	61	156	5	0	0	0	114	15	0	.132

LEAGUE CHAMPIONSHIP SERIES

	W	L	PCT	ERA	G	GS	CG	IP	H	BB	SO	ShO	W	L	SV	AB	H	HR	BA
1980 HOU N	0	0	–	0.00	1	0	0	1	0	1	0	0	0	0	1	0	0	0	
1982 STL N	1	0	1.000	2.70	1	1	0	6.2	6	2	4	0	0	0	0	1	0	0	.000
2 yrs.	1	0	1.000	2.35	2	1	0	7.2	6	3	4	0	0	0	1	1	0	0	.000

WORLD SERIES

	W	L	PCT	ERA	G	GS	CG	IP	H	BB	SO	ShO	W	L	SV	AB	H	HR	BA
1982 STL N	2	0	1.000	1.35	2	2	0	13.1	10	1	4	0	0	0	0	0	0	0	–

Luis Arroyo

ARROYO, LUIS ENRIQUE (Yo-Yo)
B. Feb. 18, 1927, Penuelas, Puerto Rico   BL TL 5'8½"   178 lbs.

	W	L	PCT	ERA	G	GS	CG	IP	H	BB	SO	ShO	W	L	SV	AB	H	HR	BA
1955 STL N	11	8	.579	4.19	35	24	9	159	162	63	68	1	1	0	0	56	13	1	.232
1956 PIT N	3	3	.500	4.71	18	2	1	28.2	36	12	17	0	2	2	0	4	2	0	.500
1957	3	11	.214	4.68	54	10	0	130.2	151	31	101	0	3	5	1	32	5	0	.156
1959 CIN N	1	0	1.000	3.95	10	0	0	13.2	17	11	8	0	1	0	0	2	0	0	.000
1960 NY A	5	1	.833	2.88	29	0	0	40.2	30	22	29	0	5	1	7	5	0	0	.000
1961	15	5	.750	2.19	65	0	0	119	83	49	87	0	15	5	29	25	7	0	.280
1962	1	3	.250	4.81	27	0	0	33.2	33	17	21	0	1	3	7	4	2	0	.500
1963	1	1	.500	13.50	6	0	0	6	12	3	5	0	1	1	0	0	0	0	–
8 yrs.	40	32	.556	3.93	244	36	10	531.1	524	208	336	1	29	17	44	128	29	1	.227
1 yr.	11	8	.579	4.19	35	24	9	159	162	63	68	1	1	0	0	56	13	1	.232

WORLD SERIES

	W	L	PCT	ERA	G	GS	CG	IP	H	BB	SO	ShO	W	L	SV	AB	H	HR	BA
1960 NY A	0	0	–	13.50	1	0	0	.2	2	0	1	0	0	0	0	1	0	0	.000
1961	1	0	1.000	2.25	2	0	0	4	4	2	3	0	1	0	0	0	0	0	–
2 yrs.	1	0	1.000	3.86	3	0	0	4.2	6	2	4	0	1	0	0	1	0	0	.000

Rudy Arroyo

ARROYO, RUDOLPH JR
B. June 19, 1950, New York, N. Y.   BR TL 6'2"   195 lbs.

	W	L	PCT	ERA	G	GS	CG	IP	H	BB	SO	ShO	W	L	SV	AB	H	HR	BA
1971 STL N	0	1	.000	5.25	9	0	0	12	18	5	5	0	0	1	0	1	0	0	.000

Dennis Aust

AUST, DENNIS KAY
B. Nov. 25, 1940, Tecumseh, Neb.   BR TR 5'11"   180 lbs.

	W	L	PCT	ERA	G	GS	CG	IP	H	BB	SO	ShO	W	L	SV	AB	H	HR	BA
1965 STL N	0	0	–	4.91	6	0	0	7.1	6	2	7	0	0	0	0	1	0	0	.000
1966	0	1	.000	6.52	9	0	0	9.2	12	6	7	0	0	1	1	1	0	0	.000
2 yrs.	0	1	.000	5.82	15	0	0	17	18	8	14	0	0	1	2	2	0	0	.000
2 yrs.	0	1	.000	5.82	15	0	0	17	18	8	14	0	0	1	2	2	0	0	.000

Les Backman

BACKMAN, LESTER JOHN
B. Mar. 20, 1888, Cleves, Ohio   BR TR 6'½"   195 lbs.

	W	L	PCT	ERA	G	GS	CG	IP	H	BB	SO	ShO	W	L	SV	AB	H	HR	BA
1909 STL N	3	12	.200	4.14	21	15	8	128.1	146	39	35	0	0	0	0	39	4	0	.103
1910	7	6	.538	3.03	26	11	6	116	117	53	41	0	5	1	1	35	4	0	.114
2 yrs.	10	18	.357	3.61	47	26	14	244.1	263	92	76	0	5	1	1	74	8	0	.108
2 yrs.	10	18	.357	3.61	47	26	14	244.1	263	92	76	0	5	1	1	74	8	0	.108

Bill Bailey

BAILEY, WILLIAM F.
B. Apr. 12, 1889, Fort Smith, Ark.   D. Nov. 2, 1926   BL TL 5'11"   165 lbs.

	W	L	PCT	ERA	G	GS	CG	IP	H	BB	SO	ShO	W	L	SV	AB	H	HR	BA
1907 STL A	4	1	.800	2.42	6	5	3	48.1	39	15	17	0	0	0	0	20	3	0	.150
1908	3	5	.375	3.04	22	12	7	106.2	85	50	42	0	0	0	0	34	3	0	.088
1909	9	12	.429	2.44	32	20	17	199	174	75	114	1	1	2	0	77	22	0	.286
1910	2	18	.100	3.32	34	20	13	192.1	186	97	90	0	2	1	1	63	13	0	.206
1911	0	3	.000	4.55	7	2	2	31.2	42	16	8	0	0	1	0	11	0	0	.000
1912	0	1	.000	9.28	3	2	1	10.2	15	10	2	0	0	0	0	2	1	0	.500
1914 BAL F	6	9	.400	3.08	19	18	10	128.2	106	68	131	1	1	0	0	43	7	0	.163
1915 2 teams			BAL	F	(36G 5–19)			CHI	F	(5G 3–1)									
" total	8	20	.286	4.27	41	28	14	223.2	202	125	122	5	1	4	0	74	17	0	.230
1918 DET A	0	2	.000	5.97	8	4	1	37.2	53	26	13	0	0	0	0	13	1	0	.077
1921 STL N	2	5	.286	4.26	19	6	3	74	95	22	20	1	1	2	0	22	2	0	.091
1922	0	2	.000	5.40	12	0	0	31.2	38	23	11	0	0	2	0	7	2	0	.286
11 yrs.	34	78	.304	3.57	203	117	71	1084.1	1035	527	570	8	6	12	1	366	71	0	.194
2 yrs.	2	7	.222	4.60	31	6	3	105.2	133	45	31	1	1	4	0	29	4	0	.138

	W	L	PCT	ERA	G	GS	CG	IP	H	BB	SO	ShO	Relief Pitching W	L	SV	BATTING AB	H	HR	BA

Doug Bair

BAIR, CHARLES DOUGLAS
B. Aug. 22, 1949, Defiance, Ohio — BR TR 6' 170 lbs.

Year/Team	W	L	PCT	ERA	G	GS	CG	IP	H	BB	SO	ShO	RW	RL	SV	AB	H	HR	BA
1976 PIT N	0	0	–	5.68	4	0	0	6.1	4	5	4	0	0	0	0	0	0	0	–
1977 OAK A	4	6	.400	3.47	45	0	0	83	78	57	68	0	4	6	8	0	0	0	–
1978 CIN N	7	6	.538	1.98	70	0	0	100	87	38	91	0	7	6	28	14	2	0	.143
1979	11	7	.611	4.31	65	0	0	94	93	51	86	0	11	7	16	8	0	0	.000
1980	3	6	.333	4.24	61	0	0	85	91	39	62	0	3	6	6	2	0	0	.000
1981 2 teams			CIN N (24G 2-2)			STL N (11G 2-0)														
" total	4	2	.667	5.10	35	0	0	54.2	55	19	30	0	4	2	1	6	1	1	.167
1982 STL N	5	3	.625	2.55	63	0	0	91.2	69	36	68	0	5	3	8	13	1	0	.077
7 yrs.	34	30	.531	3.50	343	0	0	514.2	477	245	409	0	34	30	67	43	4	1	.093
2 yrs.	7	3	.700	2.68	74	0	0	107.1	82	38	82	0	7	3	9	16	1	0	.063

LEAGUE CHAMPIONSHIP SERIES

Year/Team	W	L	PCT	ERA	G	GS	CG	IP	H	BB	SO	ShO	RW	RL	SV	AB	H	HR	BA
1979 CIN N	0	1	.000	9.00	1	0	0	1	2	1	0	0	0	1	0	0	0	0	–
1982 STL N	0	0	–	0.00	1	0	0	1	2	3	0	0	0	0	0	0	0	0	–
2 yrs.	0	1	.000	4.50	2	0	0	2	4	4	0	0	0	1	0	0	0	0	–

WORLD SERIES

Year/Team	W	L	PCT	ERA	G	GS	CG	IP	H	BB	SO	ShO	RW	RL	SV	AB	H	HR	BA
1982 STL N	0	1	.000	9.00	3	0	0	2	2	2	3	0	0	1	0	0	0	0	–

Dave Bakenhaster

BAKENHASTER, DAVID LEE
B. Mar. 5, 1945, Columbus, Ohio — BR TR 5'10" 168 lbs.

Year/Team	W	L	PCT	ERA	G	GS	CG	IP	H	BB	SO	ShO	RW	RL	SV	AB	H	HR	BA
1964 STL N	0	0	–	6.00	2	0	0	3	9	1	0	0	0	0	0	0	0	0	–

O. F. Baldwin

BALDWIN, O. F.
B. Youngstown, Ohio

Year/Team	W	L	PCT	ERA	G	GS	CG	IP	H	BB	SO	ShO	RW	RL	SV	AB	H	HR	BA
1908 STL N	1	3	.250	6.14	4	4	0	14.2	16	11	5	0	0	0	0	6	0	0	.000

Jimmy Bannon

BANNON, JAMES HENRY (Foxy Grandpa)
Brother of Tom Bannon.
B. May 5, 1871, Amesbury, Mass.   D. Mar. 24, 1948, Glenrock, N. J. — BR TR 5'5" 160 lbs.

Year/Team	W	L	PCT	ERA	G	GS	CG	IP	H	BB	SO	ShO	RW	RL	SV	AB	H	HR	BA
1893 STL N	0	1	.000	22.50	1	1	0	4	10	5	1	0	0	0	0	107	36	0	.336
1894 BOS N	0	0	–	0.00	1	0	0	2	4	1	0	0	0	0	0	494	166	13	.336
1895	0	0	–	6.00	1	0	0	3	4	2	1	0	0	0	0	489	171	6	.350
3 yrs.	0	1	.000	12.00	3	1	0	9	18	8	2	0	0	0	0	*			
1 yr.	0	1	.000	22.50	1	1	0	4	10	5	1	0	0	0	0	107	36	0	.336

Ray Bare

BARE, RAYMOND DOUGLAS
B. Apr. 15, 1949, Miami, Fla. — BR TR 6'2" 185 lbs.

Year/Team	W	L	PCT	ERA	G	GS	CG	IP	H	BB	SO	ShO	RW	RL	SV	AB	H	HR	BA
1972 STL N	0	1	.000	0.54	14	0	0	16.2	18	6	5	0	0	1	0	0	0	0	–
1974	1	2	.333	6.00	10	3	0	24	25	9	6	0	1	0	0	5	1	0	.200
1975 DET A	8	13	.381	4.48	29	21	6	150.2	174	47	71	1	2	0	0	0	0	0	–
1976	7	8	.467	4.63	30	21	3	134	157	51	59	2	0	0	0	0	0	0	–
1977	0	2	.000	12.86	5	4	0	14	24	7	4	0	0	0	0	0	0	0	–
5 yrs.	16	26	.381	4.80	88	49	9	339.1	398	120	145	3	3	1	1	5	1	0	.200
2 yrs.	1	3	.250	3.76	24	3	0	40.2	43	15	11	0	1	1	1	5	1	0	.200

Clyde Barfoot

BARFOOT, CLYDE RAYMOND
B. July 8, 1891, Richmond, Va.   D. Mar. 11, 1971, Highland Park, Calif. — BR TR 6' 170 lbs.

Year/Team	W	L	PCT	ERA	G	GS	CG	IP	H	BB	SO	ShO	RW	RL	SV	AB	H	HR	BA
1922 STL N	4	5	.444	4.21	42	2	1	117.2	139	30	19	0	3	4	2	34	12	0	.353
1923	3	3	.500	3.73	33	2	1	101.1	112	27	23	1	2	3	1	37	7	0	.189
1926 DET A	1	2	.333	4.88	11	0	0	31.1	42	9	7	0	1	1	2	5	1	0	.200
3 yrs.	8	10	.444	4.10	86	5	2	250.1	293	66	49	1	6	8	5	76	20	0	.263
2 yrs.	7	8	.467	3.99	75	4	2	219	251	57	42	1	5	7	3	71	19	0	.268

Mike Barlow

BARLOW, MICHAEL ROSWELL
B. Apr. 30, 1948, Stamford, N. Y. — BL TL 6'6" 210 lbs.

Year/Team	W	L	PCT	ERA	G	GS	CG	IP	H	BB	SO	ShO	RW	RL	SV	AB	H	HR	BA
1975 STL N	0	0	–	4.50	9	0	0	8	11	3	2	0	0	0	0	0	0	0	–
1976 HOU N	2	2	.500	4.50	16	0	0	22	27	17	11	0	2	2	0	3	0	0	.000
1977 CAL A	4	2	.667	4.58	20	1	0	59	53	27	25	0	3	1	1	0	0	0	–
1978	0	0	–	4.50	1	0	0	2	3	1	0	0	0	0	0	0	0	0	–
1979	1	1	.500	5.13	35	0	0	86	106	30	33	0	1	1	0	0	0	0	–
1980 TOR A	3	1	.750	4.09	40	1	0	55	57	21	19	0	2	1	5	0	0	0	–
1981	0	0	–	4.20	12	0	0	15	22	6	5	0	0	0	0	0	0	0	–
7 yrs.	10	6	.625	4.63	133	2	0	247	279	104	96	0	8	5	6	3	0	0	.000
1 yr.	0	0	–	4.50	9	0	0	8	11	3	2	0	0	0	0	0	0	0	–

LEAGUE CHAMPIONSHIP SERIES

Year/Team	W	L	PCT	ERA	G	GS	CG	IP	H	BB	SO	ShO	RW	RL	SV	AB	H	HR	BA
1979 CAL A	0	0	–	0.00	1	0	0	1	0	0	0	0	0	0	0	0	0	0	–

Frank Barnes

BARNES, FRANK
B. Aug. 26, 1928, Longwood, Miss. — BR TR 6' 170 lbs.

Year/Team	W	L	PCT	ERA	G	GS	CG	IP	H	BB	SO	ShO	RW	RL	SV	AB	H	HR	BA
1957 STL N	0	1	.000	4.50	3	1	0	10	13	9	5	0	0	0	0	2	0	0	.000
1958	1	1	.500	7.58	8	1	0	19	19	16	17	0	1	1	0	6	1	0	.167
1960	0	1	.000	3.52	4	1	0	7.2	8	9	8	0	0	0	1	2	0	0	.000
3 yrs.	1	3	.250	5.89	15	3	0	36.2	40	34	30	0	1	1	1	10	1	0	.100
3 yrs.	1	3	.250	5.89	15	3	0	36.2	40	34	30	0	1	1	1	10	1	0	.100

Frank Barrett

BARRETT, FRANCIS JOSEPH (Red)
B. July 1, 1913, Fort Lauderdale, Fla. — BR TR 6'2" 173 lbs.

Year/Team	W	L	PCT	ERA	G	GS	CG	IP	H	BB	SO	ShO	RW	RL	SV	AB	H	HR	BA
1939 STL N	0	1	.000	5.40	4	0	0	1.2	1	1	3	0	1	0	0	0	0	0	–
1944 BOS A	8	7	.533	3.69	38	2	0	90.1	93	42	40	0	7	6	8	28	4	0	.143
1945	4	3	.571	2.62	37	0	0	86	77	29	35	0	4	3	3	20	5	0	.250
1946 BOS A	2	4	.333	5.09	23	0	0	35.1	35	17	12	0	2	4	1	6	0	0	.000
1950 PIT N	1	2	.333	4.15	5	0	0	4.1	5	1	0	0	1	2	0	0	0	0	–

	W	L	PCT	ERA	G	GS	CG	IP	H	BB	SO	ShO	Relief Pitching W	L	SV	BATTING AB	H	HR	BA

Frank Barrett continued

| 5 yrs. | 15 | 17 | .469 | 3.51 | 104 | 2 | 0 | 217.2 | 211 | 90 | 90 | 0 | 14 | 16 | 12 | 54 | 9 | 0 | .167 |
| 1 yr. | 0 | 1 | .000 | 5.40 | 1 | 0 | 0 | 1.2 | 1 | 1 | 3 | 0 | 0 | 1 | 0 | 0 | 0 | 0 | – |

Red Barrett

BARRETT, CHARLES HENRY   BR TR 5'11" 183 lbs.
B. Feb. 14, 1915, Santa Barbara, Calif.

1937 CIN N	0	0	–	1.42	1	0	0	6.1	5	2	1	0	0	0	0	3	0	0	.000
1938	2	0	1.000	3.14	6	2	2	28.2	28	15	5	0	0	0	0	7	1	0	.143
1939	0	0	–	1.69	2	0	0	5.1	5	1	1	0	0	0	0	1	0	0	.000
1940	1	0	1.000	6.75	3	0	0	2.2	5	1	0	0	1	0	0	0	0	0	–
1943 BOS N	12	18	.400	3.18	38	31	14	255	240	63	64	3	0	2	0	81	11	0	.136
1944	9	16	.360	4.06	42	30	11	230.1	257	63	54	1	0	3	2	75	13	0	.173
1945 2 teams			BOS N	(9G 2–3)			STL N	(36G 21–9)											
" total	23	12	.657	3.00	45	34	24	284.2	287	54	76	3	1	3	2	98	12	0	.122
1946 STL N	3	2	.600	4.03	23	9	1	67	75	24	22	1	1	0	2	17	1	0	.059
1947 BOS N	11	12	.478	3.55	36	30	12	210.2	200	53	53	3	0	1	1	72	8	0	.111
1948	7	8	.467	3.65	34	13	3	128.1	132	26	40	0	2	3	0	39	7	0	.179
1949	1	1	.500	5.68	23	0	0	44.1	58	10	17	0	1	0	0	5	1	0	.200
11 yrs.	69	69	.500	3.53	253	149	67	1263.1	1292	312	333	11	6	13	7	398	54	0	.136
2 yrs.	24	11	.686	3.01	59	38	23	313.2	319	62	85	4	1	2	2	106	11	0	.104

WORLD SERIES
| 1948 BOS N | 0 | 0 | – | 0.00 | 2 | 0 | 0 | 3.2 | 1 | 0 | 1 | 0 | 0 | 0 | 0 | 0 | 0 | 0 | – |

Frank Bates

BATES, FRANK CHARLES
B. Chattanooga, Tenn.   Deceased.

1898 CLE N	2	1	.667	3.10	4	4	4	29	30	11	5	0	0	0	0	9	1	0	.111
1899 2 teams			STL N	(2G 0–0)			CLE N	(20G 1–18)											
" total	1	18	.053	6.90	22	19	17	161.2	246	110	13	0	0	0	0	68	15	0	.221
2 yrs.	3	19	.136	6.33	26	23	21	190.2	276	121	18	0	0	0	0	77	16	0	.208
1 yr.	0	0	–	1.04	2	0	0	8.2	7	5	0	0	0	0	0	3	1	0	.333

Ed Bauta

BAUTA, EDUARDO GALVEZ   BR TR 6'3" 200 lbs.
B. Jan. 6, 1935, Florida Camaguey, Cuba

1960 STL N	0	0	–	6.32	9	0	0	15.2	14	11	6	0	0	0	1	1	0	0	.000
1961	2	0	1.000	1.40	13	0	0	19.1	12	5	12	0	2	0	5	4	2	0	.500
1962	1	0	1.000	5.01	20	0	0	32.1	28	21	25	0	1	0	1	4	1	0	.250
1963 2 teams			STL N	(38G 3–4)			NY N	(9G 0–0)											
" total	3	4	.429	4.27	47	0	0	71.2	77	30	43	0	3	4	3	8	0	0	.000
1964 NY N	0	2	.000	5.40	8	0	0	10	17	3	3	0	0	2	1	0	0	0	–
5 yrs.	6	6	.500	4.35	97	0	0	149	148	70	89	0	6	6	11	17	3	0	.176
4 yrs.	6	4	.600	4.13	80	0	0	120	109	58	73	0	6	4	10	14	3	0	.214

Ralph Beard

BEARD, RALPH WILLIAM   BR TR 6'5" 200 lbs.
B. Feb. 11, 1929, Cincinnati, Ohio

| 1954 STL N | 0 | 4 | .000 | 3.72 | 13 | 10 | 0 | 58 | 62 | 28 | 17 | 0 | 0 | 0 | 0 | 17 | 1 | 0 | .059 |

Johnny Beazley

BEAZLEY, JOHN ANDREW   BR TR 6'1½" 190 lbs.
B. May 25, 1918, Nashville, Tenn.

1941 STL N	1	0	1.000	1.00	1	1	1	9	10	3	4	0	0	0	0	3	0	0	.000
1942	21	6	.778	2.13	43	23	13	215.1	181	73	91	3	6	3	3	73	10	0	.137
1946	7	5	.583	4.46	19	18	5	103	109	55	36	0	0	0	0	33	8	0	.242
1947 BOS N	2	0	1.000	4.40	9	2	2	28.2	30	19	12	0	0	0	0	7	0	0	.000
1948	0	1	.000	4.50	3	2	0	16	19	7	4	0	0	0	0	4	0	0	.000
1949	0	0	–	0.00	1	0	0	2	0	0	0	0	0	0	0	0	0	0	–
6 yrs.	31	12	.721	3.01	76	46	21	374	349	157	147	3	6	3	3	120	18	0	.150
3 yrs.	29	11	.725	2.83	63	42	19	327.1	300	131	131	3	6	3	3	109	18	0	.165

WORLD SERIES
1942 STL N	2	0	1.000	2.50	2	2	2	18	17	3	6	0	0	0	0	7	1	0	.143
1946	0	0	–	0.00	1	0	0	1	1	0	1	0	0	0	0	0	0	0	–
2 yrs.	2	0	1.000	2.37	3	2	2	19	18	3	7	0	0	0	0	7	1	0	.143

Jake Beckley

BECKLEY, JACOB PETER (Eagle Eye)   BL TL 5'10" 200 lbs.
B. Aug. 4, 1867, Hannibal, Mo.   D. June 25, 1918, Kansas City, Mo.
Hall of Fame 1971.

| 1902 CIN N | 0 | 1 | .000 | 6.75 | 1 | 1 | 0 | 4 | 9 | 1 | 2 | 0 | 0 | 0 | 0 | * | | | |

Bill Beckmann

BECKMANN, WILLIAM ALOYS   BR TR 6' 175 lbs.
B. Dec. 8, 1907, Clayton, Mo.

1939 PHI A	7	11	.389	5.39	27	19	7	155.1	199	41	20	2	2	0	0	52	13	0	.250
1940	8	4	.667	4.17	34	9	6	127.1	132	35	47	2	3	2	1	39	8	0	.205
1941	5	9	.357	4.57	22	15	4	130	141	33	28	0	3	0	1	47	9	0	.191
1942 2 teams			PHI A	(5G 0–1)			STL N	(2G 1–0)											
" total	1	1	.500	5.27	7	1	0	27.1	28	10	13	0	1	0	0	5	2	0	.400
4 yrs.	21	25	.457	4.79	90	44	17	440	499	119	108	4	9	2	2	143	32	0	.224
1 yr.	1	0	1.000	0.00	2	1	0	4	1	3	1	0	1	0	0	1	0	0	.000

Fred Beebe

BEEBE, FREDERICK LEONARD   BR TR 6'1" 190 lbs.
B. Dec. 31, 1880, Lincoln, Neb.   D. Oct. 30, 1957, LaGrange, Ill.

1906 2 teams			CHI N	(14G 7–1)			STL N	(20G 9–9)											
" total	16	10	.615	2.93	34	25	20	230.2	171	100	171	1	3	0	1	87	13	0	.149
1907 STL N	7	19	.269	2.72	31	29	24	238.1	192	109	141	4	1	0	0	86	11	0	.128

	W	L	PCT	ERA	G	GS	CG	IP	H	BB	SO	ShO	Relief Pitching W	L	SV	BATTING AB	H	HR	BA

Fred Beebe continued

Year	W	L	PCT	ERA	G	GS	CG	IP	H	BB	SO	ShO	W	L	SV	AB	H	HR	BA
1908	5	13	.278	2.63	29	19	12	174.1	134	66	72	0	0	1	0	56	7	0	.125
1909	15	21	.417	2.82	44	35	18	287.2	256	104	105	1	2	3	1	108	18	0	.167
1910 CIN N	12	14	.462	3.07	35	26	11	214.1	193	94	93	2	2	0	0	73	12	0	.164
1911 PHI N	3	3	.500	4.47	9	8	3	48.1	52	24	20	0	0	0	0	19	5	0	.263
1916 CLE A	5	3	.625	2.41	20	12	5	100.2	92	37	32	1	0	0	2	28	6	0	.214
7 yrs.	63	83	.432	2.86	202	154	93	1294.1	1090	534	634	9	8	4	4	457	72	0	.158
4 yrs.	36	62	.367	2.79	124	102	70	861	697	347	434	6	3	4	1	308	46	0	.149
				6th															

Clarence Beers

BEERS, CLARENCE SCOTT BR TR 6' 175 lbs.
B. Dec. 9, 1918, Eldorado, Kans.

Year	W	L	PCT	ERA	G	GS	CG	IP	H	BB	SO	ShO	W	L	SV	AB	H	HR	BA
1948 STL N	0	0	–	13.50	1	0	0	.2	3	1	0	0	0	0	0	0	0	0	–

Hi Bell

BELL, HERMAN S BR TR 6' 185 lbs.
B. July 16, 1895, Louisville, Ky. D. June 7, 1949, Glendale, Calif.

Year	W	L	PCT	ERA	G	GS	CG	IP	H	BB	SO	ShO	W	L	SV	AB	H	HR	BA
1924 STL N	3	8	.273	4.92	28	11	5	113.1	124	29	29	0	0	1	1	31	2	0	.065
1926	6	6	.500	3.18	27	8	3	85	82	17	27	0	3	2	2	25	3	0	.120
1927	1	3	.250	3.92	25	1	0	57.1	71	22	31	0	1	2	0	11	1	0	.091
1929	0	2	.000	6.92	7	0	0	13	19	4	4	0	0	2	0	3	0	0	.000
1930	4	3	.571	3.90	39	9	2	115.1	143	23	42	0	3	1	8	26	2	0	.077
1932 NY N	8	4	.667	3.68	35	10	3	120	132	16	25	0	3	1	2	34	3	0	.088
1933	6	5	.545	2.05	38	7	1	105.1	100	20	24	1	4	2	5	29	4	0	.138
1934	4	3	.571	3.67	22	2	0	54	72	12	9	0	4	2	6	19	2	0	.105
8 yrs.	32	34	.485	3.69	221	48	14	663.1	743	143	191	1	18	13	24	178	17	0	.096
5 yrs.	14	22	.389	4.15	126	29	10	384	439	95	133	0	7	8	11	96	8	0	.083

WORLD SERIES

Year	W	L	PCT	ERA	G	GS	CG	IP	H	BB	SO	ShO	W	L	SV	AB	H	HR	BA
1926 STL N	0	0	–	9.00	1	0	0	2	4	1	1	0	0	0	0	0	0	0	–
1930	0	0	–	0.00	1	0	0	1	0	0	0	0	0	0	0	0	0	0	–
1933 NY N	0	0	–	0.00	1	0	0	1	0	0	0	0	0	0	0	0	0	0	–
3 yrs.	0	0	–	4.50	3	0	0	4	4	1	1	0	0	0	0	0	0	0	–

Sid Benton

BENTON, SIDNEY WRIGHT BR TR 6'1" 170 lbs.
B. Aug. 4, 1895, Buckner, Ark. D. Mar. 8, 1977, Fayetteville, Ark.

Year	W	L	PCT	ERA	G	GS	CG	IP	H	BB	SO	ShO	W	L	SV	AB	H	HR	BA
1922 STL N	0	0	–	0.00	1	0	0	2	0	2	0	0	0	0	0	*			

Jack Berly

BERLY, JOHN CHAMBERS BR TR 5'11½" 190 lbs.
B. May 24, 1903, Natchitoches, La. D. June 26, 1977, Houston, Tex.

Year	W	L	PCT	ERA	G	GS	CG	IP	H	BB	SO	ShO	W	L	SV	AB	H	HR	BA
1924 STL N	0	0	–	5.63	4	0	0	8	8	4	2	0	0	0	0	2	0	0	.000
1931 NY N	7	8	.467	3.88	27	11	4	111.1	114	51	45	1	2	4	0	35	6	0	.171
1932 PHI N	1	2	.333	7.63	21	1	1	46	61	21	15	0	1	1	2	10	0	0	.000
1933	2	3	.400	5.04	13	6	1	50	62	22	4	1	0	0	0	13	4	0	.308
4 yrs.	10	13	.435	5.02	65	18	6	215.1	245	98	66	2	3	5	2	60	10	0	.167
1 yr.	0	0	–	5.63	4	0	0	8	8	4	2	0	0	0	0	2	0	0	.000

Joe Bernard

BERNARD, JOSEPH
B. Unknown.

Year	W	L	PCT	ERA	G	GS	CG	IP	H	BB	SO	ShO	W	L	SV	AB	H	HR	BA
1909 STL N	0	0	–	0.00	1	0	0	1	1	2	2	0	0	0	0	0	0	0	–

Frank Bertaina

BERTAINA, FRANK LOUIS BL TL 5'11" 177 lbs.
B. Apr. 14, 1944, San Francisco, Calif.

Year	W	L	PCT	ERA	G	GS	CG	IP	H	BB	SO	ShO	W	L	SV	AB	H	HR	BA
1964 BAL A	1	0	1.000	2.77	6	4	1	26	18	13	18	1	0	0	0	5	0	0	.000
1965	0	0	–	6.00	2	1	0	6	9	4	5	0	0	0	0	1	0	0	.000
1966	2	5	.286	3.13	16	9	0	63.1	52	36	46	0	1	0	0	19	2	0	.105
1967 2 teams			BAL	A	(5G 1-1)		WAS	A	(18G 6-5)										
" total	7	6	.538	2.99	23	19	4	117.1	107	51	86	4	0	0	0	44	3	0	.068
1968 WAS A	7	13	.350	4.66	27	23	1	127.1	133	69	81	0	0	0	0	38	5	0	.132
1969 2 teams			WAS	A	(14G 1-3)		BAL	A	(3G 0-0)										
" total	1	3	.250	5.62	17	5	0	41.2	44	26	30	0	0	3	0	12	5	1	.417
1970 STL N	1	2	.333	3.19	8	5	0	31	36	15	14	0	0	0	0	7	1	0	.143
7 yrs.	19	29	.396	3.84	99	66	6	412.2	399	214	280	5	1	3	0	126	16	1	.127
1 yr.	1	2	.333	3.19	8	5	0	31	36	15	14	0	0	0	0	7	1	0	.143

Hal Betts

BETTS, HAROLD MATTHEW BR TR 5'10" 200 lbs.
B. June 19, 1881, Alliance, Ohio D. May 22, 1946, San Antonio, Tex.

Year	W	L	PCT	ERA	G	GS	CG	IP	H	BB	SO	ShO	W	L	SV	AB	H	HR	BA
1903 STL N	0	1	.000	10.00	1	1	1	9	11	5	2	0	0	0	0	3	0	0	.000
1913 CIN N	0	0	–	2.70	1	0	0	3.1	1	3	0	0	0	0	0	1	0	0	.000
2 yrs.	0	1	.000	8.03	2	1	1	12.1	12	8	2	0	0	0	0	4	0	0	.000
1 yr.	0	1	.000	10.00	1	1	1	9	11	5	2	0	0	0	0	3	0	0	.000

Jim Bibby

BIBBY, JAMES BLAIR BR TR 6'5" 235 lbs.
B. Oct. 29, 1944, Franklinton, N. C.

Year	W	L	PCT	ERA	G	GS	CG	IP	H	BB	SO	ShO	W	L	SV	AB	H	HR	BA
1972 STL N	1	3	.250	3.35	6	6	0	40.1	29	19	28	0	0	0	0	8	1	0	.125
1973 2 teams			STL	N	(6G 0-2)		TEX	A	(26G 9-10)										
" total	9	12	.429	3.77	32	26	11	196	140	123	167	2	0	0	1	2	0	0	.000
1974 TEX A	19	19	.500	4.74	41	41	11	264	255	113	149	5	0	0	0	0	0	0	–
1975 2 teams			TEX	A	(12G 2-6)		CLE	A	(24G 5-9)										
" total	7	15	.318	3.88	36	24	6	181	172	78	93	1	1	3	1	0	0	0	–
1976 CLE A	13	7	.650	3.20	34	21	4	163	162	56	84	3	1	1	0	0	0	0	–
1977	12	13	.480	3.57	37	30	9	207	197	73	141	2	0	1	0	0	0	0	–
1978 PIT N	8	7	.533	3.53	34	14	3	107	100	39	72	2	3	2	1	31	4	1	.129
1979	12	4	.750	2.80	34	17	4	138	110	47	103	1	4	0	0	45	8	2	.178

	W	L	PCT	ERA	G	GS	CG	IP	H	BB	SO	ShO	W	L	SV	AB	H	HR	BA
													Relief Pitching			**BATTING**			

Jim Bibby continued

	W	L	PCT	ERA	G	GS	CG	IP	H	BB	SO	ShO	W	L	SV	AB	H	HR	BA
1980	19	6	.760	3.33	35	34	6	238	210	88	144	1	1	0	0	77	12	1	.156
1981	6	3	.667	2.49	14	14	2	94	79	26	48	2	0	0	0	28	4	1	.143
10 yrs.	106	89	.544	3.61	303	227	56	1628.1	1454	662	1029	19	10	8	6	191	29	5	.152
2 yrs.	1	5	.167	5.11	12	9	0	56.1	48	36	40	0	0	0	0	10	1	0	.100

LEAGUE CHAMPIONSHIP SERIES
| 1979 PIT N | 0 | 0 | — | 1.29 | 1 | 1 | 0 | 7 | 4 | 4 | 5 | 0 | 0 | 0 | 0 | 0 | 0 | 0 | — |

WORLD SERIES
| 1979 PIT N | 0 | 0 | — | 2.61 | 2 | 2 | 0 | 10.1 | 10 | 2 | 10 | 0 | 0 | 0 | 0 | 4 | 0 | 0 | .000 |

Lou Bierbauer

BIERBAUER, LOUIS W.   BR TR
Also appeared in box score as Bauer
B. Sept. 28, 1865, Erie, Pa.   D. Jan. 31, 1926, Erie, Pa.

	W	L	PCT	ERA	G	GS	CG	IP	H	BB	SO	ShO	W	L	SV	AB	H	HR	BA
1886 PHI AA	0	0	—	4.22	2	0	0	10.2	8	5	1	0	0	0	0	522	118	2	.226
1887	0	0	—	0.00	1	0	0	1	0	0	1	0	0	0	1	530	144	1	.272
1888	0	0	—	0.00	1	0	0	3	5	0	3	0	0	0	0	535	143	0	.267
3 yrs.	0	0	—	3.07	4	0	0	14.2	13	5	5	0	0	0	1	*			

Sheriff Blake

BLAKE, JOHN FREDERICK   BL TR 6' 180 lbs.
B. Sept. 17, 1899, Ansted, W. Va.   BR 1920,1925-27, BB 1937

	W	L	PCT	ERA	G	GS	CG	IP	H	BB	SO	ShO	W	L	SV	AB	H	HR	BA
1920 PIT N	0	0	—	8.10	6	0	0	13.1	21	6	7	0	0	0	0	4	1	0	.250
1924 CHI N	6	6	.500	4.57	29	11	4	106.1	123	44	42	0	2	2	1	31	9	0	.290
1925	10	18	.357	4.86	36	31	14	231.1	260	114	93	0	0	1	2	79	12	0	.152
1926	11	12	.478	3.60	39	27	11	197.2	204	92	95	4	1	1	1	65	14	0	.215
1927	13	14	.481	3.29	32	27	13	224.1	238	82	64	2	0	3	0	83	16	0	.193
1928	17	11	.607	2.47	34	29	16	240.2	209	101	78	4	3	0	1	88	19	0	.216
1929	14	13	.519	4.29	35	30	13	218.1	244	103	70	1	0	0	1	81	14	0	.173
1930	10	14	.417	4.82	34	24	7	186.2	213	99	80	0	2	2	0	66	15	0	.227
1931 2 teams					CHI N (16G 0-4)			PHI N (14G 4-5)											
" total	4	9	.308	5.43	30	14	1	121	154	61	60	0	0	3	1	41	14	0	.341
1937 2 teams					STL A (15G 2-2)			STL N (14G 0-3)											
" total	2	5	.286	5.49	29	3	2	80.1	100	38	32	0	2	3	1	20	4	0	.200
10 yrs.	87	102	.460	4.13	304	196	81	1620	1766	740	621	11	10	15	8	558	118	0	.211
1 yr.	0	3	.000	3.71	14	2	2	43.2	45	18	20	0	0	1	0	10	3	0	.300

WORLD SERIES
| 1929 CHI N | 0 | 1 | .000 | 13.50 | 2 | 0 | 0 | 1.1 | 4 | 0 | 1 | 0 | 0 | 1 | 0 | 1 | 1 | 0 | 1.000 |

Bob Blaylock

BLAYLOCK, ROBERT EDWARD   BR TR 6'1" 185 lbs.
B. June 28, 1935, Chattanooga, Okla.

	W	L	PCT	ERA	G	GS	CG	IP	H	BB	SO	ShO	W	L	SV	AB	H	HR	BA
1956 STL N	1	6	.143	6.37	14	6	0	41	45	24	39	0	1	1	0	11	1	0	.091
1959	0	1	.000	4.00	3	1	0	9	8	3	3	0	0	1	0	1	0	0	.000
2 yrs.	1	7	.125	5.94	17	7	0	50	53	27	42	0	1	2	0	12	1	0	.083
2 yrs.	1	7	.125	5.94	17	7	0	50	53	27	42	0	1	2	0	12	1	0	.083

Gary Blaylock

BLAYLOCK, GARY NELSON   BR TR 6' 196 lbs.
B. Oct. 11, 1931, Clarkton, Mo.

	W	L	PCT	ERA	G	GS	CG	IP	H	BB	SO	ShO	W	L	SV	AB	H	HR	BA
1959 2 teams					STL N (26G 4-5)			NY A (15G 0-1)											
" total	4	6	.400	4.80	41	13	3	125.2	147	58	81	0	1	1	0	36	5	2	.139

Charlie Boardman

BOARDMAN, CHARLES LOUIS   BL TL 6'2½" 194 lbs.
B. Mar. 27, 1893, Seneca Falls, N. Y.   D. Aug. 10, 1968, Sacramento, Calif.

	W	L	PCT	ERA	G	GS	CG	IP	H	BB	SO	ShO	W	L	SV	AB	H	HR	BA
1913 PHI A	0	2	.000	2.00	2	2	1	9	10	6	4	0	0	0	0	3	0	0	.000
1914	0	0	—	4.91	2	0	0	7.1	10	4	2	0	0	0	0	2	0	0	.000
1915 STL N	1	0	1.000	1.42	3	1	1	19	12	15	7	0	0	0	0	7	2	0	.286
3 yrs.	1	2	.333	2.29	7	3	2	35.1	32	25	13	0	0	0	0	12	2	0	.167
1 yr.	1	0	1.000	1.42	3	1	1	19	12	15	7	0	0	0	0	7	2	0	.286

Dick Bokelmann

BOKELMANN, RICHARD WERNER   BR TR 6'½" 180 lbs.
B. Oct. 26, 1926, Arlington Heights, Ill.

	W	L	PCT	ERA	G	GS	CG	IP	H	BB	SO	ShO	W	L	SV	AB	H	HR	BA
1951 STL N	3	3	.500	3.78	20	1	0	52.1	49	31	22	0	3	2	3	14	0	0	.000
1952	0	1	.000	9.24	11	0	0	12.2	20	7	5	0	0	1	0	0	0	0	—
1953	0	0	—	6.00	3	0	0	3	4	0	0	0	0	0	0	0	0	0	—
3 yrs.	3	4	.429	4.90	34	1	0	68	73	38	27	0	3	3	3	14	0	0	.000
3 yrs.	3	4	.429	4.90	34	1	0	68	73	38	27	0	3	3	3	14	0	0	.000

Bill Bolden

BOLDEN, WILLIAM HORACE (Big Bill)   BR TR 6'4" 200 lbs.
B. May 9, 1893, Dandridge, Tenn.   D. Dec. 8, 1966, Jefferson City, Tenn.

	W	L	PCT	ERA	G	GS	CG	IP	H	BB	SO	ShO	W	L	SV	AB	H	HR	BA
1919 STL N	0	1	.000	5.25	3	1	0	12	17	4	4	0	0	0	0	3	1	0	.333

Pedro Borbon

BORBON, PEDRO   BR TR 6'2" 185 lbs.
B. Dec. 2, 1946, Valverde De Mao, Dominican Republic

	W	L	PCT	ERA	G	GS	CG	IP	H	BB	SO	ShO	W	L	SV	AB	H	HR	BA
1969 CAL A	2	3	.400	6.15	22	0	0	41	55	11	20	0	2	3	0	3	0	0	.000
1970 CIN N	0	2	.000	6.88	12	1	0	17	21	6	6	0	0	1	0	3	0	0	.000
1971	0	0	—	4.50	3	0	0	4	3	1	4	0	0	0	0	0	0	0	—
1972	8	3	.727	3.17	62	2	0	122	115	32	48	0	8	3	11	21	1	0	.048
1973	11	4	.733	2.15	80	0	0	121.1	137	35	60	0	11	4	14	15	5	0	.333
1974	10	7	.588	3.24	73	0	0	139	133	32	53	0	10	7	14	26	5	0	.192
1975	9	5	.643	2.95	67	0	0	125	145	21	29	0	9	5	5	24	7	0	.292
1976	4	3	.571	3.35	69	0	0	121	135	31	53	0	4	2	8	18	4	0	.222

	W	L	PCT	ERA	G	GS	CG	IP	H	BB	SO	ShO	Relief Pitching W	L	SV	BATTING AB	H	HR	BA

Pedro Borbon continued

	W	L	PCT	ERA	G	GS	CG	IP	H	BB	SO	ShO	W	L	SV	AB	H	HR	BA
1977	10	5	.667	3.19	73	0	0	127	131	24	48	0	10	5	18	22	4	0	.182
1978	8	2	.800	5.00	62	0	0	99	102	27	35	0	8	2	4	11	2	0	.182
1979 2 teams			CIN N	(30G 2–2)			SF N	(30G 4–3)											
" total	6	5	.545	4.17	60	0	0	90.2	104	21	49	0	6	5	5	9	3	0	.333
1980 STL N	1	0	1.000	3.79	10	0	0	19	17	10	4	0	1	0	1	4	1	0	.250
12 yrs.	69	39	.639	3.52	593	4	0	1026	1098	251	409	0	69	37	80	156	32	0	.205
1 yr.	1	0	1.000	3.79	10	0	0	19	17	10	4	0	1	0	1	4	1	0	.250

LEAGUE CHAMPIONSHIP SERIES

	W	L	PCT	ERA	G	GS	CG	IP	H	BB	SO	ShO	W	L	SV	AB	H	HR	BA
1972 CIN N	0	0	–	2.08	3	0	0	4.1	2	0	1	0	0	0	0	0	0	0	–
1973	1	0	1.000	0.00	4	0	0	4.2	3	0	3	0	1	0	1	0	0	0	–
1975	0	0	–	0.00	1	0	0	1	0	0	1	0	0	0	0	0	0	0	–
1976	0	0	–	0.00	2	0	0	4.1	4	1	0	0	0	0	1	2	0	0	.000
4 yrs.	1	0	1.000	0.63	10	0	0	14.1	9	1	5	0	1	0	2	2	0	0	.000

WORLD SERIES

	W	L	PCT	ERA	G	GS	CG	IP	H	BB	SO	ShO	W	L	SV	AB	H	HR	BA
1972 CIN N	0	1	.000	3.86	6	0	0	7	7	2	4	0	0	1	0	0	0	0	–
1975	0	0	–	6.00	3	0	0	3	3	2	1	0	0	0	0	1	0	0	.000
1976	0	0	–	0.00	1	0	0	1.2	0	0	0	0	0	0	0	0	0	0	–
3 yrs.	0	1	.000	3.86	10	0	0	11.2	10	4	5	0	0	1	0	1	0	0	.000

Bob Bowman

BOWMAN, ROBERT JAMES   BR TR 5'10½" 160 lbs.
B. Oct. 3, 1910, Keystone, W. Va.   D. Sept. 4, 1972, Bluefield, W. Va.

	W	L	PCT	ERA	G	GS	CG	IP	H	BB	SO	ShO	W	L	SV	AB	H	HR	BA
1939 STL N	13	5	.722	2.60	51	15	4	169.1	141	60	78	2	7	0	9	47	4	0	.085
1940	7	5	.583	4.33	28	17	7	114.1	118	43	43	0	0	2	0	33	2	0	.061
1941 NY N	6	7	.462	5.71	29	6	2	80.1	100	36	25	0	4	4	1	21	1	1	.048
1942 CHI N	0	0	–	0.00	1	0	0	1	1	0	0	0	0	0	0	0	0	0	–
4 yrs.	26	17	.605	3.82	109	38	13	365	360	139	146	2	11	6	10	101	7	1	.069
2 yrs.	20	10	.667	3.30	79	32	11	283.2	259	103	121	2	7	2	9	80	6	0	.075

Cloyd Boyer

BOYER, CLOYD VICTOR (Junior)   BR TR 6'1" 188 lbs.
Brother of Ken Boyer.   Brother of Clete Boyer.
B. Sept. 1, 1927, Alba, Mo.

	W	L	PCT	ERA	G	GS	CG	IP	H	BB	SO	ShO	W	L	SV	AB	H	HR	BA
1949 STL N	0	0	–	10.80	3	1	0	3.1	5	7	0	0	0	0	0	0	0	0	–
1950	7	7	.500	3.52	36	14	6	120.1	105	49	82	2	2	1	1	33	6	0	.182
1951	2	5	.286	5.26	19	8	1	63.1	68	46	40	0	1	2	1	20	4	0	.200
1952	6	6	.500	4.24	23	14	4	110.1	108	47	44	2	0	0	0	38	8	0	.211
1955 KC A	5	5	.500	6.22	30	11	2	98.1	107	69	32	0	1	0	1	29	2	0	.069
5 yrs.	20	23	.465	4.73	111	48	13	395.2	393	218	198	4	4	4	2	120	20	0	.167
4 yrs.	15	18	.455	4.24	81	37	11	297.1	286	149	166	4	3	3	2	91	18	0	.198

Harvey Branch

BRANCH, HARVEY ALFRED   BR TL 6' 175 lbs.
B. Feb. 8, 1939, Memphis, Tenn.

	W	L	PCT	ERA	G	GS	CG	IP	H	BB	SO	ShO	W	L	SV	AB	H	HR	BA
1962 STL N	0	1	.000	5.40	1	1	0	5	5	5	2	0	0	0	0	1	0	0	.000

Al Brazle

BRAZLE, ALPHA EUGENE (Cotton)   BL TL 6'2" 185 lbs.
B. Oct. 19, 1914, Loyal, Okla.   D. Oct. 24, 1973, Grand Junction, Colo.

	W	L	PCT	ERA	G	GS	CG	IP	H	BB	SO	ShO	W	L	SV	AB	H	HR	BA
1943 STL N	8	2	.800	1.53	13	9	8	88	74	29	26	1	1	0	0	32	9	0	.281
1946	11	10	.524	3.29	37	15	6	153.1	152	55	58	2	4	2	0	52	11	0	.212
1947	14	8	.636	2.84	44	19	7	168	186	48	85	0	4	1	4	64	14	0	.219
1948	10	6	.625	3.80	42	23	6	156.1	171	50	55	3	3	0	1	55	8	0	.145
1949	14	8	.636	3.18	39	25	9	206.1	208	61	75	1	3	0	0	82	11	0	.134
1950	11	9	.550	4.10	46	12	3	164.2	188	80	47	0	5	4	6	61	13	0	.213
1951	6	5	.545	3.09	56	8	5	154.1	139	61	66	0	2	2	7	46	5	0	.109
1952	12	5	.706	2.72	46	6	3	109.1	75	42	55	2	8	3	16	32	4	0	.125
1953	6	7	.462	4.21	60	0	0	92	101	43	57	0	6	7	18	15	5	0	.333
1954	5	4	.556	4.16	58	0	0	84.1	93	24	30	0	5	4	8	14	0	0	.000
10 yrs.	97	64	.602	3.31	441	117	47	1376.2	1387	493	554	9	41	23	60	453	80	0	.177
10 yrs.	97	64	.602	3.31	441	117	47	1376.2	1387	493	554	9	41	23	60	453	80	0	.177
				6th		4th								2nd	3rd				

WORLD SERIES

	W	L	PCT	ERA	G	GS	CG	IP	H	BB	SO	ShO	W	L	SV	AB	H	HR	BA
1943 STL N	0	1	.000	3.68	1	1	0	7.1	5	2	4	0	0	0	0	3	0	0	.000
1946	0	1	.000	5.40	1	0	0	6.2	7	6	4	0	0	1	0	2	0	0	.000
2 yrs.	0	2	.000	4.50	2	1	0	14	12	8	8	0	0	1	0	5	0	0	.000

Harry Brecheen

BRECHEEN, HARRY DAVID (The Cat)   BL TL 5'10" 160 lbs.
B. Oct. 14, 1914, Broken Bow, Okla.

	W	L	PCT	ERA	G	GS	CG	IP	H	BB	SO	ShO	W	L	SV	AB	H	HR	BA
1940 STL N	0	0	–	0.00	3	0	0	3.1	2	4	0	0	0	0	0	0	0	0	–
1943	9	6	.600	2.26	29	13	8	135.1	98	39	68	1	4	1	4	42	8	0	.190
1944	16	5	.762	2.85	30	22	13	189.1	174	46	88	3	3	0	0	68	11	0	.162
1945	14	4	.778	2.52	24	18	13	157.1	136	44	63	3	2	1	2	57	7	0	.123
1946	15	15	.500	2.49	36	30	14	231.1	212	67	117	5	0	0	3	83	11	0	.133
1947	16	11	.593	3.30	29	28	18	223.1	220	66	89	1	0	0	1	83	20	0	.241
1948	20	7	.741	2.24	33	30	21	233.1	193	49	149	7	0	0	0	82	12	0	.146
1949	14	11	.560	3.35	32	31	14	214.2	207	65	88	2	0	0	1	77	21	0	.273
1950	8	11	.421	3.80	27	23	12	163.1	151	45	80	2	0	2	1	58	14	1	.241
1951	8	4	.667	3.25	24	16	5	138.2	134	54	57	0	1	1	1	55	12	1	.218
1952	7	5	.583	3.32	25	13	4	100.1	82	28	54	1	2	1	2	29	6	0	.207
1953 STL A	5	13	.278	3.07	26	16	3	117.1	122	31	44	0	2	3	1	39	7	0	.179
12 yrs.	132	92	.589	2.92	318	240	125	1907.2	1731	536	901	25	15	8	18	673	129	2	.192
11 yrs.	127	79	.617	2.91	292	224	122	1790.1	1609	505	857	25	13	5	17	634	122	2	.192
			6th 10th	5th		8th			7th	7th				7th 4th					

WORLD SERIES

	W	L	PCT	ERA	G	GS	CG	IP	H	BB	SO	ShO	W	L	SV	AB	H	HR	BA
1943 STL N	0	1	.000	2.45	3	0	0	3.2	5	3	4	0	0	1	0	0	0	0	–

	W	L	PCT	ERA	G	GS	CG	IP	H	BB	SO	ShO	Relief Pitching W	L	SV	BATTING AB	H	HR	BA

Harry Brecheen continued

	W	L	PCT	ERA	G	GS	CG	IP	H	BB	SO	ShO	W	L	SV	AB	H	HR	BA
1944	1	0	1.000	1.00	1	1	1	9	9	4	4	0	0	0	0	4	0	0	.000
1946	3	0	1.000	0.45	3	2	2	20	14	5	11	1	1	0	0	8	1	0	.125
3 yrs.	4	1	.800	0.83	7	3	3	32.2	28	12	18	1	1	1	0	12	1	0	.083
				2nd															

Ted Breitenstein

BREITENSTEIN, THEODORE P.
B. June 1, 1869, St. Louis, Mo.   D. May 3, 1935, St. Louis, Mo.
BL TL 5'9"   167 lbs.

	W	L	PCT	ERA	G	GS	CG	IP	H	BB	SO	ShO	W	L	SV	AB	H	HR	BA
1891 STL AA	2	0	1.000	2.20	6	1	1	28.2	15	14	13	1	1	0	1	12	0	0	.000
1892 STL N	14	20	.412	4.69	39	32	28	282.1	280	148	126	1	0	0	0	131	16	0	.122
1893	19	20	.487	3.18	48	42	38	382.2	359	156	102	1	0	3	1	160	29	1	.181
1894	27	25	.519	4.79	56	50	46	447.1	497	191	140	1	2	0	0	182	40	0	.220
1895	18	30	.375	4.44	54	50	46	429.2	458	178	127	1	0	1	1	218	42	0	.193
1896	18	26	.409	4.48	44	43	37	339.2	376	138	114	1	1	0	0	162	42	0	.259
1897 CIN N	23	12	.657	3.62	40	39	32	320.1	345	91	98	2	0	0	0	124	33	0	.266
1898	21	14	.600	3.42	39	37	32	315.2	313	123	68	3	1	0	0	121	26	0	.215
1899	14	10	.583	3.59	26	24	21	210.2	219	71	59	0	1	0	0	105	37	1	.352
1900	10	10	.500	3.65	24	20	18	192.1	205	79	39	1	1	1	0	126	24	2	.190
1901 STL N	0	3	.000	6.60	3	3	1	15	24	14	3	0	0	0	0	6	2	0	.333
11 yrs.	166	170	.494	4.04	379	341	300	2964.1	3091	1203	889	12	7	5	3	*			.199
6 yrs.	96	124	.436	4.33	244	220	196	1896.2	1994	825	612	5	3	4	2	859	171	1	.199
				5th				3rd		6th		3rd							

Roger Bresnahan

BRESNAHAN, ROGER PHILIP (The Duke of Tralee)
B. June 11, 1879, Toledo, Ohio   D. Dec. 4, 1944, Toledo, Ohio
Manager 1909-12, 1915.
Hall of Fame 1945.
BR TR 5'9"   200 lbs.

	W	L	PCT	ERA	G	GS	CG	IP	H	BB	SO	ShO	W	L	SV	AB	H	HR	BA
1897 WAS N	4	0	1.000	3.95	6	5	3	41	52	10	12	1	0	0	0	16	6	0	.375
1901 BAL A	0	1	.000	6.00	2	1	0	6	10	4	3	0	0	0	0	295	79	1	.268
1910 STL N	0	0	—	0.00	1	0	0	3.1	6	1	0	0	0	0	0	234	65	0	.278
3 yrs.	4	1	.800	3.93	9	6	3	50.1	68	15	15	1	0	0	0	*			.275
1 yr.	0	0	—	0.00	1	0	0	3.1	6	1	0	0	0	0	0	803	221	4	.275

Rube Bressler

BRESSLER, RAYMOND BLOOM
B. Oct. 23, 1894, Coder, Pa.   D. Nov. 7, 1966, Cincinnati, Ohio
BR TL 6'   187 lbs.

	W	L	PCT	ERA	G	GS	CG	IP	H	BB	SO	ShO	W	L	SV	AB	H	HR	BA
1914 PHI A	10	3	.769	1.77	29	10	8	147.2	112	56	96	1	4	1	2	51	11	0	.216
1915	4	17	.190	5.20	32	20	7	178.1	183	118	69	1	0	4	0	55	8	1	.145
1916	0	2	.000	6.60	4	2	0	15	16	14	8	0	0	0	0	5	1	0	.200
1917 CIN N	0	0	—	6.00	2	1	0	9	15	5	2	0	0	0	0	5	1	0	.200
1918	8	5	.615	2.46	17	13	10	128	124	39	37	0	1	0	0	62	17	0	.274
1919	2	4	.333	3.46	13	4	1	41.2	37	8	13	0	2	1	0	165	34	2	.206
1920	2	0	1.000	1.77	10	2	1	20.1	24	2	4	1	1	0	0	30	8	0	.267
7 yrs.	26	31	.456	3.40	107	52	27	540	511	242	229	3	8	6	2	*			

Marshall Bridges

BRIDGES, MARSHALL (Sheriff)
B. June 2, 1931, Jackson, Miss.
BR TL 6'1"   165 lbs.
BB 1959-61

	W	L	PCT	ERA	G	GS	CG	IP	H	BB	SO	ShO	W	L	SV	AB	H	HR	BA
1959 STL N	6	3	.667	4.26	27	4	1	76	67	37	76	0	4	2	1	23	5	1	.217
1960 2 teams				STL N (20G 2-2)			CIN N	(14G 4-0)											
" total	6	2	.750	2.38	34	1	0	56.2	47	23	53	0	6	1	3	10	1	0	.100
1961 CIN N	0	1	.000	7.84	13	0	0	20.2	26	11	17	0	0	1	0	2	0	0	.000
1962 NY A	8	4	.667	3.14	52	0	0	71.2	49	48	66	0	8	4	18	14	0	0	.000
1963	2	0	1.000	3.82	23	0	0	33	27	30	35	0	2	0	1	0	0	0	—
1964 WAS A	0	3	.000	5.70	17	0	0	30	37	17	16	0	0	3	2	3	0	0	.000
1965	1	2	.333	2.67	40	0	0	57.1	62	25	39	0	1	2	0	7	1	0	.143
7 yrs.	23	15	.605	3.75	206	5	1	345.1	315	191	302	0	21	13	25	59	7	1	.119
2 yrs.	8	5	.615	4.02	47	5	1	107.1	100	53	103	0	6	3	2	29	5	1	.172

WORLD SERIES

	W	L	PCT	ERA	G	GS	CG	IP	H	BB	SO	ShO	W	L	SV	AB	H	HR	BA
1962 NY A	0	0	—	4.91	2	0	0	3.2	4	2	3	0	0	0	0	0	0	0	—

Nellie Briles

BRILES, NELSON KELLEY (Nellie)
B. Aug. 5, 1943, Dorris, Calif.
BR TR 5'11"   195 lbs.

	W	L	PCT	ERA	G	GS	CG	IP	H	BB	SO	ShO	W	L	SV	AB	H	HR	BA
1965 STL N	3	3	.500	3.50	37	2	0	82.1	79	26	52	0	2	2	4	15	2	0	.133
1966	4	15	.211	3.21	49	17	0	154	162	54	100	0	1	6	6	38	3	0	.079
1967	14	5	.737	2.43	49	14	4	155.1	139	40	94	2	4	3	6	40	6	0	.150
1968	19	11	.633	2.81	33	33	13	243.2	251	55	141	4	0	0	0	80	11	0	.138
1969	15	13	.536	3.51	36	33	10	228	218	63	126	3	0	0	0	76	8	1	.105
1970	6	7	.462	6.22	30	19	1	107	129	36	59	1	1	2	0	39	7	0	.179
1971 PIT N	8	4	.667	3.04	37	14	4	136	131	35	76	2	1	2	1	39	10	1	.256
1972	14	11	.560	3.08	28	27	9	195.2	185	43	120	2	1	0	0	70	11	0	.157
1973	14	13	.519	2.84	33	33	7	218.2	201	51	94	1	0	0	0	72	14	1	.194
1974 KC A	5	7	.417	4.02	18	17	3	103	118	21	41	0	0	0	0	0	0	0	—
1975	6	6	.500	4.26	24	16	3	112	127	25	73	0	1	0	2	0	0	0	—
1976 TEX A	11	9	.550	3.26	32	31	7	210	224	47	98	1	0	0	0	0	0	0	—
1977 2 teams				TEX A (30G 6-4)			BAL A	(2G 0-0)											
" total	6	4	.600	4.17	32	15	1	112.1	119	30	59	1	2	0	2	0	0	0	—
1978 BAL A	4	4	.500	4.64	16	8	1	54.1	58	21	30	0	3	0	0	0	0	0	—
14 yrs.	129	112	.535	3.43	454	279	64	2112.1	2141	547	1163	17	16	15	22	469	72	3	.154
6 yrs.	61	54	.530	3.41	234	118	28	970.1	978	274	572	10	8	13	16	288	37	1	.128

LEAGUE CHAMPIONSHIP SERIES

	W	L	PCT	ERA	G	GS	CG	IP	H	BB	SO	ShO	W	L	SV	AB	H	HR	BA
1972 PIT N	0	0	—	3.00	1	1	0	6	6	1	3	0	0	0	0	2	0	0	.000

WORLD SERIES

	W	L	PCT	ERA	G	GS	CG	IP	H	BB	SO	ShO	W	L	SV	AB	H	HR	BA
1967 STL N	1	0	1.000	1.64	2	1	1	11	7	1	4	0	0	0	0	0	0	0	.000

	W	L	PCT	ERA	G	GS	CG	IP	H	BB	SO	ShO	Relief Pitching W	L	SV	BATTING AB	H	HR	BA

Nellie Briles continued

	W	L	PCT	ERA	G	GS	CG	IP	H	BB	SO	ShO	W	L	SV	AB	H	HR	BA
1968	0	1	.000	5.56	2	2	0	11.1	13	4	7	0	0	0	0	4	0	0	.000
1971 PIT N	1	0	1.000	0.00	1	1	1	9	2	2	2	1	0	0	0	2	1	0	.500
3 yrs.	2	1	.667	2.59	5	4	2	31.1	22	7	13	1	0	0	0	9	1	0	.111

Ernie Broglio

BROGLIO, ERNEST GILBERT
B. Aug. 27, 1935, Berkeley, Calif.   BR TR 6'2"   200 lbs.

	W	L	PCT	ERA	G	GS	CG	IP	H	BB	SO	ShO	W	L	SV	AB	H	HR	BA
1959 STL N	7	12	.368	4.72	35	25	6	181.1	174	89	133	3	0	3	0	61	6	0	.098
1960	21	9	.700	2.74	52	24	9	226.1	172	100	188	3	7	2	0	68	14	0	.206
1961	9	12	.429	4.12	29	26	7	174.2	166	75	113	2	0	1	0	62	9	0	.145
1962	12	9	.571	3.00	34	30	11	222.1	193	93	132	4	1	1	0	72	10	0	.139
1963	18	8	.692	2.99	39	35	11	250	202	90	145	5	2	1	0	89	10	0	.112
1964 2 teams					STL	N	(11G 3–5)		CHI	N	(18G 4–7)								
" total	7	12	.368	3.82	29	27	6	169.2	176	56	82	1	0	0	1	56	12	0	.214
1965 CHI N	1	6	.143	6.93	26	6	0	50.2	63	46	22	0	1	3	0	4	0	0	.000
1966	2	6	.250	6.35	15	11	2	62.1	70	38	34	0	0	0	1	19	7	0	.368
8 yrs.	77	74	.510	3.74	259	184	52	1337.1	1216	587	849	18	11	11	2	431	68	0	.158
6 yrs.	70	55	.560	3.43	200	151	47	1124	972	473	747	18	10	8	0	373	51	0	.137
												9th							

Jim Brosnan

BROSNAN, JAMES PATRICK (Professor)
B. Oct. 24, 1929, Cincinnati, Ohio   BR TR 6'4"   197 lbs.

	W	L	PCT	ERA	G	GS	CG	IP	H	BB	SO	ShO	W	L	SV	AB	H	HR	BA
1954 CHI N	1	0	1.000	9.45	18	0	0	33.1	44	18	17	0	1	0	0	8	1	0	.125
1956	5	9	.357	3.79	30	10	1	95	95	45	51	1	3	4	1	22	4	0	.182
1957	5	5	.500	3.38	41	5	1	98.2	79	46	73	0	4	4	0	20	5	0	.250
1958 2 teams					CHI	N	(8G 3–4)		STL	N	(33G 8–4)								
" total	11	8	.579	3.35	41	20	4	166.2	148	79	89	0	4	1	7	50	5	0	.100
1959 2 teams					STL	N	(20G 1–3)		CIN	N	(26G 8–3)								
" total	9	6	.600	3.79	46	10	1	116.1	113	41	74	1	5	3	4	30	3	0	.100
1960 CIN N	7	2	.778	2.36	57	0	0	99	79	22	62	0	7	2	12	15	3	1	.200
1961	10	4	.714	3.04	53	0	0	80	77	18	40	0	10	4	16	13	2	0	.154
1962	4	4	.500	3.34	48	0	0	64.2	76	18	51	0	4	4	13	6	0	0	.000
1963 2 teams					CIN	N	(6G 0–1)		CHI	A	(45G 3–8)								
" total	3	9	.250	3.13	51	0	0	77.2	79	25	50	0	3	9	14	13	4	0	.308
9 yrs.	55	47	.539	3.54	385	47	7	831.1	790	312	507	2	41	31	67	177	27	1	.153
2 yrs.	9	7	.563	3.77	53	13	2	148	141	65	83	0	5	4	9	38	5	0	.132

WORLD SERIES

	W	L	PCT	ERA	G	GS	CG	IP	H	BB	SO	ShO	W	L	SV	AB	H	HR	BA
1961 CIN N	0	0	—	7.50	3	0	0	6	9	4	5	0	0	0	0	0	0	0	—

Buster Brown

BROWN, CHARLES EDWARD
B. Aug. 31, 1881, Boone, Iowa   D. Feb. 9, 1914, Sioux City, Iowa   BR TR

	W	L	PCT	ERA	G	GS	CG	IP	H	BB	SO	ShO	W	L	SV	AB	H	HR	BA
1905 STL N	8	11	.421	2.97	23	21	17	179	172	62	57	1	0	0	0	65	6	0	.092
1906	8	16	.333	2.64	32	27	21	238.1	208	112	109	0	0	1	0	85	14	1	.165
1907 2 teams					STL	N	(9G 1–6)		PHI	N	(21G 9–6)								
" total	10	12	.455	2.74	30	24	19	193.2	175	101	55	4	0	0	0	79	17	0	.215
1908 PHI N	0	0	—	2.74	5	0	0	7	9	5	3	0	0	0	0	5	1	0	.200
1909 2 teams					PHI	N	(7G 0–0)		BOS	N	(18G 4–11)								
" total	4	11	.267	3.16	25	18	8	148.1	130	72	42	2	0	0	0	57	7	0	.123
1910 BOS N	8	22	.267	2.67	46	29	16	263	251	94	88	1	2	4	2	81	16	1	.198
1911	7	18	.280	4.29	42	25	13	241	258	116	76	0	1	1	2	84	21	1	.250
1912	3	15	.167	4.01	31	21	13	168.1	146	66	68	1	0	1	0	61	13	0	.213
1913	0	0	—	4.73	2	0	0	13.1	19	3	3	0	0	0	0	5	0	0	.000
9 yrs.	48	105	.314	3.20	234	165	107	1452	1368	631	501	11	3	7	4	522	95	3	.182
3 yrs.	17	33	.340	2.86	64	56	44	481	437	219	183	3	0	1	0	176	27	1	.153

Three Finger Brown

BROWN, MORDECAI PETER CENTENNIAL (Miner)   BB TR 5'10"   175 lbs.
B. Oct. 19, 1876, Nyesville, Ind.   D. Feb. 14, 1948, Terre Haute, Ind.
Manager 1914.
Hall of Fame 1949.

	W	L	PCT	ERA	G	GS	CG	IP	H	BB	SO	ShO	W	L	SV	AB	H	HR	BA
1903 STL N	9	13	.409	2.60	26	24	19	201	231	59	83	1	0	0	0	77	15	0	.195
1904 CHI N	15	10	.600	1.86	26	23	21	212.1	155	50	81	4	2	0	1	89	19	0	.213
1905	18	12	.600	2.17	30	24	24	249	219	44	89	4	2	2	0	93	13	1	.140
1906	26	6	.813	1.04	36	32	27	277.1	198	61	144	9	1	0	3	98	20	0	.204
1907	20	6	.769	1.39	34	27	21	233	180	40	107	6	2	0	3	85	13	1	.153
1908	29	9	.763	1.47	44	31	27	312.1	214	49	123	9	4	1	5	121	25	0	.207
1909	27	9	.750	1.31	50	34	32	342.2	246	53	172	8	1	1	7	125	22	0	.176
1910	25	14	.641	1.86	46	31	27	295.1	256	64	143	8	2	3	7	103	18	0	.175
1911	21	11	.656	2.80	53	27	21	270	267	55	129	6	5	3	13	91	23	0	.253
1912	5	6	.455	2.64	15	8	5	88.2	92	20	34	2	2	3	0	31	9	0	.290
1913 CIN N	11	12	.478	2.91	39	16	11	173.1	174	44	41	1	4	3	6	54	11	0	.204
1914 2 teams					STL	F	(26G 12–6)		BKN	F	(9G 2–5)								
" total	14	11	.560	3.52	35	26	18	232.2	235	61	113	2	1	2	0	78	19	0	.244
1915 CHI F	17	8	.680	2.09	35	25	18	236.1	189	64	95	3	3	3	3	82	24	0	.293
1916 CHI N	2	3	.400	3.91	12	4	2	48.1	52	9	21	0	1	0	0	16	4	0	.250
14 yrs.	239	130	.648	2.06	481	332	273	3172.1	2708	673	1375	63	30	20	48	1143	235	2	.206
				3rd							6th								
1 yr.	9	13	.409	2.60	26	24	19	201	231	59	83	1	0	0	0	77	15	0	.195

WORLD SERIES

	W	L	PCT	ERA	G	GS	CG	IP	H	BB	SO	ShO	W	L	SV	AB	H	HR	BA
1906 CHI N	1	2	.333	3.66	3	3	2	19.2	14	4	12	1	0	0	0	6	2	0	.333
1907	1	0	1.000	0.00	1	1	1	9	7	1	4	1	0	0	0	3	0	0	.000
1908	2	0	1.000	0.00	2	1	1	11	6	1	5	1	1	0	0	4	0	0	.000
1910	1	2	.333	5.00	3	2	1	18	23	2	14	0	1	0	0	7	0	0	.000
4 yrs.	5	4	.556	2.81	9	7	5	57.2	50	13	35	3	2	0	0	20	2	0	.100
	8th	7th					10th						2nd	2nd					

	W	L	PCT	ERA	G	GS	CG	IP	H	BB	SO	ShO	Relief Pitching W	L	SV	BATTING AB	H	HR	BA

Tom Brown

BROWN, THOMAS T. BL TR 5'10" 168 lbs.
B. Sept. 21, 1860, Liverpool, England   D. Oct. 27, 1927, Washington, D. C.
Manager 1897-98.

	W	L	PCT	ERA	G	GS	CG	IP	H	BB	SO	ShO	W	L	SV	AB	H	HR	BA
1883 COL AA	0	1	.000	5.79	3	1	1	14	14	10	6	0	0	0	0	420	115	5	.274
1884	2	1	.667	7.11	4	0	0	19	27	7	5	0	2	1	0	451	123	5	.273
1885 PIT AA	0	0	–	3.00	2	0	0	6	0	3	2	0	0	0	0	437	134	4	.307
1886	0	0	–	9.00	1	0	0	2	2	5	1	0	0	0	0	460	131	1	.285
4 yrs.	2	2	.500	6.15	10	1	1	41	43	25	14	0	2	1	0	*			

Cal Browning

BROWNING, CALVIN DUANE BL TL 5'11" 190 lbs.
B. Mar. 16, 1938, Burns Flat, Okla.

	W	L	PCT	ERA	G	GS	CG	IP	H	BB	SO	ShO	W	L	SV	AB	H	HR	BA
1960 STL N	0	0	–	40.50	1	0	0	.2	5	1	0	0	0	0	0	0	0	0	–

Pete Browning

BROWNING, LOUIS ROGERS (The Gladiator) BR TR 6' 180 lbs.
B. July 17, 1858, Louisville, Ky.   D. Sept. 10, 1905, Louisville, Ky.

	W	L	PCT	ERA	G	GS	CG	IP	H	BB	SO	ShO	W	L	SV	AB	H	HR	BA
1884 LOU AA	0	1	.000	54.00	1	1	0	.1	2	2	0	0	0	0	0	*			

George Brunet

BRUNET, GEORGE STUART (Lefty) BR TL 6'1" 195 lbs.
B. June 8, 1935, Houghton, Mich.

	W	L	PCT	ERA	G	GS	CG	IP	H	BB	SO	ShO	W	L	SV	AB	H	HR	BA
1956 KC A	0	0	–	7.00	6	1	0	9	10	11	5	0	0	0	0	2	0	0	.000
1957	0	1	.000	5.56	4	2	0	11.1	13	4	3	0	0	0	0	2	0	0	.000
1959	0	0	–	11.57	2	0	0	4.2	10	7	7	0	0	0	0	0	0	0	–
1960 2 teams			KC	A	(3G 0–2)			MIL	N	(17G 2–0)									
" total	2	2	.500	4.95	20	8	0	60	65	32	43	0	1	0	0	14	1	0	.071
1961 MIL N	0	0	–	5.40	5	0	0	5	7	2	0	0	0	0	0	0	0	0	–
1962 HOU N	2	4	.333	4.50	17	11	2	54	62	21	36	0	0	0	0	17	1	0	.059
1963 2 teams			HOU	N	(5G 0–3)			BAL	A	(16G 0–1)									
" total	0	4	.000	6.06	21	2	0	32.2	49	15	24	0	0	2	1	4	0	0	.000
1964 LA A	2	2	.500	3.61	10	7	0	42.1	38	25	36	0	0	0	1	11	2	0	.182
1965 CAL A	9	11	.450	2.56	41	26	8	197	149	69	141	3	1	1	2	56	3	0	.054
1966	13	13	.500	3.31	41	32	8	212	183	106	148	2	1	2	0	68	7	1	.103
1967	11	19	.367	3.31	40	37	7	250	203	90	165	2	0	1	1	78	6	0	.077
1968	13	17	.433	2.86	39	36	8	245.1	191	68	132	5	0	1	0	74	6	0	.081
1969 2 teams			CAL	A	(23G 6–7)			SEA	A	(12G 2–5)									
" total	8	12	.400	4.44	35	30	4	164.1	168	67	93	2	0	0	0	47	4	1	.085
1970 2 teams			WAS	A	(24G 5–8)			PIT	N	(12G 1–1)									
" total	9	7	.563	4.20	36	21	2	135	143	57	84	1	2	2	0	42	6	1	.143
1971 STL N	0	1	.000	6.00	7	0	0	9	12	7	4	0	0	1	0	3	1	0	.333
15 yrs.	69	93	.426	3.62	324	213	39	1431.2	1303	581	921	15	5	10	4	418	37	3	.089
1 yr.	0	1	.000	6.00	7	0	0	9	12	7	4	0	0	1	0	3	1	0	.333

Tom Bruno

BRUNO, THOMAS MICHAEL BR TR 6'5" 210 lbs.
B. Jan. 26, 1953, Chicago, Ill.

	W	L	PCT	ERA	G	GS	CG	IP	H	BB	SO	ShO	W	L	SV	AB	H	HR	BA
1976 KC A	1	0	1.000	6.88	12	0	0	17	20	9	11	0	1	0	0	0	0	0	–
1977 TOR A	0	1	.000	8.00	12	0	0	18	30	13	9	0	0	1	0	0	0	0	–
1978 STL N	4	3	.571	1.98	18	3	0	50	38	17	33	0	3	2	1	12	1	0	.083
1979	2	3	.400	4.26	27	1	0	38	37	22	27	0	2	2	0	5	1	0	.200
4 yrs.	7	7	.500	4.24	69	4	0	123	125	61	80	0	6	5	1	17	2	0	.118
2 yrs.	6	6	.500	2.97	45	4	0	88	75	39	60	0	5	4	1	17	2	0	.118

Ron Bryant

BRYANT, RONALD RAYMOND (Bear) BB TL 6' 190 lbs.
B. Nov. 12, 1947, Redlands, Calif.

	W	L	PCT	ERA	G	GS	CG	IP	H	BB	SO	ShO	W	L	SV	AB	H	HR	BA
1967 SF N	0	0	–	4.50	1	0	0	4	3	0	2	0	0	0	0	1	0	0	.000
1969	4	3	.571	4.34	16	8	0	58	60	25	30	0	0	0	1	16	3	0	.188
1970	5	8	.385	4.78	34	11	1	96	103	38	66	0	3	2	0	27	3	0	.111
1971	7	10	.412	3.79	27	22	3	140	146	49	79	2	1	0	0	50	10	0	.200
1972	14	7	.667	2.90	35	28	11	214	176	77	107	4	0	1	0	70	12	0	.171
1973	24	12	.667	3.54	41	39	8	269.2	240	115	143	0	1	0	0	95	16	0	.168
1974	3	15	.167	5.60	41	23	0	127	142	68	75	0	0	0	0	31	4	0	.129
1975 STL N	0	1	.000	16.00	10	1	0	9	20	7	7	0	0	0	0	0	0	0	.000
8 yrs.	57	56	.504	4.02	205	132	23	917.2	890	379	509	6	5	3	1	291	48	0	.165
1 yr.	0	1	.000	16.00	10	1	0	9	20	7	7	0	0	0	0	0	0	0	.000

LEAGUE CHAMPIONSHIP SERIES

	W	L	PCT	ERA	G	GS	CG	IP	H	BB	SO	ShO	W	L	SV	AB	H	HR	BA
1971 SF N	0	0	–	4.50	1	0	0	2	1	1	2	0	0	0	0	0	0	0	–

Lew Burdette

BURDETTE, SELVA LEWIS BR TR 6'2" 180 lbs.
B. Nov. 22, 1926, Nitro, W. Va.

	W	L	PCT	ERA	G	GS	CG	IP	H	BB	SO	ShO	W	L	SV	AB	H	HR	BA
1950 NY A	0	0	–	6.75	2	0	0	1.1	3	0	0	0	0	0	0	0	0	0	–
1951 BOS N	0	0	–	6.23	3	0	0	4.1	6	5	1	0	0	0	0	1	0	0	.000
1952	6	11	.353	3.61	45	9	5	137	138	47	47	0	2	8	7	35	4	0	.114
1953 MIL N	15	5	.750	3.24	46	13	6	175	177	56	58	1	8	0	8	53	9	0	.170
1954	15	14	.517	2.76	38	32	13	238	224	62	79	4	1	1	0	81	7	0	.089
1955	13	8	.619	4.03	42	33	11	230	253	73	70	2	2	1	0	86	20	0	.233
1956	19	10	.655	2.70	39	35	16	256.1	234	52	110	6	0	0	1	86	16	0	.186
1957	17	9	.654	3.72	37	33	14	256.2	260	59	78	1	2	0	0	88	13	2	.148
1958	20	10	.667	2.91	40	36	19	275.1	279	50	113	3	2	0	0	99	24	3	.242
1959	21	15	.583	4.07	41	39	20	289.2	312	38	105	4	0	0	1	104	21	0	.202
1960	19	13	.594	3.36	45	32	18	275.2	277	35	83	4	3	2	4	91	16	2	.176
1961	18	11	.621	4.00	40	36	14	272.1	295	33	92	3	2	0	0	103	21	3	.204
1962	10	9	.526	4.89	37	19	6	143.2	172	23	59	0	3	1	2	51	9	0	.176
1963 2 teams			MIL	N	(15G 6–5)			STL	N	(21G 3–8)									
" total	9	13	.409	3.70	36	27	7	182.2	177	40	73	1	1	2	2	57	4	0	.070

	W	L	PCT	ERA	G	GS	CG	IP	H	BB	SO	ShO	Relief Pitching W	L	SV	BATTING AB	H	HR	BA

Lew Burdette continued

	W	L	PCT	ERA	G	GS	CG	IP	H	BB	SO	ShO	W	L	SV	AB	H	HR	BA
1964 2 teams			STL	N	(8G 1–0)	CHI	N	(28G 9–9)											
" total	10	9	.526	4.66	36	17	8	141	162	22	43	2	2	1	0	44	12	2	.273
1965 2 teams			CHI	N	(7G 0–2)	PHI	N	(19G 3–3)											
" total	3	5	.375	5.44	26	12	1	91	121	21	28	1	0	0	0	26	8	0	.308
1966 CAL A	7	2	.778	3.39	54	0	0	79.2	80	12	27	0	7	2	5	8	1	0	.125
1967	1	0	1.000	4.91	19	0	0	18.1	16	0	8	0	1	0	1	0	0	0	—
18 yrs.	203	144	.585	3.66	626	373	158	3068	3186	628	1074	33	36	19	31	1011	185	12	.183
2 yrs.	4	8	.333	3.57	29	14	3	108.1	116	19	48	0	1	1	2	32	3	0	.094
WORLD SERIES																			
1957 MIL N	3	0	1.000	0.67	3	3	3	27	21	4	13	2	0	0	0	8	0	0	.000
1958	1	2	.333	5.64	3	3	1	22.1	22	4	12	0	0	0	0	9	1	1	.111
2 yrs.	4	2	.667	2.92	6	6	4	49.1	43	8	25	2	0	0	0	17	1	1	.059
												4th							

Sandy Burk

BURK, CHARLES SANFORD
B. Apr. 22, 1887, Columbus, Ohio D. Oct. 11, 1934, Brooklyn, N. Y. BR TR

	W	L	PCT	ERA	G	GS	CG	IP	H	BB	SO	ShO	W	L	SV	AB	H	HR	BA
1910 BKN N	0	3	.000	6.05	4	3	1	19.1	17	27	14	0	0	0	0	5	0	0	.000
1911	1	3	.250	5.12	13	7	1	58	54	47	15	0	0	0	0	19	2	0	.105
1912 2 teams			BKN	N	(2G 0–0)	STL	N	(12G 1–3)											
" total	1	3	.250	2.55	14	4	2	53	46	15	19	0	0	1	1	15	1	0	.067
1913 STL N	1	2	.333	5.14	19	4	0	70	81	33	29	0	0	2	1	22	2	0	.091
1915 PIT F	2	0	1.000	1.00	2	2	1	18	8	11	9	0	0	0	0	6	1	0	.167
5 yrs.	5	11	.313	4.25	52	20	5	218.1	206	133	86	0	0	3	2	67	6	0	.090
2 yrs.	2	5	.286	4.08	31	8	2	114.2	118	45	46	0	0	3	2	33	2	0	.061

John Burke

BURKE, JOHN PATRICK
B. Jan. 27, 1877, Hazleton, Pa. D. Aug. 4, 1950, Jersey City, N. J.

	W	L	PCT	ERA	G	GS	CG	IP	H	BB	SO	ShO	W	L	SV	AB	H	HR	BA
1902 NY N	0	1	.000	5.79	2	1	1	14	21	3	3	0	0	0	0	*			

Jesse Burkett

BURKETT, JESSE CAIL (The Crab)
B. Dec. 4, 1868, Wheeling, W. Va. D. May 27, 1953, Worcester, Mass. BL TL 5'8" 155 lbs.
Hall of Fame 1946.

	W	L	PCT	ERA	G	GS	CG	IP	H	BB	SO	ShO	W	L	SV	AB	H	HR	BA
1890 NY N	3	10	.231	5.57	21	12	6	118	134	92	82	0	2	0	0	401	124	4	.309
1894 CLE N	0	0	—	4.50	1	0	0	4	6	1	0	0	0	0	0	523	187	8	.358
1902 STL A	0	1	.000	9.00	1	0	0	1	4	1	2	0	0	1	0	553	169	5	.306
3 yrs.	3	11	.214	5.56	23	12	6	123	144	94	84	0	2	1	0	*			

Ken Burkhart

BURKHART, KENNETH WILLIAM
Born Kenneth William Burkhardt.
B. Nov. 18, 1916, Knoxville, Tenn. BR TR 6'1" 190 lbs.

	W	L	PCT	ERA	G	GS	CG	IP	H	BB	SO	ShO	W	L	SV	AB	H	HR	BA
1945 STL N	19	8	.704	2.90	42	22	12	217.1	206	66	67	4	6	1	2	72	13	0	.181
1946	6	3	.667	2.88	25	13	5	100	111	36	32	2	1	1	2	34	5	0	.147
1947	3	6	.333	5.21	34	6	1	95	108	23	44	0	1	3	1	24	3	0	.125
1948 2 teams			STL	N	(20G 0–0)	CIN	N	(16G 0–3)											
" total	0	3	.000	6.27	36	0	0	79	92	30	30	0	0	3	1	13	4	1	.308
1949 CIN N	0	0	—	3.18	11	0	0	28.1	29	10	8	0	0	1	1	7	2	0	.286
5 yrs.	28	20	.583	3.84	148	41	18	519.2	546	165	181	6	8	8	7	150	27	1	.180
4 yrs.	28	17	.622	3.60	121	41	18	449.2	475	139	159	6	8	5	6	134	22	0	.164

Farmer Burns

BURNS, JAMES
B. Ashtabula, Ohio TR

	W	L	PCT	ERA	G	GS	CG	IP	H	BB	SO	ShO	W	L	SV	AB	H	HR	BA
1901 STL N	0	0	—	9.00	1	0	0	2	1	0	0	0	0	0	0	0	0	0	—

Guy Bush

BUSH, GUY TERRELL (The Mississippi Mudcat)
B. Aug. 23, 1901, Aberdeen, Miss. BR TR 6' 175 lbs.

	W	L	PCT	ERA	G	GS	CG	IP	H	BB	SO	ShO	W	L	SV	AB	H	HR	BA
1923 CHI N	0	0	—	0.00	1	0	0	1	1	0	2	0	0	0	0	0	0	0	—
1924	2	5	.286	4.02	16	8	4	80.2	91	24	36	0	0	1	0	26	4	0	.154
1925	6	13	.316	4.30	42	15	5	182	213	52	76	0	4	2	4	57	11	0	.193
1926	13	9	.591	2.86	35	16	7	157.1	149	42	32	2	6	2	2	48	8	0	.167
1927	10	10	.500	3.03	36	22	9	193.1	177	79	62	1	3	0	0	65	8	0	.123
1928	15	6	.714	3.83	42	24	9	204.1	229	86	61	2	4	0	2	73	6	0	.082
1929	18	7	.720	3.66	50	29	18	270.2	277	107	82	2	2	1	8	91	15	0	.165
1930	15	10	.600	6.20	46	25	11	225	291	86	75	0	3	2	3	78	22	0	.282
1931	16	8	.667	4.49	39	24	14	180.1	190	66	54	1	4	0	2	57	7	0	.123
1932	19	11	.633	3.21	40	30	15	238.2	262	70	73	1	4	2	0	84	15	0	.179
1933	20	12	.625	2.75	41	32	20	258.1	261	68	84	4	1	1	2	88	11	0	.125
1934	18	10	.643	3.83	40	27	15	209.1	213	54	75	1	3	1	2	70	16	0	.229
1935 PIT N	11	11	.500	4.32	41	25	8	204.1	237	40	42	1	5	1	2	63	8	0	.127
1936 2 teams			PIT	N	(16G 1–3)	BOS	N	(15G 4–5)											
" total	5	8	.385	4.10	31	11	5	125	147	31	38	0	2	3	2	34	6	0	.176
1937 BOS N	8	15	.348	3.54	32	20	11	180.2	201	48	56	1	2	3	1	54	6	0	.111
1938 STL N	0	1	.000	5.06	6	0	0	5.1	6	3	1	0	1	1	0	0	0	0	—
1945 CIN N	0	0	—	8.31	4	0	0	4.1	5	3	1	0	0	0	0	0	0	0	—
17 yrs.	176	136	.564	3.86	542	308	151	2721	2950	859	850	16	43	20	34	888	143	0	.161
1 yr.	0	1	.000	5.06	6	0	0	5.1	6	3	1	0	1	1	0	0	0	0	—
WORLD SERIES																			
1929 CHI N	1	0	1.000	0.82	2	1	1	11	12	2	4	0	0	0	0	3	0	0	.000
1932	0	1	.000	14.29	2	2	0	5.2	5	6	2	0	0	0	0	1	0	0	.000
2 yrs.	1	1	.500	5.40	4	3	1	16.2	17	8	6	0	0	0	0	4	0	0	.000

	W	L	PCT	ERA	G	GS	CG	IP	H	BB	SO	ShO	Relief Pitching W	L	SV	BATTING AB	H	HR	BA

Bud Byerly

BYERLY, ELDRED WILLIAM   BR TR 6'2½" 185 lbs.
B. Oct. 26, 1920, Webster Groves, Mo.

	W	L	PCT	ERA	G	GS	CG	IP	H	BB	SO	ShO	W	L	SV	AB	H	HR	BA
1943 STL N	1	0	1.000	3.46	2	2	0	13	14	5	6	0	0	0	0	3	0	0	.000
1944	2	2	.500	3.40	9	4	2	42.1	37	20	13	0	1	0	0	12	2	0	.167
1945	4	5	.444	4.74	33	8	2	95	111	41	39	0	2	1	0	23	5	0	.217
1950 CIN N	0	1	.000	2.45	4	1	0	14.2	12	4	5	0	0	0	0	3	0	0	.000
1951	2	1	.667	3.27	40	0	0	66	69	25	28	0	2	1	0	6	0	0	.000
1952	0	1	.000	5.11	12	2	0	24.2	29	7	14	0	0	0	1	5	1	0	.200
1956 WAS A	2	4	.333	2.96	25	0	0	51.2	45	14	19	0	2	4	4	11	1	0	.091
1957	6	6	.500	3.13	47	0	0	95	94	22	39	0	6	6	6	15	1	0	.067
1958 2 teams		WAS	A	(17G 2–0)	BOS	A	(18G 1–2)												
" total	3	2	.600	3.98	35	0	0	54.1	65	18	29	0	3	2	1	6	0	0	.000
1959 SF N	1	0	1.000	1.38	11	0	0	13	11	5	4	0	1	0	0	0	0	0	—
1960	1	0	1.000	5.32	19	0	0	22	32	6	13	0	1	0	2	1	0	0	.000
11 yrs.	22	22	.500	3.70	237	17	4	491.2	519	167	209	0	18	14	14	85	10	0	.118
3 yrs.	7	7	.500	4.25	44	14	4	150.1	162	66	58	0	3	1	0	38	7	0	.184
WORLD SERIES																			
1944 STL N	0	0	—	0.00	1	0	0	1.1	0	0	1	0	0	0	0	0	0	0	—

Jim Callahan

CALLAHAN, JAMES W.
B. Moberly, Mo.   Deceased.

	W	L	PCT	ERA	G	GS	CG	IP	H	BB	SO	ShO	W	L	SV	AB	H	HR	BA
1898 STL N	0	2	.000	16.20	2	2	1	8.1	18	7	2	0	0	0	0	4	0	0	.000

Harry Camnitz

CAMNITZ, HENRY RICHARDSON   BR TR 6'1" 168 lbs.
Brother of Howie Camnitz.
B. Oct. 26, 1884, McKinney, Ky.   D. Jan. 6, 1951, Louisville, Ky.

	W	L	PCT	ERA	G	GS	CG	IP	H	BB	SO	ShO	W	L	SV	AB	H	HR	BA
1909 PIT N	0	0	—	4.50	1	0	0	4	6	1	1	0	0	0	0	2	0	0	.000
1911 STL N	1	0	1.000	0.00	2	0	0	2	0	1	2	0	1	0	0	0	0	0	—
2 yrs.	1	0	1.000	3.00	3	0	0	6	6	2	3	0	1	0	0	2	0	0	.000
1 yr.	1	0	1.000	0.00	2	0	0	2	0	1	2	0	1	0	0	0	0	0	—

Billy Campbell

CAMPBELL, WILLIAM JAMES   BL TL 5'10" 165 lbs.
B. Nov. 4, 1873, Pittsburgh, Pa.   D. Oct. 7, 1957, Cincinnati, Ohio

	W	L	PCT	ERA	G	GS	CG	IP	H	BB	SO	ShO	W	L	SV	AB	H	HR	BA
1905 STL N	1	1	.500	7.41	2	2	2	17	27	7	2	0	0	0	0	7	1	0	.143
1907 CIN N	3	0	1.000	2.14	3	3	3	21	19	3	4	0	0	0	0	8	2	0	.250
1908	13	13	.500	2.60	35	24	19	212.1	203	44	73	2	3	1	1	72	6	0	.083
1909	7	9	.438	2.67	30	15	7	148.1	162	39	37	0	1	4	2	43	6	0	.140
4 yrs.	24	23	.511	2.80	70	44	31	407.2	411	93	116	2	4	5	3	130	15	0	.115
1 yr.	1	1	.500	7.41	2	2	2	17	27	7	2	0	0	0	0	7	1	0	.143

Sal Campisi

CAMPISI, SAL JOHN   BR TR 6'2" 210 lbs.
B. Aug. 11, 1942, Brooklyn, N. Y.

	W	L	PCT	ERA	G	GS	CG	IP	H	BB	SO	ShO	W	L	SV	AB	H	HR	BA
1969 STL N	1	0	1.000	0.90	7	0	0	10	4	6	7	0	1	0	0	0	0	0	—
1970	2	2	.500	2.94	37	0	0	49	53	37	26	0	2	2	4	1	0	0	.000
1971 MIN A	0	0	—	4.50	6	0	0	4	5	4	2	0	0	0	0	0	0	0	—
3 yrs.	3	2	.600	2.71	50	0	0	63	62	47	35	0	3	2	4	1	0	0	.000
2 yrs.	3	2	.600	2.59	44	0	0	59	57	43	33	0	3	2	4	1	0	0	.000

Doug Capilla

CAPILLA, DOUGLAS EDMUND   BL TL 5'11" 160 lbs.
B. Jan. 7, 1952, Honolulu, Hawaii

	W	L	PCT	ERA	G	GS	CG	IP	H	BB	SO	ShO	W	L	SV	AB	H	HR	BA
1976 STL N	1	0	1.000	5.40	7	0	0	8.1	8	4	5	0	1	0	0	0	0	0	—
1977 2 teams		STL	N	(2G 0–0)	CIN	N	(22G 7–8)												
" total	7	8	.467	4.47	24	16	1	108.2	96	61	75	0	0	0	0	34	2	0	.059
1978 CIN N	0	1	.000	9.82	6	3	0	11	14	11	9	0	0	0	0	2	0	0	.000
1979 2 teams		CIN	N	(5G 1–0)	CHI	N	(13G 0–1)												
" total	1	1	.500	4.18	18	1	0	23.2	21	12	10	0	1	0	0	1	1	0	1.000
1980 CHI N	2	8	.200	4.10	39	11	0	90	82	51	51	0	1	0	0	21	4	0	.190
1981	1	0	1.000	3.18	42	0	0	51	52	34	28	0	1	0	0	3	0	0	.000
6 yrs.	12	18	.400	4.34	136	31	1	292.2	273	173	178	0	4	0	0	61	7	0	.115
2 yrs.	1	0	1.000	7.59	9	0	0	10.2	10	6	6	0	1	0	0	0	0	0	—

Tex Carleton

CARLETON, JAMES OTTO   BB TR 6'1½" 180 lbs.
B. Aug. 19, 1906, Comanche, Tex.   BR 1933-34
D. Jan. 11, 1977, Fort Worth, Tex.

	W	L	PCT	ERA	G	GS	CG	IP	H	BB	SO	ShO	W	L	SV	AB	H	HR	BA
1932 STL N	10	13	.435	4.08	44	22	9	196.1	198	70	113	3	3	2	0	60	9	1	.150
1933	17	11	.607	3.38	44	33	15	277	263	97	147	4	1	1	3	91	17	1	.187
1934	16	11	.593	4.26	40	31	16	240.2	260	52	103	0	0	1	2	88	17	1	.193
1935 CHI N	11	8	.579	3.89	31	22	8	171	169	60	84	0	2	2	1	62	8	0	.129
1936	14	10	.583	3.65	35	26	12	197.1	204	67	88	4	2	1	1	60	14	3	.233
1937	16	8	.667	3.15	32	27	18	208.1	183	94	105	4	0	1	0	71	12	0	.169
1938	10	9	.526	5.42	33	24	9	167.2	213	74	80	0	2	1	0	65	15	0	.231
1940 BKN N	6	6	.500	3.81	34	17	4	149	140	47	88	1	2	1	2	43	8	0	.186
8 yrs.	100	76	.568	3.91	293	202	91	1607.1	1630	561	808	16	12	10	9	540	100	6	.185
3 yrs.	43	35	.551	3.87	128	86	40	714	721	219	363	7	4	4	5	239	43	3	.180
WORLD SERIES																			
1934 STL N	0	0	—	7.36	2	1	0	3.2	5	2	2	0	0	0	0	1	0	0	.000
1935 CHI N	0	1	.000	1.29	1	1	0	7	6	7	4	0	0	0	0	1	0	0	.000
1938	0	0	—	∞	1	0	0		1	2	0	0	0	0	0	0	0	0	—
3 yrs.	0	1	.000	5.06	4	2	0	10.2	12	11	6	0	0	0	0	2	0	0	.000

	W	L	PCT	ERA	G	GS	CG	IP	H	BB	SO	ShO	Relief Pitching W	L	SV	BATTING AB	H	HR	BA

Steve Carlton

CARLTON, STEPHEN NORMAN (Lefty)
B. Dec. 22, 1944, Miami, Fla.   BL TL 6'4"   210 lbs.

Year Team	W	L	PCT	ERA	G	GS	CG	IP	H	BB	SO	ShO	W	L	SV	AB	H	HR	BA
1965 STL N	0	0	–	2.52	15	2	0	25	27	8	21	0	0	0	0	2	0	0	.000
1966	3	3	.500	3.12	9	9	2	52	56	18	25	1	0	0	0	15	4	0	.267
1967	14	9	.609	2.98	30	28	11	193	173	62	168	2	0	1	1	72	11	0	.153
1968	13	11	.542	2.99	34	33	10	232	214	61	162	5	0	1	0	73	12	2	.164
1969	17	11	.607	2.17	31	31	12	236	185	93	210	2	0	0	0	80	17	1	.213
1970	10	19	.345	3.72	34	33	13	254	239	109	193	2	0	0	0	80	16	0	.200
1971	20	9	.690	3.56	37	36	18	273	275	98	172	4	0	0	0	96	17	0	.177
1972 PHI N	27	10	.730	1.97	41	41	30	346.1	257	87	310	8	0	0	0	117	23	1	.197
1973	13	20	.394	3.90	40	40	18	293.1	293	113	223	3	0	0	0	100	16	2	.160
1974	16	13	.552	3.22	39	39	17	291	249	136	240	1	0	0	0	102	25	0	.245
1975	15	14	.517	3.56	37	37	14	255	217	104	192	3	0	0	0	90	14	0	.156
1976	20	7	.741	3.13	35	35	13	252.2	224	72	195	2	0	0	0	92	20	0	.217
1977	23	10	.697	2.64	36	36	17	283	229	89	198	2	0	0	0	97	26	3	.268
1978	16	13	.552	2.84	34	34	12	247	228	63	161	3	0	0	0	86	25	0	.291
1979	18	11	.621	3.62	35	35	13	251	202	89	213	4	0	0	0	94	21	0	.223
1980	24	9	.727	2.34	38	38	13	304	243	90	286	3	0	0	0	101	19	0	.188
1981	13	4	.765	2.42	24	24	10	190	152	62	179	1	0	0	0	67	9	0	.134
1982	23	11	.676	3.10	38	38	19	295.2	253	86	286	6	0	0	0	101	22	2	.218
18 yrs.	285	184	.608	3.00	587	569	242	4274	3716	1440 9th	3434 4th	52	0	2	1	1465	297	11	.203
7 yrs.	77	62	.554	3.10	190	172	66	1265	1169	449	951 4th	16	0	2	1	418	77	3	.184

DIVISIONAL PLAYOFF SERIES
| 1981 PHI N | 0 | 2 | .000 | 3.86 | 2 | 2 | 0 | 14 | 14 | 8 | 13 | 0 | 0 | 0 | 0 | 4 | 1 | 0 | .250 |

LEAGUE CHAMPIONSHIP SERIES
1976 PHI N	0	1	.000	5.14	1	1	0	7	8	5	6	0	0	0	0	2	0	0	.000
1977	0	1	.000	6.94	2	2	0	11.2	13	8	6	0	0	0	0	4	2	0	.500
1978	1	0	1.000	4.00	1	1	1	9	8	2	8	0	0	0	0	4	2	1	.500
1980	1	0	1.000	2.19	2	2	0	12.1	11	8	6	0	0	0	0	4	0	0	.000
4 yrs.	2	2	.500	4.50	6	6	1	40	40	23	26	0	0	0	0	14	4	1	.286

WORLD SERIES
1967 STL N	0	1	.000	0.00	1	1	0	6	3	2	5	0	0	0	0	1	0	0	.000
1968	0	0	–	6.75	2	0	0	4	7	1	3	0	0	0	0	0	0	0	–
1980 PHI N	2	0	1.000	2.40	2	2	0	15	14	9	17	0	0	0	0	0	0	0	–
3 yrs.	2	1	.667	2.52	5	3	0	25	24	12	25	0	0	0	0	1	0	0	.000

Clay Carroll

CARROLL, CLAY PALMER (Hawk)
B. May 2, 1941, Clanton, Ala.   BR TR 6'1"   178 lbs.

Year Team	W	L	PCT	ERA	G	GS	CG	IP	H	BB	SO	ShO	W	L	SV	AB	H	HR	BA
1964 MIL N	2	0	1.000	1.77	11	1	0	20.1	15	3	17	0	2	0	1	2	0	0	.000
1965	0	1	.000	4.41	19	1	0	34.2	35	13	16	0	0	1	1	5	0	0	.000
1966 ATL N	8	7	.533	2.37	73	3	0	144.1	127	29	67	0	8	7	11	30	3	0	.100
1967	6	12	.333	5.52	42	7	1	93	111	29	35	0	3	8	0	16	1	0	.063
1968 2 teams			ATL N (10G 0–1)				CIN N	(58G 7–7)											
" total	7	8	.467	2.69	68	1	0	144	128	38	71	0	7	8	17	29	6	0	.207
1969 CIN N	12	6	.667	3.52	71	4	0	151	149	78	90	0	11	6	7	29	6	1	.207
1970	9	4	.692	2.60	65	0	0	104	104	27	63	0	9	4	16	14	1	0	.071
1971	10	4	.714	2.49	61	0	0	94	78	42	64	0	10	4	15	10	1	0	.100
1972	6	4	.600	2.25	65	0	0	96	89	32	51	0	6	4	37	11	2	0	.182
1973	8	8	.500	3.69	53	5	0	92.2	111	34	41	0	6	8	14	14	3	0	.214
1974	12	5	.706	2.14	57	3	0	101	96	30	46	0	10	4	6	18	3	0	.167
1975	7	5	.583	2.63	56	2	0	96	93	32	44	0	7	5	7	19	0	0	.000
1976 CHI A	4	4	.500	2.57	29	0	0	77	67	24	38	0	4	4	6	0	0	0	–
1977 2 teams			CHI A (8G 1–3)				STL N	(51G 4–2)											
" total	5	5	.500	2.76	59	1	0	101	91	28	38	0	5	5	5	11	1	0	.091
1978 PIT N	0	0	–	2.25	2	0	0	4	2	3	0	0	0	0	0	0	0	0	–
15 yrs.	96	73	.568	2.94	731	28	1	1353	1296	442	681 8th	0	88	68	143	208	27	1	.130
1 yr.	4	2	.667	2.50	51	1	0	90	77	24	34	0	4	2	4	11	1	0	.091

LEAGUE CHAMPIONSHIP SERIES
1970 CIN N	0	0	–	0.00	2	0	0	1.1	2	0	2	0	0	0	1	0	0	0	–
1972	1	1	.500	3.38	2	0	0	2.2	2	3	0	0	1	1	0	0	0	0	–
1973	1	0	1.000	1.29	3	0	0	7	5	1	2	0	1	0	0	0	0	0	–
1975	0	0	–	0.00	1	0	0	1	1	1	0	0	0	0	1	0	0	0	–
4 yrs.	2	1	.667	1.50	8	0	0	12	9	5	4	0	2	1	1	0	0	0	–

WORLD SERIES
1970 CIN N	1	0	1.000	0.00	4	0	0	9	5	2	11	0	1	0	0	1	0	0	.000
1972	0	1	.000	1.59	5	0	0	5.2	6	4	3	0	0	1	1	0	0	0	–
1975	1	0	1.000	3.18	5	0	0	5.2	4	2	3	0	1	0	0	0	0	0	–
3 yrs.	2	1	.667	1.33	14 5th	0	0	20.1	15	8	17	0	2 2nd	1	1	1	0	0	.000

Kid Carsey

CARSEY, WILFRED
B. Oct. 22, 1870, New York, N. Y.   Deceased.   BR TR 5'7"   168 lbs.

Year Team	W	L	PCT	ERA	G	GS	CG	IP	H	BB	SO	ShO	W	L	SV	AB	H	HR	BA
1891 WAS AA	14	37	.275	4.99	54	53	46	415	513	161	174	1	1	0	0	187	28	0	.150
1892 PHI N	19	16	.543	3.12	43	36	30	317.2	320	104	76	1	2	0	1	131	20	1	.153
1893	20	15	.571	4.81	39	35	30	318.1	375	124	50	1	1	2	0	145	27	0	.186
1894	18	12	.600	5.56	35	31	26	277	349	102	41	0	0	1	0	125	34	0	.272
1895	24	16	.600	4.92	44	40	35	342.1	460	118	64	0	1	1	1	141	41	0	.291
1896	11	11	.500	5.62	27	21	18	187.1	273	72	36	1	1	2	0	81	18	0	.222
1897 2 teams			PHI N (4G 2–1)				STL N	(12G 3–8)											
" total	5	9	.357	5.81	16	15	13	127	168	47	15	0	0	0	0	56	16	0	.286
1898 STL N	2	12	.143	6.33	20	13	10	123.2	177	37	10	0	0	0	0	105	21	1	.200

	W	L	PCT	ERA	G	GS	CG	IP	H	BB	SO	ShO	Relief Pitching W	L	SV	BATTING AB	H	HR	BA

Kid Carsey continued

		W	L	PCT	ERA	G	GS	CG	IP	H	BB	SO	ShO	W	L	SV	AB	H	HR	BA
1899 2 teams	CLE N (10G 1-8)					WAS	N	(4G 1-2)												
" total		2	10	.167	5.15	14	12	10	106.2	136	28	14	0	1	0	0	65	16	0	.246
1901 BKN N		1	0	1.000	10.29	2	0	0	7	9	3	4	0	1	0	0	2	0	0	.000
10 yrs.		116	138	.457	4.95	294	256	218	2222	2780	796	484	4	9	5	3	148	34	1	.230
2 yrs.		5	20	.200	6.18	32	24	21	222.2	310	68	24	0	0	1	0				

Bob Caruthers

CARUTHERS, ROBERT LEE (Parisian Bob)   BL TR 5'7"   138 lbs.
B. Jan. 5, 1864, Memphis, Tenn.   D. Aug. 5, 1911, Peoria, Ill.

		W	L	PCT	ERA	G	GS	CG	IP	H	BB	SO	ShO	W	L	SV	AB	H	HR	BA
1884 STL AA		7	2	.778	2.61	13	7	7	82.2	61	15	58	0	3	0	0	82	21	2	.256
1885		40	13	.755	2.07	53	53	53	482.1	430	57	190	6	0	0	0	222	50	1	.225
1886		30	14	.682	2.32	44	43	42	387.1	323	86	166	2	1	0	0	317	106	4	.334
1887		29	9	.763	3.30	39	39	39	341	337	61	74	2	0	0	0	364	130	8	.357
1888 BKN AA		29	15	.659	2.39	44	43	42	391.2	337	53	140	4	1	0	0	335	77	5	.230
1889		40	11	.784	3.13	56	50	46	445	444	104	118	7	4	0	1	172	43	2	.250
1890 BKN N		23	11	.676	3.09	37	33	30	300	292	87	64	2	1	0	0	238	63	1	.265
1891		18	14	.563	3.12	38	32	29	297	323	107	69	2	1	0	1	171	48	2	.281
1892 STL N		2	8	.200	5.84	16	10	10	101.2	131	27	21	0	0	2	1	513	142	3	.277
9 yrs.		218	97	.692 1st	2.83	340	310	298	2828.2	2678	597	900	25	11	2	3	*			
1 yr.		2	8	.200	5.84	16	10	10	101.2	131	27	21	0	0	2	1	513	142	3	.277

Ted Cather

CATHER, THEODORE P   BR TR 5'10½" 178 lbs.
B. May 20, 1889, Chester, Pa.   D. Apr. 9, 1945, Charlestown, Md.

		W	L	PCT	ERA	G	GS	CG	IP	H	BB	SO	ShO	W	L	SV	AB	H	HR	BA
1913 STL N		0	0	—	54.00	1	0	0	.1	1	2	0	0	0	0	0	*			

Bill Chambers

CHAMBERS, WILLIAM CHRISTOPHER   BR TR 5'9"   185 lbs.
B. Sept. 13, 1889, Cameron, W. Va.   D. Mar. 27, 1962, Fort Wayne, Ind.

		W	L	PCT	ERA	G	GS	CG	IP	H	BB	SO	ShO	W	L	SV	AB	H	HR	BA
1910 STL N		0	0	—	0.00	1	0	0	1	0	1	0	0	0	0	0	0	0	0	—

Cliff Chambers

CHAMBERS, CLIFFORD DAY (Lefty)   BL TL 6'3"   208 lbs.
B. Jan. 10, 1922, Portland, Ore.

		W	L	PCT	ERA	G	GS	CG	IP	H	BB	SO	ShO	W	L	SV	AB	H	HR	BA
1948 CHI N		2	9	.182	4.43	29	12	3	103.2	100	48	51	1	0	2	0	30	4	0	.133
1949 PIT N		13	7	.650	3.96	34	21	10	177.1	186	58	93	1	1	0	0	55	13	0	.236
1950		12	15	.444	4.30	37	33	11	249.1	262	92	93	2	1	2	0	90	26	2	.289
1951 2 teams	PIT N (10G 3-6)					STL	N	(21G 11-6)												
" total		14	12	.538	4.38	31	26	11	189	184	87	64	2	1	2	0	70	15	1	.214
1952 STL N		4	4	.500	4.12	26	13	2	98.1	110	33	47	1	0	0	1	32	9	0	.281
1953		3	6	.333	4.86	32	8	0	79.2	82	43	26	0	2	2	0	17	2	0	.118
6 yrs.		48	53	.475	4.29	189	113	37	897.1	924	361	374	7	5	8	1	294	69	3	.235
3 yrs.		18	16	.529	4.19	79	37	11	307.1	312	132	118	2	3	4	1	98	19	0	.194

John Chambers

CHAMBERS, JOHN MONROE   BL TR 6'   185 lbs.
B. Sept. 10, 1911, Copperhill, Tenn.   D. May 11, 1977, Palatka, Fla.

		W	L	PCT	ERA	G	GS	CG	IP	H	BB	SO	ShO	W	L	SV	AB	H	HR	BA
1937 STL N		0	0	—	18.00	2	0	0	2	5	2	1	0	0	0	0	0	0	0	—

Tom Cheney

CHENEY, THOMAS EDGAR   BR TR 5'11"   170 lbs.
B. Oct. 14, 1934, Morgan, Ga.

		W	L	PCT	ERA	G	GS	CG	IP	H	BB	SO	ShO	W	L	SV	AB	H	HR	BA
1957 STL N		0	1	.000	5.00	4	3	0	9	6	15	10	0	0	0	0	2	0	0	.000
1959		0	1	.000	6.94	11	2	0	11.2	17	11	8	0	0	1	0	0	0	0	—
1960 PIT N		2	2	.500	3.98	11	8	1	52	44	33	35	1	0	0	0	17	3	0	.176
1961 2 teams	PIT N (1G 0-0)					WAS	A	(10G 1-3)												
" total		1	3	.250	10.01	11	7	0	29.2	33	30	20	0	0	1	1	8	4	0	.500
1962 WAS A		7	9	.438	3.17	37	23	4	173.1	134	97	147	3	0	0	0	48	3	0	.063
1963		8	9	.471	2.71	23	21	7	136.1	99	40	97	4	0	0	0	46	5	0	.109
1964		1	3	.250	3.70	15	6	1	48.2	45	13	25	0	0	0	1	12	3	0	.250
1966		0	1	.000	5.06	3	1	0	5.1	4	4	3	0	0	0	0	0	0	0	—
8 yrs.		19	29	.396	3.77	115	71	13	466	382	245	345	8	0	2	2	133	18	0	.135
2 yrs.		0	2	.000	6.10	15	5	0	20.2	23	26	18	0	0	1	0	2	0	0	.000

| WORLD SERIES | | | | | | | | | | | | | | | | | | | | |
| 1960 PIT N | | 0 | 0 | — | 4.50 | 3 | 0 | 0 | 4 | 4 | 1 | 6 | 0 | 0 | 0 | 0 | 0 | 0 | 0 | — |

Nels Chittum

CHITTUM, NELSON BOYD   BR TR 6'1"   180 lbs.
B. Mar. 25, 1933, Harrisonburg, Va.

		W	L	PCT	ERA	G	GS	CG	IP	H	BB	SO	ShO	W	L	SV	AB	H	HR	BA
1958 STL N		0	1	.000	6.44	13	2	0	29.1	31	7	13	0	0	0	0	4	1	0	.250
1959 BOS A		3	0	1.000	1.19	21	0	0	30.1	29	11	12	0	3	0	0	5	1	0	.200
1960		0	0	—	4.32	6	0	0	8.1	8	6	5	0	0	0	0	1	0	0	.000
3 yrs.		3	1	.750	3.84	40	2	0	68	68	24	30	0	3	0	0	10	2	0	.200
1 yr.		0	1	.000	6.44	13	2	0	29.1	31	7	13	0	0	0	0	4	1	0	.250

Bob Chlupsa

CHLUPSA, ROBERT JOSEPH   BR TR 6'7"   215 lbs.
B. Sept. 16, 1945, New York, N. Y.

		W	L	PCT	ERA	G	GS	CG	IP	H	BB	SO	ShO	W	L	SV	AB	H	HR	BA
1970 STL N		0	2	.000	9.00	14	0	0	16	26	9	10	0	0	2	0	0	0	0	—
1971		0	0	—	9.00	1	0	0	2	3	0	1	0	0	0	0	0	0	0	—
2 yrs.		0	2	.000	9.00	15	0	0	18	29	9	11	0	0	2	0	0	0	0	—
2 yrs.		0	2	.000	9.00	15	0	0	18	29	9	11	0	0	2	0	0	0	0	—

Al Cicotte

CICOTTE, ALVA WARREN (Bozo)   BR TR 6'3"   185 lbs.
B. Dec. 23, 1929, Melvindale, Mich.

		W	L	PCT	ERA	G	GS	CG	IP	H	BB	SO	ShO	W	L	SV	AB	H	HR	BA
1957 NY A		2	2	.500	3.03	20	2	0	65.1	57	30	36	0	2	0	2	20	3	0	.150
1958 2 teams	WAS A (8G 0-3)					DET	A	(14G 3-1)												
" total		3	4	.429	4.06	22	6	0	71	86	29	35	0	2	1	0	27	5	0	.185

	W	L	PCT	ERA	G	GS	CG	IP	H	BB	SO	ShO	Relief Pitching W	L	SV	BATTING AB	H	HR	BA

Al Cicotte continued

	W	L	PCT	ERA	G	GS	CG	IP	H	BB	SO	ShO	W	L	SV	AB	H	HR	BA
1959 CLE A	3	1	.750	5.32	26	1	0	44	46	25	23	0	3	1	1	3	1	0	.333
1961 STL N	2	6	.250	5.28	29	7	0	75	83	34	51	0	2	3	1	21	6	0	.286
1962 HOU N	0	0	—	3.86	5	0	0	4.2	8	1	4	0	0	0	0	0	0	0	—
5 yrs.	10	13	.435	4.36	102	16	0	260	280	119	149	0	9	5	4	71	15	0	.211
1 yr.	2	6	.250	5.28	29	7	0	75	83	34	51	0	2	3	1	21	6	0	.286

Mike Clark

CLARK, MICHAEL JOHN   BR TR 6'4"   190 lbs.
B. Feb. 12, 1922, Camden, N. J.

	W	L	PCT	ERA	G	GS	CG	IP	H	BB	SO	ShO	W	L	SV	AB	H	HR	BA
1952 STL N	2	0	1.000	6.04	12	4	0	25.1	32	14	10	0	2	0	0	5	0	0	.000
1953	1	0	1.000	4.79	23	2	0	35.2	46	21	17	0	0	0	1	6	0	0	.000
2 yrs.	3	0	1.000	5.31	35	6	0	61	78	35	27	0	2	0	1	11	0	0	.000
2 yrs.	3	0	1.000	5.31	35	6	0	61	78	35	27	0	2	0	1	11	0	0	.000

Phil Clark

CLARK, PHILIP JAMES   BR TR 6'3"   210 lbs.
B. Oct. 3, 1932, Albany, Ga.

	W	L	PCT	ERA	G	GS	CG	IP	H	BB	SO	ShO	W	L	SV	AB	H	HR	BA
1958 STL N	0	1	.000	3.52	7	0	0	7.2	11	3	1	0	0	1	0	1	0	0	.000
1959	0	1	.000	12.86	7	0	0	7	8	8	5	0	0	1	0	0	0	0	—
2 yrs.	0	2	.000	7.98	14	0	0	14.2	19	11	6	0	0	2	1	1	0	0	.000
2 yrs.	0	2	.000	7.98	14	0	0	14.2	19	11	6	0	0	2	1	1	0	0	.000

Dad Clarkson

CLARKSON, ARTHUR HAMILTON   BR TR 5'10"   165 lbs.
Brother of Walter Clarkson.   Brother of John Clarkson.
B. Aug. 31, 1866, Cambridge, Mass.   D. Feb. 6, 1911, Cambridge, Mass.

	W	L	PCT	ERA	G	GS	CG	IP	H	BB	SO	ShO	W	L	SV	AB	H	HR	BA
1891 NY N	1	2	.333	2.89	5	2	1	28	24	18	11	0	1	0	0	9	4	0	.444
1892 BOS N	1	0	1.000	1.29	1	1	1	7	5	3	0	0	0	0	0	3	0	0	.000
1893 STL N	12	9	.571	3.48	24	21	17	186.1	194	79	37	1	1	0	0	75	10	0	.133
1894	8	17	.320	6.36	32	24	233.1	318	117	46	1	0	0	0	88	16	0	.182
1895 2 teams						STL N (7G 1–6)		BAL N (20G 12–3)											
" total	13	9	.591	4.92	27	21	17	203	260	90	32	0	2	1	0	80	9	1	.113
1896 BAL N	4	2	.667	4.98	7	4	3	47	72	18	7	0	2	0	0	18	5	0	.278
6 yrs.	39	39	.500	4.90	96	81	63	704.2	873	325	133	2	6	1	0	273	44	1	.161
3 yrs.	21	32	.396	5.37	63	60	48	480.2	603	222	92	2	1	0	0	186	27	0	.145

Lance Clemons

CLEMONS, LANCE LEVIS   BL TL 6'2"   205 lbs.
B. July 6, 1947, Philadelphia, Pa.

	W	L	PCT	ERA	G	GS	CG	IP	H	BB	SO	ShO	W	L	SV	AB	H	HR	BA
1971 KC A	1	0	1.000	4.13	10	3	0	24	26	12	20	0	1	0	0	7	2	1	.286
1972 STL N	0	1	.000	10.13	3	1	0	5.1	8	5	2	0	0	0	0	1	0	0	.000
1974 BOS A	1	0	1.000	10.50	6	0	0	6	8	4	1	0	1	0	0	0	0	0	—
3 yrs.	2	1	.667	6.11	19	4	0	35.1	42	21	23	0	2	0	0	8	2	1	.250
1 yr.	0	1	.000	10.13	3	1	0	5.1	8	5	2	0	0	0	0	1	0	0	.000

Reggie Cleveland

CLEVELAND, REGINALD LESLIE   BR TR 6'1"   195 lbs.
B. May 23, 1948, Swift Current, Sask., Canada

	W	L	PCT	ERA	G	GS	CG	IP	H	BB	SO	ShO	W	L	SV	AB	H	HR	BA
1969 STL N	0	0	—	9.00	1	1	0	4	7	1	3	0	0	0	0	1	0	0	.000
1970	0	4	.000	7.62	16	1	0	26	31	18	22	0	0	3	0	4	1	0	.250
1971	12	12	.500	4.01	34	34	10	222	238	53	148	2	0	0	0	82	14	0	.171
1972	14	15	.483	3.94	33	33	11	230.2	229	60	153	3	0	0	0	71	17	0	.239
1973	14	10	.583	3.01	32	32	6	224	211	61	122	3	0	0	0	74	17	0	.230
1974 BOS A	12	14	.462	4.32	41	27	10	221	234	69	103	0	2	1	0	0	0	0	—
1975	13	9	.591	4.43	31	20	3	170.2	173	52	78	1	3	1	0	0	0	0	—
1976	10	9	.526	3.07	41	14	3	170	159	61	76	0	4	4	2	0	0	0	—
1977	11	8	.579	4.26	36	27	9	190.1	211	43	85	1	0	0	0	0	0	0	—
1978 2 teams						BOS A (1G 0–1)		TEX A (53G 5–7)											
" total	5	8	.385	3.08	54	0	0	76	66	23	46	0	5	8	12	0	0	0	—
1979 MIL A	1	5	.167	6.71	29	1	0	55	77	23	22	0	1	4	4	0	0	0	—
1980	11	9	.550	3.74	45	13	5	154	150	49	54	2	7	4	4	0	0	0	—
1981	2	3	.400	5.12	35	0	0	65	57	30	18	0	2	3	1	0	0	0	—
13 yrs.	105	106	.498	4.02	428	203	57	1808.2	1843	543	930	12	24	28	25	232	49	0	.211
5 yrs.	40	41	.494	3.83	116	101	27	706.2	716	193	448	8	0	3	0	232	49	0	.211

LEAGUE CHAMPIONSHIP SERIES

	W	L	PCT	ERA	G	GS	CG	IP	H	BB	SO	ShO	W	L	SV	AB	H	HR	BA
1975 BOS A	0	0	—	5.40	1	1	0	5	7	1	2	0	0	0	0	0	0	0	—

WORLD SERIES

	W	L	PCT	ERA	G	GS	CG	IP	H	BB	SO	ShO	W	L	SV	AB	H	HR	BA
1975 BOS A	0	1	.000	6.75	3	1	0	6.2	7	3	5	0	0	0	0	2	0	0	.000

Tony Cloninger

CLONINGER, TONY LEE   BR TR 6'   210 lbs.
B. Aug. 13, 1940, Lincoln, N. C.

	W	L	PCT	ERA	G	GS	CG	IP	H	BB	SO	ShO	W	L	SV	AB	H	HR	BA
1961 MIL N	7	2	.778	5.25	19	10	3	84	84	33	51	0	2	0	0	30	5	0	.167
1962	8	3	.727	4.30	24	15	4	111	113	46	69	1	0	0	0	39	4	0	.103
1963	9	11	.450	3.78	41	18	4	145.1	131	63	100	2	2	4	1	37	5	0	.135
1964	19	14	.576	3.56	38	34	15	242.2	206	82	163	3	1	0	2	87	21	0	.241
1965	24	11	.686	3.29	40	38	16	279	247	119	211	1	0	0	1	105	17	1	.162
1966 ATL N	14	11	.560	4.12	39	38	11	257.2	253	116	178	1	0	0	0	111	26	5	.234
1967	4	7	.364	5.17	16	16	1	76.2	85	31	55	0	0	0	0	25	5	0	.200
1968 2 teams						ATL N (8G 1–3)		CIN N (17G 4–3)											
" total	5	6	.455	4.08	25	18	2	110.1	96	59	72	2	1	2	0	38	7	2	.184
1969 CIN N	11	17	.393	5.02	35	34	6	190	184	103	103	2	0	0	0	72	12	1	.167
1970	9	7	.563	3.83	30	18	0	148	136	78	56	0	1	1	1	47	10	2	.213
1971	3	6	.333	3.90	28	8	1	97	79	49	51	1	0	2	0	27	7	0	.259
1972 STL N	0	2	.000	5.19	17	0	0	26	29	19	11	0	0	2	0	3	0	0	.000
12 yrs.	113	97	.538	4.07	352	247	63	1767.2	1643	798	1120	13	7	11	6	621	119	11	.192
1 yr.	0	2	.000	5.19	17	0	0	26	29	19	11	0	0	2	0	3	0	0	.000

	W	L	PCT	ERA	G	GS	CG	IP	H	BB	SO	ShO	Relief Pitching W	L	SV	BATTING AB	H	HR	BA

Tony Cloninger continued

LEAGUE CHAMPIONSHIP SERIES
| 1970 CIN N | 0 | 0 | – | 3.60 | 1 | 1 | 0 | 5 | 7 | 4 | 1 | 0 | 0 | 0 | 0 | 1 | 0 | 0 | .000 |

WORLD SERIES
| 1970 CIN N | 0 | 1 | .000 | 7.36 | 2 | 1 | 0 | 7.1 | 10 | 5 | 4 | 0 | 0 | 0 | 0 | 2 | 0 | 0 | .000 |

Ed Clough

CLOUGH, EDGAR GEORGE (Spec)   BL TL 6'   188 lbs.
B. Oct. 11, 1905, Wiconisco, Pa.   D. Jan. 30, 1944, Harrisburg, Pa.

1925 STL N	0	1	.000	8.10	3	1	0	10	11	5	3	0	0	0	0	4	1	0	.250
1926	0	0	–	22.50	1	0	0	2	5	3	0	0	0	0	0	1	0	0	.000
2 yrs.	0	1	.000	10.50	4	1	0	12	16	8	3	0	0	0	0	*			
2 yrs.	0	1	.000	10.50	4	1	0	12	16	8	3	0	0	0	0	19	2	0	.105

John Coleman

COLEMAN, JOHN
B. 1870, Jefferson City, Mo.   Deceased.

| 1895 STL N | 0 | 1 | .000 | 13.50 | 1 | 1 | 1 | 8 | 12 | 8 | 5 | 0 | 0 | 0 | 0 | 5 | 1 | 0 | .200 |

Percy Coleman

COLEMAN, PIERCE D.
B. Cincinnati, Ohio   Deceased.

1897 STL N	1	3	.250	8.16	12	4	2	57.1	99	32	10	0	0	0	0	28	6	0	.214
1898 CIN N	0	1	.000	3.00	1	1	1	9	13	3	2	0	0	0	0	3	0	0	.000
2 yrs.	1	4	.200	7.46	13	5	3	66.1	112	35	12	0	0	0	0	31	6	0	.194
1 yr.	1	3	.250	8.16	12	4	2	57.1	99	32	10	0	0	0	0	28	6	0	.214

Phil Collins

COLLINS, PHILIP EUGENE (Fidgety Phil)   BR TR 5'11"   175 lbs.
B. Aug. 27, 1900, Rockford, Ill.   D. Aug. 14, 1948, Chicago, Ill.

1923 CHI N	1	0	1.000	3.60	1	1	0	5	8	1	2	0	0	0	0	2	0	0	.000
1929 PHI N	9	7	.563	5.75	43	11	3	153.1	172	83	61	0	7	2	5	58	11	1	.190
1930	16	11	.593	4.78	47	25	17	239	287	86	87	1	3	1	3	87	22	3	.253
1931	12	16	.429	3.86	42	27	16	240.1	268	83	73	2	0	2	4	95	16	0	.168
1932	14	12	.538	5.27	43	21	6	184.1	231	65	66	0	5	3	3	68	18	0	.265
1933	8	13	.381	4.11	42	13	5	151	178	57	40	1	3	6	6	53	7	0	.132
1934	13	18	.419	4.18	45	32	15	254	277	87	72	0	4	1	1	88	15	0	.170
1935 2 teams			PHI	N	(3G 0-2)		STL	N	(26G 7-6)										
" total	7	8	.467	5.64	29	11	2	97.1	120	35	22	0	3	2	2	31	4	0	.129
8 yrs.	80	85	.485	4.66	292	141	64	1324.1	1541	497	423	4	25	17	24	482	93	4	.193
1 yr.	7	6	.538	4.57	26	8	2	82.2	96	26	18	0	3	2	2	25	4	0	.160

Jackie Collum

COLLUM, JACK DEAN   BL TL 5'7½"   160 lbs.
B. June 21, 1927, Victor, Iowa

1951 STL N	2	1	.667	1.59	3	2	1	17	11	10	5	1	0	1	0	7	3	0	.429
1952	0	0	–	0.00	2	0	0	3	2	1	0	0	0	0	0	0	0	0	–
1953 2 teams			STL	N	(7G 0-0)		CIN	N	(30G 7-11)										
" total	7	11	.389	3.97	37	12	4	136	138	43	56	1	3	3	3	39	10	0	.256
1954 CIN N	7	3	.700	3.74	36	2	1	79.1	86	32	28	0	7	2	0	13	3	1	.231
1955	9	8	.529	3.63	32	17	5	134	128	37	49	0	2	1	1	40	10	0	.250
1956 STL N	6	2	.750	4.20	38	1	0	60	63	27	17	0	6	2	7	14	3	0	.214
1957 2 teams			CHI	N	(9G 1-1)		BKN	N	(3G 0-0)										
" total	1	1	.500	7.20	12	0	0	15	15	10	10	0	1	1	1	0	0	0	–
1958 LA N	0	0	–	8.10	2	0	0	3.1	4	2	0	0	0	0	0	1	0	0	.000
1962 2 teams			MIN	A	(8G 0-2)		CLE	A	(1G 0-0)										
" total	0	2	.000	11.34	9	3	0	16.2	33	11	6	0	0	0	0	4	0	0	.000
9 yrs.	32	28	.533	4.15	171	37	11	464.1	480	173	171	2	19	10	12	118	29	1	.246
4 yrs.	8	3	.727	3.84	50	3	1	91.1	91	42	27	1	6	3	7	24	6	0	.250

Mort Cooper

COOPER, MORTON CECIL   BR TR 6'2"   210 lbs.
Brother of Walker Cooper.
B. Mar. 2, 1913, Atherton, Mo.   D. Nov. 17, 1958, Little Rock, Ark.

1938 STL N	2	1	.667	3.04	4	3	1	23.2	17	12	11	0	0	0	1	9	2	0	.222
1939	12	6	.667	3.25	45	26	7	210.2	208	97	130	2	2	0	4	69	16	2	.232
1940	11	12	.478	3.63	38	29	16	230.2	225	86	95	3	1	0	3	83	13	0	.157
1941	13	9	.591	3.91	29	25	12	186.2	175	69	118	0	1	0	0	70	13	0	.186
1942	22	7	.759	1.78	37	35	22	278.2	207	68	152	10	0	1	0	103	19	0	.184
1943	21	8	.724	2.30	37	32	24	274	228	79	141	6	1	1	3	100	17	1	.170
1944	22	7	.759	2.46	34	33	22	252.1	227	60	97	7	0	0	1	94	19	0	.202
1945 2 teams			STL	N	(4G 2-0)		BOS	N	(20G 7-4)										
" total	9	4	.692	2.92	24	14	5	101.2	97	34	59	1	3	2	1	32	8	1	.250
1946 BOS N	13	11	.542	3.12	28	27	15	199	181	39	83	4	0	1	1	67	14	1	.209
1947 2 teams			BOS	N	(10G 2-5)		NY	N	(8G 1-5)										
" total	3	10	.231	5.40	18	15	4	83.1	99	26	27	0	1	0	0	27	6	1	.222
1949 CHI N	0	0	–	∞	1	0	0	0	2	1	0	0	0	0	0	0	0	0	–
11 yrs.	128	75	.631	2.97	295	239	128	1840.2	1666	571	913	33	9	4	14	654	127	6	.194
8 yrs.	105	50	.677	2.77	228	186	105	1480.1	1307	478	758	28	5	2	12	534	101	3	.189
			8th	**1st**		**5th**			**9th**				**3rd**							

WORLD SERIES
1942 STL N	0	1	.000	5.54	2	2	0	13	17	4	9	0	0	0	0	5	1	0	.200
1943	1	1	.500	2.81	2	2	1	16	11	3	10	0	0	0	0	5	0	0	.000
1944	1	1	.500	1.13	2	2	1	16	9	5	16	1	0	0	0	4	0	0	.000
3 yrs.	2	3	.400	3.00	6	6	2	45	37	12	35	1	0	0	0	14	1	0	.071

	W	L	PCT	ERA	G	GS	CG	IP	H	BB	SO	ShO	Relief Pitching W	L	SV	BATTING AB	H	HR	BA

Mays Copeland

COPELAND, MAYS
B. Aug. 31, 1913, Mt. View, Ark.　　　　　　　　　　BR TR 6'　　　180 lbs.

	W	L	PCT	ERA	G	GS	CG	IP	H	BB	SO	ShO	W	L	SV	AB	H	HR	BA
1935 STL N	0	0	–	13.50	1	0	0	.2	2	0	0	0	0	0	0	0	0	0	–

Joe Corbett

CORBETT, JOSEPH A.
B. Dec. 4, 1875, San Francisco, Calif.　　D. May 2, 1945, San Francisco, Calif.　　BR TR

	W	L	PCT	ERA	G	GS	CG	IP	H	BB	SO	ShO	W	L	SV	AB	H	HR	BA
1895 WAS N	0	2	.000	5.68	3	3	3	19	26	9	3	0	0	0	0	15	2	0	.133
1896 BAL N	3	0	1.000	2.20	8	3	3	41	31	17	28	0	0	0	1	22	6	0	.273
1897	24	8	.750	3.11	37	37	34	313	330	115	149	1	0	0	0	150	37	0	.247
1904 STL N	5	9	.357	4.39	14	14	12	108.2	110	51	68	0	0	0	0	43	9	0	.209
4 yrs.	32	19	.627	3.42	62	57	52	481.2	497	192	248	1	0	0	1	230	54	0	.235
1 yr.	5	9	.357	4.39	14	14	12	108.2	110	51	68	0	0	0	0	43	9	0	.209

Frank Corridon

CORRIDON, FRANK J. (Fiddler)
B. Nov. 25, 1880, Newport, R. I.　　D. Feb. 21, 1941, Syracuse, N. Y.　　BR TR

	W	L	PCT	ERA	G	GS	CG	IP	H	BB	SO	ShO	W	L	SV	AB	H	HR	BA
1904 2 teams		CHI N	(12G 5–5)			PHI N	(12G 6–5)												
" total	11	10	.524	2.64	24	21	20	194.2	176	65	78	1	1	1	0	93	19	0	.204
1905 PHI N	10	13	.435	3.48	35	26	18	212	203	57	79	1	1	1	1	72	15	1	.208
1907	19	14	.576	2.46	37	32	23	274	228	89	131	3	1	1	1	97	16	0	.165
1908	14	10	.583	2.51	27	24	18	208.1	178	48	50	2	0	0	1	73	9	0	.123
1909	11	7	.611	2.11	27	19	11	171	147	61	69	3	1	1	0	59	11	0	.186
1910 STL N	7	15	.318	3.81	30	18	9	156	168	55	51	0	2	3	2	51	10	0	.196
6 yrs.	72	69	.511	2.80	180	140	99	1216	1100	375	458	10	6	7	5	445	80	1	.180
1 yr.	7	15	.318	3.81	30	18	9	156	168	55	51	0	2	3	2	51	10	0	.196

Jim Cosman

COSMAN, JAMES HENRY
B. Feb. 19, 1943, Brockport, N. Y.　　　　　　　　　BR TR 6'4½"　　211 lbs.

	W	L	PCT	ERA	G	GS	CG	IP	H	BB	SO	ShO	W	L	SV	AB	H	HR	BA
1966 STL N	1	0	1.000	0.00	1	1	1	9	2	2	5	1	0	0	0	3	0	0	.000
1967	1	0	1.000	3.16	10	5	0	31.1	21	24	11	0	0	0	0	8	1	0	.125
1970 CHI N	0	0	–	27.00	1	0	0	1	3	1	0	0	0	0	0	0	0	0	–
3 yrs.	2	0	1.000	3.05	12	6	1	41.1	26	27	16	1	0	0	0	11	1	0	.091
2 yrs.	2	0	1.000	2.45	11	6	1	40.1	23	26	16	1	0	0	0	11	1	0	.091

Bill Cox

COX, WILLIAM DONALD
B. June 23, 1913, Ashmore, Ill.　　　　　　　　　　BR TR 6'1"　　185 lbs.

	W	L	PCT	ERA	G	GS	CG	IP	H	BB	SO	ShO	W	L	SV	AB	H	HR	BA
1936 STL N	0	0	–	6.75	2	0	0	2.2	4	1	1	0	0	0	0	0	0	0	–
1937 CHI A	1	0	1.000	0.71	3	2	1	12.2	9	5	8	0	0	0	0	4	1	0	.250
1938 2 teams		CHI A	(7G 0–2)			STL A	(22G 1–4)												
" total	1	6	.143	6.99	29	8	1	74.2	92	48	21	0	0	1	0	19	1	0	.053
1939 STL A	0	2	.000	9.64	4	2	1	9.1	10	8	8	0	0	0	0	1	0	0	.000
1940	0	1	.000	7.27	12	0	0	17.1	23	12	7	0	0	1	0	1	0	0	.000
5 yrs.	2	9	.182	6.56	50	12	3	116.2	138	74	45	0	0	2	0	25	2	0	.080
1 yr.	0	0	–	6.75	2	0	0	2.2	4	1	1	0	0	0	0	0	0	0	–

Roger Craig

CRAIG, ROGER LEE
B. Feb. 17, 1931, Durham, N. C.　　　　　　　　　　BR TR 6'4"　　185 lbs.
Manager 1978-79.

	W	L	PCT	ERA	G	GS	CG	IP	H	BB	SO	ShO	W	L	SV	AB	H	HR	BA
1955 BKN N	5	3	.625	2.78	21	10	3	90.2	81	43	48	0	0	1	2	26	2	0	.077
1956	12	11	.522	3.71	35	32	8	199	169	87	109	2	0	2	1	61	1	0	.016
1957	6	9	.400	4.61	32	13	1	111.1	102	47	69	0	4	2	0	29	4	0	.138
1958 LA N	2	1	.667	4.50	9	2	1	32	30	12	16	0	0	1	0	9	0	0	.000
1959	11	5	.688	2.06	29	17	7	152.2	122	45	76	4	2	0	0	52	3	0	.058
1960	8	3	.727	3.27	21	15	6	115.2	99	43	69	1	1	0	0	36	2	0	.056
1961	5	6	.455	6.15	40	14	2	112.2	130	52	63	0	2	1	2	27	4	0	.148
1962 NY N	10	24	.294	4.51	42	33	13	233.1	261	70	118	0	4	2	3	76	4	0	.053
1963	5	22	.185	3.78	46	31	14	236.	249	58	108	0	0	1	2	69	6	0	.087
1964 STL N	7	9	.438	3.25	39	19	3	166	180	35	84	0	2	1	5	48	10	0	.208
1965 CIN N	1	4	.200	3.64	40	0	0	64.1	74	25	30	0	1	4	3	11	2	0	.182
1966 PHI N	2	1	.667	5.56	14	0	0	22.2	31	5	13	0	2	1	1	4	0	0	.000
12 yrs.	74	98	.430	3.83	368	186	58	1536.1	1528	522	803	7	18	16	19	448	38	0	.085
1 yr.	7	9	.438	3.25	39	19	3	166	180	35	84	0	2	1	5	48	10	0	.208

WORLD SERIES

	W	L	PCT	ERA	G	GS	CG	IP	H	BB	SO	ShO	W	L	SV	AB	H	HR	BA
1955 BKN N	1	0	1.000	3.00	1	1	0	6	4	5	4	0	0	0	0	0	0	0	–
1956	0	1	.000	12.00	2	1	0	6	10	3	4	0	0	0	0	2	1	0	.500
1959 LA N	0	1	.000	8.68	2	2	0	9.1	15	5	8	0	0	0	0	3	0	0	.000
1964 STL N	1	0	1.000	0.00	2	0	0	5	2	3	9	0	1	0	0	1	0	0	.000
4 yrs.	2	2	.500	6.49	7	4	0	26.1	31	16	25	0	1	0	0	6	1	0	.167

Doc Crandall

CRANDALL, JAMES OTIS
B. Oct. 8, 1887, Wadena, Ind.　　D. Aug. 17, 1951, Bell, Calif.　　BR TR 5'10½" 180 lbs.

	W	L	PCT	ERA	G	GS	CG	IP	H	BB	SO	ShO	W	L	SV	AB	H	HR	BA
1908 NY N	12	12	.500	2.93	32	24	13	214.2	198	59	77	0	2	1	0	72	16	2	.222
1909	6	4	.600	2.88	30	8	4	122	117	33	55	0	5	1	4	41	10	1	.244
1910	17	4	.810	2.56	42	18	13	207.2	194	43	73	2	7	1	4	73	25	1	.342
1911	15	5	.750	2.63	41	15	9	198.2	199	51	94	2	7	0	5	113	27	2	.239
1912	13	7	.650	3.61	37	10	7	162	181	35	60	0	6	5	2	80	25	0	.313
1913	4	4	.500	2.86	35	3	2	97.2	102	24	42	0	3	3	5	49	15	0	.306
1914 STL F	21	12	.571	3.54	27	21	18	196	194	52	84	1	1	0	0	278	86	2	.309
1915	21	15	.583	2.59	51	33	22	312.2	307	77	117	4	6	3	0	141	40	1	.284
1916 STL A	0	0	–	27.00	2	0	0	1.1	7	1	0	0	0	0	0	12	1	0	.083
1918 BOS N	1	2	.333	2.38	5	3	3	34	39	4	4	0	0	0	0	28	8	0	.286
10 yrs.	101	62	.620	2.92	302	135	91	1546.2	1538	379	606	9	37	14	21	*			

WORLD SERIES

	W	L	PCT	ERA	G	GS	CG	IP	H	BB	SO	ShO	W	L	SV	AB	H	HR	BA
1911 NY N	1	0	1.000	0.00	2	0	0	4	2	0	2	0	1	0	0	2	1	0	.500

	W	L	PCT	ERA	G	GS	CG	IP	H	BB	SO	ShO	Relief Pitching W	L	SV	BATTING AB	H	HR	BA

Doc Crandall continued

	W	L	PCT	ERA	G	GS	CG	IP	H	BB	SO	ShO	W	L	SV	AB	H	HR	BA
1912	0	0	–	0.00	1	0	0	2	1	0	2	0	0	0	0	1	0	0	.000
1913	0	0	–	3.86	2	0	0	4.2	4	0	2	0	0	0	0	4	0	0	.000
3 yrs.	1	0	1.000	1.69	5	0	0	10.2	7	0	6	0	1	0	0	7	1	0	.143

Jack Creel

CREEL, JACK DALTON (Tex)
B. Apr. 23, 1916, Kyle, Tex.   BR TR 6'   165 lbs.

	W	L	PCT	ERA	G	GS	CG	IP	H	BB	SO	ShO	W	L	SV	AB	H	HR	BA
1945 STL N	5	4	.556	4.14	26	8	2	87	78	45	34	0	2	0	2	26	2	0	.077

Jack Crimian

CRIMIAN, JOHN MELVIN
B. Feb. 17, 1926, Philadelphia, Pa.   BR TR 5'10"   180 lbs.

	W	L	PCT	ERA	G	GS	CG	IP	H	BB	SO	ShO	W	L	SV	AB	H	HR	BA
1951 STL N	1	0	1.000	9.00	11	0	0	17	24	8	5	0	1	0	1	3	1	0	.333
1952	0	0	–	9.72	5	0	0	8.1	15	4	4	0	0	0	0	1	0	0	.000
1956 KC A	4	8	.333	5.51	54	7	0	129	129	49	59	0	3	3	3	22	5	0	.227
1957 DET A	0	1	.000	12.71	4	0	0	5.2	9	4	1	0	0	1	0	0	0	0	–
4 yrs.	5	9	.357	6.36	74	7	0	160	177	65	69	0	4	4	4	26	6	0	.231
2 yrs.	1	0	1.000	9.24	16	0	0	25.1	39	12	9	0	1	0	1	4	1	0	.250

Bill Crouch

CROUCH, WILLIAM ELMER
Son of Bill Crouch.
B. Aug. 20, 1910, Wilmington, Del.   D. Dec. 26, 1980, Howell, Mich.   BB TR 6'1"   180 lbs.

	W	L	PCT	ERA	G	GS	CG	IP	H	BB	SO	ShO	W	L	SV	AB	H	HR	BA
1939 BKN N	4	0	1.000	2.58	6	3	3	38.1	37	14	10	0	1	0	0	15	2	0	.133
1941 2 teams			PHI N	(20G 2–3)		STL N	(18G 1–2)												
" total	3	5	.375	3.81	38	9	1	104	110	31	41	0	0	2	7	24	1	0	.042
1945 STL N	1	0	1.000	3.38	6	0	0	13.1	12	7	4	0	1	0	0	2	0	0	.000
3 yrs.	8	5	.615	3.47	50	12	4	155.2	159	52	55	0	2	2	7	41	3	0	.073
2 yrs.	2	2	.500	3.09	24	4	0	58.1	57	21	19	0	1	2	6	15	0	0	.000

Mike Cuellar

CUELLAR, MIGUEL SANTANA
B. May 8, 1937, Las Villas, Cuba   BL TL 6'   165 lbs.

	W	L	PCT	ERA	G	GS	CG	IP	H	BB	SO	ShO	W	L	SV	AB	H	HR	BA
1959 CIN N	0	0	–	15.75	2	0	0	4	7	4	5	0	0	0	0	1	0	0	.000
1964 STL N	5	5	.500	4.50	32	7	1	72	80	33	56	0	3	0	4	18	0	0	.000
1965 HOU N	1	4	.200	3.54	25	4	0	56	55	21	46	0	1	1	2	12	0	0	.000
1966	12	10	.545	2.22	38	28	11	227.1	193	52	175	1	3	1	2	71	8	1	.113
1967	16	11	.593	3.03	36	32	16	246.1	233	63	203	3	1	0	1	93	13	0	.140
1968	8	11	.421	2.74	28	24	11	170.2	152	45	133	2	0	1	1	57	11	1	.193
1969 BAL A	23	11	.676	2.38	39	39	18	290.2	213	79	182	5	0	0	0	103	12	0	.117
1970	24	8	.750	3.47	40	40	21	298	273	69	190	4	0	0	0	112	10	2	.089
1971	20	9	.690	3.08	38	38	21	292	250	78	124	4	0	0	0	107	11	1	.103
1972	18	12	.600	2.57	35	35	17	248.1	197	71	132	4	0	0	0	87	11	2	.126
1973	18	13	.581	3.27	38	38	17	267	265	84	140	2	0	0	0	0	0	0	–
1974	22	10	.688	3.11	38	38	20	269	253	86	106	5	0	0	0	0	0	0	–
1975	14	12	.538	3.66	36	36	17	256	229	84	105	5	0	0	0	0	0	0	–
1976	4	13	.235	4.96	26	19	2	107	129	50	32	1	0	2	1	0	0	0	–
1977 CAL A	0	1	.000	18.90	2	1	0	3.1	9	3	3	0	0	0	0	0	0	0	–
15 yrs.	185	130	.587	3.14	453	379	172	2807.2	2538	822	1632	36	8	5	11	661	76	7	.115
1 yr.	5	5	.500	4.50	32	7	1	72	80	33	56	0	3	0	4	18	0	0	.000

LEAGUE CHAMPIONSHIP SERIES

	W	L	PCT	ERA	G	GS	CG	IP	H	BB	SO	ShO	W	L	SV	AB	H	HR	BA
1969 BAL A	0	0	–	2.25	1	1	0	8	3	1	7	0	0	0	0	2	0	0	.000
1970	0	0	–	12.46	1	1	0	4.1	10	1	2	0	0	0	0	2	1	1	.500
1971	1	0	1.000	1.00	1	1	1	9	6	1	2	0	0	0	0	3	1	0	.333
1973	0	1	.000	1.80	1	1	1	10	4	3	11	0	0	0	0	0	0	0	–
1974	1	1	.500	2.84	2	2	0	12.2	9	13	6	0	0	0	0	0	0	0	–
5 yrs.	2	2	.500	3.07	6	6	2	44	32	19	28	0	0	0	0	7	2	1	.286

WORLD SERIES

	W	L	PCT	ERA	G	GS	CG	IP	H	BB	SO	ShO	W	L	SV	AB	H	HR	BA
1969 BAL A	1	0	1.000	1.13	2	2	1	16	13	4	13	0	0	0	0	5	2	0	.400
1970	1	0	1.000	3.18	2	2	1	11.1	10	2	5	0	0	0	0	4	0	0	.000
1971	0	2	.000	3.86	2	2	0	14	11	6	10	0	0	0	0	3	0	0	.000
3 yrs.	2	2	.500	2.61	6	6	2	41.1	34	12	28	0	0	0	0	12	2	0	.167

George Culver

CULVER, GEORGE RAYMOND
B. July 8, 1943, Salinas, Calif.   BR TR 6'2"   185 lbs.

	W	L	PCT	ERA	G	GS	CG	IP	H	BB	SO	ShO	W	L	SV	AB	H	HR	BA
1966 CLE A	0	2	.000	8.38	5	1	0	9.2	15	7	6	0	0	1	0	2	0	0	.000
1967	7	3	.700	3.96	53	1	0	75	71	31	41	0	7	2	3	4	1	0	.250
1968 CIN N	11	16	.407	3.23	42	35	5	226	229	84	114	2	2	0	2	66	8	0	.121
1969	5	7	.417	4.28	32	13	0	101	117	52	58	0	0	0	4	31	3	0	.097
1970 2 teams			STL N	(11G 3–3)		HOU N	(32G 3–3)												
" total	6	6	.500	3.98	43	7	2	101.2	108	45	54	0	3	6	3	21	4	0	.190
1971 HOU N	5	8	.385	2.65	59	0	0	95	89	38	57	0	5	8	7	11	1	0	.091
1972	6	2	.750	3.05	45	0	0	97.1	73	43	82	0	6	2	2	19	3	0	.158
1973 2 teams			LA N	(28G 4–4)		PHI N	(14G 3–1)												
" total	7	5	.583	3.56	42	0	0	60.2	71	36	30	0	7	5	2	4	0	0	.000
1974 PHI N	1	0	1.000	6.55	14	0	0	22	20	16	9	0	1	0	0	3	0	0	.000
9 yrs.	48	49	.495	3.62	335	57	7	788.1	793	352	451	2	31	24	23	161	20	0	.124
1 yr.	3	3	.500	4.61	11	7	2	56.2	64	24	23	0	0	3	0	17	3	0	.176

John Cumberland

CUMBERLAND, JOHN SHELDON
B. May 10, 1947, Westbrook, Me.   BR TL 6'   185 lbs.

	W	L	PCT	ERA	G	GS	CG	IP	H	BB	SO	ShO	W	L	SV	AB	H	HR	BA
1968 NY A	0	0	–	9.00	1	0	0	2	3	1	1	0	0	0	0	0	0	0	–
1969	0	0	–	4.50	2	0	0	4	3	4	0	0	0	0	0	0	0	0	–
1970 2 teams			NY A	(15G 3–4)		SF N	(7G 2–0)												
" total	5	4	.556	3.48	22	8	1	75	68	19	44	0	3	0	0	18	1	0	.056

		W	L	PCT	ERA	G	GS	CG	IP	H	BB	SO	ShO	Relief Pitching W	L	SV	BATTING AB	H	HR	BA

John Cumberland continued

		W	L	PCT	ERA	G	GS	CG	IP	H	BB	SO	ShO	W	L	SV	AB	H	HR	BA
1971 SF	N	9	6	.600	2.92	45	21	5	185	153	55	65	2	2	0	2	59	7	0	.119
1972 2 teams	SF N (9G 0–4)								STL N (14G 1–1)											
" total		1	5	.167	7.71	23	7	0	46.2	61	14	15	0	1	0	0	14	1	0	.071
1974 CAL	A	0	1	.000	3.68	17	0	0	22	24	10	12	0	0	1	0	0	0	0	–
6 yrs.		15	16	.484	3.82	110	36	6	334.2	312	103	137	2	6	1	2	91	9	0	.099
1 yr.		1	1	.500	6.65	14	1	0	21.2	23	7	7	0	1	0	0	5	0	0	.000

LEAGUE CHAMPIONSHIP SERIES

		W	L	PCT	ERA	G	GS	CG	IP	H	BB	SO	ShO	W	L	SV	AB	H	HR	BA
1971 SF	N	0	1	.000	9.00	1	1	0	3	7	4	0	0	0	0	0	0	0	0	–

Nig Cuppy

CUPPY, GEORGE JOSEPH BR TR 5'7" 160 lbs.
Born George Maceo Koppe.
B. July 3, 1869, Logansport, Ind. D. July 27, 1922, Elkhart, Ind.

		W	L	PCT	ERA	G	GS	CG	IP	H	BB	SO	ShO	W	L	SV	AB	H	HR	BA
1892 CLE	N	28	13	.683	2.51	47	42	38	376	333	121	103	1	0	0	1	168	36	0	.214
1893		17	10	.630	4.47	31	30	24	243.2	316	75	39	0	0	0	0	109	27	0	.248
1894		24	15	.615	4.56	43	33	29	316	381	128	65	3	8	0	0	135	35	0	.259
1895		26	14	.650	3.54	47	40	36	353	384	95	91	1	3	0	2	140	40	0	.286
1896		25	14	.641	3.12	46	40	35	358	388	75	86	1	2	0	1	141	38	1	.270
1897		10	6	.625	3.18	19	17	13	138.2	150	26	23	1	0	0	0	55	8	0	.145
1898		9	8	.529	3.30	18	15	13	128	147	25	27	1	1	2	0	48	5	0	.104
1899 STL	N	11	8	.579	3.15	21	21	18	171.2	203	26	25	1	0	0	0	70	13	0	.186
1900 BOS	N	8	4	.667	3.08	17	13	9	105.1	107	24	23	0	1	0	1	42	11	0	.262
1901 BOS	A	4	6	.400	4.15	13	11	9	93.1	111	14	22	0	0	0	0	49	10	0	.204
10 yrs.		162	98	.623	3.48	302	262	224	2283.2	2520	609	504	9	15	2	5	957	223	1	.233
1 yr.		11	8	.579	3.15	21	21	18	171.2	203	26	25	1	0	0	0	70	13	0	.186

Clarence Currie

CURRIE, CLARENCE F. BR TR
B. Dec. 30, 1878, Glencoe, Ont., Canada D. July 15, 1941, Appleton, Wis.

		W	L	PCT	ERA	G	GS	CG	IP	H	BB	SO	ShO	W	L	SV	AB	H	HR	BA
1902 2 teams	CIN N (10G 3–4)								STL N (14G 6–5)											
" total		9	9	.500	3.10	24	18	15	183	192	48	49	2	0	0	0	70	11	0	.157
1903 2 teams	STL N (22G 4–12)								CHI N (6G 1–2)											
" total		5	14	.263	3.82	28	19	15	181.1	190	69	61	1	2	1	2	59	9	0	.153
2 yrs.		14	23	.378	3.46	52	37	30	364.1	382	117	110	3	2	1	2	129	20	0	.155
2 yrs.		10	17	.370	3.46	36	27	22	265.2	277	91	81	2	1	1	1	93	13	0	.140

Murphy Currie

CURRIE, MURPHY ARCHIBALD BR TR 5'11½" 185 lbs.
B. Aug. 31, 1893, Fayetteville, N. C. D. June 22, 1939, Asheboro, N. C.

		W	L	PCT	ERA	G	GS	CG	IP	H	BB	SO	ShO	W	L	SV	AB	H	HR	BA
1916 STL	N	0	0	–	1.88	6	0	0	14.1	7	9	8	0	0	0	0	3	0	0	.000

John Curtis

CURTIS, JOHN DUFFIELD II BL TL 6'1" 175 lbs.
D. Mar. 9, 1948, Newton, Mass.

		W	L	PCT	ERA	G	GS	CG	IP	H	BB	SO	ShO	W	L	SV	AB	H	HR	BA
1970 BOS	A	0	0	–	13.50	1	0	0	2	4	1	1	0	0	0	0	0	0	0	–
1971		2	2	.500	3.12	5	3	1	26	30	6	19	0	1	0	0	9	1	0	.111
1972		11	8	.579	3.73	26	21	8	154.1	161	50	106	3	1	0	0	53	5	0	.094
1973		13	13	.500	3.58	35	30	10	221	225	83	101	4	0	0	0	0	0	0	–
1974 STL	N	10	14	.417	3.78	33	29	5	195	199	83	89	2	0	1	1	63	10	0	.159
1975		8	9	.471	3.43	39	18	4	147	151	65	67	0	0	1	1	38	8	0	.211
1976		6	11	.353	4.50	37	15	3	134	139	65	52	1	0	3	1	35	7	0	.200
1977 SF	N	3	3	.500	5.49	43	9	1	77	95	48	47	1	1	1	1	13	3	0	.231
1978		4	3	.571	3.71	46	0	0	63	60	29	38	0	4	3	1	2	0	0	.000
1979		10	9	.526	4.17	27	18	3	121	121	42	85	2	1	2	0	34	5	0	.147
1980 SD	N	10	8	.556	3.51	30	27	6	187	184	67	71	0	0	0	0	62	12	0	.194
1981		2	6	.250	5.10	28	8	0	67	70	30	31	0	2	4	0	13	1	0	.077
1982 2 teams	SD N (26G 8–6)								CAL A (8G 0–1)											
" total		8	7	.533	4.28	34	11	1	128.1	137	49	44	1	1	2	1	37	11	0	.297
13 yrs.		87	93	.483	3.96	384	196	42	1522.2	1576	618	771	14	11	17	6	359	63	0	.175
3 yrs.		24	34	.414	3.88	109	62	12	476	489	213	208	3	0	5	3	136	25	0	.184

John D'Acquisto

D'ACQUISTO, JOHN FRANCIS BR TR 6'2" 205 lbs.
B. Dec. 24, 1951, San Diego, Calif.

		W	L	PCT	ERA	G	GS	CG	IP	H	BB	SO	ShO	W	L	SV	AB	H	HR	BA
1973 SF	N	1	1	.500	3.54	7	3	1	28	23	19	29	0	0	0	0	9	0	0	.000
1974		12	14	.462	3.77	38	36	5	215	182	124	167	1	0	0	0	71	8	1	.113
1975		2	4	.333	10.29	10	6	0	28	29	34	22	0	1	0	0	7	0	0	.000
1976		3	8	.273	5.35	28	19	0	106	93	102	53	0	0	0	0	26	7	0	.269
1977 2 teams	STL N (3G 0–0)								SD N (17G 1–2)											
" total		1	2	.333	6.54	20	14	0	52.1	54	57	54	0	1	0	0	8	0	0	.000
1978 SD	N	4	3	.571	2.13	45	3	0	93	60	56	104	0	3	2	10	21	4	0	.190
1979		9	13	.409	4.90	51	11	1	134	140	86	97	1	5	7	2	31	4	0	.129
1980 2 teams	SD N (39G 2–3)								MON N (11G 0–2)											
" total		2	5	.286	3.38	50	0	0	88	81	45	59	0	2	5	3	8	0	0	.000
1981 CAL	A	0	0	–	10.89	6	0	0	19	26	12	8	0	0	0	0	0	0	0	–
1982 OAK	A	0	1	.000	5.29	11	0	0	17	20	9	7	0	0	1	0	0	0	0	–
10 yrs.		34	51	.400	4.56	266	92	7	780.1	708	544	600	2	12	15	15	181	23	1	.127
4 yr.					4.32	3	2	0	5	5	10	9	0	0	0	0	0	0	0	.000

Gene Dale

DALE, EMMETT EUGENE BR TR 6'3" 179 lbs.
B. June 16, 1889, St. Louis, Mo. D. Mar. 20, 1958, St. Louis, Mo.

		W	L	PCT	ERA	G	GS	CG	IP	H	BB	SO	ShO	W	L	SV	AB	H	HR	BA
1911 STL	N	1	2	.333	6.75	5	2	0	14.2	13	16	13	0	1	0	0	5	2	0	.400
1912		0	5	.000	6.57	19	3	1	61.2	76	51	37	0	0	2	0	22	6	0	.273
1915 CIN	N	18	17	.514	2.46	49	35	20	296.2	256	107	104	4	3	2	3	91	20	0	.220
1916		3	4	.429	5.17	17	5	2	69.2	80	33	23	0	2	1	0	21	3	0	.143
4 yrs.		22	28	.440	3.60	90	45	23	442.2	425	207	177	4	6	5	3	139	31	0	.223
2 yrs.		1	7	.125	6.60	24	5	1	76.1	89	67	50	0	1	2	0	27	8	0	.296

	W	L	PCT	ERA	G	GS	CG	IP	H	BB	SO	ShO	Relief Pitching W	L	SV	BATTING AB	H	HR	BA

Pete Daniels

DANIELS, PETER J.
B. Apr. 8, 1864, County Cavan, Ireland   D. Feb. 13, 1928, Indianapolis, Ind.

	W	L	PCT	ERA	G	GS	CG	IP	H	BB	SO	ShO	W	L	SV	AB	H	HR	BA
1890 PIT N	1	2	.333	7.07	4	4	3	28	40	12	8	0	0	0	0	12	4	0	.333
1898 STL N	1	6	.143	3.62	10	6	3	54.2	62	14	13	0	1	0	0	17	3	0	.176
2 yrs.	2	8	.200	4.79	14	10	6	82.2	102	26	21	0	1	0	0	29	7	0	.241
1 yr.	1	6	.143	3.62	10	6	3	54.2	62	14	13	0	1	0	0	17	3	0	.176

Alvin Dark

DARK, ALVIN RALPH (Blackie)   BR TR 5'11" 185 lbs.
B. Jan. 7, 1922, Comanche, Okla.
Manager 1961-64, 1966-71, 1974-75, 1977

	W	L	PCT	ERA	G	GS	CG	IP	H	BB	SO	ShO	W	L	SV	AB	H	HR	BA
1953 NY N	0	0	—	18.00	1	1	0	1	1	1	1	0	0	0	0	0	*		

Vic Davalillo

DAVALILLO, VICTOR JOSE   BL TL 5'7" 150 lbs.
Brother of Yo-Yo Davalillo.
B. July 31, 1939, Cabimas, Venezuela

	W	L	PCT	ERA	G	GS	CG	IP	H	BB	SO	ShO	W	L	SV	AB	H	HR	BA
1969 STL N	0	0	—	∞	2	0	0		2	2	0	0	0	0	0		*		

Curt Davis

DAVIS, CURTIS BENTON (Coonskin)   BR TR 6'2" 185 lbs.
B. Sept. 7, 1903, Greenfield, Mo.   D. Oct. 13, 1965, Covina, Calif.

	W	L	PCT	ERA	G	GS	CG	IP	H	BB	SO	ShO	W	L	SV	AB	H	HR	BA
1934 PHI N	19	17	.528	2.95	51	31	18	274.1	283	60	99	3	6	2	5	95	20	1	.211
1935	16	14	.533	3.66	44	27	19	231	264	47	74	3	2	2	2	75	13	1	.173
1936 2 teams			PHI	N	(10G 2-4)		CHI	N	(24G 11-9)										
" total	13	13	.500	3.46	34	28	13	213.1	217	50	70	0	1	2	1	79	12	0	.152
1937 CHI N	10	5	.667	4.08	28	14	8	123.2	138	30	32	0	1	1	1	40	12	1	.300
1938 STL N	12	8	.600	3.63	40	21	8	173.1	187	27	36	2	4	0	3	57	13	3	.228
1939	22	16	.579	3.63	49	31	13	248	279	48	70	3	3	5	7	105	40	1	.381
1940 2 teams			STL	N	(14G 0-4)		BKN	N	(22G 8-7)										
" total	8	11	.421	4.19	36	25	9	191	208	38	58	0	1	1	3	66	6	1	.091
1941 BKN N	13	7	.650	2.97	28	16	10	154.1	141	27	50	5	2	3	2	59	11	2	.186
1942	15	6	.714	2.36	32	26	13	206	179	51	60	5	1	0	2	68	12	0	.176
1943	10	13	.435	3.78	31	21	8	164.1	182	39	47	2	3	1	3	55	9	0	.164
1944	10	11	.476	3.34	31	23	12	194	207	39	49	1	1	0	4	63	10	0	.159
1945	10	10	.500	3.25	24	18	10	149.2	171	21	39	0	0	2	0	51	7	1	.137
1946	0	0	—	13.50	1	0	0	2	3	2	0	0	0	0	0	0	0	0	—
13 yrs.	158	131	.547	3.42	429	281	141	2325	2459	479	684	24	25	19	33	813	165	11	.203
3 yrs.	34	28	.548	3.81	103	59	21	475.1	539	94	118	5	7	5	11	181	53	4	.293

WORLD SERIES
	W	L	PCT	ERA	G	GS	CG	IP	H	BB	SO	ShO	W	L	SV	AB	H	HR	BA
1941 BKN N	0	1	.000	5.06	1	1	0	5.1	6	3	1	0	0	0	0	2	0	0	.000

Jim Davis

DAVIS, JAMES BENNETT   BB TL 6' 180 lbs.
B. Sept. 15, 1924, Red Bluff, Calif.

	W	L	PCT	ERA	G	GS	CG	IP	H	BB	SO	ShO	W	L	SV	AB	H	HR	BA
1954 CHI N	11	7	.611	3.52	46	12	2	127.2	114	51	58	0	6	2	4	32	2	0	.063
1955	7	11	.389	4.44	42	16	0	133.2	122	58	62	0	5	3	3	37	1	0	.027
1956	5	7	.417	3.66	46	11	2	120.1	116	59	66	1	3	2	2	28	5	0	.179
1957 2 teams			STL	N	(10G 0-1)		NY	N	(10G 1-0)										
" total	1	1	.500	5.84	20	0	0	24.2	31	11	11	0	1	1	1	2	1	0	.500
4 yrs.	24	26	.480	4.01	154	39	4	406.1	383	179	197	1	15	8	10	99	9	0	.091
1 yr.	0	1	.000	5.27	10	0	0	13.2	18	6	5	0	0	1	1	1	0	0	.000

Pea Ridge Day

DAY, CLYDE HENRY   BR TR 6' 190 lbs.
B. Aug. 27, 1899, Pea Ridge, Ark.   D. Mar. 21, 1934, Kansas City, Mo.

	W	L	PCT	ERA	G	GS	CG	IP	H	BB	SO	ShO	W	L	SV	AB	H	HR	BA
1924 STL N	1	1	.500	4.58	3	3	1	17.2	22	6	3	0	0	0	0	8	1	0	.125
1925	2	4	.333	6.30	17	4	1	40	53	7	13	0	1	1	1	13	2	0	.154
1926 CIN N	0	0	—	7.36	4	0	0	7.1	13	2	2	0	0	0	0	2	0	0	.000
1931 BKN N	2	2	.500	4.55	22	2	1	57.1	75	13	30	0	2	0	1	18	4	0	.222
4 yrs.	5	7	.417	5.30	46	9	3	122.1	163	28	48	0	3	1	2	41	7	0	.171
2 yrs.	3	5	.375	5.77	20	7	2	57.2	75	13	16	0	1	1	1	21	3	0	.143

Cot Deal

DEAL, ELLIS FERGASON   BB TR 5'10½" 185 lbs.
B. Jan. 23, 1923, Arapaho, Okla.   BL 1947-48

	W	L	PCT	ERA	G	GS	CG	IP	H	BB	SO	ShO	W	L	SV	AB	H	HR	BA
1947 BOS A	0	1	.000	9.24	5	2	0	12.2	20	7	6	0	0	0	0	4	2	0	.500
1948	1	0	1.000	0.00	4	0	0	4	3	3	2	0	1	0	0	0	0	0	—
1950 STL N	0	0	—	18.00	3	0	0	1	3	2	1	0	0	0	0	0	0	0	—
1954	2	3	.400	6.28	33	0	0	71.2	85	36	25	0	2	3	1	20	2	1	.100
4 yrs.	3	4	.429	6.55	45	2	0	89.1	111	48	34	0	3	3	1	24	4	1	.167
2 yrs.	2	3	.400	6.44	36	0	0	72.2	88	38	26	0	2	3	1	20	2	1	.100

Dizzy Dean

DEAN, JAY HANNA   BR TR 6'2" 182 lbs.
Brother of Paul Dean.
B. Jan. 16, 1911, Lucas, Ark.   D. July 17, 1974, Reno, Nev.
Hall of Fame 1953.

	W	L	PCT	ERA	G	GS	CG	IP	H	BB	SO	ShO	W	L	SV	AB	H	HR	BA
1930 STL N	1	0	1.000	1.00	1	1	1	9	3	3	5	0	0	0	0	3	1	0	.333
1932	18	15	.545	3.30	46	33	16	286	280	102	191	4	0	3	2	97	25	2	.258
1933	20	18	.526	3.04	48	34	26	293	279	64	199	3	1	3	4	105	19	1	.181
1934	30	7	.811	2.66	50	33	24	311.2	288	75	195	7	4	2	7	118	29	2	.246
1935	28	12	.700	3.11	50	36	29	324.1	326	82	182	3	4	3	5	128	30	2	.234
1936	24	13	.649	3.17	51	34	28	315	310	53	195	2	2	3	11	121	27	0	.223
1937	13	10	.565	2.69	27	25	17	197.1	206	33	120	4	1	1	1	66	15	1	.227
1938 CHI N	7	1	.875	1.81	13	10	3	74.2	63	8	22	1	0	0	0	26	5	0	.192

	W	L	PCT	ERA	G	GS	CG	IP	H	BB	SO	ShO	Relief Pitching W	L	SV	BATTING AB	H	HR	BA

Dizzy Dean continued

	W	L	PCT	ERA	G	GS	CG	IP	H	BB	SO	ShO	W	L	SV	AB	H	HR	BA
1939	6	4	.600	3.36	19	13	7	96.1	98	17	27	2	0	1	0	34	5	0	.147
1940	3	3	.500	5.17	10	9	3	54	68	20	18	0	0	0	0	18	4	0	.222
1941	0	0	—	18.00	1	1	0	1	3	0	1	0	0	0	0	0	0	0	—
1947 STL A	0	0	—	0.00	1	1	0	4	3	1	0	0	0	0	0	1	1	0	1.000
12 yrs.	150	83	.644	3.03	317	230	154	1966.1	1927	458	1155	26	11	16	30	717	161	8	.225
7 yrs.	134	75	.641	3.00	273	196	141	1736.1	1692	412	1087	23	11	15	30	638	146	8	.229
	5th		**2nd**				**6th**	**9th**			**2nd**	**6th**			**6th**				

WORLD SERIES

	W	L	PCT	ERA	G	GS	CG	IP	H	BB	SO	ShO	W	L	SV	AB	H	HR	BA
1934 STL N	2	1	.667	1.73	3	3	2	26	20	5	17	1	0	0	0	12	3	0	.250
1938 CHI N	0	1	.000	6.48	2	1	0	8.1	8	1	2	0	0	0	0	3	2	0	.667
2 yrs.	2	2	.500	2.88	5	4	2	34.1	28	6	19	1	0	0	0	15	5	0	.333

Paul Dean

DEAN, PAUL DEE (Daffy)   BR TR 6' 175 lbs.
Brother of Dizzy Dean.
B. Aug. 14, 1913, Lucas, Ark.   D. Mar. 17, 1981, Springdale, Ark.

	W	L	PCT	ERA	G	GS	CG	IP	H	BB	SO	ShO	W	L	SV	AB	H	HR	BA
1934 STL N	19	11	.633	3.43	39	26	16	233.1	225	52	150	5	2	4	2	83	20	0	.241
1935	19	12	.613	3.37	46	33	19	269.2	261	55	143	2	3	1	5	90	12	0	.133
1936	5	5	.500	4.60	17	14	5	92	113	20	28	0	0	1	1	34	2	0	.059
1937	0	0	—	∞	1	0	0	1	2	0	0	0	0	0	0	0	0	0	—
1938	3	1	.750	2.61	5	4	2	31	37	5	14	1	0	0	0	11	2	0	.182
1939	0	1	.000	6.07	16	2	0	43	54	10	16	0	0	0	0	9	1	0	.111
1940 NY N	4	4	.500	3.90	27	7	2	99.1	110	29	32	0	2	3	0	26	3	0	.115
1941	0	0	—	3.18	5	0	0	5.2	8	3	3	0	0	0	0	0	0	0	—
1943 STL A	0	0	—	3.38	3	1	0	13.1	16	3	1	0	0	0	0	3	0	0	.000
9 yrs.	50	34	.595	3.75	159	87	44	787.1	825	179	387	8	7	9	8	256	40	0	.156
6 yrs.	46	30	.605	3.74	124	79	42	669	691	144	351	8	5	6	8	227	37	0	.163

WORLD SERIES

	W	L	PCT	ERA	G	GS	CG	IP	H	BB	SO	ShO	W	L	SV	AB	H	HR	BA
1934 STL N	2	0	1.000	1.00	2	2	2	18	15	7	11	0	0	0	0	6	1	0	.167

Art Delaney

DELANEY, ARTHUR DEWEY   BR TR 5'10½" 178 lbs.
Born Arthur Dewey Helenius.
B. Jan. 5, 1897, Chicago, Ill.   D. May 2, 1970, Hayward, Calif.

	W	L	PCT	ERA	G	GS	CG	IP	H	BB	SO	ShO	W	L	SV	AB	H	HR	BA
1924 STL N	1	0	1.000	1.80	8	1	1	20	19	6	2	0	0	0	0	7	2	0	.286
1928 BOS N	9	17	.346	3.79	39	22	8	192.1	197	56	45	0	4	3	2	63	9	0	.143
1929	3	5	.375	6.12	20	8	3	75	103	35	17	1	1	1	0	21	3	1	.143
3 yrs.	13	22	.371	4.26	67	31	12	287.1	319	97	64	1	5	4	2	91	14	1	.154
1 yr.	1	0	1.000	1.80	8	1	1	20	19	6	2	0	0	0	0	7	2	0	.286

Luis DeLeon

DeLEON, LUIS   BR TR 6'1" 153 lbs.
B. Aug. 19, 1958, Ponce, Puerto Rico

	W	L	PCT	ERA	G	GS	CG	IP	H	BB	SO	ShO	W	L	SV	AB	H	HR	BA
1981 STL N	0	1	.000	2.40	10	0	0	15	11	3	8	0	0	1	0	1	0	0	.000
1982 SD N	9	5	.643	2.03	61	0	0	102	77	16	60	0	9	5	15	11	1	0	.091
2 yrs.	9	6	.600	2.08	71	0	0	117	88	19	68	0	9	6	15	12	1	0	.083
1 yr.	0	1	.000	2.40	10	0	0	15	11	3	8	0	0	1	0	1	0	0	.000

Wheezer Dell

DELL, WILLIAM GEORGE   BR TR 6'4" 210 lbs.
B. June 11, 1887, Tuscarora, Nev.   D. Aug. 24, 1966, Independence, Calif.

	W	L	PCT	ERA	G	GS	CG	IP	H	BB	SO	ShO	W	L	SV	AB	H	HR	BA
1912 STL N	0	0	—	11.57	3	0	0	2.1	3	3	0	0	0	0	0	0	0	0	—
1915 BKN N	11	10	.524	2.34	40	24	12	215	166	100	94	4	2	0	1	66	10	0	.152
1916	8	9	.471	2.26	32	16	9	155	143	43	76	2	2	1	1	44	4	0	.091
1917	0	4	.000	3.72	17	4	0	58	55	25	28	0	1	1	1	16	1	0	.063
4 yrs.	19	23	.452	2.55	92	44	21	430.1	367	171	198	6	4	2	3	126	15	0	.119
1 yr.	0	0	—	11.57	3	0	0	2.1	3	3	0	0	0	0	0	0	0	0	—

WORLD SERIES

	W	L	PCT	ERA	G	GS	CG	IP	H	BB	SO	ShO	W	L	SV	AB	H	HR	BA
1916 BKN N	0	0	—	0.00	1	0	0	1	1	0	1	0	0	0	0	0	0	0	—

Don Dennis

DENNIS, DONALD RAY   BR TR 6'2" 190 lbs.
B. Mar. 3, 1942, Uniontown, Kans.

	W	L	PCT	ERA	G	GS	CG	IP	H	BB	SO	ShO	W	L	SV	AB	H	HR	BA
1965 STL N	2	3	.400	2.29	41	0	0	55	47	16	29	0	2	3	6	5	2	0	.400
1966	4	2	.667	4.98	38	1	0	59.2	73	17	25	0	4	2	2	12	1	0	.083
2 yrs.	6	5	.545	3.69	79	1	0	114.2	120	33	54	0	6	5	8	17	3	0	.176
2 yrs.	6	5	.545	3.69	79	1	0	114.2	120	33	54	0	6	5	8	17	3	0	.176

John Denny

DENNY, JOHN ALLEN   BR TR 6'3" 185 lbs.
B. Nov. 8, 1952, Prescott, Ariz.

	W	L	PCT	ERA	G	GS	CG	IP	H	BB	SO	ShO	W	L	SV	AB	H	HR	BA
1974 STL N	0	0	—	0.00	2	0	0	2	3	0	1	0	0	0	0	0	0	0	—
1975	10	7	.588	3.97	25	24	3	136	149	51	72	2	0	0	0	44	10	0	.227
1976	11	9	.550	2.52	30	30	8	207	189	74	74	3	0	0	0	67	15	0	.224
1977	8	8	.500	4.50	26	26	3	150	165	62	60	1	0	0	0	51	5	0	.098
1978	14	11	.560	2.96	33	33	11	234	200	74	103	2	0	0	0	73	13	0	.178
1979	8	11	.421	4.85	31	31	5	206	206	100	99	2	0	0	0	70	9	0	.129
1980 CLE A	8	6	.571	4.38	16	16	4	109	116	47	59	1	0	0	0	0	0	0	—
1981	10	6	.625	3.14	19	19	6	146	139	66	94	3	0	0	0	0	0	0	—
1982 2 teams			CLE A	(21G 6–11)			PHI N	(4G 0–2)											
" total	6	13	.316	4.87	25	25	5	160.2	144	83	113	0	0	0	0	6	1	0	.167
9 yrs.	75	71	.514	3.81	207	204	45	1350.2	1311	557	675	14	0	0	0	311	53	0	.170
6 yrs.	51	46	.526	3.67	147	144	30	935	912	361	409	10	0	0	0	305	52	0	.170

	W	L	PCT	ERA	G	GS	CG	IP	H	BB	SO	ShO	Relief Pitching W	L	SV	BATTING AB	H	HR	BA

Paul Derringer

DERRINGER, PAUL (Duke, 'Oom Paul)
B. Oct. 17, 1906, Springfield, Ky.　　　　　BR TR 6'3½" 205 lbs.

	W	L	PCT	ERA	G	GS	CG	IP	H	BB	SO	ShO	W	L	SV	AB	H	HR	BA
1931 STL N	18	8	.692	3.36	35	23	15	211.2	225	65	134	4	4	0	2	72	7	0	.097
1932	11	14	.440	4.05	39	30	14	233.1	296	67	78	1	1	1	0	73	13	0	.178
1933 2 teams			STL	N	(3G 0–2)		CIN	N	(33G 7–25)										
" total	7	27	.206	3.30	36	33	17	248	264	60	89	2	0	1	1	81	14	0	.173
1934 CIN N	15	21	.417	3.59	47	31	18	261	297	59	122	1	2	4	4	92	18	0	.196
1935	22	13	.629	3.51	45	33	20	276.2	295	49	120	3	3	2	2	93	13	0	.140
1936	19	19	.500	4.02	51	37	13	282.1	331	42	121	2	1	3	5	90	18	0	.200
1937	10	14	.417	4.04	43	26	12	222.2	240	55	94	1	1	4	1	80	16	0	.200
1938	21	14	.600	2.93	41	37	26	307	315	49	132	4	0	0	3	119	21	2	.176
1939 CIN N	25	7	.781	2.93	38	35	28	301	321	35	128	5	1	0	0	110	23	0	.209
1940	20	12	.625	3.06	37	37	26	296.2	280	48	115	3	0	0	0	108	18	0	.167
1941	12	14	.462	3.31	29	28	17	228.1	233	54	76	2	0	0	1	84	13	0	.155
1942	10	11	.476	3.06	29	27	13	208.2	203	49	68	1	0	0	0	68	9	0	.132
1943 CHI N	10	14	.417	3.57	32	22	10	174	184	39	75	2	1	2	3	58	13	0	.224
1944	7	13	.350	4.15	42	16	7	180	205	39	69	0	2	5	3	57	9	0	.158
1945	16	11	.593	3.45	35	30	15	213.2	223	51	86	1	1	0	4	75	15	0	.200
15 yrs.	223	212	.513	3.46	579	445	251	3645	3912	761	1507	32	17	22	29	1260	220	2	.175
3 yrs.	29	24	.547	3.74	77	55	30	462	545	141	215	5	5	1	2	150	20	0	.133
WORLD SERIES																			
1931 STL N	0	2	.000	4.26	3	2	0	12.2	14	7	14	0	0	0	0	2	0	0	.000
1939 CIN N	0	1	.000	2.35	2	2	1	15.1	9	3	9	0	0	0	0	5	1	0	.200
1940	2	1	.667	2.79	3	3	2	19.1	17	10	6	0	0	0	0	7	0	0	.000
1945 CHI N	0	0	–	6.75	3	0	0	5.1	5	7	1	0	0	0	0	0	0	0	–
4 yrs.	2	4	.333	3.42	11	7	3	52.2	45	27	30	0	0	0	0	14	1	0	.071
			7th				10th					6th							

Leo Dickerman

DICKERMAN, LEO LOUIS
B. Oct. 31, 1896, DeSoto, Mo.　　　D. Apr. 30, 1982, Atkins, Ark.　　　BR TR 6'4" 192 lbs.

	W	L	PCT	ERA	G	GS	CG	IP	H	BB	SO	ShO	W	L	SV	AB	H	HR	BA
1923 BKN N	8	12	.400	3.59	35	20	7	165.2	185	71	57	1	2	1	0	52	13	2	.250
1924 2 teams			BKN	N	(7G 0–0)		STL	N	(18G 7–4)										
" total	7	4	.636	2.84	25	15	8	139.1	128	67	37	1	0	0	0	45	10	0	.222
1925 STL N	4	11	.267	5.58	29	20	7	130.2	135	79	40	2	0	0	1	44	5	0	.114
3 yrs.	19	27	.413	3.95	89	55	22	435.2	448	217	134	4	2	1	1	141	28	2	.199
2 yrs.	11	15	.423	4.06	47	33	15	250.1	243	130	68	3	0	0	1	83	14	0	.169

Murry Dickson

DICKSON, MURRY MONROE
B. Aug. 21, 1916, Tracy, Mo.　　　　　BR TR 5'10½" 157 lbs.

	W	L	PCT	ERA	G	GS	CG	IP	H	BB	SO	ShO	W	L	SV	AB	H	HR	BA
1939 STL N	0	0	–	0.00	1	0	0	3.2	1	1	2	0	0	0	0	1	0	0	.000
1940	0	0	–	16.20	1	1	0	1.2	5	1	0	0	0	0	0	0	0	0	–
1942	6	3	.667	2.91	36	7	2	120.2	91	61	66	0	4	1	2	42	8	0	.190
1943	8	2	.800	3.58	31	7	2	115.2	114	49	44	0	2	2	0	34	9	0	.265
1946	15	6	.714	2.88	47	19	12	184.1	160	56	82	2	4	2	1	65	18	0	.277
1947	13	16	.448	3.07	47	25	11	231.2	211	88	111	4	3	2	3	80	17	0	.213
1948	12	16	.429	4.14	42	29	11	252.1	257	85	113	1	2	4	1	96	27	0	.281
1949 PIT N	12	14	.462	3.29	44	20	11	224.1	216	80	89	2	3	5	0	84	17	0	.202
1950	10	15	.400	3.80	51	22	8	225	227	83	76	0	5	3	3	82	21	0	.256
1951	20	16	.556	4.02	45	35	19	288.2	294	101	112	3	4	2	2	110	30	1	.273
1952	14	21	.400	3.57	43	34	21	277.2	278	76	112	2	2	0	2	107	24	0	.224
1953	10	19	.345	4.53	45	26	10	200.2	240	58	88	1	2	4	4	61	7	0	.115
1954 PHI N	10	20	.333	3.78	40	31	12	226.1	256	73	64	4	1	1	3	79	15	0	.190
1955	12	11	.522	3.50	36	28	12	216	190	82	92	4	1	1	0	82	18	1	.220
1956 2 teams			PHI	N	(3G 0–3)		STL	N	(28G 13–8)										
" total	13	11	.542	3.28	31	30	12	219.1	195	69	110	3	0	1	0	86	22	0	.256
1957 STL N	5	3	.625	4.14	14	13	3	74	87	25	29	1	0	0	0	27	6	0	.222
1958 2 teams			KC	A	(27G 9–5)		NY	A	(6G 1–2)										
" total	10	7	.588	3.70	33	11	3	119.1	117	43	55	0	7	3	2	42	11	1	.262
1959 KC A	2	1	.667	4.94	38	0	0	71	85	27	36	0	2	1	0	17	3	0	.176
18 yrs.	172	181	.487	3.66	625	338	149	3052.1	3024	1058	1281	27	42	32	23	1095	253	3	.231
9 yrs.	72	54	.571	3.38	247	128	53	1180.1	1101	423	556	11	15	12	7	422	104	0	.246
WORLD SERIES																			
1943 STL N	0	0	–	0.00	1	0	0	.2	0	1	0	0	0	0	0	0	0	0	–
1946	0	1	.000	3.86	2	2	0	14	11	4	7	0	0	0	0	5	2	0	.400
1958 NY A	0	0	–	4.50	2	0	0	4	4	0	1	0	0	0	0	0	0	0	–
3 yrs.	0	1	.000	3.86	5	2	0	18.2	15	5	8	0	0	0	0	5	2	0	.400

Larry Dierker

DIERKER, LAWRENCE EDWARD
B. Sept. 22, 1946, Hollywood, Calif.　　　　BR TR 6'4" 190 lbs.

	W	L	PCT	ERA	G	GS	CG	IP	H	BB	SO	ShO	W	L	SV	AB	H	HR	BA
1964 HOU N	1	1	.000	2.00	3	1	0	9	7	3	5	0	0	0	0	3	0	0	.000
1965	7	8	.467	3.50	26	19	1	146.2	135	37	109	0	1	0	0	50	5	1	.100
1966	10	8	.556	3.18	29	28	8	187	173	45	108	2	0	0	0	67	10	1	.149
1967	6	5	.545	3.36	15	15	4	99	95	25	68	0	0	0	0	31	7	0	.226
1968	12	15	.444	3.31	32	32	10	233.2	206	89	161	1	0	0	0	73	5	0	.068
1969	20	13	.606	2.33	39	37	20	305	240	72	232	4	0	0	0	118	17	1	.144
1970	16	12	.571	3.87	37	36	17	270	263	82	191	2	0	0	1	92	16	0	.174
1971	12	6	.667	2.72	24	23	6	159	150	33	91	2	0	0	0	54	4	0	.074
1972	15	8	.652	3.40	31	31	12	214.2	209	51	115	5	0	0	0	78	13	0	.167
1973	1	1	.500	4.33	14	3	0	27	27	13	18	0	1	0	0	4	0	0	.000
1974	11	10	.524	2.89	33	33	7	224	189	82	150	3	0	0	0	71	14	0	.197
1975	14	16	.467	4.00	34	34	14	232	225	91	127	2	0	0	0	76	7	0	.092
1976	13	14	.481	3.69	28	28	7	188	171	72	112	4	0	0	0	64	9	1	.141
1977 STL N	2	6	.250	4.62	11	9	0	39	40	16	6	0	0	0	0	8	0	0	.000
14 yrs.	139	123	.531	3.30	356	329	106	2334	2130	711	1493	25	2	0	1	789	107	4	.136
1 yr.	2	6	.250	4.62	11	9	0	39	40	16	6	0	0	0	0	8	0	0	.000

	W	L	PCT	ERA	G	GS	CG	IP	H	BB	SO	ShO	Relief Pitching W	L	SV	BATTING AB	H	HR	BA

Bill Doak

DOAK, WILLIAM LEOPOLD (Spittin' Bill) BR TR 6'½" 165 lbs.
B. Jan. 28, 1891, Pittsburgh, Pa. D. Nov. 26, 1954, Bradenton, Fla.

	W	L	PCT	ERA	G	GS	CG	IP	H	BB	SO	ShO	W	L	SV	AB	H	HR	BA
1912 CIN N	0	0	—	4.50	1	1	0	2	4	1	0	0	0	0	0	0	0	0	—
1913 STL N	2	8	.200	3.10	15	12	5	93	79	39	51	1	0	0	1	31	1	0	.032
1914	20	6	.769	1.72	36	33	16	256	193	87	118	7	1	0	0	85	10	0	.118
1915	16	18	.471	2.64	38	36	19	276	263	85	124	3	0	0	1	86	15	0	.174
1916	12	8	.600	2.63	29	26	11	192	177	55	82	3	0	0	0	62	8	0	.129
1917	16	20	.444	3.10	44	37	16	281.2	257	85	111	3	2	1	2	95	12	0	.126
1918	9	15	.375	2.43	31	23	16	211	191	60	74	1	0	2	1	66	12	0	.182
1919	13	14	.481	3.11	31	29	13	202.2	182	55	69	3	1	0	0	64	7	0	.109
1920	20	12	.625	2.53	39	37	20	270	256	80	90	5	0	0	1	88	10	0	.114
1921	15	6	.714	2.59	32	28	13	208.2	224	37	83	1	1	0	1	70	10	0	.143
1922	11	13	.458	5.54	37	29	8	180.1	222	69	73	2	1	1	2	54	7	0	.130
1923	8	13	.381	3.26	30	26	7	185	199	69	53	3	0	3	0	67	3	0	.045
1924 2 teams		STL	N	(11G 2-1)		BKN	N	(21G 11-5)											
" total	13	6	.684	3.10	32	17	8	171.1	155	49	39	2	4	2	3	61	11	1	.180
1927 BKN N	11	8	.579	3.48	27	20	6	145	153	40	32	1	3	0	0	47	6	0	.128
1928	3	8	.273	3.26	28	12	4	99.1	104	35	12	1	1	2	3	27	3	0	.111
1929 STL N	1	2	.333	12.00	3	2	0	9	17	5	3	0	0	1	0	2	0	0	.000
16 yrs.	170	157	.520	2.98	453	368	162	2782.2	2676	851	1014	36	14	12	15	905	115	1	.127
13 yrs.	145	136	.516	2.93	376	319	144	2387	2285	740	938	32	8	9	12	775	96	0	.124
	4th	3rd		10th	5th		4th	4th		4th	5th	2nd							

George Dockins

DOCKINS, GEORGE WOODROW (Lefty) BL TL 6' 175 lbs.
B. May 5, 1917, Clyde, Kans.

	W	L	PCT	ERA	G	GS	CG	IP	H	BB	SO	ShO	W	L	SV	AB	H	HR	BA
1945 STL N	8	6	.571	3.21	31	12	5	126.1	132	38	33	2	3	4	0	34	6	0	.176
1947 BKN N	0	0	—	11.81	4	0	0	5.1	10	2	1	0	0	0	0	1	0	0	.000
2 yrs.	8	6	.571	3.55	35	12	5	131.2	142	40	34	2	3	4	0	35	6	0	.171
1 yr.	8	6	.571	3.21	31	12	5	126.1	132	38	33	2	3	4	0	34	6	0	.176

John Dolan

DOLAN, JOHN TR
B. Sept. 12, 1867, Newport, Ky. D. May 8, 1948, Springfield, Ohio

	W	L	PCT	ERA	G	GS	CG	IP	H	BB	SO	ShO	W	L	SV	AB	H	HR	BA
1890 CIN N	1	1	.500	4.50	2	2	2	18	17	10	9	0	0	0	0	8	1	0	.125
1891 COL AA	12	11	.522	4.16	27	24	19	203.1	216	84	68	0	0	0	0	78	7	1	.090
1892 WAS N	2	2	.500	4.38	5	4	3	37	39	15	8	0	0	1	0	13	3	0	.231
1893 STL N	0	2	.000	4.15	3	1	1	17.1	26	7	1	0	0	0	1	7	1	1	.143
1895 CHI N	0	1	.000	6.55	2	2	1	11	16	6	1	0	0	0	0	3	0	0	.000
5 yrs.	15	17	.469	4.30	39	33	26	286.2	314	122	87	0	0	1	1	109	12	2	.110
1 yr.	0	2	.000	4.15	3	1	1	17.1	26	7	1	0	0	0	1	7	1	1	.143

Red Donahue

DONAHUE, FRANCIS ROSTELL BR TR
B. Jan. 23, 1873, Waterbury, Conn. D. Aug. 25, 1913, Philadelphia, Pa.

	W	L	PCT	ERA	G	GS	CG	IP	H	BB	SO	ShO	W	L	SV	AB	H	HR	BA
1893 NY N	0	0	—	9.00	2	0	0	8	3	1	0	0	0	0	0	2	0	0	.000
1895 STL N	0	1	.000	6.75	1	1	1	8	9	3	2	0	0	0	0	3	0	0	.000
1896	7	24	.226	5.80	32	32	28	267	376	98	70	0	0	0	0	107	17	0	.159
1897	11	33¹	.250	6.13	46	42	38		106	64	1	1	2	1		155	33	1	.213
1898 PHI N	17	17	.500	3.55	35	35	33	284.1	327	80	57	1	0	0	0	112	16	0	.143
1899	21	8	.724	3.39	35	31	27	279	292	63	51	4	1	1	0	111	20	0	.180
1900	15	10	.600	3.60	32	24	21	240	299	50	41	2	3	1	0	90	20	0	.222
1901	22	13	.629	2.60	35	34	34	304.1	307	60	89	1	1	0	0	117	11	0	.094
1902 STL A	22	11	.667	2.76	35	34	33	316.1	322	65	63	2	1	0	0	118	11	0	.093
1903 2 teams		STL	A	(16G 8-7)		CLE	A	(16G 7-9)											
" total	15	16	.484	2.59	32	30	28	267.2	287	34	96	4	1	1	0	104	16	0	.154
1904 CLE A	19	14	.576	2.40	35	32	30	277	281	49	127	6	1	1	0	101	17	0	.168
1905	6	12	.333	3.40	20	18	13	137.2	132	25	45	1	0	0	0	53	4	0	.075
1906 DET A	14	14	.500	2.73	28	28	26	241	260	54	82	3	0	0	0	81	10	0	.123
13 yrs.	169	173	.494	3.61	368	341	312	2975.1	3384	690	788	25	9	6	2	1154	175	1	.152
3 yrs.	18	58	.237	6.00	79	75	67	623	869	207	136	1	1	2	1	265	50	1	.189

Mike Donlin

DONLIN, MICHAEL JOSEPH (Turkey Mike) BL TL 5'9" 170 lbs.
B. May 30, 1878, Erie, Pa. D. Sept. 24, 1933, Hollywood, Calif.

	W	L	PCT	ERA	G	GS	CG	IP	H	BB	SO	ShO	W	L	SV	AB	H	HR	BA
1899 STL N	0	1	.000	7.63	3	1	0	15.1	15	14	6	0	0	0	0	267	88	6	.330
1902 CIN N	0	0	—	0.00	1	0	0	1	1	0	0	0	0	0	0	143	42	0	.294
2 yrs.	0	1	.000	7.16	4	1	0	16.1	16	14	6	0	0	0	0	*			
1 yr.	0	1	.000	7.63	3	1	0	15.1	15	14	6	0	0	0	0	543	178	16	.328

Blix Donnelly

DONNELLY, SYLVESTER URBAN BR TR 5'10" 166 lbs.
B. Jan. 21, 1914, Olivia, Minn. D. June 20, 1976, Olivia, Minn.

	W	L	PCT	ERA	G	GS	CG	IP	H	BB	SO	ShO	W	L	SV	AB	H	HR	BA
1944 STL N	2	1	.667	2.12	27	4	2	76.1	61	34	45	1	0	1	2	16	1	0	.063
1945	8	10	.444	3.52	31	23	9	166.1	157	87	76	4	0	1	2	54	7	0	.130
1946 2 teams		STL	N	(13G 1-2)		PHI	N	(12G 3-4)											
" total	4	6	.400	3.10	25	8	2	90	81	34	49	0	1	2	1	25	7	0	.280
1947 PHI N	4	6	.400	2.98	38	10	5	120.2	113	46	31	1	0	3	5	32	2	0	.063
1948	5	7	.417	3.69	26	19	8	131.2	125	49	46	1	0	0	2	45	10	0	.222
1949	2	1	.667	5.06	23	10	1	78.1	84	40	36	0	1	0	1	23	4	0	.174
1950	2	4	.333	4.29	14	1	0	21	30	10	10	0	2	3	0	5	1	0	.200
1951 BOS N	0	1	.000	7.36	6	0	0	7.1	8	6	3	0	0	1	0	1	0	0	.000
8 yrs.	27	36	.429	3.49	190	75	27	691.2	659	306	296	7	4	11	12	201	32	0	.159
3 yrs.	11	13	.458	3.12	71	27	11	256.1	235	131	132	5	1	4	4	70	8	0	.114

WORLD SERIES

	W	L	PCT	ERA	G	GS	CG	IP	H	BB	SO	ShO	W	L	SV	AB	H	HR	BA
1944 STL N	1	0	1.000	0.00	2	0	0	6	2	1	9	0	1	0	0	1	0	0	.000

	W	L	PCT	ERA	G	GS	CG	IP	H	BB	SO	ShO	Relief Pitching W	L	SV	BATTING AB	H	HR	BA

Dave Dowling

DOWLING, DAVID BARCLAY
B. Aug. 23, 1942, Baton Rouge, La.   BR TL 6'2"   181 lbs.

	W	L	PCT	ERA	G	GS	CG	IP	H	BB	SO	ShO	W	L	SV	AB	H	HR	BA
1964 STL N	0	0	–	0.00	1	0	0	1	2	0	0	0	0	0	0	0	0	0	
1966 CHI N	1	0	1.000	2.00	1	1	1	9	10	0	3	0	0	0	0	2	0	0	.000
2 yrs.	1	0	1.000	1.80	2	1	1	10	12	0	3	0	0	0	0	2	0	0	.000
1 yr.	0	0	–	0.00	1	0	0	1	2	0	0	0	0	0	0	0	0	0	

Carl Doyle

DOYLE, WILLIAM CARL
B. July 30, 1912, Knoxville, Tenn.   D. Sept. 4, 1951, Knoxville, Tenn.   BR TR 6'1"   185 lbs.

	W	L	PCT	ERA	G	GS	CG	IP	H	BB	SO	ShO	W	L	SV	AB	H	HR	BA
1935 PHI A	2	7	.222	5.99	14	9	3	79.2	86	72	34	0	0	1	0	30	4	0	.133
1936	0	3	.000	10.94	8	6	1	38.2	66	29	12	0	0	0	0	15	4	0	.267
1939 BKN N	1	2	.333	1.02	5	1	1	17.2	8	7	7	1	0	2	1	6	1	0	.167
1940 2 teams			BKN	N	(3G 0–0)		STL	N	(21G 3–3)										
" total	3	3	.500	7.27	24	5	1	86.2	117	47	48	0	2	2	1	31	7	1	.226
4 yrs.	6	15	.286	6.95	51	21	6	222.2	277	155	101	1	2	5	2	82	16	1	.195
1 yr.	3	3	.500	5.89	21	5	1	81	99	41	44	0	2	2	0	30	6	1	.200

Moe Drabowsky

DRABOWSKY, MYRON WALTER
B. July 21, 1935, Ozanna, Poland   BR TR 6'3"   190 lbs.

	W	L	PCT	ERA	G	GS	CG	IP	H	BB	SO	ShO	W	L	SV	AB	H	HR	BA
1956 CHI N	2	4	.333	2.47	9	7	3	51	37	39	36	0	0	0	0	16	4	0	.250
1957	13	15	.464	3.53	36	33	12	239.2	214	94	170	2	0	0	0	82	15	1	.183
1958	9	11	.450	4.51	22	20	4	125.2	118	73	77	1	1	1	0	45	7	0	.156
1959	5	10	.333	4.13	31	23	3	141.2	138	75	70	1	0	0	0	45	5	0	.111
1960	3	1	.750	6.44	32	7	0	50.1	71	23	26	0	2	0	1	6	0	0	.000
1961 MIL N	0	2	.000	4.62	16	0	0	25.1	26	18	5	0	0	2	2	4	1	0	.250
1962 2 teams			CIN	N	(23G 2–6)		KC	A	(10G 1–1)										
" total	3	7	.300	5.03	33	3	1	111	113	41	75	0	1	1	1	23	1	0	.043
1963 KC A	7	13	.350	3.05	26	22	9	174.1	135	64	109	2	0	0	0	62	10	2	.161
1964	5	13	.278	5.29	53	21	1	168.1	176	72	119	0	1	2	1	43	1	0	.023
1965	1	5	.167	4.42	14	5	0	38.2	44	18	25	0	1	2	0	11	1	0	.091
1966 BAL A	6	0	1.000	2.81	44	3	0	96	62	29	98	0	5	0	7	22	8	0	.364
1967	7	5	.583	1.60	43	0	0	95.1	66	25	96	0	7	5	12	20	7	0	.350
1968	4	4	.500	1.91	45	0	0	61.1	35	25	46	0	4	4	7	7	2	0	.286
1969 KC A	11	9	.550	2.94	52	0	0	98	68	30	76	0	11	9	11	17	4	0	.235
1970 2 teams			KC	A	(24G 1–2)		BAL	A	(21G 4–2)										
" total	5	4	.556	3.52	45	0	0	69	58	27	59	0	5	4	3	9	1	0	.111
1971 STL N	6	1	.857	3.45	51	0	0	60	45	33	49	0	6	1	8	6	1	0	.167
1972 2 teams			STL	N	(30G 1–1)		CHI	A	(7G 0–0)										
" total	1	1	.500	2.57	37	0	0	35	35	16	26	0	1	1	2	2	0	0	.000
17 yrs.	88	105	.456	3.71	589	154	33	1640.2	1441	702	1162	6	45	32	55	420	68	3	.162
2 yrs.	7	2	.778	3.18	81	0	0	87.2	74	47	71	0	7	2	10	7	1	0	.143

WORLD SERIES

	W	L	PCT	ERA	G	GS	CG	IP	H	BB	SO	ShO	W	L	SV	AB	H	HR	BA
1966 BAL A	1	0	1.000	0.00	1	0	0	6.2	1	2	11	0	1	0	0	2	0	0	.000
1970	0	0	–	2.70	2	0	0	3.1	2	1	1	0	0	0	0	1	0	0	.000
2 yrs.	1	0	1.000	0.90	3	0	0	10	3	3	12	0	1	0	0	3	0	0	.000

Rob Dressler

DRESSLER, ROBERT ALAN
B. Feb. 2, 1954, Portland, Ore.   BR TR 6'3"   180 lbs.

	W	L	PCT	ERA	G	GS	CG	IP	H	BB	SO	ShO	W	L	SV	AB	H	HR	BA
1975 SF N	1	0	1.000	1.13	3	2	1	16	17	4	6	0	0	0	0	4	0	0	.000
1976	3	10	.231	4.43	25	19	0	107.2	125	35	33	0	1	0	0	31	4	0	.129
1978 STL N	0	1	.000	2.08	3	2	0	13	12	4	4	0	0	0	0	3	0	0	.000
1979 SEA A	3	2	.600	4.93	21	11	2	104	134	22	36	0	0	0	0	0	0	0	–
1980	4	10	.286	3.99	30	14	3	149	161	33	50	0	0	3	0	0	0	0	–
5 yrs.	11	23	.324	4.18	82	48	6	389.2	449	98	129	0	1	3	0	38	4	0	.105
1 yr.	0	1	.000	2.08	3	2	0	13	12	4	4	0	0	0	0	3	0	0	.000

Carl Druhot

DRUHOT, CARL A.
B. Sept. 1, 1882, Ohio   D. Feb. 11, 1918, Portland, Ore.   BL TL 5'7"   150 lbs.

	W	L	PCT	ERA	G	GS	CG	IP	H	BB	SO	ShO	W	L	SV	AB	H	HR	BA
1906 2 teams			CIN	N	(4G 2–2)		STL	N	(15G 6–8)										
" total	8	10	.444	2.90	19	16	13	155.1	144	53	59	1	2	0	0	65	15	0	.231
1907 STL N	0	1	.000	15.43	1	1	0	2.1	3	4	1	0	0	0	0	0	0	0	–
2 yrs.	8	11	.421	3.08	20	17	13	157.2	147	57	60	1	2	0	0	65	15	0	.231
2 yrs.	6	9	.400	2.85	16	14	12	132.2	120	50	46	1	1	0	0	56	13	0	.232

Bob Duliba

DULIBA, ROBERT JOHN
B. Jan. 9, 1935, Glen Lyon, Pa.   BR TR 5'10"   180 lbs.

	W	L	PCT	ERA	G	GS	CG	IP	H	BB	SO	ShO	W	L	SV	AB	H	HR	BA
1959 STL N	0	1	.000	2.78	11	0	0	22.2	19	12	14	0	0	1	1	4	0	0	.000
1960	4	4	.500	4.20	27	0	0	40.2	49	16	23	0	4	4	0	5	1	0	.200
1962	2	0	1.000	2.06	28	0	0	39.1	33	17	22	0	2	0	2	4	0	0	.000
1963 LA N	1	1	.500	1.17	6	0	0	7.2	3	6	4	0	1	1	1	1	0	0	.000
1964	6	4	.600	3.59	58	0	0	72.2	80	22	33	0	6	4	9	5	0	0	.000
1965 BOS A	4	2	.667	3.78	39	0	0	64.1	60	22	27	0	4	2	1	7	0	0	.000
1967 KC A	0	0	–	6.52	7	0	0	9.2	13	1	6	0	0	0	0	0	0	0	–
7 yrs.	17	12	.586	3.47	176	0	0	257	257	96	129	0	17	12	14	26	1	0	.038
3 yrs.	6	5	.545	3.07	66	0	0	102.2	101	45	59	0	6	5	3	13	1	0	.077

Wiley Dunham

DUNHAM, WILEY H.
B. Piketon, Ohio

	W	L	PCT	ERA	G	GS	CG	IP	H	BB	SO	ShO	W	L	SV	AB	H	HR	BA
1902 STL N	2	3	.400	5.68	7	5	3	38	47	13	15	0	0	0	1	12	1	0	.083

	W	L	PCT	ERA	G	GS	CG	IP	H	BB	SO	ShO	Relief Pitching W	L	SV	BATTING AB	H	HR	BA

John Dunleavy

DUNLEAVY, JOHN FRANCIS
B. Sept. 14, 1879, Harrison, N. J.   D. Apr. 12, 1944, South Norwalk, Conn.

	W	L	PCT	ERA	G	GS	CG	IP	H	BB	SO	ShO	W	L	SV	AB	H	HR	BA
1903 STL N	6	8	.429	4.06	14	13	9	102	101	57	51	0	1	0	0	193	48	0	.249
1904	1	4	.200	4.42	7	5	5	55	63	23	28	0	0	0	0	172	40	1	.233
2 yrs.	7	12	.368	4.18	21	18	14	157	164	80	79	0	1	0	0	*			
2 yrs.	7	12	.368	4.18	21	18	14	157	164	80	79	0	1	0	0	800	193	2	.241

Don Durham

DURHAM, DONALD GARY (Bull)   BR TR 6'   170 lbs.
B. Mar. 21, 1949, Yosemite, Ky.

	W	L	PCT	ERA	G	GS	CG	IP	H	BB	SO	ShO	W	L	SV	AB	H	HR	BA
1972 STL N	2	7	.222	4.34	10	8	1	47.2	42	22	35	0	0	1	0	14	7	2	.500
1973 TEX A	0	4	.000	7.65	15	4	0	40	49	23	23	0	0	0	1	0	0	0	-
2 yrs.	2	11	.154	5.85	25	12	1	87.2	91	45	58	0	0	1	1	14	7	2	.500
1 yr.	2	7	.222	4.34	10	8	1	47.2	42	22	35	0	0	1	0	14	7	2	.500

Erv Dusak

DUSAK, ERVIN FRANK (Four Sack)   BR TR 6'2"   185 lbs.
B. July 29, 1920, Chicago, Ill.

	W	L	PCT	ERA	G	GS	CG	IP	H	BB	SO	ShO	W	L	SV	AB	H	HR	BA
1948 STL N	0	0	-	0.00	1	0	0	1	0	1	0	0	0	0	0	311	65	6	.209
1950	0	2	.000	3.72	14	2	0	36.1	27	27	16	0	0	0	1	12	1	0	.083
1951 2 teams		STL N (5G 0-0)				PIT N (3G 0-1)													
" total	0	1	.000	9.18	8	1	0	16.2	24	16	10	0	0	0	0	41	13	2	.317
3 yrs.	0	3	.000	5.33	23	3	0	54	51	44	26	0	0	0	1	*			
3 yrs.	0	2	.000	4.37	20	2	0	47.1	41	35	24	0	0	0	1	969	233	22	.240

Frank Dwyer

DWYER, JOHN FRANCIS   BR TR 5'8"   145 lbs.
B. Mar. 25, 1868, Lee, Mass.   D. Feb. 4, 1943, Pittsfield, Mass.
Manager 1902.

	W	L	PCT	ERA	G	GS	CG	IP	H	BB	SO	ShO	W	L	SV	AB	H	HR	BA
1888 CHI N	4	1	.800	1.07	5	5	5	42	32	9	17	1	0	0	0	21	4	0	.190
1889	16	13	.552	3.59	32	30	27	276	307	72	63	0	1	0	0	135	27	1	.200
1890 CHI P	3	6	.333	6.23	12	6	6	69.1	98	25	17	0	2	1	1	53	14	0	.264
1891 C-M AA	19	23	.452	3.98	45	41	39	375	424	145	128	1	0	1	0	181	49	0	.271
1892 2 teams		STL N (10G 2-8)				CIN N (33G 19-10)													
" total	21	18	.538	2.98	43	37	30	323.1	341	73	61	3	2	1	1	154	23	0	.149
1893 CIN N	18	15	.545	4.13	37	30	28	287.1	332	93	53	1	2	2	2	120	24	1	.200
1894	19	22	.463	5.07	45	40	34	348	471	106	49	1	1	1	1	172	46	2	.267
1895	18	15	.545	4.24	37	31	23	280.1	355	74	46	2	2	3	0	113	30	1	.265
1896	24	11	.686	3.15	36	34	30	288.2	321	60	57	3	1	0	1	110	29	0	.264
1897	18	13	.581	3.78	37	31	22	247.1	315	56	41	0	3	1	0	94	25	0	.266
1898	16	10	.615	3.04	31	28	24	240	257	42	29	0	1	0	0	85	12	0	.141
1899	0	5	.000	5.51	5	5	2	32.2	48	9	2	0	0	0	0	11	4	0	.364
12 yrs.	176	152	.537	3.85	365	318	270	2810	3301	764	563	12	15	10	6	*			
1 yr.	2	8	.200	5.63	10	10	6	64	90	24	16	0	0	0	0	25	2	0	.080

Eddie Dyer

DYER, EDWIN HAWLEY   BL TL 5'11½"   168 lbs.
B. Oct. 11, 1900, Morgan City, La.   D. Apr. 20, 1964, Houston, Tex.
Manager 1946-50.

	W	L	PCT	ERA	G	GS	CG	IP	H	BB	SO	ShO	W	L	SV	AB	H	HR	BA
1922 STL N	0	0	-	2.45	2	0	0	3.2	7	0	3	0	0	0	0	3	1	0	.333
1923	2	1	.667	4.09	4	3	2	22	30	5	7	1	0	0	0	45	12	2	.267
1924	8	11	.421	4.61	29	15	7	136.2	174	51	23	1	3	2	0	76	18	0	.237
1925	4	3	.571	4.15	27	5	1	82.1	93	24	25	0	3	2	3	31	3	0	.097
1926	1	0	1.000	11.57	6	0	0	9.1	7	14	4	0	1	0	0	2	1	0	.500
1927	0	0	-	18.00	1	0	0	2	5	2	1	0	0	0	0	0	0	0	-
6 yrs.	15	15	.500	4.75	69	23	10	256	316	96	63	2	7	4	3	*			
6 yrs.	15	15	.500	4.75	69	23	10	256	316	96	63	2	7	4	3	157	35	2	.223

George Earnshaw

EARNSHAW, GEORGE LIVINGSTON (Moose)   BR TR 6'4"   210 lbs.
B. Feb. 15, 1900, New York, N. Y.   D. Dec. 1, 1976, Little Rock, Ark.

	W	L	PCT	ERA	G	GS	CG	IP	H	BB	SO	ShO	W	L	SV	AB	H	HR	BA
1928 PHI A	7	7	.500	3.81	26	22	7	158.1	143	100	117	3	0	0	1	57	14	0	.246
1929	24	8	.750	3.29	44	33	13	254.2	233	125	149	3	3	0	1	87	15	1	.172
1930	22	13	.629	4.44	49	39	20	296	299	139	193	3	2	2	2	114	26	0	.228
1931	21	7	.750	3.67	43	30	23	281.2	255	75	152	3	1	0	6	114	30	2	.263
1932	19	13	.594	4.77	36	33	21	245.1	262	94	109	1	1	1	0	91	26	0	.286
1933	5	10	.333	5.97	21	18	4	117.2	153	58	37	0	1	0	0	44	8	0	.182
1934 CHI A	14	11	.560	4.52	33	30	16	227	242	104	97	2	0	1	0	79	16	0	.203
1935 2 teams		CHI A (3G 1-2)				BKN N (25G 8-12)													
" total	9	14	.391	4.60	28	25	6	184	201	64	80	2	1	1	0	67	15	0	.224
1936 2 teams		BKN N (19G 4-9)				STL N (20G 2-1)													
" total	6	10	.375	5.73	39	19	5	150.2	193	50	71	1	3	0	2	51	12	0	.235
9 yrs.	127	93	.577	4.38	319	249	115	1915.1	1981	809	1005	18	12	5	12	704	162	3	.230
1 yr.	2	1	.667	6.40	20	6	1	57.2	80	20	28	0	2	0	1	18	4	0	.222
WORLD SERIES																			
1929 PHI A	1	1	.500	2.63	2	2	1	13.2	14	6	17	0	0	0	0	5	0	0	.000
1930	2	0	1.000	0.72	3	3	2	25	13	7	19	0	0	0	0	9	0	0	.000
1931	1	2	.333	1.88	3	3	2	24	12	4	20	1	0	0	0	8	0	0	.000
3 yrs.	4	3	.571	1.58	8	8	5	62.2	39	17	56	1	0	0	0	22	0	0	.000
	10th	10th		10th							7th								

Jack Easton

EASTON, JOHN E.
B. 1867, Bridgeport, Ohio   D. Nov., 1903, Steubenville, Ohio

	W	L	PCT	ERA	G	GS	CG	IP	H	BB	SO	ShO	W	L	SV	AB	H	HR	BA
1889 COL AA	1	0	1.000	3.50	4	1	1	18	13	21	7	0	0	1	0	7	0	0	.000
1890	15	14	.517	*3.52*	37	29	23	255.2	213	125	147	0	2	1	1	107	19	0	.178
1891 2 teams		COL AA (20G 5-12)				STL AA (7G 3-2)													
" total	8	14	.364	4.59	27	24	19	198	208	86	87	0	0	0	0	102	20	0	.196
1892 STL N	2	0	1.000	6.39	5	2	2	31	38	26	4	0	0	0	0	17	3	0	.176
1894 PIT N	0	1	.000	4.12	3	1	1	19.2	26	4	1	0	0	0	0	5	0	0	.000

	W	L	PCT	ERA	G	GS	CG	IP	H	BB	SO	ShO	Relief Pitching W	L	SV	BATTING AB	H	HR	BA

Jack Easton continued

	W	L	PCT	ERA	G	GS	CG	IP	H	BB	SO	ShO	W	L	SV	AB	H	HR	BA
5 yrs.	26	29	.473	4.12	76	57	46	522.1	498	262	246	0	2	1	2	238	42	0	.176
1 yr.	2	0	1.000	6.39	5	2	2	31	38	26	4	0	0	0	0	17	3	0	.176

Rawley Eastwick

EASTWICK, RAWLINS JACKSON   BR TR 6'3"   180 lbs.
B. Oct. 24, 1950, Camden, N. J.

	W	L	PCT	ERA	G	GS	CG	IP	H	BB	SO	ShO	W	L	SV	AB	H	HR	BA
1974 CIN N	0	0	—	2.00	8	0	0	18	12	5	14	0	0	0	2	1	0	0	.000
1975	5	3	.625	2.60	58	0	0	90	77	25	61	0	5	3	22	15	1	0	.067
1976	11	5	.688	2.08	71	0	0	108	93	27	70	0	11	5	26	17	0	0	.000
1977 2 teams			CIN N (23G 2–2)			STL N (41G 3–7)													
" total	5	9	.357	3.90	64	1	0	97	114	29	47	0	4	7	11	11	3	0	.273
1978 2 teams			NY A (8G 2–1)			PHI N (22G 2–1)													
" total	4	2	.667	3.76	30	0	0	64.2	53	22	27	0	4	2	0	3	0	0	.000
1979 PHI N	3	6	.333	4.88	51	0	0	83	90	25	47	0	3	6	6	7	0	0	.000
1980 KC A	0	1	.000	5.32	14	0	0	22	37	8	5	0	0	1	0	0	0	0	—
1981 CHI N	0	1	.000	2.30	30	0	0	43	43	15	24	0	0	1	1	2	0	0	.000
8 yrs.	28	27	.509	3.30	326	1	0	525.2	519	156	295	0	27	25	68	56	4	0	.071
1 yr.	3	7	.300	4.70	41	1	0	53.2	74	21	30	0	2	5	4	5	2	0	.400

LEAGUE CHAMPIONSHIP SERIES

	W	L	PCT	ERA	G	GS	CG	IP	H	BB	SO	ShO	W	L	SV	AB	H	HR	BA
1975 CIN N	1	0	1.000	0.00	2	0	0	3.2	2	2	1	0	1	0	1	0	0	0	—
1976	1	0	1.000	12.00	2	0	0	3	7	2	1	0	1	0	0	0	0	0	—
1978 PHI N	0	0	—	9.00	1	0	0	1	3	0	1	0	0	0	0	0	0	0	—
3 yrs.	2	0	1.000	5.87	5	0	0	7.2	12	4	3	0	2	0	1	0	0	0	—

WORLD SERIES

	W	L	PCT	ERA	G	GS	CG	IP	H	BB	SO	ShO	W	L	SV	AB	H	HR	BA
1975 CIN N	2	0	1.000	2.25	5	0	0	8	6	3	4	0	2	0	1	1	0	0	.000

2nd

Al Eckert

ECKERT, ALBERT GEORGE (Obbie)   BL TL 5'10"   174 lbs.
B. May 17, 1906, Milwaukee, Wis.

	W	L	PCT	ERA	G	GS	CG	IP	H	BB	SO	ShO	W	L	SV	AB	H	HR	BA
1930 CIN N	0	1	.000	7.20	2	1	0	5	7	4	1	0	0	0	0	1	0	0	.000
1931	0	1	.000	9.16	14	1	0	18.2	26	9	5	0	0	0	0	3	1	0	.333
1935 STL N	0	0	—	12.00	2	0	0	3	7	1	1	0	0	0	0	0	0	0	—
3 yrs.	0	2	.000	9.11	18	2	0	26.2	40	14	7	0	0	0	0	4	1	0	.250
1 yr.	0	0	—	12.00	2	0	0	3	7	1	1	0	0	0	0	0	0	0	—

Joe Edelen

EDELEN, BENNY JOE   BR TR 6'   165 lbs.
B. Sept. 16, 1955, Durant, Okla.

	W	L	PCT	ERA	G	GS	CG	IP	H	BB	SO	ShO	W	L	SV	AB	H	HR	BA
1981 2 teams			STL N (13G 1–0)			CIN N (5G 1–0)													
" total	2	0	1.000	5.70	18	0	0	30	34	3	15	0	2	0	0	5	1	0	.200
1982 CIN N	0	0	—	8.80	9	0	0	15.1	22	8	11	0	0	0	0	2	1	0	.500
2 yrs.	2	0	1.000	6.75	27	0	0	45.1	56	11	26	0	2	0	0	7	2	0	.286
1 yr.	1	0	1.000	9.35	13	0	0	17.1	29	3	10	0	1	0	0	3	1	0	.333

Wish Egan

EGAN, ALOYSIUS JEROME   BR TR 6'3"   185 lbs.
B. June 16, 1881, Evart, Mich.   D. Apr. 13, 1951, Detroit, Mich.

	W	L	PCT	ERA	G	GS	CG	IP	H	BB	SO	ShO	W	L	SV	AB	H	HR	BA
1902 DET A	1	2	.333	2.86	3	3	2	22	23	6	0	0	0	0	0	8	2	0	.250
1905 STL N	6	15	.286	3.58	23	19	18	171	189	39	29	0	0	2	0	59	6	0	.102
1906	2	9	.182	4.59	16	12	7	86.1	97	27	23	0	0	1	0	29	2	0	.069
3 yrs.	9	26	.257	3.83	42	34	27	279.1	309	72	52	0	0	3	0	96	10	0	.104
2 yrs.	8	24	.250	3.92	39	31	25	257.1	286	66	52	0	0	3	0	88	8	0	.091

Red Ehret

EHRET, PHILIP SYDNEY   BR TR 6'   175 lbs.
B. Aug. 31, 1868, Louisville, Ky.   D. July 28, 1940, Cincinnati, Ohio

	W	L	PCT	ERA	G	GS	CG	IP	H	BB	SO	ShO	W	L	SV	AB	H	HR	BA
1888 KC AA	3	2	.600	3.98	7	6	5	52	58	22	12	0	0	0	0	63	12	0	.190
1889 LOU AA	10	29	.256	4.80	45	38	35	364	441	115	135	1	0	2	0	258	65	1	.252
1890	25	14	.641	2.53	43	38	35	359	351	79	174	4	1	1	2	146	31	0	.212
1891	13	13	.500	3.47	26	24	23	220.2	225	70	76	2	0	2	0	91	22	0	.242
1892 PIT N	16	20	.444	2.65	39	36	32	316	290	83	101	0	0	1	0	132	34	0	.258
1893	18	18	.500	3.44	39	35	32	314.1	322	115	70	4	1	2	0	136	24	1	.176
1894	19	21	.475	5.14	46	38	31	346.2	441	128	102	1	5	0	0	135	23	0	.170
1895 STL N	6	19	.240	6.02	37	32	18	231.2	360	88	55	0	1	0	0	96	21	1	.219
1896 CIN N	18	14	.563	3.42	34	33	29	276.2	298	74	60	2	1	0	0	102	20	1	.196
1897	8	10	.444	4.78	34	19	11	184.1	256	47	43	0	2	1	2	66	13	0	.197
1898 LOU N	3	7	.300	5.76	12	10	9	89	130	20	20	0	0	0	0	40	9	0	.225
11 yrs.	139	167	.454	4.02	362	309	260	2754.1	3172	841	848	14	11	9	4	*			
1 yr.	6	19	.240	6.02	37	32	18	231.2	360	88	55	0	1	0	0	96	21	1	.219

Jim Ellis

ELLIS, JAMES RUSSELL   BR TL 6'2"   185 lbs.
B. Mar. 25, 1945, Tulare, Calif.

	W	L	PCT	ERA	G	GS	CG	IP	H	BB	SO	ShO	W	L	SV	AB	H	HR	BA
1967 CHI N	1	1	.500	3.24	8	1	0	16.2	20	9	8	0	0	1	0	5	1	0	.200
1969 STL N	0	0	—	1.80	2	1	0	5	7	3	0	0	0	0	0	0	0	0	—
2 yrs.	1	1	.500	2.91	10	2	0	21.2	27	12	8	0	0	1	0	5	1	0	.200
1 yr.	0	0	—	1.80	2	1	0	5	7	3	0	0	0	0	0	0	0	0	—

Bones Ely

ELY, FREDERICK WILLIAM   BR TR 6'1"   155 lbs.
B. June 7, 1863, Girard, Pa.   D. Jan. 10, 1952, Imola, Calif.

	W	L	PCT	ERA	G	GS	CG	IP	H	BB	SO	ShO	W	L	SV	AB	H	HR	BA
1884 BUF N	0	1	.000	14.40	1	1	0	5	17	5	4	0	0	0	0	4	0	0	.000
1886 LOU AA	0	4	.000	5.32	6	4	4	44	53	26	28	0	0	0	1	32	5	0	.156
1890 SYR AA	0	0	—	22.50	1	0	0	2	7	0	0	0	0	0	0	496	130	0	.262
1892 BAL N	0	1	.000	7.71	1	1	1	7	14	7	0	0	0	0	0	3	0	0	.000
1894 STL N	0	0	—	0.00	1	0	0	1	0	3	0	0	0	0	0	510	156	12	.306
5 yrs.	0	6	.000	6.86	10	6	5	59	91	41	32	0	0	0	1	*			.279
1 yr.	0	0	—	0.00	1	0	0	1	0	3	0	0	0	0	0	1155	322	13	.279

	W	L	PCT	ERA	G	GS	CG	IP	H	BB	SO	ShO	Relief Pitching W	L	SV	BATTING AB	H	HR	BA

Eddie Erautt

ERAUTT, JOSEPH MICHAEL   BR TR 5'11½" 185 lbs.
Brother of Joe Erautt.
B. Sept. 26, 1924, Portland, Ore.   D. Oct. 6, 1976, Portland, Ore.

	W	L	PCT	ERA	G	GS	CG	IP	H	BB	SO	ShO	W	L	SV	AB	H	HR	BA
1947 CIN N	4	9	.308	5.07	36	10	2	119	146	53	43	0	3	2	0	29	2	0	.069
1948	0	0	—	6.00	2	0	0	3	3	1	0	0	0	0	0	0	0	0	—
1949	4	11	.267	3.36	39	9	1	112.2	99	61	43	0	3	5	1	23	4	0	.174
1950	4	2	.667	5.65	33	2	1	65.1	82	22	35	0	3	1	1	13	2	0	.154
1951	0	0	—	5.72	30	0	0	39.1	50	23	20	0	1	0	0	3	0	0	.000
1953 2 teams	CIN N	(4G 0–0)		STL	N	(20G 3–1)													
" total	3	1	.750	6.25	24	1	0	40.1	54	19	16	0	3	0	0	7	1	0	.143
6 yrs.	15	23	.395	4.86	164	22	4	379.2	434	179	157	0	12	8	2	75	9	0	.120
1 yr.	3	1	.750	6.31	20	1	0	35.2	43	16	15	0	3	0	0	6	1	0	.167

Duke Esper

ESPER, CHARLES H.   TL 5'11½" 185 lbs.
B. July 28, 1868, Salem, N. J.   D. Aug. 31, 1910, Philadelphia, Pa.

	W	L	PCT	ERA	G	GS	CG	IP	H	BB	SO	ShO	W	L	SV	AB	H	HR	BA
1890 3 teams	PHI AA	(18G 8–9)		PIT	N	(2G 0–2)		PHI	N	(5G 5–0)									
" total	13	11	.542	4.55	25	23	20	201.2	234	93	88	1	1	0	0	87	22	0	.253
1891 PHI N	20	15	.571	3.56	39	36	35	296	302	121	108	1	1	0	1	123	27	0	.220
1892 2 teams	PHI N	(21G 12–6)		PIT	N	(3G 2–0)													
" total	14	6	.700	3.63	24	21	15	178.2	189	70	50	0	1	0	1	79	17	1	.215
1893 WAS N	12	28	.300	4.71	42	36	34	334.1	442	156	78	0	2	2	0	143	41	0	.287
1894 2 teams	WAS N	(19G 5–10)		BAL	N	(16G 10–2)													
" total	15	12	.556	5.86	35	24	15	224.1	298	76	52	0	3	2	2	102	26	1	.255
1895 BAL N	10	12	.455	3.92	34	25	16	218.1	248	79	39	1	1	4	1	90	16	0	.178
1896	14	5	.737	3.58	20	18	14	155.2	168	39	19	1	2	0	0	66	13	0	.197
1897 STL N	1	6	.143	5.28	8	8	7	61.1	95	12	8	0	0	0	0	25	8	0	.320
1898	3	5	.375	5.98	10	8	6	64.2	86	22	14	0	0	0	0	27	10	0	.370
9 yrs.	102	100	.505	4.40	237	199	152	1735	2062	668	456	4	11	8	5	742	180	2	.243
2 yrs.	4	11	.267	5.64	18	16	13	126	181	34	22	0	0	0	0	52	18	0	.346

LeRoy Evans

EVANS, LeROY   BR TR 6' 180 lbs.
B. Mar. 19, 1874, Knoxville, Tenn.   Deceased.

	W	L	PCT	ERA	G	GS	CG	IP	H	BB	SO	ShO	W	L	SV	AB	H	HR	BA
1897 2 teams	STL N	(3G 0–0)		LOU	N	(9G 5–4)													
" total	5	4	.556	5.10	12	8	6	72.1	99	37	24	0	1	0	0	26	3	0	.115
1898 WAS N	3	3	.500	3.38	7	4	4	50.2	50	25	11	0	1	0	0	19	1	0	.053
1899	3	4	.429	5.67	7	6	6	54	60	25	27	0	0	0	0	20	4	0	.200
1902 2 teams	NY N	(23G 8–13)		BKN	N	(13G 5–6)													
" total	13	19	.406	3.00	36	28	28	273.1	277	91	83	2	2	3	0	88	17	0	.193
1903 2 teams	BKN N	(15G 4–8)		STL	A	(7G 1–4)													
" total	5	12	.294	3.57	22	19	13	164	187	55	66	0	1	0	0	48	7	0	.146
5 yrs.	29	42	.408	3.66	84	68	57	614.1	673	233	211	2	3	5	0	201	32	0	.159
1 yr.	0	0	—	9.69	3	0	0	13	13	13	4	0	0	0	0	3	0	0	.000

Bob Ewing

EWING, GEORGE LEMUEL (Long Bob)   BR TR 6'1½" 170 lbs.
B. Apr. 24, 1873, New Hampshire, Ohio   D. June 20, 1947, Wapakoneta, Ohio

	W	L	PCT	ERA	G	GS	CG	IP	H	BB	SO	ShO	W	L	SV	AB	H	HR	BA
1902 CIN N	6	6	.500	2.98	15	12	10	117.2	126	47	44	0	0	0	0	71	12	0	.169
1903	14	13	.519	2.77	29	28	27	246.2	254	64	104	1	0	0	0	95	24	0	.253
1904	11	13	.458	2.46	26	24	22	212	198	58	99	0	1	0	0	97	25	1	.258
1905	20	11	.645	2.51	40	34	30	312	284	79	164	4	3	0	0	122	32	0	.262
1906	13	14	.481	2.38	33	32	26	287.2	248	60	145	2	0	1	0	101	14	1	.139
1907	17	19	.472	1.73	41	37	32	332.2	279	85	147	2	1	1	0	123	19	1	.154
1908	15	15	.500	2.21	37	32	23	293.2	247	57	95	4	0	0	0	94	14	0	.149
1909	11	13	.458	2.43	31	29	14	218.1	195	63	86	2	0	2	0	73	8	0	.110
1910 PHI N	16	14	.533	3.00	34	32	20	255.1	235	86	102	4	0	1	0	90	20	0	.222
1911	0	1	.000	7.88	4	3	1	24	29	14	12	0	0	0	0	6	2	0	.333
1912 STL N	0	0	—	0.00	1	1	0	1.1	2	1	0	0	0	0	0	0	0	0	—
11 yrs.	123	119	.508	2.49	291	264	205	2301.1	2097	614	998	19	5	6	4	872	170	3	.195
1 yr.	0	0	—	0.00	1	1	0	1.1	2	1	0	0	0	0	0	0	0	0	—

Pete Falcone

FALCONE, PETER   BL TL 6'2" 185 lbs.
B. Oct. 1, 1953, Brooklyn, N. Y.

	W	L	PCT	ERA	G	GS	CG	IP	H	BB	SO	ShO	W	L	SV	AB	H	HR	BA
1975 SF N	12	11	.522	4.17	34	32	3	190	171	111	131	1	0	0	0	65	4	0	.062
1976 STL N	12	16	.429	3.23	32	32	9	212	173	93	138	2	0	0	0	62	8	0	.129
1977	4	8	.333	5.44	27	22	1	124	130	61	75	1	0	1	1	41	10	0	.244
1978	2	7	.222	5.76	19	14	0	75	94	48	28	0	1	0	0	21	5	0	.238
1979 NY N	6	14	.300	4.16	33	31	1	184	194	76	113	1	0	0	0	52	9	0	.173
1980	7	10	.412	4.53	37	23	1	157	163	58	109	1	1	1	0	41	6	0	.146
1981	5	3	.625	2.56	35	9	3	95	84	36	56	1	1	2	4	22	4	1	.182
1982	8	10	.444	3.84	40	23	3	171	159	71	101	0	1	1	0	53	6	0	.113
8 yrs.	56	79	.415	4.11	257	186	21	1208	1168	554	751	6	4	5	5	357	52	1	.146
3 yrs.	18	31	.367	4.36	78	68	10	411	397	202	241	1	1	0	0	124	23	0	.185

Harry Fanok

FANOK, HARRY MICHAEL (The Flame Thrower)   BB TR 6' 180 lbs.
B. May 11, 1940, Whippany, N. J.

	W	L	PCT	ERA	G	GS	CG	IP	H	BB	SO	ShO	W	L	SV	AB	H	HR	BA
1963 STL N	2	1	.667	5.26	12	0	0	25.2	24	21	25	0	2	1	1	5	2	0	.400
1964	0	0	—	5.87	4	0	0	7.2	5	3	10	0	0	0	0	1	0	0	.000
2 yrs.	2	1	.667	5.40	16	0	0	33.1	29	24	35	0	2	1	1	6	2	0	.333
2 yrs.	2	1	.667	5.40	16	0	0	33.1	29	24	35	0	2	1	1	6	2	0	.333

	W	L	PCT	ERA	G	GS	CG	IP	H	BB	SO	ShO	Relief Pitching W	L	SV	BATTING AB	H	HR	BA

Jack Faszholz

FASZHOLZ, JOHN EDWARD (Preacher)
B. Apr. 11, 1927, St. Louis, Mo.   BR TR 6'3"   205 lbs.

	W	L	PCT	ERA	G	GS	CG	IP	H	BB	SO	ShO	W	L	SV	AB	H	HR	BA
1953 STL N	0	0	–	6.94	4	1	0	11.2	16	1	7	0	0	0	0	3	0	0	.000

Don Ferrarese

FERRARESE, DONALD HUGH (Midget)
B. June 19, 1929, Oakland, Calif.   BR TL 5'9"   170 lbs.

	W	L	PCT	ERA	G	GS	CG	IP	H	BB	SO	ShO	W	L	SV	AB	H	HR	BA
1955 BAL A	0	0	–	3.00	6	0	0	9	8	11	5	0	0	0	0	1	0	0	.000
1956	4	10	.286	5.03	36	14	3	102	86	64	81	1	2	2	2	28	1	0	.036
1957	1	1	.500	4.74	8	2	0	19	14	12	13	0	1	0	0	3	0	0	.000
1958 CLE A	3	4	.429	3.71	28	10	2	94.2	91	46	62	0	2	1	1	26	3	0	.115
1959	3	2	.625	3.20	15	10	4	76	58	51	45	0	0	0	·0	27	7	0	.259
1960 CHI A	0	1	.000	18.00	5	0	0	4	8	9	4	0	0	1	0	2	1	0	.500
1961 PHI N	5	12	.294	3.76	42	14	3	138.2	120	68	89	1	2	3	1	35	6	0	.171
1962 2 teams			PHI N	(5G 0–1)		STL	N	(38G 1–4)											
" total	1	5	.167	3.27	43	0	0	63.1	64	34	51	0	1	5	1	6	2	1	.333
8 yrs.	19	36	.345	4.00	183	50	12	506.2	449	295	350	2	8	12	5	128	20	1	.156
1 yr.	1	4	.200	2.70	38	0	0	56.2	55	31	45	0	1	4	1	5	1	1	.200

Chauncey Fisher

FISHER, CHAUNCEY BURR (Peach)   BR TR 5'11"   175 lbs.
Brother of Tom Fisher.
B. Jan. 8, 1872, Anderson, Ind.   D. Apr. 27, 1939, Los Angeles, Calif.

	W	L	PCT	ERA	G	GS	CG	IP	H	BB	SO	ShO	W	L	SV	AB	H	HR	BA
1893 CLE N	0	2	.000	5.50	2	2	1	18	26	9	9	0	0	0	0	8	2	0	.250
1894 2 teams			CLE N	(3G 0–2)		CIN	N	(11G 2–8)											
" total	2	10	.167	7.76	14	13	10	102	156	49	14	0	0	0	0	47	10	1	.213
1896 CIN N	10	7	.588	4.45	27	15	13	159.2	199	36	25	2	2	2	2	57	14	0	.246
1897 BKN N	9	7	.563	4.23	20	13	11	149	184	43	31	1	2	1	1	59	12	0	.203
1901 2 teams			NY N	(1G 0–0)		STL	N	(1G 0–0)											
" total	0	0	–	15.43	2	1	0	7	18	3	1	0	0	0	0	3	0	0	.000
5 yrs.	21	26	.447	5.37	65	44	36	435.2	583	140	80	3	4	3	3	174	38	1	.218
1 yr.	0	0	–	15.00	1	0	0	3	7	1	0	0	0	0	0	1	0	0	.000

Eddie Fisher

FISHER, EDDIE GENE   BR TR 6'2½"   200 lbs.
B. July 16, 1936, Shreveport, La.

	W	L	PCT	ERA	G	GS	CG	IP	H	BB	SO	ShO	W	L	SV	AB	H	HR	BA
1959 SF N	2	6	.250	7.88	17	5	0	40	57	8	15	0	0	4	1	8	0	0	.000
1960	1	0	1.000	3.55	3	1	1	12.2	11	2	7	0	0	0	0	5	3	0	.600
1961	0	2	.000	5.35	15	1	0	33.2	36	9	16	0	0	2	1	7	1	0	.143
1962 CHI A	9	5	.643	3.10	57	12	2	182.2	169	45	88	1	4	3	5	46	6	0	.130
1963	9	8	.529	3.95	33	15	2	120.2	114	28	67	1	2	3	0	36	5	0	.139
1964	6	3	.667	3.02	59	2	0	125	86	32	74	0	0	0	9	18	3	0	.167
1965	15	7	.682	2.40	82	0	0	165.1	118	43	90	0	15	7	24	29	4	0	.138
1966 2 teams			CHI A	(23G 1–3)		BAL	A	(44G 5–3)											
" total	6	6	.500	2.52	67	0	0	107	87	36	57	0	6	6	19	15	2	0	.133
1967 BAL A	4	3	.571	3.61	46	0	0	89.2	82	26	53	0	4	3	1	5	1	0	.200
1968 CLE A	4	2	.667	2.85	54	0	0	94.2	87	17	42	0	4	2	4	12	0	0	.000
1969 CAL A	3	2	.600	3.63	52	1	0	96.2	100	28	47	0	2	2	2	13	0	0	.000
1970	4	4	.500	3.05	67	2	0	130	117	35	74	0	4	4	8	11	1	0	.091
1971	10	8	.556	2.72	57	3	0	119	92	50	82	0	9	6	3	16	1	0	.063
1972 2 teams			CAL A	(43G 4–5)		CHI	A	(6G 0–1)											
" total	4	6	.400	3.91	49	5	0	103.2	104	40	42	0	4	3	4	24	2	0	.083
1973 2 teams			CHI A	(26G 6–7)		STL	N	(6G 2–1)											
" total	8	8	.500	4.67	32	16	2	117.2	138	39	58	0	2	1	0	1	1	0	1.000
15 yrs.	85	70	.548	3.41	690	63	7	1538.1	1398	438	812	2	56	46	81	246	30	0	.122
1 yr.	2	1	.667	1.29	6	0	0	7	3	1	1	0	2	1	0	1	1	0	1.000

Tom Flanigan

FLANIGAN, THOMAS ANTHONY   BR TL 6'3"   175 lbs.
B. Sept. 6, 1934, Cincinnati, Ohio

	W	L	PCT	ERA	G	GS	CG	IP	H	BB	SO	ShO	W	L	SV	AB	H	HR	BA
1954 CHI A	0	0	–	0.00	2	0	0	1.2	1	1	0	0	0	0	0	0	0	0	–
1958 STL N	0	0	–	9.00	1	0	0	1	2	1	0	0	0	0	0	0	0	0	–
2 yrs.	0	0	–	3.38	3	0	0	2.2	3	2	0	0	0	0	0	0	0	0	–
1 yr.	0	0	–	9.00	1	0	0	1	2	1	0	0	0	0	0	0	0	0	–

Ben Flowers

FLOWERS, BENNETT   BR TR 6'4"   195 lbs.
B. June 15, 1927, Wilson, N. C.

	W	L	PCT	ERA	G	GS	CG	IP	H	BB	SO	ShO	W	L	SV	AB	H	HR	BA
1951 BOS A	0	0	–	0.00	1	0	0	3	2	1	2	0	0	0	0	1	0	0	.000
1953	1	4	.200	3.86	32	6	1	79.1	87	24	36	1	0	0	3	19	3	0	.158
1955 2 teams			DET A	(4G 0–0)		STL	N	(4G 1–0)											
" total	1	0	1.000	4.05	8	4	0	33.1	32	14	21	0	0	0	0	11	1	0	.091
1956 2 teams			STL N	(3G 1–1)		PHI	N	(32G 0–2)											
" total	1	3	.250	5.98	35	3	0	52.2	69	15	27	0	0	2	0	5	0	0	.000
4 yrs.	3	7	.300	4.49	76	13	1	168.1	190	54	86	1	0	2	3	36	4	0	.111
2 yrs.	2	1	.667	4.62	7	7	0	39	42	17	24	0	0	0	0	13	1	0	.077

Rich Folkers

FOLKERS, RICHARD NEVIN   BL TL 6'2"   180 lbs.
B. Oct. 17, 1946, Waterloo, Iowa

	W	L	PCT	ERA	G	GS	CG	IP	H	BB	SO	ShO	W	L	SV	AB	H	HR	BA
1970 NY N	0	2	.000	6.52	16	1	0	29	36	25	15	0	0	1	2	6	2	0	.333
1972 STL N	1	0	1.000	3.38	9	0	0	13.1	12	5	7	0	1	0	0	1	0	0	.000
1973	4	4	.500	3.61	34	9	1	82.1	74	34	44	0	1	0	3	20	2	0	.100
1974	6	2	.750	3.00	55	0	0	90	65	38	57	0	6	2	5	10	1	0	.100
1975 SD N	6	11	.353	4.18	45	15	4	142	155	39	87	0	1	3	0	36	6	0	.167
1976	2	3	.400	5.28	33	3	0	59.2	67	25	26	0	2	0	0	4	0	0	.000
1977 MIL A	0	1	.000	4.50	3	0	0	6	7	4	6	0	0	1	0	0	0	0	–
7 yrs.	19	23	.452	4.11	195	28	5	422.1	416	170	242	0	11	7	7	77	11	0	.143
1 yr.	11	6	.647	3.30	98	9	1	185.2	151	77	108	0	8	2	5	31	3	0	.097

	W	L	PCT	ERA	G	GS	CG	IP	H	BB	SO	ShO	Relief Pitching W	L	SV	BATTING AB	H	HR	BA

Bob Forsch

FORSCH, ROBERT HERBERT
Brother of Ken Forsch.
B. Jan. 13, 1950, Sacramento, Calif.   BR TR 6'4" 200 lbs.

	W	L	PCT	ERA	G	GS	CG	IP	H	BB	SO	ShO	W	L	SV	AB	H	HR	BA
1974 STL N	7	4	.636	2.97	19	14	5	100	84	34	39	2	0	0	0	29	7	0	.241
1975	15	10	.600	2.86	34	34	7	230	213	70	108	4	0	0	0	78	24	1	.308
1976	8	10	.444	3.94	33	32	2	194	209	71	76	0	0	1	0	62	11	1	.177
1977	20	7	.741	3.48	35	35	8	217	210	69	95	2	0	0	0	72	12	0	.167
1978	11	17	.393	3.69	34	34	7	234	205	97	114	3	0	0	0	83	15	1	.181
1979	11	11	.500	3.82	33	32	7	219	215	52	92	1	0	0	0	73	8	0	.110
1980	11	10	.524	3.77	31	31	8	215	225	33	87	0	0	0	0	78	23	3	.295
1981	10	5	.667	3.19	20	20	1	124	106	29	41	0	0	0	0	41	5	0	.122
1982	15	9	.625	3.48	36	34	6	233	238	54	69	2	0	0	0	73	15	0	.205
9 yrs.	108	83	.565	3.51	275	266	51	1766	1705	509	721	14	0	1	1	589	120	6	.204
9 yrs.	108	83	.565	3.51	275	266	51	1766	1705	509	721	14	0	1	1	589	120	6	.204
	7th	8th						8th		10th									

LEAGUE CHAMPIONSHIP SERIES
| 1982 STL N | 1 | 0 | 1.000 | 0.00 | 1 | 1 | 1 | 9 | 3 | 0 | 6 | 1 | 0 | 0 | 0 | 3 | 2 | 0 | .667 |

WORLD SERIES
| 1982 STL N | 0 | 2 | .000 | 4.97 | 2 | 2 | 0 | 12.2 | 18 | 3 | 4 | 0 | 0 | 0 | 0 | 0 | 0 | 0 | .000 |

Alan Foster

FOSTER, ALAN BENTON
B. Dec. 8, 1946, Pasadena, Calif.   BR TR 6' 180 lbs.

	W	L	PCT	ERA	G	GS	CG	IP	H	BB	SO	ShO	W	L	SV	AB	H	HR	BA
1967 LA N	0	1	.000	2.16	4	2	0	16.2	10	3	15	0	0	0	0	4	0	0	.000
1968	1	1	.500	1.72	3	3	0	15.2	11	2	10	0	0	0	0	4	1	0	.250
1969	3	9	.250	4.37	24	15	2	103	119	29	59	2	0	0	0	27	2	0	.074
1970	10	13	.435	4.25	33	33	7	199	200	81	83	1	0	0	0	64	7	0	.109
1971 CLE A	8	12	.400	4.15	36	26	3	182	158	82	97	0	1	0	0	51	2	0	.039
1972 CAL A	0	1	.000	4.85	8	0	0	13	12	6	11	0	0	1	0	0	0	0	—
1973 STL N	13	9	.591	3.14	35	29	6	203.2	195	63	106	2	0	2	0	68	13	0	.191
1974	7	10	.412	3.89	31	25	5	162	167	61	78	1	0	0	0	48	8	0	.167
1975 SD N	3	1	.750	2.40	17	4	1	45	41	21	20	0	1	0	0	11	1	0	.091
1976	3	6	.333	3.22	26	11	2	86.2	75	35	22	0	0	0	0	18	1	0	.056
10 yrs.	48	63	.432	3.73	217	148	26	1026.2	988	383	501	6	2	3	0	295	35	0	.119
2 yrs.	20	19	.513	3.47	66	54	11	365.2	362	124	184	3	0	2	0	116	21	0	.181

Jack Fournier

FOURNIER, JOHN FRANK (Jacques)
B. Sept. 28, 1892, Au Sable, Mich.   D. Sept. 5, 1973, Tacoma, Wash.   BL TR 6' 195 lbs.

	W	L	PCT	ERA	G	GS	CG	IP	H	BB	SO	ShO	W	L	SV	AB	H	HR	BA
1922 STL N	0	0	—	0.00	1	0	0	1	0	0	0	0	0	0	0	*			

Jesse Fowler

FOWLER, JESSE (Pete)
Brother of Art Fowler.
B. Oct. 30, 1898, Spartanburg, S. C.   D. Sept. 23, 1973, Columbia, S. C.   BR TL 5'10½" 158 lbs.

	W	L	PCT	ERA	G	GS	CG	IP	H	BB	SO	ShO	W	L	SV	AB	H	HR	BA
1924 STL N	1	1	.500	4.41	13	3	0	32.2	28	18	5	0	1	0	0	9	2	0	.222

Earl Francis

FRANCIS, EARL COLEMAN
B. July 14, 1936, Slab Fork, W. Va.   BR TR 6'2" 210 lbs.

	W	L	PCT	ERA	G	GS	CG	IP	H	BB	SO	ShO	W	L	SV	AB	H	HR	BA
1960 PIT N	1	0	1.000	2.00	7	0	0	18	14	4	8	0	1	0	0	5	0	0	.000
1961	2	8	.200	4.21	23	15	0	102.2	110	47	53	0	0	1	0	28	3	0	.107
1962	9	8	.529	3.07	36	23	5	176	153	83	121	1	2	0	0	61	10	1	.164
1963	4	6	.400	4.53	33	13	0	97.1	107	43	72	0	2	0	0	26	8	0	.308
1964	0	1	.000	8.53	2	1	0	6.1	7	1	6	0	0	0	0	1	0	0	.000
1965 STL N	0	0	—	5.06	2	0	0	5.1	7	3	3	0	0	0	0	1	0	0	.000
6 yrs.	16	23	.410	3.77	103	52	5	405.2	398	181	263	1	5	1	0	122	21	1	.172
1 yr.	0	0	—	5.06	2	0	0	5.1	7	3	3	0	0	0	0	1	0	0	.000

Charlie Frank

FRANK, CHARLES
B. May 30, 1870, Mobile, Ala.   D. May 24, 1922, Memphis, Tenn.

	W	L	PCT	ERA	G	GS	CG	IP	H	BB	SO	ShO	W	L	SV	AB	H	HR	BA
1894 STL N	0	0	—	15.00	2	0	0	3	6	7	1	0	0	0	0	*			

Fred Frankhouse

FRANKHOUSE, FREDRICK MELOY
B. Apr. 9, 1904, Port Royal, Pa.   BR TR 5'11" 175 lbs.

	W	L	PCT	ERA	G	GS	CG	IP	H	BB	SO	ShO	W	L	SV	AB	H	HR	BA
1927 STL N	5	1	.833	2.70	6	6	5	50	41	16	20	1	0	0	0	20	5	0	.250
1928	3	2	.600	3.96	21	10	1	84	91	36	29	0	0	0	1	27	5	0	.185
1929	7	2	.778	4.12	30	12	6	133.1	149	43	37	0	1	0	1	52	15	1	.288
1930 2 teams			STL N (8G 2–3)			BOS N (27G 7–6)													
" total	9	9	.500	5.87	35	12	3	130.1	169	54	34	1	5	3	0	44	14	0	.318
1931 BOS N	8	8	.500	4.03	26	15	6	127.1	125	43	50	0	0	1	1	40	6	0	.150
1932	4	6	.400	3.56	37	6	3	108.2	113	45	35	0	2	3	0	30	3	0	.100
1933	16	15	.516	3.16	43	30	14	244.2	249	77	83	2	2	2	2	80	19	0	.238
1934	17	9	.654	3.20	37	31	13	233.2	239	77	78	2	0	0	1	85	17	0	.200
1935	11	15	.423	4.76	40	29	10	230.2	278	81	64	1	0	0	0	76	20	0	.263
1936 BKN N	13	10	.565	3.65	41	31	9	234.1	236	89	84	1	1	1	2	91	13	0	.143
1937	10	13	.435	4.27	33	26	9	179.1	214	78	64	1	2	1	0	58	11	0	.190
1938	3	5	.375	4.04	30	8	2	93.2	92	44	32	1	1	2	1	26	4	0	.154
1939 BOS N	0	2	.000	2.61	23	0	0	38	37	18	12	0	0	2	4	7	0	0	.000
13 yrs.	106	97	.522	3.92	402	216	81	1888	2033	701	622	10	15	14	12	636	132	1	.208
4 yrs.	17	8	.680	4.05	65	29	12	287	312	106	90	1	3	2	2	104	25	1	.240

George Frazier

FRAZIER, GEORGE ALLEN
B. Oct. 13, 1954, Oklahoma City, Okla.   BR TR 6'5" 205 lbs.

	W	L	PCT	ERA	G	GS	CG	IP	H	BB	SO	ShO	W	L	SV	AB	H	HR	BA
1978 STL N	0	3	.000	4.09	14	0	0	22	22	6	8	0	0	3	0	3	1	0	.333
1979	2	4	.333	4.50	25	0	0	32	35	12	14	0	2	4	0	1	0	0	.000

	W	L	PCT	ERA	G	GS	CG	IP	H	BB	SO	ShO	Relief Pitching W	L	SV	BATTING AB	H	HR	BA

George Frazier continued

	W	L	PCT	ERA	G	GS	CG	IP	H	BB	SO	ShO	W	L	SV	AB	H	HR	BA
1980	1	4	.200	2.74	22	0	0	23	24	7	11	0	1	4	3	0	0	0	—
1981 NY A	0	1	.000	1.61	16	0	0	28	26	11	17	0	0	1	3	0	0	0	—
1982	4	4	.500	3.47	63	0	0	111.2	103	39	69	0	4	4	1	0	0	0	—
5 yrs.	7	16	.304	3.36	140	0	0	216.2	210	75	119	0	7	16	7	4	1	0	.250
3 yrs.	3	11	.214	3.86	61	0	0	77	81	25	33	0	3	11	3	4	1	0	.250
LEAGUE CHAMPIONSHIP SERIES																			
1981 NY A	1	0	1.000	0.00	1	0	0	5.2	5	1	5	0	1	0	0	0	0	0	—
WORLD SERIES																			
1981 NY A	0	3	.000	17.18	3	0	0	3.2	9	3	2	0	0	3 (1st)	0	2	0	0	.000

Benny Frey

FREY, BENJAMIN RUDOLPH   BR TR 5'10"   165 lbs.
B. Apr. 6, 1906, Dexter, Mich.   D. Nov. 1, 1937, Jackson, Mich.

	W	L	PCT	ERA	G	GS	CG	IP	H	BB	SO	ShO	W	L	SV	AB	H	HR	BA
1929 CIN N	1	2	.333	4.13	3	3	2	24	29	8	1	0	0	0	0	8	3	0	.375
1930	11	18	.379	4.70	44	28	14	245	295	62	43	2	2	2	1	88	25	0	.284
1931	8	12	.400	4.92	34	17	7	133.2	166	36	19	1	3	0	2	44	14	0	.318
1932 2 teams			STL N	(2G 0-2)			CIN N	(28G 4-10)											
" total	4	12	.250	4.49	30	15	5	134.1	165	32	27	0	1	2	0	45	9	0	.200
1933 CIN N	6	4	.600	3.82	37	9	1	132	144	21	12	1	4	0	0	42	11	0	.262
1934	11	16	.407	3.52	39	30	12	245.1	288	42	33	2	1	1	2	82	14	0	.171
1935	6	10	.375	6.85	38	13	3	114.1	164	32	24	1	3	2	2	32	11	0	.344
1936	10	8	.556	4.25	31	12	5	131.1	164	30	20	0	4	2	0	44	11	0	.250
8 yrs.	57	82	.410	4.50	256	127	49	1160	1415	263	179	7	18	9	7	385	98	0	.255
1 yr.	0	2	.000	12.00	2	0	0	3	6	2	0	0	0	2	0	1	0	0	.000

Danny Frisella

FRISELLA, DANIEL VINCENT (Bear)   BL TR 6'   185 lbs.
B. Mar. 4, 1946, San Francisco, Calif.   D. Jan. 1, 1977, Phoenix, Ariz.

	W	L	PCT	ERA	G	GS	CG	IP	H	BB	SO	ShO	W	L	SV	AB	H	HR	BA
1967 NY N	1	6	.143	3.41	14	11	0	74	68	33	51	0	0	0	0	23	2	0	.087
1968	2	4	.333	3.91	19	4	0	50.2	53	17	47	0	0	2	2	12	1	0	.083
1969	0	0	—	7.71	3	0	0	4.2	8	3	5	0	0	0	0	1	0	0	.000
1970	8	3	.727	3.00	30	1	0	66	49	34	54	0	7	3	1	13	4	0	.308
1971	8	5	.615	1.98	53	0	0	91	76	30	93	0	8	5	12	13	3	0	.231
1972	5	8	.385	3.34	39	0	0	67.1	63	20	46	0	5	8	9	7	2	0	.286
1973 ATL N	1	2	.333	4.20	42	0	0	45	40	23	27	0	1	2	8	2	1	0	.500
1974	3	4	.429	5.14	36	1	0	42	37	28	27	0	3	4	6	1	0	0	.000
1975 SD N	1	6	.143	3.12	65	0	0	98	86	51	67	0	1	6	9	5	1	0	.200
1976 2 teams			STL N	(18G 0-0)			MIL A	(32G 5-2)											
" total	5	2	.714	3.13	50	0	0	72	49	47	54	0	5	2	10	1	0	0	.000
10 yrs.	34	40	.459	3.32	351	17	0	610.2	529	286	471	0	30	32	57	78	14	0	.179
1 yr.	0	0	—	3.97	18	0	0	22.2	19	13	11	0	0	0	1	1	0	0	.000

Art Fromme

FROMME, ARTHUR HENRY   BR TR 6'   178 lbs.
B. Sept. 3, 1883, Quincy, Ill.   D. Aug. 24, 1956, Los Angeles, Calif.

	W	L	PCT	ERA	G	GS	CG	IP	H	BB	SO	ShO	W	L	SV	AB	H	HR	BA
1906 STL N	1	2	.333	1.44	3	3	3	25	19	10	11	1	0	0	0	9	2	0	.222
1907	5	13	.278	2.90	23	16	13	145.2	138	67	67	2	1	1	0	55	10	0	.182
1908	5	13	.278	2.72	20	14	9	116	102	50	62	2	1	3	0	36	5	0	.139
1909 CIN N	19	14	.576	1.90	37	34	22	279.1	195	101	126	4	1	0	2	94	18	0	.191
1910	2	4	.333	2.92	11	5	1	49.1	44	39	10	0	1	1	0	15	2	0	.133
1911	10	11	.476	3.46	38	26	11	208	190	79	107	1	0	0	0	74	14	0	.189
1912	16	18	.471	2.74	43	37	23	296	285	88	120	3	0	1	0	103	9	0	.087
1913 2 teams			CIN N	(9G 1-4)			NY N	(26G 10-6)											
" total	11	10	.524	4.06	35	19	5	168.1	167	50	74	0	6	1	0	56	9	0	.161
1914 NY N	9	5	.643	3.20	38	12	3	138	142	44	57	1	4	0	2	31	7	0	.226
1915	0	1	.000	5.84	4	1	0	12.1	15	2	4	0	0	1	0	3	1	0	.333
10 yrs.	78	91	.462	2.90	252	167	90	1438	1297	530	638	14	14	8	4	476	77	0	.162
3 yrs.	11	28	.282	2.70	46	33	25	286.2	259	127	140	5	2	4	0	100	17	0	.170

John Fulgham

FULGHAM, JOHN THOMAS   BR TR 6'2"   205 lbs.
B. June 9, 1956, St. Louis, Mo.

	W	L	PCT	ERA	G	GS	CG	IP	H	BB	SO	ShO	W	L	SV	AB	H	HR	BA
1979 STL N	10	6	.625	2.53	20	19	10	146	123	26	75	2	0	0	0	42	6	0	.143
1980	4	6	.400	3.39	15	14	4	85	66	32	48	1	0	0	0	27	0	0	.000
2 yrs.	14	12	.538	2.84	35	33	14	231	189	58	123	3	0	0	0	69	6	0	.087
2 yrs.	14	12	.538	2.84	35	33	14	231	189	58	123	3	0	0	0	69	6	0	.087

Fred Gaiser

GAISER, FREDERICK JACOB
B. Apr. 8, 1885, Stuttgart, Germany   D. Oct. 14, 1918, Trenton, N. J.

	W	L	PCT	ERA	G	GS	CG	IP	H	BB	SO	ShO	W	L	SV	AB	H	HR	BA
1908 STL N	0	0	—	7.71	1	0	0	2.1	4	3	2	0	0	0	0	1	0	0	.000

Pud Galvin

GALVIN, JAMES FRANCIS (Gentle Jeems, The Little Steam Engine)   BR TR 5'8"   190 lbs.
Brother of Lou Galvin.
B. Dec. 25, 1855, St. Louis, Mo.   D. Mar. 7, 1902, Pittsburgh, Pa.
Manager 1885.
Hall of Fame 1965.

	W	L	PCT	ERA	G	GS	CG	IP	H	BB	SO	ShO	W	L	SV	AB	H	HR	BA
1879 BUF N	37	27	.578	2.28	66	66	65	593	585	31	136	6	0	0	0	265	66	0	.249
1880	20	37	.351	2.71	58	54	46	458.2	528	32	128	5	0	2	0	241	51	0	.212
1881	29	24	.547	2.37	56	53	48	474	546	46	136	5	0	0	0	236	50	0	.212
1882	28	23	.549	3.17	52	51	48	445.1	476	40	162	3	0	0	0	206	44	0	.214
1883	46	29	.613	2.72	76	75	72	656.1	676	50	279	5	1	0	0	322	71	1	.220
1884	46	22	.676	1.99	72	72	71	636.1	566	63	369	12	0	0	0	274	49	0	.179
1885 2 teams			BUF N	(33G 13-19)			PIT AA	(11G 3-7)											
" total	16	26	.381	3.99	44	43	40	372.1	453	44	120	3	0	0	1	160	27	1	.169

	W	L	PCT	ERA	G	GS	CG	IP	H	BB	SO	ShO	Relief Pitching W	L	SV	BATTING AB	H	HR	BA

Pud Galvin continued

	W	L	PCT	ERA	G	GS	CG	IP	H	BB	SO	ShO	W	L	SV	AB	H	HR	BA
1886 PIT AA	29	21	.580	2.67	50	50	49	434.2	457	75	72	2	0	0	0	194	49	0	.253
1887 PIT N	28	21	.571	3.29	49	48	47	440.2	490	67	76	3	1	0	0	193	41	2	.212
1888	23	25	.479	2.63	50	50	49	437.1	446	53	107	6	0	0	0	175	25	1	.143
1889	23	16	.590	4.17	41	40	38	341	392	78	77	4	0	0	0	150	28	0	.187
1890 PIT P	12	13	.480	4.35	26	25	23	217	275	49	35	1	1	0	0	97	20	0	.206
1891 PIT N	14	13	.519	2.88	33	31	23	246.2	256	62	46	2	0	0	0	109	18	0	.165
1892 2 teams			PIT	N	(12G 5–6)		STL	N	(12G 5–7)										
" total	10	13	.435	2.92	24	24	20	188	206	54	56	0	0	0	0	80	7	0	.088
14 yrs.	361	310	.538	2.87	697	682	639	5941.1	6352	744	1799	57	3	2	1	*			
	6th	2nd					2nd		2nd			9th							
1 yr.	5	7	.417	3.23	12	12	10	92	102	26	27	0	0	0	0	39	2	0	.051

Bill Gannon

GANNON, WILLIAM G.
B. New Haven, Conn.   D. Apr. 26, 1927, Ft. Worth, Tex.

	W	L	PCT	ERA	G	GS	CG	IP	H	BB	SO	ShO	W	L	SV	AB	H	HR	BA
1898 STL N	0	1	.000	11.00	1	1	1	9	13	5	2	0	0	0	0	*			

Glenn Gardner

GARDNER, MILES GLENN   BR TR 5'11" 180 lbs.
B. Jan. 25, 1916, Burnsville, N. C.   D. July 7, 1964, Rochester, N. Y.

	W	L	PCT	ERA	G	GS	CG	IP	H	BB	SO	ShO	W	L	SV	AB	H	HR	BA
1945 STL N	3	1	.750	3.29	17	4	2	54.2	50	27	20	1	1	1	1	21	7	0	.333

Mike Garman

GARMAN, MICHAEL DOUGLAS   BR TR 6'3" 195 lbs.
B. Sept. 16, 1949, Caldwell, Ida.

	W	L	PCT	ERA	G	GS	CG	IP	H	BB	SO	ShO	W	L	SV	AB	H	HR	BA
1969 BOS A	1	0	1.000	4.38	2	2	0	12.1	13	10	10	0	0	0	0	5	2	0	.400
1971	1	1	.500	3.79	3	3	0	19	15	9	6	0	0	0	0	6	2	0	.333
1972	0	1	.000	12.00	3	1	0	3	4	2	1	0	0	0	0	0	0	0	—
1973	0	0	—	5.32	12	0	0	22	32	15	9	0	0	0	0	0	0	0	—
1974 STL N	7	2	.778	2.63	64	0	0	82	66	27	45	0	7	2	6	10	1	0	.100
1975	3	8	.273	2.39	66	0	0	79	73	48	48	0	3	8	10	2	0	0	.000
1976 CHI N	2	4	.333	4.97	47	2	0	76	79	35	37	0	2	2	1	7	0	0	.000
1977 LA N	4	4	.500	2.71	49	0	0	63	60	22	29	0	4	4	12	7	0	0	.000
1978 2 teams			LA	N	(10G 0–1)		MON	N	(47G 4–6)										
" total	4	7	.364	4.40	57	0	0	77.2	69	34	28	0	4	7	13	5	0	0	.000
9 yrs.	22	27	.449	3.63	303	8	0	434	411	202	213	0	20	23	42	42	5	0	.119
2 yrs.	10	10	.500	2.52	130	0	0	161	139	75	93	0	10	10	16	12	1	0	.083

LEAGUE CHAMPIONSHIP SERIES

	W	L	PCT	ERA	G	GS	CG	IP	H	BB	SO	ShO	W	L	SV	AB	H	HR	BA
1977 LA N	0	0	—	0.00	2	0	0	1.1	0	0	1	0	0	0	1	0	0	0	—

WORLD SERIES

	W	L	PCT	ERA	G	GS	CG	IP	H	BB	SO	ShO	W	L	SV	AB	H	HR	BA
1977 LA N	0	0	—	0.00	2	0	0	4	2	1	3	0	0	0	0	0	0	0	—

Charley Gelbert

GELBERT, CHARLES MAGNUS   BR TR 5'11" 170 lbs.
B. Jan. 26, 1906, Scranton, Pa.   D. Jan. 13, 1967, Easton, Pa.

	W	L	PCT	ERA	G	GS	CG	IP	H	BB	SO	ShO	W	L	SV	AB	H	HR	BA
1940 BOS A	0	0	—	9.00	2	0	0	4	5	3	1	0	0	0	0	*			

Al Gettel

GETTEL, ALLEN JONES   BR TR 6'3½" 200 lbs.
B. Sept. 17, 1917, Norfolk, Va.

	W	L	PCT	ERA	G	GS	CG	IP	H	BB	SO	ShO	W	L	SV	AB	H	HR	BA
1945 NY A	9	8	.529	3.90	27	17	9	154.2	141	53	67	0	0	0	3	57	16	0	.281
1946	6	7	.462	2.97	26	11	5	103	89	40	54	2	3	0	0	32	4	0	.125
1947 CLE A	11	10	.524	3.20	31	21	9	149	122	62	64	2	1	2	0	51	15	0	.294
1948 2 teams			CLE	A	(5G 0–1)		CHI	A	(22G 8–10)										
" total	8	11	.421	4.68	27	21	7	155.2	169	70	53	0	0	2	1	57	13	0	.228
1949 2 teams			CHI	A	(19G 2–5)		WAS	A	(16G 0–2)										
" total	2	7	.222	6.08	35	8	1	97.2	112	50	29	1	1	4	2	26	3	0	.115
1951 NY A	1	2	.333	4.87	30	1	0	57.1	52	25	36	0	1	2	0	12	1	0	.083
1955 STL N	1	0	1.000	9.00	8	0	0	17	26	10	7	0	1	0	0	6	3	0	.500
7 yrs.	38	45	.458	4.28	184	79	31	734.1	711	310	310	5	7	10	6	241	55	0	.228
1 yr.	1	0	1.000	9.00	8	0	0	17	26	10	7	0	1	0	0	6	3	0	.500

Charlie Getzein

GETZEIN, CHARLES H. (Pretzels)   BR TR
B. Feb. 14, 1864, Chicago, Ill.   D. June 19, 1932, Chicago, Ill.

	W	L	PCT	ERA	G	GS	CG	IP	H	BB	SO	ShO	W	L	SV	AB	H	HR	BA
1884 DET N	5	12	.294	1.95	17	17	17	147.1	118	25	107	1	0	0	0	55	6	0	.109
1885	12	25	.324	3.03	37	37	37	330	360	92	110	1	0	0	0	137	29	0	.212
1886	30	11	.732	3.03	43	43	42	386.2	388	85	172	1	0	0	0	165	29	0	.176
1887	29	13	.690	3.73	43	42	41	366.2	373	106	135	2	1	0	0	156	29	1	.186
1888	19	25	.432	3.05	46	46	45	404	411	54	202	2	0	0	0	167	41	1	.246
1889 IND N	18	22	.450	4.54	45	44	36	349	395	100	139	0	0	0	1	139	25	2	.180
1890 BOS N	23	17	.575	3.19	40	40	39	350	342	86	140	4	0	0	0	147	34	2	.231
1891 2 teams			BOS	N	(11G 4–5)		CLE	N	(1G 0–1)										
" total	4	6	.400	4.22	12	10	8	98	124	27	33	0	0	0	0	45	7	1	.156
1892 STL N	5	8	.385	5.67	13	13	12	108	159	31	32	0	0	0	0	45	9	1	.200
9 yrs.	145	139	.511	3.46	296	292	277	2539.2	2670	602	1070	11	1	0	1	1056	209	8	.198
1 yr.	5	8	.385	5.67	13	13	12	108	159	31	32	0	0	0	0	45	9	1	.200

Rube Geyer

GEYER, JACOB BOWMAN   TR
B. Mar. 22, 1885, Pittsburgh, Pa.   D. Oct. 12, 1962, Wahkon, Minn.

	W	L	PCT	ERA	G	GS	CG	IP	H	BB	SO	ShO	W	L	SV	AB	H	HR	BA
1910 STL N	0	0	—	4.50	4	0	0	4	5	3	5	0	0	0	0	1	0	0	.000
1911	9	6	.600	3.27	29	11	7	148.2	141	56	46	1	3	2	0	57	13	0	.228
1912	7	14	.333	3.28	41	18	6	181	191	84	61	0	4	3	0	53	11	0	.208
1913	1	5	.167	5.26	30	4	2	78.2	83	38	21	0	0	2	1	22	2	0	.091
4 yrs.	17	25	.405	3.67	104	33	15	412.1	420	181	133	1	7	7	1	133	26	0	.195
4 yrs.	17	25	.405	3.67	104	33	15	412.1	420	181	133	1	7	7	1	133	26	0	.195

THE 1982 WORLD SERIES

GAME 1: Fredbird welcomes you to the first World Series game in St. Louis in fourteen years. Stan Musial, standing next to club president August A. Busch, Jr., prepares to throw out the first ball.

Left: The frustration of the evening is clear in Ken Oberkfell's face, as the Cards fell 10-0. Jim Kaat (*below*) got into the game in the sixth, ending a seventeen-year gap between World Series appearances for the veteran southpaw.

GAME 2: Darrell Porter cracked a two-run double in the sixth inning to tie the score, added a single in the eighth, and threw out Paul Molitor trying to steal in the ninth to preserve the Cardinals' 5-4 victory.

GAME 3: Willie's game—rookie centerfielder Willie McGee hit two homers for four RBIs and made two great catches at the wall as the Cards won 6-2 in Milwaukee for a two games to one lead in the Series. (*Photo courtesy of St. Louis Cardinals*)

Right: Joaquin Andujar was breezing along with a three-hitter in the seventh when Ted Simmons smashed a hard grounder off his right leg. He was carried off the field in pain (*below*) and Cardinal fans had to wonder if he'd be available to pitch again in the Series.

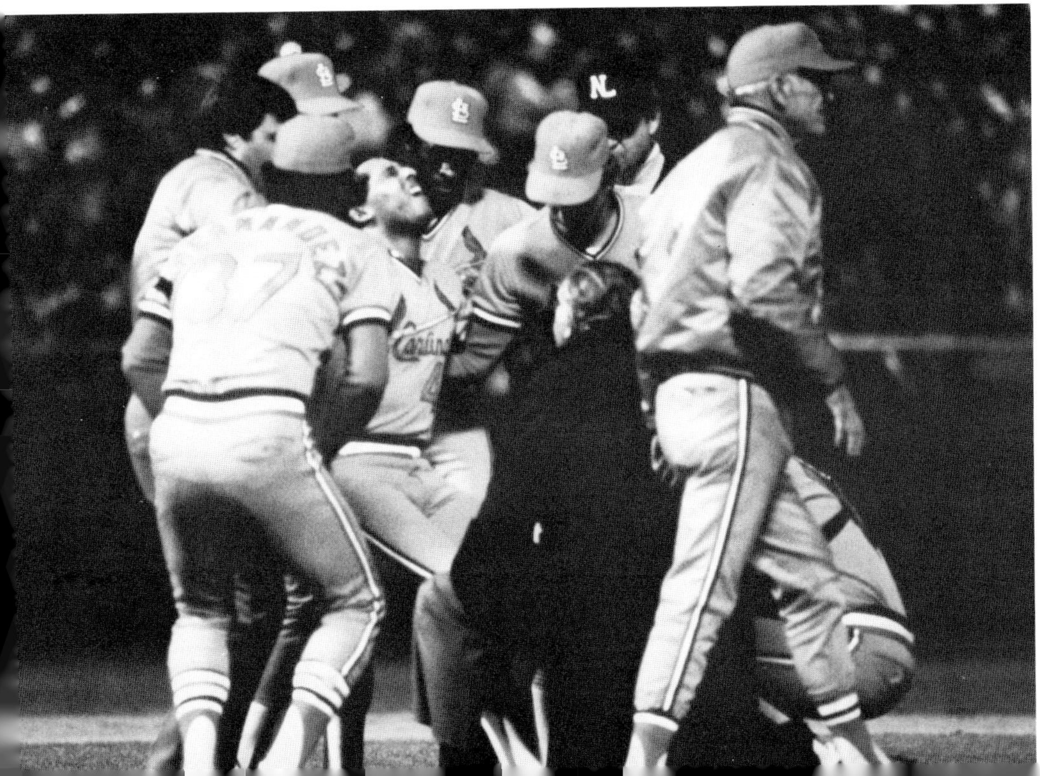

Ozzie Smith, making a fast pivot on a Game 3 double-play (*above*), was a standout in the field throughout the Series. Bruce Sutter, accepting congratulations from Keith Hernandez (*right*), worked two and two-thirds innings for the save. Had Herzog gone to him too early?

GAME 4: Ozzie Smith scored from second on Tommy Herr's sacrifice fly to center in the second (*above*), putting St. Louis up 3-0. But the Brewers rallied from a 5-1 deficit for six runs in the seventh, leading to the too-frequent sight of Whitey Herzog walking to the mound to change pitchers (*below*).

GAME 5: The Brewers finally broke through against Sutter (*left*), reaching him for three hits and two runs to break open a 4-2 game. *Below:* The only bright spot for the Cards was Keith Hernandez's snapping of an 0-for-15 slump with three hits in the 6-4 loss. (*Photo courtesy of St. Louis Cardinals*)

GAME 6: Before the rains came—Lonnie Smith crosses the plate on his attempted steal of home in the third as Ted Simmons applies the tag and George Hendrick looks on. Evans raises his arm to call him out, as Lonnie looks on in disbelief.

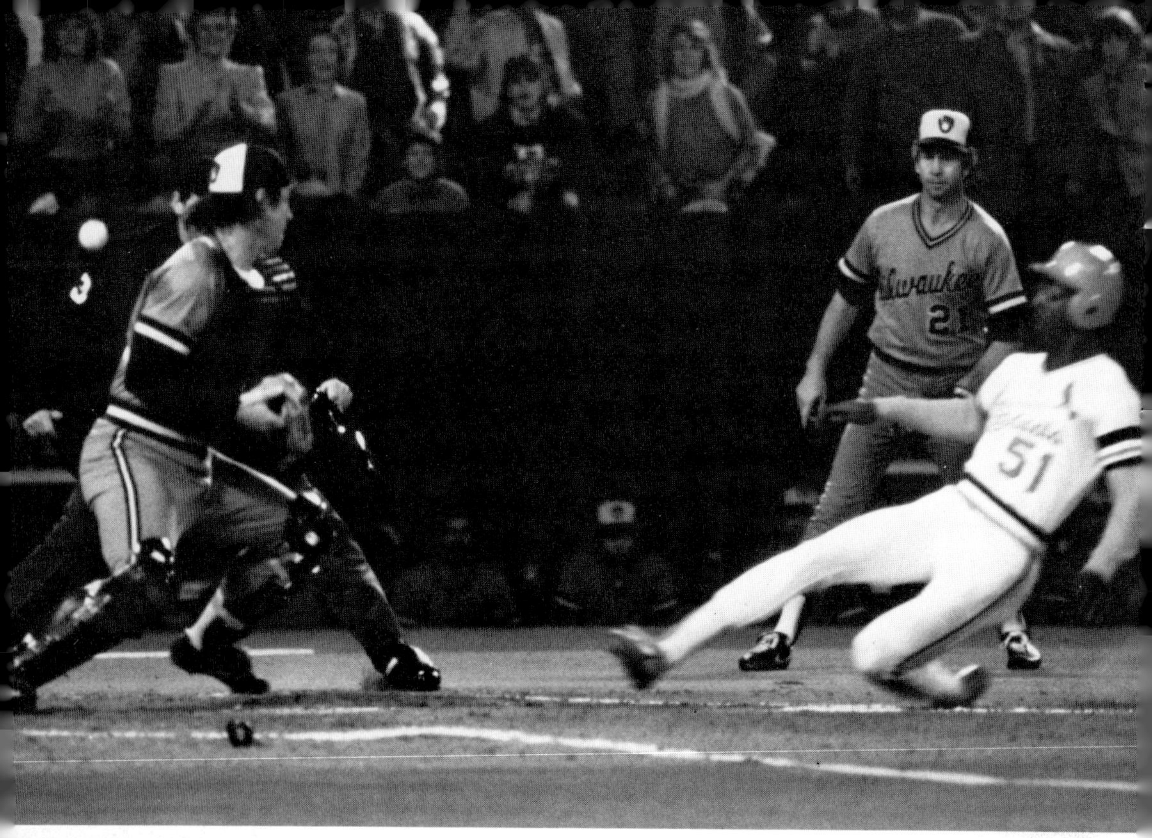
21
51

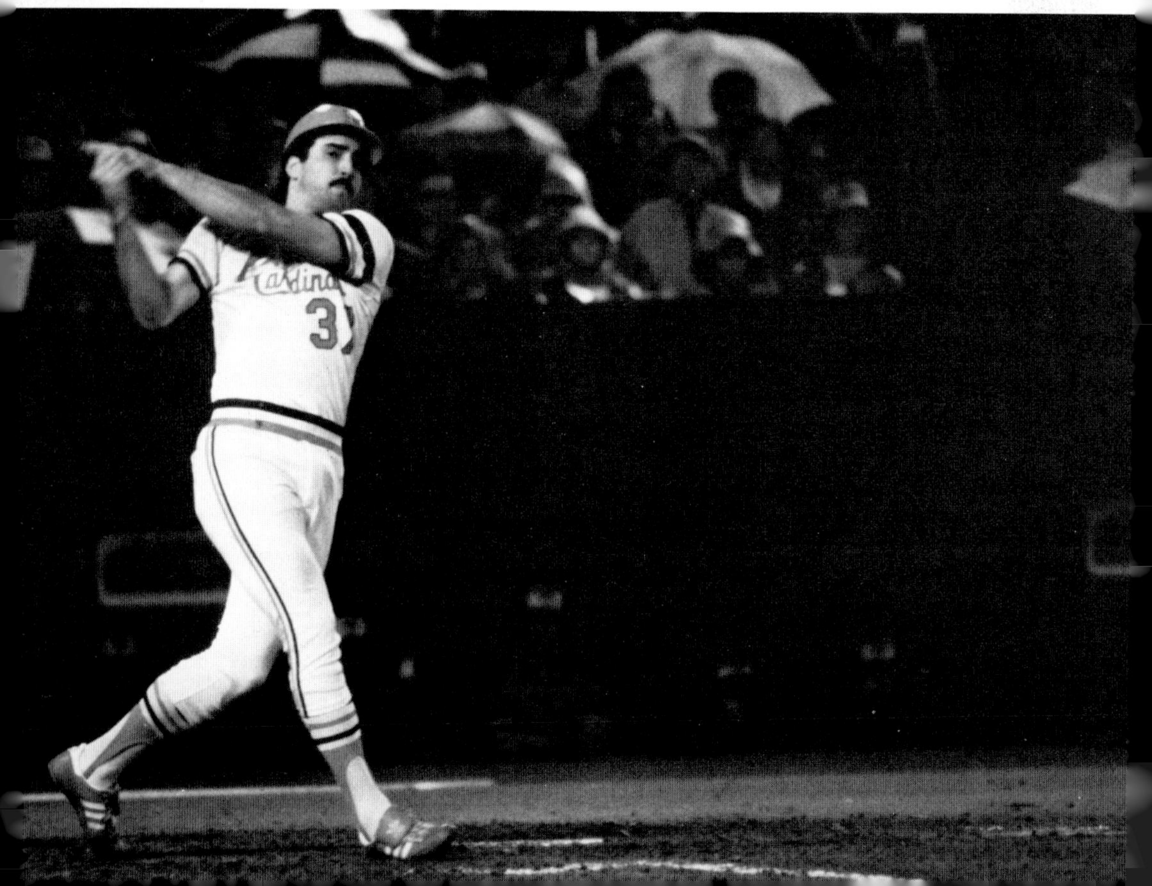

Top left: The ball bounces away from Ted Simmons as Willie McGee scores the Cardinals' second run in the second. Keith Hernandez's home run through the pouring rain stretched the lead to 7-0 before the first of two rain delays (*bottom left*).

Below: Through the long wait, John Stuper stayed calm and loose and was rewarded with a complete-game victory in the Cardinals' long, wet, 13-1 laugher.

GAME 7: His leg healed and his arm rested, Andujar (*left*) threw bullets at the Brewers for seven innings before yielding to Sutter. He also threw some angry words back at the Brewers' Jim Gantner, and had to be restrained by the big arms of umpire Lee Weyer, as Tommy Herr and Hub Kittle look on (*below*).

George Hendrick (*right*) delivered the game-winning hit in the Cardinals' three-run sixth, and threw a strike to Ken Oberkfell to nail Robin Yount trying to advance from first to third on Cecil Cooper's single in the fourth (*below*).

Bruce Sutter, finally given his big chance in the Series after all those years with the Cubs, delivered a win and two saves, retiring the last six batters in order to nail down the 6-3 clincher.

The last batter retired, his fist raised high, Sutter charges off the mound into the arms of Porter and Hernandez as the fans stream onto the field to celebrate St. Louis's ninth World Championship.

	W	L	PCT	ERA	G	GS	CG	IP	H	BB	SO	ShO	Relief Pitching W	L	SV	BATTING AB	H	HR	BA

Bob Gibson

GIBSON, ROBERT (Hoot)
B. Nov. 9, 1935, Omaha, Neb.
Hall of Fame 1981.

BR TR 6'1"   189 lbs.

	W	L	PCT	ERA	G	GS	CG	IP	H	BB	SO	ShO	W	L	SV	AB	H	HR	BA
1959 STL N	3	5	.375	3.33	13	9	2	75.2	77	39	48	1	1	0	0	26	3	0	.115
1960	3	6	.333	5.61	27	12	2	86.2	97	48	69	0	1	0	0	28	5	0	.179
1961	13	12	.520	3.24	35	27	10	211.1	186	119	166	2	0	1	1	66	13	1	.197
1962	15	13	.536	2.85	32	30	15	233.2	174	95	208	5	1	0	1	76	20	2	.263
1963	18	9	.667	3.39	36	33	14	254.2	224	96	204	2	1	0	0	87	18	3	.207
1964	19	12	.613	3.01	40	36	17	287.1	250	86	245	2	1	1	1	96	15	0	.156
1965	20	12	.625	3.07	38	36	20	299	243	103	270	6	0	0	1	104	25	5	.240
1966	21	12	.636	2.44	35	35	20	280.1	210	78	225	5	0	0	0	100	20	1	.200
1967	13	7	.650	2.98	24	24	10	175.1	151	40	147	2	0	0	0	60	8	0	.133
1968	22	9	.710	1.12	34	34	28	304.2	198	62	268	13	0	0	0	94	16	0	.170
1969	20	13	.606	2.18	35	35	28	314	251	95	269	4	0	0	0	118	29	1	.246
1970	23	7	.767	3.12	34	34	23	294	262	88	274	3	0	0	0	109	33	2	.303
1971	16	13	.552	3.04	31	31	20	246	215	76	185	5	0	0	0	87	15	2	.172
1972	19	11	.633	2.46	34	34	23	278	226	88	208	4	0	0	0	103	20	5	.194
1973	12	10	.545	2.77	25	25	13	195	159	57	142	1	0	0	0	65	12	2	.185
1974	11	13	.458	3.83	33	33	9	240	236	104	129	1	0	0	0	81	17	0	.210
1975	3	10	.231	5.04	22	14	1	109	120	62	60	0	1	2	2	28	5	0	.179
17 yrs.	251	174	.591	2.91	528	482	255	3884.2	3279	1336	3117	56	6	4	6	1328	274	24	.206
												6th 10th							
17 yrs.	251	174	.591	2.91	528	482	255	3884.2	3279	1336	3117	56	6	4	6	1328	274	24	.206
	1st	1st		10th	9th	2nd		1st	1st		1st	1st 1st							

WORLD SERIES

	W	L	PCT	ERA	G	GS	CG	IP	H	BB	SO	ShO	W	L	SV	AB	H	HR	BA
1964 STL N	2	1	.667	3.00	3	3	2	27	23	8	31	0	0	0	0	9	2	0	.222
1967	3	0	1.000	1.00	3	3	3	27	14	5	26	1	0	0	0	11	1	1	.091
1968	2	1	.667	1.67	3	3	3	27	18	4	35	1	0	0	0	8	1	1	.125
3 yrs.	7	2	.778	1.89	9	9	8	81	55	17	92	2	0	0	0	28	4	2	.143
		2nd				6th	3rd	6th		9th		2nd 4th							

George Gilpatrick

GILPATRICK, GEORGE F.
B. Feb. 28, 1875, Holden, Mo.   D. Dec. 15, 1941, Kansas City, Mo.

	W	L	PCT	ERA	G	GS	CG	IP	H	BB	SO	ShO	W	L	SV	AB	H	HR	BA
1898 STL N	0	2	.000	6.94	7	3	1	35	42	19	12	0	0	0	0	16	2	0	.125

Hal Gilson

GILSON, HAROLD (Lefty)
B. Feb. 9, 1942, Los Angeles, Calif.

BR TL 6'5"   195 lbs.

	W	L	PCT	ERA	G	GS	CG	IP	H	BB	SO	ShO	W	L	SV	AB	H	HR	BA
1968 2 teams	STL N	(13G 0–2)		HOU	N	(2G 0–0)													
" total	0	2	.000	4.97	15	0	0	25.1	34	12	20	0	0	2	2	4	0	0	.000

Dave Giusti

GIUSTI, DAVID JOHN
B. Nov. 27, 1939, Seneca Falls, N. Y.

BR TR 5'11"   190 lbs.

	W	L	PCT	ERA	G	GS	CG	IP	H	BB	SO	ShO	W	L	SV	AB	H	HR	BA
1962 HOU N	2	3	.400	5.62	22	5	0	73.2	82	30	43	0	2	0	0	24	7	0	.292
1964	0	0	—	3.16	8	0	0	25.2	24	8	16	0	0	0	0	7	2	0	.286
1965	8	7	.533	4.32	38	13	4	131.1	132	46	92	1	4	3	3	35	6	1	.171
1966	15	14	.517	4.20	34	33	9	210	215	54	131	4	0	0	0	74	17	0	.230
1967	11	15	.423	4.18	37	33	8	221.2	231	58	157	1	0	1	1	84	13	3	.155
1968	11	14	.440	3.19	37	34	12	251	226	67	186	2	0	0	1	82	15	0	.183
1969 STL N	3	7	.300	3.60	22	12	2	100	96	37	62	1	0	0	0	25	5	0	.200
1970 PIT N	9	3	.750	3.06	66	1	0	103	98	39	85	0	9	3	26	16	3	0	.188
1971	5	6	.455	2.93	58	0	0	86	79	31	55	0	5	6	30	17	1	0	.059
1972	7	4	.636	1.93	54	0	0	74.2	59	20	54	0	7	4	22	10	0	0	.000
1973	9	2	.818	2.37	67	0	0	98.2	89	37	64	0	9	2	20	13	4	0	.308
1974	7	5	.583	3.31	64	2	0	106	101	40	53	0	6	5	12	9	1	0	.111
1975	5	4	.556	2.93	61	0	0	92	79	42	38	0	5	4	17	10	3	0	.300
1976	5	4	.556	4.32	40	0	0	58.1	59	27	24	0	5	4	6	4	0	0	.000
1977 2 teams	CHI	N	(20G 0–2)		OAK	A	(40G 3–3)												
" total	3	5	.375	3.92	60	0	0	85	84	34	43	0	3	5	7	2	0	0	.000
15 yrs.	100	93	.518	3.60	668	133	35	1717	1654	570	1103	9	55	37	145	412	77	4	.187
1 yr.	3	7	.300	3.60	22	12	2	100	96	37	62	1	0	0	0	25	5	0	.200

LEAGUE CHAMPIONSHIP SERIES

	W	L	PCT	ERA	G	GS	CG	IP	H	BB	SO	ShO	W	L	SV	AB	H	HR	BA
1970 PIT N	0	0	—	3.86	2	0	0	2.1	3	1	1	0	0	0	0	0	0	0	—
1971	0	0	—	0.00	4	0	0	5.1	1	2	3	0	0	0	3	1	0	0	.000
1972	0	1	.000	6.75	3	0	0	2.2	5	0	3	0	0	1	1	1	0	0	.000
1974	0	1	.000	21.60	3	0	0	3.1	13	5	1	0	0	1	0	0	0	0	—
1975	0	0	—	0.00	1	0	0	1.1	0	0	1	0	0	0	0	0	0	0	—
5 yrs.	0	2	.000	6.60	13	0	0	15	22	8	9	0	0	2	4	2	0	0	.000

WORLD SERIES

	W	L	PCT	ERA	G	GS	CG	IP	H	BB	SO	ShO	W	L	SV	AB	H	HR	BA
1971 PIT N	0	0	—	0.00	3	0	0	5.1	3	2	4	0	0	0	1	0	0	0	—

Jack Glasscock

GLASSCOCK, JOHN WESLEY (Pebbly Jack)
B. July 22, 1859, Wheeling, W. Va.   D. Feb. 24, 1947, Wheeling, W. Va.
Manager 1889.

BR TR 5'8"   160 lbs.

	W	L	PCT	ERA	G	GS	CG	IP	H	BB	SO	ShO	W	L	SV	AB	H	HR	BA
1884 CLE N	0	0	—	5.40	2	0	0	5	8	2	1	0	0	0	0	453	142	3	.313
1887 IND N	0	0	—	0.00	1	0	0	1	0	0	1	0	0	0	0	483	142	0	.294
1888	0	0	—	54.00	1	0	0	.1	1	2	1	0	0	0	0	442	119	1	.269
1889	0	0	—	0.00	1	0	0	.2	3	3	0	0	0	0	0	582	205	7	.352
4 yrs.	0	0	—	6.43	5	0	0	7	12	7	3	0	0	0	0	*			

Kid Gleason

GLEASON, WILLIAM J. BL TR 5'7" 158 lbs.
Brother of Harry Gleason.
B. Oct. 26, 1866, Camden, N. J.   D. Jan. 2, 1933, Philadelphia, Pa.
Manager 1919-23.

	W	L	PCT	ERA	G	GS	CG	IP	H	BB	SO	ShO	W	L	SV	AB	H	HR	BA
1888 PHI N	7	16	.304	2.84	24	23	23	199.2	199	53	89	1	0	0	0	83	17	0	.205
1889	9	15	.375	5.58	29	21	15	205	242	97	64	0	2	2	1	99	25	0	.253
1890	38	17	.691	2.63	60	55	54	506	479	167	222	6	1	0	2	224	47	0	.210
1891	24	22	.522	3.51	53	44	40	418	431	165	100	1	1	2	1	214	53	0	.248
1892 STL N	16	24	.400	3.33	47	45	43	400	389	151	133	2	0	0	0	233	50	3	.215
1893	21	25	.457	4.61	48	45	37	380.1	436	187	86	1	1	1	1	199	51	0	.256
1894 2 teams								STL N (8G 2-6)		BAL N (21G 15-5)									
" total	17	11	.607	4.85	29	28	25	230	299	65	44	0	0	0	0	114	37	0	.325
1895 BAL N	2	4	.333	6.97	9	5	3	50.1	77	21	6	0	1	2	1	421	130	0	.309
8 yrs.	134	134	.500	3.79	299	266	240	2389.1	2552	906	744	11	6	7	6	*			.235
3 yrs.	39	55	.415	4.10	103	98	86	838.1	900	359	228	3	1	1	1	460	108	3	.235

Bob Glenn

GLENN, BURDETTE
B. June 16, 1894, West Sunbury, Pa.

	W	L	PCT	ERA	G	GS	CG	IP	H	BB	SO	ShO	W	L	SV	AB	H	HR	BA
1920 STL N	0	0	-	0.00	2	0	0	2	0	0	0	0	0	0	0	0	0	0	-

Roy Golden

GOLDEN, ROY K. TR
B. July 12, 1888, Chicago, Ill.   D. Oct. 4, 1961, Cincinnati, Ohio

	W	L	PCT	ERA	G	GS	CG	IP	H	BB	SO	ShO	W	L	SV	AB	H	HR	BA
1910 STL N	2	3	.400	4.43	7	6	3	42.2	44	33	31	0	0	0	0	15	4	0	.267
1911	4	9	.308	5.02	30	25	6	148.2	127	129	81	0	0	0	0	44	5	0	.114
2 yrs.	6	12	.333	4.89	37	31	9	191.1	171	162	112	0	0	0	0	59	9	0	.153
2 yrs.	6	12	.333	4.89	37	31	9	191.1	171	162	112	0	0	0	0	59	9	0	.153

Hal Goldsmith

GOLDSMITH, HAROLD EUGENE BR TR 6' 174 lbs.
B. Aug. 18, 1898, Peconic, N. Y.

	W	L	PCT	ERA	G	GS	CG	IP	H	BB	SO	ShO	W	L	SV	AB	H	HR	BA
1926 BOS N	5	7	.417	4.37	19	15	5	101	135	28	16	0	1	1	0	38	8	0	.211
1927	1	3	.250	3.52	22	5	1	71.2	83	26	13	0	0	1	1	21	5	0	.238
1928	0	0	-	3.24	4	0	0	8.1	14	1	1	0	0	0	0	2	0	0	.000
1929 STL N	0	0	-	6.75	2	0	0	4	3	1	0	0	0	0	0	1	0	0	.000
4 yrs.	6	10	.375	4.04	47	20	6	185	235	56	30	0	1	2	1	62	13	0	.210
1 yr.	0	0	-	6.75	2	0	0	4	3	1	0	0	0	0	0	1	0	0	.000

Marv Goodwin

GOODWIN, MARVIN MARDO BR TR 5'11" 168 lbs.
B. Jan. 16, 1893, Richmond, Vt.   D. Oct. 22, 1925, Houston, Tex.

	W	L	PCT	ERA	G	GS	CG	IP	H	BB	SO	ShO	W	L	SV	AB	H	HR	BA
1916 WAS A	0	0	-	3.18	3	0	0	5.2	5	3	1	0	0	0	0	1	0	0	.000
1917 STL N	6	4	.600	2.21	14	12	6	85.1	70	19	38	3	0	1	0	23	4	0	.174
1919	11	9	.550	2.51	33	17	7	179	163	33	48	0	3	3	0	60	12	0	.200
1920	3	8	.273	4.95	32	12	3	116.1	153	28	23	0	1	1	1	35	7	0	.200
1921	1	2	.333	3.72	14	4	1	36.1	47	9	7	0	0	0	1	6	0	0	.000
1922	0	0		2.25	2	0	0	4	3	3	0	0	0	0	0	0	0	0	-
1925 CIN N	0	2	.000	4.79	4	3	2	20.2	26	5	4	0	0	0	0	4	1	0	.250
7 yrs.	21	25	.457	3.30	102	48	19	447.1	467	100	121	3	4	5	2	129	24	0	.186
5 yrs.	21	23	.477	3.23	95	45	17	421	436	92	116	3	4	5	2	124	23	0	.185

Hank Gornicki

GORNICKI, FRANK TED BR TR 6'1" 145 lbs.
B. Jan. 14, 1911, Niagara, N. Y.

	W	L	PCT	ERA	G	GS	CG	IP	H	BB	SO	ShO	W	L	SV	AB	H	HR	BA
1941 2 teams								STL N (4G 1-0)		CHI N (1G 0-0)									
" total	1	0	1.000	3.38	5	1	1	13.1	9	9	8	1	0	0	0	4	1	0	.250
1942 PIT N	5	6	.455	2.57	25	14	7	112	89	40	48	2	0	0	2	35	4	1	.114
1943	9	13	.409	3.98	42	18	4	147	165	47	63	1	3	3	4	40	7	0	.175
1946	0	0	-	3.55	7	0	0	12.2	12	11	4	0	0	0	0	3	0	0	.000
4 yrs.	15	19	.441	3.38	79	33	12	285	275	107	123	4	3	3	6	82	12	1	.146
1 yr.	1	0	1.000	3.18	5	1	1	11.1	6	9	6	1	0	0	0	4	1	0	.250

Al Grabowski

GRABOWSKI, ALFONS FRANCIS (Hook) BL TL 5'11½" 175 lbs.
Brother of Reggie Grabowski.
B. Sept. 4, 1901, Syracuse, N. Y.   D. Oct. 29, 1966, Memphis, N. Y.

	W	L	PCT	ERA	G	GS	CG	IP	H	BB	SO	ShO	W	L	SV	AB	H	HR	BA
1929 STL N	3	2	.600	2.52	6	6	4	50	44	8	22	2	0	0	0	16	4	0	.250
1930	6	4	.600	4.84	33	8	1	106	121	50	45	0	2	3	1	33	12	0	.364
2 yrs.	9	6	.600	4.10	39	14	5	156	165	58	67	2	2	3	1	49	16	0	.327
2 yrs.	9	6	.600	4.10	39	14	5	156	165	58	67	2	2	3	1	49	16	0	.327

Wayne Granger

GRANGER, WAYNE ALLAN BR TR 6'2" 165 lbs.
B. Mar. 15, 1944, Springfield, Mass.

	W	L	PCT	ERA	G	GS	CG	IP	H	BB	SO	ShO	W	L	SV	AB	H	HR	BA
1968 STL N	4	2	.667	2.25	34	0	0	44	40	12	27	0	4	2	4	5	1	0	.200
1969 CIN N	9	6	.600	2.79	90	0	0	145	143	40	68	0	9	6	27	21	2	0	.095
1970	6	5	.545	2.65	67	0	0	85	79	27	38	0	6	5	35	10	1	0	.100
1971	7	6	.538	3.33	70	0	0	100	94	28	51	0	7	6	11	7	1	1	.143
1972 MIN A	2	6	.400	3.00	63	0	0	90	83	28	45	0	4	6	19	10	2	0	.200
1973 2 teams								STL N (33G 2-4)		NY A (7G 0-1)									
" total	2	5	.286	3.63	40	0	0	62	69	24	24	0	2	5	5	0	0	0	.000
1974 CHI N	0	0	-	7.88	5	0	0	8	16	3	4	0	0	0	0	0	0	0	-
1975 HOU N	2	5	.286	3.65	50	0	0	74	76	23	30	0	2	5	5	9	0	0	.000
1976 MON N	1	0	1.000	3.66	27	0	0	32	32	16	16	0	1	0	2	3	0	0	.000
9 yrs.	35	35	.500	3.14	451	0	0	640	632	201	303	0	35	35	108	68	7	1	.103
2 yrs.	5	6	.500	3.28	67	0	0	90.2	90	33	41	0	6	6	5	8	1	0	.125

LEAGUE CHAMPIONSHIP SERIES

	W	L	PCT	ERA	G	GS	CG	IP	H	BB	SO	ShO	W	L	SV	AB	H	HR	BA
1970 CIN N	0	0	-	0.00	1	0	0	.2	1	0	0	0	0	0	0	0	0	0	-

WORLD SERIES

	W	L	PCT	ERA	G	GS	CG	IP	H	BB	SO	ShO	W	L	SV	AB	H	HR	BA
1968 STL N	0	0	-	0.00	1	0	0	2	0	1	1	0	0	0	0	0	0	0	-

	W	L	PCT	ERA	G	GS	CG	IP	H	BB	SO	ShO	Relief Pitching W	L	SV	BATTING AB	H	HR	BA

Wayne Granger continued

	W	L	PCT	ERA	G	GS	CG	IP	H	BB	SO	ShO	W	L	SV	AB	H	HR	BA
1970 CIN N	0	0	—	33.75	2	0	0	1.1	7	1	1	0	0	0	0	0	0	0	—
2 yrs.	0	0	—	13.50	3	0	0	3.1	7	2	2	0	0	0	0	0	0	0	—

Mudcat Grant

GRANT, JAMES TIMOTHY   BR TR 6'1"   186 lbs.
B. Aug. 13, 1935, Lacoochee, Fla.

	W	L	PCT	ERA	G	GS	CG	IP	H	BB	SO	ShO	W	L	SV	AB	H	HR	BA
1958 CLE A	10	11	.476	3.84	44	28	11	204	173	104	111	1	2	2	4	66	5	0	.076
1959	10	7	.588	4.14	38	19	6	165.1	140	81	85	1	1	1	3	55	11	1	.200
1960	9	8	.529	4.40	33	19	5	159.2	147	78	75	0	1	3	0	57	16	0	.281
1961	15	9	.625	3.86	35	35	11	244.2	207	109	146	3	0	0	0	88	15	1	.170
1962	7	10	.412	4.27	26	23	6	149.2	128	81	90	1	0	0	0	53	8	0	.151
1963	13	14	.481	3.69	38	32	10	229.1	213	87	157	2	1	0	1	69	13	1	.188
1964 2 teams				CLE	A	(13G 3–4)		MIN	A	(26G 11–9)									
" total	14	13	.519	3.67	39	32	11	228	244	61	118	1	1	0	1	82	16	2	.195
1965 MIN A	21	7	.750	3.30	41	39	14	270.1	252	61	142	6	0	1	0	97	15	0	.155
1966	13	13	.500	3.25	35	35	10	249	248	49	110	3	0	0	0	78	15	0	.192
1967	5	6	.455	4.72	27	14	2	95.1	121	17	50	0	0	0	0	28	5	0	.179
1968 LA N	6	4	.600	2.08	37	4	1	95	77	19	35	0	5	2	3	31	4	1	.129
1969 2 teams				MON	N	(11G 1–6)		STL	N	(30G 7–5)									
" total	8	11	.421	4.42	41	13	2	114	126	36	55	0	1	0	7	33	7	0	.212
1970 2 teams				OAK	A	(72G 6–2)		PIT	N	(8G 2–1)									
" total	8	3	.727	1.87	80	0	0	135	112	32	58	0	8	3	24	11	2	0	.182
1971 2 teams				PIT	N	(42G 5–3)		OAK	A	(15G 1–0)									
" total	6	3	.667	3.18	57	0	0	102	104	34	35	0	6	3	10	11	3	0	.273
14 yrs.	145	119	.549	3.63	571	293	89	2441.1	2292	849	1267	18	25	15	53	759	135	6	.178
1 yr.	7	5	.583	4.12	30	3	1	63.1	62	22	35	0	0	0	7	17	5	0	.294

LEAGUE CHAMPIONSHIP SERIES

	W	L	PCT	ERA	G	GS	CG	IP	H	BB	SO	ShO	W	L	SV	AB	H	HR	BA
1971 OAK A	0	0	—	0.00	1	0	0	2	3	0	2	0	0	0	0	0	0	0	—

WORLD SERIES

	W	L	PCT	ERA	G	GS	CG	IP	H	BB	SO	ShO	W	L	SV	AB	H	HR	BA
1965 MIN A	2	1	.667	2.74	3	3	2	23	22	2	12	0	0	0	0	8	2	1	.250

Bill Greason

GREASON, WILLIAM HENRY (Booster)   BR TR 5'10"   170 lbs.
B. Sept. 3, 1924, Atlanta, Ga.

	W	L	PCT	ERA	G	GS	CG	IP	H	BB	SO	ShO	W	L	SV	AB	H	HR	BA
1954 STL N	0	1	.000	13.50	3	2	0	4	8	4	2	0	0	0	0	1	0	0	.000

Bill Greif

GREIF, WILLIAM BRILEY   BB TR 6'4"   196 lbs.
B. Apr. 25, 1950, Ft Stockton, Tex.

	W	L	PCT	ERA	G	GS	CG	IP	H	BB	SO	ShO	W	L	SV	AB	H	HR	BA
1971 HOU N	1	1	.500	5.06	7	3	0	16	18	8	14	0	1	0	0	3	1	0	.333
1972 SD N	5	16	.238	5.60	34	22	2	125.1	143	47	91	1	1	0	2	33	1	0	.030
1973	10	17	.370	3.21	36	31	9	199.1	181	62	120	3	0	0	1	61	6	0	.098
1974	9	19	.321	4.66	43	35	7	226	244	95	137	1	0	0	1	56	4	0	.071
1975	4	6	.400	3.88	59	1	0	72	74	38	43	0	4	6	9	1	0	0	.000
1976 2 teams				SD	N	(5G 1–3)		STL	N	(47G 1–5)									
" total	2	8	.200	5.26	52	5	0	77	87	37	37	0	1	5	6	12	0	0	.000
6 yrs.	31	67	.316	4.41	231	97	18	715.2	747	287	442	5	7	11	19	166	12	0	.072
1 yr.	1	5	.167	4.12	47	0	0	54.2	60	26	32	0	1	5	6	4	0	0	.000

Bob Grim

GRIM, ROBERT ANTON   BR TR 6'1"   175 lbs.
B. Mar. 8, 1930, New York, N. Y.

	W	L	PCT	ERA	G	GS	CG	IP	H	BB	SO	ShO	W	L	SV	AB	H	HR	BA
1954 NY A	20	6	.769	3.26	37	20	8	199	175	85	108	1	8	0	0	70	10	1	.143
1955	7	5	.583	4.19	26	11	1	92.1	81	42	63	1	3	3	4	25	3	0	.120
1956	6	1	.857	2.77	26	6	1	74.2	64	31	48	0	3	0	5	16	1	0	.063
1957	12	8	.600	2.63	46	0	0	72	60	36	52	0	12	8	19	9	1	1	.111
1958 2 teams				NY	A	(11G 0–1)		KC	A	(26G 7–6)									
" total	7	7	.500	3.81	37	14	5	130	130	51	65	1	0	3	0	33	6	0	.182
1959 KC A	6	10	.375	4.09	40	9	3	125.1	124	57	65	1	2	6	4	32	3	1	.094
1960 3 teams				CLE A (3G 0–1)		CIN	N	(26G 2–2)	STL	N	(15G 1–0)								
" total	3	3	.500	4.22	44	0	0	53.1	60	20	39	0	3	3	2	2	0	0	.000
1962 KC A	0	1	.000	6.23	12	0	0	13	14	8	3	0	0	1	3	2	0	0	.000
8 yrs.	61	41	.598	3.61	268	60	18	759.2	708	330	443	4	31	24	37	189	24	3	.127
1 yr.	1	0	1.000	3.05	15	0	0	20.2	22	9	15	0	1	0	0	1	0	0	.000

WORLD SERIES

	W	L	PCT	ERA	G	GS	CG	IP	H	BB	SO	ShO	W	L	SV	AB	H	HR	BA
1955 NY A	0	1	.000	4.15	3	1	0	8.2	8	5	8	0	0	0	1	2	0	0	.000
1957	0	1	.000	7.71	2	0	0	2.1	3	0	2	0	0	0	0	0	0	0	—
2 yrs.	0	2	.000	4.91	5	1	0	11	11	5	10	0	0	1	1	2	0	0	.000

Burleigh Grimes

GRIMES, BURLEIGH ARLAND (Ol' Stubblebeard)   BR TR 5'10"   175 lbs.
B. Aug. 18, 1893, Clear Lake, Wis.
Manager 1937-38.
Hall of Fame 1964.

	W	L	PCT	ERA	G	GS	CG	IP	H	BB	SO	ShO	W	L	SV	AB	H	HR	BA
1916 PIT N	2	3	.400	2.36	6	5	4	45.2	40	10	20	0	1	0	0	17	3	0	.176
1917	3	16	.158	3.53	37	17	8	194	186	70	72	1	1	4	0	69	16	0	.232
1918 BKN N	19	9	.679	2.14	40	28	19	269.2	210	76	113	7	1	1	0	90	18	0	.200
1919	10	11	.476	3.47	25	21	13	181.1	179	60	82	1	1	1	0	69	17	0	.246
1920	23	11	.676	2.22	40	33	25	303.2	271	67	131	5	2	1	2	111	34	0	.306
1921	22	13	.629	2.83	37	35	30	302.1	313	76	136	2	0	1	0	114	27	1	.237
1922	17	14	.548	4.76	36	34	18	259	324	84	99	1	1	0	1	93	22	0	.237
1923	21	18	.538	3.58	39	38	33	327	356	100	119	2	0	1	0	126	30	0	.238
1924	22	13	.629	3.82	38	36	30	310.2	351	91	135	1	0	1	0	124	37	0	.298
1925	12	19	.387	5.04	33	31	19	246.2	305	102	73	0	1	0	0	96	24	1	.250
1926	12	13	.480	3.71	30	29	18	225.1	238	88	64	1	1	0	1	81	18	0	.222
1927 NY N	19	8	.704	3.54	39	34	15	259.2	274	87	102	2	1	0	2	96	18	0	.188

			W	L	PCT	ERA	G	GS	CG	IP	H	BB	SO	ShO	Relief Pitching W	L	SV	BATTING AB	H	HR	BA

Burleigh Grimes continued

1928	PIT	N	25	14	.641	2.99	48	37	28	330.2	311	77	97	4	4	1	3	131	42	0	.321
1929			17	7	.708	3.13	33	29	18	232.2	245	70	62	2	0	1	2	91	26	0	.286
1930	2 teams		BOS	N	(11G 3–5)		STL	N	(22G 13–6)												
"	total		16	11	.593	4.07	33	28	11	201.1	246	65	73	1	2	2	0	73	18	0	.247
1931	STL	N	17	9	.654	3.65	29	28	17	212.1	240	59	67	3	1	0	0	76	14	0	.184
1932	CHI	N	6	11	.353	4.78	30	18	5	141.1	174	50	36	1	0	2	1	44	11	0	.250
1933	2 teams		CHI	N	(17G 3–6)		STL	N	(4G 0–1)												
"	total		3	7	.300	3.78	21	10	3	83.1	86	37	16	1	1	1	4	25	4	0	.160
1934	3 teams		STL	N	(4G 2–1)		PIT	N	(8G 1–2)		NY	A	(10G 1–2)								
"	total		4	5	.444	6.11	22	4	0	53	63	26	15	0	4	3	1	9	1	0	.111
	19 yrs.		270	212	.560	3.53	616	495	314	4179.2	4412	1295	1512	35	21	19	17	1535	380	2	.248
	4 yrs.		32	17	.653	3.45	59	50	27	386	434	112	130	4	4	3	1	138	30	0	.217

WORLD SERIES

1920	BKN	N	1	2	.333	4.19	3	3	1	19.1	23	9	4	1	0	0	0	6	2	0	.333
1930	STL	N	0	2	.000	3.71	2	2	2	17	10	6	13	0	0	0	0	5	2	0	.400
1931			2	0	1.000	2.04	2	2	1	17.2	9	9	11	0	0	0	0	7	2	0	.286
1932	CHI	N	0	0	—	23.63	2	0	0	2.2	7	2	0	0	0	0	0	1	0	0	.000
	4 yrs.		3	4	.429	4.29	9	7	4	56.2	49	26	28	1	0	0	0	19	6	0	.316
					7th								8th								

John Grimes

GRIMES, JOHN THOMAS
B. Apr. 17, 1869, Woodstock, Md.   D. Jan. 17, 1964, San Francisco, Calif.
BR TR 5'11"   160 lbs.

| 1897 | STL | N | 0 | 2 | .000 | 5.95 | 3 | 1 | 1 | 19.2 | 24 | 8 | 4 | 0 | 0 | 1 | 0 | 7 | 2 | 0 | .286 |

Dan Griner

GRINER, DONALD DEXTER (Rusty)
B. Mar. 7, 1888, Centerville, Tenn.   D. June 3, 1950, Bishopville, S. C.
BL TR 6'1½"   200 lbs.

1912	STL	N	3	4	.429	3.17	12	7	2	54	59	15	20	0	0	0	0	13	1	0	.077
1913			10	22	.313	5.08	34	34	18	225	279	66	79	1	0	0	0	81	21	0	.259
1914			9	13	.409	2.51	37	16	11	179	163	57	74	2	1	1	2	55	14	0	.255
1915			5	11	.313	2.81	37	18	9	150.1	137	46	46	3	0	3	3	52	14	0	.269
1916			0	0	—	4.09	4	0	0	11	15	3	3	0	0	0	0	4	1	0	.250
1918	BKN	N	1	5	.167	2.15	11	6	3	54.1	47	15	22	1	0	0	0	14	1	0	.071
	6 yrs.		28	55	.337	3.49	135	81	43	673.2	700	202	244	7	1	4	6	219	52	0	.237
	5 yrs.		27	50	.351	3.60	124	75	40	619.1	653	187	222	6	1	4	6	205	51	0	.249

Marv Grissom

GRISSOM, MARVIN EDWARD
Brother of Lee Grissom.
B. Mar. 31, 1918, Los Molinos, Calif.
BR TR 6'3"   190 lbs.

1946	NY	N	0	2	.000	4.34	4	3	0	18.2	17	13	9	0	0	0	0	5	1	0	.200
1949	DET	A	2	4	.333	6.41	27	2	0	39.1	56	34	17	0	2	3	0	9	2	0	.222
1952	CHI	A	12	10	.545	3.74	28	24	4	166	156	79	97	1	0	1	0	53	8	0	.151
1953	2 teams		BOS	A	(13G 2–6)		NY	N	(21G 4–2)												
"	total		6	8	.429	4.26	34	18	4	143.2	144	61	77	0	1	0	0	45	2	0	.044
1954	NY	N	10	7	.588	2.35	56	3	1	122.1	100	50	64	1	9	7	19	32	5	0	.156
1955			5	4	.556	2.92	55	0	0	89.1	76	41	49	0	5	4	8	13	2	0	.154
1956			1	1	.500	1.56	43	0	0	80.2	71	16	49	0	1	1	7	11	1	0	.091
1957			4	4	.500	2.61	55	0	0	82.2	74	23	51	0	4	4	14	12	2	0	.167
1958	SF	N	7	5	.583	3.99	51	0	0	65.1	71	26	46	0	7	5	10	9	0	0	.000
1959	STL	N	0	0	—	22.50	3	0	0	2	6	0	0	0	0	0	0	0	0	0	—
	10 yrs.		47	45	.511	3.41	356	52	12	810	771	343	459	3	28	26	58	189	23	0	.122
	1 yr.		0	0	—	22.50	3	0	0	2	6	0	0	0	0	0	0	0	0	0	—

WORLD SERIES

| 1954 | NY | N | 1 | 0 | 1.000 | 0.00 | 1 | 0 | 0 | 2.2 | 1 | 3 | 2 | 0 | 1 | 0 | 0 | 1 | 0 | 0 | .000 |

Johnny Grodzicki

GRODZICKI, JOHN
B. Feb. 26, 1917, Nanticoke, Pa.
BR TR 6'1½"   200 lbs.

1941	STL	N	2	1	.667	1.35	5	1	0	13.1	6	11	10	0	2	0	0	2	0	0	.000
1946			0	0	—	9.00	3	0	0	4	4	4	2	0	0	0	0	0	0	0	—
1947			0	1	.000	5.40	16	0	0	23.1	21	19	8	0	0	1	0	1	0	0	.000
	3 yrs.		2	2	.500	4.43	24	1	0	40.2	31	34	20	0	2	1	0	3	0	0	.000
	3 yrs.		2	2	.500	4.43	24	1	0	40.2	31	34	20	0	2	1	0	3	0	0	.000

Joe Grzenda

GRZENDA, JOSEPH CHARLES
B. June 8, 1937, Scranton, Pa.
BR TL 6'2"   180 lbs.

1961	DET	A	1	0	1.000	7.94	4	0	0	5.2	9	2	0	0	1	0	0	1	1	0	1.000
1964	KC	A	0	2	.000	5.40	20	0	0	25	34	13	17	0	0	2	0	2	0	0	.000
1966			0	2	.000	3.27	21	0	0	22	28	12	14	0	0	2	0	0	0	0	—
1967	NY	N	0	0	—	2.16	11	0	0	16.2	14	8	9	0	0	0	0	0	0	0	.000
1969	MIN	A	4	1	.800	3.88	38	0	0	48.2	52	17	24	0	4	1	3	5	0	0	.000
1970	WAS	A	3	6	.333	4.98	49	3	0	85	86	34	38	0	2	5	6	12	0	0	.000
1971			5	2	.714	1.93	46	0	0	70	54	17	56	0	5	2	5	7	1	0	.143
1972	STL	N	1	0	1.000	5.71	30	0	0	34.2	46	17	15	0	1	0	1	3	0	0	.000
	8 yrs.		14	13	.519	4.01	219	3	0	307.2	323	120	173	0	13	12	14	30	2	0	.067
	1 yr.		1	0	1.000	5.71	30	0	0	34.2	46	17	15	0	1	0	1	3	0	0	.000

LEAGUE CHAMPIONSHIP SERIES

| 1969 | MIN | A | 0 | 0 | — | 0.00 | 1 | 0 | 0 | .2 | 0 | 1 | 0 | 0 | 0 | 0 | 0 | 0 | 0 | 0 | — |

Harry Gumbert

GUMBERT, HARRY EDWARD (Gunboat)
B. Nov. 5, 1909, Elizabeth, Pa.
BR TR 6'2"   185 lbs.

| 1935 | NY | N | 1 | 2 | .333 | 6.08 | 6 | 3 | 1 | 23.2 | 35 | 10 | 11 | 0 | 0 | 0 | 0 | 8 | 0 | 0 | .000 |
| 1936 | | | 11 | 3 | .786 | 3.90 | 39 | 15 | 3 | 140.2 | 157 | 54 | 52 | 0 | 4 | 0 | 0 | 44 | 11 | 0 | .250 |

	W	L	PCT	ERA	G	GS	CG	IP	H	BB	SO	ShO	Relief Pitching W	L	SV	BATTING AB	H	HR	BA

Harry Gumbert continued

	W	L	PCT	ERA	G	GS	CG	IP	H	BB	SO	ShO	W	L	SV	AB	H	HR	BA
1937	10	11	.476	3.68	34	24	10	200.1	194	62	65	1	0	0	1	72	13	1	.181
1938	15	13	.536	4.01	38	33	14	235.2	238	84	84	1	0	0	0	84	13	0	.155
1939	18	11	.621	4.32	36	34	14	243.2	257	81	81	2	0	1	0	90	18	0	.200
1940	12	14	.462	3.76	35	30	14	237	230	81	77	2	2	0	2	87	17	1	.195
1941 2 teams			NY	N	(5G 1–1)		STL	N	(33G 11–5)										
" total	12	6	.667	3.06	38	22	9	176.2	173	48	62	3	4	0	1	65	19	2	.292
1942 STL N	9	5	.643	3.26	38	19	5	163	156	59	52	0	4	0	5	54	6	0	.111
1943	10	5	.667	2.84	21	19	7	133	115	32	40	2	0	0	0	45	7	0	.156
1944 2 teams			STL	N	(10G 4–2)		CIN	N	(24G 10–8)										
" total	14	10	.583	3.07	34	26	14	216.2	217	59	56	2	1	2	3	73	9	0	.123
1946 CIN N	6	8	.429	3.24	36	10	5	119.1	112	42	44	0	4	0	4	32	8	0	.250
1947	10	10	.500	3.89	46	0	0	90.1	88	47	43	0	10	10	10	22	6	0	.273
1948	10	8	.556	3.47	61	0	0	106.1	123	34	25	0	10	8	17	25	1	1	.040
1949 2 teams			CIN	N	(29G 4–3)		PIT	N	(16G 1–4)										
" total	5	7	.417	5.64	45	0	0	68.2	88	26	17	0	5	7	5	6	1	0	.167
1950 PIT N	0	0	—	5.40	1	0	0	1.2	3	2	0	0	0	0	0	1	1	0	1.000
15 yrs.	143	113	.559	3.68	508	235	94	2156.2	2186	721	709	13	44	28	48	708	130	5	.184
4 yrs.	34	17	.667	2.91	102	62	23	501.2	470	140	161	5	8	0	7	173	34	2	.197
WORLD SERIES																			
1936 NY N	0	0	—	36.00	2	0	0	2	7	4	2	0	0	0	0	0	0	0	—
1937	0	0	—	27.00	2	0	0	1.1	4	1	1	0	0	0	0	0	0	0	—
1942 STL N	0	0	—	0.00	2	0	0	.2	1	0	0	0	0	0	0	0	0	0	—
3 yrs.	0	0	—	27.00	6	0	0	4	12	5	3	0	0	0	0	0	0	0	—

Santiago Guzman

GUZMAN, SANTIAGO DONOVAN   BR TR 6'2"   180 lbs.
B. July 25, 1949, San Piedro De Macoris, Dominican Republic

	W	L	PCT	ERA	G	GS	CG	IP	H	BB	SO	ShO	W	L	SV	AB	H	HR	BA
1969 STL N	0	1	.000	5.14	1	1	0	7	9	3	7	0	0	0	0	3	1	0	.333
1970	1	1	.500	7.07	8	3	1	14	14	13	9	0	0	1	0	5	1	0	.200
1971	0	0	—	0.00	2	1	0	10	6	2	13	0	0	0	0	1	0	0	.000
1972	0	0	—	9.00	1	0	0	1	1	0	0	0	0	0	0	0	0	0	—
4 yrs.	1	2	.333	4.50	12	5	1	32	30	18	29	0	0	1	0	9	2	0	.222
4 yrs.	1	2	.333	4.50	12	5	1	32	30	18	29	0	0	1	0	9	2	0	.222

Bob Habenicht

HABENICHT, ROBERT JULIUS (Hobby)   BR TR 6'2"   185 lbs.
B. Feb. 13, 1926, St. Louis, Mo.   D. Dec. 24, 1980, Richmond, Va.

	W	L	PCT	ERA	G	GS	CG	IP	H	BB	SO	ShO	W	L	SV	AB	H	HR	BA
1951 STL N	0	0	—	7.20	3	0	0	5	5	9	1	0	0	0	0	1	0	0	.000
1953 STL A	0	0	—	5.40	1	0	0	1.2	1	1	1	0	0	0	0	0	0	0	—
2 yrs.	0	0	—	6.75	4	0	0	6.2	6	10	2	0	0	0	0	1	0	0	.000
1 yr.	0	0	—	7.20	3	0	0	5	5	9	1	0	0	0	0	1	0	0	.000

Jim Hackett

HACKETT, JAMES JOSEPH (Sunny Jim)   BR TR 6'2"   185 lbs.
B. Oct. 1, 1877, Jacksonville, Ill.   D. Mar. 28, 1961, Douglas, Mich.

	W	L	PCT	ERA	G	GS	CG	IP	H	BB	SO	ShO	W	L	SV	AB	H	HR	BA
1902 STL N	0	3	.000	6.23	4	3	3	30.1	46	16	7	0	0	0	0	21	6	0	.286
1903	1	4	.200	3.72	7	6	5	48.1	47	18	21	0	0	0	1	351	80	0	.228
2 yrs.	1	7	.125	4.69	11	9	8	78.2	93	34	28	0	0	0	1	*			
2 yrs.	1	7	.125	4.69	11	9	8	78.2	93	34	28	0	0	0	1	372	86	0	.231

Harvey Haddix

HADDIX, HARVEY (The Kitten)   BL TL 5'9½"   170 lbs.
B. Sept. 18, 1925, Medway, Ohio

	W	L	PCT	ERA	G	GS	CG	IP	H	BB	SO	ShO	W	L	SV	AB	H	HR	BA
1952 STL N	2	2	.500	2.79	7	6	3	42	31	10	31	0	0	0	0	14	3	0	.214
1953	20	9	.690	3.06	36	33	19	253	220	69	163	6	0	0	1	97	28	1	.289
1954	18	13	.581	3.57	43	35	13	259.2	247	77	184	3	1	1	4	93	18	0	.194
1955	12	16	.429	4.46	37	30	9	208	216	62	150	2	1	1	1	73	12	1	.164
1956 2 teams			STL	N	(4G 1–0)		PHI	N	(31G 12–8)										
" total	13	8	.619	3.67	35	30	12	230.1	224	65	170	3	0	0	2	102	24	0	.235
1957 PHI N	10	13	.435	4.06	27	25	8	170.2	176	39	136	1	1	0	0	68	21	0	.309
1958 CIN N	8	7	.533	3.52	29	26	8	184	191	43	110	1	0	0	0	61	11	1	.180
1959 PIT N	12	12	.500	3.13	31	29	14	224.1	189	49	149	2	0	0	1	83	12	0	.145
1960	11	10	.524	3.97	29	28	4	172.1	189	38	101	0	0	0	0	67	17	0	.254
1961	10	6	.625	4.10	29	22	5	156	159	41	99	2	3	0	0	56	8	0	.143
1962	9	6	.600	4.20	28	20	4	141.1	146	42	101	0	2	1	0	52	13	1	.250
1963	3	4	.429	3.34	49	1	0	70	67	20	70	0	3	4	1	11	2	0	.182
1964 BAL A	5	5	.500	2.31	49	0	0	89.2	68	23	90	0	5	5	10	19	0	0	.000
1965	3	2	.600	3.48	24	0	0	33.2	31	23	21	0	3	2	1	2	0	0	.000
14 yrs.	136	113	.546	3.63	453	285	99	2235	2154	601	1575	20	19	14	21	*			
5 yrs.	53	40	.570	3.65	127	108	45	786.1	742	228	544	12	2	2	6	286	63	2	.220
WORLD SERIES																			
1960 PIT N	2	0	1.000	2.45	2	1	0	7.1	6	2	6	0	1	0	0	3	1	0	.333

Casey Hageman

HAGEMAN, KURT MORITZ   BR TR 5'10½" 186 lbs.
B. May 12, 1887, Mt. Oliver, Pa.   D. Apr. 1, 1964, New Bedford, Pa.

	W	L	PCT	ERA	G	GS	CG	IP	H	BB	SO	ShO	W	L	SV	AB	H	HR	BA
1911 BOS A	0	2	.000	2.12	2	2	2	17	16	5	8	0	0	0	0	4	0	0	.000
1912	0	0	—	27.00	2	1	0	1.1	5	3	1	0	0	0	0	0	0	0	—
1914 2 teams			STL	N	(12G 1–4)		CHI	N	(16G 2–1)										
" total	3	5	.375	2.91	28	8	1	102	87	32	38	0	2	1	1	31	9	0	.290
3 yrs.	3	7	.300	3.07	32	11	3	120.1	108	40	47	0	2	1	1	35	9	0	.257
1 yr.	1	4	.200	2.44	12	7	1	55.1	43	20	21	0	0	0	0	16	2	0	.125

Fred Hahn

HAHN, FREDERICK ALOYS   BR TL 6'3"   174 lbs.
B. Feb. 16, 1929, Nyack, N. Y.

	W	L	PCT	ERA	G	GS	CG	IP	H	BB	SO	ShO	W	L	SV	AB	H	HR	BA
1952 STL N	0	0	—	0.00	1	0	0	2	2	1	0	0	0	0	0	0	0	0	—

	W	L	PCT	ERA	G	GS	CG	IP	H	BB	SO	ShO	Relief Pitching W	L	SV	BATTING AB	H	HR	BA

Hal Haid

HAID, HAROLD AUGUSTINE   BR TR 5'10½" 150 lbs.
B. Dec. 21, 1897, Barberton, Ohio   D. Aug. 13, 1952, Beverly Hills, Calif.

	W	L	PCT	ERA	G	GS	CG	IP	H	BB	SO	ShO	W	L	SV	AB	H	HR	BA
1919 STL A	0	0	–	18.00	1	0	0	2	5	3	1	0	0	0	0	0	0	0	–
1928 STL N	2	2	.500	2.30	27	0	0	47	39	11	21	0	2	2	5	8	3	0	.375
1929	9	9	.500	4.07	38	12	8	154.2	171	66	41	0	4	3	4	49	4	0	.082
1930	3	2	.600	4.09	20	0	0	33	38	14	13	0	3	2	2	3	0	0	.000
1931 BOS N	0	2	.000	4.50	27	0	0	56	59	16	20	0	0	2	1	8	1	0	.125
1933 CHI A	0	0	–	7.98	6	0	0	14.2	18	13	7	0	0	0	0	4	1	0	.250
6 yrs.	14	15	.483	4.16	119	12	8	307.1	330	123	103	0	9	9	12	72	9	0	.125
3 yrs.	14	13	.519	3.72	85	12	8	234.2	248	91	75	0	9	7	11	60	7	0	.117

Jesse Haines

HAINES, JESSE JOSEPH (Pop)   BR TR 6' 190 lbs.
B. July 22, 1893, Clayton, Ohio   D. Aug. 5, 1978, Dayton, Ohio
Hall of Fame 1970.

	W	L	PCT	ERA	G	GS	CG	IP	H	BB	SO	ShO	W	L	SV	AB	H	HR	BA
1918 CIN N	0	0	–	1.80	1	0	0	5	5	1	2	0	0	0	0	1	1	0	1.000
1920 STL N	13	20	.394	2.98	47	37	19	301.2	303	80	120	4	2	2	2	108	19	1	.176
1921	18	12	.600	3.50	37	29	14	244.1	261	56	84	3	3	0	0	94	17	0	.181
1922	11	9	.550	3.84	29	26	11	183	207	45	62	2	0	1	0	72	12	0	.167
1923	20	13	.606	3.11	37	36	23	266	283	75	73	1	1	0	0	99	20	0	.202
1924	8	19	.296	4.41	35	31	16	222.2	275	66	69	1	0	1	0	74	14	0	.189
1925	13	14	.481	4.57	29	25	15	207	234	52	63	0	1	1	0	74	13	0	.176
1926	13	4	.765	3.25	33	21	14	183	186	48	46	3	0	0	1	61	13	0	.213
1927	24	10	.706	2.72	38	36	25	300.2	273	77	89	6	1	0	1	114	23	0	.202
1928	20	8	.714	3.18	33	28	20	240.1	238	72	77	1	1	1	0	87	16	0	.184
1929	13	10	.565	5.71	28	25	12	179.2	230	73	59	0	0	0	0	69	11	1	.159
1930	13	8	.619	4.30	29	24	14	182	215	54	68	0	0	0	1	65	16	0	.246
1931	12	3	.800	3.02	19	17	8	122.1	134	28	27	2	1	0	0	45	6	0	.133
1932	3	5	.375	4.75	20	10	4	85.1	116	16	27	1	0	1	0	27	5	1	.185
1933	9	6	.600	2.50	32	10	5	115.1	113	37	37	0	5	2	1	30	2	0	.067
1934	4	4	.500	3.50	37	6	0	90	86	19	17	0	4	2	1	19	3	0	.158
1935	6	5	.545	3.59	30	12	3	115.1	110	28	24	0	1	2	2	33	9	0	.273
1936	7	5	.583	3.90	25	9	4	99.1	110	21	19	0	4	1	1	30	5	0	.167
1937	3	3	.500	4.52	16	6	2	65.2	81	23	18	0	1	0	0	22	4	0	.182
19 yrs.	210	158	.571	3.64	555	388	209	3208.2	3460	871	981	24	25	14	10	1124	209	3	.186
18 yrs.	210	158	.571	3.64	554	388	209	3203.2	3455	870	979	24	25	14	10	1123	208	3	.185
	2nd	2nd			1st		2nd	2nd		2nd	3rd	5th	6th						

WORLD SERIES

	W	L	PCT	ERA	G	GS	CG	IP	H	BB	SO	ShO	W	L	SV	AB	H	HR	BA
1926 STL N	2	0	1.000	1.08	3	2	1	16.2	13	9	5	1	0	0	0	5	3	1	.600
1928	0	1	.000	4.50	1	1	0	6	6	3	3	0	0	0	0	2	0	0	.000
1930	1	0	1.000	1.00	1	1	1	9	4	4	2	0	0	0	0	2	1	0	.500
1934	0	0	–	0.00	1	0	0	.2	1	0	2	0	0	0	0	0	0	0	–
4 yrs.	3	1	.750	1.67	6	4	2	32.1	24	16	12	1	0	0	0	9	4	1	.444

Charley Hall

HALL, CHARLES LOUIS (Sea Lion)   BL TR 6'1" 187 lbs.
Born Carlos Clolo.
B. July 27, 1885, Ventura, Calif.   D. Dec. 6, 1943, Ventura, Calif.

	W	L	PCT	ERA	G	GS	CG	IP	H	BB	SO	ShO	W	L	SV	AB	H	HR	BA
1906 CIN N	4	7	.364	3.32	14	9	9	95	86	50	49	1	0	2	1	47	6	0	.128
1907	4	2	.667	2.51	11	8	5	68	51	43	25	0	1	0	0	26	7	0	.269
1909 BOS A	6	4	.600	2.56	11	7	3	59.2	59	17	27	0	3	0	0	19	3	0	.158
1910	10	9	.526	1.91	35	16	13	188.2	142	73	95	0	4	1	5	82	17	0	.207
1911	7	7	.500	3.73	32	10	6	147.1	149	72	83	0	3	3	5	64	9	1	.141
1912	15	8	.652	3.02	34	21	10	191	178	70	83	2	6	0	2	75	20	1	.267
1913	5	5	.500	3.43	35	4	2	105	97	46	48	0	5	1	4	42	9	0	.214
1916 STL N	0	4	.000	5.48	10	5	2	42.2	45	14	15	0	0	0	1	14	2	0	.143
1918 DET A	0	1	.000	6.75	6	1	0	13.1	14	6	2	0	0	0	0	2	0	0	.000
9 yrs.	51	47	.520	3.08	188	81	50	910.2	821	391	427	3	22	7	18	*			
1 yr.	0	4	.000	5.48	10	5	2	42.2	45	14	15	0	0	0	1	14	2	0	.143

WORLD SERIES

	W	L	PCT	ERA	G	GS	CG	IP	H	BB	SO	ShO	W	L	SV	AB	H	HR	BA
1912 BOS A	0	0	–	3.38	2	0	0	10.2	11	9	1	0	0	0	0	4	3	0	.750

Bill Hallahan

HALLAHAN, WILLIAM ANTHONY (Wild Bill)   BR TL 5'10½" 170 lbs.
B. Aug. 4, 1902, Binghamton, N. Y.   D. July 8, 1981, Binghamton, N. Y.

	W	L	PCT	ERA	G	GS	CG	IP	H	BB	SO	ShO	W	L	SV	AB	H	HR	BA
1925 STL N	1	0	1.000	3.52	6	0	0	15.1	14	11	8	0	1	0	0	3	1	0	.333
1926	1	4	.200	3.65	19	3	0	56.2	45	32	28	0	1	2	0	16	4	0	.250
1929	4	4	.500	4.42	20	12	5	93.2	94	60	52	0	0	0	0	26	4	0	.154
1930	15	9	.625	4.66	35	32	13	237.1	233	126	177	2	0	0	2	81	10	0	.123
1931	19	9	.679	3.29	37	30	16	248.2	242	112	159	3	1	1	4	81	8	0	.099
1932	12	7	.632	3.11	25	22	13	176.1	169	69	108	1	1	0	1	56	12	0	.214
1933	16	13	.552	3.50	36	32	16	244.1	245	98	93	2	1	1	0	80	12	0	.150
1934	8	12	.400	4.26	32	26	10	162.2	195	66	70	2	0	0	0	55	10	0	.182
1935	15	8	.652	3.42	40	23	8	181.1	196	57	73	2	3	2	1	56	8	1	.143
1936 2 teams		STL N	(9G 2–2)		CIN N	(23G 5–9)													
" total	7	11	.389	4.76	32	25	6	172	178	77	48	0	2	0	0	56	14	1	.250
1937 CIN N	3	9	.250	6.14	21	9	2	63	90	29	18	0	1	3	0	21	2	0	.095
1938 PHI N	1	8	.111	5.46	21	10	1	89	107	45	22	0	0	3	0	26	5	0	.192
12 yrs.	102	94	.520	4.03	324	224	90	1740.1	1808	782	856	14	9	14	8	557	90	2	.162
10 yrs.	93	68	.578	3.82	259	186	82	1453.1	1461	651	784	12	8	6	8	463	74	1	.160
										5th	9th								

WORLD SERIES

	W	L	PCT	ERA	G	GS	CG	IP	H	BB	SO	ShO	W	L	SV	AB	H	HR	BA
1926 STL N	0	0	–	4.50	1	0	0	2	2	2	1	0	0	0	0	0	0	0	–
1930	1	1	.500	1.64	2	2	1	11	9	8	8	1	0	0	0	2	0	0	.000
1931	2	0	1.000	0.49	3	2	2	18.1	12	8	12	1	0	0	0	6	0	0	.000
1934	0	0	–	2.16	1	1	0	8.1	6	4	6	0	0	0	0	3	0	0	.000
4 yrs.	3	1	.750	1.36	7	5	3	39.2	29	23	27	2	0	0	0	11	0	0	.000
											4th								

	W	L	PCT	ERA	G	GS	CG	IP	H	BB	SO	ShO	Relief Pitching W	L	SV	BATTING AB	H	HR	BA

Bill Hallman

HALLMAN, WILLIAM WHITE   BR TR
B. Mar. 30, 1867, Pittsburgh, Pa.   D. Sept. 11, 1920, Philadelphia, Pa.
Manager 1897.

	W	L	PCT	ERA	G	GS	CG	IP	H	BB	SO	ShO	RP W	L	SV	AB	H	HR	BA
1896 PHI N	0	0	—	18.00	1	0	0	2	4	2	0	0	0	0	0	0	*		

Dave Hamilton

HAMILTON, DAVID EDWARD   BL TL 6'   180 lbs.
B. Dec. 14, 1947, Seattle, Wash.

	W	L	PCT	ERA	G	GS	CG	IP	H	BB	SO	ShO	RP W	L	SV	AB	H	HR	BA
1972 OAK A	6	6	.500	2.93	25	14	1	101.1	94	31	55	0	0	1	0	26	4	0	.154
1973	6	4	.600	4.39	16	11	1	69.2	74	24	34	0	1	0	0	0	0	0	—
1974	7	4	.636	3.15	29	18	1	117	104	48	69	1	1	0	0	0	0	0	—
1975 2 teams			OAK A (11G 1–2)		CHI A (30G 6–5)														
" total	7	7	.500	3.25	41	5	0	105.1	105	47	71	0	7	4	6	0	0	0	—
1976 CHI A	6	6	.500	3.60	45	1	0	90	81	45	62	0	5	6	10	0	0	0	—
1977	4	5	.444	3.63	55	0	0	67	71	33	45	0	4	5	9	0	0	0	—
1978 2 teams			STL N (13G 0–0)		PIT N (16G 0–2)														
" total	0	2	.000	4.46	29	0	0	40.1	39	18	23	0	0	2	1	7	0	0	.000
1979 OAK A	3	4	.429	3.69	40	7	1	83	80	43	52	0	2	0	5	0	0	0	—
1980	0	3	.000	11.40	21	1	0	30	44	28	23	0	0	3	0	0	0	0	—
9 yrs.	39	41	.488	3.85	301	57	4	703.2	692	317	434	1	20	21	31	33	4	0	.121
1 yr.	0	0	—	6.43	13	0	0	14	16	6	8	0	0	0	0	1	0	0	.000
LEAGUE CHAMPIONSHIP SERIES																			
1972 OAK A	0	0	—	0.00	1	0	0	1	1	0	0	0	0	0	0	0	0	—
WORLD SERIES																			
1972 OAK A	0	0	—	27.00	2	0	0	1.1	3	1	1	0	0	0	0	0	0	—

Bob Harmon

HARMON, ROBERT GREENE (Hickory Bob)   BB TR 6'   187 lbs.
B. Oct. 15, 1887, Liberal, Mo.   D. Nov. 27, 1961, Monroe, La.

	W	L	PCT	ERA	G	GS	CG	IP	H	BB	SO	ShO	RP W	L	SV	AB	H	HR	BA
1909 STL N	5	12	.294	3.68	21	17	10	159	155	65	48	0	0	1	0	51	13	0	.255
1910	11	15	.423	4.46	43	33	15	236	227	133	87	0	2	1	2	76	14	0	.184
1911	23	15	.605	3.13	51	41	28	348	290	181	144	2	1	1	4	111	17	0	.153
1912	18	18	.500	3.93	43	34	15	268	284	116	73	3	3	2	0	99	23	0	.232
1913	8	21	.276	3.92	42	27	16	273.1	291	99	66	1	3	6	1	92	24	0	.261
1914 PIT N	12	17	.414	2.53	37	30	19	245	226	55	61	2	1	0	3	86	12	1	.140
1915	15	17	.469	2.50	37	32	25	269.2	242	62	86	5	0	1	1	95	14	0	.147
1916	8	11	.421	2.81	31	17	10	172.2	175	39	62	2	1	3	0	55	6	0	.109
1918	2	7	.222	2.62	16	9	5	82.1	76	12	7	0	0	1	0	27	4	0	.148
9 yrs.	102	133	.434	3.33	321	240	143	2054	1966	762	634	15	11	16	11	692	127	1	.184
5 yrs.	65	81	.445	3.78	200	152	84	1284.1	1247	418	416	6	9	11	7	429	91	0	.212
			9th								7th								

Jack Harper

HARPER, CHARLES WILLIAM   BR TR 6'   178 lbs.
B. Apr. 2, 1878, Franklin, Pa.   D. Sept. 30, 1950, Jamestown, N. Y.

	W	L	PCT	ERA	G	GS	CG	IP	H	BB	SO	ShO	RP W	L	SV	AB	H	HR	BA
1899 CLE N	1	4	.200	3.89	5	5	5	37	44	12	14	0	0	0	0	11	2	0	.182
1900 STL N	1	0	1.000	12.00	1	1	0	3	4	2	0	0	0	0	0	1	0	0	.000
1901	23	13	.639	3.62	39	37	28	308.2	294	99	128	1	1	0	0	116	20	1	.172
1902 STL A	15	11	.577	4.13	29	26	20	222.1	224	81	74	2	1	1	0	83	17	0	.205
1903 CIN N	6	8	.429	4.33	17	15	13	135	143	70	45	0	0	2	0	56	14	0	.250
1904	23	9	.719	2.37	35	35	31	284.2	262	85	125	6	0	0	0	113	18	0	.159
1905	10	13	.435	3.87	26	23	15	179	189	69	70	1	1	0	0	60	10	0	.167
1906 2 teams			CIN N (5G 1–4)		CHI N (1G 0–0)														
" total	1	4	.200	4.06	6	6	3	37.2	38	20	10	0	0	0	0	11	3	0	.273
8 yrs.	79	63	.556	3.58	158	148	115	1207.1	1198	438	466	10	3	3	0	451	84	1	.186
2 yrs.	23	14	.622	3.70	40	38	28	311.2	298	101	128	1	1	0	0	117	20	1	.171

Ray Harrell

HARRELL, RAYMOND JAMES (Cowboy)   BR TR 6'1"   185 lbs.
B. Feb. 16, 1912, Petrolia, Tex.

	W	L	PCT	ERA	G	GS	CG	IP	H	BB	SO	ShO	RP W	L	SV	AB	H	HR	BA
1935 STL N	1	1	.500	6.67	11	1	0	29.2	39	11	13	0	1	0	0	4	0	0	.000
1937	3	7	.300	5.87	35	15	1	96.2	99	59	41	1	1	0	1	22	1	0	.045
1938	2	3	.400	4.86	32	3	1	63	78	29	32	0	1	3	2	10	0	0	.000
1939 2 teams			CHI N (4G 0–2)		PHI N (22G 3–7)														
" total	3	9	.250	5.87	26	12	4	112	127	62	40	0	1	0	0	31	3	0	.097
1940 PIT N	0	0	—	8.10	3	0	0	3.1	5	2	3	0	0	0	0	5	1	0	.200
1945 NY N	0	0	—	4.97	12	0	0	25.1	34	14	7	0	0	0	0	0	0	0	.069
6 yrs.	9	20	.310	5.70	119	31	6	330	382	177	136	1	4	4	3	72	5	0	.069
3 yrs.	6	11	.353	5.66	78	19	2	189.1	216	99	86	1	3	4	3	36	1	0	.028

Bill Hart

HART, WILLIAM FRANKLIN   BR TR 6'
B. July 19, 1865, Louisville, Ky.   D. Sept. 19, 1936, Cincinnati, Ohio

	W	L	PCT	ERA	G	GS	CG	IP	H	BB	SO	ShO	RP W	L	SV	AB	H	HR	BA
1886 PHI AA	9	13	.409	3.19	22	22	22	186	183	66	78	2	0	0	0	73	10	0	.137
1887	1	2	.333	4.50	3	3	3	26	28	17	4	0	0	0	0	13	1	0	.077
1892 BKN N	9	4	.429	3.28	23	16	16	195	188	96	65	2	1	1	1	125	24	2	.192
1895 PIT N	14	17	.452	4.75	36	29	24	261.2	293	135	85	0	1	1	1	106	25	0	.236
1896 STL N	12	29	.293	5.12	42	41	37	336	411	141	65	0	0	1	0	161	30	0	.186
1897	9	27	.250	6.26	39	38	31	294.2	395	148	67	0	0	0	0	156	39	2	.250
1898 PIT N	5	9	.357	4.82	16	15	13	125	141	44	19	1	0	0	0	50	12	0	.240
1901 CLE A	7	11	.389	3.77	20	19	16	157.2	180	57	48	0	0	0	0	64	14	0	.219
8 yrs.	66	120	.465	4.65	206	190	162	1582	1819	704	431	5	2	3	3	*			
2 yrs.	21	56	.273	5.65	81	79	68	630.2	806	289	132	0	0	1	0	317	69	2	.218

Chuck Hartenstein

HARTENSTEIN, CHARLES OSCAR (Twiggy)   BR TR 5'11"   165 lbs.
B. May 26, 1942, Seguin, Tex.

	W	L	PCT	ERA	G	GS	CG	IP	H	BB	SO	ShO	RP W	L	SV	AB	H	HR	BA
1965 CHI N	0	0	—	0.00	0	0	0	0	0	0	0	0	0	0	0	0	0	0	—
1966	0	0	—	1.93	5	0	0	9.1	8	3	4	0	0	0	0	0	0	0	—

	W	L	PCT	ERA	G	GS	CG	IP	H	BB	SO	ShO	Relief Pitching W	L	SV	BATTING AB	H	HR	BA

Chuck Hartenstein continued

	W	L	PCT	ERA	G	GS	CG	IP	H	BB	SO	ShO	W	L	SV	AB	H	HR	BA
1967	9	5	.643	3.08	45	0	0	73	74	17	20	0	9	5	10	16	1	0	.063
1968	2	4	.333	4.54	28	0	0	35.2	41	11	17	0	2	4	1	2	0	0	.000
1969 PIT N	5	4	.556	3.94	56	0	0	96	84	27	44	0	5	4	10	14	1	0	.071
1970 3 teams			PIT N	(17G 1–1)		STL N	(6G 0–0)		BOS A	(17G 0–3)									
" total	1	4	.200	6.75	40	0	0	56	70	25	35	0	1	4	2	5	0	0	.000
1977 TOR A	0	2	.000	6.67	13	0	0	27	40	6	15	0	0	2	0	0	0	0	–
7 yrs.	17	19	.472	4.52	187	0	0	297	317	89	135	0	17	19	23	37	2	0	.054
1 yr.	0	0	–	8.78	6	0	0	13.1	24	5	9	0	0	0	0	0	0	0	.000

Bill Hawke

HAWKE, WILLIAM VICTOR (Dick)
B. Apr. 28, 1870, Wilmington, Del.   D. Dec. 12, 1902, Wilmington, Del.

	W	L	PCT	ERA	G	GS	CG	IP	H	BB	SO	ShO	W	L	SV	AB	H	HR	BA
1892 STL N	4	5	.444	3.70	14	11	10	97.1	108	45	55	1	0	1	0	45	4	0	.089
1893 2 teams			STL N	(1G 0–1)		BAL N	(29G 11–16)												
" total	11	17	.393	4.77	30	30	22	230.1	257	111	70	0	0	0	0	96	17	1	.177
1894 BAL N	16	9	.640	5.84	32	25	17	205	264	78	68	0	2	0	3	92	28	1	.304
3 yrs.	31	31	.500	4.98	76	66	49	532.2	629	234	193	2	2	1	3	233	49	2	.210
2 yrs.	4	6	.400	3.77	15	12	10	102.2	117	48	56	1	0	1	0	48	5	0	.104

Pink Hawley

HAWLEY, EMERSON P.   BL TR 5'10" 185 lbs.
B. Dec. 5, 1872, Beaver Dam, Wis.   D. Sept. 19, 1938, Beaver Dam, Wis.

	W	L	PCT	ERA	G	GS	CG	IP	H	BB	SO	ShO	W	L	SV	AB	H	HR	BA
1892 STL N	6	14	.300	3.19	20	20	18	166.1	160	63	63	0	0	0	0	71	12	1	.169
1893	5	17	.227	4.60	31	24	21	227	249	103	73	0	0	0	1	91	26	0	.286
1894	19	26	.422	4.90	53	41	36	392.2	481	149	120	0	2	5	0	163	43	2	.264
1895 PIT N	32	21	.604	3.18	56	50	44	444.1	449	122	142	4	3	2	1	185	57	5	.308
1896	22	21	.512	3.57	49	43	37	378	382	157	137	2	3	1	0	163	39	1	.239
1897	18	18	.500	4.80	40	39	33	311.1	362	94	88	0	0	0	0	130	30	1	.231
1898 CIN N	27	11	.711	3.37	43	37	32	331	357	91	69	3	4	0	0	130	24	1	.185
1899	14	17	.452	4.24	34	29	25	250.1	289	65	46	0	1	3	1	101	22	0	.218
1900 NY N	18	18	.500	3.53	41	38	34	329.1	377	89	80	1	0	0	0	123	25	1	.203
1901 MIL A	7	14	.333	4.59	26	23	17	182.1	228	41	50	0	0	0	0	73	19	0	.260
10 yrs.	168	177	.487	3.96	393	344	297	3012.2	3334	974	868	10	13	12	3	1230	297	11	.241
3 yrs.	30	57	.345	4.45	104	85	75	786	890	315	256	0	2	5	1	325	81	3	.249

Bunny Hearn

HEARN, BUNN   BL TL 5'11" 190 lbs.
B. May 21, 1891, Chapel Hill, N. C.   D. Oct. 10, 1959, Wilson, N. C.

	W	L	PCT	ERA	G	GS	CG	IP	H	BB	SO	ShO	W	L	SV	AB	H	HR	BA
1910 STL N	1	3	.250	5.08	5	5	4	39	49	16	14	0	0	0	0	15	2	1	.133
1911	0	0	–	13.50	2	0	0	2.2	7	0	1	0	0	0	0	1	0	0	.000
1913 NY N	1	1	.500	2.77	2	2	1	13	13	7	8	0	0	0	0	5	2	0	.400
1915 PIT F	6	11	.353	3.38	29	17	8	175.2	187	37	49	1	1	1	0	53	10	0	.189
1918 BOS N	5	6	.455	2.49	17	12	9	126.1	119	29	30	1	0	0	0	45	8	0	.178
1920	0	3	.000	5.65	11	4	2	43	54	11	9	0	0	0	0	14	2	0	.143
6 yrs.	13	24	.351	3.56	66	40	24	399.2	429	100	111	2	1	1	0	133	24	1	.180
2 yrs.	1	3	.250	5.62	7	5	4	41.2	56	16	15	0	0	0	0	16	2	1	.125

Jim Hearn

HEARN, JAMES TOLBERT   BR TR 6'3" 205 lbs.
B. Apr. 11, 1921, Atlanta, Ga.

	W	L	PCT	ERA	G	GS	CG	IP	H	BB	SO	ShO	W	L	SV	AB	H	HR	BA
1947 STL N	12	7	.632	3.22	37	21	8	162	151	63	57	1	3	2	1	55	8	0	.145
1948	8	6	.571	4.22	34	13	3	89.2	92	35	27	0	5	2	1	25	5	0	.200
1949	1	3	.250	5.14	17	4	0	42	48	23	18	0	1	1	0	10	1	0	.100
1950 2 teams			STL N	(6G 0–1)		NY N	(16G 11–3)												
" total	11	4	.733	2.49	22	16	11	134	84	44	58	5	0	0	0	45	7	0	.156
1951 NY N	17	9	.654	3.62	34	34	11	211.1	204	82	66	0	0	0	0	74	12	1	.162
1952	14	7	.667	3.78	37	34	11	223.2	208	97	89	1	0	0	1	77	14	3	.182
1953	9	12	.429	4.53	36	32	6	196.2	206	84	77	0	0	0	0	66	9	0	.136
1954	8	8	.500	4.15	29	18	3	130	137	66	45	2	1	1	1	45	5	1	.111
1955	14	16	.467	3.73	39	33	11	226.2	225	66	86	1	2	1	0	77	12	4	.156
1956	5	11	.313	3.97	30	19	2	129.1	124	44	66	0	0	0	0	41	4	0	.098
1957 PHI N	5	1	.833	3.65	36	4	1	74	79	18	46	0	4	0	3	17	0	0	.000
1958	5	3	.625	4.17	39	1	0	73.1	88	27	33	0	4	3	0	14	0	0	.000
1959	0	2	.000	5.73	6	0	0	11	15	6	1	0	0	2	0	2	0	0	.000
13 yrs.	109	89	.551	3.81	396	229	63	1703.2	1661	655	669	10	20	15	8	548	77	9	.141
4 yrs.	21	17	.553	3.98	94	38	7	302.2	303	127	106	1	9	6	2	91	15	0	.165

WORLD SERIES

	W	L	PCT	ERA	G	GS	CG	IP	H	BB	SO	ShO	W	L	SV	AB	H	HR	BA
1951 NY N	1	0	1.000	1.04	1	1	0	8.2	5	8	1	1	0	0	0	3	0	0	.000

John Heidrick

HEIDRICK, JOHN EMMETT (Snags)
B. July 6, 1876, Queenstown, Pa.   D. Jan. 20, 1916, Clarion, Pa.

	W	L	PCT	ERA	G	GS	CG	IP	H	BB	SO	ShO	W	L	SV	AB	H	HR	BA
1902 STL A	0	0	–	0.00	1	0	0	1	0	0	0	0	0	0	0	*			

Clarence Heise

HEISE, CLARENCE EDWARD (Lefty)   BL TL 5'10" 172 lbs.
B. Aug. 7, 1907, Topeka, Kans.

	W	L	PCT	ERA	G	GS	CG	IP	H	BB	SO	ShO	W	L	SV	AB	H	HR	BA
1934 STL N	0	0	–	4.50	1	0	0	2	3	0	1	0	0	0	0	0	0	0	–

Roy Henshaw

HENSHAW, ROY K   BR TL 5'8" 155 lbs.
B. July 29, 1911, Chicago, Ill.

	W	L	PCT	ERA	G	GS	CG	IP	H	BB	SO	ShO	W	L	SV	AB	H	HR	BA
1933 CHI N	2	1	.667	4.19	21	0	0	38.2	32	20	16	0	2	1	0	10	2	0	.200
1935	13	5	.722	3.28	31	18	7	142.2	135	68	53	3	4	0	1	51	13	0	.255
1936	6	5	.545	3.97	39	14	6	129.1	152	56	69	0	2	1	3	44	6	0	.136
1937 BKN N	5	12	.294	5.07	42	16	5	156.1	176	69	98	0	1	3	2	48	8	0	.167
1938 STL N	5	11	.313	4.02	27	15	4	130	132	48	34	0	1	2	0	41	9	0	.220
1942 DET A	2	4	.333	4.09	23	2	0	61.2	63	27	24	0	2	3	1	12	1	0	.083

	W	L	PCT	ERA	G	GS	CG	IP	H	BB	SO	ShO	Relief Pitching W	L	SV	BATTING AB	H	HR	BA

Roy Henshaw continued

	W	L	PCT	ERA	G	GS	CG	IP	H	BB	SO	ShO	W	L	SV	AB	H	HR	BA
1943	0	2	.000	3.79	26	3	0	71.1	75	33	33	0	0	1	2	18	2	0	.111
1944	0	0	–	8.76	7	1	0	12.1	17	6	10	0	0	0	0	5	0	0	.000
8 yrs.	33	40	.452	4.16	216	69	22	742.1	782	327	337	5	12	12	7	229	41	0	.179
1 yr.	5	11	.313	4.02	27	15	4	130	132	48	34	0	2	1	0	41	9	0	.220
WORLD SERIES																			
1935 CHI N	0	0	–	7.36	1	0	0	3.2	2	5	2	0	0	0	0	1	0	0	.000

Ed Heusser

HEUSSER, EDWARD BURLETON (The Wild Elk of the Wasatch)
B. May 7, 1909, Murray, Utah
D. Mar. 1, 1956, Aurora, Colo.
BB TR 6'½" 187 lbs.
BR 1935-38

	W	L	PCT	ERA	G	GS	CG	IP	H	BB	SO	ShO	W	L	SV	AB	H	HR	BA
1935 STL N	5	5	.500	2.92	33	11	2	123.1	125	27	39	0	2	1	2	34	4	0	.118
1936	7	3	.700	5.43	42	3	0	104.1	130	38	26	0	6	2	3	26	7	1	.269
1938 PHI N	0	0	–	27.00	1	0	0	1	2	1	0	0	0	0	0	0	0	0	–
1940 PHI A	6	13	.316	4.99	41	6	2	110	144	42	39	0	4	9	5	30	5	1	.167
1943 CIN N	4	3	.571	3.46	26	10	2	91	97	23	28	1	2	0	0	27	5	0	.185
1944	13	11	.542	2.38	30	23	17	192.2	165	42	42	4	2	1	2	69	15	0	.217
1945	11	16	.407	3.71	31	30	18	223	248	60	56	4	0	0	1	77	19	1	.247
1946	7	14	.333	3.22	29	21	9	167.2	167	39	47	1	0	1	2	53	11	0	.208
1948 PHI N	3	2	.600	4.99	33	0	0	74	89	28	22	0	3	2	3	19	3	0	.158
9 yrs.	56	67	.455	3.69	266	104	50	1087	1167	300	299	10	19	16	18	335	69	3	.206
2 yrs.	12	8	.600	4.07	75	14	2	227.2	255	65	65	0	8	3	5	60	11	1	.183

Jim Hickman

HICKMAN, JAMES LUCIUS
B. May 10, 1937, Henning, Tenn.
BR TR 6'3" 192 lbs.

	W	L	PCT	ERA	G	GS	CG	IP	H	BB	SO	ShO	W	L	SV	AB	H	HR	BA
1967 LA N	0	0	–	4.50	1	0	0	2	2	0	0	0	0	0	0	*			

Irv Higginbotham

HIGGINBOTHAM, IRVING CLINTON
B. Apr. 26, 1882, Homer, Neb.   D. June 12, 1959, Seattle, Wash.
BR TR

	W	L	PCT	ERA	G	GS	CG	IP	H	BB	SO	ShO	W	L	SV	AB	H	HR	BA
1906 STL N	1	4	.200	3.23	7	6	4	47.1	50	11	14	0	0	0	0	18	4	0	.222
1908	4	8	.333	3.20	19	11	7	107	113	33	38	1	0	1	0	38	5	0	.132
1909 2 teams		STL N	(3G 1–0)		CHI N	(19G 5–2)													
" total	6	2	.750	2.12	22	7	5	89.1	69	22	34	0	3	1	0	29	6	0	.207
3 yrs.	11	14	.440	2.81	48	24	16	243.2	232	66	86	1	3	2	0	85	15	0	.176
3 yrs.	6	12	.333	3.10	29	18	12	165.2	168	46	54	1	0	1	0	59	9	0	.153

Dennis Higgins

HIGGINS, DENNIS DEAN
B. Aug. 4, 1939, Jefferson City, Mo.
BR TR 6'3" 180 lbs.

	W	L	PCT	ERA	G	GS	CG	IP	H	BB	SO	ShO	W	L	SV	AB	H	HR	BA
1966 CHI A	1	0	1.000	2.52	42	1	0	93	66	33	86	0	0	0	5	17	3	0	.176
1967	1	2	.333	5.84	9	0	0	12.1	13	10	8	0	1	2	0	1	0	0	.000
1968 WAS A	4	4	.500	3.25	59	0	0	99.2	81	46	66	0	4	4	13	15	2	0	.133
1969	10	9	.526	3.48	55	0	0	85.1	79	56	71	0	10	9	16	11	1	0	.091
1970 CLE A	4	6	.400	4.00	58	0	0	90	82	54	82	0	4	6	11	12	3	0	.250
1971 STL N	1	0	1.000	3.86	3	0	0	7	6	2	6	0	1	0	0	1	0	0	.000
1972	1	2	.333	3.97	15	1	0	22.2	19	22	20	0	1	1	1	1	0	0	.000
7 yrs.	22	23	.489	3.42	241	2	0	410	346	223	339	0	21	22	46	58	9	0	.155
2 yrs.	2	2	.500	3.94	18	1	0	29.2	25	24	26	0	2	1	1	2	0	0	.000

Festus Higgins

HIGGINS, FESTUS EDWARD
B. 1893, Cincinnati, Ohio   D. Oct. 4, 1924, Minooka, Pa.
BR TR

	W	L	PCT	ERA	G	GS	CG	IP	H	BB	SO	ShO	W	L	SV	AB	H	HR	BA
1909 STL N	3	3	.500	4.50	16	5	5	66	68	17	15	0	1	0	0	21	4	0	.190
1910	0	1	.000	4.35	2	0	0	10.1	15	7	1	0	0	1	0	5	2	0	.400
2 yrs.	3	4	.429	4.48	18	5	5	76.1	83	24	16	0	1	1	0	26	6	0	.231
2 yrs.	3	4	.429	4.48	18	5	5	76.1	83	24	16	0	1	1	0	26	6	0	.231

Tom Hilgendorf

HILGENDORF, THOMAS EUGENE
B. Mar. 10, 1942, Clinton, Iowa
BB TL 6'1½" 187 lbs.

	W	L	PCT	ERA	G	GS	CG	IP	H	BB	SO	ShO	W	L	SV	AB	H	HR	BA
1969 STL N	0	0	–	1.50	6	0	0	6	3	2	2	0	0	0	2	1	1	0	1.000
1970	0	4	.000	3.86	23	0	0	21	22	13	13	0	0	4	3	1	0	0	.000
1972 CLE A	3	1	.750	2.68	19	5	1	47	51	21	25	0	1	0	0	13	1	0	.077
1973	5	3	.625	3.14	48	1	1	94.2	87	36	58	0	5	2	6	0	0	0	–
1974	4	3	.571	4.88	35	0	0	48	58	17	23	0	4	3	0	12	3	0	.250
1975 PHI N	7	3	.700	2.13	53	0	0	97	82	38	52	0	7	3	3	27	5	0	.185
6 yrs.	19	14	.576	3.04	184	6	2	313.2	303	127	173	0	17	12	14	27	5	0	.185
2 yrs.	0	4	.000	3.33	29	0	0	27	25	15	15	0	0	4	5	2	1	0	.500

Carmen Hill

HILL, CARMEN PROCTOR (Specs, Bunker)
B. Oct. 1, 1895, Royalton, Minn.
BR TR 6'1" 180 lbs.

	W	L	PCT	ERA	G	GS	CG	IP	H	BB	SO	ShO	W	L	SV	AB	H	HR	BA
1915 PIT N	2	1	.667	1.15	8	3	2	47	42	13	24	1	0	0	0	13	2	0	.154
1916	0	0	–	8.53	2	0	0	6.1	11	5	5	0	0	0	0	0	0	0	–
1918	2	3	.400	1.24	6	4	3	43.2	24	17	15	0	1	0	0	12	2	0	.167
1919	0	0	–	9.00	4	0	0	5	12	1	1	0	0	0	0	0	0	0	–
1922 NY N	2	1	.667	4.76	8	4	0	28.1	33	5	6	0	1	0	0	11	2	0	.182
1926 PIT N	3	3	.500	3.40	6	6	4	39.2	42	9	8	1	0	0	0	17	3	0	.176
1927	22	11	.667	3.24	43	31	22	277.2	260	80	95	2	4	0	3	104	22	0	.212
1928	16	10	.615	3.53	36	31	16	237	229	81	73	1	1	1	2	86	20	0	.233
1929 2 teams		PIT N	(27G 2–3)		STL N	(3G 0–0)													
" total	2	3	.400	4.41	30	2	0	87.2	104	43	29	0	2	1	3	31	1	0	.032
1930 STL N	0	1	.000	7.36	4	2	0	14.2	12	13	8	0	0	0	0	1	0	0	.333
10 yrs.	49	33	.598	3.44	147	85	47	787	769	267	264	5	9	2	8	277	53	0	.191
2 yrs.	0	1	.000	7.71	7	3	0	23.1	22	21	9	0	0	0	0	6	1	0	.167

	W	L	PCT	ERA	G	GS	CG	IP	H	BB	SO	ShO	Relief Pitching W	L	SV	BATTING AB	H	HR	BA

Carmen Hill continued

WORLD SERIES
	W	L	PCT	ERA	G	GS	CG	IP	H	BB	SO	ShO	RW	RL	SV	AB	H	HR	BA
1927 PIT N	0	0	–	4.50	1	1	0	6	9	1	6	0	0	0	0	1	0	0	.000

Bruce Hitt

HITT, BRUCE SMITH   BR TR 6'1"   190 lbs.
B. Mar. 14, 1898, Comanche, Tex.   D. Nov. 10, 1973, Portland, Ore.

	W	L	PCT	ERA	G	GS	CG	IP	H	BB	SO	ShO	RW	RL	SV	AB	H	HR	BA
1917 STL N	0	0	–	9.00	2	0	0	4	7	1	1	0	0	0	0	1	0	0	.000

Glen Hobbie

HOBBIE, GLEN FREDERICK   BR TR 6'2"   195 lbs.
B. Apr. 24, 1936, Witt, Ill.

	W	L	PCT	ERA	G	GS	CG	IP	H	BB	SO	ShO	RW	RL	SV	AB	H	HR	BA
1957 CHI N	0	0		10.38	2	0	0	4.1	6	5	3	0	0	0	0	2	0	0	.000
1958	10	6	.625	3.74	55	16	2	168.1	163	93	91	1	6	1	2	48	7	0	.146
1959	16	13	.552	3.69	46	33	10	234	204	106	138	3	0	1	0	79	9	0	.114
1960	16	20	.444	3.97	46	36	16	258.2	253	101	134	4	2	3	1	86	13	1	.151
1961	7	13	.350	4.26	36	29	7	198.2	207	54	103	2	1	0	2	66	11	2	.167
1962	5	14	.263	5.22	42	23	5	162	198	62	87	0	0	2	0	49	6	0	.122
1963	7	10	.412	3.92	36	24	4	165.1	172	49	94	1	1	0	0	50	4	0	.080
1964 2 teams	CHI	N	(8G 0–3)		STL	N	(13G 1–2)												
" total	1	5	.167	5.65	21	9	1	71.2	80	25	32	0	0	0	1	18	2	1	.111
8 yrs.	62	81	.434	4.20	284	170	45	1263	1283	495	682	11	10	7	6	398	52	4	.131
1 yr.	1	2	.333	4.26	13	5	1	44.1	41	15	18	0	0	0	1	13	2	1	.154

Art Hoelskoetter

HOELSKOETTER, ARTHUR H.   TR
Played as Art Hostetter 1907-08.
B. Sept. 30, 1882, St. Louis, Mo.   D. Aug. 3, 1954, St. Louis, Mo.

	W	L	PCT	ERA	G	GS	CG	IP	H	BB	SO	ShO	RW	RL	SV	AB	H	HR	BA
1905 STL N	0	1	.000	1.50	1	1	1	6	6	5	4	0	0	0	0	83	20	0	.241
1906	2	4	.333	4.63	12	3	2	58.1	53	34	20	0	1	0	0	317	71	0	.224
1907	0	0		5.73	2	0	0	11	9	10	8	0	0	0	0	396	98	2	.247
3 yrs.	2	5	.286	4.54	15	4	3	75.1	68	49	32	0	1	0	0	*			
3 yrs.	2	5	.286	4.54	15	4	3	75.1	68	49	32	0	1	0	0	951	225	2	.237

Joe Hoerner

HOERNER, JOSEPH WALTER   BR TL 6'1"   200 lbs.
B. Nov. 12, 1936, Dubuque, Iowa

	W	L	PCT	ERA	G	GS	CG	IP	H	BB	SO	ShO	RW	RL	SV	AB	H	HR	BA
1963 HOU N	0	0	–	0.00	1	0	0	3	2	0	2	0	0	0	0	1	0	0	.000
1964	0	0	–	4.91	7	0	0	11	13	6	4	0	0	0	0	1	0	0	.000
1966 STL N	5	1	.833	1.54	57	0	0	76	57	21	63	0	5	1	13	8	1	1	.125
1967	4	4	.500	2.59	57	0	0	66	52	20	50	0	4	4	15	11	2	0	.182
1968	8	2	.800	1.47	47	0	0	49	34	12	42	0	8	2	17	6	0	0	.000
1969	2	3	.400	2.89	45	0	0	53	44	9	35	0	2	3	15	5	0	0	.000
1970 PHI N	9	5	.643	2.64	44	0	0	58	53	20	39	0	9	5	9	10	2	0	.200
1971	4	5	.444	1.97	49	0	0	73	57	21	57	0	4	5	9	10	1	0	.100
1972 2 teams	PHI	N	(15G 0–2)		ATL	N	(25G 1–3)												
" total	1	5	.167	4.40	40	0	0	45	55	13	31	0	1	5	5	5	0	0	.000
1973 2 teams	ATL	N	(20G 2–2)		KC	A	(22G 2–0)												
" total	4	2	.667	5.63	42	0	0	32	45	17	25	0	4	2	6	0	0	0	–
1974 KC A	2	3	.400	3.86	30	0	0	35	32	12	24	0	2	3	2	0	0	0	–
1975 PHI N	0	0	–	2.57	25	0	0	21	25	8	20	0	0	0	2	0	0	0	.000
1976 TEX A	0	4	.000	5.14	41	0	0	35	41	19	15	0	0	4	8	0	0	0	–
1977 CIN N	0	0	–	12.00	8	0	0	6	9	5	5	0	0	0	0	0	0	0	–
14 yrs.	39	34	.534	2.99	493	0	0	563	519	181	412	0	39	34	99	59	6	1	.102
4 yrs.	19	10	.655	2.10	206	0	0	244	187	62	190	0	19	10	60	30	3	1	.100
													8th		3rd				

WORLD SERIES
	W	L	PCT	ERA	G	GS	CG	IP	H	BB	SO	ShO	RW	RL	SV	AB	H	HR	BA
1967 STL N	0	0	–	40.50	2	0	0	.2	4	1	0	0	0	0	0	0	0	0	–
1968	0	1	.000	3.86	3	0	0	4.2	5	5	3	0	0	1	1	2	1	0	.500
2 yrs.	0	1	.000	8.44	5	0	0	5.1	9	6	3	0	0	1	1	2	1	0	.500

Mul Holland

HOLLAND, HOWARD ARTHUR   BR TR 6'4"   185 lbs.
B. Jan. 6, 1903, Franklin, Va.   D. Feb. 16, 1969, Winchester, Va.

	W	L	PCT	ERA	G	GS	CG	IP	H	BB	SO	ShO	RW	RL	SV	AB	H	HR	BA
1926 CIN N	0	0	–	1.35	3	0	0	6.2	3	5	0	0	0	0	0	2	1	0	.500
1927 NY N	1	0	1.000	0.00	2	0	0	2	0	3	0	0	1	0	0	0	0	0	–
1929 STL N	0	1	.000	9.42	8	0	0	14.1	13	7	5	0	0	1	0	4	1	0	.250
3 yrs.	1	1	.500	6.26	13	0	0	23	16	15	5	0	1	1	0	6	2	0	.333
1 yr.	0	1	.000	9.42	8	0	0	14.1	13	7	5	0	0	1	0	4	1	0	.250

Ducky Holmes

HOLMES, JAMES WILLIAM   BL TR 5'6"   170 lbs.
B. Jan. 28, 1869, Des Moines, Iowa   D. Aug. 6, 1932, Truro, Iowa

	W	L	PCT	ERA	G	GS	CG	IP	H	BB	SO	ShO	RW	RL	SV	AB	H	HR	BA
1895 LOU N	1	0	1.000	5.79	2	1	1	14	16	4	0	0	0	0	0	161	60	3	.373
1896	0	1	.000	7.50	2	1	0	12	26	8	3	0	0	0	0	141	38	0	.270
2 yrs.	1	1	.500	6.58	4	2	1	26	42	12	3	0	0	0	0	*			

Don Hood

HOOD, DONALD HARRIS   BL TL 6'2"   180 lbs.
B. Oct. 16, 1949, Florence, S. C.

	W	L	PCT	ERA	G	GS	CG	IP	H	BB	SO	ShO	RW	RL	SV	AB	H	HR	BA
1973 BAL A	3	2	.600	3.94	8	4	1	32	31	6	18	1	2	0	1	0	0	0	–
1974	1	1	.500	3.47	20	2	0	57	47	20	26	0	1	0	1	0	0	0	–
1975 CLE A	6	10	.375	4.39	29	19	2	135.1	136	57	51	0	1	1	0	0	0	0	–
1976	3	5	.375	4.85	33	6	0	78	89	41	32	0	2	1	1	0	0	0	–
1977	2	1	.667	3.00	41	5	1	105	87	49	62	0	1	0	0	0	0	0	–
1978	5	6	.455	4.47	36	19	1	155	166	77	73	0	1	0	0	0	0	0	–
1979 2 teams	CLE	A	(13G 1–0)		NY	A	(27G 3–1)												
" total	4	1	.800	3.24	40	6	0	89	75	44	29	0	2	1	2	0	0	0	–

	W	L	PCT	ERA	G	GS	CG	IP	H	BB	SO	ShO	Relief Pitching W	L	SV	BATTING AB	H	HR	BA

Don Hood continued

	W	L	PCT	ERA	G	GS	CG	IP	H	BB	SO	ShO	W	L	SV	AB	H	HR	BA
1980 STL N	4	6	.400	3.40	33	8	1	82	90	34	35	0	1	4	0	20	4	0	.200
1982 KC A	4	0	1.000	3.51	30	3	0	66.2	71	22	31	0	1	0	1	0	0	0	—
9 yrs.	32	32	.500	3.88	270	72	6	800	792	350	357	1	11	8	6	20	4	0	.200
1 yr.	4	6	.400	3.40	33	8	1	82	90	34	35	0	1	4	0	20	4	0	.200

Bill Hopper

HOPPER, WILLIAM BOOTH (Bird Dog)   BR TR 6'   175 lbs.
B. Aug. 26, 1890, Jackson, Tenn.   D. Jan. 14, 1965, Allen Park, Mich.

	W	L	PCT	ERA	G	GS	CG	IP	H	BB	SO	ShO	W	L	SV	AB	H	HR	BA
1913 STL N	0	3	.000	3.75	3	3	2	24	20	8	3	0	0	0	0	8	3	0	.375
1914	0	0	—	3.60	3	0	0	5	6	5	1	0	0	0	0	0	0	0	—
1915 WAS A	0	1	.000	4.60	13	0	0	31.1	39	16	8	0	0	1	1	5	1	0	.200
3 yrs.	0	4	.000	4.18	19	3	2	60.1	65	29	12	0	0	1	1	13	4	0	.308
2 yrs.	0	3	.000	3.72	6	3	2	29	26	13	4	0	0	0	0	8	3	0	.375

Oscar Horstmann

HORSTMANN, OSCAR THEODORE   BR TR 5'11"   165 lbs.
B. June 2, 1891, Alma, Mo.   D. May 11, 1977, Salina, Kans.

	W	L	PCT	ERA	G	GS	CG	IP	H	BB	SO	ShO	W	L	SV	AB	H	HR	BA
1917 STL N	9	4	.692	3.45	35	11	4	138.1	111	54	50	0	4	0	1	46	9	0	.196
1918	0	2	.000	5.48	9	2	0	23	29	14	6	0	0	1	0	4	0	0	.000
1919	0	1	.000	3.00	6	2	0	15	14	12	5	0	0	0	0	2	1	0	.500
3 yrs.	9	7	.563	3.67	50	15	4	176.1	154	80	61	1	4	1	1	52	10	0	.192
3 yrs.	9	7	.563	3.67	50	15	4	176.1	154	80	61	1	4	1	1	52	10	0	.192

Earl Howard

HOWARD, EARL N.   BR TR 6'1"   160 lbs.
B. June 25, 1896, Everett, Pa.   D. Apr., 1937, Bedford, Pa.

	W	L	PCT	ERA	G	GS	CG	IP	H	BB	SO	ShO	W	L	SV	AB	H	HR	BA
1918 STL N	0	0	—	0.00	1	0	0	2	0	0	2	0	0	0	0	0	0	0	—

Roland Howell

HOWELL, ROLAND BOATNER (Billiken)   BR TR 6'4"   210 lbs.
B. Jan. 3, 1892, Napoleonville, La.   D. Mar. 31, 1973

	W	L	PCT	ERA	G	GS	CG	IP	H	BB	SO	ShO	W	L	SV	AB	H	HR	BA
1912 STL N	0	0	—	27.00	3	0	0	1.2	5	5	0	0	0	0	0	0	0	0	—

Al Hrabosky

HRABOSKY, ALAN THOMAS (The Mad Hungarian)   BR TL 5'11"   185 lbs.
B. July 21, 1949, Oakland, Calif.

	W	L	PCT	ERA	G	GS	CG	IP	H	BB	SO	ShO	W	L	SV	AB	H	HR	BA
1970 STL N	2	1	.667	4.74	16	1	0	19	22	7	12	0	2	1	0	3	0	0	.000
1971	0	0	—	0.00	1	0	0	2	2	0	2	0	0	0	0	0	0	0	—
1972	1	0	1.000	0.00	5	0	0	7	2	3	9	0	1	0	0	1	0	0	.000
1973	2	4	.333	2.09	44	0	0	56	45	21	57	0	2	4	5	4	0	0	.000
1974	8	1	.889	2.97	65	0	0	88	71	38	82	0	8	1	9	13	4	0	.308
1975	13	3	.813	1.67	65	0	0	97	72	33	82	0	13	3	22	15	3	0	.200
1976	8	6	.571	3.30	68	0	0	95.1	89	39	73	0	8	6	13	7	0	0	.000
1977	6	5	.545	4.40	65	0	0	86	82	41	68	0	6	5	10	8	0	0	.000
1978 KC A	8	7	.533	2.88	58	0	0	75	52	35	60	0	8	7	20	0	0	0	—
1979	9	4	.692	3.74	58	0	0	65	67	41	39	0	9	4	11	0	0	0	—
1980 ATL N	4	2	.667	3.60	45	0	0	60	50	31	31	0	4	2	3	1	0	0	.000
1981	1	1	.500	1.06	24	0	0	34	24	9	13	0	1	1	1	1	0	0	.000
1982	2	1	.667	5.54	31	0	0	37.1	41	17	20	0	2	1	3	3	1	0	.333
13 yrs.	64	35	.646	3.11	545	1	0	721.2	619	315	548	0	64	35	97	56	8	0	.143
8 yrs.	40	20	.667	2.94	329	1	0	450.1	385	182	385	0	40	20	59	51	7	0	.137
				8th									3rd		5th				

LEAGUE CHAMPIONSHIP SERIES

	W	L	PCT	ERA	G	GS	CG	IP	H	BB	SO	ShO	W	L	SV	AB	H	HR	BA
1978 KC A	0	0	—	3.00	3	0	0	3	3	1	2	0	0	0	0	0	0	0	—

Charles Hudson

HUDSON, CHARLES   BL TL 6'3"   185 lbs.
B. Aug. 18, 1949, Ada, Okla.

	W	L	PCT	ERA	G	GS	CG	IP	H	BB	SO	ShO	W	L	SV	AB	H	HR	BA
1972 STL N	1	0	1.000	5.11	12	0	0	12.1	10	7	4	0	1	0	0	0	0	0	—
1973 TEX A	4	2	.667	4.65	25	4	1	62	59	31	34	1	2	1	1	0	0	0	—
1975 CAL A	0	1	.000	9.53	3	1	0	5.2	7	4	0	0	0	0	0	0	0	0	—
3 yrs.	5	3	.625	5.06	40	5	1	80	76	42	38	1	3	1	1	0	0	0	—
1 yr.	1	0	1.000	5.11	12	0	0	12.1	10	7	4	0	1	0	0	0	0	0	—

Dick Hughes

HUGHES, RICHARD HENRY   BR TR 6'3"   195 lbs.
B. Feb. 13, 1938, Stephens, Ark.

	W	L	PCT	ERA	G	GS	CG	IP	H	BB	SO	ShO	W	L	SV	AB	H	HR	BA
1966 STL N	2	1	.667	1.71	6	2	1	21	12	7	20	1	1	1	1	5	2	0	.400
1967	16	6	.727	2.67	37	27	12	222.1	164	48	161	3	1	0	3	78	10	0	.128
1968	2	2	.500	3.53	25	5	0	63.2	45	21	49	0	1	1	4	15	0	0	.000
3 yrs.	20	9	.690	2.79	68	34	13	307	221	76	230	4	3	2	8	98	12	0	.122
3 yrs.	20	9	.690	2.79	68	34	13	307	221	76	230	4	3	2	8	98	12	0	.122

WORLD SERIES

	W	L	PCT	ERA	G	GS	CG	IP	H	BB	SO	ShO	W	L	SV	AB	H	HR	BA
1967 STL N	0	1	.000	5.00	2	2	0	9	9	3	7	0	0	0	0	3	0	0	.000
1968	0	0	—	0.00	1	0	0	.1	2	0	0	0	0	0	0	0	0	0	—
2 yrs.	0	1	.000	4.82	3	2	0	9.1	11	3	7	0	0	0	0	3	0	0	.000

Tom Hughes

HUGHES, THOMAS EDWARD   BL TR 6'2"   180 lbs.
B. Sept. 13, 1934, Ancon, Canal Zone

	W	L	PCT	ERA	G	GS	CG	IP	H	BB	SO	ShO	W	L	SV	AB	H	HR	BA
1959 STL N	0	2	.000	15.75	3	0	0	4	9	2	2	0	0	0	0	1	0	0	.000

Jim Hughey

HUGHEY, JAMES ULYSSES (Cold Water Jim)   TR
B. Mar. 8, 1869, Coldwater, Mich.   D. Mar. 29, 1945, Coldwater, Mich.

	W	L	PCT	ERA	G	GS	CG	IP	H	BB	SO	ShO	W	L	SV	AB	H	HR	BA
1891 C-M AA	1	0	1.000	3.00	2	1	1	15	18	3	9	0	0	0	0	7	1	0	.143
1893 CHI N	0	1	.000	11.00	2	2	1	9	14	3	4	0	0	0	0	2	0	0	.000
1896 PIT N	6	8	.429	4.99	25	14	11	155	171	67	48	0	2	0	0	65	14	0	.215

	W	L	PCT	ERA	G	GS	CG	IP	H	BB	SO	ShO	Relief Pitching W	L	SV	BATTING AB	H	HR	BA

Jim Hughey continued

	W	L	PCT	ERA	G	GS	CG	IP	H	BB	SO	ShO	W	L	SV	AB	H	HR	BA
1897	6	10	.375	5.06	25	17	13	149.1	193	45	38	0	1	1	1	63	8	0	.127
1898 STL N	7	24	.226	3.93	35	33	31	283.2	325	71	74	0	0	0	0	97	11	1	.113
1899 CLE N	4	30	.118	5.41	36	34	32	283	403	88	54	0	0	2	0	111	18	0	.162
1900 STL N	5	7	.417	5.19	20	12	11	112.2	147	40	23	0	0	0	0	41	7	0	.171
7 yrs.	29	80	.266	4.87	145	113	100	1007.2	1271	317	250	0	3	3	1	386	59	1	.153
2 yrs.	12	31	.279	4.29	55	45	42	396.1	472	111	97	0	0	0	0	138	18	1	.130

Bob Humphreys

HUMPHREYS, ROBERT WILLIAM
B. Aug. 18, 1935, Covington, Va.   BR TR 5'11"   165 lbs.

	W	L	PCT	ERA	G	GS	CG	IP	H	BB	SO	ShO	W	L	SV	AB	H	HR	BA
1962 DET A	0	1	.000	7.20	4	0	0	5	8	2	3	0	0	1	1	0	0	0	–
1963 STL N	0	0	.000	5.06	9	0	0	10.2	11	7	8	0	0	1	0	0	0	0	–
1964	2	0	1.000	2.53	28	0	0	42.2	32	15	36	0	2	0	2	4	1	0	.250
1965 CHI N	2	0	1.000	3.15	41	0	0	65.2	59	27	38	0	2	0	0	3	0	0	.000
1966 WAS A	7	3	.700	2.82	58	1	0	111.2	91	28	88	0	6	3	3	12	2	0	.167
1967	6	2	.750	4.17	48	2	0	105.2	93	41	54	0	5	1	4	15	2	0	.133
1968	5	7	.417	3.69	56	0	0	92.2	78	30	56	0	5	7	2	5	2	0	.400
1969	3	3	.500	3.05	47	0	0	79.2	69	38	43	0	3	3	5	13	1	0	.077
1970 2 teams		WAS A	(5G 0–0)			MIL A	(23G 2–4)												
" total	2	4	.333	2.92	28	1	0	52.1	41	31	38	0	2	4	3	9	0	0	.000
9 yrs.	27	21	.563	3.36	319	4	0	566	482	219	364	0	25	20	20	61	8	0	.131
2 yrs.	2	1	.667	3.04	37	0	0	53.1	43	22	44	0	2	1	2	4	1	0	.250

WORLD SERIES

	W	L	PCT	ERA	G	GS	CG	IP	H	BB	SO	ShO	W	L	SV	AB	H	HR	BA
1964 STL N	0	0	–	0.00	1	0	0	1	0	0	1	0	0	0	0	0	0	0	–

Ben Hunt

HUNT, BENJAMIN FRANKLIN (Highpockets)
B. 1888, Eufaula, Okla.   BL TL

	W	L	PCT	ERA	G	GS	CG	IP	H	BB	SO	ShO	W	L	SV	AB	H	HR	BA
1910 BOS A	2	4	.333	4.05	7	7	3	46.2	45	20	19	0	0	0	0	18	1	0	.056
1913 STL N	0	1	.000	3.38	2	1	0	8	6	9	6	0	0	0	0	2	0	0	.000
2 yrs.	2	5	.286	3.95	9	8	3	54.2	51	29	25	0	0	0	0	20	1	0	.050
1 yr.	0	1	.000	3.38	2	1	0	8	6	9	6	0	0	0	0	2	0	0	.000

Walter Huntzinger

HUNTZINGER, WALTER HENRY (Shakes)
B. Feb. 6, 1899, Pottsville, Pa.   D. Aug. 11, 1981, Upper Darby, Pa.   BR TR 6'   150 lbs.

	W	L	PCT	ERA	G	GS	CG	IP	H	BB	SO	ShO	W	L	SV	AB	H	HR	BA
1923 NY N	0	1	.000	7.88	2	1	0	8	12	4	2	0	0	0	0	2	0	0	.000
1924	1	1	.500	4.45	12	2	0	32.1	41	9	6	0	0	0	0	8	4	0	.500
1925	5	1	.833	3.50	26	1	0	64.1	68	17	19	0	5	1	0	11	1	0	.091
1926 2 teams		STL N	(9G 0–4)			CHI N	(11G 1–1)												
" total	1	5	.167	2.73	20	2	2	62.2	61	22	13	0	1	2	2	15	1	0	.067
4 yrs.	7	8	.467	3.60	60	6	2	167.1	179	49	40	0	6	4	3	36	6	0	.167
1 yr.	0	4	.000	4.24	9	4	2	34	35	14	9	0	0	1	0	8	0	0	.000

Fred Hutchinson

HUTCHINSON, FREDERICK CHARLES
B. Aug. 12, 1919, Seattle, Wash.   D. Nov. 12, 1964, Bradenton, Fla.   BL TR 6'2"   190 lbs.
Manager 1952-54, 1956-64.

	W	L	PCT	ERA	G	GS	CG	IP	H	BB	SO	ShO	W	L	SV	AB	H	HR	BA
1939 DET A	3	6	.333	5.21	13	12	8	84.2	95	51	22	0	0	0	0	34	13	0	.382
1940	3	7	.300	5.68	17	10	1	76	85	26	32	0	1	2	0	30	8	0	.267
1941	0	0	–	0.00	0	0	0	0	0	0	0	0	0	0	0	2	0	0	.000
1946	14	11	.560	3.09	28	26	16	207	184	66	138	3	0	0	0	89	28	0	.315
1947	18	10	.643	3.03	33	25	18	219.2	211	61	113	3	2	1	2	106	32	2	.302
1948	13	11	.542	4.32	33	28	15	221	223	48	92	0	0	0	0	112	23	1	.205
1949	15	7	.682	2.96	33	21	9	188.2	167	52	54	4	3	2	1	73	18	0	.247
1950	17	8	.680	3.96	39	26	10	231.2	269	48	71	1	4	1	0	95	31	0	.326
1951	10	10	.500	3.68	31	20	9	188.1	204	27	53	2	4	1	2	85	16	0	.188
1952	2	1	.667	3.38	12	1	0	37.1	40	9	12	0	2	0	0	18	1	0	.056
1953	0	0	–	2.79	3	0	0	9.2	9	0	4	0	0	0	0	6	1	1	.167
11 yrs.	95	71	.572	3.73	242	169	81	1464	1487	388	591	13	16	7	7	*			

WORLD SERIES

	W	L	PCT	ERA	G	GS	CG	IP	H	BB	SO	ShO	W	L	SV	AB	H	HR	BA
1940 DET A	0	0	–	9.00	1	0	0	1	1	1	1	0	0	0	0	0	0	0	–

Ira Hutchinson

HUTCHINSON, IRA KENDALL
B. Aug. 31, 1910, Chicago, Ill.   D. Aug. 21, 1973, Chicago, Ill.   BR TR 5'10½" 180 lbs.

	W	L	PCT	ERA	G	GS	CG	IP	H	BB	SO	ShO	W	L	SV	AB	H	HR	BA
1933 CHI A	0	0	–	13.50	1	1	0	4	7	3	2	0	0	0	0	2	1	0	.500
1937 BOS N	4	6	.400	3.73	31	8	1	91.2	99	35	29	0	4	0	0	26	3	0	.115
1938	9	8	.529	2.74	36	12	4	151	150	61	38	1	5	3	4	52	9	0	.173
1939 BKN N	5	2	.714	4.34	41	1	0	105.2	103	51	46	0	5	2	1	27	1	0	.037
1940 STL N	4	2	.667	3.13	20	2	1	63.1	68	19	19	0	2	2	1	18	4	0	.222
1941	1	5	.167	3.86	29	0	0	46.2	32	19	19	0	1	5	5	8	2	0	.250
1944 BOS N	9	7	.563	4.21	40	8	1	119.2	136	53	22	1	6	4	1	29	4	0	.138
1945	2	3	.400	5.02	11	0	0	28.2	33	8	4	0	2	3	1	9	0	0	.000
8 yrs.	34	33	.507	3.76	209	32	7	610.2	628	249	179	2	25	19	13	171	24	0	.140
2 yrs.	5	7	.417	3.44	60	2	1	110	100	38	38	0	3	7	6	26	6	0	.231

Bill Hutchison

HUTCHISON, WILLIAM FORREST (Wild Bill)
B. Dec. 17, 1859, New Haven, Conn.   D. Mar. 19, 1926, Kansas City, Mo.   BR TR 5'9"   175 lbs.

	W	L	PCT	ERA	G	GS	CG	IP	H	BB	SO	ShO	W	L	SV	AB	H	HR	BA
1889 CHI N	16	17	.485	3.54	37	36	33	318	306	117	136	3	0	0	0	133	21	1	.158
1890	42	25	.627	2.70	71	66	65	603	505	199	289	5	1	1	2	261	53	2	.203
1891	43	19	.694	2.81	66	58	56	561	508	178	261	4	7	1	1	243	45	0	.185
1892	37	34	.521	2.74	75	71	67	627	572	187	316	5	1	2	0	263	57	1	.217
1893	16	23	.410	4.75	44	40	38	348.1	420	156	80	2	1	0	0	162	41	0	.253
1894	14	15	.483	6.06	36	34	28	277.2	373	140	59	0	1	0	0	136	42	6	.309

	W	L	PCT	ERA	G	GS	CG	IP	H	BB	SO	ShO	Relief Pitching W	L	SV	BATTING AB	H	HR	BA

Bill Hutchison continued

	W	L	PCT	ERA	G	GS	CG	IP	H	BB	SO	ShO	W	L	SV	AB	H	HR	BA
1895	13	21	.382	4.73	38	35	30	291	371	129	85	2	0	0	0	126	25	0	.198
1897 STL N	1	4	.200	6.08	6	5	2	40	55	22	5	0	0	0	0	18	5	0	.278
8 yrs.	182	158	.535	3.59	373	345	319	3066	3110	1128	1231	21	10	4	3	1342	289	12	.215
1 yr.	1	4	.200	6.08	6	5	2	40	55	22	5	0	0	0	0	18	5	0	.278

Pat Hynes

HYNES, PATRICK J.
B. Mar. 12, 1884, St. Louis, Mo.   D. Mar. 12, 1907, St. Louis, Mo.

	W	L	PCT	ERA	G	GS	CG	IP	H	BB	SO	ShO	W	L	SV	AB	H	HR	BA
1903 STL N	0	1	.000	4.00	1	1	1	9	10	6	1	0	0	0	0	3	0	0	.000
1904 STL A	1	1	.500	6.23	5	2	1	26	35	7	6	0	0	1	0	254	60	0	.236
2 yrs.	1	2	.333	5.66	6	3	2	35	45	13	7	0	0	1	0	*			
1 yr.	0	1	.000	4.00	1	1	1	9	10	6	1	0	0	0	0	3	0	0	.000

Al Jackson

JACKSON, ALVIN NEAL
B. Dec. 25, 1935, Waco, Tex.

BL TL 5'10"   169 lbs.

	W	L	PCT	ERA	G	GS	CG	IP	H	BB	SO	ShO	W	L	SV	AB	H	HR	BA
1959 PIT N	0	0	—	6.50	8	3	0	18	30	8	13	0	0	0	0	5	1	0	.200
1961	1	0	1.000	3.42	3	2	1	23.2	20	4	15	0	0	0	0	8	0	0	.000
1962 NY N	8	20	.286	4.40	36	33	12	231.1	244	78	118	4	0	0	0	73	5	0	.068
1963	13	17	.433	3.96	37	34	11	227	237	84	142	0	0	0	0	79	16	0	.203
1964	11	16	.407	4.26	40	31	11	213.1	229	60	112	3	2	0	1	72	11	1	.153
1965	8	20	.286	4.34	37	31	7	205.1	217	61	120	3	0	0	1	60	7	0	.117
1966 STL N	13	15	.464	2.51	36	30	11	232.2	222	45	90	3	1	1	0	74	13	0	.176
1967	9	4	.692	3.95	38	11	1	107	117	29	43	1	4	1	1	31	8	0	.258
1968 NY N	3	7	.300	3.69	25	9	0	92.2	88	17	59	0	1	1	3	28	7	0	.250
1969 2 teams							NY N (9G 0-0)				CIN N (33G 1-0)								
" total	1	0	1.000	6.81	42	0	0	38.1	45	21	26	0	1	0	3	5	1	0	.200
10 yrs.	67	99	.404	3.98	302	184	54	1389.1	1449	407	738	14	9	3	10	435	69	1	.159
2 yrs.	22	19	.537	2.97	74	41	12	339.2	339	74	133	4	5	2	1	105	21	0	.200

Larry Jackson

JACKSON, LAWRENCE CURTIS
B. June 2, 1931, Nampa, Ida.

BR TR 6'1½"   175 lbs.

	W	L	PCT	ERA	G	GS	CG	IP	H	BB	SO	ShO	W	L	SV	AB	H	HR	BA
1955 STL N	9	14	.391	4.31	37	25	4	177.1	189	72	88	1	4	2	2	57	3	0	.053
1956	2	2	.500	4.11	51	1	0	85.1	75	45	50	0	2	1	9	11	1	0	.091
1957	15	9	.625	3.47	41	22	6	210.1	196	57	96	2	7	2	1	72	13	0	.181
1958	13	13	.500	3.68	49	23	11	198	211	51	124	1	2	5	8	60	9	0	.150
1959	14	13	.519	3.30	40	37	12	256	271	64	145	3	0	1	0	80	9	0	.113
1960	18	13	.581	3.48	43	38	14	282	277	70	171	3	0	2	0	95	20	0	.211
1961	14	11	.560	3.75	33	28	12	211	203	56	113	3	0	1	0	74	13	0	.176
1962	16	11	.593	3.75	36	35	11	252.1	267	64	112	2	0	0	0	89	15	0	.169
1963 CHI N	14	18	.438	2.55	37	37	13	275	256	54	153	4	0	0	0	87	17	0	.195
1964	24	11	.686	3.14	40	38	19	297.2	265	58	148	3	0	1	0	114	20	0	.175
1965	14	21	.400	3.85	39	39	12	257.1	268	57	131	4	0	0	0	86	11	1	.128
1966 2 teams							CHI N (3G 0-2)				PHI N (35G 15-13)								
" total	15	15	.500	3.32	38	35	12	255	257	62	112	5	1	0	0	92	13	1	.141
1967 PHI N	13	15	.464	3.10	40	37	11	261.2	242	54	139	4	1	0	0	87	14	0	.161
1968	13	17	.433	2.77	34	34	12	243.2	229	60	127	2	0	0	0	85	12	0	.141
14 yrs.	194	183	.515	3.40	558	429	149	3262.2	3206	824	1709	37	17	15	20	1089	170	2	.156
8 yrs.	101	86	.540	3.67	330	209	70	1672.1	1689	479	899	15	15	14	20	538	83	0	.154
	10th	7th				7th					6th								

Mike Jackson

JACKSON, MICHAEL WARREN
B. Mar. 27, 1946, Paterson, N. J.

BL TL 6'3"   190 lbs.

	W	L	PCT	ERA	G	GS	CG	IP	H	BB	SO	ShO	W	L	SV	AB	H	HR	BA
1970 PHI N	1	1	.500	1.50	5	0	0	6	6	4	4	0	1	1	0	1	1	0	1.000
1971 STL N	0	0	—	0.00	1	0	0	1	1	1	0	0	0	0	0	1	0	0	.000
1972 KC A	1	2	.333	6.30	7	3	0	20	24	14	15	0	0	1	0	5	0	0	.000
1973 2 teams							KC A (9G 0-0)				CLE A (1G 0-0)								
" total	0	0	—	6.65	10	0	0	23	26	20	14	0	0	0	0	0	0		—
4 yrs.	2	3	.400	5.76	23	3	0	50	57	39	33	0	1	2	0	7	1	0	.143
1 yr.	0	0	—	0.00	1	0	0	1	1	1	0	0	0	0	0	1	0	0	.000

Elmer Jacobs

JACOBS, WILLIAM ELMER
B. Aug. 10, 1892, Salem, Mo.   D. Feb. 10, 1958, Salem, Mo.

BR TR 6'   165 lbs.

	W	L	PCT	ERA	G	GS	CG	IP	H	BB	SO	ShO	W	L	SV	AB	H	HR	BA
1914 PHI N	1	3	.250	4.80	14	7	1	50.2	65	20	17	0	0	0	0	14	0	0	.000
1916 PIT N	6	10	.375	2.94	34	17	8	153	151	38	46	0	2	1	0	40	3	0	.075
1917	6	19	.240	2.81	38	25	10	227.1	214	76	58	1	1	3	2	67	12	0	.179
1918 2 teams							PIT N (8G 0-1)				PHI N (18G 9-5)								
" total	9	6	.600	2.95	26	18	12	146.1	122	56	35	4	0	1	1	45	8	0	.178
1919 2 teams							PHI N (17G 6-10)				STL N (17G 2-6)								
" total	8	16	.333	3.32	34	23	17	214	231	69	68	1	1	1	1	68	16	0	.235
1920 STL N	4	8	.333	5.21	23	9	1	77.2	91	33	21	0	2	2	1	26	5	0	.192
1924 CHI N	11	12	.478	3.74	38	22	13	190.1	181	72	50	1	2	2	1	54	6	0	.111
1925	2	3	.400	5.17	18	4	1	55.2	63	22	19	1	1	2	1	13	3	0	.231
1927 CHI A	2	4	.333	4.60	25	8	2	74.1	105	37	22	1	0	0	0	20	3	0	.150
9 yrs.	49	81	.377	3.55	250	133	65	1189.1	1223	423	336	9	9	12	7	347	56	0	.161
2 yrs.	6	14	.300	3.81	40	17	5	163	172	58	52	1	3	2	2	49	13	0	.265

Tony Jacobs

JACOBS, ANTHONY ROBERT
B. Aug. 5, 1925, Dixmoor, Ill.   D. Dec. 21, 1980, Nashville, Tenn.

BB TR 5'9"   150 lbs.

	W	L	PCT	ERA	G	GS	CG	IP	H	BB	SO	ShO	W	L	SV	AB	H	HR	BA
1948 CHI N	0	0	—	4.50	1	0	0	2	3	0	2	0	0	0	0	0	0	0	—
1955 STL N	0	0	—	18.00	1	0	0	2	6	1	1	0	0	0	0	1	0	0	.000
2 yrs.	0	0	—	11.25	2	0	0	4	9	1	3	0	0	0	0	1	0	0	.000
1 yr.	0	0	—	18.00	1	0	0	2	6	1	1	0	0	0	0	1	0	0	.000

	W	L	PCT	ERA	G	GS	CG	IP	H	BB	SO	ShO	Relief Pitching W	L	SV	BATTING AB	H	HR	BA

Hi Jasper

JASPER, HARRY W.
B. May 24, 1887, St. Louis, Mo.   D. May 22, 1937, St. Louis, Mo.   BR TR 5'11" 180 lbs.

	W	L	PCT	ERA	G	GS	CG	IP	H	BB	SO	ShO	W	L	SV	AB	H	HR	BA
1914 CHI A	1	0	1.000	3.34	16	0	0	32.1	22	20	19	0	1	0	0	5	0	0	.000
1915	0	1	.000	4.60	3	2	1	15.2	8	9	15	0	0	0	0	7	2	0	.286
1916 STL N	5	6	.455	3.28	21	9	2	107	97	42	37	0	3	1	1	33	7	1	.212
1919 CLE A	4	5	.444	3.59	12	10	5	82.2	83	28	25	0	1	0	0	29	3	0	.103
4 yrs.	10	12	.455	3.48	52	21	8	237.2	210	99	96	0	5	1	1	74	12	1	.162
1 yr.	5	6	.455	3.28	21	9	2	107	97	42	37	0	3	1	1	33	7	1	.212

Larry Jaster

JASTER, LARRY EDWARD
B. Jan. 13, 1944, Midland, Mich.   BL TL 6'3" 190 lbs.

	W	L	PCT	ERA	G	GS	CG	IP	H	BB	SO	ShO	W	L	SV	AB	H	HR	BA
1965 STL N	3	0	1.000	1.61	4	3	3	28	21	7	10	0	0	0	0	10	2	0	.200
1966	11	5	.688	3.26	26	21	6	151.2	124	45	92	5	1	0	0	45	8	1	.178
1967	9	7	.563	3.01	34	23	2	152.1	141	44	87	1	1	0	3	50	5	0	.100
1968	9	13	.409	3.51	31	23	3	153.2	153	38	70	1	2	1	0	43	6	1	.140
1969 MON N	1	6	.143	5.49	24	11	1	77	95	28	39	0	0	0	0	19	8	0	.421
1970 ATL N	1	1	.500	6.95	14	0	0	22	33	8	9	0	1	1	0	3	0	0	.000
1972	1	1	.500	5.25	5	0	0	12	12	8	6	0	1	0	0	0	0	0	.000
7 yrs.	35	33	.515	3.65	138	80	15	596.2	579	178	313	7	6	2	3	171	29	2	.170
4 yrs.	32	25	.561	3.17	95	68	14	485.2	439	134	259	7	4	1	3	148	21	2	.142
WORLD SERIES																			
1967 STL N	0	0	—	0.00	1	0	0	.1	2	0	0	0	0	0	0	0	0	0	—
1968	0	0	—	∞	1	0	0		2	1	0	0	0	0	0	0	0	0	—
2 yrs.	0	0	—	81.00	2	0	0	.1	4	1	0	0	0	0	0	0	0	0	—

Hal Jeffcoat

JEFFCOAT, HAROLD BENTLEY
Brother of George Jeffcoat.
B. Sept. 6, 1924, West Columbia, S. C.   BR TR 5'10½" 185 lbs.

	W	L	PCT	ERA	G	GS	CG	IP	H	BB	SO	ShO	W	L	SV	AB	H	HR	BA
1954 CHI N	5	6	.455	5.19	43	3	1	104	110	58	35	0	4	4	7	31	8	1	.258
1955	8	6	.571	2.95	50	1	0	100.2	107	53	32	0	8	6	6	23	4	1	.174
1956 CIN N	8	2	.800	3.84	38	16	2	171	189	55	55	0	2	0	2	54	8	0	.148
1957	12	13	.480	4.52	37	31	10	207	236	46	63	1	0	1	0	69	14	4	.203
1958	6	8	.429	3.72	49	0	0	75	76	26	35	0	6	8	9	9	5	0	.556
1959 2 teams								CIN N (17G 0–1)			STL N (11G 0–1)								
" total	0	2	.000	5.95	28	0	0	39.1	54	19	19	0	0	1	1	4	1	0	.250
6 yrs.	39	37	.513	4.22	245	51	13	697	772	257	239	1	20	21	25	*			
1 yr.	0	1	.000	9.17	11	0	0	17.2	33	9	7	0	0	1	0	3	0	0	.000

Adam Johnson

JOHNSON, ADAM RANKIN, SR. (Tex)
Father of Adam Johnson.
B. Feb. 4, 1888, Burnet, Tex.   D. July 2, 1972, Williamsport, Pa.   BR TR 6'1½" 185 lbs.

	W	L	PCT	ERA	G	GS	CG	IP	H	BB	SO	ShO	W	L	SV	AB	H	HR	BA
1914 2 teams								BOS A (16G 4–9)			CHI F (16G 9–5)								
" total	13	14	.481	2.26	32	27	16	219.1	180	63	84	4	1	1	0	67	8	0	.119
1915 2 teams								CHI F (11G 2–4)			BAL F (23G 7–11)								
" total	9	15	.375	3.64	34	25	15	207.2	201	81	81	2	1	2	2	73	9	0	.123
1918 STL N	1	1	.500	2.74	6	1	0	23	20	7	4	0	1	0	0	4	1	0	.250
3 yrs.	23	30	.434	2.92	72	53	31	450	401	151	169	6	3	3	2	144	18	0	.125
1 yr.	1	1	.500	2.74	6	1	0	23	20	7	4	0	1	0	0	4	1	0	.250

Jerry Johnson

JOHNSON, JERRY MICHAEL
B. Dec. 3, 1943, Miami, Fla.   BR TR 6'3" 200 lbs.

	W	L	PCT	ERA	G	GS	CG	IP	H	BB	SO	ShO	W	L	SV	AB	H	HR	BA
1968 PHI N	4	4	.500	3.24	16	11	2	80.2	82	29	40	0	0	0	0	25	2	0	.080
1969	6	13	.316	4.29	33	21	4	147	151	57	82	2	0	0	1	43	9	0	.209
1970 2 teams								STL N (7G 2–0)			SF N (33G 3–4)								
" total	5	4	.556	4.11	40	1	0	76.2	73	41	49	0	5	3	4	16	1	0	.063
1971 SF N	12	9	.571	2.97	67	0	0	109	93	48	85	0	12	9	18	13	2	0	.154
1972	8	6	.571	4.44	48	0	0	73	73	40	57	0	8	6	8	9	0	0	.000
1973 CLE A	5	6	.455	6.18	39	1	0	59.2	70	39	45	0	5	6	5	0	0		—
1974 HOU N	2	1	.667	4.80	14	0	0	45	47	24	32	0	2	1	0	1	0	0	.000
1975 SD N	3	1	.750	5.17	21	4	0	54	60	31	18	0	1	1	0	12	1	0	.083
1976	1	3	.250	5.31	24	1	0	39	39	26	27	0	0	2	0	3	0	0	.000
1977 TOR A	2	4	.333	4.60	43	0	0	86	91	54	54	0	2	4	5	0	0		—
10 yrs.	48	51	.485	4.31	365	39	6	770	779	389	489	2	36	31	41	122	15	0	.123
1 yr.	2	0	1.000	3.18	7	0	0	11.1	6	3	5	0	2	0	1	1	0	0	.000
LEAGUE CHAMPIONSHIP SERIES																			
1971 SF N	0	0	—	13.50	1	0	0	1.1	1	1	2	0	0	0	0	0	0	0	—

Ken Johnson

JOHNSON, KENNETH CARSTENSEN (Hooks)
B. Jan. 14, 1923, Topeka, Kans.   BL TL 6'1" 185 lbs.

	W	L	PCT	ERA	G	GS	CG	IP	H	BB	SO	ShO	W	L	SV	AB	H	HR	BA
1947 STL N	1	0	1.000	0.00	2	1	1	10	2	5	8	0	0	0	0	4	2	0	.500
1948	2	4	.333	4.76	13	4	0	45.1	43	30	20	0	2	1	0	20	6	0	.300
1949	0	1	.000	6.42	14	0	0	33.2	29	35	18	0	0	0	0	8	2	0	.250
1950 2 teams								STL N (2G 0–0)			PHI N (14G 4–1)								
" total	4	1	.800	3.88	16	8	0	62.2	62	46	33	1	1	0	0	19	3	0	.158
1951 PHI N	5	8	.385	4.57	20	18	4	106.1	103	68	58	3	0	0	0	35	5	0	.143
1952 DET A	0	0	—	6.35	9	1	0	11.1	12	11	10	0	0	0	0	3	1	0	.333
6 yrs.	12	14	.462	4.58	74	34	8	269.1	251	195	147	4	3	1	0	89	19	0	.213
4 yrs.	3	5	.375	4.75	31	7	1	91	75	73	47	0	2	1	0	32	10	0	.313

Si Johnson

JOHNSON, SILAS KENNETH
B. Oct. 5, 1906, Marseilles, Ill.   BR TR 5'11½" 185 lbs.

	W	L	PCT	ERA	G	GS	CG	IP	H	BB	SO	ShO	W	L	SV	AB	H	HR	BA
1928 CIN N	0	0	—	4.35	3	0	0	10.1	9	5	1	0	0	0	0	4	1	0	.250
1929	0	0	—	4.50	3	0	0	2	2	1	1	0	0	0	0	0	0	0	—

	W	L	PCT	ERA	G	GS	CG	IP	H	BB	SO	ShO	Relief Pitching W	L	SV	BATTING AB	H	HR	BA

Si Johnson continued

	W	L	PCT	ERA	G	GS	CG	IP	H	BB	SO	ShO	W	L	SV	AB	H	HR	BA
1930	3	1	.750	4.94	35	3	0	78.1	86	31	47	0	2	1	0	17	4	0	.235
1931	11	19	.367	3.77	42	33	14	262.1	273	74	95	0	0	2	0	87	13	0	.149
1932	13	15	.464	3.27	42	27	14	245	246	57	94	2	1	0	2	80	10	0	.125
1933	7	18	.280	3.49	34	28	14	211.1	212	54	51	4	0	0	1	72	3	0	.042
1934	7	22	.241	5.22	46	31	9	215.2	264	84	89	0	0	2	3	72	10	0	.139
1935	5	11	.313	6.23	30	20	4	130	155	59	40	1	0	0	0	41	1	0	.024
1936 2 teams			CIN N (2G 0–0)			STL N (12G 5–3)													
" total	5	3	.625	4.93	14	9	3	65.2	89	11	23	1	1	1	0	21	4	0	.190
1937 STL N	12	12	.500	3.32	38	21	12	192.1	222	43	64	1	3	3	1	65	9	0	.138
1938	0	3	.000	7.47	6	3	0	15.2	27	6	4	0	0	0	0	1	0	0	.000
1940 PHI N	5	14	.263	4.88	37	14	5	138.1	145	42	58	0	1	6	1	43	6	0	.140
1941	5	12	.294	4.52	39	21	6	163.1	207	54	80	1	0	3	2	47	7	0	.149
1942	8	19	.296	3.69	39	26	10	195.1	198	72	78	1	1	1	0	58	6	0	.103
1943	8	3	.727	3.27	21	14	9	113	110	25	46	1	0	0	2	33	6	0	.182
1946 2 teams			PHI N (1G 0–0)			BOS N (28G 6–5)													
" total	6	5	.545	2.77	29	12	5	130	141	35	43	1	0	0	1	38	6	0	.158
1947 BOS N	6	8	.429	4.23	36	10	3	112.2	124	34	27	0	2	2	2	30	1	0	.033
17 yrs.	101	165	.380	4.09	492	272	108	2281.1	2510	687	840	13	11	21	15	709	87	0	.123
3 yrs.	17	18	.486	3.80	56	33	15	269.2	331	60	89	2	4	4	1	87	13	0	.149

Syl Johnson

JOHNSON, SYLVESTER W.   BR TR 5'11½" 180 lbs.
B. Dec. 31, 1900, Portland, Ore.

	W	L	PCT	ERA	G	GS	CG	IP	H	BB	SO	ShO	W	L	SV	AB	H	HR	BA
1922 DET A	7	3	.700	3.71	29	8	3	97	99	30	29	0	3	1	1	36	8	0	.222
1923	12	7	.632	3.98	37	18	7	176.1	181	47	93	1	5	2	0	62	10	1	.161
1924	5	4	.556	4.93	29	9	2	104	117	42	55	0	2	2	3	34	7	0	.206
1925	0	2	.000	3.46	6	0	0	13	11	10	5	0	0	2	0	3	0	0	.000
1926 STL N	0	3	.000	4.22	19	6	1	49	54	15	10	0	0	0	1	12	0	0	.000
1927	0	0	—	6.00	2	0	0	3	3	0	2	0	0	0	0	0	0	0	—
1928	8	4	.667	3.90	34	6	2	120	117	33	66	0	4	2	3	38	6	0	.158
1929	13	7	.650	3.60	42	19	12	182.1	186	56	80	3	3	2	3	60	7	1	.117
1930	12	10	.545	4.65	32	24	9	187.2	215	38	92	2	2	1	2	70	15	0	.214
1931	11	9	.550	3.00	32	24	12	186	186	29	82	2	1	0	2	60	14	0	.233
1932	5	14	.263	4.92	32	22	7	164.2	199	35	70	1	1	1	2	51	10	0	.196
1933	3	3	.500	4.29	35	1	0	84	89	16	28	0	2	3	3	21	5	0	.238
1934 2 teams			CIN N (2G 0–0)			PHI N (42G 5–9)													
" total	5	9	.357	3.46	44	10	4	140.1	131	24	54	3	2	5	3	43	9	1	.209
1935 PHI N	10	8	.556	3.56	37	18	8	174.2	182	31	89	1	3	1	6	58	14	1	.241
1936	5	7	.417	4.30	39	8	1	111	129	29	48	0	1	4	7	36	9	0	.250
1937	4	10	.286	5.02	32	15	4	138	155	22	46	0	1	2	3	48	7	0	.146
1938	2	7	.222	4.23	22	6	2	83	87	11	21	0	1	3	0	29	1	0	.034
1939	8	8	.500	3.81	22	14	6	111	112	15	37	0	2	0	2	33	5	0	.152
1940	2	2	.500	4.20	17	2	2	40.2	37	5	13	0	2	2	2	8	0	0	.000
19 yrs.	112	117	.489	4.06	542	210	82	2165.2	2290	488	920	13	33	33	43	702	127	4	.181
8 yrs.	52	50	.510	4.05	228	102	43	976.2	1049	222	430	8	13	9	16	312	57	1	.183

WORLD SERIES

	W	L	PCT	ERA	G	GS	CG	IP	H	BB	SO	ShO	W	L	SV	AB	H	HR	BA
1928 STL N	0	0	—	4.50	2	0	0	2	4	1	1	0	0	0	0	0	0	0	—
1930	0	0	—	7.20	2	0	0	5	4	3	4	0	0	0	0	0	0	0	—
1931	0	1	.000	3.00	3	1	0	9	10	1	6	0	0	0	0	2	0	0	.000
3 yrs.	0	1	.000	4.50	7	1	0	16	18	5	11	0	0	0	0	2	0	0	.000

Cowboy Jones

JONES, ALBERT EDWARD (Bronco)   BL TL 5'11" 160 lbs.
B. Aug. 23, 1874, Golden, Colo.   D. Feb. 8, 1958, Inglewood, Calif.

	W	L	PCT	ERA	G	GS	CG	IP	H	BB	SO	ShO	W	L	SV	AB	H	HR	BA
1898 CLE N	4	4	.500	3.00	9	9	7	72	76	29	26	0	0	0	0	28	2	0	.071
1899 STL N	6	5	.545	3.59	12	12	9	85.1	111	22	28	0	0	0	0	29	5	0	.172
1900	13	19	.406	3.54	39	36	29	292.2	334	82	68	3	0	2	0	117	21	0	.179
1901	2	6	.250	4.48	10	9	7	76.1	97	22	25	0	0	0	0	27	4	0	.148
4 yrs.	25	34	.424	3.61	70	66	52	526.1	618	155	147	3	0	2	0	201	32	0	.159
3 yrs.	21	30	.412	3.70	61	57	45	454.1	542	126	121	3	0	2	0	173	30	0	.173

Gordon Jones

JONES, GORDON BASSETT   BR TR 6' 185 lbs.
B. Apr. 2, 1930, Portland, Ore.

	W	L	PCT	ERA	G	GS	CG	IP	H	BB	SO	ShO	W	L	SV	AB	H	HR	BA
1954 STL N	4	4	.500	2.00	11	10	4	81	78	19	48	2	0	0	0	24	3	0	.125
1955	1	4	.200	5.84	15	9	0	57	66	28	46	0	0	1	0	14	1	0	.071
1956	0	2	.000	5.56	5	1	0	11.1	14	5	6	0	0	1	0	2	0	0	.000
1957 NY N	0	1	.000	6.17	10	0	0	11.2	16	3	5	0	0	1	0	2	1	0	.500
1958 SF N	3	1	.750	2.37	11	1	0	30.1	33	5	8	0	2	1	1	7	0	0	.000
1959	3	2	.600	4.33	31	0	0	43.2	45	19	29	0	3	2	2	4	0	0	.000
1960 BAL A	1	1	.500	4.42	29	0	0	55	59	13	30	0	1	1	2	5	2	0	.400
1961	0	0	—	5.40	3	0	0	5	5	0	4	0	0	0	1	0	0	0	—
1962 KC A	3	2	.600	6.34	21	0	0	32.2	31	14	28	0	3	2	6	5	0	0	.000
1964 HOU N	0	1	.000	4.14	34	0	0	50	58	14	28	0	0	0	0	4	1	0	.250
1965	0	0	—	0.00	1	0	0	1	0	0	0	0	0	0	0	0	0	0	—
11 yrs.	15	18	.455	4.16	171	21	4	378.2	405	120	232	2	9	10	12	67	8	0	.119
3 yrs.	5	10	.333	3.74	31	20	4	149.1	158	52	100	2	0	2	0	40	4	0	.100

Sam Jones

JONES, SAMUEL (Toothpick Sam, Sad Sam)   BR TR 6'4" 192 lbs.
B. Dec. 14, 1925, Stewartsville, Ohio   D. Nov. 5, 1971, Morgantown, W. Va.

	W	L	PCT	ERA	G	GS	CG	IP	H	BB	SO	ShO	W	L	SV	AB	H	HR	BA
1951 CLE A	0	1	.000	2.08	2	1	0	8.2	4	5	4	0	0	0	0	2	0	0	.000
1952	2	3	.400	7.25	14	4	0	36	38	37	28	0	1	0	1	10	1	0	.100
1955 CHI N	14	20	.412	4.10	36	34	12	241.2	175	185	198	4	1	1	0	77	14	0	.182
1956	9	14	.391	3.91	33	28	8	188.2	155	115	176	2	1	0	0	57	10	0	.175
1957 STL N	12	9	.571	3.60	28	27	10	182.2	164	71	154	2	1	0	0	63	10	0	.159

	W	L	PCT	ERA	G	GS	CG	IP	H	BB	SO	ShO	Relief Pitching W	L	SV	BATTING AB	H	HR	BA

Sam Jones continued

	W	L	PCT	ERA	G	GS	CG	IP	H	BB	SO	ShO	W	L	SV	AB	H	HR	BA
1958	14	13	.519	2.88	35	35	14	250	204	107	225	2	0	0	0	90	9	0	.100
1959 SF N	21	15	.583	2.83	50	35	16	270.2	232	109	209	4	4	1	4	85	11	0	.129
1960	18	14	.563	3.19	39	35	13	234	200	91	190	3	2	1	0	80	16	0	.200
1961	8	8	.500	4.49	37	17	2	128.1	134	57	105	0	2	1	1	36	5	0	.139
1962 DET A	2	4	.333	3.65	30	6	1	81.1	77	35	73	0	1	1	1	21	2	1	.095
1963 STL N	2	0	1.000	9.00	11	0	0	11	15	5	8	0	2	0	2	1	0	0	.000
1964 BAL A	0	0	–	2.61	7	0	0	10.1	5	5	6	0	0	0	0	0	0	0	–
12 yrs.	102	101	.502	3.59	322	222	76	1643.1	1403	822	1376	17	15	5	9	522	78	1	.149
3 yrs.	28	22	.560	3.33	74	62	24	443.2	383	183	387	4	3	0	2	154	19	0	.123

Al Jurisich

JURISICH, ALVIN JOSEPH
B. Aug. 25, 1921, New Orleans, La.   BR TR 6'2" 193 lbs.

	W	L	PCT	ERA	G	GS	CG	IP	H	BB	SO	ShO	W	L	SV	AB	H	HR	BA
1944 STL N	7	9	.438	3.39	30	14	5	130	102	65	53	2	2	0	1	45	8	0	.178
1945	3	3	.500	5.15	27	6	1	71.2	61	41	42	0	1	1	0	23	2	0	.087
1946 PHI N	4	3	.571	3.69	13	10	2	68.1	71	31	34	1	0	0	1	23	3	0	.130
1947	1	7	.125	4.94	34	12	5	118.1	110	52	48	0	1	2	3	31	1	0	.032
4 yrs.	15	22	.405	4.24	104	42	13	388.1	344	189	177	3	4	3	5	122	14	0	.115
2 yrs.	10	12	.455	4.02	57	20	6	201.2	163	106	95	2	3	1	1	68	10	0	.147

WORLD SERIES
| 1944 STL N | 0 | 0 | – | 27.00 | 1 | 0 | 0 | .2 | 2 | 1 | 0 | 0 | 0 | 0 | 0 | 0 | 0 | 0 | – |

Jim Kaat

KAAT, JAMES LEE
B. Nov. 7, 1938, Zeeland, Mich.   BL TL 6'4½" 205 lbs.

	W	L	PCT	ERA	G	GS	CG	IP	H	BB	SO	ShO	W	L	SV	AB	H	HR	BA
1959 WAS A	0	2	.000	12.60	3	2	0	5	7	4	2	0	0	0	0	1	0	0	.000
1960	1	5	.167	5.58	13	9	0	50	48	31	25	0	0	0	0	14	2	0	.143
1961 MIN A	9	17	.346	3.90	36	29	8	200.2	188	82	122	1	0	1	0	63	15	0	.238
1962	18	14	.563	3.14	39	35	16	269	243	75	173	5	1	0	1	100	18	1	.180
1963	10	10	.500	4.19	31	27	7	178.1	195	38	105	1	0	1	1	61	8	1	.131
1964	17	11	.607	3.22	36	34	13	243	231	60	171	0	0	0	1	83	14	3	.169
1965	18	11	.621	2.83	45	42	7	264.1	267	63	154	2	0	0	2	93	23	1	.247
1966	25	13	.658	2.75	41	41	19	304.2	271	55	205	3	0	0	0	118	23	2	.195
1967	16	13	.552	3.04	42	38	13	263.1	269	42	211	2	0	0	0	99	17	1	.172
1968	14	12	.538	2.94	30	29	9	208	192	40	130	2	0	0	0	77	12	0	.156
1969	14	13	.519	3.49	40	32	10	242.1	252	75	139	0	3	1	1	87	18	2	.207
1970	14	10	.583	3.56	45	34	4	230	244	58	120	1	1	0	0	76	15	1	.197
1971	13	14	.481	3.32	39	38	10	260	275	47	137	4	0	0	0	93	15	0	.161
1972	10	2	.833	2.07	15	15	5	113	94	20	64	0	0	0	0	45	13	2	.289
1973 2 teams					MIN	A	(29G 11–12)		CHI	A	(7G 4–1)								
" total	15	13	.536	4.37	36	35	10	224.1	250	43	109	3	1	0	0	0	0	0	–
1974 CHI A	21	13	.618	2.92	42	39	15	277	263	63	142	3	1	0	0	1	0	0	.000
1975	20	14	.588	3.11	43	41	12	303.2	321	77	142	1	0	0	0	0	0	0	–
1976 PHI N	12	14	.462	3.48	38	35	7	227.2	241	32	83	1	0	1	0	79	14	1	.177
1977	6	11	.353	5.40	35	27	2	160	211	40	55	0	0	0	0	53	10	0	.189
1978	8	5	.615	4.11	26	24	2	140	150	32	48	1	0	0	0	48	7	0	.146
1979 2 teams					PHI	N	(3G 1–0)		NY	A	(40G 2–3)								
" total	3	3	.500	3.95	43	2	0	66	73	19	25	0	3	3	2	1	0	0	.000
1980 2 teams					NY	A	(4G 0–1)		STL	N	(49G 8–7)								
" total	8	8	.500	3.93	53	14	6	135	148	37	37	1	3	3	4	35	5	1	.143
1981 STL N	6	6	.500	3.40	41	1	0	53	60	17	8	0	6	5	4	8	3	0	.375
1982	5	3	.625	4.08	62	2	0	75	79	23	35	0	5	3	2	12	0	0	.000
24 yrs.	283	237	.544	3.45	874	625	180	4493.1	4572	1073	2442	31	24	19	18	1247	232	16	.186
			10th								5th								
3 yrs.	19	16	.543	3.80	152	17	6	258	279	73	79		14	10	10	55	8	1	.145

LEAGUE CHAMPIONSHIP SERIES
1970 MIN A	0	1	.000	9.00	1	1	0	2	6	2	1	0	0	0	0	1	0	0	.000
1976 PHI N	0	0	–	3.00	1	1	0	6	2	2	1	0	0	0	0	2	1	0	.500
2 yrs.	0	1	.000	4.50	2	2	0	8	8	4	2	0	0	0	0	3	1	0	.333

WORLD SERIES
1965 MIN A	1	2	.333	3.77	3	3	1	14.1	18	4	6	0	0	0	0	6	1	0	.167
1982 STL N	0	0	–	3.86	4	0	0	2.1	4	2	2	0	0	0	0	0	0	0	–
2 yrs.	1	2	.333	3.78	7	3	1	16.2	22	4	8	0	0	0	0	6	1	0	.167

Ed Karger

KARGER, EDWIN
B. May 6, 1883, San Angelo, Tex.   D. Sept. 9, 1957, Delta, Colo.   BL TL 5'11" 185 lbs.

	W	L	PCT	ERA	G	GS	CG	IP	H	BB	SO	ShO	W	L	SV	AB	H	HR	BA
1906 2 teams					PIT	N	(6G 2–3)		STL	N	(25G 5–16)								
" total	7	19	.269	2.62	31	22	17	219.2	214	52	81	0	1	4	1	84	18	1	.214
1907 STL N	15	19	.441	2.03	38	31	28	310	251	64	132	6	1	2	1	111	19	2	.171
1908	4	8	.333	3.06	22	15	9	141.1	148	50	34	1	0	0	0	54	13	0	.241
1909 2 teams					CIN	N	(9G 1–3)		BOS	A	(12G 4–2)								
" total	5	5	.500	3.61	21	11	4	102.1	97	52	25	0	1	2	0	35	6	0	.171
1910 BOS A	12	7	.632	3.19	27	25	16	183.1	162	53	81	0	0	0	1	68	20	2	.294
1911	6	8	.429	3.37	25	18	6	131	134	42	57	0	0	0	0	47	11	1	.234
6 yrs.	49	66	.426	2.79	164	122	80	1087.2	1006	313	410	8	3	8	3	399	87	6	.218
3 yrs.	24	43	.358	2.46	85	66	54	643	592	157	239	7	1	4	2	238	49	3	.206

Tony Kaufmann

KAUFMANN, ANTHONY CHARLES
B. Dec. 16, 1900, Chicago, Ill.   D. June 4, 1982, Elgin, Ill.   BR TR 5'11" 165 lbs.

	W	L	PCT	ERA	G	GS	CG	IP	H	BB	SO	ShO	W	L	SV	AB	H	HR	BA
1921 CHI N	1	0	1.000	4.15	2	1	1	13	12	3	6	0	0	0	1	5	2	0	.400
1922	7	13	.350	4.06	37	9	4	153	161	57	45	1	1	6	3	45	9	1	.200
1923	14	10	.583	3.10	33	24	18	206.1	209	67	72	2	1	0	3	74	16	2	.216
1924	16	11	.593	4.02	34	26	16	208.1	218	66	79	3	1	2	0	76	24	1	.316
1925	13	13	.500	4.50	31	23	14	196	221	77	49	2	2	3	2	78	15	2	.192

	W	L	PCT	ERA	G	GS	CG	IP	H	BB	SO	ShO	Relief Pitching W	L	SV	AB	H	HR	BA

Tony Kaufmann continued

	W	L	PCT	ERA	G	GS	CG	IP	H	BB	SO	ShO	W	L	SV	AB	H	HR	BA
1926	9	7	.563	3.02	26	21	14	169.2	169	44	52	1	0	0	2	60	15	1	.250
1927 3 teams					CHI N (9G 3-3)			PHI N (5G 0-3)			STL N (1G 0-0)								
" total	3	6	.333	7.84	15	11	4	72.1	116	28	25	0	0	0	0	23	6	2	.261
1928 STL N	0	0	—	9.64	4	1	0	4.2	8	4	2	0	0	0	0	0	0	0	—
1929 NY N	0	0	—	0.00	1	0	0	0	0	0	0	0	0	0	0	32	1	0	.031
1930 STL N	0	1	.000	7.84	2	1	0	10.1	15	4	2	0	0	0	0	3	1	0	.333
1931	1	1	.500	6.06	15	1	0	49	65	17	13	0	1	1	1	18	2	0	.111
1935	0	0	—	2.45	3	0	0	3.2	4	1	0	0	0	0	0	0	0	0	—
12 yrs.	64	62	.508	4.18	202	118	71	1086.1	1198	368	345	9	6	12	12	414	91	9	.220
5 yrs.	1	2	.333	6.75	25	3	0	68	96	27	17	0	1	1	1	21	3	0	.143

Vic Keen

KEEN, HOWARD VICTOR BR TR 5'9" 165 lbs.
B. Mar. 16, 1899, Belair, Md.   D. Dec. 10, 1976, Salisbury, Md.

	W	L	PCT	ERA	G	GS	CG	IP	H	BB	SO	ShO	W	L	SV	AB	H	HR	BA
1918 PHI A	0	1	.000	3.38	1	1	0	8	9	1	1	0	0	0	0	5	0	0	.000
1921 CHI N	0	3	.000	4.68	5	4	1	25	29	9	9	0	0	0	0	5	0	0	.000
1922	1	2	.333	3.89	7	3	2	34.2	36	10	11	0	0	1	1	12	4	0	.333
1923	12	8	.600	3.00	35	17	10	177	169	57	46	0	3	2	1	53	8	0	.151
1924	15	14	.517	3.80	40	28	15	234.2	242	80	75	0	2	1	3	77	12	0	.156
1925	2	6	.250	6.26	30	8	1	83.1	125	41	19	0	2	1	1	25	6	0	.240
1926 STL N	10	9	.526	4.56	26	21	12	152	179	42	29	1	0	1	0	53	3	0	.057
1927	2	1	.667	4.81	21	0	0	33.2	39	8	12	0	2	1	0	4	1	0	.250
8 yrs.	42	44	.488	4.11	165	82	41	748.1	828	248	202	1	9	7	6	230	34	0	.148
2 yrs.	12	10	.545	4.61	47	21	12	185.2	218	50	41	1	2	2	0	57	4	0	.070

WORLD SERIES
	W	L	PCT	ERA	G	GS	CG	IP	H	BB	SO	ShO	W	L	SV	AB	H	HR	BA
1926 STL N	0	0	—	0.00	1	0	0	1	0	0	0	0	0	0	0	0	0	0	—

Jeff Keener

KEENER, JEFFREY BRUCE BL TR 6' 180 lbs.
B. Jan. 14, 1959, Pana, Ill.

	W	L	PCT	ERA	G	GS	CG	IP	H	BB	SO	ShO	W	L	SV	AB	H	HR	BA
1982 STL N	1	1	.500	1.61	19	0	0	22.1	19	19	25	0	1	1	0	0	0	0	—

Alex Kellner

KELLNER, ALEXANDER RAYMOND BR TL 6' 200 lbs.
Brother of Walt Kellner.
B. Aug. 26, 1924, Tucson, Ariz.

	W	L	PCT	ERA	G	GS	CG	IP	H	BB	SO	ShO	W	L	SV	AB	H	HR	BA
1948 PHI A	0	0	—	7.83	13	1	0	23	21	16	14	0	0	0	0	5	0	0	.000
1949	20	12	.625	3.75	38	27	19	245	243	129	94	0	4	2	1	92	20	0	.217
1950	8	20	.286	5.47	36	29	15	225.1	253	112	85	0	0	1	2	80	16	0	.200
1951	11	14	.440	4.46	33	29	11	209.2	218	93	94	1	0	1	2	79	18	0	.228
1952	12	14	.462	4.36	34	33	14	231.1	223	86	105	2	0	0	0	82	17	1	.207
1953	11	12	.478	3.93	25	25	14	201.2	210	51	81	2	0	0	0	69	15	0	.217
1954	6	17	.261	5.39	27	27	8	173.2	204	88	69	1	0	0	0	55	10	0	.182
1955 KC A	11	8	.579	4.20	30	24	6	162.2	164	60	75	3	0	1	0	56	12	0	.214
1956	4	3	.636	4.32	20	17	5	91.2	103	33	44	0	1	0	0	30	6	0	.200
1957	6	5	.545	4.27	28	21	3	132.2	141	41	72	0	0	0	0	47	11	3	.234
1958 2 teams					KC A (7G 0-2)			CIN N (18G 7-3)											
" total	7	5	.583	3.35	25	13	4	115.2	114	28	64	0	3	0	0	39	11	0	.282
1959 STL N	2	1	.667	3.16	12	4	0	37	31	10	19	0	1	0	0	9	2	0	.222
12 yrs.	101	112	.474	4.41	321	250	99	1849.1	1925	747	816	9	9	5	5	643	138	4	.215
1 yr.	2	1	.667	3.16	12	4	0	37	31	10	19	0	1	0	0	9	2	0	.222

Win Kellum

KELLUM, WINFORD ANSLEY BL TL 5'10" 190 lbs.
B. Apr. 11, 1876, Waterford, Ont., Canada   D. Aug. 10, 1951, Big Rapids, Mich.

	W	L	PCT	ERA	G	GS	CG	IP	H	BB	SO	ShO	W	L	SV	AB	H	HR	BA
1901 BOS A	2	3	.400	6.38	6	6	5	48	61	7	8	0	0	0	0	18	3	0	.167
1904 CIN N	15	10	.600	2.60	31	24	22	224.2	206	46	70	1	2	1	2	82	13	0	.159
1905 STL N	3	3	.500	2.92	11	7	5	74	70	10	19	1	0	1	0	25	5	0	.200
3 yrs.	20	16	.556	3.19	48	37	32	346.2	337	63	97	2	2	2	2	125	21	0	.168
1 yr.	3	3	.500	2.92	11	7	5	74	70	10	19	1	0	1	0	25	5	0	.200

Newt Kimball

KIMBALL, NEWELL W. BR TR 6'2½" 190 lbs.
B. Mar. 27, 1915, Logan, Utah

	W	L	PCT	ERA	G	GS	CG	IP	H	BB	SO	ShO	W	L	SV	AB	H	HR	BA
1937 CHI N	0	0	—	10.80	2	0	0	5	12	1	0	0	0	0	0	1	0	0	.000
1938	0	0	—	9.00	1	0	0	1	3	0	1	0	0	0	0	0	0	0	—
1940 2 teams					BKN N (21G 3-1)			STL N (2G 1-0)											
" total	4	1	.800	3.02	23	1	1	47.2	40	21	27	0	3	1	1	11	2	0	.182
1941 BKN N	3	1	.750	3.63	15	5	1	52	43	29	17	0	1	0	1	14	3	0	.214
1942	2	0	1.000	4.91	14	1	0	29.1	27	19	8	0	1	0	0	5	1	0	.200
1943 2 teams					BKN N (5G 1-1)			PHI N (34G 1-6)											
" total	2	7	.222	3.84	39	6	2	100.2	94	47	35	0	1	4	3	19	3	0	.158
6 yrs.	11	9	.550	3.78	94	13	4	235.2	219	117	88	0	6	5	5	50	9	0	.180
1 yr.	1	0	1.000	2.57	2	1	1	14	11	6	6	0	0	0	0	6	2	0	.333

Hal Kime

KIME, HAROLD LEE (Lefty) BL TL 5'9" 160 lbs.
B. Mar. 15, 1899, West Salem, Ohio   D. May 16, 1939, Columbus, Ohio

	W	L	PCT	ERA	G	GS	CG	IP	H	BB	SO	ShO	W	L	SV	AB	H	HR	BA
1920 STL N	0	0	—	2.57	4	0	0	7	9	2	1	0	0	0	0	1	0	0	.000

Ellis Kinder

KINDER, ELLIS RAYMOND (Old Folks) BR TR 6' 195 lbs.
B. July 26, 1914, Atkins, Ark.   D. Oct. 16, 1968, Jackson, Tenn.

	W	L	PCT	ERA	G	GS	CG	IP	H	BB	SO	ShO	W	L	SV	AB	H	HR	BA
1946 STL A	3	3	.500	3.32	33	7	1	86.2	78	36	59	0	0	0	1	19	1	0	.053
1947	8	15	.348	4.49	34	26	10	194.1	201	82	110	2	0	0	0	62	8	0	.129
1948 BOS A	10	7	.588	3.74	28	22	10	178	183	63	53	1	1	2	0	62	6	0	.097
1949	23	6	.793	3.36	43	30	19	252	251	99	138	6	2	1	4	92	12	0	.130
1950	14	12	.538	4.26	48	23	11	207	212	78	95	1	3	4	9	83	15	1	.183

	W	L	PCT	ERA	G	GS	CG	IP	H	BB	SO	ShO	Relief Pitching W	L	SV	BATTING AB	H	HR	BA

Ellis Kinder continued

	W	L	PCT	ERA	G	GS	CG	IP	H	BB	SO	ShO	W	L	SV	AB	H	HR	BA
1951	11	2	.846	2.55	**63**	2	1	127	108	46	84	0	**10**	1	**14**	34	4	0	.118
1952	5	6	.455	2.58	23	10	4	97.2	85	28	50	0	1	2	4	32	0	0	.000
1953	10	6	.625	1.85	**69**	0	0	107	84	38	39	0	**10**	6	**27**	29	11	0	.379
1954	8	8	.500	3.62	48	2	0	107	106	36	67	0	7	8	15	27	5	0	.185
1955	5	5	.500	2.84	43	0	0	66.2	57	15	31	0	5	5	18	12	3	0	.250
1956 2 teams		STL	N	(22G 2–0)		CHI	A	(29G 3–1)											
" total	5	1	.833	3.09	51	0	0	55.1	56	17	23	0	5	1	9	4	0	0	.000
1957 CHI A	0	0	–	0.00	1	0	0	1	0	1	0	0	0	0	0	0	0	0	–
12 yrs.	102	71	.590	3.43	484	122	56	1479.2	1421	539	749	10	44	30	102	444	63	1	.142
1 yr.	2	0	1.000	3.51	22	0	0	25.2	23	9	4	0	2	0	6	2	0	0	.000

Mike Kircher

KIRCHER, MICHAEL ANDREW
B. Sept. 30, 1897, Rochester, N. Y.   D. June 26, 1972, Rochester, N. Y.   BR TL 6'   180 lbs.

	W	L	PCT	ERA	G	GS	CG	IP	H	BB	SO	ShO	W	L	SV	AB	H	HR	BA
1919 PHI A	0	0	–	7.88	2	0	0	8	15	3	2	0	0	0	0	3	0	0	.000
1920 STL N	2	1	.667	5.40	9	3	1	36.2	50	5	5	0	1	0	0	11	3	0	.273
1921	0	1	.000	8.10	3	0	0	3.1	4	1	2	0	0	1	0	0	0	0	–
3 yrs.	2	2	.500	6.00	14	3	1	48	69	9	9	0	1	1	0	14	3	0	.214
2 yrs.	2	2	.500	5.63	12	3	1	40	54	6	7	0	1	1	0	11	3	0	.273

Bill Kissinger

KISSINGER, WILLIAM FRANCIS (Shang)
B. Aug. 15, 1871, Dayton, Ky.   D. Apr. 20, 1929, Cincinnati, Ohio   BR TR

	W	L	PCT	ERA	G	GS	CG	IP	H	BB	SO	ShO	W	L	SV	AB	H	HR	BA
1895 2 teams		BAL	N	(2G 1–0)		STL	N	(24G 4–12)											
" total	5	12	.294	6.51	26	16	10	152	240	53	34	0	2	2	0	102	25	0	.245
1896 STL N	2	9	.182	6.49	20	12	11	136	209	55	22	0	0	0	1	73	22	0	.301
1897	0	4	.000	11.49	7	4	2	31.1	51	15	5	0	0	0	0	39	13	0	.333
3 yrs.	7	25	.219	6.99	53	32	23	319.1	500	123	61	0	2	2	1	*			
3 yrs.	6	25	.194	7.10	51	30	22	308	482	121	58	0	2	2	1	209	59	0	.282

Nub Kleinke

KLEINKE, NORBERT GEORGE
B. May 19, 1912, Fond du Lac, Wis.   D. Mar. 16, 1950, Off Marin Coast, Calif.   BR TR 6'1"   170 lbs.

	W	L	PCT	ERA	G	GS	CG	IP	H	BB	SO	ShO	W	L	SV	AB	H	HR	BA
1935 STL N	0	0	–	4.97	4	2	0	12.2	19	3	5	0	0	0	0	2	0	0	.000
1937	1	1	.500	4.79	5	2	1	20.2	25	7	9	0	1	0	0	8	0	0	.000
2 yrs.	1	1	.500	4.86	9	4	1	33.1	44	10	14	0	1	0	0	10	0	0	.000
2 yrs.	1	1	.500	4.86	9	4	1	33.1	44	10	14	0	1	0	0	10	0	0	.000

Ron Kline

KLINE, RONALD LEE
B. Mar. 9, 1932, Callery, Pa.   BR TR 6'3"   205 lbs.

	W	L	PCT	ERA	G	GS	CG	IP	H	BB	SO	ShO	W	L	SV	AB	H	HR	BA
1952 PIT N	0	7	.000	5.49	27	11	0	78.2	74	66	27	0	0	1	0	19	0	0	.000
1955	6	13	.316	4.15	36	19	2	136.2	161	53	48	1	2	0	2	38	5	0	.132
1956	14	18	.438	3.38	44	39	9	264	263	81	125	2	0	0	2	79	10	0	.127
1957	9	16	.360	4.04	40	31	11	205	214	61	88	2	0	0	0	66	4	0	.061
1958	13	16	.448	3.53	32	32	11	237.1	220	92	109	2	0	0	0	74	2	0	.027
1959	11	13	.458	4.26	33	29	7	186	186	70	91	0	1	0	0	59	8	0	.136
1960 STL N	4	9	.308	6.04	34	17	1	117.2	133	43	54	0	1	2	1	35	5	0	.143
1961 2 teams		LA	A	(26G 3–6)		DET	A	(10G 5–3)											
" total	8	9	.471	4.14	36	20	3	161	172	61	97	1	1	3	1	49	6	0	.122
1962 DET A	3	6	.333	4.31	36	4	0	77.1	88	28	47	0	3	3	2	16	2	0	.125
1963 WAS A	3	8	.273	2.79	62	1	0	93.2	85	30	49	0	3	8	17	11	1	0	.091
1964	10	7	.588	2.32	61	0	0	81.1	81	21	40	0	10	7	14	6	1	0	.167
1965	7	6	.538	2.63	74	0	0	99.1	106	32	52	0	7	6	**29**	7	0	0	.000
1966	6	4	.600	2.39	63	0	0	90.1	79	17	46	0	6	4	23	6	1	0	.167
1967 MIN A	7	1	.875	3.77	54	0	0	71.2	71	15	36	0	7	1	5	5	0	0	.000
1968 PIT N	12	5	.706	1.68	56	0	0	112.2	94	31	48	0	**12**	5	7	16	0	0	.000
1969 3 teams		PIT	N	(20G 1–3)		SF	N	(7G 0–2)		BOS	A	(16G 0–1)							
" total	1	6	.143	5.19	43	0	0	59	77	28	29	0	1	6	4	5	0	0	.000
1970 ATL N	0	0	–	7.50	5	0	0	6	9	2	3	0	0	0	1	0	0	0	–
17 yrs.	114	144	.442	3.75	736	203	44	2077.2	2113	731	989	8	54	47	108	491	45	0	.092
1 yr.	4	9	.308	6.04	34	17	1	117.2	133	43	54	0	1	2	1	35	5	0	.143

Jack Knight

KNIGHT, ELMER RUSSELL
B. Jan. 12, 1895, Pittsboro, Miss.   D. July 30, 1976, San Antonio, Tex.   BL TR 6'   175 lbs.

	W	L	PCT	ERA	G	GS	CG	IP	H	BB	SO	ShO	W	L	SV	AB	H	HR	BA
1922 STL N	0	0	–	9.00	1	1	0	4	9	3	1	0	0	0	0	2	1	0	.500
1925 PHI A	7	6	.538	6.84	33	11	4	105.1	161	36	19	0	3	3	3	44	9	0	.205
1926	3	12	.200	6.62	35	15	5	142.2	206	48	29	0	1	1	2	56	12	2	.214
1927 BOS N	0	0	–	15.00	3	0	0	3	6	2	0	0	0	0	0	0	0	0	–
4 yrs.	10	18	.357	6.85	72	27	9	255	382	89	49	0	4	3	5	102	22	2	.216
1 yr.	0	0	–	9.00	1	1	0	4	9	3	1	0	0	0	0	2	1	0	.500

Darold Knowles

KNOWLES, DAROLD DUANE
B. Dec. 9, 1941, Brunswick, Mo.   BL TL 6'   180 lbs.

	W	L	PCT	ERA	G	GS	CG	IP	H	BB	SO	ShO	W	L	SV	AB	H	HR	BA
1965 BAL A	0	1	.000	9.20	5	0	0	14.2	14	10	12	0	0	1	0	4	0	0	.000
1966 PHI N	6	5	.545	3.05	69	0	0	100.1	98	46	88	0	6	5	13	16	4	0	.250
1967 WAS A	6	8	.429	2.70	61	1	0	113.1	91	52	85	0	6	7	14	16	1	0	.063
1968	1	1	.500	2.18	32	0	0	41.1	38	12	37	0	1	1	4	4	1	0	.250
1969	9	2	.818	2.24	53	0	0	84.1	73	31	59	0	9	2	13	13	1	0	.077
1970	2	14	.125	2.04	71	0	0	119	100	58	71	0	2	**14**	27	20	1	0	.050
1971 2 teams		WAS	A	(12G 2–2)		OAK	A	(43G 5–2)											
" total	7	4	.636	3.57	55	0	0	68	57	22	56	0	7	4	9	10	1	0	.100
1972 OAK A	5	1	.833	1.36	54	0	0	66	49	37	36	0	5	1	11	12	3	0	.250
1973	6	8	.429	3.09	52	5	1	99	87	49	46	0	4	5	9	0	0	0	–
1974	3	3	.500	4.25	46	1	0	53	61	35	18	0	3	3	5	0	0	0	–
1975 CHI N	6	9	.400	5.83	58	0	0	88	107	36	63	0	6	9	15	15	1	0	.067

	W	L	PCT	ERA	G	GS	CG	IP	H	BB	SO	ShO	Relief Pitching W	L	SV	BATTING AB	H	HR	BA

Darold Knowles continued

	W	L	PCT	ERA	G	GS	CG	IP	H	BB	SO	ShO	W	L	SV	AB	H	HR	BA
1976	5	7	.417	2.88	58	0	0	72	61	22	39	0	5	7	9	7	1	0	.143
1977 TEX A	5	2	.714	3.24	42	0	0	50	50	23	14	0	5	2	4	0	0	0	—
1978 MON N	3	3	.500	2.38	60	0	0	72	63	30	34	0	3	3	6	6	1	0	.167
1979 STL N	2	5	.286	4.04	48	0	0	49	54	17	22	0	2	5	6	2	0	0	.000
1980	0	1	.000	9.00	2	0	0	2	3	0	1	0	0	1	0	0	0	0	—
16 yrs.	66	74	.471	3.12	765	8	1	1092	1006	480	681	1	63	69	143	125	15	0	.120
					10th														
2 yrs.	2	6	.250	4.24	50	0	0	51	57	17	23	0	2	6	6	2	0	0	.000

LEAGUE CHAMPIONSHIP SERIES
| 1971 OAK A | 0 | 0 | — | 0.00 | 1 | 0 | 0 | .1 | 1 | 0 | 0 | 0 | 0 | 0 | 0 | 0 | 0 | 0 | — |

WORLD SERIES
| 1973 OAK A | 0 | 0 | — | 0.00 | 7 | 0 | 0 | 6.1 | 4 | 5 | 5 | 0 | 0 | 0 | 2 | 0 | 0 | 0 | — |

Willis Koenigsmark

KOENIGSMARK, WILLIE THOMAS   BR TR 6'4"   180 lbs.
B. Feb. 27, 1896, Waterloo, Ill.   D. July 1, 1972, Waterloo, Ill.

| 1919 STL N | 0 | 0 | — | ∞ | 1 | 0 | 0 | 2 | 1 | 0 | 0 | 0 | 0 | 0 | 0 | 0 | 0 | 0 | — |

Ed Konetchy

KONETCHY, EDWARD JOSEPH (Big Ed)   BR TR 6'2½"   195 lbs.
Also appeared in box score as Koney
B. Sept. 3, 1885, LaCrosse, Wis.   D. May 27, 1947, Fort Worth, Tex.

1910 STL N	0	0	—	4.50	1	0	0	4	4	1	0	0	0	0	0	520	157	3	.302
1913	1	0	1.000	0.00	1	0	0	4.2	1	4	3	0	1	0	0	502	137	7	.273
1918 BOS N	0	1	.000	6.75	1	1	1	8	14	2	3	0	0	0	0	437	103	2	.236
3 yrs.	1	1	.500	4.32	3	1	1	16.2	19	7	6	0	1	0	0	*			
2 yrs.	1	0	1.000	2.08	2	0	0	8.2	5	5	3	0	1	0	0	3582	1011	36	.282

Jim Konstanty

KONSTANTY, CASIMIR JAMES   BR TR 6'1½"   202 lbs.
B. Mar. 2, 1917, Strykersville, N. Y.   D. June 11, 1976, Oneonta, N. Y.

1944 CIN N	6	4	.600	2.80	20	12	5	112.2	113	33	19	0	2	1	0	34	10	0	.294
1946 BOS N	0	1	.000	5.28	10	1	0	15.1	17	7	9	0	0	0	0	2	0	0	.000
1948 PHI N	1	0	1.000	0.93	6	0	0	9.2	7	2	7	0	1	0	2	3	0	0	.000
1949	9	5	.643	3.25	53	0	0	97	98	29	43	0	9	5	7	17	3	0	.176
1950	16	7	.696	2.66	74	0	0	152	108	50	56	0	16	7	22	37	4	0	.108
1951	4	11	.267	4.05	58	1	0	115.2	127	31	27	0	4	10	9	19	3	0	.158
1952	5	3	.625	3.94	42	2	2	80	87	21	16	1	4	2	6	14	1	0	.071
1953	14	10	.583	4.43	48	19	7	170.2	198	42	45	0	4	3	5	50	11	0	.220
1954 2 teams				PHI N (33G 2–3)				NY A (9G 1–1)											
" total	3	4	.429	3.01	42	1	0	68.2	73	18	14	0	3	4	5	16	0	0	.000
1955 NY A	7	2	.778	2.32	45	0	0	73.2	68	24	19	0	7	2	11	8	1	0	.125
1956 2 teams				NY A (8G 0–0)				STL N (27G 1–1)											
" total	1	1	.500	4.65	35	0	0	50.1	61	12	13	0	1	1	7	2	0	0	.000
11 yrs.	66	48	.579	3.46	433	36	14	945.2	957	269	268	2	51	35	74	202	33	0	.163
1 yr.	1	1	.500	4.58	27	0	0	39.1	46	6	7	0	1	1	5	0	0	0	—

WORLD SERIES
| 1950 PHI N | 0 | 1 | .000 | 2.40 | 3 | 1 | 0 | 15 | 9 | 4 | 3 | 0 | 0 | 0 | 0 | 4 | 1 | 0 | .250 |

Lew Krausse

KRAUSSE, LOUIS BERNARD, JR.   BR TR 6'   175 lbs.
Son of Lew Krausse.
B. Apr. 25, 1943, Media, Pa.

1961 KC A	2	5	.286	4.85	12	8	2	55.2	49	46	32	1	0	0	0	17	2	0	.118
1964	0	2	.000	7.36	5	4	0	14.2	22	9	9	0	0	0	0	2	0	0	.000
1965	2	4	.333	5.04	7	5	0	25	29	8	22	0	0	1	0	7	0	0	.000
1966	14	9	.609	2.99	36	22	4	177.2	144	63	87	1	1	3	3	52	8	0	.154
1967	7	17	.292	4.28	48	19	0	160	140	67	96	0	3	3	6	41	6	1	.146
1968 OAK A	10	11	.476	3.11	36	25	2	185	147	62	105	0	2	1	4	56	9	0	.161
1969	7	7	.500	4.44	43	16	4	140	134	48	85	2	1	3	7	48	8	4	.167
1970 MIL A	13	18	.419	4.75	37	35	8	216	235	67	130	1	0	0	0	65	9	0	.138
1971	8	12	.400	2.95	43	22	1	180	164	62	92	0	1	2	0	44	1	0	.023
1972 BOS A	1	3	.250	6.34	24	7	0	61	74	28	35	0	0	0	1	16	2	0	.125
1973 STL N	0	0	—	0.00	1	0	0	2	2	1	1	0	0	0	0	0	0	0	—
1974 ATL N	4	3	.571	4.16	29	4	0	67	65	32	27	0	3	1	0	6	2	1	.333
12 yrs.	68	91	.428	4.00	321	167	21	1284	1205	493	721	5	11	14	21	354	47	6	.133
1 yr.	0	0	—	0.00	1	0	0	2	2	1	1	0	0	0	0	0	0	0	—

Kurt Krieger

KRIEGER, KURT FERDINAND (Dutch)   BR TR 6'3"   212 lbs.
B. Sept. 16, 1926, Traisen, Austria   D. Aug. 16, 1970, St. Louis, Mo.

1949 STL N	0	0	—	0.00	1	0	0	1	0	1	0	0	0	0	0	0	0	0	—
1951	0	0	—	15.75	2	0	0	4	6	5	3	0	0	0	0	0	0	0	—
2 yrs.	0	0	—	12.60	3	0	0	5	6	6	3	0	0	0	0	0	0	0	—
2 yrs.	0	0	—	12.60	3	0	0	5	6	6	3	0	0	0	0	0	0	0	—

Howie Krist

KRIST, HOWARD WILBUR (Spud)   BL TR 6'1"   175 lbs.
B. Feb. 28, 1916, West Henrietta, N. Y.

1937 STL N	3	1	.750	4.23	6	4	1	27.2	34	10	6	0	1	0	0	9	0	0	.000
1938	0	0	—	0.00	2	0	0	1.1	1	0	1	0	0	0	0	0	0	0	—
1941	10	0	1.000	4.03	37	8	2	114	107	35	36	0	6	0	2	38	9	0	.237
1942	13	3	.813	2.51	34	8	3	118.1	103	43	47	0	8	2	1	42	6	0	.143
1943	11	5	.688	2.90	34	17	9	164.1	141	62	57	3	2	1	3	60	10	0	.167
1946	0	2	.000	6.75	15	0	0	18.2	22	8	3	0	0	2	0	0	0	0	—
6 yrs.	37	11	.771	3.32	128	37	15	444.1	408	158	150	3	17	5	6	149	25	0	.168
6 yrs.	37	11	.771	3.32	128	37	15	444.1	408	158	150	3	17	5	6	149	25	0	.168
												10th							

WORLD SERIES
| 1943 STL N | 0 | 0 | — | 0.00 | 1 | 0 | 0 | 1 | 1 | 0 | 0 | 0 | 0 | 0 | 0 | 0 | 0 | 0 | — |

	W	L	PCT	ERA	G	GS	CG	IP	H	BB	SO	ShO	Relief Pitching W	L	SV	BATTING AB	H	HR	BA

Ryan Kurosaki

KUROSAKI, RYAN YOSHITOMO
B. July 3, 1952, Honolulu, Hawaii

BR TR 5'10" 160 lbs.

	W	L	PCT	ERA	G	GS	CG	IP	H	BB	SO	ShO	W	L	SV	AB	H	HR	BA
1975 STL N	0	0	–	7.62	7	0	0	13	15	7	6	0	0	0	0	1	0	0	.000

Bob Kuzava

KUZAVA, ROBERT LeROY (Sarge)
B. May 28, 1923, Wyandotte, Mich.

BB TL 6'2" 202 lbs.
BR 1946

	W	L	PCT	ERA	G	GS	CG	IP	H	BB	SO	ShO	W	L	SV	AB	H	HR	BA
1946 CLE A	1	0	1.000	3.00	2	2	0	12	9	11	4	0	0	0	0	5	1	0	.200
1947	1	1	.500	4.15	4	4	1	21.2	22	9	9	1	0	0	0	9	1	0	.111
1949 CHI A	10	6	.625	4.02	29	18	9	156.2	139	91	83	1	2	0	0	56	2	0	.036
1950 2 teams			CHI	A	(10G 1–3)		WAS	A	(22G 8–7)										
" total	9	10	.474	4.33	32	29	9	199.1	199	102	105	1	0	0	0	62	6	1	.097
1951 2 teams			WAS	A	(8G 3–3)		NY	A	(23G 8–4)										
" total	11	7	.611	3.61	31	16	7	134.2	133	55	72	1	5	1	5	39	6	0	.154
1952 NY A	8	8	.500	3.45	28	12	6	133	115	63	67	1	3	2	3	43	4	0	.093
1953	6	5	.545	3.31	33	6	2	92.1	92	34	48	2	4	1	4	21	1	0	.048
1954 2 teams			NY	A	(20G 1–3)		BAL	A	(4G 1–3)										
" total	2	6	.250	4.97	24	7	0	63.1	76	29	37	0	1	1	1	13	0	0	.000
1955 2 teams			BAL	A	(6G 0–1)		PHI	N	(17G 1–0)										
" total	1	1	.500	6.25	23	5	0	44.2	57	16	18	0	0	0	0	8	1	0	.125
1957 2 teams			PIT	N	(4G 0–0)		STL	N	(3G 0–0)										
" total	0	0	–	6.23	7	0	0	4.1	7	5	3	0	0	0	0	0	0	0	–
10 yrs.	49	44	.527	4.05	213	99	34	862	849	415	446	7	15	5	13	256	22	1	.086
1 yr.	0	0	–	3.86	3	0	0	2.1	4	2	2	0	0	0	0	0	0	0	–

WORLD SERIES

	W	L	PCT	ERA	G	GS	CG	IP	H	BB	SO	ShO	W	L	SV	AB	H	HR	BA
1951 NY A	0	0	–	0.00	1	0	0	1	0	0	0	0	0	0	1	0	0	0	–
1952	0	0	–	0.00	1	0	0	2.2	0	0	2	0	0	0	1	1	0	0	.000
1953	0	0	–	13.50	1	0	0	.2	2	0	1	0	0	0	0	1	0	0	.000
3 yrs.	0	0	–	2.08	3	0	0	4.1	2	0	3	0	0	0	2	2	0	0	.000

Lerrin LaGrow

LaGROW, LERRIN HARRIS
B. July 8, 1948, Phoenix, Ariz.

BR TR 6'5" 220 lbs.

	W	L	PCT	ERA	G	GS	CG	IP	H	BB	SO	ShO	W	L	SV	AB	H	HR	BA
1970 DET A	0	1	.000	7.50	10	0	0	12	16	6	7	0	0	1	0	1	0	0	.000
1972	0	1	.000	1.33	16	0	0	27	22	6	9	0	0	1	2	1	0	0	–
1973	1	5	.167	4.33	21	3	0	54	54	23	33	0	0	3	3	0	0	0	–
1974	8	19	.296	4.67	37	34	11	216	245	80	85	0	0	0	0	0	0	0	–
1975	7	14	.333	4.38	32	26	7	164.1	183	66	75	2	0	0	0	0	0	0	–
1976 STL N	0	1	.000	1.48	8	2	1	24.1	21	7	10	0	0	0	0	5	0	0	.000
1977 CHI A	7	3	.700	2.45	66	0	0	99	81	35	63	0	7	3	25	0	0	0	–
1978	6	5	.545	4.40	42	0	0	88	85	38	41	0	6	5	16	0	0	0	–
1979 2 teams			CHI	A	(11G 0–3)		LA	N	(31G 5–1)										
" total	5	4	.556	5.24	42	2	0	55	65	34	31	0	5	2	5	3	1	0	.333
1980 PHI N	2	2	.000	4.15	25	0	0	39	42	17	21	0	0	2	3	4	1	0	.250
10 yrs.	34	55	.382	4.11	309	67	19	778.2	814	312	375	2	18	17	54	13	2	0	.154
1 yr.	0	1	.000	1.48	8	2	1	24.1	21	7	10	0	0	0	0	5	0	0	.000

LEAGUE CHAMPIONSHIP SERIES

	W	L	PCT	ERA	G	GS	CG	IP	H	BB	SO	ShO	W	L	SV	AB	H	HR	BA
1972 DET A	0	0	–	0.00	1	0	0	1	0	0	1	0	0	0	0	0	0	0	–

Jeff Lahti

LAHTI, JEFFREY ALLEN
B. Oct. 8, 1956, Oregon City, Ore.

BR TR 6' 180 lbs.

	W	L	PCT	ERA	G	GS	CG	IP	H	BB	SO	ShO	W	L	SV	AB	H	HR	BA
1982 STL N	5	4	.556	3.81	33	1	0	56.2	53	21	22	0	5	3	0	13	1	0	.077

WORLD SERIES

	W	L	PCT	ERA	G	GS	CG	IP	H	BB	SO	ShO	W	L	SV	AB	H	HR	BA
1982 STL N	0	0	–	10.80	2	0	0	1.2	4	1	1	0	0	0	0	0	0	0	–

Eddie Lake

LAKE, EDWARD ERVING
B. Mar. 18, 1916, Antioch, Calif.

BR TR 5'7" 159 lbs.

	W	L	PCT	ERA	G	GS	CG	IP	H	BB	SO	ShO	W	L	SV	AB	H	HR	BA
1944 BOS A	0	0	–	4.19	6	0	0	19.1	20	11	7	0	0	0	0	*			

Jack Lamabe

LAMABE, JOHN ALEXANDER
B. Oct. 3, 1936, Farmingdale, N. Y.

BR TR 6'1" 198 lbs.

	W	L	PCT	ERA	G	GS	CG	IP	H	BB	SO	ShO	W	L	SV	AB	H	HR	BA
1962 PIT N	3	1	.750	2.88	46	0	0	78	70	40	56	0	3	1	2	9	0	0	.000
1963 BOS A	7	4	.636	3.15	65	2	0	151.1	139	46	93	0	7	3	6	32	3	1	.094
1964	9	13	.409	5.89	39	26	3	177.1	235	57	109	0	1	2	1	52	6	0	.115
1965 2 teams			BOS	A	(14G 0–3)		HOU	N	(3G 0–2)										
" total	0	5	.000	6.87	17	2	0	38	51	17	23	0	0	0	0	8	1	0	.125
1966 CHI A	7	9	.438	3.93	34	17	3	121.1	116	35	67	2	2	0	0	35	2	0	.057
1967 3 teams			CHI	A	(3G 1–0)		NY	N	(16G 0–3)		STL	N	(23G 3–4)						
" total	4	7	.364	3.20	42	3	1	84.1	74	19	56	1	3	5	5	15	2	0	.133
1968 CHI N	3	2	.600	4.30	42	0	0	60.2	68	24	30	0	3	2	1	5	1	0	.200
7 yrs.	33	41	.446	4.24	285	49	7	711	753	238	434	3	19	16	15	156	15	1	.096
1 yr.	3	4	.429	2.83	23	1	1	47.2	43	10	30	1	2	4	4	10	2	0	.200

WORLD SERIES

	W	L	PCT	ERA	G	GS	CG	IP	H	BB	SO	ShO	W	L	SV	AB	H	HR	BA
1967 STL N	0	1	.000	6.75	3	0	0	2.2	5	0	4	0	0	1	0	0	0	0	–

	W	L	PCT	ERA	G	GS	CG	IP	H	BB	SO	ShO	Relief Pitching W	L	SV	BATTING AB	H	HR	BA

Fred Lamline

LAMLINE, FREDERICK ARTHUR (Dutch)
B. Aug. 14, 1891, Port Huron, Mich.   D. Sept. 20, 1970, Port Huron, Mich.
BR TR 5'11" 171 lbs.

	W	L	PCT	ERA	G	GS	CG	IP	H	BB	SO	ShO	W	L	SV	AB	H	HR	BA
1912 CHI A	0	0	—	31.50	1	0	0	2	7	2	1	0	0	0	0	0	0	0	—
1915 STL N	0	0	—	2.84	4	0	0	19	21	3	11	0	0	0	0	8	1	0	.125
2 yrs.	0	0	—	5.57	5	0	0	21	28	5	12	0	0	0	0	8	1	0	.125
1 yr.	0	0	—	2.84	4	0	0	19	21	3	11	0	0	0	0	8	1	0	.125

Max Lanier

LANIER, HUBERT MAX
Father of Hal Lanier.
B. Aug. 18, 1915, Denton, N. C.
BR TL 5'11" 180 lbs.

	W	L	PCT	ERA	G	GS	CG	IP	H	BB	SO	ShO	W	L	SV	AB	H	HR	BA
1938 STL N	0	3	.000	4.20	18	3	1	45	57	28	14	0	0	2	0	10	1	0	.100
1939	2	1	.667	2.39	7	6	2	37.2	29	13	14	0	0	0	0	14	4	0	.286
1940	9	6	.600	3.34	35	11	4	105	113	38	49	2	5	3	3	30	6	0	.200
1941	10	8	.556	2.82	35	18	8	153	126	59	93	2	2	3	3	52	10	0	.192
1942	13	8	.619	2.98	34	20	8	160	137	60	93	2	5	0	2	47	12	0	.255
1943	15	7	.682	1.90	32	25	14	213.1	195	75	123	2	2	0	3	73	12	0	.164
1944	17	12	.586	2.65	33	30	16	224.1	192	71	141	5	3	0	0	77	14	0	.182
1945	2	2	.500	1.73	4	3	3	26	22	8	16	0	0	1	0	11	2	0	.182
1946	6	0	1.000	1.93	6	6	6	56	45	19	36	2	0	0	0	25	5	0	.200
1949	5	4	.556	3.82	15	15	4	92	92	35	37	1	0	0	0	27	2	0	.074
1950	11	9	.550	3.13	27	27	10	181.1	173	68	89	2	0	0	0	68	11	0	.162
1951	11	9	.550	3.26	31	23	9	160	149	50	59	2	1	0	1	53	8	0	.151
1952 NY N	7	12	.368	3.94	37	16	6	137	124	65	47	1	2	3	5	41	11	0	.268
1953 2 teams	NY N (3G 0–0)				STL A (10G 0–1)														
" total	0	1	.000	7.16	13	1	0	27.2	36	22	10	0	0	0	0	7	1	0	.143
14 yrs.	108	82	.568	3.01	327	204	91	1618.1	1490	611	821	21	20	12	17	535	99	0	.185
12 yrs.	101	69	.594	2.84	277	187	85	1453.2	1330	524	764	20	18	9	12	487	87	0	.179
			10th					9th			7th								9th 7th 9th

WORLD SERIES																			
1942 STL N	1	0	1.000	0.00	2	0	0	4	3	1	1	0	1	0	0	1	1	0	1.000
1943	0	1	.000	1.76	3	2	0	15.1	13	3	13	0	0	0	0	4	1	0	.250
1944	1	0	1.000	2.19	2	2	0	12.1	8	8	11	0	0	0	0	4	2	0	.500
3 yrs.	2	1	.667	1.71	7	4	0	31.2	24	12	25	0	1	0	0	9	4	0	.444

Paul LaPalme

LaPALME, PAUL EDMORE (Lefty)
B. Dec. 14, 1923, Springfield, Mass.
BL TL 5'10" 175 lbs.

	W	L	PCT	ERA	G	GS	CG	IP	H	BB	SO	ShO	W	L	SV	AB	H	HR	BA
1951 PIT N	1	5	.167	6.29	22	8	1	54.1	79	31	24	1	0	2	0	10	1	0	.100
1952	1	2	.333	3.92	31	2	0	59.2	56	37	25	0	1	2	0	10	1	0	.100
1953	8	16	.333	4.59	35	24	7	176.1	191	64	86	1	1	1	2	59	5	0	.085
1954	4	10	.286	5.52	33	15	2	120.2	147	54	57	0	1	1	0	35	5	0	.143
1955 STL N	4	3	.571	2.75	56	0	0	91.2	76	34	39	0	4	3	3	19	4	0	.211
1956 3 teams	STL N (1G 0–0)			CIN N (11G 2–4)			CHI A (29G 3–1)												
" total	5	5	.500	3.93	41	2	0	73.1	61	33	27	0	4	4	2	10	2	0	.200
1957 CHI A	1	4	.200	3.35	35	0	0	40.1	35	19	19	0	1	4	7	4	2	0	.500
7 yrs.	24	45	.348	4.42	253	51	10	616.1	645	272	277	2	12	17	14	147	20	0	.136
2 yrs.	4	3	.571	3.31	57	0	0	92.1	80	36	39	0	4	3	3	19	4	0	.211

Dave LaPoint

LaPOINT, DAVID JEFFREY
B. July 29, 1959, Glens Falls, N. Y.
BL TL 6'3" 205 lbs.

	W	L	PCT	ERA	G	GS	CG	IP	H	BB	SO	ShO	W	L	SV	AB	H	HR	BA
1980 MIL A	1	0	1.000	6.00	5	3	0	15	17	13	5	0	1	0	1	0	0	0	—
1981 STL N	1	0	1.000	4.09	3	2	0	11	12	2	4	0	0	0	0	5	0	0	.000
1982	9	3	.750	3.42	42	21	0	152.2	170	52	81	0	1	0	0	38	2	0	.053
3 yrs.	11	3	.786	3.68	50	26	0	178.2	199	67	90	0	2	0	1	43	2	0	.047
2 yrs.	10	3	.769	3.46	45	23	0	163.2	182	54	85	0	1	0	0	43	2	0	.047

WORLD SERIES																			
1982 STL N	0	0	—	3.24	2	1	0	8.1	10	2	3	0	0	0	0	0	0	0	—

Brooks Lawrence

LAWRENCE, ULYSSES BROOKS (Bull)
B. Jan. 30, 1925, Springfield, Ohio
BR TR 6' 205 lbs.

	W	L	PCT	ERA	G	GS	CG	IP	H	BB	SO	ShO	W	L	SV	AB	H	HR	BA
1954 STL N	15	6	.714	3.74	35	18	8	158.2	141	72	72	0	6	4	1	53	10	0	.189
1955	3	8	.273	6.56	46	10	2	96	102	58	52	1	1	3	1	21	2	0	.095
1956 CIN N	19	10	.655	3.99	49	30	11	218.2	210	71	96	1	6	1	0	70	11	0	.157
1957	16	13	.552	3.52	49	32	12	250.1	234	76	121	1	1	2	4	82	14	0	.171
1958	8	13	.381	4.13	46	23	6	181	194	55	74	2	2	5	5	53	6	0	.113
1959	7	12	.368	4.77	43	14	3	128.1	144	45	64	0	4	5	10	40	6	0	.150
1960	1	0	1.000	10.57	7	0	0	7.2	9	8	2	0	1	0	1	0	0	0	—
7 yrs.	69	62	.527	4.25	275	127	42	1040.2	1034	385	481	5	21	20	22	319	49	0	.154
2 yrs.	18	14	.563	4.81	81	28	10	254.2	243	130	124	1	7	7	2	74	12	0	.162

Barry Lersch

LERSCH, BARRY LEE
B. Sept. 7, 1944, Denver, Colo.
BR TR 6' 175 lbs.

	W	L	PCT	ERA	G	GS	CG	IP	H	BB	SO	ShO	W	L	SV	AB	H	HR	BA
1969 PHI N	0	3	.000	7.00	10	0	0	18	20	10	13	0	0	3	2	3	0	0	.000
1970	6	3	.667	3.26	42	11	3	138	119	47	92	0	2	0	3	31	2	0	.065
1971	5	14	.263	3.79	38	30	3	214	203	50	113	0	0	0	0	59	10	0	.169
1972	4	6	.400	3.04	36	8	3	100.2	86	33	48	1	0	2	0	23	0	0	.000
1973	3	6	.333	4.39	42	4	0	98.1	105	27	51	0	3	4	1	17	3	0	.176
1974 STL N	0	0	—	54.00	1	0	0	1	3	5	0	0	0	0	0	0	0	0	—
6 yrs.	18	32	.360	3.82	169	53	9	570	536	172	317	1	5	9	6	133	15	0	.113
1 yr.	0	0	—	54.00	1	0	0	1	3	5	0	0	0	0	0	0	0	0	—

	W	L	PCT	ERA	G	GS	CG	IP	H	BB	SO	ShO	Relief Pitching W	L	SV	BATTING AB	H	HR	BA

Dan Lewandowski

LEWANDOWSKI, DANIEL WILLIAM　　　　BR TR 6'　180 lbs.
B. Jan. 6, 1928, Buffalo, N. Y.

	W	L	PCT	ERA	G	GS	CG	IP	H	BB	SO	ShO	W	L	SV	AB	H	HR	BA
1951 STL N	0	1	.000	9.00	2	0	1	1	1	1	1	0	0	1	0	0	0	0	—

Don Liddle

LIDDLE, DONALD EUGENE　　　　BL TL 5'10"　165 lbs.
B. May 25, 1925, Mt. Carmel, Ill.

	W	L	PCT	ERA	G	GS	CG	IP	H	BB	SO	ShO	W	L	SV	AB	H	HR	BA
1953 MIL N	7	6	.538	3.08	31	15	4	128.2	119	55	63	0	3	1	2	34	3	0	.088
1954 NY N	9	4	.692	3.06	28	19	4	126.2	100	55	44	3	1	1	0	37	7	0	.189
1955	10	4	.714	4.23	33	13	4	106.1	97	61	56	0	4	1	1	27	5	0	.185
1956 2 teams			.333	5.59	NY N (11G 1–2)		STL N (14G 1–2)												
" total	2	4	.333	5.59	25	7	1	66	81	32	35	0	1	0	1	14	2	0	.143
4 yrs.	28	18	.609	3.75	117	54	13	427.2	397	203	198	3	9	3	4	112	17	0	.152
1 yr.	1	2	.333	8.39	14	2	0	24.2	36	18	14	0	1	0	0	2	0	0	.000
WORLD SERIES																			
1954 NY N	1	0	1.000	1.29	2	1	0	7	5	1	2	0	0	0	0	3	0	0	.000

Gene Lillard

LILLARD, ROBERT EUGENE　　　　BR TR 5'10½" 178 lbs.
Brother of Bill Lillard.
B. Nov. 12, 1913, Santa Barbara, Calif.

	W	L	PCT	ERA	G	GS	CG	IP	H	BB	SO	ShO	W	L	SV	AB	H	HR	BA
1939 CHI N	3	5	.375	6.55	20	7	2	55	68	36	31	0	1	1	0	10	1	0	.100
1940 STL N	0	1	.000	13.50	2	1	0	4.2	8	4	2	0	0	1	0	0	0	0	—
2 yrs.	3	6	.333	7.09	22	8	2	59.2	76	40	33	0	1	2	0	44	8	0	.182
1 yr.	0	1	.000	13.50	2	1	0	4.2	8	4	2	0	0	1	0	0	0	0	—

Johnny Lindell

LINDELL, JOHN HARLAN　　　　BR TR 6'4½"　217 lbs.
B. Aug. 30, 1916, Greeley, Colo.

	W	L	PCT	ERA	G	GS	CG	IP	H	BB	SO	ShO	W	L	SV	AB	H	HR	BA
1942 NY A	2	1	.667	3.76	23	2	0	52.2	52	22	28	0	2	0	1	24	6	0	.250
1953 2 teams					PIT N (27G 5–16)		PHI N (5G 1–1)												
" total	6	17	.261	4.66	32	26	15	199	195	139	118	1	1	0	0	109	33	4	.303
2 yrs.	8	18	.308	4.47	55	28	15	251.2	247	161	146	1	3	0	1	*			

Jim Lindsey

LINDSEY, JAMES KENDRICK　　　　BR TR 6'1"　175 lbs.
B. Jan. 24, 1898, Greensburg, La.　D. Oct. 25, 1963, Jackson, La.

	W	L	PCT	ERA	G	GS	CG	IP	H	BB	SO	ShO	W	L	SV	AB	H	HR	BA
1922 CLE A	4	5	.444	6.02	29	5	0	83.2	105	24	29	0	4	2	1	24	4	0	.167
1924	0	0	—	21.00	3	0	0	3	8	3	0	0	0	0	0	0	0	0	—
1929 STL N	1	1	.500	5.51	2	2	1	16.1	20	2	8	0	0	0	0	5	1	0	.200
1930	7	5	.583	4.43	39	6	3	105.2	131	46	50	0	4	2	5	28	8	0	.286
1931	6	4	.600	2.77	35	2	1	74.2	77	45	32	1	5	4	7	9	1	0	.111
1932	3	3	.500	4.94	33	5	0	89.1	96	38	31	0	3	3	3	21	3	0	.143
1933	0	0	—	4.50	1	0	0	2	2	1	1	0	0	0	0	0	0	0	—
1934 2 teams					CIN N (4G 0–0)		STL N (11G 0–1)												
" total	0	1	.000	6.00	15	0	0	18	25	5	9	0	0	1	1	1	0	0	.000
1937 BKN N	0	1	.000	3.52	20	0	0	38.1	43	12	15	0	0	1	2	6	1	0	.167
9 yrs.	21	20	.512	4.70	177	20	5	431	507	176	175	1	16	12	19	94	18	0	.191
6 yrs.	17	14	.548	4.32	121	15	5	302	347	135	129	1	12	9	16	64	13	0	.203
WORLD SERIES																			
1930 STL N	0	0	—	1.93	2	0	0	4.2	1	1	2	0	0	0	0	1	1	0	1.000
1931	0	0	—	5.40	2	0	0	3.1	4	3	2	0	0	0	0	0	0	0	—
2 yrs.	0	0	—	3.38	4	0	0	8	5	4	4	0	0	0	0	1	1	0	1.000

Royce Lint

LINT, ROYCE JAMES　　　　BL TL 6'1"　165 lbs.
B. Jan. 1, 1921, Birmingham, Ala.

	W	L	PCT	ERA	G	GS	CG	IP	H	BB	SO	ShO	W	L	SV	AB	H	HR	BA
1954 STL N	2	3	.400	4.86	30	4	1	70.1	75	30	36	1	1	3	0	10	1	0	.100

Frank Linzy

LINZY, FRANK ALFRED　　　　BR TR 6'1"　190 lbs.
B. Sept. 15, 1940, Fort Gibson, Okla.

	W	L	PCT	ERA	G	GS	CG	IP	H	BB	SO	ShO	W	L	SV	AB	H	HR	BA
1963 SF N	0	0	—	4.86	8	1	0	16.2	22	10	14	0	0	0	0	3	0	0	.000
1965	9	3	.750	1.43	57	0	0	81.2	76	23	35	0	9	3	21	18	4	1	.222
1966	7	11	.389	2.96	51	0	0	100.1	107	34	57	0	7	11	16	20	3	0	.150
1967	7	7	.500	1.51	57	0	0	95.2	67	34	38	0	7	7	17	15	0	0	.000
1968	9	8	.529	2.08	57	0	0	95.1	76	27	36	0	9	8	12	11	0	0	.000
1969	14	9	.609	3.65	58	0	0	116	129	38	62	0	14	9	11	30	8	0	.267
1970 2 teams					SF N (20G 2–1)		STL N (47G 3–5)												
" total	5	6	.455	4.66	67	0	0	87	99	34	35	0	5	6	3	11	0	0	.000
1971 STL N	4	3	.571	2.14	58	0	0	59	49	27	24	0	4	3	6	4	2	0	.500
1972 MIL A	2	2	.500	3.04	47	0	0	77	70	27	24	0	2	2	12	9	1	0	.111
1973	2	6	.250	3.57	42	0	0	63	68	21	21	0	2	6	13	0	0	0	—
1974 PHI N	3	2	.600	3.24	22	0	0	25	27	7	12	0	3	2	0	0	0	0	—
11 yrs.	62	57	.521	2.85	516	2	0	816.2	790	282	358	0	62	57	111	121	18	1	.149
2 yrs.	7	8	.467	2.92	97	0	0	120.1	115	50	43	0	7	8	8	11	2	0	.182

Mark Littell

LITTELL, MARK ALAN　　　　BL TR 6'3"　210 lbs.
B. Jan. 17, 1953, Gideon, Mo.

	W	L	PCT	ERA	G	GS	CG	IP	H	BB	SO	ShO	W	L	SV	AB	H	HR	BA
1973 KC A	1	3	.250	5.68	8	7	1	38	44	23	16	0	0	0	0	0	0	0	—
1975	1	2	.333	3.70	7	3	1	24.1	19	15	19	0	1	0	0	0	0	0	—
1976	8	4	.667	2.08	60	1	0	104	68	60	92	0	8	3	16	1	0	0	.000
1977	8	4	.667	3.60	48	5	0	105	73	55	106	0	6	4	12	1	0	0	.000
1978 STL N	4	8	.333	2.80	72	2	0	106	80	59	130	0	4	8	11	7	0	0	.000
1979	9	4	.692	2.20	63	0	0	82	60	39	67	0	9	4	13	14	0	0	.000
1980	0	2	.000	9.00	14	0	0	11	14	7	7	0	0	2	0	2	0	0	.000
1981	1	3	.250	4.39	28	1	0	41	36	31	22	0	1	2	5	8	2	0	.250
1982	0	1	.000	5.23	16	0	0	20.2	22	15	7	0	0	1	0	0	0	0	.000

	W	L	PCT	ERA	G	GS	CG	IP	H	BB	SO	ShO	Relief Pitching W	L	SV	BATTING AB	H	HR	BA

Mark Littell continued

	W	L	PCT	ERA	G	GS	CG	IP	H	BB	SO	ShO	W	L	SV	AB	H	HR	BA
9 yrs.	32	31	.508	3.32	316	19	2	532	416	304	466	0	29	24	56	34	2	0	.059
5 yrs.	14	18	.438	3.31	193	3	0	260.2	212	151	233	0	14	17	28	32	2	0	.063
															8th				

LEAGUE CHAMPIONSHIP SERIES

	W	L	PCT	ERA	G	GS	CG	IP	H	BB	SO	ShO	W	L	SV	AB	H	HR	BA
1976 KC A	0	1	.000	1.93	3	0	0	4.2	4	1	3	0	0	1	0	0	0	0	—
1977	0	0	—	3.00	2	0	0	3	5	3	1	0	0	0	0	0	0	0	—
2 yrs.	0	1	.000	2.35	5	0	0	7.2	9	4	4	0	0	1	0	0	0	0	—

Jeff Little

LITTLE, DONALD JEFFREY
B. Dec. 25, 1954, Fremont, Ohio   BR TL 6'6"   220 lbs.

	W	L	PCT	ERA	G	GS	CG	IP	H	BB	SO	ShO	W	L	SV	AB	H	HR	BA
1980 STL N	1	1	.500	3.79	7	2	0	19	18	9	17	0	0	0	0	6	1	0	.167
1982 MIN A	2	0	1.000	4.21	33	0	0	36.1	33	27	26	0	2	0	0	0	0	0	—
2 yrs.	3	1	.750	4.07	40	2	0	55.1	51	36	43	0	2	0	0	6	1	0	.167
1 yr.	1	1	.500	3.79	7	2	0	19	18	9	17	0	0	0	0	6	1	0	.167

Dick Littlefield

LITTLEFIELD, RICHARD BERNARD
B. Mar. 18, 1926, Detroit, Mich.   BL TL 6'   180 lbs.

	W	L	PCT	ERA	G	GS	CG	IP	H	BB	SO	ShO	W	L	SV	AB	H	HR	BA
1950 BOS A	2	2	.500	9.26	15	2	0	23.1	27	24	13	0	2	0	1	4	0	0	.000
1951 CHI A	1	1	.500	8.38	4	2	0	9.2	9	17	7	0	1	0	0	1	0	0	.000
1952 2 teams	DET A (28G 0–3)	STL A (7G 2–3)																	
" total	2	6	.250	3.54	35	6	3	94	81	42	66	0	1	3	1	23	2	0	.087
1953 STL A	7	12	.368	5.08	36	22	2	152.1	153	84	104	0	2	1	0	42	8	0	.190
1954 2 teams	BAL A (3G 0–0)	PIT N (23G 10–11)																	
" total	10	11	.476	3.86	26	21	7	161	148	91	97	1	1	0	0	50	8	0	.160
1955 PIT N	5	12	.294	5.12	35	17	4	130	148	68	70	1	1	3	0	34	6	0	.176
1956 3 teams	PIT N (6G 0–0)	STL N (3G 0–2)	NY N (31G 4–4)																
" total	4	6	.400	4.37	40	11	0	119.1	101	49	80	0	1	2	2	28	2	0	.071
1957 CHI N	2	3	.400	5.35	48	2	0	65.2	76	37	51	0	2	1	4	11	2	0	.182
1958 MIL N	0	1	.000	4.26	4	0	0	6.1	7	1	7	0	0	1	0	0	0	0	—
9 yrs.	33	54	.379	4.71	243	83	16	761.2	750	413	495	2	11	11	9	193	28	0	.145
1 yr.	0	2	.000	7.45	3	2	0	9.2	9	4	5	0	0	0	0	2	0	0	.000

John Littlefield

LITTLEFIELD, JOHN ANDREW
B. Jan. 5, 1954, Covina, Calif.   BR TR 6'2"   200 lbs.

	W	L	PCT	ERA	G	GS	CG	IP	H	BB	SO	ShO	W	L	SV	AB	H	HR	BA
1980 STL N	5	5	.500	3.14	52	0	0	66	71	20	22	0	5	5	9	11	0	0	.000
1981 SD N	2	3	.400	3.66	42	0	0	64	53	28	21	0	2	3	2	1	0	0	.000
2 yrs.	7	8	.467	3.39	94	0	0	130	124	48	43	0	7	8	11	12	0	0	.000
1 yr.	5	5	.500	3.14	52	0	0	66	71	20	22	0	5	5	9	11	0	0	.000

Carlisle Littlejohn

LITTLEJOHN, CHARLES CARLISLE
B. Oct. 6, 1901, Mertens, Tex.   BR TR 5'10"   175 lbs.

	W	L	PCT	ERA	G	GS	CG	IP	H	BB	SO	ShO	W	L	SV	AB	H	HR	BA
1927 STL N	3	1	.750	4.50	14	2	1	42	47	14	16	0	2	0	0	12	5	0	.417
1928	2	1	.667	3.66	12	2	1	32	36	14	6	0	1	1	0	11	0	0	.000
2 yrs.	5	2	.714	4.14	26	4	2	74	83	28	22	0	3	1	0	23	5	0	.217
2 yrs.	5	2	.714	4.14	26	4	2	74	83	28	22	0	3	1	0	23	5	0	.217

Larry Locke

LOCKE, LAWRENCE DONALD (Bobby)
B. Mar. 3, 1934, Rowe's Run, Pa.   BR TR 5'11"   185 lbs.

	W	L	PCT	ERA	G	GS	CG	IP	H	BB	SO	ShO	W	L	SV	AB	H	HR	BA
1959 CLE A	3	2	.600	3.13	24	7	0	77.2	66	41	40	0	1	0	2	24	8	1	.333
1960	3	5	.375	3.37	32	11	2	123	121	37	53	2	0	3	2	38	9	0	.237
1961	4	4	.500	4.53	37	4	0	95.1	112	40	37	0	3	4	2	19	4	0	.211
1962 2 teams	STL N (1G 0–0)	PHI N (5G 1–0)																	
" total	1	0	1.000	5.09	6	0	0	17.2	17	12	10	0	1	0	0	7	2	0	.286
1963 PHI N	0	0	—	5.91	9	0	0	10.2	10	5	7	0	0	0	0	1	0	0	.000
1964	0	0	—	2.79	8	0	0	19.1	21	6	11	0	0	0	0	2	0	0	.000
1965 CIN N	0	1	.000	5.71	11	0	0	17.1	20	8	8	0	0	1	0	3	2	0	.667
1967 CAL A	3	0	1.000	2.33	9	1	0	19.1	14	3	7	0	2	0	3	3	0	0	.000
1968	2	3	.400	6.44	29	0	0	36.1	51	13	21	0	2	3	2	1	0	0	—
9 yrs.	16	15	.516	4.02	165	23	2	416.2	432	165	194	2	9	11	10	98	25	1	.255
1 yr.	0	0	—	0.00	1	0	0	2	1	2	1	0	0	0	0	0	0	0	—

Bill Lohrman

LOHRMAN, WILLIAM LeROY
B. May 22, 1913, Brooklyn, N. Y.   BR TR 6'1"   185 lbs.

	W	L	PCT	ERA	G	GS	CG	IP	H	BB	SO	ShO	W	L	SV	AB	H	HR	BA
1934 PHI N	0	1	.000	4.50	4	0	0	6	5	1	2	0	0	0	1	2	1	0	.500
1937 NY N	1	0	1.000	0.90	2	1	1	10	5	2	3	0	0	0	1	2	0	0	.000
1938	9	6	.600	3.32	31	14	3	152	152	33	52	0	4	0	0	49	4	0	.082
1939	12	13	.480	4.07	38	24	9	185.2	200	45	70	1	2	2	1	60	14	2	.233
1940	10	15	.400	3.78	31	27	11	195	200	43	73	5	1	0	1	65	8	0	.123
1941	9	10	.474	4.02	33	20	6	159	184	40	61	2	1	3	3	48	11	0	.229
1942 2 teams	STL N (5G 1–1)	NY N (26G 13–4)																	
" total	14	5	.737	2.48	31	19	12	170.2	154	35	47	2	2	1	0	61	9	0	.148
1943 2 teams	NY N (17G 5–6)	BKN N (6G 0–2)																	
" total	5	8	.385	4.75	23	14	5	108	139	35	21	0	1	1	1	34	2	0	.059
1944 2 teams	BKN N (3G 0–0)	CIN N (2G 0–1)																	
" total	0	1	.000	10.38	5	1	0	4.1	9	6	1	0	0	0	0	0	0	0	—
9 yrs.	60	59	.504	3.69	198	120	47	990.2	1048	240	330	10	11	8	8	321	49	2	.153
1 yr.	1	1	.500	1.42	5	0	0	12.2	10.1	11	2	6	0	1	0	0	3	2	0	.667

Art Lopatka

LOPATKA, ARTHUR JOSEPH
B. May 28, 1920, Chicago, Ill.   BL TL 5'10"   170 lbs.
BB 1946

	W	L	PCT	ERA	G	GS	CG	IP	H	BB	SO	ShO	W	L	SV	AB	H	HR	BA
1945 STL N	1	0	1.000	1.54	4	1	0	11.2	7	3	5	0	0	0	0	4	1	0	.250
1946 PHI N	0	1	.000	16.88	4	1	0	5.1	13	4	4	0	0	0	0	0	0	0	—
2 yrs.	1	1	.500	6.35	8	2	0	17	20	7	9	0	0	0	0	4	1	0	.250
1 yr.	1	0	1.000	1.54	4	1	0	11.2	7	3	5	0	0	0	0	4	1	0	.250

	W	L	PCT	ERA	G	GS	CG	IP	H	BB	SO	ShO	Relief Pitching W	L	SV	BATTING AB	H	HR	BA

Aurelio Lopez

LOPEZ, AURELIO
Also known as Aurelio Rios.
B. Sept. 21, 1948, Tecamachoico Pue., Mexico
BR TR 6' 185 lbs.

	W	L	PCT	ERA	G	GS	CG	IP	H	BB	SO	ShO	W	L	SV	AB	H	HR	BA
1974 KC A	0	0	—	5.63	8	1	0	16	21	10	5	0	0	0	0	0	0	0	—
1978 STL N	4	2	.667	4.29	25	4	0	65	52	32	46	0	2	1	0	14	3	0	.214
1979 DET A	10	5	.667	2.41	61	0	0	127	95	51	106	0	10	5	21	0	0	0	—
1980	13	6	.684	3.77	67	1	0	124	125	45	97	0	13	5	21	0	0	0	—
1981	5	2	.714	3.62	29	3	0	82	70	31	53	0	3	2	3	0	0	0	—
1982	3	1	.750	5.27	19	0	0	41	41	19	26	0	3	1	3	0	0	0	—
6 yrs.	35	16	.686	3.64	209	9	0	455	404	188	333	0	31	14	48	14	3	0	.214
1 yr.	4	2	.667	4.29	25	4	0	65	52	32	46	0	2	1	0	14	3	0	.214

Joe Lotz

LOTZ, JOSEPH PETER (Smokey)
B. Jan. 2, 1891, Remsen, Iowa   D. Jan. 1, 1971, Castro Valley, Calif.
BR TR 5'8½" 175 lbs.

	W	L	PCT	ERA	G	GS	CG	IP	H	BB	SO	ShO	W	L	SV	AB	H	HR	BA
1916 STL N	0	3	.000	4.28	12	3	1	40	31	17	18	0	0	0	0	12	4	0	.333

Lynn Lovenguth

LOVENGUTH, LYNN RICHARD
B. Nov. 29, 1922, Camden, N. Y.
BL TR 5'10½" 170 lbs.

	W	L	PCT	ERA	G	GS	CG	IP	H	BB	SO	ShO	W	L	SV	AB	H	HR	BA
1955 PHI N	0	1	.000	4.50	14	0	0	18	17	10	14	0	0	1	0	2	0	0	.000
1957 STL N	0	1	.000	2.00	2	1	0	9	6	6	6	0	0	0	0	2	0	0	.000
2 yrs.	0	2	.000	3.67	16	1	0	27	23	16	20	0	0	1	0	4	0	0	.000
1 yr.	0	1	.000	2.00	2	1	0	9	6	6	6	0	0	0	0	2	0	0	.000

John Lovett

LOVETT, JOHN
B. May 6, 1878, Monday, Ohio   D. Dec. 5, 1937, Murray City, Iowa

	W	L	PCT	ERA	G	GS	CG	IP	H	BB	SO	ShO	W	L	SV	AB	H	HR	BA
1903 STL N	0	1	.000	5.40	3	1	0	5	6	5	3	0	0	0	0	3	1	0	.333

Grover Lowdermilk

LOWDERMILK, GROVER CLEVELAND (Slim)
Brother of Lou Lowdermilk.
B. Jan. 15, 1885, Sandborn, Ind.   D. Mar. 31, 1968, Odin, Ill.
BR TR 6'4" 190 lbs.

	W	L	PCT	ERA	G	GS	CG	IP	H	BB	SO	ShO	W	L	SV	AB	H	HR	BA
1909 STL N	0	2	.000	6.21	7	3	0	29	28	30	14	0	0	0	0	10	1	0	.100
1911	0	1	.000	7.29	11	2	1	33.1	37	33	15	0	0	0	0	9	1	0	.111
1912 CHI N	0	1	.000	9.69	2	1	1	13	17	14	8	0	0	0	0	4	0	0	.000
1915 2 teams			STL	A (38G 9–17)			DET	A (7G 4–1)											
" total	13	18	.419	3.24	45	34	14	250.1	200	157	148	1	3	2	0	80	10	0	.125
1916 2 teams			DET	A (1G 0–0)			CLE	A (10G 1–5)											
" total	1	5	.167	5.75	11	9	2	51.2	52	48	28	0	0	0	0	18	3	0	.167
1917 STL A	2	1	.667	1.42	3	2	2	19	16	4	9	1	0	1	0	7	0	0	.000
1918	2	6	.250	3.15	13	11	4	80	74	38	25	0	1	0	0	28	7	0	.250
1919 2 teams			STL	A (7G 0–0)			CHI	A (20G 5–5)											
" total	5	5	.500	2.57	27	11	5	108.2	101	47	49	0	2	0	0	35	3	0	.086
1920 CHI A	0	0	—	6.75	3	0	0	5.1	9	5	0	0	0	0	0	0	0	0	—
9 yrs.	23	39	.371	3.81	122	73	30	590.1	534	376	296	2	3	5	0	191	25	0	.131
2 yrs.	0	3	.000	6.79	18	5	2	62.1	65	63	29	0	0	0	0	19	2	0	.105

WORLD SERIES

	W	L	PCT	ERA	G	GS	CG	IP	H	BB	SO	ShO	W	L	SV	AB	H	HR	BA
1919 CHI A	0	0	—	9.00	1	0	0	1	2	1	0	0	0	0	0	0	0	0	—

Lou Lowdermilk

LOWDERMILK, LOUIS BAILEY
Brother of Grover Lowdermilk.
B. Feb. 23, 1887, Sandborn, Ind.   D. Dec. 27, 1975, Centralia, Ill.
BR TL 6'1" 180 lbs.

	W	L	PCT	ERA	G	GS	CG	IP	H	BB	SO	ShO	W	L	SV	AB	H	HR	BA
1911 STL N	3	4	.429	3.46	16	3	3	65	72	29	20	0	2	2	0	18	2	0	.111
1912	1	1	.500	3.00	4	1	1	15	14	9	2	0	0	1	1	4	1	0	.250
2 yrs.	4	5	.444	3.38	20	4	4	80	86	38	22	0	2	3	1	22	3	0	.136
2 yrs.	4	5	.444	3.38	20	4	4	80	86	38	22	0	2	3	1	22	3	0	.136

Con Lucid

LUCID, CORNELIUS CONRAD
B. Feb. 24, 1869, Dublin, Ireland   Deceased.

	W	L	PCT	ERA	G	GS	CG	IP	H	BB	SO	ShO	W	L	SV	AB	H	HR	BA
1893 LOU N	0	1	.000	15.00	2	1	0	6	10	10	0	0	0	0	0	3	1	0	.333
1894 BKN N	5	3	.625	6.56	10	9	7	71.1	87	44	15	0	0	0	0	33	7	0	.212
1895 2 teams			BKN	N (21G 10–7)			PHI	N (10G 6–3)											
" total	16	10	.615	5.66	31	29	19	206.2	244	107	43	3	1	0	0	82	23	0	.280
1896 PHI N	1	4	.200	8.36	5	5	5	42	75	17	3	0	0	0	0	16	2	0	.125
1897 STL N	1	5	.167	3.67	6	6	5	49	66	26	4	0	0	0	0	17	3	0	.176
5 yrs.	23	23	.500	6.02	54	50	36	375	482	204	65	3	1	0	0	151	36	0	.238
1 yr.	1	5	.167	3.67	6	6	5	49	66	26	4	0	0	0	0	17	3	0	.176

Memo Luna

LUNA, GUILLERMO ROMERO
B. June 25, 1930, Tacubaya, Mexico
BL TL 6' 168 lbs.

	W	L	PCT	ERA	G	GS	CG	IP	H	BB	SO	ShO	W	L	SV	AB	H	HR	BA
1954 STL N	0	1	.000	27.00	1	1	0	.2	2	2	0	0	0	0	0	0	0	0	—

Johnny Lush

LUSH, JOHN CHARLES
B. Oct. 8, 1885, Williamsport, Pa.   D. Nov. 18, 1946, Beverly Hills, Calif.
BL TL 5'9½" 165 lbs.

	W	L	PCT	ERA	G	GS	CG	IP	H	BB	SO	ShO	W	L	SV	AB	H	HR	BA
1904 PHI N	0	6	.000	3.59	7	6	3	42.2	52	27	27	0	0	0	0	369	102	2	.276
1905	1	0	1.000	1.59	2	2	1	17	12	8	8	0	0	0	0	16	5	0	.313
1906	18	15	.545	2.37	37	35	24	281	254	119	151	5	0	0	0	212	56	0	.264
1907 2 teams			PHI	N (8G 3–5)			STL	N (20G 7–10)											
" total	10	15	.400	2.64	28	27	20	201.1	180	63	91	6	0	0	0	122	31	0	.254
1908 STL N	11	19	.367	2.12	38	32	23	250.2	221	57	93	3	1	0	0	89	15	0	.169
1909	11	18	.379	3.13	34	28	21	221.1	215	69	66	2	0	1	0	92	22	0	.239
1910	14	13	.519	3.20	36	25	13	225.1	235	70	54	1	4	1	0	93	21	0	.226

	W	L	PCT	ERA	G	GS	CG	IP	H	BB	SO	ShO	Relief Pitching W	L	SV	BATTING AB	H	HR	BA

Johnny Lush continued

	W	L	PCT	ERA	G	GS	CG	IP	H	BB	SO	ShO	W	L	SV	AB	H	HR	BA
7 yrs.	66	86	.434	2.68	182	155	105	1239.1	1169	413	490	17	5	4	2	*			.228
4 yrs.	43	60	.417	2.74	128	104	72	841.1	803	238	284	10	5	4	2	356	81	0	.228
				3rd															

George Lyons

LYONS, GEORGE TONY (Smooth)
B. Jan. 25, 1891, Bible Grove, Ill.   D. Aug. 12, 1981, Nevada, Mo.   BR TR 5'11"   180 lbs.

	W	L	PCT	ERA	G	GS	CG	IP	H	BB	SO	ShO	W	L	SV	AB	H	HR	BA
1920 STL N	2	1	.667	3.09	7	2	1	23.1	21	9	5	0	1	0	0	7	1	0	.143
1924 STL A	3	2	.600	4.93	25	6	2	76.2	95	44	25	0	1	0	0	20	5	0	.250
2 yrs.	5	3	.625	4.50	32	8	3	100	116	53	30	0	2	0	0	27	6	0	.222
1 yr.	2	1	.667	3.09	7	2	1	23.1	21	9	5	0	1	0	0	7	1	0	.143

Hersh Lyons

LYONS, HERSHEL ENGLEBERT
B. July 23, 1915, Fresno, Calif.   BR TR 5'11"   195 lbs.

	W	L	PCT	ERA	G	GS	CG	IP	H	BB	SO	ShO	W	L	SV	AB	H	HR	BA
1941 STL N	0	0	–	0.00	1	0	0	1.1	1	3	1	0	0	0	0	0	0	0	–

Bob Mabe

MABE, ROBERT LEE
B. Oct. 8, 1929, Danville, Va.   BR TR 5'11"   165 lbs.

	W	L	PCT	ERA	G	GS	CG	IP	H	BB	SO	ShO	W	L	SV	AB	H	HR	BA
1958 STL N	3	9	.250	4.51	31	13	4	111.2	113	41	74	0	1	1	0	24	1	0	.042
1959 CIN N	4	2	.667	5.46	18	1	0	29.2	29	19	8	0	4	2	3	7	0	0	.000
1960 BAL A	0	0	–	27.00	2	0	0	.2	4	1	0	0	0	0	0	0	0	0	–
3 yrs.	7	11	.389	4.82	51	14	4	142	146	61	82	0	5	3	3	31	1	0	.032
1 yr.	3	9	.250	4.51	31	13	4	111.2	113	41	74	0	1	1	0	24	1	0	.042

Ken MacKenzie

MacKENZIE, KENNETH PURVIS
B. Mar. 10, 1934, Gore Bay, Ont., Canada   BR TL 6'   185 lbs.

	W	L	PCT	ERA	G	GS	CG	IP	H	BB	SO	ShO	W	L	SV	AB	H	HR	BA
1960 MIL N	0	1	.000	6.48	9	0	0	8.1	9	3	9	0	0	1	0	1	0	0	.000
1961	0	1	.000	5.14	5	0	0	7	8	2	5	0	0	1	0	2	0	0	.000
1962 NY N	5	4	.556	4.95	42	1	0	80	87	34	51	0	5	3	1	12	1	0	.083
1963 2 teams					NY	N	(34G 3–1)			STL	N	(8G 0–0)							
" total	3	1	.750	4.88	42	0	0	66.1	72	15	48	0	3	1	3	10	0	0	.000
1964 SF N	0	0	–	5.00	10	0	0	9	9	3	3	0	0	0	1	0	0	0	–
1965 HOU N	0	3	.000	3.86	21	0	0	37.1	46	6	26	0	0	3	0	11	3	0	.273
6 yrs.	8	10	.444	4.80	129	1	0	208	231	63	142	0	8	9	5	36	4	0	.111
1 yr.	0	0	–	4.15	8	0	0	8.2	9	3	7	0	0	0	0	0	0	0	–

Johnny Mackinson

MACKINSON, JOHN JOSEPH
B. Oct. 29, 1923, Orange, N. J.   BR TR 5'10½" 160 lbs.

	W	L	PCT	ERA	G	GS	CG	IP	H	BB	SO	ShO	W	L	SV	AB	H	HR	BA
1953 PHI A	0	0	–	0.00	1	0	0	1.1	1	2	0	0	0	0	0	0	0	0	–
1955 STL N	0	1	.000	7.84	8	1	0	20.2	24	10	8	0	0	1	0	4	0	0	.000
2 yrs.	0	1	.000	7.36	9	1	0	22	25	12	8	0	0	1	0	4	0	0	.000
1 yr.	0	1	.000	7.84	8	1	0	20.2	24	10	8	0	0	1	0	4	0	0	.000

Max Macon

MACON, MAX CULLEN
B. Oct. 14, 1915, Pensacola, Fla.   BL TL 6'3"   175 lbs.

	W	L	PCT	ERA	G	GS	CG	IP	H	BB	SO	ShO	W	L	SV	AB	H	HR	BA
1938 STL N	4	11	.267	4.11	38	12	5	129.1	133	61	39	1	2	2	2	36	11	0	.306
1940 BKN N	1	0	1.000	22.50	2	0	0	2	5	0	1	0	1	0	0	1	1	0	1.000
1942	5	3	.625	1.93	14	8	4	84	67	33	27	1	2	0	1	43	12	0	.279
1943	7	5	.583	5.96	25	9	0	77	89	32	21	0	3	2	0	55	9	0	.164
1944 BOS N	0	0	–	21.00	1	0	0	3	10	1	1	0	0	0	0	366	100	3	.273
1947	0	0	–	0.00	1	0	0	2	1	1	1	0	0	0	0	1	0	0	.000
6 yrs.	17	19	.472	4.24	81	29	9	297.1	305	128	90	2	8	4	3	*			
1 yr.	4	11	.267	4.11	38	12	5	129.1	133	61	39	1	2	2	2	36	11	0	.306

Bill Magee

MAGEE, WILLIAM M.
B. Jan. 11, 1868, Boston, Mass.   Deceased.   TR 5'10"   154 lbs.

	W	L	PCT	ERA	G	GS	CG	IP	H	BB	SO	ShO	W	L	SV	AB	H	HR	BA
1897 LOU N	4	12	.250	5.39	22	16	13	155.1	186	99	44	1	0	1	0	62	13	0	.210
1898	16	15	.516	4.05	38	33	29	295.1	294	129	55	3	0	1	0	111	14	0	.126
1899 3 teams					LOU	N	(12G 3–7)			PHI	N	(9G 3–5)		WAS N	(8G 1–4)			
" total	7	16	.304	6.15	29	26	17	183	227	88	28	1	0	1	0	73	13	0	.178
1901 2 teams					STL	N	(1G 0–0)			NY	N	(6G 0–4)							
" total	0	4	.000	5.72	7	6	4	50.1	64	15	17	0	0	0	0	18	4	0	.222
1902 2 teams					NY	N	(2G 0–0)			PHI	N	(8G 2–4)							
" total	2	4	.333	3.68	10	7	6	58.2	66	19	17	0	0	0	0	20	4	0	.200
5 yrs.	29	51	.363	4.93	106	88	69	742.2	837	350	161	5	0	3	0	284	48	0	.169
1 yr.	0	0	–	4.50	1	1	0	8	8	4	3	0	0	0	0	4	2	0	.500

Sal Maglie

MAGLIE, SALVATORE ANTHONY (The Barber)
B. Apr. 26, 1917, Niagara Falls, N. Y.   BR TR 6'2"   180 lbs.

	W	L	PCT	ERA	G	GS	CG	IP	H	BB	SO	ShO	W	L	SV	AB	H	HR	BA
1945 NY N	5	4	.556	2.35	13	10	7	84.1	72	22	32	3	0	1	0	30	5	0	.167
1950	18	4	.818	2.71	47	16	12	206	169	86	96	5	5	2	1	66	8	0	.121
1951	23	6	.793	2.93	42	37	22	298	254	86	146	3	1	0	4	112	17	1	.152
1952	18	8	.692	2.92	35	31	12	216	199	75	112	3	1	1	1	69	5	0	.072
1953	8	9	.471	4.15	27	24	9	145.1	158	47	80	3	0	0	0	48	13	0	.271
1954	14	6	.700	3.26	34	32	9	218.1	222	70	117	1	0	0	2	63	8	0	.127
1955 2 teams					NY	N	(23G 9–5)			CLE	A	(10G 0–2)							
" total	9	7	.563	3.77	33	23	6	155.1	168	55	82	0	1	0	2	45	5	0	.111
1956 2 teams					CLE	A	(2G 0–0)			BKN	N	(28G 13–5)							
" total	13	5	.722	2.89	30	26	9	196	160	54	110	3	0	0	0	70	9	0	.129
1957 2 teams					BKN	N	(19G 6–6)			NY	A	(6G 2–0)							
" total	8	6	.571	2.69	25	20	5	127.1	116	33	59	2	0	0	4	37	3	0	.081
1958 2 teams					NY	A	(7G 1–1)			STL	N	(10G 2–6)							
" total	3	7	.300	4.72	17	13	2	76.1	73	34	28	0	0	0	0	23	3	1	.130

	W	L	PCT	ERA	G	GS	CG	IP	H	BB	SO	ShO	Relief Pitching W	L	SV	BATTING AB	H	HR	BA

Sal Maglie continued

	W	L	PCT	ERA	G	GS	CG	IP	H	BB	SO	ShO	W	L	SV	AB	H	HR	BA
10 yrs.	119	62	.657 9th	3.15	303	232	93	1723	1591	562	862	25	8	4	14	563	76	2	.135
1 yr.	2	6	.250	4.75	10	10	2	53	46	25	21	0	0	0	0	16	2	0	.125

WORLD SERIES

	W	L	PCT	ERA	G	GS	CG	IP	H	BB	SO	ShO	W	L	SV	AB	H	HR	BA
1951 NY N	0	1	.000	7.20	1	1	0	5	8	2	3	0	0	0	0	1	0	0	.000
1954	0	0	–	2.57	1	1	0	7	7	2	2	0	0	0	0	3	0	0	.000
1956 BKN N	1	1	.500	2.65	2	2	2	17	14	6	15	0	0	0	0	5	0	0	.000
3 yrs.	1	2	.333	3.41	4	4	2	29	29	10	20	0	0	0	0	9	0	0	.000

Art Mahaffey

MAHAFFEY, ARTHUR
B. June 4, 1938, Cincinnati, Ohio   BR TR 6'1" 185 lbs.

	W	L	PCT	ERA	G	GS	CG	IP	H	BB	SO	ShO	W	L	SV	AB	H	HR	BA
1960 PHI N	7	3	.700	2.31	14	12	5	93.1	78	34	56	1	0	0	0	30	3	0	.100
1961	11	19	.367	4.10	36	32	12	219.1	205	70	158	3	0	1	0	63	8	0	.127
1962	19	14	.576	3.94	41	39	20	274	253	81	177	2	0	1	0	92	13	2	.141
1963	7	10	.412	3.99	26	22	6	149	143	48	97	1	1	0	0	50	10	0	.200
1964	12	9	.571	4.52	34	29	2	157.1	161	82	80	2	1	0	0	50	6	1	.120
1965	2	5	.286	6.21	22	9	1	71	82	32	52	0	0	0	0	21	2	0	.095
1966 STL N	1	4	.200	6.43	12	5	0	35	37	21	19	0	0	0	1	7	0	0	.000
7 yrs.	59	64	.480	4.17	185	148	46	999	959	368	639	9	2	2	1	313	42	3	.134
1 yr.	1	4	.200	6.43	12	5	0	35	37	21	19	0	0	0	1	7	0	0	.000

Mike Mahoney

MAHONEY, GEORGE W.
B. Dec. 5, 1873, Boston, Mass.   D. Jan. 3, 1940, Boston, Mass.

	W	L	PCT	ERA	G	GS	CG	IP	H	BB	SO	ShO	W	L	SV	AB	H	HR	BA
1897 BOS N	0	0	–	18.00	1	0	0	3	1	3	1	0	0	0	0	*			

Duster Mails

MAILS, JOHN WALTER (The Great)
B. Oct. 1, 1895, San Quentin, Calif.   D. July 5, 1974, San Francisco, Calif.   BL TL 6' 195 lbs.

	W	L	PCT	ERA	G	GS	CG	IP	H	BB	SO	ShO	W	L	SV	AB	H	HR	BA
1915 BKN N	0	1	.000	3.60	2	0	0	5	6	5	3	0	0	1	0	1	0	0	.000
1916	0	1	.000	3.63	11	0	0	17.1	15	9	13	0	0	1	0	4	1	0	.250
1920 CLE A	7	0	1.000	1.85	9	8	6	63.1	54	18	25	2	0	0	0	20	4	0	.200
1921	14	8	.636	3.94	34	24	10	194.1	210	89	87	2	2	1	2	64	6	0	.094
1922	4	7	.364	5.28	26	13	4	104	122	40	54	1	1	1	0	31	5	0	.161
1925 STL N	7	7	.500	4.60	21	14	9	131	145	58	49	0	0	1	0	45	6	0	.133
1926	0	1	.000	0.00	1	0	0	1	2	1	1	0	0	1	0	0	0	0	–
7 yrs.	32	25	.561	4.10	104	59	29	516	554	220	232	5	3	6	2	165	22	0	.133
2 yrs.	7	8	.467	4.57	22	14	9	132	147	59	50	0	0	2	0	45	6	0	.133

WORLD SERIES

	W	L	PCT	ERA	G	GS	CG	IP	H	BB	SO	ShO	W	L	SV	AB	H	HR	BA
1920 CLE A	1	0	1.000	0.00	2	1	1	15.2	6	6	6	1	0	0	0	5	0	0	.000

Walt Marbet

MARBET, WALTER WILLIAM
B. Sept. 13, 1890, Plymouth County, Iowa   D. Sept. 24, 1956, Hohenwald, Tenn.   BR TR 6'1" 175 lbs.

	W	L	PCT	ERA	G	GS	CG	IP	H	BB	SO	ShO	W	L	SV	AB	H	HR	BA
1913 STL N	0	1	.000	16.20	3	1	0	3.1	9	4	1	0	0	0	0	0	0	0	–

Freddie Martin

MARTIN, FRED TURNER
B. June 27, 1915, Williams, Okla.   D. June 11, 1979, Chicago, Ill.   BR TR 6'1" 185 lbs.

	W	L	PCT	ERA	G	GS	CG	IP	H	BB	SO	ShO	W	L	SV	AB	H	HR	BA
1946 STL N	2	1	.667	4.08	6	3	2	28.2	29	8	19	0	0	1	0	11	3	0	.273
1949	6	0	1.000	2.44	21	5	3	70	65	20	30	0	2	0	0	20	6	0	.300
1950	4	2	.667	5.12	30	2	0	63.1	87	30	19	0	4	0	0	15	4	0	.267
3 yrs.	12	3	.800	3.78	57	10	5	162	181	58	68	0	6	1	0	46	13	0	.283
3 yrs.	12	3	.800	3.78	57	10	5	162	181	58	68	0	6	1	0	46	13	0	.283

John Martin

MARTIN, JOHN ROBERT
B. Apr. 11, 1956, Wyandotte, Minn.   BB TL 6' 190 lbs.

	W	L	PCT	ERA	G	GS	CG	IP	H	BB	SO	ShO	W	L	SV	AB	H	HR	BA
1980 STL N	2	3	.400	4.29	9	5	1	42	39	9	23	0	0	0	0	11	3	0	.273
1981	8	5	.615	3.41	17	15	4	103	85	26	36	0	0	0	0	33	7	0	.212
1982	4	5	.444	4.23	24	7	0	66	56	30	21	0	1	2	0	11	1	0	.091
3 yrs.	14	13	.519	3.84	50	27	5	211	180	65	80	0	1	3	0	55	11	0	.200
3 yrs.	14	13	.519	3.84	50	27	5	211	180	65	80	0	1	3	0	55	11	0	.200

Morrie Martin

MARTIN, MORRIS WEBSTER
B. Sept. 3, 1922, Dixon, Mo.   BL TL 6' 173 lbs.

	W	L	PCT	ERA	G	GS	CG	IP	H	BB	SO	ShO	W	L	SV	AB	H	HR	BA
1949 BKN N	1	3	.250	7.04	10	4	0	30.2	39	15	15	0	1	0	0	10	2	0	.200
1951 PHI A	11	4	.733	3.78	35	13	3	138	139	63	35	1	5	0	0	50	11	0	.220
1952	0	2	.000	6.39	5	5	0	25.1	32	15	13	0	0	0	0	9	1	0	.111
1953	10	12	.455	4.43	58	11	2	156.1	158	59	64	0	8	5	7	42	4	0	.095
1954 2 teams		PHI A	(13G 2–4)		CHI A	(35G 5–4)													
" total	7	8	.467	3.52	48	8	3	122.2	109	43	55	0	4	5	5	32	6	0	.188
1955 CHI A	2	3	.400	3.63	37	0	0	52	50	22	20	0	2	3	2	10	3	0	.300
1956 2 teams		CHI A	(10G 1–0)		BAL A	(9G 1–1)													
" total	2	1	.667	6.17	19	0	0	23.1	31	9	12	0	2	1	0	5	1	0	.200
1957 STL N	0	0	–	2.53	4	1	0	10.2	5	4	7	0	0	0	0	2	0	0	.000
1958 2 teams		STL N	(17G 3–1)		CLE A	(14G 2–0)													
" total	5	1	.833	3.74	31	0	0	43.1	39	20	21	0	5	1	1	5	0	0	.000
1959 CHI A	0	0	–	19.29	3	0	0	2.1	5	1	1	0	0	0	0	0	0	0	–
10 yrs.	38	34	.528	4.29	250	42	8	604.2	607	251	245	1	27	15	15	165	28	0	.170
2 yrs.	3	1	.750	4.08	21	0	0	35.1	24	16	23	0	3	1	0	5	0	0	.000

	W	L	PCT	ERA	G	GS	CG	IP	H	BB	SO	ShO	W	L	SV	AB	H	HR	BA

Pepper Martin

MARTIN, JOHNNY LEONARD ROOSEVELT (The Wild Hoss Of The Osage)
BR TR 5'8" 170 lbs.
B. Feb. 29, 1904, Temple, Okla. D. Mar. 5, 1965, McAlester, Okla.

	W	L	PCT	ERA	G	GS	CG	IP	H	BB	SO	ShO	W	L	SV	AB	H	HR	BA
1934 STL N	0	0	–	4.50	1	0	0	2	1	0	0	0	0	0	0	454	131	5	.289
1936	0	0	–	0.00	1	0	0	2	1	2	0	0	0	0	0	572	177	11	.309
2 yrs.	0	0	–	2.25	2	0	0	4	2	2	0	0	0	0	0	*			
2 yrs.	0	0	–	2.25	2	0	0	4	2	2	0	0	0	0	0	4117	1227	59	.298

Marty Martinez

MARTINEZ, ORLANDO OLIVO
BB TR 6' 170 lbs.
BR 1962
B. Aug. 23, 1941, Havana, Cuba

	W	L	PCT	ERA	G	GS	CG	IP	H	BB	SO	ShO	W	L	SV	AB	H	HR	BA
1969 HOU N	0	0	–	9.00	1	0	0	1	1	0	0	0	0	0	0	*			

Silvio Martinez

MARTINEZ, SILVIO RAMON
BR TR 5'10" 170 lbs.
B. Aug. 31, 1955, Santiago, Dominican Republic

	W	L	PCT	ERA	G	GS	CG	IP	H	BB	SO	ShO	W	L	SV	AB	H	HR	BA
1977 CHI A	0	1	.000	5.57	10	0	0	21	28	12	10	0	0	1	1	0	0	0	–
1978 STL N	9	8	.529	3.65	22	22	5	138	114	71	45	2	0	0	0	47	8	0	.170
1979	15	8	.652	3.26	32	29	7	207	204	67	102	2	0	0	0	62	8	0	.129
1980	5	10	.333	4.80	25	20	2	120	127	48	39	0	1	0	0	35	3	0	.086
1981	2	5	.286	3.99	18	16	0	97	95	39	34	0	0	0	0	35	7	0	.200
5 yrs.	31	32	.492	3.87	107	87	14	583	568	237	230	4	1	1	1	179	26	0	.145
4 yrs.	31	31	.500	3.81	97	87	14	562	540	225	220	4	1	0	0	179	26	0	.145

Ernie Mason

MASON, ERNEST
B. New Orleans, La. D. July 30, 1904, Covington, La.

	W	L	PCT	ERA	G	GS	CG	IP	H	BB	SO	ShO	W	L	SV	AB	H	HR	BA
1894 STL N	0	2	.000	7.15	4	2	2	22.2	34	10	3	0	0	1	0	12	3	0	.250

Harry Maupin

MAUPIN, HENRY CARR
B. July 11, 1872, Wellesville, Mo. D. Aug. 23, 1952

	W	L	PCT	ERA	G	GS	CG	IP	H	BB	SO	ShO	W	L	SV	AB	H	HR	BA
1898 STL N	0	2	.000	5.50	2	2	2	18	22	3	3	0	0	0	0	7	3	0	.429
1899 CLE N	0	3	.000	12.60	5	3	2	25	55	7	3	0	0	0	0	10	0	0	.000
2 yrs.	0	5	.000	9.63	7	5	4	43	77	10	6	0	0	0	0	17	3	0	.176
1 yr.	0	2	.000	5.50	2	2	2	18	22	3	3	0	0	0	0	7	3	0	.429

Jakie May

MAY, FRANK SPRUIELL
BR TL 5'8" 178 lbs.
B. Nov. 25, 1895, Youngville, N. C. D. June 3, 1970, Wendell, N. C.

	W	L	PCT	ERA	G	GS	CG	IP	H	BB	SO	ShO	W	L	SV	AB	H	HR	BA
1917 STL N	0	0	–	3.38	15	1	0	29.1	29	11	18	0	0	0	0	4	0	0	.000
1918	5	6	.455	3.83	29	16	6	152.2	149	69	61	0	2	0	0	45	3	1	.067
1919	3	12	.200	3.22	28	19	8	125.2	99	87	58	1	0	1	0	37	6	0	.162
1920	1	4	.200	3.06	16	5	3	70.2	65	37	33	0	0	1	0	22	5	0	.227
1921	1	3	.250	4.71	5	5	1	21	29	12	5	0	0	0	0	6	2	0	.333
1924 CIN N	3	3	.500	3.00	38	4	2	99	104	29	59	0	2	2	6	27	3	1	.111
1925	8	9	.471	3.87	36	12	7	137.1	146	45	74	1	2	4	2	43	8	0	.186
1926	13	9	.591	3.22	45	15	9	167.2	175	44	103	1	5	4	3	48	7	0	.146
1927	15	12	.556	3.51	44	28	17	235.2	242	70	121	2	2	0	1	76	14	0	.184
1928	3	5	.375	4.42	21	11	1	79.1	99	35	39	1	2	2	1	27	8	0	.296
1929	10	14	.417	4.61	41	24	10	199	219	75	92	0	4	1	3	64	13	0	.203
1930	3	11	.214	5.77	26	18	5	112.1	147	41	44	1	0	1	0	39	5	0	.128
1931 CHI N	5	5	.500	3.87	31	4	1	79	81	43	38	0	3	4	2	22	5	0	.227
1932	2	2	.500	4.36	35	0	0	53.2	61	19	20	0	2	2	1	8	1	0	.125
14 yrs.	72	95	.431	3.88	410	162	70	1562.1	1645	617	765	7	24	22	19	468	80	2	.171
5 yrs.	10	25	.286	3.52	93	46	18	399.1	371	216	175	1	2	2	0	114	16	1	.140

WORLD SERIES

	W	L	PCT	ERA	G	GS	CG	IP	H	BB	SO	ShO	W	L	SV	AB	H	HR	BA
1932 CHI N	0	1	.000	11.57	2	0	0	4.2	9	3	4	0	0	1	0	2	0	0	.000

Jack McAdams

McADAMS, GEORGE D.
BR TR 6'1½" 170 lbs.
B. Dec. 17, 1886, Benton, Ark. D. May 21, 1937, San Francisco, Calif.

	W	L	PCT	ERA	G	GS	CG	IP	H	BB	SO	ShO	W	L	SV	AB	H	HR	BA
1911 STL N	0	0	–	3.72	6	0	0	9.2	7	5	4	0	0	0	0	1	0	0	.000

Pete McBride

McBRIDE, PETER WILLIAM
BR TR 5'10" 170 lbs.
B. July 9, 1875, Adams, Mass. D. July 3, 1944, North Adams, Mass.

	W	L	PCT	ERA	G	GS	CG	IP	H	BB	SO	ShO	W	L	SV	AB	H	HR	BA
1898 CLE N	0	1	.000	6.43	1	1	1	7	9	4	6	0	0	0	0	2	2	0	1.000
1899 STL N	2	4	.333	4.08	11	6	4	64	65	40	26	0	0	0	0	27	5	1	.185
2 yrs.	2	5	.286	4.31	12	7	5	71	74	44	32	0	0	0	0	29	7	1	.241
1 yr.	2	4	.333	4.08	11	6	4	64	65	40	26	0	0	0	0	27	5	1	.185

Billy McCool

McCOOL, WILLIAM JOHN
BR TL 6'2" 195 lbs.
B. July 14, 1944, Batesville, Ind.

	W	L	PCT	ERA	G	GS	CG	IP	H	BB	SO	ShO	W	L	SV	AB	H	HR	BA
1964 CIN N	6	5	.545	2.42	40	3	0	89.1	66	29	87	0	5	2	7	17	0	0	.000
1965	9	10	.474	4.27	62	2	0	105.1	93	47	120	0	9	8	21	27	1	0	.037
1966	8	8	.500	2.48	57	0	0	105.1	76	41	104	0	8	8	18	18	3	0	.167
1967	3	7	.300	3.42	31	11	0	97.1	92	56	83	0	0	3	2	26	2	0	.077
1968	3	4	.429	4.97	30	4	0	50.2	59	41	30	0	2	3	2	8	1	0	.125
1969 SD N	3	5	.375	4.27	54	0	0	59	59	42	35	0	3	5	7	1	0	0	.000
1970 STL N	0	3	.000	6.14	18	0	0	22	20	16	12	0	0	3	1	4	0	0	.000
7 yrs.	32	42	.432	3.59	292	20	0	529	465	272	471	0	27	32	58	101	7	0	.069
1 yr.	0	3	.000	6.14	18	0	0	22	20	16	12	0	0	3	1	4	0	0	.000

Lindy McDaniel

McDANIEL, LYNDALL DALE
Brother of Von McDaniel.
BR TR 6'3" 195 lbs.
B. Dec. 13, 1935, Hollis, Okla.

	W	L	PCT	ERA	G	GS	CG	IP	H	BB	SO	ShO	W	L	SV	AB	H	HR	BA
1955 STL N	0	0	–	4.74	4	2	0	19	22	7	7	0	0	0	0	5	1	0	.200

	W	L	PCT	ERA	G	GS	CG	IP	H	BB	SO	ShO	Relief Pitching W	L	SV	BATTING AB	H	HR	BA

Lindy McDaniel continued

	W	L	PCT	ERA	G	GS	CG	IP	H	BB	SO	ShO	W	L	SV	AB	H	HR	BA
1956	7	6	.538	3.40	39	7	1	116.1	121	42	59	0	5	2	0	32	7	0	.219
1957	15	9	.625	3.49	30	26	10	191	196	53	75	1	3	0	0	74	19	1	.257
1958	5	7	.417	5.80	26	17	2	108.2	139	31	47	1	0	2	0	30	2	0	.067
1959	14	12	.538	3.82	62	7	1	132	144	41	86	0	13	8	15	29	1	0	.034
1960	12	4	.750	2.09	65	2	1	116.1	85	24	105	0	12	2	26	26	6	0	.231
1961	10	6	.625	4.87	55	0	0	94.1	117	31	65	0	10	6	9	17	4	0	.235
1962	3	10	.231	4.12	55	2	0	107	96	29	79	0	2	9	14	21	2	0	.095
1963 CHI N	13	7	.650	2.86	57	0	0	88	82	27	75	0	13	7	22	22	2	1	.091
1964	1	7	.125	3.88	63	0	0	95	104	23	71	0	1	7	15	16	2	0	.125
1965	5	6	.455	2.59	71	0	0	128.2	115	47	92	0	5	6	2	8	0	0	.000
1966 SF N	10	5	.667	2.66	64	0	0	121.2	103	35	93	0	10	5	6	22	2	0	.091
1967	2	6	.250	3.72	41	3	0	72.2	69	24	48	0	2	4	3	11	1	0	.091
1968 2 teams			SF N (12G 0–0)		NY A (24G 4–1)														
" total			.800	3.31	36	0	0	70.2	60	17	52	0	4	1	10	15	0	0	.000
1969 NY A	5	6	.455	3.55	51	0	0	83.2	84	23	60	0	5	6	5	8	0	0	.000
1970	9	5	.643	2.01	62	0	0	112	88	23	81	0	9	5	29	24	4	0	.167
1971	5	10	.333	5.01	44	0	0	70	82	24	39	0	5	10	4	9	1	0	.111
1972	3	1	.750	2.25	37	0	0	68	54	25	47	0	3	1	0	7	2	1	.286
1973	12	6	.667	2.81	47	3	1	160.1	148	49	93	0	12	3	10	0	0	0	—
1974 KC A	1	4	.200	3.45	38	5	2	107	109	24	47	0	0	2	1	0	0	0	—
1975	5	1	.833	4.15	40	0	0	78	81	24	40	0	5	1	1	0	0	0	—
21 yrs.	141	119	.542	3.45	987 2nd	74	18	2140.1	2099	623	1361	2	119 2nd	87	172 10th	376	56	3	.149
8 yrs.	66	54	.550	3.88	336 6th	63	15	884.2	920	258	523	2	45 1st	29	64 1st	234	42	1	.179

Von McDaniel

McDANIEL, MAX VON
Brother of Lindy McDaniel.
B. Apr. 18, 1939, Hollis, Okla.

BR TR 6'2½" 180 lbs.

	W	L	PCT	ERA	G	GS	CG	IP	H	BB	SO	ShO	W	L	SV	AB	H	HR	BA
1957 STL N	7	5	.583	3.22	17	13	4	86.2	71	31	45	2	1	0	0	26	0	0	.000
1958	0	0	—	13.50	2	1	0	2	5	5	0	0	0	0	0	0	0	0	—
2 yrs.	7	5	.583	3.45	19	14	4	88.2	76	36	45	2	1	0	0	26	0	0	.000
2 yrs.	7	5	.583	3.45	19	14	4	88.2	76	36	45	2	1	0	0	26	0	0	.000

Mickey McDermott

McDERMOTT, MAURICE JOSEPH
B. Aug. 29, 1928, Poughkeepsie, N. Y.

BL TL 6'2" 170 lbs.

	W	L	PCT	ERA	G	GS	CG	IP	H	BB	SO	ShO	W	L	SV	AB	H	HR	BA
1948 BOS A	0	0	—	6.17	7	0	0	23.1	16	35	17	0	0	0	0	8	3	0	.375
1949	5	4	.556	4.05	12	12	6	80	63	52	50	2	0	0	0	33	7	0	.212
1950	7	3	.700	5.19	38	15	4	130	119	124	96	0	3	0	5	44	16	0	.364
1951	8	8	.500	3.35	34	19	9	172	141	92	127	1	0	1	3	66	18	1	.273
1952	10	9	.526	3.72	30	21	7	162	139	92	117	2	2	3	0	62	14	1	.226
1953	18	10	.643	3.01	32	30	8	206.1	169	109	92	4	0	0	0	93	28	1	.301
1954 WAS A	7	15	.318	3.44	30	26	11	196.1	172	110	95	1	0	0	1	95	19	0	.200
1955	10	10	.500	3.75	31	20	8	156	140	102	78	1	2	1	1	95	25	1	.263
1956 NY A	2	6	.250	4.24	23	9	1	87	85	47	38	0	0	0	0	52	11	1	.212
1957 KC A	1	4	.200	5.48	29	4	0	69	68	50	29	0	1	2	0	49	12	4	.245
1958 DET A	0	0	—	9.00	2	0	0	2	6	2	0	0	0	0	0	3	1	0	.333
1961 2 teams			STL N (19G 1–0)		KC A (4G 0–0)														
" total	1	0	1.000	5.51	23	0	0	32.2	43	25	18	0	1	0	4	19	2	0	.105
12 yrs.	69	69	.500	3.91	291	156	54	1316.2	1161	840	757	11	9	7	14	*			
1 yr.	1	0	1.000	3.67	19	0	0	27	29	15	15	0	1	0	4	14	1	0	.071

WORLD SERIES

	W	L	PCT	ERA	G	GS	CG	IP	H	BB	SO	ShO	W	L	SV	AB	H	HR	BA
1956 NY A	0	0	—	3.00	1	0	0	3	2	3	3	0	0	0	0	1	1	0	1.000

Mike McDermott

McDERMOTT, MICHAEL JOSEPH
B. Sept. 7, 1862, St. Louis, Mo.   D. June 30, 1943, St. Louis, Mo.

TR

	W	L	PCT	ERA	G	GS	CG	IP	H	BB	SO	ShO	W	L	SV	AB	H	HR	BA
1889 LOU AA	1	8	.111	4.16	9	9	9	84.1	108	34	22	0	0	0	0	33	6	0	.182
1895 LOU N	4	19	.174	5.99	33	26	18	207.1	258	103	42	0	0	0	0	82	13	0	.159
1896	2	7	.222	7.34	12	10	4	65	87	44	12	1	0	0	0	27	8	0	.296
1897 2 teams			CLE N (9G 4–5)		STL N (4G 1–2)														
" total	5	7	.417	5.72	13	11	5	83.1	98	44	15	0	2	0	0	34	10	0	.294
4 yrs.	12	41	.226	5.79	67	56	36	440	551	225	91	2	2	0	0	176	37	0	.210
1 yr.	1	2	.333	9.28	4	4	1	21.1	23	19	3	0	0	0	0	9	2	0	.222

John McDougal

McDOUGAL, JOHN H.
B. Sept. 19, 1871, Aledo, Ill.   D. Apr. 28, 1936, Galesburg, Ill.

	W	L	PCT	ERA	G	GS	CG	IP	H	BB	SO	ShO	W	L	SV	AB	H	HR	BA
1895 STL N	4	10	.286	8.32	18	14	10	114.2	187	46	23	0	0	1	0	41	6	0	.146
1896	0	1	.000	8.10	3	1	0	10	13	4	0	0	0	0	0	3	0	0	.000
2 yrs.	4	11	.267	8.30	21	15	10	124.2	200	50	23	0	0	1	0	44	6	0	.136
2 yrs.	4	11	.267	8.30	21	15	10	124.2	200	50	23	0	0	1	0	44	6	0	.136

Sandy McDougal

McDOUGAL, JAMES A
B. Feb. 18, 1878, Buffalo, N. Y.   D. Oct. 4, 1910, Buffalo, N. Y.

	W	L	PCT	ERA	G	GS	CG	IP	H	BB	SO	ShO	W	L	SV	AB	H	HR	BA
1905 STL N	1	4	.200	3.43	5	5	5	44.2	50	12	10	0	0	0	0	15	2	0	.133

Will McEnaney

McENANEY, WILLIAM HENRY
B. Feb. 14, 1952, Springfield, Ohio

BL TL 6' 180 lbs.

	W	L	PCT	ERA	G	GS	CG	IP	H	BB	SO	ShO	W	L	SV	AB	H	HR	BA
1974 CIN N	2	1	.667	4.33	24	0	0	27	24	9	13	0	2	1	2	0	0	0	—
1975	5	2	.714	2.47	70	0	0	91	92	23	48	0	5	2	15	14	0	0	.000
1976	2	6	.250	4.88	55	0	0	72	97	23	28	0	2	6	7	6	1	0	.167

	W	L	PCT	ERA	G	GS	CG	IP	H	BB	SO	ShO	Relief Pitching W	L	SV	BATTING AB	H	HR	BA

Will McEnaney continued

	W	L	PCT	ERA	G	GS	CG	IP	H	BB	SO	ShO	W	L	SV	AB	H	HR	BA
1977 MON N	3	5	.375	3.93	69	0	0	87	92	22	38	0	3	5	3	8	0	0	.000
1978 PIT N	0	0	–	10.00	6	0	0	9	15	2	6	0	0	0	0	0	0	0	–
1979 STL N	0	3	.000	2.95	45	0	0	64	60	16	15	0	0	3	2	3	0	0	.000
6 yrs.	12	17	.414	3.75	269	0	0	350	380	95	148	0	12	17	29	31	1	0	.032
1 yr.	0	3	.000	2.95	45	0	0	64	60	16	15	0	0	3	2	3	0	0	.000
LEAGUE CHAMPIONSHIP SERIES																			
1975 CIN N	0	0	–	6.75	1	0	0	1.1	1	0	1	0	0	0	0	0	0	0	–
WORLD SERIES																			
1975 CIN N	0	0	–	2.70	5	0	0	6.2	3	2	5	0	0	0	1	1	1	0	1.000
1976	0	0	–	0.00	2	0	0	4.2	2	1	2	0	0	0	2	0	0	0	–
2 yrs.	0	0	–	1.59	7	0	0	11.1	5	3	7	0	0	0	3 (4th)	1	1	0	1.000

Chappie McFarland

McFARLAND, CHARLES EDWARD
Brother of Monte McFarland.
D. Dec. 15, 1924, Houston, Tex.　　　　　　　　　　TR

	W	L	PCT	ERA	G	GS	CG	IP	H	BB	SO	ShO	W	L	SV	AB	H	HR	BA
1902 STL N	0	1	.000	5.73	2	1	1	11	11	3	3	0	0	0	0	4	0	0	.000
1903	9	18	.333	3.07	28	26	25	229	253	48	76	1	0	2	0	74	8	0	.108
1904	14	17	.452	3.21	32	31	28	269.1	266	56	111	1	0	0	0	99	13	0	.131
1905	8	18	.308	3.82	31	28	22	250	281	65	85	3	0	0	1	85	14	0	.165
1906 3 teams				STL N (6G 2–1)				PIT N (1G 0–1)				BKN N (1G 0–1)							
" total	3	5	.375	2.87	13	10	5	81.2	82	20	32	1	0	0	1	31	7	0	.226
5 yrs.	34	59	.366	3.35	106	96	81	841	893	192	307	6	0	2	2	293	42	0	.143
5 yrs.	33	55	.375	3.33	99	90	78	796.2	844	180	291	5	0	2	2	277	37	0	.134

Bill McGee

McGEE, WILLIAM HENRY (Fiddler Bill)
B. Nov. 16, 1909, Batchtown, Ill.　　　　　　　BR TR 6'1"　　215 lbs.

	W	L	PCT	ERA	G	GS	CG	IP	H	BB	SO	ShO	W	L	SV	AB	H	HR	BA
1935 STL N	1	0	1.000	1.00	1	1	1	9	3	1	2	0	0	0	0	3	1	0	.333
1936	1	1	.500	8.04	7	2	0	15.2	23	4	8	0	0	0	0	4	1	0	.250
1937	1	0	1.000	2.63	4	1	1	13.2	13	4	9	0	0	0	0	5	1	0	.200
1938	7	12	.368	3.21	47	25	10	216	216	78	104	1	1	2	5	67	14	0	.209
1939	12	5	.706	3.81	43	17	5	156	155	59	56	4	4	3	0	55	8	0	.145
1940	16	10	.615	3.80	38	31	11	217.2	222	96	78	3	1	2	0	73	13	0	.178
1941 2 teams				STL N (4G 0–1)				NY N (22G 2–9)											
" total	2	10	.167	4.92	26	17	1	120.2	134	67	43	0	0	1	0	35	5	0	.143
1942 NY N	6	3	.667	2.93	31	8	2	104.1	95	46	40	1	4	3	1	29	3	0	.103
8 yrs.	46	41	.529	3.74	197	102	31	853	861	355	340	9	10	11	6	271	46	0	.170
7 yrs.	38	29	.567	3.67	144	80	28	642.1	649	255	259	8	6	7	5	211	38	0	.180

Jim McGinley

McGINLEY, JAMES WILLIAM
B. Oct. 2, 1878, Groveland, Mass.　　D. Sept. 20, 1961, Haverhill, Mass.　　BR TR 5'9½" 165 lbs.

	W	L	PCT	ERA	G	GS	CG	IP	H	BB	SO	ShO	W	L	SV	AB	H	HR	BA
1904 STL N	2	1	.667	2.00	3	3	3	27	28	6	6	0	0	0	0	11	1	0	.091
1905	0	1	.000	15.00	1	1	0	3	5	2	0	0	0	0	0	1	1	0	1.000
2 yrs.	2	2	.500	3.30	4	4	3	30	33	8	6	0	0	0	0	12	2	0	.167
2 yrs.	2	2	.500	3.30	4	4	3	30	33	8	6	0	0	0	0	12	2	0	.167

Lynn McGlothen

McGLOTHEN, LYNN EVERATT
B. Mar. 27, 1950, Monroe, La.　　　　　　　BL TR 6'2"　　185 lbs.

	W	L	PCT	ERA	G	GS	CG	IP	H	BB	SO	ShO	W	L	SV	AB	H	HR	BA
1972 BOS A	8	7	.533	3.41	22	22	4	145.1	135	59	112	1	0	0	0	53	10	0	.189
1973	1	2	.333	8.22	6	3	0	23	39	8	16	0	0	0	0	0	0	0	–
1974 STL N	16	12	.571	2.70	31	31	8	237	212	89	142	3	0	0	0	83	15	0	.181
1975	15	13	.536	3.92	35	34	9	239	231	97	146	2	0	0	0	80	7	0	.088
1976	13	15	.464	3.91	33	32	10	205	209	68	106	4	0	0	0	71	15	0	.211
1977 SF N	2	9	.182	5.63	21	15	2	80	94	52	42	0	0	1	0	19	2	0	.105
1978 2 teams				SF N (5G 0–0)				CHI N (49G 5–3)											
" total	5	3	.625	5.30	54	2	0	92.2	92	43	69	0	5	2	6	16	3	0	.188
1979 CHI N	13	14	.481	4.12	42	29	6	212	236	55	147	1	3	1	2	71	16	0	.225
1980	12	14	.462	4.80	39	27	2	182	211	64	119	2	0	1	0	51	10	0	.196
1981 2 teams				CHI N (20G 1–4)				CHI A (11G 0–0)											
" total	1	4	.200	4.56	31	6	0	77	85	35	38	0	1	1	0	12	1	0	.083
1982 NY A	0	0	–	10.80	4	0	0	5	9	2	2	0	0	0	0	0	0	0	–
11 yrs.	86	93	.480	3.98	318	201	41	1498	1553	572	939	13	9	6	2	456	79	0	.173
3 yrs.	44	40	.524	3.49	99	97	27	681	652	254	394	9	0	0	0	234	37	0	.158

Stoney McGlynn

McGLYNN, ULYSSES SIMPSON GRANT
B. May 26, 1872, Lancaster, Pa.　　D. Aug. 26, 1941, Manitowoc, Wis.

	W	L	PCT	ERA	G	GS	CG	IP	H	BB	SO	ShO	W	L	SV	AB	H	HR	BA
1906 STL N	2	2	.500	2.44	6	6	6	48	43	15	25	0	0	0	0	17	1	0	.059
1907	14	25	.359	2.91	45	39	33	352.1	329	112	109	3	1	1	1	125	25	0	.200
1908	1	6	.143	3.45	16	6	4	75.2	76	17	23	0	1	0	1	26	2	0	.077
3 yrs.	17	33	.340	2.95	67	51	43	476	448	144	157	3	2	1	2	168	28	0	.167
3 yrs.	17	33	.340	2.95	67	51	43	476	448	144	157	3	2	1	2	168	28	0	.167

Bob McGraw

McGRAW, ROBERT EMMETT
B. Apr. 10, 1895, La Veta, Colo.　　D. June 2, 1978, Seal Beach, Calif.　　BR TR 6'2"　　160 lbs.

	W	L	PCT	ERA	G	GS	CG	IP	H	BB	SO	ShO	W	L	SV	AB	H	HR	BA
1917 NY A	0	1	.000	0.82	2	2	1	11	9	3	3	0	0	0	0	3	0	0	.000
1918	0	1	.000	∞	1	1	0	0	0	4	0	0	0	0	0	0	0	0	–
1919 2 teams				NY A (6G 1–0)				BOS A (10G 0–2)											
" total	1	2	.333	5.44	16	1	0	43	44	27	9	0	1	1	0	13	1	0	.077
1920 NY A	0	0	–	4.67	15	0	0	27	24	20	11	0	0	0	0	7	0	0	.000
1925 BKN N	0	0	–	3.20	2	2	2	19.2	14	13	3	0	0	0	0	6	1	0	.167
1926	9	13	.409	4.59	33	21	10	174.1	197	67	49	0	1	2	1	55	8	0	.145
1927 2 teams				BKN N (1G 0–1)				STL N (18G 4–5)											
" total	4	6	.400	5.23	19	13	4	98	126	32	39	1	0	1	0	34	6	1	.176

	W	L	PCT	ERA	G	GS	CG	IP	H	BB	SO	ShO	Relief Pitching W	L	SV	BATTING AB	H	HR	BA

Bob McGraw continued

	W	L	PCT	ERA	G	GS	CG	IP	H	BB	SO	ShO	W	L	SV	AB	H	HR	BA
1928 PHI N	7	8	.467	4.64	39	3	0	132	150	56	28	0	5	8	1	36	4	0	.111
1929	5	5	.500	5.73	41	4	0	86.1	113	43	22	0	4	4	4	20	4	0	.200
9 yrs.	26	38	.406	4.89	168	47	17	591.1	677	265	164	1	11	16	6	174	24	1	.138
1 yr.	4	5	.444	5.07	18	12	4	94	121	30	37	1	0	1	0	33	6	1	.182

Lee Meadows

MEADOWS, HENRY LEE (Specs)
B. July 12, 1894, Oxford, N. C.
D. Jan. 29, 1963, Daytona Beach, Fla.
BL TR 5'9" 190 lbs. BR 1920-21, BB 1926,1929

	W	L	PCT	ERA	G	GS	CG	IP	H	BB	SO	ShO	W	L	SV	AB	H	HR	BA
1915 STL N	13	11	.542	2.99	39	26	14	244	232	88	104	1	3	0	0	83	8	0	.096
1916	12	23	.343	2.58	51	36	11	289	261	119	120	1	5	3	2	95	15	0	.158
1917	15	9	.625	3.09	43	37	18	265.1	253	90	100	4	3	0	2	89	9	0	.101
1918	8	14	.364	3.59	30	22	12	165.1	176	56	49	0	1	2	1	55	7	0	.127
1919 2 teams			STL	N	(22G 4-10)		PHI	N	(18G 8-10)										
" total	12	20	.375	2.69	40	29	18	241.1	228	79	116	4	2	2	0	80	9	0	.113
1920 PHI N	16	14	.533	2.84	35	33	19	247	249	90	95	3	1	0	0	82	14	0	.171
1921	11	16	.407	4.31	28	27	15	194.1	226	62	52	2	1	0	0	62	13	3	.210
1922	12	18	.400	4.03	33	33	19	237	264	71	62	0	0	0	0	86	27	0	.314
1923 2 teams			PHI	N	(8G 1-3)		PIT	N	(31G 16-10)										
" total	17	13	.567	3.83	39	30	17	246.2	290	59	76	1	1	1	1	98	26	1	.265
1924 PIT N	13	12	.520	3.26	36	30	15	229.1	240	51	61	3	1	1	0	82	16	0	.195
1925	19	10	.655	3.67	35	31	20	255.1	272	67	87	1	1	2	1	97	17	1	.175
1926	20	9	.690	3.97	36	31	15	226.2	254	52	54	1	3	0	0	88	20	0	.227
1927	19	10	.655	3.40	40	38	25	299.1	315	66	84	2	0	0	0	115	18	0	.157
1928	1	1	.500	8.10	4	2	1	10	18	5	3	0	0	0	0	4	2	0	.500
1929	0	0	–	13.50	1	0	0	.2	2	1	0	0	0	0	0	1	0	0	.000
15 yrs.	188	180	.511	3.38	490	405	219	3151.1	3280	956	1063	25	22	11	7	1117	201	5	.180
5 yrs.	52	67	.437	3.00	185	133	58	1055.2	1022	383	401	7	13	7	5	351	42	0	.120

WORLD SERIES

	W	L	PCT	ERA	G	GS	CG	IP	H	BB	SO	ShO	W	L	SV	AB	H	HR	BA
1925 PIT N	0	1	.000	3.38	1	1	0	8	6	0	4	0	0	0	0	1	0	0	.000
1927	0	1	.000	9.95	1	1	0	6.1	7	1	6	0	0	0	0	2	0	0	.000
2 yrs.	0	2	.000	6.28	2	2	0	14.1	13	1	10	0	0	0	0	3	0	0	.000

Sam Mejias

MEJIAS, SAMUEL ELIAS
B. May 9, 1953, Santiago, Dominican Republic
BR TR 6' 170 lbs.

	W	L	PCT	ERA	G	GS	CG	IP	H	BB	SO	ShO	W	L	SV	AB	H	HR	BA
1978 MON N	0	0	–	0.00	1	0	0	1	0	0	0	0	0	0	0	*			

Steve Melter

MELTER, STEPHEN BLASIUS
D. Jan. 28, 1962, Mishawaka, Ind.
TR

	W	L	PCT	ERA	G	GS	CG	IP	H	BB	SO	ShO	W	L	SV	AB	H	HR	BA
1909 STL N	2	1	.667	3.50	23	1	0	64.1	79	20	24	0	2	1	1	15	2	0	.133

John Mercer

MERCER, JOHN LOCKE
B. June 22, 1890, Taylortown, La.
BL TL 5'10½" 155 lbs.

	W	L	PCT	ERA	G	GS	CG	IP	H	BB	SO	ShO	W	L	SV	AB	H	HR	BA
1910 PIT N	0	0	–	0.00	1	0	0	2	1	2	1	0	0	0	0	0	0	0	–

Lloyd Merritt

MERRITT, LLOYD WESLEY .
B. Apr. 8, 1933, St. Louis, Mo.
BR TR 6' 189 lbs.

	W	L	PCT	ERA	G	GS	CG	IP	H	BB	SO	ShO	W	L	SV	AB	H	HR	BA
1957 STL N	1	2	.333	3.31	44	0	0	65.1	60	28	35	0	1	2	7	7	0	0	.000

Sam Mertes

MERTES, SAMUEL BLAIR (Sandow)
B. Aug. 6, 1872, San Francisco, Calif. D. Mar. 11, 1945, San Francisco, Calif.
BR TR 5'10" 185 lbs.

	W	L	PCT	ERA	G	GS	CG	IP	H	BB	SO	ShO	W	L	SV	AB	H	HR	BA
1902 CHI A	1	0	1.000	1.17	1	0	0	7.2	6	0	0	0	1	0	0	*			

Clarence Metzger

METZGER, CLARENCE EDWARD (Butch)
B. May 23, 1952, Lafayette, Ind.
BR TR 6'1" 185 lbs.

	W	L	PCT	ERA	G	GS	CG	IP	H	BB	SO	ShO	W	L	SV	AB	H	HR	BA
1974 SF N	1	0	1.000	3.46	10	0	0	13	11	12	5	0	1	0	0	0	0	0	–
1975 SD N	1	0	1.000	7.20	4	0	0	5	6	4	6	0	1	0	0	0	0	0	–
1976	11	4	.733	2.92	77	0	0	123.1	119	52	89	0	11	4	16	8	0	0	.000
1977 2 teams			SD	N	(17G 0-0)		STL	N	(58G 4-2)										
" total	4	2	.667	3.59	75	1	0	115.1	105	50	54	0	4	2	7	7	0	0	.000
1978 NY N	1	3	.250	6.57	25	0	0	37	48	22	21	0	1	3	0	0	0	0	–
5 yrs.	18	9	.667	3.74	191	1	0	293.2	289	140	175	0	18	9	23	15	0	0	.000
1 yr.	4	2	.667	3.11	58	0	0	92.2	78	38	48	0	4	2	7	4	0	0	.000

Pete Mikkelsen

MIKKELSEN, PETER JAMES
B. Oct. 25, 1939, Staten Island, N. Y.
BR TR 6'2" 210 lbs.

	W	L	PCT	ERA	G	GS	CG	IP	H	BB	SO	ShO	W	L	SV	AB	H	HR	BA
1964 NY A	7	4	.636	3.56	50	0	0	86	79	41	63	0	7	4	12	16	1	0	.063
1965	4	9	.308	3.28	41	3	0	82.1	78	36	69	0	4	6	1	10	1	0	.100
1966 PIT N	9	8	.529	3.07	71	0	0	126	106	51	76	0	9	8	14	20	3	0	.150
1967 2 teams			PIT	N	(32G 1-2)		CHI	N	(7G 0-0)										
" total	1	2	.333	4.55	39	0	0	63.1	59	24	30	0	1	2	2	4	0	0	.000
1968 2 teams			CHI	N	(3G 0-0)		STL	N	(5G 0-0)										
" total	0	0		2.61	8	0	0	20.2	17	8	13	0	0	0	0	4	1	0	.250
1969 LA N	7	5	.583	2.78	48	0	0	81	57	30	51	0	7	5	4	6	1	0	.167
1970	4	2	.667	2.76	33	0	0	62	48	20	47	0	4	2	6	6	2	0	.333
1971	8	5	.615	3.65	41	0	0	74	67	17	46	0	8	5	5	10	2	0	.200
1972	5	5	.500	4.06	33	0	0	57.2	65	23	41	0	5	5	5	7	0	0	.000
9 yrs.	45	40	.529	3.38	364	3	0	653	576	250	436	0	45	37	49	83	11	0	.133
1 yr.	0	0	–	1.13	5	0	0	16	10	7	8	0	0	0	0	0	0	0	.000

WORLD SERIES

	W	L	PCT	ERA	G	GS	CG	IP	H	BB	SO	ShO	W	L	SV	AB	H	HR	BA
1964 NY A	0	1	.000	5.79	4	0	0	4.2	4	2	4	0	0	1	0	0	0	0	–

	W	L	PCT	ERA	G	GS	CG	IP	H	BB	SO	ShO	Relief Pitching W	L	SV	AB	H	HR	BA

Bob Miller

MILLER, ROBERT LANE
B. Feb. 18, 1939, St. Louis, Mo.
BR TR 6'1"   180 lbs.

	W	L	PCT	ERA	G	GS	CG	IP	H	BB	SO	ShO	W	L	SV	AB	H	HR	BA
1957 STL N	0	0	—	7.00	5	0	0	9	13	5	7	0	0	0	0	0	0	0	—
1959	4	3	.571	3.31	11	10	3	70.2	66	21	43	0	0	0	0	24	5	0	.208
1960	4	3	.571	3.42	15	7	0	52.2	53	17	33	0	1	0	0	14	2	0	.143
1961	1	3	.250	4.24	34	5	0	74.1	82	46	39	0	1	1	3	14	5	0	.357
1962 NY N	1	12	.077	4.89	33	21	1	143.2	146	62	91	0	0	1	1	41	5	0	.122
1963 LA N	10	8	.556	2.89	42	23	2	187	171	65	125	0	4	2	1	57	4	0	.070
1964	7	7	.500	2.62	74	2	0	137.2	115	63	94	0	6	7	9	19	3	0	.158
1965	6	7	.462	2.97	61	1	0	103	82	26	77	0	6	6	9	16	0	0	.000
1966	4	2	.667	2.77	46	0	0	84.1	70	29	58	0	4	2	5	13	1	0	.077
1967	2	9	.182	4.31	52	4	0	85.2	88	27	32	0	2	6	0	8	1	0	.125
1968 MIN A	0	3	.000	2.74	45	0	0	72.1	65	24	41	0	0	3	2	7	1	0	.143
1969	5	5	.500	3.02	48	11	1	119.1	118	32	57	0	0	4	3	31	0	0	.000
1970 3 teams				CLE A (15G 2–2)			CHI N (7G 0–0)			CHI A (15G 4–6)									
" total	6	8	.429	4.79	37	15	0	107	129	54	55	0	2	0	3	28	5	0	.179
1971 3 teams				CHI N (2G 0–0)			SD N (38G 7–3)			PIT N (16G 1–2)									
" total	8	5	.615	1.64	56	0	0	98.2	83	40	51	0	8	5	10	12	0	0	.000
1972 PIT N	5	2	.714	2.65	36	0	0	54.1	54	24	18	0	5	2	3	4	0	0	.000
1973 3 teams				DET A (22G 4–2)			SD N (18G 0–0)			NY N (1G 0–0)									
" total	4	2	.667	3.67	41	0	0	73.2	63	34	39	0	4	2	1	2	0	0	.000
1974 NY N	2	2	.500	3.58	58	0	0	78	89	39	35	0	2	2	2	9	1	0	.111
17 yrs.	69	81	.460	3.37	694	99	7	1551.1	1487	608	895	0	45	43	52	299	33	0	.110
4 yrs.	9	9	.500	3.83	65	22	3	206.2	214	89	122	0	2	1	3	52	12	0	.231

LEAGUE CHAMPIONSHIP SERIES

	W	L	PCT	ERA	G	GS	CG	IP	H	BB	SO	ShO	W	L	SV	AB	H	HR	BA
1969 MIN A	0	1	.000	5.40	1	1	0	1.2	5	0	0	0	0	0	0	0	0	0	—
1971 PIT N	0	0	—	6.00	1	0	0	3	3	3	3	0	0	0	0	1	0	0	.000
1972	0	0	—	0.00	1	0	0	1	0	0	1	0	0	0	0	0	0	0	—
3 yrs.	0	1	.000	4.76	3	1	0	5.2	8	3	4	0	0	0	0	1	0	0	.000

WORLD SERIES

	W	L	PCT	ERA	G	GS	CG	IP	H	BB	SO	ShO	W	L	SV	AB	H	HR	BA
1965 LA N	0	0	—	0.00	2	0	0	1.1	0	0	0	0	0	0	0	0	0	0	—
1966	0	0	—	0.00	1	0	0	3	2	2	1	0	0	0	0	0	0	0	—
1971 PIT N	0	1	.000	3.86	3	0	0	4.2	7	1	2	0	0	0	0	0	0	0	—
3 yrs.	0	1	.000	2.00	6	0	0	9	9	3	3	0	0	0	0	0	0	0	—

Stu Miller

MILLER, STUART LEONARD
B. Dec. 26, 1927, Northampton, Mass.
BR TR 5'11½" 165 lbs.

	W	L	PCT	ERA	G	GS	CG	IP	H	BB	SO	ShO	W	L	SV	AB	H	HR	BA
1952 STL N	6	3	.667	2.05	12	11	6	88	63	26	64	2	1	0	0	25	3	0	.120
1953	7	8	.467	5.56	40	18	8	137.2	161	47	79	2	0	1	4	43	8	0	.186
1954	2	3	.400	5.79	19	4	0	46.2	55	29	22	0	1	2	2	13	4	0	.308
1956 2 teams				STL N (3G 0–1)			PHI N (24G 5–8)												
" total	5	9	.357	4.50	27	15	2	114	121	56	60	0	2	1	1	26	4	0	.154
1957 NY N	7	9	.438	3.63	38	13	0	124	110	45	60	0	6	3	1	35	2	0	.057
1958 SF N	6	9	.400	2.47	41	20	4	182	160	49	119	1	0	2	0	50	6	0	.120
1959	8	7	.533	2.84	59	9	2	167.2	164	57	95	0	7	4	8	45	2	0	.044
1960	7	6	.538	3.90	47	3	2	101.2	100	31	65	0	5	5	2	25	5	0	.200
1961	14	5	.737	2.66	63	0	0	122	95	37	89	0	14	5	17	20	4	0	.200
1962	5	8	.385	4.12	59	0	0	107	107	42	78	0	5	8	19	16	2	0	.125
1963 BAL A	5	8	.385	2.24	71	0	0	112.1	93	53	114	0	5	8	27	16	5	0	.313
1964	7	7	.500	3.06	66	0	0	97	77	34	87	0	7	7	23	9	1	0	.111
1965	14	7	.667	1.89	67	0	0	119.1	87	32	104	0	14	7	24	16	1	0	.063
1966	9	4	.692	2.25	51	0	0	92	65	22	67	0	9	4	18	19	2	0	.105
1967	3	10	.231	4.12	42	0	0	81.1	63	36	60	0	3	10	8	11	0	0	.000
1968 ATL N	0	0	—	54.00	2	0	0	.2	1	4	1	0	0	0	0	0	0	0	—
16 yrs.	105	103	.505	3.24	704	93	24	1693.1	1522	600	1164	5	79 10th	67	154	369	49	0	.133
4 yrs.	15	15	.500	4.47	74	33	14	279.2	291	107	170	4	2	4	7	82	15	0	.183

WORLD SERIES

	W	L	PCT	ERA	G	GS	CG	IP	H	BB	SO	ShO	W	L	SV	AB	H	HR	BA
1962 SF N	0	0	—	0.00	2	0	0	1.1	1	2	0	0	0	0	0	0	0	0	—

Larry Milton

MILTON, S. LAWRENCE
B. Pittsburg, Kans.

	W	L	PCT	ERA	G	GS	CG	IP	H	BB	SO	ShO	W	L	SV	AB	H	HR	BA
1903 STL N	0	0	—	2.25	1	0	0	4	3	1	0	0	0	0	0	2	1	0	.500

Clarence Mitchell

MITCHELL, CLARENCE ELMER
B. Feb. 22, 1891, Franklin, Neb.   D. Nov. 6, 1963, Grand Island, Neb.
BL TL 5'11½" 190 lbs.

	W	L	PCT	ERA	G	GS	CG	IP	H	BB	SO	ShO	W	L	SV	AB	H	HR	BA
1911 DET A	1	0	1.000	8.16	5	1	0	14.1	20	7	4	0	1	0	0	4	2	0	.500
1916 CIN N	11	10	.524	3.14	29	24	17	194.2	211	45	52	1	0	1	0	117	28	0	.239
1917	9	15	.375	3.22	32	20	10	159.1	166	34	37	2	2	3	1	90	25	0	.278
1918 BKN N	0	1	.000	108.00	1	1	0	.1	4	0	0	0	0	0	0	24	6	0	.250
1919	7	5	.583	3.06	23	11	9	108.2	123	23	43	0	1	0	0	49	18	1	.367
1920	5	2	.714	3.09	19	7	3	78.2	85	23	18	1	0	1	1	107	25	0	.234
1921	11	9	.550	2.89	37	18	13	190	206	46	39	3	2	2	2	91	24	0	.264
1922	0	3	.000	14.21	5	3	0	12.2	28	7	1	0	0	0	0	155	45	3	.290
1923 PHI N	9	10	.474	4.72	29	19	8	139.1	170	46	42	1	1	0	0	78	21	1	.269
1924	6	13	.316	5.62	30	26	9	165	223	58	36	1	0	1	0	102	26	0	.255
1925	10	17	.370	5.28	32	26	12	199.1	245	51	46	1	0	1	1	92	18	0	.196
1926	9	14	.391	4.58	28	25	12	178.2	232	55	52	0	1	0	1	78	19	0	.244
1927	6	3	.667	4.09	13	12	8	94.2	99	28	17	1	0	0	0	42	10	1	.238
1928 2 teams				PHI N (3G 0–0)			STL N (19G 8–9)												
" total	8	9	.471	3.53	22	18	9	155.2	162	40	31	1	1	0	0	60	8	0	.133
1929 STL N	8	11	.421	4.27	25	22	16	173	221	60	39	0	0	0	0	66	18	0	.273
1930 2 teams				STL N (1G 1–0)			NY N (24G 10–3)												
" total	11	3	.786	4.02	25	17	5	132	156	38	41	0	1	2	0	49	13	0	.265

	W	L	PCT	ERA	G	GS	CG	IP	H	BB	SO	ShO	Relief Pitching W	L	SV	BATTING AB	H	HR	BA

Clarence Mitchell continued

	W	L	PCT	ERA	G	GS	CG	IP	H	BB	SO	ShO	W	L	SV	AB	H	HR	BA
1931 NY N	13	11	.542	4.07	27	25	13	190.1	221	52	39	0	0	0	0	73	16	1	.219
1932	1	3	.250	4.15	8	3	1	30.1	41	11	7	0	0	1	2	10	2	0	.200
18 yrs.	125	139	.473	4.12	390	278	145	2217	2613	624	544	12	10	13	9	*			
3 yrs.	17	20	.459	3.84	45	41	25	326	375	100	71	1	1	0	0	124	26	0	.210

WORLD SERIES

	W	L	PCT	ERA	G	GS	CG	IP	H	BB	SO	ShO	W	L	SV	AB	H	HR	BA
1920 BKN N	0	0	–	0.00	1	0	0	4.2	3	3	1	0	0	0	0	3	1	0	.333
1928 STL N	0	0	–	1.59	1	0	0	5.2	2	2	2	0	0	0	0	2	0	0	.000
2 yrs.	0	0	–	0.87	2	0	0	10.1	5	5	3	0	0	0	0	5	1	0	.200

Vinegar Bend Mizell

MIZELL, WILMER DAVID
B. Aug. 13, 1930, Leakesville, Miss.   BR TL 6'3½" 205 lbs.

	W	L	PCT	ERA	G	GS	CG	IP	H	BB	SO	ShO	W	L	SV	AB	H	HR	BA
1952 STL N	10	8	.556	3.65	30	30	7	190	171	**103**	146	2	0	0	0	68	3	0	.044
1953	13	11	.542	3.49	33	33	10	224.1	193	114	173	1	0	0	0	83	7	1	.084
1956	14	14	.500	3.62	33	33	11	208.2	172	92	153	3	0	0	0	75	8	0	.107
1957	8	10	.444	3.74	33	21	7	149.1	136	51	87	2	1	1	0	45	4	0	.089
1958	10	14	.417	3.42	30	29	8	189.2	178	91	80	2	0	0	0	61	7	0	.115
1959	13	10	.565	4.20	31	30	8	201.1	196	89	108	1	1	0	0	75	14	0	.187
1960 2 teams			STL N	(9G 1-3)		PIT	N	(23G 13-5)											
" total	14	8	.636	3.59	32	32	8	211	205	74	113	3	0	0	0	69	9	0	.130
1961 PIT N	7	10	.412	5.04	25	17	2	100	120	31	37	1	1	0	0	23	3	0	.130
1962 2 teams			PIT	N	(4G 1-1)		NY	N	(17G 0-2)										
" total	1	3	.250	6.63	21	5	0	54.1	63	35	21	0	0	2	0	14	2	0	.143
9 yrs.	90	88	.506	3.85	268	230	61	1528.2	1434	680	918	15	3	3	0	513	57	1	.111
7 yrs.	69	70	.496	3.72	199	185	51	1218.2	1110	568	789	11	2	1	0	425	45	1	.106
										8th	**8th**								

WORLD SERIES

	W	L	PCT	ERA	G	GS	CG	IP	H	BB	SO	ShO	W	L	SV	AB	H	HR	BA
1960 PIT N	0	1	.000	15.43	2	1	0	2.1	4	2	1	0	0	0	0	0	0	0	–

Herb Moford

MOFORD, HERBERT
B. Aug. 6, 1928, Brooksville, Ky.   BR TR 6'1" 175 lbs.

	W	L	PCT	ERA	G	GS	CG	IP	H	BB	SO	ShO	W	L	SV	AB	H	HR	BA
1955 STL N	1	1	.500	7.88	14	1	0	24	29	15	8	0	1	0	2	2	0	0	.000
1958 DET A	4	9	.308	3.61	25	11	6	109.2	83	42	58	0	0	2	1	37	1	0	.027
1959 BOS A	0	2	.000	11.42	4	2	0	8.2	10	6	7	0	0	0	0	1	0	0	.000
1962 NY N	0	1	.000	7.20	7	0	0	15	21	1	5	0	0	1	0	4	1	0	.250
4 yrs.	5	13	.278	5.03	50	14	6	157.1	143	64	78	0	1	3	3	44	2	0	.045
1 yr.	1	1	.500	7.88	14	1	0	24	29	15	8	0	1	0	2	2	0	0	.000

Jim Mooney

MOONEY, JAMES IRVING
B. Sept. 4, 1906, Mooresburg, Tenn.   D. Apr. 27, 1979, Johnson City, Tenn.   BR TL 5'11" 168 lbs.

	W	L	PCT	ERA	G	GS	CG	IP	H	BB	SO	ShO	W	L	SV	AB	H	HR	BA
1931 NY N	7	1	.875	2.01	10	8	6	71.2	71	16	38	2	1	0	0	25	4	0	.160
1932	6	10	.375	5.05	29	18	4	124.2	154	42	37	1	0	1	0	41	5	0	.122
1933 STL N	2	5	.286	3.72	21	8	2	77.1	87	26	14	0	0	1	1	20	1	0	.050
1934	2	4	.333	5.47	32	7	1	82.1	114	49	27	0	2	0	1	19	1	0	.053
4 yrs.	17	20	.459	4.25	92	41	13	356	426	133	116	3	3	2	2	105	11	0	.105
2 yrs.	4	9	.308	4.62	53	15	3	159.2	201	75	41	0	2	1	2	39	2	0	.051

WORLD SERIES

	W	L	PCT	ERA	G	GS	CG	IP	H	BB	SO	ShO	W	L	SV	AB	H	HR	BA
1934 STL N	0	0	–	0.00	1	0	0	1	1	1	0	0	0	0	0	0	0	0	–

Donnie Moore

MOORE, DONNIE ROY
B. Feb. 13, 1954, Lubbock, Tex.   BL TR 6' 170 lbs.

	W	L	PCT	ERA	G	GS	CG	IP	H	BB	SO	ShO	W	L	SV	AB	H	HR	BA
1975 CHI N	0	0	–	4.00	4	1	0	9	12	4	8	0	0	0	0	3	0	0	.000
1977	4	2	.667	4.04	27	1	0	49	51	18	34	0	3	2	0	10	3	0	.300
1978	9	7	.563	4.11	71	1	0	103	117	31	50	0	9	7	4	15	4	0	.267
1979	1	4	.200	5.18	39	1	0	73	95	25	43	0	1	3	1	13	2	0	.154
1980 STL N	1	1	.500	6.14	11	0	0	22	25	5	10	0	1	1	0	4	3	0	.750
1981 MIL A	0	0	–	6.75	3	0	0	4	4	4	2	0	0	0	0	0	0	0	–
1982 ATL N	3	1	.750	4.23	16	0	0	27.2	32	7	17	0	3	1	1	1	0	0	.000
7 yrs.	18	15	.545	4.57	171	4	0	287.2	336	94	164	0	17	14	6	46	12	0	.261
1 yr.	1	1	.500	6.14	11	0	0	22	25	5	10	0	1	1	0	4	3	0	.750

LEAGUE CHAMPIONSHIP SERIES

	W	L	PCT	ERA	G	GS	CG	IP	H	BB	SO	ShO	W	L	SV	AB	H	HR	BA
1982 ATL N	0	0	–	0.00	2	0	0	2.2	2	0	1	0	0	0	0	0	0	0	–

Terry Moore

MOORE, TERRY BLUFORD
B. May 27, 1912, Vernon, Ala.
Manager 1954.   BR TR 5'11" 195 lbs.

	W	L	PCT	ERA	G	GS	CG	IP	H	BB	SO	ShO	W	L	SV	AB	H	HR	BA
1939 STL N	0	0	–	0.00	1	0	0	1	0	0	1	0	0	0	0	*			

Tommy Moore

MOORE, TOMMY JOE
B. July 7, 1948, Lynwood, Calif.   BR TR 5'11" 175 lbs.

	W	L	PCT	ERA	G	GS	CG	IP	H	BB	SO	ShO	W	L	SV	AB	H	HR	BA
1972 NY N	0	0	–	2.92	3	1	0	12.1	12	1	5	0	0	0	0	3	1	0	.333
1973	0	1	.000	10.80	3	1	0	3.1	6	3	1	0	0	0	0	0	0	0	–
1975 2 teams			STL N	(10G 0-0)		TEX	A	(12G 0-2)											
" total	0	2	.000	6.08	22	0	0	40	46	24	21	0	0	2	0	2	1	0	.500
1977 SEA A	2	1	.667	4.91	14	1	0	33	36	21	13	0	2	0	0	0	0	0	–
4 yrs.	2	4	.333	5.38	42	3	0	88.2	100	49	40	0	2	2	0	5	2	0	.400
1 yr.	0	0	–	3.79	10	0	0	19	15	12	6	0	0	0	0	2	1	0	.500

	W	L	PCT	ERA	G	GS	CG	IP	H	BB	SO	ShO	W	L	SV	AB	H	HR	BA

Whitey Moore

MOORE, LLOYD ALBERT   BR TR 6'1"   195 lbs.
B. June 10, 1912, Tuscarawas, Ohio

	W	L	PCT	ERA	G	GS	CG	IP	H	BB	SO	ShO	W	L	SV	AB	H	HR	BA
1936 CIN N	1	0	1.000	5.40	1	0	0	5	3	3	4	0	1	0	0	2	0	0	.000
1937	0	3	.000	4.89	13	6	0	38.2	32	39	27	0	0	0	0	8	0	0	.000
1938	6	4	.600	3.49	19	11	3	90.1	66	42	38	1	2	0	0	26	2	0	.077
1939	13	12	.520	3.45	42	24	9	187.2	177	95	81	2	4	0	3	61	6	0	.098
1940	8	8	.500	3.63	25	15	5	116.2	100	56	60	1	2	2	1	39	5	0	.128
1941	2	1	.667	4.38	23	4	1	61.2	62	45	17	0	1	0	0	18	3	0	.167
1942 2 teams				CIN N (1G 0–0)			STL N (9G 0–1)												
" total	0	1	.000	4.05	10	0	0	13.1	10	12	1	0	0	1	0	2	0	0	.000
7 yrs.	30	29	.508	3.75	133	60	18	513.1	450	292	228	4	10	3	4	156	16	0	.103
1 yr.	0	1	.000	4.38	9	0	0	12.1	10	11	1	0	0	1	0	2	0	0	.000
WORLD SERIES																			
1939 CIN N	0	0	–	0.00	1	0	0	3	0	0	2	0	0	0	0	1	0	0	.000
1940	0	0	–	3.24	1	0	0	8.1	8	6	7	0	0	0	0	2	0	0	.000
2 yrs.	0	0	–	2.38	2	0	0	11.1	8	6	9	0	0	0	0	3	0	0	.000

Charley Moran

MORAN, CHARLES BARTHELL (Uncle Charlie)   BR TR 5'8"   180 lbs.
B. Feb. 22, 1878, Nashville, Tenn.   D. June 13, 1949, Horse Cave, Ky.

	W	L	PCT	ERA	G	GS	CG	IP	H	BB	SO	ShO	W	L	SV	AB	H	HR	BA
1903 STL N	0	1	.000	5.25	3	2	2	24	30	19	7	0	0	0	0	*			

Forrest More

MORE, FORREST T.   BR TR 6'   180 lbs.
B. Sept. 30, 1883, Hayden, Ind.   D. Aug. 17, 1968, Columbus, Ind.

	W	L	PCT	ERA	G	GS	CG	IP	H	BB	SO	ShO	W	L	SV	AB	H	HR	BA
1909 2 teams				STL N (15G 1–5)			BOS N (10G 0–4)												
" total	1	9	.100	4.74	25	7	4	98.2	95	40	27	0	0	5	0	28	3	0	.107

Gene Moriarity

MORIARITY, EUGENE JOHN   5'8"   190 lbs.
B. Holyoke, Mass.   Deceased.

	W	L	PCT	ERA	G	GS	CG	IP	H	BB	SO	ShO	W	L	SV	AB	H	HR	BA
1884 BOS N	0	2	.000	5.27	2	2	2	13.2	16	7	4	1	0	0	0	53	9	0	.170
1885 DET N	0	0	–	9.00	1	0	0	2	3	1	1	0	0	0	0	39	1	0	.026
2 yrs.	0	2	.000	5.74	3	2	2	15.2	19	8	5	1	0	0	0	*			

Billy Muffett

MUFFETT, BILLY ARNOLD (Muff)   BR TR 6'1"   198 lbs.
B. Sept. 21, 1930, Hammond, Ind.

	W	L	PCT	ERA	G	GS	CG	IP	H	BB	SO	ShO	W	L	SV	AB	H	HR	BA
1957 STL N	3	2	.600	2.25	23	0	0	44	35	13	21	0	3	2	8	7	0	0	.000
1958	4	6	.400	4.93	35	6	1	84	107	42	41	0	3	3	5	20	4	0	.200
1959 SF N	0	0	–	5.40	5	0	0	6.2	11	3	3	0	0	0	0	0	0	0	–
1960 BOS A	6	4	.600	3.24	23	14	4	125	116	36	75	1	1	1	0	41	11	0	.268
1961	3	11	.214	5.67	38	11	2	112.2	130	36	47	0	2	3	2	23	5	1	.217
1962	0	0	–	9.00	1	1	0	4	8	2	1	0	0	0	0	1	0	0	.000
6 yrs.	16	23	.410	4.33	125	32	7	376.1	407	132	188	1	9	9	15	92	20	1	.217
2 yrs.	7	8	.467	4.01	58	6	1	128	142	55	62	0	6	5	13	27	4	0	.148

George Munger

MUNGER, GEORGE DAVID (Red)   BR TR 6'2"   200 lbs.
B. Oct. 4, 1918, Houston, Tex.

	W	L	PCT	ERA	G	GS	CG	IP	H	BB	SO	ShO	W	L	SV	AB	H	HR	BA
1943 STL N	9	5	.643	3.95	32	9	5	93.1	101	42	45	0	4	2	2	28	6	0	.214
1944	11	3	.786	1.34	21	12	7	121	92	41	55	2	2	1	2	44	5	0	.114
1946	2	2	.500	3.33	10	7	2	48.2	47	12	28	0	0	0	1	16	4	0	.250
1947	16	5	.762	3.37	40	31	13	224.1	218	76	123	6	0	0	3	81	15	0	.185
1948	10	11	.476	4.50	39	25	7	166	179	74	72	2	0	2	0	50	8	0	.160
1949	15	8	.652	3.87	35	28	12	188.1	179	87	82	2	0	2	2	66	17	1	.258
1950	7	8	.467	3.90	32	20	5	154.2	158	70	61	1	1	1	0	51	7	0	.137
1951	4	6	.400	5.32	23	11	3	94.2	106	46	44	0	2	2	0	29	5	0	.172
1952 2 teams				STL N (1G 0–1)			PIT N (5G 0–3)												
" total	0	4	.000	7.92	6	5	0	30.2	37	11	9	0	0	0	0	9	0	0	.000
1956 PIT N	3	4	.429	4.04	35	13	0	107	126	41	45	0	1	1	2	28	3	0	.107
10 yrs.	77	56	.579	3.83	273	161	54	1228.2	1243	500	564	13	10	11	12	402	70	1	.174
9 yrs.	74	49	.602	3.73	233	144	54	1095.1	1087	449	511	13	9	10	10	367	67	1	.183
				7th															
WORLD SERIES																			
1946 STL N	1	0	1.000	1.00	1	1	1	9	9	3	2	0	0	0	0	4	1	0	.250

Les Munns

MUNNS, LESLIE ERNEST (Nemo, Big Ed)   BR TR 6'5"   212 lbs.
B. Dec. 1, 1908, Grand Forks, N. D.

	W	L	PCT	ERA	G	GS	CG	IP	H	BB	SO	ShO	W	L	SV	AB	H	HR	BA
1934 BKN N	3	7	.300	4.71	33	9	4	99.1	106	60	41	0	1	1	0	29	7	0	.241
1935	1	3	.250	5.55	21	5	0	58.1	74	33	13	0	1	0	1	16	3	0	.188
1936 STL N	0	3	.000	3.00	7	1	0	24	23	12	4	0	0	3	1	9	1	0	.111
3 yrs.	4	13	.235	4.76	61	15	4	181.2	203	105	58	0	2	4	2	54	11	0	.204
1 yr.	0	3	.000	3.00	7	1	0	24	23	12	4	0	0	3	1	9	1	0	.111

Steve Mura

MURA, STEPHEN ANDREW   BR TR 6'2"   188 lbs.
B. Dec. 2, 1955, New Orleans, La.

	W	L	PCT	ERA	G	GS	CG	IP	H	BB	SO	ShO	W	L	SV	AB	H	HR	BA
1978 SD N	0	2	.000	11.25	5	2	0	8	15	5	5	0	0	0	0	1	0	0	.000
1979	4	4	.500	3.08	38	5	0	73	57	37	59	0	3	2	2	10	0	0	.000
1980	8	7	.533	3.67	37	23	3	169	149	86	109	1	0	0	2	51	7	0	.137
1981	5	14	.263	4.27	23	22	2	139	156	50	70	0	0	0	0	44	6	0	.136
1982 STL N	12	11	.522	4.05	35	30	7	184.1	196	80	84	1	0	0	0	53	3	0	.057
5 yrs.	29	38	.433	3.97	138	82	12	573.1	573	258	327	2	3	3	4	159	16	0	.101
1 yr.	12	11	.522	4.05	35	30	7	184.1	196	80	84	1	0	0	0	53	3	0	.057

	W	L	PCT	ERA	G	GS	CG	IP	H	BB	SO	ShO	Relief Pitching W	L	SV	BATTING AB	H	HR	BA

Tim Murchison

MURCHISON, THOMAS MALCOLM
B. Oct. 8, 1896, Liberty, N. C.   D. Oct. 20, 1962, Liberty, N. C.   BR TL 6'   185 lbs.

	W	L	PCT	ERA	G	GS	CG	IP	H	BB	SO	ShO	W	L	SV	AB	H	HR	BA
1917 STL N	0	0	–	0.00	1	0	0	1	0	2	0	0	0	0	0	0	0	0	–
1920 CLE A	0	0	–	0.00	2	0	0	5	3	4	0	0	0	0	0	1	0	0	.000
2 yrs.	0	0	–	0.00	3	0	0	6	3	6	2	0	0	0	0	1	0	0	.000
1 yr.	0	0	–	0.00	1	0	0	1	0	2	2	0	0	0	0	0	0	0	–

Ed Murphy

MURPHY, EDWARD J.
B. Jan. 22, 1877, Auburn, N. Y.   D. Jan. 29, 1935, Weedsport, N. Y.   TR

	W	L	PCT	ERA	G	GS	CG	IP	H	BB	SO	ShO	W	L	SV	AB	H	HR	BA
1898 PHI N	1	2	.333	5.10	7	3	2	30	41	10	8	0	0	0	0	14	5	0	.357
1901 STL N	10	9	.526	4.20	23	21	16	165	201	32	42	0	0	0	0	64	16	1	.250
1902	9	7	.563	3.02	23	17	12	164	187	31	37	1	1	0	1	61	16	0	.262
1903	4	8	.333	3.31	15	12	9	106	108	38	16	0	1	1	0	64	13	0	.203
4 yrs.	24	26	.480	3.64	68	53	39	465	537	111	103	1	2	1	1	203	50	1	.246
3 yrs.	23	24	.489	3.54	61	50	37	435	496	101	95	1	2	1	1	189	45	1	.238

Tom Murphy

MURPHY, THOMAS ANDREW
B. Dec. 30, 1945, Cleveland, Ohio   BR TR 6'3"   185 lbs.

	W	L	PCT	ERA	G	GS	CG	IP	H	BB	SO	ShO	W	L	SV	AB	H	HR	BA
1968 CAL A	5	6	.455	2.17	15	15	3	99.1	67	28	56	0	0	0	0	28	0	0	.000
1969	10	16	.385	4.21	36	35	4	215.2	213	69	100	0	0	0	0	71	10	0	.141
1970	16	13	.552	4.24	39	38	5	227	223	81	99	2	0	0	0	76	14	1	.184
1971	6	17	.261	3.78	37	36	7	243	228	82	89	0	0	0	0	75	13	0	.173
1972 2 teams					CAL A	(6G 0–0)		KC A	(18G 4–4)										
" total	4	4	.500	3.36	24	9	1	80.1	90	24	36	1	1	0	1	14	0	0	.000
1973 STL N	3	7	.300	3.76	19	13	2	88.2	89	22	42	0	0	0	0	23	4	0	.174
1974 MIL A	10	10	.500	1.90	70	0	0	123	97	51	47	0	10	10	20	2	1	0	.500
1975	1	9	.100	4.60	52	0	0	72.1	85	27	32	0	1	9	20	0	0	0	–
1976 2 teams					MIL A	(15G 0–1)		BOS A	(37G 4–5)										
" total	4	6	.400	4.17	52	0	0	99.1	116	34	39	0	4	6	9	0	0	0	–
1977 2 teams					BOS A	(16G 0–1)		TOR A	(19G 2–1)										
" total	2	2	.500	4.79	35	1	0	82.2	107	30	39	0	1	2	2	0	0	0	–
1978 TOR A	6	9	.400	3.93	50	0	0	94	87	37	36	0	6	9	7	0	0	0	–
1979	1	2	.333	5.50	10	0	0	18	23	8	6	0	1	2	0	0	0	0	–
12 yrs.	68	101	.402	3.78	439	147	22	1443.1	1425	493	621	3	24	38	59	289	42	1	.145
1 yr.	3	7	.300	3.76	19	13	2	88.2	89	22	42	0	0	0	0	23	4	0	.174

Stan Musial

MUSIAL, STANLEY FRANK (Stan the Man)
B. Nov. 21, 1920, Donora, Pa.
Hall of Fame 1969.   BL TL 6'   175 lbs.

	W	L	PCT	ERA	G	GS	CG	IP	H	BB	SO	ShO	W	L	SV	AB	H	HR	BA
1952 STL N	0	0	–	0.00	1	0	0	0	0	0	0	0	0	0	0	*			

Mike Nagy

NAGY, MICHAEL TIMOTHY
B. Mar. 25, 1948, Bronx, N. Y.   BR TR 6'3"   195 lbs.

	W	L	PCT	ERA	G	GS	CG	IP	H	BB	SO	ShO	W	L	SV	AB	H	HR	BA
1969 BOS A	12	2	.857	3.11	33	28	7	196.2	183	106	84	1	0	0	0	65	5	0	.077
1970	6	5	.545	4.47	23	20	4	129	138	64	56	0	0	0	0	44	11	0	.250
1971	1	3	.250	6.63	12	7	0	38	46	20	9	0	0	1	0	12	1	0	.083
1972	0	0	–	9.00	1	0	0	2	3	0	2	0	0	0	0	0	0	0	–
1973 STL N	0	2	.000	4.20	9	7	0	40.2	44	15	14	0	0	0	0	11	1	0	.091
1974 HOU N	1	1	.500	8.53	9	0	0	12.2	17	5	5	0	1	1	0	1	0	0	.000
6 yrs.	20	13	.606	4.15	87	62	11	419	431	210	170	1	1	2	0	133	18	0	.135
1 yr.	0	2	.000	4.20	9	7	0	40.2	44	15	14	0	0	0	0	11	1	0	.091

Sam Nahem

NAHEM, SAMUEL RALPH
B. Oct. 19, 1915, New York, N. Y.   BR TR 6'1½"   190 lbs.

	W	L	PCT	ERA	G	GS	CG	IP	H	BB	SO	ShO	W	L	SV	AB	H	HR	BA
1938 BKN N	1	0	1.000	3.00	1	1	1	9	6	4	2	0	0	0	0	5	2	0	.400
1941 STL N	5	2	.714	2.98	26	8	2	81.2	76	38	31	0	1	1	1	23	4	0	.174
1942 PHI N	1	3	.250	4.94	35	2	0	74.2	72	40	38	0	1	2	0	20	2	0	.100
1948	3	3	.500	7.02	28	1	0	59	68	45	30	0	3	2	0	13	2	0	.154
4 yrs.	10	8	.556	4.69	90	12	3	224.1	222	127	101	0	5	5	1	61	10	0	.164
1 yr.	5	2	.714	2.98	26	8	2	81.2	76	38	31	0	1	1	1	23	4	0	.174

Mike Naymick

NAYMICK, MICHAEL JOHN
B. Sept. 6, 1917, Berlin, Pa.   BR TR 6'8"   225 lbs.

	W	L	PCT	ERA	G	GS	CG	IP	H	BB	SO	ShO	W	L	SV	AB	H	HR	BA
1939 CLE A	0	1	.000	1.93	2	1	1	4.2	3	5	3	0	0	0	0	3	0	0	.000
1940	1	2	.333	5.10	13	4	0	30	36	17	15	0	0	0	0	6	1	0	.167
1943	4	4	.500	2.30	29	4	0	62.2	47	47	41	0	4	1	2	16	3	0	.188
1944 2 teams					CLE A	(7G 0–0)		STL N	(1G 0–0)										
" total	0	0	–	9.00	8	0	0	15	18	11	5	0	0	0	0	1	0	0	.000
4 yrs.	5	7	.417	3.93	52	9	1	112.1	89	80	64	0	4	1	2	26	4	0	.154
1 yr.	0	0	–	4.50	1	0	0	2	2	1	0	0	0	0	0	0	0	0	–

Mel Nelson

NELSON, MELVIN FREDERICK
B. May 30, 1936, San Diego, Calif.   BR TL 6'   185 lbs.

	W	L	PCT	ERA	G	GS	CG	IP	H	BB	SO	ShO	W	L	SV	AB	H	HR	BA
1960 STL N	0	1	.000	3.38	2	1	0	8	7	2	7	0	0	0	0	2	1	0	.500
1963 LA A	2	3	.400	5.30	36	3	0	52.2	55	32	41	0	2	0	1	11	1	0	.091
1965 MIN A	0	4	.000	4.12	28	3	0	54.2	57	23	31	0	0	3	3	9	1	0	.111
1967	0	0	–	54.00	1	0	0	.1	3	0	0	0	0	0	0	0	0	0	–
1968 STL N	2	1	.667	2.91	18	4	1	52.2	49	9	16	0	0	1	1	12	2	0	.167
1969	0	1	.000	12.60	8	0	0	5	13	3	3	0	0	1	0	0	0	0	–
6 yrs.	4	10	.286	4.41	93	11	1	173.1	184	69	98	0	2	5	5	34	5	0	.147
3 yrs.	2	3	.400	3.70	28	4	1	65.2	69	14	26	0	2	2	1	14	3	0	.214
WORLD SERIES																			
1968 STL N	0	0	–	0.00	1	0	0	1	0	0	1	0	0	0	0	0	0	0	–

	W	L	PCT	ERA	G	GS	CG	IP	H	BB	SO	ShO	Relief Pitching W	L	SV	BATTING AB	H	HR	BA

Kid Nichols

NICHOLS, CHARLES AUGUSTUS
B. Sept. 14, 1869, Madison, Wis.   D. Apr. 11, 1953, Kansas City, Mo.
Manager 1904-05.
Hall of Fame 1949.
BR TR 5'10½" 175 lbs.

	W	L	PCT	ERA	G	GS	CG	IP	H	BB	SO	ShO	W	L	SV	AB	H	HR	BA
1890 BOS N	27	19	.587	2.21	48	47	47	427	374	112	222	7	0	0	0	174	43	0	.247
1891	30	17	.638	2.39	52	48	45	425.2	413	103	240	5	0	1	3	183	36	0	.197
1892	35	16	.686	2.83	53	51	50	454	404	121	187	5	1	0	0	197	39	2	.198
1893	33	13	.717	3.52	52	45	44	425	426	127	94	1	3	1	1	177	39	2	.220
1894	32	13	.711	4.75	50	46	40	407	488	121	113	3	1	1	0	170	50	0	.294
1895	30	14	.682	3.29	48	42	42	394	417	82	146	1	0	0	3	157	37	0	.236
1896	30	15	.667	2.81	49	43	37	375	387	101	102	3	2	1	1	147	28	1	.190
1897	30	11	.732	2.64	46	40	37	368	362	72	136	2	2	0	3	147	39	3	.265
1898	29	12	.707	2.13	50	42	40	388	316	85	138	5	3	0	3	158	38	2	.241
1899	21	17	.553	2.94	42	37	37	349	326	86	109	4	1	2	1	136	26	1	.191
1900	13	15	.464	3.07	29	27	25	231.1	215	73	54	4	0	2	0	90	18	1	.200
1901	18	15	.545	3.17	38	34	33	326	306	90	143	4	2	1	0	163	46	4	.282
1904 STL N	21	13	.618	2.02	36	35	35	317	268	50	134	3	0	0	1	109	17	0	.156
1905 2 teams		STL	N	(7G 1-5)	PHI	N	(17G 10-6)												
" total	11	11	.500	3.11	24	23	20	191	193	46	66	1	0	0	0	75	15	0	.200
1906 PHI N	0	1	.000	9.82	4	2	1	11	17	13	1	0	0	0	0	3	0	0	.000
15 yrs.	360	202	.641	2.94	621	562	533	5089	4912	1282	1885	48	15	9	16	*			
		7th																	
2 yrs.	22	18	.550	2.49	43	42	40	369	332	68	150	3	0	0	1	131	22	0	.168

Dick Niehaus

NIEHAUS, RICHARD J.
B. Oct. 24, 1892, Covington, Ky.   D. Mar. 12, 1957, Atlanta, Ga.
BL TL 5'11" 165 lbs.

	W	L	PCT	ERA	G	GS	CG	IP	H	BB	SO	ShO	W	L	SV	AB	H	HR	BA
1913 STL N	0	2	.000	4.13	3	3	2	24	20	13	4	0	0	0	0	7	2	0	.286
1914	1	0	1.000	3.12	8	1	1	17.1	18	8	6	0	0	0	0	4	1	0	.250
1915	2	1	.667	3.97	15	2	0	45.1	48	22	21	0	1	0	0	14	1	0	.071
1920 CLE A	1	2	.333	3.60	19	3	0	40	42	16	12	0	1	0	2	9	4	0	.444
4 yrs.	4	5	.444	3.77	45	9	3	126.2	128	59	43	0	2	0	2	34	8	0	.235
3 yrs.	3	3	.500	3.84	26	6	3	86.2	86	43	31	0	1	0	0	25	4	0	.160

Fred Norman

NORMAN, FREDIE HUBERT
B. Aug. 20, 1942, San Antonio, Tex.
BL TL 5'8" 155 lbs.

	W	L	PCT	ERA	G	GS	CG	IP	H	BB	SO	ShO	W	L	SV	AB	H	HR	BA
1962 KC A	0	0	—	2.25	2	0	0	4	4	1	2	0	0	0	0	0	0	0	—
1963	0	1	.000	11.37	2	2	0	6.1	9	7	6	0	0	0	0	1	0	0	.000
1964 CHI N	0	4	.000	6.54	8	5	0	31.2	34	21	20	0	0	0	0	11	1	0	.091
1966	0	0	—	4.50	2	0	0	4	5	2	6	0	0	0	0	0	0	0	—
1967	0	0	—	0.00	1	0	0	1	0	0	3	0	0	0	0	0	0	0	—
1970 2 teams		LA	N	(30G 2-0)	STL	N	(1G 0-0)												
" total	2	0	1.000	5.14	31	0	0	63	66	33	47	0	2	0	1	7	1	0	.143
1971 2 teams		STL	N	(4G 0-0)	SD	N	(20G 3-12)												
" total	3	12	.200	3.57	24	18	5	131	121	63	81	0	0	0	0	38	9	0	.237
1972 SD N	9	11	.450	3.44	42	28	10	211.2	195	88	167	6	1	0	2	64	8	0	.125
1973 2 teams		SD	N	(12G 1-7)	CIN	N	(24G 12-6)												
" total	13	13	.500	3.60	36	35	8	240.1	208	101	161	3	0	0	0	80	6	0	.075
1974 CIN N	13	12	.520	3.15	35	26	8	186	170	68	141	2	0	2	0	61	8	0	.131
1975	12	4	.750	3.73	34	26	2	188	163	84	119	0	1	0	0	60	7	0	.117
1976	12	7	.632	3.10	33	24	8	180	153	70	126	3	1	0	0	50	7	0	.140
1977	14	13	.519	3.38	35	34	8	221	200	98	160	1	0	0	0	73	8	0	.110
1978	11	9	.550	3.71	36	31	0	177	173	82	111	0	1	0	1	50	7	0	.140
1979	11	13	.458	3.65	34	31	5	195	193	57	95	0	0	1	0	59	9	0	.153
1980 MON N	4	4	.500	4.05	48	8	0	98.6	96	40	58	0	1	0	4	20	1	0	.050
16 yrs.	104	103	.502	3.64	403	268	56	1938.6	1790	815	1303	15	6	4	8	574	72	0	.125
2 yrs.	0	0	—	9.64	5	0	0	4.2	8	7	4	0	0	0	0	0	0	0	—

LEAGUE CHAMPIONSHIP SERIES

	W	L	PCT	ERA	G	GS	CG	IP	H	BB	SO	ShO	W	L	SV	AB	H	HR	BA
1973 CIN N	0	0	—	1.80	1	1	0	5	1	3	3	0	0	0	0	1	0	0	.000
1975	1	0	1.000	1.50	1	1	0	6	4	5	4	0	0	0	0	1	0	0	.000
1979	0	0	—	18.00	1	0	0	2	4	1	1	0	0	0	0	1	0	0	.000
3 yrs.	1	0	1.000	4.15	3	2	0	13	9	9	8	0	0	0	0	3	0	0	.000

WORLD SERIES

	W	L	PCT	ERA	G	GS	CG	IP	H	BB	SO	ShO	W	L	SV	AB	H	HR	BA
1975 CIN N	0	1	.000	9.00	2	1	0	4	8	3	2	0	0	0	0	1	0	0	.000
1976	0	0	—	4.26	1	1	0	6.1	9	2	2	0	0	0	0	0	0	0	—
2 yrs.	0	1	.000	6.10	3	2	0	10.1	17	5	4	0	0	0	0	1	0	0	.000

Lou North

NORTH, LOUIS ALEXANDER
B. June 15, 1891, Elgin, Ill.   D. May 16, 1974, Shelton, Conn.
BR TR 5'11" 175 lbs.

	W	L	PCT	ERA	G	GS	CG	IP	H	BB	SO	ShO	W	L	SV	AB	H	HR	BA
1913 DET A	0	1	.000	15.00	1	1	0	6	10	9	3	0	0	0	0	2	0	0	.000
1917 STL N	0	0	—	3.97	5	0	0	11.1	14	4	4	0	0	0	0	3	0	0	.000
1920	3	2	.600	3.27	24	6	3	88	90	32	37	0	1	1	1	31	7	0	.226
1921	4	4	.500	3.54	40	6	0	86.1	81	32	28	0	4	4	7	19	3	0	.158
1922	10	3	.769	4.45	53	11	4	149.2	164	64	84	0	5	1	4	47	11	0	.234
1923	3	4	.429	5.15	34	3	0	71.2	90	31	24	0	2	4	1	22	4	0	.182
1924 2 teams		STL	N	(6G 0-0)	BOS	N	(9G 1-2)												
" total	1	2	.333	5.76	15	4	1	50	60	28	19	0	0	0	0	13	2	0	.154
7 yrs.	21	16	.568	4.43	172	25	8	463	509	200	199	0	12	10	13	137	27	1	.197
6 yrs.	20	13	.606	4.20	162	20	7	421.2	454	172	185	0	12	10	13	126	26	1	.206

Howie Nunn

NUNN, HOWARD RALPH
B. Oct. 18, 1935, Westfield, N. C.
BR TR 6' 173 lbs.

	W	L	PCT	ERA	G	GS	CG	IP	H	BB	SO	ShO	W	L	SV	AB	H	HR	BA
1959 STL N	2	2	.500	7.59	16	0	0	21.1	23	15	20	0	2	2	0	1	0	0	.000
1961 CIN N	2	1	.667	3.58	24	0	0	37.2	35	24	26	0	2	1	0	8	2	0	.250
1962	0	0	—	5.59	6	0	0	9.2	15	3	4	0	0	0	0	1	0	0	.000

	W	L	PCT	ERA	G	GS	CG	IP	H	BB	SO	ShO	W	L	SV	AB	H	HR	BA
													Relief Pitching			**BATTING**			

Howie Nunn continued

	W	L	PCT	ERA	G	GS	CG	IP	H	BB	SO	ShO	W	L	SV	AB	H	HR	BA
3 yrs.	4	3	.571	5.11	46	0	0	68.2	73	42	50	0	4	3	0	10	2	0	.200
1 yr.	2	2	.500	7.59	16	0	0	21.1	23	15	20	0	2	2	0	1	0	0	.000

Rich Nye

NYE, RICHARD RAYMOND
B. Aug. 4, 1944, Oakland, Calif. BL TL 6'4" 185 lbs.

	W	L	PCT	ERA	G	GS	CG	IP	H	BB	SO	ShO	W	L	SV	AB	H	HR	BA
1966 CHI N	0	2	.000	2.12	3	2	0	17	16	7	9	0	0	0	0	4	1	0	.250
1967	13	10	.565	3.20	35	30	7	205	179	52	119	0	0	1	0	75	16	0	.213
1968	7	12	.368	3.80	27	20	6	132.2	145	34	74	1	1	0	1	44	8	0	.182
1969	3	5	.375	5.09	34	5	1	69	72	21	39	0	0	0	3	16	1	0	.063
1970 2 teams					MON N (8G 3–2)				STL N (6G 0–0)										
" total	3	2	.600	4.14	14	6	2	54.1	60	26	26	0	0	0	0	19	4	0	.211
5 yrs.	26	31	.456	3.71	113	63	16	478	472	140	267	1	1	1	4	158	30	0	.190
1 yr.	0	0	–	4.50	6	0	0	8	13	6	5	0	0	0	0	2	1	0	.500

Dan O'Brien

O'BRIEN, DANIEL JOSEPH
B. Apr. 22, 1954, St. Petersburg, Fla. BR TR 6'4" 215 lbs.

	W	L	PCT	ERA	G	GS	CG	IP	H	BB	SO	ShO	W	L	SV	AB	H	HR	BA
1978 STL N	0	2	.000	4.50	7	2	0	18	22	8	12	0	0	1	0	3	0	0	.000
1979	1	1	.500	8.18	6	0	0	11	21	3	5	0	1	1	0	2	0	0	.000
2 yrs.	1	3	.250	5.90	13	2	0	29	43	11	17	0	1	2	0	5	0	0	.000
2 yrs.	1	3	.250	5.90	13	2	0	29	43	11	17	0	1	2	0	5	0	0	.000

Johnny O'Brien

O'BRIEN, JOHN THOMAS
Brother of Eddie O'Brien.
B. Dec. 11, 1930, South Amboy, N. J. BR TR 5'9" 170 lbs.

	W	L	PCT	ERA	G	GS	CG	IP	H	BB	SO	ShO	W	L	SV	AB	H	HR	BA
1956 PIT N	1	0	1.000	2.84	8	0	0	19	8	9	9	0	1	0	0	104	18	0	.173
1957	0	3	.000	6.08	16	1	0	40	46	24	19	0	0	2	0	35	11	0	.314
1958	0	0	–	22.50	1	0	0	2	7	2	2	0	0	0	0	3	0	0	.000
3 yrs.	1	3	.250	5.61	25	1	0	61	61	35	30	0	1	2	0	*			
1 yr.	0	0	–	22.50	1	0	0	2	7	2	2	0	0	0	0	2	0	0	.000

Bill O'Hara

O'HARA, WILLIAM ALEXANDER
B. Aug. 14, 1883, Toronto, Ont., Canada D. June 15, 1931, Jersey City, N. J. BL

	W	L	PCT	ERA	G	GS	CG	IP	H	BB	SO	ShO	W	L	SV	AB	H	HR	BA
1910 STL N	0	0	–	0.00	1	0	0	1	0	0	0	0	0	0	0	*			

Diomedes Olivo

OLIVO, DIOMEDES ANTONIO
Brother of Chi Chi Olivo.
B. Jan. 22, 1919, Guayubin, Dominican Republic D. Feb. 15, 1977, Santo Domingo, Dominican Republic BL TL 6'1" 195 lbs.

	W	L	PCT	ERA	G	GS	CG	IP	H	BB	SO	ShO	W	L	SV	AB	H	HR	BA
1960 PIT N	0	0	–	2.79	4	0	0	9.2	8	5	10	0	0	0	0	1	0	0	.000
1962	5	1	.833	2.77	62	1	0	84.1	88	25	66	0	5	1	7	16	3	0	.188
1963 STL N	0	5	.000	5.40	19	0	0	13.1	16	9	9	0	0	5	0	0	0	0	–
3 yrs.	5	6	.455	3.10	85	1	0	107.1	112	39	85	0	5	6	7	17	3	0	.176
1 yr.	0	5	.000	5.40	19	0	0	13.1	16	9	9	0	0	5	0	0	0	0	–

Alan Olmsted

OLMSTED, ALAN RAY
B. Mar. 18, 1957, St. Louis, Mo. BR TL 6'2" 195 lbs.

	W	L	PCT	ERA	G	GS	CG	IP	H	BB	SO	ShO	W	L	SV	AB	H	HR	BA
1980 STL N	1	1	.500	2.83	5	5	0	35	32	14	14	0	0	0	0	11	2	0	.182

Jack O'Neill

O'NEILL, JOHN JOSEPH
Brother of Jim O'Neill. Brother of Steve O'Neill.
Brother of Mike O'Neill.
B. Jan. 10, 1873, Maam, Ireland D. June 29, 1935, Scranton, Pa. BR TR 5'10" 165 lbs.

	W	L	PCT	ERA	G	GS	CG	IP	H	BB	SO	ShO	W	L	SV	AB	H	HR	BA
1902 STL N	1	1	.500	5.00	2	2	2	18	21	8	6	0	0	0	0	*			

Mike O'Neill

O'NEILL, MICHAEL JOYCE
Played as Mike Joyce 1901. Brother of Jim O'Neill.
Brother of Jack O'Neill. Brother of Steve O'Neill.
B. Sept. 7, 1877, Galway, Ireland D. Aug. 12, 1959, Scranton, Pa. BL TL 5'11" 185 lbs.

	W	L	PCT	ERA	G	GS	CG	IP	H	BB	SO	ShO	W	L	SV	AB	H	HR	BA
1901 STL N	2	2	.500	1.32	5	4	4	41	29	10	16	1	0	0	0	15	6	0	.400
1902	17	13	.567	2.76	34	30	27	270.1	276	58	99	2	2	0	0	135	43	2	.319
1903	4	13	.235	4.77	19	17	12	115	184	43	39	0	0	0	0	110	25	0	.227
1904	10	14	.417	2.09	25	24	23	220	229	50	68	1	0	0	0	91	21	0	.231
1907 CIN N	0	0	–	0.00	0	0	0	0	0	0	0	0	0	0	0	29	2	0	.069
5 yrs.	33	42	.440	2.80	83	75	66	646.1	718	161	222	4	2	0	0	*			
4 yrs.	33	42	.440	2.80	83	75	66	646.1	718	161	222	4	2	0	0	351	95	2	.271

Claude Osteen

OSTEEN, CLAUDE WILSON
B. Aug. 9, 1939, Caney Springs, Tenn. BL TL 5'11" 160 lbs.

	W	L	PCT	ERA	G	GS	CG	IP	H	BB	SO	ShO	W	L	SV	AB	H	HR	BA
1957 CIN N	0	0	–	2.25	3	0	0	4	4	3	3	0	0	0	0	1	0	0	.000
1959	0	0	–	7.04	2	0	0	7.2	11	9	3	0	0	0	0	2	0	0	.000
1960	0	1	.000	5.03	20	3	0	48.1	53	30	15	0	0	0	0	12	1	0	.083
1961 2 teams					CIN N (1G 0–0)				WAS A (3G 1–1)										
" total	1	1	.500	4.82	4	3	0	18.2	14	9	14	0	0	0	0	7	1	0	.143
1962 WAS A	8	13	.381	3.65	28	22	7	150.1	140	47	59	2	0	0	1	48	10	0	.208
1963	9	14	.391	3.35	40	29	8	212.1	222	60	109	2	1	1	0	70	12	1	.171
1964	15	13	.536	3.33	37	36	13	257	256	64	133	0	0	0	0	90	14	1	.156
1965 LA N	15	15	.500	2.79	40	40	9	287	253	78	162	1	0	0	0	99	12	0	.121
1966	17	14	.548	2.85	39	38	8	240.1	238	65	137	3	0	0	0	76	16	1	.211
1967	17	17	.500	3.22	39	39	14	288.1	298	52	152	5	0	0	0	101	18	2	.178
1968	12	18	.400	3.08	39	36	5	254	267	54	119	3	0	0	0	84	15	0	.179

	W	L	PCT	ERA	G	GS	CG	IP	H	BB	SO	ShO	Relief Pitching W	L	SV	BATTING AB	H	HR	BA

Claude Osteen continued

	W	L	PCT	ERA	G	GS	CG	IP	H	BB	SO	ShO	W	L	SV	AB	H	HR	BA
1969	20	15	.571	2.66	41	41	16	321	**293**	74	183	7	0	0	0	111	24	1	.216
1970	16	14	.533	3.82	37	37	11	259	280	52	114	4	0	0	0	93	19	1	.204
1971	14	11	.560	3.51	38	38	11	259	262	63	109	4	0	0	0	86	16	0	.186
1972	20	11	.645	2.64	33	33	14	252	232	69	100	4	0	0	0	88	24	1	.273
1973	16	11	.593	3.31	33	33	12	236.2	227	61	86	3	0	0	0	78	12	0	.154
1974 2 teams			HOU	N	(23G 9–9)		STL	N	(8G 0–2)										
" total	9	11	.450	3.80	31	23	7	161	184	58	51	2	0	1	0	53	13	0	.245
1975 CHI A	7	16	.304	4.36	37	37	5	204.1	237	92	63	0	0	0	0	0	0	0	—
18 yrs.	196	195	.501	3.30	541	488	140	3461	3471	940	1612	40	1	2	1	1099	207	8	.188
1 yr.	0	2	.000	4.37	8	2	0	22.2	26	11	6	0	0	0	0	7	0	0	.000
WORLD SERIES																			
1965 LA N	1	1	.500	0.64	2	2	1	14	9	5	4	1	0	0	0	3	1	0	.333
1966	0	1	.000	1.29	1	1	0	7	3	1	3	0	0	0	0	2	0	0	.000
2 yrs.	1	2	.333	0.86	3	3	1	21	12	6	7	1	0	0	0	5	1	0	.200

Jim Otten

OTTEN, JAMES EDWARD
B. July 1, 1951, Lewiston, Mont.   BR TR 6'2"   195 lbs.

	W	L	PCT	ERA	G	GS	CG	IP	H	BB	SO	ShO	W	L	SV	AB	H	HR	BA
1974 CHI A	0	1	.000	5.63	5	1	0	16	22	12	11	0	0	0	0	0	0	0	—
1975	0	0	—	6.75	2	0	0	5.1	4	7	3	0	0	0	0	0	0	0	—
1976	0	0	—	4.50	2	0	0	6	9	2	3	0	0	0	0	0	0	0	—
1980 STL N	0	5	.000	5.56	31	4	0	55	71	26	38	0	0	1	0	5	1	0	.200
1981	1	0	1.000	5.25	24	0	0	36	44	20	20	0	1	0	0	2	0	0	.000
5 yrs.	1	6	.143	5.48	64	5	0	118.1	150	67	75	0	1	1	0	7	1	0	.143
2 yrs.	1	5	.167	5.44	55	4	0	91	115	46	58	0	1	1	0	7	1	0	.143

Gene Packard

PACKARD, EUGENE MILO
B. July 13, 1887, Colorado Springs, Colo.   D. May 19, 1959, Riverside, Calif.   BL TL 5'10"   155 lbs.

	W	L	PCT	ERA	G	GS	CG	IP	H	BB	SO	ShO	W	L	SV	AB	H	HR	BA
1912 CIN N	1	0	1.000	3.00	1	1	1	9	7	4	2	0	0	0	0	4	1	0	.250
1913	7	11	.389	2.97	39	22	9	190.2	208	64	73	2	1	2	0	61	11	0	.180
1914 KC F	21	13	.618	2.89	42	34	24	302	282	88	154	4	3	0	4	116	28	1	.241
1915	20	11	.645	2.68	42	31	21	281.2	250	74	108	5	2	2	2	95	22	1	.232
1916 CHI N	10	6	.625	2.78	37	15	5	155.1	154	38	36	2	4	1	5	54	7	0	.130
1917 2 teams			CHI	N	(2G 0–0)		STL	N	(34G 9–6)										
" total	9	6	.600	2.55	36	11	6	155	141	25	45	0	6	0	2	52	15	0	.288
1918 STL N	12	12	.500	3.50	30	23	10	182.1	184	33	46	1	3	1	2	69	12	0	.174
1919 PHI N	6	8	.429	4.15	21	16	10	134.1	167	30	24	1	0	1	1	51	7	0	.137
8 yrs.	86	67	.562	3.01	248	153	86	1410.1	1393	356	488	15	19	7	16	502	103	2	.205
2 yrs.	21	18	.538	3.03	64	34	16	335.2	322	58	90	1	9	1	4	121	27	0	.223

Phil Paine

PAINE, PHILLIPS STEERE (Flip)
B. June 8, 1930, Chepachet, R. I.   D. Feb. 19, 1978, Lebanon, Pa.   BR TR 6'2"   180 lbs.

	W	L	PCT	ERA	G	GS	CG	IP	H	BB	SO	ShO	W	L	SV	AB	H	HR	BA
1951 BOS N	2	0	1.000	3.06	21	0	0	35.1	36	20	17	0	2	0	0	4	0	0	.000
1954 MIL N	1	0	1.000	3.86	11	0	0	14	14	12	11	0	1	0	0	0	0	0	—
1955	2	0	1.000	2.49	15	0	0	25.1	20	14	26	0	2	0	0	3	1	0	.333
1956	0	0	—	∞	1	0	0	0	3	0	0	0	0	0	0	0	0	0	—
1957	0	0	—	0.00	1	0	0	2	1	3	2	0	0	0	0	0	0	0	—
1958 STL N	5	1	.833	3.56	46	0	0	73.1	70	31	45	0	5	1	1	7	2	0	.286
6 yrs.	10	1	.909	3.36	95	0	0	150	144	80	101	0	10	1	1	14	3	0	.214
1 yr.	5	1	.833	3.56	46	0	0	73.1	70	31	45	0	5	1	1	7	2	0	.286

Lowell Palmer

PALMER, LOWELL RAYMOND
B. Aug. 18, 1947, Sacramento, Calif.   BR TR 6'1"   190 lbs.

	W	L	PCT	ERA	G	GS	CG	IP	H	BB	SO	ShO	W	L	SV	AB	H	HR	BA
1969 PHI N	2	8	.200	5.20	26	9	1	90	91	47	68	1	0	0	0	22	3	1	.136
1970	1	2	.333	5.47	38	5	0	102	98	55	85	0	1	1	0	27	4	0	.148
1971	0	0	—	6.00	3	1	0	15	13	13	6	0	0	0	0	5	1	0	.200
1972 2 teams			CLE	A	(1G 0–0)		STL	N	(16G 0–3)										
" total	0	3	.000	3.89	17	2	0	37	32	28	28	0	0	1	0	5	0	0	.000
1974 SD N	2	5	.286	5.67	22	8	1	73	68	59	52	0	1	2	0	23	2	0	.087
5 yrs.	5	18	.217	5.28	106	25	2	317	302	202	239	1	2	4	0	82	10	1	.122
1 yr.	0	3	.000	3.86	16	2	0	35	30	26	25	0	0	1	0	5	0	0	.000

Al Papai

PAPAI, ALFRED THOMAS
B. May 7, 1919, Divernon, Ill.   BR TR 6'3"   185 lbs.

	W	L	PCT	ERA	G	GS	CG	IP	H	BB	SO	ShO	W	L	SV	AB	H	HR	BA
1948 STL N	0	1	.000	5.06	10	0	0	16	14	7	8	0	0	1	0	2	0	0	.000
1949 STL A	4	11	.267	5.06	42	15	6	142.1	175	81	31	0	2	3	2	38	3	0	.079
1950 2 teams			BOS	A	(16G 4–2)		STL	N	(13G 1–0)										
" total	5	2	.714	6.33	29	3	2	69.2	82	42	26	0	4	0	2	20	3	0	.150
1955 CHI A	0	0	—	3.86	7	0	0	11.2	10	8	5	0	0	0	0	2	0	0	.000
4 yrs.	9	14	.391	5.37	88	18	8	239.2	281	138	70	0	6	4	4	62	6	0	.097
2 yrs.	1	1	.500	5.14	23	0	0	35	35	21	15	0	1	1	0	5	0	0	.000

Harry Parker

PARKER, HARRY WILLIAM
B. Sept. 14, 1947, Highland, Ill.   BR TR 6'3"   190 lbs.

	W	L	PCT	ERA	G	GS	CG	IP	H	BB	SO	ShO	W	L	SV	AB	H	HR	BA
1970 STL N	1	1	.500	3.27	7	4	0	22	24	15	9	0	1	1	0	8	2	0	.250
1971	0	0	—	7.20	4	0	0	5	6	2	2	0	0	0	0	0	0	0	—
1973 NY N	8	4	.667	3.35	38	9	0	96.2	79	36	63	0	4	2	5	23	4	0	.174
1974	4	12	.250	3.92	40	16	1	131	145	46	58	0	2	4	2	36	0	0	.000
1975 2 teams			NY	N	(18G 2–3)		STL	N	(14G 0–1)										
" total	2	4	.333	5.06	32	1	0	53.1	58	29	35	0	2	3	3	3	0	0	.000
1976 CLE A	0	0	—	3.00	3	0	0	7	3	0	5	0	0	0	0	0	0	0	—
6 yrs.	15	21	.417	3.86	124	30	1	315	315	128	172	0	7	8	12	70	6	0	.086
3 yrs.	1	2	.333	4.93	25	4	0	45.2	51	27	24	0	1	2	1	9	2	0	.222
LEAGUE CHAMPIONSHIP SERIES																			
1973 NY N	0	1	.000	9.00	1	0	0	1	1	1	0	0	0	1	0	0	0	0	—

	W	L	PCT	ERA	G	GS	CG	IP	H	BB	SO	ShO	Relief Pitching W	L	SV	BATTING AB	H	HR	BA

Harry Parker continued

WORLD SERIES
| 1973 NY N | 0 | 1 | .000 | 0.00 | 3 | 0 | 0 | 3.1 | 2 | 2 | 2 | 0 | 0 | 1 | 0 | 0 | 0 | 0 | – |

Roy Parker

PARKER, ROY W.
B. 1897   BR TR 6'2"   185 lbs.

| 1919 STL N | 0 | 0 | – | 31.50 | 2 | 0 | 0 | 2 | 6 | 1 | 0 | 0 | 0 | 0 | 0 | 0 | 0 | 0 | – |

Roy Parmelee

PARMELEE, LeROY EARL (Tarzan)   BR TR 6'1"   190 lbs.
B. Apr. 25, 1907, Lambertville, Mich.   D. Aug. 31, 1981, San Francisco, Calif.

1929 NY N	1	0	1.000	9.00	2	1	0	7	13	3	1	0	0	0	0	2	1	0	.500
1930	0	1	.000	9.43	11	1	0	21	18	26	19	0	0	0	0	4	1	0	.250
1931	2	2	.500	3.68	13	5	4	58.2	47	33	30	0	0	0	0	20	4	0	.200
1932	0	3	.000	3.91	8	3	0	25.1	25	14	23	0	0	0	0	5	2	0	.400
1933	13	8	.619	3.17	32	32	14	218.1	191	77	132	3	0	0	0	81	19	1	.235
1934	10	6	.625	3.42	22	20	7	152.2	134	60	83	3	0	0	0	55	11	2	.200
1935	14	10	.583	4.22	34	31	13	226	214	97	79	0	1	0	0	86	18	0	.209
1936 STL N	11	11	.500	4.56	37	28	9	221	226	107	79	0	0	1	2	76	15	0	.197
1937 CHI N	7	8	.467	5.13	33	18	8	145.2	165	79	55	0	0	1	0	52	9	2	.173
1939 PHI A	1	6	.143	6.45	14	5	0	44.2	42	35	13	0	1	2	1	15	2	0	.133
10 yrs.	59	55	.518	4.27	206	144	55	1120.1	1075	531	514	6	2	4	3	396	82	5	.207
1 yr.	11	11	.500	4.56	37	28	9	221	226	107	79	0	0	1	2	76	15	0	.197

Tom Parrott

PARROTT, THOMAS WILLIAM (Tacky Tom)   BR TR 5'10½"   170 lbs.
Brother of Jiggs Parrott.
B. Apr. 10, 1868, Portland, Ore.   D. Jan. 1, 1932, Newberg, Ore.

1893 2 teams			CHI N	(4G 0–3)		CIN N	(22G 10–7)											
" total	10	10	.500	4.48	26	20	13	181	209	87	40	1	3	0	0	95	20	1	.211
1894 CIN N	17	19	.472	5.60	41	36	31	308.2	402	126	61	1	0	1	1	229	74	4	.323
1895	11	18	.379	5.47	41	31	23	263.1	382	76	57	0	3	1	3	201	69	3	.343
1896 STL N	1	1	.500	6.21	7	2	2	42	62	18	8	0	0	0	0	474	138	7	.291
4 yrs.	39	48	.448	5.33	115	89	69	795	1055	307	166	2	6	2	4	*			
1 yr.	1	1	.500	6.21	7	2	2	42	62	18	8	0	0	0	0	474	138	7	.291

Stan Partenheimer

PARTENHEIMER, STANWOOD WENDELL (Party)   BB TL 5'11"   175 lbs.
Son of Steve Partenheimer.   BL 1944
B. Oct. 21, 1922, Chicopee Falls, Mass.

1944 BOS A	0	0	–	18.00	1	1	0	1	3	2	0	0	0	0	0	1	0	0	.000
1945 STL N	0	0	–	6.08	8	2	0	13.1	12	16	6	0	0	0	0	3	0	0	.000
2 yrs.	0	0	–	6.91	9	3	0	14.1	15	18	6	0	0	0	0	4	0	0	.000
1 yr.	0	0	–	6.08	8	2	0	13.1	12	16	6	0	0	0	0	3	0	0	.000

Daryl Patterson

PATTERSON, DARYL ALAN   BL TR 6'4"   192 lbs.
B. Nov. 21, 1943, Coalinga, Calif.

1968 DET A	2	3	.400	2.12	38	1	0	68	53	27	49	0	0	0	7	13	0	0	.000
1969	0	2	.000	2.82	18	0	0	22.1	15	19	12	0	0	2	0	1	0	0	.000
1970	7	1	.875	4.85	43	0	0	78	81	39	55	0	7	1	2	11	0	0	.000
1971 3 teams			DET A	(12G 0–1)		OAK A	(4G 0–0)		STL N	(13G 0–1)								
" total	0	2	.000	4.93	29	2	0	42	39	25	18	0	0	2	1	6	0	0	.000
1974 PIT N	2	1	.667	7.29	14	0	0	21	35	9	8	0	2	1	1	4	0	0	.000
5 yrs.	11	9	.550	4.09	142	3	0	231.1	223	119	142	0	9	6	11	35	0	0	.000
1 yr.	0	1	.000	4.33	13	2	0	27	20	15	11	0	0	1	1	5	0	0	.000

WORLD SERIES
| 1968 DET A | 0 | 0 | – | 0.00 | 2 | 0 | 0 | 3 | 1 | 1 | 0 | 0 | 0 | 0 | 0 | 0 | 0 | 0 | – |

Harry Patton

PATTON, HARRY C.
B. Davenport, Iowa

| 1910 STL N | 0 | 0 | – | 2.25 | 1 | 0 | 0 | 4 | 4 | 2 | 2 | 0 | 0 | 0 | 0 | 0 | 0 | 0 | – |

Gene Paulette

PAULETTE, EUGENE EDWARD   BR TR 6'   150 lbs.
B. May 26, 1891, Centralia, Ill.   D. Feb. 8, 1966, Little Rock, Ark.

| 1918 STL N | 0 | 0 | – | 0.00 | 1 | 0 | 0 | .1 | 1 | 1 | 0 | 0 | 0 | 0 | 0 | * | | | |

Gil Paulsen

PAULSEN, GUILFORD PAUL HANS   BR TR 6'2½"   190 lbs.
B. Nov. 14, 1902, Graettinger, Iowa

| 1925 STL N | 0 | 0 | – | 0.00 | 1 | 0 | 0 | 2 | 1 | 0 | 1 | 0 | 0 | 0 | 0 | 0 | 0 | 0 | – |

George Pearce

PEARCE, GEORGE THOMAS   BL TL 5'10½"   175 lbs.
B. Jan. 10, 1888, Aurora, Ill.   D. Oct. 11, 1935, Joliet, Ill.

1912 CHI N	0	0	–	5.52	3	2	0	14.2	15	12	9	0	0	0	0	6	1	0	.167
1913	13	5	.722	2.31	25	21	14	163.1	137	59	73	3	1	0	0	55	4	0	.073
1914	6	12	.333	3.51	30	17	4	141	122	65	78	0	2	3	1	45	4	0	.089
1915	13	9	.591	3.32	36	20	8	176	158	77	96	2	4	1	0	56	11	0	.196
1916	0	0	–	2.08	4	0	0	4.1	6	1	0	0	0	0	0	0	0	0	–
1917 STL N	1	1	.500	3.48	5	0	0	10.1	7	3	4	0	1	1	0	4	0	0	.000
6 yrs.	33	27	.550	3.11	103	61	26	509.2	445	217	260	5	8	5	1	166	20	0	.120
1 yr.	1	1	.500	3.48	5	0	0	10.1	7	3	4	0	1	1	0	4	0	0	.000

	W	L	PCT	ERA	G	GS	CG	IP	H	BB	SO	ShO	W	L	SV	AB	H	HR	BA
													Relief Pitching			BATTING			

Frank Pears

PEARS, FRANK T.
B. 1866, St. Louis, Mo.   Deceased.

	W	L	PCT	ERA	G	GS	CG	IP	H	BB	SO	ShO	W	L	SV	AB	H	HR	BA
1889 KC AA	0	2	.000	4.91	3	2	2	22	21	9	5	0	0	0	0	11	1	0	.091
1893 STL N	0	0	–	13.50	1	0	0	4	9	2	0	0	0	0	0	2	0	0	.000
2 yrs.	0	2	.000	6.23	4	2	2	26	30	11	5	0	0	0	0	13	1	0	.077
1 yr.	0	0	–	13.50	1	0	0	4	9	2	0	0	0	0	0	2	0	0	.000

Alex Pearson

PEARSON, ALEXANDER FRANKLIN   BR TR 5'10½" 160 lbs.
B. Mar. 9, 1877, Greensboro, Pa.   D. Oct. 30, 1966, Rochester, Pa.

	W	L	PCT	ERA	G	GS	CG	IP	H	BB	SO	ShO	W	L	SV	AB	H	HR	BA
1902 STL N	2	6	.250	3.95	11	10	8	82	90	22	24	0	0	0	0	34	9	0	.265
1903 CLE A	1	2	.333	3.56	4	3	2	30.1	34	3	12	0	0	0	0	12	1	0	.083
2 yrs.	3	8	.273	3.85	15	13	10	112.1	124	25	36	0	0	0	0	46	10	0	.217
1 yr.	2	6	.250	3.95	11	10	8	82	90	22	24	0	0	0	0	34	9	0	.265

Heinie Peitz

PEITZ, HENRY CLEMENT   BR TR 5'11" 165 lbs.
Brother of Joe Peitz.
B. Nov. 28, 1870, St. Louis, Mo.   D. Oct. 23, 1943, Cincinnati, Ohio

	W	L	PCT	ERA	G	GS	CG	IP	H	BB	SO	ShO	W	L	SV	AB	H	HR	BA
1894 STL N	0	0	–	9.00	1	0	0	3	7	2	0	0	0	0	0	338	89	3	.263
1897 CIN N	0	1	.000	7.88	2	1	1	8	9	4	0	0	0	0	0	266	78	1	.293
1899	0	0	–	5.40	1	0	0	5	6	1	3	0	0	0	0	290	79	1	.272
3 yrs.	0	1	.000	7.31	4	1	1	16	22	7	3	0	0	0	0	1041	277	6	.266
1 yr.	0	0	–	9.00	1	0	0	3	7	2	0	0	0	0	0	*			

Orlando Pena

PENA, ORLANDO GREGORY   BR TR 5'11" 154 lbs.
B. Nov. 17, 1933, Victoria de las Tunas, Cuba

	W	L	PCT	ERA	G	GS	CG	IP	H	BB	SO	ShO	W	L	SV	AB	H	HR	BA
1958 CIN N	1	0	1.000	0.60	9	0	0	15	10	4	11	0	1	0	3	0	0	0	–
1959	5	9	.357	4.76	46	8	1	136	150	39	76	0	2	4	5	34	3	0	.088
1960	0	1	.000	2.89	4	0	0	9.1	8	3	9	0	0	1	0	1	0	0	.000
1962 KC A	6	4	.600	3.01	13	12	6	89.2	71	27	56	1	0	0	0	31	5	0	.161
1963	12	20	.375	3.69	35	33	9	217	218	53	128	3	1	0	0	62	9	1	.145
1964	12	14	.462	4.43	40	32	5	219.1	231	73	184	0	0	0	0	75	12	1	.160
1965 2 teams	KC A	(12G 0–6)		DET A	(30G 4–6)														
" total	4	12	.250	4.18	42	5	0	92.2	96	33	79	0	4	7	4	17	3	0	.176
1966 DET A	4	2	.667	3.08	54	0	0	108	105	35	79	0	4	2	7	18	2	0	.111
1967 2 teams	DET A	(2G 0–1)		CLE A	(48G 0–3)														
" total	0	4	.000	3.59	50	1	0	90.1	72	22	74	0	3	8	0	8	0	0	.000
1970 PIT N	2	1	.667	4.74	23	0	0	38	38	7	25	0	2	1	2	6	0	0	.000
1971 BAL A	0	1	.000	3.00	5	0	0	15	16	5	4	0	0	1	0	3	0	0	.000
1973 2 teams	BAL A	(11G 1–1)		STL N	(42G 4–4)														
" total	5	5	.500	2.94	53	0	0	107	96	22	61	0	5	5	7	7	1	0	.143
1974 2 teams	STL N	(42G 5–2)		CAL A	(4G 0–0)														
" total	5	2	.714	2.21	46	0	0	53	51	21	28	0	5	2	4	2	1	0	.500
1975 CAL A	0	2	.000	2.13	7	0	0	12.2	13	8	4	0	0	2	0	0	0	0	–
14 yrs.	56	77	.421	3.70	427	93	21	1203	1175	352	818	4	24	28	40	264	36	2	.136
2 yrs.	9	6	.600	2.36	84	0	0	107	105	34	61	0	9	6	7	9	2	0	.222

Hub Perdue

PERDUE, HERBERT RODNEY (The Gallatin Squash)   BR TR 5'10½" 192 lbs.
B. June 7, 1882, Gallatin, Tenn.   D. Oct. 31, 1968, Gallatin, Tenn.

	W	L	PCT	ERA	G	GS	CG	IP	H	BB	SO	ShO	W	L	SV	AB	H	HR	BA
1911 BOS N	6	9	.400	4.98	24	19	9	137.1	180	41	40	0	0	0	1	48	10	0	.208
1912	13	16	.448	3.80	37	30	20	249	295	54	101	1	0	2	3	87	12	0	.138
1913	16	13	.552	3.26	38	32	16	212.1	201	39	91	3	2	0	1	67	7	0	.104
1914 2 teams	BOS N	(9G 2–5)		STL N	(22G 8–8)														
" total	10	13	.435	3.57	31	28	14	204.1	220	46	56	0	0	0	1	62	9	0	.145
1915 STL N	6	12	.333	4.21	31	13	5	115.1	141	19	29	1	3	5	1	36	4	0	.111
5 yrs.	51	63	.447	3.85	161	122	64	918.1	1037	199	317	5	5	7	7	300	42	0	.140
2 yrs.	14	20	.412	3.42	53	32	17	268.2	301	54	72	1	3	5	2	84	12	0	.143

Pol Perritt

PERRITT, WILLIAM DAYTON   BR TR 6'2" 168 lbs.
B. Aug. 30, 1892, Arcadia, La.   D. Oct. 15, 1947, Shreveport, La.

	W	L	PCT	ERA	G	GS	CG	IP	H	BB	SO	ShO	W	L	SV	AB	H	HR	BA
1912 STL N	1	1	.500	3.19	6	3	1	31	25	10	13	0	0	0	0	9	2	0	.222
1913	6	14	.300	5.25	36	21	8	175	205	64	64	0	3	0	0	59	12	0	.203
1914	16	13	.552	2.36	41	32	18	286	248	93	115	3	2	1	2	92	13	0	.141
1915 NY N	12	18	.400	2.66	35	30	16	220	226	59	91	4	1	1	0	68	11	0	.162
1916	17	11	.607	2.62	40	28	17	251	243	56	115	5	2	5	2	83	7	0	.084
1917	17	7	.708	1.88	35	26	14	215	186	45	72	5	2	3	1	70	11	0	.157
1918	18	13	.581	2.74	35	31	19	233	212	38	60	6	1	1	0	80	14	0	.175
1919	1	1	.500	7.11	11	3	0	19	27	12	2	0	1	0	1	4	0	0	.000
1920	0	0	–	1.80	9	0	0	15	9	4	3	0	0	0	0	4	0	0	.000
1921 2 teams	NY N	(5G 2–0)		DET A	(4G 1–0)														
" total	3	0	1.000	4.38	9	3	0	24.2	35	9	8	0	2	0	0	8	2	0	.250
10 yrs.	91	78	.538	2.89	256	177	93	1469.2	1416	390	543	23	14	11	8	477	72	0	.151
3 yrs.	23	28	.451	3.44	83	56	27	492	478	167	192	3	5	1	2	160	27	0	.169

WORLD SERIES

	W	L	PCT	ERA	G	GS	CG	IP	H	BB	SO	ShO	W	L	SV	AB	H	HR	BA
1917 NY N	0	0	–	2.16	3	0	0	8.1	9	3	3	0	0	0	0	2	2	0	1.000

Bill Pertica

PERTICA, WILLIAM ANDREW   BR TR 5'9" 165 lbs.
B. Aug. 17, 1898, Santa Barbara, Calif.   D. Dec. 28, 1967, Los Angeles, Calif.

	W	L	PCT	ERA	G	GS	CG	IP	H	BB	SO	ShO	W	L	SV	AB	H	HR	BA
1918 BOS A	0	0	–	3.00	1	0	0	3	0	1	0	0	0	0	0	0	0	0	.000
1921 STL N	14	10	.583	3.37	38	31	15	208.1	212	70	67	2	0	1	2	70	10	0	.143
1922	8	8	.500	5.91	34	14	2	117.1	153	65	30	0	4	2	0	33	6	0	.182
1923	0	0	–	3.86	1	1	0	2.1	2	3	0	0	0	0	0	2	0	0	.000
4 yrs.	22	18	.550	4.27	74	46	17	331	370	138	98	2	4	3	2	105	16	0	.152
3 yrs.	22	18	.550	4.28	73	46	17	328	367	138	97	2	4	3	2	104	16	0	.154

	W	L	PCT	ERA	G	GS	CG	IP	H	BB	SO	ShO	Relief Pitching W	L	SV	BATTING AB	H	HR	BA

Jeff Pfeffer

PFEFFER, EDWARD JOSEPH
Brother of Big Jeff Pfeffer.
B. Mar. 4, 1888, Seymour, Ill.   D. Aug. 15, 1972, Chicago, Ill.   BR TR 6'3"   210 lbs.

	W	L	PCT	ERA	G	GS	CG	IP	H	BB	SO	ShO	RW	RL	SV	AB	H	HR	BA
1911 STL A	0	0	–	7.20	2	0	0	10	11	4	4	0	0	0	0	4	0	0	.000
1913 BKN N	0	1	.000	3.33	5	2	1	24.1	28	13	13	0	0	0	0	7	0	0	.000
1914	23	12	.657	1.97	43	34	27	315	264	91	135	3	0	2	4	116	23	0	.198
1915	19	14	.576	2.10	40	34	26	291.2	243	76	84	6	1	2	3	106	27	0	.255
1916	25	11	.694	1.92	41	37	30	328.2	274	63	128	6	1	0	1	122	34	0	.279
1917	11	15	.423	2.23	30	30	24	266	225	66	115	3	0	0	0	100	13	0	.130
1918	1	0	1.000	0.00	1	1	1	9	2	3	1	1	0	0	0	4	1	0	.250
1919	17	13	.567	2.66	30	30	26	267	270	49	92	4	0	0	0	97	20	0	.206
1920	16	9	.640	3.01	30	28	20	215	225	45	80	2	1	0	0	74	18	0	.243
1921 2 teams		BKN	N (6G 1–5)		STL	N	(18G 9–3)												
" total	10	8	.556	4.35	24	18	9	130.1	151	37	30	1	2	0	0	40	4	0	.100
1922 STL N	19	12	.613	3.58	44	32	19	261.1	286	58	83	1	3	1	2	98	24	0	.245
1923	8	9	.471	4.02	26	18	7	152.1	171	40	32	1	1	1	0	55	7	0	.127
1924 2 teams		STL	N (16G 4–5)		PIT	N	(15G 5–3)												
" total	9	8	.529	4.35	31	16	4	136.2	170	47	39	0	4	3	0	51	9	0	.176
13 yrs.	158	112	.585	2.77	347	280	194	2407.1	2320	592	836	28	13	9	10	874	180	0	.206
4 yrs.	40	29	.580	4.04	104	75	36	590.1	674	156	157	3	7	3	2	208	38	0	.183
WORLD SERIES																			
1916 BKN N	0	1	.000	2.53	3	1	0	10.2	7	4	5	0	0	0	1	4	1	0	.250
1920	0	0	–	3.00	1	0	0	3	4	2	1	0	0	0	0	1	0	0	.000
2 yrs.	0	1	.000	2.63	4	1	0	13.2	11	6	6	0	0	0	1	5	1	0	.200

Bill Phyle

PHYLE, WILLIAM JOSEPH
B. June 25, 1875, Duluth, Minn.   D. Aug. 7, 1953, Los Angeles, Calif.   TR

	W	L	PCT	ERA	G	GS	CG	IP	H	BB	SO	ShO	RW	RL	SV	AB	H	HR	BA
1898 CHI N	2	1	.667	0.78	3	3	3	23	24	6	4	2	0	0	0	9	1	0	.111
1899	1	8	.111	4.20	10	9	9	83.2	92	29	10	0	0	0	1	34	6	0	.176
1901 NY N	7	9	.438	4.27	24	19	16	168.2	208	54	62	0	0	0	1	66	12	0	.182
3 yrs.	10	18	.357	3.96	37	31	28	275.1	324	89	76	2	0	0	2	*			

Ron Piche

PICHE, RONALD JACQUES
B. May 22, 1935, Verdun, Que., Canada   BR TR 5'11"   165 lbs.

	W	L	PCT	ERA	G	GS	CG	IP	H	BB	SO	ShO	RW	RL	SV	AB	H	HR	BA
1960 MIL N	3	5	.375	3.56	37	0	0	48	48	23	38	0	3	5	9	7	0	0	.000
1961	2	2	.500	3.47	12	1	1	23.1	20	16	16	0	1	2	1	5	0	0	.000
1962	3	2	.600	4.85	14	8	2	52	54	29	28	0	0	0	0	18	1	0	.056
1963	1	1	.500	3.40	37	1	0	53	53	25	40	0	1	1	0	7	0	0	.000
1965 CAL A	0	3	.000	6.86	14	1	0	19.2	20	12	14	0	0	2	0	1	0	0	.000
1966 STL N	1	3	.250	4.26	20	0	0	25.1	21	18	21	0	1	3	2	4	0	0	.000
6 yrs.	10	16	.385	4.19	134	11	3	221.1	216	123	157	0	6	13	12	42	1	0	.024
1 yr.	1	3	.250	4.26	20	0	0	25.1	21	18	21	0	1	3	2	4	0	0	.000

Charlie Pickett

PICKETT, CHARLES A.
B. Columbus, Ohio

	W	L	PCT	ERA	G	GS	CG	IP	H	BB	SO	ShO	RW	RL	SV	AB	H	HR	BA
1910 STL N	0	0	–	1.50	2	0	0	6	7	2	2	0	0	0	0	0	0	0	–

George Pinckney

PINCKNEY, GEORGE BURTON
B. Jan. 11, 1862, Peoria, Ill.   D. Nov. 9, 1926, Peoria, Ill.   BR TR

	W	L	PCT	ERA	G	GS	CG	IP	H	BB	SO	ShO	RW	RL	SV	AB	H	HR	BA
1886 BKN AA	0	0	–	4.50	1	0	0	2	2	0	0	0	0	0	0	*			

Cotton Pippen

PIPPEN, HENRY HAROLD
B. Apr. 2, 1910, Cisco, Tex.   BR TR 6'2"   180 lbs.

	W	L	PCT	ERA	G	GS	CG	IP	H	BB	SO	ShO	RW	RL	SV	AB	H	HR	BA
1936 STL N	0	2	.000	7.71	6	3	0	21	37	8	8	0	0	0	0	6	1	0	.167
1939 2 teams		PHI	A (25G 4–11)		DET	A	(3G 0–1)												
" total	4	12	.250	6.11	28	19	5	132.2	187	46	38	0	0	1	1	40	5	0	.125
1940 DET A	1	2	.333	6.75	4	3	0	21.1	29	10	9	0	0	0	0	8	0	0	.000
3 yrs.	5	16	.238	6.38	38	25	5	175	253	64	55	0	0	1	1	54	6	0	.111
1 yr.	0	2	.000	7.71	6	3	0	21	37	8	8	0	0	0	0	6	1	0	.167

Tim Plodinec

PLODINEC, TIMOTHY ALFRED
B. Jan. 27, 1947, Aliquippa, Pa.   BR TR 6'4"   190 lbs.

	W	L	PCT	ERA	G	GS	CG	IP	H	BB	SO	ShO	RW	RL	SV	AB	H	HR	BA
1972 STL N	0	0	–	27.00	1	0	0	.1	3	0	0	0	0	0	0	0	0	0	–

Tom Poholsky

POHOLSKY, THOMAS GEORGE
B. Aug. 26, 1929, Detroit, Mich.   BR TR 6'3"   205 lbs.

	W	L	PCT	ERA	G	GS	CG	IP	H	BB	SO	ShO	RW	RL	SV	AB	H	HR	BA
1950 STL N	0	0	–	3.68	5	1	0	14.2	16	3	2	0	0	0	0	2	0	0	.000
1951	7	13	.350	4.43	38	26	10	195	204	68	70	1	1	2	1	67	14	0	.209
1954	5	7	.417	3.06	25	13	4	106	101	20	55	0	0	2	0	27	4	0	.148
1955	9	11	.450	3.81	30	24	8	151	143	35	66	2	0	0	0	44	8	0	.182
1956	9	14	.391	3.59	33	29	7	203	210	44	95	2	0	0	0	69	11	0	.159
1957 CHI N	1	7	.125	4.93	28	11	1	84	117	22	28	0	0	0	0	19	2	0	.105
6 yrs.	31	52	.373	3.93	159	104	30	753.2	791	192	316	5	1	4	1	228	39	0	.171
5 yrs.	30	45	.400	3.80	131	93	29	669.2	674	170	288	5	1	4	1	209	37	0	.177

Howie Pollet

POLLET, HOWARD JOSEPH
B. June 26, 1921, New Orleans, La.   D. Aug. 8, 1974, Houston, Tex.   BL TL 6'1½"   175 lbs.

	W	L	PCT	ERA	G	GS	CG	IP	H	BB	SO	ShO	RW	RL	SV	AB	H	HR	BA
1941 STL N	5	2	.714	1.93	9	8	6	70	55	27	37	2	0	0	0	28	5	0	.179
1942	7	5	.583	2.88	27	13	5	109.1	102	39	42	2	0	1	0	31	7	0	.226
1943	8	4	.667	1.75	16	14	12	118.1	83	32	61	5	0	0	0	43	7	0	.163
1946	21	10	.677	2.10	40	32	22	266	228	86	107	4	0	0	5	87	14	0	.161

	W	L	PCT	ERA	G	GS	CG	IP	H	BB	SO	ShO	Relief Pitching W	L	SV	BATTING AB	H	HR	BA

Howie Pollet *continued*

	W	L	PCT	ERA	G	GS	CG	IP	H	BB	SO	ShO	W	L	SV	AB	H	HR	BA
1947	9	11	.450	4.34	37	24	9	176.1	195	87	73	0	1	0	2	65	15	0	.231
1948	13	8	.619	4.54	36	26	11	186.1	216	67	80	0	2	0	0	68	8	0	.118
1949	20	9	.690	2.77	39	28	17	230.2	228	59	108	5	3	1	1	82	16	0	.195
1950	14	13	.519	3.29	37	30	14	232.1	228	68	117	2	1	1	2	84	12	0	.143
1951 2 teams	STL	N	(6G 0–3)		PIT	N	(21G 6–10)												
" total	6	13	.316	4.98	27	23	4	141	151	59	57	1	0	2	1	37	5	0	.135
1952 PIT N	7	16	.304	4.12	31	30	9	214	217	71	90	1	0	0	0	68	13	0	.191
1953 2 teams	PIT	N	(5G 1–1)		CHI	N	(25G 5–6)												
" total	6	7	.462	4.79	30	18	2	124	147	50	53	0	0	1	1	34	5	0	.147
1954 CHI N	8	10	.444	3.58	20	20	4	128.1	131	54	58	2	0	0	0	47	13	0	.277
1955	4	3	.571	5.61	24	7	1	61	62	27	27	1	3	0	5	15	6	0	.400
1956 2 teams	CHI	A	(11G 3–1)		PIT	N	(19G 0–4)												
" total	3	5	.375	3.62	30	4	0	49.2	45	19	24	0	3	4	3	9	3	0	.333
14 yrs.	131	116	.530	3.51	403	277	116	2107.1	2088	745	934	25	13	10	20	698	129	0	.185
9 yrs.	97	65	.599	3.06	247	177	96	1401.2	1345	473	635	20	7	5	11	489	84	0	.172
				8th								7th							

WORLD SERIES

	W	L	PCT	ERA	G	GS	CG	IP	H	BB	SO	ShO	W	L	SV	AB	H	HR	BA
1942 STL N	0	0	–	0.00	1	0	0	.1	0	0	0	0	0	0	0	0	0	0	–
1946	0	1	.000	3.48	2	2	1	10.1	12	4	3	0	0	0	0	4	0	0	.000
2 yrs.	0	1	.000	3.38	3	2	1	10.2	12	4	3	0	0	0	0	4	0	0	.000

Bill Popp

POPP, WILLIAM PETER   TR
B. June 7, 1877, St. Louis, Mo.   D. Sept. 5, 1909, St. Louis, Mo.

	W	L	PCT	ERA	G	GS	CG	IP	H	BB	SO	ShO	W	L	SV	AB	H	HR	BA
1902 STL N	2	6	.250	4.92	9	7	5	60.1	87	26	20	0	0	1	0	21	1	0	.048

Nels Potter

POTTER, NELSON THOMAS   BL TR 5'11"   180 lbs.
B. Aug. 23, 1911, Mt. Morris, Ill.

	W	L	PCT	ERA	G	GS	CG	IP	H	BB	SO	ShO	W	L	SV	AB	H	HR	BA
1936 STL N	0	0	–	0.00	1	0	0	1	0	0	0	0	0	0	0	0	0	0	–
1938 PHI A	2	12	.143	6.47	35	9	4	111.1	139	49	43	0	1	3	5	39	10	0	.256
1939	8	12	.400	6.60	41	25	9	196.1	258	88	60	0	0	2	2	67	12	0	.179
1940	9	14	.391	4.44	31	25	13	200.2	213	71	73	0	1	1	0	71	18	0	.254
1941 2 teams	PHI	A	(10G 1–1)		BOS	A	(10G 2–0)												
" total	3	1	.750	7.06	20	3	1	43.1	56	32	13	0	2	0	2	9	1	0	.111
1943 STL A	10	5	.667	2.78	33	13	8	168.1	146	54	80	0	2	0	1	55	8	0	.145
1944	19	7	.731	2.83	32	29	16	232	211	70	91	3	0	2	0	82	13	0	.159
1945	15	11	.577	2.47	32	32	21	255.1	212	68	129	3	0	0	0	92	28	0	.304
1946	8	9	.471	3.72	23	19	10	145	152	59	72	0	0	0	0	52	12	0	.231
1947	4	10	.286	4.04	32	10	3	122.2	130	44	65	0	2	2	2	35	9	0	.257
1948 3 teams	STL	A	(2G 1–1)		PHI	A	(8G 2–2)		BOS	N	(18G 5–2)								
" total	8	5	.615	2.86	28	9	3	113.1	105	17	64	0	3	2	3	37	14	0	.378
1949 BOS N	6	11	.353	4.19	41	3	1	96.2	99	30	57	0	5	11	7	23	3	0	.130
12 yrs.	92	97	.487	3.99	349	177	89	1686	1721	582	747	6	16	23	22	562	128	0	.228
1 yr.	0	0	–	0.00	1	0	0	1	0	0	0	0	0	0	0	0	0	0	–

WORLD SERIES

	W	L	PCT	ERA	G	GS	CG	IP	H	BB	SO	ShO	W	L	SV	AB	H	HR	BA
1944 STL A	0	1	.000	0.93	2	2	0	9.2	10	3	6	0	0	0	0	4	0	0	.000
1948 BOS N	0	0	–	8.44	2	1	0	5.1	6	2	1	0	0	0	0	2	1	0	.500
2 yrs.	0	1	.000	3.60	4	3	0	15	16	5	7	0	0	0	0	6	1	0	.167

Jack Powell

POWELL, JOHN JOSEPH   BR TR
B. July 9, 1874, Bloomington, Ill.   D. Oct. 17, 1944, Chicago, Ill.

	W	L	PCT	ERA	G	GS	CG	IP	H	BB	SO	ShO	W	L	SV	AB	H	HR	BA
1897 CLE N	15	9	.625	3.16	27	26	24	225	245	62	61	2	0	0	0	97	20	0	.206
1898	24	15	.615	3.00	42	41	36	342	328	112	93	6	0	1	0	136	18	0	.132
1899 STL N	23	21	.523	3.52	48	43	40	373	433	85	87	2	2	0	0	134	27	0	.201
1900	17	17	.500	4.44	38	37	28	287.2	325	77	77	3	1	0	0	109	31	1	.284
1901	19	19	.500	3.54	45	37	33	338.1	351	50	133	2	2	2	3	119	21	2	.176
1902 STL A	22	17	.564	3.21	42	39	36	328.1	320	93	137	3	0	0	3	127	26	1	.205
1903	15	19	.441	2.91	38	34	33	306.1	294	58	169	4	1	0	2	120	25	0	.208
1904 NY A	23	19	.548	2.44	47	45	38	390.1	340	92	202	3	1	0	0	146	26	0	.178
1905 2 teams	NY	A	(36G 9–13)		STL	A	(3G 2–1)												
" total	11	14	.440	3.29	39	26	16	230	236	62	96	1	2	3	1	75	13	1	.173
1906 STL A	13	14	.481	1.77	28	26	25	244	196	55	132	3	2	0	0	94	22	1	.234
1907	14	16	.467	2.68	32	31	27	255.2	229	62	96	4	1	0	0	91	12	0	.132
1908	16	13	.552	2.11	33	32	23	256	208	47	85	6	0	0	0	89	21	0	.236
1909	12	16	.429	2.11	34	27	18	239	221	42	82	4	2	0	0	78	14	0	.179
1910	7	11	.389	2.30	21	18	9	129.1	121	28	52	3	2	1	0	43	7	0	.163
1911	8	19	.296	3.29	31	27	18	207.2	224	44	52	1	0	0	1	73	12	0	.164
1912	9	16	.360	3.10	32	28	21	235.1	248	52	67	0	0	0	0	82	15	1	.183
16 yrs.	248	255	.493	2.97	577	517	424	4388	4319	1021	1621	47	16	7	13	1613	310	7	.192
				4th															
3 yrs.	59	57	.509	3.79	131	117	101	999	1109	212	297	7	5	2	3	362	79	3	.218
								10th											

Joe Presko

PRESKO, JOSEPH EDWARD (Little Joe)   BR TR 5'9½"   165 lbs.
B. Oct. 7, 1928, Kansas City, Mo.

	W	L	PCT	ERA	G	GS	CG	IP	H	BB	SO	ShO	W	L	SV	AB	H	HR	BA
1951 STL N	7	4	.636	3.45	15	12	5	88.2	86	20	38	0	1	0	2	37	6	0	.162
1952	7	10	.412	4.05	28	18	5	146.2	140	57	63	1	2	1	0	43	4	0	.093
1953	6	13	.316	5.01	34	25	4	161.2	165	65	56	0	0	0	1	59	13	0	.220
1954	4	9	.308	6.91	37	6	1	71.2	97	41	36	1	3	5	0	16	4	0	.250
1957 DET A	1	1	.500	1.64	7	0	0	11	10	4	3	0	1	0	0	1	0	0	.000
1958	0	0	–	3.38	7	0	0	10.2	13	1	6	0	0	2	0	0	0	0	–
6 yrs.	25	37	.403	4.61	128	61	15	490.1	511	188	202	2	7	7	5	156	27	0	.173
4 yrs.	24	36	.400	4.70	114	61	15	468.2	488	183	193	2	6	6	3	155	27	0	.174

	W	L	PCT	ERA	G	GS	CG	IP	H	BB	SO	ShO	Relief Pitching W	L	SV	BATTING AB	H	HR	BA

Mike Proly

PROLY, MICHAEL JAMES
B. Dec. 15, 1950, Jamaica, N. Y.   BR TR 6'   185 lbs.

Year	Tm	W	L	PCT	ERA	G	GS	CG	IP	H	BB	SO	ShO	RW	RL	SV	AB	H	HR	BA
1976 STL N		1	0	1.000	3.71	14	0	0	17	21	6	4	0	1	0	0	0	0	0	—
1978 CHI A		5	2	.714	2.74	14	6	2	65.2	63	12	19	0	0	0	1	0	0	0	—
1979		3	8	.273	3.89	38	6	0	88	89	40	32	0	3	4	9	0	0	0	—
1980		5	10	.333	3.06	62	3	0	147	136	58	56	0	4	4	8	0	0	0	—
1981 PHI N		2	1	.667	3.86	35	2	0	63	66	19	19	0	2	1	2	7	0	0	.000
1982 CHI N		5	3	.625	2.30	44	1	0	82	77	22	24	0	5	3	1	14	4	0	.286
6 yrs		21	24	.467	3.17	207	18	2	462.2	452	157	154	0	15	12	21	21	4	0	.190
1 yr		1	0	1.000	3.71	14	0	0	17	21	6	4	0	1	0	0	0	0	0	—

Bob Purkey

PURKEY, ROBERT THOMAS
B. July 14, 1929, Pittsburgh, Pa.   BR TR 6'2"   175 lbs.

Year	Tm	W	L	PCT	ERA	G	GS	CG	IP	H	BB	SO	ShO	RW	RL	SV	AB	H	HR	BA
1954 PIT N		3	8	.273	5.07	36	11	0	131.1	145	62	38	0	1	1	0	26	2	0	.077
1955		2	7	.222	5.32	14	10	2	67.2	77	25	24	0	0	0	1	19	6	1	.316
1956		0	0	—	2.25	2	0	0	4	2	0	1	0	0	0	0	0	0	0	—
1957		11	14	.440	3.86	48	21	6	179.2	194	38	51	1	5	3	2	45	5	0	.111
1958 CIN N		17	11	.607	3.60	37	34	17	250	259	49	70	3	0	0	0	81	9	1	.111
1959		13	18	.419	4.25	38	33	9	218	241	43	78	1	2	1	1	66	11	1	.167
1960		17	11	.607	3.60	41	33	11	252.2	259	59	97	1	0	0	0	83	11	0	.133
1961		16	12	.571	3.73	36	34	13	246.1	245	51	116	1	0	0	1	80	8	1	.100
1962		23	5	.821	2.81	37	37	18	288.1	260	64	141	2	0	0	0	107	11	2	.103
1963		6	10	.375	3.55	21	21	4	137	143	33	55	1	0	0	0	41	4	0	.098
1964		11	9	.550	3.04	34	25	9	195.2	181	49	78	2	1	1	1	58	3	0	.052
1965 STL N		10	9	.526	5.79	32	17	3	124.1	148	33	39	1	3	2	2	35	1	0	.029
1966 PIT N		0	1	—	1.37	10	0	0	19.2	16	4	5	0	0	1	1	4	0	0	.000
13 yrs		129	115	.529	3.79	386	276	92	2114.2	2170	510	793	13	12	9	9	645	71	6	.110
1 yr		10	9	.526	5.79	32	17	3	124.1	148	33	39	1	3	2	2	35	1	0	.029

WORLD SERIES

Year	Tm	W	L	PCT	ERA	G	GS	CG	IP	H	BB	SO	ShO	RW	RL	SV	AB	H	HR	BA
1961 CIN N		0	1	.000	1.64	2	1	1	11	6	3	5	0	0	0	0	3	0	0	.000

Ambrose Puttman

PUTTMAN, AMBROSE NICHOLAS
B. Sept. 9, 1880, Cincinnati, Ohio   D. June 21, 1936, Jamaica, N. Y.   TL

Year	Tm	W	L	PCT	ERA	G	GS	CG	IP	H	BB	SO	ShO	RW	RL	SV	AB	H	HR	BA
1903 NY A		2	0	1.000	0.95	3	2	1	19	16	4	8	0	0	0	0	7	1	0	.143
1904		2	0	1.000	2.74	9	3	2	49.1	40	17	26	1	0	0	0	18	5	0	.278
1905		2	7	.222	4.27	17	9	5	86.1	79	37	39	1	1	0	1	32	10	0	.313
1906 STL N		1	2	.333	5.30	4	4	0	18.2	23	9	12	0	0	0	0	6	2	0	.333
4 yrs		7	9	.438	3.58	33	18	8	173.1	158	67	85	2	1	0	1	63	18	0	.286
1 yr		1	2	.333	5.30	4	4	0	18.2	23	9	12	0	0	0	0	6	2	0	.333

Roy Radebaugh

RADEBAUGH, ROY
B. Feb. 22, 1884, Champaign, Ill.   D. Jan. 17, 1945, Cedar Rapids, Iowa   BR TR 5'7"   160 lbs.

Year	Tm	W	L	PCT	ERA	G	GS	CG	IP	H	BB	SO	ShO	RW	RL	SV	AB	H	HR	BA
1911 STL N		0	0	—	2.70	2	1	0	10	6	4	1	0	0	0	0	3	0	0	.000

Ken Raffensberger

RAFFENSBERGER, KENNETH DAVID
B. Aug. 8, 1917, York, Pa.   BR TL 6'2"   185 lbs.

Year	Tm	W	L	PCT	ERA	G	GS	CG	IP	H	BB	SO	ShO	RW	RL	SV	AB	H	HR	BA
1939 STL N		0	0	—	0.00	1	0	0	1	2	0	1	0	0	0	0	0	0	0	—
1940 CHI N		7	9	.438	3.38	43	10	3	114.2	120	29	55	0	4	4	3	30	5	0	.167
1941		0	1	.000	4.50	10	1	0	18	17	7	5	0	0	1	0	5	0	0	.000
1943 PHI N		0	1	.000	1.13	1	1	1	8	7	2	3	0	0	0	0	3	0	0	.000
1944		13	20	.394	3.06	37	31	18	258.2	257	45	136	3	1	2	0	80	11	0	.138
1945		0	3	.000	4.44	5	4	1	24.1	28	14	6	0	0	0	0	8	0	0	.000
1946		8	15	.348	3.63	39	23	14	196	203	39	73	2	0	0	6	60	10	0	.167
1947 2 teams	PHI N (10G 2–6)					CIN N		(19G 6–5)												
" total		8	11	.421	4.51	29	22	10	147.2	182	37	54	1	1	2	1	52	10	0	.192
1948 CIN N		11	12	.478	3.84	40	24	7	180.1	187	37	57	4	3	0	0	62	7	0	.113
1949		18	17	.514	3.39	41	38	20	284	289	80	103	5	1	1	0	90	16	1	.178
1950		14	19	.424	4.26	38	35	18	239	271	40	87	4	0	0	0	82	11	1	.134
1951		16	17	.485	3.44	42	33	14	248.2	232	38	81	5	2	2	5	82	10	0	.122
1952		17	13	.567	2.81	38	33	10	247	247	45	93	6	0	0	0	75	8	1	.107
1953		7	14	.333	3.93	26	26	9	174	200	33	47	1	0	0	0	57	8	1	.140
1954		0	2	.000	7.84	6	1	0	10.1	15	3	5	0	0	2	0	2	1	0	.500
15 yrs		119	154	.436	3.60	396	282	133	2151.2	2257	449	806	31	12	16	16	688	97	4	.141
1 yr		0	0	—	0.00	1	0	0	1	2	0	1	0	0	0	0	0	0	0	—

John Raleigh

RALEIGH, JOHN AUSTIN
B. Apr. 21, 1890, Elkhorn, Wis.   D. Aug. 24, 1955, Escondido, Calif.   BR TL

Year	Tm	W	L	PCT	ERA	G	GS	CG	IP	H	BB	SO	ShO	RW	RL	SV	AB	H	HR	BA
1909 STL N		1	9	.100	3.79	15	10	3	80.2	85	21	26	0	0	0	0	23	2	0	.087
1910		0	0	—	9.00	3	1	0	5	8	0	2	0	0	0	0	1	0	0	.000
2 yrs		1	9	.100	4.10	18	11	3	85.2	93	21	28	0	0	0	0	24	2	0	.083
2 yrs		1	9	.100	4.10	18	11	3	85.2	93	21	28	0	0	0	0	24	2	0	.083

Vic Raschi

RASCHI, VICTOR JOHN ANGELO (The Springfield Rifle)
B. Mar. 28, 1919, West Springfield, Mass.   BR TR 6'1"   205 lbs.

Year	Tm	W	L	PCT	ERA	G	GS	CG	IP	H	BB	SO	ShO	RW	RL	SV	AB	H	HR	BA
1946 NY A		2	0	1.000	3.94	2	2	2	16	14	5	11	0	0	0	0	4	1	0	.250
1947		7	2	.778	3.87	15	14	6	104.2	89	38	51	1	0	0	0	40	10	0	.250
1948		19	8	.704	3.84	36	31	18	222.2	208	74	124	6	0	1	1	81	19	0	.235
1949		21	10	.677	3.34	38	37	21	274.2	247	138	124	3	1	0	0	83	13	0	.157
1950		21	8	.724	4.00	33	32	17	256.2	232	116	155	2	0	0	0	86	17	1	.198
1951		21	10	.677	3.27	35	34	15	258.1	233	103	164	4	0	0	0	85	15	0	.176
1952		16	6	.727	2.78	31	31	13	223	174	91	127	4	0	1	0	69	13	0	.188
1953		13	6	.684	3.33	28	26	7	181	150	55	76	1	0	1	0	63	9	0	.143

	W	L	PCT	ERA	G	GS	CG	IP	H	BB	SO	ShO	Relief Pitching W	L	SV	BATTING AB	H	HR	BA

Vic Raschi continued

	W	L	PCT	ERA	G	GS	CG	IP	H	BB	SO	ShO	W	L	SV	AB	H	HR	BA
1954 STL N	8	9	.471	4.73	30	29	6	179	182	71	73	2	0	0	0	64	9	0	.141
1955 2 teams			STL	N	(1G 0–1)			KC	A	(20G 4–6)									
" total	4	7	.364	5.68	21	19	1	103	137	36	39	0	0	0	0	33	6	0	.182
10 yrs.	132	66	.667 5th	3.72	269	255	106	1819	1666	727	944	26	2	1	3	608	112	1	.184
2 yrs.	8	10	.444	4.88	31	30	6	180.2	187	72	74	2	0	0	0	64	9	0	.141
WORLD SERIES																			
1947 NY A	0	0	–	6.75	2	0	0	1.1	2	0	1	0	0	0	0	0	0	0	–
1949	1	1	.500	4.30	2	2	0	14.2	15	5	11	0	0	0	0	5	1	0	.200
1950	1	0	1.000	0.00	1	1	1	9	2	1	5	1	0	0	0	3	1	0	.333
1951	1	1	.500	0.87	2	2	0	10.1	12	8	4	0	0	0	0	2	0	0	.000
1952	2	0	1.000	1.59	3	2	1	17	12	8	18	0	0	0	0	6	1	0	.167
1953	0	1	.000	3.38	1	1	1	8	9	3	4	0	0	0	0	2	0	0	.000
6 yrs.	5	3	.625 8th	2.24	11	8	3	60.1	52	25	43 10th	1	0	0	0	18	3	0	.167

Eric Rasmussen

RASMUSSEN, HAROLD RALPH   BR TR 6'3"   205 lbs.
B. Mar. 22, 1952, Racine, Wis.

	W	L	PCT	ERA	G	GS	CG	IP	H	BB	SO	ShO	W	L	SV	AB	H	HR	BA
1975 STL N	5	5	.500	3.78	14	13	2	81	86	20	59	1	0	0	0	26	4	0	.154
1976	6	12	.333	3.53	43	17	2	150.1	139	54	76	1	3	5	0	38	4	0	.105
1977	11	17	.393	3.48	34	34	11	233	223	63	120	3	0	0	0	72	10	0	.139
1978 2 teams			STL	N	(10G 2–5)			SD	N	(27G 12–10)									
" total	14	15	.483	4.09	37	34	5	206.2	215	63	91	3	0	0	0	64	9	0	.141
1979 SD N	6	9	.400	3.27	45	20	5	157	142	42	54	3	0	0	3	36	2	0	.056
1980	4	11	.267	4.38	40	14	0	111	130	33	50	0	3	2	1	21	2	0	.095
1982 STL N	1	2	.333	4.42	8	3	0	18.1	21	8	15	0	1	0	0	3	0	0	.000
7 yrs.	47	71	.398	3.73	221	135	25	957.1	956	283	465	11	7	7	4	260	31	0	.119
5 yrs.	25	41	.379	3.65	109	77	17	543	530	165	302	6	4	5	0	157	20	0	.127

Bugs Raymond

RAYMOND, ARTHUR LAWRENCE   BR TR
B. Feb. 24, 1882, Chicago, Ill.   D. Sept. 7, 1912, Chicago, Ill.

	W	L	PCT	ERA	G	GS	CG	IP	H	BB	SO	ShO	W	L	SV	AB	H	HR	BA
1904 DET A	0	1	.000	3.07	5	2	1	14.2	14	6	7	0	0	0	0	5	0	0	.000
1907 STL N	2	4	.333	1.67	8	6	6	64.2	56	21	34	1	0	0	0	22	2	0	.091
1908	14	25	.359	2.03	48	37	23	324.1	236	95	145	5	2	1	2	90	17	0	.189
1909 NY N	18	12	.600	2.47	39	31	18	270	239	87	121	.2	3	1	0	89	13	0	.146
1910	4	9	.308	3.81	19	11	6	99.1	106	40	55	0	1	2	0	32	5	0	.156
1911	6	3	.667	3.31	17	9	4	81.2	73	33	39	1	2	1	0	25	5	0	.200
6 yrs.	44	54	.449	2.49	136	96	58	854.2	724	282	401	9	8	5	2	263	42	0	.160
2 yrs.	16	29	.356	1.97	56	43	29	389	292	116	179	6	2	1	2	112	19	0	.170

Phil Redding

REDDING, PHILIP HAYDEN   BL TR 5'11½" 190 lbs.
B. Jan. 25, 1890, Crystal Springs, Miss.   D. Mar. 31, 1928, Greenwood, Miss.

	W	L	PCT	ERA	G	GS	CG	IP	H	BB	SO	ShO	W	L	SV	AB	H	HR	BA
1912 STL N	2	1	.667	4.97	3	3	2	25.1	31	11	9	0	0	0	0	8	0	0	.000
1913	0	0	–	6.75	1	0	0	2.2	2	1	1	0	0	0	0	1	0	0	.000
2 yrs.	2	1	.667	5.14	4	3	2	28	33	12	10	0	0	0	0	9	0	0	.000
2 yrs.	2	1	.667	5.14	4	3	2	28	33	12	10	0	0	0	0	9	0	0	.000

Ron Reed

REED, RONALD LEE   BR TR 6'6"   215 lbs.
B. Nov. 2, 1942, La Porte, Ind.

	W	L	PCT	ERA	G	GS	CG	IP	H	BB	SO	ShO	W	L	SV	AB	H	HR	BA
1966 ATL N	1	1	.500	2.16	2	2	0	8.1	7	4	6	0	0	0	0	2	0	0	.000
1967	1	1	.500	2.95	3	3	0	21.1	21	3	11	0	0	0	0	8	0	0	.000
1968	11	10	.524	3.35	35	28	6	201.2	189	49	111	1	0	0	0	62	10	0	.161
1969	18	10	.643	3.47	36	33	7	241	227	56	160	1	0	0	0	80	10	0	.125
1970	7	10	.412	4.40	21	18	6	135	140	39	68	0	0	1	0	44	4	0	.091
1971	13	14	.481	3.73	32	32	8	222	221	54	129	1	0	0	0	74	11	0	.149
1972	11	15	.423	3.93	31	30	11	213	222	60	111	1	0	0	0	73	13	0	.178
1973	4	11	.267	4.42	20	19	2	116	133	31	64	0	0	0	1	45	9	0	.200
1974	10	11	.476	3.39	28	28	6	186	171	41	78	2	0	0	0	57	6	0	.105
1975 2 teams			ATL	N	(10G 4–5)			STL	N	(24G 9–8)									
" total	13	13	.500	3.52	34	34	8	250.1	274	53	139	2	0	0	0	82	15	0	.183
1976 PHI N	8	7	.533	2.46	59	4	1	128	88	32	96	0	6	6	14	24	4	0	.167
1977	7	5	.583	2.76	60	3	0	124	101	37	84	0	7	4	15	18	2	0	.111
1978	3	4	.429	2.23	66	0	0	109	87	23	85	0	3	4	17	6	0	0	.000
1979	13	8	.619	4.15	61	0	0	102	110	32	58	0	13	8	5	10	3	0	.300
1980	7	5	.583	4.05	55	0	0	91	88	30	54	0	7	5	9	10	3	0	.300
1981	5	3	.625	3.10	39	0	0	61	54	17	40	0	5	3	8	6	3	0	.500
1982	5	5	.500	2.66	57	2	0	98	85	24	57	0	4	4	14	12	4	0	.333
17 yrs.	137	133	.507	3.47	639	236	55	2307.2	2218	585	1351	8	45	35	83	613	97	0	.158
1 yr.	9	8	.529	3.23	24	24	7	175.2	181	37	99	2	0	0	0	56	9	0	.161
DIVISIONAL PLAYOFF SERIES																			
1981 PHI N	0	0	–	3.00	4	0	0	6	5	3	4	0	0	0	0	0	0	0	–
LEAGUE CHAMPIONSHIP SERIES																			
1969 ATL N	0	1	.000	21.60	1	1	0	1.2	5	3	3	0	0	0	0	0	0	0	–
1976 PHI N	0	0	–	7.71	2	0	0	4.2	6	2	2	0	0	0	0	1	0	0	.000
1977	0	0	–	1.80	3	0	0	5	3	2	5	0	0	0	0	0	0	0	–
1978	0	0	–	2.25	2	0	0	4	6	0	2	0	0	0	0	0	0	0	–
1980	0	1	.000	18.00	3	0	0	2	3	1	1	0	0	0	0	0	0	0	–
5 yrs.	0	2	.000	7.27	11	1	0	17.1	23	8	13	0	0	1	0	1	0	0	.000
WORLD SERIES																			
1980 PHI N	0	0	–	0.00	2	0	0	2	2	0	2	0	0	0	1	0	0	0	–

	W	L	PCT	ERA	G	GS	CG	IP	H	BB	SO	ShO	Relief Pitching W	L	SV	BATTING AB	H	HR	BA

Bill Reeder
REEDER, WILLIAM EDGAR
B. Feb. 20, 1922, Dike, Tex.   BR TR 6'5"   205 lbs.

	W	L	PCT	ERA	G	GS	CG	IP	H	BB	SO	ShO	RW	RL	SV	AB	H	HR	BA
1949 STL N	1	1	.500	5.08	21	1	0	33.2	33	30	21	0	1	0	0	3	0	0	.000

Art Reinhart
REINHART, ARTHUR CONRAD
B. May 29, 1899, Ackley, Iowa   D. Nov. 11, 1946, Houston, Tex.   BL TL 6'1"   170 lbs.

	W	L	PCT	ERA	G	GS	CG	IP	H	BB	SO	ShO	RW	RL	SV	AB	H	HR	BA
1919 STL N	0	0	–	0.00	1	0	0		0	0	0	0	0	0	0	0	0	0	–
1925	11	5	.688	3.05	20	16	15	144.2	149	47	26	1	0	0	0	67	22	0	.328
1926	10	5	.667	4.22	27	11	9	143	159	47	26	0	2	2	0	63	20	0	.317
1927	5	2	.714	4.19	21	9	4	81.2	82	36	15	2	0	0	1	32	10	0	.313
1928	4	6	.400	2.87	23	9	3	75.1	80	27	12	1	2	2	2	24	4	0	.167
5 yrs.	30	18	.625	3.60	92	45	31	444.2	470	157	79	4	4	4	3	186	56	0	.301
5 yrs.	30	18	.625	3.60	92	45	31	444.2	470	157	79	4	4	4	3	186	56	0	.301

WORLD SERIES
| 1926 STL N | 0 | 1 | .000 | ∞ | 1 | 0 | 0 | | 1 | 4 | 0 | 0 | 0 | 1 | 0 | 0 | 0 | 0 | – |

Jack Reis
REIS, HARRIE CRANE
B. June 14, 1890, Cincinnati, Ohio   D. July 20, 1939, Cincinnati, Ohio   BR TR 5'10½" 160 lbs.

	W	L	PCT	ERA	G	GS	CG	IP	H	BB	SO	ShO	RW	RL	SV	AB	H	HR	BA
1911 STL N	0	0	–	0.96	3	0	0	9.1	5	8	4	0	0	0	0	2	0	0	.000

Jerry Reuss
REUSS, JERRY
B. June 19, 1949, St. Louis, Mo.   BL TL 6'5"   200 lbs.

	W	L	PCT	ERA	G	GS	CG	IP	H	BB	SO	ShO	RW	RL	SV	AB	H	HR	BA
1969 STL N	1	0	1.000	0.00	1	1	0	7	2	3	3	0	0	0	0	3	1	0	.333
1970	7	8	.467	4.11	20	20	5	127	132	49	74	2	0	0	0	40	2	0	.050
1971	14	14	.500	4.78	36	35	7	211	228	109	131	2	0	0	0	65	8	0	.123
1972 HOU N	9	13	.409	4.17	33	30	4	192	177	83	174	1	0	0	1	66	7	0	.106
1973	16	13	.552	3.74	41	40	12	279.1	271	117	177	3	1	0	0	95	13	0	.137
1974 PIT N	16	11	.593	3.50	35	35	14	260	259	101	105	1	0	0	0	86	13	0	.151
1975	18	11	.621	2.54	32	32	15	237	224	78	131	6	0	0	0	71	14	0	.197
1976	14	9	.609	3.53	31	29	11	209.1	209	51	108	3	0	0	2	66	16	0	.242
1977	10	13	.435	4.11	33	33	8	208	225	71	116	2	0	0	0	70	12	0	.171
1978	3	2	.600	4.88	23	12	3	83	97	23	42	0	0	0	0	27	5	0	.185
1979 LA N	7	14	.333	3.54	39	21	4	160	178	60	83	1	2	4	3	42	7	0	.167
1980	18	6	.750	2.52	37	29	10	229	193	40	111	6	3	0	3	68	6	1	.088
1981	10	4	.714	2.29	22	22	8	153	138	27	51	2	0	0	0	51	10	0	.196
1982	18	11	.621	3.11	39	37	8	254.2	232	50	138	4	1	0	0	77	17	0	.221
14 yrs.	161	129	.555	3.51	422	376	109	2610.1	2565	862	1444	33	7	4	9	827	131	1	.158
3 yrs.	22	22	.500	4.43	57	56	12	345	362	161	208	4	0	0	0	108	11	0	.102

DIVISIONAL PLAYOFF SERIES
| 1981 LA N | 1 | 0 | 1.000 | 0.00 | 2 | 2 | 1 | 18 | 10 | 5 | 7 | 1 | 0 | 0 | 0 | 8 | 0 | 0 | .000 |

LEAGUE CHAMPIONSHIP SERIES
1974 PIT N	0	2	.000	3.72	2	2	0	9.2	7	8	3	0	0	0	0	4	0	0	.000
1975	0	1	.000	13.50	1	1	0	2.2	4	4	1	0	0	0	0	1	0	0	.000
1981 LA N	0	1	.000	5.14	1	1	0	7	7	1	2	0	0	0	0	2	0	0	.000
3 yrs.	0	4	.000	5.59	4	4	0	19.1	18	13	6	0	0	0	0	5	0	0	.000

WORLD SERIES
| 1981 LA N | 1 | 1 | .500 | 3.86 | 2 | 2 | 1 | 11.2 | 10 | 3 | 8 | 0 | 0 | 0 | 0 | 3 | 0 | 0 | .000 |

Bob Reynolds
REYNOLDS, ROBERT ALLEN
B. Jan. 21, 1947, Seattle, Wash.   BR TR 6'   205 lbs.

	W	L	PCT	ERA	G	GS	CG	IP	H	BB	SO	ShO	RW	RL	SV	AB	H	HR	BA
1969 MON N	0	0	–	20.25	1	1	0	1.1	3	3	2	0	0	0	0	0	0	0	–
1971 2 teams				MIL A (3G 0–1)			STL N	(4G 0–0)											
" total	0	1	.000	6.92	7	0	0	13	19	9	8	0	0	1	0	2	0	0	.000
1972 BAL A	0	0	–	1.80	3	0	0	10	8	7	5	0	0	0	0	2	0	0	.000
1973	7	5	.583	1.86	42	1	0	111	88	31	77	0	7	5	9	0	0	0	–
1974	7	5	.583	2.74	54	0	0	69	75	14	43	0	7	5	7	0	0	0	–
1975 3 teams				BAL A (7G 0–1)			DET A	(21G 0–2)			CLE	A	(5G 0–2)						
" total	0	5	.000	5.19	33	0	0	50.1	62	18	32	0	0	5	5	0	0	0	–
6 yrs.	14	16	.467	3.11	140	2	0	254.2	255	82	167	0	14	16	21	4	0	0	.000
1 yr.	0	0	–	10.29	4	0	0	7	15	6	4	0	0	0	0	1	0	0	.000

LEAGUE CHAMPIONSHIP SERIES
1973 BAL A	0	0	–	3.18	2	0	0	5.2	5	3	5	0	0	0	0	0	0	0	–
1974	0	0	–	0.00	1	0	0	1.1	0	3	1	0	0	0	0	0	0	0	–
2 yrs.	0	0	–	2.57	3	0	0	7	5	6	6	0	0	0	0	0	0	0	–

Ken Reynolds
REYNOLDS, KENNETH LEE
B. Jan. 4, 1947, Trevose, Pa.   BL TL 6'   180 lbs.

	W	L	PCT	ERA	G	GS	CG	IP	H	BB	SO	ShO	RW	RL	SV	AB	H	HR	BA
1970 PHI N	0	0	–	0.00	4	0	0	2	3	4	1	0	0	0	0	0	0	0	–
1971	5	9	.357	4.50	35	25	2	162	163	82	81	1	0	0	0	50	10	0	.200
1972	2	15	.118	4.26	33	23	2	154.1	149	60	87	0	0	1	0	40	8	0	.200
1973 MIL A	0	1	.000	7.36	2	1	0	7.1	5	10	3	0	0	0	0	0	0	0	–
1975 STL N	0	1	.000	1.59	10	0	0	17	12	11	7	0	0	1	0	2	0	0	.000
1976 SD N	0	3	.000	6.40	19	2	0	32.1	38	29	18	0	0	2	1	5	0	0	.000
6 yrs.	7	29	.194	4.46	103	51	4	375	370	196	197	1	0	4	1	97	18	0	.186
1 yr.	0	1	.000	1.59	10	0	0	17	12	11	7	0	0	1	0	2	0	0	.000

Flint Rhem
RHEM, CHARLES FLINT (Shad)
B. Jan. 24, 1901, Rhems, S. C.   D. July 30, 1969, Columbia, S. C.   BR TR 6'2"   180 lbs.

	W	L	PCT	ERA	G	GS	CG	IP	H	BB	SO	ShO	RW	RL	SV	AB	H	HR	BA
1924 STL N	2	2	.500	4.45	6	3	3	32.1	31	17	20	0	0	1	1	12	2	0	.167
1925	8	13	.381	4.92	30	23	8	170	204	58	66	1	0	0	1	59	14	1	.237
1926	20	7	.741	3.21	34	34	20	258	241	75	72	1	0	0	0	96	18	1	.188
1927	10	12	.455	4.41	27	26	9	169.1	189	54	51	2	0	0	0	59	4	0	.068

	W	L	PCT	ERA	G	GS	CG	IP	H	BB	SO	ShO	Relief Pitching W	L	SV	BATTING AB	H	HR	BA

Flint Rhem continued

	W	L	PCT	ERA	G	GS	CG	IP	H	BB	SO	ShO	W	L	SV	AB	H	HR	BA
1928	11	8	.579	4.14	28	22	9	169.2	199	71	47	0	0	0	3	67	11	1	.164
1930	12	8	.600	4.45	26	19	9	139.2	173	37	47	0	1	4	0	52	12	0	.231
1931	11	10	.524	3.56	33	26	10	207.1	214	60	72	2	1	0	1	69	9	0	.130
1932 2 teams			STL	N	(6G 4–2)		PHI	N	(26G 11–7)										
" total	15	9	.625	3.58	32	26	15	218.2	225	59	53	1	1	0	1	78	10	0	.128
1933 PHI N	5	14	.263	6.57	28	19	3	126	182	33	27	0	1	2	2	46	4	0	.087
1934 2 teams			STL	N	(5G 1–0)		BOS	N	(25G 8–8)										
" total	9	8	.529	3.69	30	21	5	168.1	190	45	62	1	3	0	1	54	3	0	.056
1935 BOS N	0	5	.000	5.31	10	6	0	40.2	61	11	10	0	0	0	0	10	0	0	.000
1936 STL N	2	1	.667	6.75	10	4	0	26.2	49	49	9	0	1	0	0	8	1	0	.125
12 yrs.	105	97	.520	4.20	294	229	91	1726.2	1958	569	536	8	8	7	10	610	88	3	.144
10 yrs.	81	63	.563	4.05	205	164	73	1238.2	1374	438	408	7	4	5	7	440	74	3	.168

WORLD SERIES

	W	L	PCT	ERA	G	GS	CG	IP	H	BB	SO	ShO	W	L	SV	AB	H	HR	BA
1926 STL N	0	0	—	6.75	1	1	0	4	7	2	4	0	0	0	0	1	0	0	.000
1928	0	0	—	0.00	1	0	0	2	0	0	1	0	0	0	0	0	0	0	—
1930	0	1	.000	10.80	1	1	0	3.1	7	2	3	0	0	0	0	1	0	0	.000
1931	0	0	—	0.00	1	0	0	1	1	0	1	0	0	0	0	2	0	0	.000
4 yrs.	0	1	.000	6.10	4	2	0	10.1	15	4	9	0	0	0	0	4	0	0	.000

Bob Rhoads

RHOADS, ROBERT BARTON (Dusty)   BR TR 6'1"   215 lbs.
B. Oct. 4, 1879, Wooster, Ohio   D. Feb. 12, 1967, San Bernardino, Calif.

	W	L	PCT	ERA	G	GS	CG	IP	H	BB	SO	ShO	W	L	SV	AB	H	HR	BA
1902 CHI N	4	8	.333	3.20	16	12	12	118	131	42	43	1	0	0	1	45	10	0	.222
1903 2 teams			STL	N	(17G 5–8)		CLE	A	(5G 2–3)										
" total	7	11	.389	4.76	22	18	17	170	209	50	73	1	0	0	0	67	9	0	.134
1904 CLE A	10	9	.526	2.87	22	19	18	175.1	175	48	72	0	0	0	0	92	18	0	.196
1905	16	9	.640	2.83	28	26	24	235	219	55	61	4	1	0	0	95	21	1	.221
1906	22	10	.688	1.80	38	34	31	315	259	92	89	7	0	0	1	118	19	0	.161
1907	16	14	.533	2.29	35	31	23	275	258	84	76	5	2	0	0	92	17	0	.185
1908	18	12	.600	1.77	37	30	20	270	229	73	62	1	2	2	0	90	20	0	.222
1909	5	8	.385	2.90	20	15	9	133.1	124	50	46	2	0	1	0	43	7	0	.163
8 yrs.	98	81	.547	2.61	218	185	154	1691.2	1604	494	522	21	5	3	2	642	121	1	.188
1 yr.	5	8	.385	4.60	17	13	12	129	154	47	52	1	0	0	0	50	7	0	.140

Charlie Rhodes

RHODES, CHARLES ANDERSON   BR TR   180 lbs.
D. Oct. 26, 1918, Caney, Kans.

	W	L	PCT	ERA	G	GS	CG	IP	H	BB	SO	ShO	W	L	SV	AB	H	HR	BA
1906 STL N	3	4	.429	3.40	9	6	3	45	37	20	32	0	1	0	0	16	3	0	.188
1908 2 teams			CIN	N	(1G 0–0)		STL	N	(4G 1–2)										
" total	1	2	.333	2.68	5	4	3	37	24	14	19	0	0	0	0	13	3	0	.231
1909 STL N	2	5	.286	3.98	12	10	4	61	55	33	25	0	0	0	0	19	4	0	.211
3 yrs.	6	11	.353	3.46	26	20	10	143	116	67	76	0	1	0	0	48	10	0	.208
3 yrs.	6	11	.353	3.56	25	20	10	139	115	65	72	0	1	0	0	47	10	0	.213

Dennis Ribant

RIBANT, DENNIS JOSEPH   BR TR 5'11"   165 lbs.
B. Sept. 20, 1941, Detroit, Mich.

	W	L	PCT	ERA	G	GS	CG	IP	H	BB	SO	ShO	W	L	SV	AB	H	HR	BA
1964 NY N	1	5	.167	5.15	14	7	1	57.2	65	9	35	1	0	0	1	20	2	0	.100
1965	1	3	.250	3.82	19	1	0	35.1	29	6	13	0	1	3	3	6	0	0	.000
1966	11	9	.550	3.20	39	26	10	188.1	184	40	84	1	0	0	3	61	12	0	.197
1967 PIT N	9	8	.529	4.08	38	22	2	172	186	40	75	0	3	2	0	60	16	0	.267
1968 2 teams			DET	A	(14G 2–2)		CHI	A	(17G 0–2)										
" total	2	4	.333	4.37	31	0	0	55.2	62	27	27	0	2	4	2	12	1	0	.083
1969 2 teams			STL	N	(1G 0–0)		CIN	N	(7G 0–0)										
" total	0	0	—	2.79	8	0	0	9.2	10	4	7	0	0	0	0	0	0	0	—
6 yrs.	24	29	.453	3.87	149	56	13	518.2	536	126	241	2	6	9	9	159	31	0	.195
1 yr.	0	0	—	13.50	1	0	0	1.1	4	1	0	0	0	0	0	0	0	0	—

Gordie Richardson

RICHARDSON, GORDON CLARK   BR TL 6'   185 lbs.
B. July 19, 1939, Colquitt, Ga.

	W	L	PCT	ERA	G	GS	CG	IP	H	BB	SO	ShO	W	L	SV	AB	H	HR	BA
1964 STL N	4	2	.667	2.30	19	6	1	47	40	15	28	0	1	0	1	13	1	0	.077
1965 NY N	2	2	.500	3.78	35	0	0	52.1	41	16	43	0	2	2	2	7	0	0	.000
1966	0	2	.000	9.16	15	1	0	18.2	24	6	15	0	0	1	1	1	0	0	.000
3 yrs.	6	6	.500	4.04	69	7	1	118	105	37	86	0	3	3	4	21	1	0	.048
1 yr.	4	2	.667	2.30	19	6	1	47	40	15	28	0	1	0	1	13	1	0	.077

WORLD SERIES

	W	L	PCT	ERA	G	GS	CG	IP	H	BB	SO	ShO	W	L	SV	AB	H	HR	BA
1964 STL N	0	0	—	40.50	2	0	0	.2	3	2	0	0	0	0	0	0	0	0	—

Pete Richert

RICHERT, PETER GERARD   BL TL 5'11"   165 lbs.
B. Oct. 29, 1939, Floral Park, N. Y.

	W	L	PCT	ERA	G	GS	CG	IP	H	BB	SO	ShO	W	L	SV	AB	H	HR	BA
1962 LA N	5	4	.556	3.87	19	12	1	81.1	77	45	75	0	1	1	0	25	2	0	.080
1963	5	3	.625	4.50	20	12	1	78	80	28	54	0	1	1	0	22	4	0	.182
1964	2	3	.400	4.15	8	6	1	34.2	38	18	25	1	0	0	0	11	1	0	.091
1965 WAS A	15	12	.556	2.60	34	29	6	194	146	84	161	0	1	0	0	64	10	0	.156
1966	14	14	.500	3.37	36	34	7	245.2	196	69	195	0	0	0	0	86	14	1	.163
1967 2 teams			WAS	A	(11G 2–6)		BAL	A	(26G 7–10)										
" total	9	16	.360	3.47	37	29	6	186.2	156	56	131	2	2	0	2	54	5	0	.093
1968 BAL A	6	3	.667	3.47	36	0	0	62.1	51	12	47	0	6	3	6	10	2	0	.200
1969	7	4	.636	2.20	44	0	0	57.1	42	14	54	0	7	4	12	8	1	0	.125
1970	7	2	.778	1.96	50	0	0	55	36	24	66	0	7	2	13	4	0	0	.000
1971	3	5	.375	3.50	36	0	0	36	26	22	35	0	3	5	4	2	0	0	.000
1972 LA N	3	4	.400	2.25	37	0	0	52	42	18	38	0	3	3	6	6	3	0	.500
1973	3	3	.500	3.18	39	0	0	51	44	19	31	0	3	3	7	5	1	0	.200
1974 2 teams			STL	N	(13G 0–0)		PHI	N	(21G 2–1)										
" total	2	1	.667	2.27	34	0	0	31.2	25	15	13	0	2	1	1	0	0	0	—

	W	L	PCT	ERA	G	GS	CG	IP	H	BB	SO	ShO	Relief Pitching W	L	SV	BATTING AB	H	HR	BA

Pete Richert continued

	W	L	PCT	ERA	G	GS	CG	IP	H	BB	SO	ShO	W	L	SV	AB	H	HR	BA
13 yrs.	80	73	.523	3.19	429	122	22	1165.2	959	424	925	3	35	23	51	297	43	1	.145
1 yr.	0	0	—	2.38	13	0	0	11.1	10	11	4	0	0	0	1	0	0	0	—
LEAGUE CHAMPIONSHIP SERIES																			
1969 BAL A	0	0	—	0.00	1	0	0	1	0	2	2	0	0	0	0	0	0	0	—
WORLD SERIES																			
1969 BAL A	0	0	—	0.00	1	0	0	.1	0	0	0	0	0	0	0	0	0	0	—
1970	0	0	—	0.00	1	0	0	.1	0	0	0	0	0	0	1	0	0	0	—
1971	0	0	—	0.00	1	0	0	.2	0	0	1	0	0	0	0	0	0	0	—
3 yrs.	0	0	—	0.00	3	0	0	1	0	0	1	0	0	0	1	0	0	0	—

Dick Ricketts

RICKETTS, RICHARD JAMES
Brother of Dave Ricketts.
B. Dec. 4, 1933, Pottstown, Pa.　　　BL TR 6'7"　215 lbs.

	W	L	PCT	ERA	G	GS	CG	IP	H	BB	SO	ShO	W	L	SV	AB	H	HR	BA
1959 STL N	1	6	.143	5.82	12	9	0	55.2	68	30	25	0	0	0	0	18	1	0	.056

Elmer Rieger

RIEGER, ELMER JAY
B. Feb. 25, 1889, Perris, Calif.　　D. Oct. 21, 1959, Los Angeles, Calif.　　BB TR 6'　175 lbs.

	W	L	PCT	ERA	G	GS	CG	IP	H	BB	SO	ShO	W	L	SV	AB	H	HR	BA
1910 STL N	0	2	.000	5.48	13	2	1	21.1	26	7	9	0	0	1	0	3	0	0	.000

Andy Rincon

RINCON, ANDREW JOHN
B. Mar. 5, 1959, Pico Rivera, Calif.　　BR TR 6'3"　195 lbs.

	W	L	PCT	ERA	G	GS	CG	IP	H	BB	SO	ShO	W	L	SV	AB	H	HR	BA
1980 STL N	3	1	.750	2.61	4	4	1	31	23	7	22	0	0	0	0	12	3	0	.250
1981	3	1	.750	1.75	5	5	1	36	27	5	13	1	0	0	0	13	3	0	.231
1982	2	3	.400	4.73	11	6	1	40	35	25	11	0	1	0	0	10	1	0	.100
3 yrs.	8	5	.615	3.11	20	15	3	107	85	37	46	1	1	0	0	35	7	0	.200
3 yrs.	8	5	.615	3.11	20	15	3	107	85	37	46	1	1	0	0	35	7	0	.200

Jimmy Ring

RING, JAMES JOSEPH
B. Feb. 15, 1895, Brooklyn, N.Y.　　D. July 6, 1965, New York, N.Y.　　BR TR 6'1"　170 lbs.

	W	L	PCT	ERA	G	GS	CG	IP	H	BB	SO	ShO	W	L	SV	AB	H	HR	BA
1917 CIN N	3	7	.300	4.40	24	7	3	88	90	35	33	0	0	3	2	26	2	0	.077
1918	9	5	.643	2.85	21	18	13	142.1	130	48	26	4	0	0	0	50	6	0	.120
1919	10	9	.526	2.26	32	18	12	183	150	51	61	2	1	1	3	62	6	0	.097
1920	17	16	.515	3.23	42	33	18	292.2	268	92	73	1	2	1	1	96	19	0	.198
1921 PHI N	10	19	.345	4.24	34	30	21	246	258	88	88	0	1	1	1	83	12	0	.145
1922	12	18	.400	4.58	40	33	17	249.1	292	103	116	0	2	1	1	88	13	1	.148
1923	18	16	.529	3.76	39	36	23	313.1	336	115	112	0	1	2	0	113	12	1	.106
1924	10	12	.455	3.97	32	31	16	215.1	236	108	72	1	0	0	0	74	17	0	.230
1925	14	16	.467	4.37	38	37	21	270	325	119	93	1	0	0	0	101	11	2	.109
1926 NY N	11	10	.524	4.57	39	23	5	183.1	207	74	76	0	2	0	2	56	8	0	.143
1927 STL N	0	4	.000	6.55	13	3	1	33	39	17	13	0	0	2	0	8	3	0	.375
1928 PHI N	4	17	.190	6.40	35	25	4	173	214	103	72	0	0	0	0	60	11	0	.183
12 yrs.	118	149	.442	4.06	389	294	154	2389.1	2545	953	835	9	9	11	11	817	120	4	.147
1 yr.	0	4	.000	6.55	13	3	1	33	39	17	13	0	0	2	0	8	3	0	.375
WORLD SERIES																			
1919 CIN N	1	1	.500	0.64	2	1	1	14	7	6	4	1	0	1	0	5	0	0	.000

Tink Riviere

RIVIERE, ARTHUR BERNARD
B. Aug. 2, 1899, Liberty, Tex.　　D. Sept. 27, 1965, Liberty, Tex.　　BR TR 5'10"　167 lbs.

	W	L	PCT	ERA	G	GS	CG	IP	H	BB	SO	ShO	W	L	SV	AB	H	HR	BA
1921 STL N	1	0	1.000	6.10	18	2	0	38.1	45	20	15	0	1	0	0	8	3	0	.375
1925 CHI A	0	0	—	13.50	3	0	0	4.2	6	7	1	0	0	0	0	1	0	0	.000
2 yrs.	1	0	1.000	6.91	21	2	0	43	51	27	16	0	1	0	0	9	3	0	.333
1 yr.	1	0	1.000	6.10	18	2	0	38.1	45	20	15	0	1	0	0	8	3	0	.375

Hank Robinson

ROBINSON, JOHN HENRY (Rube)
Born John Henry Robertson.
B. Aug. 16, 1889, Floyd, Ark.　　D. July 2, 1965, North Little Rock, Ark.　　BR TL 5'11½"　160 lbs.

	W	L	PCT	ERA	G	GS	CG	IP	H	BB	SO	ShO	W	L	SV	AB	H	HR	BA
1911 PIT N	0	1	.000	2.77	5	0	0	13	13	5	8	0	0	1	0	3	0	0	.000
1912	12	7	.632	2.26	33	16	11	175	146	30	79	0	3	1	2	59	15	0	.254
1913	14	9	.609	2.38	43	23	8	196.1	184	41	50	1	4	4	0	61	11	0	.180
1914 STL N	6	8	.429	3.00	26	16	6	126	128	32	30	1	2	1	0	35	6	0	.171
1915	7	8	.467	2.45	32	15	6	143	128	35	57	1	3	4	0	47	5	0	.106
1918 NY A	2	4	.333	3.00	11	3	1	48	47	16	14	0	1	3	0	13	0	0	.000
6 yrs.	41	37	.526	2.53	150	73	32	701.1	646	159	238	3	13	14	2	218	37	0	.170
2 yrs.	13	16	.448	2.71	58	31	12	269	256	67	87	2	5	5	0	82	11	0	.134

Preacher Roe

ROE, ELWIN CHARLES
B. Feb. 26, 1915, Ashflat, Ark.　　BR TL 6'2"　170 lbs.

	W	L	PCT	ERA	G	GS	CG	IP	H	BB	SO	ShO	W	L	SV	AB	H	HR	BA
1938 STL N	0	0	—	13.50	1	0	0	2.2	6	2	1	0	0	0	0	1	0	0	.000
1944 PIT N	13	11	.542	3.11	39	25	7	185.1	182	59	88	1	0	0	0	53	7	0	.132
1945	14	13	.519	2.87	33	31	15	235	228	46	148	3	5	1	1	75	8	0	.107
1946	3	8	.273	5.14	21	10	1	70	83	25	28	0	2	1	2	15	1	0	.067
1947	4	15	.211	5.25	38	22	4	144	156	63	59	1	1	1	0	40	5	0	.125
1948 BKN N	12	8	.600	2.63	34	22	8	177.2	156	33	86	2	2	0	2	51	5	0	.098
1949	15	6	.714	2.79	30	27	13	212.2	201	44	109	3	0	1	1	70	8	0	.114
1950	19	11	.633	3.30	36	32	16	250.2	245	66	125	2	1	0	0	91	14	0	.154
1951	22	3	.880	3.04	34	33	19	257.2	247	64	113	2	1	0	0	89	10	0	.112
1952	11	2	.846	3.12	27	25	8	158.2	163	39	83	2	1	0	0	57	4	0	.070
1953	11	3	.786	4.36	25	24	9	157	171	40	85	1	0	0	0	57	3	0	.053
1954	3	4	.429	5.00	15	10	1	63	69	23	31	0	0	0	0	21	3	1	.143

	W	L	PCT	ERA	G	GS	CG	IP	H	BB	SO	ShO	Relief Pitching W	L	SV	BATTING AB	H	HR	BA

Preacher Roe continued

	W	L	PCT	ERA	G	GS	CG	IP	H	BB	SO	ShO	W	L	SV	AB	H	HR	BA
12 yrs.	127	84	.602	3.43	333	261	101	1914.1	1907	504	956	17	14	3	10	620	68	1	.110
1 yr.	0	0	–	13.50	1	0	0	2.2	6	2	1	0	0	0	0	1	0	0	.000
WORLD SERIES																			
1949 BKN N	1	0	1.000	0.00	1	1	1	9	6	0	3	1	0	0	0	3	0	0	.000
1952	1	0	1.000	3.18	3	1	1	11.1	9	6	7	0	0	0	0	2	0	0	.000
1953	0	1	.000	4.50	1	1	1	8	5	4	4	0	0	0	0	3	0	0	.000
3 yrs.	2	1	.667	2.54	5	3	3	28.1	20	10	14	1	0	0	0	8	0	0	.000

Cookie Rojas

ROJAS, OCTAVIO RIVAS
B. Mar. 6, 1939, Havana, Cuba

BR TR 5'10" 160 lbs.

	W	L	PCT	ERA	G	GS	CG	IP	H	BB	SO	ShO	W	L	SV	AB	H	HR	BA
1967 PHI N	0	0	–	0.00	1	0	0	1	1	0	0	0	0	0	0	*			

John Romonosky

ROMONOSKY, JOHN
B. July 7, 1929, Harrisburg, Ill.

BR TR 6'2" 195 lbs.

	W	L	PCT	ERA	G	GS	CG	IP	H	BB	SO	ShO	W	L	SV	AB	H	HR	BA
1953 STL N	0	0	–	4.70	2	2	0	7.2	9	4	3	0	0	0	0	2	0	0	.000
1958 WAS A	2	4	.333	6.51	18	5	1	55.1	52	28	38	0	1	0	0	13	4	1	.308
1959	1	0	1.000	3.29	12	2	0	38.1	36	19	22	0	0	0	0	11	2	0	.182
3 yrs.	3	4	.429	5.15	32	9	1	101.1	97	51	63	0	1	0	0	26	6	1	.231
1 yr.	0	0	–	4.70	2	2	0	7.2	9	4	3	0	0	0	0	2	0	0	.000

Jack Rothrock

ROTHROCK, JOHN HOUSTON
B. Mar. 14, 1905, Long Beach, Calif.
D. Feb. 2, 1980, San Bernardino, Calif.

BB TR 5'11½" 165 lbs.
BR 1925-27

	W	L	PCT	ERA	G	GS	CG	IP	H	BB	SO	ShO	W	L	SV	AB	H	HR	BA
1928 BOS A	0	0	–	0.00	1	0	0	1	0	0	0	0	0	0	0	*			

Jack Russell

RUSSELL, JACK ERWIN
B. Oct. 24, 1905, Paris, Tex.

BR TR 6'1½" 178 lbs.

	W	L	PCT	ERA	G	GS	CG	IP	H	BB	SO	ShO	W	L	SV	AB	H	HR	BA
1926 BOS A	0	5	.000	3.58	36	5	1	98	94	24	17	0	0	2	0	21	4	0	.190
1927	4	9	.308	4.10	34	15	4	147	172	40	25	1	1	1	0	48	6	0	.125
1928	11	14	.440	3.84	32	26	10	201.1	233	41	27	2	1	0	0	62	13	0	.210
1929	6	18	.250	3.94	35	32	13	226.1	263	40	37	0	0	0	0	70	9	0	.129
1930	9	20	.310	5.45	35	30	15	229.2	302	53	35	0	0	0	0	79	14	1	.177
1931	10	18	.357	5.16	36	31	13	232	298	65	45	0	0	1	0	82	16	0	.195
1932 2 teams		BOS	A	(11G 1–7)	CLE	A	(18G 5–7)												
" total	6	14	.300	5.25	29	17	7	152.2	207	42	34	0	0	3	1	51	13	0	.255
1933 WAS A	12	6	.667	2.69	50	3	2	124	119	32	28	0	11	4	13	34	5	0	.147
1934	5	10	.333	4.17	54	9	3	157.2	179	56	30	0	2	7	7	44	7	0	.159
1935	4	9	.308	5.71	43	7	2	126	170	37	30	0	4	5	3	35	7	0	.200
1936 2 teams		WAS	A	(18G 3–2)	BOS	A	(23G 0–3)												
" total	3	5	.375	6.02	41	7	1	89.2	123	41	15	0	1	4	3	22	2	0	.091
1937 DET A	2	5	.286	7.59	25	0	0	40.1	63	20	10	0	2	5	4	7	0	0	.000
1938 CHI N	6	1	.857	3.34	42	0	0	102.1	100	30	29	0	6	1	3	32	7	0	.219
1939	4	3	.571	3.67	39	0	0	68.2	78	24	32	0	4	3	3	17	0	0	.000
1940 STL N	3	4	.429	3.55	26	0	0	54	53	26	16	0	3	4	1	13	0	0	.000
15 yrs.	85	141	.376	4.47	557	182	71	2049.2	2454	571	418	3	35	40	38	617	103	1	.167
1 yr.	3	4	.429	2.50	26	0	0	54	53	26	16	0	3	4	1	13	0	0	.000
WORLD SERIES																			
1933 WAS A	0	1	.000	0.87	3	0	0	10.1	8	0	7	0	0	1	0	2	0	0	.000
1938 CHI N	0	0	–	0.00	2	0	0	1.2	1	1	0	0	0	0	0	0	0	0	–
2 yrs.	0	1	.000	0.75	5	0	0	12	9	1	7	0	0	1	0	2	0	0	.000

John Ryan

RYAN, JOHN BENNETT
B. Nov. 12, 1868, Haverhill, Mass. Deceased.

BR TR 5'10½" 165 lbs.

	W	L	PCT	ERA	G	GS	CG	IP	H	BB	SO	ShO	W	L	SV	AB	H	HR	BA
1902 STL N	1	0	1.000	0.00	1	1	1	7	3	4	1	1	0	0	0	*			

Mike Ryba

RYBA, DOMINIC JOSEPH
B. June 9, 1903, DeLancey, Pa.   D. Dec. 13, 1971, Springfield, Mo.

BR TR 5'11½" 180 lbs.

	W	L	PCT	ERA	G	GS	CG	IP	H	BB	SO	ShO	W	L	SV	AB	H	HR	BA
1935 STL N	1	1	.500	3.38	2	1	1	16	15	1	6	0	1	0	0	5	2	0	.400
1936	5	1	.833	5.40	14	0	0	45	55	16	25	0	5	1	0	18	3	0	.167
1937	9	6	.600	4.13	38	8	5	135	152	40	57	0	6	3	0	48	15	0	.313
1938	1	1	.500	5.40	3	0	0	5	8	1	0	0	1	1	0	0	0	0	–
1941 BOS A	7	3	.700	4.46	40	3	0	121	143	42	54	0	6	2	6	37	8	0	.216
1942	3	3	.500	3.86	18	0	0	44.1	49	13	16	0	3	3	3	17	5	0	.294
1943	7	5	.583	3.26	40	8	4	143.2	142	57	50	1	4	4	2	43	8	0	.186
1944	12	7	.632	3.33	42	7	2	138	119	39	50	0	9	5	2	41	6	0	.146
1945	7	6	.538	2.49	34	9	4	123	122	33	44	1	4	2	2	36	9	0	.250
1946	0	1	.000	3.55	9	0	0	12.2	12	5	5	0	0	1	1	2	2	0	1.000
10 yrs.	52	34	.605	3.66	240	36	16	783.2	817	247	307	2	39	22	16	247	58	0	.235
4 yrs.	16	9	.640	4.39	57	9	6	201	230	58	88	0	13	5	0	71	20	0	.282
WORLD SERIES																			
1946 BOS A	0	0	–	13.50	1	0	0	.2	2	1	0	0	0	0	0	0	0	0	–

Ray Sadecki

SADECKI, RAYMOND MICHAEL
B. Dec. 26, 1940, Kansas City, Kans.

BL TL 5'11" 180 lbs.

	W	L	PCT	ERA	G	GS	CG	IP	H	BB	SO	ShO	W	L	SV	AB	H	HR	BA
1960 STL N	9	9	.500	3.78	26	26	7	157.1	148	86	95	1	0	0	0	57	12	0	.211
1961	14	10	.583	3.72	31	31	13	222.2	196	102	114	0	0	0	0	87	22	0	.253
1962	6	8	.429	5.54	22	17	4	102.1	121	43	50	1	1	0	1	37	3	1	.081
1963	10	10	.500	4.10	36	28	4	193.1	198	78	136	1	1	0	0	64	9	0	.141
1964	20	11	.645	3.68	37	32	9	220	232	60	119	2	0	2	1	75	12	0	.160
1965	6	15	.286	5.21	36	28	4	172.2	192	64	122	0	0	0	0	55	11	0	.200

	W	L	PCT	ERA	G	GS	CG	IP	H	BB	SO	ShO	Relief Pitching W	L	SV	BATTING AB	H	HR	BA

Ray Sadecki continued

	W	L	PCT	ERA	G	GS	CG	IP	H	BB	SO	ShO	W	L	SV	AB	H	HR	BA
1966 2 teams STL N (5G 2–1) SF N (26G 3–7)																			
" total	5	8	.385	4.80	31	22	4	129.1	141	48	83	1	0	0	0	41	14	3	.341
1967 SF N	12	6	.667	2.78	35	24	10	188	165	58	145	2	1	0	0	73	18	0	.247
1968	12	18	.400	2.91	38	36	13	253.2	225	70	206	6	0	0	0	85	8	0	.094
1969	5	8	.385	4.24	29	17	4	138	137	53	104	3	0	0	0	40	5	1	.125
1970 NY N	8	4	.667	3.88	28	19	4	139	134	52	89	0	0	0	0	39	8	0	.205
1971	7	7	.500	2.93	34	20	5	163	139	44	120	2	1	0	0	50	10	0	.200
1972	2	1	.667	3.09	34	2	0	75.2	73	31	38	0	1	0	0	13	2	0	.154
1973	5	4	.556	3.39	31	11	1	116.2	109	41	87	0	1	0	1	31	7	0	.226
1974	8	8	.500	3.48	34	10	3	101	107	35	46	1	4	3	0	27	7	0	.259
1975 3 teams STL N (8G 1–0) ATL N (25G 2–3) KC A (5G 1–0)																			
" total	4	3	.571	4.03	38	1	0	80.1	91	31	32	0	3	1	1	15	3	0	.200
1976 2 teams KC A (3G 0–0) MIL A (36G 2–0)																			
" total	2	0	1.000	3.86	39	0	0	42	45	23	28	0	2	0	1	0	0	0	–
1977 NY N	0	1	.000	6.00	4	0	0	3	3	3	0	0	0	1	0	0	0	0	–
18 yrs.	135	131	.508	3.79	563	328	85	2498	2456	922	1614	20	15	7	7	789	151	5	.191
8 yrs.	68	64	.515	4.15	201	165	42	1103.2	1116	449	665	5	3	2	4	382	72	2	.188
WORLD SERIES																			
1964 STL N	1	0	1.000	8.53	2	2	0	6.1	12	5	2	0	0	0	0	2	1	0	.500
1973 NY N	0	0	–	1.93	4	0	0	4.2	5	1	6	0	0	0	1	0	0	0	–
2 yrs.	1	0	1.000	5.73	6	2	0	11	17	6	8	0	0	0	1	2	1	0	.500

Slim Sallee

SALLEE, HARRY FRANKLIN BL TL 6'3" 180 lbs.
B. Feb. 3, 1885, Higginsport, Ohio   D. Mar. 22, 1950, Higginsport, Ohio

	W	L	PCT	ERA	G	GS	CG	IP	H	BB	SO	ShO	W	L	SV	AB	H	HR	BA
1908 STL N	3	8	.273	3.15	25	12	7	128.2	144	36	39	1	1	0	0	41	2	0	.049
1909	10	10	.500	2.42	32	27	12	219	223	59	55	1	0	2	0	71	8	0	.113
1910	7	9	.438	2.97	18	13	9	115	112	24	46	1	1	2	2	37	4	0	.108
1911	16	9	.640	2.76	36	30	18	245	234	64	74	1	1	1	2	89	15	0	.169
1912	15	17	.469	2.60	48	32	20	294	289	72	108	3	4	3	6	103	14	0	.136
1913	18	15	.545	2.70	49	30	17	273	254	59	105	3	2	1	5	94	19	2	.202
1914	18	17	.514	2.10	46	30	18	282.1	252	72	105	3	2	5	6	91	21	0	.231
1915	13	17	.433	2.84	46	33	17	275.1	245	57	91	2	0	2	3	92	11	0	.120
1916 2 teams STL N (16G 5–5) NY N (15G 9–4)																			
" total	14	9	.609	2.18	31	18	11	181.2	171	33	63	4	4	1	1	53	12	0	.226
1917 NY N	18	7	.720	2.17	34	24	18	215.2	199	34	54	1	2	3	4	77	17	0	.221
1918	8	8	.500	2.25	18	16	12	132	122	12	33	1	0	0	2	41	5	0	.122
1919 CIN N	21	7	.750	2.06	29	28	22	227.2	221	20	24	4	1	0	0	74	14	0	.189
1920 2 teams CIN N (21G 5–6) NY N (5G 1–0)																			
" total	6	6	.500	3.11	26	13	7	133	145	16	15	0	0	1	2	38	7	0	.184
1921 NY N	6	4	.600	3.64	37	0	0	96.1	115	14	23	0	6	4	2	22	8	0	.364
14 yrs.	173	143	.547	2.56	475	306	188	2818.2	2726	572	835	25	24	25	35	923	157	2	.170
9 yrs.	105	107	.495	2.67	316	214	122	1902.1	1828	466	651	17	13	17	25	636	97	2	.153
	8th	6th		1st				9th		7th	5th				10th				10th
WORLD SERIES																			
1917 NY N	0	2	.000	4.70	2	2	1	15.1	20	4	4	0	0	0	0	6	1	0	.167
1919 CIN N	1	1	.500	1.35	2	2	1	13.1	19	1	2	0	0	0	0	4	0	0	.000
2 yrs.	1	3	.250	3.14	4	4	2	28.2	39	5	6	0	0	0	0	10	1	0	.100

War Sanders

SANDERS, WARREN WILLIAMS BR TL 5'10" 160 lbs.
B. Aug. 2, 1877, Maynardville, Tenn.   D. Aug. 3, 1962, Chattanooga, Tenn.

	W	L	PCT	ERA	G	GS	CG	IP	H	BB	SO	ShO	W	L	SV	AB	H	HR	BA
1903 STL N	1	5	.167	6.08	8	6	3	40	48	21	9	0	0	0	0	15	1	0	.067
1904	1	2	.333	4.74	4	3	1	19	25	1	11	0	0	0	0	6	0	0	.000
2 yrs.	2	7	.222	5.64	12	9	4	59	73	22	20	0	0	1	0	21	1	0	.048
2 yrs.	2	7	.222	5.64	12	9	4	59	73	22	20	0	0	1	0	21	1	0	.048

Al Santorini

SANTORINI, ALAN JOEL BR TR 6' 190 lbs.
B. May 19, 1948, Irvington, N. J.

	W	L	PCT	ERA	G	GS	CG	IP	H	BB	SO	ShO	W	L	SV	AB	H	HR	BA
1968 ATL N	0	1	.000	0.00	1	0	0	3	4	0	0	0	0	0	0	0	0	0	–
1969 SD N	8	14	.364	3.94	32	30	2	185	194	73	111	0	0	0	0	63	7	1	.111
1970	1	8	.111	6.04	21	12	0	76	91	43	41	0	0	0	1	18	0	0	.000
1971 2 teams SD N (18G 0–2) STL N (19G 0–2)																			
" total	0	4	.000	3.78	37	8	0	88	94	30	42	0	0	0	2	15	5	0	.333
1972 STL N	8	11	.421	4.11	30	19	3	133.2	136	46	72	3	2	3	0	40	3	0	.075
1973	0	0	–	5.40	6	0	0	8.1	14	2	2	0	0	0	0	1	0	0	.000
6 yrs.	17	38	.309	4.28	127	70	5	494	533	194	268	4	2	3	3	137	15	1	.109
3 yrs.	8	13	.381	4.09	55	24	3	191.2	201	67	95	3	2	3	2	51	6	0	.118

Carl Scheib

SCHEIB, CARL ALVIN BR TR 6'1" 192 lbs.
B. Jan. 1, 1927, Gratz, Pa.

	W	L	PCT	ERA	G	GS	CG	IP	H	BB	SO	ShO	W	L	SV	AB	H	HR	BA
1943 PHI A	0	1	.000	4.34	6	0	0	18.2	24	3	3	0	0	1	0	5	0	0	.000
1944	0	0	–	4.10	15	0	0	37.1	36	11	13	0	0	0	0	10	3	0	.300
1945	0	0	–	3.12	4	0	0	8.2	6	4	2	0	0	0	0	2	0	0	.000
1947	4	6	.400	5.04	21	12	6	116	121	55	26	0	1	0	0	45	6	0	.133
1948	14	8	.636	3.94	32	24	15	198.2	219	76	44	1	3	1	0	104	31	2	.298
1949	9	12	.429	5.12	38	23	11	182.2	191	118	43	2	2	0	0	72	17	0	.236
1950	3	10	.231	7.22	43	8	1	106	138	70	37	0	1	9	3	52	13	1	.250
1951	1	12	.077	4.47	46	11	3	143	132	71	49	0	1	3	10	53	21	2	.396
1952	11	7	.611	4.39	30	19	8	158	153	50	42	1	3	2	2	82	18	0	.220
1953	3	7	.300	4.88	28	8	3	96	99	29	25	0	1	2	0	41	8	0	.195
1954 2 teams PHI A (1G 0–1) STL N (3G 0–1)																			
" total	0	2	.000	14.85	4	2	0	6.2	11	6	6	0	0	0	0	2	0	0	.000
11 yrs.	45	65	.409	4.88	267	107	47	1071.2	1130	493	290	6	11	22	17	*			
1 yr.	0	1	.000	11.57	3	1	0	4.2	6	5	5	0	0	0	0	0	0	0	.000

	W	L	PCT	ERA	G	GS	CG	IP	H	BB	SO	ShO	Relief Pitching W	L	SV	BATTING AB	H	HR	BA

Freddy Schmidt

SCHMIDT, FREDERICK ALBERT
B. Feb. 9, 1916, Hartford, Conn.   BR TR 6'1"   185 lbs.

	W	L	PCT	ERA	G	GS	CG	IP	H	BB	SO	ShO	RP W	L	SV	AB	H	HR	BA
1944 STL N	7	3	.700	3.15	37	9	3	114.1	94	58	58	2	3	0	5	34	7	0	.206
1946	1	0	1.000	3.29	16	0	0	27.1	27	15	14	0	1	0	0	1	0	0	.000
1947 3 teams	STL N	(2G 0-0)		PHI N	(29G 5-8)		CHI N	(1G 0-0)											
" total	5	8	.385	4.73	32	6	0	83.2	85	49	26	0	5	4	0	22	1	0	.045
3 yrs.	13	11	.542	3.75	85	15	3	225.1	206	122	98	2	9	4	5	57	8	0	.140
3 yrs.	8	3	.727	3.15	55	9	3	145.2	126	74	74	2	4	0	5	35	7	0	.200
WORLD SERIES																			
1944 STL N	0	0	–	0.00	1	0	0	3.1	1	1	1	0	0	0	0	1	0	0	.000

Willard Schmidt

SCHMIDT, WILLARD RAYMOND
B. May 29, 1928, Hays, Kans.   BR TR 6'1"   187 lbs.

	W	L	PCT	ERA	G	GS	CG	IP	H	BB	SO	ShO	RP W	L	SV	AB	H	HR	BA
1952 STL N	2	3	.400	5.19	18	3	0	34.2	36	18	30	0	1	1	1	8	1	0	.125
1953	0	2	.000	9.17	6	2	0	17.2	21	13	11	0	0	0	0	4	0	0	.000
1955	7	6	.538	2.78	20	15	8	129.2	89	57	86	1	0	0	0	42	5	0	.119
1956	6	8	.429	3.84	33	21	2	147.2	131	78	52	0	0	0	1	43	10	0	.233
1957	10	3	.769	4.78	40	8	1	116.2	146	49	63	0	5	3	0	33	7	0	.212
1958 CIN N	3	5	.375	2.86	41	2	0	69.1	60	33	41	0	3	5	0	11	1	0	.091
1959	3	2	.600	3.95	36	4	0	70.2	80	30	40	0	2	0	0	12	1	0	.083
7 yrs.	31	29	.517	3.93	194	55	11	586.1	563	278	323	1	11	9	2	153	25	0	.163
5 yrs.	25	22	.532	4.09	117	49	11	446.1	423	215	242	1	6	4	2	130	23	0	.177

Barney Schultz

SCHULTZ, GEORGE WARREN
B. Aug. 15, 1926, Beverly, N. J.   BR TR 6'2"   200 lbs.

	W	L	PCT	ERA	G	GS	CG	IP	H	BB	SO	ShO	RP W	L	SV	AB	H	HR	BA
1955 STL N	1	2	.333	7.89	19	0	0	29.2	28	15	19	0	1	2	4	4	0	0	.000
1959 DET A	1	2	.333	4.42	13	0	0	18.1	17	14	17	0	1	2	0	2	2	0	1.000
1961 CHI N	7	6	.538	2.70	41	0	0	66.2	57	25	59	0	7	6	7	10	1	0	.100
1962	5	5	.500	3.82	51	0	0	77.2	66	23	58	0	5	5	5	5	0	0	.000
1963 2 teams	CHI N	(15G 1-0)		STL N	(24G 2-0)														
" total	3	0	1.000	3.59	39	0	0	62.2	61	17	44	0	3	0	3	4	0	0	.000
1964 STL N	1	3	.250	1.64	30	0	0	49.1	35	11	29	0	1	3	14	6	1	0	.167
1965	2	2	.500	3.83	34	0	0	42.1	39	11	38	0	2	2	2	2	0	0	.000
7 yrs.	20	20	.500	3.63	227	0	0	346.2	303	116	264	0	20	20	35	33	4	0	.121
4 yrs.	6	7	.462	3.85	107	0	0	156.2	138	45	112	0	6	7	21	12	1	0	.083
WORLD SERIES																			
1964 STL N	0	1	.000	18.00	4	0	0	4	9	3	1	0	0	1	1	1	0	0	.000

Buddy Schultz

SCHULTZ, CHARLES BUDD
B. Sept. 19, 1950, Cleveland, Ohio   BR TL 6'   170 lbs.

	W	L	PCT	ERA	G	GS	CG	IP	H	BB	SO	ShO	RP W	L	SV	AB	H	HR	BA
1975 CHI N	2	0	1.000	6.00	6	0	0	6	11	5	4	0	2	0	0	0	0	0	–
1976	1	1	.500	6.00	29	0	0	24	37	9	15	0	1	1	2	4	0	0	.000
1977 STL N	6	1	.857	2.33	40	3	0	85	76	24	66	0	4	1	1	12	2	0	.167
1978	2	4	.333	3.80	62	0	0	83	68	36	70	0	2	4	6	5	1	0	.200
1979	4	3	.571	4.50	31	0	0	42	40	14	38	0	4	3	3	4	0	0	.000
5 yrs.	15	9	.625	3.68	168	3	0	240	232	88	193	0	13	9	12	25	3	0	.120
3 yrs.	12	8	.600	3.34	133	3	0	210	184	74	174	0	10	8	10	21	3	0	.143

Walt Schulz

SCHULZ, WALTER FREDERICK
B. Apr. 16, 1900, St. Louis, Mo.   D. Feb. 27, 1928, Prescott, Ariz.   BR TR 6'   170 lbs.

	W	L	PCT	ERA	G	GS	CG	IP	H	BB	SO	ShO	RP W	L	SV	AB	H	HR	BA
1920 STL N	0	0	–	6.00	2	0	0	6	10	2	0	0	0	0	0	2	0	0	.000

Ferdie Schupp

SCHUPP, FERDINAND MAURICE
B. Jan. 16, 1891, Louisville, Ky.   D. Dec. 16, 1971, Los Angeles, Calif.   BR TL 5'10"   150 lbs.

	W	L	PCT	ERA	G	GS	CG	IP	H	BB	SO	ShO	RP W	L	SV	AB	H	HR	BA
1913 NY N	0	0	–	0.75	5	1	0	12	10	3	2	0	0	0	0	3	1	0	.333
1914	0	0	–	5.82	8	0	0	17	19	9	9	0	0	0	1	2	0	0	.000
1915	1	0	1.000	5.10	23	1	0	54.2	57	29	28	0	1	0	0	10	2	0	.200
1916	10	3	.769	0.90	30	11	8	140.1	79	37	86	4	2	1	0	41	4	0	.098
1917	21	7	.750	1.95	36	32	25	272	202	70	147	6	0	1	0	93	15	0	.161
1918	0	1	.000	7.56	10	2	1	33.1	42	27	22	0	0	0	0	9	1	0	.111
1919 2 teams	NY N	(9G 1-3)		STL N	(10G 4-4)														
" total	5	7	.417	4.34	19	13	6	101.2	87	48	54	0	1	0	1	26	3	1	.115
1920 STL N	16	13	.552	3.52	38	37	17	250.2	246	127	119	0	0	0	0	86	22	0	.256
1921 2 teams	STL N	(9G 2-0)		BKN N	(20G 3-4)														
" total	5	4	.556	4.39	29	11	2	98.1	117	48	48	0	3	0	3	26	5	0	.192
1922 CHI A	4	4	.500	6.08	18	12	3	74	79	66	38	1	1	0	0	25	5	0	.200
10 yrs.	62	39	.614	3.32	216	120	62	1054	938	464	553	11	8	2	5	321	58	1	.181
3 yrs.	22	17	.564	3.62	57	50	24	357.2	343	178	178	0	1	0	1	120	27	1	.225
WORLD SERIES																			
1917 NY N	1	0	1.000	1.74	2	2	1	10.1	11	2	9	1	0	0	0	4	1	0	.250

George Scott

SCOTT, GEORGE WILLIAM
B. Nov. 17, 1896, Trenton, Mo.   BR TR 6'1"   175 lbs.

	W	L	PCT	ERA	G	GS	CG	IP	H	BB	SO	ShO	RP W	L	SV	AB	H	HR	BA
1920 STL N	0	0	–	4.50	2	0	0	4	3	1	1	0	0	0	0	1	0	0	.000

Kim Seaman

SEAMAN, KIM MICHAEL
B. May 6, 1957, Moss Point, Miss.   BL TL 6'4"   205 lbs.

	W	L	PCT	ERA	G	GS	CG	IP	H	BB	SO	ShO	RP W	L	SV	AB	H	HR	BA
1979 STL N	0	0	–	0.00	1	0	0	2	0	2	3	0	0	0	0	0	0	0	–
1980	3	2	.600	3.38	26	0	0	24	16	13	10	0	3	2	4	1	0	0	.000
2 yrs.	3	2	.600	3.12	27	0	0	26	16	15	13	0	3	2	4	1	0	0	.000
2 yrs.	3	2	.600	3.12	27	0	0	26	16	15	13	0	3	2	4	1	0	0	.000

	W	L	PCT	ERA	G	GS	CG	IP	H	BB	SO	ShO	Relief Pitching W	L	SV	BATTING AB	H	HR	BA

Diego Segui

SEGUI, DIEGO GONZALES
B. Aug. 17, 1937, Holguin, Cuba — BR TR 6' 190 lbs.

Year/Team	W	L	PCT	ERA	G	GS	CG	IP	H	BB	SO	ShO	RP W	RP L	RP SV	AB	H	HR	BA
1962 KC A	8	5	.615	3.86	37	13	2	116.2	89	46	71	0	3	2	6	34	8	1	.235
1963	9	6	.600	3.77	38	23	4	167	173	73	116	1	1	0	0	55	12	0	.218
1964	8	17	.320	4.56	40	35	5	217	219	94	155	2	0	0	0	71	11	1	.155
1965	5	15	.250	4.64	40	25	5	163	166	67	119	1	0	2	0	47	9	1	.191
1966 WAS A	3	7	.300	5.00	21	13	1	72	82	24	54	1	1	0	0	18	2	0	.111
1967 KC A	3	4	.429	3.09	36	3	0	70	62	31	52	0	3	1	1	9	0	0	.000
1968 OAK A	6	5	.545	2.39	52	0	0	83	51	32	72	0	6	5	6	9	1	0	.111
1969 SEA A	12	6	.667	3.35	66	8	2	142.1	127	61	113	0	8	4	12	27	4	0	.148
1970 OAK A	10	10	.500	2.56	47	19	3	162	130	68	95	2	2	3	2	43	5	0	.116
1971	10	8	.556	3.14	26	21	5	146	122	63	81	0	1	0	0	47	4	1	.085
1972 2 teams			OAK A	(7G 0-1)		STL N	(33G 3-1)												
" total	3	2	.600	3.20	40	3	0	78.2	72	39	65	0	3	2	9	14	2	0	.143
1973 STL N	7	6	.538	2.78	65	0	0	100.1	78	53	93	0	7	6	17	10	0	0	.000
1974 BOS A	6	8	.429	4.00	58	0	0	108	106	49	76	0	6	8	10	0	0	0	—
1975	2	5	.286	4.82	33	1	1	71	71	43	45	0	2	4	6	0	0	0	—
1977 SEA A	0	7	.000	5.68	40	7	0	111	108	43	91	0	0	2	2	0	0	0	—
15 yrs.	92	111	.453	3.81	639	171	28	1808	1656	786	1298	7	43	39	71	384	58	4	.151
2 yrs.	10	7	.588	2.88	98	0	0	156	125	85	147	0	10	7	26 9th	17	1	0	.059

LEAGUE CHAMPIONSHIP SERIES

1971 OAK A	0	1	.000	5.79	1	0	0	4.2	6	6	4	0	0	0	0	2	0	0	.000

WORLD SERIES

1975 BOS A	0	0	—	0.00	1	0	0	1	0	0	0	0	0	0	0	0	0	0	—

Epp Sell

SELL, ELWOOD LESTER
B. Apr. 26, 1897, Llewellyn, Pa. D. Feb. 19, 1961, Reading, Pa. — BR TR 6' 175 lbs.

Year/Team	W	L	PCT	ERA	G	GS	CG	IP	H	BB	SO	ShO	RP W	RP L	RP SV	AB	H	HR	BA
1922 STL N	4	2	.667	6.82	7	5	0	33	47	6	5	0	2	0	0	12	4	0	.333
1923	0	1	.000	6.00	5	1	0	15	16	8	2	0	0	1	0	7	0	0	.000
2 yrs.	4	3	.571	6.56	12	6	0	48	63	14	7	0	2	1	0	19	4	0	.211
2 yrs.	4	3	.571	6.56	12	6	0	48	63	14	7	0	2	1	0	19	4	0	.211

Bobby Shantz

SHANTZ, ROBERT CLAYTON
Brother of Billy Shantz.
B. Sept. 26, 1925, Pottstown, Pa. — BR TL 5'6" 139 lbs.

Year/Team	W	L	PCT	ERA	G	GS	CG	IP	H	BB	SO	ShO	RP W	RP L	RP SV	AB	H	HR	BA
1949 PHI A	6	8	.429	3.40	33	7	4	127	100	74	58	1	3	4	2	37	7	0	.189
1950	8	14	.364	4.61	36	23	6	214.2	251	85	93	1	2	0	0	66	11	1	.167
1951	18	10	.643	3.94	32	25	13	205.1	213	70	77	4	2	1	0	72	18	0	.250
1952	24	7	.774	2.48	33	33	27	279.2	230	63	152	5	0	0	0	96	19	0	.198
1953	5	9	.357	4.09	16	16	6	105.2	107	26	58	0	0	0	0	38	9	0	.237
1954	1	0	1.000	7.88	2	1	0	8	12	3	3	0	0	0	0	3	1	0	.333
1955 KC A	5	10	.333	4.54	23	17	4	125	124	66	58	1	2	0	0	41	6	0	.146
1956	2	7	.222	4.35	45	2	1	101.1	95	37	67	0	1	6	9	22	2	0	.091
1957 NY A	11	5	.688	2.45	30	21	9	173	157	40	72	1	1	0	5	56	10	0	.179
1958	7	6	.538	3.36	33	13	3	126	127	35	80	0	5	5	0	35	8	0	.229
1959	7	3	.700	2.38	33	4	2	94.2	64	33	66	2	5	1	3	23	5	0	.217
1960	5	4	.556	2.79	42	0	0	67.2	57	24	54	0	5	4	0	10	1	0	.100
1961 PIT N	6	3	.667	3.32	43	6	2	89.1	91	26	61	1	3	1	2	16	7	0	.438
1962 2 teams			HOU N	(3G 1-1)		STL N	(28G 5-3)												
" total	6	4	.600	1.95	31	3	1	78.1	60	25	61	0	5	3	4	21	2	0	.095
1963 STL N	6	4	.600	2.61	55	0	0	79.1	55	17	70	0	6	4	11	7	1	0	.143
1964 3 teams			STL N	(16G 1-3)		CHI N	(20G 0-1)	PHI N	(14G 1-1)										
" total	2	5	.286	3.12	50	0	0	60.2	52	19	42	0	2	5	1	5	0	0	.000
16 yrs.	119	99	.546	3.38	537	171	78	1935.2	1795	643	1072	16	42	34	48	548	107	1	.195
3 yrs.	12	10	.545	2.51	99	0	0	154.1	114	44	129	0	12	10	15	20	3	0	.150

WORLD SERIES

1957 NY A	0	1	.000	4.05	3	1	0	6.2	8	2	7	0	0	0	0	1	0	0	.000
1960	0	0	—	4.26	3	0	0	6.1	4	1	1	0	0	0	1	3	1	0	.333
2 yrs.	0	1	.000	4.15	6	1	0	13	12	3	8	0	0	0	1	4	1	0	.250

Don Shaw

SHAW, DONALD WELLINGTON
B. Feb. 23, 1944, Pittsburgh, Pa. — BL TL 6' 180 lbs.

Year/Team	W	L	PCT	ERA	G	GS	CG	IP	H	BB	SO	ShO	RP W	RP L	RP SV	AB	H	HR	BA
1967 NY N	4	5	.444	2.98	40	0	0	51.1	40	23	44	0	4	5	3	3	0	0	.000
1968	0	0	—	0.75	7	0	0	12	3	5	11	0	0	0	0	0	0	0	—
1969 MON N	2	5	.286	5.21	35	1	0	65.2	61	37	45	0	2	4	0	10	0	0	.000
1971 STL N	7	2	.778	2.65	45	0	0	51	45	31	19	0	7	2	2	1	0	0	.000
1972 2 teams			STL N	(8G 0-1)		OAK A	(3G 0-1)												
" total	0	2	.000	14.63	11	0	0	8	17	5	4	0	0	2	0	1	0	0	.000
5 yrs.	13	14	.481	4.02	138	1	0	188	166	101	123	0	13	13	5	15	0	0	.000
2 yrs.	7	3	.700	3.00	53	0	0	54	50	34	19	0	7	3	2	2	0	0	.000

Bill Sherdel

SHERDEL, WILLIAM HENRY (Wee Willie)
B. Aug. 15, 1896, McSherrystown, Pa. D. Nov. 14, 1968, McSherrystown, Pa. — BL TL 5'10" 160 lbs.

Year/Team	W	L	PCT	ERA	G	GS	CG	IP	H	BB	SO	ShO	RP W	RP L	RP SV	AB	H	HR	BA
1918 STL N	6	12	.333	2.71	35	17	9	182.1	174	49	40	1	1	4	0	62	15	1	.242
1919	5	9	.357	3.47	36	10	7	137.1	137	42	52	0	3	1	1	48	13	0	.271
1920	11	10	.524	3.28	43	7	4	170	183	40	74	0	8	8	6	63	14	1	.222
1921	9	8	.529	3.18	38	8	5	144.1	137	38	57	1	4	6	1	44	5	0	.114
1922	17	13	.567	3.88	47	31	15	241.1	298	62	79	3	2	1	2	88	17	1	.193
1923	15	13	.536	4.32	39	26	14	225	270	59	78	0	3	2	2	83	28	1	.337
1924	8	9	.471	3.42	35	10	6	168.2	188	38	57	0	6	3	1	75	15	0	.200
1925	15	6	.714	3.11	32	21	17	200	216	42	53	0	2	0	0	73	15	1	.205
1926	16	12	.571	3.49	34	29	17	234.2	255	49	59	3	1	2	0	90	22	1	.244
1927	17	12	.586	3.53	39	28	18	232.1	241	48	59	0	3	0	6	72	14	1	.194
1928	21	10	.677	2.86	38	27	20	248.2	251	56	72	0	3	2	5	84	19	1	.226

	W	L	PCT	ERA	G	GS	CG	IP	H	BB	SO	ShO	Relief Pitching W	L	SV	BATTING AB	H	HR	BA

Bill Sherdel continued

	W	L	PCT	ERA	G	GS	CG	IP	H	BB	SO	ShO	W	L	SV	AB	H	HR	BA
1929	10	15	.400	5.93	33	22	11	195.2	278	58	69	1	3	2	0	70	16	1	.229
1930 2 teams					STL N (13G 3–2)			BOS N (21G 6–5)											
" total	9	7	.563	4.71	34	21	8	183.1	217	43	55	1	1	0	1	61	6	0	.098
1931 BOS N	6	10	.375	4.25	27	16	8	137.2	163	35	34	0	1	1	0	46	14	0	.304
1932 2 teams					BOS N (1G 0–0)			STL N (3G 0–0)											
" total	0	0	–	3.68	4	0	0	7.1	10	2	1	0	0	0	0	1	1	0	1.000
15 yrs.	165	146	.531	3.72	514	273	159	2708.2	3018	661	839	12	39	32	26	960	214	9	.223
14 yrs.	153	131	.539	3.64	465	243	144	2450	2721	595	779	12	38	31	25	872	196	9	.225
	3rd	4th				3rd			4th	3rd			6th	10th		4th		10th	

WORLD SERIES

	W	L	PCT	ERA	G	GS	CG	IP	H	BB	SO	ShO	W	L	SV	AB	H	HR	BA
1926 STL N	0	2	.000	2.12	2	2	1	17	15	8	3	0	0	0	0	5	0	0	.000
1928	0	2	.000	4.73	2	2	0	13.1	15	3	3	0	0	0	0	5	0	0	.000
2 yrs.	0	4	.000	3.26	4	4	1	30.1	30	11	6	0	0	0	0	10	0	0	.000
		7th																	

Charlie Shields

SHIELDS, CHARLES JESSAMINE   BL TL
B. Dec. 10, 1879, Jackson, Tenn.   D. Aug. 27, 1953, Memphis, Tenn.

	W	L	PCT	ERA	G	GS	CG	IP	H	BB	SO	ShO	W	L	SV	AB	H	HR	BA
1902 2 teams					BAL A (23G 5–11)			STL A (4G 3–0)											
" total	8	11	.421	4.07	27	19	13	172.1	238	39	34	1	2	1	0	61	14	0	.230
1907 STL N	0	2	.000	9.45	3	2	0	6.2	12	7	1	0	0	0	0	2	0	0	.000
2 yrs.	8	13	.381	4.27	30	21	13	179	250	46	35	1	2	1	0	63	14	0	.222
1 yr.	0	2	.000	9.45	3	2	0	6.2	12	7	1	0	0	0	0	2	0	0	.000

Vince Shields

SHIELDS, VINCENT WILLIAM   BL TR 5'11" 185 lbs.
B. Nov. 18, 1900, Fredericton, N. B., Canada   D. Oct. 17, 1952, Plaster Rock, N. B., Canada

	W	L	PCT	ERA	G	GS	CG	IP	H	BB	SO	ShO	W	L	SV	AB	H	HR	BA
1924 STL N	1	1	.500	3.00	2	1	0	12	10	3	4	0	1	0	0	5	2	0	.400

Bob Shirley

SHIRLEY, ROBERT CHARLES   BL TL 5'11" 180 lbs.
B. June 25, 1954, Oklahoma City, Okla.

	W	L	PCT	ERA	G	GS	CG	IP	H	BB	SO	ShO	W	L	SV	AB	H	HR	BA
1977 SD N	12	18	.400	3.70	39	35	1	214	215	100	146	0	0	1	0	74	9	0	.122
1978	8	11	.421	3.69	50	20	2	166	164	61	102	0	1	2	5	40	5	0	.125
1979	8	16	.333	3.38	49	25	4	205	196	59	117	1	2	4	0	55	5	0	.091
1980	11	12	.478	3.55	59	12	3	137	143	54	67	0	7	6	7	30	1	0	.033
1981 STL N	6	4	.600	3.60	28	11	1	79	78	34	36	0	1	0	1	22	3	0	.136
1982 CIN N	8	13	.381	3.60	41	20	1	152.2	138	73	89	0	2	4	0	42	6	0	.143
6 yrs.	53	74	.417	3.62	266	123	12	953.2	934	381	557	1	13	17	13	263	29	0	.110
1 yr.	6	4	.600	4.10	28	11	1	79	78	34	36	0	1	0	1	22	3	0	.136

Clyde Shoun

SHOUN, CLYDE MITCHELL (Hardrock)   BL TL 6'1" 188 lbs.
B. Mar. 20, 1912, Mountain City, Tenn.   D. Mar. 20, 1968, Mountain Home, Tenn.

	W	L	PCT	ERA	G	GS	CG	IP	H	BB	SO	ShO	W	L	SV	AB	H	HR	BA
1935 CHI N	1	0	1.000	2.84	5	1	0	12.2	14	5	5	0	0	0	0	3	0	0	.000
1936	0	0	–	12.46	4	0	0	4.1	3	6	1	0	0	0	0	0	0	0	–
1937	7	7	.500	5.61	37	9	2	93	118	45	43	0	3	3	0	29	4	0	.138
1938 STL N	6	6	.500	4.14	40	12	3	117.1	130	43	37	0	2	2	1	31	8	0	.258
1939	3	1	.750	3.76	53	2	0	103	98	42	50	0	3	1	9	26	3	0	.115
1940	13	11	.542	3.92	54	19	13	197.1	193	46	82	1	3	4	5	63	12	0	.190
1941	3	5	.375	5.66	26	6	0	70	98	20	34	0	3	1	0	22	4	0	.182
1942 2 teams					STL N (2G 0–0)			CIN N (34G 1–3)											
" total	1	3	.250	2.18	36	0	0	74.1	56	24	32	0	1	3	0	13	4	0	.308
1943 CIN N	14	5	.737	3.06	45	5	2	147	131	46	61	0	13	3	7	42	13	0	.310
1944	13	10	.565	3.02	38	21	12	202.2	193	42	55	1	3	2	2	67	15	0	.224
1946	1	6	.143	4.10	27	5	0	79	87	26	20	0	1	3	0	21	2	0	.095
1947 2 teams					CIN N (10G 0–0)			BOS N (26G 5–3)											
" total	5	3	.625	4.50	36	3	1	88	89	26	30	1	4	1	1	19	3	0	.158
1948 BOS N	5	1	.833	4.01	36	2	1	74	77	20	25	0	4	1	4	21	4	0	.190
1949 2 teams					BOS N (1G 0–0)			CHI A (16G 1–1)											
" total	1	1	.500	5.55	17	0	0	24.1	38	13	8	0	1	1	0	5	1	0	.200
14 yrs.	73	59	.553	3.91	454	85	34	1287	1325	404	483	3	41	25	29	362	73	0	.202
5 yrs.	25	23	.521	4.18	175	39	16	489.1	520	151	203	1	11	8	15	142	27	0	.190

Sonny Siebert

SIEBERT, WILFRED CHARLES   BR TR 6'3" 190 lbs.
B. Jan. 14, 1937, St. Mary's, Mo.

	W	L	PCT	ERA	G	GS	CG	IP	H	BB	SO	ShO	W	L	SV	AB	H	HR	BA
1964 CLE A	7	9	.438	3.23	41	14	3	156	142	57	144	1	1	2	3	49	13	2	.265
1965	16	8	.667	2.43	39	27	4	188.2	139	46	191	1	4	0	1	66	7	1	.106
1966	16	8	**.667**	2.80	34	32	11	241	193	62	163	1	0	0	1	85	11	0	.129
1967	10	12	.455	2.38	34	26	7	185.1	136	54	136	1	1	1	4	52	7	1	.135
1968	12	10	.545	2.97	31	30	8	206	145	88	146	4	0	0	0	70	11	0	.157
1969 2 teams					CLE A (2G 0–1)			BOS A (43G 14–10)											
" total	14	11	.560	3.76	45	24	2	177.1	161	76	133	0	5	5	1	57	9	1	.158
1970 BOS A	15	8	.652	3.43	33	33	7	223	207	60	142	2	0	0	0	77	10	0	.130
1971	16	10	.615	2.91	32	32	12	235	220	60	131	4	0	0	0	79	21	6	.266
1972	12	12	.500	3.80	32	30	7	196.1	204	59	123	3	0	0	0	72	17	0	.236
1973 2 teams					BOS A (2G 0–1)			TEX A (25G 7–11)											
" total	7	12	.368	4.06	27	20	1	122	125	38	81	1	0	2	2	0	0	0	–
1974 STL N	8	8	.500	3.22	28	20	3	134	150	51	68	3	1	0	0	44	5	0	.114
1975 2 teams					SD N (6G 3–2)			OAK A (17G 4–4)											
" total	7	6	.538	3.89	23	19	0	88	97	41	54	0	0	0	0	9	3	0	.333
12 yrs.	140	114	.551	3.21	399	307	67	2152.2	1919	692	1512	21	12	6	16	660	114	12	.173
1 yr.	8	8	.500	3.83	28	20	5	134	150	51	68	3	1	0	0	44	5	0	.114

			W	L	PCT	ERA	G	GS	CG	IP	H	BB	SO	ShO	Relief W	Relief L	Relief SV	AB	H	HR	BA

Curt Simmons

SIMMONS, CURTIS THOMAS
B. May 19, 1929, Egypt, Pa. BL TL 5'11" 175 lbs.

Year	Team	Lg	W	L	PCT	ERA	G	GS	CG	IP	H	BB	SO	ShO	RW	RL	SV	AB	H	HR	BA
1947	PHI	N	1	0	1.000	1.00	1	1	1	9	5	6	9	0	0	0	0	2	1	0	.500
1948			7	13	.350	4.87	31	22	7	170	169	108	86	0	0	0	0	51	7	0	.137
1949			4	10	.286	4.59	38	14	2	131.1	133	55	83	0	1	3	1	41	7	0	.171
1950			17	8	.680	3.40	31	27	11	214.2	178	88	146	2	0	0	1	77	12	0	.156
1952			14	8	.636	2.82	28	28	15	201.1	170	70	141	6	0	0	0	67	11	1	.164
1953			16	13	.552	3.21	32	30	19	238	211	82	138	4	0	0	0	93	13	0	.140
1954			14	15	.483	2.81	34	33	21	253	226	98	125	3	0	0	1	91	16	0	.176
1955			8	8	.500	4.92	25	22	3	130	148	50	58	0	1	1	0	46	8	0	.174
1956			15	10	.600	3.36	33	27	14	198	186	65	88	0	1	0	0	72	17	0	.236
1957			12	11	.522	3.44	32	29	9	212	214	50	92	2	0	0	0	71	17	0	.239
1958			7	14	.333	4.38	29	27	7	168.1	196	40	78	1	0	0	1	59	12	0	.203
1959			0	0	–	4.50	7	0	0	10	16	0	4	0	0	0	0	0	0	0	–
1960 2 teams	PHI	N (4G 0-0)					STL	N	(23G 7-4)												
" total			7	4	.636	3.06	27	19	3	156	162	37	67	1	0	0	0	47	10	0	.213
1961	STL	N	9	10	.474	3.13	30	29	6	195.2	203	64	99	2	0	0	0	66	20	0	.303
1962			10	10	.500	3.51	31	22	9	154	167	32	74	4	0	3	0	50	8	0	.160
1963			15	9	.625	2.48	32	32	11	232.2	209	48	127	6	0	0	0	81	13	0	.160
1964			18	9	.667	3.43	34	34	12	244	233	49	104	3	0	0	0	94	10	0	.106
1965			9	15	.375	4.08	34	32	5	203	229	54	96	0	0	0	0	64	3	0	.047
1966 2 teams	STL	N (10G 1-1)					CHI	N	(19G 4-7)												
" total			5	8	.385	4.23	29	15	4	110.2	114	35	38	1	2	2	0	26	3	0	.115
1967 2 teams	CHI	N (17G 3-7)					CAL	A	(14G 2-1)												
" total			5	8	.385	4.24	31	18	4	116.2	144	32	44	1	1	0	0	37	6	0	.162
20 yrs.			193	183	.513	3.54	569	461	163	3348.1	3313	1063	1697	36	8	9	5	1135	194	1	.171
7 yrs.			69	58	.543	3.25	194	171	47	1214.2	1225	292	577	16	0	3	0	410	65	0	.159

WORLD SERIES

Year	Team	Lg	W	L	PCT	ERA	G	GS	CG	IP	H	BB	SO	ShO	RW	RL	SV	AB	H	HR	BA
1964	STL	N	0	1	.000	2.51	2	2	0	14.1	11	3	8	0	0	0	0	4	2	0	.500

Bill Smith

SMITH, WILLIAM GARLAND
B. June 8, 1934, Washington, D. C. BL TL 6' 190 lbs.

Year	Team	Lg	W	L	PCT	ERA	G	GS	CG	IP	H	BB	SO	ShO	RW	RL	SV	AB	H	HR	BA
1958	STL	N	0	1	.000	6.52	2	1	0	9.2	12	4	4	0	0	0	0	2	0	0	.000
1959			0	0	–	1.08	6	0	0	8.1	11	3	4	0	0	0	1	1	0	0	.000
1962	PHI	N	1	5	.167	4.29	24	5	0	50.1	59	10	26	0	1	1	0	11	2	0	.182
3 yrs.			1	6	.143	4.21	32	6	0	68.1	82	17	34	0	1	1	1	14	2	0	.143
2 yrs.			0	1	.000	4.00	8	1	0	18	23	7	8	0	0	0	1	3	0	0	.000

Bob Smith

SMITH, ROBERT GILCHRIST
B. Feb. 1, 1931, Woodsville, N. H. BR TL 6'1½" 190 lbs.

Year	Team	Lg	W	L	PCT	ERA	G	GS	CG	IP	H	BB	SO	ShO	RW	RL	SV	AB	H	HR	BA
1955	BOS	A	0	0	–	0.00	1	0	0	1.2	1	1	1	0	0	0	0	0	0	0	–
1957 2 teams	STL	N (6G 0-0)					PIT	N	(20G 2-4)												
" total			2	4	.333	3.34	26	4	2	64.2	60	31	46	0	0	3	1	15	1	0	.067
1958	PIT	N	2	2	.500	4.43	35	4	0	61	61	31	24	0	2	0	1	11	1	0	.091
1959 2 teams	PIT	N (20G 0-0)					DET	A	(9G 0-3)												
" total			0	3	.000	4.81	29	0	0	39.1	52	20	22	0	0	3	0	3	0	0	.000
4 yrs.			4	9	.308	4.05	91	8	2	166.2	174	83	93	0	2	6	2	29	2	0	.069
1 yr.			0	0	–	4.66	6	0	0	9.2	12	6	11	0	0	0	1	2	0	0	.000

Frank Smith

SMITH, FRANK THOMAS
B. Apr. 4, 1928, Pierrepont Manor, N. Y. BR TR 6'3" 195 lbs.

Year	Team	Lg	W	L	PCT	ERA	G	GS	CG	IP	H	BB	SO	ShO	RW	RL	SV	AB	H	HR	BA
1950	CIN	N	2	7	.222	3.87	38	4	0	90.2	73	39	55	0	2	4	3	21	2	0	.095
1951			5	5	.500	3.20	50	0	0	76	65	22	34	0	5	5	11	10	0	0	.000
1952			12	11	.522	3.75	53	2	1	122.1	109	41	77	0	12	9	7	29	5	0	.172
1953			8	1	.889	5.49	50	1	0	83.2	89	45	42	0	8	1	2	13	2	0	.154
1954			5	8	.385	2.67	50	0	0	81	60	29	51	0	5	8	20	10	1	0	.100
1955	STL	N	3	1	.750	3.23	28	0	0	39	27	23	17	0	3	1	1	4	0	0	.000
1956	CIN	N	0	0	–	12.00	2	0	0	3	3	2	1	0	0	0	0	0	0	0	–
7 yrs.			35	33	.515	3.81	271	7	1	495.2	426	181	277	0	35	28	44	87	10	0	.115
1 yr.			3	1	.750	3.23	28	0	0	39	27	23	17	0	3	1	1	4	0	0	.000

Germany Smith

SMITH, GEORGE J.
B. Apr. 21, 1863, Pittsburgh, Pa. D. Dec. 1, 1927, Altoona, Pa. BR TR 6' 175 lbs.

Year	Team	Lg	W	L	PCT	ERA	G	GS	CG	IP	H	BB	SO	ShO	RW	RL	SV	AB	H	HR	BA
1884	CLE	N	0	0	–	9.00	1	0	0	3	3	0	1	0	0	0	0	*			

Tom Smith

SMITH, THOMAS E.
B. Dec. 5, 1871, Boston, Mass. D. Mar. 2, 1929, Dorchester, Mass.

Year	Team	Lg	W	L	PCT	ERA	G	GS	CG	IP	H	BB	SO	ShO	RW	RL	SV	AB	H	HR	BA
1894	BOS	N	0	0	–	15.00	2	0	0	6	8	6	2	0	0	0	1	2	0	0	.000
1895	PHI	N	2	3	.400	6.88	11	7	4	68	76	53	21	0	0	0	0	33	8	0	.242
1896	LOU	N	2	3	.400	5.40	11	5	4	55	73	25	14	0	1	0	0	39	8	0	.205
1898	STL	N	0	1	.000	2.00	1	1	1	9	9	5	1	0	0	0	0	2	1	0	.500
4 yrs.			4	7	.364	6.33	25	13	9	138	166	89	38	0	1	0	0	76	17	0	.224
1 yr.			0	1	.000	2.00	1	1	1	9	9	5	1	0	0	0	0	2	1	0	.500

Eddie Solomon

SOLOMON, EDDIE JR.
B. Feb. 9, 1952, Houston County, Ga. BR TR 6'2" 185 lbs.

Year	Team	Lg	W	L	PCT	ERA	G	GS	CG	IP	H	BB	SO	ShO	RW	RL	SV	AB	H	HR	BA
1973	LA	N	0	0	–	7.11	4	0	0	6.1	10	4	6	0	0	0	0	1	0	0	.000
1974			0	0	–	1.35	4	0	0	6.2	5	2	2	0	0	0	0	0	0	0	–
1975	CHI	N	0	0	–	1.29	6	0	0	7	7	6	3	0	0	0	0	0	0	0	–
1976	STL	N	1	1	.500	4.86	26	2	0	37	45	16	19	0	0	1	0	5	2	0	.400
1977	ATL	N	6	6	.500	4.55	18	16	0	89	110	34	54	0	0	0	0	31	4	0	.129
1978			4	6	.400	4.08	37	8	0	106	98	50	64	0	1	3	2	29	4	0	.138

	W	L	PCT	ERA	G	GS	CG	IP	H	BB	SO	ShO	Relief Pitching W	L	SV	BATTING AB	H	HR	BA

Eddie Solomon continued

	W	L	PCT	ERA	G	GS	CG	IP	H	BB	SO	ShO	W	L	SV	AB	H	HR	BA
1979	7	14	.333	4.21	31	30	4	186	184	51	96	0	0	0	0	64	13	0	.203
1980 PIT N	7	3	.700	2.70	26	12	2	100	96	37	35	0	2	0	0	32	7	0	.219
1981	8	6	.571	3.12	22	17	2	127	133	27	38	0	1	1	1	43	7	0	.163
1982 2 teams				PIT N (11G 2-6)				CHI A (6G 1-0)											
" total	3	6	.333	6.33	17	10	0	54	76	20	20	0	2	0	0	15	2	0	.133
10 yrs.	36	42	.462	3.99	191	95	8	719	764	247	337	0	6	5	4	220	39	0	.177
1 yr.	1	1	.500	4.86	26	2	0	37	45	16	19	0	0	1	0	5	2	0	.400

LEAGUE CHAMPIONSHIP SERIES

	W	L	PCT	ERA	G	GS	CG	IP	H	BB	SO	ShO	W	L	SV	AB	H	HR	BA
1974 LA N	0	0	—	0.00	1	0	0	2	2	1	1	0	0	0	0	0	0	0	—

SORENSEN, LARY ALAN   BR TR 6'2"   200 lbs.
B. Oct. 4, 1955, Detroit, Mich.

Lary Sorensen

	W	L	PCT	ERA	G	GS	CG	IP	H	BB	SO	ShO	W	L	SV	AB	H	HR	BA
1977 MIL A	7	10	.412	4.37	23	20	9	142	147	36	57	0	0	1	0	0	0	0	—
1978	18	12	.600	3.21	37	36	17	280.2	277	50	78	3	0	0	1	0	0	0	—
1979	15	14	.517	3.98	34	34	16	235	250	42	63	2	0	0	0	0	0	0	—
1980	12	10	.545	3.67	35	29	8	196	242	45	54	2	0	1	1	0	0	0	—
1981 STL N	7	7	.500	3.28	23	23	3	140	149	26	52	1	0	0	0	46	3	0	.065
1982 CLE A	10	15	.400	5.61	32	30	6	189.1	251	55	62	1	0	0	0	0	0	0	—
6 yrs.	69	68	.504	3.97	184	172	59	1183	1316	254	366	9	0	2	2	46	3	0	.065
1 yr.	7	7	.500	3.28	23	23	3	140	149	26	52	1	0	0	0	46	3	0	.065

SOSA, ELIAS MARTINEZ   BR TR 6'2"   186 lbs.
B. June 10, 1950, La Vega, Dominican Republic

Elias Sosa

	W	L	PCT	ERA	G	GS	CG	IP	H	BB	SO	ShO	W	L	SV	AB	H	HR	BA
1972 SF N	0	1	.000	2.25	8	0	0	16	10	12	10	0	1	0	3	4	0	0	.000
1973	10	4	.714	3.28	71	1	0	107	95	41	70	0	10	3	18	14	1	0	.071
1974	9	7	.563	3.48	68	0	0	101	94	45	48	0	9	7	6	15	1	0	.067
1975 2 teams				STL N (14G 0-3)				ATL N (43G 2-2)											
" total	2	5	.286	4.32	57	1	0	89.2	92	43	46	0	2	4	2	15	2	0	.133
1976 2 teams				ATL N (21G 4-4)				LA N (24G 2-4)											
" total	6	8	.429	4.43	45	0	0	69	71	25	52	0	6	8	4	7	1	0	.143
1977 LA N	2	2	.500	1.97	44	0	0	64	42	12	47	0	2	2	14	4	1	0	.250
1978 OAK A	8	2	.800	2.64	68	0	0	109	106	44	61	0	8	2	14	0	0	0	—
1979 MON N	8	7	.533	1.95	62	0	0	97	77	37	59	0	8	7	18	13	2	0	.154
1980	9	6	.600	3.06	67	0	0	94	104	19	58	0	9	6	9	11	1	0	.091
1981	1	2	.333	3.69	32	0	0	39	46	8	18	0	1	2	3	2	2	0	1.000
1982 DET A	3	3	.500	4.43	38	0	0	61	64	18	24	0	3	3	4	0	0	0	—
11 yrs.	58	47	.552	3.23	560	2	0	846.2	801	304	493	0	58	45	82	85	11	0	.129
1 yr.	0	3	.000	3.95	14	1	0	27.1	22	14	15	0	0	2	0	8	1	0	.125

DIVISIONAL PLAYOFF SERIES

	W	L	PCT	ERA	G	GS	CG	IP	H	BB	SO	ShO	W	L	SV	AB	H	HR	BA
1981 MON N	0	0	—	3.00	2	0	0	3	4	0	1	0	0	0	0	0	0	0	—

LEAGUE CHAMPIONSHIP SERIES

	W	L	PCT	ERA	G	GS	CG	IP	H	BB	SO	ShO	W	L	SV	AB	H	HR	BA
1977 LA N	0	1	.000	10.13	2	0	0	2.2	5	0	0	0	0	1	0	1	0	0	.000
1981 MON N	0	0	—	0.00	1	0	0	.1	1	1	0	0	0	0	0	0	0	0	—
2 yrs.	0	1	.000	9.00	3	0	0	3	6	1	0	0	0	1	0	1	0	0	.000

WORLD SERIES

	W	L	PCT	ERA	G	GS	CG	IP	H	BB	SO	ShO	W	L	SV	AB	H	HR	BA
1977 LA N	0	0	—	11.57	2	0	0	2.1	3	1	1	0	0	0	0	0	0	0	—

SOTHORON, ALLEN SUTTON   BB TR 5'11"   182 lbs.
B. Apr. 29, 1893, Laura, Ohio   BR 1924-26
D. June 17, 1939, St. Louis, Mo.
Manager 1933.

Allen Sothoron

	W	L	PCT	ERA	G	GS	CG	IP	H	BB	SO	ShO	W	L	SV	AB	H	HR	BA
1914 STL A	0	0	—	6.00	1	0	0	6	6	4	3	0	0	0	0	2	0	0	.000
1915	0	1	.000	7.36	3	1	0	3.2	8	5	2	0	0	0	0	1	0	0	.000
1917	14	19	.424	2.83	48	33	17	276.2	259	96	85	3	1	3	4	91	19	0	.209
1918	13	12	.520	1.94	29	24	14	209	152	67	71	2	1	1	0	63	10	0	.159
1919	20	13	.606	2.20	40	30	21	270	256	87	106	3	5	0	3	97	17	0	.175
1920	8	15	.348	4.70	36	26	12	218.1	263	89	81	1	0	1	2	72	16	0	.222
1921 3 teams				STL A (5G 1-2)				BOS A (2G 0-2)				CLE A (22G 12-4)							
" total	13	8	.619	3.89	29	22	11	178.1	194	71	72	2	2	0	0	69	18	0	.261
1922 CLE A	1	3	.250	6.39	6	4	2	25.1	26	14	8	0	0	1	0	9	4	0	.444
1924 STL N	10	16	.385	3.57	29	28	16	196.2	209	84	62	4	0	1	0	72	14	0	.194
1925	10	10	.500	4.05	28	23	8	155.2	173	63	67	2	1	1	0	56	11	0	.196
1926	3	3	.500	4.22	15	4	1	42.2	37	16	19	0	2	2	0	13	3	0	.231
11 yrs.	92	100	.479	3.31	264	195	102	1582.1	1583	596	576	17	12	10	9	545	112	0	.206
3 yrs.	23	29	.442	3.83	72	55	25	395	419	163	148	6	3	4	0	141	28	0	.199

SPINKS, SCIPIO RONALD   BR TR 6'1"   183 lbs.
B. July 12, 1947, Chicago, Ill.

Scipio Spinks

	W	L	PCT	ERA	G	GS	CG	IP	H	BB	SO	ShO	W	L	SV	AB	H	HR	BA
1969 HOU N	0	0	—	0.00	1	0	0	1	1	4	1	0	0	0	0	0	0	0	—
1970	0	1	.000	9.64	5	2	0	14	17	9	6	0	0	0	0	3	0	0	.000
1971	1	0	1.000	3.72	5	3	1	29	22	13	26	0	0	0	0	9	2	0	.222
1972 STL N	5	5	.500	2.67	16	16	6	118	96	59	93	0	0	0	0	42	7	0	.167
1973	1	5	.167	4.89	8	8	0	38.2	39	25	25	0	0	0	0	11	2	1	.182
5 yrs.	7	11	.389	3.70	35	29	7	201.2	175	107	154	0	0	0	0	65	11	1	.169
2 yrs.	6	10	.375	3.22	24	24	6	156.2	135	84	118	0	0	0	0	53	9	1	.170

SPRAGUE, EDWARD NELSON   BR TR 6'4"   195 lbs.
B. Sept. 16, 1945, Boston, Mass.

Ed Sprague

	W	L	PCT	ERA	G	GS	CG	IP	H	BB	SO	ShO	W	L	SV	AB	H	HR	BA
1968 OAK A	3	4	.429	3.28	47	1	0	68.2	51	34	34	0	3	3	4	7	0	0	.000
1969	1	1	.500	4.47	27	0	0	46.1	47	31	20	0	1	1	2	5	1	0	.200
1971 CIN N	1	0	1.000	0.00	7	0	0	11	8	1	7	0	1	0	0	1	0	0	.000

	W	L	PCT	ERA	G	GS	CG	IP	H	BB	SO	ShO	Relief Pitching W	L	SV	BATTING AB	H	HR	BA

Ed Sprague continued

Year	Team		W	L	PCT	ERA	G	GS	CG	IP	H	BB	SO	ShO	W	L	SV	AB	H	HR	BA
1972			3	3	.500	4.13	33	1	0	56.2	55	26	25	0	2	3	0	7	0	0	.000
1973	3 teams	CIN N (28G 1-3) STL N (8G 0-0) MIL A (7G 0-1)																			
"	total		1	4	.200	5.43	43	0	0	56.1	56	40	24	0	1	4	2	2	0	0	.000
1974	MIL A		7	2	.778	2.39	20	10	3	94	94	31	57	0	0	0	0	0	0	0	–
1975			1	7	.125	4.68	18	11	0	67.1	81	40	21	0	0	2	1	0	0	0	–
1976			0	2	.000	6.75	3	0	0	8	14	3	0	0	0	0	0	0	0	0	–
8 yrs.			17	23	.425	3.84	198	23	3	408.1	406	206	188	0	8	15	9	22	1	0	.045
1 yr.			0	0	–	2.25	8	0	0	8	8	4	2	0	0	0	0	0	0	0	–

Jack Spring

SPRING, JACK RUSSELL B. Mar. 11, 1933, Spokane, Wash. BR TL 6'1" 175 lbs.

Year	Team		W	L	PCT	ERA	G	GS	CG	IP	H	BB	SO	ShO	W	L	SV	AB	H	HR	BA
1955	PHI N		0	1	.000	6.75	2	0	1	2.2	2	1	2	0	0	1	0	1	0	0	.000
1957	BOS A		0	0	–	0.00	1	0	0	1	0	0	2	0	0	0	0	0	0	0	–
1958	WAS A		0	0	–	14.14	3	1	0	7	16	7	1	0	0	0	0	0	0	0	–
1961	LA A		3	0	1.000	4.26	18	4	0	38	35	15	27	0	0	0	0	2	0	0	.000
1962			4	2	.667	4.02	57	0	0	65	66	30	31	0	4	2	6	11	1	0	.091
1963			3	0	1.000	3.05	45	0	0	38.1	40	9	13	0	3	0	2	3	1	0	.333
1964	3 teams	LA A (6G 1-0) CHI N (7G 0-0) STL N (2G 0-0)																			
"	total		1	0	1.000	4.38	15	0	0	12.1	15	6	1	0	1	0	0	0	0	0	–
1965	CLE A		1	2	.333	3.74	14	0	0	21.2	21	10	9	0	1	2	0	3	1	0	.333
8 yrs.			12	5	.706	4.26	155	5	0	186	195	78	86	0	9	5	8	28	3	0	.107
1 yr.			0	0	–	3.00	2	0	0	3	8	1	0	0	0	0	0	0	0	0	–

Gerry Staley

STALEY, GERALD LEE B. Aug. 21, 1920, Brush Prairie, Wash. BR TR 6' 195 lbs.

Year	Team		W	L	PCT	ERA	G	GS	CG	IP	H	BB	SO	ShO	W	L	SV	AB	H	HR	BA
1947	STL N		1	0	1.000	2.76	18	1	1	29.1	33	8	14	0	0	0	0	6	0	0	.000
1948			4	4	.500	6.92	31	3	0	52	61	21	23	0	4	3	0	9	2	1	.222
1949			10	10	.500	2.73	45	17	5	171.1	154	41	55	2	4	2	6	41	5	0	.122
1950			13	13	.500	4.99	42	22	7	169.2	201	61	62	1	6	1	3	55	8	0	.145
1951			19	13	.594	3.81	42	30	10	227	244	74	67	4	6	1	3	81	13	0	.160
1952			17	14	.548	3.27	35	33	15	239.2	238	52	93	0	0	2	0	85	13	0	.153
1953			18	9	.667	3.99	40	32	10	230	243	54	88	1	0	4	0	78	8	0	.103
1954			7	13	.350	5.26	48	20	3	155.2	198	47	50	1	3	6	2	36	5	0	.139
1955	2 teams	CIN N (30G 5-8) NY A (2G 0-0)																			
"	total		5	8	.385	4.81	32	18	2	121.2	151	29	40	0	0	1	0	36	2	0	.056
1956	2 teams	NY A (1G 0-0) CHI A (26G 8-3)																			
"	total		8	3	.727	3.26	27	10	5	102	102	20	26	0	1	1	0	33	3	0	.091
1957	CHI A		5	1	.833	2.06	47	0	0	105	95	27	44	0	5	1	7	22	1	0	.045
1958			4	5	.444	3.16	50	0	0	85.1	81	24	27	0	4	5	8	11	0	0	.000
1959			8	5	.615	2.24	67	0	0	116.1	111	25	54	0	8	5	14	13	2	0	.154
1960			13	8	.619	2.42	64	0	0	115.1	94	25	52	0	13	8	10	17	4	0	.235
1961	3 teams	CHI A (16G 0-3) KC A (23G 1-1) DET A (13G 1-1)																			
"	total		2	5	.286	3.96	52	0	0	61.1	64	21	32	0	2	5	4	2	0	0	.000
15 yrs.			134	111	.547	3.70	640	186	58	1981.2	2070	529	727	9	56	41	61	525	66	1	.126
										10th											
8 yrs.			89	76	.539	4.03	301	158	51	1274.2	1372	358	452	9	23	15	18	391	54	1	.138
													7th								

WORLD SERIES

Year	Team		W	L	PCT	ERA	G	GS	CG	IP	H	BB	SO	ShO	W	L	SV	AB	H	HR	BA
1959	CHI A		0	1	.000	2.16	4	0	0	8.1	8	0	3	0	0	1	1	1	0	0	.000

Harry Staley

STALEY, HENRY E. B. Nov. 3, 1866, Jacksonville, Ill. D. Jan. 12, 1910, Battle Creek, Mich. BR TR

Year	Team		W	L	PCT	ERA	G	GS	CG	IP	H	BB	SO	ShO	W	L	SV	AB	H	HR	BA
1888	PIT N		12	12	.500	2.69	25	24	24	207.1	185	53	89	2	0	0	0	85	11	0	.129
1889			21	26	.447	3.51	49	47	46	420	433	116	159	1	0	0	1	186	30	0	.161
1890	PIT P		21	25	.457	3.23	48	46	44	387.2	392	74	145	3	0	0	0	164	34	1	.207
1891	2 teams	PIT N (9G 4-5) BOS N (31G 20-8)																			
"	total		24	13	.649	2.58	40	37	32	324	313	80	139	1	2	1	0	133	24	1	.180
1892	BOS N		22	10	.688	3.03	37	35	31	299.2	273	97	93	3	0	0	0	122	16	1	.131
1893			18	10	.643	5.13	36	31	23	263	344	81	61	0	2	0	0	113	30	2	.265
1894			13	10	.565	6.81	27	21	18	208.2	305	61	32	0	1	3	0	85	20	2	.235
1895	STL N		6	13	.316	5.22	23	16	13	158.2	223	39	28	0	2	1	0	67	9	0	.134
8 yrs.			137	119	.535	3.80	283	257	231	2269	2468	601	746	10	7	5	1	955	174	7	.182
1 yr.			6	13	.316	5.22	23	16	13	158.2	223	39	28	0	2	1	0	67	9	0	.134

Tracy Stallard

STALLARD, EVAN TRACY B. Aug. 31, 1937, Coeburn, Va. BR TR 6'5" 204 lbs.

Year	Team		W	L	PCT	ERA	G	GS	CG	IP	H	BB	SO	ShO	W	L	SV	AB	H	HR	BA
1960	BOS A		0	0	–	0.00	4	0	0	2	2	6	0	0	0	0	0	0	0	0	–
1961			2	7	.222	4.88	43	14	1	132.2	110	96	109	0	0	0	2	36	3	0	.083
1962			0	0	–	0.00	1	0	0	1	0	0	0	0	0	0	0	0	0	0	–
1963	NY N		6	17	.261	4.71	39	23	5	154.2	156	77	110	0	0	3	1	48	3	0	.063
1964			10	20	.333	3.79	36	34	11	225.2	213	73	118	2	0	1	0	79	15	0	.190
1965	STL N		11	8	.579	3.38	40	26	4	194.1	172	70	99	1	0	0	0	68	6	0	.088
1966			1	5	.167	5.68	20	7	0	52.1	65	25	35	0	0	2	1	14	0	0	–
7 yrs.			30	57	.345	4.17	183	104	21	764.2	716	343	477	3	0	6	4	245	27	0	.110
2 yrs.			12	13	.480	3.87	60	33	4	246.2	237	95	134	1	0	2	1	82	6	0	.073

Pete Standridge

STANDRIDGE, ALFRED PETER B. Apr. 25, 1891, Seattle, Wash. D. Aug. 2, 1963, San Francisco, Calif. BR TR 5'10½" 165 lbs.

Year	Team		W	L	PCT	ERA	G	GS	CG	IP	H	BB	SO	ShO	W	L	SV	AB	H	HR	BA
1911	STL N		0	0	–	9.64	2	0	0	4.2	10	4	3	0	0	0	0	1	0	0	.000
1915	CHI N		4	1	.800	3.61	29	3	2	112.1	120	36	42	0	2	1	0	40	9	0	.225
2 yrs.			4	1	.800	3.85	31	3	2	117	130	40	45	0	2	1	0	41	9	0	.220
1 yr.			0	0	–	9.64	2	0	0	4.2	10	4	3	0	0	0	0	1	0	0	.000

	W	L	PCT	ERA	G	GS	CG	IP	H	BB	SO	ShO	Relief Pitching W	L	SV	BATTING AB	H	HR	BA

Ray Starr

STARR, RAYMOND FRANCIS (Iron Man) BR TR 6'1" 178 lbs.
B. Apr. 23, 1906, Nowata, Okla. D. Feb. 9, 1963, Baylis, Ill.

	W	L	PCT	ERA	G	GS	CG	IP	H	BB	SO	ShO	W	L	SV	AB	H	HR	BA
1932 STL N	1	1	.500	2.70	3	2	1	20	19	10	6	1	0	0	0	4	1	0	.250
1933 2 teams					NY N (6G 0-1)					BOS N (9G 0-1)									
" total	0	2	.000	4.35	15	3	0	41.1	51	19	17	0	0	1	0	10	1	0	.100
1941 CIN N	3	2	.600	2.65	7	4	3	34	28	6	11	2	1	1	0	11	2	0	.182
1942	15	13	.536	2.67	37	33	17	276.2	228	106	83	4	0	0	0	88	8	0	.091
1943	11	10	.524	3.64	36	33	9	217.1	201	91	42	2	1	0	1	74	9	0	.122
1944 PIT N	6	5	.545	5.02	27	12	5	89.2	116	36	25	0	2	3	3	22	3	0	.136
1945 2 teams					PIT N (4G 0-2)					CHI N (9G 1-0)									
" total	1	2	.333	8.10	13	1	0	20	27	11	5	0	1	2	0	3	2	0	.667
7 yrs.	37	35	.514	3.53	138	88	35	699	670	279	189	9	5	6	4	212	26	0	.123
1 yr.	1	1	.500	2.70	3	2	1	20	19	10	6	1	0	0	0	4	1	0	.250

Bill Steele

STEELE, WILLIAM MITCHELL (Big Bill) BR TR
B. Oct. 5, 1885, Milford, Pa. D. Oct. 19, 1949, Overland, Mo.

	W	L	PCT	ERA	G	GS	CG	IP	H	BB	SO	ShO	W	L	SV	AB	H	HR	BA
1910 STL N	4	4	.500	3.27	9	8	8	71.2	71	24	25	0	0	0	1	31	8	0	.258
1911	16	19	.457	3.73	43	34	23	287.1	287	113	115	1	2	3	3	101	21	0	.208
1912	10	13	.435	4.69	40	25	7	194	245	66	67	0	5	2	1	61	11	0	.180
1913	4	4	.500	5.00	12	9	2	54	58	18	10	0	0	0	0	18	1	0	.056
1914 2 teams					STL N (17G 2-2)					BKN N (8G 1-1)									
" total	3	3	.500	3.36	25	3	0	69.2	72	14	19	0	3	0	0	20	6	0	.300
5 yrs.	37	43	.463	4.02	129	79	40	676.2	733	235	236	1	10	7	5	231	47	0	.203
5 yrs.	36	42	.462	3.98	121	78	40	660.1	716	228	233	1	9	6	5	228	46	0	.202

Bob Steele

STEELE, ROBERT WESLEY BR TL 5'10½" 175 lbs.
B. Mar. 29, 1894, Cassburn, Ont., Canada D. Jan. 27, 1962, Ocala, Fla.

	W	L	PCT	ERA	G	GS	CG	IP	H	BB	SO	ShO	W	L	SV	AB	H	HR	BA
1916 STL N	5	15	.250	3.41	29	27	7	148	156	42	67	1	0	1	0	51	10	0	.196
1917 2 teams					STL N (12G 1-3)					PIT N (27G 5-11)									
" total	6	14	.300	2.84	39	25	14	221.2	191	72	105	1	2	1	1	89	22	0	.247
1918 2 teams					PIT N (10G 2-3)					NY N (12G 3-5)									
" total	5	8	.385	2.90	22	11	7	115	100	28	45	2	1	3	2	37	8	0	.216
1919 NY N	0	1	.000	6.00	1	0	0	3	3	2	0	0	0	1	0	1	0	0	.000
4 yrs.	16	38	.296	3.05	91	58	28	487.2	450	144	217	4	3	6	3	178	40	0	.225
2 yrs.	6	18	.250	3.36	41	28	8	190	189	61	90	1	0	1	0	64	15	0	.234

Chuck Stobbs

STOBBS, CHARLES KLEIN BL TL 6'1" 185 lbs.
B. July 2, 1929, Wheeling, W. Va.

	W	L	PCT	ERA	G	GS	CG	IP	H	BB	SO	ShO	W	L	SV	AB	H	HR	BA
1947 BOS A	0	1	.000	6.00	4	1	0	9	10	10	5	0	0	0	0	1	0	0	.000
1948	0	0	—	6.43	6	0	0	7	9	7	4	0	0	0	0	1	0	0	.000
1949	11	6	.647	4.03	26	19	10	152	145	75	70	0	1	1	1	53	11	0	.208
1950	12	7	.632	5.10	32	21	6	169.1	158	88	78	0	0	0	0	57	14	0	.246
1951	10	9	.526	4.76	34	25	6	170	180	74	75	0	0	0	0	61	11	0	.180
1952 CHI A	7	12	.368	3.13	38	17	2	135	118	72	73	0	3	1	1	38	3	0	.079
1953 WAS A	11	8	.579	3.29	27	20	8	153	146	44	67	0	0	0	0	44	10	0	.227
1954	11	11	.500	4.10	31	24	10	182	189	67	67	3	1	0	0	51	7	0	.137
1955	4	14	.222	5.00	41	16	2	140.1	169	57	60	0	3	3	3	35	6	0	.171
1956	15	15	.500	3.60	37	33	15	240	264	54	97	1	1	0	1	84	15	0	.179
1957	8	20	.286	5.36	42	31	5	211.2	235	80	114	2	1	2	1	76	16	0	.211
1958 2 teams					WAS A (19G 2-6)					STL N (17G 1-3)									
" total	3	9	.250	5.04	36	8	0	96.1	127	30	48	0	2	3	1	16	1	0	.063
1959 WAS A	1	8	.111	2.98	41	7	0	90.2	82	24	50	0	0	3	7	19	2	0	.105
1960	12	7	.632	3.32	40	13	0	119.1	115	38	72	1	6	2	2	34	3	0	.088
1961 MIN A	2	3	.400	7.46	24	3	0	44.2	56	15	17	0	2	1	2	8	3	0	.375
15 yrs.	107	130	.451	4.29	459	238	65	1920.1	2003	735	897	7	20	18	19	578	102	0	.176
1 yr.	1	3	.250	3.63	17	0	0	39.2	40	14	25	0	1	3	1	4	1	0	.250

Dean Stone

STONE, DARRAH DEAN BL TL 6'4" 205 lbs.
B. Sept. 1, 1930, Moline, Ill.

	W	L	PCT	ERA	G	GS	CG	IP	H	BB	SO	ShO	W	L	SV	AB	H	HR	BA
1953 WAS A	0	1	.000	8.31	3	1	0	8.2	13	5	5	0	0	0	0	2	0	0	.000
1954	12	10	.545	3.22	31	23	10	178.2	161	69	87	2	1	0	0	52	5	1	.096
1955	6	13	.316	4.15	43	24	5	180	180	114	84	1	0	2	1	46	2	0	.043
1956	5	7	.417	6.27	41	21	2	132	148	93	86	0	0	1	3	34	3	0	.088
1957 2 teams					WAS A (3G 0-0)					BOS A (17G 1-3)									
" total	1	3	.250	5.27	20	8	0	54.2	61	37	35	0	0	0	0	14	0	0	.000
1959 STL N	0	1	.000	4.20	18	0	0	30	30	16	17	0	0	0	1	4	0	0	.000
1962 2 teams					HOU N (15G 3-2)					CHI A (27G 1-0)									
" total	4	2	.667	4.03	42	7	2	82.2	89	29	54	2	2	0	5	18	5	0	.278
1963 BAL A	1	2	.333	5.12	17	0	0	19.1	23	10	12	0	1	2	1	0	0	0	
8 yrs.	29	39	.426	4.47	215	85	19	686	705	373	380	5	4	5	12	170	15	1	.088
1 yr.	0	1	.000	4.20	18	0	0	30	30	16	17	0	0	0	1	4	0	0	.000

Tige Stone

STONE, WILLIAM ARTHUR BR TR 5'8" 145 lbs.
B. Sept. 18, 1901, Macon, Ga. D. Jan. 1, 1960, Jacksonville, Fla.

	W	L	PCT	ERA	G	GS	CG	IP	H	BB	SO	ShO	W	L	SV	AB	H	HR	BA
1923 STL N	0	0	—	12.00	1	0	0	3	5	3	1	0	0	0	0	*			

Allyn Stout

STOUT, ALLYN McCLELLAND (Fish Hook) BR TR 5'10" 167 lbs.
B. Oct. 31, 1904, Peoria, Ill. D. Dec. 22, 1974, Sikeston, Mo.

	W	L	PCT	ERA	G	GS	CG	IP	H	BB	SO	ShO	W	L	SV	AB	H	HR	BA
1931 STL N	6	0	1.000	4.21	30	3	1	72.2	87	34	40	0	4	0	3	19	2	0	.105
1932	4	5	.444	4.40	36	3	1	73.2	87	28	32	0	4	3	1	20	2	0	.100
1933 2 teams					STL N (1G 0-0)					CIN N (23G 2-3)									
" total	2	3	.400	3.68	24	5	2	73.1	86	27	30	0	0	0	0	22	4	0	.182
1934 CIN N	6	8	.429	4.86	41	16	4	140.2	170	47	51	0	1	3	1	43	8	0	.186
1935 NY N	1	4	.200	4.91	40	2	0	88	99	37	29	0	1	0	1	15	2	0	.133
1943 BOS N	1	0	1.000	6.75	9	0	0	9.1	17	4	3	0	1	0	1	0	0	0	.000

	W	L	PCT	ERA	G	GS	CG	IP	H	BB	SO	ShO	Relief Pitching W	L	SV	BATTING AB	H	HR	BA

Allyn Stout continued

	W	L	PCT	ERA	G	GS	CG	IP	H	BB	SO	ShO	W	L	SV	AB	H	HR	BA
6 yrs.	20	20	.500	4.54	180	29	8	457.2	546	177	185	0	11	10	11	121	18	1	.149
3 yrs.	10	5	.667	4.25	67	6	2	148.1	175	63	73	0	8	3	4	39	4	0	.103

Cub Stricker

STRICKER, JOHN A.   BR TR
Born John A. Streaker.
B. June 8, 1859, Philadelphia, Pa.   Deceased.

	W	L	PCT	ERA	G	GS	CG	IP	H	BB	SO	ShO	W	L	SV	AB	H	HR	BA
1882 PHI AA	1	0	1.000	1.29	2	0	0	7	3	1	2	0	1	0	0	272	59	0	.217
1884	0	0	–	6.00	1	0	0	3	6	1	1	0	0	0	0	399	92	1	.231
1887 CLE AA	0	0	–	3.18	3	0	0	5.2	5	7	2	0	0	0	1	534	141	2	.264
1888	1	0	1.000	4.50	2	0	0	12	16	2	5	0	1	0	0	493	115	1	.233
4 yrs.	2	0	1.000	3.58	8	0	0	27.2	30	11	10	0	2	0	1	*			

Johnny Stuart

STUART, JOHN DAVIS (Stud)   BR TR 5'11" 170 lbs.
B. Apr. 27, 1901, Clinton, Tenn.   D. May 13, 1970, Charleston, W. Va.

	W	L	PCT	ERA	G	GS	CG	IP	H	BB	SO	ShO	W	L	SV	AB	H	HR	BA
1922 STL N	0	0	–	9.00	2	1	0	2	2	2	1	0	0	0	0	0	0	0	–
1923	9	5	.643	4.27	37	10	7	149.2	139	70	55	1	2	3	3	57	14	0	.246
1924	9	11	.450	4.75	28	22	13	159	167	60	54	0	0	1	0	54	11	0	.204
1925	2	2	.500	6.13	15	1	1	47	52	24	14	0	1	2	0	16	4	0	.250
4 yrs.	20	18	.526	4.76	82	34	21	357.2	360	156	124	1	3	6	3	127	29	0	.228
4 yrs.	20	18	.526	4.76	82	34	21	357.2	360	156	124	1	3	6	3	127	29	0	.228

John Stuper

STUPER, JOHN ANTON   BR TR 6'2" 200 lbs.
B. May 9, 1957, Butler, Pa.

	W	L	PCT	ERA	G	GS	CG	IP	H	BB	SO	ShO	W	L	SV	AB	H	HR	BA
1982 STL N	9	7	.563	3.36	23	21	2	136.2	137	55	53	0	0	0	0	42	5	0	.119

LEAGUE CHAMPIONSHIP SERIES

	W	L	PCT	ERA	G	GS	CG	IP	H	BB	SO	ShO	W	L	SV	AB	H	HR	BA
1982 STL N	0	0	–	3.00	1	1	0	6	4	1	4	0	0	0	0	1	0	0	.000

WORLD SERIES

	W	L	PCT	ERA	G	GS	CG	IP	H	BB	SO	ShO	W	L	SV	AB	H	HR	BA
1982 STL N	1	0	1.000	3.46	2	2	1	13	10	5	5	0	0	0	0	0	0	0	–

Willie Sudhoff

SUDHOFF, JOHN WILLIAM (Wee Willie)   BR TR 5'7" 165 lbs.
B. Sept. 17, 1874, St. Louis, Mo.   D. May 25, 1917, St. Louis, Mo.

	W	L	PCT	ERA	G	GS	CG	IP	H	BB	SO	ShO	W	L	SV	AB	H	HR	BA
1897 STL N	1	8	.111	4.47	11	9	9	92.2	126	21	19	0	0	0	0	42	10	0	.238
1898	11	27	.289	4.34	41	38	35	315	355	102	65	0	1	0	1	120	19	0	.158
1899 2 teams			CLE N (11G 3–8)				STL N (26G 13–10)												
" total	16	18	.471	4.67	37	34	26	275.2	334	92	43	0	2	0	0	99	16	0	.162
1900 STL N	6	8	.429	2.76	16	14	13	127	128	37	29	2	0	1	0	106	20	0	.189
1901	17	11	.607	3.52	38	26	25	276.1	281	92	78	1	1	0	2	108	19	1	.176
1902 STL A	13	13	.500	2.86	30	25	20	220	213	67	42	1	2	1	0	77	13	0	.169
1903	20	15	.571	2.27	38	35	30	293.2	262	56	104	5	1	1	1	110	20	0	.182
1904	8	15	.348	3.76	27	24	20	222.1	232	54	63	1	2	1	0	85	14	0	.165
1905	10	19	.345	2.99	32	30	23	244	222	78	70	1	1	0	0	86	16	0	.186
1906 WAS A	0	2	.000	9.15	9	5	0	19.2	30	9	7	0	0	0	0	7	3	0	.429
10 yrs.	102	136	.429	3.56	279	240	201	2086.1	2183	608	520	11	10	4	4	*			
5 yrs.	48	64	.429	3.79	132	111	100	1000.1	1093	319	224	3	3	1	3	444	82	1	.185

Joe Sugden

SUGDEN, JOSEPH   BB TR 5'10" 180 lbs.
B. July 31, 1870, Philadelphia, Pa.   D. June 28, 1959, Philadelphia, Pa.

	W	L	PCT	ERA	G	GS	CG	IP	H	BB	SO	ShO	W	L	SV	AB	H	HR	BA
1902 STL A	0	0	–	0.00	1	0	0	1	1	0	0	0	0	0	0	*			

Harry Sullivan

SULLIVAN, HARRY ANDREW   BL TL
B. Apr. 12, 1888, Rockford, Ill.   D. Sept. 22, 1919, Rockford, Ill.

	W	L	PCT	ERA	G	GS	CG	IP	H	BB	SO	ShO	W	L	SV	AB	H	HR	BA
1909 STL N	0	0	–	36.00	2	1	0	1	4	2	1	0	0	0	0	1	0	0	.000

Suter Sullivan

SULLIVAN, SUTER G.
B. 1872, Baltimore, Md.   Deceased.

	W	L	PCT	ERA	G	GS	CG	IP	H	BB	SO	ShO	W	L	SV	AB	H	HR	BA
1898 STL N	0	0	–	1.50	1	0	0	6	10	4	3	0	0	0	0	*			

Tom Sunkel

SUNKEL, THOMAS JACOB (Lefty)   BL TL 6'1" 190 lbs.
B. Aug. 9, 1912, Paris, Ill.

	W	L	PCT	ERA	G	GS	CG	IP	H	BB	SO	ShO	W	L	SV	AB	H	HR	BA
1937 STL N	0	0	–	2.06	9	1	0	39.1	24	11	9	0	0	0	1	9	1	0	.111
1939	4	4	.500	4.22	20	11	2	85.1	79	56	54	1	0	0	0	28	9	0	.321
1941 NY N	1	1	.500	2.93	2	2	1	15.1	7	12	14	1	0	0	0	6	2	0	.333
1942	3	6	.333	4.81	19	11	3	63.2	65	41	29	0	0	0	0	19	2	0	.105
1943	0	1	.000	10.13	1	1	0	2.2	4	3	0	0	0	0	0	0	0	0	–
1944 BKN N	1	3	.250	7.50	12	3	0	24	39	10	6	0	1	1	1	4	0	0	.000
6 yrs.	9	15	.375	4.34	63	29	6	230.1	218	133	112	2	1	1	2	66	14	0	.212
2 yrs.	4	4	.500	3.54	29	12	2	124.2	103	67	63	1	0	0	1	37	10	0	.270

Max Surkont

SURKONT, MATTHEW CONSTANTINE   BR TR 6'1" 195 lbs.
B. June 16, 1922, Central Falls, R. I.

	W	L	PCT	ERA	G	GS	CG	IP	H	BB	SO	ShO	W	L	SV	AB	H	HR	BA
1949 CHI A	3	5	.375	4.78	44	2	0	96	92	60	38	0	3	4	4	22	1	0	.045
1950 BOS N	5	2	.714	3.23	9	6	0	55.2	63	20	21	0	2	0	0	23	10	1	.435
1951	12	16	.429	3.99	37	33	11	237	230	89	110	2	1	0	1	73	11	0	.151
1952	12	13	.480	3.77	31	29	12	215	201	76	125	3	0	0	0	63	7	0	.111
1953 MIL N	11	5	.688	4.18	28	24	11	170	168	64	83	2	0	0	0	56	16	0	.286
1954 PIT N	9	18	.333	4.41	33	29	11	208.1	216	78	78	0	1	0	0	60	10	0	.167
1955	7	14	.333	5.57	35	22	5	166.1	194	78	84	0	1	1	2	50	7	0	.140
1956 3 teams			PIT N (1G 0–0)				STL N (5G 0–0)				NY N (8G 2–2)								
" total	2	2	.500	5.45	14	4	1	39.2	36	14	24	0	0	0	0	10	1	0	.100

	W	L	PCT	ERA	G	GS	CG	IP	H	BB	SO	ShO	Relief Pitching W	L	SV	BATTING AB	H	HR	BA

Max Surkont continued

	W	L	PCT	ERA	G	GS	CG	IP	H	BB	SO	ShO	W	L	SV	AB	H	HR	BA
1957 NY N	0	1	.000	9.95	5	0	0	6.1	9	2	8	0	0	1	0	0	0	0	—
9 yrs.	61	76	.445	4.38	236	149	53	1194.1	1209	481	571	7	8	6	8	357	63	1	.176
1 yr.	0	0	—	9.53	5	0	0	5.2	10	2	5	0	0	0	0	1	0	0	—

Bruce Sutter

SUTTER, HOWARD BRUCE
B. Jan. 8, 1953, Lancaster, Pa.   BR TR 6'2"   190 lbs.

	W	L	PCT	ERA	G	GS	CG	IP	H	BB	SO	ShO	W	L	SV	AB	H	HR	BA
1976 CHI N	6	3	.667	2.71	52	0	0	83	63	26	73	0	6	3	10	8	0	0	.000
1977	7	3	.700	1.35	62	0	0	107	69	23	129	0	7	3	31	20	3	0	.150
1978	8	10	.444	3.18	64	0	0	99	82	34	106	0	8	10	27	13	1	0	.077
1979	6	6	.500	2.23	62	0	0	101	67	32	110	0	6	6	37	12	3	0	.250
1980	5	8	.385	2.65	60	0	0	102	90	34	76	0	5	8	28	9	1	0	.111
1981 STL N	3	5	.375	2.63	48	0	0	82	64	24	57	0	3	5	25	9	0	0	.000
1982	9	8	.529	2.90	70	0	0	102.1	88	34	61	0	9	8	36	8	1	0	.125
7 yrs.	44	43	.506	2.50	418	0	0	676.1	523	207	612	0	44	43	194 4th	79	9	0	.114
2 yrs.	12	13	.480	2.78	118	0	0	184.1	152	58	118	0	12	13	61 2nd	17	1	0	.059

LEAGUE CHAMPIONSHIP SERIES

	W	L	PCT	ERA	G	GS	CG	IP	H	BB	SO	ShO	W	L	SV	AB	H	HR	BA
1982 STL N	1	0	1.000	0.00	2	0	0	4.1	0	0	1	0	1	0	1	1	0	0	.000

WORLD SERIES

	W	L	PCT	ERA	G	GS	CG	IP	H	BB	SO	ShO	W	L	SV	AB	H	HR	BA
1982 STL N	1	0	1.000	4.70	4	0	0	7.2	6	3	6	0	1	0	2	0	0	0	—

Jack Sutthoff

SUTTHOFF, JOHN GERHARD (Sunny Jack)
B. June 29, 1873, Cincinnati, Ohio   D. Aug. 3, 1942, Cincinnati, Ohio   BR TR 5'9"   175 lbs.

	W	L	PCT	ERA	G	GS	CG	IP	H	BB	SO	ShO	W	L	SV	AB	H	HR	BA
1898 WAS N	0	0	—	12.96	2	1	0	8.1	16	8	3	0	0	0	0	3	1	0	.333
1899 STL N	1	1	.500	10.38	2	2	1	13	19	10	4	0	0	0	0	6	0	0	.000
1901 CIN N	1	3	.250	5.50	10	4	4	70.1	82	39	12	0	0	0	0	28	3	0	.107
1903	16	10	.615	2.80	30	27	21	224.2	207	79	76	3	0	0	0	84	12	0	.143
1904 2 teams			CIN	N	(12G	5–6)		PHI	N	(19G	6–13)								
" total	11	19	.367	3.19	31	28	25	253.2	255	114	73	0	2	1	0	94	16	0	.170
1905 PHI N	3	4	.429	3.81	13	6	4	78	82	36	26	1	0	1	0	25	2	0	.080
6 yrs.	32	37	.464	3.65	88	68	55	648	661	286	194	4	2	2	0	240	34	0	.142
1 yr.	1	1	.500	10.38	2	2	1	13	19	10	4	0	0	0	0	6	0	0	.000

Johnny Sutton

SUTTON, JOHNNY IKE
B. Nov. 13, 1952, Dallas, Tex.   BR TR 5'11"   185 lbs.

	W	L	PCT	ERA	G	GS	CG	IP	H	BB	SO	ShO	W	L	SV	AB	H	HR	BA
1977 STL N	2	1	.667	2.63	14	0	0	24	28	9	9	0	2	1	0	1	0	0	.000
1978 MIN A	0	0	—	3.48	17	0	0	44	46	15	18	0	0	0	0	0	0	0	—
2 yrs.	2	1	.667	3.18	31	0	0	68	74	24	27	0	2	1	0	1	0	0	.000
1 yr.	2	1	.667	2.63	14	0	0	24	28	9	9	0	2	1	0	1	0	0	.000

Bob Sykes

SYKES, ROBERT JOSEPH
B. Dec. 11, 1954, Neptune, N. J.   BL TL 6'1"   195 lbs.

	W	L	PCT	ERA	G	GS	CG	IP	H	BB	SO	ShO	W	L	SV	AB	H	HR	BA
1977 DET A	5	7	.417	4.40	32	20	3	133	141	50	58	0	0	1	0	0	0	0	—
1978	6	6	.500	3.94	22	10	3	93.2	99	34	58	2	3	1	2	21	2	0	.095
1979 STL N	4	3	.571	6.18	13	11	0	67	86	34	35	0	0	0	0	39	4	0	.103
1980	6	10	.375	4.64	27	19	4	126	134	54	50	3	0	3	0	2	0	0	.000
1981	2	0	1.000	4.62	22	1	0	37	37	18	14	0	2	0	0	0	0	0	—
5 yrs.	23	26	.469	4.65	116	61	10	456.2	497	190	215	5	5	5	2	62	6	0	.097
3 yrs.	12	13	.480	5.09	62	31	4	230	257	106	99	3	2	3	0	62	6	0	.097

Chuck Taylor

TAYLOR, CHARLES GILBERT
B. Apr. 18, 1942, Murfreesboro, Tenn.   BR TR 6'2"   195 lbs.

	W	L	PCT	ERA	G	GS	CG	IP	H	BB	SO	ShO	W	L	SV	AB	H	HR	BA
1969 STL N	7	5	.583	2.55	27	13	5	127	108	30	62	1	0	0	0	39	7	0	.179
1970	6	7	.462	3.12	56	7	1	124	116	31	64	1	3	5	8	26	3	0	.115
1971	3	1	.750	3.55	43	1	0	71	72	25	46	0	3	2	3	12	2	0	.167
1972 2 teams			NY	N	(20G	0–0)		MIL	A	(5G	0–0)								
" total	0	0	—	4.40	25	0	0	43	52	12	14	0	0	0	3	5	1	0	.200
1973 MON N	2	0	1.000	1.77	8	0	0	20.1	17	2	10	0	2	0	2	4	0	0	.000
1974	6	2	.750	2.17	61	0	0	108	101	25	43	0	6	2	11	10	3	0	.300
1975	2	2	.500	3.53	54	0	0	74	72	24	29	0	2	2	6	2	0	0	.000
1976	2	3	.400	4.50	31	0	0	40	38	13	14	0	2	3	0	3	0	0	.000
8 yrs.	28	20	.583	3.07	305	21	6	607.1	576	162	282	2	18	14	31	101	16	0	.158
3 yrs.	16	13	.552	2.99	126	21	6	322	296	86	172	2	6	7	11	77	12	0	.156

Ed Taylor

TAYLOR, EDWARD
B. Unknown.

	W	L	PCT	ERA	G	GS	CG	IP	H	BB	SO	ShO	W	L	SV	AB	H	HR	BA
1903 STL N	0	0	—	0.00	1	0	0	3	0	0	1	0	0	0	0	1	0	0	.000

Jack Taylor

TAYLOR, JOHN B. (Brewery Jack)
B. May 27, 1873, Staten Island, N. Y.   D. Feb. 7, 1900, Staten Island, N. Y.   BR TR 6'1"   190 lbs.

	W	L	PCT	ERA	G	GS	CG	IP	H	BB	SO	ShO	W	L	SV	AB	H	HR	BA
1891 NY N	0	1	.000	1.13	1	1	1	8	4	3	3	0	0	0	0	2	0	0	.000
1892 PHI N	1	0	1.000	1.38	3	3	2	26	28	10	7	0	0	0	0	12	2	0	.167
1893	10	9	.526	4.24	25	16	14	170	189	77	41	0	3	2	1	93	20	0	.215
1894	23	13	.639	4.08	41	34	31	298	347	96	76	1	1	2	1	144	48	0	.333
1895	26	14	.650	4.49	41	37	33	335	403	83	93	1	0	1	0	155	45	3	.290
1896	20	21	.488	4.79	45	41	35	359	459	112	97	1	0	1	1	157	29	0	.185
1897	16	20	.444	4.23	40	37	35	317.1	376	76	88	2	0	1	2	139	35	1	.252
1898 STL N	15	29	.341	3.90	50	47	42	397.1	465	83	89	0	0	0	1	68	17	0	.250
1899 CIN N	9	10	.474	4.12	24	18	15	168.1	197	41	34	2	1	1	2	157	38	1	.242
9 yrs.	120	117	.506	4.23	270	234	208	2079	2468	581	528	7	6	9	1	927	234	6	.252
1 yr.	15	29	.341	3.90	50	47	42	397.1	465	83	89	0	0	0	1	157	38	1	.242

	W	L	PCT	ERA	G	GS	CG	IP	H	BB	SO	ShO	Relief Pitching W	L	SV	BATTING AB	H	HR	BA

Jack Taylor

TAYLOR, JOHN W.
B. Sept. 13, 1873, Straightville, Ohio   D. Mar. 4, 1938, Columbus, Ohio
BR TR 5'10"   170 lbs.

	W	L	PCT	ERA	G	GS	CG	IP	H	BB	SO	ShO	W	L	SV	AB	H	HR	BA
1898 CHI N	5	0	1.000	2.20	5	5	5	41	32	10	11	0	0	0	0	15	3	0	.200
1899	18	21	.462	3.76	41	39	39	354.2	380	84	67	1	1	0	0	139	37	0	.266
1900	10	17	.370	2.55	28	26	25	222.1	226	58	57	2	1	0	1	81	19	1	.235
1901	13	19	.406	3.36	33	31	30	275.2	341	44	68	0	1	0	0	106	23	0	.217
1902	22	11	.667	1.33	36	33	33	324.2	271	43	83	8	0	0	1	186	44	0	.237
1903	21	14	.600	2.45	37	33	33	312.1	277	57	83	1	1	1	1	126	28	0	.222
1904 STL N	21	19	.525	2.22	41	39	39	352	297	82	103	2	0	0	1	133	28	1	.211
1905	15	21	.417	3.44	37	34	34	309	302	85	102	3	1	1	1	121	23	0	.190
1906 2 teams		STL	N	(17G 8–9)		CHI	N	(17G 12–3)											
" total	20	12	.625	1.99	34	33	32	302.1	249	86	61	3	0	0	0	106	22	0	.208
1907 CHI N	6	5	.545	3.29	18	13	8	123	127	33	22	0	1	0	0	47	9	0	.191
10 yrs.	151	139	.521	2.66	310	286	278	2617	2502	582	657	20	7	2	5	*			
3 yrs.	44	49	.473	2.67 2nd	95	90	90	816	732	214	232	6	1	1	2	307	62	1	.202

Ron Taylor

TAYLOR, RONALD WESLEY
B. Dec. 13, 1937, Toronto, Ont., Canada
BR TR 6'1"   195 lbs.

	W	L	PCT	ERA	G	GS	CG	IP	H	BB	SO	ShO	W	L	SV	AB	H	HR	BA
1962 CLE A	2	2	.500	5.94	8	4	1	33.1	36	13	15	0	1	0	0	11	3	0	.273
1963 STL N	9	7	.563	2.84	54	9	2	133.1	119	30	91	0	7	3	11	32	1	0	.031
1964	8	4	.667	4.62	63	2	0	101.1	109	33	69	0	8	2	7	15	2	0	.133
1965 2 teams		STL	N	(25G 2–1)		HOU	N	(32G 1–5)											
" total	3	6	.333	5.60	57	1	0	101.1	111	31	63	0	2	1	5	18	2	0	.111
1966 HOU N	2	3	.400	5.71	36	1	0	64.2	89	10	29	0	2	3	0	12	2	0	.167
1967 NY N	4	6	.400	2.34	50	0	0	73	60	23	46	0	4	6	8	7	0	0	.000
1968	1	5	.167	2.70	58	0	0	76.2	64	18	49	0	1	5	13	9	0	0	.000
1969	9	4	.692	2.72	59	0	0	76	61	24	42	0	9	4	13	4	1	0	.250
1970	5	4	.556	3.95	57	0	0	66	65	16	28	0	5	4	13	4	0	0	.000
1971	2	2	.500	3.65	45	0	0	69	71	11	32	0	2	2	2	4	1	0	.250
1972 SD N	0	0	–	12.60	4	0	0	5	9	0	0	0	0	0	0	0	0	0	–
11 yrs.	45	43	.511	3.93	491	17	3	799.2	794	209	464	0	41	30	72	116	12	0	.103
3 yrs.	19	12	.613	3.75	142	11	2	278.1	271	78	186	0	17 10th	6	19	52	5	0	.096

LEAGUE CHAMPIONSHIP SERIES

	W	L	PCT	ERA	G	GS	CG	IP	H	BB	SO	ShO	W	L	SV	AB	H	HR	BA
1969 NY N	1	0	1.000	0.00	2	0	0	3.1	3	0	4	0	1	0	1	0	0	0	–

WORLD SERIES

	W	L	PCT	ERA	G	GS	CG	IP	H	BB	SO	ShO	W	L	SV	AB	H	HR	BA
1964 STL N	0	0		0.00	2	0	0	4.2	0	1	2	0	0	0	1	1	0	0	.000
1969 NY N	0	0		0.00	2	0	0	2.1	0	1	3	0	0	0	1	0	0	0	–
2 yrs.	0	0		0.00	4	0	0	7	0	2	5	0	0	0	2	1	0	0	.000

Bud Teachout

TEACHOUT, ARTHUR JOHN
B. Feb. 27, 1904, Los Angeles, Calif.
BR TL 6'2"   183 lbs.

	W	L	PCT	ERA	G	GS	CG	IP	H	BB	SO	ShO	W	L	SV	AB	H	HR	BA
1930 CHI N	11	4	.733	4.06	40	16	6	153	178	48	59	0	4	1	0	63	17	0	.270
1931	1	2	.333	5.72	27	3	1	61.1	79	28	14	0	1	0	0	21	5	0	.238
1932 STL N	0	0	–	0.00	1	0	0	1	2	0	0	0	0	0	0	0	0	0	–
3 yrs.	12	6	.667	4.51	68	19	7	215.1	259	76	73	0	5	1	0	84	22	0	.262
1 yr.	0	0	–	0.00	1	0	0	1	2	0	0	0	0	0	0	0	0	0	–

Patsy Tebeau

TEBEAU, OLIVER WENDELL
Brother of White Wings Tebeau.
B. Dec. 5, 1864, St. Louis, Mo.   D. May 15, 1918, St. Louis, Mo.
Manager 1890-1900.
BR TR

	W	L	PCT	ERA	G	GS	CG	IP	H	BB	SO	ShO	W	L	SV	AB	H	HR	BA
1896 CLE N	0	0	–	0.00	1	0	0	1	1	0	0	0	0	0	0	*			

Greg Terlecky

TERLECKY, GREGORY JOHN
B. Mar. 20, 1952, Culver City, Calif.
BR TR 6'3"   200 lbs.

	W	L	PCT	ERA	G	GS	CG	IP	H	BB	SO	ShO	W	L	SV	AB	H	HR	BA
1975 STL N	0	1	.000	4.50	20	0	0	30	38	12	13	0	0	1	0	3	1	0	.333

Dick Terwilliger

TERWILLIGER, RICHARD MARTIN
B. June 27, 1906, Sand Lake, Mich.
BR TR 5'11"   178 lbs.

	W	L	PCT	ERA	G	GS	CG	IP	H	BB	SO	ShO	W	L	SV	AB	H	HR	BA
1932 STL N	0	0	–	0.00	1	0	0	3	1	2	2	0	0	0	0	1	0	0	.000

Jake Thielman

THIELMAN, JOHN PETER
Brother of Henry Thielman.
B. Mar. 20, 1879, St. Cloud, Minn.   D. Jan. 28, 1928, Minneapolis, Minn.

	W	L	PCT	ERA	G	GS	CG	IP	H	BB	SO	ShO	W	L	SV	AB	H	HR	BA
1905 STL N	15	16	.484	3.50	32	29	26	242	265	62	87	0	1	1	0	91	21	0	.231
1906	0	1	.000	3.60	1	1	0	5	5	2	0	0	0	0	0	2	1	0	.500
1907 CLE A	11	8	.579	2.33	20	18	18	166	151	34	56	3	1	0	0	59	12	0	.203
1908 2 teams		CLE	A	(11G 4–3)		BOS	A	(1G 0–0)											
" total	4	3	.571	4.04	12	8	5	62.1	62	9	15	0	0	0	0	23	8	0	.348
4 yrs.	30	28	.517	3.16	65	56	49	475.1	483	107	158	3	2	1	0	175	42	0	.240
2 yrs.	15	17	.469	3.50	33	30	26	247	270	64	87	0	1	1	0	93	22	0	.237

Roy Thomas

THOMAS, ROY JUSTIN
B. June 22, 1953, Quantico, Va.
BR TR 6'5"   215 lbs.

	W	L	PCT	ERA	G	GS	CG	IP	H	BB	SO	ShO	W	L	SV	AB	H	HR	BA
1977 HOU N	0	0	–	3.00	4	0	0	6	5	3	4	0	0	0	0	0	0	0	–
1978 STL N	1	1	.500	3.86	16	1	0	28	21	16	16	0	1	0	3	4	1	0	.250
1979	3	4	.429	2.92	26	6	0	77	66	24	44	0	2	2	1	17	1	0	.059
1980	2	3	.400	4.75	24	5	0	55	59	25	22	0	0	2	0	13	2	0	.154
4 yrs.	6	8	.429	3.69	70	12	0	166	151	68	86	0	3	4	4	34	4	0	.118
3 yrs.	6	8	.429	3.71	66	12	0	160	146	65	82	0	3	4	4	34	4	0	.118

	W	L	PCT	ERA	G	GS	CG	IP	H	BB	SO	ShO	Relief Pitching W	L	SV	BATTING AB	H	HR	BA

Tom Thomas

THOMAS, THOMAS W. (Savage Tom)   BR TR 6'4"   195 lbs.
B. Dec. 27, 1873, Syracuse, Ohio   D. Sept. 22, 1942, Shawnee, Ohio

	W	L	PCT	ERA	G	GS	CG	IP	H	BB	SO	ShO	RW	RL	SV	AB	H	HR	BA
1899 STL N	1	1	.500	2.52	4	2	2	25	22	4	8	0	0	0	0	12	3	0	.250
1900	1	1	.500	3.76	5	1	1	26.1	38	4	7	0	1	0	0	11	1	0	.091
2 yrs.	2	2	.500	3.16	9	3	3	51.1	60	8	15	0	1	0	0	23	4	0	.174
2 yrs.	2	2	.500	3.16	9	3	3	51.1	60	8	15	0	1	0	0	23	4	0	.174

Gus Thompson

THOMPSON, JOHN GUSTAV   BR TR 6'2"   185 lbs.
B. June 22, 1877, Humboldt, Iowa   D. Mar. 28, 1958, Kalispell, Mont.

	W	L	PCT	ERA	G	GS	CG	IP	H	BB	SO	ShO	RW	RL	SV	AB	H	HR	BA
1903 PIT N	2	3	.400	3.56	5	4	3	43	52	16	22	0	0	1	0	16	4	0	.250
1906 STL N	2	10	.167	4.28	17	12	8	103	111	25	36	0	0	3	0	34	6	0	.176
2 yrs.	4	13	.235	4.07	22	16	11	146	163	41	58	0	0	4	0	50	10	0	.200
1 yr.	2	10	.167	4.28	17	12	8	103	111	25	36	0	0	3	0	34	6	0	.176

WORLD SERIES

	W	L	PCT	ERA	G	GS	CG	IP	H	BB	SO	ShO	RW	RL	SV	AB	H	HR	BA
1903 PIT N	0	0	—	4.50	1	0	0	2	3	0	1	0	0	0	0	1	0	0	.000

Mike Thompson

THOMPSON, MICHAEL WAYNE   BR TR 6'3"   190 lbs.
B. Sept. 6, 1949, Denver, Colo.

	W	L	PCT	ERA	G	GS	CG	IP	H	BB	SO	ShO	RW	RL	SV	AB	H	HR	BA
1971 WAS A	1	6	.143	4.84	16	12	0	67	53	54	41	0	0	0	0	17	2	0	.118
1973 STL N	0	0	—	0.00	2	2	0	4	1	5	3	0	0	0	0	1	0	0	.000
1974 2 teams			STL N	(19G 0-3)		ATL	N	(1G 0-0)											
" total	0	3	.000	5.53	20	4	0	42.1	44	37	27	0	0	0	0	9	1	0	.111
1975 ATL N	0	6	.000	4.67	16	10	0	52	60	32	42	0	0	0	0	14	1	0	.071
4 yrs.	1	15	.063	4.84	54	28	0	165.1	158	128	113	0	0	0	0	41	4	0	.098
2 yrs.	0	3	.000	5.10	21	6	0	42.1	38	40	28	0	0	0	0	9	0	0	.000

John Thornton

THORNTON, JOHN   5'10½" 175 lbs.
B. 1870, Washington, D. C.   D. Aug. 31, 1893, Pensacola, Fla.

	W	L	PCT	ERA	G	GS	CG	IP	H	BB	SO	ShO	RW	RL	SV	AB	H	HR	BA
1889 WAS N	1	0	1.000	5.00	1	1	1	9	8	7	3	0	0	0	0	4	0	0	.000
1891 PHI N	15	16	.484	3.68	37	32	23	269	268	115	52	1	0	0	2	123	17	0	.138
1892	0	2	.000	12.75	3	2	1	12	16	17	2	0	0	0	0	16	5	0	.313
3 yrs.	15	19	.441	4.10	41	35	25	290	292	139	57	1	0	0	2	143	22	0	.154

Bobby Tiefenauer

TIEFENAUER, BOBBY GENE   BR TR 6'2"   185 lbs.
B. Oct. 10, 1929, Desloge, Mo.

	W	L	PCT	ERA	G	GS	CG	IP	H	BB	SO	ShO	RW	RL	SV	AB	H	HR	BA
1952 STL N	0	0	—	7.88	6	0	0	8	12	7	3	0	0	0	0	1	0	0	.000
1955	1	4	.200	4.41	18	0	0	32.2	31	10	16	0	1	4	0	5	0	0	.000
1960 CLE A	0	1	.000	2.00	6	0	0	9	8	3	2	0	0	1	0	1	0	0	.000
1961 STL N	0	0	—	6.23	3	0	0	4.1	9	4	3	0	0	0	0	0	0	0	—
1962 HOU N	2	4	.333	4.34	43	0	0	85	91	21	60	0	2	4	1	9	1	0	.111
1963 MIL N	1	1	.500	1.21	12	0	0	29.2	20	4	22	0	1	1	2	5	0	0	.000
1964	4	6	.400	3.21	46	0	0	73	61	15	48	0	4	6	13	14	0	0	.000
1965 3 teams			MIL N	(6G 0-1)		NY	A	(10G 1-1)		CLE	A	(15G 0-5)							
" total	1	7	.125	4.71	31	0	0	49.2	51	18	35	0	1	7	6	3	0	0	.000
1967 CLE A	0	1	.000	0.79	5	0	0	11.1	9	3	6	0	0	1	0	0	0	0	—
1968 CHI N	0	1	.000	6.08	9	0	0	13.1	20	2	9	0	0	1	1	1	0	0	.000
10 yrs.	9	25	.265	3.84	179	0	0	316	312	87	204	0	9	25	23	39	1	0	.026
3 yrs.	1	4	.200	5.20	27	0	0	45	52	21	22	0	1	4	0	6	0	0	.000

Bud Tinning

TINNING, LYLE FORREST   BB TR 5'11"   198 lbs.
B. Mar. 12, 1906, Pilger, Neb.   BR 1934-35
D. Jan. 17, 1961, Evansville, Ind.

	W	L	PCT	ERA	G	GS	CG	IP	H	BB	SO	ShO	RW	RL	SV	AB	H	HR	BA
1932 CHI N	5	3	.625	2.80	24	7	2	93.1	93	24	30	0	4	0	0	23	2	0	.087
1933	13	6	.684	3.18	32	21	10	175.1	169	60	59	3	1	0	1	67	14	0	.209
1934	4	6	.400	3.34	39	7	1	129.1	134	46	44	1	3	1	3	39	7	0	.179
1935 STL N	0	0	—	5.87	4	0	0	7.2	9	5	2	0	0	0	0	1	0	0	.000
4 yrs.	22	15	.595	3.19	99	35	13	405.2	405	135	135	4	8	1	4	130	23	0	.177
1 yr.	0	0	—	5.87	4	0	0	7.2	9	5	2	0	0	0	0	1	0	0	.000

WORLD SERIES

	W	L	PCT	ERA	G	GS	CG	IP	H	BB	SO	ShO	RW	RL	SV	AB	H	HR	BA
1932 CHI N	0	0	—	0.00	2	0	0	2.1	0	0	3	0	0	0	0	0	0	0	

Fred Toney

TONEY, FREDERICK ARTHUR   BR TR 6'1"   195 lbs.
B. Dec. 11, 1887, Nashville, Tenn.   D. Mar. 11, 1953, Nashville, Tenn.

	W	L	PCT	ERA	G	GS	CG	IP	H	BB	SO	ShO	RW	RL	SV	AB	H	HR	BA
1911 CHI N	1	1	.500	2.42	18	4	1	67	55	35	27	0	0	0	0	18	2	0	.111
1912	1	2	.333	5.25	9	2	0	24	21	11	9	0	1	0	0	4	0	0	.000
1913	2	2	.500	6.00	7	5	2	39	52	22	12	0	0	0	0	12	3	0	.250
1915 CIN N	15	6	.714	1.58	36	23	18	222.2	160	73	108	6	1	1	2	74	7	0	.095
1916	14	17	.452	2.28	41	38	21	300	247	78	146	3	0	0	1	99	12	0	.121
1917	24	16	.600	2.20	43	42	31	339.2	300	77	123	7	0	0	1	116	13	0	.112
1918 2 teams			CIN N	(21G 6-10)		NY	N	(11G 6-2)											
" total	12	12	.500	2.43	32	28	16	222	203	38	51	2	0	0	3	74	15	0	.203
1919 NY N	13	6	.684	1.84	24	20	14	181	157	35	40	4	0	1	1	66	15	0	.227
1920	21	11	.656	2.65	42	37	17	278.1	266	57	81	4	2	0	1	96	23	0	.240
1921	18	11	.621	3.61	42	32	16	249.1	274	65	63	1	3	0	3	86	18	3	.209
1922	5	6	.455	4.17	13	12	6	86.1	91	31	10	0	0	0	0	30	2	0	.067
1923 STL N	11	12	.478	3.84	29	28	16	196.2	211	61	48	1	0	0	0	69	8	0	.116
12 yrs.	137	102	.573	2.69	336	271	158	2206	2037	583	718	28	7	2	12	744	118	3	.159
1 yr.	11	12	.478	3.84	29	28	16	196.2	211	61	48	1	0	0	0	69	8	0	.116

WORLD SERIES

	W	L	PCT	ERA	G	GS	CG	IP	H	BB	SO	ShO	RW	RL	SV	AB	H	HR	BA
1921 NY N	0	0	—	23.63	2	2	0	2.2	7	3	1	0	0	0	0	0	0	0	

	W	L	PCT	ERA	G	GS	CG	IP	H	BB	SO	ShO	Relief Pitching W	L	SV	BATTING AB	H	HR	BA

Mike Torrez

TORREZ, MICHAEL AUGUSTINE
B. Aug. 28, 1946, Topeka, Kans.   BR TR 6'5"   220 lbs.

Year Team	W	L	PCT	ERA	G	GS	CG	IP	H	BB	SO	ShO	RW	RL	SV	AB	H	HR	BA
1967 STL N	0	1	.000	3.18	3	1	0	5.2	5	1	5	0	0	1	0	1	0	0	.000
1968	2	1	.667	2.84	5	2	0	19	20	12	6	0	1	0	0	7	2	0	.286
1969	10	4	.714	3.58	24	15	3	108	96	62	61	0	0	0	0	41	3	0	.073
1970	8	10	.444	4.22	30	28	5	179	168	103	100	1	0	0	0	63	17	0	.270
1971 2 teams			STL N	(9G 1–2)		MON N	(1G 0–0)												
" total	1	2	.333	5.54	10	6	0	39	45	31	10	0	0	0	0	7	1	0	.143
1972 MON N	16	12	.571	3.33	34	33	13	243.1	215	103	112	0	0	0	0	85	15	0	.176
1973	9	12	.429	4.46	35	34	3	208	207	115	90	1	0	0	0	69	12	0	.174
1974	15	8	.652	3.58	32	30	6	186	184	84	92	1	0	0	0	64	8	0	.125
1975 BAL A	20	9	.690	3.06	36	36	16	270.2	238	133	119	2	0	0	0	0	0	0	–
1976 OAK A	16	12	.571	2.50	39	39	13	266	231	87	115	4	0	0	0	0	0	0	–
1977 2 teams			OAK A	(4G 3–1)		NY A	(31G 14–12)												
" total	17	13	.567	3.92	35	35	17	243.1	235	86	102	2	0	0	0	0	0	0	–
1978 BOS A	16	13	.552	3.96	36	36	15	250	272	99	120	2	0	0	0	0	0	0	–
1979	16	13	.552	4.50	36	36	12	252	254	121	125	1	0	0	0	0	0	0	–
1980	9	16	.360	5.09	36	32	6	207	256	75	97	1	0	2	0	0	0	0	–
1981	10	3	.769	3.69	22	22	2	127	130	51	54	0	0	0	0	0	0	0	–
1982	9	9	.500	5.23	31	31	1	175.2	196	74	84	0	0	0	0	0	0	0	–
16 yrs.	174	138	.558	3.90	444	416	112	2779.2	2752	1237	1292	15	1	3	0	337	58	0	.172
5 yrs.	21	18	.538	4.12	71	52	8	347.2	330	208	180	1	1	1	0	119	23	0	.193
LEAGUE CHAMPIONSHIP SERIES																			
1977 NY A	0	1	.000	4.09	2	1	0	11	11	5	5	0	0	0	0	0	0	0	–
WORLD SERIES																			
1977 NY A	2	0	1.000	2.50	2	2	2	18	16	5	15	0	0	0	0	6	0	0	.000

Paul Toth

TOTH, PAUL LOUIS
B. June 30, 1935, McRoberts, Ky.   BR TR 6'1"   175 lbs.

Year Team	W	L	PCT	ERA	G	GS	CG	IP	H	BB	SO	ShO	RW	RL	SV	AB	H	HR	BA
1962 2 teams			STL N	(6G 1–0)		CHI N	(6G 3–1)												
" total	4	1	.800	4.62	12	5	2	50.2	47	14	16	0	0	0	0	16	4	0	.250
1963 CHI N	5	9	.357	3.10	27	14	3	130.2	115	35	66	2	1	3	0	39	1	0	.026
1964	0	2	.000	8.44	4	2	0	10.2	15	5	0	0	0	0	0	3	1	0	.333
3 yrs.	9	12	.429	3.80	43	21	5	192	177	54	82	2	1	3	0	58	6	0	.103
1 yr.	1	0	1.000	5.40	6	1	1	16.2	18	4	5	0	0	0	0	5	2	0	.400

Harry Trekell

TREKELL, HARRY ROY
B. Nov. 18, 1892, Breda, Ill.   D. Nov. 4, 1965, Spokane, Wash.   BR TR 6'1½"   170 lbs.

Year Team	W	L	PCT	ERA	G	GS	CG	IP	H	BB	SO	ShO	RW	RL	SV	AB	H	HR	BA
1913 STL N	0	1	.000	4.50	7	1	1	30	25	8	15	0	0	0	0	9	1	0	.111

Bill Trotter

TROTTER, WILLIAM FELIX
B. Aug. 10, 1908, Cisne, Ill.   BR TR 6'2"   195 lbs.

Year Team	W	L	PCT	ERA	G	GS	CG	IP	H	BB	SO	ShO	RW	RL	SV	AB	H	HR	BA
1937 STL A	2	9	.182	5.81	34	12	3	122.1	150	50	37	0	0	2	1	33	1	0	.030
1938	0	1	.000	5.63	1	1	0	8	8	0	1	0	0	0	0	2	0	0	.000
1939	6	13	.316	5.34	41	13	4	156.2	205	54	61	0	3	2	0	37	4	0	.108
1940	7	6	.538	3.77	36	4	1	98	117	31	29	0	6	3	2	22	1	0	.045
1941	4	2	.667	5.98	29	0	0	49.2	68	19	17	0	4	2	0	6	0	0	.000
1942 2 teams			STL A	(3G 0–1)		WAS A	(17G 3–1)												
" total	3	2	.600	6.33	20	0	0	42.2	57	16	13	0	3	2	0	8	0	0	.000
1944 STL N	0	1	.000	13.50	2	0	0	6	14	4	0	0	0	0	0	1	0	0	–
7 yrs.	22	34	.393	5.40	163	31	9	483.1	619	174	158	0	16	11	3	109	6	0	.055
1 yr.	0	1	.000	13.50	2	0	0	6	14	4	0	0	0	0	0	1	0	0	–

Tommy Tucker

TUCKER, THOMAS JOSEPH
B. Oct. 28, 1863, Holyoke, Mass.   D. Oct. 22, 1935, Montague, Mass.   BB TR 5'11"   165 lbs.

Year Team	W	L	PCT	ERA	G	GS	CG	IP	H	BB	SO	ShO	RW	RL	SV	AB	H	HR	BA
1888 BAL AA	0	0	–	3.86	1	0	0	2.1	4	0	2	0	0	0	0	520	149	6	.287
1891 BOS N	0	0	–	9.00	1	0	0	1	3	0	0	0	0	0	0	548	148	2	.270
2 yrs.	0	0	–	5.40	2	0	0	3.1	7	0	2	0	0	0	0	*			

Oscar Tuero

TUERO, OSCAR MONZON
B. Dec. 17, 1892, Havana, Cuba   BR TR 5'8½"   158 lbs.

Year Team	W	L	PCT	ERA	G	GS	CG	IP	H	BB	SO	ShO	RW	RL	SV	AB	H	HR	BA
1918 STL N	1	2	.333	1.02	11	3	2	44.1	32	10	13	0	0	0	0	12	3	0	.250
1919	5	7	.417	3.20	45	15	4	154.2	137	42	45	0	1	1	4	39	8	0	.205
1920	0	0	–	54.00	2	0	0	.2	5	1	0	0	0	0	0	0	0	0	–
3 yrs.	6	9	.400	2.88	58	18	6	199.2	174	53	58	0	1	1	4	51	11	0	.216
3 yrs.	6	9	.400	2.88	58	18	6	199.2	174	53	58	0	1	1	4	51	11	0	.216

Tuck Turner

TURNER, GEORGE A.
B. 1870, Staten Island, N. Y.   D. July 16, 1945, Staten Island, N. Y.   BL

Year Team	W	L	PCT	ERA	G	GS	CG	IP	H	BB	SO	ShO	RW	RL	SV	AB	H	HR	BA
1894 PHI N	0	0	–	7.50	1	0	0	6	9	2	3	0	0	0	0	*			

Tom Underwood

UNDERWOOD, THOMAS GERALD
Brother of Pat Underwood.
B. Dec. 22, 1953, Kokomo, Ind.   BR TL 5'11"   170 lbs.

Year Team	W	L	PCT	ERA	G	GS	CG	IP	H	BB	SO	ShO	RW	RL	SV	AB	H	HR	BA
1974 PHI N	1	0	1.000	4.85	7	0	0	13	15	5	8	0	1	0	0	1	0	0	.000
1975	14	13	.519	4.15	35	35	7	219	221	84	123	2	0	0	0	74	9	0	.122
1976	10	5	.667	3.53	33	25	3	155.2	154	63	94	0	1	0	2	46	5	0	.109
1977 2 teams			PHI N	(14G 3–2)		STL N	(19G 6–9)												
" total	9	11	.450	5.01	33	17	1	133	148	75	86	0	3	3	1	33	4	0	.121
1978 TOR A	6	14	.300	4.10	31	30	7	197.2	201	87	139	1	0	1	0	0	0	0	–
1979	9	16	.360	3.69	33	32	12	227	213	95	127	1	0	0	0	0	0	0	–
1980 NY A	13	9	.591	3.66	38	27	2	187	163	66	116	2	2	2	2	0	0	0	–

	W	L	PCT	ERA	G	GS	CG	IP	H	BB	SO	ShO	Relief Pitching W	L	SV	BATTING AB	H	HR	BA

Tom Underwood continued

		W	L	PCT	ERA	G	GS	CG	IP	H	BB	SO	ShO	W	L	SV	AB	H	HR	BA
1981 2 teams	NY A (9G 1–4)					OAK A (16G 3–2)														
" total		4	6	.400	3.64	25	11	1	84	69	38	75	0	2	2	1	0	0	0	–
1982 OAK A		10	6	.625	3.29	56	10	2	153	136	68	79	0	5	3	7	0	0	0	–
9 yrs.		76	80	.487	3.89	291	187	35	1369.1	1320	581	847	6	14	11	13	154	18	0	.117
1 yr.		6	9	.400	4.95	19	17	1	100	104	57	66	0	0	1	0	30	4	0	.133

DIVISIONAL PLAYOFF SERIES

		W	L	PCT	ERA	G	GS	CG	IP	H	BB	SO	ShO	W	L	SV	AB	H	HR	BA
1981 OAK A		0	0	–	0.00	1	0	0	.1	0	0	1	0	0	0	0	0	0	0	–

LEAGUE CHAMPIONSHIP SERIES

		W	L	PCT	ERA	G	GS	CG	IP	H	BB	SO	ShO	W	L	SV	AB	H	HR	BA
1976 PHI N		0	0	–	0.00	1	0	0	.1	1	2	0	0	0	0	0	0	0	0	–
1980 NY A		0	0	–	0.00	2	0	0	3	3	0	3	0	0	0	0	0	0	0	–
1981 OAK A		0	0	–	13.50	2	0	0	1.1	4	2	2	0	0	0	0	0	0	0	–
3 yrs.		0	0	–	3.86	5	0	0	4.2	8	4	5	0	0	0	0	0	0	0	–

Jack Urban

URBAN, JACK ELMER
B. Dec. 5, 1928, Omaha, Neb.   BR TR 5'8"   155 lbs.

		W	L	PCT	ERA	G	GS	CG	IP	H	BB	SO	ShO	W	L	SV	AB	H	HR	BA
1957 KC A		7	4	.636	3.34	31	13	3	129.1	111	45	55	0	1	0	0	39	11	0	.282
1958		8	11	.421	5.93	30	24	5	132	150	51	54	1	0	0	1	46	7	0	.152
1959 STL N		0	0	–	9.28	8	0	0	10.2	18	7	4	0	0	0	0	1	0	0	.000
3 yrs.		15	15	.500	4.83	69	37	8	272	279	103	113	1	1	0	1	86	18	0	.209
1 yr.		0	0	–	9.28	8	0	0	10.2	18	7	4	0	0	0	0	1	0	0	.000

John Urrea

URREA, JOHN GOODY
B. Feb. 9, 1955, Los Angeles, Calif.   BR TR 6'3"   200 lbs.

		W	L	PCT	ERA	G	GS	CG	IP	H	BB	SO	ShO	W	L	SV	AB	H	HR	BA
1977 STL N		7	6	.538	3.15	41	12	2	140	126	35	81	1	2	3	4	29	4	0	.138
1978		4	9	.308	5.36	27	12	1	99	108	47	61	0	0	2	0	24	3	0	.125
1979		0	0	–	4.09	3	2	0	11	13	9	5	0	0	0	0	4	1	0	.250
1980		4	1	.800	3.46	30	1	0	65	57	41	36	0	3	1	3	13	3	0	.231
1981 SD N		2	2	.500	2.39	38	0	0	49	43	28	19	0	2	2	2	4	1	0	.250
5 yrs.		17	18	.486	3.73	139	27	3	364	347	160	202	1	7	8	9	74	12	0	.162
4 yrs.		15	16	.484	3.94	101	27	3	315	304	132	183	1	5	6	7	70	11	0	.157

Dazzy Vance

VANCE, CLARENCE ARTHUR
B. Mar. 4, 1891, Orient, Iowa   D. Feb. 16, 1961, Homosassa Springs, Fla.
Hall of Fame 1955.   BR TR 6'2"   200 lbs.

		W	L	PCT	ERA	G	GS	CG	IP	H	BB	SO	ShO	W	L	SV	AB	H	HR	BA
1915 2 teams	PIT N (1G 0–1)					NY A (8G 0–3)														
" total		0	4	.000	4.11	9	4	1	30.2	26	21	18	0	0	0	0	4	2	0	.500
1918 NY A		0	0	–	15.43	2	0	0	2.1	9	2	0	0	0	0	0	0	0	0	–
1922 BKN N		18	12	.600	3.70	36	30	16	245.2	259	94	134	5	0	1	0	89	20	0	.225
1923		18	15	.545	3.50	37	35	21	280.1	263	100	197	3	2	0	0	83	7	1	.084
1924		28	6	.824	2.16	35	34	30	308.2	238	77	262	3	1	0	0	106	16	2	.151
1925		22	9	.710	3.53	31	31	26	265.1	247	66	221	4	0	0	0	98	14	3	.143
1926		9	10	.474	3.89	24	22	12	169	172	58	140	1	0	0	1	55	10	0	.182
1927		16	15	.516	2.70	34	32	25	273.1	242	69	184	2	0	0	1	90	15	0	.167
1928		22	10	.688	2.09	38	32	24	280.1	226	72	200	4	1	1	2	96	17	0	.177
1929		14	13	.519	3.89	31	26	17	231.1	244	47	126	1	1	2	0	74	10	0	.135
1930		17	15	.531	2.61	35	31	20	258.2	241	55	173	4	1	1	0	89	12	0	.135
1931		11	13	.458	3.38	30	29	12	218.2	221	53	150	2	1	0	0	67	9	0	.134
1932		12	11	.522	4.20	27	24	9	175.2	171	57	103	1	1	0	1	56	5	0	.089
1933 STL N		6	2	.750	3.55	28	11	2	99	105	28	67	0	3	0	3	28	5	0	.179
1934 2 teams	STL N (19G 1–1)					CIN N (6G 0–2)														
" total		1	3	.250	4.56	25	6	1	77	90	25	42	0	0	0	1	19	3	1	.158
1935 BKN N		3	2	.600	4.41	20	0	0	51	55	16	28	0	3	2	2	17	1	0	.059
16 yrs.		197	140	.585	3.24	442	347	216	2967	2809	840	2045	30	14	7	11	971	146	7	.150
2 yrs.		7	3	.700	3.59	47	15	3	158	167	42	100	0	3	0	4	43	7	1	.163

WORLD SERIES

		W	L	PCT	ERA	G	GS	CG	IP	H	BB	SO	ShO	W	L	SV	AB	H	HR	BA
1934 STL N		0	0	–	0.00	1	0	0	1.1	2	1	3	0	0	0	0	0	0	0	–

Bob Vines

VINES, ROBERT EARL
B. Feb. 25, 1897, Waxahachie, Tex.   BR TR 6'4"   184 lbs.

		W	L	PCT	ERA	G	GS	CG	IP	H	BB	SO	ShO	W	L	SV	AB	H	HR	BA
1924 STL N		0	0	–	9.28	2	0	0	10.2	23	0	0	0	0	0	0	4	0	0	.000
1925 PHI N		0	0	–	11.25	3	0	0	4	9	3	0	0	0	0	0	0	0	0	–
2 yrs.		0	0	–	9.82	5	0	0	14.2	32	3	0	0	0	0	0	4	0	0	.000
1 yr.		0	0	–	9.28	2	0	0	10.2	23	0	0	0	0	0	0	4	0	0	.000

Pete Vuckovich

VUCKOVICH, PETER DENNIS
B. Oct. 27, 1952, Johnstown, Pa.   BR TR 6'4"   215 lbs.

		W	L	PCT	ERA	G	GS	CG	IP	H	BB	SO	ShO	W	L	SV	AB	H	HR	BA
1975 CHI A		0	1	.000	13.06	4	2	0	10.1	17	7	5	0	0	0	0	0	0	0	–
1976		7	4	.636	4.66	33	7	1	110	122	60	62	0	2	2	0	0	0	0	–
1977 TOR A		7	7	.500	3.47	53	8	3	148	143	59	123	1	4	3	8	0	0	0	–
1978 STL N		12	12	.500	2.55	40	23	6	198	187	59	149	2	1	4	1	58	8	0	.138
1979		15	10	.600	3.59	34	32	9	233	229	64	145	0	0	1	0	79	12	0	.152
1980		12	9	.571	3.41	32	30	7	222	203	68	132	3	0	0	1	71	13	0	.183
1981 MIL A		14	4	.778	3.54	24	23	2	150	137	57	84	0	0	0	0	0	0	0	–
1982		18	6	.750	3.34	30	30	9	223.2	234	102	105	0	0	0	0	0	0	0	–
8 yrs.		85	53	.616	3.50	255	155	37	1295	1272	476	805	8	7	10	10	208	33	0	.159
4 yrs.		39	31	.557	3.21	111	85	22	653	619	191	426	5	1	5	2	208	33	0	.159

DIVISIONAL PLAYOFF SERIES

		W	L	PCT	ERA	G	GS	CG	IP	H	BB	SO	ShO	W	L	SV	AB	H	HR	BA
1981 MIL A		1	0	1.000	0.00	2	1	0	5.1	2	3	4	0	0	0	0	0	0	0	–

LEAGUE CHAMPIONSHIP SERIES

		W	L	PCT	ERA	G	GS	CG	IP	H	BB	SO	ShO	W	L	SV	AB	H	HR	BA
1982 MIL A		0	1	.000	4.40	2	2	1	14.1	15	7	8	0	0	0	0	0	0	0	–

	W	L	PCT	ERA	G	GS	CG	IP	H	BB	SO	ShO	W	L	SV	AB	H	HR	BA
													Relief Pitching			BATTING			

Pete Vuckovich continued

	W	L	PCT	ERA	G	GS	CG	IP	H	BB	SO	ShO	W	L	SV	AB	H	HR	BA
WORLD SERIES																			
1982 MIL A	0	1	.000	4.50	2	2	0	14	16	5	4	0	0	0	0	0	0	0	–

Ben Wade

WADE, BENJAMIN STYRON
Brother of Jake Wade.
B. Nov. 26, 1922, Morehead City, N. C.   BR TR 6'3"   195 lbs.

	W	L	PCT	ERA	G	GS	CG	IP	H	BB	SO	ShO	W	L	SV	AB	H	HR	BA
1948 CHI N	0	1	.000	7.20	2	0	0	5	4	4	1	0	0	1	0	2	0	0	.000
1952 BKN N	11	9	.550	3.60	37	24	5	180	166	94	118	1	2	0	3	60	7	3	.117
1953	7	5	.583	3.79	32	0	0	90.1	79	33	65	0	7	5	3	24	4	1	.167
1954 2 teams		BKN	N	(23G 1–1)		STL	N	(13G 0–0)											
" total	1	1	.500	7.28	36	0	0	68	89	36	44	0	1	1	3	8	0	0	.000
1955 PIT N	0	1	.000	3.21	11	1	0	28	26	14	7	0	0	1	1	4	0	0	.000
5 yrs.	19	17	.528	4.34	118	25	5	371.1	364	181	235	1	10	8	10	98	11	4	.112
1 yr.	0	0	–	5.48	13	0	0	23	27	15	19	0	0	0	0	3	0	0	.000
WORLD SERIES																			
1953 BKN N	0	0	–	15.43	2	0	0	2.1	4	1	2	0	0	0	0	0	0	0	–

Bill Walker

WALKER, WILLIAM HENRY
B. Oct. 7, 1903, East St. Louis, Ill.   D. June 14, 1966, East St. Louis, Ill.   BR TL 6'   175 lbs.

	W	L	PCT	ERA	G	GS	CG	IP	H	BB	SO	ShO	W	L	SV	AB	H	HR	BA
1927 NY N	0	0	–	9.00	3	0	0	4	6	5	4	0	0	0	0	0	0	0	–
1928	3	6	.333	4.72	22	8	1	76.1	79	31	39	0	1	1	0	22	2	0	.091
1929	14	7	.667	3.09	29	23	13	177.2	188	57	65	1	1	1	0	61	7	1	.115
1930	17	15	.531	3.93	39	34	13	245.1	258	88	105	2	2	1	1	86	16	2	.186
1931	17	9	.654	2.26	37	28	19	239.1	212	64	121	6	1	0	3	77	5	0	.065
1932	8	12	.400	4.14	31	22	9	163	177	55	74	0	1	1	2	52	7	0	.135
1933 STL N	9	10	.474	3.42	29	20	6	158	168	67	41	2	3	1	0	53	7	1	.132
1934	12	4	.750	3.12	24	19	10	153	160	66	76	1	0	0	0	54	5	0	.093
1935	13	8	.619	3.82	37	25	8	193.1	222	78	79	2	4	1	1	59	6	0	.102
1936	5	6	.455	5.87	21	13	4	79.2	106	27	22	1	1	1	1	25	7	0	.280
10 yrs.	98	77	.560	3.59	272	192	83	1489.2	1576	538	626	15	14	7	8	489	62	4	.127
4 yrs.	39	28	.582	3.81	111	77	28	584	656	238	218	6	8	3	2	191	25	1	.131
WORLD SERIES																			
1934 STL N	0	2	.000	7.11	2	0	0	6.1	6	6	2	0	0	2	0	2	0	0	.000
														2nd					

Roy Walker

WALKER, JAMES ROY (Dixie)
B. Apr. 13, 1893, Lawrenceburg, Tenn.
D. Feb. 10, 1962, New Orleans, La.   BR TR 6'1½"   180 lbs.
BB 1922

	W	L	PCT	ERA	G	GS	CG	IP	H	BB	SO	ShO	W	L	SV	AB	H	HR	BA
1912 CLE A	0	0	–	0.00	2	0	0	3	0	3	1	0	0	0	0	0	0	0	–
1915	4	9	.308	3.98	25	15	4	131	122	65	57	0	0	1	1	38	5	0	.132
1917 CHI N	0	1	.000	3.86	2	1	0	7	8	5	4	0	0	0	0	1	0	0	.000
1918	1	3	.250	2.70	13	7	2	43.1	50	15	20	0	0	0	1	11	0	0	.000
1921 STL N	11	12	.478	4.22	38	24	11	170.2	194	53	52	0	2	0	3	54	11	0	.204
1922	1	2	.333	4.78	12	2	0	32	34	15	14	0	1	1	0	7	1	0	.143
6 yrs.	17	27	.386	3.98	92	49	17	387	408	156	148	0	3	2	5	111	17	0	.153
2 yrs.	12	14	.462	4.31	50	26	11	202.2	228	68	66	0	3	1	3	61	12	0	.197

Tom Walker

WALKER, ROBERT THOMAS
B. Nov. 7, 1948, Tampa, Fla.   BR TR 6'1"   188 lbs.

	W	L	PCT	ERA	G	GS	CG	IP	H	BB	SO	ShO	W	L	SV	AB	H	HR	BA
1972 MON N	2	2	.500	2.89	46	0	0	74.2	71	22	42	0	2	2	2	3	0	0	.000
1973	7	5	.583	3.63	54	0	0	91.2	95	42	68	0	7	5	4	7	0	0	.000
1974	4	5	.444	3.82	33	8	1	92	96	28	70	0	2	1	2	16	3	0	.188
1975 DET A	3	8	.273	4.45	36	9	1	115.1	116	40	60	0	1	3	0	0	0	0	–
1976 STL N	1	2	.333	4.12	10	0	0	19.2	22	3	11	0	1	2	3	5	2	0	.400
1977 2 teams		MON	N	(11G 1–1)		CAL	A	(1G 0–0)											
" total	1	1	.500	5.14	12	0	0	21	18	7	11	0	1	1	0	2	0	0	.000
6 yrs.	18	23	.439	3.87	191	17	3	414.1	418	142	262	0	14	14	11	33	5	0	.152
1 yr.	1	2	.333	4.12	10	0	0	19.2	22	3	11	0	1	2	3	5	2	0	.400

Bobby Wallace

WALLACE, RODERICK JOHN (Rhody)
B. Nov. 4, 1873, Pittsburgh, Pa.   D. Nov. 3, 1960, Torrance, Calif.   BR TR 5'8"   170 lbs.
Manager 1911-12, 1937.
Hall of Fame 1953.

	W	L	PCT	ERA	G	GS	CG	IP	H	BB	SO	ShO	W	L	SV	AB	H	HR	BA
1894 CLE N	2	1	.667	5.47	4	3	3	26.1	28	22	10	0	0	0	0	13	2	0	.154
1895	12	14	.462	4.09	30	28	23	228.2	271	87	63	1	0	1	0	98	21	0	.214
1896	10	7	.588	3.34	22	16	13	145.1	167	49	46	2	1	1	0	149	35	1	.235
1902 STL A	0	0	–	0.00	1	1	0	2	3	0	1	0	0	0	0	495	142	1	.287
4 yrs.	24	22	.522	3.89	57	48	38	402.1	469	158	120	3	1	2	1	*			

Mike Wallace

WALLACE, MICHAEL SHERMAN
B. Feb. 3, 1951, Gastonia, N. C.   BL TL 6'2"   190 lbs.

	W	L	PCT	ERA	G	GS	CG	IP	H	BB	SO	ShO	W	L	SV	AB	H	HR	BA
1973 PHI N	1	1	.500	3.78	20	3	1	33.1	38	15	20	0	0	0	1	0	0	0	.000
1974 2 teams		PHI	N	(8G 1–0)		NY	A	(23G 6–0)											
" total	7	0	1.000	2.85	31	1	0	60	54	37	35	0	6	0	0	0	0	0	–
1975 2 teams		NY	A	(3G 0–0)		STL	N	(9G 0–0)											
" total	0	0	–	6.23	12	0	0	13	20	6	8	0	0	0	0	0	0	0	–
1976 STL N	3	2	.600	4.07	49	0	0	66.1	66	39	40	0	3	2	2	3	1	0	.333
1977 TEX A	0	0	–	7.88	5	0	0	8	10	10	2	0	0	0	0	0	0	0	–
5 yrs.	11	3	.786	3.94	117	4	1	180.2	188	107	105	0	9	2	3	7	1	0	.143
3 yrs.	3	2	.600	3.82	58	0	0	75.1	75	44	46	0	3	2	2	3	1	0	.333

	W	L	PCT	ERA	G	GS	CG	IP	H	BB	SO	ShO	Relief Pitching W	L	SV	BATTING AB	H	HR	BA

Dick Ward

WARD, RICHARD (Ole) BR TR 6'1" 198 lbs.
B. May 21, 1909, Herrick, S. D.   D. May 31, 1966, Freeland, Wash.

	W	L	PCT	ERA	G	GS	CG	IP	H	BB	SO	ShO	W	L	SV	AB	H	HR	BA
1934 CHI N	0	0	—	3.18	3	0	0	5.2	9	2	1	0	0	0	0	1	0	0	.000
1935 STL N	0	0	—	0.00	1	0	0	0	0	1	0	0	0	0	0	0	0	0	—
2 yrs.	0	0	—	3.18	4	0	0	5.2	9	3	1	0	0	0	0	1	0	0	.000
1 yr.	0	0	—	0.00	1	0	0	0	0	1	0	0	0	0	0	0	0	0	—

Cy Warmoth

WARMOTH, WALLACE WALTER BL TL 5'11" 158 lbs.
B. Feb. 2, 1893, Bone Gap, Ill.   D. June 20, 1957, Mt. Carmel, Ill.

	W	L	PCT	ERA	G	GS	CG	IP	H	BB	SO	ShO	W	L	SV	AB	H	HR	BA
1916 STL N	0	0	—	14.40	3	0	0	5	12	4	1	0	0	0	0	2	0	0	.000
1922 WAS A	1	0	1.000	1.42	5	1	1	19	15	9	8	0	1	0	0	7	1	0	.143
1923	7	4	.636	4.29	21	13	4	105	103	76	45	0	1	0	0	36	8	0	.222
3 yrs.	8	4	.667	4.26	29	14	5	129	130	89	54	0	2	0	0	45	9	0	.200
1 yr.	0	0	—	14.40	3	0	0	5	12	4	1	0	0	0	0	2	0	0	.000

Lon Warneke

WARNEKE, LONNIE (The Arkansas Humming Bird) BR TR 6'2" 185 lbs.
B. Mar. 28, 1909, Mt. Ida, Ark.   D. June 23, 1976, Hot Springs, Ark.

	W	L	PCT	ERA	G	GS	CG	IP	H	BB	SO	ShO	W	L	SV	AB	H	HR	BA
1930 CHI N	0	0	—	33.75	1	0	0	1.1	2	5	0	0	0	0	0	0	0	0	—
1931	2	4	.333	3.22	20	7	3	64.1	67	37	27	0	0	1	0	19	5	0	.263
1932	22	6	.786	2.37	35	32	25	277	247	64	106	4	0	0	0	99	19	0	.192
1933	18	13	.581	2.00	36	34	26	287.1	262	75	133	4	0	0	1	100	30	2	.300
1934	22	10	.688	3.21	43	35	23	291.1	273	66	143	3	2	1	3	113	22	0	.195
1935	20	13	.606	3.06	42	30	20	261.2	257	50	120	1	4	3	4	91	20	0	.220
1936	16	13	.552	3.44	40	29	13	240.2	246	76	113	4	1	5	1	84	17	1	.202
1937 STL N	18	11	.621	4.53	36	33	18	238.2	280	69	87	2	0	0	0	80	21	0	.263
1938	13	8	.619	3.97	31	26	12	197	199	64	89	4	2	0	0	71	23	0	.324
1939	13	7	.650	3.78	34	21	6	162	160	49	59	3	3	1	2	52	10	0	.192
1940	16	10	.615	3.14	33	31	17	232	235	47	85	1	0	0	0	86	18	1	.209
1941	17	9	.654	3.15	37	30	12	246	227	82	83	4	3	1	0	77	9	0	.117
1942 2 teams		STL	N	(12G 6–4)		CHI	N	(15G 5–7)											
" total	11	11	.500	2.73	27	24	13	181	173	36	59	1	0	0	2	62	16	0	.258
1943 CHI N	4	5	.444	3.16	21	10	4	88.1	82	18	30	0	1	0	0	26	5	0	.192
1945	1	1	.500	3.86	9	1	0	14	16	1	6	0	1	0	0	2	0	0	.000
15 yrs.	193	121	.615	3.18	445	343	192	2782.2	2726	739	1140	31	17	12	13	962	215	4	.223
6 yrs.	83	49	.629	3.67	183	153	70	1157.2	1177	326	434	14	8	2	2	396	91	1	.230
				3rd															

WORLD SERIES

	W	L	PCT	ERA	G	GS	CG	IP	H	BB	SO	ShO	W	L	SV	AB	H	HR	BA
1932 CHI N	0	1	.000	5.91	2	1	1	10.2	15	5	8	0	0	0	0	4	0	0	.000
1935	2	0	1.000	0.54	3	2	1	16.2	9	4	5	1	0	0	0	5	1	0	.200
2 yrs.	2	1	.667	2.63	5	3	2	27.1	24	9	13	1	0	0	0	9	1	0	.111

Ray Washburn

WASHBURN, RAY CLARK BR TR 6'1" 205 lbs.
B. May 31, 1938, Pasco, Wash.

	W	L	PCT	ERA	G	GS	CG	IP	H	BB	SO	ShO	W	L	SV	AB	H	HR	BA
1961 STL N	1	1	.500	1.77	3	2	1	20.1	10	7	12	1	0	0	0	8	1	0	.125
1962	12	9	.571	4.10	34	25	2	175.2	187	58	109	1	1	2	0	56	10	0	.179
1963	5	3	.625	3.08	11	11	4	64.1	50	14	47	2	0	0	0	19	1	0	.053
1964	3	4	.429	4.05	15	10	0	60	60	17	28	0	0	0	2	15	2	0	.133
1965	9	11	.450	3.62	28	16	1	119.1	114	28	67	1	5	0	2	33	5	0	.152
1966	11	9	.550	3.76	27	26	4	170	183	44	98	1	0	0	0	54	5	1	.093
1967	10	7	.588	3.53	27	27	3	186.1	190	42	98	1	0	0	0	66	6	0	.091
1968	14	8	.636	2.26	31	30	8	215.1	191	47	124	4	1	0	0	60	5	0	.083
1969	3	8	.273	3.07	28	16	2	132	133	49	80	0	0	0	1	37	3	0	.081
1970 CIN N	4	4	.500	6.95	35	3	0	66	90	48	37	0	4	2	0	13	0	0	.000
10 yrs.	72	64	.529	3.54	239	166	25	1209.1	1208	354	700	10	11	4	5	361	38	1	.105
9 yrs.	68	60	.531	3.34	204	163	25	1143.1	1118	306	663	10	7	2	5	348	38	1	.109

WORLD SERIES

	W	L	PCT	ERA	G	GS	CG	IP	H	BB	SO	ShO	W	L	SV	AB	H	HR	BA
1967 STL N	0	0	—	0.00	2	0	0	2.1	1	1	2	0	0	0	0	0	0	0	—
1968	1	1	.500	9.82	2	2	0	7.1	7	7	6	0	0	0	0	3	0	0	.000
1970 CIN N	0	0	—	13.50	1	0	0	1.1	2	2	0	0	0	0	0	0	0	0	—
3 yrs.	1	1	.500	8.18	5	2	0	11	10	10	8	0	0	0	0	3	0	0	.000

Gary Waslewski

WASLEWSKI, GARY LEE BR TR 6'4" 190 lbs.
B. July 21, 1941, Meriden, Conn.

	W	L	PCT	ERA	G	GS	CG	IP	H	BB	SO	ShO	W	L	SV	AB	H	HR	BA
1967 BOS A	2	2	.500	3.21	12	8	0	42	34	20	20	0	0	0	0	11	1	0	.091
1968	4	7	.364	3.67	34	11	2	105.1	108	40	59	0	1	1	2	26	1	0	.038
1969 2 teams		STL	N	(12G 0–2)		MON	N	(30G 3–7)											
" total	3	9	.250	3.39	42	14	3	130	121	71	79	1	0	2	2	31	1	0	.032
1970 2 teams		MON	N	(6G 0–2)		NY	A	(26G 2–2)											
" total	2	4	.333	3.71	32	9	0	80	65	42	46	0	1	0	0	16	1	0	.063
1971 NY A	0	1	.000	3.25	24	0	0	36	28	16	17	0	0	1	1	1	0	0	.000
1972 OAK A	0	3	.000	2.00	8	0	0	18	12	8	8	0	0	1	0	3	0	0	.000
6 yrs.	11	26	.297	3.44	152	42	5	411.1	368	197	229	1	2	7	5	88	4	0	.045
1 yr.	0	2	.000	3.92	12	0	0	20.2	19	8	16	0	0	2	1	0	0	0	—

WORLD SERIES

	W	L	PCT	ERA	G	GS	CG	IP	H	BB	SO	ShO	W	L	SV	AB	H	HR	BA
1967 BOS A	0	0	—	2.16	2	1	0	8.1	4	2	7	0	0	0	0	1	0	0	.000

Steve Waterbury

WATERBURY, STEVEN CRAIG BR TR 6'5" 190 lbs.
B. Apr. 6, 1952, Marion, Ill.

	W	L	PCT	ERA	G	GS	CG	IP	H	BB	SO	ShO	W	L	SV	AB	H	HR	BA
1976 STL N	0	0	—	6.00	5	0	0	6	7	3	4	0	0	0	0	0	0	0	—

	W	L	PCT	ERA	G	GS	CG	IP	H	BB	SO	ShO	Relief Pitching W	L	SV	BATTING AB	H	HR	BA

Milt Watson

WATSON, MILTON W.
B. 1893, Paris, Tex. BR TR 6' 185 lbs.

	W	L	PCT	ERA	G	GS	CG	IP	H	BB	SO	ShO	W	L	SV	AB	H	HR	BA
1916 STL N	4	6	.400	3.06	18	13	5	103	109	33	27	2	0	0	0	32	7	0	.219
1917	10	13	.435	3.51	41	20	5	161.1	149	51	45	3	3	3	0	51	5	0	.098
1918 PHI N	5	7	.417	3.43	23	11	6	112.2	126	36	29	0	2	1	0	40	3	0	.075
1919	2	4	.333	5.17	8	4	3	47	51	19	12	0	1	1	0	16	1	0	.063
4 yrs.	21	30	.412	3.57	90	48	19	424	435	139	113	5	6	5	0	139	16	0	.115
2 yrs.	14	19	.424	3.34	59	33	10	264.1	258	84	72	5	3	3	0	83	12	0	.145

Herm Wehmeier

WEHMEIER, HERMAN RALPH
B. Feb. 18, 1927, Cincinnati, Ohio D. May 21, 1973, Dallas, Tex. BR TR 6'2" 185 lbs.

	W	L	PCT	ERA	G	GS	CG	IP	H	BB	SO	ShO	W	L	SV	AB	H	HR	BA
1945 CIN N	0	1	.000	12.60	2	2	0	5	10	4	0	0	0	0	0	1	0	0	.000
1947	0	0	–	0.00	1	0	0	1	0	0	0	0	0	0	0	0	0	0	
1948	11	8	.579	5.86	33	24	6	147.1	179	75	56	0	1	1	0	55	5	0	.091
1949	11	12	.478	4.68	33	29	11	213.1	202	117	80	1	1	1	0	78	20	0	.256
1950	10	18	.357	5.67	41	32	12	230	255	135	121	0	0	0	4	92	14	0	.152
1951	7	10	.412	3.70	39	22	10	184.2	167	89	93	2	0	0	2	59	17	0	.288
1952	9	11	.450	5.15	33	26	6	190.1	197	103	83	1	0	2	0	64	12	1	.188
1953	1	6	.143	7.16	28	10	2	81.2	100	47	32	0	0	0	0	20	4	0	.200
1954 2 teams			CIN N (12G 0-3)				PHI N (25G 10-8)												
" total	10	11	.476	4.40	37	29	11	171.2	153	72	62	2	1	0	2	59	6	0	.102
1955 PHI N	10	12	.455	4.41	31	29	10	193.2	176	67	85	1	0	0	0	72	20	0	.278
1956 2 teams			PHI N (3G 0-2)				STL N (34G 12-9)												
" total	12	11	.522	3.73	37	22	7	190.2	168	82	76	2	5	1	1	66	13	2	.197
1957 STL N	10	7	.588	4.31	36	18	5	165	165	54	91	0	2	2	0	59	12	0	.203
1958 2 teams			STL N (3G 0-1)				DET A (7G 1-0)												
" total	1	1	.500	4.71	10	6	0	28.2	34	7	15	0	0	0	0	8	1	0	.125
13 yrs.	92	108	.460	4.80	361	240	79	1803	1806	852	794	9	10	7	9	633	124	3	.196
3 yrs.	22	17	.564	4.16	73	40	12	341.2	328	127	163	2	7	3	1	119	26	2	.218

Bob Weiland

WEILAND, ROBERT GEORGE (Lefty)
Brother of Ed Weiland.
B. Dec. 14, 1905, Chicago, Ill. BL TL 6'4" 215 lbs.

	W	L	PCT	ERA	G	GS	CG	IP	H	BB	SO	ShO	W	L	SV	AB	H	HR	BA
1928 CHI A	1	0	1.000	0.00	1	1	0	9	7	5	9	1	0	0	0	3	1	0	.333
1929	2	4	.333	5.81	15	9	1	62	62	43	25	0	0	0	1	18	2	0	.111
1930	0	4	.000	6.61	14	3	0	32.2	38	21	15	0	0	0	0	8	0	0	.000
1931	2	7	.222	5.16	15	8	3	75	75	46	38	0	0	1	0	22	4	0	.182
1932 BOS A	6	16	.273	4.51	43	27	7	195.2	231	97	63	0	0	1	1	61	9	0	.148
1933	8	14	.364	3.87	39	27	12	216.1	197	100	97	0	0	3	1	65	7	0	.108
1934 2 teams			BOS A (11G 1-5)				CLE A (16G 1-5)												
" total	2	10	.167	4.73	27	14	4	125.2	134	57	71	0	0	1	0	43	5	1	.116
1935 STL A	0	2	.000	9.56	14	4	0	32	39	31	11	0	0	0	0	8	0	0	.000
1937 STL N	15	14	.517	3.54	41	34	21	264.1	283	94	105	2	0	2	0	89	15	2	.169
1938	16	11	.593	3.59	35	29	11	228.1	248	67	117	1	0	0	1	80	11	0	.138
1939	10	12	.455	3.57	32	23	6	146.1	146	50	63	3	2	1	1	46	3	0	.065
1940	0	0	–	40.50	1	0	0	.2	3	0	0	0	0	0	0	0	0	0	–
12 yrs.	62	94	.397	4.24	277	179	66	1388	1463	611	614	7	2	6	7	443	57	3	.129
4 yrs.	41	37	.526	3.60	109	86	38	639.2	680	211	285	6	2	3	2	215	29	2	.135

Perry Werden

WERDEN, PERCIVAL WHERITT
B. July 21, 1865, St. Louis, Mo. D. Jan. 9, 1934, Minneapolis, Minn. BR TR

	W	L	PCT	ERA	G	GS	CG	IP	H	BB	SO	ShO	W	L	SV	AB	H	HR	BA
1884 STL U	12	1	.923	1.97	16	16	12	141.1	113	22	51	1	0	0	0	*			

Bill Werle

WERLE, WILLIAM GEORGE (Bugs)
B. Dec. 21, 1920, Oakland, Calif. BL TL 6'2½" 182 lbs.

	W	L	PCT	ERA	G	GS	CG	IP	H	BB	SO	ShO	W	L	SV	AB	H	HR	BA
1949 PIT N	12	13	.480	4.24	35	29	10	221	243	51	106	2	2	1	0	77	9	0	.117
1950	8	16	.333	4.60	48	22	6	215.1	249	65	78	0	2	5	8	67	13	0	.194
1951	8	6	.571	5.65	59	9	2	149.2	181	51	59	0	4	2	6	40	12	0	.300
1952 2 teams			PIT N (5G 0-0)				STL N (19G 1-2)												
" total	1	2	.333	5.23	24	0	0	43	49	16	24	0	1	2	1	9	1	0	.111
1953 BOS A	0	1	.000	1.54	5	0	0	11.2	7	1	4	0	0	1	0	2	0	0	.000
1954	0	1	.000	4.38	14	0	0	24.2	41	10	14	0	0	1	0	4	0	0	.000
6 yrs.	29	39	.426	4.69	185	60	18	665.1	770	194	285	2	9	12	15	199	35	0	.176
1 yr.	1	2	.333	4.85	19	0	0	39	40	15	23	0	1	2	1	9	1	0	.111

Gus Weyhing

WEYHING, AUGUST
Brother of John Weyhing.
B. Sept. 29, 1866, Louisville, Ky. D. Sept. 3, 1955, Louisville, Ky. BR TR 5'10" 145 lbs.

	W	L	PCT	ERA	G	GS	CG	IP	H	BB	SO	ShO	W	L	SV	AB	H	HR	BA
1887 PHI AA	26	28	.481	4.27	55	55	53	466.1	465	167	193	2	0	0	0	209	42	0	.201
1888	28	18	.609	2.25	47	47	45	404	314	111	204	3	0	0	0	184	40	1	.217
1889	30	21	.588	2.95	54	53	50	449	382	212	213	4	0	0	0	191	25	0	.131
1890 BKN P	30	16	.652	3.60	49	46	38	390	419	179	177	3	1	1	0	165	27	1	.164
1891 PHI AA	31	20	.608	3.18	52	51	51	450	428	161	219	3	0	0	0	198	22	0	.111
1892 PHI N	32	21	.604	2.66	59	49	46	469.2	411	168	202	6	4	0	3	214	29	0	.136
1893	23	16	.590	4.74	42	40	33	345.1	399	145	101	2	1	0	0	147	22	0	.150
1894	16	14	.533	5.81	38	34	25	266.1	365	116	81	2	1	0	1	115	20	0	.174
1895 3 teams			PHI N (2G 0-2)			PIT N (1G 1-0)			LOU N (28G 7-19)										
" total	8	21	.276	5.81	31	28	23	231	318	84	61	1	1	0	0	97	21	1	.216
1896 LOU N	3	2	.400	6.64	5	5	4	42	42	15	9	0	0	0	0	15	2	0	.133
1898 WAS N	15	26	.366	4.51	45	42	39	361	428	84	92	0	1	0	0	141	25	0	.177
1899	17	23	.425	4.54	43	38	34	334.2	414	76	96	2	1	0	0	126	26	0	.206
1900 2 teams			STL N (7G 3-4)				BKN N (8G 3-4)												
" total	6	8	.429	4.47	15	13	6	94.2	126	41	14	0	1	0	0	39	6	0	.154
1901 2 teams			CLE A (2G 0-0)				CIN N (1G 0-1)												
" total	0	1	.000	5.75	2	2	1	20.1	31	7	3	0	0	0	0	8	0	0	.000

	W	L	PCT	ERA	G	GS	CG	IP	H	BB	SO	ShO	W	L	SV	AB	H	HR	BA
													Relief Pitching			**BATTING**			

Gus Weyhing continued

	W	L	PCT	ERA	G	GS	CG	IP	H	BB	SO	ShO	W	L	SV	AB	H	HR	BA
14 yrs.	264	236	.528	3.89	538	503	448	4324.1	4562	1566	1665	28	10	3	4	1849	307	3	.166
										6th									
1 yr.	3	4	.429	4.63	7	5	3	46.2	60	21	6	0	1	0	0	21	2	0	.095

Abe White

WHITE, ADEL   BR TL 6'   185 lbs.
B. May 16, 1906, Winder, Ga.

	W	L	PCT	ERA	G	GS	CG	IP	H	BB	SO	ShO	W	L	SV	AB	H	HR	BA
1937 STL N	0	1	.000	6.75	5	0	0	9.1	14	3	2	0	0	1	0	1	1	0	1.000

Ernie White

WHITE, ERNEST DANIEL   BR TL 5'11½" 175 lbs.
B. Sept. 5, 1916, Pacolet Mills, S. C.   D. May 22, 1974, Augusta, Ga.

	W	L	PCT	ERA	G	GS	CG	IP	H	BB	SO	ShO	W	L	SV	AB	H	HR	BA
1940 STL N	1	1	.500	4.15	8	1	0	21.2	29	14	15	0	1	0	0	7	3	0	.429
1941	17	7	.708	2.40	32	25	12	210	169	70	117	3	3	0	2	79	15	0	.190
1942	7	5	.583	2.52	26	19	7	128.1	113	41	67	1	1	0	2	41	8	0	.195
1943	5	5	.500	3.78	14	10	5	78.2	78	33	28	1	0	1	0	28	6	0	.214
1946 BOS N	0	1	.000	4.18	12	1	0	23.2	22	12	8	0	0	0	0	4	1	0	.250
1947	0	0	–	0.00	1	1	0	4	1	1	1	0	0	0	0	1	1	0	1.000
1948	0	2	.000	1.96	15	0	0	23	13	17	8	0	0	2	2	3	0	0	.000
7 yrs.	30	21	.588	2.78	108	57	24	489.1	425	188	244	5	5	3	6	163	34	0	.209
4 yrs.	30	18	.625	2.77	80	55	24	438.2	389	158	227	5	5	1	4	155	32	0	.206

WORLD SERIES

	W	L	PCT	ERA	G	GS	CG	IP	H	BB	SO	ShO	W	L	SV	AB	H	HR	BA
1942 STL N	1	0	1.000	0.00	1	1	1	9	6	0	6	1	0	0	0	2	0	0	.000

Hal White

WHITE, HAROLD GEORGE   BL TR 5'10"   165 lbs.
B. Mar. 18, 1919, Utica, N. Y.

	W	L	PCT	ERA	G	GS	CG	IP	H	BB	SO	ShO	W	L	SV	AB	H	HR	BA
1941 DET A	0	0	–	6.00	4	0	0	9	11	6	2	0	0	0	0	2	0	0	.000
1942	12	12	.500	2.91	34	25	12	216.2	212	82	93	4	1	3	1	77	13	0	.169
1943	7	12	.368	3.39	32	24	7	177.2	150	71	58	2	0	2	2	57	8	0	.140
1946	1	1	.500	5.60	11	1	1	27.1	34	15	12	0	0	1	0	7	0	0	.000
1947	4	5	.444	3.61	35	5	0	84.2	91	47	33	0	4	2	2	18	3	0	.167
1948	2	1	.667	6.12	27	0	0	42.2	46	26	17	0	2	1	1	13	2	0	.154
1949	1	0	1.000	0.00	9	0	0	12	5	4	4	0	1	0	2	3	1	0	.333
1950	9	6	.600	4.54	42	8	3	111	96	65	53	1	6	3	1	33	4	0	.121
1951	3	4	.429	4.74	38	4	0	76	74	49	23	0	2	1	4	16	4	0	.250
1952	1	8	.111	3.69	41	0	0	63.1	53	39	18	0	1	8	5	11	2	0	.182
1953 2 teams			STL A	(10G 0–0)			STL N	(49G 6–5)											
" total	6	5	.545	2.94	59	0	0	95	92	42	34	0	6	5	7	17	0	0	.000
1954 STL N	0	0	–	19.80	4	0	0	5	11	4	2	0	0	0	0	1	0	0	.000
12 yrs.	46	54	.460	3.78	336	67	23	920.1	875	450	349	7	23	26	25	255	37	0	.145
2 yrs.	6	5	.545	3.91	53	0	0	89.2	95	43	34	0	6	5	7	17	0	0	.000

Bob Wicker

WICKER, ROBERT KITRIDGE   BR TR 5'11½" 180 lbs.
B. May 25, 1878, Lawrence County, Ind.   D. Jan. 22, 1955, Evanston, Ill.

	W	L	PCT	ERA	G	GS	CG	IP	H	BB	SO	ShO	W	L	SV	AB	H	HR	BA
1901 STL N	0	0	–	0.00	1	0	0	3	4	1	2	0	0	0	0	3	1	0	.333
1902	5	13	.278	3.19	22	16	14	152.1	159	45	78	1	1	2	0	77	18	0	.234
1903 2 teams			STL N	(1G 0–0)			CHI N	(32G 19–10)											
" total	19	10	.655	2.96	33	27	24	252	240	77	113	1	1	1	1	100	24	0	.240
1904 CHI N	17	8	.680	2.67	30	27	23	229	201	58	99	4	0	1	0	155	34	0	.219
1905	13	7	.650	2.02	22	22	17	178	139	47	86	4	0	0	0	72	10	0	.139
1906 2 teams			CHI N	(10G 3–4)			CIN N	(20G 7–11)											
" total	10	15	.400	2.79	30	25	19	222.1	220	65	94	0	2	2	0	70	11	0	.157
6 yrs.	64	53	.547	2.73	138	117	97	1036.2	963	293	472	10	4	6	1	*			
3 yrs.	5	13	.278	3.03	24	16	14	160.1	167	49	83	1	1	2	0	82	19	0	.232

Bill Wight

WIGHT, WILLIAM ROBERT (Lefty)   BL TL 6'1"   180 lbs.
B. Apr. 12, 1922, Rio Vista, Calif.

	W	L	PCT	ERA	G	GS	CG	IP	H	BB	SO	ShO	W	L	SV	AB	H	HR	BA
1946 NY A	2	2	.500	4.46	14	4	1	40.1	44	30	11	0	0	0	0	9	0	0	.000
1947	1	0	1.000	1.00	1	1	1	9	8	2	3	0	0	0	0	2	0	0	.000
1948 CHI A	9	20	.310	4.80	34	32	7	223.1	238	135	68	1	0	0	1	73	6	0	.082
1949	15	13	.536	3.31	35	33	14	245	254	96	78	3	0	0	1	85	14	0	.165
1950	10	16	.385	3.58	30	28	13	206	213	79	62	3	0	1	0	61	0	0	.000
1951 BOS A	7	7	.500	5.10	34	17	4	118.1	128	63	38	2	2	0	0	41	3	0	.073
1952 2 teams			BOS A	(10G 2–1)			DET A	(23G 5–9)											
" total	7	10	.412	3.75	33	21	8	168	181	69	70	3	1	0	0	57	12	0	.211
1953 2 teams			DET A	(13G 0–3)			CLE A	(20G 2–1)											
" total	2	4	.333	6.23	33	4	0	52	64	30	24	0	2	2	1	12	3	0	.250
1955 2 teams			CLE A	(17G 0–0)			BAL A	(19G 6–8)											
" total	6	8	.429	2.48	36	14	8	141.1	135	48	63	2	0	1	3	36	3	0	.083
1956 BAL A	9	12	.429	4.02	35	26	7	174.2	198	72	84	1	1	0	0	60	12	0	.200
1957	6	6	.500	3.64	27	17	2	121	122	54	50	0	0	0	0	34	1	0	.029
1958 2 teams			CIN N	(7G 0–1)			STL N	(28G 3–0)											
" total	3	1	.750	4.92	35	1	0	64	71	36	23	0	2	1	2	10	1	0	.100
12 yrs.	77	99	.438	3.95	347	198	66	1563	1656	714	574	15	8	5	8	480	55	0	.115
1 yr.	3	0	1.000	5.02	28	1	1	57.1	64	32	18	0	2	0	2	10	1	0	.100

Fred Wigington

WIGINGTON, FREDERICK THOMAS   BR TR 5'10½" 168 lbs.
B. Dec. 16, 1897, Rogers, Neb.

	W	L	PCT	ERA	G	GS	CG	IP	H	BB	SO	ShO	W	L	SV	AB	H	HR	BA
1923 STL N	0	0	–	3.24	4	0	0	8.1	11	5	2	0	0	0	0	1	0	0	.000

	W	L	PCT	ERA	G	GS	CG	IP	H	BB	SO	ShO	Relief Pitching W	L	SV	BATTING AB	H	HR	BA

Hoyt Wilhelm

WILHELM, JAMES HOYT
B. July 26, 1923, Huntersville, N. C.   BR TR 6'   190 lbs.

Year	Team	W	L	PCT	ERA	G	GS	CG	IP	H	BB	SO	ShO	RP W	RP L	RP SV	AB	H	HR	BA
1952	NY N	15	3	.833	2.43	71	0	0	159.1	127	57	108	0	15	3	11	38	6	1	.158
1953		7	8	.467	3.04	68	0	0	145	127	77	71	0	7	8	15	33	5	0	.152
1954		12	4	.750	2.10	57	0	0	111.1	77	52	64	0	12	4	7	21	1	0	.048
1955		4	1	.800	3.93	59	0	0	103	104	40	71	0	4	1	0	19	3	0	.158
1956		4	9	.308	3.83	64	0	0	89.1	97	43	71	0	4	9	8	9	2	0	.222
1957 2 teams	STL N (40G 1–4)					CLE	A	(2G 1–0)												
" total		2	4	.333	4.14	42	0	0	58.2	54	22	29	0	2	4	12	6	0	0	.000
1958 2 teams	CLE A (30G 2–7)					BAL	A	(9G 1–3)												
" total		3	10	.231	2.34	39	10	4	131	95	45	92	1	2	4	5	32	3	0	.094
1959	BAL A	15	11	.577	2.19	32	27	13	226	178	77	139	3	0	1	0	76	4	0	.053
1960		11	8	.579	3.31	41	11	3	147	125	39	107	1	7	5	7	42	3	0	.071
1961		9	7	.563	2.30	51	1	0	109.2	89	41	87	0	9	7	18	20	1	0	.050
1962		7	10	.412	1.94	52	0	0	93	64	34	90	0	7	10	15	16	2	0	.125
1963	CHI A	5	8	.385	2.64	55	3	0	136.1	106	30	111	0	5	7	21	29	2	0	.069
1964		12	9	.571	1.99	73	0	0	131.1	94	30	95	0	12	9	27	21	3	0	.143
1965		7	7	.500	1.81	66	0	0	144	88	32	106	0	7	7	20	22	0	0	.000
1966		5	2	.714	1.66	46	0	0	81.1	50	17	61	0	5	2	6	8	1	0	.125
1967		8	3	.727	1.31	49	0	0	89	58	34	76	0	8	3	12	13	1	0	.077
1968		4	4	.500	1.73	72	0	0	93.2	69	24	72	0	4	4	12	3	0	0	.000
1969 2 teams	CAL A (44G 5–7)					ATL	N	(8G 2–0)												
" total		7	7	.500	2.20	52	0	0	77.2	50	22	67	0	7	7	14	9	0	0	.000
1970 2 teams	ATL N (50G 6–4)					CHI	N	(3G 0–1)												
" total		6	5	.545	3.40	53	0	0	82	73	42	68	0	6	5	13	11	1	0	.091
1971 2 teams	ATL N (3G 0–0)					LA	N	(9G 0–1)												
" total		0	1	.000	2.70	12	0	0	20	12	5	16	0	0	1	3	3	0	0	.000
1972	LA N	0	1	.000	4.62	16	0	0	25.1	20	15	9	0	0	1	1	1	0	0	.000
21 yrs.		143	122	.540	2.52	1070	52	20	2254	1757	778	1610	5	123	102	227	432	38	1	.088
					1st									1st		3rd				
1 yr.		1	4	.200	4.25	40	0	0	55	52	21	29	0	1	4	11	6	0	0	.000

WORLD SERIES

Year	Team	W	L	PCT	ERA	G	GS	CG	IP	H	BB	SO	ShO	RP W	RP L	RP SV	AB	H	HR	BA
1954	NY N	0	0	–	0.00	2	0	0	2.1	1	0	3	0	0	0	1	1	0	0	.000

Ted Wilks

WILKS, TEDDY (Cork)
B. Nov. 13, 1915, Fulton, N. Y.   BR TR 5'9½"   178 lbs.

Year	Team	W	L	PCT	ERA	G	GS	CG	IP	H	BB	SO	ShO	RP W	RP L	RP SV	AB	H	HR	BA
1944	STL N	17	4	.810	2.65	36	21	16	207.1	173	49	70	4	2	1	0	64	9	0	.141
1945		4	7	.364	2.93	18	16	4	98.1	103	29	28	1	0	0	0	30	4	0	.133
1946		8	0	1.000	3.41	40	4	0	95	88	38	40	0	6	0	1	24	5	0	.208
1947		4	0	1.000	5.01	37	0	0	50.1	57	11	28	0	4	0	5	6	1	0	.167
1948		6	6	.500	2.62	57	2	1	130.2	113	39	71	0	4	4	13	30	5	0	.167
1949		10	3	.769	3.73	59	0	0	118.1	105	38	71	0	10	3	9	27	1	0	.037
1950		2	0	1.000	6.66	18	0	0	24.1	27	9	15	0	2	0	0	4	0	0	.000
1951 2 teams	STL N (17G 0–0)					PIT	N	(48G 3–5)												
" total		3	5	.375	2.86	65	1	1	100.2	88	29	48	1	2	5	13	13	1	0	.077
1952 2 teams	PIT N (44G 5–5)					CLE	A	(7G 0–0)												
" total		5	5	.500	3.64	51	0	0	84	73	38	30	0	5	5	5	8	1	0	.125
1953	CLE A	0	0	–	7.36	4	0	0	3.2	5	3	2	0	0	0	0	0	0	0	–
10 yrs.		59	30	.663	3.26	385	44	22	912.2	832	283	403	5	35	18	46	206	27	0	.131
8 yrs.		51	20	.718	3.25	282	43	21	742.1	685	218	328	5	28	8	29	186	25	0	.134
														5th		7th				

WORLD SERIES

Year	Team	W	L	PCT	ERA	G	GS	CG	IP	H	BB	SO	ShO	RP W	RP L	RP SV	AB	H	HR	BA
1944	STL N	0	1	.000	5.68	2	1	0	6.1	5	3	7	0	0	0	1	2	0	0	.000
1946		0	0	–	0.00	1	0	0	1	2	0	0	0	0	0	0	0	0	0	–
2 yrs.		0	1	.000	4.91	3	1	0	7.1	7	3	7	0	0	0	1	2	0	0	.000

Stan Williams

WILLIAMS, STANLEY WILSON
B. Sept. 14, 1936, Enfield, N. H.   BR TR 6'5"   230 lbs.

Year	Team	W	L	PCT	ERA	G	GS	CG	IP	H	BB	SO	ShO	RP W	RP L	RP SV	AB	H	HR	BA
1958	LA N	9	7	.563	4.01	27	21	3	119	99	65	80	2	1	1	0	40	2	1	.050
1959		5	5	.500	3.97	35	15	2	124.2	102	86	89	0	2	2	0	36	7	0	.194
1960		14	10	.583	3.00	38	30	9	207.1	162	72	175	2	0	0	0	64	9	2	.141
1961		15	12	.556	3.90	41	35	6	235.1	213	108	205	2	1	0	0	78	13	0	.167
1962		14	12	.538	4.46	40	28	4	185.2	184	98	108	1	1	1	1	66	5	2	.076
1963	NY A	9	8	.529	3.20	29	21	6	146.1	137	57	98	1	2	2	0	49	5	0	.102
1964		1	5	.167	3.84	21	10	1	82	76	38	54	0	1	1	0	21	3	0	.143
1965	CLE A	0	0	–	6.23	3	0	0	4.1	6	3	1	0	0	0	0	0	0	0	–
1967		6	4	.600	2.62	16	8	2	79	64	24	75	1	3	0	1	22	2	0	.091
1968		13	11	.542	2.50	44	24	6	194.1	163	51	147	2	2	0	9	56	9	0	.161
1969		6	14	.300	3.94	61	15	3	178.1	155	67	139	0	2	9	12	40	4	0	.100
1970	MIN A	10	1	.909	1.99	68	0	0	113	85	32	76	0	10	1	15	19	0	0	.000
1971 2 teams	MIN A (46G 4–5)					STL	N	(10G 3–0)												
" total		7	5	.583	3.76	56	0	0	91	76	46	55	0	7	5	4	11	0	0	.000
1972	BOS A	0	0	–	6.75	3	0	0	4	5	3	3	0	0	0	0	0	0	0	–
14 yrs.		109	94	.537	3.48	482	208	42	1764.1	1527	748	1305	11	32	22	43	502	59	5	.118
1 yr.		3	0	1.000	1.38	10	0	0	13	13	2	8	0	3	0	0	1	0	0	.000

LEAGUE CHAMPIONSHIP SERIES

Year	Team	W	L	PCT	ERA	G	GS	CG	IP	H	BB	SO	ShO	RP W	RP L	RP SV	AB	H	HR	BA
1970	MIN A	0	0	–	0.00	2	0	0	6	2	1	0	0	0	0	0	0	0	0	–

WORLD SERIES

Year	Team	W	L	PCT	ERA	G	GS	CG	IP	H	BB	SO	ShO	RP W	RP L	RP SV	AB	H	HR	BA
1959	LA N	0	0	–	0.00	1	0	0	2	0	2	1	0	0	0	0	0	0	0	–
1963	NY A	0	0	–	0.00	1	0	0	3	1	0	5	0	0	0	0	0	0	0	–
2 yrs.		0	0	–	0.00	2	0	0	5	1	2	6	0	0	0	0	0	0	0	–

	W	L	PCT	ERA	G	GS	CG	IP	H	BB	SO	ShO	Relief Pitching W	L	SV	BATTING AB	H	HR	BA

Steamboat Williams

WILLIAMS, REES GEPHARDT   BL TR 5'11" 170 lbs.
B. Jan. 31, 1892, Cascade, Mont.   D. June 29, 1979, Deer River, Minn.

	W	L	PCT	ERA	G	GS	CG	IP	H	BB	SO	ShO	W	L	SV	AB	H	HR	BA
1914 STL N	0	1	.000	6.55	5	1	0	11	13	6	2	0	0	0	0	1	0	0	.000
1916	6	7	.462	4.20	36	8	5	105	121	27	25	0	4	2	1	24	5	0	.208
2 yrs.	6	8	.429	4.42	41	9	5	116	134	33	27	0	4	2	1	25	5	0	.200
2 yrs.	6	8	.429	4.42	41	9	5	116	134	33	27	0	4	2	1	25	5	0	.200

Joe Willis

WILLIS, JOSEPH DENK   BR TL 6'1" 185 lbs.
B. Apr. 9, 1890, Ironton, Ohio   D. Dec. 3, 1966, Ironton, Ohio

	W	L	PCT	ERA	G	GS	CG	IP	H	BB	SO	ShO	W	L	SV	AB	H	HR	BA
1911 2 teams			STL A (1G 0–1)		STL N	(2G 0–1)													
" total	0	2	.000	4.50	3	3	1	22	21	7	5	0	0	0	0	7	0	0	.000
1912 STL N	4	9	.308	4.44	31	17	4	129.2	143	62	55	0	1	2	2	38	6	0	.158
1913	0	0	—	7.45	7	0	0	9.2	9	11	6	0	0	0	1	3	0	0	.000
3 yrs.	4	11	.267	4.63	41	20	5	161.1	173	80	66	0	1	2	3	48	6	0	.125
3 yrs.	4	10	.286	4.61	40	19	5	154.1	165	77	66	0	1	2	3	46	6	0	.130

Ron Willis

WILLIS, RONALD EARL   BR TR 6'2" 185 lbs.
B. July 12, 1943, Willisville, Tenn.   D. Nov. 21, 1977, Memphis, Tenn.

	W	L	PCT	ERA	G	GS	CG	IP	H	BB	SO	ShO	W	L	SV	AB	H	HR	BA
1966 STL N	0	0	—	0.00	4	0	0	3	1	1	2	0	0	0	1	0	0	0	—
1967	6	5	.545	2.67	65	0	0	81	76	43	42	0	6	5	10	8	3	0	.375
1968	2	3	.400	3.39	48	0	0	63.2	50	28	39	0	2	3	4	11	0	0	.000
1969 2 teams			STL N (26G 1–2)		HOU N	(3G 0–0)													
" total	1	2	.333	3.89	29	0	0	34.2	29	19	25	0	1	2	0	1	1	0	1.000
1970 SD N	2	2	.500	4.02	42	0	0	56	53	28	20	0	2	2	4	5	0	0	.000
5 yrs.	11	12	.478	3.32	188	0	0	238.1	209	119	128	0	11	12	19	25	4	0	.160
4 yrs.	9	10	.474	3.15	143	0	0	180	153	91	106	0	9	10	15	20	4	0	.200
WORLD SERIES																			
1967 STL N	0	0	—	27.00	3	0	0	1	2	4	1	0	0	0	0	0	0	0	—
1968	0	0	—	8.31	3	0	0	4.1	2	4	3	0	0	0	0	0	0	0	—
2 yrs.	0	0	—	11.81	6	0	0	5.1	4	8	4	0	0	0	0	0	0	0	—

Vic Willis

WILLIS, VICTOR GAZAWAY   BR TR 6'2" 185 lbs.
B. Apr. 12, 1876, Wilmington, Del.   D. Aug. 3, 1947, Elkton, Md.

	W	L	PCT	ERA	G	GS	CG	IP	H	BB	SO	ShO	W	L	SV	AB	H	HR	BA
1898 BOS N	24	13	.649	2.84	41	38	29	311	264	148	160	1	1	1	0	117	17	0	.145
1899	27	10	.730	2.50	41	38	35	342.2	277	117	120	5	0	0	2	134	29	0	.216
1900	10	17	.370	4.19	32	29	22	236	258	106	53	2	1	0	0	88	12	0	.136
1901	20	17	.541	2.36	38	35	33	305.1	262	78	133	6	2	0	0	107	20	1	.187
1902	27	20	.574	2.20	51	46	45	410	372	101	225	4	1	1	3	150	23	0	.153
1903	12	18	.400	2.98	33	32	29	278	256	88	125	2	0	0	0	128	24	0	.188
1904	18	25	.419	2.85	43	43	39	350	357	109	196	2	0	0	0	148	27	0	.182
1905	11	29	.275	3.21	41	41	36	342	340	107	149	4	0	0	0	131	20	0	.153
1906 PIT N	22	13	.629	1.73	41	36	32	322	295	76	124	6	1	0	1	115	20	0	.174
1907	21	12	.636	2.34	39	37	27	292.2	234	69	107	6	0	0	1	103	14	0	.136
1908	24	11	.686	2.07	41	38	25	304.2	239	69	97	7	1	0	0	103	17	0	.165
1909	23	11	.676	2.24	39	35	24	289.2	243	83	95	4	3	1	0	103	14	0	.136
1910 STL N	9	12	.429	3.35	33	23	12	212	224	61	67	1	3	0	3	66	11	0	.167
13 yrs.	248	208	.544	2.63	513	471	388	3996	3621	1212	1651	50	13	3	10	1493	248	1	.166
1 yr.	9	12	.429	3.35	33	23	12	212	224	61	67	1	3	0	3	66	11	0	.167
WORLD SERIES																			
1909 PIT N	0	1	.000	4.76	2	1	0	11.1	10	8	3	0	0	0	0	4	0	0	.000

Zeke Wilson

WILSON, FRANK EALTON
B. Dec. 24, 1869, Benton, Ala.   D. Apr. 26, 1928, Montgomery, Ala.

	W	L	PCT	ERA	G	GS	CG	IP	H	BB	SO	ShO	W	L	SV	AB	H	HR	BA
1895 2 teams			BOS N (6G 2–4)		CLE N	(8G 3–1)													
" total	5	5	.500	4.72	14	13	7	89.2	117	47	21	0	1	0	0	37	8	1	.216
1896 CLE N	17	9	.654	4.01	33	29	20	240	265	81	56	1	1	0	1	100	27	0	.270
1897	16	11	.593	4.16	34	30	26	263.2	323	83	69	1	0	0	0	116	26	0	.224
1898	13	18	.419	3.60	33	31	28	254.2	307	51	45	1	0	0	0	118	21	0	.178
1899 STL N	1	1	.500	4.50	5	2	2	26	30	4	3	0	0	0	0	10	0	0	.000
5 yrs.	52	44	.542	4.03	119	105	83	874	1042	266	194	3	2	0	1	381	82	1	.215
1 yr.	1	1	.500	4.50	5	2	2	26	30	4	3	0	0	0	0	10	0	0	.000

Jim Winford

WINFORD, JAMES HEAD (Cowboy)   BR TR 6'1" 180 lbs.
B. Oct. 9, 1909, Shelbyville, Tenn.   D. Dec. 16, 1970, Oakland, Calif.

	W	L	PCT	ERA	G	GS	CG	IP	H	BB	SO	ShO	W	L	SV	AB	H	HR	BA
1932 STL N	1	1	.500	6.48	4	1	0	8.1	9	5	4	0	1	0	0	3	2	0	.667
1934	0	2	.000	7.82	5	1	0	12.2	17	6	3	0	0	1	0	1	0	0	.000
1935	0	0	—	3.97	2	1	0	11.1	13	5	7	0	0	0	0	2	0	0	.000
1936	11	10	.524	3.80	39	23	10	192	203	68	72	1	1	2	3	59	5	0	.085
1937	2	4	.333	5.83	16	4	0	46.1	56	27	19	0	2	0	0	8	1	0	.125
1938 BKN N	0	1	.000	11.12	2	1	0	5.2	9	4	4	0	0	0	0	1	0	0	.000
6 yrs.	14	18	.438	4.56	68	31	10	276.1	307	115	109	1	4	3	3	74	8	0	.108
5 yrs.	14	17	.452	4.42	66	30	10	270.2	298	111	105	1	4	3	3	73	8	0	.110

Tom Winsett

WINSETT, JOHN THOMAS (Long Tom)   BL TR 6'2" 190 lbs.
B. Nov. 24, 1909, McKenzie, Tenn.

	W	L	PCT	ERA	G	GS	CG	IP	H	BB	SO	ShO	W	L	SV	AB	H	HR	BA
1937 BKN N	0	0	—	18.00	1	0	0	1	3	2	0	0	0	0	0	*			

Rick Wise

WISE, RICHARD CHARLES   BR TR 6'1" 180 lbs.
B. Sept. 13, 1945, Jackson, Mich.

	W	L	PCT	ERA	G	GS	CG	IP	H	BB	SO	ShO	W	L	SV	AB	H	HR	BA
1964 PHI N	5	3	.625	4.04	25	8	0	69	78	25	39	0	1	1	0	17	5	0	.294
1966	5	6	.455	3.71	22	13	3	99.1	100	24	58	0	0	2	0	30	0	0	.000
1967	11	11	.500	3.28	36	25	6	181.1	177	45	111	3	2	0	0	53	11	0	.208
1968	9	15	.375	4.54	30	30	7	182.1	210	37	97	1	0	0	0	58	14	2	.241

	W	L	PCT	ERA	G	GS	CG	IP	H	BB	SO	ShO	W	L	SV	AB	H	HR	BA
													Relief Pitching			**BATTING**			

Rick Wise continued

		W	L	PCT	ERA	G	GS	CG	IP	H	BB	SO	ShO	W	L	SV	AB	H	HR	BA
1969		15	13	.536	3.23	33	31	14	220	215	61	144	4	0	0	0	74	20	1	.270
1970		13	14	.481	4.17	35	34	5	220	253	65	113	1	0	0	0	75	15	2	.200
1971		17	14	.548	2.88	38	37	17	272	261	70	155	4	0	0	0	97	23	6	.237
1972 STL N		16	16	.500	3.11	35	35	20	269	250	71	142	2	0	0	0	93	16	1	.172
1973		16	12	.571	3.37	35	34	14	259	259	59	144	5	1	0	0	88	17	3	.193
1974 BOS A		3	4	.429	3.86	9	9	1	49	47	16	25	0	0	0	0	0	0	0	–
1975		19	12	.613	3.95	35	35	17	255.1	262	72	141	1	0	0	0	0	0	0	–
1976		14	11	.560	3.54	34	34	11	224	218	48	93	4	0	0	0	0	0	0	–
1977		11	5	.688	4.78	26	20	4	128	151	28	85	2	0	2	0	0	0	0	–
1978 CLE A		9	19	.321	4.32	33	31	9	212.2	226	59	106	1	0	0	0	0	0	0	–
1979		15	10	.600	3.72	34	34	9	232	229	68	108	2	0	0	0	0	0	0	–
1980 SD N		6	8	.429	3.68	27	27	1	154	172	37	59	0	0	0	0	58	8	0	.138
1981		4	8	.333	3.77	18	18	0	98	116	19	27	0	0	0	0	25	1	0	.040
1982		0	0	–	9.00	1	0	0	2	3	0	0	0	0	0	0	0	0	0	–
18 yrs.		188	181	.509	3.69	506	455	138	3127	3227	804	1647	30	4	5	0	668	130	15	.195
2 yrs.		32	28	.533	3.24	70	69	34	528	509	130	286	7	1	0	0	181	33	4	.182

LEAGUE CHAMPIONSHIP SERIES

		W	L	PCT	ERA	G	GS	CG	IP	H	BB	SO	ShO	W	L	SV	AB	H	HR	BA
1975 BOS A		1	0	1.000	2.45	1	1	0	7.1	6	3	2	0	0	0	0	0	0	0	–

WORLD SERIES

		W	L	PCT	ERA	G	GS	CG	IP	H	BB	SO	ShO	W	L	SV	AB	H	HR	BA
1975 BOS A		1	0	1.000	8.44	2	1	0	5.1	6	2	2	0	1	0	0	2	0	0	.000

Chicken Wolf

WOLF, WILLIAM VAN WINKLE BR TR
B. May 12, 1862, Louisville, Ky.   D. May 16, 1903, Louisville, Ky.
Manager 1889.

		W	L	PCT	ERA	G	GS	CG	IP	H	BB	SO	ShO	W	L	SV	AB	H	HR	BA
1882 LOU AA		0	0	–	9.00	1	0	0	6	11	3	1	0	0	0	0	318	95	0	.299
1885		0	0	–	9.00	1	0	0	1	1	0	1	0	0	0	0	483	141	1	.292
1886		0	0	–	15.00	1	0	0	3	7	0	0	0	0	0	0	545	148	3	.272
3 yrs.		0	0	–	10.80	3	0	0	10	19	3	2	0	0	0	0	*			

Harry Wolter

WOLTER, HARRY MEIGS BL TL 5'10" 175 lbs.
B. July 11, 1884, Monterey, Calif.   D. July 7, 1970, Palo Alto, Calif.

		W	L	PCT	ERA	G	GS	CG	IP	H	BB	SO	ShO	W	L	SV	AB	H	HR	BA
1907 2 teams	STL N	(3G 1–2)		PIT	N	(1G 0–0)														
" total		1	2	.333	4.32	4	3	1	25	30	20	8	0	0	0	0	63	18	0	.286
1909 BOS A		3	3	.500	3.91	10	6	0	53	53	28	20	0	0	0	1	119	29	2	.244
2 yrs.		4	5	.444	4.04	14	9	1	78	83	48	28	0	0	0	1	*			
1 yr.		1	2	.333	4.30	3	3	1	23	27	18	8	0	0	0	0	47	16	0	.340

John Wood

WOOD, JOHN B.
Deceased.

		W	L	PCT	ERA	G	GS	CG	IP	H	BB	SO	ShO	W	L	SV	AB	H	HR	BA
1896 STL N		0	0	–	∞	1	0	0		1	2	0	0	0	0	0	0	0	0	–

Gene Woodburn

WOODBURN, EUGENE STEWART BR TR 6' 175 lbs.
B. Aug. 20, 1886, Bellaire, Ohio   D. Jan. 18, 1961, Sandusky, Ohio

		W	L	PCT	ERA	G	GS	CG	IP	H	BB	SO	ShO	W	L	SV	AB	H	HR	BA
1911 STL N		1	6	.143	5.40	11	6	1	38.1	22	40	23	0	0	2	0	6	1	0	.167
1912		1	4	.200	5.59	20	5	1	48.1	60	42	25	0	1	0	0	13	0	0	.000
2 yrs.		2	10	.167	5.50	31	11	2	86.2	82	82	48	0	1	2	0	19	1	0	.053
2 yrs.		2	10	.167	5.50	31	11	2	86.2	82	82	48	0	1	2	0	19	1	0	.053

Hal Woodeshick

WOODESHICK, HAROLD JOSEPH BR TL 6'3" 200 lbs.
B. Aug. 24, 1932, Wilkes-Barre, Pa.

		W	L	PCT	ERA	G	GS	CG	IP	H	BB	SO	ShO	W	L	SV	AB	H	HR	BA
1956 DET A		0	2	.000	13.50	2	2	0	5.1	12	3	1	0	0	0	0	0	0	0	–
1958 CLE A		6	6	.500	3.64	14	9	3	71.2	71	25	27	0	3	0	0	24	4	0	.167
1959 WAS A		2	4	.333	3.69	31	3	0	61	58	36	30	0	2	1	0	8	0	0	.000
1960		4	5	.444	4.70	41	14	1	115	131	60	46	0	2	1	4	29	2	0	.069
1961 2 teams	WAS	A	(7G 3–2)	DET	A	(12G 1–1)														
" total		4	3	.571	5.22	19	8	1	58.2	63	41	37	0	1	0	0	20	2	0	.100
1962 HOU N		5	16	.238	4.39	31	26	2	139.1	161	54	82	1	0	1	0	37	3	0	.081
1963		11	9	.550	1.97	55	0	0	114	75	42	94	0	11	9	10	23	3	0	.130
1964		2	9	.182	2.76	61	0	0	78.1	73	32	58	0	2	9	23	10	0	0	.000
1965 2 teams	HOU	N	(27G 3–4)	STL	N	(51G 3–2)														
" total		6	6	.500	2.25	78	0	0	92	74	45	59	0	6	6	18	14	1	0	.071
1966 STL N		2	1	.667	1.92	59	0	0	70.1	57	23	30	0	2	1	4	5	1	0	.200
1967		2	1	.667	5.18	36	0	0	41.2	41	28	20	0	2	1	2	4	0	0	.000
11 yrs.		44	62	.415	3.56	427	62	7	847.1	816	389	484	1	31	29	61	174	16	0	.092
3 yrs.		7	4	.636	2.67	146	0	0	171.2	145	78	87	0	7	4	21	17	1	0	.059

WORLD SERIES

		W	L	PCT	ERA	G	GS	CG	IP	H	BB	SO	ShO	W	L	SV	AB	H	HR	BA
1967 STL N		0	0	–	0.00	1	0	0	1	1	0	0	0	0	0	0	0	0	0	–

Frank Woodward

WOODWARD, FRANK RUSSELL BR TR 5'10" 175 lbs.
B. May 17, 1894, New Haven, Conn.   D. June 11, 1961, New Haven, Conn.

		W	L	PCT	ERA	G	GS	CG	IP	H	BB	SO	ShO	W	L	SV	AB	H	HR	BA
1918 PHI N		0	0	–	6.00	2	0	0	6	6	4	4	0	0	0	0	3	1	0	.333
1919 2 teams	PHI	N	(17G 6–9)	STL	N	(17G 4–5)														
" total		10	14	.417	3.86	34	19	8	172.2	174	63	45	0	4	2	0	50	7	0	.140
1921 WAS A		0	0	–	5.91	3	1	0	10.2	11	3	4	0	0	0	0	3	1	0	.333
1922		0	0	–	11.57	1	0	0	2.1	5	3	2	0	0	0	0	1	0	0	.000
1923 CHI A		0	1	.000	13.50	2	1	0	2	5	1	0	0	0	0	0	0	0	0	–
5 yrs.		10	15	.400	4.23	42	21	8	193.2	199	74	55	0	4	2	0	57	9	0	.158
1 yr.		4	5	.444	2.63	17	7	2	72	65	28	18	0	3	0	0	21	1	0	.048

	W	L	PCT	ERA	G	GS	CG	IP	H	BB	SO	ShO	Relief Pitching W	L	SV	BATTING AB	H	HR	BA

Floyd Wooldridge

WOOLDRIDGE, FLOYD LEWIS
B. Aug. 25, 1928, Jerico Springs, Mo.   BR TR 6'1"   185 lbs.

	W	L	PCT	ERA	G	GS	CG	IP	H	BB	SO	ShO	RP W	L	SV	AB	H	HR	BA
1955 STL N	2	4	.333	4.84	18	8	2	57.2	64	27	14	0	0	1	0	18	4	0	.222

Mel Wright

WRIGHT, MELVIN JAMES
B. May 11, 1928, Manila, Ark.   BR TR 6'3"   210 lbs.

	W	L	PCT	ERA	G	GS	CG	IP	H	BB	SO	ShO	RP W	L	SV	AB	H	HR	BA
1954 STL N	0	0	—	10.45	9	0	0	10.1	16	11	4	0	0	0	0	1	0	0	.000
1955	2	2	.500	6.19	29	0	0	36.1	44	9	18	0	2	2	1	6	0	0	.000
1960 CHI N	0	1	.000	4.96	9	0	0	16.1	17	3	8	0	0	1	2	2	0	0	.000
1961	0	1	.000	10.71	11	0	0	21	42	4	6	0	0	1	0	2	0	0	.000
4 yrs.	2	4	.333	7.61	58	0	0	84	119	27	36	0	2	4	3	11	0	0	.000
2 yrs.	2	2	.500	7.14	38	0	0	46.2	60	20	22	0	2	2	1	7	0	0	.000

Stan Yerkes

YERKES, STANLEY LEWIS
B. Boston, Mass.   D. July 28, 1940, Boston, Mass.

	W	L	PCT	ERA	G	GS	CG	IP	H	BB	SO	ShO	RP W	L	SV	AB	H	HR	BA
1901 2 teams	BAL A (1G 0–1)				STL N	(4G 3–1)													
" total	3	2	.600	3.86	5	5	5	42	47	8	19	0	0	0	0	15	2	0	.133
1902 STL N	11	20	.355	3.66	39	37	27	272.2	341	79	81	1	0	0	0	91	12	0	.132
1903	0	1	.000	1.80	1	1	0	5	8	0	3	0	0	0	0	2	0	0	.000
3 yrs.	14	23	.378	3.66	45	43	32	319.2	396	87	103	1	0	0	0	108	14	0	.130
3 yrs.	14	22	.389	3.58	44	42	31	311.2	384	85	99	1	0	0	0	105	13	0	.124

Ray Yochim

YOCHIM, RAYMOND AUSTIN ALOYSIUS
Brother of Len Yochim.
B. July 19, 1922, New Orleans, La.   BR TR 6'1"   170 lbs.

	W	L	PCT	ERA	G	GS	CG	IP	H	BB	SO	ShO	RP W	L	SV	AB	H	HR	BA
1948 STL N	0	0	—	0.00	1	0	0	1	0	3	1	0	0	0	0	0	0	0	—
1949	0	0	—	15.43	3	0	0	2.1	3	4	3	0	0	0	0	0	0	0	—
2 yrs.	0	0	—	10.80	4	0	0	3.1	3	7	4	0	0	0	0	0	0	0	—
2 yrs.	0	0	—	10.80	4	0	0	3.1	3	7	4	0	0	0	0	0	0	0	—

Cy Young

YOUNG, DENTON TRUE
B. Mar. 29, 1867, Gilmore, Ohio   D. Nov. 4, 1955, Peoli, Ohio   BR TR 6'2"   210 lbs.
Manager 1907.
Hall of Fame 1937.

	W	L	PCT	ERA	G	GS	CG	IP	H	BB	SO	ShO	RP W	L	SV	AB	H	HR	BA
1890 CLE N	9	7	.563	3.47	17	16	16	147.2	145	30	36	0	0	0	0	65	8	0	.123
1891	27	20	.574	2.85	55	46	44	423.2	431	140	147	0	1	3	2	174	29	1	.167
1892	36	11	.766	1.93	53	49	48	453	363	118	167	9	1	1	0	196	31	1	.158
1893	32	16	.667	3.36	53	46	42	422.2	442	103	102	1	4	1	1	187	44	1	.235
1894	25	22	.532	3.94	52	47	44	408.2	488	106	101	2	1	1	1	186	40	2	.215
1895	35	10	.778	3.24	47	40	36	369.2	363	75	121	4	7	0	0	140	30	0	.214
1896	29	16	.644	3.24	51	46	42	414.1	477	62	137	5	0	1	3	180	52	3	.289
1897	21	18	.538	3.79	46	38	35	335	391	49	87	2	1	4	0	153	34	0	.222
1898	25	14	.641	2.53	46	41	40	377.2	387	41	107	1	0	1	0	154	39	2	.253
1899 STL N	26	15	.634	2.58	44	42	40	369.1	368	44	111	4	0	1	1	148	32	1	.216
1900	20	18	.526	3.00	41	35	32	321.1	337	36	119	4	2	2	0	124	22	1	.177
1901 BOS A	33	10	.767	1.62	43	41	38	371.1	324	37	158	5	2	0	0	153	32	0	.209
1902	32	10	.762	2.15	45	43	41	384.2	350	53	166	3	0	0	0	148	34	1	.230
1903	28	10	.737	2.08	40	35	34	341.2	294	37	183	7	1	2	2	137	44	1	.321
1904	26	16	.619	1.97	43	41	40	380	327	29	203	10	2	0	0	148	33	1	.223
1905	18	19	.486	1.82	38	34	32	320.2	248	30	208	5	4	0	0	120	18	2	.150
1906	13	21	.382	3.19	39	34	28	287.2	288	25	140	0	0	0	2	104	16	0	.154
1907	22	15	.595	1.99	43	37	33	343.1	286	51	147	6	1	0	3	125	27	1	.216
1908	21	11	.656	1.26	36	33	30	299	230	37	150	3	0	1	2	107	21	0	.196
1909 CLE A	19	15	.559	2.26	35	34	30	295	267	59	109	3	0	0	0	55	8	0	.145
1910	7	10	.412	2.53	21	20	14	163.1	149	27	58	1	0	0	0	41	3	0	.073
1911 2 teams	CLE	A (7G 3–4)			BOS	N (11G 4–5)													
" total	7	9	.438	3.78	18	18	12	126.1	137	28	55	2	0	0	0	41	3	0	.210
22 yrs.	511	313	.620	2.63	906	816	751	7356	7092	1217	2812	77	28	18	17	2960	623	18	.210
	1st	1st			3rd		1st	1st				4th							
2 yrs.	46	33	.582	2.78	85	77	72	690.2	705	80	230	8	2	3	1	272	54	2	.199
WORLD SERIES																			
1903 BOS A	2	1	.667	1.59	4	3	3	34	31	4	17	0	0	0	0	15	2	0	.133

J. D. Young

YOUNG, J. D.
B. Mt. Carmel, Pa.   Deceased.

	W	L	PCT	ERA	G	GS	CG	IP	H	BB	SO	ShO	RP W	L	SV	AB	H	HR	BA
1892 STL N	0	0	—	22.50	1	0	0	2	9	2	1	0	0	0	0	1	0	0	.000

Eddie Yuhas

YUHAS, JOHN EDWARD
B. Aug. 5, 1924, Youngstown, Ohio   BR TR 6'1"   180 lbs.

	W	L	PCT	ERA	G	GS	CG	IP	H	BB	SO	ShO	RP W	L	SV	AB	H	HR	BA
1952 STL N	12	2	.857	2.72	54	2	0	99.1	90	35	39	0	11	1	6	21	4	0	.190
1953	0	0	—	18.00	2	0	0	1	3	0	0	0	0	0	0	0	0	0	—
2 yrs.	12	2	.857	2.87	56	2	0	100.1	93	35	39	0	11	1	6	21	4	0	.190
2 yrs.	12	2	.857	2.87	56	2	0	100.1	93	35	39	0	11	1	6	21	4	0	.190

Chris Zachary

ZACHARY, WILLIAM CHRIS
B. Feb. 19, 1944, Knoxville, Tenn.   BL TR 6'2"   200 lbs.

	W	L	PCT	ERA	G	GS	CG	IP	H	BB	SO	ShO	RP W	L	SV	AB	H	HR	BA
1963 HOU N	2	2	.500	4.89	22	7	0	57	62	22	42	0	0	0	0	13	0	0	.000
1964	0	1	.000	9.00	1	1	0	4	6	1	2	0	0	0	0	1	0	0	.000
1965	0	2	.000	4.22	4	2	0	10.2	12	6	4	0	0	0	0	2	0	0	.000
1966	3	5	.375	3.44	10	8	0	55	44	32	37	0	0	0	0	18	4	0	.222
1967	1	6	.143	5.70	9	7	0	36.1	42	12	18	0	0	0	0	10	1	0	.100
1969 KC A	0	1	.000	7.85	8	2	0	18.1	27	7	6	0	0	0	0	2	1	0	.500

	W	L	PCT	ERA	G	GS	CG	IP	H	BB	SO	ShO	Relief Pitching W	L	SV	BATTING AB	H	HR	BA

Chris Zachary continued

		W	L	PCT	ERA	G	GS	CG	IP	H	BB	SO	ShO	W	L	SV	AB	H	HR	BA
1971	STL N	3	10	.231	5.30	23	12	1	90	114	26	48	1	1	2	0	33	8	0	.242
1972	DET A	1	1	.500	1.42	25	1	0	38	27	15	21	0	1	0	1	2	1	0	.500
1973	PIT N	0	1	.000	3.00	6	0	0	12	10	1	6	0	0	1	1	2	0	0	.000
9 yrs.		10	29	.256	4.57	108	40	1	321.1	344	122	184	1	2	4	2	83	15	0	.181
1 yr.		3	10	.231	5.30	23	12	1	90	114	26	48	1	1	2	0	33	8	0	.242
LEAGUE CHAMPIONSHIP SERIES																				
1972	DET A	0	0	—	∞	1	0	0		0	1	0	0	0	0	0	0	0	0	—

George Zackert

ZACKERT, GEORGE CARL   BL TL 6'   177 lbs.
B. Dec. 24, 1884, St. Joseph, Mo.   D. Feb. 18, 1977, Burlington, Iowa

		W	L	PCT	ERA	G	GS	CG	IP	H	BB	SO	ShO	W	L	SV	AB	H	HR	BA
1911	STL N	0	2	.000	11.05	4	1	0	7.1	17	6	6	0	0	1	0	1	0	0	.000
1912		0	0	—	18.00	1	0	0	1	2	1	0	0	0	0	0	1	0	0	.000
2 yrs.		0	2	.000	11.88	5	1	0	8.1	19	7	6	0	0	1	0	2	0	0	.000
2 yrs.		0	2	.000	11.88	5	1	0	8.1	19	7	6	0	0	1	0	2	0	0	.000

Ed Zmich

ZMICH, EDWARD ALBERT (Ike)   BL TL 6'   180 lbs.
B. Oct. 1, 1884, Cleveland, Ohio   D. Aug. 20, 1950, Cleveland, Ohio

		W	L	PCT	ERA	G	GS	CG	IP	H	BB	SO	ShO	W	L	SV	AB	H	HR	BA
1910	STL N	0	5	.000	6.25	9	6	2	36	38	29	19	0	0	0	0	13	1	0	.077
1911		1	0	1.000	2.13	4	0	0	12.2	8	8	4	0	1	0	0	4	0	0	.000
2 yrs.		1	5	.167	5.18	13	6	2	48.2	46	37	23	0	1	0	0	17	1	0	.059
2 yrs.		1	5	.167	5.18	13	6	2	48.2	46	37	23	0	1	0	0	17	1	0	.059

Manager Register

The Manager Register is an alphabetical listing of every man who has managed the St. Louis Cardinals. Included are facts about the managers and their year-by-year managerial records for the regular season, League Championship Series, and the World Series.

Most of the information in this section is self-explanatory. That which is not is explained as follows:

Games Managed includes tie games.

Lifetime Total. The first total shown after the regular season's statistics is the manager's total lifetime record in the major leagues.

Cardinals Lifetime Total. The second line is the manager's total lifetime record with the Cardinals.

Blank space appearing beneath a team and league means that the team and league are the same.

Standing. The figures in this column indicate the standing of the team at the end of the season and when there was a managerial change. The four possible cases are as follows:

> *Only Manager for the Team That Year.* Indicated by a single bold-faced figure that appears in the extreme left-hand column and shows the final standing of the team.
>
> *Manager Started Season, But Did Not Finish.* Indicated by two figures: the first is bold-faced and shows the standing of the team when this manager left; the second shows the final standing of the team.

Manager Finished Season, But Did Not Start. Indicated by two figures: the first shows the standing of the team when this manager started; the second is bold-faced and shows the final standing of the team.

Manager Did Not Start or Finish Season. Indicated by three figures: the first shows the standing of the team when this manager started; the second is bold-faced and shows the standing of the team when this manager left; the third shows the final standing of the team.

1981 Split Season Indicator. The managers' records for the 1981 split season are given separately for each half. "(1st)" or "(2nd)" will appear to the right of the standings to indicate which half.

| | G | W | L | PCT | Standing |

Ray Blades

BLADES, FRANCIS RAYMOND
B. Aug. 6, 1896, Mt. Vernon, Ill.
D. May 18, 1979, Lincoln, Ill.

		G	W	L	PCT	Standing	
1939	STL N	155	92	61	.601	2	
1940		40	15	24	.385	7	3
2 yrs.		195	107	85	.557		
2 yrs.		195	107	85	.557		

Ken Boyer

BOYER, KENTON LLOYD
Brother of Cloyd Boyer.
Brother of Clete Boyer.
B. May 20, 1931, Liberty, Mo.
D. Sept. 7, 1982, St. Louis, Mo.

		G	W	L	PCT	Standing	
1978	STL N	144	62	82	.431	5	5
1979		162	86	76	.531	3	
1980		51	18	33	.353	6	4
3 yrs.		357	166	191	.465		
3 yrs.		357	166	191	.465		

Roger Bresnahan

BRESNAHAN, ROGER PHILIP (The Duke of Tralee)
B. June 11, 1879, Toledo, Ohio
D. Dec. 4, 1944, Toledo, Ohio
Hall of Fame 1945.

		G	W	L	PCT	Standing
1909	STL N	154	54	98	.355	7
1910		153	63	90	.412	7
1911		158	75	74	.503	5
1912		153	63	90	.412	6
1915	CHI N	156	73	80	.477	4
5 yrs.		774	328	432	.432	
4 yrs.		618	255	352	.420	

Al Buckenberger

BUCKENBERGER, ALBERT C.
B. Jan. 31, 1861, Detroit, Mich.
D. July 1, 1917

		G	W	L	PCT	Standing	
1889	COL AA	140	60	78	.435	6	
1890		84	42	42	.500	5	2
1892	PIT N	99	55	43	.561	9	6
1893		131	81	48	.628	2	
1894		109	53	55	.491	7	7
1895	STL N	49	16	32	.333	11	11
1902	BOS N	142	73	64	.533	3	
1903		140	58	80	.420	6	
1904		155	55	98	.359	7	
9 yrs.		1049	493	540	.477		
1 yr.		49	16	32	.333		

Jimmy Burke

BURKE, JAMES TIMOTHY (Sunset Jimmy)
B. Oct. 12, 1874, St. Louis, Mo.
D. Mar. 26, 1942, St. Louis, Mo.

		G	W	L	PCT	Standing		
1905	STL N	49	17	32	.347	6	6	6
1918	STL A	62	29	32	.475	6	5	
1919		140	67	72	.482	5		
1920		154	76	77	.497	4		
4 yrs.		405	189	213	.470			
1 yr.		49	17	32	.347			

Roger Connor

CONNOR, ROGER
Brother of Joe Connor.
B. July 1, 1857, Waterbury, Conn.
D. Jan. 4, 1931, Waterbury, Conn.
Hall of Fame 1976.

		G	W	L	PCT	Standing		
1896	STL N	46	9	37	.196	11	11	11

Harry Diddlebock

DIDDLEBOCK, HENRY H.
B. June 27, 1854, Philadelphia, Pa.
D. Feb. 5, 1900, Philadelphia, Pa.

		G	W	L	PCT	Standing		
1896	STL N	18	7	11	.389	10	11	

Patsy Donovan

DONOVAN, PATRICK JOSEPH
Brother of Wild Bill Donovan.
B. Mar. 16, 1865, County Cork, Ireland
D. Dec. 25, 1953, Lawrence, Mass.

		G	W	L	PCT	Standing	
1897	PIT N	135	60	71	.458	8	
1899		129	68	57	.544	10	7
1901	STL N	142	76	64	.543	4	
1902		140	56	78	.418	6	
1903		139	43	94	.314	8	
1904	WAS A	139	37	97	.276	8	8
1906	BKN N	153	66	86	.434	5	
1907		153	65	83	.439	5	
1908		154	53	101	.344	7	
1910	BOS A	158	81	72	.529	4	
1911		153	78	75	.510	5	
11 yrs.		1595	683	878	.438		
3 yrs.		421	175	236	.426		

Tommy Dowd

DOWD, THOMAS JEFFERSON (Buttermilk Tommy)
B. Apr. 20, 1869, Holyoke, Mass.
D. July 2, 1933, Holyoke, Mass.

		G	W	L	PCT	Standing	
1896	STL N	62	24	38	.387	11	11
1897		32	6	25	.194	12	12
2 yrs.		94	30	63	.323		
2 yrs.		94	30	63	.323		

Eddie Dyer

DYER, EDWIN HAWLEY
B. Oct. 11, 1900, Morgan City, La.
D. Apr. 20, 1964, Houston, Tex.

		G	W	L	PCT	Standing
1946	STL N	156	98	58	.628	1
1947		156	89	65	.578	2
1948		155	85	69	.552	2
1949		157	96	58	.623	2
1950		153	78	75	.510	5
5 yrs.		777	446	325	.578	
5 yrs.		777	446	325	.578	

WORLD SERIES		G	W	L	PCT
1946	STL N	7	4	3	.571

Frankie Frisch

FRISCH, FRANK FRANCIS (The Fordham Flash)
B. Sept. 9, 1898, Queens, N. Y.
D. Mar. 12, 1973, Wilmington, Del.
Hall of Fame 1947.

		G	W	L	PCT	Standing	
1933	STL N	63	36	26	.581	5	5
1934		154	95	58	.621	1	
1935		154	96	58	.623	2	
1936		155	87	67	.565	2	
1937		157	81	73	.526	4	
1938		138	62	72	.463	6	6
1940	PIT N	156	78	76	.506	4	
1941		156	81	73	.526	4	
1942		151	66	81	.449	5	
1943		157	80	74	.519	4	
1944		158	90	63	.588	2	
1945		155	82	72	.532	4	
1946		152	62	89	.411	7	7
1949	CHI N	104	42	62	.404	8	8
1950		154	64	89	.418	7	
1951		81	35	45	.438	7	8
16 yrs.		2245	1137	1078	.513		
6 yrs.		821	457	354	.564		

WORLD SERIES		G	W	L	PCT
1934	STL N	7	4	3	.571

	G	W	L	PCT	Standing			G	W	L	PCT	Standing

Mike Gonzalez

GONZALEZ, MIGUEL ANGEL
B. Sept. 24, 1890, Havana, Cuba
D. Havana, Cuba

		G	W	L	PCT	Standing	
1938	STL N	18	9	8	.529	6	6
1940		5	0	5	.000	7 6	3
2 yrs.		23	9	13	.409		
2 yrs.		23	9	13	.409		

Stan Hack

HACK, STANLEY CAMFIELD (Smiling Stan)
B. Dec. 6, 1909, Sacramento, Calif.
D. Dec. 15, 1979, Dickson, Ill.

		G	W	L	PCT	Standing	
1954	CHI N	154	64	90	.416	7	
1955		154	72	81	.471	6	
1956		157	60	94	.390	8	
1958	STL N	10	3	7	.300	5	5
4 yrs.		475	199	272	.423		
1 yr.		10	3	7	.300		

Bill Hallman

HALLMAN, WILLIAM WHITE
B. Mar. 30, 1867, Pittsburgh, Pa.
D. Sept. 11, 1920, Philadelphia, Pa.

		G	W	L	PCT	Standing		
1897	STL N	59	13	46	.220	12	12	12

Louie Heilbroner

HEILBRONER, LOUIS WILBUR
B. July 4, 1861, Ft. Wayne, Ind.
D. Dec. 21, 1933

		G	W	L	PCT	Standing	
1900	STL N	38	17	20	.459	7	5

Solly Hemus

HEMUS, SOLOMON JOSEPH
B. Apr. 17, 1923, Phoenix, Ariz.

		G	W	L	PCT	Standing	
1959	STL N	154	71	83	.461	7	
1960		155	86	68	.558	3	
1961		75	33	41	.446	6	5
3 yrs.		384	190	192	.497		
3 yrs.		384	190	192	.497		

Jack Hendricks

HENDRICKS, JOHN CHARLES
B. Apr. 9, 1875, Joliet, Ill.
D. May 13, 1943, Chicago, Ill.

		G	W	L	PCT	Standing
1918	STL N	131	51	78	.395	8
1924	CIN N	153	83	70	.542	4
1925		153	80	73	.523	3
1926		157	87	67	.565	2
1927		153	75	78	.490	5
1928		153	78	74	.513	5
1929		155	66	88	.429	7
7 yrs.		1055	520	528	.496	
1 yr.		131	51	78	.395	

Whitey Herzog

HERZOG, DORREL NORMAN ELVERT
B. Nov. 9, 1931, New Athens, Ill.

		G	W	L	PCT	Standing		
1973	TEX A	138	47	91	.341	6	6	
1975	KC A	66	41	25	.621	2	2	
1976		162	90	72	.556	1		
1977		162	102	60	.630	1		
1978		162	92	70	.568	1		
1979		162	85	77	.525	2		
1980	STL N	73	38	35	.521	6 5	4	
1981		51	30	20	.600	2		(1st)
1981		52	29	23	.558	2		(2nd)
1982		162	92	70	.568	1		
9 yrs.		1190	646	543	.543			
3 yrs.		338	189	148	.561			

LEAGUE CHAMPIONSHIP SERIES

		G	W	L	PCT	Standing
1976	KC A	5	2	3	.400	
1977		5	2	3	.400	
1978		4	1	3	.250	
1982	STL N	3	3	0	1.000	
4 yrs.		17	8	9	.471	
			4th	4th	3rd	4th
1 yr.		3	3	0	.000	

WORLD SERIES

		G	W	L	PCT
1982	STL N	7	4	3	.571

Rogers Hornsby

HORNSBY, ROGERS (Rajah)
B. Apr. 27, 1896, Winters, Tex.
D. Jan. 5, 1963, Chicago, Ill.
Hall of Fame 1942.

		G	W	L	PCT	Standing	
1925	STL N	115	64	51	.557	8	4
1926		156	89	65	.578	1	
1928	BOS N	122	39	83	.320	7	7
1930	CHI N	4	4	0	1.000	2	2
1931		156	84	70	.545	3	
1932		97	53	44	.546	2	1
1933	STL A	56	20	34	.370	8	8
1934		154	67	85	.441	6	
1935		155	65	87	.428	7	
1936		155	57	95	.375	7	
1937		76	25	50	.333	8	8
1952		50	22	28	.440	7	7
1952	CIN N	51	27	24	.529	7	6
1953		147	64	82	.438	6	6
13 yrs.		1494	680	798	.460		
2 yrs.		271	153	116	.569		

WORLD SERIES

		G	W	L	PCT
1926	STL N	7	4	3	.571

Miller Huggins

HUGGINS, MILLER JAMES (Hug, The Mighty Mite)
B. Mar. 27, 1879, Cincinnati, Ohio
D. Sept. 25, 1929, New York, N. Y.
Hall of Fame 1964.

		G	W	L	PCT	Standing	
1913	STL N	152	51	99	.340	8	
1914		157	81	72	.529	3	
1915		157	72	81	.471	6	
1916		153	60	93	.392	7	
1917		154	82	70	.539	3	
1918	NY A	126	60	63	.488	4	
1919		141	80	59	.576	3	
1920		154	95	59	.617	3	
1921		153	98	55	.641	1	
1922		154	94	60	.610	1	
1923		152	98	54	.645	1	
1924		153	89	63	.586	2	
1925		156	69	85	.448	7	
1926		155	91	63	.591	1	
1927		155	110	44	.714	1	
1928		154	101	53	.656	1	
1929		143	82	61	.573	2	2
17 yrs.		2569	1413	1134	.555		
5 yrs.		773	346	415	.455		

WORLD SERIES

		G	W	L	PCT
1921	NY A	8	3	5	.375
1922		5	0	4	.000
1923		6	4	2	.667
1926		7	3	4	.429

	G	W	L	PCT	Standing

Miller Huggins continued

	G	W	L	PCT	Standing
1927	4	4	0	1.000	
1928	4	4	0	1.000	
6 yrs.	34	18	15	.545	
	6th	6th	5th		5th

Tim Hurst
HURST, TIMOTHY CARROLL
B. June 30, 1865, Ashland, Pa.
D. June 4, 1915

1898 STL N	154	39	111	.260	12

Fred Hutchinson
HUTCHINSON, FREDERICK CHARLES
B. Aug. 12, 1919, Seattle, Wash.
D. Nov. 12, 1964, Bradenton, Fla.

1952 DET A	83	27	55	.329	8	8
1953	158	60	94	.390	6	
1954	155	68	86	.442	5	
1956 STL N	156	76	78	.494	4	
1957	154	87	67	.565	2	
1958	144	69	75	.479	5	5
1959 CIN N	74	39	35	.527	7	5
1960	154	67	87	.435	6	
1961	154	93	61	.604	1	
1962	162	98	64	.605	3	
1963	162	86	76	.531	5	
1964	110	60	49	.550	3	2
12 yrs.	1666	830	827	.501		
3 yrs.	454	232	220	.513		
WORLD SERIES						
1961 CIN N	5	1	4	.200		

Johnny Keane
KEANE, JOHN JOSEPH
B. Nov. 3, 1911, St. Louis, Mo.
D. Jan. 6, 1967, Houston, Tex.

1961 STL N	80	47	33	.588	6	5
1962	163	84	78	.519	6	
1963	162	93	69	.574	2	
1964	162	93	69	.574	1	
1965 NY A	162	77	85	.475	6	
1966	20	4	16	.200	10	10
6 yrs.	749	398	350	.532		
4 yrs.	567	317	249	.560		
WORLD SERIES						
1964 STL N	7	4	3	.571		

Jack Krol
KROL, JOHN THOMAS
B. July 5, 1936, Chicago, Ill.

1978 STL N	3	2	1	.667	6	5	5
1980	1	0	1	.000	6	6	4
2 yrs.	4	2	2	.500			
2 yrs.	4	2	2	.500			

Arlie Latham
LATHAM, WALTER ARLINGTON (The Freshest Man on Earth)
B. Mar. 15, 1859, W. Lebanon, N. H.
D. Nov. 29, 1952, Garden City, N. Y.

1896 STL N	2	0	2	.000	10	10	11

Marty Marion
MARION, MARTIN WHITFORD (Slats, The Octopus)
Brother of Red Marion.
B. Dec. 1, 1917, Richburg, S. C.

1951 STL N	156	81	73	.526	3

Marty Marion continued

1952 STL A	105	42	62	.404	7	7
1953	154	54	100	.351	8	
1954 CHI A	9	3	6	.333	3	3
1955	155	91	63	.591	3	
1956	154	85	69	.552	3	
6 yrs.	733	356	373	.488		
1 yr.	156	81	73	.526		

John McCloskey
McCLOSKEY, JOHN JAMES (Honest John)
B. Apr. 4, 1862, Louisville, Ky.
D. Nov. 17, 1940

1895 LOU N	133	35	96	.267	12	
1896	44	9	34	.209	12	12
1906 STL N	154	52	98	.347	7	
1907	155	52	101	.340	8	
1908	154	49	105	.318	8	
5 yrs.	640	197	434	.312		
3 yrs.	463	153	304	.335		

Bill McKechnie
McKECHNIE, WILLIAM BOYD (Deacon)
B. Aug. 7, 1886, Wilkinsburg, Pa.
D. Oct. 29, 1965, Bradenton, Fla.
Hall of Fame 1962.

1915 NWK F	102	54	45	.545	6	5
1922 PIT N	90	53	36	.596	5	3
1923	154	87	67	.565	3	
1924	153	90	63	.588	3	
1925	153	95	58	.621	1	
1926	157	84	69	.549	3	
1928 STL N	154	95	59	.617	1	
1929	62	33	29	.532	4	4
1930 BOS N	154	70	84	.455	6	
1931	156	64	90	.416	7	
1932	155	77	77	.500	5	
1933	156	83	71	.539	4	
1934	152	78	73	.517	4	
1935	153	38	115	.248	8	
1936	157	71	83	.461	6	
1937	152	79	73	.520	5	
1938 CIN N	151	82	68	.547	4	
1939	156	97	57	.630	1	
1940	155	100	53	.654	1	
1941	154	88	66	.571	3	
1942	154	76	76	.500	4	
1943	155	87	67	.565	2	
1944	155	89	65	.578	3	
1945	154	61	93	.396	7	
1946	156	67	87	.435	6	
25 yrs.	3650	1898	1724	.524		
	7th	8th	6th			
2 yrs.	216	128	88	.593		
WORLD SERIES						
1925 PIT N	7	4	3	.571		
1928 STL N	4	0	4	.000		
1939 CIN N	4	0	4	.000		
1940	7	4	3	.571		
4 yrs.	22	8	14	.364		
	9th		6th			
1 yr.	4	0	4	.000		

George Miller
MILLER, GEORGE
B. Feb. 19, 1853, Newport, Ky.
D. July 25, 1929, Cincinnati, Ohio

1894 STL N	132	56	76	.424	9

	G	W	L	PCT	Standing				G	W	L	PCT	Standing

Kid Nichols

NICHOLS, CHARLES AUGUSTUS
B. Sept. 14, 1869, Madison, Wis.
D. Apr. 11, 1953, Kansas City, Mo.
Hall of Fame 1949.

		G	W	L	PCT	Standing
1904	STL N	155	75	79	.487	5
1905		48	19	29	.396	6 6
2 yrs.		203	94	108	.465	
2 yrs.		203	94	108	.465	

Hugh Nicol

NICOL, HUGH N.
B. Jan. 1, 1858, Campsie, Scotland
D. June 27, 1921, Lafayette, Ind.

		G	W	L	PCT	Standing
1897	STL N	38	9	29	.237	12 **12** 12

Bob O'Farrell

O'FARRELL, ROBERT ARTHUR
B. Oct. 19, 1896, Waukegan, Ill.

		G	W	L	PCT	Standing
1927	STL N	153	92	61	.601	2
1934	CIN N	85	26	58	.310	8 8
2 yrs.		238	118	119	.498	
1 yr.		153	92	61	.601	

Lew Phelan

PHELAN, LEWIS G.
Deceased.

		G	W	L	PCT	Standing
1895	STL N	31	8	21	.276	11 **11** 11

Joe Quinn

QUINN, JOSEPH J.
B. Dec. 25, 1864, Sydney, Australia
D. Nov. 12, 1940, St. Louis, Mo.

		G	W	L	PCT	Standing
1895	STL N	41	13	27	.325	11 **11** 11
1899	CLE N	116	12	104	.103	12 **12**
2 yrs.		157	25	131	.160	
1 yr.		41	13	27	.325	

Vern Rapp

RAPP, VERNON FRED
B. May 11, 1928, St. Louis, Mo.

		G	W	L	PCT	Standing
1977	STL N	162	83	79	.512	3
1978		15	5	10	.333	6 5
2 yrs.		177	88	89	.497	
2 yrs.		177	88	89	.497	

Branch Rickey

RICKEY, WESLEY BRANCH (The Mahatma)
B. Dec. 20, 1881, Stockdale, Ohio
D. Dec. 9, 1965, Columbia, Mo.
Hall of Fame 1967.

		G	W	L	PCT	Standing
1913	STL A	12	5	6	.455	8 8
1914		159	71	82	.464	5
1915		159	63	91	.409	6
1919	STL N	138	54	83	.394	7
1920		155	75	79	.487	5
1921		154	87	66	.569	3
1922		154	85	69	.552	3
1923		154	79	74	.516	5
1924		154	65	89	.422	6
1925		38	13	25	.342	8 4
10 yrs.		1277	597	664	.473	
7 yrs.		947	458	485	.486	

Stanley Robison

ROBISON, MATTHEW STANLEY
B. 1857, Dubuque, Iowa
D. Mar. 24, 1911

		G	W	L	PCT	Standing
1905	STL N	57	22	35	.386	6 6

Red Schoendienst

SCHOENDIENST, ALBERT FRED
B. Feb. 2, 1923, Germantown, Ill.

		G	W	L	PCT	Standing
1965	STL N	162	80	81	.497	7
1966		162	83	79	.512	6
1967		161	101	60	.627	1
1968		162	97	65	.599	1
1969		162	87	75	.537	4
1970		162	76	86	.469	4
1971		163	90	72	.556	2
1972		156	75	81	.481	4
1973		162	81	81	.500	2
1974		161	86	75	.534	2
1975		163	82	80	.506	3
1976		162	72	90	.444	5
1980		37	18	19	.486	5 4
13 yrs.		1975	1028	944	.521	
13 yrs.		1975	1028	944	.521	

WORLD SERIES						
1967	STL N	7	4	3	.571	
1968		7	3	4	.429	
2 yrs.		14	7	7	.500	
2 yrs.		14	7	7	.500	

Billy Southworth

SOUTHWORTH, WILLIAM HARRISON
B. Mar. 9, 1893, Harvard, Neb.
D. Nov. 15, 1969, Columbus, Ohio

		G	W	L	PCT	Standing
1929	STL N	89	43	45	.489	4 4
1940		111	69	40	.633	6 3
1941		155	97	56	.634	2
1942		156	106	48	.688	1
1943		157	105	49	.682	1
1944		157	105	49	.682	1
1945		155	95	59	.617	2
1946	BOS N	154	81	72	.529	4
1947		154	86	68	.558	3
1948		154	91	62	.595	1
1949		157	75	79	.487	4
1950		156	83	71	.539	4
1951		60	28	31	.475	5 4
13 yrs.		1815	1064	729	.593	
						6th
7 yrs.		980	620	346	.642	

WORLD SERIES						
1942	STL N	5	4	1	.800	
1943		5	1	4	.200	
1944		6	4	2	.667	
1948	BOS N	6	2	4	.333	
4 yrs.		22	11	11	.500	
		9th	8th			9th
3 yrs.		16	9	7	.563	

Eddie Stanky

STANKY, EDWARD RAYMOND (The Brat, Muggsy)
B. Sept. 3, 1916, Philadelphia, Pa.

		G	W	L	PCT	Standing
1952	STL N	154	88	66	.571	3
1953		157	83	71	.539	3
1954		154	72	82	.468	6
1955		36	17	19	.472	5 7
1966	CHI A	163	83	79	.512	4
1967		162	89	73	.549	4
1968		79	34	45	.430	9 9
1977	TEX A	1	1	0	1.000	4 2 2
8 yrs.		906	467	435	.518	
4 yrs.		501	260	238	.522	

Gabby Street

STREET, CHARLES EVARD (Old Sarge)
B. Sept. 30, 1882, Huntsville, Ala.
D. Feb. 6, 1951, Joplin, Mo.

		G	W	L	PCT	Standing
1929	STL N	2	2	0	1.000	4 4 4
1930		154	92	62	.597	1
1931		154	101	53	.656	1
1932		156	72	82	.468	6
1933		91	46	45	.505	5 5
1938	STL A	156	55	97	.362	7
6 yrs.		713	368	339	.521	
5 yrs.		557	313	242	.564	

	G	W	L	PCT	Standing		

Gabby Street continued

WORLD SERIES

		G	W	L	PCT	Standing
1930 **STL N**		6	2	4	.333	
1931		7	4	3	.571	
2 yrs.		13	6	7	.462	
2 yrs.		13	6	7	.462	

Patsy Tebeau

TEBEAU, OLIVER WENDELL
Brother of White Wings Tebeau.
B. Dec. 5, 1864, St. Louis, Mo.
D. May 15, 1918, St. Louis, Mo.

		G	W	L	PCT	Standing	
1890 **CLE P**		36	18	17	.514	7	7
1891 **CLE N**		76	34	40	.459	6	5
1892		153	93	56	.624	2	
1893		129	73	55	.570	3	
1894		130	68	61	.527	6	
1895		131	84	46	.646	2	
1896		135	80	48	.625	2	
1897		132	69	62	.527	5	
1898		156	81	68	.544	5	
1899 **STL N**		155	84	67	.556	5	
1900		104	48	55	.466	7	5
11 yrs.		1337	732	575	.560		
2 yrs.		259	132	122	.520		

Chris Von Der Ahe

**VON DER AHE, CHRISTIAN FREDERICK
WILHELM**
B. Nov. 7, 1851, Hille, Germany
D. June 7, 1913

		G	W	L	PCT	Standing		
1892 **STL N**		155	56	94	.373	11		
1895		14	2	12	.143	11	11	
1896		3	0	2	.000	10	11	11
1897		3	1	2	.333	12	12	
4 yrs.		175	59	110	.349			
4 yrs.		175	59	110	.349			

Harry Walker

WALKER, HARRY WILLIAM (The Hat)
Son of Dixie Walker.
Brother of Dixie Walker.
B. Oct. 22, 1918, Pascagoula, Miss.

		G	W	L	PCT	Standing	
1955 **STL N**		118	51	67	.432	5	7
1965 **PIT N**		163	90	72	.556	3	
1966		162	92	70	.568	3	
1967		84	42	42	.500	6	6
1968 **HOU N**		101	49	52	.485	10	10
1969		162	81	81	.500	5	
1970		162	79	83	.488	4	
1971		162	79	83	.488	4	
1972		121	67	54	.554	3	2
9 yrs.		1235	630	604	.511		
1 yr.		118	51	67	.432		

Bill Watkins

WATKINS, WILLIAM HENRY
B. May 5, 1859, Brantford, Ont., Canada
D. June 9, 1937, Port Huron, Mich.

		G	W	L	PCT	Standing	
1884 **IND AA**		24	4	19	.174	11	12
1885 **DET N**		51	23	28	.451	7	6
1886		126	87	36	.707	2	
1887		127	79	45	.637	1	
1888		96	49	45	.521	3	5
1888 **KC AA**		14	3	11	.214	8	8
1889		139	55	82	.401	7	
1893 **STL N**		135	57	75	.432	10	
1898 **PIT N**		152	72	76	.486	8	
1899		25	8	16	.333	10	7
9 yrs.		889	437	433	.502		
1 yr.		135	57	75	.432		

Cardinal World Series Highlights and Summaries

THE WORLD SERIES AND NATIONAL LEAGUE CHAMPIONSHIP SERIES

This section provides information on the thirteen World Series the Cardinals have played in through 1982. Included are facts about the individual games; most of the information is self-explanatory. That which may appear unfamiliar is listed below.

INDIVIDUAL GAME INFORMATION

Innings Pitched. Pitchers are listed in the order of appearance. In parentheses, following each pitcher's name, are the number of innings he pitched in the game. For example: Doe (2.1) would mean that he pitched 2⅓ innings.

Winning and Losing Pitchers. Indicated by bold-faced print.

Saves. The pitcher who is credited with a Save is indicated by the abbreviation SV, which appears in bold-faced print after his innings pitched.

Home Runs. Players are listed in the order their home runs were hit.

	R H E	PITCHERS (inn. pit.)	HOME RUNS (men on)	HIGHLIGHTS

St. Louis (N.L.) defeats New York (A.L.) 4 games to 3

GAME 1 - OCTOBER 2

STL N 1 3 1 **Sherdel** (7), Haines (1)

NY A 2 6 0 **Pennock** (9)

Gehrig's single in the sixth sends Ruth home to break a 1-1 tie. Bottomley collects two of the Cardinals' three hits in the loss.

GAME 2 - OCTOBER 3

STL N 6 12 1 **Alexander** (9)

NY A 2 4 0 **Shocker** (7), Shawkey (1), Jones (1)

Southworth (2 on), Thevenow

Alexander checks the Yankees as he strikes out ten and retires the last 21 men in succession. Southworth's three-run homer in the seventh ices the game.

GAME 3 - OCTOBER 5

NY A 0 5 1 **Ruether** (4.1), Shawkey (2.2), Thomas (1)

STL N 4 8 0 **Haines** (9)

Haines (1 on)

The Cardinals put together three runs in the fourth to break open the game as Haines aids his own cause with a two-run homer to start the scoring.

GAME 4 - OCTOBER 6

NY A 10 14 1 **Hoyt** (9)

STL N 5 14 0 **Rhem** (4), Reinhart (0), H. Bell (2), Hallahan (2), Keen (1)

Ruth, Ruth, Ruth (1 on)

Ruth unloads for a record three home runs in leading the Yankee bombardment which knots the Series.

GAME 5 - OCTOBER 7

NY A 3 9 1 **Pennock** (10)

STL N 2 7 1 **Sherdel** (10)

Lazzeri's sacrifice fly in the tenth scores Koenig with the winning tally of the game after Sherdel's wild pitch sets up the run. O'Farrell makes three hits in the losing cause.

GAME 6 - OCTOBER 9

STL N 10 13 2 **Alexander** (9)

NY A 2 8 1 **Shawkey** (6.1), Shocker (0.2), Thomas (2)

L. Bell (1 on)

St. Louis scores three in the first and adds five more in the seventh to break open the game. Les Bell's three hits and four RBI's feature the Cardinals' attack.

GAME 7 - OCTOBER 10

STL N 3 8 0 **Haines** (6.2), Alexander (2.1) **SV**

NY A 2 8 3 **Hoyt** (6), Pennock (3)

Ruth

The Cardinals score three unearned runs in the fourth and Alexander saves the victory in the seventh, when, with two out and the bases loaded, he strikes out Lazzeri.

Team Totals

		W	AB	H	2B	3B	HR	R	RBI	BA	BB	SO	ERA
STL	N	4	239	65	12	1	4	31	30	.272	11	30	2.57
NY	A	3	223	54	10	1	4	21	19	.242	31	31	3.14

Individual Batting

ST. LOUIS (N.L.)

	AB	H	2B	3B	HR	R	RBI	BA
J. Bottomley, 1b	29	10	3	0	0	4	5	.345
B. Southworth, of	29	10	1	1	1	6	4	.345
R. Hornsby, 2b	28	7	1	0	0	2	4	.250
L. Bell, 3b	27	7	1	0	1	4	6	.259
C. Hafey, of	27	5	2	0	0	2	0	.185
T. Thevenow, ss	24	10	1	0	1	5	4	.417
B. O'Farrell, c	23	7	1	0	0	2	2	.304
W. Holm, of	16	2	0	0	0	1	1	.125
T. Douthit, of	15	4	2	0	0	3	1	.267
G. Alexander, p	7	0	0	0	0	1	0	.000
J. Haines, p	5	3	0	0	1	1	2	.600
B. Sherdel, p	5	0	0	0	0	0	0	.000
J. Flowers	3	0	0	0	0	0	0	.000
F. Rhem, p	1	0	0	0	0	0	0	.000
S. Toporcer	0	0	0	0	0	0	1	—

Errors: L. Bell (2), T. Thevenow (2), G. Alexander

Stolen bases: R. Hornsby, B. Southworth

NEW YORK (A.L.)

	AB	H	2B	3B	HR	R	RBI	BA
M. Koenig, ss	32	4	1	0	0	2	2	.125
E. Combs, of	28	10	2	0	0	3	2	.357
T. Lazzeri, 2b	26	5	1	0	0	2	3	.192
J. Dugan, 3b	24	8	1	0	0	2	2	.333
L. Gehrig, 1b	23	8	2	0	0	1	3	.348
H. Severeid, c	22	6	1	0	0	1	1	.273
B. Meusel, of	21	5	1	1	0	3	0	.238
B. Ruth, of	20	6	0	0	4	6	5	.300
H. Pennock, p	7	1	1	0	0	1	0	.143
W. Hoyt, p	6	0	0	0	0	0	0	.000
B. Paschal	4	1	0	0	0	0	1	.250
D. Ruether, p	4	0	0	0	0	0	0	.000
P. Collins, c	2	0	0	0	0	0	0	.000
B. Shawkey, p	2	0	0	0	0	0	0	.000
U. Shocker, p	2	0	0	0	0	0	0	.000
S. Adams	0	0	0	0	0	0	0	—
M. Gazella, 3b	0	0	0	0	0	0	0	—

Errors: M. Koenig (4), J. Dugan, T. Lazzeri, B. Meusel

Stolen bases: B. Ruth

Individual Pitching

ST. LOUIS (N.L.)

	W	L	ERA	IP	H	BB	SO	SV
G. Alexander	2	0	0.89	20.1	12	4	17	1
B. Sherdel	0	2	2.12	17	15	8	3	0
J. Haines	2	0	1.08	16.2	13	9	5	0
F. Rhem	0	0	6.75	4	7	2	4	0
H. Bell	0	0	9.00	2	4	1	1	0
B. Hallahan	0	0	4.50	2	2	3	1	0
V. Keen	0	0	0.00	1	0	0	0	0
A. Reinhart	0	1	∞	0.0	1	4	0	0

NEW YORK (A.L.)

	W	L	ERA	IP	H	BB	SO	SV
H. Pennock	2	0	1.23	22	13	4	8	0
W. Hoyt	1	1	1.20	15	19	1	10	0
B. Shawkey	0	1	5.40	10	8	2	7	0
U. Shocker	0	1	5.87	7.2	13	0	3	0
D. Ruether	0	1	8.31	4.1	7	2	1	0
M. Thomas	0	0	3.00	3	3	0	0	0
S. Jones	0	0	9.00	1	2	2	1	0

	R H E	PITCHERS (inn. pit.)	HOME RUNS (men on)	HIGHLIGHTS

New York (A.L.) defeats St. Louis (N.L.) 4 games to 0

GAME 1 - OCTOBER 4

		R H E	PITCHERS (inn. pit.)	HOME RUNS	HIGHLIGHTS
STL	N	1 3 1	**Sherdel** (7), Johnson (1)	Bottomley	Hoyt opens with a win for the second year in a row, notching a three-hitter over Sherdel. Meusel's homer in the fourth scores two and Bottomley's blast spoils a shutout.
NY	A	4 7 0	**Hoyt** (9)	Meusel (1 on)	

GAME 2 - OCTOBER 5

		R H E	PITCHERS (inn. pit.)	HOME RUNS	HIGHLIGHTS
STL	N	3 4 1	**Alexander** (2.1), Mitchell (5.2)		Gehrig's homer in the first leads the Yankees to a revenge win over Alexander, the hero of the 1926 classic. Pipgras, relying on curve balls, goes the distance despite a shaky start in which the Cardinals score three in the second.
NY	A	9 8 2	**Pipgras** (9)	Gehrig (2 on)	

GAME 3 - OCTOBER 7

		R H E	PITCHERS (inn. pit.)	HOME RUNS	HIGHLIGHTS
NY	A	7 7 2	**Zachary** (9)	Gehrig, Gehrig (1 on)	Zachary, a surprise southpaw starter, has an easy task when Gehrig connects twice for homers, batting in three as the Yankees dispose of Haines in six.
STL	N	3 9 3	**Haines** (6), Johnson (1), Rhem (2)		

GAME 4 - OCTOBER 9

		R H E	PITCHERS (inn. pit.)	HOME RUNS	HIGHLIGHTS
NY	A	7 15 2	**Hoyt** (9)	Ruth, Ruth, Gehrig, Durst, Ruth	Ruth rises to heights with three homers, aided by the umpire's ruling depriving Sherdel of striking him out on a "quick-pitch," as Hoyt wins for the second time.
STL	N	3 11 0	**Sherdel** (6.1), Alexander (2.2)		

Team Totals

		W	AB	H	2B	3B	HR	R	RBI	BA	BB	SO	ERA
NY	A	4	134	37	7	0	9	27	25	.276	13	12	2.00
STL	N	0	131	27	5	1	1	10	8	.206	11	29	6.09

Individual Batting

NEW YORK (A.L.)

	AB	H	2B	3B	HR	R	RBI	BA
M. Koenig, ss	19	3	0	0	0	1	0	.158
B. Ruth, of	16	10	3	0	3	9	4	.625
B. Meusel, of	15	3	1	0	1	5	3	.200
B. Bengough, c	13	3	0	0	0	1	1	.231
T. Lazzeri, 2b	12	3	1	0	0	2	0	.250
L. Gehrig, 1b	11	6	1	0	4	5	9	.545
B. Paschal, of	10	2	0	0	0	0	1	.200
C. Durst, of	8	3	0	0	1	3	2	.375
G. Robertson, 3b	8	1	0	0	0	1	2	.125
W. Hoyt, p	7	1	0	0	0	0	0	.143
J. Dugan, 3b	6	1	0	0	0	0	1	.167
T. Zachary, p	4	0	0	0	0	0	0	.000
L. Durocher, 2b	2	0	0	0	0	0	0	.000
G. Pipgras, p	2	0	0	0	0	0	1	.000
P. Collins, c	1	1	1	0	0	0	0	1.000
E. Combs	0	0	0	0	0	0	1	–

Errors: M. Koenig (2), T. Lazzeri (2), W. Hoyt, G. Robertson
Stolen bases: T. Lazzeri (2), B. Meusel (2)

ST. LOUIS (N.L.)

	AB	H	2B	3B	HR	R	RBI	BA
A. High, 3b	17	5	2	0	0	1	1	.294
C. Hafey, of	15	3	0	0	0	0	0	.200
J. Bottomley, 1b	14	3	0	1	1	1	3	.214
F. Frisch, 2b	13	3	0	0	0	1	1	.231
R. Maranville, ss	13	4	1	0	0	2	0	.308
T. Douthit, of	11	1	0	0	0	1	0	.091
J. Wilson, c	11	1	1	0	0	1	1	.091
G. Harper, of	9	1	0	0	0	0	0	.111
E. Orsatti, of	7	2	1	0	0	1	0	.286
W. Holm, of	6	1	0	0	0	0	1	.167
B. Sherdel, p	5	0	0	0	0	0	0	.000
E. Smith, c	4	3	0	0	0	0	0	.750
J. Haines, p	2	0	0	0	0	0	0	.000
C. Mitchell, p	2	0	0	0	0	0	0	.000
G. Alexander, p	1	0	0	0	0	0	1	.000
R. Blades	1	0	0	0	0	0	0	.000
P. Martin	0	0	0	0	0	1	0	–
T. Thevenow, ss	0	0	0	0	0	0	0	–

Errors: J. Wilson (2), C. Hafey, R. Maranville, C. Mitchell
Stolen bases: F. Frisch (2), R. Maranville

Individual Pitching

NEW YORK (A.L.)

	W	L	ERA	IP	H	BB	SO	SV
W. Hoyt	2	0	1.50	18	14	6	14	0
G. Pipgras	1	0	2.00	9	4	4	8	0
T. Zachary	1	0	3.00	9	9	1	7	0

ST. LOUIS (N.L.)

	W	L	ERA	IP	H	BB	SO	SV
B. Sherdel	0	2	4.73	13.1	15	3	3	0
J. Haines	0	1	4.50	6	6	3	3	0
G. Alexander	0	1	19.80	5	10	4	2	0
C. Mitchell	0	0	1.59	5.2	2	2	2	0
S. Johnson	0	0	4.50	2	4	1	1	0
F. Rhem	0	0	0.00	2	0	0	1	0

	R	H	E	PITCHERS (inn. pit.)	HOME RUNS (men on)	HIGHLIGHTS

Philadelphia (A.L.) defeats St. Louis (N.L.) 4 games to 2

GAME 1 - OCTOBER 1

STL N 2 9 0 Grimes (8)
PHI A 5 5 0 Grove (9) — Simmons, Cochrane — The Athletics get only five hits in five different innings off Grimes but all are for extra bases and each produces a run.

GAME 2 - OCTOBER 2

STL N 1 6 2 Rhem (3.1), Lindsey (2.2), Johnson (2) — Watkins
PHI A 6 7 2 Earnshaw (9) — Cochrane — The Athletics score six runs off Rhem in the first four innings to win easily as Earnshaw walks one and strikes out eight.

GAME 3 - OCTOBER 4

PHI A 0 7 0 Walberg (4.2), Shores (1.1), Quinn (2)
STL N 5 10 0 Hallahan (9) — Douthit — Hallahan has an easy shutout after escaping from a first inning jam by striking out Dykes, Simmons, and Miller.

GAME 4 - OCTOBER 5

PHI A 1 4 1 Grove (8)
STL N 3 5 1 Haines (9) — Dykes' error allows the Cardinals to score twice in the fourth and win the game as Haines doesn't allow a hit for the last six innings.

GAME 5 - OCTOBER 6

PHI A 2 5 0 Earnshaw (7), **Grove** (2) — Foxx (1 on)
STL N 0 3 1 Grimes (9) — Foxx's homer wins for the Athletics in the ninth as Earnshaw and Grove prevent any Cardinal runners from reaching third base.

GAME 6 - OCTOBER 8

STL N 1 5 1 Hallahan (2), Johnson (3), Lindsey (2), Bell (1)
PHI A 7 7 0 Earnshaw (9) — Simmons, Dykes (1 on) — Once again the Athletics get only extra base hits and turn each one into a run as Earnshaw, with only one day's rest, pitches a strong five-hitter.

Team Totals

		W	AB	H	2B	3B	HR	R	RBI	BA	BB	SO	ERA
PHI	A	4	178	35	10	2	6	21	20	.197	24	32	1.73
STL	N	2	190	38	10	1	2	12	11	.200	11	33	3.35

Individual Batting

PHILADELPHIA (A.L.)

	AB	H	2B	3B	HR	R	RBI	BA
A. Simmons, of	22	8	2	0	2	4	4	.364
J. Boley, ss	21	2	0	0	0	1	1	.095
J. Foxx, 1b	21	7	2	1	1	3	3	.333
B. Miller, of	21	3	2	0	0	0	3	.143
M. Bishop, 2b	18	4	0	0	0	5	0	.222
M. Cochrane, c	18	4	1	0	2	5	3	.222
J. Dykes, 3b	18	4	3	0	1	2	5	.222
M. Haas, of	18	2	0	1	0	1	1	.111
G. Earnshaw, p	9	0	0	0	0	0	0	.000
L. Grove, p	6	0	0	0	0	0	0	.000
J. Moore, of	3	1	0	0	0	0	0	.333
R. Walberg, p	2	0	0	0	0	0	0	.000
E. McNair	1	0	0	0	0	0	0	.000

Errors: J. Boley, M. Cochrane, J. Dykes

ST. LOUIS (N.L.)

	AB	H	2B	3B	HR	R	RBI	BA
T. Douthit, of	24	2	0	0	1	0	2	.083
F. Frisch, 2b	24	5	2	0	0	0	0	.208
J. Bottomley, 1b	22	1	1	0	0	1	0	.045
C. Hafey, of	22	6	5	0	0	2	2	.273
S. Adams, 3b	21	3	0	0	0	0	1	.143
C. Gelbert, ss	17	6	0	1	0	2	2	.353
J. Wilson, c	15	4	1	0	0	0	2	.267
G. Watkins, of	12	2	0	0	1	2	1	.167
R. Blades, of	9	1	0	0	0	2	0	.111
G. Mancuso, c	7	2	0	0	0	1	0	.286
B. Grimes, p	5	2	0	0	0	0	0	.400
S. Fisher	2	1	1	0	0	0	0	.500
J. Haines, p	2	1	0	0	0	0	1	.500
B. Hallahan, p	2	0	0	0	0	0	0	.000
A. High, 3b	2	1	0	0	0	1	0	.500
J. Lindsey, p	1	1	0	0	0	0	0	1.000
E. Orsatti	1	0	0	0	0	0	0	.000
G. Puccinelli	1	0	0	0	0	0	0	.000
F. Rhem, p	1	0	0	0	0	0	0	.000

Errors: F. Frisch (3), F. Rhem, G. Watkins
Stolen bases: F. Frisch

Individual Pitching

PHILADELPHIA (A.L.)

	W	L	ERA	IP	H	BB	SO	SV
G. Earnshaw	2	0	0.72	25	13	7	19	0
L. Grove	2	1	1.42	19	15	3	10	0
R. Walberg	0	1	3.86	4.2	4	1	3	0
J. Quinn	0	0	4.50	2	3	0	1	0
B. Shores	0	0	13.50	1.1	3	0	0	0

ST. LOUIS (N.L.)

	W	L	ERA	IP	H	BB	SO	SV
B. Grimes	0	2	3.71	17	10	6	13	0
B. Hallahan	1	1	1.64	11	9	8	8	0
J. Haines	1	0	1.00	9	4	4	2	0
S. Johnson	0	0	7.20	5	4	3	4	0
J. Lindsey	0	0	1.93	4.2	4	1	1	2
F. Rhem	0	1	10.80	3.1	7	2	3	0
H. Bell	0	0	0.00	1	0	0	0	0

		R	H	E	PITCHERS (inn. pit.)	HOME RUNS (men on)	HIGHLIGHTS

St. Louis (N.L.) defeats Philadelphia (A.L.) 4 games to 3

GAME 1 - OCTOBER 1

PHI A 6 11 0 **Grove (9)**

STL N 2 12 0 **Derringer (7), Johnson (2)**   Simmons (1 on)   The Cardinals score twice in the first but the Athletics come back to score four in the third, capped by Foxx's two-run single.

GAME 2 - OCTOBER 2

PHI A 0 3 0 **Earnshaw (8)**

STL N 2 6 1 **Hallahan (9)**   Pepper Martin, with two hits and two stolen bases, scores both Cardinal runs to support Hallahan's shutout pitching.

GAME 3 - OCTOBER 5

STL N 5 12 0 **Grimes (9)**

PHI A 2 2 0 **Grove (8), Mahaffey (1)**   Simmons (1 on)   Grimes supports his two-hitter with a two-run single in the fourth.

GAME 4 - OCTOBER 6

STL N 0 2 1 **Johnson (5.2), Lindsey (1.1), Derringer (1)**   Simmons doubles home Bishop in the first to give Earnshaw the only run he needs as Martin gets the only two Cardinal hits.

PHI A 3 10 0 **Earnshaw (9)**   Foxx

GAME 5 - OCTOBER 7

STL N 5 12 0 **Hallahan (9)**   Martin (1 on)   Martin, with three hits and a long fly, bats in four runs to lead the Cardinal attack.

PHI A 1 9 0 **Hoyt (6), Walberg (2), Rommel (1)**

GAME 6 - OCTOBER 9

PHI A 8 8 1 **Grove (9)**   The Athletics break a scoreless tie with four runs in the fifth on two singles, four walks and an error.

STL N 1 5 2 **Derringer (4.2), Johnson (1.1), Lindsey (2), Rhem (1)**

GAME 7 - OCTOBER 10

PHI A 2 7 1 **Earnshaw (7), Walberg (1)**   Watkins (1 on)   Watkins' two-run homer in the third gives the Cardinals a 4-0 lead and enables them to withstand a two-run Athletics rally in the ninth as Grimes tires.

STL N 4 5 0 **Grimes (8.2), Hallahan (0.1) SV**

Team Totals

		W	AB	H	2B	3B	HR	R	RBI	BA	BB	SO	ERA
STL	N	4	229	54	11	0	2	19	17	.236	9	41	2.32
PHI	A	3	227	50	5	0	3	22	20	.220	28	46	2.66

Individual Batting

ST. LOUIS (N.L.)

	AB	H	2B	3B	HR	R	RBI	BA
F. Frisch, 2b	27	7	2	0	0	2	1	.259
J. Bottomley, 1b	25	4	1	0	0	2	2	.160
C. Hafey, of	24	4	0	0	0	1	0	.167
P. Martin, of	24	12	4	0	1	5	5	.500
C. Gelbert, ss	23	6	1	0	0	0	3	.261
J. Wilson, c	23	5	0	0	0	0	2	.217
A. High, 3b	15	4	0	0	0	3	0	.267
W. Roettger, of	14	4	1	0	0	1	0	.286
G. Watkins, of	14	4	1	0	1	4	2	.286
J. Flowers, 3b	11	1	1	0	0	1	0	.091
B. Grimes, p	7	2	0	0	0	0	2	.286
B. Hallahan, p	6	0	0	0	0	0	0	.000
S. Adams, 3b	4	1	0	0	0	0	0	.250
E. Orsatti, of	3	0	0	0	0	0	0	.000
R. Blades	2	0	0	0	0	0	0	.000
R. Collins	2	0	0	0	0	0	0	.000
P. Derringer, p	2	0	0	0	0	0	0	.000
S. Johnson, p	2	0	0	0	0	0	0	.000
G. Mancuso, c	1	0	0	0	0	0	0	.000

Errors: J. Bottomley, J. Flowers, C. Hafey, J. Wilson

Stolen bases: P. Martin (5), F. Frisch, C. Hafey, G. Watkins

PHILADELPHIA (A.L.)

	AB	H	2B	3B	HR	R	RBI	BA
M. Bishop, 2b	27	4	0	0	0	4	0	.148
A. Simmons, of	27	9	2	0	2	4	8	.333
B. Miller, of	26	7	1	0	0	3	1	.269
M. Cochrane, c	25	4	0	0	0	2	1	.160
D. Williams, ss	25	8	1	0	0	2	1	.320
J. Foxx, 1b	23	8	0	0	1	3	3	.348
M. Haas, of	23	3	1	0	0	1	2	.130
J. Dykes, 3b	22	5	0	0	0	2	2	.227
L. Grove, p	10	0	0	0	0	0	0	.000
G. Earnshaw, p	8	0	0	0	0	0	0	.000
J. Moore, of	3	1	0	0	0	0	0	.333
D. Cramer	2	1	0	0	0	0	2	.500
W. Hoyt, p	2	0	0	0	0	0	0	.000
E. McNair, 2b	2	0	0	0	0	1	0	.000
J. Boley	1	0	0	0	0	0	0	.000
J. Heving	1	0	0	0	0	0	0	.000
P. Todt	0	0	0	0	0	0	0	—

Errors: M. Cochrane, J. Foxx

Individual Pitching

ST. LOUIS (N.L.)

	W	L	ERA	IP	H	BB	SO	SV
B. Hallahan	2	0	0.49	18.1	12	8	12	1
B. Grimes	2	0	2.04	17.2	9	9	11	0
P. Derringer	0	2	4.26	12.2	14	7	14	0
S. Johnson	0	1	3.00	9	10	1	6	0
J. Lindsey	0	0	5.40	3.1	4	3	2	0
F. Rhem	0	0	0.00	1	1	0	1	0

PHILADELPHIA (A.L.)

	W	L	ERA	IP	H	BB	SO	SV
L. Grove	2	1	2.42	26	28	2	16	0
G. Earnshaw	1	2	1.88	24	12	4	20	0
W. Hoyt	0	1	4.50	6	7	0	1	0
R. Walberg	0	0	3.00	3	3	2	4	0
R. Mahaffey	0	0	9.00	1	1	1	0	0
E. Rommel	0	0	9.00	1	3	0	0	0

R H E	PITCHERS (inn. pit.)	HOME RUNS (men on)	HIGHLIGHTS

St. Louis (N.L.) defeats Detroit (A.L.) 4 games to 3

GAME 1 - OCTOBER 3

STL N 8 13 2 **D. Dean** (9) — Medwick / Greenberg — The Cardinals capitalize on five errors by the Tigers' infield as Medwick leads the attack with four hits.
DET A 3 8 5 **Crowder** (5), Marberry (0.2), Hogsett (3.1)

GAME 2 - OCTOBER 4

STL N 2 7 3 Hallahan (8.1), **B. Walker** — Gee Walker, given a chance when Collins and Delancey fail to catch his pop foul, singles in the tieing run for the Tigers in the ninth. They go on to win in the twelfth when Goslin singles following walks to Gehringer and Greenberg.
DET A 3 7 0 **Rowe** (12)

GAME 3 - OCTOBER 5

DET A 1 8 2 **Bridges** (4), Hogsett (4) — The Tigers leave 13 men on base as Martin's double and triple, and the two runs he scores leads the Cardinals.
STL N 4 9 1 **P. Dean** (9)

GAME 4 - OCTOBER 6

DET A 10 13 1 **Auker** (9) — Led by Greenberg's four hits, good for three RBI's, and Rogell's four RBI's, the Tigers even the Series.
STL N 4 10 5 Carleton (2.2), Vance (1.1), **B. Walker** (3.1), Haines (0.2), Mooney (1)

GAME 5 - OCTOBER 7

DET A 3 7 0 **Bridges** (9) — Gehringer / Delancey — Bridges returns after a day's rest and subdues the Cardinals behind Gehringer's game-deciding homer in the sixth.
STL N 1 7 1 **D. Dean** (8), Carleton (1)

GAME 6 - OCTOBER 8

STL N 4 10 2 **P. Dean** (9) — Paul Dean aids his own cause with a single in the seventh that sends in what proves to be the winning run.
DET A 3 7 1 **Rowe** (9)

GAME 7 - OCTOBER 9

STL N 11 17 1 **D. Dean** (9) — The Cardinals easily win the Series on a seven-run third-inning barrage which features Frisch's three-run double
DET A 0 6 3 **Auker** (2.1), Rowe (0.1), Hogsett (0), Bridges (4.1), Marberry (1), Crowder (1)

Team Totals

		W	AB	H	2B	3B	HR	R	RBI	BA	BB	SO	ERA
STL	N	4	262	73	14	5	2	34	32	.279	11	31	2.34
DET	A	3	250	56	12	1	2	23	20	.224	25	43	3.74

Individual Batting

ST. LOUIS (N.L.)

	AB	H	2B	3B	HR	R	RBI	BA
F. Frisch, 2b	31	6	1	0	0	2	4	.194
P. Martin, 3b	31	11	3	1	0	8	3	.355
R. Collins, 1b	30	11	1	0	0	4	4	.367
J. Rothrock, of	30	7	3	1	0	3	6	.233
B. DeLancey, c	29	5	3	0	1	3	4	.172
J. Medwick, of	29	11	0	1	1	4	5	.379
L. Durocher, ss	27	7	1	1	0	4	0	.259
E. Orsatti, of	22	7	0	1	0	3	2	.318
D. Dean, p	12	3	2	0	0	3	1	.250
P. Dean, p	6	1	0	0	0	0	2	.167
C. Fullis, of	5	2	0	0	0	0	0	.400
B. Hallahan, p	3	0	0	0	0	0	0	.000
P. Crawford	2	0	0	0	0	0	0	.000
S. Davis	2	2	0	0	0	0	1	1.000
B. Walker, p	2	0	0	0	0	0	0	.000
T. Carleton, p	1	0	0	0	0	0	0	.000
B. Whitehead, ss	0	0	0	0	0	0	0	

Errors: P. Martin (4), F. Frisch (2), E. Orsatti (2), R. Collins, P. Dean, B. DeLancey, C. Fullis, B. Hallahan, J. Rothrock, B. Walker
Stolen bases: P. Martin (2)

DETROIT (A.L.)

	AB	H	2B	3B	HR	R	RBI	BA
C. Gehringer, 2b	29	11	1	0	1	5	2	.379
G. Goslin, of	29	7	1	0	0	2	2	.241
M. Owen, 3b	29	2	0	0	0	0	1	.069
B. Rogell, ss	29	8	1	0	0	3	4	.276
M. Cochrane, c	28	6	1	0	0	2	1	.214
P. Fox, of	28	8	6	0	0	1	2	.286
H. Greenberg, 1b	28	9	2	1	1	4	7	.321
J. White, of	23	3	0	0	0	6	0	.130
T. Bridges, p	7	1	0	0	0	0	0	.143
S. Rowe, p	7	0	0	0	0	0	0	.000
E. Auker, p	4	0	0	0	0	0	0	.000
C. Hogsett, p	3	0	0	0	0	0	0	.000
G. Walker	3	1	0	0	0	0	1	.333
F. Doljack, of	2	0	0	0	0	0	0	.000
G. Crowder, p	1	0	0	0	0	0	0	.000
R. Hayworth, c	0	0	0	0	0	0	0	

Errors: C. Gehringer (3), B. Rogell (3), G. Goslin (2), M. Owen (2), H. Greenberg, J. White
Stolen bases: C. Gehringer, H. Greenberg, M. Owen, J. White

Individual Pitching

ST. LOUIS (N.L.)

	W	L	ERA	IP	H	BB	SO	SV
D. Dean	2	1	1.73	26	20	5	17	0
P. Dean	2	0	1.00	18	15	7	11	0
B. Hallahan	0	0	2.16	8.1	6	4	6	0
B. Walker	0	0	7.11	6.1	6	6	2	0
T. Carleton	0	0	7.36	3.2	5	2	2	0
J. Mooney	0	0	0.00	1	1	0	0	0
D. Vance	0	0	0.00	1.1	2	1	3	0
J. Haines	0	0	0.00	0.2	1	0	2	0

DETROIT (A.L.)

	W	L	ERA	IP	H	BB	SO	SV
S. Rowe	1	1	2.95	21.1	19	0	12	0
T. Bridges	1	1	3.63	17.1	21	1	12	0
E. Auker	1	1	5.56	11.1	16	5	2	0
C. Hogsett	0	0	1.23	7.1	6	3	3	0
G. Crowder	0	1	1.50	6	6	1	2	0
F. Marberry	0	0	21.60	1.2	5	1	0	0

	R H E	PITCHERS (inn. pit.)	HOME RUNS (men on)	HIGHLIGHTS

St. Louis (N.L.) defeats New York (A.L.) 4 games to 1

GAME 1 - SEPTEMBER 30

		R H E	PITCHERS	HOME RUNS	
NY	A	7 11 0	**Ruffing** (8.2), Chandler (0.1) **SV**		The Yankees make an early lead stand up, but four in the ninth by the Cardinals flash an omen of things to come. Ruffing does not allow a hit until there are two out in the eighth and becomes the first pitcher to win seven World Series games.
STL	N	4 7 4	M. Cooper (7.2), Gumbert (0.1) Lanier (1)		

GAME 2 - OCTOBER 1

		R H E		HOME RUNS	
NY	A	3 10 2	Bonham (8)	, Keller (1 on)	A two-run homer by Keller ties the score in the eighth, but the Cardinals eke out a win in the home half when Slaughter doubles and Musial singles. Slaughter then saves the day with a great throw to choke Stainback at third in the ninth.
STL	N	4 6 0	**Beazley** (9)		

GAME 3 - OCTOBER 3

		R H E			
STL	N	2 5 1	**White** (9)		The Yankees are blanked for the first time since 1926 when White holds New York to six singles in the game without an extra-base hit. The runs score on Brown's infield out in the third and Slaughter's single in the ninth.
NY	A	0 6 1	**Chandler** (8), Breuer (0), Turner (1)		

GAME 4 - OCTOBER 4

		R H E		HOME RUNS	
STL	N	9 12 1	M. Cooper (5.1), Gumbert (0.1), Pollet (0.1), **Lanier** (3)		The score stands at 6-6, when the Cardinals erupt in the seventh and win. Walker Cooper's single scores Slaughter, and Marion hits a long fly, scoring Musial after the catch.
NY	A	6 10 1	Borowy (3), **Donald** (3), Bonham (3)	Keller (2 on)	

GAME 5 - OCTOBER 5

		R H E		HOME RUNS	
STL	N	4 9 4	**Beazley** (9)	Slaughter, Kurowski (1 on) Rizzuto	A thriller is tied in the ninth, 2-2, when Kurowski homers scoring Walker Cooper ahead of him.
NY	A	2 7 1	**Ruffing** (9)		

Team Totals

		W	AB	H	2B	3B	HR	R	RBI	BA	BB	SO	ERA
STL	N	4	163	39	4	2	2	23	23	.239	17	19	2.60
NY	A	1	178	44	6	0	3	18	14	.247	8	22	4.50

Individual Batting

ST. LOUIS (N.L.)

	AB	H	2B	3B	HR	R	RBI	BA
W. Cooper, c	21	6	1	0	0	3	4	.286
J. Brown, 2b	20	6	0	0	0	2	1	.300
E. Slaughter, of	19	5	1	0	1	3	2	.263
M. Marion, ss	18	2	0	1	0	2	3	.111
S. Musial, of	18	4	1	0	0	2	2	.222
J. Hopp, 1b	17	3	0	0	0	0	0	.176
T. Moore, of	17	5	1	0	0	2	0	.294
W. Kurowski, 3b	15	4	0	1	1	3	5	.267
J. Beazley, p	7	1	0	0	0	0	0	.143
M. Cooper, p	5	1	0	0	0	1	2	.200
E. White, p	2	0	0	0	0	0	0	.000
M. Lanier, p	1	1	0	0	0	0	1	1.000
K. O'Dea	1	1	0	0	0	0	1	1.000
R. Sanders	1	0	0	0	0	1	0	.000
H. Walker	1	0	0	0	0	0	0	.000
C. Crespi	0	0	0	0	0	1	0	

Errors: J. Brown (3), M. Lanier (2), J. Beazley, W. Cooper, J. Hopp, W. Kurowski, E. Slaughter

NEW YORK (A.L.)

	AB	H	2B	3B	HR	R	RBI	BA
J. DiMaggio, of	21	7	0	0	0	3	3	.333
J. Gordon, 2b	21	2	1	0	0	1	0	.095
P. Rizzuto, ss	21	8	0	0	1	2	1	.381
C. Keller, of	20	4	0	0	2	2	5	.200
R. Cullenbine, of	19	5	1	0	0	3	2	.263
B. Dickey, c	19	5	0	0	0	1	0	.263
R. Rolfe, 3b	17	6	2	0	0	5	0	.353
G. Priddy, 1b, 3b	10	1	1	0	0	0	1	.100
B. Hassett, 1b	9	3	1	0	0	1	2	.333
R. Ruffing, p	9	2	0	0	0	0	0	.222
F. Crosetti, 3b	3	0	0	0	0	0	0	.000
E. Bonham, p	2	0	0	0	0	0	0	.000
S. Chandler, p	2	0	0	0	0	0	0	.000
A. Donald, p	2	0	0	0	0	0	0	.000
H. Borowy, p	1	0	0	0	0	0	0	.000
B. Rosar	1	1	0	0	0	0	0	1.000
G. Selkirk	1	0	0	0	0	0	0	.000
T. Stainback	0	0	0	0	0	0	0	—

Errors: M. Breuer, B. Dickey, B. Hassett, G. Priddy, P. Rizzuto
Stolen bases: P. Rizzuto (2), R. Cullenbine

Individual Pitching

ST. LOUIS (N.L.)

	W	L	ERA	IP	H	BB	SO	SV
J. Beazley	2	0	2.50	18	17	3	6	0
M. Cooper	0	1	5.54	13	17	4	9	0
E. White	1	0	0.00	9	6	0	6	0
M. Lanier	1	0	0.00	4	3	1	1	0
H. Gumbert	0	0	0.00	0.2	1	0	0	0
H. Pollet	0	0	0.00	0.1	0	0	0	0

NEW YORK (A.L.)

	W	L	ERA	IP	H	BB	SO	SV
R. Ruffing	1	1	4.08	17.2	14	7	11	0
E. Bonham	0	1	4.09	11	9	3	3	0
S. Chandler	0	1	1.08	8.1	5	1	3	1
H. Borowy	0	0	18.00	3	6	3	1	0
A. Donald	0	1	6.00	3	2	1	0	0
J. Turner	0	0	0.00	1	0	1	0	0
M. Breuer	0	0	—	0.0	2	0	0	0

R	H	E	PITCHERS (inn. pit.)	HOME RUNS (men on)	HIGHLIGHTS

New York (A.L.) defeats St. Louis (N.L.) 4 games to 1

GAME 1 - OCTOBER 5

		R	H	E	PITCHERS	HOME RUNS	HIGHLIGHTS
STL	N	2	7	2	**Lanier** (7), Brecheen (1)	Gordon	The Yankees break a 2-2 tie in the sixth with two runs on singles by Crosetti, Johnson and Dickey and a wild pitch by Lanier.
NY	A	4	8	2	**Chandler** (9)		

GAME 2 - OCTOBER 6

		R	H	E	PITCHERS	HOME RUNS	HIGHLIGHTS
STL	N	4	7	2	**M. Cooper** (9)	Marion, Sanders(1 on)	The Cardinals win in the fourth on singles by Musial and Kurowski and a home run by Sanders.
NY	A	3	6	0	**Bonham** (8), Murphy (1)		

GAME 3 - OCTOBER 7

		R	H	E	PITCHERS	HOME RUNS	HIGHLIGHTS
STL	N	2	6	4	**Brazle** (7.1), Krist (0), Brecheen (0.2)		The Yankees erase a 2-1 deficit with five runs in the eighth as Johnson drives in three with a bases loaded triple.
NY	A	6	8	0	**Borowy** (8), Murphy (1) **SV**		

GAME 4 - OCTOBER 10

		R	H	E	PITCHERS	HOME RUNS	HIGHLIGHTS
NY	A	2	6	2	**Russo** (9)		Russo allows one unearned run and scores the winning run in the eighth on his double and a long fly by Crosetti.
STL	N	1	7	1	Lanier (7), **Brecheen** (2)		

GAME 5 - OCTOBER 11

		R	H	E	PITCHERS	HOME RUNS	HIGHLIGHTS
NY	A	2	7	1	**Chandler** (9)	Dickey (1 on)	Dickey's homer following Keller's single in the sixth accounts for the only runs as the Cardinals leave 11 men on base.
STL	N	0	10	1	**M. Cooper** (7), Lanier (1.1), Dickson (0.2)		

Team Totals

		W	AB	H	2B	3B	HR	R	RBI	BA	BB	SO	ERA
NY	A	4	159	35	5	2	2	17	14	.220	12	30	1.40
STL	N	1	165	37	5	0	2	9	8	.224	11	26	2.51

Individual Batting

NEW YORK (A.L.)

	AB	H	2B	3B	HR	R	RBI	BA
B. Johnson, 3b	20	6	1	1	0	3	3	.300
N. Etten, 1b	19	2	0	0	0	0	2	.105
F. Crosetti, ss	18	5	0	0	0	4	1	.278
B. Dickey, c	18	5	0	0	1	1	4	.278
C. Keller, of	18	4	0	1	0	3	2	.222
J. Gordon, 2b	17	4	1	0	1	2	2	.235
T. Stainback, of	17	3	0	0	0	0	0	.176
J. Lindell, of	9	1	0	0	0	1	0	.111
B. Metheny, of	8	1	0	0	0	0	0	.125
S. Chandler, p	6	1	0	0	0	0	0	.167
M. Russo, p	3	2	2	0	0	1	0	.667
E. Bonham, p	2	0	0	0	0	0	0	.000
H. Borowy, p	2	1	1	0	0	1	0	.500
S. Stirnweiss	1	0	0	0	0	1	0	.000
R. Weatherly	1	0	0	0	0	0	0	.000

Errors: F. Crosetti (3), N. Etten, B. Johnson
Stolen bases: F. Crosetti, C. Keller

ST. LOUIS (N.L.)

	AB	H	2B	3B	HR	R	RBI	BA
L. Klein, 2b	22	3	0	0	0	0	0	.136
W. Kurowski, 3b	18	4	1	0	0	2	1	.222
S. Musial, of	18	5	0	0	0	2	0	.278
H. Walker, of	18	3	1	0	0	0	0	.167
W. Cooper, c	17	5	0	0	0	1	0	.294
R. Sanders, 1b	17	5	0	1	3	2		.294
D. Litwhiler, of	15	4	1	0	0	0	2	.267
M. Marion, ss	14	5	2	0	1	1	2	.357
M. Cooper, p	5	0	0	0	0	0	0	.000
D. Garms, of	5	0	0	0	0	0	0	.000
J. Hopp, of	4	0	0	0	0	0	0	.000
M. Lanier, p	4	1	0	0	0	0	1	.250
A. Brazle, p	3	0	0	0	0	0	0	.000
K. O'Dea, c	3	2	0	0	0	0	0	.667
F. Demaree	1	0	0	0	0	0	0	.000
S. Narron	1	0	0	0	0	0	0	.000
E. White	0	0	0	0	0	0	0	–

Errors: W. Cooper (2), L. Klein (2), W. Kurowski (2), H. Walker (2), M. Lanier, M. Marion
Stolen bases: M. Marion

Individual Pitching

NEW YORK (A.L.)

	W	L	ERA	IP	H	BB	SO	SV
S. Chandler	2	0	0.50	18	17	3	10	0
M. Russo	1	0	0.00	9	7	1	2	0
E. Bonham	0	1	4.50	8	6	3	9	0
H. Borowy	1	0	2.25	8	6	3	4	0
J. Murphy	0	0	0.00	2	1	1	1	1

ST. LOUIS (N.L.)

	W	L	ERA	IP	H	BB	SO	SV
M. Cooper	1	1	2.81	16	11	3	10	0
M. Lanier	0	1	1.76	15.1	13	3	13	0
A. Brazle	0	1	3.68	7.1	5	2	4	0
H. Brecheen	0	1	2.45	3.2	5	3	3	0
M. Dickson	0	0	0.00	0.2	0	1	0	0
H. Krist	0	0	–	0.0	1	0	0	0

		R	H	E	PITCHERS (inn. pit.)	HOME RUNS (men on)	HIGHLIGHTS

St. Louis (N.L.) defeats St. Louis (A.L.) 4 games to 2

GAME 1 - OCTOBER 4

		R	H	E	PITCHERS	HOME RUNS	HIGHLIGHTS
STL	A	2	2	0	Galehouse (9)	McQuinn (1 on)	Cooper loses a two-hitter when Moore
STL	N	1	7	0	M. Cooper (7), Donnelly (2)		singles and McQuinn homers in the fourth.

GAME 2 - OCTOBER 5

		R	H	E	PITCHERS		HIGHLIGHTS
STL	A	2	7	4	Potter (6), Muncrief (4.1)		Donnelly strikes out seven and allows
STL	N	3	7	0	Lanier (7), Donnelly (4)		only three balls to be hit out of the infield in four innings as the Cardinals win in the eleventh on O'Dea's pinch-hit single with two on.

GAME 3 - OCTOBER 6

		R	H	E	PITCHERS		HIGHLIGHTS
STL	N	2	7	0	Wilks (2.2), Schmidt (3.1), Jurisich (0.2), Byerly (1.1)		The Browns score four runs on five hits after two are out in the third.
STL	A	6	8	2	Kramer (9)		

GAME 4 - OCTOBER 7

		R	H	E	PITCHERS	HOME RUNS	HIGHLIGHTS
STL	N	5	12	0	Brecheen (9)	Musial (1 on)	Musial's three hits pace the Cardinals to
STL	A	1	9	1	Jakucki (3), Hollingsworth (4), Shirley (2)		a 5-0 lead as the Brown's only rally is stopped in the eighth by a spectacular double play started by Marion.

GAME 5 - OCTOBER 8

		R	H	E	PITCHERS	HOME RUNS	HIGHLIGHTS
STL	N	2	6	1	M. Cooper (9)	Sanders, Litwhiler	Homers by Sanders and Litwhiler decide
STL	A	0	7	1	Galehouse (9)		a pitching duel as Cooper strikes out 12 and Galehouse 10.

GAME 6 - OCTOBER 9

		R	H	E	PITCHERS		HIGHLIGHTS
STL	A	1	3	2	Potter (3.2), Muncrief (2.1), Kramer (2)		Wilks enters the game in the sixth, with one out and men on second and third, and
STL	N	3	10	0	Lanier (5.1), Wilks (3.2) **SV**		retires the last 11 batters in a row to preserve the 3-1 margin.

Team Totals

		W	AB	H	2B	3B	HR	R	RBI	BA	BB	SO	ERA
STL	N	4	204	49	9	1	3	16	15	.240	19	43	1.96
STL	A	2	197	36	9	1	1	12	9	.183	23	49	1.49

Individual Batting

ST. LOUIS (N.L.)

	AB	H	2B	3B	HR	R	RBI	BA
J. Hopp, of	27	5	0	0	0	2	0	.185
W. Kurowski, 3b	23	5	1	0	0	2	1	.217
S. Musial, of	23	7	2	0	1	2	2	.304
W. Cooper, c	22	7	2	1	0	1	2	.318
M. Marion, ss	22	5	3	0	0	1	2	.227
R. Sanders, 1b	21	6	0	0	1	5	1	.286
D. Litwhiler, of	20	4	1	0	1	2	1	.200
E. Verban, 2b	17	7	0	0	0	1	2	.412
A. Bergamo, of	6	0	0	0	0	0	1	.000
H. Brecheen, p	4	0	0	0	0	0	0	.000
M. Cooper, p	4	0	0	0	0	0	0	.000
M. Lanier, p	4	2	0	0	0	0	1	.500
K. O'Dea	3	1	0	0	0	0	2	.333
G. Fallon, 2b	2	0	0	0	0	0	0	.000
D. Garms	2	0	0	0	0	0	0	.000
T. Wilks, p	2	0	0	0	0	0	0	.000
B. Donnelly, p	1	0	0	0	0	0	0	.000
F. Schmidt, p	1	0	0	0	0	0	0	.000

Errors: S. Musial

ST. LOUIS (A.L.)

	AB	H	2B	3B	HR	R	RBI	BA
M. Kreevich, of	26	6	3	0	0	0	0	.231
M. Christman, 3b	22	2	0	0	0	0	1	.091
G. Moore, of	22	4	0	0	0	4	0	.182
V. Stephens, ss	22	5	1	0	0	2	0	.227
D. Gutteridge, 2b	21	3	1	0	0	1	0	.143
R. Hayworth, c	17	2	1	0	0	1	1	.118
G. McQuinn, 1b	16	7	2	0	1	2	5	.438
C. Laabs, of	15	3	1	1	0	1	0	.200
A. Zarilla, of	10	1	0	0	0	1	1	.100
D. Galehouse, p	5	1	0	0	0	0	0	.200
J. Kramer, p	4	0	0	0	0	0	0	.000
N. Potter, p	4	0	0	0	0	0	0	.000
F. Mancuso, c	3	2	0	0	0	0	1	.667
F. Baker, 2b	2	0	0	0	0	0	0	.000
M. Byrnes	2	0	0	0	0	0	0	.000
M. Chartak	2	0	0	0	0	0	0	.000
E. Clary	1	0	0	0	0	0	0	.000
Hollingsworth, p	1	0	0	0	0	0	0	.000
B. Muncrief, p	1	0	0	0	0	0	0	.000
T. Turner	1	0	0	0	0	0	0	.000

Errors: D. Gutteridge (3), V. Stephens (3), N. Potter (2), M. Christman, R. Hayworth

Individual Pitching

ST. LOUIS (N.L.)

	W	L	ERA	IP	H	BB	SO	SV
M. Cooper	1	1	1.13	16	9	5	16	0
M. Lanier	1	0	2.19	12.1	8	8	11	0
H. Brecheen	1	0	1.00	9	9	4	4	0
B. Donnelly	1	0	0.00	6	2	1	9	0
T. Wilks	0	1	5.68	6.1	5	3	7	1
F. Schmidt	0	0	0.00	3.1	1	1	1	0
B. Byerly	0	0	0.00	1.1	0	0	1	0
A. Jurisich	0	0	27.00	0.2	2	1	0	0

ST. LOUIS (A.L.)

	W	L	ERA	IP	H	BB	SO	SV
D. Galehouse	1	1	1.50	18	13	5	15	0
J. Kramer	1	0	0.00	11	9	4	12	0
N. Potter	0	1	0.93	9.2	10	3	6	0
B. Muncrief	0	1	1.35	6.2	5	4	4	0
Hollingsworth	0	0	2.25	4	5	2	1	0
S. Jakucki	0	1	9.00	3	5	0	4	0
T. Shirley	0	0	0.00	2	2	1	1	0

	R	H	E	PITCHERS (inn. pit.)	HOME RUNS (men on)	HIGHLIGHTS

St. Louis (N.L.) defeats Boston (A.L.) 4 games to 3

GAME 1 - OCTOBER 6

		R	H	E	PITCHERS	HOME RUNS	HIGHLIGHTS
BOS	A	3	9	2	Hughson (8), **Johnson (2)**	York	The Red Sox tie the score in the ninth when a ground ball takes a freak bounce through Marion's legs, setting the stage for York, who homers in the tenth.
STL	N	2	7	0	Pollet (10)		

GAME 2 - OCTOBER 7

		R	H	E	PITCHERS	HOME RUNS	HIGHLIGHTS
BOS	A	0	4	1	**Harris (7)**, Dobson (1)		Brecheen drives in the first run of the game and allows only four singles.
STL	N	3	6	0	**Brecheen (9)**		

GAME 3 - OCTOBER 9

		R	H	E	PITCHERS	HOME RUNS	HIGHLIGHTS
STL	N	0	6	1	Dickson (7), Wilks (1)		The Red Sox break the game open in the first on York's three-run homer. Ferriss' shutout is 50th in World Series history.
BOS	A	4	8	0	**Ferriss (9)**	York (2 on)	

GAME 4 - OCTOBER 10

		R	H	E	PITCHERS	HOME RUNS	HIGHLIGHTS
STL	N	12	20	1	**Munger (9)**	Slaughter	Slaughter, Kurowski, and Garagiola each get four hits in leading the Cardinals as they tie a Series record with 20 hits.
BOS	A	3	9	4	Hughson (2), Bagby (3), Zuber (2), Brown (1), Ryba (0.2), Dreisewerd (0.1)	Doerr (1 on)	

GAME 5 - OCTOBER 11

		R	H	E	PITCHERS	HOME RUNS	HIGHLIGHTS
STL	N	3	5	1	Pollet (0.1), **Brazle (6.2)**, Beazley (1)		Higgins' double in the seventh scores DiMaggio for the deciding run of the game. Walker leads the hitters with three RBI's.
BOS	A	6	11	3	**Dobson (9)**	Culberson	

GAME 6 - OCTOBER 13

		R	H	E	PITCHERS	HOME RUNS	HIGHLIGHTS
BOS	A	1	7	0	**Harris (2.2)**, Hughson (4.1), Johnson (1)		With their backs to the wall, the Cardinals score three times in the third to break open the game and even the Series.
STL	N	4	8	0	**Brecheen (9)**		

GAME 7 - OCTOBER 15

		R	H	E	PITCHERS	HOME RUNS	HIGHLIGHTS
BOS	A	3	8	0	Ferriss (4.1), Dobson (2.2), **Klinger (0.2)**, Johnson (0.1)		Pesky hesitates throwing the ball in after Walker's hit in the eighth and Slaughter races home from first with the deciding run. Brecheen records his third victory of the Series.
STL	N	4	9	1	Dickson (7), **Brecheen (2)**		

Team Totals

		W	AB	H	2B	3B	HR	R	RBI	BA	BB	SO	ERA
STL	N	4	232	60	19	2	1	28	27	.259	19	30	2.32
BOS	A	3	233	56	7	1	4	20	18	.240	22	28	2.95

Individual Batting

ST. LOUIS (N.L.)

	AB	H	2B	3B	HR	R	RBI	BA
Schoendienst, 2b	30	7	1	0	0	3	1	.233
W. Kurowski, 3b	27	8	3	0	0	5	2	.296
T. Moore, of	27	4	0	0	0	1	2	.148
S. Musial, 1b	27	6	4	1	0	3	4	.222
E. Slaughter, of	25	8	1	1	0	5	2	.320
M. Marion, ss	24	6	2	0	0	1	4	.250
J. Garagiola, c	19	6	2	0	0	2	4	.316
H. Walker, of	17	7	2	0	0	3	6	.412
H. Brecheen, p	8	1	0	0	0	2	1	.125
D. Rice, c	6	3	1	0	0	2	0	.500
M. Dickson, p	5	2	2	0	0	1	1	.400
E. Dusak, of	4	1	1	0	0	0	0	.250
G. Munger, p	4	1	0	0	0	0	0	.250
H. Pollet, p	4	0	0	0	0	0	0	.000
A. Brazle, p	2	0	0	0	0	0	0	.000
D. Sisler	2	0	0	0	0	0	0	.000
N. Jones	1	0	0	0	0	0	0	.000

Errors: M. Marion (2), W. Kurowski, Schoendienst
Stolen bases: S. Musial, Schoendienst, E. Slaughter

BOSTON (A.L.)

	AB	H	2B	3B	HR	R	RBI	BA
J. Pesky, ss	30	7	0	0	0	2	0	.233
D. DiMaggio, of	27	7	3	0	0	2	3	.259
T. Williams, of	25	5	0	0	0	2	1	.200
P. Higgins, 3b	24	5	1	0	0	1	2	.208
R. York, 1b	23	6	1	1	2	6	5	.261
B. Doerr, 2b	22	9	1	0	1	1	3	.409
H. Wagner, c	13	0	0	0	0	0	0	.000
T. McBride, of	12	2	0	0	0	0	1	.167
W. Moses, of	12	5	0	0	0	1	0	.417
R. Partee, c	10	1	0	0	0	1	0	.100
L. Culberson, of	9	2	0	0	1	1	1	.222
B. Ferriss, p	6	0	0	0	0	0	0	.000
D. Gutteridge, 2b	5	2	0	0	0	1	1	.400
J. Dobson, p	3	0	0	0	0	0	0	.000
M. Harris, p	3	1	0	0	0	0	0	.333
T. Hughson, p	3	1	0	0	0	1	0	.333
C. Metkovich	2	1	1	0	0	1	0	.500
R. Russell, 3b	2	2	0	0	0	1	0	1.000
J. Bagby, p	1	0	0	0	0	0	0	.000
E. Johnson, p	1	0	0	0	0	0	0	.000
P. Campbell	0	0	0	0	0	0	0	—

Errors: J. Pesky (4), P. Higgins (2), T. Hughson, T. McBride, M. Ryba, R. York
Stolen bases: L. Culberson, J. Pesky

Individual Pitching

ST. LOUIS (N.L.)

	W	L	ERA	IP	H	BB	SO	SV
H. Brecheen	3	0	0.45	20	14	5	11	0
M. Dickson	0	1	3.86	14	11	4	7	0
H. Pollet	0	1	3.48	10.1	12	4	3	0
G. Munger	1	0	1.00	9	9	3	2	0
A. Brazle	0	1	5.40	6.2	7	6	4	0
J. Beazley	0	0	0.00	1	1	0	1	0
T. Wilks	0	0	0.00	1	2	0	0	0

BOSTON (A.L.)

	W	L	ERA	IP	H	BB	SO	SV
T. Hughson	0	1	3.14	14.1	14	3	8	0
B. Ferriss	1	0	2.03	13.1	13	2	4	0
J. Dobson	1	0	0.00	12.2	4	3	10	0
M. Harris	0	2	3.72	9.2	11	4	5	0
J. Bagby	0	0	3.00	3	6	1	1	0
E. Johnson	1	0	2.70	3.1	1	2	1	0
B. Zuber	0	0	4.50	2	3	1	1	0
M. Brown	0	0	27.00	1	4	1	0	0
C. Dreiseverd	0	0	0.00	0.1	0	0	0	0
B. Klinger	0	1	13.50	0.2	2	1	0	0
M. Ryba	0	0	13.50	0.2	1	0	0	0

	R	H	E	PITCHERS (inn. pit.)	HOME RUNS (men on)	HIGHLIGHTS

St. Louis (N.L.) defeats New York (A.L.) 4 games to 3

GAME 1 - OCTOBER 7

		R	H	E	PITCHERS (inn. pit.)	HOME RUNS (men on)	HIGHLIGHTS
NY	A	5	12	2	Ford (5.1), Downing (1.2), Sheldon (0.2), Mikkelsen (0.1)	Tresh (1 on)	The Cardinals erase a 4-2 deficit with four runs in the sixth as Shannon homers to tie and Warwick's pinch-single and Flood's triple drive in the go-ahead runs.
STL	N	9	12	0	Sadecki (6), Schultz (3) **SV**	Shannon (1 on)	

GAME 2 - OCTOBER 8

		R	H	E	PITCHERS	HOME RUNS	HIGHLIGHTS
NY	A	8	12	0	**Stottlemyre** (9)	Linz	The Yankees break the game open with four runs in the ninth after Gibson is removed for a pinch-hitter.
STL	N	3	7	0	Gibson (8), Schultz (0.1), G. Richardson (0.1), Craig (0.1)		

GAME 3 - OCTOBER 10

		R	H	E	PITCHERS	HOME RUNS	HIGHLIGHTS
STL	N	1	6	0	Simmons (8), **Schultz** (0)		Mantle leads off the bottom of the ninth with a home run off Schultz's first pitch after Simmons is removed for a pinch-hitter.
NY	A	2	5	2	**Bouton** (9)	Mantle	

GAME 4 - OCTOBER 11

		R	H	E	PITCHERS	HOME RUNS	HIGHLIGHTS
STL	N	4	6	1	Sadecki (0.1) **Craig** (4.2) Taylor (4) **SV**	K. Boyer (3 on)	A grand-slam homer by Ken Boyer in the fifth wipes out a 3-0 Yankee lead as Craig and Taylor allow only one hit in 8.2 innings of relief pitching.
NY	A	3	6	1	**Downing** (6), Mikkelsen (1), terry (2)		

GAME 5 - OCTOBER 12

		R	H	E	PITCHERS	HOME RUNS	HIGHLIGHTS
STL	N	5	10	1	**Gibson** (10)	McCarver (2 on)	McCarver's three-run homer in the tenth wins after Tresh's two-run homer ties the game with two out in the ninth. Gibson strikes out 13.
NY	A	2	6	2	Stottlemyre (7), Reniff (0.1), **Mikkelsen** (2.2)	Tresh (1 on)	

GAME 6 - OCTOBER 14

		R	H	E	PITCHERS	HOME RUNS	HIGHLIGHTS
NY	A	8	10	0	**Bouton** (8.1), Hamilton (0.2) **SV**	Maris, Mantle, Pepitone (3 on)	Consecutive homers by Maris and Mantle give the Yankees a 3-1 lead in the sixth. Pepitone's grand slam in the eighth insures the victory.
STL	N	3	10	1	**Simmons** (6.1), Taylor (0.2), Schultz (0.2), G. Richardson (0.1), Humphreys (1)		

GAME 7 - OCTOBER 15

		R	H	E	PITCHERS	HOME RUNS	HIGHLIGHTS
NY	A	5	9	2	**Stottlemyre** (4), Downing (0), Sheldon (2), Hamilton (1.1), Mikkelsen (0.2)	Mantle (2 on), C. Boyer Linz	Gibson pitches his second complete game of the Series and strikes out nine for a Series total of 31, Richardson sets an all-time Series record with 13 hits.
STL	N	7	10	1	**Gibson** (9)	Brock, K. Boyer	

Team Totals

		W	AB	H	2B	3B	HR	R	RBI	BA	BB	SO	ERA
STL	N	4	240	61	8	3	5	32	29	.254	18	39	4.29
NY	A	3	239	60	11	0	10	33	33	.251	25	54	3.77

Individual Batting

ST. LOUIS (N.L.)

	AB	H	2B	3B	HR	R	RBI	BA
L. Brock, of	30	9	2	0	1	2	5	.300
C. Flood, of	30	6	0	1	0	5	3	.200
M. Shannon, of	28	6	0	0	1	6	2	.214
K. Boyer, 3b	27	6	1	0	2	5	6	.222
B. White, 1b	27	3	1	0	0	2	2	.111
D. Groat, ss	26	5	1	1	0	3	1	.192
T. McCarver, c	23	11	1	1	1	4	5	.478
D. Maxvill, 2b	20	4	1	0	0	0	1	.200
B. Gibson, p	9	2	0	0	0	1	0	.222
C. Simmons, p	4	2	0	0	0	1	1	.500
C. Warwick	4	3	0	0	0	2	1	.750
C. James	3	0	0	0	0	0	0	.000
B. Skinner	3	2	1	0	0	0	1	.667
R. Sadecki, p	2	1	0	0	0	0	1	.500
J. Buchek	1	1	0	0	1	0	0	1.000
R. Craig, p	1	0	0	0	0	0	0	.000
B. Schultz, p	1	0	0	0	0	0	0	.000
R. Taylor, p	1	0	0	0	0	0	0	.000
J. Javier, 2b	0	0	0	0	0	1	0	

Errors: D. Groat (2), K. Boyer, L. Brock
Stolen bases: T. McCarver, M. Shannon, B. White

NEW YORK (A.L.)

	AB	H	2B	3B	HR	R	RBI	BA
B. Richardson, 2b	32	13	2	0	0	3	3	.406
P. Linz, ss	31	7	1	0	2	5	2	.226
R. Maris, of	30	6	0	0	1	4	1	.200
J. Pepitone, 1b	26	4	1	0	1	1	5	.154
C. Boyer, 3b	24	5	1	0	1	2	3	.208
E. Howard, c	24	7	1	0	0	5	2	.292
M. Mantle, of	24	8	2	0	3	8	8	.333
T. Tresh, of	22	6	2	0	2	4	7	.273
Stottlemyre, p	8	1	0	0	0	0	0	.125
J. Bouton, p	7	1	0	0	0	0	1	.143
J. Blanchard	4	1	1	0	0	0	0	.250
A. Downing, of	2	0	0	0	0	0	0	.000
H. Lopez, of	2	0	0	0	0	0	0	.000
W. Ford, p	1	1	0	0	0	0	1	1.000
P. Gonzalez, 3b	1	0	0	0	0	0	0	.000
M. Hegan	1	0	0	0	0	1	0	.000

Errors: C. Boyer (2), P. Linz (2), M. Mantle (2), B. Richardson (2), E. Howard
Stolen bases: C. Boyer, B. Richardson

Individual Pitching

ST. LOUIS (N.L.)

	W	L	ERA	IP	H	BB	SO	SV
B. Gibson	2	1	3.00	27	23	8	31	0
C. Simmons	0	1	2.51	14.1	11	3	8	0
R. Sadecki	1	0	8.53	6.1	12	5	2	0
R. Craig	1	0	0.00	5	2	3	9	0
B. Schultz	0	1	18.00	4	9	3	1	1
R. Taylor	0	0	0.00	4.2	0	1	2	1
B. Humphreys	0	0	0.00	1	0	0	1	0
G. Richardson	0	0	40.50	0.2	3	2	0	0

NEW YORK (A.L.)

	W	L	ERA	IP	H	BB	SO	SV
Stottlemyre	1	1	3.15	20	18	6	12	0
J. Bouton	2	0	1.56	17.1	15	5	7	0
A. Downing	0	1	8.22	7.2	9	2	5	0
W. Ford	0	1	8.44	5.1	8	1	4	0
P. Mikkelsen	0	1	5.79	4.2	4	2	4	0
S. Hamilton	0	0	4.50	2	3	0	2	1
R. Sheldon	0	0	0.00	2.2	0	2	2	0
R. Terry	0	0	0.00	2	2	0	3	0
H. Reniff	0	0	0.00	0.1	2	0	0	0

	R	H	E	PITCHERS (inn. pit.)	HOME RUNS (men on)	HIGHLIGHTS

St. Louis (N.L.) defeats Boston (A.L.) 4 games to 3

GAME 1 - OCTOBER 4

		R	H	E	PITCHERS	HOME RUNS	HIGHLIGHTS
STL	N	2	10	0	B. Gibson (9)	Santiago	Gibson scatters six hits and strikes out ten as Brock collects four singles and two stolen bases to pace the Cardinal attack.
BOS	A	1	6	0	Santiago (7), Wyatt (2)		

GAME 2 - OCTOBER 5

		R	H	E	PITCHERS	HOME RUNS	HIGHLIGHTS
STL	N	0	1	1	Hughes (5.1), Willis (0.2), Hoerner (0.2), Lamabe (1.1)		Lonborg retires the first 20 batters in a row until Javier doubles for the only Cardinal hit of the game. Yastrzemski's homers pace the Red Sox attack.
BOS	A	5	9	0	Lonborg (9)	Yastrzemski, Yastrzemski (2 on)	

GAME 3 - OCTOBER 7

		R	H	E	PITCHERS	HOME RUNS	HIGHLIGHTS
BOS	A	2	7	1	Bell (2), Waslewski (3), Stange (2), Osinski (1)	Smith	Shannon homers with Maxvill on base in the second for the deciding runs as Briles holds Boston to seven hits.
STL	N	5	10	0	Briles (9)	Shannon (1 on)	

GAME 4 - OCTOBER 8

		R	H	E	PITCHERS	HOME RUNS	HIGHLIGHTS
BOS	A	0	5	0	Santiago (0.2), Bell (1.1), Stephenson (2), Morehead (3), Brett (1)		Gibson allows five hits and coasts to a 6-0 shutout as the Cardinals score four times in the first and twice in the third.
STL	N	6	9	0	B. Gibson (9)		

GAME 5 - OCTOBER 9

		R	H	E	PITCHERS	HOME RUNS	HIGHLIGHTS
BOS	A	3	6	1	Lonborg (9)	Maris	Howard's single in the ninth inning with the bases filled scores the deciding run. Maris homers in the bottom of the inning for the Cardinals' only run.
STL	N	1	3	2	Carlton (6), Washburn (2), Willis (0), Lamabe (1)		

GAME 6 - OCTOBER 11

		R	H	E	PITCHERS	HOME RUNS	HIGHLIGHTS
STL	N	4	8	0	Hughes (3.2), Willis (0.1), Briles (2), Lamabe (0.1), Hoerner (0), Jaster (0.1), Washburn (0.1), Woodeshick (1)	Brock (1 on)	Three fourth inning home runs by Yastrzemski, Smith, and Petrocelli for a World Series record provides the punch in an 8-4 victory.
BOS	A	8	12	1	Waslewski (5.1), Wyatt (1.2), Bell (2) SV	Petrocelli, Yastrzemski, Smith, Petrocelli	

GAME 7 - OCTOBER 12

		R	H	E	PITCHERS	HOME RUNS	HIGHLIGHTS
STL	N	7	10	1	B. Gibson (9)	B. Gibson, Javier (2 on)	Gibson allows three hits and strikes out ten as St. Louis routs Lonborg for the Series victory.
BOS	A	2	3	1	Lonborg (6), Santiago (2), Morehead (0.1), Osinski (0.1), Brett (0.1)		

Team Totals

		W	AB	H	2B	3B	HR	R	RBI	BA	BB	SO	ERA
STL	N	4	229	51	11	2	5	25	24	.223	17	30	2.66
BOS	A	3	222	48	6	1	8	21	19	.216	17	49	3.39

Individual Batting

ST. LOUIS (N.L.)

	AB	H	2B	3B	HR	R	RBI	BA
L. Brock, of	29	12	2	1	1	8	3	.414
O. Cepeda, 1b	29	3	2	0	0	1	1	.103
C. Flood, of	28	5	1	0	0	2	3	.179
R. Maris, of	26	10	1	0	1	3	7	.385
J. Javier, 2b	25	9	3	0	1	2	4	.360
T. McCarver, c	24	3	1	0	0	3	2	.125
M. Shannon, 3b	24	5	1	0	1	3	2	.208
D. Maxvill, ss	19	3	0	1	0	1	1	.158
B. Gibson, p	11	1	0	0	1	1	1	.091
N. Briles, p	3	0	0	0	0	0	0	.000
D. Hughes, p	3	0	0	0	0	0	0	.000
D. Ricketts	3	0	0	0	0	0	0	.000
B. Tolan	2	0	0	0	0	1	0	.000
S. Carlton, p	1	0	0	0	0	0	0	.000
P. Gagliano	1	0	0	0	0	0	0	.000
E. Spiezio	1	0	0	0	0	0	0	.000
E. Bressoud, ss	0	0	0	0	0	0	0	—

Errors: M. Shannon (2), J. Javier, R. Maris
Stolen bases: L. Brock (7)

BOSTON (A.L.)

	AB	H	2B	3B	HR	R	RBI	BA
G. Scott, 1b	26	6	1	1	0	3	0	.231
Yastrzemski, of	25	10	2	0	3	4	5	.400
R. Smith, of	24	6	1	0	2	3	3	.250
R. Petrocelli, ss	20	4	1	0	2	3	3	.200
E. Howard, c	18	2	0	0	0	0	1	.111
D. Jones, 3b	18	7	0	0	0	2	1	.389
J. Adair, 2b	16	2	0	0	0	0	1	.125
J. Foy, 3b	15	2	1	0	0	2	1	.133
M. Andrews, 2b	13	4	0	0	0	2	1	.308
K. Harrelson, of	13	1	0	0	0	0	1	.077
J. Tartabull, of	13	2	0	0	0	1	0	.154
J. Lonborg, p	9	0	0	0	0	0	0	.000
N. Siebern, of	3	1	0	0	0	0	1	.333
M. Ryan, c	2	0	0	0	0	0	0	.000
J. Santiago, p	2	1	0	0	1	1	1	.500
G. Thomas, of	2	0	0	0	0	0	0	.000
R. Gibson, c	2	0	0	0	0	0	0	.000
G. Waslewski, p	1	0	0	0	0	0	0	.000

Errors: R. Petrocelli (2), J. Foy, L. Stange
Stolen bases: J. Adair

Individual Pitching

ST. LOUIS (N.L.)

	W	L	ERA	IP	H	BB	SO	SV
B. Gibson	3	0	1.00	27	14	5	26	0
N. Briles	1	0	1.64	11	7	1	4	0
D. Hughes	0	1	5.00	9	9	3	7	0
S. Carlton	0	1	0.00	6	3	2	5	0
J. Lamabe	0	1	6.75	2.2	5	0	4	0
R. Washburn	0	0	0.00	2.1	1	1	2	0
R. Willis	0	0	27.00	1	2	4	1	0
H. Woodeshick	0	0	0.00	1	1	0	0	0
J. Hoerner	0	0	40.50	0.2	4	1	0	0
L. Jaster	0	0	0.00	0.1	2	0	0	0

BOSTON (A.L.)

	W	L	ERA	IP	H	BB	SO	SV
J. Lonborg	2	1	2.63	24	14	2	11	0
J. Santiago	0	2	5.59	9.2	16	3	6	0
G. Waslewski	0	0	2.16	8.1	4	2	7	0
G. Bell	0	1	5.06	5.1	8	1	1	1
D. Morehead	0	0	0.00	3.1	0	4	3	0
J. Wyatt	1	0	4.91	3.2	1	3	1	0
L. Stange	0	0	0.00	2	3	0	0	0
J. Stephenson	0	0	9.00	2	3	1	0	0
D. Osinski	0	0	6.75	1.1	2	0	0	0
K. Brett	0	0	0.00	1.1	0	1	1	0

R H E	PITCHERS (inn. pit.)	HOME RUNS (men on)	HIGHLIGHTS

Detroit (A.L.) defeats St. Louis (N.L.) 4 games to 3

GAME 1 - OCTOBER 2

		R H E	PITCHERS	HOME RUNS	HIGHLIGHTS
DET	A	0 5 3	McLain (5), Dobson (2), McMahon (1)		Gibson subdues the Tigers on a Series record 17-strike-out performance as McLain, the first 30-game winner since 1931, lasts only until the sixth.
STL	N	4 6 0	Gibson (9)	Brock	

GAME 2 - OCTOBER 3

| DET | A | 8 13 1 | Lolich (9) | Horton, Lolich, Cash | Lolich hits his first homer in the majors, aiding his own cause as he allows the Cardinals six singles. |
| STL | N | 1 6 1 | Briles (5), Carlton (1), Willis (2), Hoerner (1) | | |

GAME 3 - OCTOBER 5

| STL | N | 7 13 0 | Washburn (5.1), Hoerner (3.2) **SV** | McCarver (2 on), Cepeda (2 on), Kaline (1 on), McAuliffe | McCarver's go-ahead three-run homer in the fifth and Cepeda's three-run homer in the seventh upends the Tigers. |
| DET | A | 3 4 0 | Wilson (4.1), Dobson (0.2), McMahon (1), Patterson (1), Hiller (2) | | |

GAME 4 - OCTOBER 6

| STL | N | 10 13 0 | Gibson (9) | Brock, Gibson, Northrup | Gibson coasts to his seventh straight victory, a Series record, striking out ten as Brock collects four RBI's. |
| DET | A | 1 5 4 | McLain (2.2), Sparma (0.1), Patterson (2), Lasher (2), Hiller (0), Dobson (2) | | |

GAME 5 - OCTOBER 7

| STL | N | 3 9 0 | Briles (6.1), **Hoerner (0)**, Willis (1.2) | Cepeda (2 on) | Lolich survives three Cardinal runs in the first as the Tigers bail him out with three runs in the seventh. |
| DET | A | 5 9 1 | Lolich (9) | | |

GAME 6 - OCTOBER 9

| DET | A | 13 12 1 | McLain (9) | Northrup (3 on), Kaline | The Tigers break open the game on a ten-run third-inning barrage which features Northrup's grand slam. |
| STL | N | 1 9 1 | Washburn (2), Jaster (0), Willis (0.2), Hughes (0.1), Carlton (3), Granger (2), Nelson (1) | | |

GAME 7 - OCTOBER 10

| DET | A | 4 8 1 | Lolich (9) | | The Tigers win the Series behind Northrup's go-ahead, two-run triple in the seventh. Gibson's eight strikeouts give him a single-Series record of 35. Key plays come in the sixth when Lolich picks Brock and Flood off first. |
| STL | N | 1 5 0 | Gibson (9) | Shannon | |

Team Totals

		W	AB	H	2B	3B	HR	R	RBI	BA	BB	SO	ERA
DET	A	4	231	56	4	3	8	34	33	.242	27	59	3.48
STL	N	3	239	61	7	3	7	27	27	.255	21	40	4.65

Individual Batting

DETROIT (A.L.)

	AB	H	2B	3B	HR	R	RBI	BA
A. Kaline, of	29	11	2	0	2	6	8	.379
J. Northrup, of	28	7	0	1	2	4	8	.250
M. Stanley, ss, of	28	6	0	1	0	4	0	.214
D. McAuliffe, 2b	27	6	0	0	1	5	3	.222
N. Cash, 1b	26	10	0	0	1	5	5	.385
B. Freehan, c	24	2	1	0	0	0	2	.083
W. Horton, of	23	7	1	1	1	6	3	.304
D. Wert, 3b	17	2	0	0	0	1	2	.118
M. Lolich, p	12	3	0	1	2	2	2	.250
D. McLain, p	6	0	0	0	0	0	0	.000
E. Mathews, 3b	3	1	0	0	0	0	0	.333
T. Matchick	3	0	0	0	0	0	0	.000
J. Price	2	0	0	0	0	0	0	.000
G. Brown	1	0	0	0	0	0	0	.000
E. Wilson, p	1	0	0	0	0	0	0	.000
W. Comer	1	1	0	0	0	0	0	1.000
R. Oyler, ss	0	0	0	0	0	0	0	—
D. Tracewski, 3b	0	0	0	0	0	0	0	—

Errors: N. Cash (2), B. Freehan (2), J. Northrup (2), M. Stanley (2), W. Horton, E. Mathews, D. McLain

ST. LOUIS (N.L.)

	AB	H	2B	3B	HR	R	RBI	BA
M. Shannon, 3b	29	8	1	0	1	3	4	.276
L. Brock, of	28	13	3	1	2	6	5	.464
O. Cepeda, 1b	28	7	0	0	2	2	6	.250
C. Flood, of	28	8	1	0	0	4	2	.286
J. Javier, 2b	27	9	1	0	0	1	3	.333
T. McCarver, c	27	9	0	2	1	3	4	.333
D. Maxvill, ss	22	0	0	0	0	1	0	.000
R. Maris, of	19	3	1	0	0	5	1	.158
B. Gibson, p	8	1	0	0	1	2	2	.125
R. Davis, of	7	0	0	0	0	0	0	.000
N. Briles, p	4	0	0	0	0	0	0	.000
P. Gagliano	3	0	0	0	0	0	0	.000
R. Washburn, p	3	0	0	0	0	0	0	.000
J. Hoerner, p	2	1	0	0	0	0	0	.500
J. Edwards	1	0	0	0	0	0	0	.000
D. Ricketts	1	1	0	0	0	0	0	1.000
E. Spiezio	1	1	0	0	0	0	0	1.000
B. Tolan	1	0	0	0	0	0	0	.000
D. Schofield	0	0	0	0	0	0	0	—

Errors: L. Brock, M. Shannon
Stolen bases: L. Brock (7), C. Flood (3), J. Javier

Individual Pitching

DETROIT (A.L.)

	W	L	ERA	IP	H	BB	SO	SV
M. Lolich	3	0	1.67	27	20	6	21	0
D. McLain	1	2	3.24	16.2	18	4	13	0
E. Wilson	0	1	6.23	4.1	4	8	3	0
P. Dobson	0	0	3.86	4.2	5	1	0	0
D. Patterson	0	0	0.00	3	1	1	0	0
J. Hiller	0	0	13.50	2	6	3	1	0
F. Lasher	0	0	0.00	2	1	0	1	0
D. McMahon	0	0	13.50	2	4	0	1	0
J. Sparma	0	0	54.00	0.1	2	1	0	0

ST. LOUIS (N.L.)

	W	L	ERA	IP	H	BB	SO	SV
B. Gibson	2	1	1.67	27	18	4	35	0
N. Briles	0	1	5.56	11.1	13	4	7	0
R. Washburn	1	1	9.82	7.1	7	7	6	0
S. Carlton	0	0	6.75	4	7	1	3	0
J. Hoerner	0	1	3.86	4.2	5	5	3	1
R. Willis	0	0	8.31	4.1	2	4	3	0
W. Granger	0	0	0.00	2	0	1	1	0
M. Nelson	0	0	0.00	1	0	1	0	0
D. Hughes	0	0	0.00	0.1	2	0	0	0
L. Jaster	0	0	∞	0.0	2	1	0	0

	R	H	E	PITCHERS (inn. pit.)	HOME RUNS (men on)	HIGHLIGHTS

St. Louis (East) defeats Atlanta (West) 3 games to 0

GAME 1 - OCTOBER 7

		R	H	E	
ATL	W	0	3	0	**Perez** (5), Bedrosian (0.2), Moore (1.1), Walk (1)
STL	E	7	13	1	**Forsch** (9)

Game One came a day late after rain washed away the previous night's effort with Atlanta leading 1-0 in the fifth. In the game that counts, the Cardinals scored five in the sixth to break open a 1-0 game. Bob Forsch scattered three hits and walked none for the win.

GAME 2 - OCTOBER 9

		R	H	E	
ATL	W	3	6	0	Niekro (6), **Garber** (2.1)
STL	E	4	9	1	Stuper (6), Bair (1), **Sutter** (2)

Another day of rain allowed Phil Niekro, who pitched in the Game One washout, to come back on two days' rest. Niekro left the game with a 3-2 lead, but Garber could not hold it. Ken Oberkfell, 6-for-10 against Garber in the season, singled home the winning run with first base open in the bottom of the ninth.

GAME 3 - OCTOBER 10

		R	H	E		
STL	E	5	12	0	**Andujar** (6.2), Sutter (2.1) SV	McGee
ATL	W	2	6	1	**Camp** (1), Perez (3.2), Moore (1.1), Mahler (1.2), Bedrosian (0.1), Garber (1)	

Five Cardinal hits, topped by rookie Willie McGee's triple, led to four runs in the second inning to chase Rick Camp. McGee added a homer in the ninth and Bruce Sutter set down seven straight hitters to nail down the Cardinals' first pennant in fourteen years.

Team Totals

		W	AB	H	2B	3B	HR	R	RBI	BA	BB	SO	ERA
STL	E	3	103	34	4	2	1	17	16	.330	12	16	1.33
ATL	W	0	89	15	1	0	0	5	3	.169	6	15	6.05

Individual Batting

ST. LOUIS (EAST)

	AB	H	2B	3B	HR	R	RBI	BA
K. Oberkfell, 3b	15	3	0	0	0	1	2	.200
G. Hendrick, of	13	4	0	0	0	2	2	.308
T. Herr, 2b	13	3	1	0	0	1	0	.231
W. McGee, of	13	4	0	2	1	4	5	.308
K. Hernandez, 1b	12	4	0	0	0	3	1	.333
L. Smith, of	11	3	0	0	0	1	1	.273
O. Smith, ss	9	5	0	0	0	3		.556
D. Porter, c	9	5	3	0	0	3	1	.556
B. Forsch, p	3	2	0	0	0	1	1	.667
S. Braun	1	0	0	0	0	0	0	.000
J. Andujar, p	1	0	0	0	0	0	0	.000
B. Sutter, p	1	0	0	0	0	0	0	.000
D. Green, of	1	1	0	0	0	1	0	1.000
J. Stuper, p	1	0	0	0	0	0	0	.000

Errors: K. Oberkfell, W. McGee

Stolen bases: O. Smith

ATLANTA (WEST)

	AB	H	2B	3B	HR	R	RBI	BA
D. Murphy, of	11	3	0	0	0	1	0	.273
B. Horner, 3b	11	1	0	0	0	0	0	.091
R. Ramirez, ss	11	2	0	0	0	1	1	.182
J. Royster, of, 3b	11	2	0	0	0	0	0	.182
C. Chambliss, 1b	10	0	0	0	0	0	0	.000
C. Washington, of	9	3	0	0	0	0	0	.333
G. Hubbard, 2b	9	2	0	0	0	1	1	.222
B. Benedict, c	8	2	1	0	0	1	0	.250
P. Perez, p	3	0	0	0	0	0	0	.000
L. Whisenton	2	0	0	0	0	0	0	.000
G. Garber, p	1	0	0	0	0	0	0	.000
B. Pocoroba	1	0	0	0	0	0	0	.000
T. Harper, of	1	0	0	0	0	1	0	.000
B. Butler, of	1	0	0	0	0	0	0	.000
P. Niekro, p	0	0	0	0	0	0	1	—

Errors: R. Ramirez

Stolen bases: D. Murphy

Individual Pitching

ST. LOUIS (EAST)

	W	L	ERA	IP	H	BB	SO	SV
B. Forsch	1	0	0.00	9	3	0	6	0
J. Andujar	1	0	2.70	6.2	6	2	4	0
J. Stuper	0	0	3.00	6	4	1	4	0
B. Sutter	1	0	0.00	4.1	0	0	1	1
D. Bair	0	0	0.00	1	2	3	0	0

ATLANTA (WEST)

	W	L	ERA	IP	H	BB	SO	SV
P. Perez	0	1	5.19	8.2	10	2	4	0
P. Niekro	0	0	3.00	6	6	4	5	0
G. Garber	0	1	8.10	3.1	4	1	3	0
D. Moore	0	0	0.00	2.2	2	0	1	0
R. Camp	0	1	36.00	1	4	1	0	0
R. Mahler	0	0	0.00	1.2	3	2	0	0
B. Walk	0	0	9.00	1	2	1	1	0
S. Bedrosian	0	0	18.00	1	3	1	2	0

	R	H	E	PITCHERS (inn. pit.)	HOME RUNS (men on)	HIGHLIGHTS

St. Louis (N.L.) defeats Milwaukee (A.L.) 4 games to 3

GAME 1 - OCTOBER 12

MIL A 10 17 0 **Caldwell (9)** — Simmons — Caldwell allowed three hits as Milwaukee hammered four Cardinal pitchers. Paul Molitor had the first five-hit game in World Series history, and Robin Yount added four of his own.

STL N 0 3 1 Forsch (5.2), Kaat (1.1), LaPoint (1.2), Lahti (0.1)

GAME 2 - OCTOBER 13

MIL A 4 10 1 Sutton (6), **McClure (1.1)**, Ladd (0.2) — Simmons — Darrell Porter doubled in two runs in the sixth and had a key single in the Cards' game-winning rally in the eighth.

STL N 5 8 0 Stuper (4), Kaat (0.2), Bair (2), **Sutter (2.1)**

GAME 3 - OCTOBER 15

STL N 6 6 1 Andujar (6.1), Kaat (0.1), Bair (0), Sutter (2.1) **SV** — McGee (2 on), McGee — Willie McGee sparkled with two home runs and a great catch at the wall, driving in four runs and saving another. Andujar was hit on the leg with a line drive, and had to leave the game, leading to an early appearance by relief ace Sutter.

MIL A 2 5 3 Vuckovich (8.2), McClure (0.1) — Cooper (1 on)

GAME 4 - OCTOBER 16

STL N 5 8 1 LaPoint (6.2), **Bair (0)**, Kaat (0), Lahti (1.1) — — With Sutter unavailable, four Cardinal pitchers could not stop the Brewers from rallying for a 7-5 win after LaPoint's error opened the door in the seventh.

MIL A 7 10 2 Haas (5.1), **Slaton (2)**, McClure (1.2) **SV**

GAME 5 - OCTOBER 17

STL N 4 15 2 Forsch (7), Sutter (1) — — Yount set an all-time Series record with his second four-hit game. Caldwell got his second win, McClure his second save.

MIL A 6 11 1 **Caldwell (8.1)**, McClure (0.2) **SV** — Yount

GAME 6 - OCTOBER 19

MIL A 1 4 4 Sutton (4.1), Slaton (0.2), Medich (2), Bernard (1) — — Rookie John Stuper earned a complete-game win despite two rain delays totalling more than two and a half hours. Dane Iorg led the way with two doubles and a triple.

STL N 13 12 1 **Stuper (9)** — Hernandez (1 on), Porter (1 on)

GAME 7 - OCTOBER 20

MIL A 3 7 0 Vuckovich (5.1), **McClure (0.1)**, Haas (2), Caldwell (0.1) — Oglivie — A three-run rally in the sixth, capped by Hendrick's go-ahead single, overcame a 3-1 deficit to give St. Louis the championship.

STL N 6 15 1 **Andujar (7)**, Sutter (2) **SV**

Team Totals

		W	AB	H	2B	3B	HR	R	RBI	BA	BB	SO	ERA
STL	N	4	245	67	16	3	4	39	34	.273	20	26	3.39
MIL	A	3	238	64	12	2	5	33	28	.269	19	28	4.80

Individual Batting

ST. LOUIS (N.L.)

	AB	H	2B	3B	HR	R	RBI	BA
G. Hendrick, of	28	9	0	0	0	5	5	.321
L. Smith, of, dh	28	9	4	1	0	6	1	.321
D. Porter, c	28	8	2	0	1	1	5	.286
K. Hernandez, 1b	27	7	2	0	1	4	8	.259
T. Herr, 2b	25	4	2	0	0	2	5	.160
W. McGee, of	25	6	0	0	2	6	5	.240
K. Oberkfell, 3b	24	7	1	0	0	4	1	.292
O. Smith, ss	24	5	0	0	0	3	1	.208
D. Iorg, dh	17	9	4	1	0	4	1	.529
D. Green, of, dh	10	2	1	1	0	3	0	.200
G. Tenace, dh	6	0	0	0	0	0	0	.000
S. Braun, dh	2	1	0	0	0	0	2	.500
M. Ramsey, 3b	1	0	0	0	0	1	0	.000
G. Brummer, c	0	0	0	0	0	0	0	—

Errors: K. Hernandez (2), B. Forsch, J. Andujar, K. Oberkfell, T. Herr, D. LaPoint

Stolen bases: K. Oberkfell (2), L. Smith (2), W. McGee (2), O. Smith

MILWAUKEE (A.L.)

	AB	H	2B	3B	HR	R	RBI	BA
P. Molitor, 3b	31	11	0	0	0	5	2	.355
R. Yount, ss	29	12	3	0	1	6	6	.414
C. Cooper, 1b	28	8	1	0	1	3	6	.286
B. Oglivie, of	27	6	0	1	1	4	1	.222
C. Moore, of	26	9	3	0	0	3	2	.346
G. Thomas, of	26	3	0	0	0	0	3	.115
J. Gantner, 2b	24	8	4	1	0	5	4	.333
T. Simmons, c	23	4	0	0	2	2	3	.174
D. Money, dh	13	3	1	0	0	4	1	.231
R. Howell, dh	11	0	0	0	0	1	0	.000
N. Yost, c	0	0	0	0	0	0	0	—
M. Edwards, of	0	0	0	0	0	0	0	—

Errors: J. Gantner (5), R. Yount (3), T. Simmons, C. Cooper, B. Oglivie

Stolen bases: P. Molitor

Individual Pitching

ST. LOUIS (N.L.)

	W	L	ERA	IP	H	BB	SO	SV
J. Andujar	2	0	1.35	13.1	10	1	4	0
J. Stuper	1	0	3.46	13	10	5	5	0
B. Forsch	0	2	4.97	12.2	18	3	4	0
D. LaPoint	0	0	3.24	8.1	10	2	3	0
B. Sutter	1	0	4.70	7.2	6	3	6	2
J. Kaat	0	0	3.86	2.1	4	2	2	0
D. Bair	0	1	9.00	2	2	2	3	0
J. Lahti	0	0	10.80	1.2	4	1	1	0

MILWAUKEE (A.L.)

	W	L	ERA	IP	H	BB	SO	SV
M. Caldwell	2	0	2.04	17.2	19	3	6	0
P. Vuckovich	0	1	4.50	14	16	5	4	0
D. Sutton	0	1	7.84	10.1	12	1	5	0
M. Haas	0	0	7.36	7.1	8	3	4	0
B. McClure	0	2	4.15	4.1	5	3	5	2
J. Slaton	1	0	0.00	2.2	1	2	1	0
D. Medich	0	0	18.00	2	5	1	0	0
D. Bernard	0	0	0.00	1	0	0	1	0
P. Ladd	0	0	0.00	0.2	1	2	0	0